S0-ATQ-610

APPLYING THE LAW

CONCEPT REVIEW

ESSENTIALS OF

BUSINESS LAW
And the Legal Environment

ESSENTIALS OF

BUSINESS LAW
And the Legal Environment

TWELFTH EDITION

Richard A. Mann
The University of North Carolina at Chapel Hill
Member of the North Carolina Bar

Barry S. Roberts
The University of North Carolina at Chapel Hill
Member of the North Carolina and Pennsylvania Bars

CENGAGE
Learning·

Australia • Brazil • Japan • Korea •Mexico • Singapore • Spain • United Kingdom • United States

CENGAGE
Learning®

Essentials of Business Law and the Legal Environment, Twelfth Edition
Richard A. Mann and Barry S. Roberts

Vice President, General Manager,
Social Science & Qualitative Business: Erin Joyner

Product Director: Michael Worls

Senior Product Manager: Vicky True-Baker

Content Developer: Sarah Blasco

Product Assistant: Ryan McAndrews

Marketing Director: Kristen Hurd

Senior Marketing Manager: Katie Jergens

Marketing Coordinator: Chris Walz

Senior Art Director: Michelle Kunkler

Sr Content Project Manager: Ann Borman

Content Digitization Project Manager: Tom Burns

Digital Content Designer: Javan Kline

Manufacturing Planner: Kevin Kluck

Production Service/Compositor: Cenveo Publisher Services

Cover and Internal Designer: Imbue Design/Kim Torbeck

Cover and case logo image is
© Pgiam/iStockphoto.com

Intellectual Property:

    Analyst: Jennifer Nonemacher

    Project Manager: Betsy Hathaway

© 2016, 2013, 2010 Cengage Learning
WCN: 01-100-101

ALL RIGHTS RESERVED. No part of this work covered by the copyright herein may be reproduced, transmitted, stored, or used in any form or by any means graphic, electronic, or mechanical, including but not limited to photocopying, recording, scanning, digitizing, taping, Web distribution, information networks, or information storage and retrieval systems, except as permitted under Section 107 or 108 of the 1976 United States Copyright Act, without the prior written permission of the publisher.

> For product information and technology assistance, contact us at
> **Cengage Learning Customer & Sales Support, 1-800-354-9706**
>
> For permission to use material from this text or product, submit all requests online at **www.cengage.com/permissions**
> Further permissions questions can be emailed to
> **permissionrequest@cengage.com**

Library of Congress Control Number: 2014952093

Student Edition ISBN: 978-1-305-07543-6

Cengage Learning
20 Channel Center Street
Boston, MA 02210
USA

Cengage Learning is a leading provider of customized learning solutions with office locations around the globe, including Singapore, the United Kingdom, Australia, Mexico, Brazil, and Japan. Locate your local office at:
www.cengage.com/global

Cengage Learning products are represented in Canada by Nelson Education, Ltd.

To learn more about Cengage Learning Solutions, visit **www.cengage.com**

Purchase any of our products at your local college store or at our preferred online store **www.cengagebrain.com**

Unless otherwise noted, all content is copyright Cengage Learning

Printed in the United States of America
Print Number: 01   Print Year: 2016

About the Authors

RICHARD A. MANN received a B.S. in mathematics from the University of North Carolina at Chapel Hill and a J.D. from Yale Law School. He is professor emeritus of Business Law at the Kenan-Flagler School of Business, University of North Carolina at Chapel Hill, and is past president of the Southeastern Regional Business Law Association. He is a member of Who's Who in America, Who's Who in American Law, and the North Carolina Bar (inactive).

Professor Mann has written extensively on a number of legal topics, including bankruptcy, sales, secured transactions, real property, insurance law, and business associations. He has received the *American Business Law Journal's* award both for the best article and for the best comment and, in addition, has served as a reviewer and staff editor for the publication. Professor Mann is a coauthor of *Smith and Roberson's Business Law* (sixteenth edition), as well as *Business Law and the Regulation of Business* (eleventh edition) and *Contemporary Business Law.*

BARRY S. ROBERTS received a B.S. in business administration from Pennsylvania State University, a J.D. from the University of Pennsylvania, and an LL.M. from Harvard Law School. He served as a judicial clerk for the Pennsylvania Supreme Court prior to practicing law in Pittsburgh. Barry Roberts is professor of business law at the Kenan-Flagler School of Business, University of North Carolina at Chapel Hill, and is a member of Who's Who in American Law and the North Carolina and Pennsylvania Bars (inactive).

Professor Roberts has written numerous articles on such topics as antitrust, products liability, constitutional law, banking law, employment law, and business associations. He has been a reviewer and staff editor for the *American Business Law Journal.* He is a coauthor *of Smith and Roberson's Business Law* (sixteenth edition), as well as *Business Law and the Regulation of Business* (eleventh edition) and *Contemporary Business Law.*

Contents in Brief

Contents

APPENDICES

Table of Cases

Table of Figures

Preface

THE TRADITION CONTINUES

The twelfth edition of *Essentials of Business Law and the Legal Environment* continues the tradition of accuracy, comprehensiveness, and authoritativeness associated with its earlier editions. This text covers its subject material in a succinct, nontechnical but authoritative manner, and provides depth sufficient to ensure easy comprehension by today's students.

Certified Public Accountant Preparation

This text is designed for use in business law and legal environment of business courses generally offered in universities, colleges, and schools of business and management. Because of its broad and deep coverage, this text may be readily adapted to specially designed courses in business law or the legal environment of business by assigning and emphasizing different combinations of chapters.

Furthermore, this text covers the following parts of the CPA Exam: (1) the legal responsibilities and liabilities of accountants section and (2) the corporate governance portion of the business environment and concepts section. See the inside back cover of this text for a listing of the CPA exam topics covered in this text as well as the chapters covering each topic.

Uniform CPA Examination Content Specifications

The American Institute of CPAs (AICPA) Board of Examiners has approved and adopted content specification outlines (CSOs) for the four sections of the new computer-based Uniform CPA Examination: Auditing and Attestation, Financial Accounting and Reporting, Regulation, and Business Environment and Concepts. As updated, effective January 1, 2015, the CSOs include the following topics, which are covered in this textbook:

Regulation Section
I. Ethics, Professional, and Legal Responsibilities
    A. Legal Duties and Responsibilities [of Accountants]
        1. Common law duties and liability to clients and third parties
        2. Federal statutory liability
        3. Privileged communications, confidentiality, and privacy acts
II. Business Law
    A. Agency
        1. Formation and termination
        2. Authority of agents and principals
        3. Duties and liabilities of agents and principals
    B. Contracts
        1. Formation
        2. Performance
        3. Third-party assignments
        4. Discharge, breach, and remedies

    C. Uniform Commercial Code
       1. Sales contracts
       2. Negotiable instruments
       3. Secured transactions
       4. Documents of title and title transfer
    D. Debtor–Creditor Relationships
       1. Rights, duties, and liabilities of debtors, creditors, and guarantors
       2. Bankruptcy and insolvency
    E. Government Regulation of Business
       1. Federal securities regulation
       2. Other federal laws and regulations (antitrust, copyright, patents, labor, and employment)
    F. Business Structure (Selection of a Business Entity)
       1. Advantages, disadvantages, implications, and constraints
       2. Formation, operation, and termination
       3. Financial structure, capitalization, profit and loss allocation, and distributions
       4. Rights, duties, legal obligations, and authority of owners and management

Business Environment and Concepts Section

I. Corporate Governance
    A. Rights, Duties, Responsibilities, Authority, and Ethics of the Board of Directors, Officers, and Other Employees

For more information, visit **www.cpa-exam.org**.

Business Ethics Emphasis

The Chapter 2 Business Ethics case studies require students to make the value trade-offs that confront business people in their professional lives. (We gratefully acknowledge the assistance of James Leis in writing the Mykon's Dilemma case.) Two-thirds of the chapters also contain an Ethical Dilemma, which presents a managerial situation involving ethical issues. A series of questions leads the student to explore the ethical dimensions of each situation. We wish to acknowledge and thank the following professors for their contributions in preparing the Ethical Dilemmas: Sandra K. Miller, professor of accounting and taxation, Widener University, and Gregory P. Cermignano, associate professor of accounting and business law, Widener University. In addition, to provide further application of ethics in different business contexts, an ethics question follows many cases. These questions are designed to encourage students to consider the ethical dimensions of the facts in the case or of the legal issue invoked by the facts.

New to This Edition

- **Going Global.** A Going Global feature has been added to fifteen chapters (Chapters 1, 3, 6, 9, 15, 19, 20, 27, 30, 34, 38, 39, 40, 41, and 42), thus integrating international business law content throughout the text. This feature enables students to consider the international aspects of legal issues as they are covered. The International Business Law chapter (Chapter 46) has been retained in its entirety.

- **Updated and Expanded Coverage.** The 2012 amendments to Uniform Commercial Code (UCC) Article 4A has been added to Chapter 27. Coverage of limited liability companies has been updated and expanded in Chapter 32. The Secured Transactions chapter (Chapter 37) covers the most significant provisions of the 2010 amendments to UCC Article 9 and the coverage of suretyship has been updated and expanded. The Employment Law chapter (Chapter 41) covers the Genetic Information Nondiscrimination Act. The chapter on Securities Regulation (Chapter 39) covers the Jumpstart Our Business Startups Act of 2012, the Stop Trading on Congressional Knowledge Act of 2012, and the U.S. Securities and Exchange Commission's new disclosure rules clarifying how companies can use social media to disseminate information. The Intellectual Property chapter (Chapter 40) includes the changes made by the Foreign and Economic Espionage Penalty Enhancement Act of 2012. The Environmental Law chapter (Chapter 45) includes coverage of the EPA's regulation of greenhouse gases. The International Business Law chapter (Chapter 46) covers the United Nations Convention on the Law of the Sea (UNCLOS).

- **New Cases.** More than thirty recent legal cases are new to this edition (see Table of Cases). The new cases include recent U.S. Supreme Court decisions such as *Mims v. Arrow Financial Services, LLC; Nitro-Lift Technologies, LLC v. Howard; Brown v. Entertainment Merchants Association; Mayo Foundation for Medical Education and Research v. United States; Sackett v. Environmental Protection Agency; Radlax Gateway Hotel, LLC v. Amalgamated Bank; Association for Molecular Pathology v. Myriad Genetics, Inc.; Matrixx Initiatives, Inc. v. Siracusano; Vance v. Ball State University; Freeman v. Quicken Loans, Inc.*; and *Environmental Protection Agency v. EME Homer City Generation, LP.*

- **Coverage of Recent U.S. Supreme Court Decisions.** The Constitutional Law chapter (Chapter 4) discusses recent U.S. Supreme Court's decisions in the cases challenging the constitutionality of (1) the Patient Protection and Affordable Care Act, (2) the Defense of Marriage Act, (3) a federal statute restricting how much money an individual donor may contribute in total to all candidates or committees during a political cycle, and (4) Michigan's constitutional amendment banning affirmative action in admissions to the state's public universities.

- **Coverage of Restatement of Restitution.** Chapters 9, 11, 13, 14, 15, 17, 18, and 50 cover the new Restatement (Third) of Restitution and Unjust Enrichment.

KEY FEATURES

Summarized Cases

The facts, decisions, and opinions for all of the cases are summarized for clarity. Each case is followed by an interpretation, which explains the significance of the case and how it relates to the textual material. We have retained the landmark cases from the prior edition. In addition, we have incorporated more than thirty recent cases, including a number of U.S. Supreme Court cases.

Case Critical Thinking Questions

Each case is also followed by a critical thinking question to encourage students to examine the legal policy or reasoning behind the legal principle of the case or to apply it in a real-world context.

Ample Illustrations

We have incorporated more than 220 classroom-tested figures, tables, diagrams, concept reviews, and chapter summaries. The figures, tables, and diagrams help the students conceptualize the many abstract concepts in the law. The Concept Reviews not only summarize prior discussions but also indicate relationships between different legal rules. Moreover, each chapter ends with a summary in the form of an annotated outline of the entire chapter, including key terms.

Applying the Law

A number of chapters include a feature that provides a systematic legal analysis of a single concept learned in that chapter. It consists of (1) the facts of a hypothetical case, (2) an identification of the broad legal issue presented by those facts, (3) a statement of the applicable rule, (4) the application of the rule to the facts, and (5) a legal conclusion in the case. We wish to acknowledge and thank Professor Ann Olazábal, University of Miami, for her contribution in preparing this feature.

Business Law in Action

A number of chapters include a scenario that illustrates the application of legal concepts in the chapter to business situations that commonly arise. We wish to acknowledge and thank Professor Ann Olazábal, University of Miami, for her contribution in preparing this feature.

Practical Advice

Each chapter contains a number of statements that illustrate how legal concepts covered in that chapter can be applied to common business situations.

Chapter Outcomes

Each chapter begins with a list of learning objectives for the student.

Enhanced Readability

To improve readability throughout the text, all unnecessary "legalese" has been eliminated, while necessary legal terms have been printed in boldface and clearly defined, explained, and illustrated. Definitions of essential legal terms and legal concepts also appear in the margins. Each chapter is carefully organized with sufficient levels of subordination to enhance the accessibility of the material. The text is enriched by numerous illustrative hypothetical and case examples that help students relate material to real-life experiences.

Classroom-Proven End-of-Chapter Materials

Classroom-proven questions and case problems appear at the end of the chapters to test the students' understanding of major concepts. We have used the questions (based on hypothetical situations) and the case problems (taken from reported court decisions) in our own classrooms and consider them excellent stimulants to classroom discussion. Students, in turn, have found the questions and case problems helpful in enabling them to apply the basic rules of law to factual situations.

Taking Sides

Each chapter—except for Chapters 1 and 2—has an end-of-chapter feature that requires students to apply critical thinking skills to a case-based fact situation. The students are asked to identify the relevant legal rules and develop arguments for both parties to the dispute. In addition, the students are asked to explain how they think a court would resolve the dispute.

Pedagogical Benefits

Classroom use and study of this book should provide for the student the following benefits and skills:

1. Perception and appreciation of the scope, extent, and importance of the law.
2. Basic knowledge of the fundamental concepts, principles, and rules of law that apply to business transactions.
3. Knowledge of the function and operation of courts and government administrative agencies.
4. Ability to recognize the potential legal problems that may arise in a doubtful or complicated situation, and the necessity of consulting a lawyer and obtaining competent professional legal advice.
5. Development of analytical skills and reasoning power.

COMPREHENSIVE LEARNING RESOURCES

Instructor's Resources

Access instructor resources by going to **login.cengage.com**, logging in with your faculty account username and password, and searching ISBN 9781305075436 to add instructor resources to your account "Bookshelf."

- The **Instructor's Manual** prepared by Richard A. Mann, Barry S. Roberts, and Beth D. Woods contains chapter outlines; teaching notes; answers to the Questions, Case Problems, and Taking Sides; and part openers that provide suggested research and outside activities for students.

- **PowerPoint® Slides** clarify course content and guide student note-taking during lectures.

- The **Test Bank** contains thousands of true/false, multiple-choice, and essay questions. The questions vary in levels of difficulty and meet a full range of tagging requirements so that instructors can tailor their testing to meet their specific needs.

- **Cengage Learning Testing Powered by Cognero** is a flexible, online system that allows you to

  - author, edit, and manage test bank content from multiple Cengage Learning solutions

  - create multiple test versions in an instant

  - deliver tests from your Learning Management Systems (LMS), your classroom, or wherever you want

ADDITIONAL COURSE TOOLS

MindTap

New for *Essentials of Business Law and the Legal Environment* (twelfth edition) MindTap is a fully online, highly personalized learning environment built on Cengage Learning content. Mind-Tap combines student-learning tools—readings, multimedia, activities, and assessments—into a singular Learning Path that guides students through their course. Instructors can personalize the experience by customizing authoritative Cengage Learning content and learning tools. MindTap offers instructors the ability to add their own content in the Learning Path with apps that integrate into the MindTap framework seamlessly with LMS.

Business Law Digital Video Library

Featuring more than ninety video clips that spark class discussion and clarify core legal principles, the Business Law Digital Video Library is organized into five series: Legal Conflicts in Business (includes specific modern business and e-commerce scenarios); Ask the Instructor (presents straightforward explanations of concepts for student review); Drama of the Law (features classic business scenarios that spark classroom participation); Real-World Legal (presents legal scenarios encountered in real businesses); and Business Ethics in Action (presents ethical dilemmas in business scenarios). For more information about the Digital Video Library, visit **www.cengage. com/blaw/dvl**.

ACKNOWLEDGMENTS

We express our gratitude to the following professors for their helpful comments:

Michael E. Adighibe, Cheyney University; Martha Agee, Baylor University; Jessica Allen, Suffolk Community College; Terence Baird, Antelope Valley College; Keith A. Beebe, SUNY-Cobleskill; Dawn Bennett-Alexander, University of Northern Florida; Janie Blankenship, DelMar College; George S. Bohler, Embry-Riddle University; Joyce Boland-DeVito, St. John's University; Steven W. Bostian, Caston College; Norman E. Bradshaw, Alvin Community College; Donald R. Brenner, American University; Carroll Burrell, San Jacinto College; Jane Campbell, Jackson Community College; Stephanie Campbell, Mineral Area College; Vic Daniels, Tallahassee Community College; Ed Dash, Pierce Junior College; Joseph P. Davey, Hartnell College; David L Davis, Tallahassee Community College; Sandra Defebaugh, Eastern Michigan University; Theodore M. Dinges, Longview Community College; Vernon P. Dorweiler, Michigan Technological University; Dora J. L. Dye, City College of San Francisco; Steve Easter, Mineral Area College; Robert Ek, Seminole Community College; Tony Enerva, Lakeland Community College; Karla Harbin Fox, University of Connecticut; Edward J. Gac, University of Colorado; George P. Generas, Jr., University of Hartford; Allan M. Gerson, Palm Beach Community College; J. P. Giovacchini, Western Nevada College; Thomson Glover, Murray State University; Douglas C. Gordon, Arapahoe Community College; Suzanne Gradisher, University of Akron; A. James Granito, Youngstown State University; Deborah C. Hanks, Cardinal Stritch University; E. Sharon Hayenga, Minneapolis Community College; James E. Holloway, East Carolina University; H. Daniel Holt,

Southeastern Illinois College; Trevor Howell, Belmont College; Gregory M. Huckabee, University of South Dakota; Dan Huss, Miami University; Robert Inama, Ricks College; Keith Kasper, University of Vermont; Michael A. Katz, Delaware State University; Julia S. Kennedy, University of St. Francis; George Kepner, Hartwick College; Edward M. Kissling, Ocean County College; Blake LeCrone, Baylor University; Daniel A. Levin, University of Colorado–Boulder; David Ludwich, Belmont College; Sarah H. Ludwig, Mary Baldwin College; Bradley Lutz, Hillsborough Community College; Richard Lynn, Belmont College; John F. Mastriani, El Paso Community College; Marian Matthews, Central New Mexico Community College; Kyle McFatter, McNeese State University; James Miles, Anoka-Ramsey Community College; Scott E. Miller, CPA, J.D., Gannon University; David J. Moser, Belmont University; Andre Nelson, Montgomery College; John H. Neu, Whittier College; Brennan Neville, Bellevue University; L. K. O'Drudy, Jr., University of Virginia; Michael J. O'Hara, University of Nebraska; Dinah Payne, University of New Orleans; Mary Ellen Perri, SUNY-Farmingdale; Todd B. Piller, SUNY-Cobleskill; Richard W. Post, College of the Desert; LeGene Quesenberry, Clarion University; Roger E. Reinsch, Emporia State University; Darlington C. Richards, Morgan State University; M. Rose, Macomb County Community College; Herbert Rossman, Drexel University; Sylvia Samuels, Skyline College; Donald E. Sanders, Southwest Texas State University; Susan Schoeffler, Central Piedmont Community College; John E. H. Sherry, Cornell University; Caroline W. Smith, College of Central Florida; Owen T. Smith, Long Island University; Michael E. Sommerville, St. Mary's College; Dan Spielmann, University of Wisconsin-Green Bay; Art Stelly, Baylor University; Larry Stephens, Gulf Coast College; Stanley H. Stone, Valencia Community College-East Campus; Mary Torma, Lorain County Community College; Patricia S. Tulin, Central Connecticut State University; Robert J. Votta, Pierce Junior College; Edward C. Wachter, Jr., Point Park College; Pamela Poole Weber, Seminole Community College; Hugh Wilkoff, Cerritos College; Kim Wong Central New Mexico Community College.

We express our thanks and appreciation to Debra Corvey for administrative assistance. For their support, we extend our thanks to Karlene Fogelin Knebel and Joanne Erwick Roberts. And we are grateful to Vicky True-Baker, Sarah Blasco, and Ann Borman of Cengage Learning for their invaluable assistance and cooperation in connection with the preparation of this text.

This text is dedicated also to our children Lilli-Marie Knebel Mann, Justin Erwick Roberts, and Matthew Charles Roberts.

Richard A. Mann
Barry S. Roberts

INTRODUCTION TO LAW AND ETHICS

Introduction to Law

CHAPTER 1

The life of the law has not been logic; it has been experience.

Oliver Wendell Holmes
The Common Law (1881)

CHAPTER OUTCOMES

After reading and studying this chapter, you should be able to:

1. Identify and describe the basic functions of law.

2. Distinguish between (a) law and justice and (b) law and morals.

3. Distinguish between (a) substantive and procedural law, (b) public and private law, and (c) civil and criminal law.

4. Identify and describe the sources of law.

5. Explain the principle of *stare decisis*.

Law concerns the relations between individuals as such relations affect the social and economic order. It is both the product of civilization and the means by which civilization is maintained. As such, law reflects the social, economic, political, religious, and moral philosophy of society.

Law is an instrument of social control. Its function is to regulate, within certain limitations, human conduct and human relations. Accordingly, the laws of the United States affect the life of every U.S. citizen. At the same time, the laws of each state influence the life of each of its citizens and the lives of many noncitizens as well. The rights and duties of all individuals, as well as the safety and security of all people and their property, depend on the law.

The law is pervasive. It permits, forbids, or regulates practically every human activity and affects all persons either directly or indirectly. Law is, in part, prohibitory: certain acts must not be committed. For example, one must not steal; one must not murder. Law is also partly mandatory: certain acts must be done or be done in a prescribed way. Thus, taxes must be paid; corporations must make and file certain reports with state or federal authorities; traffic must keep to the right. Finally, law is permissive: certain acts may be done. For instance, one may or may not enter into a contract; one may or may not dispose of one's estate by will.

Because the areas of law are so highly interrelated, you will find it helpful to begin the study of the different areas of business law by first considering the nature, classification, and sources of law. This will enable you not only to understand better each specific area of law but also to understand its relationship to other areas of law.

NATURE OF LAW [1-1]

The law has evolved slowly, and it will continue to change. It is not a pure science based on unchanging and universal truths. Rather, it results from a continuous striving to develop a workable set of rules that balance the individual and group rights of a society.

Definition of Law [1-1a]

Definition of law

"a rule of civil conduct prescribed by the supreme power in a state, commanding what is right, and prohibiting what is wrong" (William Blackstone)

Scholars and citizens in general often ask a fundamental but difficult question regarding law: what is it? Numerous philosophers and jurists (legal scholars) have attempted to define it. American jurists and Supreme Court Justices Oliver Wendell Holmes and Benjamin Cardozo defined law as predictions of the way in which a court will decide specific legal questions. The English jurist William Blackstone, on the other hand, defined law as "a rule of civil conduct prescribed by the supreme power in a state, commanding what is right, and prohibiting what is wrong."

Because of its great complexity, many legal scholars have attempted to explain the law by outlining its essential characteristics. Roscoe Pound, a distinguished American jurist and former dean of the Harvard Law School, described law as having multiple meanings:

> First we may mean the legal order, that is, the régime of ordering human activities and relations through systematic application of the force of politically organized society, or through social pressure in such a society backed by such force. We use the term "law" in this sense when we speak of "respect for law" or for the "end of law."
>
> Second we may mean the aggregate of laws or legal precepts; the body of authoritative grounds of judicial and administrative action established in such a society. We may mean the body of received and established materials on which judicial and administrative determinations proceed. We use the term in this sense when we speak of "systems of law" or of "justice according to law."
>
> Third we may mean what Justice Cardozo has happily styled "the judicial process." We may mean the process of determining controversies, whether as it actually takes place, or as the public, the jurists, and the practitioners in the courts hold it ought to take place.

Functions of Law [1-1b]

Functions of law

to maintain stability in the social, political, and economic system through dispute resolution, protection of property, and the preservation of the state, while simultaneously permitting ordered change

At a general level the primary **function of law** is to maintain stability in the social, political, and economic system while simultaneously permitting change. The law accomplishes this basic function by performing a number of specific functions, among them dispute resolution, protection of property, and preservation of the state.

Disputes, which arise inevitably in any modern society, may involve criminal matters, such as theft, or noncriminal matters, such as an automobile accident. Because disputes threaten social stability, the law has established an elaborate and evolving set of rules to resolve them. In addition, the legal system has instituted societal remedies, usually administered by the courts, in place of private remedies such as revenge.

A second crucial function of law is to protect the private ownership of property and to assist in the making of voluntary agreements (called contracts) regarding exchanges of property and services. Accordingly, a significant portion of law, as well as this text, involves property and its disposition, including the law of property, contracts, sales, commercial paper, and business associations.

A third essential function of the law is preservation of the state. In our system, law ensures that changes in political structure and leadership are brought about by political action, such as elections, legislation, and referenda, rather than by revolution, sedition, and rebellion.

Law and Morals [1-1c]

Laws and morals

are different but overlapping: law provides sanctions while morals do not

Although moral concepts greatly influence the law, morals and law are not the same. You might think of them as two intersecting circles (see Figure 1-1). The area common to both circles includes the vast body of ideas that are both moral and legal. For instance, "Thou shall not kill" and "Thou shall not steal" are both moral precepts and legal constraints.

On the other hand, the part of the legal circle that does not intersect the morality circle includes many rules of law that are completely unrelated to morals, such as the rules stating that you must drive on the right side of the road and that you must register before you can vote. Likewise, the part of the morality circle that does not intersect the legal circle includes moral precepts not enforced by legal sanctions, such as the idea that you should not silently stand by and watch a blind man walk off a cliff or that you should provide food to a starving child.

Figure 1-1 Law and Morals

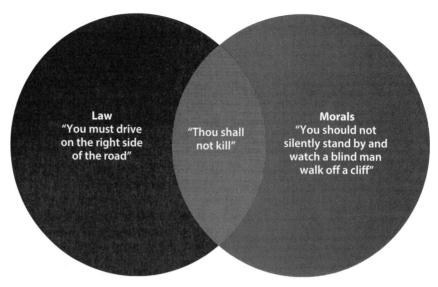

Law and Justice [1-1d]

Law and justice
are separate and distinct
concepts; justice is the fair,
equitable, and impartial
treatment of competing
interests with due regard
for the common good

Law and justice represent separate and distinct concepts. Without law, however, there can be no justice. Although defining justice is at least as difficult as defining law, justice generally may be defined as the fair, equitable, and impartial treatment of the competing interests and desires of individuals and groups with due regard for the common good.

On the other hand, law is no guarantee of justice. Some of history's most monstrous acts have been committed pursuant to "law." Examples include the actions of Nazi Germany during the 1930s and 1940s and the actions of the South African government under apartheid from 1948 until 1994. Totalitarian societies often have shaped formal legal systems around the atrocities they have sanctioned.

CLASSIFICATION OF LAW [1-2]

Because the subject is vast, classifying the law into categories is helpful. Though a number of categories are possible, the most useful ones are (1) substantive and procedural, (2) public and private, and (3) civil and criminal. See Figure 1-2, which illustrates a classification of law.

Right
legal capacity to require
another person to perform
or refrain from performing
an act

Basic to understanding these classifications are the terms *right* and *duty*. A **right** is the capacity of a person, with the aid of the law, to require another person or persons to perform, or to refrain from performing, a certain act. Thus, if Alice sells and delivers goods to Bob for the

Figure 1-2 Classification of Law

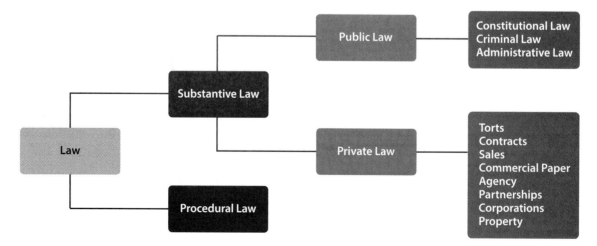

Duty
legal obligation requiring a person to perform or refrain from performing an act

Substantive law
the basic law creating rights and duties

Procedural law
rules for enforcing substantive law

Public law
the law dealing with the relationship between government and individuals

Private law
the law involving relationships among individuals and legal entities

Civil law
the law dealing with the rights and duties of individuals among themselves

Criminal law
the law that involves offenses against the entire community

Sue
to begin a lawsuit in a court

Defendant
the person against whom a legal action is brought

Plaintiff
the person who initiates a civil suit

Prosecute
to bring a criminal proceeding

agreed price of $500 payable at a certain date, Alice is capable, with the aid of the courts, of enforcing the payment by Bob of the $500. A **duty** is the obligation the law imposes upon a person to perform, or to refrain from performing, a certain act. Duty and right are correlatives: no right can rest upon one person without a corresponding duty resting upon some other person, or in some cases upon all other persons.

Substantive and Procedural Law [1-2a]

Substantive law creates, defines, and regulates legal rights and duties. Thus, the rules of contract law that determine a binding contract are rules of substantive law. On the other hand, **procedural law** sets forth the rules for enforcing those rights that exist by reason of the substantive law. Thus, procedural law defines the method by which to obtain a remedy in court.

Public and Private Law [1-2b]

Public law is the branch of substantive law that deals with the government's rights and powers and its relationship to individuals or groups. Public law consists of constitutional, administrative, and criminal law. **Private law** is that part of substantive law governing individuals and legal entities (such as corporations) in their relationships with one another. Business law is primarily private law.

Civil and Criminal Law [1-2c]

The **civil law** defines duties, the violation of which constitutes a wrong against the party injured by the violation. In contrast, the **criminal law** establishes duties, the violation of which is a wrong against the whole community. Civil law is a part of private law, whereas criminal law is a part of public law. (The term *civil law* should be distinguished from the concept of a civil law *system*, which is discussed later in this chapter.) In a civil action the injured party **sues** to recover *compensation* for the damage and injury sustained as a result of the **defendant's** wrongful conduct. The party bringing a civil action (the **plaintiff**) has the burden of proof, which the plaintiff must sustain by a *preponderance* (greater weight) *of the evidence*. The purpose of the civil law is to compensate the injured party, not, as in the case of criminal law, to punish the wrongdoer. The principal forms of relief the civil law affords are a judgment for money damages and a decree ordering the defendant to perform a specified act or to desist from specified conduct.

A crime is any act prohibited or omission required by public law in the interest of protecting the public and made punishable by the government in a judicial proceeding brought (**prosecuted**) by it. The government must prove criminal guilt *beyond a reasonable doubt*, which is a significantly higher burden of proof than that required in a civil action. Crimes are prohibited and punished on the grounds of public policy, which may include the safeguarding of government, human life, or private property. Additional purposes of criminal law include deterrence and rehabilitation. See Concept Review 1-1 for a comparison of civil and criminal law.

CONCEPT REVIEW 1-1

Comparison of Civil and Criminal Law

	Civil Law	Criminal Law
Commencement of Action	Aggrieved individual (plaintiff) sues	State or federal government prosecutes
Purpose	Compensation Deterrence	Punishment Deterrence Rehabilitation Preservation of peace
Burden of Proof	Preponderance of the evidence	Beyond a reasonable doubt
Principal Sanctions	Monetary damages Equitable remedies	Capital punishment Imprisonment Fines

SOURCES OF LAW [1-3]

The sources of law in the U.S. legal system are the federal and state constitutions, federal treaties, interstate compacts, federal and state statutes and executive orders, the ordinances of countless local municipal governments, the rules and regulations of federal and state administrative agencies, and an ever-increasing volume of reported federal and state court decisions.

The *supreme law* of the land is the U.S. Constitution, which provides in turn that federal statutes and treaties shall be paramount to state constitutions and statutes. Federal legislation is of great significance as a source of law. Other federal actions having the force of law are executive orders by the President and rules and regulations set by federal administrative officials, agencies, and commissions. The federal courts also contribute considerably to the body of law in the United States.

The same pattern exists in every state. The paramount law of each state is contained in its written constitution. (Although a state constitution cannot deprive citizens of federal constitutional rights, it can guarantee rights beyond those provided in the U.S. Constitution.) State constitutions tend to be more specific than the U.S. Constitution and, generally, have been amended more frequently. Subordinate to the state constitution are the statutes enacted by the state's legislature and the case law developed by its judiciary. Likewise, rules and regulations of state administrative agencies have the force of law, as do executive orders issued by the governors of most states. In addition, cities, towns, and villages have limited legislative powers to pass ordinances and resolutions within their respective municipal areas. See Figure 1-3, which illustrates this hierarchy.

Constitutional Law [1-3a]

Constitution
fundamental law of a government establishing its powers and limitations

A **constitution**—the fundamental law of a particular level of government—establishes the governmental structure and allocates power among governmental levels, thereby defining political relationships. One of the fundamental principles on which our government is founded is that of separation of powers. As incorporated into the U.S. Constitution, this means that government consists of three distinct and independent branches—the federal judiciary, the Congress, and the executive branch.

A constitution also restricts the powers of government and specifies the rights and liberties of the people. For example, the Constitution of the United States not only specifically states what rights and authority are vested in the national government but also specifically enumerates certain rights and liberties of the people. Moreover, the Ninth Amendment to the U.S. Constitution makes it clear that this enumeration of rights does not in any way deny or limit other rights that the people retain.

Judicial review
authority of the courts to determine the constitutionality of legislative and executive acts

All other law in the United States is subordinate to the federal Constitution. No law, federal or state, is valid if it violates the federal Constitution. Under the principle of **judicial review**, the Supreme Court of the United States determines the constitutionality of *all* laws.

Judicial Law [1-3b]

Common law system
body of law originating in England and derived from judicial decisions

The U.S. legal system, a **common law system** like the system first developed in England, relies heavily on the judiciary as a source of law and on the adversary system for settling disputes. In an **adversary system** the parties, not the court, must initiate and conduct litigation. This approach is based on the belief that the truth is more likely to emerge from the investigation and presentation of evidence by two opposing parties, both motivated by self-interest, than from judicial investigation motivated only by official duty. In addition to the United States and England, the common law system is used in other English-speaking countries, including Canada and Australia.

Adversary system
system in which opposing parties initiate and present their cases

Civil law system
body of law derived from Roman law and based upon comprehensive legislative enactments

In distinct contrast to the common law system are civil law systems, which are based on Roman law. **Civil law systems** depend on comprehensive legislative enactments (called codes) and an inquisitorial system of determining disputes. In the **inquisitorial system**, the judiciary initiates litigation, investigates pertinent facts, and conducts the presentation of evidence. The civil law system prevails in most of Europe, Scotland, the state of Louisiana, the province of Quebec, Latin America, and parts of Africa and Asia.

Inquisitorial system
system in which the judiciary initiates, conducts, and decides cases

Figure 1-3 Hierarchy of Law

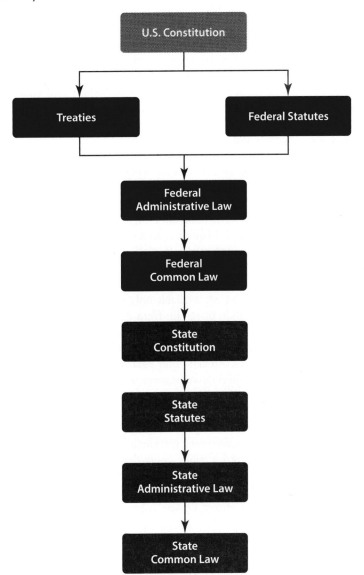

Common Law   The courts in common law systems have developed a body of law that serves as precedent for determining later controversies. In this sense, common law, also called case law or judge-made law, is distinguished from other sources of law, such as legislation and administrative rulings.

To evolve in a stable and predictable manner, the common law has developed by application of *stare decisis* ("to stand by the decisions"). Under the principle of **stare decisis**, courts adhere to and rely on rules of law that they or superior courts relied on and applied in prior similar decisions. Judicial decisions thus have two uses: (1) to determine with finality the case currently being decided and (2) to indicate how the court will decide similar cases in the future. *Stare decisis* does not, however, preclude courts from correcting erroneous decisions or from choosing among conflicting precedents. Thus, the doctrine allows sufficient flexibility for the common law to change. The strength of the common law is its ability to adapt to change without losing its sense of direction.

Equity   As the common law developed in England, it became overly rigid and beset with technicalities. As a consequence, in many cases no remedies were provided because the judges insisted that a claim must fall within one of the recognized forms of action. Moreover, courts of common law could provide only limited remedies; the principal type of relief obtainable was a

Stare decisis

principle that courts should apply rules decided in prior cases in deciding substantially similar cases monetary judgment. Consequently, individuals who could not obtain adequate relief from monetary awards began to petition the king directly for justice. He, in turn, came to delegate these petitions to his chancellor.

Gradually, there evolved what was in effect a new and supplementary system of needed judicial relief for those who could not receive adequate remedies through the common law. This new system, called **equity**, was administered by a court of chancery presided over by the chancellor. The chancellor, deciding cases on "equity and good conscience," regularly provided relief where common law judges had refused to act or where the remedy at law was inadequate. Thus, there grew up, side by side, two systems of law administered by different tribunals, the common law courts and the courts of equity.

An important difference between common law and equity is that the chancellor could issue a **decree**, or order, compelling a defendant to do, or refrain from doing, a specified act. A defendant who did not comply with this order could be held in contempt of court and punished by fine or imprisonment. This power of compulsion available in a court of equity opened the door to many needed remedies not available in a court of common law.

Courts of equity in some cases recognized rights that were enforceable at common law, but they provided more effective remedies. For example, in a court of equity, for breach of a land contract the buyer could obtain a decree of **specific performance** commanding the defendant seller to perform his part of the contract by transferring title to the land. Another powerful and effective remedy available only in the courts of equity was the **injunction**, a court order requiring a party to do or refrain from doing a specified act. Another remedy not available elsewhere was **reformation**, where, upon the ground of mutual mistake, an action could be brought to reform or change the language of a written agreement to conform to the actual intention of the contracting parties. An action for **rescission** of a contract, which allowed a party to invalidate a contract under certain circumstances, was another remedy.

Although courts of equity provided remedies not available in courts of law, they granted such remedies only at their discretion, not as a matter of right. This discretion was exercised according to the general legal principles, or **maxims**, formulated by equity courts over the years.

In nearly every jurisdiction in the United States, courts of common law and equity have merged into a single court that administers both systems of law. Vestiges of the old division remain, however. For example, the right to a trial by jury applies only to actions at law, but not, under federal law and in almost every state, to suits filed in equity.

See Concept Review 1-2 for a comparison of law and equity.

Restatements of Law   The common law of the United States results from the independent decisions of the state and federal courts. The rapid increase in the number of decisions by these courts led to the establishment of the American Law Institute (ALI) in 1923. The ALI is composed of a distinguished group of lawyers, judges, and law professors who set out to prepare

Equity
body of law based upon principles distinct from common law and providing remedies not available at law

Decree
decision of a court of equity

Specific performance
decree ordering a party to perform a contractual duty

Injunction
decree ordering a party to do or refrain from doing a specified act

Reformation
equitable remedy rewriting a contract to conform with the original intent of the contracting parties

Rescission
an equitable remedy invalidating a contract

Maxim
a general legal principle

CONCEPT REVIEW 1-2

Comparison of Law and Equity

	Law	Equity
Availability	Generally	Discretionary: if remedy at law is inadequate
Precedents	*Stare decisis*	Equitable maxims
Jury	If either party demands	None in federal and almost all states
Remedies	Judgment for monetary damages	Decree of specific performance, injunction, reformation, rescission

an orderly restatement of the general common law of the United States, including in that term not only the law developed solely by judicial decision, but also the law that has grown from the application by the courts of statutes that were generally enacted and were in force for many years.

Currently the ALI is made up of more than 4,300 lawyers, judges, and law professors.

Regarded as the authoritative statement of the common law of the United States, the Restatements cover many important areas of the common law, including torts, contracts, agency, property, and trusts. Although not law in themselves, they are highly persuasive, and courts frequently have used them to support their opinions. Because they provide a concise and clear statement of much of the common law, relevant portions of the Restatements are relied on frequently in this book.

Legislative Law [1-3c]

Since the end of the nineteenth century, legislation has become the primary source of new law and ordered social change in the United States. The annual volume of legislative law is enormous. Justice Felix Frankfurter's remarks to the New York City Bar in 1947 are even more appropriate in the twenty-first century:

> Inevitably the work of the Supreme Court reflects the great shift in the center of gravity of lawmaking. Broadly speaking, the number of cases disposed of by opinions has not changed from term to term. But even as late as 1875 more than 40 percent of the controversies before the Court were common-law litigation, fifty years later only 5 percent, while today cases not resting on statutes are reduced almost to zero. It is therefore accurate to say that courts have ceased to be the primary makers of law in the sense in which they "legislated" the common law. It is certainly true of the Supreme Court that almost every case has a statute at its heart or close to it.

This emphasis on legislative or statutory law has occurred because common law, which develops evolutionarily and haphazardly, is not well suited for making drastic or comprehensive changes. Moreover, while courts tend to be hesitant about overruling prior decisions, legislatures commonly repeal prior enactments. In addition, legislatures may choose the issues they wish to address, whereas courts may deal only with those issues presented by actual cases. As a result, legislatures are better equipped to make the dramatic, sweeping, and relatively rapid changes in the law that technological, social, and economic innovations compel.

While some business law topics, such as contracts, agency, property, and trusts, still are governed principally by the common law, most areas of commercial law, including partnerships, corporations, sales, commercial paper, secured transactions, insurance, securities regulation, antitrust, and bankruptcy have become largely statutory. Because most states enacted their own statutes dealing with these branches of commercial law, a great diversity developed among the states and hampered the conduct of commerce on a national scale. The increased need for greater uniformity led to the development of a number of proposed uniform laws that would reduce the conflicts among state laws.

The most successful example is the *Uniform Commercial Code (UCC)*, which was prepared under the joint sponsorship and direction of the ALI and the Uniform Law Commission (ULC), which is also known as the National Conference of Commissioners on Uniform State Laws (NCCUSL). All fifty states (although Louisiana has adopted only Articles 1, 3, 4, 5, 7, and 8), the District of Columbia, and the Virgin Islands have adopted the UCC.

The ULC has drafted more than three hundred uniform laws, including the Uniform Partnership Act, the Uniform Limited Partnership Act, and the Uniform Probate Code. The ALI has developed a number of model statutory formulations, including the Model Code of Evidence, the Model Penal Code, and a Model Land Development Code. In addition, the American Bar Association has promulgated the Model Business Corporation Act.

Treaties   A **treaty** is an agreement between or among independent nations. The U.S. Constitution authorizes the President to enter into treaties with the advice and consent of the Senate, "providing two thirds of the Senators present concur."

Treaties may be entered into only by the federal government, not by the states. A treaty signed by the President and approved by the Senate has the legal force of a federal statute. Accordingly, a federal treaty may supersede a prior federal statute, while a federal statute may

Treaty
an agreement between or among independent nations

GOING GLOBAL

What is the WTO?

Nations have entered into bilateral and multilateral treaties to facilitate and regulate trade and to protect their national interests. Probably the most important multilateral trade treaty is the General Agreement on Tariffs and Trade (GATT), which the *World Trade Organization (WTO)* replaced as an international organization. The WTO officially commenced on January 1, 1995, and has at least 160 members, including the United States, accounting for more than 97 percent of world trade. (Approximately twenty-five countries are observers and are seeking membership.) Its basic purpose is to facilitate the flow of trade by establishing agreements on potential trade barriers, such as import quotas, customs, export regulations, antidumping restrictions (the prohibition against selling goods for less than their fair market value), subsidies, and import fees. The WTO administers trade agreements, acts as a forum for trade negotiations, handles trade disputes, monitors national trade policies, and provides technical assistance and training for developing countries.

supersede a prior treaty. Like statutes, treaties are subordinate to the federal Constitution and subject to judicial review.

Executive order
legislation issued by the President or a governor

Executive Orders In addition to the executive functions, the President of the United States also has authority to issue laws, which are called **executive orders**. This authority typically derives from specific delegation by federal legislation. An executive order may amend, revoke, or supersede a prior executive order. An example of an executive order is the one issued by President Johnson in 1965 prohibiting discrimination by federal contractors on the basis of race, color, sex, religion, or national origin in employment on any work the contractor performed during the period of the federal contract.

The governors of most states enjoy comparable authority to issue executive orders.

Administrative Law [1-3d]

Administrative law
law dealing with the establishment, duties, and powers of agencies in the executive branch of government

Administrative law is the branch of public law that is created by administrative agencies in the form of rules, regulations, orders, and decisions to carry out the regulatory powers and duties of those agencies. It also deals with controversies arising among individuals and these public officials and agencies. Administrative functions and activities concern general matters of public health, safety, and welfare, including the establishment and maintenance of military forces, police, citizenship and naturalization, taxation, environmental protection, and the regulation of transportation, interstate highways, waterways, television, radio, and trade and commerce.

Because of the increasing complexity of the nation's social, economic, and industrial life, the scope of administrative law has expanded enormously. In 1952 Justice Jackson stated, "the rise of administrative bodies has been the most significant legal trend of the last century, and perhaps more values today are affected by their decisions than by those of all the courts, review of administrative decisions apart." This is evidenced by the great increase in the number and activities of federal government boards, commissions, and other agencies. Certainly, agencies create more legal rules and decide more controversies than all the legislatures and courts combined.

LEGAL ANALYSIS [1-4]

Decisions in state trial courts generally are not reported or published. The precedent a trial court sets is not sufficiently weighty to warrant permanent reporting. Except in New York and a few other states where selected opinions of trial courts are published, decisions in trial courts are simply filed in the office of the clerk of the court, where they are available for public inspection. Decisions of state courts of appeals are published in consecutively numbered volumes called "reports." In most states, court decisions are found in the official state reports of that state. In addition, state reports are published by West Publishing Company in a regional reporter called the National Reporter System, composed of the following: Atlantic (A., A.2d, or A.3d); South Eastern (S.E. or S.E.2d); South Western (S.W., S.W.2d, or S.W.3d); New York Supplement

(N.Y.S. or N.Y.S.2d); North Western (N.W. or N.W.2d); North Eastern (N.E. or N.E.2d); Southern (So., So.2d, or So.3d); Pacific (P., P.2d, or P.3d); and California Reporter (Cal.Rptr., Cal.Rptr.2d, or Cal.Rptr.3d). At least twenty states no longer publish official reports and have designated a commercial reporter as the authoritative source of state case law.

After they are published, these opinions, or "cases," are referred to ("cited") by giving (1) the name of the case; (2) the volume, name, and page of the official state report, if any, in which it is published; (3) the volume, name, and page of the particular set and series of the National Reporter System; and (4) the volume, name, and page of any other selected case series. For instance, *Lefkowitz v. Great Minneapolis Surplus Store, Inc.*, 251 Minn. 188, 86 N.W.2d 689 (1957), indicates that the opinion in this case may be found in Volume 251 of the official Minnesota Reports at page 188 and in Volume 86 of the North Western Reporter, Second Series, at page 689, and that the opinion was delivered in 1957.

The decisions of courts in the federal system are found in a number of reports. U.S. District Court opinions appear in the Federal Supplement (F.Supp. or F.Supp.2d). Decisions of the U.S. Court of Appeals are found in the Federal Reporter (Fed., F.2d, or F.3d), and the U.S. Supreme Court's opinions are published in the U.S. Supreme Court Reports (U.S.), Supreme Court Reporter (S.Ct.), and Lawyers Edition (L.Ed.). While all U.S. Supreme Court decisions are reported, not every case decided by the U.S. District Courts and the U.S. Courts of Appeals is reported. Each circuit has established rules determining which decisions are published.

In reading the title of a case, such as "*Jones v. Brown*," the "v." or "vs." means versus or against. In the trial court, Jones is the ***plaintiff***, the person who filed the suit, and Brown is the ***defendant***, the person against whom the suit was brought. When the case is appealed, some, but not all, courts of appeals or appellate courts place the name of the party who appeals, or the **appellant**, first, so that "*Jones v. Brown*" in the trial court becomes, if Brown loses and hence becomes the appellant, "*Brown v. Jones*" in the appellate court. Therefore, it is not always possible to determine from the title itself who was the plaintiff and who was the defendant. You must carefully read the facts of each case and clearly identify each party in your mind to understand the discussion by the appellate court. In a criminal case the caption in the trial court will first designate the prosecuting government unit and then will indicate the defendant, as in "*State v. Jones*" or "*Commonwealth v. Brown*."

The study of reported cases requires an understanding and application of legal analysis. Normally, the reported opinion in a case sets forth (1) the essential facts, the nature of the action, the parties, what happened to bring about the controversy, what happened in the lower court, and what pleadings are material to the issues; (2) the issues of law or fact; (3) the legal principles involved; (4) the application of these principles; and (5) the decision.

Appellant
party who appeals

APPLYING THE LAW

Introduction to Law

Facts Jackson bought a new car and planned to sell his old one for about $2,500. But before he did so, he happened to receive a call from his cousin, Trina, who had just graduated from college. Among other things, Trina told Jackson she needed a car but did not have much money. Feeling generous, Jackson told Trina he would give her his old car. But the next day a coworker offered Jackson $3,500 for his old car, and Jackson sold it to the coworker.

Issue Did Jackson have the right to sell his car to the coworker, or legally had he already made a gift of it to Trina?

Rule of Law A gift is the transfer of ownership of property from one person to another without anything in return. The person making the gift is called the donor, and the person receiving it is known as the donee. A valid gift requires (1) the donor's present intent to transfer the property and (2) delivery of the property.

Application In this case, Jackson is the would-be donor and Trina is the would-be donee. To find that Jackson had already made a gift of the car to Trina, both Jackson's intent to give it to her and delivery of the car to Trina would need to

be demonstrated. It is evident from their telephone conversation that Jackson did intend at that point to give the car to Trina. It is equally apparent from his conduct that he later changed his mind, because he sold it to someone else the next day. Consequently, he did not deliver the car to Trina.

Conclusion Because the donor did not deliver the property to the donee, legally no gift was made. Jackson was free to sell the car.

You can and should use this same legal analysis when learning the substantive concepts presented in this text and applying them to the end-of-chapter questions and case problems. By way of example, in a number of chapters throughout the text we have included a boxed feature called "**Applying the Law**," which provides a systematic legal analysis of a single concept learned in the chapter. This feature begins with the **facts** of a hypothetical case, followed by an identification of the broad legal **issue** presented by those facts. We then state the **rule of law**—or applicable legal principles, including definitions, which aid in resolving the legal issue—and **apply** it to the facts. Finally we state a legal **conclusion**, or decision in the case. An example of this type of legal analysis appears on the previous page.

CHAPTER SUMMARY

Nature of Law

Definition of Law "a rule of civil conduct prescribed by the supreme power in a state, commanding what is right, and prohibiting what is wrong" (William Blackstone)

Functions of Law to maintain stability in the social, political, and economic system through dispute resolution, protection of property, and the preservation of the state, while simultaneously permitting ordered change

Laws and Morals are different but overlapping; law provides sanctions while morals do not

Law and Justice are separate and distinct concepts; justice is the fair, equitable, and impartial treatment of competing interests with due regard for the common good

Classification of Law

Substantive and Procedural
- *Substantive Law* law creating rights and duties
- *Procedural Law* rules for enforcing substantive law

Public and Private
- *Public Law* law dealing with the relationship between government and individuals
- *Private Law* law governing the relationships among individuals and legal entities

Civil and Criminal
- *Civil Law* law dealing with rights and duties, the violation of which constitutes a wrong against an individual or other legal entity
- *Criminal Law* law establishing duties that, if violated, constitute a wrong against the entire community

Sources of Law

Constitutional Law fundamental law of a government establishing its powers and limitations

Judicial Law
- *Common Law* body of law developed by the courts that serves as precedent for determination of later controversies
- *Equity* body of law based upon principles distinct from common law and providing remedies not available at law

Legislative Law statutes adopted by legislative bodies
- *Treaties* agreements between or among independent nations
- *Executive Orders* laws issued by the President or by the governor of a state

Administrative Law law created by administrative agencies in the form of rules, regulations, orders, and decisions to carry out the regulatory powers and duties of those agencies

Business Ethics

CHAPTER 2

Our characters are the result of our conduct.

Aristotle
Nicomachean Ethics (c. 335 BCE)

CHAPTER OUTCOMES

After reading and studying this chapter, you should be able to:

1. Describe the difference between law and ethics.

2. Compare the various ethical theories.

3. Describe cost-benefit analysis and explain when it should be used and when it should be avoided.

4. Explain Kohlberg's stages of moral development.

5. Explain the ethical responsibilities of business.

Ethics
study of what is right or good for human beings

Business ethics
study of what is right and good in a business setting; includes the moral issues that arise from business practices, institutions, and decision making

Business ethics is a subset of ethics: no special set of ethical principles applies only to the world of business. Immoral acts are immoral, whether or not a businessperson has committed them. In the last few years, countless business wrongs, such as insider trading, fraudulent earnings statements and other accounting misconduct, price-fixing, concealment of dangerous defects in products, reckless lending and improper foreclosures in the housing market, and bribery, have been reported almost daily. Companies such as Enron, WorldCom, Adelphia, Parmalat, Arthur Andersen, and Global Crossing have violated the law, and some of these firms no longer exist as a result of these ethical lapses. In 2004, Martha Stewart was convicted of obstructing justice and lying to investigators about a stock sale. More recently, Bernie Madoff perpetrated the largest Ponzi scheme in history with an estimated loss of $20 billion in principal and approximately $65 billion in paper losses. In May 2011, Galleon Group (a hedge fund) billionaire, Raj Rajaratnam, was found guilty of fourteen counts of conspiracy and securities fraud. In 2013, large international banks faced a widening scandal—and substantial fines—over attempts to rig benchmark interest rates, including the London Interbank Offered Rate (LIBOR).

Ethics can be defined broadly as the study of what is right or good for human beings. It attempts to determine what people ought to do, or what goals they should pursue. **Business ethics**, as a branch of applied ethics, is the study and determination of what is right and good in business settings. Business ethics seeks to understand the moral issues that arise from business practices, institutions, and decision making, and their relationship to generalized human values. Unlike legal analyses, analyses of ethics have no central authority, such as courts or legislatures, upon which to rely; nor do they follow clear-cut universal standards. Nonetheless, despite these inherent limitations, it still may be possible to make meaningful ethical judgments. To improve ethical decision making, it is important to understand how others have approached the task.

Some examples of the many business ethics questions may clarify the definition of business ethics. In the employment relationship, countless ethical issues arise regarding the safety and compensation of workers, their civil rights (such as equal treatment, privacy, and freedom from sexual harassment), and the legitimacy of whistle-blowing. In the relationship between business and its customers, ethical issues permeate marketing techniques, product safety, and consumer protection. The relationship between business and its owners bristles with ethical questions involving corporate governance, shareholder voting, and management's duties to the shareholders. The relationship among competing businesses involves numerous ethical matters, including fair competition and the effects of collusion. The interaction between business and society at large presents additional ethical dimensions: pollution of the physical environment, commitment to the community's economic and social infrastructure, and depletion of natural resources. Not only do all of these issues recur at the international level, but also additional ones present themselves, such as bribery of foreign officials, exploitation of developing countries, and conflicts among differing cultures and value systems.

In resolving the ethical issues raised by business conduct, it is helpful to use a seeing-knowing-doing model. First, the decision maker should *see* (identify) the ethical issues involved in the proposed conduct, including the ethical implications of the various available options. Second, the decision maker should **know** (resolve) what to do by choosing the best option. Finally, the decision maker should **do** (implement) the chosen option by developing and implementing strategies.

This chapter first surveys the most prominent ethical theories (the knowing part of the decision, on which the great majority of philosophers and ethicists have focused). The chapter then examines ethical standards in business and the ethical responsibilities of business. It concludes with five ethical business cases, which give the student the opportunity to apply the seeing-knowing-doing model. The student (1) identifies the ethical issues presented in these cases; (2) resolves these issues by using one of the ethical theories described in the chapter, some other ethical theory, or a combination of the theories; and (3) develops strategies for implementing the ethical resolution.

LAW VERSUS ETHICS [2-1]

As discussed in Chapter 1, moral concepts strongly affect the law, but law and morality are not the same. Although it is tempting to say that "if it's legal, it's moral," such a proposition is generally too simplistic. For example, it would seem gravely immoral to stand by silently while a blind man walks off a cliff if one could prevent the fall by shouting a warning, even though one would not be legally obligated to do so. Similarly, moral questions arise concerning "legal" business practices, such as failing to fulfill a promise that is not legally binding; exporting products banned in the United States to developing countries where they are not prohibited; or slaughtering baby seals for fur coats. The mere fact that these practices are legal does not prevent them from being challenged on moral grounds.

Just as it is possible for legal acts to be immoral, it is equally possible for illegal acts to seem morally preferable to following the law. For example, it is the moral conviction of the great majority of people that those who sheltered Jews in violation of Nazi edicts during World War II and those who committed acts of civil disobedience in the 1950s and 1960s to challenge segregation laws in the United States were acting properly and that the laws themselves were immoral.

ETHICAL THEORIES [2-2]

Philosophers have sought for centuries to develop dependable and universal methods for making ethical judgments. In earlier times, some thinkers analogized the discovery of ethical principles with the derivation of mathematical proofs. They asserted that people could discover fundamental ethical rules by applying careful reasoning a priori. (A priori reasoning is based on theory rather than experimentation and deductively draws conclusions from cause to effect and from generalizations to particular instances.) In more recent times, many philosophers have concluded that although careful reasoning and deep thought assist substantially in moral reasoning, experience reveals that the complexities of the world defeat most attempts to fashion precise, a priori guidelines. Nevertheless, a review of the most significant ethical theories can aid the analysis of business ethics issues.

Ethical Fundamentalism [2-2a]

Ethical fundamentalism
individuals look to a central authority or set of rules to guide them in ethical decision making

Under **ethical fundamentalism**, or absolutism, individuals look to a central authority or set of rules to guide them in ethical decision making. Some look to the Bible; others look to the Koran or to the writings of Karl Marx or to any number of living or deceased prophets. The essential characteristic of this approach is a reliance on a central repository of wisdom. In some cases, such reliance is total. In others, followers of a religion or a spiritual leader may believe that all members of the group are obligated to assess moral dilemmas independently, according to each person's understanding of the dictates of the fundamental principles.

Ethical Relativism [2-2b]

Ethical relativism
actions must be judged by what individuals subjectively feel is right or wrong for themselves

Ethical relativism is a doctrine asserting that actions must be judged by what individuals feel is right or wrong for themselves. It holds that when any two individuals or cultures differ regarding the morality of a particular issue or action, they are both correct because morality is relative. However, although ethical relativism promotes open-mindedness and tolerance, it has limitations. If each person's actions are always correct for that person, then his behavior is, by definition, moral and therefore exempt from criticism. Once a person concludes that criticizing or punishing behavior in some cases is appropriate, he abandons ethical relativism and faces the task of developing a broader ethical methodology.

Situational ethics
judging a person's actions by first putting oneself in the actor's situation

Although bearing a surface resemblance to ethical relativism, situational ethics actually differs substantially. **Situational ethics** holds that developing precise guidelines for effectively navigating ethical dilemmas is difficult because real-life decision making is so complex. To judge the morality of someone's behavior, the person judging must actually put herself in the other person's shoes to understand what motivated the other to choose a particular course of action. Situational ethics, however, does not cede the ultimate judgment of the propriety of an action to the actor; rather, it insists that, prior to evaluation, a person's decision or act be viewed from the actor's perspective.

Utilitarianism [2-2c]

Utilitarianism
moral actions are those that produce the greatest net pleasure compared with net pain

Utilitarianism is a doctrine that assesses good and evil in terms of the consequences of actions. Those actions that produce the greatest net pleasure compared with net pain are better in a moral sense than those that produce less net pleasure. As Jeremy Bentham, one of the most influential proponents of utilitarianism, proclaimed, a good or moral act is one that results in "the greatest happiness for the greatest number."

Act utilitarianism
each separate act must be assessed according to whether it maximizes pleasure over pain

The two major forms of utilitarianism are act utilitarianism and rule utilitarianism. **Act utilitarianism** assesses each separate act according to whether it maximizes pleasure over pain. For example, if telling a lie in a particular situation produces more overall pleasure than pain, then an act utilitarian would support lying as the moral thing to do. Rule utilitarians, disturbed by the unpredictability of act utilitarianism and its potential for abuse, follow a different approach. **Rule utilitarianism** holds that general rules must be established and followed even though, in some instances, following rules may produce less overall pleasure than not following them. It applies utilitarian principles in developing rules; thus, it supports rules that on balance produce the greatest satisfaction. Determining whether telling a lie in a given instance would produce greater pleasure than telling the truth is less important to the rule utilitarian than deciding whether a general practice of lying would maximize society's pleasure. If lying would not maximize pleasure generally, then one should follow a rule of not lying even though on occasion telling a lie would produce greater pleasure than would telling the truth.

Rule utilitarianism
supports rules that on balance produce the greatest good

Cost-benefit analysis
quantifies in monetary terms the benefits and costs of alternatives

Utilitarian notions underlie cost-benefit analysis, an analytical tool used by many business and government managers today. **Cost-benefit analysis** first quantifies in monetary terms and then compares the direct and indirect costs and benefits of program alternatives for meeting a specified objective. Cost-benefit analysis seeks the greatest economic efficiency according to the underlying notion that, given two potential acts, the act achieving the greatest output at the least cost promotes the greatest marginal happiness over the less-efficient act, other things being equal.

The chief criticism of utilitarianism is that in some important instances it ignores justice. A number of situations would maximize the pleasure of the majority at great social cost to a minority. Another major criticism of utilitarianism is that measuring pleasure and pain in the fashion its supporters advocate is extremely difficult, if not impossible.

Deontology [2-2d]

Deontology

holds that actions must be judged by their motives and means as well as their results

Deontological theories (from the Greek word *deon*, meaning duty or obligation) address the practical problems of utilitarianism by holding that certain underlying principles are right or wrong regardless of any pleasure or pain calculations. Believing that actions cannot be measured simply by their results but rather must be judged by means and motives as well, deontologists judge the morality of acts not so much by their consequences but by the motives that lead to them. A person not only must achieve just results but also must employ the proper means.

The eighteenth-century philosopher Immanuel Kant proffered the best-known deontological theory. Under Kant's **categorical imperative**, for an action to be moral it (1) must potentially be a universal law that could be applied consistently and (2) must respect the autonomy and rationality of all human beings and not treat them as an expedient. That is, one should not do anything that he or she would not have everyone do in a similar situation. For example, you should not lie to colleagues unless you support the right of all colleagues to lie to one another. Similarly, you should not cheat others unless you advocate everyone's right to cheat. We apply Kantian reasoning when we challenge someone's behavior by asking: what if everybody acted that way?

Under Kant's approach, it would be improper to assert a principle to which one claimed personal exception, such as insisting that it was acceptable for you to cheat but not for anyone else to do so. This principle could not be universalized because everyone would then insist on similar rules from which only they were exempt.

Kant's philosophy also rejects notions of the end justifying the means. To Kant, every person is an end in himself or herself. Each person deserves respect simply because of his or her humanity. Thus, any sacrifice of a person for the greater good of society would be unacceptable to Kant.

In many respects, Kant's categorical imperative is a variation of the Golden Rule; and, like the Golden Rule, the categorical imperative appeals to the individual's self-centeredness.

As does every theory, Kantian ethics has its critics. Just as deontologists criticize utilitarians for excessive pragmatism and flexible moral guidelines, utilitarians and others criticize deontologists for rigidity and excessive formalism. For example, if one inflexibly adopts as a rule to tell the truth, one ignores situations in which lying might well be justified. A person hiding a terrified wife from her angry, abusive husband would seem to be acting morally by falsely denying that the wife is at the person's house. Yet a deontologist, feeling bound to tell the truth, might ignore the consequences of truthfulness, tell the husband where his wife is, and create the possibility of a terrible tragedy. Another criticism of deontological theories is that the proper course may be difficult to determine when values or assumptions conflict.

Social Ethics Theories [2-2e]

Social ethical theories

focus on a person's obligations to other members in society and on the individual's rights and obligations

Social ethics theories assert that special obligations arise from the social nature of human beings. Such theories focus not only on each person's obligations to other members of society but also on the individual's rights and obligations within the society. For example, **social egalitarians** believe that society should provide each person with equal amounts of goods and services regardless of the contribution each makes to increase society's wealth.

Social egalitarians

believe that society should provide all members with equal amounts of goods and services irrespective of their relative contributions

Two other ethics theories have received widespread attention in recent years. One is the theory of **distributive justice** proposed by Harvard philosopher John Rawls, which seeks to analyze the type of society that people in a "natural state" would establish if they could not determine in advance whether they would be talented, rich, healthy, or ambitious, relative to other members of society. According to distributive justice, the society contemplated through this "veil of ignorance" is the one that should be developed because it considers the needs and rights of all its members. Rawls did not argue that such a society would be strictly egalitarian and that it would unfairly penalize those who turned out to be the most talented and ambitious. Instead, Rawls suggested that such a society would stress equality of opportunity, not of results. On the other hand, Rawls stressed that society would pay heed to the least advantaged to ensure that they did not suffer unduly and that they enjoyed society's benefits. To Rawls, society must be premised on justice. Everyone is entitled to his or her fair share in society, a fairness all must work to guarantee.

Distributive justice

stresses equality of opportunity rather than of results

In contrast to Rawls, another Harvard philosopher, Robert Nozick, stressed liberty, not justice, as the most important obligation that society owes its members. **Libertarians** stress market outcomes as the basis for distributing society's rewards. Only to the extent that one meets market demands does one deserve society's benefits. Libertarians oppose social interference in the lives of those who do not violate the rules of the marketplace; that is, in the lives of those who do not cheat others and who disclose honestly the nature of their transactions with others. The fact that some end up with fortunes while others accumulate little simply proves that some can play in the market effectively while others cannot. To libertarians, this is not unjust. What is unjust to them is any attempt by society to take wealth earned by citizens and distribute it to those who did not earn it.

These theories and others (e.g., Marxism) judge society in moral terms by its organization and by the way in which it distributes goods and services. They demonstrate the difficulty of ethical decision making in the context of a social organization: behavior that is consistently ethical from individual to individual may not necessarily produce a just society.

Other Theories [2-2f]

The preceding theories do not exhaust the possible approaches to evaluating ethical behavior; several other theories also deserve mention. **Intuitionism** holds that a rational person possesses inherent powers to assess the correctness of actions. Though an individual may refine and strengthen these powers, they are just as basic to humanity as our instincts for survival and self-defense. Just as some people are better artists or musicians, some people have more insight into ethical behavior than others. Consistent with intuitionism is the **good person philosophy**, which declares that if individuals wish to act morally, they should seek out and emulate those who always seem to know the right choice in any given situation and who always seem to do the right thing. One variation of these ethical approaches is the *Television Test*, which directs us to imagine that every ethical decision we make is being broadcast on nationwide television. An appropriate decision is one we would be comfortable broadcasting on national television for all to witness.

ETHICAL STANDARDS IN BUSINESS [2-3]

In this section, we explore the application of the theories of ethical behavior to the world of business.

Choosing an Ethical System [2-3a]

In their efforts to resolve the moral dilemmas facing humankind, philosophers and other thinkers have struggled for years to refine the various systems previously discussed. All of the systems are limited, however, in terms of applicability and tend to produce unacceptable prescriptions for action in some circumstances. But to say that each system has limits is not to say it is useless. On the contrary, a number of these systems provide insight into ethical decision making and help us formulate issues and resolve moral dilemmas. Furthermore, concluding that moral standards are difficult to articulate and that moral boundaries are imprecise is not the same as concluding that moral standards are unnecessary or nonexistent.

Research by the noted psychologist Lawrence Kohlberg provides some insight into ethical decision making and lends credibility to the notion that moral growth, like physical growth, is part of the human condition. **Kohlberg** observed that people progress through sequential **stages of moral development** according to two major variables: age and reasoning. During the first level—the *preconventional level*—a child's conduct is a reaction to the fear of punishment and, later, to the pleasure of reward. Although people who operate at this level may behave in a moral manner, they do so without understanding why their behavior is moral. The rules are imposed upon them. During adolescence—Kohlberg's *conventional level*—people conform their behavior to meet the expectations of groups, such as family, peers, and eventually society. The motivation for conformity is loyalty, affection, and trust. Most adults operate at this level. According to Kohlberg, some reach the third level—the *postconventional level*—at which they accept and conform to moral principles because they understand *why* the principles are right and binding. At this level, moral principles are voluntarily internalized, not externally imposed. Moreover, individuals at this stage develop their own universal ethical principles and may even question the

Libertarians
stress market outcomes as the basis for distributing society's rewards

Intuitionism
a rational person possesses inherent powers to assess the correctness of actions

Good person philosophy
holds that individuals seek out and emulate good role models

Kohlberg's stages of moral development
see Figure 2-1

Figure 2-1 Kohlberg's Stages of Moral Development

Levels	Perspective	Justification
Preconventional (Childhood)	Self	Punishment/Reward
Conventional (Adolescent)	Group	Group Norms
Postconventional (Adult)	Universal	Moral Principles

laws and values that society and others have adopted (see Figure 2-1 for Kohlberg's stages of moral development).

Kohlberg believed that not all people reach the third, or even the second, stage. He therefore argued that essential to the study of ethics was the exploration of ways to help people achieve the advanced stage of postconventional thought. Other psychologists assert that individuals do not pass sequentially from stage to stage but rather function in all three stages simultaneously.

Whatever the source of our ethical approach, we cannot avoid facing moral dilemmas that challenge us to recognize and do the right thing. Moreover, for those who plan business careers, such dilemmas necessarily will have implications for many others—employees, shareholders, suppliers, customers, and society at large.

Corporations as Moral Agents [2-3b]

Corporations as moral agents

because a corporation is a statutory entity, it is difficult to resolve whether it should be morally accountable

Because corporations are not persons but rather artificial entities created by the state, whether they can or should be held morally accountable is difficult to determine. Though, clearly, individuals within corporations can be held morally responsible, the corporate entity presents unique problems.

Commentators are divided on the issue. Some insist that only people can engage in behavior that can be judged in moral terms. Opponents of this view concede that corporations are not persons in any literal sense but insist that the attributes of responsibility inherent in corporations are sufficient to justify judging corporate behavior from a moral perspective.

ETHICAL RESPONSIBILITIES OF BUSINESS [2-4]

Many people assert that the only responsibility of business is to maximize profit and that this obligation overrides any ethical or social responsibility. Although our economic system of modified capitalism is based on the pursuit of self-interest, it also contains components to check this motivation of greed. Our system always has recognized the need for some form of regulation, whether by the "invisible hand" of competition, the self-regulation of business, or government regulation.

Regulation of Business [2-4a]

As explained and justified by Adam Smith in *The Wealth of Nations* (1776), the capitalistic system is composed of six "institutions": economic motivation, private productive property, free enterprise, free markets, competition, and limited government. As long as all these constituent institutions continue to exist and operate in balance, the factors of production—land, capital, and labor—combine to produce an efficient allocation of resources for individual consumers and for the economy as a whole. To achieve this outcome, however, Smith's model requires that a number of conditions be satisfied: "standardized products, numerous firms in markets, each firm with a small share and unable by its actions alone to exert significant influence over price, no barriers to entry, and output carried to the point where each seller's marginal cost equals the going market price." E. Singer, *Antitrust Economics and Legal Analysis*.

History has demonstrated that the actual operation of the economy has satisfied almost none of these assumptions. More specifically, the actual competitive process falls considerably short of the assumptions of the classic economic model of perfect competition:

> Competitive industries are never perfectly competitive in this sense. Many of the resources they employ cannot be shifted to other employments without substantial cost and delay. The allocation of those resources, as between industries or as to relative proportions within a single industry, is unlikely to have been made in a way that affords the best possible expenditure of economic effort. Information is incomplete, motivation confused, and decision therefore ill informed and often

unwise. Variations in efficiency are not directly reflected in variations of profit. Success is derived in large part from competitive selling efforts, which in the aggregate may be wasteful, and from differentiation of products, which may be undertaken partly by methods designed to impair the opportunity of the buyer to compare quality and price.

C. Edwards, *Maintaining Competition*

In addition to capitalism's failure to allocate resources efficiently, it cannot be relied on to achieve all of the social and public policy objectives a pluralistic democracy requires. For example, the free enterprise model simply does not address equitable distribution of wealth, national defense, conservation of natural resources, full employment, stability in economic cycles, protection against economic dislocations, health and safety, social security, and other important social and economic goals. Increased **regulation of business** has occurred not only to preserve the competitive process in our economic system but also to achieve social goals extrinsic to the efficient allocation of resources, the "invisible hand" and self-regulation by business having failed to bring about these desired results. Such intervention attempts (1) to regulate both "legal" monopolies, such as those conferred by law through copyrights, patents, and trade symbols, and "natural" monopolies, such as utilities, transportation, and communications; (2) to preserve competition by correcting imperfections in the market system; (3) to protect specific groups, especially labor and agriculture, from marketplace failures; and (4) to promote other social goals. Successful government regulation involves a delicate balance between regulations that attempt to preserve competition and those that attempt to advance other social objectives. The latter should not undermine the basic competitive processes that provide an efficient allocation of economic resources.

Regulation of business
government regulation is necessary because all the conditions for perfect competition have not been satisfied and free competition cannot by itself achieve other social goals

Corporate Governance [2-4b]

In addition to the broad demands of maintaining a competitive and fair marketplace, another factor demanding the ethical and social responsibility of business is the sheer size and power of individual corporations. The five thousand largest U.S. firms currently produce more than half of the nation's gross national product.

In a classic study published in 1932, Adolf Berle and Gardner Means concluded that great amounts of economic power had been concentrated in a relatively few large corporations, that the ownership of these corporations had become widely dispersed, and that the shareholders had become far removed from active participation in management. Since their original study, these trends have continued steadily. The five hundred to one thousand large publicly held corporations own the great bulk of the industrial wealth of the United States. Moreover, these corporations are controlled by a small group of corporate officers.

Historically, the boards of many publicly held corporations consisted mainly or entirely of inside directors (corporate officers who also serve on the board of directors). During the past two decades, however, as a result of regulations by the U.S. Securities and Exchange Commission and the stock exchanges, the number and influence of outside directors has increased substantially. Now the boards of the great majority of publicly held corporations consist primarily of outside directors, and these corporations have audit committees consisting entirely of outside directors. Nevertheless, a number of instances of corporate misconduct have been revealed in the first years of this century. In response to these business scandals—involving companies such as Enron, WorldCom, Global Crossing, Adelphia, and Arthur Andersen—in 2002 Congress passed the Sarbanes-Oxley Act. This legislation seeks to prevent these types of scandals by increasing corporate responsibility through the imposition of additional corporate governance requirements on publicly held corporations. (This statute is discussed further in Chapters 6, 35, 39, and 43.)

Moreover, in July 2010, the Dodd-Frank Wall Street Reform and Consumer Protection Act (Dodd-Frank Act) was enacted, representing the most significant change to U.S. financial regulation since the New Deal. Its purposes include improving accountability and transparency in the financial system, protecting consumers from abusive financial services practices, and improving corporate governance in publicly held companies. (The Dodd-Frank Act is discussed further in Chapters 27, 34, 35, 36, 39, 44, and 49.) These developments raise a large number of social, policy, and ethical issues about the governance of large, publicly owned corporations. Many observers insist that companies playing such an important economic role should have a responsibility

Corporate governance
vast amounts of wealth and power have become concentrated in a small number of corporations, which in turn are controlled by a small group of people, and it is argued that they therefore have a responsibility to undertake projects to benefit society

to undertake projects that benefit society in ways that go beyond mere financial efficiency in producing goods and services. In some instances, the idea of corporate obligations comes from industrialists themselves.

Arguments Against Social Responsibility [2-4c]

A number of arguments oppose business involvement in socially responsible activities: profitability, unfairness, accountability, and expertise.

Profitability
the business of business should be to return as much money as possible to shareholders

Profitability As Milton Friedman and others have argued, businesses are artificial entities established to permit people to engage in profit-making, not social, activities. Without profits, they assert, there is little reason for a corporation to exist and no real way to measure the effectiveness of corporate activities. Businesses are not organized to engage in social activities; they are structured to produce goods and services for which they receive money. Their social obligation is to return as much of this money as possible to their direct stakeholders. In a free market with significant competition, the selfish pursuits of corporations will lead to maximizing output, minimizing costs, and establishing fair prices. All other concerns distract companies and interfere with achieving these goals.

Unfairness
whenever corporations engage in social activities, they divert funds rightfully belonging to shareholders and/or employees

Unfairness Whenever companies stray from their designated role of profit-maker, they take unfair advantage of company employees and shareholders. For example, a company may support the arts or education or spend excess funds on health and safety; however, these funds rightfully belong to the shareholders or employees. The company's decision to disburse these funds to others who may well be less deserving than the shareholders and employees is unfair. Furthermore, consumers can express their desires through the marketplace, and shareholders and employees can decide privately whether they wish to make charitable contributions. In most cases, senior management consults the board of directors about supporting social concerns but does not seek the approval of the company's major stakeholders, thereby effectively disenfranchising these shareholders from actions that reduce their benefits from the corporation.

Accountability
a corporation is subject to less public accountability than public bodies

Accountability Corporations, as previously noted, are private institutions that are subject to a lower standard of **accountability** than are public bodies. Accordingly, a company may decide to support a wide range of social causes and yet submit to little public scrutiny. But a substantial potential for abuse exists in such cases. For one thing, a company could provide funding for a variety of causes its employees or shareholders did not support. It also could provide money "with strings attached," thereby controlling the recipients' agendas for less than socially beneficial purposes. For example, a drug company that contributes to a consumer group might implicitly or explicitly condition its assistance on the group's agreement never to criticize the company or the drug industry.

This lack of accountability warrants particular concern because of the enormous power corporations wield in modern society. Many large companies, like Walmart, Toyota, or ExxonMobil, generate and spend more money in a year than all but a handful of the world's countries. If these companies suddenly began to vigorously pursue their own social agendas, their influence might well rival, and perhaps undermine, that of their national government. In a country like the United States, founded on the principles of limited government and the balance of powers, too much corporate involvement in social affairs might well present substantial problems. Without clear guidelines and accountability, companies pursuing their private visions of socially responsible behavior might well distort the entire process of governance.

There is a clear alternative to corporations engaging in socially responsible action. If society wishes to increase the resources devoted to needy causes, it has the power to do so. Let the corporations seek profits without the burden of a social agenda, let the consumers vote in the marketplace for the products and services they desire, and let the government tax a portion of corporate profits for socially beneficial causes.

Expertise
although a corporation may have a high level of expertise in selling its goods and services, there is absolutely no guarantee that any promotion of social activities will be carried on with the same degree of competence

Expertise Even though a corporation has an **expertise** in producing and selling its product, it may not possess a talent for recognizing or managing socially useful activities. Corporations become successful in the market because they can identify and meet the needs of their customers.

Nothing suggests that this talent spills over into nonbusiness arenas. In fact, critics of corporate participation in social activities worry that corporations will prove unable to distinguish the true needs of society from their own narrow self-interests.

Arguments in Favor of Social Responsibility [2-4d]

First, it should be recognized that even the critics of business acknowledge that the prime responsibility of business is to make a reasonable return on its investment by producing a quality product at a reasonable price. They do not suggest that business entities be charitable institutions. They do assert, however, that business has certain obligations beyond making a profit or not harming society. Such critics contend that business must help to resolve societal problems, and they offer a number of arguments in support of their position.

The social contract
because society allows for the creation of corporations and gives them special rights, including a grant of limited liability, corporations owe a responsibility to society

Stakeholder model
corporations have fiduciary duty to all of their stakeholders, not just their stockholders

The Social Contract   Society creates corporations and gives them a special social status, including the granting of limited liability, which insulates owners from liability for debts their organizations incur. Supporters of social roles for corporations assert that limited liability and other rights granted to companies carry a responsibility: corporations, just like other members of society, must contribute to its betterment. Therefore, companies owe a moral debt to society to contribute to its overall well-being. Society needs a host of improvements, such as pollution control, safe products, a free marketplace, quality education, cures for illness, and freedom from crime. Corporations can help in each of these areas. Granted, deciding which social needs deserve corporate attention is difficult; however, this challenge does not lessen a company's obligation to choose a cause. Corporate America cannot ignore the multitude of pressing needs that remain, despite the efforts of government and private charities.

A derivative of the social contract theory is the **stakeholder model** for the societal role of the business corporation. Under the stakeholder model, a corporation has fiduciary responsibilities—duty of utmost loyalty and good faith—to all of its stakeholders, not just its stockholders. Historically, the stockholder model for the role of business has been the norm. Under this theory, a corporation is viewed as private property owned by and for the benefit of its owners—the stockholders of the corporation. (For a full discussion of this legal model, see Chapter 35.) The stakeholder model, on the other hand, holds that corporations are responsible to society at large and more directly to all those constituencies on which they depend for their survival. Thus, it is argued that a corporation should be managed for the benefit of all of its stakeholders—stockholders, employees, customers, suppliers, and managers, as well as the local communities in which it operates. (See Figure 2-2 for the stakeholder model of corporate responsibility; compare it with Figure 35-1.)

Figure 2-2 The Stakeholder Model

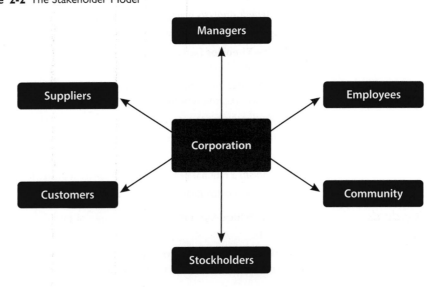

Less government regulation
by taking a more proactive role in addressing society's problems, corporations create a climate of trust and respect that has the effect of reducing government regulation

Less Government Regulation   According to another argument in favor of corporate social responsibility, the more responsibly companies act, the less the government must regulate them. This idea, if accurate, would likely appeal to those corporations that typically view regulation with distaste, perceiving it as a crude and expensive way of achieving social goals. To them, regulation often imposes inappropriate, overly broad rules that hamper productivity and require extensive recordkeeping procedures to document compliance. If companies can use more flexible, voluntary methods of meeting a social norm, such as pollution control, then government will be less tempted to legislate norms.

The argument can be taken further. Not only does anticipatory corporate action lessen the likelihood of government regulation, but also social involvement by companies creates a climate of trust and respect that reduces the overall inclination of government to interfere in company business. For example, a government agency is much more likely to show some leniency toward a socially responsible company than toward one that ignores social plights.

Long-run profits
corporate involvement in social causes creates goodwill, which simply makes good business sense

Long-Run Profits   Perhaps the most persuasive argument in favor of corporate involvement in social causes is that such involvement actually makes good business sense. Consumers often support good corporate images and avoid bad ones. For example, consumers generally prefer to patronize stores with "easy return" policies. Even though the law does not require such policies, companies institute them because they create goodwill—an intangible though indispensable asset for ensuring repeat customers. In the long run, enhanced goodwill often rebounds to stronger profits. Moreover, corporate actions to improve the well-being of their communities make these communities more attractive to citizens and more profitable for business.

CHAPTER SUMMARY

Definitions

Ethics study of what is right or good for human beings

Business Ethics study of what is right and good in a business setting

Ethical Theories

Ethical Fundamentalism individuals look to a central authority or set of rules to guide them in ethical decision making

Ethical Relativism asserts that actions must be judged by what individuals subjectively feel is right or wrong for themselves

Situational Ethics one must judge a person's actions by first putting oneself in the actor's situation

Utilitarianism moral actions are those that produce the greatest net pleasure compared with net pain

- *Act Utilitarianism* assesses each separate act according to whether it maximizes pleasure over pain
- *Rule Utilitarianism* supports rules that on balance produce the greatest pleasure for society
- *Cost-Benefit Analysis* quantifies the benefits and costs of alternatives

Deontology holds that actions must be judged by their motives and means as well as their results

Social Ethics Theories focus on a person's obligations to other members in society and on the individual's rights and obligations within society

- *Social Egalitarians* believe that society should provide all its members with equal amounts of goods and services regardless of their relative contributions
- *Distributive Justice* stresses equality of opportunity rather than results
- *Libertarians* stress market outcomes as the basis for distributing society's rewards

Other Theories

- *Intuitionism* a rational person possesses inherent power to assess the correctness of actions
- *Good Person* individuals should seek out and emulate good role models

Ethical Standards in Business

Choosing an Ethical System Kohlberg's stages of moral development is a widely accepted model (see Figure 2-1)

Corporations as Moral Agents because a corporation is a statutorily created entity, it is not clear whether it should be held morally responsible

Ethical Responsibilities of Business

Regulation of Business government regulation has been necessary because all the conditions for perfect competition have not been satisfied and free competition cannot by itself achieve other societal objectives

Corporate Governance vast amounts of wealth and power have become concentrated in a small number of corporations, which in turn are controlled by a small group of corporate officers

Arguments Against Social Responsibility

- *Profitability* because corporations are artificial entities established for profit-making activities, their only social obligation should be to return as much money as possible to shareholders
- *Unfairness* whenever corporations engage in social activities, such as supporting the arts or education, they divert funds rightfully belonging to shareholders and/or employees to unrelated third parties
- *Accountability* a corporation is subject to less public accountability than public bodies are
- *Expertise* although a corporation may have a high level of expertise in selling its goods and services, there is absolutely no guarantee that any promotion of social activities will be carried on with the same degree of competence

Arguments in Favor of Social Responsibility

- *The Social Contract* because society allows for the creation of corporations and gives them special rights, including a grant of limited liability, corporations owe a responsibility to society
- *Less Government Regulation* by taking a more proactive role in addressing society's problems, corporations create a climate of trust and respect that has the effect of reducing government regulation
- *Long-Run Profits* corporate involvement in social causes creates goodwill, which simply makes good business sense

QUESTIONS

1. You have an employee who has a chemical imbalance in the brain that causes him to be severely unstable. The medication that is available to deal with this schizophrenic condition is extremely powerful and decreases the taker's life span by one to two years for every year that the user takes it. You know that his doctors and family believe that it is in his best interest to take the medication. What course of action should you follow?

2. You have a very shy employee who is from another country. After a time, you notice that the quality of her performance is deteriorating rapidly. You find an appropriate time to speak with her and determine that she is extremely distraught. She tells you that her family has arranged a marriage for her and that she refuses to obey their contract. She further states to you that she is thinking about committing suicide. Two weeks later, after her poor performance continues, you determine that she is on the verge of a nervous breakdown; and once again she informs you that she is going to commit suicide.

   What should you do? Consider further that you can petition a court to have her involuntarily committed to a mental hospital. You know, however, that her family would consider such a commitment an extreme insult and that they might seek retribution. Does this prospect alter your decision?

3. You receive a telephone call from a company you never do business with requesting a reference on one of your employees, Mary Sunshine. You believe Mary performs in a generally incompetent manner, and you would be delighted to see her take another job. You give her a glowing reference. Is this right? Explain.

4. You have just received a report suggesting that a chemical your company uses in its manufacturing process is very dangerous. You have not read the report, but you are generally aware of its contents. You believe that the chemical can be replaced fairly easily, but that if word gets out, panic may set in among employees and community members. A reporter asks if you have seen the report, and you say no. Is your behavior right or wrong? Explain.

5. You and Joe Jones, your neighbor and friend, bought lottery tickets at the corner drugstore. While watching the lottery drawing on television with you that night, Joe leaped from the couch, waved his lottery ticket, and shouted, "I've got the winning number!" Suddenly, he clutched his chest, keeled over, and died on the spot. You are the only living person who knows that Joe, not you, bought the winning ticket. If you substitute his ticket for yours, no one will know of the switch and you will be $10 million richer. Joe's only living relative is a rich aunt whom he despised. Will you switch his ticket for yours? Explain.

6. Omega, Inc., a publicly held corporation, has assets of $100 million and annual earnings in the range of $13 to $15 million. Omega owns three aluminum plants, which are profitable, and one plastics plant, which is losing $4 million a year. Because of its very high operating costs, the plastics plant shows no sign of ever becoming profitable, and there is no evidence that the plant and the underlying real estate will increase in value. Omega decides to sell the plastics plant. The only bidder for the plant is Gold, who intends to use the plant for a new purpose: to introduce automation, and to replace all existing employees. Would it be ethical for Omega to turn down Gold's bid and keep the plastics plant operating indefinitely, for the purpose of preserving the employees' jobs? Explain.

7. You are the sales manager of a two-year-old electronics firm. At times, the firm has seemed on the brink of failure, but recently it has begun to be profitable. In large part, the profitability is due to the aggressive and talented sales force you have recruited. Two months ago, you hired Alice North, an honors graduate from the State University, who decided that she was tired of the Research Department and wanted to try sales.

Almost immediately after you sent Alice out for training with Brad West, your best salesperson, he began reporting to you an unexpected turn of events. According to Brad, "Alice is terrific: she's confident, smooth, and persistent. Unfortunately, a lot of our buyers are good old boys who just aren't comfortable around young, bright women. Just last week, Hiram Jones, one of our biggest customers, told me that he simply won't continue to do business with 'young chicks' who think they invented the world. It's not that Alice is a know-it-all. She's not. It's just that these guys like to booze it up a bit, tell some off-color jokes, and then get down to business. Alice doesn't drink, and, although she never objects to the jokes, it's clear she thinks they're offensive." Brad felt that several potential deals had fallen through "because the mood just wasn't right with Alice there." Brad added, "I don't like a lot of these guys' styles myself, but I go along to make the sales. I just do not think Alice is going to make it."

When you call Alice in to discuss the situation, she concedes the accuracy of Brad's report but indicates that she's not to blame and insists that she be kept on the job. You feel committed to equal opportunity but don't want to jeopardize your company's ability to survive. What should you do?

8. Major Company subcontracted the development of part of a large technology system to Start-up Company, a small corporation specializing in custom computer systems. The contract, which was a major breakthrough for Start-up Company and crucial to its future, provided for an initial development fee and subsequent progress payments, as well as a final date for completion.

Start-up Company provided Major Company with periodic reports indicating that everything was on schedule. After several months, however, the status reports stopped coming, and the company missed delivery of the schematics, the second major milestone. As an in-house technical consultant for Major Company, you visited Start-up Company and found not only that it was far behind schedule but also that it had lied about its previous progress. Moreover, you determined that this slippage put the schedule for the entire project in severe jeopardy. The cause of Start-up's slippage was the removal of personnel from your project to work on short-term contracts to obtain money to meet the weekly payroll.

Your company decided that you should stay at Start-up Company to monitor its work and to assist in the design of the project. After six weeks and some progress, Start-up is still way behind its delivery dates. Nonetheless, you are now familiar enough with the project to complete it in-house with Major's personnel.

Start-up is still experiencing severe cash flow problems and repeatedly requests payment from Major. But your CEO, furious with Start-up's lies and deceptions, wishes to "bury" Start-up and finish the project using Major Company's internal resources. She knows that withholding payment to Start-up will put it out of business. What do you do? Explain.

9. A customer requested certain sophisticated tests on equipment he purchased from your factory. Such tests are very expensive and must be performed by a third party. The equipment was tested as requested and met all of the industry standards, but showed anomalies that could not be explained. Though the problem appeared to be very minor, you decided to inspect the unit to try to understand the test data—a very expensive and time-consuming process. You informed the customer of this decision. A problem was found, but it was minor and was highly unlikely ever to cause the unit to fail. Rebuilding the equipment would be very expensive and time-consuming; moreover, notifying the customer that you were planning to rebuild the unit would also put your overall manufacturing procedures in question. Should you fix the problem, ship the equipment as is, or inform the customer?

10. You are a project manager for a company making a major proposal to a Middle Eastern country. Your major competition is from Japan.
a. Your local agent, who is closely tied to a very influential sheikh, would receive a 5 percent commission if the proposal were accepted. Near the date for the decision, the agent asks you for $150,000 to grease the skids so that your proposal is accepted. What do you do?
b. What do you do if, after you say no, the agent goes to your vice president, who provides the money?
c. Your overseas operation learns that most other foreign companies in this Middle Eastern location bolster their business by exchanging currency on the gray market. You discover that your division is twice as profitable as budgeted due to the amount of domestic currency you have received on the gray market. What do you do?

BUSINESS ETHICS CASES

The business ethics cases that follow are based on the kinds of situations that companies regularly face when conducting business. You should first read each case carefully and in its entirety before attempting to analyze it. Second, you should identify the most important ethical issues arising from the situation. Often it is helpful to prioritize these issues. Third, you should identify the viable options for addressing these issues and the ethical implications of the identified options. This might include examining the options from the perspectives of the various ethical theories as well as the affected stakeholders. Fourth, you should reach a definite resolution of the ethical issues by choosing what you think is the best option. You should have a well-articulated rationale for your resolution. Finally, develop a strategy for implementing your resolution.

PHARMAKON DRUG COMPANY

Background

William Wilson, senior vice president of research, development, and medical (RD&M) at Pharmakon Drug Company, received both his Ph.D. in biochemistry and his M.D. from the University of Oklahoma. Upon completion of his residency, Dr. Wilson joined the faculty at Harvard Medical School. He left Harvard after five years to join the research group at Merck & Co. Three years later, he went to Burroughs-Wellcome as director of RD&M, and, after eight years, Dr. Wilson joined Pharmakon in his current position.

William Wilson has always been highly respected as a scientist, a manager, and an individual. He has also been an outstanding leader in the scientific community, particularly in the effort to attract more minorities into the field.

Pharmakon concentrates its research efforts in the areas of antivirals (with a focus on HIV), cardiovascular, respiratory, muscle relaxants, gastrointestinal, the central nervous system, and consumer health care (i.e., nonprescription or over-the-counter [OTC] medicines). Dr. Wilson is on the board of directors of Pharmakon and the company's executive committee. He reports directly to the chairman of the board and CEO, Mr. Jarred Swenstrum.

Declining Growth

During the previous eight years, Pharmakon experienced tremendous growth: 253 percent overall with yearly growth ranging from 12 percent to 25 percent. During this period, Pharmakon's RD&M budget grew from $79 million to $403 million, and the number of employees rose from 1,192 to 3,273 (see Figure 2-3). During the previous two years, however, growth in revenue and earnings had slowed considerably. Moreover, in the current year, Pharmakon's revenues of $3.55 billion and earnings before taxes of $1.12 billion were up only 2 percent from the previous year. Furthermore, both revenues and earnings are projected to be flat or declining for the next five years.

The cessation of this period's tremendous growth and the likelihood of future decline have been brought about principally by two causes. First, a number of Pharmakon's most important patents have expired and competition from generics has begun and could continue to erode its products' market shares. Second, as new types of health-care delivery organizations evolve, pharmaceutical companies' revenues and earnings will in all likelihood be adversely affected.

Problem and Proposed Solutions

In response, the board of directors has decided that the company must emphasize two conflicting goals: increase the number of new drugs brought to market and cut back on the workforce in anticipation of rising labor and marketing costs and declining revenues. Accordingly, Dr. Wilson has been instructed to cut costs significantly and to reduce his workforce by 15 percent over the next six months.

Dr. Wilson called a meeting with his management team to discuss the workforce reduction. One of his managers, Leashia Harmon, argued that the layoffs should be made "so that recent gains in minority hiring are not wiped out." The percentage of minority employees had increased from 2.7 percent eight years ago to 8.3 percent in the previous year (see Figure 2-3). The minority population in communities in which Pharmakon has major facilities has remained over the

Figure 2-3 Pharmakon Employment

Attribute/Years Ago	1	2	3	4	5	6	7	8
Total Employment	3,273	3,079	2,765	2,372	1,927	1,619	1,306	1,192
Minority	272	238	196	143	109	75	53	32
Employment	(8.35%)	(7.7%)	(7.15%)	(6.0%)	(5.7%)	(4.6%)	(4.1%)	(2.7%)
Revenue ($ million)	3,481	3,087	2,702	2,184	1,750	1,479	1,214	986
Profit ($ million)	1,106	1,021	996	869	724	634	520	340
RD&M Budget ($ million)	403	381	357	274	195	126	96	79

Figure 2-4 Pharmakon Affirmative Action Program

Pharmakon Drug Company

Equal Employment Opportunity Affirmative Action Program

POLICY

It is the policy of Pharmakon Drug Co. to provide equal employment opportunities without regard to race, color, religion, sex, national origin, sexual orientation, disability, and veteran status. The Company will also take affirmative action to employ and advance individual applicants from all segments of our society. This policy relates to all phases of employment, including, but not limited to, recruiting, hiring, placement, promotion, demotion, layoff, recall, termination, compensation, and training. In communities where Pharmakon has facilities, it is our policy to be a leader in providing equal employment for all of its citizens.

RESPONSIBILITY FOR IMPLEMENTATION

The head of each division is ultimately responsible for initiating, administering, and controlling activities within all areas of responsibility necessary to ensure full implementation of this policy.

The managers of each location or area are responsible for the implementation of this policy.

All other members of management are responsible for conducting day-to-day activities in a manner to ensure compliance with this policy.

---

years at approximately 23 percent. About 20 percent of the RD&M workforce have a Ph.D. in a physical science or in pharmacology, and another 3 percent have an M.D.

Dr. Harmon, a Ph.D. in pharmacology and head of clinical studies, is the only minority on Dr. Wilson's seven-member management team. Dr. Harmon argued that RD&M has worked long and hard to increase minority employment and has been a leader in promoting Pharmakon's affirmative action plan (see Figure 2-4). Therefore, she asserted, all layoffs should reflect this commitment, even if it meant disproportionate layoffs of nonminorities.

Dr. Anson Peake, another member of Dr. Wilson's management team and director of new products, argued that Pharmakon's RD&M division has never discharged a worker except for cause and should adhere as closely as possible to that policy by terminating individuals solely based on merit. Dr. Rachel Waugh, director of product development, pointed out that the enormous growth in employment over the last eight years—almost a trebling of the workforce—had made the company's employee performance evaluation system less than reliable. Consequently, she contended that because laying off 15 percent of her group would be extremely difficult and subjective, she preferred to follow a system of seniority.

Dr. Wilson immediately recognized that any system of reducing the workforce would be difficult to implement. Moreover, he was concerned about fairness to employees and maintaining the best qualified group to carry out the area's mission. He was very troubled by a merit or seniority system if it could not maintain the minority gains. In fact, he had even thought about the possibility of using this difficult situation to increase the percentage of minorities to bring it more in line with the minority percentage of the communities in which Pharmakon had major facilities.

MYKON'S DILEMMA

Jack Spratt, the newly appointed CEO of Mykon Pharmaceuticals, Inc., sat at his desk and scratched his head for the thousandth time that night. His friends never tired of telling him that unless he stopped this habit he would remove what little hair he had left. Nevertheless, he had good reason to be perplexed—the decisions he made would determine the future of the company and, literally, the life or death of thousands of people.

As a young, ambitious scientist, Spratt had gained international fame and considerable fortune while rising quickly through the ranks of the scientists at Mykon. After receiving a degree from the Executive MBA program at the Kenan-Flagler Business School, University of North Carolina at Chapel Hill, he assumed, in rapid succession, a number of administrative positions at the company, culminating in his appointment as CEO. But no one had told him that finding cures for previously incurable diseases would be fraught with moral dilemmas. Although it was 3:00 A.M., Spratt remained at his desk, unable to stop thinking about his difficult choices. His preoccupation was made worse by the knowledge that pressure from governments and consumers would only increase each day he failed to reach a decision. This pressure had mounted relentlessly since the fateful day he announced that Mykon had discovered the cure for AIDS. But the cure brought with it a curse: there was not enough to go around.

Background

Mykon, a major international research-based pharmaceutical group, engages in the research, development, manufacture, and marketing of human health-care products for sale in both the prescription and over-the-counter (OTC) markets. The company's principal prescription medicines include a range of products in the following areas: antiviral, neuromuscular blocking, cardiovascular, anti-inflammatory, immunosuppressive, systemic antibacterial, and central nervous system. Mykon also manufactures other products such as muscle relaxants, antidepressants, anticonvulsants, and respiratory stimulants. In addition, the company markets drugs for the treatment of congestive heart failure and the prevention of organ rejection following transplant.

Mykon's OTC business primarily consists of cough and cold preparations and several topical antibiotics. The company seeks to expand its OTC business in various ways, including the reclassification of some of its prescription drugs to OTC status. Mykon's OTC sales represented 14 percent of the company's sales during last year.

Mykon has a long tradition of excellence in research and development (R&D). The company's expenditures on R&D for the last three financial years constituted 15 percent of its sales.

Mykon focuses its R&D on the following selected therapeutic areas, listed in descending order of expenditure amount: antivirals and other antibiotics, cardiovascular, central nervous system, anticancer, anti-inflammatory, respiratory, and neuromuscular.

Mykon sells its products internationally in more than 120 countries and has a significant presence in two of the largest pharmaceutical markets—the United States and Europe—and a growing presence in Japan. It generated approximately 43 percent and 35 percent of the company's sales from the previous year in the United States and Europe, respectively. The company sells essentially the same range of products throughout the world.

Production

Mykon carries out most of its production in Rotterdam in the Netherlands and in Research Triangle Park, North Carolina, in the United States. The latter is the company's world headquarters. The company's manufacturing processes typically consist of three stages: the manufacture of active chemicals, the incorporation of these chemicals into products designed for use by the consumer, and packaging. The firm has an ongoing program of capital expenditure to provide up-to-date production facilities and relies on advanced technology, automation, and computerization of its manufacturing capability to help maintain its competitive position.

Production facilities are also located in ten other countries to meet the needs of local markets and to overcome legal restrictions on the importation of finished products. These facilities principally engage in product formulation and packaging, although plants in certain countries manufacture active chemicals. Last year, Mykon had more than seventeen thousand employees, 27 percent of whom were in the United States. Approximately 21 percent of Mykon's employees were engaged in R&D, largely in the Netherlands and the United States. Although unions represent a number of the firm's employees, the firm has not experienced any significant labor disputes in recent years, and it considers its employee relations to be good.

Research and Development

In the pharmaceutical industry, R&D is both expensive and prolonged, entailing considerable uncertainty. The process of producing a commercial drug typically takes between eight and twelve years as it proceeds from discovery through development to regulatory approval and finally to the product launch. No assurance exists that new compounds will survive the development process or obtain the requisite regulatory approvals. In addition, research conducted by other pharmaceutical companies may lead at any time to the introduction of competing or improved treatments.

Last year Mykon incurred approximately 95 percent of its R&D expenditures in the Netherlands and the United States. Figure 2-5 sets out the firm's annual expenditure on R&D in dollars and as a percentage of sales for each of the last three financial years.

Figure 2-5 Mykon R&D Expenditures

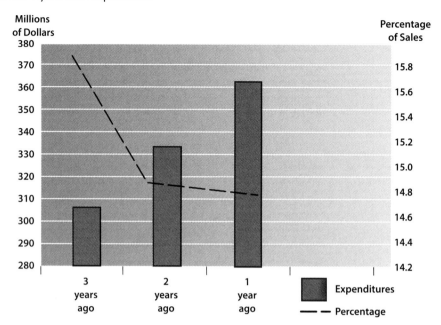

Jack Spratt

> Every society, every institution, every company, and most important, every individual should follow those precepts that society holds most dear. The pursuit of profits must be consistent with and subordinate to these ideals, the most important of which is the Golden Rule. To work for the betterment of humanity is the reason I became a scientist in the first place. As a child, Banting and Best were my heroes. I could think of no vocation that held greater promise to help mankind. Now that I am CEO I intend to have these beliefs included in our company's mission statement.

These sentiments, expressed by Jack Spratt in a newsmagazine interview, capture the intensity and drive that animate the man. None who knew him was surprised when he set out years ago—fueled by his prodigious energy, guided by his brilliant mind, and financed by Mykon—for the inner reaches of the Amazon Basin to find naturally occurring medicines. Spratt considered it to be his manifest destiny to discover the cure for some dread disease.

His search was not totally blind. Some years earlier, Frans Berger, a well-known but eccentric scientist, had written extensively about the variety of plant life and fungi that flourished in the jungles of the Bobonaza River region deep in the Amazon watershed. Although he spent twenty years there and discovered nothing of medical significance, the vast number and intriguing uniqueness of his specimens convinced Spratt that it was just a matter of time before a major breakthrough would occur.

Spratt also had some scientific evidence. While working in Mykon's laboratory to finance his graduate education in biology and genetics, Spratt and his supervisors had noticed that several fungi could not only restore damaged skin but, when combined with synthetic polymers, had significant effects on internal cells. Several more years of scientific expeditions and investigations proved promising enough for Mykon to send Spratt and a twenty-person exploration team to the Amazon Basin for two years. Two years became five, and the enormous quantity of specimens sent back eventually took over an entire wing of the company's sizable laboratories in Research Triangle Park, North Carolina.

Upon Spratt's return, he headed up a group of Mykon scientists who examined the Amazonian fungi for pharmacological activity. After several years of promising beginnings and disappointing endings, they discovered that one fungus destroyed the recently identified virus HIV. Years later, the company managed to produce enough of the drug (code named Sprattalin) derived from the fungus to inform the Food and Drug Administration (FDA) that it was testing what appeared to be a cure for HIV. It was the happiest moment of Jack Spratt's life. The years of determined effort, not to mention the $800 million Mykon had invested, would now be more than fully rewarded.

Spratt's joy was short-lived, though. Public awareness of the drug quickly spread, and groups pressured the FDA to shorten or eliminate its normal approval process, which ordinarily takes more than seven years. People dying from the virus's effects demanded immediate access to the drug.

The Drug

Mirroring the insidiousness of HIV itself, the structure of Sprattalin is extraordinarily complex. Consequently, it takes four to seven months to produce a small quantity, only 25 percent of which is usable. It is expensive; each unit of Sprattalin costs Mykon $20,000 to produce. The projected dosage ranges from ten units for asymptomatic HIV-positive patients who have normal white blood cell counts to fifty units for patients with low white blood cell counts and full-blown AIDS. The drug appears to eliminate the virus from all patients regardless of their stage of the disease. However, it does not have any restorative effect on patients' compromised immune systems. Accordingly, it is expected that asymptomatic HIV-positive patients will revert to their normal life expectancies. It is not clear what the life expectancy will be of patients with full-blown AIDS, although it is almost certain that their life expectancy would be curtailed.

Supply of Sprattalin The company has estimated that the first two years of production would yield enough Sprattalin to cure 6 percent of all asymptomatic HIV-positive patients. Alternatively, the supply would be sufficient to treat 4 percent of all patients with full-blown AIDS. Children constitute 10 percent of all people living with HIV/AIDS. See Figures 2-6 and 2-7 for statistics on the HIV/AIDS epidemic.

Interested parties have argued that the solution to production problems is clear: build larger facilities. However, even with production levels as low as they are, the bottleneck in supply occurs elsewhere. The fungus on which the whole process depends is incredibly rare, growing only in two small regions near Jatun Molino, Ecuador, along the Bobonaza River. At current

Figure 2-6 Global Summary of the AIDS Epidemic

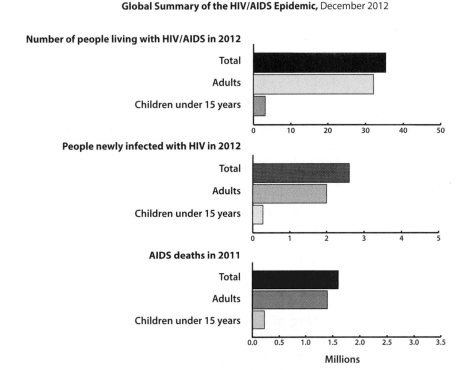

Global Summary of the HIV/AIDS Epidemic, December 2012

Source: World Health Organization, HIV/AIDS Department (March 2014).

Figure 2-7 Regional Statistics for HIV and AIDS End of 2012

Region	Adults and Children Living with HIV/AIDS	Adults and Children Newly Infected	Adult Prevalence	AIDS-Related Deaths in Adults and Children
Sub-Saharan Africa	25.0 million	1.6 million	4.7%	1.2 million
North Africa & Middle East	260,000	32,000	0.1%	17,000
South and South-East Asia	3.9 million	270,000	0.3%	220,000
East Asia	880,000	81,000	0.1%	41,000
Oceania	51,000	2,100	0.2%	1,200
Latin America	1.5 million	86,000	0.4%	52,000
Caribbean	250,000	12,000	1.0%	11,000
Eastern Europe & Central Asia	1.3 million	130,000	0.7%	91,000
North America	1.3 million	48,000	0.5%	20,000
Western & Central Europe	860,000	29,000	0.2%	7,600
Global Total	35.3 million	2.3 million	0.8%	1.6 million

Source: World Health Organization, HIV/AIDS Department (March 2014).

harvesting rates, scientists predict that all known deposits will be depleted in three years, and many of them insist that production should be scaled back to allow the fungus to regenerate itself.

Presently there are no known methods of cultivating the fungus in the laboratory. Apparently, the delicate ecology that allows it to exist in only one region of the earth is somehow distressed enough by either transport or lab conditions to render it unable to grow and produce the drug's precursor. Scientists are feverishly trying to discover those factors that will support successful culture. However, with limited quantities of the starting material and most of that pressured into production, the company has enjoyed no success in this endeavor. Because of Sprattalin's complexity, attempts to synthesize the drug have failed completely, mainly because it is not known how the drug works; thus, Sprattalin's effectiveness remains shrouded in mystery.

Allocation of Sprattalin In response to the insufficient supply, a number of powerful consumer groups have made public their suggestions regarding the allocation of Sprattalin. One proposition advanced would use medical records to establish a waiting list of possible recipients based on the length of time they have been in treatment for the virus. The argument is that those people who have waited the longest and are most in danger of dying should be the first to find relief.

Other groups propose an opposite approach, arguing that because supply is so drastically short, Mykon should make Sprattalin available only to asymptomatic HIV patients. They require the least concentrations of the drug to become well, thus extending the drug's supply. They also have the greatest likelihood of returning to full life expectancies. Under this proposal, people who have full-blown AIDS would be ineligible for treatment. Such patients have previously come to terms with their impending mortality, have fewer psychological adjustments to make, and represent, on a dosage basis, two to five healthier patients. In meting the drug out in this manner, proponents argue, the drug can more readily meet the highest public health objectives to eradicate the virus and prevent further transmission.

Others propose that only patients who contracted the virus through no fault of their own should have priority. This approach would first make Sprattalin available to children who were born with the virus, hemophiliacs and others who got the virus from blood transfusions, rape victims, and health-care workers.

One member of Sprattalin's executive committee has suggested a free market approach: the drug should go to the highest bidder.

Pricing of Sprattalin In addition to supply problems, Mykon has come under considerable criticism for its proposed pricing structure. Because of extraordinarily high development and production costs, the company has tentatively priced the drug at levels unattainable for most people afflicted with HIV. Perhaps never before in the history of medicine has the ability to pay been so starkly presented as those who can pay will live, while those who cannot pay will die.

Even at these prices, though, demand far exceeds supply. Jack Spratt and the rest of the Mykon executives predict that the company could easily sell available supplies at twice the proposed price.

A growing number of Mykon executives disagree with the passive stance the company has taken in pricing the product. In their view, a 20 percent markup represents a meager return for the prolonged risk and high levels of spending that the company incurred to develop the drug. Moreover, it leaves little surplus for future investment. Furthermore, eight years is too long to amortize the R&D expenses because Sprattalin, though the first, is unlikely to be the last anti-HIV drug, now that Mykon has blazed a path. Other, more heavily capitalized companies are racing to reverse engineer the drug, and the availability of competing drugs remains only a matter of time. Accordingly, the company cannot realistically count on an eight-year window of opportunity.

Foreign markets further exacerbate the pricing perplexity. Other countries, with less privatized health care, have already promised their citizens access to Sprattalin at any price. Some industrial countries, for instance, are willing to pay up to $2 million per patient. They do not, however, wish to subsidize the drug for the United States. At the same time, some voices in the United States insist that supplies should go first to U.S. citizens.

On the other hand, countries with the most severe concentration of the HIV infection cannot afford to pay even Mykon's actual costs. Jack Spratt feels a very real moral obligation to help at least some of these people, whether they can pay or not.

Making the Decision

In the past few months, Jack Spratt had seen many aspects of the most important project in his life become not only public knowledge but also public domain. Because of the enormous social and political consequences of the discovery, it is unlikely that the government will allow Mykon to control the destiny of either Sprattalin or ultimately the company.

Addressing the public's concern over access to the drug while ensuring future prosperity of his company had become like walking a tightrope with strangers holding each end of the rope. He knew of no way to satisfy everyone. As Jack Spratt sat at his desk, sleep remained an eon away.

OLIVER WINERY, INC.

Background

Paul Oliver, Sr., immigrated to the United States from Greece. After working for several wineries, he started Oliver Winery, Inc., which eventually found a market niche in nonvarietal jug wines. Through mass-marketing techniques, the company established a substantial presence in this segment of the market. Ten years ago, Paul, Jr., joined the firm after receiving a degree in enology (the study of wine making). He convinced his father of the desirability of entering a different segment of the wine market: premium varietals. To do this, the company needed a large infusion of capital to purchase appropriate vineyards. Reluctantly, Paul, Sr., agreed to take the company public. The initial public offering succeeded, and 40 percent of the company's stock went into outsiders' hands. Also, for the first time, outsiders served on the board of directors. Although Paul, Jr., wanted to use a new name for the premium varietal to appeal to a more upscale market, his father insisted on using the name Oliver.

Board Meeting

The board of directors met, along with Janet Stabler, the director of marketing of Oliver Winery, Inc. The following directors were in attendance:

Paul Oliver, Sr.,
    chairman of the board, founder of the company
Paul Oliver, Jr., CEO,
    has an advanced degree in enology

Cyrus Abbott, CFO,
    has an MBA
Arlene Dale, comptroller,
    has a CPA with a master's degree in accounting
Raj Ray, COO,
    has a master's degree in industrial engineering
LaTasha Lane, vice president legal,
    has a J.D. degree
Elisabeth Constable, union representative to the board,
    has a GED degree
Rev. John W. Calvin, outside director,
    has a Doctor of Divinity degree
Carlos Menendez, outside director,
    has an MFA degree

Oliver, Sr.: The next item on the agenda is a proposal to develop a new line of wines. Janet Stabler will briefly present the proposal.

Stabler: Thank you. The proposal is to enter the fortified wine market. It's the only type of wine in which unit sales are increasing. We'll make the wines cheaply and package them in pint bottles with screw-on caps. Our chief competitors are Canandaigua with Richard's Wild Irish Rose, Gallo with Thunderbird and Night Train Express, and Mogen David with MD 20/20. We'll market the wine with little or no media advertising by strategically sampling the product to targeted consumers. That's it in a nutshell.

Oliver, Sr.: Any questions before we vote?

Menendez: Who'll buy this wine?

Calvin: From what I know about the consumers of your competitors, it appears to me that it's bought by homeless winos.

Stabler: Not entirely. For example, pensioners on a fixed income would find the price of the wine appealing. Thunderbird has been recently introduced into England and has become very popular with the yuppie crowd.

Calvin: Then why put it in pint bottles?

Stabler: For the convenience of consumers.

Menendez: Why would pensioners want a small bottle?

Calvin: Homeless people want it in pints so they can fit it in their hip pockets. They obviously don't have a wine cellar to lay away their favorite bottles of Mad Dog.

Stabler: The pint size also keeps the price as low as possible.

Calvin: Translation: The homeless don't have to panhandle as long before they can make a purchase. Also, why would you increase the alcoholic content to 18 percent and make it so sweet if it weren't for the wino market?

Stabler: Many people like sweet dessert wines and 18 percent is not that much more than other types of wines that have 12 percent alcohol.

Menendez: Is it legal?

Lane: Sure. We sell to the retailers. It may be against the law to sell to intoxicated persons, but that's the retailers' business. We cannot control what they do.

Calvin: Isn't this product intended for a perpetually intoxicated audience that many people consider to be ill? Wouldn't we be taking advantage of their illness by selling highly sugared alcohol that suppresses their appetite? I've spoken to drinkers who claim to live on a gallon of this type of product a day.

Oliver, Jr.: What will this do to our image? We're still trying to get our premium wines accepted.

Stabler: Of course we won't use the Oliver name on these wines. We will use another name.

Menendez: Is it okay to do that?

Stabler: Why not? Canandaigua, Gallo, and Mogen David all do the same thing. None of them put their corporate name on this low-end product.

Abbott: We're getting away from the crux of the matter. Profit margins would be at least 10 percent higher on this line than our others. Moreover, unit sales might increase over time. Our other lines are stagnant or decreasing. The public shareholders are grousing.

Dale: Not to mention that our stock options have become almost worthless. I'm only a few years from retirement. We need to increase the profitability of the company.

Ray: Operationally, this proposal is a great fit. We can use the grapes we reject from the premium line. It will also insulate us from bad grape years because any grape will do for this wine. We can fill a lot of our unused capacity.

Constable: And hire back some of the workers who were laid off!

Stabler: It's a marketing dream. Just give out some samples to "bell cows."

Menendez: What are bell cows?

Stabler: Opinion leaders who will induce other consumers to switch to our brand.

Calvin: You mean wino gurus?

Oliver, Sr.: Look, if we don't do it, others will. In fact, they already have.

Abbott: And they'll get richer and we'll get poorer.

Lane: Gallo pulled out of several of these skid-row markets as did Canandaigua. Little good it did. The alcoholics just switched to malt liquor, vodka, or anything they could get their hands on.

Dale: I think our concern is misplaced. These people are the dregs of society. They contribute nothing.

Calvin: They're human beings who need help. We're profiting off their misfortune and misery.

Oliver, Sr.: We can take that up when we decide on what charities to support. Anyone opposed to the proposal?

Calvin: Is this a done deal? I believe we should contribute half of our profits from this product to support homeless shelters and other programs that benefit indigent and homeless people. If not, I must resign from this board.

Sources

Carrie Dolan, "Gallo Conducts Test to Placate Critics of Its Cheap Wine," *The Wall Street Journal*, June 16, 1989, p. B3.

Alix M. Freedman, "Winos and Thunderbird Are a Subject Gallo Doesn't Like to Discuss," *The Wall Street Journal*, February 25, 1988, p. 1.

Frank J. Prial, "Experiments by a Wine Maker Fails to Thwart Street Drunks," *The New York Times*, February 11, 1990, p. A29.

JLM, Inc.

Background

Sitting in her office, Ellen Fulbright, director of human resources (HR) for JLM, Inc., thought over the decisions confronting her. To help her decide, she mentally reviewed how they had arisen.

After receiving her MBA and J.D. degrees from a highly regarded university, she joined a prestigious New York law firm where she specialized in employment law. After seven years at the law firm, she was hired by one of the firm's clients as general counsel. When that company was acquired by JLM, she joined its legal staff and within a few years had been promoted to her current position.

Fulbright's rapid advancement resulted from her having made a positive impression on Rasheed Raven, JLM's CEO. Raven is a hard-driving, bottom-line-oriented pragmatist in his early forties. Raven, a graduate of Howard University, had begun his business career on Wall Street, which he astounded with his aggressive but successful takeover strategies. After acquiring fifteen unrelated manufacturing companies, he decided to try his hand at the turnaround business. He organized JLM as an umbrella for his acquired companies. Soon he earned the reputation as the best in the business by transforming JLM into the leader in the industry.

JLM is a highly successful turnaround company. Typically, JLM purchases companies that are in serious financial trouble and manages them until they become successful companies. At that time, JLM either retains them in its own portfolio of companies or sells them off to other enterprises.

Reference Letter Policy

About a year after Fulbright had become HR director, Raven called her into his office and showed her a newspaper article. It reported, in somewhat sensational fashion, that several defamation suits had resulted in multimillion-dollar judgments against companies that had written negative letters of references about former employees. Raven told her that he was concerned about this and that he wanted her to develop an HR policy covering letters of reference.

In researching the issue, she discovered several articles in which the authors decried the recent spate of companies that had decided to stop writing letters of reference. According to their data, they believed that these companies had overreacted to the actual risk posed by defamation suits. Based on these articles and her own inclination toward full disclosure, she proposed that the company continue to permit letters of reference but that all letters with negative comments must be reviewed by her.

Raven did not receive her proposal favorably and sought a second opinion from her old law firm. His analysis of the firm's advice was: "We get nothing but brownie points for writing reference letters, but we face the possibility of incurring the cost of a legal defense or, worse yet, a court judgment. This is a 'no-brainer.' We have no upside and all downside." Raven ordered that, henceforth, company employees would no longer write letters of reference but would simply verify dates of employment.

Although Fulbright was personally and professionally miffed by his decision, she drew up the policy statement as directed. Fulbright believed that because JLM frequently took over companies that needed immediate downsizing, this policy would be unfair and extremely detrimental to longtime employees of newly purchased companies.

Takeover of Diversified Manufacturing, Inc.

After a number of years of steady growth, Diversified Manufacturing began experiencing huge financial losses and its immediate survival was in serious doubt. After careful consideration, Raven decided that Diversified was an ideal takeover target in that its core businesses were extremely strong and presented great long-term economic viability.

Upon acquiring Diversified, JLM quickly decided that it had to rid Diversified of some of its poorly performing companies and that it had to reduce the size of Diversified's home office staff by 25 percent. Raven relentlessly orchestrated the reduction in force, but at Fulbright's urging he provided the discharged executives with above-average severance packages, including excellent outplacement services.

The Problem

The reduction in force was disruptive and demoralizing in all the usual ways. But for Fulbright there was a further complication: the "no reference letter" policy. She was extremely troubled by its application to three discharged Diversified employees and to one discharged JLM employee.

The Salacious Sales Manager Soon after taking over Diversified, Fulbright became all too aware of the story of Ken Byrd, Diversified's then national sales manager. Ken is an affable man of fifty who had been an unusually effective sales manager. Throughout his career, his sales figures had always doubled those of his peers. He achieved rapid advancement despite a fatal flaw: he is an inveterate and indiscreet womanizer. He could not control his hands, which slapped backs so well, nor his tongue, which persuaded so eloquently. He had two approaches to women. With a woman of equal or superior rank in the company, he would politely, but inexorably, attempt to sweep her off her feet. With these women, he would be extremely charming and attentive, taking great care to avoid being offensive or harassing. In contrast, with a woman of subordinate rank, he would physically harass her. Less openly, but much too often, he would come up behind a woman, reach around her, and grab her. He invariably found this amusing—his victims, however, did not.

Fulbright could not believe that such a manager had stayed employed at Diversified so long, let alone been continually promoted to positions of greater responsibility and power. As Fulbright investigated the situation, she discovered that numerous sexual harassment complaints had been filed with Diversified concerning Byrd's behavior. To protect Byrd, Diversified dealt with these complaints by providing money and undeserved promotions to the complainants to smooth over their anger. Thus, Diversified successfully kept the complaints in-house and away from the courts and the Equal Employment Opportunity Commission.

After JLM's takeover of Diversified, Fulbright quickly discharged Byrd. Her satisfaction in getting rid of him was short-lived, however. His golden tongue and stellar sales record had landed him several job offers. Her dilemma was that she was uncomfortable about unleashing this deviant on an unsuspecting new employer. But JLM's policy forbade her from writing any letters or answering questions from prospective employers.

The Fruitless Juice Melissa Cuthbertson had been a vice president in procurement for Diversified's Birch-Wood division with direct responsibility over the ordering of supplies and raw materials. Birch-Wood manufactured a full line of baby food products, including fruit juices that were labeled "100% fruit juice." To cut costs, Stanley Aker, the division's president, had arranged for an unscrupulous supplier to provide high-fructose corn syrup labeled as juice concentrate. Because standard testing in the industry was unable to detect the substitution, the company did not get caught. Emboldened, Aker gradually increased the proportion of corn syrup until there were only trace amounts of fruit juice left in the "juice." A company employee discovered the practice and after the takeover brought the matter to Fulbright's attention through JLM's internal whistle-blowing channel, which Fulbright had established. She referred the matter to Raven, who called in Aker and Cuthbertson and confronted them with the accusation. They admitted it all, explaining that nutritionally the corn syrup was equivalent to the fruit juice. But at 60 percent of the cost of fruit juice, the corn syrup made a big difference to the bottom line. Raven told them that such conduct was not permitted and that they must properly dispose of the adulterated juice.

That night Aker and Cuthbertson had the juice moved from Birch-Wood's New York warehouse and shipped to its Puerto Rico warehouse. Over the course of the next few days, the "juice" was sold in Latin America as "apple juice." Aker reported to Raven that the juice had been properly disposed of and that Birch-Wood had sustained only a small loss during that quarter. When Raven discovered the truth, he immediately discharged Aker and Cuthbertson, telling them "that if he had anything to do with it, neither of them would ever work again." Fulbright was to meet soon with Raven to discuss what should be done about Aker and Cuthbertson.

The Compassionate CFO Jackson Cobb, JLM's former chief financial officer, is a brilliant analyst. Through hard work, he had earned an excellent education that honed his innate mathematical gifts. His natural curiosity led him to read widely, and this enabled him to bring disparate facts and concepts to bear on his often-novel analyses of financial matters. But he had no interest in implementing his insights, for his only enjoyment was the process of discovering connections. Fortune—or fate—had brought him together with Raven, who is twenty years younger than Cobb. Theirs was definitely a case of opposites attracting. Raven cared little about ideas; he cared primarily about money. Cobb cared little about money; he cared primarily about ideas. Raven took Cobb's insights and translated them into action with spectacular success. Their relationship brought new meaning to the concept of synergy. When Raven formed JLM, he brought Cobb on as CFO and installed him in an adjoining office.

Their relationship continued to flourish, as did JLM's bottom line, until Cobb's wife became terminally ill. During the eighteen months she languished, Cobb spent as much time as he could taking care of her. After forty years of marriage, he was unwilling to leave her welfare to the "kindness of strangers." At his own expense, he installed a state-of-the-art communication center in his home. By virtue of computers, modems, video cameras, faxes, copiers, mobile telephones, and the like, he had available to him the same data and information as he had at his office. He could be reached by telephone at all times. But he was not in the office next to Raven; he was not present at Raven's daily breakfast meetings; he was not on the corporate jet en route to business meetings. After their many years of working together, Raven was enraged at the loss of immediate access to Cobb. He felt that Cobb had betrayed him and demanded that Cobb resume his old working hours. Cobb refused, and Raven fired him. Because of his age, Cobb was experiencing difficulty in finding new employment, and Fulbright wanted to write a letter on his behalf.

SWORD TECHNOLOGY, INC.

Background

Sitting in his office, Stephen Hag, CEO of Sword Technology, Inc., contemplated the problems that had been perplexing him for some time. They had begun when he took his company international, and they kept coming. But today he was no more successful in devising a solution than he had been previously. Slowly, his thoughts drifted to those early days years ago when he and his sister Marian started the company.

The company's first product was an investment newsletter stressing technical analysis in securities investing. A few years later, he developed what became a "killer app": a computer program that defines an entirely new market and through customer loyalty substantially dominates that market. His software program enabled investors to track their investments in stocks, bonds, and futures. By combining powerful analytical tools with an accessible graphical interface, it appealed to both professional and amateur investors. Moreover, it required users to download information from the company's database. With one of the most extensive databases and the cheapest downloading rates in the industry, the company soon controlled the U.S. market. Sword then went public through a highly successful IPO (an initial public offering of the company's common stock), and its stock is traded on the NASDAQ Stock Market. The company is required to file periodic reports with the Securities and Exchange Commission.

The company used cash from sales of software, online charges, and the IPO to try to enter the hardware side of the computer industry. It began manufacturing modems and other computer peripherals. A nagging problem, however, plagued the company's manufacturing efforts. Although Sword's modem could convert data more quickly and efficiently than most of its competitors, because of high labor costs it was unable to market its modem successfully. To reduce manufacturing costs, especially labor costs, the company decided to move its manufacturing facilities overseas. And that's when the trouble began.

Stephen's thoughts returned to the present. He reopened the folder labeled "Confidential: International Issues" and began perusing its contents.

Transfer Pricing

The first item he saw was an opinion letter from the company's tax attorney. It dealt with Excalibur Technology, the first overseas company Sword established. Excalibur, a wholly owned subsidiary of Sword, is incorporated in Tolemac, an emerging country with a rapidly growing economy. To encourage foreign investment, Tolemac taxes corporate profits at a significantly lower rate than the United States and other industrial nations. Excalibur manufactures modems for Sword pursuant to a licensing agreement under which Excalibur pays Sword a royalty equal to a specified percentage of the modems' gross sales. Excalibur sells all of its output at a fair market price to Sword, which then markets the modems in the United States. Stephen had been closely involved in structuring this arrangement and had insisted on keeping the royalty rate low to minimize taxable income for Sword. Stephen reread the opinion letter:

> Section 482 of the Internal Revenue Code authorizes the Internal Revenue Service to allocate gross income, deductions, credits, and other common allowances among two or more organizations, trades, or businesses under common ownership or control whenever it determines that this action is necessary "in order to prevent evasion of taxes or clearly to reflect the income of any such

organizations, trades, or businesses." IRS Regulation 1.482-2(e) governing the sale or trade of intangibles between related persons mandates an appropriate allocation to reflect the price that an unrelated party under the same circumstances would have paid, which normally includes profit to the seller. The Regulations provide four methods for determining an arm's-length price. In our opinion, under the only method applicable to the circumstances of Sword Technology, Inc., and Excalibur Technology, the royalty rate should be at least three times the current one. If the IRS were to reach the same conclusion, then the company would be liable for the taxes it underpaid because of the understatement of income. Moreover, the company would be liable for a penalty of either 20 percent or 40 percent of the tax deficiency, unless the company can show that it had reasonable cause and acted in good faith.

Stephen had spoken to the tax attorney at length and learned that the probability of an audit was about 10 percent and that many multinational companies play similar "games" with their transfer pricing. The attorney also told him that he believed that if the company were audited, there was at least a 90 percent probability that the IRS would agree with his conclusion and at least a 70 percent probability that it would impose a penalty. Because the dollar amount of the contingent tax liability was not an insignificant amount, Stephen had been concerned about it for the six weeks since he had received the letter.

Customs and Customs

Soon after Excalibur had manufactured the first shipment of modems, a new problem arose: getting them out of Tolemac. It took far too long to clear customs, thus undermining their carefully planned just-in-time manufacturing schedules. Stephen hired a local export broker, who distributed cash gifts to customs officials. Miraculously, the clearance time shortened and manufacturing schedules were maintained. The export broker billed the company for his services and the amount of the cash gifts. Although the broker assured Stephen that such gifts were entirely customary, Stephen was not entirely comfortable with the practice.

The Thorn in His Side

Tolemac was not Stephen's only problem. Six months after commencing operations in Tolemac, Sword began serious negotiations to enter the Liarg market. Liarg is a developing country with a large population and a larger national debt. Previously, Sword had encountered great difficulties in exporting products to Liarg. Stephen's sister, Marian, COO of Sword, took on the challenge of establishing a Liarg presence.

They decided that setting up a manufacturing facility in Liarg would achieve two objectives: greater access to the Liarg marketplace and lower-cost modems. At first, the Liarg government insisted that Sword enter into a joint venture, with the government having a 51 percent interest. Sword was unwilling to invest in such an arrangement, countering with a proposal for a wholly owned subsidiary. Marian conducted extensive negotiations with the government, assisted by a Liarg consulting firm that specialized in lobbying governmental officials. As part of these negotiations, Sword made contributions to the reelection campaigns of key Liarg legislators who were opposed to wholly owned subsidiaries of foreign corporations. After the legislators' reelection, the negotiations quickly reached a successful conclusion. On closing the contract, Sword flew several Liarg officials and their wives to Lake Tahoe for a lavish three-day celebration. All of these expenses were reported in the company's financial statements as payments for legal and consulting fees.

Marian then hired an international engineering firm to help design the manufacturing plant. Two weeks later, they submitted plans for the plant and its operations that fully complied with Liarg regulations regarding worker health and safety as well as environmental protection. But, as Marian had explained to Stephen, the plant's design fell far short of complying with U.S. requirements. Marian noted that, under the proposed design, the workers would face exposure to moderately high levels of toxic chemicals and hazardous materials. The design also would degrade the water supply of nearby towns. However, the design would generate significant savings in capital and operational costs as compared with the design used in their U.S. facility. Marian assured Stephen that all quality control systems were in place so the modems produced in this plant would be indistinguishable from their U.S. counterparts. Stephen and Marian have had long discussions about what to do about the plant.

Stephen then took from the folder an article that had appeared in a number of U.S. newspapers.

Children and Chips

A twelve-year-old Liarg child recently spoke at an international conference in New York denouncing the exploitation of children in the Liarg computer chip industry. The child informed the outraged audience that he had worked in such a plant from age four to age ten. He asserted that he was just one of many children who were so employed. He described the deplorable working conditions: poor ventilation, long hours, inadequate food, and substandard housing. The pay was low. But, because their families could not afford to keep them at home, the children were hired out to the factory owners, who especially wanted young children because their small fingers made them adept at many assembly processes.

Stephen had read the article countless times, thinking about his own children. He knew that if they set up a plant in Liarg, they would have to buy chip components from Liarg suppliers. He also knew that there would be no way for Sword to ensure that the chips had not been made with child labor.

Another labor issue also troubled Stephen. Marian told him that she had met considerable resistance from the Liarg executives they had hired when she suggested that women should be hired at the supervisory level. They maintained that it was not done and would make it impossible to hire and control a satisfactory workforce at the plant. Moreover, they insisted on hiring their relatives as supervisors. When Marian protested this nepotism, they assured her that it was customary and asserted that they could not trust anyone not related to them.

To Outsource or Not to Outsource

Once again Stephen glanced over the cost data. Sword's labor costs for supporting its database services and hardware were eviscerating the company's profits. After racking his brain endlessly, he had concluded that wherever it made financial and strategic sense Sword should utilize business process outsourcing (BPO); that is, long-term contracting out of non-core business processes to an outside provider in order to lower costs and thereby increase shareholder value.

Stephen had examined a number of potential countries on the basis of many factors, including time zone, communications infrastructure, technical training, English language skills of the workforce, and—most critically—costs. Liarg had emerged as the optimal choice. He anticipated reducing labor and associated overhead costs by 45 to 50 percent.

He planned to start by offshoring half of the call center operations, soon to be followed by a third of the low-end software development such as maintenance and coding. Assuming all went as he envisioned, he expected to move offshore back-office operations and higher-level software development. As his imagination soared, he saw the potential to amplify the company's operations with round-the-clock development.

Stephen realized that embarking on this course would result in reducing the staffing at the company's U.S. call centers. He expected he could achieve some reductions through attrition and reassignment, but considerable layoffs would be necessary. He hoped that outsourcing the low-end software development would enable the company to redeploy its software developers to higher-level and more profitable assignments. Moreover, the recent rollback in the number of visas had resulted in difficulty in hiring sufficient numbers of software developers with the necessary skills. If Sword were to offshore back-office operations, Stephen expected an impact on current employees comparable to offshoring the call centers.

On top of all these concerns had come a letter from the company's outside legal counsel regarding payments made to foreign officials.

Memorandum of Law

The Foreign Corrupt Practices Act makes it unlawful for any person, and certain foreign issuers of securities, or any of its officers, directors, employees, or agents or its stockholders acting on its behalf to offer or give anything of value directly or indirectly to any foreign official, political party, or political official for the purpose of

1. influencing any act or decision of that person or party in his or its official capacity,
2. inducing an act or omission in violation of his or its lawful duty, or
3. inducing such person or party to use its influence to affect a decision of a foreign government in order to assist the domestic concern in obtaining or retaining business.

An offer or promise to make a prohibited payment is a violation even if the offer is not accepted or the promise is not performed. The 1988 amendments explicitly excluded facilitating or expediting payments made to expedite or secure the performance of routine governmental actions by a foreign official, political party, or party official. Routine government action does not include any decision by a foreign official regarding the award of new business or the continuation of old business. The amendments also added an affirmative defense for payments that are lawful under the written laws or regulations of the foreign official's country. Violations are punishable by fines of up to $2 million for companies; individuals may be fined a maximum of $100,000 or imprisoned up to five years, or both. Moreover, under the Alternative Fines Act, the actual fine may be up to twice the benefit that the person sought to obtain by making the corrupt payment. Fines imposed upon individuals may not be paid directly or indirectly by the domestic company or other business entity on whose behalf the individuals acted. In addition, the courts may impose civil penalties of up to $16,000.

The statute also imposes internal control requirements on all reporting companies. Such companies must

1. make and keep books, records, and accounts, that in reasonable detail, accurately and fairly reflect the transactions and dispositions of the assets of the company; and
2. devise and maintain a system of internal controls that ensure that transactions are executed as authorized and recorded in conformity with generally accepted accounting principles, thereby establishing accountability with regard to assets and ensuring that access to those assets is permitted only with management's authorization.

Any person who knowingly circumvents or knowingly fails to implement a system of internal accounting controls or knowingly falsifies any book, record, or account is subject to criminal liability.

VULCAN, INC.

The Company

Vulcan, Inc., is a multinational *Fortune* 200 company engaging principally in the exploration for and extraction of minerals. It is listed on the New York Stock Exchange and has more than 615 million shares outstanding.

The Meeting (March 7)

On March 5, Stewart Myer, the company's CEO, personally telephoned Martha Bordeaux, the vice president for finance; Lamont Johnson, the chief geologist; and Natasha Bylinski, the vice president for acquisitions, to arrange a March 7 meeting at the Atlanta airport. He emphasized to each of them the need for the utmost secrecy, directing them to arrange their travel to Atlanta as a connection to other and different destinations. When they all arrived at the meeting room, Myer reemphasized the need for complete secrecy. He then asked Johnson to present his report.

The Report

Johnson read his report:

> Over the past few years we have conducted extensive aerial geophysical surveys of the areas west of the Great Plains. These revealed numerous anomalies or extreme variations in the conductivity of rocks. One appeared particularly encouraging, so late last year we began a ground geophysical survey of the southwest portion of the Z segment in Montana. This survey confirmed the presence of anomalies. Accordingly, on January 14 we drilled some core samples and sent them to our lab. The results were so extraordinarily promising that on February 10 we obtained more core samples and

had them chemically assayed. On February 25, we received the assay, which revealed an average mineral content of 1.17 percent copper and 8.6 percent zinc over 600 feet of the sample's 650-foot length.

Johnson then commented, "In my forty years in the business I have never seen such remarkable test results. On a scale of one to ten, this is an eleven."

The Reaction

Bordeaux exclaimed, "Our stock price will go through the roof!" Bylinski retorted, "So will land prices!"

The Strategy

Myer interrupted, "Look, we're not here to celebrate. There are a lot of better places to do that. We can't keep a lid on this for very long so we have to strike soon. We need to line up the right agents to acquire the land. We must fragment the acquisitions to keep the sellers in the dark. Most critical is maintaining absolute secrecy. No one else in the company must know this. I will decide who needs to know and I will tell them. It is your duty to the company to keep totally quiet. Now, let's discuss the acquisition plan."

When asked how he had managed to obtain core samples without tipping off the owners of the land, Johnson explained, "We pretended to be a motion picture company looking for locations to remake the movie *High Noon*. We drilled the samples in isolated areas and quickly filled the holes. To further cover our tracks we drilled some barren core samples from land we owned and hid the cores on our land."

The Plan

Bylinski outlined the plan to acquire the land. "We only own about 20 percent of the land we want and we have options on another 15 percent. However, we currently own none of the principal portion. So we have a lot of work to do. We will employ several agents to negotiate the purchases. We will instruct them not to disclose that they are acting for us. In fact, we will order them not to disclose they are acting for anyone. We need to acquire approximately twenty square miles of additional land."

Bordeaux asked, "What if the locals start getting curious?"

Myer replied, "I'll deal with that later if it arises."

Stock Options

On March 15, Vulcan issued stock options at $23.50 per share to thirty of its executives, including Myer, Bordeaux, Johnson, and Bylinski. At this time neither the stock option committee nor the board of directors had been informed of the strike or the pending land acquisition program.

The Rumors

While the land acquisition plan was nearing completion, rumors about a major strike by Vulcan began circulating throughout the business community. On the morning of March 20, Bordeaux read an account in a national newspaper reporting that ore samples had been sent out of Montana and inferring from that fact that Vulcan had made a rich strike. Bordeaux called Myer and told him about the article.

The Press Release

Myer prepared the following press release, which appeared in morning newspapers of general circulation on March 21:

> During the past few days the press has reported drilling activities by Vulcan and rumors of a substantial copper discovery. These reports greatly exaggerate. Vulcan has engaged in normal geophysical explorations throughout the West. We routinely send core samples to verify our visual examinations. Most of the areas drilled have been barren or marginal. When we have additional information we will issue a statement to shareholders and the public.

Figure 2-8 Stock Price of Vulcan, Inc. (note irregular intervals on time axis)

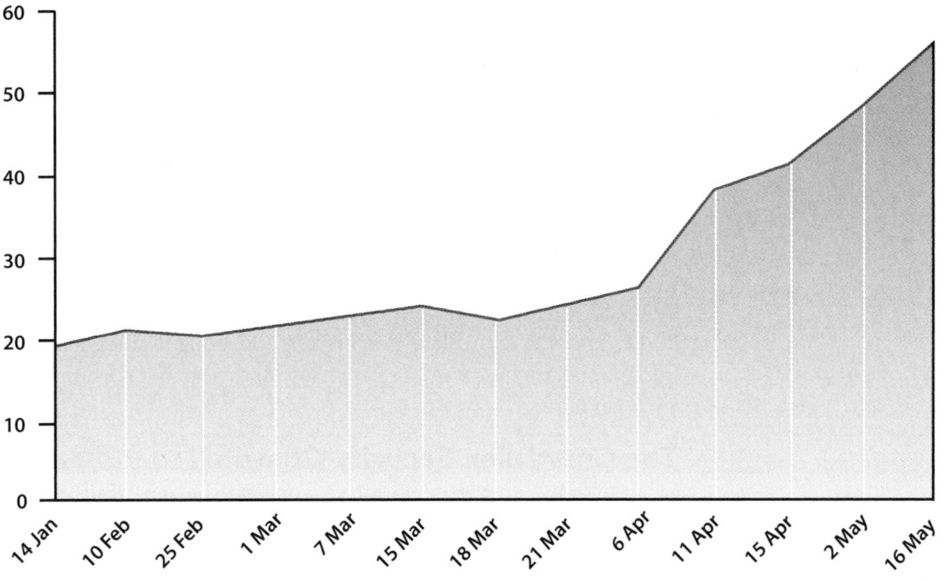

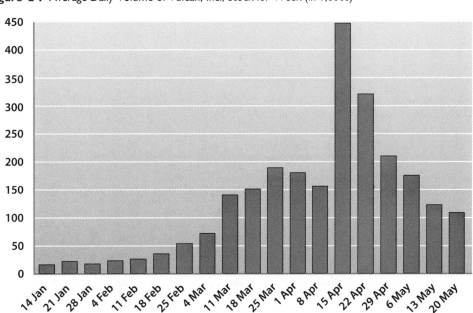

Land Acquired

On April 6, Vulcan completed its land acquisition program. It had employed seven different agents. In total, it had acquired thirty-seven parcels from twenty-two different sellers at prices ranging from $300 to $600 per acre. The land cost a total of approximately $6 million.

Official Announcement

At 10:00 A.M. on April 11, Myer released on behalf of Vulcan an official announcement of a strike in Montana containing at least 30 million tons of high-grade copper and zinc ore. The release appeared on the wire services at 10:30 A.M. The price of Vulcan stock shot up eleven points to $38 by the close of business that day and continued to rise, reaching a price of $56 on May 16. (Figures 2-8 and 2-9 show the price and volume of Vulcan stock.)

Figure 2-9 Average Daily Volume of Vulcan, Inc., Stock for Week (in 1,000s)

Loose Lips

Prior to the April 11 official announcement, a number of people purchased Vulcan stock with knowledge of the mineral discovery. Some people also purchased land adjacent to Vulcan's holdings in Montana. These purchasers included the following:

The Vulcan Executives Myer, Bordeaux, Johnson, and Bylinski each purchased shares or calls on several occasions during this time period. See Figure 2-10 for a listing of their purchases.

The Eager Eavesdropper After leaving the March 7 meeting, Bordeaux and Bylinski went to the airport lounge to wait for their flights. They excitedly—and loudly—discussed what they had learned at the meeting. Several people overheard their remarks, and one of them, Rae Bodie, immediately called her broker and bought fifteen hundred shares of Vulcan stock. Ms. Bodie also purchased a large tract of land next to Vulcan's site in Montana for approximately $600 per acre.

The Crestfallen Security Guard On March 9, Johnson went into the home office very early to finish up the exploratory work on the new find. At the elevator he encountered Celia Tidey, one of the company's security guards. Johnson knew her fairly well since they both had worked for Vulcan for more than fifteen years. Noting her despondent visage, Johnson asked her what was wrong. She related to him her tale of woe: her husband had become disabled and lost his job while her son needed an expensive medical procedure and their health insurance did not cover it. Johnson felt great empathy for her plight. He told her that big doings were afoot at Vulcan and that if she bought Vulcan stock soon she would make a lot of money in a month or so. She took her savings and bought two hundred shares of Vulcan stock, which were as many shares as she could buy.

The Avaricious Agent William Baggio, one of the agents hired to acquire the land, inferred that whatever was up had to be good for Vulcan. Accordingly, on March 21, he purchased twenty-five hundred shares of Vulcan and five thousand acres of land adjacent to the Vulcan property.

The Trusted Tippee On March 8, Myer called Theodore Griffey, his oldest and dearest friend. After getting Griffey to swear absolute confidentiality, Myer told him all the details of the strike. After hanging up the telephone, Griffey immediately purchased fifteen thousand shares of Vulcan stock. Griffey then told his father and sister about the land; both of them bought fifteen thousand shares.

Figure 2-10 Purchases of Vulcan Stock by Selected Executives

Purchaser	Date	Shares	Price	Calls	Price
Myer	Jan. 20	10,000	18.00		
	Feb. 25	10,000	20.00		
	March 2	15,000	21.25		
	March 7			5,000	22.25
	March 15			5,000	23.75
Bordeaux	March 7	10,000	22.00		
	March 15			7,500	23.75
	March 18	5,000	24.00		
Johnson	Jan. 20	5,000	18.00		
	Feb. 25	8,000	20.00		
	March 1	12,000	21.00		
	March 7	6,000	22.00		
	March 15	4,000	23.50		
Bylinski	March 7	5,000	22.00		
	March 15	3,000	23.50		
	March 18			4,000	24.25

The Scampering Stockbroker Morris Lynch, Myer's stockbroker, was intrigued by Myer's purchases of an unusually large volume of Vulcan shares. During the last two weeks of March, he put a number of his other clients into Vulcan, telling them, "I've looked at this stock and it's good for you." About a dozen of his clients purchased a total of eight thousand shares.

The Land Grab

After the official announcement on April 11, several of Vulcan's competitors began exploring the area and purchased large tracks of land, bidding up the price of land to $2,250 per acre. Both Bodie and Baggio sold their newly acquired land to Vulcan competitors at this higher price.

THE LEGAL ENVIRONMENT OF BUSINESS

Civil Dispute Resolution

Laws are a dead letter without courts to expound and define their true meaning and operation.

Alexander Hamilton
The Federalist (1787)

CHAPTER OUTCOMES

After reading and studying this chapter, you should be able to:

1. List and describe the courts in the federal court system and in a typical state court system.

2. Distinguish among exclusive federal jurisdiction, concurrent federal jurisdiction, and exclusive state jurisdiction.

3. Distinguish among (a) subject matter jurisdiction and jurisdiction over the parties and (b) the three types of jurisdiction over the parties.

4. List and explain the various stages of a civil proceeding.

5. Compare and contrast litigation, arbitration, conciliation, and mediation.

A s discussed in Chapter 1, substantive law sets forth the rights and duties of individuals and other legal entities, whereas procedural law determines how these rights are asserted. Procedural law attempts to accomplish two competing objectives: (1) to be fair and impartial and (2) to operate efficiently. The judicial process in the United States represents a balance between these two objectives as well as a commitment to the adversary system.

In the first part of this chapter, we will describe the structure and function of the federal and state court systems. The second part of this chapter deals with jurisdiction; the third part discusses civil dispute resolution, including the procedure in civil lawsuits.

THE COURT SYSTEM

Courts are impartial tribunals (seats of judgment) established by government bodies to settle disputes. A court may render a binding decision only when it has jurisdiction over the dispute and the parties to that dispute; that is, when it has a right to hear and make a judgment in a case. The United States has a dual court system: the federal government has its own independent system, as does each of the fifty states and the District of Columbia.

THE FEDERAL COURTS [3-1]

Article III of the U.S. Constitution states that the judicial power of the United States shall be vested in one Supreme Court and such lower courts as Congress may establish. Congress has established a lower federal court system consisting of a number of special courts, district courts, and courts of appeals. Judges in the federal court system are appointed for life by the President, subject to confirmation by the Senate. The structure of the federal court system is illustrated in Figure 3-1.

Figure 3-1 Federal Judicial System

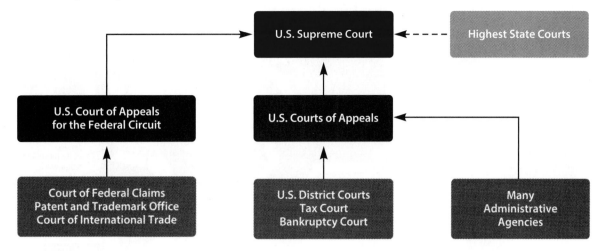

District Courts [3-1a]

District Courts

trial courts of general jurisdiction that can hear and decide most legal controversies in the federal system

The **district courts** are general trial courts in the federal system. Most federal cases begin in the district court, and it is here that issues of fact are decided. The district court is generally presided over by *one* judge, although in certain cases three judges preside. In a few cases, an appeal from a judgment or decree of a district court is taken directly to the Supreme Court. In most cases, however, appeals go to the Circuit Court of Appeals of the appropriate circuit, the decision of which is final in most cases.

Congress has established ninety-four federal judicial districts, each of which is located entirely in a particular state. All states have at least one district; about half of the states contain more than one district. For instance, California and New York each have four districts, Illinois has three, and Wisconsin has two, while about half of the states each make up a single district.

Courts of Appeals [3-1b]

Courts of Appeals

hear appeals from the district courts and review orders of certain administrative agencies

Congress has established twelve judicial circuits (eleven numbered circuits plus the D.C. circuit), each having a court known as the **Court of Appeals**, which primarily hears appeals from the district courts located within its circuit (see Figure 3-2). In addition, these courts review decisions of many administrative agencies, the Tax Court, and the Bankruptcy Courts. Congress has also established the U.S. Court of Appeals for the Federal Circuit, which is discussed later in the section on "Special Courts." The U.S. Courts of Appeals generally hear cases in panels of three judges, although in some instances all judges of the circuit will sit *en banc* to decide a case.

Reverse

set aside the lower court's judgment

Modify

change the lower court's judgment

Remand

send the case back to the lower court

Affirm

uphold the lower court's judgment

The function of appellate courts is to examine the record of a case on appeal and to determine whether the trial court committed prejudicial error (error substantially affecting the appellant's rights and duties). If so, the appellate court will **reverse** or **modify** the judgment of the lower court and, if necessary, **remand** or send it back to the lower court for further proceeding. If there is no prejudicial error, the appellate court will **affirm** the decision of the lower court.

The Supreme Court [3-1c]

The Supreme Court

the nation's highest court whose principal function is to review decisions of the Federal Courts of Appeals and the highest state courts

The nation's highest tribunal is the U.S. **Supreme Court**, which consists of nine justices (a Chief Justice and eight Associate Justices) who sit as a group in Washington, D.C. A quorum consists of any six justices. In certain types of cases, the U.S. Supreme Court has original jurisdiction (the right to hear a case first). The Court's principal function, nonetheless, is to review decisions of the Federal Courts of Appeals and, in some instances, decisions involving federal law resolved by

Figure 3-2 Circuit Courts of the United States

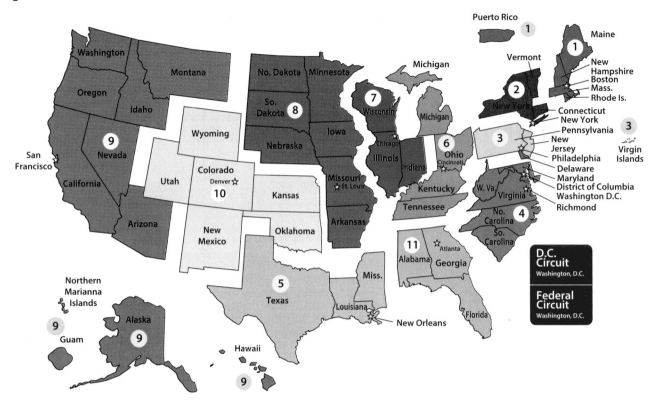

Source: Administrative Office of The United States Courts, January 1983.

the highest state courts. Cases reach the Supreme Court under its appellate jurisdiction by one of two routes. Very few come by way of **appeal by right**. The Court must hear these cases if one of the parties requests the review. In 1988, Congress enacted legislation that almost completely eliminated the right to appeal to the U.S. Supreme Court.

The second way in which the Supreme Court may review a decision of a lower court is by the discretionary **writ of *certiorari***, which requires a lower court to produce the records of a case it has tried. Now almost all cases reaching the Supreme Court come to it by means of writs of *certiorari*. If four Justices vote to hear the case, the Court grants writs when there is a federal question of substantial importance or a conflict in the decisions of the U.S. Circuit Courts of Appeals. Only a small percentage of the petitions to the Supreme Court for review by *certiorari* are granted, however, because the Court uses the writ as a device to choose which cases it wishes to hear.

Appeal by right
mandatory review by a higher court

Writ of *certiorari*
discretionary review by a higher court

Special Courts [3-1d]

Special courts
have jurisdiction over cases in a particular area of federal law and include the U.S. Court of Federal Claims, the Tax Court, the U.S. Bankruptcy Courts, and the U.S. Court of Appeals for the Federal Circuit

The **special courts** in the federal judicial system include the U.S. Court of Federal Claims, the U.S. Bankruptcy Courts, the U.S. Tax Court, and the U.S. Court of Appeals for the Federal Circuit. These courts have jurisdiction over particular subject matter. The U.S. Court of Federal Claims has national jurisdiction to hear claims against the United States. The U.S. Bankruptcy Courts have jurisdiction to hear and decide certain matters under the Federal Bankruptcy Code, subject to review by the U.S. District Court. The U.S. Tax Court has national jurisdiction over certain cases involving federal taxes. The U.S. Court of Appeals for the Federal Circuit has national jurisdiction and reviews decisions of the Court of Federal Claims, the Patent and Trademark Office, the U.S. Court of International Trade, the Merit Systems Protection Board, and the U.S. Court of Veterans Appeals, as well as patent cases decided by U.S. District Courts.

Figure 3-3 State Court System

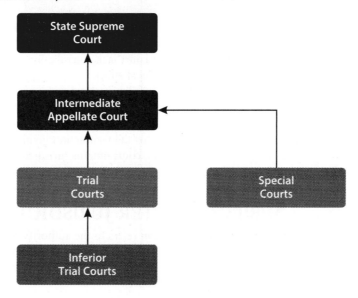

STATE COURTS [3-2]

Each of the fifty states and the District of Columbia has its own independent court system. In most states, the voters elect judges for a stated term. The structure of state court systems varies from state to state. Figure 3-3 shows a typical system.

Inferior Trial Courts [3-2a]

At the bottom of the state court system are the **inferior trial courts**, which decide the least serious criminal and civil matters. Usually, inferior trial courts do not keep a complete written record of trial proceedings. Minor criminal cases such as traffic offenses are heard in inferior trial courts, which are referred to as municipal courts, justice of the peace courts, or traffic courts. These courts also conduct preliminary hearings in more serious criminal cases.

Small claims courts are inferior trial courts that hear civil cases involving a limited amount of money. Usually there is no jury, the procedure is informal, and neither side employs an attorney. An appeal from a small claims court is taken to the trial court of general jurisdiction, where a new trial (called a trial *de novo*, in which the small claims court's decision is given no weight, is begun.

Trial Courts [3-2b]

Each state has **trial courts** of general jurisdiction, which may be called county, district, superior, circuit, or common pleas courts. (In New York the trial court is called the Supreme Court.) These courts do not have a dollar limitation on their jurisdiction in civil cases and hear all criminal cases other than minor offenses. Unlike the inferior trial courts, these trial courts of general jurisdiction maintain formal records of their proceedings as procedural safeguards.

Many states have **special trial courts** that have jurisdiction over particular areas. For example, many states have probate courts with jurisdiction over the administration of wills and estates as well as family courts with jurisdiction over divorce and child custody cases.

Appellate Courts [3-2c]

At the summit of the state court system is the state's court of last resort, a reviewing court generally called the supreme court of the state. Except for those cases in which review by the U.S. Supreme Court is available, the decision of the highest state tribunal is final. In addition, most states also have created intermediate **appellate courts** to handle the large volume of cases in which review is sought. Review by such a court is usually by right. Further review is in most cases at the highest court's discretion.

Inferior trial courts
hear minor criminal cases such as traffic offenses and civil cases involving small amounts of money and conduct preliminary hearings in more serious criminal cases

Small claims courts
inferior trial courts with jurisdiction over civil cases involving a limited dollar amount

Trial courts
have general jurisdiction over civil and criminal cases

Special trial courts
trial courts, such as probate courts and family courts, which have jurisdiction over a particular area of state law

Appellate courts
include one or two levels; the highest court's decisions are final except in those cases reviewed by the U.S. Supreme Court

JURISDICTION

Jurisdiction
authority of a court to hear
and decide a case

Jurisdiction means the power or authority of a court to hear and decide a given case. To resolve a lawsuit, a court must have two kinds of jurisdiction. The first is jurisdiction over the subject matter of the lawsuit. If a court lacks jurisdiction over the subject matter of a case, no action it takes in the case will have legal effect.

The second kind of jurisdiction is over the parties to a lawsuit. This jurisdiction is required for the court to render an enforceable judgment that affects the parties' rights and duties. A court usually may obtain jurisdiction over the defendant in a lawsuit if the defendant lives and is present in the court's territory or the transaction giving rise to the case has a substantial connection to the court's territory. The court obtains jurisdiction over the plaintiff when the plaintiff voluntarily submits to the court's power by filing a complaint with the court.

SUBJECT MATTER JURISDICTION [3-3]

**Subject matter
jurisdiction**
authority of a court to
decide a particular kind of
case

Subject matter jurisdiction refers to the authority of a particular court to judge a controversy of a particular kind. Federal courts have *limited* subject matter jurisdiction. State courts have jurisdiction over *all* matters that the Constitution or the Congress neither denies them nor gives exclusively to the federal courts.

Federal Jurisdiction [3-3a]

**Exclusive federal
jurisdiction**
jurisdiction that permits
only the federal courts to
hear a case

The federal courts have, to the exclusion of the state courts, subject matter jurisdiction over some areas. Such jurisdiction is called **exclusive federal jurisdiction**. Federal jurisdiction is exclusive only if Congress so provides, either explicitly or implicitly. If Congress does not so provide and the area is one over which federal courts have subject matter jurisdiction, they share this jurisdiction with the state courts. Such jurisdiction is known as **concurrent federal jurisdiction**.

**Concurrent federal
jurisdiction**
authority of federal or state
courts to hear the same
case

Exclusive Federal Jurisdiction   The federal courts have exclusive jurisdiction over federal criminal prosecutions; admiralty, bankruptcy, antitrust, patent, trademark, and copyright cases; suits against the United States; and cases arising under certain federal statutes that expressly provide for exclusive federal jurisdiction.

Concurrent Federal Jurisdiction   The two types of concurrent federal jurisdiction are federal question jurisdiction and diversity jurisdiction. The first arises whenever there is a federal question over which the federal courts do not have exclusive jurisdiction. A **federal question** is any case arising under the Constitution, statutes, or treaties of the United States. There is no minimum dollar requirement in federal question cases. When a state court hears a concurrent federal question case, it applies *federal* substantive law but its own procedural rules.

Federal question
any case arising under the
Constitution, statutes, or
treaties of the United
States

The second type of concurrent federal jurisdiction occurs in a civil suit in which there is diversity of citizenship and the amount in controversy exceeds $75,000. As the following case explains, the jurisdictional requirement is satisfied if the claim for the amount is made in good faith, unless it is clear to a legal certainty that the claim does not meet or exceed the required amount. *Diversity of citizenship* exists (1) when the plaintiffs are citizens of a state or states different from the state or states of which the defendants are citizens; (2) when a foreign country brings an action against citizens of the United States; or (3) when the controversy is between citizens of a state and citizens of a foreign country. The citizenship of an individual litigant (party in a lawsuit) is the state in which the individual resides or is domiciled, whereas that of a corporate litigant is both the state of incorporation and the state in which its principal place of business is located. For example, if the amount in controversy exceeds $75,000, then diversity of citizenship jurisdiction would be satisfied if Ada, a citizen of California, sues Bob, a citizen of Idaho. If, however, Carol, a citizen of Virginia, and Dianne, a citizen of North Carolina, sue Evan, a citizen of Georgia, and Farley, a citizen of North Carolina, there is *not* diversity of citizenship, because both Dianne, a plaintiff, and Farley, a defendant, are citizens of North Carolina.

Practical Advice

If you have the option,
consider whether you want
to bring your lawsuit in a
federal or state court.

When a federal district court hears a case solely under diversity of citizenship jurisdiction, no federal question is involved; and, accordingly, the federal courts must apply *state* substantive law. The conflict of law rules of the state in which the district court is located determine which state's substantive law is to be used in the case. (Conflict of laws is discussed later.) Federal courts apply federal procedural rules in diversity cases.

In any case involving concurrent jurisdiction, the plaintiff has the choice of bringing the action in either an appropriate federal court or state court. If the plaintiff brings the case in a state court, however, the defendant usually may have it removed (shifted) to a federal court for the district in which the state court is located.

Mims v. Arrow Financial Services, LLC
Supreme Court of the United States, 2012
565 U.S. ___, 132 S.Ct. 740, 181 L.Ed.2d 881
http://scholar.google.com/scholar_case?case=15936914266018909724&q=132+S.Ct.+740&hl=en&as_sdt=2,34

FACTS Numerous consumer complaints about abuses of telephone technology—for example, computerized calls to private homes—prompted Congress to pass the Telephone Consumer Protection Act of 1991 (TCPA). Congress determined that federal legislation was needed because telemarketers, by operating interstate, were escaping state-law prohibitions on intrusive nuisance calls. The TCPA bans certain practices invasive of privacy and directs the Federal Communications Commission (FCC or Commission) to establish implementing regulations. It authorizes the states to bring civil actions to enjoin prohibited practices and to recover damages on their residents' behalf. The TCPA provides that jurisdiction over state-initiated TCPA suits lies exclusively in the U.S. district courts. Congress also provided for civil actions by private parties seeking redress for violations of the TCPA or of the Commission's regulations.

Marcus D. Mims, complaining of multiple violations of the TCPA by Arrow Financial Services, LLC (Arrow), a debt-collection agency, commenced an action for damages against Arrow in the U.S. District Court for the Southern District of Florida. Mims invoked the court's "federal question" jurisdiction, *i.e.*, its authority to adjudicate claims "arising under the ... laws ... of the United States," 28 U.S.C. §1331. The District Court, affirmed by the U.S. Court of Appeals for the Eleventh Circuit, dismissed Mims's complaint for want of subject-matter jurisdiction. Both courts relied on Congress' specification in Section 227(b)(3) of the TCPA that a private person may seek redress for violations of the Act (or of the Commission's regulations thereunder) "in an appropriate court of [a] State," "if [such an action is] otherwise permitted by the laws or rules of court of [that] State." The U.S. Supreme Court granted *certiorari*.

DECISION The judgment of the United States Court of Appeals for the Eleventh Circuit is reversed, and the case is remanded.

OPINION Federal courts, although "courts of limited jurisdiction," in the main "have no more right to decline the exercise of jurisdiction which is given, then to usurp that which is not given." "The district courts shall have original [federal-question] jurisdiction of all civil actions arising under the Constitution, laws, or treaties of the United States." 28 U.S.C. §1331. Recognizing the responsibility of federal courts to decide claims, large or small, arising under federal law, Congress in 1980 eliminated the amount-in-controversy requirement in federal-question (but not diversity) cases.

Because federal law creates the right of action and provides the rules of decision, Mims's TCPA claim, in 28 U.S.C. §1331's words, plainly "aris[es] under" the "laws ... of the United States." Arrow agrees that this action arises under federal law but urges that Congress vested exclusive adjudicatory authority over private TCPA actions in state courts. In cases "arising under" federal law there is a "deeply rooted presumption in favor of concurrent state court jurisdiction," rebuttable if "Congress affirmatively ousts the state courts of jurisdiction over a particular federal claim." The presumption of concurrent state-court jurisdiction can be overcome "by an explicit statutory directive, by unmistakable implication from legislative history, or by a clear incompatibility between state-court jurisdiction and federal interests."

Arrow's arguments do not persuade that Congress has eliminated §1331 jurisdiction over private actions under the TCPA. Nothing in the permissive language of Section 227(b)(3) of the TCPA makes state-court jurisdiction exclusive, or otherwise purports to oust federal courts of their 28 U.S.C. §1331 jurisdiction over federal claims. Section 227(b)(3) of the TCPA does not state that a private plaintiff may bring an action under the TCPA "only" in state court, or "exclusively" in state court. Nothing in the text, structure, purpose, or legislative history of the TCPA calls for displacement of the federal-question jurisdiction U.S. district courts ordinarily have under 28 U.S.C. §1331. In the absence of direction from Congress stronger than any Arrow has advanced, the familiar default rule applies: Federal courts have §1331 jurisdiction over claims that arise under federal law. Because federal law gives rise to the claim for relief Mims has stated and specifies the substantive rules of decision, the Eleventh Circuit erred in dismissing Mims's case for lack of subject-matter jurisdiction.

INTERPRETATION Federal courts retain jurisdiction over causes of action created by federal law, unless the federal law in question, expressly or by fair implication, excludes federal court jurisdiction.

CRITICAL THINKING QUESTION Why would Congress have specifically granted private party TCPA jurisdiction to the state courts when those courts already had concurrent jurisdiction in federal question cases?

Figure 3-4 Federal and State Jurisdiction

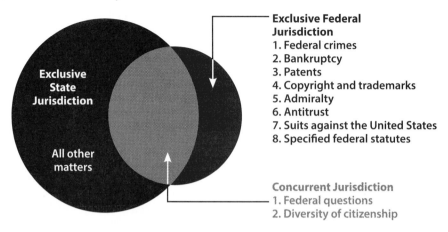

Exclusive State Jurisdiction [3-3b]

Practical Advice

Consider including in your contracts a choice-of-law provision specifying which jurisdiction's law will apply.

The state courts have exclusive jurisdiction over all other matters. All matters not granted to the federal courts in the Constitution or by Congress are solely within the jurisdiction of the states. Accordingly, exclusive state jurisdiction would include cases involving diversity of citizenship in which the amount in controversy is $75,000 or less. In addition, the state courts have exclusive jurisdiction over all cases to which the federal judicial power does not reach, including, but by no means limited to, property, torts, contract, agency, commercial transactions, and most crimes.

A court in one state may be a proper forum for a case even though some or all of the relevant events occurred in another state. For example, a California plaintiff may sue a Washington defendant in Washington over a car accident that occurred in Oregon. Because of Oregon's connections to the accident, Washington may choose, under its **conflict of laws** rules, to apply the substantive law of Oregon. Conflict of laws rules vary from state to state.

The jurisdiction of the federal and state courts is illustrated in Figure 3-4. Also, see Concept Review 3-1.

Stare Decisis in the Dual Court System [3-3c]

The doctrine of *stare decisis* presents certain problems when there are two parallel court systems. As a consequence, in the United States, *stare decisis* works approximately as follows (also illustrated in Figure 3-5):

1. The U.S. Supreme Court has never held itself to be bound rigidly by its own decisions, and lower federal courts and state courts have followed that course with respect to their own decisions.
2. A decision of the U.S. Supreme Court on a federal question is binding on all other courts, federal or state.
3. On a federal question, although a decision of a federal court other than the Supreme Court may be persuasive in a state court, it is not binding.
4. A decision of a state court may be persuasive in the federal courts, but it is not binding except in cases in which federal jurisdiction is based on diversity of citizenship. In such a case, the federal courts must apply state law as determined by the highest state court.
5. Decisions of the federal courts (other than the U.S. Supreme Court) are not binding on other federal courts of equal or inferior rank unless the latter owe obedience to the deciding court. For example, a decision of the Fifth Circuit Court of Appeals binds district courts in the Fifth Circuit but binds no other federal court.
6. A decision of a state court is binding on all courts inferior to it in its jurisdiction. Thus, the decision of the highest court in a state binds all other courts in that state.
7. A decision of a state court is not binding on courts in another state except in cases in which the latter courts are required, under their conflict of laws rules, to apply the law of the first state as determined by the highest court in that state. For example, if a North Carolina court is required to apply Virginia law, it must follow decisions of the Supreme Court of Virginia.

CONCEPT REVIEW 3-1

Subject Matter Jurisdiction

Type of Jurisdiction	Court	Substantive Law Applied	Procedural Law Applied
Exclusive federal	Federal	Federal	Federal
Concurrent: federal question	Federal	Federal	Federal
	State	Federal	State
Concurrent: diversity	Federal	State	Federal
	State	State	State
Exclusive state	State	State	State

JURISDICTION OVER THE PARTIES [3-4]

Jurisdiction over the parties

power of a court to bind the parties to a suit

Practical Advice

Consider including in your contracts a choice-of-forum provision specifying what court will have jurisdiction over any litigation arising from the contract.

In addition to subject matter jurisdiction, a court also must have **jurisdiction over the parties**, which is the power to bind the parties involved in the dispute. The court obtains jurisdiction over the *plaintiff* when she voluntarily submits to the court's power by filing a complaint with the court. A court may obtain jurisdiction over the *defendant*, in three possible ways: (1) *in personam* jurisdiction, (2) *in rem* jurisdiction, or (3) attachment jurisdiction. In addition, the exercise of jurisdiction over a defendant must satisfy the constitutionally imposed requirements of reasonable notification and a reasonable opportunity to be heard. Moreover, the court's exercise of jurisdiction over a defendant is valid under the Due Process Clause of the U.S. Constitution only if the defendant has minimum contacts with the state sufficient to prevent the court's assertion of jurisdiction from offending "traditional notions of fair play and substantial justice." For a court constitutionally to assert jurisdiction over a defendant, the defendant must have engaged in either purposeful acts in the state or acts outside the state that are of such a nature that the defendant could reasonably foresee being sued in that state, as discussed in the next case.

Figure 3-5 *Stare Decisis* in the Dual Court System

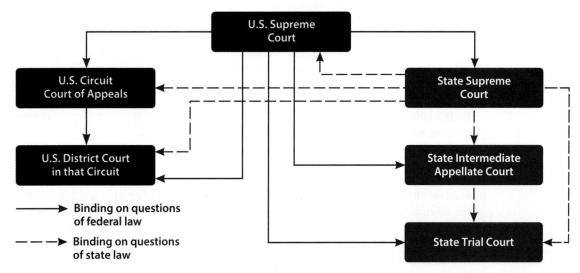

World-Wide Volkswagen Corp. v. Woodson
Supreme Court of the United States, 1980
444 U.S. 286, 100 S.Ct. 559, 62 L.Ed.2d 490
http://scholar.google.com/scholar_case?q=100+S.CT.+559&hl=en&as_sdt=2,34&case=2649456870546423871&scilh=0

FACTS Harry and Kay Robinson purchased a new Audi automobile from Seaway Volkswagen, Inc. (Seaway) in Massena, New York. The Robinsons, who had resided in New York for years, left for a new home in Arizona. As they drove through Oklahoma, another car struck their Audi from behind, causing a fire that severely burned Kay and her two children.

The Robinsons brought a products-liability suit in the District Court in Oklahoma, claiming their injuries resulted from defective design of the Audi gas tank and fuel system. They joined as defendants the manufacturer (Audi), the regional distributor (World-Wide Volkswagen Corp.), and the retail distributor (Seaway).

World-Wide and Seaway entered special appearances, asserting that Oklahoma's exercise of jurisdiction over them offended limitations on state jurisdiction imposed by the Due Process Clause of the Fourteenth Amendment. The Oklahoma Supreme Court upheld the assertion of state jurisdiction, and World-Wide and Seaway appealed.

DECISION Judgment of Oklahoma Supreme Court reversed.

OPINION The Due Process Clause of the Fourteenth Amendment limits the power of a state court to render a valid personal judgment against a nonresident defendant. A judgment rendered in violation of due process is void in the rendering state and is not entitled to full faith and credit elsewhere. A state court may exercise personal jurisdiction over a nonresident defendant only so long as there exist "minimum contacts" between the defendant and the forum state. The defendant's contacts with the forum state must be such that maintenance of the suit does not offend traditional notions of fair play and justice.

World-Wide is incorporated and has its place of business in New York. It distributes vehicles, parts, and accessories to retail dealers in New York, New Jersey, and Connecticut. Seaway, one of those retail dealers, is incorporated and has its place of business in New York. There is no evidence that either World-Wide or Seaway does any business in Oklahoma, ships or sells any products to or in that state, has an agent to receive process there, or purchases advertisements in any media calculated to reach Oklahoma. In fact, there is no showing that any automobile sold by World-Wide or Seaway has ever entered Oklahoma with the single exception of the Robinsons' Audi. Thus, in this case, there is a total absence of those affiliating circumstances, or minimum contacts, that are a necessary predicate to any exercise of state court jurisdiction.

INTERPRETATION Sufficient minimal contacts between the defendant and the state must exist for a state to exercise jurisdiction.

CRITICAL THINKING QUESTION Explain the public policy reasons for subjecting nonresidents doing business in a state to the *in personam* jurisdiction of the courts within that state.

In Personam Jurisdiction [3-4a]

In personam jurisdiction
jurisdiction based upon
claims against a person in
contrast to jurisdiction
over his property

In personam **jurisdiction**, or personal jurisdiction, is the jurisdiction of a court over the parties to a lawsuit, in contrast to its jurisdiction over their property. A court obtains *in personam* jurisdiction over a defendant either (1) by serving process on the party within the state in which the court is located or (2) by reasonable notification to a party outside the state in those instances where a "long-arm statute" applies. To *serve process* means to deliver a summons, which is an order to respond to a complaint lodged against a party. (The terms *summons* and *complaint* are explained more fully later in this chapter.)

Personal jurisdiction may be obtained by personally serving process upon a defendant within a state if that person is domiciled in that state. The U.S. Supreme Court has held that a state may exercise personal jurisdiction over a nonresident defendant who is temporarily present if the defendant is personally served in that state. Personal jurisdiction also may arise from a party's consent. For example, parties to a contract may agree that any dispute concerning that contract will be subject to the jurisdiction of a specific court.

Most states have adopted **long-arm statutes** to expand their jurisdictional reach beyond those persons who may be personally served within the state. These statutes allow courts to obtain jurisdiction over nonresident defendants under the following conditions, as long as the exercise of jurisdiction does not offend traditional notions of fair play and substantial justice: if the defendant (1) has committed a tort (civil wrong) within the state, (2) owns property within the state and if that property is the subject matter of the lawsuit, (3) has entered into a contract within the state, or (4) has transacted business within the state and if that business is the subject matter of the lawsuit.

Figure 3-6 Jurisdiction

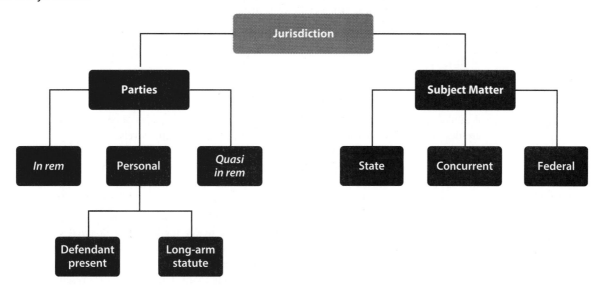

In Rem Jurisdiction [3-4b]

In rem jurisdiction
jurisdiction based on claims
against property

Courts in a state have the jurisdiction to adjudicate claims to property situated within the state if the plaintiff gives those persons who have an interest in the property reasonable notice and an opportunity to be heard. Such jurisdiction over property is called *in rem* **jurisdiction**. For example, if Carpenter and Miller are involved in a lawsuit over property located in Kansas, then an appropriate court in Kansas would have *in rem* jurisdiction to adjudicate claims over this property as long as both parties are given notice of the lawsuit and a reasonable opportunity to contest the claim.

Attachment Jurisdiction [3-4c]

**Attachment or *quasi
in rem* jurisdiction**
jurisdiction over property
not based on claims against it

Attachment jurisdiction, or *quasi in rem* **jurisdiction**, like *in rem* jurisdiction, is jurisdiction over property rather than over a person. But attachment jurisdiction is invoked by seizing the defendant's property located within the state to obtain payment of a claim against the defendant that is *unrelated* to the property seized. For example, Allen, a resident of Ohio, has obtained a valid judgment in the amount of $20,000 against Bradley, a citizen of Kentucky. Allen can attach Bradley's automobile, which is located in Ohio, to satisfy his court judgment against Bradley.

See Figure 3-6, which outlines the concepts of subject matter and party jurisdiction.

Venue [3-4d]

Venue
particular geographic place
where a court with
jurisdiction may hear a case

Venue, which often is confused with jurisdiction, concerns the geographic area in which a lawsuit *should* be brought. The purpose of venue is to regulate the distribution of cases within a specific court system and to identify a convenient forum. In the federal court system, venue determines the district or districts in a given state in which suit may be brought. State rules of venue typically require that a suit be initiated in a county where one of the defendants lives. In matters involving real estate, most venue rules require that a suit be initiated in the county where the property is situated.

CIVIL DISPUTE RESOLUTION

As mentioned in Chapter 1, one of the primary functions of law is to provide for the peaceful resolution of disputes. Accordingly, our legal system has established an elaborate set of government mechanisms to settle disputes. The most prominent of these is judicial dispute resolution, called *litigation*. Judicial resolution of civil disputes is governed by the rules of civil procedure, which we will discuss in the first part of this section. Judicial resolution of criminal cases is governed by the rules of criminal procedure, which are covered in Chapter 6. Dispute resolution by administrative agencies, which is also common, is discussed in Chapter 5.

As an alternative to government dispute resolution, several nongovernmental methods of dispute resolution, such as arbitration, have developed. We will discuss these in the second part of this section.

CIVIL PROCEDURE [3-5]

A civil dispute that enters the judicial system must follow the rules of civil procedure. These rules are designed to resolve the dispute justly, promptly, and inexpensively.

To acquaint you with civil procedure, we will carry a hypothetical action through the trial court to the highest court of review in the state. Although there are technical differences in trial and appellate procedure among the states and the federal courts, the following illustration will give you a general understanding of the trial and appeal of cases. Assume that Pam Pederson, a pedestrian, is struck while crossing a street in Chicago by an automobile driven by David Dryden. Pederson suffers serious personal injuries, incurs heavy medical and hospital expenses, and is unable to work for several months. She desires that Dryden pay her for the loss and damages she sustained. After attempts at settlement fail, Pederson brings an action at law against Dryden. Thus, Pederson is the plaintiff and Dryden the defendant. Each party is represented by a lawyer. Let us follow the progress of the case.

The Pleadings [3-5a]

The **pleadings** are a series of responsive, formal, written statements in which each side to a lawsuit states its claims and defenses. The purpose of pleadings is to give notice and to establish the issues of fact and law the parties dispute. An "issue of fact" is a dispute between the parties regarding the events that gave rise to the lawsuit. In contrast, an "issue of law" is a dispute between the parties as to what legal rules apply to these facts. Issues of fact are decided by the jury, or by the judge when there is no jury, whereas issues of law are decided by the judge.

Complaint and Summons
A lawsuit begins when Pederson, the plaintiff, files with the clerk of the trial court a **complaint** against Dryden that contains (1) a statement of the claim and supporting facts showing that she is entitled to relief and (2) a demand for that relief. Pederson's complaint alleges that while exercising due and reasonable care for her own safety, she was struck by Dryden's automobile, which was being driven negligently by Dryden, causing her personal injuries and damages of $50,000, for which Pederson requests judgment.

Once the plaintiff has filed a complaint, the clerk issues a **summons** to be served upon the defendant to notify him that a suit has been brought against him. If the defendant has contacts with the state sufficient to show that the state's assertion of jurisdiction over the defendant is constitutional, proper service of the summons establishes the court's jurisdiction over the person of the defendant. The county sheriff or a deputy sheriff serves a summons and a copy of the complaint on Dryden, the defendant, commanding him to file his appearance and answer with the clerk of the court within a specific time, usually thirty days from the date the summons was served.

Responses to Complaint
At this point, Dryden has several options. If he fails to respond at all, a **default judgment** will be entered against him. He may make *pretrial motions* contesting the court's jurisdiction over him or asserting that the action is barred by the statute of limitations, which requires suits to be brought within a specified time. Dryden also may move, or request, that the complaint be made more definite and certain, or he may instead move that the complaint be dismissed for failure to state a claim on which relief may be granted. Such a motion is sometimes called a **demurrer**; it essentially asserts that even if all of Pederson's allegations were true, she still would not be entitled to the relief she seeks and that therefore there is no need for a trial of the facts. The court rules on this motion as a matter of law. If it rules in favor of the defendant, the plaintiff may appeal the ruling.

If he does not make any pretrial motions, or if they are denied, Dryden will respond to the complaint by filing an **answer**, which may contain denials, admissions, affirmative defenses, and counterclaims. Dryden might answer the complaint by denying its allegations of negligence and

---

Practical Advice

If you become involved in litigation, make full disclosure to your attorney and do not discuss the lawsuit without consulting your attorney.

Pleadings
series of responsive, formal, written statements by each side to a lawsuit

Complaint
initial pleading by the plaintiff stating his case

Summons
notice given to inform a person of a lawsuit against her

Default judgment
judgment against a defendant who fails to respond to a complaint

Demurrer
motion to dismiss for failure to state a claim

Answer
defendant's pleading in response to the plaintiff's complaint

stating that he was driving his car at a low speed and with reasonable care (a **denial**) when his car struck Pederson (an **admission**), who had dashed across the street in front of his car without looking in any direction to see whether cars or other vehicles were approaching; that, accordingly, Pederson's injuries were caused by her own negligence (an **affirmative defense**); and that, therefore, she should not be permitted to recover any damages. Dryden might further state that Pederson caused damage to his car and request a judgment for $2,000 (a **counterclaim**). These pleadings create an issue of fact regarding whether Dryden or Pederson, or both, failed to exercise due and reasonable care under the circumstances and were thus negligent and liable for their carelessness.

If the defendant counterclaims, the plaintiff must respond through a **reply**, which also may contain admissions, denials, and affirmative defenses.

Pretrial Procedure [3-5b]

Judgment on the Pleadings
After the pleadings, either party may move for **judgment on the pleadings**, which requests the judge to rule as a matter of law whether the facts as alleged in the pleadings of the nonmoving party are sufficient to warrant granting the requested relief.

Discovery
In preparation for trial and even before completion of the pleadings stage, each party has the right to obtain relevant evidence, or information that may lead to evidence, from the other party. This procedure, known as **discovery**, includes (1) pretrial *depositions* consisting of sworn testimony, taken out of court, of the opposing party or other witnesses; (2) sworn answers by the opposing party to *written interrogatories*, or questions; (3) *production* of documents and physical objects in the possession of the opposing party or, by a court-ordered subpoena, in the possession of nonparties; (4) *court-ordered examination* by a physician of the opposing party, as needed; and (5) admissions of facts obtained by a *request for admissions* submitted to the opposing party. By using discovery properly, each party may become fully informed of relevant evidence and avoid surprise at trial. Another purpose of this procedure is to facilitate settlements by giving both parties as much relevant information as possible.

Pretrial Conference
Also furthering these objectives is the pretrial conference between the judge and the attorneys representing the parties. The basic purposes of the **pretrial conference** are (1) to simplify the issues in dispute by amending the pleadings, admitting or stipulating facts, and identifying witnesses and documents to be presented at trial; and (2) to encourage settlement of the dispute without trial. (More than 90 percent of all cases are settled before going to trial.) If no settlement occurs, the judge will enter a pretrial order containing all of the amendments, stipulations, admissions, and other matters agreed to during the pretrial conference. The order supersedes the pleadings and controls the remainder of the trial.

Summary Judgment
The evidence disclosed by discovery may be so clear that a trial to determine the facts becomes unnecessary. If this is so, either party may move for a summary judgment, which requests the judge to rule that, because there are no issues of fact to be determined by trial, the party thus moving should prevail as a matter of law. A **summary judgment** is a final binding determination on the merits made by the judge before a trial. The following case involving actress Shirley MacLaine explains the rules courts use to determine whether to grant summary judgment.

Reply
plaintiff's pleading in response to the defendant's answer

Pretrial procedure
process requiring the parties to disclose what evidence is available to prove the disputed facts; designed to encourage settlement of cases or to make the trial more efficient

Judgment on the pleadings
final binding determination on the merits made by the judge after the pleadings

Discovery
pretrial exchange of information between opposing parties to a lawsuit

Pretrial conference
a conference between the judge and the attorneys to simplify the issues in dispute and to attempt to settle the dispute without trial

Summary judgment
binding determinations on the merits made by the judge before trial

---

Parker v. Twentieth Century-Fox Film Corp.
Supreme Court of California, 1970
3 Cal.3d 176, 89 Cal.Rptr. 737, 474 P.2d 689
http://scholar.google.com/scholar_case?q=474+P.2d+689&hl=en&as_sdt=2,34&case=8204943341098207403&scilh=0

FACTS Shirley MacLaine Parker, a well-known actress, contracted with Twentieth Century-Fox Film Corporation in August 1965 to play the female lead in Fox's upcoming production of *Bloomer Girl*, a motion picture musical that was to be filmed in

California. Fox agreed to pay Parker $750,000 for fourteen weeks of her services. Fox decided to cancel its plans for *Bloomer Girl* before production had begun and, instead, offered Parker the female lead in another film, *Big Country, Big Man*, a dramatic western to be filmed in Australia. The compensation offered was identical, but Parker's right to approve the director and screenplay would have been eliminated or altered by the *Big Country* proposal. She refused to accept and brought suit to recover the $750,000 for Fox's breach of the *Bloomer Girl* contract. Fox's sole defense in its answer was that it owed no money to Parker because she had deliberately failed to mitigate or reduce her damages by unreasonably refusing to accept the *Big Country* lead. Parker filed a motion for summary judgment. Fox, in opposition to the motion, claimed, in effect, only that the *Big Country* offer was not employment different from or inferior to that under the *Bloomer Girl* contract. The trial court granted Parker a summary judgment and Fox appealed.

DECISION   Summary judgment affirmed.

OPINION   The matter to be determined by a trial court on a motion for summary judgment is whether facts have been presented which give rise to a triable factual issue. The trial court may not pass upon the issue itself. Summary judgment is proper only if the affidavits or declarations in support of Parker, the

moving party, would be sufficient to sustain a judgment in her favor and her opponent does not by affidavit show facts sufficient to present a triable issue of fact. The affidavits of the moving party are strictly construed, and doubts as to the propriety of summary judgment should be resolved against granting the motion. Such summary procedure is drastic and should be used with caution so that it does not become a substitute for the open trial method of determining facts.

Here, it is clear that the trial court correctly ruled that Parker's failure to accept Fox's tendered substitute employment could not be applied in mitigation of damages because the offer of the *Big Country* lead was of employment both different and inferior, and that no factual dispute was presented on that issue. Therefore, summary judgment in favor of Parker is granted for $750,000.

INTERPRETATION   A court will grant summary judgment when there are no issues of fact to be determined by trial.

CRITICAL THINKING QUESTION   When should a court grant summary judgment? Explain.

Trial [3-5c]

Trial
determines the facts and the outcome of the case

In all federal civil cases at common law involving more than $20.00, the U.S. Constitution guarantees the right to a jury **trial**. In addition, nearly every state constitution provides a similar right. In addition, federal and state statutes may authorize jury trials in cases not within the constitutional guarantees. Under federal law and in almost all states, jury trials are *not* available in equity cases. Even in cases in which a jury trial is available, the parties may waive (choose not to have) a trial by jury. When a trial is conducted without a jury, the judge serves as the fact finder and will make separate findings of fact and conclusions of law. When a trial is conducted *with* a jury, the judge determines issues of law and the jury determines questions of fact.

Voir dire
preliminary examination of potential jurors

Jury Selection   Assuming a timely demand for a jury has been made, the trial begins with the selection of a jury. The jury selection process involves a **voir dire**, an examination by the parties' attorneys (or in some courts by the judge) of the potential jurors. Each party has an unlimited number of *challenges for cause*, which allow the party to prevent a prospective juror from serving if the juror is biased or cannot be fair and impartial. In addition, each party has a limited number of *peremptory challenges* for which no cause is required to disqualify a prospective juror. The Supreme Court has held that the U.S. Constitution prohibits discrimination in jury selection on the basis of race or gender.

Edmonson v. Leesville Concrete Company, Inc.
Supreme Court of the United States, 1991
500 U.S. 614, 111 S.Ct. 2077, 114 L.Ed.2d 660
http://scholar.google.com/scholar_case?case=15015557139421049892&q=111+S.Ct.+2077&hl=en&as_sdt=6,34

FACTS   Thaddeus Donald Edmonson, a construction worker, was injured in a job-site accident at Fort Polk, Louisiana. Edmonson sued Leesville Concrete Company for negligence in the U.S. District Court for the Western District of Louisiana, claiming that a Leesville employee permitted one of the company's trucks to roll backward and pin him against some construction equipment. Edmonson invoked his Seventh Amendment right to a trial by jury. During *voir dire*, Leesville used two of its three peremptory challenges authorized by statute to remove black persons from the prospective jury. When Edmonson, who is himself black,

requested that the District Court require Leesville to articulate a race-neutral explanation for striking the two jurors, the District Court ruled that the precedent on which Edmonson's request relied applied only to criminal cases and allowed the strikes to stand. A jury of eleven whites and one black brought in a verdict for Edmonson, assessing total damages at $90,000. It also attributed 80 percent of the fault to Edmonson's contributory negligence and awarded him only $18,000. On appeal, a divided *en banc* panel affirmed the judgment of the District Court, concluding that the use of peremptory challenges by private litigants did not constitute state action and, as a result, did not violate constitutional guarantees against racial discrimination. The U.S. Supreme Court granted *certiorari*.

DECISION Judgment for Edmonson.

OPINION Although the conduct of private parties lies beyond the Constitution's scope in most instances, governmental authority may dominate an activity to such an extent that its participants must be deemed to act with the authority of the government and, as a result, be subject to Constitutional constraints. In determining whether a particular course of action is governmental in character, it is relevant to examine (1) the extent to which the actor relies on government assistance and benefits, (2) whether the actor is performing a traditional government function, and (3) whether the injury caused is aggravated in a unique way by the incidents of government authority. The Court held that, based on these three principles, the exercise of peremptory challenges by the defendant in the district court was pursuant to a course of state action and therefore subject to Constitutional protection against discrimination on the basis of race.

Without significant participation of the government, the whole jury trial system, of which the peremptory challenge is a part, could not exist. In fact, peremptory challenges have no utility outside the jury system. Furthermore, government statutes prescribe the qualifications for jury service, the procedures for jury selection, and lawful excuse from jury service. Trials are held in government buildings and presided over by judges who are state actors charged to use the utmost care to see that justice is done. And in all jurisdictions, a verdict will be incorporated in a judgment, which is enforceable by the state. When private litigants participate in the judicial process—including the selection of jurors—they serve an important function within the government and act with its substantial assistance. Finally, the injury caused by discrimination in peremptory challenges is made more severe because it has occurred within the courthouse, where the law itself unfolds in an ongoing expression of Constitutional authority. To permit racial exclusion in this official forum offends the integrity of the court and compounds the racial insult inherent in judging a citizen by the color of his or her skin.

INTERPRETATION The U.S. Constitution imposes restrictions against racial discrimination in the jury selection process.

ETHICAL QUESTION What are ethical grounds for an attorney to exercise a peremptory challenge? Explain.

CRITICAL THINKING QUESTION What grounds should be disallowed in the exercise of peremptory challenges? Explain.

Conduct of trial consists of opening statements by attorneys, direct and cross-examination of witnesses, and closing arguments

Conduct of Trial

After the jury has been selected, both attorneys make an ***opening statement*** about the facts that they expect to prove in the trial. The plaintiff and plaintiff's witnesses then testify on ***direct examination*** by the plaintiff's attorney. Each is subject to ***cross-examination*** by the defendant's attorney. Pederson and her witnesses testify that the traffic light at the street intersection where she was struck was green for traffic in the direction in which she was crossing but changed to yellow when she was about one-third of the way across the street.

During the trial, the judge rules on the admission and exclusion of evidence on the basis of its relevance and reliability. If the judge does not allow certain evidence to be introduced or certain testimony to be given, the attorney must make an ***offer of proof*** to preserve for review on appeal the question of its admissibility. The offer of proof consists of oral statements of counsel or witnesses showing for the record the evidence that the judge has ruled inadmissible; it is not regarded as evidence and is not heard by the jury.

Directed verdict final binding determination on the merits made by the judge after a trial has begun but before the jury renders a verdict

After cross-examination, followed by redirect examination of each of her witnesses, Pederson rests her case. At this time, Dryden may move for a directed verdict in his favor. A **directed verdict** is a final binding determination on the merits made by the judge after a trial has begun but before the jury renders a verdict. If the judge concludes that the evidence introduced by Pederson, which is assumed for the purposes of the motion to be true, would not be sufficient for the jury to find in favor of the plaintiff, then the judge will grant the directed verdict in favor of the defendant. In some states, the judge will deny the motion for a directed verdict if there is *any* evidence on which the jury might possibly render a verdict for the plaintiff.

If the judge denies the motion for a directed verdict, however, the defendant then has the opportunity to present evidence. Dryden and his witnesses testify that he was driving his car at a low speed when it struck Pederson and that Dryden at the time had the green light at the intersection. After the defendant has presented his evidence, the plaintiff and the defendant may be permitted to introduce rebuttal evidence. Once both parties have rested (concluded), then either party may move for a directed verdict. By this motion, the party contends that the evidence is so clear that reasonable persons could not differ about the outcome of the case. If the judge grants the motion for a directed verdict, he takes the case away from the jury and enters a judgment for the party making the motion.

If these motions are denied, then Pederson's attorney makes a ***closing argument*** to the jury, reviewing the evidence and urging a verdict in favor of Pederson. Then Dryden's attorney makes a closing argument, summarizing the evidence and urging a verdict in favor of Dryden. Peder-son's attorney is permitted to make a short argument in rebuttal.

Jury Instructions   The attorneys previously have given possible written jury instructions on the applicable law to the trial judge, who gives to the jury those instructions that he approves and denies those that he considers incorrect. The judge also may give the jury instructions of his own. **Jury instructions** (called "charges" in some states) advise the jury of the particular rules of law that apply to the facts the jury determines from the evidence.

Verdict   The jury then retires to the jury room to deliberate and to reach its **verdict** in favor of one party or the other. If the jury finds the issues in favor of Dryden, its verdict is that he is not liable. If, however, it finds the issues for Pederson and against Dryden, its verdict will be that the defendant is liable and will specify the amount of the plaintiff's damages. In this case, the jury found that Pederson's damages were $35,000. On returning to the jury box, the foreperson either announces the verdict or hands it in written form to the clerk to give to the judge, who reads the verdict in open court. In some jurisdictions, a *special verdict*, by which the jury makes specific written findings on each factual issue, is used. The judge then applies the law to these findings and renders a judgment. In the United States the prevailing litigant is ordinarily *not* entitled to collect attorneys' fees from the losing party, unless otherwise provided by statute or an enforcea-ble contract allocating attorneys' fees.

Motions Challenging Verdict   The unsuccessful party may then file a written motion for a new trial or for judgment notwithstanding the verdict. A *motion for a new trial* may be granted if (1) the judge committed prejudicial error during the trial, (2) the verdict is against the weight of the evidence, (3) the damages are excessive, or (4) the trial was not fair. The judge has the discretion to grant a motion for a new trial (on grounds 1, 3, or 4) even if the verdict is supported by substantial evidence. On the other hand, the motion for judgment notwithstanding the verdict (also called a judgment n.o.v.) must be denied if any substantial evidence supports the verdict. This motion is similar to a motion for a directed verdict, only it is made *after* the jury's verdict. To grant the motion for **judgment notwithstanding the verdict**, the judge must decide that the evidence is so clear that reasonable people could not differ as to the outcome of the case. If a judgment n.o.v. is reversed on appeal, a new trial is *not* necessary, and the jury's verdict is entered. If the judge denies the motions for a new trial and for a judgment notwith-standing the verdict, he enters *judgment on the verdict* for $35,000 in favor of the plaintiff.

Appeal [3-5d]

The purpose of an **appeal** is to determine whether the trial court committed prejudicial error. Most jurisdictions permit an appeal only from a final judgment. As a general rule, only errors of law are reviewed by an appellate court. Errors of law include the judge's decisions to admit or exclude evidence; the judge's instructions to the jury; and the judge's actions in denying or grant-ing a motion for a demurrer, a summary judgment, a directed verdict, or a judgment n.o.v. Appellate courts review errors of law *de novo*. Errors of fact will be reversed only if they are so clearly erroneous that they are considered to be an error of law.

Let us assume that Dryden directs his attorney to appeal. The attorney files a notice of appeal with the clerk of the trial court within the prescribed time. Later, Dryden, as appellant, files in the reviewing court the record on appeal, which contains the pleadings, a transcript of the testimony, rulings by the judge on motions made by the parties, arguments of counsel, jury instructions, the verdict, posttrial motions, and the judgment from which the appeal is taken. In states having an intermediate court of appeals, such court usually will be the reviewing court. In states having no intermediate court of appeal, a party may appeal directly from the trial court to the state supreme court.

Dryden, as appellant, is required to prepare a condensation of the record, known as an abstract, or pertinent excerpts from the record, which he files with the reviewing court together with a brief and argument. His *brief* contains a statement of the facts, the issues, the rulings by the trial court that Dryden contends are erroneous and prejudicial, grounds for reversal of the judgment, a statement of the applicable law, and arguments on his behalf. Pederson, the appellee,

Jury instructions
judge gives the jury the particular rules of law that apply to the case

Verdict
formal decision by the jury on questions submitted to it

Motions challenging verdict
include motions for a new trial and a motion for judgment notwithstanding the verdict

Judgment notwithstanding the verdict
a final binding determination on the merits made by the judge after and contrary to the jury's verdict

Appeal
determines whether the trial court committed prejudicial error

files an answering brief and argument. Dryden may, but is not required to, file a reply brief. The case is now ready to be considered by the reviewing court.

The appellate court does not hear any evidence; rather, it decides the case on the record, abstracts, and briefs. After *oral argument* by the attorneys, if the court elects to hear one, the court takes the case under advisement, or begins deliberations. Then, having made a decision based on majority rule, the appellate court prepares a written opinion containing the reasons for its decision, the rules of law that apply, and its judgment. The judgment may affirm the judgment of the trial court, or, if the appellate court finds that reversible error was committed, the judgment may be reversed or modified or returned to the lower court (remanded) for a new trial. In some instances the appellate court will affirm the lower court's decision in part and will reverse it in part. The losing party may file a petition for rehearing, which is usually denied.

If the reviewing court is an intermediate appellate court, the party losing in that court may decide to seek a reversal of its judgment by filing within a prescribed time a notice of appeal, if the appeal is by right, or a petition for leave to appeal to the state supreme court, if the appeal is by discretion. This petition corresponds to a petition for a writ of *certiorari* in the U.S. Supreme Court. The party winning in the appellate court may file an answer to the petition for leave to appeal. If the petition is granted, or if the appeal is by right, the record is certified to the Supreme Court, where each party files a new brief and argument. The Supreme Court may hear oral argument or simply review the record; it then takes the case under advisement. If the Supreme Court concludes that the judgment of the appellate court is correct, it affirms. If it decides otherwise, it reverses the judgment of the appellate court and enters a reversal or an order of remand. The unsuccessful party may again file a petition for a rehearing, which is likely to be denied. Barring the remote possibility of an application for still further review by the U.S. Supreme Court, the case either has reached its termination or, on remand, is about to start its second journey through the courts, beginning, as it did originally, in the trial court.

Enforcement [3-5e]

Enforcement

plaintiff with an unpaid judgment may resort to a writ of execution to have the sheriff seize property of the defendant and to garnishment to collect money owed to the defendant by a third party

If Dryden does not appeal, or if the reviewing court affirms the judgment if he does appeal, and Dryden does not pay the judgment, the task of enforcement will remain. Pederson must request the clerk to issue a *writ of execution* demanding payment of the judgment, which is served by the sheriff on the defendant. If the writ is returned "unsatisfied," that is, if Dryden still does not pay, Pederson may post bond or other security and order a levy on and sale of specific nonexempt property belonging to the defendant, which is then seized by the sheriff, advertised for sale, and sold at a public sale under the writ of execution. If the sale does not produce enough money to pay the judgment, Pederson's attorney may begin another proceeding in an attempt to locate money or other property belonging to Dryden. In an attempt to collect the judgment, Pederson's attorney may also proceed by *garnishment* against Dryden's employer to collect from his wages or against a bank in which he has an account.

If Pederson cannot satisfy the judgment with Dryden's property located within Illinois (the state where the judgment was obtained), Pederson will have to bring an action on the original judgment in other states where Dryden owns property. Because the U.S. Constitution requires each state to accord judgments of other states *full faith and credit*, Pederson will be able to obtain a local judgment that may be enforced by the methods described previously.

The various stages in civil procedure are illustrated in Figure 3-7.

ALTERNATIVE DISPUTE RESOLUTION [3-6]

Litigation is complex, time consuming, and expensive. Furthermore, court adjudications involve long delays, lack special expertise in substantive areas, and provide only a limited range of remedies. Additionally, litigation is structured so that one party takes all with little opportunity for compromise and often causes animosity between the disputants. Consequently, in an attempt to overcome some of the disadvantages of litigation, several nonjudicial methods of dealing with disputes have developed. The most important of these alternatives to litigation is arbitration. Others include conciliation, mediation, and "mini-trials."

Figure 3-7 Stages in Civil Procedure

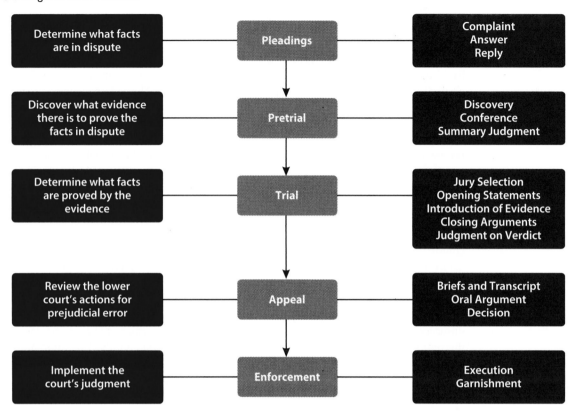

The various techniques differ in a number of ways, including (1) whether the process is voluntary, (2) whether the process is binding, (3) whether the disputants represent themselves or are represented by attorneys, (4) whether the decision is made by the disputants or by a third party, (5) whether the procedure used is formal or informal, and (6) whether the basis for the decision is law or some other criterion.

Which method of civil dispute resolution—litigation or one of the nongovernmental methods—is better for a particular dispute depends on several factors, including the financial circumstances of the disputants, the nature of the relationship (commercial or personal, ongoing or limited) between them, and the urgency of a quick resolution. Alternative dispute resolution methods are especially suitable in cases in which privacy, speed, preservation of continuing relations, and control over the process—including the flexibility to compromise—are important to the parties. Nevertheless, the disadvantages of using alternative dispute mechanisms may make court adjudication more appropriate. For example, with the exception of arbitration, only courts can compel participation and provide a binding resolution. In addition, only courts can establish precedents and create public duties. Furthermore, the courts provide greater due process protections and uniformity of outcome. Finally, the courts are independent of the parties and are publicly funded.

See Concept Review 3-2 for a comparison of adjudication, arbitration, and mediation/conciliation.

Arbitration [3-6a]

In **arbitration**, the parties select a *neutral* third person or persons—the arbitrator(s)—who render(s) a binding decision after hearing arguments and reviewing evidence. Because the presentation of the case is less formal and the rules of evidence are more relaxed, arbitration usually takes less time and costs less than litigation. Moreover, in many arbitration cases, the parties are able to select an arbitrator with special expertise concerning the subject of the dispute. Thus, the quality of the arbitrator's decision may be higher than that available through the court system. In addition, arbitration normally is conducted in private, thus avoiding unwanted publicity. Arbitration is commonly used in commercial and labor management disputes.

Practical Advice

Consider including in your contracts a provision specifying what means of dispute resolution will apply to the contract.

Arbitration

nonjudicial proceeding in which a neutral third party selected by disputants renders a binding decision

CONCEPT REVIEW 3-2

Comparison of Court Adjudication, Arbitration, and Mediation/Conciliation

	Court Adjudication	Arbitration	Mediation/Conciliation
Binding	Yes	Yes	No
Public proceedings	Yes	No	No
Special expertise	No	Yes	Yes
Publicly funded	Yes	No	No
Precedents established	Yes	No	No
Time consuming	Yes	No	No
Long delays	Yes	No	No
Expensive	Yes	No	No

Consensual arbitration
arbitration voluntarily entered into by the parties

Types of Arbitration   There are two basic types of arbitration—consensual, which is by far the most common, and compulsory. **Consensual arbitration** occurs whenever the parties to a dispute agree to submit the controversy to arbitration. They may do this in advance by agreeing in their contract that disputes arising out of their contract will be resolved by arbitration. Or they may do so after a dispute arises by then agreeing to submit the dispute to arbitration. In either instance, such agreements are enforceable under the Federal Arbitration Act (FAA) and state statutes. Forty-nine states have adopted the Uniform Arbitration Act (UAA). (In 2000, the Uniform Law Commission, also known as the National Conference of Commissioners on Uniform State Laws, promulgated the Revised UAA to provide state legislatures with a more up-to-date statute to resolve disputes through arbitration. To date, at least seventeen states have adopted the Revised UAA.) In **compulsory arbitration**, which is relatively infrequent, a federal or state statute requires arbitration for specific types of disputes, such as those involving public employees, including police officers, teachers, and firefighters.

Compulsory arbitration
arbitration required by statute for specific types of disputes

Procedure   Usually the parties' agreement to arbitrate specifies how the arbitrator or arbitrators will be chosen. If it does not, the FAA and state statutes provide methods for selecting arbitrators. Although the requirements for arbitration hearings vary from state to state, they generally consist of opening statements, case presentation, and closing statements. Case presentations may include witnesses, documentation, and site inspections. The parties may cross-examine witnesses and may be represented by attorneys.

Award
the decision of an arbitrator

The decision of the arbitrator, called an **award**, is binding on the parties. Nevertheless, it is subject to *very* limited judicial review. Under the FAA and the Revised UAA these include (1) the award was procured by corruption, fraud, or other undue means; (2) the arbitrators were partial or corrupt; (3) the arbitrators were guilty of misconduct prejudicing the rights of a party to the arbitration proceeding; and (4) the arbitrators exceeded their powers. Historically, the courts were unfriendly to arbitration; however, they have dramatically changed their attitude and now favor arbitration.

Court-Annexed Arbitration   A growing number of federal and state courts have adopted court-annexed arbitration in civil cases in which the parties seek limited amounts of damages. The arbitrators are usually attorneys. Appeal from this type of *nonbinding* arbitration is by trial *de novo*. Many states have enacted statutes requiring the arbitration of medical malpractice disputes.

Nitro-Lift Technologies, L.L.C. v. Howard
Supreme Court of the United States, 2012
568 U.S. ___, 133 S.Ct. 500, 184 L.Ed.2d 328
http://scholar.google.com/scholar_case?q=133+S.Ct.+500&hl=en&as_sdt=4,60&as_ylo=2012
&case=12798986269666351327&scilh=0

FACTS This dispute arises from a contract between Nitro-Lift Technologies, L.L.C., and two of its former employees. Nitro-Lift contracts with operators of oil and gas wells to provide services that enhance production. The plaintiffs Eddie Lee Howard and Shane D. Schneider entered a confidentiality and noncompetition agreement with Nitro-Lift that contained the following arbitration clause:

> Any dispute, difference or unresolved question between Nitro-Lift and the Employee (collectively the "Disputing Parties") shall be settled by arbitration by a single arbitrator mutually agreeable to the Disputing Parties in an arbitration proceeding conducted in Houston, Texas in accordance with the rules existing at the date hereof of the American Arbitration Association.

After working for Nitro-Lift on wells in Oklahoma, Texas, and Arkansas, the plaintiffs quit and began working for one of Nitro-Lift's competitors. Claiming that the plaintiffs had breached their noncompetition agreements, Nitro-Lift served them with a demand for arbitration. The plaintiffs then filed suit in the District Court of Johnston County, Oklahoma, asking the court to declare the noncompetition agreements null and void and to enjoin their enforcement. The court dismissed the complaint, finding that the contracts contained valid arbitration clauses under which an arbitrator, and not the court, must settle the parties' disagreement.

The plaintiffs appealed, and the Oklahoma Supreme Court held that despite the "[U.S.] Supreme Court cases on which the employers rely," the "existence of an arbitration agreement in an employment contract does not prohibit judicial review of the underlying agreement." Finding the arbitration clauses no obstacle to its review, the Oklahoma Supreme Court held that the noncompetition agreements were "void and unenforceable as against Oklahoma's public policy," expressed in an Oklahoma statute.

DECISION The judgment of the Supreme Court of Oklahoma is vacated, and the case is remanded.

OPINION State courts rather than federal courts are most frequently called upon to apply the Federal Arbitration Act (FAA), including the Act's national policy favoring arbitration. It is a matter of great importance, therefore, that state supreme courts adhere to a correct interpretation of the legislation.

The Oklahoma Supreme Court's decision disregards the U.S. Supreme Court's precedents on the FAA. That Act, which "declare[s] a national policy favoring arbitration," provides that a "written provision in … a contract evidencing a transaction involving commerce to settle by arbitration a controversy thereafter arising out of such contract or transaction … shall be valid, irrevocable, and enforceable, save upon such grounds as exist at law or in equity for the revocation of any contract." It is well settled that "the substantive law the Act created [is] applicable in state and federal courts." Moreover, when parties commit to arbitrate contractual disputes, it is a mainstay of the Act's substantive law that attacks on the validity of the contract, as distinct from attacks on the validity of the arbitration clause itself, are to be resolved "by the arbitrator in the first instance, not by a federal or state court."

This principle requires that the decision below be vacated. The trial court found that the contract contained a valid arbitration clause, and the Oklahoma Supreme Court did not hold otherwise. It nonetheless assumed the arbitrator's role by declaring the noncompetition agreements null and void. The Oklahoma Supreme Court insisted that its "[own] jurisprudence controls this issue" and permits review of a "contract submitted to arbitration where one party assert[s] that the underlying agreement [is] void and unenforceable." But the Oklahoma Supreme Court must abide by the FAA, which under the U.S. Constitution is "the supreme Law of the Land," and by the opinions of the U.S. Supreme Court interpreting the FAA. It is the U.S. Supreme Court's responsibility to say what a statute means, and once the Court has spoken, it is the duty of other courts to respect that understanding of the governing rule of law.

The U.S. Supreme Court's cases hold that the FAA forecloses precisely this type of "judicial hostility towards arbitration." When state law prohibits outright the arbitration of a particular type of claim, that state law is displaced by the FAA. Hence, it is for the arbitrator to decide whether the covenants not to compete are valid as a matter of applicable state law.

INTERPRETATION When parties commit to arbitrate contractual disputes, the FAA requires that attacks on the validity of the contract, as distinct from attacks on the validity of the arbitration clause itself, are to be resolved by the arbitrator in the first instance, not by a federal or state court.

CRITICAL THINKING QUESTION Why should attacks on the validity of a contract calling for arbitration be treated differently than attacks on the validity of the arbitration clause?

Conciliation [3-6b]

Conciliation
nonbinding process in which a third party acts as an intermediary between the disputing parties

Conciliation is a nonbinding, informal process in which a third party (the conciliator) selected by the disputing parties attempts to help them reach a mutually acceptable agreement. The duties of the conciliator include improving communications, explaining issues, scheduling meetings, discussing differences of opinion, and serving as an intermediary between the parties when they are unwilling to meet.

BUSINESS LAW **IN ACTION**

In any given year, a large company like Dobashi Motors has lots of litigation exposure. In its vehicle manufacturing division it employs thousands of workers, who bring numerous claims arising out of such matters as workplace injuries and alleged employment discrimination. Nationwide it has a network of hundreds of dealers, who may have contract disagreements with Dobashi, some of which inevitably escalate to the point they end up in court.

Naturally the company also regularly contends with payment disputes involving its many service providers and parts suppliers, sometimes initiating suit and other times finding itself on the other side as a defendant. And together with its financing division, Dobashi Motors deals with

thousands of buyers and potential buyers, who sue not so infrequently, typically based on state deceptive practices statutes or federal laws governing access to credit. Every year, adverse judgments arise from at least some of each of these types of legal disputes. Judgments aside, even if Dobashi were to win every case, the company still would spend millions of dollars in attorneys' fees and other litigation expenses annually.

Legal disagreement is inherent in a business's contractual relationships. Recognizing this, Dobashi can choose to include predispute arbitration agreements in its employment contracts, written distribution and vendor arrangements, and financing deals. The regular use of such clauses would divert most of Dobashi's litigation out of

the court system and into what has been acknowledged to be a much more inexpensive, faster, more private, and more flexible dispute resolution environment. Indeed, studies have shown that a company like Dobashi can save 50 percent or more in litigation expenses by choosing arbitration as its primary vehicle for resolving disputes.

Critics contend that arbitration results often are inconsistent with the law and that they can deprive the parties of certain remedies available only in court. Good drafting can eliminate the latter and, even if the former is true, it will operate rather evenhandedly: Dobashi may lose some cases it would have won in court, and vice versa. In the end, the cost savings are not inconsequential, both in the short term and over time.

Mediation

nonbinding process in which a third party acts as an intermediary between the disputing parties and proposes solutions for them to consider

Med-arb

binding process in which a third party serves first as a mediator and then as an arbitrator for those issues not resolved through mediation

Mediation [3-6c]

Mediation is a process in which a third party (the mediator) selected by the disputants helps them to reach a voluntary agreement resolving their disagreement. In addition to employing conciliation techniques to improve communications, the mediator, unlike the conciliator, proposes possible solutions for the parties to consider. Like the conciliator, the mediator does not have the power to render a binding decision. Because it is a voluntary process and has lower costs than a formal legal proceeding or arbitration, mediation has become one of the most widespread forms of dispute resolution in the United States. Mediation commonly is used by the judicial system in such tribunals as small claims courts, housing courts, family courts, and neighborhood justice centers. In 2001, the Uniform Law Commission promulgated the Uniform Mediation Act, which was amended in 2003. The Act establishes a privilege of confidentiality for mediators and participants. To date at least eleven states have adopted it.

Sometimes the techniques of arbitration and mediation are combined in a procedure called "med-arb." In **med-arb**, the neutral third party serves first as a mediator and, if all issues are not

---

GOING GLOBAL

What about international dispute resolution?

Laws vary greatly from country to country: what one nation requires by law, another may forbid. To complicate matters, there is no single authority in international law that can compel countries to act. When the laws of two or more nations conflict, or when one party has violated an agreement and the other party wishes to enforce it or to recover damages, establishing who will adjudicate the matter, which laws will be applied, what remedies will be available, or where the matter should be decided often

is very confusing and uncertain. Unlike domestic law, international law generally cannot be enforced. Consequently, international courts do not have compulsory jurisdiction, though they do have authority to resolve an international dispute if the parties to the dispute accept the court's jurisdiction over the matter.

Accordingly, arbitration is a commonly used means for resolving international disputes. The United Nations Committee on International Trade Law (UNCITRAL) and

the International Chamber of Commerce have promulgated arbitration rules that have won broad international adherence. The FAA has provisions implementing the United Nations Convention on the Recognition and Enforcement of Foreign Arbitral Awards. A number of states have enacted laws specifically governing international arbitration; some of the statutes have been based on the Model Law on International Arbitration drafted by UNCITRAL.

Mini-trial
nonbinding process in which attorneys for the disputing parties present evidence to managers of the disputing parties and a neutral third party, and then the managers attempt to negotiate a settlement in consultation with the third party

Summary jury trial
mock trial followed by negotiations

Negotiation
consensual bargaining process in which the parties attempt to reach an agreement resolving their dispute without the involvement of third parties

resolved through such mediation, then serves as an arbitrator authorized to render a binding decision on the remaining issues.

Mini-Trial [3-6d]

A mini-trial is a structured settlement process that combines elements of negotiation, mediation, and trials. Mini-trials are most commonly used when both disputants are corporations. In a **mini-trial**, attorneys for the two corporations conduct limited discovery and then present evidence to a panel consisting of managers from each company, as well as to a neutral third party, who may be a retired judge or other attorney. After the lawyers complete their presentations, the managers try to negotiate a settlement without the attorneys. The managers may consult the third party on how a court might resolve the issues in dispute.

Summary Jury Trial [3-6e]

A **summary jury trial** is a mock trial in which the parties present their case to a jury. Though not binding, the jury's verdict does influence the negotiations in which the parties must participate following the mock trial. If the parties do not reach a settlement, they may have a full trial *de novo*.

Negotiation [3-6f]

Negotiation is a consensual bargaining process in which the parties attempt to reach an agreement resolving their dispute. Negotiation differs from other methods of alternate dispute resolution in that no third parties are involved.

CHAPTER SUMMARY

The Court System

Federal Courts

District Courts trial courts of general jurisdiction that can hear and decide most legal controversies in the federal system

Courts of Appeals hear appeals from the district courts and review orders of certain administrative agencies

The Supreme Court the nation's highest court, whose principal function is to review decisions of the federal Courts of Appeals and the highest state courts

Special Courts have jurisdiction over cases in a particular area of federal law and include the U.S. Court of Federal Claims, the U.S. Tax Court, the U.S. Bankruptcy Courts, and the U.S. Court of Appeals for the Federal Circuit

State Courts

Inferior Trial Courts hear minor criminal cases such as traffic offenses and civil cases involving small amounts of money and conduct preliminary hearings in more serious criminal cases

Trial Courts have general jurisdiction over civil and criminal cases

Special Trial Courts trial courts, such as probate courts and family courts, which have jurisdiction over a particular area of state law

Appellate Courts include one or two levels; the highest court's decisions are final except in those cases reviewed by the U.S. Supreme Court

Jurisdiction

Subject Matter Jurisdiction

Definition authority of a court to decide a particular kind of case

Federal Jurisdiction

- *Exclusive Federal Jurisdiction* federal courts have sole jurisdiction over federal crimes, bankruptcy, antitrust, patent, trademark, copyright, and other special cases

- *Concurrent Federal Jurisdiction* authority of more than one court to hear the same case; state and federal courts have concurrent jurisdiction over (1) federal question cases (cases arising under the Constitution, statutes, or treaties of the United States) which do not involve exclusive federal jurisdiction and (2) diversity of citizenship cases involving more than $75,000

Exclusive State Jurisdiction state courts have exclusive jurisdiction over all matters to which the federal judicial power does not reach

Jurisdiction over the Parties

Definition the power of a court to bind the parties to a suit

In Personam **Jurisdiction** jurisdiction based on claims against a person, in contrast to jurisdiction over property

In Rem **Jurisdiction** jurisdiction based on claims against property

Attachment Jurisdiction jurisdiction over a defendant's property to obtain payment of a claim not related to the property

Venue geographic area in which a lawsuit should be brought

Civil Dispute Resolution

Civil Procedure

Pleadings series of statements that give notice and establish the issues of fact and law presented and disputed

- *Complaint* initial pleading by the plaintiff stating his case
- *Summons* notice given to inform a person of a lawsuit against her
- *Answer* defendant's pleading in response to the plaintiff's complaint
- *Reply* plaintiff's pleading in response to the defendant's answer

Pretrial Procedure process requiring the parties to disclose what evidence is available to prove the disputed facts; designed to encourage settlement of cases or to make the trial more efficient

- *Judgment on Pleadings* a final ruling in favor of one party by the judge based on the pleadings
- *Discovery* right of each party to obtain evidence from the other party
- *Pretrial Conference* a conference between the judge and the attorneys to simplify the issues in dispute and to attempt to settle the dispute without trial
- *Summary Judgment* final ruling by the judge in favor of one party based on the evidence disclosed by discovery

Trial determines the facts and the outcome of the case

- *Jury Selection* each party has an unlimited number of challenges for cause and a limited number of peremptory challenges
- *Conduct of Trial* consists of opening statements by attorneys, direct and cross-examination of witnesses, and closing arguments
- *Directed Verdict* final ruling by the judge in favor of one party based on the evidence introduced at trial
- *Jury Instructions* judge gives the jury the particular rules of law that apply to the case
- *Verdict* the jury's decision based on those facts the jury determines the evidence proves
- *Motions Challenging Verdict* include motions for a new trial and a motion for judgment notwithstanding the verdict

Appeal determines whether the trial court committed prejudicial error

Enforcement plaintiff with an unpaid judgment may resort to a writ of execution to have the sheriff seize property of the defendants and to garnishment to collect money owed to the defendant by a third party

Alternative Dispute Resolution

Arbitration nonjudicial proceeding in which a neutral third party selected by the disputants renders a binding decision (award)

Conciliation nonbinding process in which a third party acts as an intermediary between the disputing parties

Mediation nonbinding process in which a third party acts as an intermediary between the disputing parties and proposes solutions for them to consider

Mini-Trial nonbinding process in which attorneys for the disputing parties (typically corporations) present evidence to managers of the disputing parties and a neutral third party, after which the managers attempt to negotiate a settlement in consultation with the third party

Summary Jury Trial mock trial followed by negotiations

Negotiation consensual bargaining process in which the parties attempt to reach an agreement resolving their dispute without the involvement of third parties

QUESTIONS

1. On June 15 a newspaper columnist predicted that the coast of State X would be flooded on the following September 1. Relying on this pronouncement, Gullible quit his job and sold his property at a loss so as not to be financially ruined. When the flooding did not occur, Gullible sued the columnist in a State X court for damages. The court dismissed the case for failure to state a cause of action under applicable state law. On appeal, the State X Supreme Court upheld the lower court. Three months after this ruling, the State Y Supreme Court heard an appeal in which a lower court had ruled that a reader could sue a columnist for falsely predicting flooding.
   a. Must the State Y Supreme Court follow the ruling of the State X Supreme Court as a matter of *stare decisis*?
   b. Should the State Y lower court have followed the ruling of the State X Supreme Court until the State Y Supreme Court issued a ruling on the issue?
   c. Once the State X Supreme Court issued its ruling, could the U.S. Supreme Court overrule the State X Supreme Court?
   d. If the State Y Supreme Court and the State X Supreme Court rule in exactly opposite ways, must the U.S. Supreme Court resolve the conflict between the two courts?

2. State Senator Bowdler convinced the legislature of State Z to pass a law requiring all professors to submit their class notes and transparencies to a board of censors to be sure that no "lewd" materials were presented to students at state universities. Professor Rabelais would like to challenge this law as being violative of his First Amendment rights under the U.S. Constitution.
   a. May Professor Rabelais challenge this law in State Z courts?
   b. May Professor Rabelais challenge this law in a federal district court?

3. While driving his car in Virginia, Carpe Diem, a resident of North Carolina, struck Butt, a resident of Alaska. As a result of the accident, Butt suffered more than $80,000 in medical expenses. Butt would like to know if he personally serves the proper papers to Diem whether he can obtain jurisdiction against Diem for damages in the following courts:
   a. Alaska state trial court

   b. Federal Circuit Court of Appeals for the Ninth Circuit (includes Alaska)
   c. Virginia state trial court
   d. Virginia federal district court
   e. Federal Circuit Court of Appeals for the Fourth Circuit (includes Virginia and North Carolina)
   f. Virginia equity court
   g. North Carolina state trial court

4. Sam Simpleton, a resident of Kansas, and Nellie Naive, a resident of Missouri, each bought $85,000 in stock at local offices in their home states from Evil Stockbrokers, Inc. (Evil), a business incorporated in Delaware with its principal place of business in Kansas. Both Simpleton and Naive believe that they were cheated by Evil and would like to sue it for fraud. Assuming that no federal question is at issue, assess the accuracy of the following statements:
   a. Simpleton can sue Evil in a Kansas state trial court.
   b. Simpleton can sue Evil in a federal district court in Kansas.
   c. Naive can sue Evil in a Missouri state trial court.
   d. Naive can sue Evil in a federal district court in Missouri.

5. The Supreme Court of State A ruled that, under the law of State A, pit bull owners must either keep their dogs fenced or pay damages to anyone bitten by the dogs. Assess the accuracy of the following statements:
   a. It is likely that the U.S. Supreme Court would issue a writ of *certiorari* in the "pit bull" case.
   b. If a case similar to the "pit bull" case were to come before the Supreme Court of State B in the future, the doctrine of *stare decisis* would leave the court no choice but to rule the same way as the Supreme Court of State A ruled in the "pit bull" case.

6. The Supreme Court of State G decided that the U.S. Constitution requires professors to warn students of their right to remain silent before questioning the students about cheating. This ruling directly conflicts with a decision of the Federal Court of Appeals for the circuit that includes State G.
   a. Must the Federal Circuit Court of Appeals withdraw its ruling?
   b. Must the Supreme Court of State G withdraw its ruling?

CASE PROBLEMS

7. Thomas Clements brought an action in a court in Illinois to recover damages for breach of warranty against defendant, Signa Corporation. (A warranty is an obligation that the seller of goods assumes with respect to the quality of the goods sold.) Clements had purchased a motorboat from Barney's Sporting Goods, an Illinois corporation. The boat was manufactured by Signa Corporation, an Indiana corporation with its principal place of business in Decatur, Indiana. Signa has no office in Illinois and no agent authorized to do business on its behalf within Illinois. Clements saw Signa's boats on display at the Chicago Boat Show. In addition, literature on Signa's boats was distributed at the Chicago Boat Show. Several boating magazines, delivered to Clements in Illinois, contained advertisements for Signa's boats. Clements had also seen Signa's boats on display at Barney's Sporting Goods Store in Palatine, Illinois, where he eventually purchased the boat. A written warranty issued by Signa was delivered to Clements in Illinois. Although Signa was served with a summons, it failed to enter an appearance in this case. A default order was entered against Signa and subsequently a judgment of $6,220 was entered against Signa. Signa appealed. Decision?

8. Vette sued Aetna under a fire insurance policy. Aetna moved for summary judgment on the basis that the pleadings and discovered evidence showed a lack of an insurable interest in Vette. An "insurable interest" exists when the insured derives a monetary benefit or advantage from the preservation or continued existence of the property or would sustain an economic loss from its destruction. Aetna provided ample evidence to infer that Vette had no insurable interest in the contents of the burned building. Vette also provided sufficient evidence to put in dispute this factual issue. The trial court granted the motion for summary judgment. Vette appealed. Decision?

9. Mark Womer and Brian Perry were members of the U.S. Navy and were stationed in Newport, Rhode Island. On April 10, Womer allowed Perry to borrow his automobile so that Perry could visit his family in New Hampshire. Later that day, while operating Womer's vehicle, Perry was involved in an accident in Manchester, New Hampshire. As a result of the accident, Tzannetos Tavoularis was injured. Tavoularis brought this action against Womer in a New Hampshire superior court, contending that Womer was negligent in lending the automobile to Perry when he knew or should have known that Perry did not have a valid driver's license. Womer sought to dismiss the action on the ground that the New Hampshire courts lacked jurisdiction over him, citing the following facts: (a) he did not live in New Hampshire, (b) he had no relatives in New Hampshire, (c) he neither owned property nor possessed investments in New Hampshire, and (d) he had never conducted business in New Hampshire. Did the New Hampshire courts have jurisdiction? Explain.

10. Mariana Deutsch worked as a knitwear mender and attended a school for beauticians. The sink in her apartment collapsed on her foot, fracturing her big toe and making it painful for her to stand. She claims that as a consequence of the injury she was compelled to abandon her plans to become a beautician because that job requires long periods of standing. She also asserts that she was unable to work at her current job for a month. She filed a tort claim against Hewes Street Realty for negligence in failing properly to maintain the sink. She brought the suit in federal district court, claiming damages of $85,000. Her medical expenses and actual loss of salary were less than $7,500; the rest of her alleged damages were for loss of future earnings as a beautician. Hewes Street moved to dismiss the suit on the basis that Deutsch's claim fell short of the jurisdictional requirement and therefore the federal court lacked subject matter jurisdiction over her claim. The district court dismissed the suit, and Deutsch appealed. Does the federal court have jurisdiction? Explain.

11. Kenneth Thomas brought suit against his former employer, Kidder, Peabody & Company, and two of its employees, Barclay Perry and James Johnston, in a dispute over commissions on sales of securities. When he applied to work at Kidder, Peabody & Company, Thomas had filled out a form, which contained an arbitration agreement clause. Thomas had also registered with the New York Stock Exchange (NYSE). Rule 347 of the NYSE provides that any controversy between a registered representative and a member company shall be settled by arbitration. Kidder, Peabody & Company is a member of the NYSE. Thomas refused to arbitrate, relying on Section 229 of the California Labor Code, which provides that actions for the collection of wages may be maintained "without regard to the existence of any private agreement to arbitrate." Perry and Johnston filed a petition in a California state court to compel arbitration under Section 2 of the Federal Arbitration Act, which was enacted pursuant to the Commerce Clause of the U.S. Constitution. Should the petition of Perry and Johnson be granted?

12. Steven Gwin bought a lifetime Termite Protection Plan for his home in Alabama from the local office of Allied-Bruce, a franchisee of Terminix International Company. The plan provided that Allied-Bruce would "protect" Gwin's house against termite infestation, reinspect periodically, provide additional treatment if necessary, and repair damage caused by new termite infestations. Terminix International guaranteed the fulfillment of these contractual provisions. The plan also provided that all disputes arising out of the contract would be settled exclusively by arbitration. Four years later, Gwin had Allied-Bruce reinspect the house in anticipation of selling it. Allied-Bruce gave the house a "clean bill of health." Gwin then sold the house and transferred the Termite Protection Plan to Dobson. Shortly thereafter, Dobson found the house to be infested with termites. Allied-Bruce attempted to treat and repair the house, using materials from out of state, but these efforts failed to satisfy Dobson. Dobson then sued Gwin, Allied-Bruce, and Terminix International in an Alabama state court. Allied-Bruce and Terminix International asked for a stay of these proceedings until arbitration could be carried out as stipulated in the contract. The trial court refused to grant the stay. The Alabama Supreme Court upheld that ruling, citing a state statute that makes predispute arbitration agreements unenforceable. The court found that the Federal Arbitration Act, which preempts conflicting state law, did not apply to this contract because its connection to interstate commerce was too slight. Was the Alabama Supreme Court correct? Explain.

TAKING SIDES

John Connelly suffered personal injuries when a tire manufactured by Uniroyal failed while his 1969 Opel Kadett was being operated on a highway in Colorado. Connelly's father had purchased the automobile from a Buick dealer in Evanston, Illinois. The tire bore the name "Uniroyal" and the legend "made in Belgium" and was manufactured by Uniroyal, sold in Belgium to General Motors, and subsequently installed on the Opel when it was assembled at a General Motors plant in Belgium. The automobile was shipped to the United States for distribution by General Motors. It appears that between the years 1968 and 1971 more than 4,000 Opels imported into the United States from Antwerp, Belgium, were delivered to dealers in Illinois each year; that in each of those years between 600 and 1,320 of the Opels delivered to Illinois dealers were equipped with tires manufactured by Uniroyal, and that the estimated number of Uniroyal tires mounted on Opels delivered in Illinois within each of those years ranged from 3,235 to 6,630. Connelly brought suit in Illinois against Uniroyal to recover damages for personal injuries. Uniroyal asserted that it was not subject to the jurisdiction of the Illinois courts because it is not registered to do business and has never had an agent, employee, representative, or salesperson in Illinois; that it has never possessed or controlled any land or maintained any office or telephone listing in Illinois; that it has never sold or shipped any products into Illinois, either directly or indirectly; and that it has never advertised in Illinois.

a. What arguments could Connelly make in support of his claim that Illinois courts have jurisdiction over Uniroyal?

b. What arguments could Uniroyal make in support of its claim that Illinois courts do not have jurisdiction over it?

c. Who should prevail? Explain.

Constitutional Law

CHAPTER 4

I have always regarded [the American] Constitution as the most remarkable work known to me in modern times to have been produced by the human intellect, at a single stroke (so to speak), in its application to political affairs.

William Gladstone
British Prime Minister (1887)

CHAPTER OUTCOMES

After reading and studying this chapter, you should be able to:

1. Explain the basic principles of constitutional law.

2. Describe the sources and extent of the power of the federal and state governments to regulate business and commerce.

3. Distinguish the three levels of scrutiny used by the courts to determine the constitutionality of government action.

4. Explain the effect of the First Amendment on (a) corporate political speech, (b) commercial speech, and (c) defamation.

5. Explain the difference between substantive and procedural due process.

Y ou will recall from Chapter 1 that a constitution is the fundamental law of a particular level of government. It establishes the structure of government and defines the political relationships within it. It also places restrictions on the powers of government and guarantees the rights and liberties of the people. The Constitution of the United States was adopted on September 17, 1787, by representatives of the thirteen newly created states. Its purpose is stated in the preamble:

> We the People of the United States, in Order to form a more perfect Union, establish Justice, insure domestic Tranquility, provide for the common defense, promote the general Welfare, and secure the Blessings of Liberty to ourselves and our Posterity, do ordain and establish this Constitution for the United States of America.

Although the framers of the U.S. Constitution stated precisely what rights and authority were vested in the new national government, they considered it unnecessary to list those liberties the people were to keep for themselves. Nonetheless, during the state conventions ratifying the document, people expressed fear that the federal government might abuse its powers. To calm these concerns, the first Congress approved ten amendments to the U.S. Constitution, now known as the Bill of Rights, which were adopted on December 15, 1791.

The Bill of Rights restricts the powers and authority of the federal government and establishes many of the civil and political rights enjoyed in the United States, including the right to due process of law and freedoms of speech, press, religion, assembly, and petition. Though the Bill of Rights does not apply directly to the states, the Supreme Court has held that the Fourteenth Amendment incorporates most of the principal guarantees of the Bill of Rights, thus making them applicable to the states.

This chapter concerns constitutional law as it applies to business and commerce. We will begin by surveying some of the basic principles of constitutional law and will then examine the allocation of power between the federal and state governments with respect to the regulation of business. Finally, we will discuss the constitutional restrictions on the power of government to regulate business.

BASIC PRINCIPLES [4-1]

Constitutional law in the United States involves several basic concepts. These fundamental principles, which apply both to the powers of and to the limitations on government, are (1) federalism, (2) federal supremacy and preemption, (3) judicial review, (4) separation of powers, and (5) state action.

Federalism [4-1a]

Federalism

governing power is divided between the federal government and the states

Federalism is the division of governing power between the federal government and the states. The U.S. Constitution enumerates the powers of the federal government and specifically reserves to the states or the people the powers not expressly delegated to the federal government. Accordingly, the federal government is a government of enumerated, or limited, powers, and a specified power must authorize each of its acts. The doctrine of enumerated powers is not, however, a significant limitation on the federal government, because a number of these enumerated powers, in particular the power to regulate interstate and foreign commerce, have been broadly interpreted.

Furthermore, the Constitution grants Congress not only specified powers but also the power "[t]o make all Laws which shall be necessary and proper for carrying into Execution the foregoing Powers, and all other Powers vested by this Constitution in the Government of the United States, or in any Department or Officer thereof." U.S. Constitution, Article I, Section 8, clause 18. In the Supreme Court's view, the Necessary and Proper Clause enables Congress to legislate in areas not mentioned in the list of enumerated powers as long as such legislation reasonably relates to some enumerated power.

Federal Supremacy and Preemption [4-1b]

Supremacy Clause

federal law takes precedence over conflicting state laws

Although under the U.S. federalist system the states retain significant powers, the **Supremacy Clause** of the U.S. Constitution provides that, within its own sphere, federal law is supreme and that state law must, in case of conflict, yield. Accordingly, any state constitutional provision or law that conflicts with the U.S. Constitution or valid federal laws or treaties is unconstitutional and may not be given effect.

Federal preemption

first right of the federal government to regulate matters within its powers to the possible exclusion of state regulation

Under the Supremacy Clause, whenever Congress enacts legislation within its constitutional powers, the federal action **preempts** (overrides) any conflicting state legislation. Even if a state regulation is not in conflict, it must still give way if Congress clearly has intended its action to preempt state legislation. This intent may be stated expressly in the legislation or inferred from the scope of the legislation, the need for uniformity, or the danger of conflict between coexisting federal and state regulation.

When Congress has *not* intended to displace all state legislation, then nonconflicting state legislation is permitted. When Congress has not acted, the fact that it has the power to act does not prevent the states from acting. Until Congress exercises its power to preempt, state regulation is permitted.

Williamson v. Mazda Motor of America, Inc.
Supreme Court of the United States, 2011
562 U.S. ___, 131 S.Ct. 1131, 179 L.Ed.2d 75
http://scholar.google.com/scholar_case?q=131+S.CT.+1131&hl=en&as_sdt=2,34&case=17793025419262348357&scilh=0

FACTS The 1989 version of Federal Motor Vehicle Safety Standard 208 (FMVSS 208) requires, among other things, that auto manufacturers install seatbelts on the rear seats of passenger vehicles. They must install lap-and-shoulder belts on seats next to a vehicle's doors or frames. But they have a choice about what to install on rear middle seats or those next to an aisle in a minivan. There they can install either lap belts or lap-and-shoulder belts.

In 2002, the Williamson family, riding in their 1993 Mazda minivan, was struck head on by another vehicle. Thanh Williamson

was sitting in a rear aisle seat, wearing a lap belt; she died in the accident. Delbert and Alexa Williamson were wearing lap-and-shoulder belts; they survived. They, along with Thanh's estate, brought this California tort suit against Mazda. They claimed that Mazda should have installed lap-and-shoulder belts on rear aisle seats in the minivan, and that Thanh died because Mazda equipped her seat with a lap belt instead.

The California trial court dismissed this tort claim on the basis of the pleadings. The California Court of Appeal affirmed, relying on a U.S. Supreme Court decision, *Geier v. American Honda Motor Co.* That case held that a different portion of an older version of FMVSS 208—which required installation of passive restraint devices—preempted a state tort suit that sought to hold an auto manufacturer liable for failure to install a particular kind of passive restraint, namely, airbags. The Williamsons sought *certiorari*, which was granted.

DECISION The judgment of the California Court of Appeal is reversed.

OPINION Did the state tort action here conflict with the federal regulation? Under ordinary conflict preemption principles, a state law that "stands as an obstacle to the accomplishment and execution of the full purposes and objectives" of a federal law is preempted. Like the regulation in *Geier*, the regulation in this case leaves the manufacturer with a choice, and the tort suit here would restrict that choice. But unlike *Geier*, the choice here is *not* a significant regulatory objective. The Department of Transportation (DOT) rejected a regulation requiring lap-and-shoulder belts in rear seats in 1984. But by 1989, changed circumstances led DOT to require manufacturers to install lap-and-shoulder belts for rear outer seats but to retain a manufacturer choice for rear inner seats. It was not concerned about consumer acceptance; it thought that lap-and-shoulder belts would increase safety and did not pose additional safety risks; and it was not seeking to use the regulation to spur development of alternative safety devices.

The more important reason why DOT did not require lap-and-shoulder belts for rear inner seats was that it thought that this requirement would not be cost-effective. But the fact that DOT made a negative judgment about cost effectiveness cannot by itself show that DOT sought to forbid common-law tort suits in which a judge or jury might reach a different conclusion.

For one thing, DOT did not believe that costs would remain frozen. Rather it pointed out that costs were falling, as manufacturers were "voluntarily equipping more and more of their vehicles with rear seat lap/shoulder belts." For another thing, many, perhaps most, federal safety regulations embody some kind of cost-effectiveness judgment. While an agency could base a decision to preempt on its cost-effectiveness judgment, the rulemaking record at issue here discloses no such preemptive intent. And to infer from the mere existence of such a cost-effectiveness judgment that the federal agency intends to bar states from imposing stricter standards would treat all such federal standards as if they were maximum standards, eliminating the possibility that the federal agency seeks only to set forth a minimum standard potentially supplemented through state tort law. This consequence cannot be reconciled with a statutory saving clause that foresees the likelihood of a continued meaningful role for state tort law.

Here the regulation's history, the agency's contemporaneous explanation, and its consistently held interpretive views indicated that the regulation did not seek to maintain manufacturer choice in order to further significant regulatory objectives. The Court therefore concluded that, even though the state tort suit may restrict the manufacturer's choice, it does not "stan[d] as an obstacle to the accomplishment … of the full purposes and objectives" of federal law. Thus, the regulation does not preempt this tort action.

INTERPRETATION Providing manufacturers with a choice of belts for rear inner seats is not a significant objective of the federal regulation, and thus the regulation does not preempt the state tort suit.

CRITICAL THINKING QUESTION How does this decision affect the extent to which manufacturers can rely on federal safety regulations? Explain.

Judicial Review [4-1c]

Judicial review
power of the courts to determine the constitutionality of any legislative or executive act

Judicial review describes the process by which the courts examine government actions to determine whether they conform to the U.S. Constitution. If government action violates the U.S. Constitution, under judicial review the courts will invalidate that action. Judicial review extends to legislation, acts of the executive branch, and the decisions of inferior courts; such review scrutinizes actions of both the federal and state governments and applies to both the same standards of constitutionality. The U.S. Supreme Court is the final authority as to the constitutionality of any federal and state law.

Separation of Powers [4-1d]

Separation of powers
allocation of powers among the legislative, executive, and judicial branches of government

Another basic principle on which the U.S. government is founded is that of **separation of powers**. The U.S. Constitution vests power in three distinct and independent branches of government—the executive, legislative, and judicial branches. The purpose of the doctrine of separation of powers is to prevent any branch of government from gaining too much power. The doctrine also permits each branch to function without interference from any other branch. Basically, the legislative branch is granted the power to make the law, the executive branch to enforce the law, and the judicial branch to interpret the law. This separation of powers is not complete, however. For example, the executive branch has veto power over legislation enacted by Congress; the legislative branch must approve a great number of executive appointments; and the judicial branch may declare both legislation and executive actions unconstitutional. Nevertheless, the U.S. government generally operates under a three-branch scheme that provides for separation of powers and places checks and balances on the power of each branch, as illustrated by Figure 4-1.

Figure 4-1 Separation of Powers: Checks and Balances

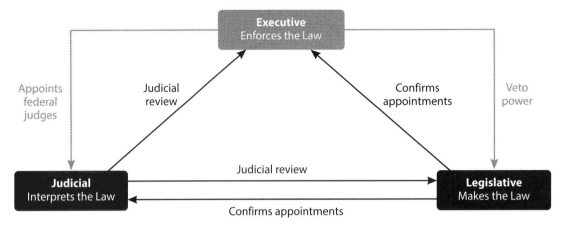

State Action [4-1e]

State action

actions by governments as opposed to actions taken by private individuals

Most of the protections provided by the U.S. Constitution and its amendments apply only to government, or state, action. **State action** includes any actions of the federal and state governments and their subdivisions, such as city or county governments and agencies. Only the Thirteenth Amendment, which abolishes slavery or involuntary servitude, applies to the actions of private individuals. The protections that guard against state action, however, may be extended by *statute* to apply to private activity.

Additionally, action taken by private citizens may constitute state action if the state exercises coercive power over the challenged private action, has encouraged the action significantly, or was substantially involved with the action. For example, the Supreme Court found state action when the Supreme Court of Missouri ordered a lower court to enforce an agreement among white property owners that prohibited the transfer of their property to nonwhites. Moreover, if "private" individuals or entities engage in public functions, their actions may be considered state action subject to constitutional limitations. For example, the U.S. Supreme Court held that a company town was subject to the First Amendment because the state had allowed the company to exercise all of the public functions and activities usually conducted by a town government. Since that case, the Supreme Court has been less willing to find state action based upon the performance of public functions by private entities; the Court now limits such a finding to those functions "traditionally exclusively reserved to the state."

 Brentwood Academy v. Tennessee Secondary School Athletic Association
Supreme Court of the United States, 2001
531 U.S. 288, 121 S.Ct. 924, 148 L.Ed.2d 807
http://scholar.google.com/scholar_case?q=121+S.Ct.+924&hl=en&as_sdt=2,34&case=2890003226740495113&scilh=0

FACTS The Tennessee Secondary School Athletic Association (Association) is a not-for-profit membership corporation organized to regulate interscholastic sport among the public and private high schools in Tennessee. No school is forced to join, but since there is no other authority regulating interscholastic athletics, it enjoys the memberships of almost all the state's public high schools (some 290 of them or 84 percent of the Association's voting membership), far outnumbering the fifty-five private schools that belong.

The Association's rulemaking arm is its legislative council, while its board of control deals with administration. The voting membership of each of these nine-person committees is limited under the Association's bylaws to high school principals, assistant

principals, and superintendents elected by the member schools, and the public school administrators who so serve typically attend meetings during regular school hours. Although the Association's staff members are not paid by the state, they are eligible to join the state's public retirement system for its employees. Member schools pay dues to the Association, though the bulk of its revenue is gate receipts at member teams' football and basketball tournaments. The constitution, bylaws, and rules of the Association set standards of school membership and the eligibility of students to play in interscholastic games. In 1997, a regulatory enforcement proceeding was brought against Brentwood Academy, a private parochial high school member of the Association. The Association's board of control found that Brentwood violated a rule prohibiting "undue influence" in recruiting athletes, when it wrote to incoming students and their parents about spring football practice. The Association placed Brentwood's athletic program on probation for four years, declared its football and boys' basketball teams ineligible to compete in playoffs for two years, and imposed a $3,000 fine.

Brentwood sued the Association and its executive director claiming that enforcement of the Rule was state action and a violation of the First and Fourteenth Amendments. The district court entered summary judgment for Brentwood and enjoined the Association from enforcing the Rule. The U.S. Court of Appeals for the Sixth Circuit reversed, saying that the district court was mistaken in seeing a symbiotic relationship between the state and the Association. It emphasized that the Association was neither engaging in a traditional and exclusive public function nor responding to state compulsion. The U.S. Supreme Court granted *certiorari* to resolve the conflict.

DECISION The judgment of the Court of Appeals for the Sixth Circuit is reversed, and the case is remanded for further proceedings consistent with this opinion.

OPINION State action may be found if, though only if, there is such a "close nexus between the State and the challenged action" that seemingly private behavior "may be fairly treated as that of the State itself." In this case, the Association is not an organization of natural persons acting on their own, but of schools, and of public schools to the extent of 84 percent of the total. Each member school is represented by its principal or a faculty member, who has a vote in selecting members of the governing legislative council and the board of control from eligible principals, assistant principals, and superintendents.

Although there is no express conclusion of law that public school officials act within the scope of their duties when they represent their institutions, no other view would be rational. Interscholastic athletics obviously play an integral part in the public education of Tennessee, requiring some mechanism to produce rules and regulate competition. The mechanism is an organization overwhelmingly composed of public school officials who select representatives (all of them public officials at the time in question here), who in turn adopt and enforce the rules that make the system work. Many of the council or board meetings are held during official school hours, and the public schools have largely provided for the Association's financial support.

In sum, to the extent of 84 percent of its membership, the Association is an organization of public schools represented by their officials acting in their official capacity to provide an integral element of secondary public schooling. There would be no recognizable Association, legal or tangible, without the public school officials, who do not merely control but overwhelmingly perform all but the purely ministerial acts by which the Association exists and functions in practical terms. Only the 16 percent minority of private school memberships prevents this entwinement of the Association and the public school system from being total and their identities totally indistinguishable.

To complement the entwinement of public school officials with the Association from the bottom up, the State of Tennessee has provided for entwinement from top down. State Board members are assigned *ex officio* to serve as members of the board of control and legislative council, and the Association's ministerial employees are treated as state employees to the extent of being eligible for membership in the state retirement system. The entwinement down from the State Board is therefore unmistakable, just as the entwinement up from the member public schools is overwhelming.

INTERPRETATION If an association involves the pervasive entwinement of state school officials in its structure, the association's regulatory activity will be treated as state action.

CRITICAL THINKING QUESTION Should the actions of private parties be immune from federal constitutional limitations? Explain.

Powers of Government [4-2]

The U.S. Constitution created a federal government of enumerated powers. Moreover, as the Tenth Amendment declares, "[t]he powers not delegated to the United States by the Constitution, nor prohibited by it to the States, are reserved to the States respectively, or to the people." Consequently, the legislation Congress enacts must be based on a specific power the Constitution grants to the federal government or be reasonably necessary to carry out an enumerated power.

Some government powers may be exercised only by the federal government. These exclusive federal powers include the power to establish laws regarding bankruptcy, to establish post offices, to grant patents and copyrights, to coin currency, to wage war, and to enter into treaties. Conversely, both the federal government and the states may exercise concurrent government powers, which include taxation, spending, and police power (regulation of public health, safety, and welfare).

In this part of the chapter, we will examine the sources and extent of the powers of the federal government—as well as the power of the states—to regulate business and commerce.

Federal Commerce Power [4-2a]

The U.S. Constitution provides that Congress has the power to regulate commerce with other nations and among the states. This Commerce Clause has two important effects: (1) it provides a

Commerce power

exclusive power granted by the U.S. Constitution to the federal government to regulate commerce with foreign countries and among the states

broad source of **commerce power** for the federal government to regulate the economy and (2) it restricts state regulations that obstruct or unduly burden interstate commerce.

The U.S. Supreme Court interprets the Commerce Clause as granting virtually complete power to Congress to regulate the economy and business. More specifically, under the Commerce Clause, Congress has the power to regulate (1) the channels of interstate commerce, (2) the instrumentalities of interstate commerce, and (3) those activities having a substantial relation to interstate commerce. A court may invalidate legislation enacted under the Commerce Clause only if it is clear that (1) the activity the legislation regulates does not affect interstate commerce *or* (2) no reasonable connection exists between the selected regulatory means and the stated ends. For example, activities conducted solely within one state, such as the practice of law or real estate brokerage agreements, are subject to federal antitrust laws under the power granted by the Commerce Clause if those activities (1) substantially affect interstate commerce or (2) are in the flow of commerce.

Because of the broad and permissive interpretation of the commerce power, Congress currently regulates a vast range of activities. Many of the activities discussed in this text are regulated by the federal government through its exercise of the commerce power; such activities include federal crimes, consumer warranties and credit transactions, electronic funds transfers, trademarks, unfair trade practices, other consumer transactions, residential real estate transactions, consumer and employee safety, labor relations, civil rights in employment, transactions in securities, and environmental protection.

In 2010, Congress enacted the Patient Protection and Affordable Care Act (commonly called "Obamacare") to increase the number of Americans covered by health insurance and decrease the cost of health care. One key provision—the *individual mandate*—requires most Americans to maintain "minimum essential" health insurance coverage or make a "shared responsibility payment" to the federal government. The constitutionality of the individual mandate was challenged as beyond the commerce and taxing powers of Congress. In deciding the Commerce Clause question, the U.S. Supreme Court explained that the Commerce Clause presupposes the existence of commercial activity to be regulated:

> The individual mandate, however, does not regulate existing commercial activity. It instead compels individuals to *become* active in commerce by purchasing a product, on the ground that their failure to do so affects interstate commerce. Construing the Commerce Clause to permit Congress to regulate individuals precisely *because* they are doing nothing would open a new and potentially vast domain to congressional authority.

Accordingly, in a 5–4 vote the Court held that the individual mandate was *not* a valid exercise of the commerce power. *National Federation of Independent Business v. Sebelius*, 567 U.S. 1 (2012). The Court's decision regarding the taxing power of Congress is covered later in this chapter.

State regulation of commerce

the Commerce Clause of the U.S. Constitution restricts the states' power to regulate activities if the result obstructs interstate commerce

State Regulation of Commerce [4-2b]

The Commerce Clause, as we have previously discussed, specifically grants to Congress the power to regulate commerce among the states. In addition to acting as a broad source of federal power, the clause also implicitly restricts the states' power to regulate activities if the result obstructs or unduly burdens interstate commerce.

Regulations   The U.S. Supreme Court ultimately decides the extent to which state regulation may affect interstate commerce. In doing so, the Court weighs and balances several factors: (1) the necessity and importance of the state regulation, (2) the burden it imposes on interstate commerce, and (3) the extent to which it discriminates against interstate commerce in favor of local concerns. The application of these factors involves case-by-case analysis. In general, in cases in which a state statute regulates evenhandedly to accomplish a legitimate state interest and its effects on interstate commerce are only incidental, the Court will uphold the statute unless the burden imposed on interstate commerce is clearly excessive compared with the local benefits. The Court will uphold a discriminatory regulation only if no other reasonable method of achieving a legitimate local interest exists.

Department of Revenue of Kentucky, et al. v. Davis
Supreme Court of the United States, 2008
553 U.S. 328, 128 S.Ct. 1801, 170 L.Ed.2d 685
http://scholar.google.com/scholar_case?q=128+S.Ct.+1801&hl=en&as_sdt=2,34&case=15768194217522904809&scilh=0

FACTS Kentucky, like forty other states, exempts from state income taxes interest on bonds issued by it or its political subdivisions but not on bonds issued by other states and their subdivisions. The differential tax scheme in Kentucky benefits its residents who buy its bonds by effectively lowering interest rates. After paying state income tax on out-of-state municipal bonds, plaintiffs sued Kentucky for a refund, claiming that Kentucky's differential tax impermissibly discriminated against interstate commerce. The trial court ruled for Kentucky. The State Court of Appeals reversed, finding that Kentucky's scheme violated the Commerce Clause. The U.S. Supreme Court granted *certiorari*.

DECISION The judgment is reversed, and the case is remanded.

OPINION The significance of the differential tax scheme is immense. Between 1996 and 2002, Kentucky and its subdivisions issued $7.7 billion in long-term bonds to pay for spending on transportation, public safety, education, utilities, and environmental protection, among other things. Across the United States during the same period, states issued over $750 billion in long-term bonds, with nearly a third of the money going to education, followed by transportation (13%) and utilities (11%). Municipal bonds currently finance roughly two-thirds of capital expenditures by state and local governments.

The "dormant" Commerce Clause implicitly restricts state regulatory measures designed to benefit in-state economic interests by burdening out-of-state competitors. Under the dormant Commerce Clause a challenged law that discriminates against interstate commerce is "virtually *per se* invalid" and will survive only if it

"advances a legitimate local purpose that cannot be adequately served by reasonable nondiscriminatory alternatives." Absent discrimination for the forbidden purpose, however, the law "will be upheld unless the burden imposed on [interstate] commerce is clearly excessive in relation to the putative local benefits."

Kentucky treats income from municipal bonds of other states just like income from bonds privately issued in Kentucky or elsewhere; no preference is given to any local issuer, and none to any local holder, beyond what is entailed in the preference Kentucky grants itself when it engages in activities serving public objectives. These facts suggest that no state perceives any local advantage or disadvantage beyond the permissible ones open to a government and to those who deal with it when that government itself enters the market. The differential tax scheme is critical to the operation of an identifiable segment of the municipal financial market as it currently functions, and this fact alone demonstrates that the unanimous desire of the states to preserve the tax feature is a far cry from the private protectionism that has driven the development of the dormant Commerce Clause.

INTERPRETATION State law exempting from state income taxes interest on bonds issued by that state or its political subdivisions but not on bonds issued by other states and their subdivisions does not impermissibly discriminate against interstate commerce.

CRITICAL THINKING QUESTION Had the Court invalidated Kentucky's taxing scheme, what would the impact have been on the states' ability to finance their operations?

Taxation   The Commerce Clause, in conjunction with the Import-Export Clause, also limits the power of the state to tax. The Import-Export Clause provides: "No State shall, without the Consent of the Congress, lay any Imposts or Duties on Imports or Exports." U.S. Constitution, Article I, Section 10, clause 2. Together, the Commerce Clause and the Import-Export Clause exempt from state taxation goods that have entered the stream of commerce, whether they are interstate or foreign and whether they are imports or exports. The purpose of this immunity is to protect goods in commerce from both discriminatory and cumulative state taxes. Once the goods enter the stream of interstate or foreign commerce, the power of the state to tax ceases and does not resume until the goods are delivered to the purchaser or the owner terminates the movement of the goods through commerce.

The Due Process Clause of the Fourteenth Amendment also restricts the power of states to tax. Under the Due Process Clause, for a state tax to be constitutional, a sufficient nexus must exist between the state and the person, thing, or activity to be taxed.

Federal Fiscal Powers [4-2c]

The federal government exerts a dominating influence over the national economy through its control of financial matters. Much of this impact results from the exercise of its regulatory powers under the Commerce Clause, as previously discussed. In addition, the government derives a substantial portion of its influence from powers that are independent of the Commerce Clause. These include (1) the power to tax, (2) the power to spend, (3) the power to borrow and coin money, and (4) the power of eminent domain.

Taxation The federal government's power to tax, although extremely broad, has three major limitations: (1) direct taxes must be apportioned among the states, (2) all custom duties and excise taxes must be uniform throughout the United States, and (3) no duties may be levied on exports from any state.

Besides raising revenues, taxes also have regulatory and socioeconomic effects. For example, import taxes and custom duties can protect domestic industry from foreign competition. Graduated or progressive tax rates and exemptions may further social policies seeking the redistribution of wealth. Tax credits encourage investment in favored enterprises to the disadvantage of unfavored businesses. A tax that does more than just raise revenue will be upheld "so long as the motive of Congress and the effect of its legislative action are to secure revenue for the benefit of the general government."

The Patient Protection and Affordable Care Act's individual mandate provision requires most Americans to maintain "minimum essential" health insurance coverage or make a "shared responsibility payment" to the federal government. The constitutionality of the individual mandate was challenged as beyond the commerce and taxing powers of Congress. In deciding the taxing power question, in a 5–4 vote the U.S. Supreme Court held that requiring certain individuals to "pay a financial penalty for not obtaining health insurance may reasonably be characterized as a tax. Because the Constitution permits such a tax, it is not our role to forbid it, or to pass upon its wisdom or fairness." *National Federation of Independent Business v. Sebelius*, 567 U.S. 1 (2012).

Spending Power The Constitution authorizes the federal government to pay debts and to spend for the common defense and general welfare of the United States. Like the power to tax, the spending power of Congress is extremely broad; this power will be upheld so long as it does not violate a specific constitutional limitation on federal power.

Furthermore, through its spending power, Congress may accomplish indirectly what it may not do directly. For example, the Supreme Court has held that Congress may condition a state's receipt of federal highway funds on that state's mandating twenty-one as the minimum drinking age, even though the Twenty-First Amendment grants the states significant powers with respect to alcohol consumption within their respective borders. As the Court noted, "Constitutional limitations on Congress when exercising its spending power are less exacting than those on its authority to regulate directly." Whether directly or indirectly, the power of the federal government to spend money represents an important regulatory force in the economy and significantly affects the general welfare of the United States.

Borrowing and Coining Money The U.S. Constitution also grants Congress the power to borrow money on the credit of the United States and to coin money. These two powers have enabled the federal government to establish a national banking system, the Federal Reserve System, and specialized federal lending programs such as the Federal Land Bank. Through these and other institutions and agencies, the federal government wields extensive control over national fiscal and monetary policies and exerts considerable influence over interest rates, the money supply, and foreign exchange rates.

Eminent Domain The government's power to take private property for public use, known as the power of **eminent domain**, is recognized, in the federal Constitution and in the constitutions of the states, as one of the inherent powers of government. At the same time, however, the power is carefully limited. The Fifth Amendment to the federal Constitution contains a Takings Clause that provides that private property shall not be taken for public use without just compensation. Although this amendment applies only to the federal government, the U.S. Supreme Court has held that the Takings Clause is incorporated through the Fourteenth Amendment and is therefore applicable to the states. Moreover, similar or identical provisions are found in the constitutions of the states.

As the language of the Takings Clause indicates, the taking must be for a public use. Public use has been held to be synonymous with public purpose. Thus, private entities, such as railroads and housing authorities, may use the government's power of eminent domain so long as the entity's use of the property benefits the public. When the government or a private entity properly

Eminent domain
the power of a government to take private property for public use upon payment of fair compensation

Figure 4-2 Powers of Government

People's Powers

States' Powers

Federal Powers

Commerce Power	Copyrights*
Taxation	Patents*
Borrowing	International Treaties*
Currency*	Waging War*
Eminent Domain	Post*
Civil Rights	Naturalization*
Bankruptcy*	Weights*
Admiralty*	Measures*

Powers not granted by the Constitution to the federal government or prohibited to the states

All powers not granted to federal or state government

*Exclusive power

takes property under the power of eminent domain, the owners of the property must receive just compensation, which has been interpreted as the fair market value of the property.

The U.S. Supreme Court has held that the Takings Clause requires just compensation only if a government taking actually occurs, not if the government regulation only reduces the value of the property. If, however, a regulation deprives the owner of all economic use of the property, then a taking has occurred. Eminent domain is discussed further in Chapter 49.

Figure 4-2 summarizes the powers granted to the federal government, the states, and the people.

LIMITATIONS ON GOVERNMENT [4-3]

As we have discussed, the U.S. Constitution grants certain specified powers to the federal government, while reserving other, unspecified powers to the states. The Constitution and its amendments, however, impose limits on the powers of both the federal government and the states. In this part of the chapter, we will discuss those limitations most applicable to business: (1) the Contract Clause, (2) the First Amendment, (3) due process, and (4) equal protection. The first of these—the Contract Clause—applies only to the actions of state governments, whereas the other three apply to both the federal government and the states.

None of these restrictions operates as an absolute limitation but instead triggers review or scrutiny by the courts to determine whether the government power exercised encroaches impermissibly upon the interest the Constitution protects. The U.S. Supreme Court has used different levels of scrutiny, depending on the interest affected and the nature of the government action. Although this differentiation among levels of scrutiny is most fully developed in the area of equal protection, it also occurs in other areas, including substantive due process and protection of free speech.

The least rigorous level of scrutiny is the **rational relationship test**, which requires that the regulation conceivably bear some rational relationship to a legitimate government interest that the regulation will attempt to further. The most exacting level of scrutiny is the **strict scrutiny test**, which requires that the regulation be necessary to promote a compelling government interest. Finally, under the **intermediate test**, the regulation must have a substantial relationship to an important government objective. These standards will be explained more fully. See Concept Review 4-1 illustrating these limitations on government.

Rational relationship test
requirement that regulation bears a rational relationship to a legitimate government interest

Strict scrutiny test
requirement that regulation be necessary to promote a compelling government interest

Intermediate test
requirement that regulation have a substantial relationship to an important government objective

CONCEPT REVIEW 4-1

Limitations on Government

Test/Interest	Equal Protection	Substantive Due Process	Free Speech
Strict Scrutiny	Fundamental Rights Suspect Classifications	Fundamental Rights	Protected Noncommercial Speech
Intermediate	Gender Legitimacy		Commercial Speech
Rational Relationship	Economic Regulation	Economic Regulation	Nonprotected Speech

Contract Clause [4-3a]

Contract Clause

prohibition against the states' retroactively modifying public and private contracts

Article I, Section 10, of the Constitution provides: "No State shall … pass any … Law impairing the Obligation of Contracts." The U.S. Supreme Court has used the **Contract Clause** to restrict states from retroactively modifying public charters and private contracts. However, the Court, holding that the Contract Clause does *not* preclude the states from exercising eminent domain or their police powers, has ruled: "No legislature can bargain away the public health or the public morals." Although the Contract Clause does not apply to the federal government, due process limits the federal government's power to impair contracts.

Practical Advice

The federal Constitution protects you from a state law that impairs a preexisting contract.

First Amendment [4-3b]

The First Amendment states:

> Congress shall make no law respecting an establishment of religion, or prohibiting the free exercise thereof; or abridging the freedom of speech, or of the press; or the right of the people peaceably to assemble, and to petition the Government for a redress of grievances.

Free speech

First Amendment protects most speech by using a strict scrutiny standard

The First Amendment's protection of **free speech** is not absolute. Some forms of speech, such as obscenity, receive no protection. Most forms of speech, however, are protected by the strict or exacting scrutiny standard, which requires the existence of a compelling and legitimate state interest to justify a restriction of speech. If such an interest exists, the legislature must use means that least restrict free speech. We will examine the application of the First Amendment's guarantee of free speech to (1) corporate political speech, (2) commercial speech, and (3) defamation.

Brown v. Entertainment Merchants Association
Supreme Court of the United States, 2011
564 U.S. ___, 131 S.Ct. 2729, 180 L.Ed.2d 708
http://scholar.google.com/scholar_case?q=131+S.Ct.+2729+(2011)&hl=en&as_sdt=3,34&case=12960598670321445636&scilh=0

FACTS A California statute (the Act) prohibits the sale or rental of violent video games to minors and requires their packaging to be labeled "18." The Act does "not apply if the violent video game is sold or rented to a minor by the minor's parent, grandparent, aunt, uncle, or legal guardian." The Act covers games "in which the range of options available to a player includes killing, maiming, dismembering, or sexually assaulting an image of a human being, if those acts are depicted" in a manner that "[a] reasonable person, considering the game as a whole, would find appeals to a deviant or morbid interest of minors," that is "patently offensive to prevailing standards in the community as to what is suitable for minors," and that "causes the game, as a whole, to lack serious literary, artistic, political, or scientific value for minors." Violation of the Act is punishable by a civil fine of up to $1,000.

The plaintiffs, representing the video-game and software industries, brought a challenge to the Act in the U.S. District Court for the Northern District of California. That court concluded that the Act violated the First Amendment's freedom of speech clause and permanently enjoined its enforcement. The Court of Appeals affirmed, and the U.S. Supreme Court granted *certiorari*.

DECISION The judgment of the Court of Appeals is affirmed.

OPINION California correctly acknowledges that video games qualify for First Amendment protection. The Free Speech Clause exists principally to protect discourse on public matters, but the U.S. Supreme Court has long recognized that it is difficult to distinguish politics from entertainment, and dangerous to try. Like the protected books, plays, and movies that preceded them, video games communicate ideas—and even social messages—through many familiar literary devices (such as characters, dialogue, plot, and music) and through features distinctive to the medium (such as the player's interaction with the virtual world). That suffices to confer First Amendment protection.

The most basic of First Amendment principles is this: "[A]s a general matter, … government has no power to restrict expression because of its message, its ideas, its subject matter, or its content." There are of course exceptions. "'From 1791 to the present,' … the First Amendment has 'permitted restrictions upon the content of speech in a few limited areas,' and has never 'include[d] a freedom to disregard these traditional limitations.'" [Citations.] These limited areas—such as obscenity, [citation], incitement, [citation], and fighting words, [citation]—represent "well-defined and narrowly limited classes of speech, the prevention and punishment of which have never been thought to raise any Constitutional problem."

The California Act does not adjust the boundaries of an existing category of unprotected speech to ensure that a definition designed for adults is not uncritically applied to children. Instead, it wishes to create a wholly new category of content-based regulation that is permissible only for speech directed at children.

That is unprecedented and mistaken. "[M]inors are entitled to a significant measure of First Amendment protection, and only in relatively narrow and well-defined circumstances may government bar public dissemination of protected materials to them." Thus, "[s]peech that is neither obscene as to youths nor subject to some other legitimate proscription cannot be suppressed solely to protect the young from ideas or images that a legislative body thinks unsuitable for them."

Because the Act imposes a restriction on the content of protected speech, it is invalid unless California can demonstrate that it passes strict scrutiny—that is, unless it is justified by a compel-ling government interest and is narrowly drawn to serve that interest. California must specifically identify an "actual problem" in need of solving, and the curtailment of free speech must be actually necessary to the solution. That is a demanding standard. "It is rare that a regulation restricting speech because of its content will ever be permissible."

California cannot meet that standard. At the outset, it acknowledges that it cannot show a direct causal link between violent video games and harm to minors.

California's legislation straddles the fence between (1) addressing a serious social problem and (2) helping concerned parents control their children. Both ends are legitimate, but when they affect First Amendment rights they must be pursued by means that are neither seriously underinclusive nor seriously overinclusive. As a means of protecting children from portrayals of violence, the legislation is seriously underinclusive, not only because it excludes portrayals other than video games, but also because it permits a parental veto. And as a means of assisting concerned parents it is seriously overinclusive because it abridges the First Amendment rights of young people whose parents (and aunts and uncles) think violent video games are a harmless pastime. And the overbreadth in achieving one goal is not cured by the underbreadth in achieving the other. Legislation such as this, which is neither fish nor fowl, cannot survive strict scrutiny.

INTERPRETATION Because video games qualify for First Amendment protection and new categories of unprotected speech may not be added, a state must show that a law restricting video game sales to minors (1) is justified by a compelling government interest and (2) is narrowly drawn to serve that interest.

CRITICAL THINKING QUESTION Is there a less restrictive alternative to California's law that would be at least as effective? Explain.

Corporate political speech

First Amendment protects a corporation's right to speak out on political issues

Corporate Political Speech   Freedom of speech is indispensable to the discovery and spread of political truth; indeed, "the best test of truth is the power of the thought to get itself accepted in the competition of the market." To promote this competition of ideas, the First Amendment's guarantee of free speech applies not only to individuals but also to corporations. Accordingly, corporations may not be prohibited from speaking out on political issues. For example, in *First National Bank v. Bellotti*, 435 U.S. 765 (1978), the U.S. Supreme Court has held unconstitutional a Massachusetts criminal statute that prohibited banks and business corporations from making contributions and expenditures with regard to most referenda issues. The Court held that if speech is otherwise protected, the fact that the speaker is a corporation does not alter the speech's protected status.

The Supreme Court retreated somewhat from its holding in *Bellotti* when it upheld a state statute prohibiting corporations, except media corporations, from using general treasury funds to make independent expenditures in elections for public office but permitting such expenditures from segregated funds used solely for political purposes. The Court held that the statute did not violate the First Amendment because the burden on corporations' exercise of political expression was justified by a compelling state interest in preventing corruption in the political arena: "the corrosive and distorting effects of immense aggregations of wealth that are accumulated with the help of the corporate form and that have little or no correlation to the public's support for the corporation's political ideas." The Court held that the statute was sufficiently narrowly tailored because it "is precisely targeted to eliminate the distortion caused by corporate spending while also allowing corporations to express their political views" by making expenditures through segregated funds. *Austin v. Michigan Chamber of Commerce*, 494 U.S. 652 (1990).

In a recent landmark 5–4 decision, *Citizens United v. Federal Election Commission*, 558 U.S. 310 (2010), the U.S. Supreme Court explicitly overruled the *Austin* case. *Citizens United* involved a First Amendment challenge to a federal law that prohibited corporations and unions from using their general treasury funds to make independent expenditures for speech defined as an "electioneering communication" or for speech expressly advocating the election or defeat of a candidate. (An electioneering communication is "any broadcast, cable, or satellite communication" that "refers to a clearly identified candidate for Federal office" and is made within thirty days of a primary election.) The Supreme Court invalidated these provisions as conflicting with the First Amendment, holding: "We return to the principle established in … *Bellotti* that the Government may not suppress political speech on the basis of the speaker's corporate identity. No sufficient governmental interest justifies limits on the political speech of nonprofit or for-profit corporations."

The ruling in *Citizens United*, however, did not apply to the two types of federal statutory limits on direct contributions by individuals to federal candidates and political parties. The first limit, called base limits, restricts how much money an individual may contribute to a particular candidate or committee. The second limit, called aggregate limits, restricts how much money an individual donor may contribute in total to all candidates or committees during a political cycle. In 2014, the U.S. Supreme Court considered a challenge to the aggregate limits in the case of *McCutcheon v. Federal Election Commission*, 572 U.S. ___ (2014). In a 5–4 decision, the Supreme Court invalidated the aggregate limits under the First Amendment. This decision did *not* involve any challenge to the base limits, which have been upheld previously as serving the permissible objective of combatting corruption. In addition, this decision concerned only contributions from *individuals*; federal law continues to ban direct contributions by corporations and unions.

Commercial speech

expression related to the economic interests of the speaker and his audience

Commercial Speech **Commercial speech** is expression related to the economic interests of the speaker and his audience, such as advertisements for a product or service. Since the mid-1970s, U.S. Supreme Court decisions have eliminated the doctrine that commercial speech is wholly outside the protection of the First Amendment. Rather, the Court has established the principle that speech proposing a commercial transaction is entitled to protection, which, although less than that accorded to political speech, is still extensive. Protection is accorded commercial speech because of the interest such communication holds for the advertiser, consumer, and general public. Advertising and other similar messages convey important information for the proper and efficient distribution of resources in a free market system. At the same time, however, commercial speech is less valuable and less vulnerable than other varieties of speech and therefore does not merit complete First Amendment protection.

In cases determining the protection to be afforded commercial speech, a four-part analysis has developed. First, the court must determine whether the expression is protected by the First Amendment. For commercial speech to come within that provision, such speech, at the least, must concern lawful activity and not be misleading. Second, the court must determine whether the asserted government interest is substantial. If both inquiries yield positive answers, then, third, the court must determine whether the regulation directly advances the government interest asserted and, fourth, whether the regulation is not more extensive than is necessary to serve that interest. The Supreme Court recently held that government restrictions of commercial speech need not be absolutely the least severe so long as they are "narrowly tailored" to achieve the government objective.

Because the constitutional protection extended to commercial speech is based on the informational function of advertising, governments may regulate or suppress commercial messages that do not accurately inform the public about lawful activity. "The government may ban forms of communication more likely to deceive the public than to inform it, or commercial speech related to illegal activity." Therefore, government regulation of false and misleading advertising is permissible under the First Amendment.

Defamation

injury of a person's reputation by publication of false statements

Defamation **Defamation** is a civil wrong or tort that consists of disgracing or diminishing a person's reputation through the communication of a false statement. An example would be the publication of a statement that a person had committed a crime or had a loathsome disease. (Defamation is also discussed in Chapter 7.)

Because defamation involves a communication, it receives the protection extended to speech by the First Amendment. Moreover, the U.S. Supreme Court has ruled that a public official who is defamed in regard to his conduct, fitness, or role as public official may not recover in a defamation action unless the statement was made with *actual malice*, which requires clear and convincing proof that the defendant had knowledge of the falsity of the communication or acted in reckless disregard of its truth or falsity. This restriction on the right to recover for defamation is based on "a profound national commitment to the principle that debate on public issues should be uninhibited, robust and wide-open, and that it may well include vehement, caustic, and sometimes unpleasantly sharp attacks on government and public officials." *New York Times Co. v. Sullivan*, 376 U.S. 254 (1964). The communication may deal with the official's qualifications for and performance in office, which would likely include most aspects of character and public conduct. In addition, the Supreme Court has extended the same rule to public figures and candidates for public office. (The Supreme Court, however, has not precisely defined the term *public figure*.)

In a defamation suit brought by a private person (one who is neither a public official nor a public figure), the plaintiff must prove that the defendant published the defamatory and false comment with either malice *or* negligence.

Due Process [4-3c]

The Fifth and Fourteenth Amendments prohibit the federal and state governments, respectively, from depriving any person of life, liberty, or property without **due process** of law. Due process has two different aspects: substantive and procedural. As discussed in Chapter 1, substantive law creates, defines, or regulates legal rights, whereas procedural law establishes the rules for enforcing those rights. Accordingly, substantive due process concerns the compatibility of a law or government action with fundamental constitutional rights such as free speech. In contrast, procedural due process involves the review of the decision-making process that enforces substantive laws and results in depriving a person of life, liberty, or property.

Substantive Due Process   **Substantive due process**, which involves a court's determination of whether a particular government action is compatible with individual liberties, addresses the constitutionality of a legal rule, not the fairness of the process by which the rule is applied. Legislation affecting economic and social interests satisfies substantive due process so long as the legislation is rationally related to legitimate government objectives. In cases in which a rule affects individuals' fundamental rights under the Constitution, however, courts will carefully scrutinize the legislation to determine whether it is necessary to promote a compelling or overriding government interest. For example, the U.S. Supreme Court overturned the federal Defense of Marriage Act (DOMA), which defines marriage as the union of a man and a woman for purposes of federal benefits. DOMA thus denies federal benefits to persons in same-sex marriages made lawful by some of the states. The Supreme Court held that

> The federal statute is invalid, for no legitimate purpose overcomes the purpose and effect to disparage and to injure those whom the State, by its marriage laws, sought to protect in personhood and dignity ... By seeking to displace this protection and treating those persons as living in marriages less respected than others, the federal statute is in violation of the Fifth Amendment. *United States v. Windsor*, 570 U.S. ___ (2013).

Procedural Due Process   **Procedural due process** pertains to the government decision-making process that results in depriving a person of life, liberty, or property. As the Supreme Court has interpreted procedural due process, the government is required to provide an individual with a fair procedure if, but only if, the person faces deprivation of life, liberty, or property. When government action adversely affects an individual but does not deny life, liberty, or property, the government is not required to give the person any hearing at all.

For the purposes of procedural due process, **liberty** generally includes the ability of individuals to engage in freedom of action and choice regarding their personal lives. **Property** includes

Due process
Fifth and Fourteenth Amendments prohibit the federal and state governments from depriving any person of life, liberty, or property without due process of law

Substantive due process
requirement that government action be compatible with individual liberties

Procedural due process
requirement that government action depriving a person of life, liberty, or property be done through a fair procedure

Liberty
ability of individuals to engage in freedom of action and choice regarding their personal lives

Property
includes real property, personal property, and certain benefits conferred by government

not only all forms of real and personal property but also certain benefits (entitlements) conferred by the government, such as social security payments and food stamps.

When applicable, procedural due process requires that a court use a fair and impartial procedure in resolving the factual and legal basis for a government action that results in a deprivation of life, liberty, or property.

Equal Protection [4-3d]

Equal protection
requirement that similarly situated persons be treated similarly by government action

The Fourteenth Amendment provides that "nor shall any State … deny to any person within its jurisdiction the equal protection of the laws." Although this amendment applies only to the actions of state governments, the Supreme Court has interpreted the Due Process clause of the Fifth Amendment to subject federal actions to the same standards of review. The most important constitutional concept protecting individual rights, the guarantee of **equal protection** basically requires that similarly situated persons be treated similarly by government actions.

When government action involves classification of people, the equal protection guarantee comes into play. In determining whether government action satisfies the equal protection guarantee, the Supreme Court uses one of three standards of review, depending on the nature of the right involved. The three standards are (1) the rational relationship test, (2) the strict scrutiny test, and (3) the intermediate test.

Rational Relationship Test

The **rational relationship test**, which applies to cases not subject to either the strict scrutiny test or the intermediate test, requires that the classification *conceivably* bear some rational relationship to a legitimate government interest the classification seeks to further. Under this standard of review, the government action is permitted to attack part of the evil to which the action is addressed. Moreover, there is a strong presumption that the action is constitutional. Therefore, the courts will overturn the government action *only* if clear and convincing evidence shows that there is *no* reasonable basis justifying the action.

For example, in *United States v. Windsor*, 570 U.S. ___ (2013), discussed earlier, the U.S. Supreme Court overturned the federal Defense of Marriage Act (DOMA) also for violating the constitutional guarantee of equal protection. By defining marriage as the union of a man and a woman, DOMA denies federal benefits to persons in same-sex marriages made lawful by some of the states. The Court held that DOMA denies equal protection of the laws, stating:

> The class to which DOMA directs its restrictions and restraints are those persons who are joined in same-sex marriages made lawful by the State. DOMA singles out a class of persons deemed by a State entitled to recognition and protection to enhance their own liberty. It imposes a disability on the class by refusing to acknowledge a status the State finds to be dignified and proper. DOMA instructs all federal officials, and indeed all persons with whom same-sex couples interact, including their own children, that their marriage is less worthy than the marriages of others. The federal statute is invalid, for no legitimate purpose overcomes the purpose and effect to disparage and to injure those whom the State, by its marriage laws, sought to protect in personhood and dignity. By seeking to displace this protection and treating those persons as living in marriages less respected than others, the federal statute is in violation of the Fifth Amendment.

Strict Scrutiny Test

Strict scrutiny test
exacting standard of review applicable to regulation affecting a fundamental right or involving a suspect classification

The strict scrutiny test is far more exacting than the rational relationship test. Under this test, the courts do not defer to the government; rather, they independently determine whether a classification of persons is constitutionally permissible. This determination requires that the classification be necessary to promote a compelling or overriding government interest.

The strict scrutiny test is applied when government action affects fundamental rights or involves suspect classifications. Fundamental rights include most of the provisions of the Bill of Rights and certain other rights, such as interstate travel, voting, and access to criminal justice. Suspect classifications include those made on the basis of race or national origin. A classic and important example of strict scrutiny applied to classifications based upon race is found in the 1954 school desegregation case of *Brown v. Board of Education of Topeka*, in which the Supreme Court ruled that segregated public school systems violated the equal protection guarantee.

Subsequently, the Court has invalidated segregation in public beaches, municipal golf courses, buses, parks, public golf courses, and courtroom seating.

A recent U.S. Supreme Court case again addressed the application of strict scrutiny to public schools. School districts in Seattle, Washington, and metropolitan Louisville, Kentucky, had voluntarily adopted student assignment plans that relied on race to determine which schools certain children may attend. In a 5–4 decision, the Court held that public school systems may not seek to achieve or maintain integration through measures that take explicit account of a student's race. The Court reaffirmed that when the government distributes burdens or benefits on the basis of individual racial classifications, that action is reviewed under strict scrutiny requiring the most exact connection between justification and classification. Therefore, the school districts must demonstrate that the use of individual racial classifications in their school assignment plans is narrowly tailored to achieve a compelling government interest. In reversing the lower courts' decisions upholding the schools' plans, the Court held: "The [school] districts have also failed to show that they considered methods other than explicit racial classifications to achieve their stated goals. Narrow tailoring requires 'serious, good faith consideration of workable race-neutral alternatives.'" *Parents Involved in Community Schools v. Seattle School District No.1*, 551 U.S. 701 (2007).

Moreover, in reviewing the use of race by the University of Texas at Austin as one of various factors in its undergraduate admissions process, the U.S. Supreme Court held that strict scrutiny must be applied to any admissions program using racial categories or classifications. In this case, the Supreme Court reaffirmed that "all racial classifications imposed by government 'must be analyzed by a reviewing court under strict scrutiny.'" *Fisher v. University of Texas at Austin*, 570 U.S. ___ (2013).

In the 2014 case of *Schuette v. BAMN*, the U.S. Supreme Court in a 6–2 ruling upheld a Michigan constitutional amendment, approved and enacted by its voters, that bans affirmative action in admissions to the state's public universities. In holding that the amendment was *not* invalid under the Equal Protection Clause of the Fourteenth Amendment, the Supreme Court stated:

> In *Fisher* [*v. University of Texas at Austin*], the Court did not disturb the principle that the consideration of race in admissions is permissible, provided that certain conditions are met. In this case, as in *Fisher*, that principle is not challenged. The question here concerns not the permissibility of race-conscious admissions policies under the Constitution but whether, and in what manner, voters in the States may choose to prohibit the consideration of racial preferences in governmental decisions, in particular with respect to school admissions.... This case is not about how the debate about racial preferences should be resolved. It is about who may resolve it. There is no authority in the Constitution of the United States or in this Court's precedents for the Judiciary to set aside Michigan laws that commit this policy determination to the voters.

Brown v. Board of Education of Topeka
Supreme Court of the United States, 1954
347 U.S. 483, 74 S.Ct. 686, 98 L.Ed. 873
http://scholar.google.com/scholar_case?q=74+S.Ct.+686&hl=en&as_sdt=2,34&case=12120372216939101759&scilh=0

FACTS These were consolidated cases from Kansas, South Carolina, Virginia, and Delaware, each with a different set of facts and local conditions but also presenting a common legal question. Black minors, through their legal representatives, sought court orders to obtain admission to the public schools in their community on a nonsegregated basis. They had been denied admission to schools attended by white children under laws requiring or permitting segregation according to race. The Supreme Court had previously upheld such laws under the "separate but equal" doctrine, which provided that there was equality of treatment of the races through substantially equal, though separate, facilities; and the lower courts had found that the white schools and the black schools involved had been or were being equalized with respect to buildings, curricula, qualifications and salaries of teachers, and other "tangible" factors. The black minors contended, however, that segregated public schools were not and could not be made "equal," and that hence they had been deprived of the equal protection of the laws guaranteed by the Fourteenth Amendment.

DECISION Judgment for plaintiffs.

OPINION Segregation of children in public schools solely on the basis of race generates a feeling of inferiority that diminishes their motivation to learn and affects "their hearts and minds in a way unlikely ever to be undone." Though the physical facilities and other "tangible" factors may be equal, segregation of the races with the sanction of law retards the educational and mental development of black children and deprives them of equal educational opportunities. Since separate educational facilities are inherently unequal, the "separate but equal" doctrine has no place in the field of public education. Therefore, segregation denies the black children the equal protection of the laws guaranteed by the Fourteenth Amendment.

INTERPRETATION When a governmentally imposed classification involves fundamental rights or suspect classifications, equal protection requires the classification to be necessary to promote a compelling or overriding government interest.

CRITICAL THINKING QUESTION Is the Equal Protection Clause of the U.S. Constitution violated when different public school districts spend significantly different amounts of money per student? Explain.

Intermediate test
standard of review applicable to regulation based on gender and legitimacy

Intermediate Test An **intermediate test** has been applied to government action based on gender and legitimacy. Under this test, the classification must have a substantial relationship to an important government objective. The intermediate standard eliminates the strong presumption of constitutionality to which the rational relationship test adheres. For example, the Supreme Court invalidated an Alabama law that allowed courts to grant alimony awards only from husbands to wives and not from wives to husbands. Similarly, where an Idaho statute gave preference to males over females in qualifying for selection as administrators of estates, the Supreme Court invalidated the statute because the preference did not bear a fair and substantial relationship to any legitimate legislative objective. Moreover, the Supreme Court invalidated a state university's (Virginia Military Institute) admission policy excluding women. *U.S. v. Virginia*, 518 U.S. 515 (1996). On the other hand, not all legislation based on gender is invalid. For example, the Supreme Court has upheld a California statutory rape law that imposed penalties only on males, as well as the federal military Selective Service Act that exempted women from registering for the draft.

ETHICAL DILEMMA

Who Is Responsible for Commercial Speech?

Facts Jane Stewart is an assistant manager of advertising for *Dazzling Magazine*, a fashion magazine aimed primarily at women between the ages of twenty-five and thirty-five. Offering regular columns on health, beauty, fashion, and current events, the magazine has a small circulation and handles its advertising internally.

Having experienced declining sales in recent years, the magazine has downsized its operations by eliminating jobs and implementing cost-cutting measures. To prevent further declines in revenue, *Dazzling*'s marketing and editorial staffs are attempting to expand the magazine's appeal to include younger audiences between the ages of sixteen and twenty-four. Jane is in charge of making recommendations to the advertising manager with regard to new advertisements. The advertising manager,

in turn, makes the final recommendation to the head of the advertising department. Because of the magazine's overall decline in sales, the advertising unit has come under increased pressure to generate revenue from advertisements. Compensation of advertising unit employees is based in part on the earning of "bonus points" related to first-year revenues from new clients.

Jane has received advertisement offers from two cigarette companies and from one swimsuit manufacturer. Although the cigarette advertisements would generate twice as much revenue as the swimsuit advertisement, Jane is concerned that the cigarette advertisements would lure young women to smoke. She has recommended to her supervisor, Agnes Scott, that the cigarette advertisements be rejected.

Scott adamantly disagrees. She strongly recommends to the head of the advertising department that the cigarette advertisements be accepted.

Social, Policy, and Ethical Considerations

1. What should Jane do? What is best for (a) her company and (b) society? Should Jane raise her concerns to the department head?
2. Identify the competing social values at stake with regard to cigarette advertising. What role should the government play in regulating speech that promotes products such as tobacco and alcohol?
3. Should the age of *Dazzling*'s prospective audience influence the choice of advertisements? Explain.

CHAPTER SUMMARY

Basic Principles

Federalism the division of governing power between the federal government and the states

Federal Supremacy federal law takes precedence over conflicting state law

Federal Preemption right of federal government to regulate matters within its power to the exclusion of regulation by the states

Judicial Review examination of government actions to determine whether they conform to the U.S. Constitution

Separation of Powers allocation of powers among executive, legislative, and judicial branches of government

State Action actions of governments to which constitutional provisions apply

Powers of Government

Federal Commerce Power exclusive power of federal government to regulate commerce with other nations and among the states

State Regulation of Commerce the Commerce Clause of the Constitution restricts the states' power to regulate activities if the result obstructs interstate commerce

Federal Fiscal Powers

- *Taxation and Spending* the Constitution grants Congress broad powers to tax and spend; such powers are important to federal government regulation of the economy

- *Borrowing and Coining Money* enables the federal government to establish a national banking system and to control national fiscal and monetary policy

- *Eminent Domain* the government's power to take private property for public use with the payment of just compensation

Limitations on Government

Contract Clause restricts states from retroactively modifying contracts

Freedom of Speech First Amendment protects most speech by using a strict scrutiny standard

- *Corporate Political Speech* First Amendment protects a corporation's right to speak out on political issues

- *Commercial Speech* expression related to the economic interests of the speaker and its audience; such expression receives a lesser degree of protection

- *Defamation* a tort consisting of a false communication that injures a person's reputation; such a communication receives limited constitutional protection

Due Process Fifth and Fourteenth Amendments prohibit the federal and state governments from depriving any person of life, liberty, or property without due process of law

- *Substantive Due Process* determination of whether a particular government action is compatible with individual liberties

- *Procedural Due Process* requires the government decision-making process to be fair and impartial if it deprives a person of life, liberty, or property

Equal Protection requires that similarly situated persons be treated similarly by government actions

- *Rational Relationship Test* standard of review used to determine whether economic regulation satisfies the equal protection guarantee

- *Strict Scrutiny Test* exacting standard of review applicable to regulation affecting a fundamental right or involving a suspect classification

- *Intermediate Test* standard of review applicable to regulation based on gender and legitimacy

QUESTIONS

1. In May, Patricia Allen left her automobile on the shoulder of a road in the city of Erehwon after the car stopped running. A member of the Erehwon city police department found the car later that day and placed on it a sticker stating that unless the car was moved, it would be towed. When after a week the car had not been removed, the police department authorized Baldwin Auto Wrecking Co. to tow it away and to store it on its property. Allen was told by a friend that her car was at Baldwin's. Allen

asked Baldwin to allow her to take possession of her car, but Baldwin refused to relinquish the car until the $70.00 towing fee was paid. Allen could not afford to pay the fee, and the car remained at Baldwin's for six weeks. At that time, Baldwin requested the police department for a permit to dispose of the

automobile. After the police department tried unsuccessfully to telephone Allen, the department issued the permit. In late July, Baldwin destroyed the automobile. Allen brings an action against the city and Baldwin for damages for loss of the vehicle, arguing that she was denied due process. Decision?

CASE PROBLEMS

2. In 1967, large oil reserves were discovered in the Prudhoe Bay area of Alaska. As a result, state revenues increased from $124 million in 1969 to $3.7 billion in 1981. In 1980, the state legislature enacted a dividend program that would distribute annually a portion of these earnings to the state's adult residents. Under the plan, each citizen eighteen years of age or older receives one unit for each year of residency subsequent to 1959, the year Alaska became a state. The state advanced three purposes justifying the distinctions made by the dividend program: (a) creation of a financial incentive for individuals to establish and maintain residence in Alaska; (b) encouragement of prudent management of the earnings; and (c) apportionment of benefits in recognition of undefined "contributions of various kinds, both tangible and intangible, which residents have made during their years of residency." Crawford, a resident since 1978, brings suit challenging the dividend distribution plan as violative of the equal protection guarantee. Did the dividend program violate the Equal Protection Clause of the Fourteenth Amendment? Explain.

3. Maryland enacted a statute prohibiting any producer or refiner of petroleum products from operating retail service stations within the state. The statute also required that any producer or refiner discontinue operating its company-owned retail service stations. Approximately 3,800 retail service stations in Maryland sell more than twenty different brands of gasoline. All of this gasoline is brought in from other states, as no petroleum products are produced or refined in Maryland. Only 5 percent of the total number of retailers are operated by a producer or refiner. Maryland enacted the statute because a survey conducted by the state comptroller indicated that gasoline stations operated by producers or refiners had received preferential treatment during periods of gasoline shortage. Seven major producers and refiners brought an action challenging the statute on the ground that it discriminated against interstate commerce in violation of the Commerce Clause of the U.S. Constitution. Are they correct? Explain.

4. The Federal Aviation Act provides that "The United States of America is declared to possess and exercise complete and exclusive national sovereignty in the airspace of the United States." The city of Orion adopted an ordinance that makes it unlawful for jet aircraft to take off from its airport between 11:00 P.M. of one day and 7:00 A.M. of the next day. Jordan Airlines, Inc., is adversely affected by this ordinance and brings suit challenging it under the Supremacy Clause of the U.S. Constitution as conflicting with the Federal Aviation Act or preempted by it. Is the ordinance valid? Explain.

5. The Public Service Commission of State X issued a regulation completely banning all advertising that "promotes the use of

electricity" by any electric utility company in State X. The commission issued the regulation to conserve energy. Central Electric Corporation of State X challenges the order in the state courts, arguing that the commission had restrained commercial speech in violation of the First Amendment. Was its freedom of speech unconstitutionally infringed? Explain.

6. E-Z-Rest Motel is a motel with 216 rooms located in the center of a large city in State Y. It is readily accessible from two interstate highways and three major state highways. The motel solicits patronage from outside State Y through various national advertising media, including magazines of national circulation. It accepts convention trade from outside State Y, and approximately 75 percent of its registered guests are from out of State Y. An action under the Federal Civil Rights Act of 1964 has been brought against E-Z-Rest Motel alleging that the motel discriminates on the basis of race and color. The motel contends that the statute cannot be applied to it because it is not engaged in interstate commerce. Can the federal government regulate this activity under the Interstate Commerce Clause? Why?

7. State Z enacted a Private Pension Benefits Protection Act requiring private employers with one hundred or more employees to pay a pension funding charge for terminating a pension plan or closing an office in State Z. Acme Steel Company closed its offices in State Z, whereupon the state assessed the company $185,000 under the vesting provisions of the Act. Acme challenged the constitutionality of the Act under the Contract Clause of the U.S. Constitution. Was the Act constitutional? Explain.

8. A state statute empowered public school principals to suspend students for up to ten days without any notice or hearing. A student who was suspended for ten days challenges the constitutionality of his suspension on the ground that he was denied due process. Was due process denied? Explain.

9. Iowa enacted a statute prohibiting the use of sixty-five-foot double-trailer-truck combinations. All of the other midwestern and western states permit such trucks to be used on their roads. Despite these restrictions, Iowa's statute permits cities abutting the state line to enact local ordinances adopting the length limitations of the adjoining state. In cases in which a city has exercised this option, otherwise-oversized trucks are permitted within the city limits and in nearby commercial zones. Consolidated Freightways is adversely affected by this statute and brings suit against Iowa, alleging that the statute violates the Commerce Clause. The District Court found that the evidence established that sixty-five-foot doubles were as safe as the shorter truck units. Does the statute violate the Commerce Clause? Explain.

10. Metropolitan Edison Company is a privately owned and operated Pennsylvania corporation subject to extensive regulation by the Pennsylvania Public Utility Commission. Under a provision of its general tariff filed with the commission, Edison had the right to discontinue electric service to any customer on reasonable notice of nonpayment of bills. Catherine Jackson had been receiving electricity from Metropolitan Edison when her account was terminated because of her delinquency in payments. Edison later opened a new account for her residence in the name of James Dodson, another occupant of Jackson's residence. In August of the following year, Dodson moved away and no further payments were made to the account. Finally, in October, Edison disconnected Jackson's service without any prior notice. Jackson brought suit claiming that her electric service could not be terminated without notice and a hearing. She further argued that such action, allowed by a provision of Edison's tariff filed with the commission, constituted "state action" depriving her of property in violation of the Fourteenth Amendment's guarantee of due process of law. Should Edison's actions be considered state action? Explain.

11. The McClungs owned Ollie's Barbecue, a restaurant located a few blocks from the interstate highway in Birmingham, Alabama, with dining accommodations for whites only and a take-out service for blacks. In the year preceding the passage of the Civil Rights Act of 1964, the restaurant had purchased a substantial portion of the food it served from outside the state. The restaurant had refused to serve blacks since its original opening in 1927 and asserted that if it were required to serve blacks it would lose much of its business. The McClungs sought a declaratory judgment to render unconstitutional the application of the Civil Rights Act to their restaurant because their admitted racial discrimination did not restrict or significantly impede interstate commerce. Decision?

12. Miss Horowitz was admitted as an advanced medical student at the University of Missouri-Kansas City. During the spring of her first year, several faculty members expressed dissatisfaction with Miss Horowitz's clinical performance, noting that it was below that of her peers, that she was erratic in attendance at her clinical sessions, and that she lacked a critical concern for personal hygiene. Upon the recommendation of the school's Council on Evaluation, she was advanced to her second and final year on a probationary basis. After subsequent unfavorable reviews during her second year and a negative evaluation of her performance by seven practicing physicians, the council recommended that Miss Horowitz be dismissed from the school for her failure to meet academic standards. The decision was approved by the dean and later affirmed by the provost after an appeal by Miss Horowitz. She brought suit against the school's Board of Curators, claiming that her dismissal violated her right to procedural due process under the Fourteenth Amendment and deprived her of "liberty" by substantially impairing her opportunities to continue her medical education or return to employment in a medically related field. Is her claim correct? Explain.

13. Drug compounding is a process by which a pharmacist or doctor combines, mixes, or alters ingredients to create a medication tailored to the needs of an individual patient. Compounding is typically used to prepare medications that are not commercially available, such as medication for a patient who is allergic to an ingredient in a mass-produced product. The Federal Food, Drug, and Cosmetic Act of 1938 (FDCA) regulates drug manufacturing, marketing, and distribution, providing that no person may sell any new drug unless approved by the Food and Drug Administration (FDA). The Food and Drug Administration Modernization Act of 1997 (FDAMA), which amends the FDCA, exempts compounded drugs from the FDCA's requirements provided the drugs satisfy a number of restrictions, including that the prescription must be "unsolicited," and the provider compounding the drug may "not advertise or promote the compounding of any particular drug, class of drug, or type of drug." The provider, however, may "advertise and promote the compounding service."

A group of licensed pharmacies that specialize in drug compounding challenged the FDAMA's requirement that they refrain from advertising and promoting their products if they wish to continue compounding on the basis that it violates the Free Speech Clause of the First Amendment. What test should the court apply in determining the validity of the FDAMA?

TAKING SIDES

Alabama was one of only sixteen states that permitted commercial hazardous waste landfills. From 1985 through 1989, the tonnage of hazardous waste received per year more than doubled. Of this, up to 90 percent of the hazardous waste was shipped in from other states. In response, Alabama imposed a fee of $97.60 per ton for hazardous waste generated outside Alabama compared with a fee of $25.60 per ton for hazardous wastes generated within Alabama.

Chemical Waste Management, Inc., which operates a commercial hazardous waste land disposal facility in Emelle, Alabama, filed suit asserting that the Alabama law violated the Commerce Clause of the U.S. Constitution.

a. What arguments could Chemical Waste Management, Inc. make in support of its claim that the statute is unconstitutional?

b. What arguments could Alabama make to defend the constitutionality of the statute?

c. Who should prevail? Explain.

Administrative Law

CHAPTER 5

In all tyrannical governments, ... the right both of making and enforcing the law is vested in ... one and the same body of men; and wherever these two powers are united together, there can be no public liberty.

William Blackstone
British Jurist (1775)

CHAPTER OUTCOMES

After reading and studying this chapter, you should be able to:

1. Explain the three basic functions of administrative agencies.

2. Distinguish among the three types of rules promulgated by administrative agencies.

3. Explain the difference between formal and informal methods of adjudication.

4. Identify (a) the questions of law determined by a court in conducting a review of a rule or order of an administrative agency and (b) the three standards of judicial review of factual determinations made by administrative agencies.

5. Describe the limitations imposed on administrative agencies by the legislative branch, the executive branch, and the legally required disclosure of information.

Administrative agency
government entity (other than a court or legislature) having authority to affect the rights of private parties

Administrative law is the branch of public law that is created by administrative agencies in the form of rules, regulations, orders, and decisions to carry out the regulatory powers and duties of those agencies. **Administrative agencies** are government entities—other than courts and legislatures—having authority to affect the rights of private parties through their operations. Administrative agencies, referred to by names such as commission, board, department, agency, administration, government corporation, bureau, or office, regulate a vast array of important matters involving national safety, welfare, and convenience. For instance, federal administrative agencies are charged with responsibility for national security, citizenship and naturalization, law enforcement, taxation, currency, elections, environmental protection, consumer protection, regulation of transportation, telecommunications, labor relations, trade, commerce, and securities markets, as well as with providing health and social services.

Because of the increasing complexity of the social, economic, and industrial life of the nation, the scope of administrative law has expanded enormously. In 1952, Justice Jackson observed that "the rise of administrative bodies has been the most significant legal trend of the last century, and perhaps more values today are affected by their decisions than by those of all the courts, review of administrative decisions apart." This observation is even truer in the twenty-first century, as evidenced by the great increase in the number and activities of federal government boards, commissions, and other agencies. Certainly, agencies create more legal rules and adjudicate more controversies than all the nation's legislatures and courts combined.

State agencies also play a significant role in the functioning of our society. Among the more important state boards and commissions are those that supervise and regulate banking, insurance, communications, transportation, public utilities, pollution control, and workers' compensation.

Much of the federal, state, and local law in this country is established by countless administrative agencies. These agencies, which many label the "fourth branch of government," possess tremendous power and have long been criticized as being "in reality miniature independent governments … which are a haphazard deposit of irresponsible agencies." Presidential Task Force Report (1937).

Despite such criticism, these administrative entities clearly play a significant and necessary role in our society. Administrative agencies relieve legislatures from the impossible burden of fashioning legislation that deals with every detail of a specific problem. As a result, Congress can enact legislation, such as the Federal Trade Commission Act, which prohibits unfair and deceptive trade practices, without having to define such a phrase specifically or to anticipate all the particular problems that may arise. Instead, Congress may pass an enabling statute that creates an agency—in this example, the Federal Trade Commission (FTC)—to which it can delegate the power to issue rules, regulations, and guidelines to carry out the statutory mandate. In addition, the establishment of separate, specialized bodies enables administrative agencies to be staffed by individuals with expertise in the field being regulated. Administrative agencies thus can develop the knowledge and devote the time necessary to provide continuous and flexible solutions to evolving regulatory problems.

In this chapter, we will discuss federal administrative agencies. Such agencies can be classified as either independent or executive. Executive agencies are those housed within the executive branch of government, whereas independent agencies are not. Many federal agencies are discussed in other parts of the text. More specifically, the FTC and Department of Justice are discussed in Chapter 42; the FTC and the Consumer Product Safety Commission (CPSC) in Chapter 44; the Department of Labor, National Labor Relations Board (NLRB) and Equal Employment Opportunity Commission (EEOC) in Chapter 41; the Securities and Exchange Commission (SEC) in Chapters 39 and 43; and the Environmental Protection Agency (EPA) in Chapter 45.

OPERATION OF ADMINISTRATIVE AGENCIES [5-1]

Most administrative agencies perform three basic functions: (1) rulemaking, (2) enforcement, and (3) adjudication of controversies. The term **administrative process** refers to the entire set of activities in which administrative agencies engage while carrying out these functions. Administrative agencies exercise powers that have been allocated by the Constitution to the three separate branches of government. More specifically, an agency exercises legislative power when it makes rules, executive power when it enforces its enabling statute and its rules, and judicial power when it adjudicates disputes. This concentration of power has raised questions regarding the propriety of having the same bodies that establish the rules also act as prosecutors and judges in determining whether those rules have been violated. To address this issue and to bring about certain additional procedural reforms, the Administrative Procedure Act (APA) was enacted in 1946.

Rulemaking [5-1a]

Rulemaking is the process by which an administrative agency enacts or promulgates rules of law. Under the APA, a **rule** is "the whole or a part of an agency statement of general or particular applicability and future effect designed to implement, interpret, or process law or policy." Once promulgated, rules are applicable to all parties. Moreover, the process of rulemaking notifies all parties that the impending rule is being considered and provides concerned individuals with an opportunity to be heard. Administrative agencies promulgate three types of rules: legislative rules, interpretative rules, and procedural rules.

Legislative Rules
Legislative rules, often called regulations, are in effect "administrative statutes." **Legislative rules** are those issued by an agency having the ability, under a legislative delegation of power, to make rules having the force and effect of law. For example, the FTC has rulemaking power with which to elaborate upon its enabling statute's prohibition of unfair or deceptive acts or practices.

Legislative rules have the force of law if they are constitutional, within the power granted to the agency by the legislature, and issued according to proper procedure. To be constitutional,

Administrative process

entire set of activities engaged in by administrative agencies while carrying out their rulemaking, enforcement, and adjudicative functions

Rulemaking

process by which an administrative agency promulgates rules of law

Rule

agency statement of general or particular applicability designed to implement, interpret, or process law or policy

Legislative rules

substantive rules issued by an administrative agency under the authority delegated to it by the legislature

Practical Advice

Keep informed of the regulations issued by administrative agencies that affect your business.

regulations must not violate any provisions of the U.S. Constitution, such as due process or equal protection. In addition, they may not involve an unconstitutional delegation of legislative power from the legislature to the agency. To be constitutionally permissible, the enabling statute granting power to an agency must establish reasonable standards to guide the agency in implementing the statute. This requirement has been met by such statutory language as "to prohibit unfair methods of competition," "fair and equitable," "public interest, convenience, and necessity," and other equally broad expressions. In any event, agencies may not exceed the actual authority granted by the enabling statute.

Legislative rules must be promulgated in accordance with the procedural requirements of the APA, although the enabling statute may impose more stringent requirements. Most legislative rules are issued in accordance with the ***informal rulemaking*** procedures of the APA, which require that the agency provide the following:

1. prior notice of a proposed rule, usually by publication in the *Federal Register*;
2. an opportunity for interested parties to participate in the rulemaking; and
3. publication of a final draft containing a concise general statement of the rule's basis and purpose at least thirty days before its effective date.

In some instances the enabling statute requires that certain rules be made only after the opportunity for an agency hearing. This formal rulemaking procedure is far more complex than the informal procedures and is governed by the same APA provisions that govern adjudication, discussed later in this chapter. In ***formal rulemaking***, the agency must consider the record of the trial-like agency hearing and include a statement of "findings and conclusions, and the reasons or basis therefore, on all the material issues of fact, law, or discretion presented on the record" when making rules.

Some enabling statutes direct that the agency, in making rules, use certain procedures that are more formal than those in informal rulemaking but do not compel the full hearing that formal rulemaking requires. This intermediate procedure, known as ***hybrid rulemaking***, results from combining the informal procedures of the APA with the additional procedures specified by the enabling statute. For example, an agency may be required to conduct a legislative-type hearing (formal) that permits no cross-examination (informal).

Practical Advice

Participate as early as possible in the rulemaking process of administrative agencies that affect your business.

In 1990, Congress enacted the Negotiated Rulemaking Act to encourage the involvement of affected parties in the initial stages of the policy-making process prior to the publication of notice of a proposed rule. The Act authorizes agencies to use negotiated rulemaking but does not require it. If an agency decides to use negotiated rulemaking, the affected parties and the agency develop an agreement and offer it to the agency. If accepted, the agreement becomes a basis for the proposed regulation, which is then published for comment.

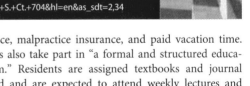

Mayo Foundation for Medical Education and Research v. United States
Supreme Court of the United States, 2011
562 U.S. ___, 131 S.Ct. 704, 178 L.Ed.2d 588
http://scholar.google.com/scholar_case?case=3055490070969307951&q=131+S.+Ct.+704&hl=en&as_sdt=2,34

FACTS Most doctors who graduate from medical school in the United States pursue additional education in a specialty to become board certified to practice in that field (e.g. orthopedics, cardiology, ophthalmology). Plaintiffs Mayo Foundation for Medical Education and Research, Mayo Clinic, and the Regents of the University of Minnesota (collectively Mayo) offer medical residency programs that provide such instruction. Mayo's residency programs, which usually last three to five years, train doctors primarily through hands-on experience. Residents often spend between fifty and eighty hours a week caring for patients supervised by more senior residents and by faculty members known as attending physicians. In 2005, Mayo paid its residents annual "stipends" ranging between $41,000 and $56,000 and provided them with

health insurance, malpractice insurance, and paid vacation time. Mayo residents also take part in "a formal and structured educational program." Residents are assigned textbooks and journal articles to read and are expected to attend weekly lectures and other conferences. Residents also take written exams and are evaluated by the attending faculty physicians. The bulk of residents' time is spent caring for patients.

Through the Social Security Act and related legislation, Congress has created a comprehensive national insurance system that provides benefits for retired workers, disabled workers, unemployed workers, and their families. Under the Federal Insurance Contributions Act (FICA), Congress funds Social Security by taxing both employers and employees on the wages employees earn.

Congress has defined "wages" to include "all remuneration for employment" and "employment" as "any service, of whatever nature, performed … by an employee for the person employing him."

In Section 3121(b)(10), Congress excluded from taxation "service performed in the employ of … a school, college, or university … if such service is performed by a student who is enrolled and regularly attending classes at such school, college, or university." In 2004, the Treasury Department adopted a rule prescribing that an employee's service is "incident" to his studies only when "[t]he educational aspect of the relationship between the employer and the employee, as compared to the service aspect of the relationship, [is] predominant." The rule categorically provides that "[t]he services of a full-time employee"—as defined by the employer's policies, but in any event including any employee normally scheduled to work forty hours or more per week—"are not incident to and for the purpose of pursuing a course of study." The rule clarifies that the Department's analysis "is not affected by the fact that the services performed … may have an educational, instructional, or training aspect." The rule also includes as an example the case of a medical resident whose "normal work schedule calls for [him] to perform services forty or more hours per week," and provides that his service is "not incident to and for the purpose of pursuing a course of study," and he accordingly is not an exempt "student" under Section 3121(b)(10).

After the Department promulgated the full-time employee rule, Mayo filed suit asserting that its residents were exempt under §3121(b)(10) and that the Treasury Department's full-time employee rule was invalid. The U.S. District Court granted Mayo's motion for summary judgment. The Government appealed, and the U.S. Court of Appeals reversed. The U.S. Supreme Court granted Mayo's petition for *certiorari*.

DECISION The judgment of the U.S. Court of Appeals is affirmed.

OPINION Analysis begins with the first step of the two-part framework announced in the U.S. Supreme Court case of *Chevron USA Inc. v. Natural Resources Defense Council, Inc.* This step asks whether Congress has "directly addressed the precise question at issue." Congress has not done so here. The statute does not define the term "student," and does not otherwise address the precise question whether medical residents are subject to FICA.

Under the second step of *Chevron* courts may not disturb an agency rule unless it is "arbitrary or capricious in substance, or manifestly contrary to the statute." The principles underlying *Chevron* apply with full force in the tax context. *Chevron* recognized that "[t]he power of an administrative agency to administer a congressionally created … program necessarily requires the formulation of policy and the making of rules to fill any gap left, implicitly or explicitly, by Congress." Filling gaps in the Internal Revenue Code plainly requires the Treasury Department to make interpretive choices for statutory implementation at least as complex as the ones other agencies must make in administering their statutes. Therefore, Supreme Court review of tax regulations should be guided by agency expertise pursuant to *Chevron* to the same extent as the Court's review of other regulations.

The *Chevron* deference to an agency rule is appropriate "when it appears that Congress delegated authority to the agency generally to make rules carrying the force of law, and that the agency interpretation claiming deference was promulgated in the exercise of that authority." The Department issued the full-time employee rule pursuant to the explicit authorization to "prescribe all needful rules and regulations for the enforcement" of the Internal Revenue Code.

The full-time employee rule easily satisfies the second step of *Chevron*, which asks whether the Department's rule is a "reasonable interpretation" of the enacted text. To begin, Mayo accepts that "the 'educational aspect of the relationship between the employer and the employee, as compared to the service aspect of the relationship, [must] be predominant'" in order for an individual to qualify for the exemption. Mayo objects, however, to the Department's conclusion that residents who work more than forty hours per week categorically cannot satisfy that requirement. Because residents' employment is itself educational, Mayo argues, the hours a resident spends working make him "more of a student, not less of one." Mayo contends that the Treasury Department should be required to engage in a case-by-case inquiry into "*what* [each] employee does [in his service] and *why*" he does it. Mayo also objects that the Department has drawn an arbitrary distinction between "hands-on training" and "classroom instruction."

Regulation, like legislation, often requires drawing lines. Mayo does not dispute that the Treasury Department reasonably sought a way to distinguish between workers who study and students who work. The Department reasonably concluded that its full-time employee rule would "improve administrability," and it thereby "has avoided the wasteful litigation and continuing uncertainty that would inevitably accompany any purely case-by-case approach" like the one Mayo advocates.

There is no doubt that Mayo's residents are engaged in a valuable educational pursuit or that they are students of their craft. The question whether they are "students" for purposes of §3121, however, is a different matter. Because it is one to which Congress has not directly spoken, and because the Treasury Department's rule is a reasonable construction of what Congress has said, the judgment of the Court of Appeals must be affirmed.

INTERPRETATION Generally, when Congress has not directly addressed the precise question at issue, courts may not disturb an agency rule that attempts to resolve the question, unless it is arbitrary or capricious in substance or manifestly contrary to statute.

CRITICAL THINKING QUESTION Do you agree that the agency's full-time employee rule is better than a case-by-case approach? Explain.

Interpretative rules
statements issued by an administrative agency indicating its construction of the statutes and rules that it administers

Interpretative Rules   **Interpretative rules** are "issued by an agency to advise the public of the agency's construction of the statutes and rules which it administers." *Attorney General's Manual on the Administrative Procedure Act.* Interpretative rules, however, which are exempt from the APA's procedural requirements of notice and comment, are *not* automatically binding on the private parties the agency regulates or on the courts, although they are given substantial weight. As the Supreme Court has stated, "The weight of such [an interpretative rule] in a particular case will depend upon the thoroughness evident in its consideration, the validity of its reasoning, its consistency with earlier and later pronouncements, and all those factors which give it power to persuade."

Procedural rules

rules issued by an administrative agency establishing its organization, method of operation, and rules of conduct for practice before it

Procedural Rules **Procedural rules** are also exempt from the notice and comment requirements of the APA and are not law. These rules establish rules of conduct for practice before the agency, identify an agency's organization, and describe its method of operation. For example, the SEC's Rules of Practice deal with matters such as who may appear before the commission; business hours and notice of proceedings and hearings; settlements, agreements, and conferences; presentation of evidence and the taking of depositions and interrogatories; and review of hearings.

See Concept Review 5-1.

Enforcement

process by which agencies determine whether their rules have been violated

Enforcement [5-1b]

Agencies also investigate conduct to determine whether the enabling statute or the agency's legislative rules have been violated. In carrying out this executive function, the agencies traditionally have been accorded great discretion, subject to constitutional limitations, to compel the disclosure of information. These limitations require that (1) the investigation is authorized by law and undertaken for a legitimate purpose, (2) the information sought is relevant, (3) the demand for information is sufficiently specific and not unreasonably burdensome, and (4) the information sought is not privileged.

For example, the following explains some of the SEC's investigative and enforcement functions:

All SEC investigations are conducted privately. Facts are developed to the fullest extent possible through informal inquiry, interviewing witnesses, examining brokerage records, reviewing trading data, and other methods. With a formal order of investigation, the Division's staff may compel witnesses by subpoena to testify and produce books, records, and other relevant documents. Following an investigation, SEC staff present their findings to the Commission for its review. The Commission can authorize the staff to file a case in federal court or bring an administrative action. In many cases, the Commission and the party charged decide to settle a matter without trial. (SEC Website, http://www.sec.gov.)

Practical Advice

When available, consider using alternative methods of dispute resolution with administrative agencies.

Adjudication [5-1c]

After concluding an investigation, the agency may use informal or formal methods to resolve the matter. Because the caseload of administrative agencies is vast, far greater than that of the judicial system, most matters are informally adjudicated. Informal procedures include advising, negotiating, and settling. In 1990 Congress enacted the Administrative Dispute Resolution Act to authorize and encourage federal agencies to use mediation, conciliation, arbitration, and other techniques for the prompt and informal resolution of disputes. The Act does not, however, require agencies to use alternative dispute resolution, and the affected parties must consent to its use.

Adjudication

formal methods by which an agency resolves disputes

Order

a final disposition made by an agency

The formal procedure by which an agency resolves a matter (called **adjudication**) involves finding facts, applying legal rules to the facts, and formulating orders. An **order** "means the

CONCEPT REVIEW 5-1

Administrative Rulemaking

Rule	Procedure	Effect
Legislative	Subject to APA	Binding
Interpretative	Exempt from APA	Persuasive
Procedural	Exempt from APA	Persuasive

whole or a part of a final disposition, whether affirmative, negative, injunctive or declaratory in form, of an agency." Adjudication, which in essence is an administrative trial, is used when the enabling statute so requires.

The procedures employed by the various administrative agencies to adjudicate cases are nearly as varied as the agencies themselves. Nevertheless, the APA does establish certain mandatory standards for those federal agencies the Act covers. For example, an agency must give notice of a hearing. The APA also requires that the agency give all interested parties the opportunity to submit and consider "facts, arguments, offers of settlement, or proposals of adjustment." In many cases this involves testimony and cross-examination of witnesses. If no settlement is reached, then a hearing must be held.

The hearing is presided over by an administrative law judge (ALJ) and is prosecuted by the agency. ALJs are appointed by the agency through a professional merit selection system and may be removed only for good cause. There are more than twice as many ALJs as there are federal judges. Juries are never used. Thus, the agency serves as both the prosecutor and decision maker. To reduce the potential for a conflict of interest, the APA provides for a separation of functions between those agency members engaged in investigation and prosecution and those involved in decision making.

Either party may introduce oral and documentary evidence, and the agency must base all sanctions, rules, and orders upon "consideration of the whole record or those parts cited by a party and supported by and in accordance with the reliable, probative, and substantial evidence." All decisions must include a statement of findings of fact and conclusions of law and the reasons or basis for them, as well as a statement of the appropriate rule, order, sanction, or relief.

If such are authorized by law and within its delegated jurisdiction, an agency may impose in its orders sanctions such as penalties; fines; the seizing of property; the assessment of damages, restitution, compensation, or fees; and the act of requiring, revoking, or suspending a license. In most instances, orders are final unless appealed, and failure to comply with an order subjects the party to a statutory penalty. If the order is appealed, the governing body of the agency may decide the case *de novo*. Thus, the agency may hear additional evidence and arguments in deciding whether to revise the findings and conclusions it made in the initial decision.

Although administrative adjudications mirror to a large extent the procedures of judicial trials, there are many differences between the two.

> Agency hearings, especially those dealing with rulemaking, often tend to produce evidence of general conditions as distinguished from facts relating solely to the respondent. Administrative agencies in rulemaking and occasionally in formal adversarial adjudications more consciously formulate policy than do courts. Consequently, administrative adjudications may require that the administrative law judge consider more consciously the impact of his decision upon the public interest as well as upon the particular respondent.... An administrative hearing is tried to an **administrative law judge**, never to a **jury**. Since many of the rules governing the admission of proof in judicial trials are designed to protect the jury from unreliable and possibly confusing evidence, it has long been asserted that such rules need not be applied at all or with the same vigor in proceedings solely before an administrative law judge.... Consequently, the technical common law rules governing the admissibility of evidence have generally been abandoned by administrative agencies. *McCormick on Evidence*, 4th ed., Section 350, p. 605.

LIMITS ON ADMINISTRATIVE AGENCIES [5-2]

An important and fundamental part of administrative law is the limits imposed by judicial review upon the activities of administrative agencies. On matters of policy, however, courts are not supposed to substitute their judgment for the agency's judgment. Additional limitations arise from the legislature and the executive branch, which, unlike the judiciary, may address the wisdom and correctness of an agency's decision or action. See Figure 5-1, which illustrates the limits on administrative agencies. Moreover, legally required disclosure of agency actions provides further protection for the public.

Figure 5-1 Limits on Administrative Agencies

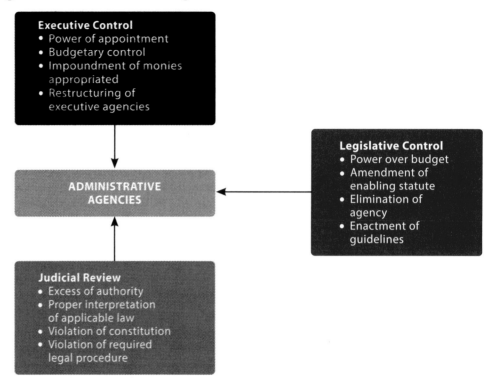

Judicial review

acts as a control or check
by a court on a particular
rule or order of an
administrative agency

Judicial Review [5-2a]

As discussed in Chapter 4, **judicial review** describes the process by which the courts examine government action. Judicial review, which is available unless a statute precludes such review or the agency action is committed to agency discretion by law, acts as a control or check on a particular rule or order of an administrative agency.

General Requirements   Parties seeking to challenge agency action must have standing and must have exhausted their administrative remedies. Standing requires that the agency action injure the party in fact and that the party assert an interest that is in the "zone of interests to be protected or regulated by the statute in question." Judicial review is ordinarily available only for *final* agency action. Accordingly, if a party seeks review while an agency proceeding is in progress, a court will usually dismiss the action because the party has failed to exhaust his administrative remedies.

Practical Advice

Be sure to exhaust all of your administrative remedies before seeking judicial review of action taken by an administrative agency.

Sackett v. Environmental Protection Agency
Supreme Court of the United States, 2012
566 U.S. ___, 132 S.Ct. 1367, 182 L.Ed.2d 367
http://scholar.google.com/scholar_case?q=132+S.Ct.+1367&hl=en&as_sdt=6,34&case=13663798285804514473&scilh=0

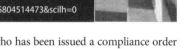

FACTS The Clean Water Act (Act) prohibits "the discharge of any pollutant by any person," without a permit, into "navigable waters," which the Act defines as "the waters of the United States." If the Environmental Protection Agency (EPA) determines that any person is in violation of this restriction, the Act directs the agency either to issue a compliance order or to initiate a civil enforcement action. When the EPA prevails in a civil action, the Act provides for a civil penalty not to exceed $37,500 per day for each violation. According to the government, when the EPA

prevails against any person who has been issued a compliance order but has failed to comply, that amount is increased to $75,000.

The Sacketts own a two-thirds-acre residential lot in Bonner County, Idaho. Their property lies just north of Priest Lake, but it is separated from the lake by several lots containing permanent structures. In preparation for constructing a house, the Sacketts filled in part of their lot with dirt and rock. Some months later, they received from the EPA a compliance order, which stated that their residential lot contained navigable waters and that their construction project violated the Act by placing fill material on the property. On that basis the order directs them immediately to restore the property pursuant to an EPA work plan and to provide the EPA with access to the site and all records and documents related to the conditions at the site.

The Sacketts, who do not believe that their property is subject to the Act, asked the EPA for a hearing, but that request was denied. They then brought an action in the U.S. District Court for the District of Idaho, seeking declaratory and injunctive relief. Their complaint contended that the EPA's issuance of the compliance order was "arbitrary [and] capricious" under the Administrative Procedure Act (APA) and that it deprived them of "life, liberty, or property, without due process of law," in violation of the Fifth Amendment. The District Court dismissed the claims for want of subject-matter jurisdiction. The U.S. Court of Appeals for the Ninth Circuit affirmed, concluding that the Act "preclude[s] pre-enforcement judicial review of compliance orders" and that such preclusion does not violate the Fifth Amendment's due process guarantee. The U.S. Supreme Court granted *certiorari*.

DECISION The judgment of the U.S. Court of Appeals is reversed, and the case is remanded.

OPINION The Sacketts brought suit under Chapter 7 of the APA, which provides for judicial review of "final agency action for which there is no other adequate remedy in a court." There is no doubt the compliance order is agency action, which the APA defines as including even a "failure to act." But is it *final*? It has all of the hallmarks of APA finality that Supreme Court opinions establish. Through the order, the EPA "determined" "rights or obligations." Also, "legal consequences … flow" from issuance of the order.

The issuance of the compliance order also marks the "consummation" of the agency's decision-making process. The "Findings and Conclusions" that the compliance order contained were not subject to further agency review. The APA's judicial review provision also requires that the person seeking APA review of final agency action have "no other adequate remedy in a court." In Clean Water Act enforcement cases, judicial review ordinarily comes by way of a civil action brought by the EPA. But the Sacketts cannot initiate that process, and each day they wait for the agency to drop the hammer, they accrue an additional $75,000 in potential liability. The other possible route to judicial review—applying to the Corps of Engineers for a permit and then filing suit under the APA if a permit is denied—will not serve either.

Nothing in the Clean Water Act *expressly* precludes judicial review under the APA or otherwise. But in determining "[w]hether and to what extent a particular statute precludes judicial review," the Court does not look only to its express language. The APA creates a "presumption favoring judicial review of administrative action," but as with most presumptions, this one may be overcome by inferences of intent drawn from the statutory scheme as a whole. The Government offered several reasons why the statutory scheme of the Clean Water Act precludes review. The Supreme Court found that these arguments did not support an inference that the Clean Water Act's statutory scheme precluded APA review.

The Supreme Court concluded that the compliance order in this case is final agency action for which there is no adequate remedy other than APA review, and that the Clean Water Act does not preclude that review. The Supreme Court therefore reversed the judgment of the Court of Appeals and remanded the case for further proceedings consistent with this opinion.

INTERPRETATION The APA provides for judicial review of final agency action for which there is no other adequate remedy in a court unless another statute precludes judicial review.

CRITICAL THINKING QUESTION What policy reasons support and which oppose the requirement for final agency action prior to judicial review?

In exercising judicial review, the court may decide either to compel agency action unlawfully withheld or to set aside impermissible agency action. In making its determination, the court must review the whole record and may set aside agency action only if the error is prejudicial.

Questions of Law   When conducting a review, a court decides all relevant questions of law, interprets constitutional and statutory provisions, and determines the meaning or applicability of the terms of an agency action. This review of questions of law includes determining whether the agency has (1) exceeded its authority, (2) properly interpreted the applicable law, (3) violated any constitutional provision, or (4) acted contrary to the procedural requirements of the law.

Questions of Fact   When reviewing factual determinations, the courts use one of three different standards. In cases in which informal rulemaking or informal adjudication has occurred, the standard generally is the ***arbitrary and capricious*** test, which requires only that the agency had a rational basis for reaching its decision. Where there has been a formal hearing, the substantial evidence test usually applies. It also applies to informal or hybrid rulemaking if the enabling statute so requires. The ***substantial evidence*** test requires the conclusions reached to be supported by "such relevant evidence as a reasonable mind might accept as adequate to support a conclusion." Finally, in rare instances, the reviewing court may apply the *unwarranted by the facts* standard, which permits the court to try the facts *de novo*. This strict review is available only when the enabling statute so provides, when the agency has conducted an adjudication with inadequate fact-finding procedures, or when issues that were not before the agency are raised in a proceeding to enforce nonadjudicative agency action.

FCC v. Fox Television Stations, Inc.
Supreme Court of the United States, 2009
556 U.S. 502, 129 S.Ct. 1800, 1 73 L.Ed.2d 738
http://scholar.google.com/scholar_case?q=129+S.CT.+1800&hl=en&as_sdt=2,34&case=2103709062574873617&scilh=0

FACTS Federal law bans the broadcasting of "any ... indecent ... language," which includes references to sexual or excretory activity or organs. Congress has given the Federal Communications Commission (FCC) various means of enforcing this indecency ban, including civil fines, license revocations, and the denial of license renewals. The Commission first invoked the statutory ban on indecent broadcasts in 1975, declaring a daytime broadcast of George Carlin's "Filthy Words" monologue actionably indecent. In the ensuing years, the Commission took a cautious, but gradually expanding, approach to enforcing the statutory prohibition against indecent broadcasts. Although the Commission had expanded its enforcement beyond the "repetitive use of specific words or phrases," it preserved a distinction between literal and nonliteral (or "expletive") uses of evocative language. The Commission explained that each literal "description or depiction of sexual or excretory functions must be examined in context to determine whether it is patently offensive," but that "deliberate and repetitive use ... is a requisite to a finding of indecency" when a complaint focuses solely on the use of nonliteral expletives. In 2004, the FCC's *Golden Globes Order* declared for the first time that an expletive (nonliteral) use of the F-Word or the Sh Word could be actionably indecent, even when the word is used only once. The first order to this effect dealt with an NBC broadcast of the Golden Globe Awards, in which the performer Bono commented, "This is really, really, f * * * ing brilliant."

This case concerns utterances in two live broadcasts aired by Fox Television Stations, Inc., and its affiliates prior to the Commission's *Golden Globes Order*. The first occurred during the 2002 Billboard Music Awards, when the singer Cher exclaimed, "I've also had critics for the last 40 years saying that I was on my way out every year. Right. So f * * * 'em." The second involved a segment of the 2003 Billboard Music Awards, during the presentation of an award by Nicole Richie and Paris Hilton, principals in a Fox television series called "The Simple Life." Ms. Hilton began their interchange by reminding Ms. Richie to "watch the bad language," but Ms. Richie proceeded to ask the audience, "Why do they even call it 'The Simple Life?' Have you ever tried to get cow s * * * out of a Prada purse? It's not so f * * * ing simple." Following each of these broadcasts, the Commission received numerous complaints from parents whose children were exposed to the language.

In 2006, the FCC found both broadcasts to have violated the prohibition against indecency. The FCC's order stated that the *Golden Globes Order* eliminated any doubt that fleeting expletives could be actionable; declared that under the new policy, a lack of repetition weighs against a finding of indecency, but is not a safe harbor; and held that both broadcasts met the new test because

one involved a literal description of excrement and both invoked the F-Word. The order did not impose sanctions for either broadcast. The Second Circuit set aside the agency action, declining to address the constitutionality of the FCC's action but finding the FCC's reasoning inadequate under the Administrative Procedure Act (APA).

DECISION The judgment of the U.S. Court of Appeals for the Second Circuit is reversed, and the case is remanded.

OPINION The APA permits the setting aside of agency action that is "arbitrary" or "capricious." Under this narrow standard of review, an agency must "examine the relevant data and articulate a satisfactory explanation for its action." However, a court is not to substitute its judgment for that of the agency and should uphold a decision of less than ideal clarity if the agency's path may reasonably be discerned.

In overturning the Commission's judgment, the Court of Appeals relied in part on Circuit precedent requiring a more substantial explanation for agency action that changes prior policy. The Second Circuit has interpreted the APA and Supreme Court precedent as requiring agencies to make clear "why the original reasons for adopting the [displaced] rule or policy are no longer dispositive" as well as "why the new rule effectuates the statute as well as or better than the old rule."

There is no basis in the APA or in Supreme Court opinions for a requirement that all agency change be subjected to more searching review. The requirement that an agency provide reasoned explanation for its action would ordinarily demand that it display awareness that it is changing position. The agency must show that there are good reasons for the new policy. But it need not demonstrate to a court's satisfaction that the reasons for the new policy are *better* than the reasons for the old one; it suffices that the new policy is permissible under the statute, that there are good reasons for it, and that the agency *believes* it to be better, which the conscious change of course adequately indicates. This means that the agency need not always provide a more detailed justification than what would suffice for a new policy created on a blank slate. Sometimes it must: for example, when its new policy rests upon factual findings that contradict those which underlay its prior policy or when its prior policy has engendered serious reliance interests that must be taken into account. It would be arbitrary or capricious to ignore such matters. In such cases it is not that further justification is demanded by the mere fact of policy change, but rather that a reasoned explanation is needed for disregarding facts and circumstances that underlay or were engendered by the prior policy.

Judged under these standards, the Commission's new enforcement policy and its order finding the broadcasts actionably indecent were neither arbitrary nor capricious. First, the Commission forthrightly acknowledged that its recent actions have broken new ground, taking account of inconsistent "prior Commission and staff action" and explicitly disavowing them as "no longer good law." There is no doubt that the Commission knew it was making a change. That is why it declined to assess penalties.

Moreover, the agency's reasons for expanding the scope of its enforcement activity were entirely rational. Even isolated utterances can be made in "pander[ing,] ... vulgar and shocking" manners and can constitute harmful "first blow[s]" to children. It is rational to

believe that a safe harbor for single words would "likely lead to more widespread use of the offensive language."

INTERPRETATION For agency action to be upheld on review under the APA's "arbitrary or capricious" standard, the agency must have examined relevant data and articulated a satisfactory explanation for its action.

CRITICAL THINKING QUESTION What policies support limitations on judicial review of agency action? Were these policies implicated in this case?

In deciding this case on remand, the Second Circuit Court of Appeals found the FCC's policy unconstitutionally vague and invalidated it in its entirety. The U.S. Supreme Court vacated the Second Circuit's decision but ruled against the FCC's imposing sanctions against Fox. The Supreme Court explained that under the Due Process Clause laws must give fair notice of conduct that is forbidden or required and laws that are impermissibly vague must be invalidated. The Court held that because the FCC failed to give Fox fair notice prior to the broadcasts in question that fleeting expletives could be found actionably indecent, the FCC's standards as applied to these broadcasts were vague, and therefore the FCC's orders must be set aside. The Supreme Court noted that its decision (1) does not address the First Amendment implications of the FCC's indecency policy, (2) leaves the FCC free to modify its current indecency policy in light of its determination of the public interest and applicable legal requirements, and (3) leaves the courts free to review the current policy or any modified policy in light of its content and application. *FCC v. Fox Television Stations, Inc.*, 567 U.S. ___, 132 S.Ct. 2307, 183 L.Ed.2d 234 (2012).

Legislative Control [5-2b]

The legislature may exercise control over administrative agencies in various ways. Through its budgetary power, it may greatly restrict or expand an agency's operations. Congress may amend an enabling statute to increase, modify, or decrease an agency's authority. Even more drastically, it may completely eliminate an agency. Or, Congress may establish general guidelines to govern agency action, as it did by enacting the APA. Moreover, it may reverse or change an agency rule or decision by specific legislation. In addition, each house of Congress has oversight committees that review the operations of administrative agencies. Finally, the Senate has the power of confirmation over some high-level appointments to administrative agencies.

In 1996 Congress enacted the Congressional Review Act, which subjects most rules to a new, extensive form of legislative control. With limited exceptions, the Act requires agencies to submit newly adopted rules to each house of Congress before they can take effect. If the rule is a major rule, it does not become final until Congress has had an opportunity to disapprove it. A *major rule* is any rule that the Office of Management and Budget (OMB) finds has resulted in or is likely to result in (1) an annual effect on the economy of at least $100 million; (2) a major increase in costs or prices; or (3) a significant adverse effect on competition, employment, investment, productivity, innovation, or international competitiveness of U.S. enterprises. If the rule is not a major rule, it takes effect as it otherwise would have after its submission to Congress; it is subject to possible disapproval by Congress. All rules covered by the Act shall not take effect if Congress adopts a joint resolution of disapproval. The President may veto the joint resolution, but Congress may then vote to override the veto. A rule that has been disapproved is treated as though it had never taken effect.

Executive Branch Control [5-2c]

By virtue of their power to appoint and remove their chief administrators, U.S. Presidents have significant control over the administrative agencies housed within the executive branch. With respect to independent agencies, however, the President has less control because commissioners serve for a fixed term that is staggered with the President's term of office. Nevertheless, his power to appoint agency chairs and to fill vacancies confers considerable control, as does his power to remove commissioners for statutorily defined cause. The President's central role in the budgeting process of agencies also enables him to exert great control over agency policy and operations. Even more extreme is the President's power to impound monies appropriated to an agency by Congress. In addition, the President may radically alter, combine, or even abolish agencies of the executive branch unless either house of Congress disapproves such an act within a prescribed time.

Disclosure of Information [5-2d]

Requiring administrative agencies to disclose information about their actions makes them more accountable to the public. Accordingly, Congress has enacted disclosure statutes to enhance public and political oversight of agency activities. These statutes include the Freedom of Information Act (FOIA), the Privacy Act, and the Government in the Sunshine Act.

Freedom of Information Act
First enacted in 1966, FOIA gives the public access to most records in the files of federal administrative agencies. Once a person has requested files, an agency must indicate within ten working days whether it intends to comply with the request and must within a reasonable time respond to the request. The agency may charge a fee for providing the records.

Practical Advice

Be aware that the Freedom of Information Act may give the public access to information you provide to administrative agencies.

FOIA permits agencies to deny access to nine categories of records: (1) records specifically authorized in the interest of national defense or foreign policy to be kept secret; (2) records that relate solely to the internal personnel rules and practices of an agency; (3) records specifically exempted by statute from disclosure; (4) trade secrets and commercial or financial information that is privileged or confidential; (5) interagency or intra-agency memorandums; (6) personnel and medical files, the disclosure of which would constitute a clearly unwarranted invasion of personal privacy; (7) investigatory records compiled for law enforcement purposes; (8) records that relate to the regulation or supervision of financial institutions; and (9) certain geological and geophysical information and data.

The Electronic FOIA Amendments require agencies to provide public access to information in an electronic format. Agencies must, within one year after their creation, make records available by computer telecommunications or other electronic means.

Privacy Act
The Privacy Act protects certain government records pertaining to individuals that a federal agency maintains and retrieves by an individual's name or other personal identifier, including social security number. In general, the Privacy Act prohibits unauthorized disclosures of those records covered by the Act. It also gives individuals the right to review and copy records about themselves, to find out whether these records have been disclosed, and to request corrections or amendments of these records, unless the records are legally exempt. It also requires agencies to maintain in their records only that information about an individual that is relevant and necessary to accomplish an agency function and to collect information to the greatest extent practicable directly from the individual.

Government in the Sunshine Act
The Government in the Sunshine Act requires meetings of many federal agencies to be open to the public. This Act applies to multimember bodies whose members the President appoints with the advice and consent of the Senate, such as the SEC, the FTC, the Federal Communications Commission, the CPSC, and the Commodity Futures Trading Commission. The Act does not cover executive agencies such as the EPA, the Food and Drug Administration (FDA), and the National Highway Safety Administration (NHTSA).

Agencies generally may close meetings on the same grounds upon which they may refuse disclosure of records under FOIA. In addition, agencies such as the SEC and the Federal Reserve Board may close meetings to protect information the disclosure of which would lead to financial speculation or endanger the stability of financial institutions. The Sunshine Act also permits agencies to close meetings that concern agency participation in pending or anticipated litigation.

ETHICAL DILEMMA

Should the Terminally Ill Be Asked to Await FDA Approval of Last-Chance Treatments?

Facts Mrs. Barnett is a seventy-three-year-old widow who has just been diagnosed with ovarian cancer. Because of the lack of adequate screening procedures for this type of cancer, Mrs. Barnett's cancer has long gone undetected and has progressed considerably.

Dr. Jason, Mrs. Barnett's doctor, will perform immediate surgery, but the surgery will not effectively cure the cancer. He has recommended that she undergo rigorous chemotherapy on a monthly basis for eighteen months following surgery. Thereafter, an exploratory operation can be conducted to assess the success of the treatment. The proposed chemotherapy will cause severe side effects, including nausea, oral lesions, and complete hair loss.

Dr. Jason has informed Mrs. Barnett and her two daughters, June and Sarina, that although chemotherapy will defer their mother's immediate death, her chances of a recovery are slim. Dr. Jason stated that while, on average, one in three patients undergoing such treatment could expect to recover, he believed Mrs. Barnett's recovery was highly unlikely. A second opinion from a reputable cancer treatment center confirmed Dr. Jason's diagnosis and recommendations for treatment.

Sarina has heard of an experimental cancer drug being tested in Europe. Thus far the results seem promising. Though the drug may be obtained in Europe, it is not yet legal in the United States. The Food and Drug Administration (FDA) has just begun to review the drug, but it will be years before the drug could receive FDA approval.

Sarina is strongly opposed to the painful regimen of chemotherapy that has been proposed, particularly because the treatment seems futile. She wants to fly to Europe, obtain the experimental drug, and return with it to the United States. Mrs. Barnett is much too ill to travel. June, on the other hand, is opposed to any course of treatment that does not have the approval of the FDA. Mrs. Barnett, who is weak and confused, is looking to her daughters for guidance.

Social, Policy, and Ethical Considerations

1. If Mrs. Barnett were your mother, what recommendation would you make? Under the circumstances, is it unethical to use a drug that has not been approved by the FDA?
2. As a policy matter, how should the FDA handle drugs for life-threatening diseases?
3. Should individuals be allowed absolute freedom to take risks with drug therapy?
4. Should the FDA apply different drug approval standards with regard to children who suffer from life-threatening diseases?
5. As policy matter, how should the government and nonprofit organizations allocate resources among research groups competing for funding? How should the government, through its administrative agencies, establish priorities for funding research on various illnesses?

CHAPTER SUMMARY

Operation of Administrative Agencies	**Rulemaking** process by which an administrative agency promulgates rules of law

- *Legislative Rules* substantive rules issued by an administrative agency under the authority delegated to it by the legislature
- *Interpretative Rules* statements issued by an administrative agency indicating how it construes the statutes and rules that it administers
- *Procedural Rules* rules issued by an administrative agency establishing its organization, method of operation, and rules of conduct for practice before the agency

Enforcement process by which agencies determine whether their rules have been violated

Adjudication formal methods by which an agency resolves disputes

Limits on Administrative Agencies	**Judicial Review** acts as a control or check by a court on a particular rule or order of an administrative agency

Legislative Control includes control over the agency's budget and enabling statute

Executive Branch Control includes the President's power to appoint members of the agency

Disclosure of Information congressionally required public disclosure enhances oversight of agency activities

CASE PROBLEMS

1. Congress passed the Emergency Price Control Act in the interest of national defense and security. The stated purpose of the Act was "to stabilize prices and to prevent speculative, unwarranted and abnormal increases in prices and rents." The Act established the Office of Price Administration, which was authorized to establish maximum prices and rents that were to be "generally fair and equitable and [were to] effectuate the purposes of this Act." Stark was convicted for selling beef at prices in excess of those set by the agency. Stark appeals on the ground that the Act unconstitutionally delegated to the agency the legislative power of Congress to control prices. Is Stark correct in this contention?

2. The Secretary of Commerce (Secretary) published a notice in the *Federal Register* inviting comments regarding flammability standards for mattresses. Statistical data were compiled, consultant studies were conducted, and seventy-five groups submitted comments. The Secretary then determined that all mattresses, including crib mattresses, must pass a cigarette test, consisting of bringing a mattress in contact with a burning cigarette. The department's staff supported this position by stating: "Exemption of youth and crib mattresses is not recommended. While members of these age groups do not smoke, their parents frequently do, and the accidental dropping of a lighted cigarette on these mattresses while attending to a child is a distinct possibility." Bunny Bear, Inc., now challenges the cigarette flammability test, asserting that the standard was not shown to be applicable to crib mattresses, as "infants and young children obviously do not smoke." Bunny Bear argues that the Secretary has not satisfied the burden of proof justifying the inclusion of crib mattresses within this general safety standard. Is Bunny Bear correct? Explain.

3. Reagan National Airport in Washington, D.C., is one of the busiest and most crowded airports in the nation. Accordingly, the Federal Aviation Administration (FAA) has restricted the number of commercial landing and takeoff slots at National to forty per hour. Allocation of the slots among the air carriers serving National had been by voluntary agreement through an airline scheduling committee (ASC). When a new carrier requested twenty slots during peak hours, National's ASC was unable to agree on a slot allocation schedule. The FAA engaged in informal rulemaking and invited public comment as a means to solve the slot allocation dilemma. The FAA then issued Special Federal Aviation Regulation 43 (SFAR 43) based on public comments and a proposal made at the last National ASC meeting, thereby decreasing the number of slots held by current carriers and shifting some slots to less desirable times. SFAR 43 also granted eighteen slots to New York Air. More specifically, SFAR 43 requires five carriers to give up one or more slots in specific hours during the day, requires twelve carriers to shift one slot to the latest hour of operations, and then reserves and allocates the yielded slots among the new entrants and several other carriers. Northwest Airlines seeks judicial review of SFAR 43, claiming that it is arbitrary, capricious, and not a product of reasoned decision making, and that it capriciously favors the Washington–New York market as well as the new carrier.

What standard would apply to the agency's actions? Should Northwest prevail? Explain.

4. Bachowski was defeated in a United Steelworkers of America union election. After exhausting his union remedies, Bachowski filed a complaint with Secretary of Labor Dunlop. Bachowski invoked the Labor-Management Reporting and Disclosure Act, which required Dunlop to investigate the complaint and determine whether to bring a court action to set aside the election. Dunlop decided such action was unwarranted. Bachowski then filed an action in a federal district court to order Dunlop to file suit to set aside the election. What standard of review would apply and what would Bachowski have to prove to prevail under that standard?

5. The Federal Crop Insurance Corporation (FCIC) was created as a wholly government-owned corporation to insure wheat producers against unavoidable crop failure. As required by law, the FCIC published in the *Federal Register* conditions for crop insurance. Specifically, the FCIC published that spring wheat reseeded on winter wheat acreage was ineligible for coverage. When farmer Merrill applied for insurance on his wheat crop, he informed the local FCIC agent that 400 of his 460 acres of spring wheat were reseeded on the winter acreage. The agent advised Merrill that his entire crop was insurable. When drought destroyed Merrill's wheat, Merrill tried to collect the insurance, but the FCIC refused to pay, asserting that Merrill is bound by the notice provided by publication of the regulation in the *Federal Register*. Is the FCIC correct? Explain.

6. The Department of Energy (DOE) issued a subpoena requesting information regarding purchases, sales, exchanges, and other transactions in crude oil from Phoenix Petroleum Company (Phoenix). The aim of the DOE audit was to uncover violations of the Emergency Petroleum Allocation Act (EPAA). The EPAA contained provisions for summary, or expedited, enforcement of DOE decisions. However, after the subpoena was issued but before Phoenix had responded, the EPAA expired. The EPAA provided that

> The authority to promulgate and amend any regulation, or to issue any order under this Chapter shall expire at midnight September 30, 1981, but such expiration shall not affect any action or pending proceedings, administrative, civil or criminal action or proceeding, whether or not pending, based upon any act committed or liability incurred prior to such expiration date.

Using the summary enforcement provisions of the now-defunct EPAA, the DOE sues to enforce the subpoena. Phoenix argues that because the EPAA has expired, the DOE lacks the authority either to issue the subpoena or to use the summary enforcement provisions. Is Phoenix correct? Why?

7. Under the Communications Act, the Federal Communications Commission may not impose common carrier obligations on cable operators. A common carrier is one that "makes a public offering to provide [communication facilities] whereby all

members of the public who choose to employ such facilities may communicate or transmit." In May 1976, the Commission issued rules requiring cable television systems of a designated size (a) to develop a minimum ten-channel capacity by 1986; (b) to make available on a first-come, nondiscriminatory basis certain channels for access by third parties; and (c) to furnish equipment and facilities for such access. The purpose of these rules was to ensure public access to the cable systems. Midwest Video Corporation claimed that the access rules exceeded the Commission's jurisdiction granted it by the Communications Act, because the rules infringe upon the cable systems' journalistic freedom by in effect treating the cable operators as "common carriers." The Commission contended that its expansive mandate under the Communications Act to supervise and regulate broadcasting encompassed the access rules. Did the Commission exceed its authority under the Act?

8. Congress enacted the National Traffic and Motor Vehicle Safety Act of 1966 (the Act) for the purpose of reducing the number of traffic accidents that result in death or personal injury. The Act directs the Secretary of Transportation to issue motor vehicle safety standards in order to improve the design and safety features of cars. The Secretary has delegated authority to promulgate safety standards to the National Highway Traffic Safety Administration (NHTSA) under the informal rulemaking procedure of the APA. The Act also authorizes judicial review under the provisions of the Administrative Procedure Act (APA) of all orders establishing, amending, or revoking a federal motor vehicle safety standard issued by the NHTSA.

   Pursuant to the Act, the NHTSA issued Motor Vehicle Safety Standard 208, which required all cars made after September 1982 to be equipped with passive restraints (either automatic seatbelts or airbags). The cost of implementing the standard was estimated to be around $1 billion. However, early in 1981, due to changes in economic circumstances and particularly due to complaints from the automotive industry,

the NHTSA rescinded Standard 208. The NHTSA had originally assumed that car manufacturers would install airbags in 60 percent of new cars and passive seatbelts in 40 percent. However, by 1981 it appeared that manufacturers were planning to install seatbelts in 99 percent of all new cars. Moreover, the majority of passive seatbelts could be easily and permanently detached by consumers. Therefore, the NHTSA felt that Standard 208 would not result in any significant safety benefits. State Farm Mutual Automobile Insurance Company (State Farm) and the National Association of Independent Insurers (NAII) filed petitions in federal court for review of the NHTSA's rescission of Standard 208. What standard of review would apply to the rescission? Should it be set aside? Explain.

9. David Diersen filed a complaint against the Chicago Car Exchange (CCE), an automobile dealership, alleging that the CCE fraudulently furnished him an inaccurate odometer reading when it sold him a 1968 Dodge Charger, in violation of the Vehicle Information and Cost Savings Act ("the Odometer Act" or "the Act"). The Odometer Act requires all persons transferring a motor vehicle to give an accurate, written odometer reading to the purchaser or recipient of the transferred vehicle. Under the Act, those who disclose an inaccurate odometer reading with the intent to defraud are subject to a private cause of action by the purchaser and may be held liable for treble damages or $1,500, whichever is greater. The trial court granted the defendant's motion for summary judgment, relying upon a regulation promulgated by the National Highway Traffic Safety Administration (NHTSA), which purports to exempt vehicles that are at least ten years old (such as the one Diersen purchased from the CCE) from the Act's odometer disclosure requirements. Diersen then filed a motion for reconsideration of the court's summary judgment order, arguing that the older-car exemption created by the NHTSA lacked any basis in the Act and was therefore invalid. What standard should the court apply in determining the validity of the NHTSA regulation?

TAKING SIDES

Section 7(a)(2) of the Endangered Species Act of 1973 (ESA) provides (in relevant part) that

> [e]ach Federal agency shall, in consultation with and with the assistance of the Secretary (of the Interior), insure that any action authorized, funded, or carried out by such agency … is not likely to jeopardize the continued existence of any endangered species or threatened species or result in the destruction or adverse modification of habitat of such species which is determined by the Secretary, after consultation as appropriate with affected States, to be critical.

In 1978, the Fish and Wildlife Service and the National Marine Fisheries Service, on behalf of the Secretary of the Interior and the Secretary of Commerce respectively, promulgated a joint regulation stating that the obligations imposed by Section 7(a)(2) extend

to actions taken in foreign nations. In 1983, the Interior Department proposed a revised joint regulation that would require consultation only for actions taken in the United States or on the high seas. Shortly thereafter, Defenders of Wildlife and other organizations filed an action against the Secretary of the Interior, seeking a declaratory judgment that the new regulation is in error as to the geographic scope of Section 7(a)(2) and an injunction requiring the Secretary to promulgate a new regulation restoring the initial interpretation. The Secretary asserted that the plaintiffs did not have standing to bring this action.

a. What arguments would support the plaintiff's standing to bring this action?

b. What arguments would support Secretary's claim that plaintiffs did not have standing to bring this action?

c. Which side's arguments are most convincing? Explain.

Criminal Law

CHAPTER 6

These guys commit their crimes with a pencil instead of a gun.

Mario Merola (Bronx District Attorney)
Speaking about corporate crime to the *New York Times* (1985)

CHAPTER OUTCOMES

After reading and studying this chapter, you should be able to:

1. Describe criminal intent and the various degrees of mental fault.

2. Identify the significant features of white-collar crimes, corporate crimes, and Racketeer Influenced and Corrupt Organizations Act (RICO).

3. List and define the crimes against business.

4. Describe the defenses of person or property, duress, mistake of fact, and entrapment.

5. List and explain the constitutional amendments affecting criminal procedure.

As discussed in Chapter 1, the civil law defines duties the violation of which constitutes a wrong against the injured party. The criminal law, on the other hand, establishes duties the violation of which is a societal wrong against the whole community. Civil law is a part of private law, whereas criminal law is a part of public law. In a civil action, the injured party sues to recover compensation for the damage and injury that he has sustained as a result of the defendant's wrongful conduct. The party bringing a civil action (the plaintiff) has the burden of proof, which he must sustain by a preponderance (greater weight) of the evidence. The purpose of the civil law is to compensate the aggrieved party.

Criminal law is designed to prevent harm to society by defining criminal conduct and establishing punishment for such conduct. In a criminal case, the defendant is prosecuted by the government, which must prove the defendant's guilt beyond a reasonable doubt, a significantly higher burden of proof than that required in a civil action. Moreover, under our legal system, guilt is never presumed. Indeed, the law presumes the innocence of the accused, and this presumption is unaffected by the defendant's failure to testify in her own defense. The government still has the burden of affirmatively proving the guilt of the accused beyond a reasonable doubt.

Of course, the same conduct may, and often does, constitute both a crime and a tort, which is a civil wrong. (We will discuss torts in Chapters 7 and 8.) But an act may be criminal without being tortious; by the same token, an act may be a tort but not a crime.

Because of the increasing use of criminal sanctions to enforce government regulation of business, criminal law is an essential part of business law. Moreover, businesses sustain considerable loss as victims of criminal actions. Accordingly, this chapter covers the general principles of criminal law and criminal procedure as well as specific crimes and defenses relevant to business.

NATURE OF CRIMES [6-1]

Crime

an act or omission in violation of a public law and punishable by the government

A **crime** is any act or omission forbidden by public law in the interest of protecting society and made punishable by the government in a judicial proceeding brought by it. Punishment for criminal conduct includes fines, imprisonment, probation, and death. In addition, some states and the federal government have enacted victim indemnification statutes, which establish funds, financed by criminal fines, to provide indemnification in limited amounts to victims of criminal activity. Crimes are prohibited and punished on grounds of public policy, which may include the protection and safeguarding of government (as in treason), human life (as in murder), or private property (as in larceny). Additional purposes for criminal law include deterrence, rehabilitation, and retribution.

Historically, criminal law was primarily common law. In the twenty-first century, however, criminal law is almost exclusively statutory. All states have enacted comprehensive criminal law statutes (or codes) covering most, if not all, of the common law crimes. Since its promulgation in 1962, the American Law Institute's Model Penal Code has played an important part in the widespread revision and codification of the substantive criminal law of the United States. Moreover, these statutes have made the number of crimes defined in criminal law far greater than the number of crimes defined under common law. Some codes expressly limit crimes to those the code includes, thus abolishing common law crimes. Nonetheless, some states do not define all crimes statutorily; therefore, the courts must rely on common law definitions. Because there are no federal common law crimes, all federal crimes are statutory.

Within recent times the scope of the criminal law has increased greatly. The scope of traditional criminal behavior has been expanded by numerous regulations and laws, pertaining to nearly every phase of modern living, that contain criminal penalties. Typical examples in the field of business law are those laws concerning the licensing and conduct of a business, antitrust laws, and laws governing the sales of securities.

Essential Elements [6-1a]

Actus reus

wrongful or overt act

Mens rea

criminal intent or mental fault

In general, a crime consists of two elements: (1) the wrongful or overt act (**actus reus**) and (2) the criminal or mental intent (**mens rea**). For example, to support a larceny conviction, it is not enough to show that the defendant stole another's goods; it also must be established that he intended to steal the goods. Conversely, criminal intent without an overt act is not a crime. For instance, Ann decides to rob the neighborhood grocery store and then really "live it up." Without more than the thought, Ann has committed no crime.

Actus reus refers to all the nonmental elements of a crime, including the physical act that must be performed, the circumstances under which it must be performed, and the consequences of that act. The *actus reus* required for specific crimes will be discussed later in this chapter.

Mens rea, or mental fault, refers to the mental element of a crime. Most common law and some statutory crimes require subjective fault, whereas other crimes require objective fault; some statutory crimes require no fault at all. The Model Penal Code and most modern criminal statutes recognize three possible types of **subjective fault**: purposeful, knowing, and reckless. A person acts *purposely* or *intentionally* if his conscious object is to engage in the prohibited conduct or to cause the prohibited result. Thus, if Arthur, with the desire to kill Donna, shoots his rifle at Donna, who is seemingly out of gunshot range, and in fact does kill her, Arthur had the purpose or intent to kill Donna. If Benjamin, desiring to poison Paula, places a toxic chemical in the water cooler in Paula's office and unwittingly poisons Gail and Ram, Benjamin will be found to have purposefully killed Gail and Ram, because Benjamin's intent to kill Paula is transferred to Gail and Ram, regardless of Benjamin's feelings toward Gail and Ram.

Subjective fault

purposeful, knowing, or reckless

A person acts *knowingly* if he is aware that his conduct is of a prohibited type or is practically certain to cause a prohibited result. A person acts *recklessly* if he consciously disregards a substantial and unjustifiable risk that his conduct is prohibited or that it will cause a prohibited result.

Objective fault

gross deviation from reasonable conduct

Objective fault involves a gross deviation from the standard of care that a reasonable person would observe under given circumstances. Criminal statutes refer to objective fault by terms such as carelessness or negligence. Such conduct occurs when a person *should* be aware of a

---

CONCEPT REVIEW 6-1

Degrees of Mental Fault

Type	Fault Required	Examples
Subjective fault	Purposeful Knowing Reckless	Larceny Embezzlement
Objective fault	Negligent Careless	Careless driving Issuing bad checks (some states)
Liability without fault	None	Sale of alcohol to a minor Sale of adulterated food

---

Liability without fault

crime to do a specific act or cause a certain result without regard to the care exercised

substantial and unjustifiable risk that his conduct is prohibited or will cause a prohibited result. Examples of crimes requiring objective fault are involuntary manslaughter (negligently causing the death of another), carelessly driving an automobile, and, in some states, issuing a bad check.

Many regulatory statutes have totally dispensed with the mental element of a crime by imposing criminal **liability without fault**. Without regard to the care that a person exercises, criminal liability without fault makes it a crime for that person to do a specified act or to bring about a certain result. Statutory crimes imposing liability without fault include the sale of adulterated food, the sale of narcotics without a prescription, and the sale of alcoholic beverages to a minor. Most of these crimes involve regulatory statutes dealing with health and safety and impose only fines for violations. See *State v. Morse* later in this chapter.

See the Concept Review 6-1 for an overview of degree of mental fault.

Mala in se

wrongs in themselves or morally wrong

Mala prohibita

not morally wrong but declared wrongful by law

Felony

serious crime

Misdemeanor

less serious crime

Vicarious liability

liability imposed on one for acts of another

CLASSIFICATION [6-2]

Historically, crimes have been classified *mala in se* (wrongs in themselves or morally wrong, such as murder) or *mala prohibita* (not morally wrong but declared wrongful by law, such as the failure to drive on the right side of the road). From the standpoint of the seriousness of the offense, crimes are also classified as a **felony**, which is a serious crime (any crime punishable by death or imprisonment in the penitentiary), or as a **misdemeanor**, which is a less serious crime (any crime punishable by a fine or imprisonment in a local jail).

Vicarious Liability [6-2a]

Vicarious liability is liability imposed upon one person for the acts of another. Employers are vicariously liable for the authorized criminal acts of their employees if the employer directed, participated in, or approved of the act. For example, if an employer directs its vice president of marketing to fix prices with its company's competitors, and the employee does so, both the employer and employee have criminally violated the Sherman Antitrust Act. On the other hand, employers ordinarily are not liable for the unauthorized criminal acts of their employees. As previously discussed, most crimes require mental fault; this element is not present, so far as criminal responsibility of the employer is concerned, where the employee's criminal act was not authorized.

Practical Advice

Because employers may be criminally liable for the acts of their employees, you should exercise due diligence in adequately checking the backgrounds of prospective employees.

Employers, however, may be subject to a criminal penalty for the unauthorized act of an adviser or manager acting in the scope of employment. Moreover, an employer may be criminally liable under a liability without fault statute for certain unauthorized acts of an employee, whether or not the employee is managerial. For example, many states have statutes that punish "every person who by himself or his employee or agent sells anything at short weight," or "whoever sells liquor to a minor and any sale by an employee shall be deemed the act of the employer as well."

Liability of a corporation

under certain circumstances a corporation may be convicted of crimes and punished by fines

Liability of a Corporation [6-2b]

Historically, corporations were not held criminally liable because, under the traditional view, a corporation could not possess the requisite criminal intent and, therefore, was incapable of committing a crime. The dramatic growth in size and importance of corporations changed this view. Under the modern approach, a corporation may be liable for violation of statutes imposing liability without fault. In addition, a corporation may be liable where the offense is perpetrated by a high corporate officer or the board of directors. The Model Penal Code provides that a corporation may be convicted of a criminal offense for the conduct of its employees if

1. the legislative purpose of the statute defining the offense is to impose liability on corporations and the conduct is within the scope of the [employee's] office or employment;
2. the offense consists of an omission to discharge a specific, affirmative duty imposed upon corporations by law; or
3. the offense was authorized, requested, commanded, performed, or recklessly tolerated by the board of directors or by a high managerial agent of the corporation.

Punishment of a corporation for crimes is necessarily by fine, not imprisonment. Nonetheless, individuals bearing responsibility for the criminal act face fines, imprisonment, or both. The Model Penal Code provides that the corporate agent having primary responsibility for the discharge of the duty imposed by law on the corporation is as accountable for a reckless omission to perform the required act as though the law imposed the duty directly upon him.

On November 1, 1991 (updated in 2004 and 2010), the Federal Organizational Corporate Sentencing Guidelines took effect. The overall purpose of the guidelines is to impose sanctions that will provide just punishment and adequate deterrence. The guidelines provide a base fine for each criminal offense, but that fine can be increased or reduced. Factors that can increase a corporate fine include the corporation's involvement in or tolerance of criminal activity, its prior history, and whether it has obstructed justice. On the other hand, corporations can reduce their punishment by implementing an effective compliance and ethics program reasonably designed to prevent potential legal violations by the corporation and its employees.

An effective compliance and ethics program should include the following:

1. standards and procedures to prevent and detect criminal conduct;
2. responsibility at all levels and adequate resources, and authority for the program;
3. personnel screening related to program goals;
4. training at all levels;
5. auditing, monitoring, and evaluating program effectiveness;
6. nonretaliatory internal reporting systems;
7. incentives and discipline to promote compliance; and
8. reasonable steps to respond to and prevent further similar offenses upon detection of a violation.

The 2010 amendments to the guidelines expanded the availability of reduced sentencing for corporations meeting additional requirements. Under the previous guidelines, convicted corporations could receive a reduced fine for having an effective compliance and ethics program *only if* no high-level personnel were involved in, or willfully ignorant of, the crime. Under the 2010 amendments, a corporation can be eligible for a reduced fine based on an effective compliance and ethics program *despite* the involvement or willful ignorance of high-level personnel if the convicted corporation satisfies four additional criteria:

1. a direct and prompt communication channel exists between compliance personnel and the organization's governing authority (e.g., the board of directors or the audit committee of the board);
2. the compliance program discovered the criminal offense before discovery outside the company was reasonably likely;
3. the corporation promptly reported the offense to appropriate government authorities; and
4. no individual with operational responsibility for the compliance program participated in, condoned, or was willfully ignorant of the offense.

Practical Advice

Companies should ensure that they have a satisfactory corporate compliance program.

WHITE-COLLAR CRIME [6-3]

White-collar crime
nonviolent crime involving
deceit, corruption, or
breach of trust

White-collar crime has been defined in various ways. The Justice Department defines it as non-violent crime involving deceit, corruption, or breach of trust. It includes crimes committed by individuals—such as embezzlement and forgery—as well as crimes committed on behalf of a corporation—such as commercial bribery, product safety and health crimes, false advertising, and antitrust violations. Regardless of the definition, white-collar crime clearly costs society billions of dollars; according to the Federal Bureau of Investigation, white-collar crime is estimated to cost the United States between $300 and $660 billion per year. Historically, prosecution of white-collar crime was deemphasized because such crime was not considered violent. Now, however, many contend that white-collar crime often inflicts violence but does so impersonally. For example, unsafe products cause injury and death to consumers, while unsafe working conditions cause injury and death to employees. Indeed, many contend that white-collar criminals should receive stiff prison sentences due to the magnitude of their crimes.

In response to the business scandals involving companies such as Enron, WorldCom, Global Crossing, Adelphia, and Arthur Andersen, in 2002, Congress passed the Sarbanes-Oxley Act. The Act, according to former President George W. Bush, constitutes "the most far-reaching reforms of American business practices since the time of Franklin Delano Roosevelt [President from 1932 until 1945]." The legislation seeks to prevent such scandals by increasing corporate responsibility; adding new financial disclosure requirements; creating new criminal offenses and increasing the penalties of existing federal crimes; and creating a powerful new five-person Accounting Oversight Board with authority to review and discipline auditors.

The Sarbanes-Oxley Act establishes new criminal penalties, including the following: (1) making it a crime to defraud any person or to obtain any money or property fraudulently in connection with any security of a public company with penalties of a fine and/or up to twenty-five years imprisonment; and (2) imposing fines and/or imprisonment of up to twenty years for knowingly altering, destroying, mutilating, or falsifying any document with the intent of impeding a federal investigation. In addition, the Act substantially increases the penalties for existing crimes, including the following: (1) mail and wire fraud (five-year maximum increased to twenty-five-year maximum) and (2) violation of the Securities and Exchange Act (ten-year maximum increased to twenty-year maximum). The Act is discussed further in Chapters 35, 39, and 43.

In December 2008, Bernard L. Madoff admitted to perpetrating a massive Ponzi scheme with estimated losses of $20 billion in principal and approximately $65 billion dollars in paper losses. As a result, in 2010 the Securities and Exchange Commission began reforming and improving the way it operates to reduce the chances that such frauds will occur or be undetected in the future.

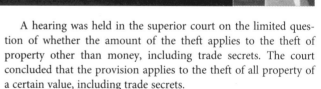

People v. Farell
Supreme Court of California, 2002
28 Cal.4th 381, 121 Cal.Rptr.2d 603, 121 Cal.Rptr.2d 603
http://scholar.google.com/scholar_case?case=12312804905483823177&q=28+Cal.4th+381&hl=en&as_sdt=40006

FACTS On April 18, 1997, the defendant, Farell, was charged with the theft of a trade secret based upon evidence that he had printed out confidential design specifications for certain computer chips on the last day of his employment as an electrical engineer at Digital Equipment Corporation. As a sentence enhancement, it was further alleged that the loss exceeded $2.5 million and, as a restriction on probation, that the theft was of an amount exceeding $100,000. Defendant pleaded no contest to the theft charge but objected to the potential application of Section 1203.044 to his sentence, which requires a ninety-day county jail sentence as condition of probation for theft of an amount exceeding $50,000. The trial court placed him on probation conditioned on the service of a term in county jail under Section 1203.044.

A hearing was held in the superior court on the limited question of whether the amount of the theft applies to the theft of property other than money, including trade secrets. The court concluded that the provision applies to the theft of all property of a certain value, including trade secrets.

The Court of Appeal reversed, holding that the statute applies only to the theft of what it termed "monetary property." The California Supreme Court granted the government's petition for review.

DECISION The judgment of the Court of Appeal is reversed.

OPINION Defendant stands convicted of theft, specifically a violation of a California statute that provides:

(b) Every person is guilty of theft who, with intent to deprive or withhold the control of a trade secret from its owner, or with an intent to appropriate a trade secret to his or her own use or to the use of another, does any of the following: (1) Steals, takes, carries away, or uses without authorization, a trade secret.

The statute defines the term "trade secret" as follows:

information, including a formula, pattern, compilation, program, device, method, technique, or process, that: (A) Derives independent economic value, actual or potential, from not being generally known to the public or to other persons who can obtain economic value from its disclosure or use; and (B) Is the subject of efforts that are reasonable under the circumstances to maintain its secrecy.

The trial court determined that Section 1203.044 applies to such a theft. This statute, entitled The Economic Crime Law of 1992, requires that a defendant who is convicted of certain theft offenses and is granted probation shall be sentenced to at least ninety days in the county jail as a condition of probation. Section 1203.044 applies only to a defendant convicted of a felony for theft of an amount exceeding fifty thousand dollars ($50,000) in a single transaction or occurrence.

In interpreting a statute a court must first turn to the words of the statute themselves, recognizing that they generally provide the most reliable indicator of legislative intent. The California Supreme Court determined that the meaning of the phrase "convicted of a felony for theft of an amount exceeding fifty thousand dollars," does not specify that the theft must involve cash— or that it must involve what is referred to by the Court of Appeal as "monetary property." In the absence of evidence to the contrary, it must be inferred that when the legislature referred in Section 1203.044 to persons "convicted of a felony for theft," it had in mind the general definition of theft, including the broad categories of property that maybe the subject of theft, including trade secrets.

As further evidence, the Court looked at the legislature's intent in regard to punishment of white-collar crime. The legislature declared in enacting Section 1203.044:

[M]ajor economic or "white collar" crime is an increasing threat to California's economy and the well-being of its citizens. The Legislature intends to deter that crime by ensuring that every offender, without exception, serves at least some time in jail and by requiring the offenders to divert a portion of their future resources to the payment of restitution to their victims.

Moreover, the term "white-collar crime" is a relatively broad one generally defined as "[a] nonviolent crime usu[ally] involving cheating or dishonesty in commercial matters. Examples include fraud, embezzlement, bribery, and insider trading."

INTERPRETATION The requirement imposing a minimum term in county jail applies to the theft of property other than money, including trade secrets.

CRITICAL THINKING QUESTION Should the penalty for theft vary depending on the dollar value of the property taken? Explain.

Computer Crime [6-3a]

Computer crime (cybercrime)

crime by, with, or at a computer

One special type of white-collar crime is computer crime. **Computer crime**, or **cybercrime**, is best categorized based on whether the computer was the instrument or the target of the crime. Examples of cybercrimes using computers as the *instrument* of the crime include the distribution of child pornography, money laundering, illegal gambling, copyright infringement, illegal communication of trade secret, and fraud involving credit cards, e-commerce, and securities. Cybercrime with a computer as a *target* of the crime attacks a computer's confidentiality, integrity, or availability; examples include theft or destruction of proprietary information, vandalism, denial of service, website defacing and interference, and implanting malicious code. Detection of crimes involving computers is extremely difficult. In addition, computer crimes often are not reported because businesses do not want to give the impression that their security is lax. Nonetheless, losses due to computer crimes are estimated to be in the tens of billions of dollars. Moreover, given society's ever-increasing dependence upon computers, this type of crime will in all likelihood continue to increase.

As a consequence, enterprises are spending large sums of money to increase computer security. In addition, every state has enacted computer crime laws. Originally passed in 1984, the federal Computer Fraud and Abuse Act protects a broad range of computers that facilitate interstate and international commerce and communications. The Act was amended in 1986, 1994, 1996, 2001, 2002, and 2008. The Act makes it a crime with respect to any computer that is used in interstate commerce or communications (1) to access or damage it without authorization, (2) to access it with the intent to commit fraud, (3) to traffic in passwords for it, and (4) to threaten to cause damage to it with the intent to extort money or anything of value. Furthermore, depending on the details of the crime, cybercriminals also may be prosecuted under other federal laws, such as copyright, mail fraud, or wire fraud laws. *Spam*—unsolicited commercial electronic mail—is currently estimated to account for well over half of all electronic mail. Congress has concluded that spam has become the most prevalent method used

Practical Advice

Adequately protect the safety and security of all company electronic data and records.

for distributing pornography; perpetrating fraudulent schemes; and introducing viruses, worms, and Trojan horses into personal and business computer systems. In response, Congress enacted the Controlling the Assault of Non-Solicited Pornography and Marketing Act of 2003, or the CAN-SPAM Act of 2003, which went into effect on January 1, 2004. In enacting the statute Congress determined that senders of spam should not mislead recipients as to the source or content of such mail and that recipients of spam have a right to decline to receive additional spam from the same source.

Racketeer Influenced and Corrupt Organizations Act [6-3b]

RICO

federal law intended to stop organized crime from infiltrating legitimate businesses

The **Racketeer Influenced and Corrupt Organizations Act (RICO)** was enacted in 1970 with the stated purpose of terminating the infiltration by organized crime into legitimate business. The Act subjects to severe civil and criminal penalties enterprises that engage in a pattern of racketeering, defined as the commission of two or more predicate acts within a period of ten years. A "predicate act" is any of several criminal offenses listed in RICO. Included are nine major categories of state crimes and more than thirty federal crimes, such as murder, kidnapping, arson, extortion, drug dealing, mail fraud, and bribery. The most controversial issue concerning RICO is its application to businesses that are not engaged in organized crime but that do meet the "pattern of racketeering" test under the Act. Criminal conviction under the law may result in (1) fines of up to $250,000 ($500,000 for an organization) or twice the amount of gross profits or other proceeds from the offense and/or (2) a prison term of up to twenty years or for life if the violation is based on a racketeering activity for which the maximum penalty includes life imprisonment. In addition, businesses forfeit any property obtained due to a RICO violation, and individuals harmed by RICO violations may invoke the statute's civil remedies, which include treble damage and attorneys' fees.

Other areas of federal law that impose both civil and criminal penalties include bankruptcy (Chapter 38), antitrust (Chapter 42), securities regulation (Chapter 43), and environmental regulation (Chapter 45).

CRIMES AGAINST BUSINESS [6-4]

Criminal offenses against property greatly affect businesses, amounting to losses worth hundreds of billions of dollars each year. In this section we will discuss the following crimes against property: (1) larceny, (2) embezzlement, (3) false pretenses, (4) robbery, (5) burglary, (6) extortion and bribery, (7) forgery, and (8) bad checks.

Larceny [6-4a]

Larceny

trespassory taking and carrying away of the goods of another with the intent to permanently deprive

The crime of **larceny** is the (1) trespassory (2) taking and (3) carrying away of (or exercising dominion or control over) (4) personal property (5) of another (6) with the intent to deprive the victim permanently of the goods. All six elements must be present for the crime to exist. Thus, if Carol takes Dan's 1968 automobile without Dan's permission, intending to use it for a joyride and to then return it to Dan, Carol has not committed larceny because she did not intend to deprive Dan permanently of the automobile. (Carol nevertheless has committed the offense of unauthorized use of an automobile, which is a crime in most states.) On the other hand, if Carol left Dan's 1968 car in a junkyard after the joyride, Carol most likely would be held to have committed a larceny because of the high risk that Dan would be permanently deprived of the car.

Embezzlement [6-4b]

Embezzlement

taking the property of one's employer in violation of a trust

Embezzlement is the fraudulent conversion of another's property by one who was in lawful possession of it. A conversion is any act that seriously interferes with the owner's rights in the property; such acts may include exhausting the resources of the property, selling it, giving it away, or refusing to return it to its rightful owner. The key distinction between larceny and embezzlement, therefore, is whether the thief is in lawful possession of the property. Although both situations concern misuse of the property of another, in embezzlement, the thief lawfully possesses the property; in larceny, she does not.

False Pretenses [6-4c]

False pretenses

obtaining title to property of another by means of materially false representations of fact made with knowledge of their falsity and with the intent to defraud

False pretenses is the crime of obtaining title to property of another by making materially false representations of an existing fact with knowledge of their falsity and with the intent to defraud. Larceny does not cover this situation because here the victim voluntarily transfers the property to the thief. For example, a con artist who goes door to door and collects money by saying he is selling stereo equipment, when he is not, is committing the crime of false pretenses.

Other specialized crimes that are similar to false pretenses include mail, wire, and bank fraud as well as securities fraud. **Mail fraud**, unlike the crime of false pretenses, does not require the victim to be actually defrauded; it simply requires the defendant to use the mails (or private carrier) to carry out a scheme that attempts to defraud others. Due to its breadth and ease of use, mail fraud has been employed extensively by federal prosecutors. The **wire fraud** statute prohibits the transmittal by wire, radio, or television in interstate or foreign commerce of any information with the intent to defraud. The federal statute prohibiting **bank fraud** makes it a crime knowingly to execute or attempt to execute a scheme to defraud a financial institution or to obtain by false pretenses funds under the control or custody of a financial institution. **Securities fraud** is discussed in Chapter 39.

APPLYING THE LAW

Criminal Law

Facts Bivens worked as an accounts payable clerk for C&N Construction. Every Wednesday morning, the site foreman would call Bivens and give her the names of the employees working on the job and the number of hours they had worked. Bivens would then convey this information to a paycheck-processing company, which would return unsigned payroll checks to C&N. After a designated officer of the company signed them, Bivens would forward the checks to the job site for distribution by the foreman. After working for the company for nearly eight years, Bivens began sending false information to the payroll service about employees and hours worked. The resulting checks were typically payable to employees who had worked for C&N in the recent past but who were not active on the current job. Bivens would intercept these "fake" checks after they were signed, forge the payees' names, and either cash them or deposit them into her bank account. Over a period of seventeen months, Bivens diverted tens of thousands of dollars to herself by forging more than one hundred fake paychecks. She spent all but a few hundred dollars of the money on meals and entertainment, jewelry, clothing, and shoes. C&N's vice president ultimately discovered Bivens's practice, fired her, and notified the authorities of her conduct.

Issue Has Bivens committed the crime of embezzlement?

Rule of Law A crime consists of two elements: (1) *actus reus*, or a wrongful act, and (2) *mens rea*, or criminal intent. The crime of embezzlement occurs when a person who is in lawful possession of another's property intentionally misuses the property or seriously interferes with the owner's rights in it. Possible defenses to a crime include defense of person or property, duress, and mistake of fact.

Application The *actus reus* in this case is exercising wrongful dominion and control over the property of another while in legal possession of it. Bivens was lawfully in possession of C&N's property in the form of the payroll checks. While her job description certainly did not authorize her to keep any of the checks or payroll funds for herself, Bivens's position at C&N did require her to record and transmit payroll information as well as to handle the checks themselves. While in legal possession of C&N paychecks, Bivens misused or seriously interfered with C&N payroll funds. Without permission or right, she cashed some of the checks and diverted to herself money that belonged to C&N. She has committed the necessary wrongful act.

The next question is whether she had the requisite state of mind. Bivens's paycheck scheme also reflects *mens rea*, or subjective fault. Her conduct with regard to the checks was clearly purposeful or intentional. While it might be possible to make an error in transmitting employee

names or hours worked occasionally, Bivens could not have negligently transmitted incorrect information about former employees in more than one hundred instances. Moreover, the fact she separated out the fake checks from the genuine paychecks, surreptitiously took them from work, falsely endorsed them with the names of the former employee payees, and then cashed them and spent the money indicates she intended to steal the funds. This series of events benefiting Bivens could not possibly have happened unintentionally or through carelessness alone. Therefore the necessary *mens rea* is present.

Moreover, none of the defenses to a crime is applicable here. Bivens was not acting to protect herself, another person, or her property. Nor was she under duress; she was not threatened with immediate, serious bodily harm when she engaged in the paycheck scam. Finally, there is nothing to indicate that Bivens was mistaken about C&N's ownership of the payroll funds, about the names or hours worked by employees any given week, or that she could have mistakenly thought she was expected to or permitted to falsify payroll records so as to cause paychecks to be issued to former employees, paychecks which she would then take and cash for herself. Thus, Bivens has no valid legal defense.

Conclusion Bivens's conduct with regard to these checks constitutes embezzlement.

State of South Dakota v. Morse
Supreme Court of South Dakota, 2008
753 N.W.2d 915, 2008 SD 66
http://scholar.google.com/scholar_case?case=4959207354232635251&q=753+N.W.2d+915,&hl=en&as_sclt=2,22

FACTS Janice Heffron orally contracted with her neighbor, Wyatt Morse, to convert her second-floor bedroom into a bathroom in five weeks for $5,000. According to Janice, Morse repeatedly stated that he could do it "easy, quick, cheap." Janice told her mother, Maxine Heffron, who would finance the project, about Morse's offer. Maxine and Janice then went to Morse's home, where he showed them the bathroom he had restored. Janice and Maxine were impressed. Morse also told them that he had plumbing experience, that his work would be above and beyond code, and that the local inspector did not inspect his work because he was so good. Maxine wanted to pay using personal checks to assure a paper trail, but Morse convinced her to pay him with cash. According to Janice, he wanted to be paid in cash to avoid the Internal Revenue Service. They agreed that Morse would convert the room into a bathroom, install an antique claw-foot tub (one that he would provide personally), put wainscoting on the walls, install an old tin ceiling like the one in his bathroom, and install crown molding.

Morse began work in January 2006. His efforts continued until the second week of March. He installed plumbing fixtures and he removed the old water heater and installed a new one. He ran a freeze-proof spigot outside the house. He put in a bathroom vent with an antique vent cover. He custom built a bathroom cabinet at no extra cost to the Heffrons. He mounted wainscoting and crafted a surrounding shelf with rope lighting. He put in a faux tin ceiling, with crown molding and trim. He installed water pipes and a new drain stack. The project took longer and cost more than originally agreed. Morse ran into difficulties when he attempted to install a tankless water heater. He was never able to install the tankless heater and ended up installing a traditional tanked water heater. Morse also experienced problems with some of the pipes he installed. Janice told him that they were leaking. He repaired them and blamed the leaks on bad batches of solder.

Maxine paid Morse somewhere between $6,000 and $6,500 cash. In March 2006, Morse fell and aggravated his already bad back. Before Janice and Maxine hired him, Morse had told them that he had a back condition. After his fall in March, he came to the job site less and less. Then, after the second week in March he stopped coming entirely. The Heffrons tried contacting him through phone calls, personal visits, and certified mail. He never responded. After Morse abandoned the project, Janice contacted a licensed plumber, who examined Morse's work and gave Janice an estimate on the cost of completing the project. The plumber pointed out several deficiencies in Morse's work. In particular, Morse incorrectly installed the water heater, the pipes for the sink, lavatory, and bathtub. He used S-traps, illegal in South Dakota, and improperly vented the floor drains. Because he installed the water heater incorrectly, carbon monoxide was leaking into Janice's home. In sum, Morse's work on the bathroom, in the opinion of the licensed plumber, had no value to the home.

On October 12, 2006, Morse was indicted for grand theft by deception in violation of South Dakota law. A jury returned a guilty verdict. Morse was sentenced to five years in prison. He appeals asserting that the evidence was insufficient to sustain the verdict.

DECISION Judgment reversed.

OPINION Morse argues that South Dakota failed to prove he had the requisite intent to defraud the Heffrons. He does not dispute that the work he did on Janice's home was faulty and resulted in the Heffrons having to pay considerably more in repairs. Nonetheless, he claims that his faulty work created a classic breach of contract claim, because when he entered into the agreement to remodel the bathroom, he believed he was capable of doing quality work and fully intended on completing the project. The state, on the other hand, argues that Morse "created and reinforced the false impression in the minds of Jan and Maxine Heffron that he was licensed to, and capable of, installing a second floor bathroom" and in his ability to do the work. Theft by deception is a specific intent crime. Intent to defraud "means to act willfully and with the specific intent to deceive or cheat, ordinarily for the purpose of either causing some financial loss to another or bringing about some financial gain to one's self." Therefore, Morse must have had the "purpose to deceive."

The record indicates that Morse (1) failed to complete the project in five weeks for $5,000 as promised; (2) performed work that was not "above and beyond code" as promised; (3) lied about obtaining a building permit; (4) lied about the reasons he could not get the tankless water heater installed and why the pipes were leaking; (5) returned the water heater and did not give the $186 refund to Maxine; (6) never provided Janice or Maxine receipts for materials purchased; (7) quit working on the project prematurely and without explanation; and (8) never responded to the Heffrons' attempts to contact him.

These facts do not prove the elements of theft by deception. There is no evidence that Morse had a purpose to deceive or intended to defraud the Heffrons when he agreed to remodel Janice's bathroom. Although his work was not above and beyond code, the state never argued that Morse *knew* he would do faulty work. Janice and Maxine both testified that Morse took them up to his house and showed him the remodeling that he did to his own bathroom. They both said they were impressed. It cannot be inferred that Morse intended to defraud the Heffrons because his work product was not up to code.

Moreover, the state never argued or presented evidence that Morse took Maxine's money with the intention of never performing under their agreement. The parties made their agreement in December 2005, and no one disputes that Morse worked regularly on the project from January 2006 until the second week of March. While Morse failed to complete the project in five weeks for $5,000 as promised, the state never claimed that he *knew* it would take longer and charge more, and tricked the Heffrons into believing him. Neither Janice nor Maxine claimed that Morse deceived them into paying him more money when the project took longer than anticipated.

INTERPRETATION An essential element of a crime is the mental intent (*mens rea*) to commit the crime.

CRITICAL THINKING QUESTION When should circumstantial evidence be permitted to prove a crime has been committed? Explain.

Robbery [6-4d]

Robbery
larceny from a person by force or threat of force

Robbery is a larceny with two additional elements: (1) the property is taken directly from the victim or in the immediate presence of the victim and (2) the act is accomplished through either force or the threat of force. The defendant's force or threat of force need not be against the person from whom the property is taken. For example, a robber threatens Sam that unless Sam opens up his employer's safe, the robber will shoot Maria.

Many statutes distinguish between simple robbery and aggravated robbery. Robbery can be aggravated by any of several factors, including (1) robbery with a deadly weapon, (2) robbery where the robber has the intent to kill or would kill if faced with resistance, (3) robbery that involves serious bodily injury, or (4) robbery by two or more persons.

Burglary [6-4e]

Burglary
breaking and entering the home of another at night with intent to commit a felony

At common law, **burglary** was defined as breaking and entering the dwelling of another at night with the intent to commit a felony. Modern statutes differ from the common law definition. Many of them simply require that there be (1) an entry (2) into a building (3) with the intent to commit a felony in the building. Nevertheless, the modern statutes vary so greatly it is nearly impossible to generalize.

Extortion and Bribery [6-4f]

Extortion
making threats to obtain property

Although extortion and bribery are frequently confused, they are two distinct crimes. **Extortion**, or blackmail as it is sometimes called, is generally held to be the making of threats for the purpose of obtaining money or property. For example, Lindsey tells Jason that unless Jason pays her $10,000, she will tell Jason's customers that Jason was once arrested for disturbing the peace. Lindsey has committed the crime of extortion. In a few jurisdictions, however, the crime of extortion occurs only if the defendant actually causes the victim to relinquish money or property.

Bribery
offering property to a public official to influence the official's decision

Bribery, on the other hand, is the offer of money or property to a public official to influence the official's decision. The crime of bribery is committed when the illegal offer is made, whether accepted or not. Thus, if Andrea offered Edward, the mayor of Allentown, a 20 percent interest in Andrea's planned real estate development if Edward would use his influence to have the development proposal approved, Andrea would be guilty of criminal bribery. In contrast, if Edward had threatened Andrea that unless he received a 20 percent interest in Andrea's development, he would use his influence to prevent the approval of the development, Edward would be guilty of criminal extortion. Bribery of foreign officials is covered by the Foreign Corrupt Practices Act, discussed in Chapters 39 and 46.

Some jurisdictions have gone beyond the traditional bribery law to adopt statutes that make *commercial bribery* illegal. Commercial bribery is the use of bribery to acquire new business, obtain secret information or processes, or obtain kickbacks.

Forgery [6-4g]

Forgery
intentional falsification of a document in order to defraud

Forgery is the intentional falsification or false making of a document with the intent to defraud. Accordingly, if William prepares a false certificate of title to a stolen automobile, he is guilty of forgery. Likewise, if an individual alters some receipts to increase her income tax deductions, she has committed the crime of forgery. The most common type of forgery is the signing of another's name to a financial document.

Bad Checks [6-4h]

Bad checks
checks issued with funds insufficient to cover them

All jurisdictions have enacted laws making it a crime to issue **bad checks**; that is, writing a check when there is not enough money in the account to cover the check. Most jurisdictions simply require that the check be issued; they do not require that the issuer receive anything in return for the check. Also, though most jurisdictions require that defendants issue a check with knowledge that they do not have enough money to cover the check, a few jurisdictions require only that there be insufficient funds.

GOING GLOBAL

What about international bribery?

In 1977, Congress enacted the Foreign Corrupt Practices Act (FCPA) prohibiting any U.S. person, and certain foreign issuers of securities, from bribing foreign government or political officials to assist in obtaining or retaining business. Since 1998, the antibribery provisions also apply to foreign firms and persons who take any act in furtherance of such a corrupt payment while in the United States. The FCPA makes it unlawful for any U.S. person, and certain foreign issuers of securities, or any of its officers, directors, employees, or agents to offer or give anything of value directly or indirectly to any foreign official, political party, or political official for the purpose of (1) influencing any act or decision of that person or party in his or its official capacity, (2) inducing an act or omission in violation of his or its lawful duty, or (3) inducing such person or party to use his or its influence to affect a decision of a foreign government to assist the person in obtaining or retaining business. An offer or promise to make a prohibited payment is a violation even if the offer is not accepted or the promise is not performed. The 1988

amendments to the FCPA explicitly excluded routine government actions not involving the discretion of the official, such as obtaining permits or processing applications. This exclusion does *not* cover any decision by a foreign official whether, or on what terms, to award new business or to continue business with a particular party. The amendments also added an affirmative defense for payments that are lawful under the written laws or regulations of the foreign official's country.

Violations can result in fines of up to $2 million for corporations and other business entities; individuals may be fined a maximum of $100,000 or imprisoned up to five years, or both. Moreover, under the Alternative Fines Act, the actual fine may be up to twice the benefit that the person sought to obtain by making the corrupt payment. Fines imposed upon individuals may not be paid directly or indirectly by the corporation or other business entity on whose behalf the individuals acted. In addition, the courts may impose civil penalties of up to $16,000, as adjusted for inflation in March 2013.

In 1997 the United States signed the Organisation for Economic Co-operation and Development Convention on Combating Bribery of Foreign Public Officials in International Business Transactions (OECD Convention). The OECD Convention has been adopted by at least forty nations. In 1998 Congress enacted the International Anti-Bribery and Fair Competition Act of 1998 to conform the FCPA to the OECD Convention. The 1998 Act expands the FCPA to include (1) payments made to "secure any improper advantage" from foreign officials, (2) all foreign persons who commit an act in furtherance of a foreign bribe while in the United States, and (3) officials of public international organizations within the definition of a "foreign official." A public international organization is defined as either an organization designated by executive order pursuant to the International Organizations Immunities Act or any other international organization designated by executive order of the President.

State v. Kelm
Superior Court of New Jersey, 1996
289 N.J. Super. 55, 672 A.2d 1261; *cert. denied*, 146 N.J. 68, 679 A.2d 655 (1996)
http://scholar.google.com/scholar_case?case=13514723993330084946&q=672+A.2d+1261&hl=en&as_sdt=40006

FACTS On February 10, 1991, defendant Kelm secured a loan for $6,000 from Ms. Joan Williams. Kelm told Williams that the loan was to finance a real estate transaction. Five days later, Ms. Williams received a check drawn by Kelm in the amount of $6,000 from Kelm's attorney. Although the check was dated February 15, 1991, Kelm claims that she delivered the check to her attorney on February 10, 1991. The following week, Ms. Williams learned the check was uncollectible. Subsequently, Williams received assurances from Kelm but was unsuccessful in her efforts to obtain money from the drawee's bank. When Williams deposited the check, it was returned with a notation that it should not be presented again and that no account was on file. Bank records show that the account was closed on March 8, 1991, and that it had negative balances since February 10, 1991. Following a jury trial, Kelm was found guilty of issuing a bad check. Kelm appeals, asserting that an intent to defraud is an element of the statutory offense of issuing a bad check and that the statutory provision exempts postdated checks.

DECISION The jury verdict is affirmed.

OPINION The principal issue on appeal is whether an intent to defraud is an element of Section 2C:21-5 [issuing a bad check] of the New Jersey statutes. The statute provides:

A person who issues or passes a check or similar sight order for the payment of money, knowing that it will not be honored by the drawee, commits an offense.... For the purposes of this section as well as in any prosecution for theft committed by means of a bad check, an issuer is presumed to know that the check or money order (other than a post-dated check or order) would not be paid, if:
* * *.
(b) Payment was refused by the drawee for lack of funds, upon presentation within 30 days after issue, and the issuer failed to make good within 10 days after receiving notice of that refusal....

This statute, unlike its predecessor, does not contain the language "with intent to defraud." Kelm's reliance on cases interpreting the prior bad check statute is misplaced. An intent to defraud is not an element of the offense of issuing a bad check. Rather, the current statute requires mere knowledge at the time the check is issued or passed that it will not be honored by the drawee.

Addressing Kelm's second assertion, the statute's reference to postdated checks does not completely exempt such checks from its operation. That reference only exempts the drawer of a post-dated check from the presumption of knowledge that the check will not be paid. In such cases, the state must prove such knowledge beyond a reasonable doubt.

The trial judge's charge to the jury correctly reflected the statutory requirement of knowledge. It also states that if the jury should find that the check was postdated, then the element of knowledge requires proof beyond a reasonable doubt. The jury was correctly instructed by this charge. Therefore, the jury's verdict is affirmed.

INTERPRETATION Under the New Jersey statute the offense of issuing a bad check requires mere knowledge at the time the check is issued or passed that the check will not be honored by the drawee.

CRITICAL THINKING QUESTION What elements do you believe are essential to a bad check law? Explain.

DEFENSES TO CRIMES [6-5]

Even though a defendant is found to have committed a criminal act, he will not be convicted if he has a valid defense. The defenses most relevant to white-collar crimes and crimes against business include defense of property, duress, mistake of fact, and entrapment. In some instances, a defense proves the absence of a required element of the crime; other defenses provide a justification or excuse that bars criminal liability.

Defense of Person or Property [6-5a]

Defense of person or property
individuals may use reasonable force to protect themselves, other individuals, and their property

Individuals may use reasonable force to protect themselves, other individuals, and their property. This defense enables a person to commit, without any criminal liability, what otherwise would be considered the crime of assault, battery, manslaughter, or murder. Under the majority rule, deadly force is never reasonable to protect property because life is deemed more important than the protection of property. For this reason, individuals cannot use a deadly mechanical device, such as a spring gun, to protect their property. If, however, the defender's use of reasonable force in protecting his property is met with an attack upon his person, he then may use deadly force if the attack threatens him with death or serious bodily harm.

Duress [6-5b]

Duress
coercion by threat of serious bodily injury

A person who is threatened with immediate, serious bodily harm to himself or another unless he engages in criminal activity has the valid defense of **duress** (sometimes referred to as compulsion or coercion) to criminal conduct other than murder. For example, Ann threatens to kill Ben if Ben does not assist her in committing larceny. Ben complies. Because of duress, he would not be guilty of the larceny.

Mistake of Fact [6-5c]

Mistake of fact
honest and reasonable belief that conduct is not criminal is a defense

If a person reasonably believes the facts surrounding an act to be such that his conduct would not constitute a crime, then the law will treat the facts as he reasonably believes them to be. Accordingly, an honest and reasonable **mistake of fact** will justify the defendant's conduct. For example, if Ann gets into a car that she reasonably believes to be hers—the car is the same color, model, and year as hers, is parked in the same parking lot, and is started by her key—she will be relieved of criminal responsibility for taking Ben's automobile.

Entrapment [6-5d]

Entrapment
the act of a government official in inducing another to commit a crime

The defense of **entrapment** arises when a law enforcement official induces a person to commit a crime when that person would not have done so without the persuasion of the police official. The rationale behind the rule, which applies only to government officials and agents, not to private individuals, is to prevent law enforcement officials from provoking crime and from engaging in improper conduct.

CRIMINAL PROCEDURE [6-6]

Each of the states and the federal government have procedures for initiating and coordinating criminal prosecutions. In addition, the first ten amendments to the U.S. Constitution (called the Bill of Rights) guarantee many defenses and rights of an accused. The Fourth Amendment prohibits unreasonable searches and seizures to obtain incriminating evidence. The Fifth Amendment requires indictment by a grand jury for capital crimes, prevents double jeopardy, protects against self-incrimination, and prohibits deprivation of life or liberty without due process of law. The Sixth Amendment requires that an accused receive a speedy and public trial by an impartial jury and that he be informed of the nature of the accusation, be confronted with the witnesses who testify against him, be given the power to obtain witnesses in his favor, and have the right to competent counsel for his defense. The Eighth Amendment prohibits excessive bail, excessive fines, and cruel or unusual punishment.

Most state constitutions have similar provisions to protect the rights of accused persons. In addition, the Fourteenth Amendment prohibits state governments from depriving any person of life, liberty, or property without due process of law. Moreover, the U.S. Supreme Court has held that most of the constitutional protections just discussed apply to the states through the operation of the Fourteenth Amendment.

Although various jurisdictions may differ in actual operational details, their criminal processes have a number of common objectives. The primary purpose of the process in any jurisdiction is the effective enforcement of the criminal law, but this purpose must be accomplished within the limitations imposed by other goals. These goals include advancing an adversary system of adjudication, requiring the government to bear the burden of proof, minimizing both erroneous convictions and the burdens of defense, respecting individual dignity, maintaining the appearance of fairness, and achieving equality in the administration of the process.

We will first discuss the steps in a criminal prosecution; we will then focus on the major constitutional protections for the accused in our system of criminal justice.

Steps in Criminal Prosecution [6-6a]

Steps in criminal prosecution generally include arrest, booking, formal notice of charges, preliminary hearing to determine probable cause, indictment or information, arraignment, and trial

Preliminary hearing determines whether there is probable cause

Indictment grand jury charge that the defendant should stand trial

Information formal accusation of a crime brought by a prosecutor

Arraignment accused is informed of the charge against him and enters a plea

Although the particulars of criminal procedure vary from state to state, the following provides a basic overview of the **steps in criminal prosecution**. After arrest, the accused is booked and appears before the magistrate, commissioner, or justice of the peace, where he is given formal notice of the charges and is advised of his rights and where bail is set. Next, a **preliminary hearing** is held to determine whether there is probable cause to believe the defendant is the one who committed the crime. The defendant is usually entitled to be represented by counsel.

If the magistrate concludes that there is probable cause, she will bind the case over to the next stage, which is either an indictment or information, depending upon the jurisdiction. The federal system and about one-third of the states require indictments for all felony prosecutions (unless waived by the defendant), while the other states permit, but do not mandate, indictments. A grand jury issues an **indictment** or true bill if it finds sufficient evidence to justify a trial on the charge brought. The grand jury, which traditionally consists of no fewer than sixteen and no more than twenty-three people, is not bound by the magistrate's decision at the preliminary hearing. Unlike the preliminary hearing, the grand jury does not hear evidence from the defendant, nor does the defendant appear before the grand jury. In contrast, an **information** is a formal accusation of a crime brought by a prosecuting officer, not a grand jury. Such a procedure is used in misdemeanor cases and in some felony cases in those states that do not require indictments. The indictment or information at times precedes the actual arrest.

At the **arraignment**, the defendant is brought before the trial court, where he is informed of the charge against him and where he enters his plea. The arraignment must be held promptly after the indictment or information has been filed. If his plea is "not guilty," the defendant must stand trial. He is entitled to a jury trial for all felonies and for misdemeanors punishable by more than six months' imprisonment. Most states also permit a defendant to request a jury trial for lesser misdemeanors. If the defendant chooses, however, he may have his guilt or innocence determined by the court sitting without a jury, which is called a "bench trial."

In the great majority of criminal cases, defendants enter into a plea bargain with the government instead of going to trial. In a 2012 case, the U.S. Supreme Court stated, "Ninety-seven percent of federal convictions and ninety-four percent of state convictions are the result of guilty pleas."

A criminal trial is similar to a civil trial, but there are some significant differences: (1) the defendant is presumed innocent, (2) the burden of proof on the prosecution is to prove criminal guilt **beyond a reasonable doubt** (proof that is entirely convincing, satisfied to a moral certainty), and (3) the defendant is not required to testify. The trial begins with the selection of the jury and the opening statements by the prosecutor and the attorney for the defense. The prosecution presents evidence first; then the defendant presents his evidence. At the conclusion of the testimony, closing statements are made and the jury is instructed as to the applicable law and retires to arrive at a verdict. If the verdict is "not guilty," the matter ends there. The state has no right to appeal from an acquittal; and the accused, having been placed in "jeopardy," cannot be tried a second time for the same offense. If the verdict is "guilty," the judge will enter a judgment of conviction and set the case for sentencing. The defendant may make a motion for a new trial, asserting that prejudicial error occurred at his original trial, thus requiring a retrial of the case. He may appeal to a reviewing court, alleging error by the trial court and asking for either his discharge or a remand of the case for a new trial.

Fourth Amendment [6-6b]

The **Fourth Amendment**, which protects all individuals against unreasonable searches and seizures, is designed to guard the privacy and security of individuals against arbitrary invasions by government officials. Although the Fourth Amendment by its terms applies only to acts of the federal government, the Fourteenth Amendment makes it applicable to state government actions as well.

When a violation of the Fourth Amendment has occurred, the general rule prohibits the introduction of the illegally seized evidence at trial. The purpose of this **exclusionary rule** is to discourage illegal police conduct and to protect individual liberty, not to hinder the search for the truth. Nonetheless, in recent years the Supreme Court has limited the exclusionary rule.

To obtain a warrant to search a particular person, place, or thing, a law enforcement official must demonstrate to a magistrate that he has probable cause to believe that the search will reveal evidence of criminal activity. **Probable cause** means "[t]he task of the issuing magistrate is simply to make a practical, common-sense decision whether, given all the circumstances set forth … before him, … there is a fair probability that contraband or evidence of a crime will be found in a particular place." *Illinois v. Gates*, 462 U.S. 213 (1983). Even though the Fourth Amendment requires that a search and seizure generally be made after a valid search warrant has been obtained, in some instances a search warrant is not necessary. For example, it has been held that a warrant is not necessary when (1) there is hot pursuit of a fugitive, (2) the subject of the search voluntarily consents, (3) an emergency requires such action, (4) there has been a lawful arrest, (5) evidence of a crime is in plain view of the law enforcement officer, or (6) delay would present a significant obstacle to the investigation.

Fifth Amendment [6-6c]

The **Fifth Amendment** protects persons against self-incrimination, double jeopardy, and being charged with a capital or infamous crime except by grand jury indictment. The prohibitions against self-incrimination and double jeopardy also apply to the states through the Due Process Clause of the Fourteenth Amendment; however, the grand jury clause does not.

The privilege against self-incrimination extends only to testimonial evidence, not to physical evidence. The Fifth Amendment privilege "protects an accused only from being compelled to testify against himself, or otherwise provide the state with evidence of a testimonial or communicative nature." Therefore, a person can be forced to stand in an identification lineup, provide a handwriting sample, or take a blood test. Significantly, the Fifth Amendment does not protect the records of a business entity, such as a corporation or partnership; it applies only to papers of individuals. Moreover, the Fifth Amendment does not prohibit examination of an individual's business records as long as the individual is not compelled to testify against himself.

Beyond a reasonable doubt

proof that is entirely convincing; satisfied to a moral certainty

Fourth Amendment

protects individuals against unreasonable searches and seizures

Exclusionary rule

prohibition against the introduction of illegally seized evidence

Probable cause

reasonable belief of the offense charged

Fifth Amendment

protects persons against self-incrimination, double jeopardy, and being charged with a capital crime except by grand jury indictment

---

CONCEPT REVIEW 6-2

Constitutional Protection for the Criminal Defendant

Amendment	Protection Conferred
Fourth	Freedom from unreasonable search and seizure
Fifth	Right to due process Right to indictment by grand jury for capital crimes* Freedom from double jeopardy Freedom from self-incrimination
Sixth	Right to speedy, public trial by jury Right to be informed of accusations Right to present witnesses Right to competent counsel
Eighth	Freedom from excessive bail Freedom from cruel and unusual punishment

*This right has *not* been applied to the states through the Fourteenth Amendment.

Practical Advice

A defendant has the right not to testify against himself and a jury cannot consider this against him.

Sixth Amendment

provides the accused with the right to a speedy and public trial, the opportunity to confront witnesses, have compulsory process for obtaining witnesses, and the right to counsel

The Fifth Amendment and the Fourteenth Amendment also guarantee due process of law, which is basically the requirement of a fair trial. All persons are entitled to have the charges or complaints against them made publicly and in writing, whether in civil or criminal proceedings, and are to be given the opportunity to defend themselves against such charges. In criminal prosecutions, due process includes the right to counsel, to confront and cross-examine adverse witnesses, to testify in one's own behalf if desired, to produce witnesses and offer other evidence, and to be free from any and all prejudicial conduct and statements.

Sixth Amendment [6-6d]

The **Sixth Amendment** provides that the federal government shall provide the accused with a speedy and public trial by an impartial jury, inform him of the nature and cause of the accusation, confront him with the witnesses against him, have compulsory process for obtaining witnesses in his favor, and allow him to obtain the assistance of counsel for his defense. The Fourteenth Amendment extends these guarantees to the states.

See Concept Review 6-2 for a presentation of the constitutional protections provided the defendant in a criminal action.

CHAPTER SUMMARY

Nature of Crimes

Definition any act or omission forbidden by public law

Essential Elements

- *Actus reus* wrongful or overt act
- *Mens rea* criminal intent or mental fault
- *Felony* a serious crime
- *Misdemeanor* a less serious crime

Classification

Vicarious Liability liability imposed for acts of his or her employees if the employer directed, participated in, or approved of the acts

Liability of a Corporation under certain circumstances a corporation may be convicted of crimes and punished by fines

White-Collar Crime	**Definition** nonviolent crime involving deceit, corruption, or breach of trust
	Computer Crime use of a computer to commit a crime
	Racketeer Influenced and Corrupt Organizations Act federal law intended to stop organized crime from infiltrating legitimate businesses
Crimes Against Business	**Larceny** trespassory taking and carrying away of personal property of another with the intent to deprive the victim permanently of the property
	Embezzlement taking of another's property by a person who was in lawful possession of the property
	False Pretenses obtaining title to property of another by means of representations one knows to be materially false, made with intent to defraud
	Robbery committing larceny with the use or threat of force
	Burglary under most modern statutes, an entry into a building with the intent to commit a felony
	Extortion the making of threats to obtain money or property
	Bribery offering money or property to a public official to influence the official's decision
	Forgery intentional falsification of a document in order to defraud
	Bad Checks knowingly issuing a check without funds sufficient to cover the check
Defenses to Crimes	**Defense of Person or Property** individuals may use reasonable force to protect themselves, other individuals, and their property
	Duress coercion by threat of serious bodily harm is a defense to criminal conduct other than murder
	Mistake of Fact honest and reasonable belief that conduct is not criminal is a defense
	Entrapment inducement by a law enforcement official to commit a crime is a defense
Criminal Procedure	**Steps in Criminal Prosecution** generally include arrest, booking, formal notice of charges, preliminary hearing to determine probable cause, indictment or information, arraignment, and trial
	Fourth Amendment protects individuals against unreasonable searches and seizures
	Fifth Amendment protects persons against self-incrimination, double jeopardy, and being charged with a capital crime except by grand jury indictment
	Sixth Amendment provides the accused with the right to a speedy and public trial, the opportunity to confront witnesses, have compulsory process for obtaining witnesses, and the right to counsel

QUESTIONS

1. Sam said to Carol, "Kim is going to sell me a good used car next Monday and then I'll deliver it to you in exchange for your computer but I'd like to have the computer now." Relying on this statement, Carol delivered the computer to Sam. Sam knew Kim had no car and would have none in the future, and he had no such arrangement with her. The appointed time of exchange passed, and Sam failed to deliver the car to Carol. Has a crime been committed? Discuss.

2. Sara, a lawyer, drew a deed for Robert by which Robert was to convey land to Rick. The deed was correct in every detail. Robert examined and verbally approved it but did not sign it. Then Sara erased Rick's name and substituted her own. Robert subsequently signed the deed with all required legal formalities without noticing the change. Was Sara guilty of forgery? Discuss.

3. Ann took Bonnie's watch without Bonnie knowing of the theft. Bonnie subsequently discovered her loss and was informed that Ann had taken the watch. Bonnie immediately pursued Ann. Ann pointed a loaded pistol at Bonnie, who, in fear of being shot, allowed Ann to escape. Was Ann guilty of robbery? Of any other crime?

4. Jones and Wilson were on trial, separately, for larceny of a $10,000 bearer bond (payable to the holder of the bond, not a named individual) issued by Brown, Inc. The commonwealth's evidence showed that the owner of the bond put it in an envelope bearing his name and address and dropped it accidentally in the street; that Jones found the envelope with the bond in it; that Jones could neither read nor write; that Jones presented the envelope and bond to Wilson, an educated man, and asked Wilson what he should do with it; that Wilson told Jones that the finder of lost property becomes the owner of it; that Wilson told Jones that the bond was worth $1,000 but that the money could be collected only at the issuer's home office; that Jones then handed the bond to Wilson, who redeemed it at the corporation's home office and received $10,000; that Wilson gave Jones $1,000 of the proceeds. What rulings?

5. Truck drivers for a hauling company, while loading a desk, found a $100 bill that had fallen out of the desk. They agreed

to get it exchanged for small bills and divide the proceeds. En route to the bank, one of them changed his mind and refused to proceed with the scheme, whereupon the other pulled a knife and demanded the bill. A police officer intervened. What crimes have been committed?

6. Peter, an undercover police agent, was trying to locate a laboratory where it was believed that methamphetamine, or "speed"—a controlled substance—was being manufactured illegally. Peter went to Mary's home and said that he represented a large organization that was interested in obtaining methamphetamine. Peter offered to supply a necessary ingredient for the manufacture of the drug, which was very difficult to obtain, in return for one-half of the drug produced. Mary agreed and processed the chemical given to her by Peter in Peter's presence. Later Peter returned with a search warrant and arrested Mary. Mary was charged with various narcotics law violations. Mary asserted the defense of entrapment. Should Mary prevail? Why?

7. The police obtained a search warrant based on an affidavit that contained the following allegations: (a) Donald was seen crossing a state line on four occasions during a five-day period and going to a particular apartment; (b) telephone records disclosed that the apartment had two telephones; (c) Donald had a reputation as a bookmaker and as an associate of gamblers; and (d) the Federal Bureau of Investigation was informed by a "confidential reliable informant" that Donald was conducting gambling operations from the apartment. The affidavit did not indicate how the informant knew of this information nor did it contain any information about the reliability of the informant. When a search was made based on the warrant, evidence was obtained that resulted in Donald's conviction of violating certain gambling laws. Donald challenged the constitutionality of the search warrant. Were Donald's constitutional rights violated? Explain your answer.

8. A national bank was robbed by a man with a small strip of tape on each side of his face. An indictment was returned against David. David was then arrested, and counsel was appointed to represent him. Two weeks later, without notice to David's lawyer, an agent with the Federal Bureau of Investigation arranged to have the two bank employees observe a lineup, including David and five or six other prisoners. Each person in the lineup wore strips of tape, as had the robber, and each was directed to repeat the words "Put the money in the bag," as had the robber. Both of the bank employees identified David as the robber. At David's trial he was again identified by the two, in the courtroom, and the prior lineup identification was elicited on cross-examination by David's counsel. David's counsel moved the court either to grant a judgment of acquittal or alternatively to strike the courtroom identifications on the ground that the lineup had violated David's Fifth Amendment privilege against self-incrimination and his Sixth Amendment right to counsel. Decision?

CASE PROBLEMS

9. Waronek owned and operated a trucking rig, transporting goods for L.T.L. Perishables, Inc., of St. Paul, Minnesota. He accepted an offer to haul a trailer load of beef from Illini Beef Packers, Inc., in Joslin, Illinois, to Midtown Packing Company in New York City. After his truck was loaded with ninety-five forequarters and ninety-five hindquarters of beef in Joslin, Waronek drove north to his home in Watertown, Wisconsin, rather than east to New York. While in Watertown, he asked employees of the Royal Meat Company to butcher and prepare four hindquarters of beef—two for himself and two for his friends. He also offered to sell ten hindquarters to one employee of the company at an alarmingly reduced rate. The suspicious employee contacted the authorities, who told him to proceed with the deal. When Waronek arrived in New York with his load short nineteen hindquarters, Waronek telephoned L.T.L. Perishables in St. Paul. He notified them "that he was short nineteen hindquarters, that he knew where the beef went, and that he would make good on it out of future settlements." L.T.L. told him to contact the New York police but he failed to do so. Shortly thereafter, he was arrested by the Federal Bureau of Investigation and indicted for the embezzlement of goods moving in interstate commerce. Explain whether Waronek was guilty of the crime of embezzlement.

10. Four separate cases involving similar fact situations were consolidated because they presented the same constitutional question. In each case, police officers, detectives, or prosecuting attorneys took a defendant into custody and interrogated him in a police station to obtain a confession. In none of these cases did the officials fully and effectively advise the defendant of his rights at the outset of the interrogation. The interrogations produced oral admissions of guilt from each defendant, as well as signed statements from three of them, which were used to convict them at their trials. The defendants appealed, arguing that the officials should have warned them of their constitutional rights and the consequences of waiving them before the questioning began. It was contended that to permit any statements obtained without such a warning violated their Fifth Amendment privilege against self-incrimination. Were the defendants' constitutional rights violated? Discuss.

11. Officer Cyril Rombach of the Burbank Police Department, an experienced and well-trained narcotics officer, applied for a warrant to search several residences and automobiles for cocaine, methaqualone, and other narcotics. Rombach supported his application with information given to another police officer by a confidential informant of unproven reliability. He also based the warrant application on his own observations made during an extensive investigation: known drug offenders visiting the residences and leaving with small packages as well as a suspicious trip to Miami by two of the suspects. A state superior court judge in good faith issued a search warrant to Rombach based on this information. Rombach's searches netted large quantities of drugs and other evidence, which produced indictments of several suspects on

charges of conspiracy to possess and distribute cocaine. The defendants moved to suppress the evidence on the grounds that the search warrant was defective in that Rombach had failed to establish the informant's credibility. Should the evidence be excluded or can it be placed into evidence since the police and courts acted in good faith? Why?

TAKING SIDES

Olivo was in the hardware area of a department store. A security guard saw him look around, take a set of wrenches, and conceal it in his clothing. Olivo looked around once more and proceeded toward an exit, passing several cash registers. The guard stopped him short of the exit.

a. What argument would support the prosecutor in finding Olivo guilty of larceny?
b. What argument would you make as Olivio's defense counsel for finding him not guilty of larceny?
c. Which side's argument do you find most convincing? Explain.

Intentional Torts

CHAPTER 7

Torts are infinitely various, not limited or confined, for there is nothing in nature but may be an instrument for mischief.

Charles Pratt
Quoted in *The Guide to American Law*, vol. 10

CHAPTER OUTCOMES

After reading and studying this chapter, you should be able to:

1. Identify and describe the torts that protect against intentional harm to personal rights.

2. Explain the application of the various privileges to defamation suits and how they are affected by whether the plaintiff is (a) a public figure, (b) a public official, or (c) a private person.

3. Describe and distinguish the four torts comprising invasion of privacy.

4. Identify and describe the torts that protect against harm to property.

5. Distinguish among interference with contractual relations, disparagement, and fraudulent misrepresentation.

Tort
a civil wrong causing injury to persons, their property, or their economic interests

All forms of civil liability are either (1) voluntarily assumed, as by contract, or (2) involuntarily assumed, as imposed by law. **Tort** liability is of the second type. Tort law gives persons relief from civil wrongs or injuries to their persons, property, and economic interests. Examples include assault and battery, automobile accidents, professional malpractice, and products liability. This law has three principal objectives: (1) to compensate persons who sustain harm or loss resulting from another's conduct, (2) to place the cost of that compensation only on those parties who should bear it, and (3) to prevent future harms and losses. Thus, the law of torts reallocates losses caused by human misconduct. In general, a tort is committed when (1) a duty owed by one person to another (2) is breached, (3) proximately causing (4) injury or damage to the owner of a legally protected interest.

Each person is legally responsible for the damages proximately caused by his tortious conduct. Moreover, as we will discuss in Chapter 29, businesses that conduct their business activities through employees are also liable for the torts their employees commit in the course of employment. The tort liability of employers makes the study of tort law essential to business managers.

Injuries may be inflicted intentionally, negligently, or without fault (strict liability). We will discuss intentional torts in this chapter and cover negligence and strict liability in Chapter 8.

The same conduct may, and often does, constitute both a crime and a tort. For example, let us assume that Johnson has committed an assault and battery against West. For the commission of this crime, the state may take appropriate action against Johnson. In addition, Johnson has violated West's right to be secure in his person, and so has committed a tort against West. Regardless of the criminal action brought by the state against Johnson, West may bring a civil tort action against Johnson for damages. But an act may be criminal without being tortious; by the same token, an act may be a tort but not a crime.

In a tort action, the injured party sues to recover compensation for the injury sustained as a result of the defendant's wrongful conduct. The purpose of tort law, unlike criminal law, is to compensate the injured party, not to punish the wrongdoer. In certain cases, however, courts may award exemplary or **punitive damages**, which are damages over and above the amount necessary to compensate the plaintiff. In cases in which the defendant's tortious conduct has been intentional—or in some states, reckless—and outrageous, showing malice or a fraudulent or evil motive, most courts permit a jury to award punitive damages. The allowance of punitive damages is designed to punish and make an example of the defendant and thus deter the defendant and others from similar conduct.

Punitive damages

damages awarded in excess of normal compensation to punish a defendant for a serious civil wrong

Philip Morris USA v. Williams
Supreme Court of the United States, 2007
549 U.S. 346, 127 S.Ct. 1057, 166 L.Ed.2d 940
http://scholar.google.com/scholar_case?case=3002949669360902078&q=549+U.S.+346&hl=en&as_sdt=2,34

FACTS This lawsuit arises out of the death of Jesse Williams, a heavy cigarette smoker. Williams' widow represents his estate in this state lawsuit for negligence and deceit against Philip Morris, the manufacturer of Marlboro, the brand that Williams smoked. A jury found that Williams' death was caused by smoking; that Williams smoked in significant part because he thought it was safe to do so; and that Philip Morris knowingly and falsely led him to believe that this was so. The jury found that both Philip Morris and Williams were negligent and that Philip Morris had engaged in deceit. In respect to deceit, it awarded compensatory damages of about $821,000 along with $79.5 million in punitive damages.

The trial judge subsequently found the $79.5 million punitive damages award "excessive" and reduced it to $32 million. Both sides appealed. The Oregon Court of Appeals rejected Philip Morris' arguments and restored the $79.5 million jury award. Subsequently, the Oregon Supreme Court rejected Philip Morris' arguments that the trial court should have instructed the jury that it could not punish Philip Morris for injury to persons not before the court and that the roughly 100:1 ratio of the $79.5 million punitive damages award to the compensatory damages amount was "grossly excessive."

The U.S. Supreme Court granted Philip Morris *certiorari* on its claims that (1) Oregon had unconstitutionally permitted it to be punished for harming nonparty victims; and (2) Oregon had in effect disregarded "the constitutional requirement that punitive damages be reasonably related to the plaintiff's harm."

DECISION The Oregon Supreme Court's judgment is vacated, and the case is remanded.

OPINION The Supreme Court has long made clear that "punitive damages may properly be imposed to further a State's legitimate interests in punishing unlawful conduct and deterring its repetition." At the same time, the Supreme Court has emphasized the need to avoid an arbitrary determination of an award's amount. Unless a state insists upon proper standards that will confine the jury's discretionary authority, its punitive damages system may deprive a defendant of "fair notice … of the severity of the penalty that a State may impose"; it may threaten "arbitrary punishments;" and, where the amounts are sufficiently large, it may impose one state's "policy choice," as to the conditions under which (or even whether) certain products can be sold, upon other states" with different public policies.

For these and similar reasons, the Supreme Court has found that the Constitution imposes certain limits, in respect both to procedures for awarding punitive damages and to amounts forbidden as "grossly excessive." These opinions have required *de novo* judicial review of the size of punitive awards; have held that excessiveness depends upon (1) the reprehensibility of the defendant's conduct, (2) whether the award bears a reasonable relationship to the actual and potential harm caused by the defendant to the plaintiff, and (3) the difference between the award and sanctions "authorized or imposed in comparable cases;" and have indicated that excessiveness is more likely where the ratio between punitive and compensatory damages exceeds single digits.

In the Court's view, the Constitution's Due Process Clause forbids a state to use a punitive damages award to punish a defendant for injury that it inflicts upon nonparties or those whom they directly represent, that is, injury that it inflicts upon those who are, essentially, strangers to the litigation.

Finally, the Court has said that it may be appropriate to consider the reasonableness of a punitive damages award in light of the *potential* harm the defendant's conduct could have caused. But the Court has made clear that the potential harm at issue was harm potentially caused *the plaintiff.*

Evidence of actual harm to nonparties can help to show that the conduct that harmed the plaintiff also posed a substantial risk of harm to the general public, and so was particularly reprehensible—although counsel may argue in a particular case that conduct resulting in no harm to others nonetheless posed a grave risk to the public, or the converse. Yet for the reasons given above, a jury may not go further than this and use a punitive damages verdict to punish a defendant directly on account of harms it is alleged to have caused nonparties. The Court concluded that the Due Process Clause requires states to provide assurance that juries are not asking the wrong question, that is, seeking, not simply to determine reprehensibility, but also to punish for harm caused strangers.

The instruction that Philip Morris said the trial court should have given distinguishes between using harm to others as part of the "reasonable relationship" equation (which it would allow) and using it directly as a basis for punishment. This case was remanded so that the Oregon Supreme Court could apply the standard the Court set forth in this opinion. Because the application of this standard may lead to the need for a new trial, or a change in the level of the punitive damages award, the Court did not consider whether the award is constitutionally "grossly excessive."

INTERPRETATION In most states, a jury may award punitive damages if a defendant's tortious conduct is intentional and outrageous, but the amount of damages must not be grossly excessive and may not punish the defendant for harm caused to parties other than the plaintiff.

ETHICAL QUESTION Is it ethical to impose punishment in a civil case without the protections provided to defendants in a criminal proceeding? Explain.

CRITICAL THINKING QUESTION Can juries be adequately instructed to make the distinction required by the U.S. Supreme Court? Explain.

Practical Advice

When bringing a lawsuit for an intentional tort, consider whether it is appropriate to ask for punitive damages.

Tort law is primarily common law, and, as we mentioned in Chapter 1, the Restatements, prepared by the American Law Institute (ALI), present many important areas of the common law, including torts. You will recall that although they are not law in themselves, the Restatements are highly persuasive in the courts. Since then, the Restatement has served as a vital force in shaping the law of torts. Between 1965 and 1978, the institute adopted and promulgated a second edition of the Restatement of Torts, which revised and superseded the First Restatement. This text will refer to the second Restatement simply as the Restatement.

In 1996, the ALI approved the development of a new Restatement, called Restatement Third, Torts: Liability for Physical and Emotional Harm, which addresses the general or basic elements of the tort action for liability for accidental personal injury, property damage, and emotional harm but does not cover liability for economic loss. This work replaces comparable provisions in the Restatement Second, Torts. The final work is published in two volumes. Volume 1 was released in 2010 and primarily covers liability for negligence causing physical harm, duty, strict liability, factual cause, and scope of liability (traditionally called proximate cause). Volume 2, published in 2012, covers affirmative duties, emotional harm, land possessors' liability, and liability of actors who retain independent contractors.

Because this new Restatement applies to nonintentional torts, it will be covered extensively in the next chapter, and it will be cited as the "Third Restatement." A few of its provisions, however, do apply to intentional torts and will be included in this chapter. Comment c to Section 5 of the Third Restatement provides that the Second Restatement remains largely authoritative in explaining the details of specific intentional torts and their related defenses. The ALI, however, has begun work on the Restatement Third, Torts: Intentional Torts to Persons, which is the latest installment of the ALI's ongoing revision of the Restatement Second of Torts. This new project will complete the work focusing on recovery for physical and emotional harm to persons.

The Restatement Third, Torts: Economic Torts and Related Wrongs will update coverage on torts that involve economic loss or pecuniary harm *not* resulting from physical harm or physical contact to a person or property. The project will update coverage of economic torts in Restatement Second, Torts and address some topics not covered in prior Restatements. The ALI began this project in 2004 and after several years of inactivity the project was resumed in 2010. In 2012, a portion of Chapter 1 of the Tentative Draft was approved.

Intent

desire to cause the consequences of an act or knowledge that the consequences are substantially certain to result from the act

Intent, as used in tort law, does not require a hostile or evil motive. Rather, it means that the actor desires to cause the consequences of his act or that he believes the consequences are substantially (almost) certain to result from it. (See Figure 7-1, which illustrates intent.) The Third Restatement provides that "[a] person acts with the intent to produce a consequence if: (a) the person acts with the purpose of producing that consequence; or (b) the person acts knowing that the consequence is substantially certain to result."

The following examples illustrate the definition of intent: (1) If Mark fires a gun in the middle of the Mojave Desert, he intends to fire the gun; but when the bullet hits Steven, who is in the desert without Mark's knowledge, Mark does not intend that result. (2) Mark throws a bomb into Steven's office in order to kill Steven. Mark knows that Carol is in Steven's office and that the bomb is substantially certain to injure Carol, although Mark has no desire to harm her. Mark is, nonetheless, liable to Carol for any injury caused Carol. Mark's intent to injure Steven is *transferred* to Carol.

Infants (persons who have not reached the age of majority, which is eighteen years in almost all states) are held liable for their intentional torts. The infant's age and knowledge, however, are critical in determining whether the infant had sufficient intelligence to form the required intent. Incompetents, like infants, are generally held liable for their intentional torts.

Figure 7-1 Intent

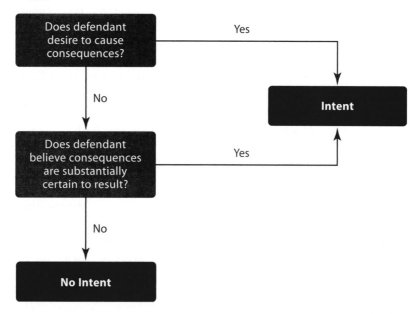

Even though the defendant has intentionally invaded the interests of the plaintiff, the defendant will not be liable if such conduct was privileged. A defendant's conduct is **_privileged_** if it furthers an interest of such social importance that the law grants immunity from tort liability for damage to others. Examples of privilege include self-defense, defense of property, and defense of others. In addition, the plaintiff's consent to the defendant's conduct is a defense to intentional torts.

HARM TO THE PERSON [7-1]

The law provides protection against harm to the person. Generally, intentional torts to the person entitle the injured party to recover damages for bodily harm, emotional distress, loss or impairment of earning capacity, reasonable medical expenses, and harm the tortious conduct caused to property or business.

Battery [7-1a]

Battery

intentional infliction of harmful or offensive bodily contact

Battery is an intentional infliction of harmful or offensive bodily contact. It may consist of contact causing serious injury, such as a gunshot wound or a blow on the head with a club. Or it may involve contact causing little or no physical injury, such as knocking a hat off of a person's head or flicking a glove in another's face. Bodily contact is offensive if it would offend a reasonable person's sense of dignity. Such contact may be accomplished through the use of objects, such as Gustav's throwing a rock at Hester with the intention of hitting her. If the rock hits Hester or any other person, Gustav has committed a battery.

Assault [7-1b]

Assault

intentional infliction of apprehension of immediate bodily harm or offensive contact

Assault is intentional conduct by one person directed at another that places the other in apprehension of imminent (immediate) bodily harm or offensive contact. It is usually committed immediately before a battery, but if the intended battery fails, the assault remains. Assault is essentially a mental rather than a physical intrusion. Accordingly, damages for it may include compensation for fright and humiliation. The person in danger of immediate bodily harm must have _knowledge_ of the danger and be apprehensive of its imminent threat to his safety.

False Imprisonment [7-1c]

False imprisonment

intentional interference with a person's freedom of movement by unlawful confinement

The tort of **false imprisonment** or _false arrest_ is the act of intentionally confining a person against her will within fixed boundaries if the person is conscious of the confinement or harmed by it. Such restraint may be brought about by physical force, the threat of physical force, or by force directed against a person's property. Damages for false imprisonment may include

Practical Advice

When detaining a suspected shoplifter, be careful to conform to the limitations of your state's statutory privilege.

compensation for loss of time, physical discomfort, inconvenience, physical illness, and mental suffering. Merely obstructing a person's freedom of movement is not false imprisonment so long as a reasonable alternative exit is available.

Merchants occasionally encounter potential liability for false imprisonment when they seek to question a suspected shoplifter. A merchant who detains an innocent person may face a lawsuit for false imprisonment. However, most states have statutes protecting the merchant, provided she detains the suspect with probable cause, in a reasonable manner, and for not more than a reasonable time.

Infliction of Emotional Distress [7-1d]

Infliction of emotional distress

extreme and outrageous conduct intentionally or recklessly causing severe emotional distress

Recklessness

conduct that evidences a conscious disregard of or an indifference to the consequences of the act committed

Under the Second and Third Restatements, a person is liable for **infliction of emotional distress** when that person by extreme and outrageous conduct intentionally or recklessly causes severe emotional distress to another. The person is liable for that emotional distress and, if the emotional distress causes bodily harm, also for the resulting bodily harm. **Recklessness** is conduct that evidences a conscious disregard of or an indifference to the consequences of the act committed. With respect to infliction of emotional distress, the Third Restatement explains that an

> actor acts recklessly when the actor knows of the risk of severe emotional disturbance (or knows facts that make the risk obvious) and fails to take a precaution that would eliminate or reduce the risk even though the burden is slight relative to the magnitude of the risk, thereby demonstrating the actor's indifference.

Damages may be recovered for severe emotional distress even in the absence of any physical injury. Liability for infliction of emotional distress, however, arises only when the person seeking recovery has suffered *severe* emotional disturbance and when a reasonable person in the same circumstances would suffer severe disturbance. Thus, the Third Restatement is imposing an objective—not a subjective—test. Accordingly, there is no liability for mental harm suffered by an unusually vulnerable plaintiff, unless the defendant knew of the plaintiff's special vulnerability. Under the "extreme and outrageous" requirement, a person is liable only if the conduct goes beyond the bounds of human decency and would be regarded as intolerable in a civilized community. Ordinary insults and indignities are not enough for liability to be imposed, even if the person desires to cause emotional disturbance. Examples of this tort include sexual harassment on the job and outrageous and prolonged bullying tactics employed by creditors or collection agencies attempting to collect a debt, or by insurance adjusters trying to force a settlement of an insurance claim.

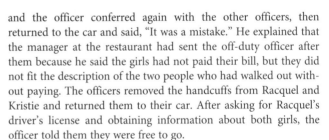

Ferrell v. Mikula
Court of Appeals of Georgia, 2008; reconsideration denied, 2008
295 Ga.App. 326, 627 S.E.2d 7
http://scholar.google.com/scholar_case?case=12901711244406213270&hl=en&as_sdt=2&as_vis=1&oi=scholarr

FACTS On Friday night, August 6, 2006, eighteen-year-old Racquel Ferrell and thirteen-year-old Kristie Ferrell went to Ruby Tuesday. After they ate and paid their bill, the girls left the restaurant, got into their car, and drove out of the parking lot. As they entered the highway, Racquel noticed a black truck following her very closely with its headlights on high. A marked police car by the side of the road pulled onto the highway between the girls' car and the following truck and pulled the car over. The officer pulled Racquel out of the car, placed her in handcuffs, and put her in the back seat of his patrol car. Another officer removed Kristie from the car, placed her in handcuffs, and put her in the back of another patrol car.

All of the police officers gathered to talk to the driver of the truck that had been following the Ferrells, who turned out to be a uniformed off-duty police officer working as a security guard for Ruby Tuesday. The officer who arrested Racquel returned to the patrol car where she was being held and told her if she had not paid her Ruby Tuesday bill, she was going to jail. She protested,

and the officer conferred again with the other officers, then returned to the car and said, "It was a mistake." He explained that the manager at the restaurant had sent the off-duty officer after them because he said the girls had not paid their bill, but they did not fit the description of the two people who had walked out without paying. The officers removed the handcuffs from Racquel and Kristie and returned them to their car. After asking for Racquel's driver's license and obtaining information about both girls, the officer told them they were free to go.

Christian Mikula had been an assistant manager for about a month, and was the only manager at Ruby Tuesday that night. One of the servers, Robert, reported that his customers at Table 24 had a complaint, so Mikula talked to the couple and told them he would "take care of the food item in question. The customers were a man and a woman in their late twenties to early thirties. Mikula left the table to discuss the matter with Robert, after which server Aaron told Mikula that the patrons at Table 24 had left without paying. Mikula looked at the table, confirmed they had not left any money for the bill, and went out the main entrance. He saw a car pulling out of the parking lot, and said to the off-duty officer, "Hey, I think they just left without paying." The officer said, "Who, them?" Mikula said, "I think so," and the officer got up and went to his vehicle.

Mikula knew the officer was going to follow the people in the car and would stop them, but did not ask the officer if he had seen who got into the car. He did not give the officer a description of the people at Table 24, and did not know the race, age, gender, or number of people in the car being followed. He did not know if there were people in any of the other cars in the parking lot. He did not ask any other people in the restaurant if they had seen the people at Table 24 leave the building, which had two exits. He did not know how long the people had been gone before Aaron told him they left, or whether another customer had picked up money from Table 24. He could have tried to obtain more information to determine whether the people in the car he pointed out were the people who had been sitting at Table 24, but did not do so.

Racquel Ferrell and the parents of Kristie Ferrell sued Ruby Tuesday, Inc. and its manager, Christian Mikula, for false imprisonment and intentional infliction of emotional distress. The trial court granted the defendants' motion for summary judgment on all counts. The Ferrells appealed.

DECISION Summary judgment on the claim for intentional infliction of emotional distress is affirmed; summary judgment on the claim for false imprisonment is reversed.

OPINION In this case, the Ferrells were detained without a warrant and thus have a claim for false imprisonment. False imprisonment is the unlawful detention of the person of another, for any length of time, whereby such person is deprived of his personal liberty. The only essential elements of the action being the detention and its unlawfulness; malice and the want of probable cause need not be shown.

The evidence in this case clearly establishes that the Ferrells were detained. Although "'imprisonment' was originally intended to have meant stone walls and iron bars, … under modern tort law an individual may be imprisoned when his movements are restrained in the open street, or in a traveling automobile." Ruby Tuesday does not argue otherwise, but instead argues that the evidence established sufficient probable cause and the plaintiffs failed to establish that Mikula acted with malice. But malice is not an element of false imprisonment. Further, the mere existence of probable cause standing alone has no real defensive bearing on the issue of liability for false imprisonment.

Arresting or causing the arrest of a person without a warrant constitutes a tort, unless he can justify under some of the exceptions in which arrest and imprisonment without a warrant are permitted by law. Generally, one who causes or directs the arrest of another by an officer without a warrant may be held liable for false imprisonment, in the absence of justification, and the burden of proving that such imprisonment lies within an exception rests upon the person causing the imprisonment.

Accordingly, as the Ferrells have established an unlawful detention, the next issue to consider is whether Mikula "caused" the arrest. It is a factual question for the jury to determine whether a party (1) is potentially liable for false imprisonment by directly or indirectly urging a law enforcement official to begin criminal proceedings or (2) is not liable because he merely relates facts to an official who then makes an independent decision to arrest. The party need not expressly request an arrest and may be liable if his conduct and acts "procured and directed the arrest."

Here, Mikula told the officer that the car leaving the parking lot contained people who left without paying for their food, although he did not know or try to ascertain who was in the car. He also knew the officer was going to detain the people in the car and could have tried to stop him, but made no attempt to do so. Accordingly, the trial court erred in granting summary judgment to the defendants on the plaintiffs' false imprisonment claim.

The Ferrells also contend that the trial court erred in granting summary judgment to the defendants on their claim for intentional infliction of emotional distress. The elements of a cause of action for intentional infliction of emotional distress are: (1) intentional or reckless conduct; (2) that is extreme and outrageous; (3) a causal connection between the wrongful conduct and the emotional distress; and (4) severe emotional distress. Further,

> [l]iability for this tort has been found only where the conduct has been so outrageous in character, and so extreme in degree, as to go beyond all possible bounds of decency, and to be regarded as atrocious, and utterly intolerable in a civilized community. Generally, the case is one in which the recitation of the facts to an average member of the community would arouse his resentment against the actor, and lead him to exclaim, "Outrageous!"

In this case, the action upon which the Ferrells base their emotional distress claim is being stopped by the police, placed in handcuffs, and held in a patrol car for a short period of time before being released. While this incident was unfortunate, the question raised by the evidence was whether the restaurant manager's actions were negligent, not whether he acted maliciously or his conduct was extreme, atrocious, or utterly intolerable. Accordingly, the trial court did not err in granting the defendants' motion for summary judgment on the Ferrells' claim for intentional infliction of emotional distress.

INTERPRETATION False imprisonment is the unlawful detention of the person of another, for any length of time, whereby such person is deprived of his personal liberty unless there is a legally recognized justification. Liability is imposed under the tort of infliction of emotional distress for intentional or reckless conduct that is extreme and outrageous and that causes severe emotional distress.

CRITICAL THINKING QUESTION Do you agree that the manager's conduct was negligent at most and thus not reckless?

Harm to the Right of Dignity [7-2]

The law also protects a person against intentional interference with, or harm to, his right of dignity. This protection covers a person's reputation, privacy, and right to freedom from unjustifiable litigation.

Defamation [7-2a]

Defamation

injury to a person's reputation by publication of false statements

As discussed in Chapter 4, the tort of **defamation** is a false communication that injures a person's reputation by disgracing him and diminishing the respect in which he is held. An example would be the publication of a false statement that a person had committed a crime or had a loathsome disease.

Elements of Defamation

The elements of a defamation action are (1) a false and defamatory statement concerning another; (2) an unprivileged publication (communication) to a third party; (3) depending on the status of the defendant, negligence or recklessness on her part in knowing or failing to ascertain the falsity of the statement; and (4) in some cases, proof of special harm caused by the publication. The burden of proof is on the plaintiff to prove the falsity of the defamatory statement.

Libel

defamation communicated by writing, television, radio, or the like

Slander

oral defamation

If the defamatory communication is handwritten, typewritten, printed, pictorial, or in any other medium with similar communicative power, such as a television or radio broadcast, it is designated as **libel**. If it is spoken or oral, it is designated as **slander**. In either case, it must be communicated to a person or persons other than the one who is defamed, a process referred to as its **publication**. Thus, if Maurice writes a defamatory letter about Pierre's character that he hands or mails to Pierre, this is not a publication because it is intended only for Pierre. The publication must have been intentional or the result of the defendant's negligence.

Practical Advice

Consider whether you should provide employment references for current and former employees, and if you decide to do so, take care in what you say. See the "Business Law in Action" feature on the next page.

Any living person, as well as corporations, partnerships, and unincorporated associations, may be defamed. Unless a statute provides otherwise, no action may be brought for defamation of a deceased person.

A significant trend affecting business has been the bringing of defamation suits against former employers by discharged employees. It has been reported that such suits account for approximately one-third of all defamation lawsuits. The following case demonstrates the consequences of failing to be careful in discharging an employee.

Frank B. Hall & Co., Inc. v. Buck
Court of Appeals of Texas, Fourteenth District, 1984
678 S.W.2d 612; *cert. denied*, 472 U.S. 1009, 105 S.Ct. 2704, 86 L.Ed.2d 720 (1985)
http://scholar.google.com/scholar_case?q=678+S.W.2d+612&hl=en&as_sdt=2,34&case=17495651340574040653&scilh=0

FACTS On June 1, 1976, Larry W. Buck, an established salesman in the insurance business, began working for Frank B. Hall & Co. In the course of the ensuing months, Buck brought several major accounts to Hall and produced substantial commission income for the firm. In October 1976, Mendel Kaliff, then president of Frank B. Hall & Co. of Texas, informed Buck that his salary and benefits were being reduced because of his failure to generate sufficient income for the firm. On March 31, 1977, Kaliff and Lester Eckert, Hall's office manager, fired Buck. Buck was unable to procure subsequent employment with another insurance firm. He hired an investigator, Lloyd Barber, to discover the true reasons for his dismissal and for his inability to find other employment.

Barber contacted Kaliff, Eckert, and Virginia Hilley, a Hall employee, and told them he was an investigator and was seeking information about Buck's employment with the firm. Barber conducted tape-recorded interviews with the three in September and October of 1977. Kaliff accused Buck of being disruptive, untrustworthy, paranoid, hostile, untruthful, and of padding his expense account. Eckert referred to Buck as "a zero" and a "classical sociopath" who was ruthless, irrational, and disliked by other employees. Hilley stated that Buck could have been charged with theft for certain materials he brought with him from his former employer to Hall. Buck sued Hall for damages for defamation and was awarded over $1.9 million by a jury—$605,000 for actual damages and $1,300,000 for punitive damages. Hall then brought this appeal.

DECISION Judgment for Buck affirmed.

OPINION Any intentional or negligent communication of defamatory matter to a third person is a publication, unless the defamed individual authorized, invited, or procured the statement or statements and knew of their contents in advance. The Hall employees intentionally communicated disparaging remarks about Buck to Barber. While it may be true that Buck could assume the employees would express their opinion of him, he did not know they would defame him. Their accusations were not mere opinions but were untrue and derogatory statements of fact. Although the comments were directed at an individual acting at Buck's request, communication to an agent of the defamed individual qualifies as a publication unless the defamed individual or his agent invited the publication. In this case, neither Buck nor Barber induced the defamatory remarks.

INTERPRETATION The key elements of defamation are that the statements made are false, injure the plaintiff's reputation, and are published.

ETHICAL QUESTION Did Hall's employees act ethically? Did Buck act ethically in hiring an investigator to obtain the information? Explain.

CRITICAL THINKING QUESTION How should a company respond to inquiries for information about former or current employees? Explain.

BUSINESS LAW **IN ACTION**

If you own or manage a business, you can expect employees to leave for a variety of reasons. When your present or former employees apply for work elsewhere, their potential new employers may well call you to verify their employment history and ask your opinion of them as employees. Should you give that information?

Many employers have stopped giving meaningful references for former employees. Some employers verify only employment dates and job titles of former employees. Others give no information at all. The reason? Fear of liability for defamation and of incurring large legal expenses to defend a lawsuit.

Are those fears justified? Does the benefit of minimizing risk outweigh the cost of shutting down a legitimate and valuable information system? Consider the following points:

- A number of the states have enacted statutes that provide varying degrees of protection against liability for defamation to companies that give job references for current or former employees.
- An employer is liable for a false statement only if she was negligent in attempting to establish its truth.
- Employment references enjoy qualified privilege, unless the employer communicates the statements to people with no need to know their contents or publishes them out of spite.
- Employment references are valuable. Employers who expect to get useful information about job applicants should also be willing to give it.

You can reduce the risk of liability when giving employment references if you …

- Endeavor to ensure that all statements you publish about an employee are true. Your effort can be used as a defense against negligence.
- Make sure you publish statements only to people with a legitimate need to know (i.e., potential employers).
- Regulate the giving of references in your company. Make sure people who work for you understand who may give references and who may not. And make sure they know that no one is ever to publish statements maliciously.
- Ask your existing employees to give you written consent to provide references for them.

Source: Ramona L. Paetzold and Steven L. Wilborn, "Employer (Ir)rationality and the Demise of Employment References," *American Business Law Journal*, May 1992, 123–42.

Privilege

immunity from tort liability

Defenses to Defamation

The defense of **privilege** is immunity from tort liability granted when the defendant's conduct furthers a societal interest of greater importance than the injury inflicted upon the plaintiff. Three kinds of privileges apply to defamation: absolute, conditional, and constitutional.

Absolute privilege, which protects the defendant regardless of his motive or intent, has been confined to those few situations in which public policy clearly favors complete freedom of speech. Such privilege includes (1) statements made by participants in a judicial proceeding regarding that proceeding, (2) statements made by members of Congress on the floor of Congress and by members of state and local legislative bodies, (3) statements made by certain executive branch officers while performing their government duties, and (4) statements regarding a third party made between spouses when they are alone.

Qualified or *conditional privilege* depends on proper use of the privilege. A person has a conditional privilege to publish defamatory matter to protect her own legitimate interests or, in some cases, the interests of another. Conditional privilege also extends to many communications in which the publisher and the recipient have a common interest, such as letters of reference. Conditional privilege, however, is forfeited by a publisher who acts in an excessive manner, without probable cause, or for an improper purpose.

The First Amendment to the U.S. Constitution guarantees freedom of speech and freedom of the press. The U.S. Supreme Court has applied these rights to the law of defamation by extending a form of *constitutional privilege* to defamatory and false statements about public officials or public figures so long as it is done without malice. For these purposes, *malice* is not ill will but clear and convincing proof of the publisher's knowledge of falsity or reckless disregard of the truth. Thus, under constitutional privilege, the public official or public figure must prove that the defendant published the defamatory and false comment with knowledge or in reckless disregard of the comment's falsity and its defamatory character. However, in a defamation suit brought by a private person (one who is neither a public official nor a public figure), the plaintiff must prove that the defendant published the defamatory and false comment with malice *or* negligence.

Congress enacted Section 230 of the *Communications Decency Act of 1996 (CDA)* granting immunity to Internet service providers (ISPs) from liability for defamation when publishing information originating from a third party. A court has interpreted this provision of the CDA as immunizing an ISP that refused to remove or retract an allegedly defamatory posting made on its bulletin board. The immunity granted by the CDA to ISPs has spawned a number of lawsuits urging ISPs to reveal the identities of subscribers who have posted allegedly defamatory statements. To date, ISPs have complied, generating additional litigation by angry ISP patrons attempting to keep their identities protected by asserting that their right to free speech is being compromised.

Because Section 230 of the CDA grants immunity only to ISPs, there is the possibility that employers will be held liable for some online defamatory statements made by an employee. Section 577(2) of the Restatement of Torts provides that a person who intentionally and unreasonably fails to remove defamatory matter that she knows is exhibited on property in her possession or under her control is liable for its continued publication. Therefore, employers in control of e-forums, such as electronic bulletin boards and chat rooms, should act quickly to remove any defamatory statement brought to their attention.

Invasion of Privacy [7-2b]

The invasion of a person's right to privacy actually consists of four distinct torts: (1) appropriation of a person's name or likeness, (2) unreasonable intrusion on the seclusion of another, (3) unreasonable public disclosure of private facts, or (4) unreasonable publicity that places another in a false light in the public eye.

It is entirely possible and not uncommon for a person's right of privacy to be invaded in a manner entailing two or more of these related torts. For example, Bart forces his way into Cindy's hospital room, takes a photograph of Cindy, and publishes it to promote his cure for Cindy's illness along with false statements about Cindy that would be highly objectionable to a reasonable person. Cindy would be entitled to recover on any or all of the four torts comprising invasion of privacy.

Appropriation The tort of **appropriation** is the unauthorized use of another person's name or likeness for one's own benefit, as, for example, in promoting or advertising a product or service. The tort of appropriation, which seeks to protect the individual's right to the exclusive use of his identity, is also known as the "right of publicity." In the previous example, Bart's use of Cindy's photograph to promote Bart's business constitutes the tort of appropriation. The following case involving Vanna White is also an example of appropriation.

Practical Advice

When using another person's identity for your own purposes, be sure to obtain that person's written consent.

Appropriation
unauthorized use of another person's name or likeness for one's own benefit

White v. Samsung Electronics
U.S. Court of Appeals, Ninth Circuit, 1992
971 F.2d 1395; *cert. denied*, 508 U.S. 951, 113 S.Ct. 2443, 124 L.Ed.2d 660 (1993)
http://scholar.google.com/scholar_case?case=15763501998860364615&q=971+F.2d+1395&hl=en&as_sdt=2,34

FACTS Plaintiff, Vanna White, is the hostess of *Wheel of Fortune*, one of the most popular game shows in television history. Samsung Electronics and David Deutsch Associates ran an advertisement for videocassette recorders that depicted a robot dressed in a wig, gown, and jewelry chosen to resemble White's hair and dress. The robot was posed in a stance, for which White is famous, next to a game board, which is instantly recognizable as the *Wheel of Fortune* game show set. The caption of the ad read: "Longest-running game show. 2012 AD." Defendants referred to the ad as the "Vanna White" ad. White neither consented to the ads, nor was she paid for them. White sued Samsung and Deutsch under the California common law right of publicity. The district court granted summary judgment against White on this claim.

DECISION Judgment reversed.

OPINION The law protects a person's exclusive right to exploit the value of her identity. To state a cause of action under the California common law right of publicity, a plaintiff must allege (1) the defendant's use of the plaintiff's identity; (2) the appropriation of the plaintiff's name or likeness to the defendant's advantage, commercially or otherwise; (3) lack of consent; and (4) resulting injury. In this case, the district court dismissed White's claim for

failure to meet the second element. Although the robot ad did not make use of White's name or likeness, the common law right of publicity is not so confined. The "name or likeness" formulation originated not as an element of the right of publicity cause of action, but as a description of the types of cases in which the cause of action had been recognized. The case law has borne out that the right of publicity is not limited to the appropriation of name or likeness. The specific means of appropriation are relevant only for determining whether the defendant has in fact appropriated the plaintiff's identity. It is not important how the defendant has appropriated the plaintiff's identity, but whether the defendant has done so.

To consider the means of appropriation as dispositive would not only weaken the right of publicity but would effectively eviscerate it. The identities of the most popular celebrities are not only the most attractive for advertisers but also the easiest to evoke without resorting to obvious means such as name, likeness, or voice. Consider a hypothetical advertisement that depicts a mechanical robot with male features, an African-American complexion, and a bald head. The robot is wearing black high-top Air Jordan basketball sneakers and a red basketball uniform with black trim, baggy shorts, and the number 23 (though not revealing

"Bulls" or "Jordan" lettering). The ad depicts the robot dunking a basketball one-handed, stiff-armed, legs extended like open scissors, and tongue hanging out. Now envision that this ad is run on television during professional basketball games. Considered individually, the robot's physical attributes, its dress, and its stance tell us little. Taken together, they lead to the only conclusion that any sports viewer who has registered a discernible pulse in the past five years would reach: the ad depicts Michael Jordan.

Viewed together, the individual aspects of the ad in the present case leave little doubt about the celebrity the ad is meant to depict.

Indeed, the defendants themselves referred to their ad as the "Vanna White" ad. Because White has alleged facts showing that Samsung and Deutsch had appropriated her identity, the district court erred by rejecting, on summary judgment, White's common law right of publicity claim.

INTERPRETATION The tort of appropriation protects a person's exclusive right to exploit the value of her identity.

CRITICAL THINKING QUESTION What are the interests protected by this tort?

Intrusion
unreasonable and highly offensive interference with the seclusion of another

Intrusion
The tort of **intrusion** is the unreasonable and highly offensive interference with the solitude or seclusion of another. Such unreasonable interference includes improper entry into another's dwelling, unauthorized eavesdropping on another's private conversations, and unauthorized examination of another's private papers and records. The intrusion must be highly offensive or objectionable to a reasonable person and must involve private matters. Thus, there is no liability if the defendant examines public records or observes the plaintiff in a public place. This form of invasion of privacy is committed once the intrusion occurs—publicity is not required.

Public disclosure of private facts
highly offensive publicity given to private information about another person

Public Disclosure of Private Facts
Under the tort of **public disclosure of private facts**, liability is imposed for publicity given to private information about another, if the matter made public would be highly offensive and objectionable to a reasonable person. Like intrusion, this tort applies only to private, not public, information about an individual; unlike intrusion, it requires publicity. Under the Restatement, the publicity required differs in degree from "publication" as used in the law of defamation. This tort requires that private facts be communicated to the public at large or that they become public knowledge, whereas publication of a defamatory statement need be made only to a single third party. Thus Kathy, a creditor of Gary, will not invade Gary's privacy by writing a letter to Gary's employer informing the employer of Gary's failure to pay the debt, but Kathy would be liable if she posted in the window of her store a statement that Gary will not pay a debt owed to her. Some courts, however, have allowed recovery where the disclosure was made to only one person. Also, unlike defamation, this tort applies to truthful private information if the matter published would be offensive and objectionable to a reasonable person of ordinary sensibilities.

False light
highly offensive publicity placing another in a false light

False Light
The tort of **false light** imposes liability for highly offensive publicity placing another in a false light if the defendant knew that the matter publicized was false or acted in reckless disregard of the truth. For example, Edgar includes Jason's name and photograph in a public "rogues' gallery" of convicted criminals. Because Jason has never been convicted of any crime, Edgar is liable to Jason for placing him in a false light.

As with defamation, the matter must be untrue; unlike defamation, it must be "publicized," not merely "published." Although the matter must be objectionable to a reasonable person, it need not be defamatory. In many instances, the same facts will give rise to actions both for defamation and for false light.

Defenses
The defenses of absolute, conditional, and constitutional privilege apply to publication of any matter that is an invasion of privacy to the same extent that such defenses apply to defamation.

Misuse of Legal Procedure [7-2c]

Misuse of legal procedure
torts protecting an individual from unjustifiable litigation

Three torts comprise the **misuse of legal procedure**: malicious prosecution, wrongful civil proceedings, and abuse of process. Each protects an individual from being subjected to unjustifiable litigation. *Malicious prosecution* and *wrongful civil proceedings* impose liability for damages caused by improperly brought proceedings, including harm to reputation, credit, or standing; emotional distress; and the expenses incurred in defending against the wrongfully brought lawsuit. *Abuse of process* consists of using a legal proceeding (criminal or civil) to accomplish a

CONCEPT REVIEW 7-1

Privacy

	Appropriation	Intrusion	Public Disclosure	False Light
Publicity	Yes	No	Yes	Yes
Private Facts	No	Yes	Yes	No
Offensiveness	No	Yes	Yes	Yes
Falsity	No	No	No	Yes

purpose for which the proceeding is not designed. This misuse of procedure applies even when there is probable cause or when the plaintiff or prosecution succeeds in the litigation.

HARM TO PROPERTY [7-3]

The law also provides protection against invasions of a person's interests in property. Intentional harm to property includes the torts of (1) trespass to real property, (2) nuisance, (3) trespass to personal property, and (4) conversion.

Real Property [7-3a]

Real property is land and anything attached to it, such as buildings, trees, and minerals. The law protects the possessor's rights to the exclusive use and quiet enjoyment of the land. Accordingly, damages for harm to land include compensation for the resulting diminution in the value of the land, the loss of use of the land, and the discomfort caused to the possessor of the land.

Real property
land and anything attached to it

Trespass   A person is liable for **trespass to real property** if he intentionally (1) enters or remains on land in the possession of another, (2) causes a thing or a third person to so enter or remain, or (3) fails to remove from the land a thing that he is under a duty to remove. Liability exists even though no actual damage is done to the land.

It is no defense that the intruder acted under the mistaken belief of law or fact that he was not trespassing. If the intruder intended to be on the particular property, his reasonable belief that he owned the land or had permission to enter on it is irrelevant. However, an intruder is not liable if his presence on the land of another is not caused by his own actions. For example, if Shirley is thrown onto Roy's land by Jimmy, Shirley is not liable to Roy for trespass, although Jimmy is.

A trespass may be committed on, beneath, or above the surface of the land, although the law regards the upper air, above a prescribed minimum altitude for flight, as a public highway. No aerial trespass occurs unless the aircraft enters into the lower reaches of the airspace and substantially interferes with the landowner's use and enjoyment.

Trespass to real property
wrongful entry onto another's land

Practical Advice

In using, manufacturing, and disposing of dangerous, noxious, or toxic materials take care not to create a nuisance.

Nuisance   A **nuisance** is a nontrespassory invasion of another's interest in the private use and enjoyment of land. In contrast to trespass, nuisance does not require interference with another's right to exclusive possession of land but imposes liability for significant and unreasonable harm to another's use or enjoyment of land. Examples of nuisances include the emission of unpleasant odors, smoke, dust, or gas, as well as the pollution of a stream, pond, or underground water supply.

Nuisance
nontrespassory invasion of another's interest in the private use and enjoyment of his land

Personal Property [7-3b]

Personal property is any type of property other than an interest in land. The law protects a number of interests in the possession of personal property, including an interest in the property's physical condition and usability, an interest in the retention of possession, and an interest in the property's availability for future use.

Personal property
any property other than an interest in land

Trespass to personal property
intentional dispossession or unauthorized use of the personal property of another

Trespass   The tort of **trespass to personal property** consists of the intentional dispossession or unauthorized use of the personal property of another. Although the interference with the right to exclusive use and possession may be direct or indirect, liability is limited to instances in which the trespasser (1) dispossesses the other of the property; (2) substantially impairs the condition, quality, or value of the property; or (3) deprives the possessor of use of the property for a substantial time. For example, Albert parks his car in front of his house. Later, Ronald pushes Albert's car around the corner. Albert subsequently looks for his car but cannot find it for several hours. Ronald is liable to Albert for trespass.

Conversion
intentional exercise of dominion or control over another's personal property

Conversion   The tort of **conversion** is an intentional exercise of dominion or control over another's personal property that so seriously interferes with the other's right of control as justly to require the payment of full value for the property. Thus, all conversions are trespasses, but not all trespasses are conversions. Conversion may consist of the intentional destruction of the personal property or the use of the property in an unauthorized manner. For example, Barbara entrusts an automobile to Ken, a dealer, for sale. After he drives the car eight thousand miles on his own business, Ken is liable to Barbara for conversion. On the other hand, in the example in which Ronald pushed Albert's car around the corner, Ronald would not be liable to Albert for conversion.

Harm to Economic Interests [7-4]

Economic interests comprise a fourth set of interests the law protects against intentional interference. Economic or pecuniary interests include a person's existing and prospective contractual relations, a person's business reputation, a person's name and likeness (previously discussed under appropriation), and a person's freedom from deception. In this section, we will discuss business torts—those torts that protect a person's economic interests.

Interference with Contractual Relations [7-4a]

Interference with contractual relations
intentionally causing one of the parties to a contract not to perform the contract

Interference with contractual relations involves interfering intentionally and improperly with the performance of a contract by inducing one of the parties not to perform it. (Contracts are discussed extensively in Part III of this text.) The injured party may recover the economic loss resulting from the breach of the contract. The law imposes similar liability for intentional and improper interference with another's prospective contractual relation, such as a lease renewal or financing for construction.

In either case, the rule requires that a person act with the purpose or motive of interfering with another's contract or with the knowledge that such interference is substantially certain to occur as a natural consequence of her actions. The interference may occur by prevention through the use of physical force or by threats. Frequently, the interference is accomplished by inducement, such as the offer of a better contract. For instance, Calvin may offer Becky, an employee of Fran under a contract that has two years left, a yearly salary of $5,000 per year more than the contractual arrangement between Becky and Fran. If Calvin is aware of the contract between Becky and Fran and of the fact that his offer to Becky will interfere with that contract, then Calvin is liable to Fran for intentional interference with contractual relations.

Practical Advice

Recognize that inducing another person's employees to breach a valid agreement not to compete or not to disclose confidential information may be improper interference with contractual relations.

Texaco, Inc. v. Pennzoil, Co.
Court of Appeals of Texas, First District, 1987
729 S.W.2d 768; *cert. denied,* 485 U.S. 994, 108 S.Ct. 1305, 99 L.Ed.2d 686 (1988)
http://scholar.google.com/scholar_case?case=11763000609638124594&q=729+S.W.2d+768&hl=en&as_sdt=2,34

FACTS Pennzoil negotiated with Gordon Getty and the J. Paul Getty Museum over the purchase by Pennzoil of all the Getty Oil stock held by each. Gordon Getty, who was also a director of Getty Oil, held about 40.2 percent of the outstanding shares of Getty Oil. The Museum held 11.8 percent. On January 2, a Memorandum of Agreement was drafted, setting forth the terms reached by Pennzoil, Gordon Getty, and the Museum. After increasing the offering price to $110 per share plus a $5 "stub" or bonus, the board of directors

of Getty Oil voted on January 3 to accept the Pennzoil deal. Accordingly, on January 4 both Getty Oil and Pennzoil issued press releases, announcing an agreement in principle on the terms of the Memorandum of Agreement but at the higher price.

Having learned of the impending sale of Getty Oil stock to Pennzoil, Texaco hurriedly called several in-house meetings, and hired an investment banker as well, to determine a feasible price range for acquiring Getty Oil. On January 5, Texaco decided on

$125 per share and authorized its officers to take any steps necessary to conclude a deal. Texaco met first with a lawyer for the Museum, then with Gordon Getty. Texaco stressed to Getty that if he hesitated in selling his shares, he might be "locked out" in a minority position. On January 6, the Getty Oil board of directors voted to withdraw from the Pennzoil deal and unanimously voted to accept the $125-per-share Texaco offer. Pennzoil sued and won an award of $7.53 billion in compensatory damages and $3 billion in punitive damages based on tortious interference with a contract. Texaco appealed.

DECISION Judgment of trial court affirmed.

OPINION New York law requires knowledge by a defendant of the existence of contractual rights as an element of the tort of inducing breach of that contract. Since there was no direct evidence of Texaco's knowledge of a contract, the question is whether there was legally and factually sufficient circumstantial evidence from which the knowledge could be inferred. Among the evidence were (1) Texaco's carefully mapped strategy to defeat Pennzoil's deal; (2) the notice of a contract in a January 5 *Wall Street Journal* article, although Texaco claimed that no one at Texaco had seen it; (3) the knowledge of an agreement that would arise from comparing the Memorandum of Agreement with the Getty press release; and (4) demands made by the Museum and Trust for full indemnity by Texaco against any claims by Pennzoil based on the Memorandum of Agreement. Clearly, the inference by the jury that

Texaco had knowledge of contractual relations between Pennzoil and Gordon Getty and the Museum is supported by the evidence.

Another necessary element is a showing that the defendant took an active part in persuading a party to a contract to breach it. Merely entering into a contract with a party with the knowledge of that party's contractual obligations to someone else is not the same as inducing a breach. For tort liability to arise, it is necessary that there be some act of interference or of persuading a party to breach, such as by offering better terms or other incentives. The evidence shows that Texaco knew it had only twenty-four hours to "stop the Pennzoil train." Furthermore, the evidence also shows that Texaco's strategy included pressure on Gordon Getty, as well as on key people at the Museum. This evidence contradicts the contention that Texaco passively accepted a deal proposed by the other parties.

INTERPRETATION The tort of interference with contractual relations protects a party to a contract from a third party who intentionally and improperly induces the other contracting party not to perform the contract.

ETHICAL QUESTION Did Getty or Texaco act unethically? Explain.

CRITICAL THINKING QUESTION Does the protection afforded by this tort conflict with society's interest in free competition? Explain.

Disparagement [7-4b]

Disparagement
publication of false statements resulting in harm to another's monetary interests

The tort of **disparagement** or injurious falsehood imposes liability upon one who publishes a false statement that results in harm to another's monetary interests if the publisher knows that the statement is false or acts in reckless disregard of its truth or falsity. This tort most commonly involves intentionally false statements that cast doubt on another's right of ownership in or on the quality of another's property or products. Thus Simon, while contemplating the purchase of a stock of merchandise that belongs to Marie, reads an advertisement in a newspaper in which Ernst falsely asserts he owns the merchandise. Ernst has disparaged Marie's property in the goods.

Absolute, conditional, and constitutional privileges apply to the same extent to the tort of disparagement as they do to defamation. In addition, a competitor has conditional privilege to compare her products favorably with those of a rival, even though she does not believe that her products are superior. No privilege applies, however, if the comparison contains false assertions of specific unfavorable facts about the competitor's property.

The pecuniary loss an injured person may recover is that which directly and immediately results from impairment of the marketability of the property disparaged. Damages also may be recovered for expenses necessary to counteract the false publication, including litigation expenses, the cost of notifying customers, and the cost of publishing denials.

Practical Advice

When commenting on the products or services offered by a competitor, take care not to make any false statements.

Fraudulent misrepresentation
false statement made with knowledge of its falsity and with intent to induce another to act

Fraudulent Misrepresentation [7-4c]

Fraudulent misrepresentation imposes liability for the monetary loss caused by a justifiable reliance on a misrepresentation of fact intentionally made for the purpose of inducing the relying party to act. For example, Smith misrepresents to Jones that a tract of land in Texas is located in an area where oil drilling has recently commenced. Smith makes this statement knowing it is not true. In reliance upon the statement, Jones purchases the land from Smith. Smith is liable to Jones for intentional or fraudulent misrepresentation. Although fraudulent misrepresentation is a tort action, it is closely connected with contractual negotiations; we will discuss its relationship to contracts in Chapter 11.

Practical Advice

When describing your products or services, take care not to make any false statements.

CONCEPT REVIEW 7-2

Intentional Torts

Interest Protected	Tort
Person	
Freedom from contact	Battery
Freedom from apprehension	Assault
Freedom of movement	False imprisonment
Freedom from distress	Infliction of emotional distress
Dignity	
Reputation	Defamation
Privacy	Appropriation
	Intrusion
	Public disclosure of private facts
	False light
Freedom from wrongful legal actions	Misuse of legal procedure
Property	
Real	Trespass
	Nuisance
Personal	Trespass
	Conversion
Economic	
Contracts	Interference with contractual rights
Goodwill	Disparagement
Freedom from deception	Fraudulent misrepresentation

ETHICAL DILEMMA

What May One Do to Attract Clients from a Previous Employer?

Facts Carl Adle and Louise Bart formed a law firm as partners, and Anne Lily, Marvin Thomas, and Tim Jones joined the newly formed firm of Adle & Bart as associates (nonpartner employees). After about five years, Lily, Thomas, and Jones became disenchanted with the law firm and decided to form their own, to be called Lily, Thomas & Jones.

Lily and Thomas suggested to Jones that they contact approximately five hundred of Adle & Bart's current clients. Lily and Thomas had prepared a model letter to inform clients about the new law firm (Lily, Thomas & Jones) and to encourage them to leave Adle & Bart and to become clients of the new firm. The letter also indicated that Lily, Thomas & Jones would offer legal services far better than those of Adle & Bart: billing rates would be more reasonable, service more prompt, and legal representation more effective and successful. The reference to success was aimed, in part, at three large clients who

recently lost lawsuits under Adle & Bart representation. Although the losses had not resulted from malpractice or mishandling by Adle & Bart, Lily and Thomas knew that significant amounts of money had been at issue and that the clients were sensitive about the results of the lengthy litigation.

The letter included two postage-paid form letters for the prospective client to sign and mail. One form letter was addressed to Adle & Bart, informing them of the client's desire to discontinue the client-attorney relationship and requesting the firm to forward all files to Lily, Thomas & Jones. The other form letter, addressed to Lily, Thomas & Jones, requested representation.

Jones is reluctant about the proposed mailing. Lily and Thomas, in turn, argue that their new firm is not doing as well as they expected. They essentially give Jones an ultimatum: join in the letter or leave the firm. Jones, who has thoroughly alienated Adle & Bart, does not believe he has any immediate alternative job opportunities.

Social, Policy, and Ethical Considerations

1. Should Jones agree to the proposed mailing? Is it ethical for those forming the new firm to use a client list of their former employer when seeking clients?

2. What practical steps could Jones take to assist him in his decision?

3. What are the competing social interests at stake in this controversy?

4. How would your answers differ, if at all, if the firms were accounting firms rather than law firms?

5. In what manner, if at all, should the law protect existing businesses from competition? Under what circumstances might competition become unfair, and how should laws be tailored to deter unfair practices?

6. Should Jones be concerned about the comparisons the letter makes between the new firm and Adle & Bart?

CHAPTER SUMMARY

Harm to the Person

Battery intentional infliction of harmful or offensive bodily contact

Assault intentional infliction of apprehension of immediate bodily harm or offensive contact

False Imprisonment intentional confining of a person against her will

Infliction of Emotional Distress extreme and outrageous conduct intentionally or recklessly causing severe emotional distress

Harm to the Right of Dignity

Defamation false communication that injures a person's reputation
* *Libel* written or electronically transmitted defamation
* *Slander* spoken defamation

Invasion of Privacy
* *Appropriation* unauthorized use of a person's identity
* *Intrusion* unreasonable and highly offensive interference with the seclusion of another
* *Public Disclosure of Private Facts* highly offensive publicity of private information
* *False Light* highly offensive and false publicity about another

Misuse of Legal Procedure torts of malicious prosecution, wrongful civil proceeding, and abuse of process that protect an individual from unjustifiable litigation

Harm to Property

Real Property land and anything attached to it
* *Trespass to Real Property* wrongfully entering on land of another
* *Nuisance* a nontrespassory interference with another's use and enjoyment of land

Personal Property any property other than land
* *Trespass to Personal Property* an intentional taking or use of another's personal property
* *Conversion* intentional exercise of control over another's personal property

Harm to Economic Interests

Interference with Contractual Relations intentionally causing one of the parties to a contract not to perform

Disparagement publication of false statements about another's property or products

Fraudulent Misrepresentation a false statement, made with knowledge of its falsity, intended to induce another to act

QUESTIONS

1. The Penguin intentionally hits Batman with his umbrella. Batman, stunned by the blow, falls backward, knocking Robin down. Robin's leg is broken in the fall, and he cries out, "Holy broken bat bones! My leg is broken." Who, if anyone, has liability to Robin? Why?

2. CEO was convinced by his employee, M. Ploy, that a coworker, A. Cused, had been stealing money from the company. At lunch that day in the company cafeteria, CEO discharged Cused from her employment, accused her of stealing from the company, searched through her purse over her objections, and finally forcibly escorted her to his office to await the arrival of the police, whom he had his secretary summon. Cused is indicted for embezzlement but subsequently is acquitted upon establishing her innocence. What rights, if any, does Cused have against CEO?

3. Ralph kisses Edith while she is asleep but does not waken or harm her. Edith sues Ralph for battery. Has a battery been committed?

4. Claude, a creditor seeking to collect a debt, calls on Dianne and demands payment in a rude and insolent manner. When Dianne says that she cannot pay, Claude calls Dianne a deadbeat and says that he will never trust Dianne again. Is Claude liable to Dianne? If so, for what tort?

5. Lana, a ten-year-old child, is run over by a car negligently driven by Mitchell. Lana, at the time of the accident, was acting reasonably and without negligence. Clark, a newspaper reporter, photographs Lana while she is lying in the street in great pain. Two years later, Perry, the publisher of a newspaper, prints Clark's picture of Lana in his newspaper as a lead to an article concerning the negligence of children. The caption under the picture reads: "They ask to be killed." Lana, who has recovered from the accident, brings suit against Clark and Perry. What is the result?

6. The *Saturday Evening Post* featured an article entitled "The Story of a College Football Fix," characterized in the subtitle as "A Shocking Report of How Wally Butts and Bear Bryant

Rigged a Game Last Fall." Butts was athletic director of the University of Georgia, and Bryant was head coach of the University of Alabama. The article was based on a claim by one George Burnett that he had accidentally overheard a long-distance telephone conversation between Butts and Bryant in the course of which Butts divulged information on plays Georgia would use in the upcoming game against Alabama. The writer assigned to the story by the *Post* was not a football expert, did not interview either Butts or Bryant, and did not personally see the notes Burnett had made of the telephone conversation. Butts admitted that he had a long-distance telephone conversation with Bryant but denied that any advance information on prospective football plays was given. Has Butts been defamed by the *Post*?

7. A patient confined in a hospital, Joan, has a rare disease that is of great interest to the public. Carol, a television reporter, requests Joan to consent to an interview. Joan refuses, but Carol, nonetheless, enters Joan's room over her objection and photographs her. Joan brings a suit against Carol. Is Carol liable? If so, for what tort?

8. Owner has a place on his land where he piles trash. The pile has been there for three months. John, a neighbor of Owner, without Owner's consent or knowledge, throws trash onto the trash pile. Owner learns that John has done this and sues him. What tort, if any, has John committed?

9. Chris leaves her car parked in front of a store. There are no signs that say Chris cannot park there. The storeowner, however, needs the car moved to enable a delivery truck to unload. He releases the brake and pushes Chris's car three or four feet, doing no harm to the car. Chris returns and sees that her car has been moved and is very angry. She threatens to sue the storeowner for trespass to her personal property. Can she recover?

10. Carr borrowed John's brand-new Ford for the purpose of going to the store. He told John he would be right back. Carr then decided, however, to go to the beach while he had the car. Can John recover from Carr the value of the automobile? If so, for what tort?

CASE PROBLEMS

11. Marcia Samms claimed that David Eccles had repeatedly and persistently called her at various hours, including late at night, from May to December, soliciting her to have illicit sexual relations with him. She also claimed that on one occasion Eccles came over to her residence to again solicit sex and indecently exposed himself to her. Mrs. Samms had never encouraged Eccles but had continuously repulsed his "insulting, indecent, and obscene" proposals. She brought suit against Eccles, claiming she suffered great anxiety and fear for her personal safety and severe emotional distress, demanding actual and punitive damages. Can she recover? If so, for what tort?

12. National Bond and Investment Company sent two of its employees to repossess Whithorn's car after he failed to complete the payments. The two repossessors located Whithorn while he was driving his car. They followed him and hailed him down in order to make the repossession. Whithorn refused to abandon his car and demanded evidence of their authority. The two repossessors became impatient and called a wrecker. They ordered the driver of the wrecker to hook Whithorn's car and move it down the street while Whithorn was still inside the vehicle. Whithorn started the car and tried to escape, but the wrecker lifted the car off the road and progressed seventy-five to one hundred feet until Whithorn managed to stall the wrecker. Has National Bond committed the tort of false imprisonment?

13. William Proxmire, a U.S. senator from Wisconsin, initiated the "Golden Fleece of the Month Award" to publicize what he believed to be wasteful government spending. The second of these awards was given to the federal agencies that had for seven years funded Dr. Hutchinson's research on stress levels in animals. The award was made in a speech Proxmire gave in the Senate; the text was also incorporated into an advance press release that was sent to 275 members of the national news media. Proxmire also referred to the research again in two subsequent newsletters sent to one hundred thousand constituents and during a television interview. Hutchinson then brought this action alleging defamation resulting in personal and economic injury. Assuming that Hutchinson proved that the statements were false and defamatory, would he prevail?

14. Capune was attempting a trip from New York to Florida on an eighteen-foot-long paddleboard. The trip was being covered by various media to gain publicity for Capune and certain products he endorsed. Capune approached a pier by water. The pier was owned by Robbins, who had posted signs prohibiting surfing and swimming around the pier. Capune was unaware of these notices and attempted to continue his journey by passing under the pier. Robbins ran up yelling and threw two bottles at Capune. Capune was frightened and tried to maneuver his paddleboard to go around the pier. Robbins then threw a third bottle that hit Capune on the head. Capune had to be helped out of the water and taken to the hospital. He suffered a physical wound that required twenty-four sutures and, as a result, had to discontinue his trip. Capune brought suit in tort against Robbins. Is Robbins liable? If so, for which tort or torts?

15. Ralph Nader, who has been a critic of General Motors Corp. for many years, claims that when General Motors learned that Nader was about to publish a book entitled *Unsafe at Any Speed*, criticizing one of its automobiles, the company decided to conduct a campaign of intimidation against him. Specifically, Nader claims that GMC (a) conducted a series of interviews with Nader's acquaintances, questioning them about his political, social, racial, and religious views; (b) kept him under surveillance in public places for an unreasonable length of time including close observation of him in a bank; (c) caused him to be accosted by women for the purpose of

entrapping him into illicit relationships; (d) made threatening, harassing, and obnoxious telephone calls to him; (e) tapped his telephone and eavesdropped by means of mechanical and electronic equipment on his private conversations with others; and (f) conducted a "continuing" and harassing investigation of him. Nader brought suit against GMC for invasion of privacy. Which, if any, of the alleged actions would constitute invasion of privacy?

16. Bill Kinsey was charged with murdering his wife while working for the Peace Corps in Tanzania. After waiting six months in jail, he was acquitted at a trial that attracted wide publicity. Five years later, while a graduate student at Stanford University, Kinsey had a brief affair with Mary Macur. He abruptly ended the affair by telling Macur he would no longer be seeing her because another woman, Sally Allen, was coming from England to live with him. A few months later, Kinsey and Allen moved to Africa and were subsequently married. Soon after Bill ended their affair, Macur began a letter-writing campaign designed to expose Bill and his mistreatment of her. Macur sent several letters to both Bill and Sally Kinsey, their parents, their neighbors, their parents' neighbors, members of Bill's dissertation committee, other faculty, and the president of Stanford University. The letters contained statements accusing Bill of murdering his first wife, spending six months in jail for the crime, being a rapist, and other questionable behavior. The Kinseys brought an action for invasion of privacy, seeking damages and a permanent injunction. Will the Kinseys prevail? If so, for what tort?

17. Plaintiff, John W. Carson, was the host and star of *The Tonight Show*, a well-known television program broadcast by the National Broadcasting Company. Carson also appeared as an entertainer in nightclubs and theaters around the country. From the time he began hosting *The Tonight Show*, he had been introduced on the show each night with the phrase "Here's Johnny." The phrase "Here's Johnny" is still generally associated with Carson by a substantial segment of the television viewing public. To earn additional income, Carson began authorizing use of this phrase by outside business ventures.

Defendant, Here's Johnny Portable Toilets, Inc., is a Michigan corporation engaged in the business of renting and selling "Here's Johnny" portable toilets. Defendant's founder was aware at the time he formed the corporation that "Here's Johnny" was the introductory slogan for Carson on *The Tonight Show*. He indicated that he coupled the phrase with a second one, "The World's Foremost Commodian," to make "a good play on a phrase." Carson brought suit for invasion of privacy. Should Carson recover? If so, for which tort?

18. Lemmie L. Ruffin, Jr., was an Alabama licensed agent for Pacific Mutual Life Insurance and for Union Fidelity Life Insurance Company. Union wrote group health insurance policies for municipalities, while Pacific did not. Plaintiffs Cleopatra Haslip, Cynthia Craig, Alma M. Calhoun, and Eddie Hargrove were employees of Roosevelt City, Alabama. Ruffin gave the city a single proposal for health and life insurance for its employees, which the city approved. Both companies provided the coverage; however, Union provided the health insurance and Pacific provided the life insurance. This packaging of coverage by two different and unrelated insurers

was not unusual. Union would send its billings for health premiums to Ruffin at Pacific Mutual's office. The city clerk each month issued a check for those premiums and sent it to Ruffin. Ruffin, however, did not remit to Union the premium payments he received from the city; instead, he misappropriated most of them. When Union did not receive payment from the city, it sent notices of lapsed health coverage to the plaintiffs, who did not know that their health policies had been canceled.

Plaintiff Haslip was subsequently hospitalized and because the hospital could not confirm her health coverage, it required her to make a partial payment on her bill. Her physician, when he was not paid, placed her account with a collection agency, which obtained against Haslip a judgment that damaged her credit. Plaintiffs sued Pacific Mutual and Ruffin for fraud. The case was submitted to a jury, which was instructed that if it found liability for fraud, it could award punitive damages. The jury returned verdicts for the plaintiffs and awarded Haslip $1,040,000, of which at least $840,000 was punitive damages. The Supreme Court of Alabama affirmed the trial court's judgment. Pacific Mutual appealed. Decision?

19. Susan Jungclaus Peterson was a twenty-one-year-old student at Moorhead State University who had lived most of her life on her family farm in Minnesota. Though Susan was a dean's list student her first year, her academic performance declined after she became deeply involved in an international religious cult organization known locally as The Way of Minnesota, Inc. The cult demanded an enormous psychological and monetary commitment from Susan. Near the end of her junior year, her parents became alarmed by the changes in Susan's physical and mental well-being and concluded that she had been "reduced to a condition of psychological bondage by The Way." They sought help from Kathy Mills, a self-styled "deprogrammer" of minds brainwashed by cults.

On May 24, Norman Jungclaus, Susan's father, picked up Susan at Moorhead State. Instead of returning home, they went to the residence of Veronica Morgel, where Kathy Mills attempted to deprogram Susan. For the first few days of her stay, Susan was unwilling to discuss her involvement. She lay curled in a fetal position in her bedroom, plugging her ears and hysterically screaming and crying while her father pleaded with her to listen. By the third day, however, Susan's demeanor changed completely. She became friendly and vivacious and communicated with her father. Susan also went roller skating and played softball at a nearby park over the following weekend. She spent the next week in Columbus, Ohio, with a former cult member who had shared her experiences of the previous week. While in Columbus, she spoke daily by telephone with her fiancé, a member of The Way, who begged her to return to the cult. Susan expressed the desire to get her fiancé out of the organization, but a meeting between them could not be arranged outside the presence of other members of The Way. Her parents attempted to persuade Susan to sign an agreement releasing them from liability for their actions, but Susan refused. After nearly sixteen days of "deprogramming" Susan left the Morgel residence and returned to her fiancé and The Way. Upon the direction of The Way ministry, she brought an action against her parents for false imprisonment. Will Susan prevail? Explain.

20. Debra Agis was a waitress in a restaurant owned by the Howard Johnson Company. On May 23, Roger Dionne, manager of the restaurant, called a meeting of all waitresses at which he informed them "there was some stealing going on." Dionne also stated that the identity of the party or parties responsible was not known and that he would begin firing all waitresses in alphabetical order until the guilty party or parties were detected. He then fired Debra Agis, who allegedly "became greatly upset, began to cry, sustained emotional distress, mental anguish, and loss of wages and earnings." Mrs. Agis brought this complaint against the Howard Johnson Company and Roger Dionne, alleging that the defendants acted recklessly and outrageously, intending to cause emotional distress and anguish. The defendants argued that damages for emotional distress are not recoverable unless physical injury occurs as a result of the distress. Will Agis be successful on her complaint?

TAKING SIDES

Edith Mitchell, accompanied by her thirteen-year-old daughter, went through the checkout at Walmart and purchased several items. As they exited, the Mitchells passed through an electronic antitheft device, which sounded an alarm. Robert Canady, employed by Walmart as a "people greeter" and security guard, forcibly stopped Edith Mitchell at the exit, grabbed her bag, and told her to step back inside. The security guard never touched Edith or her daughter and never threatened to touch either of them. Nevertheless, Edith Mitchell described the security guard's actions in her affidavit as "gruff, loud, rude behavior." The security guard removed every item Mitchell had just purchased and ran it through the security gate. One of the items still had a security code unit on it, which an employee admitted could have been overlooked by the cashier. When the security guard finished examining the contents of Mitchell's bag, he put it on the checkout counter. This examination of her bag took ten or fifteen minutes. Once her bag had been checked, no employee of Walmart ever told Mitchell she could not leave. Mitchell was never threatened with arrest. Mitchell brought a tort action against Walmart.

a. Explain on which torts should Mitchell base her claim against Walmart?

b. What arguments would support Walmart denial of liability for these torts?

c. Which party should prevail? Explain.

Negligence and Strict Liability

CHAPTER 8

Nothing is so easy as to be wise after the event.

Quoted by Baron Bramwell (1859)

CHAPTER OUTCOMES

After reading and studying this chapter, you should be able to:

1. List and describe the three required elements of an action for negligence.

2. Explain the duty of care that is imposed on (a) adults, (b) children, (c) persons with a physical disability, (d) persons with a mental deficiency, (e) persons with superior knowledge, and (f) persons acting in an emergency.

3. Differentiate among the duties that possessors of land owe to trespassers, licensees, and invitees.

4. Identify the defenses that are available to a tort action in negligence and those that are available to a tort action in strict liability.

5. Identify and describe those activities giving rise to a tort action in strict liability.

Whereas intentional torts deal with conduct that has a substantial certainty of causing harm, negligence involves conduct that creates an unreasonable risk of harm. The basis of liability for negligence is the failure to exercise reasonable care under the circumstances for the safety of another person or his property, which failure proximately causes injury to such person or damage to his property, or both. Thus, if the driver of an automobile intentionally runs down a person, she has committed the intentional tort of battery. If, on the other hand, the driver hits and injures a person while driving with no reasonable regard for the safety of others, she is negligent.

Strict liability is not based on the negligence or intent of the defendant but rather on the nature of the activity in which he is engaging. Under this doctrine, defendants who engage in certain activities, such as keeping animals or carrying on abnormally dangerous conditions, are held liable for injuries they cause, even if they have exercised the utmost care. The law imposes this liability to bring about a just reallocation of loss, given that the defendant engaged in the activity for his own benefit and probably is better prepared than the plaintiff is to manage the risk inherent in the activity through insurance or otherwise.

As mentioned in Chapter 7, the American Law Institute (ALI) has published the Restatement Third, Torts: Liability for Physical and Emotional Harm (the "Third Restatement"). This new Restatement addresses the general or basic elements of the tort action for liability for accidental personal injury, property damage, and emotional harm, but it does not cover liability for economic loss. "Physical harm" is defined as bodily harm (physical injury, illness, disease, and death) or property damage (physical impairment of real property or tangible personal property). The Third Restatement replaces comparable provisions in the Restatement Second, Torts. However, the Third Restatement does not cover the following matters, which remain governed by the

Second Restatement: protection of reputation or privacy, economic loss, or domestic relations; determination of the recoverable damages and their amount; and the standards for liability of professionals for malpractice. Otherwise, this chapter reflects the Third Restatement's provisions.

The ALI's Restatement Third, Torts: Economic Torts and Related Wrongs will update coverage on torts that involve economic loss or pecuniary harm *not* resulting from physical harm or physical contact to a person or property. This project will update coverage of economic torts in Restatement Second, Torts and address some topics not covered in prior Restatements. The ALI began this project in 2004, and after several years of inactivity, the project was resumed in 2010. In 2012, a portion of Chapter 1 of the Tentative Draft was approved.

NEGLIGENCE

Negligence

conduct that falls below the standard established by law for the protection of others against unreasonable risk of harm

A person acts negligently if the person does not exercise reasonable care under all the circumstances. Moreover, the general rule is that a person is under a duty to all others at all times to exercise reasonable care for the safety of other persons and their property.

As the comments to the Third Restatement explain, an action for **negligence** consists of five elements, each of which the plaintiff must prove:

1. **Duty of care:** that a legal duty required the defendant to conform to the standard of conduct established for the protection of others;
2. **Breach of duty:** that the defendant failed to exercise reasonable care;
3. **Factual cause:** that the defendant's failure to exercise reasonable care in fact caused the harm the plaintiff sustained;
4. **Harm:** that the harm sustained is of a type protected against negligent conduct; and
5. **Scope of liability:** that the harm sustained is within the "scope of liability," which historically has been referred to as "proximate cause."

We will discuss the first two elements in the next section, "Breach of Duty of Care"; we will cover the last three elements in subsequent sections.

BREACH OF DUTY OF CARE [8-1]

Negligence consists of conduct that creates an unreasonable risk of harm. In determining whether a given risk of harm was unreasonable, the following factors are considered: (1) the foreseeable probability that the person's conduct will result in harm, (2) the foreseeable gravity or severity of any harm that may follow, and (3) the burden of taking precautions to eliminate or reduce the risk of harm. Thus, the standard of conduct, which is the basis for the law of negligence, is usually determined by a cost-benefit or risk-benefit analysis.

Reasonable Person Standard [8-1a]

Reasonable person standard

degree of care that a reasonable person would exercise under all the circumstances

The duty of care imposed by law is measured by the degree of carefulness that a reasonable person would exercise in a given situation. The **reasonable person** is a fictitious individual who is always careful and prudent and never negligent. What the judge or jury determines a reasonable person would have done in light of the facts revealed by the evidence in a particular case sets the standard of conduct for that case. The reasonable person standard is thus *external* and *objective*.

Children

must conform to conduct of a reasonable person of the same age, intelligence, and experience

Children   A child is a person below the age of majority, which in almost all states has been lowered from twenty-one to eighteen. The standard of conduct to which a child must conform to avoid being negligent is that of a reasonably careful person of the same age, intelligence, and experience under all the circumstances. The law applies a test that acknowledges these three factors, because children do not have the judgment, intelligence, knowledge, and experience of adults. Moreover, children as a general rule do not engage in activities entailing high risk to others, and their conduct normally does not involve a potential for harm as great as that of adult conduct. A child who engages in a dangerous activity that is characteristically undertaken by adults, however, such as flying an airplane or driving a boat or car, is held in almost all states to the standard of care applicable to adults.

Physical disability
a disabled person's conduct
must conform to that of a
reasonable person under
the same disability

Mental disability
a mentally disabled person
is held to the reasonable
person standard of a
reasonable person who is
not mentally deficient

**Superior skill or
knowledge**
if a person has skills or
knowledge beyond those
possessed by most others,
these skills or knowledge
are circumstances to be
taken into account in
determining whether the
person has acted with
reasonable care

**Standard for
emergencies**
the reasonable person
standard applies, but an
unexpected emergency is
considered part of the
circumstances

Emergency
sudden, unexpected event
calling for immediate action

Violation of statute
if the statute applies, the
violation is negligence *per se*
in most states

Negligence *per se*
conclusive on the issue of
negligence (duty of care and
breach)

Practical Advice

Assess the potential liability
for negligence arising from
your activities and obtain
adequate liability insurance
to cover your exposure.

Physical Disability

If a person is ill or otherwise physically disabled, the standard of conduct to which he or she must conform to avoid being negligent is that of a reasonably careful person with the same disability. Thus, a blind person must act as a reasonable person who is blind. However, the conduct of a person during a period of sudden incapacitation or loss of consciousness resulting from physical illness is negligent only if the sudden incapacitation or loss of consciousness was reasonably foreseeable to the actor. Examples of sudden incapacitation include heart attack, stroke, epileptic seizure, and diabetes.

Mental Disability

A person's mental or emotional disability is not considered in determining whether conduct is negligent unless the person is a child. The defendant is held to the standard of conduct of a reasonable person who is not mentally or emotionally disabled, even though the defendant is, in fact, incapable of conforming to the standard. When a person's intoxication is voluntary, it is not considered as an excuse for conduct that is otherwise lacking in reasonable care.

Superior Skill or Knowledge

If a person has skills or knowledge beyond those possessed by most others, these skills or knowledge are circumstances to be taken into account in determining whether the person has acted with reasonable care. Thus, persons who are qualified and who practice a profession or trade that requires special skill and expertise are required to use the same care and skill that members of their profession or trade normally possess. This standard applies to such professionals as physicians, dentists, attorneys, pharmacists, architects, accountants, and engineers and to those who perform a skilled trade such as an airline pilot, electrician, carpenter, and plumber. If a member of a profession or skilled trade possesses greater skill than that common to the profession or trade, she is required to exercise that greater degree of skill.

Standard for Emergencies

An **emergency** is a sudden and unexpected event that calls for immediate action and permits no time for deliberation. In determining whether a defendant's conduct was reasonable, the fact that he was at the time confronted with a sudden and unexpected emergency is taken into consideration. The standard is still that of a reasonable person under the circumstances—the emergency is simply part of the circumstances. If, however, the defendant's own negligent or tortious conduct created the emergency, he is liable for the consequences of this conduct even if he acted reasonably in the resulting emergency situation. Moreover, failure to anticipate an emergency may itself constitute negligence.

Violation of Statute

The reasonable person standard of conduct may be established by legislation or administrative regulation. Some statutes do so by expressly imposing civil liability on violators. In cases in which a statute does not expressly provide for civil liability, courts may adopt the requirements of the statute as the standard of conduct if the statute is designed to protect against the type of accident the defendant's conduct causes and the accident victim is within the class of persons the statute is designed to protect.

If the statute is found to apply, the great majority of the courts hold that an unexcused violation is **negligence *per se***, that is, the violation conclusively shows negligent conduct (breach of duty of care). In a minority of states, the violation is considered merely to be evidence of negligence. In either event, the plaintiff must also prove legal causation and injury.

For example, a statute enacted to protect employees from injuries requires that all factory elevators be equipped with specified safety devices. Arthur, an employee in Leonard's factory, and Marian, a business visitor to the factory, are injured when the elevator fails because the safety devices have not been installed. The court may adopt the statute as a standard of conduct as to Arthur, and hold Leonard negligent *per se* as to Arthur, but not as to Marian, because Arthur, not Marian, is within the class of persons the statute is intended to protect. Marian would have to establish that a reasonable person in the position of Leonard under the circumstances would have installed the safety device. (See Figure 8-1 illustrating negligence and negligence *per se*.)

On the other hand, compliance with a legislative enactment or administrative regulation does not prevent a finding of negligence if a reasonable person would have taken additional precautions. For instance, driving at the speed limit may not constitute due care when traffic or road conditions require a lower speed. Legislative or administrative rules normally establish *minimum* standards.

Figure 8-1 Negligence and Negligence *Per Se*

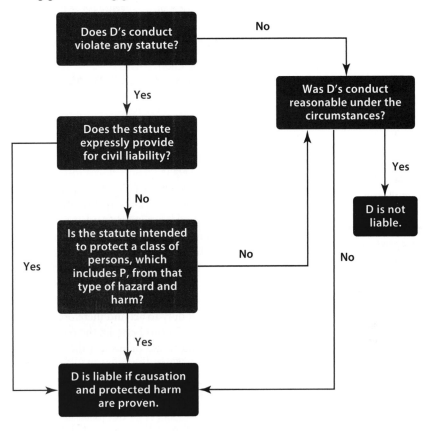

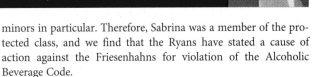

Ryan v. Friesenhahn
Court of Appeals of Texas, 1995
911 S.W.2d 113; aff'd, 41 Tex. Sup. J. 261, 960 S.W.2d 656 (1998)
http://scholar.google.com/scholar_case?case=5075518384525866053&q=911+S.W.2d+113&hl=en&as_sdt=2,34

FACTS Todd Friesenhahn, son of Nancy and Frederick Friesenhahn, held an "open invitation" party at his parents' home that encouraged guests to "bring your own bottle." Sabrina Ryan attended the party, became intoxicated, and was involved in a fatal accident after she left the party. Sandra and Stephen Ryan, Sabrina's parents, sued the Friesenhahns for negligence, alleging that the Friesenhahns were aware of the underage drinking at the party and of Sabrina's condition when she left the party. The trial court granted summary judgment for the Friesenhahns.

DECISION Judgment reversed.

OPINION Accepting the Ryans' allegations as true, the Friesenhahns were aware that minors possessed and consumed alcohol on their property and specifically allowed Sabrina to become intoxicated. The Texas Alcoholic Beverage Code provides that a person commits an offense if, with criminal negligence, that person "makes available an alcoholic beverage to a minor." A violation of a statute constitutes negligence *per se* if the injured party is a member of the class protected by the statute. The Alcoholic Beverage Code was designed to protect the general public and

minors in particular. Therefore, Sabrina was a member of the protected class, and we find that the Ryans have stated a cause of action against the Friesenhahns for violation of the Alcoholic Beverage Code.

In considering common-law negligence as a basis for social host liability, courts have relied on *Graff v. Board*, a prior Texas Supreme Court decision in which it was held that no third party liability should be imposed on social hosts who provide alcohol to adult guests. The Texas Supreme Court gave two reasons for its holding in *Graff*: first, the host cannot reasonably know the extent of his guests' alcohol consumption level; second, the host cannot reasonably be expected to control his guests' conduct. However, this rationale does not apply where the guest is a minor. The adult social host need not estimate the extent of a minor's alcohol consumption, because serving minors any amount of alcohol is a criminal offense. Furthermore, the social host may control the minor, with whom there is a special relationship, in a manner analogous to that of parent–child.

Although one adult has no general duty to control the behavior of another adult, one would hope that adults would exercise special diligence in supervising minors. When a party is for the purpose of engaging in the consumption of alcohol by minors, adults certainly have a greater duty of care. Moreover, in view of the legislature's determination that minors are not competent to understand the effects of alcohol, the court found sufficient legislative intent to support its holding that a duty exists between the adult social host and the minor guest. Accordingly, the court found that the Ryans' petition stated a common-law cause of action.

INTERPRETATION A violation of a statute constitutes negligence *per se* if the injured party is a member of the class protected by the statute.

ETHICAL QUESTION When should a parent be held liable for her child's negligence? Explain.

CRITICAL THINKING QUESTION Should a court extend social host liability for providing alcohol to an adult guest? Explain?

Duty to act

a person is under a duty to all others at all times to exercise reasonable care for the safety of the others' person and property; however, except in special circumstances, no one is required to aid another in peril

Duty to Act [8-1b]

As stated previously, the general rule is that a person is under a duty to all others at all times to exercise reasonable care for the safety of the others' person and property. On the other hand, subject to several exceptions, a person (Andrea) does not have a duty of care when the other's (Bennie's) person or property is at risk for reasons other than the conduct of Andrea. This rule applies even though the person may be in a position to help another in peril. For example, Anthony, an adult standing at the edge of a steep cliff, observes a baby carriage with a crying infant in it slowly heading toward the edge and certain doom. Anthony could easily prevent the baby's fall at no risk to his own safety. Nonetheless, Anthony does nothing, and the baby falls to its death. Anthony is under no legal duty to act and therefore incurs no liability for failing to do so.

Nonetheless, special relations between the parties may impose an affirmative duty of reasonable care on the defendant to aid or protect the other with respect to risks that arise within the scope of the relationship. Thus, in the previous example, if Anthony were the baby's parent or babysitter, Anthony would be under a duty to act and therefore would be liable for not taking action. The special relations giving rise to an affirmative duty to aid or protect another include (1) a common carrier with its passengers, (2) an innkeeper with its guest, (3) an employer with its employees, (4) a school with its students, (5) a landlord with its tenants with respect to common areas under the landlord's control, (6) a business open to the public with its customers, and (7) custodian with those in its custody including parents with their children. The Third Restatement leaves it to the courts whether to recognize additional relationships as sufficient to impose an affirmative duty. Furthermore, state and federal statutes and administrative regulations as well as local ordinances may impose an affirmative duty to act for the protection of another.

In addition, when a person's prior conduct, even though not tortious, creates a continuing risk of physical harm, the person has a duty to exercise reasonable care to prevent or minimize the harm. For example, Alice innocently drives her car into Frank, rendering him unconscious. Alice leaves Frank lying in the middle of the road, where he is run over by a second car driven by Rebecca. Alice is liable to Frank for the additional injuries inflicted by Rebecca. Moreover, a person who begins a rescue by taking charge of another who is imperiled and unable to protect himself incurs a duty to exercise reasonable care under the circumstances. Furthermore, a person who discontinues aid or protection is under a duty of reasonable care not to leave the other in a worse position. For example, Ann finds Ben drunk and stumbling along a dark sidewalk. Ann leads Ben halfway up a steep and unguarded stairway, where she then abandons him. Ben attempts to climb the stairs but trips and falls, suffering serious injury. Ann is liable to Ben for having left him in a worse position. Most states have enacted Good Samaritan statutes to encourage voluntary emergency care. These statutes vary considerably, but they typically limit or disallow liability for some rescuers under specified circumstances.

There are special relationships in which one person has some degree of control over another person, including (1) a parent with dependent children, and (2) an employer with employees when the employment facilitates the employee's causing harm to third parties. The parent and the employer each owe a duty of reasonable care under the circumstances to third persons with regard to foreseeable risks that arise within the scope of the relationship. Depending on the circumstances, reasonable care may require controlling the activities of the other person or merely providing a warning. Generally, the duty of parents is limited to dependent children; thus when children reach majority or are no longer dependent, parents no longer have control and the duty of reasonable care ceases. The duty of employers includes the duty to exercise reasonable care in the hiring, training, supervision, and retention of employees. This duty of employers is independent of the vicarious liability of an employer for an employee's tortious conduct during the course of employment, and extends to conduct by the employee that occurs both inside and outside the scope of employment so long as the employment facilitates the employee causing harm to third parties. The Third Restatement provides the following example of an employer's duty:

> Don is employed by Welch Repair Service, which knows that Don had several episodes of assault in his previous employment. Don goes to Traci's residence, where he had previously been dispatched by Welch, and misrepresents to Traci that he is there on Welch business to check repairs that had previously been made in Traci's home. After Traci admits Don, he assaults Traci. Welch is subject to a duty under this subsection with regard to Don's assault on Traci.

Soldano v. O'Daniels
California Court of Appeals, Fifth District, 1983
141 Cal.App.3d 443, 190 Cal.Rptr. 310
http://scholar.google.com/scholar_case?case=636498466656533477&q=190+Cal.Rptr.+310&hl=en&as_sdt=2,34

FACTS On August 9, the plaintiff's father, Darrell Soldano, was shot and killed at the Happy Jack Saloon. The defendant owns and operates the Circle Inn, an eating establishment across the street from the Happy Jack Saloon. On the night of the shooting, a patron of the Happy Jack Saloon came into the Circle Inn and informed the Circle Inn bartender that a man had been threatened at Happy Jack's. The patron requested that the Circle Inn bartender either call the police or allow the patron to use the Circle Inn phone to call the police. The bartender refused either to make the call or to allow the Happy Jack patron to use the phone. The plaintiff alleges that the actions of the Circle Inn employee were a breach of the legal duty that the Circle Inn owed to the decedent. The defendant maintains that there was no legal obligation to take any action, and therefore there was no duty owed to the decedent. The trial court dismissed the case on the defendant's motion for summary judgment.

DECISION The appellate court reversed and remanded the case for trial.

OPINION Defendant points to the established rule that one who has not created a peril ordinarily does not have a duty to take affirmative action to assist an imperiled person. The courts have increased the instances in which affirmative duties are imposed, not by direct rejection of the common law rule but by expanding the list of special relationships that will justify departure from that rule. In this case, however, there was no special relationship between the defendant and the deceased. Nonetheless, the court

determined to reexamine the common law rule of nonliability for nonfeasance in the special circumstances of this case. Imposing such a duty to third parties requires an examination and balancing of foreseeability of harm, certainty that the plaintiff would suffer injury, the connection between defendant's conduct and the injury, moral blame attached to defendant's conduct, the prevention of future harm, extent of the burden to the defendant, consequences to the community of imposing a duty to exercise care, and the availability, cost, and prevalence of insurance for the particular risk involved. The court concluded, on these facts, that the Circle Inn's employee's conduct displayed a disregard for human life in that the burden on the defendant to respond was minimal. Balancing these factors, the court concluded that there was an affirmative duty on the defendant's part to respond and that his failure to respond resulted in a legal breach of duty of care. It bears emphasizing that the duty in this case does not require that one go to the aid of another. Rather, the use of a telephone, in the public portion of a business open to the public, during business hours, should not be refused for a legitimate emergency call.

INTERPRETATION Although a person may not have a duty to help another, in a case such as this, a person has a duty not to hinder others who are trying to help.

CRITICAL THINKING QUESTION Should the courts go beyond the rule of this case and impose an affirmative duty to go to the aid of another person who is in peril if it can be done without endangerment? Explain.

Duties of Possessors of Land [8-1c]

The right of possessors of land to use that land for their own benefit and enjoyment is limited by their duty to do so in a reasonable manner. By the use of their land, possessors of land cannot cause unreasonable risks of harm to others. Liability for breach of this obligation may arise from conduct in any of the three areas of torts discussed in this and the preceding chapter: intentional harm, negligence, or strict liability. Most of these cases fall within the classification of negligence.

In conducting activities on her land, the possessor of land is required to exercise reasonable care to protect others who are not on her property. For example, a property owner who constructs a factory on her premises must take reasonable care that it is not unreasonably dangerous to people off the site. Moreover, a business or other possessor of land that holds its premises open to the public owes those who are lawfully on the premises a duty of reasonable care with regard to risks that arise within the scope of the relationship.

In most states and under the Second Restatement, the duty of a possessor of land to persons who come on the land usually depends on whether those persons are trespassers, licensees, or invitees. In about fifteen states, however, licensees and invitees are owed the same duty. In addition, at least nine states have abandoned these distinctions and simply apply ordinary negligence principles of foreseeable risk and reasonable care to all entrants on the land including trespassers. The Third Restatement has adopted this last—the unitary—approach.

Second Restatement

Second Restatement
a land possessor owes the following duties: (1) not to injure intentionally *trespassers*, (2) to warn *licensees* of known dangerous conditions licensees are unlikely to discover for themselves, and (3) to exercise reasonable care to protect *invitees* against dangerous conditions land possessor should know of but invitees are unlikely to discover

Second Restatement   In accordance with the historical—and still majority—approach to the duties of possessors of land, the **Second Restatement** provides for varying duties depending on the status of the entrant on the land.

A **trespasser** is a person who enters or remains on the land of another without the possessor's consent or a legal privilege to do so. The possessor of the land is *not* liable to adult trespassers for his failure to maintain the land in a reasonably safe condition. Nonetheless, the possessor is not free to inflict intentional injury on a trespasser. Moreover, most courts hold that upon discovery of the presence of trespassers on the land, the lawful possessor is required to exercise reasonable care for their safety in carrying on her activities and to warn the trespassers of potentially dangerous conditions that the trespassers are not likely to discover.

Trespasser
person who enters or remains on the land of another without permission or privilege to do so

A **licensee** is a person who is privileged to enter or remain on land only by virtue of the lawful possessor's consent. Licensees include members of the possessor's household, social guests, and salespersons calling at private homes. A licensee will become a trespasser, however, if he enters a portion of the land to which he is not invited or remains on the land after his invitation has expired. The possessor owes a higher duty of care to licensees than to trespassers. The possessor must warn the licensee of dangerous activities and conditions (1) of which the possessor has knowledge or reason to know and (2) the licensee does not and is not likely to discover. If he is not warned, the licensee may recover if the activity or dangerous condition resulted from the possessor's failure to exercise reasonable care to protect him from the danger. To illustrate: Henry invites a friend, Anne, to his place in the country at 8:00 P.M. on a winter evening. Henry knows that a bridge in his driveway is in a dangerous condition that is not noticeable in the dark. Henry does not inform Anne of this fact. The bridge gives way under Anne's car, causing serious harm to Anne. Henry is liable to Anne.

Licensee
person privileged to enter or remain on land by virtue of the consent of the lawful possessor

An **invitee** is a person invited upon land as a member of the public or for a business purpose. A *public invitee* is a person who is invited to enter or remain on land as a member of the public for a purpose for which the land is held open to the public. Such invitees include those who use public parks, beaches, or swimming pools, as well as those who use government facilities, such as a post office or an office of the recorder of deeds, where business with the public is transacted openly. A *business visitor* is a person invited to enter or remain on premises for a purpose directly or indirectly concerning business dealings with the possessor of the land, such as one who enters a store or a worker who enters a residence to make repairs. With respect to the condition of the premises, the possessor of land is under a duty to exercise reasonable care to protect invitees against dangerous conditions they are unlikely to discover. This liability extends not only to those conditions of which the possessor actually knows but also to those of which she would discover by the exercise of reasonable care. For example, David's store has a large glass front door that is well lighted and plainly visible. Maxine, a customer, mistakes the glass for an open doorway and walks into the glass, injuring herself. David is not liable to Maxine. If, on the other hand, the glass was difficult to see and a person foreseeably might have mistaken the glass for an open doorway, then David would be liable to Maxine if Maxine crashed into the glass while exercising reasonable care.

Invitee
person invited upon land as a member of the public or for a business purpose

Third Restatement
adopts a unitary duty of reasonable care to all entrants on the land except for flagrant trespassers: a land possessor must use reasonable care to investigate and discover dangerous conditions and must use reasonable care to eliminate or improve those dangerous conditions that are known or should have been discovered by the exercise of reasonable care

Third Restatement

Third Restatement   The status-based duty rules just discussed have been rejected by the **Third Restatement**, which adopts a unitary duty of reasonable care to persons coming onto the land.

[Except for "flagrant trespassers,"] a land possessor owes a duty of reasonable care to entrants on the land with regard to:

1. conduct by the land possessor that creates risks to entrants on the land;
2. artificial conditions on the land that pose risks to entrants on the land;
3. natural conditions on the land that pose risks to entrants on the land; ...

This rule is similar to the duty land possessors owed to invitees under the Second Restatement except that it extends the duty to all who enter the land, including trespassers, with the exception of "flagrant trespassers." This rule requires a land possessor to use reasonable care to investigate and discover dangerous conditions and to use reasonable care to eliminate or improve those dangerous conditions that are known or should have been discovered by the exercise of reasonable care. However, some risks cannot reasonably be discovered, and the land possessor is not subject to liability for those risks. In addition, a land possessor is not liable to an ordinary trespasser whose unforeseeable presence results in an unforeseeable risk.

A different rule applies to "flagrant trespassers." The Third Restatement requires that a land possessor only (1) refrain from intentional, willful, or wanton conduct that harms a flagrant trespasser and (2) exercise reasonable care on behalf of flagrant trespassers who are imperiled and helpless. The Third Restatement does not define "flagrant trespassers" but instead leaves it to each state to determine at what point an ordinary trespasser becomes a "flagrant trespasser." The comments to the Third Restatement explain:

> The idea behind distinguishing particularly egregious trespassers for different treatment is that their presence on another's land is so antithetical to the rights of the land possessor to exclusive use and possession of the land that the land possessor should not be subject to liability for failing to exercise the ordinary duty of reasonable care otherwise owed to them as entrants on the land. It stems from the idea that when a trespass is sufficiently offensive to the property rights of the land possessor it is unfair to subject the possessor to liability for mere negligence.

The Third Restatement provides an illustration of a flagrant trespasser: "Herman engaged in a late-night burglary of the Jacob liquor store after it had closed. While leaving the store after taking cash from the store's register, Herman slipped on a slick spot on the floor, fell, and broke his arm. Herman is a flagrant trespasser...."

Practical Advice

Take care to inspect your premises regularly to detect any dangerous conditions and either remedy the danger or post prominent warnings of any dangerous conditions you discover.

Love v. Hardee's Food Systems, Inc.
Court of Appeals of Missouri, Eastern District, Division Two, 2000
16 S.W.3d 739
http://scholar.google.com/scholar_case?case=12304910341505965816&hl=en&as_sdt=2&as_=1&oi=scholarr

FACTS At about 3:15 P.M. on November 15, 1995, plaintiff, Jason Love, and his mother, Billye Ann Love, went to the Hardee's Restaurant in Arnold, Missouri, owned by defendant, Hardee's Food Systems, Inc. There were no other customers in the restaurant between 3:00 P.M. and 4:00 P.M., but two or three workmen were in the back doing construction. The workmen reported that they did not use the restroom and did not see anyone use the restroom. When Jason went to use the restroom, he slipped on water on the restroom floor. He fell backwards, hit his head, and felt a shooting pain down his right leg. He found himself lying in an area of dirty water, which soaked his clothes. There were no barricades, warning cones, or anything else that would either restrict access to the bathroom or warn of the danger.

Jason stated after the fall that his back and leg were "hurting pretty bad." His mother reported the fall. The supervisor filled out an accident report form, which reported that the accident occurred at 3:50 P.M. The supervisor testified that the water appeared to have come from someone shaking his hands after washing them. The supervisor could not recall the last time the restroom had been checked. Jason was taken to a hospital emergency room. As a result of his injuries, he underwent two back surgeries, missed substantial time from work, and suffered from continuing pain and limitations on his physical activities.

Hardee's had a policy requiring that the restroom be checked and cleaned every hour by a maintenance person, who was scheduled to work until 3:00 P.M., but normally left at 1:00 P.M. The supervisor could not recall whether the maintenance person left at 1:00 P.M. or 3:00 P.M. on November 15, and the defendant was unable to produce the time clock report for that day.

It was also a store policy that whenever employees cleaned the tables, they would check the restroom. If an employee had to use the restroom, then that employee was also supposed to check the restroom. The restaurant supervisor did not ask if any employees had been in the restroom, or if they had checked it in the hour prior to the accident, and did not know if the restroom was actually inspected or cleaned at 3:00 P.M. The restaurant had shift inspection checklists on which the manager would report on the cleanliness of the restrooms and whether the floors were clean and dry. However, the checklists for November 15 were thrown away.

Jason Love filed a lawsuit against Hardee's Food Systems, Inc. to recover damages for negligence. The jury returned a verdict in the plaintiff's favor in the amount of $125,000.

DECISION The judgment of the trial court is affirmed.

OPINION In order to have made a submissible case, the plaintiff had to show that defendant knew or, by using ordinary care, could have known of the dangerous condition and failed to use ordinary care to remove it, barricade it, or warn of it, and plaintiff sustained damage as a direct result of such failure. In order to establish constructive notice, the condition must have existed for a sufficient length of time or the facts must be such that the defendant should have reasonably known of its presence.

In this case the accident took place in the restaurant's restroom, which is provided for the use of employees and customers. The cause of the accident was water, which is provided in the restroom. The restaurant owner could reasonably foresee that anyone using the restroom, customers or employees, would use the tap water provided in the restroom and could spill, drop, or splash water on the floor. Accordingly, the restaurant owner was under a duty to use due care to guard against danger from water on the floor.

There was substantial evidence to support the plaintiff's case. First, there was evidence that the water was on the floor of the restroom and the supervisor testified it appeared that someone had shaken water from his hands on the floor. If the water was caused by a nonemployee, the water was on the floor for at least fifty minutes, or longer, because no other customers were in the store to use the restroom after 3:00 P.M. and the workmen on the site had not used the restroom. In addition, the defendant's employees had the opportunity to observe the hazard. The restroom was to be used by the employees and was supposed to be checked by them when they used it; employees cleaning tables were supposed to check the restroom when they cleaned the tables; and a maintenance man was supposed to check and clean the restroom every hour.

There was evidence that the maintenance man charged with cleaning the restroom every hour did not clean the restroom at 3:00 P.M. as scheduled on the day of the accident. There was testimony that the maintenance man usually left at 1:00 P.M. This could have created a span of two hours and fifty minutes during which there was no employee working at the restaurant whose primary responsibility was to clean the restroom.

INTERPRETATION The owner or possessor of property is liable to an invitee if the owner knew or, by using ordinary care, could have known of the dangerous condition and failed to use ordinary care to remove it, barricade it, or warn of it, and the invitee sustained damage as a direct result of such failure.

CRITICAL THINKING QUESTION Should customers be required to look for dangers?

Res Ipsa Loquitur [8-1d]

Res ipsa loquitur
"the thing speaks for itself;" permits the jury to infer both negligent conduct and causation

A rule of circumstantial evidence has developed that permits the jury to infer both negligent conduct and causation from the mere occurrence of certain types of events. This rule, called **res ipsa loquitur**, meaning "the thing speaks for itself," applies when the accident causing the plaintiff's physical harm is a type of accident that ordinarily happens as a result of the negligence of a class of actors of which the defendant is the relevant member. For example, Camille rents a room in Leo's motel. During the night, a large piece of plaster falls from the ceiling and injures Camille. In the absence of other evidence, the jury may infer that the harm resulted from Leo's negligence in permitting the plaster to become defective. Leo is permitted, however, to introduce evidence to contradict the inference of negligence.

FACTUAL CAUSE [8-2]

Factual cause
liability for the negligent conduct of a defendant requires that his conduct in fact caused harm to the plaintiff

But-for test
the defendant's conduct is a factual cause of the harm when the harm would not have occurred absent the conduct

Liability for the negligent conduct of a defendant requires that the conduct in fact caused harm to the plaintiff. The Third Restatement states: "Tortious conduct must be a factual cause of physical harm for liability to be imposed." A widely applied test for causation in fact is the **but-for test**: A person's conduct is a cause of an event if the event would not have occurred but for the person's negligent conduct. That is, conduct is a factual cause of harm when the harm would not have occurred absent the conduct. For instance, Arnold fails to erect a barrier around an excavation. Doyle is driving a truck when its accelerator becomes stuck. Arnold's negligence is not a cause in fact of Doyle's death if the runaway truck would have crashed through the barrier even if it had been erected. Similarly, failure to install a proper fire escape to a hotel is not the cause in fact of the death of a person who is suffocated by the smoke while sleeping in bed during a hotel fire.

If the tortious conduct of Adam is *insufficient* by itself to cause Paula's harm, but when Adam's conduct is combined with the tortious conduct of Barry, the combined conduct is sufficient to cause Paula's harm, then Adam and Barry are each considered a factual cause of Paula's harm.

The but-for test, however, is not satisfied when there are two or more causes, each of which is *sufficient* to bring about the harm in question and each of which is active at the time harm occurs. For example, Wilson and Hart negligently set fires that combine to destroy Kennedy's property. Either fire would have destroyed the property. Under the but-for test, either Wilson or Hart, or both, could argue that the fire caused by the other would have destroyed the property and that he, therefore, is not liable. The Third Restatement addresses this problem of multiple *sufficient* causes by providing, "If multiple acts exist, each of which alone would have been a factual cause under [the but-for test] of the physical harm at the same time, each act is regarded as a factual cause of the harm." Under this rule the conduct of both Wilson and Hart would be found to be a factual cause of the destruction of Kennedy's property.

SCOPE OF LIABILITY (PROXIMATE CAUSE) [8-3]

Scope of liability
liability is limited to those harms that result from the risks that made the defendant's conduct tortious

As a matter of social policy, legal responsibility has not followed all the consequences of a negligent act. Tort law does not impose liability on a defendant for all harm factually caused by the defendant's negligent conduct. Liability has been limited—to a greater extent than with intentional torts—to those harms that result from the risks that made the defendant's conduct tortious. This "risk standard" limitation on liability also applies to strict liability cases. The Third Restatement provides the following example: Richard, a hunter, finishes his day in the field and stops at a friend's house while walking home. His friend's nine-year-old daughter, Kim, greets Richard, who hands his loaded shotgun to her as he enters the house. Kim drops the shotgun, which lands on her toe, breaking it. Although Richard was negligent for giving Kim his shotgun, the risk that made Richard negligent was that Kim might shoot someone with the gun, not that she would drop it and hurt herself (the gun was neither especially heavy nor unwieldy). Kim's broken toe is outside the scope of Richard's liability, even though Richard's tortious conduct was a factual cause of Kim's harm.

Foreseeability [8-3a]

Determining the liability of a negligent defendant for unforeseeable consequences has proved to be troublesome and controversial. The Second Restatement and many courts have adopted the following position:

1. If the actor's conduct is a substantial factor in bringing about harm to another, the fact that the actor neither foresaw nor should have foreseen the extent of the harm or the manner in which it occurred does *not* prevent him from being liable.
2. The actor's conduct may be held not to be a legal cause of harm to another where, after the event and looking back from the harm to the actor's negligent conduct, it appears to the court highly extraordinary that it should have brought about the harm.

A comment to the Third Restatement explains that

the foreseeability test for proximate cause is essentially consistent with the standard set forth in this [Restatement]. Properly understood, both the risk standard and a foreseeability test exclude liability for harms that were sufficiently unforeseeable at the time of the actor's tortious conduct that they were not among the risks—potential harms—that made the actor negligent. Negligence limits the requirement of reasonable care to those risks that are foreseeable.

For example, Steven, while negligently driving an automobile, collides with a car carrying dynamite. Steven is unaware of the contents of the other car and has no reason to know about them. The collision causes the dynamite to explode, shattering glass in a building a block away. The shattered glass injures Doria, who is inside the building. The explosion also injures Walter, who is walking on the sidewalk near the collision. Steven would be liable to Walter because

Steven should have realized that his negligent driving might result in a collision that would endanger pedestrians nearby. Doria's harm, however, was beyond the risks posed by Steven's negligent driving and he, accordingly, is not liable to Doria.

Palsgraf v. Long Island Railroad Co.
Court of Appeals of New York, 1928
248 N.Y. 339, 162 N.E. 99
http://www.nycourts.gov/reporter/archives/palsgraf_lirr.htm

FACTS Palsgraf was on the railroad station platform buying a ticket when a train stopped at the station. As it began to depart, two men ran to catch it. After the first was safely aboard, the second jumped onto the moving car. When he started to fall, a guard on the train reached to grab him and another guard on the platform pushed the man from behind. They helped the man to regain his balance, but in the process they knocked a small package out of his arm. The package, which contained fireworks, fell onto the rails and exploded. The shock from the explosion knocked over a scale resting on the other end of the platform, and it landed on Mrs. Palsgraf. She then brought an action against the Long Island Railroad Company to recover for the injuries she sustained. The railroad appealed from the trial and appellate courts' decisions in favor of Palsgraf.

DECISION Judgment for Palsgraf reversed.

OPINION Negligence is not actionable unless it involves the invasion of a legally protected interest or the violation of a right.

In other words, in order for a given act to be held negligent, it must be shown that the charged party owed a duty to the complaining individual, the observance of which would have averted or avoided the injury.

Here, then, Palsgraf cannot recover because the railroad, although perhaps negligent as to the man carrying the package, was not negligent as to her. This was because the harm to her was not foreseeable. She cannot recover for injuries sustained merely because the railroad's agents were negligent as to the man they assisted.

INTERPRETATION Even if the defendant's negligent conduct in fact caused harm to the plaintiff, the defendant is not liable if the defendant could not have foreseen injuring the plaintiff or a class of persons to which the plaintiff belonged.

CRITICAL THINKING QUESTION Should a person be held liable for all injuries that her negligence in fact causes? Explain.

Superseding Cause [8-3b]

An intervening cause is an event or act that occurs after the defendant's negligent conduct and with that negligence causes the plaintiff's harm. If the intervening cause is deemed a **superseding cause**, it relieves the defendant of liability for that harm.

Superseding cause intervening event that occurs after the defendant's negligent conduct and relieves her of liability

For example, Carol negligently leaves in a public sidewalk a substantial excavation without a fence or warning lights, into which Gary falls at night. Darkness is an intervening, but not a superseding, cause of harm to Gary because it is a normal consequence of the situation caused by Carol's negligence. Therefore, Carol is liable to Gary. In contrast, if Carol negligently leaves an excavation in a public sidewalk into which Barbara intentionally shoves Gary, under the Second Restatement as a matter of law Carol is not liable to Gary because Barbara's conduct is a superseding cause that relieves Carol of liability. The Third Restatement rejects this exception to liability, stating,

> Whether Gary's harm is within the scope of Carol's liability for her negligence is an issue for the factfinder. The factfinder will have to determine whether the appropriate characterization of the harm to Gary is falling into an unguarded excavation site or being deliberately pushed into an unguarded excavation site and, if the latter, whether it is among the risks that made Carol negligent.

An intervening cause that is a foreseeable or normal consequence of the defendant's negligence is not a superseding cause. Thus, a person who negligently places another person or his property in imminent danger is liable for the injury sustained by a third-party rescuer who attempts to aid the imperiled person or his property. The same is true of attempts by the endangered person to escape the peril, as, for example, when a person swerves off the road to avoid a head-on collision with an automobile driven negligently on the wrong side of the road. It is commonly held that a negligent defendant is liable for the results of necessary medical treatment of the injured party, even if the treatment itself is negligent.

Petition of Kinsman Transit Co.
United States Court of Appeals, Second Circuit, 1964
338 F.2d 708
http://scholar.google.com/scholar_case?case=7870539560920231106&q=338+F.2d+708&hl=en&as_sdt=2,34

FACTS The *MacGilvray Shiras* was a ship owned by the Kinsman Transit Company. During the winter months when Lake Erie was frozen, the ship and others moored at docks on the Buffalo River. As oftentimes happened, one night an ice jam disintegrated upstream, sending large chunks of ice downstream. Chunks of ice began to pile up against the *Shiras*, which at that time was without power and manned only by a shipman. The ship broke loose when a negligently constructed "deadman" to which one mooring cable was attached pulled out of the ground. The "deadman" was operated by Continental Grain Company. The ship began moving down the S-shaped river stern first and struck another ship, the *Tewksbury*. The *Tewksbury* also broke loose from its mooring, and the two ships floated down the river together. Although the crew manning the Michigan Avenue Bridge downstream had been notified of the runaway ships, they failed to raise the bridge in time to avoid a collision because of a mix-up in the shift changeover. As a result, both ships crashed into the bridge and were wedged against the bank of the river. The two vessels substantially dammed the flow of the river, causing ice and water to back up and flood installations as far as three miles upstream. The injured parties brought this action for damages against Kinsman, Continental, and the city of Buffalo. The trial court found the three defendants liable, and they appealed from that decree.

DECISION Decree of trial court affirmed as to liability.

OPINION A ship insecurely moored in a fast-flowing river is a known danger to the owners of all ships and structures down the river and to persons upon them. Kinsman and Continental, then, owed a duty of care to all within the foreseeable reach of the ships' destructive path. Similarly, the city is liable to those who foreseeably could have been injured by its negligent failure to raise the bridge in time to prevent the collision. Finally, although the exact type of harm that occurred was not foreseeable, this does not prevent liability. The damage resulted from the same physical forces whose existence required the exercise of greater care than was displayed and was of the same general type that was foreseeable. In short, the unforeseeability of the exact developments and of the extent of the loss will not limit liability where the persons injured and the general nature of the damage done were foreseeable.

INTERPRETATION The unforeseeability of the exact manner and extent of a loss will not limit liability where the persons injured and the general nature of the damage were foreseeable.

CRITICAL THINKING QUESTION Compare this decision with that in the *Palsgraf* case and attempt to reconcile the two decisions.

HARM [8-4]

Harm to legally protected interest
courts determine which interests are protected from negligent interference

The plaintiff must *prove* that the defendant's negligent conduct proximately caused **harm to a legally protected interest**. Certain interests receive little or no protection against such conduct, while others receive full protection. The courts determine the extent of protection for a particular interest as a matter of law on the basis of social policy and expediency. For example, negligent conduct that is the proximate cause of harmful contact with the person of another is actionable. Thus, if Bob while driving his car negligently runs into Julie, a pedestrian, who is carefully crossing the street, Bob is liable for physical injuries Julie sustains as a result of the collision. On the other hand, if Bob's careless driving causes the car's side view mirror to brush Julie's coat but results in no physical injuries to her or damage to the coat, thus causing only offensive contact with Julie's person, Bob is not liable because Julie did not sustain harm to a legally protected interest.

The courts traditionally have been reluctant to allow recovery for negligently inflicted emotional distress. This view has gradually changed, and the majority of courts now hold a person liable for negligently causing emotional distress if bodily harm—such as a heart attack—results from the distress. And though, in the majority of states, a defendant is not liable for conduct resulting solely in emotional disturbance, some courts have recently allowed recovery of damages for negligently inflicted emotional distress even in the absence of physical harm when a person's negligent conduct places another in immediate danger of bodily harm. The Third Restatement follows the minority approach: a person whose negligent conduct places another in immediate danger of bodily harm is subject to liability to the other for serious emotional disturbance caused by reaction to the danger even though the negligent conduct did not cause any impact or bodily harm to the other. Furthermore, in a majority of states and under the Third Restatement liability for negligently inflicted emotional distress arises in the following situation: A negligently causes serious bodily injury to B. If C is a close family member of B and witnesses the injury to B, then A is liable to C for serious emotional disturbance C suffers from witnessing the event.

DEFENSES TO NEGLIGENCE [8-5]

Although a plaintiff has established by a preponderance of the evidence all the required elements of a negligence action, he may nevertheless fail to recover damages if the defendant proves a valid defense. As a general rule, any defense to an intentional tort is also available in an action in negligence. In addition, certain defenses are available in negligence cases that are not defenses to intentional torts. These are contributory negligence, comparative negligence, and assumption of risk. (See Figure 8-2 illustrating the defenses to a negligence action.)

Contributory Negligence [8-5a]

Contributory negligence is defined as conduct on the part of the plaintiff that falls below the standard to which he should conform for his own protection and that is a legal cause of the plaintiff's harm. The Third Restatement's definition of negligence as the failure of a person to exercise reasonable care under all the circumstances applies to the contributory negligence of the plaintiff. In those few jurisdictions that have not adopted comparative negligence (Alabama, Maryland, North Carolina, Virginia, and Washington, D.C.), the contributory negligence of the plaintiff, whether slight or extensive, prevents him from recovering *any* damages from the defendant.

Notwithstanding the contributory negligence of the plaintiff, if the defendant had a **last clear chance** to avoid injury to the plaintiff but did not avail himself of such a chance, the contributory negligence of the plaintiff does not bar his recovery of damages.

Contributory negligence
failure of a plaintiff to exercise reasonable care such that her failure is a legal cause of the plaintiff's harm

Last clear chance
final opportunity to avoid an injury

Figure 8-2 Defenses to a Negligence Action

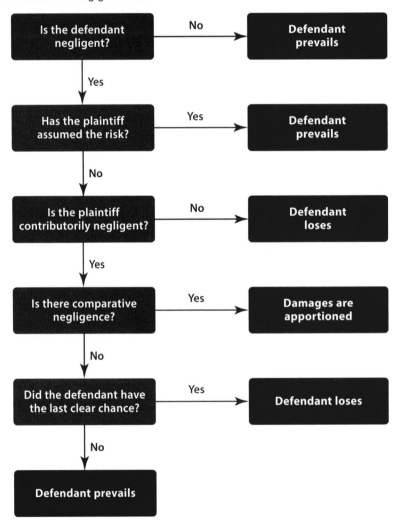

Comparative Negligence [8-5b]

Comparative negligence
doctrine dividing damages
between the plaintiff and
defendant where the
negligence of each has
caused the harm

The harshness of the contributory negligence doctrine has caused all but a few states to reject its all-or-nothing rule and to substitute the doctrine of **comparative negligence**, which is also called comparative fault or comparative responsibility. (In states adopting comparative negligence, the doctrine of last clear chance has been abandoned.)

Approximately a dozen states have judicially or legislatively adopted "pure" comparative negligence systems. (The ALI's Third Restatement of Torts: Apportionment of Liability advocates this form of comparative negligence.) Under ***pure comparative negligence*** damages are divided between the parties in proportion to the degree of fault or negligence found against them. For instance, Matthew negligently drives his automobile into Nancy, who is crossing against the light. Nancy sustains damages in the amount of $10,000 and sues Matthew. If the trier of fact (the jury or judge, depending on the case) determines that Matthew's negligence contributed 70 percent to Nancy's injury and that Nancy's contributory negligence contributed 30 percent to her injury, then Nancy would recover $7,000.

Most states have adopted the doctrine of "modified" comparative negligence. Under ***modified comparative negligence*** the plaintiff recovers as in pure comparative negligence unless her contributory negligence was equal to or greater than that of the defendant, in which case the plaintiff recovers nothing. Thus, in the previous example, if the trier of fact determined that Matthew's negligence and Nancy's contributory negligence contributed 40 percent and 60 percent, respectively, to her injury, then Nancy would not recover anything from Matthew.

Moore v. Kitsmiller
Court of Appeals of Texas, Twelfth District, Tyler, 2006
201 S.W.3d 147, *review denied*
http://scholar.google.com/scholar_case?q=201+S.W.3D+147&hl=en&as_sdt=2,34&case=5663712118613187322&scilh=0

FACTS In the spring of 2001, Kitsmiller purchased a house in Van Zandt County to use as rental property. In mid-June, he hired B & H Shaw Company, Inc. (B & H) to install a replacement septic tank in the back yard. The septic tank was located about two or three feet from a concrete stoop at the back door of the garage. B & H mounded dirt over the septic tank and the lateral lines going out from it upon completion. Sometime after B & H installed the septic tank, Kitsmiller smoothed out the mounds of dirt over the septic tank and lateral lines. Kitsmiller then leased the property to Moore and his wife on July 27. Kitsmiller testified that he viewed the back yard about a week or ten days prior to leasing the property to the Moores and stated that the dirt around the septic system looked firm.

On August 7, the Moores moved in. On August 11, Moore and his wife went into the back yard for the first time, and as he stepped off the stoop, he was unable to see the ground and could only see his wife and the bag of trash in his left arm. His wife testified that the ground looked flat. Moore testified that he had only taken a few steps off the stoop when his left leg sank into a hole, causing him to fall forward into his wife. As he tried to steady himself with his right foot, it hung and then sank, causing him to fall backward on his head and back. Moore testified that the injury to his back required surgery and affected his ability to earn a living.

Moore filed suit against Kitsmiller and B & H. He sought damages for past and future pain and suffering, past and future mental anguish, past and future physical impairment, and past and future loss of earning capacity. In their answers to Moore's suit, both Kitsmiller and B & H pleaded the affirmative defense of contributory negligence.

During the jury trial, Moore testified Kitsmiller should have notified him where the septic tank and lateral lines were located and that the dirt should have remained mounded over the tank and lines. Martin, an on-site septic tank complaint investigator for both the Texas Commission on Environmental Quality and Van Zandt County, testified that dirt should have been mounded over the septic tank and lateral lines, so that when the dirt settled, there would be no holes in the ground around the septic tank or lateral lines.

The jury determined that (1) both Kitsmiller and Moore were negligent, but B & H was not; (2) Kitsmiller was 51 percent negligent and Moore was 49 percent negligent; and (3) Moore was entitled to $210,000 in damages. On September 29, 2004, the trial court entered a judgment in favor of Moore and against Kitsmiller in the amount of $210,000 plus interest and costs. Applying comparative negligence, the trial court entered a modified final judgment on November 1, 2004, awarding Moore $107,100 plus interest and costs based upon Moore's contributory negligence. Moore appealed all issues involving his contributory negligence.

DECISION The judgment of the trial court is affirmed.

OPINION Contributory negligence contemplates an injured person's failure to use ordinary care regarding his or her own safety. This affirmative defense requires proof that the plaintiff was negligent and that the plaintiff's negligence proximately caused his or her injuries. Negligence requires proof of proximate cause. Proximate cause requires proof of both cause in fact and foreseeability. The test for cause in fact is whether the negligent act or omission was a substantial factor in bringing about an injury without which the harm would not have occurred. Foreseeability requires that a person of ordinary intelligence should have anticipated the danger created by a negligent act or omission.

Because comparative responsibility involves measuring the party's comparative fault in causing the plaintiff's injuries, it requires a preliminary finding that the plaintiff was in fact contributorily negligent. The standards and tests for determining contributory negligence ordinarily are the same as those for determining negligence. The burden of proof on the whole case is on the plaintiff. However, the burden of proof is on the defendant to prove the defense contributory negligence by a preponderance of the evidence.

The trier of fact may draw reasonable and logical inferences from the evidence. It is within the province of the jury to draw one reasonable inference from the evidence although another inference could have been made.

Moore testified that when he stepped off the stoop into the back yard for the first time on August 11, 2001, he could only see his wife and the plastic bag of trash he was carrying in his left hand. The jury was allowed to draw an inference from this evidence that Moore was not watching where he was walking. An individual must keep a proper lookout where he is walking, and a jury is allowed to make a reasonable inference that failure to do so was the proximate cause of his injuries. It was reasonable for the jury to make an inference from Moore's testimony that his failure to keep a proper lookout where he was walking contributed to the occurrence.

Moore contends that the only reasonable inference the jury could have made was that, even if he had been watching where he was walking, he would not have been able to avoid stepping in the holes because they were not visible to the naked eye. The jury could have made that inference, but chose not to do so. Thus the jury made a reasonable inference from the evidence in finding Moore contributorily negligent.

INTERPRETATION In cases in which both the plaintiff and defendant are negligent, under comparative negligence the law apportions damages between the parties in proportion to the degree of fault or negligence found against them.

CRITICAL THINKING QUESTION Is it fair that the plaintiff recovers damages despite being contributorily negligent? Explain.

Assumption of Risk [8-5c]

Express assumption of the risk
plaintiff's express consent to encounter a known danger

A plaintiff who has voluntarily and knowingly assumed the risk of harm arising from the negligent or reckless conduct of the defendant cannot recover for such harm. In **express assumption of the risk**, the plaintiff expressly agrees to assume the risk of harm from the defendant's conduct. Usually, but not always, such an agreement is by contract. Courts usually construe these exculpatory contracts strictly and will hold that the plaintiff has assumed the risk only if the terms of the agreement are clear and unequivocal. Moreover, some contracts for assumption of risk are considered unenforceable as a matter of public policy. See Chapter 13.

In *implied assumption of the risk*, the plaintiff voluntarily proceeds to encounter a known danger. Thus, a spectator entering a baseball park may be regarded as consenting that the players may proceed with the game without taking precautions to protect him from being hit by the ball. Most states have abolished or modified the defense of implied assumption of risk. Some have abandoned it entirely while others have merged implied assumption of risk into their comparative negligence systems.

Practical Advice

Consider having customers and clients sign waivers of liability and assumption of risk forms, but realize that many courts limit their effectiveness.

Reflecting this general trend the Third Restatement of Torts: Apportionment of Liability has abandoned the doctrine of implied voluntary assumption of risk: it is no longer a defense that the plaintiff was aware of a risk and voluntarily confronted it. But if a plaintiff's conduct in the face of a known risk is unreasonable, it might constitute contributory negligence, thereby reducing the plaintiff's recovery under comparative negligence. This new Restatement limits the defense of assumption of risk to express assumption of risk, which consists of a contract between the plaintiff and another person to absolve the other person from liability for future harm. Contractual assumption of risk may occur by written agreement, express oral agreement, or conduct that creates an implied-in-fact contract, as determined by the applicable rules of contract law. Some contractual assumptions of risk, however, are not enforceable under other areas of substantive law or as against public policy.

STRICT LIABILITY

Strict liability
liability for nonintentional and nonnegligent conduct

In some instances a person may be held liable for injuries he has caused even though he has not acted intentionally or negligently. Such liability is called **strict liability**, absolute liability, or liability without fault. The courts have determined that certain types of otherwise socially desirable activities pose sufficiently high risks of harm regardless of how carefully they are conducted, and that therefore those who carry on these activities should bear the cost of any harm that such activities cause. The doctrine of strict liability is not based on any particular fault of the defendant but on the nature of the activity in which he is engaging.

ACTIVITIES GIVING RISE TO STRICT LIABILITY [8-6]

We will discuss in this section the following activities that give rise to strict liability: (1) performing abnormally dangerous activities and (2) keeping animals. In addition, strict liability is imposed upon other activities. For example, nearly all states have imposed a limited form of strict product liability upon manufacturers and merchants who sell goods in a *defective condition* unreasonably dangerous to the user or consumer. This topic is covered in Chapter 22.

Abnormally dangerous activity

strict liability is imposed for any activity that (1) creates a foreseeable and highly significant risk of harm and (2) is not one of common usage

Practical Advice

Determine if any of your activities involve abnormally dangerous activities for which strict liability is imposed and be sure to obtain adequate insurance.

Abnormally Dangerous Activities [8-6a]

A person who carries on an abnormally dangerous activity is subject to strict liability for physical harm resulting from the activity. The Third Restatement provides that an activity is an **abnormally dangerous activity** if: "(1) the activity creates a foreseeable and highly significant risk of physical harm even when reasonable care is exercised by all actors; and (2) the activity is not one of common usage." The court determines whether an activity is abnormally dangerous by applying these factors. Activities to which the rule has been applied include collecting water or sewage in such quantity and location as to make it dangerous; storing explosives or flammable liquids in large quantities; blasting or pile driving; crop dusting; drilling for or refining oil in populated areas; and emitting noxious gases or fumes into a settled community. On the other hand, courts have refused to apply the rule where the activity is a "natural" use of the land, such as drilling for oil in the oil fields of Texas or transmitting gas through a gas pipe or electricity through electric wiring.

Klein v. Pyrodyne Corporation
Supreme Court of Washington, 1991
117 Wash.2d 1, 810 P.2d 917, as corrected 817 P.2d 1359
http://scholar.google.com/scholar_case?case=7983277736024137446&q=810+P.2d+917&hl=en&as_sclt=2,34

FACTS Pyrodyne Corporation contracted to conduct the fireworks display at the Western Washington State Fairgrounds in Puyallup, Washington, on July 4, 1987. During the fireworks display, one of the five-inch mortars was knocked into a horizontal position. A shell inside ignited and discharged, flying five hundred feet parallel to the earth and exploding near the crowd of onlookers. Danny and Marion Klein were injured by the explosion. Mr. Klein suffered facial burns and serious injuries to his eyes. The parties provided conflicting explanations for the improper discharge, and because all the evidence had exploded, there was no means of proving the cause of the misfire. The Kleins brought suit against Pyrodyne under the theory of strict liability for participating in an abnormally dangerous activity.

DECISION Judgment for the Kleins.

OPINION Under the modern doctrine of strict liability for abnormally dangerous activities, a defendant will be liable when he damages another by a thing or activity unduly dangerous and inappropriate to the place where it is maintained, in light of the character of that place and its surroundings. The Restatement of Torts provides that any party carrying on an "abnormally dangerous activity" is strictly liable and lists six factors that courts are to consider in determining whether an activity is "abnormally dangerous." These factors are (1) the existence of a high degree of risk of some harm to the person, land, or chattels of others; (2) the likelihood that the harm resulting from the activity will be great; (3) the inability to eliminate the risk by the exercise of reasonable care; (4) the extent to which the activity is not a matter of common usage; (5) the inappropriateness of the activity to the place

where it is carried on; and (6) the extent to which the activity's dangerous attributes outweigh its value to the community. Any one of these is not necessarily sufficient, and ordinarily a finding of strict liability will require several of them. The essential question is whether the risk the activity creates is so unusual as to justify the imposition of strict liability even though the activity is conducted with all reasonable care.

Factors (1), (2), and (3) are present in this case. Any time a person ignites aerial shells or rockets with the intention of sending them aloft in the presence of large crowds of people, a high risk of serious personal injury or property damage is created. That risk arises because of the possibility that a shell or rocket will malfunction or be misdirected. Furthermore, no matter how much care pyrotechnicians exercise, they cannot entirely eliminate the high risk inherent in setting off powerful explosives, such as fireworks, near crowds. Moreover, since relatively few persons conduct public fireworks displays, factor (4) is also present. Since the fairgrounds were an appropriate place for the fireworks and we as a society value fireworks on the Fourth of July more than we fear the risks, factors (5) and (6) are not present. Finding that four of the six conditions were present, the court holds that conducting public fireworks displays is an abnormally dangerous activity justifying strict liability.

INTERPRETATION The courts impose strict liability for harm resulting from an abnormally dangerous activity, as determined in light of the place, time, and manner in which the activity was conducted.

CRITICAL THINKING QUESTION If an activity is abnormally dangerous, should the law abolish it? Explain.

Keeping of animals

strict liability is imposed for wild animals and usually for trespassing domestic animals

Keeping of Animals [8-6b]

Strict liability for harm caused by animals existed at common law and continues today with some modification. As a general rule, those who possess animals for their own purposes do so at their peril and must protect against harm those animals may cause to people and property.

Trespassing Animals   Owners and possessors of animals, except for dogs and cats, are subject to strict liability for any physical harm their animals cause by trespassing on the property of another. There are two exceptions to this rule: (1) keepers of animals are not strictly liable for animals incidentally straying upon land immediately adjacent to a highway on which they are being lawfully driven, although the owner may be liable for negligence if he fails to control them properly and (2) in some western states, keepers of farm animals, typically cattle, are not strictly liable for harm caused by their trespassing animals that are allowed to graze freely.

Nontrespassing Animals   Owners and possessors of wild animals are subject to strict liability for physical harm caused by such animals, whether or not they are trespassing. Accordingly the owner or possessor is liable even if she has exercised reasonable care in attempting to restrain the wild animal. *Wild animals* are defined as those that, in the particular region in which they are kept, are known to be likely to inflict serious damage and that cannot be considered safe, no matter how domesticated they are. The Third Restatement has a similar definition: "A wild animal is an animal that belongs to a category of animals that have not been generally domesticated and that are likely, unless restrained, to cause personal injury." The court determines whether a category of animals is wild. Animals included in this category are bears, lions, elephants, monkeys, tigers, deer, and raccoons. On the other hand, iguanas, pigeons, and manatees are not considered wild animals because they do not pose a risk of causing substantial personal injury.

Domestic animals are those animals that are traditionally devoted to the service of humankind and that as a class are considered safe. Examples of domestic animals are dogs, cats, horses, cattle, and sheep. Owners and possessors of domestic animals are subject to strict liability if they knew, or had reason to know, of an animal's dangerous tendencies abnormal for the animal's category. The animal's dangerous propensity must be the cause of the harm. For example, a keeper is not liable for a dog that bites a human merely because he knows that the dog has a propensity to fight with other dogs. On the other hand, a person whose 150-pound Old English sheepdog has a propensity to jump enthusiastically on visitors would be liable for any damage caused by the dog's playfulness. About half of the states statutorily impose strict liability in dog cases even where the owner or possessor does not know, and did not have reason to know, of the dog's dangerous tendencies.

Palumbo v. Nikirk

Supreme Court, Appellate Division, Second Department, New York, 2009

59 A.D.3d 691, 874 N.Y.S.2d 222, 2009 N.Y. Slip Op. 01454

http://scholar.google.com/scholar_case?case=7266290354304468850&q=2009+NY+Slip+Op+1454&hl=en&as_sdt=2,34

FACTS The plaintiff (Palumbo), a mail carrier, sustained injuries when he allegedly was bitten and attacked by a dog on the front steps of the defendants' (Nikirk's) house as he attempted to deliver the mail. The plaintiff, who crossed over the defendants' lawn and driveway from the house next door, and whose view of the dog was obstructed by a bush, did not see the dog or hear it bark until he opened the lid of the mailbox and was bitten. The plaintiff brought an action to recover damages for personal injuries. The trial court granted the defendants' motion for summary judgment dismissing the complaint. The plaintiff appealed.

DECISION Summary judgment is affirmed.

OPINION To recover upon a theory of strict liability in tort for a dog bite or attack, a plaintiff must prove that the dog had vicious propensities and that the owner of the dog, or person in control of the premises where the dog was, knew or should have known of such propensities. Vicious propensities include the "propensity to do any act that might endanger the safety of the persons and property of others in a given situation."

Here, the defendants established their *prima facie* entitlement to judgment as a matter of law by presenting evidence that the dog had never bitten, jumped, or growled at anyone prior to the incident in question, nor had the dog exhibited any other aggressive or vicious behavior. In opposition, the plaintiff failed to come forward with any proof that the dog had ever previously bitten anyone or exhibited any vicious propensities. Furthermore, the presence of a "Beware of Dog" sign on the premises, the breed of the dog, and the owner's testimony that the dog was always on a leash were insufficient to raise a triable issue of fact as to the dog's vicious propensities in the absence of any evidence that prior to this incident the dog exhibited any fierce or hostile tendencies.

INTERPRETATION Owners and possessors of domestic animals are subject to strict liability if they knew, or had reason to know, of the animal's vicious propensities.

CRITICAL THINKING QUESTION Is the burden on the plaintiff to establish the animal's prior vicious propensities too difficult to sustain?

DEFENSES TO STRICT LIABILITY [8-7]

Contributory negligence
is *not* a defense to strict liability

Comparative negligence
some states apply this doctrine to some strict liability cases

Assumption of risk
express assumption of risk is a defense to an action based upon strict liability; some states apply implied assumption of risk to strict liability cases

Because the strict liability of one who carries on an abnormally dangerous activity or keeps animals is not based on his negligence, the ordinary **contributory negligence** of the plaintiff is *not* a defense to such liability. The law in imposing strict liability places the full responsibility for preventing harm on the defendant. Nevertheless, some states apply the doctrine of **comparative negligence** to some types of strict liability. The Third Restatement provides that if the plaintiff has been contributorily negligent in failing to take reasonable precautions, the plaintiff's recovery in a strict-liability claim for physical harm caused by abnormally dangerous activities or keeping of animals is reduced in accordance with the share of comparative responsibility assigned to the plaintiff.

Under the Second Restatement of Torts voluntary **assumption of risk** is a defense to an action based on strict liability. If the owner of an automobile knowingly and voluntarily parks the vehicle in a blasting zone, he may not recover for harm to his automobile. The assumption of risk, however, must be voluntary. Where blasting operations are established, for example, the possessor of nearby land is not required to move away and may recover for harm suffered.

The more recent Third Restatement of Torts: Apportionment of Liability has abandoned the doctrine of implied voluntary assumption of risk in tort actions generally: it is no longer a defense that the plaintiff was aware of a risk and voluntarily confronted it. This new Restatement limits the defense of assumption of risk to express assumption of risk, which consists of a contract between the plaintiff and another person to absolve the other person from liability for future harm.

ETHICAL DILEMMA

What Are the Obligations of a Bartender to His Patrons?

Facts John Campbell, age twenty-two, was recently hired as a management trainee for the Stanton Hotel. The Stanton features a health club, swimming pool, ski slopes, and boating facilities. The management trainee program is an eighteen-month program during which the trainees rotate jobs to gain exposure to all phases of hotel operations. There is no formal orientation, and each trainee is randomly assigned to jobs.

John's first assignment was at the restaurant/bar working with Mr. Arnold, a bartender who was fifty years old and quite experienced. Mr. Arnold commented to John that John was lucky to be working the bar during the skiing season. Mr. Arnold explained that skiers frequently come in from the slopes to warm up. He told John that all tips are shared equally and that the

more it snows and the colder it gets, the better the bar business.

One day, John observed that Mr. Arnold was serving drinks to two young men who appeared to be about twenty-two or twenty-three. John overheard the men planning to ski an hour or so more and then drive over to meet friends at a neighboring hotel. One of the men appeared self-contained and unaffected by the drinks. His friend, however, was gradually getting louder, although he was not making a disturbance.

John noticed that Mr. Arnold had already served three rounds of bourbon to the men. When Mr. Arnold was preparing the fourth round, John said to him, "Don't you think they've had enough? They're going back on the slopes."

Mr. Arnold replied, "Kid, you've got a lot to learn."

Social, Policy, and Ethical Considerations
1. What action, if any, should John take?
2. What are the potential risks to the two men who are drinking? Are public safety issues involved?
3. What management policies should the hotel institute with regard to its liquor policies and athletic operations?
4. Do the drinking companions bear an ethical responsibility for each other's drinking?
5. How should society balance the interests of freedom of business and individual conduct (i.e., drinking) with the competing interests of protecting public safety?

The Third Restatement: Liability for Physical and Emotional Harm recognizes a limitation on strict liability for abnormally dangerous activities and keeping of animals when the victim suffers harm as a result of exposure to the animal or activity resulting from the victim's securing some benefit from that exposure. The Third Restatement gives the following example: "if the plaintiff is a veterinarian or a groomer who accepts an animal such as a dog from the defendant, the plaintiff is deriving financial benefits from the acceptance of the animal, and is beyond the scope of strict liability, even if the dog can be deemed abnormally dangerous."

CHAPTER SUMMARY

Negligence

Breach of Duty of Care

Definition of Negligence conduct that falls below the standard established by law for the protection of others against unreasonable risk of harm

Reasonable Person Standard degree of care that a reasonable person would exercise under all the circumstances

- *Children* must conform to conduct of a reasonable person of the same age, intelligence, and experience under all the circumstances
- *Physical Disability* a disabled person's conduct must conform to that of a reasonable person under the same disability
- *Mental Disability* a mentally disabled person is held to the reasonable person standard of a reasonable person who is not mentally deficient
- *Superior Skill or Knowledge* if a person has skills or knowledge beyond those possessed by most others, these skills or knowledge are circumstances to be taken into account in determining whether the person has acted with reasonable care
- *Standard for Emergencies* the reasonable person standard applies, but an unexpected emergency is considered part of the circumstances
- *Violation of Statute* if the statute applies, the violation is negligence *per se* in most states

Duty to Act a person is under a duty to all others at all times to exercise reasonable care for the safety of the others' person and property; however, except in special circumstances, no one is required to aid another in peril

Duties of Possessors of Land

- *Second Restatement* a land possessor owes the following duties: (1) not to injure intentionally *trespassers*, (2) to warn *licensees* of known dangerous conditions licensees are unlikely to discover for themselves, and (3) to exercise reasonable care to protect *invitees* against dangerous conditions land possessor should know of but invitees are unlikely to discover
- *Third Restatement* adopts a unitary duty of reasonable care to all entrants on the land except for flagrant trespassers: a land possessor must use reasonable care to investigate and discover dangerous conditions and must use reasonable care to eliminate or improve those dangerous conditions that are known or should have been discovered by the exercise of reasonable care

Res Ipsa Loquitur permits the jury to infer both negligent conduct and causation

Factual Cause and Scope of Liability

Factual Cause the defendant's conduct is a factual cause of the harm when the harm would not have occurred absent the conduct

Scope of Liability (Proximate Cause) Liability is limited to those harms that result from the risks that made the defendant's conduct tortious

- *Foreseeability* excludes liability for harms that were sufficiently unforeseeable at the time of the defendant's tortious conduct that they were not among the risks that made the defendant negligent
- *Superseding Cause* an intervening act that relieves the defendant of liability

Harm

Burden of Proof plaintiff must prove that defendant's negligent conduct caused harm to a legally protected interest

Harm to Legally Protected Interest courts determine which interests are protected from negligent interference

Defenses to Negligence	**Contributory Negligence** failure of a plaintiff to exercise reasonable care for his own protection, which in a few states prevents the plaintiff from recovering anything
	Comparative Negligence damages are divided between the parties in proportion to their degree of negligence; applies in almost all states
	Assumption of Risk plaintiff's express consent to encounter a known danger; some states still apply implied assumption of the risk

Strict Liability

Activities Giving Rise to Strict Liability	**Definition of Strict Liability** liability for nonintentional and nonnegligent conduct
	Abnormally Dangerous Activity strict liability is imposed for any activity that (1) creates a foreseeable and highly significant risk of harm and (2) is not one of common usage
	Keeping of Animals strict liability is imposed for wild animals and usually for trespassing domestic animals
Defenses to Strict Liability	**Contributory Negligence** is not a defense to strict liability
	Comparative Negligence some states apply this doctrine to some strict liability cases
	Assumption of Risk express assumption of risk is a defense to an action based upon strict liability; some states apply implied assumption of risk to strict liability cases

QUESTIONS

1. A statute that requires railroads to fence their tracks is construed as intended solely to prevent injuries to animals straying onto the right-of-way. B & A Railroad Company fails to fence its tracks. Two of Calvin's cows wander onto the track. Nellie is hit by a train. Elsie is poisoned by weeds growing beside the track. For which cow(s), if any, is B & A Railroad Company liable to Calvin? Why?

2. Martha invites John to come to lunch. Martha knows that her private road is dangerous to travel, having been heavily eroded by recent rains. She doesn't warn John of the condition, reasonably believing that he will notice the deep ruts and exercise sufficient care. John's attention, while driving over, is diverted from the road by the screaming of his child, who has been stung by a bee. He fails to notice the condition of the road, hits a rut, and skids into a tree. If John is not contributorily negligent, is Martha liable to John?

3. Nathan is run over by a car and left lying in the street. Sam, seeing Nathan's helpless state, places him in his car for the purpose of taking him to the hospital. Sam drives negligently into a ditch, causing additional injury to Nathan. Is Sam liable to Nathan?

4. Vance was served liquor while he was an intoxicated patron of the Clear Air Force Station Noncommissioned Officers' Club. He later injured himself as a result of his intoxication. An Alaska state statute makes it a crime to give or to sell liquor to intoxicated persons. Vance has brought an action seeking damages for the injuries he suffered. Could Vance successfully argue that the United States was negligent *per se* by its employee's violation of the statute?

5. A statute requires all vessels traveling on the Great Lakes to provide lifeboats. One of Winston Steamship Company's boats is sent out of port without a lifeboat. Perry, a sailor, falls overboard in a storm so heavy that had there been a lifeboat it could not have been launched. Perry drowns. Is Winston liable to Perry's estate?

6. Lionel is negligently driving an automobile at excessive speed. Reginald's negligently driven car crosses the center line of the highway and scrapes the side of Lionel's car, damaging its fenders. As a result, Lionel loses control of his car, which goes into the ditch, wrecking the car and causing personal injuries to Lionel. What can Lionel recover?

7. Ellen, the owner of a baseball park, is under a duty to the entering public to provide a reasonably sufficient number of screened seats to protect those who desire such protection against the risk of being hit by batted balls. Ellen fails to do so.
   a. Frank, a customer entering the park, is unable to find a screened seat and, although fully aware of the risk, sits in an unscreened seat. Frank is struck and injured by a batted ball. Is Ellen liable?
   b. Gretchen, Frank's wife, has just arrived from Germany and is viewing baseball for the first time. Without asking any questions, she follows Frank to a seat. After the batted ball hits Frank, it caroms into Gretchen, injuring her. Is Ellen liable to Gretchen?

8. CC Railroad is negligent in failing to give warning of the approach of its train to a crossing and thereby endangers Larry, a blind man who is about to cross. Mildred, a bystander, in a reasonable effort to save Larry, rushes onto the track to push Larry out of danger. Although Mildred acts as carefully as possible, she is struck and injured by the train.
   a. Can Mildred recover from Larry?
   b. Can Mildred recover from CC Railroad?

9. Two thugs in an alley in Manhattan held up an unidentified man. When the thieves departed with his possessions, the man quickly gave chase. He had almost caught one when the thief managed to force his way into an empty taxicab stopped at a traffic light. The Peerless Transport Company owned the cab. The thief pointed his gun at the driver's head and ordered him to drive on. The driver started to follow the directions while closely pursued by a posse of good citizens, but then suddenly jammed on the brakes and jumped out of the car to safety. The thief also jumped out, but the car traveled on, injuring Mrs. Cordas and her two children. The Cordases then brought an action for damages, claiming that the cab driver was negli-gent in jumping to safety and leaving the moving vehicle uncontrolled. Was the cab driver negligent? Explain.

10. Timothy keeps a pet chimpanzee that is thoroughly tamed and accustomed to playing with its owner's children. The chimpanzee escapes, despite every precaution to keep it on the owner's premises. It approaches a group of children. Wanda, the mother of one of the children, erroneously think-ing the chimpanzee is about to attack the children, rushes to her child's assistance. In her hurry and excitement, she stum-bles and falls, breaking her leg. Can Wanda recover from Timothy for her personal injuries?

CASE PROBLEMS

11. Hawkins slipped and fell on a puddle of water just inside the automatic door to the H. E. Butt Grocery Company's store. The water had been tracked into the store by customers and blown through the door by a strong wind. The store manager was aware of the puddle and had mopped it up several times earlier in the day. Still, no signs had been placed to warn store patrons of the danger. Hawkins brought an action to recover damages for injuries sustained in the fall. Was the store negli-gent in its conduct?

12. Escola, a waitress, was injured when a bottle of soda exploded in her hand while she was putting it into the restaurant's cooler. The bottle came from a shipment that had remained under the counter for thirty-six hours after being delivered by the bottling company. The bottler had subjected the bottle to the method of testing for defects commonly used in the industry, and there is no evidence that Escola or anyone else did anything to damage the bottle between its delivery and the explosion. Escola brought an action against the bottler for damages. Because she is unable to show any specific acts of negligence on its part, she seeks to rely on the doctrine of *res ipsa loquitur*. Should she be able to recover on this theory? Explain.

13. Hunn injured herself when she slipped and fell on a loose plank while walking down some steps. The night before, while entering the hotel, she had noticed that the steps were dan-gerous, and although she knew from her earlier stays at the hotel that another exit was available, she chose that morning to leave via the dangerous steps. The hotel was aware of the hazard, as one of three other guests who had fallen that night had reported his accident to the desk clerk then on duty. Still, the hotel did not place cautionary signs on the steps to warn of the danger, and the steps were not roped off or otherwise excluded from use. Hunn brought an action against the hotel for injuries she sustained as a result of her fall. Should she recover? Explain.

14. Fredericks, a hotel owner, had a dog named Sport that he had trained as a watchdog. When Vincent Zarek, a guest at the hotel, leaned over to pet the dog, it bit him. Although Sport had never bitten anyone before, Fredericks was aware of the dog's violent tendencies and, therefore, did not allow it to roam around the hotel alone. Vincent brought an action for injuries sustained when the dog bit him. Is Fredericks liable for the actions of his dog? Explain.

15. Led Foot drives his car carelessly into another car. The second car contains dynamite, a fact which Led had no way of know-ing. The collision causes an explosion that shatters a window of a building half a block away on another street. The flying glass inflicts serious cuts on Sally, who is working at a desk near the window. The explosion also harms Vic, who is walk-ing on the sidewalk near the point of the collision. Toward whom is Led Foot negligent?

16. A foul ball struck Marie Uzdavines on the head while she was watching the Metropolitan Baseball Club (The Mets) play the Philadelphia Phillies at the Mets' home stadium in New York. The ball came through a hole in a screen designed to protect spectators sitting behind home plate. The screen contained several holes that had been repaired with baling wire, a lighter weight wire than that used in the original screen. Although the manager of the stadium makes no formal inspections of the screen, his employees do try to repair the holes as they find them. Weather conditions, rust deterioration, and base-balls hitting the screen are the chief causes of these holes. The owner of the stadium, the city of New York, leases the sta-dium to the Mets and replaces the entire screen every two years. Uzdavines sued the Mets for negligence under the doc-trine of *res ipsa loquitur*. Is this an appropriate case for *res ipsa loquitur*? Explain.

17. Two-year-old David Allen was bitten by Joseph Whitehead's dog while he was playing on the porch at the Allen residence. Allen suffered facial cuts, a severed muscle in his left eye, a hole in his left ear, and scarring over his forehead. Through his father, David sued Whitehead, claiming that, as owner, Whitehead is responsible for his dog's actions. Whitehead admitted that (a) the dog was large, mean-looking, and fre-quently barked at neighbors; (b) the dog was allowed to roam wild; and (c) the dog frequently chased and barked at cars. He stated, however, that (a) the dog was friendly and often played with his and neighbors' children; (b) he had not received previous complaints about the dog; (c) the dog was neither aggressive nor threatening; and (d) the dog had never bitten anyone before this incident. Is Whitehead liable?

18. Larry VanEgdom, in an intoxicated state, bought alcoholic beverages from the Hudson Municipal Liquor Store in Hudson, South Dakota. An hour later, VanEgdom, while driving a car, struck and killed Guy William Ludwig, who was stopped on his motorcycle at a stop sign. Lela Walz, as special administrator of Ludwig's estate, brought an action against the city of Hudson, which operated the liquor store, for the wrongful death of Ludwig. Walz alleged that the store employee was negligent in selling intoxicating beverages to VanEgdom when he knew or could have observed that VanEgdom was drunk. Decision?

19. Carolyn Falgout accompanied William Wardlaw as a social guest to Wardlaw's brother's camp. After both parties had consumed intoxicating beverages, Falgout walked onto a pier that was then only partially completed. Wardlaw had requested that she not go on the pier. Falgout said, "Don't tell me what to do," and proceeded to walk on the pier. Wardlaw then asked her not to walk past the completed portion of the pier. She ignored his warnings and walked to the pier's end. When returning to the shore, Falgout got her shoe caught between the boards. She fell, hanging by her foot, with her head and arms in the water. Wardlaw rescued Falgout, who had seriously injured her knee and leg. She sued Wardlaw for negligence. Decision?

20. Joseph Yania, a coal strip-mine operator, and Boyd Ross visited a coal strip-mining operation owned by John Bigan to discuss a business matter with Bigan. On Bigan's property there were several cuts and trenches he had dug to remove the coal underneath. While there, Bigan asked the two men to help him pump water from one of these cuts in the earth. This particular cut contained water eight to ten feet in depth with sidewalls or embankments sixteen to eighteen feet in height. The two men agreed, and the process began with Ross and Bigan entering the cut and standing at the point where the pump was located. Yania stood at the top of one of the cut's sidewalls. Apparently, Bigan taunted Yania into jumping into the water from the top of the sidewall—a height of sixteen to eighteen feet. As a result, Yania drowned. His widow brought a negligence action against Bigan. She claims that Bigan was negligent "(1) by urging, enticing, taunting, and inveigling Yania to jump into the water; (2) by failing to warn Yania of a dangerous condition on the land; and (3) by failing to go to Yania's rescue after he jumped into the water." Was Bigan negligent?

TAKING SIDES

Rebecca S. Dukat arrived at Mockingbird Lanes, a bowling alley in Omaha, Nebraska, at approximately 6:00 P.M. to bowl in her league game. The bowling alley's parking lot and adjacent sidewalk were covered with snow and ice. Dukat proceeded to walk into the bowling alley on the only sidewalk provided in and out of the building. She testified that she noticed the sidewalk was icy. After bowling three games and drinking three beers, Dukat left the bowling alley at approximately 9:00 P.M. She retraced her steps on the same sidewalk, which was still covered with ice and in a condition that, according to Frank Jameson, general manager of Mockingbird Lanes, was "unacceptable" if the bowling alley were open to customers. As Dukat proceeded along the sidewalk to her car, she slipped, attempted to catch herself by reaching toward a car, and fell. She suffered a fracture of both bones in her left ankle as well as a ruptured ligament. Dukat sued Mockingbird Lanes, seeking damages for her for personal injuries. Mockingbird denied liability for Dukat's personal injuries.

a. What arguments would support Dukat's claim for her personal injuries?

b. What arguments would support Mockingbird's denial of liability for Dukat's personal injuries?

c. Which side should prevail? Explain.

Introduction to Contracts

A promise is a debt, and I certainly wish to keep all my promises to the letter; I can give no better advice.

Geoffrey Chaucer
The Man of Law in the *Canterbury Tales*
(1387)

CHAPTER OUTCOMES

After reading and studying this chapter, you should be able to:

1. Distinguish between contracts that are covered by the Uniform Commercial Code and those covered by the common law.

2. List the essential elements of a contract.

3. Distinguish among (a) express and implied contracts; (b) unilateral and bilateral contracts; (c) valid, void, voidable, and unenforceable agreements; and (d) executed and executory contracts.

4. Explain the doctrine of promissory estoppel.

5. Identify the three elements of enforceable quasi contract and explain how it differs from a contract.

Every business enterprise, whether large or small, must enter into contracts with its employees, its suppliers of goods and services, and its customers in order to conduct its business operations. Thus, contract law is an important subject for the business manager. Contract law is also basic to fields of law treated in other parts of this book, such as agency, partnerships, corporations, sales of personal property, negotiable instruments, and secured transactions.

Even the most common transaction may involve many contracts. For example, in a typical contract for the sale of land, the seller promises to transfer title, or right of ownership, to the land; and the buyer promises to pay an agreed-upon purchase price. In addition, the seller may promise to pay certain taxes, and the buyer may promise to assume a mortgage on the property or to pay the purchase price to a creditor of the seller. If the parties have lawyers, they very likely have contracts with these lawyers. If the seller deposits the proceeds of the sale in a bank, he enters into a contract with the bank. If the buyer rents the property, he enters into a contract with the tenant. When one of the parties leaves his car in a parking lot to attend to any of these matters, he assumes a contractual relationship with the owner of the lot. In short, nearly every business transaction is based on contract and the expectations the agreed-upon promises create. It is, therefore, essential that you know the legal requirements for making binding contracts.

DEVELOPMENT OF THE LAW OF CONTRACTS [9-1]

Contract law, like the law as a whole, is not static. It has undergone—and is still undergoing—enormous changes. In the nineteenth century, almost total freedom in forming contracts was the rule. However, contract formation also involved many technicalities, and the courts imposed contract liability only when the parties complied strictly with the required formalities.

During the twentieth century, many of the formalities of contract formation were relaxed, and as a result, contractual obligations usually are recognized whenever the parties clearly intend to be bound. In addition, an increasing number of promises are now enforced in certain circumstances, even though such promises do not comply strictly with the basic requirements of a contract. In brief, the twentieth century left its mark on contract law by limiting the absolute freedom of contract and, at the same time, by relaxing the requirements of contract formation. Accordingly, we can say that it is considerably easier now both to get into a contract and to get out of one.

Common Law [9-1a]

Contracts are primarily governed by state common law. As we mentioned in Chapter 1, the Restatements, prepared by the American Law Institute (ALI), present many important areas of the common law, including contracts. Although the Restatements are not law in themselves, they are highly persuasive in the courts. An orderly presentation of the common law of contracts is found in the Restatements of the Law of Contracts, valuable authoritative reference works extensively relied on and quoted in reported judicial opinions. Between 1959 and 1981, the ALI adopted and promulgated a second edition of the Restatement of the Law of Contracts, which revised and superseded the first Restatement of the Law of Contracts. This text will refer to the second Restatement of the Law of Contracts simply as the "Restatement."

There are two principal types of contracts: (1) business-to-business contracts (commercial contracts) and (2) business-to-consumer contracts (consumer contracts). The common law and the Restatement generally apply the same rules to both commercial and consumer contracts. (The Uniform Commercial Code's Article 2, discussed in the following paragraphs, for the most part also does not distinguish between sales of goods to consumers and sales between commercial parties.)

In 2012 the ALI began a new project: the Restatement of the Law of Consumer Contracts. This new project will focus on the rules of contract law that treat consumer contracts differently from commercial contracts. It includes regulatory rules that are prominently applied in consumer protection law. The project will cover common law as well as statutory and regulatory law.

The Uniform Commercial Code [9-1b]

Uniform Commercial Code (UCC)
Article 2 of the UCC governs the sales of goods

Sale
the transfer of title from seller to buyer

Goods
tangible personal property

Personal property
property other than an interest in land

The sale of personal property is a large part of commercial activity. Article 2 of the **Uniform Commercial Code** (the Code, or UCC) governs such sales in all states except Louisiana. A **sale** consists of the passing of title to goods from seller to buyer for a price. A contract for sale includes both a present sale of goods and a contract to sell goods at a future time. The Code essentially defines **goods** as tangible personal property. **Personal property** is any property other than an interest in real property (land). For example, the purchase of a television set, an automobile, or a textbook is a sale of goods. All such transactions are governed by Article 2 of the Code, but in cases in which the Code has not specifically modified general contract law, the common law of contracts continues to apply. In other words, the law of sales is a specialized part of the general law of contracts, and the law of contracts governs unless specifically displaced by the Code. See *Pittsley v. Houser* in Chapter 19.

Amendments to Article 2 were promulgated in 2003 to accommodate electronic commerce and to reflect development of business practices, changes in other law, and other practical issues. Because no states had adopted them and prospects for enactment in the near future were bleak, the 2003 amendments to UCC Articles 2 and 2A were withdrawn in 2011. However, at least forty-five states have adopted the 2001 Revisions to Article 1, which applies to all of the articles of the Code.

Figure 9-1 Law Governing Contracts

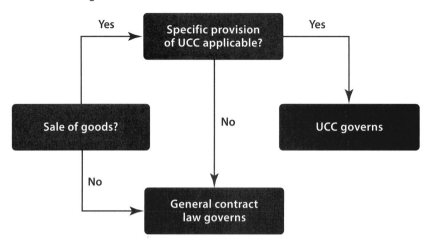

Common law

most contracts are primarily governed by state common law, including contracts involving employment, services, insurance, real property, patents, and copyrights

Real property

land and anything attached to it

Types of Contracts Outside the Code [9-1c]

General contract law (**common law**) governs all contracts outside the scope of the Code. Such contracts play a significant role in commercial activities. For example, the Code does *not* apply to employment contracts, service contracts, insurance contracts, contracts involving **real property** (land and anything attached to it, including buildings, as well as any right, privilege, or power in the real property, including leases, mortgages, options, and easements), and contracts for the sale of intangibles such as patents and copyrights. These transactions continue to be governed by general contract law. Figure 9-1 summarizes the types of law governing contracts.

See *Fox v. Mountain West Electric, Inc.*, later in this chapter.

GOING GLOBAL

What about international contracts?

The legal issues inherent in domestic commercial contracts also arise in international contracts. Moreover, certain additional issues, such as differences in language, customs, legal systems, and currency, are peculiar to international contracts. An international contract should specify its official language and define all of the significant legal terms it incorporates. In addition, it should specify the acceptable currency (or currencies) and payment method. The contract should include a choice of law clause designating what law will govern any breach or dispute regarding the contract, and a choice of forum clause designating whether the parties will resolve disputes through one nation's court system or through third-party arbitration. (The United Nations

Committee on International Trade Law and the International Chamber of Commerce have promulgated arbitration rules that have won broad international acceptance.) Finally, the contract should include a *force majeure* (unavoidable superior force) clause apportioning the liabilities and responsibilities of the parties in the event of an unforeseeable occurrence, such as a typhoon, tornado, flood, earthquake, nuclear disaster, or war, including civil war.

The United Nations Convention on Contracts for the International Sales of Goods (CISG), which has been ratified by the United States and at least seventy-nine other countries, governs all contracts for the international sales of goods between parties located in different nations that have ratified the CISG. Because treaties are

federal law, the CISG supersedes the Uniform Commercial Code in any situation to which either could apply. The CISG includes provisions dealing with interpretation, trade usage, contract formation, obligations, and remedies of sellers and buyers, and risk of loss. Parties to an international sales contract may, however, expressly exclude CISG governance from their contract. The CISG specifically excludes sales of (1) goods bought for personal, family, or household use; (2) ships or aircraft; and (3) electricity. In addition, it does not apply to contracts in which the primary obligation of the party furnishing the goods consists of supplying labor or services. The CISG is discussed in Chapters 19 through 23.

Figure 9-2 Contractual and Noncontractual Promises

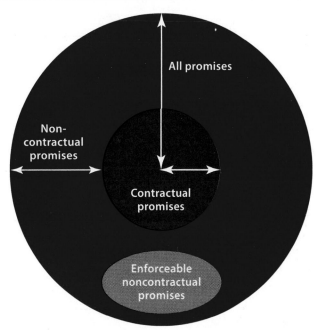

DEFINITION OF CONTRACT [9-2]

Contract

binding agreement that the courts will enforce

Put simply, a **contract** is a binding agreement that the courts will enforce. The Restatement Second, Contracts more precisely defines a contract as "a promise or a set of promises for the breach of which the law gives a remedy, or the performance of which the law in some way recognizes a duty." A *promise* manifests or demonstrates the intention to act or to refrain from acting in a specified manner.

Those promises that meet *all* of the essential requirements of a binding contract are contractual and will be enforced. All other promises are *not* contractual, and usually no legal remedy is available for a **breach** of, or a failure to properly perform, these promises. (The remedies provided for breach of contract—which include compensatory damages, equitable remedies, reliance damages, and restitution—are discussed in Chapter 18.) Thus, a promise may be contractual (and therefore binding) or noncontractual. In other words, all contracts are promises, but not all promises are contracts, as illustrated by Figure 9-2.

Breach

failure to properly perform a contractual obligation

REQUIREMENTS OF A CONTRACT [9-3]

The four basic requirements of a contract are as follows:

1. **Mutual assent.** The parties to a contract must manifest by words or conduct that they have agreed to enter into a contract. The usual method of showing mutual assent is by offer and acceptance.
2. **Consideration.** Each party to a contract must intentionally exchange a legal benefit or incur a legal detriment as an inducement to the other party to make a return exchange.
3. **Legality of object.** The purpose of a contract must not be criminal, tortious, or otherwise against public policy.
4. **Capacity.** The parties to a contract must have contractual capacity. Certain persons, such as adjudicated incompetents, have no legal capacity to contract, whereas others, such as minors, incompetent persons, and intoxicated persons, have limited capacity to contract. All others have full contractual capacity.

In addition, though in a limited number of instances a contract must be evidenced by a writing to be enforceable, in most cases an oral contract is binding and enforceable. Moreover, there must be an *absence* of invalidating conduct, such as duress, undue influence, misrepresentation,

Figure 9-3 Validity of Agreements

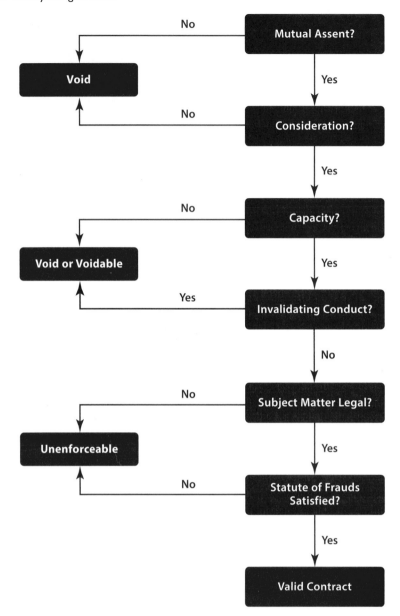

or mistake. (See Figure 9-3.) As the *Steinberg v. Chicago Medical School* case shows, a promise meeting all of these requirements is contractual and legally binding. However, if any requirement is unmet, the promise is noncontractual. We will consider these requirements separately in succeeding chapters.

Steinberg v. Chicago Medical School
Illinois Court of Appeals, 1976
41 Ill.App.3d 804, 354 N.E.2d 586
http://scholar.google.com/scholar_case?case=13765816040578352414&q=354+N.E.2d+586&hl=en&as_sdt=2,34

FACTS Robert Steinberg applied for admission to the Chicago Medical School as a first-year student and paid an application fee of $15. The school, a private educational institution, rejected his application. Steinberg brought an action against the school, claiming that it did not evaluate his and other applications according to the academic entrance criteria printed in the school's bulletin. Instead, he argues, the school based its decisions primarily on nonacademic considerations, such as family connections between the applicant and the school's faculty and members of its board of trustees and the ability of the applicant or his family to donate large sums of money to the school. Steinberg asserts that by evaluating his application according to these unpublished criteria, the school breached the contract it had created when it accepted his application fee. The trial court granted the defendant's motion to dismiss, and Steinberg appealed.

DECISION Trial court's dismissal reversed and case remanded.

OPINION A contract is a promise or set of promises for the breach of which the law gives a remedy. "A contract's essential requirements are: competent parties, valid subject matter, legal consideration, mutuality of obligation and mutuality of agreement." Generally, parties may contract in any situation where there is no legal prohibition. To be binding, however, the terms must be "reasonably certain and definite." The contract must also be supported by consideration. Defined in its most general terms, consideration is some benefit accruing to one party or some detriment undertaken by the other, such as the payment of or promise to pay money. In addition, the parties must mutually agree to the contract's essential terms and conditions to make the contract binding. Mutual consent is gathered from the language employed by the parties or manifested by their words or acts.

In this situation, the school's promise to evaluate the applications according to academic standards is stated in a "definitive manner" in its bulletin. Steinberg accepted this in good faith, and his $15 application fee served as valid consideration. When the school accepted this money, it bound itself to honor the obligations stated in its bulletin. Therefore, its failure to use the stated academic criteria in evaluating applications constituted a breach of its contractual obligation to Steinberg.

INTERPRETATION An agreement meeting all of the requirements of a contract is binding and legally enforceable.

ETHICAL QUESTION Is it ethical for a school to consider any factors other than an applicant's merit? Explain.

CRITICAL THINKING QUESTION Should the courts resolve this type of dispute on the basis of contract law? Explain.

Practical Advice

Whenever possible, try to use written express contracts that specify all of the important terms rather than using implied in fact contracts.

Implied in fact contract
contract in which agreement of the parties is inferred from their conduct

Express contract
agreement of parties that is stated in words either in writing or orally

CLASSIFICATION OF CONTRACTS [9-4]

Contracts can be classified according to various characteristics, such as method of formation, content, and legal effect. The standard classifications are (1) express or implied contracts; (2) bilateral or unilateral contracts; (3) valid, void, voidable, or unenforceable contracts; and (4) executed or executory contracts. These classifications are not mutually exclusive. For example, a contract may be express, bilateral, valid, and executory.

Express and Implied Contracts [9-4a]

Parties to a contract may indicate their assent either in words or by conduct implying such willingness. For instance, a regular customer known to have an account at a drugstore might pick up an item at the drugstore, show it to the clerk, and walk out. This is a perfectly valid contract. The clerk knows from the customer's conduct that she is buying the item at the specified price and wants it charged to her account. Her actions speak as effectively as words. Such a contract, formed by conduct, is an implied or, more precisely, an **implied in fact contract**; in contrast, a contract in which the parties manifest assent in words is an **express contract**. Both are contracts, equally enforceable. The difference between them is merely the manner in which the parties manifest their assent.

Fox v. Mountain West Electric, Inc.
Supreme Court of Idaho, 2002
137 Idaho 703, 52 P.3d 848; rehearing denied, 2002
http://scholar.google.com/scholar_case?q=52+P.3D+848&hl=en&as_sdt=2,34&case=12020421688825080366&scilh=0

FACTS Lockheed Martin Idaho Technical Company (LMITCO) requested bids for a comprehensive fire alarm system in its twelve buildings located in Idaho Falls. Mountain West Electric (MWE) was in the business of installing electrical wiring, conduit and related hookups, and attachments. Fox provided services in designing, drafting, testing, and assisting in the installation of fire alarm systems. The parties decided that it would be better for them to work together with MWE taking the lead on the project. The parties prepared a document defining each of their roles and jointly prepared a bid. MWE was awarded the LMITCO fixed-price contract. In May 1996, Fox began performing various services at the direction of MWE's manager.

During the course of the project, many changes and modifications to the LMITCO contract were made. MWE and Fox disagreed on the procedure for the compensation of the change orders. MWE proposed a flow-down procedure, whereby Fox would receive whatever compensation LMITCO decided to pay MWE. Fox found this unacceptable and suggested a bidding procedure to which MWE objected. Fox and MWE could not reach an agreement upon a compensation arrangement with respect to change orders. Fox left the project on December 9, 1996, after delivering the remaining equipment and materials to MWE. MWE contracted with Life Safety Systems to complete the LMITCO project.

Fox filed a complaint in July 1998 seeking money owed for materials and services provided to MWE by Fox. MWE answered and counterclaimed seeking monetary damages resulting from the alleged breach of the parties' agreement by Fox. The district court found in favor of MWE holding that an implied in fact contract existed. Fox appealed.

DECISION The decision of the district court is affirmed.

OPINION The Court recognizes three types of contractual relationships: (1) an express contract in which the parties expressly agree regarding a transaction; (2) an implied in fact contract in which there is no express agreement, but the conduct of the parties implies an agreement from which an obligation in contract exists; and (3) an implied in law contract, or quasi contract, which is not a contract at all, but an obligation imposed by law for the purpose of bringing about justice and equity without reference to the intent or the agreement of the parties.

An implied in fact contract is one in which the terms and existence of the contract are manifested by the conduct of the parties with the request of one party and the performance by the other often being inferred from the circumstances attending the performance. An implied in fact contract is grounded in the parties' agreement and tacit understanding.

Using the district court's finding that pricings submitted by Fox were used by MWE as estimates for the change orders, the Court held that the district court did not err in finding that there was an implied in fact contract using the industry standard's flow-down method of compensation for the change orders rather than a series of fixed price contracts between MWE and Fox.

A second question that was raised is whether this contract should be governed by the Uniform Commercial Code (UCC). For that to be the case, the contract would have to be predominantly for the sale of goods. Fox argued the predominant factor of this transaction was the fire alarm system, not the methodology of how the system was installed, and, therefore, the UCC should govern.

MWE contended that the UCC should not be used, despite the fact that goods accounted for one-half of the contract price, because the predominant factor at issue is services and not the sale of goods. MWE points out that the primary issue is the value of Fox's services under the change orders and the cost of obtaining replacement services after Fox left the job.

The Court held that the predominant factor test should be used to determine whether the UCC applies to transactions involving the sale of both goods and services as explained in *Pittsley v. Houser* (see Chapter 19).

The test for inclusion or exclusion is not whether they are mixed, but, granting that they are mixed, whether their predominant factor, their thrust, and their purpose, reasonably stated, is the rendition of service, with goods incidentally involved (e.g., contract with artist for painting) or is a transaction of sale, with labor incidentally involved (e.g., installation of a water heater in a bathroom). This test essentially involves consideration of the contract in its entirety, applying the UCC to the entire contract or not at all.

The district court found that the contract at issue in this case contained both goods and services; however, the predominant factor was Fox's services while the goods provided by Fox were merely incidental to the services he provided. The Court held that the district court did not err in finding that the predominant factor of the underlying transaction was services and that the UCC did not apply.

INTERPRETATION An implied in fact contract is formed by the conduct of the parties; in cases in which a contract provides for both goods and services, the common law applies if the predominant factor of the contract is the provision of services.

CRITICAL THINKING QUESTION Why should the legal rights of contracting parties depend on whether a contract is or is not for the sale of goods?

Bilateral and Unilateral Contracts [9-4b]

Bilateral contract

contract in which both parties exchange promises

Promisor

person making a promise

Promisee

person to whom a promise is made

In the typical contractual transaction, each party makes at least one promise. For example, if Adelle says to Byron, "If you promise to mow my lawn, I will pay you $10," and Byron agrees to mow Adelle's lawn, Adelle and Byron have made mutual promises, each agreeing to do something in exchange for the promise of the other. When a contract is formed by the exchange of promises, each party is under a duty to the other. This kind of contract is called a **bilateral contract**, because each party is both a **promisor** (a person making a promise) and a **promisee** (the person to whom a promise is made).

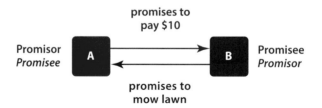

But suppose that only one of the parties makes a promise. Adelle says to Byron, "If you will mow my lawn, I will pay you $10." A contract will be formed when Byron has finished mowing the lawn and not before. At that time, Adelle becomes contractually obligated to pay $10 to Byron. Adelle's offer was in exchange for Byron's act of mowing the lawn, not for his promise to

Unilateral contract
contract in which only one party makes a promise

Practical Advice

Because it is uncertain whether the offeree in a unilateral contract will choose to perform, use bilateral contracts wherever possible.

Valid contract
contract that meets all of the requirements of a binding contract

Void contract
an agreement without legal effect

Voidable contract
contract capable of being made void

Unenforceable contract
contract for the breach of which the law does not provide a remedy

---

Practical Advice

Be careful to avoid entering into void, voidable, and unenforceable contracts.

Executed contract
contract fully performed by all of the parties

Executory contract
contract not fully performed

Promissory estoppel
doctrine enforcing noncontractual promises for which there has been justifiable reliance on the promise and justice requires enforcement

mow it. Because Byron never made a promise to mow the lawn, he was under no duty to mow it. This is a **unilateral contract** because only one of the parties has made a promise.

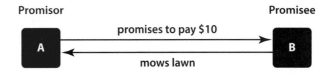

Promisor   Promisee

A ——— promises to pay $10 ———▶ B
A ◀——— mows lawn ——— B

Thus, whereas a bilateral contract results from the exchange of a promise for a return promise, a unilateral contract results from the exchange of a promise either for performing an act or for refraining from doing an act. In cases in which it is not clear whether a unilateral or bilateral contract has been formed, the courts presume that the parties intended a bilateral contract. Thus, if Adelle says to Byron, "If you will mow my lawn, I will pay you $10," and Byron replies, "OK, I will mow your lawn," a bilateral contract is formed.

Valid, Void, Voidable, and Unenforceable Contracts [9-4c]

By definition a **valid contract** is one that meets all of the requirements of a binding contract. It is an enforceable promise or agreement.

A **void contract** is an agreement that does not meet all of the requirements of a binding contract. Thus, it is no contract at all; it is merely a promise or an agreement that has no legal effect. An example of a void agreement is an agreement entered into by a person whom the courts have declared incompetent.

A **voidable contract**, on the other hand, though defective, is not wholly lacking in legal effect. A voidable contract is a contract; however, because of the manner in which the contract was formed or a lack of capacity of a party to it, the law permits one or more of the parties to avoid the legal duties the contract creates. If the contract is voided, both of the parties are relieved of their legal duties under the agreement. For instance, through intentional misrepresentation of a material fact (fraud), Thomas induces Regina to enter into a contract. Regina may, upon discovery of the fraud, notify Thomas that by reason of the misrepresentation, she will not perform her promise, and the law will support Regina. Although the contract induced by fraud is not void, it is voidable at the election of Regina, the defrauded party. Thomas, the fraudulent party, may make no such election. If Regina elects to avoid the contract, Thomas will be released from his promise under the agreement, although he may be liable for damages under tort law for fraud.

A contract that is neither void nor voidable may nonetheless be unenforceable. An **unenforceable contract** is one for the breach of which the law provides no remedy. For example, a contract may be unenforceable because of a failure to satisfy the requirements of the statute of frauds, which requires certain kinds of contracts to be evidenced by a writing to be enforceable. Also, the statute of limitations imposes restrictions on the time during which a party has the right to bring a lawsuit for breach of contract. After the statutory time period has passed, a contract is referred to as unenforceable, rather than void or voidable. Figure 9-3 lists the requirements of a binding contract and the consequences of failing to satisfy each requirement.

Executed and Executory Contracts [9-4d]

A contract that has been fully carried out by all of the parties to it is an **executed contract**. Strictly speaking, an executed contract is no longer a contract, because all of the duties under it have been performed, but having a term for such a completed contract is useful. By comparison, the term **executory contract** applies to contracts that are still partially or entirely unperformed by one or more of the parties.

PROMISSORY ESTOPPEL [9-5]

As a general rule, promises are not enforceable if they do not meet all the requirements of a contract. Nevertheless, in certain circumstances, the courts enforce noncontractual promises under the doctrine of **promissory estoppel** to avoid injustice. A noncontractual promise is enforceable when it is made under circumstances that should lead the promisor reasonably to expect that the

Practical Advice

Take care not to make promises on which others may detrimentally rely.

promisee, in reliance on the promise, would be induced by it to take definite and substantial action or to forbear, and the promisee does take such action or does forbear (see Figure 9-2). For example, Gordon promises Constance not to foreclose for a period of six months on a mortgage Gordon owns on Constance's land. Constance then expends $100,000 to construct a building on the land. His promise not to foreclose is binding on Gordon under the doctrine of promissory estoppel.

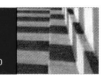

Skebba v. Kasch
Court of Appeals of Wisconsin, 2006
2006 WI App 232, 724 N.W.2d 408; review denied, 2007 WI 59
http://scholar.google.com/scholar_case?q=724+N.W.2d+408&hl=en&as_sdt=2,34&case=17278464423229519438&scilh=0

FACTS Kasch and his brother owned M.W. Kasch Co. Kasch hired Skebba as a sales representative, and over the years promoted him first to account manager, then to customer service manager, field sales manager, vice president of sales, senior vice president of sales and purchasing, and finally to vice president of sales. When M.W. Kasch Co. experienced serious financial problems in 1993, Skebba was approached by another company to leave Kasch and work for them. When Skebba told Kasch he was accepting the new opportunity, Kasch asked what it would take to get him to stay. Skebba told Kasch that he needed security for his retirement and family and would stay if Kasch agreed to pay Skebba $250,000 if one of these three conditions occurred: (1) the company was sold; (2) Skebba was lawfully terminated; or (3) Skebba retired. Kasch agreed to this proposal and promised to have the agreement drawn up. Skebba turned down the job opportunity and stayed with Kasch from December 1993 through 1999 when the company assets were sold.

Over the years, Skebba repeatedly but unsuccessfully asked Kasch for a written summary of this agreement. Eventually, Kasch sold the business receiving $5.1 million dollars for his fifty-one percent share of the business. Upon the sale of the business, Skebba asked Kasch for the $250,000 Kasch had previously promised to him. Kasch refused and denied ever having made such an agreement. Instead, Kasch gave Skebba a severance agreement, which had been drafted by Kasch's lawyers in 1993. This agreement promised two years of salary continuation on the sale of the company, but only if Skebba was not hired by the successor company. The severance agreement also required a set-off against the salary continuation of any sums Skebba earned from any activity during the two years of the severance agreement. Skebba sued, alleging breach of contract and promissory estoppel.

The jury found there was no contract, but that Kasch had made a promise upon which Skebba relied to his detriment, that the reliance was foreseeable, and that Skebba was damaged in the amount of $250,000. The trial court concluded that, based on its reading of applicable case law, it could not specifically enforce the promise the jury found Kasch made to Skebba because there were other ways to measure damages. The trial court held that since Skebba could not establish what he had lost by relying on Kasch's promise he had not proved his damages.

DECISION Order of trial court reversed and case remanded.

OPINION Kasch did not promise to pay Skebba more than Skebba would have earned at the job Skebba turned down. Kasch did not promise that total income to Skebba would be greater than

in the turned-down job, no matter how long he remained with Kasch. Kasch only promised that if Skebba stayed, Kasch would pay Skebba $250,000 (the sum Skebba wanted for his retirement), at the time the earliest of three conditions occurred. Kasch sold the business while Skebba was still employed by Kasch. Kasch refused to pay as promised.

The purpose of promissory estoppel is to enforce promises where the failure to do so is unjust. The requirements of promissory estoppel follow: (1) Was the promise one which the promisor should reasonably expect to induce action or forbearance of a definite and substantial character on the part of the promisee? (2) Did the promise induce such action or forbearance? (3) Can injustice be avoided only by enforcement of the promise? The first two of these requirements are facts to be found by a jury or other factfinder, while the third is a policy decision to be made by the court.

A court, in fashioning a remedy, can consider any equitable or legal remedy, which will "prevent injustice." Moreover, the

> amount allowed as damages may be determined by the plaintiff's expenditures or change of position in reliance as well as by the value to him of the promised performance.... In determining what justice requires, the court must remember all of its powers, derived from equity, law merchant, and other sources, as well as the common law. Its decree should be molded accordingly.

Wisconsin is one of a small group of states which recognizes that to fulfill the purpose of promissory estoppel (i.e., prevent injustice) a court must be able to fashion a remedy that restores the promisee to where he or she would be if the promisor had fulfilled the promise. In this case, Skebba performed in reliance on Kasch's promise to pay $250,000 to him if one of three conditions occurred. Kasch enjoyed the fruits of Skebba's reliance—he kept on a top salesperson to help the company through tough financial times and he avoided the damage that he believed Skebba's leaving could have had on M.W. Kasch's reputation in the industry. Accordingly, to prevent injustice, the equitable remedy for Skebba to receive is Kasch's specific performance: the promised payment of the $250,000.

INTERPRETATION The courts will enforce a promise that the promisor should reasonably expect to induce detrimental reliance by the promisee if the promisee takes such action and justice requires enforcement.

ETHICAL QUESTION Did Kasch act ethically? Explain.

CRITICAL THINKING QUESTION What could Skebba have done to better protect his interests? Explain.

<table>
<tr><td colspan="4" align="center">**CONCEPT REVIEW 9-1**</td></tr>
<tr><td colspan="4" align="center">*Contracts, Promissory Estoppel, and Quasi Contracts (Restitution)*</td></tr>
<tr><td></td><td>**Contract**</td><td>**Promissory Estoppel**</td><td>**Quasi Contract (Restitution)**</td></tr>
<tr><td>**Type of Promise**</td><td>Contractual</td><td>Noncontractual</td><td>None
Void
Unenforceable
Invalidated</td></tr>
<tr><td>**Requirements**</td><td>All of the essential elements of a contract</td><td>Detrimental and justifiable reliance</td><td>Benefit conferred and knowingly accepted</td></tr>
<tr><td>**Remedies**</td><td>Equitable
Compensatory
Reliance
Restitution</td><td>Promise enforced to the extent necessary to avoid injustice</td><td>Reasonable value of benefit conferred</td></tr>
</table>

QUASI CONTRACTS OR RESTITUTION [9-6]

Quasi contract or restitution
obligation *not* based upon contract that is imposed to avoid injustice

In addition to express and implied in fact contracts, there are implied in law or **quasi contracts**, which were not included in the previous classification of contracts for the reason that a quasi (meaning "as if") contract is not a contract at all but is based in restitution. **Restitution** is an obligation imposed by law to avoid injustice. The basic rule of restitution is that a person who is unjustly enriched at the expense of another is subject to liability in restitution, which usually requires the unjustly enriched person to restore the benefit received or pay money in an amount necessary to eliminate the unjust enrichment. In 2011, the ALI promulgated the Restatement (Third) of Restitution and Unjust Enrichment, which will be referred to as the "Restatement of Restitution."

Restitution is not a contract because it is based neither on an express nor on an implied promise. Rather, restitution is an independent basis of liability, in addition to contract or tort liability. The comments to the Restatement of Restitution explain

> Restitution is the law of nonconsensual and nonbargained benefits in the same way that torts is the law of nonconsensual and nonlicensed harms. Both subjects deal with the consequences of transactions in which the parties have not specified for themselves what the consequences of their interaction should be. … [T]he law of restitution identifies those circumstances in which a person is liable for benefits received, measuring liability by the extent of the benefit.

For example, Willard by mistake delivers to Roy a plain, unaddressed envelope containing $100 intended for Lucia. Roy is under no contractual obligation to return it, but Willard is permitted to recover the $100 from Roy. The law imposes a quasi-contractual obligation of restitution on Roy to prevent his unjust enrichment at the expense of Willard. Such a recovery requires three essential elements: (1) a benefit conferred upon the defendant (Roy) by the plaintiff (Willard); (2) the defendant's (Roy's) appreciation or knowledge of the benefit; and (3) acceptance or retention of the benefit by the defendant (Roy) under circumstances making it inequitable for him to retain the benefit without compensating the plaintiff for its value.

The law of restitution provides a remedy when the parties enter into a void contract, an unenforceable contract, or a voidable contract that is avoided. In such a case, the law of restitution will determine what recovery is permitted for any performance rendered by the parties under the invalid, unenforceable, or invalidated agreement. Restitution also provides a remedy for the breach of a contractual obligation as discussed in Chapter 18.

Jasdip Properties SC, LLC v. Estate of Richardson

Court of Appeals of South Carolina, 2011

395 S.C. 633, 720 S.E.2d 485

http://scholar.google.com/scholar_case?q=395+S.C.+633&hl=en&as_sdt=6,34&case=460584843454513831&scilh=0

FACTS On May 5, 2006, Stewart Richardson (Seller) and JASDIP Properties SC, LLC (Buyer) entered into an agreement for the purchase of certain property in Georgetown, South Carolina. The purchase price for the property was to be $537,000. Buyer paid an initial earnest money deposit of $10,000. The balance was due at the closing on or before July 28, 2006. Thereafter Seller granted Buyer extensions to the closing date in return for additional payments of $175,000 and $25,000, each to be applied to the purchase price. Buyer was unable to close in a timely fashion, and Seller rescinded the contract.

Thereafter, Buyer brought suit against the seller (1) contending that Seller would be unjustly enriched if allowed to keep the money paid despite the rescission of the agreement and (2) requesting $210,000. The $210,000 consisted of the $10,000 earnest money deposit and $200,000 in subsequent payments. Buyer later filed an amended complaint requesting $205,000, stating that the agreement permitted Seller to retain half of the $10,000 earnest money deposit.

A jury determined that neither party had breached the contract and awarded no damages on that basis. Buyer then requested a ruling by the trial court on its action for unjust enrichment. The trial court denied Buyer's claim for unjust enrichment. Buyer appealed arguing that all the evidence presented at trial, as well as the jury's verdict, supports a finding that the agreement was rescinded or abandoned and that this requires restitution of $205,000 to Buyer.

DECISION Judgment of the trial court is reversed, and the case is remanded.

OPINION Restitution is a remedy designed to prevent unjust enrichment. The terms "restitution" and "unjust enrichment" are modern designations for the older doctrine of quasi-contract. *Quantum meruit*, quasi-contract, and implied by law contract are equivalent terms for this remedy.

Implied in law or quasi contracts are not considered contracts at all but are akin to restitution, which permits recovery of that amount the defendant has been benefitted at the expense of the plaintiff in order to preclude unjust enrichment.

To recover on a theory of restitution, the plaintiff must show that (1) the plaintiff conferred a non-gratuitous benefit on the defendant, (2) the defendant realized some value from the benefit, and (3) it would be inequitable for the defendant to retain the benefit without paying the plaintiff for the value of the benefit. Unjust enrichment is usually a prerequisite for enforcement of the doctrine of restitution; if there is no basis for unjust enrichment, there is no basis for restitution.

Buyer seeks the $175,000 and $25,000 payments as well as half of the $10,000 earnest money. The $175,000 and $25,000 payments both explicitly stated that they were towards the purchase price. Additionally, Buyer paid $10,000 in an earnest money deposit. Based on the unappealed jury's finding that Buyer did not breach, Buyer is entitled to the money paid towards the purchase price as well as half of the earnest money under the theory of restitution. Buyer met the requirements to recover under the theory of restitution: (1) Buyer paid Seller $205,000 towards the purchase price, and the sale did not go through despite the fact that neither party breached; (2) Seller kept the $205,000 although he also retained the Property; and (3) Seller's keeping the $205,000 is inequitable because the Seller still has the Property, the jury found neither party had breached, and the evidence supports that Buyer intended to go forward with the purchase. Therefore, the trial court erred in failing to find for Buyer for its claim of unjust enrichment. Accordingly, the trial court's determination that Buyer was not entitled to restitution is reversed, and Buyer is awarded $205,000.

INTERPRETATION Implied in law or quasi contracts are not considered contracts at all, but are akin to restitution which permits recovery of that amount the defendant has been benefited at the expense of the plaintiff in order to prevent unjust enrichment.

CRITICAL THINKING QUESTION Why does the law allow a recovery in restitution or quasi contract?

BUSINESS LAW **IN ACTION**

Armed with a hastily scribbled work order, Jonas, an employee of Triton Painting Service, heads to 109 Millard Road. He works for two full days power cleaning, priming, and painting the exterior of the house. Satisfied with his work, Jonas moves on to his next job. When the homeowners, the Prestons, return from their vacation several days later, they are shocked to see their formerly "Palatial Peach" home painted "Santa Fe Sand." They are even more surprised when they receive a call from Triton demanding payment for the paint job.

Errors such as this sometimes occur in business. It was the homeowners at 104

Millard Road who had contracted to pay Triton $1,200 for an exterior paint job using Santa Fe Sand. But Jonas felt sure enough he had the correct house number, and no one stopped him from doing the work. And even though the Prestons had not chosen the color, they now have a freshly painted house because of Triton's error. Should the Prestons have to pay? If so, how much? What does the law say about this?

To begin with, there was no contract between Triton and the Prestons. Therefore Triton cannot sue the Prestons for breach of contract. A suit in quasi contract or restitution is Triton's best bet, but to prevail, Triton

must prove unjust enrichment. One factor affecting Triton's success is whether the Prestons, in good faith, dislike the new color. However, even if they do not dislike Santa Fe Sand, another factor is whether the house needed repainting. It would be unfair to require the Prestons to pay for an unnecessary service. Moreover, because the Prestons were out of town they could not have stopped Jonas from doing the work. Finally, because they received services rather than goods, they cannot now give back the service. Under these circumstances, it is hardly equitable to make the Prestons pay for what was clearly Triton's mistake.

CHAPTER SUMMARY

Development of the
Law of Contracts

Common Law most contracts are primarily governed by state common law, including contracts involving employment, services, insurance, real property (land and anything attached to it), patents, and copyrights

The Uniform Commercial Code (UCC) Article 2 of the UCC governs the sales of goods

- *Sale* the transfer of title from seller to buyer
- *Goods* tangible personal property (personal property is all property other than an interest in land)

Definition of a
Contract

Contract binding agreement that the courts will enforce

Breach failure to properly perform a contractual obligation

Requirements of
a Contract

Mutual Assent the parties to a contract must manifest by words or conduct that they have agreed to enter into a contract

Consideration each party to a contract must intentionally exchange a legal benefit or incur a legal detriment as an inducement to the other party to make a return exchange

Legality of Object the purpose of a contract must not be criminal, tortious, or otherwise against public policy

Capacity the parties to a contract must have contractual capacity

Classification of
Contracts

Express and Implied Contracts

- *Implied in Fact Contract* contract in which the agreement of the parties is inferred from their conduct
- *Express Contract* an agreement that is stated in words either orally or in writing

Bilateral and Unilateral Contracts

- *Bilateral Contract* contract in which both parties exchange promises
- *Unilateral Contract* contract in which only one party makes a promise

Valid, Void, Voidable, and Unenforceable Contracts

- *Valid Contract* one that meets all of the requirements of a binding contract
- *Void Contract* no contract at all; without legal effect
- *Voidable Contract* contract capable of being made void
- *Unenforceable Contract* contract for the breach of which the law provides no remedy

Executed and Executory Contracts

- *Executed Contract* contract that has been fully performed by all of the parties
- *Executory Contract* contract that has yet to be fully performed

Promissory Estoppel

Definition a doctrine enforcing some noncontractual promises

Requirements a promise made under circumstances that should lead the promisor reasonably to expect that the promise would induce the promisee to take definite and substantial action, and the promisee does take such action

Remedy a court will enforce the promise to the extent necessary to avoid injustice

Quasi Contract or
Restitution

Definition an obligation not based upon contract that is imposed by law to avoid injustice; also called an implied in law contract

Requirements a court will impose a quasi contract or restitution when (1) the plaintiff confers a benefit upon the defendant, (2) the defendant knows or appreciates the benefit, and (3) the defendant's retention of the benefit is inequitable

Remedy the plaintiff recovers the reasonable value of the benefit she conferred upon the defendant

QUESTIONS

1. Owen telephones an order to Hillary's store for certain goods, which Hillary delivers to Owen. Nothing is said by either party about price or payment terms. What are the legal obligations of Owen and Hillary?

2. Minth is the owner of the Hiawatha Supper Club, which he leased for two years to Piekarski. During the period of the lease, Piekarski contracted with Puttkammer for the resurfacing of the access and service areas of the supper club. Puttkammer performed the work satisfactorily. Minth knew about the contract and the performance of the work. The work, including labor and materials, had a reasonable value of $2,540, but Puttkammer was never paid because Piekarski went bankrupt. Puttkammer brought an action against Minth to recover the amount owed to him by Piekarski. Will Puttkammer prevail? Explain.

3. Jonathan writes to Willa, stating, "I'll pay you $150 if you reseed my lawn." Willa reseeds Jonathan's lawn as requested. Has a contract been formed? If so, what kind?

4. Calvin uses fraud to induce Maria to promise to pay money in return for goods he has delivered to her. Has a contract been formed? If so, what kind? What are the rights of Calvin and Maria?

5. Anna is about to buy a house on a hill. Prior to the purchase, she obtains a promise from Betty, the owner of the adjacent property, that Betty will not build any structure that would block Anna's view. In reliance on this promise, Anna buys the house. Is Betty's promise binding? Why or why not?

CASE PROBLEMS

6. Mary Dobos was admitted to Boca Raton Community Hospital in serious condition with an abdominal aneurysm. The hospital called upon Nursing Care Services, Inc., to provide around-the-clock nursing services for Mrs. Dobos. She received two weeks of in-hospital care, forty-eight hours of postrelease care, and two weeks of at-home care. The total bill was $3,723.90. Mrs. Dobos refused to pay, and Nursing Care Services, Inc., brought an action to recover. Mrs. Dobos maintained that she was not obligated to render payment in that she never signed a written contract, nor did she orally agree to be liable for the services. The necessity for the services, reasonableness of the fee, and competency of the nurses were undisputed. After Mrs. Dobos admitted that she or her daughter authorized the forty-eight hours of postrelease care, the trial court ordered compensation of $248 for that period. It did not allow payment of the balance, and Nursing Care Services, Inc., appealed. Decision?

7. St. Charles Drilling Co. contracted with Osterholt to install a well and water system that would produce a specified quantity of water. The water system failed to meet its warranted capacity, and Osterholt sued for breach of contract. Does the Uniform Commercial Code apply to this contract?

8. Helvey brought suit against the Wabash County REMC (REMC) for breach of implied and express warranties. He alleged that REMC furnished electricity in excess of 135 volts to Helvey's home, damaging his 110-volt household appliances. This incident occurred more than four years before Helvey brought this suit. In defense, REMC pleads that the Uniform Commercial Code's (UCC's) Article 2 statute of limitations of four years has passed, thereby barring Helvey's suit. Helvey argues that providing electrical energy is not a transaction in goods under the UCC but rather a furnishing of services that would make applicable the general contract six-year statute of limitations. Is the contract governed by the UCC? Why?

9. Jack Duran, president of Colorado Carpet Installation, Inc., began negotiations with Fred and Zuma Palermo for the sale and installation of carpeting, carpet padding, tile, and vinyl floor covering in their home. Duran drew up a written proposal that referred to Colorado Carpet as "the seller" and to the Palermos as the "customer." The proposal listed the quantity, unit cost, and total price of each item to be installed. The total price of the job was $4,777.75. Although labor was expressly included in this figure, Duran estimated the total labor cost at $926. Mrs. Palermo in writing accepted Duran's written proposal soon after he submitted it to her. After Colorado Carpet delivered the tile to the Palermo home, however, Mrs. Palermo had a disagreement with Colorado Carpet's tile man and arranged for another contractor to perform the job. Colorado Carpet brought an action against the Palermos for breach of contract. Does the Uniform Commercial Code apply to this contract?

10. On November 1, the Kansas City Post Office Employees Credit Union merged into the Kansas City Telephone Credit Union to form the Communications Credit Union (Credit Union). Systems Design and Management Information (SDMI) develops computer software programs for credit unions, using Burroughs (now Unisys) hardware. SDMI and Burroughs together offered to sell to Credit Union both a software package, called the Generic System, and Burroughs hardware. Later in November, a demonstration of the software was held at SDMI's offices, and the Credit Union agreed to purchase the Generic System software. This agreement was oral. After Credit Union was converted to the SDMI Generic System, major problems with the system immediately became apparent, so SDMI filed suit against Credit Union to recover the outstanding contract price for the software. Credit Union counterclaimed for damages based upon breach of contract and negligent and fraudulent misrepresentation. Does the Uniform Commercial Code apply to this contract?

11. Insul-Mark is the marketing arm of Kor-It Sales, Inc. Kor-It manufactures roofing fasteners and Insul-Mark distributes them nationwide. In late 1985, Kor-It contracted with Modern Materials, Inc., to have large volumes of screws coated with a rust-proofing agent. The contract specified that the coated screws must pass a standard industry test and that Kor-It would pay according to the pound and length of the screws coated. Kor-It had received numerous complaints from customers that the coated screws were rusting, and Modern Materials unsuccessfully attempted to remedy the problem. Kor-It terminated its relationship with Modern Materials and brought suit for the deficient coating. Modern Materials counterclaimed for the labor and materials it had furnished to Kor-It. The trial court held that the contract (a) was for performance of a service, (b) not governed by the Uniform Commercial Code, (c) governed by the common law of contracts, and (d) therefore, barred by a two-year statute of limitations. Insul-Mark appealed. Decision?

12. Max E. Pass, Jr., and his wife, Martha N. Pass, departed in an aircraft owned and operated by Mr. Pass from Plant City, Florida, bound for Clarksville, Tennessee. Somewhere over Alabama the couple encountered turbulence, and Mr. Pass lost control of the aircraft. The plane crashed, killing both Mr. and Mrs. Pass. Approximately four and a half months prior to the flight in which he was killed, Mr. Pass had taken his airplane to Shelby Aviation, an aircraft service company, for inspection and service. In servicing the aircraft, Shelby Aviation replaced both rear wing attach point brackets on the plane. Three and one half years after the crash, Max E. Pass, Sr., father of Mr. Pass and administrator of his estate, and Shirley Williams, mother of Mrs. Pass and administratrix of her estate, filed suit against Shelby Aviation. The lawsuit alleged that the rear wing attach point brackets sold and installed by Shelby Aviation were defective because they lacked the bolts necessary to secure them properly to the airplane. The plaintiffs asserted claims against the defendant for breach of express and implied warranties under Article 2 of the Uniform Commercial Code (UCC), which governs the sale of goods. Shelby Aviation contended that the transaction with Mr. Pass had been primarily for the sale of services, rather than of goods, and that consequently Article 2 of the UCC did not cover the transaction. Does the UCC apply to this transaction? Explain.

13. In March, William Tackaberry, a real estate agent for the firm of Weichert Co. Realtors (Weichert), informed Thomas Ryan, a local developer, that he knew of property Ryan might be interested in purchasing. Ryan indicated he was interested in knowing more about the property. Tackaberry disclosed the property's identity and the seller's proposed price. Tackaberry also stated that the purchaser would have to pay Weichert a 10 percent commission. Tackaberry met with the property owner and gathered information concerning the property's current leases, income, expenses, and development plans. Tackaberry also collected tax and zoning documents relevant to the property. In a face-to-face meeting on April 4, Tackaberry gave Ryan the data he had gathered and presented Ryan with a letter calling for a 10 percent finder's fee to be paid to Weichert by Ryan upon "successfully completing and closing of title." Ryan refused to agree to the 10 percent figure during this meeting. Tackaberry arranged a meeting, held three days later, where Ryan contracted with the owner to buy the land. Ryan refused, however, to pay the 10 percent finder's fee to Weichert. What, if anything, is Weichert entitled to recover from Ryan? Explain.

TAKING SIDES

Richardson hired J. C. Flood Company, a plumbing contractor, to correct a stoppage in the sewer line of her house. The plumbing company's "snake" device, used to clear the line leading to the main sewer, became caught in the underground line. To release it, the company excavated a portion of the sewer line in Richardson's backyard. In the process, the company discovered numerous leaks in a rusty, defective water pipe that ran parallel with the sewer line. To meet public regulations, the water pipe, of a type no longer approved for such service, had to be replaced either then or later, when the yard would have to be excavated again. The plumbing company proceeded to repair the water pipe. Though Richardson inspected the company's work daily and did not express any objection to the extra work involved in replacing the water pipe, she refused to pay any part of the total bill after the company completed the entire operation. J. C. Flood Company then sued Richardson for the costs of labor and material it had furnished.

a. What arguments would support J. C. Flood's claim for the costs of labor and material it had furnished?

b. What arguments would support Richardson's refusal to pay the bill?

c. For what, if anything, should Richardson be liable? Explain.

Mutual Assent

It is elementary that for a contract to exist there must be an offer and acceptance.

Zeller v. First National Bank & Trust, Tales, 79 Ill.App.3d 170, 34 Ill. Dec. 473, 398 N.E.2d 148 (1979)

CHAPTER 10

CHAPTER OUTCOMES

After reading and studying this chapter, you should be able to:

1. Identify the three essentials of an offer and explain briefly the requirements associated with each.

2. State the seven ways by which an offer may be terminated other than by acceptance.

3. Compare the traditional and modern theories of definiteness of acceptance of an offer, as shown by the common law "mirror image" rule and by the rule of the Uniform Commercial Code.

4. Describe the five situations limiting an offeror's right to revoke her offer.

5. Explain the various rules that determine when an acceptance takes effect.

Though each of the requirements for forming a contract is essential to its existence, mutual assent is so basic that frequently a contract is referred to as an agreement between the parties. Enforcing the contract means enforcing the agreement; indeed, the agreement between the parties is the very core of the contract. As we discussed in Chapter 9, a contractual agreement always involves either a promise exchanged for a promise (*bilateral contract*) or a promise exchanged for a completed act or forbearance to act (*unilateral contract*).

The way in which parties usually show mutual assent is by offer and acceptance. One party makes a proposal (offer) by words or conduct to the other party, who agrees by words or conduct to the proposal (acceptance).

A contract may be formed by conduct. Thus, though there may be no definite offer and acceptance, or definite acceptance of an offer, a contract exists if both parties' actions manifest (indicate) a recognition by each of them of the existence of a contract. To form a contract, the agreement must be objectively manifested. The important thing is what the parties indicate to one another by spoken or written words or by conduct. The law applies an *objective* standard and, therefore, is concerned only with the assent, agreement, or intention of a party as it reasonably appears from his words or actions. The law of contracts is not concerned with what a party may have actually thought or the meaning that he intended to convey even if his subjective understanding or intention differed from the meaning he objectively indicated by word or conduct. For example, if Joanne seemingly offers to sell to Bruce her Chevrolet automobile but intended to offer and believes that she is offering her Ford automobile, and Bruce accepts the offer, reasonably believing it was for the Chevrolet, a contract has been formed for the sale of the Chevrolet. Subjectively, Joanne and Bruce are not in agreement as to the subject matter. Objectively, however, there is agreement, and the objective manifestation is binding.

The Uniform Commercial Code's (UCC's or Code's) treatment of mutual assent is covered in greater detail in Chapter 19.

OFFER

Offer

a proposal indicating a willingness to enter into a contract

Offeror

person making the offer

Offeree

person to whom the offer is made

An **offer** is a definite undertaking or proposal made by one person to another indicating a willingness to enter into a contract. The person making the proposal is the **offeror**. The person to whom it is made is the **offeree**. When it is received, the offer confers on the offeree the power to create a contract by acceptance, which is an expression of the offeree's willingness to comply with the terms of the offer. Until the offeree exercises this power, the outstanding offer creates neither rights nor liabilities.

ESSENTIALS OF AN OFFER [10-1]

An offer need not take any particular form to have legal effect. To be effective, however, it must (1) be communicated to the offeree; (2) manifest an intent to enter into a contract; and (3) be sufficiently definite and certain. If these essentials are present and the offer has not terminated, the offer gives the offeree the power to form a contract by accepting the offer.

Communication [10-1a]

Communication

offeree must have knowledge of the offer and the offer must be made by the offeror or her authorized agent to the offeree

To provide his part of the mutual assent required to form a contract, the offeree must know about the offer; he cannot agree to something about which he has no knowledge. Accordingly, the offeror must communicate the offer in an intended manner. For example, Oscar signs a letter containing an offer to Ellen and leaves it on top of the desk in his office. Later that day, Ellen, without prearrangement, goes to Oscar's office, discovers that he is away, notices the letter on his desk, reads it, and then writes on it an acceptance that she dates and signs. No contract is formed because the offer never became effective: Ellen became aware of the offer by chance, not by Oscar's intentional communication of it.

Not only must the offer be communicated to the offeree, but the communication must also be made or authorized by the offeror. If Jones tells Black that she plans to offer White $600 for a piano, and Black promptly informs White of Jones's intention, no offer has been made. There was no authorized communication of any offer by Jones to White. By the same token, if David should offer to sell to Lou his diamond ring, an acceptance of this offer by Tia would not be effective, as David made no offer to Tia.

An offer need not be stated or communicated by words. Conduct from which a reasonable person may infer a proposal in return for either an act or a promise amounts to an offer.

An offer may be made to the general public. No person can accept such an offer, however, until and unless he knows that the offer exists. For example, if a person, without knowing of an advertised reward for information leading to the return of a lost watch, gives information leading to the return of the watch, he is not entitled to the reward. His act was not an acceptance of the offer because he could not accept something of which he had no knowledge.

Intent [10-1b]

Intent

determined by an objective standard of what a reasonable offeree would have believed

To have legal effect, an offer must manifest an intent to enter into a contract. The **intent** of an offer is determined objectively from the words or conduct of the parties. The meaning of either party's manifestation is based on what a reasonable person in the other party's position would have believed.

Occasionally, a person exercises her sense of humor by speaking or writing words that—taken literally and without regard to context or surrounding circumstances—could be construed as an offer. The promise is intended as a joke, however, and the promisee as a reasonable person should understand it to be such. Therefore, it is not an offer. Because the person to whom it is made realizes or should realize that it is not made in earnest, it should not create a reasonable expectation in his mind. No contractual intent exists on the part of the promisor, and the promisee is or reasonably ought to be aware of that fact. If, however, the intended joke is so real that the promisee as a reasonable person under all the circumstances believes that the joke is in fact an offer, and so believing accepts, the objective standard applies and the parties have entered into a contract.

A promise made under obvious excitement or emotional strain is likewise not an offer. For example, Charlotte, after having her month-old Cadillac break down for the third time in two days, screams in disgust, "I will sell this car to anyone for $10.00!" Lisa hears Charlotte and hands her a $10.00 bill. Under the circumstances, Charlotte's statement was not an offer if a reasonable person in Lisa's position would have recognized it merely as an excited, nonbinding utterance.

It is important to distinguish language that constitutes an offer from that which merely solicits or invites offers. Such proposals, although made in earnest, lack the intent to enter into a contract and therefore are not deemed offers. As a result, a purported acceptance does not bring about a contract but operates only as an offer. Proposals that invite offers include preliminary negotiations, advertisements, and auctions.

Practical Advice

Make sure that you indicate by words or conduct what agreement you wish to enter.

Catamount Slate Products, Inc. v. Sheldon
Supreme Court of Vermont, 2004
2003 VT 112, 845 A.2d 324
http://scholar.google.com/scholar_case?case=12161607133389120155&q=2003+VT+112&hl=en&as_sdt=2,22

FACTS The Reed Family owns and operates Catamount Slate Products, Inc. (Catamount), a slate quarry and mill, on 122 acres in Fair Haven, Vermont. The Sheldons own neighboring property. Since 1997, the parties have been litigating the Reeds' right to operate their slate business and to use the access road leading to the quarry. In 2000, the parties agreed to try to resolve their disputes in a state-funded mediation with retired Judge Arthur O'Dea serving as mediator. Prior to the mediation, Judge O'Dea sent each party a Mediation Agreement outlining the rules governing the mediation. Paragraph nine of the Mediation Agreement stated that—

> i. all statements, admissions, confessions, acts, or exchanges … are acknowledged by the parties to be offers in negotiation of settlement and compromise, and as such inadmissible in evidence, and not binding upon either party unless reduced to a final agreement of settlement. Any final agreement of settlement must be in writing and signed by every party sought to be charged.

The mediation was held on September 5, 2000. Judge O'Dea began the session by reaffirming the statements made in the Mediation Agreement. After ten hours, the parties purportedly reached an agreement on all major issues. Judge O'Dea then orally summarized the terms of the resolution with the parties and counsel present. The attorneys took notes on the terms of the agreement with the understanding that they would prepare the necessary documents for signature in the coming days.

The resolution required the Reeds to pay the Sheldons $250 a month for the right to use the access road, with payments to commence on October 1, 2000. The parties also agreed to a series of terms governing the operation of the slate quarry. These terms were to be memorialized in two distinct documents, a Lease Agreement and a Settlement Agreement.

On September 7, 2000, two days after the mediation, the Sheldons' attorney, Emily Joselson, drafted a letter outlining the terms of the settlement and sent copies to James Leary, the Reeds' attorney, and Judge O'Dea. Within a week, Leary responded by letter concurring in some respects and outlining the issues on which the Reeds disagreed with Joselson's characterization of the settlement.

On October 1, 2000, the Reeds began paying the $250 monthly lease payments, but, since the settlement agreement was not final, the parties agreed that the money would go into an escrow account maintained by the Sheldons' counsel. The check was delivered to the Sheldons' attorney with a cover memo stating, "This check is forwarded to you with the understanding that the funds will be disbursed to your clients only after settlement agreement becomes

final. Of course, if the settlement agreement does not come to fruition, then the funds must be returned to my clients." The parties continued to exchange letters actively negotiating the remaining details of the Lease and Settlement Agreements for the better part of the next five months.

In February 2001, while drafts were still being exchanged, Christine Stannard, the Reeds' daughter, saw a deed and map in the Fair Haven Town Clerk's Office, which led her to believe that the disputed road was not owned by the Sheldons, but was a town highway. The Reeds then refused to proceed any further with negotiating the settlement agreement. A written settlement agreement was never signed by either party.

The Sheldons then filed a motion to enforce the settlement agreement. The trial court granted the option, finding that the attorneys' notes taken at the end of the mediation and the unsigned drafts of the Lease and Settlement Agreements sufficiently memorialized the agreement between the parties and thus constituted an enforceable settlement agreement.

DECISION Judgment of the trial is reversed and remanded.

OPINION The question is whether the oral agreement reached at mediation, when combined with the unexecuted documents drafted subsequently, constituted a binding, enforceable settlement agreement. Parties are free to enter into a binding contract without memorializing their agreement in a fully executed document. In such an instance, the mere intention or discussion to commit their agreement to writing will not prevent the formation of a contract prior to the document's execution.

"On the other hand, if either party communicates an intent not to be bound until he achieves a fully executed document, no amount of negotiation or oral agreement to specific terms will result in the formation of a binding contract." The freedom to determine the exact moment in which an agreement becomes binding encourages the parties to negotiate as candidly as possible, secure in the knowledge that they will not be bound until the execution of what both parties consider to be a final, binding agreement.

We look to the intent of the parties to determine the moment of contract formation. Intent to be bound is a question of fact. "To discern that intent a court must look to the words and deeds [of the parties] which constitute objective signs in a given set of circumstances." In determining whether the parties intended to be bound in the absence of a fully executed document the court will "consider (1) whether there has been an express reservation of the right not to be bound in the absence of a writing; (2) whether there has been partial performance of the contract; (3) whether all of the terms of the alleged contract have been agreed upon; and (4) whether the agreement at issue is the type of contract that is usually committed to writing." The language of the parties' correspondence and other documentary evidence presented reveals an intent by the mediation participants not to be bound prior to the execution of a final document. The Mediation Agreement Judge O'Dea sent to the parties prior to the mediation clearly contemplates that any settlement agreement emanating from the mediation would be binding only after being put in writing and signed. Further, Judge O'Dea reminded the parties of these ground rules at the outset of the mediation. The Reeds testified that they relied on these statements and assumed that, as indicated, they would not be bound until they signed a written agreement. Even more compelling evidence of the Reeds' lack of intent to be bound in the absence of a writing is the statement in the cover letter accompanying the Reeds' $250 payments to the Sheldons' attorney saying, "This check is forwarded to you with the understanding that the funds will be disbursed to your clients only after settlement agreement becomes final. Of course, if the settlement agreement does not come to fruition, then the funds must be returned to my clients."

No evidence was presented of partial performance of the settlement agreement. The third factor is whether there is anything left to negotiate. The lengthy correspondence in this case makes clear that several points of disagreement and ambiguity arose during

the drafting process. Resolution of these issues was clearly important enough to forestall final execution until the language of the documents could be agreed upon. In such a case, where the parties intend to be bound only upon execution of a final document, for the court to determine that, despite continuing disagreement on substantive terms, the parties reached a binding, enforceable settlement agreement undermines their right to enter into the specific settlement agreement for which they contracted.

The fourth and final factor, whether the agreement at issue is the type of contract usually put into writing, also weighs in the Reeds' favor. Being a contract for an interest in land, the Lease Agreement is subject to the Statute of Frauds and thus generally must be in writing.

In conclusion, three of the four factors indicate that the parties here did not intend to be bound until the execution of a final written document, and therefore the parties never entered into a binding settlement agreement.

INTERPRETATION The intent of the parties to be bound to a contract is determined by an objective standard of what a reasonable person would have believed based on the words and conduct of the parties.

CRITICAL THINKING QUESTION Does the decision rendered by the court establish a policy that is best for society? Explain.

Preliminary Negotiations If a communication creates in the mind of a reasonable person in the position of the offeree an expectation that his acceptance will conclude a contract, then the communication is an offer. If it does not, then the communication is a preliminary negotiation. Initial communications between potential parties to a contract often take the form of preliminary negotiations, through which the parties either request or supply the terms of an offer that may or may not be made. A statement that may indicate a willingness to make an offer is not in itself an offer. For instance, if Brown writes to Young, "Will you buy my automobile for $3,000?" and Young replies, "Yes," there is no contract. Brown has not made an offer to sell her automobile to Young for $3,000. The offeror must demonstrate an intent to enter into a contract, not merely a willingness to enter into a negotiation.

Advertisements Merchants desire to sell their merchandise and thus are interested in informing potential customers about the goods, terms of sale, and price. But if they make widespread promises to sell to each person on their mailing list, the number of acceptances and resulting contracts might conceivably exceed their ability to perform. Consequently, a merchant might refrain from making offers by merely announcing that he has goods for sale, describing the goods, and quoting prices. He is simply inviting his customers and, in the case of published advertisements, the public, to make offers to him to buy his goods. His advertisements, circulars, quotation sheets, and displays of merchandise are *not* offers because (1) they do not contain a promise and (2) they leave unexpressed many terms that would be necessary to the making of a contract. Accordingly, his customers' responses are not acceptances because no offer to sell has been made.

Nonetheless, a seller is not free to advertise goods at one price and then raise the price once demand has been stimulated. Although as far as contract law is concerned, the seller has made no offer, such conduct is prohibited by the Federal Trade Commission as well as by legislation in most states. Moreover, in some circumstances a public announcement or advertisement may constitute an offer if the advertisement or announcement contains a definite promise of something in exchange for something else and confers a power of acceptance on a specified person or class of persons. The typical offer of a reward is an example of a definite offer, as is the situation presented in the landmark *Lefkowitz v. Great Minneapolis Surplus Store, Inc.* case, which follows.

Lefkowitz v. Great Minneapolis Surplus Store, Inc.
Supreme Court of Minnesota, 1957
251 Minn. 188, 86 N.W.2d 689
http://scholar.google.com/scholar_case?case=1365398257799813577&q=251+Minn.+188&hl=en&as_sdt=2,22

FACTS On April 6, 1956, Great Minneapolis Surplus Store published an advertisement in a Minneapolis newspaper reporting that "Saturday, 9:00 A.M. sharp; 3 brand new fur coats worth up to $100; first come, first served, $1.00 each." Lefkowitz was the first to arrive at the store, but the store refused to sell him the fur coats because the "house rule" was that the offers were intended for women only and sales would not be made to men. The following week, Great Minneapolis published a similar advertisement for the sale of two mink scarves and a black lapin stole. Again Lefkowitz was the first to arrive at the store on Saturday morning, and once again the store refused to sell to him, this time because Lefkowitz knew of the house rule. This appeal was from a judgment awarding the plaintiff the sum of $138.50 as damages for breach of contract.

DECISION Judgment for Lefkowitz affirmed.

OPINION Whether a newspaper advertisement constitutes an offer, rather than a mere invitation to make an offer, depends upon the intention of the parties and the surrounding circumstances. If the facts show that some performance was promised in positive terms in return for something requested, then a newspaper advertisement addressed to the general public may lead to a binding obligation. Here the newspaper advertisements were clear, definite, and explicit, and left nothing open for negotiation. Lefkowitz was the first to arrive at the store and to offer to purchase the furs and, therefore, was entitled to performance on the part of the store.

INTERPRETATION Although advertisements generally do not constitute offers, under some circumstances they do.

ETHICAL QUESTION Should Lefkowitz be entitled to damages? Why?

CRITICAL THINKING QUESTION Should an advertisement generally be construed as *not* constituting an offer? Explain.

Auction Sales The auctioneer at an auction sale does not make offers to sell the property being auctioned but invites offers to buy. The classic statement by the auctioneer is, "How much am I offered?" The persons attending the auction may make progressively higher bids for the property, and each bid or statement of a price or a figure is an offer to buy at that figure. If the bid is accepted, customarily indicated by the fall of the hammer in the auctioneer's hand, a contract results. A bidder is free to withdraw his bid at any time prior to its acceptance. The auctioneer is likewise free to withdraw the goods from sale *unless* the sale is advertised or announced to be without reserve.

Without reserve
auctioneer may not withdraw the goods from the auction

If the auction sale is advertised or announced in explicit terms to be **without reserve**, the auctioneer may not withdraw an article or lot put up for sale unless no bid is made within a reasonable time. Unless so advertised or announced, the sale is with reserve. A bidder at either type of sale may retract his bid at any time prior to its acceptance by the auctioneer; such retraction, however, does not revive any previous bid.

Definiteness [10-1c]

Definiteness
offer's terms must be clear enough to provide a court with a basis for giving an appropriate remedy

The terms of a contract, all of which are usually contained in the offer, must be clear enough to provide a court with a reasonable basis for determining the existence of a breach and for giving an appropriate remedy. It is a fundamental policy that contracts should be made by the parties, not by the courts; accordingly, remedies for a breach must in turn have their basis in the parties' contract. Where the parties have intended to form a contract, the courts will attempt to find a basis for granting a remedy. Missing terms may be supplied by course of dealing, usage of trade, or inference. Thus, uncertainty as to incidental matters seldom will be fatal so long as the parties intended to form a contract. Nevertheless, the more terms the parties leave open, the less likely it is that they have intended to form a contract. Moreover, given the great variety of contracts, stating the terms that are essential to all contracts is impossible. In most cases, however, material terms would include the parties, subject matter, price, quantity, quality, and time of performance. (See *DiLorenzo v. Valve and Primer Corporation* in Chapter 12.)

Practical Advice

To make an offer that will result in an enforceable contract, make sure you include all the necessary terms.

Open Terms With respect to agreements for the sale of goods, the UCC provides standards by which the courts may determine omitted terms, provided the parties intended to enter into a binding contract. The Code provides missing terms in a number of instances, where, for example, the contract fails to specify the price, the time or place of delivery, or payment terms.

The Restatement has adopted an approach similar to the Code's in supplying terms omitted from the parties' contract.

Under the Code, an offer for the purchase or sale of goods may leave open particulars of performance to be specified by one of the parties. Any such specification must be made in good faith and within limits set by commercial reasonableness. **Good faith** is defined as honesty in fact and the observance of reasonable commercial standards of fair dealing under the 2001 Revised UCC Article 1 adopted by at least forty-five states. (Under the original UCC, good faith means honesty in fact in the conduct or transaction concerned.) **Commercial reasonableness** is a standard determined in terms of the business judgment of reasonable persons familiar with the practices customary in the type of transaction involved and in terms of the facts and circumstances of the case. (See *DiLorenzo v. Valve and Primer Corporation* in Chapter 12.)

Output and Requirements Contracts   An **output contract** is an agreement of a buyer to purchase a seller's entire output for a stated period. In comparison, a **requirements contract** is an agreement of a seller to supply a buyer with all his requirements for certain goods. Even though the exact quantity of goods is not specified and the seller may have some degree of control over his output and the buyer over his requirements, under the Code and the Restatement, such agreements are enforceable by the application of an objective standard based on the good faith of both parties. Thus, a seller who operated a factory only eight hours a day before the agreement was made cannot operate the factory twenty-four hours a day and insist that the buyer take all of the output. Nor can the buyer expand his business abnormally and insist that the seller still supply all of his requirements.

Duration of Offers [10-2]

An offer confers upon the offeree a power of acceptance, which continues until the offer terminates. The ways in which an offer may be terminated, other than by acceptance, are through (1) lapse of time, (2) revocation, (3) rejection, (4) counteroffer, (5) death or incompetency of the offeror or offeree, (6) destruction of the subject matter to which the offer relates, and (7) subsequent illegality of the type of contract the offer proposes.

Lapse of Time [10-2a]

The offeror may specify the time within which the offer is to be accepted, just as he may specify any other term or condition in the offer. Unless otherwise terminated, the offer remains open for the *specified* time. Upon the expiration of that time, the offer no longer exists and cannot be accepted. Any purported acceptance of an expired offer will serve only as a new offer.

If the offer does not state the time within which the offeree may accept, the offer will terminate after a *reasonable* time. Determining a "reasonable" time is a question of fact, depending on the nature of the contract proposed, the usages of business, and other circumstances of the case (including whether the offer was communicated by electronic means). For instance, an offer to sell a perishable good would be open for a far shorter period of time than an offer to sell undeveloped real estate.

Good faith
honesty in fact and the observance of reasonable commercial standards of fair dealing

Commercial reasonableness
judgment of reasonable persons familiar with the business transaction

Output contract
an agreement of a buyer to purchase the entire output of a seller's factory

Requirements contract
an agreement of a seller to supply a buyer with all his requirements for certain goods

Lapse of time
offer remains open for the time period specified or, if no time is stated, for a reasonable period of time

Practical Advice

Because of the uncertainty as to what is a "reasonable time," it is advisable to specify clearly the duration of offers you make.

Sherrod v. Kidd
Court of Appeals of Washington, Division 3, 2007
155 P.3d 976
http://scholar.google.com/scholar_case?case=7607426217314840344&q=155+P.3d+976&hl=en&as_sclt=2,22

FACTS David and Elizabeth Kidd's dog bit Mikaila Sherrod. Mikaila through her guardian ad litem (GAL) made a claim for damages against the Kidds (defendants). On June 14, 2005, the Kidds offered to settle the claim for $31,837. On July 12, Mikaila through her GAL sued the Kidds. On July 20, the Kidds raised their settlement offer to $32,843. The suit was subject to mandatory arbitration. The parties proceeded to arbitration on April 28, 2006. On May 5, the arbitrator awarded Mikaila $25,069.47. On May 9, the GAL wrote to the Kidds and purported to accept their last offer of $32,843, made the year before. The GAL on Mikaila's behalf moved to enforce the settlement agreement. The court concluded the offer was properly accepted because it had not been withdrawn and it entered judgment in the amount of the first written offer.

DECISION The decision of the trial judge is reversed.

OPINION An offer to form a contract is open only for a reasonable time, unless the offer specifically states how long it is open for acceptance. How much time is reasonable is usually a question of fact. A reasonable time "is the time that a reasonable person in the exact position of the offeree would believe to be satisfactory to the offeror." A reasonable time for an offeree to accept an offer depends on the "nature of the contract and the character of the business in which the parties were engaged."

Implicit in an offer (and an acceptance) to settle a personal injury suit is the party's intent to avoid a less favorable result at the hands of a jury, a judge or, in this case, an arbitrator. The defendant runs the risk that the award might be more than the offer. The plaintiff, of course, runs the risk that the award might be less than the offer. Both want to avoid that risk. And it is those risks that settlements avoid. In this case the offer expired when the arbitrator announced the award and thus was not subject to being accepted.

INTERPRETATION An offer is open for a reasonable period of time.

CRITICAL THINKING QUESTION Should the courts consider the social and public policy in a case such as this? Explain.

Revocation [10-2b]

Revocation

cancellation of an offer by an offeror; generally, an offer may be terminated at any time before it is accepted

The offeror generally may cancel or *revoke* an offer (**revocation**) at any time *prior* to its acceptance. If the offeror originally promises that the offer will be open for thirty days but wishes to terminate it after five days, he may do so merely by giving the offeree notice that he is withdrawing the offer. This notice may be given by any means of communication and effectively terminates the offer when *received* by the offeree. A very few states, however, have adopted a rule that treats revocations the same as acceptances, thus making them effective upon dispatch. An offer made to the general public is revoked only by giving to the revocation publicity equivalent to that given the offer.

Notice of revocation may be communicated indirectly to the offeree through reliable information from a third person that the offeror has disposed of the property he has offered for sale or has otherwise placed himself in a position indicating an unwillingness or inability to perform the promise contained in the offer. For example, Aaron offers to sell his portable television set to Ted and tells Ted that he has ten days in which to accept. One week later, Ted observes the television set in Celia's house and is informed that Celia purchased it from Aaron. The next day, Ted sends to Aaron an acceptance of the offer. There is no contract because Aaron's offer was effectively revoked when Ted learned of Aaron's inability to sell the television set to Ted because he had sold it to Celia.

Certain limitations, however, restrict the offeror's power to revoke the offer at any time prior to its acceptance. These limitations apply to the following five situations.

Option

contract providing that an offer will stay open for a specified period of time

Consideration

the inducement to enter into a contract, consisting of an act or promise that has legal value

Option Contracts An **option** is a contract by which the offeror is bound to hold open an offer for a specified period of time. It must comply with all of the requirements of a contract, including the offeree's giving of consideration to the offeror. (**Consideration**, or the inducement to enter into a contract consisting of an act or promise that has legal value, is discussed in Chapter 12.) For example, if Ellen, in return for the payment of $500 to her by Barry, grants Barry an option, exercisable at any time within thirty days, to buy Blackacre at a price of $80,000, Ellen's offer is irrevocable. Ellen is legally bound to keep the offer open for thirty days, and any communication by Ellen to Barry giving notice of withdrawal of the offer is ineffective. Though Barry is not bound to accept the offer, the option contract entitles him to thirty days in which to accept.

Firm offer

irrevocable offer by a merchant to sell or buy goods, made in a signed writing that gives assurance that it will not be revoked for up to three months

Firm Offers Under the Code The Code provides that a *merchant* is bound to keep an offer to buy or sell *goods* open for a stated period (or, if no time is stated, for a reasonable time) not exceeding three months if the merchant gives assurance in a *signed writing* that the offer will be held open. The Code, therefore, makes a merchant's **firm offer** (written promise not to revoke an offer for a stated period of time) enforceable even though no consideration is given to the offeror for that promise (i.e., an option contract does not exist). A *merchant* is defined as a person (1) who is a dealer in a given type of goods, or (2) who by his occupation holds himself out as having knowledge or skill peculiar to the goods or practices involved, or (3) who employs an agent or broker whom he holds out as having such knowledge or skill.

Statutory irrevocability

offer made irrevocable by statute

Statutory Irrevocability Certain offers, such as bids made to the state, municipality, or other government body for the construction of a building or some public work, are made irrevocable by statute. Another example is preincorporation stock subscription agreements, which are irrevocable for a period of six months under many state corporation statutes.

Irrevocable Offers of Unilateral Contracts

Irrevocable offer of unilateral contracts a unilateral offer may not be revoked for a reasonable time after performance is begun

Irrevocable Offers of Unilateral Contracts Where the offer contemplates a *unilateral* contract—that is, a promise for an act—injustice to the offeree may result if revocation is permitted after the offeree has started to perform the act requested in the offer and has substantially but not completely accomplished it. Such an offer is not accepted and no contract is formed until the offeree has completed the requested act. By simply starting performance, the offeree does not bind himself to complete performance; historically, he did not bind the offeror to keep the offer open, either. Thus, the offeror could revoke the offer at any time before the offeree's completion of performance. For example, Jordan offers Karlene $300 if Karlene will climb to the top of the flagpole in the center of campus. Karlene starts to climb, but when she is five feet from the top, Jordan yells to her, "I revoke."

The Restatement deals with this problem by providing that where the performance of the requested act necessarily requires the offeree to expend time and effort, the offeror is obligated not to revoke the offer for a reasonable time. This obligation arises when the offeree begins performance. If, however, the offeror does not know of the offeree's performance and has no adequate means of learning of it within a reasonable time, the offeree must exercise reasonable diligence to notify the offeror of the performance.

Practical Advice

When making an offer, be careful to make it irrevocable only if you so desire.

APPLYING THE LAW

Mutual Assent

Facts Taylor and Arbuckle formed a partnership for the purpose of practicing pediatric medicine together. They found new medical office space to lease and thereafter, among other things, they set about furnishing the waiting room in a way that children would find inviting. In addition to contracting with a mural painter, they decided to purchase a high-definition flat-panel television on which they could show children's programming. On a Monday, Taylor and Arbuckle visited a local retailer with a reputation for competitive pricing, called Today's Electronics. In addition to comparing the pictures on the various models on display, the doctors discussed the pros and cons of LCD (liquid crystal display) versus plasma with the store's owner, Patel.

While they were able to narrow their options down significantly, Taylor and Arbuckle nonetheless could not decide on the exact size set to purchase because they had not yet determined the configuration of the seating to be installed in the waiting room. Sensing that the doctors were considering shopping around, Patel offered them a sizeable discount: only $999 for the forty-inch LCD screen they had chosen, or the fifty-inch plasma model they favored for only $1,299. As they were leaving the store, Patel gave the doctors his business card, on which he had jotted the model

numbers and discount prices, his signature, and the notation "we assure you this offer is open through Sun., April 27."

Anxious to have the waiting room completed, Taylor and Arbuckle quickly agreed on a feasible seating arrangement for the waiting room, ordered the necessary furniture, and decided that the fifty-inch television would be too big. On Friday, April 25, Taylor returned to Today's Electronics. But before she could tell Patel that they had decided on the forty-inch LCD, Patel informed her that he could not honor the discounted prices because he no longer had in stock either model the doctors were considering.

Issue Is Patel free to revoke his offer notwithstanding having agreed to hold it open through the weekend?

Rule of Law The general rule is that an offeror may revoke, or withdraw, an offer any time before it has been accepted. However, there are several limitations on an offeror's power to revoke an offer before acceptance. One of these is the Uniform Commercial Code's (UCC's) "merchant's firm offer" rule. Under the UCC, a merchant's offer to buy or sell goods is irrevocable for the stated period (or, if no period is stated, for a reasonable time) not exceeding three months, when he has signed a writing assuring the offeree that

the offer will be kept open for that period. The Code defines a merchant as one who trades in the types of goods in question or who holds himself out, either personally or by way of an agent, to be knowledgeable regarding the goods or practices involved in the transaction.

Application The proposed contract between the doctors and Today's Electronics is governed by Article 2 of the Code because it involves a sale of goods, in this case a television set. Both Patel and Today's Electronics are considered merchants of televisions under the Code's definition, because Patel and his store regularly sell electronics, including television sets. Patel offered to sell to Taylor and Arbuckle either the forty-inch LCD television for $999 or the fifty-inch plasma for $1,299. By reducing his offer to a signed writing, and by promising in that writing that the stated prices were assured to be open through Sun., April 27, Patel has made a firm offer that he cannot revoke during that six-day period. Whether he still has either model in stock does not affect the irrevocability of the offer.

Conclusion Patel's offer is irrevocable through Sunday, April 27. Therefore Patel's attempt to revoke it is ineffective, and Taylor may still accept it.

Promissory estoppel

noncontractual promise that binds the promisor because she should reasonably expect that the promise will induce the promisee (offeree) to take action in reliance on it

Promissory Estoppel   As discussed in the previous chapter, a noncontractual promise may be enforced when it is made under circumstances that should lead the promisor reasonably to expect that the promise will induce the promisee to take action in reliance on it. This doctrine has been used in some cases to prevent an offeror from revoking an offer prior to its acceptance.

Thus, Ramanan Plumbing Co. submits a written offer for plumbing work to be used by Resolute Building Co. as part of Resolute's bid as a general contractor. Ramanan knows that Resolute is relying on Ramanan's bid, and in fact Resolute submits Ramanan's name as the plumbing subcontractor in the bid. Ramanan's offer is irrevocable until Resolute has a reasonable opportunity to notify Ramanan that Resolute's bid has been accepted.

Rejection [10-2c]

Rejection

the refusal to accept an offer

An offeree is at liberty to accept or reject the offer as he sees fit. If he decides not to accept it, he is not required to reject it formally but may simply wait until the offer terminates by lapse of time. A **rejection** of an offer is a manifestation by the offeree of his unwillingness to accept. A communicated rejection terminates the power of acceptance. From the effective moment of rejection, which is the receipt of the rejection by the offeror, the offeree may no longer accept the offer. Rejection by the offeree may consist of express language or may be implied from language or conduct.

Counteroffer [10-2d]

Counteroffer

counterproposal to an offer

A **counteroffer** is a counterproposal from the offeree to the offeror that indicates a willingness to contract but on terms or conditions different from those contained in the original offer. It is not an unequivocal acceptance of the original offer, and by indicating an unwillingness to agree to the terms of the offer, it generally operates as a rejection. It also operates as a new offer. To illustrate further, assume that Worthy writes Joanne a letter stating that he will sell to Joanne a secondhand color television set for $300. Joanne replies that she will pay Worthy $250 for the set. This is a counteroffer that, on *receipt* by Worthy, terminates the original offer. Worthy may, if he wishes, accept the counteroffer and thereby create a contract for $250. If, on the other hand, Joanne in her reply states that she wishes to consider the $300 offer but is willing to pay $250 at once for the set, she is making a counteroffer that does *not* terminate Worthy's original offer. In the first instance, after making the $250 counteroffer, Joanne may not accept the $300 offer. In the second instance, she may do so, because the counteroffer was stated in such a manner as not to indicate an unwillingness to accept the original offer; Joanne therefore did not terminate it. In addition, a mere inquiry about the possibility of obtaining different or new terms is not a counteroffer and does not terminate the original offer.

Practical Advice

Consider whether you want to make a counterproposal that terminates the original offer or whether you merely wish to discuss alternative possibilities.

Conditional acceptance

acceptance of an offer contingent upon the acceptance of an additional or different term

Another common type of counteroffer is the **conditional acceptance**, which claims to accept the offer but expressly makes the acceptance contingent on the offeror's assent to additional or different terms. Nonetheless, it is a counteroffer and generally terminates the original offer. The Code's treatment of acceptances containing terms that vary from the offer is discussed later in this chapter.

Giannetti v. Cornillie
Court of Appeals of Michigan, 1994
204 Mich. App. 234, 514 N.W.2d 221
http://scholar.google.com/scholar_case?case=17128858960507849357&q=514+N.W.2d+221&hl=en&as_sdt=2,34

FACTS Defendants listed with a real estate agent a home for sale. Plaintiffs, Patrick and Anne Giannetti, offered $155,000 for the home and submitted a deposit in the amount of $2,500. The defendants countered the offer with an offer to sell the house for $160,000. The plaintiffs then inquired whether certain equipment and items of furniture could be included with the sale of the house. The defendants refused to include the questioned items in the sale. The plaintiffs then accepted the $160,000 offer, but changed the mortgage amount from $124,000 to $128,000. The agent failed to show this change to the defendants but instead told

the defendants that the plaintiffs had accepted their counteroffer. Defendants then signed all papers, but before the closing sought to invalidate the agreement. The plaintiffs brought this action for specific performance to enforce the sale. The trial court granted plaintiffs' motion and the defendants appealed.

DECISION Judgment for the defendants.

OPINION Defendants' argue that, "[a]n offer is a unilateral declaration of intention, and is not a contract. A contract is made when both parties have executed or accepted it, and not before.

A counter proposition is not an acceptance." An acceptance must be "unambiguous and in strict conformance with an offer." Moreover, "[A] proposal to accept, or an acceptance, upon terms varying from those offered, is a rejection of the offer, and puts an end to the negotiation, unless the party who made the original offer renews it, or assents to the modification suggested." Thus, "[a]ny material departure from the terms of an offer invalidates the offer as made and results in a counter proposition, which, unless accepted, cannot be enforced." Before the change, plaintiffs were obligated to buy the property if they obtained a mortgage for $124,000; after the change, no obligation to buy arose unless they obtained a $128,000 mortgage. Thus, the modification changed the contract and it was therefore material.

INTERPRETATION A counteroffer generally operates as a rejection and thus terminates the power of acceptance.

ETHICAL QUESTION Was the defendant morally obligated to sell the property? Explain.

CRITICAL THINKING QUESTION What could the plaintiffs have done to protect themselves while at the same time seeking different terms?

Death or Incompetency [10-2e]

Death or incompetency of either the offeror or the offeree terminates the offer

The **death or incompetency** of either the offeror or the offeree ordinarily terminates an offer. On his death or incompetency, the offeror no longer has the legal capacity to enter into a contract; thus, all outstanding offers are terminated. Death or incompetency of the offeree also terminates the offer, because an ordinary offer is not assignable (transferable) and may be accepted only by the person to whom it was made. When the offeree dies or ceases to have legal capability to enter into a contract, no one else has the power to accept the offer. Therefore, the offer necessarily terminates.

The death or incompetency of the offeror or offeree, however, does *not* terminate an offer contained in an option.

Destruction of Subject Matter [10-2f]

Destruction of subject matter of an offer terminates the offer

Destruction of the specific subject matter of an offer terminates the offer. Suppose that Sarah, owning a Buick, offers to sell the car to Barbara and allows Barbara five days in which to accept. Three days later the car is destroyed by fire. On the following day, Barbara, without knowledge of the destruction of the car, notifies Sarah that she accepts Sarah's offer. There is no contract. The destruction of the car terminated Sarah's offer.

Subsequent Illegality [10-2g]

Subsequent illegality of the purpose or subject matter of the offer terminates the offer

One of the essential requirements of a contract, as we previously mentioned, is legality of purpose or subject matter. If performance of a valid contract is subsequently made illegal, the obligations of both parties under the contract are discharged. Illegality taking effect after the making of an offer but prior to acceptance has the same effect: the offer is legally terminated. For an illustration of the duration of revocable offers, see Figure 10-1.

ACCEPTANCE OF OFFER

Acceptance manifestation of a willingness to enter into a contract on the terms of the offer

The acceptance of an offer is essential to the formation of a contract. Once an effective acceptance has been given, the contract is formed. **Acceptance** of an offer for a bilateral contract is some overt act by the offeree that manifests his assent to the terms of the offer, such as speaking or sending a letter, or other explicit or implicit communication to the offeror. If the offer is for a unilateral contract, acceptance is the performance of the requested act with the intention of accepting. For example, if Joy publishes an offer of a reward to anyone who returns the diamond ring that she has lost (an offer to enter into a unilateral contract) and Bob, with knowledge of the offer, finds and returns the ring to Joy, Bob has accepted the offer.

COMMUNICATION OF ACCEPTANCE [10-3]
General Rule [10-3a]

Because acceptance is the manifestation of the offeree's assent to the offer, it must necessarily be communicated to the offeror. This is the rule as to all offers to enter into bilateral contracts. In the case of unilateral offers, however, notice of acceptance to the offeror usually is not required. If, however, the offeree in a unilateral contract has reason to know that the offeror has no

Figure 10-1 Duration of Revocable Offers

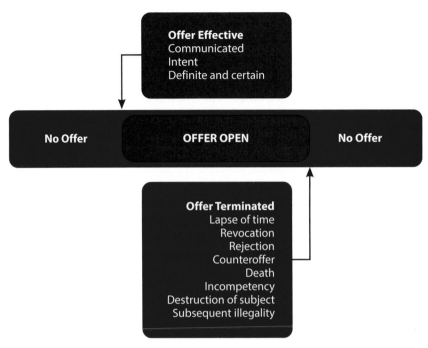

adequate means of learning of the offeree's performance with reasonable promptness and certainty, then the offeree must make reasonable efforts to notify the offeror of acceptance or lose the right to enforce the contract.

Silence as Acceptance [10-3b]

An offeree is generally under no legal duty to reply to an offer. Silence or inaction therefore does *not* indicate acceptance of the offer. By custom, usage, or course of dealing, however, the offeree's silence or inaction may operate as an acceptance. Thus, the silence or inaction of an offeree who fails to reply to an offer operates as an acceptance and causes a contract to be formed. Through previous dealings, for example, the offeree has given the offeror reason to understand that the offeree will accept all offers unless the offeree sends notice to the contrary. Another example of silence operating as an acceptance occurs when the prospective member of a mail-order club agrees that his failure to return a notification card rejecting offered goods will constitute his acceptance of the club's offer to sell the goods.

Furthermore, if an offeror sends unordered or unsolicited merchandise to a person, stating that the goods may be purchased at a specified price and that the offer will be deemed to have been accepted unless the goods are returned within a stated period of time, the offer is one for an inverted unilateral contract (i.e., an act for a promise). This practice has led to abuse, however, prompting the federal government as well as most states to enact statutes that provide that in such cases the offeree-recipient of the goods may keep them as a gift and is under no obligation either to return them or to pay for them.

Effective Moment [10-3c]

As we discussed previously, an offer, a revocation, a rejection, and a counteroffer are effective when they are *received*. An acceptance is generally effective upon *dispatch*. This is true unless the offer specifically provides otherwise, the offeree uses an unauthorized means of communication, or the acceptance follows a prior rejection.

Stipulated Provisions in the Offer   If the offer specifically stipulates the means of communication to be used by the offeree, the acceptance must conform to that specification. Thus, if an offer states that acceptance must be made by registered mail, any purported acceptance not made by registered mail would be ineffective. Moreover, the rule that an acceptance is effective when dispatched or sent does not apply in cases in which the offer provides that the

Effective moment
acceptance effective upon dispatch unless the offer specifically provides otherwise or the offeree uses an unauthorized means of communication

Stipulated provisions in the offer
the communication of acceptance must conform to the specifications in the offer

Practical Advice

Consider whether you should specify in your offers that acceptances are valid only upon receipt.

acceptance must be received by the offeror. If the offeror states that a reply must be received by a certain date or that he must hear from the offeree or uses other language indicating that the acceptance must be received by him, the effective moment of the acceptance is when the offeror receives it, not when the offeree sends or dispatches it.

Authorized Means   Historically, an authorized means of communication was either the means the offeror expressly authorized in the offer or, if none was authorized, the means the offeror used in presenting the offer. If in reply to an offer by mail, the offeree places in the mail a letter of acceptance properly stamped and addressed to the offeror, a contract is formed at the time and place that the offeree mails the letter. This assumes, of course, that the offer was open at that time and had not been terminated by any of the methods previously discussed. The reason for this rule is that the offeror, by using the mail, impliedly authorized the offeree to use the same means of communication. It is immaterial if the letter of acceptance goes astray in the mail and is never received.

The Restatement and the Code both now provide that where the language in the offer or the circumstances do not otherwise indicate, an offer to make a contract shall be construed as authorizing acceptance in any reasonable manner. Thus, an **authorized means** is usually any *reasonable* means of communication. These provisions are intended to allow flexibility of response and the ability to keep pace with new modes of communication.

See Figure 10-2 for an overview of offer and acceptance.

Authorized means
usually any reasonable means of communication

Osprey L.L.C. v. Kelly-Moore Paint Co., Inc.
Supreme Court of Oklahoma, 1999
1999 OK 50, 984 P.2d 194
http://scholar.google.com/scholar_case?case=15066374301719252497&q=1999+OK+50&hl=en&as_sdt=2,22

FACTS In 1977, the defendant, Kelly-Moore Paint Company, entered into a fifteen-year commercial lease with the plaintiff, Osprey, for a property in Edmond, Oklahoma. The lease contained two five-year renewal options. The lease required that the lessee give notice of its intent to renew at least six months prior to its expiration. It also provided that the renewal "may be delivered either personally or by depositing the same in United States mail, first class postage prepaid, registered or certified mail, return receipt requested." Upon expiration of the original fifteen-year lease, Kelly-Moore timely informed the lessor by certified letter of its intent to extend the lease an additional five years. The first five-year extension was due to expire on August 31, 1997. On the last day of the six-month notification deadline, Kelly-Moore faxed a letter of renewal notice to Osprey's office at 5:28 P.M. In addition, Kelly-Moore sent a copy of the faxed renewal notice letter by Federal Express that same day. Osprey denies ever receiving the fax, but it admits receiving the Federal Express copy of the notice on the following business day. Osprey rejected the notice, asserting that it was late, and it filed an action to remove the defendant from the premises. After a trial on the merits, the trial court granted judgment in favor of Kelly-Moore, finding that the faxed notice was effective. Osprey appealed. The Court of Civil Appeals reversed, determining that the plain language of the lease required that it be renewed by delivering notice either personally or by mail, and that Kelly-Moore had done neither. Kelly-Moore appealed.

DECISION The decision of the Court of Appeals is vacated and the decision of the trial court is affirmed.

OPINION A lease is a contract and, in construing a lease, the usual rules for the interpretation of contractual writings apply. Language in a contract is given its plain and ordinary meaning, unless some technical term is used in a manner meant to convey a specific technical concept. A contract term is ambiguous only if it can be interpreted as

having two different meanings. The lease does not appear to be ambiguous. "Shall" is ordinarily construed as mandatory and "may" is ordinarily construed as permissive. The contract clearly requires that notice "shall" be in writing. The provision for delivery, either personally or by certified or registered mail, uses the permissive "may" and it does not bar other modes of transmission which are just as effective.

The purpose of providing notice by personal delivery or registered mail is to ensure the delivery of the notice and to settle any dispute which might arise between the parties concerning whether the notice was received. A substituted method of notice that performs the same function and serves the same purpose as an authorized method of notice is not defective. Here, the contract provided that time was of the essence. Although Osprey denies that it ever received the fax, the fax activity report and telephone company records confirm that the fax was transmitted successfully and that it was sent to Osprey's correct facsimile number on the last day of the deadline to extend the lease. The fax provided immediate written communication similar to personal delivery and would be timely if it were properly transmitted before the deadline. Kelly-Moore's use of the fax served the same function and the same purpose as the two methods suggested by the lease, and it was transmitted before the expiration of the deadline to renew. Under these facts, the faxed or facsimile delivery of the written notice to renew the commercial lease was sufficient to exercise timely the renewal option of the lease.

INTERPRETATION Where the language in the offer or the circumstances does not otherwise indicate, an offer to make a contract shall be construed as authorizing acceptance in any reasonable manner.

CRITICAL THINKING QUESTION Are there instances in which an offeror should require a certain mode for acceptance? When?

Figure 10-2 Mutual Assent

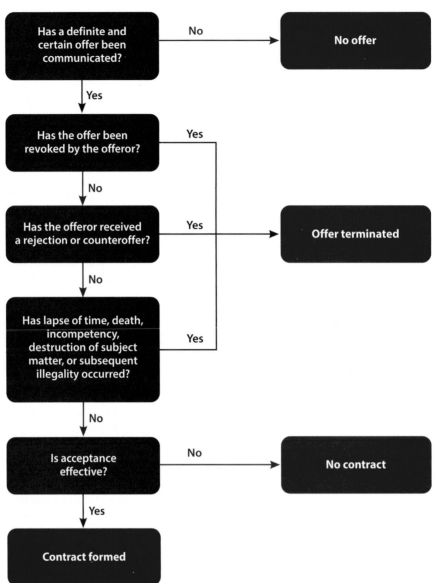

Unauthorized means
acceptance effective when
received, provided that it is
received within the time
within which the authorized
means would have arrived

**Acceptance following
a prior rejection**
first communication
received by the offeror is
effective

Unauthorized Means   When the method of communication used by the offeree is unauthorized, the traditional rule is that acceptance is effective when and if received by the offeror, provided that it is received within the time during which the authorized means would have arrived. The Restatement goes further by providing that if these conditions are met, then the effective time for the acceptance is the moment of dispatch.

Acceptance Following a Prior Rejection   An acceptance sent after a prior rejection is not effective when sent by the offeree, but only when and if *received* by the offeror before he receives the rejection. Thus, when an acceptance follows a prior rejection, *the first communication* the offeror receives is the effective one. For example, Carlos in New York sends by mail to Paula in San Francisco an offer that is expressly stated to be open for ten days. On the fourth day, Paula sends to Carlos by mail a letter of rejection, which is delivered on the morning of the seventh day. At noon on the fifth day, Paula dispatches an overnight letter of acceptance that Carlos receives before the close of business on the sixth day. A contract was formed when Carlos received Paula's overnight letter of acceptance, as it was received before the letter of rejection.

Defective Acceptances [10-3d]

Defective acceptance does not create a contract but serves as a new offer

A late or **defective acceptance** does not create a contract. After the offer has expired, it cannot be accepted. However, a late or defective acceptance does manifest a willingness on the part of the offeree to enter into a contract and therefore constitutes a new offer. To create a contract based on this offer, the original offeror must accept the new offer by manifesting his assent to it.

VARIANT ACCEPTANCES [10-4]

A variant acceptance—one that contains terms different from or additional to those in the offer—receives distinctly different treatment under the common law and under the Code.

Common Law [10-4a]

Mirror image rule an acceptance cannot deviate from the terms of the offer

An acceptance must be *positive* and *unequivocal*. It may not change, add to, subtract from, or qualify in any way the provisions of the offer. In other words, it must be the **mirror image** of the offer. Any communication by the offeree that attempts to modify the offer is not an acceptance but a counteroffer, which does not create a contract.

Code [10-4b]

The common law mirror image rule, by which the acceptance cannot vary or deviate from the terms of the offer, is modified by the Code. This modification is necessitated by the realities of modern business practices. A vast number of business transactions use standardized business forms. For example, a merchant buyer sends to a merchant seller on the buyer's order form a purchase order for one thousand cotton shirts at $60.00 per dozen with delivery by October 1 at the buyer's place of business. On the reverse side of this standard form are twenty-five numbered paragraphs containing provisions generally favorable to the buyer. When the seller receives the buyer's order, he agrees to the buyer's quantity, price, and delivery terms and sends to the buyer on his acceptance form an unequivocal acceptance of the offer. However, on the back of his acceptance form, the seller has thirty-two numbered paragraphs generally favorable to himself and in significant conflict with the provisions on the buyer's form. Under the common law's *mirror image* rule, no contract would exist; for the seller has not accepted unequivocally all of the material terms of the buyer's offer.

The Code attempts to alleviate this **battle of the forms** by focusing on the intent of the parties. If the offeree does not expressly make her acceptance conditional upon the offeror's assent to the additional or different terms, a contract is formed. The issue then becomes whether the offeree's different or additional terms become part of the contract. If both offeror and offeree are merchants, such *additional* terms may become part of the contract provided that they do not materially alter the agreement and are not objected to either in the offer itself or within a reasonable period of time. If either of the parties is not a merchant or if the additional terms materially alter the offer, then the additional terms are merely construed as proposals to the contract. *Different* terms proposed by the offeree will not become part of the contract unless accepted by the offeror. The courts are divided over what terms to include when the terms differ or conflict. Most courts hold that the offeror's terms govern; other courts hold that the terms cancel each other out and look to the Code to provide the missing terms. Some states follow a third alternative and apply the additional terms test to different terms. (See Figure 19-1 in Chapter 19.)

Let us apply the Code to the previous example involving the seller and the buyer: because both parties are merchants and the seller's acceptance was not conditional upon assent to the seller's additional or different terms, then either (1) the contract will be formed without the seller's different terms unless the buyer specifically accepts them; (2) the contract will be formed without the seller's additional terms (unless they are specifically accepted by the buyer) because the additional terms materially alter the offer; or (3) depending upon the jurisdiction, either (a) the buyer's conflicting terms will be included in the contract; (b) the Code will provide the missing terms, because the conflicting terms cancel each other out; or (c) the additional terms test is applied.

See Concept Review 10-1 explicating the effective time and effect of communications involved in offers and acceptances.

CONCEPT REVIEW 10-1

Offer and Acceptance

	Time Effective	Effect
Communications by Offeror		
• Offer	Received by offeree	Creates power to form a contract
• Revocation	Received by offeree	Terminates power
Communications by Offeree		
• Rejection	Received by offeror	Terminates offer
• Counteroffer	Received by offeror	Terminates offer
• Acceptance	Sent by offeree	Forms a contract
• Acceptance after prior rejection	Received by offeror	If received before rejection forms a contract

BUSINESS LAW IN ACTION

Business-to-consumer, or "B2C," transactions on the Internet allow buyers to purchase goods for delivery as quickly as overnight—everything from sports equipment and welding tools to bath towels and fresh cut flowers. And increasingly consumers can buy services in cyberspace, too, like vacation packages and movie theater tickets.

The contracting process is easy. In addition to requiring the purchaser to input data like payment details and shipping and billing addresses, Web-based providers use radio buttons or check boxes for the customer to make various selections. In some cases the customer must uncheck or deselect items, and in others, the consumer must affirmatively click on a button or series of buttons labeled "I agree," or "I

accept." These cybercontracts are sometimes called "clickwrap" or "click on" agreements.

By filling in the required blanks, selecting or deselecting various options, and otherwise completing the transaction, the purchaser is indicating his or her assent to be bound by the seller's offer. Sales of goods can be relatively simple and straightforward. But services available on the Internet, particularly those that involve an ongoing relationship between the user and the provider, usually require more complex contract provisions.

Offers for video rental club memberships and software licenses, for example, frequently contain restrictions on use and such other terms as warranty disclaimers and arbitration clauses as well as privacy

policy disclosures, all written primarily in legalese and taking up multiple screens of text. The reality is that many buyers simply do not read them. Nonetheless, depending on how the agreement process is set up, these terms are likely binding.

Whether a buyer's nonverbal assent to these lengthy contract provisions will pass legal muster is dependent on the online contracting process. Even if the buyer does not read the proposed terms, they will be enforced if the buyer has had the opportunity to review them, either by way of an automatic screen or a link. And, equally as important, the cyberoffer's terms will be binding when the site requires the buyer to actively select them or to click on a button or type words affirmatively indicating his or her assent.

CHAPTER SUMMARY

Offer

Essentials of an Offer

Definition indication of willingness to enter into a contract

Communication offeree must have knowledge of the offer and the offer must be made by the offeror or her authorized agent to the offeree

Intent determined by an objective standard of what a reasonable offeree would have believed

Definiteness offer's terms must be clear enough to provide a court with a basis for giving an appropriate remedy

Duration of Offers

Lapse of Time offer remains open for the time period specified or, if no time is stated, for a reasonable period of time

Revocation generally, an offer may be terminated at any time before it is accepted, subject to the following exceptions

- *Option Contracts* contract that binds offeror to keep an offer open for a specified time
- *Firm Offer* a merchant's irrevocable offer to sell or buy goods in a signed writing that ensures that the offer will not be terminated for up to three months
- *Statutory Irrevocability* offer made irrevocable by statute
- *Irrevocable Offer of Unilateral Contracts* a unilateral offer may not be *revoked* for a reasonable time after performance is begun
- *Promissory Estoppel* noncontractual promise that binds the promisor because she should reasonably expect that the promise will induce the promisee (offeree) to take action in reliance on it

Rejection refusal to accept an offer terminates the power of acceptance

Counteroffer counterproposal to an offer that generally terminates the original offer

Death or Incompetency of either the offeror or the offeree terminates the offer

Destruction of Subject Matter of an offer terminates the offer

Subsequent Illegality of the purpose or subject matter of the offer terminates the offer

---

Acceptance of Offer

Requirements

Definition positive and unequivocal expression of a willingness to enter into a contract on the terms of the offer

Mirror Image Rule except as modified by the Code, an acceptance cannot deviate from the terms of the offer

Communication of Acceptance

General Rule acceptance effective upon dispatch unless the offer specifically provides otherwise or the offeree uses an unauthorized means of communication

Silence as Acceptance generally does not indicate acceptance of the offer

Effective Moment generally upon dispatch

- *Stipulated Provisions in the Offer* the communication of acceptance must conform to the specifications in the offer
- *Authorized Means* the Restatement and the Code provide that, unless the offer provides otherwise, acceptance is authorized to be in any reasonable manner
- *Unauthorized Means* acceptance effective when received, provided that it is received within the time within which the authorized means would have arrived
- *Acceptance Following a Prior Rejection* first communication received by the offeror is effective

Defective Acceptance does not create a contract but serves as a new offer

QUESTIONS

1. Ames, seeking business for his lawn maintenance firm, posted the following notice in the meeting room of the Antlers, a local lodge: "To the members of the Antlers—Special this month. I will resod your lawn for $4.00 per square foot using Fairway brand sod. This offer expires July 15."

   The notice also included Ames's name, address, and signature and specified that the acceptance was to be in writing.

   Bates, a member of the Antlers, and Cramer, the janitor, read the notice and were interested. Bates wrote a letter to Ames saying he would accept the offer if Ames would use Putting Green brand sod. Ames received this letter July 14 and wrote to Bates saying he would not use Putting Green

   sod. Bates received Ames's letter on July 16 and promptly wrote Ames that he would accept Fairway sod. Cramer wrote to Ames on July 10 saying he accepted Ames's offer.

   By July 15, Ames had found more profitable ventures and refused to resod either lawn at the specified price. Bates and Cramer brought an appropriate action against Ames for breach of contract. Decisions as to the respective claims of Bates and Cramer?

2. Justin owned four speedboats named *Porpoise, Priscilla, Providence,* and *Prudence.* On April 2, Justin made written offers to sell the four boats in the order named for $14,200 each to Charles, Diane, Edward, and Fran, respectively, allowing ten

days for acceptance. In which, if any, of the following four situations was a contract formed?

a. Five days later, Charles received notice from Justin that he had contracted to sell *Porpoise* to Mark. The next day, April 8, Charles notified Justin that he accepted Justin's offer.

b. On the third day, April 5, Diane mailed a rejection to Justin that reached Justin on the morning of the sixth day. At 10:00 A.M. on the fourth day, Diane sent an acceptance by overnight letter to Justin, who received it at noon the fifth day.

c. Edward, on April 3, replied that he was interested in buying *Providence* but declared the price appeared slightly excessive and wondered if, perhaps, Justin would be willing to sell the boat for $13,900. Five days later, having received no reply from Justin, Edward accepted Justin's offer by letter, and enclosed a certified check for $14,200.

d. Fran was accidentally killed in an automobile accident on April 9. The following day, the executor of her estate mailed an acceptance of Justin's offer to Justin.

3. Alpha Rolling Mill Corporation (Alpha Corporation), by letter dated June 8, offered to sell Brooklyn Railroad Company (Brooklyn Company) two thousand to five thousand tons of fifty-pound iron rails on certain specified terms and added that, if the offer was accepted, Alpha Corporation would expect to be notified prior to June 20. Brooklyn Company, on June 16, by fax, referring to Alpha Corporation's offer of June 8, directed Alpha Corporation to enter an order for one thousand two hundred tons of fifty-pound iron rails on the terms specified. The same day, June 16, Brooklyn Company, by letter to Alpha Corporation, confirmed the fax. On June 18, Alpha Corporation, by telephone, declined to fulfill the order. Brooklyn Company, on June 19, wrote Alpha Corporation: "Please enter an order for two thousand tons of rails as per your letter of the eighth. Please forward written contract. Reply." In reply to Brooklyn Company's repeated inquiries concerning whether the order for two thousand tons of rails had been entered, Alpha denied the existence of any contract between Brooklyn Company and itself. Thereafter, Brooklyn Company sued Alpha Corporation for breach of contract. Decision?

4. On April 8, Crystal received a telephone call from Akers, a truck dealer, who told Crystal that a new model truck in which Crystal was interested would arrive in one week. Although Akers initially wanted $10,500, the conversation ended after Akers agreed to sell and Crystal agreed to purchase the truck for $10,000, with a $1,000 down payment and the balance on delivery. The next day, Crystal sent Akers a check for $1,000, which Akers promptly cashed.

One week later, when Crystal called Akers and inquired about the truck, Akers informed Crystal he had several prospects looking at the truck and would not sell for less than $10,500. The following day Akers sent Crystal a properly executed check for $1,000 with the following notation thereon: "Return of down payment on sale of truck."

After notifying Akers that she will not cash the check, Crystal sues Akers for damages. Should Crystal prevail? Explain.

5. On November 15, Gloria, Inc., a manufacturer of crystalware, mailed to Benny Buyer a letter stating that Gloria would sell to Buyer one hundred crystal "A" goblets at $100 per goblet and that "the offer would remain open for fifteen (15) days."

On November 18, Gloria, noticing the sudden rise in the price of crystal "A" goblets, decided to withdraw her offer to Buyer and so notified Buyer. Buyer chose to ignore Gloria's letter of revocation and gleefully watched as the price of crystal "A" goblets continued to skyrocket. On November 30, Buyer mailed to Gloria a letter accepting Gloria's offer to sell the goblets. The letter was received by Gloria on December 4. Buyer demands delivery of the goblets. What is the result?

6. On May 1, Melforth Realty Company offered to sell Greenacre to Dallas, Inc., for $1 million. The offer was made by a letter sent by overnight delivery and stated that the offer would expire on May 15. Dallas decided to purchase the property and sent a letter by registered first-class mail to Melforth on May 10 accepting the offer. As a result of unexplained delays in the postal service, the letter was not received by Melforth until May 22. Melforth wishes to sell Greenacre to another buyer who is offering $1.2 million for the tract of land. Has a contract resulted between Melforth and Dallas?

7. Rowe advertised in newspapers of wide circulation and otherwise made known that she would pay $5,000 for a complete set, consisting of ten volumes, of certain rare books. Ford, not knowing of the offer, gave Rowe all but one volume of the set of rare books as a Christmas present. Ford later learned of the offer, obtained the one remaining book, tendered it to Rowe, and demanded the $5,000. Rowe refused to pay. Is Ford entitled to the $5,000?

8. Scott, manufacturer of a carbonated beverage, entered into a contract with Otis, owner of a baseball park, whereby Otis rented to Scott a large signboard on top of the center field wall. The contract provided that Otis should letter the sign as Scott desired and would change the lettering from time to time within forty-eight hours after receipt of written request from Scott. As directed by Scott, the signboard originally stated in large letters that Scott would pay $100 to any ball player hitting a home run over the sign.

In the first game of the season, Hume, the best hitter in the league, hit one home run over the sign. Scott immediately served written notice on Otis instructing Otis to replace the offer on the signboard with an offer to pay $50.00 to every pitcher who pitched a no-hit game in the park. A week after receipt of Scott's letter, Otis had not changed the wording on the sign; and on that day, Perry, a pitcher for a scheduled game, pitched a no-hit game and Todd, one of his teammates, hit a home run over Scott's sign.

Scott refuses to pay any of the three players. What are the rights of Scott, Hume, Perry, and Todd?

9. Barney accepted Clark's offer to sell to him a portion of Clark's coin collection. Clark forgot at the time of the offer and acceptance that her prized $20.00 gold piece was included in the portion that she offered to sell to Barney. Clark did not intend to include the gold piece in the sale. Barney, at the time of inspecting the offered portion of the collection, and prior to accepting the offer, saw the gold piece. Is Barney entitled to the $20.00 gold piece?

10. Small, admiring Jasper's watch, asked Jasper where and at what price he had purchased it. Jasper replied, "I bought it at West Watch Shop about two years ago for around $85.00, but I am not certain as to that." Small then said, "Those fellows at

West are good people and always sell good watches. I'll buy that watch from you." Jasper replied, "It's a deal." The next morning, Small telephoned Jasper and said he had changed his mind and did not wish to buy the watch.

Jasper sued Small for breach of contract. In defense, Small has pleaded that he made no enforceable contract with Jasper because (a) the parties did not agree on the price to be paid for the watch and (b) the parties did not agree on the place and time of delivery of the watch to Small. Are either, or both, of these defenses good?

11. Jeff says to Brenda, "I offer to sell you my PC for $900." Brenda replies, "If you do not hear otherwise from me by Thursday, I have accepted your offer." Jeff agrees and does not hear from Brenda by Thursday. Does a contract exist between Jeff and Brenda? Explain.

12. On November 19, Hoover Motor Express Company sent to Clements Paper Company a written offer to purchase certain real estate. Sometime in December, Clements authorized Williams to accept the offer. Williams, however, attempted to bargain with Hoover to obtain a better deal, specifically that Clements would retain easements on the property. In a telephone conversation on January 13 of the following year, Williams first told Hoover of his plan to obtain the easements. Hoover replied, "Well, I don't know if we are ready. We have not decided, we might not want to go through with it." On January 20, Clements sent a written acceptance of Hoover's offer. Hoover refused to buy, claiming it had revoked its offer through the January 13 phone conversation. Clements then brought suit to compel the sale or obtain damages. Did Hoover successfully revoke its offer?

13. Walker leased a small lot to Keith for ten years at $100 a month, with a right for Keith to extend the lease for another ten-year term under the same terms except as to rent. The renewal option provided:

> Rental will be fixed in such amount as shall actually be agreed upon by the lessors and the lessee with the monthly rental fixed on the comparative basis of rental values as of the date of the renewal with rental values at this time reflected by the comparative business conditions of the two periods.

Keith sought to exercise the renewal right and, when the parties were unable to agree on the rent, brought suit against Walker. Who prevails? Why?

CASE PROBLEMS

14. The Brewers contracted to purchase Dower House from McAfee. Then, several weeks before the May 7 settlement date for the purchase of the house, the two parties began to negotiate for the sale of certain items of furniture in the house. On April 30, McAfee sent the Brewers a letter containing a list of the furnishings to be purchased at specific prices; a payment schedule including a $3,000 payment due on acceptance; and a clause reading: "If the above is satisfactory, please sign and return one copy with the first payment."

On June 3, the Brewers sent a letter to McAfee stating that enclosed was a $3,000 check; that the original contract had been misplaced and could another be furnished; that they planned to move into Dower House on June 12; and that they wished that the red desk also be included in the contract. McAfee then sent a letter dated June 8 to the Brewers listing the items of furniture they had purchased.

The Brewers moved into Dower House in the middle of June. Soon after they moved in, they tried to contact McAfee at his office to tell him that there had been a misunderstanding relating to their purchase of the listed items. They then refused to pay him any more money, and he brought this action to recover the outstanding balance unless the red desk was also included in the sale. Will McAfee be able to collect the additional money from the Brewers?

15. The Thoelkes were owners of real property located in Florida, which the Morrisons agreed to purchase. The Morrisons signed a contract for the sale of that property and mailed it to the Thoelkes in Texas on November 26. Subsequently, the Thoelkes executed the contract and placed it in the mail addressed to the Morrisons' attorney in Florida. After the executed contract was mailed but before it was received in Florida, the Thoelkes called the Morrisons' attorney in Florida and attempted to repudiate the contract. Does a contract exist between the Thoelkes and the Morrisons? Discuss.

16. Lucy and Zehmer met while having drinks in a restaurant. During the course of their conversation, Lucy apparently offered to buy Zehmer's 471.6-acre farm for $50,000 cash. Although Zehmer claims that he thought the offer was made in jest, he wrote the following on the back of a pad: "We hereby agree to sell to W. O. Lucy the Ferguson Farm complete for $50,000, title satisfactory to buyer." Zehmer then signed the writing and induced his wife Ida to do the same. She claims, however, that she signed only after Zehmer assured her that it was only a joke. Finally, Zehmer claims that he was "high as a Georgia pine" at the time but admits that he was not too drunk to make a valid contract. Explain whether the contract is enforceable.

17. On July 31, Lee Calan Imports advertised a used Volvo station wagon for sale in the *Chicago Sun-Times*. As part of the information for the advertisement, Lee Calan Imports instructed the newspaper to print the price of the car as $1,795. However, due to a mistake made by the newspaper, without any fault on the part of Lee Calan Imports, the printed ad listed the price of the car as $1,095. After reading the ad and then examining the car, O'Brien told a Lee Calan Imports salesman that he wanted to purchase the car for the advertised price of $1,095. Calan Imports refuses to sell the car to O'Brien for $1,095. Is there a contract? If so, for what price?

18. On May 20, cattle rancher Oliver visited his neighbor Southworth, telling him, "I know you're interested in buying the

land I'm selling." Southworth replied, "Yes, I do want to buy that land, especially because it adjoins my property." Although the two men did not discuss the price, Oliver told Southworth he would determine the value of the property and send that information to Southworth so that he would have "notice" of what Oliver "wanted for the land." On June 13, Southworth called Oliver to ask if he still planned to sell the land. Oliver answered, "Yes, and I should have the value of the land determined soon." On June 17, Oliver sent a letter to Southworth listing a price quotation of $324,000. Southworth then responded to Oliver by letter on June 21, stating that he accepted Oliver's offer. However, on June 24 Oliver wrote back to Southworth saying, "There has never been a firm offer to sell, and there is no enforceable contract between us." Oliver maintains that a price quotation alone is not an offer. Southworth claims a valid contract has been made. Who wins? Discuss.

19. On August 12, Mr. and Mrs. Mitchell, the owners of a small secondhand store, attended Alexander's Auction, where they bought a used safe for $50.00. The safe, part of the Sumstad estate, contained a locked inside compartment. Both the auctioneer and the Mitchells knew this fact. Soon after the auction, the Mitchells had the compartment opened by a locksmith, who discovered $32,207 inside. The Everett Police Department impounded the money. The city of Everett brought an action against the Sumstad estate and the Mitchells to determine the owner of the money. Who should receive the money? Why?

20. Irwin Schiff is a self-styled "tax rebel" who has made a career, and substantial profit, out of his tax protest activities. On February 7, Schiff appeared live on CBS News *Nightwatch*, a late-night program with a viewer participation format. During the broadcast Schiff repeated his assertion that nothing in the Internal Revenue Code stated that an individual was legally required to pay federal income tax. Schiff then challenged, "If anybody calls this show—I have the Code—and cites any section of this Code that says an individual is required to file a tax return, I will pay them $100,000." Call-in telephone numbers were periodically flashed on the screen. John Newman, an attorney, did not see Schiff's live appearance on *Nightwatch*. Newman did, however, see a two-minute videotaped segment, including Schiff's challenge, which was rebroadcast several hours later on the *CBS Morning News*. Newman researched the matter that same day, and on the following day, February 9, placed a call using directory assistance to *CBS Morning News* stating that the call was performance of the consideration requested by Mr. Schiff in exchange for his promise to pay $100,000. When Schiff refused to pay, Newman sued. Should Newman prevail? Explain.

TAKING SIDES

Cushing filed an application with the office of the Adjutant General of the State of New Hampshire for the use of the Portsmouth Armory to hold a dance on the evening of April 29. The application, made on behalf of the Portsmouth Area Clamshell Alliance, was received by the Adjutant General's office on or about March 30. On March 31 the Adjutant General mailed a signed contract after agreeing to rent the armory for the evening requested. The agreement required acceptance by the renter affixing his signature to the agreement and then returning the copy to the Adjutant General within five days after receipt. Cushing received the contract offer, signed it on behalf of the Alliance, and placed it in the outbox for mailing on April 3. At 6:30 on the evening of April 4, Cushing received a telephone call from the Adjutant General revoking the rental offer. Cushing stated during the conversation that he had already signed and mailed the contract. The Adjutant General sent a written confirmation of the withdrawal on April 5. On April 6 the Adjutant General's office received by mail from Cushing the signed contract dated April 3 and postmarked April 5.

a. What are the arguments that a binding contract exists?

b. What are the arguments that a contract does not exist or should not exist?

c. What is the proper outcome? Explain.

Conduct Invalidating Assent

CHAPTER 11

Fraud—A generic term embracing all multifarious means which human ingenuity can devise, and which are resorted to by one individual to get advantage over another by false suggestion or by suppression of the truth.

Johnson v. McDonald, 170 Okl. 117, 39 P.2d 150

CHAPTER OUTCOMES

After reading and studying this chapter, you should be able to:

1. Identify the types of duress and describe the legal effect of each.

2. Define undue influence and identify some of the situations giving rise to a confidential relationship.

3. Identify the types of fraud and the elements that must be shown to establish the existence of each.

4. Define the two types of nonfraudulent misrepresentation.

5. Identify and explain the situations involving voidable mistakes.

I n addition to requiring offer and acceptance, the law requires that the agreement be voluntary and knowing. If these requirements are not met, then the agreement is either voidable or void. This chapter deals with situations in which the consent manifested by one of the parties to the contract is not effective because it was not knowingly and voluntarily given. We consider five such situations in this chapter: duress, undue influence, fraud, nonfraudulent misrepresentation, and mistake.

DURESS [11-1]

A person should not be held to an agreement he has not entered voluntarily. Accordingly, the law will not enforce any contract induced by **duress**, which in general is any wrongful or unlawful act or threat that overcomes the free will of a party.

Physical Compulsion [11-1a]

Duress is of two basic types. The first type, **physical duress**, occurs when one party compels another to manifest assent to a contract through actual physical force, such as pointing a gun at a person or taking a person's hand and compelling him to sign a written contract. This type of duress, while extremely rare, renders the agreement *void*, and the party exerting the duress is liable in restitution as necessary to avoid unjust enrichment.

Improper Threats [11-1b]

The second and more common type of duress involves the use of **improper threats** or acts, including economic and social coercion, to compel a person to enter into a contract. Though the threat may be explicit or may be inferred from words or conduct, in either case it must leave the victim with no reasonable alternative. This type of duress makes the contract *voidable* at the option of the coerced party, and the party exerting the duress is liable in restitution as necessary to avoid unjust enrichment (see Chapter 18).

Duress
wrongful or unlawful act or threat that overcomes the free will of a party

Physical duress
coercion involving physical force renders the agreement void

Improper threats
improper threats or acts, including economic and social coercion, render the contract voidable

For example, if Ellen, a landlord, induces Vijay, an infirm, bedridden tenant, to enter into a new lease on the same apartment at a greatly increased rent by wrongfully threatening to terminate Vijay's lease and evict him, Vijay can escape or *avoid* the new lease by reason of the duress exerted on him.

The fact that the act or threat would not affect a person of average strength and intelligence is not important if it places fear in the person actually affected and induces her to act against her will. The test is *subjective*, and the question is this: did the threat actually induce assent on the part of the person claiming to be the victim of duress?

Ordinarily, the acts or threats constituting duress are themselves crimes or torts. But this is not true in all cases. The acts need not be criminal or tortious to be *wrongful*; they merely need to be contrary to public policy or morally reprehensible. For example, if the threat involves a breach of a contractual duty of good faith and fair dealing, it is improper.

Practical Advice

If you entered into a contract due to improper threats, consider whether you wish to void the contract. If you decide to do so, act promptly.

Moreover, it generally has been held that contracts induced by threats of criminal prosecution are voidable, regardless of whether the coerced party had committed an unlawful act. Similarly, threatening the criminal prosecution of a close relative is also duress. To be distinguished from such threats of prosecution are threats that resort to ordinary civil remedies to recover a debt due from another. It is not wrongful to threaten a civil suit against an individual to recover a debt. What is prohibited is threatening to bring a civil suit when bringing such a suit would be abuse of process.

Berardi v. Meadowbrook Mall Company
Supreme Court of Appeals of West Virginia, 2002
212 W.Va. 377, 572 S.E.2d 900
http://scholar.google.com/scholar_case?case=1600684206457698039&q=572+S.E.2d+900&hl=en&as_sdt=6,34

FACTS Between 1985 and 1987, Jerry A. Berardi, Betty J. Berardi, and Bentley Corporation (the Berardis) leased space for three restaurants from Meadowbrook Mall Company. In 1990, the Berardis were delinquent in their rent. Meadowbrook informed Mr. Berardi that a lawsuit would be filed in Ohio requesting judgment for the total amount owed. Mr. Berardi then entered into a consent judgment with Meadowbrook granting judgment for the full amount owed. Meadowbrook in return promised that no steps to enforce the judgment would be undertaken provided the Berardis continued to operate their three restaurants.

In April 1996, Meadowbrook filed in the Circuit Court of Harrison County, West Virginia, the judgment of the Ohio lawsuits and obtained a lien on a building that was owned by the Berardis, the Goff Building. By so doing, Meadowbrook impeded the then-pending refinancing of the building by the Berardis.

In June 1997, the Berardis and Meadowbrook signed a "Settlement Agreement and Release" settling the 1990 Ohio judgments. In this document, the Berardis acknowledged the validity of the 1990 Ohio judgments and that the aggregate due under them was $814,375.97. The Berardis agreed to pay Meadowbrook $150,000 on the date the Goff Building refinancing occurred, and also to pay Meadowbrook $100,000 plus 8.5 percent interest per year on the third anniversary of the initial $150,000 payment. These payments would discharge the Berardis from all other amounts owed. The payment of the initial $150,000 would also result in Meadowbrook releasing the lien against the Goff Building.

The agreement additionally recited:

> Berardis hereby release and forever discharge Meadowbrook, its employees, agents, successors, and assigns from any and all claims, demands, damages, actions, and causes of action of any kind or nature that have arisen or may arise as a result of the leases.

Nevertheless, on October 2, 2000, the Berardis filed a complaint against Meadowbrook alleging that Meadowbrook breached the October 1990 agreement by attempting to enforce the 1990 Ohio judgments and that Meadowbrook extorted by duress and coercion the 1997 agreement. Meadowbrook filed a motion to dismiss under the 1997 settlement. Meadowbrook sought summary judgment, which the circuit court granted. Berardi now appeals.

DECISION Summary judgment affirmed.

OPINION Courts are generally reluctant to overturn settlement agreements as long as they are legally sound. The law favors and encourages the resolution of controversies by contracts of compromise and settlement rather than by litigation; and it is the policy of the law to uphold and enforce such contracts if they are fairly made and are not in contravention of some law or public policy.

The concept of "economic duress" may be generally stated as follows: Where the plaintiff is forced into a transaction as a result of unlawful threats or wrongful, oppressive, or unconscionable conduct on the part of the defendant which leaves the plaintiff no reasonable alternative but to acquiesce, the plaintiff may void the transaction and recover any economic loss.

Duress is not readily accepted as an excuse to avoid a contract. Thus, to establish economic duress, in addition to their own statements, the plaintiffs must produce objective evidence of their duress. Evidence of duress is not shown just because one party to the contract has driven a hard bargain or that market or other conditions now make the contract more difficult to perform by one of the parties or that financial circumstances may have caused one party to make concessions.

Mr. Berardi is a sophisticated businessman who has operated a number of commercial enterprises. Typically, "where an experienced businessman takes sufficient time, seeks the advice of counsel and understands the content of what he is signing he cannot claim the execution of the release was a product of duress."

Given the facts, the law's disfavor of economic duress, its support of settlements, the sophisticated nature of the parties, and the extremely high evidentiary burden the Berardis must overcome, the circuit court rendered the correct decision.

INTERPRETATION Economic duress consists of unlawful threats or wrongful, oppressive, or unconscionable conduct by one party which leaves the other party no reasonable alternative but to acquiesce to the terms of a contract.

ETHICAL QUESTION Did Meadowbrook act in a proper manner? Explain.

CRITICAL THINKING QUESTION Did Berardi really have a reasonable alternative to signing the release? Explain.

UNDUE INFLUENCE [11-2]

Undue influence
the unfair persuasion of a person by a party in a dominant position based on a relationship of trust and confidence

Practical Advice

If you are in a confidential relationship with another person, when you enter into a contract with that person, make sure that (1) you fully disclose all relevant information about that transaction, (2) the contract is fair, and (3) the other party obtains independent advice about the transaction.

Undue influence is the unfair persuasion of a person by a party in a dominant position based on a *confidential relationship*. The law very carefully scrutinizes contracts between those in a relationship of trust and confidence that is likely to permit one party to take unfair advantage of the other. Examples are the relationships of guardian–ward, trustee–beneficiary, agent–principal, spouses, parent–child, attorney–client, physician–patient, and clergy–parishioner.

A transaction induced by undue influence on the part of the dominant party is *voidable*, and the dominant party is liable in restitution as necessary to avoid unjust enrichment (see Chapter 18). The ultimate question in undue influence cases is whether the transaction was induced by dominating either or both the mind or emotions of a submissive party. The weakness or dependence of the person persuaded is a strong indicator of whether the persuasion may have been unfair. For example, Abigail, a person without business experience, has for years relied on Boris, who is experienced in business, for advice on business matters. Boris, without making any false representations of fact, induces Abigail to enter into a contract with Boris's confederate, Cassius. The contract, however, is disadvantageous to Abigail, as both Boris and Cassius know. The transaction is voidable on the grounds of undue influence.

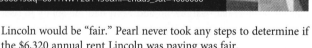

Neugebauer v. Neugebauer
Supreme Court of South Dakota, 2011
804 N.W.2d 450, 2011 S.D. 64
http://scholar.google.com/scholar_case?case=1062309080412566845&q=804+NW+2d+450&hl=en&as_sdt=4000006

FACTS Harold and Pearl Neugebauer owned a 159-acre farm they called the "Home Place." The farm included a house, garage, granary, machine sheds, barns, silos, and a dairy barn. During their marriage, Harold handled all of the legal and financial affairs of the farm and family. In 1980, Harold died, leaving Pearl as the sole owner of the Home Place and another farm property. Following Harold's death, Lincoln, the youngest of Harold and Pearl's seven children, began farming both properties. Lincoln also lived with his mother on the Home Place. In 1984, Lincoln and Dennis, one of Pearl's other sons, formed L & D Farms partnership to manage the farming operation on Pearl's land. L & D Farms entered into an oral ten-year lease with Pearl that included an option to purchase the Home Place for $117,000, the appraised value in 1984. In 1985, Pearl moved from the farm to a home in town. In 1989, Lincoln and Dennis dissolved L & D Farms without exercising the option to purchase the Home Place. After dissolution of the partnership, Lincoln farmed Pearl's land by himself. He paid annual rent, but Lincoln and Pearl never put their oral farm lease in writing. Pearl trusted Lincoln and left it to him to determine how much rent to pay. Pearl did, however, expect that

Lincoln would be "fair." Pearl never took any steps to determine if the $6,320 annual rent Lincoln was paying was fair.

On several occasions from 2004 to 2008, Lincoln privately consulted with an attorney, Keith Goehring, about purchasing the Home Place. On December 3, 2008, Lincoln took Pearl to Goehring's office to discuss the purchase. Pearl, who had only an eighth-grade education, was almost eighty-four years old and was hard of hearing. Although Lincoln and Goehring discussed details of Lincoln's proposed purchase, Pearl said virtually nothing. She later testified that she could not keep up with the conversation and did not understand the terms discussed. A few days later, Pearl and Lincoln executed a contract for deed that had been drafted by Goehring. Goehring had been retained and his fees were paid by Lincoln. Neither Lincoln nor Goehring advised Pearl that Goehring represented only Lincoln, and neither suggested that Pearl could or should retain her own legal counsel.

There is no dispute that the fair market value of the Home Place was $697,000 in 2008 when the contract for deed was executed. Under the terms of the contract, Lincoln was to pay Pearl $117,000, the farm's 1984 appraised value. The contract price was to be paid over thirty years by making annual payments of $6,902.98. After executing the contract, Lincoln told Pearl not to tell the rest of her children about the agreement. Pearl later became suspicious that something may have been wrong with the contract. In January 2009, Pearl revealed the contract to the rest of her children, and they explained the contract to her. She began to cry and wanted the contract torn up. Pearl personally and through her children asked Lincoln to tear up the contract. Lincoln refused.

Pearl then brought an action for rescission of the contract on the ground of undue influence. The trial court found that Lincoln had exerted undue influence and rescinded the contract. Lincoln appealed.

DECISION Judgment of the trial court is affirmed.

OPINION The elements of undue influence are: (1) a person susceptible to undue influence; (2) another's opportunity to exert undue influence on that person to effect a wrongful purpose; (3) another's disposition to do so for an improper purpose; and (4) a result clearly showing the effects of undue influence. The party alleging undue influence must prove these elements by a preponderance of the evidence.

Lincoln argues that no evidence supported the court's finding that Pearl was susceptible to undue influence. Lincoln contends that in the absence of medical evidence of mental deficits, the court erred in finding that Pearl was susceptible to undue influence.

Obviously, an aged and infirm person with impaired mental faculties would be more susceptible to influence than a mentally alert younger person in good health. But it is not required that medical evidence be presented to prove susceptibility to undue influence. There was substantial non-medical evidence demonstrating Pearl's susceptibility to undue influence. Pearl had an eighth-grade education, and she lacked experience in business and legal transactions. When she signed the contract for deed, Pearl was almost eighty-four and hard of hearing. Lincoln further admitted that Pearl had some mental impairment.

Lincoln contends that the court's finding of opportunity to exert undue influence was erroneous because Lincoln and Pearl had no confidential relationship and Pearl had the ability to seek independent advice between the two meetings with Goehring, but

chose not to do so. In this case, Pearl testified that Lincoln was her son and someone with whom she had previously lived for many years, someone she trusted to "do right." Lincoln conceded that on the date Pearl signed the contract, he knew Pearl trusted him and had confidence that he would treat her fairly in his business dealings with her. This type of trust and confidence by a mother in her son is sufficient to prove opportunity.

The court's finding that Lincoln had a disposition to exert undue influence for an improper purpose was also supported. Lincoln had substantial experience in farmland transactions and real estate appreciation. He collaborated with an attorney a number of times over four years to purchase the farm and draft the necessary documents. Yet Lincoln did not have the farm appraised as he had previously done when farming the property with his brother. Instead, Lincoln set the price at a value for which it had appraised twenty-four years earlier, a price that was one-sixth of its then current value. He also took no steps to ensure that his elderly mother understood the contract terms, including the fact that considering her age and the thirty-year amortization, she would likely never receive a substantial portion of the payments. Neither Lincoln nor his attorney advised Pearl to seek legal representation. Finally, Lincoln's conduct after execution of the contract was also relevant to show disposition to exercise undue influence at the time the contract was executed.

By executing the contract for deed, Pearl sold her property for $580,000 less than its value. Not only was the contract price of $117,000 substantially below the market value of $697,000, the thirty-year payment term would have required Pearl to live to 114 years-of-age to receive the payments.

INTERPRETATION A transaction induced by undue influence on the part of the dominant party is voidable by the unduly influenced party.

ETHICAL QUESTION Did Lincoln act in a proper manner? Explain.

CRITICAL THINKING QUESTION Explain who should have the burden of proof in undue influence cases: the party alleging undue influence or the party alleged to have exerted undue influence.

FRAUD [11-3]

Another factor affecting the validity of consent given by a contracting party is fraud, which prevents assent from being knowingly given. There are two distinct types of fraud: fraud in the execution and fraud in the inducement.

Fraud in the Execution [11-3a]

Fraud in the execution
a misrepresentation that deceives the other party as to the very nature of the contract; renders the agreement void

Fraud in the execution, which is extremely rare, consists of a misrepresentation that deceives the defrauded person as to the very nature of the contract. Such fraud occurs when a person does not know, or does not have reasonable opportunity to know, the character or essence of a proposed contract because the other party misrepresents its character or essential terms. Fraud in the execution renders the transaction *void*.

For example, Melody delivers a package to Ray, requests that Ray sign a receipt for it, holds out a simple printed form headed "Receipt," and indicates the line on which Ray is to sign. This line, which appears to Ray to be the bottom line of the receipt, is actually the signature line of a promissory note cleverly concealed underneath the receipt. Ray signs where directed without knowing that he is signing a note. This is fraud in the execution. The note is void and of no legal effect, for, although the signature is genuine and appears to manifest Ray's assent to the terms of the note, there is no actual assent. The nature of Melody's fraud precluded consent to the signing of the note because it prevented Ray from reasonably knowing what he was signing.

Fraud in the Inducement [11-3b]

Fraud in the inducement

misrepresentation regarding the subject matter of a contract that induces the other party to enter into the contract; renders the contract voidable

Fraud in the inducement, generally referred to as fraud or deceit, is an intentional misrepresentation of material fact by one party to the other, who consents to enter into a contract in justifiable reliance on the misrepresentation. Fraud in the inducement renders the contract *voidable* by the defrauded party and makes the fraudulent party liable in restitution as necessary to avoid unjust enrichment. For example, Alice, in offering to sell her dog to Bob, tells Bob that the dog won first prize in its class in the recent national dog show. In truth, the dog had not even been entered in the show. However, Alice's statement induces Bob to accept the offer and pay a high price for the dog. There is a contract, but it is voidable by Bob because Alice's fraud induced his assent.

The requisites for fraud in the inducement are as follows:

1. a false representation
2. of a fact
3. that is material and
4. made with knowledge of its falsity and the intention to deceive (scienter) and
5. which representation is justifiably relied on.

The remedies that may be available for fraud in the inducement are rescission, restitution, and damages, as discussed in Chapter 18.

Misrepresentation

some positive statement or conduct that is not in accord with the facts

Concealment

action taken to keep another from learning of a fact

False Representation   A basic element of fraud is a false representation or a **misrepresentation** (i.e., misleading conduct or an assertion not in accord with the facts, made through a positive statement). In contrast, **concealment** is an action intended or known to be likely to keep another from learning a fact he otherwise would have learned. Active concealment can form the basis for fraud, as, for example, when a seller puts heavy oil or grease in a car engine to conceal a knock. Truth may be suppressed by concealment as much as by misrepresentation. Expressly denying knowledge of a fact that a party knows to exist is a misrepresentation if it leads the other party to believe that the fact does not exist or cannot be discovered. Moreover, a statement of misleading half-truth is considered the equivalent of a false representation.

Generally, *silence* or nondisclosure alone does not amount to fraud when the parties deal at arm's length. An *arm's-length transaction* is one in which the parties owe each other no special duties and each is acting in his or her self-interest. In most business or market transactions, the parties deal at arm's length and generally have no obligation to tell the other party everything they know about the subject of the contract. Thus, it is not fraud when a buyer possesses advantageous information about the seller's property, information of which he knows the seller to be ignorant, and does not disclose such information to the seller. A buyer is under no duty to inform the seller of the greater value or other advantages of the property for sale. Assume, for example, that Sid owns a farm that, as a farm, is worth $100,000. Brenda, who knows that there is oil under Sid's farm, also knows that Sid is ignorant of this fact. Without disclosing this information to Sid, Brenda makes an offer to Sid to buy the farm for $100,000. Sid accepts the offer, and a contract is duly made. Sid, on later learning the facts, can do nothing about the matter, either at law or in equity. As one case puts it, "a purchaser is not bound by our laws to make the man he buys from as wise as himself."

Practical Advice

Consider bargaining with the other party to promise to give you full disclosure.

Although nondisclosure usually does not constitute a misrepresentation, in certain situations it does. One such situation arises when (1) a person fails to disclose a fact known to him; (2) he knows that the disclosure of that fact would correct a mistake of the other party as to a basic assumption on which that party is making the contract; and (3) nondisclosure of the fact amounts to a failure to act in good faith and in accordance with reasonable standards of fair dealing. Accordingly, if the property at issue in the contract contains a substantial latent (hidden) defect, one that would not be discovered through an ordinary examination, the seller may be obliged to reveal it. Suppose, for example, that Judith owns a valuable horse, which she knows is suffering from a disease discoverable only by a competent veterinary surgeon. Judith offers to sell

Practical Advice

When entering into contract negotiations, first determine what duty of disclosure you owe to the other party.

Fiduciary

person who owes a duty of trust, loyalty, and confidence to another

Fact

an event that took place or a thing that exists

Opinion

belief in the existence of a fact or a judgment as to value

Puffing

sales talk that is considered general bragging or overstatement

this horse to Curt but does not inform him about the condition of her horse. Curt makes a reasonable examination of the horse and, finding it in apparently normal condition, purchases it from Judith. Curt, on later discovering the disease in question, can have the sale set aside. Judith's silence, under the circumstances, was a misrepresentation.

In other situations, the law also imposes a duty of disclosure. For example, one may have a duty of disclosure because of prior representations innocently made before entering into the contract, which are later discovered to be untrue. Another instance in which silence may constitute fraud is a transaction involving a fiduciary. A **fiduciary** is a person in a confidential relationship who owes a duty of trust, loyalty, and confidence to another. For example, an agent owes a fiduciary duty to his principal, as does a trustee to the beneficiary of the trust and a partner to her copartners. A fiduciary may not deal at arm's length, as a party in most everyday business or market transactions may, but owes a duty to disclose fully all relevant facts when entering into a transaction with the other party to the relationship.

Fact   The basic element of fraud is the misrepresentation of a material fact. A **fact** is an event that actually took place or a thing that actually exists. Suppose that Dale induces Mike to purchase shares in a company unknown to Mike at a price of $100 per share by representing that she had paid $150 per share for them during the preceding year, when in fact she had paid only $50.00. This representation of a past event is a misrepresentation of fact.

Actionable fraud rarely can be based on what is merely a statement of **opinion**. A representation is one of opinion if it expresses only the uncertain belief of the representer as to the existence of a fact or his judgment as to quality, value, authenticity, or other matters of judgment.

The line between fact and opinion is not an easy one to draw and in close cases presents an issue for the jury. The solution often will turn on the superior knowledge of the person making the statement and the information available to the other party. Thus, if Dale said to Mike that the shares were "a good investment," she was merely stating her opinion; and normally Mike ought to regard it as no more than that. Other common examples of opinion are statements of value, such as "This is the best car for the money in town" or "This deluxe model will give you twice the wear of a cheaper model." Such exaggerations and commendations of articles offered for sale are to be expected from dealers, who are merely **puffing** their wares with "sales talk." If the representer is a professional advising a client, the courts are more likely to regard an untrue statement of opinion as actionable. Such a statement expresses the opinion of one holding himself out as having expert knowledge, and the tendency is to grant relief to those who have sustained loss by reasonable reliance on expert evaluation, as the next case shows.

Also to be distinguished from a representation of fact is a *prediction*. Predictions are similar to opinions, as no one can know with certainty what will happen in the future, and normally they are not regarded as factual statements. Likewise, promissory statements ordinarily do not constitute a basis of fraud, because a breach of promise does not necessarily indicate that the promise was fraudulently made. However, a promise that the promisor, at the time of making, had no intention of keeping is a misrepresentation of fact.

Historically, courts held that representations of *law* were not statements of fact but of opinion. The present trend is to recognize that a statement of law may have the effect of either a statement of fact or a statement of opinion. For example, a statement asserting that a particular statute has been enacted or repealed has the effect of a statement of fact. On the other hand, a statement as to the legal consequences of a particular set of facts is a statement of opinion.

Maroun v. Wyreless Systems, Inc.
Supreme Court of Idaho, 2005
141 Idaho 604, 114 P.3d 974
http://scholar.google.com/scholar_case?case=18286843461461582750&hl=en&as_sdt=2&as_vis=1&oi=scholarr

FACTS Tony Y. Maroun (Maroun) was employed by Amkor when he accepted an offer to work for Wyreless, a start-up company. Wyreless promised Maroun, among other items, the following: (1) annual salary of $300,000; (2) $300,000 bonus for successful organization of Wyreless Systems, Inc.; (3) 15 percent of the issued equity in Wyreless Systems, Inc.; (4) the equity and "organization bonus" will need to be tied to agreeable milestones; (5) full medical benefits; and (6) the position of chief executive officer, president, and board member. Maroun began working for Wyreless but was terminated a few months later. Maroun then filed suit alleging he had not received 15 percent of issued equity and had not received $429,145, which represented the remainder of the $600,000. Wyreless filed a motion for summary judgment. The district court granted the motion, and Maroun appealed.

DECISION Judgment of the district court affirmed.

OPINION Maroun argues the district court erred in granting summary judgment on the fraud claim. In opposition to the defendants' motion for summary judgment, Maroun filed an affidavit that stated Robinson (representing Wyreless) made the following representations to Maroun:

1. That Wyreless was to be a corporation of considerable size, with initial net revenues in excess of several hundred million dollars.
2. That Robinson would soon acquire one and one-half million dollars in personal assets, which Robinson would make available to personally guaranty payment of my compensation from Wyreless.
3. That he would have no difficulty in obtaining the initial investments required to capitalize Wyreless as a large, world leading corporation with initial net revenues in excess of several hundred million dollars.
4. That he had obtained firm commitments from several investors and that investment funds would be received in Wyreless' bank account in the near future.

An action for fraud or misrepresentation will not lie for statements of future events. A promise or a statement as to a future event will not serve as a basis for fraud. Statements numbered one and two both address future events. The representation forming the basis of a claim for fraud must concern past or existing material facts. Neither of these statements constitutes a statement or a representation of past or existing fact. A promise or statement that an act will be undertaken, however, is actionable, if it is proven that the speaker made the promise without intending to keep it. There is no indication that Robinson did not intend to fulfill those representations to Maroun at the time he made the statements.

Opinions or predictions about the anticipated profitability of a business are generally not actionable as fraud. Statement number three is merely Robinson's opinion. As to statement number four, no evidence was submitted that Robinson had not received commitments at the time he made the statement to Maroun. Accordingly, the district court's grant of summary judgment against Maroun on the fraud claim is affirmed.

INTERPRETATION Fraud generally must be based on a material fact and not on predictions or a person's opinion.

ETHICAL QUESTION Did Wyreless act in an ethical manner?

CRITICAL THINKING QUESTION When should an employer be held to its "promises"?

Material

of substantial importance; likely to induce a reasonable person to enter into the contract

Materiality In addition to the requirement that a misrepresentation be one of fact, it must also be material. A misrepresentation is **material** if (1) it would be likely to induce a reasonable person to manifest assent or (2) the maker knows that it would be likely to induce the recipient to do so. Thus, in the sale of a racehorse, it may not be material whether the horse was ridden in its most recent race by a certain jockey, but its running time for the race probably would be. The Restatement of Contracts and the Restatement of Restitution provide that a contract justifiably induced by a misrepresentation is voidable if the misrepresentation is either fraudulent or material. Therefore, a fraudulent misrepresentation does not have to be material to obtain rescission, but it must be material to recover damages.

The *Reed v. King* case presents an unusual factual situation involving the duty to disclose a "material" fact.

Reed v. King
California Court of Appeals, 1983
145 Cal.App.3d 261, 193 Cal.Rptr. 130
http://scholar.google.com/scholar_case?case=575864357603110085&q=193+Cal.Rptr.+130&hl=en&as_sdt=2,34

FACTS Dorris Reed bought a house from Robert King for $76,000. King and his real estate agent knew that a woman and her four children had been murdered in the house ten years earlier and allegedly knew that the event had materially affected the market value of the house. They said nothing about the murders to Reed, and King asked a neighbor not to inform her of them. After the sale, neighbors told Reed about the murders and informed her that the house was consequently worth only $65,000. Reed brought an action against King and the real estate agent, alleging

fraud and seeking rescission and damages. The complaint was dismissed, and Reed appealed.

DECISION Judgment reversed.

OPINION The requisite elements of fraud are "(1) *a false representation* or concealment of a material fact (or, in some cases, an opinion) susceptible of knowledge, (2) made with *knowledge* of its falsity or without sufficient knowledge on the subject to warrant a representation, (3) with the *intent* to induce the person to whom it is made to act upon it; and such person must (4) act in *reliance* upon the representation (5) to his *damage*." The trial court determined that Reed failed to allege concealment of a material fact. Concealment, however, may include mere silence when a party has a duty to disclose. This duty falls upon the seller of real property where he (1) knows of facts that have a material effect upon the value or desirability of the property and (2) knows that these facts are unknown to the buyer and inaccessible to the buyer through the exercise of ordinary diligence. The second of these conditions clearly applies. King knew that Reed was unaware of the murders, and Reed cannot reasonably be expected to anticipate and discover such an unlikely possibility. The issue therefore turns upon the question of materiality. Material nondisclosures in real property cases generally pertain to physical defects of the property or to legal impediments to its use. Murder, however, is a particularly

disturbing event that may cause a buyer to be unable to live in a house where it has occurred and may thus deprive the buyer of the intended use of the property. Moreover, the content of the information not disclosed by the seller need not be the crucial factor. If Reed can prove that the murders significantly and measurably affected the market value of the premises, she should receive a favorable judgment on the issue of materiality and duty to disclose.

INTERPRETATION A representation is material if it is likely to influence or affect a reasonable person.

ETHICAL QUESTION Should King have revealed the information to Reed? Explain.

CRITICAL THINKING QUESTION What is material information, and how should it be determined?

Scienter
guilty knowledge

Knowledge of Falsity and Intention to Deceive To establish fraud, the misrepresentation must have been known by the one making it to be false and must be made with an intent to deceive. This element of fraud is known as **scienter**. Knowledge of falsity can consist of (1) actual knowledge, (2) lack of belief in the statement's truthfulness, or (3) reckless indifference as to its truthfulness.

Justifiable reliance
reasonably influenced by
the misrepresentation

Justifiable Reliance A person is not entitled to relief unless she has **justifiably relied** on the misrepresentation. If the complaining party's decision was in no way influenced by the misrepresentation, she must abide by the terms of the contract. She is not deceived if she does not rely on the misrepresentation. Justifiable reliance requires that the misrepresentation contribute substantially to the misled party's decision to enter into the contract. If the complaining party knew or it was obvious that the representation of the defendant was untrue, but she still entered into the contract, she has not justifiably relied on that representation. Moreover, where the misrepresentation is fraudulent, the party who relies on it is entitled to relief even though she does not investigate the statement or is contributorily negligent in relying on it. Not knowing or discovering the facts before making a contract does not make a person's reliance unjustified unless her reliance amounts to a failure to act in good faith and in accordance with reasonable standards of fair dealing. Thus, most courts will not allow a person who concocts a deliberate and elaborate scheme to defraud—one that the defrauded party should readily detect—to argue that the defrauded party did not justifiably rely upon the misrepresentation.

NONFRAUDULENT MISREPRESENTATION [11-4]

Negligent misrepresentation
made without knowledge of
its falsity *and* without due
care

Innocent misrepresentation
misrepresentation made
without knowledge of its
falsity but with due care

Nonfraudulent misrepresentation is a material, false statement that induces another to rely justifiably but is made *without* scienter. Such representation may occur in one of two ways. **Negligent misrepresentation** is a false representation that is made without knowledge of its falsity *and* without due care in ascertaining its truthfulness; such representation renders an agreement voidable. **Innocent misrepresentation**, which also renders a contract voidable, is a false representation made without knowledge of its falsity but with due care. To obtain relief for nonfraudulent misrepresentation, all of the other elements of fraud must be present *and* the misrepresentation must be material. The remedies that may be available for nonfraudulent misrepresentation are rescission, restitution, and damages (see Chapter 18).

MISTAKE [11-5]

Mistake
an understanding that is not
in accord with existing fact

A **mistake** is a belief that is not in accord with the facts. Where the mistaken facts relate to the basis of the parties' agreement, the law permits the adversely affected party to avoid or reform

CONCEPT REVIEW 11-1

Misrepresentation

	Fraudulent	Negligent	Innocent
False Statement of Fact	Yes	Yes	Yes
Materiality	Yes for damages No for rescission	Yes	Yes
Fault	With knowledge and intent (scienter)	Without knowledge and without due care	Without knowledge but with due care
Reliance	Yes	Yes	Yes
Injury	Yes for damages No for rescission	Yes for damages No for rescission	Yes for damages No for rescission
Remedies	Damages Rescission	Damages Rescission	Damages Rescission

the contract under certain circumstances. But because permitting avoidance for mistake undermines the objective approach to mutual assent, the law has experienced considerable difficulty in specifying those circumstances that justify permitting the subjective matter of mistake to invalidate an otherwise objectively satisfactory agreement. As a result, establishing clear rules to govern the effect of mistake has proven elusive.

The Restatement and modern cases treat mistakes of law in existence at the time of making the contract *no* differently than mistakes of fact. For example, Susan contracts to sell a parcel of land to James with the mutual understanding that James will build an apartment house on the land. Both Susan and James believe that such a building is lawful. Unknown to them, however, three days before they entered into their contract, the town in which the land was located had enacted an ordinance precluding such use of the land. In states that regard mistakes of law and fact in the same light, this mistake of law would be treated as a mistake of fact that would lead to the consequences discussed in the following section.

Mutual Mistake [11-5a]

Mutual mistake
both parties have a
common but erroneous
belief forming the basis of
a contract

Mutual mistake occurs when *both* parties are mistaken as to the same set of facts. If the mistake relates to a basic assumption on which the contract is made and has a material effect on the agreed exchange, then it is *voidable* by the adversely affected party unless he bears the risk of the mistake. In addition, the adversely affected party is entitled to restitution as necessary to avoid unjust enrichment.

Usually, market conditions and the financial situation of the parties are not considered basic assumptions. Thus, if Gail contracts to purchase Pete's automobile under the belief that she can sell it at a profit to Jesse, she is not excused from liability if she is mistaken in this belief. Nor can she rescind the agreement simply because she was mistaken as to her estimate of what the automobile was worth. These are the ordinary risks of business, and courts do not undertake to relieve against them. But suppose that the parties contract upon the assumption that the automobile is a 2010 Cadillac with fifteen thousand miles of use, when in fact the engine is that of a cheaper model and has been run in excess of fifty thousand miles. Here, a court likely would allow a rescission because of mutual mistake of a material fact. In a New Zealand case, the plaintiff purchased a "stud bull" at an auction. There were no express warranties as to "sex, condition, or otherwise." Actually, the bull was sterile. Rescission was allowed, the court observing that it was a "bull in name only."

APPLYING THE LAW

Conduct Invalidating Assent

Facts Gillian bought a two-year-old used car from a luxury automobile dealer for $36,000. At the time of her purchase, the odometer and title documentation both indicated that the car had 21,445 miles on it. But after just a little more than a year, the engine failed, and Gillian had to take the car to a mechanic. The problem was the water pump, which needed to be replaced. Surprised that a water pump should fail in a car with so few miles on it, the mechanic more closely examined the odometer and determined that someone had cleverly tampered with it. According to the mechanic, the car probably had about sixty thousand miles on it when Gillian bought it. At the time Gillian bought the car, the retail value for the same vehicle with sixty thousand miles on it was approximately $30,000.

Gillian decided that under these conditions she no longer wanted the car. She contacted the dealership, which strenuously denied having tampered with the odometer. In fact, the dealership's records reflect that it purchased Gillian's car at auction for $34,000, after a thorough inspection that revealed no mechanical deficiencies or alteration of the car's odometer.

Issue Is Gillian's contract voidable by her?

Rule of Law Innocent misrepresentation renders a contract voidable. Innocent misrepresentation is proven when the following elements are established: (1) a false representation, (2) of fact, (3) that is material, (4) made without knowledge of its falsity but with due care, and (5) the representation is justifiably relied upon.

Application Gillian can prove all five elements of innocent misrepresentation. First, the dealership's false representation was that the mileage on the car was 21,445, when the car actually had about sixty thousand miles on it. Second, the mileage of the car at the time of sale is an actual event not an opinion or prediction. Third, as the mileage of a used car is probably the most critical determinant of its value, this misrepresentation was material to the parties' agreed sale price, inducing the formation of the contract. Indeed, while Gillian might still have purchased this car with sixty thousand miles on it, she most certainly would have done so only at a lower price. Fourth, it is highly unlikely that the dealership was aware of the incorrect odometer reading.

We know this because it paid $34,000 for the car, which should have sold for something less than $30,000 in the wholesale market if the true mileage had been known. Moreover, the dealership appears to have conducted appropriate due diligence to support both its own purchase price and the price at which it offered the car to Gillian. The odometer tampering was cleverly concealed, so much so that neither the dealerships' inspection before purchase nor Gillian's mechanic's initial inspection revealed it. Fifth, Gillian's reliance on the ostensible odometer reading is justified. The car was only two years old when she bought it, and 21,445 miles is within an average range of mileage for a used car of that age. Unless the car's physical condition or something in the title paperwork should have alerted her to an inconsistency between the stated mileage and the car's actual mileage, Gillian was entitled to rely on what appeared to be a correct odometer reading.

Conclusion Because all the elements of innocent misrepresentation can be shown, Gillian's contract is voidable by Gillian.

Lesher v. Strid
Court of Appeals of Oregon, 2000
165 Or.App. 34, 996 P.2d 988
http://scholar.google.com/scholar_case?q=996+P.2d+988&hl=en&as_sdt=6,34&case=3643927747561854317&scilh=0

FACTS In May 1995, the plaintiffs, Vernon and Janene Lesher, agreed to purchase an eighteen-acre parcel of real property from defendant with the intention of using it to raise horses. In purchasing the property, the plaintiffs relied on their impression that at least four acres of the subject property had a right to irrigation from Slate Creek. The earnest money agreement to the contract provided:

> **D. Water Rights** are being conveyed to Buyer at the close of escrow…. Seller will provide Buyer with a written explanation of the operation of the irrigation system, water right certificates, and inventory of irrigation equipment included in sale.

The earnest money agreement also provided:

> **THE SUBJECT PROPERTY IS BEING SOLD "AS IS"** subject to the Buyer's approval of the tests and conditions as stated herein.

> Buyer declares that Buyer is not depending on any other statement of the Seller or licensees that is not incorporated by reference in this earnest money contract [Bold in original].

Before signing the earnest money agreement, the defendants presented to the plaintiffs a 1977 Water Resources Department water rights certificate and a map purporting to show an area of the subject property to be irrigated ("area to be irrigated" map), which indicated that the property carried a four-acre water right. Both parties believed that the property carried the irrigation rights and that the plaintiffs needed such rights for their horse farm. The plaintiffs did not obtain the services of an attorney or a water rights examiner before purchasing the property.

After purchasing the property and before establishing a pasture, the plaintiffs learned that the property did not carry a four-acre water right. The plaintiffs sought rescission of the contract for sale, alleging mutual mistake of fact or innocent misrepresentation regarding the existence of water rights. The trial court ruled in favor of the plaintiffs and the defendant appeals.

DECISION Judgment of the trial court affirmed.

OPINION Grounds for rescission on the basis of a mutual mistake of fact or innocent misrepresentation must be proved by clear and convincing evidence. An innocent misrepresentation of fact renders a contract voidable by a party if the party is relying on the material misrepresentation by the other party. A mutual mistake of fact renders a contract voidable by the adversely affected party, if the mistake is so fundamental that it frustrates the purpose of the contract. Even though it appears that the trial court did not apply the clear and convincing standard, the plaintiffs' evidence meets that standard. Both defendant and plaintiffs testified that they believed that the four acres of water rights were appurtenant to the subject property. Defendant does not dispute that the 1977 water rights certificate and the "area to be irrigated" map are her representation about the water right. Plaintiffs also established by clear and convincing evidence that the existence of the four-acre water right was material and essential to the contract. Vernon testified that the motivation for the purchase was to expand his ability to raise horses from property they already owned where they had a two-acre irrigation right and that the subject property's water right was essential to the contract. Certainly, a smaller water right would limit, not expand, the plaintiffs' ability to raise horses. The mistake, therefore, goes to the very essence of the contract.

The defendant argues that the plaintiffs bore the risk of that mistake. The Restatement (Second) of Contracts § 154 explains that a party bears the risk of a mistake, in part, if the risk is allocated to the party by agreement of the parties, or if the risk is allocated to the party "by the court on the ground that it is reasonable in the circumstances to do so." There is nothing in the contract that would allocate to plaintiffs the risk of a mistake as to the existence of a four-acre water right. Defendant argues in the alternative that the plaintiffs' mistake of fact is the result of the defendant's misrepresentation, on which plaintiffs could not reasonably rely. An "innocent misrepresentation may support a claim for rescission of a real estate agreement if the party who relied on the misrepresentations of another establishes a right to have done so." Defendant argues that her representations about the four-acre water right were extrinsic to the contract and that the contract's "as is" clause expressly excluded reliance on such extrinsic representations. The "as is" clause specifically contemplated reliance on any statements by the seller that were "incorporated by reference" in the earnest money agreement. The earnest money agreement specifically referred to the conveyance of water rights.

INTERPRETATION If both parties to a contract have a common but erroneous belief as to a basic assumption on which the contract is made, the contract is voidable.

CRITICAL THINKING QUESTION Should all contracts provide for this type of situation? If so, how? Explain.

Unilateral Mistake [11-5b]

Unilateral mistake
erroneous belief on the part of only one of the parties to a contract

Unilateral mistake occurs when only one of the parties is mistaken. Courts have been hesitant to grant relief for unilateral mistake, even though it relates to a basic assumption on which a party entered into the contract and has a material effect on the agreed exchange. Nevertheless, relief will be granted in cases in which (1) the nonmistaken party knows, or reasonably should know, that such a mistake has been made (palpable unilateral mistake) or (2) the mistake was caused by the fault of the nonmistaken party. For example, suppose a building contractor makes a serious error in his computations and consequently submits a job bid that is one-half the amount it should be. If the other party knows that the contractor made such an error, or reasonably should have known it, she cannot, as a general rule, take advantage of the other's mistake by accepting the offer. In addition, many courts and the Restatement allow rescission in cases in which the effect of unilateral mistake makes enforcement of the contract unconscionable.

Assumption of Risk of Mistake [11-5c]

Assumption of risk of mistake
a party may assume the risk of a mistake

A party who has undertaken to bear the risk of a mistake will not be able to avoid the contract, even though the mistake (which may be either mutual or unilateral) would have otherwise permitted the party to do so. This allocation of risk may occur by agreement of the parties. For instance, a ship at sea may be sold "lost or not lost." In such case the buyer is liable whether the ship was lost or not lost at the time the contract was made. There is no mistake; instead, there is a conscious allocation of risk.

Practical Advice

If you are unsure about the nature of a contract, consider allocating the risk of the uncertainties in your contract.

The risk of mistake also may be allocated by conscious ignorance when the parties recognize that they have limited knowledge of the facts. For example, the Supreme Court of Wisconsin refused to set aside the sale of a stone for which the purchaser paid $1.00 but that was subsequently discovered to be an uncut diamond valued at $700. The parties did not know at the time of sale what the stone was and knew they did not know. Each consciously assumed the risk that the value might be more or less than the selling price.

> ### CONCEPT REVIEW 11-2
>
> *Conduct Invalidating Assent*
>
> | Conduct | Effect |
> |---|---|
> | Duress by physical force | Void |
> | Duress by improper threat | Voidable |
> | Undue influence | Voidable |
> | Fraud in the execution | Void |
> | Fraud in the inducement | Voidable |

Effect of fault upon mistake

not a bar to avoidance unless the fault amounts to a failure to act in good faith

Effect of Fault upon Mistake [11-5d]

The Restatement provides that a mistaken party's fault in not knowing or discovering a fact before making a contract does not prevent him from avoiding the contract "unless his fault amounts to a failure to act in good faith and in accordance with reasonable standards of fair dealing." This rule does not, however, apply to a failure to read a contract. As a general proposition, a party is held to what she signs. Her signature authenticates the writing, and she cannot repudiate that which she has voluntarily approved. Generally, one who assents to a writing is presumed to know its contents and cannot escape being bound by its terms merely by contending that she did not read them; her assent is deemed to cover unknown as well as known terms.

Mistake in Meaning of Terms [11-5e]

Somewhat related to mistakes of fact is the situation in which the parties misunderstand their manifestations of mutual assent. A famous case involving this problem is *Raffles v. Wichelhaus*, 2 Hurlstone & Coltman 906 (1864), popularly known as the *Peerless* case. A contract of purchase was made for 125 bales of cotton to arrive on the *Peerless* from Bombay. It happened, however, that there were two ships by the name of *Peerless* each sailing from Bombay, one in October and the other in December. The buyer had in mind the ship that sailed in October, whereas the seller reasonably believed the agreement referred to the *Peerless* sailing in December. Neither party was at fault, but both believed in good faith that a different ship was intended. The English court held that no contract existed.

The Restatement is in accord: there is no manifestation of mutual assent in cases in which the parties attach materially different meanings to their manifestations and neither party knows or has reason to know the meaning attached by the other. If blame can be ascribed to either party, however, that party will be held responsible. Thus, if the seller knew of the sailing from Bombay of two ships by the name of *Peerless*, then he would be at fault, and the contract would be for the ship sailing in October as the buyer expected. If neither party is to blame or both are to blame, there is no contract at all; that is, the agreement is void.

CHAPTER SUMMARY

Duress

Definition wrongful act or threat that overcomes the free will of a party

Physical Compulsion coercion involving physical force renders the agreement void

Improper Threats improper threats or acts, including economic and social coercion, render the contract voidable

Undue Influence	**Definition** taking unfair advantage of a person by reason of a dominant position based on a confidential relationship
	Effect renders the contract voidable
Fraud	**Fraud in the Execution** a misrepresentation that deceives the other party as to the nature of a document evidencing the contract; renders the agreement void
	Fraud in the Inducement renders the agreement voidable if the following elements are present:

- *False Representation* positive statement or conduct that misleads
- *Fact* an event that occurred or thing that exists
- *Materiality* of substantial importance
- *Knowledge of Falsity and Intention to Deceive* (called scienter) and includes (1) actual knowledge, (2) lack of belief in statement's truthfulness, or (3) reckless indifference to its truthfulness
- *Justifiable Reliance* a defrauded party is reasonably influenced by the misrepresentation

Nonfraudulent Misrepresentation	**Negligent Misrepresentation** misrepresentation made without knowledge of its falsity *and* without due care in ascertaining its truthfulness; renders the contract voidable
	Innocent Misrepresentation misrepresentation made without knowledge of its falsity but with due care; renders the contract voidable
Mistake	**Definition** an understanding that is not in accord with existing fact
	Mutual Mistake both parties have a common but erroneous belief forming the basis of the contract; renders the contract voidable by either party
	Unilateral Mistake courts are unlikely to grant relief unless the error is known or should be known by the nonmistaken party
	Assumption of Risk of Mistake a party may assume the risk of a mistake
	Effect of Fault upon Mistake not a bar to avoidance unless the fault amounts to a failure to act in good faith

QUESTIONS

1. Anita and Barry were negotiating, and Anita's attorney prepared a long and carefully drawn contract that was given to Barry for examination. Five days later and prior to its execution, Barry's eyes became so infected that it was impossible for him to read. Ten days thereafter and during the continuance of the illness, Anita called Barry and urged him to sign the contract, telling him that time was running out. Barry signed the contract despite the fact he was unable to read it. In a subsequent action by Anita, Barry claimed that the contract was not binding on him because it was impossible for him to read and he did not know what it contained prior to his signing it. Should Barry be held to the contract?

2. **a.** William tells Carol that he paid $150,000 for his farm in 2008, and that he believes it is worth twice that at the present time. Relying upon these statements, Carol buys the farm from William for $225,000. William did pay $150,000 for the farm in 2008, but its value has increased only slightly, and it is presently not worth $300,000. On discovering this, Carol offers to reconvey the farm to William and sues for the return of her $225,000. Result?

    b. Modify the facts in (a) by assuming that William had paid $100,000 for the property in 2008. What is the result?

3. On September 1, Adams in Portland, Oregon, wrote a letter to Brown in New York City offering to sell to Brown one thousand tons of chromite at $48.00 per ton, to be shipped by *S.S. Malabar* sailing from Portland, Oregon, to New York City via the Panama Canal. Upon receiving the letter on September 5, Brown immediately mailed to Adams a letter stating that she accepted the offer. There were two ships by the name of *S.S. Malabar* sailing from Portland to New York City via the Panama Canal, one sailing in October and the other sailing in December. At the time of mailing her letter of acceptance, Brown knew of both sailings and further knew that Adams knew only of the December sailing. Is there a contract? If so, to which *S.S. Malabar* does it relate?

4. Adler owes Perreault, a police captain, $500. Adler threatens Perreault that unless Perreault gives him a discharge from the debt, Adler will disclose the fact that Perreault has on several occasions become highly intoxicated and has been seen in the company of certain disreputable persons. Perreault, induced by fear that such a disclosure would cost him his position or in any event lead to social disgrace, gives Adler a release but subsequently sues to set it aside and recover on his claim. Will Adler be able to enforce the release?

5. Harris owned a farm that was worth about $600 an acre. By false representations of fact, Harris induced Pringle to buy the farm at $1,500 an acre. Shortly after taking possession of the farm, Pringle discovered oil under the land. Harris, on learning this, sues to have the sale set aside on the ground that it was voidable because of fraud. Result?

6. On February 2, Phillips induced Mallor to purchase from her fifty shares of stock in the XYZ Corporation for $10,000, representing that the actual book value of each share was $200. A certificate for fifty shares was delivered to Mallor. On February 16, Mallor discovered that the February 2 book value was only $50.00 per share. Thereafter, Mallor sues Phillips. Will Mallor be successful in a lawsuit against Phillips? Why?

7. Dorothy mistakenly accused Fred's son, Steven, of negligently burning down Dorothy's barn. Fred believed that his son was guilty of the wrong and that he, Fred, was personally liable for the damage, because Steven was only fifteen years old. Upon demand made by Dorothy, Fred paid Dorothy $25,000 for the damage to Dorothy's barn. After making this payment, Fred learned that his son had not caused the burning of Dorothy's barn and was in no way responsible for its burning. Fred then sued Dorothy to recover the $25,000 that he had paid her. Will he be successful?

8. Jones, a farmer, found an odd-looking stone in his fields. He went to Smith, the town jeweler, and asked him what he thought it was. Smith said he did not know but thought it might be a ruby. Jones asked Smith what he would pay for it, and Smith said $200, whereupon Jones sold it to Smith for $200. The stone turned out to be an uncut diamond worth $3,000. Jones brought an action against Smith to recover the stone. On trial, it was proved that Smith actually did not know the stone was a diamond when he bought it, but he thought it might be a ruby. Can Jones void the sale? Explain.

9. Decedent, Joan Jones, a bedridden, lonely woman, eighty-six years old, owned outright Greenacre, her ancestral estate. Biggers, her physician and friend, visited her weekly and was held in the highest regard by Joan. Joan was extremely fearful of pain and suffering and depended on Biggers to ease her anxiety and pain. Several months before her death, Joan deeded Greenacre to Biggers for $10,000. The fair market value of Greenacre at this time was $250,000. Joan was survived by two children and six grandchildren. Joan's children challenged the validity of the deed. Should the deed be declared invalid due to Biggers' undue influence? Explain.

CASE PROBLEMS

10. In February, Gardner, a schoolteacher with no experience in running a tavern, entered into a contract to purchase for $40,000 the Punjab Tavern from Meiling. The contract was contingent upon Gardner's obtaining a five-year lease for the tavern's premises and a liquor license from the state. Prior to the formation of the contract, Meiling had made no representations to Gardner concerning the gross income of the tavern. Approximately three months after the contract was signed, Gardner and Meiling met with an inspector from the Oregon Liquor Control Commission (OLCC) to discuss transfer of the liquor license. Meiling reported to the agent, in Gardner's presence, that the tavern's gross income figures for February, March, and April were $5,710, $4,918, and $5,009, respectively. The OLCC granted the required license, the transaction was closed, and Gardner took possession on June 10. After discovering that the tavern's income was very low and that the tavern had very few female patrons, Gardner contacted Meiling's bookkeeping service and learned that the actual gross income for those three months had been approximately $1,400 to $2,000. Will a court grant Gardner rescission of the contract? Explain.

11. Dorothy and John Huffschneider listed their house and lot for sale with C. B. Property. The asking price was $165,000, and the owners told C. B. that the property contained 6.8 acres. Dean Olson, a salesman for C. B., advertised the property in local newspapers as consisting of six acres. James and Jean Holcomb signed a contract to purchase the property through Olson after first inspecting the property with Olson and being assured by Olson that the property was at least 6.6 acres. The Holcombs never asked for nor received a copy of the survey. In actuality, the lot was only 4.6 acres. Can the Holcombs rescind the contract? Explain.

12. Christine Boyd was designated as the beneficiary of a life insurance policy issued by Aetna Life Insurance Company on the life of Christine's husband, Jimmie Boyd. The policy insured against Jimmie's permanent total disability and provided for a death benefit to be paid on Jimmie's death. Several years after the policy was issued, Jimmie and Christine separated. Jimmie began to travel extensively, and, therefore, Christine was unable to keep track of his whereabouts or his state of health. Jimmie nevertheless continued to pay the premiums on the policy until Christine tried to cash in the policy to alleviate her financial distress. A loan previously had been made on the policy, however, leaving its cash surrender value, and thus the amount Christine received, at only $4.19. Shortly thereafter, Christine learned that Jimmie had been permanently and totally disabled before the surrender of the policy. Aetna also was unaware of Jimmie's condition, and Christine requested the surrendered policy be reinstated and that the disability payments be made. Jimmie died soon thereafter, and Christine then requested that Aetna pay the death benefit. Decision?

13. Treasure Salvors and the state of Florida entered into a series of four annual contracts governing the salvage of the *Nuestra Senora de Atocha*. The *Atocha* is a Spanish galleon that sank in 1622, carrying a treasure now worth well over $250 million. Both parties had contracted under the impression that the seabed on which the *Atocha* lay was land owned by Florida. Treasure Salvors agreed to relinquish 25 percent of the items recovered in return for the right to salvage on state lands. In accordance with these contracts, Treasure Salvors delivered to Florida its share of the salvaged artifacts. Subsequently the U.S. Supreme Court held that the part of the continental shelf on which the *Atocha* was resting had *never* been owned by Florida. Treasure Salvors then brought suit to rescind the contracts and to recover the artifacts it had delivered to the state of Florida. Should Treasure Salvors prevail?

14. Jane Francois married Victor H. Francois. At the time of the marriage, Victor was a fifty-year-old bachelor living with his elderly mother, and Jane was a thirty-year-old, twice-divorced mother of two. Victor had a relatively secure financial portfolio; Jane, on the other hand, brought no money or property to the marriage.

   The marriage deteriorated quickly over the next couple of years, with disputes centered on financial matters. During this period, Jane systematically gained a joint interest and took control of most of Victor's assets. Three years after they married Jane contracted Harold Monoson, an attorney, to draw up divorce papers. Victor was unaware of Jane's decision until he was taken to Monoson's office, where Monoson presented for Victor's signature a "Property Settlement and Separation Agreement." Monoson told Victor that he would need an attorney, but Jane vetoed Victor's choice. Monoson then asked another lawyer, Gregory Ball, to come into the office. Ball read the agreement and strenuously advised Victor not to sign it because it would commit him to financial suicide. The agreement transferred most of Victor's remaining assets to Jane. Victor, however, signed it because Jane and Monoson persuaded him that it was the only way that his marriage could be saved. In October of the following year, Jane informed Victor that she had sold most of his former property and that she was leaving him permanently. Can Victor have the agreement set aside as a result of undue influence?

15. Iverson owned Iverson Motor Company, an enterprise engaged in the repair and sale of Oldsmobile, Rambler, and International Harvester Scout automobiles. Forty percent of the business's sales volume and net earnings came from the Oldsmobile franchise. Whipp contracted to buy Iverson Motors, which Iverson said included the Oldsmobile franchise. After the sale, however, General Motors refused to transfer the franchise to Whipp. Whipp then returned the property to Iverson and brought this action seeking rescission of the contract. Should the contract be rescinded? Explain.

16. On February 10, Mrs. Sunderhaus purchased a diamond ring from Perel & Lowenstein for $6,990. She was told by the company's salesman that the ring was worth its purchase price, and she also received at that time a written guarantee from the company attesting to the diamond's value, style, and trade-in value. When Mrs. Sunderhaus went to trade the ring for another, however, she was told by two jewelers that the ring was valued at $3,000 and $3,500, respectively. Mrs. Sunderhaus knew little about the value of diamonds and claims to have relied on the oral representation of the Perel & Lowenstein's salesman and the written representation as to the ring's value. Mrs. Sunderhaus seeks rescission of the contract or damages in the amount of the sales price over the ring's value. Will she prevail? Explain.

17. Division West Chinchilla Ranch advertised on television that a five-figure income could be earned by raising chinchillas with an investment of only $3.75 per animal per year and only thirty minutes of maintenance per day. The minimum investment was $2,150 for one male and six female chinchillas. Division West represented to the plaintiffs that chinchilla ranching would be easy and that no experience was required to make ranching profitable. The plaintiffs, who had no experience raising chinchillas, each invested $2,150 or more to purchase Division's chinchillas and supplies. After three years without earning a profit, the plaintiffs sued Division West for fraud. Do these facts sustain an action for fraud in the inducement?

18. William Schmalz entered into an employment contract with Hardy Salt Company. The contract granted Schmalz six months' severance pay for involuntary termination but none for voluntary separation or termination for cause. Schmalz was asked to resign from his employment. He was informed that if he did not resign he would be fired for alleged misconduct. When Schmalz turned in his letter of resignation, he signed a release prohibiting him from suing his former employer as a consequence of his employment. Schmalz consulted an attorney before signing the release and, upon signing it, received $4,583.00 (one month's salary) in consideration. Schmalz now sues his former employer for the severance pay, claiming that he signed the release under duress. Is Schmalz correct in his assertion?

19. Glen Haumont, who owned an equipment retail business in Broken Bow, Nebraska, owed the Security State Bank more than $628,000 due to improper selling practices as well as business and inventory loans. Several times Glen tried to persuade his parents, Lee and Letha Haumont, to financially back his business debts, but each time they refused. Glen then told his parents that, according to his attorney and the bank, Glen could be prosecuted and sent to jail. Soon afterwards, David Schweitz, the president of the bank, drove out to the elder Haumonts' farm to convince them to sign as guarantors of Glen's debt. Both Schweitz and Glen stressed to the Haumonts that unless they agreed to guarantee his debt, Glen would go to jail. Letha asked that her attorney be allowed to read over the guarantee agreement, but Schweitz told her that he did not have time to wait and that she must decide right then whether Glen was to go to jail. As a result, the Haumonts signed the agreement, encumbering their previously debt-free family farm for more than $628,000. Should the guarantee agreement be set aside due to duress?

20. Conrad Schaneman was a Russian immigrant who could neither read nor write the English language. In 2011, Conrad deeded (conveyed) a farm he owned to his eldest son, Laurence, for $23,500, which was the original purchase price of the property in 1981. The value of the farm in 2011 was between $145,000 and $160,000. At the time he executed the deed, Conrad was an eighty-two-year-old invalid, severely ill, and completely dependent on others for his personal needs. He weighed between 325 and 350 pounds, had difficulty breathing, could not walk more than fifteen feet, and needed a special jackhoist to get in and out of the bathtub. Conrad enjoyed a long-standing, confidential relationship with Laurence, who was

his principal adviser and handled Conrad's business affairs. Laurence also obtained a power of attorney from Conrad and made himself a joint owner of Conrad's bank account and $20,000 certificate of deposit. Conrad brought this suit to cancel the deed, claiming it was the result of Laurence's undue influence. Explain whether the deed was executed as a result of undue influence.

21. At the time of her death Olga Mestrovic was the owner of a large number of works of art created by her late husband, Ivan Mestrovic, an internationally known sculptor and artist whose works were displayed throughout Europe and the United States. By the terms of Olga's will, all the works of art created by her husband were to be sold and the proceeds distributed to members of the Mestrovic family. Also included in the estate of Olga Mestrovic was certain real property which 1st Source Bank (the Bank), as personal representative of the estate of Olga Mestrovic, agreed to sell to Terrence and Antoinette Wilkin. The agreement of purchase and sale made no mention of any works of art, although it did provide for the sale of such personal property as a dishwasher, drapes, and French doors stored in the attic. Immediately after closing on the real estate, the Wilkins complained to the Bank of the clutter left on the premises; the Bank gave the Wilkins an option of cleaning the house themselves and keeping any personal property they desired, to which the Wilkins agreed. At the time these arrangements were made, neither the Bank nor the Wilkins suspected that any works of art remained on the premises. During cleanup, however, the Wilkins found eight drawings and a sculpture created by Ivan Mestrovic to which the Wilkins claimed ownership based upon their agreement with the Bank that, if they cleaned the real property, they could keep such personal property as they desired. Who is entitled to ownership of the works of art?

22. Frank Berryessa stole funds from his employer, the Eccles Hotel Company. His father, W. S. Berryessa (Berryessa), learned of his son's trouble and, thinking the amount involved was about $2,000, gave the hotel a promissory note for $2,186 to cover the shortage. In return, the hotel agreed not to publicize the incident or notify the bonding company. (A bonding company is an insurer that is paid a premium for agreeing to reimburse an employer for thefts by an employee.) Before this note became due, however, the hotel discovered that Frank had actually misappropriated $6,865. The hotel then notified its bonding company, Great American Indemnity Company, to collect the entire loss. W. S. Berryessa claims that the agent for Great American told him that unless he paid them $2,000 in cash and signed a note for the remaining $4,865, Frank would be prosecuted (which note would replace the initial note). Berryessa agreed, signed the note, and gave the agent a cashier's check for $1,500 and a personal check for $500. He requested that the agent not cash the personal check for about a month. Subsequently, Great American sued Berryessa on the note. He defends against the note on the grounds of duress and counterclaims for the return of the $1,500 and the cancellation of the uncashed $500 check. Who should prevail?

23. Ronald D. Johnson is a former employee of International Business Machines Corporation (IBM). As part of a downsizing effort, IBM discharged Johnson. In exchange for an enhanced severance package, Johnson signed a written release and covenant not to sue IBM. IBM's downsizing plan provided that surplus personnel were eligible to receive benefits, including outplacement assistance, career counseling, job retraining, and an enhanced separation allowance. These employees were eligible, at IBM's discretion, to receive a separation allowance of two weeks' pay. However, employees who signed a release could be eligible for an enhanced severance allowance equal to one week's pay for each six months of accumulated service with a maximum of twenty-six weeks' pay. Surplus employees could also apply for alternate, generally lower-paying, manufacturing positions. Johnson opted for the release and received the maximum twenty-six weeks' pay. He then alleged, among other claims, that IBM subjected him to economic duress when he signed the release and covenant-not-to-sue, and he sought to rescind both. What will Johnson need to show in order to prove his cause of action?

24. Etta Mae Paulson died on January 31, 2014, leaving four children: Ken, Donald, Barbara, and Larry. She had purchased a home in Rainier in 2009, for $21,300. At that time, she had a will that she had executed in 1993, leaving all of her property to her four children in equal shares. That will was never changed. After she moved into the house in Rainier, Ken, Ken's wife, Barbara, and Don helped Etta, who suffered from arthritis in both hands, renal failure, congestive heart failure, and diabetes. As a result of these conditions, Etta had trouble getting around and, during the last part of her life, she used an electric cart. She was taking several medications, including Prozac, Prednisone, Zantac, and Procardia, and was receiving insulin daily and dialysis an average of three times a week. Although there is no evidence that she was mentally incompetent, the medications and treatments made her drowsy, tired, and depressed, and caused mood swings. It is undisputed that she was dependent on the help of others in her daily living.

Larry was not in the Rainier area when his mother moved there and did not visit her. The other children and her neighbor helped her. The other children reroofed the house, picked fruit and stored it, and mowed the lawn; her daughter helped her with her finances and had a joint account with her, which the daughter never used. All of those children visited her frequently, and at least one of them saw her every day. Etta expressed concern about losing the house because of her medical bills and suggested that she put the house in Ken's name; he and Barbara looked into the situation and concluded that it was not necessary, and so advised their mother. At some point—it is not clear when—Larry was told by state welfare authorities, as Ken and Barbara had learned, that so long as his mother maintained her house as her primary residence and was not receiving Medicaid, she was not in danger of losing her house to the state.

Some time in early 2013, Larry and his then girlfriend (later his wife) moved in with Etta and took over her care. Larry expressed his concern to his mother that the state might take her house. Not long thereafter, Larry rented a house in Longview in his name and persuaded his mother to move in with him, his girlfriend, and her child. After Etta moved to Longview, she rented her house in Rainier; the rent was used to maintain the house in Longview. At that time, Etta had a savings account with approximately $2,000 in it; Larry held his mother's power of attorney. At the time of her death in January 2014, that account was exhausted, although her medical expenses were being paid by Medicare. Larry admitted that he used some of that money to buy a bicycle and a guitar. He had also used her credit card, on which there was a substantial balance after her death, which he did not pay. He said that that debt "died with his mother." On numerous occasions, Larry expressed to his mother his concern that the state would take her house if she kept it in her name. She was fearful of that, in spite of what she had been told by Ken and Barbara. Larry told her that they were wrong, and frequently urged her to make up her mind "about the deed." Etta was hospitalized three times during 2013. Finally, on September 30, 2013, Larry suggested to his mother that they go to a title company in Rainier to get a deed. Etta signed the deed and gave up all of her rights in the property. Larry then had it recorded. He did not mention it to any of his half-brothers or -sister until two months later when he boasted of it to his half-sister. Is the deed voidable? Explain.

TAKING SIDES

Mrs. Audrey E. Vokes, a widow of fifty-one years and without family, purchased fourteen separate dance courses from J. P. Davenport's Arthur Murray, Inc., School of Dance. The fourteen courses totaled in the aggregate 2,302 hours of dancing lessons at a cost to Mrs. Vokes of $31,090.45. Mrs. Vokes was induced continually to reapply for new courses by representations made by Mr. Davenport that her dancing ability was improving, that she was responding to instruction, that she had excellent potential, and that they were developing her into an accomplished dancer. In fact, she had no dancing ability or aptitude and had trouble "hearing the musical beat." Mrs. Vokes brought action to have the contracts set aside.

a. What are the arguments that the contract should be set aside?

b. What are the arguments that the contract should be enforced?

c. What is the proper outcome? Explain.

Consideration

CHAPTER 12

Nuda pactio obligationem non parit. (A naked agreement, that is, one without consideration, does not beget an obligation.)

Legal Maxim

CHAPTER OUTCOMES

After reading and studying this chapter, you should be able to:

1. Define *consideration* and explain what is meant by legal sufficiency.

2. Describe illusory promises, output contracts, requirements contracts, exclusive dealing contracts, and conditional contracts.

3. Explain whether preexisting public and contractual obligations satisfy the legal requirement of consideration.

4. Explain the concept of bargained-for exchange and whether this element is present with past consideration and third-party beneficiaries.

5. Identify and discuss those contracts that are enforceable even though they are not supported by consideration.

Consideration
inducement to make a promise enforceable

Gratuitous promise
promise made without consideration

onsideration is the primary—but not the only—basis for the enforcement of promises in our legal system. **Consideration** is the inducement to make a promise enforceable. The doctrine of consideration ensures that promises are enforced only in cases in which the parties have exchanged something of value in the eye of the law. **Gratuitous** (gift) **promises**—those made without consideration—are not legally enforceable, except under certain circumstances, which are discussed later in the chapter.

Consideration, or that which is exchanged for a promise, is present only when the parties intend an exchange. The consideration exchanged for the promise may be an act, a forbearance to act, or a promise to do either of these. Thus, there are two basic elements to consideration: (1) legal sufficiency (something of value in the eye of the law) and (2) bargained-for exchange. Both must be present to satisfy the requirement of consideration.

LEGAL SUFFICIENCY [12-1]

Legal sufficiency
benefit to the promisor or detriment to the promisee

Legal detriment
(1) doing an act that one is not legally obligated to do or; (2) refraining from doing an act that one has a legal right to do

Legal benefit
obtaining something to which one had no legal right

To be **legally sufficient**, the consideration for the promise must be either a legal detriment to the promisee or a legal benefit to the promisor. In other words, in return for the promise, the promisee must give up something of legal value or the promisor must receive something of legal value.

Legal detriment means (1) the doing of (or the undertaking to do) that which the promisee was under no prior legal obligation to do or (2) the refraining from the doing of (or the undertaking to refrain from doing) that which he was previously under no legal obligation to refrain from doing. On the other hand, **legal benefit** means the obtaining by the promisor of that which he had no prior legal right to obtain. In most, if not all, cases in which there is legal detriment to the promisee, there is also a legal benefit to the promisor. However, the presence of either is sufficient.

Adequacy [12-1a]

Legal sufficiency has nothing to do with *adequacy of consideration*. The items or actions that the parties agree to exchange do not need to have the same value. Rather, the law will regard the consideration as adequate if the parties have freely agreed to the exchange. The requirement of legally sufficient consideration, therefore, is not at all concerned with whether the bargain was good or bad or whether one party received disproportionately more or less than what he gave or promised in exchange. (Such facts, however, may be relevant to the availability of certain defenses—such as fraud, duress, or undue influence—or certain remedies—such as specific performance.) The requirement of legally sufficient consideration is simply (1) that the parties have agreed to an exchange and (2) that, with respect to each party, the subject matter exchanged, or promised in exchange, either imposed a legal detriment on the promisee or conferred a legal benefit on the promisor. If the purported consideration is clearly without value, however, such that the transaction is a sham, many courts would hold that consideration is lacking.

Unilateral Contracts [12-1b]

In a unilateral contract, a promise is exchanged for a completed act or a forbearance to act. Because only one promise exists, only one party, the *offeror*, makes a promise, and is therefore the *promisor* while the other party, the *offeree*, is the person receiving the promise and, thus, is the *promisee*. For example, A promises to pay B $2,000 if B paints A's house. B paints A's house.

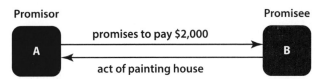

A's promise is binding only if it is supported by consideration consisting of either a legal detriment to B, the promisee (offeree), or a legal benefit to A, the promisor (offeror). B's painting the house is a legal detriment to B, the promisee, because she was under no prior legal duty to paint A's house. Also, B's painting of A's house is a legal benefit to A, the promisor, because A had no prior legal right to have his house painted by B.

A unilateral contract also may consist of a promise exchanged for a forbearance. To illustrate, A negligently injures B, for which B may recover damages in a tort action. A promises B $5,000 if B forbears from bringing suit. B accepts by not suing.

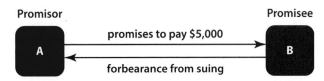

A's promise to pay B $5,000 is binding because it is supported by consideration; B, the promisee (offeree), has incurred a legal detriment by refraining from bringing suit, which he was under no prior legal obligation to refrain from doing. A, the promisor (offeror), has received a legal benefit because she had no prior legal right to B's forbearance from bringing suit.

Bilateral Contracts [12-1c]

In a bilateral contract there is an exchange of promises. Thus, each party is *both* a promisor and a promisee. For example, if A (the offeror) promises (offers) to purchase an automobile from B for $20,000, and B (the offeree) promises to sell the automobile to A for $20,000 (accepts the offer), the following relationship exists:

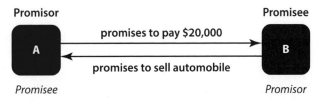

A (offeror) as promisor: *A's promise (the offer)* to pay B $20,000 is binding if that promise is supported by legal consideration from B (offeror), which may consist of either a legal detriment to B, the *promisee*, or a legal benefit to A, the *promisor*. B's promise to sell A the automobile is a legal detriment to B because he was under no prior legal duty to sell the automobile to A. Moreover, B's promise is also a legal benefit to A because A had no prior legal right to that automobile. Consequently, A's promise to pay $20,000 to B is supported by consideration and is enforceable.

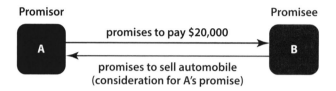

B (offeree) as promisor: For *B's promise (the acceptance)* to sell the automobile to A to be binding, it likewise must be supported by consideration from A (offeror), which may be either a legal detriment to A, the *promisee*, or a legal benefit to B, the *promisor*. A's promise to pay B $20,000 is a legal detriment to A because he was under no prior legal duty to pay $20,000 to B. At the same time, A's promise is also a legal benefit to B because B had no prior legal right to the $20,000. Thus, B's promise to sell the automobile is supported by consideration and is enforceable.

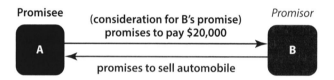

To summarize, for A's *promise* to B to be binding, it must be supported by legally sufficient consideration, which requires that the promise A receives from B in exchange either provides a legal benefit to A or constitutes a legal detriment to B. B's return promise to A must also be supported by consideration. Thus, in a bilateral contract, each promise is the consideration for the other, a relationship that has been referred to as *mutuality of obligation*. A general consequence of mutuality of obligation is that each promisor in a bilateral contract must be bound or neither is bound. See Concept Review 12-1 for an overview of consideration in both unilateral and bilateral contracts. Also see the Ethical Dilemma at the end of the chapter for a situation dealing with the disputed enforceability of a promise.

CONCEPT REVIEW 12-1

Consideration in Unilateral and Bilateral Contracts

Type of Contract	Offer	Acceptance	Consideration
Unilateral	Promise by A	Performance of requested act or forbearance by B	*Promise* by A *Performance* of requested act or forbearance by B
Bilateral	Promise by A	Return promise by B to perform requested act or forbearance	*Promise* by A *Return promise* by B to perform requested act or forbearance

Illusory Promises [12-1d]

Words of promise that make the performance of the purported promisor entirely optional do not constitute a promise at all. Consequently, they cannot serve as consideration. In this section, we will distinguish such illusory promises from promises that do impose obligations of performance upon the promisor and thus can be legally sufficient consideration.

Illusory promise
promise imposing no obligation on the promisor

An **illusory promise** is a statement that is in the form of a promise but imposes no obligation upon the maker of the statement. An illusory promise is not consideration for a return promise. Thus, a statement committing the promisor to purchase such quantity of goods as he may "desire" or "want" or "wish to buy" is an illusory promise because its performance is entirely optional. For example, if ExxonMobil offers to sell to Gasco as many barrels of oil as Gasco shall choose at $40.00 per barrel, there is no consideration. An offer containing such a promise, although accepted by the offeree, does not create a contract because the promise is illusory— Gasco's performance is entirely optional and no constraint is placed on its freedom. It is not bound to do anything, nor can ExxonMobil reasonably expect it to do anything. Thus, Gasco, by its promise, suffers no legal detriment and confers no legal benefit.

Practical Advice

Because an agreement under which one party may perform at his discretion is not a binding contract, be sure that you make a promise and receive a promise that is not optional.

Vanegas v. American Energy Services
Supreme Court of Texas, 2009
302 S.W.3d 299
http://scholar.google.com/scholar_case?case=3293885797327227839&q=302+S.W.3d+299+&hl=en&as_sdt=2,34

FACTS American Energy Services (AES or employer) was formed in the summer of 1996. Employees, hired in 1996, allege that in an operational meeting in June 1997, they voiced concerns to John Carnett, a vice president of AES, about the continued viability of the company. The employees allege that, in an effort to provide an incentive for them to stay with the company, Carnett promised the employees, who were at-will employees and therefore free to leave the company at any time, that "in the event of sale or merger of AES, the original [eight] employees remaining with AES at that time would get 5% of the value of any sale or merger of AES." AES Acquisition, Inc. acquired AES in 2001. Seven of the eight original employees were still with AES at the time of the acquisition. These remaining employees demanded their proceeds, and when the company refused to pay, the employees sued, claiming AES had breached the oral agreement.

AES moved for summary judgment on the ground that the agreement was illusory. The employees argued that the promise represented a unilateral contract, and by remaining employed for the stated period, the employees performed, thereby making the promise enforceable. The trial court granted AES's motion for summary judgment, and the employees appealed. The court of appeals affirmed, holding that the alleged unilateral contract failed because it was not supported by at least one nonillusory promise.

DECISION Judgment of the court of appeals reversed, and case remanded.

OPINION The issue turns on the distinction between bilateral and unilateral contracts. "A bilateral contract is one in which there are mutual promises between two parties to the contract, each party being both a promisor and a promisee." A unilateral contract, on the other hand, is "created by the promisor promising a benefit if the promisee performs. The contract becomes enforceable when the promisee performs." This case involves a unilateral contract and does not depend upon a bilateral promise.

The court of appeals held that even if AES promised to pay the employees the five percent, that promise was illusory at the time it was made because the employees were at-will, and AES could have fired all of them prior to the acquisition. But whether the promise was illusory at the time it was made is irrelevant; what matters is whether the promise became enforceable by the time of the breach. Almost all unilateral contracts begin as illusory promises. Take, for instance, the classic textbook example of a unilateral contract: "I will pay you $50 if you paint my house." The offer to pay the individual to paint the house can be withdrawn at any point prior to performance. But once the individual accepts the offer by performing, the promise to pay the $50 becomes binding. The employees allege that AES made an offer to split five percent of the proceeds of the sale or merger of the company among any remaining original employees. Assuming that allegation is true, the seven remaining employees accepted this offer by remaining employed for the requested period of time. At that point, AES's promise became binding. AES then breached its agreement with the employees when it refused to pay the employees their five percent share.

AES allegedly promised to pay any remaining original employees five percent of the proceeds when AES was sold. Assuming AES did make such an offer, the seven remaining employees accepted the offer by staying with AES until the sale. Regardless of whether the promise was illusory at the time it was made, the promise became enforceable upon the employees' performance.

INTERPRETATION An illusory promise is a statement that is in the form of a promise but imposes no obligation upon the maker of the statement.

ETHICAL QUESTION Did AES act ethically by inducing the employees to continue working in return for a promise that AES considered to be not binding? Explain.

CRITICAL THINKING QUESTION Do you agree with this decision? Explain.

Output and Requirements Contracts The agreement of a seller to sell her entire production to a particular purchaser is called an **output contract**. It gives the seller an ensured market for her product. Conversely, a purchaser's agreement to purchase from a particular seller all the materials of a particular kind that the purchaser needs is called a **requirements contract**. It ensures the buyer of a ready source of inventory or supplies. These contracts are *not* illusory. The buyer under a requirements contract does not promise to buy as much as she desires to buy, but to buy as much as she *needs*. Similarly, under an output contract, the seller promises to sell to the buyer the seller's entire production, not merely as much as the seller desires.

Furthermore, the Code imposes a good faith limitation upon the quantity to be sold or purchased under an output or requirements contract. Thus, this type of contract involves such actual output or requirements as may occur in good faith, except that no quantity unreasonably disproportionate to any stated estimate or, in the absence of a stated estimate, to any normal prior output or requirements may be tendered or demanded. Therefore, after contracting to sell to Adler, Inc., its entire output, Benevito Company cannot increase its production from one eight-hour shift per day to three eight-hour shifts per day.

Exclusive Dealing Contracts An **exclusive dealing** agreement is a contract in which a manufacturer of goods grants to a distributor an exclusive right to sell its products in a designated market. Unless otherwise agreed, an implied obligation is imposed on the manufacturer to use its best efforts to supply the goods and on the distributor to use her best efforts to promote their sale. These implied obligations are sufficient consideration to bind both parties to the exclusive dealing contract.

Conditional Promises A **conditional promise** is a promise the performance of which depends upon the happening or nonhappening of an event not certain to occur (the condition). A conditional promise is sufficient consideration *unless* the promisor knows at the time of making the promise that the condition cannot occur.

Thus, if Joanne offers to pay Barry $8,000 for Barry's automobile, provided that Joanne receives such amount as an inheritance from the estate of her deceased uncle, and Barry accepts the offer, the duty of Joanne to pay $8,000 to Barry is *conditioned* on her receiving $8,000 from her deceased uncle's estate. The consideration moving from Barry to Joanne is the transfer of title to the automobile. The consideration moving from Joanne to Barry is the promise of $8,000 subject to the condition.

Preexisting Public Obligations [12-1e]

The law does not regard the performance of, or the promise to perform, a preexisting legal duty, public or private, as either a legal detriment or a legal benefit. A *public duty* does not arise out of a contract; rather, it is imposed on members of society by force of the common law or by statute. Illustrations, as found in the law of torts, include the duty not to commit assault, battery, false imprisonment, or defamation. The criminal law also imposes many public duties. Thus, if Norton promises to pay Holmes, the village ruffian, $100 not to injure him, Norton's promise is unenforceable because both tort and criminal law impose a preexisting public obligation on Holmes to refrain from such abuse.

Public officials, such as the mayor of a city, members of a city council, police, and firefighters, are under a preexisting obligation to perform their duties by virtue of their public office. See the following case *Denney v. Reppert*.

The performance of, or the promise to perform, a **preexisting contractual duty**, a duty the terms of which are neither doubtful nor the subject of honest dispute, is also legally insufficient consideration because the doing of what one is legally bound to do is neither a detriment to a promisee nor a benefit to the promisor. For example, if Anita employs Ben for one year at a salary of $1,000 per month, and at the end of six months promises Ben that in addition to the salary

---

Output contract
agreement to sell all of one's production

Requirements contract
agreement to buy all of one's needs

Practical Advice

If you use an output or requirements contract, be sure to act in good faith and do not take unfair advantage of the situation.

Exclusive dealing
sole right to sell goods in a defined market

Conditional promise
obligations contingent upon a stated event

Preexisting public obligations
performance of public duties such as those imposed by tort or criminal law is neither a legal detriment nor a legal benefit

Preexisting contractual duty
performance of a preexisting contractual duty is not consideration

she will pay Ben $3,000 if Ben remains on the job for the remainder of the period originally agreed on, Anita's promise is not binding for lack of legally sufficient consideration. However, if Ben's duties were by agreement changed in nature or amount, Anita's promise would be binding because Ben's new duties are a legal detriment to Ben and a legal benefit to Anita.

The following case deals with both preexisting public and contractual obligations.

Denney v. Reppert
Court of Appeals of Kentucky, 1968
432 S.W.2d 647
http://scholar.google.com/scholar_case?case=14895092933351248292&q=432+S.W.2d+647&hl=en&as_sclt=2,34

FACTS In June, three armed men entered and robbed the First State Bank of Eubank, Kentucky, of $30,000. Acting on information supplied by four employees of the bank, Denney, Buis, McCollum, and Snyder, three law enforcement officials apprehended the robbers. Two of the arresting officers, Godby and Simms, were state policemen, and the third, Reppert, was a deputy sheriff in a neighboring county. All seven claimed the reward for the apprehension and conviction of the bank robbers. The trial court held that only Reppert was entitled to the reward, and Denney appealed.

DECISION Judgment affirmed.

OPINION In general, when a reward is offered to the general public for the performance of some specified act, the reward may be claimed by the person who performs that act unless that person is an agent, employee, or public official acting within the scope of his employment or official duties. For this reason, the bank employees cannot recover. At the time of the robbery, they were under a duty to protect the bank's resources and to safeguard the institution furnishing them employment Thus, in assisting the police officers in apprehending the bank robbers, the bank employees were merely doing their duty and, therefore, are not entitled to share in the reward.

Similarly, the state policemen, Godby and Simms, were exercising their duty as police officers in arresting the bank robbers and, thus, are not entitled to share in the reward. Reppert, on the other hand, was out of his jurisdiction at the time and, thus, was under no legal duty to arrest the bank robbers.

INTERPRETATION The law does not regard the performance of a preexisting duty as either a legal detriment or a legal benefit.

ETHICAL QUESTION Did the court treat all the parties fairly? Explain.

CRITICAL THINKING QUESTION Do you agree with the preexisting duty rule? Explain.

Modification of a preexisting contract
under the common law, a modification of a preexisting contract must be supported by mutual consideration; under the Uniform Commercial Code a contract can be modified without new consideration

---

Practical Advice

If you modify a contract governed by the common law, be sure to provide additional consideration to make the other party's new promise enforceable.

Modification of a Preexisting Contract   A **modification of a preexisting contract** occurs when the parties to the contract mutually agree to change one or more of its terms. Under the common law, as shown in the following case, a modification of an existing contract must be supported by mutual consideration to be enforceable. In other words, the modification must be supported by some new consideration beyond that which is already owed under the original contract. Thus, there must be a separate and distinct modification contract. For example, Diane and Fred agree that Diane shall put in a gravel driveway for Fred at a cost of $2,000. Subsequently, Fred agrees to pay an additional $3,000 if Diane will blacktop the driveway. Because Diane was not bound by the original contract to provide blacktop, she would incur a legal detriment in doing so and is therefore entitled to the additional $3,000. Similarly, consideration may consist of the promisee's refraining from exercising a legal right.

The Code has modified the common law rule for contract modification by providing that the parties can effectively modify a contract for the sale of goods without new consideration, provided they both intend to modify the contract and act in good faith. Moreover, the Restatement has moved toward this position by providing that a modification of an executory contract is binding if it is fair and equitable in the light of surrounding facts that the parties had not anticipated when the contract was made. Figure 12-1 demonstrates when consideration is required to modify an existing contract.

Figure 12-1 Modification of a Preexisting Contract

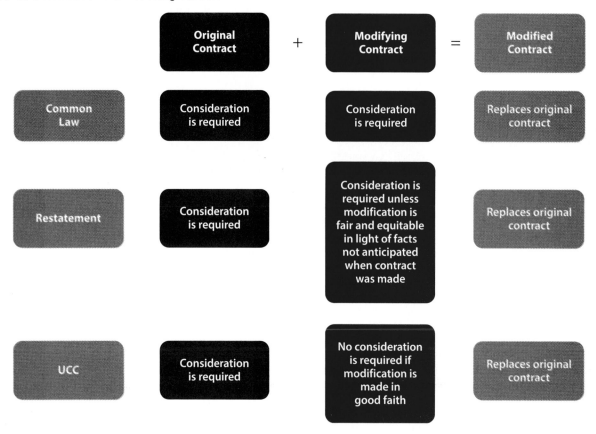

New England Rock Services, Inc. v. Empire Paving, Inc.
Appellate Court of Connecticut, 1999
53 Conn.App. 771, 731 A.2d 784; *cert. denied*, 250 Conn. 921, 738 A.2d 658
http://scholar.google.com/scholar_case?case=2815205762460431873&q=731+A.2d+784&hl=en&as_sdt=2,34

FACTS On October 26, 1995, the defendant, Empire Paving, Inc., entered into a contract with Rock Services under which Rock Services would provide drilling and blasting services as a subcontractor on the Niles Hill Road sewer project on which Empire was the general contractor and the city of New London was the owner. Rock Services was to be paid an agreed-upon price of $29 per cubic yard with an estimated amount of five thousand cubic yards, or on a time and materials basis, whichever was less. From the outset, Rock Services experienced problems on the job, the primary problem being the presence of a heavy concentration of water on the site. The water problem hindered Rock Services' ability to complete its work as anticipated. It is the responsibility of the general contractor to control the water on the work site and, on this particular job, Empire failed to control the water on the site properly. Rock Services attempted alternative methods of dealing with the problem, but was prevented from using them by the city. Thereafter, to complete its work, Rock Services was compelled to use a more costly and time-consuming method.

In late November 1995, Rock Services advised Empire that it would be unable to complete the work as anticipated because of the conditions at the site and requested that Empire agree to amend the contract to allow Rock Services to complete the project

on a time and materials basis. On December 8, Empire signed a purchase order that so modified the original agreement. Upon completion of the work, Empire refused to pay Rock Services for the remaining balance due on the time and materials agreement in the amount of $58,686.63, and Rock Services instituted this action. The trial court concluded that the modified agreement was valid and ruled in favor of Rock Services. Empire brings this appeal.

DECISION Judgment in favor of Rock Services affirmed.

OPINION The general rule of contracts is that in the absence of consideration an executory promise is unenforceable. A modification of an agreement must be supported by valid consideration and requires a party to do, or promise to do, something further than, or different from, that which he is already bound to do. So, when a party negotiates a modification resulting in greater pay for the same, already-owed work, that modification is not valid without additional consideration. However, an exception to the preexisting duty rule occurs:

> [W]here a contract must be performed under burdensome conditions not anticipated, and not within the contemplation of the parties at the time when the contract was made, and the promisee

measures up to the right standard of honesty and fair dealing, and agrees, in view of the changed conditions, to pay what is then reasonable, just, and fair, such new contract is not without consideration within the meaning of that term, either in law or in equity.

Empire argues that the water conditions on the site cannot qualify as a new circumstance that was not anticipated at the time the original contract was signed. The court, however, ruled that Empire's duty to control or remove the water on the job site arose in accordance with the custom and practice in the industry and, therefore, Empire's failure to control or remove the water on the

site constituted a new circumstance that Rock Services did not anticipate at the time the original contract was signed.

INTERPRETATION The Restatement provides that a modification of an executory contract is binding if it is fair and equitable in the light of surrounding facts that the parties had not anticipated when the contract was made.

CRITICAL THINKING QUESTION Which rule for contract modification do you believe is the best: the common law, the Restatement's, or the Uniform Commercial Code's? Why?

Substituted contract
parties rescind their original contract and enter into a new one

Substituted Contracts

A **substituted contract** results when the parties to a contract mutually agree to rescind their original contract and enter into a new one. This situation actually involves three separate contracts: the original contract, the contract of rescission, and the substitute contract. Substituted contracts are perfectly valid, allowing the parties to effectively discharge the original contract and to impose obligations under the new one. The rescission is binding in that, as long as each party still had rights under the original contract, each has, by giving up those rights, provided consideration to the other.

Settlement of an undisputed debt
payment of a lesser sum of money to discharge an undisputed debt does not constitute legally sufficient consideration

Undisputed debt
obligation whose existence and amount are not contested

Settlement of an Undisputed Debt

An **undisputed debt** is an obligation that is not contested as to its existence and its amount. Under the common law, the payment of a lesser sum of money than is owed in consideration of a promise to discharge a fully matured, undisputed debt is legally insufficient to support the promise of discharge. To illustrate, assume that Barbara owes Arnold $100, and in consideration of Barbara's paying him $50.00, Arnold agrees to discharge the debt. In a subsequent suit by Arnold against Barbara to recover the remaining $50.00, at common law Arnold is entitled to a judgment for $50.00 on the ground that Arnold's promise of discharge is not binding, because Barbara's payment of $50.00 was no legal detriment to the promisee, Barbara, because she was under a *preexisting legal obligation* to pay that much and more. Consequently, the consideration for Arnold's promise of discharge was legally insufficient, and Arnold is not bound by his promise. If, however, Arnold had accepted from Barbara any new or different consideration, such as the sum of $40.00 and a fountain pen worth $10.00 or less, or even the fountain pen with no payment of money, in full satisfaction of the $100 debt, the consideration moving from Barbara would be legally sufficient because Barbara was under no legal obligation to give a fountain pen to Arnold. In this example, consideration would also exist if Arnold had agreed to accept $50.00 *before* the debt became due, in full satisfaction of the debt. Barbara was under no legal obligation to pay any of the debt before its due date. Consequently, Barbara's early payment would constitute a legal detriment to Barbara as well as a legal benefit to Arnold. The common law is not concerned with the amount of the discount, because that is simply a question of adequacy. Likewise, Barbara's payment of a lesser amount on the due date at an agreed-upon different place of payment would be legally sufficient consideration. The Restatement, however, requires that the new consideration "differ[s] from what was required by the duty in a way which reflects more than a pretense of bargain."

Settlement of a disputed debt
payment of a lesser sum of money to discharge a disputed debt is legally sufficient consideration

Disputed debt
obligation whose existence or amount is contested

Settlement of a Disputed Debt

A **disputed debt** is an obligation whose existence or amount is contested. A promise to settle a validly disputed claim in exchange for an agreed payment or other performance is supported by consideration. Where the dispute is based on contentions without merit or not made in good faith, the debtor's surrender of such contentions is not a legal detriment to the claimant. The Restatement adopts a different position by providing that the settlement of a claim that proves invalid is consideration if at the time of the settlement (1) the claimant honestly believed that the claim was valid or (2) the claim was in fact doubtful because of uncertainty as to the facts or the law.

For example, in situations in which a person has requested professional services from an accountant or a lawyer and no agreement has been made about the amount of the fee to be charged, the client has a legal obligation to pay the reasonable value of the services performed. Because no definite amount was agreed on, the client's obligation is uncertain. When the accountant or lawyer sends the client a bill for services rendered, even though the amount stated in the bill is an estimate of the reasonable value of the services, the debt does not become undisputed until and unless the client agrees to pay the amount of the bill. If the client honestly disputes the amount that is owed and offers in full settlement an amount less than the bill, acceptance of the lesser amount by the accountant or lawyer discharges the debt. Thus, if Andy sends to Bess, an accountant, a check for $120 in full payment of his debt to Bess for services rendered, which services Andy considered worthless but for which Bess billed Andy $600, Bess's acceptance (cashing) of the check releases Andy from any further liability. Andy has given up his right to dispute the billing further, and Bess has forfeited her right to further collection. Thus, there is mutuality of consideration.

Practical Advice

If your contract is validly disputed, carefully consider whether to accept any payment marked "payment in full."

Bargained-for exchange
mutually agreed-upon exchange

Practical Advice

Because a promise to make a gift is generally not legally enforceable, obtain delivery of something that shows your control or ownership of the item to make it an executed gift.

Past consideration
unbargained-for past events

Bargained-for Exchange [12-2]

The central idea behind consideration is that the parties have intentionally entered into a **bargained-for exchange** with each other and have each given to the other something in a mutually agreed-upon exchange for his promise or performance. Thus, a promise to give someone a birthday present is without consideration, because the promisor received nothing in exchange for her promise of a present.

Past Consideration [12-2a]

Consideration, as previously defined, is the inducement for a promise or performance. The element of exchange is absent where a promise is given for an act already done. Therefore, unbargained-for past events are not consideration, despite their designation as **past consideration**. A promise made on account of something that the promisee has already done is not enforceable. For example, Diana installs Tom's complex new car stereo and speakers. Tom subsequently promises to reimburse Diana for her expenses, but his promise is not binding because there is no bargained-for exchange. See *DiLorenzo v. Valve and Primer Corporation* later in this chapter.

Third Parties [12-2b]

Consideration to support a promise may be given to a person other than the promisor if the promisor bargains for that exchange. For example, A promises to pay B $15.00 if B delivers a specified book to C.

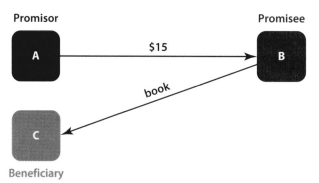

A's promise is binding because B incurred a legal detriment by delivering the book to C, because B was under no prior legal obligation to do so, and A had no prior legal right to have the book given to C. A and B have bargained for A to pay B $15.00 in return for B's delivering the book to C. A's promise to pay $15.00 is also consideration for B's promise to give C the book.

Conversely, consideration may be given by some person other than the promisee. For example, A promises to pay B $25.00 in return for D's promise to give a radio to A. A's promise to pay $25.00 to B is consideration for D's promise to give a radio to A and *vice versa*.

Contracts Without Consideration [12-3]

Certain transactions are enforceable even though they are not supported by consideration.

Promises to Perform Prior Unenforceable Obligations [12-3a]

In certain circumstances the courts will enforce new promises to perform an obligation that originally was not enforceable or that has become unenforceable by operation of law. These situations include promises to pay debts barred by the statute of limitations, debts discharged in bankruptcy, and voidable obligations. In addition, some courts will enforce promises to pay moral obligations.

Promise to pay debt barred by the statute of limitations
a new promise by the debtor to pay the debt renews the running of the statute of limitations for a second statutory period

Statute of limitation
time period within which a lawsuit must be initiated

Promise to Pay Debt Barred by the Statute of Limitations   Every state has
a **statute of limitations** stating that legal actions to enforce a debt must be brought within a prescribed period of time after the rights to bring the action arose. Actions not begun within the specified period—such periods vary among the states and also with the nature of the legal action—will be dismissed.

An exception to the past consideration rule extends to promises to pay all or part of a contractual or quasi-contractual debt barred by the statute of limitations. The new promise is binding according to its terms, without consideration, for a second statutory period. Any recovery under the new promise is limited to the terms contained in the new promise. Most states require that new promises falling under this rule, except those partially paid, must be in writing to be enforceable.

Promise to pay debt discharged in bankruptcy
may be enforceable without consideration

Promise to Pay Debt Discharged in Bankruptcy   A promise to pay a debt that
has been discharged in bankruptcy is also enforceable without consideration. The Bankruptcy Code, however, imposes a number of requirements that must be met before such a promise may be enforced. These requirements are discussed in Chapter 38.

Voidable promises
a new promise to perform a voidable obligation that has not been previously avoided is enforceable

Voidable Promises   Another promise that is enforceable without new consideration is a
new promise to perform a voidable obligation that has not previously been avoided. The power of avoidance may be based on lack of capacity, fraud, misrepresentation, duress, undue influence, or mistake. For instance, a promise to perform an antecedent obligation made by a minor upon reaching the age of majority is enforceable without new consideration. To be enforceable, the promise itself must not be voidable. For example, if the new promise is made without knowledge of the original fraud or by a minor before reaching the age of majority, then the new promise is not enforceable.

Moral obligation
a promise made to satisfy a preexisting moral obligation is generally unenforceable for lack of consideration

Moral Obligation   Under the common law and in most states, a promise made to satisfy a
preexisting moral obligation is made for past consideration and therefore is unenforceable for lack of consideration. Instances involving such moral obligations include promises to pay another for board and lodging previously furnished to one's needy relative and promises to pay debts owed by a relative.

The Restatement and a minority of states recognize moral obligations as consideration. The Restatement provides that a promise made for "a benefit previously received by the promisor from the promisee is binding to the extent necessary to prevent injustice." For instance, under the Restatement, Tim's subsequent promise to Donna to reimburse her for expenses she incurred in rendering emergency services to Tim's son is binding even though it is not supported by new consideration.

Promissory estoppel
doctrine that prohibits a party from denying his promise when the promisee takes action or forbearance to his detriment reasonably based upon the promise

Promissory Estoppel [12-3b]

As discussed in Chapter 9, in certain circumstances in which there has been detrimental reliance, the courts enforce noncontractual promises under the doctrine of promissory estoppel. When applicable, the doctrine makes gratuitous promises enforceable to the extent necessary to avoid injustice. The doctrine applies when a promise that the promisor should reasonably expect to induce detrimental reliance does induce such action or forbearance.

Promissory estoppel does not mean that a promise given without consideration is binding simply because it is followed by a change of position on the part of the promisee. Such a change of position in justifiable reliance on the promise creates liability if injustice can be avoided only by the enforcement of the promise. For example, Ann promises Larry not to foreclose for a period of six months on a mortgage Ann owns on Larry's land. Larry then changes his position by spending $100,000 to construct a building on the land. Ann's promise not to foreclose is binding on her under the doctrine of promissory estoppel.

The most common application of the doctrine of promissory estoppel is to charitable subscriptions. Numerous churches, memorials, college buildings, stadiums, hospitals, and other structures used for religious, educational, or charitable purposes have been built with the assistance of contributions made through fulfillment of pledges or promises to contribute to particular worthwhile causes. Although the pledgor regards herself as making a gift for a charitable purpose and gift promises tend not to be enforceable, the courts have generally enforced charitable subscription promises. Although various reasons and theories have been advanced in support of liability, the one most commonly accepted is that the subscription has induced a change of position by the promisee (the church, school, or charitable organization) in reliance on the promise. The Restatement, moreover, has relaxed the reliance requirement for charitable subscriptions so that actual reliance need not be shown; the probability of reliance is sufficient.

DiLorenzo v. Valve & Primer Corporation
Appellate Court of Illinois, First District, Fifth Division, 2004
807 N.E.2d 673, 283 Ill.Dec. 68
http://scholar.google.com/scholar_case?case=258399757685586555&q=807+N.E.2d+673&hl=en&as_sdt=2,34

FACTS DiLorenzo, a forty-year employee of Valve & Primer, was also an officer, director, and shareholder of one hundred shares of stock. DiLorenzo claims that in 1987 Valve & Primer offered him a ten-year stock option that would allow DiLorenzo to purchase an additional three hundred shares at the fixed price of $250 per share. DiLorenzo claims that in reliance on that employment agreement, he stayed in his job for over nine additional years and did not follow up on any of several recruitment offers from other companies. Valve & Primer claims the 1987 employment agreement between it and DiLorenzo did not contain a stock purchase agreement. The only purported proof of the agreement is an unsigned copy of board meeting minutes of which DiLorenzo had the only copy.

In January 1996, DiLorenzo entered into a semi-retirement agreement with Valve & Primer, and he attempted to tender his remaining one hundred shares pursuant to a stock redemption agreement. Shortly thereafter, Valve & Primer fired DiLorenzo. DiLorenzo argued before the trial court that, even if the purported agreement was not found to be valid, it should be enforced on promissory estoppel grounds. Valve & Primer's moved for summary judgment, which the trial court granted for lack of consideration. The trial court denied the promissory estoppel claim because of insufficient reliance. DiLorenzo appealed.

DECISION The trial court's grant of Valve & Primer's motion for summary judgment is affirmed.

OPINION Whether the 1987 corporate minutes are authentic is not an issue on appeal. The purported minutes of the June 8, 1987, special meeting contain the following relevant language:

> That in order to retain and reward such dedication … that Ralph DiLorenzo be given an option to purchase additional shares not to exceed 300. Said option to be exercised within 10 years from below date at the price of $250.00 per share.

The first question is whether there was consideration for the stock options. DiLorenzo could have exercised the option the moment it was purportedly made, then immediately quit, thereby giving nothing to the employer. Though the exercise of the option would require the transfer of money for the stock, the option itself carries with it no detriment to DiLorenzo. Therefore, there was no consideration for the option.

The second issue is whether DiLorenzo is entitled to the value of the shares of stock based upon the theory of promissory estoppel. DiLorenzo argues that he detrimentally relied upon Valve & Primer's promise in that he worked at Valve & Primer for an additional period in excess of nine years in reliance on the stock option agreement.

There is nothing in the language of the corporate minutes or any other source to be found in this record to suggest that Valve & Primer conditioned the alleged stock option on DiLorenzo's promise to remain in his employment. Since the corporate minutes lack a mandatory obligation on which DiLorenzo could have reasonably detrimentally relied, and he could have elected to buy the shares of stock immediately, DiLorenzo's decision to remain on the job for the additional period of over nine years must be viewed as a voluntary act. Under those circumstances, promissory estoppel would not apply.

INTERPRETATION Past consideration is not legal consideration to support a promise; promissory estoppel requires detrimental reliance.

ETHICAL QUESTION Did the parties act ethically? Explain.

CRITICAL THINKING QUESTION What would have satisfied the consideration requirement in this case?

Contracts Under Seal [12-3c]

Contracts under seal where still recognized, the seal acts as a substitute for consideration

Under the common law, when a person desired to bind himself by bond, deed, or solemn promise, he executed his promise under seal. He did not have to sign the document; rather, his delivery of a document to which he had affixed his seal was sufficient. No consideration for his promise was necessary. In some states a promise under seal is still binding without consideration.

Nevertheless, most states have abolished by statute the distinction between contracts under seal and written unsealed contracts. In these states, the seal is no longer recognized as a substitute for consideration. The Code also has adopted this position, specifically eliminating the use of seals in contracts for the sale of goods.

Promises Made Enforceable by Statute [12-3d]

Some gratuitous promises that otherwise would be unenforceable have been made binding by statute. Most significant among these are (1) contract modifications, (2) renunciations, and (3) irrevocable offers.

Contract Modifications   As mentioned previously, the Uniform Commercial Code (UCC) has abandoned the common law rule requiring that a modification of an existing contract be supported by consideration to be valid. Instead, the Code provides that a contract for the sale of goods can be effectively modified without new consideration, provided the modification is made in good faith.

Renunciations   Under the Revised UCC Article 1, a claim or right arising out of an alleged breach may be discharged in whole or in part without consideration by agreement of the aggrieved party in an authenticated record. Under the original Code, any claim or right arising out of an alleged breach of contract can be discharged in whole or in part without consideration by a written waiver or renunciation signed and delivered by the aggrieved party. Under both versions of the Code, this provision is subject to the obligation of good faith and, as with all sections of Article 1, applies to a transaction to the extent that it is governed by one of the other articles of the UCC.

Firm Offers   Under the Code, a firm offer, a written offer signed by a merchant offeror to buy or sell goods, is not revocable for lack of consideration during the time within which it is stated to be open, not to exceed three months or, if no time is stated, for a reasonable time. For a summary of consideration, see Figure 12-2.

ETHICAL DILEMMA

Should a Spouse's Promise Be Legally Binding?

Facts Joan Kantor is a social worker for the employees of Surf & Co., a towel manufacturer. Stan Koronetsky, a Surf employee, has confided the following problems to Kantor.

Koronetsky and his wife, Paula, have been married for ten years. Koronetsky states that three years ago his wife was unfaithful and Koronetsky began a divorce proceeding. When Paula Koronetsky promised to refrain from further infidelity and to attend marital counseling sessions, Koronetsky agreed to stop the divorce proceeding. However, although Stan dropped the divorce proceeding, his wife never attended counseling.

Koronetsky is also upset because he and his wife had agreed that she would attend medical school while he worked to support her. In exchange for his promise to put her through medical school, Paula promised that she would support him while he obtained his MBA degree. But after Paula became a doctor, she refused to support him; consequently, Stan never got his master's degree.

Social, Policy, and Ethical Considerations

1. What should Joan Kantor do in this situation? What is the scope of her counseling responsibilities?

2. Should agreements between married parties be enforced in a court of law? If so, what types of agreements should be enforceable?

3. What are the individual interests at stake in this situation? Is it reasonable to assume that spouses make many private agreements, and that generally these agreements are made without the intention of their being legally binding?

Figure 12-2 Consideration

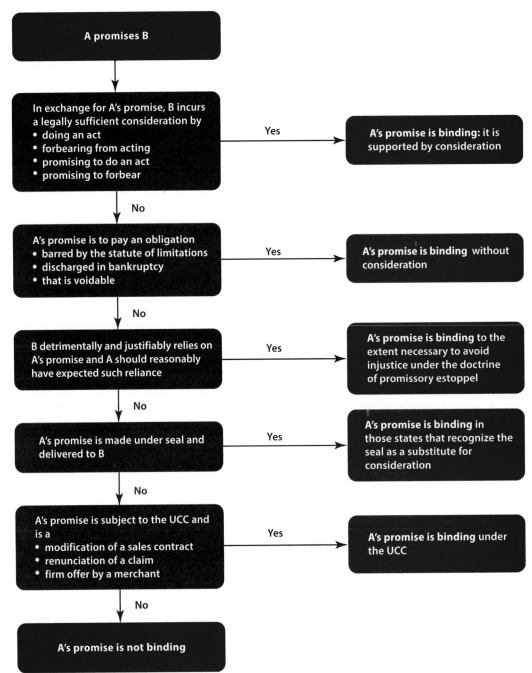

BUSINESS LAW **IN ACTION**

Computer Castle agreed to custom configure seventy-five personal computers and deliver them to Delber Data Corp. within ninety days. The price of each computer was $899, and Delber Data also agreed to a "Service-Pak" extended warranty plan for each unit purchased.

Computer Castle's employees worked diligently to get the order ready and had only five computers left to configure when a next-generation operating system hit the market. Prices for computers carrying the old operating system plummeted. Delber Data quickly sought to change its order, but Computer Castle had already built nearly all the computers. Delber admitted

it could still use the computers with the old operating system but felt that at a minimum Computer Castle should grant a price concession.

The computers Delber Data had agreed to buy could now be sold for only $699 each at most. Not wanting to lose a possible long-term business relationship, Computer Castle agreed to lower the price of the Delber Data computers to $799 each. Computer Castle faxed a short note to Delber confirming the new price. Thus, Delber Data has given no consideration to support the new contract price—indeed Delber is getting the very same computers for *less* than it originally agreed to pay.

Whether Computer Castle's price reduction will be enforceable depends on what law governs the parties' contract. Though Delber did purchase the warranty plan, a service, the contract is clearly one for the sale of goods—the predominant purpose of the contract is the purchase of configured personal computers. The price reduction, then, is a modification of a sales contract and is governed by the Uniform Commercial Code. Despite the lack of consideration, the Code permits enforcement of this contract modification, as the change was agreed to by both parties and sought by Delber in good faith, here based on the unanticipated emergence of newer technology.

CHAPTER SUMMARY

Consideration

Definition the inducement to enter into a contract

Elements legal sufficiency and bargained-for exchange

Legal Sufficiency of Consideration

Definition consists of either a benefit to the promisor or a detriment to the promisee

- *Legal Benefit* obtaining something to which one had no prior legal right
- *Legal Detriment* doing an act one is not legally obligated to do or not doing an act that one has a legal right to do

Adequacy of Consideration not required where the parties have freely agreed to the exchange

Illusory Promise promise that imposes no obligation on the promisor; the following promises are not illusory

- *Output Contract* agreement to sell all of one's production to a single buyer
- *Requirements Contract* agreement to buy all of one's needs from a single producer
- *Exclusive Dealing Contract* grant to a franchisee or licensee by a manufacturer of the sole right to sell goods in a defined market
- *Conditional Contract* a contract in which the obligations are contingent upon the occurrence of a stated event

Preexisting Public Obligations public duties such as those imposed by tort or criminal law are neither a legal detriment nor a legal benefit

Preexisting Contractual Obligation performance of a preexisting contractual duty is not consideration

- *Modification of a Preexisting Contract* under the common law a modification of a preexisting contract must be supported by mutual consideration; under the Code a contract can be modified without new consideration
- *Substituted Contracts* the parties agree to rescind their original contract and to enter into a new one; rescission and new contract are supported by consideration
- *Settlement of an Undisputed Debt* payment of a lesser sum of money to discharge an undisputed debt (one whose existence and amount are not contested) does not constitute legally sufficient consideration
- *Settlement of a Disputed Debt* payment of a lesser sum of money to discharge a disputed debt (one whose existence or amount is contested) is legally sufficient consideration

| *Bargained-for Exchange* | **Definition** a mutually agreed-upon exchange |
| | **Past Consideration** an act done before the contract is made is not consideration |

Contracts Without Consideration

Promises to Perform Prior Unenforceable Obligations

- *Promise to Pay Debt Barred by the Statute of Limitations* a new promise by the debtor to pay the debt renews the running of the statute of limitations for a second statutory period
- *Promise to Pay Debt Discharged in Bankruptcy* may be enforceable without consideration
- *Voidable Promises* a new promise to perform a voidable obligation that has not been previously avoided is enforceable
- *Moral Obligation* a promise made to satisfy a preexisting moral obligation is generally unenforceable for lack of consideration

Promissory Estoppel doctrine that prohibits a party from denying his promise when the promisee takes action or forbearance to his detriment reasonably based upon the promise

Contracts Under Seal where still recognized, the seal acts as a substitute for consideration

Promises Made Enforceable by Statute some gratuitous promises have been made enforceable by statute; the Code makes enforceable (1) contract modifications, (2) renunciations, and (3) firm offers

QUESTIONS

1. In consideration of $1,800 paid to him by Joyce, Hill gave Joyce a written option to purchase his house for $180,000 on or before April 1. Prior to April 1, Hill verbally agreed to extend the option until July 1. On May 18, Hill, known to Joyce, sold the house to Gray, who was ignorant of the unrecorded option. On May 20 Joyce sent an acceptance to Hill who received it on May 25. Is there a contract between Joyce and Hill? Explain.

2. **a.** Ann owed $2,500 to Barry for services Barry rendered to Ann. The debt was due June 30, 2014. In March 2015, the debt was still unpaid. Barry was in urgent need of ready cash and told Ann that if she would pay $1,500 on the debt at once, Barry would release her from the balance. Ann paid $1,500 and stated to Barry that all claims had been paid in full. In August 2015, Barry demanded the unpaid balance and subsequently sued Ann for $1,000. Result?

   b. Modify the facts in (a) by assuming that Barry gave Ann a written receipt stating that all claims had been paid in full. Result?

   c. Modify the facts in (a) by assuming that Ann owed Barry the $2,500 on Ann's purchase of a motorcycle from Barry. Result?

3. **a.** Judy orally promises her daughter, Liza, that she will give her a tract of land for her home. Liza, as intended by Judy, gives up her homestead and takes possession of the land. Liza lives there for six months and starts construction of a home. Is Judy bound to convey the real estate?

   b. Ralph, knowing that his son, Ed, desires to purchase a tract of land, promises to give him the $25,000 he needs for the purchase. Ed, relying on this promise, buys an option on the tract of land. Can Ralph rescind his promise?

4. George owed Keith $800 on a personal loan. Neither the amount of the debt nor George's liability to pay the $800 was disputed. Keith had also rendered services as a carpenter to George without any agreement as to the price to be paid. When the work was completed, an honest and reasonable difference of opinion developed between George and Keith with respect to the value of Keith's services. Upon receiving Keith's bill for the carpentry services for $600, George mailed in a properly stamped and addressed envelope his check for $800 to Keith. In an accompanying letter, George stated that the enclosed check was in full settlement of both claims. Keith endorsed and cashed the check. Thereafter, Keith unsuccessfully sought to collect from George an alleged unpaid balance of $600. May Keith recover the $600 from George?

5. The Snyder Mfg. Co., being a large user of coal, entered into separate contracts with several coal companies. In each contract, it was agreed that the coal company would supply coal during the year in such amounts as the manufacturing company might desire to order, at a price of $55.00 per ton. In February of that year, the Snyder Company ordered one thousand tons of coal from Union Coal Company, one of the contracting parties. Union Coal Company delivered five hundred tons of the order and then notified Snyder Company that no more deliveries would be made and that it denied any obligation under the contract. In an action by Union Coal to collect $55.00 per ton for the five hundred tons of coal delivered, Snyder files a counterclaim, claiming damages of $1,500 for failure to deliver the additional five hundred tons of the order and damages of $4,000 for breach of agreement to deliver coal during the balance of the year. What contract, if any, exists between Snyder and Union?

6. On February 5, Devon entered into a written agreement with Gordon whereby Gordon agreed to drill a well on Devon's property for the sum of $5,000 and to complete the well on or before April 15. Before entering into the contract, Gordon had made test borings and had satisfied himself as to the character of the subsurface. After two days of drilling, Gordon struck hard rock. On February 17, Gordon removed his equipment and advised Devon that the project had proved

unprofitable and that he would not continue. On March 17, Devon went to Gordon and told Gordon that he would assume the risk of the enterprise and would pay Gordon $100 for each day required to drill the well, as compensation for labor, the use of Gordon's equipment, and Gordon's services in supervising the work, provided Gordon would furnish certain special equipment designed to cut through hard rock. Gordon said that the proposal was satisfactory. The work was continued by Gordon and completed in an additional fifty-eight days. Upon completion of the work, Devon failed to pay, and Gordon brought an action to recover $5,800. Devon answered that he had never become obligated to pay $100 a day and filed a counterclaim for damages in the amount of $500 for the month's delay based on an alleged breach of contract by Gordon. Explain who will prevail and why.

7. Discuss and explain whether there is valid consideration for each of the following promises:

   a. A and B entered into a contract for the purchase and sale of goods. A subsequently promised to pay a higher price for the goods when B refused to deliver at the contract price.

   b. A promised in writing to pay a debt, which was due from B to C, on C's agreement to extend the time of payment for one year.

   c. A orally promised to pay $150 to her son, B, solely in consideration of past services rendered to A by B, for which there had been no agreement or request to pay.

8. Alan purchased shoes from Barbara on open account. Barbara sent Alan a bill for $10,000. Alan wrote back that two hundred pairs of the shoes were defective and offered to pay $6,000 and give Barbara his promissory note for $1,000. Barbara accepted the offer, and Alan sent his check for $6,000 and his note in accordance with the agreement. Barbara cashed the check, collected on the note, and one month later sued Alan for $3,000. Is Barbara bound by her acceptance of the offer?

9. Nancy owed Sharon $1,500, but Sharon did not initiate a lawsuit to collect the debt within the time period prescribed by the statute of limitations. Nevertheless, Nancy promises Sharon that she will pay the barred debt. Thereafter, Nancy refuses to pay. Sharon brings suit to collect on this new promise. Is Nancy's new promise binding? Explain.

10. Anthony lends money to Frank, who dies without having repaid the loan. Frank's widow, Carol, promises Anthony to repay the loan. Upon Carol's refusal to pay the loan, Anthony brings suit against Carol for payment. Is Carol bound by her promise to pay the loan?

11. The parties entered into an oral contract in June under which the plaintiff agreed to construct a building for the defendant on a time and materials basis, at a maximum cost of $56,146, plus sales tax and extras ordered by the defendant. When the building was 90 percent completed, the defendant told the plaintiff he was unhappy with the whole job as "the thing just wasn't being run right." The parties then, on October 17, signed a written agreement lowering the maximum cost to $52,000 plus sales tax. The plaintiff thereafter completed the building at a cost of $64,155. The maximum under the June oral agreement, plus extras and sales tax, totaled $61,040. Explain whether the defendant is obligated to pay only the lower maximum fixed by the October 17 agreement.

CASE PROBLEMS

12. Taylor assaulted his wife, who then took refuge in Ms. Harrington's house. The next day, Mr. Taylor entered the house and began another assault on his wife. Taylor's wife knocked him down and, while he was lying on the floor, attempted to cut his head open or decapitate him with an ax. Harrington intervened to stop the bloodshed and was hit by the ax as it was descending. The ax fell upon her hand, mutilating it badly, but sparing Taylor his life. Afterwards, Taylor orally promised to compensate Harrington for her injury. Is Taylor's promise enforceable? Explain.

13. Jonnel Enterprises, Inc., contracted to construct a student dormitory at Clarion State College. On May 6, Jonnel entered into a written agreement with Graham and Long as electrical contractors to perform the electrical work and to supply materials for the dormitory. The contract price was $70,544.66. Graham and Long claim that they believed the May 6 agreement obligated them to perform the electrical work on only one wing of the building, but that three or four days after work was started, a second wing of the building was found to be in need of wiring. At that time, Graham and Long informed Jonnel that they would not wire both wings of the building under the present contract, so the parties orally agreed upon a new contract. Under the new contract, Graham and Long were obligated to wire both wings and were to be paid only $65,000, but they were relieved of the obligations to supply entrances and a heating system. Graham and Long resumed their work, and Jonnel made seven of the eight progress payments called for. When Jonnel did not pay the final payment, Graham and Long brought this action. Jonnel claims that the May 6 contract is controlling. Is Jonnel correct in its assertion? Why?

14. Baker entered into an oral agreement with Healey, the state distributor of Ballantine & Sons' liquor products, that Ballantine would supply Baker with its products on demand and that Baker would have the exclusive agency for Ballantine within a certain area of Connecticut. Shortly thereafter, the agreement was modified to give Baker the right to terminate at will. Eight months later, Ballantine & Sons revoked its agency. May Baker enforce the oral agreement? Explain.

15. PLM, Inc., entered into an oral agreement with Quaintance Associates, an executive "headhunter" service, for the recruitment of qualified candidates to be employed by PLM. As agreed, PLM's obligation to pay Quaintance did not depend on PLM actually hiring a qualified candidate presented by Quaintance. After several months Quaintance sent a letter to PLM, admitting that it had so far failed to produce a suitable

candidate, but included a bill for $9,806.61, covering fees and expenses. PLM responded that Quaintance's services were only worth $6,060.48, and that payment of the lesser amount was the only fair way to handle the dispute. Accordingly, PLM enclosed a check for $6,060.48, writing on the back of the check "IN FULL PAYMENT OF ANY CLAIMS QUAINTANCE HAS AGAINST PLM, INC." Quaintance cashed the check and then sued PLM for the remaining $3,746.13. Decision?

16. Red Owl Stores told the Hoffman family that upon the payment of approximately $518,000 a grocery store franchise would be built for them in a new location. On the advice of Red Owl, the Hoffmans bought a small grocery store in their hometown to get management experience. After the Hoffmans operated at a profit for three months, Red Owl advised them to sell the small grocery, assuring them that Red Owl would find them a larger store elsewhere. Although selling at that point would cost them much profit, the Hoffmans followed Red Owl's directions. Additionally, to raise the required money for the deal, the Hoffmans sold their bakery business in their hometown. The Hoffmans also sold their house and moved to a new home in the city where their new store was to be located. Red Owl then informed the Hoffmans that it would take $524,100, not $518,000, to complete the deal. The family scrambled to find the additional funds. However, when told by Red Owl that it would now cost them $534,000 to get their new franchise, the Hoffmans decided to sue instead. Should Red Owl be held to its promises? Explain.

17. The plaintiff, Brenner, entered into a contract with the defendant, Little Red School House, Ltd., which stated that in return for a nonrefundable tuition of $1,080, Brenner's son could attend the defendant's school for a year. When Brenner's ex-wife refused to enroll their son, the plaintiff sought and received a verbal promise of a refund. The defendant now refuses to refund the plaintiff's money for lack of consideration. Did mutual consideration exist between the parties? Explain.

18. Tender Loving Care, Inc. (TLC), a corporation owned and operated by Virginia Bryant, eventually went out of business. The Secretary of State canceled its corporate charter, and a check drawn on TLC's account made out to the Department of Human Resources (DHR) to pay state unemployment taxes was returned for insufficient funds. Subsequently, Bryant filed individually for bankruptcy, listing the DHR as a creditor. This claim was not allowed, because Bryant was held not to be personally liable on the debts of TLC to the DHR. The DHR later called Bryant to its offices, where she was told that she needed to pay the debt owed to the DHR by TLC. Unable to contact her lawyer, Bryant was persuaded to sign a personal guarantee to cover the debt. Later, when Bryant refused to pay, the DHR filed suit. Decision?

19. Ben Collins was a full professor with tenure at Wisconsin State University in 2010. In March 2010, Parsons College, in an attempt to lure Dr. Collins from Wisconsin State, offered him a written contract promising him the rank of full professor with tenure and a salary of $65,000 for the 2010–11 academic year. The contract further provided that the College would increase his salary by $2,000 each year for the next five

years. In return, Collins was to teach two trimesters of the academic year beginning in October 2010. In addition, the contract stipulated, by reference to the College's faculty bylaws, that tenured professors could be dismissed only for just cause and after written charges were filed with the Professional Problems Committee. The two parties signed the contract, and Collins resigned his position at Wisconsin State.

In February 2012, the College tendered a different contract to Collins to cover the following year. This contract reduced his salary to $55,000 with no provision for annual increments, but left his rank of full professor intact. It also required that Collins waive any and all rights or claims existing under any previous employment contracts with the College. Collins refused to sign this new contract and Parsons College soon notified him that he would not be employed the following year. The College did not give any grounds for his dismissal; nor did it file charges with the Professional Problems Committee. As a result, Collins was forced to take a teaching position at the University of North Dakota at a substantially reduced salary. He sued to recover the difference between the salary Parsons College promised him until 2016 and the amount he earned. Will he prevail? Explain.

20. Rodney and Donna Mathis (Mathis) filed a wrongful death action against St. Alexis Hospital and several physicians, arising out of the death of their mother, Mary Mathis. Several weeks before trial, an expert consulted by Mathis notified the trial court and Mathis's counsel that, in his opinion, Mary Mathis's death was not proximately caused by the negligence of the physicians. Shortly thereafter, Mathis voluntarily dismissed the wrongful death action. Mathis and St. Alexis entered into a covenant-not-to-sue in which Mathis agreed not to pursue any claims against St. Alexis or its employees in terms of the medical care of Mary Mathis. St. Alexis, in return, agreed not to seek sanctions, including attorney fees and costs incurred in defense of the previously dismissed wrongful death action. Subsequently, Mathis filed a second wrongful death action against St. Alexis Hospital, among others. Mathis asked the court to rescind the covenant-not-to-sue, arguing that because St. Alexis was not entitled to sanctions in connection with the first wrongful death action, there was no consideration for the covenant-not-to-sue. Is this contention correct? Explain.

21. Harold Pearsall and Joe Alexander were friends for more than twenty-five years. About twice a week they would get together after work and proceed to a liquor store, where they would purchase what the two liked to refer to as a "package"—a half-pint of vodka, orange juice, two cups, and two lottery tickets. Occasionally, these lottery tickets would yield modest rewards of two or three dollars, which the pair would then "plow back" into the purchase of additional tickets. On December 16, Pearsall and Alexander visited the liquor store twice, buying their normal "package" on both occasions. For the first package, Pearsall went into the store alone, and when he returned to the car, he said to Alexander, in reference to the tickets, "Are you in on it?" Alexander said, "Yes." When Pearsall asked him for his half of the purchase price, though, Alexander replied that he had no money. When they went to Alexander's home, Alexander snatched the tickets from Pearsall's hand and

"scratched" them, only to find that they were both worthless. Later that same evening Alexander returned to the liquor store and bought a second "package." This time, Pearsall snatched the tickets from Alexander and said that he would "scratch" them. Instead, he gave one to Alexander, and each man scratched one of the tickets. Alexander's was a $20,000 winner. Alexander cashed the ticket and refused to give Pearsall anything. Can Pearsall recover half of the proceeds from Alexander? Explain.

TAKING SIDES

Anna Feinberg began working for the Pfeiffer Company in 1968 at age seventeen. By 2005, she had attained the position of book-keeper, office manager, and assistant treasurer. In appreciation for her skill, dedication, and long years of service, the Pfeiffer board of directors resolved to increase Feinberg's monthly salary to $4,000 and to create for her a retirement plan. The plan allowed that Feinberg would be given the privilege of retiring from active duty at any time she chose and that she would receive retirement pay of $2,000 per month for life, although the Board expressed the hope that Feinberg would continue to serve the company for many years. Feinberg, however, chose to retire two years later. The Pfeiffer Company paid Feinberg her retirement pay until 2014. The company thereafter discontinued payments.

a. What are the arguments that the company's promise to pay Feinberg $2,000 per month for life is enforceable?

b. What are the arguments that the company's promise is not enforceable?

c. What is the proper outcome? Explain.

Illegal Bargains

CHAPTER 13

Pactis privatorum juri publico non derogatur. (Private contracts do not take away from public law.)

Legal Maxim

CHAPTER OUTCOMES

After reading and studying this chapter, you should be able to:

1. Identify and explain the types of contracts that may violate a statute and distinguish between the two types of licensing statutes.

2. Describe when a covenant not to compete will be enforced and identify the two situations in which these types of covenants most frequently arise.

3. Explain when exculpatory agreements, agreements involving the commitment of a tort, and agreements involving public officials will be held to be illegal.

4. Distinguish between procedural and substantive unconscionability.

5. Explain the usual effects of illegality and the major exceptions to this rule.

A legal objective is essential for a promise or agreement to be binding. When the formation or performance of an agreement is criminal, tortious, or otherwise contrary to public policy, the agreement is illegal and ***unenforceable*** (as opposed to being void). The law does *not* provide a remedy for the breach of an unenforceable agreement and thus "leaves the parties where it finds them." (It is preferable to use the term *illegal bargain* or *illegal agreement* rather than *illegal contract*, because the word *contract*, by definition, denotes a legal and enforceable agreement.) The illegal bargain is made unenforceable (1) to discourage such undesirable conduct in the future and (2) to avoid the inappropriate use of the judicial process in carrying out the socially undesirable bargain.

In this chapter, we will discuss (1) agreements in violation of a statute, (2) agreements contrary to public policy, and (3) the effect of illegality on agreements.

VIOLATIONS OF STATUTES [13-1]

Violations of statutes
the courts will not enforce agreements declared illegal by statute

The courts will not enforce an agreement declared illegal by statute. For example, "wagering or gambling contracts" are specifically declared unenforceable in most states. Likewise, an agreement induced by criminal conduct will not be enforced. For example, if Alice enters into an agreement with Brent Co. through the bribing of Brent Co.'s purchasing agent, the agreement would be unenforceable.

Licensing Statutes [13-1a]

License
formal authorization to engage in certain practices

Every jurisdiction has laws requiring a **license** for those who engage in certain trades, professions, or businesses. Common examples are licensing statutes that apply to lawyers, doctors, dentists, accountants, brokers, plumbers, and contractors. Some licensing statutes mandate schooling and/or examination, while others require only financial responsibility and/or good moral character. Whether a person who has failed to comply with a licensing requirement may recover for services rendered depends on the terms or type of licensing statute.

The statute itself may expressly provide that an unlicensed person engaged in a business or profession for which a license is required shall not recover for services rendered. Where there is no express statutory provision, the courts commonly distinguish between regulatory statutes and those enacted merely to raise revenue through the issuance of licenses. If the statute is regulatory, a person cannot recover for professional services unless he has the required license as long as the public policy behind the regulatory purpose clearly outweighs the person's interest in being paid for his services. Some courts balance the penalty suffered by the unlicensed party against the benefit received by the other party. In contrast, if the law is for revenue purposes only, agreements for unlicensed services are enforceable.

A **regulatory license** is a measure designed to protect the public from unqualified practitioners. Examples are licenses issued under statutes prescribing standards for those who seek to practice law or medicine or, as demonstrated by the following case, to engage in the construction business. A **revenue license**, on the other hand, does not seek to protect against incompetent or unqualified practitioners but serves simply to raise money. An example is a statute requiring a license of plumbers but not establishing standards of competence for those who practice the trade. The courts regard this as a taxing measure lacking any expression of legislative intent to prevent unlicensed plumbers from enforcing their business contracts.

Practical Advice

Obtain all necessary licenses before beginning to operate your business.

Regulatory license
measure to protect the public interest

Revenue license
measure to raise money

Alcoa Concrete & Masonry v. Stalker Bros.

Court of Special Appeals of Maryland, 2010

993 A.2d 136, 191 Md.App. 596

http://scholar.google.com/scholar_case?case=16829939965873776087&q=993+A.2d+136&hl=en&as_sdt=2,34

FACTS General contractor Stalker Brothers, Inc. (Stalker) from 2004 through 2007 hired a subcontractor Alcoa Concrete and Masonry, Inc. (Alcoa). Alcoa was unlicensed until March 26, 2008. In 2004, all of Alcoa's invoices were fully and timely paid. When payments in 2005 became less regular, Stalker promised to pay Alcoa when a building owned by Stalker was sold, but full payment was not made. Alcoa continued to perform subcontract work for Stalker based on an agreement that Stalker would pay Alcoa $1,500 per week against invoices for past work and new work. In November 2006, Alcoa performed the cement and masonry work for Stalker on the "Cahill" job. In the summer of 2007, Stalker ceased paying Alcoa entirely.

Alcoa sued Stalker for $53,000 plus interest and attorneys' fees. Stalker was granted a summary judgment on the ground that because Alcoa was not licensed, the series of subcontracts were illegal and could not be enforced. The circuit court's decision was based on a line of Maryland cases dealing with licensing, which is illustrated in the home improvement field principally by *Harry Berenter, Inc. v. Berman*. If the purpose of a business licensing statute is to raise revenue, courts will enforce a contract for compensation for business activity that requires a license, even if made by an unlicensed person. But, if the purpose of the licensing requirement is to protect the public, then the Maryland cases relied upon by the circuit court do not enforce contracts made by unlicensed persons who seek compensation for business activity for which a license is required.

DECISION The judgment of the circuit court is reversed, and the case remanded.

OPINION At issue is whether a home improvement general contractor is contractually obligated to pay a subcontractor who was not licensed under the Maryland Home Improvement Law (Act), either at the time of entering into the subcontract or when the

subcontract was properly performed, but who was licensed when this suit was brought.

Maryland appellate decisions have applied the revenue/regulation rule in a number of contexts. All of the cases under the Act have dealt with the relationship between a contractor and a homeowner. The members of the public who were protected by the regulatory licensing requirement were the owners of the home. This court recently again has held, applying *Harry Berenter*, that a contract between the owner of the improved premises and an unlicensed contractor would not be enforced.

This court's review fails to disclose any Maryland appellate decision directly answering whether the regulatory license rule applies to a subcontract between a licensed contractor and an unlicensed subcontractor. *Harry Berenter* does recognize that, pursuant to provisions of the Act, the failure to comply with certain formal contractual requirements in a home improvement contract does not invalidate the contract.

The authors of *Corbin on Contracts*, after reviewing the revenue/regulatory rule, state:

Even when the purpose of a licensing statute is regulatory, courts do not always deny enforcement to the unlicensed party. The statute clearly may protect against fraud and incompetence. Yet, in very many cases the situation involves neither fraud nor incompetence. The unlicensed party may have rendered excellent service or delivered goods of the highest quality. The noncompliance with the statute may be nearly harmless. The real defrauder may be the defendant who will be enriched at the unlicensed party's expense by a court's refusal to enforce the contract. Although courts have yearned for a mechanically applicable rule, most have not made one in the present instance. Justice requires that the penalty should fit the crime. Justice and sound policy do not always require the enforcement of licensing statutes by large forfeitures going not to the state but to repudiating defendants.

In most cases, the statute itself does not require such forfeitures. The statute fixes its own penalties, usually a fine or imprisonment of a minor character with a degree of discretion in the court. The added penalty of unenforceability of bargains is a judicial creation. In many cases, the court may be wise to apply this additional penalty. But when nonenforcement of the contract causes great and disproportionate hardship, a court must avoid nonenforcement.

This court finds no indication in the Act or in the Maryland cases that a policy of the Act is to protect general contractors from unlicensed subcontractors. Consequently, the fact that the Act is a regulatory measure does not bar Alcoa from recovering on its subcontracts with Stalker.

INTERPRETATION A regulatory license is a measure to protect the public from unqualified practitioners; the failure to comply with such a regulation prevents the noncomplying party from recovering for services rendered if (1) the statute provides that a noncomplying agreement is unenforceable or (2) the public policy behind the regulatory purpose clearly outweighs the noncomplying party's interest in being paid for services rendered.

CRITICAL THINKING QUESTION When should the failure to obtain a license to operate a business prevent the owner or operator from receiving compensation for services?

Gambling Statutes [13-1b]

Wager (gambling)
agreement that one party will win and the other lose depending upon the outcome of an event in which their only interest is the possible gain or loss

In a **wager**, the parties stipulate that one shall win and the other lose depending on the outcome of an event in which their only "interest" is the possibility of such gain or loss. All states have legislation on gambling or wagering, and U.S. courts generally refuse to recognize the enforceability of a gambling agreement. Thus, if Smith makes a bet with Brown on the outcome of a ball game, the agreement is unenforceable by either party. Some states, however, now permit certain kinds of regulated gambling. Wagering conducted by government agencies, principally state-operated lotteries, has come to constitute an increasingly important source of public revenues.

Usury Statutes [13-1c]

Practical Advice

Make sure that your promotions that offer prizes do not fall under state gambling statutes.

Usury statute
law establishing a maximum rate of interest

A **usury statute** is a law establishing a maximum rate of permissible interest for which a lender and borrower of money may contract. Although historically every state had a usury statute, the recent trend is to limit or relax such statutes. Maximum permitted rates vary greatly from state to state and among types of transactions. These statutes typically are general in their application, and certain types of transactions are exempted altogether. For example, many states impose no limit on the rate of interest that may be charged on loans to corporations. Furthermore, some states permit the parties to contract for any rate of interest on loans made to individual proprietorships or partnerships for the purpose of carrying on a business. Moreover, there are not many protections remaining for typical consumer transactions, including those involving credit cards. More than half of the states have no interest rate limits on credit card transactions. Furthermore, under federal law, a national bank may charge the interest rate allowed in the state in which the bank is located to customers living anywhere in the United States, including states with more restrictive interest caps.

In addition to the exceptions affecting certain designated types of borrowers, a number of states have exempted specific lenders. For example, the majority of states have enacted installment loan laws, which permit eligible lenders a higher return on installment loans than otherwise would be permitted under the applicable general interest statute. These specific lender usury statutes, which have all but eliminated general usury statutes, vary greatly but generally encompass small consumer loans, retail installment sales acts, corporate loans, loans by small lenders, real estate mortgages, and numerous other transactions.

Practical Advice

When calculating interest, consider all charges, including service fees, that exceed the actual reasonable expense of making the loan.

For a transaction to be usurious, courts usually require evidence of the following factors: (1) a loan (2) of money (3) that is repayable absolutely and in all events (4) for which an interest charge is exacted in excess of the interest rate allowed by law. Nevertheless, the law does permit certain expenses or charges in addition to the maximum legal interest, such as payments made by a borrower to the lender for expenses incurred or for services rendered in good faith in making a loan or in obtaining security for its repayment. Permissible expenses commonly incurred by a lender include the costs of examining title, investigating the borrower's credit rating, drawing necessary documents, and inspecting the property. If not excessive, such expenses are not considered in determining the rate of interest under the usury statutes. As shown in the following case, however, payments made to the lender from which he derives an advantage are considered if they exceed the reasonable value of services he actually rendered.

Dunnam v. Burns
Court of Appeals of Texas, El Paso, 1995
901 S.W.2d 628
http://scholar.google.com/scholar_case?case=1178913169644146691 &q=901+S.W.2d+628&hl=en&as_sdt=2,34

FACTS Defendant (Louis Dunnam) and Steve Oualline jointly borrowed $35,000 from plaintiff (Ken Burns) and agreed to repay the principal plus $5,000 six months later. After defendant defaulted on the loan, plaintiff sued to recover. Dunnam defended by claiming the loan was usurious. The trial court ruled in favor of the plaintiff, and defendant appealed.

DECISION Judgment for defendant.

OPINION Defendant claims the trial court erred by refusing to submit his usury defense to the jury. Usury is interest in excess of the amount permitted by law. For most transactions between private persons, the maximum allowable rate of interest is 18 percent if the parties agree on a rate of interest and 6 percent if they do not. Persons who contract for or collect usurious interest are subject to penalties that may exceed the total value of the contract.

When money is advanced in exchange for an obligation to repay the advance plus an additional amount, the added amount

is interest that may not exceed the statutory maximum. Thus, defendant's absolute obligation to pay $5,000 in addition to the principal renders the additional amount interest. Plaintiff argues that he did not "charge" such interest because the instrument was drafted by defendant and because plaintiff was actually interested in collecting only the principal amount. However, a document that contains an absolute obligation to repay a loan together with interest in excess of the amount permitted by statute is usurious on its face. The specific intent of the lender is immaterial because it is presumed to be reflected in the document he signs. The drafter of the usurious promissory note is simply irrelevant. The instrument embodies a usurious transaction, and plaintiff, as the lender, contracted for usurious interest.

INTERPRETATION Usury statutes establish a maximum rate of interest for which a lender may charge a borrower.

CRITICAL THINKING QUESTION Should the law establish maximum rates of interest? If so, in what situations?

The legal effect of a usurious loan varies from state to state. In a few states, the lender forfeits both principal and interest. In some jurisdictions, the lender can recover the principal but forfeits all interest. In other states, only that portion of interest exceeding the permitted maximum is forfeited, whereas in still other states, the amount forfeited is a multiple (double or treble) of the interest charged. How the states deal with usurious interest already paid also varies. Some states do not allow the borrower to recover any of the usurious interest she has paid; others allow recovery of such interest or a multiple of it.

Violations of Public Policy [13-2]

The reach of a statute may extend beyond its language. Sometimes the courts, by analogy, use a statute and the policy it embodies as a guide in determining a person's rights under a private contract. Conversely, the courts frequently must express the "public policy" of the state without significant help from statutory sources. This judicially declared public policy is very broad in scope, it often being said that agreements having "a tendency to be injurious to the public or the public good" are contrary to public policy. Contracts raising questions of public policy include agreements that (1) restrain trade, (2) excuse or exculpate a party from liability for his own negligence, (3) are unconscionable, (4) involve tortious conduct, (5) tend to corrupt public officials or impair the legislative process, (6) tend to obstruct the administration of justice, or (7) impair family relationships. This section will focus on the first five of these types of agreements.

Restraint of trade
agreement that eliminates or tends to eliminate competition

Covenant not to compete
agreement to refrain from entering into a competing trade, profession, or business

Common Law Restraint of Trade [13-2a]

A **restraint of trade** is any contract or agreement that eliminates or tends to eliminate competition or otherwise obstructs trade or commerce. One type of restraint of trade is a **covenant not to compete**, which is an agreement to refrain from entering into a competing trade, profession, or business.

An agreement to refrain from a particular trade, profession, or business is enforceable if (1) the purpose of the restraint is to protect a property interest of the promisee and (2) the restraint is no more extensive than is reasonably necessary to protect that interest. Restraints typically arise in two situations: (1) the sale of a business and (2) employment contracts.

**Covenant in sale of
a business**

the promise by the seller of
a business not to compete
in that particular business in
a reasonable geographic
area for a reasonable period
of time is enforceable

Sale of a Business

As part of an agreement to sell a business, the seller frequently promises not to compete in that particular type of business in a defined area for a stated period of time to protect the business's goodwill (an asset that the buyer has purchased). The courts will enforce such a covenant (promise) if the restraint is within reasonable limitations. The reasonableness of the restraint depends on the geographic area the restraint covers, the period for which it is to be effective, and the hardship it imposes on the promisor and the public.

For example, the promise of a person selling a service station business in Detroit not to enter the service station business in Michigan for the next twenty-five years is unreasonable as to both area and time. The business interest would not include the entire state, so the protection of the purchaser does not require that the seller be prevented from engaging in the service station business in all of Michigan or perhaps, for that matter, in the entire city of Detroit. Limiting the area to the neighborhood in which the station is located or to a radius of a few miles probably would be adequate protection. However, in the case of a citywide business, such as a laundry or cleaning establishment with neighborhood outlets, a covenant restraining competition anywhere in the city might well be reasonable.

The same type of inquiry must be made about time limitations. In the sale of a service station, a twenty-five-year ban on competition from the seller would be unreasonable, but a one-year ban probably would not. The courts consider each case on its own facts to determine what is reasonable under the particular circumstances.

**Covenant in
employment contracts**

an employment contract
prohibiting an employee
from competing with his
employer for a reasonable
period following
termination is enforceable
provided the restriction
is necessary to protect
legitimate interests of the
employer

Employment Contracts

Salespeople, management personnel, and other employees are frequently required to sign employment contracts prohibiting them from competing with their employers during their employment and for some additional stated period after their termination. The same is also frequently true among corporations or partnerships involving professionals such as accountants, lawyers, investment brokers, stockbrokers, or doctors. Though the courts readily enforce a covenant not to compete during the period of employment, they subject the promise not to compete after termination of employment to a test of reasonableness stricter even than that applied to noncompetition promises included in a contract for the sale of a business.

A court order enjoining (prohibiting) a former employee from competing in a described territory for a stated period of time is the usual way in which an employer seeks to enforce an employee's promise not to compete. However, before the courts will grant such injunctions, the employer must demonstrate that the restriction is necessary to protect his legitimate interests, such as trade secrets or customer lists. Because the injunction may have the practical effect of placing the employee out of work, the courts must carefully balance the public policy favoring the employer's right to protect his business interests against the public policy favoring full opportunity for individuals to gain employment. Some courts, rather than refusing to enforce an unreasonable restraint, will modify the restrictive covenant to make it reasonable under the circumstances.

Thus, one court has held unreasonable a contract covenant requiring a travel agency employee after termination of her employment to not engage in a like business in any capacity in either of two named towns or within a sixty-mile radius of those towns for two years. There was no indication that the employee had enough influence over customers to cause them to move their business to her new agency, nor was it shown that any trade secrets were involved.

Due to the rapid evolution of business practices in the Internet industry, it has been argued that noncompetition agreements for Internet company employees need their own rules. *National Business Services, Inc. v. Wright* addressed the geographic scope of an Internet noncompetition agreement, upholding a one-year time restriction and a territorial clause that prevented the employee from taking another Internet-related job anywhere in the United States. The court stated, "Transactions involving the Internet, unlike traditional 'sales territory' cases, are not limited by state boundaries."

Practical Advice

If you include a covenant
not to compete to protect
your property interests, be
careful to select a reasonable
duration and geographic
scope.

Payroll Advance, Inc. v. Yates
Missouri Court of Appeals, 2008
270 S.W.3d 428
http://scholar.google.com/scholar_case?case=12029870438647495616&q=270+S.W.3d+428&hl=en&as_sclt=2,22

FACTS In June of 1998, Payroll Advance, Inc. entered into an employment contract with Barbara Yates, which contained a covenant not to compete. It is customary for each of Payroll's branch offices to employ a sole employee at each branch and that sole employee is the manager of that particular branch. On November 19, 1999, as a condition of her continued employment, Payroll presented Yates with the Employment Agreement which included a provision entitled "NON-COMPETE" This provision provided:

> [Yates] agrees not to compete with [Payroll] as owner, manager, partner, stockholder, or employee in any business that is in competition with [Payroll] and within a fifty-mile radius of [Payroll's] business for a period of two (2) years after termination of employment or [Yates] quits or [Yates] leaves employment of [Payroll].

On November 8, 2007, Yates was fired for cause. Approximately thirty-two days after being terminated Yates obtained employment with Check Please, one of the Payroll's competitors. At Check Please, Yates performed basically the same duties as she had when employed with Payroll.

On February 7, 2008, Payroll filed a complaint against Yates for: (1) injunctive relief to prevent Yates from soliciting its clients for her new employer, and to stop her from using client information she purportedly obtained from her time with Payroll and (2) damages for breach of contract for violation of the covenant not to compete together with attorney fees and costs. The trial court found

> [n]o evidence exists that, following [Payroll's] termination of [Yates'] ten year period of employment, [Yates] removed any customer list or other documents from [Payroll's] place of business [or] … made any personal or other contact with any previous or present customer of [Payroll's] business or intends to do so.

The trial court further determined that if the covenant not to compete were enforced as requested, Yates would be prohibited from engaging in employment with any payday loan business in at least 126 cities situated in Missouri, Arkansas, and Tennessee. Further, Yates could also be prohibited from employment at a bank, savings and loan company, credit union, pawnshop, or title-loan company within Missouri, Arkansas, and Tennessee. Accordingly, the trial court found in favor of Yates holding that the Employment Agreement's noncompete covenant signed by the parties was not valid in that it was "unreasonable under the facts and circumstances of the particular industry, agreement, and geographic location here involved." Payroll appealed.

DECISION Judgment affirmed.

OPINION Because covenants not to compete are generally considered to be restraints on trade, they are presumptively void and

are enforceable only to the extent that they are demonstratively reasonable. Thus, covenants not to compete are not favored in the law, and the party attempting to enforce a noncompetition agreement has the burden of demonstrating both the necessity to protect the claimant's legitimate interests and that the agreement is reasonable as to time and space. Non-compete agreements are typically enforceable so long as they are reasonable. In practical terms, a non-compete agreement is reasonable if it is no more restrictive than is necessary to protect the legitimate interests of the employer. In order to obtain an injunction it is not necessary for the employer to show that actual damage has occurred.

In this case, it is clear the trial court took umbrage with the covenant's restrictive provisions and geographical limitations on Yates' ability to find employment. The question of reasonableness of a restraint is to be determined according to the facts of the particular case and hence requires a thorough consideration of all surrounding circumstances, including the subject matter of the contract, the purpose to be served, the situation of the parties, the extent of the restraint, and the specialization of the business. Here, the covenant not to compete grandly declares that Yates cannot "compete with Appellant [Payroll] as owner, manager, partner, stockholder, or employee *in any business* that is in competition with [Payroll] and within a fifty-mile radius of [Payroll's] business.…" There was evidence from Payroll's representative at trial that Payroll has seventeen branch offices in Missouri and still other locations in Arkansas. Thus under the plain meaning of the covenant not to compete as written, the covenant not to compete would prevent Yates not only from working at a competing business within fifty miles of the branch office in Kennett, Missouri, but Yates would also be barred from working in a competing business within fifty miles of *any* of Payroll's branch offices. Under this interpretation, Yates would be greatly limited in the geographic area she could work.

Additionally, the covenant not to compete bars Yates from working at "any business that is in competition with [Payroll]." Yet, it fails to set out with precision what is to be considered a competing business and certainly does not specify that it only applies to other payday loan businesses.

INTERPRETATION Noncompete clauses in employment agreements can be enforced only to the extent necessary to protect the employer's legitimate interests and only if reasonably limited in duration and geographic scope.

CRITICAL THINKING QUESTION How should courts balance the protection of employers with the freedom of employees to change jobs? Explain.

Exculpatory Clauses [13-2b]

Exculpatory clause
a provision excusing one party from fault or liability

Some contracts contain an **exculpatory clause** that excuses one party from liability for her own tortious conduct. Although there is general agreement that exculpatory clauses relieving a person from tort liability for harm caused intentionally or recklessly are unenforceable as violating public policy, exculpatory clauses that excuse a party from liability for harm caused by negligent

Practical Advice

Because many courts do
not favor exculpatory
clauses, carefully limit
its applicability, make
sure that it is clear and
understandable, put it in
writing, and have it signed.

conduct undergo careful scrutiny by the courts, which often require that the clause be conspicuously placed in the contract and clearly written. Accordingly, an exculpatory clause on the reverse side of a parking lot claim check, which attempts to relieve the parking lot operator of liability for negligently damaging the customer's automobile, generally will be held unenforceable as against public policy.

Where one party's superior bargaining position has enabled him to impose an exculpatory clause upon the other party, the courts are inclined to nullify the provision. Such a situation may arise in residential leases exempting a landlord from liability for his negligence. Moreover, an exculpatory clause may be unenforceable for unconscionability.

Anderson v. McOskar Enterprises, Inc.
Court of Appeals of Minnesota, 2006
712 N.W.2d 796
http://scholar.google.com/scholar_case?q=712+N.W.+2d+796&hl=en&as_sdt=6,34&case=14986343261318628809&scilh=0

FACTS Plaintiff, Tammey J. Anderson, on April 2, 2003, joined the fitness club Curves for Women, which was owned and operated by McOskar Enterprises. As part of the registration requirements, Anderson read an "AGREEMENT AND RELEASE OF LIABILITY," initialed each of the three paragraphs in the document, and dated and signed it. The first paragraph purported to release Curves from liability for injuries Anderson might sustain in participating in club activities or using club equipment:

> In consideration of being allowed to participate in the activities and programs of Curves for Women and to use its facilities, equipment and machinery in addition to the payment of any fee or charge, I do hereby waive, release and forever discharge Curves International Inc., Curves for Women, and their officers, agents, employees, representatives, executors, and all others (Curves representatives) from any and all responsibilities or liabilities from injuries or damages arriving [sic] out of or connected with my attendance at Curves for Women, my participation in all activities, my use of equipment or machinery, or any act or omission, including negligence by Curves representatives.

The second paragraph provided for Anderson's acknowledgment that fitness activities "involve a risk of injury" and her agreement "to expressly assume and accept any and all risks of injury or death."

After completing the registration, Anderson began a workout under the supervision of a trainer. About fifteen or twenty minutes later, having used four or five machines, Anderson developed a headache in the back of her head. She contends that she told the trainer, who suggested that the problem was likely just a previous lack of use of certain muscles and that Anderson would be fine. Anderson continued her workout and developed pain in her neck, shoulder, and arm. She informed the trainer but continued to exercise until she completed the program for that session. The pain persisted when Anderson returned home. She then sought medical attention and, in June 2003, underwent a cervical diskectomy. She then filed this lawsuit for damages, alleging that Curves had been negligent in its acts or omissions during her workout at the club. Curves moved for summary judgment on the ground that Anderson had released the club from liability for negligence. The district court agreed and granted the motion. Anderson appealed.

DECISION Judgment of the district court is affirmed.

OPINION It is settled law that, under certain circumstances, "parties to a contract may, without violation of public policy, protect themselves against liability resulting from their own negligence."

The public interest in freedom of contract is preserved by recognizing release and exculpatory clauses as valid.

Releases of liability, however, are not favored by the law and are strictly construed against the benefited party. "If the clause is either ambiguous in scope or purports to release the benefited party from liability for intentional, willful or wanton acts, it will not be enforced." Furthermore, even if a release clause is unambiguous in scope and is limited only to negligence, courts must still ascertain whether its enforcement will contravene public policy. On this issue, a two-prong test is applied:

> Before enforcing an exculpatory clause, both prongs of the test are examined, to-wit: (1) whether there was a disparity of bargaining power between the parties (in terms of a compulsion to sign a contract containing an unacceptable provision and the lack of ability to negotiate elimination of the unacceptable provision) … and (2) the types of services being offered or provided (taking into consideration whether it is a public or essential service).

The two-prong test describes what is generally known as a "contract of adhesion." There is nothing in the Curves release that expressly exonerates the club from liability for any intentional, willful, or wanton act. Thus, the question is whether the release is ambiguous in scope. In the context of a release in connection with an athletic, health, or fitness activity, the consumer surely is entitled to know precisely what liability is being exonerated. A release that is so vague, general, or broad as to fail to specifically designate the particular nature of the liability exonerated is not enforceable. It is clear from this release that the unmistakable intent of the parties is that Curves would not be held liable for acts of negligence.

Even if a release is unambiguously confined to liability for negligence, it still will be unenforceable if it contravenes public policy. Anderson contends that the Curves contract is one of adhesion characterized by such a disparity in bargaining power that she was compelled to sign it without any ability to negotiate. In this case there was neither proof of disparity in bargaining ability nor was there a showing that the services provided by Curves were necessary and unobtainable elsewhere.

INTERPRETATION An exculpatory clause is valid if it is limited in scope, not ambiguous, and not contrary to public policy.

ETHICAL QUESTION Did Curves act unethically? Explain.

CRITICAL THINKING QUESTION When should an exculpatory clause be held invalid? Explain.

Unconscionable Contracts [13-2c]

Unconscionable
unfair or unduly harsh

The Uniform Commercial Code provides that a court may scrutinize every contract for the sale of goods to determine whether in its commercial setting, purpose, and effect the contract is unconscionable, or unfair. The court may refuse to enforce an **unconscionable** contract or any part of the contract it finds to be unconscionable. The Restatement has a similar provision.

Though neither the Code nor the Restatement defines the word *unconscionable*, the term is defined in the *New Webster's Dictionary* (Deluxe Encyclopedic Edition) as "contrary to the dictates of conscience; unscrupulous or unprincipled; exceeding that which is reasonable or customary; inordinate, unjustifiable."

The doctrine of unconscionability has been justified on the basis that it permits the courts to resolve issues of unfairness explicitly in terms of that unfairness without recourse to formalistic rules or legal fictions. In policing contracts for fairness, the courts have again demonstrated their willingness to limit freedom of contract to protect the less advantaged from overreaching by dominant contracting parties. The doctrine of unconscionability has evolved through its application by the courts to include both procedural and substantive unconscionability. **Procedural unconscionability** involves scrutiny for the presence of "bargaining naughtiness." In other words, was the negotiation process fair? Or were there procedural irregularities, such as burying important terms of the agreement in fine print or obscuring the true meaning of the contract with impenetrable legal jargon?

Procedural unconscionability
unfair or irregular bargaining

Substantive unconscionability
oppressive or grossly unfair contractual terms

By comparison, in searching for **substantive unconscionability**, the courts examine the actual terms of a contract for oppressive or grossly unfair provisions such as exorbitant prices or unfair exclusions or limitations of contractual remedies. An all-too-common example of such a provision involves a buyer in pressing need who is in an unequal bargaining position with a seller who consequently obtains an exorbitant price for his product or service. In one case, a price of $749 ($920 if the purchaser wished to pay on credit over time) for a vacuum cleaner that cost the seller $140 was held unconscionable. In another case, the buyers, welfare recipients, purchased by a time payment contract a home freezer unit for $900 that, when time credit charges, credit life insurance, credit property insurance, and sales tax were added, cost $1,235. The purchase resulted from a visit to the buyers' home by a salesperson representing Your Shop At Home Service, Inc.; the maximum retail value of the freezer unit at the time of purchase was $300. The court held the contract unconscionable and reformed it by reducing the price to the total payment ($620) the buyers had managed to make.

Practical Advice

When negotiating a contract, keep in mind that if your bargaining techniques or the contract terms are oppressive, a court may refuse to enforce the contract in part or in full.

Some courts hold that for a contract to be unenforceable both substantive and procedural unconscionability must be present. Nevertheless, they need not exist to the same degree; the more oppressive one is, the less evidence of the other is required.

Sanchez v. Western Pizza Enterprises, Inc.
Court of Appeals of California, Second District, Division Three, 2009
172 Cal.App.4th 154
http://scholar.google.com/scholar_case?case=18161264297915300969&q=172+Cal.+App.+4th+154&hl=en&as_sdt=2,34

FACTS Octavio Sanchez worked as a delivery driver at a Domino's Pizza restaurant owned by Western Pizza. He drove his own car in making deliveries. His hourly wage ranged from the legal minimum wage to approximately $0.50 above minimum wage. Western Pizza reimburses him at a fixed rate of $0.80 per delivery regardless of the number of miles driven or actual expenses incurred. Sanchez brought this class action against Western Pizza alleging that the flat rate at which drivers were reimbursed for delivery expenses violated wage and hour laws and that the drivers were paid less than the legal minimum wage.

Sanchez and Western Pizza are parties to an undated arbitration agreement. The agreement states that (1) the execution of the agreement "is not a mandatory condition of employment"; (2) any dispute that the parties are unable to resolve informally

will be submitted to binding arbitration before an arbitrator approved by both parties and "selected from the then-current Employment Arbitration panel of the Dispute Eradication Services"; (3) the parties waive the right to a jury trial; (4) the arbitration fees will be borne by Western Pizza and, except as otherwise required by law, each party will bear its own attorney fees and costs; (5) small claims may be resolved by a summary small claims procedure; and (6) the parties waive the right to bring class arbitration. The Superior Court of Los Angeles County denied the restaurant's motion to compel arbitration, and the restaurant appealed.

DECISION The denial of the motion to compel arbitration is affirmed.

OPINION Western Pizza contends the arbitration agreement is neither procedurally nor substantively unconscionable.

Procedural and substantive unconscionability must both be present to justify the refusal to enforce a contract or clause based on unconscionability. Procedural unconscionability focuses on oppression or unfair surprise, while substantive unconscionability focuses on overly harsh or one-sided terms. The more procedural unconscionability is present, the less substantive unconscionability is required to justify a determination that a contract or clause is unenforceable. Conversely, the less procedural unconscionability is present, the more substantive unconscionability is required to justify such a determination.

A finding of procedural unconscionability does not mean that a contract will not be enforced, but rather that courts will scrutinize the substantive terms of the contract to ensure they are not manifestly unfair or one-sided. There are degrees of procedural unconscionability. At one end of the spectrum are contracts that have been freely negotiated by roughly equal parties, in which there is no procedural unconscionability. Although certain terms in these contracts may be construed strictly, courts will not find these contracts substantively unconscionable, no matter how one-sided the terms appear to be. Contracts of adhesion that involve surprise or other sharp practices lie on the other end of the spectrum. A contract that contains no element of procedural unconscionability is tantamount to saying that, no matter how one-sided the contract terms, a court will not disturb the contract because of its confidence that the contract was negotiated or chosen freely, that the party subject to a seemingly one-sided term is presumed to have obtained some advantage from conceding the term or that, if one party negotiated poorly, it is not the court's place to rectify these kinds of errors or asymmetries.

The Arbitration Agreement Is Procedurally Unconscionable
Procedural unconscionability focuses on oppression or unfair surprise. Oppression results from unequal bargaining power when a contracting party has no meaningful choice but to accept the contract terms. Unfair surprise results from misleading bargaining conduct or other circumstances indicating that a party's consent was not an informed choice.

The record indicates a degree of procedural unconscionability in two respects. First, the inequality in bargaining power between the low-wage employees and their employer makes it likely that the employees felt at least some pressure to sign the arbitration agreement. Second, the arbitration agreement suggests that there are multiple arbitrators to choose from ("the then-current Employment Arbitration panel of the Dispute Eradication Services") and fails to mention that the designated arbitration provider includes only one arbitrator. This renders the arbitrator selection process illusory and creates a significant risk that Western Pizza as a "repeat player" before the same arbitrator will reap a significant advantage. These circumstances indicate that the employees' decision to enter into the arbitration agreement likely was not a free and informed decision but was marked by some degree of oppression and unfair surprise, i.e., procedural unconscionability. Thus the court must scrutinize the terms of the arbitration agreement to determine whether it is so unfairly one-sided as to be substantively unconscionable.

The Arbitrator Selection Provision Is Substantively Unconscionable
Substantively unconscionable terms may take various forms, but may generally be described as unfairly one-sided. "Given the lack of choice and the potential disadvantages that even a fair arbitration system can harbor for employees, we must be particularly attuned to claims that employers with superior bargaining power have imposed one-sided, substantively unconscionable terms as part of an arbitration agreement. 'Private arbitration may resolve disputes faster and cheaper than judicial proceedings. Private arbitration, however, may also become an instrument of injustice imposed on a "take it or leave it" basis.'"

Sanchez contends the arbitration agreement is substantively unconscionable in several respects. He cites the class arbitration waiver, the small claims provision, the absence of any provision requiring a written arbitration award, the designation of an arbitration provider consisting of a single arbitrator, and the absence of any express provision for discovery. An arbitration agreement must provide for a neutral arbitrator. Here, the designation of a "panel" of arbitrators consisting of a single arbitrator selected by Western Pizza created a false appearance of mutuality in the selection of an arbitrator. Moreover, the effective designation of a single arbitrator in what appears to be a standard arbitration agreement applicable to a large number of corporate employees gives rise to a significant risk of financial interdependence between Western Pizza and the arbitrator, and an opportunity for Western Pizza to gain an advantage through its knowledge of and experience with the arbitrator. Thus, this provision is unfairly one-sided and substantively unconscionable.

The Entire Arbitration Agreement Is Unenforceable
The arbitration agreement here includes a class arbitration waiver that is contrary to public policy and an unconscionable arbitrator selection clause. These are important provisions that, if they were not challenged in litigation, could create substantial disadvantages for an employee seeking to arbitrate a modest claim. Although it may be true that neither of these provisions alone would justify the refusal to enforce the entire arbitration agreement, together these provisions indicate an effort to impose on an employee a forum with distinct advantages for the employer. Thus, the arbitration agreement is permeated by an unlawful purpose. Accordingly, the denial of the motion to compel arbitration was proper.

INTERPRETATION The doctrine of unconscionability includes both procedural and substantive unconscionability.

ETHICAL QUESTION Did Western Pizza act unethically? Explain.

CRITICAL THINKING QUESTION When should a court modify a challenged clause and when should it refuse to enforce the entire clause in question?

Closely akin to the concept of unconscionability is the doctrine of contracts of adhesion. An *adhesion contract*, a standard-form contract prepared by one party, generally involves the preparer offering the other party the contract on a "take-it-or-leave-it" basis. Such contracts are not automatically unenforceable but are subject to greater scrutiny for procedural or substantive unconscionability. See the earlier case *Anderson v. McOskar Enterprises, Inc.* and the Ethical Dilemma at the end of this chapter.

Tortious Conduct [13-2d]

Tortious conduct
an agreement that requires a person to commit a tort is unenforceable

An agreement that requires a person to commit a tort is an illegal agreement and thus is unenforceable. The courts will not permit contract law to violate the law of torts. Any agreement attempting to do so is considered contrary to public policy. For example, Ada and Bernard enter into an agreement under which Ada promises Bernard that in return for $5,000, she will disparage the product of Bernard's competitor, Cone, in order to provide Bernard with a competitive advantage. Ada's promise is to commit the tort of disparagement and is unenforceable as contrary to public policy.

Corrupting Public Officials [13-2e]

Agreements that may adversely affect the public interest through the corruption of public officials or the impairment of the legislative process are unenforceable. Examples include using improper means to influence legislation, to secure some official action, or to procure a government contract. Contracts to pay lobbyists for services to obtain or defeat official action by means of persuasive argument are to be distinguished from illegal influence-peddling agreements. (Chapters 39 and 46 cover the Foreign Corrupt Practices Act, which prohibits any U.S. person—and certain foreign issuers of securities—from bribing foreign government or political officials to assist in obtaining or retaining business.)

For example, a bargain by a candidate for public office to make a certain appointment following his election is illegal. In addition, an agreement to pay a public officer something extra for performing his official duty, such as promising a bonus to a police officer for strictly enforcing the traffic laws on her beat, is illegal. The same is true of an agreement in which a citizen promises to perform, or to refrain from performing, duties imposed on her by citizenship. Thus, a promise by Carl to pay $50.00 to Rachel if she will register and vote is opposed to public policy and illegal.

BUSINESS LAW **IN ACTION**

Southwestern Casualty Insurance (SCI) has issued automobile insurance policies in the southwestern United States for a number of years. Its standard-form policies historically have covered its policyholders for accidents occurring in Mexico. After reassessing the company's liabilities, SCI determined that inserting an exclusion for accidents occurring within Mexico's borders would both assist in keeping premiums in check and contribute positively to the company's bottom line. It therefore issued a new standard-form policy that was the same in all respects as its old policy, but which now contained the Mexico exclusion in a long paragraph of other policy exclusions.

Rather than simply send the new form to its customers along with a premium notice when their policies are up for renewal, SCI must take pains to make its customers aware of the change in coverage. If it does not, there is a good chance in many jurisdictions that SCI will be stopped from enforcing the exclusion, and therefore will be required to provide coverage according to its customers' reasonable expectations.

Standard-form insurance policies generally are contracts of adhesion. This is because, while some provisions regarding limits and types of coverage may be bargained for, these agreements consist largely of boilerplate provisions that are

not negotiated and that often are not, nor are they expected to be, read or fully understood by the insured. Standard-form insurance contracts are useful in commerce; by narrowing the consumer's choice from a limited number of meaningful features rather than an endless combination of possible coverages, they focus the time and effort of the insurer and insured, thereby reducing costs to the benefit of all. The adhesive nature of the agreement, however, imposes an obligation of good faith on the insurer, which has been translated into a rule that insureds do not assent to standard-form terms the insurer has reason to believe that the consumer would not have accepted.

EFFECT OF ILLEGALITY [13-3]

With few exceptions, illegal contracts are ***unenforceable***. In most cases, neither party to an illegal agreement can sue the other for breach or recover for any performance rendered. It is often said that where parties are *in pari delicto*—in equal fault—a court will leave them where it finds them. The law will provide neither with any remedy. This strict rule of unenforceability is subject to certain exceptions, however, which are discussed as follows.

Party Withdrawing Before Performance [13-3a]

A party to an illegal agreement may withdraw, before performance, from the transaction and recover whatever she has contributed, if the party has not engaged in serious misconduct. A common example is recovery of money left with a stakeholder for a wager before it is paid over to the winner.

Party Protected by Statute [13-3b]

Sometimes an agreement is illegal because it violates a statute designed to protect persons from the effects of the prohibited agreement. For example, state and federal statutes prohibiting the sale of unregistered securities are designed primarily to protect investors. In such case, even though there is an unlawful agreement, the statutes usually expressly give the purchaser a right to withdraw from the sale and recover the money paid.

Party Not Equally at Fault [13-3c]

Where one of the parties is less at fault than the other, he may be allowed to recover payments made or property transferred. For example, this exception would apply in cases in which one party induces the other to enter into an illegal bargain through the exercise of fraud, duress, or undue influence.

Excusable Ignorance [13-3d]

An agreement that appears to be entirely permissible on its face, nevertheless, may be illegal by reason of facts and circumstances of which one of the parties is completely unaware. For example, a man and woman make mutual promises to marry, but unknown to the woman, the man is already married. This is an agreement to commit the crime of bigamy, and the marriage, if entered into, is void. In such case, the courts permit the party who is ignorant of the illegality to maintain a lawsuit against the other party for damages.

A party also may be excused for ignorance of legislation of a minor character. For instance, Jones and Old South Building Co. enter into a contract to build a factory that contains specifications in violation of the town's building ordinance. Jones did not know of the violation and had no reason to know. Old South's promise to build would not be rendered unenforceable on grounds of public policy, and Jones consequently would have a claim against Old South for damages for breach of contract.

Partial Illegality [13-3e]

A contract may be partly unlawful and partly lawful. The courts view such a contract in one of two ways. First, the partial illegality may be held to taint the entire contract with illegality, so that it is wholly unenforceable. Second, the court may determine it possible to separate the illegal from the legal part, in which case the illegal part only will be held unenforceable, whereas the legal part will be enforced. For example, if a contract contains an illegal covenant not to compete, the covenant will not be enforced, though the rest of the contract may be.

Restitution [13-3f]

The Restatement of Restitution provides that a person who renders performance under an agreement that is illegal or otherwise unenforceable for reasons of public policy may obtain restitution from the other party, as necessary to prevent unjust enrichment, if the allowance of restitution will not defeat or frustrate the policy of the underlying prohibition. However, a claim in restitution is not allowed if it is foreclosed by the claimant's inequitable conduct.

ETHICAL DILEMMA

When Is a Bargain Too Hard?

Facts Between 2009 and 2014, Williams purchased a number of household items on credit from the Penguin Furniture Co., a retail furniture store. Penguin retained the right in its contracts to repossess an item if Williams defaulted on an installment payment. Each contract also provided that each installment payment by Williams would be credited *pro rata* to all outstanding accounts or bills owed to Penguin. As a result of this provision, an unpaid balance would remain on every item purchased until the entire balance due on all items, whenever purchased, was paid in full. Williams defaulted on a monthly installment payment in 2014, and Penguin sought to repossess all the items that Williams had purchased since 2009.

Social, Policy, and Ethical Considerations

1. Is the bargaining power of Penguin too great to assume that the terms of the agreement resulted from a fair negotiation process?
2. Do the terms of this agreement appear fair and reasonable to both parties?
3. Has Penguin acted unethically?

CHAPTER SUMMARY

Violations of Statutes

General Rule the courts will not enforce agreements declared illegal by statute

Licensing Statutes require formal authorization to engage in certain trades, professions, or businesses

- *Regulatory License* licensing statute that is intended to protect the public against unqualified persons; an unlicensed person may not recover for services he has performed
- *Revenue License* licensing statute that seeks to raise money; an unlicensed person may recover for services he has performed

Gambling Statutes prohibit wagers, which are agreements that one party will win and the other lose depending on the outcome of an event in which their only interest is the gain or loss

Usury Statutes establish a maximum rate of interest

Violations of Public Policy

Common Law Restraint of Trade unreasonable restraints of trade are not enforceable

- *Sale of a Business* the promise by the seller of a business not to compete in that particular business in a reasonable geographic area for a reasonable period of time is enforceable
- *Employment Contracts* an employment contract prohibiting an employee from competing with his employer for a reasonable period following termination is enforceable provided the restriction is necessary to protect legitimate interests of the employer

Exculpatory Clauses the courts generally disapprove of contractual provisions excusing a party from liability for his own tortious conduct

Unconscionable Contracts unfair or unduly harsh agreements are not enforceable

- *Procedural Unconscionability* unfair or irregular bargaining
- *Substantive Unconscionability* oppressive or grossly unfair contractual terms

Tortious Conduct an agreement that requires a person to commit a tort is unenforceable

Corrupting Public Officials agreements that corrupt public officials are not enforceable

Effect of Illegality

Unenforceability neither party may recover (unenforceable) under an illegal agreement where both parties are *in pari delicto* (in equal fault)

Exceptions permit one party to recover payments

- *Party Withdrawing Before Performance*
- *Party Protected by Statute*
- *Party Not Equally at Fault*
- *Excusable Ignorance*
- *Partial Illegality*
- *Restitution*

QUESTIONS

1. Johnson and Wilson were the principal shareholders in Matthew Corporation, located in the city of Jonesville, Wisconsin. This corporation was engaged in the business of manufacturing paper novelties, which were sold over a wide area in the Midwest. The corporation was also in the business of binding books. Johnson purchased Wilson's shares in Matthew Corporation and, in consideration thereof, Wilson agreed that for a period of two years he would not (a) manufacture or sell in Wisconsin any paper novelties of any kind that would compete with those sold by Matthew Corporation or (b) engage in the bookbinding business in the city of Jonesville. Discuss the validity and effect, if any, of this agreement.

2. Wilkins, a Texas resident licensed by that state as a certified public accountant (CPA), rendered service in his professional capacity in Louisiana to Coverton Cosmetics Company. He was not registered as a CPA in Louisiana. His service under his contract with the cosmetics company was not the only occasion on which he had practiced his profession in that state. The company denied liability and refused to pay him, relying on a Louisiana statute declaring it unlawful for any person to perform or offer to perform services as a CPA for compensation until he has been registered by the designated agency of the state and holds an unrevoked registration card. The statute provides that a CPA certificate may be issued without examination to any applicant who holds a valid unrevoked certificate as a CPA under the laws of any other state. The statute provides further that rendering services of the kind performed by Wilkins, without registration, is a misdemeanor punishable by a fine or imprisonment in the county jail or by both fine and imprisonment. Discuss whether Wilkins would be successful in an action against Coverton seeking to recover a fee in the amount of $1,500 as the reasonable value of his services.

3. Michael is interested in promoting the passage of a bill in the state legislature. He agrees with Christy, an attorney, to pay Christy for her services in writing the required bill, obtaining its introduction in the legislature, and making an argument for its passage before the legislative committee to which it will be referred. Christy renders these services. Subsequently, on Michael's refusal to pay Christy, Christy sues Michael for damages for breach of contract. Will Christy prevail? Explain.

4. Anthony promises to pay McCarthy $100,000 if McCarthy reveals to the public that Washington is a communist. Washington is not a communist and never has been. McCarthy successfully persuades the media to report that Washington is a communist and now seeks to recover the $100,000 from Anthony, who refuses to pay. McCarthy initiates a lawsuit against Anthony. What will be the result?

5. The Dear Corporation was engaged in the business of making and selling harvesting machines. It sold everything pertaining to its business to the HI Company, agreeing "not again to go into the manufacture of harvesting machines anywhere in the United States." The Dear Corporation, which had a national and international goodwill in its business, now begins the manufacture of such machines contrary to its agreement. Should the court stop it from doing so? Explain.

6. Charles Leigh, engaged in the industrial laundry business in Central City, employed Tim Close, previously employed in the home laundry business, as a route salesperson. Leigh rents linens and industrial uniforms to commercial customers; the soiled linens and uniforms are picked up at regular intervals by the route drivers and replaced with clean ones. Every employee is assigned a list of customers whom she services. The contract of employment stated that in consideration of being employed, on termination of his employment, Close would not "directly or indirectly engage in the linen supply business or any competitive business within Central City, Illinois, for a period of one year from the date when his employment under this contract ceases." On May 10 of the following year, Close's employment was terminated by Leigh for valid reasons. Close then accepted employment with Ajax Linen Service, a direct competitor of Leigh in Central City. He began soliciting former customers he had called on for Leigh and obtained some of them as customers for Ajax. Will Leigh be able to enforce the provisions of the contract?

7. On July 5, 2014, Bill and George entered into a bet on the outcome of the 2014 congressional election. On January 28, 2015, Bill, who bet on the winner, approached George, seeking to collect the $3,000 George had wagered. George paid Bill the wager but now seeks to recover the funds from Bill. Result?

8. Carl, a salesperson for Smith, comes to Benson's home and sells him a complete set of "gourmet cooking utensils" that are worth approximately $300. Benson, an eighty-year-old man who lives alone in a one-room efficiency apartment, signs a contract to buy the utensils for $1,450 plus a credit charge of $145 and to make payments in ten equal monthly installments. Three weeks after Carl leaves with the signed contract, Benson decides he cannot afford the cooking utensils and has no use for them. What can Benson do? Explain.

9. Consider the facts in Question 8 but assume that the price was $350. Assume further that Benson wishes to avoid the contract based on the allegation that Carl befriended and tricked him into the purchase. Discuss.

10. Adrian rents a bicycle from Barbara. The bicycle rental contract Adrian signed provides that Barbara is not liable for any injury to the renter caused by any defect in the bicycle or the negligence of Barbara. Adrian is injured when she is involved in an accident due to Barbara's improper maintenance of the bicycle. Adrian sues Barbara for damages. Will Barbara be protected from liability by the provision in their contract?

11. Emily was a Java programmer employed with Sun Microsystems in Palo Alto, California. Upon beginning employment, Emily signed a contract that included a noncompetition clause that prevented her from taking another Java programming position with any of five companies Sun listed as "direct competitors" within three months of terminating her employment. Later

that year Emily resigned and two months later accepted a position with Hewlett-Packard (HP) in Houston, Texas. HP was listed in Emily's contract as a "direct competitor," but she argues that due to the significant geographic distance between both jobs, the contract is not enforceable. Explain whether the contract is enforceable.

CASE PROBLEMS

12. Merrill Lynch employed Post and Maney as account executives. Both men elected to be paid a salary and to participate in the firm's pension and profit-sharing plans rather than take a straight commission. Thirteen years later, Merrill Lynch terminated the employment of both Post and Maney without cause. Both men began working for a competitor of Merrill Lynch. Merrill Lynch then informed them that all of their rights in the company-funded pension plan had been forfeited pursuant to a provision of the plan that permitted forfeiture in the event an employee directly or indirectly competed with the firm. Is Merrill Lynch correct in its assertion?

13. Tovar applied for the position of resident physician in Paxton Community Memorial Hospital. The hospital examined his background and licensing and assured him that he was qualified for the position. Relying upon the hospital's promise of permanent employment, Tovar resigned from his job and began work at the hospital. He was discharged two weeks later, however, because he did not hold a license to practice medicine in Illinois as required by state law. He had taken the examination but had never passed it. Tovar claims that the hospital promised him a position of permanent employment and that by discharging him, it breached their employment contract. Who is correct? Discuss.

14. Carolyn Murphy, a welfare recipient with very limited education and with four minor children, responded to an advertisement that offered the opportunity to purchase televisions without a deposit or credit history. She entered into a rent-to-own contract for a twenty-five-inch television set that required seventy-eight weekly payments of $16.00 (a total of $1,248, which was two and one-half times the retail value of the set). Under the contract, the renter could terminate the agreement by returning the television and forfeiting any payments already made. After Murphy had paid $436 on the television, she read a newspaper article criticizing the lease plan. She stopped payment and sued the television company. In response, the television company has attempted to take possession of the set. What will be the outcome?

15. Albert Bennett, an amateur cyclist, participated in a bicycle race conducted by the United States Cycling Federation. During the race, Bennett was hit by an automobile. He claims that employees of the Federation improperly allowed the car onto the course. The Federation claims that it cannot be held liable to Bennett because Bennett signed a release exculpating the Federation from responsibility for any personal injury resulting from his participation in the race. Is the exculpatory clause effective?

16. In February, Brady, a general contractor, signed a written contract with the Fulghums to build for them a house in North Carolina. The contract price of the house was $206,850, and construction was to begin in March of that year. Neither during the contract negotiations nor during the commencement of construction was Brady licensed as a general contractor as required by North Carolina law. In fact, Brady did not obtain his license until late October of that year, at which time he had completed more than two-thirds of the construction on the Fulghums' house. The Fulghums submitted to Brady total payments of $204,000 on the house. Brady sues for $2,850 on the original contract and $29,000 for additions and changes requested by the Fulghums during construction. Is Fulghum liable to Brady? Explain.

17. Robert McCart owned and operated an H&R Block tax preparation franchise. When Robert became a district manager for H&R Block, he was not allowed to continue operating a franchise. So, in accordance with company policy, he signed over his franchise to his wife June. June signed the new franchise agreement, which included a covenant not to compete for a two-year period within a fifty-mile radius of the franchise territory should the H&R Block franchise be terminated, transferred, or otherwise disposed of. June and Robert were both aware of the terms of this agreement, but June chose to terminate her franchise agreement anyway. Shortly thereafter, June sent out letters to H&R Block customers, criticizing H&R Block's fees and informing them that she and Robert would establish their own tax preparation services at the same address as the former franchise location. Each letter included a separate letter from Robert detailing the tax services to be offered by the McCart's new business. Should H&R Block be able to obtain an injunction against June? Against Robert?

18. Michelle Marvin and actor Lee Marvin began living together, holding themselves out to the general public as man and wife without actually being married. The two orally agreed that while they lived together they would share equally any and all property and earnings accumulated as a result of their individual and combined efforts. In addition, Michelle promised to render her services as "companion, homemaker, housekeeper, and cook" to Lee. Shortly thereafter, she gave up her lucrative career as an entertainer to devote her full time to being Lee's companion, homemaker, housekeeper, and cook. In return he agreed to provide for all of her financial support and needs for the rest of her life. After living together for six years, Lee compelled Michelle to leave his household but continued to provide for her support. One year later, however, he refused to provide further support. Michelle sued to recover support payments and half of their accumulated property. Lee contends that their agreement is so closely related to the supposed "immoral" character of their relationship that its enforcement would violate public policy. The trial court granted Lee's motion for judgment on the pleadings. Decision?

19. Richard Brobston was hired by Insulation Corporation of America (ICA) in 2005. Initially, he was hired as a territory sales manager but was promoted to national account manager in 2009 and to general manager in 2013. In 2015, ICA was planning to acquire computer-assisted design (CAD) technology to upgrade its product line. Prior to acquiring this technology, ICA required that Brobston and certain other employees sign employment contracts that contained restrictive covenants or be terminated and changed their employment status to "at will" employees. These restrictive covenants provided that in the event of Brobston's termination for any reason, Brobston would not reveal any of ICA's trade secrets or sales information and would not enter into direct competition with ICA within three hundred miles of Allentown, Pennsylvania, for a period of two years from the date of termination. The purported consideration for Brobston's agreement was a $2,000 increase in his base salary and proprietary information concerning the CAD system, customers, and pricing. Brobston signed the proffered employment contract. In October 2015, Brobston became vice president of special products, which included responsibility for sales of the CAD system products as well as other products. Over the course of the next year, Brobston failed in several respects to properly perform his employment duties and on August 13, 2016, ICA terminated Brobston's employment. In December 2013, Brobston was hired by a competitor of ICA who was aware of ICA's restrictive covenants. Can ICA enforce the employment agreement by enjoining Brobston from disclosing proprietary information about ICA and by restraining him from competing with ICA? If so, for what duration and over what geographic area?

20. Henrioulle, an unemployed widower with two children, received public assistance in the form of a rent subsidy. He entered into an apartment lease agreement with Marin Ventures that provided "INDEMNIFICATION: Owner shall not be liable for any damage or injury to the tenant, or any other person, or to any property, occurring on the premises, or any part thereof, and Tenant agrees to hold Owner harmless for any claims for damages no matter how caused." Henrioulle fractured his wrist when he tripped over a rock on a common stairway in the apartment building. At the time of the accident, the landlord had been having difficulty keeping the common areas of the apartment building clean. Will the exculpatory clause effectively bar Henrioulle from recovery? Explain.

21. Universal City Studios, Inc. (Universal) entered into a general contract with Turner Construction Company (Turner) for the construction of the Jurassic Park ride. Turner entered into a subcontract with Pacific Custom Pools, Inc. (PCP), for PCP to furnish and install all water treatment work for the project for the contract price of $959,131. PCP performed work on the project from April 2012 until June 2013 for which it was paid $897,719. PCP's contractor's license, however, was under suspension from October 12, 2012 to March 14, 2013. In addition, PCP's license had expired as of January 31, 2013, and it was not renewed until May 5. California Business and Professions Code Section 7031 provides that no contractor may bring an action to recover compensation for the performance of any work requiring a license unless he or she was "a duly licensed contractor at all times during the performance of that [work], regardless of the merits of the cause of action brought by the contractor." The purpose of this licensing law is to protect the public from incompetence and dishonesty in those who provide building and construction services. PCP brought suit against Universal and Turner, the defendants, for the remainder of the contract price. Explain who should prevail.

TAKING SIDES

EarthWeb provided online products and services to business professionals in the information technology (IT) industry. EarthWeb operated through a family of websites offering information, products, and services for IT professionals to use for facilitating tasks and solving technology problems in a business setting. EarthWeb obtained this content primarily through licensing agreements with third parties. Schlack began his employment with EarthWeb in its New York City office. His title at EarthWeb was Vice President, Worldwide Content, and he was responsible for the content of all of EarthWeb's websites. Schlack's employment contract stated that he was an employee at will and included a section titled "Limited Agreement Not To Compete." That section provided:

(c) For a period of twelve (12) months after the termination of Schlack's employment with EarthWeb, Schlack shall not, directly or indirectly:

   (1) work as an employee … or in any other … capacity for any person or entity that directly competes with EarthWeb. For the purpose of this section, the term "directly competing" is defined as a person or entity or division on an entity that is

   (i) an online service for Information Professionals whose primary business is to provide Information Technology Professionals with a directory of third party technology, software, and/or developer resources; and/or an online reference library, and or

   (ii) an online store, the primary purpose of which is to sell or distribute third party software or products used for Internet site or software development.

About one year later, Schlack tendered his letter of resignation to EarthWeb. Schlack revealed at this time that he had accepted a position with ITworld.com.

a. What arguments would support EarthWeb's enforcement of the covenant not to compete?

b. What arguments would support Schlack's argument that the covenant is not enforceable?

c. Which side should prevail? Explain.

Contractual Capacity

CHAPTER 14

Youth is a blunder, manhood a struggle, old age a regret.

Benjamin Disraeli (1804–1881)
Coningsby (Book III, Ch. 1)

CHAPTER OUTCOMES

After reading and studying this chapter, you should be able to:

1. Explain how and when a minor may ratify a contract.

2. Describe the liability of a minor who (a) disaffirms a contract or (b) misrepresents his age.

3. Define as necessary and explain how it affects the contracts of a minor.

4. Distinguish between the legal capacity of a person under guardianship and a mentally incompetent person who is not under guardianship.

5. Explain the rule governing an intoxicated person's capacity to enter into a contract and contrast this rule with the law governing minors and incompetent persons.

A binding promise or agreement requires that the parties to the agreement have contractual capacity. Everyone is regarded as having such capacity unless the law, for public policy reasons, holds that the individual lacks such capacity. We will consider this essential ingredient of a contract by discussing those classes and conditions of persons who are legally limited in their capacity to contract: minors, incompetent persons, and intoxicated persons.

MINORS [14-1]

Almost without exception a minor's contract, whether executory or executed, is *voidable* unless the contract has been ratified. A **minor**, also called an infant, is a person who has not attained the age of legal majority. At common law, a minor was an individual who had not reached the age of twenty-one years. Today the age of majority has been changed by statute in nearly all jurisdictions, usually to age eighteen.

Thus, the minor is in a favored position by having the option to disaffirm the contract or to enforce it. The adult party to the contract cannot avoid her contract with a minor. Even an "emancipated" minor, one who, because of marriage or other reasons, is no longer subject to strict parental control, may nevertheless avoid contractual liability in most jurisdictions. Consequently, business people deal at their peril with minors and in situations of consequence generally require an adult to cosign or guarantee the performance of the contract. Nevertheless, most states recognize special categories of contracts that cannot be avoided (such as student loans or contracts for medical care) or that have a lower age for capacity (such as bank accounts, marriage, and insurance contracts).

Minor

person under age of legal majority

Liability on contracts
minor's contracts are
voidable at the minor's
option

Disaffirmance
avoidance of a contract

Ratification
affirmation of a contract

Liability on Contracts [14-1a]

A minor's contract is not entirely void and of no legal effect; rather, as we have said, it is voidable at the minor's option. The exercise of this power of avoidance, called a **disaffirmance**, releases the minor from any liability on the contract. On the other hand, after the minor comes of age, he may choose to adopt or ratify the contract, in which case he surrenders his power of avoidance and becomes bound by his **ratification**.

Disaffirmance   As stated earlier, a minor has the power to avoid liability. The minor or, in some jurisdictions, her guardian, may exercise the power to disaffirm a contract through words or conduct showing an intention not to abide by it.

A minor may disaffirm a contract at any time before reaching the age of majority. Moreover, a minor generally may disaffirm a contract within a reasonable time after coming of age as long as she has not already ratified the contract. A notable exception is that a minor cannot disaffirm a sale of land until *after* reaching her majority.

In most states, determining a reasonable time depends on circumstances such as the nature of the transaction, whether either party has caused the delay, and the extent to which either party has been injured by the delay. Some states, however, statutorily prescribe a time period, generally one year, in which the minor may disaffirm the contract.

Disaffirmance may be either *express* or *implied*. No particular form of language is essential, so long as it shows an intention not to be bound. This intention also may be manifested by acts or by conduct. For example, a minor agrees to sell property to Andy and then sells the property to Betty. The sale to Betty constitutes a disaffirmance of the contract with Andy.

Restitution
a minor who has
disaffirmed a contract is
entitled to restitution from
the other party for any
benefit the minor has
conferred on the other
party; the courts differ
regarding the obligation
of the minor to make
restitution to the other
party

Restitution   Disaffirmance of an executory contract releases the minor from any liability on the contractual obligation. In cases in which either or both of the parties have performed partially or fully, however, the issue of **restitution** arises. A minor who has disaffirmed a contract is entitled to restitution from the other party for any benefit the minor has conferred on the other party.

A troublesome yet important problem in this area pertains to the minor's duty to make restitution to the other party upon disaffirmance. The courts do not agree on this question. The majority hold that the minor must return any property received from the other party to the contract, provided she is in possession of it at the time of disaffirmance. Nothing more is required. Under this approach, if a minor disaffirms the purchase of an automobile and the vehicle has been wrecked, the minor need only return the wrecked vehicle. Other states require at least the payment of a reasonable amount for the use of the property or of the amount by which the property depreciated while in the hands of the minor. (See the following case *Berg v. Traylor*.) Some states, however, either by statute or court ruling, recognize a duty on the part of the minor to make *restitution*—that is, to return an equivalent of what has been received so that the seller will be in approximately the same position he would have occupied had the sale not occurred.

The newly adopted Restatement of Restitution adopts the last position: if the other party has dealt with the minor in good faith on reasonable terms, rescission leaves the minor liable in restitution for benefits the minor received in the transaction. The Restatement of Restitution provides the following example:

> Minor purchases a used car from Dealer, paying $5,000 cash and making no misrepresentation of age. Dealer acts in good faith, and the sale is on reasonable terms. Several months later the car develops mechanical problems. Minor continues to drive the car without obtaining the necessary repairs; the car becomes inoperable; Minor repudiates the purchase. Minor is entitled to rescind the transaction on the ground of incapacity. In the two-way restoration consequent on rescission, Minor's claim is to $5,000 plus interest; Dealer recovers the car, with a credit (against Dealer's liability to Minor) equal to the car's depreciation in value while in Minor's possession.

Finally, can a minor disaffirm and recover property that he has sold to a buyer who in turn has sold it to a good-faith purchaser for value? Traditionally, the minor could avoid the contract and recover the property, even though the third person gave value for it and had no notice of the minority. Thus, in the case of the sale of real estate, a minor could take back a deed of

Practical Advice

In all significant contracts entered into with a minor, have an adult cosign or guarantee the written agreement.

conveyance even against a third-party good-faith purchaser of the land who did not know of the minority. The Uniform Commercial Code (UCC), however, has changed this principle in connection with sales of goods by providing that a person with voidable title (e.g., the person buying goods from a minor) has power to transfer valid title to a good-faith purchaser for value. For example, a minor sells his car to an individual who resells it to a used-car dealer, a good-faith purchaser for value. The used-car dealer would acquire legal title even though he bought the car from a seller who had only voidable title.

Berg v. Traylor
Court of Appeal, Second District, Division 2, California, 2007
148 Cal.App.4th 809, 56 Cal.Rptr.3d 140
http://scholar.google.com/scholar_case?case=15409397777753786246&q=56+Cal.Rptr.3d + 140&hl=en&as_sclt=2,22

FACTS Sharyn Berg (Berg), plaintiff, brought this action against Meshiel Cooper Traylor (Meshiel) and her minor son Craig Lamar Traylor (Craig) for unpaid commissions under a contract between Berg, Meshiel, and Craig for Berg to serve as the personal manager of Craig. On January 18, 1999, Berg entered into a two-page "Artist's Manager's Agreement" (agreement) with Meshiel and Craig, who was then ten years old. Meshiel signed the agreement and wrote Craig's name on the signature page where he was designated "Artist." Craig did not sign the agreement. The agreement provided that Berg was to act as Craig's exclusive personal manager in exchange for a commission of 15 percent of all monies paid to him as an artist during the three-year term of the agreement. The agreement expressly provided that any action Craig "may take in the future pertaining to disaffirmance of this agreement, whether successful or not," would not affect Meshiel's liability for any commissions due Berg. The agreement also provided that any disputes concerning payment or interpretation of the agreement would be determined by arbitration in accordance with the rules of Judicial Arbitration and Mediation Services, Inc. (JAMS).

In June 2001, Craig obtained a role on the Fox Television Network show "Malcolm in the Middle" (show). On September 11, 2001, four months prior to the expiration of the agreement, Meshiel sent a certified letter to Berg stating that while she and Craig appreciated her advice and guidance, they no longer needed her management services and could no longer afford to pay Berg her 15 percent commission because they owed a "huge amount" of taxes. On September 28, 2001, Berg responded, informing appellants that they were in breach of the agreement.

The arbitration hearing was held in February 2005. The arbitrator awarded Berg commissions and interest of $154,714.15, repayment of personal loans and interest of $5,094, and attorneys' fees and costs of $13,762. He also awarded Berg $405,000 "for future earnings projected on a minimum of six years for national syndication earnings." The defendants then filed a petition with the state trial court to vacate the arbitration award. Following a hearing, the trial court trial court entered a judgment in favor of Berg against Meshiel and Craig consistent with the arbitrator's award.

DECISION The decision against Craig is reversed but the judgment against Meshiel is affirmed.

OPINION One who provides a minor with goods and services does so at her own risk. The agreement here in question expressly contemplated this risk, requiring that Meshiel remain obligated

for commissions due under the agreement regardless of whether Craig disaffirmed the agreement. Thus, Craig is permitted to and did disaffirm the agreement and any of its obligations, while Meshiel is liable under the agreement and resulting judgment. Craig's minority status entitled him to disaffirm the agreement and the arbitration award and judgment.

"As a general proposition, parental consent is required for the provision of services to minors for the simple reason that minors may disaffirm their own contracts to acquire such services." A contract of a minor may be disaffirmed by the minor before majority or within a reasonable time afterwards. The law shields minors from their lack of judgment and experience. This is so even though in many instances such disaffirmance may be a hardship upon those who deal with an infant, the right to avoid his contracts is conferred by law upon a minor for his protection against his own improvidence and the designs of others. It is the policy of the law to protect a minor against himself and his indiscretions and immaturity as well as against the machinations of other people and to discourage adults from contracting with an infant. No specific language is required to communicate an intent to disaffirm. Express notice to the other party is unnecessary. Craig disaffirmed both the agreement and the arbitration award.

Berg offers two reasons this rule is inapplicable. First, she without justification or legal support argues that a minor may not disaffirm an agreement signed by a parent. Second, Berg argues that Craig cannot disaffirm the agreement because it was for his and his family's necessities. This agreement, however, is not a contract to pay for the necessities of life for Craig or his family. A contract to secure personal management services for the purpose of advancing Craig's acting career does not constitute a necessity. Moreover, there is no evidence that Meshiel was unable to provide for the family in 1999 at the time of the agreement.

A disaffirmance of an agreement by a minor does not operate to terminate the contractual obligations of the parent who signed the agreement. There is no legal reason for Meshiel to avoid her independent obligations under the agreement.

INTERPRETATION A minor may disaffirm his contracts during minority and for a reasonable time thereafter; nevertheless, the minor's right to disaffirm does not extend to an adult party to the agreement.

CRITICAL THINKING QUESTION Under what circumstances should minors be able to disaffirm their contracts and receive their full consideration? Explain.

BUSINESS LAW IN ACTION

Using his own money, fifteen-year-old Zach bought $160 worth of video games and DVDs at a local electronics warehouse. His parents were furious about the purchase, but initially they did nothing. Several months later Zach's father learned about the so-called infancy doctrine and insisted that Zach return the games and movies. Zach took the items back to the store and asked for a refund. But the clerk refused, pointing to the store's "Return Policy," which permitted returns on opened items like those Zach had bought only within thirty days of purchase and only for the same title when necessary to replace defects. After speaking to the manager and getting a similar result, Zach's father considered filing suit against the store in small claims court. Does

a minor's right of disaffirmation override the store's return policy in a case like this?

Generally speaking, minors may disaffirm contracts entered into during their minority. In a majority of jurisdictions this is true even if the child or teenager cannot return the consideration he or she received and even if the minor misrepresented his or her age when entering into the transaction with the adult. However, this rule of incapacity does not excuse minors from paying the reasonable value of any necessaries for which they may have contracted. There is little question here that the purchases Zach made do not qualify as necessaries, things that supply his basic needs. Therefore, Zach is entitled

to disaffirm his contract and receive a refund, although some states perhaps would subject the refund to a deduction of some amount representing depreciation of the items or the use or benefit he received.

Nonetheless, retailers need not fear or refuse transactions with minors, especially relatively insignificant ones. Most people will not go to the trouble and expense of bringing litigation to recover a small amount of money. It is also foreseeable that many courts, if given the opportunity, would not allow a minor to take unfair advantage of her minority. Moreover, teens make up a growing and lucrative segment of the retail market, with their purchases tallying in the billions of dollars each year.

Ratification   A minor has the option of ratifying a contract after reaching the age of majority. Ratification makes the contract binding *ab initio* (from the beginning). That is, the result is the same as if the contract had been valid and binding from its inception. Ratification, once effected, is final and cannot be withdrawn; furthermore, it must be in total, validating the entire contract. The minor can ratify the contract only as a whole, both as to burdens and benefits. He cannot, for example, ratify so as to retain the consideration received and escape payment or other performance on his part; nor can the minor retain part of the contract and disaffirm another part.

Note that a minor has *no* power to ratify a contract while still a minor. A ratification based on words or conduct occurring while the minor is still underage is no more effective than his original contractual promise. The ratification must take place after the individual has acquired contractual capacity by attaining his majority.

Ratification can occur in three ways: (1) through express language, (2) as implied from conduct, and (3) through failure to make a timely disaffirmance. Suppose that a minor makes a contract to buy property from an adult. The contract is voidable by the minor, and she can escape liability. But suppose that after reaching her majority she promises to go through with the purchase. The minor has *expressly* ratified the contract she entered when she was a minor. Her promise is binding, and the adult can recover for breach if the minor fails to carry out the terms of the contract.

Ratification also may be *implied* from a person's conduct. Suppose that the minor, after attaining majority, uses the property involved in the contract, undertakes to sell it to someone else, or performs some other act showing an intention to affirm the contract. She may not thereafter disaffirm the contract but is bound by it. Perhaps the most common form of implied ratification occurs when a minor, after attaining majority, continues to use the property purchased as a minor. This use is obviously inconsistent with the nonexistence of a contract. Whether the contract is performed or still partly executory, the continued use of the property amounts to a ratification and prevents a disaffirmance by the minor. Simply keeping the goods for an unreasonable time after attaining majority has also been construed as a ratification.

In re The Score Board, Inc.
United States District Court, District of New Jersey, 1999
238 B.R. 585
http://scholar.google.com/scholar_case?case=9690754193230293303&q=238+B.R.+585+&hl=en&as_sdt=2,34

FACTS During the spring of 1996, Kobe Bryant (Bryant), then a seventeen-year-old star high school basketball player, declared his intention to forgo college and enter the 1996 National Basketball Association (NBA) lottery draft. The Score Board Inc., a company in the business of licensing, manufacturing, and distributing sports and entertainment-related memorabilia, entered into negotiations with Bryant's agent, Arn Tellem (Agent) and Bryant's father, former NBA star Joe "Jelly Bean" Bryant, to sign Bryant to a contract. In early July 1996, Score Board sent Bryant a signed written licensing agreement (agreement). The agreement granted Score Board the right to produce licensed products, such as trading cards, with Bryant's image. Bryant was obligated to make two personal appearances on behalf of Score Board and provide between a minimum of 15,000 and a maximum of 32,500 autographs. Bryant was to receive a $2 stipend for each autograph, after the first 7,500. Under the agreement, Bryant could receive a maximum of $75,000 for the autographs. In addition to being compensated for the autographs, Bryant was entitled to receive a base compensation of $10,000.

Bryant rejected this proposed agreement, and on July 11, 1996, while still a minor, made a counteroffer (counteroffer), signed it, and returned it to Score Board. The counteroffer made several changes to Score Board's agreement, including the number of autographs. Score Board claimed that they signed the counteroffer and placed it into its files. The copy signed by Score Board was subsequently misplaced and has never been produced by Score Board during these proceedings. Rather, Score Board has produced a copy signed only by Bryant.

On August 23, 1996, Bryant turned eighteen. Three days later, Bryant deposited the check for $10,000 into his account. Bryant subsequently performed his contractual duties for about a year and a half. By late 1997, Bryant grew reluctant to sign any more autographs under the agreement and his Agent came to the conclusion that a fully executed contract did not exist. By this time, Agent became concerned with Score Board's financial condition because it failed to make certain payments to several other players. Score Board claims that the true motivation for Bryant's reluctance stems from his perception that he was becoming a "star" player, and that his autograph was "worth" more than $2.

On March 17, 1998, Score Board mistakenly sent Bryant a check for $1,130 as compensation for unpaid autographs. Bryant was actually entitled to $10,130 and the check for $1,130 was based on a miscalculation.

On March 18, 1998, Score Board filed a voluntary Chapter 11 bankruptcy petition. On March 23, 1998, Agent returned the $1,130 check. Included with the check was a letter that directed Score Board to "immediately cease and desist from any use of" Kobe Bryant's name, likeness, or other publicity rights. Subsequently, Score Board began to sell its assets, including numerous executory contracts with major athletes, including Bryant. Bryant argued that Score Board could not do this, because he believed that a contract never existed. In the alternative, if a contract had been created, Bryant contended that it was voidable because it had been entered into while he was a minor. The Bankruptcy Court ruled in favor of Score Board. Bryant appealed.

DECISION Judgment affirmed.

OPINION Bryant challenges the Bankruptcy Court's finding that he ratified the agreement upon attaining majority. Contracts made during minority are voidable at the minor's election within a reasonable time after the minor attains the age of majority. The infant's conduct upon reaching the age of majority may amount to ratification.

After Bryant deposited the $10,000 check sent to him from Score Board, he performed his contractual duties by signing autographs. It is clear that Bryant ratified the contract from the facts. Bryant asserts, however, that he acted at the insistence of his Agent, who believed that he was contractually obligated to perform. Yet, neither Bryant nor his Agent disputed the existence of a contract until the March 23, 1998, letter by the Agent. That Bryant may have relied on his Agent is irrelevant to this Court's inquiry and is proper evidence only in a suit against the Agent. To the contrary, by admitting that he acted because he was under the belief that a contract existed, Bryant confirms the existence of the contract. Moreover, it was Bryant who deposited the check, signed the autographs, and made personal appearances.

INTERPRETATION Ratification of a contract may be implied from a person's conduct after the person attains his majority.

CRITICAL THINKING QUESTION What criteria should a court employ in determining what is a reasonable period of time for disaffirmance by a person who has attained majority?

Liability for necessaries
a minor is liable for the reasonable value of necessary items

Necessaries
items that reasonably supply a person's needs

Liability for Necessaries [14-1b]

Contractual incapacity does not excuse a minor from an obligation to pay for **necessaries**, those things, such as food, shelter, medicine, and clothing, that suitably and reasonably supply his personal needs. Even here, however, the minor is not contractually liable for the agreed price but for the *reasonable* value of the items furnished. Recovery is based on quasi-contract. Thus, if a clothier sells a minor a suit that the minor needs, the clothier can successfully sue the minor. The clothier's recovery, however, is limited to the reasonable value of the suit only, even if this amount is much less than the agreed-upon selling price. In addition, a minor is not liable for anything on the ground that the item is a necessary, unless it has been actually furnished to him and used or consumed by him. In other words, a minor may disaffirm his executory contracts for necessaries and refuse to accept such clothing, lodging, or other items.

Defining "necessaries" is a difficult task. In general, the states regard as necessary those things that the minor needs to maintain himself in his particular station in life. Items necessary for subsistence and health, such as food, lodging, clothing, medicine, and medical services, are included. But other less essential items, such as textbooks, school instruction, and legal advice, may be included as well. Furthermore, some states enlarge the concept of necessaries to include articles of property and services that a minor needs to earn the money required to provide the necessities of life for himself and his dependents. Nevertheless, many states limit necessaries to items that are not provided to the minor. Thus, if a minor's guardian provides her with an adequate wardrobe, a blouse the minor purchased would *not* be considered a necessary.

Ordinarily, luxury items, such as cameras, tape recorders, stereo equipment, television sets, and motorboats, do not qualify as necessaries. The question concerning whether automobiles and trucks are necessaries has caused considerable controversy, but some courts have recognized that under certain circumstances, an automobile may be a necessary where it is used by the minor for his business activities.

Zelnick v. Adams
Supreme Court of Virginia, 2002
263 Va. 601, 561 S.E.2d 711
http://scholar.google.com/scholar_case?case=13963993610436500611&q=561+S.E.2d+711+&hl=en&as_sdt=2,34

FACTS Jonathan Ray Adams (Jonathan) was born on April 5, 1980, the son of Mildred A. Adams (Adams or mother) and Cecil D. Hylton, Jr. (Hylton or father). Jonathan's parents were never married. Nevertheless, the Florida courts did determine Hylton's paternity of Jonathan. Jonathan's grandfather, Cecil D. Hylton, Sr. (Hylton Sr.), died in 1989 and had established certain trusts under his will, which provided that the trustees had sole discretion to determine who qualified as "issue" under the will.

In 1996, Adams met with an attorney, Robert J. Zelnick (Zelnick), about protecting Jonathan's interest as a beneficiary of the trusts after she had unsuccessfully attempted to get Jonathan recognized as an heir. Adams explained that she could not afford to pay Zelnick's hourly fee and requested legal services on her son's behalf on a contingency fee basis. Zelnick subsequently informed Adams that he had examined a copy of the will and that he was willing to accept the case. Adams went to Zelnick's office the next day, where Zelnick explained that the gross amount of the estate was very large. Adams signed a retainer agreement (the contract) for Zelnick's firm to represent Jonathan on a one-third contingency fee.

In May 1997, Zelnick initiated a legal action on Jonathan's behalf. A consent decree was entered on January 23, 1998, which ordered that Jonathan was "declared to be the grandchild and issue of Cecil D. Hylton" and was entitled to all benefits under the Will and Trusts of Cecil D. Hylton.

In March 1998, Jonathan's father brought suit against Adams and Zelnick, on Jonathan's behalf, to have the contract with Zelnick declared void. Upon reaching the age of majority, Jonathan filed a petition to intervene, in which he disaffirmed the contract. Jonathan filed a motion for summary judgment asserting that the contract was "void as a matter of law" because it was not a contract for necessaries. Jonathan argued that the 1997 suit was unnecessary due to the Florida paternity decree which conclusively established Hylton's paternity.

The trial court granted Jonathan's motion for summary judgment and ruled that the contingency fee agreement was not binding on Jonathan because he was "in his minority" when the contract was executed. This appeal followed.

DECISION Judgment reversed and remanded.

OPINION Under well- and long-established Virginia law, a contract with an infant is not void, only voidable by the infant upon attaining the age of majority. When a court is faced with a defense of infancy, the court has the initial duty to determine, as a matter of law, whether the "things supplied" to the infant under a contract may fall within the general class of necessaries, and were in fact necessary in the instant case. If not, the provider of the goods cannot recover under the disaffirmed contract.

If a necessary, the party who provided the goods or services to the infant is entitled to the "reasonable value" of the things furnished. "Things supplied," which fall into the class of necessaries, include "board, clothing, and education." Things that are "necessary to [an infant's] subsistence and comfort, and to enable [an infant] to live according to his real position in society" are also considered part of the class of necessaries.

Certainly, the provision of legal services may fall within the class of necessaries for which an infant may not be avoided or disaffirmed on the grounds of infancy. Generally, contracts for legal services related to prosecuting personal injury actions and protecting an infant's personal liberty, security, or reputation are considered contracts for necessaries. Other states have also broadened the definition of "necessaries" to include contracts for legal services for the protection of an infant's property rights.

The trier of fact must also conclude that "under all the circumstances, the things furnished were actually necessary to the position and condition of the infant … and whether the infant was already sufficiently supplied." If the contract does fall within the "general classes of necessaries," but upon consideration of all of the circumstances, the trier of fact determines that the provision of the particular services or things was not actually necessary, the plea of infancy must be sustained.

Because the trial court erred in its determination, on this record, on summary judgment, that the doctrine of necessaries did not apply, the decision must be reversed and remanded for further proceedings, including the taking of evidence on the issue of the factual determination of necessity "under all of the circumstances." Should the trial court upon remand hold that the evidence is sufficient to defeat Jonathan's plea of infancy, the trial

court shall receive evidence of the reasonable value of the services rendered.

INTERPRETATION Contractual incapacity does not excuse a minor from an obligation to pay the reasonable value of a necessary.

ETHICAL QUESTION Did Jonathan act ethically? Explain.

CRITICAL THINKING QUESTION What factors should a court use in determining whether goods or services are necessary? Explain.

Liability for misrepresentation of age
prevailing view is that a minor may disaffirm the contract

Practical Advice

In all significant contracts, if you have doubts about the age of your customers, have them prove that they are of legal age.

Liability for Misrepresentation of Age [14-1c]

The states do not agree whether a minor who fraudulently misrepresents her age when entering into a contract has the power to disaffirm. Suppose a contracting minor says that she is eighteen years of age (or twenty-one, if that is the year of attaining majority) and actually looks at least that age. By the prevailing view in this country, despite her misrepresentation, the minor may nevertheless disaffirm the contract. Some states, however, prohibit disaffirmance if a minor misrepresented her age to an adult who, in good faith, reasonably relied on the misrepresentation. As shown in the case of *Keser v. Chagnon*, other states not following the majority rule either (1) require the minor to restore the other party to the position he occupied before making the contract or (2) allow the defrauded party to recover damages against the minor in tort.

 **Keser v. Chagnon**
Supreme Court of Colorado, 1966
159 Colo. 209, 410 P.2d 637
http://scholar.google.com/scholar_case?case=4554012522196124668&q=410+P.2d+637&hl=en&as_sdt=2,34

FACTS On June 11, 1964, Chagnon bought a 1959 Ford Edsel from Keser for $995. Chagnon, who was then a twenty-year-old minor, obtained the contract by falsely advising to Keser that he was over twenty-one years old, the age of majority. On September 25, 1964, two months and four days after his twenty-first birthday, Chagnon disaffirmed the contract and, ten days later, returned the Edsel to Keser. He then brought suit to recover the money he had paid for the automobile. Keser counterclaimed that he suffered damages as the direct result of Chagnon's false representation of his age. A trial was had to the court, sitting without a jury, all of which culminated in a judgment in favor of Chagnon against Keser in the sum of $655.78. This particular sum was arrived at by the trial court in the following manner: the trial court found that Chagnon initially purchased the Edsel for the sum of $995 and that he was entitled to the return of his $995; and then, by way of setoff, the trial court subtracted from the $995 the sum of $339.22, apparently representing the difference between the purchase price paid for the vehicle and the reasonable value of the Edsel on October 5, 1964, the date when the Edsel was returned to Keser.

DECISION Judgment affirmed except as to the calculation of damages for misrepresentation.

OPINION If a minor does not exercise his right to disaffirm a contract within a "reasonable time" after he reaches the age of

majority, he loses that right. Here, however, Chagnon's disaffirmance just two months after reaching majority was within a reasonable time. Under the general rule, once he returned the car—the only consideration in his possession—he was entitled to recover the full $995. While a false representation of his age does not destroy a minor's right to disaffirm, it does permit the seller to deduct from the buyer's compensation any damages that the seller suffered due to the false representation. The measure of damages for the seller is the difference between the reasonable value of the property on the date of delivery and its reasonable value on the date of return. Since Chagnon obtained the contract by false representation of his age, he will not recover his full $995. Instead, his recovery is decreased by the amount of Keser's damages—the loss of the Edsel's reasonable value.

INTERPRETATION States vary on the rights of a minor and a defrauded party when a minor fraudulently misrepresents her age when entering into a contract.

ETHICAL QUESTION If a minor misrepresents his age, should he forfeit the right to avoid the contract? Explain.

CRITICAL THINKING QUESTION What rule would you apply in this case? Explain.

Liability for Tort Connected with Contract [14-1d]

Liability for tort connected with contract

if a tort and a contract are so intertwined that to enforce the tort the court must enforce the contract, the minor is not liable in tort

It is well settled that minors are generally liable for their torts. There is, however, a legal doctrine that if a tort and a contract are so "interwoven" that the court must enforce the contract to enforce the tort action, the minor is not liable in tort. Thus, a minor who rents an automobile from an adult enters into a contractual relationship obliging him to exercise reasonable care to protect the property from injury. By negligently damaging the automobile, he breaches that contractual undertaking. But his contractual immunity protects him from an action by the adult based on the contract. By the majority view, the adult cannot successfully sue the minor for damages on a tort theory. For, it is reasoned, a tort recovery would, in effect, be an enforcement of the contract and would defeat the protection that contract law gives the minor. Should the minor depart, however, from the terms of the agreement (e.g., by using a rental automobile for an unauthorized purpose) and in so doing negligently cause damage to the automobile, most courts would hold that the tort is independent and that the adult can collect from the minor.

INCOMPETENT PERSONS [14-2]

In this section, we will discuss the contract status of mentally incompetent persons who are under court-appointed guardianship and persons with mental incapacity who are not adjudicated incompetents.

Person Under Guardianship [14-2a]

Person under guardianship

contracts made by a person placed under guardianship by court order are void

Guardianship

the relationship under which a person (the guardian) is appointed by a court to preserve and control the property of another (the ward)

If a person is under **guardianship** by *court order*, her contracts are *void* and of no legal effect. A court appoints a *guardian*, generally under the terms of a statute, to control and preserve the property of a person (the *ward* or *adjudicated incompetent*) whose impaired capacity prevents her from managing her own property. Nonetheless, a party dealing with an individual under guardianship may be able to recover the fair value of any necessaries provided to the incompetent. Moreover, the contracts of the ward may be ratified by her guardian during the period of guardianship or by the ward on termination of the guardianship.

Mental Illness or Defect [14-2b]

Mental illness or defect

a contract entered into by a nonadjudicated mentally incompetent person (one who is unable to understand the nature and consequences of his acts) is voidable

Mentally incompetent

a person whose mental incapacity has not been adjudicated but is unable to understand the nature and effect of his acts

Because a contract is a consensual transaction, the parties to a valid contract must have a certain level of mental capacity. If a person lacks such mental capacity, or is **mentally incompetent**, the agreement is *voidable*.

Under the traditional cognitive ability test, a person is mentally incompetent if he is unable to comprehend the subject of the contract, its nature, and its probable consequences. Though he need not be proved permanently incompetent to avoid the contract, his mental defect must be something more than a weakness of intellect or a lack of average intelligence. In short, a person is competent unless he is unable to understand the nature and effect of his actions, in which case he may disaffirm the contract even if the other party did not know or had no reason to know of the incompetent's mental condition.

A second type of mental incompetence recognized by the Restatement of Contracts and some states is a mental condition that impairs a person's ability to act in a reasonable manner. In other words, the person understands what he is doing but cannot control his behavior in order to act in a reasonable and rational way.

The newly adopted Restatement of Restitution provides that a transfer by a person lacking mental capacity is subject to rescission unless ratified. Upon disaffirmance by the mentally incompetent person, the other party to the contract is liable in restitution as necessary to avoid unjust enrichment. If the other party has dealt with the mentally incompetent person in good faith on reasonable terms, rescission leaves the mentally incompetent person liable in restitution for benefits the mentally incompetent person received in the transaction.

Like minors and persons under guardianship, an incompetent person is liable on the principle of quasi-contract for *necessaries* furnished him, the amount of recovery being the reasonable value of the goods or services. Moreover, an incompetent person may *ratify* or *disaffirm* voidable contracts during a lucid period or when he becomes competent.

Practical Advice

If you have doubts about the capacity of the other party to a contract, have an individual with full legal capacity cosign the contract.

INTOXICATED PERSONS [14-3]

Intoxicated persons

a contract entered into by an intoxicated person (one who cannot understand the nature and consequence of her actions) is voidable

A person may *avoid* any contract that he enters into if the other party has reason to know that the person, because of his intoxication, is unable to understand the nature and consequences of his actions or unable to act in a reasonable manner. Such contracts, as in the case that follows, are **voidable**, although they may be ratified when the intoxicated person regains his capacity. Slight intoxication will not destroy one's contractual capacity; on the other hand, to make a contract voidable, a person need not be so drunk that he is totally without reason or understanding.

The effect that the courts allow intoxication to have on contractual capacity is similar to the effect they allow contracts that are voidable because of incompetency, although the courts are even more strict with intoxication due to its voluntary nature. Most courts, therefore, require that, to avoid a contract, the intoxicated person on regaining his capacity must act promptly to disaffirm and generally must offer to restore the consideration he has received. Individuals who are taking prescribed medication or who are involuntarily intoxicated are treated the same as those who are incompetent under the cognitive ability test. As with incompetent persons, intoxicated persons are liable in quasi-contract for necessaries furnished during their incapacity.

First State Bank of Sinai v. Hyland
Supreme Court of South Dakota, 1987
399 N.W.2d 894
http://scholar.google.com/scholar_case?case=9646538788520684587&q=399+N.W.2d+894&hl=en&as_sclt=2,34

FACTS Randy Hyland, unable to pay two promissory notes due September 19, 1981, negotiated with The First State Bank of Sinai (Bank) for an extension. The Bank agreed on the condition that Randy's father, Mervin, act as cosigner. Mervin, a good customer of the Bank, had executed and paid on time over sixty promissory notes within a seven-year period. Accordingly, the Bank drafted a new promissory note with an April 20, 1982, due date, which Randy took home for Mervin to sign. On April 20, 1982, the new note was unpaid. Randy, on May 5, 1982, brought the Bank a check signed by Mervin to cover the interest owed on the unpaid note and asked for another extension. The Bank agreed to a second extension, again on the condition that Mervin act as cosigner. Mervin, however, refused to sign the last note; and Randy subsequently declared bankruptcy. The Bank sued Mervin on December 19, 1982. Mervin responded that he was not liable since he had been incapacitated by liquor at the time he signed the note. He had been drinking heavily throughout this period, and in fact had been involuntarily committed to an alcoholism treatment hospital twice during the time of these events. In between commitments, however, Mervin had executed and paid his own promissory note with the Bank and had transacted business in connection with his farm. The trial court held that Mervin's contract as cosigner was void due to alcohol-related incapacity, and the Bank appealed.

DECISION Judgment for the Bank.

OPINION Mervin's obligation on the note was voidable, not void, due to his alcohol-related incapacity. Voidable contracts may be disaffirmed by the temporarily disabled party. Disaffirmance, however, must be prompt upon the recovery of the intoxicated person, or upon notice of the agreement if the once-disabled person has forgotten it. A voidable contract may also be ratified by the party who contracted while disabled, resulting in a fully valid legal obligation. Ratification may be either express or implied by conduct. Furthermore, failure to disaffirm over a period of time may itself ripen into ratification, especially when voiding the contract will significantly prejudice the other party. Mervin had notice, both from Randy and the Bank, that the note he cosigned was overdue. Nevertheless, Mervin wrote a check paying the interest due. Such action amounts to ratification by conduct. Mervin also ratified the contract by waiting several months before attempting to disaffirm. The Bank has been significantly prejudiced by Mervin's delay since Randy has now been discharged through bankruptcy. Through his failure to disaffirm and subsequent ratification, the once-voidable contract is now fully binding on Mervin.

INTERPRETATION An intoxicated party ratifies a contract by not disaffirming it when she is not intoxicated and learns of its existence and by making interest payments on it when she is not intoxicated.

CRITICAL THINKING QUESTION When should a person be allowed to invalidate an agreement because of intoxication? Explain.

Figure 14-1 summarizes the voidability of contracts made by persons with contractual incapacity.

Figure 14-1 Incapacity: Minors, Nonadjudicated Incompetents, and Intoxicated

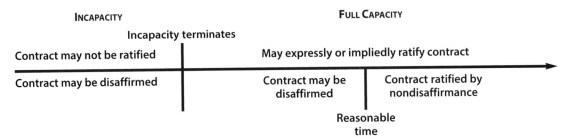

ETHICAL DILEMMA

Should a Merchant Sell to One Who Lacks Capacity?

Facts Alice Richards is a salesclerk for an exclusive department store in Connecticut. She was working in the children's clothing department when an elderly woman, Carrie Johnson, entered the area and began to browse. Because part of her compensation is based on commissions and it had been a slow season, Richards was eager to help her. However, when Richards asked Johnson if she needed any help, Johnson replied, "No, I'm just looking for a new pocketbook." When Richards attempted to direct Johnson to the pocketbooks, Johnson did not appear to respond. Puzzled, Richards began to wonder whether the woman was mentally alert.

Johnson picked out infant's clothing and accessories worth approximately $250. At the cashier's counter she exclaimed how lovely everything was and explained that the jumpers and bath toys would go well with the other new clothes she had purchased for her son, who would soon be back from a cruise in the Bahamas.

Worried that the woman did not know what she was purchasing, Richards asked her manager for assistance. The manager said that the sale should be completed, as long as the store's credit policies were satisfied.

Social, Policy, and Ethical Considerations
1. What would you do?
2. What responsibility does a retail store have in stopping a sale where a reasonable person would assume that the customer lacks capacity? What business policies are appropriate?
3. What are the dangers in assuming a protective position? How can a retailer avoid discrimination and extend appropriate protection?
4. What alternatives does a family have when an elderly member begins to lose capacity?

CHAPTER SUMMARY

Minors

Definition person who is under the age of majority (usually eighteen years)

Liability on Contracts minor's contracts are voidable at the minor's option

- *Disaffirmance* avoidance of the contract; may be done during minority and for a reasonable time after reaching majority
- *Restitution* a minor who has disaffirmed a contract is entitled to restitution from the other party for any benefit the minor has conferred on the other party; the courts differ regarding the obligation of the minor to make restitution to the other party
- *Ratification* affirmation of the entire contract; may be done upon reaching majority

Liability for Necessaries a minor is liable for the reasonable value of necessary items (those that reasonably supply a person's needs)

Liability for Misrepresentation of Age prevailing view is that a minor may disaffirm the contract

Liability for Tort Connected with Contract a minor is not liable in tort if a tort and a contract are so intertwined that to enforce the tort the court must enforce the contract

Incompetent and Intoxicated Persons

Person Under Guardianship a contract made by a mentally incompetent person placed under guardianship by court order is void

Mental Illness or Defect a contract entered into by a nonadjudicated mentally incompetent person (one who is unable to understand the nature and consequences of his acts) is voidable

Intoxicated Persons a contract entered into by an intoxicated person (one who cannot understand the nature and consequence of her actions) is voidable

QUESTIONS

1. Mark, a minor, operates a one-man automobile repair shop. Rose, having heard of Mark's good work on other cars, takes her car to Mark's shop for a thorough engine overhaul. Mark, while overhauling Rose's engine, carelessly fits an unsuitable piston ring on one of the pistons, with the result that Rose's engine is seriously damaged. Mark offers to return the sum that Rose paid him for his work, but refuses to pay for the damage. Rose sues Mark in tort for the damage to her engine. Can Rose recover from Mark in tort for the damage to her engine? Why?

2. Explain the outcome of each of the following transactions.
   a. On March 20, Andy Small turned seventeen years old, but he appeared to be at least twenty-one. On April 1, he moved into a rooming house in Chicago and orally agreed to pay the landlady $800 a month for room and board, payable at the end of each month. On April 30, he refused to pay his landlady for his room and board for the month of April.
   b. On April 4, he went to Honest Hal's Carfeteria and signed a contract to buy a used car on credit with a small down payment. He made no representation as to his age, but Honest Hal represented the car to be in top condition, which it subsequently turned out not to be. On April 25, he returned the car to Honest Hal and demanded a refund of his down payment.
   c. On April 7, Andy sold and conveyed to Adam Smith a parcel of real estate that he owned. On April 28, he demanded that Adam Smith reconvey the land although the purchase price, which Andy received in cash, had been spent in riotous living.

3. Jones, a minor, owned a 2013 automobile. She traded it to Stone for a 2014 car. Jones went on a three-week trip and found that the 2014 car was not as good as the 2013 car. She asked Stone to return the 2013 car but was told that it had been sold to Tate, who did not know that the car had been obtained by Stone from a minor. Jones thereupon sued Tate for the return of the 2013 car. Is Jones entitled to regain ownership of the 2013 car? Explain.

4. On May 7, Roy, a minor, a resident of Smithton, purchased an automobile from Royal Motors, Inc., for $12,750 in cash. On the same day, he bought a motor scooter from Marks, also a minor, for $1,750 and paid him in full. On June 5, two days before attaining his majority, Roy disaffirmed the contracts and offered to return the car and the motor scooter to the respective sellers. Royal Motors and Marks each refused the offers. On June 16, Roy brought separate appropriate actions against Royal Motors and Marks to recover the purchase price of the car and the motor scooter. By agreement on July 30, Royal Motors accepted the automobile. Royal then filed a counterclaim against Roy for the reasonable rental value of the car between June 5 and July 30. The car was not damaged during this period. Royal knew that Roy lived twenty-five miles from his place of employment in Smithton and that he

probably used the car, as he did, for transportation. What is the decision as to
   a. Roy's action against Royal Motors, Inc., and its counterclaim against Roy; and
   b. Roy's action against Marks?

5. On October 1, George Jones entered into a contract with Johnson Motor Company, a dealer in automobiles, to buy a car for $10,600. He paid $1,100 down and agreed to make monthly payments thereafter of $325 each. Although he made the first payment on November 1, he failed to make any more payments. Jones was seventeen years old at the time he made the contract, but he represented to the company that he was twenty-one years old because he was afraid the company would not sell the car to him if it knew his real age. His appearance was that of a man of twenty-one years of age. On December 15, the company repossessed the car under the terms provided in the contract. At that time, the car had been damaged and was in need of repairs. On December 20, George Jones became of age and at once disaffirmed the contract and demanded the return of the $1,425 paid on the contract. When the company refused to do so, Jones brought an action to recover the $1,425, and the company set up a counterclaim of $1,500 for expenses it incurred in repairing the car. Who will prevail? Why?

6. Rebecca entered into a written contract to sell certain real estate to Mary, a minor, for $80,000, payable $4,000 on the execution of the contract and $800 on the first day of each month thereafter until paid. Mary paid the $4,000 down payment and eight monthly installments before attaining her majority. Thereafter, Mary made two additional monthly payments and caused the contract to be recorded in the county where the real estate was located. Mary was then advised by her lawyer that the contract was voidable. After being so advised, Mary immediately tendered the contract to Rebecca, together with a deed reconveying all of Mary's interest in the property to Rebecca. Also, Mary demanded that Rebecca return the money paid under the contract. Rebecca refused the tender and declined to repay any portion of the money paid to her by Mary. Can Mary cancel the contract and recover the amount paid to Rebecca? Explain.

7. Anita sold and delivered an automobile to Marvin, a minor. Marvin, during his minority, returned the automobile to Anita, saying that he disaffirmed the sale. Anita accepted the automobile and said she would return the purchase price to Marvin the next day. Later in the day, Marvin changed his mind, took the automobile without Anita's knowledge, and sold it to Chris. Anita had not returned the purchase price when Marvin took the car. On what theory, if any, can Anita recover from Marvin? Explain.

8. Ira, who in 2012 had been found not guilty of a criminal offense because of insanity, was released from a hospital for the criminally insane during the summer of 2013 and since that time has been a reputable and well-respected citizen and businessperson. On February 1, 2014, Ira and Shirley entered

into a contract in which Ira would sell his farm to Shirley for $300,000. Ira now seeks to void the contract. Shirley insists that Ira is fully competent and has no right to avoid the contract. Who will prevail? Why?

9. Daniel, while under the influence of alcohol to the extent that he did not know the nature and consequences of his acts, agreed to sell his 2013 automobile to Belinda for $13,000. The next morning when Belinda went to Daniel's house with the $13,000 in cash, Daniel stated that he did not remember the transaction but that "a deal is a deal." One week after completing the sale, Daniel decides that he wishes to avoid the contract. What is the result?

CASE PROBLEMS

10. Langstraat, age seventeen, owned a motorcycle that he insured against liability with Midwest Mutual Insurance Company. He signed a notice of rejection attached to the policy indicating that he did not desire to purchase uninsured motorists' coverage from the insurance company. Later he was involved in an accident with another motorcycle owned and operated by a party who was uninsured. Langstraat now seeks to recover from the insurance company, asserting that his rejection was not valid because he is a minor. Can Langstraat recover from Midwest? Explain.

11. G.A.S. married his wife, S.I.S., on January 19, 1997. He began to have mental health problems in 2010; that year, he was hospitalized at the Delaware State Hospital for eight weeks. Similar illnesses occurred in 2008 and in the early part of 2014, with G.A.S. suffering from symptoms such as paranoia and loss of a sense of reality. In early 2015, G.A.S. was still committed to the Delaware State Hospital, attending a regular job during the day and returning to the hospital at night. G.A.S., however, was never adjudicated to be incompetent by any court. During this time, he entered into a separation agreement prepared by his wife's attorney which was grossly unfair to G.A.S. However, G.A.S. never spoke with the attorney about the contents of the agreement, nor did he read it prior to signing. Moreover, G.A.S. was not independently represented by counsel when he executed this agreement. Can G.A.S. disaffirm the separation agreement? Explain.

12. L. D. Robertson bought a pickup truck from King and Julian, who did business as the Julian Pontiac Company. At the time of purchase, Robertson was seventeen years old, living at home with his parents, and driving his father's truck around the county to different construction jobs. According to the sales contract, he traded in a passenger car for the truck and was given $723 credit toward the truck's $1,743 purchase price, agreeing to pay the remainder in monthly installments. After he paid the first month's installment, the truck caught fire and was rendered useless. The insurance agent, upon finding that Robertson was a minor, refused to deal with him. Consequently, Robertson sued to exercise his right as a minor to rescind the contract and to recover the purchase price he had already paid ($723 credit for the car traded in plus the one month's installment). The defendants argue that Robertson, even as a minor, cannot rescind the contract because it was for a necessary item. Are they correct?

13. A fifteen-year-old minor was employed by Midway Toyota, Inc. On August 18, 2013, the minor, while engaged in lifting heavy objects, injured his lower back. In October 2013 he underwent surgery to remove a herniated disk. Midway Toyota paid him the appropriate amount of temporary total disability payments ($153.36 per week) from August 18, 2013, through November 15, 2014. In February 2015 a final settlement was reached for 150 weeks of permanent partial disability benefits totaling $18,403.40. Tom Mazurek represented Midway Toyota in the negotiations leading up to the agreement and negotiated directly with the minor and his mother, Hermoine Parrent. The final settlement agreement was signed by the minor only. Mrs. Parrent was present at the time and did not object to the signing, but neither she nor anyone else of "legal guardian status" cosigned the agreement. The minor later sought to disaffirm the agreement and reopen his workers' compensation case. The workers' compensation court denied his petition, holding that Mrs. Parrent "participated fully in consideration of the offered final settlement and … ratified and approved it on behalf of her ward … to the same legal effect as if she had actually signed [it]…." The minor appealed. Decision?

14. Rose, a minor, bought a new Buick Riviera from Sheehan Buick. Seven months later, while still a minor, he attempted to disaffirm the purchase. Sheehan Buick refused to accept the return of the car or to refund the purchase price. Rose, at the time of the purchase, gave all the appearance of being of legal age. The car had been used by him to carry on his school, business, and social activities. Can Rose successfully disaffirm the contract?

15. Haydocy Pontiac sold Jennifer Lee a used automobile for $7,500, of which $6,750 was financed with a note and security agreement. At the time of the sale, Lee, age twenty, represented to Haydocy that she was twenty-one years old, the age of majority then, and capable of contracting. After receiving the car, Lee allowed John Roberts to take possession of it. Roberts took the car and has not returned. Lee has failed to make any further payments on the car. Haydocy has sued to recover on the note, but Lee disaffirms the contract, claiming that she was too young to enter into a valid contract. Can Haydocy recover the money from Lee? Explain.

16. Carol White ordered a $225 pair of contact lenses through an optometrist. White, an emancipated minor, paid $100 by check and agreed to pay the remaining $125 at a later time. The doctor ordered the lenses, incurring a debt of $110. After the lenses were ordered, White called to cancel her order and stopped payment on the $100 check. The lenses could be used by no one but White. The doctor sued White for the value of the lenses. Will the doctor be able to recover the money from White? Explain.

17. Halbman, a minor, purchased a 2010 Mercury from Lemke for $11,250. Under the terms of the contract, Halbman would pay $1,000 down and the balance in $250 weekly installments. Halbman purchased the car as a way to get around and have some fun. Upon making the down payment, Halbman received possession of the car, but Lemke retained the title until the balance was paid. After Halbman had made his first four payments, a connecting rod in the car's engine broke. Lemke denied responsibility but offered to help Halbman repair the engine if Halbman would provide the parts. Halbman, however, placed the car in a garage where the repairs cost $1,637.40. Halbman never paid the repair bill.

Hoping to avoid any liability for the vehicle, Lemke transferred title to Halbman even though Halbman never paid the balance owed. Halbman returned the title with a letter disaffirming the contract and demanded return of the money paid. Lemke refused. As the repair bill remained unpaid, the garage removed the car's engine and transmission and towed the body to Halbman's father's house. Vandalism during the period of storage rendered the car unsalvageable. Several times Halbman requested Lemke to remove the car. Lemke refused. Halbman sued Lemke for the return of his consideration, and Lemke countersued for the amount still owed on the contract. Decision?

18. On April 29, 2013, Kirsten Fletcher and John E. Marshall III jointly signed a lease to rent an apartment for the term beginning on July 1, 2013, and ending on June 30, 2014, for a monthly rent of $525 per month. At the time the lease was signed, Marshall was not yet eighteen years of age. Marshall turned eighteen on May 30, 2013. The couple moved into the apartment. About two months later, Marshall moved out to attend college, but Fletcher remained. She paid the rent herself for the remaining ten months of the lease and then sought contribution for Marshall's share of the rent plus court costs in the amount of $2,500. Can Fletcher collect from Marshall?

19. Rogers was a nineteen-year-old (the age of majority then being twenty-one) high school graduate pursuing a civil engineering degree when he learned that his wife was expecting a child. As a result, he quit school and sought assistance from Gastonia Personnel Corporation in finding a job. Rogers signed a contract with the employment agency providing that he would pay the agency a service charge if it obtained suitable employment for him. The employment agency found him such a job, but Rogers refused to pay the service charge, asserting that he was a minor when he signed the contract. Gastonia sued to recover the agreed-upon service charge from Rogers. Should Rogers be liable under his contract? If so, for how much?

TAKING SIDES

Joseph Eugene Dodson, age sixteen, purchased a used pickup truck from Burns and Mary Shrader. The Shraders owned and operated Shrader's Auto Sales. Dodson paid $14,900 in cash for the truck. At the time of sale, the Shraders did not question Dodson's age, but thought he was eighteen or nineteen. Dodson made no misrepresentation concerning his age. Nine months after the date of purchase, the truck began to develop mechanical problems. A mechanic diagnosed the problem as a burnt valve but could not be certain. Dodson, who could not afford the repairs, continued to drive the truck until one month later, when the engine "blew up." Dodson parked the vehicle in the front yard of his parents' home and contacted the Shraders to rescind the purchase of the truck and to request a full refund.

a. What arguments would support Dodson's termination of the contract?

b. What arguments would support Shrader's position that the contract is not voidable?

c. Which side should prevail? Explain.

Contracts in Writing

CHAPTER 15

To break an oral agreement which is not legally binding is morally wrong.

The Talmud

CHAPTER OUTCOMES

After reading and studying this chapter, you should be able to:

1. Identify and explain the five types of contracts covered by the general contract statute of frauds and the contracts covered by the Uniform Commercial Code (UCC) statute of frauds provision.

2. Describe the writings that are required to satisfy the general contract and the UCC statute of frauds provisions.

3. Identify and describe the other methods of complying with the general contract and the UCC statute of frauds provisions.

4. Explain the parol evidence rule and identify the situations to which the rule does not apply.

5. Discuss the rules that aid in the interpretation of a contract.

A n *oral* contract, that is, one not in writing, is in every way as enforceable as a written contract *unless* otherwise provided by statute. Although most contracts do not need to be in writing to be enforceable, it is highly desirable that significant contracts be written. Written contracts avoid many problems that proving the terms of oral contracts inevitably involve. The process of setting down the contractual terms in a written document also tends to clarify the terms and bring to light problems the parties might not otherwise foresee. Moreover, the terms of a written contract do not change over time, whereas the parties' recollections of the terms might.

When the parties do reduce their agreement to a complete and final written expression, the law (under the parol evidence rule) honors this document by not allowing the parties to introduce any evidence in a lawsuit that would alter, modify, or vary the terms of the written contract. Nevertheless, the parties may differ as to the proper or intended meaning of language contained in the written agreement where such language is ambiguous or susceptible to different interpretations. To determine the proper meaning requires an interpretation, or construction, of the contract. The rules of construction permit the parties to introduce evidence to resolve ambiguity and to show the meaning of the language employed and the sense in which both parties used it.

In this chapter, we will examine (1) the types of contracts that must be in writing to be enforceable, (2) the parol evidence rule, and (3) the rules of contractual interpretation.

STATUTE OF FRAUDS

Statute of frauds
specifies those contracts
that must be in writing to
be enforceable

The **statute of frauds** requires that certain designated types of contracts be evidenced by a writing to be enforceable. Many more types of contracts are not subject to the statute of frauds than are subject to it. Most oral contracts, as previously indicated, are as enforceable and valid as written contracts. If, however, a given contract subject to the statute of frauds is said to be within the statute, to be enforceable it must comply with the requirements of the statute. All other types of contracts are said to be "not within" or "outside" the statute and need not comply with its requirements to be enforceable.

The statute of frauds has no relation whatever to any kind of fraud practiced in the making of contracts. The rules relating to such fraud are rules of common law and are discussed in Chapter 11. The purpose of the statute is to prevent fraud in the proof of certain oral contracts by perjured testimony in court. This purpose is accomplished by requiring certain contracts to be proved by a signed writing. On the other hand, the statute does not prevent the performance of oral contracts if the parties are willing to perform. In brief, the statute relates only to the proof or evidence of a contract. It has nothing to do with the circumstances surrounding the making of a contract or with the validity of a contract.

Practical Advice

Significant contracts should be memorialized in a writing signed by both parties.

Contracts Within the Statute of Frauds [15-1]

The following five kinds of contracts are within the statute of frauds as most states have adopted it. Compliance requires a writing signed by the party to be charged (the party against whom the contract is to be enforced).

1. Promises to answer for the duty of another
2. Promises of an executor or administrator to answer personally for a duty of the decedent whose funds he is administering
3. Agreements upon consideration of marriage
4. Agreements for the transfer of an interest in land
5. Agreements not to be performed within one year

A sixth type of contract within the original English statute of frauds applied to contracts for the sale of goods. The Uniform Commercial Code (UCC) now governs the enforceability of contracts of this kind.

The various provisions of the statute of frauds apply independently. Accordingly, a contract for the sale of an interest in land also may be a contract in consideration of marriage, a contract not to be performed in one year, *and* a contract for the sale of goods.

In addition to those contracts specified in the original statute, most states require that other contracts be evidenced by a writing as well—for example, a contract to make a will, to authorize an agent to sell real estate, or to pay a commission to a real estate broker. In addition, UCC Article 9 requires that contracts creating certain types of security interests be in writing. On the other hand, UCC Revised Article 8, which all states have adopted, provides that the statute of frauds does *not* apply to contracts for the sale of securities. Finally, Article 1 of the UCC requires that contracts for the sale of other personal property for more than $5,000 be in writing. The 2001 Revisions to Article 1, however, has deleted this requirement.

Electronic Records [15-1a]

One significant impediment to e-commerce has been the questionable enforceability of contracts entered into through electronic means such as the Internet or e-mail because of the writing requirements under contract and sales law (statute of frauds). In response, the ***Uniform Electronic Transactions Act (UETA)*** was promulgated by the National Conference of Commissioners on Uniform State Laws (NCCUSL) in July 1999 and has been adopted by at least forty-seven states. UETA applies only to transactions between parties each of which has agreed to conduct transactions by electronic means. It gives full effect to electronic contracts, encouraging their widespread use, and develops a uniform legal framework for their implementation. UETA protects electronic signatures and contracts from being denied enforcement because of the statute of frauds. Section 7 of UETA accomplishes this by providing the following:

1. A record or signature may not be denied legal effect or enforceability solely because it is in electronic form.
2. A contract may not be denied legal effect or enforceability solely because an electronic record was used in its formation.
3. If a law requires a record to be in writing, an electronic record satisfies the law.
4. If a law requires a signature, an electronic signature satisfies the law.

Section 14 of UETA further validates contracts formed by machines functioning as electronic agents for parties to a transaction: "A contract may be formed by the interaction of electronic agents of the parties, even if no individual was aware of or reviewed the electronic agents' actions or the resulting terms and agreements." The Act excludes from its coverage wills, codicils, and testamentary trusts as well as all Articles of the UCC except Articles 2 and 2A.

In addition, Congress in 2000 enacted the ***Electronic Signatures in Global and National Commerce (E-Sign)***. The Act, which uses language very similar to that of UETA, makes electronic records and signatures valid and enforceable across the United States for many types of transactions in or affecting interstate or foreign commerce. E-Sign does not generally preempt UETA. E-Sign does not require any person to agree to use or accept electronic records or electronic signatures. The Act defines transactions quite broadly to include the sale, lease, exchange, and licensing of personal property and services, as well as the sale, lease, exchange, or other disposition of any interest in real property. E-Sign defines an electronic record as "a contract or other record created, generated, sent, communicated, received, or stored by electronic means." It defines an electronic signature as "an electronic sound, symbol, or process, attached to or logically associated with a contract or other record and executed or adopted by a person with the intent to sign the record." Like UETA, E-Sign ensures that Internet and e-mail agreements will not be unenforceable because of the statute of frauds by providing that

1. a signature, contract, or other record relating to such transaction may not be denied legal effect, validity, or enforceability solely because it is in electronic form; and
2. a contract relating to such transaction may not be denied legal effect, validity, or enforceability solely because an electronic signature or electronic record was used in its formation.

To protect consumers, E-Sign provides that they must consent *electronically* to conducting transactions with electronic records after being informed of the types of hardware and software required. Prior to consent, consumers must also receive a "clear and conspicuous" statement informing consumers of their right to (1) have the record provided on paper or in nonelectronic form; (2) after consenting to electronic records, receive paper copies of the electronic record; and (3) withdraw consent to receiving electronic records.

As defined by E-Sign, an electronic agent is a computer program or other automated means used independently to initiate an action or respond to electronic records or performances in whole or in part without review or action by an individual at the time of the action or response. The Act validates contracts or other records relating to a transaction in or affecting interstate or foreign commerce formed by electronic agents so long as the action of each electronic agent is legally attributable to the person to be bound.

E-Sign specifically excludes certain transactions, including (1) wills, codicils, and testamentary trusts; (2) adoptions, divorces, and other matters of family law; and (3) the UCC other than sales and leases of goods.

GOING GLOBAL

What about electronic commerce and electronic signatures in international contracts?

The United Nations Commission on International Trade Law (UNCITRAL) was established by the U.N. General Assembly to further the progressive harmonization and unification of the law of international trade. The Commission is composed of sixty member states elected by the General Assembly and is structured to be representative of the world's various geographic regions and its principal economic and legal systems. One of its primary functions is to develop conventions, model laws, and rules that are acceptable worldwide.

The UNCITRAL Model Law on Electronic Commerce, adopted in 1996, is intended to facilitate the use of modern means of communications and storage of information. Legislation based on it has been adopted in more than fifty nations and, in the United States, it has influenced the Uniform Electronic Transactions Act, promulgated by the Uniform Law Commission (ULC) in 1999 and adopted by nearly all of the states.

In 2001 the UNCITRAL Model Law on Electronic Signatures was adopted to bring additional legal certainty regarding the use of electronic signatures. Following a technology-neutral approach, the Act establishes a presumption that electronic signatures, which meet certain criteria of technical reliability, shall be treated as equivalent to handwritten signatures. Legislation based on it has been adopted in at least twenty-five nations.

Suretyship Provision [15-1b]

Suretyship provision
promise to pay the debts of another

Surety
person who promises to pay the debt of another

Principal debtor
person whose debt is being supported

Collateral promise
undertaking to be secondarily liable; that is, liable if the principal debtor does not perform

The **suretyship provision** applies to a contractual promise by a **surety** (*promisor*) to a *creditor* (*promisee*) to perform the duties or obligations of a third person (**principal debtor**) if the principal debtor does not perform. Thus, if a mother tells a merchant to extend $1,000 worth of credit to her son and says, "If he doesn't pay, I will," the promise is a suretyship and must be evidenced by a writing (or have a sufficient electronic record) to be enforceable. The factual situation can be reduced to the simple idea that, "If X doesn't pay, I will." The promise is said to be a **collateral promise**, in that the promisor is not primarily liable. The mother does not promise to pay in any event; her promise is to pay only if the one primarily obligated, the son, defaults.

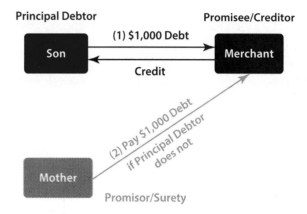

Thus, a suretyship involves three parties and two contracts. The primary contract, between the principal debtor and the creditor, creates the indebtedness. The collateral contract is made by the third person (surety) directly with the creditor, whereby the surety promises to pay the debt to the creditor in case the principal debtor fails to do so. For a complete discussion of suretyship, see Chapter 37. See *Rosewood Care Center, Inc. v. Caterpillar, Inc.* later in this chapter.

Original promise
promise to become primarily liable

Original Promise   If the promisor makes an **original promise** by undertaking to become primarily liable, then the statute of frauds does not apply. For example, a father tells a merchant to deliver certain items to his daughter and says, "I will pay $400 for them." The father is not promising to answer for the debt of another; rather, he is making the debt his own. It is to the father, and to the father alone, that the merchant extends credit; to the father alone the creditor may look for payment. The statute of frauds does not apply, and the promise may be oral.

Practical Advice

When entering into a contract with two parties promising you that they will perform, make them both original promisors and avoid having a surety. In any event, if the contract is for a significant amount of money, have both parties sign a written agreement.

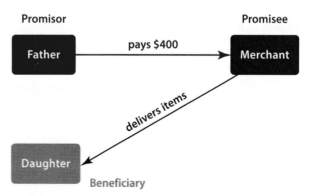

Main purpose
object of promisor/surety is to provide an economic benefit for herself

Main Purpose Doctrine   The courts have developed an exception to the suretyship provision called the "main purpose doctrine" or "leading object rule." In cases in which the **main purpose** of the promisor is to obtain an economic benefit for herself that she did not previously have, then the promise comes within the exception and is *outside* the statute. The expected benefit to the surety "must be such as to justify the conclusion that his main purpose in making the promise is to advance his own interest." The fact that the surety received consideration for his promise or that he might receive a slight and indirect advantage is insufficient to bring the promise within the main purpose doctrine.

Suppose that a supply company has refused to furnish materials on the credit of a building contractor. Faced with a possible slowdown in the construction of his building, the owner of the land promises the supplier that if the supplier will extend credit to the contractor, the owner will pay if the contractor does not. Here, the purpose of the promisor was to serve an economic interest of his own, even though the performance of the promise would discharge the duty of another. The intent to benefit the contractor was at most incidental, and courts will enforce oral promises of this type.

Rosewood Care Center, Inc., v. Caterpillar, Inc.
Supreme Court of Illinois, 2007
226 Ill.2d 559, 877 N.E.2d 1091, 315 Ill.Dec. 762
http://scholar.google.com/scholar_case?case=1422781429709921037&q=877+N.E.2d+1091&hl=en&as_sclt=2,22

FACTS On January 3, 2002, Caterpillar contacted HSM Management Services (HSM), the management agent for Plaintiff, Rosewood Care Center, Inc. (Rosewood), a skilled nursing facility. Caterpillar requested that Rosewood admit Betty Jo Cook, an employee of Caterpillar, on a "managed care basis (fixed rate)." HSM advised Caterpillar that Rosewood would not admit Cook on those terms. Shortly thereafter, on January 10, Dr. Norma Just, Caterpillar's employee in charge of medical care relating to workers' compensation claims, contacted HSM. Just told HSM that Cook had sustained a work-related injury and was receiving medical care at Caterpillar's expense under the workers' compensation laws. Just requested that Cook be admitted to Rosewood for skilled nursing care and therapy, and stated that the cost of Cook's care would be 100 percent covered and paid directly by Caterpillar to Rosewood with a zero deductible and no maximum limit. Just further advised HSM that Cook had been precertified for four weeks of care. Just asked that Rosewood send the bills for Cook's care to Caterpillar's workers' compensation division. On January 20, "Sue" from Dr. Just's office telephoned HSM and confirmed approval for Cook's transfer from the hospital to Rosewood. On January 30, Sue reconfirmed, via telephone, Caterpillar's authorization for Cook's care and treatment in accordance with the January 10 agreement, except that Sue now advised HSM that Cook was precertified for two weeks of care instead of the original four weeks. On January 30, Cook was admitted to Rosewood. Upon her admission, Cook signed a document entitled "Assignment of Insurance Benefits" as required by law. In this document, Cook assigned any insurance benefits she might receive to Rosewood and acknowledged her liability for any unpaid services. Caterpillar, through its health care management company, continued to orally "authorize" care for Cook and did so on February 8, February 25, March 11, March 21, April 8, April 18, May 16, and June 4. Cook remained at Rosewood until June 13, 2002. The total of Rosewood's charges for Cook's care amounted to $181,857. Caterpillar never objected to the bills being sent to it for Cook's care, nor did it ever advise Rosewood that treatment was not authorized. However, Caterpillar ultimately refused to pay for services rendered to Cook.

The plaintiff filed an action against Caterpillar seeking reimbursement for the services provided to Cook while she was a patient at Rosewood. In response, Caterpillar moved to dismiss the complaint, arguing that the alleged promise to pay for Cook's care was not enforceable because it was not in writing as required by the statute of frauds. The trial court granted Caterpillar's motion for summary judgment and Rosewood appealed. The appellate court reversed and remanded.

DECISION Judgment of the appellate court affirmed and remanded.

OPINION In general, the statute of frauds provides that a promise to pay the debt of another, that is, a suretyship agreement, is unenforceable unless it is in writing. According to Rosewood, Caterpillar's promise falls outside the statute of frauds pursuant to the "main purpose" or "leading object" rule. Under this rule, when the "main purpose" or "leading object" of the promisor/surety is to advance its own pecuniary or business interests, the promise does not fall within the statute. Caterpillar contended that the "main purpose" rule did not apply to its promises to Rosewood because the promises were not to promote its own interest. The question of whether Caterpillar's promise was within Caterpillar's "main purpose" or "leading object," is a factual one to be made based on evidence to be presented by the parties. Accordingly, this issue must be resolved by the trial court on remand.

INTERPRETATION When the "main purpose" or "leading object" of the surety is to advance its own pecuniary or business interests, the promise does not fall within the statute.

CRITICAL THINKING QUESTION Should the contracts of a surety have to be in writing? Explain.

Promise Made to Debtor The suretyship provision has been interpreted *not* to include promises made to a *debtor*. For example, D owes a debt to C. S promises D to pay D's debt. Because the promise of S was made to the debtor (D), not the creditor (C), the promise is enforceable even if it is oral.

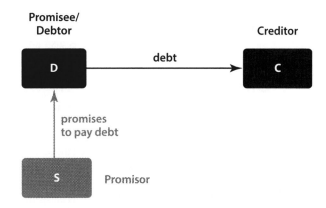

Executor-Administrator Provision [15-1c]

Executor-administrator provision
applies to promises to answer personally for a duty of the decedent

Executor-administrator
person appointed to settle a decedent's estate

The **executor-administrator provision** applies to the promises of an executor of a decedent's will, or to those of the administrator of the estate if there is no will, to answer personally for a duty of the decedent. An **executor** or **administrator** is a person appointed by a court to carry out, subject to order of court, the administration of the estate of a deceased person. If the will of a decedent nominates a certain person as executor, the court usually appoints that person. (For a more detailed discussion of executors, administrators, and the differences between the two, see Chapter 50.) If an executor or administrator promises to answer personally for a duty of the decedent, the promise is unenforceable unless it is in writing or in proper electronic form. For example, Edgar, who is Donna's son and executor of Donna's will, recognizes that Donna's estate will not have enough funds to pay all of the decedent's debts. He orally promises Clark, one of Donna's creditors, that he will personally pay all of his mother's debts in full. Edgar's oral promise is not enforceable. This provision does not apply, however, to promises to pay debts of the deceased out of assets of the estate.

The executor-administrator provision is thus a specific application of the suretyship provision. Accordingly, the exceptions to the suretyship provision also apply to this provision.

Marriage Provision [15-1d]

Marriage provision
applies to promises in consideration of marriage but not to mutual promises to marry

The notable feature of the **marriage provision** is that it does not apply to mutual promises to marry. Rather, the provision applies only if a promise to marry is made in consideration for some promise other than a mutual promise to marry. Therefore, this provision covers Adams's promise to convey title to a certain farm to Barnes if Barnes accepts Adams's proposal of marriage.

Land Contract Provision [15-1e]

Land contract provision
applies to promises to transfer any right, privilege, power, or immunity in real property

Interest in land
any right, privilege, power, or immunity in real property

The **land contract provision** covers promises to transfer any **interest in land**, which includes any right, privilege, power, or immunity in real property. Thus, all promises to transfer, buy, or pay for an interest in land, including ownership interests, leases, mortgages, options, and easements, are within the provision.

The land contract provision does not include contracts to transfer an interest in personal property. It also does not cover short-term leases, which by statute in most states are those for one year or less; contracts to build a building on a piece of land; contracts to do work on the land; or contracts to insure a building.

An oral contract for the transfer of an interest in land may be enforced if the party seeking enforcement has so changed his position in reasonable reliance on the contract that a court can prevent injustice only by enforcing the contract. In applying this *part performance* exception, many states require that the transferee has paid a portion or all of the purchase price *and* either has taken possession of the real estate or has started to make valuable improvements on the land. Payment of part or all of the price is not sufficient in itself to make the contract enforceable under this exception. For example, Jane orally agrees to sell land to Jack for $30,000. With Jane's consent, Jack takes possession of the land, pays Jane $10,000, builds a house on the land, and occupies it. Several years later, Jane repudiates the contract. The courts will enforce the contract against Jane.

An oral promise by a purchaser is also enforceable if the seller fully performs by conveying the property to the purchaser.

One-Year Provision [15-1f]

One-year provision

applies to contracts that cannot be performed within one year

The statute of frauds requires that all contracts that *cannot* be fully performed within one year of the making of the contract be in writing or in proper electronic form.

The Possibility Test   To determine whether a contract falls within the one-year provision, the courts ask whether it is *possible* for the performance of the contract to be completed within a year. Under the majority rule, the **possibility test** does not ask whether the agreement is likely to be performed within one year from the date it was formed; nor does it ask whether the parties think that performance will occur within the year. The enforceability of the contract depends *not* on probabilities or on actual subsequent events but on whether the terms of the contract make it possible for performance to occur within one year. For example, an oral contract between Alice and Bill for Alice to build a bridge, which should reasonably take three years, is generally enforceable if it is possible, although extremely unlikely and difficult, for Alice to perform the contract in one year. Similarly, if Alice agrees to employ Bill for life, this contract is also not within the statute of frauds. It is possible that Bill may die within the year, in which case the contract would be completely performed. The contract is therefore one that is *fully performable* within a year. Contracts of indefinite duration are likewise excluded from the provision. On the other hand, an oral contract to employ another person for thirteen months could not possibly be performed within a year and is therefore unenforceable.

Possibility test

if it is possible for the agreement to be performed within one year, it is not within the statute of frauds

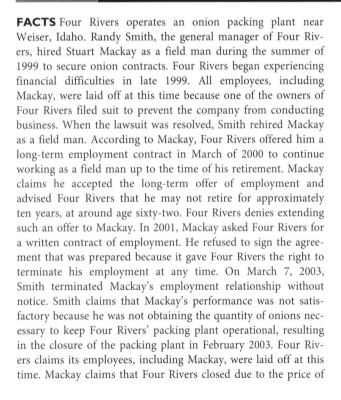

Mackay v. Four Rivers Packing Co.
Supreme Court of Idaho, 2008
179 P.3d 1064
http://scholar.google.com/scholar_case?case=3479455732652915832&q=179+P.+3d+1064+&hl=en&as_sdt=2,34

FACTS Four Rivers operates an onion packing plant near Weiser, Idaho. Randy Smith, the general manager of Four Rivers, hired Stuart Mackay as a field man during the summer of 1999 to secure onion contracts. Four Rivers began experiencing financial difficulties in late 1999. All employees, including Mackay, were laid off at this time because one of the owners of Four Rivers filed suit to prevent the company from conducting business. When the lawsuit was resolved, Smith rehired Mackay as a field man. According to Mackay, Four Rivers offered him a long-term employment contract in March of 2000 to continue working as a field man up to the time of his retirement. Mackay claims he accepted the long-term offer of employment and advised Four Rivers that he may not retire for approximately ten years, at around age sixty-two. Four Rivers denies extending such an offer to Mackay. In 2001, Mackay asked Four Rivers for a written contract of employment. He refused to sign the agreement that was prepared because it gave Four Rivers the right to terminate his employment at any time. On March 7, 2003, Smith terminated Mackay's employment relationship without notice. Smith claims that Mackay's performance was not satisfactory because he was not obtaining the quantity of onions necessary to keep Four Rivers' packing plant operational, resulting in the closure of the packing plant in February 2003. Four Rivers claims its employees, including Mackay, were laid off at this time. Mackay claims that Four Rivers closed due to the price of onions at the time. Mackay applied for unemployment benefits in 2003, stating in his application that he was laid off due to company financial difficulties. Smith states he offered to rehire Mackay in a different position later that year, and Mackay declined.

Mackay sued Four Rivers on August 24, 2004, claiming that Four Rivers breached his oral long-term employment contract. Four Rivers answered by alleging that a contract such as that claimed by Mackay is unenforceable under the Idaho Statute of Frauds because the agreement could not be performed within one year of its making and therefore Mackay was an "at will" employee. Four Rivers moved for summary judgment in October 2006, and the district court granted its motion.

DECISION The decision of the trial court is vacated, and the case is remanded.

OPINION The parties disagree regarding the proper application of Idaho's Statute of Frauds. The longstanding rule in Idaho is that where an agreement depends upon a condition that may ripen within a year, even though it may not mature until much later, the agreement does not fall within the Statute. Since the alleged contract here contains a term that it will last until Mackay retires, and Mackay could have retired within the first year, the oral contract does not violate the Statute. Under the prevailing interpretation of the one-year rule, the enforceability of a contract under the provision does not turn on the actual course of subsequent events, nor on the expectations of the parties as to the probabilities. Contracts of uncertain duration are simply excluded, and the provision covers only those contracts whose performance cannot possibly be completed within a year.

It is well settled that the oral contracts invalidated by the Statute because they are not to be performed within a year include only those that *cannot* be performed within that period. A promise which is not likely to be performed within a year, and which in fact is not performed within a year, is not within the Statute, if at the time the contract is made there is a possibility in law and in fact that full performance such as the parties intended may be completed before the expiration of a year. The question is not what the probable, or expected, or actual, performance of the contract was, but whether the contract, according to the reasonable

interpretation of its terms, required that it could not be performed within the year.

Idaho cases are in accord. A contract which is capable of being performed and might have been fully performed and terminated within a year does not fall within the Statute. Thus, the district court erred when it precluded enforcement of the contract alleged in this case. Since Mackay could have retired within one year under the terms of the alleged contract, this contract is outside Idaho's Statute of Frauds provision.

INTERPRETATION If it is possible to perform fully a contract within one year, the contract does not fall within the statute of frauds.

CRITICAL THINKING QUESTION Do you agree with the one-year provision? Explain.

Computation of time

the year runs from the time the agreement is made

Computation of Time
The year runs from the time the *agreement is made*, not from the time when the performance is to begin. For example, on January 1, 2014, A hires B to work for eleven months starting on May 1, 2014, under the terms of an oral contract. That contract will be fully performed on March 31, 2015, which is more than one year after January 1, 2014, the date the contract was made. Consequently, the contract is *within* the statute of frauds and unenforceable because it is oral.

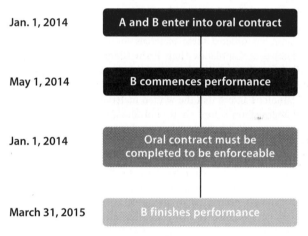

Jan. 1, 2014	A and B enter into oral contract
May 1, 2014	B commences performance
Jan. 1, 2014	Oral contract must be completed to be enforceable
March 31, 2015	B finishes performance

Similarly, a contract for a year's performance that is to begin three days after the date of the making of the contract is within the statute and, if oral, is unenforceable. If, however, the performance is to begin the day following the making or, under the terms of the agreement, *could* have begun the following day, it is not within the statute and need not be in writing.

Full performance by one party

makes the promise of the other party enforceable under majority view

Full Performance by One Party
Where a contract has been fully performed by one party, most courts hold that the promise of the other party is enforceable even though by its terms its performance was not possible within one year. For example, Jane borrows $4,800 from Tom. Jane orally promises to pay Tom $4,800 in three annual installments of $1,600. Jane's promise is enforceable, despite the one-year provision, because Tom has fully performed by making the loan.

Sale of goods

a contract for the sale of goods for the price of $500 or more must be evidenced by a writing to be enforceable

Sale of Goods [15-1g]
The English statute of frauds, which applied to contracts for the sale of goods, has been used as a prototype for the UCC, Article 2, statute of frauds provision. The UCC provides that a contract

for the sale of goods for the price of **$500 or more** is not enforceable unless there is some writing or record sufficient to indicate that a contract for sale has been made between the parties. The Code defines *goods* as movable personal property.

Admission

Admission
an admission in pleadings, testimony, or otherwise in court makes the contract enforceable for the quantity of goods admitted

Admission The Code permits an oral contract for the sale of goods to be enforced against a party who, in his pleading, testimony, or otherwise, admits in court that a contract was made; but the Code limits enforcement to the quantity of goods he admits. Moreover, some courts hold that, by performing over a period of time, for example, a party may implicitly admit the existence of a contract. Some courts now apply this exception to other statute of frauds provisions.

Specially manufactured goods
an oral contract for specially manufactured goods is enforceable

Specially Manufactured Goods The Code permits enforcement of an oral contract for goods specially manufactured for a buyer, but only if evidence indicates that the goods were made for the buyer and the seller can show that he has made a *substantial beginning* of their manufacture before receiving any notice of repudiation. If the goods, although manufactured on special order, may be readily resold in the ordinary course of the seller's business, this exception does not apply.

Kalas v. Cook
Appellate Court of Connecticut, 2002
70 Conn.App. 477, 800 A.2d 553, 47 UCC Rep.Serv.2d 1307
http://scholar.google.com/scholar_case?case=9737435026218396545&q=800+A.2d+553&hl=en&as_sdt=2,34

FACTS The plaintiff, Barbara H. Kalas, doing business as Clinton Press, operated a printing press and, for several decades, provided written materials, including books and pamphlets, for Adelma G. Simmons. Simmons ordered these materials for use and sale at her farm, known as Caprilands Herb Farm (Caprilands). The defendant has not suggested that these materials could have been sold on the open market. Due to limited space at Caprilands, the plaintiff and Simmons agreed that the written materials would remain stored at the plaintiff's print shop until Simmons decided that delivery was necessary. The materials were delivered either routinely or upon request by Simmons and were paid for according to the invoice from plaintiff.

In early 1997, the plaintiff decided to close her business. The plaintiff and Simmons agreed that the materials printed for Caprilands and stored at the plaintiff's print shop would be delivered and paid for upon delivery. On December 3, 1997, Simmons died. The plaintiff submitted a claim against the estate for $24,599.38 for unpaid deliveries to Caprilands. (The defendant, Edward W. Cook, is the executor of the estate of Simmons.) The defendant denied these allegations and raised a defense under the statute of frauds.

The trial ruled that as a contract for the sale of goods, its enforcement was not precluded by the Uniform Commercial Code (UCC) statute of frauds provision. Accordingly, the court rendered a judgment in favor of the plaintiff in the amount of $24,599.38. The defendant appealed.

DECISION Judgment affirmed.

OPINION On appeal, the defendant argued that the oral contract was invalid because a writing was required by the UCC. Contracts for the sale of goods at a price of $500 or more are presumptively unenforceable. However, under the Code, an oral contract for the sale of goods is enforceable if the goods in question are "specially manufactured." In determining whether goods are specially manufactured, courts generally apply a four-part standard:

(1) the goods must be specially made for the buyer; (2) the goods must be unsuitable for sale to others in the ordinary course of the seller's business; (3) the seller must have substantially begun to have manufactured the goods or to have a commitment for their procurement; and (4) the manufacture or commitment must have been commenced under circumstances reasonably indicating that the goods are for the buyer and prior to the seller's receipt of notification of contractual repudiation.

The term "specially manufactured," therefore, refers to the nature of the particular goods in question and not to whether the goods were made in an unusual, as opposed to the regular, business operation or manufacturing process of the seller. Printed material, particularly that, as in this case, names the buyer, has been deemed by both state and federal courts to fall within the exception set out for specially manufactured goods.

The printed materials in this case were specially manufactured goods. The materials were printed specifically for Caprilands. The materials included brochures and labels with the Caprilands' name, as well as books that were written and designed by Simmons. The plaintiff testified that the books were printed, as Simmons had requested, in a rustic style with typed inserts and hand-drawn pictures. Therefore, none of these materials was suitable for sale to others. Thus, the agreement for their production was not required to be in writing.

INTERPRETATION An oral contract for the sale of goods is enforceable if the goods in question are specially manufactured.

ETHICAL QUESTION Did the executor of Simmons' estate act ethically? Explain.

CRITICAL THINKING QUESTION Do you agree with the court's decision? Explain.

Delivery or payment and acceptance validates the contract only for the goods that have been accepted or for which payment has been accepted

Delivery or Payment and Acceptance   Under the Code, delivery and acceptance of part of the goods, or payment and acceptance of part of the price, validates the contract but only for the goods that have been accepted or for which payment has been accepted. To illustrate, Liz orally agrees to buy one thousand watches from David for $15,000. David delivers three hundred watches to Liz, who receives and accepts the watches. The oral contract is enforceable to the extent of three hundred watches ($4,500)—those received and accepted—but is unenforceable to the extent of seven hundred watches ($10,500).

A summary of the contracts within, and the exceptions to, the statute of frauds is provided in Concept Review 15-1.

Modification or rescission of contracts within the statute of frauds oral contracts modifying existing contracts are unenforceable if the resulting contract is within the statute of frauds

Modification or Rescission of Contracts Within the Statute of Frauds [15-1h]

Oral contracts modifying previously existing contracts are unenforceable if the resulting contract is within the statute of frauds. The reverse is also true: an oral modification of a prior contract is enforceable if the new contract is not within the statute of frauds.

Thus, examples of unenforceable oral contracts include an oral promise to guarantee the additional duties of another, an oral agreement to substitute different land for that described in the original contract, and an oral agreement to extend an employee's contract for six months to a total of two years. On the other hand, an oral agreement to modify an employee's contract from two years to six months at a higher salary is not within the statute of frauds and is enforceable.

Under the UCC, the decisive point is the contract price after modification. If the parties enter into an oral contract to sell for $450 a motorcycle to be delivered to the buyer and later, prior to delivery, orally agree that the seller shall paint the motorcycle and install new tires and that the buyer shall pay a price of $550, the modified contract is unenforceable. Conversely, if the parties have a written contract for the sale of two hundred bushels of wheat at a price of $4.00 per bushel and later orally agree to decrease the quantity to one hundred bushels at the same price per bushel, the agreement as modified is for a total price of $400 and thus is enforceable.

Practical Advice

When significantly modifying an existing common law contract, make sure that consideration is given and that the modification is in writing and signed by both parties.

CONCEPT REVIEW 15-1

The Statute of Frauds

Contracts Within the Statute of Frauds	Exceptions
Suretyship—a promise to answer for the duty of another	• Main purpose rule • Original promise • Promise made to debtor
Executor-Administrator—a promise to answer personally for debt of decedent	• Main purpose rule • Original promise • Promise made to debtor
Agreements made upon consideration of marriage	• Mutual promises to marry
Agreements for the transfer of an interest in land	• Part performance plus detrimental reliance • Seller conveys property
Agreements not to be performed within one year	• Full performance by one party • Possibility of performance within one year
Sale of goods for $500 or more	• Admission • Specially manufactured goods • Delivery or payment and acceptance

An oral rescission is effective and discharges all unperformed duties under the original contract. For example, Jones and Brown enter into a written contract of employment for a two-year term. Later they orally agree to rescind the contract. The oral agreement is effective, and the written contract is rescinded. Where land has been transferred, however, an agreement to rescind the transaction is a contract to retransfer the land and is within the statute of frauds.

COMPLIANCE WITH THE STATUTE OF FRAUDS [15-2]

Even a contract within the statute of frauds will be enforced if it is contained in a *writing, memorandum,* or *record* sufficient to satisfy the statute's requirements. As long as the writing or record meets those requirements, it need not be in any specific form, nor be an attempt by the parties to enter into a binding contract, nor represent their entire agreement.

General Contract Provisions [15-2a]

The English statute of frauds and most modern statutes of frauds require that the agreement be evidenced by a writing or record to be enforceable. The statute's purpose in requiring a writing or record is to ensure that the parties have actually entered into a contract. It is, therefore, not necessary that the writing or record be in existence when the parties initiate litigation; it is sufficient to show that the memorandum existed at one time. The note, memorandum, or record, which may be formal or informal, must

1. specify the parties to the contract,
2. specify with reasonable certainty the subject matter and the essential terms of the unperformed promises, and
3. be signed by the party to be charged or by her agent.

The memorandum may be such that the parties themselves view it as having no legal significance whatever. For example, a personal letter between the parties, an interdepartmental communication, an advertisement, or the record books of a business may serve as a memorandum. The writing need not have been delivered to the party who seeks to take advantage of it, and it may even contain a repudiation of the oral agreement. For example, Sid and Gail enter into an oral agreement that Sid will sell Blackacre to Gail for $5,000. Sid subsequently receives a better offer and sends Gail a signed letter, which begins by reciting all the material terms of the oral agreement. The letter concludes: "Because my agreement to sell Blackacre to you for $5,000 was oral, I am not bound by my promise. I have since received a better offer and will accept that one." Sid's letter constitutes a sufficient memorandum for Gail to enforce Sid's promise to sell Blackacre. Because Gail did not sign the memorandum, however, the writing does not bind her. Thus, a contract may be enforceable against only one of the parties.

The "signature" may be initials or may even be typewritten or printed, as long as the party intended it to authenticate the writing or record. Furthermore, the signature need not be at the bottom of the page or at the customary place for a signature.

The memorandum may consist of several papers or documents, none of which would be sufficient by itself. The several memoranda, however, must together satisfy all of the requirements of a writing to comply with the statute of frauds and must clearly indicate that they relate to the same transaction. The latter requirement can be satisfied if (1) the writings are physically connected, (2) the writings refer to each other, or (3) an examination of the writings shows them to be in reference to each other.

Compliance: general contract law

the writing or writings must (1) specify the parties to the contract; (2) specify the subject matter and essential terms; and (3) be signed by the party to be charged or by her agent

Practical Advice

To avoid becoming solely liable by signing a contract before the other party signs, include a provision to the effect that no party is bound to the contract until all parties sign the contract.

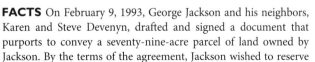

Estate of Jackson v. Devenyns
Supreme Court of Wyoming, 1995
892 P.2d 786
http://scholar.google.com/scholar_case?case=11233159489095516955&q=892+P.2d.786&hl=en&as_sdt=2,34

FACTS On February 9, 1993, George Jackson and his neighbors, Karen and Steve Devenyn, drafted and signed a document that purports to convey a seventy-nine-acre parcel of land owned by Jackson. By the terms of the agreement, Jackson wished to reserve a 1.3 acre portion of the parcel. Although the agreement contained a drawing and dimensions of the conveyance, it did not contain a specific description of the parcel. Jackson died on May 8, 1993, and his estate refused to honor the agreement. The Devenyns then filed a petition with the probate court to order a conveyance. Based on the parol evidence rule, the estate of Jackson objected to the admission of the witnesses' testimony that they could point out the specific area based on conversations with Jackson. However, the probate court heard the testimony and determined that, with the witnesses' testimony, a sufficient description of the parcel could be determined. Accordingly, it granted the petition. The estate appeals.

DECISION Judgment reversed.

OPINION A written memorandum purporting to convey real estate must sufficiently describe the property to comply with the requirements of the statute of frauds and permit specific performance. A valid contract to convey land must expressly contain a description of the land, certain in itself or capable of being rendered certain by reference to an extrinsic source that the writing itself designates. It is expressly prohibited to supply the writing's essential provisions by inferences or presumptions deduced from oral testimony. This writing insufficiently describes the property it purports to convey, to reserve, and for which it grants an option

to purchase. The writing's description of the property to be conveyed states: "George Jackson agrees to sell 79 acres...." Such a description is insufficiently definite to identify the land without recourse to extrinsic evidence. When a writing states only the total acreage without any description of the location of the land involved, the statute of frauds' requirement that the subject matter be reasonably certain is not satisfied and the contract is void. The present description provides only the total acreage and does not provide any certainty that this particular tract was intended to be conveyed. Therefore, this agreement is too uncertain to be enforced.

INTERPRETATION A writing to comply with the general contract statute of frauds must (1) specify the parties to the contract, (2) specify with reasonable certainty the subject matter and the essential terms of the promises, and (3) be signed by the party to be charged or by her agent.

CRITICAL THINKING QUESTION Should the statute of frauds provision mandate that the writing contain a reasonably certain description of the land? Explain.

Compliance: sale of goods

the writing or writings must (1) be sufficient to indicate that a contract has been made between the parties, (2) be signed by the party against whom enforcement is sought or by her authorized agent, and (3) specify the quantity of goods to be sold

Practical Advice

Merchants should examine written confirmations carefully and promptly to make certain that they are accurate.

Sale of Goods [15-2b]

The statute of frauds provision under Article 2 (Sales) of the UCC is more liberal. For a sale of goods, the Code requires merely a writing or record (1) sufficient to indicate that a contract has been made between the parties, (2) signed by the party against whom enforcement is sought or by her authorized agent or broker, and (3) specifying the *quantity* of goods or securities to be sold. The writing or record is sufficient even if it omits or incorrectly states an agreed-upon term; however, if the quantity term is misstated, the contract can be enforced only to the extent of the quantity stated in the writing or record.

As with general contracts, several related documents may satisfy the writing requirement. Moreover, the "signature" may be by initials or even typewritten or printed, so long as the party intended to authenticate the writing or record.

In addition, between merchants, if one party, within a reasonable time after entering into the oral contract, sends a written confirmation of the contract for a sale of goods to the other party and the written confirmation is sufficient against the sender, it is also sufficient against the recipient of the confirmation unless the recipient gives written notice of his objection within ten days after receiving the confirmation. This means that if these requirements have been met, the recipient of the writing or record is in the same position he would have assumed by signing it, and the confirmation, therefore, is enforceable against him.

For example, Brown Co. and ANM Industries enter into an oral contract that provides that ANM will deliver twelve thousand shirts to Brown at $6.00 per shirt. Brown sends a letter to ANM acknowledging the agreement. The letter is signed by Brown's president, contains the quantity term but not the price, and is mailed to ANM's vice president for sales. Brown is bound by the contract once its authorized agent signs the letter, while ANM cannot raise the defense of the statute of frauds ten days after receiving the letter if it does not object within that time.

EFFECT OF NONCOMPLIANCE [15-3]

Under both the statute of frauds and the Code, the basic legal effect is the same: a contracting party has a defense to an action by the other party for enforcement of an *unenforceable* oral contract—that is, an oral contract that falls within the statute and does not comply with its requirements. For example, if Kirkland, a painter, and Riggsbee, a homeowner, make an oral contract under which Riggsbee is to give Kirkland a certain tract of land in return for the painting of Riggsbee's house, the contract is unenforceable under the statute of frauds. It is a contract for the

BUSINESS LAW **IN ACTION**

When *should* a writing or record be used to memorialize a contract? The statute of frauds identifies those categories of contracts that must be evidenced by a writing or record to be enforced, but it does not prevent us from using written contracts when they are not legally called for nor does it preclude us from entering into an agreement without one.

Any time there is a doubt about the other party's ability to perform or a likelihood of future dispute over terms, the parties should have a writing—however brief or informal. For example, one should consider putting in writing service contracts that will be completed in less than a year, such as construction contracts, professional contracts, or other contracts for personal service, even though they typically do not fall within the statute of frauds.

On the other hand, there are times when insisting on a writing might actually undermine an agreement. The most common reason for disregarding the statute of frauds is business expediency. Even though goods valued at greater than $500 may be involved, the seller may not want to "bother" with the formality of a writing, and there may be a buyer who is equally motivated to consummate the transaction. Waiting for a written agreement might mean losing out on the deal. In such a case, however, both parties must understand that if the other party fails to perform, the agreement will be unenforceable.

Commerce is dynamic: depending on the type of agreement involved, it can be fast paced and fluid or it can be deliberate and painstaking. Understanding the statute of frauds is important, but one may also wish to consider other factors in deciding whether to put a contract in writing.

sale of an interest in land. Either party can repudiate and has a defense to an action by the other to enforce the contract.

Full Performance [15-3a]

Full performance

statute does not apply to executed contracts

After *all* the promises of an oral contract have been *performed* by all the parties, the statute of frauds no longer applies. Accordingly, neither party may ask the court to rescind the executed oral contract on the basis that it did not meet the statute's requirements. Thus, the statute applies to executory contracts only.

Restitution [15-3b]

Restitution

when a contract is unenforceable because of the statute of frauds, a party may recover in restitution the benefits conferred on the other party in performance of the contract

A party to a contract that is unenforceable because of the statute of frauds may have, nonetheless, acted in reliance upon the contract. In such a case, the party may recover in **restitution** the benefits he conferred upon the other in relying upon the unenforceable contract. Most courts require, however, that the party seeking restitution not be in default.

The Restatement of Restitution provides that a person who renders performance under an agreement that cannot be enforced by reason of the failure to satisfy the statute of frauds has a claim in restitution to prevent unjust enrichment. In such a case, that party may recover in restitution the benefits he directly conferred on the other as the performance required or invited by the unenforceable contract.

Thus, if Matthew makes an oral contract to furnish services to Rachel that are not to be performed within a year, and Rachel discharges Matthew after three months, Matthew may recover in restitution the value of the services rendered during the three months. Similarly, Lenny enters into an oral contract to sell land to Elaine, and Elaine pays a portion of the price as a down payment. Lenny subsequently repudiates the oral contract. Elaine may recover in restitution the portion of the price she paid.

Promissory Estoppel [15-3c]

Promissory estoppel

oral contracts will be enforced where the party seeking enforcement has reasonably and justifiably relied on the promise and the court can avoid injustice only by enforcement

A growing number of courts have used the doctrine of **promissory estoppel** to displace the requirement of a writing by enforcing oral contracts within the statute of frauds in cases in which the party seeking enforcement has reasonably and foreseeably relied upon a promise in such a way that the court can avoid injustice only by enforcing the promise. The remedy granted is limited, as justice requires, and depends on such factors as the availability of other remedies; the foreseeability, reasonableness, and substantiality of the reliance; and the extent to which reliance corroborates evidence of the promise. The use of promissory estoppel, however, to avoid the writing requirement of the statute of frauds has gained little acceptance in cases involving the sale of goods.

PAROL EVIDENCE RULE

A contract reduced to writing and signed by the parties is frequently the result of many conversations, conferences, proposals, counterproposals, letters, and memoranda; sometimes it is also the product of negotiations conducted, or partly conducted, by agents of the parties. At some stage in the negotiations, the parties or their agents may have reached tentative agreements that were superseded (or regarded as such by one of the parties) by subsequent negotiations. Offers may have been made and withdrawn, either expressly or by implication, or forgotten in the give-and-take of negotiations. Ultimately, though, the parties prepare and sign a final draft of the written contract, which may or may not include all of the points that they discussed and agreed on in the course of the negotiations. By signing the agreement, despite its potential omissions, the parties have declared it to be their contract, and the terms as contained in it represent the contract they have made. As a rule of substantive law, neither party is later permitted to show that the contract they made is different from the terms and provisions that appear in the written agreement. This rule, which also applies to wills and deeds, is called the "parol evidence" rule.

THE RULE [15-4]

Parol evidence rule
excludes inconsistent prior and contemporaneous oral and written agreements not incorporated into an integrated contract

Integrated contract
complete and exclusive agreement of the parties

Practical Advice

If your contract is intended to be the complete and final agreement, make sure that all terms are included and state your intention that the writing is complete and final. If you do not intend the writing to be complete or final, make sure that you so indicate in the writing itself.

When the parties express their contract in a writing that is intended to be the complete and final expression of their rights and duties, the **parol evidence rule** excludes *prior* oral or written negotiations or agreements of the parties or their *contemporaneous* oral agreements that *vary* or *change* an integrated written contract. The word *parol* literally means "speech" or "words." The term *parol evidence* refers to any evidence, whether oral or in writing, that is outside the written contract and not incorporated into it either directly or by reference.

The parol evidence rule applies only to an **integrated contract**, that is, one contained in a certain writing or writings to which the parties have assented as being the statement of the complete and exclusive agreement or contract between them. When there is such an integration of a contract, the courts will not permit parol evidence of any prior or contemporaneous agreement to vary, change, alter, or modify any of the terms or provisions of the written contract.

The reason for the rule is that the parties, by reducing their entire agreement to writing, are regarded as having intended the writing that they signed to include the whole of their agreement. The terms and provisions contained in the writing are there because the parties intended them to be in their contract. Conversely, the courts regard the parties as having omitted intentionally any provision not in the writing. The rule, by excluding evidence that would tend to change, alter, vary, or modify the terms of the written agreement, safeguards the contract as made by the parties. The rule, which applies to all integrated written contracts, deals with what terms are part of the contract. The rule differs from the statute of frauds, which governs what contracts must be evidenced by a writing to be enforceable. Does the parol evidence rule or the statute of frauds apply to the situation presented in the Ethical Dilemma at the end of this chapter?

Jenkins v. Eckerd Corporation
District Court of Appeal of Florida, First District, 2005
913 So.2d 43
http://scholar.google.com/scholar_case?case=12402686802007965629&hl=en&as_sdt=2&as_vis=1&oi=scholarr

FACTS In January 1991, Sandhill entered into a lease agreement with K & B Florida Corporation (K & B), a pharmaceutical retailer, providing for the rental of a parcel of real property located in the Gulf Breeze Shopping Center in Gulf Breeze, Florida. Shortly before the execution of the K & B Lease, Sandhill had leased space in the shopping center to Delchamps, Inc., a regional supermarket chain, as the "anchor" tenant in the shopping center.

Article 2B of the K & B Lease referred to the Delchamps lease and provided:

> ARTICLE 2
> B. Lessor represents to Lessee that Lessor has entered into leases with the following named concerns: with Delchamps, Inc. (Delchamps) for a minimum of 45,000 square feet for supermarket grocery store and that Lessor will construct and offer for lease

individual retail shops for a minimum of 21,000 square feet for various retail uses, all located and dimensioned shown on the attached Plot Plan, … The continued leasing and payment of rent for their store in the Shopping Center by Delchamps is part of the consideration to induce Lessee to lease and pay rent for its store, … Accordingly, should Delchamps fail or cease to lease and pay rent for its store in the Shopping Center during the Lease Term as hereinafter set out, Lessee shall have the right and privilege of: (a) canceling this Lease and of terminating all of its obligations hereunder at any time thereafter upon written notice by Lessee to Lessor, and such cancellation and termination shall be effective ninety (90) days after the mailing of such written notice; …

The K & B Lease contained an integration clause which provided that "[t]his lease contains all of the agreements made between the parties hereto and may not be modified orally or in any manner other than by an agreement in writing." The Delchamps' lease included an assignment provision which granted Delchamps "the right, at any time after the commencement of the term hereof, to assign this lease."

In September 1997, Jitney Jungle Stores of America, Inc. (Jitney Jungle), another grocery store operator, acquired Delchamps and continued the operation of the Delchamps' grocery store in the shopping center. In 1998, Eckerd acquired the K & B drugstore. The K & B Lease was assigned to Eckerd, which began operating an Eckerd drugstore in the leased premises. In October 1999, Jitney Jungle filed for bankruptcy protection under Chapter 11 of the U.S. Bankruptcy Code. Thereafter, an order was entered in the bankruptcy proceeding approving Delchamps' assignment of its lease in the shopping center to Bruno's Supermarkets, Inc. (Bruno's). Since the assignment, Bruno's has occupied the leased premises under the assigned Delchamps' lease and has operated a Bruno's grocery store. Sandhill did not provide notice to, or obtain consent from, Eckerd of this assignment. On June 22, 2001, Eckerd notified Sandhill that, because Delchamps had ceased to lease and pay rent for its store in the shopping center, pursuant to the K & B Lease, Eckerd was canceling its lease effective September 20, 2001. Sandhill filed suit against Eckerd for an alleged breach of the shopping center lease. At trial, Sandhill sought to introduce testimony relating to its negotiations of the K & B Lease to explain the parties' intent in drafting the allegedly ambiguous language in article 2B. The trial court prohibited the introduction of this evidence under the parol evidence rule. The district court entered a judgment in favor of Eckerd. This appeal was filed.

DECISION Judgment affirmed.

OPINION It is a fundamental rule of contract interpretation that a contract which is clear, complete, and unambiguous does not require judicial construction. The K & B Lease (article 2B) clearly and unambiguously gave the lessee the option to cancel the lease if Delchamps ceased to lease its store.

Sandhill argues that the trial court erred in applying the parol evidence rule and refusing to allow the introduction of extrinsic evidence in interpreting article 2B of the Lease. However, if a contract provision is "clear and unambiguous," a court may not consider extrinsic or "parol" evidence to change the plain meaning set forth in the contract. Sandhill contends that parol evidence was admissible below since the lease is incomplete and contains a latent ambiguity. A latent ambiguity arises when a contract on its face appears clear and unambiguous, but fails to specify the rights or duties of the parties in certain situations. Sandhill incorrectly argues that, while the reference in article 2B of the K & B Lease to the Delchamps' lease may be "unambiguous" when read literally, this reference was not "clear" or "complete" with regard to the operation of the lease should the Delchamps' lease be assigned. The operation of the parol evidence rule encourages parties to embody their complete agreement in a written contract and fosters reliance upon the written contract. "The parol evidence rule serves as a shield to protect a valid, complete and unambiguous written instrument from any verbal assault that would contradict, add to, or subtract from it, or affect its construction." The terms of an integrated (complete and exclusive) written contract can be varied by extrinsic evidence only to the extent that the terms are ambiguous and are given meaning by the extrinsic evidence. The K & B Lease is an integrated agreement complete in all essential terms.

Furthermore, article 2B is not in the least unclear or incomplete. It contains no latent or patent ambiguity. Although article 2B does not mention assignment by Delchamps, it unambiguously grants the lessee the right to terminate the K & B Lease if Delchamps ceases to lease and pay rent for its store in the shopping center *for any reason.*

INTERPRETATION The parol evidence rule encourages parties to embody their complete agreement in an integrated written contract and fosters reliance upon the written contract.

CRITICAL THINKING QUESTION Do you agree with the parol evidence rule? Explain.

SITUATIONS TO WHICH THE RULE DOES NOT APPLY [15-5]

The parol evidence rule, in spite of its name, is not an exclusionary rule of evidence; nor is it a rule of construction or interpretation. Rather, it is a rule of substantive law that defines the limits of a contract. Bearing this in mind, as well as the reason underlying the rule, you will readily understand that the rule does *not* apply to any of the following situations (see Figure 15-1 for an overview of the parol evidence rule):

1. A contract that is *partly* written and partly oral—that is, a contract in which the parties do not intend the writing to be their entire agreement.
2. A clerical or *typographical error* that obviously does not represent the agreement of the parties. Where, for example, a written contract for the services of a skilled mining engineer provides that his rate of compensation is to be $8.00 per day, a court of equity would

Figure 15-1 Parol Evidence Rule

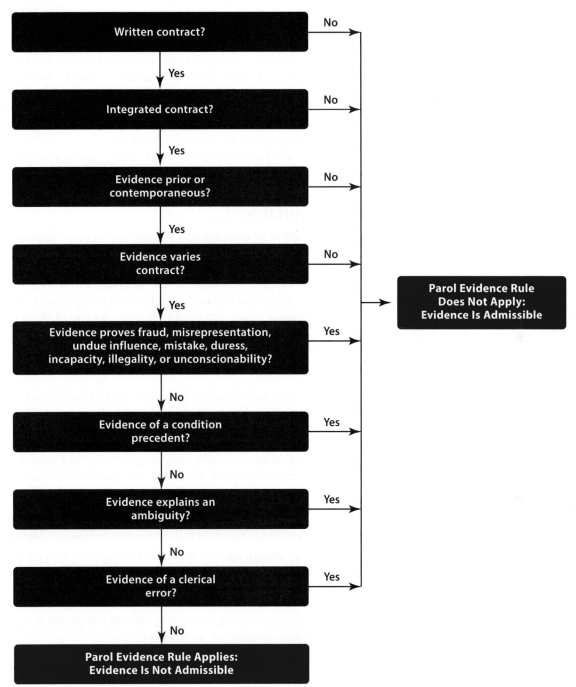

permit reformation (correction) of the contract to correct the mistake if both parties intended the rate to be $800 per day.

3. The lack of *contractual capacity* of one of the parties through, for instance, minority, intoxication, or mental incompetency. Such evidence would not tend to vary, change, or alter any of the terms of the written agreement but rather would show that the written agreement was voidable or void.

4. A *defense* of fraud, misrepresentation, duress, undue influence, mistake, illegality, lack of consideration, or other invalidating cause. Evidence establishing any of these defenses would not purport to vary, change, or alter any of the terms of the written agreement but rather would show such agreement to be voidable, void, or unenforceable.

5. A *condition precedent* to which the parties agreed orally at the time of the execution of the written agreement and to which the entire agreement was made subject. Such evidence does not tend to vary, alter, or change any of the terms of the agreement; rather, it shows whether the entire unchanged written agreement ever became effective.

6. A *subsequent mutual rescission* or *modification* of the written contract. Parol evidence of a later agreement does not tend to show that the integrated writing did not represent the contract between the parties at the time the writing was made.

7. Parol evidence is admissible to explain *ambiguous* terms in the contract. To enforce a contract, it is necessary to understand its intended meaning. Nevertheless, such interpretation is not to alter, change, or vary the terms of the contract.

8. A *separate contract;* the rule does not prevent a party from proving the existence of a separate, distinct contract between the same parties.

SUPPLEMENTAL EVIDENCE [15-6]

Although a written agreement cannot be contradicted by evidence of a prior agreement or of a contemporaneous agreement, under the Restatement and the Code, a written contract may be explained or supplemented by (1) course of dealing between the parties; (2) usage of trade; (3) course of performance; or (4) evidence of consistent additional terms, unless the writing was intended by the parties to be a complete and exclusive statement of their agreement.

Course of dealing
previous conduct between the parties

A **course of dealing** is a sequence of previous conduct between the parties that a court may fairly regard as having established a common basis of understanding for interpreting their expressions and other conduct.

Usage of trade
practice engaged in by the trade or industry

A **usage of trade** is a practice or method of dealing regularly observed and followed in a place, vocation, or trade.

Course of performance
conduct between the parties concerning performance of the particular contract

Course of performance refers to the manner in which and the extent to which the respective parties to a contract have accepted without objection successive tenders of performance by the other party.

The Restatement and the Code permit *supplemental consistent evidence* to be introduced into a court proceeding. Such evidence, however, is admissible only if it does not contradict a term or terms of the original agreement and probably would not have been included in the original contract.

INTERPRETATION OF CONTRACTS

Although parol evidence may not change the written words or language in which the parties embodied their agreement or contract, the ascertainment (determination) of the meaning to be given to the written language is outside the scope of the parol evidence rule. Though the written words embody the terms of the contract, these words are but symbols; and, if their meaning is ambiguous, the courts may clarify this meaning by applying rules of interpretation or construction and by using extrinsic (external) evidence where necessary.

Interpretation
construction or meaning given the contract

The Restatement defines **interpretation** as the ascertainment of the meaning of a promise or agreement or of a term of the promise or agreement. Where the language in a contract is unambiguous, a court will not accept extrinsic evidence tending to show a meaning different from that which the words clearly convey. To perform its function of interpreting and construing written contracts and documents, the court adopts rules of interpretation to apply a legal standard to the words contained in the agreement. These are among the rules that aid interpretation:

1. Words and other conduct are interpreted in the light of all the circumstances, and if the principal purpose of the parties is ascertainable, it is given great weight.

2. A writing is interpreted as a whole, and all writings that are part of the same transaction are interpreted together.

3. Unless the parties manifest a different intention, language that has a commonly accepted meaning is interpreted in accordance with that meaning.

4. Unless a different intention is manifested, technical terms and words of art are given their technical meanings.

5. Wherever reasonable, the parties' manifestations of intention regarding a promise or agreement are interpreted as consistent with each other and with any relevant course of performance, course of dealing, or usage of trade.

6. An interpretation that gives a reasonable, lawful, and effective meaning to all the terms is preferred over an interpretation that leaves a part unreasonable, unlawful, or of no effect.

7. Specific and exact terms are given greater weight than general language.

8. Separately negotiated or added terms are given greater weight than standardized terms or other terms not separately negotiated.

9. Express terms, course of performance, course of dealing, and usage of trade are weighted in that order.

10. Where a term or promise has several possible meanings, it will be interpreted against the party who supplied the contract or the term.

11. Where written provisions are inconsistent with typed or printed provisions, the written provision is given preference. Likewise, typed provisions are given preference to printed provisions.

12. If the amount payable is set forth in both figures and words and the amounts differ, the words control the figures.

Practical Advice

Take care to ensure that your contracts are complete and understandable, especially if you drafted the contract.

We may observe that, through the application of the parol evidence rule (where properly applicable) and the previous rules of interpretation and construction, the law not only enforces a contract but also, in so doing, exercises great care both that the contract being enforced is the one the parties made and that the sense and meaning of the parties' intentions are carefully ascertained and given effect.

ETHICAL DILEMMA

What's (Wrong) in a Contract?

Facts Rick Davidson was an All-American point guard on Donaldson University's varsity basketball team. He was a four-year starter and, through the cooperation of several accommodating professors, was able to graduate on time—with one small catch: he really couldn't read or write. But his classroom experiences helped convince him that he could handle any situation, and when he was drafted in the first round by a National Basketball Association (NBA) team, he decided to act as his own agent.

During the negotiations, John Stock, general manager for the team, made Rick an offer of $2.4 million to play for the team for three years. After seeing that other first-round draft choices were receiving closer to $3 million for the same three years, Rick made it known to Stock that the team's offer was unacceptable. Stock told Rick that

because of the salary cap (each NBA team has a limit on the total amount of salaries it can pay its players), he would be willing to raise the offer to $2.8 million but that the extra $400,000 could not be written into the contract. This would be an oral agreement that would avoid disclosing the salary cap violation to the league. After considering the offer, Rick signed the contract for $2.4 million for three years' service, and he and Stock shook hands on the deal for the additional $400,000 for the same three years. The contract stated that it was the complete and final agreement between the parties.

After Rick's first year, it was obvious to the team that Rick was not worth the money, and Stock decided not to pay him the first year's portion of the extra $400,000. Stock claimed that because this

agreement was not in writing, it was not enforceable.

Social, Policy, and Ethical Considerations
1. What would you do?
2. Is the team legally obligated to pay the additional $400,000? Is it ethically obligated to do so?
3. What policy interests are served by the team's decision not to pay Rick the extra money? Would the fact that NBA policy makes it impossible for a player to leave a team and play for another NBA team change your answer?
4. What responsibility does the university bear in this situation?
5. What is the nature of Rick's responsibility with respect to these facts? What should he do?

CHAPTER SUMMARY

Statute of Frauds

Contracts Within the Statute of Frauds

Rule contracts within the statute of frauds must be evidenced by a writing to be enforceable

Electronic Records full effect is given to electronic contracts and signatures

Suretyship Provision applies to promises to pay the debt of another

- *Promise Must Be Collateral* promisor must be secondarily, not primarily, liable
- *Main Purpose Doctrine* if primary object is to provide an economic benefit to the surety, then the promise is not within the statute

Executor-Administrator Provision applies to promises to answer personally for a duty of the decedent

Marriage Provision applies to promises in consideration of marriage but not to mutual promises to marry

Land Contract Provision applies to promises to transfer any right, privilege, power, or immunity in real property

One-Year Provision applies to contracts that cannot be performed within one year

- *The Possibility Test* the criterion is whether it is possible, not likely, for the agreement to be performed within one year
- *Computation of Time* the year runs from the time the agreement is made
- *Full Performance by One Party* makes the promise of the other party enforceable under majority view

Sale of Goods a contract for the sale of goods for the price of $500 or more must be evidenced by a writing or record to be enforceable

- *Admission* an admission in pleadings, testimony, or otherwise in court makes the contract enforceable for the quantity of goods admitted
- *Specially Manufactured Goods* an oral contract for specially manufactured goods is enforceable
- *Delivery or Payment and Acceptance* validates the contract only for the goods that have been accepted or for which payment has been accepted

Modification or Rescission of Contracts Within the Statute of Frauds oral contracts modifying existing contracts are unenforceable if the resulting contract is within the statute of frauds

Methods of Compliance

General Contract Provisions the writing(s) or record must

- specify the parties to the contract
- specify the subject matter and essential terms
- be signed by the party to be charged or by her agent

Sale of Goods provides a general method of compliance for all parties and an additional one for merchants

- *Writing(s) or Record* must (1) be sufficient to indicate that a contract has been made between the parties, (2) be signed by the party against whom enforcement is sought or by her authorized agent, and (3) specify the quantity of goods to be sold
- *Written Confirmation* between merchants, a written confirmation that is sufficient against the sender is also sufficient against the recipient unless the recipient gives written notice of his objection within ten days

Effect of Noncompliance

Oral Contract Within Statute of Frauds is unenforceable

Full Performance statute does not apply to executed contracts

Restitution when a contract is unenforceable because of the statute of frauds, a party may recover in restitution the benefits conferred on the other party in performance of the contract

Promissory Estoppel oral contracts will be enforced in cases in which the party seeking enforcement has reasonably and justifiably relied on the promise and the court can avoid injustice only by enforcement

Parol Evidence Rule and Interpretation of Contracts

The Parol Evidence Rule

Statement of Rule when parties express a contract in a writing that they intend to be the final expression of their rights and duties, evidence of their prior oral or written negotiations or agreements of their contemporaneous oral agreements that vary or change the written contract are not admissible

Situations to Which the Rule Does Not Apply

- a contract that is not an integrated document
- correction of a typographical error
- showing that a contract was void or voidable
- showing whether a condition has in fact occurred
- showing a subsequent mutual rescission or modification of the contract

Supplemental Evidence may be admitted

- *Course of Dealing* previous conduct between the parties
- *Usage of Trade* practice engaged in by the trade or industry
- *Course of Performance* conduct between the parties concerning performance of the particular contract
- *Supplemental Consistent Evidence*

Interpretation of Contracts

Definition the ascertainment of the meaning of a promise or agreement or a term of the promise or agreement

Rules of Interpretation include

- all the circumstances are considered and the principal purpose of the parties is given great weight
- a writing is interpreted as a whole
- commonly accepted meanings are used unless the parties manifest a different intention
- wherever possible, the intentions of the parties are interpreted as consistent with each other and with course of performance, course of dealing, or usage of trade
- technical terms are given their technical meaning
- specific terms are given greater weight than general language
- separately negotiated terms are given greater weight than standardized terms or those not separately negotiated
- the order for interpretation is express terms, course of performance, course of dealing, and usage of trade
- where a term has several possible meanings, the term will be interpreted against the party who supplied the contract or term
- written provisions are given preference over typed or printed provisions and typed provisions are given preference over printed provisions
- if an amount is set forth in both words and figures and they differ, words control the figures

QUESTIONS

1. Rafferty was the principal shareholder in Continental Corporation, and, as a result, he received the lion's share of Continental Corporation's dividends. Continental Corporation was anxious to close an important deal for iron ore products to use in its business. A written contract was on the desk of Stage Corporation for the sale of the iron ore to Continental Corporation. Stage Corporation, however, was cautious about signing the contract, and it did not sign until Rafferty called Stage Corporation on the telephone and stated that if Continental Corporation did not pay for the ore, he would pay. Business reversals struck Continental Corporation, and it failed. Stage Corporation sued Rafferty. What defense, if any, has Rafferty?

2. Green was the owner of a large department store. On Wednesday, January 26, he talked to Smith and said, "I will hire you to act as sales manager in my store for one year at a salary of $48,000. You are to begin work next Monday." Smith accepted and started work on Monday, January 31. At the end of three months, Green discharged Smith. On May 15, Smith brought an action against Green to recover the unpaid portion of the $48,000 salary. Is Smith's employment contract enforceable?

3. Rowe was admitted to the hospital suffering from a critical illness. He was given emergency treatment and later underwent surgery. On at least four occasions, Rowe's two sons discussed with the hospital the payment for services to be rendered by the hospital. The first of these four conversations took place the day after Rowe was admitted. The sons informed the treating physician that their father had no financial means but that they themselves would pay for such services. During the other conversations, the sons authorized whatever treatment their father needed, assuring the hospital that they would pay for the services. After Rowe's discharge, the hospital brought this action against the sons to recover the unpaid bill for the services rendered to their father. Are the sons' promises to the hospital enforceable? Explain.

4. Ames, Bell, Cain, and Dole each orally ordered LCD (liquid crystal display) televisions from Marvel Electronics Company, which accepted the orders. Ames's television was to be encased in a specially designed ebony cabinet. Bell, Cain, and Dole ordered standard televisions described as "Alpha Omega Theatre." The price of Ames's television was $1,800, and the televisions ordered by Bell, Cain, and Dole were $700 each. Bell paid the company $75.00 to apply on his purchase; Ames, Cain, and Dole paid nothing. The next day, Marvel sent Ames, Bell, Cain, and Dole written confirmations captioned "Purchase Memorandum," numbered 12345, 12346, 12347, and 12348, respectively, containing the essential terms of the oral agreements. Each memorandum was sent in duplicate with the request that one copy be signed and returned to the company. None of the four purchasers returned a signed copy. Ames promptly called the company and repudiated the oral contract, which it received before beginning manufacture of the set for Ames or making commitments to carry out the contract. Cain sent the company a letter reading in part, "Referring to your Contract No. 12347, please be advised I have canceled this contract. Yours truly, (Signed) Cain." The four televisions were duly tendered by Marvel to Ames, Bell, Cain, and Dole, all of whom refused to accept delivery. Marvel brings four separate actions against Ames, Bell, Cain, and Dole for breach of contract. Decide each claim.

5. Moriarity and Holmes enter into an oral contract by which Moriarity promises to sell and Holmes promises to buy Blackacre for $10,000. Moriarity repudiates the contract by writing a letter to Holmes in which she states accurately the terms of the bargain, but adds "our agreement was oral. It, therefore, is not binding upon me, and I shall not carry it out." Thereafter, Holmes sues Moriarity for specific performance of the contract. Moriarity interposes the defense of the statute of frauds, arguing that the contract is within the statute and hence unenforceable. What will be the result? Discuss.

6. On March 1, Lucas called Craig on the telephone and offered to pay him $90,000 for a house and lot that Craig owned. Craig accepted the offer immediately on the telephone. Later in the same day, Lucas told Annabelle that if she would marry him, he would convey to her the property then owned by Craig that was the subject of the earlier agreement. On March 2 Lucas called Penelope and offered her $16,000 if she would work for him for the year commencing March 15, and she

agreed. Lucas and Annabelle were married on June 25. By this time, Craig had refused to convey the house to Lucas. Thereafter, Lucas renounced his promise to convey the property to Annabelle. Penelope, who had been working for Lucas, was discharged without cause on July 5; Annabelle left Lucas and instituted divorce proceedings in July.

What rights, if any, has
  a. Lucas against Craig for his failure to convey the property;
  b. Annabelle against Lucas for failure to convey the house to her; and
  c. Penelope against Lucas for discharging her before the end of the agreed term of employment?

7. Blair orally promises Clay to sell him five crops of potatoes to be grown on Blackacre, a farm in Idaho, and Clay promises to pay a stated price for them on delivery. Is the contract enforceable?

8. Rachel leased an apartment to Bertha for a one-year term beginning May 1, at $800 a month, "payable in advance on the first day of each and every month of said term." At the time the lease was signed, Bertha told Rachel that she received her salary on the tenth of the month, and that she would be unable to pay the rent before that date each month. Rachel replied that would be satisfactory. On June 2, Bertha not having paid the June rent, Rachel sued Bertha for the rent. At the trial, Bertha offered to prove the oral agreement as to the date of payment each month. Explain whether Rachel should succeed.

9. Ann bought a car from the Used Car Agency (Used) under a written contract. She purchased the car in reliance on Used's agent's oral representations that it had never been in a wreck and could be driven at least two thousand miles without adding oil. Thereafter, Ann discovered that the car had, in fact, been previously wrecked and rebuilt, that it used excessive quantities of oil, and that Used's agent was aware of these facts when the car was sold. Ann brought an action to rescind the contract and recover the purchase price. Used objected to the introduction of oral testimony concerning representations of its agent, contending that the written contract alone governed the rights of the parties. Should Ann succeed?

10. In a contract drawn up by Goldberg Company, it agreed to sell and Edwards Contracting Company agreed to buy wood shingles at $650. After the shingles were delivered and used, Goldberg Company billed Edwards Company at $650 per bunch of nine hundred shingles. Edwards Company refused to pay because it thought the contract meant $650 per thousand shingles. Goldberg Company brought action to recover on the basis of $650 per bunch. The evidence showed that there was no applicable custom or usage in the trade and that each party held its belief in good faith. Decision?

11. Amos orally agrees to hire Elizabeth for an eight-month trial period. Elizabeth performs the job magnificently, and after several weeks Amos orally offers Elizabeth a six-month extension at a salary increase of 20 percent. Elizabeth accepts the offer. At the end of the eight-month trial period, Amos discharges Elizabeth, who brings suit against Amos for breach of contract. Is Amos liable? Why?

CASE PROBLEMS

12. Halsey, a widower, was living without family or housekeeper in his house in Howell, New York. Burns and his wife claim that Halsey invited them to give up their house and business in Andover, New York, to live in his house and care for him. In return, they allege, he promised them the house and its furniture upon his death. Acting upon this proposal, the Burnses left Andover, moved into Halsey's house, and cared for him until he died five months later. No deed, will, or memorandum exists to authenticate Halsey's promise. McCormick, the administrator of the estate, claims the oral promise is unenforceable under the statute of frauds. Explain whether McCormick is correct.

13. Ethel Greenberg acquired the ownership of the Carlyle Hotel on Miami Beach but had little experience in the hotel business. She asked Miller to participate in and counsel her operation of the hotel, which he did. He claims that, because his efforts produced a substantial profit, Ethel made an oral agreement for the continuation of his services. Miller alleges that in return for his services, Ethel promised to marry him and to share the net income resulting from the operation of the hotel. Miller maintains that he rendered his services to Ethel in reliance upon her promises and that the couple planned to wed in the fall. Ethel, due to physical illness, decided not to marry. Miller sued for damages for Ethel's breach of agreement. Is the oral contract enforceable? Discuss.

14. Dean was hired on February 12 as a sales manager of the Co-op Dairy for a minimum period of one year with the dairy agreeing to pay his moving expenses. By February 26, Dean had signed a lease, moved his family from Oklahoma to Arizona, and reported for work. After he worked for a few days, he was fired. Dean then brought this action against the dairy for his salary for the year, less what he was paid. The dairy argues that the statute of frauds bars enforcement of the oral contract because the contract was not to be performed within one year. Is the dairy correct in its assertion?

15. Yokel, a grower of soybeans, had sold soybeans to Campbell Grain and Seed Company and other grain companies in the past. Campbell entered into an oral contract with Yokel to purchase soybeans from him. Promptly after entering into the oral contract, Campbell signed and mailed to Yokel a written confirmation of the oral agreement. Yokel received the written confirmation but did not sign it or object to its content. Campbell now brings this action against Yokel for breach of contract upon Yokel's failure to deliver the soybeans. Is the agreement binding?

16. Presti claims that he reached an oral agreement with Wilson by telephone in October to buy a horse for $60,000. Presti asserts that he sent Wilson a bill of sale and a postdated check, which Wilson retained. Presti also claims that Wilson told him that for tax reasons he wished not to consummate the transaction until January 1 of the following year. The check was neither deposited nor negotiated. Wilson denies that he ever agreed to sell the horse or that he received the check and bill of sale from Presti. Presti's claim is supported by a copy of his check stub and by the affidavit of his executive assistant, who says that he monitored the telephone call and prepared and mailed both the bill of sale and the check. Wilson argues that the statute of frauds governs this transaction and that because there was no writing, the contract claim is barred. Is Wilson correct? Explain.

17. Louie E. Brown worked for the Phelps Dodge Corporation under an oral contract for approximately twenty-three years. In 2011, he was suspended from work for unauthorized possession of company property. In 2012, Phelps Dodge fired Brown after discovering that he was using company property without permission and building a trailer on company time. Brown sued Phelps Dodge for benefits under an unemployment benefit plan. According to the plan, "in order to be eligible for unemployment benefits, a laid-off employee must: (1) Have completed 2 or more years of continuous service with the company, and (2) Have been laid off from work because the company had determined that work was not available for him." The trial court held that the wording of the second condition was ambiguous and should be construed against Phelps Dodge, the party who chose the wording. A reading of the entire contract, however, indicates that the plan was not intended to apply to someone who was fired for cause. What is the correct interpretation of this contract?

18. Katz offered to purchase land from Joiner, and, after negotiating the terms, Joiner accepted. On October 13, over the telephone, both parties agreed to extend the time period for completing and mailing the written contract until October 20. Although the original paperwork deadline in the offer was October 14, Katz stated he had inserted that provision "for my purpose only." All other provisions of the contract remained unchanged. Accordingly, Joiner completed the contract and mailed it on October 20. Immediately after, however, Joiner sent Katz an overnight letter stating that "I have signed and returned contract, but have changed my mind. Do not wish to sell property." Joiner now claims an oral modification of a contract within the statute of frauds is unenforceable. Katz counters that the modification is not material and therefore does not affect the underlying contract. Explain who is correct.

19. When Mr. McClam died, he left the family farm, heavily mortgaged, to his wife and children. To save the farm from foreclosure, Mrs. McClam planned to use insurance proceeds and her savings to pay off the debts. She was unwilling to do so, however, unless she had full ownership of the property. Mrs. McClam wrote her daughter, stating that the daughter should deed over her interest in the family farm to her mother. Mrs. McClam promised that upon her death all the children would inherit the farm from their mother equally. The letter further explained that if foreclosure occurred, each child would receive very little, but if they complied with their mother's plan, each would eventually receive a valuable property interest upon her death. Finally, the letter stated that all the other children had agreed to this plan. The daughter also agreed. Years later, Mrs. McClam tried to convey the farm to her son Donald. The daughter challenged, arguing that the mother was contractually bound to convey the land equally to all children. Donald says this was an oral agreement to sell land and is unenforceable. The daughter says the letter satisfies the statute of frauds, making the contract enforceable. Who gets the farm? Explain.

20. Butler Brothers Building Company sublet all of the work in a highway construction contract to Ganley Brothers, Inc. Soon thereafter, Ganley brought this action against Butler for fraud in the inducement of the contract. The contract, however, provided: "The contractor [Ganley] has examined the said contracts …, knows all the requirements, and is not relying upon any statement made by the company in respect thereto." Can Ganley introduce into evidence the oral representations made by Butler?

21. Alice solicited an offer from Robett Manufacturing Company to manufacture certain clothing that Alice intended to supply to the government. Alice contends that in a telephone conversation Robett made an oral offer that she immediately accepted. She then received the following letter from Robett, which, she claims, confirmed their agreement:

> Confirming our telephone conversation, we are pleased to offer the 3,500 shirts at $14.00 each and the trousers at $13.80 each with delivery approximately ninety days after receipt of order. We will try to cut this to sixty days if at all possible.
>
> This, of course, is quoted f.o.b. Atlanta and the order will not be subject to cancellation, domestic pack only. Thanking you for the opportunity to offer these garments, we are
>
> Very truly yours,
> ROBETT MANUFACTURING CO., INC.

Is the agreement enforceable against Robett?

22. Enrique Gittes was a financial consultant for NCC, an English holding company that invested capital in other businesses in return for a stake in those businesses. One of NCC's investments was a substantial holding in Simplicity Pattern Company. Gittes's consulting contract was subsequently transferred to Simplicity, and Gittes was elected to the Simplicity board of directors.

When NCC fell into serious financial straits, it became imperative that it sell its interest in Simplicity. Accordingly, a buyer was found. The buyer insisted that before closing the deal all current Simplicity directors, including Gittes, must resign. Gittes, however, refused to resign. Edward Cook, the largest shareholder of NCC and the one with the most to lose if the Simplicity sale was not completed, orally offered Gittes a five-year, $50,000-per-year consulting contract with Cook International if Gittes would resign from the Simplicity board.

Gittes and Cook never executed a formal contract. However, Cook International did issue two writings, a prospectus and a memo, that mentioned the employment of Gittes for five years at $50,000 per year. Neither writing described the nature of Gittes's job or any of his duties. In fact, Gittes was given no responsibilities, and was never paid. Gittes sued to enforce the employment contract. Cook International contended that the statute of frauds made the oral contract unenforceable. Decision?

23. Shane Quadri contacted Don Hoffman, an employee of Al J. Hoffman & Co. (Hoffman Agency), to procure car insurance. Later, Quadri's car was stolen. Quadri contacted Hoffman, who arranged with Budget Rent-a-Car for a rental car for Quadri until his car was recovered. Hoffman authorized Budget Rent-a-Car to bill the Hoffman Agency. Later, when the stolen car was recovered, Hoffman telephoned Goodyear and arranged to have four new tires put on Quadri's car to replace those damaged during the theft. Budget and Goodyear sued Hoffman for payment of the car rental and tires. Is Hoffman liable on his oral promise to pay for the car rental and the four new tires?

24. On July 5, 2003, Richard Price signed a written employment contract as a new salesman with the Mercury Supply Company. The contract was of indefinite duration and could be terminated by either party for any reason upon fifteen days' notice. Between 2003 and 2011, Price was promoted several times. In 2005, Price was made vice president of sales. In September of 2011, however, Price was told that his performance was not satisfactory and that if he did not improve he would be fired. In February of 2014, Price received notice of termination. Price claims that in 2008 he entered into a valid oral employment contract with Mercury Supply Company in which he was made vice president of sales for life or until he should retire. Is the alleged oral contract barred by the one-year provision of the statute of frauds?

25. Thomson Printing Company is a buyer and seller of used machinery. On April 10, the president of the company, James Thomson, went to the surplus machinery department of B.F. Goodrich Company in Akron, Ohio, to examine some used equipment that was for sale. Thomson discussed the sale, including a price of $9,000, with Ingram Meyers, a Goodrich employee and agent. Four days later, on April 14, Thomson sent a purchase order to confirm the oral contract for purchase of the machinery and a partial payment of $1,000 to Goodrich in Akron. The purchase order contained Thomson Printing's name, address, and telephone number, as well as certain information about the purchase, but did not specifically mention Meyers or the surplus equipment department. Goodrich sent copies of the documents to a number of its divisions, but Meyers never learned of the confirmation until weeks later, by which time the equipment had been sold to another party. Thomson Printing brought suit against Goodrich for breach of contract. Goodrich claimed that no contract had existed and that at any rate the alleged oral contract could not be enforced because of the statute of frauds. Is the contract enforceable? Why?

26. Plaintiffs leased commercial space from the defendant to open a florist shop. After the lease was executed, the plaintiffs learned that they could not place a freestanding sign along the highway to advertise their business because the Deschutes County Code allowed only one freestanding sign on the property, and the defendant already had one in place. The plaintiffs filed this action, alleging that defendant had breached the lease by failing to provide them with space in which they

could erect a freestanding sign. Paragraph 16 of the lease provides as follows: "Tenant shall not erect or install any signs … visible from outside the leased premises with out [sic] the previous written consent of the Landlord." Explain whether this evidence is admissible.

27. Jesse Carter and Jesse Thomas had an auto accident with a driver insured by Allstate. Carter and Thomas hired an attorney, Joseph Onwuteaka, to represent them. Mr. Onwuteaka sent a demand letter for settlement of the plaintiffs' claims to Allstate's adjustor, Ms. Gracie Weatherly. Mr. Onwuteaka claims Ms. Weatherly made, and he orally accepted, settlement terms on behalf of the plaintiffs. When Allstate did not honor the agreements, Carter and Thomas filed a suit for breach of contract. Discuss the enforceability of the oral agreement.

28. Mary Iacono and Carolyn Lyons had been friends for almost thirty-five years. Mary suffers from advanced rheumatoid arthritis and is in a wheelchair. Carolyn invited Mary to join her on a trip to Las Vegas, Nevada, for which Carolyn paid. Mary contended that she was invited to Las Vegas by Carolyn because Carolyn thought Mary was lucky. Sometime before the trip, Mary had a dream about winning on a Las Vegas slot machine. Mary's dream convinced her to go to Las Vegas, and she accepted Carolyn's offer to split "50–50" any gambling winnings. Carolyn provided Mary with money for gambling. Mary and Carolyn started to gamble but after losing $47.00, Carolyn wanted to leave to see a show. Mary begged Carolyn to stay, and Carolyn agreed on the condition that Carolyn put the coins into the machines because doing so took Mary too long. Mary agreed and led Carolyn to a dollar slot machine that looked like the machine in her dream. The machine did not pay on the first try. Mary then said, "Just one more time," and Carolyn looked at Mary and said, "This one's for you, Puddin." They hit the jackpot, winning $1,908,064 to be paid over a period of twenty years. Carolyn refused to share the winnings with Mary. Is Mary entitled to one-half of the proceeds? Explain.

TAKING SIDES

Stuart Studio, an art studio, prepared a new catalog for the National School of Heavy Equipment, a school run by Gilbert and Donald Shaw. When the artwork was virtually finished, Gilbert Shaw requested Stuart Studio to purchase and supervise the printing of twenty-five thousand catalogs. Shaw told the art studio that payment of the printing costs would be made within ten days after billing and that if the "National School would not pay the full total that he would stand good for the entire bill." Shaw was chairman of the board of directors of the school, and he owned 100 percent of its voting stock and 49 percent of its nonvoting stock. The school became bankrupt, and Stuart Studio was unable to recover the sum from the school. Stuart Studio then brought an action against Shaw on the basis of his promise to pay the bill.

a. What are the arguments that Shaw is not liable on his promise?

b. What are the arguments that Shaw is liable on his promise?

c. Is Shaw obligated to pay the debt in question? Explain.

Third Parties to Contracts

CHAPTER 16

The establishment of [the third-party beneficiary] doctrine ... is a victory of practical utility over theory, of equity over technical subtlety.

Brantly on Contracts, 2nd edition

CHAPTER OUTCOMES

After reading and studying this chapter, you should be able to:

1. Distinguish between an assignment of rights and a delegation of duties.

2. Identify (a) the requirements of an assignment of contract rights and (b) those rights that are not assignable.

3. Identify those situations in which a delegation of duties is not permitted.

4. Distinguish between an intended beneficiary and an incidental beneficiary.

5. Explain when the rights of an intended beneficiary vest.

I n prior chapters, we considered situations that essentially involved only two parties. In this chapter, we deal with the rights and duties of third parties, namely, persons who are not parties to the contract but who have a right to or an obligation for its performance. These rights and duties arise either by (1) an assignment of the rights of a party to the contract, (2) a delegation of the duties of a party to the contract, or (3) the express terms of a contract entered into for the benefit of a third person. In an assignment or delegation, the third party's rights or duties arise after the original contract is made, whereas in the third situation, the third-party beneficiary's rights arise at the time the contract is formed. We will consider these three situations in that order.

ASSIGNMENT OF RIGHTS [16-1]

Obligor
party owing a duty under original contract

Obligee
party to whom a contractual duty of performance is owed

Every contract creates both rights and duties. A person who owes a duty under a contract is an **obligor**, while a person to whom a contractual duty is owed is an **obligee**. For instance, Ann promises to sell to Bart an automobile for which Bart promises to pay $10,000 by monthly installments over the next three years. Ann's right under the contract is to receive payment from Bart, whereas Ann's duty is to deliver the automobile. Bart's right is to receive the automobile; his duty is to pay for it.

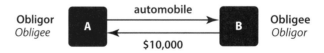

Assignment of rights
voluntary transfer to a third party of the rights arising from a contract

An **assignment of rights** is the voluntary transfer to a third party of the rights arising from the contract. In the previous example, if Ann were to transfer her right

Assignor

party making an assignment

Assignee

party to whom contractual rights are assigned

under the contract (the installment payments due from Bart) to Clark for $8,500 in cash, this would constitute a valid assignment of rights. In this case, Ann would be the **assignor**, Clark would be the **assignee**, and Bart would be the *obligor*.

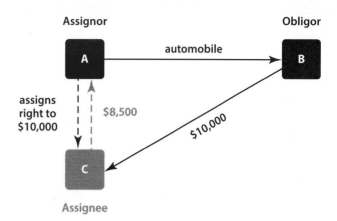

An effective assignment terminates the assignor's right to receive performance by the obligor. After an assignment, only the assignee has a right to the obligor's performance.

On the other hand, if Ann and Doris agree that Doris should deliver the automobile to Bart, this would constitute a delegation, not an assignment, of duties between Ann and Doris. A **delegation of duties** is a transfer to a third party of a contractual obligation. In this instance, Ann would be the **delegator**, Doris would be the **delegatee**, and Bart would be the *obligee*.

Delegation of duties

transfer to a third party of a contractual obligation

Delegator

party delegating his duty to a third party

Delegatee

third party to whom the delegator's duty is delegated

Requirements of an Assignment [16-1a]

The Restatement defines an assignment of a right as a manifestation of the assignor's intention to transfer the right so that the assignor's right to the performance of the obligor is extinguished either in whole or in part and the assignee acquires a right to such performance. No special form or particular words are necessary to create an assignment. Any words that fairly indicate an intention to make the assignee the owner of the right are sufficient.

Unless otherwise provided by statute, an assignment may be oral. The Uniform Commercial Code (UCC) imposes a writing requirement on all assignments beyond $5,000. The 2001 Revision to Article 1, however, has deleted this requirement. In addition, Article 9 requires certain assignments to be in writing.

Consideration is not required for an effective assignment. Consequently, gratuitous assignments are valid and enforceable. By giving value, or consideration, for the assignment, the assignee indicates his assent to the assignment as part of the bargained-for exchange. On the other hand, when the assignment is gratuitous, the assignee's assent is not always required. Any assignee who has not assented to an assignment, however, may disclaim the assignment within a reasonable time after learning of its existence and terms.

Revocability of assignment

when the assignee gives consideration, the assignor may not revoke the assignment without the assignee's consent

---

Practical Advice

Be sure to make irrevocable assignments of only those rights you wish to transfer.

Revocability of Assignments   When the assignee gives consideration in exchange for an assignment, a contract exists between the assignor and the assignee. Consequently, the assignor may not revoke the assignment without the assignee's assent. In contrast, a gratuitous assignment is revocable by the assignor and is terminated by the assignor's death, incapacity, or subsequent assignment of the right, unless the assignor has made an effective delivery of the assignment to the assignee, as in the case of *Speelman v. Pascal*. Such delivery can be accomplished by transferring a deed or other document evidencing the right, such as a stock certificate or savings passbook. Delivery also may consist of physically delivering a signed, written assignment of the contract right. A gratuitous assignment is also made irrevocable if, before the attempted revocation, the donee-assignee receives payment of the claim from the obligor, obtains a judgment against the obligor, or obtains a new contract with the obligor.

Speelman v. Pascal
Court of Appeals of New York, 1961
10 N.Y.2d 313, 222 N.Y.S.2d 324, 178 N.E.2d 723
http://scholar.google.com/scholar_case?q=178+N.E.2d+723&hl=en&as_sdt=6,34&case=18121890776629170977&scilh=0

FACTS In 1952, the estate of George Bernard Shaw granted to Gabriel Pascal Enterprises, Limited, the exclusive rights to produce a musical play and a motion picture based on Shaw's play *Pygmalion*. The agreement contained a provision terminating the license if Gabriel Pascal Enterprises did not arrange for well-known composers, such as Lerner and Loewe, to write the musical and produce it within a specified period of time. George Pascal, owner of 98 percent of Gabriel Pascal Enterprises' stock, attempted to meet these requirements but died in July 1954 before negotiations had been completed. In February 1954, however, while the license had two years yet to run, Pascal had sent a letter to Kingman, his executive secretary, granting to her certain percentages of his share of the profits from the expected stage and screen productions of *Pygmalion*. Subsequently, Pascal's estate arranged for the writing and production of the highly successful *My Fair Lady*, based on Shaw's *Pygmalion*. Kingman then sued to enforce Pascal's gift assignment of the future royalties. The trial court entered judgment for Kingman.

DECISION Judgment for Kingman affirmed.

OPINION Assignments of rights to sums that are expected to become due to the assignor are enforceable. To make a gift of such an assignment, the donor need only demonstrate a present intent to transfer irrevocably his right to the donee. Although at the time of the delivery of the letter there was no musical play or motion picture in existence, Pascal's letter was intended to transfer irrevocably by assignment a percentage of the royalties from the future productions to Kingman. Therefore, the assignment is enforceable as a valid gift.

INTERPRETATION A gratuitous assignment becomes irrevocable upon the assignor's making an effective delivery of the assignment to the assignee.

CRITICAL THINKING QUESTION Should the law enforce assignments of contractual rights not in existence at the time of the assignment? Explain.

Partial assignment
transfer of a portion of contractual rights to one or more assignees

Partial Assignments   A **partial assignment** is a transfer of a portion of the contractual rights to one or more assignees, as in *Speelman v. Pascal*. The obligor, however, may require all the parties entitled to the promised performance to litigate the matter in one action, thus ensuring that all parties are present and avoiding the undue hardship of multiple lawsuits. For example, Jack owes Richard $2,500. Richard assigns $1,000 to Mildred. Neither Richard nor Mildred can maintain an action against Jack if Jack objects, unless the other is joined in the proceeding against Jack.

Rights That Are Assignable [16-1b]

As a general rule, most contract rights, including rights under an option contract, are assignable. The most common contractual right that may be assigned is the right to the payment of money. A contract right to other property, such as land or goods, is likewise assignable.

Rights That Are Not Assignable [16-1c]

To protect the obligor or the public interest, some contract rights are not assignable. These nonassignable contract rights include those that (1) materially increase the duty, risk, or burden upon the obligor; (2) transfer highly personal contract rights; (3) are expressly prohibited by the contract; or (4) are prohibited by law.

Assignments That Materially Increase the Duty, Risk, or Burden   An assignment is ineffective if performance by the obligor to the assignee would differ materially from the obligor's performance to the assignor, that is, if the assignment would significantly change the nature or extent of the obligor's duty. Thus, an automobile liability insurance policy issued to Alex is not assignable by Alex to Betty. The risk assumed by the insurance company was liability for Alex's negligent operation of the automobile. Liability for Betty's operation of the same automobile would be a risk entirely different from the one the insurance company had assumed. Similarly, Candice would not be allowed to assign to Eunice, the owner of a twenty-five-room mansion, Candice's contractual right to have David paint her small, two-bedroom house. Clearly, such an assignment would materially increase David's duty of performance. By comparison, the right to receive monthly payments under a contract may be assigned, for mailing the check to the assignee costs no more than mailing it to the assignor. Moreover, if a contract explicitly provides that it may be assigned, then rights under it are assignable even if the assignment would change the duty, risk, or burden of performance on the obligor.

Assignments of Personal Rights When the rights under a contract are highly personal, in that they are limited to the person of the obligee, such rights are not assignable. An extreme example of such a contract is an agreement of two persons to marry one another. The prospective groom obviously may not transfer the prospective bride's promise to marry to some third party. A more typical example of a contract involving personal rights would be a contract between a teacher and a school. The teacher could not assign her right to a faculty position to another teacher. Similarly, a student who is awarded a scholarship cannot assign his right to some other person. The *Magness* case involves another example.

In re Magness
United States Court of Appeals, Sixth Circuit, 1992
972 F.2d 689
http://scholar.google.com/scholar_case?case=6023421001644754391&q=972+F.2d+689&hl=en&as_sdt=2,34

FACTS The Dayton Country Club Company (the Club) offers many social activities to its members. The privilege to play golf at the Club, however, is reserved to a special membership category for which additional fees are charged. The Club chooses golfing memberships from a waiting list of members according to detailed rules, regulations, and procedures. Magness and Redman were golfing members of the Club. Upon their filing for bankruptcy, their trustee sought to assign by sale their golf rights to (1) other members on the waiting list, (2) other members not on the waiting list, or (3) the general public, provided the purchaser first acquired membership in the Club. The bankruptcy court found that the Club's rules governing golf membership were essentially anti-assignment provisions and therefore the estate could not assign rights contained in the membership agreement. On appeal to the district court, the bankruptcy court's ruling was affirmed. The district court added that this case was not a lease but rather a "non-commercial dispute over the possession of a valuable membership in a recreational and social club."

DECISION Judgment affirmed.

OPINION The court of appeals found that the memberships of Magness and Redman were personal contracts that are not assignable. A personal contract is one in which "the personality of one of the parties is material." The determination of whether a contract is personal is a question of intent as shown by the language used in the contract and the nature of the contract. In this case, "[t]he contracts creating the complex relationships among the parties and others are not in any way commercial. They create personal relationships among individuals who play golf, who are waiting to play golf, who eat together, swim and play together." Therefore, the parties intended these contracts to be personal and thus they are nonassignable.

INTERPRETATION When rights under a contract are personal, they may not be assigned.

ETHICAL QUESTION Is the court's decision fair to the creditors of Magness and Redman? Explain.

CRITICAL THINKING QUESTION Which type of contracts should not be assignable because of their personal nature? Explain.

Express Prohibition Against Assignment Though contract terms prohibiting assignment of rights under the contract are strictly construed, most courts interpret a general prohibition against assignments as a mere promise not to assign. As a consequence, the general prohibition, if violated, gives the obligor a right to damages for breach of the terms forbidding assignment but does not render the assignment ineffective.

The Restatement provides that, unless circumstances indicate the contrary, a contract term prohibiting assignment of the *contract* bars only the delegation to the assignee (delegatee) of the assignor's (delegator's) duty of performance, not the assignment of *rights*. Thus, Norman and Lucy contract for the sale of land by Lucy to Norman for $300,000 and provide in their contract that Norman may not assign the contract. Norman pays Lucy $300,000, thereby fulfilling his duty of performance under the contract. Norman then assigns his rights to George, who consequently is entitled to receive the land from Lucy (the obligor) despite the contractual prohibition of assignment.

Article 2 of the Code provides that a right to damages for breach of the whole contract or a right arising out of the assignor's due performance of his entire obligation can be assigned despite a contractual provision to the contrary. Article 2 also provides that, unless circumstances indicate the contrary, a contract term prohibiting assignment of the *contract* bars only the delegation to the assignee (delegatee) of the assignor's (delegator's) *duty* of performance, not the assignment of *rights*. Article 9 of the Code makes generally ineffective any term in a security agreement restricting the assignment of a security interest in any right to payment for goods sold or leased or for services rendered.

Practical Advice

Consider including in your contract a provision prohibiting the assignment of any contractual rights without your written consent and making ineffective any such assignment.

Aldana v. Colonial Palms Plaza, Inc.
District Court of Appeal of Florida, Third District, 1991
591 So.2d 953; rehearing denied, 1992
http://scholar.google.com/scholar_case?case=1977050164764776625&q=591+So.2d+953&hl=en&as_sdt=2,34

FACTS Colonial Palms Plaza, Inc. (Landlord) entered into a lease agreement with Abby's Cakes On Dixie, Inc. (Tenant). The lease included a provision in which Landlord agreed to pay Tenant a construction allowance of up to $11,250 after Tenant completed certain improvements. Prior to completion of the improvements, Tenant assigned its right to receive the first $8,000 of the construction allowance to Robert Aldana in return for a loan of $8,000 to finance the construction. Aldana sent notice of the assignment to Landlord. When Tenant completed the improvements, Landlord ignored the assignment and paid Tenant the construction allowance. Aldana sued Landlord for the money due pursuant to the assignment. Landlord relied on an anti-assignment clause in the lease to argue that the assignment was void. That clause states in part:

> TENANT agrees not to assign, mortgage, pledge, or encumber this Lease, in whole or in part, to sublet in whole or any part of the DEMISED PREMISES … without first obtaining the prior, specific written consent of the LANDLORD at LANDLORD'S sole discretion…. Any such assignment … without such consent shall be void.

The trial court granted Landlord summary judgment.

DECISION Summary judgment reversed and case remanded.

OPINION Aldana argued that under ordinary contract principles the lease provision does not prevent the assignment of the right to receive contractual payments. The appellate court agreed. Tenant did not assign the lease but instead assigned a right to receive the construction allowance. The law in this area is summarized in the Restatement of Contracts as follows: "Unless the circumstances indicate the contrary, a contract term prohibiting assignment of 'the contract' bars only the delegation to an assignee of the performance by the assignor of a duty or condition." As a rule of construction, a prohibition against assignment of a contract (in this case, the lease) will prevent assignment of contractual duties but does not prevent assignment of the right to receive payments due—unless circumstances indicate otherwise. Having received notice of the assignment, Landlord was bound by the assignment.

INTERPRETATION Unless circumstances indicate the contrary, a contract term prohibiting assignment of the contract bars only delegation of the assignor's contractual duties.

ETHICAL QUESTION If the landlord had inadvertently ignored the notice of assignment, would the outcome of the case have been fair? Explain.

CRITICAL THINKING QUESTION Should the courts honor contractual prohibitions of assignments by rendering such assignments ineffective? Explain.

Assignments Prohibited by Law Various federal and state statutes, as well as public policy, prohibit or regulate the assignment of certain types of contract rights. For instance, assignments of future wages are subject to such statutes, some of which prohibit these assignments altogether, whereas others require the assignments to be in writing and subject them to certain restrictions. Moreover, an assignment that violates public policy will be unenforceable even in the absence of a prohibiting statute.

Rights of the assignee
assignee stands in the shoes of the assignor

Rights of the Assignee [16-1d]

Obtains Rights of Assignor
The general rule is that an assignee *stands in the shoes* of the assignor. She acquires the rights of the assignor but no new or additional rights, and she takes with the assigned rights all of the defenses, defects, and infirmities to which they would be subject in an action against the obligor by the assignor. Thus, in an action brought by the assignee against the obligor, the obligor may plead fraud, duress, undue influence, failure of consideration, breach of contract, or any other defense arising out of the original contract against the assignor. The obligor may also assert rights of **setoff** or counterclaim arising out of entirely separate matters that he may have against the assignor, as long as they arose before he had notice of the assignment.

Setoff
claim by obligor against assignor arising out of an entirely separate transaction

The Code permits the buyer under a contract of sale to agree as part of the contract that he will not assert against an assignee any claim or defense that the buyer may have against the seller if the assignee takes the assignment for value, in good faith, and without notice of conflicting claims or of certain defenses. Such a provision in an agreement renders the seller's rights more marketable. The Federal Trade Commission, however, has invalidated such waiver of defense provisions in consumer credit transactions. This rule is discussed more fully in Chapter 25. Article 9 reflects this rule by essentially rendering waiver-of-defense clauses ineffective in consumer transactions. Most states also have statutes protecting buyers in consumer transactions by prohibiting waiver of defenses.

Mountain Peaks Financial Services, Inc. v. Roth-Steffen
Court of Appeals of Minnesota, 2010
778 N.W.2d 380
http://scholar.google.com/scholar_case?q=778+N.W.2d+380&hl=en&as_sdt=2,34&case=11662901939297878943&scilh=0

FACTS In May 1998, Catherine Roth-Steffen graduated from law school with over $100,000 in school loans from more than a dozen lenders. Of this total, Roth-Steffen received $20,350 from the Missouri Higher Education Loan Authority (MOHELA) CASH Loan program. As of November 5, 1998, Roth-Steffen had incurred interest on these loans (MOHELA loan) in the amount of $3,043.28. Roth-Steffen listed the balance of $23,401.28 in a loan consolidation application she submitted in December 1998. She requested that the MOHELA loan not be consolidated with her other loans.

In February 2003, MOHELA assigned ownership of the MOHELA loan to Guarantee National Insurance Company (GNIC), which, in turn, assigned the loan for collection to respondent Mountain Peaks Financial Services, Inc. (Mountain Peaks). Mountain Peaks commenced a collection action claiming that it holds the MOHELA loan and that it is entitled to judgment in the amount of the outstanding balance, $23,120.52, and additional interest at the rate of 2.54% from July 19, 2007. In response, Roth-Steffen asserted that the action is barred by Minnesota's six-year statute of limitations for collection on promissory notes. The district court granted summary judgment in favor of Mountain Peaks, determining that Mountain Peaks (1) owns Roth-Steffen's loan, (2) is a valid assignee of MOHELA's right, and (3) under the federal Higher Education Act is not to be subject to any state statutes of limitation.

DECISION Summary judgment is affirmed.

OPINION The Higher Education Act of 1965 (Act) was the first comprehensive government program designed to provide scholarships, grants, work-study funding, and loans for students to attend college and graduate school. Pursuant to the Act, the federal government makes loans and guarantees loans made by private lenders. In response to rising loan defaults and an unfavorable legal ruling, Congress adopted the Higher Education Technical Amendments of 1991.

The amendments eliminate all statutes of limitation on actions to recover on defaulted student loans for certain "named lenders."

Mountain Peaks argues that it is exempt from Minnesota's statutes of limitation because it is a valid assignee of MOHELA, a named lender. Roth-Steffen acknowledges that MOHELA is a named lender but argues that because Congress did not expressly identify assignees as named lenders, the Act does not preempt state statutes of limitation for claims asserted by assignees of named lenders.

The Act does not, by its terms, extend its statutes-of-limitation exemption to assignees of named lenders. Nor does the Act expressly preclude application of the exemption to assignees. But courts interpreting federal statutes must also presume that Congress intended to preserve the common law.

The common law of most states, including Minnesota, has long recognized that "[a]n assignment operates to place the assignee in the shoes of the assignor, and provides the assignee with the same legal rights as the assignor had before assignment." Contractual rights and duties are generally assignable, including the rights to receive payment on debts, obtain nonmonetary performance, and recover damages. Restatement (Second) of Contracts § 316. But an assignor may not transfer rights that are personal, such as recovery for personal injuries or performance under contracts that involve personal trust or confidences. Restatement (Second) of Contracts § 317, Comment c. Under the common law, a contractual right to recover student-loan debt is assignable and does not fall within the personal-rights exclusion to the assignment rule.

Because Congress legislated with a full knowledge of the common law of assignment, all contractual rights of the named lenders, including the protection from state statutes of limitations, should transfer to their assignees.

INTERPRETATION An assignment places the assignee in the shoes of the assignor and provides the assignee with the same legal rights as the assignor had before the assignment.

CRITICAL THINKING QUESTION If assignees of student loans were made subject to state statutes of limitations what would be the probable effect on the availability of student loans? Explain.

Practical Advice

Upon receiving an assignment of a contractual right, promptly notify the obligor of the assignment.

Notice   The obligor need not receive notice for an assignment to be valid. Giving notice of assignment is advisable, however, because an assignee will lose his rights against the obligor if the obligor, without notice of the assignment, pays the assignor. Compelling an obligor to pay a claim a second time, when she was unaware that a new party was entitled to payment, would be unfair. For example, Donald owes Gary $1,000 due on September 1. Gary assigns the debt to Paula on August 1, but neither Gary nor Paula informs Donald. On September 1, Donald pays Gary. Donald is fully discharged from his obligation, whereas Gary is liable for $1,000 to Paula. On the other hand, if Paula had given notice of the assignment to Donald before September 1 and Donald had paid Gary nevertheless, Paula would then have the right to recover the $1,000 from either Donald or Gary. Furthermore, notice cuts off any defenses based on subsequent agreements between the obligor and assignor and, as already indicated, subsequent setoffs and counterclaims of the obligor that may arise out of entirely separate matters.

Implied Warranties of Assignor [16-1e]

Implied warranty

obligation imposed by law upon the transferor of property or contract rights

An **implied warranty** is an obligation imposed by law upon the transferor of property or contract rights. In the absence of an express intention to the contrary, an assignor who receives value makes the following implied warranties to the assignee with respect to the assigned right:

1. that he will do nothing to defeat or impair the assignment;
2. that the assigned right actually exists and is subject to no limitations or defenses other than those stated or apparent at the time of the assignment;
3. that any writing that evidences the right and that is delivered to the assignee or exhibited to him as an inducement to accept the assignment is genuine and what it purports to be; and
4. that the assignor has no knowledge of any fact that would impair the value of the assignment.

Thus, Eric has a right against Julia and assigns it for value to Gwen. Later, Eric gives Julia a release. Gwen may recover damages from Eric for breach of the first implied warranty.

Express Warranties of Assignor [16-1f]

Express warranty

explicitly made contractual promise regarding the property or contract rights transferred

An **express warranty** is an explicitly made contractual promise regarding the property or contract rights transferred. The assignor is further bound by any specific express warranties he makes to the assignee about the right assigned. Unless he explicitly states as much, however, the assignor does not guarantee that the obligor will pay the assigned debt or otherwise perform.

Practical Advice

Consider obtaining from the assignor an express warranty that the contractual right is assignable and guaranteeing that the obligor will perform the assigned obligation.

Successive Assignments of the Same Right [16-1g]

Successive assignments of the same right

the majority rule is that the first assignee in point of time prevails over later assignees; minority rule is that the first assignee to notify the obligor prevails

The owner of a right could conceivably make successive assignments of the same claim to different persons. Although this action is morally and legally inappropriate, it raises the question of what rights successive assignees have. Assume, for example, that B owes A $1,000. On June 1, A for value assigns the debt to C. Thereafter, on June 15, A assigns it to D, who in good faith gives value and has no knowledge of the prior assignment by A to C. If the assignment is subject to Article 9, then the article's priority rules will control, as discussed in Chapter 37. Otherwise, the priority is determined by the common law. The majority rule in the United States is that the first assignee in point of time (C) prevails over later assignees. By way of contrast, in England and in a minority of the states, the first assignee to notify the obligor prevails.

The Restatement adopts a third view. A prior assignee is entitled to the assigned right and its proceeds to the exclusion of a subsequent assignee, *except* where the prior assignment is revocable or voidable by the assignor or the subsequent assignee in good faith and without knowledge of the prior assignment gives value and obtains one of the following: (1) payment or satisfaction of the obligor's duty, (2) a judgment against the obligor, (3) a new contract with the obligor, or (4) possession of a writing of a type customarily accepted as a symbol or evidence of the right assigned.

DELEGATION OF DUTIES [16-2]

Delegation of duty

transfer to a third party of a contractual obligation

As we indicated, contractual **duties** are not assignable, but their performance generally may be delegated to a third person. A delegation of duties is a transfer of a contractual obligation to a third party. For example, A promises to sell B a new automobile, for which B promises to pay $10,000 by monthly installments over the next three years. If A and D agree that D should deliver the automobile to B, this would not constitute an assignment but would be a delegation of duties between A and D. In this instance, A would be the **delegator**, D would be the **delegatee**, and B would be the **obligee**. A delegation of duty does not extinguish the delegator's obligation to perform because A remains liable to B. When the delegatee accepts, or **assumes**, the delegated duty, *both* the delegator and delegatee are liable for performance of the contractual duty to the obligee.

Assumes

delegatee agrees to perform the contractual obligation of the delegator

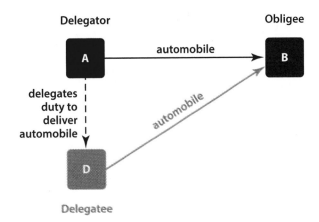

Delegator   **Obligee**

A ──automobile──▶ B

delegates
duty to
deliver
automobile

automobile

D

Delegatee

Delegable Duties [16-2a]

Though contractual duties generally are delegable, a delegation will not be permitted if

1. the nature of the duties is personal in that the obligee has a substantial interest in having the delegator perform the contract;
2. the performance is expressly made nondelegable; or
3. the delegation is prohibited by statute or public policy.

Practical Advice

When it is important that the other party to a contract personally perform his contractual obligations, consider including a term in the contract prohibiting any delegation of duties without written consent.

The courts will examine a delegation more closely than an assignment because a delegation compels the nondelegating party to the contract (the obligee) to receive performance from a party with whom she has not dealt.

For example, a schoolteacher may not delegate her performance to another teacher, even if the substitute is equally competent, for this contract is personal in nature. On the other hand, under a contract in which performance by a party involves no special skill and in which no personal trust or confidence is involved, the party may delegate performance of his duty. For example, the duty to pay money, to deliver fungible goods such as corn, or to mow a lawn is usually delegable. The next case deals with this type of delegation.

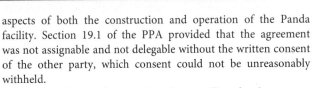

Public Service Commission of Maryland v. Panda-Brandywine, L.P.

Court of Appeals of Maryland, 2003
375 Md. 185, 825 A.2d 462
http://scholar.google.com/scholar_case?case=14283409950595264869&q=825+a.2d+462&hl=en&as_sdt=2,34

FACTS Potomac Electric Power Company (PEPCO) is an electric utility serving the metropolitan Washington, D.C., area. Panda-Brandywine, L.P. (Panda) is a "qualified facility" under the Public Utility Regulatory Policies Act of 1978. In August, 1991, PEPCO and Panda entered into a power purchase agreement (PPA) calling for (1) the construction by Panda of a new 230-megawatt cogenerating power plant in Prince George's County, Maryland; (2) connection of the facility to PEPCO's high-voltage transmission system by transmission facilities to be built by Panda but later transferred without cost to PEPCO; and (3) upon commencement of the commercial operation of the plant, for PEPCO to purchase the power generated by that plant for a period of twenty-five years. The plant was built at a cost of $215 million.

The PPA is 113 pages in length, single-spaced, and is both detailed and complex. It gave PEPCO substantial authority to review, influence, and, in some instances, determine important

aspects of both the construction and operation of the Panda facility. Section 19.1 of the PPA provided that the agreement was not assignable and not delegable without the written consent of the other party, which consent could not be unreasonably withheld.

In 1999, Maryland enacted legislation calling for the restructuring of the electric industry in an effort to promote competition in the generation and delivery of electricity. PEPCO's proposed restructuring involved a complete divestiture of its electric generating assets and its various PPAs, to be accomplished by an auction. The sale to the winning bidder was to be accomplished by an Asset Purchase and Sale Agreement (APSA) that included the PPA to which PEPCO and Panda were parties. Under the APSA the buyer was authorized to take all actions that PEPCO could lawfully take under the PPA with Panda.

On June 7, 2000, Southern Energy, Inc. (SEI) was declared the winning bidder. On September 27, 2000, the Public Service

Commission (PSC) entered an order declaring, among other things, that the provisions in the APSA did not constitute an assignment or transfer within the meaning of Section 19.1 of the Panda PPA, that PEPCO was not assigning "significant obligations and rights under the PPA," that Panda would not be harmed by the transaction, and that the APSA did not "fundamentally alter" the contract between Panda and PEPCO. The PSC thus concluded that Panda's consent to the proposed APSA was not required.

Panda disagreed and brought this lawsuit. The trial court ruled that the APSA effected an assignment of Panda's PPA and reversed the PSC order. PEPCO appealed and the appellate court concluded that, through the APSA, PEPCO effectively and improperly delegated its duties under the PPA to SEI.

DECISION Judgment affirmed.

OPINION In a bilateral contract, each party ordinarily has both rights and duties—the right to expect performance from the other party to the contract and the duty to perform what the party has agreed to perform. Although both are often the subjects of transfer, the law does distinguish between them, using the term "assignment" to refer to the transfer of contractual rights and the term "delegation" to refer to the transfer of contractual duties.

The Restatement (Second) of Contracts permits a contractual right to be assigned unless

(1) the substitution of a right of the assignee for the right of the assignor would materially change the duty of the obligor, or materially increase the burden or risk imposed on him by his contract, or materially impair his chance of obtaining return performance, or materially reduce its value to him,

(2) the assignment is forbidden by statute or is inoperative on grounds of public policy, or

(3) "assignment is validly precluded by contract."

Section 19.1 of the PPA very clearly prohibits both the assignment of rights and the delegation of duties of performance, absent express written consent. The issue, then, is not whether PEPCO can make such an assignment or delegation but only whether it has, in fact, done so. The answer to that lies in the effect that the provisions of the APSA have on the contractual relationship between PEPCO and Panda.

The APSA involves a great deal more than merely a resale of electricity purchased from Panda and even more than the effective substitution of one customer for another. Much of Panda's control over its own facility and business was subject to the approval and cooperation of PEPCO; indeed, to a large extent, the operation of the facility was, in many important respects, almost a joint venture. In agreeing to that kind of arrangement, Panda necessarily was relying on its perceptions of PEPCO's competence and managerial style. One does not ordinarily choose a business partner by auction or lottery, and there is no evidence that Panda did so in this case. Panda has "a substantial interest in having [PEPCO] perform or control the acts promised." Under the APSA that control has been delegated irrevocably to SEI—a stranger to Panda—with the ability of SEI to delegate it to others. Virtually none of the rights and responsibilities transferred to SEI under the APSA are permitted under Section 19.1 of the PPA. Thus the APSA constitutes an assignment of rights and obligations under the PPA in contravention of Section 19.1 of that agreement and it is therefore invalid and unenforceable.

INTERPRETATION The extent to which contractual rights may be assigned and duties of performance delegated are subject to any valid contractual provision prohibiting assignment or delegation.

CRITICAL THINKING QUESTION If the APSA had involved only the resale of electricity purchased from Panda would the court have permitted the delegation?

Duties of the Parties [16-2b]

Delegation

delegator is still bound to perform original obligation

Novation

contract, to which the promisee is a party, substituting a new promisor for an existing promisor, who is consequently no longer liable on the original contract and is not liable as a delegator

Even when permitted, a **delegation** of a duty to a third person leaves the delegator bound to perform. If the delegator desires to be discharged of the duty, she may enter into an agreement by which she obtains the consent of the obligee to substitute a third person (the delegatee) in her place. This is a **novation**, whereby the delegator is discharged and the third party becomes directly bound on his promise to the obligee.

Though a delegation authorizes a third party to perform a duty for the delegator, the delegatee becomes liable for performance only if he assents to perform the delegated duties. Thus, if Frank owes a duty to Grace, and Frank delegates that duty to Henry, Henry is not obligated to either Frank or Grace to perform the duty unless Henry agrees to do so. If, however, Henry promises either Frank (the delegator) or Grace (the obligee) that he will perform Frank's duty, Henry is said to have **assumed the delegated duty** and becomes liable for nonperformance to both Frank and Grace. Accordingly, when there is both a delegation of duties *and* an assumption of the delegated duties, *both* the delegator and the delegatee are liable to the obligee for proper performance of the original contractual duty. The delegatee's promise to perform creates contract rights in the obligee, who may bring an action against the delegatee as a third-party beneficiary of the contract between the delegator and the delegatee. (Third-party contracts are discussed in the next section in this chapter.)

APPLYING THE LAW

Third Parties to Contracts

Facts Monica signed a twelve-month lease with Grandridge Apartments in Grand City. But after only two months she received a promotion that required her to move to Lakeville, three hundred miles away. Mindful of her lease obligation, she found an acquaintance, Troy, to rent the apartment for the remaining ten months. Troy promised Monica he would pay the rent directly to the landlord each month and would clean the place up before moving out at the end of the lease term.

After moving in, Troy personally delivered a check for the rent to the landlord each month until four months later when he lost his job, at which point he stopped paying rent altogether. The landlord evicted Troy and, as he was unable to find another suitable tenant, he sued Monica for the rent owed on the remainder of the lease. Monica claimed the landlord should have sued Troy.

Issue Is Monica liable for the remaining lease payments?

Rule of Law Performance of a contract obligation generally may be delegated to a third person who is willing to assume the liability. However, such a delegation by the obligor does not extinguish the obligor-delegator's duty to perform the contract. If the delegator wishes to be discharged from the contract prospectively, she should enter into a new agreement with the obligee, in which the obligee consents to the substitution of a third party (the delegatee) in the delegator's place. This is called a novation.

Application The lease is a contract obligation. Monica is the obligor, and the landlord is the obligee. Here, Monica delegated her performance under the lease to Troy. Troy assumed liability for the lease payments by agreeing to pay the rent. However, even though a valid delegation has been made, Monica is not relieved of her duty to pay the rent. Instead, both Troy and Monica are now obligated to the landlord for the remaining lease term.

Had Monica entered into a novation with the landlord, only Troy would be liable for the remaining rent. But the facts do not support finding a novation. Troy made the rent payments directly to the landlord, who ultimately evicted Troy from the apartment. Therefore, the landlord was aware that Troy had taken possession of the apartment and that Troy may have taken on some responsibility for rent payments. At most, the landlord tacitly consented to the informal assignment and delegation of the lease to Troy. However, the landlord never agreed to substitute Troy for Monica and thereby to release Monica from her legal obligations under the lease.

Conclusion In a suit by the landlord, Monica is responsible for the remaining rent payments.

The question of whether a party has assumed contractual duties frequently arises in the following ambiguous situation: Marty and Carol agree to an assignment of Marty's contract with Bob. The Restatement and the Code clearly resolve this ambiguity by providing that unless the language or circumstances indicate the contrary, an assignment of "the contract" or of "all my rights under the contract" or an assignment in similar general terms is an assignment of rights *and* a delegation of performance of the duties of the assignor, and its acceptance by the assignee constitutes a promise to perform those duties. For example, Cooper Oil Company has a contract to deliver oil to Halsey. Cooper makes a written assignment to Lowell Oil Company "of all Cooper's rights under the contract." Lowell is under a duty to Halsey to deliver the oil called for by the contract, and Cooper is liable to Halsey if Lowell does not perform. You should also recall that the Restatement and the Code provide that a clause prohibiting an assignment of "the contract" is to be construed as barring only the delegation to the assignee (delegatee) of the assignor's (delegator's) performance, unless the circumstances indicate the contrary.

Third-party beneficiary contract
contract in which one party promises to render a performance to a third person

Intended beneficiary
third party intended by the two contracting parties to receive a benefit from their contract

THIRD-PARTY BENEFICIARY CONTRACTS [16-3]

A contract in which a party (the *promisor*) promises to render a certain performance not to the other party (the promisee) but to a third person (the beneficiary) is called a **third-party beneficiary contract**. The third person is merely a beneficiary of the contract, not a party to it. The law divides such contracts into two types: (1) intended beneficiary contracts and (2) incidental beneficiary contracts. An **intended beneficiary** is intended by the two parties to the contract (the promisor and promisee) to receive a benefit from the performance of their agreement. Accordingly, the courts generally permit intended beneficiaries to enforce third-party contracts. For example, Abbot promises Baldwin to deliver an automobile to Carson if Baldwin promises to pay $10,000. Carson is the intended beneficiary.

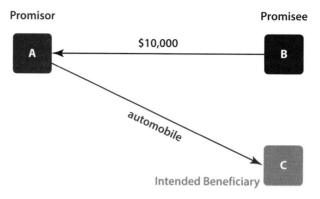

Incidental beneficiary
third party whom the two parties to the contract have no intention of benefiting by their contract and who acquires no rights under the contract

In an **incidental beneficiary** contract the third party is not intended to receive a benefit under the contract. Accordingly, courts do not enforce the third party's right to the benefits of the contract. For example, Abbot promises to purchase and deliver to Baldwin an automobile for $10,000. In all probability Abbot would acquire the automobile from Davis. Davis would be an incidental beneficiary and would have no enforceable rights against either Abbot or Baldwin.

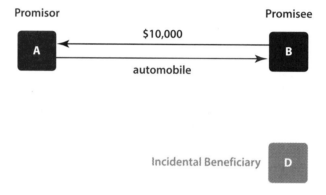

Intended Beneficiary [16-3a]

Unless otherwise agreed between the promisor and promisee, a beneficiary of a promise is an intended beneficiary if the parties intended this to be the result of their agreement. Thus, there are two types of intended beneficiaries: (1) donee beneficiaries and (2) creditor beneficiaries.

Donee beneficiary
a third party intended to receive a benefit from the contract as a gift

Donee Beneficiary
A third party is an intended **donee beneficiary** if the promisee's purpose in bargaining for and obtaining the contract with the promisor was to make a gift of the promised performance to the beneficiary. The ordinary life insurance policy illustrates this type of intended beneficiary third-party contract. The insured (the promisee) makes a contract with an insurance company (the promisor), which promises, in consideration of premiums paid to it by the insured, to pay upon the death of the insured a stated sum of money to the named beneficiary (generally a relative or close friend), who is an intended donee beneficiary.

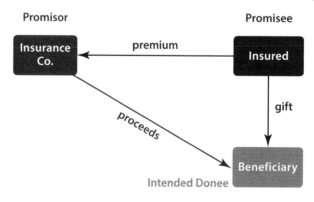

Creditor beneficiary

a third person intended to receive a benefit from the agreement to satisfy a legal duty owed to him

Creditor Beneficiary A third person is an intended **creditor beneficiary** if the promisee intends the performance of the promise to satisfy a legal duty owed to the beneficiary, who is a creditor of the promisee. The contract involves consideration moving from the promisee to the promisor in exchange for the promisor's engaging to pay a debt or to discharge an obligation the promisee owes to the third person.

To illustrate: in the contract for the sale by Wesley of his business to Susan, she promises Wesley that she will pay all of his outstanding business debts, as listed in the contract. Wesley's creditors are intended creditor beneficiaries.

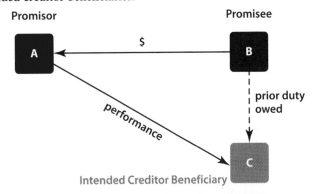

Stine v. Stewart
Supreme Court of Texas, 2002
80 S.W.3d 586; rehearing denied, 2002
http://scholar.google.com/scholar_case?q=80+S.W.3D+586&hl=en&as_sdt=2,34&case=11787409436171520113&scilh=0

FACTS On April 26, 1984, Mary Stine (Stine) loaned her daughter (Mary Ellen) and son-in-law William Stewart $100,000 to purchase a home. In return, the Stewarts jointly executed a promissory note for $100,000, payable on demand to Stine. The Stewarts did not give a security interest or mortgage to secure the note. The Stewarts eventually paid $50,000 on the note, leaving $50,000, plus unpaid interest, due.

The Stewarts divorced on October 2, 1992. The couple executed an Agreement Incident to Divorce, which disposed of marital property, including the home (the agreement identifies the home as the Lago Vista property). The agreement provided that if Stewart sold the home, he agreed that "any monies owing to [Stine] are to be paid in the current principal sum of $50,000.00." The agreement further states:

> The parties agree that with regard to the note to Mary Nelle Stine, after application of the proceeds of the [Lago Vista property], if there are any amounts owing to [Stine] the remaining balance owing to her will be appropriated 50% to NANCY KAREN STEWART and 50% to WILLIAM DEAN STEWART, JR. and said 50% from each party will be due and payable upon the determination that the proceeds from the sale of said residence are not sufficient to repay said $50,000.00 in full.

Stine did not sign the agreement.

On November 17, 1995, Stewart sold the Lago Vista property for $125,000, leaving $6,820.21 in net proceeds. Stewart did not pay these proceeds to Stine and did not make any further payments on the $50,000 principal. Consequently, on July 27, 1998, Stine sued Stewart for breaching the agreement.

The trial court concluded that Stine was an intended third-party beneficiary of the agreement and that Stewart breached the agreement when he refused to pay Stine. The trial court awarded Stine $28,410 in damages from Stewart. The court of appeals reversed the judgment, concluding that Stine was neither an

intended third-party donee beneficiary of the agreement nor an intended third-party creditor beneficiary of the agreement.

DECISION The court of appeals' judgment is reversed and case remanded.

OPINION A third party may recover on a contract made between other parties only if the parties intended to secure a benefit to that third party, and only if the contracting parties entered into the contract directly for the third party's benefit. A third party does not have a right to enforce the contract if she received only an incidental benefit. An agreement must clearly and fully express an intent to confer a direct benefit to the third party. To determine the parties' intent, courts must examine the entire agreement and give effect to all the contract's provisions so that none are rendered meaningless.

To qualify as an intended third-party beneficiary, a party must show that she is either a "donee" or "creditor" beneficiary of the contract. An agreement benefits a "donee" beneficiary if "the performance promised will, when rendered, come to him as a pure donation." In contrast, an agreement benefits a "creditor" beneficiary if "that performance will come to him in satisfaction of a legal duty owed to him by the promisee." This duty may be an indebtedness, contractual obligation, or other legally enforceable commitment owed to the third party.

The Court agreed with the court of appeals' determination that Stine was not an intended third-party donee beneficiary of the agreement. But, it concluded that Stine is a third-party creditor beneficiary. The agreement expressly provides that the Stewarts intended to satisfy an obligation to repay Stine the $50,000 that the Stewarts owed her. Specifically, the agreement refers to the monies owed to Stine as "the current principal sum of $50,000." Then, the agreement states that Stewart agreed to pay the property sale net proceeds "with regard to the note" to Stine. The agreement further provides that, if the property sale net proceeds did not cover the amount owed to Stine, the remainder would be immediately due and payable from the Stewarts, with each owing one half. Thus, the agreement expressly requires the Stewarts to satisfy their obligation to pay Stine.

The agreement's language clearly shows that Stewart intended to secure a benefit to Stine as a third-party creditor beneficiary. Consequently, Stewart breached the agreement when he refused to pay Stine the money owed to her as the agreement requires.

INTERPRETATION An intended third-party beneficiary of a contract may enforce that contract.

CRITICAL THINKING QUESTION Why did the court conclude that Stine was not an intended third-party donee beneficiary?

Rights of intended beneficiary

an intended donee beneficiary may enforce the contract against the promisor; an intended creditor beneficiary may enforce the contract against either or both the promisor and the promisee

Vesting of rights

if the beneficiary's rights vest, the promisor and promisee may not thereafter vary or discharge these vested rights

---

Practical Advice

To avoid uncertainty, consider specifying in the contract whether there are any third-party beneficiaries and, if so, who they are, what their rights are, and when their rights vest.

Defenses against beneficiary

in an action by the intended beneficiary to enforce the promise, the promisor may assert any defense that would be available to her if the action had been brought by the promisee

Incidental beneficiary

third party whom the two parties to a contract have no intention of benefiting by their contract

Rights of Intended Beneficiary

Though an intended creditor beneficiary may sue either or both parties, an intended donee beneficiary may enforce the contract against the promisor only. He cannot maintain an action against the promisee, as the promisee was under no legal obligation to him.

Vesting of Rights

A contract for the benefit of an intended beneficiary confers upon that beneficiary rights that the beneficiary may enforce. Until these rights vest (take effect), however, the promisor and promisee may, by later agreement, vary or completely discharge them. There is considerable variation among the states as to when vesting occurs. Some states hold that vesting takes place immediately upon the making of the contract. In other states, vesting occurs when the third party learns of the contract and assents to it. In another group of states, vesting requires the third party to change his position in reliance upon the promise made for his benefit. The Restatement has adopted the following position: if the contract between the promisor and promisee provides that its terms may not be varied without the consent of the beneficiary, such a provision will be upheld. If there is no such provision, the parties to the contract may rescind or vary the contract unless the intended beneficiary (1) has brought an action on the promise, (2) has changed her position in reliance on it, or (3) has assented to the promise at the request of the promisor or promisee.

On the other hand, the promisor and promisee may provide that the benefits will never vest. For example, Mildred purchases an insurance policy on her own life, naming her husband as beneficiary. The policy, as such policies commonly do, reserves to Mildred the right to change her beneficiary or even to cancel the policy entirely.

Defenses Against Beneficiary

In an action by the intended beneficiary to enforce the promise, the promisor may assert any defense that would be available to her if the action had been brought by the promisee. The rights of the third party are based upon the promisor's contract with the promisee. Thus, the promisor may assert the absence of mutual assent or consideration, lack of capacity, fraud, mistake, and the like against the intended beneficiary. Once an intended beneficiary's rights have vested, however, the promisor may not assert the defense of contractual modification or rescission entered into with the promisee.

Incidental Beneficiary [16-3b]

An incidental third-party beneficiary is a person to whom the parties to a contract did not intend a benefit but who nevertheless would derive some benefit by its performance. For instance, a contract to raze an old, unsightly building and to replace it with a costly modern house would benefit the owner of the adjoining property by increasing his property's value. He would have no rights under the contract, however, as the benefit to him would be unintended and incidental.

A third person who may benefit incidentally by the performance of a contract to which he is not a party has no rights under the contract, as neither the promisee nor the promisor intended that the third person benefit. Assume that for a stated consideration Charles promises Madeline that he will purchase and deliver to Madeline a new Sony television of the latest model. Madeline pays in advance for the television. Charles does not deliver the television to Madeline. Reiner, the local exclusive Sony dealer, has no rights under the contract, although performance by Charles would produce a sale from which Reiner would derive a benefit, for Reiner is only an incidental beneficiary.

CHAPTER SUMMARY

Assignment of Rights

Definition of Assignment voluntary transfer to a third party of the rights arising from a contract so that the assignor's right to performance is extinguished

- *Assignor* party making an assignment
- *Assignee* party to whom contract rights are assigned
- *Obligor* party owing a duty to the assignor under the original contract
- *Obligee* party to whom a duty of performance is owed under a contract

Requirements of an Assignment include intent but not consideration

- *Revocability of Assignment* when the assignee gives consideration, the assignor may not revoke the assignment without the assignee's consent
- *Partial Assignment* transfer of a portion of contractual rights to one or more assignees

Assignability most contract rights are assignable except

- Assignments that materially increase the duty, risk, or burden upon the obligor
- Assignments of personal rights
- Assignments expressly forbidden by the contract
- Assignments prohibited by law

Rights of Assignee the assignee stands in the shoes of the assignor

- *Defenses of Obligor* may be asserted against the assignee
- *Notice* is not required but is advisable

Implied Warranties obligation imposed by law upon the assignor of a contract right

Express Warranty explicitly made contractual promise regarding contract rights transferred

Successive Assignments of the Same Right the majority rule is that the first assignee in point of time prevails over later assignees; minority rule is that the first assignee to notify the obligor prevails

Delegation of Duties

Definition of Delegation transfer to a third party of a contractual obligation

- *Delegator* party delegating his duty to a third party
- *Delegatee* third party to whom the delegator's duty is delegated
- *Obligee* party to whom a duty of performance is owed by the delegator and delegate

Delegable Duties most contract duties may be delegated except

- Duties that are personal
- Duties that are expressly nondelegable
- Duties whose delegation is prohibited by statute or public policy

Duties of the Parties

- *Delegation* delegator is still bound to perform original obligation
- *Novation Contract* a substituted contract to which the promisee is a party, which substitutes a new promisor for an existing promisor, who is consequently no longer liable on the original contract and is not liable as a delegator

Third-Party Beneficiary Contracts

Definition a third-party beneficiary contract is one in which one party promises to render a performance to a third person (the beneficiary)

Intended Beneficiaries third parties intended by the two contracting parties to receive a benefit from their contract

- *Donee Beneficiary* a third party intended to receive a benefit from the contract as a gift
- *Creditor Beneficiary* a third person intended to receive a benefit from the contract to satisfy a legal duty owed to him
- *Rights of Intended Beneficiary* an intended donee beneficiary may enforce the contract against the promisor; an intended creditor beneficiary may enforce the contract against either or both the promisor and the promisee
- *Vesting of Rights* if the beneficiary's rights vest, the promisor and promisee may not thereafter vary or discharge these vested rights

Defenses Against Beneficiary in an action by the intended beneficiary to enforce the promise, the promisor may assert any defense that would be available to her if the action had been brought by the promisee

Incidental Beneficiary third party whom the two parties to the contract have no intention of benefiting by their contract and who acquires no rights under the contract

QUESTIONS

1. On December 1, Euphonia, a famous singer, contracted with Boito to sing at Boito's theater on December 31 for a fee of $45,000 to be paid immediately after the performance.
   a. Euphonia, for value received, assigns this fee to Carter.
   b. Euphonia, for value received, assigns this contract to sing to Dumont, an equally famous singer.
   c. Boito sells his theater to Edmund and assigns his contract with Euphonia to Edmund.
   State the effect of each of these assignments.

2. The Smooth Paving Company entered into a paving contract with the city of Chicago. The contract contained the clause "contractor shall be liable for all damages to buildings resulting from the work performed." In the process of construction, one of the bulldozers of the Smooth Paving Company struck and broke a gas main, causing an explosion and a fire that destroyed the house of John Puff. Puff brought an action for breach of the paving contract against the Smooth Paving Company to recover damages for the loss of his house. Can Puff recover under this contract? Explain.

3. Anne, who was unemployed, registered with the Speedy Employment Agency. A contract was then made under which Anne, in consideration of such position as the agency would obtain for her, agreed to pay the agency one half of her first month's salary. The contract also contained an assignment by Anne to the agency of one half of her first month's salary. Two weeks later, the agency obtained a permanent position for Anne with the Bostwick Co. at a monthly salary of $1,900. The agency also notified Bostwick Co. of the assignment by Anne. At the end of the first month, Bostwick Co. paid Anne her salary in full. Anne then quit and disappeared. The agency now sues Bostwick Co. for $950 under the assignment. Who will prevail? Explain.

4. Georgia purchased an option on Greenacre from Pamela for $10,000. The option contract contained a provision by which Georgia promised not to assign the option contract without Pamela's permission. Georgia, without Pamela's permission, assigned the contract to Michael. Michael now seeks to exercise the option, and Pamela refuses to sell Greenacre to him. Must Pamela sell the land to Michael?

5. Julia contracts to sell to Hayden, an ice cream manufacturer, the amount of ice Hayden may need in his business for the ensuing three years to the extent of not more than 250 tons a week at a stated price per ton. Hayden makes a corresponding promise to Julia to buy such an amount of ice. Hayden sells his ice cream plant to Reed and assigns to Reed all Hayden's rights under the contract with Julia. On learning of the sale,

Julia refuses to furnish ice to Reed. Can Reed successfully collect damages from Julia? Explain.

6. Brown enters into a written contract with Ideal Insurance Company under which, in consideration of Brown's payment of her premiums, the insurance company promises to pay Williams College the face amount of the policy, $100,000, on Brown's death. Brown pays the premiums until her death. Thereafter, Williams College makes demand for the $100,000, which the insurance company refuses to pay on the ground that Williams College was not a party to the contract. Can Williams successfully enforce the contract?

7. Grant and Debbie enter into a contract binding Grant personally to do some delicate cabinetwork. Grant assigns his rights and delegates performance of his duties to Clarence.
   a. On being informed of this, Debbie agrees with Clarence, in consideration of Clarence's promise to do the work, that Debbie will accept Clarence's work, if properly done, instead of the performance promised by Grant. Later, without cause, Debbie refuses to allow Clarence to proceed with the work, though Clarence is ready to do so, and makes demand on Grant that Grant perform. Grant refuses. Can Clarence recover damages from Debbie? Can Debbie recover from Grant?
   b. Instead, assume that Debbie refuses to permit Clarence to do the work, employs another carpenter, and brings an action against Grant, claiming as damages the difference between the contract price and the cost to employ the other carpenter. Explain whether Debbie will prevail.

8. Rebecca owes Lewis $2,500 due on November 1. On August 15, Lewis assigns this right for value received to Julia, who gives notice on September 10 of the assignment to Rebecca. On August 25, Lewis assigns the same right to Wayne, who in good faith gives value and has no prior knowledge of the assignment by Lewis to Julia. Wayne gives Rebecca notice of the assignment on August 30. What are the rights and obligations of Rebecca, Lewis, Julia, and Wayne?

9. Lisa hired Jay in the spring, as she had for many years, to set out in beds the flowers Lisa had grown in her greenhouses during the winter. The work was to be done in Lisa's absence for $300. Jay became ill the day after Lisa departed and requested his friend, Curtis, to set out the flowers, promising to pay Curtis $250 when Jay received his payment. Curtis agreed. On completion of the planting, an agent of Lisa's, who had authority to dispense the money, paid Jay, and Jay paid Curtis. Within two days, it became obvious that the planting was a disaster. Because he did not operate Lisa's

automatic watering system properly, everything set out by Curtis had died of water rot. May Lisa recover damages from Curtis? May Lisa recover damages from Jay, and, if so, does Jay have an action against Curtis?

10. Caleb, operator of a window-washing business, dictated a letter to his secretary addressed to Apartments, Inc., stating, "I will wash the windows of your apartment buildings at $4.10 per window to be paid on completion of the work." The secretary typed the letter, signed Caleb's name, and mailed it to Apartments, Inc. Apartments, Inc., replied, "Accept your offer."

Caleb wrote back, "I will wash them during the week starting July 10 and direct you to pay the money you will owe me to my son, Bernie. I am giving it to him as a wedding present." Caleb sent a signed copy of the letter to Bernie.

Caleb washed the windows during the time stated and demanded payment to him of $8,200 (2,000 windows at $4.10 each), informing Apartments, Inc., that he had changed his mind about having the money paid to Bernie.

What are the rights of the parties?

CASE PROBLEMS

11. On April 1, members of Local 100, Transport Workers Union of America (TWU), began an eleven-day mass transit strike that paralyzed the life and commerce of the city of New York. Jackson, Lewis, Schnitzler & Krupman, a Manhattan law firm, brought a class action suit against the TWU for the direct and foreseeable damages it suffered as a result of the union's illegal strike. The law firm sought to recover as a third-party beneficiary of the collective bargaining agreement between the union and New York City. The agreement contains a no-strike clause and states that the TWU agreed to cooperate with the city to provide a safe, efficient, and dependable mass transit system. The law firm argues that its members are a part of the general public that depends on the mass transit system to go to and from work. Therefore, they are in the class of persons for whose benefit the union has promised to provide dependable transportation service. Are the members of the class action suit entitled to recover? Explain.

12. Northwest Airlines leased space in the terminal building at the Portland Airport from the Port of Portland. Crosetti entered into a contract with the Port to furnish janitorial services for the building, which required Crosetti to keep the floor clean, to indemnify the Port against loss due to claims or lawsuits based upon Crosetti's failure to perform, and to provide public liability insurance for the Port and Crosetti. A patron of the building who was injured by a fall caused by a foreign substance on the floor at Northwest's ticket counter brought suit for damages against Northwest, the Port, and Crosetti. Upon settlement of this suit, Northwest sued Crosetti to recover the amount of its contribution to the settlement and other expenses on the grounds that Northwest was a third-party beneficiary of Crosetti's contract with the Port to keep the floors clean and, therefore, within the protection of Crosetti's indemnification agreement. Will Northwest prevail? Why?

13. Tompkins-Beckwith, as the contractor on a construction project, entered into a subcontract with a division of Air Metal Industries. Air Metal procured American Fire and Casualty Company to be surety on certain bonds in connection with contracts it was performing for Tompkins-Beckwith and others. As security for these bonds, on January 3, Air Metal executed an assignment to American Fire of all accounts receivable under the Tompkins-Beckwith subcontract. On

November 26 of that year, Boulevard National Bank lent money to Air Metal. To secure the loans, Air Metal purported to assign to the bank certain accounts receivable it had under its subcontract with Tompkins-Beckwith.

In June of the following year, Air Metal defaulted on various contracts bonded by American Fire. On July 1, American Fire served formal notice on Tompkins-Beckwith of Air Metal's assignment. Tompkins-Beckwith acknowledged the assignment and agreed to pay. In August, Boulevard National Bank notified Tompkins-Beckwith of its assignment. Tompkins-Beckwith refused to recognize the bank's claim and, instead, paid all remaining funds that had accrued to Air Metal to American Fire. The bank then sued to enforce its claim under Air Metal's assignment. Is the assignment effective? Why?

14. The International Association of Machinists (the union) was the bargaining agent for the employees of Powder Power Tool Corporation. On August 24, the union and the corporation executed a collective bargaining agreement providing for retroactively increased wage rates for the corporation's employees effective as of the previous April 1. Three employees who were working for Powder before and for several months after April 1, but who were not employed by the corporation when the agreement was executed on August 24, were paid to the time their employment terminated at the old wage scale. The three employees assigned their claims to Springer, who brought this action against the corporation for the extra wages. Decision?

15. In March, Adrian Saylor sold government bonds owned exclusively by him and with $6,450 of the proceeds opened a savings account in a bank in the name of "Mr. or Mrs. Adrian M. Saylor." In June of the following year, Saylor deposited the additional sum of $2,132 of his own money in the account. There were no other deposits and no withdrawals prior to the death of Saylor in May a year later. Is the balance of the account on Saylor's death payable wholly to Adrian Saylor's estate, wholly to his widow, or half to each?

16. Linda King was found liable to Charlotte Clement as the result of an automobile accident. King, who was insolvent at the time, declared bankruptcy and directed her attorney, Prestwich, to list Clement as an unsecured creditor. The attorney

failed to carry out this duty, and consequently King sued him for legal malpractice. When Clement pursued her judgment against King, she received a written assignment of King's legal malpractice claim against Prestwich. Clement has attempted to bring the claim, but Prestwich alleges that a claim for legal malpractice is not assignable. Decision?

17. Rensselaer Water Company contracted with the city of Rensselaer to provide water to the city for use in homes, public buildings, industry, and fire hydrants. During the term of the contract, a building caught fire. The fire spread to a nearby warehouse and destroyed it and its contents. The water company knew of the fire but failed to supply adequate water pressure at the fire hydrant to extinguish the fire. The warehouse owner sued the water company for failure to fulfill its contract with the city. Can the owner of the warehouse enforce the contract? Explain.

18. McDonald's has an undeviating policy of retaining absolute control over who receives new franchises. McDonald's granted to Copeland a franchise in Omaha, Nebraska. In a separate letter, it also granted him a right of first refusal for future franchises to be developed in the Omaha-Council Bluffs area. Copeland then sold all rights in his six McDonald's franchises to Schupack. When McDonald's offered a new franchise in the Omaha area to someone other than Schupack, he attempted to exercise the right of first refusal. McDonald's would not recognize the right in Schupack, claiming that it was personal to Copeland and, therefore, nonassignable without its consent. Schupack brought an action for specific performance, requiring McDonald's to accord him the right of first refusal. Is Schupack correct in his contention?

19. While under contract to play professional basketball for the Philadelphia 76ers, Billy Cunningham, an outstanding player, negotiated a three-year contract with the Carolina Cougars, another professional basketball team. The contract with the Cougars was to begin at the expiration of the contract with the 76ers. In addition to a signing bonus of $125,000, Cunningham was to receive under the new contract a salary of $100,000 for the first year, $110,000 for the second, and $120,000 for the third. The contract also stated that Cunningham "had special, exceptional and unique knowledge, skill and ability as a basketball player" and that Cunningham therefore agreed the Cougars could enjoin him from playing basketball for any other team for the term of the contract. In addition, the contract contained a clause prohibiting its assignment to another club without Cunningham's consent. In 1971, the ownership of the Cougars changed, and Cunningham's contract was assigned to Munchak Corporation, the new owners, without his consent. When Cunningham refused to play for the Cougars, Munchak Corporation sought to enjoin his playing for any other team. Cunningham asserts that his contract was not assignable. Was the contract assignable? Explain.

20. Pauline Brown was shot and seriously injured by an unknown assailant in the parking lot of National Supermarkets. Pauline and George Brown brought a negligence action against National, Sentry Security Agency, and T. G. Watkins, a security guard and Sentry employee. The Browns maintained that the defendants have a legal duty to protect National's customers, both in the store and in the parking lot, and that this duty was breached. The defendants denied this allegation. What will the Browns have to prove to prevail? Explain.

TAKING SIDES

Pizza of Gaithersburg and The Pizza Shops (Pizza Shops) contracted with Virginia Coffee Service (Virginia) to install vending machines in each of their restaurants. One year later, the Macke Company (a provider of vending machines) purchased Virginia's assets, and the vending machine contracts were assigned to Macke. Pizza Shops had dealt with Macke before but had chosen Virginia because they preferred the way it conducted its business. When Pizza Shops attempted to terminate their contracts for vending services, Macke brought suit for damages for breach of contract.

a. What arguments would support Pizza Shops' termination of the contracts?

b. What arguments would support Macke's suit for breach of contract?

c. Which side should prevail? Explain.

Performance, Breach, and Discharge

CHAPTER 17

Because contracting parties ordinarily expect that they will perform their obligations, they are usually more explicit in defining those obligations than in stating the consequences of their nonperformance.

Restatement of Contracts, Introductory Note

CHAPTER OUTCOMES

After reading and studying this chapter, you should be able to:

1. Identify and distinguish among the various types of conditions.

2. Distinguish between full performance and tender of performance.

3. Explain the difference between material breach and substantial performance.

4. Distinguish among a mutual rescission, substituted contract, accord and satisfaction, and novation.

5. Identify and explain the ways discharge may be brought about by operation of law.

The subject of discharge of contracts concerns the termination of contractual duties. In earlier chapters we saw how parties may become contractually bound by their promises. It is also important to know how a person may become unbound from a contract. Although contractual promises are made for a purpose and the parties reasonably expect this purpose to be fulfilled by performance, performance of a contractual duty is only one method of discharge.

Whatever causes a binding promise to cease to be binding is a discharge of the contract. In general, there are four kinds of discharge: (1) performance by the parties, (2) material breach by one or both of the parties, (3) agreement of the parties, and (4) operation of law. Moreover, many contractual promises are not absolute promises to perform but are conditional—that is, they depend on the happening or nonhappening of a specific event. After we discuss the subject of conditions, we will cover the four kinds of discharge.

CONDITIONS [17-1]

Condition
an uncertain event that affects the duty of performance

A **condition** is an event whose happening or nonhappening affects a duty of performance under a contract. Some conditions must be satisfied before any duty to perform arises; others terminate the duty to perform; still others either limit or modify the duty to perform. A condition is inserted in a contract to protect and benefit the promisor. The more conditions to which a promise is subject, the less content the promise has. For example, a promise to pay $8,000 provided that such sum is realized from the sale of an automobile, provided the automobile is sold within sixty days, and provided that the automobile, which has been stolen, can be found, is clearly different from, and worth considerably less than, an unconditional promise by the same promisor to pay $8,000.

A fundamental difference exists between the breach or nonperformance of a contractual promise and the failure or nonhappening of a condition. A breach of contract

Practical Advice

Consider using conditions to place the risk of the nonoccurrence of critical, uncertain events on the other party to the contract.

Express condition

performance is explicitly made contingent on the happening or nonhappening of a stated event

Satisfaction

express condition making performance contingent upon one party's approval of the other's performance

Subjective satisfaction

approval based upon a party's honestly held opinion

Objective satisfaction

approval based upon whether a reasonable person would be satisfied

Practical Advice

In your contracts based on satisfaction, specify which standard—subjective satisfaction or objective satisfaction—should apply to each contractual duty of performance.

subjects the promisor to liability. It may or may not, depending on its materiality, excuse the nonbreaching party's nonperformance of his duty under the contract. The happening or non-happening of a condition, on the other hand, either prevents a party from acquiring a right or deprives him of a right but subjects neither party to any liability.

Conditions may be classified by *how* they are imposed: express conditions, implied-in-fact conditions, or implied-in-law conditions (also called constructive conditions). They also may be classified by *when* they affect a duty of performance: conditions concurrent, conditions precedent, or conditions subsequent. These two ways of classifying conditions are not mutually exclusive; for example, a condition may be constructive and concurrent or express and precedent.

Express Conditions [17-1a]

An **express condition** is explicitly set forth in language. No particular form of words is necessary to create an express condition, as long as the event to which the performance of the promise is made subject is clearly expressed. An express condition is usually preceded by words such as "provided that," "on condition that," "if," "subject to," "while," "after," "upon," or "as soon as."

The basic rule applied to express conditions is that they must be fully and literally performed before the conditional duty to perform arises. However, when application of the full and literal performance test would result in a forfeiture, the courts usually apply to the completed portion of the condition a substantial satisfaction test, as discussed in this chapter under "Substantial Performance."

Satisfaction of a Contracting Party
The parties to a contract may agree that performance by one of them shall be to the **satisfaction** of the other, who will not be obligated to perform unless he is satisfied. This is an express condition to the duty to perform. Assume that tailor Ken contracts to make a suit of clothes to Dick's satisfaction, and that Dick promises to pay Ken $850 for the suit if he is satisfied with it when completed. Ken completes the suit using materials ordered by Dick. The suit fits Dick beautifully, but Dick tells Ken that he is not satisfied with it and refuses to accept or pay for it. Ken is not entitled to recover $850 or any amount from Dick because the express condition did not happen. This is so if Dick's dissatisfaction is honest and in good faith, even if it is unreasonable. Where satisfaction relates to a matter of personal taste, opinion, or judgment, the law applies the **subjective satisfaction** standard, and the condition has not occurred if the promisor is in good faith dissatisfied.

If the contract does not clearly indicate that satisfaction is subjective, or if the performance contracted for relates to mechanical fitness or utility, the law assumes an **objective satisfaction** standard. For example, the objective standard of satisfaction would apply to the sale of a building or standard goods. In such cases, the question would not be whether the promisor was actually satisfied with the performance by the other party but whether, as a reasonable person, he ought to be satisfied.

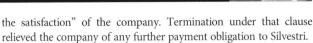

Michael Silvestri v. Optus Software, Inc.
Supreme Court of New Jersey, 2003
175 N.J. 113, 814 A.2d 602
http://scholar.google.com/scholar_case?q=814+A.2d+602&hl=en&as_sdt=2,34&case=3846111007491599697&scilh=0

FACTS Optus Software, Inc. (Optus), a small computer software company, hired Michael Silvestri as its director of support services at an annual salary of $70,000. Silvestri was responsible for supervising technical customer support services. More specifically, Silvestri was charged with supervision of the support services staff, responsibility for communication with resellers of the Optus computer software, and coordination of ongoing training for support staff and resellers. Silvestri's two-year employment contract began on January 4, 1999, and contained a satisfaction clause that reserved to the company the right to terminate his employment for "failure or refusal to perform faithfully, diligently or completely his duties ... to

the satisfaction" of the company. Termination under that clause relieved the company of any further payment obligation to Silvestri.

During the first six months of his employment Silvestri enjoyed the full support of Joseph Avellino, the CEO of Optus. Avellino's attitude started to change during the summer months of 1999, when several clients and resellers communicated to Avellino their disappointment with the performance and attitude of the support services staff generally, and several complaints targeted Silvestri specifically. Avellino informed Silvestri of those criticisms. On September 17, 1999, Avellino terminated Silvestri under the satisfaction clause.

Silvestri filed an action for breach of contract. Silvestri did not assert that there was any reason for his termination other than Avellino's genuine dissatisfaction with his performance. Rather, Silvestri challenged the reasonableness of that dissatisfaction. He portrayed Avellino as a meddling micromanager who overreacted to any customer criticism and thus could not reasonably be satisfied.

The trial court granted summary judgment in favor of Optus, refusing to substitute its judgment for that of the president and CEO of Optus. The Appellate Division reversed, holding that an employer must meet an objective, reasonable-person test when invoking a satisfaction clause permitting termination of employment. The Supreme Court of New Jersey granted review.

DECISION The judgment of the Appellate Division is reversed, and the case remanded for entry of summary judgment in favor of Optus.

OPINION Agreements containing a promise to perform in a manner satisfactory to another are a common form of enforceable contract. Such "satisfaction" contracts are generally divided into two categories: (1) contracts that involve matters of personal taste, sensibility, judgment, or convenience and (2) contracts that contain a requirement of satisfaction as to mechanical fitness, utility, or marketability. The standard for evaluating satisfaction depends on the type of contract. Satisfaction contracts of the first type are interpreted on a subjective basis, with satisfaction dependent on the personal, honest evaluation of the party to be satisfied. Absent language to the contrary, however, contracts of the second type—involving operative fitness or mechanical utility—are subject to an objective test of reasonableness, because in those cases the extent and quality of performance can be measured by objective tests.

A subjective standard typically is applied to satisfaction clauses in employment contracts because "there is greater reason and a greater tendency to interpret the contract as involving personal satisfaction," rather than the satisfaction of a hypothetical "reasonable" person. In the case of a high-level business manager, a subjective test is particularly appropriate to the flexibility needed by the owners and higher-level officers operating a competitive enterprise. When a manager has been hired to share responsibility for the success of a business entity, an employer is entitled to be highly personal and idiosyncratic in judging the employee's satisfactory performance in advancing the enterprise.

The Court held that a subjective test of performance governs the employer's resort to a satisfaction clause in an employment contract unless there is some language in the contract to suggest that the parties intended an objective standard. There is no such language here. Although the subjective standard obliges the employer to act "honestly in accordance with his duty of good faith and fair dealing," genuine dissatisfaction of the employer, honestly held, is sufficient for discharge.

INTERPRETATION A subjective test of performance governs an employer's use of a satisfaction clause in an employment contract unless language in the contract suggests that the parties intended an objective standard.

CRITICAL THINKING QUESTION Could an employee discharged under a satisfaction clause demonstrate that the employer was not honestly dissatisfied? Explain.

Satisfaction of a Third Party   A contract may condition the duty of one contracting party to accept and pay for the performance of the other contracting party upon the approval of a third party who is not a party to the contract. For example, building contracts commonly provide that before the owner is required to pay, the builder shall furnish the architect's certificate stating that the building has been constructed according to the plans and specifications on which the builder and the owner agreed. Although the price is being paid for the building, not for the certificate, the owner must have both the building and the certificate before she will be obliged to pay. The duty of payment was made expressly conditional on the presentation of the certificate.

Implied-in-Fact Conditions [17-1b]

Implied-in-fact condition
contingency understood but not expressed by the parties

Implied-in-fact conditions are similar to express conditions in that they must fully and literally occur and in that they are understood by the parties to be part of the agreement. They differ in that they are not stated in express language; rather, they are necessarily inferred from the terms of the contract, the nature of the transaction, or the conduct of the parties. Thus, if Edna, for $1,750, contracts to paint Sy's house any color Sy desires, it is necessarily implied in fact that Sy will inform Edna of the desired color before Edna begins to paint. The notification of choice of color is an implied-in-fact condition, an operative event that must occur before Edna is subject to the duty of painting the house.

Implied-in-Law Conditions [17-1c]

Implied-in-law condition
contingency that arises from operation of law

An **implied-in-law condition**, or a constructive condition, is imposed by law to accomplish a just and fair result. It differs from an express condition and an implied-in-fact condition in two ways: (1) it is not contained in the language of the contract or necessarily inferred from the contract and (2) it need only be substantially performed. For example, Fernando contracts to sell a certain tract of land to Marie for $18,000, but the contract is silent as to the time of delivery of the deed and payment of the price. According to the law, the contract implies that payment and delivery of the deed are not independent of each other. The courts will treat the promises as mutually dependent and therefore will hold that a delivery or tender of the deed by Fernando to Marie is a condition to the duty of Marie to pay the price. Conversely, payment or tender of $18,000 by Marie to Fernando is a condition to the duty of Fernando to deliver the deed to Marie.

Concurrent Conditions [17-1d]

Concurrent condition

performance by the parties is to occur simultaneously

Concurrent conditions occur when the mutual duties of performance are to take place simultaneously. As we indicated in the discussion of implied-in-law conditions, in the absence of agreement to the contrary, the law assumes that the respective performances under a contract are concurrent conditions.

Condition Precedent [17-1e]

Condition precedent

an event that must or must not occur before performance is due

A **condition precedent** is an event that must occur before performance is due under a contract. In other words, the immediate duty of one party to perform is subject to the condition that some event must first occur. For instance, Steve is to deliver shoes to Nancy on June 1, and Nancy is to pay for the shoes on July 15. Steve's delivery of the shoes is a condition precedent to Nancy's performance. Similarly, if Rachel promises to buy Justin's land for $50,000, provided Rachel can obtain financing in the amount of $40,000 at 10 percent or less for thirty years within sixty days of signing the contract, Rachel's obtaining the specified financing is a condition precedent to her duty. If the condition is satisfied, Rachel is bound to perform; if it is not met, she is not bound to perform. Rachel, however, is under an implied-in-law duty to use her best efforts to obtain financing under these terms.

Condition Subsequent [17-1f]

Condition subsequent

an event that terminates a duty of performance

A **condition subsequent** is an event that terminates an existing duty. For example, when goods are sold under terms of "sale or return," the buyer has the right to return the goods to the seller within a stated period but is under an immediate duty to pay the price unless the parties have agreed on credit. The duty to pay the price is terminated by a return of the goods, which operates as a condition subsequent. Conditions subsequent occur very infrequently in contract law; conditions precedent are quite common.

DISCHARGE BY PERFORMANCE [17-2]

Discharge

termination of a contractual duty

Performance

fulfillment of a contractual obligation

Tender

offer of performance

Discharge is the termination of a contractual duty. **Performance** is the fulfillment of a contractual obligation. Discharge by performance is undoubtedly the most frequent method of discharging a contractual duty. If a promisor exactly performs his duty under the contract, the promisor is no longer subject to that duty.

Every contract imposes upon each party a duty of good faith and fair dealing in its performance and its enforcement. As discussed in Chapter 19, the Uniform Commercial Code imposes a comparable duty.

Tender is an offer by one party—who is ready, willing, and able to perform—to the other party to perform his obligation according to the terms of the contract. Under a bilateral contract, the refusal or rejection of a tender, or offer of performance, by one party may be treated as a repudiation, excusing or discharging the tendering party from further duty of performance under the contract.

DISCHARGE BY BREACH [17-3]

Breach

wrongful failure to perform the terms of a contract

A **breach** of a contract is a wrongful failure to perform its terms. Breach of contract always gives rise to a cause of action for damages by the aggrieved (injured) party. It may, however, have a more important effect: an uncured (uncorrected) *material* breach by one party operates as an excuse for nonperformance by the other party and discharges the aggrieved party from any further duty under the contract. If, on the other hand, the breach is not material, the aggrieved party is not discharged from the contract, although she may recover money damages. Under the Code's perfect tender rule, which applies only to sales transactions, *any* deviation discharges the aggrieved party.

APPLYING THE LAW

Performance, Breach, and Discharge

Facts Davis manages commercial real estate. In April, Davis contracted with Bidley to acquire and plant impatiens in the flowerbeds outside fourteen office properties that Davis manages. Bidley verbally agreed to buy and plant the impatiens by May 31, for a total of $10,000. Bidley purchased the necessary plants from Ackerman, who delivered them to Bidley on May 26. Bidley completed the planting at thirteen of the office buildings by May 29, but because another job took much longer than anticipated, Bidley was unable to finish planting the flowers outside the fourteenth office building until June 1. When he received Bidley's invoice, Davis refused to pay any of the $10,000.

Issue Has Bidley's committed a material breach of the contract so as to discharge Davis's performance under the contract?

Rule of Law Breach of contract is defined as a wrongful failure to perform. An uncured material breach discharges the aggrieved

party's performance, serving as an excuse for the aggrieved party's nonperformance of his obligations under the contract. A breach is material if it significantly impairs the aggrieved party's contract rights. When a breach relates to timing of performance, failure to promptly perform a contract as promised is considered a material breach only if the parties have agreed that "time is of the essence," in other words that the failure to perform on time is material. If, on the other hand, the aggrieved party does get substantially that for which he bargained, the breach is not material. In such a case the aggrieved party is not discharged from the contract but has a right to collect damages for the injury sustained as a result of the breach.

Application Bidley failed to plant all of the flowers by May 31 as he promised. Therefore, he has breached the contract. However, Bidley's breach is not material. There is no indication that the parties agreed that time

was of the essence nor that there was any compelling reason the plants had to be in the ground by May 31. They simply agreed on May 31 as the date for performance.

Furthermore, Davis has gotten substantially that for which he bargained. In fact, as of May 31, Bidley had completed the planting at thirteen of the office buildings and had commenced the work at the fourteenth. One day later, the entire job was done. Given that Bidley's late performance did not significantly impair Davis's rights under the contract, the breach is not material. Therefore, Davis is entitled only to recover any damages he can prove were suffered as a result of Bidley's late performance.

Conclusion Bidley's breach is not material. Davis is not discharged from performance and must pay the $10,000 owed under the contract, less the value of any damages caused by the one-day delay in planting flowers at one office building.

Material breach
nonperformance that significantly impairs the aggrieved party's rights under the contract; discharges the injured party from any further duty under the contract

---

Practical Advice

If the timely performance of a contractual duty is important, use a "time-is-of-the-essence" clause to make failure to perform promptly a material breach.

Prevention of performance
one party's substantial interference with or prevention of performance by the other constitutes a material breach and discharges the other party to the contract

Material Breach [17-3a]

An unjustified failure to perform *substantially* the obligations promised in a contract is a **material breach**. The key is whether the aggrieved party obtained substantially what he had bargained for, despite the breach, or whether the breach significantly impaired his rights under the contract. A material breach discharges the aggrieved party from his duty of performance. For instance, Joe orders a custom-made, tailored suit from Peggy to be made of wool, but Peggy makes the suit of cotton instead. Assuming that the labor component of this contract predominates and thus the contract is not considered a sale of goods, Peggy has materially breached the contract. Consequently, Joe is discharged from his duty to pay for the suit, and he may also recover money damages from Peggy for her breach.

Although there are no clear-cut rules as to what constitutes a material breach, several basic principles apply. First, partial performance is a material breach of a contract if it omits some essential part of the contract. Second, the courts will consider a breach material if it is quantitatively or qualitatively serious. Third, an intentional breach of contract is generally held to be material. Fourth, a failure to perform a promise promptly is a material breach if time is of the essence; that is, if the parties have clearly indicated that a failure to perform by a stated time is material; otherwise, the aggrieved party may recover damages only for loss caused by the delay. Fifth, the parties to a contract may, within limits, specify what breaches are to be considered material.

Prevention of Performance

One party's substantial interference with, or prevention of, performance by the other generally constitutes a material breach that discharges the other party to the contract. For instance, Dale prevents an architect from giving Lucy a certificate that is a condition to Dale's liability to pay Lucy a certain sum of money. Dale may not then use Lucy's failure to produce a certificate as an excuse for nonpayment. Likewise, if Matthew has contracted to grow a certain crop for Richard and Richard plows the field and destroys the seedlings Matthew has planted, his interference with Matthew's performance discharges Matthew from his duty under the contract. It does not, however, discharge Richard from his duty under the contract.

Perfect tender rule
standard under the Uniform Commercial Code that performance must comply strictly with contractual duties and that any deviation discharges the injured party

Substantial performance
performance that is incomplete but does not defeat the purpose of the contract; does not discharge the injured party but entitles him to damages

Anticipatory repudiation
breach of a contract before performance is due by a party announcing that he will not perform or by committing an act that makes it impossible to perform; it is treated as a breach, allowing the nonrepudiating party to bring suit immediately

Practical Advice

If the other party to a contract commits an anticipatory breach, carefully consider whether it is better to sue immediately or to wait until the time performance is due.

Perfect Tender Rule   The Code greatly alters the common law doctrine of material breach by adopting what is known as the **perfect tender rule**. The perfect tender rule, which we will discuss more fully in Chapter 20, essentially provides that *any* deviation from the promised performance in a sales contract under the Code constitutes a material breach of the contract and discharges the aggrieved party from his duty of performance.

Substantial Performance [17-3b]

Substantial performance is performance that, though incomplete, does not defeat the purpose of the contract. If a party substantially, but not completely, performs her obligations under a contract, the common law generally will allow her to obtain the other party's performance, less any damages the partial performance caused. If no harm has been caused, the breaching party will obtain the other party's full contractual performance. Thus, in the specially ordered suit illustration, if Peggy, the tailor, used the correct fabric but improperly used black buttons instead of blue, she would be permitted to collect from Joe the contract price of the suit less the damage, if any, caused to Joe by the substitution of the wrongly colored buttons. The doctrine of substantial performance assumes particular importance in the construction industry in cases in which a structure is built on the aggrieved party's land. Consider the following: Adam builds a $300,000 house for Betty but deviates from the specifications, causing Betty $10,000 in damages. If the courts considered this a material breach, Betty would not have to pay for the house that is now on her land, a result that would clearly constitute an unjust forfeiture on Adam's part. Therefore, because Adam's performance has been substantial, the courts would probably not deem the breach material, and he would be able to collect $290,000 from Betty.

Anticipatory Repudiation [17-3c]

A breach of contract, as discussed, is a failure to perform the terms of a contract. Although it is logically and physically impossible to fail to perform a duty before the date on which that performance is due, a party may announce before the due date that she will not perform, or she may commit an act that makes her unable to perform. Either act is a repudiation of the contract, which notifies the other party that a breach is imminent. Such repudiation before the date fixed by the contract for performance is called an **anticipatory repudiation**. The courts, as shown in the leading case that follows, view it as a breach that discharges the nonrepudiating party's duty to perform and permits her to bring suit immediately. Nonetheless, the nonbreaching party may wait until the time the performance is due, to see whether the repudiator will retract his repudiation and perform his contractual duties. To be effective, the retraction must come to the attention of the injured party before she materially changes her position in reliance on the repudiation or before she indicates to the other party that she considers the repudiation to be final. If the retraction is effective and the repudiator does perform, then there is a discharge by performance; if the repudiator does not perform, there is a material breach.

 Hochster v. De La Tour
Queen's Bench of England, 1853
2 Ellis and Blackburn Reports 678

FACTS On April 12, 1852, Hochster contracted with De La Tour to serve as a guide for De La Tour on his three-month trip to Europe, beginning on June 1 at an agreed-upon salary. On May 11, De La Tour notified Hochster that he would not need Hochster's services. He also refused to pay Hochster any compensation. Hochster brought this action to recover damages for breach of contract.

DECISION Judgment for Hochster.

OPINION Hochster may treat the repudiation by De La Tour as a breach of contract and immediately bring suit. Otherwise, Hochster would have to remain ready to perform and to refrain from accepting other employment in order to tender his services on June 1. It is far more rational, upon repudiation of the contract by one of the parties, to allow the other party to consider his performance under the contract as excused and seek other employment while retaining his right to sue for damages.

INTERPRETATION An anticipatory breach discharges the injured party and entitles her to bring suit immediately.

CRITICAL THINKING QUESTION What policy reasons support an injured party's right to bring suit immediately upon an anticipatory repudiation? Explain.

Unauthorized material alteration of written contract
a material and fraudulent alteration of a written contract by a party to the contract discharges the entire contract

Unauthorized Material Alteration of Written Contract [17-3d]

An unauthorized alteration or change of any of the material terms or provisions of a written contract or document is a discharge of the entire contract. An alteration is material if it would vary any party's legal relations with the maker of the alteration or would adversely affect that party's legal relations with a third person. To constitute a discharge, the alteration must be material and fraudulent and must be the act of either a party to the contract or someone acting on his behalf. An unauthorized change in the terms of a written contract by a person who is not a party to the contract does not discharge the contract.

DISCHARGE BY AGREEMENT OF THE PARTIES [17-4]

By agreement, the parties to a contract may discharge each other from performance under the contract. They may do this by rescission, substituted contract, accord and satisfaction, or novation.

Mutual rescission
agreement of the parties to terminate their contractual duties

Mutual Rescission [17-4a]

A **mutual rescission** is an agreement between the parties to terminate their respective duties under the contract. It is, literally, a contract to end a contract; and it must contain all of the essentials of a contract. In rescinding an executory, bilateral contract, each party furnishes consideration in giving up his rights under the contract in exchange for the other party's doing the same. If one party has already fully performed, however, a mutual rescission is not binding at common law because of lack of consideration.

Substituted contract
a new contract accepted in satisfaction of the parties' duties under the original contract

Substituted Contracts [17-4b]

A **substituted contract** is a new contract accepted by both parties in satisfaction of the parties' duties under the original contract. A substituted contract immediately discharges the original contract and imposes new obligations under its own terms.

Accord and satisfaction
substituted performance (accord) and the discharge of the prior contractual obligation by performance of the new duty (satisfaction)

Accord and Satisfaction [17-4c]

An **accord** is a contract by which an obligee promises to accept a stated performance in satisfaction of the obligor's existing contractual duty. The performance of the accord, called a **satisfaction**, discharges the original duty. Thus, if Dan owes Sara $500, and the parties agree that Dan will paint Sara's house in satisfaction of the debt, the agreement is an executory accord. When Dan performs the accord by painting Sara's house, he will by satisfaction discharge the $500 debt.

McDowell Welding & Pipefitting, Inc. v. United States Gypsum Co.
Supreme Court of Oregon, 2008
345 Or. 272, 193 P.3d 9
http://scholar.google.com/scholar_case?q=193+P.3d+9&hl=en&as_sdt=2,34&case=8212741394978818508&scilh=0

FACTS Defendant United States Gypsum (U.S. Gypsum) hired BE & K as general contractor on a new plant U.S. Gypsum was building in Columbia County. BE & K subcontracted with the plaintiff (McDowell Welding & Pipefitting, Inc.) to perform work on the project. During construction, the defendants asked the plaintiff to perform additional tasks, over and above the plaintiff's contractual obligations, and the defendants promised to pay the plaintiff for the additional work. After the plaintiff completed its work on the project, the parties disagreed over the amount that the defendants owed the plaintiff for the additional work.

The plaintiff filed an action against the defendants, alleging breach of contract. All of the plaintiff's claims arose out of the modification to the construction contract. BE & K's asserted an affirmative defense alleging that the plaintiff had agreed to settle its claims for a total payment of $896,000.

The trial court granted BE & K's motion to try its counterclaim before trying the plaintiff's claims against it. The plaintiff then filed a demand for a jury trial, which BE & K moved to strike, arguing that because its counterclaim was equitable, the plaintiff had no right to a jury trial on the counterclaim. The trial court granted BE & K's motion to strike the plaintiff's jury trial demand and, sitting as the trier of fact, found that the plaintiff had accepted the defendants' offer to settle its claims in return for the defendants' promise to pay the plaintiff $800,000. Although the defendants alleged that they promised to pay the plaintiff $896,000 in return for the plaintiff's promise to release its claims against them, the trial court found that the defendants had promised to pay only $800,000.

Based on its resolution of the defendants' counterclaim, the trial court entered a limited judgment directing the defendants to tender $800,000 to the court clerk and directing the plaintiff, after the defendants tendered that sum, to execute releases of its claims against the defendants. The plaintiff appealed, claiming a state constitutional right to a jury trial on the factual issues that the defendant's counterclaim had raised. A divided Court of Appeals affirmed the trial court's judgment. The Oregon Supreme Court allowed the plaintiff's petition for review.

DECISION Judgment of the Court of Appeals is affirmed in part, reversed in part, and remanded.

OPINION A settlement agreement may take one of three forms: an executory accord, an accord and satisfaction, or a substituted contract. When the Oregon Constitution was adopted, only a court of equity would enforce an executory accord. The law courts would not enforce executory accords because they suspended the underlying obligation; they did not discharge it. By contrast, an accord and satisfaction and a substituted contract discharged the underlying obligation, and both were enforceable in the law courts.

An executory accord is "an agreement for the future discharge of an existing claim by a substituted performance." Usually, an executory accord is a bilateral agreement; the debtor promises to pay an amount in return for the creditor's promise to release the underlying claim. When the parties enter into an executory accord, the underlying claim "is not [discharged] until the new agreement is performed. The right to enforce the original claim is merely suspended, and is revived by the debtor's breach of the new agreement."

Because an executory accord does not discharge the underlying claim but merely suspends it, the law courts refused to allow it to be pleaded as a bar to the underlying claim. Once the promised performance occurs, the accord has been executed or satisfied and the underlying claim is discharged, resulting in an accord and satisfaction. An accord and satisfaction may occur in one of two ways:

> The two parties may first make an executory accord, that is, a contract for the future discharge of the existing claim by a substituted performance still to be rendered. When this executory contract is fully performed as agreed, there is said to be an accord and satisfaction, and

the previously existing claim is discharged. It is quite possible, however, for the parties to make an accord and satisfaction without any preliminary executory accord or any other executory contract of any kind. [For example, a] debtor may offer the substituted performance in satisfaction of his debt and the creditor may receive it, without any binding promise being made by either party.

Because an accord and satisfaction discharges the underlying claim, that defense is legal, not equitable.

Finally, the parties may enter into a substituted contract; that is, the parties may agree to substitute the new agreement for the underlying obligation. A substituted contract differs from an executory accord in that the parties intend that entering into the new agreement will immediately discharge the underlying obligation. A substituted contract discharges the underlying obligation and could be asserted as a bar to an action at law.

In this case the defendants alleged that they agreed to pay the plaintiff $896,000 in exchange for a release of the plaintiff's claims against them. The defendants did not allege that they had paid the plaintiff the promised sum—an allegation necessary for an accord and satisfaction. Nor did they allege that, by entering into the settlement agreement, they extinguished the underlying obligation—an allegation necessary to allege a substituted contract. Rather, the defendants alleged that the plaintiff agreed to release its claims only after the defendants made the promised payment. Thus, the defendants alleged an executory accord.

The Oregon constitutional right to a jury trial in civil cases does not extend to the defendants' counterclaim of an executory accord.

INTERPRETATION When a debtor and a creditor enter into an executory accord, the underlying claim is not discharged until the new agreement is performed; the right to enforce the original claim is merely suspended, and is revived by the debtor's breach of the new agreement.

CRITICAL THINKING QUESTION In settling a contract dispute, what are the advantages and disadvantages of using an executory accord compared with using a substituted contract?

Novation [17-4d]

Novation

substituted contract involving a new third-party promisor or promisee

A **novation** is a substituted contract that involves an agreement among *three* parties to substitute a new promisee for the existing promisee or to replace the existing promisor with a new one. A novation discharges the old obligation by creating a new contract in which there is either a new promisee or a new promisor. Thus, if B owes A $500, and A, B, and C agree that C will pay the debt and B will be discharged, the novation is the substitution of the new promisor C for B. Alternatively, if the three parties agree that B will pay $500 to C instead of to A, the novation is the substitution of a new promisee (C for A). In each instance, the debt B owes A is discharged.

DISCHARGE BY OPERATION OF LAW [17-5]

In this chapter, we have considered various ways by which contractual duties may be discharged. In all of these cases, the discharge resulted from the action of one or both of the parties to the contract. In this section, we will examine discharge brought about by the operation of law.

Impossibility [17-5a]

Subjective impossibility

the promisor—but not all promisors—cannot perform; does not discharge the promisor

If a particular contracting party is unable to perform because of financial inability or lack of competence, for instance, this **subjective impossibility** does *not* excuse the promisor from

Objective impossibility

performance cannot be done by anyone; generally discharges the promisor

___

Practical Advice

Use a clause in your contract specifying which events will excuse the nonperformance of the contract.

___

liability for breach of contract, as the next case shows. Historically, the common law excused a party from contractual duties only for **objective impossibility**, that is, for situations in which no one could render performance. Thus, the death or illness of a person who has contracted to render personal services is a discharge of his contractual duty. Furthermore, the contract is discharged if, for example, a jockey contracts to ride a certain horse in the Kentucky Derby and the horse dies prior to the derby, for it is objectively impossible for this or any other jockey to perform the contract. Also, if Ken contracts to lease to Karlene a certain ballroom for a party on a scheduled future date, destruction of the ballroom by fire without Ken's fault before the scheduled event discharges the contract. Destruction of the subject matter or of the agreed-upon means of performance of a contract, without the fault of the promisor, is excusable impossibility.

Christy v. Pilkinton
Supreme Court of Arkansas, 1954
224 Ark. 407, 273 S.W.2d 533
http://scholar.google.com/scholar_case?q=273+S.W.2d+533&hl=en&as_sdt=6,34&case=17719371089791667280&scilh=0

FACTS The Christys entered into a written contract to purchase an apartment house from Pilkinton for $30,000. Pilkinton tendered a deed to the property and demanded payment of the unpaid balance of $29,000 due on the purchase price. As a result of a decline in the Christy's used car business, the Christys did not possess and could not borrow the unpaid balance and, thus, asserted that it was impossible for them to perform their contract. This suit was brought by Pilkinton to enforce the sale of the apartment house.

DECISION Judgment for Pilkinton.

OPINION There is an important distinction between objective impossibility, which amounts to saying, "the thing cannot be done," and subjective impossibility—"I cannot do it." The latter, which is well illustrated by a promisor's financial inability to pay, does not discharge the contractual duty.

INTERPRETATION Subjective impossibility (the promisor, but not all promisors, cannot perform) does not discharge the promisor's contractual duty.

ETHICAL QUESTION Is it fair to make contracting parties strictly liable for breach of contract? Explain.

CRITICAL THINKING QUESTION What type of fact situation would have excused the Christys' duty to perform? Explain.

___

Subsequent illegality

if performance becomes illegal or impractical as a result of a change in the law, the duty of performance is discharged

Frustration of purpose

principal purpose of a contract cannot be fulfilled because of a subsequent event

___

Practical Advice

Clearly state the basic assumptions of your contract and which risks are assumed by each of the parties.

___

Subsequent Illegality   If the performance of a contract that was legal when formed becomes illegal or impractical because of a subsequently enacted law, the duty of performance is discharged. For example, Linda contracts to sell and deliver to Carlos ten cases of a certain whiskey each month for one year. A subsequent prohibition law makes the manufacture, transportation, or sale of intoxicating liquor unlawful. The contractual duties that Linda has yet to perform are discharged.

Frustration of Purpose   Where, after a contract is made, a party's principal purpose is substantially frustrated without his fault by the occurrence of an event whose nonoccurrence was a basic assumption on which the contract was made, his remaining duties to render performance are discharged, unless the party has assumed the risk. This rule developed from the so-called coronation cases. When, on the death of his mother, Queen Victoria, Edward VII became King of England, impressive coronation ceremonies were planned, including a procession along a designated route through London. Owners and lessees of buildings along the route made contracts to permit the use of rooms on the day scheduled for the procession. The king became ill, however, and the procession did not take place. Consequently, the rooms were not used. Numerous suits were filed, some by landowners seeking to hold the would-be viewers liable on their promises, and some by the would-be viewers seeking to recover money they had paid in advance for the rooms. Though the principle involved was novel, from these cases evolved the frustration of purpose doctrine, under which a contract is discharged if supervening circumstances make impossible the fulfillment of the purpose that both parties had in mind, unless one of the parties has contractually assumed that risk.

Commercial impracticability

where performance can be accomplished only under unforeseen and unjust hardship, the contract is discharged under the Code and the Restatement

Commercial Impracticability   The Restatement and Code have relaxed the traditional test of objective impossibility by providing that performance need not be actually or literally impossible; rather, **commercial impracticability**, or unforeseen and unjust hardship, will excuse nonperformance. This does not mean mere hardship or an unexpectedly increased cost of performance. A party will be discharged from performing her duty only when her performance is made impracticable by a supervening event not caused by her own fault. Moreover, the non-occurrence of the subsequent event must have been a "basic assumption" made by both parties when entering into the contract, neither party having assumed the risk that the event would occur.

Northern Corporation v. Chugach Electrical Association
Supreme Court of Alaska, 1974
518 P.2d 76
http://scholar.google.com/scholar_case?q=518+P.2d+76&hl=en&as_sdt=2,34&case=2017068664150967540&scilh=0

FACTS Northern Corporation (Northern) entered into a contract with Chugach Electrical Association (Chugach) in August 1966 to repair and upgrade the upstream face of Cooper Lake Dam in Alaska. The contract required Northern to obtain rock from a quarry site at the opposite end of the lake and to transport the rock to the dam during the winter across the ice on the lake. In December 1966, Northern cleared a road on the ice to permit deeper freezing, but thereafter water overflowed on the ice, preventing use of the road. Northern complained of the unsafe conditions of the lake ice, but Chugach insisted on performance. In March 1967, one of Northern's loaded trucks broke through the ice and sank. Northern continued to encounter difficulties and ceased operations with the approval of Chugach. However, on January 8, 1968, Chugach notified Northern that it would be in default unless all rock was hauled by April 1. After two more trucks broke through the ice, causing the deaths of the drivers, Northern ceased operations and notified Chugach that it would make no more attempts to haul across the lake. Northern advised Chugach that it considered the contract terminated for impossibility of performance and commenced suit to recover the cost incurred in attempting to complete the contract. The trial court found for Northern.

DECISION Judgment for Northern affirmed.

OPINION Northern's contract to perform was discharged by impossibility of performance. The particular method of performance specified in the contract presupposed the existence of ice frozen to sufficient depth to permit hauling of rock across the lake. This expectation by both parties was never fulfilled. A party is discharged from its contractual obligation, even if it is technically possible to perform, if the cost of performance would be so greatly disproportionate to that reasonably contemplated by the parties that performance would be commercially impracticable. In addition, a serious risk to life or health will excuse nonperformance.

INTERPRETATION Commercial impracticability (unforeseen and unjust hardship) will excuse performance.

ETHICAL QUESTION Did Chugach act ethically in insisting on performance by Northern in face of dangerous conditions? Explain.

CRITICAL THINKING QUESTION Do you think that the court used the proper standard in this case? Explain.

Availability of restitution

a person who renders more advanced performance under a contract that is discharged for impossibility, subsequent illegality, frustration, or impracticability is entitled to restitution to prevent unjust enrichment of the other party

Availability of Restitution   In cases in which impossibility, subsequent illegality, frustration, or impracticability apply, contract law permits the avoidance of a contract obligation. If the contract is wholly executory, discharge of the contract obligations resolves the legal issues. However, if the contract has been partially or wholly performed, the legal issues include not only the enforceability of the contract but also restitution. The Restatement of Restitution provides that a person who renders more advanced performance under a contract that is discharged for impossibility, subsequent illegality, frustration, or impracticability is entitled to restitution to prevent unjust enrichment of the other party. Thus, for example, if the seller has performed prior to receiving payment, the seller would have a claim in restitution. On the other hand, if the buyer has paid part or all of the price in advance, the buyer would be entitled to restitution.

Bankruptcy [17-5b]

Bankruptcy

discharge available to a debtor who obtains an order of discharge by the bankruptcy court

Bankruptcy is a discharge of a contractual duty by operation of law available to a debtor who, by compliance with the requirements of the Bankruptcy Code, obtains an order of discharge by the bankruptcy court. It applies only to obligations that the Bankruptcy Code provides are dischargeable in bankruptcy. (We will treat the subject of bankruptcy in Chapter 38.)

Figure 17-1 Discharge of Contracts

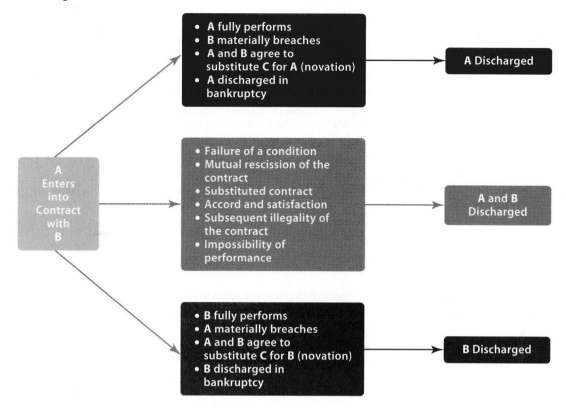

Statute of limitations

after the statute of
limitations has run, the debt
is not discharged, but the
creditor cannot maintain an
action against the debtor

Statute of Limitations [17-5c]

At common law a plaintiff was not subject to any time limitation within which to bring an action. Now, however, all states have statutes providing such a limitation. The majority of courts hold that the running of the period of the statute of limitations does not operate to discharge the obligation but only to bar the creditor's right to bring an action.

For a summary of discharge of contracts, see Figure 17-1.

CHAPTER SUMMARY

Conditions

Definition of a Condition an event whose happening or nonhappening affects a duty of performance

Express Condition contingency explicitly set forth in language

- *Satisfaction* express condition making performance contingent on one party's approval of the other's performance

- *Subjective Satisfaction* approval based on a party's honestly held opinion

- *Objective Satisfaction* approval based on whether a reasonable person would be satisfied

Implied-in-Fact Condition contingency understood by the parties to be part of the agreement, though not expressed

Implied-in-Law Condition contingency not contained in the language of the contract but imposed by law; also called a constructive condition

Concurrent Conditions conditions that are to take place at the same time

Condition Precedent an event that must or must not occur before performance is due

Condition Subsequent an event that terminates a duty of performance

Discharge by Performance	**Discharge** termination of a contractual duty
	Performance fulfillment of a contractual obligation resulting in a discharge

Discharge by Breach

Definition of Breach a wrongful failure to perform the terms of a contract that gives rise to a right to damages by the injured party

Material Breach nonperformance that significantly impairs the injured party's rights under the contract and discharges the injured party from any further duty under the contract

- *Prevention of Performance* one party's substantial interference with or prevention of performance by the other constitutes a material breach and discharges the other party to the contract
- *Perfect Tender Rule* standard under the Uniform Commercial Code that a seller's performance under a sales contract must strictly comply with contractual duties and that any deviation discharges the injured party

Substantial Performance performance that is incomplete but that does not defeat the purpose of the contract; does not discharge the injured party but entitles him to damages

Anticipatory Repudiation an inability or refusal to perform, before performance is due, that is treated as a breach, allowing the nonrepudiating party to bring suit immediately

Unauthorized Material Alteration of Written Contract a material and fraudulent alteration of a written contract by a party to the contract discharges the entire contract

Discharge by Agreement of the Parties

Mutual Rescission an agreement between the parties to terminate their respective duties under the contract

Substituted Contract a new contract accepted by both parties in satisfaction of the parties' duties under the original contract

Accord and Satisfaction substituted duty under a contract (accord) and the discharge of the prior contractual obligation by performance of the new duty (satisfaction)

Novation a substituted contract involving a new third-party promisor or promisee

Discharge by Operation of Law

Impossibility performance of contract cannot be done

- *Subjective Impossibility* the promisor—but not all promisors—cannot perform; does not discharge the promisor
- *Objective Impossibility* no promisor is able to perform; generally discharges the promisor
- *Subsequent Illegality* if performance becomes illegal or impractical as a result of a change in the law, the duty of performance is discharged
- *Frustration of Purpose* principal purpose of a contract cannot be fulfilled because of a subsequent event
- *Commercial Impracticability* where performance can be accomplished only under unforeseen and unjust hardship, the contract is discharged under the Code and the Restatement
- *Availability of Restitution* a person who renders more advanced performance under a contract that is discharged for impossibility, subsequent illegality, frustration, or impracticability is entitled to restitution to prevent unjust enrichment of the other party

Bankruptcy discharge available to a debtor who obtains an order of discharge by the bankruptcy court

Statute of Limitations after the statute of limitations has run, the debt is not discharged, but the creditor cannot maintain an action against the debtor

QUESTIONS

1. A-1 Roofing Co. entered into a written contract with Jaffe to put a new roof on the latter's residence for $1,800, using a specified type of roofing, and to complete the job without unreasonable delay. A-1 undertook the work within a week thereafter, and when all the roofing material was at the site and the labor 50 percent completed, the premises were totally destroyed by fire caused by lightning. A-1 submitted a bill to Jaffe for $1,200 for materials furnished and labor performed up to the time of the destruction of the premises. Jaffe refused to pay the bill, and A-1 now seeks payment from Jaffe. Should A-1 prevail? Explain.

2. By contract dated January 5, Rebecca agreed to sell to Nancy, and Nancy agreed to buy from Rebecca, a certain parcel of land then zoned commercial. The specific intent of Nancy, which was known to Rebecca, was to erect a manufacturing plant on the land; and the contract stated that the agreement was conditioned on Nancy's ability to construct such a plant on the land. The closing date for the transaction was set for April 1. On February 15, the city council rezoned the land from commercial to residential, which precluded the erection of the plant. As the closing date drew near, Nancy made it

known to Rebecca that she did not intend to go through with the purchase because the land could no longer be used as intended. On April 1, Rebecca tendered the deed to Nancy, who refused to pay Rebecca the agreed purchase price. Rebecca brought an action against Nancy for breach of contract. Can Rebecca enforce the contract?

3. The Perfection Produce Company entered into a written contract with Hiram Hodges for the purchase of three hundred tons of potatoes to be grown on Hodges's farm in Maine at a stipulated price per ton. Though the land would ordinarily produce one thousand tons and although the planting and cultivation were properly done, Hodges was able to deliver only one hundred tons because an unprecedented drought caused a partial crop failure. Perfection accepted the one hundred tons but paid only 80 percent of the stipulated price per ton. Hodges sued the produce company to recover the unpaid balance of the agreed price for the one hundred tons of potatoes accepted by Perfection. Perfection counterclaimed against Hodges for his failure to deliver the additional two hundred tons. Who will prevail? Why?

4. On November 23, Sally agreed to sell to Bart her Buick automobile for $7,000, delivery and payment to be made on December 1. On November 26, Bart informed Sally that he wished to rescind the contract and would pay Sally $350 if Sally agreed. Sally agreed and took the $350 in cash. On December 1, Bart tendered to Sally $6,650 and demanded that Sally deliver the automobile. Sally refused, and Bart initiated a lawsuit. May Bart enforce the original contract?

5. Webster, Inc., dealt in automobile accessories at wholesale. Although it manufactured a few items in its own factory, among them windshield wipers, Webster purchased most of its inventory from a large number of other manufacturers. In January, Webster entered into a written contract to sell Hunter two thousand windshield wipers for $1,900, delivery to be made June 1. In April, Webster's factory burned to the ground and Webster failed to make delivery on June 1. Hunter, forced to buy windshield wipers elsewhere at a higher price, is now trying to recover damages from Webster. Will Hunter be successful in its claim?

6. Erwick Construction Company contracted to build a house for Charles. The specifications called for the use of Karlene Pipe for all plumbing. Erwick, nevertheless, got a better price on Boynton Pipe and substituted the equally good Boynton Pipe for Karlene Pipe. Charles's inspection revealed the change, and Charles now refuses to make the final payment. The contract price was for $200,000, and the final payment is $20,000. Erwick now brings suit seeking the $20,000. Will Erwick succeed in its claim?

7. Green owed White $3,500, which was due and payable on June 1. White owed Brown $3,500, which was due and payable on August 1. On May 25, White received a letter signed by Green stating, "If you will cancel my debt to you, in the amount of $3,500, I will pay, on the due date, the debt you owe Brown, in the amount of $3,500." On May 28, Green received a letter signed by White stating, "I received your letter and agree to the proposals recited therein. You may consider your debt to me canceled as of the date of this letter." On June 1, White, needing money to pay his income taxes, made a demand upon Green to pay him the $3,500 due on that date. Is Green obligated to pay the money demanded by White?

8. By written contract, Ames agreed to build a house on Bowen's lot for $145,000, commencing within ninety days of the date of the contract. Prior to the date for beginning construction, Ames informed Bowen that he was repudiating the contract and would not perform. Bowen refused to accept the repudiation and demanded fulfillment of the contract. Eighty days after the date of the contract, Bowen entered into a new contract with Curd for $142,000. The next day, without knowledge or notice of Bowen's contract with Curd, Ames began construction. Bowen ordered Ames from the premises and refused to allow him to continue. Will Ames be able to collect damages from Bowen? Explain.

9. Judy agreed in writing to work for Northern Enterprises, Inc., for three years as superintendent of Northern's manufacturing establishment and to devote herself entirely to the business, giving it her full time, attention, and skill, for which she was to receive $72,000 per annum in monthly installments of $6,000. Judy worked and was paid for the first twelve months, when, through no fault of her own or Northern's, she was arrested and imprisoned for one month. It became imperative for Northern to employ another, and it treated the contract with Judy as breached and abandoned, refusing to permit Judy to resume work on her release from jail. What rights, if any, does Judy have under the contract?

10. The Park Plaza Hotel awarded its valet and laundry concession to Larson for a three-year term. The contract contained the following provision: "It is distinctly understood and agreed that the services to be rendered by Larson shall meet with the approval of the Park Plaza Hotel, which shall be the sole judge of the sufficiency and propriety of the services." After seven months, the hotel gave a month's notice to discontinue services based on the failure of the services to meet its approval. Larson brought an action against the hotel, alleging that its dissatisfaction was unreasonable. The hotel defended on the ground that subjective or personal satisfaction may be the sole justification for termination of the contract. Who is correct? Explain.

11. Schlosser entered into an agreement to purchase a cooperative apartment from Flynn Company. The written agreement contained the following provision: "This entire agreement is conditioned on Purchaser's being approved for occupancy by the board of directors of the Cooperative. In the event approval of the Purchaser shall be denied, this agreement shall thereafter be of no further force or effect." When Schlosser unilaterally revoked her "offer," Flynn sued for breach of contract. Schlosser claims the approval provision was a condition precedent to the existence of a binding contract and, thus, she was free to revoke. Decision?

12. Jacobs, owner of a farm, entered into a contract with Earl Walker in which Walker agreed to paint the buildings on the farm. As authorized by Jacobs, Walker acquired the paint from Jones with the bill to be sent to Jacobs. Before the work was completed, however, Jacobs without good cause ordered Walker to stop. Walker made offers to complete the job, but Jacobs declined to permit Walker to fulfill his contract. Jacobs refused to pay Jones for the paint Walker had acquired for the job. Explain whether Jones and Walker would be successful in an action against Jacobs for breach of contract.

CASE PROBLEMS

13. Barta entered into a written contract to buy the K&K Pharmacy, located in a local shopping center. Included in the contract was a provision stating "this Agreement shall be contingent upon Buyer's ability to obtain a new lease from Landlord for the premises presently occupied by Seller. In the event Buyer is unable to obtain a lease satisfactory to Buyer, this Agreement shall be null and void." Barta planned to sell "high-traffic" grocery items, such as bread, milk, and coffee, to attract customers to his drugstore. A grocery store in the shopping center, however, already held the exclusive right to sell grocery items. Barta, therefore, could not obtain a leasing agreement meeting his approval. Barta refused to close the sale. In a suit by K&K Pharmacy against Barta for breach of contract, who will prevail? Explain.

14. Victor Packing Co. (Victor) contracted to supply Sun Maid Raisin Growers 1,800 tons of raisins from the current year's crop. After delivering 1,190 tons of raisins by August, Victor refused to supply any more. Although Victor had until the end of the crop season to ship the remaining 610 tons of raisins, Sun Maid treated Victor's repeated refusals to ship any more raisins as a repudiation of the contract. To prevent breaching its own contracts, Sun Maid went into the marketplace to "cover" and bought the raisins needed. Unfortunately, between the time Victor refused delivery and Sun Maid entered the market, disastrous rains had caused the price of raisins to skyrocket. May Sun Maid recover from Victor the difference between the contract price and the market price before the end of the current crop year?

15. On August 20, Hildebrand entered into a written contract with the city of Douglasville whereby he was to serve as community development project engineer for three years at a monthly fee of $1,583.33. This salary figure could be changed without affecting the other terms of the contract. One of the provisions for termination of the contract was written notice by either party to the other at any time at least ninety days prior to the intended date of termination. The contract listed a substantial number of services and duties Hildebrand was to perform for the city; among the lesser duties were (a) keeping the community development director (Hildebrand's supervisor) informed at all times of his whereabouts and how he could be contacted and (b) attending meetings at which his presence was requested. Two years later, by which time Hildebrand's fee had risen to $1,915.83 per month, the city fired Hildebrand effective immediately, citing "certain material breaches … of the … agreement." The city specifically charged that he did not attend the necessary meetings although requested to do so and seldom if ever kept his supervisor informed of his whereabouts and how he could be contacted. Will Hildebrand prevail in a suit against the mayor and city for the amount of $5,747.49 for breach of his employment contract because of the city's failure to give him ninety days' notice prior to termination?

16. Walker & Co. contracted to provide a sign for Harrison to place above his dry cleaning business. According to the contract, Harrison would lease the sign from Walker, making monthly payments for thirty-six months. In return, Walker agreed to maintain and service the sign at its own expense. Walker installed the sign in July, and Harrison made the first rental payment. Shortly thereafter, someone hit the sign with a tomato. Harrison also claims he discovered rust on its chrome and little spider webs in its corners. Harrison repeatedly called Walker for the maintenance work promised under the contract, but Walker did not respond immediately. Harrison then notified Walker that, due to Walker's failure to perform the maintenance services, he held Walker in material breach of the contract. A week later, Walker sent out a crew, which did all of the requested maintenance services. Has Walker committed a material breach of contract? Explain.

17. In May, Watts was awarded a construction contract, based on its low bid, by the Cullman County Commission. The contract provided that it would not become effective until approved by the state director of the Farmers Home Administration (now part of the U.S. Department of Agriculture Rural Development Office). In September, construction still had not been authorized and Watts wrote to the County Commission requesting a 5 percent price increase to reflect seasonal and inflationary price increases. The County Commission countered with an offer of 3.5 percent. Watts then wrote the commission, insisting on a 5 percent increase and stating that if this was not agreeable, it was withdrawing its original bid. The commission obtained another company to perform the project, and on October 14, informed Watts that it had accepted the withdrawal of the bid. Watts sued for breach of contract. Explain whether Watts will prevail and why or why not.

18. K & G Construction Co. was the owner of and the general contractor for a housing subdivision project. Harris contracted with the company to do excavating and earth-moving work on the project. Certain provisions of the contract stated that (a) K & G was to make monthly progress payments to Harris, (b) no such payments were to be made until Harris obtained liability insurance, and (c) all of Harris's work on the project must be performed in a workmanlike manner. On August 9, a bulldozer operator, working for Harris, drove too close to one of K & G's houses, causing the collapse of a wall and other damage. When Harris and his insurance carrier denied liability and refused to pay for the damage, K & G refused to make the August monthly progress payment. Harris, nonetheless, continued to work on the project until mid-September, when the excavator ceased its operations due to K & G's refusal to make the progress payment. K & G had another excavator finish the job at an added cost of $450. It then sued Harris for the bulldozer damage, alleging negligence, and for the $450 damages for breach of contract. Harris claims that K & G defaulted first, having no legal right to refuse the August progress payment. Did K & G default first? Explain.

19. Mountain Restaurant Corporation (Mountain) leased commercial space in the ParkCenter Mall to operate a restaurant called Zac's Grill. The lease specified that the lessee shall

"at all times have a nonexclusive and nonrevocable right, together with the other tenants and occupants of … the shopping center, to use the parking area … for itself, its customers and employees." Zac's Grill was to be a fast-food restaurant where tables were anticipated to "turn over" twice during lunch. Zac's operated successfully until parking close to the restaurant became restricted. Two other restaurants opened and began competing for parking spaces, and the parking lot would become full between 12:00 and 12:30 P.M. Parking, however, was always available at other areas of the mall. Business declined for Zac's, which fell behind on the rent due to ParkCenter until finally the restaurant closed. Mountain claims that it was discharged from its obligations under the lease because of material breach. Is Mountain correct? Explain.

20. In late 2011 or early 2012, the plaintiff, Lan England, agreed to sell 258,363 shares of stock to the defendant, Eugene Horbach, for $2.75 per share, for a total price of $710,498.25. Although the purchase money was to be paid in the first quarter of 2012, the defendant made periodic payments on the stock at least through September 2012. The parties met in May of 2013 to finalize the transaction. At this time, the plaintiff believed that the defendant owed at least $25,000 of the original purchase price. The defendant did not dispute that amount. The parties then reached a second agreement whereby the defendant agreed to pay to the plaintiff an additional $25,000 and to hold in trust 2 percent of the stock for the plaintiff. In return, the plaintiff agreed to transfer the stock and to forgo his right to sue the defendant for breach of the original agreement.

In December 2014, the plaintiff made a demand for the 2 percent stock, but the defendant refused, contending that the 2 percent agreement was meant only to secure his payment of the additional $25,000. The plaintiff sued for breach of the 2 percent agreement. Prior to trial, the defendant discovered additional business records documenting that he had, before entering into the second agreement, actually overpaid the plaintiff for the purchase of the stock. The defendant asserts the plaintiff could not enforce the second agreement

as an accord and satisfaction because (a) it was not supported by consideration and (b) it was based upon a mutual mistake that the defendant owed additional money on the original agreement. Is the defendant correct in his assertions? Explain.

21. An artist once produced a painting now called *The Plains of Meudon*. For a while, the parties in this case thought that the artist was Theodore Rousseau, a prominent member of the Barbizon school, and that the painting was quite valuable. With this idea in mind, the Kohlers consigned the painting to Leslie Hindman, Inc. (Hindman), an auction house. Among other things, the consignment agreement between the Kohlers and Hindman defined the scope of Hindman, Inc.'s authority as agent. First, Hindman was obliged to sell the painting according to the conditions of sale spelled out in the auction catalog. Those conditions provided that neither the consignors nor Hindman made any warranties of authenticity. Second, the consignment agreement gave Hindman extensive and exclusive discretionary authority to rescind sales if in its "sole discretion" it determined that the sale subjected the company or the Kohlers to any liability under a warranty of authenticity.

Despite having some doubts about its authenticity, Thune was still interested in the painting but wanted to have it authenticated before committing to its purchase. Unable to obtain an authoritative opinion about its authenticity before the auction, Leslie Hindman and Thune made a verbal agreement that Thune could return the painting within approximately thirty days of the auction if he was the successful bidder and if an expert then determined that Rousseau had not painted it. Neither Leslie Hindman nor anyone else at Hindman told the Kohlers about the questions concerning the painting or about the side agreement between Thune and Hindman. At the auction, Thune prevailed in the bidding with a high bid of $90,000, and he took possession of the painting without paying. He then sent it to an expert in Paris who decided that it was not a Rousseau. Thune returned the painting to Hindman within the agreed-upon period. Explain whether the Kohlers would be successful in a lawsuit against either Hindman or Thune.

TAKING SIDES

Associated Builders, Inc., provided labor and materials to William M. Coggins and Benjamin W. Coggins, doing business as Ben & Bill's Chocolate Emporium, to complete a structure on Main Street in Bar Harbor, Maine. After a dispute arose regarding compensation, Associated and the Cogginses executed an agreement stating that there existed an outstanding balance of $70,000 and setting forth the following terms of repayment:

It is agreed that, two payments will be made by the Cogginses to Associated Builders as follows: Twenty Five Thousand Dollars ($25,000.00) on or before June 1, 2013, and Twenty Five Thousand Dollars ($25,000.00) on or before June 1, 2014. No interest will be charged or paid providing payments are made as agreed. If the payments are not made as agreed then interest shall accrue at 10%

per annum figured from the date of default. It is further agreed that Associated Builders will forfeit the balance of Twenty Thousand Dollars and No Cents ($20,000.00) providing the above payments are made as agreed.

The Cogginses made their first payment in accordance with the agreement. The second payment, however, was delivered three days late on June 4, 2014. Claiming a breach of the contract, Associated contended that the remainder of the original balance of $20,000, plus interest and cost, were now due.

a. What arguments would support Associated's claim for $20,000?

b. What arguments would support the claim by the Cogginses that they were not liable for $20,000?

c. For what damages, if any, are the Cogginses liable? Explain.

Contract Remedies

CHAPTER 18

The traditional goal of the law of contract remedies has not been the compulsion of the promisor to perform his promise but compensation of the promisee for the loss resulting from breach.

Restatement of Contracts

CHAPTER OUTCOMES

After reading and studying this chapter, you should be able to:

1. Explain how compensatory damages and reliance damages are computed.

2. Define (a) nominal damages, (b) incidental damages, (c) consequential damages, (d) foreseeability of damages, (e) punitive damages, (f) liquidated damages, and (g) mitigation of damages.

3. Define the various types of equitable relief and explain when the courts will grant such relief.

4. Explain how restitutionary damages are computed and identify the situations in which restitution is available as a contractual remedy.

5. Identify and explain the limitations on contractual remedies.

Practical Advice

Consider including in your contracts a provision for the recovery of attorneys' fees in the event of breach of contract.

Practical Advice

Consider including in your contracts a provision for the arbitration of contract disputes.

When one party to a contract breaches the contract by failing to perform his contractual duties, the law provides a remedy for the injured party. Although the primary objective of contract remedies is to compensate the injured party for the loss resulting from the breach, it is impossible for any remedy to equal the promised performance. The relief a court can give an injured party is what it regards as an *equivalent* of the promised performance.

In this chapter, we will examine the most common remedies available for breach of contract: (1) monetary damages, (2) the equitable remedies of specific performance and injunction, and (3) restitution. Article 2 of the Uniform Commercial Code (UCC), which provides specialized remedies that we will discuss in Chapter 23, governs the sale of goods. Contract remedies are available to protect one or more of the following interests of the injured parties:

1. their *expectation interest*, which is their interest in having the benefit of their bargain by being put in a position as good as the one they would have been in had the contract been performed;
2. their *reliance interest*, which is their interest in being reimbursed for loss caused by reliance on the contract by being put in a position as good as the one they would have been in had the contract not been made; or
3. their *restitution interest*, which is their interest in having restored to them any benefit that they had conferred on the other party.

The contract remedies of compensatory damages, specific performance, and injunction protect the expectation interest. The contractual remedy of reliance damages protects the reliance interest, while the contractual remedy of restitution protects the restitution interest.

MONETARY DAMAGES [18-1]

A judgment awarding monetary damages is the most frequently granted judicial remedy for breach of contract. Monetary damages, however, will be awarded only for losses that are foreseeable, established with reasonable certainty, and not avoidable. The equitable remedies discussed in this chapter are discretionary and are available only if monetary damages are inadequate.

Compensatory Damages [18-1a]

The right to recover compensatory damages for breach of contract is always available to the injured party. The purpose in allowing **compensatory damages** is to place the injured party in a position as good as the one he would have been in had the other party performed under the contract. This involves compensating the injured party for the dollar value of the benefits he would have received had the contract been performed less any savings he experienced by not having to perform his own obligations under the contract. These damages are intended to protect the injured party's *expectation interest*, which is the value he expected to derive from the contract. Thus, the amount of compensatory damages is the loss of value to the injured party caused by the other party's failure to perform or by the other party's deficient performance *minus* the loss or cost avoided by the injured party *plus* incidental damages *plus* consequential damages.

Loss of Value
In general, **loss of value** is the *difference between the value of the promised performance* of the breaching party *and the value of the actual performance* rendered by the breaching party. If no performance is rendered at all, the loss of value is the value of the promised performance. If defective or partial performance is rendered, the loss of value is the difference between the value that the full performance would have had and the value of the performance actually rendered. Thus, when there has been a breach of warranty, the injured party may recover the difference between the value the goods would have had, had they been as warranted, and the value of the goods in the condition in which the buyer actually received them. To illustrate, Jacob sells an automobile to Juliet, expressly warranting that it will get forty-five miles per gallon; but the automobile gets only twenty miles per gallon. The automobile would have been worth $24,000 if as warranted, but it is worth only $20,000 as delivered. Juliet would recover $4,000 in damages for loss of value.

Cost Avoided
The recovery by the injured party is reduced, however, by any cost or loss she has avoided by not having to perform. For example, Clinton agrees to build a hotel for Debra for $11 million by September 1. Clinton breaches by not completing construction until October 1. As a consequence, Debra loses revenues for one month in the amount of $400,000 but saves operating expenses of $60,000. Therefore, she may recover damages for $340,000. Similarly, in a contract in which the injured party has not fully performed, the injured party's recovery is reduced by the value to the injured party of the performance the injured party promised but did not render. For example, Victor agrees to convey land to Joan in return for Joan's promise to work for Victor for two years. Joan repudiates the contract before Victor has conveyed the land to Joan. Victor's recovery for loss from Joan is reduced by the value to Victor of the land.

Incidental Damages
Incidental damages are damages that arise directly out of the breach, such as costs incurred to acquire the nondelivered performance from some other source. For example, Agnes employs Benton for nine months for $40,000 to supervise construction of a factory. She then fires Benton without cause after three weeks. Benton, who spends $850 in reasonable fees attempting to find comparable employment, may recover $850 in incidental damages in addition to any other actual loss he has suffered.

Consequential Damages
Consequential damages are damages not arising directly out of a breach but arising as a foreseeable result of the breach. Consequential damages include lost profits and injury to person or property. Thus, if Tracy leases to Sean a defective machine that causes $40,000 in property damage and $120,000 in personal injuries, Sean may recover, in addition to damages for loss of value and incidental damages, $160,000 as consequential damages.

Compensatory damages contract damages placing the injured party in a position as good as the one he would have held had the other party performed; equals loss of value minus loss avoided by injured party plus incidental damages plus consequential damages

Loss of value value of promised performance minus value of actual performance

Cost avoided loss or costs the injured party avoids by not having to perform

Incidental damages damages arising directly out of a breach of contract

Consequential damages damages not arising directly out of a breach but as a foreseeable result of the breach

---

Practical Advice

If you are the provider of goods or services, consider including a contractual provision for the limitation or exclusion of consequential damages. If you are the purchaser of goods or services, avoid such limitations.

BUSINESS LAW **IN ACTION**

When contracting parties litigate over a breach, does the losing party have to pay the winner's attorneys' fees? These fees may appear to qualify as consequential damages, direct consequences of the breach of contract. However, courts in this country follow what is known as the "American Rule," which provides that each party pays its own attorneys' fees, regardless of who wins. This rule holds true unless there is an applicable statute or express contract clause to the contrary. (Some states have statutes that specifically provide for an award of reasonable attorneys'

fees and costs to the prevailing party in certain suits arising out of contract.)

Even though the general rule is that attorneys' fees are not awarded in breach of contract suits, proactive contracting parties can expressly provide in their contract that the losing party will pay the reasonable attorneys' fees of the prevailing party. Many written contracts, particularly those that are drafted by lawyers, contain so-called attorneys' fees provisions. An example of the language used follows: "In the event of any dispute arising out of the performance or breach of this agreement, the

prevailing party will be entitled to an award of reasonable attorneys' fees." Then if the parties end up litigating over the contract, the judge will be able to make the non-breaching party whole by requiring the losing party to pay the winner's reasonable attorneys' fees, in addition to any other damages or relief granted.

However, absent an attorneys' fees clause in the parties' written agreement and without an attorneys' fees statute in place, the general rule applies and attorneys' fees will not be considered part of a litigating party's damages.

Reliance Damages [18-1b]

Reliance damages

contract damages placing the injured party in as good a position as he would have been in had the contract not been made

Instead of seeking compensatory damages, a party injured by total breach or repudiation may seek reimbursement for foreseeable loss caused by her reliance on the contract as measured by the cost or the value of the injured party's performance. The purpose of **reliance damages** is to place the injured party in a position as good as the position she would have been in had the contract *not been made*. The Restatement of Restitution provides that reliance damages for *cost* of performance include the injured party's uncompensated expenses incurred in preparing to perform, in actually performing, or in forgoing opportunities to enter into other contracts. Recovery based on cost of performance, however, is reduced by any loss the breaching party can prove with reasonable certainty that the injured party would have suffered had the contract been performed. Alternatively, reliance damages may be the market *value* of the injured party's uncompensated contractual performance, not exceeding the contract price of such performance. Limiting damages for the value of performance to the contract price prevents injured parties from choosing reliance damages to escape from an unfavorable bargain. In addition to recovering the cost or value of her performance, the injured party may also recover for any other loss, including incidental or consequential loss, caused by the breach.

An injured party may prefer damages for reliance to compensatory damages when she is unable to establish her lost profits with reasonable certainty. For example, Donald agrees to sell his retail store to Gary, who spends $750,000 in acquiring inventory and fixtures. Donald then repudiates the contract, and Gary sells the inventory and fixtures for $735,000. Because neither party can establish with reasonable certainty what profit Gary would have made, Gary may recover from Donald as damages the loss of $15,000 he sustained on the sale of the inventory and fixtures plus any other costs he incurred in entering into the contract.

Nominal Damages [18-1c]

Nominal damages

a small sum awarded when a contract has been breached but the loss is negligible or unproved

An action to recover damages for breach of contract may be maintained even though the plaintiff has not sustained or cannot prove any injury or loss resulting from the breach. In such case he will be permitted to recover **nominal damages**—a small sum fixed without regard to the amount of loss. Such a judgment may also include an award of court costs.

Damages for Misrepresentation [18-1d]

The basic remedy for misrepresentation is rescission (avoidance) of the contract. When appropriate, restitution will also be required. At common law, an alternative remedy to rescission is a suit for damages. The Code liberalizes the common law by not restricting a defrauded party to an election of remedies. That is, the injured party may both rescind the contract by restoring the other party to the status quo and recover damages or obtain any other remedy available under the Code. In most states, the measure of damages for misrepresentation depends on whether the misrepresentation was fraudulent or nonfraudulent.

Out-of-pocket damages
difference between the value received and the value given

Benefit-of-the-bargain damages
difference between the value received and the value of the fraudulent party's performance as represented

Fraud A party who has been induced by fraud to enter into a contract may recover general damages in a tort action. A minority of states allow the injured party to recover, under the "**out-of-pocket**" rule, general damages equal to the difference between the value of what she has received and the value of what she has given for it. The great majority of states, however, permit the intentionally defrauded party to recover, under the "**benefit-of-the-bargain**" rule, general damages that are equal to the difference between the value of what she has received and the value of the fraudulent party's performance as represented. The Restatement of Torts provides the fraudulently injured party with the option of either out-of-pocket or benefit-of-the-bargain damages. To illustrate, Emily intentionally misrepresents the capabilities of a printing press and thereby induces Melissa to purchase the machine for $20,000. Though the value of the press as delivered is $14,000, the machine would be worth $24,000 if it performed as represented. Under the out-of-pocket rule, Melissa would recover $6,000, whereas under the benefit-of-the-bargain rule, she would recover $10,000. In addition to a recovery of general damages under one of the measures just discussed, consequential damages may be recovered to the extent they are proved with reasonable certainty and to the extent they do not duplicate general damages. Moreover, where the fraud is gross, oppressive, or aggravated, punitive damages are permitted. See *Merritt v. Craig* later in this chapter.

Nonfraudulent Misrepresentation When the misrepresentation is negligent, the deceived party may recover general damages (under the out-of-pocket measure) and consequential damages. Furthermore, some states permit the recovery of general damages under the benefit-of-the-bargain measure. When the misrepresentation is neither fraudulent nor negligent, however, the Restatement of Torts limits damages to the out-of-pocket measure.

Punitive Damages [18-1e]

Punitive damages
are generally not recoverable for breach of contract

Punitive damages are monetary damages in addition to compensatory damages awarded to a plaintiff in certain situations involving willful, wanton, or malicious conduct. Their purpose is to punish the defendant and thus discourage him, and others, from similar wrongful conduct. The purpose of allowing contract damages, on the other hand, is to compensate the plaintiff for the loss sustained because of the defendant's breach of contract. Accordingly, the Restatement provides that punitive damages are not recoverable for a breach of contract unless the conduct constituting the breach is also a tort for which the plaintiff may recover punitive damages. See *Merritt v. Craig* later in this chapter.

Liquidated Damages [18-1f]

Liquidated damages
reasonable damages agreed to in advance by the parties to a contract

Practical Advice

Consider including a contractual provision for reasonable liquidated damages, especially where damages will be difficult to prove.

A contract may contain a **liquidated damages** provision by which the parties agree in advance to the damages to be paid in event of a breach. Such a provision will be enforced if it amounts to a reasonable forecast of the loss that may or does result from the breach. If, however, the sum agreed on as liquidated damages bears no reasonable relationship to the amount of probable loss, it is unenforceable as a penalty. (A penalty is a contractual provision designed to deter a party from breaching her contract and to punish her for doing so.) Such equivalence is required because the objective of contract remedies is compensatory, not punitive. By examining the substance of the provision, the nature of the contract, and the extent of probable harm that a breach may reasonably be expected to cause the promisee, the courts will determine whether the agreed amount is proper as liquidated damages or unenforceable as a penalty. If a liquidated damages provision is not enforceable, the injured party nevertheless is entitled to the ordinary remedies for breach of contract.

Arrowhead School District No. 75, Park County, Montana, v. Klyap

Supreme Court of Montana, 2003

318 Mont. 103, 79 P.3d 250

http://scholar.google.com/scholar_case?case=643756738100095281 &q=79+p.3d+250&hl=en&as_sdt=2,34

FACTS Arrowhead School District No. 75 is located in Park County, Montana, and consists of one school, Arrowhead School (School). For the 1997–98 school year, the School employed eleven full-time teachers and several part-time teachers. During that school year, the School employed James Klyap as a new teacher instructing math, language arts, and physical education for the sixth, seventh, and eighth grades. In addition, Klyap helped start a sports program and coached flag football, basketball, and volleyball. In June 1998, the School offered Klyap a contract for the 1998–99 school year, which he accepted. This contract provided for a $20,500 salary and included a liquidated damages clause. The clause calculated liquidated damages as a percentage of annual salary determined by the date of breach; a breach of contract after July 20, 1998, required payment of 20 percent of salary as damages. Klyap also signed a notice indicating he accepted responsibility for familiarizing himself with the information in the teacher's handbook which also included the liquidated damages clause. On August 12, Klyap informed the School that he would not be returning for the 1998-99 school year even though classes were scheduled to start on August 26. The School then sought to enforce the liquidated damages clause in Klyap's teaching contract for the stipulated amount of $4,100.

After Klyap resigned, the School attempted to find another teacher to take Klyap's place. Although at the time that Klyap was offered his contract the School had eighty potential applicants, only two viable applicants remained available. Right before classes started, the School was able to hire one of those applicants, a less-experienced teacher, at a salary of $19,500.

After a bench trial, the District Court determined the clause was enforceable because the damages suffered by the School were impractical and extremely difficult to fix. Specifically, the court found the School suffered damages because it had to spend additional time setting up an interview committee, conducting interviews, training the new, less-experienced teacher, and reorganizing the sports program. After concluding that the School took appropriate steps to mitigate its damages, the court awarded judgment in favor of the School in the amount of $4,100. Klyap appealed.

DECISION Judgment affirmed.

OPINION The fundamental tenet of modern contract law is freedom of contract: parties are free to mutually agree to terms governing their private conduct as long as those terms do not conflict with public laws or policies. This tenet presumes that parties are in the best position to make decisions in their own interest. When one party breaches the contract, judicial enforcement of the contract ensures the nonbreaching party receives expectancy damages, compensation equal to what that party would receive if the contract were performed. By only awarding expectancy damages rather than additional damages intended to punish the breaching party for failure to perform the contract, court enforcement of private contracts supports the theory of efficient breach. In other words, if it is more efficient for a party to breach a contract and pay expectancy damages in order to enter a superior contract, courts will not interfere by requiring the breaching party to pay more than was due under their contract.

Liquidated damages are, in theory, an extension of these principles. Rather than wait until the occurrence of breach, the parties to a contract are free to agree in advance on a specific damage amount to be paid upon breach. This amount is intended to predetermine expectancy damages. Ideally, this predetermination is intended to make the agreement between the parties more efficient. Rather than requiring a postbreach inquiry into damages between the parties, the breaching party simply pays the nonbreaching party the stipulated amount. Furthermore, in this way, liquidated damages clauses allow parties to estimate damages that are impractical or difficult to prove, as courts cannot enforce expectancy damages without sufficient proof.

To determine whether a clause should be declared a penalty, courts attempt to measure the reasonableness of a liquidated damages clause. The threshold indicator of reasonableness is whether the situation involves damages of a type that are impractical or extremely difficult to prove. According to Restatement, damages must be reasonable in relation to the damages the parties anticipated when the contract was executed or in relation to actual damages resulting from the breach. Liquidated damages in a personal service contract induce performance by an employee by predetermining compensation to an employer if the employee leaves. However, the employer clearly prefers performance by the specific employee because that employee was chosen for hire. Furthermore, because personal service contracts are not enforceable by specific performance, liquidated damages are an appropriate way for employers to protect their interests.

After reviewing the facts of this case, the court held that while the 20 percent liquidated damages clause is definitely harsher than most, it is still within Klyap's reasonable expectations and is not unduly oppressive. First, as the School pointed out during testimony, at such a small school teachers are chosen in part depending on how their skills complement those of the other teachers. Therefore, finding someone who would provide services equivalent to Klyap at such a late date would be virtually impossible. Second, besides the loss of equivalent services, the School lost time for preparation for other activities in order to attempt to find equivalent services. Because Klyap was essential to the sports program, the School had to spend additional time reorganizing the sports program as one sport had to be eliminated with Klyap's loss. Therefore, because as a teacher Klyap would know teachers are typically employed for an entire school year and would know how difficult it is to replace equivalent services at such a small rural school, it was within Klyap's reasonable expectations to agree to a contract with a 20 percent of salary liquidated damages provision for a departure so close to the start of the school year.

INTERPRETATION A liquidated damages provision is enforceable if it is a reasonable forecast of the harm caused by the breach.

CRITICAL THINKING QUESTION What limitations, if any, should the law impose upon liquidated damages? Explain.

Limitations on Damages [18-1g]

To accomplish the basic purposes of contract remedies, the limitations of foreseeability, certainty, and mitigation have been imposed upon monetary damages. These limitations are intended to ensure that damages can be taken into account at the time of contracting, that they are compensatory and not speculative, and that they do not include loss that could have been avoided by reasonable efforts.

Foreseeability of Damages   Contracting parties are generally expected to consider foreseeable risks at the time they enter into the contract. Therefore, compensatory or reliance damages are recoverable only for loss that the party in breach had reason to foresee as a *probable* result of a breach when the contract was made. The breaching party is not liable for loss that was not foreseeable at the time of entering into the contract. The test of **foreseeable damages** is *objective*, based on what the breaching party had reason to foresee. Loss may be deemed foreseeable as a probable result of a breach because it followed from the breach (1) in the ordinary course of events or (2) as a result of special circumstances, beyond the ordinary course of events, about which the party in breach had reason to know.

> **Foreseeable damages**
> loss that the party in breach had reason to anticipate when the contract was made

A leading case on the subject of foreseeability of damages is *Hadley v. Baxendale*, decided in England in 1854.

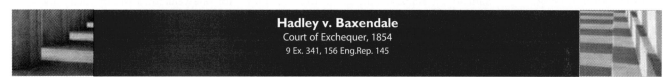

Hadley v. Baxendale
Court of Exchequer, 1854
9 Ex. 341, 156 Eng.Rep. 145

FACTS The plaintiffs operated a flour mill at Gloucester. They had to stop operating the mill because of a broken crankshaft attached to the steam engine that furnished power to the mill. It was necessary to send the broken shaft to a foundry in Greenwich so that a new shaft could be made. The plaintiffs delivered the broken shaft to the defendants, who were common carriers, for immediate transportation from Gloucester to Greenwich but did not inform the defendants that the mill had ceased operating because of the broken crankshaft. The defendants received the shaft, collected the freight charges in advance, and promised the plaintiffs to deliver the shaft for repairs the following day. The defendants did not make prompt delivery as promised. As a result, the plaintiffs could not operate the mill for several days, thus losing profits that they otherwise would have received. The defendants contended that the loss of profits was too remote, and therefore unforeseeable, to be recoverable. In awarding damages to the plaintiffs, the jury was permitted to consider the loss of these profits.

DECISION Judgment for defendants.

OPINION The appellate court reversed the decision and ordered a new trial on the ground that the special circumstances that caused the loss of profits, namely, the continued stoppage of the mill while awaiting the return of the new crankshaft, had never been communicated by the plaintiffs to the defendants. A common carrier would not reasonably foresee that the plaintiff's mill would be shut down as a result of delay in transporting the broken crankshaft. Damages for

> breach of contract should be such as may fairly and reasonably be considered either arising naturally, i.e., according to the usual course of things, from such breach … or such as may reasonably be supposed to have been in the contemplation of both parties at the time they made the contract, as the probable result of the breach of it.

INTERPRETATION Damages are recoverable only for those damages that were foreseeable at the time of entering into the contract.

ETHICAL QUESTION Is the court's decision fair? Explain.

CRITICAL THINKING QUESTION Should damages be limited to those that are foreseeable? Explain.

On the other hand, if the defendants in *Hadley v. Baxendale* had been informed that the shaft was necessary for the operation of the mill, or otherwise had reason to know this fact, they would be liable for the plaintiffs' loss of profit during that period of the shutdown caused by their delay. Under these circumstances, the loss would be the "foreseeable" and "natural" result of the breach.

Should a plaintiff's expected profit be extraordinarily large, the general rule is that the breaching party will be liable for such special loss only if he had reason to know of it. In any event, the plaintiff may recover for any ordinary loss resulting from the breach. Thus, if Madeline breaches a contract with Jane, causing Jane, due to special circumstances, $10,000 in damages when ordinarily such a breach would result in only $6,000 in damages, Madeline would be liable to Jane for $6,000, not $10,000, provided that Madeline was unaware of the special circumstances causing Jane the unusually large loss.

Practical Advice

Be sure to inform the other party to the contract of any "special circumstances" beyond the ordinary course of events that could result from a breach of contract.

Certainty of damages
damages are not recoverable beyond an amount that can be established with reasonable certainty

Certainty of Damages
Damages are not recoverable for loss beyond an amount that the injured party can establish with reasonable certainty. If the injured party cannot prove a particular element of her loss with reasonable certainty, she nevertheless will be entitled to recover the portion of her loss that she can prove with reasonable certainty. The certainty requirement creates the greatest challenge for plaintiffs seeking the recovery of consequential damages for lost profits on related transactions. Similar difficulty arises in proving lost profits caused by breach of a contract to produce a sporting event or to publish a new book, for example.

Mitigation of damages
the injured party may not recover damages for loss he could have avoided by reasonable effort

Mitigation of Damages
Under the doctrine of **mitigation of damages**, the injured party may not recover damages for loss that he could have avoided with reasonable effort and without undue risk, burden, or humiliation. Thus, if Earl is under a contract to manufacture goods for Karl and Karl repudiates the contract after Earl has begun performance, Earl will not be allowed to recover for losses he sustains by continuing to manufacture the goods, if to do so would increase the amount of damages. The amount of loss that reasonably could have been avoided is deducted from the amount that otherwise would be recoverable as damages. On the other hand, if the goods were almost completed when Karl repudiated the contract, completing the goods might reduce the damages, because the finished goods may be resalable whereas the unfinished goods may not.

Practical Advice

If the other party to the contract breaches, be sure to make reasonable efforts to avoid or mitigate damages.

Similarly, if Harvey contracts to work for Olivia for one year for a weekly salary and after two months is wrongfully discharged by Olivia, Harvey must use reasonable efforts to mitigate his damages by seeking other employment. If, after such effort, he cannot obtain other employment of the same general character, he is entitled to recover full pay for the contract period during which he is unemployed. He is not obliged to accept a radically different type of employment or to accept work at a distant place. For example, a person employed as a schoolteacher or accountant who is wrongfully discharged is not obliged to accept employment as a chauffeur or truck driver. If Harvey does *not* seek other employment, then if Olivia proves with reasonable certainty that employment of the same general character was available, Harvey's damages are reduced by the amount he could have earned. The next case involving Shirley MacLaine turns on whether acting in a western is employment equivalent to singing and dancing in a musical.

Parker v. Twentieth Century-Fox Film Corp.
Supreme Court of California, 1970
3 Cal.3d 176, 89 Cal.Rptr. 737, 474 P.2d 689
http://scholar.google.com/scholar_case?q=474+P.2d+689&hl=en&as_sdt=2,34&case=8204943341098207403&scilh=0

FACTS Shirley MacLaine Parker, a well-known actress, contracted with Twentieth Century-Fox Film Corporation (Fox) in August 1965 to play the female lead in Fox's upcoming production of *Bloomer Girl*, a motion picture musical that was to be filmed in California. The contract provided that Fox would pay Parker a minimum "guaranteed compensation" of $750,000 for fourteen weeks of Parker's services, beginning May 23, 1966. By letter dated April 4, 1966, Fox notified Parker of its intention not to produce the film and, instead, offered to employ Parker in the female lead of another film entitled *Big Country, Big Man*, a dramatic western to be filmed in Australia. The compensation offered and most of the other provisions in the substitute contract were identical to the *Bloomer Girl* provisions, except that Parker's right to approve the director and screenplay would have been eliminated or reduced under the *Big Country* contract. Parker refused to accept and brought suit against Fox to recover $750,000 for breach of the *Bloomer Girl* contract. Fox contended that it owed no money to Parker because she had deliberately failed to mitigate or reduce her damages by unreasonably refusing to accept the *Big Country* lead. The trial court granted Parker a summary judgment. (The court's opinion with respect to the rules for determining whether to grant summary judgment appears in Chapter 3.)

DECISION Judgment for Parker affirmed.

OPINION A wrongfully discharged employee generally has a duty to mitigate her damages either by attempting to find or by actually finding substitute employment. The measure of recovery is typically the amount of salary promised under the original contract minus the amount the employer proves the employee has earned, or with reasonable effort might have earned, from other, "substantially similar" employment. The employee's rejection of or failure to seek other employment of a different or inferior kind cannot be used to mitigate damages.

Bloomer Girl was to be a musical revue calling upon Parker's talents as a dancer as well as an actress and was to be filmed in Los Angeles. On the other hand, *Big Country, Big Man* was a straight acting, western-type motion picture taking place in an opal mine in Australia. In addition, Parker would have had her right to approve the director and screenplay eliminated or impaired by the *Big Country* contract. Such disparities between the two projects render the substitute *Big Country* lead of a kind different and inferior to the *Bloomer Girl* role. Therefore, Parker need not accept or seek such inferior employment and could reject

Fox's substitute offer with no reduction in her award for failure to mitigate.

INTERPRETATION An injured party's damages may not be reduced by mitigation for her failure to accept or seek other employment of a different or inferior kind.

ETHICAL QUESTION Was it fair for Twentieth Century-Fox Film Corporation to expect Parker to act in the substitute film? Explain.

CRITICAL THINKING QUESTION Why should an injured party be required to mitigate damages? Explain.

REMEDIES IN EQUITY [18-2]

At times, damages will not adequately compensate an injured party. In these cases, equitable relief in the form of specific performance or an injunction may be available to protect the injured party's interest. Such remedies are not a matter of right but rest in the discretion of the court. Consequently, they will not be granted when there is an adequate remedy at law; when it is impossible to enforce them, as when the seller has already transferred the subject matter of the contract to an innocent third person; when the terms of the contract are unfair; when the consideration is grossly inadequate; when the contract is tainted with fraud, duress, undue influence, mistake, or unfair practices; or when the relief would cause the defendant unreasonable hardship. See *Real Estate Analytics, LLC. v. Vallas* in this chapter.

On the other hand, a court may grant specific performance or an injunction despite a provision for liquidated damages. Moreover, a court will grant specific performance or an injunction even though a term of the contract prohibits equitable relief, if denying such relief would cause the injured party unreasonable hardship.

Reformation

equitable remedy correcting a written contract to conform with the original intent of the contracting parties

Another equitable remedy is **reformation**, a process whereby the court "rewrites" or "corrects" a written contract to make it conform to the true agreement of the parties. The purpose of reformation is not to make a new contract for the parties but to express adequately the contract they have made for themselves. The remedy of reformation is granted when the parties agree on a contract but write it in a way that inaccurately reflects their actual agreement. For example, Acme Insurance Co. and Bell agree that for good consideration, Acme will issue an annuity paying $500 per month. Because of a clerical error, the annuity policy is issued for $50 per month. A court of equity, upon satisfactory proof of the mistake, will reform the policy to provide for the correct amount—$500 per month. In addition, as discussed in Chapter 13, in cases in which a covenant not to compete is unreasonable, some courts will reform the agreement to make it reasonable and enforceable.

Specific Performance [18-2a]

Specific performance

court decree ordering a breaching party to render promised performance

Specific performance is the equitable remedy that compels the defaulting party to perform her contractual obligations. As with all equitable remedies, it is available only when there is no adequate remedy at law. Ordinarily, for instance, in a case in which a seller breaches a contract for the sale of personal property, the buyer has a sufficient remedy at law. When, however, the personal property contracted for is rare or unique, this remedy is inadequate. Examples of such property would include a famous painting or statue, an original manuscript or a rare edition of a book, a patent, a copyright, shares of stock in a closely held corporation, or an heirloom. Articles of this kind cannot be purchased elsewhere. Accordingly, on breach by the seller of the contract for the sale of any such article, money damages will not adequately compensate the buyer. Consequently, the buyer may avail herself of the equitable remedy of specific performance.

Although courts of equity will grant specific performance in connection with contracts for the sale of personal property only in exceptional circumstances, they will always grant it in case of breach of contract for the sale of real property. The reason for this is that every parcel of land is regarded as unique. Consequently, if the seller refuses to convey title to the real estate contracted for, the buyer may seek the aid of a court of equity to compel the seller to convey the title. Most courts of equity will likewise compel the buyer in a real estate contract to perform at the suit of the seller.

Courts of equity will not grant specific performance of contracts for personal services. In the first place, there is the practical difficulty, if not impossibility, of enforcing such a decree. In the second place, it is against the policy of the courts to force one person to work for or to serve another against his will, even though the person has contracted to do so. Such enforcement would closely resemble involuntary servitude. For example, if Carmen, an accomplished concert pianist, agrees to appear at a certain time and place to play a specified program for Rudolf, a court would not issue a decree of specific performance upon her refusal to appear.

Real Estate Analytics, LLC v. Vallas
Court of Appeal, Fourth District, Division 1, California, 2008
160 Cal.App.4th 463, 72 Cal.Rptr.3d 835; review denied, 2008
http://scholar.google.com/scholar_case?case=16761955053572987435&q=72+cal.rptr.3d+835&hl=en&as_sdt=2,34

FACTS Real Estate Analytics, LLC (REA) is a limited liability company formed by Troy Shadian. In January 2004, Shadian and his business partner, Roshan Bhakta, became interested in Theodore Tee Vallas's 14.13-acre Lanikai Lane property located in Carlsbad, California. The property contained a mobile home park with 147 individual mobile homes and numerous amenities, including a pool, playground, laundry facilities, and a long winding street. Vallas leased the property to a mobile home park operator, which managed the park and subleased the spaces to residents who owned their mobile homes. The lease began in 1951 and terminates in 2013.

REA's primary goal in purchasing the property was to make a profit for its investors and themselves. One proposed business model was to subdivide the property and sell the subdivided lots to the property's mobile home park residents. In March 2004, REA and Vallas entered into a written agreement for Vallas to sell the property to REA. Under the agreement, the sales price was $8.5 million, with REA to pay an immediate $100,000 deposit, and then pay $2.9 million at closing. In return, Vallas agreed to finance the remaining $5.5 million, with the unpaid balance to be paid over a five-year period, with the balance due on April 1, 2009. On June 14, Vallas cancelled the contract. The next day REA brought a breach of contract action seeking specific performance. The court, sitting without a jury, found Vallas breached the contract but refused to grant specific performance and instead awarded REA damages of $500,000, reflecting the difference between the contract price and the fair market value at the time of the breach. The court declined to award specific performance on the basis of its finding that damages would provide REA adequate relief.

DECISION Judgment is reversed, and the trial court is ordered to enter a new judgment granting specific performance.

OPINION To obtain specific performance after a breach of contract, a plaintiff must generally show the following: (1) the inadequacy of his legal remedy, (2) an underlying contract that is both reasonable and supported by adequate consideration, (3) the existence of a mutuality of remedies, (4) contractual terms which are sufficiently definite to enable the court to know what it is to enforce, and (5) a substantial similarity of the requested performance to that promised in the contract.

In this case, the trial court refused to specifically enforce the contract based on its finding that the first element (inadequacy of legal remedy) was not satisfied because REA sought to purchase the property as an investment, and not for some particular use of the land. A damage award is generally an inadequate remedy for a breach of real estate contract, and therefore courts generally grant a plaintiff's request for specific performance. Most jurisdictions have rules requiring special treatment of land sale contracts, reflecting the enduring view that (1) each parcel of land is unique and therefore there can be no adequate replacement after a breach and (2) monetary damages are difficult to calculate after a party refuses to complete a land sales contract, particularly expectation damages. In California, these principles are statutorily embodied in section 3387, which states the following:

> It is to be presumed that the breach of an agreement to transfer real property cannot be adequately relieved by pecuniary compensation. In the case of a single-family dwelling which the party seeking performance intends to occupy, this presumption is conclusive. In all other cases, this presumption is a presumption affecting the burden of proof.

By imposing a conclusive presumption for certain residential transactions, the California legislature decided that monetary damages can never be satisfactory compensation for a buyer who intends to live at a single-family home, regardless of the circumstances. But by establishing a rebuttable presumption with respect to other property, the legislature left open the possibility that damages can be an adequate remedy for a breach of a real estate contract. Given the statutory presumption that damages were inadequate and the largely undisputed evidence strongly supporting this presumption, Vallas had a high threshold to satisfy his burden to show damages would be an adequate remedy. Thus, although REA did not necessarily intend to benefit from its personal or commercial *use* of the land, the land did have a particular unique value because of the manner in which it could be used to earn profits upon a resale. Missing from the trial court's analysis was the recognition that to rebut the presumption that damages are an inadequate remedy, the defendant must come forward with evidence showing that damages will fully compensate the plaintiff for the breach. The record in this case was bereft of any such evidence.

INTERPRETATION Specific performance is an appropriate remedy when there is no adequate remedy at law.

CRITICAL THINKING QUESTION Should specific performance be available for all breaches of contract? Explain.

Injunction [18-2b]

Injunction
court order prohibiting a
party from doing a specific
act

An **injunction**, as used as a contract remedy, is a formal court order enjoining (commanding) a person to refrain from doing a specific act or to cease engaging in specific conduct. A court of equity, at its discretion, may grant an injunction against breach of a contractual duty when damages for a breach would be inadequate. For example, Clint enters into a written contract to give Janice the right of first refusal on a tract of land owned by Clint. Clint, however, subsequently offers the land to Blake without first offering it to Janice. A court of equity may properly enjoin Clint from selling the land to Blake. Similarly, valid covenants not to compete may be enforced by an injunction.

An employee's promise of exclusive personal services may be enforced by an injunction against serving another employer as long as the probable result will not deprive the employee of other reasonable means of making a living. Suppose, for example, that Allan makes a contract with Marlene, a famous singer, under which Marlene agrees to sing at Allan's theater on certain dates for an agreed-upon fee. Before the date of the first performance, Marlene makes a contract with Craig to sing for Craig at his theater on the same dates. Although, as we have discussed, Allan cannot obtain specific performance of his contract by Marlene, a court of equity will, on suit by Allan against Marlene, issue an injunction against her ordering her not to sing for Craig. This is the situation in the case of *Madison Square Garden Corp., Ill. v. Carnera*.

In cases in which the services contracted for are *not* unusual or extraordinary in character, the injured party cannot obtain injunctive relief. His only remedy is an action at law for damages.

 Madison Square Garden Corp., Ill. v. Carnera
United States Court of Appeals, Second Circuit, 1931
52 F.2d 47
http://scholar.google.com/scholar_case?q=52+F.2d+47&hl=en&as_sdt=2,34&case=133326573442361100&scilh=0

FACTS Carnera (defendant) agreed with Madison Square Garden (plaintiff) to render services as a boxer in his next contest with the winner of the Schmeling-Stribling contest for the heavyweight championship title. The contract also provided that prior to the match Carnera would not engage in any major boxing contest without the permission of Madison Square Garden. Without obtaining such permission, Carnera contracted to engage in a major boxing contest with Sharkey. Madison Square Garden brought suit requesting an injunction against Carnera's performing his contract to box Sharkey. The trial court granted a preliminary injunction.

DECISION Order for Madison Square Garden affirmed.

OPINION The affidavits in support of the request for a preliminary injunction adequately show that Carnera's services are unique and extraordinary. While specific performance will not be ordered to compel Carnera to render personal services, the court will specifically enforce a negative covenant by injunctive order when damages are not readily ascertainable.

INTERPRETATION When damages are not adequate, an injunction may be used to enforce an agreement to perform exclusive services that are unusual and extraordinary.

CRITICAL THINKING QUESTION Should money damages have been an adequate remedy in this case? Explain.

RESTITUTION [18-3]

Restitution
restoration of the injured
party to the position he
was in before the contract
was made

One of the remedies that may be available to a party to a contract is restitution. **Restitution** is the act of returning to the aggrieved party the consideration, or its value, that he gave to the other party. The purpose of restitution is to restore the injured party to the position he was in before the contract was made. Therefore, the party seeking restitution must return what has been received from the other party.

Restitution is available in several contractual situations: (1) for a party injured by breach, as an alternative remedy, (2) for a party in default, (3) for a party who may not enforce a contract because of the statute of frauds, and (4) for a party wishing to rescind (avoid) a voidable contract.

Party Injured by Breach [18-3a]

Party injured by breach
may recover in restitution if
the other party totally
breaches the contract by
nonperformance or
repudiation

The Restatement of Restitution provides that a party is entitled to restitution if the other party totally breaches the contract by nonperformance or repudiation. For example, Benedict agrees to sell land to Beatrice for $60,000. After Beatrice makes a partial payment of $15,000, Benedict wrongfully refuses to transfer title. As an alternative to damages or specific performance, Beatrice may recover the $15,000 in restitution. The Restatement of Restitution provides, however, that restitution as a remedy for breach of contract is *not* available against a defendant whose defaulted obligation is exclusively an obligation to pay money. Thus, restitution as an alternative contract remedy is available to a prepaying buyer but not to a credit seller.

Party in Default [18-3b]

Party in default
may recover in restitution any benefit conferred in excess of the loss caused by that party's breach

The Restatement of Restitution provides that a partly performing party whose material breach prevents a recovery on the contract has a claim in restitution against the recipient of performance, as necessary to prevent unjust enrichment. Thus, if a party, after having partly performed, commits a breach by nonperformance or repudiation that discharges the other party's duty to perform, the party in default is entitled to restitution for any benefit she has conferred in excess of the loss she has caused by the breach. For example, Nathan agrees to sell land to Milly for $160,000, and Milly makes a partial payment of $15,000. Milly then repudiates the contract. Nathan sells the land to Murray in good faith for $155,000. Milly may recover from Nathan in restitution the part payment of the $15,000 less the $5,000 damages Nathan sustained because of Milly's breach, which equals $10,000.

Statute of Frauds [18-3c]

Statute of frauds
when a contract is unenforceable because of the statute of frauds, a party may recover in restitution the benefits conferred on the other party in performance of the contract

The Restatement of Restitution provides that a person who renders performance under an agreement that cannot be enforced by reason of the failure to satisfy the **statute of frauds** has a claim in restitution to prevent unjust enrichment. In such a case, that party may recover in restitution the benefits he directly conferred on the other as the performance required or invited by the unenforceable contract. Thus, if Wilton makes an oral contract to furnish services to Rochelle that are not to be performed within a year, and Rochelle discharges Wilton after three months, Wilton may recover in restitution the value of the services rendered during the three months. Similarly, Sanford enters into an oral contract to sell land to Betty, and Betty pays a portion of the price as a down payment. Sanford subsequently repudiates the oral contract. Betty may recover in restitution the portion of the price she paid.

Voidable Contracts [18-3d]

Voidable contracts
a party who has rightfully avoided a contract is entitled to restitution for any benefit conferred on the other party but generally must return any benefit that he has received under the contract

A party who has rescinded or avoided a contract for lack of capacity, duress, undue influence, fraud in the inducement, nonfraudulent misrepresentation, or mistake is entitled to restitution for any benefit he has conferred on the other party. Generally, the party seeking restitution must return any benefit that he has received under the agreement; however, as we found in our discussion of contractual capacity (Chapter 14), this is not always the case. The Restatement of Restitution provides

> Rescission requires a mutual restoration and accounting in which each party (a) restores property received from the other, to the extent such restoration is feasible, (b) accounts for additional benefits obtained at the expense of the other as a result of the transaction and its subsequent avoidance, as necessary to prevent unjust enrichment, and (c) compensates the other for loss from related expenditure as justice may require.

For example, Samuel fraudulently induces Jessica to sell land for $160,000. Samuel pays the purchase price, and Jessica conveys the land. Jessica then discovers the fraud. Jessica may disaffirm the contract and recover the land as restitution but she must return the $160,000 purchase price to Samuel.

Figure 18-1 summarizes the remedies for breach of contract.

LIMITATIONS ON REMEDIES [18-4]

Election of Remedies [18-4a]

Election of remedies
if remedies are not inconsistent, a party injured by a breach of contract may seek more than one remedy

If a party injured by a breach of contract has more than one remedy available, her manifestation of a choice of one remedy, such as bringing suit, does not prevent seeking another unless the

Figure 18-1 Contract Remedies

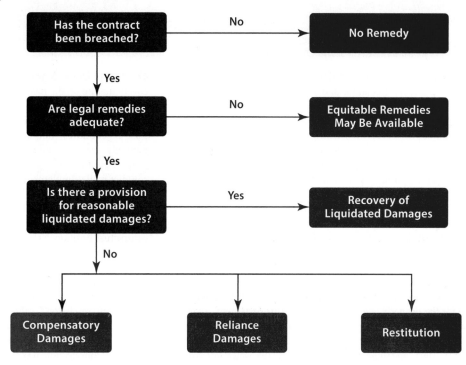

remedies are inconsistent and the other party materially changes his position in reliance on the manifestation. For example, a party who seeks specific performance, an injunction, or restitution may be entitled to incidental damages, such as those brought about by delay in performance. Damages for total breach, however, are inconsistent with the remedies of specific performance, injunction, and restitution. Likewise, the remedy of specific performance or an injunction is inconsistent with that of restitution.

With respect to contracts for the sale of goods, the Code rejects any doctrine of election of remedies. Thus, the remedies it provides, which are essentially cumulative, include all of the remedies available for breach. Under the Code, whether one remedy prevents the use of another depends on the facts of the individual case.

Loss of Power of Avoidance [18-4b]

A party with a power of avoidance for lack of capacity, duress, undue influence, fraud, misrepresentation, or mistake may lose that power if (1) she affirms the contract, (2) she delays unreasonably in exercising the power of disaffirmance, or (3) the rights of third parties intervene.

Affirmance A party who has the power to avoid a contract for lack of capacity, duress, undue influence, fraud in the inducement, nonfraudulent misrepresentation, or mistake will lose that power by affirming the contract. Affirmance occurs when the party, with full knowledge of the facts, either declares the intention to proceed with the contract or takes some other action from which such intention may reasonably be inferred. Thus, suppose that Pam was induced to purchase a ring from Sally through Sally's fraudulent misrepresentation. If, after learning the truth, Pam undertakes to sell the ring to Janet or does something else that is consistent only with her ownership of the ring, she may no longer rescind the transaction with Sally. In the case of incapacity, duress, or undue influence, affirmance is effective only after the circumstances that made the contract voidable cease to exist. In cases in which there has been fraudulent misrepresentation, the defrauded party may affirm only after he knows of the misrepresentation; if the misrepresentation is nonfraudulent or a mistake is involved, affirmance may occur only after the defrauded party knows or should know of the misrepresentation or mistake.

Loss of power of avoidance

a party with the power to avoid a contract may lose that power by (1) affirming the contract, (2) delaying unreasonably in exercising the power of avoidance, or (3) being subordinated to the intervening rights of third parties

---

Practical Advice

If you have the power to avoid a contract, do not affirm the contract unless you are sure you wish to relinquish your right to rescind the contract.

Merritt v. Craig
Court of Special Appeals of Maryland, 2000
130 Md.App. 350, 746 A.2d 923; *cert. denied*, 359 Md. 29, 753 A.2d 2, 2000
http://scholar.google.com/scholar_case?case=10339288125936808164&q=746+a.2d+923&hl=en&as_sdt=2,34

FACTS In the fall of 1995, during their search for a new residence, the plaintiffs, Benjamin and Julie Merritt, advised the defendant, Virginia Craig, that they were interested in purchasing Craig's property contingent upon a satisfactory home inspection. On November 5, 1995, the plaintiffs, their inspector, and the defendant's husband Mark Craig conducted an inspection of the cistern and water supply pipes in the basement. The examination revealed that the cistern had been used to store a water supply reserve, but was not currently utilized. There were also two water lines that entered into the basement. One of the lines came from an eight-hundred-foot well that was located on the property, and the other line came from a well located on the adjacent property. The well located on the adjacent property supplied water to both the residence and a guesthouse owned by Craig. The existence of the adjacent well was not disclosed to the plaintiffs.

On December 2, 1995, plaintiffs and Craig executed a contract of sale for the property, along with a "Disclosure Statement" signed by Craig and acknowledged by the plaintiffs affirming that there were no problems with the water supply to the house. Between November 5, 1995, and June 1996, Craig caused the water line from the guesthouse to the house purchased by the plaintiffs to be cut, and the cistern reactivated to store water from the existing well. On May 18, 1996, Craig's husband advised Dennis Hannibal, one of the real estate agents involved in the deal, that he had spent $4,196.79 to upgrade the water system on the property. On June 14, 1996, the plaintiffs and Craig closed the sale of the property. Later that afternoon, Craig's husband, without the plaintiffs' knowledge, excavated the inside wall of the house and installed a cap to stop a leaking condition on the water line that he had previously cut.

Upon taking possession of the house the plaintiffs noticed that the water supply in their well had depleted. The plaintiffs met with Craig to discuss a solution to the water failure problem, agreeing with Craig to conduct a flow test to the existing well and to contribute money for the construction of a new well. On October 29, 1996, the well was drilled and produced only one-half gallon of water per minute. Subsequently plaintiffs paid for the drilling of a second well on their property, but it failed to produce water. In January 1997, appellants contacted a plumber, who confirmed that the line from the guesthouse well had been cut flush with the inside surface of the basement wall and cemented closed. Plaintiffs continued to do further work on the house in an effort to cure the water problem. The plaintiffs brought suit against Craig, seeking rescission of the deed to the property and contract of sale, along with compensatory and punitive damages. The trial judge dismissed plaintiffs' claim for rescission on the ground that they had effectively waived their right to rescission. The jury returned a verdict in favor of the plaintiffs, awarding compensatory damages in the amount of $42,264.76 and punitive damages in the amount of $150,000. The plaintiffs appealed the trial court's judgment denying their right to rescind the contract. The defendant cross-appealed on the award of punitive damages.

DECISION Judgment of the trial court reversed, and the case is remanded.

OPINION Under Maryland law, when a party to a contract discovers that he or she has been defrauded, the party defrauded has either a right to retain the contract and collect damages for its breach, or a right to rescind the contract and recover his or her own expenditures, not both. These rights are inconsistent and mutually exclusive, and the discovery puts the purchaser to a prompt election. The plaintiffs may not successfully rescind the contract while simultaneously recovering compensatory and punitive damages. Restitution is "a party's unilateral unmaking of a contract for a legally sufficient reason, such as the other party's material breach" and it in effect "restores the parties to their pre-contractual position." The restoration of the parties to their original position is incompatible with the windfall of compensatory and punitive damages beyond incidental expenses.

Maryland law asserts, "A plaintiff seeking rescission must demonstrate that he [or she] acted promptly after discovery of the ground for rescission," otherwise the right to rescind is waived. Under the facts of this case, the plaintiffs must elect between damages or rescission. Because the plaintiffs were led to believe by the court that no election was required, the case is remanded to the lower court for the plaintiffs to make the proper election and for the case to be retried, pursuant to that election.

On the question whether the trial court erred by allowing the jury verdict awarding the plaintiffs punitive damages in the amount of $150,000 to stand, the plaintiffs are entitled to be awarded punitive damages resulting from Craig's actions. The jury believed that the representations made by Craig were undertaken with actual knowledge that the representations were false and with the intention to deceive the plaintiffs, which constitutes the actual malice required to support an award for punitive damages. The jury could reasonably infer Craig's intention to defraud the plaintiffs by her representation that there were no problems with the water supply, and by subsequently making substantial changes in the water system by cutting off a water line which supplied water to the plaintiffs' residence immediately after the plaintiffs' inspector examined the system.

Craig also challenges the punitive damages award on the basis that the amount of the award was excessive, but Craig's conduct toward the plaintiffs was reprehensible and fully warranted punitive damages. Her conduct in willfully misrepresenting the condition of the water system, coupled with the actions of interfering and diverting the water flow subsequent to the inspection and sale of the property, constitute egregious conduct. As a result of Craig's conduct, the plaintiffs were forced to employ extreme water conservation practices due to an insufficient water supply and they attempted to ameliorate the problem by having two new wells drilled on the property, which proved to be unproductive.

INTERPRETATION A defrauded party may rescind a contract induced by fraud but may lose that power if he affirms the contract or delays unreasonably in exercising the power of rescission.

CRITICAL THINKING QUESTION What is the policy reason for requiring a defrauded party to elect between rescission and damages? Explain.

Practical Advice

If you have the power to avoid a contract, be sure to rescind within a reasonable time or you will forfeit your right to do so.

Delay   The power of avoidance may be lost if the party who has the power to do so does not rescind within a reasonable time after the circumstances that made the contract voidable have ceased to exist. Determining a reasonable time depends on all the circumstances, including the extent to which the delay enables the party with the power of avoidance to speculate at the other party's risk. To illustrate, a defrauded purchaser of stock cannot wait unduly to see whether the market price or value of the stock appreciates sufficiently to justify retaining the stock.

Rights of Third Parties   The intervening rights of third parties further limit the power of avoidance and the accompanying right to restitution. If A transfers property to B in a transaction that is voidable by A, and B sells the property to C (a good faith purchaser for value) before A exercises the power of avoidance, A will lose the right to recover the property.

Thus, if a third party (C), who is a good faith purchaser for value, acquires an interest in the subject matter of the contract before A has elected to rescind, no rescission is permitted. Because the transaction is voidable, B acquires a voidable title to the property. Upon a sale of the property by B to C, who is a purchaser in good faith and for value, C obtains good title and is allowed to retain the property. Because both A and C are innocent, the law will not disturb the title held by C, the good faith purchaser. In this case, as in all cases in which rescission is not available, A's only recourse is against B.

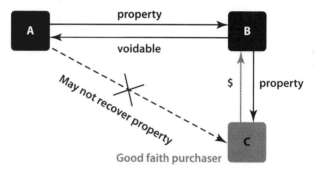

The one notable exception to this rule is the situation involving a sale, *other than a sale of goods*, by a minor who subsequently wishes to avoid the transaction, in which the property has been retransferred to a good faith purchaser. Under this special rule, a good faith purchaser is deprived of the protection generally provided such third parties. Therefore, the third party in a transaction not involving goods, real property being the primary example, is no more protected from the minor's disaffirmance than is the person dealing directly with the minor.

CHAPTER SUMMARY

Monetary Damages

Compensatory Damages contract damages placing the injured party in a position as good as the one he would have held had the other party performed; equals loss of value minus loss avoided by injured party plus incidental damages plus consequential damages

- *Loss of Value* value of promised performance minus value of actual performance
- *Cost Avoided* loss or costs the injured party avoids by not having to perform
- *Incidental Damages* damages arising directly out of a breach of contract
- *Consequential Damages* damages not arising directly out of a breach but arising as a foreseeable result of the breach

Reliance Damages contract damages placing the injured party in as good a position as she would have been in had the contract not been made

Nominal Damages a small sum awarded when a contract has been breached but the loss is negligible or unproved

Damages for Misrepresentation

- *Out-of-Pocket Damages* difference between the value given and the value received
- *Benefit-of-the-Bargain Damages* difference between the value of the fraudulent party's performance as represented and the value the defrauded party received

Punitive Damages are generally not recoverable for breach of contract

Liquidated Damages reasonable damages agreed to in advance by the parties to a contract

Limitations on Damages

- *Foreseeability of Damages* potential loss that the party now in default had reason to know of when the contract was made
- *Certainty of Damages* damages are not recoverable beyond an amount that can be established with reasonable certainty
- *Mitigation of Damages* injured party may not recover damages for loss he could have avoided by reasonable effort

Remedies in Equity

Availability only in cases in which there is no adequate remedy at law

Types

- *Specific Performance* court decree ordering the breaching party to render promised performance
- *Injunction* court order prohibiting a party from doing a specific act
- *Reformation* court order correcting a written contract to conform with the intent of the contracting parties

Restitution

Definition of Restitution restoration of the injured party to the position she was in before the contract was made

Availability

- *Party Injured by Breach* if the other party totally breaches the contract by nonperformance or repudiation
- *Party in Default* for any benefit conferred in excess of the loss caused by the party in default's breach
- *Statute of Frauds* where a contract is unenforceable because of the statute of frauds, a party may recover the benefits conferred on the other party in performance of the contract
- *Voidable Contracts* a party who has rightfully avoided a contract is entitled to restitution for any benefit conferred on the other party but generally must return any benefit that he has received under the contract

Limitations on Remedies

Election of Remedies if remedies are not inconsistent, a party injured by a breach of contract may seek more than one remedy

Loss of Power of Avoidance a party with the power to avoid a contract may lose that power by

- Affirming the contract
- Delaying unreasonably in exercising the power of avoidance
- Being subordinated to the intervening rights of third parties

QUESTIONS

1. Edward, a candy manufacturer, contracted to buy one thousand barrels of sugar from Marcia. Marcia failed to deliver, and Edward was unable to buy any sugar in the market. As a direct consequence he was unable to make candies to fulfill unusually lucrative contracts for the Christmas trade. (a) What damages is Edward entitled to recover? (b) Would it make any difference if Marcia had been told by Edward that he wanted the sugar to make candies for the Christmas trade and that he had accepted lucrative contracts for delivery for the Christmas trade?

2. Daniel agreed to erect an apartment building for Steven for $12 million, and that Daniel would suffer a deduction of $12,000 per day for every day of delay. Daniel was twenty days late in finishing the job, losing ten days because of a strike and ten days because the material suppliers were late in furnishing him with materials. Daniel claims that he is entitled to payment in full (a) because the agreement as to $12,000 a day is a penalty and (b) because Steven has not shown that he has sustained any damage. Discuss each contention and decide.

3. Sharon contracted with Jane, a shirtmaker, for one thousand shirts for men. Jane manufactured and delivered five hundred shirts, for which Sharon paid. At the same time, Sharon notified Jane that she could not use or dispose of the other five hundred shirts and directed Jane not to manufacture any more under the contract. Nevertheless, Jane made up the other five hundred shirts and tendered them to Sharon. Sharon refused to accept the shirts. Jane then sued for the purchase price. Is she entitled to the purchase price? If not, is she entitled to any damages? Explain.

4. Stuart contracts to act in a comedy for Charlotte and to comply with all theater regulations for four seasons. Charlotte promises to pay Stuart $1,800 for each performance and to allow Stuart one benefit performance each season. It is expressly agreed "Stuart shall not be employed in any other production for the period of the contract." Stuart and Charlotte, during the first year of the contract, have a terrible quarrel. Thereafter, Stuart signs a contract to perform in Elaine's production and ceases performing for Charlotte. Charlotte seeks (a) to prevent Stuart from performing for Elaine and (b) to require Stuart to perform his contract with Charlotte. What result?

5. Louis leased a building to Pam for five years at a rental of $1,000 per month. Pam was to deposit $10,000 as security for performance of all her promises in the lease, which was to be retained by Louis in case of any breach on Pam's part. Pam defaulted in the payment of rent for the last two months of the lease. Louis refused to return any of the deposit, claiming it as liquidated damages. Pam sued Louis to recover $8,000 (the $10,000 deposit less the amount of rent due Louis for the last two months). What amount of damages should Pam be allowed to collect from Louis? Explain.

6. In which of the following situations is specific performance available as a remedy?
   a. Mary and Anne enter into a written agreement under which Mary agrees to sell and Anne agrees to buy for $100 per share one hundred shares of the three hundred shares outstanding of the capital stock of the Infinitesimal Steel Corporation, whose shares are not listed on any exchange and are closely held. Mary refuses to deliver when tendered the $10,000.
   b. Modifying (a), assume that the subject matter of the agreement is stock of the U.S. Steel Corporation, which is traded on the New York Stock Exchange.
   c. Modifying (a), assume that the subject matter of the agreement is undeveloped farmland of little commercial value.

7. On March 1, Joseph sold to Sandra fifty acres of land in Oregon that Joseph at the time represented to be fine black loam, high, dry, and free of stumps. Sandra paid Joseph the agreed price of $140,000 and took from Joseph a deed to the land. Sandra subsequently discovered that the land was low, swampy, and not entirely free of stumps. Sandra, nevertheless, undertook to convert the greater part of the land into cranberry bogs. After one year of cranberry culture, Sandra became entirely dissatisfied, tendered the land back to Joseph, and demanded from Joseph the return of the $140,000. On Joseph's refusal to repay the money, Sandra brought an action at law against him to recover the $140,000. What judgment?

8. James contracts to make repairs to Betty's building in return for Betty's promise to pay $12,000 on completion of the repairs. After partially completing the repairs, James is unable to continue. Betty refuses to pay James and hires another builder, who completes the repairs for $5,000. The building's value to Betty has increased by $10,000 as a result of the repairs by James, but Betty has lost $500 in rents because of the delay caused by James's breach. James sues Betty. How much, if any, may James recover in restitution from Betty?

9. Linda induced Sally to enter into a purchase of a home theater receiver by intentionally misrepresenting the power output to be seventy-five watts at rated distortion, when in fact it delivered only forty watts. Sally paid $450 for the receiver. Receivers producing forty watts generally sell for $200, whereas receivers producing seventy-five watts generally sell for $550. Sally decides to keep the receiver and sue for damages. How much may Sally recover in damages from Linda?

10. Virginia induced Charles to sell Charles's boat to Virginia by misrepresentation of material fact on which Charles reasonably relied. Virginia promptly sold the boat to Donald, who paid fair value for it and knew nothing concerning the transaction between Virginia and Charles. Upon discovering the misrepresentation, Charles seeks to recover the boat. What are Charles's rights against Virginia and Donald?

CASE PROBLEMS

11. Felch was employed as a member of the faculty of Findlay College under a contract that permitted dismissal only for cause. He was dismissed by action of the President and Board of Trustees, which did not comply with a contractual provision for dismissal that requires a hearing. Felch requested the court to grant specific performance of the contract and require Findlay College to continue Felch as a member of the faculty and to pay him the salary agreed upon. Is Felch entitled to specific performance? Explain.

12. Copenhaver, the owner of a laundry business, contracted with Berryman, the owner of a large apartment complex, to allow Copenhaver to own and operate the laundry facilities within the apartment complex. Berryman terminated the five-year contract with Copenhaver with forty-seven months remaining. Within six months, Copenhaver placed the equipment into use in other locations and generated at least as much income as he would have earned at Berryman's apartment complex. He then filed suit, claiming that he was entitled to conduct the laundry operations for an additional forty-seven months and that, through such operations, he would have earned a profit of $13,886.58, after deducting Berryman's share of the gross receipts and other operating expenses. Decision?

13. Billy Williams Builders and Developers (Williams) entered into a contract with Hillerich under which Williams agreed to sell to Hillerich a certain lot and to construct on it a house according to submitted plans and specifications. The house built by Williams was defectively constructed. Hillerich brought suit for specific performance of the contract and for damages resulting from the defective construction and delay in performance. Williams argued that Hillerich was not entitled to have both specific performance and damages for breach of the contract because the remedies were inconsistent and Hillerich had to elect one or the other. Explain whether Williams is correct in this assertion.

14. Developers under a plan approved by the city of Rye had constructed six luxury cooperative apartment buildings and were to construct six more. To obtain certificates of occupancy for the six completed buildings, the developers were required to post a bond with the city to insure completion of the remaining buildings. The developers posted a $100,000 bond upon which Public Service Mutual Insurance Company, as guarantor or surety, agreed to pay $200 for each day after the contractual deadline that the remaining buildings were not completed. After the contractual deadline, more than five hundred days passed without completion of the buildings. The city claims that its inspectors and employees will be required to devote more time to the project than anticipated because it has taken extra years to complete. It also claims that it will lose tax revenues for the years the buildings are not completed. Should the city prevail in its suit against the developers and the insurance company to recover $100,000 on the bond? Explain.

15. Kerr Steamship Company sent a telegram at a cost of $26.78 to the Philippines through the Radio Corporation of America. The telegram, which contained instructions in unintelligible code for loading cargo on one of Kerr's ships, was mislaid and never delivered. Consequently, the ship was improperly loaded and the cargo was lost. Kerr sued the Radio Corporation for the $6,675.29 in profits the company lost on the cargo because of the Radio Corporation's failure to deliver the telegram. Should Kerr be allowed to recover damages from Radio? Explain.

16. El Dorado Tire Company fired Bill Ballard, a sales executive. Ballard had a five-year contract with El Dorado but was fired after only two years of employment. Ballard sued El Dorado for breach of contract. El Dorado claimed that any damages due to breach of the contract should be mitigated because of Ballard's failure to seek other employment after he was fired. El Dorado did not provide any proof showing the availability of comparable employment. Explain whether El Dorado is correct in its contention.

17. California and Hawaiian Sugar Company (C and H) is an agricultural cooperative in the business of growing sugarcane in Hawaii and transporting the raw sugar to its refinery in California for processing. Because of the seasonal nature of the sugarcane crop, availability of ships to transport the raw sugar immediately after harvest is imperative. After losing the services of the shipping company it had previously used, C and H decided to build its own ship, a Macababoo, which had two components, a tug and a barge. C and H contracted with Halter Marine to build the tug and with Sun Ship to build the barge. In finalizing the contract for construction of the barge, both C and H and Sun Ship were represented by senior management and by legal counsel. The resulting contract called for a liquidated damages payment of $17,000 per day that delivery of the completed barge was delayed. Delivery of both the barge and the tug was significantly delayed. Sun Ship paid the $17,000 per day liquidated damages amount and then sued to recover it, claiming that without the liquidated damages provision, C and H's legal remedy for money damages would have been significantly less than that paid by Sun Ship pursuant to the liquidated damages provision. Decision?

18. Bettye Gregg offered to purchase a house from Head & Seeman, Inc. (seller). Though she represented in writing that she had between $15,000 and $20,000 in equity in another home that she would pay to the seller after she sold the other home, she knew that she did not have such equity. In reliance upon these intentionally fraudulent representations, the seller accepted Gregg's offer and the parties entered into a land contract. After taking occupancy, Gregg failed to make any of the contract payments. The seller's investigations then revealed the fraud. Head & Seeman then brought suit seeking rescission of the contract, return of the real estate, and restitution. Restitution was sought for the rental value for the five months of lost use of the property and the seller's out-of-pocket expenses made in reliance upon the bargain. Gregg contends that under the election of remedies doctrine, the seller cannot both rescind the contract and recover damages for its breach. Is Gregg correct? Explain.

19. Watson agreed to buy Ingram's house for $355,000. The contract provided that Watson deposit $15,000 as earnest money and that "in the event of default by the Buyer, earnest money shall be forfeited to Seller as liquidated damages, unless Seller elects to seek actual damages or specific performance." Because Watson did not timely comply with all of the terms of the contract, nine months after the Watson sale was to occur, Ingram sold the house to a third party for $355,000. Is Ingram entitled to Watson's $15,000 earnest money as liquidated damages? Explain.

TAKING SIDES

Sanders agreed in writing to write, direct, and produce a motion picture on the subject of lithography (a method for printing using stone or metal) for the Tamarind Lithography Workshop. After the completion of this film, *Four Stones for Kanemitsu*, litigation arose concerning the parties' rights and obligations under their agreement. Tamarind and Sanders resolved this dispute by a written settlement agreement that provided for Tamarind to give Sanders a screen credit stating: "A Film by Terry Sanders." Tamarind did not comply with this agreement and failed to include the agreed-upon screen credit for Sanders. Sanders sued Tamarind seeking damages for breach of the settlement agreement and specific performance to compel Tamarind's compliance with its obligation to provide the screen credit.

a. What arguments would support Sanders's claim for specific performance in addition to damages?

b. What arguments would support Tamarind's claim that Sanders was not entitled to specific performance in addition to damages?

c. Which side's arguments are most convincing? Explain.

Introduction to Sales and Leases

The propensity to truck, barter, and exchange one thing for another ... is common to all men, and to be found in no other race of animals.

Adam Smith (1723–1790)
The Wealth of Nations, 1776

CHAPTER OUTCOMES

After reading this chapter you should be able to:

1. Distinguish a sale from a lease and describe the governing law for both.

2. Identify and explain the fundamental principles of Article 2 and Article 2A of the Uniform Commercial Code (UCC).

3. Compare and contrast the manifestation of mutual assent under both the common law and under Article 2.

4. Determine how Article 2 deals with (a) the necessity of consideration to modify a contract and (b) irrevocable offers.

5. Describe the UCC's approach to requiring that certain contracts be in writing and identify the alternative methods of compliance under the Code.

Sales are the most common and important of all commercial transactions. In an exchange economy such as ours, sales are the essential means by which the various units of production exchange their outputs, thereby providing the opportunity for specialization and enhanced productivity. An advanced, complex, industrialized economy with highly coordinated manufacturing and distribution systems requires a reliable mechanism for ensuring that *future* exchanges can be entered into today and fulfilled later. Because practically everyone in our economy is a purchaser of both durable and consumable goods, the manufacture and distribution of goods involve numerous sales transactions. The critical role of the law of sales is to establish a framework in which these present and future exchanges may take place in a predictable, certain, and orderly fashion with a minimum of transaction costs. Article 2 of the Uniform Commercial Code (the Code, or UCC) governs such sales in all states except Louisiana.

Leases of personal property are also of great economic significance. Leases range from a consumer renting an automobile or a lawn mower to a Fortune 500 corporation leasing heavy industrial machinery. Despite the frequent and widespread use of personal property leases, the law governing these transactions had been patched together from the common law of personal property, real estate leasing law, and Articles 2 and 9 of the UCC. Although containing several applicable provisions, the UCC did not directly relate to leases.

To fill this void, the drafters of the Code approved Article 2A—Leases in 1987 and subsequently amended the Article in 1990. An analogue of Article 2, the new Article adopts many of the rules contained in Article 2. Article 2A is an attempt to codify in one statute all the rules governing the leasing of personal property. South Dakota has enacted the 1987 version of Article 2A while the District of Columbia and all the other states except Louisiana have adopted the 1990 version.

Amendments to UCC Articles 2 and 2A were promulgated in 2003 to accommodate electronic commerce and to reflect development of business practices, changes in other law, and interpretive difficulties of practical significance. Because no states had adopted them and prospects for enactment in the near future were bleak, the 2003 amendments to UCC Articles 2 and 2A were withdrawn in 2011. However, at least forty-five states have adopted the 2001 Revisions to Article 1, which applies to all of the articles of the Code.

This part of the book covers sales and leases of goods. All chapters in this part will cover Article 2A in addition to Article 2 by stating "Article 2A" wherever Article 2A's provision is either identical to or essentially the same as the Article 2 provision. When Article 2A significantly deviates from Article 2, both rules will be discussed. In this chapter we will discuss the nature and formation of sales and lease contracts and the fundamental principles of sales and leases of goods.

NATURE OF SALES AND LEASES

The law of sales, which governs contracts involving the sale of goods, is a specialized branch of both the law of contracts (discussed in Chapters 9–18) and the law of personal property (discussed in Chapter 47). This section will cover the definition of sales and leases and the fundamental principles of Article 2 and Article 2A of the UCC.

DEFINITIONS [19-1]
Goods [19-1a]

Goods
movable personal property

Goods are essentially defined as movable, tangible, personal property. For example, the sale of a bicycle, stereo set, or this textbook is considered a sale of goods. Goods also include the unborn young of animals, growing crops, and, if removed by the seller, timber, minerals, or a building attached to real property. Under Article 2A, minerals cannot be leased prior to their extraction.

Sale [19-1b]

Sale
transfer of title to goods from seller to buyer for a price

The Code defines a **sale** as the transfer of title to goods from seller to buyer for a price. The price can be money, other goods, real estate, or services.

Lease [19-1c]

Lease
a transfer of right to possession and use of goods in return for consideration

Article 2A defines a **lease** of goods as a "transfer of the right to possession and use of goods for a term in return for consideration, but … retention or creation of a security interest is not a lease." A transaction within this definition of a lease is governed by Article 2A, but if the transaction is a security interest disguised as a lease, it is governed by Article 9. Categorizing a transaction as a lease has significant implications not only for the parties to the lease but for third parties as well. If the transaction is deemed to be a lease, the residual interest in the goods belongs to the lessor, who need not file publicly to protect this interest. On the other hand, if the transaction is a security interest, then the provisions of Article 9 regarding enforceability, perfection, priority, and remedies apply. UCC Section 1-201(37) and Revised Section 1-203 provide rules that govern the determination of whether a transaction in the form of a lease creates a security interest.

Consumer leases
leases by a merchant to an individual who leases for personal, family, or household purposes for no more than $25,000

Consumer Leases   Article 2A affords special treatment for consumer leases. The definition of a **consumer lease** requires that (1) the transaction meet the definition of a lease under Article 2A; (2) the lessor be regularly engaged in the business of leasing *or* selling goods; (3) the lessee be an individual, not an organization; (4) the lessee take the lease interest primarily for a personal, family, or household purpose; and (5) the total payments under the lease do not exceed $25,000. Although consumer protection for lease transactions is primarily left to other state and federal law, Article 2A does contain a number of provisions that apply to consumer leases and that may *not* be varied by agreement of the parties.

Finance lease
special type of lease transaction generally involving three parties: the lessor, the supplier, and the lessee

Finance Leases   A **finance lease** is a special type of lease transaction generally involving three parties instead of two. Whereas in the typical lease situation the lessor also supplies the goods, in a finance lease arrangement, the lessor and the supplier are separate parties. The lessor's primary function in a finance lease is to provide financing to the lessee for a lease of goods provided by the supplier. For example, under a finance lease arrangement, a manufacturer supplies goods pursuant to the lessee's instructions or specifications. The party functioning as the lessor will then either purchase those goods from the supplier or act as the prime lessee in leasing them from the supplier. In turn, the lessor will lease or sublease the goods to the lessee. Because the finance lessor functions merely as a source of credit, she typically will have no special expertise as to the goods. Due to the limited role the finance lessor usually plays, Article 2A treats finance leases differently from ordinary leases.

 Carter v. Tokai Financial Services, Inc.
Court of Appeals of Georgia, 1998
231 Ga.App. 755, 500 S.E.2d 638
http://scholar.google.com/scholar_case?case=1919852511859232954&q=500+S.E.2d+638&hl=en&as_sdt=2,34

FACTS On January 3, 1996, Tokai's (now part of De Lage Landen Leasing and Trade Finance) predecessor in interest, Mitel Financial, entered into a "Master Equipment Lease Agreement" (Agreement) with Applied Radiological Control, Inc. (ARC) for the lease of certain telephone equipment valued at $42,000. Randy P. Carter of ARC personally guaranteed ARC's obligations under the Agreement. ARC made four rental payments and then defaulted on its obligations. Thereafter, Tokai repossessed the telephone equipment and sold it for $5,900. Tokai then brought this suit against Carter, and the trial court awarded Tokai $56,765.74. Carter appeals.

DECISION Judgment reversed.

OPINION Carter contends that the true intent of the parties was to enter into a security agreement. Whether a transaction creates a lease or security interest is determined by the facts of each case. A transaction, however,

creates a security interest if the consideration the lessee is to pay the lessor for the right to possession and use of the goods is an obligation for the term of the lease not subject to termination by the lessee, and (a) the original term of the lease is equal to or greater than the remaining economic life of the goods, (b) the lessee is bound to renew the lease for the remaining economic life

of the goods or is bound to become the owner of the goods, (c) the lessee has an option to renew the lease for the remaining economic life of the goods for no additional consideration or nominal additional consideration upon compliance with the lease agreement, or (d) the lessee has an option to become the owner of the goods for no additional consideration or nominal additional consideration upon compliance with the lease agreement. (Section 1-201(37))

Here, the Agreement's initial term was for five years, ARC was not required to renew the lease or purchase the telephone equipment at the end of the term, and ARC did not have the option to renew the lease or purchase the property at the end of the term for nominal consideration. Therefore, the Agreement does not fit within the definition of a secured transaction provided by the Uniform Commercial Code and is a true finance lease. Thus, the agreement is governed by Article 2A, not by Article 9.

INTERPRETATION A lease will be governed by Article 2A unless, in compliance with the terms of the "lease," the lessee has the option to become the owner of the property for no additional or for a nominal consideration, in which case, the lease is deemed to be intended for security and governed by Article 9.

CRITICAL THINKING QUESTION Why might the parties attempt to disguise a security agreement as a lease?

Governing Law [19-1d]

Sales transactions governed by Article 2 of the Code, except when general contract law has not been specifically modified by the Code, general contract law continues to apply

Transactions outside the Code include employment contracts, service contracts, insurance contracts, contracts involving real property, and contracts for the sale of tangibles

Although **sales transactions** are governed by Article 2 of the Code, general contract law continues to apply in cases in which the Code has not specifically modified such law. Nevertheless, although principles of common law and equity may supplement provisions of the Code, they may not be used to supplant its provisions. Thus, the law of sales is a specialized part of the general law of contracts, and the law of contracts continues to govern unless specifically displaced by the Code.

General contract law also continues to govern all **contracts outside the scope of the Code**. Transactions not within the scope of Article 2 include employment contracts; service contracts; insurance contracts; contracts involving real property; and contracts for the sale of intangibles such as stocks, bonds, patents, and copyrights. For an illustration of the law governing contracts, see Figure 9-1. In determining whether a contract containing both a sale of goods and a service is a UCC contract or general contract, the majority of states follow the predominant purpose test. This test, as in *Pittsley v. Houser*, which follows, and in *Fox v. Mountain West Electric, Inc.* in Chapter 9 holds that if the predominant purpose of the whole transaction is a sale of goods, Article 2 applies to the entire transaction. If, on the other hand, the predominant purpose is the nongood or service portion, Article 2 does not apply. A few states apply Article 2 only to the goods part of a transaction and general contract law to the nongoods or service part of the transaction.

GOING GLOBAL

What law governs international sales?

The United Nations Convention on Contracts for the International Sale of Goods (CISG), which has been ratified by the United States and at least seventy-nine other countries, governs all contracts for the international sales of goods between parties located in different nations that have ratified the CISG. Because treaties are federal law, the CISG supersedes the

UCC in any situation to which either could apply. The CISG includes provisions dealing with interpretation, trade usage, contract formation, obligations and remedies of sellers and buyers, and risk of loss. Parties to an international sales contract may, however, expressly exclude CISG governance from their contract. The CISG specifically excludes sales of

(1) goods bought for personal, family, or household use; (2) ships or aircraft; and (3) electricity. In addition, it does not apply to contracts in which the primary obligation of the party furnishing the goods consists of supplying labor or services. The chapters on Sales (19 through 23) include the comparable provisions of the CISG.

Practical Advice

Because it is unclear which law will govern certain contracts, be careful to specify the particulars of your agreement in your written contract.

Although Article 2 governs sales, the drafters of the article have invited the courts to extend Code principles to nonsale transactions in goods. To date, a number of courts have accepted this invitation and have applied Code provisions by analogy to other transactions in goods not expressly included within the Act, most frequently to leases and bailments. The Code has also greatly influenced the revision of the Restatement, Second, Contracts, which, as previously discussed, has great effect upon all contracts.

Pittsley v. Houser
Idaho Court of Appeals, 1994
875 P.2d 232
http://scholar.google.com/scholar_case?case=1225385276065420693&hl=en&as_sdt=2&as_vis=1&oi=scholarr

FACTS Jane Pittsley contracted with Donald Houser, who was doing business as Hilton Contract Co. (Hilton), to install carpet in her home. The total contract price was $4,402. From this sum, Hilton paid the installers $700 to put the carpet in Pittsley's home. Following installation, Pittsley complained to Hilton that the installation was defective in several respects. Hilton attempted to fix the installation but was unable to satisfy Pittsley. Eventually, Pittsley refused any further efforts to fix the carpet. She sued for rescission of the contract and return of the $3,500 she had previously paid on the contract plus incidental damages. Hilton counterclaimed for the balance due on the contract. The magistrate determined that the breach was not so material as to justify rescission of the contract and awarded Pittsley $250 in repair costs plus $150 in expenses. The magistrate also awarded Hilton the balance of $902 remaining on the contract. Pittsley appealed to the district court, which reversed and remanded the case to the magistrate for additional findings of fact and to apply the Uniform Commercial Code (UCC) to the transaction. Hilton appeals this ruling, asserting that application of the UCC is inappropriate because the only defects alleged were in the installation of the carpet, not in the carpet itself.

DECISION The judgment of the magistrate is vacated and the case remanded.

OPINION The subject transaction is a hybrid transaction, involving both the sale of goods (carpet) and services (installation). There are two lines of authority addressing the question of whether such transactions are governed by the UCC or by common law. The majority position utilizes the "predominant factor" test. This test essentially involves consideration of the contract in its entirety, applying the UCC to the entire contract or not at all. In considering

the applicability of the UCC to a hybrid transaction, a court must determine whether its predominant factor, its purpose, is the rendition of service, with goods incidentally involved, or is a transaction of sale, with labor incidentally involved. The second line of authority, which Hilton urged, allows the contract to be severed into different parts, applying the UCC to the goods involved in the contract but not to the nongoods involved. Thus an action focusing on defects or problems with the goods themselves would be covered by the UCC, whereas a suit based on the service or other nongoods provided would not be covered by the UCC.

The predominant factor test is the more prudent rule. Severing contracts into various parts, attempting to label each as goods or nongoods and applying different law to each separate part clearly contravenes the UCC's declared purpose to simplify, clarify, and modernize the law governing commercial transactions. Under the predominant factor test, the UCC is applicable to the subject transaction in the present case. It appears that Pittsley entered into this contract for the purpose of obtaining carpet of a certain quality and color. The installation service does not appear to have been a factor in inducing Pittsley to choose Hilton as the carpet supplier. Pittsley specified neither who would provide the service or the nature of the work. Since the sale of carpet was the predominant factor in this transaction, the UCC applies to the entire transaction.

INTERPRETATION If the predominant purpose of the whole transaction is a sale of goods, then Article 2 applies to the whole transaction; if the predominant purpose is the nongood or service component, then Article 2 does not apply.

CRITICAL THINKING QUESTION Which test do you prefer? Explain.

Lease transactions
governed by Article 2A of the Code, but when general contract law has not been specifically modified by the Code, general contract law continues to apply

Although **lease transactions** are governed by Article 2A of the Code, general contract law continues to apply in cases in which the Code has not specifically modified such law. In other words, the law of leases is a specialized part of the general law of contracts, and the law of contracts continues to govern unless specifically displaced by the Code.

FUNDAMENTAL PRINCIPLES OF ARTICLE 2 AND ARTICLE 2A [19-2]

Fundamental principles of Article 2 and Article 2A
to modernize, clarify, simplify, and make uniform the law of sales

The purpose of Article 2 is to modernize, clarify, simplify, and make uniform the law of sales. Furthermore, the article is to be interpreted according to these principles and not according to some abstraction such as the passage of title. The Code

> is drawn to provide flexibility so that, since it is intended to be a semi-permanent piece of legislation, it will provide its own machinery for expansion of commercial practices. It is intended to make it possible for the law embodied in this Act to be developed by the courts in the light of unforeseen and new circumstances and practices. However, the proper construction of the Act requires that its interpretation and application be limited to its reason. (*General Provisions* in Comment to Section 1-102)

This open-ended drafting includes the following fundamental concepts.

CISG   *The CISG governs only the formation of the contract of sales and the rights and obligations of the seller and buyer arising from such contract. It does not cover the validity of the contract or any of its provisions. In addition, one of the purposes of the CISG is to promote uniformity of the law of sales.*

Good faith
honesty in fact in conduct or transaction; in the case of a merchant (and a nonmerchant under Revised Article 1), it also includes the observance of reasonable commercial standards of fair dealing

Good Faith [19-2a]

All parties who enter into a contract or duty within the scope of the Code must perform their obligations in good faith. The original Code defines **good faith** as "honesty in fact in the conduct or transaction concerned." For a merchant, good faith also requires the observance of reasonable commercial standards of fair dealing in the trade. Revised UCC Section 1–201(20) provides that "good faith means honesty in fact and the observance of reasonable commercial standards of fair dealing," thus adopting the broader definition of good faith and making it applicable to both merchants and nonmerchants. For instance, if the parties agree that the seller is to set the price term, the seller must establish the price in good faith.

CISG   *The CISG is also designed to promote the observation of good faith in international trade.*

Unconscionability
a court may refuse to enforce an unconscionable contract or any part of a contract found to be unconscionable

Unconscionability [19-2b]

The courts may scrutinize every contract of sale to determine whether in its commercial setting, purpose, and effect it is unconscionable. The reviewing court may refuse to enforce a contract (or any part of it) found to be unconscionable or may limit its application to prevent an unconscionable result. The Code does not define ***unconscionable***; however, the term is defined in the *New Webster's Dictionary* (Deluxe Encyclopedic Edition) as "contrary to the dictates of conscience; unscrupulous or unprincipled; exceeding that which is reasonable or customary; inordinate, unjustifiable."

The Code denies or limits enforcement of an unconscionable contract for the sale of goods to promote fairness and decency and to correct harshness or oppression in contracts resulting from the unequal bargaining positions of the parties.

The doctrine of **unconscionability** permits the courts to resolve issues of unfairness explicitly on that basis without recourse to formalistic rules or legal fictions. In policing contracts for fairness, the courts have demonstrated their willingness to limit freedom of contract to protect the less advantaged from the overreaching of dominant contracting parties.

The doctrine of unconscionability has evolved through its application by the courts to include both procedural and substantive unconscionability. **Procedural unconscionability** involves scrutiny for the presence of "bargaining naughtiness." In other words, was the negotiation process fair? Or were there procedural irregularities such as burying important terms of the agreement in fine print or obscuring the true meaning of the contract with impenetrable legal jargon?

In the search for **substantive unconscionability**, the court examines the actual terms of the contract, seeking oppressive or grossly unfair provisions such as an exorbitant price or an unfair exclusion or limitation of contractual remedies. An all-too-common example involves a necessitous buyer in an unequal bargaining position with a seller who consequently has obtained an exorbitant price for his product or service.

As to *all* leases, Article 2A provides that a court faced with an unconscionable contract or clause may refuse to enforce either the entire contract or just the unconscionable clause or may limit the application of the unconscionable clause to avoid an unconscionable result. This is similar to Article 2's treatment of unconscionable clauses in sales contracts. A lessee under a consumer lease, however, is provided with additional protection against unconscionability. In the case of a consumer lease, if a court as a matter of law finds that any part of the lease contract has been induced by unconscionable conduct, the court is expressly empowered to grant appropriate relief. The same is true when unconscionable conduct occurs in the collection of a claim arising from a consumer lease contract. The explicit availability of relief for consumers subjected to unconscionable conduct (procedural unconscionability)—in addition to a provision regarding unconscionable contracts (substantive unconscionability)—represents a departure from Article 2. An additional remedy that Article 2A provides for consumers is the award of attorneys' fees. If the court finds unconscionability with respect to a consumer lease, it shall award reasonable attorneys' fees to the lessee.

Procedural unconscionability
unreasonable bargaining process

Substantive unconscionability
grossly unfair contractual terms

Practical Advice

Refrain from entering into contracts with provisions that are oppressively harsh or that were negotiated under unfair circumstances.

Construction Associates, Inc. v. Fargo Water Equipment Co.
North Dakota Supreme Court, 1989
446 N.W.2d 237
http://scholar.google.com/scholar_case?case=10357932109621482420&q=446+N.W.2D+237&hl=en&as_sdt=6,34

FACTS Construction Associates (CA) was the successful bidder to construct a water supply line for the city of Breckenridge, Minnesota. CA purchased a large amount of polyvinyl chloride pipe manufactured by the Johns-Manville Sales Corporation (J-M) to construct the pipeline. CA, however, did not have any direct contact with J-M; instead, it purchased the pipe through a supply company (Fargo Water Equipment). J-M shipped the pipe directly to the work site, and included with each shipment an installation guide written for those who actually directed the installation of the pipe. On page three of the installation guide, J-M expressly warranted the pipe to be free from defects in workmanship and materials. In addition, J-M set forth a limitation of liability clause, which stated there would be no liability except for breach of the express warranty, and that J-M would be responsible only for resupplying a like quantity of nondefective pipe. J-M stated that it would not be liable for any incidental, consequential, or other damages.

Eventually the Breckenridge pipeline developed more than seventy leaks. The only way these leaks could be repaired was to remove the defective joints and replace them with stainless steel sleeves. After incurring more than $140,000 in repairs to the pipeline, CA sued J-M and Fargo. CA won a jury award of more than $140,000 in damages from J-M. J-M appealed, claiming that the limitation of liability clause should be enforced.

DECISION Judgment for CA affirmed.

OPINION The Uniform Commercial Code (UCC) expressly allows a party to a contract to limit or exclude consequential damages, unless the limitation or exclusion is unconscionable. The UCC, however, also states that

> if the court as a matter of law finds the contract or any clause of the contract to have been unconscionable at the time it was made the court may refuse to enforce the contract, or it may enforce the remainder of the contract without the unconscionable clause, or it may limit the application of any unconscionable clause as to avoid any unconscionable result.

Courts will determine whether the unconscionability in question is procedural or substantive in nature. Procedural unconscionability includes unfair surprise, oppression, and inequality of bargaining power, while harshness or one-sidedness of contractual provisions are types of substantive unconscionability. From a procedural viewpoint, the limitation of liability clause was never negotiated, and in fact was only seen by lower-level CA employees at the work site. In addition, even though this is a commercial setting, there is significant inequality of bargaining power between the local contractor CA and the international conglomerate J-M. Substantively, all J-M is required to do under the limitation of liability clause is resupply more pipe. Since the only way to repair the installed pipe is with stainless steel sleeves, this remedy is virtually worthless. Given both the procedural and substantive unconscionability in this instance, the decision of the trial court is affirmed.

INTERPRETATION A court can override a term of a contract if it finds that term to be unconscionable or the result of an unconscionable negotiation process.

ETHICAL QUESTION Is unconscionable conduct always unethical? Explain.

CRITICAL THINKING QUESTION How active should courts be in finding contracts or clauses to be unconscionable? Explain.

Expansion of Commercial Practices [19-2c]

Course of dealing
sequence of previous conduct between parties establishing a basis for interpreting their agreement

Usage of trade
practice or method of dealing regularly observed and followed in a place, vocation, or trade

An underlying policy of the Code is "to permit the continued expansion of commercial practices through custom, usage and agreement of the parties." In particular, the Code emphasizes the course of dealing and the usage of trade in interpreting agreements.

A **course of dealing** is a sequence of previous conduct between the parties that may fairly be regarded as establishing a common basis of understanding for interpreting their expressions and agreement.

A **usage of trade** is a practice or method of dealing regularly observed and followed in a place, vocation, or trade. To illustrate: Connie contracts to sell Ward one thousand feet of San Domingo mahogany. By usage of dealers in mahogany, known to Connie and Ward, good-figured mahogany of a certain density is known as San Domingo mahogany, though it does not come from San Domingo. Unless otherwise agreed, the usage is part of the contract.

CISG *The parties are bound by any usage or practices that they have agreed to or established between themselves. In addition, the parties are considered, unless otherwise agreed, to be bound by any usage of international trade that is widely known and regularly observed in the particular trade.*

Sales By and Between Merchants [19-2d]

Merchant
dealer in goods or person who by his occupation holds himself out as having knowledge or skill peculiar to the goods

The Code establishes some separate rules that apply to transactions between merchants or to transactions involving a merchant as a party. A **merchant** is defined as a person (1) who is a dealer in a particular type of goods, (2) who by his occupation holds himself out as having knowledge or skill peculiar to certain goods or practices, or (3) who employs an agent or broker whom he holds out as having such knowledge or skill. (Article 2A.) These rules exact higher standards of conduct from merchants because of their knowledge of trade and commerce and because merchants as a class generally set these standards for themselves. The more significant of these merchant provisions are good faith, confirmation of oral contracts, firm offers, "battle of the forms," warranty of title, warranty of merchantability, sales on approval, retention of possession of goods by seller, entrusting of goods, risk of loss, and duties after rightful rejection.

Liberal Administration of Remedies [19-2e]

The Code provides that its remedies shall be liberally administered to place the aggrieved party in a position as good as the one she would have held, had the defaulting party fully performed. The Code does make it clear, however, that remedies are limited to compensation and may not include consequential or punitive damages, unless specifically provided by the Code. According to its provisions, for cases in which the Code itself does not expressly provide a remedy for a right or obligation, the courts should provide an appropriate remedy. Remedies are discussed in Chapter 23.

Freedom of Contract [19-2f]

Freedom of contract
most provisions of the Code may be varied by agreement

Most of the Code's provisions are not mandatory but permit the parties by agreement to vary or displace them altogether. However, the obligations of good faith, diligence, reasonableness, and

Validation and preservation of sales contract
the Code reduces formal requisites to the bare minimum and attempts to preserve agreements whenever the parties manifest an intention to enter into a contract

care may not be disclaimed by agreement, although the parties may by agreement determine the standards by which to measure the performance of these obligations, as long as the standards are not obviously unreasonable.

Validation and Preservation of Sales Contracts [19-2g]

One of the requirements of commercial law is the establishment of rules that determine when an agreement is valid. The Code approaches this requirement by reducing formal requisites to the bare minimum and by attempting to preserve agreements whenever the parties manifest an intent to enter into a contract.

FORMATION OF SALES AND LEASE CONTRACTS

As we have stated previously, the Code's basic approach to validation is to recognize contracts whenever the parties manifest such an intent. This is so whether or not the parties can identify the precise moment at which they formed the contract. (Article 2A.)

MANIFESTATION OF MUTUAL ASSENT [19-3]

For a contract to exist, there must be an objective manifestation of mutual assent: an offer and an acceptance. In this section, we will examine the UCC rules that affect offers and acceptances.

Definiteness of an offer
the Code provides that a contract does not fail for indefiniteness even though one or more terms may have been omitted; the Code provides standards by which missing essential terms may be supplied

Definiteness of an Offer [19-3a]

At common law, the terms of a contract were required to be definite and complete. The Code has rejected the strict approach of the common law by recognizing an agreement as valid, despite missing terms, if there is any reasonably certain basis for granting a remedy. Accordingly, the Code provides that even though a contract may omit one or more terms, the contract need not fail for indefiniteness. (Article 2A.) The Code provides standards by which the courts may ascertain and supply omitted essential terms, provided the parties intended to enter into a binding agreement. Nevertheless, the more terms the parties leave open, the less likely their intent to enter into a binding contract. Article 2A generally does not provide the same gap-filling provisions.

CISG   *An offer to contract is sufficiently definite if it indicates the goods and fixes or makes provision, expressly or implicitly, for determining price and quality.*

Open Price   The parties may enter into a contract for the sale of goods even though they have reached no agreement on the price. In such a case, the price is reasonable at the time for delivery. A contract has an open price term if the agreement (1) says nothing as to price; (2) provides that the parties shall agree later as to the price and they fail to so agree; or (3) fixes the price in terms of some agreed market or other standard, as set by a third person or agency, and the price is not so set. An agreement that the price is to be fixed by the seller or buyer means that it must be fixed in good faith.

Open Quantity: Output and Requirements Contracts   As we discussed in Chapters 10 and 12, an output contract is the agreement of a buyer to purchase the entire output of a seller for a stated period, whereas a requirements contract is an agreement of a seller to supply a buyer with all her requirements for certain goods. Even though the exact quantity of goods is not specified and even though the seller may have some control over his output and the buyer over her requirements, such agreements are enforceable through the application of an objective standard based on the good faith of both parties. Moreover, the parties may not produce or request quantities disproportionate to any stated estimate of need or production or to prior output or requirements.

Option

contract to hold open an offer

Firm offer

signed writing by merchant to hold open an offer for the sale or purchase of goods or the lease of goods

Irrevocable Offer   An offeror generally may withdraw an offer at any time prior to its acceptance. To be effective, the notice revoking the offer must reach the offeree before he has accepted.

An **option** is a contract by which the offeror is bound to hold open an offer for a specified time. It must comply with all of the requirements of a contract, including consideration. Option contracts apply to all types of contracts, including sales of goods.

The Code has made certain offers—called **firm offers**—irrevocable without the offeree giving any consideration for the promise to keep the offer open. The Code provides that a merchant is bound to keep an offer open for a maximum of three months if the merchant gives assurance in a signed writing that it will be held open. (Article 2A.) The Code, therefore, makes a merchant's written promise not to revoke an offer for a stated period of time enforceable even though no consideration is given the merchant–offeror for that promise.

CISG   *An offer may not be revoked if it indicates, whether by stating a fixed time for acceptance or otherwise, that it is irrevocable; it need not be in writing.*

Variant acceptances

the inclusion of different or additional terms in an acceptance is addressed by focusing on the intent of the parties

Variant Acceptances [19-3b]

The common law *mirror image* rule, by which the acceptance cannot vary or deviate from the terms of the offer, has been modified by the Code. This modification has been necessitated by the realities of modern business practices, notably by the fact that a vast number of businesses use standardized business forms. For example, a buyer sends to the seller on the buyer's order form a purchase order for 1,000 dozen cotton shirts at $60.00 per dozen with delivery by October 1 at the buyer's place of business. On the reverse side of this standard form are twenty-five numbered paragraphs containing provisions generally favorable to the buyer. When the seller receives the buyer's order and agrees to the buyer's quantity, price, and delivery terms, he sends to the buyer an unequivocal acceptance of the offer on his acceptance form. On the back of his acceptance form, however, the seller has thirty-two numbered paragraphs generally favorable to himself and in significant conflict with the provisions in the buyer's form. Under the common law's mirror image rule, no contract would exist, for the seller has not accepted unequivocally all of the material terms of the buyer's offer.

The Code attempts to reconcile this *battle of the forms* by focusing on the intent of the parties. If the offeree expressly makes his acceptance conditional upon assent to the additional or different terms, no contract is formed. If, however, the offeree does not expressly require such a condition, a contract is formed. The issue then becomes whether the offeree's different or *additional* terms become part of the contract. If both offeror and offeree are merchants, additional terms (terms the offeree proposed for the contract for the first time) will become part of the contract if they do not materially alter the agreement and are not objected to either in the offer itself or within a reasonable time. If either of the parties is not a merchant, or if the terms materially alter the offer, the additional terms are merely construed as proposals for addition to the contract. *Different* terms (terms that contradict or conflict with terms of the offer) proposed by the offeree generally will not become part of the contract unless specifically accepted by the offeror.

The courts are divided over what terms are included when the terms conflict. The majority of courts hold that the terms cancel each other out and look to the Code to provide the missing terms; other courts hold that the offeror's terms govern. Some states follow a third alternative and apply the additional terms test to different terms. See Figure 19-1 for a summary of the battle of the forms.

Applying Section 2–207 to the previous example: Because both parties are merchants and the seller did not condition acceptance upon the buyer's assent to the additional or different terms, (1) the contract will be formed without the *seller's different terms* unless the buyer specifically accepts them; (2) the contract will be formed without the *seller's additional terms* unless (a) the buyer specifically accepts or (b) the additional terms do not materially alter the offer and the buyer does not object to them; and (3) depending on the jurisdiction, (a) the *conflicting terms* cancel each other out and the Code provides the missing terms, (b) the *buyer's conflicting terms* are included in the contract, or (c) the additional terms test is applied.

Practical Advice

In negotiating a contract, try to be the offeror and consider providing in your offer that your terms control and that any new or different terms will be made part of the contract only if you specifically agree to them in a signed writing.

Figure 19-1 Battle of the Forms

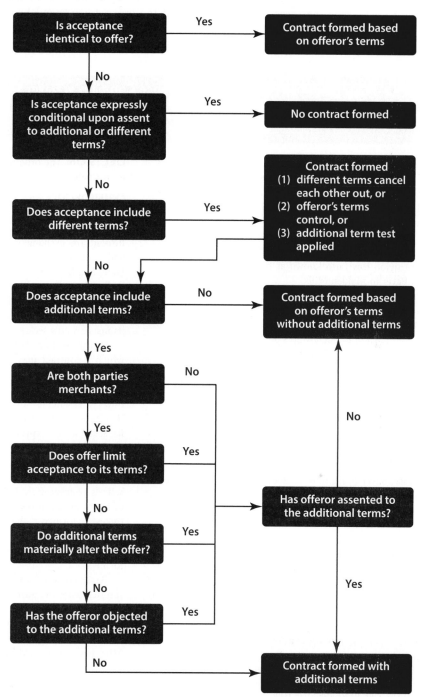

CISG   *A reply to an offer that contains additions, limitations, or other modifications is a counteroffer that rejects the original offer. Nevertheless, a purported acceptance that contains additional or different terms acts as an acceptance if the terms do not materially alter the contract unless the offeror objects to the change. Changes in price, payment, quality, quantity, place and time of delivery, terms of delivery, liability of the parties, and settlement of a dispute are always considered to be material alterations.*

Finally, subsection (3) of 2–207 deals with those situations in which the writings do not form a contract, but the conduct of the parties recognizes the existence of one. For instance,

Ernest makes an offer to Gwen, who replies with a conditional acceptance. Although no contract has been formed, Gwen ships the ordered goods and Ernest accepts the goods. Subsection (3) provides that in this instance the contract consists of the written terms to which both parties agreed together with supplementary provisions of the Code.

Commerce & Industry Insurance Company v. Bayer Corporation
Supreme Judicial Court of Massachusetts, 2001
433 Mass. 388, 742 N.E.2d 567, 44 UCC Rep.Serv.2d 50
http://scholar.google.com/scholar_case?case=8104304470024394019&q=742+N.E.2d+567&hl=en&as_sdt=2,22

FACTS On December 11, 1995, an explosion and fire destroyed several of Malden Mills's buildings at its manufacturing facility. Malden Mills and its property insurers, the plaintiffs Commerce & Industry Insurance Company and Federal Insurance Company, brought suit in the Superior Court against numerous defendants, including Bayer Corporation. In their complaint, the plaintiffs allege that the cause of the fire was the ignition, by static electrical discharge, of nylon tow (also known as bulk nylon fiber), which was sold by Bayer to Malden Mills.

Malden Mills initiated purchases of nylon tow from Bayer either by sending its standard form purchase order to Bayer, or by placing a telephone order to Bayer, followed by a standard form purchase order. Each of Malden Mills's purchase orders contained, on the reverse side, as one of its "terms and conditions," an arbitration provision.

Another "term and condition" appearing in paragraph one on the reverse side of each purchase order provides:

> This purchase order represents the entire agreement between both parties, not withstanding any Seller's order form, and this document cannot be modified except in writing and signed by an authorized representative of the buyer.

In response, Bayer transmitted Malden Mills's purchase orders to the manufacturer with instructions, in most instances, that the nylon tow was to be shipped directly to Malden Mills. Thereafter, Bayer prepared and sent Malden Mills an invoice. Each of the Bayer invoices contained the following language on its face, located at the bottom of the form in capital letters:

> TERMS AND CONDITIONS: NOTWITHSTANDING ANY CONTRARY OR INCONSISTENT CONDITIONS THAT MAY BE EMBODIED IN YOUR PURCHASE ORDER, YOUR ORDER IS ACCEPTED SUBJECT TO THE PRICES, TERMS AND CONDITIONS OF THE MUTUALLY EXECUTED CONTRACT BETWEEN US, OR, IF NO SUCH CONTRACT EXISTS, YOUR ORDER IS ACCEPTED SUBJECT TO OUR REGULAR SCHEDULED PRICE AND TERMS IN EFFECT AT TIME OF SHIPMENT AND SUBJECT TO THE TERMS AND CONDITIONS PRINTED ON THE REVERSE SIDE HEREOF.

The following "condition" appears on the reverse side of each invoice:

> This document is not an Expression of Acceptance or a Confirmation document as contemplated in Section 2-207 of the Uniform Commercial Code. The acceptance of any order entered by [Malden Mills] is expressly conditioned on [Malden Mills's] assent to any additional or conflicting terms contained herein.

Based on the arbitration provision in Malden Mills's purchase orders, Bayer demanded that Malden Mills arbitrate its claims against Bayer. After Malden Mills refused, Bayer moved to compel arbitration. The court ruled in favor of Malden Mills.

DECISION The order denying the motion to compel arbitration is affirmed.

OPINION This case presents a dispute arising from what has been styled a typical "battle of the forms" sale, in which a buyer and a seller each attempt to complete a commercial transaction through the exchange of self-serving preprinted forms that clash, and contradict each other, on both material and minor terms. Here, Malden Mills's form, a purchase order, contains an arbitration provision, and Bayer's form, a seller's invoice, is silent on how the parties will resolve any disputes. Oddly enough, the buyer (Malden Mills), the party proposing the arbitration provision, and its insurers now seek to avoid an arbitral forum.

Under Section 2-207, there are essentially three ways by which a contract may be formed. First, if the parties exchange forms with divergent terms, but the seller's invoice does not state that its acceptance is made expressly conditional on the buyer's assent to any additional or different terms in the invoice, a contract is formed. Second, if the seller does make its acceptance "expressly conditional" on the buyer's assent to any additional or divergent terms in the seller's invoice, the invoice is merely a counteroffer, and a contract is formed only when the buyer expresses its affirmative acceptance of the seller's counteroffer. Third, where for any reason the exchange of forms does not result in contract formation, a contract nonetheless is formed if their subsequent conduct—for instance, the seller ships and the buyer accepts the goods—demonstrates that the parties believed that a binding agreement had been formed.

Bayer correctly concedes that its contract with Malden Mills resulted from the parties' conduct, and, thus, was formed pursuant to subsection (3) of Section 2-207. The reverse side of Bayer's invoices expressly conditioned acceptance on Malden Mills's assent to "additional or different" terms, and Malden Mills never expressed "affirmative acceptance" of any of Bayer's invoices. In addition, the exchange of forms between Malden Mills and Bayer did not result in a contract because Malden Mills, by means of language in paragraph one of its purchase orders, expressly limited Bayer's acceptance to the terms of Malden Mills's offers.

Although Bayer acknowledges that its contract with Malden Mills was formed through its conduct, it nonetheless argues that the terms of the contract are determined through an application of the principles in subsection (2) of Section 2-207. Under this analysis, Bayer asserts that the arbitration provision became part of the parties' contract because it was not a "material alteration." This analysis is incorrect because subsection (2) instructs on how to ascertain the terms of a contract only when the contract is formed either by the parties' writings or by a party's written confirmation of an oral contract.

In cases in which a contract is formed by the parties' conduct (as opposed to writings), as is the case here, the terms of the contract are determined exclusively by subsection (3) of Section 2-207: "the terms of the particular contract consist of those terms on which the writings of the parties agree, together with any supplementary terms incorporated under any other provisions of this chapter." Section 2-207 subsection (3). Under this rule, the Code accepts "common terms but rejects all the rest."

INTERPRETATION In cases in which a contract is formed by the parties' conduct (as opposed to writings), all conflicting written terms are invalid.

ETHICAL QUESTION Is it unethical for Malden Mills to try to avoid a term from its own forms? Explain.

CRITICAL THINKING QUESTION Do you agree with how the Code deals with the battle of the forms?

Manner of acceptance

an acceptance can be made in any reasonable manner and is effective upon dispatch

Manner of Acceptance [19-3c]

As is true of contracts under common law, the offeror may specify the manner in which the offer must be accepted. If the offeror does not so specify and the circumstances do not otherwise clearly indicate, an offer to make a sales contract invites acceptance, effective upon dispatch, in any manner and in any medium reasonable in the circumstances. (Article 2A.) The Code therefore allows flexibility of response and the ability to keep pace with new modes of communication.

An offer to buy goods for prompt or current shipment may be accepted either by a prompt promise to ship or by prompt shipment. Acceptance by performance requires notice within a reasonable time, or the offer may be treated as lapsed. (Article 2A.)

Auction

auction sales are generally with reserve, permitting the auctioneer to withdraw the goods at any time prior to sale

Auctions [19-3d]

The Code provides that if an auction sale is advertised or announced in explicit terms to be *without reserve*, the auctioneer may not withdraw the article put up for sale unless no bid is made within a reasonable time. Unless the sale is advertised as being without reserve, the sale is *with reserve*, and the auctioneer may withdraw the goods at any time until he announces completion of the sale. Whether with or without reserve, a bidder may retract his bid at any time prior to acceptance by the auctioneer. Such retraction, however, does not revive any previous bid.

If the auctioneer knowingly receives a bid by or on behalf of the seller, and notice has not been given that the seller reserves the right to bid at the auction sale, the bidder to whom the goods are sold can either avoid the sale or take the goods at the price of the last good faith bid.

CISG   *The CISG does not apply to sales by auctions.*

Contractual modifications

the Code provides that a contract for the sale or lease of goods may be modified without new consideration if the modification is made in good faith

CONSIDERATION [19-4]

In several respects, the Code has relaxed the common law requirements regarding consideration. For example, the Code provides that a contract for the sale of goods can be modified without new consideration, provided the **modification** is made in good faith. (Article 2A.) In addition, any claim of right arising out of an alleged breach of contract can be discharged in whole or in part without consideration by a written waiver or renunciation signed and delivered by the aggrieved party. Under Revised UCC Article 1, a claim or right arising out of an alleged breach may be discharged in whole or in part without consideration by agreement of the aggrieved party in an authenticated record. Moreover, a firm offer is not revocable for lack of consideration.

CISG   *Consideration is not needed to modify a contract.*

FORM OF THE CONTRACT [19-5]
Statute of Frauds [19-5a]

Statute of frauds

sale of goods costing $500 or more (or lease of goods for $1,000 or more) must be evidenced by a signed writing to be enforceable

The original **statute of frauds**, which applied to contracts for the sale of goods, has been used as a prototype for the Article 2 statute of frauds provision. The Code provides that a contract for the sale of goods costing *$500 or more* is not enforceable unless there is some writing or record sufficient to evidence the existence of a contract between the parties ($1,000 or more for leases—Article 2A). As discussed in Chapter 15, at least forty-seven states have adopted the *Uniform Electronic Transactions Act (UETA)*, which gives full effect to contracts formed by electronic records and signatures. The Act applies to contracts governed by Articles 2 and 2A. In addition, Congress in 2000 enacted the *Electronic Signatures in Global and National Commerce (E-Sign)*. The Act, which uses language very similar to that of UETA, makes electronic records and signatures valid and enforceable across the United States for many types of transactions in or affecting interstate or foreign commerce.

CISG *A contract need not be evidenced by a writing, unless one of the parties has its place of business in a country that provides otherwise.*

Modification of Contracts An agreement modifying a contract must be in writing if the resulting contract is within the statute of frauds (Article 2A omits this provision). Conversely, if a contract that was previously within the statute of frauds is modified so as to no longer fall within it, the modification is enforceable even if it is oral. Thus, if the parties enter into an oral contract to sell for $450 a dining room table, to be delivered to the buyer, and later, prior to delivery, *orally* agree that the seller shall stain the table and that the buyer shall pay a price of $550, the modified contract is unenforceable. In contrast, if the parties have a written contract for the sale of one hundred and fifty bushels of wheat at a price of $4.50 per bushel and, later, orally agree to decrease the quantity to one hundred bushels at the same price per bushel, the agreement, as modified, is enforceable.

A signed agreement that requires modifications or rescissions of it to be in a signed writing cannot be otherwise modified or rescinded. (Article 2A.) If this requirement is on a form provided by a merchant, the other party must separately sign it unless the other party is a merchant.

Written compliance

the Code requires some writing or writings sufficient to indicate that a contract has been made between the parties, signed by the party against whom enforcement is sought or by her authorized agent or broker, and including a term specifying the quantity of goods

Writing(s) or Record The statute of frauds **compliance** provisions under the Code are more liberal than the rules under general contract law. The Code requires merely some writing or record (1) sufficient to indicate that a contract has been made between the parties, (2) signed by the party against whom enforcement is sought or by her authorized agent or broker, and (3) including a term specifying the quantity of goods to be exchanged. Whereas general contract law requires that the writing include all essential terms, under the Code a writing or record may be sufficient even if it omits or incorrectly states an agreed-upon term. This is consistent with other provisions of the Code that permit contracts to be enforced even though material terms are omitted. Nevertheless, the contract is enforceable only to the extent of the quantity of goods stated. Given proof that a contract was intended and that a signed writing or record describes the goods, the quantity of goods, and the names of the parties, the court, under the Code, can supply omitted terms such as price and particulars of performance. Moreover, several related documents together may satisfy the writing or record requirement.

Between merchants, a written confirmation, if sufficient against the sender, is also sufficient against the recipient unless the recipient gives written notice of her objection within ten days after receiving the confirmation. (Article 2A does not have a comparable rule.) This means that if these requirements have been met, the recipient of the writing or record is in the same position he would have assumed by signing it; and the confirmation, therefore, is enforceable against him. For example, Brown Co. and ATM Industries enter into an oral contract providing that ATM will deliver 1,000 dozen shirts to Brown at $6.00 per shirt. The next day, Brown sends to ATM a letter signed by Brown's president confirming the agreement. The letter contains the quantity

BUSINESS LAW **IN ACTION**

Between buyers and sellers of goods, many contracts are created via preprinted forms, like pro forma invoices, purchase orders, order confirmations, and invoices. These forms typically contain legal terms not expressly negotiated by the parties. The question often arises as to whether a term appearing in only one of the two preprinted forms binds the parties.

Say Bi-Rite Systems ordered $325,000 of component parts from Kruger Corp. on account, agreeing to pay within ten days of receipt of Kruger's invoice. Bi-Rite used a standard form purchase order that accurately reflected the price, quantity, and delivery terms to which the parties had agreed but said nothing about interest on

overdue balances. Kruger delivered the goods along with its standard form invoice, which stated: "Accounts not paid within 10 days from the date of billing will be subject to a finance charge of 1-1/2% per month." Bi-Rite paid Kruger's invoice twenty-five days after the date of billing. Does Bi-Rite owe the finance charge?

Code Section 2-207 provides that in contracts between merchants "additional terms" found in a form contract acceptance generally become an enforceable part of the bargain, unless (1) the offer expressly limits acceptance to the terms of the offer, (2) the additional term materially alters the offer, or (3) there is prompt objection to the proposed additional term.

Bi-Rite's purchase order is the offer and Kruger's invoice the acceptance. The invoice's finance charge provision is an "additional term." Since there is no indication that either the offer was expressly limited to its terms or that Bi-Rite made any objection to the proposed finance charge clause, the question is whether it "materially alters" the offer. Courts have routinely held that interest provisions, arbitration clauses, and even remedy limitations set out in form acceptances do *not* materially alter the terms of the offer. Therefore the finance charge clause in Kruger's preprinted form invoice is enforceable.

Practical Advice

Be aware that if you receive a signed written confirmation of a contract, you have ten business days to object if the confirmation is inaccurate.

Parol evidence

contractual terms that are set forth in a writing intended by the parties as a final expression of their agreement may not be contradicted by evidence of any prior agreement or of a contemporaneous oral agreement, but such terms may be explained or supplemented by course of dealing, usage of trade, course of performance, or consistent additional evidence

term but does not mention the price. Brown is bound by the contract when its authorized agent sends the letter, whereas ATM is bound by the oral contract ten days after receiving the letter, unless it objects in writing within that time. Therefore, it is essential that merchants examine their mail carefully and promptly to make certain that any written confirmations conform to their understanding of their outstanding contractual agreements. Where one or both of the parties is not a merchant, however, this rule does not apply.

Exceptions   A contract that does not satisfy the writing requirement but is otherwise valid is enforceable in the following instances:

The Code permits an oral contract for the sale of goods to be enforced against a party who in his pleading, testimony, or otherwise in court **admits** that a contract was made; but the Code limits enforcement to the quantity of goods he admits. (Article 2A.) This provision recognizes that the policy behind the statute of frauds does not apply when the party seeking to avoid the oral contract admits under oath the existence of the contract.

The Code also permits enforcement of an oral contract for goods **specially manufactured** for the buyer. (Article 2A.) Nevertheless, if the goods are readily marketable in the ordinary course of the seller's business, even though they were manufactured on special order, the contract is not enforceable unless it is in writing.

Under the Code, delivery and acceptance of part of the goods or payment and acceptance of part of the price validates the contract, but only for the goods that have been **delivered and accepted** or for which **payment** has been **accepted**. (Article 2A.) To illustrate, Debra orally agrees to buy one thousand watches from Brian for $15,000. Brian delivers three hundred watches to Debra, who receives and accepts them. The oral contract is enforceable to the extent of three hundred watches ($4,500)—those received and accepted—but is unenforceable to the extent of seven hundred watches ($10,500).

Parol Evidence [19-5b]

Contractual terms that are set forth in a writing intended by the parties as a final expression of their agreement may not be contradicted by evidence of any prior agreement or of a contemporaneous oral agreement, but, under the Code, the terms may be explained or supplemented by (1) course of dealing, usage of trade, or course of performance and (2) evidence of consistent additional terms, unless the writing was intended as the complete and exclusive statement of the terms of the agreement. (Article 2A.)

CONCEPT REVIEW 19-1

Contract Law Compared with Law of Sales

Section of UCC	Contract Law	Law of Sales
Definiteness	Contract must include all material terms.	Open terms permitted if parties intend to make a contract. (Article 2, 2A)
Counteroffers	Acceptance must be a mirror image of offer. Counteroffer and conditional acceptance are rejections.	Battle of the Forms. See Figure 19-1. (Article 2)
Modification of Contract	Consideration is required.	Consideration is not required. (Article 2, 2A)
Irrevocable Offers	Options.	Options. Firm offers up to three months' binding without consideration. (Article 2, 2A)
Statute of Frauds	Writing must include all material terms.	Writing must include quantity term. Specially manufactured goods. Confirmation by merchants. Delivery or payment and acceptance. Admissions. (Article 2, Article 2A *except* merchant confirmation.)

ETHICAL DILEMMA

What Constitutes Unconscionability in a Business?

Facts Frank's Maintenance and Repair, Inc., orally placed with C. A. Roberts Co. an order for steel tubing to use in manufacturing front fork tubes for motorcycles. Front fork tubes bear the bulk of a motorcycle's weight, so Frank's had to use high-quality steel.

Soon, Frank's received from Roberts Co. an acknowledgment of the order. This acknowledgment included the conditions of sale, which limited consequential damages, as well as a description of restricted remedies that were available upon the contract's breach. The sale conditions required that the buyer make any claim for defective equipment promptly upon receipt of the goods. These conditions were printed on the back of the acknowledgment. On the front, a legend that read "conditions of sale on reverse side" had been stamped over in such a way that the words at first appeared to read "No conditions of sale on reverse side."

Roberts delivered the steel to Frank's in December. The steel had no visible defects. When Frank's began using the material in its manufacturing process in the summer of the following year, however, the company discovered that the steel was hopelessly pitted and cracked. Frank's Maintenance and Repair informed Roberts Co. of the defects, revoked its acceptance of the steel, and sued for breach of the warranty of merchantability.

Social, Policy, and Ethical Considerations

1. Did Frank's Maintenance and Repair have a reasonable opportunity to understand the terms of its contract with C. A. Roberts Co.? Given the contract that Frank's received, was the company able to make a meaningful choice with regard to the terms of the agreement? Why or why not?

2. Who bears the responsibility in a situation such as this when both parties are businesspersons and thus should know enough to read all contracts carefully and thoroughly?

3. With or without the stamp, did Roberts act unconscionably in drawing up its contract? Moreover, should Roberts have the right to restrict a buyer's remedies if its steel may have a latent defect?

CHAPTER SUMMARY

Nature of Sales and Leases

Definitions

Goods movable personal property

Sale transfer of title to goods from seller to buyer for a price

Lease a transfer of right to possession and use of goods in return for consideration

- *Consumer Leases* leases by a merchant to an individual who leases for personal, family, or household purposes for no more than $25,000
- *Finance Leases* special type of lease transaction generally involving three parties: the lessor, the supplier, and the lessee

Governing Law

- *Sales Transactions* governed by Article 2 of the Code, except where general contract law has not been specifically modified by the Code, general contract law continues to apply
- *Lease Transactions* governed by Article 2A of the Code, but where general contract law has not been specifically modified by the Code, general contract law continues to apply
- *Transactions Outside the Code* include employment contracts, service contracts, insurance contracts, contracts involving real property, and contracts for the sale of tangibles

Fundamental Principles of Article 2 and Article 2A

Purpose to modernize, clarify, simplify, and make uniform the law of sales and leases

Good Faith the Code requires all sales and lease contracts to be performed in good faith, which means honesty in fact in the conduct or transaction concerned; in the case of a merchant (and a nonmerchant under Revised Article 1), it also includes the observance of reasonable commercial standards of fair dealing

Unconscionability a court may refuse to enforce an unconscionable contract or any part of a contract found to be unconscionable

- *Procedural Unconscionability* unfairness of the bargaining process
- *Substantive Unconscionability* oppressive or grossly unfair contractual provisions

Expansion of Commercial Practices

- *Course of Dealing* a sequence of previous conduct between the parties establishing a common basis for interpreting their agreement
- *Usage of Trade* a practice or method of dealing regularly observed and followed in a place, vocation, or trade

Sales By and Between Merchants the Code establishes separate rules that apply to transactions between merchants or involving a merchant (a dealer in goods or a person who by his occupation holds himself out as having knowledge or skill peculiar to the goods or practices involved, or who employs an agent or broker whom he holds out as having such knowledge or skill)

Liberal Administration of Remedies

- *Freedom of Contract* most provisions of the Code may be varied by agreement
- *Validation and Preservation of Sales Contracts* the Code reduces formal requisites to the bare minimum and attempts to preserve agreements whenever the parties manifest an intention to enter into a contract

Formation of Sales and Lease Contracts

Manifestation of Mutual Assent

Definiteness of an Offer the Code provides that a contract does not fail for indefiniteness even though one or more terms may have been omitted; the Code provides standards by which missing essential terms may be supplied

Irrevocable Offers

- *Option* a contract to hold open an offer
- *Firm Offer* a signed writing by a merchant to hold open an offer for the purchase or sale of goods (or lease of goods) for a maximum of three months

Variant Acceptances the inclusion of different or additional terms in an acceptance is addressed by focusing on the intent of the parties

Manner of Acceptance an acceptance can be made in any reasonable manner and is effective upon dispatch

Auction auction sales are generally with reserve, permitting the auctioneer to withdraw the goods at any time prior to sale

Consideration

Contractual Modifications the Code provides that a contract for the sale or lease of goods may be modified without new consideration if the modification is made in good faith

Firm Offers are not revocable for lack of consideration

Form of the Contract

Statute of Frauds sale of goods costing $500 or more (or lease of goods for $1,000 or more) must be evidenced by a signed writing or record to be enforceable; full effect is given to electronic contracts and signatures

- *Writing(s) or Record* the Code requires some writing(s) or record sufficient to indicate that a contract has been made between the parties, signed by the party against whom enforcement is sought or by her authorized agent or broker, and including a term specifying the quantity of goods
- *Alternative Methods of Compliance* written confirmation between merchants, admission, specially manufactured goods, and delivery or payment and acceptance

Parol Evidence contractual terms that are set forth in a writing intended by the parties as a final expression of their agreement may not be contradicted by evidence of any prior agreement or of a contemporaneous oral agreement, but such terms may be explained or supplemented by course of dealing, usage of trade, course of performance, or consistent additional evidence

QUESTIONS

1. Dickinson orders one thousand widgets at $5.00 per widget from International Widget to be delivered within sixty days. After the contract is consummated and signed, Dickinson orally requests that International deliver the widgets within thirty days rather than sixty days. International agrees. Is the contractual modification binding?

2. In Question 1, what effect, if any, would the following letter have?

   International Widget:

   In accordance with our agreement of this date you will deliver the one thousand previously ordered widgets within thirty days. Thank you for your cooperation in this matter.

   (signed) Dickinson

3. Hicks, a San Francisco company, orders from U.S. Electronics, a New York company, ten thousand electronic units. Hicks's order form provides that any dispute would be resolved by an arbitration panel located in San Francisco. U.S. Electronics executes and delivers to Hicks its acknowledgment form accepting the order and containing the following provision: "All disputes will be resolved by the state courts of New York." A dispute arises concerning the workmanship of the parts, and Hicks wishes the case to be arbitrated in San Francisco. What would be the result?

4. Explain how the result in Question 3 might change if the U.S. Electronics form contained the following provisions:
   a. "The seller's acceptance of the purchase order to which this acknowledgment responds is expressly made conditional on the buyer's assent to any or different terms contained in this acknowledgment."

   b. "The seller's acceptance of the purchase order is subject to the terms and conditions on the face and reverse side hereof, which the buyer accepts by accepting the goods described herein."
   c. "The seller's terms govern this agreement—this acknowledgment merely constitutes a counteroffer."

5. Reinfort executed a written contract with Bylinski to purchase an assorted collection of shoes for $3,000. A week before the agreed shipment date, Bylinski called Reinfort and said, "We cannot deliver at $3,000; unless you agree to pay $4,000, we will cancel the order." After considerable discussion, Reinfort agreed to pay $4,000 if Bylinski would ship as agreed in the contract. After the shoes had been delivered and accepted by Reinfort, Reinfort refused to pay $4,000 and insisted on paying only $3,000. Is the contractual modification binding? Explain.

6. On November 23, Blackburn, a dress manufacturer, mailed to Conroy a written and signed offer to sell one thousand sun dresses at $50 per dress. The offer stated that it would "remain open for ten days" and that it could "not be withdrawn prior to that date."

   Two days later, Blackburn, noting a sudden increase in the price of sundresses, changed his mind. Blackburn therefore sent Conroy a letter revoking the offer. The letter was sent on November 25 and received by Conroy on November 28.

   Conroy chose to disregard the letter of November 25; instead, she happily continued to watch the price of sundresses rise. On December 1, Conroy sent a letter accepting the original offer. The letter, however, was not received by Blackburn until December 9, due to a delay in the mail.

Conroy has demanded delivery of the goods according to the terms of the offer of November 23, but Blackburn has refused. Does a contract exist between Conroy and Blackburn? Explain.

7. Henry and Wilma, an elderly immigrant couple, agreed to purchase from Harris a refrigerator with a fair market value of $450 for twenty-five monthly installments of $60.00 per month. Henry and Wilma now wish to void the contract, asserting that they did not realize the exorbitant price they were paying. Result?

8. Courts Distributors needed two hundred compact refrigerators on a rush basis. It contacted Eastinghouse Corporation, a manufacturer of refrigerators. Eastinghouse said it would take some time to quote a price on an order of that size. Courts replied, "Send the refrigerators immediately and bill us later." The refrigerators were delivered three days later, and the invoice arrived ten days after that. The invoice price was $140,000. Courts believes that the wholesale market price of the refrigerators is only $120,000. Do the parties have a contract? If so, what is the price? Explain.

CASE PROBLEMS

9. While adjusting a television antenna beside his mobile home and underneath a high-voltage electric transmission wire, Prince received an electric shock resulting in personal injury. He claims the high-voltage electric current jumped from the transmission wire to the antenna. The wire, which carried some 7,200 volts of electricity, did not serve his mobile home but ran directly above it. Prince sued the Navarro County Electric Co-Op, the owner and operator of the wire, for breach of implied warranty of merchantability under the Uniform Commercial Code (UCC). He contends that the Code's implied warranty of merchantability extends to the container of a product—in this instance, the wiring—and that the escape of the current shows that the wiring was unfit for its purpose of transporting electricity. The electric company argues that the electricity passing through the transmission wire was not being sold to Prince and that, therefore, there was no sale of goods to Prince. Is the contract covered by the UCC?

10. HMT, already in the business of marketing agricultural products, decided to try its hand at marketing potatoes for processing. Nine months before the potato harvest, HMT contracted to supply Bell Brand with one hundred thousand sacks of potatoes. At harvest time, Bell Brand would accept only sixty thousand sacks. HMT sues for breach of contract. Bell Brand argues that custom and usage in marketing processing potatoes allows buyers to give estimates in contracts, not fixed quantities, as the contracts are established so far in advance. HMT responds that the quantity term in the contract was definite and unambiguous. Can custom and trade usage be used to interpret an unambiguous contract? Discuss.

11. Schreiner, a cotton farmer, agreed over the telephone to sell 150 bales of cotton to Loeb & Co. Schreiner had sold cotton to Loeb & Co. for the past five years. Written confirmation of the date, parties, price, and conditions was mailed to Schreiner, who did not respond to the confirmation in any way. Four months later, when the price of cotton had doubled, Loeb & Co. sought to enforce the contract. Schreiner argues that he is not a merchant. Is the contract enforceable?

12. American Sand & Gravel, Inc., agreed to sell sand to Clark at a special discount if twenty to twenty-five thousand tons were ordered. The discount price was $9.45 per ton, compared with the normal price of $10.00 per ton. Two years later, Clark orders, and receives, 1,600 tons of sand from American Sand & Gravel. Clark refuses to pay more than $9.45 per ton.

American Sand & Gravel sues for the remaining $0.55 per ton. Decision?

13. In September, Auburn Plastics submitted price quotations to CBS for the manufacture of eight cavity molds to be used in making parts for CBS's toys. Each quotation specified that the offer would not be binding unless accepted within fifteen days. Furthermore, CBS would be subject to an additional 30 percent charge for engineering services upon delivery of the molds. In December and January of the following year, CBS sent detailed purchase orders to Auburn Plastics for cavity molds. The purchase order forms stated that CBS reserved the right to remove the molds from Auburn Plastics without an additional or "withdrawal" charge. Auburn Plastics acknowledged the purchase order and stated that the sale would be subject to all conditions contained in the price quotation. CBS paid Auburn for the molds, and Auburn began to fabricate toy parts from the molds for CBS. Later, Auburn announced a price increase, and CBS demanded delivery of the molds. Auburn refused to deliver the molds unless CBS paid the additional charge for engineering services. CBS claimed that the contract did not provide for a withdrawal charge. Who will prevail? Why?

14. The defendant, Gray Communications, desired to have a television tower built. After a number of negotiation sessions conducted by telephone between the defendant and the plaintiff, Kline Iron, the parties allegedly reached an oral agreement under which the plaintiff would build a tower for the defendant for a total price of $1,485,368. A few days later, the plaintiff sent a written document, referred to as a proposal, for execution by the defendant. The proposal indicated that it had been prepared for immediate acceptance by the defendant and that prior to formal acceptance by the defendant it could be modified or withdrawn without notice. A few days later, without having executed the proposal, the defendant advised the plaintiff that a competitor had provided a lower bid for construction of the tower. The defendant requested that the plaintiff explain its higher bid price, which the plaintiff failed to do. The defendant then advised the plaintiff by letter that it would not be retained to construct the tower. The plaintiff then commenced suit, alleging breach of an oral contract, and asserting that the oral agreement was enforceable because the common law of contracts, not the Uniform Commercial Code (UCC), governed the transaction and that

under the common law a writing is not necessary to cover this type of transaction. Even if the transaction was subject to the UCC, the plaintiff alternatively argued, the contract was within the UCC "merchant's exception." Is the contract enforceable?

15. Dorton, as a representative for The Carpet Mart, purchased carpets from Collins & Aikman that were supposedly manufactured of 100 percent Kodel polyester fiber but were, in fact, made of cheaper and inferior fibers. Dorton then brought suit for compensatory and punitive damages against Collins & Aikman for its fraud, deceit, and misrepresentation in the sale of the carpets. Collins & Aikman moved for a stay pending arbitration, claiming that Dorton was bound to an arbitration agreement printed on the reverse side of Collins & Aikman's printed sales acknowledgment form. A provision printed on the face of the acknowledgment form stated that its acceptance was "subject to all of the terms and conditions on the face and reverse side thereof, including arbitration, all of which are accepted by buyer." Holding that there existed no binding arbitration agreement between the parties, the district court denied the stay. Collins & Aikman appealed. Is the arbitration clause enforceable?

16. Emery Industries (Emery) contracted with Mechanicals, Inc. (Mechanicals), to install a pipe system to carry chemicals and fatty acids under high pressure and temperature. The system required stainless steel "stub ends" (used to connect pipe segments), which Mechanicals ordered from McJunkin Corporation (McJunkin). McJunkin in turn ordered the stub ends from the Alaskan Copper Companies, Inc. (Alaskan). McJunkin's purchase order required the seller to certify the goods and to relieve the buyer of liabilities that might arise from defective goods. After shipment of the goods to McJunkin, Alaskan sent written acknowledgment of the order, containing terms and conditions of sale different from those in McJunkin's purchase order. The acknowledgment provided a disclaimer of warranty and a requirement for inspection of the goods within ten days of receipt. The acknowledgment also contained a requirement that the buyer accept all of the seller's terms.

The stub ends were delivered to Mechanicals in several shipments over a five-month period. Each shipment included a document reciting terms the same as those on Alaskan's initial acknowledgment. Apparently, McJunkin never objected to any of the terms contained in any of Alaskan's documents.

After the stub ends were installed, they were found to be defective. Mechanicals had to remove and replace them, causing Emery to close its plant for several days. McJunkin filed a complaint alleging that Mechanicals had failed to pay $26,141.88 owed on account for the stub ends McJunkin supplied. Mechanicals filed an answer and counterclaim against McJunkin, alleging $93,586.13 in damages resulting from the replacement and repair of the defective stub ends. McJunkin filed a third-party complaint against Alaskan, alleging that Alaskan was liable for any damages Mechanicals incurred as a result of the defective stub ends. What result? Explain.

TAKING SIDES

Terminal Grain Corporation brought an action against Glen Freeman, a farmer, to recover damages for breach of an oral contract to deliver grain. According to Terminal Grain, Freeman orally agreed to two sales of wheat to Terminal Grain of four thousand bushels each at $6.21 a bushel and $6.41 a bushel, respectively. Dwayne Maher, merchandising manager of Terminal Grain, sent two written confirmations of the agreements to Freeman. Freeman never made any written objections to the confirmations. After the first transaction had occurred, the price of wheat rose to between $6.75 and $6.80 per bushel, and Freeman refused to deliver the remaining four thousand bushels at the agreed-upon price. Freeman denies entering into any agreement to sell the second four thousand bushels of wheat to Terminal Grain but admits that he received the two written confirmations sent by Maher.

a. What arguments support considering Freeman to be a merchant who is bound by the written confirmations?

b. What arguments support considering Freeman not to be a merchant seller and thus not bound by the written confirmations?

c. What is the appropriate decision?

Performance

CHAPTER 20

*The buyer needs a hundred eyes, the
seller not one.*

George Herbert (1593–1633)

CHAPTER OUTCOMES

After reading and studying this chapter, you should be able to:

1. Explain the requirements of tender of delivery with respect to time, manner, and place of delivery.

2. Explain the perfect tender rule and the three limitations on it.

3. Explain when the buyer has the right to reject the goods and what obligations the buyer has upon rejection.

4. Explain what constitutes acceptance by the buyer and the buyer's right to revoke acceptance.

5. Identify and describe the excuses for nonperformance and the Uniform Commercial Code's provisions for protecting the parties' expectations of performance by the other party.

Performance
fulfillment of a contractual
obligation

Performance is the process of discharging contractual obligations by carrying out those obligations according to a contract's terms. The basic obligation of the seller in a contract for the sale of goods is to transfer and deliver goods that conform to the terms of the contract. The basic obligation of the buyer is to accept and pay for conforming goods in accordance with the contract. In a lease, the basic obligation of the lessor is to transfer possession of the goods for the lease term and that of the lessee is to pay the agreed rent. A contract of sale also requires that each party not impair the other party's expectation of having the contract performed.

The obligations of the parties are determined by their contractual agreement. Thus, the contract of sale may expressly state, for example, whether the seller must deliver the goods before receiving payment of the price or whether the buyer must pay the price before receiving the goods. If the contract does not sufficiently cover the particulars of performance, these terms will be supplied by the Uniform Commercial Code (UCC), common law, course of dealings, usage of trade, and course of performance. (Article 2A provides only a few gap fillers.) In all events, both parties to the sales contract must perform their contractual obligations in good faith.

In this chapter, we will examine the performance obligations of the seller and the buyer as well as the contractual obligations that apply to both of them.

PERFORMANCE BY THE SELLER [20-1]

Unless the parties have agreed otherwise, tender (offer) of performance by one party is a condition to performance by the other party. Tender of conforming goods by the seller entitles him to acceptance of them by the buyer and to payment of the contractually agreed-upon price. Nonetheless, the terms of the contract may establish other rights for the parties. For example, if the seller has agreed to sell goods on sixty or ninety days' credit, he is required to perform his part of the contract by delivering the goods before the buyer performs.

Tender of delivery
seller makes available to buyer goods conforming to the contract and so notifies the buyer

Tender of delivery requires that the seller put and hold goods that conform to the contract at the buyer's disposition and that the seller give the buyer reasonable notification to enable her to take delivery. Tender must also be made at a reasonable time and be kept open for a reasonable period. For example, Jim agrees to sell Joan a home theater system composed of a speaker system (consisting of four identical speakers for the front and rear, a center channel speaker, and a subwoofer speaker), a Blu-Ray disc player, and an audio-video receiver. Each component is specified by manufacturer and model number, and delivery is to be at Jim's store. Jim obtains the ordered equipment in accordance with the contractual specifications and notifies Joan that she may pick up the system at her convenience. Jim has now tendered and thus has performed his obligations under the sales contract: he holds goods that conform to the contract, he has placed them at the buyer's disposition, and he has notified the buyer of their readiness.

CISG   *According to the United Nations Convention on Contracts for the International Sales of Goods (CISG), the seller must deliver the goods, hand over any documents relating to them, and transfer the property in the goods, as required by the contract and the CISG.*

Time of Tender [20-1a]

Time of tender
tender must be made at a reasonable time and kept open for a reasonable period of time

Tender must be at a reasonable time, and the goods tendered must be kept available for the period reasonably necessary to enable the buyer to take possession of them. If the contract terms set no definite time for delivery, the seller is allowed a reasonable time after entering into the contract within which to tender the goods to the buyer. Likewise, the buyer has a reasonable time within which to accept delivery. What length of time is reasonable depends on the facts and circumstances of each case.

A contract may not be performed piecemeal or in installments unless the parties specifically so agree. Otherwise, all of the goods called for by a contract must be tendered in a single delivery, with payment due at the time of such tender.

CISG   *The seller must deliver the goods: (1) if a date is fixed by or determinable from the contract, on that date; (2) if a period of time is fixed by or determinable from the contract, at any time within that period unless circumstances indicate that the buyer is to choose a date; or (3) in any other case, within a reasonable time after the conclusion of the contract.*

Place of Tender [20-1b]

Place of tender
if none is specified, place for delivery is the seller's place of business or, if he has no such place, his residence

If the contract does not specify the place for delivery of the goods, the place for delivery is the seller's place of business or, if he has no place of business, his residence. If the contract is for the sale of identified goods that the parties know at the time of making the contract are not located either at the seller's place of business or residence, the location of the goods is then the place for delivery.

The parties frequently agree expressly on the place of tender, typically by using one of the various delivery terms. These terms specify whether the contract is a shipment or destination contract and determine where the seller must tender delivery of the goods.

CISG   *If the seller is not bound to deliver the goods at any other particular place and the contract of sale does not involve carriage of the goods, his obligation to deliver consists (1) if the contract relates to specific goods, or unidentified goods to be drawn from a specific stock or to be manufactured or produced, and at the time of the conclusion of the contract the parties knew that the goods were at, or were to be manufactured or produced at, a particular place, in placing the goods at the buyer's disposal at that place; and (2) in other cases, in placing the goods at the buyer's disposal at the place where the seller had his place of business at the time of the conclusion of the contract.*

Shipment Contracts   The delivery terms *F.O.B. (free on board) place of shipment, F.A.S. (free alongside ship) seller's port, C.I.F. (cost, insurance, and freight)*, and *C. & F. (cost and freight)* are all shipment contracts. Under a **shipment contract**, the seller is required or authorized to send the goods to the buyer, but the contract does not obligate her to deliver them at a particular destination. In these cases, the seller's tender of performance occurs at the point of shipment, provided the seller meets certain specified conditions designed to protect the interests of the absent buyer.

Under the Code, the initials **F.O.B.** and **F.A.S.** are delivery terms, even though they are used only in connection with a stated price. A contract providing that the sale is **F.O.B.** *place of shipment* or **F.A.S.** *port of shipment* is a shipment contract. Under a **C.I.F.** contract, in consideration for an agreed unit price for the goods, the seller pays all costs of transportation, insurance, and freight to the destination. Under a **C. & F.** contract, he will pay "cost and freight." A seller under a shipment contract is required to (1) deliver the goods to a carrier, (2) make a contract for their transportation that is reasonable according to the nature of the goods and other circumstances, (3) obtain and promptly deliver or tender to the buyer any document necessary to enable the buyer to obtain possession of the goods from the carrier, and (4) promptly notify the buyer of the shipment.

CISG   *If the seller is not bound to deliver the goods at any other particular place and if the contract of sale involves carriage of the goods, his obligation to deliver consists in handing the goods over to the first carrier for delivery to the buyer.*

Destination Contracts   The delivery terms *F.O.B. city of buyer, ex-ship*, and *no arrival, no sale* are destination contracts. Because a **destination contract** requires the seller to tender delivery of conforming goods at a specified destination, the seller must place the goods at the buyer's disposition and give the buyer reasonable notice to enable him to take delivery. In addition, if the destination contract involves documents of title, the seller must tender the necessary documents.

When the contract provides that the sale is **F.O.B.** *place of destination*, the seller must at his own expense and risk transport the goods to that place and there tender delivery of them to the buyer. For example, if the buyer is in Boston and the seller is in Chicago, a contract providing F.O.B. Boston is a destination contract under which the seller must tender the goods at the designated place in Boston at his own expense and risk. A contract that provides for delivery **ex-ship**, or "from the ship," is also a destination contract, requiring the seller to unload the goods from the carrier at a named destination. Finally, if the contract contains the terms **no arrival, no sale**, the title and risk of loss do not pass to the buyer until the seller makes a tender of the goods after they arrive at their destination.

Goods Held by Bailee   When goods are in the possession of a bailee and are to be delivered without being moved, in most instances the seller may either tender to the buyer a document of title or obtain an acknowledgment by the bailee of the buyer's right to possess the goods. This acknowledgment permits the buyer to obtain the goods directly from the bailee.

For a summary of performance by the seller, see Figure 20-1.

Perfect Tender Rule [20-1c]

The Code's **perfect tender rule** imposes on the seller the obligation to conform her tender of goods *exactly* to the terms of the contract. If either the tender of delivery or the goods fail in any respect to conform to the contract, the buyer may (1) reject the whole lot, (2) accept the whole lot, or (3) accept any commercial unit or units and reject the rest. (Article 2A.) A **commercial unit** means such a unit of goods that by commercial usage is a single unit and that, if divided, would be materially impaired in character or value. (Article 2A.)

Thus, a buyer may rightfully reject the delivery of 110 dozen shirts under an agreement calling for delivery of 100 dozen shirts. The size or extent of the breach does not affect the right to reject. The following case further illustrates the perfect tender rule.

Shipment contract

seller is required to tender delivery of the goods to a carrier for delivery to buyer

Destination contract

seller is required to tender delivery of the goods at a named destination

Practical Advice

In your sales contracts clearly specify by use of the correct shipment term or specific language which party pays the shipping costs and where the seller must tender delivery of the goods.

Perfect tender rule

seller's tender of performance must conform exactly to the contract subject to (1) agreement of the parties, (2) cure by seller, and (3) installment contracts

Figure 20-1 Tender of Performance by the Seller

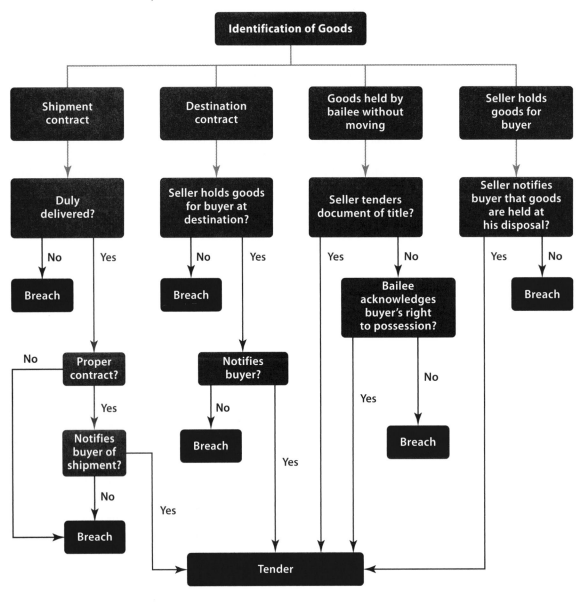

Moulton Cavity & Mold Inc. v. Lyn-Flex Ind.
Supreme Court of Maine, 1979
396 A.2d 1024
http://scholar.google.com/scholar_case?case=7850526598237666882&q=396+A.2d+1024&hl=en&as_sclt=2,34

FACTS Moulton Cavity & Mold Inc. agreed to manufacture twenty-six innersole molds to be purchased by Lyn-Flex. Moulton delivered the twenty-six molds to Lyn-Flex after Lyn-Flex allegedly approved the sample molds. However, Lyn-Flex rejected the molds, claiming that they did not satisfy the specifications exactly, and denied that it had ever approved the sample molds. Moulton then sued, contending that Lyn-Flex wrongfully rejected the molds. Lyn-Flex, arguing that the Code's perfect tender rule permitted its rejection of the imperfect molds, regardless of Moulton's substantial performance, appealed from a judgment entered by the trial court in favor of Moulton.

DECISION Judgment for Moulton reversed and a new trial ordered.

OPINION Under the Code's perfect tender provision, "if the goods or the tender of delivery fail in any respect to conform to the contract, the buyer may reject the whole." Therefore, Moulton's substantial performance does not obligate Lyn-Flex to accept the molds. If they failed to meet the contract's specifications in any respect, Lyn-Flex was entitled to reject them without liability.

INTERPRETATION If the seller does not perform his contractual obligations exactly, the buyer may rightfully reject the seller's performance.

CRITICAL THINKING QUESTION Do you agree with the Code's perfect tender rule? Explain.

CISG *The CISG does not follow the perfect tender rule. The buyer may declare the contract avoided if the failure by the seller to perform any of his obligations under the contract or the CISG amounts to a* fundamental *breach of contract. A breach of contract committed by one of the parties is fundamental if it results in such detriment to the other party as substantially to deprive him of what he is entitled to expect under the contract, unless the party in breach did not foresee and a reasonable person of the same kind in the same circumstances would not have foreseen such a result.*

Three basic conditions qualify the buyer's right to reject the goods upon the seller's failure to comply with the perfect tender rule: (1) agreement between the parties limiting the buyer's right to reject nonconforming goods, (2) cure by the seller, and (3) the existence of an installment contract. In addition, the perfect tender rule does not apply to a seller's breach of her obligation under a shipment contract to make a proper contract for transportation or to give proper notice of the shipment. A failure to perform either of these obligations is a ground for rejection only if material loss or delay results.

Agreement Between the Parties

The parties may contractually agree to limit the operation of the perfect tender rule. For example, they may agree that the seller shall have the right to repair or replace any defective parts or goods. We will discuss these contractual limitations in Chapter 23.

Cure by the Seller

The Code recognizes two situations in which a seller may **cure**, or correct, a nonconforming tender of goods. This relaxation of the seller's obligation to make a perfect tender gives the seller an opportunity either to make a second delivery or to make a substitute tender. The first opportunity for cure occurs when the time for performance under the contract has not expired. The second opportunity for cure is available after the time for performance has expired but only if the seller had reasonable grounds to believe that the nonconforming tender would be acceptable to the buyer with or without a monetary adjustment.

In cases in which the buyer refuses to accept a tender of goods that do not conform to the contract, the seller, by acting promptly and within the time allowed for performance, may make a proper tender or delivery of conforming goods and thereby cure the defective tender or performance. (Article 2A.) Upon notice of the buyer's rightful rejection, the seller must first give the buyer reasonable notice of her intention to cure the defect and must then make a proper tender according to the original contract. This rule gives the seller the full contractual period in which to perform but does not cause any harm to the buyer, who receives full performance within the time agreed to in the contract. For example, Neal is to deliver to Jessica twenty-five blue shirts and fifty white shirts by October 15. On October 1, Neal delivers twenty-nine blue shirts and forty-six white shirts, which Jessica rejects as not conforming to the contract. Jessica notifies Neal of her rejection and the reasons for it. Neal has until October 15 to cure the defect by making a perfect tender, provided he seasonably notifies Jessica of his intention to do so.

The Code also provides the seller an opportunity to cure a nonconforming tender that the seller had reasonable grounds to believe would be acceptable to the buyer with or without a money allowance. (Article 2A.) If, on the buyer's notice of rejection, the seller seasonably notifies the buyer of his intention to cure, the seller is permitted a reasonable time in which to substitute a conforming tender. For example, Tim orders from Noel a model 110X television to be delivered on January 20. The 110X is unavailable, but Noel can obtain a model 110, which is last year's model of the same television and which lists for 5 percent less than the 110X. On January 20, Noel delivers to Tim the 110 at a discount price of 10 percent less than the contract price for the 110X. Tim rejects the substituted television set. Noel, who promptly notifies Tim that she will obtain and deliver a model 110X, will have a reasonable time beyond the January 20 deadline in which to deliver the 110X television set to Tim, because under these facts she had reasonable grounds to believe the model 110 would be acceptable with the money allowance in Tim's favor.

Agreement between the parties
the parties may contractually limit the operation of the perfect tender rule

Practical Advice

If you are the seller, consider using a contractual term to limit the operation of the perfect tender rule; if you are the buyer, carefully scrutinize such a limitation.

Cure
when the time for performance under the contract has not expired or when the seller has shipped nonconforming goods in the belief that the nonconforming tender would be acceptable, a seller may cure or correct his nonconforming tender

Practical Advice

If you want to exercise the seller's right to cure, be sure to give the buyer timely notice of your intent to cure.

CISG

If the seller has delivered goods before the date for delivery, he may, up to that date, cure any deficiency, provided that the exercise of this right does not cause the buyer unreasonable inconvenience or unreasonable expense. However, the buyer retains any right to claim damages as provided for in the CISG. If the seller does not perform on time, the buyer may fix an additional period of time of reasonable length for performance by the seller of his obligations. Unless the buyer has received notice from the seller that the seller will not perform within the period so fixed, the buyer may not, during that period, resort to any remedy for breach of contract. However, the buyer retains any right he may have to claim damages for delay in performance. If the seller does not deliver the goods within the additional period of time or declares that he will not deliver within the period so fixed, the buyer may declare the contract avoided.

The seller may, even after the date for delivery, cure a defective performance, if he can do so without unreasonable delay and without causing the buyer unreasonable inconvenience. However, the buyer retains any right to claim damages for delay in performance. If the seller requests the buyer to make known whether he will accept performance and the buyer does not comply with the request within a reasonable time, the seller may perform within the time indicated in his request.

Installment contract

when the contract calls for the goods to be delivered in separate lots, the buyer may reject a nonconforming installment if it substantially impairs the value of that installment and cannot be cured; but if nonconformity or default of one or more of the installments substantially impairs the value of the whole contract, the buyer can treat the breach as a breach of the whole contract

Installment Contracts Unless the parties have otherwise agreed, the buyer does not have to pay any part of the price of the goods until the seller has delivered or tendered to her the entire quantity specified in the contract. An **installment contract** represents an instance in which the parties have otherwise agreed. It expressly provides for delivery of the goods in separate lots or installments and usually provides for payment of the price in installments. If the contract is silent about payment, the Code provides that the seller may demand the price, if it can be apportioned, for each lot.

The buyer may reject any nonconforming installment if the nonconformity substantially impairs the value of that installment and cannot be cured. When, however, the nonconforming installment substantially impairs the value of the installment but not the value of the entire contract, the buyer cannot reject the installment if the seller gives adequate assurance of the installment's cure. (Article 2A.) On the other hand, whenever the nonconformity or default with respect to one or more of the installments substantially impairs the value of the whole contract, the buyer can treat the breach as a breach of the whole contract. (Article 2A.)

CISG

When a contract calls for delivery of goods by installments, if the seller's failure to perform any of his obligations with respect to any installment constitutes a fundamental breach of contract with respect to that installment, the buyer may declare the contract avoided with respect to that installment. A buyer who declares the contract avoided with respect to any delivery may, at the same time, declare it avoided with respect to deliveries already made or to future deliveries if, by reason of their interdependence, those deliveries could not be used for the purpose contemplated by the parties at the time of the conclusion of the contract. If the seller's failure to perform any of his obligations with respect to any installment gives the buyer good grounds to conclude that a fundamental breach of contract will occur with respect to future installments, he may declare the contract avoided for the future, provided that he does so within a reasonable time.

PERFORMANCE BY THE BUYER [20-2]

A buyer is obliged to accept conforming goods and to pay for them according to the contract terms. (Article 2A.) Payment or tender of payment by the buyer, unless otherwise agreed, is a condition of the seller's duty to tender and to complete any delivery. The buyer is not obliged to accept a tender or delivery of goods that do not conform to the contract. Upon determining that the tender or delivery is nonconforming, the buyer has three choices. He may (1) reject all of the goods, (2) accept all of the goods, or (3) accept any commercial unit or units of the goods and reject the rest. (Article 2A.) The buyer must pay the contract rate for the commercial units he accepts.

CISG   *The buyer must pay the price for the goods and take delivery of them as required by the contract and the CISG.*

Inspection

unless otherwise agreed, the buyer has a reasonable time in which to inspect the goods before payment or acceptance to determine whether they conform

Inspection [20-2a]

Unless the parties agree otherwise, the buyer has a right to inspect the goods before payment or acceptance. (Article 2A provides for the right to inspect before acceptance.) This **inspection** enables the buyer to determine whether the goods tendered or delivered conform to the contract. If the contract requires payment before acceptance (e.g., when the contract provides for shipment C.O.D., collect on delivery), payment must be made prior to inspection; however, such payment is not an acceptance of the goods and impairs neither the buyer's right to inspect nor any of her remedies.

Practical Advice

If you are the buyer, carefully inspect tendered goods before accepting them. If this is not feasible, inspect the goods as soon as possible.

The buyer, allowed a reasonable time to inspect the goods, may lose the right to reject or revoke acceptance of nonconforming goods by failing to inspect them within such time. Nevertheless, although the buyer must bear the expenses of inspection, she may recover them from the seller if the goods do not conform and are rightfully rejected. (Article 2A.)

CISG   *The buyer is not bound to pay the price until he has had an opportunity to examine the goods, unless the parties have agreed otherwise. The buyer must examine the goods within as short a period of time as is practicable in the circumstances. The buyer loses the right to rely on a lack of conformity of the goods if he does not give notice to the seller of the nonconformity within a reasonable time after he has discovered it or ought to have discovered it.*

Rejection [20-2b]

Rejection is a manifestation by the buyer of her unwillingness to become the owner of the goods. It must be made within a reasonable time after the goods have been tendered or delivered and is not effective unless the buyer reasonably notifies the seller. (Article 2A.)

Rejection

buyer's manifestation of unwillingness to become the owner of the goods; must be made within a reasonable time after the goods have been tendered or delivered and gives the buyer the right to (1) reject all of the goods, or (2) accept all of the goods, or (3) accept any commercial unit(s) and reject the rest

Rejection of the goods may be rightful or wrongful, depending on whether the goods tendered or delivered conform to the contract. The buyer's rejection of nonconforming goods or tender is rightful under the perfect tender rule.

If the buyer refuses a tender of goods or rejects it as nonconforming without disclosing to the seller the nature of the defect, she may not assert such defect as an excuse for not accepting the goods or as a breach of contract by the seller if the defect is curable. (Article 2A.)

After the buyer has rejected the goods, the Code allows her to exercise no ownership of them. (Since the lessor retains title in a lease, this does not apply to leases.) If the buyer possesses the rejected goods but has no security interest in them, she is obliged to hold them with reasonable care for a time sufficient to permit the seller to remove them. (Article 2A.) The buyer who is not a merchant is under no further obligation with regard to goods rightfully rejected. (Article 2A.)

Practical Advice

If you have rejected nonconforming goods, be sure to notify the seller in a timely manner and do not exercise ownership of the rejected goods.

If the seller gives no instructions within a reasonable time after notification of rejection, the buyer may (1) store the goods for the seller's account, (2) reship them to the seller, or (3) resell them for the seller's account. Such action is not an acceptance or conversion of the goods. (Article 2A.) A merchant buyer of goods who has rightfully rejected them has additional duties: she is obligated to follow reasonable instructions from the seller regarding disposal of the goods in her possession or control when the seller has no agent or business at the place of rejection. (Article 2A.) If the merchant buyer receives no instructions from the seller within a reasonable time after giving notice of the rejection, and if the rejected goods are perishable or threaten to decline in value speedily, she is obligated to make reasonable efforts to sell them for the seller's account. (Article 2A.)

When the buyer sells the rejected goods, she is entitled to reimbursement for the reasonable expenses of caring for and selling them and to a reasonable selling commission not to exceed 10 percent of the gross proceeds. (Article 2A.)

CISG *If the goods do not conform with the contract and the nonconformity constitutes a fundamental breach of contract, the buyer may require delivery of substitute goods. If the buyer has received the goods and intends to exercise any right under the contract or the CISG to reject them, he must take such steps to preserve them as are reasonable in the circumstances. He is entitled to retain them until he has been reimbursed his reasonable expenses by the seller.*

Furlong v. Alpha Chi Omega Sorority
Bowling Green County Municipal Court, 1993
73 Ohio Misc.2d 26, 657 N.E.2d 866
http://scholar.google.com/scholar_case?case=13710936984230391946&q=657+N.E.2d+866&hl=en&as_sdt=2,34

FACTS Alpha Chi Omega (AXO) entered into an oral contract with Furlong to buy 168 "custom-designed" sweaters for the Midnight Masquerade III. The purchase price of $3,612 was to be paid as follows: $2,000 down payment and $1,612 upon delivery. During phone conversations with Furlong, Emily, the AXO social chairperson, described the design to be imprinted on the sweater. She also specified the colors to be used in the lettering (hunter green on top of maroon outlined in navy blue) and the color of the mask design (hunter green). Furlong promised to have a third party imprint the sweaters as specified. Furlong later sent to Emily a sweater with maroon letters to show her the color. He then sent her a fax illustrating the sweater design with arrows indicating where each of the three colors was to appear. On the day before delivery was due, Argento, Furlong's supplier, requested design changes, which Furlong approved without the consent of AXO. These changes included deleting the navy blue outline, reducing the number of colors from three to two, changing the maroon lettering to red, and changing the color of the masks from hunter green to red. Upon delivery, AXO gave a check for the balance of the purchase price. Later that day, Emily inspected the sweaters and was dismayed at the design changes. AXO immediately stopped payment on the check. Amy, the president of AXO, phoned Furlong, stating that the sweaters were not what AXO had ordered. She gave the specifics as to why the sweaters were not as ordered and offered to return them. Furlong refused but offered to reduce the unit price of the sweaters if AXO agreed to accept them. AXO refused this offer. Furlong then filed suit against AXO for the unpaid portion of the sweaters' purchase price ($1,612) and AXO counterclaimed for return of the down payment ($2,000).

DECISION Judgment for AXO. The court ordered Furlong to pay $2,000 plus interest and costs and AXO to return the sweaters upon such payment.

OPINION Because this is a sale of goods, the provisions of the Uniform Commercial Code apply. The design specifications were part of the basis of the bargain and as such became an express warranty. This warranty was created in three ways that are consistent and, therefore, cumulative. First, Furlong's promise during the phone call to have the sweaters printed as specified was sufficient to have created an express warranty. Second, the sweater with maroon lettering that Furlong sent was sufficient to create an express warranty as a sample. Third, Furlong's fax to Emily was sufficient to create an express warranty as a description. By delivering nonconforming goods, Furlong breached the express warranty to meet the bargained-for specifications and, therefore, breached the contract. Since AXO seasonably notified the seller of the nonconformity by phone "within a reasonable time" (on the same day as delivery), its rejection of the goods was rightful. AXO was within its rights to reject the whole lot of sweaters if the goods failed in any respect to conform to the contract. Here, the goods materially failed to conform in many respects. Since AXO never accepted the goods, the duty to pay the purchase price never arose. Therefore, AXO did not breach the contract. Moreover, although the law allowed AXO to accept Furlong's offer of compromise, it did not require AXO to do so. Finally, because Furlong breached the contract, AXO may cancel the contract and recover the partial payment of the contract price.

INTERPRETATION If the goods fail in any respect to conform to the contract, the buyer may reject the whole lot.

ETHICAL QUESTION Did Furlong act in bad faith by not seeking AXO's consent to the changes? Explain.

CRITICAL THINKING QUESTION Does the court's decision remedy the situation in which the seller's breach left the sorority? Explain.

Acceptance [20-2c]

Acceptance

buyer's manifestation of a willingness to become the owner of the goods

Acceptance of goods means a willingness by the buyer to become the owner of the goods tendered or delivered to her by the seller. Acceptance of the goods, which precludes any later rejection of them, includes overt acts or conduct that manifest such willingness. (Article 2A.) Such acts or conduct may include express words, the presumed intention of the buyer through her failure to act, or conduct of the buyer inconsistent with the seller's ownership of the goods. More specifically, acceptance occurs when the buyer, after a reasonable opportunity to inspect the goods (1) signifies to the seller that the goods conform to the contract, (2) signifies to the seller that she will take the goods or retain them in spite of their nonconformity to the contract, or (3) fails to make an effective rejection of the goods. (Article 2A.)

Acceptance of any part of a commercial unit is acceptance of the entire unit. (Article 2A.) The buyer must pay at the contract rate for any goods she accepts but may recover damages for any nonconformity of the goods, provided the buyer reasonably notifies the seller of any breach. (Article 2A, except for finance leases in some situations.) For example, Nancy agrees to deliver to Paul five hundred light bulbs, one hundred watts each, for $300 and one thousand light bulbs, sixty watts each, for $500. Nancy delivers on time, but the shipment contains only four hundred of the hundred-watt bulbs and seven hundred fifty of the sixty-watt bulbs. If Paul accepts the shipment, he must pay Nancy $240 for the hundred-watt bulbs accepted and $375 for the sixty-watt bulbs accepted, less the amount of damages Nancy's nonconforming delivery caused him.

Revocation of Acceptance [20-2d]

Revocation of acceptance

rescission of buyer's acceptance of the goods if nonconformity of the goods substantially impairs their value, provided that the acceptance was (1) premised on the assumption that the nonconformity would be cured by the seller and it was not or (2) the nonconformity was an undiscovered hidden defect

A buyer might accept defective goods either because it is difficult to discover the defect by inspection or because the buyer reasonably assumes that the seller will correct the defect. In either instance, the buyer may revoke his acceptance of the goods if the uncorrected defect substantially impairs the value of the goods to him. **Revocation of acceptance** gives the buyer the same rights and duties with respect to the goods as he would have acquired by rejecting them. (Article 2A.)

More specifically, the buyer may revoke acceptance of goods that do not conform to the contract if the nonconformity *substantially* impairs the value of the goods to him, provided that his acceptance was (1) premised on the reasonable assumption that the seller would cure the nonconformity, and it was not seasonably cured or (2) made without discovery of the nonconformity, and such acceptance was reasonably induced by the difficulty of discovery before acceptance or by the seller's assurances. (Article 2A.)

Revocation of acceptance is not effective until notification is given to the seller. This must be done within a reasonable time after the buyer discovers or should have discovered the grounds for revocation and before the goods have undergone any substantial change not caused by their own defects. (Article 2A.)

Practical Advice

If you have cause to revoke your acceptance of goods, be sure to notify the seller within a reasonable time after discovering the grounds for revocation.

Waddell v. L.V.R.V. Inc.
Supreme Court of Nevada, 2006
125 P.3d 1160
http://scholar.google.com/scholar_case?q=125+P.3D+1160+&hl=en&as_sdt=2,34&case=13475809545477317507&scilh=0

FACTS L.V.R.V. Inc., doing business as Wheeler's Las Vegas RV (Wheeler's) sold a 1996 Coachmen Santara motor home (RV) to Arthur R. Waddell and Roswitha M. Waddell. Before they took possession of the RV, the Waddells requested that Wheeler's perform various repairs, including service on the RV's engine cooling system, new batteries, and alignment of the door frames. Wheeler's told Arthur Waddell that the repairs had been performed, and the Waddells took delivery of the RV on September 1, 1997.

The Waddells first noticed a problem with the RV's engine shortly after they took possession. They drove the RV from Las Vegas to Hemet, California. On the return trip, while climbing a moderate grade, the RV's engine overheated so much that Mr. Waddell had to pull over to the side of the road and wait for the engine to cool down. When the Waddells returned from California, they took the RV back to Wheeler's for repairs. Despite Wheeler's attempts to repair the RV, the Waddells continually experienced further episodes of engine overheating. Between September 1997 and March 1999, Wheeler's service department spent a total of seven months attempting to repair the RV.

On June 9, 2000, the Waddells filed a complaint in district court seeking both equitable relief and money damages. The district court concluded that the RV's nonconformities substantially impaired its value to the Waddells and allowed the Waddells to revoke their acceptance of the RV.

DECISION Affirmed in relevant part.

OPINION The Code provides that a buyer may revoke his acceptance if the item suffers from a nonconformity that substantially impairs its value *to the buyer* and (1) the buyer accepted the goods on the understanding that the seller would cure the nonconformity or (2) the buyer was unaware of the nonconformity and the nonconformity was concealed by the difficulty of discovery or by the seller's assurances that the good was conforming.

To determine whether a nonconformity substantially impairs the value of the goods to the buyer a two-part test is applied. The test has both an objective and a subjective prong. The value of conforming goods *to the plaintiff* must first be determined. This is a subjective question because it calls for a consideration of the needs and circumstances of the plaintiff who seeks to revoke, not the needs and circumstances of an average buyer. The second inquiry is whether the nonconformity in fact substantially impairs the value of the goods to the buyer, having in mind his particular needs. This is an objective question in that it requires evidence from which it can be inferred that plaintiff's needs were not met because of the nonconformity.

Mr. Waddell's testimony demonstrates that the RV's *subjective* value to the Waddells was based on their ability to spend two or three years driving the RV around the country. Mr. Waddell also testified that as a result of the RV's defects, he and his wife were unable to enjoy the RV as they had intended. Mr. Waddell further testified that the RV's engine would overheat within ten miles of embarking if the travel included any climbing. Consequently, the RV spent a total of 213 days, or seven months and one day, at Wheeler's service department during the eighteen months immediately following the purchase. This testimony is sufficient to demonstrate an *objective*, substantial impairment of value. Accordingly, substantial evidence exists to support revocation of acceptance under the Code.

The Waddells gave Wheeler's several opportunities to repair the defects before revoking their acceptance. Because Wheeler's was unable to repair the defects after a total of seven months, the Waddells were entitled to say, "that's all" and revoke their acceptance, despite Wheeler's good-faith attempts to repair the RV.

INTERPRETATION A buyer may revoke his acceptance if the goods suffer from a nonconformity that substantially impairs their value to him subject to the seller's right to cure the nonconformity; however, the seller's attempts to cure do not count against the buyer regarding timely revocation.

CRITICAL THINKING Do you agree with the requirements for revocation of acceptance? Explain.

Obligation of payment
in the absence of an agreement, payment is due at the time and place the buyer is to receive the goods

Practical Advice

Specify in your sales contract the time and other terms of payment.

Obligation of Payment [20-2e]

The terms of the contract may expressly state the time and place at which the buyer is obligated to pay for the goods. If so, these terms are controlling. Thus, if the buyer has agreed to pay either the seller or a carrier for the goods in advance of delivery, his duty to pay is not conditional on performance or a tender of performance by the seller. Furthermore, when the sale is on credit, the buyer is not obligated to pay for the goods when he receives them. The credit provision in the contract will control the time of payment.

In the absence of agreement, payment is due at the time and place the buyer is to receive the goods, even though the place of shipment is the place of delivery. This rule is understandable in view of the right of the buyer, in the absence of agreement to the contrary, to inspect the goods before being obliged to pay for them. Tender of payment is sufficient when made by any means or in any manner current, such as a check, in the ordinary course of business, unless the seller demands cash and allows the buyer a reasonable time within which to obtain it.

For a summary of performance by the buyer, see Figure 20-2.

CISG

Unless the buyer is bound to pay the price at any other specific time, he must pay it when the seller places either the goods or documents controlling their disposition at the buyer's disposal in accordance with the contract and the CISG. The seller may make such payment a condition for handing over the goods or documents. If the buyer is not bound to pay the price at any other particular place, he must pay it to the seller (1) at the seller's place of business or (2) if the payment is to be made against the handing over of the goods or of documents, at the place where the handing over takes place.

OBLIGATIONS OF BOTH PARTIES [20-3]

Contracts for the sale of goods necessarily involve risks concerning future events that may or may not occur. Though in some instances the parties explicitly allocate these risks, in most instances they do not. The Code contains three sections that allocate these risks when the parties fail to do so. Each provision, when applicable, relieves the parties from the obligation of full performance under the sales contract. (See also the Ethical Dilemma at the end of this chapter.)

Related to the subject of whether the Code will excuse performance is the question of whether both parties will be able and willing to perform. In such instances, the Code allows the insecure party to seek reasonable assurance of the potentially defaulting party's willingness and ability to perform. In addition, if one of the parties clearly indicates an unwillingness or inability to perform, the Code protects the other party.

Casualty to identified goods
if the contract is for goods that were identified when the contract was made and those goods are *totally* lost or damaged without fault of either party and before the risk of loss has passed to the buyer, the contract is avoided

Casualty to Identified Goods [20-3a]

If goods are destroyed before an offer to sell or to buy them is accepted, the offer is terminated by general contract law. But what if the goods are destroyed after the sales contract is formed?

Figure 20-2 Performance by the Buyer

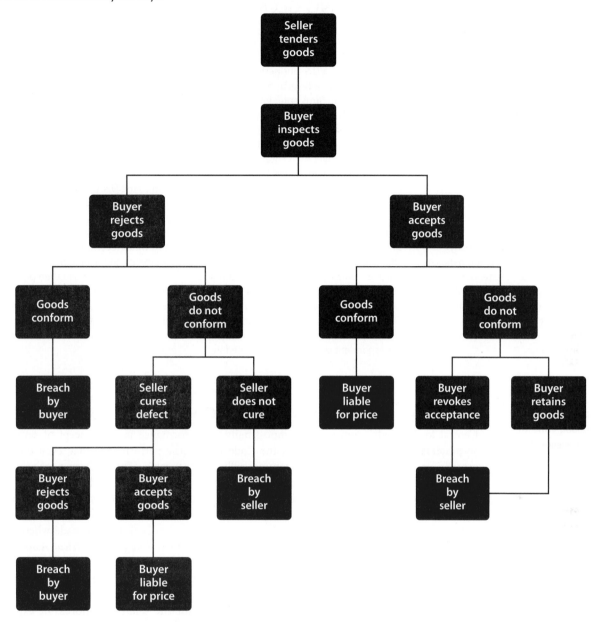

Identified goods

goods designated as a part
of a particular contract

Practical Advice

Specify in your contract
which events will excuse the
nonperformance of the
contract, the basic
assumptions of your
contract, and which risks
are assumed by each of the
parties.

The rules for the passage of risk of loss, as discussed in Chapter 21, apply with one exception: the contract is for goods that are **identified** when the contract was made and the goods suffer damage without fault of either party *before* the risk of loss passes to the buyer. The outcome of this situation depends upon the degree of damage. (1) If these goods are totally lost or damaged, the contract is avoided. (Article 2A.) This means that each party is excused from his obligation to perform under the contract: the seller is no longer obligated to deliver, and the buyer need not pay the price. (2) In the case of a partial destruction or deterioration of the goods, the buyer has the option to avoid the contract or to accept the goods with due allowance or deduction from the contract price sufficient to account for the deterioration or deficiency in quantity. (Article 2A, except in a finance lease that is not a consumer lease.)

On the other hand, if the destruction or damage to the goods, whether total or partial, occurs *after* risk of loss has passed to the buyer, then the buyer has no option but must pay the entire contract price of the goods.

GOING GLOBAL

What about letters of credit?

International trade involves a number of risks not generally encountered in domestic trade, most notably government controls over the export or import of goods and currency. The most effective means of managing these risks—as well as the ordinary trade risks of nonperformance by seller and buyer—is the irrevocable documentary letter of credit. Most international letters of credit are governed by the Uniform Customs and Practices for Documentary Credits, a document drafted by commercial law experts from many countries and adopted by the International Chamber of Commerce. A letter of credit is a promise by a buyer's bank to pay the seller, provided certain conditions are met. The letter of credit transaction involves three or four different parties and three underlying contracts.

To illustrate: a U.S. business wishes to sell computers to a Belgian company. The U.S. and Belgian firms enter into a sales agreement that includes details such as the number of computers, the features they will have, and the date they will be shipped. The buyer then enters into a second contract with a local bank, called an issuer, committing the bank to pay the agreed price upon receiving specified documents. These documents normally include a bill of lading (proving that the seller has delivered the goods for shipment), a commercial invoice listing the purchase terms, proof of insurance, and a customs certificate indicating that customs officials have cleared the goods for export. The buyer's bank's commitment to pay is the irrevocable letter of credit. Typically, a correspondent or paying bank located in

the seller's country makes payment to the seller. Here, the Belgian issuing bank arranges to pay the U.S. correspondent bank the agreed sum of money in exchange for the documents. The issuer then sends the U.S. computer firm the letter of credit. When the U.S. firm obtains all the necessary documents, it presents them to the U.S. correspondent bank, which verifies the documents, pays the computer company in U.S. dollars, and sends the documents to the Belgian issuing bank. Upon receiving the required documents, the issuing bank pays the correspondent bank and then presents the documents to the buyer. In our example, the Belgian buyer pays the issuing bank in Belgian francs for the letter of credit when the buyer receives the specified documents from the bank.

Nonhappening of presupposed condition
the seller is excused from the duty of performance on the nonoccurrence of presupposed conditions that were a basic assumption of the contract, unless the seller has expressly assumed the risk

Commercial impracticability
performance is impracticable as a result of an unforeseen supervening event

Nonhappening of Presupposed Condition [20-3b]

Central to the Code's approach to impossibility of performance is the concept of **commercial impracticability**. Under this concept, the Code will excuse performance that, even though not actually or literally impossible, is commercially impracticable. This, however, requires more than mere hardship or increased cost of performance. For a party to be discharged, performance must be rendered impracticable as a result of an unforeseen supervening event not within the contemplation of the parties at the time of contracting. Moreover, the nonoccurrence of the event must have been a "basic assumption" that both parties made when entering into the contract. (Article 2A.) See *Northern Corporation v. Chugach Electrical Association* in Chapter 17.

Increased production cost alone does not excuse performance by the seller, nor does a collapse of the market for the goods excuse the buyer. But a party to a contract for the sale of programs for a scheduled Super Bowl that is called off, for the sale of tin horns for export that become subject to embargo, or for the production of goods at a designated factory that becomes damaged or destroyed by fire would be excused.

Although the nonhappening of presupposed conditions may relieve the seller of her contractual duty, if the contingency affects only a part of the seller's capacity to perform, the seller must, to the extent of her remaining capacity, allocate delivery and production in a fair and reasonable manner among her customers. (Article 2A.)

CISG   *A party is not liable for a failure to perform any of his obligations if he proves that the failure was due to an impediment beyond his control and that he could not reasonably be expected to have taken the impediment into account at the time of the conclusion of the contract or to have avoided or overcome it or its consequences.*

Substituted Performance [20-3c]

Substituted performance when neither party is at fault and the agreed manner of delivery of goods becomes commercially impracticable, a substituted manner of performance must be tendered and accepted

The Code provides that when neither party is at fault and the agreed-upon manner of delivering the goods becomes commercially impracticable—because of the failure of loading or unloading facilities or the unavailability of an agreed-upon type of carrier, for example—a substituted manner of performance, if commercially reasonable, must be tendered and accepted. (Article 2A.) When a practical alternative or substitute exists, the Code excuses neither seller nor buyer on the ground that delivery in the express manner provided in the contract is impossible.

Right to Adequate Assurance of Performance [20-3d]

Right to adequate assurance of performance when reasonable grounds for insecurity arise regarding either party's performance, the other party may demand written assurance and suspend his own performance until he receives that assurance

A contract of sale also requires that each party not impair the other party's expectation of having the contract performed. Therefore, when reasonable grounds for insecurity arise regarding either party's performance, the other party may demand written assurance and suspend his own performance until he receives that assurance. The failure to provide adequate assurance of performance within a reasonable time, not exceeding thirty days, constitutes a repudiation of the contract. (Article 2A.)

CISG *A party may suspend the performance of his obligations if, after the conclusion of the contract, it becomes apparent that the other party will not perform a substantial part of his obligations. A party suspending performance must immediately notify the other party of the suspension and must continue with performance if the other party provides adequate assurance of his performance.*

Right to Cooperation [20-3e]

Right to cooperation if one party's required cooperation is untimely, the other party is excused from any resulting delay in her own performance

When one party's cooperation is necessary to the agreed performance but is not timely forthcoming, the other party is excused with regard to any resulting delay in her own performance. The nonbreaching party either may proceed to perform in any reasonable manner or, if the time for her performance has occurred, may treat the other's failure to cooperate as a breach. In either event, the nonbreaching party has access to any other remedies the Code may provide, as discussed in Chapter 23.

Anticipatory Repudiation [20-3f]

Anticipatory repudiation if either party clearly indicates an unwillingness or inability to perform before the performance is due, the other party may await performance for a reasonable time or resort to any remedy for breach

Although a repudiation in itself is a clear indication by either party to a contract that he is unwilling or unable to perform his obligations under the contract, an **anticipatory repudiation** is a repudiation made *before* the time to perform occurs. It may occur by express communication or by the repudiating party's taking an action that makes performance impossible, such as selling unique goods to a third party. It also may result from the failure of a party to give timely assurance of performance after a justifiable demand. If an anticipatory repudiation substantially impairs the value of the contract, the aggrieved party may (1) await performance for a commercially reasonable time or (2) resort to any remedy for breach. In either case, he may suspend his own performance. (Article 2A.) The repudiating party may retract his anticipatory repudiation and thereby reinstate the contract unless the aggrieved party has canceled the contract, has materially changed her position, or has otherwise indicated that she considers the anticipatory repudiation final. (Article 2A.)

CISG *If prior to the date for performance of the contract it is clear that one of the parties will commit a fundamental breach of contract, the other party may declare the contract avoided.*

Hessler v. Crystal Lake Chrysler-Plymouth, Inc.
Appellate Court of Illinois, Second District, 2003
788 N.E.2d 405, 273 Ill.Dec. 96, 50 UCC Rep.Serv.2d 330
http://scholar.google.com/scholar_case?case=8385072036048572860&q=788+n.e.2d+405&hl=en&as_sclt=2,34

FACTS In February 1997, Chrysler Corporation introduced a new promotional vehicle called the Plymouth Prowler but did not reveal whether it would manufacture any of the vehicles. Donald Hessler (the plaintiff), aware of the vehicle and of its uncertain production, contacted several dealerships to inquire about purchasing a Prowler. On February 5, 1997, plaintiff met with Gary Rosenberg, co-owner of Crystal Lake Chrysler-Plymouth, Inc. (defendant) and signed a "Retail Order for a Motor Vehicle" (Agreement). The Agreement, which was filled out primarily by Rosenberg, stated that the order was for a 1997, V6, two-door, purple Plymouth Prowler and provided "Customer to pay $5,000 00/100 over list price by manufacturer. Money refundable if cannot [deliver] by 12/30/97. Dealer to keep car 2 weeks."

The order noted that plaintiff had deposited $5,000 for the car. The Agreement contained a box labeled "TO BE DELIVERED ON OR ABOUT." Inside the box was written "ASAP," which term Rosenberg stated is used in his business "in lieu of a stock number. Just line it up in order. As soon as you can get it done, do it." Rosenberg testified that Hessler was the first person to place an order for a Prowler and that Rosenberg was "pretty sure" that plaintiff's order was the first order on which he received a deposit. On May 11, 1997, Rosenberg and Hessler agreed that the information they had received was that the manufacturer's list price would be $39,000.

On May 23, 1997, Salvatore Palandri entered into a contract with defendant to purchase a 1997 Plymouth Prowler. His contract reflected a purchase price of "50,000 + tax + lic + doc" and a $10,000 deposit. It also stated that Palandri would receive the "first one delivered to [the] dealership."

Plaintiff testified that on August 11, 1997, Rosenberg informed plaintiff that no Prowlers would be delivered to the Midwest and that he would be returning plaintiff's check. Defendant, according to the plaintiff, nevertheless, stated that should defendant receive a vehicle, it would be plaintiff's. Defendant denies having stated this.

Plaintiff testified that he attended a Chrysler customer appreciation event at Great America on September 19 and spoke to a company representative about the Prowler. Two days later, the representative sent him a fax that contained a tentative list of dealers who were to receive Prowlers. Defendant's name was on the list. Plaintiff testified that he called Rosenberg on September 22 to notify him that his dealership was on a list of dealers due to receive Prowlers. Rosenberg informed plaintiff that he would not sell plaintiff a car because plaintiff had gone behind Rosenberg's back and that contacting Chrysler would cause Rosenberg problems. Rosenberg also stated that plaintiff was not the first person with whom he contracted to sell a Prowler. Plaintiff protested, and Rosenberg informed him that he would not sell plaintiff the car.

Beginning on September 23, 1997, plaintiff contacted thirty-eight Chrysler-Plymouth dealerships to inquire about purchasing a 1997 Prowler, but did not obtain one. On October 24, 1997, plaintiff attended a Prowler coming-out party at the Hard Rock Cafe and saw a purple Prowler in the parking lot with a sign in its window that had defendant's name written on it. On October 25, plaintiff went to defendant's showroom and saw a Prowler parked there. He found Rosenberg and informed him that he was there to pick up his car. Rosenberg stated that he was not going to sell plaintiff the car and that he did not want to do business with him. Later that day, plaintiff purchased a Prowler from another dealer for $77,706. On October 27, 1997, defendant sold the only Prowler it received in that year to Palandri for a total sale price of $54,859, including his $10,000 deposit.

On April 23, 1998, plaintiff sued defendant for breach of contract. The trial court entered judgment for plaintiff and awarded him $29,853 in damages. It concluded that defendant breached the Agreement and that plaintiff properly covered by purchasing a replacement vehicle for $29,853 more than the contract price. The trial court also concluded that defendant repudiated its contract in September and October of 1997 when Rosenberg told plaintiff that he would not sell him a car. It found plaintiff "ready, willing, and able to perform the contract." The court found that the price plaintiff paid for the car at another dealership was the best price he could receive for a Prowler after Rosenberg's refusal to sell to him a car.

DECISION The judgment of the trial court is affirmed.

OPINION Under the Uniform Commercial Code (UCC), certain actions by a party to a contract may constitute an anticipatory repudiation of the contract if the actions are sufficiently clear manifestations of intent not to perform under the contract.

Comment 1 to Section 2–610 provides:

Anticipatory repudiation centers upon an overt communication of intention or an action which renders performance impossible or demonstrates a clear determination not to continue with performance.... When such a repudiation substantially impairs the value of the contract, the aggrieved party may at any time resort to his remedies for breach....

The appellate court held that the trial court did not err in finding that defendant's actions reasonably indicated to plaintiff that defendant would not deliver to him a Prowler under the Agreement. The defendant contracted to deliver a Prowler to plaintiff as soon as possible. It was not against the manifest weight of the evidence for the trial court to find that defendant repudiated the Agreement when it repeatedly informed plaintiff that it would not deliver to him the first Prowler it received. Such actions made it sufficiently clear to plaintiff that defendant would not perform under the Agreement.

With respect to plaintiff's actions, Section 2-610(b) of the UCC provides that an aggrieved party may "resort to any remedy for breach" of the contract "even though he has notified the repudiating party that he would await the latter's performance." One such remedy is to cover by purchasing substitute goods from another seller.

INTERPRETATION If an anticipatory repudiation substantially impairs the value of the contract, the injured party may await performance for a commercially reasonable time or resort to any remedy for breach.

CRITICAL THINKING QUESTION At what point should a buyer have a reasonable basis for believing the seller had repudiated? Explain.

ETHICAL DILEMMA

Should a Buyer Refuse to Perform a Contract Because a Legal Product May Be Unsafe?

Facts Carson and Olson are partners in a landscape and gardening business that operates out of three major locations and employs approximately thirty people. The business provides general lawn care predominately for residential homes; its services include grass cutting, fertilizing, and trimming of shrubbery. Carson and Olson also provide landscape design services.

One year ago, Carson and Olson entered into a two-year contract with Chem-Care, which manufactures chemical-based fertilizers effective in weed control. Because the contract was for a long term and because Carson and Olson have been excellent Chem-Care customers for the past fifteen years, they obtained an extremely favorable price of $40,000 for a two-year supply of Chem-Care fertilizers.

Chem-Care fertilizers have been approved by the government and do not violate any standards currently in place. Nevertheless, due to publicity concerning health problems associated with certain chemical lawn treatments, the majority of Carson and Olson's customers now have decided that they no longer want chemical lawn treatments. Concerned by the health hazards associated with chemical fertilizers, the customers insist upon natural fertilizers.

Carson wants to cancel the contract with Chem-Care. But Olson feels a sense of loyalty to Chem-Care and wants to honor the contract by trying to find new customers who would be willing to use the Chem-Care products.

Social, Policy, and Ethical Considerations

1. Should Carson and Olson attempt to invalidate the contract? Compare the social value of enforcing promises made with the good faith intention of being legally bound against the value of protecting the public from health or environmental threats.

2. Is it premature to characterize Chem-Care products as a threat to health or the environment?

3. Should the law excuse the performance of contracts that involve products that are under investigation for posing health or environmental problems?

4. As a practical matter, what should Carson and Olson do? Given the question as to the safety of Chem-Care products, does Olson's suggestion of getting new customers for Chem-Care products make sense from an ethical or a business standpoint?

CHAPTER SUMMARY

Performance by the Seller

Tender of Delivery the seller makes available to the buyer goods conforming to the contract and so notifies the buyer

- Buyer is obligated to accept conforming goods
- Seller is entitled to receive payment of the contract price

Time of Tender tender must be made at a reasonable time and kept open for a reasonable period of time

Place of Tender if none is specified, place for delivery is the seller's place of business or, if he has no such place, his residence

- *Shipment Contracts* seller is required to tender delivery of the goods to a carrier for delivery to buyer; shipment terms include F.O.B. (free on board) place of shipment, F.A.S. (free alongside ship) port of shipment, C.I.F. (cost, insurance, and freight), and C. & F. (cost and freight).
- *Destination Contracts* seller is required to tender delivery of the goods at a named destination; destination terms include F.O.B. place of destination, ex-ship, and no arrival, no sale
- *Goods Held by Bailee* seller must either tender to the buyer a document of title or obtain an acknowledgment from the bailee

Perfect Tender Rule the seller's tender of performance must conform exactly to the contract, subject to the following qualifications:

- *Agreement Between the Parties* the parties may contractually limit the operation of the perfect tender rule
- *Cure by the Seller* when the time for performance under the contract has not expired or when the seller has shipped nonconforming goods in the belief that the nonconforming tender would be acceptable, a seller may cure or correct his nonconforming tender
- *Installment Contracts* when the contract calls for delivery of goods in separate lots, the buyer may reject a nonconforming installment if it substantially impairs the value of that installment and cannot be cured; but if nonconformity or default of one or more of the installments substantially impairs the value of the whole contract, the buyer can treat the breach as a breach of the whole contract

Performance by the Buyer

Inspection unless otherwise agreed, the buyer has a reasonable time in which to inspect the goods before payment or acceptance to determine whether they conform

Rejection buyer's manifestation of unwillingness to become the owner of the goods; must be made within a reasonable time after the goods have been tendered or delivered and gives the buyer the right to (1) reject all of the goods, (2) accept all of the goods, or (3) accept any commercial unit(s) and reject the rest

Acceptance buyer's express or implied manifestation of a willingness to become the owner of the goods

Revocation of Acceptance rescission of buyer's acceptance of the goods if nonconformity of the goods substantially impairs their value, provided that the acceptance was (1) premised on the assumption that the nonconformity would be cured by the seller and it was not, or (2) the nonconformity was an undiscovered hidden defect

Obligation of Payment in the absence of an agreement, payment is due at the time and place the buyer is to receive the goods

Obligations of Both Parties

Casualty to Identified Goods if the contract is for goods that were identified when the contract was made and those goods are *totally* lost or damaged without fault of either party and before the risk of loss has passed to the buyer, the contract is avoided

Nonhappening of Presupposed Condition the seller is excused from the duty of performance on the nonoccurrence of presupposed conditions that were a basic assumption of the contract, unless the seller has expressly assumed the risk

Substituted Performance when neither party is at fault and the agreed manner of delivery of goods becomes commercially impracticable, a substituted manner of performance must be tendered and accepted

Right to Adequate Assurance of Performance when reasonable grounds for insecurity arise regarding either party's performance, the other party may demand written assurance and suspend his own performance until he receives that assurance

Right to Cooperation if one party's required cooperation is untimely, the other party is excused from any resulting delay in her own performance

Anticipatory Repudiation if either party clearly indicates an unwillingness or inability to perform before the performance is due, the other party may await performance for a reasonable time or resort to any remedy for breach

QUESTIONS

1. Tammie contracted with Kristine to manufacture, sell, and deliver to Kristine and put in running order a certain machine. After Tammie set up the machine and put it in running order, Kristine found it unsatisfactory and notified Tammie that she rejected the machine. She continued to use it for three months but continually complained of its defective condition. At the end of the three months, she notified Tammie to come and get it. Has Kristine lost her right (a) to reject the machine? (b) to revoke acceptance of the machine?

2. Smith, having contracted to sell to Beyer thirty tons of described fertilizer, shipped to Beyer by carrier thirty tons of fertilizer that he stated conformed to the contract. Nothing was stated in the contract as to time of payment, but Smith demanded payment as a condition of handing over the fertilizer to Beyer. Beyer refused to pay unless he was given the opportunity to inspect the fertilizer. Who is correct? Explain.

3. Benny and Sheree entered into a contract for the sale of one hundred barrels of flour. No mention was made of any place of delivery. Thereafter, Sheree demanded that Benny deliver

the flour at her place of business, and Benny demanded that Sheree come and take the flour from his place of business. Neither party acceded to the demand of the other. Has either one a right of action against the other?

4. Johnson, a manufacturer of air-conditioning units, made a written contract with Maxwell to sell to Maxwell forty units at a price of $200 each and to deliver them at a certain apartment building owned by Maxwell for installation by Maxwell. On the arrival of Johnson's truck for delivery at the apartment building, Maxwell examined the units on the truck, counted only thirty units, and asked the driver if that was the total delivery. The driver replied that it was as far as he knew. Maxwell told the driver that she would not accept delivery of the units. The next day, Johnson telephoned Maxwell and inquired why delivery was refused. Maxwell stated that the units on the truck were not what she ordered, that she ordered forty units, that only thirty were tendered, and that she was going to buy air-conditioning units elsewhere. In an action by Johnson against Maxwell for breach of contract, Maxwell

defends on the ground that the tender of thirty units was improper, because the contract called for delivery of forty units. Is this a valid defense?

5. Edwin sells a sofa to Jack for $800. Edwin and Jack both know that the sofa is in Edwin's warehouse, located approximately ten miles from Jack's home. The contract does not specify the place of delivery, and Jack insists that the place of delivery is either his house or Edwin's store. Is Jack correct?

6. On November 4, Kim contracted to sell to Lynn five hundred sacks of flour at $4.00 each to be delivered to Lynn by December 12. On November 27, Kim shipped the flour. By December 5, when the shipment arrived, containing only 450 sacks, the market price of flour had fallen. Lynn refused to accept delivery or to pay. Kim shipped fifty more sacks of flour, which arrived December 10. Lynn refused delivery. Kim resold the five hundred sacks of flour for $3.00 per sack. What are Kim's rights against Lynn?

7. Farley and Trudy entered into a written contract whereby Farley agreed to sell and Trudy agreed to buy six thousand bushels of wheat at $10.33 per bushel, deliverable at the rate of one thousand bushels a month commencing June 1, the price for each installment being payable ten days after delivery thereof. Though Farley delivered and received payment for the June installment, he defaulted by failing to deliver the July and August installments. By August 15, the market price

of wheat had increased to $12.00 per bushel. Trudy thereupon entered into a contract with Albert to purchase five thousand bushels of wheat at $12.00 per bushel deliverable over the ensuing four months. In late September, the market price of wheat started to decline and by December 1 was $9.25 per bushel. Explain whether Trudy would succeed in a legal action against Farley for breach of contract.

8. Bain ordered from Marcum a carload of lumber, which he intended to use in the construction of small boats for the U.S. Navy, pursuant to contract. The order specified that the lumber was to be free from knots, wormholes, and defects. The lumber was shipped, and immediately on receipt Bain looked into the door of the fully loaded car, ascertained that there was a full carload of lumber, and acknowledged to Marcum that the carload had been received. On the same day, Bain moved the car to his private siding and sent to Marcum full payment in accordance with the terms of the order.

A day later, the car was moved to the work area and unloaded in the presence of the Navy inspector, who refused to allow three-fourths of it to be used because of excessive knots and wormholes in the lumber. Bain then informed Marcum that he was rejecting the order and requested refund of the payment and directions on disposition of the lumber. Marcum replied that because Bain had accepted the order and unloaded it, he was not entitled to return of the purchase price. Who is correct? Explain.

CASE PROBLEMS

9. The plaintiff, a seller of milk, had for ten years bid on contracts to supply milk to the defendant school district and had supplied milk to other school districts in the area. On June 15, the plaintiff contracted to supply the defendant's requirements of milk for the next school year, at a price of $0.0759 per half-pint. The price of raw milk delivered from the farm had for years been controlled by the U.S. Department of Agriculture. On June 15, the department's administrator for the New York/New Jersey area had mandated a price for raw milk of $8.03 per hundredweight. By December, the mandated price had been raised to $9.31 per hundredweight, an increase of nearly 20 percent. If required to complete deliveries at the contract price, the plaintiff would lose $7,350.55 on its contract with the defendant and would face similar losses on contracts with two other school districts. Is the plaintiff correct in its assertion (a) that its performance had become impracticable through unforeseen events and (b) that it is entitled to relief from performance?

10. In April, F. W. Lang Company (Lang) purchased an ice cream freezer and refrigeration compressor unit from Fleet for $2,160. Although the parties agreed to a written installment contract providing for an $850 down payment and eighteen installment payments, Lang made only one $200 payment upon receipt of the goods. One year later, Lang moved to a new location and took the equipment along without notifying Fleet. Then, in May or June of the following year, Lang disconnected

the compressor from the freezer and used it to operate an air conditioner. Lang continued to use the compressor for that purpose until the sheriff seized the equipment and returned it to Fleet pursuant to a court order. Fleet then sold the equipment for $500 in what both parties conceded was a fair sale. Lang then brought an action charging that the equipment was defective and unusable for its intended purpose and sought to recover the down payment and expenses incurred in repairing the equipment. Fleet counterclaimed for the balance due under the installment contract less the proceeds from the sale. Who will prevail? Why?

11. Deborah McCullough bought a new car from Bill Swad Chrysler, Inc. The car was protected by both a limited warranty and an extended warranty. McCullough immediately encountered problems with the automobile's brakes, transmission, and air-conditioning and discovered a number of cosmetic defects as well. She returned the car to Swad for repairs, but Swad did not fix the brakes properly or perform any of the cosmetic work. Moreover, new problems appeared with respect to the car's steering mechanism. McCullough returned the car twice more for repairs, but on each occasion, old problems persisted and new ones emerged. After the engine abruptly shut off on a short trip away from home and the brakes again failed on a more extensive excursion, McCullough presented Swad with a list of thirty-two of the car's defects and demanded their correction. When Swad failed to remedy more than a few of the

problems, McCullough wrote a letter to Swad calling for rescission of the purchase agreement and a refund of the purchase price and offering to return the car upon receiving from Swad instructions regarding where to return it. Swad did not respond to the letter, and McCullough brought an action against Swad. She continued to operate the vehicle until the time of trial, some seventeen and one-half months (and twenty-three thousand miles) later. Can McCullough rescind the agreement?

12. On March 17, Peckham bought a new car from Larsen Chevrolet for $16,400. During the first one and one-half months after the purchase, Peckham discovered that the car's hood was dented, its gas tank contained no baffles, its emergency brake was inoperable, the car did not have a jack or a spare tire, and neither the clock nor the speedometer worked. Larsen claimed that Peckham knew of the defects at the time of the purchase. Peckham, on the other hand, claimed that he did not know the extent of the defects and that despite his repeated efforts the defects were not repaired until June 11. Then, on July 15, the car's dashboard caught fire, leaving the car's interior damaged and the car itself inoperable. Peckham then returned to Larsen Chevrolet and told Larsen that Larsen had to repair the car at its own expense or that he, Peckham, would either rescind the contract or demand a new automobile. Peckham also claimed that at the end of their conversation, he notified Larsen Chevrolet that he was electing to rescind the contract and demanded the return of the purchase price. Larsen denied having received that oral notification. On October 12, Peckham sent a written notice of revocation of acceptance to Larsen. What are the rights of the parties?

13. Joc Oil bought a cargo of fuel oil for resale. The certificate from the foreign refinery stated the sulfur content of the oil was 0.5 percent. Joc Oil entered into a written contract with Con Ed for the sale of this oil. The contract specified a sulfur content of 0.5 percent. Joc Oil knew, however, that Con Ed was authorized to buy and burn oil of up to 1 percent sulfur content and that Con Ed often bought and mixed oils of varying contents to stay within this limit. The oil under contract was delivered to Con Ed, but independent testing revealed a sulfur content of 0.92 percent. Con Ed promptly rejected the nonconforming shipment. Joc Oil immediately offered to substitute a conforming shipment of oil, although the time for performance had expired after the first shipment of oil. Con Ed refused to accept the substituted shipment. Joc Oil sues Con Ed for breach of contract. Judgment?

14. The plaintiff, a German wine producer and exporter, contracted to ship 620 cases of wine to the defendant, a distributor in North Carolina. The contract was silent as to the shipment destination. During the next several months, the defendant called repeatedly to find out the status of the shipment. Later, without notifying the defendant, the plaintiff delivered the wine to a shipping line in Rotterdam, destined for Wilmington, North Carolina. The ship and the wine were lost at sea en route to Wilmington. When the defendant refused to pay on the contract, the plaintiff sued. Decision?

15. Can-Key Industries, Inc., manufactured a turkey-hatching unit, which it sold to Industrial Leasing Corporation (ILC), which leased it to Rose-A-Linda Turkey Farms. ILC conditioned its obligation to pay on Rose-A-Linda's acceptance of the equipment. Rose-A-Linda twice notified Can-Key that the equipment was unacceptable and asked that it be removed. Over a period of fifteen months Can-Key made several unsuccessful attempts to solve the problems with the equipment. During this time, Can-Key did not instruct Rose-A-Linda to refrain from using the equipment. Rose-A-Linda indicated its dissatisfaction with the equipment, and ILC refused to perform its obligations under the contract. Can-Key then brought suit against ILC for breach of contract. It argued that Rose-A-Linda accepted the equipment, because it used it for fifteen months. ILC countered that the equipment was unacceptable and asked that it be removed. It claimed that Can-Key refused and failed to instruct Rose-A-Linda to refrain from using the equipment. Therefore, ILC argued, Rose-A-Linda effectively rejected the turkey-hatching unit, relieving ILC of its contractual obligations. Who is correct? Explain.

16. Frederick Manufacturing Corporation ordered 500 dozen units of Import Traders' rubber pads for $2,580. The order indicated that the pads should be "as soft as possible." Import Traders delivered the rubber pads to Frederick Manufacturing on November 19. Frederick failed to inspect the goods upon delivery, even though the parties recognized that there might be a problem with the softness. Frederick finally complained about the nonconformity of the pads in April of the following year, when Import Traders requested the contract price for the goods. Can Import Traders recover the contract price from Frederick?

17. Neptune Research & Development, Inc. (the buyer), manufacturer of solar-operated valves used in scientific instruments, saw advertised in a trade journal a hole-drilling machine with a very high degree of accuracy, manufactured and sold by Teknics Industrial Systems, Inc. (the seller). Because the machine's specifications met the buyer's needs, the buyer contacted the seller in late March and ordered one of the machines to be delivered in mid-June. There was no "time-is-of-the-essence" clause in the contract.

Although the buyer made several calls to the seller throughout the month of June, the seller never delivered the machine and never gave the buyer any reasons for the nondelivery. By late August, the buyer desperately needed the machine. The buyer went to the seller's place of business to examine the machine and discovered that the still-unbuilt machine had been redesigned, omitting a particular feature that the buyer had wanted. Nonetheless, the buyer agreed to take the machine, and the seller promised that it would be ready on September 5. The seller also agreed to call the buyer on September 3 to give the buyer two days to arrange for transportation of the machine.

The seller failed to telephone the buyer on September 3 as agreed. On September 4 the buyer called the seller to find out the status of the machine and was told by the seller that "under no circumstances" could the seller have the machine ready by September 5. At this point, the buyer notified the seller that the order was canceled. One hour later, still on September 4, the seller called the buyer, retracted its earlier statement, and indicated that the machine would be ready by the agreed September 5 date. The buyer sued for the return of its $3,000 deposit. Should the buyer prevail? Explain.

18. ALPAC and Eagon are corporations that import and export raw logs. In April, Setsuo Kimura, ALPAC's president, and C. K. Ahn, Eagon's vice president, entered into a contract for ALPAC to ship about fifteen thousand cubic meters of logs between the end of July and the end of August. Eagon agreed to purchase them. Subsequently, the market for logs began to soften, making the contract less attractive to Eagon. ALPAC became concerned that Eagon would try to cancel the contract. Kimura and Ahn began a series of meetings and letters, apparently to assure ALPAC that Eagon would purchase the logs.

Eagon was troubled by the drop in timber prices and initially withheld approval of the shipment. Ahn sent numerous internal memoranda to the home office indicating that it might not wish to complete the deal, but that accepting the logs was "inevitable" under the contract.

On August 23, Eagon received a fax from ALPAC suggesting a reduction in price and volume of the contract, but Eagon did not respond. Soon after, Kimura asked Ahn whether he intended to accept the logs; Ahn admitted that he was having trouble getting approval. On August 30, Ahn informed the home office that he would attempt to avoid accepting the logs but that it would be difficult and suggested holding ALPAC responsible for shipment delay. Kimura thereafter believed that Eagon would not accept the shipment and eventually canceled the vessel reserved to ship the logs, believing that Eagon was canceling the contract. The logs were not loaded or shipped by August 31, but Ahn and Kimura continued to discuss the contract. On September 7, Ahn told Kimura that he would try to convince the firm to accept the delivery and indicated that he did not want Kimura to sell the logs to another buyer. The same day, Ahn informed Eagon that it should consider accepting the shipment in September or October.

By September 27, ALPAC had not shipped the logs and sent a final letter to Eagon stating that because it failed to take delivery of the logs, it had breached the contract. Eagon responded to the letter, stating that there was "no contract" because ALPAC's breach (not shipping by the deadline) excused Eagon's performance. Explain whether either party breached the agreement.

TAKING SIDES

On February 26, 2014, William Stem purchased a used BMW from Gary Braden for $26,600. Stem's primary purpose for buying the car was to use it to drive his child to school and various activities. Braden indicated to Stem that the car had not been wrecked and that it was in good condition. Stem thought the car had been driven only seventy thousand miles. Less than a week after the purchase, Stem discovered a disconnected plug that, when plugged in, caused the oil warning light to turn on. When Stem then took his car to a mechanic, the mechanic discovered that the front end was that of a 2005 BMW and the rear end was that of a 2001 BMW. Further investigation revealed that the front half had been driven one hundred and seventy thousand miles. On March 10, 2014, Stem sent a letter informing Braden that he refused the automobile and that he intended to rescind the sale. Braden refused. Stem then drove the automobile for seven months and nearly nine thousand miles before filing an action against Braden, seeking to revoke his acceptance and to obtain the return of the purchase price.

a. What arguments would support Stem's revocation of his acceptance and the return of the purchase price?
b. What arguments would support Braden's denial of Stem's claim?
c. Who should prevail? Explain.

Transfer of Title and Risk of Loss

CHAPTER 21

Aliud est possidere, aliud esse in possessione. (It is one thing to possess; it is another to be in possession.)

Legal Maxim

CHAPTER OUTCOMES

After reading and studying this chapter, you should be able to:

1. Explain the relative importance of title under the common law and Article 2.

2. Explain when the seller has a right or power to transfer title and when the transfer is void or voidable.

3. Distinguish between a shipment contract and a destination contract and explain when title and risk of loss pass under each.

4. Identify and explain the rules covering (a) risk of loss in the absence of a breach and (b) risk of loss when there is a breach.

5. Explain how bulk transfers concern creditors and how the Uniform Commercial Code attempts to regulate such transfers.

Historically, the principle of title governed nearly every aspect of the rights and duties of the buyer and seller arising from a sales contract. In an attempt to add greater precision and certainty to sales contracts, the Uniform Commercial Code (UCC or the Code) has abandoned the common law's reliance on title. Instead, the Code approaches each legal issue arising from a sales contract on its own merits and provides separate and specific rules to control various transactional situations. In this chapter, we will cover the Code's approach to the transfer of title and other property rights, the passage of risk of loss, and the transfer of goods sold in bulk.

TRANSFER OF TITLE [21-1]

As previously stated, a sale of goods is defined as the transfer of title from the seller to the buyer for a consideration known as the price. Transfer of title is, therefore, fundamental to a sale of goods. Title, however, cannot pass under a contract for sale until existing goods have been identified as those to which the contract refers. Future goods (goods that are not both existing and identified) cannot constitute a present sale. If the buyer rejects the goods, whether justifiably or not, title reverts to the seller.

In a lease, title does not pass. Instead, the lessee obtains the right to possess and use the goods for a period of time in return for consideration.

Identification [21-1a]

Identification is the designation of specific goods as goods to which the contract of sale refers. Identification may be made by either the seller or the buyer and may be made at any time and in any manner agreed upon by the parties. To illustrate, suppose Barringer contracts to purchase a particular Buick automobile from Stevenson's car lot.

Identification
designation of specific goods as goods to which the contract of sale refers

Fungible

the equivalent of any other unit

Security interest

interest in personal property or fixtures that ensures payment or performance of an obligation

Insurable interest

interest in property that may be insured against loss

Lien

a nonconsensual claim against property

Passage of title

title passes when the parties intend it to pass; when the parties do not specifically agree, the Code provides rules to determine when title passes

Physical movement of the goods

when delivery is to be made by moving the goods, title passes at the time and place that the seller completes his performance with reference to delivery

Shipment contract

seller is required to deliver the goods to a carrier for delivery to buyer

Destination contract

seller is required to tender delivery of the goods at a particular destination

Tender

seller offers conforming goods to buyer and gives buyer notice that the goods are available

Power to transfer title

the purchaser of goods obtains such title as his transferor either has or had the power to transfer; however, to encourage and make secure good faith acquisitions of goods, it is necessary to protect certain third parties under certain circumstances

Identification occurs as soon as the parties enter the contract. If, however, Barringer agreed to purchase a television set from Stevenson, who has his storeroom filled with such televisions, identification will not occur until either Barringer or Stevenson selects a particular television to fulfill the contract. (Article 2A is similar.)

If the goods are **fungible** (the equivalent of any other unit), identification of a share of undivided goods occurs when the contract is entered into. Thus, if Barringer agreed to purchase one thousand gallons of gasoline from Stevenson, who owns a five-thousand-gallon tank of gasoline, identification occurs as soon as the contract is formed.

Security Interest   The Code defines a **security interest** as an interest in personal property or fixtures that ensures payment or performance of an obligation. Any reservation by the seller of a title to goods *delivered* to the buyer is limited in effect to a reservation of a security interest. Security interests in goods are governed by Article 9 of the Code (discussed in Chapter 37).

Insurable Interest   For a contract or policy of insurance to be valid, the insured must have an **insurable interest** in the subject matter. At common law, only a person with title or a **lien** (a legal claim of a creditor on property) could insure his interest in specific goods. The Code extends an insurable interest to a buyer's interest in goods that have been identified as goods to which the contract refers. (Article 2A.) This *special property interest* of the buyer, which arises upon identification, enables her to purchase insurance protection on goods that she does not presently own but will own upon delivery by the seller. The seller also has an insurable interest in the goods, as long as he has title to them or any security interest in them. In a lease, the lessor retains an insurable interest in the goods until an option to buy, if included in the lease, has been exercised by the lessee.

Passage of Title [21-1b]

Title passes when the parties *intend* it to pass, provided the goods are in existence and have been identified. When the parties have no explicit agreement as to transfer of title, the Code provides rules that determine when title passes to the buyer.

Physical Movement of the Goods   When delivery is to be made by moving the goods, title passes at the time and place the seller completes his performance with reference to delivery of the goods. When and where delivery occurs depends on whether the contract is a shipment contract or a destination contract.

A **shipment contract** requires or authorizes the seller to send the goods to the buyer but does not require the seller to deliver them to a particular destination. Under a shipment contract, title passes to the buyer at the time and place the seller delivers the goods to the carrier for shipment to the buyer.

A **destination contract** requires the seller to deliver the goods to a particular destination. Under a destination contract, title passes to the buyer on tender of the goods at that destination. **Tender**, as discussed in Chapter 20, requires that the seller, at a reasonable time, (1) put and hold conforming goods at the buyer's disposition, (2) give notice to the buyer that the goods are available, and (3) keep the goods available for a reasonable period of time.

No Movement of the Goods   When delivery is to be made without moving the goods, unless otherwise agreed, title passes (1) on delivery of a document of title, when the contract calls for delivery of such document (documents of title are documents that evidence a right to receive specified goods; they are discussed more fully in Chapter 47); or (2) at the time and place of contracting, if the goods at that time have been identified by either the seller or the buyer as the goods to which the contract refers and no documents are to be delivered. When the goods are not identified at the time of contracting, title passes when the goods are identified.

Power to Transfer Title [21-1c]

It is important to understand under what circumstances a seller has the right or **power to transfer title** to a buyer. If the seller is the rightful owner of goods or is authorized to sell the goods for the rightful owner, the seller has the *right* to transfer title. But when a seller possesses goods that he neither owns nor has authority to sell, the sale is not rightful. In some situations, however, unauthorized sellers may have the *power* to transfer good title to certain buyers. This section pertains to such sales by a person in possession of goods that he neither owns nor has authority to sell.

The rule of property law protecting existing ownership of goods is the starting point for any discussion of a sale of goods by a nonowner. One of the law's most basic tenets, expressly stated in the Code, is that a purchaser of goods obtains such title as his transferor had or had power to transfer. (Article 2A.) Likewise, the purchaser of a limited interest in goods acquires rights only to the extent of the interest that he purchased. By the same token, no one can transfer what he does not have. A purported sale by a thief or finder or ordinary bailee of goods does not transfer title to the purchaser.

The principal reason underlying the policy of the law in protecting existing ownership of goods is that a person should not be required to retain possession at all times of all the goods that he owns to maintain ownership of them. One valuable incident of the ownership of goods is the freedom of the owner to make a bailment of his goods as desired; the mere possession of goods by a bailee does not authorize the bailee to sell them.

Another legal policy conflicts, however, with the policy protecting existing ownership of goods; this latter protection, the protection of the good faith purchaser, is based on the importance in trade and commerce of ensuring the security of good faith transactions in goods. To encourage and make secure good faith acquisitions of goods, bona fide (good faith) purchasers for value must be protected under certain circumstances. A **good faith purchaser** is defined as one who acts honestly, gives value, and takes the goods without notice or knowledge of any defect in the title of the transferor.

Void and Voidable Title to Goods

A **void title** is no title. A person claiming ownership of goods by an agreement that is void obtains no title to the goods. Thus, a thief or a finder of goods or a person who acquires goods from someone under physical duress or under guardianship has no title to them and can transfer none.

A **voidable title** is one acquired under circumstances that permit the former owner to rescind the transfer and revest herself with title, as in the case of mistake, common duress, undue influence, fraud in the inducement, misrepresentation, mistake, or sale by a person without contractual capacity (other than an individual under guardianship). In these situations, the buyer has acquired legal title to the goods, which may be divested by action of the seller. If, however, the buyer were to resell the goods to a good faith purchaser for value, before the seller has rescinded the transfer of title, the right of rescission in the seller is cut off, and the good faith purchaser acquires good title. The Code defines **good faith** as "honesty in fact in the conduct or transaction concerned"; for merchants, and all parties under Revised Article 1, good faith also requires the observance of reasonable commercial standards of fair dealing. The Code defines value to include a consideration sufficient to support a simple contract.

The distinction between a void and voidable title is, therefore, extremely important in determining the rights of good faith purchasers of goods. The good faith purchaser always believes that she is buying the goods from the owner or from one with authority to sell. Otherwise, she would not be acting in good faith. In each situation, the party selling the goods appears to be the owner, whether his title is valid, void, or voidable. Given a case involving two innocent persons—the true owner who has done nothing wrong and the good faith purchaser who has done nothing wrong—the law will not disturb the legal title but will rule in favor of the one who has it. Thus, when A transfers possession of goods to B under such circumstances that B acquires no title or a void title, and B thereafter sells the goods to C, a good faith purchaser for value, B has nothing to transfer to C except possession. In a lawsuit between A and C involving the right to the goods, A will win because she has the legal title. (See Figure 21-1 for a diagram of void title.) C's only recourse is against B for breach of warranty of title, which we will discuss in Chapter 22. If, however, B acquired a voidable title from A and resold the goods to C, in a suit between A and C over the goods, C would win. In this case, B had title, though voidable, which she transferred to the good faith purchaser. The title thus acquired by C will be protected. The voidable title in B is title until it has been avoided, and, after transfer to a good faith purchaser, it may not be avoided. (See Figure 21-2 for a diagram of voidable title.) A's only recourse is against B for restitution or damages.

Good faith purchaser
buyer who acts honestly, gives value, and takes the goods without notice or knowledge of any defect in the title of his transferor

Practical Advice

Be sure you give value and act honestly so as to obtain the protection the law grants a good faith purchaser.

Void title
no title can be transferred

Voidable title
the good faith purchaser acquires good title

Good faith
honesty in fact in the conduct or transaction concerned; in the case of a merchant, and all parties under Revised Article 1, it also includes the observance of reasonable commercial standards of fair dealing

Figure 21-1 Void Title

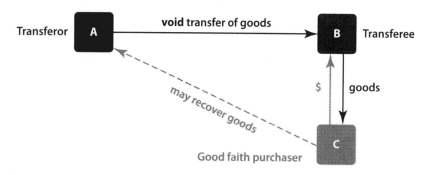

Figure 21-2 Voidable Title

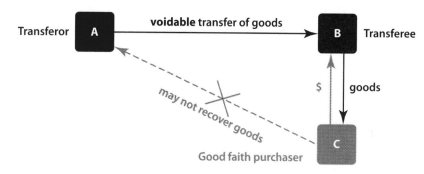

Robinson v. Durham
Alabama Court of Civil Appeals, 1988
537 So.2d 966
http://scholar.google.com/scholar_case?case=15758867258525788627&hl=en&as_sdt=2&as_vis=1&oi=scholarr

FACTS Mike Durham bought a used 1968 Chevrolet Camaro from Ronald and Wyman Robinson, owners of Friendly Discount Auto Sales. Unknown to either Durham or the Robinsons, the car had been stolen. In fact, when he first bought the car, Wyman Robinson had obtained tag receipts from what turned out to be the car thief and had subsequently registered the car in his name. Durham had received all prior documentation upon purchase of the car. However, the Federal Bureau of Investigation seized the car from Durham and returned it to the original owner. Durham sued the Robinsons, alleging, among other things, breach of the warranty of title. The jury awarded Durham $5,200, the amount he had paid for the car. The Robinsons appealed.

DECISION Judgment for Durham.

OPINION The Robinsons assert that since they were good faith purchasers for value when they bought the car for their business, they had good title and therefore passed good title to Durham. Alternatively, the Robinsons maintain that they had at least a voidable title and thus could pass good title to Durham, who was himself a good faith purchaser for value. Both arguments are without merit. It is clear that a thief gets only void title, and without more, cannot pass *any* title to a subsequent purchaser, not even to a good faith purchaser for value. Since the Robinsons obtained no title from the thief, they could not pass good title to Durham. This clearly constitutes a breach of warranty of title between the Robinsons and Durham.

INTERPRETATION A void title is no title.

ETHICAL QUESTION Did either of the parties act unethically? Explain.

CRITICAL THINKING QUESTION Who should bear the loss between the Robinsons and Durham? Explain.

The Code has enlarged the common law voidable title doctrine by providing that a good faith purchaser for value obtains valid title from one possessing voidable title even if that person obtained voidable title by (1) fraud as to her identity; (2) exchange for a subsequently dishonored check; (3) an agreement that the transaction was to be a cash sale, and the sales price has not been paid; or (4) criminal fraud punishable as larceny. (Article 2A is similar.)

Practical Advice

A buyer should obtain a written express warranty that the seller has ownership of the property or the authority to transfer ownership.

Entrusting of goods to a merchant

buyers in the ordinary course of business acquire good title when buying from merchants

Buyer in ordinary course of business

person who buys in ordinary course of business, in good faith, and without knowledge that the sale to him is in violation of anyone's ownership rights

Entrusting

transfer of possession of goods

Practical Advice

Properly mark and identify goods you entrust to a merchant who is in the business of selling used goods of that type.

In addition, the Code has expanded the rights of good faith purchasers with respect to sales by *minors*. Although the common law permitted a minor seller of goods to disaffirm the sale and to recover the goods from a third person who had purchased them in good faith from the party who had acquired the goods from the minor, the Code changed this rule by no longer permitting a minor seller to prevail over a good faith purchaser for value.

Entrusting of Goods to a Merchant Frequently, an owner of goods entrusts (transfers possession of) goods to a bailee for resale, repair, or some other use. In some instances, the bailee violates this entrusting by selling the goods to a third party without the owner's permission or by keeping the proceeds of such a sale. Although the "true" owner has a right of recourse against the bailee for the value of the goods, what right, if any, should the true owner of the goods have against the third party? Once again, the law must balance the right of ownership against the rights of market transactions.

The Code protects buyers of goods in the ordinary course of business from merchants who deal in goods of that kind, when the owner has entrusted possession of the goods to the merchant. The Code defines a **buyer in the ordinary course of business** as a person who in good faith and without knowledge that the sale to him is in violation of the ownership rights or security interest of another buys the goods in the ordinary course of business from a person, other than a pawnbroker, in the business of selling goods of that kind. Because the merchant who deals in goods of that kind is cloaked with the appearance of ownership or apparent authority to sell, the Code seeks to protect the innocent third-party purchaser. Any such **entrusting** of possession bestows on the merchant the power to transfer all rights of the entruster to a buyer in the ordinary course of business. (Article 2A is similar.) For example, A brings his stereo for repair to B, who also sells both new and used stereo equipment. C purchases A's stereo from B in good faith and in the ordinary course of business. The Code protects the rights of C and defeats the rights of A, whose only recourse is against B.

The Code, however, does not go so far as to protect the buyer in the ordinary course of business from a merchant to whom the goods have been entrusted by a thief, a finder, or a completely unauthorized person. It merely grants the buyer in the ordinary course of business the rights of the entruster.

When a buyer of goods to whom title has passed leaves the seller in possession of the goods, the buyer has "entrusted the goods" to the seller. If that seller is a merchant and resells and delivers the goods to another buyer in the ordinary course of business, this second buyer acquires good title to the goods. Thus, Dennis sells certain goods to Sylvia, who pays the price but allows possession to remain with Dennis. Dennis thereafter sells the same goods to Karen, a buyer in the ordinary course of business. Karen takes delivery of the goods. Sylvia does not have any rights against Karen or to the goods. Sylvia's only remedy is against Dennis.

Heinrich v. Titus-Will Sales, Inc.
Court of Appeals of Washington, 1994
73 Wash.App. 147, 868 P.2d 169
http://scholar.google.com/scholar_case?case=18393426036611380515&q=868+P.2d+169&hl=en&as_sdt=2,34

FACTS In 1989, Michael Heinrich retained James Wilson to purchase a new Ford pickup truck for him. Wilson had held himself out as a dealer/broker, but unbeknownst to Heinrich, Wilson had lost his vehicle dealer license. Wilson negotiated with Titus-Will Ford Sales, Inc. (Titus-Will) to purchase the truck for Heinrich. Titus-Will had dealt with Wilson as a dealer before but did not know that he had lost his license. All payments for the truck went through Wilson, and the purchase order indicated that the truck was being sold to Wilson as a dealer for resale. Wilson agreed to deliver the truck to Heinrich at Titus-Will on Saturday, October 21. Wilson delivered to a clerk at Titus-Will a postdated check for the balance of the purchase price, which the clerk accepted, and in return delivered to Wilson a packet containing the keys to the truck, the owner's manual, an odometer disclosure statement, and the warranty card. The odometer statement showed that Wilson was the transferor, and Titus-Will did not fill out the warranty card as the sale appeared to be dealer to dealer. Wilson's check, however, did not clear, and Titus-Will demanded the return of the truck. On November 6, Wilson picked up the truck from Heinrich, telling him he would have Titus-Will make certain repairs under the warranty, and returned the truck to Titus-Will. On November 9, Wilson admitted to Heinrich that he did not have funds to cover his check and that Titus-Will would not release the truck without payment. Heinrich then asked Titus-Will for the truck but was refused. Heinrich sued Titus-Will and Wilson, seeking return of the truck and damages for his loss of use. By pretrial arrangement, Heinrich regained possession of, but not clear title to, the truck. After a bench trial, the court awarded Heinrich title to the truck and $3,050 in damages for loss of its use. Titus-Will appeals.

DECISION Judgment affirmed.

OPINION Titus-Will argues that the trial court erroneously applied the entrustment doctrine of Uniform Commercial Code (UCC) Section 2-403. To prevail under this provision, Heinrich must show (1) Titus-Will "entrusted" the truck to Wilson and, thus, empowered Wilson subsequently to transfer all rights of Titus-Will in the truck to Heinrich; (2) Wilson was a merchant dealing in automobiles; and (3) Heinrich bought the truck from Wilson as a "buyer in the ordinary course of business."

Titus-Will did entrust the truck to Wilson, who was a merchant dealing in automobiles. The UCC does not require proper state licensing for merchant status. Wilson held himself out as a dealer in automobiles and appeared to be a dealer in automobiles. There is also substantial evidence that Heinrich was a "buyer in the ordinary course of business." A buyer in the ordinary course of business is a person who in good faith and without knowledge that the sale to him is in violation of the ownership rights or security interest of a third party in the goods buys in ordinary course from a person in the business of selling goods of that kind.

Good faith is "honesty in fact in the conduct or transaction concerned." There was no showing that Heinrich acted other than in good faith. He gave substantial value for the truck, more than Wilson agreed to pay Titus-Will. Nor did Heinrich know or have a basis to believe that Wilson's sale of the truck to him violated Titus-Will's ownership or security interest rights. Therefore, Wilson's illegal fraudulent activity does not taint Heinrich's status as a buyer.

Titus-Will not only entrusted Wilson with the truck but also with the signed odometer disclosure statement, the owner's manual, the warranty card, and the keys. By doing so, Titus-Will enabled Wilson to complete the sales transaction. In addition, the entrustment allowed Wilson to continue to deceive Heinrich from the date of delivery to the date when Wilson finally admitted the truth. Under these circumstances, application of the entrustment doctrine furthers the policy of protecting the buyer who relies on the merchant's apparent legal ability to sell goods in the merchant's possession.

INTERPRETATION A buyer in the ordinary course of business acquires good title when buying from a merchant seller who was entrusted with possession of the goods.

CRITICAL THINKING QUESTION Should Titus-Will be held responsible in this situation? Explain.

RISK OF LOSS [21-2]

Risk of loss

allocation of loss between seller and buyer where the goods have been damaged, destroyed, or lost

Risk of loss, as the term is used in the law of sales, addresses the allocation of loss between seller and buyer when the goods have been damaged, destroyed, or lost without the fault of either the seller or the buyer. If the loss is placed on the buyer, he is under a duty to pay the price for the goods even though they were damaged or never received. If placed on the seller, she has no right to recover the purchase price from the buyer, although she does have a right to the return of the damaged goods.

CISG   *According to the United Nations Convention on CISG, loss of or damage to the goods after the risk of loss has passed to the buyer does not discharge the buyer from his obligation to pay the purchase price.*

In determining who has the risk of loss, the Code provides definite rules for specific situations—a sharp departure from the common law concept, which essentially determined risk of loss according to who had ownership of the goods and which depended on whether title had been transferred. The Code's transactional approach is necessarily detailed and for this reason is probably more understandable and meaningful than the common law's reliance on the abstract concept of title. The Code has adopted rules for determining the risk of loss in the absence of breach separate from those that apply where a breach of the sales contract has occurred.

Except in a finance lease, risk of loss is retained by the lessor and does not pass to the lessee. In a finance lease, risk of loss passes to the lessee as discussed later.

Risk of Loss Where There Is a Breach [21-2a]

When one party breaches the contract, the Code places the risk of loss on that party, even though this allocation differs from the passage of risk of loss in the absence of a breach. Nevertheless, when the nonbreaching party is in control of the goods, the Code places the risk of loss on him to the extent of his insurance coverage.

Breach by the seller

if the seller ships to the buyer goods that do not conform to the contract, the risk of loss remains on the seller until the buyer has accepted the goods or until the seller has remedied the defect

Breach by the Seller

If the seller ships to the buyer goods that do not conform to the contract, the risk of loss remains on the seller until the buyer has accepted the goods or until the seller has remedied the defect. (Article 2A.)

When the buyer has accepted nonconforming goods but thereafter by timely notice to the seller rightfully revokes his acceptance (discussed in Chapter 20), he may treat the risk of loss as resting from the beginning on the seller, to the extent of any deficiency in the buyer's effective insurance coverage. (Article 2A.) For example, Stuart delivers to Bernard nonconforming goods, which Bernard accepts. Subsequently, Bernard discovers a hidden defect in the goods and rightfully revokes his prior acceptance. If the goods are destroyed through no fault of either party, and Bernard has insured the goods for 60 percent of their fair market value of $10,000, then the insurance company will cover $6,000 of the loss and Stuart will cover the remainder, or $4,000. Had the buyer's insurance coverage been $10,000, Stuart would not bear any of the loss.

Breach by the buyer

the seller may treat the risk of loss as resting on the buyer for a commercially reasonable time to the extent of any deficiency in the seller's effective insurance coverage

Breach by the Buyer

When conforming goods have been identified to a contract that the buyer repudiates or breaches before risk of loss has passed to him, the seller may treat the risk of loss as resting on the buyer "for a commercially reasonable time" to the extent of any deficiency in the seller's effective insurance coverage. (Article 2A.) For example, Susan agrees to sell forty thousand pounds of plastic resin to Bella, F.O.B. (free on board) Bella's factory, delivery by March 1. On February 1, Bella wrongfully repudiates the contract by telephoning Susan and telling her that she does not want the resin. Susan immediately seeks another buyer, but before she is able to locate one, and within a commercially reasonable time, the resin is destroyed by a fire through no fault of Susan's. The fair market value of the resin is $35,000. Because Susan's insurance covers only $15,000 of the loss, Bella is liable for $20,000.

Risk of Loss in Absence of a Breach [21-2b]

When there is no breach, the parties may allocate the risk of loss by agreement. Where there is no breach and the parties have not otherwise agreed, the Code places the risk of loss, for the most part, on the party who is more likely to have greater control over the goods, is more likely to insure the goods, or is better able to prevent the loss of the goods.

Agreement of the Parties

The parties, by agreement, not only may shift the allocation of risk of loss but also may divide the risk between them. Such agreement is controlling. Thus, for example, the parties may agree that a seller shall retain the risk of loss even though the buyer is in possession of the goods or has title to them. Furthermore, the agreement may provide that the buyer bears 60 percent of the risk and that the seller bears 40 percent.

Practical Advice

Specify in your contract of sale how risk of loss should be allocated.

Trial Sales

Some sales are made with the understanding that the buyer can return the goods even though they conform to the contract. These trial sales permit the buyer to try the goods for a period of time to determine if she wishes either to keep them or to try to resell them. The Code recognizes two types of trial sales—a sale on approval and a sale or return—and provides a test for distinguishing between them: unless otherwise agreed, if the goods are delivered primarily for the buyer's use, the transaction is a sale on approval; if they are delivered primarily for resale by the buyer, it is a sale or return.

In a **sale on approval**, possession of, but not title to, the goods is transferred to the buyer for a stated period of time. If no time is stated, the buyer may use the goods for a reasonable time to determine whether she wishes to accept them. Both title and risk of loss remain with the *seller* until the buyer "approves," or accepts, the goods. Until acceptance by the buyer, the sale is a bailment with an option to purchase.

Although use of the goods consistent with the purpose of approval by the buyer is not acceptance, the buyer's failure to notify the seller within a reasonable time of her election to return the goods *is* an acceptance. The buyer also may manifest approval by exercising any dominion or control over the goods inconsistent with the seller's ownership. On approval, title and risk of loss

Sale or return

sale for which buyer has option to return goods to seller

Consignment

delivery of possession of personal property to an agent for sale

Contracts involving carriers

in shipment contracts, the seller bears the risk of loss and expense until the goods are delivered to the carrier for shipment; in destination contracts, the seller bears the risk of loss and expense until tender of the goods at a particular destination

---

Practical Advice

Select the shipment term that passes the risk of loss when you desire it to pass.

---

pass to the buyer, who then becomes liable to the seller for the purchase price of the goods. If, however, the buyer then decides to return the goods and so notifies the seller, the return is at the seller's risk and expense.

In a **sale or return**, the goods are sold and delivered to the buyer with an option to return them to the seller. The risk of loss is on the *buyer*, who has title until she revests it in the seller by returning the goods. The return of the goods is at the buyer's risk and expense.

A **consignment** is a delivery of possession of personal property to an agent for sale by the agent. Under the Code, a sale on consignment is regarded as a sale or return. Therefore, the creditors of the consignee (the agent who receives the merchandise for sale) prevail over the consignor and may obtain possession of the consigned goods, provided the consignee maintains a place of business where he deals in goods of the kind involved under a name other than the name of the consignor. Nevertheless, the consignor will prevail if she (1) complies with applicable state law requiring a consignor's interest to be evidenced by a sign, (2) establishes that the consignee is generally known by his creditors to be substantially engaged in selling the goods of others, or (3) complies with the filing provisions of Article 9 (Secured Transactions).

Contracts Involving Carriers Sales contracts frequently contain terms indicating the agreement of the parties as to delivery by a carrier. These terms identify the contract as a shipment contract or as a destination contract and, by implication, indicate the time at which the risk of loss passes. If the contract does not require the seller to deliver the goods to a particular destination but merely to the common carrier (a shipment contract), risk of loss passes to the buyer when the seller delivers the goods to the carrier. If the seller is required to deliver them to a particular destination (a destination contract), risk of loss passes to the buyer at destination when the goods are tendered to the buyer. (Article 2A.)

CISG   *If the sales contract involves the carriage of the goods and the seller is not obligated to hand them over at a particular destination, the risk of loss passes to the buyer when the goods are handed over to the first carrier. If the contract requires the seller to deliver the goods to a carrier at a particular destination, the risk of loss passes when the goods are handed over to the carrier at that place.*

The following case deals with the question of when the risk of loss passes between parties whose sales contract contains no specific provision or any delivery term. The case demonstrates that if the contract is not clearly a destination contract or a shipment contract, the law assumes that it is a shipment contract.

Windows, Inc. v. Jordan Panel Systems Corp.
United States Court of Appeals, Second Circuit, 1999
177 F.3d 114
http://scholar.google.com/scholar_case?case=11386214941351710507&q=177+F.3d+114&hl=en&as_sdt=6,34

FACTS Jordan Panel Systems, Inc. ordered custom-made windows from Windows, Inc. The purchase contract provided that the windows were to be shipped properly packaged for motor freight transit and "delivered to New York City." Windows constructed the windows according to Jordan's specifications and arranged to have them shipped to Jordan by a common carrier, Consolidated Freightways Corp. Windows delivered them to Consolidated intact and properly packaged. During the course of shipment, however, the goods sustained extensive damage. Much of the glass was broken and many of the window frames were gouged and twisted. Jordan's president signed a delivery receipt noting that approximately two-thirds of the shipment was damaged due to "load shift." Jordan made a claim with Consolidated

for damages it had sustained and also ordered a new shipment from Windows, which was delivered without incident. Jordan did not pay for either shipment of windows, and Windows brought suit. Jordan cross-claimed for incidental and consequential damages resulting from the damaged shipment. The parties resolved the claim by Windows, and the only issue that remains is Jordan's counterclaim. The district court granted Windows' motion for summary judgment on this matter. Jordan brings this appeal.

DECISION Judgment affirmed in favor of Windows.

OPINION Jordan seeks to recover incidental and consequential damages pursuant to Uniform Commercial Code Section 2-715.

Under that provision, Jordan is entitled to recover incidental and consequential damages if those damages "result[ed] from the seller's breach." A destination contract is covered by Section 2-503(3); it arises where "the seller is required to deliver at a particular destination." In contrast, a shipment contract arises where "the seller is required … to send the goods to the buyer and the contract does not require him to deliver them at a particular destination." Section 2-504. Under a shipment contract, the seller must "put the goods in the possession of such a carrier and make such a contract for their transportation as may be reasonable having regard to the nature of the goods and other circumstances of the case." Section 2-504(a).

Unless the parties "expressly specify" that the contract requires the seller to deliver to a particular destination, the contract is generally considered to be a shipment contract.

Jordan's confirmation of its purchase order, by letter to Windows dated September 22, 1993, provided, "All windows to be shipped properly crated/packaged/boxed suitable for cross country motor freight transit and delivered to New York City." This is a shipment contract rather than a destination contract.

Thus, under the terms of its contract, Windows satisfied its obligations to Jordan when it put the goods, properly packaged, into the possession of the carrier for shipment. Upon Windows' proper delivery to the carrier, Jordan assumed the risk of loss and cannot recover incidental or consequential damages from the seller caused by the carrier's negligence.

INTERPRETATION Unless specifically designated as a destination contract, a sales contract that involves shipment by a carrier is a shipment contract.

ETHICAL QUESTION Did the court fairly decide this case? Explain.

CRITICAL THINKING QUESTION What factors should be taken into consideration in deciding whether a contract is a shipment or a destination contract? Explain.

Goods in Possession of Bailee In some sales, the goods, at the time the contract is made, are held by a bailee and are to be delivered without being moved. For instance, a seller may contract with a buyer to sell grain that is located in a grain elevator and that the buyer intends to leave in the same elevator. In such situations, the time at which the risk of loss passes to the buyer depends on the document of title involved—or, as the case may be, on whether the transaction involves such a document at all: (1) if a negotiable document of title (discussed in Chapter 48) is involved, the risk of loss passes when the buyer *receives* the document; (2) if a nonnegotiable document of title is involved, the risk passes when the document is *tendered* to the buyer; and (3) if no documents of title are employed, it passes either (a) when the seller *tenders* to the buyer written directions to the bailee to deliver the goods to the buyer or (b) when the bailee acknowledges the buyer's right to possession of the goods. (Article 2A.)

In situations 2 and 3a, if the buyer seasonably objects, the risk of loss remains upon the seller until the buyer has had a reasonable time to present the document or direction to the bailee.

CISG   *If the buyer is bound to take over the goods at a place other than the seller's place of business, the risk of loss passes when the buyer is aware of the fact that the goods are placed at her disposal at that location.*

All other sales

for merchant seller, risk of loss passes to buyer on the buyer's receipt of the goods; for nonmerchant seller, risk of loss passes to buyer upon tender of goods

All Other Sales If the buyer possesses the goods when the contract is formed, risk of loss passes to the buyer at that time. (Article 2A.)

All other sales not involving breach are covered by the Code's catchall provision, which applies to those instances in which the buyer picks up the goods at the seller's place of business or those in which the seller delivers the goods using her own transportation. In these cases, risk of loss depends on whether the seller is a merchant. If the seller is a **merchant**, risk of loss passes to the buyer on the buyer's receipt of the goods. If the seller is **not a merchant**, it passes on tender of the goods from the seller to the buyer. (Article 2A.) The policy behind this rule is that so long as the merchant seller is making delivery at her place of business or with her own vehicle, she continues to control the goods and can be expected to insure them. The buyer, on the other hand, has no control over the goods and is not likely to have insurance on them.

Suppose Ted goes to Jack's furniture store, selects a particular set of dining room furniture, and pays Jack the agreed price of $800 on Jack's agreement to stain the set a darker color and to deliver it. Jack stains the furniture and notifies Ted that he will deliver it the next day. That night, the furniture is accidentally destroyed by fire. Ted can recover the $800 payment from Jack. The risk of loss is on the seller, Jack, because he is a merchant and the goods were not received by Ted but were only tendered to him.

On the other hand, suppose Debra, an accountant, having moved to a different city, contracts to sell her household furniture to Dwight for $3,000 by a written agreement signed by Dwight. Though she notifies Dwight that the furniture is available for Dwight to pick up, he delays picking it up for several days; in the interim, the furniture is stolen from Debra's residence through no fault of Debra's. Debra may recover the $3,000 purchase price from Dwight. The risk of loss is on the buyer, Dwight, because, the seller, Debra, is not a merchant and tender is sufficient to transfer the risk of loss.

CISG   *If the sales contract does not involve the carriage of the goods, the risk of loss passes to the buyer when he takes over the goods, or, if the buyer does not take over the goods in due time, from the time when the goods are placed at his disposal and he commits a breach of contract by failing to take delivery.*

Martin v. Melland's Inc.
Supreme Court of North Dakota, 1979
283 N.W.2d 76
http://scholar.google.com/scholar_case?q=283+N.W.2d+76+&hl=en&as_sdt=6,34&case=283656012940553957&scilh=0

FACTS Martin entered into a written agreement with Melland's, Inc., a farm implement dealer, to purchase a truck and attached haystack mover. According to the contract, Martin was to trade in his old truck and haystack mover unit, to mail or bring the certificate of title to the old unit to Melland's within a week, and to retain the use and possession of the old unit until Melland's had the new one ready. The contract contained no provision allocating the risk of loss of the trade-in unit. After Martin mailed the certificate to Melland's, but while he still had possession of the trade-in unit itself, the unit was destroyed by fire. Martin then sued to compel Melland's to bear the loss of the trade-in, claiming that title had passed to Melland's before the destruction of the old unit. The district court dismissed the cause of action, and Martin appealed.

DECISION Judgment for Melland's Inc. affirmed.

OPINION Under the Code, the passage of title is irrelevant to the determination of who bears the risk of loss. The risk of loss is determined by specific provisions of the Code. The provision

applicable here states: "The risk of loss passes to the buyer on his receipt of the goods if the seller is a merchant; otherwise the risk passes to the buyer on tender of delivery." Because Martin was the original owner of the trade-in unit, he is considered the seller of it. Moreover, Martin, by his own admission, is not a merchant-seller. Thus, the risk of loss would shift to Melland's only after Martin had tendered delivery of the unit. Since both parties agreed that Martin would keep the old unit until the new one was ready, tender of delivery had not been made when the unit was destroyed. Consequently, Martin must bear the loss.

INTERPRETATION In a sale involving a nonmerchant seller, the risk of loss stays with the seller until the goods are tendered to the buyer.

ETHICAL QUESTION Did the court fairly decide this case? Explain.

CRITICAL THINKING QUESTION When should risk of loss pass in this type of situation? Explain.

See Figure 21-3 for an illustration of risk of loss in the absence of breach. See also the Ethical Dilemma at the end of this chapter.

BULK SALES [21-3]

A sale of goods in bulk occurs when a merchant sells all or a major portion of his inventory at once. Creditors have an obvious interest in such a bulk disposal of merchandise made not in the ordinary course of business, for a debtor may secretly liquidate all or a major part of his tangible assets by a bulk sale and conceal or divert the proceeds of the sale without paying his creditors. The central purpose of bulk sales law is to deter two common forms of commercial fraud. These occur (1) when the merchant, owing debts, sells out his stock in trade to a friend for a low price, pays his creditors less than he owes them, and hopes to come back into the business "through the back door" sometime in the future; and (2) when the merchant, owing debts, sells out his stock in trade to anyone for any price, pockets the proceeds, and disappears without paying his creditors.

Article 6 of the Code, which applies to such sales, defines a **bulk transfer** as "any transfer in bulk and not in the ordinary course of the transferor's business of a major part of the materials,

Bulk transfer
transfer of a major part of the transferor's inventory made not in the ordinary course of his business

Figure 21-3 Passage of Risk of Loss in Absence of Breach

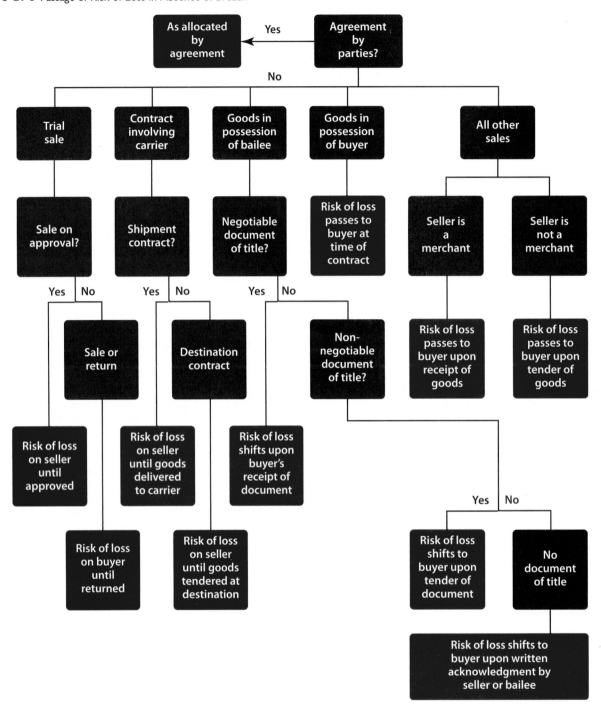

supplies, merchandise, or other inventory." The transfer of a substantial part of equipment is a bulk transfer only if made in connection with a bulk transfer of inventory. Those subject to Article 6 of the Code are merchants whose principal business is the sale of merchandise from stock, including those who manufacture what they sell.

The Code provides that a bulk transfer of assets is ineffective against any creditor of the transferor, unless the transfer meets certain **Article 6 requirements** designed to give the creditor notice of the bulk transfer. Should the transferor fail to comply with these requirements, the goods in the possession of the transferee continue to be subject to the claims of the transferor's unpaid creditors.

Article 6 requirements
transfer is ineffective against any creditor of the transferor, unless certain requirements are met

CISG *If the sales contract does not involve the carriage of the goods, the risk of loss passes to the buyer when he takes over the goods, or, if the buyer does not take over the goods in due time, from the time when the goods are placed at his disposal and he commits a breach of contract by failing to take delivery.*

In 1988, the Uniform Law Commission and the American Law Institute jointly issued a recommendation stating "that changes in the business and legal contexts in which sales are conducted have made regulation of bulk sales unnecessary." They therefore recommended the repeal of Article 6 or, for those states that felt the need to continue the regulation of bulk sales, the adoption of a revised Article 6 designed to afford better protection to creditors while minimizing the obstacles to good faith transactions. Nearly every state has repealed Article 6; only a few states have adopted Revised Article 6.

ETHICAL DILEMMA

Who Should Bear the Loss?

Facts Stratton Corporation, a regional pharmaceutical company located in Smithville, has embarked on a policy that encourages its employees to become computer literate. Accordingly, it has made a deal with BMI, a computer manufacturer, to have computers available for purchase by Stratton's employees at considerable savings from the standard retail price. The computers, which Stratton purchases in bulk, are delivered to the home office in Smithville.

The state in which Smithville is located imposes a 7 percent sales tax on any sale that takes place in the state. For state tax purposes, the place of sale is the point of delivery. To help reduce the costs to its employees, Stratton has arranged for its personnel to pick up their purchased computers at its Somerton office, located about twenty-five miles from Smithville in a neighboring state that does not impose a sales tax.

Arthur Johnson, a Stratton employee, took advantage of the offer and purchased

a computer through Stratton on December 1. The computer arrived in Smithville on December 18, and was immediately placed on a Stratton pickup truck for transfer to Somerton. Johnson, however, wanting the computer home by Christmas, suggested that he put the unit in his car and deliver it to Somerton himself, where he would immediately pick it up. Stratton, seeing a chance to save time and money, agreed to the suggestion.

On December 19, in a heavy snowfall, Johnson left Smithville with the computer bound for Somerton. As he turned onto the highway, the snowfall became a whiteout. Hearing on his car radio that blizzard conditions had already made the roads into Somerton impassable, Johnson brought the computer to his home, planning to hold it there until he could deliver it to Somerton. On the night of December 21, when snow still blocked the Somerton roads, the Johnson home and many of its furnishings were destroyed by fire. Unfortunately, Johnson had no fire insurance at the time.

The computer was among the items that were destroyed. Stratton refused to accept the loss on the computer and demanded that Johnson pay for it in full. Johnson refuses.

Social, Policy, and Ethical Considerations

1. From a legal standpoint, who must bear the risk of loss for the computer? From an ethical standpoint, who should bear the loss?

2. What social responsibility did Stratton violate in setting up the computer delivery scheme? Did it have a legitimate reason for implementing the plan?

3. Do cost savings ever give a business the right to violate a social or ethical responsibility?

4. Are there any similarities between Stratton's actions in this case and a company's decision to close one of its plants?

CHAPTER SUMMARY

Transfer of Title   **Identification** designation of specific goods as goods to which the contract of sale refers

- *Security Interest* an interest in personal property or fixtures that ensures payment or performance of an obligation
- *Insurable Interest* buyer obtains an insurable interest and specific remedies in the goods by the identification of existing goods as goods to which the contract of sale refers

Passage of Title title passes when the parties intend it to pass; when the parties do not specifically agree, the Code provides rules to determine when title passes

- *Physical Movement of the Goods* when delivery is to be made by moving the goods, title passes at the time and place where the seller completes his performance with reference to delivery
- *No Movement of the Goods*

Power to Transfer Title the purchaser of goods obtains such title because his transferor either has or had the power to transfer; however, to encourage and make secure good faith acquisitions of goods, it is necessary to protect certain third parties under certain circumstances

- *Void Title* no title can be transferred
- *Voidable Title* the good faith purchaser acquires good title
- *Entrusting of Goods to a Merchant* buyers in the ordinary course of business acquire good title when buying from merchants

Risk of Loss

Definition allocation of loss between seller and buyer when the goods have been damaged, destroyed, or lost without the fault of either party

Risk of Loss Where There Is a Breach

- *Breach by the Seller* if the seller ships to the buyer goods that do not conform to the contract, the risk of loss remains on the seller until the buyer has accepted the goods or until the seller has remedied the defect
- *Breach by the Buyer* the seller may treat the risk of loss as resting on the buyer for a commercially reasonable time to the extent of any deficiency in the seller's effective insurance coverage

Risk of Loss in Absence of a Breach

- *Agreement of the Parties* the parties may by agreement allocate the risk of loss
- *Trial Sales* unless otherwise agreed, if the goods are delivered primarily for the buyer's use, the transaction is a sale on approval (risk of loss remains with the seller until "approval" or acceptance of the goods by the buyer); if they are delivered primarily for resale by the buyer, it is a sale or return (the risk of loss is on the buyer until she returns the goods)
- *Contracts Involving Carriers* in shipment contracts, the seller bears the risk of loss and expense until the goods are delivered to the carrier for shipment; in destination contracts, the seller bears the risk of loss and expense until tender of the goods at a particular destination
- *Goods in Possession of Bailee*
- *All Other Sales* for merchant seller, risk of loss passes to buyer on the buyer's receipt of the goods; for nonmerchant seller, risk of loss passes to buyer upon tender of goods

Bulk Sales

Definition a transfer, not in the ordinary course of the transferor's business, of a major part of inventory

Article 6 Requirements transfer is ineffective against any creditor of the transferor, unless certain requirements are met

---

QUESTIONS

1. Stein, a mechanic, and Beal, a life insurance agent, entered into a written contract for the sale of Stein's tractor to Beal for $6,800 cash. It was agreed that Stein would tune the motor on the tractor. Stein fulfilled this obligation and on the night of July 1 telephoned Beal that the tractor was ready to be picked up on Beal's making payment. Beal responded, "I'll be there in the morning with the money." On the next morning, however, Beal was approached by an insurance prospect and decided to get the tractor at a later date. On the night of July 2, the tractor was destroyed by fire of unknown origin. Neither Stein nor Beal had any fire insurance. Who must bear the loss?

2. Regan received a letter from Chase, the material portion of which stated, "Chase hereby places an order with you for fifty cases of Red Top Tomatoes. Ship them C.O.D." As soon as he received the letter, Regan shipped the tomatoes to Chase. While en route, the railroad car carrying the tomatoes was wrecked. When Chase refused to pay for the tomatoes, Regan started an action to recover the purchase price. Chase defended on the ground that because the shipment was C.O.D., neither title to the tomatoes nor risk of loss passed until their delivery to Chase. Who has title? Who has the risk of loss? Explain.

3. On May 10, the Adair Company, acting through Brown, entered into a contract with Clark for the installation of a milking machine at Clark's farm. Following the enumeration of the articles to be furnished, together with the price of each article, the written contract provided: "This machinery is subject to thirty days' free trial and is to be installed about June 1." Within thirty days after installation, all the purchased machinery, except for a double utility unit, was destroyed by fire through no fault of Clark's. The Adair Company sued Clark to recover the value of the articles destroyed. Explain who bears the risk of loss.

4. Brown contracted to buy sixty cases of Lovely Brand canned corn from Smith, a Toledo seller, at a contract price of $1,260. Based on the contract, Smith selected and set aside sixty cases of Lovely Brand canned corn and tagged them "For Brown." The contract required Smith to ship the corn to Brown via T Railroad, F.O.B. Toledo. Before Smith delivered the corn to the railroad, the sixty cases were stolen from Smith's warehouse.
   a. Who is liable for the loss of the sixty cases of corn, Brown or Smith?
   b. Suppose Smith had delivered the corn to the railroad in Toledo. After the corn was loaded on a freight car but before the train left the yard, the car was broken open and its contents, including the corn, were stolen. Who is liable for the loss, Brown or Smith?
   c. Would your answer in Question 4(b) be the same if this contract were F.O.B. Brown's warehouse, and all other facts remained the same?

5. Farber owned a quantity of corn that was stored in a corncrib located on Farber's farm. On March 12, Farber wrote a letter to Barber stating that he would sell to Barber all of the corn in this crib, which Barber estimated at between nine hundred and one thousand bushels, for $3.60 per bushel. Barber received this letter on March 13, and on the same day immediately wrote and mailed a letter to Farber stating that he would buy the corn. The corncrib and contents were accidentally destroyed by a fire that broke out about 3:00 A.M. on March 14. What are the rights and liabilities of the parties? What difference, if any, in result would there be if Farber were a merchant?

6. Franco, a New York dealer, purchased twenty-five barrels of specially graded and packed apples from a producer at Hood River, Oregon, under a contract that specified an agreed price on delivery at Franco's place of business in New York. The apples were shipped to Franco from Oregon but, through no fault of Franco, were totally destroyed before reaching New York. Does any liability rest on Franco?

7. Smith was approached by a man who introduced himself as Brown of Brown & Co. Smith, who did not know Brown, asked Dun & Bradstreet for a credit report on Brown. He thereupon sold Brown some expensive gems and billed Brown & Co. "Brown" turned out to be a clever jewel thief, who later sold the gems to Brown & Co. for valuable consideration. Brown & Co. was unaware of "Brown's" transaction with Smith. Can Smith successfully sue Brown & Co. for either the return of the gems or the price as billed to Brown & Co.?

8. Charlotte, the owner of a new Cadillac automobile, agreed to loan the car to Ellen for the month of February while she (Charlotte) went to Florida for a winter vacation. It was understood that Ellen, who was a small-town Cadillac dealer, would merely place Charlotte's car in her showroom for exhibition and sales promotion purposes. While Charlotte was away, Ellen sold the car to Bob. When Charlotte returned from Florida, she sued to recover the car from Bob. Who has title to the automobile? Explain.

9. Steven offered to sell his used automobile to Benito for $7,600 cash. Benito agreed to buy the car, gave Steven a check for $7,600, and drove away in the car. The next day, Benito sold the car for $8,000 to Jose, a good faith purchaser. The bank returned Benito's $7,600 check to Steven because of insufficient funds in Benito's account. Steven brings an action against Jose to recover the automobile. What is the judgment? Explain.

10. Justin told Jennifer he wished to buy Jennifer's collection of antique watches. He told Jennifer he wanted to take the watches to his partner for evaluation. Justin then left with the watches and never returned. Justin sold the watches in another state to Thomas and gave him a bill of sale. Can Jennifer recover the watches from Thomas? Explain.

11. On February 7, Pillsbury purchased eight thousand bushels of wheat from Landis. The wheat was being stored at the Greensville Grain Company. Pillsbury also intended to store the wheat with Greensville. On February 10, the wheat was destroyed. Landis demands payment for the wheat from Pillsbury. Who prevails? Who has title? Who has the risk of loss? Explain.

12. Johnson, who owns a hardware store, was indebted to Hutchinson, one of his suppliers. Johnson sold his business to Lockhart, one of Johnson's previous competitors. Lockhart combined the inventory from Johnson's store with his own and moved the combined inventory to a new, larger store. Hutchinson claims that Lockhart must pay Johnson's debt because the sale of the business had been made without complying with the requirements of the bulk sales law. Discuss whether Lockhart is obligated to pay Hutchinson's debt to Johnson.

13. A seller had manufactured forty thousand pounds of plastic resin pellets especially for a buyer, who agreed to accept them at the rate of one thousand pounds per day upon his issuance of shipping instructions. Despite numerous requests by the seller, the buyer issued no such instructions. On August 18, the seller, after warehousing the goods for forty days, demanded by letter that the buyer issue instructions. The buyer agreed to issue them beginning August 20, but never did. On September 22, a fire destroyed the seller's plant containing the goods, which were not covered by insurance. Who bears the risk of loss? Why?

14. McCoy, an Oklahoma cattle dealer, orally agreed with Chandler, a Texas cattle broker, to ship cattle to a New Mexico feedlot for delivery to Chandler. The agreement was for six lots of cattle valued at $119,000. After McCoy delivered the cattle, he presented invoices to Chandler that described the cattle and set forth the sales price. McCoy then

demanded payment, which Chandler refused. Unknown to McCoy, Chandler had obtained a loan from First National Bank and had pledged the subject cattle as collateral. The bank had no knowledge of any interest that McCoy may have had in the cattle. McCoy sued to recover the cattle. The bank counter-claimed that it had a perfected security interest in the cattle that was superior to any interest of McCoy's. Who has title to the cattle? Explain.

CASE PROBLEMS

15. Home Indemnity, an insurance company, paid one of its insureds after the theft of his car. The car reappeared in another state and was sold to Michael Schrier for $8,300 by a used car dealer. The dealer promised to give Mr. Schrier a certificate of title. One month later, the car was seized by the police on behalf of Home Indemnity. Explain who is entitled to possession of the car.

16. Fred Lane, who sells boats, motors, and trailers, sold a boat, motor, and trailer to John Willis in exchange for a check for $6,285. The check was not honored when Lane attempted to use the funds. Willis subsequently left the boat, motor, and trailer with John Garrett, who sold the items to Jimmy Honeycutt for $2,500. Considering the boat's quality, Honeycutt was surprised at how inexpensive it was. He did not know where Garrett had obtained the boat, but he had dealt with Garrett before and described him as a "sly businessman." Garrett did not sell boats; normally, he sold fishing tackle and provisions. Honeycutt also received a forged certificate for the boat, on which he had observed Garrett forge the purported owner's signature. Can Lane compel Honeycutt to return the boat, motor, and trailer? Explain.

17. Mike Moses purchased a mobile home, including installation, from Gary Newman. Newman delivered the home to Moses's lot. Upon inspection of the home, Moses's fiancée found a broken window and water pipe. Moses also had not received keys to the front door. Before Newman corrected these problems, a windstorm destroyed the home. Who bears the risk for the loss of the home? Why?

TAKING SIDES

Harrison, a men's clothing retailer located in Westport, Connecticut, ordered merchandise from Ninth Street East, Ltd., a Los Angeles-based clothing manufacturer. Ninth Street delivered the merchandise to Denver-Chicago Trucking Company (Denver) in Los Angeles and then sent four invoices to Harrison that bore the notation "F.O.B. Los Angeles." Denver subsequently transferred the merchandise to a connecting carrier, Old Colony Transportation Company, for final delivery to Harrison's Westport store. When Old Colony tried to deliver the merchandise, Harrison's wife asked the truck driver to deliver the boxes inside the store, but the driver refused. The dispute remained unresolved, and the truck departed with Old Colony still in possession of the goods. By letter, Harrison then notified Ninth Street of the nondelivery, but Ninth Street was unable to locate the shipment. Ninth Street then sought to recover the contract purchase price from Harrison. Harrison refused, contending that risk of loss remained with Ninth Street because of its refusal to deliver the merchandise to Harrison's place of business.

a. What are the arguments that the risk of loss remained with Ninth Street?

b. What are the arguments that the risk of loss passed to Harrison?

c. What is the appropriate outcome?

Product Liability: Warranties and Strict Liability

CHAPTER 22

The explosion of [product liability] lawsuits—and the cost of insuring against them—is forcing managers to react. Some have pulled goods off the market. Other responses: raising prices, redesigning products, educating customers, and finding new ways of settling claims.

Michael Brody
Fortune

CHAPTER OUTCOMES

After reading and studying this chapter, you should be able to:

1. Identify and describe the types of warranties.

2. List and explain the various defenses that may be successfully raised to a warranty action.

3. Describe the elements of an action based on strict liability in tort.

4. List and explain the obstacles to an action based on strict liability in tort.

5. Compare strict liability in tort with the implied warranty of merchantability.

Practical Advice

Thoroughly test your products prior to releasing them into the channels of distribution to ensure that they are safe and properly designed. In addition, include all necessary warnings and instructions and be sure that they are clear and conspicuous.

I n this chapter, we will consider the liability of manufacturers and sellers of goods to buyers, users, consumers, and bystanders for damages caused by defective products. The rapidly expanding development of case law has established product liability as a distinct field of law that combines and enforces rules and principles of contracts, sales, negligence, strict liability, and statutory law.

One reason for the expansion of such liability has been the modern method of distributing goods. In the twenty-first century, retailers serve principally as a conduit of goods that are prepackaged in sealed containers and that are widely advertised by the manufacturer or distributor. This has hastened the extension of product liability coverage to include manufacturers and other parties within the chain of distribution. The extension of product liability to manufacturers, however, has not noticeably lessened the liability of a seller to his immediate purchaser. Rather, it has broadened the base of liability through the development and application of new principles of law.

Products liability has attracted a great deal of public attention. According to the U.S. Consumer Product Safety Commission, deaths, injuries, and property damage from consumer product incidents cost the United States more than $1 trillion annually. The resultant cost of maintaining product liability insurance has skyrocketed, causing great concern in the business community. In response to the clamor over this insurance crisis, almost all of the states have revised their tort laws to make successful tort (including product liability) lawsuits more difficult to bring. These tort reforms include legislation dealing with joint and several liability, punitive damages, non-economic damages, and class actions. Nevertheless, repeated efforts to pass federal product liability legislation have been unsuccessful.

The liability of manufacturers and sellers of goods for a defective product, or for its failure to perform adequately, may be based on one or more of the following: (1) negligence, (2) misrepresentation, (3) violation of statutory duty, (4) warranty, and (5) strict liability in tort. We covered the first three of these causes of actions in Chapters 8 and 11. Chapter 8 also covered traditional strict liability—where liability is imposed regardless of the defendant's negligence or intent to cause harm. In this chapter we will cover a specialized type of strict liability—strict liability in tort for products. This chapter will also explore warranty liability.

WARRANTIES

Warranty
obligation of the seller concerning title, quality, characteristics, or condition of goods

A **warranty**, under the Uniform Commercial Code (UCC or the Code), creates a duty on the part of the seller to ensure that the goods he sells will conform to certain qualities, characteristics, or conditions. A seller, however, is not required to warrant the goods; and, in general, he may, by appropriate words, disclaim (exclude) or modify a particular warranty or even all warranties.

In bringing a warranty action, the buyer must prove that (1) a warranty existed, (2) the warranty has been breached, (3) the breach of the warranty proximately caused the loss suffered, and (4) notice of the breach of warranty was given to the seller. The seller has the burden of proving defenses based on the buyer's conduct. If the seller breaches his warranty, the buyer may reject or revoke acceptance of the goods. Moreover, whether the goods have been accepted or rejected, the buyer may recover a judgment against the seller for damages. Harm for which damages are recoverable includes personal injury, damage to property, and economic loss. Economic loss most commonly involves damages for loss of bargain and consequential damages for lost profits. (Damages for breach of warranty are discussed in detail in the next chapter.) In this section, we will examine the various types of warranties, as well as the obstacles to a cause of action for breach of warranty.

TYPES OF WARRANTIES [22-1]

A warranty may arise out of the mere existence of a sale (a warranty of title), out of any affirmation of fact or promise made by the seller to the buyer (an express warranty), or out of the circumstances under which the sale is made (an implied warranty). In a contract for the sale of goods, it is possible to have both express and implied warranties, as well as a warranty of title. All warranties are construed as consistent with each other and cumulative, unless such construction is unreasonable. A purchaser, under Revised Article 1, means a person who takes by sale, lease, lien, security interest, gift, or any other voluntary transaction creating an interest in property. (Prior Article 1 did not include leases.)

Article 2A carries over the warranty provisions of Article 2 with relatively minor revision to reflect differences in style, leasing terminology, or leasing practices. The creation of express warranties and, except for finance leases, the imposition of the implied warranties of merchantability and fitness for a particular purpose are virtually identical to their Article 2 analogues. Article 2 and Article 2A diverge somewhat in their treatment of the warranties of title and infringement as well as in their provisions for the exclusion and modification of warranties.

Warranty of Title [22-1a]

Warranty of title
obligation to convey the right of ownership without any lien

Under the UCC's **warranty of title**, the seller implicitly warrants that (1) the title conveyed is good and its transfer rightful and (2) the goods are subject to no security interest or other lien (a claim on property by another for payment of debt) of which the buyer did not know at the time of contracting. In a lease, title does not transfer to the lessee. Accordingly, Article 2A's analogous provision protects the lessee's right to possession and use of the goods from the claims of other parties arising from an act or omission of the lessor.

Let us assume that Steven acquires goods from Nancy in a transaction that is void and then sells the goods to Rachel. Nancy brings an action against Rachel and recovers the goods. Steven has breached the warranty of title because he did not have good title to the goods and, therefore, his transfer of the goods to Rachel was not rightful. Accordingly, Steven is liable to Rachel for damages.

The Code does not label the warranty of title an implied warranty, even though it arises out of the sale and not out of any particular words or conduct. Instead, the Code has a separate disclaimer provision for warranty of title; thus, the Code's general disclaimer provision for implied warranties does not apply.

Express Warranties [22-1b]

Express warranty
affirmation of fact or promise about the goods, which may consist of a description or a sample, which becomes part of the basis of the bargain

An **express warranty** is an explicit undertaking by the seller with respect to the quality, description, condition, or performability of the goods. The undertaking may consist of an affirmation of fact or a promise that relates to the goods, a description of the goods, or a sample or model of the goods. In each of these instances, for an express warranty to be created, the undertaking must become or be made part of the basis of the bargain. It is not necessary, however, that the seller have a specific intention to make a warranty or use formal words such as "warrant" or "guarantee." Moreover, it is not necessary that, to be liable for breach of express warranty, a seller know of the falsity of a statement she makes; the seller may be acting in good faith. For example, if John mistakenly asserts to Sam that a rope will easily support two hundred pounds and Sam is injured when the rope breaks while supporting only two hundred pounds, John is liable for breach of an express warranty.

Creation

A seller can create an express warranty either orally or in writing. One way in which the seller may create such a warranty is by an affirmation of fact or a promise that relates to the goods. (Article 2A.) For example, a statement made by a seller that an automobile will get forty-two miles to the gallon of gasoline or that a camera has automatic focus is an express warranty.

Practical Advice

Make only those affirmations of fact or promises about the goods being sold that you wish to stand behind. Moreover, recognize that advertising claims and the statements made by salespeople can give rise to express warranties.

The Code further provides that an affirmation of the *value* of the goods or a statement purporting merely to be the seller's *opinion* or recommendation of the goods does not create a warranty. (Article 2A.) Such statements are not factual and do not deceive the ordinary buyer, who accepts them merely as opinions or as *puffery* (sales talk). A statement of value, however, may be an express warranty in cases in which the seller states the price at which the goods were purchased from a former owner, or in which she gives market figures relating to sales of similar goods. These are affirmations of facts. They are statements of events, not mere opinions; and the seller is liable for breach of warranty if they are untrue. Also, although a statement of opinion by the seller is not ordinarily a warranty, the seller who is an expert and who gives an opinion as such may be liable for breach of warranty.

A seller also can create an express warranty by the use of a *description* of the goods that becomes a part of the basis of the bargain. (Article 2A.) Under such a warranty, the seller expressly warrants that the goods shall conform to the description. Examples include statements regarding a particular brand or type of goods, technical specifications, and blueprints.

The use of a *sample* or model is another means of creating an express warranty. (Article 2A.) When a sample or model is a part of the basis of the bargain, the seller expressly warrants that the entire lot of goods sold shall conform to the sample or model. A sample is a good that is actually drawn from the bulk of goods that is the subject matter of the sale. By comparison, a model is offered for inspection when the subject matter is not at hand; it is not drawn from the bulk. See the case that follows, as well as *In Re L. B. Trucking, Inc.* later in this chapter.

CISG   *According to the United Nations Convention on CISG, the seller must deliver goods that conform to the quality and description required by the contract. In addition, the goods must possess the qualities of any sample or model used by the seller.*

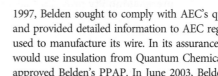

Belden, Inc. v. American Electronic Components, Inc.
Court of Appeals of Indiana, 2008
885 N.E.2d 751, 66 UCC Rep.Serv.2d 399
http://scholar.google.com/scholar_case?q=885+N.E.2d+751&hl=en&as_sdt=2,34&case=6981122239976535930&scilh=0

FACTS Belden, Inc., and Belden Wire & Cable Company (Belden) manufactures wire, and American Electronic Components, Inc. (AEC) manufactures automobile sensors. Since 1989, AEC has repeatedly purchased wire from Belden to use in its sensors. In 1994, AEC indicated to its suppliers that it was adopting a quality control program to satisfy the requirements of AEC's purchasers, automobile manufacturers. Part of AEC's quality control program included an extensive production part approval process (PPAP). In 1996 and

1997, Belden sought to comply with AEC's quality control program and provided detailed information to AEC regarding the materials it used to manufacture its wire. In its assurances, Belden stated that it would use insulation from Quantum Chemical Corp. In 1997, AEC approved Belden's PPAP. In June 2003, Belden began using insulation supplied by Dow Chemical Company. The Dow insulation had different physical properties than the insulation provided by Quantum. In October 2003, Belden sold AEC wire manufactured with the

Dow insulation. AEC used this wire to make its sensors, and the insulation ultimately cracked. Chrysler had installed AEC's sensors containing the faulty wire in approximately eighteen thousand vehicles. Chrysler recalled fourteen thousand vehicles and repaired the remaining four thousand prior to sale. Pursuant to an agreement with Chrysler, AEC was required to reimburse Chrysler for expenses associated with the recall. In 2004, AEC filed a complaint against Belden seeking damages for the changes in the insulation that resulted in the recall. In 2007, the trial court entered an order granting AEC's motion for partial summary judgment and denying Belden's cross-motion for summary judgment. Belden appealed on the basis that it did not create an express warranty regarding compliance with AEC's quality control program.

DECISION The trial court's granting AEC's partial motion for summary judgment and denying Belden's partial motion for summary judgment is affirmed.

OPINION Where an agreement is entirely in writing, the existence of express warranties is a question of law. An express warranty requires some representation, term, or statement as to how the product is warranted. There does not seem to be a dispute that in 1996 and 1997 Belden made express warranties regarding its wire. Instead, the issue is whether the 1996 and 1997 statements by Belden regarding certification created an express warranty that extended to the October 2003 contract. Belden's compliance with AEC's quality control program was essential to its contracts with AEC and was

intended to extend to the parties' repeated contracts. The sole question is whether the language or samples or models are fairly to be regarded as part of the contract. Thus, although Belden made its initial representations in 1996 and 1997, there is no indication that those representations were limited in time, that Belden subsequently disclaimed its compliance with AEC's quality control standards, or that AEC changed those standards. It is illogical to believe that AEC intended to rely on this representation for only one shipment of wire and then to understand that Belden would follow whatever quality procedures it wanted as to future shipments. A course of dealing is conduct fairly to be regarded as establishing a common basis of understanding for interpreting the parties' expressions and other conduct. It is undisputed that Belden's wire complied with the AEC's quality control requirements for more than one hundred transactions between the parties, until October 2003, when Belden switched from Quantum insulation to the Dow insulation without informing AEC of the changes. The very point of a course of dealing is to allow the parties' prior actions to create a basis of common understanding. This is exactly what Belden's 1996 and 1997 assertions taken with its continued use of Quantum insulation did.

INTERPRETATION An express warranty is created by an affirmation of fact or promise about the goods.

CRITICAL THINKING QUESTION How long should an express warranty last between merchants who continue to do business with each other over many years?

Basis of the bargain
part of the buyer's assumption underlying the sale

Implied warranty
contractual obligation arising out of certain circumstances of the sale

Merchantability
warranty by a merchant seller that the goods are fit for their ordinary purpose

---

Practical Advice

Because the warranty of merchantability applies only to merchant sellers, when purchasing goods from a nonmerchant seller, attempt to obtain a written express warranty that the goods will be, at a minimum, of average quality and fit for ordinary purposes.

Basis of Bargain   The Code does not require that the affirmations, promises, descriptions, samples, or models the seller makes or uses be relied on by the buyer but only that they constitute a part of the **basis of the bargain**. In other words, if they are part of the buyer's assumption underlying the sale, reliance by the buyer is presumed. Some courts merely require that the buyer know of the affirmation or promise for it to be presumed to be part of the basis of the bargain, while others require some showing of reliance. See the case *In Re L. B. Trucking, Inc.*

Like statements in advertisements or catalogs, statements or promises made by the seller to the buyer prior to the sale may be express warranties, as they may form a part of the basis of the bargain. In addition, under the Code, statements or promises made by the seller subsequent to the making of the contract of sale may become express warranties even though no new consideration is given. (Article 2A.)

Implied Warranties [22-1c]

An implied warranty, unlike an express warranty, is not found in the language of the sales contract or in a specific affirmation or promise by the seller. Instead, it exists by operation of law. An **implied warranty** arises out of the circumstances under which the parties enter into their contract and depends on factors such as the type of contract or sale entered into, the seller's merchant or nonmerchant status, the conduct of the parties, and the applicability of other statutes.

Merchantability   Under the Code, a *merchant seller* makes an implied warranty of the merchantability of goods that are of the kind in which he deals. The implied warranty of **merchantability** provides that the goods are reasonably fit for the *ordinary* purposes for which they are used; pass without objection in the trade under the contract description; and are of fair, average quality. (Article 2A.)

CISG   *The seller must deliver goods, unless otherwise agreed, that are fit for the purposes for which goods of the same description would ordinarily be used.*

Fitness for Particular Purpose   Unlike the warranty of merchantability, the implied warranty of fitness for a particular purpose applies to *any* seller, whether he is a merchant or not. The implied warranty of **fitness for a particular purpose** arises if at the time of contracting the seller had reason to know the buyer's particular purpose and to know that the buyer was relying on the seller's skill and judgment to select suitable goods. (Article 2A.)

The implied warranty of fitness for a particular purpose does not require any specific statement by the seller. Rather, it requires only that the seller know that the buyer, in selecting a product for her specific purpose, is relying on the seller's expertise. The buyer need not specifically inform the seller of her particular purpose; it is sufficient if the seller has reason to know it. On the other hand, the implied warranty of fitness for a particular purpose would not arise if the buyer were to insist on a particular product and the seller simply conveyed it to her because the buyer must be able to demonstrate that she relied on the seller's skill or judgment in selecting or furnishing suitable goods.

In contrast to the implied warranty of merchantability, the implied warranty of fitness for a particular purpose pertains to a specific purpose for, rather than the ordinary purpose of, the goods. A particular purpose may be a specific use or may relate to a special situation in which the buyer intends to use the goods. Thus, if the seller has reason to know that the buyer is purchasing a pair of shoes for mountain climbing and that the buyer is relying on the seller's judgment to furnish suitable shoes for this purpose, a sale of shoes suitable only for ordinary walking purposes would be a breach of this implied warranty. Likewise, if a buyer indicates to a seller that she needs a stamping machine to stamp ten thousand packages in an eight-hour period and that she relies upon the seller to select an appropriate machine, the seller, by selecting a machine, impliedly warrants that the machine selected will stamp ten thousand packages in an eight-hour period.

CISG   *The seller must deliver goods, unless otherwise agreed, that are fit for any particular purpose expressly or impliedly made known to the seller by the buyer, except when the buyer did not rely on the seller's skill and judgment or when it was unreasonable for the buyer to rely on the seller.*

Fitness for a particular purpose

warranty that goods are fit for a stated purpose, provided the seller selects the product knowing the buyer's intended use and that the buyer is relying on the seller's judgment

Frequently, as in the case that follows, a seller's conduct may involve both the implied warranty of merchantability *and* the implied warranty of fitness for a particular purpose.

In Re L. B. Trucking, Inc.
U.S. Bankruptcy Court, 1994
163 BR 709, 23 UCC Rep.Serv.2d 1093
http://scholar.google.com/scholar_case?case=6401409485061780661&q=163+BR+709&hl=en&as_sdt=2,34

FACTS Dudley B. Durham, Jr., and his wife, Barbara Durham, owned and operated a trucking company, L. B. Trucking, Inc., and a farm, Double-D Farms, Inc. In April 1983, Dudley Durham met with Richard Thomas of Southern States Cooperative—which is in the business of supplying various agricultural supplies to farmers—about arranging for the application of herbicides to the Durhams' fields.

At a subsequent meeting in early May, Durham met with Thomas to complete credit arrangements and to arrange the application of herbicides. Durham told Thomas, "I want it done the cheapest way, the best way it can be done." Thomas responded, "Will do." Thomas then outlined with some specificity the chemicals he proposed to use on the Durhams' fields. The plan included the use of a water-based carrier that was recommended by local experts, rather than a more expensive nitrogen solution. Durham had no experience or expertise on herbicidal chemicals and relied on Thomas's briefing on the various herbicide mixtures in choosing which ones to apply.

When the herbicides were actually to be applied, Southern States herbicide applicator, Gilbert McClements, received from

Mr. Thomas instructions concerning which chemicals to apply and would mix the chemicals each day prior to spraying. Apparently, though, Mr. McClements used a nitrogen solution to prepare the herbicides and did not make extensive prespraying inspections of the grass and weeds in the fields to be sprayed. When Durham noticed a significant number of weeds and grasses had survived the herbicidal treatment, he promptly notified Southern States. Southern States attempted to remedy the problem, but the harvest was dismal and far below the county average.

In 1983, the Durhams and both their businesses filed for bankruptcy. Southern States brought a claim against the consolidated bankruptcy estate to collect payment for the herbicides as well as application and other services provided. The trustee of the estate asserted counterclaims against Southern States for negligence and breach of warranties in the application of herbicides that caused severe damage to the Durhams' 1983 crop.

DECISION Judgment for the trustee.

OPINION The warranty provisions of the UCC are applicable in this case since the predominant purpose of the contract was the sale of herbicides and the service of their application was merely incidental to that sale. Furthermore, the facts of the case lead to the conclusion that Southern States breached both express and implied warranties in its sale of herbicides to the Durhams.

Thomas created at least two express warranties by his statements to Durham. First, he warranted that water would be the carrier used to distribute the herbicides. Second, Thomas made statements about the effectiveness of the herbicides in removing weeds and grass. These statements became a part of the basis of the bargain. They were not puffing or mere "seller's talk" but rather specific statements about the product. Moreover, Durham, because of his limited knowledge, relied on these statements in deciding to purchase from Southern States. The first express warranty was breached by the use of the nitrogen solution, notwithstanding Southern States' argument that the use of nitrogen solution was common trade usage in 1983. The standard for evaluating whether conduct is a breach of warranty is the affirmation of fact or promise made by the seller, not common trade usage. The second express warranty was breached since the herbicide failed to kill weeds effectively. Expert testimony established that these breaches were a proximate cause of the damage to the 1983 crop.

In addition to express warranties, Southern States also breached implied warranties created by the UCC. Under the implied warranty of merchantability, a merchant warrants that goods are merchantable at the time of sale. There is no doubt that Southern States is a merchant as defined under the UCC, because it "deals in goods of the kind." To be merchantable, goods must pass without objection in the trade and be fit for the ordinary pur-

poses for which they were intended. Herbicides are intended to be used as chemical agents that will kill weeds without damaging the primary crops. The herbicides in this case failed to control 85 percent of the weeds. Instead, the weeds flourished and the crops died. Therefore, the herbicides were not merchantable as they were unfit for the ordinary purpose for which they were intended to be used.

Southern States also breached the implied warranty that the herbicides were fit for a particular purpose. Under this warranty, if a seller "has reason to know of a particular purpose for which the goods are required and that the buyer is relying on the seller's skill or judgment to select or furnish suitable goods, the seller warrants that the goods sold shall be fit for such purpose." Durham relied on Thomas's skill and judgment in selecting suitable herbicides to conduct no-till farming on his farms. However, the herbicides did not effectively do their job. As a result, the herbicides' failure to do their intended task coupled with Durham's reliance on Southern States' judgment and skill in formulating, mixing, and applying the herbicidal chemicals breached the implied warranty of fitness for a particular purpose.

INTERPRETATION In a contract for a sale of goods, it is possible to breach multiple warranties.

ETHICAL QUESTION Did any of the parties act unethically? Explain.

CRITICAL THINKING QUESTION Did the court correctly decide this case? Explain.

OBSTACLES TO WARRANTY ACTIONS [22-2]

A number of technical obstacles, which vary considerably from jurisdiction to jurisdiction, limit the effectiveness of warranty as a basis for recovery. These include disclaimers of warranties, limitations or modifications of warranties, privity, notice of breach, and the conduct of the plaintiff.

Disclaimer of Warranties [22-2a]

To be effective, a **disclaimer** (negation of warranty) must be positive, explicit, unequivocal, and conspicuous. The Code calls for a reasonable construction of words or conduct to disclaim or limit warranties. (Article 2A.)

Express Exclusions In general, a seller cannot provide an **express warranty** and then disclaim it. A seller can, however, avoid making an express warranty by carefully refraining from making any promise or affirmation of fact relating to the goods, by refraining from making a description of the goods, or by refraining from using a sample or model in a sale. (Article 2A.) Oral warranties made before the execution of a written agreement containing an express disclaimer are subject to the parol evidence rule, however. Thus, as discussed in Chapter 15, if the parties intend the written contract to be the final and complete statement of the agreement between them, parol evidence of a warranty that contradicts the terms of the written contract is inadmissible.

A **warranty of title** may be excluded only by specific language or by certain circumstances, including a judicial sale or sales by sheriffs, executors, or foreclosing lienors. (Article 2A.) In the latter cases, the seller is clearly offering to sell only such right or title as he or a third person might have in the goods, because it is apparent that the goods are not the property of the person selling them.

To exclude or to modify an **implied warranty of merchantability**, the language of disclaimer or modification must mention *merchantability* and, in the case of a writing, must

---

Disclaimer
negation of a warranty

Express warranty
not usually possible to disclaim

Practical Advice

Recognize that once you make an express warranty, it is very difficult to disclaim the warranty.

Warranty of title
may be excluded or modified by specific language or by certain circumstances, including judicial sale or a sale by a sheriff, executor, or foreclosing lienor

Implied warranty of merchantability
the disclaimer must mention "merchantability" and, in the case of a writing, must be conspicuous (in a lease the disclaimer must be in writing and conspicuous)

Other disclaimers of implied warranties

the implied warranties of merchantability and fitness for a particular purpose may also be disclaimed (1) by expressions like "as is," "with all faults," or other similar language; (2) by course of dealing, course of performance, or usage of trade; or (3) as to defects an examination ought to have revealed in cases in which good the buyer has examined the goods or in which the buyer has refused to examine the goods

Implied warranty of fitness for a particular purpose

the disclaimer must be in writing and conspicuous

Practical Advice

If you want to disclaim the implied warranties, be sure to use large, conspicuous type; use the appropriate language; and place the disclaimer on the first page of the agreement.

be *conspicuous.* Article 2A requires that a **disclaimer of an implied warranty** of merchantability mention merchantability, be in writing, and be conspicuous. For example, Bart wishes to buy a used refrigerator from Ben's Used Appliances Store for $100. Given the low purchase price, Ben is unwilling to guarantee the refrigerator's performance. Bart agrees to buy it with no warranty protection. To exclude the warranty, Ben writes conspicuously on the contract, "This refrigerator carries no warranties, including no warranty of MERCHANTABILITY." Ben has effectively disclaimed the implied warranty of merchantability. Some courts, however, do not require the disclaimer to be conspicuous in cases in which a *commercial* buyer has actual knowledge of the disclaimer. The Code's test for whether a provision is *conspicuous* is whether a reasonable person against whom the disclaimer is to operate ought to have noticed it. Revised Article 1 provides that conspicuous terms include (1) a heading in capitals equal to or greater in size than the surrounding text; or in contrasting type, font, or color to the surrounding text of the same or lesser size; and (2) language in the body of a record or display in larger type than the surrounding text; or in contrasting type, font, or color to the surrounding text of the same size; or set off from surrounding text of the same size by symbols or other marks that call attention to the language. Whether a term is conspicuous is an issue for the court.

To exclude or to modify an **implied warranty of fitness for the particular purpose** of the buyer, the disclaimer must also be in *writing* and *conspicuous.* (Article 2A.)

All implied warranties, unless the circumstances indicate otherwise, are excluded by expressions like "*as is*" or "*with all faults*" or by other language plainly calling the buyer's attention to the exclusion of warranties. (Article 2A.) Most courts require the "as is" clause to be conspicuous. (At least twelve states do not permit "as is" sales of consumer products.) Implied warranties may also be excluded by course of dealing, course of performance, or usage of trade. (Article 2A.)

The courts will invalidate disclaimers they consider unconscionable. The Code, as discussed in Chapter 19, permits a court to limit the application of any contract or contractual provision that it finds unconscionable. (Article 2A.)

Womco, Inc. v. Navistar International Corporation
Court of Appeals of Texas, Twelfth District, Tyler, 2002
84 S.W.3d 272, 48 UCC Rep.Serv.2d 130
http://scholar.google.com/scholar_case?case=377667224667598367&q=84+S.W.3d+272&hl=en&as_sdt=2,22

FACTS In 1993, Womco, Inc. purchased through Price, a dealer, thirty 1993 International model 9300 tractor trucks manufactured by Navistar. Also, in 1993, C. L. Hall purchased sixteen 1994 International model 9300 tractor trucks also manufactured by Navistar through Mahaney, another dealer. Almost immediately after the trucks were put into service, Womco and Hall (plaintiffs) each had problems with their trucks' engines overheating. As the problems occurred, plaintiffs took their trucks, which were still covered under warranty, to their dealerships for service related to the overheating problem. Although repeated attempts were made, the dealerships were unable to correct the problem. Subsequently it was discovered that the trucks' radiators were unusually small and were insufficient to cool the engine.

Womco and Hall filed suit against Navistar, Price, and Mahaney (defendants). The trial court granted the defendants' motion for summary judgment based on their affirmative defenses of disclaimer of warranty. Womco and Hall appealed.

DECISION Summary judgment for defendants is reversed, and case remanded.

OPINION The Uniform Commercial Code (UCC) allows sellers to disclaim both the implied warranty of merchantability as well as the implied warranty of fitness for particular purpose. In order to disclaim an implied warranty of merchantability in a sales transaction, the disclaimer must mention the word "merchantability." The disclaimer may be oral or written, but if in writing, the disclaimer must be conspicuous. To disclaim an implied warranty of fitness for a particular purpose, the disclaimer must be in writing and must be conspicuous. A term or clause is conspicuous if it is written so that a reasonable person should have noticed it. Language is "conspicuous" if it is in larger type or other contrasting font or color. Nevertheless, conspicuousness is not required if the buyer has actual knowledge of the disclaimer.

The plaintiffs argue that the defendants were required to offer proof of the context of the purported disclaimers, contending that for a disclaimer of an implied warranty to be effective, the plaintiffs must have had an opportunity to examine it prior to consummation of the contract. One of the underlying purposes of UCC Section 2-316 is to protect a buyer from surprise by permitting the exclusion of implied warranties. Section 2-316 can only fulfill such a purpose if the disclaimer is required to be communicated to the buyer before the contract of sale has been completed. In support of their motion for summary judgment, the defendants offered six disclaimers. However, it is not clear whether any of these six disclaimers were communicated prior to the completion of the contract of sale. Thus, it is a question of fact to be determined by the jury as to when the disclaimers were communicated.

INTERPRETATION A disclaimer of warranties of merchantability and fitness for a particular purpose must be communicated clearly to the buyer.

ETHICAL QUESTION Did any of the parties act unethically? Explain.

CRITICAL THINKING QUESTION Do you agree with the court's decision? Explain.

Practical Advice

If you are a seller, offer the buyer an opportunity to examine the goods to avoid an implied warranty for any defects that should be detected upon inspection. If you are a buyer and are offered an opportunity to examine the goods, make sure that you make a reasonable inspection of the goods.

Buyer's Examination or Refusal to Examine If the buyer inspects the goods before entering into the contract, implied warranties do not apply to defects that are apparent on examination. Moreover, there is no implied warranty on defects that an examination ought to have revealed, not only when the buyer has examined the goods as fully as desired, but also when the buyer has refused to examine the goods. (Article 2A.)

CISG

If at the time of entering into the sales contract, the buyer knew or could not have been unaware of the lack of conformity, the seller is not liable for the warranty of particular purpose, ordinary purpose, or sale by sample or model.

Federal legislation relating to warranties of consumer goods the Magnuson-Moss Warranty Act protects purchasers of consumer goods by providing that warranty information be clear and useful and that a seller who makes a written warranty cannot disclaim any implied warranty

Consumer goods goods normally used for personal, family, or household purposes

Limitation or modification of warranties permitted as long as it is not unconscionable

Privity contractual relationship

Federal Legislation Relating to Warranties of Consumer Goods To protect purchasers of **consumer goods** (defined as "tangible personal property normally used for personal, family or household purposes"), Congress enacted the Magnuson-Moss Warranty Act. The purpose of the Act is to prevent deception and to make sure that consumer purchasers are adequately informed about warranties. Some courts have applied the Act to leases.

The Federal Trade Commission administers and enforces the Act. The Commission's guidelines for the type of consumer product warranty information a seller must supply are aimed at providing the consumer with clear and useful information. More significantly, the Act provides that a seller who makes a written warranty cannot disclaim any implied warranty. For a complete discussion of the Act, see Chapter 44.

Limitation or Modification of Warranties [22-2b]

The Code permits a seller to *limit* or *modify* the buyer's remedies for breach of warranty. One important exception to this right is the prohibition against a seller's "unconscionable" limitations or exclusions of consequential damages. (Article 2A.) Specifically, the "[l]imitation of consequential damages for injury to the person in the case of consumer goods is prima facie unconscionable." In some cases, a seller may seek to impose time limits within which the warranty is effective. Except when such clauses result in unconscionability, the Code permits them; it does not, however, permit any attempt to shorten the time period for filing an action for personal injury to less than one year.

Privity of Contract [22-2c]

Because of the close association between warranties and contracts, a principle of law in the nineteenth century established that a plaintiff could not recover for breach of warranty unless he was in a contractual relationship with the defendant. This relationship is known as **privity** of contract.

Under this rule, a warranty by seller Ingrid to buyer Sylvester, who resells the goods to purchaser Lyle under a similar warranty, gives Lyle no rights against Ingrid. There is no privity of contract between Ingrid and Lyle. In the event of breach of warranty, Lyle may recover only from his seller, Sylvester, who in turn may recover from Ingrid.

Horizontal privity
determines who benefits from a warranty and therefore may bring a cause of action

Practical Advice

If you are a seller of consumer goods and wish to disclaim the implied warranties, make sure that you do not provide any written express warranties.

Horizontal privity determines who benefits from a warranty and who may therefore sue for its breach. Horizontal privity pertains to noncontracting parties who are injured by the defective goods; this group would include users, consumers, and bystanders who are not the contracting purchaser.

The Code, however, relaxes the requirement of horizontal privity of contract by permitting recovery on a seller's warranty, at a minimum, to members of the buyer's family or household or to a guest in his home. The Code provides three alternative sections from which the states may select. Alternative A, the least comprehensive and most widely adopted alternative, provides that a seller's warranty, whether express or implied, extends to any natural person who is in the family or household of the buyer or who is a guest in his home, if it is reasonable to expect that such person may use, consume, or be affected by the goods, and who is injured in person by breach of the warranty. Alternative B extends Alternative A to "any natural person who may reasonably be expected to use, consume, or be affected by the goods." Alternative C further expands the coverage of the section to any person, not just natural persons, and to property damage as well as personal injury. (A natural person would not include artificial entities such as corporations, for example.) A seller, however, may not exclude or limit the operation of this section for injury to a person. Article 2A provides the same alternatives with slight modifications.

Nonetheless, the Code was not intended to establish outer boundaries for third-party recovery for injuries caused by defective goods. Rather, it sets a minimum standard that the states may expand through case law. Most states have judicially accepted the Code's invitation to relax the requirements of horizontal privity and, for all practical purposes, have eliminated horizontal privity in warranty cases.

Vertical privity
determines who is liable for breach of warranty

Vertical privity, in determining who is liable for breach of warranty, pertains to remote sellers within the chain of distribution, such as manufacturers and wholesalers, with whom the consumer purchaser has not entered into a contract. Although the Code adopts a neutral position regarding vertical privity, the courts in most states have *eliminated* the requirement of vertical privity in warranty actions.

Notice of Breach of Warranty [22-2d]

Notice of breach of warranty
if the buyer fails to notify the seller of any breach within a reasonable time, she is barred from any remedy against the seller

When a buyer has accepted a tender of goods that are not as warranted by the seller, she is required to notify the seller of any breach of warranty, express or implied, as well as any other breach, within a reasonable time after she has discovered or should have discovered it. If the buyer fails to notify the seller of any breach within a reasonable time, she is barred from any remedy against the seller. (Article 2A.) In determining whether notice was provided in a reasonable period of time, commercial standards apply to a merchant buyer while different standards apply to a retail consumer, so as not to deprive a good faith consumer of her remedy.

Plaintiff's Conduct [22-2e]

Contributory negligence
is not a defense in the majority of states

Voluntary assumption of the risk
is a defense

Because of the development of warranty liability in the law of sales and contracts, **contributory negligence** of the buyer is no defense to an action against the seller for breach of warranty. Comparative negligence statutes do apply, however, to warranty actions in a number of states. (Comparative negligence is discussed later in this chapter.)

If the buyer discovers a defect in the goods that may cause injury and nevertheless proceeds to make use of them, he will not be permitted to recover damages from the seller for loss or injuries caused by such use. This is not contributory negligence but **voluntary assumption of the risk**.

STRICT LIABILITY IN TORT

Section 402A
imposes strict liability in tort

The most recent and far-reaching development in the field of product liability is that of strict liability in tort. All but a very few states have now accepted the concept, which is embodied in **Section 402A** of the Restatement (Second) of Torts. A new Restatement of the Law (Third) Torts: Products Liability (the Restatement Third) was promulgated. It is far more comprehensive than the second Restatement in dealing with the liability of commercial sellers and distributors of goods for harm caused by their products. (We will discuss this revision more fully later in this chapter.)

CONCEPT REVIEW 22-1

Warranties

Type of Warranty	How Created	What Is Warranted	How Disclaimed
Title (Article 2) Use and Possession (Article 2A)	• Seller contracts to sell goods	• Good title • Rightful transfer • Not subject to lien	• Specific language • Circumstances giving buyer reason to know that seller does not claim title
Express (Article 2 and 2A)	• Affirmation of fact • Promise • Description • Sample or model	• Conform to affirmation • Conform to promise • Conform to description • Conform to sample or model	• Specific language (extremely difficult)
Merchantability (Article 2 and 2A)	• Merchant sells goods	• Fit for ordinary purposes • Adequately contained, packaged, and labeled	• Must mention "merchantability" • If in writing must be conspicuous/in lease must be in writing and conspicuous • "As is" sale • Buyer examination • Course of dealing, course of performance, usage of trade
Fitness for a Particular Purpose (Article 2 and 2A)	• Seller knows buyer is relying upon seller to select goods suitable to buyer's particular purpose	• Fit for particular purpose	• No buzzwords necessary • Must be in writing and conspicuous • "As is" sale • Buyer examination • Course of dealing, course of performance, usage of trade

Strict liability in tort merchant seller is liable for selling a product in a defective condition, unreasonably dangerous to the user

Section 402A imposes **strict liability in tort** on merchant sellers both for personal injuries and for property damage that result from selling a product in a ***defective condition, unreasonably dangerous*** to the user or consumer. Section 402A applies even though "the seller has exercised all possible care in the preparation and sale of his product." Thus, negligence is not the basis of liability in strict liability cases. The essential distinction between the two doctrines is that actions in strict liability do not require the plaintiff to prove that the injury-producing defect resulted from any specific act of negligence of the seller. Strict liability actions focus on the *product*, not on the *conduct* of the manufacturer. Courts in strict liability cases are interested in the fact that a product defect arose—not in *how* it arose. Thus, even an "innocent" manufacturer—one who has not been negligent—may be liable if his product turns out to contain a defect that injures a consumer. Although liability for personal injuries caused by a defective condition that makes goods unreasonably dangerous is usually associated with sales of such goods, this type of liability also exists with respect to ***leases*** and ***bailments*** of defective goods.

REQUIREMENTS OF STRICT LIABILITY IN TORT [22-3]

Section 402A imposes strict liability in tort if (1) the defendant was engaged in the business of selling a product such as the defective one; (2) the defendant sold the product in a defective condition; (3) the defective condition made the product unreasonably dangerous to the user or consumer or to his property; (4) the defect in the product existed when it left the defendant's hands; (5) the plaintiff sustained physical harm or property damage by using or consuming the product; and (6) the defective condition was the proximate cause of the injury or damage.

This liability is imposed by tort law as a matter of public policy; it does not depend on contract, either express or implied, and is not governed by the UCC. Nor does it require reliance by the injured user or consumer on any statements made by the manufacturer or seller. It is not limited to persons in a buyer–seller relationship; thus, neither vertical nor horizontal privity is required. No notice of the defect is required to have been given by the injured user or consumer. The liability, furthermore, generally is not subject to disclaimer, exclusion, or modification by contractual agreement. The majority of courts considering the question, however, have held that Section 402A imposes liability only for injury to person and damage to property, not for commercial loss (such as loss of bargain or profits), which is recoverable in an action for breach of warranty.

Merchant Sellers [22-3a]

Section 402A imposes liability only upon a person who is in the *business* of selling the product involved. It does not apply to an occasional seller, such as a person who trades in his used car or who sells his lawn mower to a neighbor. In this respect, the section is similar to the implied warranty of merchantability, which applies only to sales by a merchant of goods that are of the type in which he deals. A growing number of jurisdictions recognize the applicability of strict liability in tort even to merchant-sellers of *used* goods.

Defective Condition [22-3b]

In an action to recover damages under the rule of strict liability in tort, though the plaintiff must prove a defective condition in the product, she is not required to prove how or why or in what manner the product became defective. The plaintiff must, however, show that at the time she was injured, the condition of the product was not substantially changed from the condition in which the manufacturer or seller sold it. In general, defects may arise through faulty manufacturing, through faulty product design, or through inadequate warnings, labeling, packaging, or instructions. Some states, however, and the Restatement Third do not impose strict liability for a design defect or a failure to provide proper warnings or instructions.

O'Neil v. Crane Co.
Supreme Court of California, 2012
53 Cal.4th 335, 135 Cal.Rptr.3d 288, 266 P.3d 987
http://scholar.google.com/scholar_case?q=O%27Neil+v.+Crane+Co&hl=en&as_sdt=2,21&case=2363858414015569521&scilh=0

FACTS The defendants Crane Co. and Warren Pumps LLC made valves and pumps used in Navy warships. They were sued for a wrongful death allegedly caused by asbestos released from external insulation and internal gaskets and packing, all of which were made by third parties and added to the pumps and valves after the sale. It is undisputed that the defendants never manufactured or sold any of the asbestos-containing materials to which the plaintiffs' decedent had been exposed. Nevertheless, the plaintiffs claim the defendants should be held strictly liable because it was foreseeable that workers would be exposed to and harmed by the asbestos in replacement parts and products used in conjunction with their pumps and valves.

The trial court dismissed all claims against Crane and Warren. On appeal, the trial court's decision was reversed by the Court of Appeals.

DECISION The decision of the Court of Appeals is reversed, and the case is remanded.

OPINION Strict liability has been imposed for three types of product defects: manufacturing defects, design defects, and "warning defects." The third category describes "products that are dangerous because they lack adequate warnings or instructions." A basic principle in strict liability law requires that the plaintiff's injury must have been caused by a defect in the defendant's product.

This case involves the limits of a manufacturer's duty to prevent foreseeable harm related to its product: When is a product manufacturer liable for injuries caused by adjacent products or replacement parts that were made by others and used in conjunction with the defendant's product? The plaintiffs argue that the defendants' products were defective because they were used in connection with asbestos-containing parts. They also contend that the defendants should be held strictly liable for failing to warn O'Neil about the potential health consequences of breathing asbestos dust released from the products used in connection with their pumps and valves. These claims lack merit. A product manufacturer may not be held liable in strict liability or negligence for harm caused by another manufacturer's product unless the defendant's own product contributed substantially to the harm, or the defendant participated substantially in creating a harmful combined use of the products. The defendants were not strictly liable for O'Neil's injuries because (a) any design defect in the *defendants' products* was not a legal cause of injury to O'Neil, and (b) the defendants had no duty to warn of risks arising from *other manufacturers'* products.

INTERPRETATION A product manufacturer is not liable in strict liability or negligence for harm caused by another manufacturer's product unless (1) the defendant's own product contributed substantially to the harm, or (2) the defendant participated substantially in creating a harmful combined use of the products.

CRITICAL THINKING QUESTION If the California Supreme Court had upheld the Court of Appeals' decision, could the manufacturer of a saw that was used by a purchaser to cut insulation containing asbestos be liable for harm caused to the purchaser by the asbestos? Explain.

Manufacturing defect

Not produced according to specifications

Manufacturing Defect
A **manufacturing defect** occurs when the product is not properly made; that is, it fails to meet its own manufacturing specifications. For instance, suppose a chair is manufactured with legs designed to be attached by four screws and glue. If the chair was produced without the appropriate screws, this would constitute a manufacturing defect.

Design defect

plans or specifications inadequate to ensure the product's safety

Design Defect
A product contains a **design defect** when, despite its being produced as specified, the product is dangerous or hazardous because its design is inadequate. Design defects can result from a number of causes, including poor engineering, poor choice of materials, and poor packaging. An example of a design defect that received great notoriety was the fuel tank assembly of the Ford Pinto. A number of courts found the car to be inadequately designed because the fuel tank had been placed too close to its rear axle, causing the tank to rupture when the car was hit from behind.

Section 402A provides no guidance in determining which injury-producing designs should give rise to strict liability and which should not. Consequently, the courts have adopted widely varying approaches in applying 402A to defective design cases. Nevertheless, virtually none of the courts has upheld a judgment in a strict liability case in which the defendant demonstrated that the "**state of the art**" was such that the manufacturer (1) neither knew nor could have known of a product hazard or (2) if he knew of the product hazard, could have designed a safer product given existing technology. Thus, almost all courts evaluate the design of a product on the basis of the dangers that the manufacturer could have known at the time he produced the product.

State of the art

the state of technology current at the time the product is made

Failure to warn

failure to provide adequate warning of possible danger or to provide appropriate directions for use of a product

Failure to Warn
A seller is under a duty to provide adequate warning of a product's possible danger, to provide appropriate directions for its safe use, and to package the product safely. Warnings do not, however, always protect sellers from liability. A seller who could have designed or manufactured a product in a safe yet cost-effective manner, but who instead chooses to produce the product cheaply and to provide a warning of the product's hazards, cannot escape liability simply by the warning. Warnings usually will avoid liability only if no cost-effective designs or manufacturing processes are available to reduce a risk of injury.

The duty to give a warning arises from a foreseeable danger of physical harm that could result from the normal or probable use of the product and from the likelihood that, unless warned, the user or consumer would not ordinarily be aware of such danger or hazard.

Practical Advice

Warn consumers of your products of any significant danger, such as toxicity or flammability.

Kelso v. Bayer Corporation
U.S. Court of Appeals, Seventh Circuit, 2005
398 F.3d 640
http://scholar.google.com/scholar_case?case=13341242500313047129&q=398+F.3d+640&hl=en&as_sdt=2,22

FACTS Plaintiff, Ted Kelso, used Neo-Synephrine 12 HourExtra Moisturizing Spray (a product manufactured by Bayer Corporation) continuously for more than three years. After learning that his continued use of the product caused permanent nasal tissue damage requiring multiple sinus surgeries, he sued Bayer alleging that Bayer had failed to adequately warn him of the dangers associated with Neo-Synephrine. Bayer moved for summary judgment, arguing that the warning it provided, as follows, was adequate:

Do not exceed recommended dosage.

… Stop use and ask a doctor if symptoms persist. Do not use this product for more than 3 days. Use only as directed. Frequent or prolonged use may cause nasal congestion to recur or worsen.

The district court granted Bayer summary judgment, and Kelso appealed arguing that he had presented sufficient evidence to recover in a product liability action against Bayer.

DECISION Judgment affirmed.

OPINION "To recover in a product liability action, a plaintiff must plead and prove that the injury resulted from a condition of the product, that the condition was an unreasonably dangerous one, and that the condition existed at the time the product left the manufacturer's control." A product may be unreasonably dangerous because of a design defect, a manufacturing defect, or a failure of a manufacturer to properly warn of a danger or instruct on the proper use of the product as to which the average consumer would not be aware.

Kelso claims the Neo-Synephrine was unreasonably dangerous because Bayer's warning was confusing as to whether or not the product could be used safely for more than three days, when such use was effective in relieving his congestion. Kelso interpreted the warning as meaning not to exceed three days use if the product failed to relieve the congestion; he only needed to see a physician if the product did not work to relieve the congestion. However, Kelso's personal reaction to the warning is not the test. Whether a warning is sufficient is determined using an objective standard, that is, the awareness of an ordinary person. Here, the plain, clear, and unambiguous language of the warning states: "**Do not use this product for more than 3 days.**" Moreover, the warning clearly informs users to "**Stop use and ask a physician if symptoms persist.**" The warning was clear. Yet Kelso continued using the product well beyond the three days. It is unreasonable to create an ambiguity that excuses extended use when the warning against such use is unequivocal.

INTERPRETATION The duty to give a warning arises from a foreseeable danger of physical harm that could result from the normal or probable use of the product and from the likelihood that, unless warned, the user or consumer would not ordinarily be aware of such danger or hazard.

CRITICAL THINKING QUESTION When should a warning be considered sufficient?

Unreasonably Dangerous [22-3c]

Unreasonably dangerous

contains a danger beyond that which would be contemplated by the ordinary consumer

Section 402A liability applies only if the defective product is unreasonably dangerous to the user or consumer. An **unreasonably dangerous** product is one that contains a danger beyond that which would be contemplated by the ordinary consumer who purchases it with common knowledge of its characteristics. Thus, Comment *i* to Section 402A describes the difference between reasonable and unreasonable dangers:

> [G]ood whiskey is not unreasonably dangerous merely because it will make some people drunk, and is especially dangerous to alcoholics; but bad whiskey, containing a dangerous amount of fuel oil, is unreasonably dangerous. Good tobacco is not unreasonably dangerous merely because the effects of smoking may be harmful; but tobacco containing something like marijuana may be unreasonably dangerous. Good butter is not unreasonably dangerous merely because, if such be the case, it deposits cholesterol in the arteries and leads to heart attacks; but bad butter, contaminated with poisonous fish oil, is unreasonably dangerous.

Most courts have left the question of reasonable consumer expectations to the jury.

Greene v. Boddie-Noell Enterprises, Inc.
United States District Court, W.D. Virginia, 1997
966 F.Supp. 416
http://scholar.google.com/scholar_case?case=14855332202624539345&q=966+F.Supp.+416&hl=en&as_sdt=2,34

FACTS The plaintiff, Katherine Greene, contends that she was badly burned by hot coffee purchased from the drive-through window of a Hardees fast food restaurant, when the coffee spilled on her after it had been handed to her by the driver of the vehicle. Greene's boyfriend, Blevins, purchased the coffee and some food and handed the food and beverages to Greene. The food was on a plate, and the beverages were in cups. Greene placed the plate on her lap and held a cup in each hand. According to Greene, the Styrofoam coffee cup was comfortable to hold, and had a lid on the top, although she did not notice whether the lid was fully attached.

Blevins drove out of the restaurant parking lot, and over a "bad dip" at the point at which the lot meets the road. When the front tires of the car went slowly across the dip, the coffee "splashed out" on Greene, burning her legs through her clothes. Blevins remembers Greene exclaiming, "The lid came off." As soon as the coffee burned her, Greene threw the food and drink to the floor of the car, and in the process stepped on the coffee cup. When the cup was later retrieved from the floor of the car, the bottom of the cup was damaged, and the lid was at least partially off of the top of the cup.

After Greene was burned by the coffee, Blevins drove her to the emergency room of a local hospital, where she was treated. She missed eleven days of work and suffered permanent scarring to her thighs.

The defendant restaurant operator moved for summary judgment on the ground that the plaintiff cannot show a *prima facie* case of liability.

DECISION Summary judgment granted in favor of defendant.

OPINION To prove a case of liability in Virginia, a plaintiff must show that a product had a defect which rendered it unreasonably dangerous for ordinary or foreseeable use and that the product violated a prevailing safety standard from business, government, or reasonable consumer expectation.

Both Greene and Blevins testified that they had heard of the "McDonalds' coffee case" prior to this incident and Greene testified that while she was not a coffee drinker, she had been aware that if coffee spilled on her, it would burn her. After the accident, Greene gave a recorded statement to a representative of the defendant in which she stated, "I know the lid wasn't on there good. It came off too easy."

There is no evidence that either the heat of the coffee or the security of the coffee cup lid violated any applicable standard. In fact, the plaintiff testified that she knew, and therefore expected, that the coffee would be hot enough to burn her if it spilled.

The plaintiff argues that the mere fact that she was burned shows that the product was dangerously defective, either by being too hot or by having a lid which came off unexpectedly. But an accident is not sufficient proof of liability, even in product liability cases.

In the present case, there has been no showing that a reasonable seller of coffee would not conclude that the beverage must be sold hot enough to be palatable to consumers, even though it is hot enough to burn other parts of the body. A reasonable seller might also conclude that patrons desire coffee lids which prevent spillage in ordinary handling, but are not tight enough to avert a spill under other circumstances, such as when driving over a bump. It was the plaintiff's obligation to demonstrate that she had proof that the defendant breached a recognizable standard, and that such proof is sufficient to justify a verdict in her favor at trial. She has not done so.

INTERPRETATION Strict liability in tort only applies if the defective product is unreasonably dangerous to the user or consumer.

CRITICAL THINKING QUESTION Do you agree with the court's decision? Explain.

OBSTACLES TO RECOVERY [22-4]

Few of the obstacles to recovery in warranty cases present serious problems to plaintiffs in strict liability actions brought pursuant to Section 402A because this section was drafted largely to avoid such obstacles.

Disclaimers and Notice [22-4a]

Comment *m* to Section 402A provides that the basis of strict liability rests solely in tort and therefore is not subject to contractual defenses. The comment specifically states that strict product liability is not governed by the Code, that it is not affected by contractual limitations or disclaimers, and that it is not subject to any requirement that notice be given to the seller by the injured party within a reasonable time. Nevertheless, most courts have *allowed* clear and specific disclaimers of Section 402A liability in *commercial* transactions between merchants of relatively equal economic power.

Privity [22-4b]

With respect to horizontal privity, the strict liability in tort of manufacturers and other sellers extends not only to buyers, users, and consumers, but also to injured bystanders.

In terms of vertical privity, strict liability in tort imposes liability on any seller who is engaged in the business of selling the product, including a wholesaler or distributor as well as the manufacturer and retailer. The rule of strict liability in tort also applies to the manufacturer of a defective component that is used in a larger product if the manufacturer of the finished product has made no essential change in the component.

Plaintiff's Conduct [22-4c]

Many product liability defenses relate to the conduct of the plaintiff. The claim common to all of them is that the plaintiff's improper conduct so contributed to the plaintiff's injury that it would be unfair to blame the product or its seller.

Contributory negligence
not a defense in the majority of states

Contributory Negligence **Contributory negligence** is conduct on the part of the plaintiff (1) that falls below the standard to which he should conform for his own protection and (2) that is the legal cause of the plaintiff's harm. Because strict liability is designed to assess liability without fault, Section 402A rejects contributory negligence as a defense. Thus, a seller cannot defend a strict liability lawsuit on the basis of a plaintiff's negligent failure to discover a defect or to guard against its possibility. But, as discussed later, contributory negligence in the form of an assumption of the risk can bar recovery under Section 402A.

Comparative negligence
most states have applied the rule of comparative negligence to strict liability in tort

Comparative Negligence Under **comparative negligence**, the court apportions damages between the parties in proportion to the degree of fault or negligence it finds against them. Despite Section 402A's bar of contributory negligence in strict liability cases, some courts apply comparative negligence to strict liability cases. (Some courts use the term *comparative responsibility* rather than *comparative negligence*.) There are two basic types of comparative negligence or comparative responsibility. One is pure comparative responsibility, which simply reduces the plaintiff's recovery in proportion to her fault, whatever that may be. Thus, the recovery of a plaintiff found to be 80 percent at fault in causing an accident in which she suffered a $100,000 loss would be limited to 20 percent of her damages, or $20,000. Under the other type of negligence, modified comparative responsibility, the plaintiff recovers according to the general principles of comparative responsibility *unless* she is more than 50 percent responsible for her injuries, in which case she recovers nothing. The majority of comparative negligence states follow the modified comparative responsibility approach.

Voluntary Assumption of the Risk Under the Second Restatement of Torts assumption of risk is a defense in an action based on strict liability in tort. Basically, **voluntary assumption of the risk** is the plaintiff's express or implied consent to encounter a known danger. Thus, a person who drives an automobile after realizing that the brakes are not working and an employee who attempts to remove a foreign object from a high-speed roller press without shutting off the power have assumed the risk of their own injuries.

To establish such a defense, the defendant must show that (1) the plaintiff actually knew and appreciated the particular risk or danger the defect created, (2) the plaintiff voluntarily encountered the risk while realizing the danger, and (3) the plaintiff's decision to encounter the known risk was unreasonable.

The Third Restatement of Torts: Apportionment of Liability has abandoned the doctrine of implied voluntary assumption of risk in tort actions generally; it is no longer a defense that the plaintiff was aware of a risk and voluntarily confronted it. This new Restatement limits the defense of assumption of risk to express assumption of risk, which consists of a contract between the plaintiff and another person to absolve the other person from liability for future harm.

Misuse or Abuse of the Product Closely connected to voluntary assumption of the risk is the valid defense of misuse or abuse of the product by the injured party. **Misuse or abuse of the product** occurs when the injured party knows, or should know, that he is using the product in a manner the seller did not contemplate. The major difference between misuse or abuse and assumption of the risk is that the former includes actions that the injured party does not know to be dangerous, whereas the latter does not include such conduct. Instances of such misuse or abuse include standing on a rocking chair to change a light bulb or using a lawn mower to trim hedges. The courts, however, have significantly limited this defense by requiring that the misuse or abuse not be foreseeable by the seller. If a use is foreseeable, then the seller must take measures to guard against it.

Subsequent Alteration [22-4d]

Section 402A provides that liability exists only if the product reaches "the user or consumer without substantial change in the condition in which it is sold." Accordingly, most, but not all, courts would not hold a manufacturer liable for a faulty carburetor if a car dealer had removed the part and made significant changes in it before reinstalling it in an automobile.

Statute of Repose [22-4e]

A number of lawsuits have been brought against manufacturers many years after a product was first sold. In response, many states have adopted statutes of repose. These enactments limit the period—typically between six and twelve years—for which a manufacturer is liable for injury caused by a defective product. After the statutory time period has elapsed, a manufacturer ceases to be liable for such harm. See the following Business Law in Action and the Ethical Dilemma at the end of this chapter.

Limitations on Damages [22-4f]

More than half of the states have limited the punitive damages that a plaintiff can collect in a product liability lawsuit. They have done this by a number of means, including the following:

1. Placing caps on the amount of damages that can be awarded—with caps ranging greatly, but generally between $250,000 and $1 million;
2. Providing for the state to receive all or a portion of any punitive damages awarded with the state's share ranging from 35 percent to 100 percent to reduce the plaintiff's incentive to bring products liability suits;
3. Providing for bifurcated trials; that is, separate hearings to determine liability and punitive damages;
4. Increasing the plaintiff's burden of proof for recovery of punitive damages with most states adopting the "clear and convincing" evidence standard; and
5. Requiring proportionality between compensatory and punitive damages by specifying an acceptable ratio between the two types of damages.

See Concept Review 22-2.

Voluntary assumption of the risk

express assumption of risk is a defense to an action based upon strict liability; some states apply implied assumption of risk to strict liability cases

Misuse or abuse of the product

is a defense

Subsequent alteration

liability exists only if the product reaches the user or consumer without substantial change in the condition in which it is sold

Statute of repose

limits the time period for which a manufacturer is liable for injury caused by its product

BUSINESS LAW **IN ACTION**

Until the 1970s, A. H. Robins of Richmond, Virginia, operated as a relatively small, essentially family-run company with a fairly wholesome image. Nearly a decade later, however, the company's name rang sourly in the public ear.

For years, the pharmaceutical firm had been headed by E. Claiborne Robins, Sr., its chairman, and his son, E. Claiborne Robins, Jr., its CEO. Both men were well respected in Richmond, and the elder Robins was known as a generous man who donated millions to education and other concerns. Initially, A. H. Robins made such popular products as Robitussin cough medicine, ChapStick lip balm, and Sergeant's flea and tick collars. Then the company decided to get into the birth-control business, and there its troubles began.

With the sexual revolution of the sixties and the advent of the birth-control pill, corporate America sensed profits to be made from any new form of birth control—potentially large profits. But the trick was to find a safe, easy-to-use, acceptable product.

At the prestigious Johns Hopkins Hospital in Baltimore in the late 1960s, Dr. Hugh J. Davis, director of the hospital's birth-control clinic, was testing a new intrauterine device (IUD), known as the Dalkon Shield. The plastic, nickel-size, crablike instrument was inserted into a woman's uterus as a way to prevent pregnancy. No one knew why or how IUDs worked.

In February 1970, Davis reported in the *American Journal of Obstetrics and Gynecology* that the pregnancy rate for his Dalkon Shield was 1.1 percent, a rate similar to or lower than that of the birth-control pill. He did not disclose, however, that he was part owner of the small Dalkon Corporation that made the new IUD.

A few months later, A. H. Robins took notice of the Dalkon Shield at a physicians' conference in Pennsylvania. By June of that year, the firm had acquired the rights to the device and had hired Davis on as a consultant. Within two weeks of the Dalkon Shield's purchase, A. H. Robins began to hear of problems. One of its own officials cited potential difficulties with the device's tail, which, unlike the tails of other IUDs, consisted of hundreds of tiny filaments enclosed in a nylon shield that was open at one end. The tail's exposed threads potentially could attract bacteria and thus cause infection.

Still, A. H. Robins rushed the Dalkon Shield into production. The company made a few design changes but conducted no more research on the device. Nor did the Food and Drug Administration (FDA) require the company to get approval for the device before introducing it, since the Dalkon Shield was classified as a medical device, not a drug.

Within six months of buying the Dalkon Shield, A. H. Robins launched a major marketing campaign. Thousands of reprints of Davis's study that included his 1.1 percent pregnancy rate were distributed across the country. Less than a year later, the Dalkon Shield had captured 60 percent of the IUD market in the United States.

Sales mounted, and the money rolled in. By February 1971, however, the company had received two reports of women developing pelvic inflammatory disease, a painful infection that can lead to sterility. Soon, more adverse evidence surfaced. New reports suggested that the pregnancy rate for the Dalkon Shield ran as high as 4.3 percent. Another study suggested that as many as one in fourteen Dalkon Shield wearers suffered from infections. But that wasn't the only danger. While some Dalkon Shield wearers were hospitalized for infection, others were admitted for perforated uteruses or, if they happened to be pregnant, for ectopic pregnancies, for septic (or infected) abortions, or for premature labor and delivery. Some became sterile. Some died. By 1973, A. H. Robins had evidence that six women wearing the Dalkon Shield had died from septic abortions—yet it did little.

Nor did the FDA respond quickly. Not until June of 1973 did the FDA write A. H. Robins to tell the company that it should stop selling the Dalkon Shield because of safety questions. Two days later, A. H. Robins voluntarily withdrew the device from the U.S. market, yet the company waited nearly another year before banning international sales of the Dalkon Shield.

By early 1974, A. H. Robins faced another threat: lawsuits from injured women. The company, however, fought back fiercely, often playing hardball with women who pressed their claims, questioning them vociferously about their sex lives and suggesting that their own behavior had led to any problems that they might be having. Until 1979, the company was able to settle many cases out of court for an average of $11,000 each.

But then things began to unravel for A. H. Robins. In 1979, a Denver jury decided against the company, awarding an injured woman more than $6.8 million, most of it in punitive damages.

By 1984, the company had paid out $314 million in some 8,300 lawsuits. It still faced three thousand eight hundred additional lawsuits, and women were filing new suits every day. Pressure was beginning to mount. Then, in February of that year, Judge Miles Lord of the U.S. District Court in Minneapolis, exasperated by the number of Dalkon Shield lawsuits that he had presided over, made national news when he summoned three top A. H. Robins executives, including CEO E. Claiborne Robins, Jr., to his courtroom and lashed out at the officers, condemning them for their hard-heartedness and begging them to take action to protect the women who still wore the Dalkon Shield.

Obviously, the company had to do something. So, by October, A. H. Robins launched a major advertising campaign to tell women that it would pay for the removal of their Dalkon Shields. But it did not issue a recall.

Then it asked the U.S. District Court in Richmond, Virginia, to set one national trial as part of a class action suit to determine whether punitive damages should be awarded to claimants and, if so, how much. The company also moved to establish a reserve fund of $615 million to pay for pending and future claims. The fund was the biggest ever to be set aside to settle liability claims for a medical device. Unfortunately, the company underestimated the Dalkon Shield's costs.

By August 1985, A. H. Robins was in deep trouble. The company and its insurer, Aetna Life and Casualty Co., had lost $530 million in nine thousand five hundred lawsuits, and they were facing five thousand two hundred more cases. Meanwhile, four hundred new cases were being filed each month. In addition, the company had been forced to stare down a shareholders' lawsuit, which it settled for $6.9 million. With nowhere else to go, A. H. Robins filed for bankruptcy.

The Committee of the Dalkon Shield Claimants estimated their claims at between $4.2 billion and $7 billion. Robins submitted an estimate at $0.8 billion to $1.3 billion. The bankruptcy judge set a $2.5 billion cap on liability for the Dalkon Shield. In January 1988 American Home Products (AHP) won the bidding war for

Robins. In July 1988 the district court approved Robins' sixth amended and restated reorganization plan (1) creating a Dalkon Shield trust fund of $2.5 billion, (2) protecting Robins executives from punitive damages, and (3) settling claims against Aetna. Robins' shareholders received $916 million in AHP stock while the Robins family received $385 million in AHP stock and other Robins executives received $280 million in that stock. In June 1989 the federal appeals court affirmed

Robins' reorganization plan. In November 1989 the U.S. Supreme Court denied an appeal from the Robins reorganization.

By the time it closed on April 30, 2000, the Dalkon Shield Claimants Trust paid out nearly $3 billion to about two hundred thousand claimants.

Shortly after the sale of A. H. Robins to AHP (now Wyeth), E. Claiborne Robins, Jr., established ECR Pharmaceuticals, a privately held firm based in Richmond, Virginia.

RESTATEMENT (THIRD) OF TORTS: PRODUCTS LIABILITY [22-5]

The Restatement (Third) of Torts: Products Liability makes some significant changes in product liability; however, many states continue to follow Section 402A of the Second Restatement of Torts.

The new Restatement expands Section 402A into an entire treatise of its own, comprising more than twenty sections. The Restatement (Third) does not use the term strict liability but instead defines separate liability standards for each type of defect. The new Restatement continues to cover anyone engaged in the business of selling or distributing a defective product if the defect causes harm to persons or property. Its major provision (Section 2) defines a product as defective "when, at the time of sale or distribution, it contains a manufacturing defect, is defective in design, or is defective because of inadequate instructions or warnings." Thus, Section 2 explicitly recognizes the three types of product defects discussed above: manufacturing defects, design defects, and failure to warn. However, as discussed below, strict liability is imposed only for manufacturing defects, while liability for inadequate design or warning is imposed only for foreseeable risks of harm that could have been avoided by the use of an alternative *reasonable* design, warning, or instruction.

Manufacturing Defects [22-5a]

Section 2(a) provides that "A product … contains a manufacturing defect when the product departs from its intended design even though all possible care was exercised in the preparation and marketing of the product." Therefore, sellers and distributors of products remain strictly liable for manufacturing defects, although a plaintiff may seek to recover based upon allegations and proof of negligent manufacture. In actions against the manufacturer, the plaintiff ordinarily must prove that the defect existed in the product when it left the manufacturer.

Design Defect [22-5b]

Section 2(b) states:

> A product … is defective in design when the foreseeable risks of harm posed by the product could have been reduced or avoided by the adoption of a reasonable alternative design by the seller or other distributor, or a predecessor in the commercial chain of distribution, and the omission of the reasonable alternative design renders the product not reasonably safe.

This rule pulls back from a strict liability standard and imposes a negligence-like standard by requiring that the defect be reasonably foreseeable and that it could have been avoided by a reasonable alternative design. The Comments explain that this standard involves resolving "whether a reasonable alternative design would, at a reasonable cost, have reduced the foreseeable risk of harm posed by the product and, if so, whether the omission of the alternative design by the seller … rendered the product not reasonably safe." The burden rests upon the plaintiff to demonstrate the existence of a reasonable alternative safer design that would have reduced the foreseeable risks of harm. However, consumer expectations do not constitute an independent standard for judging the defectiveness of product designs.

Failure to Warn [22-5c]

Section 2(c) provides:

> A product ... is defective because of inadequate instructions or warnings when the foreseeable risks of harm posed by the product could have been reduced or avoided by the provision of reasonable instructions or warnings by the seller or other distributor, or a predecessor in the commercial chain of distribution and the omission of the instructions or warnings renders the product not reasonably safe.

Commercial product sellers must provide reasonable instructions and warnings about risks of injury associated with their products. The omission of warnings sufficient to allow informed decisions by reasonably foreseeable users or consumers renders the product not reasonably safe at time of sale. A seller, however, is under a duty to warn only if he knew or should have known of the risks involved. Moreover, warning about risks is effective only if an alternative design to avoid the risk cannot reasonably be implemented. Whenever safer products can be reasonably designed at a reasonable cost, adoption of the safer design is required rather than using a warning or instructions.

CONCEPT REVIEW 22-2

Product Liability

	Merchantability*	Strict Liability in Tort (Section 402A)
Condition of Goods Creating Liability	Not fit for ordinary purposes	Defective condition, unreasonably dangerous
Type of Transactions	Sales and leases; some courts apply to bailments of goods	Sales, leases, and bailments of goods
Disclaimer	Must mention "merchantability." If in writing, must be conspicuous; must not be unconscionable. Sales subject to Magnuson-Moss Act.	Not possible in consumer transactions; may be permitted in commercial transactions
Notice to Seller	Required within reasonable time	Not required
Causation	Required	Required
Who May Sue	In some states, buyer and the buyer's family or guests in home; in other states, any person who may be expected to use, consume, or be affected by goods	Any user or consumer of product; also, in most states, any bystander
Compensable Harms	Personal injury, property damage, economic loss	Personal injury, property damage
Who May Be Sued	Seller or lessor who is a merchant with respect to the goods sold	Seller who is engaged in business of selling such a product

*The warranty of fitness for a particular purpose differs from the warranty of merchantability in the following respects: (1) the condition that triggers liability is the failure of the goods to perform according to the particular purpose described in the warranty, and (2) a disclaimer need not mention "fitness for a particular purpose."

ETHICAL DILEMMA

When Should a Company Order a Product Recall?

Facts Walter Jones was feeding his five-month-old daughter Millie plums from a jar of Winkler baby food when she suddenly began to choke on a piece of aluminum foil that had come from the jar. Walter rushed her to the hospital, where more foil was found in her stomach. Although the amount of aluminum found was not in itself deadly, Millie was nauseous for several hours, and her parents had trouble getting her to eat for many days thereafter.

Walter sued Winkler. A number of similar incidents involving Winkler products had

occurred at about the same time. Although the incidents covered a wide geographic area, their total number was not great, and the Food and Drug Administration (FDA) decided not to require a recall of the baby food. Winkler faced two choices: (1) to do nothing and settle the cases as they arose or (2) to recall all jars of the same lot to protect other children from the possibility of ingesting foreign substances.

Social, Policy, and Ethical Considerations

1. What are the social and ethical issues Winkler must consider in choosing its

course of action? Should the fact that none of the incidents had been fatal affect the company's decision? What should Winkler do?

2. Would the first option be good for business? Who eventually bears the cost of the lawsuits or recalls? Who should bear the cost?

3. What actions should be taken by the baby's parents? Do they have any social responsibility in this case to seek publicity sufficient to warn others?

CHAPTER SUMMARY

Warranties

Types of Warranties

Definition of Warranty an obligation of the seller to the buyer (or lessor to lessee) concerning title, quality, characteristics, or condition of goods

Warranty of Title the obligation of a seller to convey the right of ownership without any lien (in a lease the warranty protects the lessee's right to possess and use the goods)

Express Warranty an affirmation of fact or promise about the goods or a description, including a sample of the goods, which becomes part of the basis of the bargain

Implied Warranty a contractual obligation, arising out of certain circumstances of the sale or lease, imposed by operation of law and not found in the language of the sales or lease contract

- *Merchantability* warranty by a merchant seller that the goods are reasonably fit for the ordinary purpose for which they are manufactured or sold; pass without objection in the trade under the contract description; and are of fair, average quality

- *Fitness for Particular Purpose* warranty by any seller that goods are reasonably fit for a particular purpose if, at the time of contracting, the seller had reason to know the buyer's particular purpose and that the buyer was relying on the seller's skill and judgment to furnish suitable goods

Obstacles to Warranty Action

Disclaimer of Warranties a negation of a warranty

- *Express Warranty* usually not possible to disclaim

- *Warranty of Title* may be excluded or modified by specific language or by certain circumstances, including judicial sale or a sale by a sheriff, executor, or foreclosing lienor

- *Implied Warranty of Merchantability* the disclaimer must mention "merchantability" and, in the case of a writing, must be conspicuous (in a lease the disclaimer must be in writing and conspicuous)

- *Implied Warranty of Fitness for a Particular Purpose* the disclaimer must be in writing and conspicuous

- *Other Disclaimers of Implied Warranties* the implied warranties of merchantability and fitness for a particular purpose may also be disclaimed (1) by expressions like "as is," "with all faults," or other similar language; (2) by course of dealing, course of performance, or usage of trade; or (3) as to defects an examination ought to have revealed in cases in which the buyer has examined the goods or in which the buyer has refused to examine the goods

- *Federal Legislation Relating to Warranties of Consumer Goods* the Magnuson-Moss Warranty Act protects purchasers of consumer goods by providing that warranty information be clear and useful and that a seller who makes a written warranty cannot disclaim any implied warranty

Limitation or Modification of Warranties permitted as long as it is not unconscionable

Privity of Contract a contractual relationship between parties that was necessary at common law to maintain a lawsuit

- *Horizontal Privity* doctrine determining who benefits from a warranty and who therefore may bring a cause of action; the Code provides three alternatives
- *Vertical Privity* doctrine determining who in the chain of distribution is liable for a breach of warranty; the Code has not adopted a position on this

Notice of Breach if the buyer fails to notify the seller of any breach within a reasonable time, she is barred from any remedy against the seller

Plaintiff's Conduct

- *Contributory Negligence* is not a defense
- *Voluntary Assumption of the Risk* is a defense

Strict Liability in Tort

Requirements of Strict Liability in Tort

General Rule imposes tort liability on merchant sellers for both personal injuries and property damage for selling a product in a defective condition unreasonably dangerous to the user or consumer

Defective Condition

- *Manufacturing Defect* by failing to meet its own manufacturing specifications, the product is not properly made
- *Design Defect* the product, though made as designed, is dangerous because the design is inadequate
- *Failure to Warn* failure to provide adequate warning of possible danger or to provide appropriate directions for use of a product

Unreasonably Dangerous contains a danger beyond that which would be contemplated by the ordinary consumer

Obstacles to Recovery

Contractual Defenses defenses such as privity, disclaimers, and notice generally do not apply to tort liability

Plaintiff's Conduct

- *Contributory Negligence* not a defense in the majority of states
- *Comparative Negligence* most states have applied the rule of comparative negligence to strict liability in tort
- *Voluntary Assumption of the Risk* express assumption of risk is a defense to an action based upon strict liability; some states apply implied assumption of risk to strict liability cases
- *Misuse or Abuse of the Product* is a defense

Subsequent Alteration liability exists only if the product reaches the user or consumer without substantial change in the condition in which it is sold

Statute of Repose limits the time period for which a manufacturer is liable for injury caused by its product

Limitations on Damages many states have limited the punitive damages that a plaintiff can collect in a product liability lawsuit

Restatement (Third) of Torts: Products Liability

General Rule One engaged in the business of selling products who sells a defective product is subject to liability for harm to persons or property caused by the defect

Defective Conditions

- *Manufacturing Defect* a seller is held to strict liability when the product departs from its intended design
- *Design Defect* a product is defective when the foreseeable risks of harm posed by the product could have been reduced or avoided by the adoption of a reasonable alternative design
- *Failure to Warn* a product is defective because of inadequate instructions or warnings when the foreseeable risks of harm posed by the product could have been reduced or avoided by the provision of reasonable instructions or warnings

QUESTIONS

1. At the start of the social season, Aunt Lavinia purchased a hula skirt in Sadie's dress shop. The salesperson told her, "This superior garment will do things for a person." Aunt Lavinia's houseguest, her niece, Florabelle, asked and obtained her aunt's permission to wear the skirt to a masquerade ball. In the midst of the festivity, where there was much dancing, drinking, and smoking, the long skirt brushed against a glimmering cigarette butt. Unknown to Aunt Lavinia and Florabelle, its wearer, the garment was made of a fine unwoven fiber that is highly flammable. It burst into flames, and Florabelle suffered severe burns. Aunt Lavinia notified Sadie of the accident and of Florabelle's intention to recover from Sadie. Can Florabelle recover damages from Sadie, the proprietor of the dress shop, and Exotic Clothes, Inc., the manufacturer from which Sadie purchased the skirt? Explain.

2. The Talent Company, manufacturer of a widely advertised and expensive perfume, sold a quantity of this product to Young, a retail druggist. Dorothy and Bird visited the store of Young, and Dorothy, desiring to make a gift to Bird, purchased a bottle of this perfume from Young, asking for it by its trade name. Young wrapped up the bottle and handed it directly to Bird. The perfume contained a foreign chemical that upon the first use of the perfume by Bird severely burned her face and caused a permanent facial disfigurement. What are the rights of Bird, if any, against Dorothy, Young, and the Talent Company?

3. John Doe purchased a bottle of "Bleach-All," a well-known brand, from Roe's combination service station and grocery store. When John used the "Bleach-All," his clothes severely deteriorated due to an error in mixing the chemicals during the detergent's manufacture. John brings an action against Roe to recover damages. Explain whether John will be successful in his lawsuit.

4. A route salesperson for Ideal Milk Company delivered a half-gallon glass jug of milk to Allen's home. The next day, when Allen grasped the milk container by its neck to take it out of his refrigerator, it shattered in his hand and caused serious injury. Allen paid Ideal on a monthly basis for the regular delivery of milk. Ideal's milk bottles each contained the legend "Property of Ideal—to be returned," and the route salesman would pick up the empty bottles when he delivered milk. Can Allen recover damages from Ideal Milk Company? Why?

5. While Butler and his wife, Wanda, were browsing through Sloan's used car lot, Butler told Sloan that he was looking for a safe but cheap family car. Sloan said, "That old Cadillac hearse ain't hurt at all, and I'll sell it to you for $5,950." Butler said, "I'll have to take your word for it because I don't know a thing about cars." Butler asked Sloan whether he would guarantee the car, and Sloan replied, "I don't guarantee used cars." Then Sloan added, "But I have checked that Caddy over, and it will run another ten thousand miles without needing any repairs." Butler replied, "It has to because I won't have an extra dime for any repairs." Butler made a down payment of $800 and signed a printed form contract, furnished by Sloan, that contained a provision: "Seller

does not warrant the condition or performance of any used automobile."

As Butler drove the car out of Sloan's lot, the left rear wheel fell off and Butler lost control of the vehicle. It veered over an embankment, causing serious injuries to Wanda. What is Sloan's liability to Butler and Wanda?

6. John purchased for cash a Revenge automobile manufactured by Japanese Motors, Ltd., from an authorized franchised dealer in the United States. The dealer told John that the car had a "twenty-four month 24,000-mile warranty." Two days after John accepted delivery of the car, he received an eighty-page manual in fine print that stated, among other things, on page 72:

> The warranties herein are expressly in lieu of any other express or implied warranty, including any implied warranty of merchantability or fitness, and of any other obligation on the part of the company or the selling dealer.
>
> Japanese Motors, Ltd., and the selling dealer warrant to the owner each part of this vehicle to be free under use and service from defects in material and workmanship for a period of twenty-four months from the date of original retail delivery of first use or until it has been driven for 24,000 miles, whichever first occurs.

Within nine months after the purchase, John was forced to return the car for repairs to the dealer on thirty different occasions; and the car has been in the dealer's custody for more than seventy days during these nine months. The dealer has been forced to make major repairs to the engine, transmission, and steering assembly. The car is now in the custody of the dealer for further major repairs, and John has demanded that it keep the car and refund his entire purchase price. The dealer has refused on the ground that it has not breached its contract and is willing to continue repairing the car during the remainder of the "twenty-four/twenty-four" period. What are the rights and liabilities of the dealer and John?

7. Fred Lyon of New York, while on vacation in California, rented a new model Home Run automobile from Hart's Drive-A-Car. The car was manufactured by the Ange Motor Company and was purchased by Hart's from Jammer, Inc., an automobile importer. Lyon was driving the car on a street in San Jose when, due to a defect in the steering mechanism, it suddenly became impossible to steer. The speed of the car at the time was thirty miles per hour, but before Lyon could bring it to a stop, the car jumped a low curb and struck Peter Wolf, who was standing on the sidewalk, breaking both of his legs and causing other injuries. What rights does Wolf have against (a) Hart's Drive-A-Car, (b) Ange Motor Company, (c) Jammer, Inc., and (d) Lyon?

8. The plaintiff brings this cause of action against a manufacturer for the loss of his leg below the hip. The leg was lost when caught in the gears of a screw auger machine sold and installed by the defendant. Shortly before the accident, the plaintiff's co-employees had removed a covering panel from the machine by use of sledgehammers and crowbars in order to do repair work. When finished with their repairs, they

replaced the panel with a single piece of cardboard instead of restoring the equipment to its original condition. The plaintiff stepped on the cardboard in the course of his work and fell, catching his leg in the moving parts. Explain what causes of action the plaintiff may have against the defendant and what defenses the defendant could raise.

9. The plaintiff, while driving a pickup manufactured by the defendant, was struck in the rear by another motor vehicle. Upon impact, the plaintiff's head was jarred backward against the rear window of the cab, causing the plaintiff serious injury. The pickup was not equipped with a headrest, and none was required at the time. Should the plaintiff prevail on a cause of action based upon strict liability in tort? Why? Why not?

10. The plaintiff, while dining at the defendant's restaurant, ordered a chicken pot pie. While she was eating, she swallowed a sliver of chicken bone, which became lodged in her throat, causing her serious injury. The plaintiff brings a cause of action. Should she prevail? Why?

11. Salem Supply Co. sells new and used gardening equipment. Ben Buyer purchased a slightly used riding lawn mower for $1,500. The price was considerably less than that of comparable used mowers. The sale was clearly indicated to be "as is."

Two weeks after Ben purchased the mower, the police arrived at his house with Owen Owner, the true owner of the lawn mower, which was stolen from his yard, and reclaimed the mower. What recourse, if any, does Ben have?

12. Seigel, a seventy-three-year-old man, was injured at one of Giant Food's retail food stores when a bottle of Coca-Cola exploded as he was placing a six-pack of Coke into his shopping cart. The explosion caused him to lose his balance and fall, with injuries resulting. Has Giant breached its implied warranty of merchantability to Seigel? Why?

13. Guarino and two others (plaintiffs) died of gas asphyxiation and five others were injured when they entered a sewer tunnel without masks to answer the cries for help of their crew leader, Rooney. Rooney had left the sewer shaft and entered the tunnel to fix a water leakage problem. Having corrected the problem, Rooney was returning to the shaft when he apparently was overcome by gas because of a defect in his oxygen mask, which was manufactured by Mine Safety Appliance Company (defendant). The plaintiffs' estates brought this action against the defendant for breach of warranty, and the defendant raised the defense of the plaintiffs' voluntary assumption of the risk. Explain who will prevail.

CASE PROBLEMS

14. Green Seed Company packaged, labeled, and marketed a quality tomato seed known as "Green's Pink Shipper" for commercial sale. Brown Seed Store, a retailer, purchased the seed from Green Seed and then sold it to Guy Jones, an individual engaged in the business of growing tomato seedlings for sale to commercial tomato growers. Williams purchased the seedlings from Jones and then transplanted and raised them in accordance with accepted farming methods. The plants, however, produced not the promised "Pink Shipper" tomatoes but an inferior variety that spoiled in the field. Williams then brought an action against Green Seed for $90,000, claiming that his crop damage had been caused by Green Seed's breach of an express warranty. Green Seed argued in defense that its warranty did not extend to remote purchasers and that the company did not receive notice of the claimed breach of warranty. Who will prevail? Why?

15. Mobley purchased from Century Dodge a car described in the contract as new. The contract also contained a disclaimer of all warranties, express or implied. Subsequently, Mobley discovered that the car had, in fact, been involved in an accident. He then sued Century Dodge to recover damages, claiming the dealer had breached its express warranty that the car was new. Century Dodge argues that it had adequately disclaimed all warranties. Decision?

16. O'Neil purchased a used diesel tractor-trailer combination from International Harvester. O'Neil claimed that International Harvester's salesman had told him that the truck had recently been overhauled and that it would be suitable for hauling logs in the mountains. The written installment contract signed by the parties provided that the truck was sold

"AS IS WITHOUT WARRANTY OF ANY CHARACTER express or implied." O'Neil admitted that he had read the disclaimer clause but claimed that he understood it to mean that the tractor-trailer would be in the condition that International Harvester's salesman had promised.

O'Neil paid the $1,700 down payment, but he failed to make any of the monthly payments. He claimed that he refused to pay because his employee had many problems with the truck when he took it to the mountains. Delays resulting from those problems, O'Neil argued, had caused him to lose his permit to cut firewood and, therefore, the accompanying business. An International Harvester representative agreed to pay for one-half of the cost of certain repairs, but the several attempts made to fix the truck were unsuccessful. O'Neil then tried to return the truck and to rescind the sale, but International Harvester refused to cooperate. Decision?

17. Mrs. Embs went into Stamper's Cash Market to buy soft drinks for her children. She had removed five bottles from an upright soft drink cooler, placed them in a carton, and turned to move away from the display when a bottle of Seven-Up in a carton at her feet exploded, cutting her leg. Apparently, several other bottles had exploded that same week. Stamper's Cash Market received its entire stock of Seven-Up from Arnold Lee Vice, the area distributor. Vice in turn received his entire stock of Seven-Up from Pepsi-Cola Bottling Co. Can Mrs. Embs recover damages from (a) Stamper, (b) Vice, or (c) Pepsi-Cola Bottling? Why?

18. Catania wished to paint the exterior of his house. He went to Brown, a local paint store owner, and asked him to recommend a paint for the job. Catania told Brown that the exterior

walls were stucco and in a chalky, powdery condition. Brown suggested Pierce's shingle and shake paint. Brown then instructed Catania how to mix the paint and how to use a wire brush to prepare the surface. Five months later, the paint began to peel, flake, and blister. Catania brings an action against Brown. Decision?

19. Robinson, a truck driver for a moving company, decided to buy a used truck from the company. Branch, the owner, told Robinson that the truck was being repaired and that Robinson should wait and inspect the truck before signing the contract. Robinson, who had driven the truck before, felt that inspection was unnecessary. Again, Branch suggested Robinson wait to inspect the truck, and again Robinson declined. Branch then told Robinson he was buying the truck "as is." Robinson then signed the contract. After the truck broke down four times, Robinson sued. Will Robinson be successful? What defenses can Branch raise?

20. Perfect Products manufactures balloons, which are then bought and resold by wholesale novelty distributors. Mego Corp. manufactures a doll called "Bubble Yum Baby." A balloon is inserted in the doll's mouth with a mouthpiece, and the doll's arm is pumped to inflate the balloon, simulating the blowing of a bubble. Mego Corp. used Perfect Products balloons in the dolls, bought through independent distributors. The plaintiff's infant daughter died after swallowing a balloon removed from the doll. Is Perfect Products liable to plaintiff under a theory of strict liability? Explain.

21. Patient was injured when the footrest of an adjustable X-ray table collapsed, causing Patient to fall to the floor. G.E. manufactured the X-ray table and the footrest. At trial, evidence was introduced that G.E. had manufactured for several years another footrest model complete with safety latches. However, there was no evidence that the footrest involved was manufactured defectively. The action is based on a theory of strict liability. Who wins? Why?

22. Vlases, a coal miner who had always raised small flocks of chickens, spent two years building a new two-story chicken coop large enough to house four thousand chickens. After its completion, he purchased two thousand two hundred one-day-old chicks from Montgomery Ward for the purpose of producing eggs for sale. He had selected them from Ward's catalog, which stated that these chicks, hybrid Leghorns, were noted for their excellent egg production. Vlases had equipped the coop with brand-new machinery and had taken further hygiene precautions for the chicks' health. Almost one month later, Vlases noticed that their feathers were beginning to fall off. A veterinarian's examination revealed signs of drug intoxication and hemorrhagic disease in a few of the chicks. Eight months later, it was determined that the chicks were suffering from visceral and avian leukosis, or bird cancer, which reduced their egg-bearing capacity to zero. Avian leukosis may be transmitted either genetically or by unsanitary conditions. Subsequently, the disease infected the entire flock. Vlases then brought suit against Montgomery Ward for its breach of the implied warranties of merchantability and of fitness for a particular purpose. Ward claimed that there was no way to detect the disease in the one-day-old chicks, nor was there medication available to prevent this disease from occur-

ring. Is Montgomery Ward liable under a warranty and/or strict liability cause of action? Explain.

23. Heckman, an employee of Clark Equipment Company, severely injured his left hand when he caught it in a power press that he was operating at work. The press was manufactured by Federal Press Company and sold to Clark eight years earlier. It could be operated either by hand controls that required the use of both hands away from the point of operation or by an optional foot pedal. When the foot pedal was used without a guard, nothing remained to keep the operator's hands from the point of operation. Federal Press did not provide safety appliances unless the customer requested them, but when it delivered the press to Clark with the optional pedal, it suggested that Clark install a guard. The press had a similar warning embossed on it. Clark did, in fact, purchase a guard for $100, but it was not mounted on the machine at the time of the injury; nor was it believed to be an effective safety device.

Heckman argued that a different type of guard, if installed, would have made the press safe in 95 percent of its customary uses. Federal, in turn, argued that the furnishing of guards was not customary in the industry; that the machine's many uses made it impracticable to design and install any one guard as standard equipment; that Clark's failure to obey Federal's warning was a superseding cause of the injury; and that state regulations placed responsibility for the safe operation of presses on employers and employees. Decision?

24. For sixteen years, the late Mrs. Dorothy Mae Palmer was married to Mr. Schultz, an insulator who worked with asbestos products. Mrs. Palmer was not exposed to asbestos dust in a factory setting; rather, she was exposed when Mr. Schultz brought his work clothes home to be washed. Mrs. Palmer died of mesothelioma. This product liability suit was brought by Mrs. Palmer's daughters to recover for the alleged wrongful death of their mother. The daughters claim that Mrs. Palmer's mesothelioma was the result of exposure to asbestos-containing products manufactured by Owens-Corning. The daughters claim that the asbestos products were defective and unreasonably dangerous and that Owens-Corning was negligent in failing to warn of the dangers associated with their products. Explain whether the plaintiffs should prevail.

25. A gasoline-powered lawn mower, which had been used earlier to cut grass, was left unattended next to a water heater that had been manufactured by Sears. Expert testimony was presented to demonstrate that vapors from the mower's gas tank accumulated under the water heater and resulted in an explosion. Three-year-old Shawn Toups was injured as a result. Evidence was also presented negating any claim that Shawn had been handling the gasoline can located nearby or the lawn mower. He was not burned on the soles of his feet or the palms of his hands. Is Sears liable to the Toups in strict product liability? Explain.

26. For more than forty years, Rose Cipollone smoked between one and two packs of cigarettes a day. Upon her death from lung cancer, Rose's husband, Antonio Cipollone, filed suit against Liggett Group, Inc., Lorillard, Inc., and Philip Morris, Inc., three of the leading firms in the tobacco industry, for the wrongful death of his wife. Many theories of liability and

defenses were asserted in this decidedly complex and protracted litigation.

One theory of liability claimed by Mr. Cipollone was breach of express warranty. It is uncontested that all three manufacturers ran multimedia ad campaigns that contained affirmations, promises, or innuendos that smoking cigarettes was safe. For example, ads for Chesterfield cigarettes boasted that a medical specialist could find no adverse health effects in subjects after six months of smoking. Chesterfields were also advertised as being manufactured with "electronic miracle" technology that made them "better and safer for you." Another ad stated that Chesterfield ingredients were tested and approved by scientists from leading universities. Another brand, L&M, publicly touted the "miracle tip" filter, claiming it was "just what the doctor ordered."

At trial, the defendant tobacco companies were not permitted to try to prove that Mrs. Cipollone disbelieved or placed no reliance on the advertisements and their safety assurances. Did the defendants breach an express warranty to the plaintiff? Explain.

27. Trans-Aire International, Inc. (TAI), converts ordinary automotive vans into recreational vehicles. TAI had been installing carpet and ceiling fabrics in the converted vans with an adhesive made by the 3M Company. Unfortunately, during the hot summer months, the 3M adhesive would often fail to hold the carpet and fabrics in place.

TAI contacted Northern Adhesive Company (Northern), seeking a "suitable" product to replace the 3M adhesive. Northern sent samples of several adhesives, commenting that hopefully one or more "might be applicable." Northern also informed TAI that one of the samples, Adhesive 7448, was a "match" for the 3M adhesive. After testing all the samples under cool plant conditions, TAI's chief engineer determined that Adhesive 7448 was better than the 3M adhesive. When TAI's president asked if the new adhesive should be tested under summerlike conditions, TAI's chief engineer responded that it was unnecessary to do so. The president then asked if Adhesive 7448 came with any warranties. A Northern representative stated that there were no warranties, except that the orders shipped would be identical to the sample.

After converting more than five hundred vans using Adhesive 7448, TAI became aware that high summer temperatures were causing the new adhesive to fail. Explain whether TAI should prevail against Northern in a suit claiming (a) breach of an implied warranty of fitness for a particular purpose, (b) breach of an implied warranty of merchantability, and (c) breach of express warranty.

28. The plaintiff's children purchased an Aero Cycle exercise bike for their mother to use in a weight-loss program. The Aero Cycle bike was manufactured by DP and purchased from Walmart. The first time the plaintiff, Judy Dunne, used the bike she used it only for a few seconds. But the second time she used it, she pedaled for three or four rotations and the rear support strut failed and the bike collapsed under her. At the time of the accident, the plaintiff weighed between 450 and 500 pounds. She fell off the bike backward, struck her head on a nearby metal file cabinet, and was knocked unconscious. When the plaintiff regained consciousness, her mouth was bleeding and her neck, left shoulder, arm, leg, knee, and ankle were injured. The plaintiff was diagnosed as having a cervical strain and multiple contusions. She filed suit against Walmart and DP. Explain whether the plaintiff should prevail.

TAKING SIDES

Brian Felley purchased a used Ford Taurus from Thomas and Cheryl Singleton for $8,800. The car had 126,000 miles on it. After test driving the car, Felley discussed the condition of the car with Thomas Singleton, who informed Felley that the only thing known to be wrong with the car was that it had a noise in the right rear and that a grommet (a connector having to do with a strut) was bad or missing. Thomas told Felley that otherwise the car was in good condition. Nevertheless, Felley soon began experiencing problems with the car. On the second day that he owned the car, Felley noticed a problem with the clutch. Over the next few days, the clutch problem worsened and Felley was unable to shift the gears. Felley presented an invoice to Thomas showing that he paid $942.76 for the removal and repair of the car's clutch. In addition, the car developed serious brake problems within the first month that Felley owned it. Felley now contends that the Singletons breached their express warranty.

a. What arguments would support Felley's contention?

b. What arguments would support the claim by the Singletons that they had not given an express warranty?

c. What is the appropriate outcome? Explain.

Sales Remedies

CHAPTER 23

Remedies ... shall be liberally administered to the end that the aggrieved party may be put in as good a position as if the other party had fully performed.

Uniform Commercial Code

CHAPTER OUTCOMES

After reading and studying this chapter, you should be able to:

1. Identify and explain the goods-oriented remedies of the seller and the buyer.

2. Identify and explain the obligation-oriented remedies of the seller and the buyer.

3. Identify and explain the money-oriented damages of the seller and the buyer.

4. Identify and explain the "specific performance" remedies of the seller and the buyer.

5. Describe the basic types of contractual provisions affecting remedies and the limitations that the Uniform Commercial Code imposes upon those provisions.

Practical Advice

Consider including in your contracts a provision for (1) the recovery of attorneys' fees in the event of breach of contract and (2) the arbitration of contract disputes.

A contract for the sale of goods may be completely performed at one time or may be performed in stages, according to the parties' agreement. At any stage, one of the parties may repudiate the contract, may become insolvent, or may breach the contract by failing to perform her obligations under it. In a sales contract, breach may consist of the seller's delivering defective goods, too few goods, the wrong goods, or no goods. The buyer may breach by not accepting conforming goods or by failing to pay for conforming goods that she has accepted. Breach may occur when the goods are in the possession of the seller, in the possession of a bailee of the buyer, in transit to the buyer, or in the possession of the buyer.

Remedies, therefore, need to address not only the type of breach of contract but also the situation with respect to the goods. Consequently, the Uniform Commercial Code (UCC) provides separate and distinct remedies for the seller and for the buyer, each specifically keyed to the type of breach and the situation of the goods.

In all events, the purpose of the Code is to put the aggrieved party in a position as good as the one she would have been in had the other party fully performed. To accomplish this purpose, the Code has provided that the courts should liberally administer its remedies. Moreover, damages do not have to be "calculable with mathematical precision"; they simply must be proved with "whatever definiteness and accuracy the facts permit, but no more." The purpose of remedies under the Code is compensation; therefore, punitive damages generally are not available.

Finally, the Code has rejected the doctrine of election of remedies. Essentially, the Code provides that remedies for breach are cumulative. Whether one remedy bars another depends entirely on the facts of the individual case.

CISG   *According to the United Nations Convention on CISG, damages for breach of contract by one party consist of a sum equal to the loss, including loss of profit, suffered by the other party as a consequence of the breach. Such damages may not exceed the loss which the party in breach foresaw or should have* *foreseen at the time of the conclusion of the contract as a possible consequence of the breach of contract. The aggrieved party must take such measures as are reasonable in the circumstances to mitigate the loss, including loss of profit, resulting from the breach. If he fails to take such measures, the party in breach may claim a reduction in the damages in the amount by which the loss should have been mitigated.*

REMEDIES OF THE SELLER [23-1]

A buyer's default in performing any of his contractual obligations deprives the seller of the rights for which he bargained. A **buyer's default** may consist of any of the following acts: wrongfully rejecting the goods, wrongfully revoking acceptance of the goods, failing to make a payment due on or before delivery, or repudiating (indicating an intention not to perform) the contract in whole or in part. (Article 2A.) The Code catalogs the seller's remedies for each of these defaults. (Article 2A has a comparable set of remedies for the lessor.) These remedies allow the seller to (1) withhold delivery of the goods, (2) stop delivery of the goods by a carrier or other bailee, (3) identify to the contract conforming goods not already identified, (4) resell the goods and recover damages, (5) recover damages for nonacceptance of the goods or repudiation of the contract, (6) recover the price, (7) recover incidental damages, (8) cancel the contract, and (9) reclaim the goods on the buyer's insolvency.

> **Buyer's default**
>
> the seller's remedies are triggered by the buyer's action in wrongfully rejecting or revoking acceptance of the goods, in failing to make payment due on or before delivery, or in repudiating the contract

Under Article 2A, a lessor also may recover compensation for any loss of or damage to the lessor's residual interest in the goods caused by the lessee's default.

The first three and the ninth remedies indexed above are *goods oriented*—that is, they relate to the seller's exercising control over the goods. The fourth through seventh remedies are *money oriented* because they provide the seller with the opportunity to recover monetary damages. The eighth remedy is *obligation oriented* because it allows the seller to avoid his obligation under the contract.

Moreover, if the seller delivers goods on credit and the buyer fails to pay the price when due, the seller's sole remedy, unless the buyer is insolvent, is to sue for the unpaid price. If, however, the buyer received the goods on credit while insolvent, the seller may be able to reclaim the goods. The Code defines insolvency to include both its equity meaning and its bankruptcy meaning. The **equity** meaning of **insolvency** is the inability to pay debts in the ordinary course of business or as they become due. The **bankruptcy** meaning of **insolvency** is that total liabilities exceed the total value of all assets.

> **Insolvency (equity)**
>
> inability to pay debts in ordinary course of business or as they become due
>
> **Insolvency (bankruptcy)**
>
> total liabilities exceed total value of assets

As noted, the Code's remedies are cumulative. Thus, by way of example, an aggrieved seller may (1) identify goods to the contract, *and* (2) withhold delivery, *and* (3) resell or recover damages for nonacceptance or recover the price, *and* (4) recover incidental damages, *and* (5) cancel the contract.

CISG   *If the buyer fails to perform any of his obligations under the contract or the CISG, the seller may (1) require the buyer to pay the price or (2) fix an additional period of time of reasonable length for the buyer to perform his obligations. Unless the seller has received notice from the buyer that she will not perform within the period so fixed, the seller may not, during that period, resort to any remedy for breach of contract. Moreover, if the buyer's breach is fundamental or the buyer fails to perform within the additional time granted by the seller, the seller may avoid the contract. In addition to these remedies, the seller also has the right to damages.*

Withhold Delivery of the Goods [23-1a]

A seller may withhold delivery of goods to a buyer who has wrongfully rejected or revoked acceptance of the goods, who has failed to make a payment due on or before delivery, or who has repudiated the contract. (Article 2A.) This right is essentially that of a seller to withhold or discontinue performance of her side of the contract because of the buyer's breach.

When the contract calls for installments, any breach of an installment that impairs the value of the *whole* contract will permit the seller to withhold the entire undelivered balance of the goods. In addition, on discovery of the buyer's insolvency, the seller may refuse to deliver the goods except for cash, including payment for all goods previously delivered under the contract. (Article 2A.)

Stop Delivery of the Goods [23-1b]

Stop delivery

if the buyer is insolvent (one who is unable to pay his debts as they become due or one whose total liabilities exceed his total assets), the seller may stop any delivery; if the buyer repudiates or otherwise breaches, the seller may stop carload, truckload, planeload, or larger shipments

An extension of the right to withhold delivery is the right of an aggrieved seller to **stop delivery** of goods in transit to the buyer or in the possession of a bailee. A seller who discovers that the buyer is insolvent may stop any delivery. If the buyer is not insolvent but repudiates or otherwise breaches the contract, the seller may stop carload, truckload, planeload, or larger shipments. (Article 2A.) To stop delivery, the seller must notify the carrier or other bailee soon enough for the bailee to prevent delivery of the goods. After this notification, the carrier or bailee must hold and deliver the goods according to the directions of the seller, who is liable to the carrier or bailee for any charges or damages incurred. If a negotiable document of title has been issued for the goods, the bailee need not obey a notification until surrender of the document.

Identify Goods to the Contract [23-1c]

On a breach of the contract by the buyer, the seller may proceed to identify to the contract conforming goods in her possession or control that were not so identified at the time she learned of the breach. (Article 2A.) This enables the seller to exercise the remedy of resale of goods (discussed in the next section). Furthermore, the seller may resell any unfinished goods that have been demonstrably intended to fulfill the particular contract. The seller may either complete the manufacture of unfinished goods and identify them to the contract or cease their manufacture and resell the unfinished goods for scrap or salvage value. (Article 2A.) In so deciding, the seller must exercise reasonable commercial judgment to minimize her loss.

Resell the Goods and Recover Damages [23-1d]

Resell the goods

the seller may resell the goods concerned or the undelivered balance of the goods and recover the difference between the contract price and the resale price, together with any incidental damages, minus expenses saved

Under the same circumstances that permit the seller to withhold delivery of goods to the buyer (i.e., wrongful rejection or revocation, repudiation, or failure to make timely payment), the seller may **resell the goods** concerned or the undelivered balance of the goods. If the resale is made in good faith and in a commercially reasonable manner, the seller may recover from the buyer the difference between the contract price and the resale price, plus any incidental damages (discussed in a later section), minus expenses saved because of the buyer's breach. For example, Floyd agrees to sell goods to Beverly for a contract price of $80,000 due on delivery. Beverly repudiates the contract and refuses to pay Floyd anything. Floyd resells the goods in strict compliance with the Code for $60,000, incurring incidental damages for sales commissions of $5,000 but saving $2,000 in transportation costs. Floyd would recover from Beverly the difference between the contract price ($80,000) and the resale price ($60,000), plus incidental damages ($5,000), minus expenses saved ($2,000), which equals $23,000.

In a lease, the comparable recovery is the *difference* between the *present values* of the *old rent* due under the original lease and the *new rent* due under the new lease. More specifically, the lessor may recover (1) the accrued and unpaid rent as of the date of commencement of the new lease; (2) *plus* the present value as of that date of total rent for the then-remaining term of the original lease *minus* the present value, as of the same date, of the rent under the new lease applicable to a comparable time period; (3) *plus* any incidental damages; (4) *minus* expenses saved because of the lessee's breach.

The resale may be a public or private sale, and the goods may be sold as a unit or in parcels. When the resale is a private sale, the seller must give the buyer reasonable notice of his intention to resell. When the resale is at a public sale (such as an auction), it must be made at a usual place or market for public sale if one is reasonably available. The seller must give the buyer reasonable notice of the time and place of the resale, unless the goods are perishable or threaten to decline in value speedily. In addition, the seller may be a purchaser of the goods at the public sale. In choosing between a public and private sale, the seller must observe relevant trade practices and usages and take into account the character of the goods.

The seller is not accountable to the buyer for any profit made on any resale of the goods. (Article 2A.) Moreover, a good faith purchaser at a resale takes the goods free of any rights of the original buyer, even if the seller has failed to comply with one or more of the requirements of the Code in making the resale. (Article 2A.)

Failure to act in good faith and in a commercially reasonable manner deprives the seller of this remedy and relegates him to the remedy of recovering damages for nonacceptance or repudiation (discussed in the next section). (Article 2A.)

CISG   *If the contract is avoided and the seller has resold the goods in a reasonable manner and within a reasonable time after avoidance, he may recover the difference between the contract price and the resale price. In addition, he may recover consequential damages.*

Recover Damages for Nonacceptance or Repudiation [23-1e]

In the event of the buyer's wrongful rejection or revocation, repudiation, or failure to make timely payment, the seller may recover damages from the buyer equal to the **market price differential**, or the difference between the unpaid contract price and the market price at the time and place of tender of the goods, plus incidental damages, minus expenses saved because of the buyer's breach. This remedy is an alternative to the remedy of reselling the goods.

In a lease, the comparable recovery is the ***difference*** between the ***present values*** of the ***old rent*** due under the original lease and the ***market rent***.

For example, Joyce in Seattle agrees to sell goods to Maynard in Chicago for $20,000 F.O.B. (free on board) Chicago, with delivery by June 15. Maynard wrongfully rejects the goods. The market price would be ascertained as of June 15 in Chicago because F.O.B. Chicago is a destination contract in which the place of tender would be Chicago. The market price of the goods on June 15 in Chicago is $15,000. Joyce, who incurred $1,000 in incidental expenses while saving $500 in expenses, would recover from Maynard the difference between the contract price ($20,000) and the market price ($15,000), plus incidental damages ($1,000), minus expenses saved ($500), which equals $5,500.

If the difference between the contract price and the market price will not place the seller in as good a position as performance would have, then the measure of damages is the **lost profit**, that is the profit, including reasonable overhead, that the seller would have realized from full performance by the buyer, plus any incidental damages, minus expenses the seller saved because of the buyer's breach. For example, Green, an automobile dealer, enters into a contract to sell a large, fuel-inefficient luxury car to Holland for $32,000. The price of gasoline increases 20 percent, and Holland repudiates. The market value of the car is still $32,000, but because Green cannot sell as many cars as he can obtain, Green's sales volume has decreased by one as a result of Holland's breach. Therefore, Green would be permitted to recover the profits he lost on the sale to Holland (computed as the contract price, minus what the car costs Green, plus an allocation of overhead), plus any incidental damages. The *Kenco Homes, Inc. v. Williams* case further explains the computation of lost profits.

Article 2A has a comparable provision, except the profit is reduced to its present value since the lessor would have received it over the term of the lease.

CISG   *If the contract is avoided and the seller has not made a resale, he may recover the difference between the contract price and the current price at the time of avoidance and at the place where delivery of goods should have been made. In addition, he may recover consequential damages.*

Market price differential the seller may recover damages from the buyer measured by the difference between the unpaid contract price and the market price at the time and place of tender of the goods, plus incidental damages, minus expenses saved

Lost profit in the alternative, the seller may recover the lost profit, including reasonable overhead, plus incidental damages, minus expenses saved

Practical Advice

Carefully consider whether you are better off reselling the goods or seeking damages for nonacceptance or repudiation.

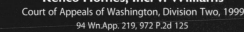

Kenco Homes, Inc. v. Williams
Court of Appeals of Washington, Division Two, 1999
94 Wn.App. 219, 972 P.2d 125
http://scholar.google.com/scholar_case?case=2280470166169778873&q=972+p.2d+125&hl=en&as_sdt=2,34

FACTS Kenco buys mobile homes from the factory and sells them to the consumer. Sometimes, it contracts to sell a home that the factory has not yet built. It has a virtually unlimited supply of product. On September 27, 1994, Kenco Homes, Inc., and Dale E. and Debi A. Williams, husband and wife, signed a written contract to buy a mobile home that had not yet been built from Kenco. The contract called for a price of $39,400, with $500 down.

The contract contained two pertinent conditions: the contract would be enforceable only if Williams (1) could obtain financing and (2) later approved a bid for site improvements. Financing was to cover the cost of the mobile home and the cost of the land on which the mobile home would be placed. The contract provided for damages. It stated, "I [Williams] understand that you [Kenco] shall have all the rights of a seller upon breach of contract under the Uniform Commercial Code [UCC], except the right to seek and collect 'liquidated damages' under Section 2-718." The contract provided for reasonable attorneys' fees. In early October, Williams accepted Kenco's bid for site improvements. As a result, the parties (1) formed a second contract and (2) fulfilled the first contract's site-improvement-approval condition. Also in early October, Williams received preliminary approval on the needed financing.

Subsequently, Williams gave Kenco a $600 check so Kenco could order an appraisal of the land on which the mobile home would be located. Before Kenco could act, however, Williams stopped payment on the check and repudiated the entire transaction. His reason was that he "had found a better deal elsewhere." When Williams repudiated, Kenco had not yet ordered the mobile home from the factory. After Williams repudiated, Kenco simply did not place the order. As a result, Kenco's only out-of-pocket expense was a minor amount of office overhead. On November 1, 1994, Kenco sued Williams for lost profits.

The trial court found that Williams had breached the contract, causing Kenco to lose profits in the amount of $11,133 ($6,720 on the mobile home, and $4,413 on the site improvements). Moreover, the trial court held that Kenco was entitled to damages, but ruled that Kenco would be adequately compensated by retaining Williams' $500 down payment. The trial court declared that Williams was the prevailing party; and that Williams should receive reasonable attorneys' fees in the amount of $1,800. Kenco appealed, claiming the trial court used an incorrect measure of damages.

DECISION Reversed with directions to enter an amended judgment awarding Kenco its lost profit of $11,133 and reasonable attorneys' fees incurred at trial and on appeal.

OPINION Under the UCC, a nonbreaching seller may recover "damages for nonacceptance" from a breaching buyer. These damages may be calculated in one of two ways. First, the seller may receive the difference between the market price (upon resale of the goods) and the unpaid contract price together with any incidental damages, but less expenses saved in consequence of the buyer's breach. If this first method of determining damages does not put

the seller in as good a position as performance would have done, then the second method of determining damages is used.

In this second method, the seller can receive any profit (including reasonable overhead) which the seller would have made from full performance by the buyer, together with incidental damages, plus allowance for costs reasonably incurred, minus any payments or proceeds of resale.

In general, the adequacy of damages under the first method depends on whether the nonbreaching seller has a readily available market on which he or she can resell the goods that the breaching buyer should have taken. The seller cannot readily resell goods in certain situations, such as (1) when the seller does not yet possess the goods, but was planning to obtain them, (2) when the goods are of a specialized nature for which there is not a ready market, and (3) when the market conditions are such that a ready buyer is not available without displacing another sale. (This is known as "lost volume.")

In this case, Kenco did not order the breached goods before Williams repudiated. After Williams repudiated, Kenco was not required to order the breached goods from the factory. It rightfully elected not to do so and it could not resell the breached goods on the open market. Thus, the measure of damages under the first method is inadequate to put Kenco in as good a position as Williams' performance would have done. Therefore, Kenco is entitled to its lost profit of $11,133.

In addition, Kenco is entitled to reasonable attorneys' fees. The parties' contract provided that the prevailing party would be entitled to such fees. Kenco is the prevailing party.

INTERPRETATION When the measure of damages based on the difference between the market price and the contract price does not put the seller in as good a position as performance would have done, then a nonbreaching seller is entitled to damages, which include the unrealized profit from the sale.

ETHICAL QUESTION Did either party act unethically? Explain.

CRITICAL THINKING QUESTION Do you agree with the Code's measure of damages for the "lost volume seller"? Explain.

Recover the Price [23-1f]

Recover the price

the seller may recover the price: (1) when the buyer has accepted the goods, (2) when the goods have been lost or damaged after the risk of loss has passed to the buyer, or (3) when the goods have been identified to the contract and there is no ready market available for their resale

The Code permits the seller to **recover the price** plus incidental damages in three situations: (1) when the buyer has accepted the goods, (2) when conforming goods have been lost or damaged after the risk of loss has passed to the buyer, and (3) when the goods have been identified to the contract and there is no ready market available for their resale at a reasonable price. For example, Kelly, in accordance with her agreement with Sally, prints ten thousand letterheads and envelopes with Sally's name and address on them. Sally wrongfully rejects the stationery, and Kelly is unable to resell it at a reasonable price. Kelly is entitled to recover the price plus incidental damages from Sally. For a case dealing with the seller's right to recover the price when the buyer has accepted the goods, see *Midwest Hatchery v. Doorenbos Poultry* later in this chapter.

Article 2A has a similar provision except that the lessor is entitled to (1) accrued and unpaid rent as of the date of the judgment, (2) the present value as of the judgment date of the rent for the then remaining lease term, *and* (3) incidental damages *less* expenses saved.

A seller who sues for the price must hold for the buyer any goods that have been identified to the contract and are still in her control. (Article 2A.) If resale becomes possible, the seller may resell the goods at any time before the collection of the judgment, and the net proceeds of such resale must be credited to the buyer. Payment of the judgment entitles the buyer to any goods not resold. In a lease, payment of the judgment entitles the lessee to the use and possession of the goods for the remaining lease term.

CISG *The seller may require the buyer to pay the price, take delivery, or perform her other obligations, unless the seller has resorted to a remedy that is inconsistent with this requirement.*

Recover Incidental Damages [23-1g]

In addition to recovering damages for the difference between the contract price and the resale price, recovering damages for nonacceptance or repudiation, or recovering the price, the seller also may recover in the same action her incidental damages to recoup expenses she reasonably incurred as a result of the buyer's breach. The Code defines a **seller's incidental damages** to include any commercially reasonable charges, expenses, or commissions incurred in stopping delivery; in the transportation, care, and custody of goods after the buyer's breach; in connection with return or resale of the goods; or otherwise resulting from the breach. Article 2A has an analogous definition.

> **Seller's incidental damages**
> commercially reasonable charges, expenses, or commissions directly resulting from breach

> *Practical Advice*
> As an aggrieved seller, maintain good records regarding incidental damages you incurred.

Cancel the Contract [23-1h]

When the buyer wrongfully rejects or revokes acceptance of the goods, fails to make a payment due on or before delivery, or repudiates the contract in whole or in part, the seller may cancel the part of the contract that concerns the goods directly affected. If the breach is of an installment contract and it substantially impairs the whole contract, the seller may cancel the entire contract. (Article 2A.)

The Code defines **cancellation** as one party's putting an end to the contract because of a breach by the other. (Article 2A.) The obligation of the canceling party for any future performance under the contract is discharged, although he retains any remedy for breach of the whole contract or for any unperformed balance. (Article 2A.) Thus, if the seller has the right to cancel, he may recover damages for breach without having to tender any further performance.

> **Cancellation**
> one party's putting an end to a contract because of a breach by the other

CISG *The seller may declare the contract avoided if (1) the buyer commits a fundamental breach or (2) the buyer does not, within the additional period of time fixed by the seller, perform his obligation to pay the price or take delivery of the goods. Avoidance of the contract releases both parties from their obligations under it, subject to any damages that may be due. Avoidance does not affect any provision of the contract for the settlement of disputes or any other provision of the contract governing the rights and obligations of the parties consequent upon the avoidance of the contract. A party who has performed the contract either wholly or in part may claim restitution from the other party. If both parties are bound to make restitution, they must do so concurrently.*

Reclaim the Goods upon the Buyer's Insolvency [23-1i]

In addition to the right of an unpaid seller to withhold and stop delivery of the goods, he may **reclaim the goods** from an insolvent buyer by demand made to the buyer within ten days after the buyer has received the goods. However, if the buyer has committed fraud by misrepresenting her solvency to the seller in writing within three months prior to delivery of the goods, the ten-day limitation does not apply.

The seller's right to reclaim the goods is subject to the rights of a buyer in the ordinary course of business or to the rights of any other good faith purchaser. In addition, a seller who successfully reclaims goods from an insolvent buyer is excluded from all other remedies with respect to those goods.

A lessor retains title to the goods and therefore has the right to recover possession of them upon default by the lessee.

> **Reclaim the goods**
> an unpaid seller may reclaim goods from an insolvent buyer under certain circumstances

> *Practical Advice*
> If you wish to exercise the seller's rights of reclamation of goods sold, you will need to act quickly.

┌───┐

CONCEPT REVIEW 23-1

Remedies of the Seller

Buyer's Breach	Seller's Remedies		
	Obligation Oriented	Goods Oriented[1]	Money Oriented[2]
Buyer Wrongfully Rejects Goods	Cancel	• Withhold delivery of goods • Stop delivery of goods in transit • Identify conforming goods to the contract	• Resell and recover damages • Recover difference between unpaid contract and market prices or lost profits • Recover price
Buyer Wrongfully Revokes Acceptance	Cancel	• Withhold delivery of goods • Stop delivery of goods in transit • Identify conforming goods to the contract	• Resell and recover damages • Recover difference between unpaid contract and market prices or lost profits • Recover price
Buyer Fails to Make Payment	Cancel	• Withhold delivery of goods • Stop delivery of goods in transit • Identify conforming goods to the contract • Reclaim goods upon buyer's insolvency	• Resell and recover damages • Recover difference between unpaid contract and market prices or lost profits • Recover price
Buyer Repudiates	Cancel	• Withhold delivery of goods • Stop delivery of goods in transit • Identify conforming goods to the contract	• Resell and recover damages • Recover difference between unpaid contract and market prices or lost profits • Recover price

[1]In a lease, the lessor has the right to recover possession of the goods upon default by the lessee.
[2]In a lease, the lessor's recovery of damages for future rent payments is reduced to their present value.

└───┘

REMEDIES OF THE BUYER [23-2]

Seller's default
the buyer's remedies arise when the seller fails to make delivery or repudiates the contract, or when the buyer rightfully rejects or justifiably revokes acceptance of goods tendered or delivered

Basically, a **seller's default** may occur in one of three different ways: she may repudiate, fail to deliver the goods without repudiation, or deliver or tender goods that do not conform to the contract. (Article 2A.) The Code provides remedies for each of these breaches. Some remedies are available for all three types of breaches, whereas others are not. Moreover, the availability of some remedies depends on the buyer's actions. For example, if the seller tenders nonconforming goods, the buyer may reject or accept them. If the buyer rejects them, he can choose from a number of remedies. On the other hand, if the buyer accepts the nonconforming goods and does not justifiably revoke his acceptance, he limits himself to recovering damages.

When the seller fails to make delivery or repudiates, or when the buyer rightfully rejects or justifiably revokes acceptance, the buyer may, with respect to any goods involved, or with respect to the whole if the breach goes to the whole contract, (1) cancel *and* (2) recover payments made. In addition, the buyer may (3) "cover" and obtain damages *or* (4) recover damages for nondelivery. When the seller fails to deliver or repudiates, the buyer, when appropriate, may also (5) recover identified goods if the seller is insolvent, *or* (6) "replevy" the goods, *or* (7) obtain specific performance. Moreover, on rightful rejection or justifiable revocation of acceptance, the buyer (8) has a security interest in the goods. When the buyer has accepted goods and notified

APPLYING THE LAW

Sales Remedies

Facts TRAC is a wholesaler of computer hardware component parts. In late February, TRAC entered into a sales contract with Gemini, a small manufacturer of custom personal computers, for the sale of $10,000 worth of component parts. The written agreement required Gemini to pay $2,000 on April 15, another $3,000 on May 15, and the remaining $5,000 on June 15, with delivery of all components to Gemini's warehouse on or before May 30.

Gemini paid the $2,000 in March, but was unable to make the second deposit payment of $3,000 on May 15. Soon thereafter, TRAC returned Gemini's $2,000 and notified Gemini in writing that it "considered the contract cancelled" and "did not intend to perform any part of the February contract." The price of the component parts began to increase steadily in early March, and the goods can now be sold for 25 percent more.

Issue What are TRAC's rights and obligations under this sales contract?

Rule of Law A buyer who fails to make a payment due on or before delivery is in default. When faced with a buyer's default, the seller has goods-oriented, money-oriented, and obligation-oriented remedies available to it, all of which are cumulative to the extent they apply. Goods-oriented remedies include identification to the contract, withholding or stopping delivery of the goods, or if the buyer is insolvent, reclamation. The seller's money-oriented remedies involve recovery of (1) damages after a commercially reasonable resale, (2) damages for nonacceptance, or (3) the contract price, and incidental and consequential damages. If the goods are resold at a profit to the seller, however, he need not account to the buyer for it. The seller's obligation-oriented remedy is cancellation, which discharges the seller from any further obligation under the contract.

Application Two of the four goods-oriented remedies are available to TRAC. It may both identify the goods to the contract, if it has not already done so, and withhold their delivery to Gemini. Neither of the other two goods-oriented remedies—stoppage in transit or reclamation—has any application here because the goods have not yet left TRAC's possession. Withholding delivery of the goods and identifying them to the contract enables TRAC to exercise its remedy of resale of the goods, which under current market conditions would yield a higher price than what Gemini had agreed to pay. As long as TRAC's incidental damages, or reasonable costs of such a sale, do not exceed the profit TRAC makes when it resells the goods, TRAC has suffered no damages. After returning Gemini's $2,000 deposit, TRAC has exercised its remaining Code remedy, the obligation-oriented remedy of cancellation. Cancellation effectively discharges TRAC of any further obligation to Gemini.

Conclusion TRAC may (1) withhold delivery of the goods to Gemini; (2) identify them to the contract; (3) resell them in a commercially reasonable manner, resulting here in a profit for which it is not accountable to Gemini; *and* (4) cancel the contract, resulting in a discharge of TRAC's performance under the contract.

---

the seller of their nonconformity, the buyer may (9) recover damages for breach of warranty. Finally, in addition to the remedies listed above, the buyer may, when appropriate, (10) recover incidental damages *and* (11) recover consequential damages. Article 2A provides for essentially the same remedies for the lessee.

The first of these remedies is ***obligation oriented***; the second through fourth and ninth through eleventh are ***money oriented***; and the fifth through eighth are ***goods oriented***.

The buyer may deduct from the price due any damages resulting from any breach of contract by the seller. The buyer must, however, give notice to the seller of her intention to withhold such damages from payment of the price due. (Article 2A.)

CISG *If the seller fails to perform any of his obligations under the contract or the CISG, the buyer may (1) require the seller to perform his contractual obligations or (2) fix an additional period of time of reasonable length for performance by the seller of his obligations. Unless the buyer has received notice from the seller that he will not perform within the period so fixed, the buyer may not, during that period, resort to any remedy for breach of contract. Moreover, if the seller's breach is fundamental or the seller fails to perform within the additional time granted by the buyer, the buyer may avoid the contract. In addition to these remedies, the buyer also has the right to damages. If the goods do not conform with the contract, the buyer may reduce the price in the same proportion as the value that the goods actually delivered had at the time of the delivery bears to the value that conforming goods would have had at that time.*

Cancel the Contract [23-2a]

When the seller fails to make delivery or repudiates the contract or when the buyer rightfully rejects or justifiably revokes acceptance of goods tendered or delivered to him, the buyer may cancel the contract with respect to any goods involved; and, if the breach by the seller concerns the whole contract, the buyer may cancel the entire contract. (Article 2A.) The buyer, who must give the seller notice of his cancellation, is excused from further performance or tender on his part. (Article 2A.)

CISG   *The buyer may declare the contract avoided if the seller (1) commits a fundamental breach or (2) does not deliver the goods within the additional period of time fixed by the buyer. Avoidance of the contract releases both parties from their obligations under it, subject to any damages that may be due. Avoidance does not affect any provision of the contract for the settlement of disputes or any other provision of the contract governing the rights and obligations of the parties consequent upon the avoidance of the contract. A party who has performed the contract either wholly or in part may claim restitution from the other party. If both parties are bound to make restitution, they must do so concurrently.*

Recover Payments Made [23-2b]

The buyer, on the seller's breach, may also recover as much of the price as he has paid. For example, Jonas and Sheila enter into a contract for a sale of goods for a contract price of $3,000, and Sheila, the buyer, has made a down payment of $600. Jonas delivers nonconforming goods to Sheila, who rightfully rejects them. Sheila may cancel the contract and recover the $600 plus whatever other damages she can prove. Under Article 2A, the lessee may recover so much of the rent and security as has been paid and is just under the circumstances.

Cover [23-2c]

Cover

the buyer may obtain cover by proceeding in good faith and without unreasonable delay to purchase substitute goods; the buyer may recover the difference between the cost of cover and the contract price, plus any incidental and consequential damages, minus expenses saved

On the seller's breach, the buyer may protect herself by obtaining cover. **Cover** means that the buyer may in good faith and without unreasonable delay proceed to purchase needed goods or make a contract to purchase such goods in substitution for those due under the contract from the seller. In a lease, the lessee may purchase or lease substitute goods.

On making a reasonable contract of cover, the buyer may recover from the seller the difference between the cost of cover and the contract price, *plus* any incidental and consequential damages (discussed later), *minus* expenses saved because of the seller's breach. For example, Phillip, whose factory is in Oakland, agrees to sell goods to Edith, in Atlanta, for $22,000 F.O.B. Oakland. Phillip fails to deliver, and Edith covers by purchasing substitute goods for $25,000, incurring $700 in sales commissions. Edith suffers no other damages as a consequence of Phillip's breach. Shipping costs from Oakland to Atlanta for the goods are $1,300. Edith would recover the difference between the cost of cover ($25,000) and the contract price ($22,000), plus incidental damages ($700 in sales commissions), plus consequential damages ($0 in this example), minus expenses saved (the $1,300 in shipping costs that Edith need not pay under the contract of cover), which equals $2,400.

In a lease, the comparable recovery is the **difference** between the **present values** of the **new rent** due under the new lease and the **old rent** due under the original lease.

The buyer is not required to obtain cover, and his failure to do so does not bar him from any other remedy the Code provides. (Article 2A.) The buyer may not, however, recover consequential damages that he could have prevented by cover. (Article 2A.)

CISG   *If the contract is avoided and the buyer has bought goods in replacement in a reasonable manner and within a reasonable time after avoidance, he may recover the difference between the contract price and the price paid in the substitute transaction. In addition, he may recover consequential damages.*

Bigelow-Sanford, Inc. v. Gunny Corp.
United States Court of Appeals, Fifth Circuit, 1981
649 F.2d 1060
http://scholar.google.com/scholar_case?case=13219527888592152337&q=649+F.2d+1060&hl=en&as_sdt=2,34

FACTS The plaintiff, Bigelow-Sanford, Inc., contracted with the defendant, Gunny Corp., for the purchase of 100,000 linear yards of jute at $0.64 per yard. Gunny delivered 22,228 linear yards in January 1979. The February and March deliveries required under the contract were not made, and eight rolls (each roll containing 66.7 linear yards) were delivered in April. With 72,265 linear yards ultimately undelivered, Gunny told Bigelow-Sanford that no more would be delivered. In mid-March, Bigelow-Sanford turned to the jute spot market to replace the balance of the order at a price of $1.21 per linear yard. As several other companies had also defaulted on their jute contracts with Bigelow-Sanford, the plaintiff purchased a total of 164,503 linear yards on the spot market. The plaintiff sued the defendant to recover losses sustained as a result of the breach of contract. Gunny appealed from a judgment in favor of Bigelow-Sanford.

DECISION Judgment for Bigelow-Sanford affirmed.

OPINION The Uniform Commercial Code permits a buyer to "cover" his damages due to the seller's breach by purchasing goods in substitution for those due from the seller. The buyer, however, must make the substitute purchases in good faith and without unreasonable delay. If he does so, the buyer may recover as damages the difference between the cost of cover and the contract price plus any incidental damages, but less expenses saved in consequence of the seller's breach.

Here, Gunny breached when it notified Bigelow-Sanford in February that no more jute would be delivered. Bigelow-Sanford made its first spot market purchases to cover by mid-March. Thus, Bigelow-Sanford covered without undue delay. Since its purchases were also reasonable and made in good faith, Bigelow-Sanford is entitled to damages. Bigelow did not specifically allocate the spot market replacements to the individual sellers' accounts. Therefore, it is reasonable to determine the cost of cover by multiplying the average cost of the spot market purchases times the amount of jute Gunny had failed to deliver.

INTERPRETATION If the buyer makes substitute purchases in good faith and without unreasonable delay, he may recover as damages the difference between the cost of cover and the contract price plus any incidental damages, but minus any expenses he saved because of the seller's breach.

CRITICAL THINKING QUESTION Do you agree with the remedy of cover? Explain.

Recover damages for nondelivery or repudiation

the buyer may recover the difference between the market price at the time the buyer learned of the breach and the contract price, plus any incidental and consequential damages, but minus expenses saved

Practical Advice

Carefully consider whether you are better off covering or seeking damages for nondelivery or repudiation.

Recover Damages for Nondelivery or Repudiation [23-2d]

If the seller repudiates the contract or fails to deliver the goods, or if the buyer rightfully rejects or justifiably revokes acceptance of the goods, the buyer is entitled to recover damages from the seller equal to the difference between the market price at the time the buyer learned of the breach and the contract price, together with incidental and consequential damages, minus expenses saved because of the seller's breach. This remedy is a complete alternative to the remedy of cover and is available only to the extent the buyer has not covered. As previously indicated, the buyer who elects this remedy may not recover consequential damages that she could have avoided by cover.

In a lease, the comparable recovery is the **difference** between the **present values** of the **market rent** and the **old rent** due under the original lease.

The market price is to be determined as of the place for tender or, in the event that the buyer has rightfully rejected the goods or has justifiably revoked his acceptance of them, as of the place of arrival. For example, Janet, in Boston, agrees to sell goods to Laura, in Denver, for $7,000 C.O.D. (collect on delivery), with delivery by November 15. Janet fails to deliver. As a consequence, Laura suffers incidental damages of $1,500 and consequential damages of $1,000. In the case of nondelivery or repudiation, market price is determined as of the place of tender. Because C.O.D. is a shipment contract, the place of tender would be the seller's city. Therefore, the market price must be the market price in Boston, the seller's city, on November 15, when Laura learned of the breach. At this time and place, the market price is $8,000. Laura would recover the difference between the market price ($8,000) and the contract price ($7,000), plus incidental damages ($1,500), plus consequential damages ($1,000), minus expenses saved ($0 in this example), which equals $3,500.

In the previous example, if Janet had instead delivered nonconforming goods that Laura rejected, the market price would be determined at Denver, Laura's place of business; if Janet had repudiated the contract on November 1, instead of November 15, then the market price would be determined as of November 1.

In a lease, market rent is to be determined as of the place for tender or, in cases of rejection after arrival or revocation of acceptance, as of the place of arrival.

CISG *If the contract is avoided and the buyer has not made a replacement purchase, he may recover the difference between the contract price and the current price at the time of avoidance and at the place where delivery of the goods should have been made. In addition, he may recover consequential damages.*

Recover identified goods on the seller's insolvency
for which the buyer has paid all or part of the price

Recover Identified Goods on the Seller's Insolvency [23-2e]

When existing goods are identified to the contract of sale, the buyer acquires a *special property interest* in the goods. This interest exists even if the goods are nonconforming and the buyer therefore has the right to return or reject them. Either the buyer or the seller may identify the goods to the contract.

The Code gives the buyer a right, which does not exist at common law, to recover from an insolvent seller the goods in which the buyer has a special property interest and for which he has paid part or all of the price. This right exists in cases in which the seller, who is in possession or control of the goods, becomes insolvent within ten days after receiving the first installment of the price. To exercise this right, the buyer must tender to the seller any unpaid portion of the price. If the special property interest exists by reason of an identification made by the buyer, he may recover the goods only if they conform to the contract for sale. (Article 2A.)

Replevin
the buyer may recover goods identified to the contract if (1) the buyer is unable to obtain cover or (2) the goods have been shipped under reservation of a security interest in the seller

Sue for Replevin [23-2f]

Replevin is an action at law to recover from a defendant's possession specific goods that are being unlawfully withheld from the plaintiff. When the seller has repudiated or breached the contract, the buyer may maintain against the seller an action for replevin for goods that have been identified to the contract if the buyer after a reasonable effort is unable to obtain cover for such goods. (Article 2A.) Article 2 also provides the buyer with the right to replevin if the goods have been shipped under reservation of a security interest in the seller and satisfaction of this security interest has been made or tendered.

Specific performance
equitable remedy compelling the party in breach to perform the contract according to its terms

Sue for Specific Performance [23-2g]

Specific performance is an equitable remedy compelling the party in breach to perform the contract according to its terms. At common law, specific performance is available only if legal remedies are inadequate. For example, when the contract is for the purchase of a unique item, such as a work of art, a famous racehorse, or an heirloom, money damages may not be an adequate remedy. In such a case, a court of equity has the discretion to order the seller specifically to deliver to the buyer, on payment of the price, the goods described in the contract.

The Code not only has continued the availability of specific performance but also has sought to promote a more liberal attitude toward its use. Accordingly, it does not expressly require that the remedy at law be inadequate. Instead, the Code states that specific performance may be granted "where the goods are unique or in other proper circumstances." (Article 2A.)

CISG *The buyer may require the seller to perform his contractual obligations. If the goods do not conform to the contract and the nonconformity constitutes a fundamental breach of contract, the buyer may require delivery of substitute goods. If the goods do not conform to the contract, the buyer may require the seller to remedy the lack of conformity by repair, unless this is unreasonable having regard to all the circumstances. Nevertheless, a court is not bound to enter a judgment for specific performance unless a court would do so under its own law with respect to similar contracts of sale not governed by the CISG.*

Enforce a security interest

a buyer who has rightfully rejected or justifiably revoked acceptance of goods that remain in her possession has a security interest in these goods for any payments made on their price and for any expenses reasonably incurred

Enforce a Security Interest in the Goods [23-2h]

A buyer who has rightfully rejected or justifiably revoked acceptance of goods that remain in her possession or control has a security interest in these goods for any payments made on their price and for any expenses reasonably incurred in their inspection, receipt, transportation, care, and custody. The buyer may hold such goods and resell them in the same manner as an aggrieved seller may resell goods. (Article 2A.) In the event of resale, the buyer is accountable to the seller for any amount of the net proceeds of the resale that exceeds the amount of her security interest. (Article 2A.)

Recover Damages for Breach in Regard to Accepted Goods [23-2i]

Recover damages for breach in regard to accepted goods

the buyer may recover damages resulting in the ordinary course of events from the seller's breach; in the case of breach of warranty, such recovery is the difference between the value the goods would have had if they had been as warranted and the value of the nonconforming goods that have been accepted

When the buyer has accepted nonconforming goods and has timely notified the seller of the breach of contract, the buyer is entitled to recover from the seller the damages resulting in the ordinary course of events from the seller's breach as determined in any reasonable manner. (Article 2A.) When appropriate, the buyer may also recover incidental and consequential damages. Nonconformity includes breaches of warranty as well as any failure of the seller to perform according to her obligations under the contract. Thus, even if a seller cures a nonconforming tender, the buyer may recover under this section for any injury suffered because the original tender was nonconforming. For a case dealing with the buyer's right to recover the damages when the buyer has accepted nonconforming goods, see *Midwest Hatchery v. Doorenbos Poultry* later in this chapter.

In the event of breach of warranty, the measure of damages is the difference at the time and place of acceptance between the value of the goods that have been accepted and the value that the goods would have had if they had been as warranted, unless special circumstances show proximate damages of a different amount. Article 2A has a comparable provision, except the recovery is for the ***present value*** of the difference between the value of the use of the goods accepted and the value if they had been as warranted for the lease term.

The contract price of the goods does not figure in this computation because the buyer is entitled to the benefit of his bargain, which is to receive goods that are as warranted. For example, Eleanor agrees to sell goods to Timothy for $1,000. Although the value of the goods accepted by Timothy is $800, if they had been as warranted, their value would have been $1,200. Timothy's damages for breach of warranty are $400, which he may deduct from any unpaid balance due on the purchase price upon notice to Eleanor of his intention to do so. (Article 2A.)

Recover Incidental Damages [23-2j]

Buyer's incidental damages

reimbursement for reasonable expenses incurred in handling rightfully rejected goods or in effecting cover

In addition to remedies such as covering, recovering damages for nondelivery or repudiation, or recovering damages for breach in regard to accepted goods, including breach of warranty, the buyer may recover incidental damages. A **buyer's incidental damages** provide reimbursement for the buyer who incurs reasonable expenses in handling rightfully rejected goods or in effecting cover. The buyer's incidental damages resulting from the seller's breach include expenses reasonably incurred in inspection, receipt, transportation, and care and custody of goods rightfully rejected; any commercially reasonable charges, expenses, or commissions in connection with obtaining cover; and any other reasonable expense connected to the delay or other breach. Article 2A has an analogous definition. For example, the buyer of a racehorse who justifiably revokes acceptance because the horse does not conform to the contract will be allowed to recover as incidental damages the cost of caring for the horse from the date the horse was delivered until the buyer returns it to the seller.

Practical Advice

As an aggrieved buyer, maintain good records regarding incidental damages you incurred.

Recover Consequential Damages [23-2k]

Consequential damages

damages resulting from buyer's requirements of which seller had reason to know at the time of contracting, as well as injury to person or property proximately resulting from breach of warranty

In many cases, the buyer's remedies previously discussed will not fully compensate the aggrieved buyer for her losses. For example, nonconforming goods that are accepted may in some way damage or destroy the buyer's warehouse and its contents, or undelivered goods may have been the subject of a lucrative contract of resale, the profits from which are now lost. The Code responds to this problem by providing the buyer with the opportunity to recover **consequential damages** resulting from the seller's breach, including (1) any loss resulting from the buyer's requirements and needs of which the seller at the time of contracting had reason to know and which the buyer could not reasonably prevent by cover or otherwise and (2) injury to person or property proximately resulting from any breach of warranty. (Article 2A.)

CONCEPT REVIEW 23-2

Remedies of the Buyer

Seller's Breach	Buyer's Remedies		
	Obligation Oriented	Goods Oriented	Money Oriented*
Buyer Rightfully Rejects Goods	Cancel	• Have a security interest	• Recover payments made • Cover and recover damages • Recover damages for nondelivery
Buyer Justifiably Revokes Acceptance	Cancel	• Have a security interest	• Recover payments made • Cover and recover damages • Recover damages for nondelivery
Seller Fails to Deliver	Cancel	• Recover identified goods if seller is insolvent • Replevy goods • Obtain specific performance	• Recover payments made • Cover and recover damages • Recover damages for nondelivery
Seller Repudiates	Cancel	• Recover identified goods if seller is insolvent • Replevy goods • Obtain specific performance	• Recover payments made • Cover and recover damages • Recover damages for nondelivery
Buyer Accepts Nonconforming Goods			• Recover damages for breach of warranty

*In a lease, the lessee's recovery of damages for future rent payments is reduced to their present value.

With respect to the first type of consequential damages, *particular* needs of the buyer usually must be made known to the seller, whereas *general* needs usually need not be. In the case of a buyer who is in the business of reselling goods, resale is one requirement of which the seller has reason to know. For example, Supreme Machine Co., a manufacturer, contracts to sell Allied Sales, Inc., a dealer in used machinery, a used machine that Allied plans to resell. After Supreme repudiates and Allied is unable to obtain a similar machine elsewhere, Allied's damages include the net profit that it would have made on resale of the machine. A buyer may not, however, recover consequential damages he could have prevented by cover. (Article 2A.) For instance, Supreme Machine Co. contracts to sell Capitol Manufacturing Co. a used machine for $10,000 to be delivered at Capitol's factory by June 1. Supreme repudiates the contract on May 1. By reasonable efforts, Capitol could buy a similar machine from United Machinery, Inc., for $11,000 in time for a June 1 delivery. Capitol fails to do so, losing a $5,000 profit that it would have made from the resale of the machine. Though it can recover $1,000 from Supreme, Capitol's damages do not include the loss of the $5,000 profit.

An example of the second type of consequential damage would be as follows: Federal Machine Co. sells a machine to Southern Manufacturing Co., warranting its suitability for Southern's purpose. However, the machine is not suitable for Southern's purpose and causes $10,000 in damage to Southern's property and $15,000 in personal injuries. Southern can recover the $25,000 in consequential damages in addition to any other loss suffered.

CONTRACTUAL PROVISIONS AFFECTING REMEDIES [23-3]

Within specified limits, the Code permits the parties to a sales contract to modify, exclude, or limit by agreement the remedies or damages that will be available for breach of that contract. Two basic types of contractual provisions affect remedies: (1) liquidation or limitation of damages and (2) modification or limitation of remedy.

Liquidation or Limitation of Damages [23-3a]

The parties may provide for liquidated damages in their contract by specifying the amount or measure of damages that either party may recover in the event of a breach by the other. The

Practical Advice

As the buyer, be sure to inform the other party to the contract of any "particular needs" beyond the ordinary course of events that could result from a breach of contract.

Liquidation or limitation of damages

the parties may specify the amount or measure of damages that may be recovered in the event of a breach if the amount is reasonable

amount of such damages must be reasonable in light of the anticipated or actual loss resulting from a breach, the difficulties of proof of loss, and the inconvenience or lack of feasibility of otherwise obtaining an adequate remedy. A contract provision that fixes unreasonably large liquidated damages is void as a penalty. By comparison, an unreasonably small amount might be stricken on the grounds of unconscionability.

Practical Advice

Both parties should consider including a contractual provision for reasonable liquidated damages, especially where damages will be difficult to prove.

To illustrate, Sterling Cabinetry Company contracts to build and install shelves and cabinets for an office building being constructed by Baron Construction Company. The contract price is $120,000, and the contract provides that Sterling would be liable for $100 per day for every day's delay beyond the completion date specified in the contract. The stipulated sum of $100 per day is reasonable and commensurate with the anticipated loss. Therefore, it is enforceable as liquidated damages. If, instead, the sum stipulated had been $5,000 per day, it would be unreasonably large and, therefore, would be void as a penalty.

Article 2A authorizes liquidated damages payable by either party for default, or any other act or omission. The amount of, or formula for, liquidated damages must be reasonable in light of the then-anticipated harm caused by default or other act or omission.

Coastal Leasing Corporation v. T-Bar S Corporation
Court of Appeals of North Carolina, 1998
128 N.C.App. 379, 496 S.E.2d 795
http://scholar.google.com/scholar_case?case=3451040025275367441&q=496+s.e.2d+795&hl=en&as_sdt=2,34

FACTS The plaintiff, Coastal Leasing Corporation (Coastal), entered into a lease agreement with the defendant, T-Bar S Corporation (T-Bar), in May 1992, whereby Coastal agreed to lease certain cash register equipment to T-Bar. Under the lease, T-Bar agreed to monthly rental payments of $289.13 each for a total of forty-eight months. Defendants George and Sharon Talbott were the officers of T-Bar and personally guaranteed payment. After making eighteen of the monthly payments, the Talbotts and T-Bar defaulted on the lease. On February 28, 1994, Coastal mailed a certified letter to the Talbotts and T-Bar advising them that the lease was in default and, pursuant to the terms of the lease, Coastal was accelerating the remaining payments due under the lease. Coastal further advised the Talbotts and T-Bar that if the entire amount due of $8,841.06 was not received within seven days, Coastal would seek to recover the balance due plus interest and reasonable attorneys' fees, as well as possession of the equipment.

On March 10, Coastal mailed a certified letter and "Notice of Public Sale of Repossessed Leased Equipment" to the Talbotts and T-Bar at the same address. This letter advised the Talbotts and T-Bar that Coastal had taken possession of the equipment and was conducting a public sale pursuant to the terms of the lease. Although the date on the notice of sale stated that the sale was to be held on March 23, the sale was actually scheduled to be held on March 25. This letter and notice of sale were returned to Coastal "unclaimed" on March 29.

Coastal conducted a public sale of the equipment on March 25, and no one appeared on behalf of the Talbotts or T-Bar. There being no other bidders, Coastal purchased the equipment at the sale for $2,000. On October 4, 1994, Coastal leased some of the same equipment to another company at a rate calculated to be $212.67 for thirty-six months. Coastal then filed this action seeking to recover the balance due under the lease, minus the net proceeds from the public sale, plus interest and reasonable attorneys' fees. The Talbotts filed an answer and counterclaim. Coastal then filed a motion for summary judgment against the Talbotts. When T-Bar failed to answer, a default judgment was entered against it. After a hearing, the trial court entered summary judgment in favor of Coastal on its complaint and the Talbotts' counterclaims and

entered judgment against the Talbotts for the sum of $7,223.56 plus interest and attorneys' fees of $1,083.54. The Talbotts appealed.

DECISION Judgment affirmed.

OPINION Since both parties agree that the transaction in this case is a lease, not a security interest, Article 2A controls. (Article 9 controls security interests and is discussed in Chapter 37.) Article 2A states, in pertinent part:

> Damages payable by either party for default, or any other act or omission … may be liquidated in the lease agreement but only at an amount or by a formula that is reasonable in light of the then-anticipated harm caused by the default or other act or omission.

This liquidated damages provision is more flexible than that provided by its statutory analogue under Article 2. The drafters of Article 2A chose not to incorporate Article 2's requirements of difficulty of proof and inconvenience or infeasibility of otherwise obtaining an adequate remedy. Moreover, the fact that there is a difference between the actual loss, as determined at or about the time of the default, and the anticipated loss or stipulated amount or formula, as stipulated at the time the lease contract was entered into, does not necessarily mean that the liquidated damage agreement is unreasonable. The basic test of the reasonableness of an agreement liquidating damages is whether the stipulated amount or amount produced by the stipulated formula represents a reasonable forecast of the probable loss. In this case, Paragraph 13 of the lease (the liquidated damages clause) reads in part as follows:

> 13. REMEDIES. If an event of default shall occur, Lessor may, at its option, at any time (a) declare the entire amount of unpaid rental for the balance of the term of this lease immediately due and payable, whereupon Lessee shall become obligated to pay to Lessor forthwith the total amount of the said rental for the balance of the said term, and (b) without demand or legal process, enter into the premises where the equipment may be found and take possession of and remove the Equipment.

The liquidated damages clause is a reasonable estimation of the then-anticipated damages in the event of default because it protects Coastal's expectation interest. The liquidated damages clause places Coastal in the position it would have occupied had the lease been fully performed by allowing it to accelerate the balance of the lease payments and repossess the equipment. Therefore, since there is no evidence that Coastal exercised a superior bargaining position in the negotiation of the liquidated damages clause, no genuine issue of material fact exists as to its reasonableness, and the trial court did not err by enforcing its provisions.

INTERPRETATION Article 2A, which governs leases, allows the parties to liquidate damages as long as the negotiated amount is reasonable in light of the anticipated loss.

CRITICAL THINKING QUESTION Do you agree with the decision by the drafters of Article 2A to omit Article 2's requirements of difficulty of proof and inconvenience or infeasibility of otherwise obtaining an adequate remedy? Explain.

Modification or limitation of remedy by agreement
the contract between the parties may expressly provide for remedies in addition to those in the Code, or it may limit or change the measure of damages recoverable for breach

Practical Advice

If you are the seller, consider including a contractual provision for the limitation or exclusion of consequential damages. If you are the buyer, avoid such limitations.

Modification or Limitation of Remedy by Agreement [23-3b]

The contract between the seller and buyer may expressly provide for remedies in addition to or instead of those provided in the Code and may limit or change the measure of damages recoverable in the event of breach. (Article 2A.) For instance, the contract may validly limit the buyer's remedy to a return of the goods and a refund of the price, or to the replacement of nonconforming goods or parts.

A contractual remedy is optional, however, unless the parties expressly agree that it is to be exclusive of other remedies, in which event it becomes the sole remedy. (Article 2A.) Moreover, when circumstances cause an exclusive or limited remedy to fail in its essential purpose, the parties may resort to the remedies provided by the Code. (Article 2A.)

The contract may expressly limit or exclude consequential damages unless such limitation or exclusion would be unconscionable. Limitation of consequential damages for personal injuries resulting from breach of warranty in the sale of consumer goods is **prima facie** unconscionable, whereas limitation of such damages for commercial loss is not. (Article 2A.) For example, Ace Motors, Inc., sells a pickup truck to Brenda, a consumer. The contract of sale excludes liability for all consequential damages. The next day, the truck explodes, causing serious personal injury to Brenda. Brenda would recover for her personal injuries unless Ace could prove that the exclusion of consequential damages was *not* unconscionable.

 Midwest Hatchery v. Doorenbos Poultry
Court of Appeals of Iowa, 2010
783 N.W.2d 56
http://scholar.google.com/scholar_case?q=783+N.W.2d+56&hl=en&as_sdt=2,34&case=17039907567362199216&scilh=0

FACTS Doorenbos Poultry, Inc., is a company that keeps approximately 150,000 chickens for egg production and sells the eggs. Hens generally do not begin laying eggs until they are seventeen or eighteen weeks old, reach their peak production at approximately twenty-six weeks, and usually continue producing eggs until they are about 110 weeks old. The practice of Doorenbos Poultry has been to keep all chickens of a single age group through their productive life and then simultaneously replace those birds with new chickens that are seventeen to eighteen weeks old. This practice maximizes production and continues some cash flow without interruption.

Midwest Hatchery & Poultry Farms, Inc. is a producer and seller of poultry products. In the fall of 2006, Doorenbos Poultry entered into a written contract with Midwest to purchase 112,000 pullets (young hens), at eighteen weeks of age, to be delivered on December 28, 2006. The contract listed a price of $1.27 per pullet, plus the cost of feed from the time of hatching to the date of delivery. The contract also provided, "If Seller breaches this Contract, at Seller's option, customer is entitled to either replacement or refund of the price paid by Customer."

By mutual agreement, delivery was delayed until January 16, 17, and 18, 2007, when Midwest delivered 115,581 pullets to Doorenbos Poultry. As the new chicks arrived, the old pullets were moved out. Scott Doorenbos, the president of Doorenbos Poultry,

thought the new chickens looked small and, based on their weight, concluded the birds delivered were thirteen to fourteen weeks of age rather than eighteen weeks. Doorenbos could not cancel the order and return the chickens because his former flock had already been removed. The barns in which the chickens are kept do not have heating and the buildings maintain their temperature from the body heat of the birds. Therefore, if Doorenbos had not kept the pullets, the water lines in the barn would have frozen.

The pullets delivered by Midwest did not start laying eggs until February 18, 2007. From the time the pullets were delivered until the pullets reached their "laying" phase, Doorenbos Poultry incurred feeding and other maintenance costs for the pullets with no egg production to generate revenue. Doorenbos Poultry kept the pullets delivered by Midwest in production and intended to keep them in production until at least 119 weeks.

On January 20, 2007, Midwest sent Doorenbos Poultry an invoice for $267,916.76, which represented $146,787.87 for the cost of 115,581 pullets, $112,460.31 for feed, and $8,668.58 for vaccine. Doorenbos Poultry did not pay for the birds Midwest delivered when it received the invoice. Within thirty days after the pullets had been delivered, Doorenbos Poultry complained to Midwest that it had not received chickens that were eighteen weeks old, as specified in the contract, sought a reduction in the contract price, and stated it lost income while the chickens were not mature enough to lay eggs. Doorenbos Poultry did not seek to have any of the pullets replaced. On August 19, 2007, Doorenbos Poultry sent Midwest a check for $184,135.18, which was what it believed should have been the cost for the younger pullets. Doorenbos Poultry never returned any chickens to Midwest.

On September 14, 2007, Midwest filed an action for a money judgment alleging breach of contract. Doorenbos Poultry responded with a counterclaim alleging breach of contract by Midwest. In a decision filed January 9, 2009, the district court concluded that about 80 percent of the pullets were three weeks too young, and about 20 percent were four weeks too young. The district court determined that (1) this action was governed by the Uniform Commercial Code (UCC); (2) because Doorenbos had accepted and kept the pullets, Midwest is entitled to the unpaid balance of the contract price; and (3) Doorenbos Poultry was liable for the full amount billed by Midwest Hatchery, meaning it still owed $83,781.58 for the pullets that had been delivered. The court also concluded that (1) Doorenbos Poultry's acceptance of the pullets did not preclude its breach of contract claim against Midwest; (2) Midwest had breached the contract by providing pullets that were not of the specified age; (3) the limitation of damages clause in the parties' contract failed in its essential purpose; and (4) Doorenbos Poultry had lost profits of $31,732.79 because it was not able to replace its existing flock with eighteen-week-old birds. The court set off the amount of the loss against the balance Doorenbos Poultry still owed Midwest and entered judgment against Doorenbos Poultry for $52,048.79 ($83,781.58 minus $31,732.79).

DECISION The decision of the district court is affirmed.

OPINION Doorenbos Poultry appealed from the decision of the district court.

Breach of Contract Under the UCC, if a buyer accepts goods, despite their nonconformity to the specifications of the contract, the buyer must pay the contract rate for the goods accepted. There is substantial evidence in the record to support the finding of the district court that Doorenbos Poultry accepted the chickens delivered by Midwest, despite their nonconformity.

Limitation of Remedies Provision The acceptance of the nonconforming goods by Doorenbos Poultry did not preclude its counterclaim for breach of contract against Midwest. Doorenbos Poultry may recover as damages for any nonconformity of tender the loss resulting in the ordinary course of events from the seller's breach as determined in any manner that is reasonable.

Under the UCC, the parties to a contract may agree to limit the remedies available if the seller breaches the contract by providing nonconforming goods, as follows:

> [T]he agreement may provide for remedies in addition to or in substitution for those provided in this Article and may limit or alter the measure of damages recoverable under this Article, as by limiting the buyer's remedies to return of the goods and repayment of the price or to repair and replacement of nonconforming goods or parts.

In this case, the parties' contract specifically provided, "If Seller breaches this Contract, at Seller's option, customer is entitled to either replacement or refund of the price paid by Customer."

The Code provides "Where circumstances cause an exclusive or limited remedy to fail of its essential purpose, remedy may be had as provided in this chapter." A remedy's essential purpose "is to give to a buyer what the seller promised him." The focus of

analysis "is not whether the remedy compensates for all damage that occurred, but that the buyer is provided with the product as seller promised."

Where repair or replacement can give the buyer what is bargained for, a limitation of remedies does not fail of its essential purpose. Here, the limited remedy provision of the parties' contract failed of its essential purpose. Doorenbos Poultry notified Midwest that the pullets were not as specified in the contract within thirty days after delivery. The reference to a replacement or refund in the contract contemplates the entire sale with Midwest taking back the entire flock of birds.

At the time Scott Doorenbos informed Midwest that the pullets delivered were not eighteen weeks old, it is clear that Doorenbos Poultry was not interested in having the pullets replaced, and Midwest made no offer to replace them. When it was notified of the breach, Midwest could have exercised its option under the contract, taken back the entire flock, and either replaced the chickens with eighteen-week-old pullets or refunded the entire purchase price. The record supports the conclusion that this did not happen because it was plainly impractical.

It would have been extremely inefficient for both parties to replace the pullets Midwest had delivered. As Scott Doorenbos testified, a simultaneous exchange would have been necessary because the birds provided the only source of heat for the barn. In addition, it does not appear that either party was interested in the option of removal and refund.

Under the circumstance presented here, the district court did not err in concluding the limitation of remedies provision in the parties' contract failed in its essential purpose.

Amount of Damages Because the limitation of remedies provision failed in its essential purpose, a consideration of damages reverts to the Code's provision for the recovery of damages for "the loss resulting in the ordinary course of events from the seller's breach as determined in any manner which is reasonable." Thus, any manner that is reasonable may be used to determine a buyer's damages for nonconforming goods. Here, the district court found a loss of profits would have been an expected loss resulting in the ordinary course of events from the nonconformity of the pullets delivered by Midwest.

Damages are measured by the difference between the value of the goods at the time of acceptance, and their value if they had been as specified in the contract, unless special circumstances show proximate damages of a different amount. The district court noted that neither party submitted any evidence as to the value of fourteen- or fifteen-week-old pullets and expressed skepticism that there would be any recognized value for pullets that were between fourteen and fifteen weeks old and did not have the ability to lay eggs. As a result, the district court concluded the "special circumstances" provision should apply.

After carefully considering the evidence presented, the district court calculated $31,732.79 as the damages to be awarded Doorenbos Poultry on its counterclaim. The appellate court affirmed this calculation.

INTERPRETATION In cases in which circumstances cause an exclusive or limited remedy to fail of its essential purpose, the general remedy provisions of the Code apply.

CRITICAL THINKING QUESTION Do you agree with the Code's policy permitting the parties to establish an exclusive remedy in place of the Code's remedies?

CHAPTER SUMMARY

Remedies of the Seller

Buyer's Default the seller's remedies are triggered by the buyer's action in wrongfully rejecting or revoking acceptance of the goods, in failing to make payment due on or before delivery, or in repudiating the contract

Withhold Delivery

Stop Delivery if the buyer is insolvent (one who is unable to pay his debts as they become due or one whose total liabilities exceed his total assets), the seller may stop any delivery; if the buyer repudiates or otherwise breaches, the seller may stop carload, truckload, planeload, or larger shipments

Identify Goods

Resell the Goods the seller may resell the goods concerned or the undelivered balance of the goods and recover the difference between the contract price and the resale price, together with any incidental damages, minus expenses saved

- *Type of Resale* may be public or private
- *Manner of Resale* must be made in good faith and in a commercially reasonable manner

Recover Damages for Nonacceptance or Repudiation

- *Market Price Differential* the seller may recover damages from the buyer measured by the difference between the unpaid contract price and the market price at the time and place of tender of the goods, plus incidental damages, minus expenses saved
- *Lost Profit* in the alternative, the seller may recover the lost profit, including reasonable overhead, plus incidental damages, minus expenses saved

Recover the Price the seller may recover the price

- when the buyer has accepted the goods
- when the goods have been lost or damaged after the risk of loss has passed to the buyer
- when the goods have been identified to the contract and there is no ready market available for their resale

Recover Incidental Damages incidental damages include any commercially reasonable charges, expenses, or commissions directly resulting from the breach

Cancel the Contract

Reclaim the Goods upon the Buyer's Insolvency an unpaid seller may reclaim goods from an insolvent buyer under certain circumstances

Remedies of the Buyer

Seller's Default the buyer's remedies arise when (1) the seller fails to make delivery or repudiates the contract or (2) the buyer rightfully rejects or justifiably revokes acceptance of goods tendered or delivered

Cancel the Contract

Recover Payments Made

Cover the buyer may obtain cover by proceeding in good faith and without unreasonable delay to purchase substitute goods; the buyer may recover the difference between the cost of cover and the contract price, plus any incidental and consequential damages, minus expenses saved

Recover Damages for Nondelivery or Repudiation the buyer may recover the difference between the market price at the time the buyer learned of the breach and the contract price, plus any incidental and consequential damages, but minus expenses saved

Recover Identified Goods on the Seller's Insolvency for which he has paid all or part of the price

Sue for Replevin the buyer may recover goods identified to the contract if (1) the buyer is unable to obtain cover or (2) the goods have been shipped under reservation of a security interest in the seller

Sue for Specific Performance the buyer may obtain specific performance when the goods are unique or in other proper circumstances

Enforce a Security Interest a buyer who has rightfully rejected or justifiably revoked acceptance of goods that remain in her possession has a security interest in these goods for any payments made on their price and for any expenses reasonably incurred

Recover Damages for Breach in Regard to Accepted Goods the buyer may recover damages resulting in the ordinary course of events from the seller's breach; in the case of breach of warranty, such recovery is the difference between the value the goods would have had if they had been as warranted and the value of the nonconforming goods that have been accepted

Recover Incidental Damages the buyer may recover incidental damages, which include any commercially reasonable expenses connected with the delay or other breach

Recover Consequential Damages the buyer may recover consequential damages resulting from the seller's breach, including (1) any loss resulting from the buyer's requirements and needs of which the seller at the time of contracting had reason to know and which the buyer could not reasonably prevent by cover or otherwise, and (2) injury to person or property proximately resulting from any breach of warranty

Contractual Provisions Affecting Remedies

Liquidation or Limitation of Damages the parties may specify the amount or measure of damages that may be recovered in the event of a breach if the amount is reasonable

Modification or Limitation of Remedy by Agreement the contract between the parties may expressly provide for remedies in addition to those in the Code, or it may limit or change the measure of damages recoverable for breach

QUESTIONS

1. Mae contracted to sell one thousand bushels of wheat to Lloyd at $10.00 per bushel. Just before Mae was to deliver the wheat, Lloyd notified her that he would not receive or accept the wheat. Mae sold the wheat for $9.60 per bushel, the market price, and later sued Lloyd for the difference of $400. Lloyd claims he was not notified by Mae of the resale and hence is not liable. Is Lloyd correct? Why?

2. On December 15, Judy wrote a letter to David stating that she would sell to David all of the mine-run coal that David might need to buy during the next calendar year for use at David's factory, delivered at the factory at a price of $50.00 per ton. David immediately replied by letter to Judy stating that he accepted the offer, that he would purchase all of his mine-run coal from Judy, and that he would need two hundred tons of coal during the first week in January. During the months of January, February, and March, Judy delivered to David a total of seven hundred tons of coal, for which David made payment to Judy at the rate of $50.00 per ton. On April 10, David ordered two hundred tons of mine-run coal from Judy, who replied to David on April 11 that she could not supply David with any more coal except at a price of $58.00 per ton delivered. David thereafter purchased elsewhere at the market price, namely $58.00 per ton, all of his factory's requirements of mine-run coal for the remainder of the year, amounting to a total of two thousand tons of coal. Can David now recover damages from Judy at the rate of $8.00 per ton for the coal thus purchased, amounting to $16,000?

3. On January 10, Betty, of Emanon, Missouri, visited the showrooms of the Forte Piano Company in St. Louis and selected a piano. A sales memorandum of the transaction signed both by Betty and by the salesman of the Forte Piano Company read as follows: "Sold to Betty one new Andover piano, factory number 46832, price $3,300, to be shipped to the buyer at Emanon, Missouri, freight prepaid, before February 1. Prior to shipment, seller will stain the case a darker color in accordance with buyer's directions and will make the tone more brilliant." On January 15, Betty repudiated the contract by letter to the Forte Piano Company. The company subsequently stained the case, made the tone more brilliant, and offered to ship the piano to Betty on January 26. Betty persisted in her refusal to accept the piano. The Forte Piano Company sued Betty to recover the contract price. To what remedy, if any, is Forte entitled?

4. Sims contracted in writing to sell Blake one hundred electric motors at a price of $100 each, freight prepaid to Blake's warehouse. By the contract of sale, Sims expressly warranted that each motor would develop twenty-five brake horsepower. The contract provided that the motors would be delivered in lots of twenty-five per week beginning January 2 and that Blake should pay for each lot of twenty-five motors as delivered, but that Blake was to have right of inspection on delivery. Immediately on delivery of the first lot of twenty-five motors on January 2, Blake forwarded Sims a check for $2,500, but on testing each of the twenty-five motors, Blake determined that none of them would develop more than fifteen brake horsepower. State all of the remedies under the Uniform Commercial Code available to Blake.

5. Henry and Mary entered into a written contract whereby Henry agreed to sell and Mary agreed to buy a certain automobile for $8,500. Henry drove the car to Mary's residence and properly parked it on the street in front of Mary's house, where he tendered it to Mary and requested payment of the price. Mary refused to take the car or pay the price. Henry informed Mary that he would hold her to the contract; but before Henry had time to enter the car and drive it away, a fire truck, answering a fire alarm and traveling at a high speed, crashed into the car and demolished it. Henry brings an action against Mary to recover the price of the car. Who is entitled to judgment? Would there be any difference in result if Henry were a dealer in automobiles?

6. Jane sells and delivers to Gerald on June 1 certain goods and receives from Gerald at the time of delivery Gerald's check in

the amount of $9,000 for the goods. The following day, Gerald is petitioned into bankruptcy; and Gerald's bank dishonors the check. On June 5, Jane serves notice on Gerald and the trustee in bankruptcy that she reclaims the goods. The trustee is in possession of the goods and refuses to deliver them to Jane. What are the rights of the parties?

7. The ABC Company, located in Chicago, contracted to sell a carload of television sets to Dodd in St. Louis, Missouri, on sixty days' credit. ABC Company shipped the carload to Dodd. On arrival of the car at St. Louis, Dodd paid the freight charges and reshipped the car to Hines of Little Rock, Arkansas, to whom he had previously contracted to sell the television sets. While the car was in transit to Little Rock, Dodd went bankrupt. ABC Company was informed of this at once and immediately telephoned XYZ Railroad Company to withhold delivery of the television sets. What should the XYZ Railroad Company do?

8. Robert in Chicago entered into a contract to sell certain machines to Terry in New York. The machines were to be manufactured by Robert and shipped F.O.B. Chicago not later than March 25. On March 24, when Robert was about to ship the machines, he received a letter from Terry wrongfully repudiating the contract. The machines cannot readily be resold for a reasonable price because they are a special kind used only in Terry's manufacturing processes. Robert sues Terry to recover the agreed price of the machines. What are the rights of the parties?

9. Calvin purchased a log home construction kit, manufactured by Boone Homes, Inc., from an authorized Boone dealer. The sales contract stated that Boone would repair or replace defective materials and that this was the exclusive remedy available against Boone. The dealer assembled the house, which was defective in a number of respects. The knotholes in the logs caused the walls and ceiling to leak. A support beam was too small and therefore cracked, causing the floor to crack also. These defects could not be completely cured by repair. Should Calvin prevail in a lawsuit against Boone for breach of warranty to recover damages for the loss in value?

10. Margaret contracted to buy a particular model Rolls-Royce from Paragon Motors, Inc. Only one hundred of these models are built each year. She paid a $30,000 deposit on the car but Paragon sold the car to Gluck. What remedy, if any, does Margaret have against Paragon?

CASE PROBLEMS

11. Technical Textile agreed by written contract to manufacture and sell 20,000 pounds of yarn to Jagger Brothers at a price of $2.15 per pound. After Technical had manufactured, delivered, and been paid for 3,723 pounds of yarn, Jagger Brothers by letter informed Technical that it was repudiating the contract and that it would refuse any further yarn deliveries. On August 12, the date of the letter, the market price of yarn was $1.90 per pound. The remaining 16,277 pounds were never manufactured. Technical sued Jagger Brothers for breach of contract. To what damages, if any, is Technical entitled? Explain.

12. Sherman Burrus, a job printer, purchased a printing press from the Itek Corporation for a price of $7,006.08. Before making the purchase, Burrus was assured by an Itek salesperson, Mr. Nessel, that the press was appropriate for the type of printing Burrus was doing. Burrus encountered problems in operating the press almost continuously from the time he received it. Burrus, his employees, and Itek representatives spent many hours in an unsuccessful attempt to get the press to operate properly. Burrus requested that the press be replaced, but Itek refused. Burrus then brought an action against Itek for (a) damages for breach of the implied warranty of merchantability and (b) consequential damages for losses resulting from the press's defective operation. Burrus was able to prove that the actual value of the press was $1,167 and, because of the defective press, that his output decreased and he sustained a great loss of paper. Itek contends that consequential damages are not recoverable in this case since Burrus elected to keep the press and continued to use it. How much should Burrus recover in damages for breach of warranty? Is he entitled to consequential damages?

13. A farmer made a contract in April to sell a grain dealer forty thousand bushels of corn to be delivered in October. On June 3, the farmer unequivocally informed the grain dealer that he was not going to plant any corn, that he would not fulfill the contract, and that if the buyer had commitments to resell the corn he should make other arrangements. The grain dealer waited in vain until October for performance of the repudiated contract. Then he bought corn at a greatly increased price on the market to fulfill commitments to his purchasers. To what damages, if any, is the grain dealer entitled? Explain.

14. Through information provided by S-2 Yachts, Inc., the plaintiff, Barr, located a yacht to his liking at the Crow's Nest marina and yacht sales company. When Barr asked the price, he was told that, although the yacht normally sold for $102,000, Crow's Nest was willing to sell this particular one for only $80,000 to make room for a new model from the manufacturer, S-2 Yachts, Inc. Barr was assured that the yacht in question came with full manufacturer's warranties. Barr asked if the yacht was new and if anything was wrong with it. Crow's Nest told him that nothing was wrong with the yacht and that there were only twenty hours of use on the engines.

Once the yacht had been delivered and Barr had taken it for a test run, he noticed several problems associated with saltwater damage, such as rusted screws, a rusted stove, and faulty electrical wiring. Barr was assured that Crow's Nest would pay for these repairs. However, as was later discovered, the yacht was in such a damaged condition that Barr experienced great personal hazard the two times that he used the boat. Examination by a marine expert revealed clearly that the boat had been sunk in salt water prior to Barr's purchase. The engines were severely damaged, and there was significant structural and equipment damage as well. According to the expert, not only was the yacht not new, it was worth at most only a half of the new value of $102,000. What should Barr be able to recover from S-2 Yachts and Crow's Nest?

15. Lee Oldsmobile sells Rolls-Royce automobiles. Mrs. Kaiden sent Lee a $25,000 deposit on a 2005 Rolls-Royce with a purchase price of $155,500. Although Lee informed Mrs. Kaiden that the car would be delivered in November, the order form did not indicate the delivery date and contained a disclaimer for delay or failure to deliver due to circumstances beyond the dealer's control. On November 21, Mrs. Kaiden purchased another car from another dealer and canceled her car from Lee. When Lee attempted to deliver a Rolls-Royce to Mrs. Kaiden on November 29, Mrs. Kaiden refused to accept delivery. Lee later sold the car for $150,495. Mrs. Kaiden sued Lee for her $25,000 deposit plus interest. Lee counterclaims, based on the terms of the contract, for liquidated damages of $25,000 (the amount of the deposit) as a result of Mrs. Kaiden's breach of contract. What are the rights of the parties?

16. Servebest contracted to sell Emessee two hundred thousand pounds of 50 percent lean beef trimmings for $105,000. Upon a substantial fall in the market price, Emessee refused to pay the contract price and informed Servebest that the contract was canceled. Servebest sues Emessee for breach of contract, including (a) damages for the difference between the contract price and the resale price of the trimmings and (b) incidental damages. Discuss.

17. Mrs. French was the highest bidder on eight antique guns at an auction held by Sotheby & Company. Mrs. French made a down payment on the guns but subsequently refused to accept the guns and refused to pay the remaining balance of $24,886.27 owed on them. Is Sotheby's entitled to collect the price of the guns from Mrs. French?

18. Teledyne Industries, Inc., entered into a contract with Teradyne, Inc., to purchase a T-347A transistor test system for the list and fair market price of $98,400 less a discount of $984. After the system was packed for shipment, Teledyne canceled the order, offering to purchase a Field Effects Transistor System for $65,000. Teradyne refused the offer and sold the T-347A to another purchaser pursuant to an order that was on hand prior to the cancellation. Can Teradyne recover from Teledyne for lost profits resulting from the breach of contract? Explain.

19. Wilson Trading Corp. agreed to sell David Ferguson a specified quantity of yarn for use in making sweaters. The written contract provided that notice of defects, to be effective, had to be received by Wilson before knitting or within ten days of receipt of the yarn. When the knitted sweaters were washed, the color of the yarn "shaded" (i.e., variations in color from piece to piece appeared). David Ferguson immediately notified Wilson of the problem and refused to pay for the yarn, claiming that the defect made the sweaters unmarketable. Wilson brought suit against Ferguson for the contract price. What result?

20. Bishop Logging Company is a large, family-owned logging contractor formed in the Lowcountry of South Carolina. Bishop Logging has traditionally harvested pine timber. However, Bishop Logging began investigating the feasibility of a fully mechanized hardwood swamp logging operation when its main customer, Stone Container Corporation, decided to expand hardwood production. In anticipating an increased demand for hardwood in conjunction with the operation of a new paper machine, Stone Container requested that Bishop Logging harvest and supply hardwood for processing at its mill. In South Carolina, most suitable hardwood is located deep in the swamplands. Because of the high accident risk in the swamp, Bishop Logging did not want to harvest hardwood by the conventional method of manual felling of trees. Because Bishop Logging had already been successful in its totally mechanized pine logging operation, it began a search for improved methods of hardwood swamp logging centered on mechanizing the process to reduce labor, minimize personal injury and insurance costs, and improve efficiency and productivity.

Bishop Logging ultimately purchased several pieces of John Deere equipment to make up the system. The gross sales price of the machinery was $608,899. All the equipment came with a written John Deere "New Equipment Warranty," whereby John Deere agreed only to repair or replace the equipment during the warranty period and did not warrant the suitability of the equipment. In the "New Equipment Warranty," John Deere expressly provided the following: (a) John Deere would repair or replace parts that were defective in material or workmanship; (b) a disclaimer of any express warranties or implied warranties of merchantability or fitness for a particular purpose; (c) an exclusion of all incidental or consequential damages; and (d) no authority for the dealer to make any representations, promises, modifications, or limitations of John Deere's written warranty. Hoping to sell more equipment if the Bishop Logging system was successful, however, John Deere agreed to assume part of the risk of the new enterprise by extending its standard equipment warranties notwithstanding the unusual use and modifications to the equipment.

Soon after being placed in operation in the swamp, the machinery began to experience numerous mechanical problems. John Deere made more than $110,000 in warranty repairs on the equipment. However, Bishop Logging contended the swamp logging system failed to operate as represented by John Deere and, as a result, it suffered a substantial financial loss. To what remedies, if any, is Bishop entitled? Explain.

21. The plaintiff contracted with the defendant to deliver liquid nitrogen to the defendant's oil refinery production facility located in Belle Chase, Louisiana. The defendant uses liquid nitrogen to ensure the safe operation of its plant. The contract was a "requirement" contract—deliveries were based on how much liquid nitrogen the defendant had in its tanks. As a result, the plaintiff typically made deliveries seven days a week, and sometimes several times a day.

The defendant claims that the plaintiff repeatedly failed to deliver the liquid nitrogen on time, thereby dropping the liquid nitrogen to dangerously low levels and compromising the safety of the plant and its personnel. The contract provided that if the plaintiff failed to deliver the liquid nitrogen as required, the defendant's sole remedy would be to purchase the product from another supplier and charge the plaintiff for the additional expenses incurred. The defendant did not exercise this right because it claims it was unable to purchase nitrogen from other suppliers. However, on the only occasion the defendant actually tried to purchase nitrogen from another supplier, it was successful. The plaintiff sued the defendant for breach of contract, and the defendant counterclaimed. What are the rights and remedies of the parties? Explain.

TAKING SIDES

Daniel Martin and John Duke contracted with J & S Distributors, Inc., to purchase a KIS Magnum Speed printer for $17,000. The parties agreed that Martin and Duke would send one-half of the money as a deposit and would pay the balance upon delivery. They also agreed to the following provision:

> In the event of nonpayment of the balance of the purchase price reflected herein on due date and in the manner recorded or on such extended date which may be caused by late delivery on the part of [the seller], the Customer shall be liable for (1) immediate payment of the full balance recorded herein; and (2) payment of interest at the rate of 12 percent per annum calculated on the balance due, when due, together with any attorney's fees, collection charges, and other necessary expenses incurred by [the seller].

When the machine arrived five days late, Martin and Duke refused to accept it, stating that the company had purchased a substitute machine elsewhere. Martin and Duke requested the return of its deposit but J & S refused. Martin and Duke sued J & S for the return of its deposit. J & S counterclaimed for full performance of the contract seeking an order that Martin and Duke accept delivery of the KIS machine and pay the entire balance of the contract.

a. What arguments would support the claim by Martin and Duke for the return of the deposit?

b. What arguments would support the claim by J & S for full performance of the contract?

c. Who should prevail? Explain.

PART V

NEGOTIABLE INSTRUMENTS

Form and Content

Money is not, properly speaking, one of the subjects of commerce; but only the instrument which men have agreed upon to facilitate the exchange of one commodity for another. It is none of the wheels of trade: It is the oil which renders the motion of the wheels more smooth and easy.

David Hume (1711–1776)
Of Money

CHAPTER OUTCOMES

After reading and studying this chapter, you should be able to:

1. Describe the concept and importance of negotiability.

2. Identify and describe the types of negotiable instruments involving an order to pay.

3. Identify and describe the types of negotiable instruments involving a promise to pay.

4. List and explain the formal requirements that an instrument must meet to be negotiable.

5. Explain the effect on negotiability of an instrument's (a) being undated, antedated, or postdated; (b) lack of completion; and (c) ambiguity.

Negotiable instruments
includes drafts, checks, promissory notes, and certificates of deposit

Negotiable instruments, also referred to simply as instruments, include drafts, checks, promissory notes, and certificates of deposit. These instruments are widely used by individuals and businesses in payment for goods and services as well as in financing numerous types of transactions.

For a number of reasons, **payment** by noncash means is preferable in many transactions. Noncash payments take two forms: *paper* (checks and drafts) and *electronic* (debit cards, credit cards, automated clearinghouse [ACH], and prepaid cards). By number of transactions, electronic payments now represent 85 percent of all noncash payments while payments by check are now less than 15 percent of all noncash payments. By value, electronic payments constitute two-thirds of all noncash payments while checks represent one-third of all noncash payments. More specifically, in the United States in 2012 (the last year data was available), the number of checks paid was approximately 18.3 billion with a value of approximately $26 trillion. (The number of paper checks has declined by more than 50 percent since 2003.) Although by number of transactions, debit cards are now the most used noncash payment in the United States, by value, debit card payments amount to only 2 percent of all noncash payments.

The *financing* or credit function of negotiable instruments is indispensable. For example, promissory notes are used extensively in financing sales of goods. In addition, corporations fund their operating expenses or current assets by issuing commercial paper in the form of short-term promissory notes; in the United States more than $1 trillion of commercial paper is outstanding. Moreover, corporations obtain long-term financing by issuing long-term promissory notes (bonds); in the United States in 2013, almost $10 trillion of corporate bonds were outstanding. Promissory notes are also used in financing sales of real estate, with more than $13 trillion of mortgage debt outstanding in the United States. A certificate of deposit (CD) is a promissory note issued by a bank and is used by many individuals as a type of deposit account that typically offers a higher rate of interest than a regular savings account.

CONCEPT REVIEW 24-1

Use of Negotiable Instruments

Instrument	Use	Chapter in Text
Check	Payment	24–27
Draft	Finance the movement of goods	24–26
Note	Commercial paper; business, personal, and real estate financing	24–26, 34, 37, 39, 49
Certificate of Deposit	Savings	24–26
Debit Card	Payment	27
Credit Card	Payment	27, 44
ACH	Payment	27
Prepaid Card	Payment	27

Accordingly, the vital importance of negotiable instruments and electronic transfers as methods of payment and financing cannot be overstated. See Concept Review 24-1 for a summary of how these instruments are commonly used and the chapters in this text that discuss them.

In 1990, the American Law Institute and the Uniform Law Commission (also known as the National Conference of Commissioners on Uniform Laws) approved a Revised Article 3 to the Uniform Commercial Code (UCC). Named "Negotiable Instruments," the new Article maintains the basic scope and content of prior Article 3 (Commercial Paper). In 2002, the American Law Institute and the Uniform Law Commission completed updates to Articles 3 and 4. All states except New York have adopted the 1990 version of Article 3 and at least eleven states have adopted the 2002 version. This part of the text will discuss the 1990 version of Revised Article 3. The 1990 version of Revised Article 3 is presented in Appendix B.

NEGOTIABILITY [24-1]

Negotiability
invests instruments with a high degree of marketability and commercial utility by conferring upon certain good faith transferees immunity from most defenses to the instrument

Negotiability is a legal concept that makes written instruments freely transferable and therefore a readily accepted form of payment in substitution for money.

Development of Law of Negotiable Instruments [24-1a]

The starting point for an understanding of negotiable instruments is recognizing that four or five centuries ago in England a contract right to the payment of money was not assignable because a contractual promise ran to the promisee. The fact that performance could be rendered only to him constituted a hardship for the owner of the right because it prevented him from selling or disposing of it. Eventually, however, the law permitted recovery upon an assignment by the assignee against the obligor.

An innocent assignee bringing an action against the obligor was subject to all defenses available to the obligor. Such an action would result in the same outcome whether it was brought by the assignee or assignor. Thus, a contract right became assignable but not very marketable because merchants had little interest in buying into a possible lawsuit. This remains the *law of assignments: The assignee stands in the shoes of his assignor.* For a discussion of assignments, see Chapter 16.

With the flourishing of trade and commerce, it became essential to develop a more effective means of exchanging contractual rights for money. For example, a merchant who sold goods for cash might use the cash to buy more goods for resale. If he were to make a sale on credit in exchange for a promise to pay money, why should he not be permitted to sell that promise to someone else for cash with which to carry on his business? One difficulty was that the buyer of the goods gave the seller only a promise to pay money to him. The seller was the only person to whom performance or payment was promised. If, however, the seller obtained from the buyer a promise in writing to pay money to anyone in possession (a *bearer*) of the writing (the *paper* or *instrument*) or to anyone the seller (or *payee* in this case) designated, then the duty of performance would run directly to the holder (the bearer of the paper or to the person to whom the payee ordered payment to be made). This is one of the essential distinctions between negotiable and nonnegotiable instruments. Although a negotiable instrument has other formal requirements, this particular one eliminates the limitations of a promise to pay money only to a named promisee.

Moreover, if the promise to pay were not subject to all of the defenses available against the assignor, a transferee would not only be more willing to acquire the promise but also would pay more for it. Accordingly, the law of negotiable instruments developed the concept of the **holder in due course**, whereby certain good faith transferees who gave value acquired the right to be paid, free of most of the defenses to which an assignee would be subject. By reason of this doctrine, a transferee of a negotiable instrument could *acquire* greater rights than his transferor, whereas an assignee would acquire *only* the rights of his assignor. With these basic innovations, negotiable instruments enabled merchants to sell their contractual rights more readily and thereby keep their capital working.

Assignment Compared with Negotiation [24-1b]

Negotiability invests negotiable instruments with a high degree of marketability and commercial utility. It allows negotiable instruments to be freely transferable and enforceable by a person with the rights of a holder in due course against any person obligated on the instrument, subject only to a limited number of defenses. To illustrate, assume that George sells and delivers goods to Elaine for $50,000 on sixty days' credit and that, a few days later, George assigns this account to Marsha. Unless Elaine is duly notified of this assignment, she may safely pay the $50,000 to George on the due date without incurring any liability to Marsha, the assignee. Assume next that the goods were defective and that Elaine, accordingly, has a defense against George to the extent of $20,000. Assume also that Marsha duly notified Elaine of the assignment. The result is that Marsha can recover only $30,000, not $50,000, from Elaine because Elaine's defense against George is equally available against George's assignee, Marsha. In other words, an assignee of contractual rights merely "steps into the shoes" of her assignor and, hence, acquires only the same rights as her assignor—and no more.

Assume, instead, that upon the sale by George to Elaine, Elaine executes and delivers her negotiable note to George for $50,000, payable to George's order in sixty days, and that, a short time later, George duly negotiates (transfers) the note to Marsha. In the first place, Marsha is not required to notify Elaine that she has acquired the note from George, because one who issues a negotiable instrument is held to know that the instrument may be negotiated and is generally obligated to pay the holder of the instrument, whoever that may be. In the second place, Elaine's defense is not available against Marsha if Marsha acquired the note in good faith and for value and had no knowledge of Elaine's defense against George and took it without reason to question its authenticity. Marsha, therefore, is entitled to hold Elaine for the full face amount of the note at maturity, namely, $50,000. In other words, Marsha, by the negotiation of the negotiable note to her, acquired rights greater than those George had, because, by keeping the note, George could have recovered only $30,000 on it because Elaine successfully could have asserted her defense in the amount of $20,000 against him.

To have the full benefit of negotiability, negotiable instruments not only must meet the requirements of negotiability but also must be acquired by a holder in due course. This chapter discusses the formal requirements that instruments must satisfy to be negotiable. Chapter 25 deals with the manner in which a negotiable instrument must be negotiated to preserve its advantages as well as the requisites and rights of a holder in due course. Chapter 26 examines the liability of all the parties to a negotiable instrument.

Figure 24-1 Order to Pay: Draft or Check

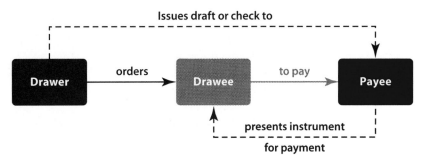

Draft

a draft involves three parties: the drawer orders the drawee to pay a fixed amount of money to a payee

Drawer

issuer of an order to pay (draft or check)

Drawee

party ordered to pay a draft or a check

Payee

person to receive payment by an instrument

Check

a specialized form of draft that is drawn on a bank and payable on demand; the drawer orders the drawee (bank) to pay the payee on demand (upon the request of the holder)

Demand

request for payment made by the holder of an instrument

TYPES OF NEGOTIABLE INSTRUMENTS [24-2]

There are four types of negotiable instruments: drafts, checks, notes, and certificates of deposit. The first two contain *orders* or directions to pay money; the last two involve *promises* to pay money.

Drafts [24-2a]

A **draft** involves three parties, each in a distinct capacity. One party, the **drawer**, *orders* a second party, the **drawee**, to pay a fixed amount of money to a third party, the **payee** (see Figure 24-1 for a three-party instrument). Thus, the drawer "draws" the draft on the drawee. The drawee is ordinarily a person or entity that either is in possession of money belonging to the drawer or owes money to him. A sample draft is reproduced in Figure 24-2. The same party may appear in more than one capacity; for instance, the drawer may also be the payee.

Drafts may be either "time" or "sight." A *time draft* is one payable at a specified future date, whereas a *sight draft* is payable on demand (i.e., immediately upon presentation to the drawee).

Checks [24-2b]

A **check** is a specialized form of draft, namely, an order to pay money drawn on a bank and payable on demand (i.e., upon the payee's request for payment). Once again, parties are involved in three distinct capacities: the *drawer* who orders the *drawee*, a bank, to pay the *payee* on **demand** (see Figure 24-3 for a check). Checks are by far the most widely used form of negotiable instruments. As previously stated, in 2012, the number of checks paid in the United States was approximately $18.3 billion with a value of approximately $26 trillion. An increasing percentage of checks are converted into an electronic payment that is processed through the ACH Network. In 2012, the percentage of checks converted to ACH-based electronic payment increased to 13 percent from 1 percent in 2003.

The Check Clearing for the 21st Century Act (also called Check 21 or the Check Truncation Act), which went into effect in late 2004, creates a new negotiable instrument called a substitute check or image replacement document (IRD). The law permits banks to truncate original checks,

Figure 24-2 Draft

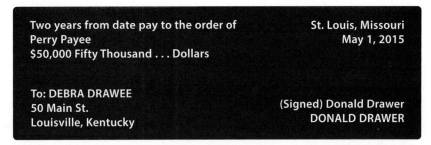

Figure 24-3 Check

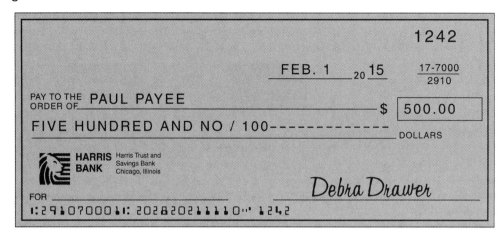

to process check information electronically, and to deliver substitute checks to banks that want to continue receiving paper checks. A substitute check would be the legal equivalent of the original check and would include all the information contained on the original check. The law does not require banks to accept checks in electronic form nor does it require banks to use the new authority granted by the act to create substitute checks. This document is more fully discussed in Chapter 27.

A *cashier's check* is a check drawn by a bank upon itself to the order of a named payee.

Notes [24-2c]

Promissory note

a written promise by a maker (issuer) to pay a payee

Maker

issuer of a promissory note or certificate of deposit

A **promissory note** is an instrument involving two parties in two capacities. One party, the **maker**, promises to pay a second party, the payee, a stated sum of money, either on demand or at a stated future date (see Figure 24-4 for a two-party promise to pay). The note may range from a simple "I promise to pay $X to the order of Y" form to more complex legal instruments such as installment notes, collateral notes, mortgage notes, and judgment notes. Figure 24-5 is a note payable at a definite time—six months from the date of April 7, 2015—and hence is referred to as a *time note*. A note payable upon the request or demand of the payee or holder is a *demand note*.

Certificates of Deposit [24-2d]

Certificate of deposit

a specialized form of note that is given by a bank or thrift association

A certificate of deposit, or CD, as it is frequently called, is a specialized form of *promise* to pay money given by a *bank*. A **certificate of deposit** is a written acknowledgment by a bank of the receipt of money that it promises to repay. The issuing party, the *maker*, which is always a bank, promises to pay a second party, the payee, who is named in the CD (see Figure 24-6 for a sample certificate of deposit).

Figure 24-4 Promise to Pay: Promissory Note or Certificate of Deposit

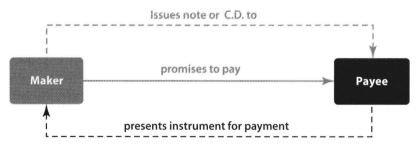

Figure 24-5 Note

$10,000	Albany, N.Y.	April 7, 2015

Six months from date I promise to pay to the order of Pat Payee ten thousand dollars.

(Signed) Matthew Maker

FORMAL REQUIREMENTS OF NEGOTIABLE INSTRUMENTS [24-3]

Formal requirements
negotiability is wholly a matter of form, and all the requirements for negotiability must be met within the "four corners" of the instrument

To perform its function in the business community effectively, a negotiable instrument must be able to pass freely from person to person. The fact that *negotiability* is wholly a matter of form makes such freedom possible. The instrument must contain within its "four corners" all the information required to determine whether it is negotiable. No reference to any other source is permitted. For this reason, a negotiable instrument is called a "courier without luggage." In addition, indorsements *cannot* create or destroy negotiability.

To be negotiable, the *instrument* must

1. be in writing,
2. be signed,
3. contain a promise or order to pay,
4. be unconditional,
5. be for a fixed amount,
6. be for money,
7. contain no other undertaking or instruction,
8. be payable on demand or at a definite time, and
9. be payable to order or to bearer.

Practical Advice

To increase the value of an undertaking, make sure that any document memorializing it qualifies as a negotiable instrument.

If these requirements are not met, the undertaking is not a negotiable instrument, and the rights of the parties are governed by the law of contract (assignment).

Writing [24-3a]

Writing
any reduction to tangible form is sufficient

The requirement that the instrument be in **writing** is broadly construed. Printing, typewriting, handwriting, or any other intentional tangible expression is sufficient to satisfy the requirement. Most negotiable instruments, of course, are written on paper, but this is not required. In one instance, a check was reportedly written on a coconut.

Figure 24-6 Certificate of Deposit

NEGOTIABLE CERTIFICATE OF DEPOSIT

The Mountain Bank

No. 13900	Mountain, N.Y.	June 1, 2015

THIS CERTIFIES THAT THERE HAS BEEN DEPOSITED

with the undersigned the sum of $200,000.00

Two Hundred Thousand .... Dollars

Payable to the order of Pablo Payee on December 1, 2015, with interest only to maturity at the rate of seven percent (7%) per annum upon surrender of this certificate properly indorsed.

The Mountain Bank
By (Signature) Malcom Maker, Vice President
Authorized Signature

Signed [24-3b]

A note or certificate of deposit must be signed by the maker; a draft or check must be signed by the drawer. As in the case of a writing, extreme latitude is granted in determining what constitutes a **signature**, which is any symbol a party executes or adopts with the present *intention* to authenticate a writing. Revised Article 1 changes the word "authenticate" to "adopt or accept." Moreover, it may consist of any word or mark used in place of a written signature, such as initials, an X, or a thumbprint. It may be a trade name or an assumed name. Even the location of the signature on the document is unimportant. Normally, a maker or drawer signs in the lower right-hand corner of the instrument, but this is not required. Negotiable instruments are frequently signed by an agent for her principal. For a discussion of the appropriate way in which an agent should sign a negotiable instrument, see Chapter 26.

Signature
any symbol executed or adopted by a party with the intention to validate a writing

Promise or Order to Pay [24-3c]

A negotiable instrument must contain either a promise to pay money, in the case of a note or certificate of deposit, or an order to pay, in the case of a draft or check.

Promise to Pay A **promise to pay** is an undertaking and must be more than the mere acknowledgment or recognition of an existing obligation or debt. The so-called due bill or IOU is not a promise but merely an acknowledgment of indebtedness. Accordingly, an instrument reciting "due Adam Brown $100" or "IOU, Adam Brown, $100" is not negotiable because it does not contain a promise to pay.

Promise to pay
an undertaking to pay, which must be more than a mere acknowledgment or recognition of an existing debt

Order to pay
instruction to pay

Order to Pay An **order to pay** is an instruction to pay. It must be more than an authorization or request and must identify with reasonable certainty the person to be paid. The usual way to express an order is by use of the word pay: "Pay to the order of John Jones" or "Pay bearer." The addition of words of courtesy, such as please pay or kindly pay, will not destroy the negotiability. Nonetheless, caution should be exercised in employing words that modify the prototypically correct "pay." For example, the use of the words "I wish you would pay" has been held to destroy the negotiability of an instrument and to render its transfer a contractual assignment.

Unconditional [24-3d]

The requirement that the promise or order be unconditional is to prevent the inclusion of any term that could reduce the promisor's obligation to pay. Conditions limiting a promise would diminish the payment and credit functions of negotiable instruments by necessitating costly and time-consuming investigations to determine the degree of risk such conditions imposed. Moreover, if the holder (transferee) had to take an instrument subject to certain conditions, her risk factor would be substantial, and this would lead to limited transferability. Substitutes for money must be capable of rapid circulation at a minimum risk.

Unconditional
an absolute promise to pay that is not subject to any contingencies

A promise or order to pay is **unconditional** if it is absolute and not subject to any contingencies or qualifications. Thus, an instrument would not be negotiable if it stated that "ABC Corp. promises to pay $100,000 to the order of Johnson provided the helicopter sold meets all contractual specifications." On the other hand, suppose that upon delivering an instrument that provided, "ABC Corp. promises to pay $100,000 to the order of Johnson," Meeker, the president of ABC, stated that the money would be paid only if the helicopter met all contractual specifications. The instrument would be negotiable because negotiability is determined solely by examining the instrument itself and is not affected by matters beyond the instrument's face.

A promise or order is unconditional unless it states: (1) that there is an express condition to payment, (2) that the promise or order is subject to or governed by another writing, or (3) that rights or obligations concerning the order or promise are stated in another writing. A mere reference to another writing, however, does not make the promise or order conditional.

An instrument is not made conditional by the fact that it is subject to implied or constructive conditions; the condition must be expressed to destroy negotiability. Implications of law or fact are not to be considered in deciding whether an instrument is negotiable. Thus, a statement in an instrument that it is given for an executory promise does *not* imply that the instrument is conditioned upon performance of that promise.

Reference to another agreement

does not destroy negotiability unless the recital makes the instrument subject to or governed by the terms of another agreement

Particular fund doctrine

an order or promise to pay only out of a particular fund is not conditional and does not destroy negotiability

Fixed amount

the holder must be assured of a determinable minimum principal payment, although provisions in the instrument may increase the amount of recovery under certain circumstances

Reference to Other Agreements   The restriction against **reference to another agreement** is to enable any person to determine the right to payment provided by the instrument without having to look beyond its four corners. If such a right is made subject to the terms of another agreement, the instrument is nonnegotiable.

A distinction is to be made between a mere recital of the *existence* of a separate agreement (this does not destroy negotiability) and a recital that makes the instrument *subject* to the terms of another agreement (this does destroy negotiability).

A statement in a note, such as "This note is given in partial payment for a television to be delivered two weeks from date in accordance with a contract of this date between the payee and the maker," does not impair negotiability. It merely describes the consideration and the transaction giving rise to the note. It does not place any restriction or condition on the maker's obligation to pay. The promise is not made subject to any other agreement. The following is an example of added words that *would* impair negotiability: "This note is subject to all terms of said contract." Such words make the promise to pay conditional upon the adequate performance of the television set in accordance with the terms of the contract and thus render the instrument nonnegotiable.

The Particular Fund Doctrine   Revised Article 3 provides that a promise or order is *not* made conditional because payment is to be made only out of a particular fund.

Fixed Amount [24-3e]

The purpose of the requirement of a **fixed amount** in money is to enable the person entitled to enforce the instrument to determine from the instrument itself the amount that he is entitled to receive.

The requirement that payment be of a "fixed amount" must be considered from the point of view of the person entitled to enforce the instrument, not the maker or drawer. The holder must be assured of a determinable minimum payment, although provisions of the instrument may increase the recovery under certain circumstances. Revised Article 3, however, applies the fixed amount requirement only to the *principal*. Thus, the fixed amount portion does not apply to interest or to the charges, such as collection fees or attorneys' fees.

Moreover, negotiability of an instrument is not affected by the inclusion or omission of a stated rate of interest. If the instrument does not state a rate of interest, it is payable without interest. If the instrument states that it is payable "with interest" but does not specify a rate, the judgment rate of interest applies.

Most significantly, Revised Article 3 provides that "Interest may be stated in an instrument as a fixed or variable amount of money or it may be expressed as a fixed or variable rate or rates." Moreover, determination of the rate of interest "may require reference to information not contained in the instrument." Variable rate mortgages, therefore, may be negotiable; this result is consistent with the rule that the fixed amount requirement applies only to the principal.

A sum payable is a fixed amount even though it is payable in installments or payable with a fixed discount, if paid before maturity, or with a fixed addition, if paid after maturity. This is because it is always possible to use the instrument itself to compute the amount due at any given time.

Heritage Bank v. Bruha
Supreme Court of Nebraska, 2012
283 Neb. 263, 812 N.W.2d 260
http://scholar.google.com/scholar_case?case=16811322925522025258&q=812+nw2d+260&hl=en&as_sdt=6,34

FACTS Jerome J. Bruha signed a promissory note on December 16, 2008, with Sherman County Bank. The note contained a promise to pay "the principal amount of Seventy-five Thousand & 00/100 ($75,000.00) or so much as may be outstanding, together with interest on the unpaid outstanding principal balance of each

advance." The note was "a revolving line of credit." The note contained a variable interest rate subject to change every month.

On this note, Bruha received advancements in the amount of $10,000 on December 16, 2008, $40,000 on December 17, and $1,000 on January 30, 2009. This totaled $51,000. Bruha then invested the money in accounts with a trading company, which allegedly shared management with Sherman County Bank.

There are a few typographical errors on the note. First, the maturity date on the note is February 1, 2008, which, read literally, means that the note would have matured about 10 months before Bruha signed it. Other notes he had signed stated maturity dates of February 1, *2009*. Second, in a section titled "COLLATERAL" the note reads: "Borrower acknowledges this Note is secured by an assignment of hedge account from Jerome Bruah [*sic*] to Sherman County Bank dated DATE [*sic*]." Thus, Bruha's name is misspelled and a line for a date is unfilled.

Sherman County Bank eventually failed, and the Federal Deposit Insurance Corporation (FDIC) was appointed as receiver. The FDIC then sold and assigned some of Sherman County Bank's assets to Heritage. These assets included the note signed by Bruha. Heritage sued Bruha to enforce the note.

Bruha admitted that he signed the note but claims that he did not do it voluntarily. He claimed that Sherman County Bank had procured his signature "by fraud and/or misrepresentation." Bruha also claims that the typographical errors destroyed the negotiability of the promissory note. Bruha admitted that he had not paid the note but denied that he was obligated to do so.

The district court granted summary judgment to Heritage and awarded it $61,384.67 ($51,000 plus interest) on the note. The court disallowed Bruha's defenses because, under federal law, for certain defenses to be asserted against the FDIC or its assignees, the defenses must be evidenced in writing. The court found that there was no evidence in writing of a defense that would invalidate the note. The court also concluded that the FDIC had become a holder in due course and thus not subject to most defenses. Bruha appealed.

DECISION Summary judgment is affirmed in part, reversed in part, and remanded for correction.

OPINION The primary issues are whether either the holder-in-due-course rule of Nebraska's Uniform Commercial Code or federal banking law bars Bruha's defenses to the enforcement of the note.

A holder in due course is, with some exceptions, "immune to defenses, claims in recoupment, and claims of title that prior parties to commercial paper might assert." So if Heritage were a holder in due course, it would enjoy an advantageous position in litigation with Bruha. However, Heritage is not a holder in due course because the note was not "negotiable" and Article 3 of the Uniform Commercial Code does not apply to this case.

Neb. U.C.C. § 3-104(a) provides: "Except as provided in subsections (c) and (d), 'negotiable instrument' means an unconditional promise or order to pay *a fixed amount of money*, with or without interest or other charges described in the promise or order...." (Emphasis supplied.) Here, the note fails to meet the definition of a "negotiable instrument" because it was not a promise "to pay a fixed amount of money."

Although the Uniform Commercial Code allows notes to have a variable interest rate, under § 3-104(a), the principal amount must be fixed. "A fixed amount is an absolute requisite to negotiability." This is because unless a purchaser can determine how much it will be paid under the instrument, it will be unable to determine a fair price to pay for it, which defeats the basic purpose for negotiable instruments.

"A guaranty is not an agreement to pay a fixed amount and is therefore not a negotiable instrument subject to Article 3 of the Nebraska Uniform Commercial Code." To meet the fixed amount requirement, the fixed amount generally must be determinable by reference to the instrument itself without any reference to any outside source. If reference to a separate instrument or extrinsic facts is needed to ascertain the principal due, the sum is not "'certain'" or fixed.

Here, the text of the note states that Bruha "promises to pay ... the principal amount of Seventy-five Thousand & 00/100 Dollars ($75,000.00) *or so much as may be outstanding....*" Further, the note states that it "evidences a revolving line of credit" and that Bruha could request advances under the obligation up to $75,000. This fails the "fixed amount of money" requirement of § 3-104(a); one looking at the instrument itself cannot tell how much Bruha has been advanced at any given time. So, the note is not negotiable. Stated simply, "[a] note given to secure a line of credit under which the amount of the obligation varies, depending on the extent to which the line of credit is used, is not negotiable...."

For a person to be a holder in due course, the instrument must be negotiable. Because the note was not a negotiable instrument, Heritage could never become a holder in due course. And further, because this note is not a negotiable instrument, Article 3 does not apply.

The Supreme Court of Nebraska reversed the district court's finding that the holder-in-due-course rule of Nebraska's Uniform Commercial Code bars Bruha's defenses. The Supreme Court, however, concluded that federal law bars Bruha's defenses and thus affirmed the district court's summary judgment in part.

INTERPRETATION To be negotiable a note must be for a fixed amount payable in money and the fixed amount generally must be determinable by reference to the instrument itself without any reference to any outside source.

CRITICAL THINKING QUESTION Do you agree with the opinion in this case? Explain.

Money [24-3f]

Money

medium of exchange currently authorized or adopted by a domestic or foreign government

The term **money** means a medium of exchange authorized or adopted by a sovereign government as part of its currency. (Revised Article 1 adds that the authorized or adopted currency must be the current official currency of the government.) Consequently, even though local custom may make gold or diamonds a medium of exchange, an instrument payable in such commodities would be nonnegotiable because of the lack of governmental sanction of such media as legal tender. On the other hand, an instrument paying a fixed amount in Swiss francs, Australian dollars, Nigerian naira, Japanese yen, or other foreign currency is negotiable.

No other undertaking or instruction

a promise or order to do an act in addition to the payment of money destroys negotiability

No Other Undertaking or Instruction [24-3g]

A negotiable instrument must contain a promise or order to pay money, but it may not "state any other undertaking or instruction by the person promising or ordering payment to do any act in addition to the payment of money." Accordingly, an instrument containing an order or promise to do an act in addition to or in lieu of the payment of money is not negotiable. For example, a promise to pay $100 "and a ton of coal" would be nonnegotiable.

The Code sets out a list of terms and provisions that may be included in instruments without adversely affecting negotiability. Among these are (1) an undertaking or power to give, maintain, or protect collateral to secure payment; (2) an authorization or power to confess judgment (written authority by the debtor to allow the holder to enter judgment against the debtor in favor of the holder) on the instrument; (3) an authorization or power to sell or dispose of collateral upon default; and (4) a waiver of the benefit of any law intended for the advantage or protection of the obligor. It is important to note that the Code does not render any of these terms legal or effective; it merely provides that their inclusion will not affect negotiability.

Practical Advice

To preserve the negotiability of an instrument, avoid including any undertaking beyond the promise or order to pay.

Payable on Demand or at a Definite Time [24-3h]

A negotiable instrument must "be payable on demand or at a definite time." This requirement, like the other formal requirements of negotiability, is designed to promote certainty in determining the present value of a negotiable instrument.

Demand paper

payable on request

Demand "Payable upon demand" means that the money owed under the instrument must be paid upon the holder's request. **Demand paper** always has been considered sufficiently certain as to time of payment to satisfy the requirements of negotiability, because it is the person entitled to enforce the instrument who makes the demand and who thus sets the time for payment. Any instrument in which no time for payment is stated—a check, for example—is payable on demand. An instrument also qualifies as being payable on demand if it is payable at sight or on presentment.

NationsBank of Virginia, N.A. v. Barnes
Virginia Circuit Court, 1994
33 Va. Cir. 184, 24 UCC Rep.Serv.2d 782

FACTS In 1991, Ad Barnes and Elaine Barnes (Barnes) executed a promissory note for $200,000 to Sovran Bank, N.A. (Sovran). The note was executed on a standard form and a box marked payable "on demand" was checked. There was no set time for repayment, only a provision requiring monthly payments of interest. Nations-Bank of Virginia, N.A. (NationsBank) became the successor by merger to Sovran and is now the holder of this note. By a letter dated February 17, 1993, NationsBank made a demand for payment on the note. Barnes did not make payment and NationsBank brought this action to recover payment. Nations-Bank filed a motion for partial summary judgment on the issue of liability. Barnes argued that NationsBank must make a showing of good faith before it may demand payment on the note.

DECISION Decision for NationsBank.

OPINION Under any contract providing for accelerated payment at will, the Uniform Commercial Code (UCC) provides that the option is to be exercised only in the good faith belief that the prospect of payment or performance is impaired. However, the Code also indicates that this rule is not applicable to a demand

note. Barnes argued that the note in this case was not a demand note and therefore NationsBank must show good faith before it can recover. To support this argument, Barnes argued that the detailed enumeration of events constituting default is inconsistent with a demand note.

UCC Revised Section 3-108(a) states that a note is payable "on demand" if it says it is payable on demand or states no time for payment. In this case, the box marked payable "on demand" was checked and no payment date was stated. The note is unambiguous and it is clearly a demand note. Therefore, no showing of good faith is required before NationsBank may demand payment. Since NationsBank has demanded payment, Barnes is liable on the note.

INTERPRETATION An instrument payable on demand must be paid upon the holder's request.

ETHICAL QUESTION Did NationsBank act in good faith? Explain.

CRITICAL THINKING QUESTION Do you agree with the court's decision? Explain.

Definite Time   Instruments payable at a definite time are called **time paper**. A promise or order is payable at a definite time if it is payable

1. at a fixed date or dates,
2. at a definite period of time after sight or acceptance, or
3. at a time readily ascertainable at the time the promise or order is issued.

An instrument is payable at a definite time if it is payable "on or before" a stated date. The person entitled to enforce the instrument is thus assured that she will have her money by the maturity date at the latest, although she may receive it sooner. This right of anticipation enables the obligor, at his option, to pay before the stated maturity date (*prepayment*) and thereby stop the further accrual of interest or, if interest rates have gone down, to refinance at a lower rate of interest. Nevertheless, it constitutes sufficient certainty so as not to impair negotiability.

Frequently, instruments are made payable at a fixed period after a stated date. For example, the instrument may be made payable "thirty days after date." This means it is payable thirty days after the date of issuance, which is recited on the instrument. Such an instrument is payable at a definite time, for its exact maturity date can be determined by simple math.

An undated instrument payable "thirty days after date" is not payable at a definite time, as the date of payment cannot be determined from its face. It is therefore nonnegotiable until it is completed.

An instrument that by its terms is otherwise payable only upon an act or event whose time of occurrence is uncertain is *not* payable at a definite time. An example would be a note providing for payment to the order "when X dies." However, as previously stated, a time that is readily ascertainable at the time the promise or order is issued is a definite time. This seemingly would permit a note reading "payable on the day of the next presidential election." As long as the scheduled event is certain to happen, Revised Article 3 appears to be satisfied.

The clause "at a fixed period after sight" is frequently used in drafts. Because a fixed period after sight means a fixed period after acceptance, a simple mathematical calculation makes the maturity date certain, and the instrument is, therefore, negotiable.

An instrument payable at a fixed time subject to *acceleration* by the holder also satisfies the requirement of being payable at a definite time. Indeed, such an instrument would seem to have a more certain maturity date than a demand instrument because it at least states a definite maturity date. In addition, the acceleration may be contingent upon the happening of some act or event.

Finally, a provision in an instrument granting the *holder* an option to extend the maturity of the instrument for a definite *or* indefinite period does not impair its negotiability. Nor does a provision permitting the *obligor* of an instrument to extend the maturity date to a further *definite* time. For example, a provision in a note, payable one year from date, that the maker may extend the maturity date six months does not impair negotiability. If the obligor is given an option to extend the maturity of the instrument for an *indefinite* period, however, his promise is illusory, and there is no certainty regarding time of payment. Such an instrument is nonnegotiable. If the obligor's right to extend is limited to a definite time, the extension clause is no more indefinite than an acceleration clause with a time limitation.

In addition, extension may be made automatic upon or after a specified act or event, provided a definite time limit is stated. An example of such an extension clause is, "I promise to pay to the order of John Doe the sum of $2,000 on December 1, 2011, but it is agreed that if the crop of sections 25 and 26 of Twp. 145 is below eight bushels per acre for the 2011 season, this note shall be extended for one year."

At a Definite Time and on Demand   If the instrument, payable at a fixed date, also provides that it is payable on demand made before the fixed date, it is still a negotiable instrument. Revised Article 3 provides that the instrument is payable on demand until the fixed date and, if demand is not made prior to the specified date, becomes payable at a definite time on the fixed date.

Payable to Order or to Bearer [24-3i]

A negotiable instrument must contain words indicating that the maker or drawer intends that it may pass into the hands of someone other than the payee. Although the "magic" words of

Payable to order or to bearer
a negotiable instrument must contain words indicating that the maker or drawer intends that it pass into the hands of someone other than the payee

Payable to order
payable to the "order of" (or other words that mean the same) a named person or anyone designated by that person

negotiability typically are **payable to order or to bearer**, other clearly equivalent words also may fulfill this requirement. The use of synonyms, however, only invites trouble. Moreover, as noted above, indorsements cannot create or destroy negotiability, which must be determined from the "face" of the instrument. Words of negotiability must be present when the instrument is issued or first comes into possession of a holder.

Revised Article 3 provides that a *check* that meets all requirements of being a negotiable instrument except that it is not payable to bearer or order is nevertheless a negotiable instrument. This rule does *not* apply to instruments other than checks.

Payable to Order   An instrument is **payable to order** if it is payable (1) to the order of an identified person or (2) to an identified person or order. If an instrument is payable to bearer, it cannot be payable to order; an instrument that is ambiguous as to this point is payable to bearer. Prior Article 3 provided that use of the word "assigns" met the requirement of words of negotiability; Revised Article 3, however, does not so provide.

Moreover, in every instance the person to whose order the instrument is payable must be designated with reasonable certainty. Within this limitation a broad range of payees is possible, including an individual, two or more payees, an office, an estate, a trust or fund, a partnership or unincorporated association, and a corporation.

This requirement should not be confused with the requirement that the instrument contain an order or promise to pay. An order to pay is an instruction to a third party to pay the instrument as drawn. The word "order" in terms of an "order instrument," on the other hand, pertains to the transferability of the instrument rather than to instructions directing a specific party to pay.

A writing, other than a *check*, that names a specified person without indicating that it is payable to order—for example, "Pay to Justin Matthew"—is not payable to order or to bearer. Such a writing is not a negotiable instrument and is not covered by Article 3. On the other hand, a check that meets all of the requirements of a negotiable instrument, except that it does not provide the words of negotiability, is still a negotiable instrument and falls within the purview of Article 3. Thus, a check "payable to Justin Matthew" is a negotiable check.

Cooperative Centrale Raiffeisen-Boerenleenbank B.A. v. Bailey
United States District Court, Central District of California, 1989
710 F.Supp. 737
http://scholar.google.com/scholar_case?case=15799376056319723245&q=710+F.SUPP.+737&hl=en&as_sdt=6,34

FACTS William Bailey, M.D., executed a promissory note to California Dreamstreet, a joint venture that invested in cattle breeding operations. California Dreamstreet subsequently sold the note to Cooperative Centrale Raiffeisen-Boerenleenbank B.A. (Bank).

The wording on the promissory note was unusual. In pertinent part it read: "DR. WILLIAM BAILEY … hereby promises to pay to the order to CALIFORNIA DREAMSTREET … the sum of Three Hundred Twenty-Nine Thousand Eight Hundred ($329,800) Dollars."

Dr. Bailey contended that the atypical wording "pay to the order to" rendered the note nonnegotiable, and refused to pay the Bank. The Bank, asserting that the note was negotiable, sued for payment.

DECISION Judgment for the Bank.

OPINION Whether an instrument is negotiable is a question of law to be determined solely from the face of the instrument, without reference to the intent of the parties. According to the Uniform Commercial Code (UCC), to be negotiable an instrument

must "be payable to order or bearer." The UCC further defines "payable to order" as follows:

> An instrument is payable to order when by its terms it is payable to the order or assigns of any person therein specified with reasonable certainty, or to him or his order, or when it is conspicuously designated on its face as 'exchange' or the like and names a payee.

It is well established that a promissory note is nonnegotiable if it states only "payable to (payee)" rather than "payable to the order of (payee)." Dr. Bailey argues that the promissory note in question falls somewhere in between and therefore should be deemed nonnegotiable. One of the basic concepts underlying the requirements of UCC Article 3 is to promote the negotiability of instruments by establishing certainty. While the wording of this particular note is unclear, it can plausibly be construed only to mean "pay to the order of." No other interpretation is realistic.

INTERPRETATION An instrument is payable to order if it is payable to the order of an identified entity.

CRITICAL THINKING QUESTION Do you agree with the court's decision? Explain.

Payable to bearer

payable to the holder of the instrument; includes instruments payable (1) to bearer (2) to an unspecified payee, or (3) to cash

Payable to Bearer The UCC states that an instrument fulfills the requirements of being **payable to bearer** if it (1) states it is payable to bearer or the order of bearer, (2) does not state a payee, or (3) states it is payable to "cash" or to the order of "cash." An instrument made payable both to order and to bearer, that is, "pay to the order of Mildred Courts or bearer," is payable to bearer.

An instrument that does not state a payee is payable to bearer. Thus, if a drawer leaves blank the "pay to order of" line of a check or the maker of a notes writes "pay to _____," the instrument is a negotiable bearer instrument.

Terms and Omissions and Their Effect on Negotiability [24-3j]

The negotiability of an instrument may be questioned because of an omission of certain provisions or because of ambiguity. Problems may also arise in connection with the interpretation of an instrument, whether or not negotiability is called into question. Accordingly, the Code contains rules of construction that apply to every instrument.

Dating of the Instrument

The negotiability of an instrument is not affected by the fact that it is antedated or postdated. If the instrument is undated, its date is the date of its issuance. If it is unissued, its date is the date it first comes into the possession of a holder.

Incomplete Instruments

Occasionally, a party will sign a paper that clearly is intended to become an instrument but that, either by intention or through oversight, is incomplete because of the omission of a necessary element such as a promise or order, a designated payee, an amount payable, or a time for payment. The Code provides that such an instrument is not negotiable until completed.

If, for example, an undated instrument is delivered on November 1, 2015, payable "thirty days after date," the payee has implied authority to fill in "November 1, 2015." Until he does so, however, the instrument is not negotiable because it is not payable at a definite time. If the payee completes the instrument by inserting an erroneous date, the rules as to material alteration, covered in Chapter 26, apply.

Ambiguous Instruments

Rather than commit the parties to the use of parol evidence to establish the interpretation of an instrument, Revised Article 3 establishes rules to resolve common ambiguities. This promotes negotiability by providing added certainty to the holder.

Where it is doubtful whether the instrument is a draft or note, the holder may treat it as either and present it for payment to the drawee or the person signing it. For example, an instrument reading

> To X: On demand, I promise to pay $500 to the order of Y.
>
> Signed, Z

may be presented for payment to X as a draft or to Z as a note.

An instrument naming no drawee but stating

> On demand, pay $500 to the order of Y.
>
> Signed, Z

although in the form of a draft, may be treated as a note and presented to Z for payment.

If a printed form of note or draft is used and the party signing it inserts handwritten or typewritten language that is inconsistent with the printed words, the handwritten words control the typewritten and the printed words, and the typewritten words control the printed words.

If the amount payable is set forth on the face of the instrument in both figures and words and the amounts differ, the words control the figures. It is presumed that the maker or drawer would be more careful with words. If the words are ambiguous, however, then the figures control.

CHAPTER SUMMARY

Negotiability

Rule invests instruments with a high degree of marketability and commercial utility by conferring upon certain good faith transferees immunity from most defenses to the instrument

Formal Requirements negotiability is wholly a matter of form, and all the requirements for negotiability must be met within the "four corners" of the instrument

Types of Negotiable Instruments

Orders to Pay

- *Drafts* a draft involves three parties: the drawer orders the drawee to pay a fixed amount of money to the payee
- *Checks* a specialized form of draft that is drawn on a bank and payable on demand; the drawer orders the drawee (bank) to pay the payee on demand (upon the request of the holder)

Promises to Pay

- *Notes* a written promise by a maker (issuer) to pay a payee
- *Certificates of Deposit* a specialized form of note that is given by a bank or thrift association

Formal Requirements of Negotiable Instruments

Writing any intentional reduction to tangible form is sufficient

Signature any symbol executed or adopted by a party with the present intention to authenticate/adopt or accept a writing

Promise or Order to Pay

- *Promise to Pay* an undertaking to pay, which must be more than a mere acknowledgment or recognition of an existing debt
- *Order to Pay* instruction to pay

Unconditional an absolute promise to pay that is not subject to any contingencies

- *Reference to Other Agreements* does not destroy negotiability unless the recital makes the instrument subject to or governed by the terms of another agreement
- *The Particular Fund Doctrine* an order or promise to pay only out of a particular fund is no longer conditional and does not destroy negotiability

Fixed Amount the holder must be assured of a determinable minimum principal payment, although provisions in the instrument may increase the amount of recovery under certain circumstances

Money medium of exchange currently authorized or adopted by a domestic or foreign government

No Other Undertaking or Instruction a promise or order to do an act in addition to the payment of money destroys negotiability

Payable on Demand or at a Definite Time an instrument is demand paper if it must be paid upon request: an instrument is time paper if it is payable at a definite time

Payable to Order or to Bearer a negotiable instrument must contain words indicating that the maker or drawer intends that it pass into the hands of someone other than the payee

- *Payable to Order* payable to the "order of" (or other words that mean the same) a named person or anyone designated by that person
- *Payable to Bearer* payable to the holder of the instrument; includes instruments
  (1) payable to bearer or the order of bearer,
  (2) that do not specify a payee, or
  (3) payable to "cash" or to order of "cash"

QUESTIONS

1. State whether the following provisions impair or preclude negotiability, the instrument in each instance being otherwise in proper form. Answer each statement with either "Negotiable" or "Nonnegotiable" and explain why.

   a. A note for $2,000 payable in twenty monthly installments of $100 each that provides the following: "In case of death of maker, all payments not due at date of death are canceled."

b. A note stating, "This note is secured by a mortgage on personal property located at 351 Maple Street, Smithton, Illinois."

c. A certificate of deposit reciting, "June 6, 2015, John Jones has deposited in the Citizens Bank of Emanon, Illinois, Two Thousand Dollars, to the credit of himself, payable upon the return of this instrument properly indorsed, with interest at the rate of 6 percent per annum from date of issue upon ninety days' written notice. (Signed) Jill Crystal, President, Citizens Bank of Emanon."

d. An instrument reciting, "IOU, Mark Noble, $1,000.00."

e. A note stating, "In accordance with our contract of December 13, 2014, I promise to pay to the order of Sam Stone $100 on March 13, 2015."

f. A draft drawn by Brown on the Acme Publishing Company for $500, payable to the order of the Sixth National Bank of Erehwon, directing the bank to "Charge this draft to my royalty account."

g. A note executed by Pierre Janvier, a resident of Chicago, for $2,000, payable in Swiss francs.

h. An undated note for $1,000 payable "six months after date."

i. A note for $500 payable to the order of Ray Rodes six months after the death of Albert Olds.

j. A note of $500 payable to the assigns of Levi Lee.

k. A check made payable "to Ketisha Johnson."

2. State whether the following provisions in a note impair or preclude negotiability, the instrument in each instance being otherwise in proper form. Answer each statement with either "Negotiable" or "Nonnegotiable" and explain why.

a. A note signed by Henry Brown in the trade name of the Quality Store.

b. A note for $850, payable to the order of TV Products Company, "If, but only if, the television set for which this note is given proves entirely satisfactory to me."

c. A note executed by Adams, Burton, and Cady Company, a partnership, for $1,000, payable to the order of Davis, payable only out of the assets of the partnership.

d. A note promising to pay $500 to the order of Leigh and to deliver ten tons of coal to Leigh.

e. A note for $10,000 executed by Eaton payable to the order of the First National Bank of Emanon, in which Eaton promises to give additional collateral if the bank deems itself insecure and demands additional security.

f. A note reading, "I promise to pay to the order of Richard Roe $2,000 on January 31, 2016, but it is agreed that if the crop of Blackacre falls below ten bushels per acre for the 2015 season, this note shall be extended indefinitely."

g. A note payable to the order of Ray Rogers fifty years from date but providing that payment shall be accelerated by the death of Silas Hughes to a point of time four months after his death.

h. A note for $4,000 calling for payments of installments of $250 each and stating, "In the event any installment hereof is not paid when due, this note shall immediately become due at the holder's option."

i. An instrument dated September 17, 2015, in the handwriting of John Henry Brown, which reads in full:
"Sixty days after date, I, John Henry Brown, promise to pay to the order of William Jones $500."

j. A note reciting, "I promise to pay Ray Reed $100 on December 24, 2014."

3. On March 10, Tolliver Tolles, also known as Thomas Towle, delivered to Alonzo Craig and Abigail Craig the following instrument, written by him in pencil:

For value received, I, Thomas Towle, promise to pay to the order of Alonzo Craig or Abigail Craig One Thousand Seventy-Five ($1,000.75) Dollars six months after my mother, Alma Tolles, dies with interest at the rate of 9 percent from date to maturity and after maturity at the rate of 9 3/4 percent. I hereby waive the benefit of all laws exempting real or personal property from levy or sale.

Is this instrument negotiable? Explain.

4. Henry Hughes, who operates a department store, executed the following instrument:

$2,600 Chicago, March 5, 2015

On July 1, 2015, I promise to pay Daniel Dalziel, or order, the sum of Twenty-Six Hundred Dollars for the privilege of one framed advertising sign, size 24 × 36 inches, at one end of each of two hundred sixty motor coaches of the New Omnibus Company for a term of three months from May 15, 2015.

Henry Hughes

Is this instrument negotiable? Explain.

5. Pablo agreed to lend Marco $500. Thereupon Marco made and delivered his note for $500 payable to Pablo or order "ten days after my marriage." Shortly thereafter Marco was married. Is the instrument negotiable? Explain.

6. For the balance due on the purchase of a tractor, Henry Brown executed and delivered to Jane Jones his promissory note containing the following language:

January 1, 2015, I promise to pay to the order of Jane Jones the sum of $7,000 to be paid only out of my checking account at the XYZ National Bank of Pinckard, Illinois, in two installments of $3,500 each, payable on May 1, 2015, and on July 1, 2015, provided that if I fail to pay the first installment on the due date, the entire sum shall become immediately due.

(Signed) Henry Brown

Is the note negotiable? Explain.

7. Sam Sharpe executed and delivered to Don Dole the following instrument:

Knoxville, Tennessee

May 29, 2015

Thirty days after date I promise to pay Don Dole or order Five Thousand Dollars. The holder of this instrument shall have the election to require the assignment and delivery to him of my 100 shares of Brookside Iron Works Corporation stock in lieu of the payment of Five Thousand Dollars in money.

(Signed) Sam Sharpe

Is this instrument negotiable? Explain.

8. Explain whether the following instrument is negotiable.

March 1, 2015

One month from date, I, James Jimson, hereby promise to pay Edmund Edwards: Six Thousand, Seven Hundred Fifty ($6,750.00) Dollars, plus 8 ³/₄ percent interest. Payment for cutting machines to be delivered on March 15, 2015.

James Jimson

CASE PROBLEMS

9. Broadway Management Corporation obtained a judgment against Briggs. The note on which the judgment was based reads in part: "Ninety Days after date, I, we, or either of us, promise to pay to the order of Three Thousand Four Hundred Ninety Eight and 45/100---Dollars." (The underlined words and symbols were typed in; the remainder was printed.) There are no blanks on the face of the instrument, any unused space having been filled in with hyphens. The note contains clauses permitting acceleration in the event the holder deems itself insecure and authorizes judgment "if this note is not paid at any stated or accelerated maturity." Explain whether the note is negotiable order paper.

10. Sandra and Thomas McGuire entered into a purchase-and-sale agreement for "Becca's Boutique" with Pascal and Rebecca Tursi. The agreement provided that the McGuires would buy the store for $75,000, with a down payment of $10,000 and the balance of $65,000 to be paid at closing on October 5, 2014. The settlement clause stated that the sale was contingent upon the McGuires obtaining a Small Business Administration loan of $65,000. On September 4, 2014, Mrs. McGuire signed a promissory note in which the McGuires promised to pay to the order of the Tursis and the Green Mountain Inn the sum of $65,000. The note specified that interest payments of $541.66 would become due and payable on the fifth days of October, November, and December 2014. The entire balance of the note, with interest, would become due and payable at the option of the holder if any installment of interest was not paid according to that schedule.

The Tursis had for several months been negotiating with Parker Perry for the purchase of the Green Mountain Inn in Stowe, Vermont. On September 7, 2014, the Tursis delivered to Perry a $65,000 promissory note payable to the order of Green Mountain Inn, Inc. This note was secured by transfer to the Green Mountain Inn of the McGuires' note to the Tursis. Subsequently, Mrs. McGuire learned that her Small Business Administration loan had been disapproved. On December 5, 2014, the Tursis defaulted on their promissory note to the Green Mountain Inn. On June 11, 2015, PP, Inc., formerly Green Mountain Inn, Inc., brought an action against the McGuires to recover on the note held as security for the Tursis' promissory note. Discuss whether the instrument is negotiable.

11. On September 2, 2011, Levine executed a mortgage bond under which she promised to pay the Mykoffs a preexisting obligation of $54,000. On October 14, 2014, the Mykoffs transferred the mortgage to Bankers Trust Co., indorsing the instrument with the words "Pay to the Order of Bankers Trust Company Without Recourse." The Lincoln First Bank, N.A., brought this action asserting that the Mykoffs' mortgage is a nonnegotiable instrument because it is not payable to order or bearer; thus it is subject to Lincoln's defense that the mortgage was not supported by consideration because an antecedent debt is not consideration. Is the instrument payable to order or bearer? Discuss.

12. Horne executed a $100,000 note in favor of R. C. Clark. On the back of the instrument was a restriction stating that the note could not be transferred, pledged, or otherwise assigned without Horne's written consent. As part of the same transaction between Horne and Clark, Horne gave Clark a separate letter authorizing Clark to pledge the note as collateral for a loan of $50,000 that Clark intended to secure from First State Bank. Clark did secure the loan and pledged the note, which was accompanied by Horne's letter authorizing Clark to use the note as collateral. First State contacted Horne and verified the agreement between Horne and Clark as to using the note as collateral. Clark defaulted on the loan. When First Bank later attempted to collect on the note, Horne refused to pay, arguing that the note was not negotiable as it could not be transferred without obtaining Horne's written consent. This suit was instituted. Is the instrument negotiable? Explain.

13. The Society National Bank (Society) agreed in a promissory note to lend U.S.A. Diversified Products, Inc. (USAD) up to $2 million in the form of an operating line of credit upon which USAD could make draws of varying amounts. The outstanding balance was to be paid on April 30 of the following year. USAD defaulted on the line of credit, and Society filed a complaint against USAD. Is the promissory note negotiable?

TAKING SIDES

Holly Hill Acres, Ltd., executed and delivered a promissory note and a purchase money mortgage to Rogers and Blythe. The note provided that it was secured by a mortgage on certain real estate and that the terms of that mortgage "are by this reference made a part hereof." Rogers and Blythe then assigned the note to Charter Bank, and the bank sought to foreclose on the note and mortgage. Holly Hill Acres refused to pay, claiming that the note was not negotiable and therefore subject to the defense that Holly Hill Acres had been defrauded by Rogers and Blythe.

a. Present the position that the note is a negotiable instrument.

b. What is the position that the note is nonnegotiable?

c. Is the note negotiable or nonnegotiable? Explain.

Transfer and Holder in Due Course

CHAPTER 25

A negotiable instrument is a courier without luggage.

Anonymous

CHAPTER OUTCOMES

After reading and studying this chapter, you should be able to:

1. Distinguish among (a) transfer, (b) negotiation, and (c) assignment.

2. Identify and explain the requirements for becoming a holder in due course.

3. Explain the shelter rule and when a payee can have the rights of a holder in due course.

4. Identify, define, and explain the real defenses.

5. Define and explain personal defenses.

The primary advantage of negotiable instruments is their ease of transferability. Nonetheless, although both negotiable instruments and nonnegotiable undertakings are transferable by assignment, only negotiable instruments can result in the transferee becoming a holder. This distinction is highly significant. If the transferee of a negotiable instrument is entitled to payment by the terms of the instrument, he is a holder of the instrument. Only holders may be holders in due course and thus may be entitled to greater rights in the instrument than the transferor may have possessed. These rights, discussed in the second part of this chapter, are the reason why negotiable instruments move freely in the marketplace.

The unique and most significant aspect of negotiability is the concept of the holder in due course. Although a mere holder acquires a negotiable instrument subject to all claims and defenses to it, a holder in due course, *except* in *consumer* credit transactions, takes the instrument free of all claims of other parties and free of all defenses to the instrument except for a very limited number. The law has conferred this preferred position upon the holder in due course to encourage the free transferability of negotiable instruments by minimizing the risks assumed by an innocent purchaser of the instrument. The transferee of a negotiable instrument wants payment for it; he does not want to be subject to any dispute between the obligor and the obligee (generally the original payee).

TRANSFER

This part of the chapter discusses the methods by which negotiable instruments may be transferred.

Holder
possessor of a negotiable instrument that is payable either to bearer or to an identified person that is the person in possession

NEGOTIATION [25-1]

Revised Article 1 of the Uniform Commercial Code (UCC or Code) broadly defines a **holder** as "the person in possession of a negotiable instrument that is payable either to bearer or to an identified person that is the person in possession." At least forty-five states have adopted the 2001 Revisions to Article 1, which applies to all of the articles of the Code. The original Article 1 has a similar definition: "a person who is in possession of … an instrument … drawn, issued, or indorsed to him or his order or to bearer or in blank." **Negotiation** is the transfer of possession, whether voluntary or involuntary, by a person other than the issuer of a negotiable instrument in such a manner that the transferee becomes a holder. An instrument is transferred when a person other than its issuer delivers it for the purpose of giving the recipient the right to enforce the instrument. Accordingly, to qualify as a holder, a person must have possession of an instrument that runs to him. Thus, there are two ways in which a person can be a holder: (1) the instrument has been issued to that person, or (2) the instrument has been transferred to that person by negotiation.

Negotiation
transfer such that transferee becomes a holder

The transfer of a nonnegotiable promise or order operates as an assignment, as does the transfer of a negotiable instrument by a means that does not render the transferee a holder. As discussed in Chapter 16, an **assignment** is the voluntary transfer to a third party of the rights arising from a contract.

Assignment
voluntary transfer to a third party of the rights arising from a contract

Whether a transfer is by *assignment* or by *negotiation*, the transferee acquires the rights the transferor had. The transfer need not be for value: if the instrument is transferred as a gift, the donee acquires all the rights of the donor. If the transferor was a holder in due course, the transferee acquires the rights of a holder in due course, which rights he in turn may transfer. This rule, sometimes referred to as the **shelter rule**, existed at common law and still exists under the UCC. The shelter rule is discussed more fully in the second part of this chapter.

Shelter rule
transferee gets rights of transferor

The requirements for negotiation depend on whether the instrument is bearer paper or order paper.

Negotiation of Bearer Paper [25-1a]

Negotiation of bearer paper
transferred by mere possession

If an instrument is payable to bearer, it may be negotiated by transfer of possession alone. Because bearer paper (an instrument payable to bearer) runs to whoever is in possession of it, a finder or a thief of bearer paper would be a holder even though he did not receive possession by voluntary transfer. For example, Poe loses an instrument payable to bearer that Igor had issued to her. Frank finds it and sells and delivers it to Barbara, who thus receives it by negotiation and is a holder. Frank also qualified as a holder because he was in possession of bearer paper. As a holder, Frank had the power to negotiate the instrument, and Barbara, the transferee, may be a holder in due course if she meets the Code's requirements for such a holder (discussed later in this chapter). See Figure 25-1 for an illustration of this example. Because a bearer instrument is transferred by mere *possession*, it is comparable to cash.

Negotiation of Order Paper [25-1b]

Negotiation of order paper
transferred by possession and indorsement by all appropriate parties

If the instrument is order paper (an instrument payable to order), both (1) transfer of its *possession* and (2) its *indorsement* (signature) by the appropriate parties are necessary for the transferee to become a holder. Figure 25-2 compares the negotiation of bearer and order paper.

Any transfer for *value* of an instrument not payable to bearer gives the transferee the specifically enforceable right to have the unqualified indorsement of the transferor, unless the parties

Figure 25-1 Bearer Paper

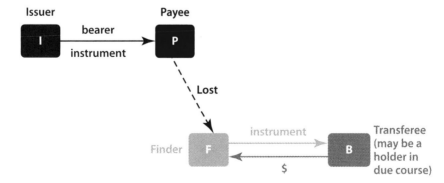

Figure 25-2 Negotiation of Bearer and Order Paper

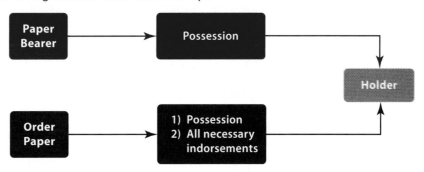

agree otherwise. The parties may agree that the transfer is to be an assignment rather than a negotiation, in which case no indorsement is required. Absent such agreement, the courts presume that negotiation was intended where value is given. When a transfer is not for value, the transaction is normally noncommercial; thus, the courts do not presume the intent to negotiate.

Until the necessary indorsement has been supplied, the transferee has nothing more than the contract rights of an assignee. Negotiation takes effect only when a proper indorsement is made, at which time the transferee becomes a holder of the instrument. Assume that a thief steals a paycheck from Poe prior to indorsement. The thief then forges Poe's signature and transfers the check to a grocer, who takes it in good faith, for value, without notice, and without reason to question its authenticity. Negotiation of an order instrument requires a valid indorsement by the person to whose order the instrument is payable, in this case, Poe. A forged indorsement is not valid. Consequently, the grocer had not taken the instrument with all necessary indorsements, and, therefore, he could not be a holder or a holder in due course. The grocer's only recourse would be to collect the amount of the check from the thief. Figure 25-3 illustrates this example.

If a customer deposits a check or other instrument for collection without properly indorsing the item, the depository bank becomes a holder when it accepts the item for deposit if the depositor is a holder. It no longer needs to supply the customer's indorsement.

 The Hyatt Corporation v. Palm Beach National Bank
Court of Appeal of Florida, Third District, 2003
840 So.2d 300, 49 UCC Rep.Serv.2d 1039
http://scholar.google.com/scholar_case?case=6827503413148655725&q=hyatt+corporation+v+palm+beach&hl=en&as_sdt=2,21

FACTS Hyatt Corporation hired Skyscraper Building Maintenance to perform maintenance work for Hyatt hotels in South Florida. Skyscraper entered into a loan agreement with J&D Financial Corp. under which Hyatt was to make checks payable for maintenance services to Skyscraper and J&D. Of the many checks issued by Hyatt to J&D and Skyscraper, two were cashed by the Palm Beach National Bank but indorsed only by Skyscraper. They were made payable as follows:

1. **Check No. 1-78671 for $22,531 payable to:**
   J&D Financial Corp.
   Skyscraper Building Maint
   P.O. Box 610250
   North Miami, Florida 33261-0250
2. **Check No. 1-75723 for $21,107 payable to:**
   Skyscraper Building Maint
   J&D Financial Corp.
   P.O. Box 610250
   North Miami, Florida 33261-0250

J&D filed a complaint against Skyscraper, Hyatt, and the bank. J&D sought damages against Skyscraper under the loan agreement

and against Hyatt and the bank for improper negotiation of the two checks. The bank, Hyatt, and J&D all moved for summary judgment. It is uncontested that the bank had a duty to negotiate the checks only on proper indorsement, and if it did not, it is liable.

The bank argued that the checks were payable to J&D and Skyscraper alternatively, and thus the bank could properly negotiate the checks based upon the indorsement of either of the two payees. The bank further argued that the checks were drafted ambiguously as to whether they were payable alternatively or jointly, and thus the checks would be construed as a matter of law to be payable alternatively.

Hyatt's and J&D's position was that the checks were not ambiguous, were payable jointly and not alternatively, and thus the checks could only be negotiated by indorsement of both of the payees. The trial court granted summary judgment for the bank. Hyatt and J&D appealed.

DECISION The trial court's summary judgment is affirmed.

OPINION The issue on appeal is whether or not a check payable to

J&D Financial Corporation
Skyscraper Building Maintenance

(stacked payees) is payable jointly to both payees requiring the indorsement of both, or whether it is ambiguous regarding whether the check was drafted payable alternatively, so that the bank could negotiate the check when it was indorsed by only one of the two payees. The Revised Uniform Commercial Code (UCC) Section 3-110(d) provides that: "If an instrument payable to two or more persons is ambiguous as to whether it is payable alternatively, the instrument is payable to the persons alternatively."

Although Florida appellate courts have not considered the issue at hand, other courts in the country have.

For example, in a case which has addressed this issue with almost identical facts the checks were made payable to

Complete Design
Allied Capital Partners, LLP.
2340 E. Trinity Mills St. 300
Carrollton, Texas 75006

Under these facts, the court found that the check was unambiguous. The court held that under Revised Article 3, when a check lists two payees without the use of the word "and" or "or," the nature of the payee is ambiguous as to whether they are alternative payees or joint payees. Therefore, they are to be treated as alternative payees, thus requiring only one of the payees' signatures. Consequently, the bank could properly negotiate the check when it was indorsed by only one of the two payees.

INTERPRETATION The listing of multiple payees on a check renders the check ambiguous as to whether alternate or joint payees were intended by the drawer and thus the payees are treated as alternative payees requiring indorsement by only one payee.

ETHICAL QUESTION Did the bank or Skyscraper act inappropriately? Explain.

CRITICAL THINKING QUESTION How would you decide this case? Explain.

Impostor rule

an indorsement of an impostor or of any other person in the name of the named payee is effective if the impostor has induced the maker or drawer to issue the instrument to him using the name of the payee

The Impostor Rule Negotiation of an order instrument requires a valid indorsement by the person to whose order the instrument is payable. The **impostor rule** governing unauthorized signatures is an *exception* to this general rule. Usually, the impostor rule comes into play in situations involving a confidence man who impersonates a respected citizen and who deceives a third party into delivering a negotiable instrument to the impostor in the name of the respected citizen. For instance, John Doe, falsely representing himself as Richard Roe, a prominent citizen, induces Ray Davis to loan him $10,000. Davis draws a check payable to the order of Richard Roe and delivers it to Doe, who then forges Roe's name to the check and presents it to the drawee for payment. The drawee pays it. Subsequently, Davis, the drawer, denies the drawee's right of reimbursement on the ground that the drawee did not pay in accordance with his order: Davis ordered payment to Roe or to Roe's order. Roe did not order payment to anyone; therefore, the drawee would not acquire a right of reimbursement against Davis. The general rule governing unauthorized signatures supports this argument in favor of the drawer.

Nevertheless, the indorsement of the impostor (Doe) or of any other person in the name of the named payee is *effective* as the indorsement of the payee if the impostor has induced the maker or drawer (Davis) to issue the instrument to him or his confederate using the name of the payee (Roe). It is as if the named payee had indorsed the instrument. The reason for this rule is that the drawer or maker is to blame for failing to detect the impersonation by the impostor. Thus, in the above example, the drawee would be able to debit the drawer's account. Moreover, Revised Article 3 extends the impostor rule to include an impostor who is impersonating an agent. Thus, if an impostor impersonates Jones and induces the drawer to draw a check to the

Figure 25-3 Stolen Order Paper

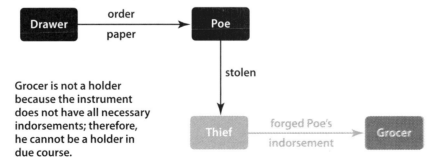

Grocer is not a holder because the instrument does not have all necessary indorsements; therefore, he cannot be a holder in due course.

order of Jones, the impostor can negotiate the check. Moreover, under the Revision, if an impostor impersonates Jones, the president of Jones Corporation, and the check is to the order of Jones Corporation, the impostor can negotiate the check.

If the person paying the instrument fails to exercise ordinary care, the issuer may recover from the payor to the extent the payor's negligence contributed to the loss. If the issuer is also negligent, comparative negligence would apply.

The Fictitious Payee Rule The rule just discussed also applies when a person who does not intend the payee to have an interest in the instrument signs as or on behalf of a maker or drawer. In such a situation, any person's indorsement in the name of the named payee is *effective* if the person identified as the payee is a fictitious person. For instance, Palmer gives Albrecht, her employee, authority to write checks in order to pay Palmer's debts. Albrecht writes a check for $2,000 to Foushee, a fictitious payee, which Albrecht takes and indorses in Foushee's name to Albrecht. Albrecht cashes the check at Palmer's bank, which can debit Palmer's account because Albrecht's signature in Foushee's name is effective against Palmer. Palmer should bear the risk of her unscrupulous employees.

In a similar situation also involving a disloyal employee, a drawer's employee falsely tells the drawer that money is owed to Leon, and the drawer writes a check payable to the order of Leon and hands it to the agent for delivery to him. The agent forges Leon's name to the check and obtains payment from the drawee bank. The drawer then denies the bank's claim to reimbursement upon the grounds that (1) the bank did not comply with her order; (2) the drawer had ordered payment to Leon or order; (3) the drawee did not make payment either to Leon or as ordered by him, inasmuch as the forgery of Leon's signature is wholly inoperative; and (4) the drawee paid in accordance with the scheme of the faithless agent and not in compliance with the drawer's order. Under the Code, an employer has liability on the instrument when one of its employees, who is entrusted with responsibility with respect to such an instrument, makes a fraudulent indorsement if (1) the instrument is payable to the employer and the employee forges the indorsement of the employer or (2) the instrument is issued by the employer and the employee forges the indorsement of the person identified as the payee. The example above falls under the second part of the rule just stated. Accordingly, the employee's indorsement is effective as that of the unintended payee, and the drawee bank will be able to debit the drawer's (employer's) account.

This rule also applies to a situation (the first part of the rule stated above) not involving a fictitious payee: a fraudulent indorsement made by an employee entrusted with responsibility with respect to an instrument payable to the employer. For example, an employee, whose job involves posting amounts of checks payable to her employer, steals some of the checks and forges her employer's indorsement. The indorsement is effective as the employer's indorsement because the employee's duties included processing checks for bookkeeping purposes.

This section provides, however, that the employer may recover from the drawee bank to the extent the loss resulted from the bank's failure to exercise ordinary care. If the employer is also negligent, a rule of comparative negligence applies.

Negotiations Subject to Rescission [25-1c]

A negotiation conforming to the requirements discussed previously is effective to transfer the instrument even if it is

1. made by an infant, a corporation exceeding its powers, or a person without capacity; or
2. obtained by fraud, duress, or mistake; or
3. made in breach of a duty or as part of an illegal transaction.

Thus, a negotiation is valid even though the transaction in which it occurs is voidable or even void. In all of these instances, the transferor loses all rights in the instrument until he regains possession of it. His right to do so, determined by state law, is valid against the immediate transferee and all subsequent holders, but not against a subsequent holder in due course or a person paying the instrument in good faith and without notice.

Fictitious payee rule an indorsement by any person in the name of the named payee is effective if an agent of the maker or drawer has supplied her with the name of the payee for fraudulent purposes

Practical Advice

Make sure that the payees of all your instruments are the appropriate parties and are being paid the appropriate amount.

Negotiations subject to rescission negotiation is valid even though a transaction is void or voidable

INDORSEMENTS [25-2]

Indorsement

signature (on the instrument) of a payee, drawee, accommodation party, or holder

An **indorsement** is

> a signature, other than that of a signer as maker, drawer, or acceptor, that alone or accompanied by other words is made on an instrument for the purpose of (i) negotiating the instrument, (ii) restricting payment of the instrument, or (iii) incurring the indorser's liability on the instrument, but regardless of the intent of the signer, a signature and its accompanying words is an indorsement unless the accompanying words, terms of the instrument, place of the signature, or other circumstances unambiguously indicate that the signature was made for a purpose other than indorsement.

An indorsement may be complex or simple. It may be dated and may indicate where it is made, but neither date nor place is required to be shown. The simplest type is merely the signature of the indorser. Because the indorser undertakes certain obligations, as explained later, an indorsement consisting of merely a signature may be said to be the shortest contract known to the law. A forged or otherwise unauthorized signature necessary to negotiation is inoperative and thus breaks the chain of title to the instrument.

The type of indorsement used in first negotiating an instrument affects its subsequent negotiation. Every indorsement is (1) either blank or special, (2) either restrictive or nonrestrictive, and (3) either qualified or unqualified. These categories are not mutually exclusive. Indeed, each indorsement may be placed within three of these six categories because all indorsements disclose three things: (1) the method to be employed in making subsequent negotiations (this depends upon whether the indorsement is blank or special); (2) the kind of interest that is being transferred (this depends upon whether the indorsement is restrictive or nonrestrictive); and (3) the liability of the indorser (this depends on whether the indorsement is qualified or unqualified). For instance, an indorser who merely signs her name on the back of an instrument is making a blank, nonrestrictive, unqualified indorsement.

Revised Article 3 identifies an additional type of indorsement—an anomalous indorsement. An anomalous indorsement is "an indorsement made by a person that is not the holder of the instrument." The only effect of an anomalous indorsement is to make the signer liable on the instrument as an indorser. Such an indorsement does not affect the manner in which the instrument may be negotiated.

The effectiveness of an indorsement as well as the rights of the transferee and transferor depend on whether the indorsement meets certain formal requirements. This section will cover the different kinds of indorsements and the formal requirements of each.

Practical Advice

It is exceedingly important that you indorse your indorsements in the appropriate manner and at the appropriate time.

Blank indorsement

one specifying no indorsee and making the instrument bearer paper

Practical Advice

Blank indorsements present a major risk and should be used judiciously.

Blank Indorsements [25-2a]

A **blank indorsement**, which specifies no indorsee, may consist solely of the signature of the indorser or an authorized agent. Such an indorsement converts order paper into bearer paper and leaves bearer paper as bearer paper. Thus, an instrument indorsed in blank may be negotiated by delivery alone without further indorsement. Hence, the holder should treat it with the same care as cash.

Special Indorsements [25-2b]

Special indorsement

one identifying an indorsee to be paid and making the instrument order paper

A **special indorsement** specifically identifies the person to whom or to whose order the instrument is to be payable. Thus, if Peter, the payee of a note, indorses it "Pay to the order of Andrea," or even "Pay Andrea," the indorsement is special because it names the transferee. Words of negotiability—"pay to order or bearer"—are *not* required in an indorsement. Thus, an indorsement reading "Pay Edward" is interpreted as meaning "Pay to the order of Edward." Any further negotiation of the instrument would require Edward's indorsement.

Moreover, a holder of an instrument with a blank indorsement may protect himself by converting the blank indorsement to a special indorsement by writing over the signature of the indorser words identifying the person to whom the instrument is payable. For example, on the

Restrictive indorsement
one attempting to limit the rights of the indorsee

Unrestrictive indorsement
one that does not attempt to restrict the rights of the indorsee

Indorsements for deposit or collection
effectively limit further negotiation to those consistent with the indorsement

---

Practical Advice

Indorsements "for deposit only" protect you as the indorser and should be used whenever necessary.

---

back of a negotiable instrument appears the blank indorsement "Sally Seller." Harry Holder, who receives the instrument from Seller, may convert this bearer instrument into order paper by inserting above Seller's signature "Pay Harry Holder" or other similar words.

Restrictive Indorsements [25-2c]

As the term implies, a **restrictive indorsement** attempts to restrict the rights of the indorsee in some fashion. It limits the purpose for which the proceeds of the instrument can be applied. The Code discusses four types of indorsements as restrictive: conditional indorsements, indorsements prohibiting further transfer, indorsements for deposit or collection, and indorsements in trust. Only the last two are effective. An **unrestrictive indorsement**, in contrast, does not attempt to restrict the rights of the indorsee.

Indorsements for Deposit or Collection
The most frequently used form of restrictive indorsement is that designed to place the instrument in the banking system for deposit or collection. Indorsements of this type, collectively referred to as "collection indorsements," include "for collection," "for deposit," and "pay any bank." Such an indorsement *effectively limits* further negotiation to those consistent with its limitation and binds (1) all nonbanking persons, (2) a depository bank that purchases the instrument or takes it for collection, and (3) a payor bank that is also the depository bank or that takes the instrument for immediate payment over the counter from a person other than a collecting bank. Thus, a collection indorsement binds all parties except an intermediary bank (discussed in Chapter 27) or a payor bank that is not also the depository bank.

 ### State of Qatar v. First American Bank of Virginia
United States District Court, E.D. Va. 1995
885 F.Supp. 849, 27 UCC Rep.Serv.2d 168
http://scholar.google.com/scholar_case?case=1102569369018879687&hl=en&as_sdt=2&as_vis=1&oi=scholarr

FACTS From 1986 to 1992, Bassam Salous defrauded his employer, the state of Qatar, by drawing checks on Qatar's account to pay false or duplicate invoices that he himself had created. He then deposited the checks into his personal account at First American Bank of Virginia (First American). At the time they were deposited, the checks bore the forged indorsement of the named payee, followed by the stamped restriction "for deposit only." Qatar has sued First American for conversion.

DECISION Judgment for Qatar.

OPINION The Uniform Commercial Code makes clear that the phrase "for deposit only" is a restrictive indorsement. Although the meaning of the term is not defined, the clear purpose of the restriction is to avoid the hazards of indorsing a check in blank. A stolen check that is indorsed in blank is essentially cash and can be freely negotiated by the bearer. To protect against the vulnerability, the payee can add the restriction "for deposit only" to the indorsement, and the depositary bank is required to handle the check in a manner consistent with that restriction.

First American contends that its action of depositing the funds into Salous's account was consistent with the restriction "for

deposit only." However, the payee's intent in adding such a restriction plainly is to direct that the funds be deposited into her own account, not simply that the funds be deposited into any account. Without such a construction, the phrase is without commercial utility. It is virtually impossible to imagine a scenario in which a payee cares only that a check be deposited and is indifferent as to the particular account to which the funds are to be credited.

By depositing the checks made payable to others and restrictively indorsed "for deposit only," into Bassam Salous's account, First American violated the restrictive indorsements on those checks. Therefore, First American is liable to Qatar for conversion in the amount of the total face values of the checks.

INTERPRETATION A "for deposit only" restrictive indorsement effectively limits the depositary bank to handle the instrument in a manner consistent with the restriction.

ETHICAL QUESTION Who should bear the risk of loss in this case? Explain.

CRITICAL THINKING QUESTION Does the use of a "for deposit only" indorsement present any risks to the indorser or indorsee? Explain.

Indorsements in trust
effectively require the indorsee to pay or apply all funds in accordance with the indorsement

Indorsements in Trust
Another common kind of restrictive indorsement is that in which the indorser creates a trust for the benefit of himself or others. If an instrument is indorsed "Pay Thelma in trust for Barbara," "Pay Thelma for Barbara," "Pay Thelma for account of Barbara," or "Pay Thelma as agent for Barbara," Thelma is a fiduciary, subject to liability for any breach of her obligation to Barbara. Trustees commonly and legitimately sell trust assets,

and, consequently, a trustee has power to negotiate an instrument. The first taker under an indorsement to her in trust (in this case Thelma) is under a duty to pay or apply, in a manner consistent with the indorsement, all the funds she receives. Thelma's immediate transferee may safely pay Thelma for the instrument if he does not have *notice* of any breach of fiduciary duty. Subsequent indorsements or transferees are not bound by such indorsement *unless* they *know* that the trustee negotiated the instrument for her own benefit or otherwise in breach of her fiduciary duty.

Indorsements with Ineffective Restrictions   A conditional indorsement is one by which the indorser makes the rights of the indorsee subject to the happening or nonhappening of a specified event. Suppose Marcin makes a note payable to Parker's order. Parker indorses it "Pay Rodriguez, but only if the good ship Jolly Jack arrives in Chicago harbor by November 15, 2016." If Marcin had used this language in the instrument itself, it would be nonnegotiable because her promise to pay must be unconditional to satisfy the formal requisites of negotiability. Revised Article 3 makes such indorsements ineffective by providing that an indorsement stating a condition to the right of a holder to receive payment does not affect the right of the indorsee to enforce the instrument.

> **Indorsements with ineffective restrictions** include conditional indorsements and indorsements attempting to prohibit further negotiation

An indorsement may by its express terms attempt to prohibit further transfer by stating "Pay [name] only" or language to similar effect. Such an indorsement, or any other purporting to prohibit further transfer, is designed to restrict the rights of the indorsee. To remove any doubt as to the effect of such a provision, the Code provides that *no* indorsement limiting payment to a particular person or otherwise prohibiting further transfer is effective. As a result, an indorsement that purports to *prohibit* further transfer of the instrument is given the same effect as an unrestricted indorsement.

Qualified and Unqualified Indorsements [25-2d]

In an **unqualified indorsement**, indorsers promise that they will pay the instrument according to its terms at the time of their indorsement to the holder or to any subsequent indorser who paid it. In short, an unqualified indorser guarantees payment of the instrument if certain conditions are met.

> **Unqualified indorsement** one that imposes liability on the indorser

An indorser may disclaim liability on the contract of indorsement, but only if the indorsement so declares and the disclaimer is written on the instrument. The customary manner of disclaiming an indorser's liability is to add the words *without recourse*, either before or after her signature. A "without recourse" indorsement, called a **qualified indorsement**, does not, however, eliminate all of an indorser's liability. As discussed in Chapter 26, a qualified indorsement disclaims contract liability but does not entirely remove the warranty liability of the indorser. A qualified indorsement and delivery is a negotiation and transfers legal title to the indorsee, but the indorser does not guarantee payment of the instrument. Furthermore, a qualified indorsement does not destroy negotiability or prevent further negotiation of the instrument. For example, assume that an attorney receives a check payable to her order in payment of a client's claim. She may indorse the check to the client without recourse, thereby disclaiming liability as a guarantor of payment of the check. The qualified indorsement plus delivery would transfer title to the client.

> **Qualified indorsement without recourse** one that limits the indorser's liability

Formal Requirements of Indorsements [25-2e]

Place of Indorsement   An indorsement must be written on the instrument or on a paper, called an **allonge**, affixed to the instrument. An allonge may be used even if the instrument contains sufficient space for the indorsement.

> **Allonge** piece of paper affixed to the instrument

Customarily, indorsements are made on the back or reverse side of the instrument, starting at the top and continuing down. Under Federal Reserve Board guidelines, indorsements of checks must be in ink of an appropriate color, such as blue or black, and must be made within one-and-one-half inches of the trailing (left) edge of the back of the check. The remaining space is reserved for bank indorsements (see Figure 25-4 for the proper placement of indorsements).

Figure 25-4 Placement of Indorsement

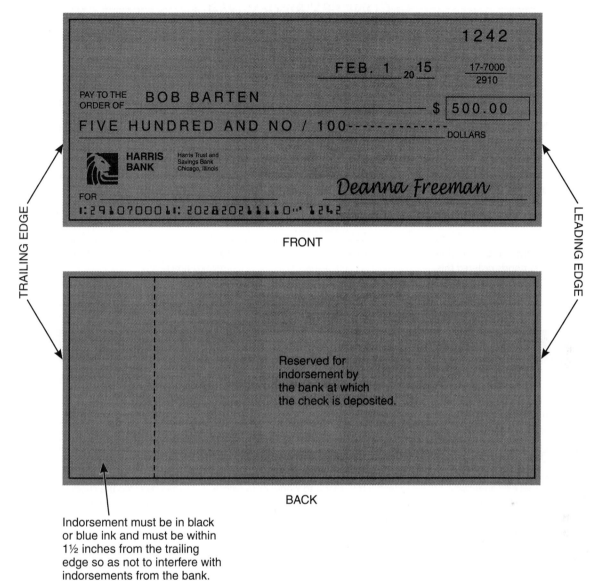

FRONT

TRAILING EDGE

LEADING EDGE

1242

FEB. 1 20 15   17-7000 / 2910

PAY TO THE ORDER OF ___ BOB BARTEN ___ $ 500.00

FIVE HUNDRED AND NO / 100--------------- DOLLARS

HARRIS BANK   Harris Trust and Savings Bank Chicago, Illinois

FOR ___

Deanna Freeman

⑈291070001⑈ 202820211110⑊ 1242

Reserved for indorsement by the bank at which the check is deposited.

BACK

Indorsement must be in black or blue ink and must be within 1½ inches from the trailing edge so as not to interfere with indorsements from the bank.

Nevertheless, failure to comply with the guidelines does not destroy negotiability, and there are no penalties for violating the standard.

Occasionally, however, a signature may appear on an instrument in such a way that it is impossible to tell with certainty the nature of the liability the signer intended to undertake. In such an event, the Code specifies that the signer is to be treated as an indorser. In keeping with the rule that a transferee must be able to determine her rights from the face of the instrument, the person who signed in an ambiguous capacity may not introduce parol evidence to establish that she intended to be something other than an indorser.

Incorrect or Misspelled Indorsements   If an instrument is payable to a payee or indorsee under a misspelled name or a name different from that of the holder, the holder may require the indorsement in the name stated or in the holder's correct name or both. Nevertheless, the person paying or taking the instrument for value may require the indorser to sign both names.

CONCEPT REVIEW 25-1

Indorsements

Indorsement	Type of Indorsement	Interest Transferred	Liability of Indorser
1. "John Doe"	Blank	Nonrestrictive	Unqualified
2. "Pay to Richard Roe, John Doe"	Special	Nonrestrictive	Unqualified
3. "Without recourse, John Doe"	Blank	Nonrestrictive	Qualified
4. "Pay to Richard Roe in trust for John Roe, without recourse, John Doe"	Special	Restrictive	Qualified
5. "For collection only, without recourse, John Doe"	Blank	Restrictive	Qualified
6. "Pay to XYZ Corp., on the condition that it delivers goods ordered this date, John Doe"	Special	Nonrestrictive (revised Article 3)	Unqualified

APPLYING THE LAW

Transfer of Negotiable Instruments

Facts On the evening of September 28, the last Friday of the month, Erica Dietz realized she had not yet made arrangements to deliver her October 1 rent payment to her landlord, Dr. Norman Toth. Though Erica's weekly after-tax earnings were $150 more than her $600 monthly rent, it was too late in the day to deposit her check and she knew she only had $212 in her checking account. Therefore, Erica indorsed her paycheck as follows: "Pay ONLY to Norman Toth, [signed] Erica Dietz" and placed it in the mail with a note asking Dr. Toth to apply the excess payment toward November's rent.

Dr. Toth's mail was stolen from his mailbox. The thief, Crawford, signed the words "Norman Toth" below Erica's indorsement on her paycheck, and deposited it in Crawford's personal bank account at Farmers' Bank, along with several thousands of dollars worth of other checks he had stolen.

Issue Is Farmer's Bank a holder of Erica's paycheck?

Rule of Law A holder is a possessor of a negotiable instrument with all necessary indorsements. An indorsement is the signature—of a payee, drawee, accommodation party, or holder—on

an instrument. There are several classifications of indorsement: blank or special, restrictive or nonrestrictive, and qualified or unqualified. Special indorsements have two effects. First, they identify the person to whom or to whose order the instrument is thereafter payable, and second, they make the instrument order paper if it is not already. Hence negotiation of specially indorsed instruments requires delivery and the further indorsement of the named person.

Indorsements that purport to limit payment to a particular person or that prohibit further negotiation are ineffective in that regard. Instead they have the same effect as unrestricted indorsements. Forged indorsements are anomalous (made by a person who is not the holder of the instrument) and are effective only to make the forger liable on the instrument as an indorser. Forged indorsements break the chain of title to a negotiable instrument and so are not effective to negotiate it.

Application In effect, Erica's indorsement of her paycheck is a special, nonrestrictive, unqualified indorsement. By adding the words "Pay ONLY to Norman Toth" above her signature, she has simply identified Dr. Toth as the person to be paid and effectively renewed the check's status as

order paper; any further negotiation of the check would require Dr. Toth's signature on it. However, Erica's attempt to restrict payment to Dr. Toth "ONLY" does not prevent further negotiation. If Dr. Toth had received the check, he could have negotiated the check simply by indorsing it and delivering it to another. But this is not what happened here.

Crawford's indorsement of Dr. Toth's name is a forgery, which operates not as Dr. Toth's signature but as Crawford's signature. Its only effect is to make Crawford liable on the instrument as an indorser. To effectively negotiate order paper, both indorsement and delivery are required. Crawford has delivered the instrument to Farmers' Bank. But Crawford's unauthorized indorsement on the stolen check breaks the chain of title and does not result in an effective negotiation to Farmer's Bank. Therefore, Crawford's transfer of the check to the Bank does not amount to a negotiation.

Conclusion Since a person in possession of a negotiable instrument can qualify as a holder only if the instrument has all necessary indorsements, and Dr. Toth has not indorsed the check Erica specially indorsed to him, Farmers' Bank cannot qualify as a holder of Erica's paycheck.

HOLDER IN DUE COURSE

This part of the chapter discusses the requirements of becoming a holder in due course and the benefits conferred upon a holder in due course.

REQUIREMENTS OF A HOLDER IN DUE COURSE [25-3]

To acquire the preferential rights of a holder in due course, a person either must meet the requirements of the UCC or must "inherit" these rights under the shelter rule (discussed later in this chapter). To satisfy the requirements of the Code, a transferee must

1. be a holder of a negotiable instrument;
2. take it for value;
3. take it in good faith; and
4. take it without notice
   a. that it is overdue or has been dishonored, or
   b. that the instrument contains an unauthorized signature or an alteration, or
   c. that any person has any defense against or claim to it; and
5. take it without reason to question its authenticity due to apparent evidence of forgery, alteration, incompleteness, or other irregularity.

Figure 25-5 illustrates the various requirements of becoming a holder in due course and the consequence of meeting or not meeting these requirements.

Holder [25-3a]

To become a holder in due course, the transferee must first be a holder. A holder, as already discussed in this chapter, is a person who is in possession of a negotiable instrument that is "payable to bearer or, in the case of an instrument payable to an identified person, if the identified person is in possession." Revised Article 1 has a similar definition: "the person in possession of a negotiable instrument that is payable either to bearer or to an identified person that is the person in possession." In other words, a holder is a person who has both possession of an instrument and all indorsements necessary to it.

Value [25-3b]

The law requires a holder in due course to give value. An obvious case of the failure to do so is when the holder makes a gift of the instrument to a third person.

The concept of value in the law of negotiable instruments is not the same as that of consideration under the law of contracts. **Value**, for purposes of negotiable instruments, is defined as (1) the actual *performing* of the agreed promise (executory promises are excluded because they have not been performed), (2) the acquiring of a security interest or other lien in the instrument other than a judicial lien, (3) the taking of the instrument in payment of or as security for an antecedent debt, (4) the giving of a negotiable instrument, and (5) the giving of an irrevocable obligation to a third party.

Executory Promise   An executory promise, though clearly valid consideration to support a contract, is *not* the giving of value to support holder in due course status because such a promise has yet to be performed. A purchaser of a note or draft who has not yet given value may rescind the transaction if she learns of a defense to the instrument. A person who has given value, however, cannot do this; to recover value, she needs the protection accorded a holder in due course.

For example, Mike executes and delivers a $1,000 note payable to the order of Pat, who negotiates it to Henry, who promises to pay Pat for it a month later. During the month, Henry learns that Mike has a defense against Pat. Henry can rescind the agreement with Pat and return or tender the note back to her. Because this makes him whole, Henry has no need to cut off Mike's defense. Assume, on the other hand, that Henry has paid Pat for the note before he

Value
differs from contractual consideration and consists of (1) the timely performance of legal consideration (excluding executory promises), (2) the acquisition of a security interest in or a lien on the instrument, (3) taking the instrument in payment of or as security for an antecedent debt, (4) the giving of a negotiable instrument, or (5) the giving of an irrevocable commitment to a third party

Figure 25-5 Rights of Transferees

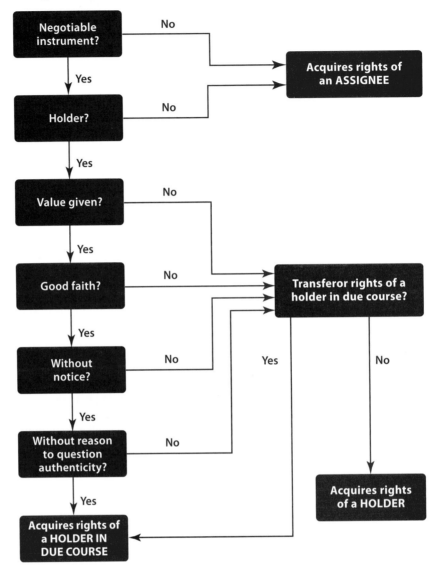

learns of Mike's defense. Because he may be unable to recover his money from Pat, Henry needs holder in due course protection, which permits him to recover on the instrument from Mike.

A holder therefore takes an instrument for value to the extent that the agreed promise of performance has been performed provided that performance was given prior to the holder's learning of any defense or claim to the instrument. Assume that in the previous example, Henry had agreed to pay Pat $900 for the note. If Henry had paid Pat $600, he could be a holder in due course to the extent of $666.67 (600/900 × $1,000), and if a defense were available, it would be valid against him only to the extent of the balance. When Henry paid the $300 balance to Pat, he would become a holder in due course as to the full $1,000 face value of the note, provided payment was made prior to Henry's discovery of Mike's defense. If he made the $300 payment after discovering the defense or claim, Henry would be a holder in due course only to the extent of $666.67. A holder in due course, to give value, need pay only the amount he agreed to pay, not the face amount of the instrument.

The Code provides an exception to the executory promise rule in two situations: (1) the giving of a negotiable instrument and (2) the making of an irrevocable obligation to a third party.

Korzenik v. Supreme Radio, Inc.
Supreme Judicial Court of Massachusetts, 1964
347 Mass. 309, 197 N.E.2d 702
http://scholar.google.com/scholar_case?case=6079193572899019477&q=347+Mass.+309&hl=en&as_sdt=2,34

FACTS Supreme Radio, Inc., issued to Southern New England Distributing Corporation (Southern) two notes worth $1,900. The two notes and others, all of a total face value of about $15,000, were transferred to Korzenik, an attorney, by his client Southern "as a retainer for services to be performed" by Korzenik. Although Korzenik was unaware of the fact, Southern had obtained the notes by fraud. Southern retained Korzenik on October 25 in connection with certain antitrust litigation, and the notes were transferred on October 31. The value of the services Korzenik performed during that time is unclear. Korzenik brought this action against Supreme Radio to recover $1,900 on the notes.

DECISION Judgment for Supreme Radio affirmed.

OPINION To qualify as a holder in due course, a holder of an instrument must take for value. A holder takes an instrument for value (1) to the extent that the agreed consideration has been performed or that he acquires a security interest in or a lien on the instrument otherwise than by legal process; or (2) when he takes the instrument in payment of or as security for an antecedent claim against any person whether or not the claim is due; or (3) when he gives a negotiable instrument for it or makes an irrevocable commitment to a third person. Value is divorced from consideration and, except as is provided in (3), an executory promise to give value is not value. Here, Korzenik has failed to show the extent to which the agreed consideration has been performed and, hence, the value that has been given.

INTERPRETATION A holder takes an instrument for value to the extent that the agreed consideration has been given, provided the consideration was given prior to the holder's learning of any defense or claim to the instrument.

CRITICAL THINKING QUESTION Should executory promises be considered value for holder in due course purposes? Explain.

Security Interest   When an instrument is given as security for an obligation, the lender is regarded as having given value to the extent of his security interest. For example, Pedro is the holder of a $1,000 note payable to his order, executed by Monica, and due in twelve months. Pedro uses the note as security for a $700 loan made to him by Larry. Larry has advanced $700; therefore, he has met the requirement of value to the extent of $700.

Likewise, a *bank* gives value when a depositor is allowed to withdraw funds against a deposited item. The provisional or temporary crediting of a depositor's account (discussed in Chapter 27) is not sufficient. If a number of checks have been deposited, and some but not all of the funds have been withdrawn, the Code traces the deposit by following the "FIFO" or "first-in, first-out" method of accounting.

Antecedent debt
preexisting obligation

Antecedent Debt   Under general contract law, an antecedent debt (a preexisting obligation) is not consideration. Under the Code, however, a holder gives value when she takes an instrument in payment of or as security for an antecedent debt. Thus, Martha makes and delivers a note for $1,000 to the order of Penny, who indorses the instrument and delivers it to Howard in payment of an outstanding debt of $970 that she owes him. Howard has given value.

Good Faith [25-3c]

Good faith
honesty in fact and the observance of reasonable commercial standards of fair dealing

Revised Article 3 defines **good faith** as "honesty in fact and the observance of reasonable commercial standards of fair dealing." Thus, Revised Article 3 adopts a definition of good faith that has both a subjective and objective component. (This is the same definition adopted by Revised Article 1.) The subjective component ("honesty in fact") measures good faith by what the purchaser knows or believes. The objective component ("the observance of reasonable commercial standards of fair dealing") is comparable to the definition of good faith applicable to *merchants* under Article 2 in that it includes the requirement of the observance of reasonable commercial standards of fairness. Buying an instrument at a discounted price does not demonstrate lack of good faith. Also see *Watson Coatings, Inc. v. American Express Travel Related Services, Inc.* later in this chapter.

Any Kind Checks Cashed, Inc. v. Talcott
Court of Appeal of Florida, Fourth District, 2002
830 So.2d 160, 48 UCC Rep.Serv.2d 800, rehearing denied
http://scholar.google.com/scholar_case?case=12205265320792531036&q=any+kind+checks+v+talcott&hl=en&as_sdt=2,21

FACTS In the mid-1990s, D. J. Rivera, a "financial advisor," sold ninety-three-year-old John G. Talcott, Jr. an investment for "somewhere in the amount of $75,000." The investment produced no returns. On December 7, 1999, Salvatore Guarino, a cohort of Rivera, established check-cashing privileges at Any Kind Checks Cashed, Inc. That day, he cashed a $450 check without incident. On January 10, 2000, Rivera telephoned Talcott and talked him into sending him a check for $10,000 made out to Guarino, which was to be used for travel expenses to obtain a return on the original $75,000 investment. Rivera received the check on January 11. On that same morning Rivera spoke to Talcott and stated that the $10,000 was more than what was needed for travel. He said that $5,700 would meet the travel costs. Talcott called his bank and stopped payment on the $10,000 check.

In spite of what Rivera told Talcott, Guarino appeared at Any Kind's Stuart, Florida, office on January 11 and presented the $10,000 check to Nancy Michael. She was a supervisor with the company with the authority to approve checks over $2,000. Guarino showed Michael his driver's license and the Federal Express envelope from Talcott in which he received the check. She asked him the purpose of the check, and he told her that he was a broker and that the maker of the check had sent it as an investment. She was unable to contact Talcott by telephone. Based on her experience, Michael believed the check was good. The Federal Express envelope was "very crucial" to her decision, because it indicated that the maker of the check had sent it to the payee trying to cash the check. After deducting the 5 percent fee, Michael cashed the check and gave Guarino $9,500.

On January 15, 2000, Rivera called Talcott and asked about the $5,700, again promising to send him a return on his investment. The same day, Talcott sent a check for $5,700. He assumed that Rivera knew that he had stopped payment on the $10,000 check. On January 17, 2000, Guarino went into the Stuart branch of the Any Kind store and presented the $5,700 check payable to him to the teller, Joanne Kochakian. He showed her the Federal Express envelope in which the check had come. Kochakian noticed that Michael had previously approved the $10,000 check. She called Michael, who was working at another location, and told her about Guarino's check. Any Kind had no written procedures that a supervisor was required to follow in deciding which checks over $2,000 to cash. Michael instructed the cashier not to cash the check until she contacted Talcott, to obtain approval. On her first attempt, Kochakian received no answer. On the second call, Talcott approved cashing the $5,700 check. There was no discussion of the $10,000 check. Any Kind cashed the second check for Guarino, and deducted a 3 percent fee.

On January 19, Rivera called Talcott to warn him that Guarino was a cheat and a thief. Talcott immediately called his bank and stopped payment on the $5,700 check. Talcott's daughter called Any Kind and told it of the stop payment on the $5,700 check.

Any Kind filed a two-count complaint against Guarino and Talcott, claiming that it was a holder in due course. Talcott's defense was that Any Kind was not a holder in due course and that his obligation on the checks was nullified because of Guarino's illegal acts.

The trial court entered final judgment in favor of Any Kind for only the $5,700 check. On the $10,000 check, the judge found for Talcott. The court held that the check-cashing store was not a holder in due course, because the procedures it followed with the $10,000 check did not comport with reasonable commercial standards of fair dealing. The court found that the circumstances surrounding the cashing of the $10,000 check were sufficient to put Any Kind on notice of potential defenses.

DECISION Judgment of the trial court affirmed.

OPINION Talcott was the drawer of the check. By sending the check via Federal Express to Guarino, Talcott issued the check to him. Guarino indorsed the check and cashed it with Any Kind. Any Kind immediately made the funds available to Guarino, less its fee. Talcott stopped payment on the check with his bank, so the check was returned to Any Kind.

When Guarino negotiated the check with Any Kind, it became a holder of the check. As the drawer of the check dishonored by his bank, Talcott's obligation was to pay the draft to a person entitled to enforce the draft according to its terms at the time it was issued. Because Talcott was fraudulently induced to issue the checks, this case turns on Any Kind's entitlement to holder in due course status. The issue of whether Any Kind qualifies as a holder in duty rests on whether Any Kind acted "in good faith."

Application of the old Uniform Commercial Code's subjective "honesty in fact" standard to Any Kind's conduct in this case would clothe it with holder in due course status. It is undisputed that Any Kind's employees were pure of heart and they acted without knowledge of Guarino's wrongdoing.

However, in 1992, the legislature adopted a new definition of "good faith" that applies to the Revised Article 3 definition of a holder in due course: "good faith" means honesty in fact and the observance of reasonable commercial standards of fair dealing.

Under this test the factfinder must determine, first, whether the conduct of the holder comported with industry or "commercial" standards applicable to the transaction and, second, whether those standards were reasonable standards intended to result in fair dealing. Each of those determinations must be made in the context of the specific transaction at hand. If the factfinder's conclusion on each point is "yes," the holder will be determined to have acted in good faith even if, in the individual transaction at issue, the result appears unreasonable. Thus a holder may be accorded holder in due course status where it acts pursuant to those reasonable commercial standards of fair dealing—even if it is negligent—but may lose that status, even where it complies with commercial standards, if those standards are not reasonably related to achieving fair dealing.

The $10,000 personal check was not the typical check cashed at a check-cashing outlet. Guarino was not the typical customer of a check-cashing outlet. As the trial judge observed, because of the 5 percent fee charged, it is unusual for a small businessman such as a broker to conduct business through a check-cashing store instead of through a traditional bank. Guarino did not have a history with Any Kind of cashing checks of similar size without incident. The need for speed in a business transaction is usually less acute than for someone cashing a paycheck or welfare check to pay for life's necessities.

Against this backdrop, the trial court did not err in finding that the $10,000 check was a red flag. To affirm the trial court is not to wreak havoc with the check-cashing industry. Verification with the maker of a check will *not* be necessary to preserve holder in due course status in the vast majority of cases arising from check-cashing outlets. This was neither the typical customer, nor the typical transaction of a check-cashing outlet.

In this case, reasonable commercial fairness required Any Kind to approach the $10,000 check with some caution and to verify it with the maker if it wanted to preserve its holder in due course status.

INTERPRETATION With respect to establishing holder in due course status, "good faith" means honesty in fact and the observance of reasonable commercial standards of fair dealing.

ETHICAL QUESTION Did any of the parties act unethically? Explain.

CRITICAL THINKING QUESTION Do you agree with the position taken by Revised Article 3? Explain.

Lack of Notice [25-3d]

To become a holder in due course, a holder must also take the instrument without notice that it is (1) overdue, (2) dishonored, (3) forged or altered, or (4) subject to any claim or defense. Notice of any of these matters should alert the purchaser that she may be buying a lawsuit and, consequently, may not be accorded the favored position of a holder in due course. Revised Article 1 defines *notice* as follows:

> [A] person has "notice" of a fact if the person: (1) has actual knowledge of it; (2) has received a notice or notification of it; or (3) from all the facts and circumstances known to the person at the time in question, has reason to know that it exists.

Original Article 1's definition is substantially the same. Whereas the first two clauses of this definition impose a wholly subjective standard, the last clause provides a partially objective one: the presence of suspicious circumstances does not adversely affect the purchaser, unless he has reason to recognize them as suspicious. Because the applicable standard is "actual notice," "notice received," or "reason to know," constructive notice through public filing or recording is not of itself sufficient notice to prevent a person from being a holder in due course.

To be effective, notice must be received at a time and in a manner that the recipient will have a reasonable opportunity to act on it.

Notice an instrument is overdue

time paper is overdue after its stated date; demand paper is overdue after demand has been made or after it has been outstanding for an unreasonable period of time

Notice an Instrument Is Overdue   To be a holder in due course, the purchaser must take the instrument without notice that it is overdue. This requirement is based on the idea that overdue paper conveys a suspicion that something is wrong. *Time paper* is due on its stated due date if the stated date is a business day or, if not, on the next business day. It "becomes overdue on the day after the due date." Thus, if an instrument is payable on July 1, a purchaser cannot become a holder in due course by buying it on July 2, provided that July 1 was a business day. In addition, in the case of an installment note or of several notes issued as part of the same transaction with successive specified maturity dates, the purchaser has notice that an instrument is overdue if he has reason to know that any part of the principal amount is overdue or that there is an uncured default in payment of another instrument of the same series.

Demand paper is overdue for purposes of preventing a purchaser from becoming a holder in due course if the purchaser has notice that she is taking the instrument on a day after demand has been made or after it has been outstanding for an unreasonably long time. The Code provides that for checks, a reasonable time is ninety days after its date. For all other demand instruments, the reasonable period of time varies, depending on the facts of the particular case. Thus, the particular situation, business custom, and other relevant factors must be considered in determining whether an instrument is overdue: no hard-and-fast rules are possible.

Acceleration clauses have caused problems. If an instrument's maturity date has been accelerated, the instrument becomes overdue on the day after the accelerated due date even though the holder may be unaware that it is past due.

Dishonor

refusal to pay or accept an instrument when it becomes due

Notice an Instrument Has Been Dishonored   **Dishonor** is the refusal to pay or accept an instrument when it becomes due. If a transferee has notice that an instrument has been dishonored, he cannot become a holder in due course. For example, a person who takes a check stamped "NSF" (not sufficient funds) or "no account" has notice of dishonor and will not be a holder in due course.

Notice of a Claim or Defense   A purchaser of an instrument cannot become a holder in due course if he purchases it with notice of "any claim to the instrument described in Section 3-306" or "a defense or claim in recoupment described in Section 3-305(a)." A **defense** protects a person from liability on an instrument, whereas a **claim** to an instrument asserts ownership to it.

Claims covered by Section 3-306 include "not only claims to ownership but also any other claim of a property or possessory right. It includes the claim to a lien or the claim of a person in rightful possession of an instrument who was wrongfully deprived of possession." Claims to instruments may be made against thieves, finders, or possessors with void or voidable title. In many instances, both a defense and claim will be involved. For example, Donna is fraudulently induced to issue a check to Pablo. Donna has a claim to ownership of the instrument as well as a defense to Pablo's demand for payment.

Section 3-305(a), which is more fully discussed later in this chapter, provides that personal defenses are valid against a holder, while real defenses are effective against both holders and holders in due course. In addition, a person without the rights of a holder in due course is subject to an obligor's claim in recoupment "against the original payee of the instrument if the claim arose from the transaction that gave rise to the instrument." For example, Buyer gives Seller a negotiable note in exchange for Seller's promise to deliver certain goods. Seller delivers non-conforming goods that Buyer elects to accept. Buyer has a cause of action under Article 2 for breach of warranty under the contract, which "claim may be asserted against Seller … to reduce the amount owing on the note. It is not relevant whether Seller knew or had notice that Buyer had the warranty claim."

Buying an instrument at a discount or for a price less than face value does not mean that the buyer had notice of any defense or claim against the instrument. Nonetheless, a court may construe an unusually large discount as notice of a claim or defense.

Without Reason to Question Its Authenticity [25-3e]

Revised Article 3 provides that a party may become a holder in due course only if the instrument issued or negotiated to the holder "does not bear such apparent evidence of forgery or alteration or is not otherwise so irregular or incomplete as to call into question its authenticity." According to the comments to this section, the term "authenticity" clarifies the idea that the irregularity or incompleteness must indicate that the instrument may not be what it purports to be. The Revision takes the position that persons who purchase such instruments do so at their own peril and should not be protected against defenses of the obligor or claims of prior owners. In addition, the Revision takes the position that it makes no difference if the holder does not have notice of such irregularity or incompleteness; it depends only on whether the instrument's defect is apparent and whether the taker should have reason to know of the problem.

HOLDER IN DUE COURSE STATUS [25-4]

A holder who meets the requirements discussed in the previous section obtains the preferred position of holder in due course status. This section discusses whether a payee may become a holder in due course. It also addresses the rights of a transferee from a holder in due course under the shelter rule. Finally, it identifies those special circumstances that prevent a transferee from acquiring holder in due course status.

A Payee May Be a Holder in Due Course [25-4a]

A **payee may be a holder in due course.** This does not mean that a payee automatically is a holder in due course but that he *may* be one if he satisfies the requirements for such status. For example, if a seller delivers goods to a buyer and accepts a current check in payment, the seller will be a holder in due course if he acted in good faith and had no notice of defenses or claims and no reason to question its authenticity. The most common example occurs in cases in which

Defense
protects a person from liability

Claim
an assertion of ownership

Without reason to question its authenticity
instrument cannot bear such apparent evidence of forgery or alteration or otherwise be so irregular or incomplete as to call into question its authenticity

Payee may be a holder in due course
the payee's rights as a holder in due course are limited to defenses of persons with whom he has not dealt

the transaction involves three parties, and the defense involves the parties other than the payee. For example, after purchasing goods from Punky, Robin fraudulently obtains a check from Clem payable to the order of Punky and forwards it to Punky. Punky takes it for value and without any knowledge that Robin had defrauded Clem into issuing the check. In such a case, the payee, Punky, is a holder in due course and takes the instrument free and clear of Clem's defense of fraud in the inducement.

Watson Coatings, Inc. v. American Express Travel Related Services, Inc.
United States Court of Appeals, Eighth Circuit, 2006
436 F.3d 1036
http://scholar.google.com/scholar_case?q=436+F.3d+1036&hl=en&as_sdt=2,34&as_vis=1&case=3703628673473138490&scilh=0

FACTS Over a ten-year period, Christine Mayfield worked for plaintiff Watson Coatings, Inc.—first as an accountant, then as the company controller, and finally as the company treasurer. Mayfield had authority to write checks on funds in Watson's corporate checking account. Watson placed no restrictions or dollar limitations regarding Mayfield's authority to sign checks. Mayfield was solely responsible for reconciling the company checkbook register with the bank statements. Although Watson received monthly bank statements with cancelled checks, Carol Watson, one of Watson's owners, delivered the unopened bank statements to Mayfield but never reviewed the bank statements or reconciled the checking account during Mayfield's tenure at Watson. Mayfield's husband, an American Express account holder, added Mayfield's name to his account in 1992. From August 1997 through October 2001, Mayfield wrote approximately forty-five to forty-seven checks (totaling more than $745,000) on Watson's corporate checking account payable to American Express for her or her husband's personal debt. Neither Mayfield's name nor her husband's name was printed on any of the checks. Each of the checks was made payable to the order of American Express and for credit to the American Express account of Mayfield's husband. American Express credited the Mayfield account for each of the checks. Watson informed American Express of Mayfield's fraud after Mayfield's employment with Watson ended. Watson filed suit to recover the funds. The district court granted American Express's motion for summary judgment. Watson filed an appeal.

DECISION Judgment affirmed.

OPINION Watson argues that American Express cannot qualify as a holder in due course because it is a payee or because it fails to meet the requirement of good faith. However, it is clear, even if unusual, that the payee of an instrument may be a holder in due course. Thus, satisfaction of the requirements of a holder in due course is all that is necessary for a payee to obtain the special protections of a holder in due course.

More specifically, the question is whether American Express fulfilled the good faith requirement. "'Good faith' means honesty in fact in the conduct of the transaction concerned." To establish a lack of good faith, that is, bad faith, Watson had to show that American Express knew, or disregarded knowledge, that Mayfield was breaching her fiduciary duty. "[M]ere suspicious circumstances" are insufficient to show bad faith. Furthermore, "many legitimate reasons [exist as to] why an agent and principal might engage in odd checking practices."

Good faith requires not only that the payee act honestly, but also that the payee act in a commercially reasonable manner. American Express processes more than a million payments a day by electronic means—the only practical means to accomplish the task. Electronic, automated check processing is commercially reasonable. Where a bank or payee electronically processes checks pursuant to its normal procedures and does not employ automated procedures that unreasonably vary from general banking usage, no genuine issue of material fact exists as to whether the payee's automated processing of checks is commercially reasonable.

Thus, American Express acted in good faith when it accepted the checks from Mayfield as payment for her husband's credit card bills because it acted honestly and in a commercially reasonable manner. American Express had no reason to suspect that it would have a problem collecting payment on the checks because they contained no facial irregularities. Finally, Mayfield drafted the checks over a four-year period without any complaint from Watson to American Express that Mayfield had no authority to pay for her husband's credit card bills with corporate checks.

INTERPRETATION A payee may be a holder in due course.

CRITICAL THINKING QUESTION Under what circumstances, if any, should a payee be permitted to be a holder in due course?

Shelter rule

the transferee of an instrument acquires the same rights that the transferor had in the instrument

The Shelter Rule [25-4b]

Through operation of the **shelter rule**, the transferee of an instrument acquires the *same* rights in the instrument as the transferor had. Therefore, even a holder who does not comply fully with the requirements for being a holder in due course nevertheless acquires all the rights of a holder in due course if some previous holder of the instrument had been a holder in due course. For example, Prosser induces Mundheim, by fraud in the inducement, to make a note payable to her

Practical Advice

If a negotiable instrument is to be transferred to you and you will not satisfy the requirements of a holder in due course, make sure that your transferor has the rights of a holder in due course.

order and then negotiates it to Henn, a holder in due course. After the note is overdue, Henn gives it to Corbin, who has notice of the fraud. Corbin is not a holder in due course, because he took the instrument when overdue, did not pay value, and had notice of Mundheim's defense. Nonetheless, through the operation of the shelter rule, Corbin acquires Henn's rights as a holder in due course, and Mundheim cannot successfully assert his defense against Corbin. The purpose of the shelter provision is not to benefit the transferee but to assure the holder in due course of a free market for the negotiable instrument he acquires.

The shelter rule, however, provides that a transferee who has himself been a party to any fraud or illegality affecting the instrument cannot subsequently acquire the rights of a holder in due course. For example, Parker induces Miles, by fraud in the inducement, to make an instrument payable to the order of Parker, who subsequently negotiates the instrument to Henson, a holder in due course. If Parker later reacquires it from Henson, Parker will not succeed to Henson's rights as a holder in due course and will remain subject to the defense of fraud.

Triffin v. Cigna Insurance Co.
Superior Court of New Jersey, Appellate Division, 1997
297 N.J.Super. 199, 687 A.2d 1045
http://scholar.google.com/scholar_case?q=687+A.2d+1045&hl=en&as_sdt=6,34&case=11522573068990632822&scilh=0

FACTS The defendant, James Mills, received a draft in the amount of $484.12, dated July 7, 1993, from one of Cigna's constituent companies, Atlantic Employers Insurance Co. (Atlantic). The draft had been issued for workers' compensation benefits. Mills falsely indicated to Atlantic that he had not received the draft due to a change in his address and requested that payment be stopped and a new draft issued by defendant. Atlantic complied and stopped payment on the initial draft. Mills nevertheless negotiated the initial draft to Sun's Market (Sun), before the stop payment notation was placed on the draft. Sun was a holder in due course. Atlantic's bank dishonored the draft in accordance with its customer's direction, stamped it "Stop Payment," and returned the draft to Sun. There is no question that had Sun at that point pressed its claim against the insurer as the issuer of the instrument, Sun would have been entitled to a judgment because of its status as a holder in due course.

Thereafter, plaintiff, who is in the business of purchasing dishonored instruments, obtained Sun's interests in this instrument and proceeded with this lawsuit. Plaintiff does not contend that he is a holder in due course of the instrument by virtue of it being negotiated to him for value, in good faith, without notice of dishonor, under the former holder in due course statute, Uniform Commercial Code (UCC) Section 3-302, nor under the present

statute: 3-302a(2). The trial court issued summary judgment in favor of Atlantic and Sun appeals.

DECISION Reversed and remanded.

OPINION Negotiation is only one way for a holder to claim the status of a holder in due course. The shelter provisions of the former UCC, which was in effect when plaintiff obtained his assignment of this instrument, state clearly that "[t]ransfer of an instrument vests in the transferee such rights as the transferor has therein." A holder in due course may thus transfer his rights.

The Revised UCC similarly states: "a holder in due course that transfers an instrument transfers those rights as a holder in due course to the purchaser." The policy is to assure the holder in due course a free market for the instrument.

Plaintiff received by negotiation the right of a holder in due course to this instrument, which has been presented and then dishonored because of defendant's stop payment order.

INTERPRETATION Through operation of the shelter rule, the transferee of an instrument acquires the same rights in the instrument as the transferor had.

CRITICAL THINKING QUESTION Do you agree with the shelter rule? Explain.

Real defenses

real defenses are available against all holders, including holders in due course

Personal (contractual) defenses

all other defenses that might be asserted in the case of any action for breach of contract

The Preferred Position of a Holder in Due Course [25-5]

In a **nonconsumer transaction**, a holder in due course takes the instrument (1) free from all *claims* on the part of any person and (2) free from all *defenses* of any party with whom he has not dealt, except for a limited number of defenses that are available against anyone, including a holder in due course. Such defenses that are available against all parties are referred to as **real defenses**. In contrast, defenses that may not be asserted against a holder in due course are referred to as **personal** (or **contractual**) **defenses**.

Real Defenses [25-5a]

The real defenses available against *all* holders, including holders in due course, are

1. infancy, to the extent that it is a defense to a simple contract;
2. any other incapacity, duress, or illegality of the transaction that renders the obligation void;
3. fraud in the execution;
4. discharge in insolvency proceedings;
5. any other discharge of which the holder has notice when he takes the instrument;
6. unauthorized signature; and
7. fraudulent alteration.

Infancy   All states have a firmly entrenched public policy of protecting minors from persons who might take advantage of them through contractual dealings. The Code does not state when minority (infancy) is available as a defense or the conditions under which it may be asserted. Rather, it provides that minority is a defense available against a holder in due course to the extent that it is a defense to a contract under the laws of the state involved. See Chapter 14.

Void Obligations   When the obligation on an instrument originates in such a way that it is *void* or null under the law of the state involved, the Code authorizes the use of this defense against a holder in due course. This follows from the idea that when the party was never obligated, it is unreasonable to permit an event over which she has no control—negotiation to a holder in due course—to convert a nullity into a valid claim against her.

Incapacity, duress, and the illegality of a transaction are defenses that may render the obligation of a party either voidable or void, depending on the law of the state involved as applied to the facts of a given transaction. To the extent the obligation is rendered void (because of duress by physical force, because the party is a person under guardianship, or, in some cases, because the contract is illegal), the defense may be asserted against a holder in due course. To the extent it is voidable, which is generally the case, the defense (other than minority, as discussed previously) is not effective against a holder in due course.

Fraud in the Execution   Fraud in the execution of the instrument renders the instrument void and therefore is a defense valid against a holder in due course. The Code describes this type of fraud as misrepresentation that induced the party to sign the instrument with neither knowledge nor reasonable opportunity to learn of its character or its essential terms. For example, Frances is asked to sign a receipt and does so without realizing or having the opportunity of learning that her signature is going on a promissory note cleverly concealed under the receipt. Because her signature has been obtained by fraud in the execution, Frances would have a valid defense against a holder in due course.

Discharge in Insolvency Proceedings   If a party's obligation on an instrument is discharged in a proceeding for bankruptcy or for any other insolvency, he has a valid defense in any action brought against him on the instrument, including one brought by a holder in due course. Thus, a debtor, whose obligation on a negotiable instrument is discharged in an insolvency proceeding, is relieved of payment, even to a holder in due course.

Discharge of Which the Holder Has Notice   Any holder, including a holder in due course, takes the instrument subject to *any* discharge of which she has notice at the time of taking. If only some, but not all, of the parties to the instrument have been discharged, the purchaser can still become a holder in due course. The discharged parties, however, have a real defense against a holder in due course who has notice of their discharge. For example, Harris, who is in possession of a negotiable instrument, strikes out the indorsement of Jones. The instrument is subsequently negotiated to Stephen, a holder in due course, against whom Jones has a real defense.

Unauthorized Signature   A person's signature on an instrument is unauthorized when it is made without express, implied, or apparent authority. Because he has not made a contract, a person whose signature is unauthorized or forged cannot be held liable on the instrument in the absence of estoppel or ratification, even if the instrument is negotiated to a holder in due course. Similarly, if Joan's signature were forged on the back of an instrument, Joan could not be held as an indorser, because she has not made a contract. Thus, any unauthorized signature is totally invalid as that of the person whose name is signed unless she ratifies it or is precluded from denying it; the unauthorized signature operates only as the signature of the unauthorized signer.

A person may be *estopped* or prevented from asserting a defense because his conduct in the matter has caused reliance by a third party to his loss or damage. Suppose Neal's son forges Neal's name to a check, which the drawee bank cashes. When the returned check reaches Neal, he learns of the forgery. Rather than subject his son to trouble, possibly including criminal prosecution, Neal says nothing. Thereafter, Neal's son continues to forge checks and to cash them at the drawee bank. Although the bank may be suspicious of the signature, the fact that Neal has not complained may induce it to believe that the signatures are proper. When he finally seeks to compel the bank to recredit his account for all the forged checks, Neal will not succeed: his conduct has estopped him from denying that his son had authority to sign his name.

A party is similarly precluded from denying the validity of his signature if his *negligence* substantially contributes to the making of the unauthorized signature. The most obvious case is that of a drawer who uses a mechanized or other automatic signing device and is negligent in safeguarding it. In such an instance, the drawer would not be permitted to assert an unauthorized signature as a defense against a holder in due course.

An unauthorized signature may be *ratified* and thereby become valid so far as its effect as a signature. Thus, Kathy forges Laura's indorsement on a promissory note and negotiates it to Allison. Laura subsequently ratifies Kathy's act. As a result, Kathy is no longer liable to Allison on the note, although Laura is. Nonetheless, Laura's ratification does *not* relieve Kathy from civil liability to Laura; nor does it in any way affect Kathy's criminal liability for the forgery.

Fraudulent Alteration   An alteration is (1) an unauthorized change that modifies the obligation of any party to the instrument or (2) an unauthorized addition or change to an incomplete instrument concerning the obligation of a party.

An alteration that is fraudulently made discharges a party whose obligation is affected by the alteration except where that party assents or is precluded by his own negligence from raising the defense. All other alterations do not discharge any party, and the instrument may be enforced according to its original terms. Thus, if an instrument has been nonfraudulently altered, it may be enforced, but only to the extent of its original tenor (i.e., according to its initially written terms). See Figure 25-6 illustrating the effects of alterations.

A discharge under the Code for fraudulent alteration, however, is not effective against a holder in due course who took the instrument without notice of the alteration. Such a subsequent holder in due course may always enforce the instrument according to its original terms and, in the case of an incomplete instrument, may enforce it as completed. (Under the Code a person taking the instrument for value, in good faith, and without notice of the alteration is accorded the same protection as a holder in due course). The following examples demonstrate the operation of these rules (Figure 25-7 illustrates these examples).

1. M executes and delivers a note to P for $2,000, which P subsequently indorses and transfers to A for $1,900. A intentionally and skillfully changes the figure on the note to $20,000 and then negotiates it to B, who takes it, in good faith, without notice of any wrongdoing and without reason to question its authenticity, for $19,000. B is a holder in due course and, therefore, can collect the original amount of the note ($2,000) from M or P and the full amount ($20,000) from A, less any amount paid by the other parties.

Figure 25-6 Effects of Alterations

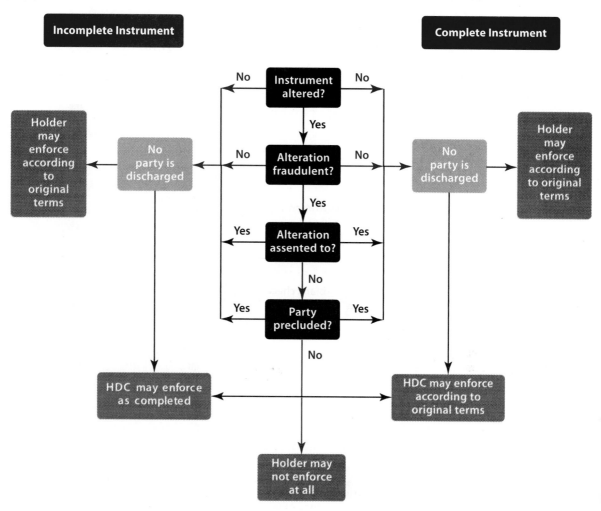

2. Assume the facts in (1), except that B is not a holder in due course. M and P are both discharged by A's fraudulent alteration. B's only recourse is against A for the full amount ($20,000).

3. M issues his blank check to P, who is to complete it when the exact amount is determined. Though the correct amount is set at $2,000, P fraudulently fills in $4,000 and then negotiates the check to T. If T is a holder in due course, she can collect the amount as completed ($4,000) from either M or P. If T is not a holder in due course, however, she has no recourse against M but may recover the full amount ($4,000) from P.

4. Assume the facts in (3), except that P filled in the $4,000 amount in good faith. No party is discharged from liability on the instrument because the alteration was not fraudulent. If T is not a holder in due course, M is liable for the correct amount ($2,000). If T is a holder in due course, T is entitled to receive $4,000 from M because she can enforce an incomplete instrument as completed. Whether or not T is a holder in due course, T may recover $4,000 from P.

Personal Defenses [25-5b]

Defenses to an instrument may arise in many ways, either when the instrument is issued or later. In general, the numerous defenses to liability on a negotiable instrument, which are similar to those that may be raised in an action for breach of contract, are available against any holder of the instrument unless she has the rights of a holder in due course. Among the

Figure 25-7 Alteration

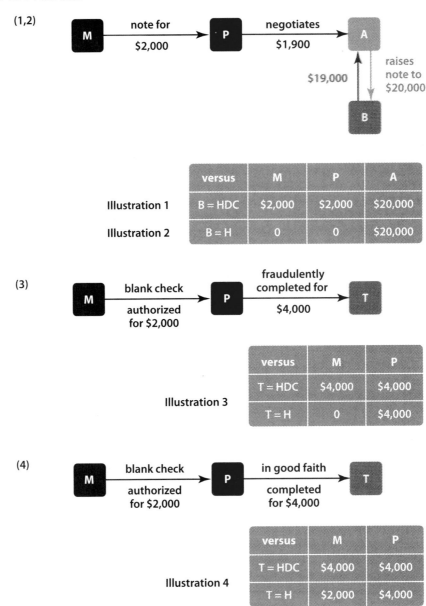

personal defenses are (1) lack of consideration; (2) failure of consideration; (3) breach of contract; (4) fraud in the inducement; (5) illegality that does not render the transaction void; (6) duress, undue influence, mistake, misrepresentation, or incapacity that does not render the transaction void; (7) setoff or counterclaim; (8) discharge of which the holder in due course does not have notice; (9) nondelivery of an instrument, whether complete or incomplete; (10) unauthorized completion of an incomplete instrument; (11) payment without obtaining surrender of the instrument; (12) theft of a bearer instrument or of an instrument payable to him; and (13) lack of authority of a corporate officer, agent, or partner as to the particular instrument, where such officer, agent, or partner had general authority to issue negotiable paper for his principal or firm.

These situations are the most common examples, but others exist. Indeed, the Code does not attempt to detail defenses that may be cut off. It can be stated that a holder in due course takes the instrument free and clear of all claims and defenses, except those listed as real

Practical Advice

When taking a negotiable instrument, make sure that you satisfy the requirements for becoming holder in due course.

Figure 25-8 Availability of Defenses Against Holders and Holders in Due Course

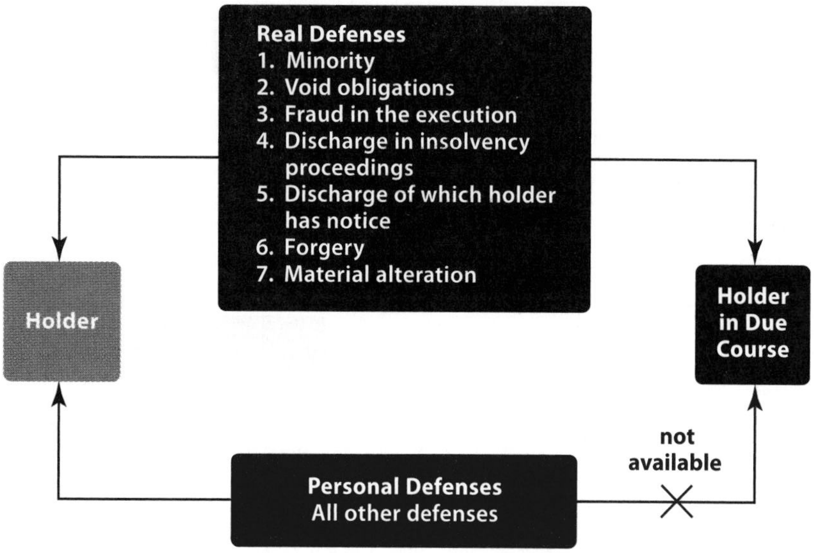

defenses. See Figure 25-8 depicting the availability of defenses against holders and holders in due course.

LIMITATIONS UPON HOLDER IN DUE COURSE RIGHTS [25-6]

Limitations upon holder in due course rights
the preferential position of a holder in due course has been severely limited by a Federal Trade Commission rule that applies to consumer credit contracts, under which a transferee of consumer credit contracts cannot take as a holder in due course

The preferential position enjoyed by a holder in due course has been severely limited by a Federal Trade Commission (FTC) rule restricting the rights of a holder in due course of an instrument concerning a debt arising out of a *consumer credit contract*, which includes negotiable instruments. The rule, entitled "Preservation of Consumers' Claims and Defenses," applies to sellers and lessors of consumer goods, which are goods for personal, household, or family use. It also applies to lenders who advance money to finance a consumer's purchase of consumer goods or services. The rule is intended to prevent consumer purchase transactions from being financed in such a manner that the purchaser is legally obligated to make full payment of the price to a third party, even though the dealer from whom she bought the goods committed fraud or the goods were defective. Such obligations arise when a purchaser executes and delivers to a seller a negotiable instrument that the seller negotiates to a holder in due course. The buyer's defense that the goods were defective or that the seller committed fraud, although valid against the seller, is not valid against the holder in due course. See Figure 25-9 illustrating the rights of holders in due course under the FTC rule.

To correct this situation, the FTC rule preserves claims and defenses of consumer buyers and borrowers against holders in due course. The rule states that no seller or creditor can take or receive a consumer credit contract unless the contract contains the conspicuous provision shown below:

Practical Advice

As a consumer, make sure that any negotiable instrument you give in a consumer credit transaction contains the notation required by the Federal Trade Commission. As a transferee of negotiable instruments arising from a consumer credit transaction, recognize that you are subject to all defenses.

NOTICE: ANY HOLDER OF THIS CONSUMER CREDIT CONTRACT IS SUBJECT TO ALL CLAIMS AND DEFENSES WHICH THE DEBTOR COULD ASSERT AGAINST THE SELLER OF THE GOODS OR SERVICES OBTAINED PURSUANT HERETO OR WITH THE PROCEEDS HEREOF. RECOVERY HEREUNDER BY THE DEBTOR SHALL NOT EXCEED AMOUNTS PAID BY THE DEBTOR HEREUNDER.

The purpose of this notice is to inform any holder in due course of a paper or negotiable instrument that he takes the instrument subject to all claims and defenses that the buyer could assert against the seller. The effect of the rule is to place the holder in due course in the position of an assignee.

Figure 25-9 Rights of Holder in Due Course Under the Federal Trade Commission Rule

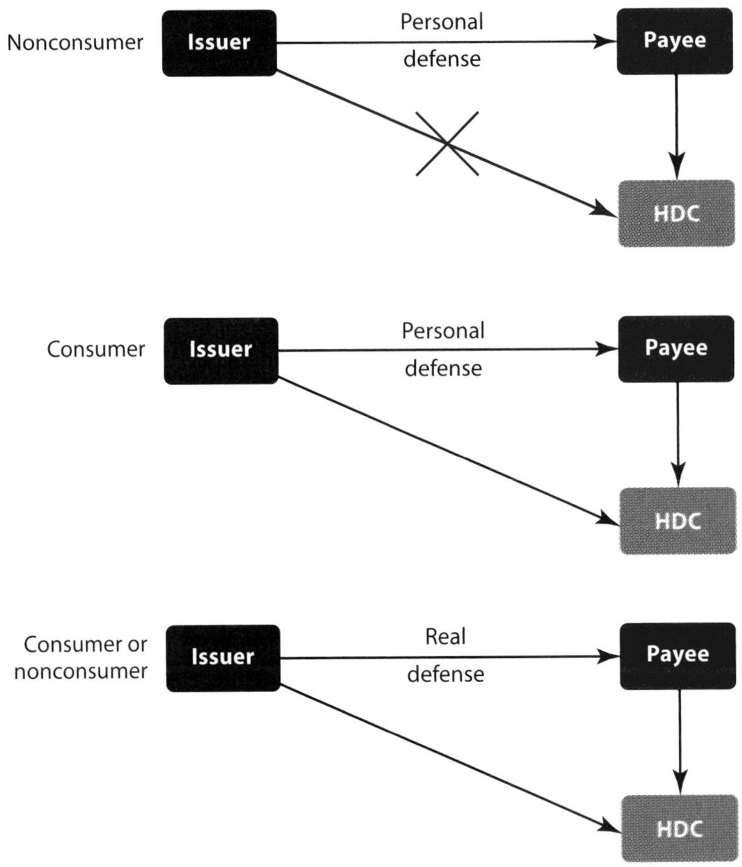

ETHICAL DILEMMA

What Responsibility Does a Holder Have in Negotiating Commercial Paper?

Facts Marcus Moore and David Arnold are subcontractors specializing in the installation of electrical wiring for commercial office space. They have incorporated their business as Moore & Arnold, Inc. Over the past two years, their business has been extremely slow. Recently, they obtained an offer to install wiring for a general contractor, Barnes & Sons, which was in charge of renovating an office to be occupied by three major tenants. The job was substantial and would pay $135,000.

Marcus and David disagreed on whether to accept the job. Marcus was concerned with the business reputation of Barnes & Sons. For years, the business had been reputably operated by Tom Barnes, the original owner, but when his son, John, assumed control of operations, problems began. The partnership was recently sued for negligence in connection with a major

construction project in a mall. It is well known that John is a gambler, and the business has gained the reputation of being slow to pay creditors.

Marcus and David finally decided to accept the job. Upon their completing the work, John Barnes handed Marcus a negotiable promissory note drawn by John Major, one of three different names Barnes & Sons has been trading under during the past year. The note was payable to Moore & Arnold, Inc., one month from date.

Marcus is instinctively nervous about accepting the note. He is aware of the cash flow problems and the litigation pending against Barnes & Sons and has become increasingly suspicious because of the different trade names the contractor uses. David, who is more trusting, wants to accept the note and negotiate it to Wire Ways, Inc., one of their major

suppliers of electrical wiring. Marcus wants to demand cash and, if Barnes refuses, to refer the account to a collection agency.

Social, Policy, and Ethical Considerations

1. Would it be ethical for Marcus and David to accept the note and negotiate it to Wire Ways, Inc.? Why?

2. What ethical responsibilities does one have to review the business reputations of prospective clients or customers and to refuse to do business with disreputable persons?

3. What risks did Moore & Arnold, Inc., assume in accepting the business? Was the risk limited to the failure to obtain payment?

4. Could Marcus and David have structured the business transaction in any way to insulate Moore & Arnold, Inc., from the risks it assumed?

CHAPTER SUMMARY

Transfer

Negotiation

Holder possessor of a negotiable instrument that is payable either to bearer or to an identified person that is the person in possession

Shelter Rule transferee gets rights of transferor

Negotiation of Bearer Paper transferred by mere possession

Negotiation of Order Paper transferred by possession and indorsement by all appropriate parties

- *The Impostor Rule* an indorsement of an impostor or of any other person in the name of the named payee is effective if the impostor has induced the maker or drawer to issue the instrument to him using the name of the payee
- *The Fictitious Payee Rule* an indorsement by any person in the name of the named payee is effective if an agent of the maker or drawer has supplied her with the name of the payee for fraudulent purposes

Negotiations Subject to Rescission negotiation is valid even though a transaction is void or voidable

Indorsements

Definition signature (on the instrument) of a payee, drawee, accommodation party, or holder

Blank Indorsement one specifying no indorsee and making the instrument bearer paper

Special Indorsement one identifying an indorsee to be paid and making the instrument order paper

Unrestrictive Indorsement one that does not attempt to restrict the rights of the indorsee

Restrictive Indorsement one attempting to limit the rights of the indorsee

- *Indorsements for Deposit or Collection* effectively limit further negotiation to those consistent with the indorsement
- *Indorsements in Trust* effectively require the indorsee to pay or apply all funds in accordance with the indorsement
- *Indorsements with Ineffective Restrictions* include conditional indorsements and indorsements attempting to prohibit further negotiation

Unqualified Indorsement one that imposes liability on the indorser

Qualified Indorsement without recourse, one that limits the indorser's liability

Formal Requirements of Indorsements

- *Place of Indorsement*
- *Incorrect or Misspelled Indorsement*

Holder in Due Course

Requirements of a Holder in Due Course

Holder possessor of a negotiable instrument that is payable either to bearer or to an identified person that is the person in possession

Value differs from contractual consideration and consists of any of the following:

- the timely performance of legal consideration (which excludes executory promises);
- the acquisition of a security interest in or a lien on the instrument;
- taking the instrument in payment of or as security for an antecedent debt;
- the giving of a negotiable instrument; or
- the giving of an irrevocable commitment to a third party

Good Faith honesty in fact and the observance of reasonable commercial standards of fair dealing

Lack of Notice

- *Notice an Instrument Is Overdue* time paper is overdue after its stated date; demand paper is overdue after demand has been made or after it has been outstanding for an unreasonable period of time

- *Notice an Instrument Has Been Dishonored* dishonor is the refusal to pay or accept an instrument when it becomes due
- *Notice of Claim or Defense* a defense protects a person from liability while a claim is an assertion of ownership

Without Reason to Question Its Authenticity instrument cannot bear such apparent evidence of forgery or alteration or otherwise be so irregular or incomplete as to call into question its authenticity

Holder in Due Course Status

A Payee May Be a Holder in Due Course the payee's rights as a holder in due course are limited to defenses of persons with whom he has not dealt

The Shelter Rule the transferee of an instrument acquires the same rights that the transferor had in the instrument

The Preferred Position of a Holder in Due Course

Real Defenses real defenses are available against all holders, including holders in due course; such defenses are as follows:

- *Infancy*
- *Void Obligations*
- *Fraud in the Execution*
- *Discharge in Insolvency Proceedings*
- *Discharge of Which the Holder Has Notice*
- *Unauthorized Signature*
- *Fraudulent Alteration*

Personal Defenses all other defenses that might be asserted in the case of any action for breach of contract

Limitations upon Holder in Due Course Rights the preferential position of a holder in due course has been severely limited by a Federal Trade Commission rule that applies to consumer credit contracts, under which a transferee of consumer credit contracts cannot take as a holder in due course

QUESTIONS

1. Roy Rand executed and delivered the following note to Sue Sims: "Chicago, Illinois, June 1, 2015; I promise to pay to Sue Sims or bearer, on or before July 1, 2015, the sum of $7,000. This note is given in consideration of Sims's transferring to the undersigned title to her 2007 Buick automobile. (signed) Roy Rand." Rand and Sims agreed that delivery of the car be deferred to July 1, 2015. On June 15, Sims sold and delivered the note, without indorsement, to Karl Kaye for $6,200. What rights, if any, has Kaye acquired?

2. Lavinia Lane received a check from Wilmore Enterprises, Inc., drawn on the Citizens Bank of Erehwon, in the sum of $10,000. Mrs. Lane indorsed the check "Mrs. Lavinia Lane for deposit only, Account of Lavinia Lane" and placed it in a "Bank by Mail" envelope addressed to the First National Bank of Emanon, where she maintained a checking account. She then placed the envelope over a tier of mailboxes in her apartment building along with other letters to be picked up by the postman the next day.

    Flora Fain stole the check, went to the Bank of Omaha, where Mrs. Lane was unknown, represented herself to be Lavinia Lane, and cashed the check. Has Bank of Omaha taken the check by negotiation? Why or why not?

3. For each of the following indorsements indicate (a) the type of indorsement and whether the indorsement is (b) blank or special, (c) restrictive or nonrestrictive, and (d) qualified or unqualified.

    a. "Pay to Monsein without recourse."
    b. "Pay to Allinore for collection."
    c. "I hereby assign all my rights, title, and interest in this note to Fullilove in full."
    d. "Pay to the Southern Trust Company."
    e. "Pay to the order of the Farmers Bank of Nicholasville for deposit only."

4. Explain whether each of the following transactions results in a valid negotiation:

    a. Arnold gives a negotiable check payable to bearer to Betsy without indorsing it.
    b. Golden indorses a negotiable promissory note payable to the order of Golden, "Pay to Chambers and Rambis, (signed) Golden."
    c. Porter lost a negotiable check payable to his order. Kersey found it and indorsed the back of the check as follows: "Pay to Drexler, (signed) Kersey."
    d. Thomas indorsed a negotiable promissory note payable to the order of Thomas, "(signed) Thomas," and delivered it to Sally. Sally then wrote above Thomas's signature, "Pay to Sally."
    e. Margarita issued to Poncho a negotiable promissory note payable to the order of Poncho. Poncho indorsed the note "Pay to Randy only, (signed) Poncho" and sold it to Randy. Randy then sold the note to Stephanie after indorsing it "Pay to Stephanie, (signed) Randy."

5. Alpha issues a negotiable check to Beta payable to the order of Beta in payment of an obligation Alpha owed Beta. Beta delivers the check to Gamma without indorsing it in exchange for one hundred shares of General Motors stock owned by Gamma. How has Beta transferred the check? What rights, if any, does Gamma have against Beta?

6. Simon Sharpe executed and delivered to Ben Bates a negotiable promissory note payable to the order of Ben Bates for $500. Bates indorsed the note, "Pay to Carl Cady upon his satisfactorily repairing the roof of my house, (signed) Ben Bates," and delivered it to Cady as a down payment on the contract price of the roofing job. Cady then indorsed the note and sold it to Timothy Tate for $450. What rights, if any, does Tate acquire in the promissory note?

7. Debbie Dean issued a check to Betty Brown payable to the order of Cathy Cain and Betty Brown. Betty indorsed the check, "Payable to Elizabeth East, (signed) Betty Brown." What rights, if any, does Elizabeth acquire in the check?

8. Marcus issues a negotiable promissory note payable to the order of Parish for the amount of $3,000. Parish raises the amount to $13,000 and negotiates it to Hilda for $12,000.
  a. If Hilda is a holder in due course, how much can she recover from Marcus? How much from Parish? If Marcus's negligence substantially contributed to the making of the alteration, how much can Hilda recover from Marcus and Parish, respectively?
  b. If Hilda is not a holder in due course, how much can she recover from Marcus? How much from Parish? If Marcus's negligence substantially contributed to the making of the alteration, how much can Hilda recover from Marcus and Parish, respectively?

9. On December 2, 2015, Miles executed and delivered to Proctor a negotiable promissory note for $1,000, payable to Proctor or order, due March 2, 2016, with interest at 14 percent from maturity, in partial payment of a printing press. On January 3, 2016, Proctor, in need of ready cash, indorsed and sold the note to Hughes for $800. Hughes paid $600 in cash to Proctor on January 3 and agreed to pay the balance of $200 one week later, namely, on January 10. On January 6, Hughes learned that Miles claimed a breach of warranty by Proctor and, for this reason, intended to refuse to pay the note when it matured. On January 10, Hughes paid Proctor $200, in conformity with their agreement of January 3. Following Miles's refusal to pay the note on March 2, 2016, Hughes sues Miles for $1,000. Is Hughes a holder in due course? If so, for what amount?

10. Thornton fraudulently represented to Daye that he would obtain for her a new car to be used in Daye's business for $17,800 from Pennek Motor Company. Daye thereupon executed her personal check for $17,800 payable to the order of Pennek Motor Company and delivered the check to Thornton, who immediately delivered it to the motor company in payment of his own prior indebtedness. The motor company had no knowledge of the representations made by Thornton to Daye. Pennek Motor Company now brings an action on the check that was not paid against Daye, who defends on the ground of failure of consideration. Is Pennek subject to this defense? Explain.

11. Adams, who reads with difficulty, arranged to borrow $2,000 from Bell. Bell prepared a note, which Adams read laboriously. As Adams was about to sign it, Bell diverted Adams's attention and substituted the following paper, which was identical to the note Adams had read except that the amounts were different:

> On June 1, 2015, I promise to pay Ben Bell or order Twelve Thousand Dollars with interest from date at 16 percent. This note is secured by certificate No. 13 for one hundred shares of stock of Brookside Mills, Inc.

Adams did not detect the substitution, signed as maker, handed the note and stock certificate to Bell, and received from Bell $2,000. Bell indorsed and sold the paper to Fore, a holder in due course, who paid him $11,000. Fore presented the note at maturity to Adams, who refused to pay. What are Fore's rights, if any, against Adams?

12. On January 2, 2015, seventeen-year-old Martin paid $2,000 for a used motorboat to use in his fishing business, after Dealer's fraudulent misrepresentation of the condition of the boat. Martin signed an installment contract for $1,500, and gave Dealer the following instrument as down payment:

> Dated: _____ 2015
>
> I promise to pay to the order of Dealer, six months after date, the sum of $500 without interest. This is given as a down payment on an installment contract for a motorboat.
>
> (signed) Martin

Dealer, on July 1, sold his business to Henry and included this note in the transaction. Dealer indorsed the note in blank and handed it to Henry, who left the note in his office safe. On July 10, Sharpie, an employee of Henry, without authority, stole the note and sold it to Bert for $300, indorsing the note "Sharpie." At the time, in Bert's presence, Sharpie filled in the date on the note as February 2, 2015. Bert demanded payment from Martin, who refused to pay.
   What are Bert's rights against Martin?

13. McLaughlin borrowed $10,000 from Adler, who, apprehensive about McLaughlin's ability to pay, demanded security. McLaughlin indorsed and delivered to Adler a negotiable promissory note executed by Topping for $12,000 payable to McLaughlin's order in twelve equal monthly installments. The note did not contain an acceleration clause, but it recited that the consideration for the note was McLaughlin's promise to paint and shingle Topping's barn. At the time McLaughlin transferred the note to Adler, the first installment was overdue and unpaid. Adler was unaware that the installment had not been paid. Topping did not pay any of the installments on the note. When the last installment became due, Adler presented the note to Topping for payment. Topping refused upon the ground that McLaughlin had not painted or reshingled her barn.
   What are Adler's rights, if any, against Topping on the note?

14. Adams, by fraudulent representations, induced Barton to purchase one hundred shares of the capital stock of the Evermore Oil Company. The shares were worthless. Barton executed and delivered to Adams a negotiable promissory note for $5,000, dated May 5, in full payment for the shares, due six months after date. On May 20, Adams indorsed and sold the note to Cooper for $4,800. On October 21, Barton, having learned that Cooper now held the note, notified Cooper of the fraud and stated he would not pay the note. On December 1, Cooper negotiated the note to Davis who, while not a party, had full knowledge of the fraud perpetrated on Barton. Upon refusal of Barton to pay the note, Davis sues Barton for $5,000. Is Davis a holder in due course or, if not, does he have the rights of a holder in due course? Explain.

15. Donna gives Peter a check for $3,000 in return for a desktop computer. The check is dated December 2. Peter transfers the check for value to Howard on December 14, and Howard deposits it in his bank on December 20. In the meantime, Donna has discovered that the computer is not what was promised and has stopped payment on the check. If Peter and Howard disappear, may the bank recover from Donna notwithstanding her defense of failure of consideration? What will be the bank's cause of action?

CASE PROBLEMS

16. The drawer, Commercial Credit Corporation (Corporation), issued two checks payable to Rauch Motor Company. Rauch indorsed the checks in blank, deposited them to its account in University National Bank, and received a corresponding amount of money. The Bank stamped "pay any bank" on the checks and initiated collection. However, the checks were dishonored and returned to the Bank with the notation "payment stopped." Rauch, through subsequent deposits, repaid the bank. Later, to compromise a lawsuit, the Bank executed a special two-page indorsement of the two checks to Lamson. Lamson then sued the Corporation for the face value of the checks, plus interest. The Corporation contends that Lamson was not a holder of the checks because the indorsement was not in conformity with the Uniform Commercial Code in that it was stapled to the checks. Is Lamson a holder? Why?

17. While assistant treasurer of Travco Corporation, Frank Mitchell caused two checks, each payable to a fictitious company, to be drawn on Travco's account with Brown City Savings Bank. In each case, Mitchell indorsed the check in his own name and then cashed it at Citizens Federal Savings & Loan Association of Port Huron. Both checks were cleared through normal banking channels and charged against Travco's account with Brown City. Travco subsequently discovered the embezzlement, and after Citizens denied its demand for reimbursement, Travco brought a suit against Citizens. Is the indorsement effective? Explain.

18. Eldon's Super Fresh Stores, Inc., is a corporation engaged in the retail grocery business. William Drexler was the attorney for and the corporate secretary of Eldon's and was also the personal attorney of Eldon Prinzing, the corporation's president and sole shareholder. From January 2015 through January 2016, Drexler maintained an active stock trading account in his name with Merrill Lynch. Eldon's had no such account. On August 12, 2015, Drexler purchased one hundred shares of Clark Oil & Refining Company stock through his Merrill Lynch stockbroker. He paid for the stock with a check drawn by Eldon's, made payable to Merrill Lynch, and signed by Prinzing. On August 15, 2015, Merrill Lynch accepted the check as payment for Drexler's stock purchase. There was no communication between Eldon's and Merrill Lynch until November 2016, fifteen months after the issuance of the check. At that time, Eldon's asked Merrill Lynch about the whereabouts of the stock certificate and asserted a claim to its ownership. Does Merrill Lynch qualify as a holder in due course? Why?

19. Walter Duester purchased a John Deere combine from St. Paul Equipment. John Deere Co. was the lender and secured party under the agreement. The combine was pledged as collateral. Duester defaulted on his debt, and the manager of St. Paul, Hansen, was instructed to repossess the combine. Hansen went to Duester's farm to accomplish this. Duester told him that he had received some payments for custom combining and would immediately purchase a cashier's check to pay the John Deere debt. Hansen followed Duester to the defendant, Boelus State Bank. Hansen remained outside, and Duester returned in a few minutes with a cashier's check in the amount of the balance of his indebtedness payable to John Deere. The check had been signed by an authorized bank employee. When John Deere, however, presented the check to the bank for payment shortly thereafter, the bank refused to pay, claiming that Duester acquired the cashier's check by theft. Is John Deere subject to this defense? Why?

20. Stephens delivered 184 bushels of corn to Aubrey, for which he was to receive $478.23. Aubrey issued a check with $478.23 typewritten in numbers, and on the line customarily used to express the amount in words appeared "$100478 and 23 cts" imprinted in red with a check-writing machine. Before Stephens cashed the check, someone crudely typed "100" in front of the typewritten $478.23. When Stephens presented this check to the State Bank of Salem, Anderson, the manager, questioned Stephens. Anderson knew that Stephens had just declared bankruptcy and was not accustomed to making such large deposits. Stephens told Anderson he had bought and sold a large quantity of corn at a great profit. Anderson accepted the explanation and applied the monies to nine promissory notes, an installment payment, and accrued interest owed by Stephens. Stephens also received $2,000 in cash, with the balance deposited in his checking account.

Later that day, Anderson reexamined the check and discovered the suspicious appearance of the typewriting. He then contacted Aubrey, who said a check in that amount was suspicious, whereupon Anderson froze the transaction. When Aubrey stopped payment on the check, the bank sustained a $28,193.91 loss because Stephens could not be located. The bank then sued Aubrey for the loss. Explain who should bear the loss.

21. L&M Home Health Corporation (L&M) had a checking account with Wells Fargo Bank. L&M engaged Gentner and Company, Inc. (Gentner) to provide consulting services, and

paid Gentner for services rendered with a check drawn on its Wells Fargo account in the amount of $60,000, dated September 23, 2014. Eleven days later, on October 4, 2014, L&M orally instructed Wells Fargo to stop payment on the check. Eleven days after that, on October 15, 2014, Gentner presented the L&M check to Wells Fargo for payment. On the same date the teller issued a cashier's check, payable to Gentner, in the amount of $60,000. On November 5, 2014, Wells Fargo placed a "stop payment order" on the cashier's check. On January 15, 2015, Gentner deposited the cashier's check at another bank, but it was not honored and was returned stamped "Payment Stopped." Gentner sues Wells Fargo for wrongful dishonor of the cashier's check. Is Gentner a holder in due course of the check? Discuss.

22. Stanley A. Erb became a vice president of the Shearson Lehman Brothers, Inc. branch office in Provo, Utah. That year, Erb was contacted by McKay Matthews, the controller for the Orem, Utah-based WordPerfect Corporation and its sister corporation, Utah Softcopy. At Matthews's request, Erb established and managed three separate investment accounts at Shearson. The accounts were for the benefit of the Word-Perfect and Utah Softcopy corporations, and one account was for the WordPerfect principals, Allen Ashton, Bruce Bastian, and Willard Peterson. In March of that year, Erb personally accepted from Matthews a check drawn by Utah Softcopy for $460,150.23 and payable to the order of "ABP Investments." At that time, there was no ABP investment account at Shearson, although the WordPerfect principals maintained accounts elsewhere in that name. Erb accepted the check, but rather than deposit it in one of the three authorized accounts, Erb opened a new account at Shearson in the name of "ABP Investments," apparently by forging the signature of Bruce Bastian on the new account documents. Over the next eleven months, Erb induced Shearson to draft thirty-seven checks on the ABP Investment account, payable to ABP Investments, by submitting falsified payment requests to Shearson's cashier.

The checks were mailed to an Orem post office box unknown to WordPerfect and its principals. Erb would obtain the checks and indorse them in the name of ABP Investments. He took the checks to Wasatch Bank for deposit into his personal account. Wasatch accepted the deposits and later allowed Erb to withdraw $504,295.30, the entire amount, from the account. Shearson discovered Erb's activities after Erb had left Shearson after two years. Shearson brought a suit against Wasatch Bank. Discuss who should prevail.

23. Turman executed a deed of trust note for $107,500 payable to Ward's Home Improvement, Inc. (Ward's). The note was in consideration of a contract for Ward's to build a house on Turman's property. On the same day, Ward's executed an assignment of the note to Robert Pomerantz for which Pomerantz paid Ward's $95,000. Although the document uses the word "assignment," no notation or indorsement was made on the note itself. Is Pomerantz a holder? Is Pomerantz a holder in due course? Explain.

24. Certain partners of the Finley Kumble law firm signed promissory notes that secured loans made to the law firm by the National Bank of Washington (NBW). When Finley Kumble subsequently declared bankruptcy and defaulted on the loans, NBW filed suit to collect on the notes. Then NBW itself became insolvent, and the Federal Deposit Insurance Corporation (FDIC) was appointed as receiver for NBW. The FDIC brought suit against the partners who had signed the note. Section 1823(e) of the Federal Deposit Insurance Act of 1950 places the FDIC in the position of a holder in due course and thus bars all personal defenses against the FDIC claims. Twenty of the Finley partners claimed that they had signed the notes under the threat that their wages and standing in the firm would decrease if they refused to sign. Such a threat constituted economic duress, which, they contended, is not a personal defense but a real defense. Discuss who should prevail.

TAKING SIDES

Wilson was employed as the office manager of Palmer & Ray Dental Supply of Abilene, Inc. Soon after an auditor discovered a discrepancy in the company's inventory, Wilson confessed to cashing thirty-five checks that she was supposed to deposit on behalf of the company. Palmer & Ray Dental Supply used a rubber stamp to indorse checks. The stamp listed the company's name and address but did not read "for deposit only." The company's president, James Ray, authorized Wilson to indorse checks with this stamp. Wilson cashed all of the checks at First National Bank.

a. What are the arguments that First National Bank is liable to Palmer & Ray Dental Supply for converting the company's funds by giving Wilson cash instead of depositing the checks into the company's bank account?

b. What are the arguments that First National Bank is not liable to Palmer & Ray Dental Supply?

c. Explain who should prevail.

Liability of Parties

CHAPTER 26

The truth shall be thy warrant ...

Sir Walter Raleigh (1552–1618)

CHAPTER OUTCOMES

After reading and studying this chapter, you should be able to:

1. Explain contractual liability, warranty liability, and liability of conversion.

2. Explain the liability of makers, acceptors, drawers, drawees, indorsers, and accommodation parties.

3. Identify and discuss the condition precedents to the liability of secondary parties.

4. Explain the methods by which liability on an instrument may be terminated.

5. Compare the warranties on transfer with the warranties on presentment.

Contractual liability
obligation on a negotiable instrument based upon signing the instrument

Warranty liability
applies to persons who transfer an instrument or receive payment for or acceptance of it

The preceding chapters discussed the requirements of negotiability, the transfer of negotiable instruments, and the preferred position of a holder in due course. When parties issue negotiable instruments, they do so with the expectation that they, either directly or indirectly, satisfy their obligation under the instrument. Likewise, when a person accepts, indorses, or transfers an instrument, he incurs liability for the instrument under certain circumstances. This chapter examines the liability of parties arising out of negotiable instruments and the ways in which liability may be terminated.

Two types of potential liability are associated with negotiable instruments: contractual liability and warranty liability. The law imposes **contractual liability** on those who *sign*, or have a representative agent sign, a negotiable instrument. Because some parties to a negotiable instrument never sign it, they never assume contractual liability.

Warranty liability, on the other hand, is not based on signature; thus, it may be imposed on both signers and nonsigners. **Warranty liability** applies (1) to persons who transfer an instrument and (2) to persons who obtain payment or acceptance of an instrument.

CONTRACTUAL LIABILITY

Primary liability
absolute obligation to pay a negotiable instrument

All parties whose signatures appear on a negotiable instrument incur certain contractual obligations, unless they disclaim liability. No person is liable on an instrument unless she signs it herself or has it signed by a person whose signature binds her. Once the person signs the instrument, the person has *prima facie* liability on the instrument. The *maker* of a promissory note and the *acceptor* of a draft assume primary, or unconditional, liability, subject to valid claims and defenses, to pay according to the terms of the instrument at the time they sign it or as completed according to the rules for incomplete instruments, discussed in Chapter 25. **Primary liability** means that a party is legally obligated to pay without the holder's having to resort first to another party.

Indorsers of all instruments incur secondary, or conditional, liability if the instrument is not paid. **Secondary liability** means that a party is legally obligated to pay only after another party, who is expected to pay, fails to do so. The liability of drawers of drafts and checks is also conditional because it is generally contingent upon the drawee's dishonor of the instrument. A *drawee* has *no* liability on the instrument until he *accepts* it.

An **accommodation party** signs the instrument to lend her credit to another party to the instrument and is a direct beneficiary of the value received. The liability of an accommodation party, who generally signs as a co-maker, or anomalous indorser, is determined by the capacity in which she signs. If the accommodation party signs as a maker, she incurs primary liability; if she signs as an anomalous indorser, she incurs secondary liability.

SIGNATURE [26-1]

The word **signature**, as discussed in Chapter 24, is broadly defined to include any name, word, or mark, whether handwritten, typed, printed, or in any other form, made with the intention of authenticating an instrument. The signature may be made by the individual herself or on her behalf by the individual's authorized agent.

Authorized Signatures [26-1a]

A person is obligated by a signature on an instrument if the signature is her own or if an agent with authority signs the instrument. Authorized agents often execute negotiable instruments on behalf of their principals. The agent is not liable if she is authorized to execute the instrument and does so properly (e.g., "Prince, principal, by Adams, agent"). If these two conditions are met, then only the principal is liable on the instrument. (For a comprehensive discussion of the principal–agent relationship, see Chapters 28 and 29.)

Occasionally, however, the agent, although fully authorized, uses an inappropriate form of signature that may mislead holders or prospective holders as to the identity of the obligor. Although incorrect signatures by agents assume many forms, they can be conveniently sorted into three groups. In each of these instances the intention of the original parties to the instrument is that the principal is to be liable on the instrument and the agent is not.

The first type occurs when an agent signs only his own name to an instrument, neither indicating that he is signing in a representative capacity nor stating the name of the principal. For example, Adams, the agent of Prince, makes a note on behalf of Prince but signs it "Adams." The signature does not indicate that Adams has signed in a representative capacity or that he has made the instrument on behalf of Prince. The second type of incorrect form occurs when an authorized agent indicates that he is signing in a representative capacity but does not disclose the name of his principal. For example, Adams, executing an instrument on behalf of Prince, merely signs it "Adams, agent." The third type of inappropriate signature occurs when an agent reveals both her name and her principal's name, but does not indicate that she has signed in a representative capacity. For example, Adams, signing an instrument on behalf of Prince, signs it "Adams, Prince."

In all three situations, the agent is liable on the instrument only to a holder in due course without notice that Adams was not intended to be liable. Because contract and agency law determine Prince's liability on the instrument, Prince is liable to all holders. Under Revised Article 3, if a representative (an agent) signs his name as the drawer of a *check* without indicating his representative status and the check is payable from an account of the represented person (the principal) who is identified on the check, the representative is not liable on the check if he is an authorized agent.

Secondary liability
obligation to pay a negotiable instrument is subject to conditions precedent

Accommodation party
signs an instrument to lend her credit to the instrument; her liability is determined by the capacity in which she signs

Signature
may be made by the individual herself or by her authorized agent

Authorized signatures
an agent who executes a negotiable instrument on behalf of his principal is not liable if the instrument is executed properly and as authorized

Practical Advice

If you are acting as an agent for another party, make sure that you properly sign any negotiable instrument by indicating your representative capacity and the identity of the principal. If you do that, you will avoid potential liability.

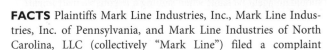

Mark Line Industries, Inc. v. Murillo Modular Group, Ltd.
United States District Court, N.D. Indiana, South Bend Division, 2011
2011 WL 1458496, 74 UCC Rep.Serv.2d 253
http://scholar.google.com/scholar_case?case=2815673533262901348&hl=en&as_sdt=6&as_vis=1&oi=scholarr

FACTS Plaintiffs Mark Line Industries, Inc., Mark Line Industries, Inc. of Pennsylvania, and Mark Line Industries of North Carolina, LLC (collectively "Mark Line") filed a complaint against defendants Murillo Modular Group, Ltd. ("MMG") and Salvador V. Murillo ("Murillo") alleging that the defendants had failed to pay the balances due on two promissory notes that they had given to Mark Line. The promissory notes, dated September 18, 2009, were for $3,802,532.00 and $743,297.50. The terms of the notes provided that they would mature on the earlier of (1) November 15, 2009 or (2) the date(s) when certain conditions were satisfied. Mark Line alleges that defendants did not pay the balance due by November 15, 2009. Mark Line further alleges that it received a payment of $79,549.51. Of this payment, $14,175.47 was applied towards accrued interest and the remaining $65,374.04 was applied to reduce the remaining principal balance.

Both notes include the following explanation for "Maker/Borrower": "Maker/Borrower: Murillo Modular Group Ltd, Salvador Murillo and Nick Mackie, (collectively and severally the "Maker or Makers or Borrower" through Murillo Modular Group, Ltd.). The Makers/Borrowers shall be jointly and severally liable."

At the end, both notes state: "IN WITNESS WHEREOF, the Maker/Borrower understands that it is liable for all obligations arising under this Note and has caused the same to be signed and delivered as of the date first written above."

The form of signature then says "Murillo Modular Group, Ltd, Maker/Borrower." Murillo's signature appears above the signature block, "By: Salvador Murillo, Owner" on the first note and "By: Salvador Murillo, Partner" on the second note. Nick Mackie has also signed the first note as "owner" and the second note as "partner." The notes then say "Accepted: Mark Line" and are signed by "L. Michael Arnold, CEO."

The parties have agreed to dismiss, without prejudice, the claim against Murillo for failure to pay the balance on the second promissory note. The defendants argue that the first promissory note for $3,802,532.00 shows that Murillo signed the note only in his representative capacity for MMG and not in his individual capacity. They argue that Murillo is not individually liable because the "form of his signature shows unambiguously" that he signed as a representative of MMG.

DECISION The motion to dismiss made by the defendants Murillo Modular Group and Murillo is denied.

OPINION Mark Line's pleadings show two different plausible theories for Murillo's individual liability for the note. First, under the UCC, Murillo may be liable on the promissory note as a matter of contract law. This part of the UCC provides:

> If a person acting, or purporting to act, as a representative signs an instrument by signing either the name of the represented person or the name of the signer, the represented person is bound by the signature to the same extent the represented person would be bound if the signature were on a simple contract. If the represented person is bound, the signature of the representative is the "authorized signature of the represented person" and the represented person is liable on the instrument, whether or not identified in the instrument.

So, for example, if Person A agreed to have Person B act as his representative as a matter of agency law, and Person B signed his own name or Person A's name to an instrument, Person A is bound to the instrument as a matter of contract law. This is because as the authorized representative of Person A, Person B's signature is an authorized signature of Person A.

The promissory note at issue states that MMG, Murillo, and Mackie are "collectively and severally the 'Maker or Makers or Borrower' through Murillo Modular Group, Ltd." The phrase "through Murillo Modular Group, Ltd." could mean that MMG was authorized to act on behalf of Murillo for this note, so that MMG was acting as Murillo's representative on the promissory note and Murillo was the represented person. In this way, Murillo could still be liable on the note even if he only signed in his representative capacity as the owner of MMG. It could be that MMG signed the note, through Murillo in his representative capacity, as Murillo's representative. Thus, the allegations paint a plausible story that MMG acted as the representative of Murillo under agency law, and by signing the note, it bound Murillo "to the same extent [he] would be bound if the signature were on a simple contract."

Second, Murillo may be liable on the note because the UCC further provides that a person is not liable on an instrument unless he has signed the instrument or his agent or representative has signed the instrument. The Code provides that a representative signing his name to an instrument as an authorized signature of a represented person is not liable on an instrument if the "form of the signature shows unambiguously that the signature is made on behalf of the represented person." If the form of signature "does not show unambiguously that the signature is made in a representative capacity," "the representative is liable on the instrument to a holder in due course that took the instrument without notice that the representative was not intended to be liable on the instrument." As to any other person "the representative is liable on the instrument unless the representative proves that the original parties did not intend the representative to be liable on the instrument."

In this case the form of signature is ambiguous. The UCC provides three examples of when the form of signature is ambiguous. One example of this is when the agent signs as an agent, but fails to identify the represented person. That is similar to the situation as alleged here because the form of signature does not clearly identify MMG as the represented party. The note identifies MMG as the "Maker/Borrower" in the form of signature. However, the note defines "Maker/Borrower" as MMG, Murillo, and Mackie "through Murillo Modular Group." It then says that the "Makers/Borrowers shall be jointly and severally liable." It could be argued that if MMG was the only Maker or Borrower, this definition would not make any sense because there would be no one for it to be jointly and severally liable with. Therefore the definition of "Maker/Borrower" in the contract confuses the identity of the represented person and makes the form of signature ambiguous.

Further, the form of signature is also ambiguous because both Murillo and Mackie signed for MMG. In sum, at this point, Mark Line has plead plausible theories for Murillo's individual liability on the note.

INTERPRETATION When the agent signs as an agent but fails to identify the represented person, the agent is liable on the instrument to a holder in due course without notice that the agent was not intended to be liable.

CRITICAL THINKING QUESTION To whom and when should an agent be liable when signing a negotiable instrument?

Unauthorized signatures

include forgeries and signatures made by an agent without proper power; are generally not binding on the person whose name appears on the instrument but are binding on the unauthorized signer

---

Practical Advice

Exercise diligence to guard against forged signatures on your negotiable instruments.

Unauthorized Signatures [26-1b]

An unauthorized signature, with two exceptions, is totally ineffective and does not bind anybody. **Unauthorized signatures** include both forgeries and signatures made by an agent without authority. Though generally not binding on the person whose name appears on the instrument, the unauthorized signature is binding upon the unauthorized signer, whether her own name appears on the instrument or not, to any person who in good faith pays or gives value for the instrument. Thus, if Adams, without authority, signed Prince's name to an instrument, Adams, not Prince, would be liable on the instrument. The rule, therefore, is an exception to the principle that only those whose names appear on a negotiable instrument can be liable on it.

Ratification of Unauthorized Signature
An unauthorized signature may be ratified by the person whose name appears on the instrument. Although the ratification may relieve the actual signer from liability on the instrument, it does not itself affect any rights the person ratifying the signature may have against the actual signer.

Negligence Contributing to Forged Signature
Any person who by his negligence substantially contributes to the making of a forged signature may not assert the lack of authority as a defense against a holder in due course or a person who in good faith pays the instrument or takes it for value or for collection. Nevertheless, if the person asserting the preclusion also fails to exercise reasonable care, Revised Article 3 adopts a comparative negligence standard.

LIABILITY OF PRIMARY PARTIES [26-2]

There is a primary party on every note: the *maker*. The maker's commitment is unconditional. No one, however, is unconditionally liable on a draft or check as issued. A *drawee* is *not* liable on the instrument unless he accepts it. If, however, the drawee accepts the draft, after which he is known as the *acceptor*, the drawee becomes primarily liable on the instrument. **Acceptance** or, in the case of a check, certification is the drawee's signed promise to pay a draft as presented. Presentment (i.e., a demand for payment) is not a condition to the holder's right to recover from parties with primary liability.

Acceptance

a drawee's signed commitment to honor the instrument

Makers [26-2a]

The **maker** of a note is obligated to pay the instrument according to its terms at the time of issuance or, if the instrument is incomplete, according to its terms when completed, as discussed in Chapter 25. The obligation of the maker is owed to a person entitled to enforce the instrument or to an indorser who paid the instrument.

Maker

person who guarantees that he will pay the note according to its original terms

Primary liability also applies to issuers of cashier's checks and to issuers of drafts drawn on the drawer (i.e., where the issuer is both the drawee and the drawer).

Acceptors [26-2b]

A drawee has no liability on the instrument until she accepts it, at which time the drawee becomes an **acceptor** and, like the maker, primarily liable. The acceptor becomes liable on the draft according to its terms at the time of acceptance or as completed according to the rules for incomplete instruments as discussed in Chapter 25. Nevertheless, if the acceptor does not state the amount accepted and the amount of the draft is later raised, a subsequent holder in due course can enforce the instrument against the acceptor according to the terms at the time the holder in due course took possession. Thus, an acceptor should always indicate on the instrument the amount that it is accepting. The acceptor owes the obligation to pay a person entitled to enforce the instrument or to the drawer or an indorser who paid the draft under drawer's or indorser's liability.

Acceptor

a drawee has no liability on the instrument until she accepts it; she then becomes primarily liable

An acceptance must be written on the draft. Having met this requirement, it may take many forms. It may be printed on the face of the draft, ready for the drawee's signature. It may consist of a rubber stamp, with the signature of the drawee added. It may be the drawee's signature, preceded by a word or phrase such as "Accepted," "Certified," or "Good." It may consist of nothing more than the drawee's signature. Normally, but by no means necessarily, an acceptance is written vertically across the face of the draft. It must not, however, contain any words indicating an intent to refuse to honor the draft. Furthermore, no writing separate from the draft and no oral statement or conduct of the drawee will convert the drawee into an acceptor.

Certification
acceptance of a check by
a bank

Checks, when accepted, are said to be certified. **Certification** is a special type of acceptance consisting of the drawee bank's promise to pay the check when subsequently presented for payment.

The drawee bank has no obligation to certify a check, and its refusal to certify does not constitute dishonor of the instrument. If the drawee refuses to accept or pay the instrument, he may be liable to the drawer for breach of contract.

See *Messing v. Bank of America, N.A.* later in this chapter.

LIABILITY OF SECONDARY PARTIES [26-3]

Parties with secondary (conditional) liability do not unconditionally promise to pay the instrument; rather, they engage to pay the instrument if the party expected to pay does not do so. The drawer is liable if the drawee dishonors the instrument. **Indorsers** (including the payee if he indorses) of an instrument are also conditionally liable; their liability is subject to the conditions of dishonor and notice of dishonor. If an instrument is *not* paid by the party expected to pay and the conditions precedent to the liability of a secondary party are satisfied, a secondary party is liable unless he has disclaimed liability or possesses a valid defense to the instrument.

Indorsers and drawers

if the instrument is not paid
by a primary party and if
the conditions precedent to
the liability of secondary
parties are satisfied,
indorsers and drawers are
secondarily (conditionally)
liable unless they have
validly disclaimed their
liability or have a valid
defense to the instrument

Drawers [26-3a]

A **drawer** of a draft orders the drawee to pay the instrument and does not expect to pay the draft personally. The drawer is obligated to pay the draft only if the drawee fails to pay the instrument. The drawer of an *unaccepted draft* is obligated to pay the instrument upon its dishonor according to its terms at the time it was issued or, in the case of an incomplete instrument, according to the rules discussed in Chapter 25. Under Revised Article 3, the drawer's liability is contingent only upon dishonor and does not require notice of dishonor. The drawer's obligation on an unaccepted draft is owed to a person entitled to enforce the instrument or to an indorser who paid the instrument under indorser's liability.

If the draft has been accepted and the acceptor is not a bank, the obligation of the drawer to pay the instrument is then contingent upon both dishonor of the instrument and notice of dishonor; the drawer's liability in this instance is equivalent to that of an indorser.

Davis v. Watson Brothers Plumbing, Inc.
Court of Civil Appeals of Texas, Dallas, 1981
615 S.W.2d 844
http://scholar.google.com/scholar_case?case=16807682647541897506&q=615+S.W.2d+844&hl=en&as_sdt=2,34

FACTS Arnett Lee presented a $152.38 check for cashing to the plaintiff, liquor store operator Troy Davis. After Davis gave Lee the cash, Lee requested a bottle of scotch and a six-pack of beer. As Davis turned to fill the order, a thief stole $110.00 of the $152.38. Lee immediately contacted the defendant-drawer of the check, Watson Brothers Plumbing, Inc., and notified them of the loss. The defendant (Watson) then issued another check for $152.38 and stopped payment on the first check held by Davis. Davis brought this action against Watson for the full amount of the check.

DECISION Judgment for Davis for $152.38.

OPINION Davis was the holder of the check, and Watson failed to raise any valid defense to enforcement of the check against it. Any party "who is in possession of … an instrument … indorsed to him … in blank" is a "holder." Since Lee indorsed the check in blank to Davis, Davis is a holder. The holder of a draft is entitled to receive its full amount from the drawer upon dishonor of the

check, unless the drawer has a valid defense to the holder's enforcement of the check against it. Watson argues that it may raise the defense of insufficiency or failure of consideration in the transaction between Davis and Lee. But the transfer of the check by Lee to Davis has no effect upon Watson's obligation to pay the check according to its tenor. "Consideration" is concerned with Lee's transaction with Watson, not with whether Davis gave anything in consideration for the check to Lee. Since Watson has no defense to enforcement of the check against Lee, it has no defense against Davis, regardless of whether Davis gave full consideration for the check.

INTERPRETATION The drawer's liability is contingent upon dishonor of the instrument.

CRITICAL THINKING QUESTION Should the drawer be permitted to raise defenses of other parties to the instrument? Explain.

Indorsers [26-3b]

An indorser promises that, upon dishonor of the instrument *and* notice of dishonor, she will pay the instrument according to the terms of the instrument at the time it was indorsed or, if an incomplete instrument when indorsed, according to its terms when completed, as discussed in Chapter 25. Once again, this obligation is owed to a person entitled to enforce the instrument or to a subsequent indorser who paid the instrument under indorser's liability.

Effect of Acceptance [26-3c]

When a *draft* is accepted by a *bank*, the drawer and all prior indorsers are discharged. The liability of indorsers subsequent to certification is not affected. When the bank accepts a draft, it should withhold from the drawer's account funds sufficient to pay the instrument. Because the bank is primarily liable on its acceptance and has the funds, whereas the drawer does not, the discharge is reasonable.

Effect of acceptance

when a draft is accepted by a bank, the drawer and all prior indorsers are discharged from contractual liability

Disclaimer of Liability by Secondary Parties [26-3d]

Both drawers and indorsers *may* disclaim their normal conditional liability by drawing or indorsing an instrument "*without recourse*." However, drawers of *checks* may not disclaim contractual liability. The use of the qualifying words *without recourse* is understood to place purchasers on notice that they may not rely on the credit of the person using this language. A person drawing or indorsing an instrument in this manner does not incur the normal contractual liability of a drawer or indorser to pay the instrument, but he may nonetheless be liable for breach of warranty.

Disclaimer by secondary parties

a drawer (except of a check) or indorser may disclaim liability by a qualified drawing or indorsing ("without recourse")

Conditions Precedent to Liability [26-3e]

A *condition precedent* is an event or events that must occur before liability arises. The condition precedent to the liability of the drawer of an *unaccepted* draft is dishonor. Conditions precedent to the liability of any indorser or the drawer of an *accepted* draft by a nonbank are dishonor and notice of dishonor. If the conditions to secondary liability are not met, a party's conditional obligation on the instrument is discharged, unless the conditions are excused.

Practical Advice

If you take an instrument from another party, make sure that she unqualifiedly indorses the instrument to add her liability to it.

Dishonor **Dishonor** generally involves the refusal to pay an instrument when it is presented. **Presentment** is a demand made by or on behalf of a person entitled to enforce the instrument for (1) *payment* by the drawee or other party obligated to pay the instrument or (2) *acceptance* by the drawee of a draft. The return of any instrument for lack of necessary indorsements or for failure of the presentment to comply with the terms of the instrument, however, is not a dishonor.

What constitutes dishonor varies depending on the type of instrument and whether presentment is required.

Dishonor

generally involves the refusal to pay an instrument when it is presented

Presentment

demand for payment or acceptance of an instrument

1. *Note:* A *demand note* is dishonored if the maker does not pay it on the day of presentment. If the note is payable at a *definite time* and (a) the terms of the note require presentment or (b) the note is payable at or through a bank, the note is dishonored if it is not paid on the date it is presented or its due date, whichever is later. All *other time notes* need not be presented and are dishonored if they are not paid on their due dates. Nevertheless, because makers are primarily liable on their notes, their liability is not affected by failure of proper presentment.

2. *Drafts:* An *unaccepted draft* (other than a check, discussed below) that is payable on *demand* is *dishonored* if presentment is made and it is not paid on the date presented. A *time draft* presented for *payment* is due on the due date or presentment date, whichever is later. A *time draft* presented for *acceptance* prior to its due date is dishonored if it is not accepted on the day presented. Refusal to *accept a demand instrument* is not a dishonor, although acceptance may be requested. Of course, if an instrument is payable at a certain time period after acceptance or sight, a refusal to accept the draft on the day presented is a dishonor.

An *accepted demand draft* is dishonored if the acceptor (who is primarily liable on the instrument) does not pay it on the day presented for payment. An *accepted time draft* is dishonored if it is not paid on the due date for payment or on the presentment date, whichever is later.

Drawers, with the exception of drafts accepted by a bank, are not discharged from liability by a delay in presentment. Once an instrument has been properly presented and dishonored, a drawer becomes liable to pay the instrument. As previously indicated, drawers and prior indorsers are discharged from liability when a draft is accepted by a bank.

3. *Checks:* If a check is presented for payment directly to the payor/drawee bank for immediate payment, a refusal to pay the check on the day presented constitutes dishonor. In the more common situation of a check being presented through the normal collection process, a check is dishonored if the payor bank makes timely return of the check, sends timely notice of dishonor or nonpayment, or becomes accountable for the amount of the check (until that payment has been made, the check is dishonored). As more fully explained in Chapter 27, under Article 4 a bank in most instances has a midnight deadline (before midnight of the next banking day) in which to decide whether to honor or dishonor an instrument. Thus, depending on the number of banks involved in the collection process, the time for dishonor can vary greatly.

Practical Advice

Make sure that you timely and properly present any negotiable instrument that you possess for acceptance or payment.

Delay in presentment discharges an *indorser* only if the instrument is a check and it is not presented for payment or given to a depositary bank for collection within thirty days after the day the indorsement was made. The same rule does not apply, however, to a drawer. If a person entitled to enforce a check fails to present a check within thirty days after its date, the drawer will be discharged only if the delay deprives the drawer of funds because of the suspension of payments by the drawee bank, such as would result from a bank failure. This discharge is quite unlikely because of federal bank insurance but would be available when an account is not fully insured because it exceeds $100,000 or because the account does not qualify for deposit insurance.

Messing v. Bank of America, N.A.
Court of Appeals of Maryland, 2003
373 Md. 672, 821 A.2d 22, 50 UCC Rep.Serv.2d 1
http://scholar.google.com/scholar_case?case=15792173749697893031 &q=821+A.2d+22&hl=en&as_sdt=2,34

FACTS Messing had a check in the amount of $976 from Toyson J. Burruss, the drawer. Instead of depositing the check into his bank account, Messing presented the check for payment at Mr. Burruss' bank, Bank of America, the drawee. The teller, by use of a computer, confirmed the availability of funds on deposit, and placed the check into the computer's printer slot. The computer stamped certain data on the back of the check, including the time, date, amount of the check, account number, and teller number. The computer also placed a hold on the amount of $976 in the customer's account. The teller gave the check back to the Messing, who indorsed it. The teller then asked for Messing's identification. He presented his driver's license and a major credit card.

At some point during the transaction, the teller counted out $976 in cash. She asked whether Messing was a customer of Bank of America. He stated that he was not. The teller returned the check to Messing and requested, consistent with bank policy when cashing checks for noncustomers, that he place his thumbprint on the check. Messing refused and the teller informed him that she would be unable to complete the transaction without his thumbprint. In response, the teller gave Messing back the check, released the hold on the customer's funds, voided the transaction in the computer, and replaced the cash.

Rather than take the check to his own bank and deposit it there, or return it to Burruss, Messing filed an action against Bank of America in the Circuit Court for Baltimore City. Messing claimed that the Bank had violated the Maryland UCC and had violated his personal privacy when the teller asked him to place an "inkless" thumbprint on the face of the check at issue.

The Circuit Court entered summary judgment in favor of the bank. The Court of Special Appeals upheld the Circuit Court's decision in favor of the bank. Messing petitioned this Court for a writ of *certiorari*, which was granted.

DECISION Judgment of the Court of Special Appeals is affirmed.

OPINION Under the UCC a check is simply an order to the drawee bank to pay the sum stated on demand. Receipt of a check does not, however, give the recipient a right against the bank. The recipient may present the check, but if the drawee bank refuses to honor it, the recipient has no recourse against the drawee.

Absent a special relationship, a noncustomer has no claim against a bank for refusing to honor a presented check. A check does not operate as an assignment of funds on deposit, and the bank only becomes obligated upon acceptance of the instrument. Once a bank accepts a check, it has primary obligation to pay the check.

Bank of America correctly argues that it did not "accept" the check. The mere fact that the teller's computer printed information on the back of the check does not, as Messing contends, amount by itself to an acceptance. The check was given back to Messing by the teller so that he could put his thumbprint signature on it, not to notify him of the purported acceptance. Thus there was never acceptance, and the bank never was obligated to pay the check.

If the thumbprint requirement is "reasonable," then the refusal of the bank to accept the check did not constitute dishonor. If, however, requiring a thumbprint is not "reasonable" then the refusal to accept the check may constitute dishonor. The issue of dishonor is relevant because Messing has no cause of action against any party, including the drawer, until the check is dishonored.

The Code itself, however, has recognized a thumbprint as a form of signature; therefore, requiring thumbprint or fingerprint identification has been found to be reasonable and not to violate privacy rights in a number of noncriminal contexts. As a result, Bank of America did not dishonor the check when it refused to accept it over the counter.

INTERPRETATION A bank is not required to accept a check from a noncustomer and, if it chooses to do so, is entitled to demand reasonable identification.

ETHICAL QUESTION Did the court fairly decide this case? Explain.

CRITICAL THINKING QUESTION What options may Messing now pursue? Explain.

Notice of Dishonor The obligation of an indorser of any instrument and of a drawer of a draft accepted by a nonbank is not enforceable unless the indorser or drawer is given notice of dishonor or the notice is otherwise excused. Thus, lack of proper notice discharges the liability of an indorser; for this purpose a drawer of a draft accepted by a party other than a bank is treated as an indorser. Notice of dishonor is *not* required to retain the liability of drawers of unaccepted drafts. In addition, as previously mentioned, a drawer is discharged when a draft is accepted by a *bank*. In short, a drawer's liability *usually* is not contingent upon receiving notice of dishonor, whereas an indorser's liability is.

Notice of dishonor is normally given by the holder or by an indorser who has received notice. For example, Michael makes a note payable to the order of Phyllis; Phyllis indorses it to Arthur; Arthur indorses it to Bambi; and Bambi indorses it to Henry, the last holder. Henry presents it to Michael within a reasonable time, but Michael refuses to pay. Henry may give notice of dishonor to all secondary parties: Phyllis, Arthur, and Bambi. If he is satisfied that Bambi will pay him or if he does not know how to contact Phyllis or Arthur, he may notify only Bambi, who then must see to it that Arthur or Phyllis is notified, or she will have no recourse. Bambi may notify either or both. If she notifies Arthur only, Arthur will have to see to it that Phyllis is notified, or Arthur will have no recourse. When properly given, notice benefits all parties who have rights on the instrument against the party notified. Thus, Henry's notification to Phyllis operates as notice to Phyllis by both Arthur and Bambi. Likewise, if Henry notifies only Bambi and Bambi notifies Arthur and Phyllis, then Henry has the benefit of Bambi's notification of Arthur and Phyllis. Nonetheless, it would be advisable for Henry to give notice to all prior parties because Bambi may be insolvent and thus may not bother to notify Arthur or Phyllis.

If, in the previous example, Henry were to notify Phyllis alone, Arthur and Bambi would be discharged. Because she has no claim against Arthur or Bambi, who indorsed after she did, Phyllis would have no ground for complaint. It cannot matter to Phyllis that she is compelled to pay Henry rather than Arthur. Therefore, subsequent parties are permitted to skip intermediate indorsers if they want to discharge them and are willing to look solely to prior indorsers for recourse.

Any necessary notice must be given by a *bank* before midnight on the *next* banking day following the banking day on which it receives notice of dishonor. Any *nonbank* with respect to an instrument taken for collection must give notice within thirty days following the day on which it received notice. In all other situations, notice of dishonor must be within thirty days following the day on which dishonor occurred. For instance, Donna draws a check on Youngstown Bank payable to the order of Pablo; Pablo indorses it to Andrea; Andrea deposits it to her account in Second Chicago National Bank; Second Chicago National Bank properly presents it to Youngstown Bank, the drawee; and Youngstown dishonors it because the drawer, Donna, has insufficient funds on deposit to cover it. Youngstown has until midnight of the following day to notify Second Chicago National,

Andrea, or Pablo of the dishonor. Second Chicago National then has until midnight on the day after receipt of notice of dishonor to notify Andrea or Pablo. That is, if Second Chicago National received the notice of dishonor on Monday, it would have until midnight on Tuesday to notify Andrea or Pablo. If it failed to notify Andrea, it could not charge the item back to her. Andrea, in turn, has thirty days after receipt of notice of dishonor to notify Pablo. Donna, a drawer of an unaccepted draft, is not discharged from liability for failure to receive notice of dishonor.

Practical Advice

Upon dishonor of any instrument that you have presented for payment or acceptance, give proper notice, wherever possible, to all prior parties.

Frequently, notice of dishonor is given by returning the unpaid instrument with an attached stamp, ticket, or memorandum stating that the item was not paid and requesting that the recipient make good on it. But because the purpose of notice is to give knowledge of dishonor and to inform the secondary party that he may be held liable on the instrument, any kind of notice that informs the recipient of potential liability is sufficient. No formal requisites are imposed—notice may be given by any commercially reasonable means, including oral, written, or electronic communication. An oral notice, while sufficient, is inadvisable because it may be difficult to prove. Notice of dishonor must reasonably identify the instrument.

Presentment and Notice of Dishonor Excused The Uniform Commercial Code (UCC) excuses *presentment* for payment or acceptance if (1) the person entitled to enforce the instrument cannot with reasonable diligence present the instrument; (2) the maker or acceptor of the instrument has repudiated the obligation to pay, is dead, or is in insolvency proceedings; (3) the terms of the instrument do not require presentment to hold the indorsers or drawer liable; (4) the drawer or indorser has waived the right of presentment; (5) the drawer instructed the drawee not to pay or accept the draft; or (6) the drawee was not obligated to the drawer to pay the draft.

Notice of dishonor is excused if the terms of the instrument do not require notice to hold the party liable or if notice has been waived by the party whose obligation is being enforced. Moreover, a waiver of presentment is also a waiver of notice of dishonor. Finally, delay in giving notice of dishonor is excused if the delay is caused by circumstances beyond the control of the person giving notice and that person exercised reasonable diligence in giving notice after the cause of the delay ceased to exist.

BUSINESS LAW **IN ACTION**

Checks made payable to "cash" are, by definition, bearer instruments. As such, they are negotiated by simple transfer of possession—their negotiation does not require an indorsement. Nonetheless, most banks instruct their tellers to obtain indorsements on all checks, including those made payable to Cash. Why?

Obtaining indorsements on all checks is a good policy for a bank to employ in order to enhance efficiency and to provide the bank extra protection in the collection process. This blanket policy makes the procedure for verifying indorsements routine, eliminating tellers' need to search the "Pay to" line on each check to ascertain whether a given check is made payable to Cash and therefore exempt from the indorsement

requirement. Further, if all checks are to be indorsed, then no *order* paper will accidentally go without indorsement.

Probably more important, though, is the bank's interest in protecting itself with the indorser liability rules. Every person who signs a check, including an indorser, is at least secondarily liable upon it. Unless an indorser qualified her indorsement by adding such language as "without recourse," she is liable to pay the check if it is dishonored.

In a worst-case scenario, the bank's customer deposits a check made payable (by a third party) to Cash, but the check is returned because the drawer's account has insufficient funds. Although the bank's depositor agreement with the customer

permits it to debit her account, her account may not have enough funds to cover the bounced check. If the dishonored check had been unqualifiedly indorsed by the customer, the bank can give notice of dishonor and seek payment from the customer's other assets by way of a lawsuit. The bank would not have this right of recourse if the check had not been unqualifiedly indorsed by the customer.

Putting sufficient funds on "hold" in the customer's account pending collection of third-party checks can provide some of the same protection. But none of these safeguards is foolproof, and several redundant policies are preferable to suffering the loss.

CONCEPT REVIEW 26-1

Contractual Liability

Party	Instrument	Liability	Conditions
Maker	Note	Unconditional	None
Acceptor	Draft	Unconditional	None
Drawer	Unaccepted draft	Conditional	Dishonor
	Draft accepted by a nonbank	Conditional	Dishonor and notice
	Cashier's check	Unconditional	None
	Draft drawn on drawer	Unconditional	None
	Draft accepted by a bank	None	
	Draft (not check) drawn without recourse	None	
Indorser	Note or draft	Conditional	Dishonor and notice
	Draft subsequently accepted by a bank	None	
	Note or draft indorsed without recourse	None	
Drawee	Draft	None	

Liability for conversion
conversion occurs (1) when an instrument is paid on a forged indorsement, (2) when a drawee refuses to return a draft that was presented for acceptance, or (3) when any person refuses to return an instrument after he dishonors it

Liability for Conversion [26-3f]

Conversion is a *tort* by which a person becomes liable in damages because of his wrongful control over the personal property of another. The law applicable to conversion of personal property applies to instruments. Revised Article 3 provides that "[a]n instrument is also converted if the instrument lacks an indorsement necessary for negotiation and it is purchased or taken for collection or the drawee takes the instrument and makes payment to a person not entitled to receive payment." Examples of conversion thus would include a drawee bank that pays an instrument containing a forged indorsement or a bank that pays an instrument containing only one of two required indorsements.

TERMINATION OF LIABILITY [26-4]

Eventually, every commercial transaction must end, terminating the potential liabilities of the parties to the instrument. The Code specifies the various methods by and extent to which the liability of *any* party, primary or secondary, is discharged. "**Discharge**" means that the obligated individual is released from liability on the instrument due to either Article 3 or contract law. The Code also specifies when the liability of *all* parties is discharged. No discharge of a party is effective against a subsequent holder in due course, however, unless she has notice of the discharge when taking the instrument. In addition, discharge of liability is not always final; liability under certain circumstances (e.g., coming into possession of a subsequent holder in due course) can be revived. Discharge applies to the individual and not the instrument, and discharge of individuals may occur at different points in time. Moreover, a person's liability may be discharged with regard to one party but not to another.

Effect of discharge
potential liability of parties to the instrument is terminated

Payment [26-4a]

The most obvious and common way for a party to discharge liability on an instrument is to pay a party entitled to enforce the instrument. An instrument is paid to the extent that payment is made by or for a person obligated to pay the instrument and to a person entitled to enforce the instrument. Subject to three exceptions, such payment results in a discharge even though it is

Practical Advice

The person making payment should take possession of the instrument or have it canceled—marked "paid" or "canceled"—so that it cannot pass to a subsequent holder in due course against whom his discharge would be ineffective.

made with knowledge of another person's claim to the instrument, unless such other person either supplies adequate indemnity or obtains an injunction in a proceeding to which the holder is made a party. It should be noted, however, that the discharge is only to the extent of the payment.

Tender of Payment [26-4b]

Any party liable on an instrument who makes proper tender of full payment to a person entitled to enforce the instrument when or after payment is due is discharged from liability for interest after the due date. If the party's tender is refused, she is not discharged from liability for the face amount of the instrument or for any interest accrued until the time of tender. Moreover, if an instrument requires presentment and the obligor is ready and able to pay the instrument when it is due at the place of payment specified in the instrument, such readiness is the equivalent of tender.

Occasionally a person entitled to enforce an instrument will refuse a tender of payment for reasons known only to himself. It may be that he believes his rights exceed the amount of the tender or that he desires to enforce payment against another party. In any event, his refusal of the tender wholly discharges to the extent of the amount of tender every party who has a right of recourse against the party making tender.

Cancellation and Renunciation [26-4c]

The Code provides that a person entitled to enforce an instrument may discharge the liability of any party to an instrument by an intentional voluntary act, such as by canceling the instrument or the signature of the party or parties to be discharged, by mutilating or destroying the instrument, by obliterating a signature, or by adding words indicating a discharge. A party entitled to enforce an instrument also may renounce his rights by a writing, signed and delivered, promising not to sue or otherwise renouncing rights against the party. Like other discharges, however, a written renunciation is of no effect against a subsequent holder in due course who takes the instrument without knowledge of the renunciation.

Cancellation or renunciation is effective even without consideration.

LIABILITY BASED ON WARRANTY

Article 3 imposes two types of implied warranties: (1) transferor's warranties and (2) presenter's warranties. Although these warranties are effective whether or not the transferor or presenter signs the instrument, the extension of the transferor's warranty to subsequent holders does depend on whether one or the other has indorsed the instrument. Like other warranties, these may be disclaimed by agreement between immediate parties. In the case of an indorser, his disclaimer of transfer warranties and presentment warranties must appear in the indorsement itself and be effective, except with respect to checks. Such disclaimers must be specific, such as "without warranty." The use of "without recourse" will only disclaim contract liability, not warranty liability.

Transferor's warranties
any person who transfers an instrument and receives consideration makes certain transferor's warranties

Beneficiary of transfer warranties
if the transfer is by delivery, the warranties run only to the immediate transferee; if the transfer is by indorsement, the warranties run to any subsequent holder who takes the instrument in good faith

Warranties on Transfer [26-5]

Any person who transfers an instrument, whether by negotiation or assignment, and receives *consideration* makes certain **transferor's warranties**. Any consideration sufficient to support a contract will support transfer warranties. If transfer is by delivery alone, warranties on transfer run only to the immediate transferee. If the transfer is made by indorsement, whether qualified or unqualified, the transfer warranty runs to "any subsequent transferee." Transfer means that the delivery of possession is voluntary. The warranties of the transferor are as follows.

Entitlement to Enforce [26-5a]

The first warranty that the Code imposes on a transferor is that the transferor is a person entitled to enforce the instrument. This warranty "is in effect a warranty that there are no unauthorized or missing indorsements that prevent the transferor from making the transferee a person entitled to enforce the instrument." The following example illustrates this rule. Mitchell makes a note payable to the order of Penelope. A thief steals the note from Penelope, forges Penelope's indorsement, and sells the instrument to Aaron. Aaron is not entitled to enforce the instrument because the break in the indorsement chain prevents him from being a holder. If Aaron transfers the instrument to Judith for consideration, Judith can hold Aaron liable for breach of warranty. The warranty action is important to Judith because it enables her to hold Aaron liable, even if Aaron indorsed the note "without recourse."

Authentic and Authorized Signatures [26-5b]

The second warranty imposed by the Code is that *all* signatures are authentic and authorized. In the previous example, this warranty also would be breached. If, however, the signature of a maker, drawer, drawee, acceptor, or indorser not in the chain of title is unauthorized, there is a breach of this warranty but no breach of the warranty of entitlement to enforce.

No Alteration [26-5c]

The third warranty is the warranty against alteration. Suppose that Maureen makes a note payable to the order of the payee in the amount of $100. The payee, without authority, alters the note so that it appears to be drawn for $1,000 and negotiates the instrument to Lois, who buys it without knowledge of the alteration. Lois, indorsing "without recourse," negotiates the instrument to Kyle for consideration. Kyle presents the instrument to Maureen, who refuses to pay more than $100 on it. Kyle can collect the difference from Lois, for although her qualified indorsement saves Lois from liability to Kyle on the indorsement contract, she is liable to him for breach of warranty. If Lois had not qualified her indorsement, Kyle would be able to recover against her on the basis of either warranty or the indorsement contract.

No Defenses [26-5d]

The fourth transferor's warranty imposed by the Code is that the instrument is not subject to a defense or claim in recoupment of any party. A claim in recoupment, as discussed in Chapter 25, is a counterclaim that arose from the transaction that gave rise to the instrument. Suppose that Madeline, a minor and a resident of a state where minors' contracts for nonnecessaries are voidable, makes a note payable to bearer in payment of a motorcycle. Pierce, the first holder, negotiates it to Iola by mere delivery. Iola indorses it and negotiates it to Justin, who unqualifiedly indorses it to Hector. All negotiations are made for consideration. Because of Madeline's minority (a real defense), Hector cannot recover upon the instrument against Iola. Hector therefore recovers against Justin or Iola on either the breach of warranty that no valid defenses exist to the instrument or the indorsement contract. Justin, if he is forced to pay Hector, can in turn recover against Iola on either a breach of warranty or the indorsement contract. Justin, however, cannot recover against Pierce. Pierce is not liable to Justin as an indorser because he did not indorse the instrument. Although Pierce, as a transferor, warrants that there are no defenses good against him, this warranty extends only to his immediate transferee, Iola. Therefore, Justin cannot hold Pierce liable. Iola, however, can recover from Pierce on either warranty or contract.

No Knowledge of Insolvency [26-5e]

Any person who transfers a negotiable instrument warrants that he has no knowledge of any insolvency proceedings instituted with respect to the maker, acceptor, or drawer of an unaccepted instrument. Insolvency proceedings include bankruptcy and "any assignment for the benefit of creditors or other proceedings intended to liquidate or rehabilitate the estate of the person involved." Thus, if Marcia makes a note payable to bearer, and the first holder, Taylor, negotiates it for consideration without indorsement to Ursula, who then negotiates it for consideration by qualified indorsement to Valerie, both Taylor and Ursula warrant that they do not know that Marcia is in bankruptcy. Valerie could not hold Taylor liable for breach of warranty, however, because Taylor's warranty runs only in favor of her immediate transferee, Ursula, because Taylor transferred the instrument without indorsement. If Valerie could hold Ursula liable on her warranty, Ursula could thereupon hold Taylor, her immediate transferor, liable. Figure 26-1 summarizes liabilities on transfer.

Figure 26-1 Liability on Transfer

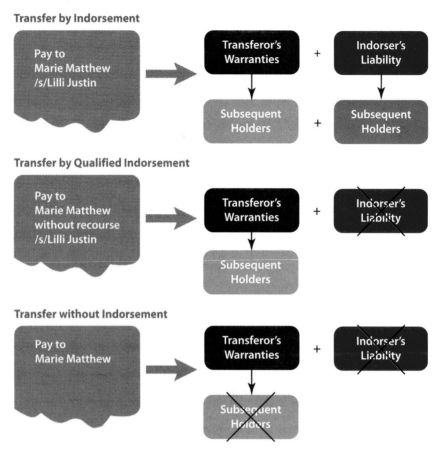

Warranties on presentment

all people who obtain payment or acceptance of an instrument as well as all prior transferors give the presenter's warranties

WARRANTIES ON PRESENTMENT [26-6]

Any party who pays or accepts an instrument must do so in strict compliance with the orders that instrument contains. For example, the payment or acceptance must be made to a person entitled to receive payment or acceptance, the amount paid or accepted must be the correct amount, and the instrument must be genuine and unaltered. If the payment or acceptance is incorrect, the payor or acceptor potentially will incur a loss. In the case of a note, a maker who pays the wrong person will not be discharged from his obligation to pay the correct person. If the maker pays too much, the excess comes out of his pocket. If a drawee pays the wrong person, he generally cannot charge the drawer's account; if the drawee pays too much, he generally cannot charge the drawer's account for the excess. Indorsers who pay an instrument may make similar incorrect payments.

After paying or accepting an instrument to the wrong person, for the wrong amount, or in some other incorrect way, does the person who incorrectly paid or accepted have any recourse against the person who received the payment or acceptance? The Code addresses this critical question by providing that

> [I]f an instrument has been paid or accepted by mistake … the person paying or accepting may recover the amount paid or revoke acceptance to the extent allowed by the law governing mistake and restitution.

Nevertheless, this payment or acceptance is *final* and may not be asserted against a person who took the instrument in good faith and for value or who in good faith changed position in reliance on the payment or acceptance, unless there has been a breach of the implied ***warranties*** *on presentment*. What warranties are given by presenters depend upon who is the payor or acceptor. The greatest protection is given to drawees of unaccepted drafts, while all other payors receive significantly less protection.

Drawees of Unaccepted Drafts [26-6a]

A drawee of an unaccepted draft (including uncertified checks), who pays or accepts in good faith, receives a presentment warranty from the person obtaining payment or acceptance and from all prior transferors of the draft. These parties warrant to the drawee making payment or accepting the draft in good faith that (1) the warrantor is a person entitled to enforce the draft, (2) the draft has not been altered, and (3) the warrantor has no knowledge that the drawer's signature is unauthorized.

Beneficiary of presentment warranties the presenter's warranties run to any person who in good faith pays or accepts an instrument

Entitled to Enforce
Presenters of unaccepted checks give the same warranty of entitlement to enforce to persons who pay or accept as is granted to transferees under the transferor's warranty. Thus, the presenter warrants that she is a person entitled to enforce the instrument. As explained above, this warranty extends to the genuineness and completeness of the indorser's signatures but not to the signature of the drawer or maker. It is "in effect a warranty that there are no unauthorized or missing indorsements."

For example, if Donnese draws a check to Peter or order, and Peter's indorsement is forged, the bank does not follow Donnese's order in paying such an item and therefore cannot charge her account (except in the impostor or fictitious payee situations discussed in Chapter 25). The bank, however, can recover for breach of the presenter's warranty of entitlement to enforce the instrument from the person who obtained payment of the check from the bank. Although it should know the signatures of its own customers, the bank should not be expected to know the signatures of payees or other indorsers of checks; the bank, therefore, should not have to bear this loss.

No Alteration
Presenters also give a warranty of no alteration. For example, if Dolores makes a check payable to Porter's order in the amount of $30, and the amount is fraudulently raised to $30,000, the drawee bank cannot charge to the drawer's account the $30,000 it pays out on the check. The drawee bank can charge the drawer's account only $30.00, because that is all the drawer ordered it to pay. Nonetheless, because the presenter's warranty of no alteration has been breached, the drawee bank can collect the difference from all warrantors.

Genuineness of Drawer's Signature
Presenters lastly warrant that they have no knowledge that the signature of the drawer is unauthorized. Thus, unless the presenter has knowledge that the drawer's signature is unauthorized, the drawee bears the risk that the drawer's signature is unauthorized.

Figure 26-2 summarizes liabilities based on warranty.

Travelers Indemnity Co. v. Stedman
U.S. District Court, Eastern District of Pennsylvania, 1995
895 F.Supp. 742, 27 UCC Rep.Serv.2d 1347
http://scholar.google.com/scholar_case?case=3305267280758542845&q=27+UCC+Rep.+Serv.2d+1347&hl=en&as_sdt=2,34

FACTS In November 1988, the plaintiff, Travelers Indemnity Co., issued a comprehensive crime insurance policy to the American Lung Association (ALA), insuring the ALA against financial losses due to employee fraud or dishonesty. In October of 1989, the ALA hired the defendant, Nancy Stedman, as the Director of Bureau Affairs. In this capacity, Stedman embezzled $129,624.23 of ALA funds by writing seventeen checks against the ALA's account with Merrill, Lynch, Pierce, Fenner & Smith (Merrill Lynch). Stedman deposited six of these checks into her personal checking account with the other defendant, Main Line Federal Savings Bank. The checks were subsequently presented to and

honored by Merrill Lynch. These checks bore two forged drawer's signatures and at least one forged indorsement. To recover its losses in paying the ALA's insurance claim, Travelers sued Stedman, Main Line, and Merrill Lynch. Merrill Lynch subsequently advanced a claim for breach of presentment warranties against Main Line. Main Line seeks judgment on the pleadings or partial summary judgment on Merrill Lynch's claims.

DECISION Judgment for Main Line.

OPINION Liability or loss allocation, under the UCC, for honoring negotiable instruments containing forged or unauthorized signatures is governed by whether the forgery at issue is that of a drawer's signature or of the indorsement of a payee or holder. Generally, a drawee bank is strictly liable to its customer, the drawer, for payment over either a forged drawer's signature or a forged indorsement. Moreover, when a drawee bank honors an instrument bearing a forged drawer's signature, that payment is final in favor of a holder in due course or one who has in good faith changed his position in reliance on the payment. As a result, when the only forgery is of the signature of the drawer and not of the indorsement, the negligence of a holder in taking the forged instrument will not allow a drawee bank to shift liability to a prior collecting or depositary bank, unless such negligence amounts to a lack of good faith, or unless the payee bank returns the instrument or sends notice of dishonor within the limited time provided. However, when the only forged signature is an indorsement, the drawee normally may pass liability back through the collection chain to the depositary or collecting bank, or to the forger herself if she is available, by a claim for breach of presentment warranties.

Regrettably, the drafters of the UCC failed to address the allocation of liability for honoring instruments containing both a forged drawer's signature and a forged indorsement, so-called double forgeries. However, court decisions have concluded that double forgeries should be treated as though only containing forged drawer's signatures. The loss incurred would be the result of the drawee bank paying the check over the forged drawer's signature. Therefore, under the UCC, checks containing both a forged drawer's signature and a forged indorsement should be treated, for loss allocation purposes, as though bearing only a forged drawer's signature. Thus, because it is uncontested that all of the checks at issue bear forged drawer's signatures, liability for honoring these checks is assessed under the loss allocation rules relevant to checks bearing only forged drawer's signatures. Therefore, Merrill Lynch is precluded by the operation of law from asserting a claim for breach of presentment warranties under the loss allocation scheme of the UCC.

INTERPRETATION Checks containing both a forged drawer's signature and a forged indorsement should be treated, for loss allocation purposes, as though bearing only a forged drawer's signature; the presentment warranties extend to the genuineness of the indorser's signatures but not to the signature of the drawer.

CRITICAL THINKING QUESTION Should the warranties for negotiable instruments treat the forgeries of drawers' signatures differently from those of indorsers? Explain.

Figure 26-2 Liability Based on Warranty

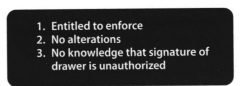

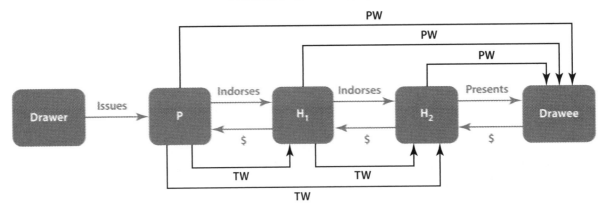

All Other Payors [26-6b]

In all instances other than a drawee of an unaccepted draft or uncertified check, the only present-ment warranty that is given is that the warrantor is a person entitled to enforce the instrument or is authorized to obtain payment on behalf of the person entitled to enforce the instrument. This warranty is given by the person obtaining payment and prior transferors and applies to the presentment of notes and accepted drafts for the benefit of any party obliged to pay the instru-ment, including an indorser. It also applies to presentment of dishonored drafts if made to the drawer or an indorser.

The warranties of no alteration and authenticity of the drawer's signature are not given to all other payors. These warranties are not necessary for makers and drawers as they should know their own signatures and the terms of their instruments. Similarly, indorsers have already war-ranted the authenticity of signatures and that the instrument was not altered. Finally, acceptors should know the terms of the instrument when they accepted it; moreover, they did receive the full presentment warranties when they as drawees accepted the draft upon presentment.

ETHICAL DILEMMA

Who Gets to Pass the Buck on a Forged Indorsement?

Facts Tom West goes to Libertyville Currency Exchange to cash a check for $3,525. The check belongs to West's friend, John Reston, who accompanies him. The check is a certified check drawn on NationsBank and made payable to the order of "Piscitello Enterprises, Inc." and indorsed on the reverse side by "Joe Piscitello."

Because West often transacts business at the currency exchange, the clerk, Rita Bosworth, recognizes him as soon as he walks in. West indorses the check and hands it to Bosworth, who dispenses the cash. West immediately turns to Reston, giving him some money.

Later, Libertyville Currency Exchange deposits the check with First National Bank, which eventually files a claim against the currency exchange because the indorsement "Joe Piscitello" has been forged. The currency exchange pays the claim, then brings an action against West.

During the trial, Bosworth testifies that she saw Reston hand some money back to West when the two men turned away from her. West vehemently denies this. He says that he received no money in exchange for helping Reston.

Libertyville Currency Exchange claims that West breached his warranty of good title under the transferor's warranty by obtaining payment for a check on which the payee's indorsement was forged. West, on the other hand, argues that he signed the check to lend his name to another party and that he is thus an accommodation party. He maintains that he is not liable to Libertyville Currency Exchange because NationsBank did not give him timely notice that the signature on the check was forged and also because

the Currency Exchange paid the check, thus releasing him from liability as an accommodation indorser.

Social, Policy, and Ethical Considerations

1. How could the bank have prevented this problem? Is a clerk responsible for knowing exactly who is cashing a check and who gave value for it? What steps, if any, could Rita Bosworth have taken to verify the check's indorsements?

2. Did Tom West have a responsibility to ensure that his friend's check was legitimate? Should he have inquired about the indorsement?

3. What issues relating to the transfer of a negotiable instrument are involved here? What liability does the bank face? What liability does Tom West face? What warranties apply to each party?

CHAPTER SUMMARY

Contractual Liability

General Principles   **Liability on the Instrument** no person has contractual liability on an instrument unless her signature appears on it

Signature a signature may be made by the individual herself or by her authorized agent

- *Authorized Signatures* an agent who executes a negotiable instrument on behalf of his principal is not liable if the instrument is executed properly and as authorized

- *Unauthorized Signatures* include forgeries and signatures made by an agent without proper power; are generally not binding on the person whose name appears on the instrument but are binding on the unauthorized signer

Liability of Primary Parties	**Primary Liability** absolute obligation to pay a negotiable instrument
	Makers the maker guarantees that he will pay the note according to its original terms
	Acceptors a drawee has no liability on the instrument until she accepts it; the drawee then becomes primarily liable
	• *Acceptance* a drawee's signed engagement to honor the instrument
	• *Certification* acceptance of a check by a bank
Liability of Secondary Parties	**Secondary (Conditional) Liability** obligation to pay a negotiable instrument that is subject to conditions precedent
	Indorsers and Drawers if the instrument is not paid by a primary party and if the conditions precedent to the liability of secondary parties are satisfied, indorsers and drawers are secondarily (conditionally) liable unless they have disclaimed their liability or have a valid defense to the instrument
	Effect of Acceptance when a draft is accepted by a bank, the drawer and all prior indorsers are discharged from contractual liability
	Disclaimer by Secondary Parties a drawer (except of a check) or indorser may disclaim liability by a qualified drawing or indorsing ("without recourse")
	Conditions Precedent to Liability
	• *Drawer* liability is generally contingent only upon dishonor and does not require notice
	• *Indorser* liability is contingent upon dishonor and notice of dishonor
Liability of Conversion	**Tort Liability** conversion occurs (1) when an instrument is paid on a forged indorsement, (2) when a drawee refuses to return a draft that was presented for acceptance, or (3) when any person refuses to return an instrument after he dishonors it
Termination of Liability	**Effect of Discharge** potential liability of parties to the instrument is terminated
	Discharge
	• *Performance*
	• *Tender of Payment* for interest, costs, and attorneys' fees
	• *Cancellation*
	• *Renunciation*

Liability Based on Warranty

Warranties on Transfer	**Parties**
	• *Warrantor* any person who transfers an instrument and receives consideration makes certain transferor's warranties
	• *Beneficiary* if the transfer is by delivery, the warranties run only to the immediate transferee; if the transfer is by indorsement, the warranties run to any subsequent holder who takes the instrument in good faith
	Warranties
	• *Entitled to Enforce*
	• *All Signatures Are Authentic and Authorized*
	• *No Alteration*
	• *No Defenses*
	• *No Knowledge of Insolvency*
Warranties on Presentment	**Parties**
	• *Warrantors* all people who obtain payment or acceptance of an instrument as well as all prior transferors give the presenter's warranties
	• *Beneficiary* the presenter's warranties run to any person who in good faith pays or accepts an instrument
	Warranties
	• *Entitled to Enforce*
	• *No Alteration*
	• *Genuineness of Drawer's Signature*

QUESTIONS

1.

November 15, 2015

The undersigned promises to pay to the order of John Doe, Nine Hundred Dollars with interest from date of note. Payment to be made in five monthly installments of One Hundred Eighty Dollars, plus accrued interest beginning on December 1, 2015. In the event of default in the payment of any installment or interest on installment date, the holder of this instrument may declare the entire obligation due and owing and proceed forthwith to collect the balance due on this instrument.

(signed) Acton, agent

On December 18, 2015, no payment having been made on the note, Doe indorsed and delivered the instrument to Todd to secure a preexisting debt in the amount of $800.

On January 18, 2016, Todd brought an action against Acton and Phi Corporation, Acton's principal, to collect the full amount of the instrument with interest. Acton defended on the basis that he signed the instrument in a representative capacity and that Doe had failed to deliver the consideration for which the instrument had been issued. Phi Corporation defended on the basis that it did not sign the instrument and that its name does not appear on the instrument.

For what amount, if any, are Acton and Phi Corporation liable?

2. While employed as a night watchman at the place of business of A. B. Cate Trucking Company, Fred Fain observed that the office safe had been left unlocked. It contained fifty payroll checks, which were ready for distribution to employees two days later. The checks had all been signed by the sole proprietor, Cate. Fain removed five of these checks and two blank checks that were also in the safe. Fain forged the indorsements of the payees on the five payroll checks and cashed them at local supermarkets. He then filled out one of the blank checks, making himself payee, and forged Cate's signature as drawer. After cashing that check at a supermarket, Fain departed by airplane to Jamaica. The six checks were promptly presented for payment to the drawee bank, the Bank of Emanon, which paid each one. Shortly thereafter, Cate learned about the missing payroll checks and forgeries and demanded that the Bank of Emanon credit his account with the amount of the six checks.

Must the Bank comply with Cate's demand? What are the Bank's rights, if any, against the supermarkets? You may assume that the supermarkets cashed all of the checks in good faith.

3. A negotiable promissory note executed and delivered by B to C passed in due course to and was indorsed in blank by C, D, E, and F.

G, the present holder, strikes out D's indorsement. What is the liability of D on her indorsement?

4. On June 15, 2007, Joanne, for consideration, executed a negotiable promissory note for $10,000, payable to Robert on or before June 15, 2015. Joanne subsequently suffered financial reverses. In January 2015, Robert, on two occasions, told Joanne that he knew she was having a difficult time, that he, Robert, did not need the money, and that the debt should be

considered completely canceled with no other act or payment being required. These conversations were witnessed by three persons, including Larry. On March 15, 2015, Robert changed his mind and indorsed the note for value to Larry. The note was not paid by June 15, 2015, and Larry sued Joanne for the amount of the note. Joanne defended on the ground that Robert had canceled the debt and renounced all rights against Joanne and that Larry had notice of this fact. Has the debt been properly canceled? Explain.

5. Tate and Fitch were longtime friends. Tate was a man of considerable means; Fitch had encountered financial difficulties. To bolster his failing business, Fitch desired to borrow $60,000 from Farmers Bank of Erehwon. To accomplish this, he persuaded Tate to aid him in the making of a promissory note by which it would appear that Tate had the responsibility of maker, but with Fitch's agreeing to pay the instrument when due. Accordingly, they executed the following instrument:

December 1, 2015

Thirty days after date and for value received, I promise to pay to the order of Frank Fitch the sum of $60,000.

(signed) Timothy Tate

On the back of the note, Fitch indorsed, "Pay to the order of Farmers Bank of Erehwon /s/ Frank Fitch" and delivered it to the bank in exchange for $60,000.

a. When the note was not paid at maturity, may the bank, without first demanding payment by Fitch, recover in an action on the note against Tate?

b. If Tate voluntarily pays the note to the bank, may he then recover on the note against Fitch, who appears as an indorser?

6. Alpha orally appointed Omega as his agent to find and purchase for him a 1930 Dodge automobile in good condition, and Omega located such a car. Its owner, Roe, agreed to sell and deliver the car on January 10, 2015, for $9,000. To evidence the purchase price, Omega mailed to Roe the following instrument:

December 1, 2015

We promise to pay to the order of bearer $9,000 with interest from date of this instrument on or before January 10, 2015. This note is given in consideration of John Roe's transferring title to and possession of his 1930 Dodge automobile.

(signed) Omega, agent

Smith stole the note from Roe's mailbox, indorsed Roe's name on the note, and promptly discounted it with Sunset Bank for $8,700. Not having received the note, Roe sold the car to a third party. On January 10, 2015, the bank, having discovered all the facts, demanded payment of the note from Alpha and Omega. Both refused payment.

a. What are Sunset Bank's rights with regard to Alpha and Omega?

b. What are Sunset Bank's rights with regard to Roe and Smith?

7. In payment of the purchase price of a used motorboat that had been fraudulently misrepresented, Young signed and delivered to Armstrong his negotiable note in the amount of $2,000 due October 1, with Selby as an accommodation co-maker. Young intended to use the boat for his fishing business. Armstrong indorsed the note in blank preparatory to discounting it. Tillman stole the note from Armstrong and delivered it to McGowan on July 1 in payment of a past-due debt in the amount of $600 that he owed to McGowan, with McGowan making up the difference by giving Tillman his check for $800 and an oral promise to pay Tillman an additional $600 on October 1.

When McGowan demanded payment of the note on December 1, both Young and Selby refused to pay the note because the note had not been presented for payment on its due date and because Armstrong had fraudulently misrepresented the motorboat for which the note had been executed.

What are McGowan's rights, if any, against Young, Selby, Tillman, and Armstrong, respectively?

8. On July 1, Anderson sold D'Aveni, a jeweler, a necklace containing imitation gems, which Anderson fraudulently represented to be diamonds. In payment for the necklace, D'Aveni executed and delivered to Anderson her promissory note for $25,000 dated July 1 and payable on December 1 to Anderson's order with interest at 12 percent per annum.

The note was thereafter successively indorsed in blank and delivered by Anderson to Bylinski, by Bylinski to Conrad, and by Conrad to Shearson, who became a holder in due course on August 10. On November 1, D'Aveni discovered Anderson's fraud and immediately notified Anderson, Bylinski, Conrad, and Shearson that she would not pay the note when it became due. Bylinski, a friend of Shearson, requested that Shearson release him from liability on the note, and Shearson, as a favor to Bylinski and for no other consideration, struck out Bylinski's indorsement.

On November 15, Shearson, who was solvent and had no creditors, indorsed the note to the order of Frederick, his father, and delivered it to Frederick as a gift. At the same time, Shearson told Frederick of D'Aveni's statement that D'Aveni would not pay the note when it became due. Frederick presented the note to D'Aveni for payment on December 1, but D'Aveni refused to pay. Thereafter, Frederick gave due notice of dishonor to Anderson, Bylinski, and Conrad.

What are Frederick's rights, if any, against Anderson, Bylinski, Conrad, and D'Aveni on the note?

CASE PROBLEMS

9. R & A Concrete Contractors, Inc., executed a promissory note that identifies both R & A Concrete and Grover Roberts as its makers. On the reverse side of the note, the following appears: "X John Ament Sec. & Treas." National Bank of Georgia, the payee, now sues both R & A Concrete and Ament on the note. What rights does National Bank have against R & A and Ament?

10. On August 10, 2013, Theta Electronic Laboratories, Inc. executed a promissory note to George and Marguerite Thomson. Six other individuals, Gerald Exten, Emil O'Neil, and James Hane, and their wives also indorsed the note. The Thomsons then transferred the note to Hane on November 26, 2015. Although a default occurred at this time, it was not until April 2016 that Hane gave notice of the dishonor and made a demand for payment on the Extens as indorsers. Are the Extens liable under their indorser's liability?

11. Attorney Eliot Disner tendered a check for $100,100 to Sidney and Lynne Cohen. In drawing the check, Disner was serving as an intermediary for his clients, Irvin and Dorothea Kipnes, who owed the money to the Cohens as part of a settlement agreement. The Kipneses had given Disner checks totaling $100,100, which he had deposited into his professional corporation's client trust account. After confirming with the Kipneses' bank that their account held sufficient funds, Disner wrote and delivered a trust account check for $100,100 to the Cohens' attorney, with this note: "Please find $100,100 in settlement (partial) of *Cohen v. Kipnes*, et al[.] Per our agreement, delivery to you constitutes timely delivery to your clients." Also typed on the check was a notation identifying the underlying lawsuit. Without Disner's knowledge, the Kipneses stopped payment on their checks, leaving insufficient funds in the trust account to cover the check to the Cohens. The trust account check therefore was not paid due to insufficient funds; the Kipneses declared bankruptcy; and the Cohens served Disner and his professional corporation with demand for payment. The Cohens sought the amount written on the check plus a $500 statutory penalty. Explain who should prevail and why.

TAKING SIDES

Saul sold goods to Bruce, warranting that the goods were of a specified quality. The goods were not of the quality warranted, however, and Saul knew this at the time of the sale. Bruce drew and delivered a check payable to Saul and drawn on Third National Bank in the amount of the purchase price. Bruce subsequently discovered the goods were faulty and stopped payment on the check. Third National refused to pay Saul on the check.

a. What are the arguments that Saul can recover (1) from Bruce and (2) from Third National?

b. What are the arguments that (1) Bruce should prevail? and (2) Third National should prevail?

c. Who should prevail? Why?

Bank Deposits, Collections, and Funds Transfers

CHAPTER 27

Money is a poor man's credit card.

Marshall McLuhan
Maclean's (June 1971)

CHAPTER OUTCOMES

After reading and studying this chapter, you should be able to:

1. Identify and explain the various stages of and parties to the collection of a check.

2. Identify and explain the duties of collecting banks.

3. Explain the relationship between a payor bank and its customers.

4. Define a consumer electronic funds transfer, identify the various types of electronic funds transfers, and outline the major provisions of the Electronic Funds Transfer Act.

5. Explain wholesale fund transfers and discuss how they operate.

I n twenty-first-century society, most goods and services are bought and sold without a physical transfer of cash. In some sales, credit is extended by the seller or a third party. In other sales, a noncash payment is made either by *paper* (checks and drafts) or *electronically* (debit cards, credit cards, automated clearinghouse [ACH], and prepaid cards). But even credit sales ultimately must be settled—when they are, payment is frequently made by check. When a check is issued, if the parties to the transaction happen to have accounts at the same bank, settlement of the check is easily accomplished. In the vast majority of checks, however, the parties have accounts at different banks. In those cases, the buyer's check must journey from the seller-payee's bank (the depositary bank), where the check is deposited by the seller for credit to his account, and then to the buyer-drawer's bank (the payor bank) for payment. In this collection process, the check frequently passes through one or more other banks (intermediary banks), each of which must accurately record its passing, before it may be collected. The U.S. banking system has developed a network to handle the collection of checks and other instruments.

In recent years, payments made by electronic funds transfers have increased at an astounding rate. The dollar amount of commercial payments made by wire transfer far exceeds the dollar amount made by checks or credit cards. In addition, electronic funds transfers have become increasingly popular with consumers. Consumer electronic funds transfers are covered by the federal Electronic Funds Transfer Act (EFTA); nonconsumer (wholesale) electronic transfers are covered by Article 4A of the Uniform Commercial Code (UCC).

This chapter will cover both the bank deposit-collection system and electronic funds transfers.

BANK DEPOSITS AND COLLECTIONS

Article 4 of the UCC, entitled "Bank Deposits and Collections," provides the principal rules governing the bank collection process. In 2002, the American Law Institute and the Uniform Law Commission completed updates to Article 4. At least eleven states have adopted the 2002 version. This part of the text will discuss the pre-2002 Article 4.

The end result of the collection process is either the payment of the check or the dishonor (refusal to pay) of the check by the drawee bank. As items in the bank collection process are essentially those covered by Article 3, "Commercial Paper," and to a lesser extent by Article 8, "Investment Securities," these Articles often apply to a bank collection problem. In addition, Articles 3 and 4 are supplemented and, at times, preempted by Federal law: the Expedited Funds Availability Act and its implementing Federal Reserve Regulation (Regulation CC). This section will cover the collection of an item through the banking system and the relationship between the payor bank and its customer.

COLLECTION OF ITEMS [27-1]

Depositary bank
the bank in which the payee or holder deposits the check for credit

When a person deposits a check in his bank (the **depositary bank**), the bank credits the individual's account by the amount of the check. This initial crediting is **provisional**. Normally, a bank does not permit a customer to draw funds against a provisional credit; by permitting its customer to thus draw, the bank will have given *value* and, provided it meets the other requirements, will be a holder in due course. Under the customer's contract with his bank, the bank is obligated to make a reasonable effort to obtain payment of all checks deposited for collection. When the amount of the check has been collected from the payor bank (the drawee), the credit becomes a **final credit**.

Provisional credit
tentative credit for the deposit of an instrument until final credit is given

Final credit
payment of the instrument by the payor bank; if the payor bank (drawee) does not pay the check, the depositary bank reverses the provisional credit

The Expedited Funds Availability Act has established maximum time periods for which a bank may hold (and thereby deny a customer access to the funds represented by) various types of instruments. Under the Act, (1) cash deposits, wire transfers, an ACH credit, government checks, the first $100 of a day's check deposits, cashier's checks, and checks deposited in one branch of a depositary institution and drawn on the same or another branch of the same institution must clear by the next business day; (2) local checks must clear within one intervening business day; and (3) nonlocal checks must clear in no more than four intervening business days.

If the payor bank (the drawee bank) does not pay the check for some reason, such as a stop payment order or insufficient funds in the drawer's account, the depositary bank reverses the provisional credit to the account, debits his account for that amount, and returns the check to him with a statement of the reason for nonpayment. If, in the meantime, the customer has been permitted to draw against the provisional credit, the bank may recover the payment from him.

Intermediary bank
a bank, other than the depositary or payor bank, involved in the collection process

In some cases, the bank involved is both the depositary bank and the payor bank. In most cases, however, the depositary and payor banks are different, in which event the bank collection aspects of Article 4 come into play. When the depositary and payor banks differ, it is necessary for the item to pass from one to the other, either directly through a clearinghouse or through one or more **intermediary banks** (banks, other than the depositary or payor bank, that are involved in the collection process, such as one of the twelve Federal Reserve Banks), as illustrated in Figure 27-1. A **clearinghouse** is an association, composed of banks or other payors, whose members settle accounts with each other on a daily basis. Each member of the clearinghouse forwards all deposited checks drawn on other members and receives from the clearinghouse all checks drawn on it. Balances are adjusted and settled each day.

Clearinghouse
an association of banks for the purpose of settling accounts on a daily basis

Collecting Banks [27-1a]

Collecting bank
any bank (other than the payor bank) handling the item for payment

A **collecting bank** is any bank, other than the payor bank, handling an item for payment. In the usual situation, when the depositary and payor banks are different, the depositary bank gives a provisional credit to its customer, transfers the item to the next bank in the chain, and receives a provisional credit or "settlement" from it; the process repeats until the item reaches the payor bank, which gives a provisional settlement to its transferor. When the item is paid, all the provisional settlements given by the respective banks in the chain become final, and the particular transaction has been completed. Because this procedure simplifies bookkeeping by necessitating only one entry if the item is paid, no adjustment is necessary on the books of any of the banks involved.

Figure 27-1 Bank Collections

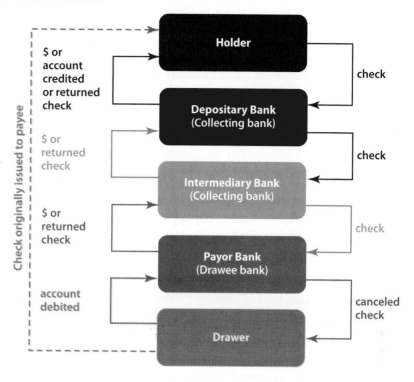

If, however, the payor bank does not pay the check, it returns the item, and each intermediary or collecting bank reverses the provisional settlement or credit it previously gave to its forwarding bank. Ultimately, the depositary bank will charge (remove the provisional credit from) the account of the customer who deposited the item. The customer must then seek recovery from the indorsers or the drawer.

A collecting bank is an **agent** or subagent of the owner of the item until the settlement becomes final. Unless otherwise provided, any credit given for the item initially is provisional. Once settled, the agency relationship changes to one of *debtor–creditor*. The effect of this agency rule is that the risk of loss remains with the owner and that any chargebacks go to her, not to the collecting bank.

All collecting banks have certain responsibilities and duties in collecting checks and other items. These will now be discussed.

Duty of Care A collecting bank must exercise ordinary care in handling an item transferred to it for collection. The steps it takes in presenting an item or sending it for presentment are of particular importance. It must act within a reasonable time after receipt of the item and must choose a reasonable method of forwarding the item for presentment. It also is responsible for using care in routing and in selecting intermediary banks or other agents.

Duty to Act Timely Closely related to the collecting bank's duty of care is its duty to act in a timely manner. A collecting bank acts timely in any event if it takes proper action, such as forwarding or presenting an item before the "midnight deadline" following its receipt of the item, notice, or payment. If the bank adheres to this standard, the timeliness of its action cannot be challenged; should it, however, take a reasonably longer time, the bank bears the burden of proof in establishing timeliness. The **midnight deadline** is the midnight of the banking day following the banking day on which the bank received the item or notice. Thus, if a bank receives a check on Monday, it must take proper action by midnight on the next banking day, or Tuesday. A banking day means the part of a day on which a bank is open to the public for carrying on substantially all of its banking functions.

Agent collecting bank
is an agent or subagent of the owner of the check until the settlement becomes final

Duty of care
a collecting bank must exercise ordinary care in handling an item

Duty to act timely
a collecting bank acts timely if it takes proper action before its midnight deadline (midnight of the next banking day)

Midnight deadline
midnight of the next banking day after receiving an item

The midnight deadline presents a problem because it takes time to process an item through a bank—whether it be the depositary, intermediary, or payor bank. If a day's transactions are to be completed without overtime work, the bank must either close early or fix an earlier cutoff time for the day's work. Accordingly, the Code provides that for the purpose of allowing time to process items, prove balances, and make the bookkeeping entries necessary to determine its position for the day, a bank may fix an afternoon hour of 2:00 P.M. or later as a cutoff point for handling money and items and for making entries on its books. Items received after the cutoff hour fixed as the close of the banking day are considered to have been received at the opening of the next banking day, and the time for taking action and for determining the bank's midnight deadline begins to run from that point.

Recognizing that everyone involved will be greatly inconvenienced if an item is not paid, the Code provides that unless otherwise instructed, a collecting bank in a good faith effort to secure payment may, in the case of a specific item drawn on a payor other than a bank, waive, modify, or extend the time limits, but not in excess of two additional banking days. This extension may be made without the approval of the parties involved and without discharging drawers or indorsers. This section does not apply to checks and other drafts drawn on a bank. The Code also authorizes delay when communications or computer facilities are interrupted as a result of

Honeycutt v. Honeycutt
Court of Special Appeals of Maryland, 2002
150 Md.App. 604; 822 A.2d 551; *cert. denied*, 376 Md. 544, 831 A.2d 4 (2003)
http://scholar.google.com/scholar_case?case=5046934000539878822&q=822+A.2d+551&hl=en&as_sdt=2,22

FACTS Ron Honeycutt was the president, treasurer, and sole stockholder of Sheldon, Inc. (Sheldon's Lounge), a bar located in Baltimore City. Christine Honeycutt was, at one time, Ron Honeycutt's wife and held the position of vice president and secretary of Sheldon. On July 1, 1984, Ron Honeycutt and Christine Honeycutt opened a business checking account with Maryland National Bank, now Bank of America, in the name of Sheldon's Lounge. At that time, Ron Honeycutt and Christine Honeycutt executed a signature card for the account, on which they checked off the box requiring only one signature to transact any business. Ron Honeycutt and Christine Honeycutt were the authorized signatories on the account.

Ron Honeycutt died February 10, 2000. On February 15, 2000, Christine Honeycutt withdrew funds in the amount of $13,066.48 from Sheldon's account. At the time of withdrawal, an employee of the bank retrieved and reviewed the signature card on file with the bank to verify Christine Honeycutt's authority to direct and conduct transactions on Sheldon's account. The bank did not inquire as to Christine Honeycutt's status with respect to Sheldon, nor did it inquire of anyone at Sheldon as to her status. At the time, the bank was unaware that Ron Honeycutt had died.

On March 13, 2000, Sheldon commenced an action against Christine Honeycutt and the bank, asserting claims for conversion, breach of contract, and negligence for permitting the allegedly unauthorized withdrawal. On May 22, 2001, the bank filed a motion for summary judgment arguing that at the time Christine Honeycutt withdrew funds from Sheldon's account, she was an authorized signatory on the account and, therefore, the bank committed no legal wrong when it permitted the withdrawal. The circuit court granted the bank's motion for summary judgment. Sheldon appealed.

DECISION The summary judgment is affirmed.

OPINION Sheldon argues that the bank breached its duty of care "by failing to make an adequate inquiry as to the authority of

Christine Honeycutt to conduct banking on behalf of the business." A bank and its customers enjoy a debtor-creditor relationship in which the rights and liabilities are contractual. The signature card was the contract between the parties which regulates their rights and duties.

The plain language of the signature card established that both Ron and Christine Honeycutt were authorized signatories able to transact business on Sheldon's account. The signature card expressly and unambiguously provided that the bank is authorized to recognize and rely upon either of Ron or Christine Honeycutt's signatures on checks, drafts, and orders for the payment of money, the withdrawal of funds, or the transaction of any business to Sheldon's account.

When Christine Honeycutt withdrew funds from Sheldon's account, the bank did not breach any standard of care owed to Sheldon. The bank exercised reasonable care when it inspected the signature card on file for Sheldon's account and verified that Christine Honeycutt was an authorized signatory on the account. Moreover, no further inquiry was required as the bank was legally entitled to release the funds to Christine Honeycutt based upon the signature card. Thus, because there was no genuine dispute as to any material fact, the lower court was correct to conclude that the signature card controlled the transaction and was correct to enter summary judgment in favor of the bank.

INTERPRETATION A bank and its customers enjoy a debtor-creditor relationship in which the rights and liabilities of each are contractual.

ETHICAL QUESTION Did any of the parties act unethically? Explain.

CRITICAL THINKING QUESTION Do you agree with the court's decision? Explain.

GOING GLOBAL

What about letters of credit?

International trade involves a number of risks not usually encountered in domestic trade, particularly the threat of government controls over the export or import of goods and currency. The most effective means of managing these risks—as well as the ordinary trade risks of nonperformance by seller and buyer—is the irrevocable documentary letter of credit. Most international letters of credit are governed by the Uniform Customs and Practices for Documentary Credits, a document drafted by commercial law experts from many countries and adopted by the International Chamber of Commerce. A letter of credit is a promise by a buyer's bank to pay the seller, provided certain conditions are met. The letter of credit transaction involves three or four different parties and three underlying contracts.

To illustrate: a U.S. business wishes to sell computers to a Belgian company. The U.S. and Belgian firms enter into a sales agreement that includes details such as the number of computers, the features they will have, and the date they will be shipped. The buyer then enters into a second contract with a local bank, called an issuer, committing the bank to pay the agreed price upon receiving specified documents. These documents normally include a bill of lading (proving that the seller has delivered the goods for shipment), a commercial invoice listing the purchase terms, proof of insurance, and a customs certificate indicating that customs officials have cleared the goods for export. The buyer's bank's commitment to pay is the irrevocable letter of credit. Typically, a correspondent or paying bank located in

the seller's country makes payment to the seller. Here, the Belgian issuing bank arranges to pay the U.S. correspondent bank the agreed sum of money in exchange for the documents. The issuer then sends the U.S. computer firm the letter of credit. When the U.S. firm obtains all the necessary documents, it presents them to the U.S. correspondent bank, which verifies the documents, pays the computer company in U.S. dollars, and sends the documents to the Belgian issuing bank. Upon receiving the required documents, the issuing bank pays the correspondent bank and then presents the documents to the buyer. In our example, the Belgian buyer pays the issuing bank in Belgian francs for the letter of credit when the buyer receives the specified documents from the bank.

blizzard, flood, hurricane, or other disaster; the suspension of payments by another bank; war; emergency conditions; failure of equipment; or other circumstances beyond the bank's control. Nevertheless, such delay will be excused only if the bank exercises such diligence as the circumstances require.

Indorsements

if an item is restrictively indorsed "for deposit only," only a bank may be a holder

Indorsements   An item restrictively indorsed with words such as "pay any bank" is locked into the bank collection system, and only a bank may acquire the rights of a holder. When forwarding an item for collection, a bank normally indorses the item "pay any bank," regardless of the type of indorsement, if any, that the item carried at the time of receipt. This protects the collecting bank by making it impossible for the item to stray from regular collection channels.

If the item had no indorsement when the depositary bank received it, the bank nonetheless becomes a holder of the item at the time it takes possession of the item for collection if the customer was a holder at the time of delivery to the bank and, if the bank satisfies the other requirements of a holder in due course, it will become a holder in due course in its own right. In return, the bank warrants to the collecting banks, the payor, and the drawer that it has paid the amount of the item to the customer or deposited that amount to the customer's account. This rule speeds up the collection process by eliminating the necessity of returning checks for indorsement when the depositary bank knows they came from its customers.

Warranties [27-1b]

Warranties

customers and collecting banks give warranties on transfer, presentment, and encoding

Customers and collecting banks give substantially the same **warranties** as those given by parties under Article 3 upon presentment and transfer, which were discussed in Chapter 26. In addition, under Article 4, customers and collecting banks may give encoding warranties. Each customer or collecting bank who transfers an item and receives a settlement or other consideration warrants to his transferee and any subsequent collecting bank that (1) the person is entitled to enforce the item, (2) all signatures are authentic and authorized, (3) the item has not been altered, (4) he is not subject to any defense or claim in recoupment, and (5) he has no knowledge of any insolvency proceeding involving the maker or acceptor or the drawer of an unaccepted draft. Moreover, each customer or collecting bank who obtains payment or acceptance from a drawee on a draft as well as each prior transferor warrants to the drawee who pays or accepts the draft in good faith that (1) she is a person entitled to enforce the draft, (2) the item has not been altered, and (3) she has no knowledge that the signature of the drawer is unauthorized.

Processing of checks is now done by Magnetic Ink Character Recognition (MICR). When a check is deposited, the depositary bank magnetically encodes the check with the amount of the check (all checks are pre-encoded with the drawer's account number and the designation of the drawee bank), after which the processing occurs automatically, without further human involvement. Despite its efficiency, the magnetic encoding of checks has created several problems. The first is the problem a bank encounters when paying a postdated instrument prior to its date. The Revision changes prior law by providing that the drawee may debit the drawer's account, unless the drawer timely informs the drawee that the check is postdated. A second difficulty arises when a depositing bank or its customer who encodes her own checks miscodes a check. Revised Article 4 provides that such an encoder warrants to any subsequent collecting bank and to the payor that information on a check is properly encoded. If the customer does the encoding, the depositary bank also makes the warranty.

Final Payment   The provisional settlements made in the collection chain are all directed toward final payment of the item by the payor bank. From this turnaround point in the collection process, the proceeds of the item begin their return flow, and provisional settlements become final. For example, a customer of the California Country State Bank may deposit a check drawn on the State of Maine Country National Bank. The check may then take a course such as follows: from the California Country State Bank to a correspondent bank in San Francisco, to the Federal Reserve Bank of San Francisco, to the Federal Reserve Bank of Boston, to the payor bank. Provisional settlements are made at each step. When the payor finally pays the item, the proceeds begin to flow back over the same course.

The critical question, then, is the point at which the payor has *paid* the item, because this not only commences the payment process but also affects questions of priority between the payment of an item and actions such as the filing of a stop payment order against it. Under the Code, **final payment** occurs when the payor bank first does any of the following: (1) pays an item in cash; (2) settles an item and does not have the right to revoke the settlement through statute, clearinghouse rule, or agreement; or (3) makes a provisional settlement and does not revoke it within the time and in the manner permitted by statute, clearinghouse rule, or agreement.

Payor Banks [27-1c]

The **payor** (or **drawee**) **bank**, under its contract of deposit with the drawer, agrees to pay to the payee or his order a check issued by the drawer, provided that the order is not countermanded, and that there are sufficient funds in the drawer's account.

The tremendous increase in volume of bank collections has necessitated deferred posting procedures, whereby items are sorted and proved on the day of receipt but are not posted to customers' accounts or returned until the next banking day. The UCC not only approves such procedures but also establishes specific standards to govern their application to the actions of payor banks.

When a payor bank that is not also a depositary bank receives a demand item other than for immediate payment over the counter, it must either return the item or give its transferor a provisional settlement before midnight of the banking day on which the item is received. Otherwise, the bank becomes liable to its transferor for the amount of the item, unless it has a valid defense, such as breach of a presentment warranty.

If the payor bank gives the provisional settlement as required, it has until the midnight deadline to return the item or, if the item is held for protest or is otherwise unavailable for return, to send written notice of dishonor or nonpayment. After doing this, the bank is entitled to revoke the settlement and recover any payment it has made. Should it fail to return the item or send notice before its midnight deadline, the payor bank will be accountable for the amount of the item unless it has a valid defense for its inaction. If a check is for $2,500 or more, federal law (Regulation CC) requires special notice of nonpayment—the paying bank must give notice

Final payment

occurs when the payor bank does any of the following, whichever happens first: (1) pays an item in cash, (2) settles and does not have the right to revoke the settlement, or (3) makes a provisional settlement and does not properly revoke it

Payor bank

under its contract with the drawer, the payor or drawee bank agrees to pay to the payee or order checks that are issued by the drawer, provided the order is not countermanded by a stop payment order and provided there are sufficient funds in the drawer's account

to the depositary bank by 4:00 P.M. on the second business day following the banking day on which the check was presented to the paying bank. This regulation does not, however, relieve the paying bank of returning the check in compliance with Article 4.

A bank may dishonor an item and return it or send notice of dishonor for innumerable reasons. The following situations are the most common: the drawer or maker may have no account or may have funds insufficient to cover the item, a signature on the item may be forged, or the drawer or maker may have stopped payment on the item.

RELATIONSHIP BETWEEN PAYOR BANK AND ITS CUSTOMER [27-2]

Contractual relationship
the relationship between a payor bank and its checking account customer is primarily the product of their contractual arrangement

The **relationship** between a payor bank and its checking account customer is primarily the product of their contractual arrangement. Although the parties have relatively broad latitude in establishing the terms of their agreement and in altering the provisions of the Code, a bank may not validly (1) disclaim responsibility for its lack of good faith, (2) disclaim responsibility for its failure to exercise ordinary care, or (3) limit its damages for a breach comprising such lack or failure. The parties by agreement, however, may determine the standards by which the bank's responsibility is to be measured, if these standards are not clearly unreasonable.

Payment of an Item [27-2a]

Payment of an item
when a payor receives an item for which the funds in the account are insufficient, the bank may either dishonor the item and return it or pay the item and charge the customer's account even though an overdraft is created

A payor owes a duty to its customer, the drawer, to pay checks properly drawn by him on an account having funds sufficient to cover the items. A check or draft, however, is not an assignment of the drawer's funds that are in the drawee's possession. Moreover, as discussed in Chapter 26, the drawee is not liable on a check until it accepts the item. Therefore, the *holder* of a check has no right to require the drawee bank to pay it, whether or not the drawer's account contains sufficient funds. But if a payor bank improperly refuses payment when presented with an item, it will incur a liability to the *customer* from whose account the item should have been paid. If the customer has adequate funds on deposit, and there is no other valid basis for the refusal to pay, the bank is liable to its customer for damages proximately caused by the *wrongful dishonor*. Liability is limited to actual damages proved and may include damages for arrest, prosecution, or other consequential damages.

When a payor bank receives an item properly payable from a customer's account but the funds in the account are insufficient to pay it, the bank may (1) dishonor the item and return it or (2) pay the item and charge its customer's account, even though the actions create an overdraft. The item authorizes or directs the bank to make the payment and hence carries with it an enforceable implied promise to reimburse the bank. Furthermore, the customer may be liable to pay the bank a service charge for its handling of the overdraft or to pay interest on the amount of the overdraft. A customer, however, is not liable for an overdraft if the customer did not sign the item or benefit from the proceeds of the item.

Practical Advice

Be sure to present checks you hold before they become stale.

A payor bank is under no obligation to its customer to pay an uncertified check that is more than six months old. This rule reflects the usual banking practice of consulting a depositor before paying a "stale" item (one more than six months old) on her account. The bank is not required to dishonor such an item, however; and if the bank makes payment in good faith, it may charge the amount of the item to its customer's account.

Substitute Check [27-2b]

The Check Clearing for the 21st Century Act (also called Check 21 or the Check Truncation Act) permits banks to truncate original checks, which means removing an original paper check from the check collection or return process and sending in lieu of it (1) a substitute check or (2) *by agreement*, information relating to the original check (including data taken from the MICR line of the original check or an electronic image of the original check). The Act sets forth a statutory framework under which a substitute check is the legal equivalent of an original check for all purposes, if the substitute check (1) accurately represents all of the information on the front and back of the original check as of the time the original check was truncated; and (2) bears the legend: "This is a legal copy of your check. You can use it the same way you would use the

Substitute check

a paper reproduction of the original check that for all purposes is the legal equivalent of an original check

original check." The Act defines a **substitute check** as a paper reproduction of the original check that (1) contains an image of the front and back of the original; (2) bears an MICR containing all the information appearing on the MICR line of the original check; (3) conforms, in paper stock, dimension, and otherwise, with generally applicable industry standards for substitute checks; and (4) is suitable for automated processing in the same manner as the original. Thus, a substitute check is basically a copy of the original check that shows both the front and back of the original check.

The law does not require banks to accept checks in electronic form, nor does it require banks to use the new authority granted by the Act to create substitute checks. On the other hand, parties cannot refuse to accept a substitute check that meets the Act's requirements. The Act permits banks to replace paper checks during the check collection process with either digital or paper substitutes. Thus, banks can employ digital images or image reduction documents (IRDs), which are documents that include the front, rear, and all MICR data in one image. However, the Act does not provide legal equivalence for electronic check or image presentment.

The ultimate objective of the Act is to make the collection process more efficient and much faster (transferring digital files within seconds rather than days) and to enhance fraud detection by accelerating return of dishonored checks.

Stop Payment Orders [27-2c]

Stop payment order

an oral stop payment order (a command for a drawer to a drawee not to pay an instrument) is binding for fourteen calendar days; a written order is effective for six months and may be renewed in writing

A check drawn on a bank is an order to pay a sum of money and an authorization to charge the amount to the drawer's account. The customer, or any person authorized to draw on the account, may countermand this order, however, by means of a **stop payment order**. If the order does not come too late, the bank is bound by it. If the bank inadvertently pays a check over a valid stop order, it is *prima facie* liable to the customer, but only to the extent of the customer's loss resulting from the payment. The burden of establishing the fact and amount of loss is on the customer.

To be effective, a stop payment order must be received in time to provide the bank a reasonable opportunity to act on it. An oral stop order is binding on the bank for only fourteen calendar days. If the customer confirms an oral stop order in writing within the fourteen-day period, the order is effective for six months and may be renewed in writing for additional six-month periods.

The fact that a drawer has filed a stop payment order does not automatically relieve her of liability. If the bank honors the stop payment order and returns the check, the holder may bring an action against the drawer. If the holder qualifies as a holder in due course, personal defenses that the drawer might have to such an action would be of no avail.

Practical Advice

If you wish to stop payment on a check, contact your bank as soon as possible, and confirm in writing an oral stop payment order within fourteen days.

Leibling, P.C. v. Mellon PSFS (NJ) National Association
Superior Court of New Jersey, Law Division, Special Civil Part, Camden County, 1998
710 A.2d 1067, 311 N.J.Super. 651, 35 UCC Rep.Serv.2d 590
http://scholar.google.com/scholar_case?case=16467934184945395960&q=710+A.2d+1067&hl=en&as_s.1067&hl=en&as_sdt=2,34

FACTS Mr. Scott D. Leibling, P.C. (hereinafter Plaintiff) is an attorney at law. Plaintiff maintains an attorney trust account (Account) at Mellon Bank (NJ) National Association (Mellon). Mellon uses a computerized system to process checks for payment.

Plaintiff represented the defendant, Fredy Winda Ramos (Ramos) in a personal injury action which resulted in a settlement. On May 19, 1995, plaintiff issued Check No. 1031 in the amount of $8,483.06 to Ramos, representing her net proceeds from the settlement. Mellon honored that check on May 26, 1995. On May 24, 1995, plaintiff mistakenly issued another check, Check No. 1043, to Ramos in the same amount of $8,483.06. Realizing his error, Plaintiff called Ramos in Puerto Rico and advised her that Check No. 1043 had been issued by mistake and instructed her to destroy the check. Plaintiff then called Mellon and ordered an oral stop payment on the check.

On December 21, 1996, some nineteen months after plaintiff issued Check No. 1043, Ramos cashed the check in Puerto Rico.

Plaintiff filed this complaint against both Ramos and Mellon. Ramos defaulted. Plaintiff's complaint against Mellon alleges breach of duty of good faith, negligence, breach of fiduciary duty, payment of a stale check, and breach of contract as a result of Mellon's honoring the second check.

DECISION Judgment for Mellon: the bank's conduct was fair and in accordance with reasonable commercial standards.

OPINION The issue turns on whether Mellon acted in good faith when it honored plaintiff's check. It appears clear that the Uniform Commercial Code acknowledges that computerized check-processing systems are common and accepted banking procedures in the United States. Therefore, it cannot be said that defendant bank acted in bad faith by using a computerized system when it honored plaintiffs "stale" check. Thus, as long as the defendant bank used an adequate computer system for processing checks, it appears to have acted in good faith even though it did not consult the Plaintiff before it honored the "stale" check that had an expired oral stop payment order on it. The obligation of a bank to stop payment on a check does not continue in perpetuity once the stop payment order expires.

INTERPRETATION It is the responsibility of the banking customer either to regain possession of the mistakenly issued check

or to renew the stop payment order in writing every six months for as long as the risk of payment exists.

CRITICAL THINKING QUESTION Do you think that banks should be required to offer a permanent stop payment option? Explain.

Bank's right to subrogation on improper payment

if a payor bank pays an item over a stop payment order or otherwise in violation of its contract, the payor bank is subrogated to (obtains) the rights of (1) any holder in due course on the item against the drawer or maker, (2) the payee or any other holder against the drawer or maker, and (3) the drawer or maker against the payee or any other holder

Bank's Right to Subrogation on Improper Payment [27-2d]

If a payor bank pays an item over a stop payment order, after an account has been closed, or otherwise in violation of its contract with the drawer or maker, the payor bank is subrogated to (obtains) the rights of (1) any holder in due course on the item against the drawer or maker, (2) the payee or any other holder against the drawer or maker, and (3) the drawer or maker against the payee or any other holder. For instance, over the drawer's stop payment order, a bank pays a check presented to the bank by a holder in due course. The drawer's defense is that the check was obtained by fraud in the inducement. The drawee bank is subrogated to the rights of the holder in due course, who would not be subject to the drawer's personal defense, and thus can debit the drawer's account. The same would be true if the presenter were the payee, against whom the drawer did not have a valid defense.

Seigel v. Merrill Lynch, Pierce, Fenner & Smith, Inc.
District of Columbia Court of Appeals, 2000
745 A.2d 301
http://scholar.google.com/scholar_case?case=13998788116535155223&q=745+A.2d+301&hl=en&as_sdt=2,34

FACTS In early 1997, the plaintiff, Walter Seigel, a Maryland resident, traveled to Atlantic City, New Jersey, to gamble. While there, he wrote a number of checks to various casinos to gamble. The checks were drawn on Seigel's cash management account with the defendant, which was established through Merrill Lynch's District of Columbia offices. There were sufficient funds in the account to cover all the checks. Seigel eventually gambled away all of the money he had received for the checks. Upon returning to Maryland, Seigel discussed the status of the outstanding checks with Merrill Lynch, informing his broker of the gambling nature of the transactions and his desire to avoid realizing the losses. Merrill Lynch informed Seigel that it was possible to escape paying the checks by placing a stop payment order and closing out his cash management account. Seigel took this advice and instructed Merrill Lynch to close his account, liquidate the assets, and not to honor any checks drawn on the account. Merrill Lynch agreed and confirmed Seigel's instructions. Many of the checks were subsequently dishonored and are not now at issue. However, Merrill Lynch accidentally paid several of the checks totaling $143,000, despite the stop payment order and the account closure. Merrill Lynch then debited Seigel's margin account to cover the payments.

Seigel brought suit in the District of Columbia against Merrill Lynch, demanding a return of the $143,000 plus interest. Merrill Lynch was granted a summary judgment. Seigel appealed.

DECISION Judgment affirmed.

OPINION The UCC provides: "The burden of establishing the fact and amount of loss resulting from the payment of an item contrary to a stop-payment order or order to close an account is on the customer." This provision, which places the burden on the customer to show actual loss, is reinforced by the extensive rights of subrogation given to the payor bank.

Therefore, Seigel is required to bear the burden of establishing that he in fact suffered a loss as a result of the payment of the checks. In assessing whether any such loss was actually incurred, Merrill Lynch must be treated as the subrogee of any rights of the casino payees against Seigel. As the payee of a dishonored check, the casino would have a prima facie right to recover its amount from Seigel as drawer.

Even if payment had been stopped, the casinos could have enforced the checks in New Jersey, where the transaction was entered into. Merrill Lynch therefore, under the Code scheme, conceptually has the same right.

Thus, Seigel failed to establish that he ultimately suffered any actual loss as a result of the payment of the checks by Merrill Lynch.

INTERPRETATION The drawer is required to bear the burden of establishing that he in fact suffered a loss as a result of the payment of a check over a stop payment order.

CRITICAL THINKING QUESTION What rule should be established for liability of a bank making a payment over a stop payment order?

Disclosure Requirements [27-2e]

Congress enacted the Truth in Savings Act, which requires all depositary institutions (including commercial banks, savings and loan associations, savings banks, and credit unions) to disclose in great detail to consumers the terms and conditions of their deposit accounts. The stated purpose of the Act is to allow consumers to make informed decisions regarding deposit accounts by mandating standardized disclosure of rates of interest and fees to facilitate meaningful comparison of different deposit products.

More specifically, the Act provides that the disclosures must be made in a clear and conspicuous writing and must be given to the consumer when an account is opened or service is provided. These disclosures must include the following: (1) the annual percentage yield (APY) and the percentage rate, (2) how variable rates are calculated and when the rates may be changed, (3) balance information (including how the balance is calculated), (4) when and how interest is calculated and credited, (5) the amount of fees that may be charged and how they are calculated, and (6) any limitation on the number or amount of withdrawals or deposits. In addition, the Act requires the depositary institution to disclose the following information with periodic statements it sends to its customers: (1) the APY earned, (2) any fees debited during the covered period, (3) the dollar amount of the interest earned during the covered period, and (4) the dates of the covered period.

Customer's Death or Incompetence [27-2f]

The general rule is that death or incompetence revokes all agency agreements. Furthermore, adjudication of incompetency by a court is regarded as notice to the world of that fact. Actual notice is not required. The Code modifies these stringent rules in several ways with respect to bank deposits and collections.

First, if either a payor or collecting bank does not know that a customer has been adjudicated incompetent, the existence of such incompetence at the time an item is issued or its collection is undertaken does not impair either bank's authority to accept, pay, or collect the item or to account for proceeds of its collection. The bank may pay the item without incurring any liability.

Second, neither death nor adjudication of incompetence of a customer revokes a payor or collecting bank's authority to accept, pay, or collect an item until the bank knows of the condition and has a reasonable opportunity to act on this knowledge.

Finally, even though a bank knows of the death of its customer, it may for ten days after the date of his death pay or certify checks drawn by the customer unless a person claiming an interest in the account, such as an heir, executor, or administrator, orders the bank to stop making such payments.

Customer's Duties [27-2g]

Customer's duties

the customer must examine bank statements and items carefully and promptly to discover any unauthorized signatures or alterations

The Code imposes certain affirmative duties on bank customers and fixes time limits within which they must assert their rights. The duties arise and the time starts to run from the point at which the bank either sends or makes available to its customer a statement of account showing payment of items against the account. The statement of account will suffice provided it describes by item the number of the item, the amount, and the date of payment. The customer must exercise reasonable promptness in examining the bank statement or the items to discover whether any payment was unauthorized due to an *unauthorized signature* on or any *alteration* of an item. Because he is not presumed to know the signatures of payees or indorsers, this duty of prompt and careful examination applies only to alterations and the customer's own signature, both of which he should be able to detect immediately. If the customer discovers an unauthorized signature or an alteration, he must notify the bank promptly. A failure to fulfill these duties of prompt examination and notice precludes the customer from asserting against the bank his unauthorized signature or any alteration if the bank establishes that it suffered a loss by reason of such failure.

Furthermore, the customer will lose his rights in a potentially more serious situation. Occasionally, a forger, possibly an employee who has access to the employer's checkbook, carries out a series of transactions involving the account of the same individual. He may forge one or more checks each month until finally detected. The bank, noticing nothing suspicious, might pay one or more of the customer's checks bearing the false signatures before the customer detects the forgery, months or even years later. The Code deals with these situations by stating that once the statement and items become available to him, the customer must examine them within a reasonable period, which in no event may exceed thirty calendar days and which may, under certain circumstances, be less, and notify the bank. Any instruments containing alterations or unauthorized signatures by the same wrongdoer that the bank pays during that period will be the bank's responsibility, but any instruments paid thereafter but before the customer notifies the bank may not be asserted against it. This rule is based on the concept that the loss involved is directly traceable to the customer's negligence and that, as a result, he should stand the loss.

Practical Advice

Promptly review your monthly bank statement to ensure that all checks and transactions were issued by you or your authorized agent and are for the correct amount.

These rules depend, however, on the bank's exercising ordinary care in paying the items involved. If it does not and that failure by the bank substantially contributed to the loss, the loss will be allocated between the bank and the customer based on their comparative negligence. But whether the bank exercised due care or not, the customer must in all events report any alteration or his unauthorized signature within one year from the time the statement or items are made available to him or be barred from asserting them against the bank. *Any unauthorized indorsement* must be asserted within three years under the Article's general Statute of Limitations provisions.

Consistent with modern automated methods for processing checks, Articles 3 and 4 provide that "ordinary care" does not require a bank to examine every check if the failure to do so does not vary unreasonably from general banking usage.

**Union Planters Bank, National Association v. Rogers**
Supreme Court of Mississippi, 2005
912 So.2d 116
http://scholar.google.com/scholar_case?q=912+So.2d+116&hl=en&as_sdt=2,34&case=1485225536307758185&scilh=0

FACTS Neal D. and Helen K. Rogers, both in their eighties, maintained four checking accounts with the Union Planters Bank in Greenville, Washington County, Mississippi. After Neal became bedridden, Helen hired Jackie Reese to help her take care of Neal, do chores, and run errands. In September 2000, Reese began writing checks on the Rogers's four accounts and forged Helen's name on the signature line. Some of the checks were made out to "cash," some to "Helen K. Rogers," and some to "Jackie Reese." The following chart summarizes the forgeries to each account:

Account Number	Beginning	Ending	Number of Checks	Amount of Checks
54282309	11/27/2000	6/18/2001	46	$ 16,635.00
0039289441	9/27/2000	1/25/2001	10	$ 2,701.00
6100110922	11/29/2000	8/13/2001	29	$ 9,297.00
6404000343	11/20/2000	8/16/2001	83	$ 29,765.00
TOTAL			**168**	**$ 58,398.00**

Neal died in late May 2001. Shortly thereafter, the Rogers's son, Neal, Jr., began helping Helen with financial matters. Together they discovered that many bank statements were missing and that there was not as much money in the accounts as they had thought. In June 2001, they contacted Union Planters and asked for copies of the missing bank statements. In September 2001, Helen was advised by Union Planters to contact the police due to forgeries made on her accounts. Subsequently, criminal charges were brought against Reese. In the meantime, Helen filed

suit against Union Planters, alleging unlawful payment of forged checks and negligence. After a trial, the jury awarded Helen $29,595 in damages, and the circuit court entered judgment accordingly.

DECISION Judgment reversed.

OPINION The relationship between Rogers and Union Planters is governed by Article 4 of the Uniform Commercial Code (UCC), which provides that a bank customer has a duty to discover and report "unauthorized signatures," that is, forgeries. Because the customer is more familiar with her own signature and should know whether or not she authorized a particular withdrawal or check, she can prevent further unauthorized activity better than a financial institution which may process thousands of transactions in a single day. In recognition that the customer is best situated to detect unauthorized transactions on her own account, the Code places the burden on the customer to exercise reasonable care to discover and report such transactions. The customer's duty to exercise this care is triggered when the bank satisfies its burden to provide sufficient information to the customer. As a result, if the bank provides sufficient information, the customer bears the loss when she fails to detect and notify the bank about unauthorized transactions. The evidence shows that all bank statements and canceled checks were sent, via U.S. mail, postage prepaid, to all customers at their "designated address" each month. Rogers introduced no evidence to the contrary. Thus, the bank fulfilled its duty of making the statements available to Rogers.

In defense of her failure to inspect the bank statements, Rogers claims that she never received the bank statements and canceled checks. Even if this allegation is true, it does not excuse Rogers from failing to fulfill her duties because the Code clearly states that a bank discharges its duty in providing the necessary information to a customer when it *"sends ... to a customer a statement of account showing payment of items."* The word "receive" is absent. The customer's duty to inspect and report does not arise when the statement is received, as Rogers claims; the customer's duty to inspect and report arises when the bank sends the statement to the customer's address. A reasonable person who has not received a monthly statement from the bank would promptly ask the bank for a copy of the statement.

A customer who has not promptly notified a bank of an irregularity may be precluded from bringing certain claims against the bank. The UCC states that a customer must report a series of forgeries within "a reasonable period of time, *not exceeding* thirty (30) days." The thirty-day period is an outside limit only. Although there is no mention of a specific date, Rogers testified that she and her son began looking for the statements in late May or early June of 2001, after her husband had died. When they discovered that statements were missing, they notified Union Planters in June of 2001 to replace the statements. At this time no mention of a possible forgery was made even though Neal, Jr. thought that something was wrong as far back as December 2000. Therefore, Rogers failed to notify Union Planters of the forgeries within thirty days of the date she should have reasonably discovered the forgeries.

INTERPRETATION A bank customer must exercise reasonable promptness in examining account statements and canceled checks to detect unauthorized signatures or alterations.

CRITICAL THINKING QUESTION Do you agree with the court's decision? Explain.

ELECTRONIC FUNDS TRANSFER

As mentioned, the use of negotiable instruments for payment has greatly reduced the use of *cash* in the United States. The advent and technological advances of interconnected computers have resulted in electronic funds transfer systems (EFTS) that have greatly reduced the use of *checks*. Financial institutions seek to substitute EFTS for checks for two principal reasons. The first is to eliminate the ever-increasing paperwork involved in processing the billions of checks issued annually. The second is to eliminate the "float" that a drawer of a check enjoys by maintaining the use of his funds during the processing period between the time at which he issues the check and final payment.

An **electronic funds transfer** (EFT) has been defined as "any transfer of funds, other than a transaction originated by check, draft, or similar paper instrument, which is initiated through an electronic terminal, telephonic instrument, or computer or magnetic tape so as to order, instruct or authorize a financial institution to debit or credit an account." For example, with an EFT, William in New York would be able to pay a debt he owes to Yvette in Illinois by entering into his computer an order to his bank to pay Yvette. The drawee bank would then instantly debit William's account and transfer the credit to Yvette's bank, where Yvette's account would immediately be credited in that amount.

The use of EFTs has generated considerable confusion concerning the legal rights of customers and financial institutions. Congress provided a partial solution to the legal issues affecting consumer EFTs by enacting the EFTA discussed later. Transactions not covered by the EFTA—primarily wholesale electronic transfers—are covered by UCC Article 4A–Funds Transfers.

Electronic funds transfer

any transfer of funds, other than a transaction originated by check, draft, or similar paper instrument, which is initiated through an electronic terminal, telephonic instrument, or computer or magnetic tape so as to order, instruct, or authorize a financial institution to debit or credit an account

TYPES OF ELECTRONIC FUNDS TRANSFER [27-3]

Although new EFTs may appear in the coming years, six main types of EFTs are currently in use: (1) automated teller machines (ATMs), (2) point-of-sale (POS) systems, (3) direct deposit and withdrawal of funds, (4) pay-by-phone systems, (5) personal computer (online) banking, and (6) wholesale wire transfers.

Automated Teller Machines [27-3a]

Automated teller machines (ATMs) permit customers to conduct various transactions with their bank through the use of electronic terminals. After activating an ATM with a plastic identification card and a personal identification number, or PIN, a customer can deposit and withdraw funds from her account, transfer funds between accounts, obtain cash advances, and make payments on loan accounts. (See Business Law in Action.)

BUSINESS LAW **IN ACTION**

What is the easiest way to rob a bank these days? Head for your local ATM, or automatic teller machine. With more than two million machines located in the United States, most of which are open virtually round the clock nationwide, ATMs offer thieves a wide new frontier; a network of thieves stole $45 million from thousands of ATM machines in twenty-six countries.

Thieves Get Sophisticated These days, you still may find yourself held up by some robber who pulls a gun and demands your ATM withdrawal, but other thieves have gotten much more sophisticated. Often, ATM robbers will use binoculars or video cameras to record your finger movements as you enter your personal identification number (PIN) at an ATM. Then they'll match your PIN with your account number on the ATM receipt that you perhaps carelessly threw away. If they encounter a problem, they'll even call you at home, posing as bank officials seeking to verify your PIN. You should know, however, that banks never do this sort of thing.

To reduce street crime around ATMs, banks have begun installing the machines in well-lighted public places such as twenty-four-hour grocery stores and shopping malls. They have also teamed up with city officials in such places as Chicago and Los Angeles to install bank machines in police stations.

Malls Become Targets Such measures, however, haven't stopped more cunning ATM robbers. One group, for example, approached mall officials at the Buckland Hills Mall in Manchester, Connecticut, about installing an ATM. Before a contract could be signed, the thieves rolled in a temporary-looking machine, which they left in the mall for two weeks, during which time shoppers who slipped in their cards and entered their PINs received an apologetic message saying that the machine was out of service. Often, a "repairman" stood by, ostensibly waiting to fix the machine. Even to mall employees, the ATM looked legitimate. Yet the machine, which rested on wheels, could have been carted away at any moment. Finally, two men dressed in uniforms came on Mother's Day and did

just that. Then, using the stolen PIN and account numbers that the machine had recorded, the robbers made fake cash cards, traveled to midtown Manhattan, and went on a shopping spree.

Another method for stealing information is a thin, transparent-plastic overlay that is placed on an ATM keypad that captures a user's identification code as it is entered. To the cardholder, it looks like some sort of cover to protect the keys. In fact, microchips in the device record every keystroke. Another transparent device inside the card slot captures the data on the ATM card. While the cardholder completes the transaction, a computer attached to the overlay records all the data necessary to clone the card.

Banks Held Liable One problem that banks face is that thieves like those in Connecticut can now buy used ATMs for as little as $6,000. Another is that customers often carelessly toss their ATM cards, PINs, or account receipts around. Many times, in fact, customers fall victim to friends or relatives who "borrow" their cards to make withdrawals.

Moreover, under the Electronic Funds Transfer Act, customers can limit their liability for unauthorized withdrawals. If, as a customer, you lose your card or it is stolen, you have two days to notify the bank from the time that you discover the problem. By acting quickly, you reduce your liability to no more than $50; if you wait four days, however, your liability shoots up to $500.

If you discover an unauthorized withdrawal on your monthly statement, you have sixty days from the postmark on the statement's envelope to report the problem. Again, your liability will be limited to $50.00. If you become the victim of a criminal who makes a fake ATM card for your account, you face no liability. Whatever the circumstance, the burden of proof rests with the bank. If your bank refuses to reimburse you in a timely manner, you can sue.

Precautions to Consider ATMs account for more than 10 billion transactions each year in the United States, and that number is growing. Increasingly, banks are using ATMs to sell everything from American

Express traveler's checks to home equity loans. The list keeps expanding. And if you travel, some ATMs in foreign countries will allow you to withdraw money from your account and receive it in the local currency. To thwart would-be robbers, then, you may want to remember these important safety tips:

- Keep your ATM card and your PIN in separate places.
- Better yet, memorize your PIN, and never give it out to anyone.
- If you must keep a record of your PIN, put it in your safe deposit box at your bank.
- Never write your PIN on your ATM card or keep your PIN in your wallet.
- Avoid using the first part of your social security number, your driver's license number, your telephone number, or your birthday for your PIN.
- Don't leave your ATM card lying around the house for someone else to pick up.
- Keep all your ATM withdrawal receipts rather than tossing them away.
- Take someone with you to the cash machine and watch out for people who are loitering nearby.
- Head for ATMs in well-lighted, protected locations, such as grocery stores or malls.
- Never let a stranger into an ATM area with you, and get in and out quickly.
- Try to use ATMs during the day and have your card ready before you approach the machine.
- Conceal your finger movements from view as you enter your PIN.
- Look for possible fraudulent devices attached to the ATM.
- Do not use the ATM if it looks different or appears to have any attachments over the card slot or keypad.
- Opt for drive-through ATMs and keep your car windows and doors locked, except for the driver's side.
- Put your money away as soon as you get it and count it later.
- Finally, regularly compare your monthly statements with your ATM receipts.

Point-of-Sale Systems [27-3b]

Computerized point-of-sale (POS) systems permit consumers to transfer funds from their bank accounts to a merchant automatically. The POS machines, located within the merchant's store and activated by the consumer's identification card and code, instantaneously debit the consumer's account and credit the merchant's account.

Direct Deposits and Withdrawals [27-3c]

Another type of EFT involves deposits, authorized in advance by a customer, that are made directly to the customer's account. Examples include direct payroll deposits, deposits of Social Security payments, and deposits of pension payments. Conversely, automatic withdrawals are pre-authorized EFTs from the customer's account for regular payments to some party other than the financial institution at which the funds are deposited. Automatic withdrawals to pay insurance premiums, utility bills, or automobile loan payments are common examples of this type of EFT.

Pay-by-Phone Systems [27-3d]

Financial institutions provide a service that permits customers to pay bills by telephoning the bank's computer system and directing a transfer of funds to a designated third party. This service also permits customers to transfer funds between accounts.

Personal Computer (Online) Banking [27-3e]

Personal computer (online) banking enables customers to execute many banking transactions via an Internet-connected computer. For instance, customers may view account balances, request transfers between accounts, and pay bills electronically.

Wholesale Electronic Funds Transfers [27-3f]

Wholesale EFTs, commonly called wholesale wire transfers, involve the movement of funds between financial institutions, between financial institutions and businesses, and between businesses. Almost $4 trillion is transferred this way each business day over the two major transfer systems—the Federal Reserve wire transfer network system (Fedwire) and the New York Clearing House Interbank Payment System (CHIPS). In addition, a number of private wholesale wire systems exist among the large banks. Limited aspects of wholesale wire transfers are governed by uniform rules promulgated by the Federal Reserve, CHIPS, and the National Automated Clearing House Association.

CONSUMER FUNDS TRANSFERS [27-4]

Electronic Funds Transfer Act
provides a basic framework establishing the rights, liabilities, and responsibilities of participants in consumer electronic funds transfers

Congress determined that the use of electronic systems to transfer funds provided the potential for substantial benefits to consumers. Existing consumer protection legislation failed to account for the unique characteristics of such systems, however, leaving the rights and obligations of consumers and financial institutions undefined. Accordingly, Congress enacted Title IX of the Consumer Protection Act, called the **Electronic Funds Transfer Act** (EFTA), to "provide a basic framework establishing the rights, liabilities, and responsibilities of participants in electronic fund transfers" with primary emphasis on "the provision of individual consumer rights." Because the EFTA deals exclusively with the protection of *consumers*, it does not govern electronic transfers between financial institutions, between financial institutions and businesses, and between businesses. The Act is similar in many respects to the Fair Credit Billing Act (see Chapter 44), which applies to credit card transactions. The EFTA is administered by the Board of Governors of the Federal Reserve System, which is mandated to prescribe regulations to carry out the purposes of the Act. Pursuant to this congressional mandate, the Federal Reserve has issued Regulation E. The Dodd-Frank Wall Street Reform and Consumer Protection Act of 2010 (Dodd-Frank Act) transferred administration of the EFTA to the Consumer Financial Protection Bureau (CFPB), an independent executive agency housed within the Federal Reserve. See Chapter 44.

The Dodd-Frank Act requires that the amount of any interchange transaction fee that an issuer may receive or charge with respect to an electronic debit transaction must be reasonable and proportional to the cost incurred by the issuer, as determined by the Federal Reserve. Debit cards issued by small banks and prepaid reloadable cards are exempt from this rule.

Disclosure [27-4a]

The EFTA is primarily a disclosure statute and as such requires that the terms and conditions of EFTs involving a consumer's account be disclosed in readily understandable language at the time the consumer contracts for such services. Included among the required disclosures are the consumer's liability for unauthorized transfers, the kinds of EFTs allowed, the charges for transfers or for the right to make transfers, the consumer's right to stop payment of preauthorized EFTs, the consumer's right to receive documentation of EFTs, rules concerning disclosure of information to third parties, procedures for correcting account errors, and the financial institution's liability to the consumer under the Act.

In addition, the Dodd-Frank Act amended the EFTA to establish new standards for remittance transfers and authorized the CFPB to issue implementing regulations. A "remittance transfer" is an electronic transfer of money from a consumer in the United States to a person or business in a foreign country through persons or financial institutions that provide such transfers in the normal course of their business. Effective on October 28, 2013, the CFPB amended Regulation E to protect consumers who make remittance transfers by generally requiring companies to disclose fees, taxes, and exchange rates to consumers before they pay for the remittance transfers.

Documentation and Periodic Statements [27-4b]

The Act requires the financial institution to provide the consumer with written documentation of each transfer made from an electronic terminal at the time of transfer—a receipt. The receipt must clearly state the amount involved, the date, the type of transfer, the identity of the account(s) involved, the identity of any third party involved, and the location of the terminal involved.

In addition, the financial institution must provide each consumer with a periodic statement for each account of the consumer that may be accessed by means of an EFT. The statement must describe the amount, date, and location for each transfer; the fee, if any, to be charged for the transaction; and an address and phone number for questions and information.

Preauthorized Transfers [27-4c]

A preauthorized transfer *from* a consumer's account must be authorized in advance and in writing by the consumer, and a copy of the authorization must be provided to the consumer when the transfer is made. Up to three business days before the scheduled date of the transfer, a consumer may stop payment of a preauthorized EFT by notifying the financial institution orally or in writing, although the financial institution may require the consumer to provide written confirmation of an oral notification within fourteen days.

Error Resolution [27-4d]

The consumer has sixty days after the financial institution sends a periodic statement in which to notify the institution of any errors appearing on that statement. The financial institution is required to investigate alleged errors within ten business days and to report its findings within three business days after completing the investigation. If the financial institution needs more than ten days to investigate, it may take up to forty-five days, provided it recredits the consumer's account for the amount alleged to be in error. The institution must correct an error within one business day after determining that the error has occurred. Failure to investigate in good faith makes the financial institution liable to the consumer for treble damages (i.e., three times the amount of provable damages).

Consumer Liability [27-4e]

A consumer's liability for an unauthorized EFT is limited to a maximum of $50.00 if the consumer notifies the financial institution within two days after he learns of the loss or theft. If the consumer does not report the loss or theft within two days, he is liable for losses up to $500 but no more than $50.00 for the first two days. If the consumer fails to report the unauthorized use

Practical Advice

Promptly and carefully
review all electronic fund
activities to ensure that they
are accurate, and if they are
not, notify your financial
institution immediately.

**Financial institution
responsibility**

liable to a consumer for all
damage proximately caused
by its failure to properly
handle an electronic funds
transfer transaction

within sixty days of transmittal of a periodic statement, he is liable for losses resulting from any unauthorized EFT that appeared on the statement if the financial institution can show that the loss would not have occurred had the consumer reported the loss within sixty days; thus there is unlimited liability on unauthorized transfers made after sixty days following the bank's sending the periodic statement.

Liability of Financial Institution [27-4f]

A **financial institution** is liable to a consumer for all damages proximately caused by its failure to make an EFT in accordance with the terms and conditions of an account, in the correct amount, or in a timely manner when properly instructed to do so by the consumer. There are, however, exceptions to such liability. The financial institution will not be liable if

1. the consumer's account has insufficient funds through no fault of the financial institution,
2. the funds are subject to legal process,
3. the transfer would exceed an established credit limit,
4. an electronic terminal has insufficient cash, or
5. circumstances beyond the financial institution's control prevent the transfer.

The financial institution is also liable for failure to stop payment of a preauthorized transfer from a consumer's account when instructed to do so in accordance with the terms and conditions of the account.

WHOLESALE FUNDS TRANSFERS [27-5]

**Wholesale funds
transfers**

the movement of funds
through the banking
system; excludes all
transactions governed by
the Electronic Funds
Transfer Act

The typical wholesale wire transfer involves sophisticated parties who seek great speed in transferring large sums of money. As mentioned, the dollar value of commercial or wholesale wire transfers over the two major transfer systems—Fedwire and CHIPS—is almost $4 trillion per business day.

Article 4A–Funds Transfers, is designed to provide a statutory framework for payment systems that are not covered by other Articles of the UCC or by the EFTA. All fifty states have adopted Article 4A. In general, "Article 4A governs a method of payment in which the person making payment (the 'originator') directly transfers an instruction to a bank to either make a payment to the person receiving the payment (the 'beneficiary') or to instruct some other bank to make payment to the beneficiary." Article 4A–102, Comment 1.

As discussed, on October 28, 2013, amended Regulation E went into effect governing consumer remittance transfers. Because these rules apply whether or not those remittance transfers are also EFTs as defined in the EFTA, neither the federal rule nor Article 4A will apply to some aspects of remittance transfers. To address this regulatory gap, in 2012 the Uniform Law Commission proposed an amendment to Article 4A to allow Article 4A to apply to a funds transfer that also is a remittance transfer, so long as that remittance transfer is not an EFT as defined in the EFTA. At least thirty-nine states have adopted the 2012 amendment to Article 4A.

Article 4A provides that the parties to a funds transfer generally may by agreement vary their rights and obligations. Moreover, funds-transfer system rules governing banks that use the system may be effective even if such rules conflict with Article 4A. Rights and obligations under Article 4A can also be changed by Federal Reserve regulations and operating circulars of Federal Reserve Banks.

Scope of Article 4A [27-5a]

Article 4A, which covers wholesale funds transfers, defines a funds transfer as a

> series of transactions, beginning with the originator's payment order, made for the purpose of making payment to the beneficiary of the order. The term includes any payment order issued by the originator's bank or an intermediary bank intended to carry out the originator's payment order. A funds transfer is completed by acceptance by the beneficiary's bank of a payment order for the benefit of the beneficiary of the originator's payment order.

The Article, therefore, covers the transfers of credit that move from an originator to a beneficiary through the banking system. If any step in the process is governed by the EFTA, however, the entire transaction is excluded from the Article's coverage except for some remittance transfers in states adopting the 2012 Amendment of Article 4A.

The following examples illustrate the coverage of the Article.

1. Johnson Co. instructs its bank, First National Bank (FNB), to pay $2 million to West Co., also a customer of FNB. FNB executes the payment order by crediting West's account with $2 million and notifying West that the credit has been made and is available.
2. Assume the same facts as those in the first example, except that West's bank is Central Bank (CB). FNB will execute the payment order of Johnson Co. by issuing to CB its own payment order instructing CB to credit the account of West.
3. Assume the facts presented in the second example with the added fact that FNB does not have a correspondent relationship with CB. In this instance, FNB will have to issue its payment order to Northern Bank (NB), a bank that does have a correspondent relationship with CB, and NB will then issue its payment order to CB.

Payment Order

A **payment order** is a sender's instruction to a receiving bank to pay, or to cause another bank to pay, a fixed or determinable amount of money to a beneficiary. The instruction may be communicated orally, electronically, or in writing. To be a payment order, the instruction must

1. not contain a condition to payment other than the time of payment;
2. be sent to a receiving bank that is to be reimbursed either by debiting an account of the sender or by otherwise receiving payment from the sender; and
3. be transmitted by the sender directly to the receiving bank or indirectly through an agent, a funds-transfer system, or a communication system.

The payment order is issued when sent and, if more than one payment is to be made, each payment represents a separate payment order. In the previous examples, one payment order is issued in the first example (from Johnson Co.), two in the second example (from Johnson Co. and from FNB), and three in the third example (from Johnson Co., from FNB, and from NB).

Parties

The **originator** is either the sender of the payment order or, in a series of payment orders, the sender of the first payment order. A **sender** is the party who gives an instruction to the **receiving bank**, or the bank to which the sender's instruction is addressed. The receiving bank may be the originator's bank, an intermediary bank, or the beneficiary's bank. The **originator's bank** is either the bank that receives the original payment order or the originator if the originator is a bank. The **beneficiary's bank**, the last bank in the chain of a funds transfer, is the bank instructed in the payment order to credit the beneficiary's account. The **beneficiary** is the person to be paid by the beneficiary bank. An **intermediary bank** is any receiving bank, other than the originator's bank or the beneficiary's bank, that receives the payment order. Thus, in the above examples,

1. Johnson Co. is the *originator* in all three examples;
2. Johnson Co. is a *sender* in all three examples, FNB is a sender in examples 2 and 3, and NB is a sender in example 3;
3. FNB is the *receiving bank* of Johnson Co.'s payment order in all three examples; in example 2, CB is the receiving bank of FNB's payment order; and, in example 3, CB is the receiving bank of NB's payment order and NB is the receiving bank of FNB's payment order;
4. FNB is the *originator's bank* in all three examples;
5. FNB is the *beneficiary's bank* in example 1; CB is the beneficiary's bank in examples 2 and 3;
6. West is the *beneficiary* in all three examples; and
7. NB is an *intermediary bank* in example 3.

In some instances, the originator and the beneficiary may be the same party. For example, a corporation may wish to transfer funds from one account to another account that is in the same or a different bank.

Payment order

an instruction of a sender to a receiving bank to pay, or to cause another bank to pay, a fixed amount of money to a beneficiary

Originator

sender of the first payment order

Sender

party who gives an instruction to the receiving bank

Receiving bank

bank that receives the sender's instructions

Originator's bank

either the bank that receives the original payment order or the originator if a bank

Beneficiary's bank

bank identified in a payment order to credit the beneficiary's account

Beneficiary

person to be paid by the beneficiary bank

Intermediary bank

any receiving bank other than an originator's or beneficiary's bank

Figure 27-2 Credit Transaction

Excluded Transactions   As mentioned, Article 4A provides that if any part of a funds transfer is governed by the EFTA, then the transfer is excluded from Article 4A coverage except for some remittance transfers in states adopting the 2012 Amendment of Article 4A. In addition, Article 4A covers only credit transactions; it therefore excludes debit transactions. If the person making the payment gives the instruction, the transfer is a credit transfer. If, however, the person receiving the payment gives the instruction, the transfer is a debit transfer. For example, a seller of goods obtains authority from the purchaser to debit the purchaser's account after the seller ships the goods. Article 4A does not cover this transaction because the instructions to make payment issue from the beneficiary (the seller), not from the party whose account is to be debited (the purchaser). See Figure 27-2 for an example of credit transaction.

Acceptance [27-5b]

Rights and obligations arise as a result of a receiving bank's acceptance of a payment order. The effect of acceptance depends on whether the payment order was issued to the beneficiary's bank or to a receiving bank other than the beneficiary's bank.

If a receiving bank is not the beneficiary's bank, the receiving bank does not subject itself to any liability until it accepts the instrument. Acceptance by a receiving bank other than the beneficiary's bank occurs when the receiving bank executes the sender's order. Such execution occurs when the receiving bank "issues a payment order intended to carry out" the sender's payment order. When the receiving bank executes the sender's payment order, the bank is entitled to payment from the sender and can debit the sender's account.

The beneficiary's bank may accept an order in any of three ways, and acceptance occurs at the earliest of these events: (1) when the bank (a) pays the beneficiary or (b) notifies the beneficiary that the bank has received the order or has credited the beneficiary's account with the funds; (2) when the bank receives payment of the sender's order; or (3) the opening of the next funds-transfer business day of the bank after the payment date of the order if the order was not rejected and funds are available for payment.

If a beneficiary's bank accepts a payment order, the bank is obliged to pay the beneficiary the amount of the order. The bank's acceptance of the payment order does not, however, create any obligation to either the sender or the originator.

Erroneous Execution of Payment Orders [27-5c]

If a receiving bank mistakenly executes a payment order for an amount greater than the amount authorized, the bank is entitled to payment only in the amount of the sender's correct order. To the extent allowed by the law governing mistake and restitution, the receiving bank may then recover from the beneficiary of the erroneous order the amount in excess of the authorized amount. If the wrong beneficiary is paid, however, the bank that issued the erroneous payment order is entitled to payment neither from its sender nor from prior senders and has the burden of recovering the payment from the improper beneficiary.

Unauthorized Payment Orders [27-5d]

If a bank wishing to prevent unauthorized transactions establishes commercially reasonable security measures, to which a customer agrees, and the bank properly follows the process it has established, the customer must pay an order even if it was unauthorized. The customer, however, can avoid liability by showing that the unauthorized order was not caused directly or indirectly by (1) a person with access to confidential security information who was acting for the customer or (2) a person who obtained such information from a source controlled by the customer.

CONCEPT REVIEW 27-1

Parties to a Funds Transfer

	Example 1	Example 2	Example 3
Originator	Johnson Co.	Johnson Co.	Johnson Co.
Sender(s)	Johnson Co.	Johnson Co. FNB	Johnson Co. FNB NB
Receiving Bank(s)	FNB	FNB CB	FNB CB NB
Originator's Bank	FNB	FNB	FNB
Beneficiary's Bank	FNB	CB	CB
Beneficiary	West	West	West
Intermediary Bank	—	—	NB

Note: CB = Central Bank; FNB = First National Bank; NB = Northern Bank.

ETHICAL DILEMMA

Can Embezzlement Ever Be a Loan?

Facts Susan Jennings was the head cashier for Pears, a highly respected discount store located in the heart of Chicago. Her job included distributing funds to each cashier, periodically collecting any large amounts from them, making a collection at the end of each shift, and depositing the previous day's receipts each morning. When a cashier brought money to Susan, the cashier would count the money and Susan would check it. At the end of each day, Susan would make out a deposit slip for the amount of cash and checks received, giving a copy of the slip to the accounting department for proper book entry. She would indorse each check with a company stamp marked "For Deposit Only."

On December 1, Alvin Troop, a new cashier, finished his shift and brought his money tray to Susan. While counting his receipts, he had noticed a check for $120 that had been made out without a payee. Alvin brought the check to Susan's attention. Matching his receipts to the cash register tape, Susan found that Alvin was exactly $120 over. Susan told him not to worry and said that she would fill in the store's name when she made the next deposit and would reconcile the receipts to the tape.

On December 2, Susan deposited the previous day's receipts in Pears's account in the First Sandy Hill Bank of Chicago, but decided to borrow $120 for her Christmas shopping. Short of cash and wanting to take advantage of a special sale, she intended to make up the difference on December 5, which was a payday. She filled her name in on the blank check, which also was drawn on the First Sandy Hill Bank, and the bank cashed it. Three days later, she replaced the money. No one knew what she had done until the customer who had written the check received his bank statement and demanded that the bank credit his account for the amount of the check that showed Susan as the payee.

Social, Policy, and Ethical Considerations

1. Were Susan's actions unethical or illegal? Explain. Would Susan's using the money for essential items, such as food or medicine, change your answer?
2. What should Susan have done?
3. What responsibility does the First Sandy Hill Bank have to its customers? In general, are banking procedures and standards established for the benefit of the bank or for that of the public?
4. If the bank teller had any idea that Susan had done something wrong, does the fact that he may have followed banking rules relieve him of any ethical responsibility?

CHAPTER SUMMARY

Bank Deposits and Collections

Collection of Items

Depositary Bank the bank in which the payee or holder deposits a check for credit

Provisional Credit tentative credit for the deposit of an instrument until final credit is given

Final Credit payment of the instrument by the payor bank; if the payor bank (drawee) does not pay the check, the depositary bank reverses the provisional credit

Intermediary Bank a bank, other than the depositary or payor bank, involved in the collection process

Collecting Bank any bank (other than the payor bank) handling the item for payment

- *Agency* a collecting bank is an agent or subagent of the owner of the check until the settlement becomes final
- *Duty of Care* a collecting bank must exercise ordinary care in handling an item
- *Duty to Act Timely* a collecting bank acts timely if it takes proper action before its midnight deadline (midnight of the next banking day)
- *Indorsements* if an item is restrictively indorsed "for deposit only," only a bank may be a holder
- *Warranties* customers and collecting banks give warranties on transfer, presentment, and encoding
- *Final Payment* occurs when the payor bank does any of the following, whichever happens first: (1) pays an item in cash; (2) settles and does not have the right to revoke the settlement; or (3) makes a provisional settlement and does not properly revoke it

Payor Bank under its contract with the drawer, the payor or drawee bank agrees to pay to the payee or his order checks that are issued by the drawer, provided the order is not countermanded by a stop payment order and provided there are sufficient funds in the drawer's account

Relationship Between Payor Bank and Its Customer

Contractual Relationship the relationship between a payor bank and its checking account customer is primarily the product of their contractual arrangement

Payment of an Item when a payor receives an item for which the funds in the account are insufficient, the bank may either dishonor the item and return it or pay the item and charge the customer's account even though an overdraft is created

Substitute Check a paper reproduction of the original check that for all purposes is the legal equivalent of an original check

Stop Payment Orders an oral stop payment order (a command from a drawer to a drawee not to pay an instrument) is binding for fourteen calendar days; a written order is effective for six months and may be renewed in writing

Bank's Right to Subrogation on Improper Payment if a payor bank pays an item over a stop payment order or otherwise in violation of its contract, the payor bank is subrogated to (obtains) the rights of (1) any holder in due course on the item against the drawer or maker, (2) the payee or any holder against the drawer or maker, and (3) the drawer or maker against the payee or any other holder

Disclosure Requirements all depositary institutions must disclose in great detail to their consumers the terms and conditions of their deposit account

Customer's Death or Incompetence a bank may pay an item if it does not know of the customer's incompetency or death

Customer's Duties the customer must examine bank statements and items carefully and promptly to discover any unauthorized signatures or alterations

Electronic Funds Transfer

Electronic Funds Transfer

Definition any transfer of funds, other than a transaction originated by check, draft, or similar paper instrument, which is initiated through an electronic terminal, telephonic instrument, or computer or magnetic tape so as to order, instruct, or authorize a financial institution to debit or credit an account

Purpose to eliminate the paperwork involved in processing checks and the "float" available to a drawer of a check

Types of Electronic Funds Transfers
- *Automated Teller Machines*
- *Point-of-Sale Systems*
- *Direct Deposits and Withdrawals*
- *Pay-by-Phone Systems*
- *Personal Computer (Online) Banking*
- *Wholesale Electronic Funds Transfers*

Consumer Funds Transfers

Electronic Funds Transfer Act provides a basic framework establishing the rights, liabilities, and responsibilities of participants in consumer electronic funds transfers

Financial Institution Responsibility liable to a consumer for all damage proximately caused by its failure to properly handle an electronic funds transfer transaction

Wholesale Funds Transfers

Scope of Article 4A
- *Wholesale Funds Transfers* the movement of funds through the banking system; excludes all transactions governed by the Electronic Funds Transfer Act except for some remittance transfers
- *Payment Order* an instruction of a sender to a receiving bank to pay, or to cause another bank to pay, a fixed amount of money to a beneficiary
- *Parties* include originator, sender, receiving bank, originator's bank, beneficiary's bank, beneficiary, and intermediary banks
- *Excluded Transactions*

Acceptance rights and obligations that arise as a result of a receiving bank's acceptance of a payment order

QUESTIONS

1. On November 9, Jane Jones writes a check for $500 payable to Ralph Rodgers in payment for goods to be received later in the month. Before the close of business on November 9, Jane notifies the bank by telephone to stop payment on the check. On December 19, Ralph gives the check to Bill Briggs for value and without notice. On December 20, Bill deposits the check in his account at Bank A. On December 21, Bank A sends the check to its correspondent, Bank B. On December 22, Bank B presents the check through the clearinghouse to Bank C. On December 23, Bank C presents the check to Bank P, the payor bank. On December 28, the payor bank makes payment of the check final. Is Jane Jones's stop payment order effective against the payor bank? Explain.

2. Howard Harrison, a longtime customer of Western Bank, operates a small department store, Harrison's Store. Because his store has few experienced employees, Harrison frequently travels throughout the United States on buying trips, although he also runs the financial operations of the business. On one of his buying trips, Harrison purchased two hundred sport shirts from Well-Made Shirt Company and paid for the transaction with a check on his store account with Western Bank in the amount of $3,000. Adams, an employee of Well-Made who deposits its checks in Security Bank, sloppily raised the amount of the check to $30,000 and indorsed the check, "Pay to the order of Adams from Pension Plan Benefits, Well-Made Shirt Company by Adams." He cashed the check and cannot be found. Western Bank processed the check, paid it, and sent it to Harrison's Store with the

monthly statement. After briefly examining the statement, Harrison left on another buying trip for three weeks.
   a. Assuming the bank acted in good faith and the alteration is not discovered and reported to the bank until an audit conducted thirteen months after the statement was received by Harrison's Store, who must bear the loss on the raised check?
   b. Assume that Harrison, who was unable to examine his statement promptly because of his buying trips, left instructions with the bank to carefully examine and to notify him of any item over $5,000 to be charged to his account; assume further that the bank nevertheless paid the item in his absence. Who bears the loss if the alteration is discovered one month after the statement was received by Harrison's Store? If the alteration is discovered thirteen months later?

3. Tom Jones owed Bank of Cleveland $10,000 on a note due November 17, with 1 percent interest due the bank for each day delinquent in payment. Jones issued a $10,000 check to Bank of Cleveland and deposited it in the night vault the evening of November 17. Several days later, he received a letter saying he owed one day's interest on the payment because of a one-day delinquency in payment. Jones refused because he said he had put the payment in the vault on November 17. Who is correct? Why?

4. Assume that Davis draws a check on Dallas Bank, payable to the order of Perkins; that Perkins indorses it to Cooper; that Cooper deposits it to her account in Houston Bank; that

Houston Bank presents it to Dallas Bank, the drawee; and that Dallas Bank dishonors it because of insufficient funds. Houston Bank receives notification of the dishonor on Monday but, because of an interruption of communication facilities, fails to notify Cooper until Wednesday. What will be the result?

5. Jones, a food wholesaler whose company has an account with City Bank in New York City, is traveling in California on business. He finds a particularly attractive offer and decides to buy a carload of oranges for delivery in New York. He gives Saltin, the seller, his company's check for $25,000 to pay for the purchase. Saltin deposits the check, with others he received that day, with his bank, the Carrboro Bank. Carrboro Bank sends the check to Downs Bank in Los Angeles, which in turn deposits it with the Los Angeles Federal Reserve Bank (L.A. Fed). The L.A. Fed sends the check, with others, to the New York Federal Reserve Bank (N.Y. Fed), which forwards the check to City Bank, Jones's bank, for collection.
   a. Is City Bank a depositary bank? A collecting bank? A payor bank?
   b. Is Carrboro a depositary bank? A collecting bank?
   c. Is the N.Y. Fed an intermediary bank?
   d. Is Downs Bank a collecting bank?

6. On April 1, Moore gave Pipkin a check properly drawn by Moore on Zebra Bank for $5,000 in payment of a painting to be framed and delivered the next day. Pipkin immediately indorsed the check and gave it to Yeager Bank as payment in full of his indebtedness to the bank on a note he previously had signed. Yeager Bank canceled the note and returned it to Pipkin.

   On April 2, upon learning that the painting had been destroyed in a fire at Pipkin's studio, Moore promptly went to Zebra Bank, signed a printed form of stop payment order, and gave it to the cashier. Zebra Bank refused payment on the check upon proper presentment by Yeager Bank.
   a. What are the rights of Yeager Bank against Zebra Bank?
   b. What are the rights of Yeager Bank against Moore?
   c. Assuming that Zebra Bank inadvertently paid the amount of the check to Yeager Bank and debited Moore's account, what are the rights of Moore against Zebra Bank?

7. As payment in advance for services to be performed, Acton signed and delivered the following instrument:

   December 1, 2015

   LAST NATIONAL BANK
   MONEYVILLE, STATE X
   Pay to the order of Olaf Owen $10,500.00 _____
   Ten Thousand Five Hundred Dollars _____ For services to be performed by Olaf Owen starting on December 6, 2015.

   (signed) Arthur Acton

   Owen requested and received Last National Bank's certification of the check even though Acton had only $9,000 on deposit. Owen indorsed the check in blank and delivered it to Dan Doty in payment of a preexisting debt.

   When Owen failed to appear for work, Acton issued a written stop payment order ordering the bank not to pay the check. Doty presented the check to Last National Bank for payment. The bank refused payment.

   What are the bank's rights and liabilities relating to the transactions described?

8. Jones drew a check for $1,000 on The First Bank and mailed it to the payee, Thrift, Inc. Caldwell stole the check from Thrift, Inc., chemically erased the name of the payee, and inserted the name of Henderson as payee. Caldwell also increased the amount of the check to $10,000 and, by using the name of Henderson, negotiated the check to Willis. Willis then took the check to The First Bank, obtained its certification on the check, and negotiated the check to Griffin, who deposited the check in The Second National Bank for collection. The Second National Bank forwarded the check to the Detroit Trust Company for collection from The First Bank, which honored the check. Griffin exhausted her account in The Second National Bank, and the account was closed. Shortly thereafter, The First Bank learned that it had paid an altered check.

   What are the rights of each of the parties?

9. On July 21, Boehmer, a customer of Birmingham Trust, secured a loan from that bank for the principal sum of $5,500 in order to purchase a boat allegedly being built for him by A. C. Manufacturing Company, Inc. After Boehmer signed a promissory note, Birmingham Trust issued a cashier's check to Boehmer and A. C. Manufacturing Company as payees. The check was given to Boehmer, who then forged A. C. Manufacturing Company's indorsement and deposited the check in his own account at Central Bank. Central Bank credited Boehmer's account and then placed the legend "P.I.G.," meaning "Prior Indorsements Guaranteed," on the check. The check was presented to and paid by Birmingham Trust on July 22. When the loan became delinquent in March of the following year, Birmingham Trust contacted A. C. Manufacturing Company to learn the location of the boat. They were informed that it had never been purchased, and they soon after learned that Boehmer had died on January 24 of that year. Can Birmingham Trust obtain reimbursement from Central Bank under Central's warranty of prior indorsements? Explain.

10. Jason, who has extremely poor vision, went to an automated teller machine (ATM) to withdraw $200 on February 1. Joshua saw that Jason was having great difficulty reading the computer screen and offered to help. Joshua obtained Jason's personal identification number and secretly exchanged one of his old credit cards for Jason's ATM card. Between February 1 and February 15, Joshua withdrew $1,600 from Jason's account. On February 15, Jason discovered that his ATM card was missing and immediately notified his bank. The bank closed Jason's ATM account on February 16, by which time Joshua had withdrawn another $150. What is Jason's liability, if any, for the unauthorized use of his account?

11. Advanced Alloys, Inc., issued a check in the amount of $2,500 to Sergeant Steel Corporation. The check was presented for payment fourteen months later to the Chase Manhattan Bank, which made payment on the check and charged Advanced Alloys's account. Can Advanced Alloys recover the payment made on the check? Why?

CASE PROBLEMS

12. Laboratory Management deposited into its account at Pulaski Bank a check issued by Fairway Farms in the amount of $150,000. The date of deposit was February 5. Pulaski, the depositary bank, initiated the collection process immediately by forwarding the check to Worthen Bank on the sixth. Worthen sent the check on for collection to M Bank Dallas, and M Bank Dallas, still on February 6, delivered the check to M Bank Fort Worth. That same day, M Bank Fort Worth delivered the check to the Fort Worth Clearinghouse. Because TAB/West Side, the drawee/payor bank, was not a clearinghouse member, it had to rely on TAB/Fort Worth for further transmittal of the check. TASI, a processing center used by both TAB/Fort Worth and TAB/West Side, received the check on the sixth and processed it as a reject item because of insufficient funds. On the seventh, TAB/West Side determined to return the check unpaid. TASI gave M Bank Dallas telephone notice of the return on February 7, but physically misrouted the check. Because of this, M Bank Dallas did not physically receive the check until February 19. However, M Bank notified Worthen by telephone on the fifteenth of the dishonor and return of the check. Worthen received the check on the twenty-first and notified Pulaski by telephone on the twenty-second. Pulaski actually received the check from Worthen on the twenty-third. On February 22 and 23, Laboratory Management's checking account with Pulaski was $46,000. Pulaski did not freeze the account because it considered the return to be too late. The Laboratory Management account was finally frozen on April 30, when it had a balance of $1,400. Pulaski brings this suit against TAB/Fort Worth, TAB/Dallas, and TASI, alleging their notice of dishonor was not timely relayed to Pulaski. Explain whether Pulaski is correct in its assertion.

13. On November 22, a $25,000 check drawn on the First National Bank of Nevada was deposited with Lincoln First Bank-Central. Lincoln forwarded the check to Nevada via Hartford National Bank and Trust Company and Wells Fargo Bank. Nevada received the check on Friday, December 10, and discovered that it was drawn on insufficient funds. That same day, Nevada informed Wells Fargo by telephone that the check had been dishonored. On Monday, December 13, Nevada mailed the check to Wells Fargo, which received it on Friday, December 17. Upon receiving the check, Wells Fargo promptly wired notice of the dishonor to Hartford and mailed the check to Hartford. Hartford received the check on December 21 and mailed it to Lincoln, which received it on December 27. Lincoln refused to accept the check, claiming that the notice of dishonor had arrived too late. Wells Fargo, which eventually ended up with the check and the $25,000 loss, brought an action to reverse the $25,000 credit it had given to Hartford in the course of handling the check. Decision?

14. On Tuesday, June 11, Siniscalchi issued a $200 check on the drawee, Valley Bank. On Saturday morning, June 15, the check was cashed. This transaction, as well as others taking place on that Saturday morning, was not recorded or processed through the bank's bookkeeping system until Monday, June 17. On that date, Siniscalchi arrived at the bank at 9:00 A.M. and asked to place a stop payment order on the check. A bank employee checked the bank records, which at that time indicated the instrument had not cleared the bank. At 9:45 A.M., she gave him a printed notice confirming his request to stop payment. May Siniscalchi recover the $200 paid on the check? Explain.

15. Tally held a savings account with American Security Bank. On seven occasions, Tally's personal secretary, who received his bank statements and had custody of his passbook, forged Tally's name on withdrawal slips that she then presented to the bank. The secretary obtained $52,825 in this manner. Three years after the secretary's last fraudulent withdrawal she confessed to Tally who promptly notified the bank of the issue. Can Tally recover the funds from American Security Bank? Explain.

16. Morvarid Kashanchi and her sister, Firoyeh Paydar, held a savings account with Texas Commerce Medical Bank. An unauthorized withdrawal of $4,900 from the account was allegedly made by means of a telephone conversation between some other unidentified individual and a bank employee. Paydar learned of the transfer of funds when she received her bank statement and notified the bank that the withdrawal was unauthorized. The bank, however, declined to recredit the account for the $4,900 transfer. Kashanchi brought an action against the bank, claiming that the bank had violated the Electronic Funds Transfer Act (EFTA). The bank defended by arguing that the Act did not apply. Does the EFTA govern the transaction? Explain.

17. During a period of almost two years, Great Lakes Higher Education Corp. (Great Lakes), a not-for-profit student loan servicer, issued 224 student loan checks totaling $273,152.88. The checks were drawn against Great Lakes's account at First Wisconsin National Bank of Milwaukee (First Wisconsin). Each of the 224 checks was presented to Austin Bank of Chicago (Austin) without indorsement of the named payee. Austin Bank accepted each check for purposes of collection and without delay forwarded each check to First Wisconsin for that purpose. First Wisconsin paid Austin Bank the face amount of each check even though the indorsement signature of the payee was not on any of the checks. Has Austin Bank breached its warranty to First Wisconsin and Great Lakes due to the absence of proper indorsements? Explain.

TAKING SIDES

Mary Mansi claims that eighteen checks on her account contain forgeries but were nevertheless paid by her bank, Sterling National Bank. The checks bore signatures that, according to the Mansi's handwriting expert, were apparently "written by another person who attempted to simulate her signature" and thus were not considered obvious forgeries. Sterling National Bank acknowledged that it did honor those eighteen checks, but nine of them were returned to the plaintiff more than one year prior to this action.

In addition, Mansi had received bank statements and failed to examine them.

a. What are the arguments that the bank is liable to Mansi for wrongfully paying the checks?

b. What are the arguments that the bank is not be liable to Mansi for paying the checks?

c. Who should prevail? Why?

Relationship of Principal and Agent

Practically all of the world's business involves agents and in most important transactions, an agent on each side.

Warren Seavey
Handbook on the Law of Agency

CHAPTER OUTCOMES

After reading and studying this chapter, you should be able to:

1. Distinguish among the following relationships: (a) agency, (b) employment, and (c) independent contractor.

2. Explain the requirements for creating an agency relationship.

3. List and explain the duties owed by an agent to her principal.

4. List and explain the duties owed by a principal to his agent.

5. Identify the ways in which an agency relationship may be terminated.

By using agents, one person (the principal) may enter into any number of business transactions as though he had carried them out personally, thus multiplying and expanding his business activities. The law of agency, like the law of contracts, is basic to almost every other branch of business law.

Practically every type of contract or business transaction can be created or conducted through an agent. Therefore, the place and importance of agency in the practical conduct and operation of business cannot be overemphasized, particularly in the case of partnerships, corporations, and other business associations. Partnership is founded on the agency of the partners. Each partner is an agent of the partnership and as such has the authority to represent and bind the partnership in all usual transactions of the partnership. Corporations, in turn, must act through the agency of their officers and employees. Limited liability companies act through the actions of their members, managers, or both. Thus, practically and legally, agency is an essential part of partnerships, corporations, and other business associations. In addition, sole proprietors also may employ agents in the operations of their businesses. Business, therefore, is conducted largely by agents or representatives, not by the owners themselves.

Although some overlap occurs, the law of agency divides broadly into two main parts: the internal and the external. An agent functions as an agent by dealing with third persons, thereby establishing legal relationships between her principal and those third persons. These relationships are the external part of agency law, which we will discuss in the next chapter. In this chapter, we will consider the nature and function of agency, as well as other topics concerning the internal part of the law of agency.

Agency is governed primarily by state common law. An orderly presentation of this law is found in the Restatement (Second) of the Law of Agency published in 1958 by the American Law Institute (ALI). Regarded as a valuable authoritative reference work, the Restatement is cited extensively and quoted in reported judicial opinions and by legal scholars. In 2006 the ALI published the Restatement of the Law Third,

Agency, which replaced the ALI's Restatement Second of Agency. This chapter and the next chapter will refer to the Third Restatement as the Restatement.

NATURE OF AGENCY [28-1]

Agency is a *consensual* relationship in which one person (the **agent**) acts as a representative of, or otherwise acts on behalf of, another person (the **principal**) with power to affect the legal rights and duties of the principal. Moreover, the principal has a right to control the actions of the agent. An agent is, therefore, one who represents another, the principal, in business dealings with a third person, and the operation of agency therefore involves three persons: the principal, the agent, and a third person who deals with the agent. In dealings with a third person, the agent acts for and in the name and place of the principal, who, along with the third person, is a party to the transaction. The result of the agent's functioning is exactly the same as if the principal had dealt directly with the third person. However, if the existence and identity of the principal are disclosed, the agent acts not as a party but simply as an intermediary.

Within the scope of the authority granted to her by her principal, the agent may negotiate the terms of contracts with others and bind her principal to such contracts. Moreover, the negligence of an agent who is an employee in conducting the business of her principal exposes the principal to tort liability for injury and loss suffered by third persons.

Scope of Agency Purposes [28-1a]

As a general rule, a person may do through an agent whatever business activity he may accomplish personally. Conversely, whatever he cannot legally do, he cannot authorize another to do for him. In addition, a person may not appoint an agent to perform acts that are so personal that their performance may not be delegated to another, as in the case of a contract for personal services.

Other Legal Relationships [28-1b]

Two other legal relationships overlap with the agency relationship: employer–employee and principal–independent contractor. In the **employment relationship**, for the purposes of vicarious liability discussed in Chapter 29, an employee is an agent whose principal controls or has the right to control the manner and means of the agent's performance of work. All employees are agents, even those employees not authorized to contract on behalf of the employer or otherwise to conduct business with third parties. Thus, an assembly-line worker in a factory is an agent of the company employing her since she is subject to the employer's control, thereby consenting to act "on behalf" of the principal, but she does not have the right to bind the principal in contracts with third parties.

Although all employees are agents, not all agents are employees. Agents who are not employees are generally referred to as **independent contractors**. (The Third Restatement does not use this term.) In these cases, although the principal has the right of control over the agent, the principal does not control the manner and means of the agent's performance. For instance, an attorney retained to handle a particular transaction would be an independent contractor–agent regarding that particular transaction because the attorney is hired by the principal to perform a service, but the manner of the attorney's performance is not controlled by the principal. Other examples are auctioneers, brokers, and factors.

Finally, not all independent contractors are agents because the person hiring the independent contractor has no right of control over the independent contractor. For example, a taxicab driver hired to carry a person to the airport is not an agent of that person. Likewise, if Pam hires Bill to build a stone wall around her property, Bill is an independent contractor who is not an agent.

The distinction between employee and independent contractor has a number of important legal consequences. For example, as we will discuss in the next chapter, a principal is liable for the torts an employee commits within the scope of her employment but ordinarily is not liable for torts committed by an independent contractor. The following case further explains the differences between an employee and an independent contractor.

Agency
consensual relationship authorizing one party (agent) to act on behalf of the other party (principal) subject to the principal's control

Agent
person authorized to act on another's behalf

Principal
person who authorizes another to act on her behalf

Scope of agency purposes
whatever business activity a person may accomplish personally he generally may do through an agent

Employment relationship
one in which the employer has the right to control the manner and means of the employee's performance of work

Independent contractor
person who contracts with another to do a particular job and is not subject to the other's control over the manner and means of conducting the work

Practical Advice

When appointing an agent, consider structuring the relationship as a principal and independent contractor.

In addition, under numerous federal and state statutes, the obligations of a principal apply only to agents who are employees. These statutes cover such matters as labor relations, employment discrimination, disability, employee safety, workers' compensation, social security, minimum wage, and unemployment compensation. We will discuss these and other statutory enactments affecting the employment relationship in Chapter 41.

Del Pilar v. DHL Global Customer Solutions (USA), Inc.
District Court of Appeal of Florida, First District, 2008
993 So.2d 142
http://scholar.google.com/scholar_case?q=993+So.2d+142&hl=en&as_sdt=2,34&case=9058638460907179646&scilh=0

FACTS Danny Del Pilar sustained injuries when his car collided with a delivery van painted in yellow, the widely recognized DHL color, and displaying the DHL name and logo. The truck was driven by a driver clad in a DHL uniform and laden with packages destined for DHL customers. The van was owned not by DHL, but by Johnny Boyd, a driver for Silver Ink, Inc., a local company that was responsible at the time for picking up, sorting, and delivering all DHL packages in metropolitan Jacksonville, Duval County, Florida. Boyd, working for Silver Ink on the DHL contract, was shuttling DHL packages when the accident occurred. DHL, whose primary business focuses on shipping packages via air around the world, has no capability to pick up or deliver local packages in Duval County and, at the time of the accident, it relied exclusively on Silver Ink to provide such local services.

DHL's agreement with Silver Ink essentially delegated to Silver Ink the responsibility to service DHL customers in the Jacksonville area. The contract identified Silver Ink as an "independent contractor" and provided that "the manner and means by which Contractor performs the services shall be at Contractor's sole discretion and control and are Contractor's sole responsibility." The agreement also, however, recited an exhaustive and detailed list of procedures that Silver Ink employees were to follow in processing, picking up, and delivering packages, and contained a provision under which Silver Ink was required to indemnify DHL in the event Silver Ink lost or damaged packages bound for DHL's customers. The agreement gave either party the power to terminate in the event of the other party's breach. Silver Ink employees were contractually required to "wear a DHL uniform and properly display the DHL Marks [sic] and uniform in a clean, professional, and businesslike manner"; the contract specified the particular articles of clothing and accessories considered part of the DHL uniform, the purchase of which was funded by DHL. Silver Ink was required to submit to unannounced operational inspections and audits at DHL's sole discretion and was required to maintain a fleet of delivery vans operated in DHL livery, designed and placed on the vehicles in strict accordance with specifications established by DHL. Silver Ink's operational hub was co-located with DHL's Duval County facility and DHL employees monitored and reviewed Silver Ink operations on a daily basis.

Danny Del Pilar sued DHL for his personal injuries arising from the auto accident. The trial court granted summary judgment for DHL after concluding that Silver Ink was an independent contractor for whose alleged negligence DHL is not vicariously liable. Danny Del Pilar appealed.

DECISION Judgment reversed, and case is remanded.

OPINION Generally, a principal is not vicariously liable for the negligence of its independent contractor, but the principal is liable for the negligence of its agent. Whether a person working on behalf of another is an agent or an independent contractor "is a question of fact … not controlled by descriptive labels employed by the parties themselves." A particularly significant factor in the determination of status is "the degree of control exercised by the employer or owner over the agent. More particularly, it is the *right* of control, and not *actual* control, which determines the relationship between the parties." In most cases, the terms of a contract between the parties is a pertinent index of the principal's right of control and should factor heavily into the inquiry, "unless other provisions of the agreement, or the parties' actual practice, demonstrate that it is not a valid indicator of status [or] … belie the creation of the status agreed to by the parties." In that case, "the actual practice and relationship of the parties should control."

Elements of control that tend to suggest a relationship in which the principal is vicariously liable for the agent's negligence include, but are not limited to (1) the principal's right to control the agent's use of the principal's trademarks; (2) reservation to the principal of the unilateral right to prohibit the agent from working on behalf of competitors; (3) a requirement that the agent's employees must undergo training before they work on the principal's behalf; (4) a requirement that the agent perform services using only equipment selected pursuant to the principal's specifications; (5) a requirement that the agent, when working on behalf of the principal, use a vehicle with the principal's logo, placed according to parameters established by the principal; (6) a requirement that the agent adhere to customer-service procedures established by the principal; and (7) a requirement that the agent submit to inspections conducted at the principal's discretion.

Here, the contract between DHL and Silver Ink certainly recites in conclusory terms the status of independent contractor. The balance of DHL's contract with Silver Ink "leaves nothing to chance." Somewhat inconsistently with the conclusory language purporting to confer broad discretion upon Silver Ink to fulfill its operational obligations, subsequent provisions list specific procedures and protocols that Silver Ink employees are to follow when picking up, sorting, and delivering DHL packages; everything from the process of scanning packages into DHL's tracking system to procedures for redelivery after unsuccessful delivery attempts is set out in detail in the agreement. Shippers and recipients are "DHL customers," and the agreement contains an indemnity provision requiring Silver Ink to indemnify DHL for damages stemming from packages lost or damaged due to Silver Ink's negligence, suggesting that DHL intends, in the first instance, to answer directly to its customers. The contract requires Silver Ink employees to "wear a DHL uniform and properly display the DHL Marks and uniform in a clean, professional, and businesslike manner," with further specification of the particular apparel considered part of the DHL uniform. Silver Ink must operate delivery vehicles painted in the DHL livery and must submit to unannounced operational inspections and audits at DHL's sole discretion. Silver Ink must pick up and deliver packages at times requested by DHL's customers pursuant to DHL's advertised guarantees.

The trial court erred in concluding, as a matter of law, that Silver Ink was DHL's independent contractor. The question of DHL's control over Silver Ink operations should go to the jury.

INTERPRETATION Whether a person is an employee or an independent contractor is a question of fact not controlled by descriptive labels employed by the parties themselves. A particularly significant factor in this determination is the degree of control exercised by the employer or owner over the agent, and it is the *right* of control, not *actual* control, which determines the relationship between the parties.

CRITICAL THINKING QUESTION Do you agree that this case requires further fact finding? Explain.

CREATION OF AGENCY [28-2]

As stated, agency is a consensual relationship that the principal and agent may form by contract or agreement. The Restatement defines an agency relationship as "the fiduciary relationship that arises when one person (a 'principal') manifests assent to another person (an 'agent') that the agent shall act on the principal's behalf and subject to the principal's control, and the agent manifests assent or otherwise consents so to act." Thus, the agency relationship involves three basic elements: assent, control by the principal, and the agent's acting on behalf of the principal. A person can manifest assent or intention through written or spoken words or other conduct. Thus, whether an agency relationship has been created is determined by an *objective* test. If the principal requests another to act for him with respect to a matter and indicates that the other is to act without further communication, and the other consents to act, the relation of principal and agent exists. For example, Paula writes to Austin, a factor whose business is purchasing goods for others, telling him to select described goods and ship them at once to Paula. Before answering Paula's letter, Austin does as directed, charging the goods to Paula. He is authorized to do this because an agency relationship exists between Paula and Austin.

The principal has the right to control the conduct of the agent with respect to the matters entrusted to the agent. The principal's right to control continues throughout the duration of the agency relationship.

The relationship of principal and agent is consensual and not necessarily contractual; therefore, it may exist without consideration. Even though the agency relationship is consensual, how the parties label the relationship does not determine whether it is an agency. An agency created without an agent's right to compensation is a **gratuitous agency**. For example, Patti asks her friend Andrew to return for credit goods recently purchased from a store. If Andrew consents, a gratuitous agency has been created. The power of a gratuitous agent to affect the principal's relationships with third persons is the same as that of a paid agent, and his liabilities to and rights against third persons are the same as well. Nonetheless, agency by contract, the most usual method of creating the relationship, must satisfy all of the requirements of a contract.

In some circumstances a person is held liable as a principal, even though no actual agency has been created, to protect third parties who justifiably rely on a reasonable belief that a person is an agent and who act on that belief to their detriment. Called **agency by estoppel**, apparent agency, or ostensible agency, this liability arises when (1) a person ("principal") intentionally or carelessly causes a third party to believe that another person (the "agent") has authority to act on the principal's behalf, (2) the principal has notice of the third party's belief and does not take reasonable steps to notify the third party, (3) the third party reasonably and in good faith relies on the appearances created by the principal, and (4) the third party justifiably and detrimentally changes her position in reliance on the agent's apparent authority. When these requirements are met, the principal is liable to the third party for the loss the third party suffered by changing her position. The doctrine is applicable when the person against whom estoppel is asserted has made no manifestation that an actor has authority as an agent, but is responsible for the third party's belief that an actor is an agent, and the third party has justifiably been induced by that belief to undergo a detrimental change in position.

Gratuitous agency
an agency created without consideration

Agency by estoppel
imposed by law when a person (P) causes a third person (T) to believe that another person (A) has authority to act on P's behalf

Miller v. McDonald's Corporation
Court of Appeals of Oregon, 1997
150 Or.App. 274, 945 P.2d 1107
http://scholar.google.com/scholar_case?case=16078633099320931234&q=945+P.2d+1107&hl=en&as_sdt

FACTS Joni Miller seeks damages from defendant McDonald's Corporation for injuries that she suffered when she bit into a heart-shaped sapphire stone while eating a Big Mac sandwich that she had purchased at a McDonald's restaurant in Tigard. McDonald's claims it is not liable because the 3K Corporation owns the restaurant. 3K owned and operated the restaurant under a License Agreement with McDonald's that required 3K to operate in a manner consistent with the "McDonald's System." This system includes proprietary rights in trademarks, "designs and color schemes" for restaurant buildings and signs, and specifications for certain food products as well as other business practices and policies. 3K, as the licensee, agreed to adopt and exclusively use the business practices of McDonald's. Despite these detailed instructions, the Agreement provided that 3K was not an agent of McDonald's for any purpose. Rather, it was an independent contractor and was responsible for all obligations and liabilities, including claims based on injury, illness, or death directly or indirectly resulting from the operation of the restaurant.

Miller was under the assumption that McDonald's owned, controlled, and managed the restaurant because its appearance and menu were similar to that of other McDonald's restaurants. In short, Miller testified, she went to the Tigard McDonald's because she relied on defendant's reputation and because she wanted to obtain the same quality of service, standard of care in food preparation, and general attention to detail that she had previously enjoyed at other McDonald's restaurants.

The trial court granted summary judgment to McDonald's on the ground that it did not own or operate the restaurant; rather, the owner and operator was a nonparty, 3K Restaurants, which held a franchise from McDonald's. Miller appeals.

DECISION Reversed and remanded.

OPINION Under these facts, 3K would be directly liable for any injuries that Miller suffered as a result of the restaurant's negligence. The issue on summary judgment is whether there is evidence to permit a jury to find McDonald's vicariously liable for those injuries because of its relationship with 3K. Miller asserts two theories of vicarious liability: actual agency and apparent agency.

Under actual agency, in order for McDonald's to be vicariously liable for 3K's negligence, McDonald's must have the right to control the method by which 3K performed its obligations under the Agreement. A number of courts have applied the right to control test to a franchise relationship. If, in practical effect, the franchise Agreement goes beyond the stage of setting standards and allocates to the franchisor the right to exercise control over the daily operations of the franchise, an agency relationship exists. We believe that a jury could find that McDonald's retained sufficient control over 3K's daily operations so that an actual agency relationship existed. The Agreement did not simply set standards that 3K had to meet. Rather, it required 3K to use the precise methods that McDonald's established, including the ways in which 3K was to handle and prepare food. McDonald's enforced the use of those methods by regularly sending inspectors and by its retained power to cancel the Agreement. That evidence would support a finding that McDonald's had the right to control the way in which 3K performed at least food handling and preparation.

Miller next asserts that McDonald's is vicariously liable for 3K's alleged negligence because 3K was an apparent agent of McDonald's. The crucial issues are whether the putative principal held the third party out as an agent and whether Miller relied on that holding out. McDonald's does not seriously dispute that a jury could find that it held 3K out as its agent. Everything about the appearance and operation of the Tigard McDonald's identified it with the common image for all McDonald's restaurants. Rather, it argues that there is insufficient evidence that Miller justifiably relied on that holding out. In this case, Miller testified that she relied on the general reputation of McDonald's in patronizing the Tigard restaurant and in her expectation of the quality of the food and service that she would receive. Especially in light of McDonald's efforts to create a public perception of a common McDonald's system at all McDonald's restaurants, whoever operated them, a jury could find that Miller's reliance was objectively reasonable. The trial court erred in granting summary judgment on the apparent agency theory.

INTERPRETATION If a franchisor exercises sufficient control over its franchisee's operations, actual agency and/or apparent agency can exist and cause the franchisor to be held vicariously liable as a principal for the acts of the franchisee even if their written agreement provides that no agency relationship exists.

CRITICAL THINKING QUESTION Do you agree that a franchise relationship should under certain circumstances be treated as an agency relationship? Explain.

Formalities

usually no particular formality is required in a contract of agency, although appointments of agents for a period of more than one year must be in writing

Formalities [28-2a]

As a general rule, a contract of agency requires no particular formality, and usually the contract either may be oral or may be inferred from the conduct of the principal. In some cases, however, the contract must be in writing. For example, the appointment of an agent for a period of more than a year comes within the one-year clause of the statute of frauds and thus must be in writing. In some states, the authority of an agent to sell land must be set down in a writing signed by the principal. Many states have "equal dignity" statutes providing that a principal must grant his agent in a written instrument the authority to enter into any contract required to be in writing.

See Chapter 15 for a discussion of state and federal legislation giving electronic records and signatures the legal effect of traditional writings and signatures.

A **power of attorney** is an instrument that states an agent's authority. A power of attorney is a formal manifestation from principal to agent, who is known as "an attorney in fact," as well as to third parties, that evidences the agent's appointment and the nature or extent of the agent's authority. Under a power of attorney, a principal may, for example, appoint an agent not only to execute a contract for the sale of the principal's real estate but also to execute the deed conveying title to the real estate to the third party. A number of states have created an optional statutory short-form power of attorney based on the Uniform Statutory Form Power of Attorney Act. In 2006, a new Uniform Power of Attorney Act (UPOAA) was promulgated to replace the Uniform Statutory Form Power of Attorney Act. At least sixteen states have adopted the 2006 Act.

Capacity [28-2b]

The capacity of an individual to be a principal, and thus to act through an agent, depends on the **capacity of the principal** to do the act. For example, contracts entered into by a minor or an incompetent not under a guardianship are voidable. Consequently, the appointment of an agent by a minor or an incompetent not under a guardianship and any resulting contracts are voidable, regardless of the agent's contractual capacity. The capacity of a person that is not an individual, such as a government or business association, to be a principal is determined by the law governing that entity.

Almost all of the states have adopted the Uniform Durable Power of Attorney Act providing for a durable power of attorney under which an agent's power survives or is triggered by the principal's loss of mental competence. (In 2006, the new UPOAA was promulgated to replace the Uniform Durable Power of Attorney Act. At least sixteen states have adopted the 2006 Act. A power of attorney created under the UPOAA is durable unless it expressly provides that it is terminated by the incapacity of the principal.) A **durable power of attorney** is a written instrument that expresses the principal's intention that the agent's authority will not be affected by the principal's subsequent incapacity or that the agent's authority will become effective upon the principal's subsequent incapacity.

On the other hand, because the act of the agent is considered the act of the principal, the incapacity of an agent to bind himself by contract does not disqualify him from making a contract that is binding on the principal. Thus, any person able to act, including individuals, corporations, partnerships, and other associations, ordinarily has the **capacity to be an agent**. The agent's liability, however, depends on the agent's capacity to contract. Therefore, although the contract of agency may be voidable, an authorized contract between the principal and the third person who dealt with the agent is valid.

An "electronic agent" is a computer program or other automated means used independently to initiate an action or respond to electronic records or performances in whole or in part without review or action by an individual. Electronic agents are not persons and, therefore, are not considered agents. In 2000 Congress enacted the Electronic Signatures in Global and National Commerce (E-Sign). The Act makes electronic records and signatures valid and enforceable across the United States for many types of transactions in or affecting interstate or foreign commerce. The Act validates contracts or other records relating to a transaction in or affecting interstate or foreign commerce formed by electronic agents so long as the action of each electronic agent is legally attributable to the person to be bound. E-Sign specifically excludes certain transactions, including (1) wills, codicils, and testamentary trusts; (2) adoptions, divorces, and other matters of family law; and (3) the Uniform Commercial Code other than sales and leases of goods.

DUTIES OF AGENT TO PRINCIPAL [28-3]

The duties of the agent to the principal are determined by the express and implied provisions of any contract between the agent and the principal. In addition to these contractual duties, the agent is subject to various other duties imposed by law, unless the parties agree otherwise. Normally, a principal bases the selection of an agent on the agent's ability, skill, and integrity. Moreover, the principal not only authorizes and empowers the agent to bind her on contracts

Power of attorney
written, formal appointment of an agent who is known as an attorney in fact

Capacity of principal
if the principal is a minor or an incompetent not under a guardianship, his appointment of another to act as an agent is voidable, as are any resulting contracts with third parties

Durable power of attorney
a written instrument that expresses the principal's intention that the agent's authority will not be affected by the principal's subsequent incapacity or that the agent's authority will become effective upon the principal's subsequent incapacity

Capacity of agent
any person able to act may act as an agent since the act of the agent is considered the act of the principal

with third persons but also often places the agent in possession of her money and other property. As a result, the agent is in a position to injure the principal, either through negligence or dishonesty. Accordingly, an agent, as a fiduciary (a person in a position of trust and confidence), owes her principal the duties of obedience, good conduct, diligence, and loyalty; the duty to inform; and the duty to provide an accounting. Moreover, an agent is liable for any loss she causes to the principal through her breach of these duties.

A gratuitous agent is subject to the same duty of loyalty that is imposed on a paid agent and is equally liable to the principal for the harm he causes by his careless performance. Although the lack of consideration usually places a gratuitous agent under no duty to perform for the principal, such an agent may be liable to the principal for failing to perform a promise on which the principal has relied if the agent should have realized that his promise would induce reliance.

Duty of Obedience [28-3a]

Duty of obedience
an agent must act in the principal's affairs only as authorized by the principal and must obey all lawful instructions and directions of the principal

The **duty of obedience** requires the agent to act in the principal's affairs only as actually authorized by the principal and to obey all lawful instructions and directions of the principal. If an agent exceeds her actual authority, she is subject to liability to the principal for loss caused to the principal. An agent is also liable to the principal for unauthorized acts that are the result of the agent's unreasonable interpretations of the principal's directions. An agent is not, however, under a duty to follow orders to perform illegal or tortious acts, such as misrepresenting the quality of his principal's goods or those of a competitor. The agent may be subject to liability to her principal for breach of the duty of obedience (1) if she entered into an unauthorized contract for which her principal is now liable, (2) if she has improperly delegated her authority, or (3) if she has committed a tort for which the principal is now liable. Thus, an agent who sells on credit in violation of his principal's explicit instructions has breached the duty of obedience and is liable to the principal for any amounts the purchaser does not pay. Moreover, an agent who violates her duty of obedience materially breaches the agency contract and loses her right to compensation.

Practical Advice

Recognize that even if you agree to serve as an agent without compensation, you owe a fiduciary duty to the principal and are liable to her for your negligence.

Duty of Good Conduct [28-3b]

Duty of good conduct
within the scope of the agency relationship, an agent must act reasonably and refrain from conduct that is likely to damage the principal's enterprise

An agent has a duty, within the scope of the agency relationship, to act reasonably and to avoid conduct that is likely to damage the principal's interests. This duty reflects the fact that the conduct of agents can have a significant effect on the principal's reputation. A breach of this duty makes the agent liable to the principal and subject to rightful discharge or termination.

Duty of Diligence [28-3c]

Duty of diligence
an agent must act with reasonable care, competence, and diligence in performing the work for which he is employed

Subject to any agreement with the principal, an agent has a duty to the principal to act with the care, competence, and diligence normally exercised by agents in similar circumstances. Special skills or knowledge possessed by an agent are circumstances to be taken into account in determining whether the agent acted with due care and diligence. Moreover, if the agent claims to possess special skill or knowledge, the agent has a duty to act with the care, competence, and diligence normally exercised by agents with such skill or knowledge. An agent who does not exercise the required care, competence, and diligence is liable to his principal for any resulting harm. For example, Peg appoints Alvin as her agent to sell goods in markets where the highest price can be obtained. Although he could have obtained a higher price in a nearby market by carefully obtaining information, Alvin sells goods in a glutted market and obtains a low price. Consequently, he is liable to Peg for breach of the duty of diligence.

A gratuitous agent owes a standard of care that is reasonable to expect under the circumstances, which include the skill and experience that the agent possesses. Thus, providing a service gratuitously may subject an agent to duties of competence and diligence to the principal that do not differ from the duties owed by a compensated agent.

Duty to Inform [28-3d]

Duty to inform
an agent must use reasonable efforts to give the principal information material to the affairs entrusted to her

An agent has a duty to use reasonable effort to provide the principal with facts that the agent knows, has reason to know, or should know if (1) the agent knows, or has reason to know, that the principal would wish to have the facts or (2) the facts are material to the agent's duties to the principal. However, this duty does not apply to facts if providing them to the principal would violate a superior duty owed by the agent to another person. The rule of agency providing that notice to an agent is notice to her principal makes this duty essential. An agent who breaches this duty is subject to liability to the principal for loss caused the principal by the agent's breach and may also be subject to termination of the agency relationship. Moreover, if the agent's breach of this duty constitutes a breach of the contract between the agent and the principal, the agent is also liable for breach of contract.

Examples of information that an agent is under a duty to communicate may include the following: (1) a customer of the principal has become insolvent; (2) a debtor of the principal has become insolvent; (3) a partner of a firm with which the principal has previously dealt, and with which the principal or agent is about to deal, has withdrawn from the firm; or (4) property that the principal has authorized the agent to sell at a specified price can be sold at a higher price.

Duty to Account [28-3e]

Duty to account

an agent must maintain and provide the principal with an accurate account of money or other property that the agent has received or expended on behalf of the principal; an agent must not mingle the principal's property with any other person's property

Subject to any agreement with the principal, an agent has a duty to keep and render accounts to the principal of money or other property received or paid out on the principal's account. Moreover, the agent may not mingle the principal's property with any other person's property and may not deal with the principal's property so that it appears to be the agent's property.

Fiduciary Duty [28-3f]

Fiduciary duty

an agent owes a duty of utmost loyalty and good faith to the principal

A **fiduciary duty**, arising out of a relationship of trust and confidence, requires the utmost loyalty and good faith. An agent has a fiduciary duty to act loyally for the principal's benefit in all matters connected with the agency relationship. This duty is imposed by law upon the agent and is also owed by an employee to his employer. The principal may agree that conduct by an agent that otherwise would constitute a breach of the fiduciary duty shall not constitute a breach of that duty provided that in obtaining the principal's consent, the agent (1) acts in good faith, (2) discloses all material facts that the agent knows, has reason to know, or should know would reasonably affect the principal's judgment, and (3) otherwise deals fairly with the principal.

An agent's fiduciary duty to a principal generally begins with the formation of the agency relationship and ends with its termination. However, as discussed later, an agent may be subject to duties after termination with respect to the agent's use of the principal's property and confidential information provided by the principal.

An agent who violates his fiduciary duty is liable to his principal for breach of contract, in tort for losses caused and possibly punitive damages, and in restitution for profits he made or property received in breach of the fiduciary duty. Moreover, he loses the right to compensation. The principal may avoid a transaction in which the agent breached his fiduciary duty, even though the principal suffered no loss. A breach of fiduciary duty may also constitute just cause for discharge of the agent. The 2011 Restatement (Third) of Restitution and Unjust Enrichment provides that benefits derived from an agent's breach of fiduciary duty may be recovered from third parties who acquire such benefits with notice of the agent's breach of fiduciary duty.

The fiduciary duty arises most frequently in the following situations involving principals and their agents, although it is by no means limited to these situations.

Conflicts of Interest

An agent has a duty not to deal with the principal as, or on behalf of, an adverse party in a transaction connected with the agency relationship. An agent must act solely in the interest of his principal, not in his own interest or in the interest of another. In addition, an agent may not represent his principal in any transaction in which the agent has a personal interest. Nor may the agent act on behalf of adverse parties to a transaction without both principals' approval to the dual agency. An agent may take a position that conflicts with the interest of his principal only if the principal, with full knowledge of all of the facts, consents. For example, A, an agent of P who desires to purchase land, agrees with C, who represents B, a seller of land, that A and C will endeavor to effect a transaction between their principals and will pool their commissions. A and C have committed a breach of fiduciary duty to P and B.

Self-Dealing

An agent has a duty not to deal with the principal as an adverse party in a transaction connected with the agency relationship. The courts scrutinize transactions between an agent and her principal. The agent may not deal at arm's length with her principal. The agent thus owes her principal a duty of full disclosure regarding all relevant facts that affect the transaction. Moreover, the transaction must be fair. Thus, Penny employs Albert to purchase for her a site suitable for a shopping center. Albert owns such a site and sells it to Penny at the fair market value but does not disclose to Penny that he had owned the land. Penny may rescind the transaction even though Albert made no misrepresentation. The agent's loyalty must be undivided, and he must devote his actions exclusively to the representation and promotion of his principal's interests.

Duty Not to Compete

During the agency relationship an agent must not compete with his principal or act on behalf or otherwise assist any of the principal's competitors. After the agency terminates without breach by the agent, however, unless otherwise agreed, the agent may compete with his former principal. The courts will enforce by injunction a contractual agreement by the agent not to compete after termination if the restriction is reasonable as to time and place and necessary to protect the principal's legitimate interest. Contractual agreements not to compete are discussed in Chapter 13 where it is noted that such noncompetition contracts may be subject to different standards for Internet companies and their employees.

Misappropriation

An agent may not use property of the principal for the agent's own purposes or for the benefit of a third party. Unless the principal consents, an agent who has possession of the principal's property has a duty to use it only on the principal's behalf even if the agent's use of the property does not cause harm to the principal. An agent is liable to the principal for any profit the agent made while using the principal's property or for the value of the agent's use of the principal's property. An agent's duties regarding the principal's property continue after the agency terminates, and a former agent has a duty to return any of the principal's property she still possesses.

Confidential Information

An agent may not use or disclose confidential information obtained in the course of the agency for her own benefit or the benefit of a third party. Confidential information is information that, if disclosed, would harm the principal's business or that has value because it is not generally known. Confidential information includes unique business methods, trade secrets, business plans, personnel, nonpublic financial results, and customer lists. An agent, however, may reveal confidential information that the principal is committing, or is about to commit, a crime. Many statutes provided protection to employees who "whistle-blow."

Unless otherwise agreed, even after the agency terminates, the agent may not use or disclose to third persons confidential information. The agent, however, may use the generally known skills, knowledge, and information she acquired during the agency relationship.

Duty to Account for Financial Benefits

Unless otherwise agreed, an agent has a duty not to acquire any financial or other material benefits in connection with transactions conducted on behalf of the principal. Such benefits would include bribes, kickbacks, and gifts. Moreover, an agent may not make a secret profit from any transaction subject to the agency. All material benefits, including secret profits, belong to the principal, to whom the agent must account. In addition, the principal may recover any damages caused by the agent's breach. Thus, if an agent, authorized to sell certain property of her principal for $1,000 sells it for $1,500, she may not secretly pocket the additional $500.

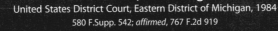
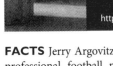

Detroit Lions, Inc. v. Argovitz
United States District Court, Eastern District of Michigan, 1984
580 F.Supp. 542; *affirmed*, 767 F.2d 919
http://scholar.google.com/scholar_case?q=580+F.Supp.+542&hl=en&as_sdt=6,34&case=17442812739569541102&scilh=0

FACTS Jerry Argovitz was employed as an agent of Billy Sims, a professional football player. Early in 1983, Argovitz informed Sims that he was awaiting the approval of his application for a U.S. Football League franchise in Houston. Sims was unaware, however, of Argovitz's extensive ownership interest in the new

Houston Gamblers organization. Meanwhile, during the spring of 1983, Argovitz continued contract negotiations on behalf of Sims with the Detroit Lions of the National Football League. By June 22, Argovitz and the Lions were very close to an agreement, although Argovitz represented to Sims that the negotiations were

---

Practical Advice

If you are the principal, consider obtaining from your agents a reasonable covenant that they will not compete with you after the agency terminates.

Practical Advice

Do not agree to become an agent if you are not willing or able to fulfill all of the duties an agent owes, unless your agency contract clearly relieves you of those duties you find unacceptable.

not proceeding well. Argovitz then sought an offer for Sims's services from the Gamblers. The Gamblers offered Sims a $3.5 million, five-year deal. Argovitz told Sims that he thought the Lions would match this figure; however, he did not seek a final offer from the Lions and then present the terms of both packages to Sims. Sims, convinced that the Lions were not negotiating in good faith, signed with the Gamblers on July 1, 1983. On December 16, 1983, Sims signed a second contract with the Lions. The Lions and Sims brought an action against Argovitz, seeking to invalidate Sims's contract with the Gamblers on the ground that Argovitz breached his fiduciary duty when negotiating the contract with the Gamblers.

DECISION Judgment for the Lions and Sims rescinding the Gamblers' contract with Sims.

OPINION Argovitz, as Sims's agent, owed Sims the fiduciary duties of loyalty, good faith, and fair and honest dealing. The duty of loyalty requires that an agent not represent his principal in a transaction in which the agent has a personal stake that conflicts with the principal's interest. Therefore, an agent may not deal on his principal's behalf with a third party in which the agent has an interest. An agent who does so is presumed to have acted fraudulently and must show that the principal freely consented to the transaction with full knowledge of every material fact known to the agent that might affect the principal. In this case, Argovitz had an ownership interest in the Gamblers and thus had a personal interest, contrary to Sims's interest, in signing Sims with the team. Fraud on Argovitz's part is therefore presumed, and Sims may rescind the contract with the Gamblers unless Argovitz can demonstrate that Sims was aware of all material facts that might have influenced his decision. Argovitz failed to show either that he informed Sims of the material facts or that these facts would have had no impact upon Sims's decision to sign the contract with the Gamblers. Indeed, Argovitz did not solicit a final contract offer from the Lions because he knew that the Lions would match the Gamblers' offer and that Sims would be lost to the Gamblers, a team that Argovitz owned.

INTERPRETATION An agent's fiduciary duty precludes the agent from acting in his own interest or in the interests of another if such action would conflict with his principal's interests.

ETHICAL QUESTION Did Argovitz act unethically? Explain.

CRITICAL THINKING QUESTION What is the appropriate relief in this situation? Explain.

DUTIES OF PRINCIPAL TO AGENT [28-4]

Although, in terms of the rights and duties arising out of the agency relationship, the duties of the agent receive more emphasis than those of the principal, an agent nonetheless has certain rights against the principal, both under the contract and by the operation of law. Connected to these rights are certain duties, based in contract and tort law, which the principal owes to the agent. For a summary of the primary duties in the principal-agent relationship, see Figure 28-1.

Figure 28-1 Duties of Principal and Agent

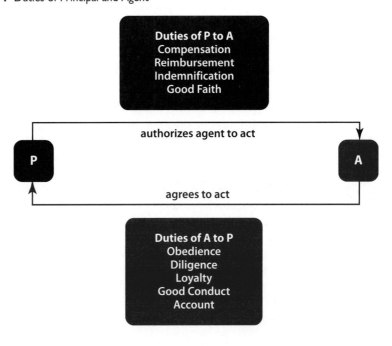

Contractual Duties [28-4a]

An agency relationship may exist in the absence of a contract between the principal and agent. However, many principals and agents do enter into contracts, in which case a principal has a duty to act in accordance with the express and implied terms of any contract between the principal and the agent. The contractual duties owed by a principal to an agent are the duties of compensation, reimbursement, and indemnification; each may be excluded or modified by agreement between the principal and agent. Although a gratuitous agent is not owed a duty of compensation, she is entitled to reimbursement and indemnification.

Depending on the particular case, the principal must furnish either the agent's means of employment or the opportunity for work. For example, a principal who employs an agent to sell his goods must supply the agent with conforming goods. It is also the duty of the principal not to terminate the agency wrongfully.

Practical Advice

Specify the compensation to be paid the agent; if none is to be paid, clearly state that the agency is intended to be gratuitous.

Compensation

a principal must compensate the agent as specified in the contract, or for the reasonable value of the services provided, if no amount is specified

Compensation   A principal has a duty to compensate her agent unless the agent has agreed to serve gratuitously. If the agreement does not specify a definite compensation, a principal is under a duty to pay the reasonable value of authorized services the agent has performed. An agent loses the right to compensation by (1) breaching the duty of obedience, (2) breaching the duty of loyalty, or (3) willfully and deliberately breaching the agency contract. Furthermore, an agent whose compensation is dependent upon her accomplishing a specific result is entitled to the agreed compensation only if she achieves the result in the time specified or in a reasonable time, if no time is stated. A common example is a listing agreement between a seller and a real estate broker providing for a commission to the broker if he finds a buyer ready, willing, and able to buy the property on the terms specified in the agreement.

Indemnification

duty owed by principal to pay for losses agent incurred while acting as directed by principal

Reimbursement

duty owed by principal to pay agent for authorized payments made on principal's behalf

Indemnification and Reimbursement   In general, a principal has an obligation to **indemnify** (compensate for a loss) an agent whenever the agent makes a payment or incurs an expense or other loss while acting as authorized on behalf of the principal. The contract between the principal and agent may specify the extent of this duty. In the absence of any contractual provisions a principal has a duty to **reimburse** the agent when the agent makes a payment within the scope of the agent's actual authority. For example, an agent who reasonably and properly pays a fire insurance premium for the protection of her principal's property is entitled to reimbursement for the payment.

A principal also has a duty to indemnify the agent when the agent suffers a loss that fairly should be borne by the principal in light of their relationship. For example, suppose that Perry, the principal, has in his possession goods belonging to Margot. Perry directs Alma, his agent, to sell these goods. Alma, believing Perry to be the owner, sells the goods to Turner. Margot then sues Alma for the conversion of her goods and recovers a judgment, which Alma pays to Margot. Alma is entitled to indemnification from Perry for her loss, including the amount she reasonably expended in defense of the lawsuit brought by Margot.

Tort and Other Duties [28-4b]

Tort duties

include the duty to provide an employee with reasonably safe conditions of employment

A principal owes to any agent the same duties under tort law that the principal owes to all parties. Moreover, a principal has a duty to deal with the agent fairly and in good faith. This duty requires that the principal provide the agent with information about risks of physical harm or monetary loss that the principal knows, has reason to know, or should know are present in the agent's work but are unknown to the agent. For instance, in directing his agent to collect rent from a tenant who is known to have assaulted rent collectors, a principal has a duty to warn the agent of this risk.

In cases in which the agent is an employee, the principal owes the agent additional duties. Among these is the duty to provide the employee with reasonably safe conditions of employment and to warn the employee of any unreasonable risk involved in the employment. A negligent employer is also liable to his employees for injury caused by the negligence of other employees and of other agents doing work for him. We will discuss the duties owed by an employer to an employee more fully in Chapter 41.

Termination of Agency [28-5]

Because the authority of an agent is based on the consent of the principal, the agency is terminated when such consent is withdrawn or otherwise ceases to exist. On termination of the agency, the agent's actual authority ends, and she is not entitled to compensation for services subsequently rendered. However, some of the agent's fiduciary duties may continue. The termination of *apparent* authority will be discussed in Chapter 29. Termination may take place by the acts of the parties or by operation of law.

Acts of the Parties [28-5a]

Termination by the acts of the parties may occur by the provisions of the original agreement, by the subsequent acts of both principal and agent, or by the subsequent act of either one.

Lapse of Time   An agent's actual authority terminates as agreed by the agent and the principal. Authority conferred upon an agent for a specified time terminates when that period expires. If no time is specified, authority terminates at the end of a reasonable period. For example, Palmer authorizes Avery to sell a tract of land for him. After ten years pass without communication between Palmer and Avery, Avery purports to sell the tract. But his authorization has terminated due to lapse of time.

Mutual Agreement of the Parties   The agency relationship is created by agreement and may be terminated at any time by mutual agreement of the principal and the agent.

Revocation of Authority   A principal may revoke an agent's authority at any time by notifying the agent. But if such revocation constitutes a breach of contract by the principal, the agent may recover damages from the principal. Nonetheless, when the agent has seriously breached the agency contract, has willfully disobeyed, or has violated the fiduciary duty, the principal is not liable for terminating the agency relationship. In addition, if the agency is gratuitous, the principal ordinarily may revoke it without liability to the agent.

Renunciation by the Agent   The agent also has the power to end the agency by notifying the principal that she renounces the authority given her by the principal. If the agency is gratuitous, the agent ordinarily may renounce it without liability to the principal. However, if the parties have contracted for the agency to continue for a specified time, an unjustified renunciation prior to the expiration of that time is a breach of contract.

Operation of Law [28-5b]

By the operation of law, the occurrence of certain events will automatically terminate an agency relationship. These events either make it impossible for the agent to perform or unlikely that the principal would want the agent to act. As a matter of law, the occurrence of any of the following events ordinarily terminates agency.

Death   Because the authority given to an agent by a principal is strictly personal, the death of an individual agent terminates the agent's actual authority. The death of an individual principal also terminates the actual authority of the agent when the agent has notice of the principal's death. This is contrary to the Second Restatement, which took the position that the principal's death terminated the agent's actual authority whether the agent had notice or not. For example, Polk employs Allison to sell Polk's line of goods under a contract that specifies Allison's commission and the one-year period for which the employment is to continue. Without Allison's knowledge, Polk dies. Under the Second Restatement, Allison no longer has authority to sell Polk's goods. The death of Polk, the principal, terminated the authority of Allison the agent. Under the Third Restatement, on the other hand, Allison would continue to have actual authority until she received notice of Polk's death. A person has *notice* of a fact if the person knows the fact, has reason to know the fact, has received an effective notification of the fact, or should know the fact to fulfill a duty owed to another person. Moreover, the Uniform Durable Power of Attorney Act and the UPOAA allow the holder of *any* power of attorney, durable or otherwise, to exercise it on the death of the principal, if its exercise is in good faith and without knowledge of the principal's death.

When an agent or principal is not an individual, the organizational statutes typically determine when authority terminates upon the cessation of the existence of that organization. (This is discussed further in Part VII of this book.) When the organizational statute does not specify, the Restatement provides the agent's actual authority terminates when the nonindividual principal or agent ceases to exist or begins a process that will lead to the cessation of its existence.

Incapacity Incapacity of the principal that occurs after the formation of the agency terminates the agent's actual authority when the agent has notice of the principal's incapacity. This is contrary to the Second Restatement, which took the position that the principal's incapacity terminated the agent's actual authority without notice to the agent. To illustrate, Powell authorizes Anna to sell in the next ten months an apartment complex for not less than $2 million. Without Anna's knowledge, Powell is adjudicated incompetent two months later. Under the Second Restatement, Anna's authority to sell the apartment complex is terminated. Under the Third Restatement, Anna would continue to have actual authority until she received notice of Powell's incapacity.

Practical Advice

A durable power of attorney is useful in families, allowing adult children to become the agents of their elderly or ill parents.

If an agent is appointed under a durable power of attorney, the authority of an agent survives, or is triggered by, the incapacity or disability of the principal. Moreover, the Uniform Durable Power of Attorney Act and the UPOAA allow the holder of a power of attorney that is *not* durable to exercise it on the incapacity of the principal, if its exercise is in good faith and without knowledge of the principal's incapacity.

Gaddy v. Douglass
Court of Appeals of South Carolina, 2004
359 S.C. 329, 597 S.E.2d 12
http://scholar.google.com/scholar_case?q=359+S.C.+329&hl=en&as_sdt=6,34&case=12426376097857542113&scilh=0

FACTS Ms. M was born in 1918. After retiring, Ms. M returned to Fairfield, South Carolina, where she lived on her family farm with her brother, a dentist, until his death in the early 1980s. Ms. M never married. Dr. Gaddy was Ms. M's physician and a close family friend. Ms. M had little contact with many of her relatives, including the appellants, who are Ms. M's third cousins. In 1988, Ms. M executed a durable general power of attorney designating Dr. Gaddy as her attorney-in-fact. Concerns about Ms. M's progressively worsening mental condition prompted Dr. Gaddy to file the 1988 durable power of attorney in November 1995. Thereafter, Dr. Gaddy began to act as Ms. M's attorney-in-fact and assumed control of her finances, farm, and health care. His responsibilities included paying her bills, tilling her garden, repairing fences, and hiring caregivers.

In March 1996, Dr. Gaddy discovered that Ms. M had fallen in her home and fractured a vertebra. Ms. M was hospitalized for six weeks. During the hospitalization, Dr. Gaddy fumigated and cleaned her home, which had become flea-infested and unclean to the point where rat droppings were found in the house. Finding that Ms. M was not mentally competent to care for herself, he arranged for full-time caretakers to attend to her after she recovered from the injuries she sustained in her fall. He made improvements in her home, including plumbing repairs adapting a bathroom to make it safer for caretakers to bathe Ms. M, who was

incapable of doing so unassisted. During Ms. M's hospitalization, neither of the appellants visited her in the hospital or sought to assist her in any manner.

Dr. Gaddy had Ms. M examined and evaluated by Dr. James E. Carnes, a neurologist, in December 1996. After examining Ms. M, Dr. Carnes found that she suffered from dementia and confirmed she was unable to handle her affairs. Ms. M's long-standing distant relationship with some members of her family, including appellants, changed in March of 1999. On March 12, 1999, appellants visited Ms. M, and with the help of a disgruntled caretaker, took her to an appointment with Columbia attorney Douglas N. Truslow to "get rid of Dr. Gaddy." On the drive to Truslow's office, Heller had to remind Ms. M several times of their destination and purpose. At Truslow's office, Ms. M signed a document revoking the 1988 will and the 1988 durable power of attorney. She also signed a new durable power of attorney naming appellants as her attorneys-in-fact. Appellants failed to disclose Ms. M's dementia to Truslow. Based on the revocation of the 1988 power of attorney and recently executed power of attorney, appellants prohibited Dr. Gaddy from contacting Ms. M. and threatened Dr. Gaddy with arrest if he tried to visit Ms. M.

On March 15, 1999, three days after Ms. M purportedly revoked the 1988 durable power of attorney and executed the 1999 durable power of attorney, Dr. Gaddy brought a legal action as her attorney-in-fact pursuant to the 1988 durable power of attorney. Medical testimony was presented from five physicians who had examined Ms. M. They concluded that Ms. M. (1) was "unable to handle her financial affairs" and "would need help managing her daily activities," and (2) would not "ever have moments of lucidity" to "understand legal documents."

The trial judge concluded that Ms. M lacked contractual capacity "from March 12, 1999 and continuously thereafter." As a result, he invalidated the 1999 revocation of the 1988 durable power of attorney and the 1999 durable power of attorney, and declared valid the 1988 durable power of attorney.

DECISION Judgment affirmed in relevant part.

OPINION Under a durable power of attorney, the attorney-in-fact retains authority to act on the principal's behalf. Courts will uphold a durable power of attorney unless the principal has contractual capacity to revoke the then existing durable power of attorney or to execute a new power of attorney.

Contractual capacity is generally defined as a person's ability to understand in a meaningful way, at the time the contract is executed, the nature, scope, and effect of the contract. Where the mental condition of the principal is of a chronic nature, evidence

of the principal's prior or subsequent condition is admissible as bearing upon his or her condition at the time the contract is executed. The credible medical testimony presented compellingly indicates that on March 12, 1999, Ms. M suffered from severe dementia caused by Alzheimer's disease, a chronic and permanent organic disease which clearly rendered her incapable of possessing contractual capacity to revoke the 1988 durable power of attorney or execute the 1999 power of attorney.

The very idea of a durable power of attorney is to protect the principal should he or she become incapacitated. Mrs. M's mental disability is precisely the situation for which the durable power of attorney is intended.

INTERPRETATION Under a durable power of attorney, the agent retains authority to act on the principal's behalf despite the principal's subsequent mental incompetence; the principal may revoke a valid power of attorney only if she possesses contractual capacity.

ETHICAL QUESTION Were the appellants' actions ethical?

CRITICAL THINKING QUESTION What are benefits and costs of authorizing durable powers of attorney?

Change in Circumstances   An agent's actual authority terminates whenever the agent should reasonably conclude that the principal no longer would assent to the agent's taking action on the principal's behalf. For example, Patricia authorizes Aaron to sell her eighty acres of farmland for $800 per acre. Subsequently, oil is discovered on nearby land, and Patricia's land greatly increases in value. Because Aaron knows of this, whereas Patricia does not, Aaron's authority to sell the land is terminated.

The Second Restatement specified a number of subsequent changes in circumstances that would terminate an agent's actual authority, including accomplishment of authorized act, bankruptcy of principal or agent, change in business conditions, loss or destruction of subject matter, disloyalty of agent, change in law, and outbreak of war. The Third Restatement takes a different approach by providing a basic rule that an agent acts with actual authority "when, *at the time of taking action* that has legal consequences for the principal, the agent reasonably believes, in accordance with the principal's manifestations to the agent, that the principal wishes the agent so to act." Thus, if circumstances have changed such that, at the time the agent takes action, it is not reasonable for the agent to believe that the principal at that time consents to the action being taken on the principal's behalf, then the agent lacks actual authority to act even though she would have had actual authority prior to the change in circumstances.

Irrevocable Powers [28-5c]

The Restatement defines a power given as security as "a power to affect the legal relations of its creator that is created in the form of a manifestation of actual authority and held for the benefit of the holder or a third person." A power given as security creates neither a relationship of agency nor actual authority, although the power enables its holder to affect the legal relations of the creator of the power. The power arises from a manifestation of assent by its creator that the holder of the power may, for example, dispose of property or other interests of the creator. The Restatement provides the following illustration: Pillsbury owns Blackacre, which is situated next to Whiteacre, on which Pillsbury operates a restaurant. To finance renovations and expansions, Pillsbury borrows money from Ashton. A written agreement between Pillsbury

APPLYING THE LAW

Relationship of Principal and Agent

Facts After Thomson's husband died in 2005, she gave a power of attorney to her niece, Surani, who was an accountant. The written power of attorney granted Surani authority to manage all of Thomson's financial affairs and specified that Surani's authority was to remain unaffected by Thomson's subsequent incapacity. Accordingly, Surani provided a copy of the power of attorney to Thomson's bank, took possession of Thomson's checkbook, and began paying all of her aunt's expenses by drawing checks on Thomson's bank account.

In 2010, Surani was involved in an accident that diminished her mental capacity. As a result, she left her job as an accountant, but she was able to continue to pay Thomson's bills. In 2014, when Thomson was ninety-two, she was hospitalized for a severe illness and subsequently adjudicated to be incompetent. Nonetheless, Surani continued to write checks for Thomson's expenses from Thomson's checking account.

Issue Was Surani's authority to issue checks from Thomson's account terminated as a matter of law—either by her own diminished capacity in 2010 or by the court's declaring Thomson incompetent in 2014?

Rule of Law The general rule is that incapacity of the principal that occurs after the formation of the agency terminates the agent's actual authority. A durable power of attorney is a formal, written appointment of an agent that provides for the agent's authority to survive, or be triggered by, the principal's subsequent incapacity.

Because the act of the agent is considered the act of the principal, the incapacity of an agent to bind himself by contract does not disqualify him from making a contract that is binding on the principal. Thus, any person able to act ordinarily has the capacity to be an agent. Thus, if the contract is authorized, it is valid despite the agent's incapacity. However, if after the creation of the agency, the agent is rendered incapable of performing the acts authorized by the principal, the agency is terminated by operation of law.

Application This case involves incapacity of both the principal, Thomson, and the agent, Surani, some years after the agency was created. The power of attorney Thomson granted to Surani by a written document in 2005 is a durable power of attorney because it expressly provided that Surani's authority to manage Thomson's financial affairs was to continue after Thomson lost her capacity to contract. Therefore, the fact that Thomson was adjudicated incompetent in 2014 did not terminate Surani's agency. Indeed, the point of a durable power of attorney is to empower the agent to act, or continue to act, on the principal's behalf after the principal's capacity is called into question.

Surani's capacity to perform the tasks required of the agency is a different question. The accident she suffered in 2010 reduced her mental capacity to some unspecified degree, but Surani was not adjudged incompetent. Instead, as a result of her disability, she either chose to, or was required to, leave her accounting practice. Nonetheless, she apparently was still capable of successfully handling Thomson's bills by issuing the necessary checks. Therefore, her accident did not terminate her authority to continue handling those expenses. This is true regardless of whether her diminished capacity may have operated to terminate other more sophisticated aspects of her written authority to "manage all of Thomson's financial affairs," such as making investment decisions, of which Surani may no longer have been capable after her accident.

Conclusion Neither Surani's accident in 2010 nor Thomson's adjudicated incompetency in 2014 terminated Surani's agency, and she retained her authority to pay Thomson's bills by drawing checks on Thomson's bank account.

and Ashton provides that Ashton shall irrevocably have Pillsbury's authority to transfer ownership of Blackacre to Ashton in the event Pillsbury defaults on the loan. Ashton has a power given as security.

The Restatement's definition includes, but is more extensive than, the rule in some states regarding an *agency coupled with an interest*, in which the holder (agent) has a security interest in the power conferred upon him by the creator (principal). For example, an agency coupled with an interest would arise in cases in which an agent has advanced funds on behalf of the principal and the agent's power to act is given as security for the loan.

Power given as security
such a power—including an agency coupled with an interest—is irrevocable

Unless otherwise agreed, a **power given as security** may *not* be revoked. In addition, the incapacity of the creator or of the holder of the power does not terminate the power. Nor will the death of the creator terminate the power, unless the duty for which the power was given terminates with the death of the creator. A power given as security *is* terminated by an event that discharges the obligation secured by it or that makes execution of the power illegal or impossible. Thus, in the previous example, when the creator repays the loan, the power is terminated.

ETHICAL DILEMMA

Is Medicaid Designed to Protect Inheritances?

Facts Mrs. Singer is a seventy-eight-year-old widow. Although she remains somewhat active and lives in her own apartment, her physical and mental abilities are declining. She fell recently and needs assistance with bathing and some routine chores.

Mrs. Singer has two children, a son, Steven, who lives within fifteen minutes of her home, and a daughter, Kate, who lives a great distance away. While Mrs. Singer sees Kate only once a year, she remains in close contact with Steven, who does her grocery shopping, takes her to the doctor, and provides transportation, thereby enabling Mrs. Singer to maintain some social life.

Steven has become increasingly concerned about his mother's declining condition and is unsure how much longer she can remain in her apartment. Steven has consulted his lawyer, who suggested that Mrs. Singer give Steven a durable power of attorney authorizing Steven to manage most of her financial affairs. It would also give Steven the power to transfer Mrs. Singer's assets to himself so that Mrs. Singer will qualify for Medicaid should she need to enter a nursing home. Steven's lawyer explained that in order to qualify for Medicaid, Mrs. Singer must meet asset and income limits that are quite low.

Mrs. Singer has substantial assets. She has a portfolio of investments in stocks, bonds, and certificates of deposit worth more than $700,000. The durable power of attorney would enable Steven to strip Mrs. Singer of her assets within the time frame necessary to allow the declining Mrs. Singer to qualify for Medicaid.

Mrs. Singer has agreed to execute the power. But Kate objects to the plan. She does not get along with Steven, does not trust his judgment, and is concerned that he will not properly share his mother's assets.

Social, Policy, and Ethical Considerations

1. Is it ethical for Steven to execute the power of attorney in an effort to enable his mother to qualify for Medicaid?
2. Should Medicaid be available only to those with low income and few assets? Could a national health care plan provide a solution?
3. What role, if any, should private insurance play in providing a safety net against the catastrophic costs of nursing home care?
4. What questions of family ethics does a plan such as Steven's raise?

CHAPTER SUMMARY

Nature of Agency

Definition of Agency consensual relationship authorizing one party (the agent) to act on behalf of the other party (the principal) subject to the principal's control

Scope of Agency Purposes whatever business activity a person may accomplish personally, he generally may do through an agent

Other Legal Relationships

- *Employment Relationship* one in which the employer has the right to control the manner and means of the employee's performance of work
- *Independent Contractor* a person who contracts with another to do a particular job and who is not subject to the other's control over the manner and means of conducting the work

Creation of Agency

Formalities though agency is a consensual relationship that may be formed by contract or agreement between the principal and agent, agency may exist without consideration

- *Requirements* no particular formality is usually required in a contract of agency, although appointments of agents for a period of more than one year must be in writing
- *Power of Attorney* written, formal appointment of an agent

Capacity

- *Principal* if the principal is a minor or an incompetent not under a guardianship, his appointment of another to act as an agent is voidable, as are any resulting contracts with third parties
- *Agent* any person able to act may act as an agent as the act of the agent is considered the act of the principal

Duties of Agent to Principal

Duty of Obedience an agent must act in the principal's affairs only as actually authorized by the principal and must obey all lawful instructions and directions of the principal

Duty of Good Conduct within the scope of the agency relationship, an agent must act reasonably and refrain from conduct that is likely to damage the principal's interests

Duty of Diligence an agent must act with reasonable care, competence, and diligence in performing the work for which he is employed

Duty to Inform an agent must use reasonable efforts to give the principal information material to the affairs entrusted to her

Duty to Account an agent must maintain and provide the principal with an accurate account of money or other property that the agent has received or expended on behalf of the principal; an agent must not mingle the principal's property with any other person's property

Fiduciary Duty an agent owes a duty of utmost loyalty and good faith to the principal; it includes—

- *Conflicts of Interest*
- *Self-Dealing*
- *Duty Not to Compete*
- *Misappropriation*
- *Confidential Information*
- *Duty to Account for Financial Benefits*

Duties of Principal to Agent

Contractual Duties

- *Compensation* a principal must compensate the agent as specified in the contract or for the reasonable value of the services provided if no amount is specified
- *Reimbursement* the principal must pay back to the agent authorized payments the agent has made on the principal's behalf
- *Indemnification* the principal must pay the agent for losses the agent incurred while acting as directed by the principal

Tort and Other Duties include (1) the duty to provide an employee with reasonably safe conditions of employment and (2) the duty to deal with the agent fairly and in good faith

Termination of Agency

Acts of the Parties

- *Lapse of Time*
- *Mutual Agreement of the Parties*
- *Revocation of Authority*
- *Renunciation by the Agent*

Operation of Law

- *Death* of either the principal or the agent
- *Incapacity* of either the principal or the agent
- *Change in Circumstances*

Irrevocable Powers a power given as security—including an agency coupled with an interest—is irrevocable

QUESTIONS

1. Parker, the owner of certain unimproved real estate in Chicago, employed Adams, a real estate agent, to sell the property for a price of $250,000 or more and agreed to pay Adams a commission of 6 percent for making a sale. Adams negotiated with Turner, who was interested in the property and willing to pay as much as $280,000 for it. Adams made an agreement with Turner that if Adams could obtain Parker's signature to a contract to sell the property to Turner for $250,000, Turner would pay Adams a bonus of $10,000. Adams prepared and Parker and Turner signed a contract for the sale of the property to Turner for $250,000. Turner refuses to pay Adams the $10,000 as promised. Parker refuses to pay Adams the 6 percent commission. In an action by Adams against Parker and Turner, what is the judgment?

2. Perry employed Alice to sell a parcel of real estate at a fixed price without knowledge that David had previously employed Alice to purchase the same property for him. Perry gave Alice no discretion as to price or terms, and Alice entered into a contract of sale with David on the exact terms authorized by Perry. After accepting a partial payment, Perry discovered that Alice was employed by David and brought an action to rescind. David resisted on the ground that Perry had suffered no damage because Alice had been given no discretion and the sale was made on the exact basis authorized by Perry. Discuss whether Perry will prevail.

3. Packer owned and operated a fruit cannery in Southton, Illinois. He stored a substantial amount of finished canned goods in a warehouse in East St. Louis, Illinois, owned and

operated by Alden, in order to have goods readily available for the St. Louis market. On March 1, he had ten thousand cans of peaches and five thousand cans of apples in storage with Alden. On the day named, he borrowed $5,000 from Alden, giving Alden his promissory note for this amount due June 1, together with a letter authorizing Alden, in the event the note was not paid at maturity, to sell any or all of his goods in storage, pay the indebtedness, and account to him for any surplus. Packer died on June 2 without having paid the note. On June 8, Alden told Taylor, a wholesale food distributor, that he had for sale, as agent of the owner, ten thousand cans of peaches and five thousand cans of apples. Taylor said he would take the peaches and would decide later about the apples. A contract for the sale of ten thousand cans of peaches for $6,000 was thereupon signed "Alden, agent for Packer, seller; Taylor, buyer." Both Alden and Taylor knew of the death of Packer. Delivery of the peaches and payment were made on June 10. On June 11, Alden and Taylor signed a similar contract covering the five thousand cans of apples, delivery and payment to be made June 30. On June 23, Packer's executor, having learned of these contracts, wrote Alden and Taylor stating that Alden had no authority to make the contracts, demanding that Taylor return the peaches, and directing Alden not to deliver the apples. Discuss the correctness of the contentions of Packer's executor.

4. Harvey Hilgendorf was a licensed real estate broker acting as the agent of the Hagues in the sale of eighty acres of farmland. The Hagues, however, terminated Hilgendorf's agency before the expiration of the listing contract when they encountered financial difficulties and decided to liquidate their entire holdings of land at one time. Hilgendorf brought this action for breach of the listing contract. The Hagues maintain that Hilgendorf's duty of loyalty required him to give up the listing contract. Are the Hagues correct in their assertion?

5. Palmer made a valid contract with Ames under which Ames was to sell Palmer's goods on commission from January 1 to June 30. Ames made satisfactory sales up to May 15 and was about to close an unusually large order when Palmer suddenly and without notice revoked Ames's authority to sell. Can Ames continue to sell Palmer's goods during the unexpired term of her contract?

6. Piedmont Electric Co. gave a list of delinquent accounts to Alexander, an employee, with instructions to discontinue electric service to delinquent customers. Among those listed was Todd Hatchery, which was then in the process of hatching chickens in a large, electrically heated incubator. Todd Hatchery told Alexander that it did not consider its account delinquent, but Alexander nevertheless cut the wires leading to the hatchery. Subsequently, Todd Hatchery recovered a judgment of $5,000 in an action brought against Alexander for the loss resulting from the interruption of the incubation process. Alexander has paid the judgment and brings a cause of action against Piedmont Electric Co. What may he recover? Explain.

7. In October 2010, Black, the owner of the Grand Opera House, and Harvey entered into a written agreement to lease the opera house to Harvey for five years at a rental of $300,000 a year. Harvey engaged Day as manager of the theater at a salary of $1,175 per week plus 10 percent of the profits. One of Day's duties was to determine the amounts of money taken in each night and, after deducting expenses, to divide the profits between Harvey and the manager of the particular attraction playing at the theater. In September 2015, Day went to Black and offered to rent the opera house from Black at a rental of $375,000 per year, whereupon Black entered into a lease with Day for five years at this figure. When Harvey learned of and objected to this transaction, Day offered to assign the lease to him for $600,000 per year. Harvey refused and brought an appropriate action against Day. Should Harvey recover? If so, on what basis and to what relief is he entitled?

8. Timothy retains Cynthia, an attorney, to bring a lawsuit upon a valid claim against Vincent. Recently enacted legislation has shortened the statute of limitations for this type of legal action. Cynthia fails to make herself aware of this new statute. Consequently, she files the complaint after the statute of limitations has run. As a result, the lawsuit is dismissed. What rights, if any, does Timothy have against Cynthia?

9. Wilson engages Ruth to sell Wilson's antique walnut chest to Harold for $2,500. The next day, Ruth learns that Sandy is willing to pay $3,000 for Wilson's chest. Ruth nevertheless sells the chest to Harold. Wilson then discovers these facts. What are Wilson's rights, if any, against Ruth?

10. Morris is a salesperson for Acme, Inc., a manufacturer of household appliances. Morris receives a commission on all sales made and no further compensation. He drives his own automobile, pays his own expenses, and calls on whom he pleases. While driving to make a call on a potential customer, Morris negligently collides with Hudson. Hudson sues Acme and Morris. Who should be held liable?

CASE PROBLEMS

11. Sierra Pacific Industries purchased various areas of timber and six other pieces of real property, including a ten-acre parcel on which five duplexes and two single-family units were located. Sierra Pacific requested the assistance of Joseph Carter, a licensed real estate broker, in selling the nontimberland properties. It commissioned him to sell the property for an asking price of $850,000, of which Sierra Pacific would receive $800,000 and Carter would receive $50,000 as a commission. Unable to find a prospective buyer, Carter finally sold the property to his daughter and son-in-law for $850,000 and retained the $50,000 commission without informing Sierra Pacific of his relationship to the buyers. After learning of these facts, Sierra Pacific brought an action against Carter. To what relief, if any, is Sierra Pacific entitled?

12. Murphy, while a guest at a motel operated by the Betsy-Len Motor Hotel Corporation, sustained injuries from a fall allegedly caused by negligence in maintaining the premises. At that time, Betsy-Len was under a license agreement with Holiday Inns, Inc. The license contained provisions permitting Holiday Inns to regulate the architectural style of the buildings as well as the type and style of the furnishings and equipment. The contract, however, did not grant Holiday Inns the power to control the day-to-day operations of Betsy-Len's motel, to fix customer rates, or to demand a share of the profits. Betsy-Len could hire and fire its employees, determine wages and working conditions, supervise the employee work routine, and discipline its employees. In return, Betsy-Len used the trade name "Holiday Inns" and paid a fee for use of the license and Holiday Inns' national advertising. Murphy sued Holiday Inns, claiming Betsy-Len was its agent. Is Murphy correct?

13. Hunter Farms contracted with Petrolia Grain & Feed Company, a Canadian company, to purchase a large supply of the farm herbicide Sencor from Petrolia for resale. Petrolia learned from the U.S. Customs Service that the import duty for the Sencor would be 5 percent but that the final rate could be determined only upon an inspection of the Sencor at the time of importation. Petrolia forwarded this information to Hunter. Meanwhile, Hunter employed F. W. Myers & Company, an import broker, to assist in moving the herbicide through customs by drafting the necessary papers. When customs later determined that certain chemicals in the herbicide, not listed on its label, would increase the customs duty from $30,000 to $128,000, Myers paid the additional amount under protest and turned to Hunter for indemnification. Explain what Myers would have to prove to recover from Hunter.

14. Tube Art was involved in moving a reader board sign to a new location. Tube Art's service manager and another employee went to the proposed site and took photographs and measurements. Later, a Tube Art employee laid out the exact size and location for the excavation by marking a four-by-four square on the asphalt surface with yellow paint. The dimensions of the hole, including its depth of six feet, were indicated with spray paint inside the square. After the layout was painted on the asphalt, Tube Art engaged a backhoe operator, Richard F. Redford, to dig the hole. Redford began digging in the early evening hours at the location designated by Tube Art. At approximately 9:30 P.M., the bucket of Redford's backhoe struck a small natural gas pipeline. After examining the pipe and finding no indication of a break or

leak, he concluded that the line was not in use and left the site. Shortly before 2:00 A.M. on the following day, an explosion and fire occurred in the building serviced by that gas pipeline. As a result, two people in the building were killed, and most of its contents were destroyed. Massey and his associates, as tenants of the building, brought an action against Tube Art and Richard Redford for the total destruction of their property. Will the plaintiffs prevail? Explain.

15. Brian Hanson sustained a paralyzing injury while playing in a lacrosse match between Ohio State University and Ashland University. Hanson had interceded in a fight between one of his teammates and an Ashland player, William Kynast. Hanson grabbed Kynast in a bear hug, but Kynast threw Hanson off his back. Hanson's head struck the ground, resulting in serious injuries. An ambulance was summoned, and after several delays, Hanson was transported to a local hospital where he underwent surgery. Doctors determined that Hanson suffered a compression fracture of his sixth spinal vertebrae. Hanson, now an incomplete quadriplegic, subsequently filed suit against Ashland University, maintaining that because Kynast was acting as the agent of Ashland, the university was therefore liable for Kynast's alleged wrongful acts. Was Kynast an agent of Ashland?

16. Tony Wilson was a member of Troop 392 of the Boy Scouts of America (BSA) and of the St. Louis Area Council (Council). Tony went on a trip with the troop to Fort Leonard Wood, Missouri. Five adult volunteer leaders accompanied the troop. The troop stayed in a building that had thirty-foot aluminum pipes stacked next to it. At approximately 10:00 P.M., Tony and other scouts were outside the building, and the leaders were inside. Tony and two other scouts picked up a pipe and raised it so that it came into contact with 7,200-volt power lines that ran over the building. All three scouts were electrocuted, and Tony died.

His parents brought a suit for wrongful death against the Council, claiming that the volunteer leaders were agents or servants of the Council and that it was vicariously liable for their negligence. The Council filed a motion for summary judgment, arguing as follows: the BSA chartered local councils in certain areas, and councils in turn granted charters to local sponsors, such as schools, churches, or civic organizations. Local councils did not administer the scouting program for the sponsor, did not select volunteers, did not prescribe training for volunteers, and did not direct or control the activities of troops. Troops were not required to get permission from local councils before participating in an activity. Are the troop leaders agents of the Council? Explain.

TAKING SIDES

Western Rivers Fly Fisher (Western) operates under license of the U.S. Forest Service as an "outfitter," a corporation in the business of arranging fishing expeditions on the Green River in Utah. Michael D. Petragallo is licensed by the Forest Service as a guide to conduct fishing expeditions but cannot do so by himself, because the Forest Service licenses only outfitters to float patrons

down the Green River. Western and several other licensed outfitters contact Petragallo to guide clients on fishing trips. Because the Forest Service licenses only outfitters to sponsor fishing expeditions, every guide must display on the boat and vehicle he uses the insignia of the outfitter sponsoring the particular trip. Petragallo may agree or refuse to take individuals Western refers to him, and Western does not restrict him from guiding expeditions for other outfitters. Western pays Petragallo a certain sum per fishing trip and does not make any deductions from his compensation. Petragallo's responsibilities include transporting patrons to the Green River, using his own boat for fishing trips, providing food and overnight needs for patrons, assisting patrons in fly fishing, and transporting them from the river to their vehicles.

Robert McMaster contacted Western and arranged for a fishing trip for him and two others. Jaeger was a member of McMaster's fishing party. McMaster paid Western, which set the price for the trip, planned the itinerary for the McMaster party, rented fishing rods to them, and arranged for Petragallo to be their guide. When Petragallo met the McMaster party, he answered affirmatively when the plaintiff asked him if he worked for Western. Petragallo provided his own vehicle and boat and supplied the food, equipment, and gasoline for the trip. Both the vehicle and the boat had signs bearing Western's identification and logo. While driving the McMaster party back to town at the conclusion of the fishing trip, Petragallo lost control of his vehicle and got into an accident, injuring Jaeger.

a. What arguments could Jaeger make for claiming that Petragallo was an employee of Western?

b. What arguments could Western make for claiming that Petragallo was an independent contactor?

c. Which side should prevail?

Relationship with Third Parties

CHAPTER 29

Qui facit per alium facit per se.
(He who acts through another, acts himself.)

Legal Maxim

CHAPTER OUTCOMES

After reading and studying this chapter, you should be able to:

1. Distinguish among actual express authority, actual implied authority, and apparent authority.

2. Explain the contractual liability of the principal, agent, and third party when the principal is (a) disclosed, (b) partially disclosed, and (c) undisclosed.

3. Explain how apparent authority is terminated and distinguish between actual and constructive notice.

4. Describe the tort liability of a principal for the (a) authorized acts of agents, (b) authorized acts of employees, and (c) unauthorized acts of independent contractors.

5. Explain the criminal liability of a principal for the acts of agents.

The purpose of an agency relationship is to allow the principal to extend his business activities by authorizing agents to enter into contracts with third persons on his behalf. Accordingly, it is important that the law balance the competing interests of principals and third persons. The principal wants to be liable only for those contracts he actually authorizes the agent to make for him. The third party, on the other hand, wishes the principal bound on all contracts that the agent negotiates on the principal's behalf. As we will discuss in this chapter, the law has adopted an intermediate outcome: the principal and the third party are bound to those contracts the principal actually authorizes plus those the principal has apparently authorized.

While pursuing the principal's business, an agent may tortiously injure third parties, who then may seek to hold the principal personally liable. Under what circumstances should the principal be held liable? Similar questions arise concerning a principal's criminal liability for an agent's violation of the criminal law. The law of agency has established rules to determine when the principal is liable for the torts and crimes his agents commit.

Finally, what liability to the third party should the agent incur and what rights should she acquire against the third party? Usually, the agent has no liability for, or rights under, contracts made on behalf of a principal. As we will discuss in this chapter, however, in some situations the agent has contractually created obligations or rights or both. We will discuss these rules in this chapter.

RELATIONSHIP OF PRINCIPAL AND THIRD PERSONS

In this section, we will first consider the contract liability of the principal; then we will examine the principal's potential tort liability.

CONTRACT LIABILITY OF THE PRINCIPAL [29-1]

Power

ability of an agent to change the legal status of his principal

Disclosed principal

one whose existence and identity are known

Unidentified (partially disclosed) principal

one whose existence is known but whose identity is not known

Undisclosed principal

one whose existence and identity are not known

The **power** of an agent is his ability to change the legal status of his principal. An agent who has either actual or apparent authority has the power to bind his principal. Thus, whenever an agent, acting within his authority, makes a contract for his principal, he creates new rights or liabilities for his principal and thus changes his principal's legal status. This power of an agent to act for his principal in business transactions is the basis of agency.

A principal's contract liability also depends on whether she is disclosed, unidentified, or undisclosed. The principal is a **disclosed principal** if, when an agent and a third party interact, the third party has notice that the agent is acting for a principal and also has notice of the principal's identity. The principal is an **unidentified principal** if, when an agent and a third party interact, the third party has notice that the agent is or may be acting for a principal but has no notice of the principal's identity. (Some courts refer to an unidentified principal as a "partially disclosed principal.") An example is an auctioneer who sells on behalf of a seller who is not identified: the seller is an unidentified principal (or a partially disclosed principal) since it is understood that the auctioneer acts as an agent. The principal is an **undisclosed principal** if, when an agent and a third party interact, the third party has no notice that the agent is acting for a principal. See Figures 29-1, 29-2, and 29-3, which explain the contract liability of disclosed principals, partially disclosed principals, and undisclosed principals.

Figure 29-1 Contract Liability of Disclosed Principal

Agent Has Actual Authority

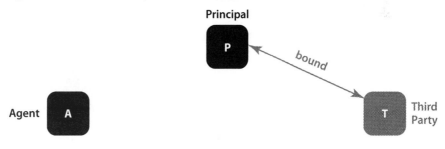

Agent Has Apparent Authority But Not Actual Authority

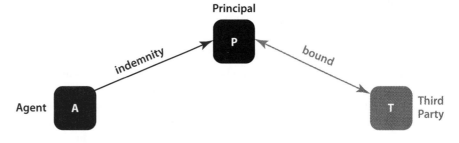

Agent Has No Actual or Apparent Authority

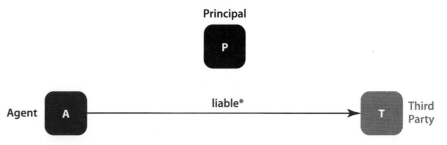

*Agent is liable for breach of implied warranty of authority or misrepresentation, as discussed later in this chapter.

Figure 29-2 Contract Liability of Unidentified Principal

Agent Has Actual Authority

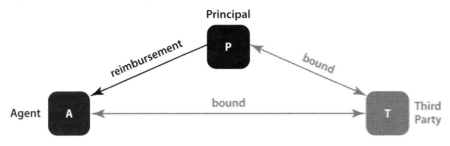

Agent Has Apparent Authority But Not Actual Authority

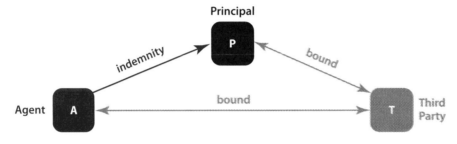

Agent Has No Actual or Apparent Authority

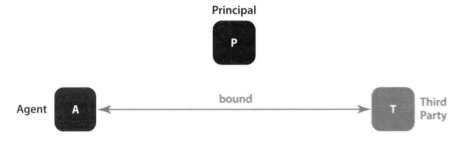

Types of Authority [29-1a]

Actual authority
power conferred upon agent by actual consent manifested by principal to the agent

Authority is of two basic types: actual and apparent. **Actual authority** exists when the principal gives actual consent to the agent. Such authority may be either express or implied. In either case, it is binding and gives the agent both the power and the right to create or to affect the principal's legal relations with third persons. Actual express authority does not depend on the third party having knowledge of the manifestations or statements made by the principal to the agent.

Apparent authority
power conferred upon agent by acts or conduct of principal that reasonably lead a third party to believe that agent has such power

Apparent authority is based on acts or conduct of the principal that lead a third person to believe that the agent, or supposed agent, has actual authority, on which belief the third person justifiably relies. This manifestation, which confers upon the agent the power to create a legal relationship between the principal and a third party, may consist of words or actions of the principal as well as other facts and circumstances that induce the third person reasonably to rely on the existence of an agency relationship.

Express authority
actual authority derived from written or spoken words of principal communicated to the agent

Actual Express Authority The **express authority** of an agent, found in the spoken or written words the principal communicates to the agent, is actual authority stated in language directing or instructing the agent to do something specific. The term "express authority" generally means actual authority that a principal has stated in very specific or detailed language. Thus, if Lee, orally or in writing, requests his agent, Anita, to sell his automobile for $6,500, Anita's authority to sell the car for this sum is actual and express.

Figure 29-3 Contract Liability of Undisclosed Principal

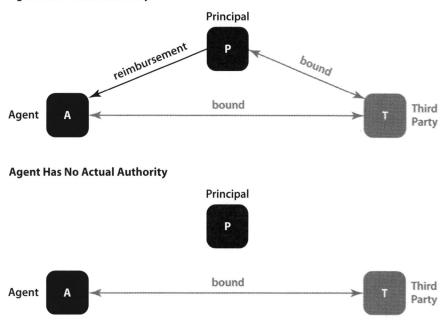

BUSINESS LAW **IN ACTION**

One of the most ambitious, successful land purchases ever made by agents for an undisclosed principal took place in Orange County, Florida, in 1964 and 1965. In just eighteen months, buyers working for a mysterious developer assembled a piece of land twice the size of Manhattan. Rumors regarding the developer's identity were rampant as agents bought up cattle ranches and road frontage, scrub woods and swampland. When the agents were finished, they had acquired about twenty-seven thousand four hundred acres at an average reported price per acre of $185, for a total expenditure of somewhat more than $5 million.

The mystery ended in 1965. Walt Disney Productions announced its intention to build Disney World, an amusement park and resort, on two thousand five hundred acres within the large tract. Disney World would be modeled on Disneyland Park, which had opened in 1955 in Anaheim, California. But Disney World would dwarf the 289 acres at Disneyland.

Disney's announcement set off the biggest wave of land speculation Florida had

seen in fifty years. David Nusbickel, an Orlando real estate broker, worked with Disney's attorneys to help buy land. Several years after Disney's announcement of its purchase had set off a buying frenzy, Nusbickel said of the land speculators, "These guys, who obviously know their business, don't even blink when you quote them a price of $75,000 to $150,000 for an acre of property that maybe went for $3,000 a few years back." *BusinessWeek* estimated that between 1965 and 1971 more than $200 million in property changed hands—confirming the wisdom of Disney's secret buying.

Walt Disney World, as the project became known, opened on October 1, 1971. While still under construction, it was called by *Newsweek* the world's largest non-governmental construction project. Despite occupying two thousand five hundred acres of land, however, phase one of Walt Disney World took up slightly less than one-tenth of the total parcel Disney had assembled. Why had Disney directed its agents to buy so much land?

In Anaheim, hotels and restaurants had sprung up on the perimeter of

Disneyland. The value of room and food revenues, which far exceeded the park's revenues, went to the owners and operators of the hotels and restaurants, not to Disney. And having developed without a plan, the hotels, restaurants, and stores gave the impression of clutter. Walt Disney's response: "It is necessary to control the environment. We learned this at Disneyland." Accordingly, Walt and his brother, Roy, decided to take their plan for Walt Disney World one step further. Not only would the company put restaurants, hotels, and golf courses inside the park, it would also buy enough land to develop housing—thus, the huge land purchase.

Said Roy Disney, who ran the financial side of the company, "I think we will make a lot more on the land than we ever will on the park. The development of this 20,000 acres can give us a future. And we will keep that future right in our own company."

Sources: *Newsweek*, November 29, 1965, 82, and April 19, 1971, 103–4; *Time*, October 18, 1971, 52–53; and *BusinessWeek*, September 11, 1971, 80.

Implied authority
actual authority inferred
from words or conduct
manifested to agent by
principal

Practical Advice

As a principal, clearly and
specifically communicate to
your agents the extent of
their actual authority. As a
third party, be sure to check
with the principal when
there is any doubt as to the
actual authority of an agent;
this is a more certain
approach than relying upon
the possibility that you will
be able to prove that the
agent had apparent authority.

Practical Advice

As a principal, be careful
how you hold out your
employees and agents
because you may create
apparent authority in them.

Actual Implied Authority

Implied authority is not found in express or explicit words of the principal but is inferred from words or conduct that the principal manifests to the agent. An agent has implied authority to do what she reasonably believes the principal wishes her to do, based on the agent's reasonable interpretation of the principal's manifestations to her and all other facts she knows or should know. Implied authority may arise from customs and usages of the principal's business. In addition, the authority granted to an agent to accomplish a particular purpose necessarily includes the implied authority to employ the means reasonably required to accomplish it. For example, Helen authorizes Jack to manage her eighty-two-unit apartment complex but says nothing about expenses. To manage the building, Jack needs to employ a janitor, purchase fuel for heating, and arrange for ordinary maintenance. Even though Helen has not expressly granted him the authority to incur such expenses, Jack may infer the authority to incur them from the express authority to manage the building because such expenses are necessary to proper management. On the other hand, suppose Paige employs Arthur, a real estate broker, to find a purchaser for her residence at a stated price. Arthur has no authority to contract for its sale. See *Schoenberger v. Chicago Transit Authority* later in this chapter.

Apparent Authority

Apparent authority is power arising from the conduct or words of a disclosed or unidentified principal that, when manifested to third persons, reasonably induce them to rely upon the assumption that actual authority exists. Apparent authority depends upon the principal's manifestations to the third party; an agent's own statements about the agent's authority do not by themselves create apparent authority. Apparent authority confers upon the agent, or supposed agent, the power to bind the disclosed or unidentified principal in contracts with third persons and prevents the principal from denying the existence of actual authority. Thus, when authority is apparent but not actual, the disclosed or unidentified principal is nonetheless bound by the act of the agent. By exceeding his actual authority, however, the agent violates his duty of obedience and is liable to the principal for any loss the principal suffers as a result of the agent's acting beyond his actual authority. See Figures 29-1 and 29-2.

Common ways in which apparent authority may arise include the following:

1. When a principal appoints an agent to a position in an organization, third parties may reasonably believe that the agent has the authority to do those acts customary of a person in such a position. (Apparent authority for agents of various business associations is discussed in Part VII.)
2. If a principal has given an agent general authority to engage in a transaction, subsequently imposed limitations or restrictions will not affect the agent's apparent authority to engage in that transaction until third parties are notified of the restrictions.
3. The principal's assent to prior similar transactions between the agent and a third party may create a basis for the third party reasonably to believe that the agent has apparent authority.
4. The agent shows the third party a document, such as a power of attorney, from the principal authorizing the agent to enter into such a transaction.
5. As discussed later, after many terminations of authority, an agent has lingering apparent authority until the third party has actual knowledge or receives notice of the termination.

For example, Peter writes a letter to Alice authorizing her to sell his automobile and sends a copy of the letter to Thomas, a prospective purchaser. On the following day, Peter writes a letter to Alice revoking the authority to sell the car but does not send a copy of the second letter to Thomas, who is not otherwise informed of the revocation. Although Alice has no actual authority to sell the car, she continues to have apparent authority with respect to Thomas. Or suppose that Arlene, in the presence of Polly, tells Thad that Arlene is Polly's agent to buy lumber. Although this statement is not true, Polly does not deny it, as she easily could. Thad, in reliance upon the statement, ships lumber to Polly on Arlene's order. Polly is obligated to pay for the lumber because Arlene had apparent authority to act on Polly's behalf. Arlene's apparent authority exists only with respect to Thad. If Arlene were to give David an order for a shipment of lumber to Polly, David would not be able to hold Polly liable. Arlene would have had neither actual authority nor, as to David, apparent authority.

Because apparent authority is the power resulting from acts that appear to the third party to be authorized by the principal, no apparent authority can exist where the principal is undisclosed. See Figure 29-3. Nor can apparent authority exist where the third party *knows* that the agent has no actual authority. See *Schoenberger v. Chicago Transit Authority* later in this chapter.

Delegation of Authority [29-1b]

Delegation of authority is usually not permitted unless actually or apparently authorized by the principal; if the agent is authorized to appoint other subagents, the acts of these subagents are as binding on the principal as those of the agent

Subagent

person appointed by agent to perform agent's duties

A **subagent** is a person appointed by an agent to perform functions that the agent has consented to perform on behalf of the agent's principal; the appointing agent is responsible to the principal for the subagent's conduct. Because the appointment of an agent reflects the principal's confidence in the agent's personal skill, integrity, and other qualifications, an agent may appoint a subagent only if the agent has actual or apparent authority to do so.

If an agent is authorized to appoint subagents, the acts of the subagent are as binding on the principal as those of the agent. The subagent, an agent of both the principal and the agent, owes a fiduciary duty to both. For example, P contracts with A, a real estate broker (agent), to sell P's house. P knows that A employs salespersons to show houses to prospective purchasers and to make representations about the property. The salespersons are A's employees and P's subagents.

If no authority exists to delegate the agent's authority, but the agent does so nevertheless, the acts of the subagent do not impose on the principal any obligations or liability to third persons. Likewise, the principal acquires no rights against such third persons.

Effect of Termination of Agency on Authority [29-1c]

Effect of termination of agency on authority

ends *actual* authority; the effect on *apparent* authority depends upon which Restatement applies and the cause of the termination of agency

As discussed in Chapter 28, when an agency terminates, the agent's *actual authority* ceases. The Second and Third Restatements differ, however, regarding when an agent's *apparent authority* ceases.

Second Restatement   In cases in which the performance of an authorized transaction becomes impossible, such as when the subject matter of the transaction is destroyed or the transaction is made illegal, the agent's *apparent authority* also expires and notice of such termination to third persons is *not* required. The bankruptcy of the principal terminates without notice the power of an agent to affect the principal's property, which has passed to the bankruptcy trustee.

BUSINESS LAW **IN ACTION**

Under typical employment arrangements, employees in a retail outlet are agents of the store owner. They, therefore, are vested with authority to conduct the store's retail business. Their actual authority will include not only that which is expressly authorized by the store owner, store manager(s), or any written manuals or policies, but also any necessary implied authority to effectuate their job of selling goods.

Actual authority in this setting might include accepting payment for goods, scheduling deliveries, and the like. Ordinarily there will be rules outlining exactly what the employee's authority includes, such as "never schedule a delivery on a Sunday" or "do not accept checks as payment." Of

necessity, these types of instructions exclude certain things from the authority of the agent-employee. So if an employee accepted a personal check for payment of a $300 purchase, this was without actual authority. The employee can be held liable to the principal—the store owner—for any resulting damage if, for example, the check cannot be collected.

However, the fact that an agent may be operating without actual authority, or contrary to express direction from the principal, does not necessarily mean the principal's liability to the third party will be affected. If a clerk schedules a Sunday delivery, the store cannot legally refuse to deliver on the appointed day simply

because the clerk was unauthorized to schedule it. Instead, the store will be bound to the customer as long as the clerk had "apparent authority."

Apparent authority arises from the principal's conduct toward the third party. In a situation such as this, providing the clerk with access to a delivery schedule that includes Sundays is probably enough to establish apparent authority. Unless there is a sign in the store or legend on the store's preprinted invoices indicating that Sunday deliveries will not be scheduled, or unless this particular customer knows of the policy, the store has led the customer reasonably to believe that the clerk may schedule Sunday deliveries, and as a result the store is bound.

When the termination is by the death or incapacity of the principal or agent, the Second Restatement provides that the agent's *apparent authority* also expires, and notice of such termination to third persons is *not* required. However, with respect to the death or incapacity of the principal, this rule has been legislatively changed in the great majority of states by the adoption of the Uniform Durable Power of Attorney Act or the Uniform Power of Attorney Act (UPOAA). Each Act provides that the death of a principal, who has executed a written power of attorney, whether or not it is durable, does not terminate the agency as to the attorney in fact (agent) or a third person who without actual knowledge of the principal's death acts in good faith under the power. Moreover, each Act provides that the incapacity of a principal, who has previously executed a written power of attorney that is *not* durable, does not terminate the agency as to the attorney in fact or a third person who without actual knowledge of the principal's incapacity acts in good faith under the power. If an agent is appointed under a durable power of attorney, the *actual* authority of an agent survives the incapacity of the principal.

In other cases, apparent authority continues until the third party has actual knowledge or receives actual notice, if the third party is one (1) with whom the agent had previously dealt on credit, (2) to whom the agent has been specially accredited, or (3) with whom the agent has begun to deal, as the principal should know. **Actual notice** requires a communication, either oral or written, to the third party. All other third parties as to whom there was apparent authority must have actual knowledge or be given **constructive notice**, through publication, for example, in a newspaper of general circulation in the area where the agency is regularly carried on.

In the next case, *Parlato v. Equitable Life Assurance Society of the United States*, the court decides whether to apply the constructive notice by publication rule just discussed.

Third Restatement Under the Third Restatement, the same rule—a reasonableness standard—applies to *all* causes of termination of agency.

(1) The termination of actual authority does not by itself end any apparent authority held by an agent.
(2) Apparent authority ends when it is no longer reasonable for the third party with whom an agent deals to believe that the agent continues to act with actual authority.

The general rule of the Third Restatement is that it is reasonable for third parties to assume that an agent's actual authority continues ("lingers"), unless and until a third party has notice of circumstances that make it unreasonable to continue that assumption. These circumstances include notice that (1) the principal has revoked the agent's actual authority, (2) the agent has renounced it, or (3) circumstances otherwise have changed such that it is no longer reasonable to believe that the principal consents to the agent's act on the principal's behalf. A person has *notice* of a fact if the person knows the fact, has reason to know the fact, has received an effective notification of the fact, or should know the fact to fulfill a duty owed to another person.

For example, if the principal tells a third party that the agent's authority has terminated, the former agent's lingering apparent authority with respect to that third party has terminated. Moreover, if a third party has notice of facts that call the agent's authority into question, and these facts would prompt a reasonable person to make an inquiry of the principal before dealing with the agent, the agent no longer acts with apparent authority. In addition, suppose that a principal has furnished an agent with a power of attorney stating the extent, nature, and duration of the agent's actual authority. Before the stated expiration of the power of attorney, the principal terminates the agent's actual authority. At this time the agent has a duty to return the power of attorney to the principal. If, however, the agent does not return the power of attorney to the principal, third parties to whom the agent shows the power of attorney would still be protected by apparent authority until the third parties have notice that actual authority had been terminated.

Consistent with this general rule—but contrary to the rule under the Second Restatement—a principal's death or loss of capacity does *not* automatically end the agent's apparent authority. In these instances, apparent authority terminates when the third party has (1) notice of the

Actual notice
knowledge actually and expressly communicated

Constructive notice
knowledge imputed by law

Practical Advice

As principal, be sure to give the appropriate notice to third parties whenever an agency relationship terminates.

principal's death or (2) has notice that the principal's loss of capacity is permanent or that the principal has been adjudicated to lack capacity. The Third Restatement's rule is consistent with the Uniform Durable Power of Attorney Act and the UPOAA.

Parlato v. Equitable Life Assurance Society of the United States
Supreme Court of New York, Appellate Division, First Department, 2002
299 A.D.2d 108, 749 N.Y.S.2d 216
http://scholar.google.com/scholar_case?case=7183003785471009812&q=749+N.Y.S.2d+216&hl=en&as_sdt=2,34

FACTS Equitable Life Assurance Society of the United States (Equitable) hired Kenneth Soule on April 1, 1990, as an agent authorized to sell Equitable financial products, such as insurance policies and annuities. Parlato, a resident of Queens, New York, began investing in Equitable financial products through Soule in May 1990, and Soule opened several Equitable accounts in Parlato's name while he was an Equitable agent. In the spring of 1992, however, Soule began criminally defrauding Parlato. Between March and May of 1992, Parlato, at Soule's urging, liquidated certain of her non-Equitable investments, and entrusted the proceeds to Soule for investment in Equitable financial products. Soule used these funds, and all additional funds that Parlato subsequently entrusted to him, for his personal use.

In 1991, Soule began soliciting plaintiff Perry, Parlato's sister and a resident of Hawaii, to invest in Equitable products. In May 1992, Perry began entrusting funds to Soule to be used to open investment accounts for her at Equitable. Perry alleges that Soule never opened any Equitable account for her and that he misappropriated all the money she entrusted to him. Equitable terminated Soule's employment in July 1992. Although Parlato allegedly still had an account with Equitable at that time, Equitable did not notify her of the termination. For approximately four years after his termination, Soule allegedly continued to represent himself to plaintiffs as an Equitable agent and to solicit their further investment in Equitable financial products. Plaintiffs do not allege, however, that Equitable made any manifestations to them of a continuing connection between Soule and Equitable after July 1992.

In August 1996, plaintiffs contacted Equitable to verify the status of their investments. At that time, Equitable informed plaintiffs that Soule had been terminated by Equitable in July 1992. Plaintiffs then alerted law enforcement authorities to Soule's misconduct. Ultimately, Soule pleaded guilty to a federal charge of mail fraud and was sentenced to twenty-seven months in prison and three years of supervised release, conditioned on his promise to make restitution in the amount of $416,000. Plaintiffs commenced this action against Equitable in December 1999. Each plaintiff asserted a cause of action for fraud, based on the contention that she entrusted her money to Soule in reliance on the appearance of authority to act for Equitable with which the company had clothed him. The trial court granted the defendant's motion to dismiss the complaint, and plaintiffs have appealed.

DECISION Judgment modified in part and affirmed in part.

OPINION It is well established that a principal may be held liable in tort for the misuse by its agent of his apparent authority to defraud a third party who reasonably relies on the appearance of authority, even if the agent commits the fraud solely for his personal benefit and to the detriment of the principal. The reason for this rule is that the principal, by virtue of its ability to select its agents and to exercise control over them, is in a better position than third parties to prevent the perpetration of fraud by such agents through the misuse of their positions. Thus, the principal should not escape liability when an innocent third person suffers a loss as the result of an agent's abuse, for his own fraudulent purposes, of the third person's reasonable reliance on the apparent authority with which the principal has invested the agent.

The plaintiffs' claims based on frauds perpetrated during the period Soule had been employed by Equitable are barred by the statute of limitations. With respect to the fraud committed after termination, the question is whether Equitable's termination of Soule's employment had the effect of immediately cutting off his apparent authority to act for Equitable vis-à-vis the two plaintiffs.

A third party who, like Parlato, is known by a principal to have previously dealt with the principal through the principal's authorized agent, is entitled to assume that the agent's authority continues until the third party receives notice the principal has revoked the agent's authority or until other circumstances render it unreasonable to believe that the agent had authority to act for the principal.

The same is not true with respect to Perry's claim against Equitable. Equitable had no way of notifying her of Soule's termination since Soule never had opened any accounts for her with Equitable. Under these circumstances, any apparent authority Soule may have had vis-à-vis Perry terminated along with his actual authority when his employment by Equitable came to an end. It is unfair to hold the principal responsible for torts its former agent commits after termination against an unknown third party, even if the former agent facilitates his wrongdoing by misrepresenting to the victim that the agency relationship is still in existence. Once the agent's employment has been terminated, the principal no longer has any power to control the agent's conduct. Moreover, the principal obviously cannot give notice of the agent's termination to a third party that is totally unknown to it.

INTERPRETATION A third party who is known by a principal to have previously dealt with the principal through the principal's authorized agent is entitled to assume that the agent's authority continues until the third party receives notice that the principal has revoked the agent's authority or until other circumstances render it unreasonable to believe that the agent had authority to act for the principal; however, a principal is not responsible for torts its former agent commits after termination against an unknown third party.

CRITICAL THINKING QUESTION How could Perry have protected herself?

Ratification [29-1d]

Ratification

affirmation by one person
of a prior unauthorized act
that another has done as
her agent or as her
purported agent

Ratification is the confirmation or affirmance by one person of a prior unauthorized act performed by another who is his agent, or who purports to be, his agent. The ratification of such act or contract binds the principal and the third party as if the agent or purported agent had been acting initially with actual authority. Once made, a valid ratification is irrevocable.

Requirements of Ratification   Ratification may relate to acts that have exceeded the authority granted to an agent, as well as to acts that a person without any authority performs on behalf of an alleged principal. To effect a ratification, the principal must manifest an intent to do so with knowledge of all material facts concerning the transaction. The principal does not need to communicate this intent, which may be manifested by express language or implied from her conduct, such as accepting or retaining the benefits of a transaction. Thus, if Amanda, without authority, contracts in Penelope's name for the purchase of goods from Tate on credit, and Penelope, having learned of Amanda's unauthorized act, accepts the goods from Tate, she thereby impliedly ratifies the contract and is bound on it. Furthermore, a principal may ratify an unauthorized action by failing to repudiate it once the principal knows the material facts about the agent's action. If formalities are required for the authorization of an act, the same formalities apply to a ratification of that act. In any event, the principal must ratify the entire act or contract.

Under the Third Restatement, a person may ratify an act if the actor acted *or* purported to act as an agent on the person's behalf. Under this provision and a number of relatively recent cases, an undisclosed principal may ratify an agent's unauthorized act. This is *contrary* to the Second Restatement's rule, which requires that the actor must have indicated to the third person that he was acting on a principal's behalf. Thus, under the Second Restatement there can be no ratification by an undisclosed principal. To illustrate: Archie, without any authority, contracts to sell to Tina an automobile belonging to Pierce. Archie states that the auto is his. Tina promises to pay $5,500 for the automobile. Pierce subsequently learns of the agreement and affirms. Under the Third Restatement, Pierce's affirmation of Archie's action *would* be a ratification because Archie had acted on behalf of Pierce. On the other hand, under the Second Restatement it would *not* be a ratification because Archie did not indicate he was acting on behalf of a principal.

To be effective, ratification must occur before the third party gives notice of his withdrawal to the principal or agent. If the affirmance of a transaction occurs when the situation has so materially changed that it would be inequitable to subject the third party to liability, the third party may elect to avoid liability. For example, Alex has no authority, but, purporting to act for Penny, he contracts to sell Penny's house to Taylor. The next day, the house burns down. Penny then affirms the sale. Taylor is not bound. Moreover, the power to ratify would be terminated by the third party's death or loss of capacity and by the lapse of a reasonable time.

Finally, for ratification to be effective, the purported principal must have been in existence when the act was done. For example, a promoter of a corporation not yet in existence may enter into contracts on behalf of the corporation. However, in the majority of states, the corporation cannot ratify these acts because the corporation did not exist when the contracts were made. Instead, the corporation may *adopt* the contract. Adoption differs from ratification because it is not retroactive and does not release the promoter from liability. See Chapter 33.

If a principal's lack of capacity entitles her to avoid transactions, the principal may also avoid any ratification made when under the incapacity. The principal, however, may ratify a contract that is voidable because of the principal's incapacity when the incapacity no longer exists. Thus, after she reaches majority, a principal may ratify an unauthorized contract made on her behalf while she was a minor. She may also avoid any ratification made prior to attaining majority.

Effect of Ratification   Ratification retroactively creates the effects of actual authority. Ratification is equivalent to prior authority, which means that the effect of ratification is

Practical Advice

As a principal, recognize that if you accept the benefits of an unauthorized contract with full knowledge, under the doctrine of ratification, you will be obliged to fulfill the contract's burdens.

substantially the same as if the agent or purported agent had been actually authorized when he performed the act. The respective rights, duties, and remedies of the principal and the third party are the same as if the agent had originally possessed actual authority. Both the principal and the agent are in the same position as the one they would have been in had the principal actually authorized the act originally. The agent is entitled to her due compensation. Moreover, she is exonerated (freed) from liability to the principal for acting as his agent without authority or for exceeding her authority, as the case may be. Between the agent and the third party, the agent is released from any liability she may have to the third party by reason of having induced the third party to enter into the contract without the principal's authority.

Schoenberger v. Chicago Transit Authority
Appellate Court of Illinois, First District, First Division, 1980
84 Ill.App.3d 1132, 39 Ill.Dec. 941, 405 N.E.2d 1076
http://scholar.google.com/scholar_case?case=2870525977617933992&q=405+N.E.2d+1076&hl=en&as_sclt=2,34

FACTS Schoenberger applied and interviewed for a position with the Chicago Transit Authority (C.T.A.). He met several times with Frank ZuChristian, who was in charge of recruiting for the C.T.A. Data Center. At the third of these meetings, ZuChristian informed Schoenberger that he wanted to employ him at a salary of $19,800 and that he was making a recommendation to that effect. When the formal offer was made by the placement department, however, the salary was stated at $19,300. Schoenberger did not accept the offer immediately but instead called ZuChristian for an explanation of the salary difference. After making inquiries, ZuChristian informed Schoenberger that a clerical error had been made and that it would take some time to correct. He urged Schoenberger to accept the job at $19,300 and said that he would see that the $500 was made up to him at one of the salary reviews in the following year. When the increase was not given, Schoenberger resigned and filed this suit to recover damages. The trial court ruled in favor of C.T.A., and Schoenberger appealed.

DECISION Judgment for C.T.A. affirmed.

OPINION ZuChristian had neither the actual nor the apparent authority to bind the C.T.A. for the additional $500. The actual authority of an agent may come only from the principal and must be founded on the words or acts of the principal, not on the acts or words of the agent. Apparent authority, in contrast, is such authority as the principal knowingly permits the agent to assume or holds out his agent as possessing. It is such authority as a reasonable, prudent person, exercising diligence and discretion, in view of the principal's conduct, would naturally suppose the agent to possess.

Here, two of ZuChristian's superiors testified that he had no actual authority to make an offer of a specific salary to Schoenberger

or to make any promise of additional compensation. Moreover, ZuChristian did not have the apparent authority to do either. The mere fact that he was allowed to interview prospective employees does not establish that the C.T.A. held him out as possessing the authority to hire or to set salaries. Furthermore, Schoenberger was told that the placement department would make the formal offer.

Finally, the plaintiff contends that irrespective of ZuChristian's actual or apparent authority, the C.T.A. is bound by ZuChristian's promise because it ratified his acts. Ratification may be express or inferred and occurs when "the principal, with knowledge of the material facts of the unauthorized transaction, takes a position inconsistent with nonaffirmation of the transaction." Ratification is the equivalent to an original authorization and confirms a transaction that was originally unauthorized. Ratification occurs where a principal attempts to seek or retain the benefits of the transaction.

Review of the evidence does not indicate that the C.T.A. acted to ratify ZuChristian's promise. According to Bonner's testimony, when he took over the supervision of ZuChristian's group in the fall of 1976 and was told of the promise, he immediately informed ZuChristian that the promise was unauthorized and consequently would not be honored. Subsequently, he informed Schoenberger of this same fact.

INTERPRETATION A principal is not bound by an agent if the agent has neither actual authority nor apparent authority, either of which must come from the conduct or words of the principal, unless the principal ratifies the unauthorized contract.

CRITICAL THINKING QUESTION Do you agree with the court's decision? Explain.

Fundamental Rules of Contractual Liability [29-1e]

The following rules summarize the contractual relations between the principal and the third party:

1. A disclosed principal and the third party are parties to the contract if the agent acts within her *actual* or *apparent* authority in making the contract on the principal's behalf. See Figure 29-1.
2. An unidentified (partially disclosed) principal and the third party are parties to the contract bound if the agent acts within her *actual* or *apparent* authority in making the contract on the principal's behalf. See Figure 29-2.

Practical Advice

As a principal, carefully consider the extent to which you want your agent to disclose your existence and identity.

3. An undisclosed principal and the third party are parties to the contract if the agent acts within her *actual* authority in making the contract on the principal's behalf unless (a) the terms of the contract exclude the principal or (b) his existence is fraudulently concealed. See Figure 29-3.

4. No principal is a party to a contract with a third party if the agent acts without any authority in making the contract on the principal's behalf, unless the principal ratifies the contract. Under the Second Restatement the principal must have been either disclosed or unidentified.

TORT LIABILITY OF THE PRINCIPAL [29-2]

In addition to being contractually liable to third persons, a principal may be liable in tort to third persons because of the acts of her agent. Tort liability may arise directly or indirectly (vicariously) from authorized or unauthorized acts of an agent. Also, a principal is liable for the unauthorized torts an agent commits in connection with a transaction that the purported principal, with full knowledge of the tort, subsequently ratifies. Cases involving unauthorized but ratified torts are extremely rare. Of course, in all of these situations, the wrongdoing agent is personally liable to the injured person because the agent committed the tort. See Figure 29-4 explaining the tort liability of the principal.

Figure 29-4 Tort Liability

Agent's Tort Authorized

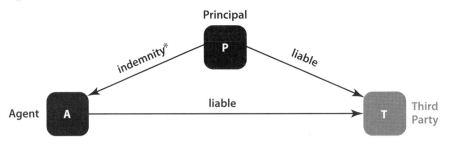

Employee's Tort Unauthorized But Within Scope of Employment

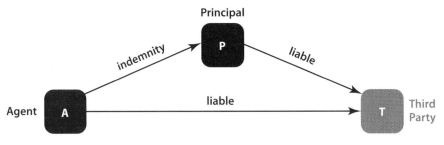

Employee's Tort Outside Authority and Scope of Employment or Independent Contractor's Tort Unauthorized

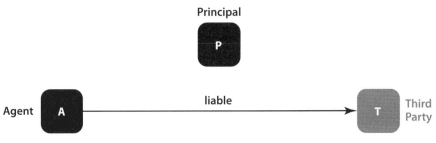

*If not illegal or known by A to be wrongful.

Direct liability of principal

a principal is liable for his own tortious conduct involving the use of agents

Direct Liability of Principal [29-2a]

A principal is liable for his *own* tortious conduct involving the use of agents. Such liability may arise in two primary ways. First, a principal is directly liable in damages for harm resulting from his directing an agent to commit a tort. Second, the principal is directly liable if he fails to exercise reasonable care in employing competent agents.

Authorized acts of agent

a principal is liable for torts that she authorizes another to commit or that she ratifies

Authorized Acts of Agent

A principal who authorizes his agent to commit a tortious act concerning the property or person of another is liable for the injury or loss that person sustains. This liability also extends to unauthorized tortious conduct that the principal subsequently ratifies. The authorized act is that of the principal. Thus, if Phillip directs his agent, Anthony, to enter Clark's land and cut timber, which neither Phillip nor Anthony has any right to do, the cutting of the timber is a trespass, and Phillip is liable to Clark. A principal may be subject to tort liability because of an agent's conduct even though the agent is not subject to liability. Phillip instructs his agent, Anthony, to make certain representations as to Phillip's property that Anthony is authorized to sell. Phillip knows these representations are false, but Anthony does not know and has no reason or duty to know. Such representations by Anthony to Tammy, who buys the property in reliance on them, constitute a deceit for which Phillip is liable to Tammy. Anthony, however, would not be liable to Tammy.

Unauthorized acts of agent

a principal is liable for failing to exercise reasonable care in employing agents whose unauthorized acts cause harm

Unauthorized Acts of Agent

A principal who negligently conducts activities through an employee or other agent is liable for harm resulting from such conduct. For example, a principal is liable if he negligently (1) selects agents, (2) retains agents, (3) trains agents, (4) supervises agents, or (5) otherwise controls agents.

The liability of a principal under this provision—called *negligent hiring*—arises when the principal does not exercise proper care in selecting an agent for the job to be done. For example, if Patricia lends to her employee, Art, a company car with which to run a business errand, knowing that Art is incapable of driving the vehicle, Patricia would be liable for her own negligence to anyone injured by Art's unsafe driving. The negligent hiring doctrine also has been used to impose liability on a principal for intentional torts committed by an agent against customers of the principal or members of the public, when the principal either knew or should have known that the agent was violent or aggressive.

Connes v. Molalla Transport System, Inc.
Supreme Court of Colorado, 1992
831 P.2d 1316
http://scholar.google.com/scholar_case?case=2485973325983137183&q=831+P.2d+1316&hl=en&as_sclt=2,34

FACTS Terry Taylor was an employee of Molalla Transport. In hiring Taylor, Molalla followed its standard hiring procedure, which includes a personal interview with each applicant and requires the applicant to fill out an extensive job application form and to produce a current driver's license and a certificate from a medical examiner. Molalla also contacts prior employers and other references about the applicant's qualifications and conducts an investigation of the applicant's driving record in the state where the applicant obtained the driver's license. Although applicants are asked whether they have been convicted of a crime, Molalla does not conduct an independent investigation to verify the statement. Approximately three months after Taylor began working for Molalla, he was assigned to transport freight from Kansas to Oregon. While traveling through Colorado, Taylor left the highway and drove by a hotel where Grace Connes was working as a night clerk. Observing that Connes was alone in the lobby, Taylor pulled his truck into the parking lot and entered the lobby. Once inside, Taylor sexually assaulted Connes at knifepoint. Although Taylor denied any prior criminal convictions on his application and during his interview, police and court records obtained since these events show that Taylor had been convicted of three felonies in Colorado and had been issued three citations for lewd conduct and another citation for simple assault in Seattle, Washington.

Connes sued Molalla on the theory of negligent hiring, claiming that Molalla knew or should have known that Taylor would come into contact with members of the public, that Molalla had a duty to hire and retain high-quality employees so as not to endanger members of the public, and that Molalla had breached its duty by failing to investigate fully and adequately Taylor's criminal background. The district court granted Molalla's motion for summary judgment. The Court of Appeals upheld the lower court's ruling, holding that Molalla had no legal duty to investigate the nonvehicular criminal record of its driver prior to hiring him as an employee. Connes appealed.

DECISION Judgment affirmed.

OPINION The tort of negligent hiring is based on the principle that a person conducting an activity through employees is subject to liability for harm resulting from negligent conduct "in the employment of improper persons or instrumentalities in work involving risk of harm to others." The tort of negligent hiring, does not impose upon an employer a duty to ensure that its employees will not engage in violent acts. On the contrary, liability is predicated on the employer's hiring of a person under circumstances which provide the employer reason to believe that the person, by reason of some attribute of character or prior conduct, would create an undue risk of harm to others in carrying out his or her employment responsibilities.

The scope of the employer's duty in exercising reasonable care in a hiring decision will depend largely on the anticipated degree of contact that the employee will have with other persons in performing his or her employment duties. When the employment calls for minimum contact between the employee and other persons, there may be no reason for an employer to conduct an investigation of the applicant's background beyond obtaining past employment information. However, when the employee will come into frequent contact with members of the public, or close contact with particular individuals with whom the employer has a special relationship, the employer's duty necessarily will be greater and may require an independent investigation of the applicant's background.

In the present case, Molalla had no reason to foresee that its hiring of Taylor under the circumstances of this case would create a risk that Taylor would sexually assault or otherwise endanger a member of the public by engaging in violent conduct. Far from requiring frequent conduct with members of the public, Taylor's duties were restricted to the hauling of freight and involved only incidental contact with third persons having no special relationship to either Molalla or Taylor. Furthermore, nothing in the hiring process gave Molalla reason to foresee that Taylor would pose an unreasonable risk of harm to members of the public. Therefore, Molalla had no legal duty to conduct an independent investigation into Taylor's nonvehicular criminal background in order to protect a member of the public from a sexual assault.

INTERPRETATION An employer's liability for negligent hiring is based on the employer's hiring a person under circumstances antecedently giving the employer reason to believe that the person would create an undue risk of harm to others in carrying out his employment duties.

ETHICAL QUESTION Was the court's decision fair? Explain.

CRITICAL THINKING QUESTION When should a prospective employer be required to check the criminal record of a job applicant? Explain.

Vicarious Liability of Principal for Unauthorized Acts of Agent [29-2b]

Vicarious liability

indirect legal responsibility for the act of another

The **vicarious liability** of a principal for unauthorized torts by an agent depends primarily on whether the agent is an employee or not. In this context, an employee is an agent whose principal controls or has the right to control the manner and means of the agent's performance of work. By comparison, if the principal does *not* control the manner and means of the agent's performance of the work, the agent is not an employee and is often referred to as an "independent contractor." The general rule is that a principal is not liable for physical harm caused by the tortious conduct of an agent who is an independent contractor if the principal did not intend or authorize the result or the manner of performance. Conversely, a principal is liable for an unauthorized tort committed by an employee acting within the scope of his employment.

Respondeat superior

let the superior (employer) respond; an employer is liable for unauthorized torts committed by an employee in the scope of his employment

Respondeat Superior An employer is subject to vicarious liability for an unauthorized tort committed by his employee, even one that is in flagrant disobedience of his instructions, if the employee committed the tort within the scope of her employment. This form of employer liability without fault is based on the doctrine of *respondeat superior*, or "let the superior respond." It does not matter how carefully the employer selected the employee if, in fact, the latter tortiously injures a third party while engaged in the scope of employment. Moreover, an *undisclosed* principal-employer is liable for the torts his employee commits within the scope of employment. Furthermore, the principal is liable even if the work is performed gratuitously so long as the principal controls or has the right to control the manner and means of the agent's performance of work.

The doctrine of *respondeat superior* is fundamental to the operation of tort law in the United States. The rationale for this doctrine is that a person who conducts his business activities through the use of employees should be liable for the employees' tortious conduct in carrying out those activities. The employer is more likely to insure against liability and is more likely to have the assets to satisfy a tort judgment than the employee. Moreover, *respondeat superior* creates an economic incentive for employers to exercise care in choosing, training, supervising, and insuring employees.

The liability of the principal under *respondeat superior* is vicarious or derivative and depends on proof of wrongdoing by the employee within the scope of his employment. The employer's vicarious liability to the third party is in *addition* to the agent's liability to the third party. Frequently, both principal and employee are defendants in the same suit. If the employee is not held liable, the principal is not liable either, because the employer's liability is based upon the employee's tortious conduct. A principal who is held liable for her employee's tort has a right of **indemnification** against the employee, which is the right to be reimbursed for the amount that she was required to pay as a result of the employee's wrongful act. Frequently, however, an employee is not able to reimburse his employer, and the principal must bear the brunt of the liability.

The wrongful act of the employee must be connected with his employment and within its scope if the principal is to be held liable for resulting injuries or damage to third persons.

The Restatement provides a general rule for determining whether the conduct of an employee is within the scope of employment:

> An employee acts within the scope of employment when performing work assigned by the employer or engaging in a course of conduct subject to the employer's control. An employee's act is not within the scope of employment when it occurs within an independent course of conduct not intended by the employee to serve any purpose of the employer.

For example, Hal, delivering gasoline for Martha, lights his pipe and negligently throws the blazing match into a pool of gasoline that has dripped on the ground during the delivery. The gasoline ignites, burning Arnold's filling station. Martha is subject to liability for the resulting harm because the negligence of the employee who delivered the gasoline relates directly to the manner in which he handled the goods in his custody. But if a chauffeur, while driving his employer's car on an errand for his employer, suddenly decides to shoot his pistol at pedestrians on the sidewalk, the employer would not be liable to the pedestrians. This willful and intentional misconduct is not related to the performance of the services for which the chauffeur was employed.

The same rule applies to an employee's tortious conduct that is unrelated to his employment. If Page employs Edward to deliver merchandise to Page's customers in a given city, and while driving a delivery truck to or from a place of delivery Edward negligently causes the truck to hit and injure Fred, Page is liable to Fred for injuries sustained. But if, after making the scheduled deliveries, Edward drives the truck to a neighboring city to visit a friend and while so doing negligently causes the truck to hit and injure Debra, Page is not liable. In the latter case, Edward is said to be on a "frolic of his own." By using the truck to accomplish his own purposes, not those of his employer, he has deviated from serving any purpose of his employer.

A principal may be held liable for the intentional torts of his employee if the commission of the tort is so reasonably connected with the employment as to be within its scope.

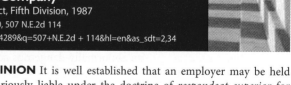

Rubin v. Yellow Cab Company
Appellate Court of Illinois, First District, Fifth Division, 1987
154 Ill.App.3d 336, 107 Ill.Dec. 450, 507 N.E.2d 114
http://scholar.google.com/scholar_case?case=2065675381460454289&q=507+N.E.2d + 114&hl=en&as_sdt=2,34

FACTS Rubin, the plaintiff, was driving on one of the city's streets when he inadvertently obstructed the path of a taxicab, causing the cab to come into contact with his vehicle. Angered by the plaintiff's sudden blocking of his traffic lane, the defendant taxi driver exited his cab, approached Rubin, and struck him about the head and shoulders with a metal pipe. Rubin filed suit against the cab driver to recover for bodily injuries resulting from the altercation. He also sued the Yellow Cab Company (Yellow Cab), asserting that the company was vicariously liable under the doctrine of *respondeat superior*. The trial court ruled in favor of Yellow Cab, and the plaintiff appealed.

DECISION Judgment for Yellow Cab affirmed.

OPINION It is well established that an employer may be held vicariously liable under the doctrine of *respondeat superior* for the negligent, willful, malicious, or criminal acts of its employees when such acts are committed in the course of employment and in furtherance of the business of the employer. However, when the acts complained of are committed solely for the benefit of the employee, the employer will not be held liable to an injured third party. The plaintiff contends that the driver's acts were committed within the course and scope of his employment and were designed to further the business purposes of Yellow Cab. The plaintiff asserts that the driver's acts (1) fulfilled his obligation to investigate and report accidents damaging company property, (2) were performed pursuant to his obligation to protect property owned by Yellow Cab, and (3) were meant to prevent the plaintiff and others from delaying his progress to obtain fares.

The court flatly rejected the plaintiff's argument. The driver's act of hitting the plaintiff has no relation whatsoever to the business of driving a cab. The nature of some jobs, such as a bouncer or bartender, makes the use of force during the course of employment highly probable. The assault on the plaintiff in this case, however, amounted to a deviation from the conduct generally associated with the enterprise of cab driving. The driver was not acting to further the business purposes of Yellow Cab. Accordingly, Yellow Cab is not vicariously liable for the battery of the plaintiff by the driver.

INTERPRETATION Under *respondeat superior*, an employer's liability for torts extends only to torts committed within the scope of employment.

CRITICAL THINKING QUESTION Do you agree that the taxi driver's conduct was outside his employment duties? If so, should it exonerate the employer from liability? Explain.

Agent acts with apparent authority

a principal is liable for torts committed by an agent in dealing with third parties while acting within the agent's apparent authority

Agent Acts with Apparent Authority   The Restatement provides that

> A principal is subject to vicarious liability for a tort committed by an agent in dealing or communicating with a third party on or purportedly on behalf of the principal when actions taken by the agent with apparent authority constitute the tort or enable the agent to conceal its commission.

This liability applies to (1) agents, whether or not they are employees, and (2) agents who are employees but whose tortious conduct is not within the scope of employment under *respondeat superior*. The torts to which this rule applies include fraudulent and negligent misrepresentations, defamation, wrongful institution of legal proceedings, and conversion of property.

Torts of independent contractor

a principal is usually not liable for the unauthorized torts of an independent contractor

---

Practical Advice

As a principal, consider hiring an independent contractor to limit your potential tort liability.

Torts of Independent Contractor   An independent contractor is not the employee of the person for whom he is performing work or rendering services. Hence, the doctrine of *respondeat superior* generally does not apply to torts committed by an independent contractor. For example, Parnell authorizes Bob, his broker, to sell land for him. Parnell, Teresa, and Bob meet in Teresa's office; and Bob arranges the sale to Teresa. While Bob is preparing a deed for Parnell to sign, he negligently knocks over an inkstand and ruins a valuable rug belonging to Teresa. Bob, not Parnell, is liable to Teresa.

Nonetheless, the principal may be *directly* liable if she fails to exercise reasonable care in selecting an independent contractor. For example, Melanie employs Gordon, whom she knows to be an alcoholic, as an independent contractor to repair her roof. Gordon attempts the repairs while heavily intoxicated and negligently drops a fifty-pound bundle of shingles upon Eric, a pedestrian walking on the sidewalk. Both Gordon and Melanie are liable to Eric.

Moreover, under some circumstances, a principal will be *vicariously* liable for torts committed by a carefully selected independent contractor. Certain duties imposed by law are nondelegable, and a person may not escape the consequences of their nonperformance by having entrusted them to another person. For example, a landowner who permits an independent contractor to maintain a dangerous condition on his premises, such as an excavation that is neither surrounded by a guardrail nor lit at night and that adjoins a public sidewalk, is liable to a member of the public who is injured by falling into the excavation.

A principal is also vicariously liable for an independent contractor's conduct in carrying on an abnormally dangerous activity, such as using fire or high explosives, or spraying crops.

CRIMINAL LIABILITY OF THE PRINCIPAL [29-3]

Authorized criminal acts

the principal is liable if he directed, participated in, or approved the criminal acts of his agents

A principal is liable for the **authorized criminal acts** of his agents only if the principal directed, participated in, or approved of the acts. For example, if an agent, at his principal's direction or with his principal's knowledge, fixes prices with the principal's competitors, both the agent and the principal have criminally violated the antitrust laws. Otherwise, a principal ordinarily is not liable for the unauthorized criminal acts of his agents. One of the elements of a crime is mental fault, and this element is absent, so far as the principal's criminal responsibility is concerned, in cases in which the principal did not authorize the agent's act.

An employer may, nevertheless, be subject to a criminal penalty for the unauthorized act of an advisory or managerial employee acting in the scope of her employment. Moreover, an

Unauthorized criminal acts

the principal may be liable either for a criminal act of a managerial person or under liability without fault statutes

employer may be criminally liable under liability without fault statutes for certain **unauthorized criminal acts** of an employee, whether the employee is managerial or not. These statutes are usually regulatory and do not require mental fault. For example, many states have statutes that punish "every person who by himself or his employee or agent sells anything at short weight," or "whoever sells liquor to a minor and any sale by an employee shall be deemed the act of the employer as well." Another example is a statute prohibiting the sale of unwholesome or adulterated food. See Chapter 6 for a more detailed discussion of this topic.

RELATIONSHIP OF AGENT AND THIRD PERSONS

The function of an agent is to assist in the conduct of the principal's business by carrying out his orders. Generally, the agent acquires no rights against third parties and likewise incurs no liabilities to them. There are, however, several exceptions to this proposition. In certain instances, an agent may become personally liable to the third party for contracts she made on behalf of her principal. Occasionally, the agent also may acquire rights against the third party. In addition, an agent who commits a tort is personally liable to the injured third party. In this section, we will cover these circumstances involving the personal liability of an agent, as well as those in which an agent may acquire rights against third persons.

CONTRACT LIABILITY OF AGENT [29-4]

The agent normally is not a party to the contract he makes with a third person on behalf of a disclosed principal. An agent who exceeds his actual and apparent authority may, however, be personally liable to the third party. In addition, an agent acting for a disclosed principal may become liable if he expressly assumes liability on the contract. When an agent enters into a contract on behalf of an unidentified (partially disclosed) principal or an undisclosed principal, the agent becomes personally liable to the third party on the contract. Furthermore, an agent who knowingly enters into a contract on behalf of a nonexistent or completely incompetent principal is personally liable to the third party on that contract.

Disclosed Principal [29-4a]

As explained, the principal is a **disclosed principal** if, when an agent and a third party interact, the third party has notice that the agent is acting for a principal and also has notice of the principal's identity. The liability of an agent acting for a disclosed principal depends on whether the agent acts within her authority in making the contract or otherwise assumes liability on the contract.

Authorized Contracts   When an agent acting with actual or apparent authority makes a contract with a third party on behalf of a disclosed principal, the agent is not a party to the contract unless she and the third party agree otherwise. The third person is on notice that he is transacting business with an agent who is acting for an identified principal and that the agent is not personally undertaking to perform the contract but is simply negotiating on behalf of her principal. The resulting contract, if within the agent's actual authority, is between the third person and the principal. The agent ordinarily incurs no liability on the contract to either party (see Figure 29-1). This is also true of unauthorized contracts that are subsequently ratified by the principal. However, if the agent has apparent authority but no actual authority, the agent has no liability to the third party but is liable to the principal for any loss the agent has caused by exceeding his actual authority.

Unauthorized Contracts   If an agent exceeds his actual and apparent authority, the principal is not bound. The fact that the principal is not bound does not, however, make the agent a party to the contract unless the agent had agreed to be a party to the contract. The agent's liability, if any, arises from express or implied representations about his authority that he

Practical Advice

When signing contracts as an agent, be sure to indicate clearly your representative capacity.

Disclosed principal

the agent is not normally a party to the contract she makes with a third person if she is authorized or if the principal ratifies an unauthorized contract

Authorized contracts

the agent is not normally a party to the contract she makes with a third person if she has actual or apparent authority or if the principal ratifies an unauthorized contract

Unauthorized contracts

if an agent exceeds her actual and apparent authority, the disclosed principal is not bound but the agent may be liable to the third party for breach of warranty or for misrepresentation makes to the third party. For example, an agent may give an *express warranty of authority* by stating that he has authority and that he will be personally liable to the third party if he does not in fact have the authority to bind his principal.

Moreover, a person who undertakes to make a contract on behalf of another gives an *implied warranty of authority* that he is in fact authorized to make the contract on behalf of the party whom he purports to represent. If the agent does not have authority to bind the principal, the agent is liable to the third party for damages unless the principal ratifies the contract or unless the third party knew that the agent was unauthorized. No implied warranty of authority exists, however, if the agent expressly states that the agent gives no warranty of authority or if the agent, acting in good faith, discloses to the third person all of the facts upon which his authority rests. For example, agent Larson has received an ambiguous letter of instruction from his principal, Dan. Larson shows it to Carol, stating that it represents all of the authority that he has to act, and both Larson and Carol rely upon its sufficiency. In this case, Larson has made to Carol no implied or express warranty of his authority.

The Restatement provides that breach of the implied warranty of authority subjects the agent to liability to the third party for damages caused by breach of that warranty, including loss of the benefit expected from performance by the principal. Some courts, however, limit the third party's recovery to the damage or loss the third party suffered and exclude the third party's expected gain from the contract.

If a purported agent *misrepresents* to a third person that he has authority to make a contract on behalf of a principal whom he has no power to bind, he is liable in a tort action to the third person for the loss she sustained in reliance upon the misrepresentation. However, if the third party knows that the representation is false, the agent is not liable.

Practical Advice

As an agent, consider disclaiming liability for any lack of authority; as a third party, consider obtaining from the agent an express warranty of authority.

Agent assumes liability

an agent may agree to become liable on a contract between the disclosed principal and the third party

Agent Assumes Liability

An agent for a disclosed principal may agree to become liable on a contract between the principal and the third party by (1) making the contract in her own name, (2) co-making the contract with the principal, or (3) guaranteeing that the principal will perform the contract between the third party and the principal. In all of these situations, the agent's liability is separate unless the parties agree otherwise. Therefore, the third party may sue the agent separately without joining the principal and may obtain a judgment against either the principal or the agent, or both. If the principal satisfies the judgment, the agent is discharged. If the agent pays the judgment, he usually will have a right of reimbursement from the principal. This right is based upon the principles of suretyship, discussed in Chapter 37.

Unidentified Principal [29-4b]

As we discussed, the principal is an unidentified principal (partially disclosed principal) if, when an agent and a third party interact, the third party has notice that the agent is acting for a principal but does not have notice of the principal's identity. Using an unidentified principal may be helpful when, for example, the third party might inflate the price of property he is selling if he knew the identity of the principal. Partial disclosure may also occur inadvertently, when the agent fails through neglect to inform the third party of the principal's identity.

Unidentified (partially disclosed) principal

an agent who acts for a partially disclosed principal is a party to the contract with the third party unless otherwise agreed

Unless otherwise agreed, when an agent makes a contract with actual or apparent authority on behalf of an **unidentified principal**, the agent is a party to the contract. For example, Ashley writes to Terrence offering to sell a rare painting on behalf of its owner, who wishes to remain unknown. Terrence accepts. Ashley is a party to the contract.

Whether the particular transaction is authorized or not, an agent for an unidentified principal is liable to the third party (see Figure 29-2). If the agent is actually or apparently authorized to make the contract, both the agent and the unidentified principal are liable. If the agent has no actual and no apparent authority, the agent is liable either as a party to the contract or for breach of the implied warranty of authority. In any event, the agent is separately liable, and the third party may sue her individually, without joining the principal, and the agent or the principal may obtain a judgment against either or both. If the principal satisfies the judgment, the agent is also discharged. If the agent pays the judgment, the principal is discharged from liability to the third party, but the agent has the right to be reimbursed by the principal.

Undisclosed Principal [29-4c]

The principal is an undisclosed principal if, when an agent and a third party interact, the third party has no notice that the agent is acting for a principal. Thus, when an agent acts for an undisclosed principal, she appears to be acting on her own behalf and the third person with whom she is dealing has no knowledge that she is acting as an agent. The principal has instructed the agent to conceal not only the principal's identity but also the agency relationship. Such concealment can also occur if the agent simply neglects to disclose the existence and identity of her principal. Thus, the third person is dealing with the agent as though the agent were a principal.

The agent is personally liable upon a contract she enters into with a third person on behalf of an **undisclosed principal** (see Figure 29-3). The agent is liable because the third person has relied upon the agent individually and has accepted the agent's personal undertaking to perform the contract. Obviously, when the principal is undisclosed, the third person does not know of the interest of anyone in the contract other than that of himself and the agent.

The Second Restatement and many cases hold that after learning the identity of the undisclosed principal, the third person may obtain performance of the contract from either the principal or the agent, but not both; and his choice, once made, binds him irrevocably. However, to avoid the risk that evidence at trial may fail to establish the agency relationship, the third person may bring suit against both the principal and agent. In most states following this approach, this act of bringing suit and proceeding to trial against both is not an election, but, before the entry of any judgment, the third person is compelled to make an election because he is not entitled to a judgment against both. A judgment against the agent by a third party who knows the identity of the previously undisclosed principal discharges the principal's liability to the third party but leaves her liable to the agent, who would have the right to be reimbursed by the principal. If the third party obtains a judgment against the agent before learning the identity of the principal, the principal is not discharged. Finally, the agent is discharged from liability if the third party obtains a judgment against the principal.

The Third Restatement and a number of states have recently rejected the election rule, holding that a third party's rights against the principal are additional and not alternative to the third party's rights against the agent. The Third Restatement provides, "When an agent has made a contract with a third party on behalf of a principal, unless the contract provides otherwise, the liability, if any, of the principal or the agent to the third party is not discharged if the third party obtains a judgment against the other." However, the liability, if any, of the principal or the agent to the third party *is* discharged to the extent a judgment against the other is satisfied.

Nonexistent or Incompetent Principal [29-4d]

Unless the third party agrees otherwise, if a person who purports to act as an agent knows or has reason to know that the person purportedly represented does not exist or completely lacks capacity to be a party to contract, the person purporting to act as agent will become a party to the contract. Complete lack of capacity to contract includes an individual person who has been adjudicated incompetent. An example of a nonexistent principal is a corporation or limited liability company (LLC) that has not yet been formed. Thus, a promoter of a corporation who enters into contracts with third persons in the name of a corporation yet to be organized is personally liable on such contracts. Not yet in existence, and therefore unable to authorize the contracts, the corporation is not liable. If, after coming into existence, the corporation affirmatively adopts a preincorporation contract made on its behalf, it, in addition to the promoter, becomes bound. If the corporation enters into a new contract with such a third person, however, the prior contract between the promoter and the third person is discharged, and the liability of the promoter is terminated. This is a novation.

An agent who makes a contract for a disclosed principal whose contracts are voidable for lack of contractual capacity is *not* liable to the third party, with two exceptions: (1) if the agent warrants or represents that the principal has capacity or (2) if the agent has reason to know both of the principal's lack of capacity and of the third party's ignorance of that incapacity.

Undisclosed principal
an agent who acts for an undisclosed principal is personally liable on the contract to the third party

Nonexistent or incompetent principal
a person who purports to act as agent for a principal whom the agent knows to be nonexistent or completely incompetent is personally liable on a contract entered into with a third person on behalf of such a principal

Plain Dealer Publishing Co. v. Worrell
Court of Appeals of Ohio, Ninth District, Summit County, 2008
178 Ohio App.3d 485, 898 N.E.2d 1009
http://scholar.google.com/scholar_case?q=Plain+Dealer+v+worrell&hl=en&as_sdt=2,34&case=13457191655705896330&scilh=0

FACTS The Plain Dealer Publishing Company brought a lawsuit in August 2005 to collect a debt for advertising placed by Frederick "Rick" Worrell, doing business as WRL Advertising. The lawsuit also named Martha J. Musil, an employee of WRL Advertising who had placed the advertising orders with the Plain Dealer at the direction of her employer. Shortly after the case was brought, Worrell filed bankruptcy, and as a result of the automatic stay, the trial court placed the case on the inactive docket. On January 24, 2006, the trial court granted the Plain Dealer's motion to reactivate the case as to Musil only. Subsequently, the Plain Dealer moved for summary judgment, asserting that Musil was personally liable on the contracts because WRL Advertising was a fictitious entity with no legal standing.

The trial court determined that although Musil communicated her agency relationship to the Plain Dealer, she did not sufficiently disclose the identity of her principal. In making this determination, the trial court noted that "[i]t is also undisputed that WRL Advertising is not a legal entity in its own right, but rather a trade name for Winfield, [sic] Bennett & Baer, LLC, which is owned and operated by Worrell." The trial court held that the use of a principal's trade name is insufficient to identify the principal. The trial court found that because she was acting, at best, on behalf of a partially disclosed principal, Musil was liable on the contracts. The trial court awarded the Plain Dealer a judgment against Musil in the amount of $8,720 plus interest. Musil appealed.

DECISION Judgment is reversed and case is remanded.

OPINION The parties do not contest the fact that Musil communicated to the Plain Dealer that she was working on behalf of a principal. In Ohio, an agent is liable to a third party when she contracts in the name of a nonexistent or fictitious principal or assumes to act as an agent for a principal who has no legal status or existence. The court held that Musil was not acting on behalf of

a fictitious entity or an entity that does not exist in Ohio, but rather that WRL Advertising was a fictitious *name* for Wingfield, Bennett, & Baer, L.L.C.

"A corporation may use a name other than its corporate name in the conduct of its business." In this case, the parties do not dispute that Wingfield, Bennett & Baer L.L.C. was registered with the Secretary of State. Therefore, Wingfield, Bennett & Baer is not a fictitious or nonexistent principal for agency law purposes. Furthermore, WRL Advertising was a fictitious *name* for Wingfield, Bennett & Baer and Musil was acting on behalf of Wingfield, Bennett & Baer, which was in turn using a fictitious name.

An agent will "avoid personal liability for debts of the corporation only if he complies with the rules which apply in all agency relationships—he must so conduct himself in dealing on behalf of the corporation with third persons that those persons are aware that he is an agent of the corporation and it is the corporation (principal) with which they are dealing, not the agent individually." In this case, Musil disclosed that she was acting on behalf of a principal, and therefore, the Plain Dealer knew that it was not dealing with Musil individually. The Plain Dealer knew it was dealing with an entity, but that entity was using the fictitious name WRL Advertising. The use of a name other than Wingfield, Bennett & Baer in the conduct of business does *not* render Musil liable as an agent of a nonexistent or fictitious principal. Because Musil was acting on behalf of a legal entity using a fictitious *name*, the trial court erred when it granted the Plain Dealer's motion for summary judgment.

INTERPRETATION To avoid personal liability on a contract, an agent must disclose both that she is acting as an agent and the identity of her principal.

CRITICAL THINKING QUESTION Should it be legally permissible for an agent not to disclose the existence and identity of his principal? Explain.

Tort liability of agent
the agent is liable to the third party for his own torts

TORT LIABILITY OF AGENT [29-5]

An agent is personally liable for his tortious acts that injure third persons, whether such acts are authorized by the principal or not and whether the principal also may be liable or not. For example, an agent is personally liable if he converts the goods of a third person to his principal's use. An agent is also liable for making representations that he knows to be fraudulent to a third person who in reliance sustains a loss.

Disclosed principal
the agent usually has no rights under the contract against the third party

Undisclosed or unidentified (partially disclosed) principal
the agent may enforce the contract against the third party

RIGHTS OF AGENT AGAINST THIRD PERSON [29-6]

An agent who makes a contract with a third person on behalf of a **disclosed principal** usually has no right of action against the third person for breach of contract. The agent is not a party to the contract. An agent for a disclosed principal may sue on the contract, however, if it provides that the agent is a party to the contract. Furthermore, an agent for an **undisclosed principal** or an **unidentified (partially disclosed) principal** may maintain in her own name an action against the third person for breach of contract.

ETHICAL DILEMMA

When Should an Agent's Power to Bind His Principal Terminate?

Facts Tim Banks was an employee of Golden Harvest Florists International (GHFI). GHFI operated a wholesale florist business on the East Coast and also maintained a small chain of retail shops in the Washington, D.C.–Baltimore area. Tim, whose responsibilities included buying large quantities of fresh cut flowers from various greenhouses along the East Coast, had established an excellent rapport with all of his suppliers and was well respected throughout the entire industry.

Because of his good reputation, Tim was shocked to discover on April 1, 2014, that he had been released by GHFI. This notice came after five years of faithful

service to the company. Though the company would not tell Tim why he had been fired, Tim learned that GHFI felt threatened by his reputation and was worried that he was becoming better known and more important than the company itself.

GHFI did not, moreover, notify any of Tim's suppliers of his release until January 1, 2015. The company was worried that notice might undermine the suppliers' confidence in the company and could possibly cause prices to rise. Meanwhile, deciding to begin his own business, Tim continued to purchase flowers from the same greenhouses. He was able to pay his

supply bills from April through November 2014, but, when his funds were low in December, he charged the flowers to GHFI. GHFI refused to pay, and the greenhouses have filed suit against Tim and GHFI.

Social, Policy, and Ethical Considerations

1. Who is legally responsible for the bills? Who is ethically responsible?
2. What is the social policy behind the requirement of notice prior to termination of a principal-agent relationship?
3. Does Tim have a responsibility to the greenhouses to notify them of the source of his funds, as long as the bill is paid?

CHAPTER SUMMARY

Relationship of Principal and Third Persons

Contract Liability of Principal

Types of Principals

- *Disclosed Principal* principal whose existence and identity are known
- *Unidentified (Partially Disclosed) Principal* principal whose existence is known but whose identity is not known
- *Undisclosed Principal* principal whose existence and identity are not known

Authority power of an agent to change the legal status of the principal

- *Actual Authority* power conferred upon the agent by actual consent manifested by the principal to the agent
- *Actual Express Authority* actual authority derived from written or spoken words of the principal communicated to the agent
- *Actual Implied Authority* actual authority inferred from words or conduct manifested to the agent by the principal
- *Apparent Authority* power conferred upon the agent by acts or conduct of the principal that reasonably lead a third party to believe that the agent has such power

Delegation of Authority is usually not permitted unless actually or apparently authorized by the principal; if the agent is authorized to appoint other subagents, the acts of these subagents are as binding on the principal as those of the agent

Effect of Termination of Agency on Authority ends *actual* authority

- *Second Restatement* if the termination is by operation of law, *apparent* authority also ends without notice to third parties; if the termination is by an act of the parties, *apparent* authority ends when third parties have actual knowledge or when appropriate notice is given to third parties; actual notice must be given to third parties with whom the agent had previously dealt on credit, has been specially accredited, or has begun to deal; all other third parties as to whom there was apparent authority need only be given constructive notice

- *Third Restatement* termination of actual authority does not by itself end any apparent authority held by an agent; *apparent* authority ends when it is no longer reasonable for the third party with whom an agent deals to believe that the agent continues to act with actual authority

Ratification affirmation by one person of a prior unauthorized act that another has done as her agent or as her purported agent

Fundamental Rules of Contractual Liability

- *Disclosed Principal* contractually bound with the third party if the agent acts within her actual or apparent authority in making the contract on the principal's behalf
- *Unidentified (Partially Disclosed) Principal* contractually bound with the third party if the agent acts within her actual or apparent authority in making the contract on the principal's behalf
- *Undisclosed Principal* contractually bound with the third party if the agent acts within her actual authority in making the contract on the principal's behalf

Tort Liability of Principal

Direct Liability of Principal a principal is liable for his own tortious conduct involving the use of agents

- *Authorized Acts of Agent* a principal is liable for torts that she authorizes another to commit or that she ratifies
- *Unauthorized Acts of Agent* a principal is liable for failing to exercise reasonable care in employing agents whose unauthorized acts cause harm

Vicarious Liability of Principal for Unauthorized Acts of Agent

- *Respondeat Superior* an employer is liable for unauthorized torts committed by an employee in the scope of his employment
- *Agent Acts with Apparent Authority* a principal is liable for torts committed by an agent in dealing with third parties while acting within the agent's apparent authority
- *Independent Contractor* a principal is usually not liable for the unauthorized torts of an independent contractor

Criminal Liability of the Principal

Authorized Acts the principal is liable if he directed, participated in, or approved the acts of his agents

Unauthorized Acts the principal may be liable either for a criminal act of a managerial person or under liability without fault statutes

---

Relationship of Agents and Third Persons

Contract Liability of Agent

Disclosed Principal

- *Authorized Contracts* the agent is not normally a party to the contract she makes with a third person if she has actual or apparent authority or if the principal ratifies an unauthorized contract
- *Unauthorized Contracts* if an agent exceeds her actual and apparent authority, the principal is not bound but the agent may be liable to the third party for breach of warranty or for misrepresentation
- *Agent Assumes Liability* an agent may agree to become liable on a contract between the principal and the third party

Unidentified (Partially Disclosed) Principal an agent who acts for a partially disclosed principal is a party to the contract with the third party unless otherwise agreed

Undisclosed Principal an agent who acts for an undisclosed principal is personally liable on the contract to the third party

Nonexistent or Incompetent Principal a person who purports to act as agent for a principal whom the agent knows to be nonexistent or completely incompetent is personally liable on a contract entered into with a third person on behalf of such a principal

Tort Liability of Agent

Authorized Acts the agent is liable to the third party for his own torts

Unauthorized Acts the agent is liable to the third party for his own torts

Rights of Agent Against Third Person

Disclosed Principal the agent usually has no rights against the third party

Unidentified (Partially Disclosed) Principal the agent may enforce the contract against the third party

Undisclosed Principal the agent may enforce the contract against the third party

QUESTIONS

1. Alice was Peter's traveling salesperson and was authorized to collect accounts. Before the agreed termination of the agency, Peter wrongfully discharged Alice. Peter did not notify anyone of Alice's termination. Alice then called on Tom, an old customer, and collected an account from Tom. She also called on Laura, a new prospect, as Peter's agent, secured a large order, collected the price of the order, sent the order to Peter, and disappeared with the collections. Peter delivered the goods to Laura per the order.
   a. What will be the result if Peter sues Tom for his account?
   b. What will be the result if Peter sues Laura for the agreed price of the goods?

2. Paula instructed Alvin, her agent, to purchase a quantity of hides. Alvin ordered the hides from Ted in his own (Alvin's) name and delivered the hides to Paula. Ted, learning later that Paula was the principal, sends the bill to Paula, who refuses to pay Ted. Ted sues Paula and Alvin. What are Ted's rights against Paula and Alvin?

3. Stan sold goods to Bill in good faith, believing him to be a principal. Bill in fact was acting as agent for Nancy and within the scope of his authority. The goods were charged to Bill, and, on his refusal to pay, Stan sued Bill for the purchase price. While this action was pending, Stan learned of Bill's relationship with Nancy. Nevertheless, thirty days after learning of that relationship, Stan obtained judgment against Bill and had an execution issued that was never satisfied. Three months after the judgment was made, Stan sued Nancy for the purchase price of the goods. Is Nancy liable? Explain.

4. Green Grocery Company employed Jones as its manager and gave her authority to purchase supplies and goods for resale. Jones had conducted business for several years with Brown Distributing Company, although her purchases had been limited to groceries. Jones contacted Brown and had it deliver a color television set to her house. She told Brown that the set was to be used in promotional advertising to increase Green's business. The advertising did not develop, and Jones disappeared from the area, taking the television set with her. Brown now seeks to recover the purchase price of the set from Green. Will Brown prevail? Explain.

5. Stone was the agent authorized to sell stock of the Turner Company at $10.00 per share and was authorized in case of sale to fill in the blanks in the certificates with the name of the purchaser, the number of shares, and the date of sale. He sold one hundred shares to Barrie, and without the knowledge or consent of the company and without reporting to the company, he indorsed the back of the certificate as follows:

   It is hereby agreed that Turner Company shall, at the end of three years after the date, repurchase the stock at $13.00 per share on thirty days' notice. Turner Company, by Stone.

   After three years, demand was made on Turner Company to repurchase. The company refused the demand and repudiated the agreement on the ground that the agent had no authority to make the agreement for repurchase. Is Turner Company liable to Barrie? Explain.

6. Helper, a delivery boy for Gunn, delivered two heavy packages of groceries to Reed's porch. As instructed by Gunn, Helper rang the bell to let Reed know the groceries had arrived. Mrs. Reed came to the door and asked Helper if he would deliver the groceries into the kitchen because the bags were heavy. Helper did so, and on leaving he observed Mrs. Reed having difficulty in moving a cabinet in the dining room. He undertook to assist her, but being more interested in watching Mrs. Reed than in noting the course of the cabinet, he failed to observe a small, valuable antique table, which he smashed into with the cabinet and totally destroyed. Does Reed have a cause of action against Gunn for the value of the destroyed antique?

7. Driver picked up Friend to accompany him on an out-of-town delivery for his employer, Speedy Service. A "No Riders" sign was prominently displayed on the windshield of the truck, and Driver violated specific instructions of his employer by permitting an unauthorized person to ride in the vehicle. While discussing a planned fishing trip with Friend, Driver ran a red light and collided with an automobile driven by Motorist. Both Friend and Motorist were injured. Is Speedy Service liable to either Friend or Motorist for the injuries they sustained?

8. Cook's Department Store advertises that it maintains a barbershop in its store and that the shop is managed by Hunter, a Cook's employee. Actually, Hunter is not an employee of the store but merely rents space in the store. While shaving Jordan in the barbershop, Hunter negligently puts a deep gash, requiring ten stitches, into one of Jordan's ears. Should Jordan be entitled to collect damages from Cook's Department Store?

9. The following contract was executed on August 22:

   Ray agrees to sell and Shaw, the representative of Todd and acting on his behalf, agrees to buy 10,000 pounds of 0.32 × 15/8 stainless steel strip type 410.

   (signed) Ray

   (signed) Shaw

   On August 26 Ray informs Shaw and Todd that the contract was in reality signed by him as agent for Upson. What are the rights of Ray, Shaw, Todd, and Upson in the event of a breach of the contract?

10. Harris, owner of certain land known as Red Bank, mailed a letter to Byron, a real estate broker in City X, stating, "I have been thinking of selling Red Bank. I have never met you, but a friend has advised me that you are an industrious and honest real estate broker. I therefore employ you to find a purchaser for Red Bank at a price of $350,000." Ten days after receiving the letter, Byron mailed the following reply to Harris: "Acting pursuant to your recent letter requesting me to find a purchaser for Red Bank, this is to advise that I have sold the property to Sims for $350,000. I enclose your copy of the contract of sale signed by Sims. Your name was signed to the contract by me as your agent." Is Harris obligated to convey Red Bank to Sims?

CASE PROBLEMS

11. While crossing a public highway in the city, Joel was struck by a horse-drawn cart driven by Morison's agent. The agent was traveling between Burton Crescent Mews and Finchley on his employer's business and was not supposed to go into the city at all. Apparently, the agent was on a detour to visit a friend when the accident occurred. Joel brought this action against Morison for the injuries he sustained as a result of the agent's negligence. Morison argues that he is not liable for his agent's negligence because the agent had strayed from his assigned path. Who is correct?

12. Serges is the owner of a retail meat marketing business. Without authority his managing agent borrowed $3,500 from David, on Serges's behalf, for use in Serges's business. Serges paid $200 on the alleged loan and on several other occasions told David that the full balance owed eventually would be paid. He then disclaimed liability on the debt, asserting that he had not authorized his agent to enter into the loan agreement. Should David succeed in an action to collect on the loan?

13. Sherwood negligently ran into the rear of Austen's car, which was stopped at a stoplight. As a result, Austen received bodily injuries and her car was damaged. Sherwood, arts editor for the *Mississippi Press Register*, was en route from a concert he had covered for the newspaper. When the accident occurred, he was on his way to spend the night at a friend's house. Austen sued Sherwood and—under the doctrine of *respondeat superior*—Sherwood's employer, the *Mississippi Press Register*. Who is liable? Explain.

14. Aretta J. Parkinson owned a two-hundred-acre farm in a state that requires written authority for an agent to sell land. Prior to her death on December 23, Parkinson deeded a one-eighth undivided interest in the farm to each of her eight children as tenants in common. On January 15 of the following year, one of the daughters, Roma Funk, approached Barbara Bradshaw about selling the Parkinson farm to the Bradshaws. They orally agreed to a selling price of $800,000. After this meeting, Funk contacted Bryant Hansen, a real estate broker, to assist her in completing the transaction. Hansen prepared an earnest money agreement that was signed by the Bradshaws but by none of the Parkinson children. Hansen also prepared warranty deeds, which were signed by three of the children. Several of the children subsequently refused to convey their interests in the farm to the Bradshaws. Explain whether the Bradshaws can get specific performance of the oral contract of sale, based on the defendants' ratification of the oral contract by their knowledge of and failure to repudiate it.

15. Chris Zulliger was a chef at the Plaza Restaurant in the Snowbird Ski Resort in Utah. The restaurant is located at the base of a mountain. As a chef for the Plaza, Zulliger was instructed by his supervisor and the restaurant manager to make periodic trips to inspect the Mid-Gad Restaurant, which was located halfway up the mountain. Because skiing helped its employees to get to work, Snowbird preferred that its employees know how to ski and gave them ski passes as part of their compensation. One day prior to beginning work at the Plaza, Zulliger went skiing. The restaurant manager asked Zulliger to stop at the Mid-Gad before beginning work that day, and Zulliger stopped at the Mid-Gad during his first run and inspected the kitchen. He then skied four runs before heading down the mountain to begin work. On the last run, Zulliger decided to take a route often taken by Snowbird employees. About midway down, Zulliger decided to jump off a crest on the side of an intermediate run. Because of the drop, a skier above the crest cannot see whether there are skiers below, and Zulliger ran into Margaret Clover, who was below the crest. The jump was well known to Snowbird; the resort's ski patrol often instructed people not to jump, and there was a sign instructing skiers to take it slow at that point. Clover sued Zulliger and, under the doctrine of *respondeat superior*, Snowbird, claiming that Zulliger had been acting within the scope of his employment. Who is liable? Explain.

16. Van D. Costas, Inc. (Costas) entered into a contract to remodel the entrance of the Magic Moment Restaurant owned by Seascape Restaurants, Inc. Rosenberg, part owner and president of Seascape, signed the contract on a line under which was typed "Jeff Rosenberg, The Magic Moment." When a dispute arose over the performance and payment of the contract, Costas brought suit against Rosenberg for breach of contract. Rosenberg contended that he had no personal liability for the contract and that only Seascape, the owner of the restaurant, was liable. Costas claimed that Rosenberg signed for an undisclosed principal and, therefore, was individually liable. Explain whether Rosenberg is liable on the contract.

17. Virginia and her husband Ronnie Hulbert were involved in an accident in Mobile County when their automobile collided with another automobile driven by Dr. Murray's nanny. The nanny's regular duties of employment included housekeeping, supervising the children, and taking the children places that they needed to go. At the time of the collision, the nanny was driving her own car and was following Dr. Murray and her family to Florida from Louisiana to accompany Dr. Murray's family on their vacation. One of Dr. Murray's daughters was in the automobile driven by the nanny. Virginia Hulbert sued Dr. Murray under the doctrine of *respondeat superior*, alleging that the nanny was acting within the scope of her employment when the automobile accident occurred. Should she be able to recover from Dr. Murray? Explain.

18. Raymond Zukaitis was a physician practicing medicine in Douglas County, Nebraska. Aetna issued a policy of professional liability insurance to Zukaitis through its agent, the Ed Larsen Insurance Agency. The policy covered the period from August 31, 2013, through August of the following year. On August 7, 2015, Dr. Zukaitis received a written notification of a claim for malpractice that had occurred on September 27, 2013. Dr. Zukaitis notified the Ed Larsen Insurance Agency immediately and forwarded the written claim to it. The claim was then mistakenly referred to St. Paul Fire and Marine

Insurance Company, the company that currently insured Dr. Zukaitis. Apparently without notice to Dr. Zukaitis, the agency contract between Larsen and Aetna had been canceled on August 1, 2014, and St. Paul had replaced Aetna as the insurance carrier. However, when St. Paul discovered it was not the carrier on the date of the alleged wrongdoing, it notified Aetna and withdrew from Dr. Zukaitis's defense. Aetna also refused to represent Dr. Zukaitis, contending that it was relieved of its obligation to Dr. Zukaitis because he had not notified Aetna immediately of the claim. Dr. Zukaitis then secured his own attorney to defend against the malpractice claim and brought an action against Aetna to recover attorneys' fees and other expenses incurred in the defense. Should Dr. Zukaitis recover? Explain.

TAKING SIDES

Sonenberg Company managed Westchester Manor Apartments through its on-site property manager, Judith. Manor Associates Limited Partnership, whose general partner is Westchester Manor, Ltd., owned the complex. The entry sign to the property did not reveal the owner's name but did disclose that Sonenberg managed the property. Judith contacted Redi-Floors and requested a proposal for installing carpet in several of the units. In preparing the proposal, Redi-Floors confirmed that Sonenberg was the managing company and that Judith was its on-site property manager. Sonenberg did not inform Redi-Floors of the owner's identity. Judith and her assistant orally ordered the carpet, and Redi-Floors installed the carpet. Redi-Floors sent invoices to the complex and received checks from "Westchester Manor Apartments." Believing that Sonenberg owned the complex, Redi-Floors did not learn of the true owner's identity until after the work had been completed when a dispute arose concerning the payment of some of its invoices.

a. What arguments would support Redi-Floors in recovering on the outstanding invoices from *both* Sonenberg and Manor Associates?

b. What arguments would limit Redi-Floors to recovering on the outstanding invoices from *either* Sonenberg or Manor Associates?

c. Explain what the outcome would be under (1) the Second Restatement and (2) the Third Restatement.

BUSINESS ASSOCIATIONS

Formation and Internal Relations of General Partnerships

CHAPTER 30

Except for marriage, it is hard to think of a voluntary legal relationship that is more intimate or complex, in human terms, than the normal partnership whose members work constantly together.

Alan Bromberg
Crane and Bromberg on Partnership

CHAPTER OUTCOMES

After reading and studying this chapter, you should be able to:

1. Identify the various types of business associations and explain the factors relevant to deciding which form to use.

2. Distinguish between a legal entity and a legal aggregate and identify those purposes for which a partnership is treated as a legal entity and those purposes for which it is treated as a legal aggregate.

3. Distinguish between a partner's rights in specific partnership property and a partner's interest in the partnership.

4. Identify and explain the duties owed by a partner to her copartners.

5. Identify and describe the rights of partners.

A business enterprise may be operated or conducted as a sole proprietorship, an unincorporated business association (such as a general partnership, a limited partnership, a limited liability company, or a limited liability partnership), or a corporation. The choice of the most appropriate form cannot be determined in a general way but depends on the particular circumstances of the owners. We will begin this chapter with a brief overview of the various types of business associations and the factors relevant to deciding which form to use. The rest of this chapter and the next chapter will examine general partnerships. Chapter 32 will cover other types of unincorporated business associations. Chapters 33 through 36 will address corporations.

CHOOSING A BUSINESS ASSOCIATION

The owners of a business enterprise determine the form of business unit they wish to use based upon their specific circumstances. In the United States there are approximately 32 million business entities, with annual receipts of approximately $33 trillion. There are approximately 23 million sole proprietorships, 5.8 million corporations, and 3.2 million unincorporated business associations (including 2.1 million limited liability companies, 585,000 general partnerships, 375,000 limited partnerships, and 125,000 limited liability partnerships). See Figure 30-1 for the number and size of these business entities.

Unincorporated business associations are common in a number of areas. General partnerships, for example, are used frequently in finance, insurance, accounting, real estate, law, and other service-related fields. Joint ventures have enjoyed popularity among major corporations planning to engage in cooperative research; in the exploitation of land and mineral rights; in the development, promotion, and sale of patents, trade names, and copyrights; and in manufacturing operations in foreign countries. Limited

Figure 30-1 Business Entities

Type of Entity	Total Number (millions)	Total Revenue ($ trillions)	Average Revenue Per Entity ($)	Percent of Total Businesses	Percent of Total Revenue
Sole Proprietorships	23.0	1.2	52,174	71.9	3.6
Partnerships and LLCs	3.2	5.5	1,718,750	10.0	16.7
Corporations	5.8	26.2	4,517,241	18.1	79.6
Totals	32.0	32.9	1,028,125	100	100

Note: LLC = limited liability company.

Source: Internal Revenue Service Statistics of Income, www.irs.gov/taxstats (accessed March 25, 2014).

Practical Advice

You should give considerable thought to choosing the best form of business association for you and your co-owners.

partnerships have been widely used for enterprises such as real estate investment and development, motion picture and theater productions, oil and gas ventures, and equipment leasing. All states have authorized the formation of limited liability companies. This form of business organization has appealed to a rapidly growing number of businesses, including real estate ventures, high-technology enterprises, businesses in which transactions involve foreign investors, professional organizations, corporate joint ventures, startup businesses, and venture capital projects. The number of limited liability companies now greatly exceeds the number of all types of partnerships combined.

First to be discussed are the most important factors to consider in choosing a form of business association. This is followed by a brief description of the various forms of business associations and how they differ with respect to these factors.

FACTORS AFFECTING THE CHOICE [30-1]

In choosing the form in which to conduct business the owners should consider a number of factors, including ease of formation, federal and state income tax laws, external liability, management and control, transferability of ownership interests, and continuity. The relative importance of each factor will vary with the specific needs and objectives of the owners.

Ease of Formation [30-1a]

Business associations differ as to the formalities and expenses of formation. Some can be created with no formality, while others require the filing of documents with the state.

Taxation [30-1b]

Most business entities are not considered to be separate *taxable* entities and taxation is on a "pass-through" basis. In these cases, the income of the business is conclusively presumed to have been distributed to the owners, who must pay taxes on that income. Losses receive comparable treatment and can be used to offset some of the owners' income. Pass-through tax treatment results in only the owners being taxed and thus avoids double taxation on the business income. In the United States, approximately 95 percent of all business entities are taxed on a pass-through basis.

In contrast, some business entities, most significantly certain corporations, are considered separate tax entities and are directly taxed. When such an entity distributes income to the owners, that income currently is separately taxed to the recipients. Thus, these funds currently are taxed twice: once to the entity and once to the owners. Unincorporated business entities can elect whether or not to be taxed as a separate entity. All businesses that have publicly traded ownership interests must be taxed as a separate entity.

External Liability [30-1c]

External liability arises in a variety of ways, but the crucial and most commonly occurring are tort and contract liability. Owners of some business forms have unlimited liability for all of the obligations of the business. Thus, if the business does not have sufficient funds to pay its debts, each and every owner has personal liability to the creditors for the full amount of the debts. In brief, owners of interests in businesses with unlimited liability place their entire estate at risk. In some types of entities, the owners have unlimited liability for some but not all of the entity's obligations. Finally, in some types of business associations, the owners enjoy limited liability, which means their liability is limited to the extent of their capital contribution. It should be noted, however, that creditors often require that the owners of small businesses guarantee personally loans made to the businesses. Moreover, an owner of *any* type of business does not have limited liability for his own tortious conduct; the person is liable as an individual tortfeasor.

Management and Control [30-1d]

In some entities, the owners can fully share in the control of the business. In other types of business associations, the owners are restricted as to their right to take part in control.

Transferability [30-1e]

An ownership interest in a business consists of a financial interest, which is the right to share in the profits of the business, and a management interest, which is the right to participate in control of the business. In some types of business associations, the owners may freely transfer their financial interest but may not transfer their management interest without the consent of all of the other owners. In other types of business associations, the entire ownership interest is freely transferable.

Continuity [30-1f]

Some business associations have low continuity, which means that the death, bankruptcy, or withdrawal of an owner results in the dissolution of the association. Other types have high continuity and are not affected by the death, bankruptcy, or withdrawal of owners.

Forms of Business Associations [30-2]

This section contains a brief description of the various types of business associations and how they differ with respect to the factors just discussed. In addition, general partnerships, limited partnerships, limited liability companies, limited liability partnerships, and corporations will be discussed more extensively in this part of the book.

Sole Proprietorship [30-2a]

Sole proprietorship
an unincorporated business consisting of one person who owns and completely controls the business

A **sole proprietorship** is an unincorporated business consisting of one person who owns and completely controls the business. It is formed without any formality, and no documents need be filed. Moreover, if one person conducts a business and does not file with the state to form a limited liability company or corporation, a sole proprietorship will result by default. A sole proprietorship is not a separate taxable entity and only the sole proprietor is taxed. Sole proprietors have unlimited liability for the sole proprietorship's debts. The sole proprietor's interest in the business is freely transferable. The death of a sole proprietor dissolves the sole proprietorship.

General Partnership [30-2b]

General partnership
an unincorporated business association of two or more persons to carry on as co-owners a business for profit

A **general partnership** is an unincorporated business association consisting of two or more persons who co-own a business for profit. It is formed without any formality and no documents need be filed. Thus, if two or more people conduct a business and do not file with the state to form another type of business organization, a general partnership will result by default. A partnership may elect not to be a separate taxable entity, in which case only the partners are taxed. Partners have unlimited liability for the partnership's debts. Each partner has an equal right to control of the partnership. Partners may assign their financial interest in the partnership, but the assignee may become a member of the partnership only if all of the members consent. Under the Revised Partnership Act the death or bankruptcy of a partner usually does not dissolve a partnership; the same is also true in a term partnership for the withdrawal of a partner.

Joint Venture [30-2c]

Joint venture
an unincorporated business association of two or more persons to carry out a particular business enterprise for profit

A **joint venture** is an unincorporated business association composed of persons who combine their property, money, efforts, skill, and knowledge for the purpose of carrying out a particular business enterprise for profit. Usually, although not always, it is of short duration. A joint venture, therefore, differs from a partnership, which is formed to carry on a business over a considerable or indefinite period of time. Nonetheless, except for a few differences, the law of partnerships generally governs a joint venture. An example of a joint venture is a securities underwriting syndicate or a syndicate formed to acquire a certain tract of land for subdivision and resale. Other common examples involve joint research conducted by corporations, the exploitation of mineral rights, and manufacturing operations in foreign countries.

Limited Partnership [30-2d]

A **limited partnership** is an unincorporated business association consisting of at least one general partner and at least one limited partner. It is formed by filing a certificate of limited partnership with the state. A limited partnership may elect not to be a separate taxable entity, in which case only the partners are taxed. Publicly traded limited partnerships, however, are subject to corporate income taxation. General partners have unlimited liability for the partnership's debts; limited partners have limited liability. Each general partner has an equal right to control of the partnership; limited partners have no right to participate in control. Partners may assign their financial interest in the partnership, but the assignee may become a limited partner only if all of the members consent. The death, bankruptcy, or withdrawal of a general partner dissolves a limited partnership; the limited partners have neither the right nor the power to dissolve the limited partnership.

Limited Liability Company [30-2e]

A **limited liability company (LLC)** is an unincorporated business association that provides limited liability to all of its owners (members) and permits all of its members to participate in management of the business. It may elect not to be a separate taxable entity, in which case only the members are taxed. As noted, publicly traded LLCs are subject to corporate income taxation. If an LLC has only one member, then it will be taxed as a sole proprietorship, unless separate entity tax treatment is elected. Thus, the LLC provides many of the advantages of a general partnership plus limited liability for all its members. Its benefits outweigh those of a limited partnership in that all members of an LLC not only enjoy limited liability but also may participate in management and control of the business. In most states members may assign their financial interest in the LLC, but the assignee may become a member of the LLC only if all of the members consent or the LLC's operating agreement provides otherwise. In some states the death, bankruptcy, or withdrawal of a member dissolves an LLC; in others they do not. Every state has adopted an LLC statute.

Limited Liability Partnership [30-2f]

A registered **limited liability partnership (LLP)** is a general partnership that, by making the statutorily required filing, limits the liability of its partners for some or all of the partnership's obligations. To become an LLP, a general partnership must file with the state an application containing specified information. All of the states have enacted LLP statutes. Except for the filing requirements and the partners' liability shield, the law governing LLPs is identical to the law governing general partnerships.

Limited Liability Limited Partnership [30-2g]

A **limited liability limited partnership (LLLP)** is a limited partnership in which the liability of the general partners has been limited to the same extent as in an LLP. A growing number of states authorize LLLPs, enabling the general partners in an LLLP to obtain the same degree of liability limitation that general partners can achieve in an LLP. Where available, a limited partnership may register as an LLLP without having to form a new organization, as would be the case in converting to an LLC.

Corporation [30-2h]

A **corporation** is a legal entity separate and distinct from its owners. It is formed by filing its articles of incorporation with the chosen state of incorporation. Some corporations are taxed as separate entities, and shareholders also are taxed on corporate earnings that are distributed to them. Most corporations, however, are eligible to elect to be taxed as Subchapter S corporations, which results in only the shareholders being taxed and thus avoids double taxation on corporate income. More than two-thirds of all corporations are taxed as Subchapter S corporations. The shareholders have limited liability for the corporation's obligations. The board of directors elected by the shareholders manages the corporation. Shares in a corporation are freely transferable. The death, bankruptcy, or withdrawal of a shareholder does not dissolve the corporation.

Limited partnership
an unincorporated business association consisting of at least one general partner and at least one limited partner

Limited liability company (LLC)
an unincorporated business association that provides limited liability to all of its owners (members) and permits all of its members to participate in management of the business

Limited liability partnership (LLP)
a general partnership that, by making the statutorily required filing, limits the liability of its partners for some or all of the partnership's obligations

Limited liability limited partnership (LLLP)
a limited partnership in which the liability of the general partners has been limited to the same extent as in an LLP

Corporation
a legal entity separate and distinct from its owners

CONCEPT REVIEW 30-1

General Partnership, Limited Partnership, Limited Liability Company, and Corporation

	General Partnership	Limited Partnership	Limited Liability Company	Corporation
Transferability	Financial interest may be assigned; Membership requires consent of all partners	Financial interest may be assigned, and assignee may become limited partner if all partners consent	Financial interest may be assigned; Membership requires consent of all members	Freely transferable unless shareholders agree otherwise
Liability	Partners have unlimited liability[1]	General partners have unlimited liability[2]; Limited partners have limited liability	All members have limited liability	Shareholders have limited liability
Control	By all partners	By general partners, not limited partners	By all members	By board of directors elected by shareholders
Continuity	RUPA: Usually unaffected by death, bankruptcy, or—in a term partnership—withdrawal of partner; UPA: Dissolved by death, bankruptcy, or withdrawal of partner	Dissolved by death, bankruptcy, or withdrawal of general partner; Unaffected by death, bankruptcy, or withdrawal of limited partner	In many states death, bankruptcy, or withdrawal of member does *not* dissolve LLC	Unaffected by death, bankruptcy, or withdrawal of shareholder
Taxation	May elect that only partners are taxed	May elect that only partners are taxed	May elect that only members are taxed	Corporation taxed unless Subchapter S applies; Shareholders taxed

[1] In an LLP, the partners' liability is limited for some or all of the partnership's obligations.
[2] In an LLLP, the partners' liability is limited for some or all of the partnership's obligations.
Note: RUPA = Revised Uniform Partnership Act; UPA = Uniform Partnership Act.

Business Trusts [30-2i]

Business trust

a trust (managed by a trustee for the benefit of a beneficiary) established to conduct a business for a profit

The **business trust**, sometimes called a Massachusetts trust, was devised to avoid the burdens of corporate regulation, particularly the formerly widespread prohibition denying to corporations the power to own and deal in real estate. The business trust is used in the twenty-first century primarily for asset securitization ventures in which income-generating assets, such as mortgages, are pooled in a trust. Like an ordinary trust between natural persons, a business trust may be created by a voluntary agreement without any authorization or consent of the state. A business trust has three distinguishing characteristics: (1) the trust estate is devoted to the conduct of a business; (2) by the terms of the agreement, each beneficiary is entitled to a certificate evidencing his ownership of a beneficial interest in the trust, which he is free to sell or otherwise transfer; and (3) the trustees have the exclusive right to manage and control the business free from control of the beneficiaries. If the third condition is not met, the trust may fail; the beneficiaries, by participating in control, would become personally liable as partners for the obligations of the business.

The trustees are personally liable for the debts of the business unless, in entering into contractual relations with others, it is expressly stated or definitely understood among the parties that the obligation is incurred solely upon the responsibility of the trust estate. To escape personal liability on the contractual obligations of the business, the trustee must obtain the agreement or consent of the other contracting party to look solely to the assets of the trust. The personal liability of the trustees for their own torts or the torts of their agents and servants employed in the operation of the business stands on a different footing. Although this liability cannot be avoided, the risk involved may be reduced substantially or eliminated altogether by insurance. In most jurisdictions, the beneficiaries of a business trust have no liability for obligations of the business trust.

GOING GLOBAL

What about multinational enterprises?

The term multinational enterprise (MNE) refers to any business that engages in transactions involving the movement of goods, information, money, people, or services across national borders. Such an enterprise may conduct its business in any of several forms: through direct sales, foreign agents, foreign distributorships, licensing, joint ventures, and wholly owned subsidiaries. A number of considerations determine which form of business organization would be best to use in conducting international transactions. These factors include financing, tax consequences, legal restrictions imposed by the host country, and the degree to which the MNE wishes to control the business.

- Under a direct export sale, the seller contracts directly with the buyer in the other country. This is the simplest and least involved MNE.
- Foreign agents often are used by MNEs seeking limited involvement in an international market. The MNE will appoint a local agent, who may be empowered to enter into contracts in the agent's country on the MNE's behalf or who may be authorized only to solicit and take orders.
- The foreign distributorship is commonly used by MNEs. Unlike an agent, a foreign distributor takes title to the merchandise it receives and thus bears many of the risks connected with commercial sales.
- Licensing is frequently used by an MNE wishing to exploit an intellectual property right, such as a patent, trademark, trade secret, or an unpatented technology. Rather than enter the foreign market itself, under licensing an MNE sells to a foreign company the right to use the intellectual property in exchange for royalties paid by the foreign company.
- In a joint venture, two or more independent businesses from different countries agree to coordinate their efforts to achieve a common result. The sharing of profits and liabilities, as well as the delegation of responsibilities, is fixed by contract.
- Creating a foreign wholly owned subsidiary corporation can offer an MNE the ability to retain authority and control over all phases of operation. This is especially attractive to MNEs wishing to safeguard their technology. Use of a foreign wholly owned subsidiary corporation, however, requires the most active participation by the MNE.

FORMATION OF GENERAL PARTNERSHIPS

The form of business association known as partnership can be traced to ancient Babylonia, classical Greece, and the Roman Empire. It was also used in Europe and England during the Middle Ages. Eventually the English common law recognized partnerships. In the nineteenth century, partnerships were widely used in England and the United States, and the common law of partnership developed considerably during this period. Partnerships are important in that they allow individuals with different expertise, backgrounds, resources, and interests to form a more competitive enterprise by combining their various skills. This part of the chapter will cover the nature of general partnerships and how they are formed. It should be recalled that except for the filing requirements and the partners' liability shield, the law governing LLPs is identical to the law governing general partnerships.

NATURE OF PARTNERSHIP [30-3]

In 1914, the Uniform Law Commission (ULC), which is also known as the National Conference of Commissioners on Uniform State Laws, promulgated the Uniform Partnership Act (UPA). Since then it had been adopted in all states (except Louisiana), as well as by the District of Columbia, the Virgin Islands, and Guam.

In August 1986, the ULC and the UPA Revision Subcommittee of the Committee on Partnerships and Unincorporated Business Organizations of the American Bar Association's Section of Corporation, Banking, and Business Law decided to undertake a complete revision of the UPA. The revision was approved in August 1992 and was amended in 1993, 1994, 1996, and 1997. At least thirty-seven states have adopted the Revised Act. This chapter will discuss the Revised Uniform Partnership Act (RUPA). Where the RUPA has made significant changes, the original 1914 UPA also will be discussed. The marginal definitions and the chapter summary reflect the RUPA.

Though fairly comprehensive, the RUPA and UPA do not cover all legal issues concerning partnerships. Accordingly, both the RUPA and the UPA provide that unless displaced by particular provisions of the Partnership Act, the principles of law and equity supplement the Partnership Act.

Definition [30-3a]

Partnership

an unincorporated business association of two or more persons to carry on as co-owners a business for profit

The RUPA defines a **partnership** as "an association of two or more persons to carry on as co-owners a business for profit." The RUPA broadly defines "person" to include "individuals, partnerships, corporations, joint ventures, business trusts, estates, trusts, and any other legal or commercial entity." The comments indicate that this definition would include an LLC. Moreover, a business includes every trade, occupation, and profession.

Entity Theory [30-3b]

Legal entity

an organization having a legal existence separate from that of its members; the Revised Act considers a partnership a legal entity for nearly all purposes

A **legal entity** is a unit capable of possessing legal rights and of being subject to legal duties. A legal entity may acquire, own, and dispose of property. It may enter into contracts, commit wrongs, sue, and be sued. For example, each business corporation is a legal entity having a legal existence separate from that of its shareholders.

A partnership was regarded by the common law as a **legal aggregate**, a group of individuals having no legal existence apart from that of its members. The Revised Act has greatly increased the extent to which partnerships are treated as entities. It applies aggregate treatment to very few aspects of partnerships, the most significant of which is that partners still have unlimited liability for the partnership's obligations. The UPA treats partnerships as legal entities for some purposes and as aggregates for others.

Legal aggregate

a group of individuals not having a legal existence separate from that of its members; the Revised Act considers a partnership a legal aggregate for a few purposes

Partnership as a Legal Entity The RUPA states: "A partnership is an entity distinct from its partners." The Revised Act embraces the entity treatment of partnerships, particularly in matters concerning title to partnership property, legal actions by and against the partnership, and continuity of existence. Examples of entity treatment include the following: (1) The assets of the firm are treated as those of the business and are considered to be distinct from the individual assets of the members. (2) A partner is accountable as a fiduciary to the partnership. (3) Every partner is considered an agent of the partnership. (4) A partnership may sue and be sued in the name of the partnership.

Partnership as a Legal Aggregate The Revised Act has retained the aggregate characteristic of a partner's unlimited liability for partnership obligations, unless the partnership has filed a statement of qualification to become an LLP. Thus, if Meg and Mike enter into a partnership that becomes insolvent, as does Meg, Mike is fully liable for the partnership's debts. Likewise, although a partner's interest in the partnership may be assigned, the assignee does not become a partner without the consent of all the partners. Moreover, a partner's dissociation results in dissolution although only in limited circumstances.

Under the UPA, because a partnership is considered an aggregate for some purposes, it can neither sue nor be sued in the firm name unless a statute specifically allows such an action. In addition, a partnership generally lacks continuity of existence: whenever any partner ceases to be associated with the partnership, it is dissolved.

FORMATION OF A PARTNERSHIP [30-4]

The RUPA provides that the association of two or more persons to carry on as co-owners a business for profit forms a partnership, whether or not the parties intend to form a partnership. The formation of a partnership is relatively simple and may be done consciously or unconsciously. A partnership may result from an oral or written agreement between the parties, from an informal arrangement, or from the conduct of the parties, who become partners by associating themselves in a business as co-owners. Consequently, if two or more individuals share the control and profits of a business, the law may deem them partners without regard to how they themselves characterize their relationship. Thus, associates frequently discover, to their chagrin, that they have inadvertently formed a partnership and have thereby subjected themselves to the duties and liabilities of partners. The legal existence of the relationship depends merely upon the parties' explicit or implicit agreement and their association in business as co-owners.

Practical Advice

Be careful that you do not unwittingly enter into a partnership: doing so will greatly increase your risk of personal liability.

Partnership Agreement [30-4a]

Partnership agreement
the agreement, whether
written, oral, or implied,
among the partners
concerning the partnership,
including amendments to
the partnership agreement

The RUPA defines a **partnership agreement** as "the agreement, whether written, oral, or implied, among the partners concerning the partnership, including amendments to the partnership agreement." This definition does not include other agreements between some or all of the partners, such as a lease or a loan agreement.

Except as otherwise provided by the RUPA, the partnership agreement governs relations among the partners and between the partners and the partnership. Thus, the RUPA gives almost total freedom to the partners to provide whatever provisions they agree upon in their partnership agreement. In essence, the RUPA is primarily a set of "default rules" that apply only when the partnership agreement does not address the issue. Nevertheless, the RUPA makes some duties mandatory; these cannot be waived or varied by the partnership agreement.

To render their understanding more clear, definite, and complete, partners are advised, though not usually required, to put their partnership agreement in writing. A partnership agreement can provide almost any conceivable arrangement of capital investment, control sharing, and profit distribution that the partners desire. Unless the agreement provides otherwise, the partners may amend it only by unanimous consent. Any partnership agreement should include the following:

Practical Advice

Partners should have a
comprehensive written
partnership agreement:
doing so brings about a
clearer and more reliable
understanding of their
respective rights and
obligations in their relations
as partners.

1. The firm name and the identity of the partners;
2. The nature and scope of the partnership business;
3. The duration of the partnership;
4. The capital contributions of each partner;
5. The division of profits and sharing of losses;
6. The managerial duties of each partner;
7. A provision for salaries, if desired;
8. Restrictions, if any, upon the authority of particular partners to bind the firm;
9. Any desired variations from the partnership statute's default provisions governing dissolution; and
10. A statement of the method or formula for determining the value of a partner's interest in the partnership.

Statute of Frauds   Because the statute of frauds does not apply expressly to a contract for the formation of a partnership, usually no writing is required to create the relationship. A contract to form a partnership to continue for a period longer than one year is within the statute, however, as is a contract for the transfer of an interest in real estate to or by a partnership; consequently, both of these contracts require a writing in order to be enforceable.

Firm Name   In the interest of acquiring and retaining goodwill, a partnership should have a firm name. Although the name selected by the partners may not be identical or deceptively similar to the name of any other existing business concern, it may be the name of the partners or of any one of them; or the partners may decide to operate the business under a fictitious or assumed name, such as "Peachtree Restaurant," "Globe Theater," or "Paradise Laundry." A partnership may not use a name that would be likely to indicate to the public that it is a corporation. Nearly all of the states have enacted statutes that require any person or persons conducting business under an assumed or fictitious name to file in a designated public office a certificate setting forth the name under which the business is conducted and the real names and addresses of all persons conducting the business as partners or proprietors.

Tests of Partnership Existence [30-4b]

**Tests of partnership
existence**
the formation of a
partnership requires all of
the following: (1) association,
(2) business for profit, and
(3) co-ownership

Partnerships can be formed without the slightest formality. Consequently, it is important that the law establish a test for determining whether or not a partnership has been formed. Two situations most often require this determination. The most common involves a creditor who has dealt only with one person but who wishes to hold another liable as well by asserting that the two were partners. Less frequently, a person seeks to share profits earned and property held by another by claiming that they are partners.

As mentioned, the RUPA provides the operative rule for formation of a partnership: an association of two or more persons to carry on as co-owners a business for profit. Thus, three components are essential to the existence of a partnership: (1) an association of two or more persons, (2) conducting a business for profit, (3) which they co-own.

Association A partnership must consist of two or more persons who have agreed to become partners. Any natural person having full *capacity* may enter into a partnership. A corporation is defined as a "person" by the RUPA and is, therefore, legally capable of entering into a partnership in those states whose incorporation statutes authorize a corporation to do so. Furthermore, as noted, a partnership, joint venture, business trust, estate, trust, and any other legal or commercial entity may be a member of a partnership.

Business for Profit The RUPA provides that co-ownership does not in itself establish a partnership, even if the co-owners share profits made by the use of the property. For a partnership to exist, there must be co-ownership of a business. Thus, passive co-ownership of property by itself, as distinguished from the carrying on of a business, does not establish a partnership. Moreover, to be a partnership, the business carried on by the association of two or more persons must be "for profit." This requirement excludes unincorporated nonprofit organizations from being partnerships. State common law and statutes govern such unincorporated nonprofit organizations. These laws, however, generally do not address the issues facing nonprofit associations in a systematic or integrated fashion. Consequently, in 1996, the ULC promulgated a Uniform Unincorporated Nonprofit Association Act (UUNAA) to reform the common law concerning unincorporated nonprofit associations in a limited number of major issues, including ownership of property, authority to sue and be sued, and the contract and tort liability of officers and members of the association. At least twelve states adopted the UUNAA. In 2008 the Revised Uniform Unincorporated Nonprofit Association Act (RUU-NAA)—a comprehensive revision of the UUNAA—was promulgated. At least four states have adopted the 2008 RUUNAA.

Nor does a partnership exist in situations in which persons associate for mutual financial gain on a temporary or limited basis involving a single transaction or a few isolated transactions: such persons are not engaged in the continuous series of commercial activities necessary to constitute a business. Co-ownership of the means or instrumentality of accomplishing a single business transaction or a limited series of transactions may result in a joint venture but not in a general partnership.

For example, Katherine and Edith have joint ownership of shares of the capital stock of a corporation, have a joint bank account, and have inherited or purchased real estate as joint tenants or tenants in common. They share the dividends paid on the stock, the interest on the bank account, and the net proceeds from the sale or lease of the real estate. Nevertheless, Katherine and Edith are not partners. Although they are co-owners and share profits, they are not engaged in carrying on a business; hence, no partnership exists. On the other hand, if Katherine and Edith continually bought and sold real estate over a period of time and conducted a business of trading in real estate, a partnership relation would exist between them, regardless of whether they considered themselves partners or not.

To illustrate further: Alec, Laura, and Shirley each inherit an undivided one-third interest in a hotel and, instead of selling the property, decide by an informal agreement to continue operating the hotel. The operation of a hotel is a business; as co-owners of a hotel business, Alec, Laura, and Shirley are partners and are subject to all of the rights, duties, and incidents arising from the partnership relation.

Co-ownership Although the co-ownership of *property* used in a business is a condition neither necessary nor sufficient for the existence of a partnership, the co-ownership of a *business* is essential. In identifying business co-ownership, the two most important factors are the sharing of profits and the right to manage and control the business.

A person who receives a share of the profits from a business is presumed to be a partner in the business. This means that persons who share profits are deemed to be partners unless they

Practical Advice

If you receive a share of a partnership's profits in a capacity other than a partner, be sure to document your actual relationship and refrain from exercising such control that would be considered that of a partner or from holding yourself out as a partner.

can prove otherwise. The RUPA, however, provides that the existence of a partnership relation shall not be presumed where such profits were received in payment

1. of a debt, by installments or otherwise;
2. for services as an independent contractor or of wages or other compensation to an employee;
3. of rent;
4. of an annuity or other retirement or health benefit to a beneficiary, representative, or designee of a deceased or retired partner;
5. of interest or other charge on a loan, even if the amount of payment varies with the profits of the business; or
6. for the sale of the goodwill of a business or other property by installments or otherwise.

These transactions do not give rise to a presumption that the party is a partner because the law assumes that the creditor, employee, landlord, or other recipient of such profits is unlikely to be a co-owner. It is possible, nonetheless, to establish that such a person is a partner by proof of other facts and circumstances, such as the sharing of control.

The sharing of *gross returns*, in contrast to profits, does *not* of itself establish a partnership. This is so whether or not the persons sharing the gross returns have a joint or common right or interest in property from which the returns are derived. Thus, two brokers who share commissions are not necessarily partners, or even presumed to be. Similarly, an author who receives royalties (a share of gross receipts from the sales of a book) is not a partner with her publisher.

By itself, evidence as to participation in the *management* or control of a business is not conclusive proof of a partnership relation, but it is persuasive. Limited voice in the management and control of a business may be accorded to an employee, a landlord, or a creditor. On the other hand, an actual partner may choose to take no active part in the affairs of the firm and may, by agreement with his copartners, forgo all right to exercise any control over the ordinary affairs of the business. In any event, the right to participate in control is an important factor considered by the courts in conjunction with other factors, particularly with profit sharing.

Figure 30-2 illustrates the tests for determining whether a partnership exists, as does the following case.

Figure 30-2 Tests for Existence of a Partnership

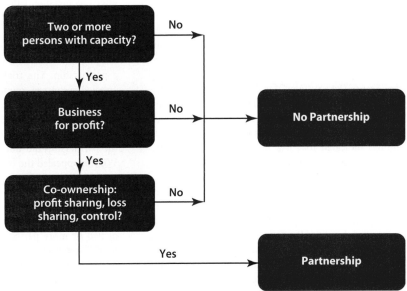

In Re KeyTronics

Supreme Court of Nebraska, 2008

274 Neb. 936, 744 N.W.2d 425

http://scholar.google.com/scholar_case?case=18315123236442947796&q=744+N.W.2d+425&hl=en&as_sdt=2,34

FACTS In 1999, King was doing business under the name of "Washco" as a sole proprietorship engaged in selling, installing, and servicing carwash systems and accessories. King offered to his customers the "QuikPay" system, a cashless vending system for carwashes that used a memory chip key that interacted with a controller at the carwash. Either a cash value can be placed on the key or the carwash usage recorded on the key would be billed monthly. Washco purchased QuikPay systems for resale from Datakey Electronics Inc. (Datakey) but it was becoming unprofitable for Datakey, partly because the keys for QuikPay could only be obtained from an attendant. According to Glen Jennings, president of Datakey, since most carwashes are unattended, this reliance on the presence of the carwash owner or employee was limiting the product's market.

As QuikPay's largest distributor, King was aware that QuikPay's limitations made the product unattractive to many of his customers. King contacted Willson, an electronics technician and computer programmer, to see if Willson could develop a combined "key dispenser" and "revalue station" for the QuikPay system that would make the system self-service. King also asked Willson if he would design and install an interface between the QuikPay system and the carwash of one of King's customers. Designing such an interface was beyond King's technical expertise. Willson individually designed and installed at least four specific customer interfaces that allowed King to sell the QuikPay system to those customers, but Willson was never paid for his work.

According to King there was an oral agreement among himself, Willson, and Scott Gardeen (an employee of Datakey who was an original designer of QuikPay) to form a corporation whenever Willson developed the key dispenser-revalue station. The three parties met in the spring of 2002 to discuss the venture in which they would design and build the key dispenser-revalue station and sell it to Datakey. It was agreed that Willson would write the software and do the firmware, hardware, and any other electrical or software work; Gardeen would contribute his knowledge of the system and his contact with Datakey; and King would contribute financial resources and his experience and contacts as QuikPay's largest distributor. Together, Willson, King, and Gardeen came up with the name "Secure Data Systems" for their business. They discussed the fact that the entity's initials, "SDS," were also the initials of their first names, Scott, Don, and Scott. By the summer, Willson had built a handheld revalue station for a meeting with Jennings. Jennings indicated that if a final, marketable key dispenser-revalue station were developed, Datakey would be interested in a business relationship with Secure Data Systems.

Around October 2002, Datakey decided to discontinue its QuikPay line and referred all of its customers to King for continued support of the system. By the beginning of 2003, King had deliberately separated his QuikPay sales, maintenance, and its future development from his Washco carwash business and had moved all QuikPay business to Secure Data Systems. Around the same time, Willson developed a website for Secure Data Systems with e-mail accounts for King and Willson.

By the spring of 2003, Willson's work for Secure Data Systems consisted primarily of dealing with QuikPay maintenance and

repair issues, although he continued to try to finish the key dispenser-revalue station whenever he had time. Willson made changes in the QuikPay software to fix problems that customers wanted fixed.

In May 2003, King and Willson went together to an international carwash convention in Las Vegas, Nevada. King suggested to Willson that he make up Secure Data Systems business cards for King and Willson. The cards presented Willson as "System Designer & Engineer" and King as "Sales." The cards described Secure Data Systems as carrying the "QuikPay Product Line."

In correspondence with clients, King often referred to Willson as the person doing technical work for QuikPay. Willson also sent e-mails communicating directly with QuikPay clients on various issues. In an e-mail dated August 12, 2003, Willson described himself as the software and hardware designer with Secure Data Systems and he referred to King as his "partner." In October 2003, King sent an e-mail to a potential customer in which King referred to Willson as "the other half of Secure Data Systems."

Willson estimated that he had put at least two thousand hours into QuikPay sales and maintenance and in developing the key dispenser-revalue station. When Willson was asked why he invested his time and expertise into QuikPay without any remuneration, he explained, "That was my contribution to the company. I mean that was my piece." Willson contacted a law firm to draw up papers to formalize the partnership. These papers were never drafted. According to Willson, when he told King he was looking into creating a written agreement for their relationship, King "assured [him] that he was having his attorneys look at it." King and Willson had another meeting around the end of December and agreed to end their relationship and any joint QuikPay or key dispenser-revalue station activities. Approximately two weeks after this meeting, King called Willson and offered to compensate him for the time he had spent in maintaining or repairing QuikPay. Willson refused.

Willson brought an action for winding up and an accounting, alleging formation of a partnership. King denied they had formed a partnership. The trial court found that King and Willson had "pooled resources, money and labor," but found no partnership existed because there was no "specific agreement." Alternatively, the trial court found that because King did not commit his preexisting business to any specifically formed partnership, the scope of the partnership did not encompass any activity garnering profits. Willson appealed the trial court's order.

DECISION Reversed and remanded.

OPINION Section 202(a) of the Revised Uniform Partnership Act (RUPA) states that a partnership is formed by "the association of two or more persons to carry on as co-owners a business for profit" and explains that this is true "whether or not the persons intend to form a partnership."

The relationship between King and Willson is "of two or more persons." A business qualifies under the "business for profit" element of Section 202(a) so long as the parties intended to carry on a business with the expectation of profits.

King argues that no partnership was formed because he never intended to form a partnership relationship with Willson. But, as Section 202(a) explicitly states, the intent necessary to form an association does not refer to the intent to form a partnership per se. There is no requirement that the parties have a "specific agreement" in order to form a partnership. People do not become partners when they attain co-ownership of a business for profit through an involuntary act. But, if the parties' voluntary actions form a relationship in which they carry on as co-owners of a business for profit, then "they may inadvertently create a partnership despite their expressed subjective intention not to do so." Intent, in such cases, is still of prime concern, but it will be ascertained objectively, rather than subjectively, from all the evidence and circumstances.

In considering the parties' intent to form an association, it is generally considered relevant how the parties characterize their relationship or how they have previously referred to one another. The joint use of a business name is evidence of an association. This is especially true when the business name is composed of the parties' names or initials.

It is undisputed that King and Willson discussed the fact that Secure Data Systems had the initials of Scott, Don, and Scott. Granted, at its inception, Secure Data Systems was an association among three parties focused on the limited task of creating a key dispenser-revalue station. King removed any QuikPay operations from his Washco business. He instead began to conduct all Quik-Pay business exclusively through Secure Data Systems. Willson was clearly associated with King in that venture.

Under RUPA Section 202(c)(3), being "co-owners" of a business for profit does not refer to the co-ownership of property but to the co-ownership of the business intended to garner profits. It is co-ownership that distinguishes partnerships from other commercial relationships such as creditor and debtor, employer and employee, franchisor and franchisee, and landlord and tenant. Co-ownership generally addresses whether the parties share the benefits, risks, and management of the enterprise such that (1) they subjectively view themselves as members of the business rather than as outsiders contracting with it and (2) they are in a better position than others dealing with the firm to monitor and obtain information about the business.

The objective indicia of co-ownership are commonly considered to be (1) profit sharing, (2) control sharing, (3) loss sharing, (4) contribution, and (5) co-ownership of property. The five indicia of co-ownership are only that; they are not all necessary to establish a partnership relationship, and no single indicium of co-ownership is either necessary or sufficient to prove co-ownership.

The record demonstrates that Willson contributed his time and expertise not only to the business of developing the key dispenser-revalue station but also to the continued operations of the regular QuikPay product line. The continuing investment of one's labor without pay is generally considered a strong indicator of co-ownership. Valid consideration for an ownership interest in a partnership may take the form of property, capital, labor, or skill, and the law does not exalt one type of contribution over another.

In this case, Willson contributed his time and expertise without any compensation for approximately one year. Conservatively, Willson estimated his contribution as totaling more than two thousand hours. Moreover, without Willson's technical assistance, King would have been unable to continue QuikPay's viability after Datakey abandoned the product. That King could have dealt with certain issues by hiring contractors or employees is irrelevant. He chose not to do so—presumably because the promise of the key dispenser-revalue station made a partnership relationship more worthwhile—and saved him the expense of paying for this labor.

The evidence shows that King and Willson shared control over QuikPay business.

Of the five indicia of co-ownership, profit sharing is possibly the most important, and the presence of profit sharing is singled out in Section 202(c)(3) as creating a rebuttable presumption of a partnership. However, what is essential to a partnership is not that profits actually be distributed, but, instead, that there be an interest in the profits. Willson's testimony that they agreed to share in the profits of the business is, in light of all the evidence, simply more credible than King's statement that compensation "was never discussed."

There is no evidence that King and Willson had an agreement for loss sharing. But this is of little import, since purported partners, expecting profits, often do not have any explicit understanding regarding loss sharing. Likewise, although King and Willson admittedly do not own any joint property, in an informal relationship, the parties may intend co-ownership of property but fail to attend to the formalities of title. Moreover, in this case, it is unclear that there is much QuikPay property at all.

In this case the objective, as well as subjective, indicia are sufficient to prove co-ownership of the business of selling, maintaining, and developing QuikPay. Since there was an association for Quik-Pay, Willson proved that he and King had formed a partnership for the business of selling, maintaining, and developing QuikPay.

INTERPRETATION If the parties' voluntary actions form a relationship in which they carry on as co-owners of a business for profit, then they may inadvertently create a partnership despite their expressed subjective intention not to do so.

CRITICAL THINKING QUESTION Do you agree with the test for the existence of a partnership?

Partnership Capital and Property [30-4c]

Partnership capital
total money and property contributed by partners for permanent use by the partnership

The total money and property that the partners contribute and dedicate to use in the enterprise is the **partnership capital**. Partnership capital represents the partners' equity in the partnership. No minimum amount of capitalization is necessary before a partnership may commence business.

Partnership property

sum of all of the partnership's assets, including all property acquired by a partnership

Partnership property is property acquired by a partnership. Property acquired by the partnership is conclusively deemed to be partnership property. Property becomes partnership property if acquired in the name of the partnership, which includes a transfer to (1) the partnership in its name or (2) one or more partners in their capacity as partners in the partnership, if the name of the partnership is indicated in the instrument transferring title to the property. Property also may be partnership property even if it is not acquired in the name of the partnership. Property is partnership property if acquired in the name of one or more of the partners with an indication in the instrument transferring title of either (1) their capacity as partners or (2) the existence of a partnership, even if the name of the partnership is not indicated.

Even if the instrument transferring title to one or more of the partners does not indicate their capacity as a partner or the existence of a partnership, the property nevertheless may be partnership property. Ultimately, the partners' intention controls whether property belongs to the partnership or to one or more of the partners in their individual capacities. The RUPA sets forth two rebuttable presumptions that apply when the partners have failed to express their intent. First, property purchased with partnership funds is presumed to be partnership property, without regard to the name in which title is held. The presumption applies not only when partnership cash or property is used for payment but also when partnership credit is used to obtain financing.

Second, property acquired in the name of one or more of the partners, without an indication of their capacity as partners and without use of partnership funds or credit, is presumed to be the partners' separate property, even if used for partnership purposes. In this last case it is presumed that only the *use* of the property is contributed to the partnership.

Practical Advice

Make clear by a written agreement whether property previously owned by one partner but used by the partnership belongs to the partnership or to the partner.

As discussed later, who owns the property—an individual partner or the partnership—determines (1) who gets it upon dissolution of the partnership, (2) who shares in any loss or gain upon its sale, (3) who shares in income from it, and (4) who may sell it or transfer it by will.

A question may arise regarding whether property that was owned by a partner before formation of the partnership and was used in the partnership business is a capital contribution and hence an asset of the partnership. For example, a partner who owns a store building may contribute to the partnership the use of the building but not the building itself. The building is, therefore, not partnership property, and the amount of capital contributed by this partner is the reasonable value of the rental of the building.

The fact that legal title to property remains unchanged is not conclusive evidence that such property has not become a partnership asset. The intent of the partners controls the question of who owns the property. Without an express agreement, an intention to consider property as partnership property may be inferred from any of the following facts: (1) the property was improved with partnership funds; (2) the property was carried on the books of the partnership as an asset; (3) taxes, liens, or expenses, such as insurance or repairs, were paid by the partnership; (4) income or proceeds of the property were treated as partnership funds; or (5) the partners declared or admitted the property to be partnership property.

Thomas v. Lloyd
Missouri Court of Appeals, Southern District, Division One, 2000
17 S.W.3d 177
http://scholar.google.com/scholar_case?case=17595001908950706244&q=17+S.W.3d+177&hl=en&as_sdt=2,34

FACTS In February 1989, the plaintiff, Mary Dean Thomas, met the defendant, Eubert Gayle Lloyd, Jr., in Mobile, Alabama, while she was traveling. Their chance meeting quickly blossomed into a romantic relationship. When the plaintiff returned to her home in Maryland, the defendant accompanied her, and they began living together. Initially, the defendant told the plaintiff he worked for a major oil company, had been outside the country for the past three years, was independently wealthy, and was not married. As the plaintiff later learned, none of these statements was true. In truth, the defendant had recently been

released from prison. He had multiple criminal convictions, including convictions for counterfeiting and stealing. In addition, the defendant's assets at the time were no more than $2,000, and he was legally married to Patricia Lloyd. Prior to the plaintiff's discovering that the defendant was not single, the parties were married on July 10, 1989, in Canada; thus this marriage was void.

The plaintiff and the defendant resided in the plaintiff's home in Maryland from late February 1989 through October 1990. During that period, the defendant made repairs and renovations to the plaintiff's house. In October 1990, the plaintiff sold her home and the parties moved to Missouri. After looking at several farm properties, they bought a six-hundred-acre farm in Crawford County, Missouri, for $150,000. The deed was dated March 8, 1991. The deed named the plaintiff, a single person, and the defendant, a single person, as joint tenants with right of survivorship. The $150,000 purchase price was paid with a $100,000 cash down payment and a $50,000 promissory note that called for one hundred and twenty monthly installments of $633.38.

After buying the farm, the plaintiff and the defendant bought cattle and farm machinery, and then began operating a cattle business on the property. The parties also made improvements to the farm. In June 1992, they began construction on a four-thousand-two-hundred-square-foot house. Later, the house was expanded to six thousand five hundred square feet. By the time of trial, the plaintiff's expenditures for labor and materials on the home exceeded $201,000.

A progressive deterioration in the parties' relationship led to the filing of this lawsuit in October 1995. The trial court found that the subject real estate was not a partnership asset and ordered it be sold at public auction and the net sale proceeds to be distributed 98 percent to the plaintiff and 2 percent to the defendant. The defendant appealed the trial court's refusal to classify farm real estate as a partnership asset.

DECISION The judgment of the trial court is affirmed.

OPINION Whether real estate titled in the names of individual partners is partnership property is a question of fact and the burden of proof is on the one alleging that the actual ownership does not match the names on the legal title. In attempting to demonstrate that the parties intended for the real estate to be a partnership asset, the defendant points to the joint ownership of the farm and the fact that the parties operated the partnership cattle business on the farm. His reliance on those facts is misplaced, however. A joint purchase of real estate by two individuals does not, in and of itself, prove the land is a partnership asset. The mere use of land by a partnership does little to show the land is owned by the partnership.

The defendant points to evidence that some real estate taxes and promissory note payments for the farm came from partnership funds. He argues such evidence indicates the parties intended the farm to be a partnership asset. Such evidence is a factor to be considered, but it is not determinative of the issue. In this case, only a small percentage of these costs were paid from partnership funds. The vast majority of payments came from the plaintiff's separate, personal funds. Such minimal partnership expenditures are more indicative of the tendency of people—particularly in family or quasi-family businesses—to intermingle personal and partnership affairs, than it is an indication of the parties' intent to include the farm as a partnership asset.

Other evidence of the parties' intent includes the following: (1) the plaintiff and the defendant signed as individuals on the $50,000 purchase money note and deed of trust securing the property, without a recital of partnership status; (2) neither party filed a partnership income tax return; (3) the plaintiff filed income tax returns as an individual; (4) the defendant never filed an income tax return after the farm was purchased; (5) the plaintiff wrote checks on her individual account for materials and labor for farm improvements; and (6) the plaintiff repeatedly testified she never intended nor agreed to a partnership with the defendant. These circumstances are sufficient to support the implicit finding and judgment of the trial court that a partnership agreement did not exist regarding the land and it was not a partnership asset. The trial court did not commit reversible error when it failed to include the farm as a partnership asset.

INTERPRETATION Whether property is partnership property depends on the intent of the parties as indicated by factors such as their express agreement; the use of the property in the partnership business; the listing of the property as an asset on the partnership's books; the improvement of the property with partnership assets; and the payment by the partnership of taxes, insurance, and other expenses of property ownership.

CRITICAL THINKING QUESTION What factors did the court use to determine whether the properties were partnership assets?

RELATIONSHIPS AMONG PARTNERS

Practical Advice

When forming a partnership, carefully consider which, if any, duties you wish to vary by agreement.

When parties enter into a partnership, the law imposes certain obligations upon them and also grants them specific rights. Except as otherwise provided by the RUPA, the partnership agreement governs relations among the partners and between the partners and the partnership. Thus, the RUPA gives almost total freedom to the partners to provide whatever provisions they agree upon in their partnership agreement. Nevertheless, the RUPA makes some duties mandatory; these cannot be waived or varied by the partnership agreement.

DUTIES AMONG PARTNERS [30-5]

The principal legal duties imposed upon partners in their relations with one another are (1) the fiduciary duty (the duty of loyalty), (2) the duty of obedience, and (3) the duty of care. In addition, each partner has a duty to inform his copartners and a duty to account to the partnership. (These additional duties are discussed later, in a section covering the rights of partners.) All of these duties correspond precisely with those duties owed by an agent to his principal and reflect the fact that much of the law of partnership is the law of agency.

Fiduciary Duty [30-5a]

Fiduciary duty

duty of utmost loyalty, fairness, and good faith owed by partners to each other and to the partnership; includes duty not to appropriate partnership opportunities, not to compete, not to have conflicts of interest, and not to reveal confidential information

The **fiduciary duty** in a partnership is the duty of utmost loyalty, fairness, and good faith owed by partners to each other and to the partnership; includes duty not to appropriate partnership opportunities, not to compete, not to have conflicts of interest, and not to reveal confidential information. The extent of the fiduciary duty has been most eloquently expressed by the often-quoted words of Judge (later Justice) Cardozo:

> Joint adventurers, like copartners, owe to one another, while the enterprise continues, the duty of the *finest loyalty*. Many forms of conduct permissible in a workaday world for those acting at arm's length, are forbidden to those bound by fiduciary ties. A trustee is held to something stricter than the morals of the market place. *Not honesty alone, but the punctilio of an honor the most sensitive, is then the standard of behavior.* As to this there has developed a tradition that is unbending and inveterate. Uncompromising rigidity has been the attitude of courts of equity when petitioned to undermine the rule of undivided loyalty by the "disintegrating erosion" of particular exceptions. Only thus has the level of conduct for fiduciaries been kept at a level higher than that trodden by the crowd. It will not consciously be lowered by any judgment of this court. *Meinhard v. Salmon,* 249 N.Y. 458, 459, 164 N.E. 545, 546 (1928) [emphasis added].

The RUPA's provision regarding the fiduciary duty is both comprehensive and exclusive. The comment to this provision explains: "In that regard, it is structurally different from the UPA which touches only sparingly on a partner's duty of loyalty and leaves any further development of the fiduciary duties of partners to the common law of agency." The RUPA completely and exclusively states the components of the duty of loyalty by specifying that a partner has a duty not to appropriate partnership benefits without the consent of her partners, to refrain from self-dealing, and to refrain from competing with the partnership. More specifically, the RUPA provides that a partner's duty of loyalty to the partnership and the other partners is limited to the following:

1. to account to the partnership and hold as trustee for it any property, profit, or benefit derived by the partner in the conduct and winding up of the partnership business or derived from a use by the partner of partnership property, including the appropriation of a partnership opportunity;
2. to refrain from dealing with the partnership in the conduct or winding up of the partnership business as, or on behalf of, a party having an interest adverse to the partnership; and
3. to refrain from competing with the partnership in the conduct of the partnership business before the dissolution of the partnership.

In addition, the Revised Act provides that a partner does not violate the duty of loyalty merely because the partner's conduct furthers the partner's own interest. For example, a partner committed a breach of fiduciary duty when he retained a secret discount on purchases of petroleum that he obtained through acquisition of a bulk plant, and the partnership was entitled to the entire amount of the discount.

Within the demands of the fiduciary duty, a partner cannot acquire for herself a partnership asset or opportunity without the consent of all the partners. Thus, a partner may not renew a partnership lease in her name alone. A partner cannot, without the permission of her partners, engage in any other business within the scope of the partnership enterprise. Should she participate in a competing or similar business, the disloyal partner not only must surrender any profit she has acquired from such business but also must compensate the existing partnership for any damage it may have suffered as a result of the competition. A partner, however, may enter into any business neither in competition with nor within the scope of the partnership's business. For example, a partner in a law firm may, without violating her fiduciary duty, act as an executor or administrator of an estate. Furthermore, she need not account for her fees in cases in which it cannot be shown that her service in this other capacity impaired her duty to the partnership (e.g., by monopolizing her attention).

The fiduciary duty does *not* extend to the formation of the partnership when, according to the comments to the RUPA, the parties are really negotiating at arm's length. The duty not to compete terminates upon dissociation, and the dissociated partner may immediately engage in a competitive business without any further consent. The partner's other fiduciary duties continue only with regard to matters arising and events occurring before the partner's dissociation, unless the partner participates in winding up the partnership's business. Thus, upon a partner's dissociation, a partner may appropriate to his own benefit any *new* business opportunity coming to his attention after dissociation, even if the partnership continues, and a partner may deal with the partnership as an adversary with respect to *new* matters or events. A dissociated partner is not, however, free to use confidential partnership information after dissociation.

The Revised Act imposes a duty of good faith and fair dealing when a partner discharges duties to the partnership and the other partners under the RUPA or under the partnership agreement and exercises any rights. The comments state:

> The obligation of good faith and fair dealing is a contract concept, imposed on the partners because of the consensual nature of a partnership.... It is not characterized, in RUPA, as a fiduciary duty arising out of the partners' special relationship. Nor is it a separate and independent obligation. It is an ancillary obligation that applies whenever a partner discharges a duty or exercises a right under the partnership agreement or the Act.

Practical Advice

As a partner, be sure to make full disclosure of all material facts regarding the partnership and your relationship to your partners.

The partnership agreement may not eliminate the duty of loyalty or the obligation of good faith and fair dealing. However, the partnership agreement may identify specific types or categories of activities that do not violate the duty of loyalty, if not clearly unreasonable. In addition, the other partners may consent to a specific act or transaction that otherwise violates the duty of loyalty, if there has been full disclosure of all material facts regarding the act or transaction as well as the partner's conflict of interest. Similarly, the partnership agreement may prescribe the standards by which the performance of the obligation of good faith and fair dealing is to be measured, if the standards are not manifestly unreasonable.

The fiduciary duty under the UPA differs in some respects from that of the RUPA. First, the partner's fiduciary duty under the UPA applies to the formation of the partnership. Second, it applies to the winding up of the partnership. The UPA states that every partner must account to the partnership for any benefit he receives and must hold as trustee for it any profits he derives without the consent of the other partners from any transaction connected with the formation, conduct, or liquidation of the partnership or from any use he makes of its property. A partner may not prefer himself over the firm, nor may he even deal at arm's length with his partners, to whom his duty is one of undivided and continuous loyalty. The fiduciary duty also applies to the purchase of a partner's interest from another partner. Each partner owes the highest duty of honesty and fair dealing to the other partners, including the obligation to disclose fully and accurately all material facts.

The next case, *Enea v. The Superior Court of Monterey County*, illustrates how rigorously the courts enforce the fiduciary duty.

Enea v. The Superior Court of Monterey County
Court of Appeal of California, Sixth Appellate District, 2005
132 Cal.App.4th 1559, 34 Cal.Rptr.3d 513
http://scholar.google.com/scholar_case?q=34+Cal.Rptr.3d+513&hl=en&as_sdt=2,34&case=5283361880886275530&scilh=0

FACTS In 1980 defendants William and Claudia Daniels, and other family members formed a general partnership: 3-D. The partnership's sole asset was a building that had been converted from a residence into offices. A portion of the property has been rented since 1981 on a month-to-month basis by the law practice of William Daniels, the firm's sole member. From time to time the property was rented on similar arrangements to others, including defendant Claudia Daniels. The partnership agreement has as its principal purpose the ownership, leasing, and sale of the only partnership assets—the building. The partnership agreement contained no provision that the property would be leased for fair market value. Defendants assert that there was no evidence of any agreement to maximize rental profits. In 1993, the plaintiff Benny

Enea, a client of William Daniels, purchased a one-third interest in the partnership from William's brother, John P. Daniels. In 2001, however, plaintiff questioned William Daniels about the rents being paid for the property, and in 2003, the plaintiff was "dissociated" from the partnership.

On August 6, 2003, Enea brought an action for damages alleging that defendants had occupied the partnership property while paying significantly less-than-fair rental value, in breach of their fiduciary duty to plaintiff. The trial court granted the defendants' motion for summary judgment, and the plaintiff appealed.

DECISION Trial court's order for summary judgment is reversed.

OPINION The question is whether defendants were entitled to lease partnership property to themselves, or to anyone, at less-than-fair market value. Partners obligate themselves to share risks and benefits and to carry out the enterprise with the highest good faith toward one another—that is, with the loyalty and care of a fiduciary. Partners may not take advantages for themselves at the expense of the partnership.

Here the defendants did take advantages for themselves from partnership property at the expense of the partnership. The advantage consisted of occupying partnership property at below-market rates. The cost to the partnership was the foregone additional rent. Defendants also argue that they had no duty to collect market rents in the absence of a contract expressly requiring them to do so. The law does not declare that partners owe each other only those duties they explicitly assume by contract. On the contrary, fiduciary duties are imposed by law, and their breach constitutes a tort.

INTERPRETATION Partnership is a fiduciary relationship, and partners may not take advantages for themselves at the expense of the partnership.

ETHICAL QUESTION Did the defendants act unethically? Explain.

CRITICAL THINKING QUESTION Explain whether the outcome of the case would have been different if the partnership agreement had explicitly stated that partnership property could be rented at below-market rates.

Duty of obedience

duty to act in accordance with the partnership agreement and any business decisions properly made by the partners

Duty of Obedience [30-5b]

A partner owes his partners a duty to act in obedience to the partnership agreement and to any business decisions properly made by the partnership. Any partner who violates this duty is liable individually to his partners for any resulting loss. For example, if a partner, in violation of a specific agreement not to extend credit to relatives, advances money from partnership funds and sells goods on credit to an insolvent relative, that partner would be held personally liable to his partners for the unpaid debt.

Duty of care

duty owed by partners to manage the partnership affairs without gross negligence, reckless conduct, intentional misconduct, or knowing violation of law

Duty of Care [30-5c]

Whereas under the fiduciary duty a partner "is held to something stricter than the morals of the market place," he is held to something less than the skill of the marketplace. Each partner owes the partnership a duty of faithful service to the best of his ability. Nonetheless, he need not possess the degree of knowledge and skill of an ordinary paid agent. Under the Revised Act a partner's duty of care to the partnership and the other partners in the conduct and winding up of the partnership business is limited to refraining from engaging in grossly negligent or reckless conduct, intentional misconduct, or a knowing violation of law. For example, a partner assigned to keep the partnership books uses an overly complicated bookkeeping system and consequently produces numerous mistakes. Because these errors result simply from poor judgment, not an intent to defraud, and are not intended to and do not operate to the personal advantage of the negligent bookkeeping partner, she is *not* liable to her copartners for any resulting loss. The duty of care may not be eliminated entirely by agreement, but the standard may be reasonably reduced. The standard may be increased by agreement to one of ordinary care or an even higher standard of care.

RIGHTS AMONG PARTNERS [30-6]

The law provides partners with certain rights, which include (1) their right to use and possess partnership property for partnership purposes, (2) their transferable interest in the partnership, (3) their right to share in distributions (part of their transferable interest), (4) their right to participate in management, (5) their right to choose associates, and (6) their enforcement rights.

Rights in Specific Partnership Property [30-6a]

In adopting the entity theory, the Revised Act abolishes the UPA's concept of tenants in partnership: partnership property is owned by the partnership entity and not by the individual partners. Moreover, the RUPA provides, "A partner is not a co-owner of partnership property and has no interest in partnership property which can be transferred, either voluntarily or involuntarily." A partner may use or possess partnership property only on behalf of the partnership.

Under the UPA a partner's ownership interest in any specific item of partnership property is that of a tenant in partnership. The UPA's tenancy in partnership reaches a similar entity result to the RUPA but states that result in aggregate terms. This type of ownership, which exists only in a partnership, has the following principal characteristics:

1. Each partner has a right equal to that of his copartners to possess partnership property for partnership purposes, but he has no right to possess it for any other purpose without his copartners' consent.
2. A partner may not make an individual assignment of his right in specific partnership property.
3. A partner's interest in specific partnership property is not subject to attachment or execution by his individual creditors. It is subject to attachment or execution only on a claim against the partnership.
4. Upon the death of a partner, his right in specific partnership property vests in the surviving partner or partners. Upon the death of the last surviving partner, his right in such property vests in his legal representative.

Partner's Interest in the Partnership [30-6b]

Each partner has an **interest in the partnership**, which is defined as "all of a partner's interests in the partnership, including the partner's transferable interest and all management and other rights." A **partner's transferable interest** is a more limited concept; it is the partner's share of the profits and losses of the partnership and the partner's right to receive distributions. This interest is personal property. A partner's transferable interest is discussed here; a partner's management and other rights are discussed later in this chapter.

Assignability   A partner may voluntarily transfer, in whole or in part, his transferable interest in the partnership. The transfer does not by itself cause the partner's dissociation or a dissolution and winding up of the partnership business. (Dissolution is discussed in Chapter 31.) The transferee, however, is not entitled to (1) participate in the management or conduct of the partnership business, (2) require access to any information concerning partnership transactions, or (3) inspect or copy the partnership books or records. She is merely entitled to receive, in accordance with the terms of the assignment, any distributions to which the assigning partner would have been entitled under the partnership agreement before dissolution. After dissolution, the transferee is entitled to receive the net amount that would have been distributed to the transferring partner upon the winding up of the business. Moreover, the assignee may apply for a court-ordered dissolution. The assigning partner remains a partner with all of a partner's other rights and duties other than the transferred interest in distributions.

However, the other partners by a unanimous vote may expel a partner who has transferred substantially all of his transferable partnership interest, other than as security for a loan. The partner may be expelled, nevertheless, upon *foreclosure* of the security interest.

The partners may agree among themselves to restrict the right to transfer their partnership interests.

Creditors' Rights   A partner's transferable interest (the right to distributions from the partnership and the right to seek court-ordered dissolution of the partnership) is subject to the claims of that partner's creditors, who may obtain a **charging order** (a type of judicial lien) against the partner's transferable interest. On application by a judgment creditor of a partner, a court may charge the transferable interest of the partner to satisfy the judgment. A charging order is also available to the judgment creditor of a *transferee* of a partnership interest. The court may appoint a receiver of the debtor's share of the distributions due or to become due. The court may order a foreclosure of the interest subject to the charging order at any time. The purchaser at the foreclosure sale has the rights of a transferee. At any time before foreclosure, an interest charged may be redeemed by (1) the partner who is the judgment debtor; (2) other partners with nonpartnership property; or (3) other partners with partnership property but only with the consent of all of the remaining partners.

The judgment creditor, the receiver, and the purchaser at foreclosure do not become a partner, and thus none of them are entitled to participate in the partnership's management or to have access to information. Furthermore, neither the charging order nor its sale upon foreclosure causes dissolution, though the other partners may dissolve the partnership or redeem the charged interest. Moreover, a partner may be expelled by a unanimous vote of the other partners upon foreclosure of a judicial lien charging a partner's interest.

Interest in the partnership

includes the partner's transferable interest and all management and other rights

Partner's transferable interest

the partner's share of the profits and losses of the partnership and the partner's right to receive distributions

Assignability

a partner may sell or assign his transferable interest in the partnership; the new owner becomes entitled to the assigning partner's right to receive distributions but does not become a partner

Creditors' rights

a partner's interest is subject to the claims of creditors, who may obtain a charging order against the partner's transferable interest

Charging order

judicial lien against a partner's transferable interest in the partnership

CONCEPT REVIEW 30-2

Partnership Property Compared with Partner's Interest

	Partnership Property		Partner's Interest
	RUPA	UPA	
Definition	A partner is *not* a co-owner of partnership property	Tenant in partnership	Share of profits and surplus
Possession	For partnership purposes, not individual ones	For partnership purposes, not individual ones	Intangible, personal property right
Assignability	Partner has *no* interest in partnership property which can be transferred	If all other partners assign their rights in the property	Assignee does not become a partner
Attachment	Only for a claim against the partnership	Only for a claim against the partnership	By a charging order
Inheritance	Partner has *no* interest in partnership property which can be transferred	Goes to surviving partner(s)	Passes to the personal representative of deceased partner

Note: RUPA = Revised Uniform Partnership Act; UPA = Uniform Partnership Act.

Right to Share in Distributions [30-6c]

Distribution

transfer of partnership property from the partnership to a partner

A **distribution** is a transfer of money or other partnership property from the partnership to a partner in the partner's capacity as a partner. Distributions include a division of profits, a return of capital contributions, a repayment of a loan or advance made by a partner to the partnership, and a payment made to compensate a partner for services rendered to the partnership. The RUPA's rules regarding distribution are subject to contrary agreement of the partners. A partner has no right to receive, and may not be required to accept, a distribution in kind. The RUPA provides that each partner is deemed to have an account that is credited with the partner's contributions and share of the partnership profits and charged with distributions to the partner and the partner's share of partnership losses.

Share in profits

each partner is entitled to an equal share of the profits unless otherwise agreed

Right to Share in Profits Because a partnership is an association to carry on a business for profit, each partner is entitled, unless otherwise agreed, to a share of the profits. Absent an agreement to the contrary, however, a partner does not have a right to receive a current distribution of the profits credited to his account, the timing of the distribution of profits being a matter arising in the ordinary course of business to be decided by majority vote of the partners. In the absence of an agreement regarding the division of profits, the partners share the profits *equally*, regardless of the ratio of their financial contributions or the degree of their participation in management. Thus, under this default rule, partners share profits per capita and not in proportion to their capital contributions.

Conversely, each partner is chargeable with a share of any losses the partnership sustains. A partner, however, is not obligated to contribute to partnership losses before his withdrawal or the liquidation of the partnership, unless the partners agree otherwise. The partners bear losses in a proportion *identical* to that in which they share profits. The partnership agreement may, however, validly provide for bearing losses in a proportion different from that in which profits are shared.

For example, Alice, Betty, and Carol form a partnership, with Alice contributing $10,000; Betty, $20,000; and Carol, $30,000. They could agree that Alice would receive 20 percent of the profits and assume 30 percent of the losses; that Betty would receive 30 percent of the profits and assume 50 percent of the losses; and that Carol would receive 50 percent of the profits and assume 20 percent of the losses. If their agreement is silent as to the sharing of profits and losses, however, each would have an equal one-third share of both profits and losses.

Right to Return of Capital

Return of capital
a partner does not have a right to receive a distribution of the capital contributions in his account before his withdrawal or the liquidation of the partnership

Absent an agreement to the contrary, a partner does not have a right to receive a distribution of the capital contributions in his account before his withdrawal or the liquidation of the partnership.

Under the UPA after all the partnership's creditors have been paid, each partner is entitled to repayment of his capital contribution during the winding up of the firm. Unless otherwise agreed, a partner is not entitled to interest on his capital contribution; however, a delay in the return of his capital contribution entitles the partner to interest at the legal rate from the date when it should have been repaid.

Right to Indemnification

Indemnification
if a partner makes an advance (loan) to the firm, he is entitled to repayment of the advance plus interest; a partner is entitled to reimbursement for payments made and indemnification for liabilities incurred by the partner in the ordinary course of the business

A partner who makes an advance beyond his agreed capital contribution is entitled to reimbursement from the partnership. An advance is treated as a loan to the partnership that accrues interest. In addition, the partnership must reimburse a partner for payments made and indemnify a partner for liabilities incurred by the partner in the ordinary course of the business of the partnership or for the protection of the partnership business or property. Under the Revised Act a loan from a partner to the partnership is treated the same as loans of a person not a partner, subject to other applicable law, such as fraudulent transfer law, the law of avoidable preferences under the Bankruptcy Act, and general debtor-creditor law. See the case of *Warnick v. Warnick* in Chapter 31.

Under the UPA a partner's claim as a creditor of the firm, though subordinate to the claims of nonpartner creditors, is superior to the partners' rights to the return of capital.

Practical Advice

If, as a partner, you advance money to your partnership, make it clear by a written agreement signed by all of the partners that your advance is to be treated as a loan, not as additional capital.

Right to Compensation

Compensation
unless otherwise agreed, no partner is entitled to payment for acting in the partnership business

The RUPA provides that, unless otherwise agreed, *no* partner is entitled to payment for services performed for the partnership. Even a partner who works disproportionately harder than the others to conduct the business is entitled to no salary but only to his share of the profits. A partner, however, may by agreement among all of the partners, receive a salary. Moreover, a partner is entitled to reasonable compensation for services rendered in winding up the business of the partnership.

Practical Advice

If, as a partner, you expect to be compensated for services you render to the partnership, make that understanding clear by a written agreement signed by all of the partners.

Right to Participate in Management [30-6d]

Management
each partner has equal rights in management unless otherwise agreed

Each of the partners, unless otherwise agreed, has *equal* rights in the **management** and conduct of the partnership business. The majority governs the actions and decisions of the partnership with respect to matters in the ordinary course of partnership business. *All* the partners must consent to any act outside the ordinary course of partnership business and to any amendment of the partnership agreement. In their partnership agreement, the partners may provide for unequal voting rights. For example, Jones, Smith, and Williams form a partnership, agreeing that Jones will have two votes, Smith four votes, and Williams five votes. Large partnerships commonly concentrate most or all management authority in a committee of a few partners or even in just one partner. Classes of partners with different management rights also may be created. This practice is common in accounting and law firms, which may have two classes (e.g., junior and senior partners) or three classes (e.g., junior, senior, and managing partners).

Right to Choose Associates [30-6e]

Choose associates
under the doctrine of *delectus personae*, no person can become a member of a partnership without the consent of all of the partners

No partner may be forced to accept as a partner any person of whom she does not approve. This is partly because of the fiduciary relationship between the partners and partly because each partner has a right to take part in the management of the business, to handle the partnership's assets for partnership purposes, and to act as an agent of the partnership. An ill-chosen partner, through negligence, poor judgment, or dishonesty, may bring financial loss

Practical Advice

Consider whether your partnership agreement should permit the admission of partners by a less-than-unanimous vote, recognizing that by doing so you forfeit veto power over new members of the partnership.

or ruin to her copartners. Because of this danger and because of the close relationship among the members, partnerships must necessarily be founded on mutual trust and confidence. All this finds expression in the term **delectus personae** (literally, "choice of the person"), which indicates the right one has to choose her partners. This principle is embodied in the RUPA, which provides: "A person may become a partner only with the consent of *all* of the partners" [emphasis added]. It is because of *delectus personae* that a purchaser (assignee) of a partner's interest does not become a partner and is not entitled to participate in management. The partnership agreement may provide, however, for admission of a new partner by a less-than-unanimous vote.

Enforcement Rights [30-6f]

As discussed, the partnership relationship creates a number of duties and rights among partners. Accordingly, partnership law provides partners and the partnership with the means to enforce these rights and duties.

Information

each partner has the right (1) without demand, to any information concerning the partnership and reasonably required for the proper exercise of the partner's rights and duties; and (2) on demand, to any other information concerning the partnership

Right to Information and Inspection of the Books The RUPA provides that if a partnership maintains books and records, they must be kept at its chief executive office. A partnership must provide partners access to its books and records to inspect and copy them during ordinary business hours. Former partners are given a similar right, although limited to the books and records pertaining to the period during which they were partners. A duly authorized agent on behalf of a partner may also exercise this right. A partnership may impose a reasonable charge, covering the costs of labor and material, for copies of documents furnished. The partnership agreement may *not* unreasonably restrict a partner's right of access to partnership books and records.

Each partner and the partnership must affirmatively disclose to a partner, *without demand*, any information concerning the partnership's business and affairs reasonably required for the proper exercise of the partner's rights and duties under the partnership agreement or the Act. (In addition, under some circumstances, a disclosure duty may arise from the obligation of good faith and fair dealing.) Moreover, *on demand*, each partner and the partnership must furnish to a partner any other information concerning the partnership's business and affairs, except to the extent the demand or the information demanded is unreasonable or otherwise improper under the circumstances. The rights to receive and demand information extend also to the legal representative of a deceased partner. They may, however, be waived or varied by agreement of the partners.

Legal action

a partner may maintain a direct suit against the partnership or another partner for legal or equitable relief to enforce the partner's rights; the partnership itself may maintain an action against a partner for any breach of the partnership agreement or for the violation of any duty owed to the partnership

Legal Action Under the RUPA a partner may maintain a direct suit against the partnership or another partner for legal or equitable relief, with or without an accounting as to partnership business, to enforce the partner's rights under the partnership agreement and the Revised Act. Thus, under the RUPA, an accounting is not a prerequisite to the availability of the other remedies a partner may have against the partnership or the other partners. Since general partners are not passive investors, the RUPA does not authorize derivative actions. Reflecting the entity theory of partnership, the RUPA provides that the partnership itself may maintain an action against a partner for any breach of the partnership agreement or for the violation of any duty owed to the partnership, such as a breach of fiduciary duty.

The UPA grants to each partner the right to an account whenever (1) his copartners wrongfully exclude him from the partnership business or possession of its property, (2) the partnership agreement so provides, (3) a partner makes a profit in violation of his fiduciary duty, or (4) other circumstances render it just and reasonable. If a partner does not receive or is dissatisfied with a requested account, she may bring an enforcement action, called an *accounting*. Designed to produce and evaluate all testimony relevant to the various claims of the partners, an accounting is an equitable proceeding for a comprehensive and effective settlement of partnership affairs.

ETHICAL DILEMMA

When Is an Opportunity a Partnership Opportunity?

Facts Ted Johnson is a real estate manager and investor. Nearly twenty years ago, Ted embarked on a partnership with Karla Jones to improve and operate an office building in New Haven, Connecticut. The building and land are owned by James Jason. James gave Ted and Karla a twenty-year lease. At the end of twenty years, the lease would terminate and the property would revert to James. Pursuant to their partnership agreement, Ted and Karla each provided 50 percent of the capital for improvements of the office space and received 50 percent of allocable net profits.

Ted has successfully managed the building and during the past twenty years has accumulated some additional capital. Six months before the twenty-year lease

was scheduled to expire, he and James had dinner together. Indicating how pleased he had been with Ted's management skills, James offered to lease the property for another twenty-year term and mentioned the idea of knocking down the present structure and building a small mall. In light of the recent building of luxury condominiums and exclusive restaurants in the neighborhood, the development of a mall appeared to be a sound idea.

Though he no longer needed Karla's capital for the project, Ted suspected that Karla would be interested in participating in the mall development. However, it was not clear whether James made the offer to renew the lease solely to Ted or to the partnership. Because Karla had not been

invited to dinner and her name had never been mentioned, Ted believed that the offer was made solely to him.

Social, Policy, and Ethical Considerations

1. Does Ted have an ethical responsibility to inform Karla of the opportunity to renew the lease?
2. Does it matter that the renewal offer for the long-term lease was initially raised in a dinner conversation between Ted and James?
3. Should Ted be free to sever relations with Karla with regard to the property? Consider that Ted has managed the property and no longer needs Karla's capital. What competing social values does his dilemma involve?

CHAPTER SUMMARY

Formation of General Partnerships

Nature of Partnership

Definition of Partnership an association of two or more persons to carry on as co-owners a business for profit

Entity Theory

- *Partnership as Legal Entity* an organization having a legal existence separate from that of its members; the Revised Act considers a partnership a legal entity for nearly all purposes
- *Partnership as Legal Aggregate* a group of individuals not having a legal existence separate from that of its members; the Revised Act considers a partnership a legal aggregate for few purposes

Formation of a Partnership

Partnership Agreement it is preferable, although not usually required, that the partners enter into a written partnership agreement

Tests of Partnership Existence the formation of a partnership requires all of the following:

- *Association* two or more persons with legal capacity who agree to become partners
- *Business for Profit*
- *Co-ownership* includes sharing of profits and control of the business

Partnership Capital total money and property contributed by the partners for use by the partnership

Partnership Property sum of all of the partnership's assets, including all property acquired by the partnership

Relationships Among Partners

Duties Among Partners

Fiduciary Duty duty of utmost loyalty, fairness, and good faith owed by partners to each other and to the partnership; includes duty not to appropriate partnership opportunities, not to compete, not to have conflicts of interest, and not to reveal confidential information

Duty of Obedience duty to act in accordance with the partnership agreement and any business decisions properly made by the partners

Duty of Care duty owed by partners to manage the partnership affairs without gross negligence, reckless conduct, intentional misconduct, or knowing violation of law

Rights Among Partners **Rights in Specific Partnership Property** partners have the right to use and possess partnership property for partnership purposes

Transferable Interest in Partnership the partner's share of the profits and losses of the partnership and the partner's right to receive distributions

- *Assignability* a partner may sell or assign his transferable interest in the partnership; the new owner becomes entitled to the assigning partner's right to receive distributions but does not become a partner
- *Creditors' Rights* a partner's transferable interest is subject to the claims of creditors, who may obtain a charging order (judicial lien) against the partner's transferable interest

Distributions transfer of partnership property from the partnership to a partner

- *Profits* each partner is entitled to an equal share of the profits unless otherwise agreed
- *Capital* a partner does not have a right to receive a distribution of the capital contributions in his account before his withdrawal or the liquidation of the partnership
- *Indemnification* if a partner makes an advance (loan) to the firm, he is entitled to repayment of the advance plus interest; a partner is entitled to reimbursement for payments made and indemnification for liabilities incurred by the partner in the ordinary course of the business
- *Compensation* unless otherwise agreed, no partner is entitled to payment for services rendered to the partnership

Management each partner has equal rights in management of the partnership unless otherwise agreed

Choice of Associates under the doctrine of *delectus personae*, no person can become a member of a partnership without the consent of all of the partners

Enforcement Rights

- *Information* each partner has the right (1) *without demand*, to any information concerning the partnership and reasonably required for the proper exercise of the partner's rights and duties and (2) *on demand*, to any other information concerning the partnership
- *Legal Actions* a partner may maintain a direct suit against the partnership or another partner for legal or equitable relief to enforce the partner's rights; the partnership itself may maintain an action against a partner for any breach of the partnership agreement or for the violation of any duty owed to the partnership

QUESTIONS

1. Lynn and Jack jointly own shares of stock of a corporation, have a joint bank account, and have purchased and own as tenants in common a piece of real estate. They share equally the dividends paid on the stock, the interest on the bank account, and the rent from the real estate. Without Lynn's knowledge, Jack makes a trip to inspect the real estate and on his way runs over Samuel. Samuel sues Lynn and Jack for his personal injuries, joining Lynn as defendant on the theory that Lynn was Jack's partner. Is Lynn a partner of Jack?

2. James and Suzanne engaged in the grocery business as partners. In one year they earned considerable money, and at the end of the year they invested a part of the profits in oil land, taking title to the land in their names as tenants in common. The investment was fortunate, for oil was discovered near the land, and its value increased many times. Is the oil land partnership property? Why?

3. Sheila owned an old roadside building that she believed could be easily converted into an antique shop. She talked to her friend Barbara, an antique fancier, and they executed the following written agreement:
   a. Sheila would supply the building, all utilities, and $100,000 capital for purchasing antiques.
   b. Barbara would supply $30,000 for purchasing antiques, Sheila to repay her when the business terminated.
   c. Barbara would manage the shop, make all purchases, and receive a salary of $500 per week plus 5 percent of the gross receipts.
   d. Fifty percent of the net profits would go into the purchase of new stock. The balance of the net profits would go to Sheila.
   e. The business would operate under the name "Roadside Antiques."

Business went poorly, and after one year a debt of $40,000 is owed to Old Fashioned, Inc., the principal supplier of antiques purchased by Barbara in the name of Roadside Antiques. Old Fashioned sues Roadside Antiques, and Sheila and Barbara as partners. Decision?

4. Clark, who owned a vacant lot, and Bird, who was engaged in building houses, entered into an oral agreement by which Bird was to erect a house on the lot. Upon the sale of the house and lot, Bird was to have his money first. Clark was then to have the agreed value of the lot, and the profits were to be equally divided. Did a partnership exist?

5. Grant, Arthur, and David formed a partnership for the purpose of betting on boxing matches. Grant and Arthur would become friendly with various boxers and offer them bribes to lose certain bouts. David would then place large bets, using money contributed by all three, and would collect the winnings. After David had accumulated a large sum of money, Grant and Arthur demanded their share, but David refused to make any split. Can Grant and Arthur compel David to account for the profits of the partnership? Why?

6. Teresa, Peter, and Walker were partners under a written agreement made in January that the partnership should continue for ten years. During the same year, Walker, being indebted to Smith, sold and conveyed his interest in the partnership to Smith. Teresa and Peter paid Smith $50,000 as Walker's share of the profits for that year but refused Smith permission to inspect the books or to come into the managing office of the partnership. Smith brings an action setting forth the above facts and asks for an account of partnership transactions and an order to inspect the books and to participate in the management of the partnership business.
 a. Does Walker's action dissolve the partnership?
 b. To what is Smith entitled with respect to (1) partnership profits, (2) inspection of partnership books, (3) an account of partnership transactions, and (4) participation in the partnership management?

7. Horn's Crane Service furnished supplies and services under a written contract to a partnership engaged in operating a quarry and rock-crushing business. Horn brought this action against Prior and Cook, the individual members of the partnership, to recover a personal judgment against them for the partnership's liability under that contract. Horn has not sued the partnership itself, nor does he claim that the partnership property is insufficient to satisfy its debts. What result? Explain.

8. Cutler worked as a bartender for Bowen until they orally agreed that Bowen would have the authority and responsibility for the entire active management and operation of the tavern business known as the Havana Club. Each was to receive $300 per week plus half of the net profits. The business continued under this arrangement for four years until the building was taken over by the Salt Lake City Redevelopment Agency. The agency paid $30,000 to Bowen as compensation for disruption. The business, however, was terminated after

Bowen and Cutler failed to find a new, suitable location. Cutler, alleging a partnership with Bowen, then brought this action against him to recover one-half of the $30,000. Bowen contends that he is entitled to the entire $30,000 because he was the sole owner of the business and that Cutler was merely his employee. Cutler argues that although Bowen owned the physical assets of the business, she, as a partner in the business, is entitled to one-half of the compensation that was paid for the business's goodwill and going-concern value. Who is correct? Explain.

9. In 2005, Gauldin and Corn entered into a partnership for the purpose of raising cattle and hogs. The two men were to share equally all costs, labor, losses, and profits. The business was started on land owned initially by Corn's parents but later acquired by Corn and his wife. No rent was ever requested or paid for use of the land. Partnership funds were used to bulldoze and clear the land, to repair and build fences, and to seed and fertilize the land. In 2009, at a cost of $2,487.50, a machine shed was built on the land. In 2011, a Cargill unit was built on the land at a cost of $8,000. When the partnership dissolved in 2015, Gauldin paid Corn $7,500 for the "removable" assets; however, the two had no agreement regarding the distribution of the barn and the Cargill unit. Is Gauldin entitled to one-half of the value of the two buildings? Explain.

10. Anita and Duncan had been partners for many years in a mercantile business. Their relationship deteriorated to the point at which Anita threatened to bring an action for an accounting and dissolution of the firm. Duncan then offered to buy Anita's interest in the partnership for $250,000. Anita refused the offer and told Duncan that she would take no less than $360,000. A short time later, James approached Duncan and informed him he had inside information that a proposed street change would greatly benefit the business and that he, James, would buy the entire business for $1 million or buy a one-half interest for $500,000. Duncan made a final offer of $350,000 to Anita for her interest. Anita accepted this offer, and the transaction was completed. Duncan then sold the one-half interest to James for $500,000. Several months later, Anita learned for the first time of the transaction between Duncan and James. What rights, if any, does Anita have against Duncan?

11. ABCD Company is a general partnership. It consists of Dianne, Greg, Knox, and Laura, whose capital contributions were as follows: Dianne, $5,000; Greg, $7,500; Knox, $10,000; and Laura, $5,000. The partnership agreement provided that the partnership would continue for three years and that no withdrawals of capital were to be made without the consent of all the partners. The agreement also provided that all advances would be entitled to interest at 10 percent per year. Six months after the partnership was formed, Dianne advanced $10,000 to the partnership. At the end of the first year, net profits totaled $11,000 before any moneys had been distributed to partners. How should the $11,000 be allocated to Dianne, Greg, Knox, and Laura? Explain.

CASE PROBLEMS

12. Donald Petersen joined his father, William Petersen, in a chicken hatchery business William had previously operated as a sole proprietorship. When the partnership was formed, William contributed the assets of the proprietorship, which included cash, equipment, and inventory having a total value of $41,000. Donald contributed nothing. They agreed to share the profits equally. For fifteen years Donald took over the operation of the hatchery with very little help from his father. When the business was terminated William contended that he was entitled to the return of his capital investment of $41,000 before Donald could recover anything. Donald asserted that he is entitled to one-half the value of the business. Explain who is correct in his contention.

13. Smith, Jones, and Brown were creditors of White, who operated a grain elevator known as White's Elevator. Heavily in debt, White was about to fail when the three creditors agreed to take title to his elevator property and pay all the debts. It was also agreed that White should continue as manager of the business at a salary of $1,500 per month and that all profits of the business were to be paid to Smith, Jones, and Brown. It was further agreed that they could dispense with White's services at any time and that he was free to quit when he pleased. White accepted the proposition and continued to operate the business as before. The agreement worked

successfully and for several years paid substantial profits, enough so that Smith, Jones, and Brown had received nearly all that they had originally advanced. Were Smith, Jones, and Brown partners? Explain.

14. Virginia, Georgia, Carolina, and Louis were partners doing business under the trade name of Morning Glory Nursery. Virginia owned a one-third interest, and Georgia, Carolina, and Louis owned two-ninths each. The partners acquired three tracts of land for the purpose of the partnership. Two of the tracts were acquired in the names of the four partners, "trading and doing business as Morning Glory Nursery." The third tract was acquired in the names of the individuals, the trade name not appearing in the deed. This third tract was acquired by the partnership out of partnership funds and for partnership purposes. Who owns each of the three tracts? Why?

15. Charles and L. W. Clement were brothers who had formed a partnership that lasted forty years until Charles discovered that his brother, who kept the partnership's books, had made several substantial personal investments with funds improperly withdrawn from the partnership. He then brought an action seeking dissolution of the partnership, appointment of a receiver, and an accounting. Should Charles succeed? Explain.

TAKING SIDES

Chaiken entered into separate but nearly identical agreements with Strazella and Spitzer to operate a barbershop. Under the terms of the "partnership" agreements, Chaiken would provide barber chairs, supplies, and licenses, while the other two would provide tools of the trade. The agreements also stated that gross returns from the partnership were to be divided on a percentage basis among the three men and that Chaiken would decide all matters of partnership policy. Finally, the agreements stated hours

of work and holidays for Strazella and Spitzer and required Chaiken to hold and distribute all receipts.

a. What are the arguments that Strazella and Spitzer are partners with Chaiken?

b. What are the arguments that Strazella and Spitzer are employees of Chaiken?

c. Explain which arguments should prevail.

Operation and Dissolution of General Partnerships

CHAPTER 31

Joint adventures, like copartners, owe to one another, while the enterprise continues, the duty of the finest loyalty.

Benjamin Cardozo
U.S. Supreme Court Justice

CHAPTER OUTCOMES

After reading and studying this chapter, you should be able to:

1. Explain the contract liability of a partnership and the partners.

2. Explain the tort liability of a partnership and the partners.

3. Distinguish between the liability of incoming partner for debts arising before his admission and those arising after admission.

4. Identify the causes of dissolution of a partnership and the conditions under which partners have the right to continue the partnership after dissociation.

5. Explain the effect of dissolution on the authority and liability of the partners and the order in which the assets of a partnership are distributed to creditors and partners.

The operation and management of a general partnership involves interactions among the partners as well as their interactions with third persons. The previous chapter covered the rights and duties of the partners among themselves. The first part of this chapter focuses on the relations among the partnership, the partners, and third persons who deal with the partnership. These relations are governed by the laws of agency, contracts, and torts as well as by the partnership statute. The second part of the chapter addresses the dissociation and dissolution of general partnerships.

RELATIONSHIP OF PARTNERSHIP AND PARTNERS WITH THIRD PARTIES

In the course of transacting business, the partnership and the partners also may acquire rights over and incur duties to third parties. For example, under the law of *agency*, a principal is liable upon contracts that his duly authorized agents make on his behalf and is liable in tort for the wrongful acts his employees commit in the course of their employment. Because much of the law of partnership is the law of agency, most problems arising between partners and third persons require the application of principles of agency law. The Revised Uniform Partnership Act (RUPA) makes this relationship explicit by stating that "[e]ach partner is an agent of the partnership for the purpose of its business." In addition, the RUPA provides that unless displaced by particular provisions of the RUPA, the principles of law and equity supplement the RUPA. The law of agency is discussed in Chapters 28 and 29.

When a partnership becomes liable to a third party, each partner has **unlimited personal liability** for that partnership obligation.

Unlimited personal liability
if the partnership is bound, each partner has joint and several unlimited personal liability

CONTRACTS OF PARTNERSHIP [31-1]

The act of every partner binds the partnership to transactions *within* the scope of the partnership business unless the partner does not have actual or apparent authority to so act. If the partnership is bound, then each general partner has unlimited personal liability for that partnership obligation unless the partnership is a limited liability partnership (LLP) and the LLP statute shields contract obligations. See Figure 31-1 for a depiction of the contract liability of partnerships. Under the Revised Act, the partners are jointly and severally liable for all contract obligations of the partnership. **Joint and several liability** means that all of the partners may be sued jointly in one action or that separate actions, leading to separate judgments, may be maintained against each of them. Judgments obtained are enforceable, however, against only property of the defendant or defendants named in the suit; and payment of any one of the judgments satisfies all of them. The Revised Act, in keeping with its entity treatment of partnerships, requires the judgment creditor to exhaust the partnership's assets before enforcing a judgment against the separate assets of a partner.

Joint and several liability a creditor may sue the partners jointly as a group or separately as individuals

The Uniform Partnership Act (UPA) provides that partners are jointly liable on all debts and contract obligations of the partnership. Under *joint liability*, a creditor must bring suit against all of the partners as a group, and the judgment must be against all of the obligors. Therefore, any suit in contract against the partners must name all of them as defendants.

Figure 31-1 Contract Liability

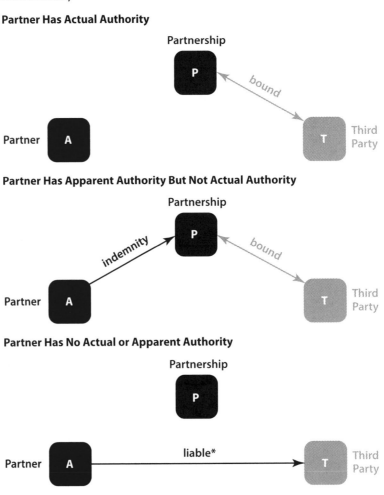

Partner Has Actual Authority

Partner Has Apparent Authority But Not Actual Authority

Partner Has No Actual or Apparent Authority

* Partner is liable for breach of implied warranty of authority or misrepresentation.

Authority to Bind Partnership [31-1a]

A partner may bind the partnership by her act if (1) she has actual authority, express or implied, to perform the act or (2) she has apparent authority to perform the act. If the act is not apparently for carrying on in the ordinary course the partnership business, then the partnership is bound only when the partner has actual authority. In such a case, the third person dealing with the partner assumes the risk that such actual authority exists. Ratification is discussed in Chapter 29.

Actual Express Authority

The **actual express authority** of partners may be written or oral; it may be specifically set forth in the partnership agreement or in an additional agreement between the partners. In addition, it may arise from decisions made by a majority of the partners regarding ordinary matters connected with the partnership business.

A partner who does not have actual authority from *all* of her partners may not bind the partnership by any act that does not apparently carry on in the ordinary course the partnership business. Acts outside the ordinary course of the partnership business would include the following: (1) execution of contracts of guaranty or suretyship in the firm name, (2) sale of partnership property not held for sale in the usual course of business, and (3) payment of an individual partner's debts out of partnership assets.

The Revised Act also authorizes the optional, central filing of a statement of partnership authority specifying the names of the partners authorized to execute instruments transferring real property held in the name of the partnership. A statement may also limit the authority of a partner or partners to transfer real property. In addition, a statement may grant extraordinary authority to some or all of the partners, or may limit their ordinary authority, to enter into transactions on behalf of the partnership. A filed statement is effective for up to five years. A partner, or other person named as a partner, may file a statement denying any fact asserted in a statement of partnership authority, including a denial of a person's status as a partner or of another person's authority as a partner. A statement of denial is a limitation on authority.

The UPA provides that the following acts do *not* bind the partnership unless authorized by *all* of the partners: (1) assignment of partnership property for the benefit of its creditors, (2) disposal of the goodwill of the business, (3) any act which would make it impossible to carry on the ordinary business of the partnership, (4) confession of a judgment, or (5) submission of a partnership claim or liability to arbitration or reference.

Actual Implied Authority

Actual implied authority is neither expressly granted nor expressly denied but is reasonably deduced from the nature of the partnership, the terms of the partnership agreement, or the relations of the partners. For example, a partner has implied authority to hire and fire employees whose services are necessary to carry on the partnership business. In addition, a partner has implied authority to purchase property necessary for the business, to receive performance of obligations due to the partnership, and to bring legal actions to enforce claims of the partnership.

Apparent Authority

Apparent authority (which may or may not be actual) is authority that a third person—in view of the circumstances, the conduct of the parties, and a lack of knowledge or notification to the contrary—may reasonably believe to exist. The RUPA provides

> Each partner is an agent of the partnership for the purpose of its business. An act of a partner, including the execution of an instrument in the partnership name, for apparently carrying on in the ordinary course the partnership business or business of the kind carried on by the partnership binds the partnership, unless the partner had no authority to act for the partnership in the particular matter and the person with whom the partner was dealing knew or had received a notification that the partner lacked authority.

This provision characterizes a partner as a general managerial agent having both actual and apparent authority within the scope of the firm's ordinary business. For example, a partner has apparent authority to indorse checks and notes, to make representations and warranties in selling goods, and to enter into contracts for advertising. A third person, however, may not rely upon apparent authority in any situation in which he already knows, or has received notification, that the partner does not have actual authority. A person knows a fact if the person has actual

---

Authority to bind partnership

a partner who has actual authority (express or implied) or apparent authority may bind the partnership

Actual express authority

authority set forth in the partnership agreement, in additional agreements among the partners, or in decisions made by a majority of the partners regarding the ordinary business of the partnership

Actual implied authority

authority that is reasonably deduced from the nature of the partnership, the terms of the partnership agreement, or the relations of the partners

Apparent authority

authority that a third person may reasonably assume to exist in light of the conduct of the partners, so long as that third person has no knowledge or notice of the lack of actual authority

knowledge of it. A person receives a notification when the notification comes to the person's attention or is duly delivered at the person's place of business or at any other place held out by the person as a place for receiving communications.

RNR Investments Limited Partnership v. Peoples First Community Bank
Court of Appeal of Florida, First District, 2002
812 So.2d 561
http://scholar.google.com/scholar_case?case=957588625820748025&q_812+so.2d+561&hl=en&as_sclt=2,34

FACTS RNR Investments is a Florida limited partnership formed to purchase land in Destin, Florida, and to construct a house on the land for resale. Bernard Roeger was RNR's general partner and Heinz Rapp, Claus North, and S.E. Waltz, Inc., were limited partners. The limited partnership agreement provided for various restrictions on the authority of the general partner: (1) it required the general partner to prepare a budget covering the cost of acquisition and construction of the project (Approved Budget); (2) it restricted the general partner's ability to borrow or spend partnership funds if not specifically provided for in the Approved Budget; and (3) it restricted the general partner's ability to exceed any line item in the Approved Budget by more than 10 percent or the total budget by more than 5 percent.

In June 1998, RNR, through its general partner, entered into a construction loan agreement, note, and mortgage in the principal amount of $990,000. From June 25, 1998, through March 13, 2000, the Bank disbursed the aggregate sum of $952,699. All draws were approved by an architect, who certified that the work had progressed as indicated and that the quality of the work was in accordance with the construction contract.

RNR defaulted under the terms of the note and mortgage by failing to make payments due in July 2000 and all monthly payments due after that. The Bank sought to foreclose. RNR defended by alleging that the Bank had negligently failed to review the limitations on the general partner's authority in RNR's limited partnership agreement and that the general partner did not have the authority to execute notes, a mortgage, and a construction loan agreement. Stephen E. Waltz alleged that the limited partners understood and orally agreed that the general partner would seek financing in the approximate amount of $650,000. RNR also asserted that a copy of the limited partnership agreement was maintained at its offices. However, the record contains no copy of an Approved Budget of the partnership or any evidence that would show that a copy of RNR's partnership agreement or any partnership budget was given to the Bank or that any notice of the general partner's restricted authority was provided to the Bank.

The trial court entered a summary judgment of foreclosure in favor of the Bank. RNR appealed.

DECISION Summary judgment is affirmed.

OPINION The Florida Revised Uniform Limited Partnership Act states that any case not provided for by that statute shall be governed by the provisions of the Florida Revised Uniform Partnership Act (FRUPA). The extent to which the partnership is bound by the acts of a partner acting within the apparent authority is thus governed by FRUPA, which provides that

> Each partner is an agent of the partnership for the purpose of its business. An act of a partner, including the execution of an instrument in the partnership name, for apparently carrying on in the ordinary scope of partnership business or business of the kind

carried on by the partnership, in the geographic area in which the partnership operates, binds the partnership unless the partner had no authority to act for the partnership in the particular manner and the person with whom the partner was dealing knew or had received notification that the partner lacked authority.

Thus, even if a general partner's actual authority is restricted by the terms of the partnership agreement, the general partner possesses the apparent authority to bind the partnership in the ordinary course of partnership business, unless the third party "knew or had received a notification that the partner lacked authority."

"Absent actual knowledge, third parties have no duty to inspect the partnership agreement or inquire otherwise to ascertain the extent of a partner's actual authority in the ordinary course of business … even if they have some reason to question it." The apparent authority provisions of FRUPA reflect a policy by the drafters that "the risk of loss from partner misconduct more appropriately belongs on the partnership than on third parties who do not knowingly participate in or take advantage of the misconduct."

The determination of whether a partner is acting with authority to bind the partnership involves a two-step analysis. The first step is to determine whether the partner purporting to bind the partnership apparently is carrying on the partnership business in the usual way or a business of the kind carried on by the partnership. An affirmative answer on this step ends the inquiry, unless it is shown that the person with whom the partner is dealing actually knew or had received a notification that the partner lacked authority. Here, it is undisputed that, in entering into the loan, the general partner was carrying on the business of RNR in the usual way. Thus, the question in this appeal is whether there are issues of material fact as to whether the Bank had actual knowledge or notice of restrictions on the general partner's authority.

While the RNR partners may have agreed upon restrictions that would limit the general partner to borrowing no more than $650,000 on behalf of the partnership, RNR does not contend and there is no evidence that would show that the Bank had actual knowledge or notice of any restrictions on the general partner's authority. Here, the partnership could have protected itself by filing a statement pursuant or by providing notice to the Bank of the specific restrictions on the authority of the general partner.

INTERPRETATION A general partner has the apparent authority to bind the partnership in the ordinary course of partnership business or in the business of the kind carried on by the partnership, unless the third party knew or had received a notification that the partner lacked authority.

CRITICAL THINKING QUESTION Do you agree with the RUPA's policy that "the risk of loss from partner misconduct more appropriately belongs on the partnership than on third parties who do not knowingly participate in or take advantage of the misconduct"? Explain.

BUSINESS LAW **IN ACTION**

Jose Miranda and Jim Troy are equal partners in a refrigeration maintenance and repair business called T&M Refrigeration. Unless they have established some other form of business entity by filing the required forms with the state, Troy and Miranda are general partners, with unlimited personal liability for the debts and liabilities of the business. Besides being unlimited, under the Revised Uniform Partnership Act, their personal liability for partnership obligations is also joint and several.

This means that each of them is liable for the entirety of any judgment that is obtained against the partnership, beyond what can be satisfied by partnership assets. If, for example, while acting within the ordinary course of T&M's business, Jim

negligently—but not grossly negligently—works on an air-conditioning unit that later explodes, causing personal injury and property damage, a lawsuit might follow. The suit likely will name as defendants Jim, T&M Refrigeration, and Jose. Even though Jose had nothing to do with the negligent conduct, he is still a proper defendant because he has joint and several liability for all partnership obligations.

Assuming the plaintiff in the personal injury suit prevails and the verdict is large, the partnership's assets may not suffice to pay the judgment. T&M Refrigeration may even be forced into bankruptcy. But that will not discharge any remaining debt, because the partners' assets are available to satisfy the

judgment. If $30,000 is still owed on the judgment after exhausting the partnership's assets, Jose and Jim each face that entire $30,000 liability, payable out of his personal assets.

The plaintiff can choose to proceed against either Jim or Jose for the entire $30,000. Or the plaintiff can choose to collect portions of the remaining judgment amount from each of the partners. Of course a plaintiff can only collect once on his or her judgment, up to its total amount. So if Jim pays $20,000, the plaintiff can collect no more than $10,000 from Jose. As they are equal partners, Jim can then pursue Jose for contribution of $5,000, making each of the partner's overall liability equal.

Partnership by Estoppel [31-1b]

Partnership by estoppel
imposes partnership duties
and liabilities on a
nonpartner who has either
represented himself or
consented to be
represented as a partner

Partnership by estoppel imposes partnership duties and liabilities upon a nonpartner who has either represented himself or consented to be represented as a partner. It extends to a third person to whom such a representation is made and who justifiably relies upon the representation.

For example, Marks and Saunders are partners doing business as Marks and Company. Marks introduces Patterson to Taylor, describing Patterson as a member of the partnership. Patterson verbally confirms the statement made by Marks. Believing that Patterson is a member of the partnership and relying upon Patterson's good credit standing, Taylor sells goods on credit to Marks and Company. In an action by Taylor against Marks, Saunders, and Patterson as partners to recover the price of the goods, Patterson is liable although he is not a partner in Marks and Company. Taylor had justifiably relied upon the representation that Patterson was a partner in Marks and Company, to which Patterson actually consented. If, however, Taylor had known at the time of the sale that Patterson was not a partner, his reliance on the representation would not have been justified, and Patterson would not be liable.

Except in situations in which the representation of membership in a partnership has been made publicly, no person is entitled to rely upon a representation of partnership unless it is made directly to him. For example, Patterson falsely tells Dillon that he is a member of the partnership Marks and Company. Dillon casually relays this statement to Taylor, who in reliance sells goods on credit to Marks and Company. Taylor cannot hold Patterson liable, as he was not justified in relying on the representation made privately by Patterson to Dillon, which Patterson did not consent to have repeated to Taylor.

Where Patterson, however, knowingly consents to his name appearing publicly in the firm name or in a list of partners, or to be used in public announcements or advertisements in a manner which indicates that he is a partner in the firm, Patterson is liable to any member of the public who relies on the purported partnership, whether or not Patterson is aware of being held out as a partner to such person.

TORTS AND CRIMES OF PARTNERSHIP [31-2]

Torts
the partnership is liable for
loss or injury caused by any
wrongful act or omission or
other actionable conduct of
any partner while acting
within the ordinary course
of the business or with the
authority of her copartners

As discussed in Chapter 29, under the doctrine of *respondeat superior* a partnership, like any employer, may be liable for an unauthorized tort committed by its employee if the employee committed the tort in the scope of his employment. With respect to a *partner's* conduct, the RUPA provides that a partnership is liable in **tort** for the loss or injury any partner causes by

Figure 31-2 Tort Liability

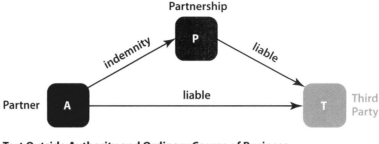

Tort Within Authority or Ordinary Course of Business

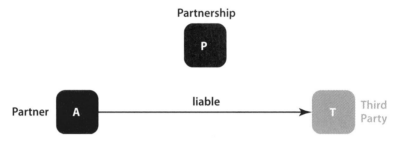

Tort Outside Authority and Ordinary Course of Business

Breach of trust

the partnership is liable if a partner in the course of the partnership's business or while acting with authority of the partnership breaches a trust by misapplying money or property entrusted by a third person

Crimes

a partner is not criminally liable for the crimes of her partners unless she authorized or participated in them

Notice to a partner

a partnership is bound by a partner's knowledge, notice, or receipt of a notification of a fact relating to the partnership

Notice

a person has notice of a fact if the person (1) knows of it, (2) has received a notification of it, or (3) has reason to know it exists from all of the facts known to the person at the time in question

any wrongful act or omission, or other actionable conduct, while acting within the ordinary course of the partnership business or with the authority of the partnership. See Figure 31-2 for the tort liability of partnerships.

Tort liability of the partnership may include not only the negligence of the partners but also trespass, fraud, defamation, and breach of fiduciary duty, so long as the tort is committed in the course of partnership business. Moreover, though the fact that a tort is intentional does not necessarily remove it from the course of business, it is a factor to be considered. The Revised Act makes the partnership liable for no-fault torts by the addition of the phrase, "or other actionable conduct." A partnership is also liable if a partner in the course of the partnership's business or while acting with authority of the partnership commits a **breach of trust** by receiving money or property of a person not a partner, and the partner misapplies the money or property.

If the partnership is liable, each partner has *unlimited personal liability* for the partnership obligation unless the partnership is an LLP. The liability of partners for a tort or breach of trust committed by any partner or by an employee of the firm in the course of partnership business is joint and several. As mentioned earlier, the Revised Act requires the judgment creditor to exhaust the partnership's assets before enforcing a judgment against the separate assets of a partner.

The partner who commits the tort or breach of trust is directly liable to the third party and must also *indemnify* the partnership for any damages it pays to the third party.

A partner is not criminally liable for the **crimes** of her partners unless she authorized or participated in them. Nor is a partnership criminally liable for the crimes of individual partners or employees unless a statute imposes vicarious liability. Even under such a statute, a partnership usually is liable only in those states that have adopted the entity theory or if the statute itself expressly imposes liability upon partnerships. Otherwise, the vicarious liability statute renders the partners liable as individuals.

NOTICE TO A PARTNER [31-3]

A partner's knowledge, notice, or receipt of a notification of a fact relating to the partnership is effective immediately as knowledge by, notice to, or receipt of a notification by the partnership, except in the case of a fraud on the partnership committed by or with the consent of that partner. A person has **notice** of a fact if the person (1) knows of it, (2) has received a notification of it, or (3) has reason to know it exists from all of the facts known to the person at the time in question.

LIABILITY OF INCOMING PARTNER [31-4]

A person admitted as a partner into an existing partnership is *not* personally liable for any partnership obligations incurred before the person's admission as a partner. This means that the liability of an incoming partner for **antecedent debts** and obligations of the firm is limited to his capital contribution. This restriction does not apply, of course, to **subsequent debts** (obligations arising after his admission into the partnership), for which obligations his liability is *unlimited*. For example, Nash is admitted to Higgins, Cooke, and Jackson Co., a partnership. Nash's capital contribution is $7,500, which she paid in cash upon her admission to the partnership. A year later, when liabilities of the firm exceed its assets by $40,000, the partnership is dissolved. Porter had lent the firm $15,000 eight months before Nash was admitted; Skinner lent the firm $20,000 two months after Nash was admitted. Nash has no liability to Porter *except* to the extent of her capital contribution, but she is *personally* liable to Skinner.

In an LLP, an incoming partner does not have personal liability for both antecedent debts *and* those subsequent debts that are shielded by that state's LLP statute.

Antecedent debts

the liability of an incoming partner for antecedent debts of the partnership is limited to his capital contribution

Subsequent debts

the liability of an incoming partner for subsequent debts of the partnership is unlimited

Conklin Farm v. Leibowitz
Supreme Court of New Jersey, 1995
140 N.J. 417, 658 A.2d 1257
http://scholar.google.com/scholar_case?q=658+A.2d+1257&hl=en&as_sdt=2,34&case=6472930221798179666&scilh=0

FACTS In December 1986, Paula Hertzberg, Elliot Leibowitz, and Joel Leibowitz formed a general partnership, LongView Estates (LongView), to acquire from plaintiff Conklin Farm (Conklin) approximately one hundred acres of land in the Township of Montville, New Jersey. Paula Hertzberg owned 40 percent of LongView; Elliot and Joel Leibowitz owned 30 percent each. They intended to build a residential condominium complex on the property.

On the same day that the partners formed the partnership, it executed a promissory note in favor of Conklin for $9 million. The three LongView partners signed the note as partners and also personally guaranteed the note. The note represented a portion of the purchase price for the land and was secured by a mortgage on the land.

On March 15, 1990, Joel Leibowitz assigned his 30 percent interest in LongView to his wife, defendant Doris Leibowitz, who agreed to be bound by all the terms and conditions of the partnership agreement. Seventeen months later, Doris assigned the interest back to her husband. During those seventeen months, the entire principal of the Conklin note of $9 million was outstanding, and interest accrued at an annual rate of nine percent.

LongView's condominium project failed, and LongView defaulted on the Conklin note. In March 1991, LongView filed a petition for bankruptcy. Eventually, Paula Hertzberg, Elliot Leibowitz, and Joel Leibowitz filed for personal bankruptcy protection, and all three were discharged of any personal liability on the Conklin note.

Conklin sued Doris Leibowitz in November 1991, claiming that she was personally liable for $547,000: 30 percent of the interest on the Conklin note that accrued during the seventeen months during which she had held her husband's partnership interest, plus interest since then and costs. Conklin asserted that, although the principal of the note was preexisting debt, the interest that accrued while Doris Leibowitz had been a partner was new debt. Doris Leibowitz filed a motion for summary judgment arguing that as an incoming partner she was not personally liable for

LongView's preexisting debt, including interest. The trial court found in favor of Doris Leibowitz holding that the interest was part of the preexisting debt, not new debt. Conklin appealed and the Appellate Division reversed, ruling that the interest on preexisting debt is new debt. Doris Leibowitz appealed.

DECISION The judgment of the Appellate Division is reversed.

OPINION Under the New Jersey Partnership Act each partner is personally liable for the debts and obligations of a partnership. However, the New Jersey Partnership Act defines the liability of new partners entering an existing partnership:

> A person admitted as a partner into an existing partnership is liable for all the obligations of the partnership arising before his admission as though he had been a partner when such obligations were incurred, except that this liability shall be satisfied only out of partnership property.
>
> Thus the Uniform Partnership Act made incoming partners personally liable for preexisting debts, but only to the extent of their investment in the partnership.

The Conklin note was executed by the partnership prior to Doris Leibowitz's having any interest in LongView. She did not sign or guarantee payment of that note. Thus, the clear language of this section resolves the issue. Because the note was a preexisting debt, and because Doris Leibowitz was an incoming partner, she was not personally liable for the debt. The parties agree that the principal of the note was preexisting debt. However, while Doris Leibowitz argues that the interest that accrued while she was a partner was part of that preexisting debt, Conklin argues that it was new debt that arose each month as it became due. Conklin argues that just as a rent obligation arises for current use of property, an interest obligation arises for current use of principal. The Appellate Division agreed, adopting Conklin's argument that interest is analogous to rent.

The Supreme Court, however, found the rent analogy faulty. Contractual interest is created by the contract and is, therefore, inseparable from the contractual debt. The interest obligation cannot be a separate debt from the principal obligation because, independent of the contract establishing the principal obligation, there is no obligation to pay interest. Because there is no obligation to pay interest independent of the promissory note, Conklin's rent analogy fails. Since the obligation to pay interest arises only as a result of the original loan instrument, interest, unlike rent, cannot be "new" debt.

Moreover, there is no prejudice to Conklin in the fact that it may look to only the original partners for payment of the preexisting debt and interest. In executing the note, Conklin considered the personal credit of only Paula Hertzberg, Elliot Leibowitz, and Joel Leibowitz, all of whom guaranteed the loan. Conklin did not rely on the personal credit of Doris Leibowitz. When lenders loan money, they rely on the financial statements of the general partners, and not of some future, unknown general partner.

Contractual interest is not new debt, and Doris Leibowitz is not personally liable for its payment.

INTERPRETATION A new partner is not personally liable for preexisting debt including interest on a preexisting note even though the interest accrues after the partner's admission.

CRITICAL THINKING QUESTION Do you agree with the court's decision? Explain.

DISSOCIATION AND DISSOLUTION OF GENERAL PARTNERSHIPS UNDER THE RUPA

Dissociation occurs when a partner ceases to be associated in the carrying on of the business. Dissolution refers to those situations in which the Revised Act requires a partnership to wind up and terminate. A dissociation of a partner results in dissolution only in limited circumstances. In many instances, dissociation will result merely in a buyout of the withdrawing partner's interest rather than a winding up of the partnership. When a dissociation or other cause results in dissolution, the partnership *is not terminated* but rather it continues until the winding up of its affairs is complete. During winding up, unfinished business is completed, receivables are collected, payments are made to creditors, and the remaining assets are distributed to the partners. Termination occurs when the process is finished.

DISSOCIATION [31-5]

Dissociation
occurs when a partner ceases to be associated in carrying on of the business

Dissociation occurs when a partner ceases to be associated in carrying on of the business. A number of events that were considered causes of dissociation or dissolution under the common law are no longer considered so under the RUPA. For example, the assignment of a partner's interest, a creditor's charging order on a partner's interest, and an accounting are not considered a dissociation or dissolution.

A partner has the *power* to dissociate at any time, rightfully or wrongfully, by expressing an intent to withdraw. A partner does not, however, always have the *right* to dissociate. A partner who wrongfully dissociates is liable to the partnership for damages caused by the dissociation. In addition, if the wrongful dissociation results in the dissolution of the partnership, the wrongfully dissociating partner is not entitled to participate in winding up the business.

Wrongful Dissociations [31-5a]

A partner's dissociation is wrongful if it breaches an express provision of the partnership agreement. In addition, dissociation is wrongful in a *term partnership* if before the expiration of the term or the completion of the undertaking (1) the partner voluntarily withdraws by express will unless the withdrawal follows within ninety days after another partner's dissociation by death, bankruptcy, or wrongful dissociation; (2) the partner is expelled for misconduct by judicial determination; (3) the partner becomes a debtor in bankruptcy; or (4) the partner is an entity (other than a trust or estate) and is expelled or otherwise dissociated because its dissolution or termination was willful. A **term partnership** is a partnership for a specific term or particular undertaking. The partnership agreement may eliminate or expand the dissociations that are wrongful or modify the effects of wrongful dissociation, except for the power of a court to expel a partner for misconduct.

Term partnership
a partnership for a specific term or particular undertaking

Rightful Dissociations [31-5b]

The RUPA provides that a partner's dissociation is wrongful only if it results from one of the events just discussed. All other dissociations are rightful, including (1) the death of partner in *any* partnership, (2) the withdrawal of a partner in a *partnership at will*, (3) in *any* partnership an event occurs that was agreed to in the partnership agreement as causing dissociation, and (4) in *any* partnership a court determines that a partner has become incapable of performing the partner's duties under the partnership agreement. The RUPA defines a **partnership at will** as a partnership in which the partners have not agreed to remain partners until the expiration of a definite term or the completion of a particular undertaking.

Partnership at will

a partnership in which the partners have not agreed to remain partners until the expiration of a definite term or the completion of a particular undertaking

Effect of dissociation

terminates dissociating partner's right to participate in the management of the partnership business and duties to partnership

Dissolution

refers to those situations when the Revised Act requires a partnership to wind up and terminate

Effect of Dissociation [31-5c]

Upon a partner's dissociation the partner's right to participate in the management and conduct of the partnership business terminates. If, however, the dissociation results in a dissolution and winding up of the business, all of the partners who have not wrongfully dissociated may participate in winding up the business. The duty not to compete terminates upon dissociation, and the dissociated partner may immediately engage in a competitive business, without any further consent. The partner's other fiduciary duties and duty of care continue only with regard to matters arising and events occurring before the partner's dissociation, unless the partner participates in winding up the partnership's business. For example, a partner who leaves a partnership providing consulting services may immediately compete with the firm for new clients, but must exercise care in completing current transactions with clients and must account to the firm for any fees received from the old clients on account of those transactions.

DISSOLUTION [31-6]

Dissolution refers to those situations in which the Revised Act requires a partnership to wind up and terminate. In accordance with the Revised Act's emphasis on the entity treatment of partnerships, only a limited subset of dissociations requires the dissolution of a partnership. In addition, some events other than dissociation can bring about the dissolution of a partnership under the RUPA. The following sections discuss the causes and effects of dissolution.

Causes of Dissolution [31-6a]

The basic rule under the RUPA is that a partnership is dissolved and its business must be wound up only if one of the events listed in Section 801 occurs. The events causing dissolution may be brought about by (1) an act of the partners (i.e., some dissociations), (2) operation of law, or (3) court order. The provisions of Section 801 that involve an act of the parties are default provisions: the partners may by agreement modify or eliminate these grounds. The partners may *not* vary or eliminate the grounds for dissolution based on operation of law or court order.

Dissolution by Act of the Partners   These causes of dissolution comprise a subset of dissociations. In a ***partnership at will***, a partner's giving notice of intent to withdraw will result in dissolution of a partnership. Thus, any member of a partnership at will has the right to force a liquidation of the partnership. (The death or bankruptcy of a partner does *not* dissolve a partnership at will.)

The Revised Act provides for three ways in which a *term partnership* will be dissolved. No partner by herself has the power to dissolve a term partnership.

1. The term of the partnership expires or the undertaking is complete. If the partners continue a term partnership after the expiration of the term or completion of the undertaking, the partnership will be treated as a partnership at will.
2. All of the partners expressly agree to dissolve. This reflects the principle that the partners can unanimously amend the partnership agreement.
3. A partner's dissociation caused by a partner's death or incapacity, bankruptcy or similar financial impairment, or wrongful dissociation will bring on a dissolution if within ninety days after dissociation at least half of the remaining partners express their will to wind up the partnership business. Thus, if a term partnership has eight partners and one of the partners wrongfully dissociates before the end of the term, the partnership will be dissolved only if four of the remaining seven partners vote in favor of liquidation.

In ***all partnerships*** dissolution occurs upon the happening of an event that was specified in the partnership agreement as resulting in dissolution. The partners may, however, agree to continue the business.

Dissolution by Operation of Law

A partnership is dissolved by operation of law if an event occurs that makes it unlawful to continue all or substantially all of the partnership's business. For example, a law prohibiting the production and sale of alcoholic beverages would dissolve a partnership formed to manufacture liquor. A cure of such illegality within ninety days after notice to the partnership of the event is effective retroactively. The partnership agreement cannot vary the requirement that an uncured illegal business must be dissolved and liquidated.

Dissolution by Court Order

On application by a *partner*, a court may order dissolution on grounds of another partner's misconduct or upon a finding that (1) the economic purpose of the partnership is likely to be unreasonably frustrated, (2) another partner has engaged in conduct relating to the partnership business that makes it not reasonably practicable to carry on the business in partnership with that partner, or (3) it is not otherwise reasonably practicable to carry on the partnership business in conformity with the partnership agreement. On application of a *transferee* of a partner's transferable interest or a purchaser at foreclosure of a charging order, a court may order dissolution if it determines that it is equitable to wind up the partnership business (1) at any time in a partnership at will or (2) after the term of a term partnership has expired. The partners may *not* by agreement vary or eliminate the court's power to wind up a partnership.

Horizon/CMS Healthcare Corporation v. Southern Oaks Health Care, Inc.
Court of Appeal of Florida, Fifth District, 1999
732 So.2d 1156; *review denied*, 744 So.2d 454
http://scholar.google.com/scholar_case?case=12151982165035491195&q=732+So.+2d+1156&hl=en&as_sdt=2,34

FACTS Horizon is a large, publicly traded provider of both nursing homes and management for nursing homes. It wanted to expand into Osceola County, Florida, in 1993. Southern Oaks was already operating in Osceola County; it owned the Southern Oaks Health Care Center and had a Certificate of Need issued by the Florida Agency for Health Care Administration for a new one-hundred-and-twenty-bed facility in Kissimmee. Horizon and Southern Oaks decided to form a partnership to own the proposed Kissimmee facility, which was ultimately named Royal Oaks, and agreed that Horizon would manage both the Southern Oaks facility and the new Royal Oaks facility. To that end, Southern Oaks and Horizon entered into twenty-year partnership and management contracts in 1993.

In 1996, Southern Oaks filed suit alleging that Horizon breached its obligations under two different partnership agreements and that Horizon had breached the various management contracts. The court ordered that the partnerships be dissolved, finding that they were incapable of continuing to operate in business together. Because it was dissolving the partnerships, the court ruled that, "there is no entitlement to future damages." In its cross-appeal, Southern Oaks asserts that because Horizon unilaterally and wrongfully sought dissolution of the partnerships, Southern Oaks should receive a damage award for the loss of the partnerships' seventeen remaining years' worth of future profits.

DECISION Dissolution affirmed and damages request denied.

OPINION First, the trial court's finding that the parties are incapable of continuing to operate together is a finding of "irreconcilable differences," a permissible reason for dissolving the partnerships under the express terms of the partnership agreements. One of the reasons the Revised Uniform Partnership Act (RUPA) gives for dissolution is "It is not otherwise reasonably practicable to carry on the partnership business in conformity

with the partnership agreement." While "reasonably practicable" is not defined in RUPA, the term is broad enough to encompass the inability of partners to continue working together, which is what the court found. Thus, dissolution was not "wrongful," and Southern Oaks was not entitled to damages for lost future profits. Additionally, the partnership contracts also permit dissolution by "judicial decree."

Second, even assuming the partnership was dissolved for a reason not provided for in the partnership agreements, damages were properly denied. Under RUPA, it is clear that wrongful dissociation triggers liability for lost future profits. However, RUPA does not contain a similar provision for dissolution. RUPA does not refer to the dissolutions as rightful or wrongful. Under RUPA only when a partner dissociates and the dissociation is wrongful can the remaining partners sue for damages.

Southern Oaks' attempt to bring the instant dissolution under the statutory provision applicable to dissociation is rejected. The trial court ordered dissolution of the partnership, not the dissociation of Horizon for wrongful conduct. There no longer appears to be "wrongful" dissolution—either dissolution is provided for by contract or statute or the dissolution was improper and the dissolution order should be reversed. In the instant case, because the dissolution either came within the terms of the partnership agreements or judicial dissolution in which case it is not reasonably practicable to carry on the partnership business, Southern Oaks' claim for lost future profits is without merit.

INTERPRETATION A court-ordered dissolution for good cause is not wrongful and does not entitle either party to damages from the other.

CRITICAL THINKING QUESTION Should the courts have placed blame on Horizon for breaching the partnership agreements and management contracts?

CONCEPT REVIEW 31-1

Dissociation and Dissolution Under the RUPA

Cause	Partnership at Will		Term Partnership	
	Dissociation	Dissolution	Dissociation	Dissolution
Acts of Partners				
Assignment of partner's interest				
Accounting				
Withdrawal	•	•	•	*
Bankruptcy	•		•	*
Incapacity	•		•	*
Death	•		•	*
Expulsion of partner	•		•	
Expiration of term				•
Event specified in partnership agreement	•	•	•	•
Unanimous agreement to dissolve	•	•	•	•
Operation of Law				
Illegality		•		•
Court Order				
Judicial expulsion of partner	•		•	*
Judicial determination of partner's incapability to perform partnership duties	•		•	*
Judicial determination of economic frustration or impracticability		•		•
Application by transferee of partner's interest if equitable		•		•

* Dissolution will occur if, within ninety days after dissociation, at least half the remaining partners express their will to wind up the partnership business.

Effects of Dissolution [31-6b]

Effects of dissolution upon dissolution a partnership is not terminated but continues until the winding up is completed

A partnership continues after dissolution only for the purpose of winding up its business. The partnership is terminated when the winding up of its business is completed. The remaining partners have the right, however, to continue the business after dissolution if *all* of the partners, including any dissociating partner other than a wrongfully dissociating partner, waive the right to have the partnership's business wound up and the partnership terminated. In that event the partnership resumes carrying on its business as if dissolution had not occurred.

Authority a partner's actual authority to act for the partnership terminates, except so far as may be appropriate to wind up partnership affairs; apparent authority continues unless notice of the dissolution is given to a third party

Authority   Upon dissolution, the *actual authority* of a partner to act for the partnership terminates, except so far as is appropriate to wind up partnership business. Actual authority to wind up includes the authority to complete existing contracts, to collect debts, to sell partnership assets, and to pay partnership obligations. A person winding up a partnership's business also has the authority to preserve the partnership business or property as a going concern for a reasonable time, bring and defend legal actions, settle and close the partnership's business, distribute the assets of the partnership pursuant to the RUPA, settle disputes by mediation or arbitration, and perform other necessary acts.

With respect to apparent authority, the partnership is bound in a transaction not appropriate for winding up only if the partner's act would have bound the partnership before dissolution and the other party to the transaction did not have notice of the dissolution. A person has notice of a fact if the person (1) knows of it, (2) has received a notification of it, or (3) has reason to know it exists from all of the facts known to the person at the time in question. Moreover, the RUPA provides that, after an event of dissolution, any partner who has not wrongfully dissociated may file a statement of dissolution on behalf of the partnership and that ninety days after the filing of the statement of dissolution nonpartners are deemed to have notice of the

Practical Advice

Be sure to give the appropriate notice to third parties whenever a partnership dissolves.

dissolution and the corresponding limitation on the authority of all partners. Thus, after ninety days, the statement of dissolution operates as constructive notice conclusively limiting the apparent authority of partners to transactions that are appropriate for winding up the business.

Existing liability
dissolution does not in itself discharge the existing liability of any partner

Liability Dissolution does not in itself discharge the **existing liability** of any partner. Partners are liable to the other partners for their share of partnership liabilities incurred after dissolution. That includes not only obligations that are appropriate for winding up the business, but also obligations that are inappropriate but within the partner's apparent authority. A partner, however, who, with knowledge of the dissolution, nevertheless incurs a liability binding on the partnership by an act that is not appropriate for winding up the partnership business, is liable to the partnership for any damage caused to the partnership by the liability.

Winding Up [31-6c]

Winding up
completing unfinished business, collecting debts, and distributing assets to creditors and partners; also called liquidation

Whenever a dissolved partnership is not to be continued, the partnership must be liquidated. The process of liquidation, called **winding up**, involves completing unfinished business, collecting debts, taking inventory, reducing assets to cash, auditing the partnership books, paying creditors, and distributing the remaining assets to the partners. During this period, the fiduciary duties of the partners continue in effect except the duty not to compete.

Right to participate in winding up
any partner who has not wrongfully dissociated may participate in winding up the partnership's business

Participation in Winding Up After dissolution, a partner who has not wrongfully dissociated has the **right to participate in winding up** the partnership's business. On application of any partner, partner's legal representative, or transferee, the court may order judicial supervision of the winding up if good cause is shown. Any partner winding up the partnership is entitled to reasonable compensation for services rendered in the winding up.

Distribution of assets
the assets of the partnership include all required contributions of partners; the liabilities of a partnership are to be paid out of partnership assets in the following order: (1) amounts owing to nonpartner and partner creditors and (2) amounts owing to partners on their partners' accounts

Distribution of Assets After all the partnership assets have been collected and reduced to cash, they are distributed to creditors and the partners. When the partnership has been profitable, the order of distribution is not critical; however, when liabilities exceed assets, the order of distribution has great importance. In winding up a partnership's business, the "assets" of the partnership include all required contributions of partners.

The RUPA provides that the partnership must apply its assets first to discharge the obligations of partners who are creditors on *parity* with other creditors, subject to any other laws, such as fraudulent conveyance laws and voidable transfers under the Bankruptcy Act Second, any surplus must be applied to pay a liquidating distribution equal to the net amount distributable to partners in accordance with their right to distributions. (This does not distinguish between amounts owing to partners for return of capital and amounts owing to partners for profits.) The partnership agreement may vary the RUPA's rules for distributing the surplus among the partners. For example, it may distinguish between capital and operating losses, as the original UPA does.

Each partner is entitled to a settlement of all partnership accounts upon winding up. In settling accounts among the partners, profits and losses that result from the liquidation of the partnership assets must be credited and charged to the partners' accounts according to their respective shares of profits and losses. Then, the partnership must make a final liquidating distribution to those partners with a positive account balance in an amount equal to any excess of the credits over the charges in the partner's account. Any partner with a negative account balance must contribute to the partnership an amount equal to any excess of the charges over the credits in the partner's account. (In an LLP a partner is *not* required to contribute for any partnership obligations for which that partner is not personally liable under the LLP statute's shield.)

Partners share proportionately in the shortfall caused by partners who fail to contribute their proportionate share. The partnership may enforce a partner's obligation to contribute. A partner is entitled to recover from the other partners any contributions in excess of that partner's share of the partnership's liabilities. After the settlement of accounts, each partner must contribute, in the proportion in which the partner shares partnership losses, the amount necessary to satisfy partnership obligations that were not known at the time of the settlement. The estate of a deceased partner is liable for the partner's obligation to contribute to the partnership.

Marshaling of Assets The Revised Act abolishes the marshaling of assets doctrine—which segregates and considers separately the assets and liabilities of the partnership and the

Partnership creditors
are entitled to be first
satisfied out of partnership
assets

Partners' creditors
share on equal footing with
unsatisfied partnership
creditors in the individually
owned assets of their
respective debtor-partners

respective assets and liabilities of the individual partners—and the dual priority rule. (These are discussed later in this chapter.) Under the RUPA, like the UPA, **partnership creditors** are entitled to be satisfied first out of partnership assets. Unlike the UPA, the Revised Act provides that unsatisfied partnership creditors may recover any deficiency out of the individually owned assets of the partners on equal footing with the **partners' creditors**.

DISSOCIATION WITHOUT DISSOLUTION [31-7]

As mentioned, the RUPA uses the term "dissociation," instead of the UPA term "dissolution," to denote the change in the relationship caused by a partner's ceasing to be associated in the carrying on of the business. Under the RUPA, a dissociation of a partner results in dissolution only in limited circumstances, discussed previously. Thus, in many instances, dissociation will result merely in a buyout of the withdrawing partner's interest rather than a winding up of the partnership.

Dissociations Not Causing Dissolution [31-7a]

In a *partnership at will*, a partner will be dissociated from the partnership without dissolution upon specified causes, including that partner's death, bankruptcy, or incapacity; the expulsion of that partner; or, in the case of an entity-partner, its termination. (As covered earlier, a partnership at will is *dissolved* upon notice of a partner's intent to withdraw.)

In a *term partnership*, if within ninety days after any specified causes of dissolution occurs, fewer than half of the remaining partners express their will to wind up the partnership business, then the partnership will not dissolve. These causes include the following: a partner's dissociation by death, bankruptcy, or incapacity; the distribution by a trust-partner of its entire partnership interest; the termination of an entity-partner; or a partner's wrongful dissociation. (A wrongful dissociation includes a partner's voluntary withdrawal in violation of the partnership agreement and the judicial expulsion of a partner.)

With three exceptions, the partners may by agreement modify or eliminate any of the grounds for dissolution. The three exceptions are (1) carrying on an illegal business, (2) a court-ordered dissolution on application of a partner, and (3) a court-ordered dissolution on application of a transferee of a partner's interest. Moreover, at any time after the dissolution of a partnership and before the winding up of its business is completed, all of the partners, including any dissociating partner other than a wrongfully dissociating partner, may waive the right to have the partnership's business wound up and the partnership terminated. In that event, the partnership resumes carrying on its business as if dissolution had never occurred.

Continuation After Dissociation [31-7b]

Continuation after dissociation
the remaining partners have
the right to continue the
partnership with a
mandatory buyout of the
dissociating partner; the
creditors of the partnership
have claims against the
continued partnership

If a partner is dissociated from a partnership without resulting in dissolution, the remaining partners have the right to continue the business. Creditors of the partnership remain creditors of the continued partnership. Moreover, the dissociated partner remains liable for partnership obligations incurred before dissociation.

The partnership must purchase the dissociated partner's interest in the partnership. The partnership agreement can vary these rights. The buyout price of a dissociated partner's interest is the amount that would have been distributable to the dissociating partner in a winding up of the partnership if, on the date of dissociation, the assets of the partnership were sold at a price equal to the greater of liquidation value or going concern value without the dissociated partner. The partnership must offset against the buyout price all other amounts owing from the dissociated partner to the partnership, including damages for wrongful dissociation. These rules, however, are merely default rules, and the partnership agreement may specify the method or formula for determining the buyout price and all of the other terms and conditions of the buyout right.

Practical Advice

Consider whether to
include a provision in your
partnership agreement
specifying a method for
valuing each partner's
interest in the partnership.

A partner in a term partnership who wrongfully dissociates before the expiration of a definite term or the completion of a particular undertaking is not entitled to payment of any portion of the buyout price until the expiration of the term or completion of the undertaking, unless the partner establishes to the satisfaction of the court that earlier payment will not cause undue hardship to the business of the partnership.

A partnership must indemnify a dissociated partner whose interest is being purchased against all partnership liabilities, whether incurred before or after the dissociation, except liabilities incurred by an act of the dissociated partner after dissociation that binds the partnership, as discussed later.

Warnick v. Warnick
Supreme Court of Wyoming, 2003
2003 WY 113, 76 P.3d 316
http://scholar.google.com/scholar_case?case=15255465738264221669&q=76+P.3d+316+&hl=en&as_sdt=2,34

FACTS In August 1978, Wilbur and Dee Warnick and their son Randall Warnick purchased a ranch in Sheridan County, Wyoming for $335,000, with $90,000 down plus $245,000 in installments over ten years at 8 percent interest. In April 1979, they formed a general partnership, Warnick Ranches, to operate the ranch and to pay off the purchase agreement. The partnership agreement recited that the initial capital contributions of the partners totaled $60,000, paid 36 percent by Wilbur, 30 percent by Dee, and 34 percent by Randall. The Warnick Ranches Partnership Agreement stated that by "unanimous agreement of all Partners, additional contributions may be made to, or withdrawals may be made from, the capital of the Partnership."

The partners over the years each contributed additional funds to the operation of the ranch and received cash distributions from the partnership. After 1983, Randall contributed very little new money, and almost all of the additional funds to pay off the mortgage came from Wilbur and Dee Warnick. Wilbur also left in the partnership account two $12,000 cash distributions that were payable to him. The net cash contributions of the partners through 1999 were as follows: Wilbur $170,112.60 (51 percent); Dee $138,834.63 (41 percent); and Randall $25,406.28 (8 percent).

In 1998, Randall Warnick began having discussions with his brother about the possibility of selling his interest in Warnick Ranches. When Randall mentioned this to his father, a dispute arose between them concerning the percentage of the partnership that Randall owned. On April 14, 1999, Randall's attorney sent a letter to Warnick Ranches proposing the sale of Randall's partnership to a third party or to the partnership, or a liquidation of the partnership.

On August 11, 1999, Warnick Ranches responded in writing, treating the letter from Randall's attorney as the expressed will of a partner to dissociate. Randall brought an action against the partnership to determine his interest in the partnership, including a buyout price if he is determined to be dissociated from the partnership.

The district court, in granting Randall Warnick's motion for summary judgment, found that dissociation of Randall as a partner was the appropriate remedy. The court awarded judgment to Randall Warnick for the amount of his cash contributions, plus 34 percent of the partnership assets' increase in value above all partners' cash contributions. As a result of that calculation, $230,819.14, or 25.24 percent, of the undisputed value of the partnership was awarded to Randall.

DECISION Judgment affirmed in part and reversed in part; case is remanded.

OPINION The partnership agreement is entirely silent as to how cash advances or payments on behalf of the business are to be treated. The partners knew that additional cash would be needed to make the mortgage payments on the ranch, and perhaps

assumed that their agreement would cover the additional funds when they would unanimously agree to adjust the capital accounts when a partner paid more money into the operation.

The partners however never entered into a unanimous agreement to amend their partnership agreement or to reflect additional capital contributions. Moreover, the advances by the partners were not anywhere documented as a loan to the partnership rather than capital contributions. The district court specifically found that there was no documentation to support a conclusion that the payments by the elder Warnicks were a loan, so they could not be treated as a loan.

The district court's decision, however, misapplies the clear provisions of the Revised Uniform Partnership Act (RUPA), which operates automatically if a partnership agreement does not have contrary provisions. RUPA provides that (1) a partner may lend money to the partnership; (2) a partnership shall repay a partner who, in aid of the partnership, makes a payment or advance beyond the amount of capital the partner agreed to contribute; and (3) such a payment or advance by a partner constitutes a loan to the partnership which accrues interest from the date of the payment or advance.

The district court's calculations in this case treat the mortgage payments as neither capital contributions nor advances, but as something else not contemplated by RUPA. The partnership agreement and RUPA are consistent in requiring that the partners must unanimously consent to any amendments of the partnership agreement. In addition, the RUPA does not require advances to the partnership or payment of partnership debts by partners to be memorialized in writing as a loan. Therefore, a partner's payment of the Warnick Ranch mortgage, without the unanimous consent required for additional capital contributions, would be an advance and a loan to the partnership.

RUPA, with the goal of avoiding unnecessary dissolutions of partnerships, contains a significant change from prior partnership law. An entirely new concept, "dissociation," is used in lieu of the original Uniform Partnership Act (UPA) term "dissolution" to denote the change in the relationship caused by a partner's ceasing to be associated in the carrying on of the business. RUPA states that a partner has the power to dissociate at any time by express will and that a partner is dissociated from a partnership upon receipt by the partnership of notice of the partner's express will to withdraw as a partner. The record supports the district court's conclusion that a dissociation occurred and that the date of the letter is the date of dissociation.

The court, however, erred in its calculation of the judgment. RUPA states that a dissociated partner's interest in the partnership shall be purchased by the partnership for a buyout price equal to the amount that would have been distributable to the dissociating partner under RUPA if, on the date of the dissociation, the partnership's assets had been sold. But RUPA provides that partnership assets must first be applied to discharge partnership liabilities to creditors, including partners who are creditors. As each partner advanced funds to pay the mortgage or other partnership expenses, that partner became a creditor of the partnership for the amount advanced, and is entitled to interest on each amount from the date of the advance. In calculating Randall's buyout price, it is therefore necessary to first calculate the amount that the partnership owes to each partner for advances to the partnership, with interest accrued from the date of each advance at the rate specified in RUPA. Moreover, these advances include the two $12,000 draws that Wilbur Warnick actually left in the partnership.

INTERPRETATION A partnership must purchase a dissociated partner's interest in the partnership for a buyout price equal to the amount that would have been distributable to the dissociating partner under RUPA if, on the date of the dissociation, the partnership's assets had been sold and first applied to discharge partnership liabilities to creditors, including partners who are creditors.

CRITICAL THINKING QUESTION Do you agree with the Wyoming Supreme Court's decision? Explain.

Dissociated partner's power to bind the partnership
a dissociated partner's actual authority to act for the partnership terminates; apparent authority continues for two years unless notice of the dissociation is given to a third party

Dissociated Partner's Power to Bind the Partnership [31-7c]

A dissociated partner has no actual authority to act for the partnership. With respect to apparent authority, the RUPA provides that for two years after a partner dissociates without resulting in a dissolution of the partnership business, the partnership is bound by an act of the dissociated partner which would have bound the partnership before dissociation but *only if* at the time of entering into the transaction the other party

1. reasonably believed that the dissociated partner was then a partner;
2. did not have notice of the partner's dissociation; *and*
3. is not deemed to have had constructive notice from a filed statement of dissociation.

A dissociated partner is liable to the partnership for any damage caused to the partnership arising from an obligation improperly incurred by the dissociated partner after dissociation for which the partnership is liable. The dissociated partner is also personally liable to the third party for the unauthorized obligation.

A person has "notice" of a fact if he knows or has reason to know it exists from all the facts that are known to him or he has received a notification of it. The RUPA provides that ninety days after a statement of dissociation is filed, nonpartners are deemed to have constructive notice of the dissociation, thereby conclusively terminating a dissociated partner's apparent authority. Thus, under the RUPA a partnership should notify all known creditors of a partner's dissociation and file a statement of dissociation, which will conclusively limit a dissociated partner's continuing agency power to ninety days after filing. Conversely, third parties dealing with a partnership should check for partnership filings at least every ninety days.

Dissociated partner's liability to third persons
a partner's dissociation does not of itself discharge the partner's liability for a partnership obligation incurred before dissociation; a dissociated partner is liable for a partnership obligation incurred within two years after a partner dissociates unless notice of the dissociation is given to a third party

Dissociated Partner's Liability to Third Persons [31-7d]

A partner's dissociation does not of itself discharge the partner's liability for a partnership obligation incurred before dissociation. A dissociated partner is not liable for a partnership obligation incurred more than two years after dissociation. For partnership obligations incurred within two years after a partner dissociates without resulting in a dissolution of the partnership business, a dissociated partner is liable for a partnership obligation if, at the time of entering into the transaction, the other party (1) reasonably believed that the dissociated partner was then a partner; (2) did not have notice of the partner's dissociation; and (3) is not deemed to have had constructive notice from a filed statement of dissociation.

By agreement with the partnership creditor and the partners continuing the business, a dissociated partner may be released from liability for a partnership obligation. Moreover, a dissociated partner is released from liability for a partnership obligation if a partnership creditor, with notice of the partner's dissociation but without the partner's consent, agrees to a material alteration in the nature or time of payment of a partnership obligation.

DISSOLUTION OF GENERAL PARTNERSHIPS UNDER THE UPA

The extinguishment of a partnership consists of three stages: (1) dissolution, (2) winding up or liquidation, and (3) termination. Dissolution occurs when the partners cease to carry on the business together. Upon dissolution, the partnership is not terminated but rather it continues until the winding up of its affairs is complete. Termination occurs when the winding up is finished.

DISSOLUTION [31-8]

The UPA defines dissolution as the change in the relation of the partners caused by any partner's ceasing to be associated in the carrying on, as distinguished from the winding up, of the business.

Causes of Dissolution [31-8a]

Dissolution may be brought about by (1) an act of the partners, (2) operation of law, or (3) court order. Because a partnership is a personal relationship, a partner always has the power to dissolve it by his actions, but whether he has the right to do so is determined by the partnership agreement. A partnership is dissolved by operation of law upon (1) the death of a partner, (2) the bankruptcy of a partner or of the partnership, or (3) the subsequent illegality of the partnership. A court-ordered dissolution may be sought by a partner, an assignee of a partner's interest, or a partner's personal creditor who has obtained a charging order against the partner's interest.

Effects of Dissolution [31-8b]

On dissolution, the partnership is not terminated but rather it continues until the winding up of its affairs is complete. Moreover, dissolution does not discharge the existing liability of any partner, though it does restrict her authority to act for the partnership.

Upon dissolution, the *actual authority* of a partner to act for the partnership terminates, except so far as may be necessary to wind up partnership affairs. Actual authority to wind up includes the authority to complete existing contracts, to collect debts, to sell partnership assets, and to pay partnership obligations.

Although actual authority terminates upon dissolution, *apparent authority* continues to bind the partnership for acts within the scope of the partnership business unless the third party is given notice of the dissolution.

WINDING UP [31-9]

Whenever a dissolved partnership is not to be continued, the partnership must be liquidated. The process of liquidation, called **winding up**, involves completing unfinished business, collecting debts, taking inventory, reducing assets to cash, auditing the partnership books, paying creditors, and distributing the remaining assets to the partners. During this period, the fiduciary duties of the partners continue in effect.

Distribution of Assets [31-9a]

The UPA sets forth the rules for settling accounts between the parties after dissolution. It states that the liabilities of a partnership are to be paid out of partnership assets in the following order: (1) amounts owing to nonpartner creditors, (2) amounts owing to partners other than for capital and profits (loans or advances), (3) amounts owing to partners for capital, and (4) amounts owing to partners for profits. The partners may by agreement among themselves change the internal priorities of distribution (numbers 2, 3, and 4) but not the preferred position of third parties (number 1). The UPA defines partnership assets to include all partnership property as well as the contributions necessary for the payment of all partnership liabilities, which consist of numbers 1, 2, and 3.

In addition, the UPA provides that, in the absence of any contrary agreement, each partner shall share equally in the profits and surplus remaining after all liabilities (numbers 1, 2, and 3) are satisfied and must contribute toward the partnership's losses, capital or otherwise, according to his share in the profits. Thus, the proportion in which the partners bear losses depends not on their relative capital contributions but on their agreement. If no specific agreement exists, the partners bear losses in the same proportion in which they share profits.

Marshaling of Assets [31-9b]

The doctrine of marshaling of assets applies only in situations in which a court of equity is administering the assets of a partnership and of its members. **Marshaling of assets** means segregating and considering separately the assets and liabilities of the partnership and the respective assets and liabilities of the individual partners. Partnership creditors are entitled to be satisfied first out of partnership assets and may recover any deficiency out of the individually owned assets of the partners. This right is subordinate, however, to the rights of nonpartnership creditors to those assets. Conversely, the nonpartnership creditors have first claim to the individually owned assets of their respective debtors, whereas their claims to partnership assets are subordinate to the claims of partnership creditors. This approach is called the "dual priority" rule.

Finally, the assets of an insolvent partner are distributed in the following order: (1) debts and liabilities owing to her nonpartnership creditors, (2) debts and liabilities owing to partnership creditors, and (3) contributions owing to other partners who have paid more than their respective share of the firm's liabilities to partnership creditors.

This rule, however, is no longer followed if the partnership is a debtor under the Bankruptcy Code. In a proceeding under the federal bankruptcy law, a trustee is appointed to administer the estate of the debtor. If the partnership property is insufficient to pay all the claims against the partnership, the statute directs the trustee to seek recovery of the deficiency first from the general partners who are not bankrupt. The trustee may then seek recovery against the estates of bankrupt partners on the same basis as other creditors of the bankrupt partner. This provision, although contrary to the UPA's doctrine of marshaling of assets, governs whenever a bankruptcy court is administering partnership assets.

CONTINUATION AFTER DISSOLUTION [31-10]

Dissolution produces one of two outcomes: either the partnership is liquidated or the remaining partners continue the partnership. Whereas liquidation sacrifices the value of a going concern, continuation of the partnership after dissolution avoids this loss. The UPA, nonetheless, gives each partner the right to have the partnership liquidated except in a few instances in which the remaining partners have the right to continue the partnership.

Right to Continue Partnership [31-10a]

After dissolution, the remaining partners have the right to continue the partnership when (1) the partnership has been dissolved in contravention of the partnership agreement, (2) a partner has been expelled in accordance with the partnership agreement, or (3) all the partners agree to continue the business.

Rights of Creditors [31-10b]

Any change in membership dissolves a partnership and forms a new one, despite the fact that the new combination may include a majority of the old partners. The creditors of the old partnership may pursue their claims against the new partnership and also may proceed to hold all of the members of the dissolved partnership personally liable. If a withdrawing partner has made arrangements with those who continue the business whereby they assume and pay all debts and obligations of the firm, the partner is still liable to creditors whose claims arose before the dissolution. If compelled to pay such debts, the withdrawing partner nonetheless has a right of indemnity against her former partners, who agreed to pay the debts but failed to do so.

A retiring partner may be discharged from his existing liabilities by entering into a *novation* with the continuing partners and the creditors. A creditor must agree to a novation, although his consent may be inferred from his course of dealing with the partnership after dissolution. Whether such dealings with a continuing partnership constitute an implied novation is a factual question of intent.

A withdrawing partner may protect herself against liability upon contracts the firm enters subsequent to her withdrawal by giving notice that she is no longer a member of the firm. Otherwise, she will be liable for debts thus incurred to creditors who had no notice or knowledge of the partner's withdrawal. Persons who had extended credit to the partnership prior to its dissolution must receive actual notice, whereas constructive notice by newspaper publication will suffice for those who knew of the partnership but had not extended credit to it before its dissolution.

ETHICAL DILEMMA

What Duty of Disclosure Is Owed to Incoming Partners?

Facts James Edwards was just appointed managing partner of the northeastern division of Banks & Borre, a prestigious national certified public accountant (CPA) firm operating as a partnership. The position is an excellent one, and James is the youngest partner ever to have served as a regional managing partner. However, although Banks & Borre is a well-established firm, it recently has been subject to several sizable lawsuits that allege the firm's misconduct in services it provided to several banks and certain tax shelters.

Robert Smith, the national manager, has given James clear guidelines on management strategy for the northeast division. Smith has emphasized the importance of expanding the client base in light of the pending lawsuits. A principal strategy is to expand through acquisition of smaller firms. Because of his position as manager of the northeastern division, James receives both a salary and a percentage of new client revenues.

Jones, Jones, & Frank is a medium-size CPA firm that provides auditing, tax, and management advisory services to a variety of clients. Brothers Ken Jones and Richard Jones began the practice twenty-five years ago. Donald Frank began as an employee but was brought into the partnership in its fifth year.

Jones, Jones, & Frank has been considering the possibility of merging its practice with that of a larger firm. Ken and Richard are in their late fifties and no longer want managerial responsibilities. Nevertheless, they wish to remain active in the practice.

James Edwards initiated discussions with Jones, Jones, & Frank regarding the possibility of a merger. James indicated that he could arrange attractive compensation packages for the partners of the smaller firm. Ken, Richard, and Donald have inquired about the lawsuits pending against Banks & Borre. Not having been involved in the services that gave rise to the lawsuits, James does not know most of the details. He does know, however, that concern about the litigation could destroy all prospects for the merger. James reassures Ken, Richard, and Donald that he does not know much about the lawsuits but is under the impression that they are not significant.

Social, Policy, and Ethical Considerations

1. Should James make a point of acquainting himself with the details of the litigation? Were his preliminary statements about the lawsuits justifiable?

2. Is it ethical for Banks & Borre to recruit new partners and to institute a policy that encourages mergers, given the pending litigation?

3. If a merger takes place, could Ken, Richard, and Donald be held liable for any judgments arising from the litigation?

4. How might a CPA firm insulate its partners from personal liability?

5. What actions should Jones, Jones, and Frank take to investigate Banks & Borre before proceeding with the merger?

CHAPTER SUMMARY

Relationship of Partnership and Partners with Third Parties

Contracts of Partnership

Partners' Liability

- *Personal Liability* if the partnership is contractually bound, each partner has joint and several unlimited personal liability

- *Joint and Several Liability* a creditor may sue the partners jointly as a group or separately as individuals

Authority to Bind Partnership a partner who has actual authority (express or implied) or apparent authority may bind the partnership

- *Actual Express Authority* authority set forth in the partnership agreement, in additional agreements among the partners, or in decisions made by a majority of the partners regarding the ordinary business of the partnership

- *Actual Implied Authority* authority that is reasonably deduced from the nature of the partnership, the terms of the partnership agreement, or the relations of the partners

- *Apparent Authority* an act of a partner for apparently carrying on in the ordinary course the partnership business or business of the kind carried on by the partnership binds the partnership, so long as that third person has no knowledge or notice of the lack of actual authority

Partnership by Estoppel imposes partnership duties and liabilities on a nonpartner who has either represented himself or consented to be represented as a partner

Torts and Crimes of Partnership	**Torts** the partnership is liable for loss or injury caused by any wrongful act or omission or other actionable conduct of any partner while acting within the ordinary course of the business or with the authority of her copartners; the partners are jointly and severally liable
	Breach of Trust the partnership is liable if a partner in the course of the partnership's business or while acting with authority of the partnership breaches a trust by misapplying money or property entrusted by a third person; the partners are jointly and severally liable
	Crimes a partner is not criminally liable for the crimes of her partners unless she authorized or participated in them
Notice to a Partner	**Binds Partnership** a partnership is bound by a partner's knowledge, notice, or receipt of a notification of a fact relating to the partnership
	Notice a person has notice of a fact if the person (1) knows of it, (2) has received a notification of it, or (3) has reason to know it exists from all of the facts known to the person at the time in question
Liability of Incoming Partner	**Antecedent Debts** the liability of an incoming partner for antecedent debts of the partnership is limited to her capital contribution
	Subsequent Debts the liability of an incoming partner for subsequent debts of the partnership is unlimited

---

Dissociation and Dissolution of General Partnerships Under the RUPA

Dissociation	**Definition of Dissociation** change in the relation of partners caused by any partner's ceasing to be associated in carrying on of the business
	• *Term Partnership* partnership for a specific term or particular undertaking
	• *Partnership at Will* partnership in which the partners have not agreed to remain partners until the expiration of a definite term or the completion of a particular undertaking
	Wrongful Dissociation a dissociation that breaches an express provision of the partnership agreement or in a term partnership if before the expiration of the term or the completion of the undertaking (1) the partner voluntarily withdraws by express will, (2) the partner is judicially expelled for misconduct, (3) the partner becomes a debtor in bankruptcy, or (4) the partner is an entity (other than a trust or estate) and is expelled or otherwise dissociated because its dissolution or termination was willful
	Rightful Dissociation all other dissociations are rightful, including the death of a partner in any partnership and the withdrawal of a partner in a partnership at will
	Effect of Dissociation terminates the dissociating partner's right to participate in the management of the partnership business and duties to partnership
Dissolution	**Definition of Dissolution** refers to those situations in which the Revised Act requires a partnership to wind up and terminate
	Causes of Dissolution
	• *Dissolution by Act of the Partners* in a *partnership at will*: withdrawal of a partner; in a *term partnership*: (1) the term ends, (2) all partners expressly agree to dissolve, or (3) a partner's dissociation is caused by a partner's death or incapacity, bankruptcy or similar financial impairment, or wrongful dissociation if within ninety days after dissociation at least half of the remaining partners express their will to wind up the partnership business; in *any partnership*: an event occurs that was specified in the partnership agreement as resulting in dissolution
	• *Dissolution by Operation of Law* a partnership is dissolved by operation of law upon the subsequent illegality of the partnership business
	• *Dissolution by Court Order* a court will order dissolution of a partnership under certain conditions
	Effects of Dissolution upon dissolution a partnership is not terminated but continues until the winding up is completed
	• *Authority* a partner's actual authority to act for the partnership terminates, except so far as may be appropriate to wind up partnership affairs; apparent authority continues unless notice of the dissolution is given to a third party
	• *Liability* dissolution does not in itself discharge the existing liability of any partner; partners are liable to the other partners for their share of partnership liabilities incurred after dissolution

Winding Up completing unfinished business, collecting debts, and distributing assets to creditors and partners; also called liquidation

- *Winding Up Required* A dissolved partnership must be wound up and terminated when the winding up of its business is completed unless all of the partners, including any rightfully dissociating partner, waive the right to have the partnership's business wound up and the partnership terminated
- *Participation in Winding Up* any partner who has not wrongfully dissociated may participate in winding up the partnership's business
- *Distribution of Assets* the assets of the partnership include all required contributions of partners; the liabilities of a partnership are to be paid out of partnership assets in the following order: (1) amounts owing to nonpartner and partner creditors and (2) amounts owing to partners on their partners' accounts
- *Partnership Creditors* are entitled to be first satisfied out of partnership assets
- *Nonpartnership Creditors* share on equal footing with unsatisfied partnership creditors in the individually owned assets of their respective debtor-partners

Dissociation Without Dissolution

Dissociations Not Causing Dissolution

- *Partnership at Will* a partner's death, bankruptcy, or incapacity; the expulsion of a partner; or the termination of an entity-partner results in a dissociation of that partner but does not result in a dissolution
- *Term Partnership* if within ninety days after any of the following causes of dissolution occur, fewer than half of the remaining partners express their will to wind up the partnership business, then the partnership will not dissolve: a partner's dissociation by death, bankruptcy, or incapacity; the distribution by a trust-partner of its entire partnership interest; the termination of an entity-partner; or a partner's wrongful dissociation

Continuation After Dissociation the remaining partners have the right to continue the partnership with a mandatory buyout of the dissociating partner; the creditors of the partnership have claims against the continued partnership

Dissociated Partner's Power to Bind the Partnership a dissociated partner's actual authority to act for the partnership terminates; apparent authority continues for two years unless notice of the dissolution is given to a third party

Dissociated Partner's Liability to Third Persons a partner's dissociation does not of itself discharge the partner's liability for a partnership obligation incurred before dissociation; a dissociated partner is liable for a partnership obligation incurred within two years after a partner dissociates unless notice of the dissolution is given to a third party

QUESTIONS

1. Albert, Betty, and Carol own and operate the Roy Lumber Company. Each contributed one-third of the capital, and they share equally in the profits and losses. Their partnership agreement provides that two partners must authorize all purchases over $2,500 in advance and that only Albert is authorized to draw checks. Unknown to Albert or Carol, Betty purchases on the firm's account a $5,500 diamond bracelet and a $5,000 forklift and orders $5,000 worth of logs, all from Doug, who operates a jewelry store and is engaged in various activities connected with the lumber business. Before Betty made these purchases, Albert told Doug that Betty is not the log buyer. Albert refuses to pay Doug for Betty's purchases. Doug calls at the mill to collect, and Albert again refuses to pay him. Doug calls Albert an unprintable name, and Albert then punches Doug in the nose, knocking him out. While Doug is lying unconscious on the ground, an employee of Roy Lumber Company negligently drops a log on Doug's leg,

breaking three bones. The firm and the three partners are completely solvent.

What are the rights of Doug against Roy Lumber Company, Albert, Betty, and Carol?

2. Paula, Fred, and Stephanie agree that Paula and Fred will form and conduct a partnership business and that Stephanie will become a partner in two years. Stephanie agrees to lend the firm $50,000 and take 10 percent of the profits in lieu of interest. Without Stephanie's knowledge, Paula and Fred tell Harold that Stephanie is a partner, and Harold, relying on Stephanie's sound financial status, gives the firm credit. The firm later becomes insolvent, and Harold seeks to hold Stephanie liable as a partner. Should Harold succeed?

3. Simmons, Hoffman, and Murray were partners doing business under the firm name of Simmons & Co. The firm borrowed money from a bank and gave the bank the firm's note for the

loan. In addition, each partner guaranteed the note individually. The firm became insolvent, and a receiver was appointed. The bank claims that it has a right to file its claim as a firm debt and also that it has a right to participate in the distribution of the assets of the individual partners before partnership creditors receive any payment from such assets.

a. Explain the principle involved in this case.

b. Is the bank correct?

4. Anthony and Karen were partners doing business as the Petite Garment Company. Leroy owned a dye plant that did much of the processing for the company. Anthony and Karen decided to offer Leroy an interest in their company, in consideration for which Leroy would contribute his dye plant to the partnership. Leroy accepted the offer and was duly admitted as a partner. At the time he was admitted as a partner, Leroy did not know that the partnership was on the verge of insolvency. About three months after Leroy was admitted to the partnership, a textile firm obtained a judgment against the partnership in the amount of $50,000. This debt represented an unpaid balance that had existed before Leroy was admitted as a partner.

The textile firm brought an action to subject the partnership property, including the dye plant, to the satisfaction of its judgment. The complaint also requested that, in the event the judgment was unsatisfied by sale of the partnership property, Leroy's home be sold and the proceeds applied to the balance of the judgment. Anthony and Karen own nothing but their interest in the partnership property.

What should be the result (a) with regard to the dye plant and (b) with regard to Leroy's home?

5. Jones and Ray formed a partnership on January 1, known as JR Construction Co., to engage in the construction business, each partner owning a one-half interest. On February 10, while conducting partnership business, Jones negligently injured Ware, who brought an action against Jones, Ray, and JR Construction Co. and obtained judgment for $250,000 against them on March 1. On April 15, Muir joined the partnership by contributing $100,000 cash, and by agreement each partner was entitled to a one-third interest. In July, the partners agreed to purchase new construction equipment for the partnership, and Muir was authorized to obtain a loan from XYZ Bank in the partnership name for $200,000 to finance the purchase. On July 10, Muir signed a $200,000 note on behalf of the partnership, and the equipment was purchased. In November, the partnership was in financial difficulty, its total assets amounting to $50,000. The note was in default, with a balance of $150,000 owing to XYZ Bank. Muir has substantial resources, while Jones and Ray each individually have assets of $20,000.

What is the extent of Muir's personal liability and the personal liability of Jones and Ray as to (a) the judgment obtained by Ware and (b) the debt owing to XYZ Bank?

6. Lauren, Matthew, and Susan form a partnership, Lauren contributing $100,000; Matthew $50,000; and Susan her time and skill. Nothing is said regarding the division of profits. The firm later dissolves. No distributions to partners have been made since the partnership was formed. The partnership sells its assets for a loss of $90,000. After payment of all firm debts, $60,000 is left. Lauren claims that she is entitled to the entire $60,000. Matthew contends that the distribution should be $40,000 to Lauren and $20,000 to Matthew. Susan claims the $60,000 should be divided equally among the partners. Who is correct? Explain.

7. Adams, a consulting engineer, entered into a partnership with three others for the practice of their profession. The only written partnership agreement is a brief document specifying that Adams is entitled to 55 percent of the profits and the others to 15 percent each. The venture is a total failure. Creditors are pressing for payment, and some have filed suit. The partners cannot agree on a course of action.

How many of the partners must agree to achieve each of the following objectives?

a. To add Jones, also an engineer, as a partner, Jones being willing to contribute a substantial amount of new capital.

b. To sell a vacant lot held in the partnership name, which had been acquired as a future office site for the partnership.

c. To move the partnership's offices to less expensive quarters.

d. To demand a formal accounting.

e. To dissolve the partnership.

f. To agree to submit certain disputed claims to arbitration, which Adams believes will prove less expensive than litigation.

g. To sell all of the partnership's personal property, Adams having what he believes to be a good offer for the property from a newly formed engineering firm.

h. To alter the respective interests of the parties in the profits and losses by decreasing Adams's share to 40 percent and increasing the others' shares accordingly.

i. To assign all the partnership's assets to a bank in trust for the benefit of creditors, hoping to work out satisfactory arrangements without filing for bankruptcy.

8. Charles and Jack orally agreed to become partners in a tool and die business. Charles, who had experience in tool and die work, was to operate the business. Jack was to take no active part but was to contribute the entire $500,000 capitalization. Charles worked ten hours a day at the plant, for which he was paid nothing. Nevertheless, despite Charles's best efforts, the business failed. The $500,000 capital was depleted, and the partnership owed $500,000 in debts. Prior to the failure of the partnership business, Jack became personally insolvent; consequently, the creditors of the partnership collected the entire $500,000 indebtedness from Charles, who was forced to sell his home and farm to satisfy the indebtedness. Jack later regained his financial responsibility, and Charles brought an appropriate action against Jack for (a) one-half of the $500,000 he had paid to partnership creditors and (b) one-half of $80,000, the reasonable value of Charles's services during the operation of the partnership. Who will prevail and why?

9. Glenn refuses an invitation to become a partner of Dorothy and Cynthia in a retail grocery business. Nevertheless, Dorothy inserts an advertisement in the local newspaper representing Glenn as their partner. Glenn takes no steps to deny the existence of a partnership between them. Ron, who extended credit to the firm, seeks to hold Glenn liable as a partner. Is Glenn liable? Explain.

10. Hanover leased a portion of his farm to Brown and Black, doing business as the Colorite Hatchery. Brown went upon the premises to remove certain chicken sheds that he and

Black had placed there for hatchery purposes. Thinking that Brown intended to remove certain other sheds, which were Hanover's property, Hanover accosted Brown, who willfully struck Hanover and knocked him down. Brown then ran to the Colorite truck, which he had previously loaded with chicken coops, and drove back to the hatchery. On the way, he picked up George, who was hitchhiking to the city to look for a job. Brown was driving at seventy miles an hour down the highway. At an open intersection with another highway, Brown in his hurry ran a stop sign, striking another vehicle. The collision caused severe injuries to George. Immediately thereafter, the partnership was dissolved, and Brown was insolvent. Hanover and George each bring separate actions against Black as copartner for the alleged tort committed by Brown against each. What judgments as to each?

11. Martin, Mark, and Marvin formed a retail clothing partner ship named M Clothiers and conducted a business for many years, buying most of their clothing from Hill, a wholesaler. On January 15, Marvin retired from the business, but Martin and Mark decided to continue it. As part of the retirement agreement, Martin and Mark agreed in writing with Marvin that Marvin would not be responsible for any of the partnership debts, either past or future. On January 15 the partnership published a notice of Marvin's retirement in a newspaper of general circulation where the partnership carried on its business.

Before January 15, Hill was a creditor of M Clothiers to the extent of $10,000, and on January 30, he extended additional credit of $5,000. Hill was not advised and did not in fact know of Marvin's retirement and the change of the partnership. On January 30, Ray, a competitor of Hill, extended credit for the first time to M Clothiers in the amount of $3,000. Ray also was not advised and did not in fact know of Marvin's retirement and the change of the partnership.

On February 1, Martin and Mark departed for parts unknown, leaving no partnership assets with which to pay the described debts. What is Marvin's liability, if any, (a) to Hill and (b) to Ray?

12. Ben, Dan, and Lilli were partners sharing profits in proportions of one-fourth, one-third, and five-twelfths, respectively. Their business failed, and the firm was dissolved. At the time of dissolution, no financial adjustments between the partners were necessary with reference to their respective partners' accounts, but the firm's liabilities to creditors exceeded its assets by $24,000. Without contributing any amount toward the payment of the liabilities, Dan moved to a destination unknown. Ben and Lilli are financially responsible. How much must each contribute?

13. Ames, Bell, and Cole were equal partners in the ABC Construction Company. Their written partnership agreement provided that the partnership would dissolve upon the death of any partner. Cole died on June 30, and his widow, Cora

Cole, qualified as executor of his will. Ames and Bell wound up the business of the partnership and on December 31 they completed the sale of all of the partnership's assets. After paying all partnership debts, they distributed the balance equally among themselves and Mrs. Cole as executor.

Subsequently, Mrs. Cole learned that Ames and Bell had made and withdrawn a net profit of $200,000 from July 1 to December 31. The profit was made through new contracts using the partnership name and assets. Ames and Bell had concealed such contracts and profit from Mrs. Cole, and she learned about them from other sources. Immediately after acquiring this information, Mrs. Cole made demand upon Ames and Bell for one-third of the profit of $200,000. They rejected her demand. What are the rights and remedies, if any, of Cora Cole as executor?

14. The articles of partnership of the firm of Wilson and Company provide the following:

> William Smith to contribute $50,000; to receive interest thereon at 13 percent per annum and to devote such time as he may be able to give; and to receive 30 percent of the profits.
>
> John Jones to contribute $50,000; to receive interest on same at 13 percent per annum; to give all of his time to the business; and to receive 30 percent of the profits.
>
> Henry Wilson to contribute all of his time to the business and to receive 20 percent of the profits.
>
> James Brown to contribute all of his time to the business and to receive 20 percent of the profits.

There is no provision for sharing losses. After six years of operation, the firm is dissolved and wound up. No distributions to partners have been made since the partnership was formed. The partnership assets are sold for $400,000 with a loss of $198,000. Liabilities to creditors total $420,000. What are the rights and liabilities of the respective parties?

15. Adam, Stanley, and Rosalind formed a partnership in State X to distribute beer and wine. Their agreement provided that the partnership would continue until December 31, 2018. Which of the following events would cause the partnership to dissolve? If so, when would the partnership be dissolved?
   a. Rosalind assigns her interest in the partnership to Mary on April 1, 2016.
   b. Stanley dies on June 1, 2018.
   c. Adam withdraws from the partnership on September 15, 2017.
   d. A creditor of Stanley obtains a charging order against Stanley's interest on October 9, 2015.
   e. In 2016, the legislature of State X enacts a statute making the sale or distribution of alcoholic beverages illegal.
   f. Stanley has a formal accounting of partnership affairs on September 19, 2017.

CASE PROBLEMS

16. Phillips and Harris are partners in a used car business. Under their oral partnership, each has an equal voice in the conduct and management of the business. Because of their irregular

business hours, the two further agreed that they could use any partnership vehicle as desired. This use includes transportation to and from work, even though the vehicles are for sale at all times. Harris conducted partnership business both at the used car lot and from his home. He was on call by Phillips or customers at his home, and he went back to the lot two or three times after going home. While driving a partnership vehicle home from the used car lot, Harris negligently hit a car driven by Cook, who brought this action against Harris and Phillips individually and as copartners for his injuries. Who is liable?

17. Voeller, the managing partner of the Pay-Out Drive-In Theater, signed a contract to sell to Hodge a small parcel of land belonging to the partnership. Except for the last twenty feet, which were necessary for the theater's driveway, the parcel was not used in theater operations. The agreement stated that it was between Hodge and the partnership, with Voeller signing for the partnership. Voeller claims that he told Hodge before signing that a plat plan would have to be approved by the other partners before the sale. Hodge denies this and sues for specific performance, claiming that Voeller had actual and apparent authority to bind the partnership. The partners argue that Voeller had no such authority and that Hodge knew this. Who is correct? Explain.

18. L. G. and S. L. Patel, husband and wife, owned and operated the City Center Motel in Eureka. On April 16, Rajeshkumar, the son of L. G. and S. L., formed a partnership with his parents and became owner of 35 percent of the City Center Motel. The partnership agreement required that Rajeshkumar approve any sale of the motel. Record title to the motel was not changed, however, to reflect his interest. On April 21, L. G. and S. L. listed their motel for sale with a real estate broker. On May 2, P. V. and Kirit Patel made an offer on the motel, which L. G. and S. L. accepted. Neither the broker nor the purchasers knew of the son's interest in the motel. When L. G. and S. L. notified Rajeshkumar of their plans, to their surprise, he refused to sell his 35 percent of the motel. On May 4, L. G. and S. L. notified P. V. and Kirit that they wished to withdraw their acceptance. They offered to pay $10,000 in damages and to give the purchasers a right of first refusal for five years. Rather than accept the offer, on May 29, P. V. and Kirit filed an action for specific performance and incidental damages. L. G., S. L., and Rajeshkumar responded that the contract could not lawfully be enforced. Discuss who will prevail and why.

19. Davis and Shipman founded a partnership under the name of Shipman & Davis Lumber Company. Seven years later, the partnership was dissolved by written agreement. Notice of the dissolution was published in a newspaper of general circulation in Merced County, where the business was conducted. No actual notice of dissolution was given to firms that previously had extended credit to the partnership. By the dissolution agreement, Shipman, who was to continue the business, was to pay all of the partnership's debts. He continued the business as a sole proprietorship for a short time until he formed a successor corporation, Shipman Lumber Servaes Co. After the partnership's dissolution, two firms that previously had done business with the partnership extended credit to Shipman for certain repair work and merchandise. The partnership also had a balance due to Valley Company for prior purchases. Five months later, two checks were drawn by Shipman Lumber Servaes Co. and accepted by Valley as partial payment on this debt. Credit Bureaus of Merced County, as assignee of these three accounts, sued the partnership as well as Shipman and Davis individually. Does the dissolution of the partnership relieve Davis of personal liability for the accounts? Explain.

20. In August Victoria Air Conditioning, Inc. (VAC), entered into a subcontract for insulation services with Southwest Texas Mechanical Insulation Company (SWT), a partnership composed of Charlie Jupe and Tommy Nabors. In February of the following year, Jupe and Nabors dissolved the partnership, but VAC did not receive notice of the dissolution at that time. Sometime later, insulation was removed from Nabors's premises to Jupe's possession and Jupe continued the insulation project with VAC. From then on, Nabors had no more involvement with SWT. One month later, Nabors informed VAC's project manager, Von Behrenfeld, that Nabors was no longer associated with SWT, had formed his own insulation company, and was interested in bidding on new jobs. Subsequently, SWT failed to perform the subcontract and Jupe could not be found. VAC brought suit for breach of contract against SWT, Jupe, and Nabors. Nabors claims that several letters and change orders introduced by both parties show that VAC knew of the dissolution and impliedly agreed to discharge Nabors from liability. These documents indicated that VAC had dealt with Jupe, but had not dealt with Nabors, after the dissolution. VAC denies that the course of dealings between VAC and Jupe was the type from which an agreement to discharge Nabors could be inferred. Who is correct? Explain.

TAKING SIDES

Stroud and Freeman are general partners in Stroud's Food Center, a grocery store. Nothing in the articles of partnership restricts the power or authority of either partner to act in respect to the ordinary business of the Food Center. In November, however, Stroud informed National Biscuit that he would not be personally responsible for any more bread sold to the partnership. Then, in the following February, at the request of Freeman, National Biscuit sold and delivered more bread to the Food Center.

a. What are the arguments that Stroud is not liable to National Biscuit for the value of the bread delivered to the Food Center?

b. What are the arguments that Stroud is liable to National Biscuit for the value of the bread delivered to the Food Center?

c. Explain which arguments should prevail.

Limited Partnerships and Limited Liability Companies

A limited partner is not liable for the obligations of a limited partnership.

Revised Uniform Limited Partnership Act

A member is not personally liable for a debt, obligation, or liability of the [limited liability] company.

Uniform Limited Liability Company Act

CHAPTER 32

CHAPTER OUTCOMES

After reading and studying this chapter, you should be able to:

1. Distinguish between a general partnership and a limited partnership.

2. Identify those activities in which a limited partner may engage without forfeiting limited liability.

3. Distinguish between a limited partnership and a limited liability company.

4. Distinguish between a member-managed limited liability company and a manager-managed limited liability company.

5. Distinguish between a limited liability partnership and a limited liability limited partnership.

I n this chapter, we will consider other types of unincorporated business associations: limited partnerships, limited liability companies, limited liability partnerships, and limited liability limited partnerships. These organizations have developed to meet special business and investment needs. Each has characteristics that make it appropriate for certain purposes.

LIMITED PARTNERSHIPS [32-1]

The limited partnership has proved to be an attractive vehicle for a variety of investments because of its tax advantages and the limited liability it confers upon the limited partners. Unlike general partnerships, limited partnerships are statutory creations. Before 1976, the governing statute in all states except Louisiana was the Uniform Limited Partnership Act (ULPA), which was promulgated in 1916. In 1976, the Uniform Law Commission (ULC) promulgated the Revised Uniform Limited Partnership Act (RULPA). In 1985, the ULC revised the RULPA; the resulting 1985 Act is substantially similar to the 1976 RULPA and does not alter its underlying philosophy or thrust. All states except Louisiana had adopted either the 1976 Act or the 1985 Act with a large majority of these states adopting the 1985 version.

In 2001, the ULC promulgated a new revision of the 1985 RULPA (the 2001 ReRULPA). The new Act has been drafted to reflect that limited liability partnerships and limited liability companies can meet many of the needs formerly met by limited partnerships. Accordingly, the 2001 ReRULPA adopts as default rules provisions that strongly favor current management and treat limited partners as passive investors with little control over or right to exit the limited partnership. At least eighteen states have adopted the 2001 ReRULPA.

In this chapter, we will discuss the 1985 RULPA. The ULPA, the 1976 RULPA, and the 1985 RULPA are supplemented by the Uniform Partnership Act, which applies to limited partnerships in any case for which the Limited Partnership Act does not provide. (The 2001 ReRULPA is a stand-alone statute and is not linked to the Uniform Partnership Act.) For a concise comparison of general and limited partnerships, see Concept Review 30-1.

In addition, limited partnership interests are almost always considered to be securities, and their sale is therefore subject to state and federal regulation, as we will discuss in Chapter 39.

Definition [32-1a]

A **limited partnership** is a partnership formed by two or more persons under the laws of a state and that has one or more general partners and one or more limited partners. A *person* includes a natural person, a partnership, a limited partnership, a trust, an estate, an association, or a corporation. Such a partnership differs from a general partnership in several respects, three of which are fundamental:

1. A statute providing for the formation of limited partnerships must be in effect.
2. The limited partnership must substantially comply with the requirements of that statute.
3. The liability of a limited partner for partnership debts or obligations is limited to the extent of the capital he has contributed or has agreed to contribute.

Formation [32-1b]

Although the **formation** of a *general* partnership requires no special procedures, the formation of a *limited* partnership requires substantial compliance with the limited partnership statute. Failure to comply may result in the limited partners not obtaining limited liability.

Filing of Certificate The RULPA provides that two or more persons desiring to form a limited partnership shall file in the office of the secretary of state of the state in which the limited partnership has its principal office a signed certificate of limited partnership. The certificate must include the following information: (1) the name of the limited partnership, (2) the address of its office and the name and address of the agent for service of process, (3) the name and the business address of each general partner, (4) the latest date upon which the limited partnership is to dissolve, and (5) any other matters the general partners decide to include in the certificate.

The certificate of limited partnership must be amended if a new general partner is admitted, a partner withdraws, or a general partner becomes aware that any statement in the certificate was or has become false. In addition, the certificate may be amended at any time for any other purpose the general partners deem proper. As discussed later, false statements in a certificate or amendment that cause loss to third parties who rely on the statements may result in liability for the general partners.

Name Including the surname of a limited partner in the partnership name is prohibited unless it is also the surname of a general partner or unless the business had been carried on under that name before the admission of that limited partner. A limited partner who knowingly permits his name to be used in violation of this provision is liable to any creditor who did not know that he was a limited partner. The RULPA also prohibits a partnership name that is the same as, or deceptively similar to, that of any corporation or other limited partnership. Finally, the name of the limited partnership must contain, unabbreviated, the words "limited partnership."

Contributions The **contribution** of a partner may be cash, property, services rendered, a promissory note, or an obligation to contribute cash or property or to perform services. A promise by a limited partner to contribute to the limited partnership is not enforceable unless it is in a signed writing. Should a partner fail to make a required capital contribution described in a signed writing, the limited partnership may hold her liable to contribute the cash value of the stated contribution.

Defective Formation A limited partnership is formed when a certificate of limited partnership that substantially complies with the statutory requirements is filed. Therefore, if no certificate is filed or if the certificate filed does not substantially meet the statutory requirements, the formation is defective. In either case, the limited liability of limited partners is jeopardized.

Limited partnership
a partnership formed by two or more persons under the laws of a state and having one or more general partners and one or more limited partners

Formation
a limited partnership can be formed only by substantial compliance with a state limited partnership statute

Filing of certificate
two or more persons must file a signed certificate of limited partnership

Name
inclusion of a limited partner's surname in the partnership name in most instances will result in the loss of the limited partner's limited liability

Contributions
may be cash; property; services; or a promise to contribute cash, property, or services

Defective formation
if no certificate is filed or if the one filed does not substantially meet the statutory requirements, the formation is defective and the limited liability of the limited partners is jeopardized

Practical Advice

To obtain limited liability as a limited partner, make sure that the limited partnership has been properly organized.

Foreign limited partnerships

a limited partnership is considered "foreign" in any state other than that in which it was formed

Rights

a general partner in a limited partnership has all the rights and powers of a partner in a general partnership

Practical Advice

When forming a limited partnership, carefully specify the rights and duties of the general and limited partners but be sure to adhere to the statutory limitations on the powers of limited partners.

Control

the general partners have almost exclusive control and management of the limited partnership; a limited partner who participates in the control of the limited partnership may lose limited liability

The RULPA provides that a person who has contributed to the capital of a business (an "equity participant"), believing erroneously and in good faith that he has become a limited partner in a limited partnership, is not liable as a general partner, provided that on ascertaining the mistake he either (1) withdraws from the business and renounces future profits or (2) files a certificate or an amendment curing the defect. However, the equity participant will be liable to any third party who transacted business with the enterprise before the withdrawal or amendment and who in good faith believed that the equity participant was a general partner at the time of the transaction.

The 1985 RULPA does not require that the limited partners be named in the certificate. This greatly reduces the risk that an inadvertent omission of such information will expose a limited partner to liability.

Foreign Limited Partnerships   A limited partnership is considered "foreign" in any state other than the one in which it was formed. The laws of the state in which a foreign limited partnership is organized govern its organization, its internal affairs, and the liability of its limited partners. In addition, the RULPA requires all foreign limited partnerships to register with the secretary of state before transacting any business in a state. Any foreign limited partnership transacting business without so registering may not bring enforcement actions in the state's courts until it registers, although it may defend itself in the state's courts.

Rights [32-1c]

Because limited partnerships are organized pursuant to statute, the rights of the parties are usually set forth in the articles of limited partnership and in the limited partnership agreement. Unless otherwise agreed or provided in the act, a general partner of a limited partnership has all the rights and powers of a partner in a partnership without limited partners. A general partner also may be a limited partner and thereby may also share in profits, losses, and distributions as a limited partner.

Control   The general partners of a limited partnership have almost exclusive control and management of the limited partnership. A limited partner, on the other hand, may not share in this management or control; if he does, he may forfeit his limited liability. A limited partner who participates in the control of the business is liable only to those persons who transact business with the limited partnership reasonably believing, based upon the limited partner's conduct, that the limited partner is a general partner.

Moreover, both versions of the RULPA provide a "safe harbor" by enumerating certain activities, any or all of which a limited partner may perform without being deemed to have participated in control of the business. They include (1) being a contractor for, or an agent or employee of, the limited partnership or a general partner; (2) consulting with and advising a general partner with respect to the business of the limited partnership; (3) acting as surety for the limited partnership; (4) approving or disapproving an amendment to the partnership agreement; and (5) voting on various fundamental changes in the limited partnership.

Alzado v. Blinder, Robinson & Company, Inc.
Supreme Court of Colorado, 1988
752 P.2d 544
http://scholar.google.com/scholar_case?case=5412987996095530695&q=752+P.2d+544&hl=en&as_sclt=2,34

FACTS   In 1979, Lyle Alzado, a former professional football player, and two business associates formed Combat Promotions, Inc., to promote an eight-round exhibition boxing match in Denver, Colorado, between Alzado and Muhammad Ali, a former world heavyweight champion boxer. Ali agreed to participate on the condition that prior to the match he would receive an irrevocable letter of credit guaranteeing payment of $250,000. Combat Promotions persuaded Blinder, Robinson & Company, Inc. (B-R) to put up the $250,000 letter of credit. B-R, however, insisted on several conditions. First, B-R required the formation of a limited partnership,

Combat Associates, with B-R as limited partner and Combat Promotions as general partner. Second, B-R required that the partnership agreement provide that the letter of credit be paid off as a partnership expense. Finally, B-R required Alzado's personal secured guarantee to reimburse B-R for any losses it might suffer. In a separate transaction Alzado signed an agreement with Combat Associates stating that he would be paid $100,000 for the match but subordinating that right to payment for expenses of the promotion.

B-R used its office as a ticket outlet, gave two parties to promote the exhibition match, and gave several promotional television interviews. Nonetheless, few tickets were sold, and the exhibition boxing match was a financial disaster. After Ali collected on the letter of credit as he was entitled to do, Combat Associates could pay B-R only $65,000, and paid nothing to Alzado or other creditors. B-R then sued Alzado for $185,000 in damages. Alzado counterclaimed, alleging that B-R should be deemed a general partner of Combat Associates and therefore liable to Alzado for $100,000. The jury awarded Alzado $92,500. B-R appealed, and the Colorado Court of Appeals reversed. Alzado then appealed to the Colorado Supreme Court.

DECISION Judgment of the Court of Appeals for Blinder, Robinson & Co., Inc., reversing the trial court's award to Alzado, affirmed.

OPINION A limited partner may become liable to partnership creditors as a general partner if the limited partner assumes control of partnership business. The Revised Uniform Limited Partnership Act (RULPA), however, allows a limited partner to participate in a number of activities without losing limited liability. Any determination of whether a limited partner's conduct

amounts to control over the partnership business requires analysis of several factors, including the purpose of the partnership, the administrative activities undertaken, the manner in which the partnership actually functioned, and the nature and frequency of the limited partner's activities.

B-R made no investment, accounting, or other financial decisions for the partnership, nor did B-R foster the appearance of being in control of the partnership. The evidence establishes at most that B-R engaged in a few promotional activities. It does not establish that B-R took part in management or control of the business affairs of Combat Associates. Rather B-R at all times remained a limited partner.

INTERPRETATION The RULPA permits limited partners to carry on certain specified activities without losing their limited liability.

CRITICAL THINKING QUESTION Do you agree that limited partners should forfeit their limited liability because they take part in control of the limited partnership? Explain.

Practical Advice

As a limited partner, exercise care not to take part in the control of the limited partnership beyond that which is legally permitted.

Choice of associates
no person may be added as a general partner or a limited partner without the consent of all partners

Withdrawal
a general partner may withdraw from a limited partnership at any time by giving written notice to the other partners; a limited partner may withdraw as provided in the limited partnership certificate

Assignment of partnership interest
unless otherwise provided in the partnership agreement, a partner may assign his partnership interest; an assignee may become a limited partner if all other partners consent

Voting Rights   The partnership agreement may grant to all or a specified group of general or limited partners the right to vote on any matter. If, however, the agreement grants limited partners voting powers beyond the Act's safe harbor provisions, a court may hold that the limited partners have participated in control of the business. The RULPA does not require that limited partners have the right to vote on matters as a class separate from the general partners, although the partnership agreement may provide such a right.

Choice of Associates   After the formation of a limited partnership, the admission of additional limited partners requires the written consent of all partners, unless the partnership agreement provides otherwise. Regarding additional general partners, the written partnership agreement determines the procedure for authorizing their admission. The written consent of all partners is required only if the partnership agreement fails to deal with this issue.

Withdrawal   A general partner may withdraw from a limited partnership at any time by giving written notice to the other partners. If the withdrawal violates the partnership agreement, the limited partnership may recover damages from the withdrawing general partner. A limited partner may withdraw as provided in the limited partnership certificate or, under the 1985 Act, the written partnership agreement. If the certificate (or written partnership agreement, under the 1985 Act) does not specify when a limited partner may withdraw or a definite time for the limited partnership's dissolution, a limited partner may withdraw upon giving at least six months' prior written notice to each general partner. Upon withdrawal, a withdrawing partner is entitled to receive any distribution to which she is entitled under the partnership agreement, subject to the amount restrictions discussed in the section on distributions. The partner is also entitled to receive the fair value of her interest in the limited partnership as of the date of withdrawal, based upon her right to share in distributions from the limited partnership, if the partnership agreement does not provide otherwise.

Assignment of Partnership Interest   A partnership interest is a partner's share of the profits and losses of a limited partnership and the right to receive distributions of partnership assets. A partnership interest is personal property. Unless the partnership agreement provides otherwise, a partner may assign his partnership interest. An assignment does not dissolve the limited partnership. The assignee does not become a partner and may not exercise any rights of a partner: the assignment entitles the assignee only to receive, to the extent of the assignment, the assigning partner's share of distributions. However, an assignee of a partnership interest, including an assignee of a general partner, may become a *limited* partner if all the other partners consent or if the assigning partner, having such power provided to her in the certificate (or in the partnership agreement, under the 1985 Act), grants the assignee this right. Except as otherwise provided in the partnership agreement, a partner ceases to be a partner upon assignment of all his partnership interest.

A creditor of a partner may obtain a charging order against a partner's interest in the partnership. To the extent of the charging order, the creditor has the rights of an assignee of the partnership interest.

Profit and Loss Sharing   The profits and losses are allocated among the partners as provided in the partnership agreement. If the partnership agreement makes no such provision in writing, the profits and losses are allocated on the basis of the value of the contributions each partner has actually made. Nonetheless, limited partners are usually not liable for losses beyond their capital contribution. The 1985 Act requires the agreement for sharing profits and losses to be in writing.

Distributions   The partners share **distributions** of cash or other assets of the limited partnership as provided in writing in the partnership agreement. The RULPA allows partners to share in distributions in a proportion different from that in which they share profits. If the partnership agreement does not allocate distributions in writing, they are made on the basis of the contributions each partner actually made. A partner who becomes entitled to a distribution has the status of a creditor with respect to that distribution. A partner may not receive a distribution from a limited partnership unless the limited partnership's assets after the distribution would be sufficient to pay all of its liabilities other than liabilities to partners on account of their partnership interests.

Loans   Both general and limited partners may be secured or unsecured creditors of the partnership with rights the same as those of a person who is not a partner, subject to applicable state and federal bankruptcy and fraudulent conveyance statutes.

Information   The partnership must continuously maintain within the state an office at which basic organizational and financial records are kept. Each partner has the right to inspect and copy any of the partnership records.

Derivative Actions   A limited partner has the right to bring an action on behalf of a limited partnership to recover a judgment in its favor if the general partners having authority to bring the action have refused to do so.

Duties and Liabilities [32-1d]

The duties and liabilities of general partners in a limited partnership are quite different from those of a limited partner. A general partner is subject to all the duties and restrictions of a partner in a partnership without limited partners, whereas a limited partner is subject to few, if any, duties and enjoys limited liability.

Duties   A *general partner* of a limited partnership has *a fiduciary* relationship to her general and limited partners. This fiduciary duty of the general partner is extremely important to the limited partners because of their circumscribed roles in the control and management of the business enterprise. Conversely, it remains unclear whether a limited partner owes a fiduciary duty to his general partners or to the limited partnership itself. The very limited judicial authority on this question seems to indicate that the limited partner does not.

The RULPA does not distinguish between the duty of care owed by a general partner to a general partnership and that owed by a general partner to a limited partnership. Thus, a general partner owes her partners a duty not to be grossly negligent, as discussed in Chapter 30. As in the next case, however, some courts have imposed upon general partners a higher duty of care toward *limited partners*. On the other hand, a limited partner owes no duty of care to a limited partnership as long as she remains a limited partner.

Profit and loss sharing
profits and losses are allocated among the partners as provided in the partnership agreement; if the partnership agreement has no such provision, then profits and losses are allocated on the basis of the contributions each partner actually made

Distributions
the partners share distributions of cash or other assets of a limited partnership as provided in the partnership agreement

Loans
both general and limited partners may be secured or unsecured creditors of the partnership

Information
each partner has the right to inspect and copy the partnership records

Derivative actions
a limited partner may sue on behalf of a limited partnership if the general partners refuse to bring the action

Duties
general partners owe a duty of care and loyalty (fiduciary duty) to the general partners, the limited partners, and the limited partnership; limited partners do not

Wyler v. Feuer
California Court of Appeal, Second District, Division 2, 1978
85 Cal.App.3d 392, 149 Cal.Rptr. 626
http://scholar.google.com/scholar_case?case=9054451800672347003&q=149+Cal.Rptr.+626&hl=en&as_sdt=2,34

FACTS Feuer and Martin, associated as Feuer and Martin Productions, Inc. (FMPI), had been successful producers of Broadway musical comedies. Their first motion picture, *Cabaret*, received eight Academy Awards in 1973. In 1972, FMPI bought the motion picture and television rights to Simone Berteaut's best-selling book about her life with her half-sister Edith Piaf. To finance a movie based on this novel, FMPI sought a substantial private investment from Wyler. In July 1973, Wyler signed a final limited partnership agreement with FMPI. The agreement stated that Wyler would provide, interest free, 100 percent financing for the proposed $1.6 million project in return for a certain portion of the profits, not to exceed 50 percent. In addition, FMPI would obtain $850,000 in production financing by September 30, 1973. The contract specifically provided that FMPI's failure to raise this amount by September 30, 1973, "shall not be deemed a breach of this agreement" and that Wyler's sole remedy would be a reduction in the producer's fee.

A year after its release in 1974, the motion picture proved less than an overwhelming success—costing $1.5 million and taking in total receipts of only $478,000. From the receipts, Wyler received $313,500 for his investment. FMPI had failed to obtain an amount even close to the required $850,000 for production financing. Wyler then sued Feuer, Martin, and FMPI for mismanagement of the limited partnership business and to recover his $1.5 million as damages. The trial court found in favor of Feuer, Martin, and FMPI.

DECISION Judgment for Feuer, Martin, and FMPI affirmed.

OPINION In a limited partnership, the limited partner restricts his liability to the amount of his capital investment. In return, the limited partner surrenders the right to manage and control the partnership business. The general partner owes to the limited partner a duty of reasonable care in his management of the business. But the general partner may not be held liable to the limited partner for mistakes made or losses incurred in the good faith exercise of reasonable business judgment.

Here, Wyler proved only that the motion picture did not make money, was not sought after by distributors, and did not live up to its producer's expectations. He failed to show that Feuer and Martin's decisions and efforts breached the standards of good faith and reasonableness. Therefore, he cannot recover damages from Feuer and Martin for an investment that simply turned sour.

INTERPRETATION A general partner is not liable for business losses if he or she conducts the business prudently and in good faith.

ETHICAL QUESTION Did the general partners act ethically? Explain.

CRITICAL THINKING QUESTION What standard of care should the general partners owe to the limited partners? Explain.

Liability of limited partners

the limited partners have limited liability (liability for partnership obligations only to the extent of the capital that the limited partner contributed or agreed to contribute)

Liabilities One of the most appealing features of a limited partnership is the limited personal liability it offers to limited partners. Limited liability means that a **limited partner** has liability for partnership obligations only to the extent of the capital that the limited partner contributed or agreed to contribute. Accordingly, a limited partner who has paid her contribution in full has no further liability to the limited partnership or its creditors. Thus, if a limited partner buys a 25 percent share of a limited partnership for $50,000 and does not forfeit limited liability, her liability is limited to the $50,000 contributed, even if the partnership suffers losses of $500,000.

This protection is subject to three conditions discussed earlier: (1) that the partnership has substantially complied in good faith with the requirement that a certificate of limited partnership be filed, (2) that the surname of the limited partner does not appear in the partnership name, and (3) that the limited partner does not take part in control of the business. In addition, if the certificate contains a false statement, anyone who suffers loss by reliance on that statement may hold liable any party to the certificate who knew the statement to be false when the certificate was executed. As long as the limited partner abides by these conditions, his liability for any and all obligations of the partnership is limited to his capital contribution.

Liability of general partners

the general partners have unlimited liability

At the same time, the **general partners** of a limited partnership have unlimited external liability, unless the limited partnership is a limited liability limited partnership, discussed later in this chapter. Also, any general partner who knew or should have known that the limited partnership certificate contained a false statement is liable to anyone who suffers loss by reliance on that false statement. Moreover, a general partner who knows or should know that a statement has become false, but who does not amend the certificate within a reasonable time, is liable as well. Accordingly, it has become a common practice for limited

---

CONCEPT REVIEW 32-1

Comparison of General and Limited Partners

	General Partner	Limited Partner
Control	Has all the rights and powers of a partner in a partnership without limited partners	Has no right to take part in management or control
Liability	Unlimited	Limited, unless partner takes part in control or partner's name is used
Agency	Is an agent of the partnership	Is not an agent of the partnership
Fiduciary Duty	Yes	No
Duty of Care	Yes	No

Practical Advice

Consider using a corporation as the sole general partner; then no natural person will be subject to unlimited, personal liability.

partnerships to be formed with a corporation or other limited liability entity as the sole general partner.

Any partner to whom any part of her contribution has been returned without violation of the partnership agreement or of the Limited Partnership Act is liable for one year to the limited partnership, to the extent necessary to pay creditors who extended credit during the period the partnership held the contribution. In contrast, any partner to whom any part of her contribution was returned in violation of the partnership agreement or the Limited Partnership Act is liable to the limited partnership for six years for the amount of the contribution wrongfully returned.

Dissolution [32-1e]

As with a general partnership, extinguishing a limited partnership involves three steps: (1) dissolution, (2) winding up or liquidation, and (3) termination. The causes of dissolution and the priorities in distributing the assets, however, differ somewhat from those in a general partnership.

Causes of dissolution the limited partners have neither the right nor the power to dissolve the partnership, except by decree of the court. The following events trigger a dissolution: (1) the expiration of the time period; (2) the withdrawal of a general partner, unless all partners agree to continue the business; or (3) a decree of judicial dissolution

Causes In a limited partnership, the limited partners have no right or power to dissolve the partnership, except by court decree. The death or bankruptcy of a limited partner does not dissolve the partnership. The RULPA specifies the events that will trigger a dissolution, after which the partnership affairs must be liquidated: (1) the expiration of the time period specified in the certificate; (2) the happening of events specified in writing in the partnership agreement; (3) the unanimous written consent of all the partners; (4) the withdrawal of a general partner, unless either (a) there is at least one other general partner and the written provisions of the partnership agreement permit the remaining general partners to continue the business or (b) within ninety days all partners agree in writing to continue the business; or (5) a decree of judicial dissolution, which may be granted whenever it is not reasonably practicable to carry on the business in conformity with the partnership agreement. A general partner's withdrawal includes his retirement, the assignment of all his general partnership interest, removal, bankruptcy, death, and adjudication of incompetency. A certificate of cancellation must be filed when the limited partnership dissolves and winding up commences.

Winding up unless otherwise provided in the partnership agreement, the general partners who have not wrongfully dissolved the partnership may wind up its affairs

Winding Up Unless otherwise provided in the partnership agreement, the general partners who have not wrongfully dissolved the limited partnership may wind up its affairs. The limited partners may wind up the limited partnership if the general partners all have wrongfully dissolved the partnership. But, by showing cause, any partner, his legal representative, or his assignee may obtain a winding up by the court.

Distribution of assets

the priorities for distribution are as follows: (1) creditors, including partners who are creditors; (2) partners and ex-partners in satisfaction of liabilities for unpaid distributions; (3) partners for the return of contributions, except as otherwise agreed; and (4) partners for their partnership interests in the proportions in which they share in distributions, except as otherwise agreed

Distribution of Assets   The priorities in distributing the assets of a limited partnership are as follows:

1. to creditors, including partners who are creditors except with respect to liabilities for distributions;
2. to partners and ex-partners in satisfaction of liabilities for unpaid distributions;
3. to partners for the return of their contributions, except as otherwise agreed; and
4. to partners for their partnership interests in the proportions in which they share in distributions, except as otherwise agreed.

General and limited partners rank equally unless the partnership agreement provides otherwise.

LIMITED LIABILITY COMPANIES [32-2]

A limited liability company (LLC) is another form of unincorporated business association. Prior to 1990, only two states had statutes permitting LLCs. By 1996 all states had enacted LLC statutes. Since then many states have amended or revised their LLC statutes. Until 1995, there was no uniform statute on which states might base their LLC legislation, and only a few states have adopted the Uniform Limited Liability Company Act (ULLCA), which was amended in 1996. In 2006 the Revised ULLCA was completed and at least ten states have adopted it. Therefore, LLC statutes vary from state to state with respect to such matters as LLC management, admission and withdrawal of members, power of members and managers to bind the LLC, duties imposed on managers and members, and the LLC's right to merge with other business entities. Nevertheless, LLC statutes generally share certain characteristics.

Limited liability company

a noncorporate business organization that provides limited liability to all of its owners (members) and permits all of its members to participate in management of the business

A **limited liability company** is a noncorporate business organization that provides limited liability to *all* of its owners (members) and permits all of its members to participate in management of the business. It may elect not to be a separate taxable entity, in which case only the members are taxed. (Publicly traded LLCs, however, are subject to corporate income taxation.) If an LLC has only one member, it will be taxed as a sole proprietorship, unless separate entity tax treatment is elected. Thus, the LLC provides many of the advantages of a general partnership plus limited liability for all its members. Its benefits outweigh those of a limited partnership in that all members of an LLC not only enjoy limited liability but also may participate in management and control of the business. (See Concept Review 30-1.) LLCs have become the most popular and widely used unincorporated business form. The most frequent use of LLCs has been in real estate transactions, professional services, construction, finance, and retail. Ownership interests in an LLC *may* be considered to be securities, especially interests in those LLCs operated by managers. If a particular LLC interest is considered a security, its sale would be subject to state and federal securities regulation, as discussed in Chapter 39.

Formation [32-2a]

Formation

the formation of a limited liability company requires substantial compliance with a state's limited liability company statute

The **formation** of an LLC requires substantial compliance with the state's LLC statute. All states permit an LLC to have only one member. Once formed, an LLC is a separate legal entity that is distinct from its members, who are normally not liable for its debts and obligations. An LLC can contract in its own name and is generally permitted to carry on any "lawful purpose," although some statutes restrict the permissible activities of LLCs.

Members   LLC statutes permit members to include individuals, corporations, general partnerships, limited partnerships, limited liability companies, trusts, estates, and other associations. LLC statutes differ concerning the procedure for adding members after an LLC has been formed.

Filing   The LLC statutes generally require the central public filing of articles of organization in a designated state office. The states vary regarding the information they require the articles to include, but all require at least the following: (1) the name of the firm, (2) the address of the principal place of business or registered office, and (3) the name and address of the agent for service of process. The articles may also include any provision consistent with law for regulating internal LLC matters.

Practical Advice

To obtain limited liability as a member of a limited liability company, make sure that the LLC has been properly organized.

Name

LLC statutes require the name of the LLC to include the words "limited liability company" or the abbreviation "LLC"

Contribution

the contribution of a member to a limited liability company may be cash, property, services rendered, a promissory note, or other obligation to contribute cash or property or to perform services

Foreign limited liability companies

a limited liability company is considered "foreign" in any state other than that in which it was formed

Rights of members

a member's interest in the LLC includes the financial interest (the right to distributions) and the management interest (which consists of all other rights granted to a member by the LLC operating agreement and the LLC statute)

Distributions

the members share distributions of cash or other assets of a limited liability company as provided in the operating agreement; if the LLC's operating agreement does not allocate distributions, in most states they are made on the basis of the contributions each member made

Most LLC statutes provide that the acceptance for filing is conclusive evidence that the LLC has been properly formed, except against the state in an involuntary dissolution or certificate revocation proceeding. Most LLC statutes require the articles to state whether the LLC will be managed by managers, who may, but need not, be members. Most states provide that LLCs have perpetual existence unless the members agree otherwise. The articles of organization may be amended by filing articles of amendment. In most states, LLCs must file annual reports with the state.

Name   LLC statutes require the **name** of the LLC to include the words "limited liability company" or the abbreviation "LLC." The name of the LLC must be distinguishable from other firms doing business within the state.

Contribution   In most states the **contribution** of a member to an LLC may be cash, property, services rendered, a promissory note, or other obligation to contribute cash or property or to perform services. Most LLC statutes require both a written agreement to make a contribution and a written record of contributions. Members are liable to the LLC for failing to make an agreed contribution.

Operating Agreement   The members of most LLCs adopt an operating agreement, which is the basic contract among the members governing the affairs of an LLC and stating the various rights and duties of the members and any managers. The operating agreement is subordinate to federal and state law. LLC statutes generally do not require the operating agreement to be in writing, although this is strongly recommended. In addition, some statutes permit modification of certain statutory rules to be only by written provision in an operating agreement. Unless the operating agreement provides otherwise, the members may amend it only by unanimous consent.

Foreign Limited Liability Companies   An LLC is considered "foreign" in any state other than that in which it was formed. LLC statutes provide that the laws of the state in which a foreign LLC is organized govern its organization, its internal affairs, and the liability of its members and managers. Foreign LLCs, however, generally are not permitted to transact business that domestic LLCs may not transact. Foreign LLCs must register with the secretary of state before transacting any business in a state. Any foreign LLC transacting business without so registering may not bring enforcement actions in the state's courts until it registers, although it may defend itself in the state's courts. Moreover, states generally impose fines and penalties on unregistered foreign LLCs that transact business in the state.

Rights of Members [32-2b]

A member has no property interest in property owned by the LLC. On the other hand, a member does have an interest in the LLC, which is personal property. A member's interest in the LLC includes two components:

1. the *financial interest*, which is the right to share profits and to receive distributions; and
2. the *management interest*, which consists of all other rights granted to a member by the LLC operating agreement and the LLC statute. The management interest typically includes the right to manage, vote, obtain information, and bring enforcement actions.

Profit and Loss Sharing   The LLC's operating agreement determines how the partners allocate the profits and losses. If the LLC's operating agreement makes no such provision, in most states the profits and losses are allocated on the basis of the value of the members' contributions. A few states follow the partnership model under which profits are divided equally.

Distributions   LLC statutes do not provide LLC members the right to distributions before withdrawal from the LLC. Therefore, the members share distributions of cash or other assets of an LLC as provided in the operating agreement. If the LLC's operating agreement does not allocate distributions, in most states they are made on the basis of the contributions each member made. All LLC statutes impose liability on members who receive wrongful distributions; some statutes also impose liability on members and managers who approved the wrongful distributions. The statutes vary in defining what constitutes a wrongful distribution, but most make a distribution wrongful if the LLC is insolvent or if the distribution would make the LLC insolvent. In most states, members are liable whether or not they knew that the distribution was wrongful.

Withdrawal

a member may withdraw and demand payment of her interest upon giving the notice specified in the statute or the LLC's operating agreement

Withdrawal   Some statutes permit a member to withdraw and demand payment of her interest upon giving the notice specified in the statute or the LLC's operating agreement. Some of the statutes permit the operating agreement to deny members the right to withdraw from the LLC.

Management

in the absence of a contrary agreement, each member has equal rights in the management of the LLC; but LLCs may be managed by one or more managers who may be members

Management   Nearly all LLC statutes provide that, in the absence of a contrary agreement, each member has equal rights in the management of the LLC. All LLC statutes permit LLCs to be managed by one or more managers who may, but need not, be members. LLC statutes generally provide that the members select the managers. In a member-managed LLC, the members have actual and apparent authority to bind the LLC. In a manager-managed LLC, the managers have this authority, while the members have no actual or apparent authority to bind the manager-managed LLC. Most statutes require a publicly filed document to elect a manager-managed structure; a few statutes permit the operating agreement to make that election.

Taghipour v. Jerez
Supreme Court of Utah, 2002
2002 UT 74, 52 P.3d 1252
http://scholar.google.com/scholar_case?case=12865993038128465710&q=52+p.3d+1252&hl=en&as_sdt=2,34

FACTS Namvar Taghipour, Danesh Rahemi, and Edgar Jerez formed a limited liability company (the LLC), on August 30, 1994, to purchase and develop a parcel of real estate. The LLC's articles of organization designated Jerez as the LLC's manager. In addition, the written operating agreement among the members of the LLC provided: "No loans may be contracted on behalf of the [LLC] … unless authorized by a resolution of the members."

On August 31, 1994, the LLC acquired the intended real estate. On January 10, 1997, Jerez, without the knowledge of the LLC's other members, entered into a loan agreement on behalf of the LLC with Mount Olympus. According to the loan agreement, Mount Olympus lent the LLC $25,000 and, as security for the loan, Jerez executed and delivered a trust deed on the LLC's real estate property. Mount Olympus then dispensed $20,000 to Jerez and retained the $5,000 balance to cover various fees. In making the loan, Mount Olympus did not investigate Jerez's authority to enter into the loan agreement beyond determining that Jerez was the manager of the LLC.

Jerez absconded with the $20,000. The LLC never made payments on the loan, since it was unaware of the loan, and consequently defaulted. Mount Olympus then foreclosed on the LLC's property giving notice of the default and pending foreclosure sale to only Jerez.

On June 18, 1999, Namvar Taghipour, Danesh Rahemi, and the LLC (collectively, Taghipour) filed suit against Mount Olympus and Jerez seeking that the loan agreement and the foreclosure be declared invalid because Jerez lacked the authority to bind the LLC. Mount Olympus moved to dismiss asserting that

the loan agreement documents are valid and binding on the LLC since they were signed by the LLC's manager. Utah Code section 48-2b-127(2) provides

> Instruments and documents providing for the acquisition, mortgage, or disposition of property of the limited liability company shall be valid and binding upon the limited liability company if they are executed by one or more managers of a limited liability company having a manager or managers or if they are executed by one or more members of a limited liability company in which management has been retained by the members.

The trial court granted Mount Olympus' motion to dismiss. Taghipour appealed to the Utah Court of Appeals. Taghipour argued that the trial court failed to consider Utah Code section 48-2b-125(2)(b), which provides that a manager's authority to bind a limited liability company can be limited by the operating agreement.

The Utah Court of Appeals affirmed the trial court, concluding that the plain language of section 48-2b-127(2) provided no limitation on a manager's authority to execute certain documents and bind a limited liability company. The Supreme Court of Utah granted Taghipour's petition for *certiorari*.

DECISION Judgment is affirmed.

OPINION When two statutory provisions purport to cover the same subject, the legislature's intent must be considered in determining which provision applies. To determine that intent, rules of statutory construction provide that "when two statutory provisions conflict in their operation, the provision more specific in application governs over the more general provision." Section 48-2b-127(2) is the more specific provision. In this case Jerez was designated as the LLC's manager in the articles of organization. Jerez, acting in his capacity as manager, executed loan agreement documents, for example, the trust deed and trust deed note, on behalf of the LLC that are specifically covered by section 48-2b-127(2). As such, these documents are valid and binding on the LLC. Therefore, the court of appeals correctly concluded that the LLC was bound by the loan agreement and, consequently, that Mount Olympus was not liable to Taghipour for Jerez's actions.

INTERPRETATION In a manager-managed LLC, the managers have actual and apparent authority to bind the LLC.

CRITICAL THINKING QUESTION Given this provision of Utah's LLC statute, is there any way that the members of the LLC could have protected themselves?

Voting

Most LLC statutes specify the voting rights of members, subject to a contrary provision in an LLC's operating agreement

Voting   Most of the LLC statutes specify the voting rights of members, subject to a contrary provision in an LLC's operating agreement. In most states the default rule for voting follows a corporate approach (voting is based on the financial interests of members), while a few states take a partnership approach (each member has equal voting rights). Typically, members have the right to vote on proposals to (1) adopt or amend the operating agreement, (2) admit any person as a member, (3) sell all or substantially all of the LLC's assets prior to dissolution, and (4) merge the LLC with another LLC or other business entity. Some LLC statutes authorize voting by proxy. A **proxy** is a member's authorization to an agent to vote for the member.

Information

LLCs must keep basic organizational and financial records; each member has the right to inspect and copy the LLC records

Information   The LLC must keep basic organizational and financial records. Each member has the right to inspect and copy the LLC records.

Derivative actions

a member has the right to bring an action on behalf of a limited liability company to recover a judgment in its favor if the managers or members with authority to bring the action have refused to do so

Derivative Actions   A member has the right to bring an action on behalf of an LLC to recover a judgment in its favor if the managers or members with authority to bring the action have refused to do so.

Assignment of LLC interest

unless otherwise provided in the LLC's operating agreement, a member may assign his financial interest in the LLC; an assignee of a financial interest in an LLC may acquire the other rights by being admitted as a member of the company if all the remaining members consent or the operating agreement so provides

Assignment of LLC Interest   Unless otherwise provided in the LLC's operating agreement, a member may assign his financial interest in the LLC. An assignment does not dissolve the LLC. The assignment entitles the assignee to receive, to the extent of the assignment, only the assigning member's share of distributions. A judgment creditor of a member may obtain a charging order against the member's financial interest in the LLC. The charging order gives the creditor the same rights as an assignee to the extent of the interest charged.

The assignee does not become a member and may not exercise any rights of a member. However, an assignee of a financial interest in an LLC may acquire the other rights by being admitted as a member of the company by all the remaining members. (Some states allow admission by majority vote.) In most states this unanimous acceptance rule is now a default rule, and the operating agreement may eliminate or modify it.

Duties [32-2c]

As with general partnerships and limited partnerships, the duties of care and loyalty also apply to LLCs. In most states, the LLC statute expressly imposes these duties. In other states, the common law imposes these duties. Many statutes also expressly impose an obligation of good faith and fair dealing. Who has these duties in an LLC depends on whether the LLC is a manager-managed LLC (analogous to a limited partnership) or a member-managed LLC (analogous to a partnership).

Manager-managed LLCs

the managers of manager-managed LLCs have a duty of care and loyalty; usually, members of a manager-managed LLC have no duties to the LLC or its members by reason of being a member

Manager-Managed LLCs   All LLC statutes either permit or require LLCs to be managed by one or more managers selected by the members. Most LLC statutes impose upon the managers of an LLC a duty of care. In some states, this is a duty to refrain from grossly negligent, reckless, or intentional conduct; in other states, it is a duty to act in good faith and as a prudent person would in similar circumstances. Managers also have a fiduciary duty, although the statutes vary in how they specify that duty. Usually, members of manager-managed LLCs have no duties to the LLC or its members by reason of being a member.

APPLYING THE LAW

Limited Partnerships and Limited Liability Companies

Facts Rustin was a member of a limited liability company (LLC) called Global Trade, LLC, which refurbished and exported used construction equipment to foreign buyers. When Rustin and his wife divorced, they entered into a property settlement agreement, which divided up their assets and liabilities in a mutually acceptable manner. As part of this contract, Rustin assigned his membership in Global Trade to his ex-wife, Fanning. Rustin's divorce lawyer notified Global Trade of the assignment to Fanning and provided a copy of the court order approving the property settlement to Global Trade's manager. The LLC's operating agreement is silent with respect to transfers of a member's interest.

Fanning subsequently declared herself a member of Global Trade. As such, she requested detailed information about a proposed merger of Global Trade with one of its primary suppliers and demanded permission to attend a meeting of Global Trade's members, at which they anticipated discussing and voting on the proposed merger. Global Trade's members declined to give her the requested information and denied her access to the meeting at which they approved the merger.

Issue Did Rustin's assignment to Fanning make her a member of the LLC?

Rule of Law Members of an LLC own an interest in the entity, which is personal property. A member's interest in the LLC consists of two components: a financial interest and a management interest. The financial interest is a right to share profits and to receive distributions only. The management interest is the bundle of remaining member rights, including the right to manage, right to be informed, and right to vote. Members may assign their financial interest unless the operating agreement provides otherwise. On the other hand, members may assign their management interest *only* if the operating agreement expressly provides members that right. Otherwise, an assignee of an interest in an LLC will become a member only if the remaining members consent to admit her.

Application As a member of Global Trade, LLC, Rustin had two distinct membership interests—the financial interest and the management interest. Because of the nature of LLCs, both of these membership rights are necessarily shaped and constrained by the terms of the relevant operating agreement and state LLC statute. In this case, the operating agreement said nothing about transfers of members' interests. Therefore, by default, Rustin's assignment is only of his financial interest.

This result is reinforced by the fact that, with notice of Rustin's assignment to her, the members denied Fanning access to their meeting. An assignee of a financial interest in an LLC, like Fanning, can acquire a management interest if the other members of the LLC consent to her membership. Here, it is unclear whether the members formally voted on the question of whether Fanning should be admitted to the LLC. Nonetheless, because they denied her request for information and excluded her from the merger meeting, it is apparent that they are unwilling to consent to her admission as a member.

Conclusion Fanning did not become a member of Global Trade, LLC, by virtue of Rustin's assignment. Instead, she gained only the right to Rustin's share of distributions from the LLC.

Member-managed LLCs members of member-managed LLCs have the same duties of care and loyalty that managers have in manager-managed LLCs

---

Practical Advice

Recognize that your rights and duties as a member of a limited liability company depend on whether the LLC is member managed or manager managed.

Member-Managed LLCs   Members of member-managed LLCs have the same duties of care and loyalty that managers have in manager-managed LLCs.

Liabilities [32-2d]

One of the most appealing features of an LLC is the limited personal liability it offers to all of its members and managers. LLC statutes typically provide that no member or manager of an LLC shall be obligated personally for any debt, obligation, or liability of the LLC solely by reason of being a member or acting as a manager of the LLC. The general rule that members and managers are not personally liable for the LLC's obligations is subject to a number of exceptions.

1. Because persons are always individually liable for their own torts, a member or manager who committed the wrongful act giving rise to the liability is personally liable for that LLC obligation.
2. A member or manager is personally liable for any LLC obligations guaranteed by the member or manager.
3. LLC statutes generally state that persons who assume to act as an LLC prior to formation or without authority to do so are jointly and severally liable for all debts and liabilities.
4. As mentioned previously, a member who fails to make an agreed contribution is liable to the LLC for the deficiency.

CONCEPT REVIEW 32-2

Comparison of Member-Managed and Manager-Managed LLCs

	Member of Member-Managed LLC Manager of Manager-Managed LLC	Member of Manager-Managed LLC
Control	Full	None
Liability	Limited	Limited
Agency	Is an agent of the LLC	Is not an agent of the LLC
Fiduciary Duty	Yes	No
Duty of Care	Yes	No

Note: LLC = limited liability company.

5. Under the doctrine of *piercing the corporate veil*, members may be held personally liable for the LLC's debts, obligations, or liabilities under certain circumstances. (This doctrine is covered more fully in Chapter 33.) Courts pierce the corporate (company) veil and hold LLC members personally liable for LLC obligations in cases in which the members (a) have not conducted the business on a company basis by failing to observe company formalities, (b) have not provided the LLC an adequate financial basis for the business, or (c) have used the LLC to defraud.

6. A member who receives a distribution or return of her contribution in violation of the LLC's operating agreement or the LLC statute is liable to the LLC for the amount of the contribution wrongfully returned.

Estate of Countryman v. Farmers Coop. Ass'n
Supreme Court of Iowa, 2004
679 N.W.2d 598
http://scholar.google.com/scholar_case?case=12820500586608385138&q=679+n.w.2d+598&hl=en&as_sdt=2,34

FACTS In the afternoon of September 6, 1999, an explosion leveled the home of Jerry Usovsky in Richland, Iowa, killing seven people who had gathered in the home to celebrate the Labor Day holiday. Six others were injured, some seriously. The likely cause of the explosion was stray propane gas. The survivors and executors of the estates of those who died filed a lawsuit based on negligence, breach of warranty, and strict liability against a number of defendants, including Iowa Double Circle, L.C. (Double Circle) and Farmers Cooperative Association of Keota (Keota).

Double Circle, is an Iowa limited liability company (LLC). It is a supplier of propane and delivered propane to Usovsky's home prior to the explosion. Keota is one of two members in Double Circle. It owns a 95 percent interest in the company. The other member is Farmland Industries, Inc. (Farmland Industries), a regional cooperative. Keota is a farm cooperative that provides a variety of farm products and services to area farmers. It is a member of Farmland Industries and is managed by Dave Hopscheidt (Hopscheidt). The executive committee of Keota's board of directors serves as the board of directors of Double Circle, along with a representative of Farmland Industries. Keota provides managerial services to Double Circle, pursuant to a management agreement

between Keota and Double Circle. Keota's duties under the agreement include "human resource and safety management." Hopscheidt oversees the daily operations of both Keota and Double Circle. However, Keota and Double Circle operate as separate entities and maintain separate finances. The plaintiffs alleged that Keota participated in the claimed wrongdoing through the management decisions it made in consumer safety matters.

The trial court found that plaintiffs failed to produce any facts to show that Keota engaged in conduct separate from its duties as director or manager of Double Circle. Consequently, it concluded Keota was protected as a matter of law from personal liability for claims of wrongful conduct attributable to Double Circle and granted summary judgment for Keota. Plaintiffs appealed.

DECISION Summary judgment is reversed and case remanded.

OPINION The LLC is a hybrid business entity that is considered to have the attributes of a partnership for federal income tax purposes and the limited liability protections of a corporation. As such, it provides for the operational advantages of a partnership by allowing the owners, called members, to participate in the management of the business. Yet, the members and managers are protected from liability in the same manner shareholders, officers, and directors of a corporation are protected.

The rules of personal liability under the Iowa Limited Liability Company Act (ILLCA) have been summarized as follows:

> Sections … of the Act generally provide that a member or manager of a limited liability company is not personally liable for acts or debts of the company solely by reason of being a member or manager, except in the following situations: (1) the ILLCA expressly provides for the person's liability; (2) the articles of organization provide for the person's liability; (3) the person has agreed in writing to be personally liable; (4) the person participates in tortious conduct; or (5) a shareholder of a corporation would be personally liable in the same situation, except that the failure to hold meetings and related formalities shall not be considered.

While liability of members and managers is limited, the statute clearly imposes liability when they participate in tortious conduct. This approach is compatible with the longstanding approach to liability in corporate settings, in which case, under general agency principles, corporate officers and directors can be liable for their torts even when committed in their capacity as an officer. The "participation in tortious conduct" standard would not impose tort liability on a manager for merely performing a general administrative duty. There must be some participation; liability is derived from individual activities. The ILLCA does not insulate a manager from liability for participation in tortious conduct merely because the conduct occurs within the scope and role as a manager. The statutory limit on liability created for members and managers of LLCs means members and managers are not liable for company torts "solely by reason of being a member or manager" of an LLC. Keota is not protected from liability if it participated in tortious conduct in performing its duties as manager of Double Circle.

INTERPRETATION Members and managers of an LLC are not liable for company torts solely by reason of being a member or manager of an LLC, but a member or manager of an LLC who takes part in the commission of a tort is liable even when the member or manager acts on behalf of the LLC.

CRITICAL THINKING QUESTION What can members and managers of LLCs do to limit their personal liability for acting on behalf of the LLC? Explain.

Dissolution

an LLC will automatically dissolve upon (1) in some states the dissociation of a member if the remaining members do *not* choose to continue the LLC, (2) the expiration of any LLC's agreed duration or the happening of any of the events specified in the articles, (3) the written consent of all the members, or (4) a decree of judicial dissolution

Dissolution [32-2e]

Extinguishing an LLC involves three steps: (1) dissolution, (2) winding up or liquidation, and (3) termination. LLC statutes require a public filing in connection with dissolution. For example, after winding up the company, some LLC statutes provide for the filing of articles of dissolution stating (1) the name of the company, (2) the date of the dissolution, and (3) that the company's business has been wound up and the legal existence of the company has been terminated. Other statutes require either (1) a public filing of the intent to dissolve at the time of dissolution or (2) filings at both the time of dissolution and after winding up.

Causes   Most LLC statutes no longer require that LLCs dissolve at the end of a stated term. Moreover, LLC statutes either (1) provide that a member's dissociation does *not* cause dissolution or (2) permit the remaining members, by either unanimous or majority vote, to avoid dissolution upon a member's disassociation. LLC statutes generally provide that an LLC will automatically dissolve upon the following:

1. the expiring of the LLC's agreed duration, if any, or the happening of any of the events specified in the articles,
2. the written consent of all the members, or
3. a decree of judicial dissolution typically on the grounds that "it is not reasonably practicable to carry on the limited liability company's activities in conformity with the articles of organization and the operating agreement" or, under some statutes, the members or managers have acted illegally, fraudulently, or oppressively.

In the Matter of 1545 Ocean Ave., LLC
Appellate Division of the Supreme Court of New York, Second Department, 2010
72 A.D.3d 121, 893 N.Y.S.2d 590
http://scholar.google.com/scholar_case?q=893+N.Y.S.2d+590&hl=en&as_sdt=2,34&case=6048414753116119174&scilh=0

FACTS 1545 LLC was formed in November 2006 by its two members Crown Royal Ventures, LLC (Crown Royal) and Ocean Suffolk Properties, LLC (Ocean Suffolk) who executed an operating agreement that provided for two managers: Walter T. Van Houten (Van Houten), who was a member of Ocean Suffolk, and John J. King, who was a member of Crown Royal. Each member of 1545 LLC contributed 50 percent of the capital, which was used to purchase premises known as 1545 Ocean Avenue in Bohemia,

New York on January 5, 2007. 1545 LLC was formed to purchase the property, rehabilitate an existing building, and build a second building for commercial rental. Van Houten, who owns a construction company, Van Houten Construction (VHC), was permitted to submit bids for the project, subject to the approval of the managers.

Article 4.1 of the operating agreement provides that "[a]t any time when there is more than one Manager, any one Manager may take any action permitted under the Agreement, unless the approval of more than one of the Managers is expressly required pursuant to the [operating agreement] or the [Limited Liability Company Law]."

Article 4.12 of the operating agreement entitled, "Regular Meetings," does not require meetings of the managers with any particular regularity. Meetings may be called without notice as the managers may "from time to time determine."

The managers disagreed about various aspects of the construction work performed on the LLC property by VHC, which billed 1545 LLC the sum of $97,322.27 for this work. King claims that he agreed 1545 LLC would pay VHC's invoice on the condition that VHC would no longer unilaterally do work on the site. Notwithstanding King's demand, VHC continued working on the site. Despite his earlier protests, King did nothing to stop it. The managers also disagreed about which company to hire to perform environmental remediation work on the site.

King contended that thereafter tensions between King and Van Houten escalated and that Van Houten refused to meet on a regular basis, proclaiming himself to be a "cowboy" and would "just get it done." Nevertheless, King acknowledged that the construction work undertaken by VHC was "awesome." By April 2007, King announced that he wanted to withdraw his investment from 1545 LLC. He proposed to have all vendors so notified telling them that Van Houten was taking over the management of 1545 LLC. As a result, Van Houten viewed King as having resigned as a manager of 1545 LLC.

Ultimately, King sought to have Ocean Suffolk buy out Crown Royal's membership in 1545 LLC or, alternatively, to have Crown Royal buy out Ocean Suffolk. Despite discussions regarding competing proposals for the buyout of the interest of each member by the other member, no satisfactory resolution was realized. During this period of disagreements, VHC continued to work unilaterally on the site so that the project was within weeks of completion when Crown Royal filed a petition to dissolve 1545 LLC. The sole ground for dissolution cited by Crown Royal was deadlock between the managing members arising from Van Houten's alleged violations of various provisions of article 4 of the operating agreement. The trial court granted the petition of Crown Royal to dissolve 1545 Ocean Avenue, LLC. Ocean Suffolk appealed.

DECISION Order of the trial court is reversed, the petition is denied, and the proceeding is dismissed.

OPINION Limited Liability Company Law § 702 is clear that the court must first examine the limited liability company's operating agreement to determine, in light of the circumstances presented, whether it is or is not "reasonably practicable" for the limited liability company to continue to carry on its business in conformity with the operating agreement.

If an operating agreement, such as that of 1545 LLC, does not address certain topics, a limited liability company is bound by the default requirements set forth in the Limited Liability Company Law. The operating agreement of 1545 LLC does not contain any specific provisions relating to dissolution.

Crown Royal argues for dissolution based on the parties' failure to hold regular meetings, failure to achieve quorums, and deadlock. The operating agreement, however, does not require regular meetings or quorums. It only provides for meetings to be held at such times as the managers may "from time to time determine." The record demonstrates that the managers, King and Van Houten, communicated with each other on a regular basis without the formality of a noticed meeting which appears to conform with the spirit and letter of the operating agreement and the continued ability of 1545 LLC to function in that context.

The only basis for dissolution can be if 1545 LLC cannot effectively operate under the operating agreement to meet and achieve the purpose for which it was created. In this case, that is the development of the property which purpose, despite the disagreements between the managing members, was being met.

Here, the operating agreement avoids the possibility of "deadlock" by permitting each managing member to operate unilaterally in furtherance of 1545 LLC's purpose.

Under the "not reasonably practicable" standard for dissolution of a limited liability company pursuant to Limited Liability Company Law § 702, the petitioning member must establish, in the context of the terms of the operating agreement, that (1) the management of the entity is unable or unwilling to reasonably permit or promote the stated purpose of the entity to be realized or achieved, or (2) continuing the entity is financially unfeasible.

Dissolution is a drastic remedy, and the petitioner has failed to meet the standard for dissolution enunciated here.

INTERPRETATION Judicial dissolution of a limited liability company requires that (1) the management of the entity is unable or unwilling reasonably to permit or promote the stated purpose of the entity to be realized or achieved, or (2) continuing the entity is financially unfeasible.

CRITICAL THINKING QUESTION When should a court grant judicial dissolution of a limited liability company? Explain.

Dissociation

Dissociation means that a member has ceased to be associated with the company and includes voluntary withdrawal, death, incompetence, expulsion, or bankruptcy

Dissociation Dissociation means that a member has ceased to be associated with the company and includes voluntary withdrawal, death, incompetence, expulsion, or bankruptcy. Some LLC states have eliminated a member's dissociation as a mandatory cause of dissolution. Other LLC statutes permit the remaining members, by either unanimous or majority vote, to avoid dissolution upon a member's disassociation.

Winding up

completing unfinished business, collecting debts, and distributing assets to creditors and members; also called liquidation

Winding Up   An LLC continues after dissolution only for the purpose of winding up its business, which involves completing unfinished business, collecting debts, taking inventory, reducing assets to cash, paying creditors, and distributing the remaining assets to the members. During this period, the fiduciary duties of members and managers continue.

Authority   Upon dissolution, the *actual authority* of a member or manager to act for the LLC terminates, except so far as is appropriate to wind up LLC business. Actual authority to wind up includes the authority to complete existing contracts, to collect debts, to sell LLC assets, and to pay LLC obligations. In addition, some statutes expressly provide that after dissolution, members and managers continue to have *apparent authority* to bind the company that they had prior to dissolution provided that the third party did not have notice of the dissolution.

Distribution of Assets   Most statutes provide default rules for distributing the assets of an LLC as follows:

1. to creditors, including members and managers who are creditors, except with respect to liabilities for distributions;
2. to members and former members in satisfaction of liabilities for unpaid distributions, except as otherwise agreed;
3. to members for the return of their contributions, except as otherwise agreed; and
4. to members for their LLC interests in the proportions in which members share in distributions, except as otherwise agreed.

Protection of Creditors   Many LLC statutes establish procedures to safeguard the interests of the LLC's creditors. Such procedures typically include the required mailing of notice of dissolution to known creditors, a general publication of notice, and the preservation of claims against the LLC for a specified time.

Mergers and Conversions [32-2f]

Merger

the combination of the assets of two or more business entities into one of the entities

Effect of merger

the surviving entity receives title to all of the assets of the merged entities and assumes all of their liabilities; the merged entities cease to exist

Most LLC statutes expressly provide for mergers. A **merger** of two or more entities is the combination of all of their assets. One of the entities, known as the *surviving entity*, receives title to all the assets. The other party or parties to the merger, known as the *merged entity* or entities, is merged into the surviving entity and ceases to exist as a separate entity. Thus, if Alpha LLC and Beta LLC combine into Alpha LLC, Alpha is the surviving LLC and Beta is the merged LLC.

The LLC statutes vary with respect to the voting rights of the members for approving mergers. Some provide for a majority or unanimous vote; others leave it to the operating agreement. Some statutes require the filing of articles of merger; others require that a merged LLC file articles of dissolution. Upon the required filing the merger is effective, and the separate existence of each merged entity terminates. All property and assets owned by each of the merged entities vests in the surviving entity, and all debts, liabilities, and other obligations of each merged entity become the obligations of the surviving entity.

Many LLC statutes provide for the conversion of another business entity into an LLC. LLC statutes and other business association statutes also provide for an LLC to be converted into another business entity. The converted entity remains the same entity that existed before the conversion.

OTHER UNINCORPORATED BUSINESS ASSOCIATIONS [32-3]

Limited Liability Partnerships [32-3a]

All of the states have enacted statutes enabling the formation of limited liability partnerships (LLPs). Until 1997 there was no uniform LLP statute, so the enabling statutes varied from state

Limited liability partnership

is a general partnership that, by making the statutorily required filing, limits the liability of its partners for some or all of the partnership's obligations

Formalities

most statutes require only a majority of the partners to authorize registration as an LLP; others require unanimous approval

Designation

the name of the LLP must include the words "limited liability partnership" or "registered limited liability partnership," or the abbreviation "LLP"

Liability limitation

some statutes limit liability only for negligent acts; others limit liability to any partnership tort or contract obligation that arose from negligence, malpractice, wrongful acts, or misconduct committed by any partner, employee, or agent of the partnership; most provide limited liability for all debts and obligations of the partnership

Practical Advice

Professionals should consider registering their partnerships as limited liability partnerships or organizing their firms as LLPs.

Limited liability limited partnership

is a limited partnership in which the liability of the general partners has been limited to the same extent as in an LLP

to state. In 1997 the Revised Uniform Partnership Act (RUPA) was amended to add provisions enabling general partnerships to elect to become LLPs, and more than thirty states have adopted this version of the RUPA. A registered **limited liability partnership** is a general partnership that, by making the statutorily required filing, limits the liability of its partners for some or all of the partnership's obligations.

Formalities   To become an LLP, a general partnership must file with the secretary of state an application containing specified information. The RUPA requires the partnership to file a statement of qualification. Most of the statutes require only a majority of the partners to authorize registration as an LLP; others require unanimous approval. Some statutes require renewal of registrations annually, other statutes require periodic reports, and a few require no renewal. The RUPA requires filing annual reports. Some statutes require a new filing after any change in membership of the partnership, but a few of the statutes do not. The RUPA does not.

Designation   All statutes require LLPs to designate themselves as such. Most statutes require the name of the LLP to include the words "limited liability partnership" or "registered limited liability partnership," or the abbreviation "LLP" or "RLLP." Most statutes provide that the laws of the jurisdiction under which a foreign LLP is registered shall govern its organization, internal affairs, and the liability and authority of its partners. Many, but not all, of the statutes require a foreign LLP to register or obtain a certificate of authenticity. The RUPA requires a foreign LLP to qualify and file annual reports.

Liability Limitation   LLP statutes have taken three different approaches to limiting the liability of partners for the partnership's obligations. The earliest statutes limited liability only for negligent acts; they retain unlimited liability for all other obligations. The next generation of statutes extended limited liability to any partnership tort or contract obligation that arose from negligence, malpractice, wrongful acts, or misconduct committed by any partner, employee, or agent of the partnership. Unlimited liability remained for ordinary contract obligations, such as those owed to suppliers, lenders, and landlords. The first two generations of LLP statutes are called "partial shield" statutes. Many of the more recent statutes, including the RUPA, have provided limited liability for all debts and obligations of the partnership. These statutes are called "full shield" statutes. Most states have now adopted full shield statutes although some states still provide only a partial shield.

The statutes, however, generally provide that the limitation on liability will not affect the liability of (1) a partner who committed the wrongful act giving rise to the liability and (2) a partner who supervised the partner, employee, or agent of the partnership who committed the wrongful act. A partner is also personally liable for any partnership obligations guaranteed by the partner. The statutes also provide that the limitations on liability will apply only to claims that arise while the partnership was a registered LLP. Accordingly, partners would have unlimited liability for obligations that arose either before registration or after registration lapses.

Limited Liability Limited Partnerships [32-3b]

A **limited liability limited partnership** (LLLP) is a limited partnership in which the liability of the general partners has been limited to the same extent as in an LLP. A growing number of states allow limited partnerships to become LLLPs. A number of states have statutes expressly providing for LLLPs. In other states, by operation of the provision in the RULPA that a general partner in a limited partnership has the liabilities of a general partner in a general partnership, the LLP statute may provide limited liability to general partners in a limited partnership that registers as an LLLP under the LLP statute. When authorized, the general partners in an LLLP will obtain the same degree of liability limitation that general partners can achieve in LLPs. When available, a limited partnership may register as an LLLP without having to form a new organization, as would be the case in converting to an LLC.

The new revision of the RULPA promulgated in 2001, which has been adopted by at least eighteen states, provides that an LLLP "means a limited partnership whose certificate of limited

---

CONCEPT REVIEW 32-3

Liability Limitations in LLPs

LLP Statutes	Limited Liability	Unlimited Liability
First Generation	Negligent acts	• All other obligations • Wrongful partner • Supervising partner
Second Generation	Tort and contract obligations arising from wrongful acts	• All other obligations • Wrongful partner • Supervising partner
Third Generation	All obligations	• Wrongful partner • Supervising partner

---

partnership states that the limited partnership is a limited liability limited partnership." The revision provides a full shield for general partners in LLLPs:

> An obligation of a limited partnership incurred while the limited partnership is a limited liability limited partnership, whether arising in contract, tort, or otherwise, is solely the obligation of the limited partnership. A general partner is not personally liable … for such an obligation solely by reason of being or acting as a general partner.

Moreover, under the revision, a *limited* partner cannot be held liable for the partnership debts even if he participates in the management and control of the limited partnership.

CHAPTER SUMMARY

Limited Partnership

Definition of a Limited Partnership a partnership formed by two or more persons under the laws of a state and having one or more general partners and one or more limited partners

Formation a limited partnership can be formed only by substantial compliance with a state limited partnership statute

- *Filing of Certificate* two or more persons must file a signed certificate of limited partnership
- *Name* inclusion of a limited partner's surname in the partnership name in most instances will result in the loss of the limited partner's limited liability
- *Contributions* may be cash, property, or services, or may be a promise to contribute cash, property, or services
- *Defective Formation* if no certificate is filed or if the one filed does not substantially meet the statutory requirements, the formation is defective and the limited liability of the limited partners is jeopardized
- *Foreign Limited Partnerships* a limited partnership is considered "foreign" in any state other than that in which it was formed

Rights a general partner in a limited partnership has all the rights and powers of a partner in a general partnership

- *Control* the general partners have almost exclusive control and management of the limited partnership; a limited partner who participates in the control of the limited partnership may lose limited liability
- *Choice of Associates* no person may be added as a general partner or a limited partner without the consent of all partners
- *Withdrawal* a general partner may withdraw from a limited partnership at any time by giving written notice to the other partners; a limited partner may withdraw as provided in the limited partnership certificate

- *Assignment of Partnership Interest* unless otherwise provided in the partnership agreement, a partner may assign his partnership interest; an assignee may become a limited partner if all other partners consent

- *Profit and Loss Sharing* profits and losses are allocated among the partners as provided in the partnership agreement; if the partnership agreement has no such provision, then profits and losses are allocated on the basis of the contributions each partner actually made

- *Distributions* the partners share distributions of cash or other assets of a limited partnership as provided in the partnership agreement

- *Loans* both general and limited partners may be secured or unsecured creditors of the partnership

- *Information* each partner has the right to inspect and copy the partnership records

- *Derivative Actions* a limited partner may sue on behalf of a limited partnership if the general partners refuse to bring the action

Duties and Liabilities

- *Duties* general partners owe a duty of care and loyalty (fiduciary duty) to the general partners, the limited partners, and the limited partnership; limited partners do not

- *Liabilities* the general partners have unlimited liability; the limited partners have limited liability (liability for partnership obligations only to the extent of the capital that the limited partner contributed or agreed to contribute)

Dissolution

- *Causes* the limited partners have neither the right nor the power to dissolve the partnership, except by decree of the court; the following events trigger a dissolution: (1) the expiration of the time period; (2) the withdrawal of a general partner, unless all partners agree to continue the business; or (3) a decree of judicial dissolution

- *Winding Up* unless otherwise provided in the partnership agreement, the general partners who have not wrongfully dissolved the partnership may wind up its affairs

- *Distribution of Assets* the priorities for distribution are as follows: (1) creditors, including partners who are creditors; (2) partners and ex-partners in satisfaction of liabilities for unpaid distributions; (3) partners for the return of contributions, except as otherwise agreed; and (4) partners for their partnership interests in the proportions in which they share in distributions, except as otherwise agreed

Limited Liability Company

Definition a limited liability company (LLC) is a noncorporate business organization that provides limited liability to all of its owners (members) and permits all of its members to participate in management of the business

Formation the formation of an LLC requires substantial compliance with a state's LLC statute

- *Members* LLC statutes permit members to include individuals, corporations, general partnerships, limited partnerships, limited liability companies, trusts, estates, and other associations

- *Filing* LLC statutes generally require the central filing of articles of organization in a designated state office

- *Name* LLC statutes generally require the name of the LLC to include the words "limited liability company" or the abbreviation "LLC"

- *Contribution* the contribution of a member to a limited liability company may be cash, property, services rendered, a promissory note, or other obligation to contribute cash or property, or to perform services

- *Operating Agreement* is the basic contract governing the affairs of a limited liability company and stating the various rights and duties of the members

- *Foreign Limited Liability Companies* a limited liability company is considered "foreign" in any state other than that in which it was formed

Rights of Members a member's interest in the LLC includes the financial interest (the right to distributions) and the management interest (which consists of all other rights granted to a member by the LLC operating agreement and the LLC statute)

- *Profit and Loss Sharing* the LLC's operating agreement determines how the partners allocate the profits and losses; if the LLC's operating agreement makes no such provision, in most states the profits and losses are allocated on the basis of the value of the members' contributions

- *Distributions* the members share distributions of cash or other assets of an LLC as provided in the operating agreement; if the LLC's operating agreement does not allocate distributions, in most states they are made on the basis of the contributions each member made

- *Withdrawal* a member may withdraw and demand payment of her interest upon giving the notice specified in the statute or the LLC's operating agreement

- *Management* in the absence of a contrary agreement, each member has equal rights in the management of the LLC; but LLCs may be managed by one or more managers who may be members

- *Voting* LLC statutes usually specify the voting rights of members, subject to a contrary provision in an LLC's operating agreement

- *Information* LLCs must keep basic organizational and financial records; each member has the right to inspect and copy the LLC records

- *Derivative Actions* a member has the right to bring an action on behalf of a limited liability company to recover a judgment in its favor if the managers or members with authority to bring the action have refused to do so

- *Assignment of LLC Interest* unless otherwise provided in the LLC's operating agreement, a member may assign his financial interest in the LLC; an assignee of a financial interest in an LLC may acquire the other rights by being admitted as a member of the company if all the remaining members consent or the operating agreement so provides

Duties

- *Manager-Managed LLCs* the managers of manager-managed LLCs have a duty of care and loyalty; usually, members of a manager-managed LLC have no duties to the LLC or its members by reason of being a member

- *Member-Managed LLCs* members of member-managed LLCs have the same duties of care and loyalty that managers have in manager-managed LLCs

Liabilities no member or manager of an LLC is obligated personally for any debt, obligation, or liability of the LLC solely by reason of being a member or acting as a manager of the LLC *unless* (1) a member or manager committed the wrongful act giving rise to the liability, (2) a member or manager personally guaranteed an LLC obligation, (3) a person assumed to act as an LLC prior to formation, (4) a member failed to make an agreed contribution, (5) the corporate veil is pierced, or (6) a member received a wrongful distribution or return of her contribution

Dissolution

- *Causes* an LLC will automatically dissolve upon (1) in some states the dissociation of a member if the remaining members do *not* choose to continue the LLC, (2) the expiration of the LLC's agreed duration or the happening of any of the events specified in the articles, (3) the written consent of all the members, or (4) a decree of judicial dissolution

- *Dissociation* means that a member has ceased to be associated with the company and includes voluntary withdrawal, death, incompetence, expulsion, or bankruptcy

- *Winding Up* completing unfinished business, collecting debts, and distributing assets to creditors and members; also called liquidation

- *Authority* the actual authority of a member or manager to act for the LLC terminates, except so far as may be appropriate to wind up LLC affairs; apparent authority continues unless notice of the dissolution is given to a third party

- *Distribution of Assets* the default rules for distributing the assets of an LLC are (1) to creditors, including members and managers who are creditors, except with respect to liabilities for distributions; (2) to members and former members in satisfaction of liabilities for unpaid distributions, except as otherwise agreed; (3) to members for the return of their contributions, except as otherwise agreed; and (4) to members for their LLC interests in the proportions in which members share in distributions, except as otherwise agreed

Mergers

- *Definition* the combination of the assets of two or more business entities into one of the entities

- *Effect* the surviving entity receives title to all of the assets of the merged entities and assumes all of their liabilities; the merged entities cease to exist

Other Unincorporated Business Associations

Limited Liability Partnership (LLP) is a general partnership that, by making the statutorily required filing, limits the liability of its partners for some or all of the partnership's obligations

- *Formalities* most statutes require only a majority of the partners to authorize registration as an LLP; others require unanimous approval

- *Designation* the name of the LLP must include the words "limited liability partnership" or "registered limited liability partnership," or the abbreviation "LLP"
- *Liability Limitation* some statutes limit liability only for negligent acts; others limit liability to any partnership tort or contract obligation that arose from negligence, malpractice, wrongful acts, or misconduct committed by any partner, employee, or agent of the partnership; most provide limited liability for all debts and obligations of the partnership

Limited Liability Limited Partnership is a limited partnership in which the liability of the general partners has been limited to the same extent as in an LLP

QUESTIONS

1. John Palmer and Henry Morrison formed the limited partnership of Palmer & Morrison for the management of the Huntington Hotel. The limited partnership agreement provided that Palmer would contribute $400,000 and be a general partner and that Morrison would contribute $300,000 and be a limited partner. Palmer was to manage the dining and cocktail rooms, and Morrison was to manage the rest of the hotel. Nanette, a popular French singer who knew nothing of the limited partnership affairs, appeared for four weeks in the Blue Room at the hotel and was not paid her fee of $8,000. Subsequently, the limited partnership became insolvent. Nanette sued Palmer and Morrison for $8,000.
   a. For how much, if anything, are Palmer and Morrison liable?
   b. If Palmer and Morrison had formed a limited liability limited partnership, for how much, if anything, would Palmer and Morrison be liable?
   c. If Palmer and Morrison had formed a limited liability company with each as members, for how much, if anything, would Palmer and Morrison be liable?
   d. If Palmer and Morrison had formed a limited liability partnership with each as general partners, for how much, if anything, would Palmer and Morrison be liable?

2. A limited partnership was formed consisting of Webster as the general partner and Stevens and Stewart as the limited partners. The limited partnership was organized in strict compliance with the limited partnership statute. Stevens was employed by the partnership as a purchasing agent. Stewart personally guaranteed a loan made to the partnership. Both Stevens and Stewart consulted with Webster about partnership business, voted on a change in the nature of the partnership business, and disapproved an amendment to the partnership agreement proposed by Webster. The partnership experienced serious financial difficulties, and its creditors seek to hold Webster, Stevens, and Stewart personally liable for the debts of the partnership. Who, if any, is personally liable?

3. Fox, Dodge, and Gilbey agreed to become limited partners in Palatine Ventures, a limited partnership. In a signed writing each agreed to contribute $20,000. Fox's contribution consisted entirely of cash; Dodge contributed $12,000 in cash and gave the partnership her promissory note for $8,000; and Gilbey's contribution was his promise to perform two hundred hours of legal services for the partnership.
   a. What liability, if any, do Fox, Dodge, and Gilbey have to the partnership by way of capital contribution?

   b. If Palatine Ventures had been formed as a limited liability company (LLC) with Fox, Dodge, and Gilbey as members, what liability, if any, would Fox, Dodge, and Gilbey have to the LLC by way of capital contribution?

4. Madison and Tilson agree to form a limited partnership with Madison as general partner and Tilson as the limited partner, each to contribute $12,500 as capital. No papers are ever filed, and after ten months the enterprise fails with liabilities exceeding assets by $30,000. Creditors of the partnership seek to hold Madison and Tilson personally liable for the $30,000. Explain whether the creditors will prevail.

5. Kraft is a limited partner of Johnson Enterprises, a limited partnership. As provided in the limited partnership agreement, Kraft decided to leave the partnership and demanded that her capital contribution of $20,000 be returned. At this time, the partnership assets were $150,000 and liabilities to all creditors totaled $140,000. The partnership returned to Kraft her capital contribution of $20,000.
   a. What liability, if any, does Kraft have to the creditors of Johnson Enterprises?
   b. If Johnson Enterprises had been formed as a limited liability company, what liability, if any, would Kraft have to the creditors of Johnson Enterprises?

6. Gordon is the only limited partner in Bushmill Ventures, a limited partnership whose general partners are Daniels and McKenna. Gordon contributed $10,000 for his limited partnership interest and loaned the partnership $7,500. Daniels and McKenna each contributed $5,000 by way of capital. After a year, the partnership is dissolved, at which time it owes $12,500 to its only creditor, Dickel, and has assets of $30,000.
   a. How should these assets be distributed?
   b. If Bushmill Ventures had been formed as a limited liability company with Gordon, Daniels, and McKenna as members, how should these assets be distributed?

7. Albert, Betty, and Carol own and operate the Roy Lumber Company, a limited liability partnership (LLP). Each contributed one-third of the capital, and they share equally in the profits and losses. Their LLP agreement provides that all purchases exceeding $2,500 must be authorized in advance by two partners and that only Albert is authorized to draw checks. Unknown to Albert or Carol, Betty purchases on the firm's account a $5,500 diamond bracelet and a $5,000 forklift and orders $5,000 worth of logs, all from Doug, who operates a jewelry store and is engaged in various activities connected

with the lumber business. Before Betty made these purchases, Albert told Doug that Betty is not the log buyer. Albert refuses to pay Doug for Betty's purchases. Doug calls at the mill to collect, and Albert again refuses to pay him. Doug calls Albert an unprintable name, and Albert then punches Doug in the nose, knocking him out. While Doug is lying unconscious on the ground, an employee of Roy Lumber Company negligently drops a log on Doug's leg, breaking three bones. The firm and the three partners are completely solvent.

What are the rights of Doug against Roy Lumber Company, Albert, Betty, and Carol?

CASE PROBLEMS

8. Dr. Vidricksen contributed $250,000 to become a limited partner in a Chevrolet car agency business with Thom, the general partner. Articles of limited partnership were drawn up, but no effort was made to comply with the state's statutory requirement of recording the certificate of limited partnership. In March, Vidricksen learned that, because of the failure to file, he might not have formed a limited partnership. At this time, the business developed financial difficulties and went into bankruptcy on September 1. Eight days later, Vidricksen filed a renunciation of the business's profits. Is Dr. Vidricksen a general partner?

9. Dale Fullerton was chairman of the board of Envirosearch and the sole stockholder in Westover Hills Management. James Anderson was president of AGFC. Fullerton and Anderson agreed to form a limited partnership to purchase certain property from WYORCO, a joint venture of which Fullerton was a member. The parties intended to form a limited partnership with Westover Hills Management as the sole general partner and AGFC and Envirosearch as limited partners. The certificate filed with the Wyoming secretary of state, however, listed all three companies as both general and limited partners of Westover Hills Ltd. Anderson and Fullerton later became aware of this error and filed an amended certificate of limited partnership, which correctly named Envirosearch and AGFC as limited partners only. Subsequently Westover Hills Ltd. became insolvent. What is the potential liability of Envirosearch and AGFC to creditors of the limited partnership?

TAKING SIDES

On April 5, Handy contracted to purchase land with the intent of forming a limited liability company (LLC) with Ginsburg and McKinley for the purpose of building a residential community on the property. On April 21, they learned from Coastal, an environmental consulting firm they had hired, that the property contained federally protected wetlands. The presence of wetlands adversely affected the property's value and development potential. Handy, Ginsburg, and McKinley abandoned construction plans and instead decided to sell the property. To advertise and promote that sale, they placed on the property a sign that stated the property had "Excellent Development Potential." Unaware of the existence of wetlands, Pepsi acquired an option to purchase the property from Handy on August 5. At that time, Willow Creek had not yet been formed and Handy had not yet purchased the property. On August 18, Handy, Ginsburg, and McKinley formed Willow Creek Estates, LLC. During the option period, Pepsi hired a soil-engineering consultant to conduct an environmental investigation of the property. In Handy's written answers to specific questions from the consultant about the property, Handy did not disclose that the property contained wetlands or that Coastal had already performed a written preliminary wetlands determination the month before. On September 4, Willow Creek, LLC took title to the property. Four months later Willow Creek, LLC sold the property to Pepsi for more than twice the amount of its purchase price and did not disclose the existence of wetlands on the property. After Pepsi learned that the property contained wetlands, it brought an action for fraud against Willow Creek, Handy, Ginsburg, and McKinley.

a. What are the arguments that Handy, Ginsburg, and McKinley are *not* individually liable to Pepsi for fraud?

b. What are the arguments that Handy, Ginsburg, and McKinley are individually liable to Pepsi for fraud?

c. Explain who should prevail.

Nature and Formation of Corporations

CHAPTER 33

A corporation is an artificial being, invisible, intangible, and existing only in contemplation of law.

Chief Justice John Marshall (1819)

CHAPTER OUTCOMES

After reading and studying this chapter, you should be able to:

1. Identify the principal attributes and classifications of corporations.

2. Explain how a corporation is formed and the role, liability, and duties of promoters.

3. Distinguish between the statutory and common law approaches to defective formation of a corporation.

4. Explain how the doctrine of piercing the corporate veil applies to closely held corporations and parent-subsidiary corporations.

5. Identify the sources of corporate powers and explain the legal consequences of a corporation's exceeding its powers.

A corporation is an entity created by law that exists separately and distinctly from the individuals whose contributions of initiative, property, and control enable it to function. The corporation is the dominant form of business organization in the United States, accounting for 85 percent of the gross revenues of all business entities. Approximately 6 million domestic corporations are currently doing business in the United States, with annual revenues exceeding $25 trillion (see Figure 30-1). Approximately 50 percent of American adults own stock directly or indirectly through institutional investors such as mutual funds, pension funds, banks, and insurance companies. Corporations have achieved this dominance because their attributes of limited liability, free transferability of shares, and continuity have attracted great numbers of widespread investors. Moreover, the centralized management of corporations has facilitated the development of large organizations that employ great quantities of invested capital, thereby taking advantage of economies of scale.

Use of the corporation as an instrument of commercial enterprise has made possible the vast concentrations of wealth and capital that have largely transformed this country's economy from an agrarian to an industrial one. Due to its size, power, and impact, the business corporation is a key institution not only in the American economy but also in the world power structure.

In 1946, a committee of the American Bar Association, after careful study and research, submitted a draft of a Model Business Corporation Act (MBCA). The Model Act has been amended frequently since then. Its provisions do not become law until a state enacts them, but the influence of the Act has been widespread: a majority of the states adopted it in whole or in part.

In 1984, the Revised Model Business Corporation Act (RMBCA) was promulgated. More than thirty states have adopted the Revised Act in whole or in part, although Delaware and seven of the ten most populous states have *not* adopted either the Model Act or the Revised Act. Moreover, many states have adopted selected provisions of the Revised Act. The Revised Act, as amended, will be used throughout the chapters on corporations in this text and will be referred to as the Revised Act or the RMBCA.

In 2009, a number of sections of the Revised Act were amended to update the Act's electronic technology provisions to bring them into alignment with Uniform Electronic Transmissions Act ("UETA") and the federal Electronic Signatures in Global and National Commerce Act ("E-Sign") both of which were discussed in Chapter 15.

NATURE OF CORPORATIONS

Creature of the state
a corporation may be formed only by substantial compliance with a state incorporation statute

A corporation is a **creature of the state**: it may be formed only by substantial compliance with a state incorporation statute. To understand corporations, it is helpful to examine the various types of corporations and their common attributes. We will discuss both of these topics in this section.

CORPORATE ATTRIBUTES [33-1]

These are the principal attributes of a corporation: (1) it is a legal entity; (2) it provides limited liability to its shareholders; (3) its shares of stock are freely transferable; (4) its existence may be perpetual; (5) its management is centralized; and it is considered, for some purposes, (6) a person and (7) a citizen. See Concept Review 30-1.

Legal Entity [33-1a]

Legal entity
a corporation is an entity apart from its shareholders, with entirely distinct rights and liabilities

A corporation is a **legal entity** separate from its shareholders, with rights and liabilities entirely distinct from theirs. It may sue or be sued by, as well as contract with, any other party, including any one of its shareholders. A transfer of stock in the corporation from one individual to another has no effect on the legal existence of the corporation. Title to corporate property belongs not to the shareholders but to the corporation. Even where a single individual owns all of the stock of the corporation, the shareholder and the corporation have distinct existences.

Limited Liability [33-1b]

Limited liability
a shareholder's liability is limited to the amount invested in the business enterprise

A corporation is a legal entity and is therefore liable out of its own assets for its debts. Generally, the shareholders have **limited liability** for the corporation's debts—their liability does not extend beyond the amount of their investment—although later in this chapter we will discuss certain circumstances under which a shareholder may be personally liable. The limitation on liability, however, will not affect the liability of a shareholder who committed the wrongful act giving rise to the liability. A shareholder is also personally liable for any corporate obligations the shareholder guarantees.

Free Transferability of Corporate Shares [33-1c]

Free transferability of corporate shares
unless otherwise specified in the charter, corporate shares are freely transferable

In the absence of contractual restrictions, shares in a corporation may be freely transferred by sale, gift, or pledge. The ability to transfer shares is a valuable right and may enhance their market value. Article 8 of the Uniform Commercial Code, Investment Securities, governs transfers of shares of stock.

Perpetual Existence [33-1d]

Perpetual existence
unless the charter provides otherwise, a corporation has perpetual existence

A corporation has **perpetual existence** unless otherwise stated in its articles of incorporation. Consequently, the death, withdrawal, or addition of a shareholder, director, or officer does not terminate its existence. A corporation's existence will terminate upon its dissolution or merger into another business.

Centralized Management [33-1e]

Centralized management
shareholders of a corporation elect the board of directors to manage its business affairs; the board appoints officers to run the day-to-day operations of the business

The shareholders of a corporation elect a board of directors that manages the business affairs of the corporation. The board must then appoint officers to run the day-to-day operations of the business. Because neither the directors nor the officers (collectively referred to as "management") need be shareholders, it is entirely possible, and in large corporations quite typical, for the ownership of the corporation to be separate from its management. We will discuss the management structure of corporations in Chapter 35.

As a Person [33-1f]

As a person
a corporation is considered a person for some but not all purposes

Whether a corporation is a "person" within the meaning of a constitution or statute is a matter of construction based on the intent of the lawmakers in using the word. For example, a corporation is considered a person within the provisions in the Fifth and Fourteenth Amendments to the U.S. Constitution that no "person" shall be "deprived of life, liberty, or property, without due process of law" and in the Fourteenth Amendment provision that no state shall "deny to any person within its jurisdiction the equal protection of the laws." A corporation also enjoys the right of a person to be secure against unreasonable searches and seizures, as provided for in the Fourth Amendment. On the other hand, a corporation is not considered to be a person within the Fifth Amendment clause that protects a "person" against self-incrimination.

As a Citizen [33-1g]

As a citizen
a corporation is considered a citizen for some but not all purposes

A corporation is considered a citizen for some purposes but not for others. For instance, a corporation is not a citizen as the term is used in the Fourteenth Amendment, which provides, "No state shall make or enforce any law which shall abridge the privileges or immunities of citizens of the United States."

A corporation is, however, regarded as a citizen of the state of its incorporation and of the state in which it has its principal office for the purpose of determining whether diversity of citizenship exists between the parties to a lawsuit, so as to provide a basis for federal court jurisdiction.

CLASSIFICATION OF CORPORATIONS [33-2]

Public corporation
one created to administer a unit of local civil government or one created by the United States to conduct public business

Private corporation
one founded by and composed of private persons for private purposes and having no government duties

Corporations may be classified as public or private, profit or nonprofit, domestic or foreign, publicly held or closely held, subchapter S, and professional. As you will see, these classifications are not mutually exclusive. For example, a corporation may be a closely held, professional, private, profit, domestic corporation.

Public or Private [33-2a]

A **public corporation** is one that is created to administer a unit of local civil government, such as a county, city, town, village, school district, or park district, or one created by the United States to conduct public business, such as the Tennessee Valley Authority or the Federal Deposit Insurance Corporation. A public corporation usually is created by specific legislation, which determines the corporation's purpose and powers. Many public corporations are also referred to as municipal corporations.

A **private corporation** is founded by and composed of private persons for private purposes and has no government duties. A private corporation may be for profit or nonprofit.

Profit corporation
one founded for the purpose of operating a business for profit

Nonprofit corporation
one whose profits must be used exclusively for the charitable, educational, or scientific purpose for which it was formed

Profit or Nonprofit [33-2b]

A **profit corporation** is one founded for the purpose of operating a business for profit from which payments are made to the corporation's shareholders in the form of dividends.

Although a **nonprofit** (or not-for-profit) **corporation** may make a profit, the profit may not be distributed to its members, directors, or officers but must be used exclusively for the charitable, educational, or scientific purpose for which the corporation was organized. Most states have special incorporation statutes governing nonprofit corporations, most of which are patterned after the Model Nonprofit Corporation Act.

Domestic corporation
corporation created under the laws of a given state

Foreign corporation
corporation created under the laws of any other state, government, or country; it must obtain a certificate of authority from each state in which it does intrastate business

Domestic or Foreign [33-2c]

A corporation is a **domestic corporation** in the state in which it is incorporated. It is a **foreign corporation** in every other state or jurisdiction. A corporation may not do business, except for acts in interstate commerce, in a state other than the state of its incorporation without the permission and authorization of the other state. Every state, however, provides for the issuance of certificates of authority, which allow foreign corporations to do business within its borders, and for the taxation of such foreign businesses. Obtaining a certificate (or "qualifying") usually involves filing certain information with the secretary of state, paying prescribed fees, and designating a resident agent. Conduct typically requiring a certificate of authority includes maintaining an office to conduct local intrastate business, selling personal property not in interstate commerce, entering into contracts relating to local business or sales, and owning or using real estate for general corporate purposes. A single agreement or isolated transaction within a state does not constitute doing business.

A foreign corporation that transacts business without having first qualified may be subject to a number of penalties. Statutes in many states provide that an unlicensed foreign corporation doing business in the state shall not be entitled to maintain a suit in a state court until it has obtained a certificate of authority. However, the failure to obtain a certificate of authority to transact business in the state does not impair the validity of a contract entered into by the corporation and does not prevent it from defending any action or proceeding brought against it in the state. In addition, most states impose fines on corporations that do not obtain certificates, and a few states also impose fines on the corporation's officers and directors, as well as holding them personally liable on contracts made within the state.

Harold Lang Jewelers, Inc. v. Johnson
Court of Appeals of North Carolina, 2003
156 N.C. App. 187, 576 S.E.2d 360; *review denied*, 357 N.C. 458, 585 S.E.2d 765
http://scholar.google.com/scholar_case?case=15826732712372931150&q=576+S.E.2d+360&hl=en&as_sdt=2,34

FACTS Harold Lang Jewelers, Inc. (Lang), a Florida corporation, through its single employee, had sold and consigned merchandise to jewelry stores in western North Carolina since 1970. Lang's employee came frequently to North Carolina for the purpose of transacting business. When the employee came to North Carolina, he always brought jewelry with him for delivery. When he visited jewelry stores in the state, he would either (1) make a direct sale on the spot without any confirmation from any other person or (2) consign the jewelry, also without any further confirmation or approval from any other person. When the employee took orders, he either shipped the ordered items to the business in North Carolina or personally delivered the merchandise. He also took returns of merchandise from customers in the state.

Lang filed suit in April 1999, alleging that Johnson owed it $160,322.90 plus interest for jewelry sold or consigned. Johnson answered in May 1999, asserting as one of its defenses that Lang could not sue in a North Carolina court because Lang had failed to obtain a certificate of authority to transact business in the state. The district court granted the motion and dismissed Lang's action. Lang appealed.

DECISION Affirmed.

OPINION Transacting business in the state "require[s] the engaging in, carrying on or exercising, in North Carolina, some of the functions for which the corporation was created." The activities carried on by the corporation in North Carolina must be substantial, continuous, systematic, and regular. Lang's business in North Carolina has been regular, systematic, and extensive. Lang has been coming to North Carolina since about 1970 to sell and consign merchandise to several jewelry stores. In fact, Lang routinely came to North Carolina as frequently as twice every four weeks during some parts of the year, and each time he brought with him merchandise to deliver. Moreover, Lang's employee finalized the sales in North Carolina.

INTERPRETATION A foreign corporation must obtain a certificate of authority in every state in which it conducts intrastate business.

ETHICAL QUESTION Is the court's decision fair to all the parties? Explain.

CRITICAL THINKING QUESTION Do you agree with the test for doing business within a state? Explain.

Publicly Held or Closely Held [33-2d]

Publicly held corporation
corporation whose shares are owned by a large number of people and are widely traded

A **publicly held corporation** is one whose shares are owned by a large number of people and are widely traded. There is no accepted minimum number of shareholders, but any corporation required to register under the federal Securities and Exchange Act of 1934 is considered to be publicly held. In addition, corporations that have issued securities subject to a registered public distribution under the federal Securities Act of 1933 usually are also considered publicly held. (The federal securities laws are discussed in Chapter 39.) To distinguish publicly held corporations from other corporations, the Revised Act was amended to define the term "public corporation" as "a corporation that has shares listed on a national securities exchange or regularly traded in a market maintained by one or more members of a national securities association."

BUSINESS LAW IN ACTION

If you owned a business and wanted to operate it as a corporation, in what state would you incorporate? Wouldn't you choose your home state?

Then why are the following companies incorporated in Delaware, even though their headquarters are elsewhere?

- Amazon (Seattle, Washington)
- McDonald's (Oak Brook, Illinois)
- Walmart (Bentonville, Arkansas)
- Microsoft (Redmond, Washington)
- Ford (Dearborn, Michigan)

Since World War I, Delaware has been the favorite state of incorporation, and more than 50 percent of all U.S. publicly traded companies and 64 percent of *Fortune* 500 companies are Delaware corporations, many of which reincorporated there. Delaware is also the leading jurisdiction for out-of-state incorporations, in which a corporation headquartered in one state chooses to incorporate in another state. This situation did not come about by accident. Corporations are chartered by the states, not by the federal government, and laws of incorporation vary significantly from state to state. New Jersey, for example, was the favorite domicile of large corporations early in the twentieth century, but later fell behind Delaware, partly because it failed to update its corporation laws often enough.

Delaware purposely has made itself attractive to corporations, and the reason is money. Franchise taxes paid by Delaware corporations are a very significant source of income for that small state. According to the Delaware Department of State:

A number of factors have led to Delaware's dominance in business formation. **First, the statute**—the Delaware General Corporation Law ("DGCL") is the foundation on which Delaware corporate law rests. The DGCL offers predictability and stability. It is shaped by corporate-law experts and protected from influence by special-interest groups. The Delaware legislature every year reviews the DGCL to ensure its ability to address current issues. * * *

Second, the courts—as important as the statute itself are the courts that interpret it. Delaware is known worldwide for its judicial system and the expert and impartial judges that decide its corporate cases. The Delaware Court of Chancery is a specialized court of equity with specific jurisdiction over corporate disputes. Without juries, and with only five expert jurists selected through a bipartisan, merit-based selection process, the Court of Chancery is flexible, responsive, focused and efficient. Cases from the Court of Chancery are appealed directly to the Delaware Supreme Court, which is the ultimate word on Delaware law. * * *

Third, the case law—the Court of Chancery and the Delaware Supreme Court both have a historical tradition of issuing reasoned written opinions supporting their decisions, thus allowing a significant body of precedent to accumulate over many decades. Judges, not juries, decide all corporate cases and must give reasons for their rulings. The resulting body of case law provides detailed and substantive guidance to corporations and their advisors. * * *

Fourth, the legal tradition—along with a sophisticated judiciary, Delaware has an ample supply of lawyers expert in Delaware corporate law. * * *

Fifth, the Delaware Secretary of State—the Division of Corporations of the Delaware Secretary of State's Office exists to provide corporations and their advisors with prompt and efficient service. Incorporations provide a major portion of the State's revenue, so Delaware takes its role seriously. * * *

Over the years Delaware's General Assembly has revised and amended the Delaware General Corporation Law to keep it clear and up to date. Delaware's courts, which have been characterized as "a judiciary of corporate specialists," are another significant attraction. Delaware judges have created a large body of case law that is "well-settled law with unique predictability" and that allows corporations to be flexible in their operations. Moreover, corporate attorneys tend to incorporate in Delaware because they are most familiar with Delaware corporate law.

Today, other states share many of Delaware's favorable provisions, but none has had so many for so long. And Delaware's great body of legal precedents has helped to give the state a head start that is hard to overcome.

Source: Robert W. Hamilton, *The Law of Corporations*, 5th ed., 2000, 66–68.

Closely held corporation

corporation that is owned by few shareholders and whose shares are not actively traded

---

Practical Advice

If you take a minority interest in a closely held corporation, attempt to provide adequate protection for your rights in the corporation's charter and bylaws as well as in shareholder agreements.

A **closely held corporation** (or close corporation) is one whose outstanding shares of stock are held by a small number of persons, frequently relatives or friends. In most closely held corporations, the shareholders are active in the management and control of the business. Accordingly, the shareholders, concerned about the identities of their fellow shareholders, frequently restrict the transfer of shares to prevent "outsiders" from obtaining the stock. Although a vast majority of corporations in the United States are closely held, they account for only a small fraction of corporate revenues and assets.

In most states, closely held corporations are subject to the general incorporation statute that governs all corporations. The Revised Act includes a number of liberalizing provisions for closely held corporations. In addition, about twenty states have enacted special legislation to accommodate the needs of closely held corporations, and a Statutory Close Corporation Supplement to the Model and Revised Acts was promulgated.

The Supplement applies only to an eligible corporation (one having fewer than fifty shareholders) that elects statutory close corporation status. A corporation may voluntarily terminate statutory close corporation status. We will discuss other provisions of the Supplement in this and other chapters.

In 1991, the Revised Act was amended to authorize shareholders in closely held corporations to adopt unanimous shareholders' agreements that depart from the statutory norms by altering (1) the governance of the corporation, (2) the allocation of the economic return from the business, and (3) other aspects of the relationship among shareholders, directors, and the corporation. Such a shareholder agreement is valid for ten years unless the agreement provides otherwise but terminates automatically if the corporation's shares become publicly traded. Moreover, shareholder agreements bind only the shareholders and the corporation; they do not bind the state, creditors, or other third parties. These provisions will be discussed in this and other chapters.

Subchapter S Corporation [33-2e]

Subchapter S corporation

eligible corporation electing to be taxed as a partnership under the Internal Revenue Code

Subchapter S of the Internal Revenue Code permits a **corporation** meeting specified requirements to elect to be taxed essentially as though it were a partnership. (More than two-thirds of all corporations in the United States are taxed as subchapter S corporations, but they account for only 20 percent of total corporate revenues and less than 5 percent of total corporate assets.) Under subchapter S, a corporation's income is taxed only once at the individual shareholder level. The requirements for a corporation to elect subchapter S treatment are (1) it must be a domestic corporation; (2) it must have no more than one hundred shareholders; (3) each shareholder must be an individual, or an estate, or certain types of trusts; (4) no shareholder may be a nonresident alien; and (5) it may have only one class of stock, although classes of common stock differing only in voting rights are permitted.

Professional Corporations [33-2f]

Professional corporation

corporate form under which duly licensed individuals may practice their professions

All of the states have **professional** association or **corporation** statutes that permit duly licensed professionals to practice in the corporate form. Some statutes apply to all professions licensed to practice within the state, whereas others apply only to specified professions. There is a Model Professional Corporation Supplement to the MBCA.

BUSINESS LAW **IN ACTION**

What is a public company? When a corporation is first formed, it is generally owned by a single person or small group of owners. At that point it is known as a "private" or "closely held" corporation. As the business expands, one of the ways it can raise needed capital is to sell additional shares of stock to the public in a process known as "going public." Usually an investment bank is engaged to analyze the prospects for a successful IPO, or initial public offering, of the company's shares. That bank or a group of banks may then agree to act as underwriters for the proposed IPO.

Since it involves the sale of securities, the IPO is strictly regulated by the federal and state securities laws as well as the rules and regulations of the U.S. Securities Exchange Commission and similar state agencies. The primary goal of these laws is to provide full and fair disclosure to the investing public about the company's financial condition and other important matters affecting investors' risk. Before shares can be issued, company financial statements and other relevant documents must be filed publicly—many of them online—so that they are easily available for potential investors to review.

Once the firm's shares have been sold to the public, it is known as a "public," "publicly held," or "publicly traded" company. Its shares can be bought and sold by investors freely, and it must now comply with a multitude of rules and regulations requiring ongoing public disclosure of important information to all existing shareholders and potential investors. Public companies, and especially those whose stock is traded on national exchanges, are also subject to significant mandates with regard to corporate governance and accounting practices.

The web of disclosure and other regulations with which a public company must comply is increasingly complex and costly. As a result, publicly held companies, especially smaller firms, are considering buying back all of their stock owned by the public and "going private" to avoid extensive regulation and its attendant expense.

FORMATION OF A CORPORATION

The formation of a corporation under a general incorporation statute requires action by various groups, individuals, and state officials.

ORGANIZING THE CORPORATION [33-3]

The procedure to organize a corporation begins with the promotion of the proposed corporation by its organizers, also known as promoters, who procure offers by interested persons, known as subscribers, to buy stock in the corporation, once created, and who also prepare the necessary incorporation papers. The incorporators then execute the articles of incorporation and file them with the secretary of state, who issues the charter or certificate of incorporation. Finally, the parties hold an organizational meeting.

Promoters [33-3a]

Promoter
person who takes the preliminary steps to organize a corporation

A **promoter** is a person who takes the preliminary steps to organize a corporation. The promoter arranges for the capital and financing of the corporation; assembles the necessary assets, equipment, licenses, personnel, leases, and services; and attends to the actual legal formation of the corporation. On incorporation, the promoter's organizational task is finished.

Promoters' contracts
promoters remain liable on preincorporation contracts made in the name of the corporation unless the contract provides otherwise or unless a novation is effected

Promoters' Contracts In addition to procuring subscriptions and preparing the incorporation papers, promoters often enter into contracts in anticipation of the creation of the corporation. The contracts may be ordinary agreements necessary for the eventual operation of the business, such as leases, purchase orders, employment contracts, sales contracts, or franchises. If the promoter executes these contracts in her own name and there is no further action, the promoter is liable on such contracts; the corporation, when created, is not liable. Moreover, a preincorporation contract made by a promoter in the name of the corporation and on its behalf does not bind the corporation. Before its formation, a corporation has no capacity to enter into contracts or to employ agents or representatives. After its formation, it is not liable at common law on any prior contract, even one made in its name, unless it adopts the contract expressly, impliedly, or by knowingly accepting benefits under it.

Practical Advice

As a promoter, obtain the agreement of the third party that the corporation's adoption of a preincorporation contract will terminate your liability; as a third party, carefully consider whether you should agree to such a provision.

A promoter who enters into a preincorporation contract in the name of the corporation usually remains liable on that contract even if the corporation adopts it. This liability results from the rule of agency law stating that a principal, in order to be able to ratify a contract, must be in existence when the contract is made. A promoter will be relieved of liability, however, if the contract itself provides that adoption shall terminate the promoter's liability or if the promoter, the third party, and the corporation enter into a novation substituting the corporation for the promoter.

Figure 33-1 summarizes the liability of the promoter and the corporation for preincorporation contracts made in the corporation's name.

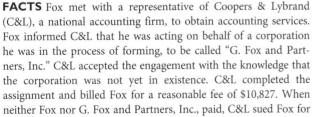

Coopers & Lybrand v. Fox
Colorado Court of Appeals, Division IV, 1988
758 P.2d 683
http://scholar.google.com/scholar_case?case=12318371943544580212&q=758+P.2d+683&hl=en&as_sdt=2,34

FACTS Fox met with a representative of Coopers & Lybrand (C&L), a national accounting firm, to obtain accounting services. Fox informed C&L that he was acting on behalf of a corporation he was in the process of forming, to be called "G. Fox and Partners, Inc." C&L accepted the engagement with the knowledge that the corporation was not yet in existence. C&L completed the assignment and billed Fox for a reasonable fee of $10,827. When neither Fox nor G. Fox and Partners, Inc., paid, C&L sued Fox for breach of express and implied contracts based on a theory of promoter liability. Fox insisted that he was acting as an agent for the future corporation. The trial court ruled for Fox after determining that there was no agreement that would obligate Fox individually to pay the fee. C&L appealed.

DECISION Judgment for Coopers & Lybrand.

OPINION We reject Fox's argument that he was acting solely as an agent for the still-unformed corporation. A person may not act as an agent of a nonexistent principal. Rather, Fox is squarely within

Figure 33-1 Promoters' Preincorporation Contracts Made in the Corporation's Name

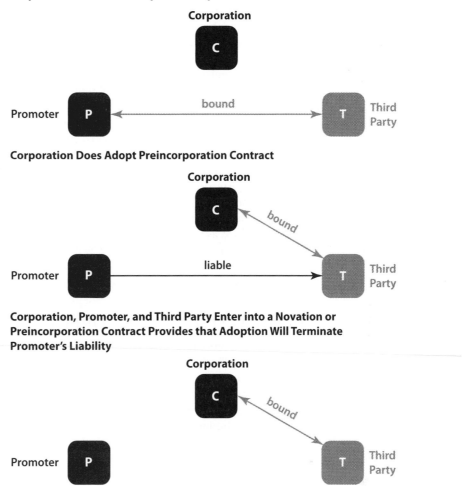

the definition of a promoter. As a general rule, promoters are personally liable for the contracts they make on behalf of a corporation to be formed. A well-recognized exception is that if the contracting party knows the corporation is not in existence but nevertheless agrees to look solely to the corporation, the promoter incurs no liability. In the absence of an express agreement, an agreement may be implied by circumstances making it reasonably certain that the parties intended to look only to the corporation. Here, the trial court found that there was no agreement, either express or implied,

regarding Fox's liability. Thus, in the absence of any agreement releasing him from liability, Fox is personally liable.

INTERPRETATION A promoter is personally liable for the contracts he makes on behalf of a future corporation unless there is an agreement releasing him from liability.

CRITICAL THINKING QUESTION Do you agree that a promoter should be liable when the corporation adopts a preincorporation contract? Explain.

Promoters' fiduciary duty

promoters owe a fiduciary duty among themselves and to the corporation, its subscribers, and its initial shareholders

Promoters' Fiduciary Duty   The promoters of a corporation have a fiduciary relationship among themselves as well as with the corporation, its subscribers, and its initial shareholders. This duty requires good faith, fair dealing, and full disclosure to an independent board of directors. If an independent board has not been elected, full disclosure must be made to all shareholders. Accordingly, the promoters are under a duty to account for any secret profit they realize. Failure to disclose also may violate federal or state securities laws.

Subscribers [33-3b]

Subscriber

a person who agrees to purchase stock in a corporation

Preincorporation subscription

offer to purchase capital stock in a corporation yet to be formed

A **subscriber** is a person who agrees to purchase stock in a corporation. A **preincorporation subscription** is an offer to purchase capital stock in a corporation yet to be formed. Courts traditionally have viewed such subscriptions in one of two ways. The majority regards a subscription as a continuing offer to purchase stock from a nonexisting entity incapable of accepting the offer until it exists. Under this view, a subscription may be revoked at any time prior to its acceptance. By comparison, a minority of jurisdictions treat a subscription as a contract among the various subscribers, making the subscription irrevocable except with all of the subscribers' consent. Most incorporation statutes have adopted an intermediate position making preincorporation subscriptions irrevocable for a stated period without regard to whether they are supported by consideration. For example, the Revised Act provides that a preincorporation subscription is irrevocable for six months, unless the subscription agreement provides a different period or all of the subscribers consent to the revocation. If the corporation accepts the subscription during the period of irrevocability, the subscription becomes a contract binding on both the subscriber and the corporation.

Practical Advice

As a preincorporation subscriber, consider how long you are willing to have your subscription be irrevocable.

A **postincorporation subscription** is a subscription agreement entered into after incorporation. It is treated as a contract between the subscriber and the corporation. Unlike preincorporation subscriptions, the subscriber may withdraw her offer to enter into a postincorporation subscription any time before the corporation accepts it. She cannot, however, withdraw the offer after the corporation has accepted it as the acceptance forms a contract.

Postincorporation subscription

a subscription agreement entered into after incorporation

FORMALITIES OF INCORPORATION [33-4]

Although the procedure involved in organizing a corporation varies somewhat from state to state, typically the incorporators execute and deliver articles of incorporation to the secretary of state or to another designated official. The Revised Act provides that, after incorporation, the board of directors named in the articles of incorporation shall hold an organizational meeting for the purpose of adopting bylaws, appointing officers, and carrying on any other business brought before the meeting. After completion of these organizational details, the corporation's business and affairs are managed by its board of directors and by its officers.

Selection of Name [33-4a]

Selection of name

the name must clearly designate the entity as a corporation

Most general incorporation laws require that the name contain a word or words that clearly designate the organization as a corporation, such as *corporation, company, incorporated, limited, Corp., Co., Inc.*, or *Ltd*. A corporate name must be distinguishable from the name of any domestic corporation or any foreign corporation authorized to do business within the state.

Incorporators [33-4b]

Incorporators

the persons who sign the articles of incorporation

The **incorporators** are the persons who sign the articles of incorporation filed in the state of incorporation with the secretary of state. Although they perform a necessary function, in many states their services as incorporators are perfunctory and short-lived, ending with the organizational meeting following incorporation. Furthermore, modern statutes have greatly relaxed the qualifications of incorporators and also have reduced the number required. The Revised Act and almost all states provide that only one person need act as the incorporator, though more may do so. The Revised Act and most states permit artificial entities to serve as incorporators. For example, the Revised Act defines a "person" to include individuals and entities, with an entity defined to include domestic and foreign corporations, not-for-profit corporations, profit and not-for-profit unincorporated associations, business trusts, estates, partnerships, and trusts.

Articles of Incorporation [33-4c]

Articles of incorporation

the charter or basic organizational document of a corporation

The **articles of incorporation** or charter is the basic organizational document of a corporation, which under the Revised Act must include the name of the corporation, the number of authorized shares, the street address of the registered office and the name of the registered agent, and the name and address of each incorporator. The Revised Act also permits the charter to include optional information, such as the identities of the corporation's initial directors, corporate purposes, management of internal affairs, powers of the corporation, par value of shares, and any provision required or permitted to be set forth in the bylaws. Some optional provisions may be elected *only* in the charter, including cumulative voting, super-majority voting requirements, preemptive rights, and limitations on the personal liability of directors for breach of their duty of care.

To form a corporation, the charter, once drawn up, must be executed and filed with the secretary of state. The charter then becomes the basic governing document of the corporation, so long as its provisions are consistent with state and federal law.

Organizational Meeting [33-4d]

The Revised Act and most states require that an **organizational meeting** be held to adopt the new corporation's bylaws, appoint officers, and carry on any other business brought before it. If the articles do not name the corporation's initial directors; the incorporators hold the organizational meeting to elect directors, and either the incorporators or the directors then complete the organization of the corporation.

Bylaws [33-4e]

The **bylaws** are the rules and regulations that govern the internal management of a corporation. Because bylaws are necessary to the organization of the corporation, their adoption is one of the first items of business at the organizational meeting held promptly after incorporation. The bylaws may contain any provision that is not inconsistent with law or the articles of incorporation. Under the Revised Act, the shareholders may amend or repeal the bylaws, which, in contrast to the certificate of incorporation embodying the articles of incorporation, do not have to be publicly filed. In addition, the board of directors may amend or repeal the bylaws, unless (1) the articles of incorporation or other sections of the RMBCA reserve that power exclusively to the shareholders in whole or in part or (2) the shareholders in amending, repealing, or adopting a bylaw expressly provide that the board of directors may not amend, repeal, or reinstate that bylaw.

The Statutory Close Corporation Supplement permits close corporations to avoid adopting bylaws by including, either in a shareholder agreement or in the articles of incorporation, all the information necessary to corporate bylaws.

Organizational meeting
the first meeting, held to adopt the bylaws and appoint officers

Bylaws
rules governing a corporation's internal management

Practical Advice

When you have the choice of placing a provision in either the charter or the bylaws, carefully consider the advantages and disadvantages of each. You may prefer the charter for provisions that protect your interests because charter provisions prevail over bylaw provisions and are more difficult to amend.

CONCEPT REVIEW 33-1

Comparison of Charter and Bylaws

	Charter	Bylaws
Filing	Publicly	Not publicly
Amendment	Requires board and shareholder approval	Requires only board approval
Availability	Must include certain mandatory provisions; May include optional provisions, although some optional provisions may be elected only in the charter	Must include certain provisions unless they are included in the charter
Validity	May include any provision not inconsistent with law	May include any provision not inconsistent with law and the charter

RECOGNITION OR DISREGARD OF CORPORATENESS

Business associates choose to incorporate to obtain one or more of the corporate attributes, primarily limited liability and perpetual existence. Because a corporation is a creature of the state, such attributes are recognized when the enterprise complies with the state's requirements for incorporation. Although the formal procedures are relatively simple, errors or omissions sometimes occur. In some cases the mistakes may be trivial, such as incorrectly stating an incorporator's address in the charter; in other instances the error may be more significant, such as a complete failure to file the articles of incorporation. The consequences of procedural noncompliance depend on the seriousness of the error. Conversely, even when a corporation has been formed in strict compliance with the incorporation statute, a court may disregard the corporateness of the enterprise if justice requires.

DEFECTIVE INCORPORATION [33-5]

Although modern corporation statutes have greatly simplified incorporation procedures, defective incorporations do occur. The possible consequences of a defective incorporation include the following: (1) the state brings an action against the association for involuntary dissolution, (2) the associates are held personally liable to a third party, (3) the association asserts that it is not liable on an obligation, or (4) a third party asserts that it is not liable to the association. Corporate statutes addressing this issue have taken an approach considerably different from that of the common law.

Common Law Approach [33-5a]

Under the common law, a defectively formed corporation was, under certain circumstances, accorded corporate attributes. The courts developed a set of doctrines granting corporateness to *de jure* (of right) corporations, *de facto* (of fact) corporations, and corporations by estoppel but denying corporateness to corporations that were too defectively formed.

Corporation de jure
one formed in substantial compliance with the incorporation statute and having all corporate attributes

Corporation de Jure A **corporation *de jure*** is one that has been formed in substantial compliance with the incorporation statute and the required organizational procedure. Once a *de jure* corporation is formed, its existence may not be challenged by anyone, even the state in a direct proceeding for this purpose.

Corporation de facto
one not formed in compliance with the statute but recognized for most purposes as a corporation

Corporation de Facto Although it fails to comply in some way with the incorporation statute and, hence, is not *de jure*, a **corporation *de facto*** is nevertheless recognized for most purposes as a corporation. A failure to form a *de jure* corporation may result in the formation of a *de facto* corporation if the following requirements are met: (1) the existence of a general corporation statute, (2) a bona fide attempt to comply with that law in organizing a corporation under the statute, and (3) the actual exercise of corporate power by conducting business in the belief that a corporation has been formed. The existence of a *de facto* corporation can be challenged only by the state in an action of *quo warranto* ("by what right").

Corporation by estoppel
prevents a person from raising the question of a corporation's existence

Corporation by Estoppel The doctrine of **corporation by estoppel** is distinct from that of corporation *de facto*. Estoppel does not create a corporation. It operates only to prevent a person or persons under the facts and circumstances of a particular case from questioning a corporation's existence or its capacity to act or to own property. Corporation by estoppel requires a holding out by a purported corporation or its associates and reliance by a third party. In addition, application of the doctrine depends on equitable considerations. A person who has dealt with a defectively organized corporation may be precluded or estopped from denying its corporate existence if the necessary elements of holding out and reliance are present. The doctrine can be applied not only to third parties but also to the purported corporation and to the associates who held themselves out as a corporation.

Defective corporation
the associates are denied the benefits of incorporation

Defective Corporation

If the associates who purported to form a corporation fail to comply with the requirements of the incorporation statute to such an extent that neither a *de jure* nor a *de facto* corporation is formed and the circumstances do not justify applying the corporation by estoppel doctrine, the courts generally deny the associates the benefits of incorporation. Some or all of the associates are then held unlimitedly liable for the obligations of the business.

Statutory Approach [33-5b]

In contrast to the common law approach to defective incorporation, which is cumbersome in both theory and application, incorporation statutes now address the issue more simply. All states provide that corporate existence begins either upon the filing of the articles of incorporation or their acceptance by the secretary of state. Moreover, under the Revised Act (**RMBCA**) and most state statutes, the filing or acceptance of the articles of incorporation by the secretary of state is conclusive proof that the incorporators have satisfied all conditions precedent to incorporation, except in a proceeding brought by the state. This applies even if the articles of incorporation contain mistakes or omissions.

RMBCA

liability is imposed only on persons who act on behalf of a defectively formed corporation knowing that there was no incorporation

MBCA

unlimited personal liability is imposed on all persons who act on behalf of a defectively formed corporation

With respect to the attribute of limited liability, the original Model Act (**MBCA**) and a few states provide that all persons who assume to act as a corporation without authority to do so shall have joint and several unlimited liability for all debts and liabilities incurred or arising as a result of their so acting. The Revised Act, however, imposes liability *only* on persons who purport to act as or on behalf of a corporation, knowing that there was no incorporation.

Consider two illustrations: First, Smith had been shown executed articles of incorporation some months before he invested in the corporation and became an officer and director. He was also told by the corporation's attorney that the articles had been filed; however, because of confusion in the attorney's office, they had not in fact been filed. Under the Revised Act and many court decisions, Smith would not be held liable for the obligations of the defective corporation. Second, knowing that no corporation has been formed because no attempt has been made to file articles of incorporation, Jones represents that a corporation exists and enters into a contract in the corporate name. Jones would be held liable for the obligations of the defective corporation under the Model Act, the Revised Act, and most court decisions involving similar situations.

Practical Advice

To obtain limited liability as a shareholder in a corporation, make sure that the corporation has been properly organized.

Harris v. Looney
Court of Appeals of Arkansas, 1993
43 Ark.App. 127, 862 S.W.2d 282
http://scholar.google.com/scholar_case?case=145280640899400887&q=862+S.W.2d+282&hl=en&as_sclt=2,34

FACTS On February 1, 1988, Robert L. Harris sold his business and its assets to J & R Construction. Joe Alexander, one of three J & R incorporators, signed the contract on behalf of J & R Construction with Harris. On the same day, the incorporators (Joe Alexander, Avanell Looney, and Rita Alexander) signed the articles of incorporation for J & R Construction, but they were not filed with the secretary of state's office until February 3, 1988. In 1991, J & R Construction defaulted on its contract and promissory note, and Harris sued the three incorporators of J & R Construction for the corporation's debt of $49,696.21. Joe Alexander and Avanell Looney stated that they were both present at the signing. Harris testified, however, that only he, his wife, and Joe Alexander were present when the contract was signed and that he does not remember Avanell Looney being present. Kathryn Harris testified that Alexander and Looney were not present when the contract was signed. The trial court held that Joe Alexander was personally liable for the debt because he was the contracting party who dealt on behalf of the corporation. The court refused to hold Avanell

Looney or Rita Alexander liable because neither of them had acted for or on behalf of the corporation. Harris appealed.

DECISION Judgment affirmed.

OPINION Revised Model Business Corporation Act Section 2.04 states, "All persons purporting to act as or on behalf of a corporation, knowing there was no incorporation under this Act, are jointly and severally liable for all liabilities created while so acting." The comment to this section explains that it seems appropriate to impose liability only on persons who act as or on behalf of corporations knowing that no corporation exists. Thus, this provision protects persons who "erroneously but in good faith believe" that a corporation existed. In adopting the Revised Act, the Arkansas General Assembly adopted a heightened standard for imposing personal liability for transactions entered into before incorporation. To be liable under Section 2.04, the persons must have acted as or on behalf of the corporation and must have known there was no incorporation under this Act.

The trial court found the evidence to show that Avanell Looney and Rita Alexander had not acted as or on behalf of the corporation. The evidence showed that the contract to purchase Harris's business and the promissory note were signed only by Joe Alexander on behalf of the corporation. There was conflicting evidence as to who else was present at the signing of the contract. Since the trial court's finding is not clearly erroneous or clearly against the preponderance of the evidence, we find no error in the court's refusal to award Harris a judgment against Rita Alexander or Avanell Looney.

INTERPRETATION The Revised Act imposes liability on all persons who purport to act as or on behalf of a corporation if they knew there was no incorporation.

ETHICAL QUESTION Was the court's decision fair to all of the parties? Explain.

CRITICAL THINKING QUESTION With which approach to recognition of corporate attributes do you agree: that taken by the Model Act or by the Revised Act? Explain.

PIERCING THE CORPORATE VEIL [33-6]

If substantial compliance with the incorporation statute results in a *de jure* or *de facto* corporation, the general rule is that the courts will recognize corporateness and its attendant attributes—including limited liability. Nonetheless, the courts will disregard the corporate entity when it is used to defeat public convenience, commit a wrongdoing, protect fraud, or circumvent the law. Reaching behind a corporate shield to prevent individuals from insulating themselves against personal accountability and the consequences of their wrongdoing is known as **piercing the corporate veil**. When they deem it necessary, courts will pierce the corporate veil to remedy wrongdoing. However, there is no commonly accepted test used by the courts. They have done so most frequently with closely held corporations and with parent-subsidiary relationships. Piercing the corporate veil is the exception, and in most cases courts uphold the separateness of the corporation.

Closely Held Corporations [33-6a]

The joint and active management by all the shareholders of closely held corporations frequently results in a tendency to forgo corporate formalities, such as holding meetings of the board and shareholders, while the small size of close corporations often renders certain creditors unable to fully satisfy their claims against the corporation. Such frustrated creditors will likely ask the court to disregard the organization's corporateness and to impose personal liability for the corporate obligations on the shareholders. Courts have responded by piercing the corporate veil in cases in which the shareholders (1) have not conducted the business on a corporate basis, (2) have not provided an adequate financial basis for the business, or (3) have used the corporation to defraud. Conducting the business on a corporate basis involves separately maintaining the corporation's and the shareholders' funds, maintaining separate financial records, holding regular directors' meetings, and generally observing corporate formalities. Adequate capitalization requires that the shareholders invest capital or purchase liability insurance sufficient to meet the reasonably anticipated requirements of the enterprise.

The Revised Act validates unanimous shareholder agreements by which the shareholders may relax traditional corporate formalities. The Revised Act further provides that the existence or performance of an agreement authorized by the Act

> [S]hall not be grounds for imposing personal liability on any shareholder for the acts or the debts of the corporation even if the agreement or its performance treats the corporation as if it were a partnership or results in failure to observe the corporate formalities otherwise applicable to the matters governed by the agreement.

Thus, this provision narrows the grounds for imposing personal liability on shareholders for the liabilities of a corporation for acts or omissions authorized by a valid shareholder agreement.

The Statutory Close Corporation Supplement validates a number of arrangements that allow the shareholders to relax traditional corporate formalities. The Supplement is intended to prevent the shareholders in a statutory close corporation from being held individually liable for the debts and torts of the business merely because the corporation does not follow the traditional corporate model. Although courts may still pierce the corporate veil of a statutory close corporation if the

Piercing the corporate veil

the courts will disregard the corporate entity when it is used to defeat public convenience, commit a wrongdoing, protect fraud, or circumvent the law

Practical Advice

If you form a closely held corporation, be sure to adhere to the required corporate formalities and adequately capitalize the corporation.

same circumstances would justify imposing personal liability on the shareholders of a general business corporation, the Supplement simply prevents a court from piercing the corporate veil just because the corporation is a statutory close corporation.

Parent-Subsidiary [33-6b]

Subsidiary corporation
corporation controlled by another corporation

Parent corporation
corporation that controls another corporation

A corporation wishing to risk only a portion of its assets in a particular enterprise may choose to form a subsidiary corporation. A **subsidiary corporation** is one in which another corporation, the **parent corporation**, owns at least a majority of the shares and over which the parent corporation therefore has control. Courts may pierce the corporate veil and hold the parent liable for the debts of its subsidiary if (1) both corporations are not adequately capitalized, *or* (2) the formalities of separate corporate procedures are not observed, *or* (3) each corporation is not held out to the public as a separate enterprise, *or* (4) the funds of the two corporations are commingled, *or* (5) the parent corporation completely dominates the subsidiary only to advance the parent's own interests. So long as a parent-subsidiary duo avoids these pitfalls, the courts generally will recognize the subsidiary as a separate entity, even if the parent owns all the subsidiary's stock and the two corporations share facilities, employees, directors, and officers.

Inter-Tel Technologies, Inc. v. Linn Station Properties, LLC
Supreme Court of Kentucky, 2012
360 S.W.3d 152
http://scholar.google.com/scholar_case?q=360+S.W.3d+152&hl=en&as_sdt=6,34&case=2563532420089966758&scilh=0

FACTS Integrated Telecom Services Corp. (ITS) was acquired by and became a wholly-owned subsidiary of Inter–Tel Technologies, Inc. (Technologies), which in turn is a wholly-owned subsidiary of Inter–Tel, Inc. (Inter–Tel). Inter–Tel designs, manufactures, sells, and services telecommunications systems through its subsidiaries and affiliates. Technologies is the retail division of Inter–Tel. ITS was the company's first retail branch in Kentucky, selling Inter–Tel's telecommunications products from an office building it leased from Linn Station Properties, LLC (Linn Station).

After ITS was acquired by Technologies, ITS was not permitted to maintain a bank account, hold any funds, or pay any bills. All of ITS's regional offices were transformed from independent dealers of communications equipment into direct sales "branches" of Inter–Tel. ITS employees became employees of Inter–Tel and were paid by Inter–Tel. When a customer purchased a telecommunications system from ITS the payment went directly into a depository account controlled by Inter–Tel. Inter–Tel paid all the vendors who provided ITS with goods and services. All of ITS's inventory was provided by another Inter–Tel subsidiary. Inter–Tel paid ITS's rent for the Linn Station Road property from the time Technologies acquired ITS until ITS abandoned the premises in 2002. Inter–Tel and Technologies were the named insureds listed on the property damage insurance for ITS's premises on Linn Station Road.

ITS did not hold an annual board of directors or shareholders meeting from 1999 through 2002. Nor did Technologies hold an annual board of directors or shareholders meeting from 1998 through 2002. During the four-year period from 1999 through 2002, ITS and Technologies had identical boards of directors and the President and CEO of Inter–Tel served on the boards of ITS, Technologies and Inter–Tel. Although all Inter–Tel business conducted in Kentucky since 2001 was performed by ITS in its own name, Inter–Tel, Technologies, and another Inter–Tel subsidiary filed sales and use tax returns with the Kentucky in 2001, 2002, and 2003.

On June 19, 2002, Linn Station filed suit against ITS, seeking damages for failure to repair and maintain the premises and for

unpaid rent. ITS failed to respond, and on August 12, 2002, a default judgment was entered against ITS for $332,900.00 plus interest. After repeated, unsuccessful attempts to satisfy the judgment against ITS, on June 20, 2003 Linn Station sued ITS, Technologies and Inter–Tel to pierce the corporate veil and establish Inter–Tel and Technologies' liability for the judgment against ITS. The trial court granted summary judgment to Linn Station, and the Court of Appeals affirmed. Technologies and Inter–Tel appealed.

DECISION The decision of the Court of Appeals is affirmed, and the case is remanded to the trial court for entry of judgment against Inter–Tel and Technologies.

OPINION Piercing the corporate veil is an equitable doctrine invoked by courts to allow a creditor recourse against the shareholders of a corporation. In short, the limited liability, which is the hallmark of a corporation, is disregarded and the debt of the pierced entity becomes enforceable against those who have exercised dominion over the corporation to the point that it has no real separate existence. A successful veil-piercing claim requires both (1) the element of domination and (2) circumstances in which continued recognition of the corporation as a separate entity would sanction a fraud or promote injustice. This two-part test is referred to as "alter ego" test. This case involves applying the piercing the corporate veil doctrine in the context of an increasingly common scenario: a creditor's attempt to collect on debt incurred by a wholly-owned subsidiary where the subsidiary has been deprived of all income and rendered asset-less by the acts of its parent (and in this case also grandparent) corporation.

The following factors are considered in applying the alter ego test: (1) inadequate capitalization, (2) failure to issue stock, (3) failure to observe corporate formalities, (4) nonpayment of dividends, (5) insolvency of the debtor corporation, (6) nonfunctioning of the other officers or directors, (7) absence of corporate records, (8) commingling of funds, (9) diversion of assets from the corporation by or to a stockholder or other person or entity to the detriment of creditors, (10) failure to maintain arm's-length relationships among related entities, and (11) whether the corporation is a mere facade for the operation of the dominant stockholders.

The alter ego test language employed by most jurisdictions expressly refers to "promoting injustice" and, indeed, piercing should not be limited to instances where all the elements of a common law fraud claim can be established. The injustice, however, must be something beyond the mere inability to collect a debt from the corporation.

The trial court and Court of Appeals were correct in concluding the undisputed facts of this case justified piercing ITS's corporate veil. ITS lost all semblance of separate corporate existence and through the joint acts of Technologies and Inter–Tel was rendered income-less and asset-less. Their diversion of ITS's corporate income and transfer of ITS's corporate assets for their own benefit provides the extra "injustice," something more than simply a creditor's inability to collect a debt from ITS. The alter ego test is thus satisfied.

Technologies was 100% owned and controlled by Inter–Tel and the two corporations acted completely in concert in dominating ITS and extracting anything of value from ITS. It is entirely appropriate to look at the larger picture of the conduct of Inter–Tel and Technologies as opposed to only the individual actions of the parent entity. To do otherwise would render the equitable piercing doctrine hopelessly inadequate, if not meaningless in some cases, based on the sheer number of business entities involved.

ITS had grossly inadequate capital for day-to-day operations because it had no funds at all, literally nothing of its own. Inter–Tel paid the employees' salaries and other expenses of ITS. ITS had no assets of its own. ITS simply had no independent financial existence. Both Technologies and Inter–Tel used the Linn Station lease premises and any other assets previously held by ITS solely for the benefit of Inter–Tel, not for ITS's benefit. Finally, the formal legal requirements of ITS were not observed. This case is clearly within the boundaries of proper application of the equitable doctrine of piercing the corporate veil. Thus, the trial court and Court of Appeals did not err in piercing ITS's veil to hold Inter–Tel and Technologies responsible for ITS's debt to Linn Station.

INTERPRETATION A court will disregard the limited liability of a corporation when (1) its owners exercise complete control and dominion to the point that it has no real separate existence and (2) circumstances in which continued recognition of the corporation as a separate entity would sanction a fraud or promote injustice.

CRITICAL THINKING QUESTION Are the standards for piercing the corporate veil sufficiently definite and predictable? Explain.

CORPORATE POWERS

Because a corporation derives its existence and all of its powers from its state of incorporation, it possesses only those powers that the state has conferred on it. Corporate powers consist of those expressly set forth in the incorporation statute unless limited by the articles of incorporation.

SOURCES OF CORPORATE POWERS [33-7]

Statutory Powers [33-7a]

Statutory powers typically include perpetual existence, right to hold property in the corporate name, and all powers necessary or convenient to effect the corporation's purposes

Typical of the general corporate powers granted by incorporation statutes are those provided by the Revised Act, which include the following: (1) to have perpetual succession; (2) to sue and be sued in the corporate name; (3) to acquire and dispose of property, including shares or other interests in, or obligations of, any other entity; (4) to make contracts, borrow money, and secure any corporate obligations; (5) to lend money; (6) to be a promoter, partner, member, associate, or manager of any partnership, joint venture, trust, or other entity; (7) to conduct business within or without the state of incorporation; (8) to establish pension plans, profit-sharing plans, share option plans, and other employee benefit plans; and (9) to make charitable donations. In most states this list is not exclusive. Moreover, the Revised Act also grants to all corporations the same powers individuals have to do all things necessary or convenient to carry out their business and affairs.

Purposes [33-7b]

All state incorporation statutes provide that a corporation may be formed for any lawful purpose. The Revised Act permits a corporation's articles of incorporation to state a more limited purpose. Many state statutes, but not the RMBCA, require that the articles of incorporation specify the corporation's purposes, although they usually permit a general statement that the corporation is formed to engage in any lawful purpose.

Ultra Vires Acts [33-8]

Ultra vires

any action or contract that
goes beyond a
corporation's express and
implied powers

Because a corporation has authority to act only within its powers, any corporate action or contract that exceeds these powers is **ultra vires**. The doctrine of *ultra vires* is less significant today because modern statutes permit incorporation for any lawful purpose and most articles of incorporation do not limit corporate powers. As a consequence, far fewer acts are *ultra vires*.

Effect of *Ultra Vires* Acts [33-8a]

Effect of *ultra vires* acts

under RMBCA, *ultra vires*
acts and conveyances are
not invalid

Traditionally, *ultra vires* contracts were unenforceable as null and void. Under the modern approach, courts allow the *ultra vires* defense in cases in which the contract is wholly executory on both sides. A corporation having received full performance from the other party to the contract is not permitted to escape liability by a plea of *ultra vires*. Conversely, the other party may not use the defense of *ultra vires* against a corporation suing for breach of a contract that has been fully performed on its side. Almost all statutes, including the Revised Act, have abolished the defense of *ultra vires* in an action by or against a corporation. These statutes do not, however, validate illegal corporate actions.

Remedies for *Ultra Vires* Acts [33-8b]

**Remedies for *ultra vires*
acts**

the RMBCA provides three
possible remedies

Although *ultra vires* under modern statutes may no longer be used as a shield against liability, corporate activities that are *ultra vires* may be redressed in any of three ways, as provided by the Revised Act:

1. in a proceeding by a shareholder against the corporation to enjoin the unauthorized act, if equitable and if all affected persons are parties to the proceeding, the court may award damages for losses suffered by the corporation or another party because of the enjoining of the unauthorized act;
2. in a proceeding by the corporation, or a shareholder derivatively (in a representative capacity), against the incumbent or former directors or officers for exceeding their authority; or
3. in a proceeding by the attorney general of the state of incorporation to dissolve the corporation or to enjoin it from the transaction of unauthorized business.

Liability for Torts and Crimes [33-9]

Torts [33-9a]

Torts

under the doctrine of
respondeat superior, a
corporation is liable for
torts committed by its
employees within the
course of their employment

A corporation is liable for the torts its agents commit in the course of their employment. The doctrine of *ultra vires*, even in those jurisdictions where it is permitted as a defense, does not apply to wrongdoing by the corporation. Rather, the doctrine of *respondeat superior* imposes full liability on a corporation for such agent and employee torts. For example, Robert, a truck driver employed by the Webster Corporation, while on a business errand negligently runs over Pamela, a pedestrian. Both Robert and the Webster Corporation are liable to Pamela in her action to recover damages for the injuries she sustained. A corporation may also be found liable for fraud, false imprisonment, malicious prosecution, libel, and other torts; but some states hold the corporation liable for *punitive* damages only if it authorized or ratified the agent's act.

Crimes [33-9b]

Crimes

a corporation may be
criminally liable for
violations of statutes
imposing liability without
fault or for an offense
perpetrated by a high
corporate officer or its
board of directors

Historically, corporations were not held criminally liable because, under the traditional view, a corporation could not possess the criminal intent requisite for committing a crime. The dramatic growth in size and importance of corporations has changed this view. Under the modern approach, a corporation may be liable for violating statutes imposing liability without fault. In addition, a corporation may be liable for an offense perpetrated by a high corporate officer or by its board of directors. Punishment of a corporation for crimes is necessarily by fine, not imprisonment.

CHAPTER SUMMARY

Nature of Corporations

Corporate Attributes

Creature of the State a corporation may be formed only by substantial compliance with a state incorporation statute

Legal Entity a corporation is an entity apart from its shareholders, with entirely distinct rights and liabilities

Limited Liability a shareholder's liability is limited to the amount invested in the business enterprise

Free Transferability of Corporate Shares unless otherwise specified in the charter

Perpetual Existence unless the charter provides otherwise

Centralized Management shareholders of a corporation elect the board of directors to manage its business affairs; the board appoints officers to run the day-to-day operations of the business

As a Person a corporation is considered a person for some but not all purposes

As a Citizen a corporation is considered a citizen for some but not all purposes

Classification of Corporations

Public or Private

- *Public Corporation* one created to administer a unit of local civil government or one created by the United States to conduct public business
- *Private Corporation* one founded by and composed of private persons for private *purposes*; has no government duties

Profit or Nonprofit

- *Profit Corporation* one founded to operate a business for profit
- *Nonprofit Corporation* one whose profits must be used exclusively for charitable, educational, or scientific purposes

Domestic or Foreign

- *Domestic Corporation* one created under the laws of a given state
- *Foreign Corporation* one created under the laws of any other state or jurisdiction; it must obtain a certificate of authority from each state in which it does intrastate business

Publicly Held or Closely Held

- *Publicly Held* corporation whose shares are owned by a large number of people and are widely traded
- *Closely Held* corporation that is owned by few shareholders and whose shares are not actively traded

Subchapter S Corporation eligible corporation electing to be taxed as a partnership under the Internal Revenue Code

Professional Corporation corporate form under which duly licensed individuals may practice their professions

Formation of a Corporation

Organizing the Corporation

Promoter person who takes the preliminary steps to organize a corporation

- *Promoters' Contracts* promoters remain liable on preincorporation contracts made in the name of the corporation unless the contract provides otherwise or unless a novation is effected
- *Promoters' Fiduciary Duty* promoters owe a fiduciary duty among themselves and to the corporation, its subscribers, and its initial shareholders

Subscribers persons who agree to purchase stock in a corporation

- *Preincorporation Subscription* an offer to purchase capital stock in a corporation yet to be formed which under many incorporation statutes is irrevocable for a specified time period
- *Postincorporation Subscription* a subscription agreement entered into after incorporation; an offer to enter into such a subscription is revocable any time before the corporation accepts it

Formalities of Incorporation

Selection of Name the name must clearly designate the entity as a corporation

Incorporators the persons who sign the articles of incorporation

Articles of Incorporation the charter or basic organizational document of a corporation

Organizational Meeting the first meeting, held to adopt the bylaws and appoint officers

Bylaws rules governing a corporation's internal management

Recognition or Disregard of Corporateness

Defective Incorporation **Common Law Approach**

- *Corporation de Jure* one formed in substantial compliance with the incorporation statute and having all corporate attributes
- *Corporation de Facto* one not formed in compliance with the statute but recognized for most purposes as a corporation
- *Corporation by Estoppel* prevents a person from raising the question of a corporation's existence
- *Defective Corporation* the associates are denied the benefits of incorporation

Statutory Approach the filing or acceptance of the articles of incorporation is generally conclusive proof of proper incorporation

- *Revised Model Business Corporation Act (RMBCA)* liability is imposed only on persons who act on behalf of a defectively formed corporation knowing that there was no incorporation
- *Model Business Corporation Act (MBCA)* unlimited personal liability is imposed on all persons who act on behalf of a defectively formed corporation

Piercing the Corporate Veil **General Rule** the courts may disregard the corporate entity when it is used to defeat public convenience, commit a wrongdoing, protect fraud, or circumvent the law

Application most frequently applied to

- *Closely Held Corporations*
- *Parent-Subsidiary Corporations*

Corporate Powers

Sources of Corporate Powers **Statutory Powers** typically include perpetual existence, right to hold property in the corporate name, and all powers necessary or convenient to effect the corporation's purposes

Purposes a corporation may be formed for any lawful purposes unless its articles of incorporation state a more limited purpose

Ultra Vires *Acts* **Definition of *Ultra Vires* Acts** any action or contract that goes beyond a corporation's express and implied powers

Effect of *Ultra Vires* Acts under the Revised Act, *ultra vires* acts and conveyances are not invalid

Remedies for *Ultra Vires* Acts the Revised Act provides three possible remedies

Liability for Torts and Crimes **Torts** under the doctrine of *respondeat superior*, a corporation is liable for torts committed by its employees within the course of their employment

Crimes a corporation may be criminally liable for violations of statutes imposing liability without fault or for an offense perpetrated by a high corporate officer or its board of directors

QUESTIONS

1. After part of the shares of a proposed corporation had been successfully subscribed, the promoter hired a carpenter to repair a building that was intended to be conveyed to the proposed corporation. The promoters subsequently secured subscriptions to the balance of the shares and completed the organization, but the corporation, finding the building to be unsuitable for its purposes, declined to use the building or to pay the carpenter. The carpenter brought suit against the corporation and the promoter for the amount that the promoter agreed would be paid to him. Who, if anyone, is liable?

2. C. A. Nimocks was a promoter engaged in organizing the Times Printing Company. On September 12, on behalf of the proposed corporation, he made a written contract with McArthur for her services as comptroller for a one-year period beginning October 1. The Times Printing Company was incorporated October 16, and on that date McArthur commenced her duties as comptroller. Neither the board of directors nor any officer took formal action on her employment, but all the shareholders, directors, and officers knew of the contract made by Nimocks. On December 1, McArthur was discharged without cause.
   a. Has she a cause of action against the Times Printing Company?
   b. Has she a cause of action against Nimocks?

3. Todd and Elaine purchased for $300,000 a building that was used for manufacturing pianos. Then, as promoters, they formed a new corporation and resold the building to the new corporation for $500,000 worth of stock. After discovering the actual purchase price paid by the promoters, the other shareholders desire to have $200,000 of the common stock canceled. Can they succeed in this action?

4. Wayne signed a subscription agreement for one hundred shares of stock of the proposed ABC Company, at a price of $18.00 per share. Two weeks later, the company was incorporated in a state that has adopted the Revised Act. A certificate was duly tendered to Wayne, but he refused to accept it. He was notified of all shareholders' meetings, but he never attended. A dividend check was sent to him, but he returned it. ABC Company brings a legal action against Wayne to recover $1,800. He defends on the ground that his subscription agreement was an unaccepted offer, that he had done nothing to ratify it, and that he was therefore not liable on it. Is he correct? Explain.

5. Julian, Cornelia, and Sheila petitioned for a corporate charter for the purpose of conducting a retail shoe business. They complied with all the statutory provisions except having their charter recorded. This was simply an oversight on their part, and they felt that they had fully complied with the law. They operated the business for three years, after which time it became insolvent. The creditors desire to hold the members personally and individually liable. May they do so?

6. Arthur, Barbara, Carl, and Debra decided to form a corporation for bottling and selling apple cider. Arthur, Barbara, and Carl were to operate the business, while Debra was to supply the necessary capital but was to have no voice in the management. They went to Jane, a lawyer, who agreed to organize a corporation for them under the name A-B-C Inc., and paid her funds sufficient to accomplish the incorporation. Jane promised that the corporation would definitely be formed by May 3. On April 27, Arthur telephoned Jane to inquire how the incorporation was progressing, and Jane said she had drafted the articles of incorporation and would send them to the secretary of state that very day. She assured Arthur that incorporation would occur before May 3.

   Relying on Jane's assurance, Arthur, with the approval of Barbara and Carl, on May 4 entered into a written contract with Grower for his entire apple crop. The contract was executed by Arthur on behalf of "A-B-C Inc." Grower delivered the apples as agreed. Unknown to Arthur, Barbara, Carl, Debra, or Grower, the articles of incorporation were never filed, through Jane's negligence. The business subsequently failed.

   What are Grower's rights, if any, against Arthur, Barbara, Carl, and Debra as individuals?

7. The Pyro Corporation has outstanding twenty thousand shares of common stock, of which nineteen thousand are owned by Peter B. Arson; five hundred shares are owned by Elizabeth Arson, his wife; and five hundred shares are owned by Joseph Q. Arson, his brother. These three individuals are the officers and directors of the corporation. The Pyro Corporation obtained a $750,000 fire insurance policy to cover a certain building it owned. Thereafter, Peter B. Arson set fire to the building, and it was totally destroyed. Can the corporation recover from the fire insurance company on the $750,000 fire insurance policy? Why?

8. A corporation is formed for the purpose of manufacturing, buying, selling, and dealing in drugs, chemicals, and similar products. The corporation, under authority of its board of directors, contracted to purchase the land and building it occupied as a factory and store. Collins, a shareholder, sues in equity to restrain the corporation from completing the contract, claiming that as the certificate of incorporation contained no provision authorizing the corporation to purchase real estate, the contract was *ultra vires*. Can Collins prevent the contract from being executed?

9. Amalgamated Corporation, organized under the laws of State S, sends several traveling salespersons into State M to solicit orders, which are accepted only at the home office of Amalgamated Corporation in State S. Riley, a resident of State M, places an order that is accepted by Amalgamated Corporation in State S. The Corporation Act of State M provides that "no foreign corporation transacting business in this state without a certificate of authority shall be permitted to maintain an action in any court of this state until such corporation shall have obtained a certificate of authority." Riley fails to pay for the goods, and when Amalgamated Corporation sues Riley in a court of State M, Riley defends on the ground that Amalgamated Corporation does not possess a certificate of authority from State M. Result?

CASE PROBLEMS

10. Dr. North, a surgeon practicing in Georgia, engaged an Arizona professional corporation consisting of twenty lawyers to represent him in a dispute with a Georgia hospital. West, a member of the law firm, flew to Atlanta and hired local counsel with Dr. North's approval. West represented Dr. North in two hearings before the hospital and in one court proceeding, as well as negotiating a compromise between Dr. North and the hospital. The total bill for the law firm's travel costs and professional services was $21,000, but Dr. North refused to pay $6,000 of it. The law firm brought an action against Dr. North for the balance owed. Dr. North argued that the action should be dismissed because the law firm failed to register as a foreign corporation in accordance with the Georgia Corporation Statute. Will the law firm be prevented from collecting on the contract? Explain.

11. An Arkansas statute provides that if any foreign corporation authorized to do business in the state should remove to the federal court any suit brought against it by an Arkansas citizen or initiate any suit in the federal court against a local citizen, without the consent of the other party, Arkansas's secretary of state should revoke all authority of the corporation to do business in the state. The Burke Construction Company, a Missouri corporation authorized to do business in Arkansas, has brought a suit in federal court and has also removed to a federal court a state suit brought against it. Burke now seeks to enjoin the secretary of state from revoking its authority to do business in Arkansas. Should the injunction be issued? Explain.

12. Little Switzerland Brewing Company was incorporated on January 28. On February 18, Ellison and Oxley were made directors of the company after they purchased some stock. Then, on September 25, Ellison and Oxley signed stock subscription agreements to purchase five thousand shares each. Under the agreement, they both issued a note that indicated that they would pay for the stock "at their discretion." Two years later in March, the board of directors passed a resolution canceling the stock subscription agreements of Ellison and Oxley. The creditors of Little Switzerland brought suit against Ellison and Oxley to recover the money owed under the subscription agreements. Are Ellison and Oxley liable? Why?

13. Oahe Enterprises was formed by the efforts of Emmick, who acted as a promoter and contributed shares of Colonial Manors, Inc. (CM), stock in exchange for stock in Oahe. The CM stock had been valued by CM's directors for internal stock option purposes at $19.00 per share. However, one month prior to Emmick's incorporation of Oahe Enterprises, CM's board reduced the stock value to $9.50 per share. Although Emmick knew of this reduction before the meeting to form Oahe Enterprises, he did not disclose this information to the Morrises, the other shareholders of the new corporation. Can Oahe Enterprises recover the shortfall?

14. In April, Cranson was asked to invest in a new business corporation that was about to be created. He agreed to purchase stock and to become an officer and director. After his attorney advised him that the corporation had been formed under the laws of Maryland, Cranson paid for and received a stock certificate evidencing his ownership of shares. The business of the new venture was conducted as if it were a corporation. Cranson was elected president, and he conducted all of his corporate actions, including those with IBM, as an officer of the corporation. At no time did he assume any personal obligation or pledge his individual credit to IBM. As a result of an oversight of the attorney, of which Cranson was unaware, the certificate of incorporation, which had been signed and acknowledged prior to May 1, was not filed until November 24. Between May 1 and November 8, the "corporation" purchased eight computers from IBM. The corporation made only partial payment. Can IBM hold Cranson personally liable for the balance due? Explain.

15. Healthwin-Midtown Convalescent Hospital, Inc. (Healthwin), was incorporated in California for the purpose of operating a health-care facility. For three years thereafter, it participated as a provider of services under the federal Medicare Act and received periodic payments from the U.S. Department of Health, Education and Welfare. Undisputed audits revealed that a series of overpayments had been made to Healthwin. The United States brought an action to recover this sum from the defendants, Healthwin and Israel Zide. Zide was a member of the board of directors of Healthwin, the administrator of its health-care facility, its president, and owner of 50 percent of its stock. Only Zide could sign the corporation's checks without prior approval of another corporate officer. Board meetings were not regularly held. In addition, Zide had a 50 percent interest in a partnership that owned both the realty in which Healthwin's health-care facility was located and the furnishings used at that facility. Healthwin consistently had outstanding liabilities in excess of $150,000, and its initial capitalization was only $10,000. Zide exercised control over Healthwin, causing its finances to become inextricably intertwined both with his personal finances and with his other business holdings. The United States contends that the corporate veil should be pierced and that Zide should be held personally liable for the Medicare overpayments made to Healthwin. Is the United States correct in its assertion? Why?

16. MPL Leasing Corporation is a California corporation that provides financing plans to dealers of Saxon Business Products. MPL invited Jay Johnson, a Saxon dealer in Alabama, to attend a sales seminar in Atlanta. MPL and Johnson entered into an agreement under which Johnson was to lease Saxon copiers with an option to buy. MPL shipped the equipment into Alabama and filed a financing statement with the secretary of state. When Johnson became delinquent with his payments to MPL, MPL brought an action against Johnson in an Alabama court. Johnson moved to dismiss the action, claiming that MPL was not qualified to conduct business in Alabama and was thus barred from enforcing its contract with Johnson in an Alabama court. Alabama law prevents foreign corporations not qualified to do business in Alabama from

enforcing their intrastate contracts in the Alabama court system. Is Johnson correct?

17. Berger was planning to produce a fashion show in Las Vegas. In April, Berger entered into a written licensing agreement with CBS Films, Inc., a wholly owned subsidiary of CBS, for presentation of the show. The next year, Stewart Cowley decided to produce a fashion show similar to Berger's and entered into a contract with CBS. CBS broadcast Cowley's show, but not Berger's. Berger brought this action against CBS to recover damages for breach of his contract with CBS Films. Berger claimed that CBS was liable because CBS Films was not operated as a separate entity, and that the court should disregard the parent-subsidiary form. In support of this claim, Berger showed that CBS Films's directors were employees of CBS, that CBS's organizational chart included CBS Films, and that all lines of employee authority from CBS Films passed through CBS employees to the CBS chairman of the board. CBS, in turn, argued that Berger had failed to justify piercing the corporate veil and disregarding the corporate identity of CBS Films to hold CBS liable. Decision?

18. Frank McAnarney and Joseph Lemon entered into an agreement to promote a corporation to engage in the manufacture of farm implements. Before the corporation was organized, McAnarney and Lemon solicited subscriptions to the stock of the corporation and presented a written agreement for the subscribers to sign. The agreement provided that the subscribers would pay $100 per share for stock in the corporation in consideration of McAnarney and Lemon's agreement to organize the corporation and advance the preincorporation expenses. Thomas Jordan signed the agreement, making application for one hundred shares of stock. After the articles of incorporation had been filed with the secretary of state but before the charter was issued to the corporation, Jordan died. The administrator of Jordan's estate notified McAnarney and Lemon that the estate would not honor Jordan's subscription.

   After the formation of the corporation, Franklin Adams signed a subscription agreement making application for one hundred shares of stock. Before the corporation accepted the subscription, Adams informed the corporation that he was canceling it.

   a. Can the corporation enforce Jordan's stock subscription against Jordan's estate?

   b. Can the corporation enforce Adams's stock subscription?

19. Green & Freedman Baking Company (Green & Freedman) was a corporation owned by the Elmans that produced and sold baked goods. The terms of a collective bargaining agreement required Green & Freedman Baking Company to make periodic payments on behalf of its unionized drivers to the New England Teamsters and Baking Industry Health Benefits and Insurance Fund (Health Fund). After sixty years of operation Green & Freedman experienced financial difficulties and ceased to make the agreed-upon contributions. The Elmans mixed their own finances with those of Green & Freedman's. The Elmans, through their domination of Green & Freedman, caused the corporation to make payments to themselves and their relatives at a time when the corporation

was known to be failing and could be expected to default, or was already in default, on its obligations to the Health Fund. It then transferred all remaining assets to a successor entity named Boston Bakers, Inc. (Boston Bakers). Boston Bakers operated essentially the same business as Green & Freedman until its demise two years later. The Health Fund sued Green & Freedman, Boston Bakers, and the two corporations' principals, Richard Elman and Stanley Elman, to recover the payments owed by Green & Freedman with interest, costs, and penalties. There was no evidence of financial self-dealing in the case of Boston Bakers. Both corporate defendants conceded liability for the delinquent contributions owed by Green & Freedman to the Health Fund. The suit against the Elmans was based on piercing the corporate veil with respect to Green & Freedman and Boston Bakers. The Elmans, however, denied they were personally liable for these corporate debts. Are the Elmans liable? Explain.

20. Ronald Nadler was a resident of Maryland and the CEO of Glenmar Cinestate, Inc., a Maryland corporation, as well as its principal stockholder. Glenmar leased certain space in the Westridge Square Shopping Center, located in Frederick, Maryland, and in Cranberry Mall, located in Westminster, Maryland. Tiller Construction Corporation and Nadler entered into two contracts for the construction of movie theaters at these locations, one calling for Tiller to do the work for Nadler at Westridge for $637,000, and the other for Tiller to do the work for Nadler at Cranberry for $688,800. Ronald Nadler requested that Tiller send all bills to Glenmar, the lessee at both shopping malls, but agreed to be personally liable to Tiller for the payment of both contracts. All inventory was bought and paid for locally, and Tiller paid sales tax in Maryland. Although there was no formal office in the state, Tiller leased a motel room for a considerable period of time, posted a sign at the job site, and maintained telephones listed in information. In addition, Tiller engaged in fairly pervasive management functions, and the value of the projects comprised a substantial part of Tiller's revenues during the period. At the time of the suit, there was a net balance due for the Cranberry project in the amount of $229,799.46, and on the Westridge project for the sum of $264,273.85, which Nadler refused to pay, even though he had approved all work and the work had been performed in a timely, good, and workmanlike manner. Tiller Construction Corporation sued Ronald Nadler and Glenmar Cinestate, Inc., for breach of contract. Nadler filed a motion to dismiss based on Maryland's business corporation statute, which prohibits a foreign corporation that conducts intrastate business in Maryland from maintaining a suit in Maryland courts if the corporation fails to register or qualify under Maryland law. Nadler asserted that Tiller was a New York corporation that had never qualified to transact business in the state of Maryland. Tiller conceded that the corporation had not qualified to do business in Maryland but argued that Tiller was not required to qualify because its activities did not constitute, in the contemplation of the statute, doing business in the state as Tiller just had occasional business in Maryland. Discuss whether Tiller could bring suit in Maryland.

TAKING SIDES

In May, Parr and Presba, while in the course of negotiations with Barker (a salesperson for Quaker Hill) to purchase plants and flowers, undertook to organize a corporation to be named the Denver Memorial Nursery, Inc. On May 14 and 16, Parr signed two orders on behalf of Denver Memorial Nursery, Inc. which, to the knowledge of Quaker Hill, was not yet formed, that fact being noted in the contract. A down payment in the amount of $1,000 was made. The corporation was not formed prior to entering into the contract because Quaker Hill insisted that the deal be concluded at once since the growing season was rapidly passing.

Under the contract, the balance of the purchase price was not due until the end of the year. The plants and flowers were shipped immediately and arrived on May 26. The Denver Memorial Nursery, Inc. was never formed. Quaker Hill seeks to recover the unpaid balance of the purchase price from Parr and Presba.

a. What are the arguments that Parr and Presba are personally liable for the unpaid balance?

b. What are the arguments that Parr and Presba are not personally liable for the unpaid balance?

c. Explain who should prevail.

Financial Structure of Corporations

CHAPTER 34

Corporation. An ingenious device for obtaining individual profit without individual responsibility.

Ambrose Bierce
The Devil's Dictionary (1881–1906)

CHAPTER OUTCOMES

After reading and studying this chapter, you should be able to:

1. Distinguish between equity and debt securities.

2. Identify and describe the principal kinds of debt securities.

3. Identify and describe the principal kinds of equity securities.

4. Explain what type and amount of consideration a corporation may validly receive for the shares it issues.

5. Explain the legal restrictions imposed upon dividends and other distributions.

Blue Sky Laws
state laws regulating the issuance and sale of securities

Practical Advice

Carefully consider the ratio between debt and equity financing, recognizing that this ratio varies considerably with the type and life cycle of a corporation.

C apital is necessary for any business to function. Two of the principal sources for corporate financing involve debt and equity investment securities. Although equity securities represent an ownership interest in the corporation and include both common and preferred stock, corporations finance most of their continued operations through debt securities. Debt securities, which include notes and bonds, do not represent an ownership interest in the corporation; rather, they create a debtor–creditor relationship between the corporation and the bondholder. The third principal way in which a corporation may meet its financial needs is through retained earnings.

All states have statutes regulating the issuance and sale of corporate shares and other securities. Popularly known as **Blue Sky Laws**, these statutes typically contain provisions prohibiting fraud in the sale of securities. In addition, a number of states require the registration of securities, and some states also regulate brokers, dealers, and others who engage in the securities business.

In 1933, Congress passed the first federal statute for the regulation of securities offered for sale and sold through the use of the mails or otherwise in interstate commerce. The statute requires a corporation to disclose certain information about a proposed security in a registration statement and in its *prospectus* (an offer a corporation makes to interest people in buying securities). Although the Securities and Exchange Commission (SEC) does not examine the merits of the proposed security and although registration does not guarantee the accuracy of the facts presented in the registration statement or prospectus, the law does prohibit false and misleading statements under penalty of fine or imprisonment or both.

Under certain conditions, a corporation may receive an exemption from the requirement of registration under the Blue Sky Laws of most states and the Securities Act of 1933. If no exemption is available, a corporation offering for sale or selling its shares of stock or other securities, as well as any person selling such securities, is subject to court injunction, possible criminal prosecution, and civil liability in damages to

GOING GLOBAL

What about foreign investment?

The financial aspects of transacting business abroad raise a number of legal issues including the taking of foreign investment property and restrictions on the flow of capital.

Investing in foreign countries involves the risk that the host nation's government may take the investment property. An *expropriation* or nationalization occurs when a government seizes foreign-owned property or assets for a public purpose and pays the owner just compensation for what is taken. In contrast, *confiscation* occurs when a government offers no payment (or a highly inadequate payment) in exchange for seized property, or seizes it for a nonpublic purpose. Confiscations violate generally observed principles of international law, whereas expropriations do not. In either case, few remedies are available to injured parties. One precaution that U.S. firms can take is to obtain insurance from a private insurer or from the Overseas Private Investment Corporation, an independent U.S. government agency.

Many nations have laws regulating foreign investment. Restrictions on the establishment of foreign investment tend to limit the amount of equity and the amount of control allowed to foreign investors. They may also restrict the way in which the investment is created, such as limiting or prohibiting investment by acquiring an existing locally owned business. At least 158 nations have signed the Convention on the Settlement of Investment Disputes Between States and Nationals of Other States. The Convention created the International Centre for the Settlement of Investment Disputes, which offers conciliation and arbitration for investment disputes between governments and foreign investors to promote increased flows of international investment.

the persons to whom securities are sold in violation of the regulatory statute. A discussion of federal regulation of securities appears in Chapter 39.

An investor has the right to transfer her investment securities by sale, gift, or pledge. The right to transfer is a valuable one, and easy transferability augments the value and marketability of investment securities. The availability of a ready market for any security affords liquidity and makes the security both attractive to investors and useful as collateral. The Uniform Commercial Code, Article 8, Investment Securities, contains the statutory rules applicable to transfers of investment securities; these rules are similar to those in Article 3, which concern negotiable instruments. In 1994 a revision to Article 8 was promulgated, which now has been adopted by all of the states. The federal securities laws also regulate several aspects of the transfer of investment securities, as discussed in Chapter 39.

In this chapter, we will discuss debt and equity securities as well as the payment of dividends and other distributions to shareholders.

DEBT SECURITIES

Debt security
source of capital creating no ownership interest and involving the corporation's promise to repay funds lent to it

Bond
a debt security

Authority to issue debt securities
each corporation has the power to issue debt securities as determined by the board of directors

Indenture
debt agreement specifying loan terms

Corporations frequently find it advantageous to use debt as a source of funds. **Debt securities** (also called **bonds**) generally involve the corporation's promise to repay the principal amount of a loan at a stated time and to pay interest, usually at a fixed rate, while the debt is outstanding. In addition to bonds, a corporation may finance its operations through other forms of debt, such as credit extended by its suppliers and short-term commercial paper. Some states, but not the Revised Act, permit articles of incorporation to confer voting rights on debt security holders; a few states allow other shareholder rights to be conferred on bondholders.

AUTHORITY TO ISSUE DEBT SECURITIES [34-1]

The Revised Act provides that every corporation has the power to borrow money and to issue its notes, bonds, and other obligations. The board of directors may issue bonds without the authorization or consent of the shareholders.

TYPES OF DEBT SECURITIES [34-2]

Depending on their characteristics, debt securities can be classified into various types, each offering numerous variants and combinations. A corporation typically issues debt securities under an **indenture** or debt agreement, which specifies in great detail the terms of the loan.

Metropolitan Life Insurance Company v. RJR Nabisco, Inc.
United States District Court, S.D. New York, 1989
716 F.Supp. 1504
http://scholar.google.com/scholar_case?case=2457879042014277410&q=716+F.Supp.+1504&hl=en&as_sdt=2,34

FACTS On October 20, 1988, F. Ross Johnson, then the CEO of RJR Nabisco (RJR), proposed a $17 billion leveraged buyout (LBO) of RJR's shareholders at $75.00 per share. (An LBO occurs when a group of investors, usually including the company's management, buy the company with little equity and significant new debt. The debt typically is financed through mortgages or high-risk/high-yield bonds, known as "junk bonds." A portion of this debt normally is secured by the company's assets. After the transaction is complete, some of these assets usually are sold to reduce the debt.) Within a few days, the investment group led by Johnson, the Kohlberg Kravis Roberts & Co. (KKR) private equity firm, and others began a bidding war. On December 1, 1988, an RJR committee recommended that RJR accept KKR's proposal of a $24 billion LBO at $109 per share. Metropolitan Life Insurance Co. (MetLife), a life insurance company with $88 billion in assets, owned $340,542,000 in principal amount of RJR Nabisco bonds purchased between July 1975 and July 1988. These bonds bore interest rates from 8 to 10.25 percent. Jefferson-Pilot Life Insurance Co., with $3 billion in assets, owned $9.34 million in principal of RJR bonds purchased between June 1978 and June 1988.

MetLife and Jefferson-Pilot (plaintiffs) argued that RJR had an implied duty of good faith and fair dealing not to incur the significant debt involved in the LBO. They asserted that RJR consistently had reassured its bondholders that it had a "mandate" from its board of directors to maintain RJR's preferred credit rating. The plaintiffs alleged that RJR's actions drastically impaired the value of their bond holdings, in effect misappropriated the value of those bonds to finance the LBO, and distributed the windfall to the company's shareholders. They declared that these actions constituted a breach of the implied duty and betrayed the fundamental basis of their bargain with RJR. The plaintiffs alleged that they unfairly suffered a multi-million dollar loss in the value of their bonds and that, therefore, RJR should redeem their bonds.

RJR defended the LBO by pointing to express provisions in the bond indentures that permitted mergers and the assumption of additional debt. These provisions, RJR pointed out, were known to the market and to the plaintiffs, who were sophisticated investors who freely bought the bonds and who were equally free to sell them at any time. RJR argued that no legal grounds supported the existence of an implied duty.

DECISION Judgment for RJR.

OPINION Although the numbers in this case are large and the financing is unprecedented, the legal principles governing the bonds are familiar: detailed bond indentures, which are in turn governed by New York contract law. The holders of public bonds often enter the market after the indentures have been negotiated and memorialized. Thus, those indentures are often not the product of face-to-face negotiations between the ultimate holders and the issuing company. Underwriters ordinarily negotiate the terms of the indentures with the issuers while keeping the buyers in mind. Moreover, the indentures in this case were not secret agreements imposed upon unwitting participants in the bond market. Indeed, sophisticated investors like the plaintiffs are well aware of indenture terms and presumably review them carefully before lending hundreds of millions of dollars to any company. Furthermore, the prospectus for the indentures contained this statement: "The Indenture contains no restrictions on the creation of unsecured short-term debt by [RJR]."

Under certain circumstances, courts will consider extrinsic evidence to evaluate the scope of an implied duty of good faith. In contracts such as bond indentures, however, an implied duty derives its substance directly from the language of the indenture and cannot give the holders of debentures any rights inconsistent with those set out in the indenture. The appropriate analysis, then, is to examine the indentures to determine the fruits of the agreement and to decide whether those "fruits" have been spoiled. The court holds that the "fruits" of these indentures do not include an implied duty that would prevent the incurrence of new debt to facilitate the LBO. The plaintiffs do not invoke an implied duty of good faith to protect a legitimate, mutually contemplated benefit of the indentures. Rather, they seek to create an additional benefit for which they did not bargain and which, if granted, would interfere with and destabilize the market.

INTERPRETATION Bond indentures are highly detailed contracts specifying the terms of the underlying loan. The courts will not imply any duties that are inconsistent with the terms of such a contract.

ETHICAL QUESTION Is the court's decision fair to the bondholders? Explain.

CRITICAL THINKING QUESTION Do you agree with the court's reluctance to impose an implied duty of good faith and fair dealing? Explain.

Unsecured bonds
also called debentures, have only the obligation of the corporation behind them

Unsecured Bonds [34-2a]

Unsecured bonds, usually called **debentures**, have only the obligation of the corporation behind them. Debenture holders are thus unsecured creditors and rank equally with other general creditors. To protect the unsecured bondholders, indentures frequently impose limitations

BUSINESS LAW **IN ACTION**

"Triple-A," "investment grade," and "junk" are familiar terms to those who invest in bonds. All three terms refer to a central concern of investors: what is the probability that the issuer of bonds will repay the principal at maturity and make scheduled interest payments on time? Put another way, what is the risk of default?

A high rating is supposed to reflect a high probability of repayment. The greater this probability, the less is the risk to the investor. Conversely, lower rated bonds are judged to be riskier. Generally, safer bonds have a lower yield, while riskier bonds have a higher yield. Investors taking greater risks demand a higher return.

Independent credit rating agencies analyze the companies and municipalities that issue bonds and assign ratings to reflect the credit-worthiness of the issuer. Credit rating agencies that are registered as such with the Securities and Exchange Commission (SEC) are known as Nationally Recognized Statistical Rating Organizations (NRSROs). In 2006, Congress passed the Credit Rating Agency Reform Act requiring the SEC to establish clear guidelines for determining which credit rating agencies qualify as NRSROs. There are ten firms currently registered as NRSROs: A.M. Best Company, Inc.; DBRS Ltd.; Egan-Jones Rating Company; Fitch, Inc.; Japan Credit Rating Agency, Ltd.; Kroll Bond Rating Agency, Inc.; Moody's Investors Service, Inc.; Rating and Investment Information, Inc.; Realpoint LLC; and Standard & Poor's Ratings Services.

In enacting the Dodd-Frank Wall Street Reform and Consumer Protection Act of 2010 (see Chapter 35), Congress found that "In the recent financial crisis, the ratings on structured financial products have proven to be inaccurate. This inaccuracy contributed significantly to the mismanagement of risks by financial institutions and investors, which in turn adversely impacted the health of the economy in the United States and around the world." Accordingly, the Dodd-Frank Act imposed additional requirements on NRSROs to enhance their accountability and transparency.

The two best-known of these NRSROs are Standard and Poor's and Moody's Investor Service. Standard and Poor's bond ratings, from highest to lowest, are AAA, AA+, AA, AA−, A+, A, A−, BBB+, BBB, BBB−, BB+, BB, BB−, B+, B, B−, CCC+, CCC, CCC−, CC, and D (in payment default). Moody's ratings are comparable: Aaa, Aa1, Aa2, Aa3, A1, A2, A3, Baa1, Baa2, Baa3, Ba1, Ba2, Ba3, B1, B2, B3, Caa1, Caa2, Caa3, Ca, C1. Moody's does not give a D.

"Investment grade" refers to the top-ten ratings, denoting bonds that are relatively safe investments for individuals and institutions. In contrast, "junk bonds" (generally anything rated below the top-ten ratings) are low rated, risky, and high yielding. Yields on junk bonds are higher than the rate of safe government bonds.

The quality of a particular bond can change over time as business conditions change for the issuer. For this reason, bond ratings have a subjective component. Analysts look not only at an issuing company's financial statements but also at trends in the industry—and adjust their ratings accordingly. A decrease in ratings will increase the companies' cost of borrowing and limit their fundraising options. Moreover, investment funds prohibited from owning junk bonds could be forced to sell corporate bonds with ratings below investment grade.

If a rating indicates how risky a bond is, then what, if anything, does it not reveal? Bond ratings relate to bond issuers, not investors. Thus, the ratings do not say whether a particular bond is an appropriate investment for a particular buyer. And ratings do not forecast the movement of interest rates, movement that causes bond prices to rise or fall. In other words, bond ratings are only a tool for investors, not a substitute for good judgment.

Secured bonds
are claims against a corporation's general assets and also a lien on specific property

Income bond
bond that conditions payment of interest on corporate earnings

Participating bond
bond that calls for a stated percentage of return regardless of earnings, with additional payments dependent upon earnings

on the corporation's borrowing, its payment of dividends, and its redemption and reacquisition of its own shares. An indenture may also require a corporation to maintain specified minimum reserves.

Secured Bonds [34-2b]

A secured creditor is one whose claim is not only enforceable against the general assets of the corporation but is also a lien on specific property. Thus, **secured** or mortgage **bonds** provide the security of specific corporate property in addition to the general obligation of the corporation. After resorting to the specified security, the holder of secured bonds becomes a general creditor for any unsatisfied amount of the debt.

Income Bonds [34-2c]

Traditionally, debt securities bear a fixed interest rate that is payable without regard to the financial condition of the corporation. **Income bonds**, on the other hand, condition the payment of interest to some extent on corporate earnings. **Participating bonds** call for a

Convertible bond

bond that may be exchanged for other securities of the corporation

Callable bond

bond that is subject to redemption (reacquisition) by the corporation

---

Practical Advice

If you purchase callable bonds, recognize that if interest rates decline, the corporation is likely to exercise its redemption privilege.

---

stated percentage of return regardless of earnings, with additional payments dependent on earnings.

Convertible Bonds [34-2d]

Usually at the option of the holder, **convertible bonds** may be exchanged, in a specified ratio, for other securities of the corporation. For example, a convertible bond may provide that the bondholder shall have the right for a specified time to exchange each bond for twenty shares of common stock.

Callable Bonds [34-2e]

Callable bonds are bonds subject to a redemption provision that permits the corporation to redeem or call (pay off) all or part of the issue before maturity at a specified redemption price.

EQUITY SECURITIES

Equity security

source of capital creating an ownership interest in the corporation

Share

a proportionate ownership interest in a corporation

An **equity security** is a source of capital creating an ownership interest in the corporation. The holders of equity securities, as owners of the corporation, occupy a position financially riskier than that of creditors, and changes in the corporation's fortunes and general economic conditions have a greater effect on shareholders than on any other class of investor.

Though a proportionate proprietary interest in a corporate enterprise can be described in terms of the **shares** a person owns, shares do not in any way vest their owner with title to any of the corporation's property. However, shares do confer on their owner a threefold interest in the corporation: (1) the right to participate in control, (2) the right to participate in the earnings of the corporation, and (3) the right to participate in the residual assets of the corporation on dissolution. The shareholder's interest is usually represented by a certificate of ownership and is recorded by the corporation.

ISSUANCE OF SHARES [34-3]

The state of incorporation regulates the issuance of shares by determining the type of shares that may be issued, the kinds and amount of consideration for which shares may be issued, and the rights of shareholders to purchase a proportionate part of additionally issued shares. Moreover, the federal government and each state in which the shares are issued or sold regulate the issuance and sale of shares.

Authority to issue shares

only those shares authorized in the articles of incorporation may be issued

---

Practical Advice

When drafting the articles of incorporation, you should authorize shares in addition to those that are to be immediately issued unless the state-imposed fees based on the number of authorized shares is prohibitive.

Authority to Issue Shares [34-3a]

The initial amount of shares to be issued is determined by the promoters or incorporators and is generally governed by practical business considerations and financial needs. A corporation is limited, however, to selling only the amount of shares that has been authorized in its articles of incorporation. Unauthorized shares of stock that are purportedly issued by a corporation are void. The rights of parties entitled to these overissued shares are governed by Article 8 of the Uniform Commercial Code, which provides that the corporation must either obtain an identical security, if one is reasonably available, for the person entitled to the security or pay that person the price he (or the last purchaser for value) paid for it, with interest from the date of that person's demand.

Once the amount of shares that the corporation is authorized to issue has been established and specified in the charter, it cannot be increased or decreased without amendment to the charter. Consequently, articles of incorporation commonly specify more shares than are to be issued immediately.

Preemptive Rights [34-3b]

Preemptive right

shareholder's right to purchase a *pro rata* share of new stock offerings

A shareholder's proportionate interest in a corporation can be changed by either a disproportionate issuance of additional shares or a disproportionate reacquisition of outstanding shares. Management is subject to fiduciary duties in both types of transactions. Moreover, when a corporation issues additional shares, a shareholder may have the **preemptive right** to purchase a proportionate part of the new issue. Preemptive rights are used far more frequently in closely held corporations than in publicly traded corporations, possibly because, without such rights, a shareholder may be unable to prevent a dilution of his ownership interest in the corporation. For example, Leonard owns two hundred shares of stock of the Fordham Company, which has a total of one thousand shares outstanding. The company decides to increase its capital stock by issuing one thousand additional shares of stock. If Leonard has preemptive rights, he and every other shareholder will be offered one share of the newly issued stock for every share they own. If he accepts the offer and buys the stock, he will have four hundred shares of a total of two thousand outstanding, and his relative interest in the corporation will be unchanged. Without preemptive rights, however, he would have only two hundred of the two thousand shares outstanding; instead of owning 20 percent of the stock, he would own 10 percent.

Most statutes expressly authorize articles of incorporation to deny or limit preemptive rights to the issuance of additionally authorized shares. In about half of the states, preemptive rights exist unless denied by the charter ("opt-out"); in about half of the states, they do not exist unless the charter so provides ("opt-in").

Practical Advice

To protect your ownership share from dilution, when organizing a close corporation you should consider including in the charter a carefully drafted provision for preemptive rights. You should recognize, however, that preemptive rights will protect you only if you can afford to purchase a proportionate part of a new issue of shares.

Certain shares are not subject to preemptive rights. In some states preemptive rights do not apply to the reissue of previously issued shares. In addition, preemptive rights generally do not apply to shares issued for noncash consideration or shares issued in connection with a merger or consolidation. Moreover, preemptive rights do not apply to the issuance of unissued shares that were originally authorized if the shares represent part of the initial capitalization.

The Revised Act adopts the opt-in approach: shareholders have no preemptive rights unless the charter provides for them. If the charter simply states that the corporation elects to have preemptive rights, the shareholders have a preemptive right to acquire proportional amounts of the corporation's unissued shares but have no such right with respect to (1) shares issued as compensation to directors, officers, and employees; (2) shares issued within six months of incorporation; and (3) shares issued for consideration other than money. In addition, holders of nonvoting preferred stock have no preemptive rights with respect to any class of shares, and holders of voting common shares have no preemptive rights with respect to preferred stock unless the preferred stock is convertible into common stock. The articles of incorporation may expressly modify any one or all of these limitations.

Amount of Consideration for Shares [34-3c]

Amount of consideration for shares

shares are deemed fully paid and nonassessable when a corporation receives the consideration for which the board of directors authorized the issuance of the shares, which in the case of par value stock must be at least par

The board of directors usually determines the price for which the corporation will issue shares, although the charter may reserve this power to the shareholders. Shares are deemed fully paid and nonassessable when the corporation receives the consideration for which the board of directors authorized their issuance. The amount of consideration depends on the kind of shares being issued.

Par Value Stock   In some states a corporation must specify in the articles of incorporation either a par value for its shares or that the shares are no par. Par value shares may be issued for any amount, not less than par, set by the board of directors or shareholders. The par value of stock must be stated in the articles of incorporation. The consideration received constitutes *stated capital* to the extent of the par value of the shares; any consideration in excess of par value constitutes *capital surplus*. It is common practice to authorize *low* or *nominal* par shares, such as $1.00 per share, and issue these shares at a considerably higher price, thereby providing ample capital surplus. By doing so, the company, in some jurisdictions, obtains greater flexibility in declaring subsequent distributions to shareholders.

The Revised Act, the 1980 amendments to the Model Business Corporation Act (MBCA), and at least twenty-eight states have eliminated the concepts of par value, stated capital, and

Figure 34-1 Issuance of Shares

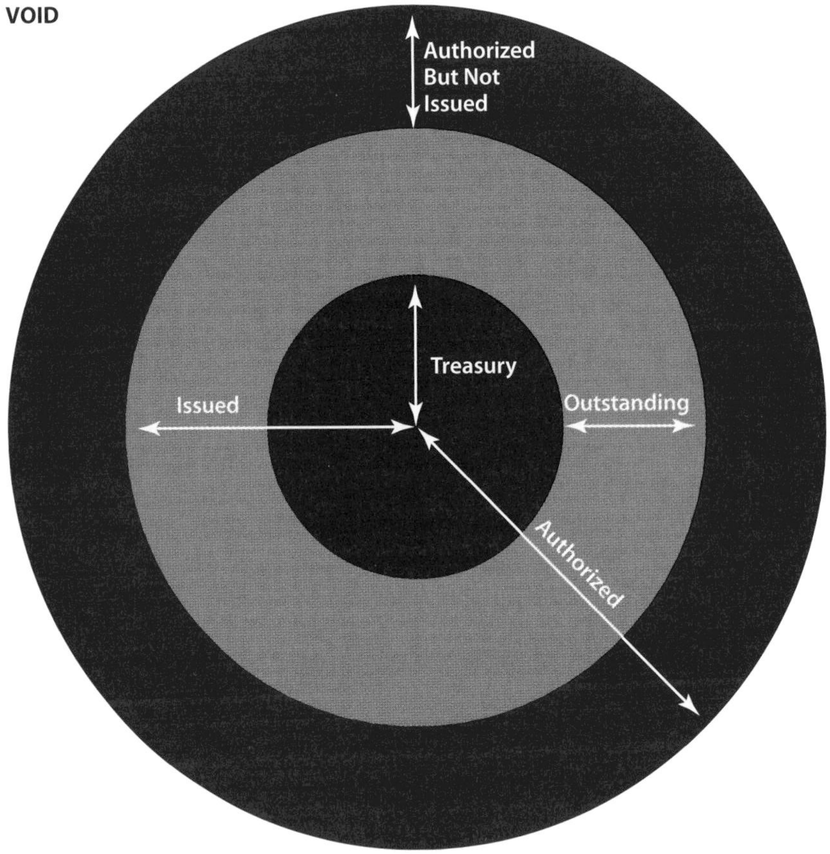

Practical Advice

Because a number of states grant more favorable tax treatment to par value stock, often it is more cost effective to issue low par value stock: this approach provides nearly the same flexibility as no par stock but with lower taxes.

capital surplus. Under these statutes, all shares may be issued for such consideration as authorized by the board of directors or, if the charter so provides, the shareholders. A corporation, however, may elect to issue shares with par value.

No Par Value Stock Shares without par value may be issued for any amount set by the board of directors or shareholders. Under incorporation statutes recognizing par value, stated capital, and capital surplus, the entire consideration a corporation receives for such stock constitutes *stated capital* unless the board of directors allocates a portion of the consideration to capital surplus. The directors are free to allocate any or all of the consideration received, unless the no par stock has a liquidation preference. In that event, only the consideration in excess of the amount of liquidation preference may be allocated to capital surplus. No par shares provide the directors great latitude in establishing capital surplus, which can, in some jurisdictions, provide greater flexibility in terms of subsequent distributions to shareholders.

Treasury stock

shares reacquired by a corporation

Treasury Stock **Treasury stock** refers to shares that a corporation buys back after it has issued them. Treasury shares are issued but not outstanding, in contrast to shares owned by shareholders, which are deemed issued and outstanding. A corporation may sell treasury shares for any amount the board of directors determines, even if the shares have a par value that is more than the sale price. Treasury shares do not provide voting rights or preemptive rights. In addition, no dividend is paid on treasury stock.

The Revised Act carries forward the 1980 amendments to the MBCA, which eliminated the concept of treasury shares. Under the Revised Act, all shares reacquired by a corporation are authorized but unissued shares, unless the articles of incorporation prohibit reissue, in which event the authorized shares are reduced by the number of shares reacquired.

Figure 34-1 illustrates the categorization of authorized shares.

Payment for shares may be cash, property, and services actually rendered, as determined by the board of directors; under the Revised Act, promises to contribute cash, property, or services are also permitted

Payment for Shares [34-3d]

Payment for shares involves two major issues. First, what type of consideration may the corporation validly accept in payment for shares? Second, who shall determine the value to be placed upon the consideration the corporation receives in payment for shares?

Type of Consideration

The definition of consideration for the issuance of capital stock is somewhat more limited than the definition of consideration under contract law. In about twenty-five states, cash, property, and services actually rendered to the corporation are generally acceptable as valid consideration, whereas promissory notes and promises regarding the performance of future services are not. Some states permit shares to be issued for preincorporation services; other states do not.

The Revised Act greatly liberalized these rules by specifically validating for the issuance of shares consideration consisting of any tangible or intangible property or benefit to the corporation, including cash, services performed, contracts for future services, and promissory notes.

Valuation of Consideration

Determining the value to be placed on the consideration that stock purchasers will exchange for shares is the responsibility of the directors. Many jurisdictions hold that this valuation is a matter of opinion and that, in the absence of fraud in the transaction, the judgment of the board of directors as to the value of the consideration the corporation receives for shares shall be conclusive. For example, assume that the directors of Elite Corporation authorize the issuance of two thousand shares of common stock for $10.00 per share to Kramer for property the directors purportedly value at $20,000. The valuation, however, is fraudulent, and the property is actually worth only $10,000. Kramer is liable to Elite Corporation and its creditors for $10,000. If, on the other hand, the directors had made the valuation without fraud and in good faith, Kramer would not be liable, even though the property is actually worth less than $20,000.

Under the Revised Act, the directors simply determine whether the consideration received (or to be received) for shares is *adequate*. Their determination is "conclusive insofar as the adequacy of consideration for the issuance of shares relates to whether the shares are validly issued, fully paid, and nonassessable." Under the Revised Act, the articles of incorporation may reserve to the shareholders the powers granted to the board regarding the issuance of shares.

Liability for Shares [34-3e]

A purchaser of shares has no liability to the corporation or its creditors with respect to shares except to pay the corporation either the consideration for which the shares were authorized to be issued or the consideration specified in the preincorporation stock subscription. When the corporation receives that consideration, the shares are fully paid and nonassessable. A transferee who acquires shares in good faith and without knowledge or notice that the full consideration had not been paid is not personally liable to the corporation or its creditors for the unpaid portion of the consideration.

CLASSES OF SHARES [34-4]

Corporations are generally authorized by statute to issue different classes of stock, which may vary with respect to their rights to dividends, their voting rights, and their right to share in the assets of the corporation on liquidation. The usual stock classifications are common and preferred shares. Although the Revised Act has eliminated the terms *preferred* and *common*, it permits the issuance of shares with different preferences, limitations, and relative rights. The Revised Act, however, explicitly requires a corporation's charter to authorize "(1) one or more classes of shares that together have unlimited voting rights, and (2) one or more classes of shares (which may be the same class or classes as those with voting rights) that together are entitled to receive the net assets of the corporation upon dissolution." In most states, however, even nonvoting shares may vote on certain mergers, share exchanges, and other fundamental changes that affect that class of shares as a class. See Chapter 36.

Practical Advice

To protect the value of your shares from dilution, when organizing a close corporation you should consider including in the charter a carefully drafted provision reserving to the shareholders the power to determine the value of consideration received for the issuance of additional shares.

Common Stock [34-4a]

Common stock
stock not having any special
contract rights

Common stock does not have any special contract rights or preferences. Frequently the only class of stock outstanding, it generally represents the greatest proportion of the corporation's capital structure and bears the greatest risk of loss should the enterprise fail.

Preferred Stock [34-4b]

Preferred stock
stock having contractual
rights superior to those of
common stock

Stock generally is considered **preferred stock** if it has contractual rights superior to those of common stock with regard to dividends, assets on liquidation, or both. (Most preferred stock has both dividend and liquidation preferences.) Other special rights or privileges generally do not remove stock from the common stock classification. The articles of incorporation must provide for the contractual rights and preferences of an issue of preferred stock.

Dividend Preferences

Dividend preference
must receive full dividends
before any dividend may be
paid on common stock

Though the holders of an issue of preferred stock with a **dividend preference** will receive full dividends before any dividend may be paid to holders of common stock, no dividend is payable on any class of stock, common or preferred, unless the board of directors has declared such dividend.

Preferred stock may provide that dividends are cumulative, noncumulative, or cumulative to the extent earned. For *cumulative* dividends, if the board does not declare regular dividends on the preferred stock, such omitted dividends cumulate, and no dividend may be declared on the common stock until all dividend arrearages on the preferred stock are declared and paid. If noncumulative, regular dividends do not cumulate on the board's failure to declare them, and all rights to a dividend for the period omitted are gone forever. Accordingly, *noncumulative* stock has priority over common stock only in the fiscal period during which a dividend on common stock is declared. Unless the charter expressly makes the dividends on preferred stock noncumulative, the courts generally hold them to be cumulative. *Cumulative-to-the-extent-earned* shares cumulate unpaid dividends only to the extent funds were legally available to pay such dividends during that fiscal period.

Preferred stock also may be participating, although generally it is not. *Participating preferred* shares are entitled to their original dividend, and after the common shares receive a specified amount, the participating preferred stock shares with the common stock in any additional dividends. The nature and extent of such participation on a specified basis with the common stock must be stated in the articles of incorporation. For example, a class of participating preferred stock could be entitled to share at the same rate with the common stock in any additional distribution of earnings for a given year *after* provision has been made for payment of the prior preferred dividend and for payment of dividends on the common stock at a rate equal to the fixed rate of the preferred.

Practical Advice

When organizing a
corporation, consider
issuing common stock to
the original shareholders
and preferred stock to
subsequent investors.

Liquidation Preferences

Liquidation preference
priority over common
stock in corporate assets
upon liquidation

After a corporation has been dissolved, its assets liquidated, and the claims of its creditors satisfied, the remaining assets are distributed *pro rata* among the shareholders according to their priority as provided in the articles of incorporation. If a class of stock with a dividend preference does not expressly provide for a preference of any kind on dissolution and liquidation, its holders share *pro rata* with the common shareholders.

When the articles provide a **liquidation preference**, preferred stock has priority over common stock to the extent the articles state. In addition, if specified, preferred shares may participate beyond the liquidation preference in a stated ratio with other classes of shares. Such shares are said to be participating preferred with reference to liquidation. Preferred shares not so specified do not participate beyond the liquidation preference.

Stock Options [34-4c]

Stock option
contractual right to
purchase stock from
a corporation

A corporation may issue **stock options** entitling their holders to purchase from the corporation shares of a specified class or classes. A *stock warrant* is a type of stock option that typically has a longer term and is freely transferable. A *stock right* is a short-term warrant. The board of directors determines the terms upon which stock rights, options, or warrants are issued; their form and content; and the consideration for which the shares are to be issued. Stock options and warrants are used in incentive compensation plans for directors, officers, and employees. Corporations also use them in raising capital to make one class of securities more attractive by including in it the right to purchase shares in another class immediately or at a later date.

CONCEPT REVIEW 34-1

Debt and Equity Securities

	Debt	Equity	
		Preferred	Common
Ownership Interest	No	Yes	Yes
Obligation to Repay Principal	Yes	No	No
Fixed Maturity	Yes	No	No
Obligation to Pay Income	Yes	No	No
Preference on Income	Yes	Yes	No
Preference on Liquidation	Yes	Yes	No
Voting Rights	Some states	Yes, unless denied	Yes, unless denied
Redeemable	Yes	Yes	In some states
Convertible	Yes	Yes	In some states

DIVIDENDS AND OTHER DISTRIBUTIONS

The board of directors, at its discretion, determines the time and amount in which to declare distributions and dividends. The corporation's working capital requirements, shareholder expectations, tax consequences, and other factors influence the board in forming distribution policy.

TYPES OF DIVIDENDS AND OTHER DISTRIBUTIONS [34-5]

Distribution

transfer of property from a corporation to any of its shareholders

The Revised Act defines a **distribution** as

> [A] direct or indirect transfer of money or other property (except its own shares) or incurrence of indebtedness by a corporation to or for the benefit of its shareholders in respect of any of its shares. A distribution may be in the form of a declaration or payment of a dividend; a purchase, redemption, or other acquisition of shares; a distribution of indebtedness; or otherwise.

Thus, a distribution includes the declaration or payment of a dividend, a purchase by a corporation of its own shares, a distribution of evidences of indebtedness or promissory notes of the corporation, and a distribution in voluntary or involuntary liquidation.

A stock or share dividend is a proportional distribution of additional shares of the corporation's capital stock to its shareholders. In a stock split, the corporation simply breaks each of the issued and outstanding shares into a larger number of shares, each representing a proportionately smaller interest in the corporation. Neither a stock dividend nor a stock split is a distribution.

The Revised Act validates in close corporations unanimous shareholder agreements by which the shareholders may relax traditional corporate formalities. This provision of the Act, for example, expressly authorizes shareholder agreements that permit making distributions not in proportion to share ownership.

Cash Dividends [34-5a]

Cash dividend

the most common type of distribution

The most customary type of dividend is a **cash dividend**, declared and paid at regular intervals from legally available funds. These dividends may vary in amount, depending on the policy of the board of directors and the earnings of the enterprise.

Property Dividends [34-5b]

Property dividend
distribution in the form of property

Although dividends are almost always paid in cash, shareholders occasionally have received a **property dividend**, a distribution of earnings in the form of property. On one occasion, a distillery declared and paid a dividend in bonded whiskey.

Liquidating Dividends [34-5c]

Liquidating dividend
a distribution of capital assets to shareholders

Although dividends ordinarily are identified with the distribution of profits, a distribution of capital assets to shareholders is referred to as a **liquidating dividend** in some jurisdictions. Incorporation statutes usually require that the shareholder be informed when a distribution is a liquidating dividend.

Redemption of Shares [34-5d]

Redemption of shares
a corporation's exercise of the right to repurchase its own shares

Redemption is the corporation's repurchase of its own shares, usually at its own option. Though the Model Act and the statutes of many states permit preferred shares to be redeemed, they do not allow the redemption of common stock; in contrast, the Revised Act does not prohibit redeemable common stock. The power of redemption must be expressly provided for in the articles of incorporation.

Acquisition of Shares [34-5e]

Acquisition of shares
a corporation's repurchase of its own shares

A corporation may acquire its own shares. As stated previously, such shares, unless canceled, are referred to as treasury shares. Under the Revised Act, such shares are considered authorized but unissued. As with redemption, the acquisition of shares constitutes a distribution to shareholders and has an effect similar to that of a dividend.

Legal restrictions on distributions
dividends and other distributions may be paid only if the cash flow and applicable balance sheet tests are satisfied

LEGAL RESTRICTIONS ON DIVIDENDS AND OTHER DISTRIBUTIONS [34-6]

A number of **legal restrictions on distributions** limit the amount of distributions the board of directors may declare. All states have statutes restricting the funds that are legally available for dividends and other distributions of corporate assets. In many instances, contractual restrictions imposed by lenders provide even more stringent limitations on the declaration of dividends and distributions.

Cash flow test
a corporation must not be or become insolvent (unable to pay its debts as they become due in the usual course of business)

States restrict the payment of dividends and other distributions to protect creditors. All states impose a **cash flow test**, the *equity insolvency test*, which prohibits the payment of any dividend or other distribution when the corporation either is insolvent or would become so through the payment of the dividend or distribution. **Insolvency in the equity sense** indicates the inability of a corporation to pay its debts as they become due in the usual course of business. In addition, almost all states impose further restrictions on what funds are legally available to pay dividends and other distributions. These additional restrictions, called the **balance sheet test**, are based on the corporation's assets or balance sheet, whereas the equity insolvency test is based on the corporation's cash flow.

Insolvency (equity)
unable to pay debts as they become due in the usual course of business

Balance sheet test
varies among the states and includes the earned surplus test (available in all states), the surplus test, and the net assets test (used by the Model and Revised Acts)

Definitions [34-6a]

The legal, asset-based restrictions on the payment of dividends or other distributions involve the concepts of earned surplus, surplus, net assets, stated capital, and capital surplus. Figure 34-2 displays the key concepts in the legal restrictions on distributions.

Earned surplus
undistributed net profits, income, gains, and losses

Earned surplus consists of the corporation's undistributed net profits, income, gains, and losses, computed from its date of incorporation.

Surplus
excess of net assets over stated capital

Surplus is the amount by which the net assets of a corporation exceed its stated capital.

Net assets
total assets minus total debts

Net assets equal the amount by which the total assets of a corporation exceed its total debts.

Figure 34-2 Key Concepts in Legal Restrictions upon Distributions

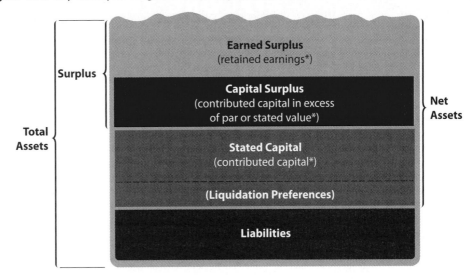

* Accounting terminology.

Stated capital
consideration, other than that allocated to capital surplus, received for issued stock

Stated capital is the sum of the consideration the corporation has received for its issued stock (except that part of the consideration properly allocated to capital surplus), including any amount transferred to stated capital when stock dividends are declared. In the case of par value shares, the amount of stated capital is the total par value of all the issued shares. In the case of no par stock, it is the consideration the corporation has received for all the no par shares it has issued, except that amount allocated in a manner permitted by law, to an account designated as capital surplus or paid-in surplus.

Capital surplus
surplus other than earned surplus

Capital surplus means the entire surplus of a corporation other than its earned surplus. It may result from an allocation of part of the consideration received for no par shares, from any consideration in excess of par value received for par shares, or from a higher reappraisal of certain corporate assets.

Legal Restrictions on Cash Dividends [34-6b]

Each state imposes an equity insolvency test on the payment of dividends. The states differ as to the asset-based or balance sheet test they apply. Some apply the earned surplus test and others use the surplus test. The Revised Act adopts a net asset test.

Earned Surplus Test Unreserved and unrestricted earned surplus is available for dividends in all jurisdictions. Many states permit dividends to be paid only from earned surplus; corporations in these jurisdictions may not pay dividends out of capital surplus or stated capital. In addition, dividends may not be paid if the corporation is or would be rendered insolvent in the equity sense by the payment. The MBCA used this test until 1980.

Surplus Test A number of less-restrictive states permit dividends to be paid out of any surplus—earned or capital. Some of these states express a surplus test by prohibiting dividends that impair stated capital. Moreover, dividends may not be paid if the corporation is or would be rendered insolvent in the equity sense by the payment.

Net Assets Test The MBCA, as amended in 1980, and the Revised Act have adopted a net asset test that permits a corporation to pay dividends unless its total assets after such payment would be less than the sum of its total liabilities and the maximum amount that then would be payable for all outstanding shares having preferential rights in liquidation.

APPLYING THE LAW

Financial Structure of Corporations

Facts Borman, Inc. is incorporated in a state that permits dividends to be paid only from unreserved and unrestricted earned surplus. It has two classes of outstanding stock: one hundred thousand shares of common stock and four thousand shares of 10 percent cumulative preferred stock with a stated value of $100. In each of 2014, 2015, and 2016, Borman had enough unreserved and unrestricted surplus earnings to pay $100,000 in dividends. However, in 2014 and 2015, the board declared no dividend. In 2016, the board declared a dividend of $10.00 per share on the preferred and $0.75 per share on the common stock.

Issue To what dividend payments are Borman's stockholders entitled?

Rule of Law The most common type of distribution is a cash dividend, which is payable from legally available funds. In all jurisdictions unreserved and unrestricted earned surplus is available for payment of dividends but in Borman's state dividends may be paid *only* from unreserved and unrestricted earned surplus. The board of directors has the discretion, but not the obligation, to declare distributions to shareholders. However, the actual amount and timing of a corporation's dividend payments depends on such factors as its working capital requirements, shareholder expectations, and tax consequences.

Corporations are statutorily authorized to issue different classes of stock, which vary in their rights to vote, to dividends, and to payments upon liquidation. The usual stock classifications are common and preferred. Common stock does not have any special contract rights or preferences. Preferred stock has a preference over common stock with respect to payment of dividends and/or with respect to distributions upon liquidation. If preferred stock has a cumulative dividend preference, no dividends may be paid to common stockholders until any current *as well as* accumulated dividends on that preferred stock have been declared and paid.

Application Borman's board of directors had no obligation in either 2014 or 2015 to declare a dividend. Nonetheless, the preferred stockholders accumulated dividends in 2014 and 2015, because their stock carries cumulative dividend rights. At its issuance, this particular preferred stock was denominated "10 percent cumulative," and it has a stated value of $100. Thus, Borman's preferred stockholders accumulated dividends of $10.00 per share in each of 2014 and 2015, despite the fact Borman's board did not declare a dividend. This means that before the 2016 dividend declaration, the preferred stockholders were already owed $20.00 per share. Before a dividend for the common stock can be declared and paid in 2016, this $80,000 ($20.00 × 4,000 shares) arrearage must be paid to the preferred stockholders. Since the earned surplus available for distribution in 2016 is only $100,000, that year's preferred stock dividend and accumulated arrearages—totaling $120,000—cannot be paid in full. If the board declares and pays this $100,000 to the preferred shareholders, the $20,000 remaining unpaid to them carries forward as an arrearage.

Because there is still an arrearage owed to preferred stockholders, the declaration of a dividend on the common stock was improper, and the common stockholders will receive no dividend payment in 2016. Unlike preferred stockholders, owners of common stock are entitled to dividends only when declared by the board of directors, and then only after dividend arrearages and any current dividend preferences on the preferred stock are declared and paid.

Conclusion The preferred dividend declaration of $10.00 per share on the preferred stock is proper. If the board chooses to pay out the remainder of the legally available funds as dividends, the preferred stockholders are entitled to that remainder resulting in a distribution to them of $25.00 per share. The remaining $5.00 per share not paid to the preferred stockholders would accumulate. Common stockholders are entitled to nothing; moreover, they will not be paid any dividend in the future until any arrearages and then-current dividends owed to the preferred stockholders have been paid in full.

Legal restrictions on liquidating distributions

states usually permit distribution in partial liquidation from capital surplus unless the company is insolvent

Legal Restrictions on Liquidating Distributions [34-6c]

Even those states that do not permit cash dividends to be paid from capital surplus usually will permit distributions, or dividends, in partial liquidation from that source. Prior to 1980, the Model Act had such a provision. A distribution paid out of such surplus returns to the shareholders' part of their investment.

No such distribution may be made, however, when the corporation is insolvent or would become insolvent by the distribution. Distributions from capital surplus are also restricted to protect the liquidation preference and cumulative dividend arrearages of preferred shareholders. Unless provided for in the articles of incorporation, a liquidating dividend must be authorized not only by the board of directors but also by the affirmative vote of the holders of a majority of the outstanding shares of stock of each class.

Because the Revised Act does not distinguish between cash and liquidating dividends, it therefore imposes the same limitations upon both.

**Legal restrictions on
redemptions of shares**

in most states, a
corporation may not
redeem shares when
insolvent or when such
redemption would render it
insolvent

**Legal restrictions on
acquisition of shares**

restrictions similar to those
on cash dividends usually
apply

Legal Restrictions on Redemption and Acquisition of Shares [34-6d]

To protect creditors and holders of other classes of shares, most states have statutory restrictions on redemption. A corporation may not redeem or purchase its redeemable shares when insolvent or when such redemption or purchase would render it insolvent or would reduce its net assets below the aggregate amount payable on shares having prior or equal rights to the corporation's assets upon involuntary dissolution.

A corporation may purchase its own shares only out of earned surplus or, if the articles of incorporation permit or if the shareholders approve, out of capital surplus. As with redemption, the corporation may make no purchase of shares when it is insolvent or when such purchase would make it insolvent.

The Revised Act permits a corporation to purchase, redeem, or otherwise acquire its own shares unless (1) the corporation's total assets after the distribution would be less than the sum of its total liabilities and the maximum amount that then would be payable for all outstanding shares having preferential rights in liquidation or (2) the corporation would be unable to pay its debts as they become due in the usual course of its business.

Additional restrictions may apply to a corporation's acquisition of its own shares. In close corporations, for example, courts may scrutinize acquisitions for compliance with the good faith and fair dealing requirements of the fiduciary duty. See *Donahue v. Rodd Electrotype Co., Inc.* in Chapter 35.

Cox Enterprises, Inc. v. Pension Benefit Guaranty Corporation
United States Court of Appeals, Eleventh Circuit, 2012
666 F.3d 697
http://scholar.google.com/scholar_case?q=666+F.3d+697&hl=en&as_sdt=6,34&case=11816251525387610788&scilh=0

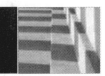

FACTS In May 2004, Cox Enterprises, Inc. (Cox), a long-time minority shareholder, sued the closely held News-Journal Corporation (News-Journal) in response to perceived abuses by News-Journal's directors in the handling of corporate assets. News-Journal elected to pursue the option provided by Florida's statute to repurchase Cox's shares. Because the parties could not agree on the fair market value of Cox's shares, the statute required that the district court determine their value. The court set the value of Cox's shares at $129.2 million and directed the terms of payment in a September 2006 order.

Between the valuation of those shares and the court ordered date for payment, News-Journal's ability to pay diminished significantly. In response, the district court appointed a receiver to manage News-Journal and prepare it for sale. After the sale of News-Journal's assets, the receiver solicited claims from News-Journal's various creditors. The district court disposed of these competing claims for News-Journal's limited assets by ordering the distribution of all the assets to Cox as payment for its shares. The Pension Benefit Guaranty Corporation (PBGC) appealed this order, contending that to distribute News-Journal's assets to Cox—a single News-Journal shareholder—pursuant to the repurchase order would render News-Journal insolvent, and that the distributions-to-shareholders provision of the Florida business corporation statute forbids this payment.

DECISION The district court's order is vacated, and the case is remanded.

OPINION The Florida election-to-purchase statute allows a corporation or other shareholders to avoid dissolution by purchasing the shares of the petitioning shareholder who initiated a dissolution proceeding. After a corporation has elected to repurchase all of the

shares owned by the petitioning shareholder, if the parties cannot agree on the value, then the court must determine the "fair value."

Payments made pursuant to a repurchase order, however, must comply with Fla. Stat. § 607.06401, which governs the distribution of corporate assets to shareholders. This distributions-to-shareholders section creates a scheme focused on the corporation's solvency to evaluate the propriety of distributions to shareholders. Subsection 3 of Fla. Stat. § 607.06401 provides in part:

> No distribution may be made if, after giving it effect: (a) The corporation would not be able to pay its debts as they become due in the usual course of business; or (b) The corporation's total assets would be less than the sum of its total liabilities plus (unless the articles of incorporation permit otherwise) the amount that would be needed, if the corporation were to be dissolved at the time of the distribution, to satisfy the preferential rights upon dissolution of shareholders whose preferential rights are superior to those receiving the distribution.

Section 607.06401, by placing restrictions on the distribution of corporate assets, maintains the fundamental tenet of corporate law that creditors' claims on corporate assets are superior to claims of shareholders. To achieve this, a distribution of corporate assets to a shareholder must not result in the violation of one of these insolvency tests.

Subsection 6 of Fla. Stat. § 607.06401 explains at what point in time must a distribution pass one of these insolvency tests:

> *Except as provided in subsection (8)*, the effect of a distribution under subsection (3) is measured:
> **(a)** In the case of distribution by purchase, redemption, or other acquisition of the corporation's shares, as of the earlier of:
>   **1.** The date money or other property is transferred or debt incurred by the corporation, or

2. The date the shareholder ceases to be a shareholder with respect to the acquired shares.

The exception contained in subsection 8 contains a different timing provision. It provides, "If the indebtedness is issued as a distribution, each payment of principal or interest is treated as a distribution, the effect of which is measured *on the date the payment is actually made*." Thus any payment made pursuant to a repurchase order must satisfy the insolvency test of the distributions-to-shareholders section judged at the time dictated by the distributions-to-shareholders section.

The parties here dispute when the court should evaluate News-Journal's insolvency. Cox asserts that News-Journal's solvency should be measured as of September 2006 based on subsection 6, which states that the effect of a distribution is generally measured on the date the corporation incurs a debt or the date a shareholder ceases to be a shareholder. PBGC claims that subsection 8 requires solvency be measured on the date of payment.

PBGC is correct in asserting that the district court's September 2006 repurchase order created an indebtedness by News-Journal to Cox and therefore News-Journal's solvency should be measured on the date of payment. Thus, on remand, the district court must consider whether a payment to Cox would comply with the insolvency test of the distributions-to-shareholders section at the time of payment to Cox. If on remand the district court finds a distribution to Cox would violate this section, News-Journal's other creditors should receive payment before any distribution is made to Cox.

INTERPRETATION Distributions by the corporation to shareholders are not permitted if those distributions would render the corporation insolvent; in cases in which indebtedness is issued as a distribution, solvency is to be determined on the date of the payment to the shareholder.

CRITICAL THINKING QUESTION Did the district court's order violate the fundamental principle of corporate law that equity should be paid last in the event of corporate insolvency? Explain.

DECLARATION AND PAYMENT OF DISTRIBUTIONS [34-7]

The board of directors of a corporation declares dividends and other distributions, and this power may not be delegated. If the charter clearly and expressly provides for mandatory dividends, however, the board must comply with the provision. Nonetheless, such provisions are extremely infrequent, and shareholders cannot assume this power in any other way, although it is in their power to elect a new board. Moreover, the board cannot discriminate in its declaration of dividends among shareholders of the same class.

Shareholders' right to compel a dividend
the declaration of dividends is within the discretion of the board of directors and only rarely will a court substitute its business judgment for that of the board

Shareholders' Right to Compel a Dividend [34-7a]

If the directors fail to declare a dividend, a shareholder may bring a suit in equity against them and the corporation to seek a mandatory injunction requiring the directors to declare a dividend. However, courts of equity are reluctant to order an injunction of this kind, for such a judgment involves substituting the court's business judgment for that of the directors elected by the shareholders. With respect to the directors' discretion regarding the declaration of dividends, a preferred shareholder having prior rights with respect to dividends is in the same position as the holder of common shares.

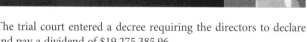

Dodge v. Ford Motor Co.
Supreme Court of Michigan, 1919
204 Mich. 459, 170 N.W. 668

FACTS Ford Motor Company had made large profits for several years. Henry Ford, Ford's president and the dominant figure on its board of directors, declared that although it had paid special dividends in the past, Ford would not, as a matter of policy, pay any special dividends in the future but instead would reinvest the profits in the proposed expansion of the company. At the conclusion of Ford's most prosperous year, John and Horace Dodge, minority shareholders in Ford, brought this action against Ford's directors to compel the declaration of dividends and to enjoin the expansion of the business. The Dodges complained that the reinvestment of the profits was not in the best interests of Ford and its shareholders and that it was an arbitrary action of the directors.

The trial court entered a decree requiring the directors to declare and pay a dividend of $19,275,385.96.

DECISION That part of the decree fixing and determining the specific amount to be distributed to stockholders affirmed; decree reversed in other respects.

OPINION In general, it is not a violation of a corporation's charter to accumulate profits for reinvestment in the company. As the managers of a corporation, the directors are impliedly invested with discretionary power as to the time and manner of distributing the company's profits. But while the court is reluctant to substitute its judgment for that of the directors, their refusal to declare and pay special dividends in light of the large surplus was not an exercise of discretion but an arbitrary refusal to do what the circumstances required to be done.

INTERPRETATION The right of shareholders to receive a share of the corporation's profits may not be arbitrarily withheld by the directors.

ETHICAL QUESTION Was the court's decision fair to all of the parties? Explain.

CRITICAL THINKING QUESTION Under what circumstances should a court override a decision by the board of directors not to declare a dividend? Explain.

Effect of declaration

once properly declared, a cash dividend is considered a debt the corporation owes to the shareholders

Effect of Declaration [34-7b]

Once lawfully and properly declared, a cash dividend is considered a debt the corporation owes to the shareholders. It follows from this debtor–creditor relationship that, once declared, a declaration of a cash dividend cannot be rescinded without the shareholders' consent; a stock dividend, however, may be revoked unless actually distributed.

LIABILITY FOR IMPROPER DIVIDENDS AND DISTRIBUTIONS [34-8]

Directors' liability

the directors who assent to an improper dividend are liable for the unlawful amount of the dividend

The Revised Act imposes personal liability on the **directors** of a corporation who vote for or assent to the declaration of a dividend or other distribution of corporate assets contrary to the incorporation statute or the articles of incorporation. The damages equal the amount of the dividend or distribution in excess of the amount that the corporation lawfully may have paid.

A director is not liable if she acted in accordance with the relevant standard of conduct: in good faith, with reasonable care, and in a manner she reasonably believed to be in the best interests of the corporation. (This standard of conduct is discussed in the next chapter.) In discharging this duty, a director is entitled to rely in good faith on financial statements presented by the corporation's officers, public accountants, or finance committee. Such statements must be prepared on the basis of "accounting practices and principles that are reasonable in the circumstances or on a fair valuation or other method that is reasonable in the circumstances." According to the Comments to the Revised Act, generally accepted accounting principles are always reasonable in the circumstances; other accounting principles may be acceptable under a general standard of reasonableness.

Shareholders' liability

a shareholder must return illegal dividends if he knew of the illegality, if the dividend resulted from his fraud, or if the corporation is insolvent

A **shareholder's** obligation to repay an illegally declared dividend depends on a variety of factors, which may include the faith, good or bad, in which the shareholder accepted the dividend; his knowledge of the facts; the solvency or insolvency of the corporation; and, in some instances, special statutory provisions. The existence of statutory liability on the part of directors does not relieve shareholders from the duty to make repayment.

A shareholder who receives illegal dividends with knowledge of their unlawful character is under a duty to refund them. When the corporation is insolvent, the shareholder may not retain even a dividend received in good faith. However, when an unsuspecting shareholder receives an illegal dividend from a solvent corporation, the majority rule is that the corporation cannot compel a refund.

CONCEPT REVIEW 34-2

Liability for Improper Distributions

	Corporation Solvent	Corporation Insolvent
Nonbreaching Director	No	No
Breaching Director	Yes	Yes
Knowing Shareholder	Yes	Yes
Innocent Shareholder	No	Yes

CHAPTER SUMMARY

Debt Securities

Authority to Issue Debt Securities

Definitions

- *Debt Security* source of capital creating no ownership interest and involving the corporation's promise to repay funds lent to it
- *Bond* a debt security

Rule each corporation has the power to issue debt securities as determined by the board of directors

Types of Debt Securities

Unsecured Bonds called debentures, have only the obligation of the corporation behind them

Secured Bonds are claims against a corporation's general assets and a lien on specific property

Income Bonds condition to some extent the payment of interest on corporate earnings

Participating Bonds call for a stated percentage of return regardless of earnings, with additional payments dependent upon earnings

Convertible Bonds may be exchanged for other securities

Callable Bonds bonds subject to redemption

Equity Securities

Issuance of Shares

Definitions

- *Equity Security* source of capital creating an ownership interest in the corporation
- *Share* a proportionate ownership interest in a corporation
- *Treasury Stock* shares reacquired by a corporation

Authority to Issue Shares only those shares authorized in the articles of incorporation may be issued

Preemptive Rights right to purchase a *pro rata* share of new stock offerings

Amount of Consideration for Shares shares are deemed fully paid and nonassessable when a corporation receives the consideration for which the board of directors authorized the issuance of the shares, which in the case of par value stock must be at least par

Payment for Newly Issued Shares may be cash, property, and services actually rendered, as determined by the board of directors; under the Revised Act, promises to contribute cash, property, or services are also permitted

Classes of Shares

Common Stock stock not having any special contract rights

Preferred Stock stock having contractual rights superior to those of common stock

- *Dividend Preferences* must receive full dividends before any dividend may be paid on common stock
- *Liquidation Preferences* priority over common stock in corporate assets upon liquidation

Stock Options contractual right to purchase stock from a corporation

Dividends and Other Distributions

Types of Dividends and Other Distributions

Distributions transfers of property by a corporation to any of its shareholders in respect of its shares; become debts of the corporation if and when declared by the board

Cash Dividends the most common type of distribution

Property Dividends distribution in form of property

Stock Dividends a proportional distribution of additional shares of stock

Stock Splits each of the outstanding shares is broken into a larger number of shares

Liquidating Dividends a distribution of capital assets to shareholders

Redemption of Shares a corporation's exercise of the right to repurchase its own shares

Acquisition of Shares a corporation's repurchase of its own shares

Legal Restrictions on Dividends and Other Distributions	**Legal Restrictions on Cash Dividends** dividends may be paid only if the cash flow and applicable balance sheet tests are satisfied
	• *Cash Flow Test* a corporation must not be or become insolvent (unable to pay its debts as they become due in the usual course of business)
	• *Balance Sheet Test* varies among the states and includes the earned surplus test (available in all states), the surplus test, and the net assets test (used by the Model and Revised Acts)
	Legal Restrictions on Liquidating Distributions states usually permit distribution in partial liquidation from capital surplus unless the company is insolvent
	Legal Restrictions on Redemptions of Shares in most states, a corporation may not redeem shares when insolvent or when such redemption would render it insolvent
	Legal Restrictions on Acquisition of Shares restrictions similar to those on cash dividends usually apply
Declaration and Payment of Distributions	**Shareholders' Right to Compel a Dividend** the declaration of dividends is within the discretion of the board of directors and only rarely will a court substitute its business judgment for that of the board
	Effect of Declaration once properly declared, a cash dividend is considered a debt the corporation owes to the shareholders
Liability for Improper Dividends and Distributions	**Directors** the directors who assent to an improper dividend are liable for the unlawful amount of the dividend
	Shareholder a shareholder must return illegal dividends if he knew of the illegality, if the dividend resulted from his fraud, or if the corporation is insolvent

QUESTIONS

1. Olympic National Agencies was organized with an authorized capitalization of preferred stock and common stock. The articles of incorporation provided for a 7 percent annual dividend for the preferred stock. The articles further stated that the preferred stock would be given priority interests in the corporation's assets up to the par value of the stock. After some years, the shareholders voted to dissolve Olympic. Olympic's assets greatly exceeded its liabilities. The liquidating trustee petitioned the court for instructions on the respective rights of the shareholders in the assets of the corporation upon dissolution. The court ordered the trustee to distribute the corporate assets remaining after the preference of the preferred stock is satisfied to the common and preferred stockholders on a *pro rata* basis. Was the court correct in rendering this decision? Explain.

2. XYZ Corporation was duly organized on July 10. Its certificate of incorporation provides for a total authorized capital of $1 million, consisting of ten thousand shares of common stock with a par value of $100 per share. The corporation issued for cash a total of five hundred certificates, numbered one to five hundred inclusive, representing various amounts of shares in the names of various individuals. All the shares had been paid for in advance, so the certificates were all dated and mailed on the same day. The five hundred certificates of stock represent a total of 10,500 shares. Certificate number 499 for 300 shares was issued to Jane Smith. Certificate number 500 for 250 shares was issued to William Jones. Is there any question concerning the validity of any of the stock thus issued? What are the rights of Smith and Jones?

3. Doris subscribed for two hundred shares of 12 percent cumulative, participating, redeemable, convertible, preferred shares of the Ritz Hotel Company with a par value of $100 per share. The subscription agreement provided that she was to receive a bonus of one share of common stock of $100 par value for each share of preferred stock. Doris fully paid her subscription agreement of $20,000 and received the two hundred shares of preferred stock and the bonus stock of two hundred shares of the par value common. The Ritz Hotel Company later becomes insolvent. Ronald, the receiver of the corporation, brings suit for $20,000, the par value of the common stock. What judgment?

4. Hyperion Company has an authorized capital stock of one thousand shares with a par value of $100 per share, of which nine hundred shares, all fully paid, were outstanding. Having an ample surplus, Hyperion Company purchased from its shareholders one hundred shares at par. Subsequently, Hyperion, needing additional working capital, issued the two hundred shares in question to Alexander at $80.00 per share. Two years later, Hyperion Company was forced into bankruptcy. How much, if any, may the trustee in bankruptcy recover from Alexander?

5. For five years, Henry and James had been engaged as partners in building houses. They owned the equipment necessary to conduct the business and had an excellent reputation. In March, Joyce, who previously had been in the same kind of business, proposed that Henry, James, and Joyce form a corporation for the purpose of constructing medium-priced houses. They engaged attorney Portia, who did all the work

required and caused the business to be incorporated under the name of Libra Corp.

The certificate of incorporation authorized one thousand shares of $100 par value stock. At the organizational meeting of the incorporators, Henry, James, and Joyce were elected directors, and Libra Corp. issued a total of six hundred and fifty shares of its stock. Henry and James each received two hundred shares in consideration for transferring to Libra Corp. the equipment and goodwill of their partnership, which had a combined value of more than $40,000. Joyce received two hundred shares as an inducement to work for Libra Corp. in the future, and Portia received fifty shares as compensation for the legal services she rendered in forming Libra Corp.

Later that year, Libra Corp. had a number of financial setbacks and in December ceased operations. What rights, if any, does Libra Corp. have against Henry, James, Joyce, and Portia in connection with the original issuance of its shares?

6. Paul Bunyan is the owner of noncumulative 8 percent preferred stock in the Broadview Corporation, which had no earnings or profits in 2013. In 2014, the corporation had large profits and a surplus from which it might properly have declared dividends. However, the directors refused to do so, using the surplus instead to purchase goods necessary for the corporation's expanding business. The corporation earned a small profit in 2015. The directors at the end of 2015 declared a 10 percent dividend on the common stock and an 8 percent dividend on the preferred stock without paying preferred dividends for 2014.
   a. Is Bunyan entitled to dividends for 2013? For 2014?
   b. Is Bunyan entitled to a dividend of 10 percent rather than 8 percent in 2015?

7. Alpha Corporation has outstanding four hundred shares of $100 par value common stock, which has been issued and sold at $105 per share for a total of $42,000. Alpha is incorporated in State X, which has adopted the earned surplus test for all distributions. At a time when the assets of the corporation amount to $65,000 and the liabilities to creditors total $10,000, the directors learn that Rachel, who holds one hundred of the four hundred shares of stock, is planning to sell her shares on the open market for $10,500. Believing that this will not be in the best interest of the corporation, the directors enter into an agreement with Rachel to buy the shares for $10,500. About six months later, when the assets of the corporation have decreased to $50,000 and its liabilities, not including its liability to Rachel, have increased to $20,000, the directors use $10,000 to pay a dividend to all of the shareholders. The corporation later becomes insolvent.

   a. Does Rachel have any liability to the corporation or its creditors in connection with the corporation's reacquisition of the one hundred shares?
   b. Was the payment of the $10,000 dividend proper?

8. Almega Corporation, organized under the laws of State S, has outstanding twenty thousand shares of $100 par value nonvoting preferred stock calling for noncumulative dividends of $5.00 per year; ten thousand shares of voting preferred stock of $50.00 par value, calling for cumulative dividends of $2.50 per year; and ten thousand shares of no par common stock. State S has adopted the earned surplus test for all distributions. As of the end of 2010, the corporation had no earned surplus. In 2011, the corporation had net earnings of $170,000; in 2012, $135,000; in 2013, $60,000; in 2014, $210,000; and in 2015, $120,000. The board of directors passed over all dividends during the four years from 2011 to 2014, as the company needed working capital for expansion purposes. In 2015, however, the directors declared a dividend of $5.00 per share on the noncumulative preferred shares, a dividend of $12.50 per share on the cumulative preferred shares, and a dividend of $30.00 per share on the common stock. The board submitted its declaration to the voting shareholders, and they ratified it. Before the dividends were paid, Payne, the record holder of five hundred shares of the noncumulative preferred stock, brought an appropriate action to restrain any payment to the cumulative preferred or common shareholders until the company paid a full dividend for the period from 2011 to 2015. Decision? What is the maximum lawful dividend that may be paid to the owner of each share of common stock?

9. Sayre learned that Adams, Boone, and Chase were planning to form a corporation for the purpose of manufacturing and marketing a line of novelties to wholesale outlets. Sayre had patented a self-locking gas tank cap but lacked the financial backing to market it profitably. He negotiated with Adams, Boone, and Chase, who agreed to purchase the patent rights for $5,000 in cash and two hundred shares of $100 par value preferred stock in a corporation to be formed.

   The corporation was formed and Sayre's stock issued to him, but the corporation has refused to make the cash payment. It has also refused to declare dividends, although the business has been very profitable because of Sayre's patent and has a substantial earned surplus with a large cash balance on hand. It is selling the remainder of the originally authorized issue of preferred shares, ignoring Sayre's demand to purchase a proportionate number of these shares. What are Sayre's rights, if any?

CASE PROBLEMS

10. Wood, the receiver of Stanton Oil Company, sued Stanton's shareholders to recover dividends paid to them for three years, claiming that at the time these dividends were declared, Stanton was in fact insolvent. Wood did not allege that the present creditors were also creditors when the dividends were paid. Were the dividends wrongfully paid? Explain.

11. International Distributing Export Company (IDE) was organized as a corporation on September 7, 2008, under the laws of New York and commenced business on November 1, 2008. IDE formerly had existed as a sole proprietorship. On October 31, 2008, the newly organized corporation had liabilities of $64,084. Its only assets, in the sum of $33,042, were those of

the former sole proprietorship. The corporation, however, set up an asset on its balance sheet in the amount of $32,000 for goodwill. As a result of this entry, IDE had a surplus at the end of each of its fiscal years from 2009 until 2014. Cano, a shareholder, received $7,144 in dividends from IDE during the period from 2010 to 2015. May Fried, the trustee in bankruptcy of IDE, recover the amount of these dividends from Cano on the basis that they had been paid when IDE was insolvent or when its capital was impaired?

12. Smith's Food & Drug Centers, Inc. (SFD) is a Delaware corporation that owns and operates a chain of supermarkets in the Southwestern United States. Jeffrey P. Smith, SFD's chief executive officer, and his family hold common and preferred stock constituting 62.1 percent voting control of SFD. On January 29, SFD entered into a merger agreement with the Yucaipa Companies that would involve a recapitalization of SFD and the repurchase by SFD of up to 50 percent of its common stock. SFD was also to repurchase 3 million shares of preferred stock from Jeffrey Smith and his family. In an April 25 proxy statement, the SFD board released a *pro forma* balance sheet showing that the merger and self-tender offer would result in a deficit to surplus on SFD's books of more than $100 million. SFD hired the investment firm of Houlihan Lokey Howard & Zukin (Houlihan) to examine the transactions, and it rendered a favorable solvency opinion based on a revaluation of corporate assets. On May 17, in reliance on the Houlihan opinion, SFD's board of directors determined that there existed sufficient surplus to consummate the transactions. On May 23, SFD's stockholders voted to approve the transactions, which closed on that day. The self-tender offer was oversubscribed, so SFD repurchased fully 50 percent of its shares at the offering price of $36.00 per share. A group of shareholders challenged the transaction alleging that the corporation's repurchase of shares violated the statutory prohibition against the impairment of capital. They argued that
   a. the negative net worth that appeared on SFD's books following the repurchase constitutes conclusive evidence of capital impairment and
   b. the SFD board was not entitled to rely on a solvency opinion based on a revaluation of corporate assets.
   Explain who should prevail.

TAKING SIDES

A closely held corporation sought to repurchase 25 percent of its outstanding shares from one of its shareholders. The corporation and the shareholder agreed that the corporation would purchase all of the shareholder's stock at a price of $500,000, payable $100,000 immediately in cash and the balance in four consecutive annual installments. The state's incorporation statute provides: "A corporation may purchase its own shares only out of earned surplus but the corporation may make no purchase of shares when it is insolvent or when such purchase would make it insolvent." At the time of the repurchase of the shares, the corporation had an earned surplus of $250,000.
a. What are the arguments that the repurchase of shares satisfied the incorporation statute?
b. What are the arguments that the repurchase of the shares did not satisfy the incorporation statute?
c. Which argument should prevail?

Management Structure
of Corporations

CHAPTER 35

*The director is really a watch-dog,
and the watch-dog has no right,
without the knowledge of his master,
to take a sop from a possible wolf.*

Chief Justice Timothy Bowen, 1892

CHAPTER OUTCOMES

After reading and studying this chapter, you should be able to:

1. Compare the actual governance of closely held corporations, the actual governance of publicly held corporations, and the statutory model of corporate governance.

2. Explain the role of shareholders in the management of a corporation.

3. Explain the role of the board of directors in the management of a corporation.

4. Explain the role of officers in the management of a corporation.

5. Explain management's duties of loyalty, obedience, and diligence.

The corporate management structure, as required by state incorporation statutes, is pyramidal. At the base of the pyramid are the **shareholders**, who are the residual owners of the corporation. Basic to their role in controlling the corporation is the right to elect representatives to manage the ordinary business matters of the corporation and the right to approve all extraordinary matters.

The **board of directors**, as the shareholders' elected representatives, are delegated the power to manage the business of the corporation. Directors exercise dominion and control over the corporation, hold positions of trust and confidence, and determine questions of operating policy. Because they are not expected to devote their full time to the corporation's affairs, directors have broad authority to delegate power to agents and to officers, who hold their offices at the will of the board. These **officers**, in turn, hire and fire all necessary operating personnel and run the day-to-day affairs of the corporation. The pyramid structure of corporate management under the statutory model is illustrated in Figure 35-1 on page 684.

CORPORATE GOVERNANCE

The statutory model of corporate management, although required by most states, accurately describes the actual governance of only a few corporations. The great majority of corporations are closely held: they have a small number of stockholders and no ready market for their shares, and most of the shareholders actively participate in the management of the business. Typically, the shareholders of a closely held corporation are also its directors and officers. Figure 35-2 on page 684 depicts the actual management structure of a typical closely held corporation.

Although the statutory model and the actual governance of closely held corporations diverge, in most states closely held corporations must adhere to the general corporate statutory model. One of the greatest burdens conventional general business corporation statutes impose on closely held corporations is a set of rigid corporate formalities. Although these formalities may be necessary and desirable in publicly held corporations having separate management and ownership, in a closely held corporation, where the owners are usually the managers, many of these formalities are unnecessary and meaningless. Consequently, shareholders in closely held corporations tend to disregard the formalities, sometimes forfeiting their limited liability as a result. In response to this problem, the 1969 amendments to the Model Business Corporation Act (MBCA), which were carried over to the Revised Act, included several liberalizing provisions for closely held corporations. Moreover, about twenty states have enacted special legislation to accommodate the needs of closely held corporations. These statutes vary considerably, but they are all optional and must be specifically elected by eligible corporations. Eligibility is generally based on the corporation's having fewer than a specified number of shareholders. These special close corporation statutes permit operation without a board of directors and authorize broad use of shareholder agreements, including their use in place of bylaws. Some prohibit courts from denying limited liability simply because an electing corporation engages in informal conduct.

As noted in Chapter 33, a Statutory Close Corporation Supplement (the Supplement) to the Model and Revised Acts has been promulgated. The Supplement relaxes most of the nonessential corporate formalities. It permits operation without a board of directors, authorizes broad use of shareholder agreements (including their use in place of bylaws), makes annual meetings optional, and authorizes one person to execute documents in more than one capacity. Most important, it prevents courts from denying limited liability simply because the corporation is a statutory close corporation. The general incorporation statute applies to closely held corporations except to the extent that it is inconsistent with the Supplement.

The Revised Act was amended to authorize shareholders in closely held corporations to adopt unanimous shareholders' agreements that depart from the statutory norms. This section of the Act requires that the agreement be set forth either (1) in the articles of incorporation or bylaws and approved by all persons who are shareholders at the time of the agreement or (2) in a written agreement that is signed by all persons who are shareholders at the time of the agreement and is made known to the corporation. Under this section, shareholder agreements are valid for ten years unless otherwise provided. The section *specifically* validates a number of provisions, including those (1) eliminating or restricting the powers of the board of directors; (2) establishing who shall be directors or officers; (3) specifying how directors or officers will be selected or removed; (4) governing the exercise or division of voting power by or between the shareholders and directors; (5) permitting the use of weighted voting rights or director proxies; and (6) transferring the authority of the board of directors to one or more shareholders or other persons. The section also *generally* authorizes any provision that governs the exercise of the corporate powers or the management of the business and affairs of the corporation or the relationship among the shareholders, the directors, and the corporation, or among any of them, so long as it is not contrary to public policy. There are limits, however, and a shareholder agreement that provides that the directors of the corporation have no duties of care or loyalty to the corporation or the shareholders would be beyond the authorization of the section. To the extent that an agreement authorized by this section limits the discretion or powers of the board of directors, it relieves the directors of liability while imposing that liability upon the person or persons in whom such discretion or powers are vested.

In sharp contrast is the large, publicly held corporation with a vast market for its shares. These shares typically are widely dispersed, and very few are owned by management. Approximately two-thirds are held by institutional investors (such as insurance companies, pension and retirement funds, mutual funds, and university endowments). The remaining shares are owned directly by individual investors. Whereas the great majority of institutional investors exercise their right to vote their shares, most individual investors do not. Nonetheless, virtually all shareholders who vote for the directors do so through the use of a proxy—an authorization by a shareholder to an agent (usually the chief executive officer of the corporation) to vote his shares. The majority of shareholders who return their proxies vote as management advises. As a result, the nominating committee of the board of directors actually determines the board's membership. Figure 35-3 illustrates the actual management structure of a typical large, publicly held corporation.

Figure 35-1 Management Structure of Corporations: The Statutory Model

Officers
Run the day-to-day
operations of the corporation

Board of Directors
Declare dividends
Delegate authority to officers
Manage the business of the corporation
Select, remove, and determine compensation
of officers

Shareholders
Elect and remove directors
Approve fundamental changes

Figure 35-2 Management Structure of Typical Closely Held Corporation

Shareholders = Directors = Officers

Figure 35-3 Management Structure of Typical Held Corporation

Shareholders
Sign and return proxies
Sell shares

Board of Directors
Delegate authority to officers
Ratify actions of officers

Officers
Control selection
of directors
Run day-to day
business
Control proxy
votes

Thus, the five hundred to one thousand largest, publicly held corporations—which own the great bulk of the industrial wealth of the United States—are controlled by a small group of corporate officers. This great concentration of the control over wealth, and the power that results from it, raises social, policy, and ethical issues concerning the governance of these corporations and the accountability of their management. The actions (or inactions) of these powerful corporations greatly affect the national economy, employment policies, the health and safety of the workplace and the environment, the quality of products, and the effects of overseas operations. Accordingly, the accountability of management is a critical issue.

In response to the business scandals involving companies such as Enron, WorldCom, Global Crossing, Adelphia, and Arthur Andersen, in 2002 Congress passed the Sarbanes-Oxley Act, which is discussed further in Chapter 39, Securities Regulation, as well as in Chapters 6 and 43. The legislation seeks to prevent these types of scandals by increasing corporate responsibility, adding new financial disclosure requirements, creating new criminal offenses, increasing the penalties for existing federal crimes, and creating a five-person Accounting Oversight Board with authority to review and discipline auditors. Several provisions of the Act impose governance requirements on publicly held corporations and will be discussed in this chapter.

In July 2010, President Obama signed into law the Dodd-Frank Wall Street Reform and Consumer Protection Act (Dodd-Frank Act), the most significant change to U.S. financial regulation since the New Deal. One of the many stand-alone statutes included in the Dodd-Frank Act is the Investor Protection and Securities Reform Act of 2010, which imposes new corporate governance rules on publicly held companies. These corporate governance provisions of the Dodd-Frank Act will be discussed in this chapter, Chapter 36, and Chapter 39.

The structure and governance of corporations must adhere to incorporation statute requirements. Therefore, in this chapter we will discuss the rights, duties, and liabilities of shareholders, directors, and officers under these statutes.

ROLE OF SHAREHOLDERS

The role of the shareholders in managing the corporation is generally restricted to the election of directors, the approval of certain extraordinary matters, the approval of corporate transactions that are void or voidable unless ratified, and the right to bring suits to enforce these rights.

VOTING RIGHTS OF SHAREHOLDERS [35-1]

The shareholder's right to vote is fundamental to the concept of the corporation and its management structure. In most states, a shareholder is entitled to one vote for each share of stock that she owns, unless the articles of incorporation provide otherwise; the articles may provide for more or less than one vote for any share. In addition, incorporation statutes generally permit the issuance of one or more classes of nonvoting stock, as long as at least one class of shares has voting rights.

Shareholder Meetings [35-1a]

Shareholder meetings
shareholders may exercise their voting rights at both annual and special shareholder meetings

Shareholders may exercise their voting rights at both annual and special **shareholder meetings**. A recent amendment to the Revised Act permits shareholders to participate in annual and special shareholder meetings by means of remote communication, such as over the Internet or through telephone conference calls. Under the Revised Act, *annual meetings* are required and must be held at a time fixed by the corporation's bylaws. If the annual shareholder meeting is not held within the earlier of six months after the end of the corporation's fiscal year or fifteen months after its last annual meeting, any shareholder may petition and obtain a court order requiring that a meeting be held. By comparison, the Close Corporation Supplement provides that no annual meeting of shareholders need be held unless a shareholder makes a written request at least thirty days in advance of the date specified for the meeting. The date may be established in the articles of incorporation, the bylaws, or a shareholder agreement.

Special meetings may be called by the board of directors, by holders of at least 10 percent of the shares, or by other persons authorized to do so in the articles of incorporation. As amended, the Revised Act permits a corporation's articles of incorporation to lower or raise the 10 percent requirement, but the corporation cannot raise the requirement to more than 25 percent of the shares.

Written notice stating the date, time, and place of the meeting and, in the case of a special meeting, the purposes for which it is called must be given in advance. Notice, however, may be waived in writing by any shareholder entitled to notice.

A number of states permit shareholders to conduct business without a meeting if all the shareholders consent in writing to the action taken. Some states have further relaxed the formalities of shareholder action by permitting shareholders to act without a meeting with the written consent of only the number of shares required to act on the matter.

Quorum and Voting [35-1b]

Quorum

minimum number necessary to be present at a meeting to transact business

A **quorum** of shares must be present at the meeting, either in person or by proxy. Unissued shares and treasury stock may not be voted or counted in determining whether a quorum exists. Decisions made at the meeting will have no effect if a quorum is not present. The majority view is that once a quorum is present at a meeting, it is deemed present for the rest of the meeting, even if shareholders withdraw in an effort to break it. Unless the articles of incorporation otherwise provide, a majority of shares entitled to vote constitutes a quorum. In most states and under the Model Act, a quorum may not consist of less than one-third of the shares entitled to vote; the Revised Act and some states do not contain a statutory minimum for a quorum. Because state statutes do not impose an upper limit upon a quorum, it may be set higher than a majority and may even require all the outstanding shares.

Practical Advice

If you are forming a close corporation and will hold a minority interest in it, consider including in the charter supermajority quorum and voting provisions for shareholder decisions to ensure that you will have veto power over specified managerial issues.

Most states require shareholder actions to be approved by a majority of the shares represented at the meeting and entitled to vote if a quorum exists. The Revised Act and some states, however, provide a different rule: if a quorum exists, a shareholder action (other than the election of directors) is approved if the votes cast for the action exceed the votes cast against it. Moreover, virtually all states permit the articles of incorporation to increase the percentage of shares required to take any action that is subject to shareholder approval. A provision that increases the voting requirements is commonly called a "supermajority provision." Close corporations frequently have used supermajority shareholder voting requirements to protect minority shareholders from oppression by the majority. Some publicly held corporations have used them to defend against hostile takeover bids as well.

Election of Directors [35-1c]

Election of directors

the shareholders elect the board at the annual meeting of the corporation

The shareholders elect directors each year at the annual shareholders' meeting. Most states provide that when a corporation's board consists of nine or more directors, the charter or bylaws may provide for a *classification* or staggering of directors, that is, a division into two or three classes to be as nearly equal in number as possible and to serve for staggered terms. Under the Revised Act as amended there is no minimum-size board required. If the directors are divided into two classes, the members of each class are elected once a year in alternate years for a two-year term; if divided into three classes, they are elected for three-year terms. This permits one-half of the board to be elected every two years or one-third to be elected every three years, thus providing continuity in the board's membership. Moreover, given two or more classes of shares and the authorization for such an action in the articles of incorporation, each class may elect a specified number of directors.

A recent amendment to the Revised Act expressly authorizes bylaws that contain one or both of the following requirements: (1) that if the corporation solicits proxies with respect to an election of directors the corporation include individuals nominated by shareholders for election as directors in its proxy statement and proxy cards and (2) that the corporation reimburse the expenses incurred by a shareholder in soliciting proxies in connection with an election of directors. The bylaws may provide procedures and conditions for the exercise of each of these rights.

Straight voting

directors are elected by a plurality of votes

Straight Voting

Normally, each shareholder has one vote for each share owned, and under the Revised Act and many state statutes, directors are elected by a *plurality* of the votes. In other states directors are elected by a *majority* of the votes. The charter may increase the percentage of shares required for the election of directors. Thus, under straight voting shareholders owning a majority of the voting shares can always elect the *entire* board of directors.

Cumulative voting

entitles shareholders to multiply the number of votes they are entitled to cast by the number of directors for whom they are entitled to vote and to cast the product for a single candidate or to distribute the product among two or more candidates

Cumulative Voting

In certain states shareholders electing directors have the right of cumulative voting. In most states, and under the Revised Act, cumulative voting is permissive, not mandatory. **Cumulative voting** entitles shareholders to multiply the number of votes they are entitled to cast by the number of directors for whom they are entitled to vote and to cast the product for a single candidate or distribute the product among two or more candidates. Cumulative voting permits a minority shareholder or a group of minority shareholders acting together to obtain minority representation on the board if they own a certain minimum number of shares. In the absence of cumulative voting, the holder or holders of 51 percent of the voting shares can elect all of the members of the board.

The formula for determining how many shares a minority shareholder with cumulative voting rights must own, or have proxies to vote, to secure representation on the board is as follows:

$$X = \frac{ac}{b+1} + 1$$

where

a = number of shares voting
b = number of directors to be elected
c = number of directors desired to be elected
X = number of shares necessary to elect the number of directors desired to be elected.

For example, Gray Corporation has two shareholders, Stephanie with sixty-four shares and Thomas with thirty-six shares. The board of directors of Gray Corporation consists of three directors. Under "straight" or noncumulative voting, Stephanie could cast sixty-four votes for each of her three candidates, and Thomas could cast thirty-six votes for his three candidates. As a result, all three of Stephanie's candidates would be elected. On the other hand, if cumulative voting were in force, Thomas could elect one director:

$$X = \frac{ac}{b+1} + 1$$

$$X = \frac{100(1)}{3+1} + 1 = 26 \text{ shares}$$

This result indicates that Thomas would need at least twenty-six shares to elect one director. Because Thomas has the right to vote thirty-six shares, he would be able to elect one director. Stephanie, of course, with her sixty-four shares, could elect the remaining two directors.

Removal of Directors [35-1d]

By a majority vote, shareholders may remove any director or the entire board of directors, with or without cause, in a meeting called for that purpose. In the case of a corporation having cumulative voting, however, removal of a director requires sufficient votes to prevent his election. We will discuss the removal of directors more fully later in this chapter.

Approval of Fundamental Changes [35-1e]

The board of directors manages the ordinary business affairs of the corporation. Extraordinary matters involving fundamental changes in the corporation require shareholder approval; such matters include amendments to the articles of incorporation, a sale or lease of all or substantially all of the corporate assets not in the regular course of business, most mergers, consolidations, compulsory share exchanges, and dissolution. We will discuss fundamental changes in Chapter 36.

Concentrations of Voting Power [35-1f]

Certain devices enable groups of shareholders to combine their voting power for purposes such as obtaining or maintaining control or maximizing the impact of cumulative voting. The most important methods of concentrating voting power are proxies, voting trusts, and shareholder agreements.

Proxies A shareholder may vote either in person or by written proxy. As we mentioned earlier, a **proxy** is a shareholder's authorization to an agent to vote his shares at a particular meeting or on a particular question. Generally, proxies must be in writing to be effective, and statutes typically limit the duration of proxies to no more than eleven months, unless the proxy specifically provides otherwise. Some states limit all proxy appointments to a period of eleven months. Because a proxy is the appointment of an agent, it is revocable, as all agencies are, unless conspicuously stated to be irrevocable and coupled with an interest, such as shares held as collateral. The solicitation of proxies by publicly held corporations is also regulated by the Securities Exchange Act of 1934, as we will discuss in Chapter 39.

As discussed, in large, publicly held corporations, virtually all shareholders who vote for the directors do so through the use of proxies. Because the majority of shareholders who return their

---

Practical Advice

If you are forming a close corporation and will hold a minority interest in it, consider including in the charter a provision for cumulative voting to ensure you a position on the board of directors.

Removal of directors

the shareholders may by majority vote remove directors with or without cause, subject to cumulative voting rights

Approval of fundamental changes

shareholder approval is required for charter amendments, most acquisitions, and dissolution

Proxy

authorization to vote another's shares at a shareholder meeting

proxies vote as management advises, the nominating committee of the board of directors almost always determines the board's membership. In 2009, the Revised Model Business Corporation Act (RMBCA) was amended to authorize the directors or shareholders of corporations to establish procedures in the corporate bylaws that (1) require the corporation to include in the corporation's proxy statement one or more individuals nominated by a shareholder in addition to individuals nominated by the board of directors and (2) require the corporation to reimburse shareholders for reasonable expenses incurred in soliciting proxies in an election of directors.

Moreover, the Dodd-Frank Act authorizes the Securities and Exchange Commission (SEC) to issue rules requiring that a publicly held company's proxy solicitation include nominations for the board of directors that have been submitted by shareholders.

Voting trust

transfer of corporate shares' voting rights to a trustee

Practical Advice

If you are forming a close corporation and will hold a minority interest in it, consider using a detailed shareholder agreement to provide fair treatment for all of the shareholders.

Shareholder voting agreement

used to provide shareholders with greater control over the election and removal of directors and other matters

Voting Trusts
Voting trusts, which are devices designed to concentrate corporate control in one or more persons, have been used in both publicly held and closely held corporations. A voting trust is a device by which one or more shareholders separate the voting rights of their shares from the ownership of them. Under a **voting trust**, one or more shareholders confer on a trustee the right to vote or otherwise act for them by signing an agreement setting out the provisions of the trust and transferring their shares to the trustee. In most states, voting trusts are permitted by statute but usually are limited in duration to ten years.

Shareholder Voting Agreements
In most jurisdictions, shareholders may agree in writing to vote in a specified manner for the election or removal of directors or on any matter subject to shareholder approval. Unlike voting trusts, shareholder voting agreements are not limited in duration. **Shareholder voting agreements** are used frequently in closely held corporations, especially in conjunction with restrictions on the transfer of shares, in order to provide each shareholder with greater control and *delectus personae* (the right to choose those who will become shareholders).

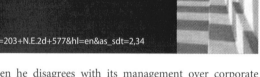

Galler v. Galler
Supreme Court of Illinois, 1964
32 Ill.2d 16, 203 N.E.2d 577
http://scholar.google.com/scholar_case?case=16188103998514121946&q=203+N.E.2d+577&hl=en&as_sdt=2,34

FACTS In 1927, two brothers, Benjamin and Isadore Galler, incorporated the Galler Drug Co., a wholesale drug business that they had operated as equal partners since 1919. The company continued to grow, and in 1955 the two brothers and their wives, Emma and Rose Galler, entered into a written shareholder agreement to leave the corporation in equal control of each family after the death of either brother. Specifically, the agreement provided that the corporation should continue to provide income for the support and maintenance of their immediate families and that the parties should vote for directors so as to give the estate and heirs of a deceased shareholder the same representation as before.

Benjamin died in 1957, and shortly thereafter his widow, Emma, requested that Isadore, the surviving brother, comply with the terms of the agreement. When he refused and proposed that certain changes be made in the agreement, Emma brought this action seeking specific performance of the agreement. Isadore and his wife Rose defended on the ground that the shareholder agreement was against public policy and the state's corporation law. The trial court entered a decree of specific performance in favor of Emma. On appeal, the decree was reversed.

DECISION Judgment of appellate court reversed.

OPINION A close corporation is one in which the stock is held in a few hands and is rarely traded. In contrast to a shareholder in a public corporation, who may easily trade his shares on the open market when he disagrees with its management over corporate policy, the shareholder of a closely held corporation often has no ready market in which to sell his shares should he wish to do so. Moreover, the shareholder in a closely held corporation often has most of his capital invested in the corporation and, therefore, views himself not only as a mere investor but also as a participant in the management of the business. Without a shareholder agreement subject to specific performance by the courts, the minority shareholder might find himself at the mercy of the controlling majority shareholder. In short, the detailed shareholder agreement is the only sound means by which the minority shareholder can protect himself. Therefore, since the agreement was reasonable in its scope and purpose of providing continuing support for the Galler brothers' families, it should be enforced.

INTERPRETATION Written shareholder agreements are an important means of enabling minority shareholders in a close corporation to maintain *delectus personae* and control as well as otherwise protecting their interest in the corporation.

ETHICAL QUESTION Did the court decide this case fairly? Explain.

CRITICAL THINKING QUESTION What limitations, if any, should the law impose upon the types of provisions that may be included in a shareholder agreement in a close corporation? Explain.

CONCEPT REVIEW 35-1

Concentrations of Voting Power

	Proxy	Voting Trust	Shareholder Agreement
Definition	Authorization of an agent to vote shares	Conferral of voting rights on trustee	Agreement among shareholders on voting of shares
Formalities	Signed writing delivered to corporation	Signed writing delivered to corporation	Signed writing
Duration	Eleven months, unless otherwise agreed	Ten years; may be extended	No limit
Revocability	Yes, unless coupled with an interest	No	Only by unanimous agreement
Prevalence	Publicly held	Publicly and closely held	Closely held

Restrictions on Transfer of Shares [35-1g]

In the absence of a specific agreement, shares of stock are freely transferable. Although free transferability of shares is usually considered an advantage of the corporate form, in some situations the shareholders may prefer to restrict the transfer of shares. In closely held corporations, for example, stock transfer restrictions are used to control who may become shareholders, thereby achieving the corporate equivalent of *delectus personae* (choice of the person). They are also used to maintain statutory close corporation status by restricting the number of persons who may become shareholders. In publicly held corporations, restrictions on the transfer of shares are used to preserve exemptions under state and federal securities laws. (These are discussed in Chapter 39.)

Most incorporation statutes have no provisions governing share transfer restrictions. The common law validates such restrictions if they are adopted for a lawful purpose and do not unreasonably restrain or prohibit transferability. In addition, the Uniform Commercial Code provides that an otherwise-valid share transfer restriction is ineffective against a person without actual knowledge of it unless the restriction is conspicuously noted on the share certificate.

The Revised Act and the statutes of several states permit the articles of incorporation, bylaws, or a shareholder agreement to impose transfer restrictions but require that the restriction be noted conspicuously on the stock certificate. The Revised Act authorizes restrictions for any reasonable purpose, including maintaining statutory close corporation status and preserving exemptions under federal and state securities law.

Practical Advice

To achieve *delectus personae* (choice of person) when organizing a close corporation, you should consider including in the charter a carefully drafted provision restricting the transfer of shares. If you do so, be sure to note such share transfer restriction on the share certificates.

ENFORCEMENT RIGHTS OF SHAREHOLDERS [35-2]

To protect a shareholder's interests in the corporation, the law provides shareholders with certain enforcement rights. These include the right to obtain information, the right to sue the corporation directly or to sue on the corporation's behalf, and the right to dissent.

Right to Inspect Books and Records [35-2a]

Right to inspect books and records

if the demand is made in good faith and for a proper purpose

Most states have enacted statutory provisions granting shareholders the right to inspect, for a *proper purpose*, books and records in person or through an agent and to copy parts of them. The right generally covers all records relevant to the shareholder's legitimate interest. The Revised Act provides that every shareholder is entitled to examine *specified* corporate records upon prior written request if the demand is made in good faith, for a proper purpose, and during regular business hours at the corporation's principal office. Many states, however, limit this right to shareholders who own a minimum number of shares or to those who have been shareholders for a minimum period of time. For example, the Model Act requires that a shareholder either must own 5 percent of the outstanding shares or must have owned his shares for at least six months (though a court may order an inspection even when neither condition is met).

A *proper purpose* for inspection is one that is reasonably relevant to that shareholder's interest in the corporation. Proper purposes include determining the financial condition of the corporation, the value of shares, the existence of mismanagement, or the names of other shareholders in order to communicate with them about corporate affairs. The right of inspection is subject to abuse and will be denied a shareholder who is seeking proprietary information for an improper purpose. Examples of improper purposes include obtaining information for use by a competing company or obtaining a list of shareholders in order to offer it for sale.

Compaq Computer Corp. v. Horton
Supreme Court of Delaware, 1993
631 A.2d 1
http://scholar.google.com/scholar_case?case=1308314219087891838&q=631+A.2d+1&hl=en&as_sdt=2,34

FACTS Charles E. Horton has beneficially owned 112 shares of common stock in Compaq Computer Corporation (Compaq), a Delaware corporation, continuously since December 6, 1990. On July 22, 1991, Horton and seventy-eight other parties sued Compaq, fifteen of its advisers, and certain management personnel, alleging that Compaq and its codefendants violated the Texas Security Act and the Texas Deceptive Trade Practices Consumer Protection Act as well as committing fraud and breaching their fiduciary duty. All these claims arise from the contention that Compaq misled the public regarding the true value of its stock at a time when members of management were selling their own shares.

On September 22, 1992, Horton delivered a letter demanding to inspect Compaq's stock ledger and related information for the period from October 1, 1990, to June 30, 1991. The demand letter stated that the purpose of the request was to enable Horton to communicate with other Compaq shareholders to inform them of the pending shareholders' suit and to ascertain whether any of them would desire to become associated with that suit or bring similar actions against Compaq and assume a *pro rata* share of the litigation expenses. On September 30, 1992, Compaq refused the demand, stating that the purpose described in the letter was not a "proper purpose" under Section 220(b) of the General Corporation Law of the state of Delaware.

Horton brought suit and the trial court concluded that the plaintiff's desire to contact other stockholders and solicit their involvement in the litigation was a purpose reasonably related to his interest as a stockholder. Accordingly, the trial court ordered Compaq to permit Horton to inspect and copy the stockholder lists and related stockholder information requested in his demand letter. Compaq appealed.

DECISION Judgment affirmed.

OPINION In Delaware, a shareholder has the statutory right during the usual hours for business to inspect *for any proper purpose* the corporation's stock ledger upon written demand under oath stating that purpose. A proper purpose is a purpose reasonably related to such person's interest as a stockholder. When a shareholder complies with the statutory requirements as to form and manner of making a demand, then the corporation bears the burden of proving that the demand is for an improper purpose. If there is any doubt, it must be resolved in favor of the stockholder's statutory right to inspect.

Essentially, Horton alleges that it is in the interests of Compaq's shareholders to know that acts of mismanagement and fraud are continuing and cannot be overlooked. Thus, it is assumed that the resultant filing of a large number of individual damage claims might well discourage further acts of misconduct by the defendants. In this specific context, the antidotal effect of the Texas litigation may indeed serve a purpose reasonably related to Horton's current interest as a Compaq stockholder.

Even though a purpose may be reasonably related to one's interest as a stockholder, it cannot be adverse to the corporation's interests. Nevertheless, because law and policy require corporations and their agents to answer for the breaches of their duties to shareholders, Compaq has no legitimate interest in avoiding the payment of compensatory damages that it, its management, or its advisers may owe to those who own the enterprise. Thus, common sense and public policy dictate that a proper purpose may be stated in these circumstances, notwithstanding the lack of a direct benefit flowing to the corporation.

Compaq's burden of showing an improper purpose is not impossible to bear. Previous cases provide valuable examples of the degree to which a stated purpose is so indefinite, doubtful, uncertain, or vexatious as to warrant denial of the right of inspection, leading to the conclusion that when the person making the demand is acting in bad faith or for reasons wholly unrelated to his or her role as a stockholder, access to the ledger will be denied. That simply is not the case here. Horton seeks in good faith to solicit the support of other similarly situated Compaq stockholders, not only to seek monetary redress for their individual economic injuries, but also to prevent further acts of fraud or mismanagement from disrupting the fair market value of Compaq's stock.

Compaq's arguments fail to meet its burden to show that Horton acts from an improper purpose. Compaq's contention that Horton's purpose is contrary to the best interests of the corporation and its current stockholders is both speculative and specious. Any harm that may accrue to the corporation as a result of releasing the list is too remote and uncertain to warrant denial of the stockholder's statutory right to inspection. If anything, the corporation and its stockholders, as well as public policy, will best be served by exposure of the fraud, if that is the case, and restoration of the stock to a value set by a properly informed market.

INTERPRETATION Upon demand, a stockholder has the right to inspect for a proper purpose the corporation's books and records. A proper purpose means a purpose reasonably related to that shareholder's interest in the corporation.

CRITICAL THINKING QUESTION Can a proper purpose ever be adverse to the corporation's interests? Explain.

Shareholder Suits [35-2b]

The ultimate recourse of a shareholder, short of selling his shares, is to bring suit against or on behalf of the corporation. Shareholder suits are essentially of two kinds: direct suits and derivative suits.

Direct suit

brought by a shareholder or a class of shareholders against the corporation based upon the ownership of shares

Direct Suits   A shareholder may bring a **direct suit** to enforce a claim that she has *against* the corporation, based on her ownership of shares. Any recovery in a direct suit goes to the shareholder plaintiff. Examples of direct suits include shareholder actions to compel payment of dividends properly declared, to enforce the right to inspect corporate records, to enforce the right to vote, to protect preemptive rights, and to compel dissolution. A ***class suit*** is a direct suit in which one or more shareholders purport to act as a representative for a class of shareholders to recover for injuries to the entire class. Such a suit is a direct suit because the representative claims that all similarly situated shareholders were injured by an act that did not injure the corporation.

Derivative suit

brought by a shareholder on behalf of the corporation to enforce a right belonging to the corporation

Derivative Suits   A **derivative suit** is a cause of action brought by one or more shareholders *on behalf of* the corporation to enforce a right belonging to it. Shareholders may bring such an action when the board of directors refuses to so act on the corporation's behalf. Recovery usually goes to the corporation's treasury, so that all shareholders can benefit proportionately. Examples of derivative suits are actions to recover damages from management for an *ultra vires* act, to recover damages for a managerial breach of duty, and to recover improper dividends. In such situations, the board of directors may well be hesitant to bring suit against the corporation's officers or directors. Consequently, a shareholder derivative suit is the only recourse.

In most states, a shareholder must have owned his shares at the time the complained-of transaction occurred in order to bring a derivative suit. In addition, under the Revised Act and some state statutes, the shareholder must first make demand on the board of directors to enforce the corporate right. In a number of states, demand is excused in limited situations.

Figure 35-4 compares direct and derivative suits.

Figure 35-4 Shareholder Suits

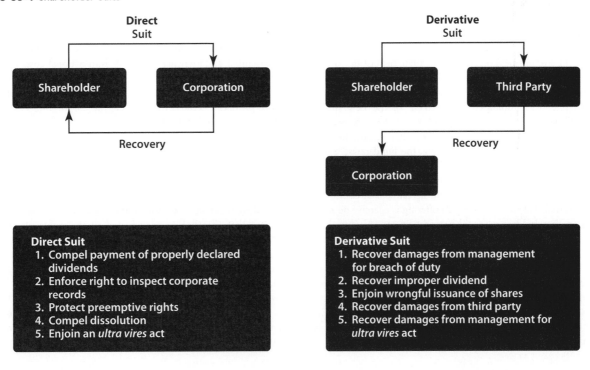

Strougo v. Bassini
United States Court of Appeals, Second Circuit, 2002
282 F.3d 162
http://scholar.google.com/scholar_case?case=3945168053066454973&q=282+F.3d+162&hl=en&as_sclt=2,34

FACTS Strougo is a shareholder of the Brazilian Equity Fund, Inc. (the Fund), a nondiversified, publicly traded, closed-end investment company incorporated under the laws of Maryland. As a closed-end fund, it has a fixed number of outstanding shares, so that investors who wish to acquire shares in the Fund ordinarily must purchase them from a shareholder rather than, as in open-end funds, directly from the Fund itself. Shares in closed-end funds are traded in the same manner as are shares of corporate stock. Shares in the Fund are listed and traded on the New York Stock Exchange. The number of outstanding shares in the Fund are "fixed" because this number does not change on a daily basis as it would were the Fund open-ended, in which case the number of outstanding shares would change each time an investor invested new money in the fund, causing issuance of new shares, and each time a shareholder divested and thereby redeemed shares.

Although closed-end funds do not sell their shares to the public in the ordinary course of their business, there are methods available to them to raise new capital after their initial public offering. One such device is a "rights offering," by which a fund offers shareholders the opportunity to purchase newly issued shares. Rights so offered may be transferable, allowing the current shareholder to sell them in the open market, or nontransferable, requiring the current shareholder to use them herself or lose their value when the rights expire.

On June 6, 1996, the Fund announced that it would issue one nontransferable "right" per outstanding share to every shareholder, and that every three rights would enable the shareholder to purchase one new share in the Fund. The subscription price per share was set at 90 percent of the lesser of (1) the average of the last reported sales price of a share of the Fund's common stock on the New York Stock Exchange on August 16, 1996, the date on which the rights expired, and the four business days preceding, and (2) the per-share net asset value at the close of business on August 16.

At the close of business on August 16, 1996, the last day of the rights offering, the closing market price for the Fund's shares was $12.38, and the Fund's per-share net asset value was $17.24. The Fund's shareholders purchased 70.3 percent of the new shares available at a subscription price set at $11.09 per share, 90 percent of the average closing price for the Fund on that and the preceding four days. Through the rights offering, the Fund raised $20.6 million in new capital.

On May 16, 1997, the plaintiff brought this class action against the Fund's directors, senior officers, and investment advisor. The plaintiff asserted that this sort of rights offering is coercive because it penalized shareholders who did not participate. The introduction of new shares at a discount diluted the value of old shares. Because the rights could not be sold on the open market, a shareholder could avoid a consequent reduction in the value of his or her net equity position in the Fund only by purchasing new shares at the discounted price. Such purchases would, in turn, have tended to increase the management fee paid to defendant BEA Associates, the Fund's investment advisor, because that fee is based on the Fund's total assets.

The plaintiff's complaint included three direct class-action claims on behalf of all shareholders. It alleges that the defendants, by approving the rights offering, breached their duties of loyalty and care at common law. It asserted that these breaches of duty resulted in four kinds of injury to shareholders: (1) loss of share value resulting from the underwriting and other transaction costs associated with the rights offering; (2) downward pressure on share prices resulting from the supply of new shares; (3) downward pressure on share prices resulting from the offering of shares at a discount; and (4) injury resulting from coercion, in that "shareholders were forced to either invest additional monies in the Fund or suffer a substantial dilution."

The district court dismissed the direct claims on the ground that the injuries alleged "applied to the shareholders as a whole" and entered judgment for the defendants. The plaintiff appealed.

DECISION The judgment of the district court is vacated, and the case is remanded.

OPINION Under Maryland law, when the shareholders of a corporation suffer an injury that is distinct from that of the corporation, the shareholders may bring direct suit for redress of that injury; there is shareholder standing. When the corporation is injured and the injury to its shareholders derives from that injury, however, only the corporation may bring suit; there is no shareholder standing. The shareholder may, at most, sue derivatively, seeking in effect to require the corporation to pursue a lawsuit to compensate for the injury to the corporation, and thereby ultimately redress the injury to the shareholders.

Applying Maryland's law of shareholder standing to the plaintiff's four alleged injuries, the court of appeals concluded that one of them does not support direct claims under Maryland law. On the other hand, the remaining alleged injuries do.

The plaintiff alleges a loss in share value resulting from the "substantial underwriting and other transactional costs associated with the Rights Offering." Underwriter fees, advisory fees, and other transaction costs incurred by a corporation decrease share price primarily because they deplete the corporation's assets, precisely the type of injury to the corporation that can be redressed under Maryland law only through a suit brought on behalf of the corporation.

The plaintiff's remaining alleged injuries can be read to describe the set of harms resulting from the coercive nature of the rights offering. The particular harm allegedly suffered by an individual shareholder as a result of the coercion depends on whether or not that shareholder participated in the rights offering. The alleged injury from the downward pressure on share prices resulting from the setting of the "exercise price of the rights … at a steep discount from the pre-rights offering net asset value" can be read to refer to the involuntary dilution in equity value suffered by the non-participating shareholders.

On the other hand, participating shareholders may have suffered harm in the form of transaction costs in liquidating other assets to purchase the new shares, and the impairment of their right to dispose of their assets as they prefer if they purchased new shares to avoid dilution.

Thus, in the case of both the participating and nonparticipating shareholders, it would appear that the alleged injuries were to the shareholders alone and not to the Fund. These harms therefore constitute "distinct" injuries supporting direct shareholder claims under Maryland law.

INTERPRETATION A class action is a direct suit *against* the corporation and seeks recovery for the shareholders as individuals. A derivative suit is brought by shareholders *on behalf of* the corporation and seeks recovery for the corporation so that all shareholders benefit proportionately.

CRITICAL THINKING QUESTION When should derivative suits be permitted? Explain.

Shareholder's right to dissent

a shareholder has the right to dissent from certain corporate actions that require shareholder approval

Shareholder's Right to Dissent [35-2c]

A shareholder has the right to dissent from certain corporate actions that require shareholder approval. These actions include most mergers, consolidations, compulsory share exchanges, and a sale or exchange of all or substantially all the assets of the corporation not in the usual and regular course of business. We will discuss the shareholder's right to dissent in Chapter 36.

ROLE OF DIRECTORS AND OFFICERS

Management of a corporation is vested by statute in its board of directors, which determines general corporate policy and appoints officers to execute that policy and to administer the day-to-day operations of the corporation. Both the directors and officers of the corporation owe certain duties to the corporate entity as well as to the corporation's shareholders and are liable for breaching these duties.

In the following sections we will discuss the roles of corporate directors and officers. In some instances, controlling shareholders (those who own a number of shares sufficient to allow them effective control over the corporation) are held to the same duties as directors and officers, which we will discuss later in this chapter. Moreover, in close corporations, many courts impose upon *all* the shareholders a fiduciary duty similar to that imposed upon partners.

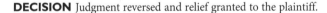

Donahue v. Rodd Electrotype Co., Inc.
Massachusetts Supreme Court, 1975
367 Mass. 578, 328 N.E.2d 505
http://scholar.google.com/scholar_case?case=10488013111081435481&q=328+N.E.2d+505&hl=en&as_sdt=2,34

FACTS Euphemia Donahue was a minority stockholder in the Rodd Electrotype Company of New England, Inc. Rodd Electrotype was, by definition, a close corporation. Members of the Rodd and Donahue families were the sole owners of the corporate stock, and no ready market for the shares existed. Moreover, the Rodds effectively controlled the corporation through their control of the chief management positions and their ownership of the majority of the stock. When Harry Rodd, a director, officer, and controlling stockholder of Rodd Electrotype, retired from the business, Rodd Electrotype purchased his shares in the corporation for $36,000. Donahue, who was not offered an equal opportunity to sell her shares to the corporation, brought an action against Rodd Electrotype, Harry Rodd, and the present directors of the corporation, claiming that the defendants breached their fiduciary duty to her in causing the corporation to purchase the shares of Harry Rodd. She sought rescission of the purchase and repayment by Harry Rodd to Rodd Electrotype of the purchase price of the shares plus interest. The trial court dismissed the case, and the appellate court affirmed.

DECISION Judgment reversed and relief granted to the plaintiff.

OPINION By definition, the close corporation strongly resembles a partnership. Moreover, just as in a partnership, all stockholders in a close corporation must have trust and confidence in one another. Specifically, the minority shareholders must rely upon the loyalty and abilities of the majority and especially of those stockholders who hold office. For instance, the majority stockholders in a corporation, through their control of the board of directors, are in a position to employ certain "freeze-out" techniques that may oppress or disadvantage the minority shareholders. The minority is unable to challenge the policies of the directors "unless a plain abuse of discretion is made to appear," and, by definition lacking 50 percent of the shares, the minority cannot cause the dissolution of the corporation. In a close corporation, a minority shareholder's recourse is further limited by the fact that no ready market for the shares is available. Therefore, the standard of duty owed by the stockholders in a close corporation is more rigorous than the general good faith and inherent fairness standard of conduct to which directors and stockholders of all corporations must adhere. Stockholders in a close corporation owe one another substantially the same fiduciary duty that partners owe to one another; the standard of duty owed by partners is the "utmost good faith and loyalty." As a result, when a close corporation purchases the shares of a controlling stockholder, the corporation must offer each stockholder an equal chance to sell a proportional number of his shares at the same price. Without such an opportunity, the purchase of shares from a member of the controlling group (1) provides an exclusive market for shares from which minority shareholders are shut out and (2) functions as a preferential distribution of the corporation's assets. This advantage is inconsistent with the strict fiduciary duty imposed upon the stockholders of close corporations. In this case, the Rodd family is a single controlling group, and the purchase of Harry Rodd's shares is a violation of the fiduciary duty owed by the controlling shareholders, the Rodds, to Donahue, a minority shareholder.

INTERPRETATION Recognizing the strong resemblance of a close corporation to a partnership, some courts impose upon all shareholders in a close corporation substantially the same fiduciary duty that partners owe each other.

ETHICAL QUESTION Did the defendant act unethically? Explain.

CRITICAL THINKING QUESTION Should close corporation law be separate and distinct from general corporation law? Explain.

Practical Advice

Do not agree to serve on a corporate board of directors unless you have sufficient time and energy to meet the requirements of the position.

FUNCTION OF THE BOARD OF DIRECTORS [35-3]

Although the shareholders elect directors to manage the corporation, the directors are neither trustees nor agents of the shareholders or the corporation. The directors are, however, fiduciaries who must perform their duties in good faith, in the best interests of the corporation, and with due care.

The Revised Act and the statutes of many states provide that "[a]ll corporate powers shall be exercised by or under the authority of, and the business and affairs of the corporation managed under the direction of, its board of directors, subject to any limitation set forth in the articles of incorporation." In some corporations, the board members are all actively involved in the management of the business. In these cases, the corporate powers are exercised *by* the board of directors. On the other hand, in publicly held corporations, a majority of board members often are not actively involved in management. Here, the corporate powers are exercised *under* the authority of the board, which formulates major management policy and monitors management's performance but does not involve itself in day-to-day management.

In publicly held corporations, the directors who are also officers or employees of the corporation are **inside directors**, while the directors who are not officers or employees are **outside directors**. Outside directors who have no business contacts with the corporation are **unaffiliated directors**; outside directors having business contacts—such as investment bankers, lawyers, or suppliers—are **affiliated directors**. Historically, the boards of many publicly held corporations consisted mainly or entirely of inside directors. During the past two decades, however, the number and influence of outside directors have increased substantially, and now boards of the great majority of publicly held corporations consist primarily of outside directors.

Under the Dodd-Frank Act, the SEC must issue rules requiring publicly held companies to disclose in annual proxy statements the reasons why the company has chosen to separate or combine the positions of chairman of the board of directors and chief executive officer.

Practical Advice

To achieve greater flexibility, when organizing a close corporation you should consider including in the charter a provision eliminating the board of directors and assigning the board's duties to designated shareholders.

In those states with special close corporation statutes, electing corporations can operate without a board of directors. Moreover, under the Revised Act, as originally enacted, a corporation having fifty or fewer shareholders may dispense with or limit the authority of a board of directors by designating in its articles of incorporation those who will perform some or all of the duties of a board. The Revised Act as amended permits any corporation to dispense with a board of directors by a written agreement executed by all of the shareholders.

Under incorporation statutes the board has the responsibility for determining corporate policy in a number of areas, including (1) selecting and removing officers, (2) determining the corporation's capital structure, (3) initiating fundamental changes, (4) declaring dividends, and (5) setting management compensation.

Selection and Removal of Officers [35-3a]

In most states, the board of directors is responsible for choosing the corporation's officers and may remove any officer at any time. Officers are corporate agents who are delegated their responsibilities by the board of directors.

Capital Structure [35-3b]

The board of directors determines the capital structure and financial policy of the corporation. For example, the board of directors has the power (1) to fix the selling price of newly issued shares, unless the articles of incorporation reserve to the shareholders the power to do so; (2) to determine the value of the consideration the corporation will receive in payment for the shares it issues; (3) to borrow money, issue notes, bonds, and other obligations, and secure any of the corporation's obligations; and (4) to sell, lease, or exchange assets of the corporation in the *usual* and *regular* course of business.

Fundamental changes

the directors have the power to make, amend, or repeal the bylaws, unless this power is exclusively reserved to the shareholders

Fundamental Changes [35-3c]

The board of directors has the power to amend or repeal the bylaws, unless the articles of incorporation reserve this power exclusively to the shareholders. In a few states directors may not repeal or amend bylaws adopted by the shareholders. In addition, the board initiates certain actions that require shareholder approval. For instance, the board initiates proceedings to amend the articles of incorporation; to effect a merger, consolidation, compulsory share exchange, or the sale or lease of all or substantially all of the assets of the corporation *other* than in the usual and regular course of business; and to dissolve the corporation.

Dividends

directors declare the amount and type of dividends

Dividends [35-3d]

The board of directors declares the amount and type of **dividends**, subject to restrictions in the state incorporation statute; the articles of incorporation; and corporate loan and preferred stock agreements. The board also may purchase, redeem, or otherwise acquire shares of the corporation's equity securities.

Management Compensation [35-3e]

The board of directors usually determines the compensation of officers. In addition, a number of states allow the board to fix the compensation of its members.

The Dodd-Frank Act requires that, at least once every three years, publicly held companies include a provision in certain proxy statements for a nonbinding shareholder vote on the compensation of executives. In a separate resolution, shareholders determine whether this "say on pay" vote should be held every one, two, or three years.

Under the Sarbanes-Oxley Act, if a publicly held company is required to issue an accounting restatement due to a material violation of securities law, the chief executive officer and the chief financial officer must forfeit certain bonuses and compensation received, as well as any profit realized from the sale of the company's securities, during the twelve-month period following the original issuance of the noncomplying financial document.

These "clawback" requirements of the Sarbanes-Oxley Act have been greatly expanded by the Dodd-Frank Act. Under the Dodd-Frank Act, the SEC must issue rules directing the national securities exchanges to require each listed company to disclose and implement a policy regarding any incentive-based compensation that is based on financial information that must be reported under the securities laws. In the event that a company is required to prepare an accounting restatement due to the material noncompliance with any financial reporting requirement under the securities laws, the company must recover from any current or former executive officers who received excess incentive-based compensation (including stock options awarded as compensation) during the three-year period preceding the date on which the company is required to prepare an accounting restatement. The amount of the recovery is the incentive-based compensation in excess of what would have been paid to the executive officer under the accounting restatement.

ELECTION AND TENURE OF DIRECTORS [35-4]

The incorporation statute, the articles of incorporation, and the bylaws determine the qualifications necessary to those who would be directors of the corporation. They also determine election procedures for and the number, tenure, and compensation of directors. Only individuals may serve as directors.

Election, Number, and Tenure of Directors [35-4a]

The initial board of directors generally is named in the articles of incorporation and serves until the first meeting of the shareholders at which directors are elected. Thereafter, directors are elected at annual meetings of the shareholders and hold office for one year unless their terms are staggered. However, if the shares represented at a meeting in person or by proxy are insufficient to constitute a quorum or if the shareholders are deadlocked and unable to elect a new board, the incumbent directors continue in office as "holdover" directors until their successors are duly elected and qualified. Although state statutes traditionally required each corporation to have three or more directors, most states permit the board to consist of one or more members. Moreover, the number of directors may be increased or decreased, within statutory limits, by amendment to the bylaws or charter.

Vacancies and Removal of Directors [35-4b]

The Revised Act provides that a vacancy in the board may be filled either by the shareholders or by the affirmative vote of a majority of the remaining directors, even if they should constitute less than a quorum of the board. The term of a director elected to fill a vacancy expires at the next shareholders' meeting at which directors are elected.

Some states have no statutory provision for the removal of directors, although a common law rule permits removal for cause by action of the shareholders. The Revised Act and an increasing number of other statutes permit the shareholders to remove one or more directors or the entire board, with or without cause, at a special meeting called for that purpose, subject to cumulative voting rights, if applicable. However, the Revised Act also permits the articles of incorporation to provide that directors may be removed only for cause.

Compensation of Directors [35-4c]

Traditionally, directors did not receive salaries for their directorial services, although they commonly received a fee or honorarium for their attendance at meetings. The Revised Act and many incorporation statutes now specifically authorize the board of directors to fix the compensation of directors, unless a contrary provision exists in the articles of incorporation or bylaws.

EXERCISE OF DIRECTORS' FUNCTIONS [35-5]

Exercise of directors' functions
directors have the power to bind the corporation only when acting as a board

Though they are powerless to bind the corporation when acting individually, directors do have this power when acting as a board. The board may act only through a meeting of the directors or through written consent signed by all of the directors, if such consent without a directors' meeting is authorized by the incorporation statute and is not contrary to the charter or bylaws.

Meetings are either held at a regular time and place fixed in the bylaws or called at special times. Notice of meetings must be given as prescribed in the bylaws. A director's attendance at any meeting is a waiver of such notice, unless the director attends only to object to the holding of the meeting or to the transaction of business at it and does not vote for or assent to action taken at the meeting. Waiver of notice also may be given in a signed writing. Most modern statutes provide that meetings of the board may be held either in or outside of the state of incorporation.

Quorum and Voting [35-5a]

Practical Advice

If you are forming a close corporation and will hold a minority interest in it, consider including in the charter supermajority quorum and voting provisions for voting by the board of directors to ensure that you will have control over specified managerial issues.

A majority of the board members constitutes a quorum (the minimum number of members that must be present at a meeting in order to transact business). Although most states do not permit a quorum to be set at less than a majority, the Revised Act and some states allow the articles of incorporation or the bylaws to authorize a quorum consisting of as few as one-third of a board's members. In contrast, however, in all states the articles of incorporation or bylaws may require a number greater than a simple majority. If a quorum is present at any meeting, the act of a majority of the directors in attendance is the act of the board, unless the articles of incorporation or bylaws require the act of a greater number.

Closely held corporations sometimes use supermajority or unanimous quorum requirements. In addition, they may require a supermajority or unanimous vote of the board for some or all matters.

By requiring a quorum to be present when "a vote is taken," the Revised Act makes it clear that the board may act only when a quorum is present. This rule is in contrast to the rule governing shareholder meetings: recall that once a quorum of shareholders is obtained, it cannot be broken by the withdrawal of shareholders. Many state statutes, however, do not have this provision. In any event, directors may not vote by proxy, although most states permit directors to participate in meetings through teleconference.

A director present at a board meeting at which action on any corporate matter is taken is deemed to have assented to such action unless, in addition to dissenting or abstaining from it, he (1) has his dissent or abstention entered in the minutes of the meeting, (2) files his written dissent or abstention to such action with the presiding officer before the meeting adjourns, or (3) delivers his written dissent or abstention to the corporation immediately after adjournment.

Action Taken Without a Meeting [35-5b]

Action taken without a meeting

permitted if a consent in writing is signed by all of the directors

The Revised Act and most states provide that unless the articles of incorporation or bylaws provide otherwise, any action the statute requires or permits to be taken at a meeting of the board may be taken without a meeting if consent in writing is signed by all of the directors.

Delegation of Board Powers [35-5c]

Delegation of board powers

committees may be appointed to perform some but not all of the board's functions

Unless otherwise provided by the articles of incorporation or the bylaws, the board of directors may, by majority vote of the full board, appoint one or more committees, all of whose members must be directors. Many state statutes permit committees only if the charter expressly authorizes their formation. The Revised Act as amended and some statutes permit a committee to have as few as one member, whereas the statutes of many states require that a committee consist of at least two directors. Committees may exercise all the authority of the board, except with regard to certain matters specified in the incorporation statute, such as declaring dividends and other distributions, filling vacancies on the board or on any of its committees, amending the bylaws, or proposing actions that require approval by shareholders. Delegating authority to a committee does not relieve any board member of his duties to the corporation. Commonly used committees include executive committees, audit committees (to recommend and oversee independent public accountants), compensation committees, finance committees, nominating committees, and investment committees.

The *Sarbanes-Oxley Act* confers on the audit committee of every publicly held corporation direct responsibility for the appointment, compensation, and oversight of the work of the public accounting firm employed by the company to perform audit services. Moreover, the public accounting firm must report directly to the audit committee, and the lead auditor must rotate every five years. Each member of the audit committee must be independent, and at least one member must qualify as a financial expert. The Act requires that the company provide appropriate funding for the audit committee to compensate the auditors, independent counsel, and other advisers. The audit committee is responsible for resolving disagreements between management and the auditor regarding the company's financial reporting. The audit committee must establish procedures for addressing complaints regarding accounting, internal accounting controls, or auditing matters.

As required by the Dodd-Frank Act, the SEC has issued rules directing the national securities exchanges to require that each member of a listed company's compensation committee be an independent member of the board of directors. The SEC has approved the exchanges' rules implementing this requirement.

Directors' Inspection Rights [35-5d]

Directors' inspection rights

directors have the right to inspect corporate books and records

So that they can perform their duties competently and fully, directors have the right to inspect corporate books and records. This right is considerably broader than a shareholder's right to inspect.

OFFICERS [35-6]

The board of directors appoints the officers of a corporation to hold the offices provided for in the bylaws, which set forth the respective duties of each officer. Statutes generally require as a minimum that the officers consist of a president; one or more vice presidents, as prescribed by the bylaws; a secretary; and a treasurer. With the exception that the same person may not hold the office of president and secretary at the same time, a person may hold more than one office.

The Revised Act and other modern statutes permit every corporation to designate whatever officers it wants. Although the Act specifies no particular number of officers, one of them must be delegated responsibility to prepare the minutes of directors' and shareholders' meetings and to authenticate corporate records. The Revised Act permits the same individual to hold *all* of the offices of a corporation.

Selection and Removal of Officers [35-6a]

Most state statutes provide that officers be appointed by the board of directors and that they serve at the pleasure of the board. Accordingly, the board may remove officers with or without cause. Of course, if the officer has an employment contract that is valid for a specified time period, removing the officer without cause before the contract expires would constitute a breach of the employment contract. The board also determines the compensation of officers.

Role of Officers [35-6b]

Role of officers
officers are agents of the corporation

The officers are, like the directors, fiduciaries to the corporation. On the other hand, unlike the directors, they are agents of the corporation. The roles of officers are set forth in the corporate bylaws.

Authority of Officers [35-6c]

Practical Advice

When signing contracts in your capacity as an officer for a corporation, be sure to indicate your representative status.

The Revised Act provides that each officer has the authority provided in the bylaws or prescribed by the board of directors, to the extent that such prescribed authority is consistent with the bylaws. Like that of other agents, the authority of an officer to bind the corporation may be (1) actual express, (2) actual implied, or (3) apparent.

Actual express authority
arises from the incorporation statute, the charter, the bylaws, and resolutions of the directors

Actual Express Authority **Actual express authority** results from the corporation's manifesting to the officer its assent that the officer should act on the corporation's behalf. Actual express authority arises from the incorporation statute, the articles of incorporation, the bylaws, and resolutions of the board of directors. The latter provide the principal source of actual express authority. The Revised Act further provides that the board of directors may authorize an officer to prescribe the duties of other officers. This provision empowers officers to delegate authority to subordinates.

Actual implied authority
authority to do what is reasonably necessary to perform actual authority

Actual Implied Authority Officers, as agents of the corporation, have **actual implied authority** to do what is reasonably necessary to perform their actual, delegated authority. In addition, a common question is whether officers possess implied authority merely by virtue of their positions. The courts have been cautious in granting such implied or inherent authority. However, any act requiring board approval, such as issuing stock, is clearly beyond the implied authority of any officer.

Apparent authority
acts of the corporation that lead a third party to believe reasonably and in good faith that an officer has the required authority

Apparent Authority **Apparent authority** arises from acts of the corporation that lead third parties to believe reasonably and in good faith that an officer has the required authority. Apparent authority might arise when a third party relies on the fact that an officer has exercised the same authority in the past with the consent of the board of directors.

Ratification
a corporation may ratify the unauthorized acts of its officers

Ratification A corporation may ratify the unauthorized acts of its officers. Equivalent to the corporation's having granted the officer prior authority, **ratification** relates back to the original transaction and may be either express or implied from the corporation's acceptance of the contract's benefits with full knowledge of the facts.

DUTIES OF DIRECTORS AND OFFICERS [35-7]

Generally, directors and officers owe the duties of obedience, diligence, and loyalty to the corporation. These duties are for the most part judicially imposed. By imposing liability upon directors and officers for specific acts, state and federal statutes supplement the common law, which nonetheless remains the most significant source of duties.

A corporation may not recover damages from its directors and officers for losses resulting from their poor business judgments or honest mistakes of judgment. Directors and officers are not duty bound to ensure business success. They are required only to be obedient, reasonably diligent, and completely loyal. In 1999, an amendment to the Revised Act was adopted refining the Act's standards of conduct and liability for directors.

Duty of obedience

must act within respective authority

Duty of Obedience [35-7a]

Directors and officers must act within their respective authority. For any loss the corporation suffers because of their unauthorized acts, they are held absolutely liable in some jurisdictions; in others, they are held liable only if they exceeded their authority intentionally or negligently.

Duty of diligence

must exercise ordinary care and prudence

Duty of Diligence [35-7b]

In discharging their duties, directors and officers must exercise ordinary care and prudence. Some states interpret this standard to mean that directors and officers must exercise "the same degree of care and prudence that [those] promoted by self-interest generally exercise in their own affairs." The great majority of states, as well as the Revised Act, however, hold that the test requires a director or officer to discharge corporate duties (1) in good faith, (2) with the care an ordinarily prudent person in a like position would exercise under similar circumstances, and (3) in a manner the director or officer reasonably believes to be in the best interests of the corporation. A director or officer whose performance of her duties complies with these requirements is not liable for any action she takes as a director or officer or for any failure to act.

So long as the directors and officers act in good faith and with due care, the courts will not substitute their judgment for that of the board or officer—the so-called business judgment rule. Directors and officers nevertheless will be held liable for bad faith or negligent conduct. Moreover, they may be liable for failing to act. In one instance, a bank director, who in the five and one-half years that he had been on the board had never attended a board meeting or examined the institution's books and records, was held liable for losses resulting from the unsupervised acts of the president and cashier, who had made various improper loans and had permitted large overdrafts.

In 1999, an amendment to the Revised Act was adopted refining the Act's standards of conduct and liability for directors. It substituted a different duty of care standard for the second point in the preceding list (prudent person): when becoming informed in connection with their decision-making function or devoting attention to their oversight function, directors shall discharge their duties with the care that a person in a like position would reasonably believe appropriate under similar circumstances. While some aspects of a director's role will be performed individually, such as preparing for meetings, this reformulation explicitly recognizes that directors perform most of their functions as a unit.

Reliance on Others   Directors and officers are permitted to entrust important work to others, and if they have selected employees with care, they are not personally liable for the negligent acts or willful wrongs of those selected. However, a reasonable amount of supervision is required; and an officer or director who knew or should have known or suspected that an employee was incurring losses through carelessness, theft, or embezzlement will be held liable for such losses.

A director also may rely in good faith on information provided him by officers and employees of the corporation; legal counsel, public accountants, or other persons as to matters the director reasonably believes are within the person's professional or expert competence; and a committee of the board of directors of which the director is not a member if the director reasonably believes the committee merits confidence. A director is not acting in good faith if he has knowledge concerning the matter in question that makes reliance unwarranted. The 1999 amendments to the Revised Act added a provision entitling a director to rely on the *performance* of board functions properly delegated by the board to officers, employees, or a committee of the board of directors of which the director is not a member unless the director has knowledge that makes reliance unwarranted.

An officer is also entitled to rely upon this information, but this right may, in many circumstances, be more limited than a director's because of the officer's greater familiarity with the affairs of the corporation.

Business Judgment Rule

Business judgment rule precludes imposing liability on directors and officers for honest mistakes in judgment if they act with due care, in good faith, and in a manner reasonably believed to be in the best interests of the corporation

Business Judgment Rule   Directors and officers are continually called on to make decisions that require balancing benefits and risks to the corporation. Although hindsight may reveal that some of these decisions were not the best, the **business judgment rule** precludes imposing liability on the directors or officers for honest mistakes of judgment if they make an informed decision (1) with due care, (2) in good faith without any conflict of interests, and (3) with a rational basis for believing the decision was in the corporation's best interests. (With respect to *directors*, the 1999 amendments to the Revised Act added a new provision codifying much of the business judgment rule and providing guidance as to its application.) Moreover, where this standard of conduct has not been met, the director's action (or inaction) must be shown to be the proximate cause of damage to the corporation.

Hasty or ill-advised action also can render directors liable. The Supreme Court of Delaware has held directors liable for approving the terms of a cash-out merger. In that case, the court found that the directors did not adequately inform themselves of the company's intrinsic value and were grossly negligent in approving the terms of the merger upon two hours' consideration and without prior notice.

Brehm v. Eisner
Supreme Court of Delaware, 2000
746 A.2d 244
http://scholar.google.com/scholar_case?q=746+A.2d+244+&hl=en&as_sdt=6,34&case=2721397479365362562&scilh=0

FACTS On October 1, 1995, Disney hired as its president Michael S. Ovitz, who was a long-time friend of Disney Chairman and CEO Michael Eisner. At the time, Ovitz was an important talent broker in Hollywood. Although he lacked experience managing a diversified public company, other companies with entertainment operations had been interested in hiring him for high-level executive positions. The employment agreement approved by the board of directors then in office (Old Board) had an initial term of five years and required that Ovitz "devote his full time and best efforts exclusively to the Company," with exceptions for volunteer work, service on the board of another company, and managing his passive investments. In return, Disney agreed to give Ovitz a base salary of $1 million per year, a discretionary bonus, and two sets of stock options (the "A" options and the "B" options) that collectively would enable Ovitz to purchase 5 million shares of Disney common stock. The "A" options were scheduled to vest in three annual increments of 1 million shares each, beginning at the end of the third full year of employment and continuing for the following two years. The agreement specifically provided that the "A" options would vest immediately if Disney granted Ovitz a nonfault termination of the employment agreement. The "B" options, consisting of 2 million shares, were scheduled to vest annually starting the year after the last "A" option would vest and were conditioned on Ovitz and Disney first having agreed to extend his employment beyond the five-year term of the employment agreement. In addition, Ovitz would forfeit the "B" options if his initial employment term of five years ended prematurely for any reason, even if from a nonfault termination.

The employment agreement provided three ways for Ovitz's employment to end. He might serve his five years and Disney might decide against offering him a new contract. If so, Disney would owe Ovitz a $10 million termination payment. Before the end of the initial term, Disney could terminate Ovitz for "good cause" only if Ovitz committed gross negligence or malfeasance, or if Ovitz resigned voluntarily. Disney would owe Ovitz no additional compensation if it terminated him for "good cause." Termination without cause (nonfault termination) would entitle Ovitz to the present value of his salary payments remaining under the agreement, a $10 million severance payment, an additional $7.5 million for each fiscal year remaining under the agreement, and the immediate vesting of the first 3 million stock options (the "A" Options).

Soon after Ovitz began work, problems surfaced and the situation continued to deteriorate during the first year of his employment. The deteriorating situation led Ovitz to begin seeking alternative employment and expressing his desire to leave the Company. On December 11, 1996, Eisner and Ovitz agreed to arrange for Ovitz to leave Disney on the nonfault basis provided for in the 1995 employment agreement. The board of directors then in office (New Board) approved this by authorizing a "non-fault termination" agreement with cash payments to Ovitz of almost $39 million and the immediate vesting of 3 million stock options with a value of $101 million.

Shareholders brought a derivative suit alleging that (1) the Old Board had breached its fiduciary duty in approving an extravagant and wasteful employment agreement and (2) the New Board had breached its fiduciary duty in agreeing to an extravagant and wasteful "nonfault" termination of the Ovitz employment agreement. The plaintiffs alleged that the Old Board had failed properly to inform itself about the total costs and incentives of the Ovitz employment agreement, especially the severance package, and failed to realize that the contract gave Ovitz an incentive to find a way to exit the Company via a non-fault termination as soon as possible because doing so would permit him to earn more than he could by fulfilling his contract. They alleged that the corporate compensation expert, Graef Crystal, who had advised the Old Board in connection with its decision to approve the Ovitz employment agreement, stated two years later that the Old Board failed to consider the incentives and the total cost of the severance provisions. The defendants moved to dismiss, and the Court of Chancery granted the motion. The shareholders appealed.

DECISION Dismissal affirmed in part, reversed in part, and remanded.

OPINION This is a case about whether there should be personal liability of the directors of a Delaware corporation to the corporation for lack of due care in the decision-making process and for waste of corporate assets. This case is not about the failure of the directors to establish and carry out ideal corporate governance practices. The inquiry here is not whether the stockholders have reason to be upset with the behavior and decisions of Disney's Old Board or New Board. The sole issue that the appellate court must determine is whether the particularized facts alleged in this complaint provide a reason to believe that the conduct of the Old Board in 1995 and the New Board in 1996 constituted a violation of their fiduciary duties.

Delaware corporate laws require that, in making business decisions, the directors (1) must be disinterested and independent relative to the decision, (2) must act in good faith, and (3) must act in a manner that can be attributed to a rational business purpose, must reach their decision without a grossly negligent process, and must consider all material facts reasonably available. The plaintiffs contend that the Disney directors on the Old Board did not avail themselves of all material information reasonably available in approving Ovitz's 1995 contract and thereby violated their fiduciary duty of care. The question is whether the trial court's formulation is consistent with the objective test of reasonableness, the test of materiality, and concepts of gross negligence The Court of Chancery is correct that the standard for judging the informational component of the directors' decision making does not mean that the Board must be informed of every fact. The Board is responsible for considering only material facts that are reasonably available, not those that are immaterial or out of the Board's reasonable reach.

Certainly in this case the economic exposure of the corporation to the payout scenarios of the Ovitz contract was material, particularly given its large size, for purposes of the directors' decision-making process. Thus, the objective tests of reasonable availability and materiality were satisfied by this complaint. But that is not the end of the inquiry for liability purposes. The complaint admits that the directors were advised by Crystal as an expert, and that they relied on his expertise. The directors are fully protected (i.e., not held liable) on the basis that they relied in good faith on a qualified expert unless the complaint can prove that (1) the directors did not in fact rely on the expert; (2) their reliance was not in good faith; (3) they did not reasonably believe that the expert's advice was within the expert's professional competence; (4) the expert was not selected with reasonable care by or on behalf of the corporation, and the faulty selection process was attributable to the directors; (5) the subject matter (in this case the cost calculation) that was material and reasonably available was so obvious that the Board's failure to consider it was grossly negligent regardless of the expert's advice or lack of advice; or (6) that the decision of the Board was so unconscionable as to constitute waste or fraud. This complaint includes no particular allegations of this nature, and therefore it was subject to dismissal as drafted.

Construed most favorably to the plaintiffs, the facts in the Complaint show that Ovitz's performance as president was disappointing at best, that Eisner admitted it had been a mistake to hire Ovitz, that Ovitz lacked commitment to the company, that he performed services for his old company, and that he negotiated for other jobs (some very lucrative) while being required under the contract to devote his full time and energy to Disney. All this shows is that the Board had arguable grounds to fire Ovitz for cause. But what is alleged is only an argument—perhaps a good one—that Ovitz's conduct constituted gross negligence or malfeasance. First, given the facts as alleged, Disney would have had to persuade a trier of fact and law of this argument in any litigated dispute with Ovitz. Second, that process of persuasion could involve expensive litigation, distraction of executive time and company resources, lost opportunity costs, more bad publicity, and an outcome that was uncertain at best and, at worst, could have resulted in damages against the company.

The Supreme Court agreed with the conclusion of the Court of Chancery. The Board made a business decision to grant Ovitz a nonfault termination. The plaintiffs may disagree with the Board's judgment as to how this matter should have been handled. But where, as here, there is no reasonable doubt as to the disinterest of or absence of fraud by the Board, mere disagreement cannot serve as grounds for imposing liability based on alleged breaches of fiduciary duty and waste.

INTERPRETATION In exercising their duties, all corporate directors must act in good faith, in the corporation's best interests, and on an informed basis with due care.

ETHICAL QUESTION Did Eisner, Ovitz, or the board of directors act unethically? Explain.

CRITICAL THINKING QUESTION Do you agree with the court's decision in this case? Explain.

Duty of loyalty

requires undeviating loyalty
to the corporation

Duty of Loyalty [35-7c]

The officers and directors of a corporation owe a duty of loyalty (a *fiduciary duty*) to the corporation and to its shareholders. The essence of a fiduciary duty is the subordination of self-interest to the interest of the person or persons to whom the duty is owed. It requires officers and directors to be constantly loyal to the corporation, which they both serve and control.

An officer or director is required to disclose fully to the corporation any financial interest he may have in any contract or transaction to which the corporation is a party. (This is a corollary to the rule that forbids fiduciaries from making secret profits.) His business conduct must be insulated from self-interest, and he may not advance his personal interest at the corporation's expense. Moreover, an officer or director may not represent conflicting interests; her duty is one of strict allegiance to the corporation.

The remedy for breach of fiduciary duty is a suit in equity by the corporation, or more often a derivative suit instituted by a shareholder, to require the fiduciary to pay to the corporation the profits she obtained through the breach. It need not be shown that the corporation could otherwise have made the profits that the fiduciary realized. The object of the rule is to discourage breaches of duty by taking from the fiduciary all of the profits she has made. Though the enforcement of the rule may result in a windfall to the corporation, this is incidental to the rule's deterrent objective. Whenever a director or officer breaches his fiduciary duty, he forfeits his right to compensation during the period he engaged in the breach.

Conflict of Interests   A contract or other transaction between an officer or a director and the corporation inherently involves a conflict of interest. Contracts between officers and the corporation are covered under the law of agency. (See Chapter 28.) Early on, the common law viewed all director-corporation transactions as automatically void or voidable but eventually recognized that this rule was unreasonable because it would prevent directors from entering into contracts beneficial to the corporation. Now, therefore, if such a contract is honest and fair, the courts will uphold it. In the case of contracts between corporations having an interlocking directorate (corporations whose boards of directors share one or more members), the courts subject the contracts to scrutiny and will set them aside unless the transaction is shown to have been entirely fair and entered in good faith.

Most states and the original version of the Revised Act address these related problems by providing that such transactions are neither void nor voidable if, after full disclosure, they are approved by either the board of disinterested directors or the shareholders or if they are fair and reasonable to the corporation.

The Revised Act was amended in 1988 to adopt a more specific approach to a director's conflict-of-interest transactions. The Revised Act establishes more clearly prescribed safe harbors to validate conflict-of-interest transactions. The Revised Act provides two alternative safe harbors, each of which is available before or after the transaction: approval by "qualified" (disinterested) directors or approval by the shareholders. In either case, the interested director must make full disclosure to the approving group. If neither of these safe harbor provisions is satisfied, then the transaction is subject to appropriate judicial action unless the transaction is fair to the corporation.

Loans to Directors and Officers   The Model Act and some states permit a corporation to lend money to its *directors* only with its shareholders' authorization for each loan. The statutes in most states permit such loans either on a general or limited basis. The Revised Act initially permitted such loans if each particular loan was approved (1) by a majority of disinterested shareholders or (2) by the board of directors after determining that the loan would benefit the corporation; however, the 1988 amendments to the Revised Act deleted this section, subjecting loans to directors to the procedure that applies to directors' conflicting-interest transactions.

The Sarbanes-Oxley Act prohibits any publicly held corporation from making personal loans to its directors or its executive officers, although it does provide certain limited exceptions.

Corporate Opportunity   Directors and officers may not usurp any corporate opportunity that in all fairness should belong to the corporation. A corporate opportunity is one in which the corporation has a right, property interest, or expectancy; whether such an opportunity exists depends on the facts and circumstances of each case. A corporate opportunity should be promptly offered to the corporation, which, in turn, should promptly accept or reject it. Rejection may be based on one or more of several factors, such as the corporation's lack of interest in the opportunity, its financial inability to acquire the opportunity, legal restrictions on its ability to accept the opportunity, or a third party's unwillingness to deal with the corporation. A provision was added to the Revised Act to deal with business opportunities and to provide safe-harbor protection for directors considering involvement with a business opportunity that might be considered a corporate opportunity.

Beam v. Stewart
Court of Chancery of Delaware, New Castle, 2003
833 A.2d 961; *affirmed*, 845 A.2d 1040
http://scholar.google.com/scholar_case?q=833+A.2d+961&hl=en&as_sdt=2,34&case=17647245391824322549&scilh=0

FACTS Monica A. Beam, a shareholder of Martha Stewart Living Omnimedia, Inc. (MSO), brings a derivative action against the defendants, all current directors and a former director of MSO, and against MSO as a nominal defendant. MSO is a Delaware corporation that operates in the publishing, television, merchandising, and Internet industries marketing products bearing the "Martha Stewart" brand name. Defendant Martha Stewart (Stewart) is a director of the company and its founder, chairman, CEO, and by far its majority shareholder controlling roughly 94.4 percent of the shareholder vote. Stewart, a former stockbroker, has in the past twenty years become a household icon, known for her advice and expertise on virtually all aspects of cooking, decorating, entertaining, and household affairs generally.

The market for MSO products is uniquely tied to the personal image and reputation of its founder, Stewart. MSO retains "an exclusive, worldwide, perpetual royalty-free license to use [Stewart's] name, likeness, image, voice and signature for its products and services." In its initial public offering prospectus, MSO recognized that impairment of Stewart's services to the company, including the tarnishing of her public reputation, would have a material adverse effect on its business. Under the terms of her employment agreement, Stewart may be terminated for gross misconduct or felony conviction that results in harm to MSO's business or reputation but is permitted discretion over the management of her personal, financial, and legal affairs to the extent that Stewart's management of her own life does not compromise her ability to serve the company.

Stewart's alleged misadventures with ImClone arise in part out of a longstanding personal friendship with Samuel D. Waksal (Waksal). Waksal is the former CEO of ImClone as well as a former suitor of Stewart's daughter. Waksal and Stewart have provided one another with reciprocal investment advice and assistance, and they share a stockbroker, Peter E. Bacanovic (Bacanovic) of Merrill Lynch. The speculative value of ImClone stock was tied quite directly to the likely success of its application for U.S. Food and Drug Administration (FDA) approval to market the cancer treatment drug Erbitux. On December 26, Waksal received information that the FDA was rejecting the application to market Erbitux. The following day, December 27, he tried to sell his own shares and tipped his father and daughter to do the same. Stewart also sold her shares on December 27. After the close of trading on December 28, ImClone publicly

announced the rejection of its application to market Erbitux. The following day the trading price closed slightly more than 20 percent lower than the closing price on the date that Stewart had sold her shares. By mid-2002, these events had attracted the interest of the *New York Times* and other news agencies, federal prosecutors, and a committee of the U.S. House of Representatives. Stewart's publicized attempts to quell any suspicion were ineffective at best because they were undermined by additional information as it came to light and by the other parties' accounts of the events. Ultimately Stewart's prompt efforts to turn away unwanted media and investigative attention failed. Stewart eventually had to discontinue her regular guest appearances on CBS's *The Early Show* because of questioning during the show about her sale of ImClone shares. After barely two months of such adverse publicity, MSO's stock price had declined by slightly more than 65 percent. In January 2002, Stewart and the Martha Stewart Family Partnership sold 3 million shares of Class A stock to an investor group.

The complaint alleges that the director defendants breached their fiduciary duties by failing to ensure that Stewart would not conduct her personal, financial, and legal affairs in a manner that would harm the Company, its intellectual property, or its business. It also alleges that Stewart breached her fiduciary duty of loyalty, usurping a corporate opportunity by selling large blocks of MSO stock.

DECISION These counts of the complaint are dismissed for failure to state a claim upon which relief can be granted.

OPINION The duty to monitor has been litigated in other circumstances, generally in cases in which directors were alleged to have been negligent in monitoring the activities of the corporation, activities that led to corporate liability. That the Company is "closely identified" with Stewart is conceded, but it does not necessarily follow that the board is required to monitor, much less control, the way Stewart handles her *personal* financial and legal affairs. Although a duty to monitor may arise when the board has reason to suspect wrongdoing, it does not burden MSO's board with a duty to monitor Stewart's *personal* affairs. Regardless of Stewart's importance to MSO, she is not the corporation. And it is unreasonable to impose a duty upon the board to monitor Stewart's personal affairs because such a requirement is neither legitimate nor feasible.

The basic requirements for establishing usurpation of a corporate opportunity were articulated by the Delaware Supreme Court in *Broz v. Cellular Information Systems, Inc.*:

> [A] corporate officer or director may not take a business opportunity for his own if: (1) the corporation is financially able to exploit the opportunity; (2) the opportunity is within the corporation's line of business; (3) the corporation has an interest or expectancy in the opportunity; and (4) by taking the opportunity for his own, the corporate fiduciary will thereby be placed in a position [inimical] to his duties to the corporation.

In this analysis, no single factor is dispositive. Instead the court must balance all factors as they apply to a particular case.

MSO was able to exploit this opportunity because the Company's certificate of incorporation had sufficient authorized, yet unissued, shares of Class A common stock to cover the sale. Therefore the first factor has been met.

An opportunity is within a corporation's line of business if it is an activity as to which the corporation has fundamental knowledge, practical experience, and ability to pursue. MSO is a consumer products company, not an investment company; selling stock is not the same line of business as selling advice to homemakers. Therefore the sale of stock by Stewart was not within MSO's line of business.

A corporation has an interest or expectancy in an opportunity if there is "some tie between that property and the nature of the corporate business." Here, plaintiff does not allege any facts that would imply that MSO was in need of additional capital, seeking additional capital, or even remotely interested in finding new investors. Thus this factor of the *Broz* test has not been met.

Given that MSO had no interest or expectancy in the issuance of new stock, Stewart's sales did not place her in a position inimical to her duties to the Company and the fourth factor has not been met. Delaware courts have recognized a policy that allows officers and directors of corporations to buy and sell shares of that corporation at will so long as they act in good faith. On balancing the four factors, the plaintiff has failed to plead facts sufficient to state a claim that Stewart usurped a corporate opportunity for herself in violation of her fiduciary duty of loyalty to MSO.

INTERPRETATION Corporate directors and officers may not usurp any opportunity in which the corporation has a right, property interest, or expectancy that in all fairness should belong to the corporation.

ETHICAL QUESTION Did the defendants act unethically? Explain.

CRITICAL THINKING QUESTION What should be the test for determining when an opportunity belongs to the corporation? Explain.

Transactions in Shares The issuance of shares at favorable prices to management by excluding other shareholders normally will constitute a violation of the fiduciary duty. So might the issuance of shares to a director at a fair price if the purpose of the issuance is to perpetuate corporate control rather than to raise capital or to serve some other corporate interest. Officers and directors have access to inside advance information, unavailable to the public, which may affect the future market value of the corporation's shares. Federal statutes have attempted to deal with this trading advantage by prohibiting officers and directors from purchasing or selling shares of their corporation's stock without adequately disclosing all material facts in their possession that may affect the stock's actual or potential value. We will discuss these matters more fully in Chapter 39.

Although state law has inconsistently imposed liability on officers and directors for secret, profitable use of inside information, the trend is toward holding them liable for breach of fiduciary duty to shareholders from whom they purchase stock without disclosing facts that give the stock added potential value. They are also held liable to the corporation for profits they realize on a sale of the stock when undisclosed conditions of the corporation make a substantial decline in value practically inevitable.

Duty Not to Compete As fiduciaries, directors and officers owe to the corporation the duty of undivided loyalty, which means that they may not compete with the corporation. A director or officer who breaches his fiduciary duty by competing with the corporation is liable for damages caused to the corporation. Although directors and officers may engage in their own business interests, courts will closely scrutinize any interest that competes with the corporation's business. Moreover, an officer or director (1) may not use corporate personnel, facilities, or funds for her own benefit and (2) may not disclose trade secrets of the corporation to others.

Indemnification

a corporation may indemnify a director or officer for liability incurred if he acted in good faith and was not adjudged negligent or liable for misconduct

Indemnification of Directors and Officers [35-7d]

Directors and officers incur personal liability for breaching any of the duties they owe to the corporation and its shareholders. Under many modern incorporation statutes, a corporation may **indemnify** a director or officer for liability incurred if he acted in good faith and in a manner he reasonably believed to be in the best interests of the corporation, so long as he has not been judged

BUSINESS LAW **IN ACTION**

In response to the spate of corporate and accounting scandals at the turn of the millennium, the Sarbanes-Oxley Act and corporate governance rules adopted by the New York Stock Exchange and the National Association of Securities Dealers (now known as the Financial Industry Regulatory Authority [FINRA]) have changed the landscape for corporate directors' accountability, at least for the vast majority of publicly traded corporations.

Boards of directors that "rubber stamp" management's decisions are no longer acceptable. Instead, recent governance reforms have the purpose of reshaping boards of directors into true corporate monitors. The primary features of today's reconfigured boards are (1) a majority of independent directors with no business or personal ties to the company, (2) specialized committees of the board to address different corporate issues, especially an audit committee consisting exclusively of independent directors that oversees the firm's outside auditors, among other duties, and (3) a clear charter of board authority that is published, usually on the firm's website.

While the business judgment rule protects corporate directors from honest mistakes in judgment when making decisions for the corporation, it does not provide a shield for their inaction, malfeasance, or lack of supervision. Inattention by the board not only fails the business judgment rule, it may amount to "abdication," which is a breach of directors' duty of loyalty. Moreover, directors who are aware that they are not devoting sufficient attention to their duties are not acting in good faith and may not be able to take advantage of exculpatory charter provisions that exonerate directors who act in good faith and without the intent to inflict harm on the corporation. In such a case, directors may also lose the indemnity protection typically accorded them when sued by shareholders or others. This will mean personal liability for any resulting civil judgments.

In this new stricter corporate governance climate, directors will need to take greater pains to establish a strong foundation for trusting the honesty, integrity, and loyalty of the executives and managers upon whom they rely, as well as the expertise and independence of the company's outside auditors and other advisors. They should also demonstrate their independence and devote substantial, meaningful time and energy to their roles as both corporate policy makers and monitors.

Practical Advice

Before agreeing to serve on a corporate board of directors, make sure that the company has sufficient director's liability insurance and determine what the policy covers.

Liability limitation statutes

many states authorize corporations—with shareholder approval—to limit or eliminate the liability of directors for some breaches of duty

negligent or liable for misconduct. The Revised Act provides for mandatory indemnification of directors and officers for reasonable expenses they incur in the wholly successful defense of any proceeding brought against them because they are or were directors or officers. These provisions, however, may be limited by the articles of incorporation. In addition, a corporation may purchase insurance to indemnify officers and directors for liability arising out of their corporate activities, including liabilities against which the corporation is not empowered to indemnify directly.

Liability Limitation Statutes [35-7e]

Virtually all states have enacted legislation limiting the liability of directors. Most of these states, including Delaware, have authorized corporations—with shareholder approval—to limit or eliminate the liability of directors for some breaches of duty. (A few states permit shareholders to limit the liability of officers.) The Delaware statute provides that the articles of incorporation may contain a provision eliminating or limiting the personal liability of a director to the corporation or its stockholders for monetary damages for breach of directorial duty, provided that such provision does not eliminate or limit the liability of a director (1) for any breach of the director's duty of loyalty to the corporation or its stockholders, (2) for acts or omissions lacking good faith or involving intentional misconduct or a knowing violation of law, (3) for liability for unlawful dividend payments or redemptions, or (4) for any transaction from which the director derived an improper personal benefit.

A few states have directly limited personal liability for directors, subject to certain exceptions, without requiring an amendment to the articles of incorporation. A third approach, taken by some states, limits the amount of money damages that may be assessed against a director or officer.

The Revised Act authorizes the articles of incorporation to include a provision eliminating or limiting—with certain exceptions—the liability of a director to the corporation or its shareholders for any action he takes, or fails to take, as a director. The exceptions, for which his liability would not be affected, are (1) the amount of any financial benefit the director receives to which he is not entitled, such as a bribe, kickback, or profits from a usurped corporate opportunity; (2) an intentional infliction of harm on the corporation or the shareholders; (3) liability under Section 8.33 for unlawful distributions; and (4) an intentional violation of the criminal law.

ETHICAL DILEMMA

Whom Does a Director Represent? What Are a Director's Duties?

Facts Maulington's, a large, publicly held food-processing company, is run by an old, dictatorial CEO, who is also chairman of the board—a board packed with inside directors and retired CEOs of other businesses. Industry analysts regard Maulington's as stodgy and unimaginative in its use of capital. Yet its profits are dependable, it pays a decent dividend, and its stock is widely held by conservative investors. In the city where the company has its headquarters, it is regarded as a good corporate citizen. Many community organizations depend on its charitable contributions.

Upon the unexpected death of a director, the remaining directors nominate a forty-year-old doctor and children's health advocate, Peter Maxwell-Deane, who has wide community connections but little business experience. The directors reason that the board could use some youth, at least for appearances. Dr. Maxwell-Deane is duly elected to the board. He knows the visibility will help his

career. He also hopes to influence the company to donate to his favorite children's health projects.

After his election, Dr. Maxwell-Deane is approached by Carola Campbell, a woman he knows from his charitable work and whom, in fact, he once dated for several months. Campbell is the granddaughter of the company's founder, owns 1 percent of the company's shares, and is feuding with the current CEO. She says that the CEO has held Maulington's back, thereby hurting its share price, and that she thinks he should have retired long ago. She tells Maxwell-Deane that the board's compensation committee has improperly given stock options to the current CEO and other inside directors. Campbell, who has no friends on the board, appeals to Maxwell-Deane for help. Specifically, she asks him to sound out other outside directors to see whether they also find the stock option deals fishy. Finally, she tells him that she is thinking about requesting a list of shareholders from the board

so that she can communicate directly with other shareholders about the management of the corporation. She wonders whether, if she has any trouble obtaining the list, Maxwell-Deane will help her.

Social, Policy, and Ethical Considerations

1. Does Dr. Maxwell-Deane, as a director, represent Carola Campbell? Should he quietly sound out the other directors as she asks? What risks would he run by doing so?
2. Does Maxwell-Deane have a duty to disclose to the board his previous relationship with Campbell? What details, if any, of his conversation with her should he report to the board?
3. What duty does Maxwell-Deane have to follow up on Campbell's allegation that stock options were improperly awarded to the CEO and other inside directors?
4. What should Maxwell-Deane do?

CHAPTER SUMMARY

Role of Shareholders

Voting Rights of Shareholders

Management Structure of Corporations see Figures 35-1, 35-2, and 35-3 for illustrations of the statutory model of corporate governance, the structure of the typical closely held corporation, and the structure of the typical publicly held corporation

Shareholder Meetings shareholders may exercise their voting rights at both annual and special shareholder meetings

Quorum minimum number necessary to be present at a meeting to transact business

Election of Directors the shareholders elect the board at the annual meeting of the corporation

- *Straight Voting* directors are elected by a plurality of votes
- *Cumulative Voting* entitles shareholders to multiply the number of votes they are entitled to cast by the number of directors for whom they are entitled to vote and to cast the product for a single candidate or to distribute the product among two or more candidates

Removal of Directors the shareholders may by majority vote remove directors with or without cause, subject to cumulative voting rights

Approval of Fundamental Changes shareholder approval is required for charter amendments, most acquisitions, and dissolution

Concentrations of Voting Power

- *Proxy* authorization to vote another's shares at a shareholder meeting
- *Voting Trust* transfer of corporate shares' voting rights to a trustee
- *Shareholder Voting Agreement* used to provide shareholders with greater control over the election and removal of directors and other matters

Restrictions on Transfer of Shares must be reasonable and conspicuously noted on stock certificate

Enforcement Right of Shareholders

Right to Inspect Books and Records if the demand is made in good faith and for a proper purpose

Shareholder Suits

- *Direct Suits* brought by a shareholder or a class of shareholders against the corporation based upon the ownership of shares
- *Derivative Suits* brought by a shareholder on behalf of the corporation to enforce a right belonging to the corporation

Shareholder's Right to Dissent a shareholder has the right to dissent from certain corporate actions that require shareholder approval

---

Role of Directors and Officers

Function of the Board of Directors

Selection and Removal of Officers

Capital Structure

Fundamental Changes the directors have the power to make, amend, or repeal the bylaws, unless this power is exclusively reserved to the shareholders

Dividends directors declare the amount and type of dividends

Management Compensation

Vacancies in the Board may be filled by the vote of a majority of the remaining directors

Exercise of Directors' Functions

Meeting directors have the power to bind the corporation only when acting as a board

Action Taken Without a Meeting permitted if a consent in writing is signed by all of the directors

Delegation of Board Powers committees may be appointed to perform some but not all of the board's functions

Directors' Inspection Rights directors have the right to inspect corporate books and records

Officers

Role of Officers officers are agents of the corporation

Authority of Officers

- *Actual Express Authority* arises from the incorporation statute, the charter, the bylaws, and resolutions of the directors
- *Actual Implied Authority* authority to do what is reasonably necessary to perform actual authority
- *Apparent Authority* acts of the principal that lead a third party to believe reasonably and in good faith that an officer has the required authority
- *Ratification* a corporation may ratify the unauthorized acts of its officers

Duties of Directors and Officers

Duty of Obedience must act within respective authority

Duty of Diligence must exercise ordinary care and prudence

Duty of Loyalty requires undeviating loyalty to the corporation

Business Judgment Rule precludes imposing liability on directors and officers for honest mistakes in judgment if they act with due care, in good faith, and in a manner reasonably believed to be in the best interests of the corporation

Indemnification a corporation may indemnify a director or officer for liability incurred if he acted in good faith and was not adjudged negligent or liable for misconduct

Liability Limitation Statutes many states now authorize corporations—with shareholder approval—to limit or eliminate the liability of directors for some breaches of duty

QUESTIONS

1. Brown, the president and director of a corporation engaged in owning and operating a chain of motels, was advised, on what seemed to be good authority, that a superhighway was to be constructed through the town of X, which would be a most desirable location for a motel. Brown presented these facts to the board of directors of the motel corporation and recommended that the corporation build a motel in the town of X at the location described. The board of directors agreed, and the new motel was constructed. However, the superhighway plans were changed after the motel was constructed, and the highway was never built. Later, a packinghouse was built on property adjoining the motel, and as a result the corporation sustained a considerable loss. The shareholders brought an appropriate action against Brown, charging that his proposal had caused the corporation a substantial loss. What is the result?

2. A, B, C, D, and E constituted the board of directors of the X Corporation. While D and E were out of town, A, B, and C held a special meeting of the board. Just as the meeting began, C became ill. He then gave a proxy to A and went home. A resolution was then adopted directing and authorizing the X Corporation's purchase of an adjoining piece of land owned by S as a site for an additional factory building. A and B voted for the resolution, and A, as C's proxy, cast C's vote in favor of the resolution. The X Corporation then made a contract with S for the purchase of the land. After the return of D and E, another special meeting of the board was held with all five directors present. A resolution was then unanimously adopted to cancel the contract with S. May S recover damages from X Corporation for breach of contract?

3. Bernard Koch was president of United Corporation, a closely held corporation. Koch, James Trent, and Henry Phillips made up the three-person board of directors. At a meeting of the board, Trent was elected president, replacing Koch. At the same meeting, Trent attempted to have the salary of the president increased. He was unable to obtain board approval of the increase because although Phillips voted for the increase, Koch voted against it. Trent was disqualified from voting by the charter. As a result, the directors, by a two-to-one vote, amended the bylaws to provide for the appointment of an executive committee composed of three reputable businesspersons to pass upon and fix all matters of salary for employees of the corporation. Subsequently, the executive committee, consisting of Jane Jones, James Black, and William Johnson, increased the salary of the president. Will Koch succeed in an appropriate action against the corporation, Trent, and Phillips to enjoin them from paying compensation to the president above that fixed by the board of directors? Explain.

4. Zenith Steel Company operates a prosperous business. In January, Zenith's CEO and president, Roe, who is also a member of the board of directors, was voted a $1 million bonus by the board of directors for valuable services he provided to the company during the previous year. Roe received an annual salary of $850,000 from the company. Black, Inc., a minority shareholder in Zenith Steel Company, brings an appropriate action to enjoin the payment by the company of the $1 million bonus. Explain whether Black will succeed in its attempt.

5. Raphael, a minority shareholder of the Sample Corporation, claims that the following sales are void and should be annulled. Explain whether Raphael is correct.
   a. Smith, a director of the Sample Corporation, sells a piece of vacant land to the Sample Corporation for $500,000. The land cost him $200,000.
   b. Jones, a shareholder of the Sample Corporation, sells a used truck to the Sample Corporation for $8,400, although the truck is worth $6,000.

6. X Corporation manufactures machine tools. Its two principal competitors are Y Corporation and Z Corporation. The five directors of X Corporation are Black, White, Brown, Green, and Crimson. At a duly called meeting of the board of directors of X Corporation in January, all five directors were present. A contract for the purchase of $10 million worth of steel from the D Company, of which Black, White, and Brown are directors, was discussed and approved by a unanimous vote. There was a lengthy discussion about entering into negotiations for the purchase of Q Corporation, which allegedly was about to be sold for around $150 million. By a 3–2 vote, it was decided not to open such negotiations.

   Three months later, Green purchased Q Corporation for $150 million. Shortly thereafter, a new board of directors for X Corporation took office. X Corporation now brings actions to rescind its contract with D Company and to compel Green to assign to X Corporation his contract for the purchase of Q Corporation. Decisions as to each action?

7. Gore had been the owner of 1 percent of the outstanding shares of the Webster Company, a corporation since its organization ten years ago. Ratliff, the president of the company, was the owner of 70 percent of the outstanding shares. Ratliff used the shareholders' list to submit to the shareholders an offer of $50.00 per share for their stock. Gore, on receiving the offer, called Ratliff and told him that the offer was inadequate and advised that she was willing to offer $60.00 per share and for that purpose demanded a shareholders' list. Ratliff knew that Gore was willing and able to supply the funds necessary to purchase the stock, but he nevertheless refused to supply the list to Gore. Furthermore, he did not offer to transmit Gore's offer to the shareholders of record. Gore then brought an action to compel the corporation to make the shareholders' list available to her. Will Gore be able to obtain a copy of the shareholders' list? Why?

8. Mitchell, Nelson, Olsen, and Parker, experts in manufacturing baubles, each owned fifteen of one hundred authorized shares of Baubles, Inc., a corporation of State X that does not permit cumulative voting. On July 7, 2008, the corporation sold forty shares to Quentin, an investor, for $1.5 million, which it used

to purchase a factory building. On July 8, 2008, Mitchell, Nelson, Olsen, and Parker contracted as follows:

> All parties will act jointly in exercising voting rights as shareholders. In the event of a failure to agree, the question shall be submitted to George Yost, whose decision shall be binding upon all parties.

Until a meeting of shareholders on April 17, 2015, when a dispute arose, all parties to the contract had voted consistently and regularly for Nelson, Olsen, and Parker as directors. At that meeting, Yost considered the dispute and decided and directed that Mitchell, Nelson, Olsen, and Parker vote their shares for the latter three as directors. Nelson, Olsen, and Parker so voted. Mitchell and Quentin voted for themselves and Olsen as directors.

a. Is the contract of July 8, 2008, valid, and, if so, what is its effect?

b. Who were elected directors of Baubles, Inc., at the meeting of its shareholders on April 17, 2015?

9. Acme Corporation's articles of incorporation require cumulative voting for the election of its directors. The board of directors of Acme Corporation consists of nine directors, each elected annually.

a. Peter owns 24 percent of the outstanding shares of Acme Corporation. How many directors can he elect with his votes?

b. If Acme Corporation were to classify its board into three classes, each consisting of three directors elected every three years, how many directors would Peter be able to elect?

10. A bylaw of Betma Corporation provides that no shareholder can sell his shares unless he first offers them for sale to the corporation or its directors. The bylaw also states that this restriction shall be printed or stamped upon each stock certificate and shall bind all present or future owners or holders. Betma Corporation did not comply with this latter provision. Shaw, having knowledge of the bylaw restriction, nevertheless purchased twenty shares of the corporation's stock from Rice, without having Rice first offer them for sale to the corporation or its directors. When Betma Corporation refused to effectuate a transfer of the shares to her, Shaw sued to compel a transfer and the issuance of a new certificate to her. What is the result?

CASE PROBLEMS

11. Neese, trustee in bankruptcy for First Trust Company, brings a suit against the directors of the company for losses the company sustained as a result of the directors' failure to use due care and diligence in the discharge of their duties. The specific acts of negligence alleged are (a) failure to give as much time and attention to the affairs of the company as its business interests required; (b) abdication of their control of the corporation by turning the entire management of the corporation over to its president, Brown; (c) failure to keep informed as to the affairs, condition, and management of the corporation; (d) failure to take action to direct or control the corporation's affairs; (e) permission of large, open, unsecured loans to affiliated but financially unsound companies that were owned and controlled by Brown; (f) failure to examine financial reports that would have shown illegal diversions and waste of the corporation's funds; and (g) failure to supervise properly the corporation's officers and directors. Which, if any, of these allegations can constitute a breach of the duty of diligence?

12. Minority shareholders of Midwest Technical Institute Development Corporation, a closed-end investment company owning assets consisting principally of securities of companies in technological fields, brought a shareholder derivative suit against officers and directors of Midwest, seeking to recover on Midwest's behalf the profits the officers and directors realized through dealings in stock held in Midwest's portfolio in breach of their fiduciary duty. Approximately three years after commencement of the action, a new corporation, Midtex, was organized to acquire Midwest's assets. May the shareholders now add Midtex as a party defendant to their suit? Why?

13. Riffe, while serving as an officer of Wilshire Oil Company, received a secret commission for work he did on behalf of a competing corporation. Can Wilshire Oil recover these secret profits and, in addition, recover the compensation Wilshire Oil paid to Riffe during the period that he acted on behalf of the competitor? Explain.

14. Muller, a shareholder of SCM, brought an action against SCM over his unsuccessful negotiations to purchase some of SCM's assets overseas. He then formed a shareholder committee to challenge the position of SCM's management in that suit. To conduct a proxy battle for management control at the next election of directors, the committee sought to obtain the list of shareholders who would be eligible to vote. At the time, however, no member of the committee had owned stock in SCM for the six-month period required to gain access to such information. Then Lopez, a former SCM executive and a shareholder for more than one year, joined the committee and demanded to be allowed to inspect the minutes of SCM shareholder proceedings and to gain access to the current shareholder list. His stated reason for making the demand was to solicit proxies in support of the committee's nominees for positions as directors. Lopez brought this action after SCM rejected his demand. Will Lopez succeed?

15. Pritchard & Baird was a reinsurance broker. A reinsurance broker arranges contracts between insurance companies so that companies that have sold large policies may sell participations in these policies to other companies in order to share the risks. Pritchard & Baird was controlled for many years by Charles Pritchard, who died in December 2012. Prior to his death, he brought his two sons, Charles, Jr. and William, into the business. The pair assumed an increasingly dominant role in the affairs of the business during the elder Charles's later years. Starting in 2009, Charles, Jr. and William began to

withdraw from the corporate account ever-increasing sums that were designated as "loans" on the balance sheet. These "loans," however, represented a significant misappropriation of funds belonging to the corporation's clients. By late 2014, Charles, Jr. and William had plunged the corporation into hopeless bankruptcy. A total of $12,333,514.47 in "loans" had accumulated by October of that year. Mrs. Lillian Pritchard, the widow of the elder Charles, was a member of the corporation's board of directors until her resignation in December 2014, the day before the corporation filed for bankruptcy. Francis, as trustee in the bankruptcy proceeding, brought suit against United Jersey Bank, the administrator of the estate of Charles, Sr. He also charged that Lillian Pritchard, as a director of the corporation, was personally liable for the misappropriated funds on the basis of negligence in discharging her duties as director. Is Francis correct?

16. Donald J. Richardson, Grove L. Cook, and Wayne Weaver were stockholders of Major Oil. They brought a direct action, individually and on behalf of all other stockholders of Major, against certain directors and other officers of the corporation. The complaint stated twelve causes of action. The first eight causes alleged some misappropriation of Major's assets by the defendants and sought to require the defendants to return the assets to Major. Three of the remaining four causes alleged breaches of fiduciary duty implicit in those fraudulent acts and sought compensatory or punitive damages for the injury that resulted. The final cause sought the appointment of a receiver. Richardson, Cook, and Weaver moved for an order certifying the suit as a class action. Decision?

17. Klinicki and Lundgren, both furloughed Pan Am pilots stationed in West Germany, decided to start their own charter airline company. They formed Berlinair, Inc., a closely held Oregon corporation. Lundgren was president and a director in charge of developing the business. Klinicki was vice president and a director in charge of operations and maintenance. Klinicki, Lundgren, and Lelco, Inc. (Lundgren's family business) each owned one-third of the stock. Klinicki and Lundgren, as representatives of Berlinair, met with BFR, a consortium of Berlin travel agents, to negotiate a lucrative air transportation contract. When Lundgren learned of the likelihood of actually obtaining the BFR contract, he formed his own solely owned company, Air Berlin Charter Company (ABC). Although he continued to negotiate for the BFR contract, he did so on behalf of ABC, not Berlinair. Eventually BFR awarded the contract to ABC. Klinicki commenced a derivative action on behalf of Berlinair and a suit against Lundgren individually for usurping a corporate opportunity of Berlinair. Lundgren claimed that Berlinair was not financially able to undertake the BFR contract and therefore no usurpation of corporate opportunity could occur. Who is correct? Explain.

TAKING SIDES

Sinclair Oil Corporation organized a subsidiary, Sinclair Venezuelan Oil Company (Sinven), for the purpose of operating in Venezuela. Sinclair owned about 97 percent of Sinven's stock. Sinclair nominates all members of Sinven's board of directors, and none of the directors were independent of Sinclair. A minority shareholder of Sinven brought a derivative action on behalf of Sinven against Sinclair seeking to recover damages sustained by Sinven. The derivative suit alleged that Sinclair had caused Sinven to pay out such excessive dividends that the industrial development of Sinven was effectively prevented.

a. What are the arguments that the transactions between Sinclair and Sinven should be subjected to judicial scrutiny and upheld only if Sinclair shows them to have been entirely fair and entered in good faith?

b. What are the arguments that the transactions between Sinclair and Sinven should be subjected to the business judgment rule and overturned only if Sinven shows that Sinclair had *not* acted with due care, in good faith, and in a manner reasonably believed to be in the best interests of Sinven?

c. Explain which standard should apply.

Fundamental Changes of Corporations

CHAPTER 36

The minority, in other words, should have the right to say to the majority, "we recognize your right to restructure the enterprise, provided you are willing to buy us out at a fair price if we object, so that we are not forced to participate in an enterprise other than the one we contemplated at the outset of our mutual association."

M. Eisenberg
The Structure of the Corporation (1976)

CHAPTER OUTCOMES

After reading and studying this chapter, you should be able to:

1. Explain the procedure for amending the charter and list which amendments give rise to the appraisal remedy.

2. Identify which combinations do not require shareholder approval and which give dissenting shareholders an appraisal remedy.

3. Distinguish between a tender offer and a compulsory share exchange.

4. Compare and contrast a cash-out combination and a management buyout.

5. Identify the ways by which voluntary and involuntary dissolution may occur.

Certain extraordinary changes affect a corporation so fundamentally that they fall outside the authority of the board of directors and require shareholder approval. Such fundamental changes include charter amendments, mergers, consolidations, compulsory share exchanges, dissolution, and the sale or lease of all or substantially all of the corporation's assets (other than those in the regular course of business), all of which alter the corporation's basic structure. Although each of these actions is authorized by state incorporation statutes that impose specific procedural requirements, they are also subject to equitable limitations imposed by the courts. In 1999 substantial revisions were made to the Revised Act's treatment of fundamental changes.

As shareholder approval for fundamental changes usually does not need to be unanimous, such changes frequently will be approved despite opposition by minority shareholders. Shareholder approval means a majority (or some other specified fraction) of *all* votes *entitled* to be cast, rather than a majority (or other fraction) of votes represented at a shareholders' meeting at which a quorum is present. (The 1999 amendments to the Revised Act significantly changed the voting rule: fundamental changes need be approved by only a majority of the shares present at a meeting at which a quorum is present.) In some instances, minority shareholders have the right to dissent and to recover the fair value of their shares if they follow the prescribed procedure for doing so. This right is called the appraisal remedy. We will discuss the legal aspects of fundamental changes in this chapter.

CHARTER AMENDMENTS [36-1]

Shareholders do not have a vested property right resulting from any provision in the articles of incorporation. Accordingly, incorporation statutes grant the **authority to amend** the corporate charter if specified procedures are followed. The amended articles of incorporation, however, may contain only those provisions that might lawfully be contained in the articles of incorporation at the time of the amendment.

Authority to amend incorporation statutes permit corporate charters to be amended

Approval by Directors and Shareholders [36-1a]

Procedure for amending
the board of directors adopts a resolution, which must be approved by a majority vote of the shareholders

Under the Revised Act and most statutes, the typical **procedure for amending** the articles of incorporation requires the board of directors to adopt a resolution setting forth the proposed amendment, which must then be approved by a majority vote of the shareholders entitled to vote, although some older statutes require a two-thirds shareholder vote. In some states shareholders may approve charter amendments without a prior board of directors' resolution. After the shareholders approve the amendment, the corporation executes articles of amendment and delivers them to the secretary of state for filing. The amendment does not affect the existing rights of nonshareholders.

Under the Revised Act, *dissenting shareholders* receive the appraisal remedy *only* if an amendment materially and adversely affects their rights by (1) altering or abolishing a preferential right of the shares; (2) creating, altering, or abolishing a right involving the redemption of the shares; (3) altering or abolishing a preemptive right of the holder of such shares; (4) excluding or limiting a shareholder's right to vote on any matter or to cumulate his votes; or (5) reducing to a fraction of a share the number of shares a shareholder owns, if the fractional share is to be acquired for cash. The 1999 amendments to the Revised Act eliminate the appraisal remedy for virtually all charter amendments.

Under the Revised Act, the shareholder approval required for an amendment depends upon the nature of the amendment. An amendment that would give rise to dissenters' rights must be approved by a majority of all votes entitled to be cast on the amendment, unless the act or the charter requires a greater vote. All other amendments must be approved by a majority of all votes cast on the amendment, unless the act or the charter requires a greater vote.

Practical Advice

If you are forming a close corporation and will hold a minority interest in it, consider including in the charter supermajority quorum and voting provisions for charter amendments to ensure that you will have veto power.

Approval by Directors [36-1b]

The Revised Act permits the board of directors to adopt certain amendments without shareholder action, unless the articles of incorporation provide otherwise. These amendments include (1) extending the duration of a corporation that was incorporated when limited duration was required by law, (2) changing each issued and unissued authorized share of an outstanding class into a greater number of whole shares if the corporation has only one class of shares, and (3) making minor name changes.

COMBINATIONS [36-2]

Acquiring all or substantially all of the assets of another corporation or corporations may be both desirable and profitable for a corporation. To accomplish this, the corporation may (1) purchase or lease other corporations' assets, (2) purchase a controlling stock interest in other corporations, (3) merge with other corporations, or (4) consolidate with other corporations. A few states and the 1999 amendments to the Revised Act contain provisions authorizing a corporation to merge into another type of business organization, such as a limited partnership, limited liability company (LLC), or a limited liability partnership.

Any method of combination that involves issuing shares, proxy solicitations, or tender offers may be subject to federal securities regulation, as we will discuss in Chapter 39. Moreover, when a combination may have a detrimental effect on competition, federal antitrust laws, as discussed in Chapter 42, may apply.

In July 2010, President Obama signed into law the Dodd-Frank Wall Street Reform and Consumer Protection Act (Dodd-Frank Act), the most significant change to U.S. financial regulation since the New Deal of the 1930s. One of the many stand-alone statutes included in the Dodd-Frank Act is the Investor Protection and Securities Reform Act of 2010, which imposes new corporate governance rules on publicly held companies. (This Act is also discussed in Chapters 34, 35, 39, and 46.) One of these provisions of the Dodd-Frank Act applies to proxy solicitations asking shareholders to approve an acquisition, merger, consolidation, or proposed sale or other disposition of all or substantially all of the assets of a publicly held company issuer. In these proxy solicitations, publicly held companies must disclose, and provide shareholders with a nonbinding vote to approve, any type of compensation that is based on or relates to these specified combinations.

Purchase or lease of all or substantially all of the assets

results in no change in the legal personality of either corporation

---

Practical Advice

Recognize that under some circumstances courts will treat the purchase of all the assets of a corporation as a de facto merger and make the purchaser liable for the debts of the seller.

Purchase or Lease of All or Substantially All of the Assets [36-2a]

When one corporation purchases or leases all or substantially all of the assets of another corporation, the legal personality of neither corporation changes. The purchaser or lessee corporation simply acquires ownership or control of additional physical assets. The selling or lessor corporation, in exchange for its physical properties, receives cash, other property, or a stipulated rental. Each corporation continues its separate existence, having altered only the form or extent of its assets.

Generally, a corporation that purchases the assets of another corporation does not assume the other's liabilities unless (1) the purchaser expressly or impliedly agrees to assume the seller's liabilities, (2) the transaction amounts to a consolidation or merger of the two corporations, (3) the purchaser is a mere continuation of the seller, or (4) the sale is for the fraudulent purpose of avoiding the seller's liabilities. Some courts, as the next case illustrates, recognize a fifth exception (called the "product line" exception), which imposes strict tort liability upon the purchaser for defects in products manufactured and distributed by the seller corporation when the purchaser corporation continues the product line.

 Ray v. Alad Corporation
Supreme Court of California, 1977
19 Cal.3d 22, 136 Cal.Rptr. 574, 560 P.2d 3
http://scholar.google.com/scholar_case?case=16480226776272933283&q=560+P.2d+3&hl=en&as_sdt=2,34

FACTS On March 24, 1969, Ray fell from a defective ladder while working for his employer. Ray brought suit in strict tort liability against the Alad Corporation (Alad II), which neither manufactured nor sold the ladder to Ray's employer. Prior to the accident, Alad II succeeded to the business of the ladder's manufacturer, the now-dissolved "Alad Corporation" (Alad I), through a purchase of Alad I's assets for an adequate cash consideration. Alad II acquired Alad I's plant, equipment, inventory, trade name, and goodwill and continued to manufacture the same line of ladders under the "Alad" name, using the same equipment, designs, and personnel. In addition, Alad II solicited through the same sales representatives with no outward indication of any change in the ownership of the business. The parties had no agreement, however, concerning Alad II's assumption of Alad I's tort liabilities. Ray appealed from a judgment for Alad II.

DECISION Judgment reversed.

OPINION Generally, a purchaser does not assume a seller's liabilities unless (1) there is an express or implied agreement of such assumption; (2) the transaction is a consolidation or merger; (3) the purchasing corporation is a mere continuation of the seller; or (4) the transfer of assets to the purchaser is for the fraudulent purpose of escaping liability for the seller's debts. Here, there was

no express or implied agreement of an assumption of tort liability, nor were the assets transferred for a fraudulent purpose. Also, the second and third exceptions were not met, because the purchase of Alad I's assets did not amount to a consolidation or merger.

Since the general rule did not render Alad II liable, the court looked to the policy considerations underlying strict tort liability—the protection of otherwise-defenseless victims of manufacturing defects and the spreading throughout society of the costs of compensating them. Justification for imposing strict liability upon Alad II rests upon (1) the virtual destruction of Ray's remedies against Alad I due to the purchase; (2) Alad II's ability to assume Alad I's risk-spreading role; and (3) the fairness of requiring Alad II to assume the responsibility for the defective product since it continued to enjoy Alad I's goodwill. The presence of these three factors renders Alad II strictly liable.

INTERPRETATION If a purchaser of all of a corporation's assets continues the seller's product line, some courts impose upon the purchaser strict tort liability for defects in products previously manufactured by the seller corporation.

CRITICAL THINKING QUESTION What are the policy arguments supporting and opposing the court's approach in this case? Explain.

Regular course of business

approval by the selling corporation's board of directors is required, but shareholder authorization is not

Regular Course of Business If the sale or lease of all or substantially all of its assets is in the selling or lessor corporation's usual and regular course of business, approval by its board of directors is required but shareholder authorization is not. In addition, a mortgage or pledge of any or all of a corporation's property and assets—whether in the usual or regular course of business or not—also requires only the approval of the board of directors. The Revised Act considers a transfer of any or all of a corporation's assets to a wholly owned subsidiary to be a sale in the regular course of business.

Other than in regular course of business

approval by the board of directors and shareholders of the selling corporation is required

Purchase of shares

a transaction by which one corporation acquires all of, or a controlling interest in, the stock of another corporation; no change occurs in the legal existence of either corporation and no formal shareholder approval of either corporation is required

Tender offer

general invitation to all of the shareholders of a target company to tender their shares for sale at a specified price

Compulsory share exchange

a transaction by which a corporation becomes the owner of all of the outstanding shares of one or more classes of stock of another corporation by an exchange that is compulsory on all owners of the acquired shares; the board of directors of each corporation and the shareholders of the corporation whose shares are being acquired must approve

Other Than in Regular Course of Business Shareholder approval is necessary only for a sale or lease of all or substantially all of a corporation's assets that is not in the usual and regular course of business. (The 1999 amendments to the Revised Act adopt an objective test for determining when shareholder approval is required.) The selling corporation, by liquidating its assets, or the lessor corporation, by placing its physical assets beyond its control, has significantly changed its position and perhaps its ability to carry on the type of business contemplated by its charter. For this reason, such a sale or lease must be approved not only by action of the directors but also by the affirmative vote of the holders of a majority of the corporation's shares entitled to be cast at a shareholders' meeting called for this purpose. In most states, dissenting shareholders of the selling corporation are given an appraisal remedy.

Purchase of Shares [36-2b]

An alternative to the purchase of another corporation's assets is the purchase of its stock. When one corporation acquires all of, or a controlling interest in, the stock of another corporation, the legal existence of neither corporation changes. The acquiring corporation acts through its board of directors, while the corporation that becomes a subsidiary does not act at all, because the decision to sell stock is made by the individual shareholders, not by the corporation itself. The capital structure of the subsidiary remains unchanged, and that of the parent is usually not altered unless financing the acquisition requires a change in capital. Because formal approval is required of neither corporation's shareholders, there is no appraisal remedy. See Figure 36-1.

Sale of Control When one or a few shareholders own a controlling interest, the shareholder(s) may privately negotiate a sale of such interest, although the courts require that these transactions be made with due care. The controlling shareholders must make a reasonable investigation so as not to transfer control to purchasers who wrongfully plan to steal or "loot" the corporation's assets or to act against its best interests. In addition, purchasers frequently are willing to pay a premium for a block of shares that conveys control. Although historically some courts required that this so-called control premium inure to the benefit of the corporation, virtually all courts now permit the controlling shareholders to retain the full amount of the control premium.

Tender Offer When one or a few shareholders do not hold a controlling interest, the acquisition of a corporation through the purchase of shares may take the form of a tender offer. A **tender offer** is a general invitation to all shareholders of a target company to tender their shares for sale at a specified price. The offer may be for all of the target company's shares or for just a controlling interest. Tender offers for publicly held companies, which are subject to federal securities regulation, will be discussed in Chapter 39.

Compulsory Share Exchange [36-2c]

The Revised Act and some states provide different procedures for a corporation to acquire shares through a **compulsory share exchange**, a transaction by which the corporation becomes the owner of all the outstanding shares of one or more classes of shares of another corporation by an exchange that is compulsory on all owners of the acquired shares. The corporation may acquire the shares with its or any other corporation's shares, obligations, or other securities, or with cash or other property. For example, if A Corporation acquires all of B Corporation's outstanding

Figure 36-1 Purchase of Shares

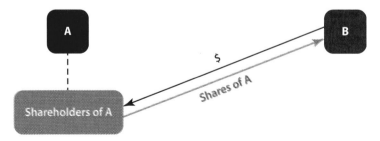

shares through a compulsory exchange, B becomes a wholly owned subsidiary of A. A compulsory share exchange does not affect the separate existence of the corporate parties to the transaction. Although their results are similar to those of mergers, as discussed in the following section, compulsory share exchanges are used instead of mergers when it is desirable that the acquired corporation remain in existence, as, for example, in the formation of holding company systems for insurance companies and banks.

A compulsory share exchange requires approval from the board of directors of each corporation and from the shareholders of the corporation whose shares are being acquired. Each class of shares included in the exchange must vote separately. The shareholders of the corporation acquiring the shares need not approve the transaction. After the shareholders adopt and approve the compulsory share exchange plan, it is binding on all who hold shares of the class to be acquired. Dissenting shareholders of the corporation whose shares are acquired are given an appraisal remedy.

Merger [36-2d]

A **merger** of two or more corporations is the combination of all of their assets. One of the corporations, known as the *surviving corporation*, receives title to all the assets. The other party or parties to the merger, known as the *merged corporation* or corporations, is merged into the surviving corporation and ceases to exist as a separate entity. Thus, if A Corporation and B Corporation combine into the A Corporation, A is the surviving corporation and B is the merged corporation. Under the Revised Act and most statutes, the shareholders of the merged corporation may receive stock or other securities issued by the surviving corporation or other consideration *including cash*, as provided in the merger agreement. Moreover, the surviving corporation assumes all debts and other liabilities of the merged corporation.

A merger requires the approval of each corporation's board of directors, as well as the affirmative vote of each corporation's holders of a majority of the shares entitled to vote. Dissenting shareholders of each corporation have an appraisal remedy. Many states and the 1999 amendments to the Revised Act permit the vote of the shareholders of the surviving corporation to be eliminated when a merger increases the number of outstanding shares by no more than 20 percent.

In a **short-form merger**, however, a corporation that owns a statutorily specified percent of the outstanding shares of each class of a subsidiary may merge the subsidiary into itself without approval by the shareholders of either corporation. The Revised Act and most states specify 90 percent. The parent's 90 percent ownership precludes the need to seek direct approval either from the shareholders or from the subsidiary's board of directors. All that is required is a resolution by the board of directors of the parent corporation.

Whereas the dissenting shareholders of the subsidiary have the right to obtain payment from the parent for their shares, the shareholders of the parent do not have this appraisal remedy, because the transaction has not materially changed their rights. Instead of indirectly owning 90 percent of the subsidiary's assets, the parent now directly owns 100 percent of the same assets.

Consolidation [36-2e]

A **consolidation** of two or more corporations is a combination of all of their assets, the title to which is taken by a newly created corporation known as the *consolidated corporation*. Each constituent corporation ceases to exist, and all of its debts and liabilities are assumed by the new corporation. The shareholders of each constituent corporation receive stock or other securities, not necessarily of the same class, issued to them by the new corporation, or other consideration provided in the plan of consolidation. A consolidation requires the approval of each corporation's board of directors, as well as the affirmative vote of each corporation's holders of a majority of the shares entitled to vote. Dissenting shareholders have an appraisal remedy. The Revised Act, however, has deleted all references to consolidations, because in modern corporate practice, ensuring the survival of one corporation is almost always advantageous.

Domestication and Conversion [36-2f]

The Revised Act was amended in 2002 to provide for domestication and conversion into other entities without a merger. The **domestication** procedures permit a corporation to change its

Merger

the combination of the assets of two or more corporations into one of the corporations

Effect of merger

the surviving corporation receives title to all of the assets of the merged corporation and assumes all of its liabilities; the merged corporation ceases to exist

Procedure for merger

requires approval by the board of directors and shareholders of each corporation

Short-form merger

a corporation that owns at least 90 percent of the outstanding shares of a subsidiary may merge the subsidiary into itself without approval by the shareholders of either corporation

Consolidation

the combination of two or more corporations into a new corporation

Effect of consolidation

each constituent corporation ceases to exist; the new corporation assumes all of their debts and liabilities

Procedure for consolidation

requires approval of the board of directors and shareholders of each corporation

Domestication

the Revised Act permits a corporation to change its state of incorporation state of incorporation, thus allowing a domestic business corporation to become a foreign business corporation or a foreign business corporation to become a domestic business corporation. The **conversion** procedures permit a domestic business corporation to become a domestic or foreign partnership, LLC, or other entity, and also permit a domestic or foreign partnership, LLC, or other entity to become a domestic business corporation. In both of these transactions a domestic business corporation must be present immediately before or after the transaction. Dissenting shareholders have an appraisal remedy in (1) a conversion of a corporation to an unincorporated entity or to nonprofit status and (2) some domestications.

Conversion

the Revised Act permits (1) a domestic business corporation to become a domestic or foreign partnership, limited liability company (LLC), or other entity; and (2) a domestic or foreign partnership, LLC, or other entity to become a domestic business corporation

Going private transactions

a combination that makes a publicly held corporation a private one; includes cash-out combinations and management buyouts

Going Private Transactions [36-2g]

Corporate combinations are sometimes used to take a publicly held corporation private to eliminate minority interests, to reduce the burdens of certain provisions of the federal securities laws, or both. One method of going private is for the corporation or its majority shareholder to acquire the corporation's shares through purchases on the open market or through a tender offer for the shares. Other methods include a cash-out combination (a merger or a sale of assets) with a corporation controlled by the majority shareholder. If the majority shareholder is a corporation, it may arrange a cash-out combination with itself or, if it owns enough shares, may use a short-form merger. In recent years, a new type of going private transaction—a management buyout—has become much more frequent. In this section, we will examine cash-out combinations and management buyouts.

Cash-Out Combinations

Cash-out combinations are used to eliminate minority shareholders by forcing them to accept cash or property for their shares. A cash-out combination often follows the acquisition, by a person, group, or company, of a large interest in a target company (T) through a tender offer. The tender offeror (TO) then seeks to eliminate all other shareholders, thereby achieving complete control of T. To do so, TO might form a new corporation (Corporation N) and take 100 percent of its stock. TO then arranges a cash-out merger of T into N, with all the shareholders of T, other than TO, to receive cash for their shares. Because TO owns all the stock of N and a controlling interest in T, the shareholders of both companies will approve the merger. Alternatively, TO could purchase for cash or notes the assets of T, leaving the minority shareholders with only an interest in the proceeds of the sale. The use of cash-out combinations has raised questions concerning both their purpose and their fairness to minority shareholders. Some states require that cash-out combinations have a valid business purpose and that they be fair to all concerned. Fairness, in this context, includes both fair dealing (which involves the procedural aspects of the transaction) and fair price (which involves the financial considerations of the merger). Other states require only that the transaction be fair.

Alpert v. 28 Williams St. Corp.
New York Court of Appeals, 1984
63 N.Y.2d 557, 483 N.Y.S.2d 667, 473 N.E.2d 19
http://scholar.google.com/scholar_case?case=6454009735176964074&q=473+N.E.2d+19&hl=en&as_sdt=2,34

FACTS 79 Realty Corporation owned a valuable seventeen-story office building in Manhattan. The plaintiffs in this action held 26 percent of the outstanding shares of 79 Realty Corporation. The defendants formed a limited partnership, Madison 28 Associates, to buy the building. This limited partnership created 28 Williams Street Corporation to act as the nominal purchaser. The defendants planned to achieve the purchase by means of a "two-step" merger in which Madison Associates would buy control of the majority shares of Realty Corporation and then merge Realty Corporation with Williams Street, "freezing out" the minority shareholders of Realty Corporation through a cash buyout. All shareholders of Realty Corporation were sent a statement of intent explaining the details of the proposed merger. Soon after the merger was approved, and in accordance with the merger plan, Realty Corporation, the surviving corporation, was dissolved, and title to the building passed to Madison Associates. The plaintiffs brought an action for equitable relief in the form of rescission of the merger. The trial court found for 28 Williams Street Corporation, and the appellate court affirmed.

DECISION Judgment for 28 Williams Street Corporation affirmed.

OPINION The directors and majority shareholders of a corporation have a fiduciary duty to treat all shareholders fairly and equally. The concept of fairness has two main components: fair dealing toward the minority shareholders and fair price. In a case such as this, fair dealing may include efforts to simulate arm's-length negotiations, the procedural fairness of the transaction, and complete and candid disclosure of all the material facts of the proposed merger. A fair price need not equal the exact "fair value" of the shares but should reflect such factors as net asset value, book value, earnings, market value, and investment value. In this case, the majority shareholders' exclusion of the minority interests through the two-step merger was, viewed as a whole, fair to the minority shareholders. The minority shareholders, however, clearly were not treated equally with other shareholders, for they had no choice but to surrender their shares in the corporation for cash. Nonetheless, in a freeze-out merger, such variant treatment of the minority shareholders is permissible when it relates to the advancement of some independent corporate purpose. Here, at least one business purpose, obtaining additional capital for building repairs, justified the exclusion of the plaintiffs'

interests. The evidence indicates that such capital would not have been available through the merger without eliminating the plaintiffs' interests in the corporation. Therefore, since the merger dealt with the minority shareholders fairly, advanced an independent corporate purpose, and was untainted by fraud or illegality, no breaches of fiduciary duty occurred and the merger may be upheld.

INTERPRETATION In a cash-out merger, the directors and majority shareholders have a fiduciary duty to treat all shareholders fairly, the merger must have an independent business purpose, and the transaction must be conducted without fraud and illegality.

CRITICAL THINKING QUESTION When, if ever, should cash-out mergers be permitted? Explain.

Management Buyout A management buyout is a transaction by which existing management increases its ownership of a corporation while eliminating the entity's public shareholders. The typical procedure is as follows. The management of an existing company (Corporation A) forms a new corporation (Corporation B), in which the management owns some of the stock and institutional investors own the rest. Corporation B issues bonds to institutional investors to raise cash, with which it purchases the assets or stock of Corporation A. The assets of Corporation A are used as security for the bonds issued by Corporation B. Because of the extensive use of borrowed funds, a management buyout is commonly called a *leveraged buyout* (LBO). The result of this transaction is twofold: the public shareholders of Corporation A no longer have any proprietary interest in the assets of Corporation A, and management's equity interest in Corporation B is greater than its interest was in Corporation A.

A critical issue is a management buyout's fairness to the shareholders of Corporation A. The transaction inherently presents a potential conflict of interest for those in management, who owe a fiduciary duty to represent the interests of the shareholders of Corporation A. As substantial shareholders of Corporation B, however, those in management have a personal and probably adverse financial interest in the transaction.

Dissenting shareholder
one who opposes a
fundamental change and has
the right to receive the fair
value of her shares

Dissenting Shareholders [36-2h]

The shareholder's right to dissent, a statutory right to obtain payment for shares, is accorded to shareholders who object to certain fundamental changes in the corporation. The Revised Act, as amended, provides this right when (1) the proposed corporate action as approved by the majority will result in a fundamental change in the shares affected by the action and (2) uncertainty about the fair value of the affected shares raises questions about the fairness of the terms of the proposed corporate action.

Practical Advice

If you wish to dissent and
obtain your appraisal
remedy, be sure to follow all
of the required procedures
and do so in a timely
manner.

Transactions Giving Rise to Dissenters' Rights States vary considerably with respect to which transactions give rise to dissenters' rights. Some include transactions not covered by the Revised Act, and other states omit transactions included in the Revised Act.

The Revised Act grants dissenters' rights to (1) dissenting shareholders of a corporation selling or leasing all or substantially all of its property or assets not in the usual or regular course of business; (2) dissenting shareholders of each corporation that is a party to a merger, except in short-form mergers, when only the dissenting shareholders of the subsidiary have dissenters' rights; (3) any plan of compulsory share exchange in which the corporation will be the one acquired; (4) any amendment to the articles of incorporation that materially and adversely affects the dissenter's rights with respect to shares; (5) conversion of a corporation to an unincorporated entity or to nonprofit status; (6) some domestications; and (7) any other corporate action taken pursuant to a shareholder vote with respect to which the articles of incorporation, the bylaws, or a resolution of the board of directors provides that shareholders shall have a right to dissent and obtain payment for their shares. The 1999 amendments to the Revised Act narrowed the scope of the appraisal remedy: in a merger, only shareholders whose shares have been exchanged have dissenters' rights and the appraisal remedy for virtually all charter amendments has been eliminated. Many states, however, have a stock market exception to the appraisal remedy. Under these statutes, the right to dissent does not exist if an established market, such as the New York Stock Exchange, exists for the shares. The Revised Act does not contain this exception, but the 1999 amendments to the Revised Act have added it.

Procedure   The corporation must notify the shareholders of the existence of dissenters' rights before taking the vote on the corporate action. A shareholder who dissents and strictly complies with the provisions of the statute is entitled to receive the fair value of his shares. However, unless he makes written demand within the prescribed time period, he is not entitled to payment for his shares.

Appraisal remedy

the right of a dissenter to receive the fair value of his shares (the value of shares immediately before the corporate action to which the dissenter objects takes place, excluding any appreciation or depreciation in anticipation of such corporate action unless such exclusion would be inequitable)

Appraisal Remedy   A dissenting shareholder who complies with all applicable requirements is entitled to an **appraisal remedy**, which is the corporation's payment of the fair value of the shares, plus accrued interest. The *fair value* is that value immediately preceding the corporate action to which the dissenter objects, excluding any appreciation or depreciation that occurs in anticipation of such corporate action, unless such exclusion would be inequitable. The 1999 amendments to the Revised Act provide that fair value is to be determined "using customary and current valuation concepts and techniques generally employed for similar businesses in the context of the transaction requiring appraisal without discounting for lack of marketability or minority status except, if appropriate, for amendments to the articles."

 Shawnee Telecom Resources, Inc. v. Brown
Supreme Court of Kentucky, 2011
354 S.W.3d 542
http://scholar.google.com/scholar_case?q=354+S.W.3d+542&hl=en&as_sdt=6,34&case=295706676174884700&scilh=0

FACTS In December 2003, Shawnee Technology, Inc. (Shawnee Tech), a Kentucky corporation, merged into Appellant Shawnee Telecom Resources, Inc. (Shawnee Tel), also a Kentucky corporation. The merger plan provided that one of Shawnee Tech's shareholders, Kathy Brown, would receive cash for her shares instead of shares in the new company, a so-called cash-out merger authorized by the Kentucky Business Corporation Act. Under that statute's dissenters' rights provisions, Brown demanded from Shawnee Tech the "fair value" for her shares. Disputing the amount of Brown's entitlement, Shawnee Tech brought an action in a Kentucky trial court for an appraisal of Brown's interest in the company.

The trial court referred the appraisal to the Master Commissioner, who heard testimony from both parties' experts concerning the value of the business and the value of Brown's shares. To arrive at the value of Brown's shares, Shawnee's expert discounted his estimate of the company's total value by 25% to account for the fact that shares of a closely held corporation do not enjoy a ready market and thus would sell for less than the more easily traded shares of a publicly held company. Thus discounted, the total value of the company's shares was $969,750, and the value of Brown's 24% interest was $232,740. Brown's expert, on the other hand, arrived at a value for Brown's interest of at least $576,232.

The Commissioner was not entirely satisfied with either expert's analysis. Instead, the Commissioner, borrowing from both

experts' analyses, found a capitalized earnings value of $2,304,178 and a net asset value of $1,343,860. The Commissioner did, however, discount the capitalized earnings value for lack of marketability. Although he acknowledged that the current version of the Model Business Corporations Act (MBCA) precludes marketability discounts, the Commissioner nevertheless ruled that such discounts are allowed under Kentucky's version of the MBCA. The Commissioner then averaged the two values, giving the net asset value twice the weight of the capitalized earnings value, and arrived at a value for Brown's 24% interest of $353,633.

The trial court adopted the Commissioner's report without change, and both parties appealed. The Court of Appeals agreed with Brown and held that marketability discounts are inappropriate in fair-value proceedings under the dissenters' rights statute and should not have been applied in this case. Shawnee appealed.

DECISION The Court of Appeals' decision is affirmed in part, reversed in part, and remanded.

OPINION Every state has adopted in some form a dissenters' rights statute that gives minority shareholders, in the event of a wide variety of fundamental corporate changes, a right to withdraw their investment for its fair value as determined by a judicial appraisal. The purpose of the appraisal remedy is twofold. It is meant to provide a sort of liquidity for the shares of investors who found themselves trapped in an altered corporate investment of which they no longer approved, and it is meant to protect minority shareholders from majority overreaching.

Under the Kentucky Business Corporation Act, which is based on the Model Business Corporation Act, "fair value" for dissenters' rights purposes is simply defined as "the value of the shares immediately before the effectuation of the corporate action to which the dissenter objects, excluding any appreciation or depreciation in anticipation of the corporate action unless exclusion would be inequitable."

As long as liquidity seemed the purpose of the appraisal remedy, courts often understood "fair value" to mean essentially fair market value and understood their task as identifying a sort of quasi-market price for the dissenting shareholder's particular shares. Since a block of shares that does not convey a controlling interest in the company would ordinarily sell for less than a block that did, in arriving at this hypothetical market price, courts sometimes applied a discount for lack of control, a so-called minority discount. Similarly, when appraising shares of a private company, courts sometimes applied a discount for lack of liquidity, a so-called marketability discount. Because these discounts apply to share value, as opposed to the value of the company as a whole, they are referred to as shareholder-level discounts.

The vast majority of states to consider the appraisal remedy for ousted minority shareholders have held that "fair value" in this context means the shareholder's proportionate interest in the company as a whole valued as a going concern according to accepted business practices. Because an award of anything less than a fully proportionate share would have the effect of transferring a portion of the minority interest to the majority, and because it is the company being valued and not the minority shares themselves as a commodity, shareholder-level discounts for lack of control or lack of marketability have also widely been disallowed.

In 1999 the American Bar Association's Committee on Corporate Laws revised the Model Business Corporation Act's definition of "fair value" to provide that value was to be determined "using customary and current valuation concepts and techniques generally employed for similar businesses in the context of the transaction requiring appraisal; and … without discounting for lack of marketability or minority status except, if appropriate, for amendments to the articles pursuant to section 13.02(a)(5)."

As of 2010, ten states had adopted the 1999 Model Act revision, but even in states, like Kentucky, that continue to use the 1984 version of the Model Act, courts have construed "fair value" as the dissenting shareholder's *pro rata* share of the company as a whole, without shareholder-level discounts for lack of control or lack of marketability. These courts have found no legislative

significance in the failure of their legislatures to adopt the 1999 revision; have emphasized the statute's use of "fair value" as distinct from "fair market value" as indicating an express rejection of a market value standard; and have endorsed the view that if the appraisal remedy is to be effective, as the legislature must have intended, then shareholder-level discounts should not be applied.

There is a broad consensus among courts, commentators, and the drafters of the Model Act that "fair value" in this context is best understood, not as a hypothetical price at which the dissenting shareholder might sell his or her particular shares, but rather as the dissenter's proportionate interest in the company as a going concern. This understanding reflects a reasonable balance of those competing interests. It does so by helping to insure that the majority's freedom to eliminate minority shareholders is not employed to transfer a portion of the minority interest to the majority, a result fully in keeping with the Kentucky General Assembly's intent. Because a hypothetical market price for the dissenter's particular shares as a commodity is thus not the value being sought, market adjustments to arrive at such a price, such as discounts for lack of control or lack of marketability, are inappropriate. This principled conclusion accounts for the broad consensus of courts writing in this area.

Although appraisers and courts remain free to consider market, income, and asset approaches to valuation and may employ a weighted average of the results of those approaches if the evidence supports such averaging, there is no suggestion in the statutes that the General Assembly meant to require that approach. It is reasonable to find instead a legislative intent that the value of the going concern be determined by any valuation technique generally recognized in the business and financial community and shown to be relevant to the circumstances of the particular company at issue. In sum, in an appraisal proceeding the dissenting shareholder is entitled to the fair value of his or her shares as measured by the proportionate interest those shares represent in the value of the company as a going concern, a value determined in accord with generally accepted valuation concepts and techniques and without shareholder-level discounts for lack of control or lack of marketability.

INTERPRETATION In an appraisal proceeding the dissenting shareholder is entitled to the fair value of his or her shares as measured by the proportionate interest those shares represent in the value of the company as a going concern, a value determined in accord with generally accepted valuation concepts and techniques and without shareholder-level discounts for lack of control or lack of marketability

CRITICAL THINKING QUESTION Do you agree that fair value is not the same as market value? Explain.

A shareholder who has a right to obtain payment for her shares does not have the right to attack the validity of the corporate action that gives rise to the right to obtain payment or to have the action set aside or rescinded, except when the corporate action is unlawful or fraudulent with regard to the complaining shareholders or to the corporation. When the corporate action is not unlawful or fraudulent, the appraisal remedy is usually exclusive, and the shareholder may not challenge the action. Some states, however, make the appraisal remedy exclusive in all cases; others, in contrast, make it nonexclusive in certain cases.

Cohen v. Mirage Resorts, Inc.
Supreme Court of Nevada, 2003
62 P.3d 720, *petition for rehearing denied 2003*
http://scholar.google.com/scholar_case?case=15507743401717772633&q=62+P.3d+720&hl=en&as_sdt=2,34

FACTS Harvey Cohen was a minority shareholder in the Boardwalk, a small, publicly held casino on Las Vegas Boulevard (The Strip). The Boardwalk had 1,200 feet of Strip frontage located between the Bellagio and the Monte Carlo, large casinos in which the Mirage Resorts had an interest. Mirage also owned twenty-three acres of land adjacent to the Boardwalk. Mirage wished to acquire the Boardwalk as well as three parcels of land surrounding the Boardwalk. The three parcels were either owned by entities connected with the Boardwalk's majority shareholders and directors or were subject to options to purchase in favor of the Boardwalk. Mirage sought to negate the Boardwalk's options and acquire the adjacent properties for purposes of expansion.

Mirage made an offer to acquire the Boardwalk's shares through a merger with a Mirage subsidiary, Acquisition. Prior to or contemporaneous with the merger, Mirage acquired the surrounding parcels. On May 27, 1998, the Boardwalk convened a special shareholder meeting to consider the offer. A majority of the shareholders approved the merger, and it was consummated on June 30, 1998. Cohen and other members of the class tendered their shares without challenging the merger's validity or claiming statutory dissenters' rights.

On September 28, 1999, a little over a year after the consummation of the merger, Cohen filed a suit for damages, alleging breach of fiduciary duty and/or loyalty by the Boardwalk's majority shareholders, board of directors, and financial advisors. Cohen asserts Mirage conspired with the Boardwalk's majority shareholders and directors to purchase the Boardwalk at an artificially low price by offering special transactions to majority shareholders and/or members of the Boardwalk's board of directors. Cohen claims that Mirage bought land or rights owned or controlled by majority shareholders or directors in properties around or involving the Boardwalk at inflated prices. Cohen contends that these shareholders and directors then agreed to approve or recommend the merger for an amount per share that was less than the fair value of the Boardwalk's stock. Finally, Cohen asserts that the directors mismanaged the Boardwalk, causing decreased profits, and that they or majority shareholders usurped corporate opportunities.

The district court dismissed the case, finding that all of Cohen's claims were derivative in nature and that Cohen and other ex-shareholders lacked standing to assert the claims. Cohen then appealed.

DECISION The order is affirmed as to the derivative causes of action; it is reversed as to the allegations of misconduct affecting the validity of the merger.

OPINION Under Nevada law, a corporate merger must be approved by a majority of the corporation's shareholders. The existing shareholders then substitute their stock ownership in the old corporation for stock ownership in the new merged corporation. Shareholders who oppose the merger have three choices: (1) accept the terms of the merger and exchange their existing shares for new shares; (2) dissent from the merger, compelling the merged corporation to purchase their shares pursuant to a judicial appraisal proceeding; and/or (3) challenge the validity of the merger based on unlawful or wrongful conduct committed during the merger process.

The states and the Model Act recognize two circumstances when minority shareholders challenge the merger process: (1) if it is unlawful, that is, procedurally deficient and (2) if fraud or material misrepresentation affected the shareholder vote on the merger. Under either theory, minority shareholders may bring suit to enjoin or rescind the merger or to recover monetary damages (compensatory and punitive) attributable to the loss of their shareholder interest caused by an invalid merger. They may also allege that the merger was accomplished through the wrongful conduct of majority shareholders, directors, or officers of the corporation and attempt to hold those individuals liable for monetary damages under theories of breach of fiduciary duty or loyalty.

A claim brought by a dissenting shareholder that questions the validity of a merger as a result of wrongful conduct on the part of majority shareholders or directors is properly classified as an individual or direct claim. The shareholder has lost unique personal property—his or her interest in a specific corporation. The district court was correct in dismissing all of the derivative claims in the complaint, but erred in not permitting Cohen to amend the complaint to clarify that he was seeking rescission of the merger and/or monetary damages based upon the invalidity of the merger.

INTERPRETATION A shareholder who has a right to obtain payment for her shares does not have the right to attack the validity of the corporate action that gives rise to the right to obtain payment or to have the action set aside or rescinded, except when the corporate action is unlawful or fraudulent with regard to the complaining shareholders or to the corporation.

ETHICAL QUESTION Did the defendants act unethically? Explain.

CRITICAL THINKING QUESTION Do you agree with the court's decision? Explain.

DISSOLUTION [36-3]

Although a corporation may have perpetual existence, its life may be terminated in a number of ways. Incorporation statutes usually provide for both voluntary and involuntary dissolution. Dissolution itself does not terminate the corporation's existence but does require that the corporation wind up its affairs and liquidate its assets.

Voluntary Dissolution [36-3a]

Voluntary dissolution

may be brought about by a resolution of the board of directors that is approved by the shareholders

A board of directors may effect a **voluntary dissolution** by a resolution approved by the affirmative vote of the holders of a majority of the corporation's shares entitled to vote at a shareholders' meeting duly called for this purpose. Although shareholders who object to dissolution usually have no right to dissent and recover the fair value of their shares, the Revised Act grants dissenters' rights in connection with a sale or exchange of all or substantially all of a corporation's assets not made in the usual or regular course of business, including a sale in dissolution. However, the Revised Act excludes such rights in sales by court order and in sales for cash on terms requiring that all or substantially all of the net proceeds be distributed to the shareholders within one year. In addition, in many states, but not the Revised Act, dissolution without action by the directors may be affected by unanimous consent of the shareholders.

The Revised Act authorizes shareholders in closely held corporations to adopt unanimous shareholders' agreements requiring dissolution of the corporation at the request of one or more shareholders or upon the occurrence of a specified event or contingency.

The Statutory Close Corporation Supplement gives shareholders who elect such a right in the articles of incorporation the power to dissolve the corporation. Unless the charter specifies otherwise, an amendment to include, modify, or delete a power to dissolve must be approved by all of the shareholders. The power to dissolve may be conferred upon any shareholder or holders of a specified number or percentage of shares of any class and may be exercised at will or upon the occurrence of a specified event or contingency.

Practical Advice

To achieve increased protection, when organizing a close corporation you should consider including in the charter a provision giving each shareholder the power to dissolve the corporation.

CONCEPT REVIEW 36-1

Fundamental Changes under Pre-1999 RMBCA

Change	Board of Directors Resolution Required	Shareholder Approval Required	Shareholders' Appraisal Remedy Available
A amends its articles of incorporation	A: Yes	A: Yes	A: No, unless amendment materially and adversely affects rights of shares
B sells its assets in usual and regular course of business to A	B: Yes	B: No	B: No
B sells its assets not in usual and regular course of business to A	B: Yes	B: Yes	B: Yes
A voluntarily purchases shares of B	A: Yes B: No	A: No B: No, individual shareholders decide	A: No B: No
A acquires shares of B through a compulsory exchange	A: Yes B: Yes	A: No B: Yes	A: No B: Yes
A and B merge	A: Yes B: Yes	A: Yes B: Yes	A: Yes B: Yes
A merges its 90 percent subsidiary B into A	A: Yes B: No	A: No B: No	A: No B: Yes
A and B consolidate	A: Yes B: Yes	A: Yes B: Yes	A: Yes B: Yes
A voluntarily dissolves	A: Yes	A: Yes	A: No (usually)

Involuntary dissolution

may occur by administrative
or judicial action taken
(1) by the attorney general,
(2) by shareholders under
certain circumstances, and
(3) by a creditor on
a showing that the
corporation has become
unable to pay its debts and
obligations as they mature
in the regular course of its
business

Involuntary Dissolution [36-3b]

A corporation may be involuntarily dissolved by administrative dissolution or by judicial dissolution.

Administrative Dissolution
The secretary of state may commence an administrative proceeding to dissolve a corporation if (1) the corporation does not pay within sixty days after they are due any franchise taxes or penalties; (2) the corporation does not deliver its annual report to the secretary of state within sixty days after it is due; (3) the corporation is without a registered agent or registered office in the state for sixty days or more; (4) the corporation does not notify the secretary of state within sixty days that it has changed its registered agent or registered office, that its registered agent has resigned, or that it has discontinued its registered office; or (5) the corporation's period of duration stated in its articles of incorporation expires.

Judicial Dissolution
The state, a shareholder, or a creditor may bring a proceeding seeking judicial dissolution. A court may dissolve a corporation in a proceeding brought by the attorney general if it is proved that the corporation obtained its charter through fraud or has continued to exceed or abuse the authority conferred upon it by law.

A court may dissolve a corporation in a proceeding brought by a shareholder if it is established that (1) the directors are deadlocked in the management of the corporate affairs, the shareholders are unable to break the deadlock, and the corporation is threatened with or is suffering irreparable injury; (2) the acts of the directors or those in control of the corporation are illegal, oppressive, or fraudulent; (3) the corporate assets are being misapplied or wasted; or (4) the shareholders are deadlocked and have failed to elect directors for at least two consecutive annual meetings. The Revised Act as amended provides a *closely held* corporation or the remaining shareholders a limited right to purchase at fair value the shares of a shareholder who has brought a proceeding for involuntary dissolution.

A creditor may bring a court action to dissolve a corporation on showing that the corporation has become unable to pay its debts and obligations as they mature in the regular course of its business and that either (1) the creditor has reduced his claim to a judgment and an execution issued on it has been returned unsatisfied or (2) the corporation has admitted in writing that the claim of the creditor is due and owing.

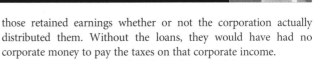

Cooke v. Fresh Express Foods Corporation, Inc.
Court of Appeals of Oregon, 2000
169 Or.App. 101, 7 P.3d 717
http://scholar.google.com/scholar_case?case=18255907503494215009&q=7+P.3d+717+&hl=en&as_sdt=2,34

FACTS Terry J. Cooke (plaintiff) is the former husband of defendant, Joni Quicker (Joni); defendant Allen John Quicker (John) is Joni's father. In the early 1980s John and Joni began a business distributing fresh produce. Terry soon left his job and began working with John and Joni full time. The business was originally a partnership, with John having a half interest and Joni and Terry together having the other half interest. The business grew throughout the 1980s. In June 1990 John, Joni, and Terry incorporated the business as Fresh Express Foods Corporation, Inc. (Fresh Express). John received 50 percent of the stock, and Joni and Terry each received 25 percent. John was the president of the corporation, Joni was the vice president, and plaintiff was the secretary and treasurer. They also constituted the three members of the board of directors.

Fresh Express was the primary source of income for all three parties. Part of that income came from their salaries, but substantial additional amounts came as loans that the corporation made to them for various purposes, including paying their individual taxes on their portions of the corporation's retained earnings. Because Fresh Express elected to be a subchapter S corporation, which for tax purposes does not pay taxes itself but passes its income through to its shareholders, plaintiff and defendants were liable for taxes on those retained earnings whether or not the corporation actually distributed them. Without the loans, they would have had no corporate money to pay the taxes on that corporate income.

Joni and Terry separated at about the time of the incorporation. The tension between them increased significantly beginning in June 1993 when, after starting a relationship with a Fresh Express employee, Terry filed for dissolution of the marriage. Terry managed the company's delivery system, which included supervising the operation of its trucks. In December 1993, while Terry was on vacation, John discovered a notice on Terry's desk from the Public Utilities Commission (PUC) that showed deficiencies resulting in a fine of $6,000 and additional penalties of $4,000. Terry had not paid those amounts, and that failure threatened Fresh Express with the loss of its PUC authority to operate. When Terry returned from vacation, John, acting as president of the company, gave him a written notice of termination that included the statement that "Fresh Express Foods Corporation has suffered monetary loss associated with [your] position and this constitutes a Breach of Fiduciary Responsibility to the Corporation." It did not refer to a threatened loss of PUC operating authority. After the termination, Terry received his unpaid wages and two weeks' severance pay. Before the termination, the corporation distributed money to all of its shareholders that it treated as shareholder loans. It continued to make those distributions to John and Joni, but it did not make them to Terry after his termination. Although Terry remained a corporate officer and director for almost two years, he was never again informed of or consulted about corporate business.

The court entered a judgment dissolving Terry's and Joni's marriage in August 1994, awarding Joni approximately $27,000. Because the corporation had never issued any stock certificates, Joni was unable to use Terry's ownership interest in the corporation to satisfy the court judgment. In order to provide Joni a stock certificate to garnish, John called a directors' meeting for November 2, 1995, for the purpose of electing officers. At the meeting John and Joni first reelected John as president and Joni as vice president; then they also elected Joni as secretary and treasurer. Terry abstained from all three votes. A few days later Joni issued a stock certificate to Terry. Instead of sending the certificate to Terry, she immediately delivered it to the sheriff under a writ of garnishment on her judgment against Terry.

In September 1996, John and Joni called a special shareholders' meeting, at which they reduced the number of directors to two, over Terry's dissenting vote, and elected John and Joni to those positions. During an informal discussion, Terry asked John's attorney if the company intended to pay the considerable amount of money it owed to him. After consulting with John, the attorney responded that John had decided not to make any more distributions to shareholders at that time. After the shareholders' meeting ended and Terry left the room at their request, John and Joni held a directors' meeting at which they first removed Terry "from all of his positions as an officer, employee and agent of the corporation." John and Joni then agreed, despite the attorney's statement to Terry, to distribute the corporation's entire accumulated adjustment account to the shareholders by using it to reduce the outstanding shareholder loans. Finally, they agreed to purchase automobiles for John and Joni and to increase John's salary from $54,000 per year to $120,000.

Terry brought suit against the corporation, John, and Joni. The trial court found that John would not have terminated Joni for a comparable error. It concluded that the purpose for firing Terry was to exclude him from participating in the corporate business or receiving any benefits from the corporation. The court found that the reason for the exclusion was the breakdown of the marriage and the animosities that followed. The trial court found that the defendants had acted oppressively toward the plaintiff in the management and control of defendant Fresh Express. As a remedy, the court ordered the defendants to purchase the plaintiff's interest in Fresh Express at a price set by the court. The defendants appealed.

DECISION Judgment for the plaintiff affirmed.

OPINION The plaintiff argues that the actions of the defendants constituted a course of oppressive conduct and that defendants breached their fiduciary duties to him by freezing him out of all participation in the corporation and depriving him of all of the benefits of being a stockholder. A number of cases make it clear that when

> [T]he majority shareholders of a closely held corporation use their control over the corporation to their own advantage and exclude the minority from the benefits of participating in the corporation, [in the absence of] a legitimate business purpose, the actions constitute a breach of their fiduciary duties of loyalty, good faith and fair dealing.

A finding that the majority shareholders have engaged in oppressive conduct under the incorporation statute permits the court either to order a dissolution of the corporation or to award lesser appropriate relief, including requiring the majority to buy out the minority's interest at a price that the court fixes.

The facts of this case show a classic squeeze-out. The defendants withheld dividends and other benefits from the plaintiff while preserving benefits for themselves.

> [W]itholding dividends can be especially devastating in an S corporation as all corporate income is passed through to the shareholders for tax purposes and shareholders are required to pay taxes on that income, but if no dividends are declared, the shareholders will have no cash from the enterprise with which to pay those taxes.

In addition, the "abrupt removal of a minority shareholder from positions of employment and management can be a devastatingly effective squeeze-out technique." Finally, majority shareholders may siphon off corporate wealth by causing a corporation to pay the majority shareholders excessively high compensation, not only in salaries but also in generous expense accounts and other fringe benefits.

The defendants acted to ensure that they would permanently receive all benefits of the corporation. They began by replacing the plaintiff as a director and reducing the number of directors to two. Although that was not necessarily improper in itself, their first actions as the sole directors of Fresh Express showed their purpose to exclude the plaintiff from any share in the corporation other than his tax liabilities. They first removed the plaintiff from any office or agency with the corporation and then took a number of actions to direct all corporate income to themselves. Despite having told the plaintiff that there would be no corporate distributions, the defendants distributed the entire retained earnings through a paper transaction that ensured that the corporate books would show no source for making any cash distribution to the plaintiff. They then more than doubled John's salary, with the result that he received his income from the corporation as an expense that would reduce its profits rather than as a distribution of profits. Finally, they had the corporation pay for their recently purchased automobiles, again adding to the corporation's expenses and reducing its profits for their benefit.

In summary, the defendants consistently acted to further their individual interests, not the interests of the corporation, and without regard to their fiduciary duties to the plaintiff. They did so either knowing or intending that their actions would harm the plaintiff, among other ways by excluding him from any benefits of his ownership of one-quarter of the corporate stock. They thereby violated their fiduciary duties to him and engaged in oppressive conduct. Under the incorporation statute, the trial court had the authority to choose a remedy for defendants' actions; requiring the defendants to purchase the plaintiff's shares is the preferable option. A purchase will disentangle the parties' affairs while keeping the corporation a going concern; dissolution would not benefit anyone, and the plaintiff did not seek it at trial.

INTERPRETATION A court may dissolve a corporation in a proceeding brought by a shareholder if it is established that the acts of the directors are oppressive.

ETHICAL QUESTION Did the directors act unethically? Explain.

CRITICAL THINKING QUESTION Do you agree with the court's decision in this case? Explain.

ETHICAL DILEMMA

What Rights Do Minority Shareholders Have?

Facts Frank, James, and Thomas were fraternity brothers who graduated from college in the same year. Shortly after graduation they began a private security company incorporated as Secure, Inc. The company specialized in providing systems and personnel to improve retail loss prevention efforts. The company also offered electronic theft detection systems for both homes and businesses.

When the company was formed, Frank put up the majority of the capital and became a 60 percent shareholder. James and Thomas had gone through college on scholarships and had little capital to invest. They received minority interests of 20 percent each.

The business became successful. Frank was excellent at customer and personnel relations, accounting, and routine business management. James and Thomas, however, were the real brains behind the business. They developed innovative techniques and systems that were highly

attractive to customers. Their innovations attracted attention in the business community, and the company was the focus of a feature article in a major newspaper.

Safety First, Inc., has made an offer that would merge Secure, Inc., into Safety First, Inc. Frank wants to accept the merger proposal, but James and Thomas are adamantly opposed. They believe that in the long run they will make considerably more money if they operate the business independently for at least five to ten more years before considering selling out. The initial intention of Secure, Inc., was to enable the three shareholders to operate an independent business. James and Thomas do not want their technology and systems sold to another company.

Social, Policy, and Ethical Considerations

1. What moral or fiduciary obligation does Frank have to James and Thomas? What

obligations do James and Thomas have to Frank?
2. To what extent should initial expectations as to business goals and operations continue to bind business associates morally? To what extent should associates spell out their expectations in advance?
3. What types of legal remedies, if any, are necessary when business associates no longer agree on fundamental business plans? To what extent should the law intervene in private management disputes among members of closely held businesses?
4. If Frank pays James and Thomas the fair value of their shares and proceeds with a merger, will this provide sufficient compensation to James and Thomas? Who owns the technological advances?

Liquidation

when a corporation is dissolved, its assets are liquidated and used first to pay its liquidation expenses and its creditors according to their respective contract or lien rights; any remainder is proportionately distributed to shareholders according to their respective contract rights

Liquidation [36-3c]

As we mentioned, dissolution requires that the corporation devote itself to winding up its affairs and liquidating its assets. After dissolution, the corporation must cease carrying on its business except as is necessary to wind up. When a corporation is dissolved, its assets are liquidated and used first to pay the expenses of liquidation and its creditors according to their respective contract or lien rights. Any remainder is proportionately distributed to shareholders according to their respective contract rights; stock with a liquidation preference has priority over common stock. The board of directors, who serve as trustees, carries out voluntary liquidation; a court-appointed receiver may conduct involuntary liquidation.

Protection of Creditors [36-3d]

The statutory provisions governing dissolution and liquidation usually prescribe procedures to safeguard the interests of the corporation's creditors. Such procedures typically include the required mailing of notice to known creditors, a general publication of notice, and the preservation of claims against the corporation.

CHAPTER SUMMARY

Charter Amendments

Authority to Amend incorporation statutes permit charters to be amended

Procedure the board of directors adopts a resolution, which must be approved by a majority vote of the shareholders

Combinations

Purchase or Lease of All or Substantially All of the Assets results in no change in the legal personality of either corporation

- *Regular Course of Business* approval by the selling corporation's board of directors is required, but shareholder authorization is not
- *Other Than in Regular Course of Business* approval by the board of directors and shareholders of the selling corporation is required

Purchase of Shares a transaction by which one corporation acquires all of, or a controlling interest in, the stock of another corporation; no change occurs in the legal existence of either corporation and no formal shareholder approval of either corporation is required

Compulsory Share Exchange a transaction by which a corporation becomes the owner of all of the outstanding shares of one or more classes of stock of another corporation by an exchange that is compulsory on all owners of the acquired shares; the board of directors of each corporation and the shareholders of the corporation whose shares are being acquired must approve

Merger the combination of the assets of two or more corporations into one of the corporations

- *Procedure* requires approval by the board of directors and shareholders of each corporation
- *Short-Form Merger* a corporation that owns at least 90 percent of the outstanding shares of a subsidiary may merge the subsidiary into itself without approval by the shareholders of either corporation
- *Effect* the surviving corporation receives title to all of the assets of the merged corporation and assumes all of its liabilities; the merged corporation ceases to exist

Consolidation the combination of two or more corporations into a new corporation

- *Procedure* requires approval of the board of directors and shareholders of each corporation
- *Effect* each constituent corporation ceases to exist; the new corporation assumes all of their debts and liabilities

Domestication the Revised Act permits a corporation to change its state of incorporation

Conversion the Revised Act permits (1) a domestic business corporation to become a domestic or foreign partnership, limited liability company (LLC), or other entity; and (2) a domestic or foreign partnership, LLC, or other entity to become a domestic business corporation

Going Private Transactions a combination that makes a publicly held corporation a private one; includes cash-out combinations and management buyouts

Dissenting Shareholder one who opposes a fundamental change and has the right to receive the fair value of her shares

- *Availability* dissenters' rights arise in (1) mergers, (2) consolidations, (3) sales or leases of all or substantially all of the assets of a corporation not in the regular course of business, (4) compulsory share exchanges, and (5) amendments that materially and adversely affect the rights of shares
- *Appraisal Remedy* the right of a dissenter to receive the fair value of his shares (the value of shares immediately before the corporate action to which the dissenter objects takes place, excluding any appreciation or depreciation in anticipation of such corporate action unless such exclusion would be inequitable)

Dissolution

Voluntary Dissolution may be brought about by a resolution of the board of directors that is approved by the shareholders

Involuntary Dissolution may occur by administrative or judicial action taken (1) by the attorney general, (2) by shareholders under certain circumstances, and (3) by a creditor on a showing that the corporation has become unable to pay its debts and obligations as they mature in the regular course of its business

Liquidation when a corporation is dissolved, its assets are liquidated and used first to pay its liquidation expenses and its creditors according to their respective contract or lien rights; any remainder is proportionately distributed to shareholders according to their respective contract rights

QUESTIONS

1. The stock in Hotel Management, Inc., a hotel management corporation, was divided equally between two families. For several years the two families had been unable to agree on or cooperate in the management of the corporation. As a result, no meeting of shareholders or directors had been held for five years. There had been no withdrawal of profits for five years, and last year the hotel operated at a loss. Although the corporation was not insolvent, such a state was imminent because the business was poorly managed and its properties were in need of repair. As a result, the owners of half the stock brought an action in equity for dissolution of the corporation. Will they succeed? Explain.

2. **a.** When may a corporation sell, lease, exchange, mortgage, or pledge all or substantially all of its assets in the usual and regular course of its business?
   b. When may a corporation sell, lease, exchange, mortgage, or pledge all or substantially all of its assets other than in the usual and regular course of its business?
   c. What are the rights of a shareholder who dissents from a proposed sale or exchange of all or substantially all of the assets of a corporation other than in the usual and regular course of its business?

3. Cutler Company was duly merged into Stone Company. Yetta, a shareholder of the former Cutler Company, having paid only one-half of her subscription, is now sued by Stone Company for the balance of the subscription. Yetta, who took no part in the merger proceedings, denies liability on the ground that, inasmuch as Cutler Company no longer exists, all her rights and obligations in connection with Cutler Company have been terminated. Explain whether she is correct.

4. Smith, while in the course of his employment with the Bee Corporation, negligently ran the company's truck into Williams, injuring him severely. Subsequently, the Bee Corporation and the Sea Corporation consolidated, forming the SeaBee Corporation. Williams filed suit against the SeaBee Corporation for damages, and the SeaBee Corporation argued the defense that the injuries Williams sustained were not caused by any of SeaBee's employees, that SeaBee was not even in existence at the time of the injury, and that the SeaBee Corporation was therefore not liable. What decision?

5. Johnson Company, a corporation organized under the laws of State X, after proper authorization by the shareholders, sold its entire assets to Samson Company, also a State X corporation. Ellen, an unpaid creditor of Johnson Company, sues Samson Company on her claim. Is Sampson liable? Explain.

6. Zenith Steel Company operates a prosperous business. The board of directors voted to spend $20 million of the company's surplus funds to purchase a majority of the stock of two other companies—Green Insurance Company and Blue Trust Company. Green Insurance Company is a thriving business whose stock is an excellent investment at the price at which it will be sold to Zenith Steel Company. The principal reasons for Zenith's purchase of Green Insurance stock are to invest surplus funds and to diversify its business. Blue Trust Company owns a controlling interest in Zenith Steel Company. The Blue Trust Company is subject to special governmental controls. The main purpose for Zenith's purchase of Blue Trust Company stock is to enable the present management and directors of Zenith Steel Company to continue their management of the company. Jones, a minority shareholder in Zenith Steel Company, brings an appropriate action to enjoin the purchase by Zenith Steel Company of the stock of either Green Insurance Company or of Blue Trust Company. What is the decision as to each purchase?

7. Mildred, Deborah, and Bob each own one-third of the stock of Nova Corporation. On Friday, Mildred received an offer to merge Nova into Buyer Corporation. Mildred, who agreed to call a shareholders' meeting to discuss the offer on the following Tuesday, telephoned Deborah and Bob and informed them of the offer and the scheduled meeting. Deborah agreed to attend. Bob was unable to attend because he was leaving on a trip on Saturday and asked if the three of them could meet Friday night to discuss the offer. Mildred and Deborah agreed. The three shareholders met informally Friday night and agreed to accept the offer only if they received preferred stock of Buyer Corporation for their shares. Bob then left on his trip. On Tuesday, at the time and place appointed by Mildred, Mildred and Deborah convened the shareholders' meeting. After discussion, they concluded that the preferred stock payment limitation was unwise and passed a formal resolution to accept Buyer Corporation's offer without any such condition. Bob files suit to enjoin Mildred, Deborah, and the Nova Corporation from implementing this resolution. Explain whether the injunction should be issued.

CASE PROBLEMS

8. Tretter alleged that his exposure over the years to asbestos products manufactured by Philip Carey Manufacturing Corporation caused him to contract asbestosis. Tretter brought an action against Rapid American Corporation, which was the surviving corporation of a merger between Philip Carey and Rapid American. Rapid American denied liability, claiming that immediately after the merger it had transferred its asbestos operations to a newly formed subsidiary corporation. Can Rapid avoid liability by such transfer? Explain.

9. Kemp & Beatley was a company incorporated under the laws of New York. Eight shareholders held the corporation's outstanding one thousand five hundred shares of stock. Dissin

and Gardstein together owned 20.33 percent of the stock, and each had been a longtime employee of the corporation. Kemp & Beatley had a longstanding practice of awarding compensation bonuses based upon stock ownership. However, when the policy was changed in 2013 to compensation based on service to the corporation, not on stock ownership, Dissin resigned. Gardstein was terminated in 2011. They commenced suit in 2015, seeking involuntary dissolution of the corporation and alleging that the corporation's board of directors had acted in a "fraudulent and oppressive" manner toward them, rendering their stock virtually worthless and frustrating their "reasonable expectations" regarding this business venture. What result? Explain.

10. All Steel Pipe and Tube is a closely held corporation engaged in the business of selling steel pipes and tubes. Leo and Scott Callier are its two equal shareholders. Scott is Leo's uncle. Leo is one of the company's two directors and is president of the corporation. Scott is the general manager. Scott's father and Leo's grandfather, Felix, is the other director. Over the years, Scott and Leo have had differences of opinion about various aspects of the operation of the business. However, despite the deterioration of their relationship, the company has flourished. When negotiations aimed at the redemption of Scott's shares by Leo began, the parties could not reach an agreement. The discussion then turned to voluntary dissolution and liquidation of the corporation, but still no agreement could be reached. Finally, Leo fired Scott and began to wind down All Steel's business and to form a new corporation, Callier Steel Pipe and Tube. Leo then brought an action seeking a dissolution and liquidation of All Steel. Should the court order dissolution? Explain.

11. The shareholders of Endicott Johnson who had dissented from a proposed merger of Endicott with McDonough Corporation brought a proceeding to fix the fair value of their stock. At issue was the proper weight to be given the market price of the stock in fixing its fair value. The shareholders argued that the market value should not be considered because McDonough controlled 70 percent of Endicott's stock and the stock had been delisted from the New York Stock Exchange. Are the shareholders correct?

12. In early 1984, Royal Dutch Petroleum Company (Royal Dutch), through various subsidiaries, controlled approximately 70 percent of the outstanding common shares of Shell Oil Co. (Shell). On January 24, 1984, Royal Dutch announced its intention to merge Shell into SPNV Holdings, Inc. (Holdings), which is now Shell Petroleum, Inc., by offering the minority shareholders $55.00 per share. Shell's board of directors, however, rejected the offer as inadequate. Royal Dutch then withdrew the merger proposal and initiated a tender offer at $58.00 per share. As a result of the tender offer, Holdings' ownership interest increased to 94.6 percent of Shell's outstanding stock. Holdings then initiated a short-form merger. Under the terms of the merger, Shell's minority stockholders were to receive $58.00 per share. However, if before July 1, 1985, a shareholder waived his right to seek an appraisal, he would receive an extra $2.00 per share. In conjunction with the short-form merger, Holdings distributed several documents to the minority, including a document entitled "Certain Information About Shell" (CIAS).

The CIAS included a table of discounted future net cash flows (DCF) for Shell's oil and gas reserves. However, due to a computer programming error, the DCF failed to account for the cash flows from approximately 295 million barrel equivalents of U.S. proved oil and gas reserves. Shell's failure to include the reserves in its calculations resulted in an understatement of its DCF of approximately $993 million to $1.1 billion or $3.00 to $3.45 per share. Moreover, as a result of the error, Shell stated in the CIAS that there had been a slight decline in the value of its oil and gas reserves from 1984 to 1985. When properly calculated, the value of the reserves had actually increased over that time period.

Shell's minority shareholders sued in the Court of Chancery, asserting that the error in the DCF along with other alleged disclosure violations constituted a breach of Holdings' fiduciary "duty of candor." Was the error in the DCF material and misleading?

TAKING SIDES

Wilcox, chief executive officer and chairman of the board of directors, owned 60 percent of the shares of Sterling Corporation. When the market price of Sterling's shares was $22.00 per share, Wilcox sold all of his shares in Sterling to Conrad for $29.00 per share. The minority shareholders of Sterling brought suit against Wilcox demanding a *pro rata* share of the amount Wilcox received in excess of the market price.

a. What are the arguments to support the minority shareholders' claim for a *pro rata* share of the amount Wilcox received in excess of the market price?

b. What are the arguments to reject the minority shareholders' claim for a *pro rata* share of the amount Wilcox received in excess of the market price?

c. Which side should prevail?

Secured Transactions and Suretyship

Neither a borrower nor a lender be: For loan oft loses both itself and friend, And borrowing dulls the edge of husbandry.

William Shakespeare
Hamlet

CHAPTER OUTCOMES

After reading and studying this chapter, you should be able to:

1. Name and define the various types of collateral.

2. Explain the purposes, methods, and requirements of attachment and perfection.

3. Discuss the priorities among the various parties who may have competing interests in collateral and the rights and remedies of the parties to a security agreement after default by the debtor.

4. Explain the requirements for the formation of a suretyship relationship.

5. Explain the rights of a creditor against a surety and the rights of a surety, including those of a cosurety.

Shakespeare's well-known lines in *Hamlet* reflect an earlier view of debt, for today borrowed funds are both essential and honorable under our economic system. In fact, the absence of loans would severely restrict the availability of goods and services and would greatly limit the quantities consumers would be able to purchase.

The public policy and social issues created by today's enormous use of debt center on certain tenets, among which are the following:

1. The means by which debt is created and transferred should be as simple and as inexpensive as possible.
2. The risks to lenders should be minimized.
3. Lenders should have a way to collect unpaid debts.

A lender typically incurs two basic collection risks: the borrower could be unwilling to repay the loan even though he is able to, or the borrower could prove to be unable to repay the loan. In addition to the remedies dealing with the first of these risks, the law has developed several devices to maximize the likelihood of repayment. These devices, which we will discuss in this chapter, include consensual security interests (also called secured transactions) and suretyships.

In addition, debtors of all sorts—wage earners, sole proprietorships, partnerships, and corporations—sometimes accumulate debts far in excess of their assets or suffer financial reverses that make it impossible for them to meet their obligations. In such an event, it is an important policy of the law to treat all creditors fairly and equitably and to provide the debtor with relief from these debts so that he may continue to contribute to society. These are the two basic purposes of the federal bankruptcy law, which we will briefly discuss in this chapter and more fully in Chapter 38.

SECURED TRANSACTIONS IN PERSONAL PROPERTY

An obligation or debt can exist without security if the creditor deems adequate the integrity, reputation, and net worth of the debtor. Often, however, businesses or individuals cannot obtain credit without giving adequate security, or, in some cases, even if the borrower can obtain an unsecured loan, he can negotiate more favorable terms by giving security.

Transactions involving security in personal property are governed by Article 9 of the Uniform Commercial Code (UCC). Article 9 was substantially revised in 1998, and the 1998 revisions have been adopted in all states. In 2010, Article 9 was amended to respond to filing issues and address other matters that have arisen in practice with the 1998 Revisions of Article 9. The 2010 Amendments took effect on July 1, 2013; this delay allowed the states to adopt the amendments uniformly and have them begin at the same time. As of May 2014, forty-seven states had adopted the 2010 Amendments and three states had introduced bills to adopt the 2010 Amendments. This chapter covers Article 9 as revised in 1998 and 2010.

Article 9 provides a simple and unified structure within which a tremendous variety of secured financing transactions can take place with less cost and with greater certainty. Moreover, the article's flexibility and simplified formalities allow new forms of secured financing to fit comfortably under its provisions. In addition, Article 9 now recognizes and provides coverage for electronic commerce.

ESSENTIALS OF SECURED TRANSACTIONS [37-1]

Article 9 governs a **secured transaction** in personal property in which the debtor *consents* to provide a security interest in personal property to secure the payment of a debt. A security interest in property cannot exist apart from the debt it secures, and discharging the debt in any manner terminates the security interest in the property. Article 9 also applies to the *sales* of certain types of collateral (accounts, chattel paper, payment intangibles, and promissory notes). Article 9 does *not* apply to nonconsensual security interests that arise by operation of law, such as mechanics' or landlords' liens, although it does cover nonpossessory statutory agricultural liens.

A common type of consensual secured transaction covered by Article 9 occurs when a person wanting to buy goods has neither the cash nor a sufficient credit standing to obtain the goods on open credit, and the seller, to secure payment of all or part of the price, obtains a security interest in the goods. Alternatively, the buyer may borrow the purchase price from a third party and pay the seller in cash. The third-party lender may then take a security interest in the goods to secure repayment of the loan.

Every consensual secured transaction involves a debtor, a secured party, collateral, a security agreement, and a security interest. Some Article 9 definitions follow:

- A **security interest** is "an interest in personal property or fixtures which secures payment or performance of an obligation."
- A **security agreement** is an agreement that creates or provides for a security interest.
- **Collateral** is the property subject to a security interest or agricultural lien.
- A **secured party** is the person in whose favor a security interest in the collateral is created or provided for under a security agreement. The definition of a secured party includes lenders, credit sellers, consignors, purchasers of certain types of collateral (accounts, chattel paper, payment intangibles, or promissory notes), and other specified persons.
- A **debtor** is a person (1) having an interest in the collateral other than a security interest or lien, whether or not the person is an obligor; (2) a seller of accounts, chattel paper, payment intangibles, or promissory notes; or (3) a consignee.
- An *obligor* is a person who, with respect to an obligation secured by a security interest in or an agricultural lien on the collateral, owes payment or other performance, has provided property other than the collateral to secure payment or performance, or is otherwise accountable for payment or performance.

Secured transaction
an agreement by which one party obtains a security interest in the personal property of another to secure the payment of a debt

Security interest
right in personal property that secures payment or performance of an obligation

Security agreement
agreement between debtor and creditor creating a security interest

Collateral
property subject to a security interest or agricultural lien

Secured party
person in whose favor a security interest in the collateral is created or provided for under the security agreement

Debtor
person who has an interest in the collateral other than a security interest; typically the person who is obligated on the debt secured by the security interest

Figure 37-1 Fundamental Rights of Secured Party and Debtor

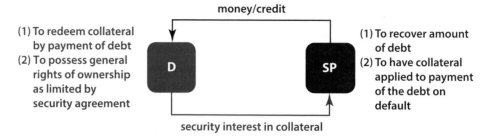

money/credit

(1) To redeem collateral by payment of debt
(2) To possess general rights of ownership as limited by security agreement

D

SP

(1) To recover amount of debt
(2) To have collateral applied to payment of the debt on default

security interest in collateral

- A *secondary obligor* is usually a guarantor or surety of the debt.
- A **purchase money security interest** (PMSI) is created in goods when a seller retains a security interest in the goods sold on credit by a security agreement. Similarly, a third-party lender who advances funds to enable the debtor to purchase goods has a PMSI in goods if she has a security agreement and the debtor in fact uses the funds to purchase the goods.

In most secured transactions, the debtor is an obligor with respect to the obligation secured by the security interest. Thus, a security interest is created when an automobile dealer sells and delivers a car to an individual (the *debtor*) under a retail installment contract (a *security agreement*) that provides that the dealer (the *secured party*) obtains a *security interest* (a *PMSI*) in the car (the *collateral*) until the price is paid. See Figure 37-1 for the fundamental rights of the secured party and the debtor.

CLASSIFICATION OF COLLATERAL [37-2]

Although most of the provisions of Article 9 apply to all kinds of personal property, some provisions state special rules that apply only to particular kinds of collateral. Under the UCC, collateral is classified according to its nature and its use. The classifications according to nature are (1) goods, (2) indispensable paper, and (3) intangibles.

Goods [37-2a]

Goods are all things that are movable when a security interest attaches and include fixtures; standing timber to be cut; the unborn young of animals; crops grown, growing, or to be grown; and manufactured homes. Goods also include computer programs embedded in goods if the software becomes part of the goods. (When software maintains its separate state it is considered a general intangible.) Goods are further classified according to their use. Goods are subdivided into (1) consumer goods, (2) farm products, (3) inventory, (4) equipment, (5) fixtures, and (6) accessions. Depending on its primary use or purpose, the same item of goods may fall into different classifications. For example, a refrigerator purchased by a physician to store medicines in his office is classified as equipment but the same refrigerator would be classified as consumer goods if the physician purchased it for home use. In the hands of a refrigerator dealer or manufacturer, the refrigerator would be classified as inventory. If goods are used for multiple purposes, such as by a physician in both his office and his home, their classification is dependent upon their predominant use.

Consumer Goods Goods used or bought for use primarily for personal, family, or household purposes are consumer goods.

Farm Products The UCC defines farm products as "goods, other than standing timber, which are part of a farming operation and which are crops grown, growing[,] or to be grown, including crops produced on trees, vines, and bushes and aquatic goods." In addition, **farm products** also include livestock, born or unborn, including aquatic goods such as fish raised on a fish farm as well as supplies used or produced in a farming operation. Thus, farm products would include wheat growing on the farmer's land; the farmer's pigs, cows, and hens; and the hens' eggs. When such products become the possessions of a person not engaged in farming operations, they cease to be farm products.

Purchase money security interest
security interest in goods purchased; interest is retained either by the seller of the goods or by a lender who advances the purchase price

Goods
things that are movable when a security interest attaches

Consumer goods
federal regulation prohibits a credit seller or lender from obtaining a consumer's grant of a nonpossessory security interest in household goods

Farm products
goods that are part of a farming operation, including crops, livestock, or supplies used or produced in farming

Inventory   The term **inventory** includes nonfarm product goods (1) held for sale, held for lease, or to be furnished under a service contract; or (2) that consist of raw materials, work in process, or materials used or consumed in a business. Thus, a retailer's or a wholesaler's merchandise, as well as a manufacturer's raw materials, are inventory.

Equipment   Goods not included in the definition of inventory, farm products, or consumer goods are classified as **equipment**. This category is broad enough to include a lawyer's library, a physician's office furniture, or a factory's machinery.

Fixtures   Goods and personal property that have become so related to particular *real property* that an interest in them arises under real estate law are called **fixtures**. Thus, state law other than the UCC determines whether and when goods become fixtures. In general terms, fixtures are goods so firmly affixed to real estate that they are considered part of such real estate. Examples are furnaces, central air-conditioning units, and plumbing fixtures. See Chapter 47 for a further discussion of fixtures. A security interest in fixtures may arise under Article 9, and, under certain circumstances, a perfected security interest in fixtures will have priority over a conflicting security interest or mortgage in the real property to which the goods are attached.

Accession   Goods installed in or firmly affixed to *personal property* are **accessions** if the identity of the original goods is not lost. Thus, a new engine placed in an old car automobile is an accession.

Indispensable Paper [37-2b]

Four kinds of collateral involve rights evidenced by **indispensable paper**: (1) chattel paper, (2) instruments, (3) documents, and (4) investment property.

Chattel Paper   **Chattel paper** is a record or records that evidence both a monetary obligation and a security interest in or a lease of specific goods. A **record** is information inscribed on a tangible medium (written on paper) or stored in an electronic or other medium and is retrievable in perceivable form (electronically stored). Thus, chattel paper can be either tangible chattel paper or electronic chattel paper.

For example, Dealer sells goods on credit to Buyer, who uses the goods as equipment. Dealer retains a PMSI in the goods. Dealer then borrows against (or sells) the security agreement of Buyer along with Dealer's security interest in the collateral. The collateral provided by Dealer to his lender in this type of transaction (consisting of the security agreement and the security interest) is chattel paper.

Instruments   The definition of an **instrument** includes negotiable instruments (drafts, checks, promissory notes, and certificate of deposits) as well as any other writing that evidences a right to payment of money that is transferable by delivery with any necessary indorsement or assignment and that is not of itself a security agreement or lease. Negotiable instruments are covered in Chapters 24 through 27. An instrument does not include an investment property, a letter of credit, or writings evidencing a right to payment from a credit or charge card.

Documents   The term **document** includes documents of title, such as bills of lading and warehouse receipts, which may be either negotiable or nonnegotiable. A document of title is negotiable if by its terms the goods it covers are deliverable to the bearer or to the order of a named person. Any other document is nonnegotiable. Documents of title are covered in Chapter 47.

Investment Property   The term **investment property** means an investment security, such as stocks and bonds, as well as securities accounts, commodity contracts, and commodity accounts. A *certificated security* is an investment security that is represented by a certificate. An *uncertificated security* is not represented by a certificate. A *security entitlement* refers to the rights and property interest of a person who holds securities or other financial assets through a securities intermediary such as a bank, broker, or clearinghouse, which in the ordinary course of business maintains security accounts for others. A security entitlement thus includes both the rights against the securities intermediary and an interest in the property held by the securities intermediary.

Intangibles [37-2c]

The UCC also recognizes two kinds of collateral that are neither goods nor indispensable paper, namely, accounts and general intangibles. These types of intangible collateral are not evidenced by any indispensable paper, such as a stock certificate or a negotiable bill of lading.

Account

right to payment for (1) goods sold, leased, licensed, or otherwise disposed of or (2) services rendered

Accounts
The term **account** includes the right to monetary payment, whether or not such right has been earned by performance, for (1) goods sold, leased, licensed, or otherwise disposed of; or (2) services rendered. Accounts include credit card receivables and health-care-insurance receivables. An example of an account is a business' accounts receivable.

General intangibles

catchall category of collateral not otherwise covered; includes software, goodwill, literary rights, and interests in patents, trademarks, and copyrights

General Intangibles
The term **general intangibles** applies to any personal property *other than* goods, accounts, chattel paper, commercial tort claims, deposit accounts, documents, instruments, investment property, letter-of-credit rights, money, and oil, gas, and other minerals before extraction. Included in the definition are software, goodwill, literary rights, and interests in patents, trademarks, and copyrights to the extent they are not regulated by federal statute. Also included is a payment intangible, which is a general intangible under which the account debtor's principal obligation is the payment of money.

Other Kinds of Collateral [37-2d]

Proceeds

whatever is received upon sale, lease, license, exchange, or other disposition of collateral; the secured party, unless the security agreement states otherwise, has rights to the proceeds

Proceeds include whatever is received upon the sale, lease, license exchange, or other disposition of collateral; whatever is collected on, or distributed on account of, collateral; or other rights arising out of collateral. For example, an automobile dealer grants a security interest in its inventory to the automobile manufacturer that sold the inventory. When the dealer sells a car to Henry and receives from Henry a used car and the remainder of the purchase price in a monetary payment, the used car and the money are both proceeds from the sale of the new car. Unless otherwise agreed, a security agreement gives the secured party (the manufacturer in this example) the rights to proceeds.

Deposit accounts

a demand, savings, time, or similar accounts maintained with a bank

Additional types of collateral include timber to be cut, minerals, motor vehicles, mobile goods (goods used in more than one jurisdiction), and money. Article 9 also includes the following kinds of collateral: commercial tort claim, letter-of-credit rights, and **deposit accounts** (a demand, savings, time, or similar account maintained with a bank). In consumer transactions, however, deposit accounts may not be taken as *original* collateral.

ATTACHMENT [37-3]

Attachment

security interest that is enforceable against the debtor

Attachment is the UCC's term to describe the creation of a security interest that is enforceable against the *debtor*. Attachment is also a prerequisite to rendering a security interest enforceable against third parties, though in some instances attachment in itself is sufficient to create such enforceability. Perfection, which provides the greatest enforceability against third parties who assert competing interests in the collateral, is discussed in the next section.

Until a security interest "attaches," it is *ineffective* against the debtor. Under the UCC, the security interest created by a security agreement attaches to the described collateral once the following events have occurred:

1. the secured party has given value;
2. the debtor has acquired rights in the collateral or has the power to transfer such rights to a secured party; and
3. the debtor and secured party have an agreement, which in most instances must be authenticated by the debtor although in some cases alternative evidence, such as possession by the secured party pursuant to agreement, will suffice.

The parties may, however, by explicit agreement postpone the time of attachment.

Value

includes consideration under contract law, a binding commitment to extend credit, or an antecedent debt

Value [37-3a]

The term **value** is broadly defined and includes consideration under contract law, a binding commitment to extend credit, and an antecedent debt. For example, Buyer purchases equipment from Seller on credit. When Buyer fails to make timely payment, Seller and Buyer enter into a security agreement that grants Seller a security interest in the equipment. By entering the agreement, Seller has given value, even though he relies upon an antecedent debt—the original transfer of goods to Buyer—instead of providing new consideration. Moreover, Seller is not limited to acquiring a security interest in the equipment he sold to Buyer but also may obtain a security interest in other personal property of Buyer.

Debtor's Rights in Collateral [37-3b]

Debtor's rights in collateral

a debtor is deemed to have rights in personal property the debtor owns, possesses, is in the process of acquiring, or has the power to transfer rights to a secured party

The elusive concept of the **debtor's rights in collateral** is not specifically defined by the UCC. As a general rule, the debtor is deemed to have rights in collateral that he owns or is in possession of as well as in those items that he is in the process of acquiring from the seller. For example, if Adrien borrows money from Richard and grants him a security interest in corporate stock that she owns, then Adrien had rights in the collateral before entering into the secured transaction. Likewise, if Sally sells goods to Benjamin on credit and he provides Sally a security interest in the goods, Benjamin will acquire rights in the collateral upon identification of the goods to the contract. In addition, the 1998 Revisions to Article 9 added the words "or the power to transfer rights in the collateral to a secured party." The comments to this section state, "[h]owever, in accordance with basic personal property conveyancing principles, the baseline rule is that a security interest attaches only to whatever rights a debtor may have, broad or limited as those rights may be."

 **Border State Bank of Greenbush v. Bagley Livestock Exchange, Inc.**
Court of Appeals of Minnesota, 2004
690 N.W.2d 326
http://scholar.google.com/scholar_case?case=11200679180282154995&q=690+N.W.2D+326&hl=en&as_sdt=40006

FACTS In December 1997, Bert Johnson, doing business as Johnson Farms, and Hal Anderson entered into an oral cattle-sharing contract. Approximately one month later, they put their oral contract into writing. Under the written agreement, Anderson agreed to care for and breed cattle owned by Johnson and in return Johnson would receive a "guaranteed" percentage of the annual calf crop. The contract further provided that the cattle Johnson placed with Anderson were "considered to be owned by Johnson Farms and any offspring is to be sold under Johnson Farms' name." The contract required Johnson Farms and Anderson mutually to agree when the calves would be sold and within thirty days of receiving money for the sale, Johnson Farms was to pay the "remainder" to Anderson "for his keeping of [the] cattle." In the fall of 1998 and 1999, calves bred under the contract were sold under the provisions of the written contract. Anderson testified that, in October 1999, Johnson asked him to care for additional cattle on the same terms. Anderson initially declined, although he claims they eventually agreed to continue based on certain modifications: (1) the share percentage would be a straight forty/sixty split, without Johnson's "guaranteed" percentage; (2) Johnson would provide feed, including beet tailings; (3) Johnson would provide additional pasture; and (4) the agreement would include approximately five hundred cattle, instead of the original 151 cattle. Johnson testified that he discussed the cattle-sharing agreement with Anderson in October 1999 and that he agreed to send Anderson beet tailings, which were free to him, so long as Anderson paid the cost of shipping. Johnson also testified that he and Anderson agreed that approximately five hundred cattle would be cared for under the cattle-sharing agreement, rather than the original 151 cattle. But Johnson denied that he had agreed to provide feed, other than the beet tailings, and denied that he had agreed

to change the provision that "guaranteed" that his percentage of the calf crop would be calculated on the initial number of cows regardless of whether each produced a calf that survived.

In March 2000, Anderson negotiated with Border State Bank for loans totaling $155,528. To secure these loans, Anderson granted Border State Bank a security interest in, among other things, all of Anderson's "rights, title, and interest" in all "livestock" then owned or thereafter acquired. In November 2000, Anderson encountered difficulty caring for the cattle due to heavy rainfall and lack of feed. The cattle were reclaimed by Johnson, but the calves remained with Anderson for sale. At trial, Anderson testified that some of the cattle that Johnson reclaimed were actually Anderson's cattle or were cattle that belonged to Evonne Stephens, another person with whom Anderson had a cattle-sharing contract.

In December 2000, 289 calves that had remained with Anderson were sold at Bagley Livestock Exchange. The livestock exchange knew of Border State's security interest in Anderson's livestock but, after discussing the agreement with Johnson, determined the security interest did not attach to the calves. The livestock exchange issued a check to Johnson Farms in the amount of $119,403. Thereafter, Johnson gave Anderson a check for $19,404, representing Anderson's share of the sale proceeds, less $55,000 that Johnson claimed as repayment for money advanced to Anderson to purchase feed. Border State Bank sued Bagley Livestock Exchange and Johnson, contending that they had converted Border State Bank's perfected security interest in the calves sold in December 2000. In addition, Anderson filed a claim against Johnson, asserting breach of contract. The district court granted Johnson's and Bagley's motion for directed verdict, finding that, under the cattle-sharing agreement, Johnson did not "grant" Anderson an "ownership interest" in the calves. Border State Bank appealed.

DECISION Reversed and remanded.

OPINION Article 9 of the UCC provides that a security interest attaches to collateral, and is enforceable against the debtor or third parties, when (1) value has been given; (2) the debtor "has rights in the collateral or the power to transfer rights"; and (3) the debtor has signed a security agreement that contains a description of the collateral. To perfect the security interest, both the security agreement and financing statement must contain an adequate description of the collateral. Descriptions in the security agreement and financing statement are liberally interpreted because their essential purpose is to provide notice, not to definitively describe each item of collateral.

The parties do not dispute that Anderson signed a security agreement and that value was given. The security agreement stated that the collateral included, in part, "all livestock owned or hereafter acquired" and Anderson's "rights, title and interest" in such livestock. The financing statements covered "all livestock," whether "now owned or hereafter acquired, together with the proceeds from the sale thereof." These descriptions are valid and include cattle and calves. The question is whether the bank's security interest attached to the 289 calves sold in December 2000 under Anderson and Johnson's cattle-sharing agreement.

The district court ruled that the cattle-sharing contract had not "granted" Anderson an "ownership interest" in the calves, specifically finding that "the modifications testified to by Mr. Anderson in the light most favorable to Border State Bank do not modify

the terms of the agreement such that an ownership interest is granted." The provisions of the UCC's Article 9, however, refer to "rights in the collateral," not solely the "ownership" of the collateral. Rights in the collateral, as the term is used in Article 9, include full ownership and limited rights that fall short of full ownership. For purposes of the UCC, "sufficient rights" arise with far less than full ownership. Ownership or title is not the relevant concern under Article 9; the issue is whether the debtor has acquired sufficient rights—beyond mere possession—in the collateral so that the security interest would attach. However, a security interest will attach to the collateral only to the extent of the debtor's rights in the collateral. Thus, the district court applied a standard of ownership that is incorrect.

INTERPRETATION A security agreement attaches to the described collateral once the following events have occurred: (1) the secured party has given value; (2) the debtor has acquired rights in the collateral or has the power to transfer such rights to a secured party; and (3) the debtor and secured party have an agreement, which in most instances must be authenticated by the debtor.

ETHICAL QUESTION Did the court fairly decide this case? Explain.

CRITICAL THINKING QUESTION What rights in collateral beyond mere possession should be considered sufficient for a security interest to attach to the collateral? Explain.

Security agreement

agreement that creates or provides for a security interest

Security Agreement [37-3c]

A security interest cannot attach unless an agreement (contract) between the debtor and creditor creates or provides the creditor with a security interest in the debtor's collateral. With certain exceptions (discussed in the following section), the agreement must (1) be authenticated by the debtor and (2) contain a reasonable description of the collateral. In addition, if the collateral is timber to be cut, the agreement must contain a reasonable description of the land concerned. A description of personal or real property is sufficient if it reasonably identifies what is described. A description of personal property may identify the collateral by specific listing, category, or in most cases, a type of collateral defined in the UCC (e.g., inventory or farm equipment). The description, however, may not be a supergeneric description, such as "all my personal property."

The UCC provides the parties with a great deal of freedom to draft the security agreement, although this freedom is limited by good faith, diligence, reasonableness, and care. Moreover, security agreements frequently contain a provision for acceleration at the secured party's option of all payments upon the default in any payment by the debtor, the debtor's bankruptcy or insolvency, or the debtor's failure to meet other requirements of the agreement. Sometimes security agreements require the debtor to furnish additional collateral if the secured party becomes insecure about the prospects of future payments.

Authenticating Record
In most instances there must be a record of the security agreement authenticated by the debtor. Authentication can occur in one of two ways. First, the debtor can sign a written security agreement. A writing can include any printing, typewriting, or other intentional reduction to tangible form. To sign includes any symbol executed or adopted by a party with the present intention to authenticate a writing. (Revised Article 1 substitutes "adopt or accept" for "authenticate.") Second, in recognition of e-commerce and electronic security agreements, Article 9 as amended provides that a debtor can authenticate a security agreement by executing or otherwise adopting a symbol, or by encrypting or similarly processing a record in whole or in part, with the present intent of the authenticating party to adopt or accept the record. As mentioned, a record means information (1) on a tangible medium or (2) that is stored

in an *electronic* or other medium and is retrievable in perceivable form. According to the UCC, "examples of current technologies commercially used to communicate or store information include, but are not limited to, magnetic media, optical discs, digital voice messaging systems, electronic mail, audio tapes, and photographic media, as well as paper. 'Record' is an inclusive term that includes all of these methods." It does not, however, include any oral or other communication that is not stored or preserved.

Authenticating Record Not Required　Under the UCC a record of a security agreement is not mandated in some situations. A record of a security agreement is not required when some types of collateral are pledged or are in the possession of the secured party pursuant to an agreement. This rule applies to a security interest in negotiable documents, goods, instruments, money, and tangible chattel paper. A **pledge** is the delivery of personal property to a creditor as security for the payment of a debt. A pledge requires that the secured party (the pledgee) and the debtor agree to the pledge of the collateral and that the collateral be *delivered* to the pledgee. Other situations in which a secured party does not need a record authenticated by the debtor include the following: (1) the collateral is a certificated security in registered form that has been delivered to the secured party, or (2) the collateral is a deposit account, electronic chattel paper, investment property, or letter-of-credit rights; the secured party has control over the collateral. Control is discussed later.

Consumer Goods　Federal regulation prohibits a credit seller or lender from obtaining a consumer's grant of a nonpossessory security interest in household goods. This rule does not apply to PMSIs or to pledges. Rather, it prevents a lender or seller from obtaining a non-PMSI covering the consumer's household goods, which are defined to include clothing, furniture, appliances, kitchenware, personal effects, wedding rings, one radio, and one television. (These hard-to-sell items are also referred to as "junk" collateral.) The definition of household goods specifically excludes works of art, other electronic entertainment equipment, antiques, and jewelry.

After-Acquired Property　Article 9 states "[A] security agreement may create or provide for a security interest in after-acquired collateral." **After-acquired property** is property that the debtor presently does not own or have rights to but may acquire at some time. For example, an after-acquired property clause in a security agreement may include all present and subsequently acquired inventory, accounts, or equipment of the debtor. This clause would provide the secured party with a valid security interest not only in the typewriter, desk, and file cabinet that the debtor currently owns, but also in a personal computer she purchases later. Article 9 therefore accepts the concept of a "continuing general lien," or a *floating lien*, though the UCC limits the operation of an after-acquired property clause against consumers by providing that no such interest can be claimed as additional security in consumer goods, except accessions, if the goods are acquired more than ten days after the secured party gives value. As discussed later, the 2010 Amendments provide added protection for a secured party having a security interest in after-acquired property when its debtor relocates to another state or merges with another entity.

Future Advances　The obligations covered by a security agreement may include **future advances**. Frequently, a debtor obtains a line of credit from a creditor for advances to be made at some later time. For instance, a manufacturer may provide a retailer with a $60,000 line of credit, only $20,000 of which the retailer initially uses. Nevertheless, the manufacturer and the retailer may enter a security agreement granting to the manufacturer a security interest in the retailer's inventory that covers not only the initial $20,000 advance but also any future advances.

PERFECTION [37-4]

To be effective against third parties who assert competing interests in the collateral (including other creditors of the debtor, the debtor's trustee in bankruptcy, and transferees of the debtor), the security interest must be perfected. **Perfection** of a security interest occurs when it has attached *and* when all the applicable steps required for perfection have been satisfied. If these

---

Pledge
delivery of collateral to creditor as security for payment of a debt

Consumer goods
goods bought or used primarily for personal, family, or household purposes

After-acquired property
property a security agreement may cover that the debtor may acquire in the future

Future advances
a security agreement may include future advances

Perfection
enforceability of a security interest against third parties

steps precede attachment, the security interest is perfected at the time it attaches. Once a security interest becomes perfected, it "may still be or become subordinate to other interests … [h]owever, in general, after perfection the secured party is protected against creditors and transferees of the debtor and, in particular, against any representative of creditors in insolvency proceedings instituted by or against the debtor." Thus, in most instances a perfected secured party will prevail over a subsequent perfected security interest, a subsequent lien creditor or a representative of creditors (e.g., a trustee in bankruptcy), and subsequent buyers of the collateral.

Depending on the type of collateral, a security interest may be perfected:

1. by the secured party filing a financing statement in the designated public office;
2. by the secured party taking or retaining possession of the collateral;
3. automatically, on the attachment of the security interest;
4. temporarily, for a period specified by the UCC; or
5. by the secured party taking control of the collateral.

A security interest or agricultural lien is perfected continuously if it is originally perfected by one method and is later perfected by another if there is no intermediate period when it was unperfected.

Many states have adopted certificate of title statutes for automobiles, trailers, mobile homes, boats, and farm tractors. A **certificate of title** is an official representation of ownership. In these states, Article 9's filing requirements do not apply to perfecting a security interest in such collateral except when the collateral is inventory held by a dealer for sale. See Concept Review 37-1 for an overview of the requisites for attachment and perfection.

Filing a Financing Statement [37-4a]

Filing a financing statement is the most common method of perfecting a security interest under Article 9. Filing is *required* to perfect a security interest in general intangibles and accounts except for assignments of isolated accounts. Filing *may* be used to perfect a security interest in any other kind of collateral, with the general *exception* of deposit accounts, letter-of-credit rights, and money. A financing statement may be filed before or after the security interest attaches. The form of the **financing statement**, which is filed to give public notice of the security interest, may vary from state to state.

What to File Article 9 uses a system of "notice filing," which indicates merely that a person may have a security interest in the collateral. Article 9 also authorizes and encourages filing financing statements electronically. Though it need not be highly detailed, the financing statement must include the name of the debtor, the name of the secured party or a representative of the secured party, and an indication of the collateral covered by the financing statement. If the financing statement substantially complies with these requirements, minor errors that do not seriously mislead will not render the financing statement ineffective. Significantly, as revised, Article 9 no longer requires the debtor's signature on the financing statement to facilitate *paperless* or *electronic filing*. Since a signature is not required, Article 9 attempts to deter unauthorized filings by imposing statutory damages of $500 in addition to damages for any loss caused.

Financing statements are indexed under the debtor's name so it is particularly important that the financing statement provide the debtor's name. The UCC provides rules for what names must appear for registered organizations (such as corporations, limited partnerships, and limited liability companies), trusts, and other organizations. If the organization does not have a name, the names of the partners, members, associates, or other persons comprising the debtor are the names used. A financing statement that includes only the trade name is insufficient. A financing statement that does not comply with these requirements is considered to be seriously misleading.

The description of the collateral is sufficient if it meets the requirements for a security agreement discussed earlier or if it indicates that the financing statement covers all assets or all personal property. Thus, the use of supergeneric descriptions is permitted in financing statements but is *not* permitted in security agreements. In *real-property-related filings* (collateral involving fixtures, timber to be cut, or minerals to be extracted), a description of the real property must be included sufficient to reasonably identify the real property.

Practical Advice

As a creditor, make sure that you properly perfect any security interest that you acquire.

Certificate of title
official representation of ownership

Financing statement
document filed by the secured party to provide notice of a security interest

The 2010 Amendments provide greater guidance as to the name of an individual debtor to be provided on a financing statement. The Amendments offer two alternative provisions:

- *Alternative A* provides that, if the debtor holds an unexpired driver's license issued by the state where the financing statement is filed, the debtor's name as it appears on the driver's license is the name required to be used on the financing statement. If the debtor does not have such a driver's license, either the debtor's actual name or the debtor's surname and first personal name may be used on the financing statement.
- *Alternative B* that the debtor's driver's license name, the debtor's actual name, or the debtor's surname and first personal name may be used on the financing statement.

The 2010 Amendments further improve the filing system for financing statements. More detailed guidance is provided for the debtor's name on a financing statement when the debtor is a corporation, limited liability company, or limited partnership as well as when the collateral is held in trust or in a decedent's estate. Moreover, some nonessential information that was provided on financing statements is no longer required.

Duration of Filing

A financing statement is generally effective for five years from the date of filing. A *continuation statement* filed by the secured party within six months prior to expiration will extend the effectiveness of the filing for another five years. If the financing statement lapses, the security interest is no longer perfected unless it is perfected by another method.

In many states, security interests in motor vehicles and other specified collateral must be perfected by making a notation on the certificate of title rather than by filing a financing statement. Nevertheless, as previously indicated, certificate of title laws do not apply if a dealer holds the collateral as inventory for sale.

Place of Filing

Except for real-estate-related collateral, financing statements must be filed in a central location designated by the state. With respect to real-estate-related collateral, the financing statement is to be filed in the office designated for the filing or recording of mortgages on the related real property, which is usually local. If the debtor is an individual, the financing statement is to be filed in the state of the individual's principal residence; for a registered organization, the place of filing is the state where the debtor is organized.

Subsequent Change of Debtor's Location

After a secured party has properly filed a financing statement, the debtor may change the place of his residence or business or the location or use of the collateral and thus render the information in the filing incorrect. A change in the use of the collateral or a move within the state (intrastate) does not impair the effectiveness of the original filing. If the debtor moves to another state after the initial filing, the security interest remains perfected until the earliest of (1) the time the security interest would have terminated in the state in which perfection occurred; (2) four months after the debtor moved to the new state; or (3) the expiration of one year after the debtor transfers the collateral to a person in another state who becomes the debtor. The 2010 Amendments also address perfection issues related to after-acquired property when a debtor moves to a new state. Under the 2010 Amendments, this four-month period of perfection applies to security interests that attach to collateral acquired *after* the debtor moves. Thus, a filed financing statement that would have been effective to perfect a security interest in the collateral if the debtor had not changed its location is effective to perfect a security interest in collateral acquired within four months after the debtor relocates.

Possession [37-4b]

Possession by the secured party perfects a security interest in goods (e.g., those in the possession of pawnbrokers), instruments, money, negotiable documents, or tangible chattel paper. Moreover, a secured party may perfect a security interest in a certificated security by taking delivery of it. Possession is *not* available, however, as a means of perfecting a security interest in accounts, commercial tort claims, deposit accounts, other types of investment property, letter-of-credit rights, or oil, gas, and other minerals before extraction.

Possession

by the secured party (a pledge); may be used for goods, instruments, money, negotiable documents, tangible chattel paper, or certificated securities

A pledge, which is a possessory security interest, is the delivery of personal property to a creditor or to a third party acting as an agent or bailee for the creditor as security for the payment of a debt. No pledge occurs in cases in which the debtor retains possession of the collateral. In making a pledge, the debtor is not legally required to sign a written security agreement; an oral agreement granting the secured party a security interest is sufficient. In any situation not involving a pledge, however, the UCC requires an authenticated record of the security agreement.

One type of pledge is the **field warehouse**. This common arrangement for financing inventory allows the debtor access to the pledged goods and provides the secured party with control over the pledged property at the same time. In this arrangement, a professional warehouseman generally establishes a warehouse on the debtor's premises—usually by enclosing a portion of those premises and posting appropriate signs—to store the debtor's unsold inventory. The warehouseman then typically issues nonnegotiable receipts for the goods to the secured party, who may then authorize the warehouseman to release a portion of the goods to the debtor as the goods are sold, at a specified quantity per week, or at any rate on which the parties agree. Thus, the secured party legally possesses the goods while allowing the debtor easy access to her inventory.

Field warehouse
secured party takes possession of the goods, but the debtor has access to them

---

Practical Advice

Field warehousing is a useful way for a creditor to perfect her security interest while providing the debtor with easy access to his inventory.

Automatic perfection
perfection upon attachment; applies to a purchase money security interest in consumer goods and isolated assignments of accounts

Automatic Perfection [37-4c]

In some situations, a security interest is automatically perfected on attachment. The most important situation to which **automatic perfection** applies is a PMSI in consumer goods. A partial or isolated assignment of accounts that transfers a less-than-significant portion of the assignor's outstanding accounts is also automatically perfected.

A PMSI in consumer goods, with the exception of motor vehicles, is perfected automatically upon attachment; filing a financing statement is unnecessary. For example, Doris purchases a refrigerator from Carol on credit for Doris's personal, family, or household use. Doris takes possession of the refrigerator and then grants Carol a security interest in the refrigerator pursuant to a written security agreement. Upon Doris's granting Carol the security interest, Carol's security interest attaches and is automatically perfected. The same would be true if Doris purchased the refrigerator for cash but borrowed the money from Logan, to whom Doris granted a security interest in the refrigerator pursuant to a written security agreement. Logan's security interest would attach and would be automatically perfected when she received the security agreement from Doris. Nevertheless, because an automatically perfected PMSI in consumer goods protects the secured party less fully than a filed PMSI, secured parties frequently file a financing statement rather than rely solely on automatic perfection.

Kimbrell's of Sanford, Inc. v. KPS, Inc.
Court of Appeals of North Carolina, 1994
113 N.C.App. 830, 440 S.E.2d 329
http://scholar.google.com/scholar_case?case=5950766689451603162&q=440+S.E.+2d+329&hl=en&as_sdt=2,34

FACTS The defendant, Burns, purchased a VCR at Kimbrell's of Sanford. At the time of sale, Burns signed a purchase money security agreement with Kimbrell's. However, Kimbrell's did not file a financing statement to perfect its purchase money security interest. Burns immediately pawned the VCR to KPS, Inc. After Burns defaulted on the security agreement, Kimbrell's filed suit in small claims court to recover the VCR. The magistrate entered judgment denying recovery. On appeal to the district court, the judgment was affirmed. Kimbrell's appeals.

DECISION Judgment reversed.

OPINION At the time the defendant purchased the VCR from Kimbrell's, he granted Kimbrell's a purchase money security

interest in the VCR. Since a VCR is a consumer good, Kimbrell's did not have to file a financing statement in order to perfect its purchase money security interest in the VCR—it automatically perfected. Therefore, when Burns defaulted on the purchase money security agreement, Kimbrell's became entitled to recover possession of the VCR.

INTERPRETATION A purchase money security interest in consumer goods, with the exception of motor vehicles, is perfected automatically on attachment.

CRITICAL THINKING QUESTION When, if ever, should the law make a security interest automatically perfected? Explain.

Temporary perfection

a security interest in
certificated securities,
instruments, and negotiable
documents is automatically
perfected for twenty days

Temporary Perfection [37-4d]

Security interests in certain types of collateral are automatically, but only temporarily, perfected. The UCC provides that a security interest in a certificated security, negotiable document, or instrument is perfected upon attachment for a period of twenty days. This provision, however, is applicable only to the extent that the security interest arises for new value given under an authenticated security agreement. A perfected security interest in a certificated security or an instrument also remains perfected for twenty days if the secured party delivers the security certificate or instrument to the debtor for the purpose of (1) sale or exchange or (2) presentation, collection, enforcement, renewal, or registration of transfer. After the temporary period expires, the security interest becomes unperfected unless it is perfected by other means.

Perfection by Control [37-4e]

Control

may be used to perfect a
security interest in
electronic chattel paper,
investment property,
nonconsumer deposit
accounts, and letter-of-
credit rights

A security interest in investment property, deposit accounts (not including consumer deposit accounts), electronic chattel paper, and letter-of-credit rights may be perfected by **control** of the collateral. A security interest in deposit accounts and letter-of-credit rights may be perfected *only* by control. What constitutes control varies with the type of collateral involved. For example, control of a commercial deposit account (e.g., a checking account) is acquired if (1) the secured party is the bank with which the checking account is maintained or (2) the debtor, secured party, and bank agree in an authenticated record that the bank will comply with the secured party's instructions. The rules for control for other collateral are somewhat different as provided in the following sections: investment property, electronic chattel paper, and letter-of-credit rights.

CONCEPT REVIEW 37-1

Applicable Method of Perfection

Collateral	Filing	Possession	Automatic	Temporary (for 20 days)	Control
Goods					
Consumer goods	•	•	PMSI		
Farm products	•	•			
Inventory	•	•			
Equipment	•	•			
Fixtures	•	•			
Indispensable Paper					
Chattel paper	•	Tangible			Electronic
Instruments	•	•		•	
Documents	Negotiable	Negotiable		Negotiable	
Investment property	•	Certificated		Certificated	•
Intangibles					
Accounts	•		Isolated Assignment		
General intangibles	•				
Deposit Accounts					Commercial
Letter-of-Credit Accounts					•
Money		•			

Note: PMSI = purchase money security interest.

CONCEPT REVIEW 37-2

Requisites for Enforceability of Security Interests

Attachment	Perfection
A. Value given by secured party	A. Secured party files a financing statement
B. Debtor has rights in collateral	B. Secured party takes possession
C. Agreement	C. Automatically
1. record authenticated by debtor (except for most pledges)	D. Temporarily, or
2. providing a security interest	E. Control
3. in described collateral	

PRIORITIES AMONG COMPETING INTERESTS [37-5]

Priority
precedence in order of
right to collateral

As previously noted, a security interest must be perfected to be most effective against the debtor's other creditors, her trustee in bankruptcy, and her transferees. Nonetheless, perfection of a security interest does *not* provide the secured party with a **priority** over *all* third parties with an interest in the collateral. On the other hand, even an unperfected but attached security interest has priority over a limited number of third parties and is enforceable against the debtor. Article 9 establishes a complex set of rules that determine the relative priorities among these parties.

Against Unsecured Creditors [37-5a]

Once a security interest *attaches*, it has priority over claims of other creditors who do not have a security interest or a lien. This priority does not depend upon perfection. If a security interest does not attach, the creditor is merely an unsecured or general creditor of the debtor.

Against Other Secured Creditors [37-5b]

The rights of a secured creditor against other secured creditors depend upon the security interests perfected, when they are perfected, and the type of collateral. Notwithstanding the rules of priority, a secured party entitled to priority may subordinate her interest to that of another secured creditor. The parties may do this by agreement, and nothing need be filed.

Perfected Versus Unperfected   A creditor with a perfected security interest or agricultural lien has superior rights in the collateral than a creditor with an unperfected security interest or agricultural lien, whether or not the unperfected security interest has attached.

Practical Advice

If perfecting by filing, file your financing statement as soon as possible.

Perfected Versus Perfected   Two parties each having a perfected security interest or agricultural lien rank according to priority in *time of filing* or *perfection*. This general rule is stated in the UCC, which provides:

> Conflicting perfected security interests and agricultural liens rank according to priority in time of filing or perfection. Priority dates from the earlier of the time a filing covering the collateral is first made or the security interest or agricultural lien is first perfected, if there is no period thereafter when there is neither filing nor perfection.

Practical Advice

Before accepting personal property as collateral, check the public records to ensure that there are no prior filings against that property.

This rule favors filing, because it can occur prior to attachment and thus grant priority from a time that may precede perfection. Generally, the original time for filing or perfection of a security interest in collateral is also the time of filing or perfection for a security interest in proceeds from that collateral.

For example, Debter Store and Leynder Bank enter into a loan agreement (assume there is no binding commitment to extend credit) under the terms of which Leynder agrees to lend $5,000 on the security of Debter's existing store equipment. A security agreement is executed and a financing statement is filed, but no funds are advanced. One week later, Debter enters into a loan agreement with Reserve Bank, and Reserve agrees to lend $5,000 on the security of the same store equipment.

The funds are advanced, a security agreement is executed, and a financing statement is filed. One week later, Leynder Bank advances the agreed sum of $5,000. Debter Store defaults on both loans. Between Leynder Bank and Reserve Bank, Leynder has priority because priority among security interests perfected by filing is determined by the order in which they were filed. Reserve Bank should have checked the financing statements on file. Had it done so, it would have discovered that Leynder Bank claimed a security interest in the equipment. Conversely, after filing its financing statement, with no prior secured party of record, Leynder had no need to check the files before advancing funds to Debter Store in accordance with its loan commitment.

To further illustrate, assume that Marc grants a security interest in a Chagall painting to Miro Bank and that the bank advances funds to Marc in accordance with the loan agreement. A financing statement is filed. Later, Marc wants more money and goes to Brague, an art dealer, who advances funds to Marc upon a pledge of the painting. Marc defaults on both loans. Between Miro and Brague, Miro has priority because its financing statement was filed before Brague's perfection by possession. By checking the financing statement on file, Brague would have discovered that Miro had a prior security interest in the painting.

There are several exceptions to the general rules just discussed:

1. A *PMSI in noninventory goods* (except livestock) takes priority over a conflicting security interest if the PMSI is perfected when the debtor receives possession of the collateral or within twenty days of receiving possession. Thus, the secured party has a twenty-day grace period in which to perfect.

   For example, Dawkins Manufacturing Co. enters into a loan contract with Larkin Bank, which loans money to Dawkins on the security (as provided in the security agreement) of Dawkins's existing and future equipment and files a financing statement stating that the collateral is "all equipment presently owned and subsequently acquired" by Dawkins. At a later date, Dawkins buys new equipment from Parker Supply Co., paying 25 percent of the purchase price, with Parker retaining a security interest (as provided in the security agreement) in the equipment to secure the remaining balance. If Parker files a financing statement within ten days of Dawkins's obtaining possession of the equipment, Parker's PMSI in the new equipment purchased from Parker has priority over Larkin's interest. If, however, Parker files one day beyond the statutory grace period, Parker's interest is subordinate to Larkin's.

2. A *PMSI in inventory* has priority over earlier-filed security interests in inventory if the following four requirements are met: (a) The purchase money security holder must perfect his interest in the inventory at the time the debtor receives the inventory; (b) the purchase money security holder must send an authenticated notification to the holder of a conflicting security interest; (c) the holder of the conflicting security interest receives the notification within five years before the debtor receives possession of the inventory; and (d) the notification states that the person sending the notification has or will acquire a PMSI in inventory of the debtor and describes the inventory.

   For example, Dodger Store and Lyons Bank enter into a loan agreement in which Lyons agrees to finance Dodger's entire inventory of stoves, refrigerators, and other kitchen appliances. A security agreement is executed and a financing statement is filed, and Lyons advances funds to Dodger. Subsequently, Dodger enters into an agreement under which Rodger Stove Co. will supply Dodger with stoves, retaining a PMSI in this inventory. Rodger will have priority as to the inventory it supplies to Dodger provided that Rodger files a financing statement by the time Dodger receives the goods and notifies Lyons that it is going to engage in this purchase money financing of the described stoves. If Rodger fails either to give the required notice or to file timely a financing statement, Lyons will have priority over Rodger as to the stoves Rodger supplies to Dodger. As noted, the UCC adopts a system of notice filing, and secured parties who fail to check the financing statements on file proceed at their peril.

3. A *security interest perfected by control* in deposit accounts, letter-of-credit rights, or investment property has priority over a conflicting perfected security interest held by a secured party who does not have control. If both conflicting security interests are perfected by control, they rank according to priority in time of obtaining control.

Unperfected Versus Unperfected If neither security interest or agricultural lien is perfected, then the first to attach has priority. If neither attaches, both of the creditors are general, unsecured creditors.

Against Buyers [37-5c]

A security interest or agricultural lien continues even in collateral that is sold, leased, licensed, exchanged, or otherwise disposed of unless the secured party authorizes the sale. Thus, following a sale, lease, license, exchange, or other disposition of collateral, a secured party who did not authorize the transaction does not have to file a new financing statement to continue her perfected interest. The security interest also attaches to any identifiable proceeds from the sale, including proceeds in consumer deposit accounts.

In many instances, however, buyers of collateral sold without the secured party's authorization take it free of an unperfected security interest. A buyer of goods, tangible chattel paper, documents, instruments, or certificated securities who gives value and receives delivery of the collateral without knowledge of the security interest and does so *before* it is perfected takes free of the security interest. Similarly, a buyer of accounts, electronic chattel paper, general intangibles, or investment property other than certificated securities takes free of a security interest if the buyer gives value without knowledge of the security interest and does so *before* it is perfected. Thus, with respect to all of these types of collateral, an unperfected security interest prevails over a buyer who does *not* give value or has *knowledge* of the security interest.

In addition, in some instances, purchasers take the collateral free of a perfected security interest. The most significant of these instances are discussed here.

Buyers in the Ordinary Course of Business A buyer in the ordinary course of business takes collateral (other than farm products) free of any security interest created by *the buyer's* seller, even if the security interest is perfected and the buyer *knows* of its existence. A **buyer in the ordinary course of business** is a person who, without knowledge that the sale violates a security interest of a third party, buys in good faith and in ordinary course from a person in the business of selling goods of that kind. Thus, this rule applies primarily to purchasers of inventory. For example, a consumer who purchases a sofa from a furniture dealer and the dealer who purchases the sofa from another dealer are both buyers in the ordinary course of business. On the other hand, a person who purchases a sofa from a dentist who used the sofa in his waiting room or from an individual who used the sofa in his home is not a buyer in the ordinary course of business.

To illustrate further, a person who in the ordinary course of business buys an automobile from an automobile dealership will take free and clear of a security interest created by the dealer from whom she purchased the car. That same buyer in the ordinary course of business will not, however, take clear of a security interest created by any person who owned the automobile prior to the dealer.

Buyers of Farm Products Buyers in the ordinary course of business of farm products, although not protected by the UCC, may be protected by the Federal Food Security Act. This Act defines a buyer in the ordinary course of business as "a person who, in the ordinary course of business, buys farm products from a person engaged in farming operations who is in the business of selling farm products." The Act provides that such a buyer shall take free of most security interests created by the seller, even if the security interest is perfected and the buyer knows of its existence.

Buyers of Consumer Goods In the case of consumer goods, a buyer who buys without knowledge of a security interest, for value, and primarily for personal, family, or household purposes takes the goods free of any PMSI *automatically* perfected but takes the goods subject to a security interest perfected by filing. For example, Ann purchases on credit a refrigerator from Sean for use in her home and grants Sean a security interest in the refrigerator. Sean does not file a financing statement but has a security interest perfected by attachment. Ann subsequently sells the refrigerator to her neighbor, Juwan, for use in his home. Juwan does not know of Sean's security interest and therefore takes the refrigerator free of that interest. If Sean had filed a financing statement, however, his security interest would continue in the collateral, even in Juwan's hands.

Buyer in the ordinary course of business

a person who buys from a merchant in good faith and in ordinary course, without knowledge that the sale violates a security interest

Buyers of Other Collateral   To the extent provided by UCC Articles 3, 7, and 8, a secured party who has a perfected security interest in a negotiable instrument, a negotiable document of title, or a security has a *subordinate* interest to a purchaser of (1) the instrument who has the rights of a holder in due course, (2) the document of title to whom it has been duly negotiated, or (3) the security who is a protected purchaser. In addition, in certain instances, a secured party who has a perfected security interest in chattel paper also may have subordinate rights to a purchaser of such collateral.

Against Lien Creditors [37-5d]

Lien creditor

a creditor who has acquired a lien on property by attachment

Trustee in bankruptcy

representative of an estate in bankruptcy who is responsible for collecting, liquidating, and distributing the debtor's assets

A **lien creditor** is a creditor who has acquired a lien in the property by judicial decree ("attachment garnishment, or the like"), an assignee for the benefit of creditors, a receiver in equity, or a trustee in bankruptcy. (A **trustee in bankruptcy** is a representative of an estate in bankruptcy who is responsible for collecting, liquidating, and distributing the debtor's assets.) Whereas a *perfected* security interest or agricultural lien has priority over lien creditors who acquire their liens after perfection, an *unperfected* security interest or agricultural lien is subordinate to the rights of one who becomes a lien creditor before (1) its perfection or (2) a financing statement covering the collateral is filed and either (a) the debtor has authenticated a properly drawn security agreement; (b) if the collateral is a certificated security, the certificate has been delivered to the secured party; or (c) if the collateral is an uncertificated security, it is in possession of the secured party. If a secured party files with respect to a *PMSI* within twenty days after the debtor receives possession of the collateral, however, the secured party takes priority over the rights of a lien creditor that arise between the time the security interest attaches and the time of filing. Nonetheless, a lien securing claims arising from services or materials furnished in the ordinary course of a person's business with respect to goods (an artisan's or mechanic's lien) has priority over a security interest in the goods unless the lien is created by a statute that expressly provides otherwise.

Against Trustee in Bankruptcy [37-5e]

The Bankruptcy Code empowers a trustee in bankruptcy to invalidate secured claims in certain instances. It also imposes some limitations on the rights of secured parties. This section will examine the power of a trustee in bankruptcy to (1) take priority over an unperfected security interest and (2) avoid preferential transfers.

Priority over Unperfected Security Interest   A trustee in bankruptcy may invalidate any security interest that is voidable by a creditor who obtained a judicial lien on the date the bankruptcy petition was filed. Under the UCC and the Bankruptcy Code, the trustee, as a hypothetical *lien creditor*, has priority over a creditor whose security interest was not perfected when the bankruptcy petition was filed. A creditor with a PMSI who files within the UCC's statutory grace period of twenty days after the debtor receives the collateral will defeat the trustee, even if the bankruptcy petition is filed before the creditor perfects and after the security interest is created. For example, David borrowed $5,000 from Cynthia on September 1 and gave her a security interest in the equipment he purchased with the borrowed funds. On October 3, before Cynthia perfected her security interest, David filed for bankruptcy. The trustee in bankruptcy can invalidate Cynthia's security interest because it was unperfected when the bankruptcy petition was filed. If, however, David had filed for bankruptcy on September 8 and Cynthia had perfected the security interest within the UCC's statutory grace period of twenty days, Cynthia would prevail.

Avoidance of Preferential Transfers   The Bankruptcy Code provides that a trustee in bankruptcy may invalidate any transfer of property—including the granting of a security interest—from the debtor, provided that the transfer (1) was to or for the benefit of a creditor; (2) was made on account of an antecedent debt; (3) was made when the debtor was insolvent; (4) was made on the date of or within ninety days before the filing of the bankruptcy petition or, if made to an insider, was made within one year before the date of the filing; and (5) enabled the transferee to receive more than he would have received in bankruptcy. (An insider includes a relative or general partner of a debtor, as well as a partnership in which the debtor is a general partner or a corporation of which the debtor is a director, officer, or person in control.) In determining whether the debtor is insolvent, the Bankruptcy Code establishes a rebuttable presumption of insolvency for the ninety days prior to the filing of the bankruptcy petition. To avoid a transfer to an insider that occurred more than one year before bankruptcy, the trustee must prove that the debtor was insolvent when the transfer was made. If a security interest is invalidated as a preferential transfer, the creditor may still make a claim for the unpaid debt, but the creditor's claim is unsecured.

To illustrate the operation of this rule, consider the following. On May 1, Debra bought and received merchandise from Stuart and gave him a security interest in the goods for the unpaid price of $20,000. On June 5, Stuart filed a financing statement. On August 1, Debra filed a petition for bankruptcy. The trustee in bankruptcy may avoid the perfected security interest as a preferential transfer because (1) the transfer of the perfected security interest on June 5 was to benefit a creditor (Stuart); (2) the transfer was on account of an antecedent debt (the $20,000 owed from the sale of the merchandise); (3) the debtor was insolvent at the time (the Bankruptcy Code presumes that the debtor is insolvent for the ninety days preceding the date the bankruptcy petition was filed—August 1); (4) the transfer was made within ninety days of bankruptcy (June 5 is less than ninety days before August 1); and (5) the transfer enabled the creditor to receive more than he would have received in bankruptcy (Stuart would have a secured claim on which he would recover more than he would on an unsecured claim).

Nevertheless, not all transfers made within ninety days of bankruptcy are voidable. As amended in 2005, the Bankruptcy Code makes exceptions for certain prebankruptcy transfers. If the creditor gives the debtor new value that the debtor uses to acquire property in which he grants the creditor a security interest, the resulting PMSI is not voidable if the creditor perfects it within thirty days after the debtor receives possession of the property. For example, if within ninety days of the filing of the petition, the debtor purchases a refrigerator on credit and grants the seller or lender a PMSI in the refrigerator, the transfer of that interest is not voidable if the secured party perfects within thirty days after the debtor receives possession of the property.

See Concept Review 37-3 for a summary of the rules of priorities.

CONCEPT REVIEW 37-3

Priorities

Versus	Unsecured Creditor	Creditor with Unperfected Security Interest	Creditor with Perfected Security Interest	Creditor with Perfected PMSI
Unsecured creditor	=	↑	↑	↑
Creditor with unperfected security interest	←	first to attach	↑	↑
Creditor with perfected security interest	←	←	first to file or perfect	↑ if PMSI perfected within grace period
Creditor with perfected PMSI	←	←	first to file or perfect	↑ if PMSI gives notice and perfects by time debtor gets possession
Buyer in ordinary course of business	←	←	← if created by immediate seller	←
Consumer buyer of consumer goods	←	←	←	← if not filed
Lien creditor (including trustee in bankruptcy)	←	←	first in time	first in time but PMSI has grace period
Trustee in bankruptcy—voidable preferences	←	←	↑ if secured party perfects when credit extended	↑ if PMSI perfects within 30 days

Note: PMSI = purchase money security interest.

BUSINESS LAW **IN ACTION**

Like many businesses, Birdwell Industrial has an operating line of credit with a bank. In addition to personal guaranties signed by Birdwell's owners, the revolving loan is collateralized by a security interest in all of Birdwell's accounts receivable, inventory, and business equipment, as well as any after-acquired property in which Birdwell may later obtain rights. The bank's lien was properly perfected.

Some time later Birdwell purchased a new telephone system for its offices, costing nearly $4,500. The telephone vendor agreed to extend credit, but only if Birdwell would grant a security interest in the telephone system until the purchase money was paid in full. Birdwell agreed, and this lien was perfected shortly after the security interest was signed and just before the equipment was delivered to Birdwell.

By granting a "purchase money security interest" in the telephone system to the vendor, Birdwell has given two liens in the same collateral. This is because by definition the telephone system is "after-acquired property," subject to the bank's preexisting security interest. In the event of Birdwell's bankruptcy or default on either creditor's loan, the two liens are competing for the same collateral. Which creditor will have a superior right to the telephone system must be determined by reference to Article 9's priority rules, which provide that a purchase money security interest in *noninventory* goods takes priority over a conflicting security interest if the purchase money security interest is perfected when the debtor receives possession of the collateral *or* within twenty days of receiving possession.

In this case, the vendor timely perfected its lien and therefore will prevail.

The rules awarding a superior interest in the collateral to one who grants credit for purchase money serve two related purposes. First, they prevent a single creditor, such as the bank in this case, from cutting off all future sources of credit for the debtor and thereby preventing the debtor from obtaining additional inventory or equipment that is needed to maintain a viable business. Second, they make it possible for a later supplier to have the first claim against only the goods it supplied and only until the purchase price is fully paid. This way, earlier creditors are protected, but not at the expense of subsequent creditors, whose purchase money enables the debtor to maintain its business and eventually to pay off all creditors.

DEFAULT [37-6]

Practical Advice

Provide in your security agreement which events place the debtor in default and what remedies the creditor will have in the event of default.

Redemption

freeing the collateral of the security interest by paying off the loan

Repossession of collateral

the secured party may take possession of the collateral on default without judicial process if it can be done without a breach of the peace

Because the UCC does not define or specify what constitutes default, general contract law or the agreement between the parties will determine when a default occurs. After default, the security agreement and the applicable provisions of the UCC govern the rights and remedies of the parties. In general, the secured party may reduce his claim to judgment, foreclose, or otherwise enforce the claim, security interest, or agricultural lien by any available judicial procedure. If the collateral consists of documents, the secured party may proceed against the documents or the goods they cover. These rights and remedies of the creditor are cumulative.

Unless the debtor has waived his rights in the collateral after default, he has a right of **redemption** (to free the collateral of the security interest by fulfilling all obligations securing the collateral and paying reasonable expenses and attorneys' fees) at any time before the secured party has collected the collateral, has disposed of the collateral, has entered a contract to dispose of it, or has discharged the obligation by accepting the collateral.

Repossession of Collateral [37-6a]

Unless the parties have agreed otherwise, the secured party may take possession of the collateral on default. If it can be done without a breach of the peace, such taking may occur without judicial process. The UCC leaves the term *breach of the peace* for the courts to define. Some states have defined such a breach to require either the use of violence or the threat of violence while others require merely an entry without consent. Most states require permission for entry to a residence or garage. On the other hand, the courts do permit the repossession of motor vehicles from driveways or streets. Some courts, however, do not permit a creditor to repossess if the debtor has orally protested the repossession.

After default, instead of removing the collateral, the secured party may render it unusable and leave it on the debtor's premises until disposing of it. Repossession also may be done without judicial process if accomplished without a breach of peace.

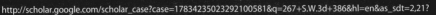

Chapa v. Traciers & Associates
Court of Appeals of Texas, Houston (14th Dist.), 2008
267 S.W.3d 386, 66 UCC Rep.Serv.2d 451
http://scholar.google.com/scholar_case?case=17834235023292100581&q=267+S.W.3d+386&hl=en&as_sdt=2,21?

FACTS Ford Motor Credit Corp. (FMCC) hired Traciers & Associates (Traciers) to repossess a white 2002 Ford Expedition owned by Marissa Chapa, who was in default on her loan. Traciers assigned the job to its field manager, Paul Chambers, and gave him an address where the vehicle could be found. FMCC, Traciers, and Chambers were unaware that the address was that of Marissa's brother, Carlos Chapa. Coincidentally, Carlos and his wife Maria Chapa also had purchased a white Ford Expedition financed by FMCC. Their vehicle, however, was a 2003 model, and Carlos and Maria were not in default. On the night of February 6, 2003, Chambers went to the address and observed a white Ford Expedition. The license number of the vehicle did not match that of the vehicle he was told to repossess, and he did not see the vehicle's vehicle identification number (VIN), which was obscured. Chambers returned early the next morning and still could not see the Expedition's VIN. He returned to his own vehicle, which was parked two houses away. Unseen by Chambers, Maria Chapa left the house and helped her two sons, ages ten and six, into the Expedition for the trip to school. Her mother-in-law's vehicle was parked behind her, so Maria backed her mother-in-law's vehicle into the street, then backed her Expedition out of the driveway and parked on the street. She left the keys to her car in the ignition with the motor running while she parked her mother-in-law's car back in the driveway and reentered the house to return her mother-in-law's keys. After Chambers saw Maria park the Expedition on the street and return to the house, it took him only thirty seconds to back his tow truck to the Expedition, hook it to his truck, and drive away. Chambers did not know the Chapa children were inside. When Maria emerged from the house, the Expedition, with her children, was gone. Maria began screaming, telephoned 911, and called her husband at work to tell him the children were gone. Shortly after taking the car, Chambers noticed that the Expedition's wheels were turning, indicating to him that the vehicle's engine was running. He stopped the tow truck and heard a sound from the Expedition. Looking inside, he discovered the two Chapa children. After he persuaded one of the boys to unlock the vehicle, Chambers drove the Expedition back to the Chapas's house. He returned the keys to Maria, who was outside her house, crying. By the time emergency personnel and Carlos Chapa arrived, the children were back home and Chambers had left the scene.

The Chapas filed suit against the financing company, the repossession company it hired, and the repossession agent who towed the vehicle. They asserted claims for mental anguish and its physical manifestations as a result of Chambers's breach of the peace. The trial court granted the defendants' motion for summary judgment.

DECISION The trial court's decision is affirmed.

OPINION The Chapas first argue that the trial court erred in granting summary judgment against them on their claim that the defendants are liable under UCC Section 9-609. This section provides in pertinent part:

(a) After default, a secured party:
   (1) may take possession of the collateral;
   (b) A secured party may proceed under Subsection (a):
   …
   (2) without judicial process, if it proceeds without breach of the peace.

This statute imposes a duty on secured creditors to take precautions for public safety when repossessing property. Thus, the creditor who elects to pursue nonjudicial repossession assumes the risk that a breach of the peace might occur. A secured creditor "remains liable for breaches of the peace committed by its independent contractor." Thus, a creditor cannot escape liability by hiring an independent contractor to repossess secured property.

Most frequently, the expression "breach of the peace" as used in the UCC "connotes conduct that incites or is likely to incite immediate public turbulence, or that leads to or is likely to lead to an immediate loss of public order and tranquility." In addition, "[b]reach of the peace … refers to conduct at or near and/or incident to seizure of property."

Here, there is no evidence that Chambers proceeded with the attempted repossession over an objection communicated to him at, near, or incident to the seizure of the property. To the contrary, Chambers immediately "desisted" repossession efforts and peaceably returned the vehicle and the children when he learned of their presence. Moreover, Chambers actively avoided confrontation. By removing an apparently unoccupied vehicle from a public street when the driver was not present, he reduced the likelihood of violence or other public disturbance.

In sum, the Chapas have not identified and the court has not found any case in which the repossession of a vehicle from a public street, without objection or confrontation, has been held to constitute a breach of the peace. The court therefore concluded that Chambers's conduct did not violate a duty imposed by UCC Section 9-609.

INTERPRETATION A secured party may take possession of the collateral on default without judicial process if it can be done without a breach of the peace.

ETHICAL QUESTION Did the court fairly decide this case? Explain.

CRITICAL THINKING QUESTION Is it important for creditors to have the right to repossess? Explain why or why not.

Sale of collateral

the secured party may sell, lease, license, or otherwise dispose of any collateral

Sale of Collateral [37-6b]

The secured party may sell, lease, license, or otherwise dispose of any collateral in its existing condition at the time of default or following any commercially reasonable preparation or processing. A secured party's disposition of the collateral after default (1) transfers to a transferee for value all of the debtor's rights in the collateral, (2) discharges the security interest under which the disposition occurred, and (3) discharges any subordinate security interests and liens.

The collateral may be disposed of at public sale (auction) or private sale, so long as all aspects of the disposition, including its method, manner, time, place, and other terms, are "commercially reasonable." The secured party may buy at a public sale and at a private sale if the collateral is customarily sold in a recognized market or is the subject of widely distributed standard price quotations. The collateral, if it is commercially reasonable, may be disposed of by one or more contracts or as a unit or in parcels. The UCC favors private sales since they generally garner a higher price for the collateral. The fact that the secured party could have received a greater amount is not of itself sufficient to establish that the sale was not made in a commercially reasonable manner. Unless the collateral is perishable or threatens to decline speedily in value or is of a type customarily sold on a recognized market, the secured party must send a reasonable authenticated notification of disposition to the debtor, any secondary obligor (surety or guarantor), and, except in the case of consumer goods, other parties who have sent an authenticated notice of a claim, or any secured party or lienholder who has filed a financing statement at least ten days before the notification date.

The UCC provides that the proceeds from the sale of the collateral are to be applied in the following order:

1. paying the reasonable expenses of retaking and disposing of the collateral,
2. paying the debt owed to the secured party,
3. paying any subordinate interests in the collateral, and
4. paying a secured party that is a consignor.

The debtor is entitled to any *surplus* and is liable for any *deficiency*, except in the case of a sale of accounts, chattel paper, payment intangibles, or promissory notes for which he is neither entitled nor liable unless the security agreement so provides. If the goods are consumer goods, the secured party must give the debtor an explanation of how the surplus or deficiency was calculated.

Acceptance of Collateral [37-6c]

Acceptance of collateral
the secured party, unless the debtor objects, may retain the collateral in full or partial satisfaction of the obligation (with the exception of the compulsory disposition of some consumer goods)

Acceptance of collateral (strict foreclosure) is a way for a secured party to acquire the debtor's interests without the need for a sale or other disposition. The secured party may, after default and repossession if the debtor consents in a record authenticated after default, keep the collateral in full or partial satisfaction of the obligation. In addition, the secured party may accept the collateral in *full* satisfaction of the obligation if she sends an unconditional proposal to the debtor to accept the collateral in full satisfaction of the obligation and if she does not receive a notice of objection authenticated by the debtor within twenty days. If there is an objection, however, the secured party must dispose of the collateral as provided in the UCC. Silence is not consent to a *partial* satisfaction of the obligation. The debtor's consent, however, will not permit the secured party to accept the collateral in satisfaction of the obligation if a person holding a junior interest (secured party or lienholder) lodges a proper objection to the proposal.

In the case of *consumer goods*, if the debtor has paid 60 percent or more of the obligation, the secured party who has taken possession of the collateral must dispose of it by sale within ninety days after repossession unless the debtor and all secondary obligors have agreed in a record authenticated after default to a longer period of time. Additionally, with a consumer debt, the secured party may not accept collateral in *partial* satisfaction of the obligation it secures.

The acceptance of collateral in full or partial satisfaction discharges the obligation to the extent consented to by the debtor, transfers all of the debtor's rights to the secured party, and terminates all subordinate interests in the collateral.

SURETYSHIP

In many business transactions, especially those involving the extension of credit, the creditor will require that someone in addition to the principal debtor promise to fulfill the

Secondary obligor

one who is obligated to perform the underlying obligation of the principal debtor if the principal debtor fails to perform

obligation. This **secondary obligor**, generally is known as a surety, is obligated to perform all or part of the underlying obligation of the principal debtor if the principal debtor fails to perform.

In a contract involving a minor, a surety commonly acts as a party with full contractual capacity who can be held responsible for the obligations arising from the contract. Sureties are often used in addition to security interests to further reduce the risks involved in the extension of credit and are used instead of security interests when security is unavailable or when the use of a secured transaction is too expensive or inconvenient. Employers frequently use sureties to protect against losses caused by employees' embezzlement, and property owners use sureties to bond the performance of contracts for the construction of commercial buildings. Similarly, statutes commonly require that contracts for work to be done for government entities have the added protection of a surety.

Suretyship is governed primarily by state common law. A comprehensive presentation of this law is found in the Restatement of the Law Third, Suretyship and Guaranty, published in 1996 by the American Law Institute. Regarded as a valuable authoritative reference work, it is cited extensively and quoted in reported judicial opinions. The rest of this chapter will refer to the Restatement of the Law Third, Suretyship and Guaranty as the Restatement.

NATURE AND FORMATION [37-7]

A secondary obligor (*surety*) promises to perform an underlying obligation owed to one person (called the *creditor*) by another (the *principal debtor*) on the principal debtor's *failure* to perform the obligation. Thus, the suretyship relationship involves three parties—the principal debtor, the creditor, and the surety—and three relationships, as illustrated by Figure 37-2.

1. *Relationship between the principal debtor and the creditor.* The creditor's rights against the principal debtor are determined by the underlying contract between them. The creditor also may take action on any collateral that the creditor or the surety holds to secure the principal debtor's performance.
2. *Relationship between the surety and the creditor.* Based on the suretyship contract, the creditor may proceed against the surety if the principal debtor defaults.
3. *Relationship between the surety and the principal debtor.* Based on the law of suretyship, a surety has rights against the principal debtor, including exoneration, reimbursement, and subrogation (see Figure 37-2). These rights of sureties, which may be modified by agreement, will be discussed later in this chapter.

Guarantor

secondary obligor who is liable to a creditor immediately upon the default of the principal debtor

Types of Sureties [37-7a]

The Restatement provides that if the secondary obligor is identified as a **guarantor**, the creditor may hold the guarantor liable as soon as the principal debtor defaults. The creditor need not proceed first against the principal debtor. In contrast, a secondary obligor who is identified as

Figure 37-2 Suretyship Relationship

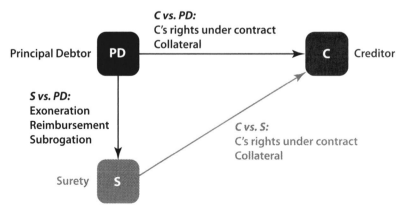

Guarantor of collection
secondary obligor who is liable to creditor only after creditor exhausts his legal remedies against the principal debtor

Surety
secondary obligor who is jointly and severally liable with the principal debtor to perform the underlying obligation

Cosureties
two or more secondary obligors who are bound for the same debt of a principal debtor

---

Practical Advice

If you sell your house and the purchaser assumes the mortgage, recognize that you are a surety and are liable to the lender if the purchaser defaults on the mortgage.

---

a **guarantor of collection** is liable only when the creditor exhausts his legal remedies against the principal debtor. Thus, a conditional guarantor of collection is liable if the creditor first obtains, but is unable to collect, a judgment against the principal debtor. A secondary obligor who is identified as a **surety** is jointly and severally liable with the principal debtor to perform the obligation set forth in the contract. Two or more secondary obligors bound for the same debt of a principal debtor are **cosureties**.

Although a distinction exists between a surety and a guarantor, these two secondary obligors are governed by the Restatement. For convenience, and because the rights and duties of a surety and a guarantor are almost indistinguishable, the term surety will be used to include both of these secondary obligors.

Particular Kinds of Suretyships [37-7b]

Creditors frequently use a suretyship arrangement to reduce the risk of default by their debtors. For example, Philco Developers, a closely held corporation, applies to Caldwell Bank, a lending institution, for a loan. After scrutinizing Philco's assets and financial prospects, the lender refuses to extend credit unless Simpson, Philco's sole shareholder, promises to repay the loan if Philco does not. Simpson agrees, and Caldwell Bank makes the loan. Simpson's undertaking is that of a surety. Similarly, Philco Developers wishes to purchase goods on credit from Bird Enterprises, the seller, who agrees to extend credit only if Philco Developers obtains an acceptable surety. Simpson agrees to pay Bird Enterprises for the goods if Philco Developers does not. Simpson is a surety. In each of these examples, the surety's promise gives the creditor recourse for payment against two persons—the principal debtor and the surety—instead of one, thereby reducing the creditor's risk of loss.

Another common suretyship relation arises when an owner of property subject to a mortgage sells the property to a purchaser who *assumes the mortgage*. Although by assuming the obligation, the purchaser becomes the principal debtor and therefore personally obligated to pay the seller's debt to the lender, the seller nevertheless remains liable to the lender and is a surety on the obligation the purchaser has assumed (see Figure 37-3).

However, a purchaser who does *not* assume the mortgage, but simply takes the property subject to the mortgage, is *not* personally liable for the mortgage; nor is he a surety for the mortgage obligation. In this case, the purchaser's potential loss is limited to the value of the property, for although the mortgagee creditor may foreclose against the property, she may not hold the purchaser personally liable for the debt.

In addition, there are numerous specialized kinds of suretyship, the most important of which are (1) fidelity, (2) performance, (3) official, and (4) judicial. A surety undertakes a ***fidelity bond*** to protect an employer against employee dishonesty. ***Performance bonds*** guarantee the performance of the terms and conditions of a contract. These bonds are used frequently in the construction industry to protect an owner from losses that may result from a contractor's failure to complete the construction in accordance with the construction contract. Statutes of the United States and of most states require performance bonds for construction contracts with government entities. ***Official bonds*** arise from statutes requiring public officers to furnish bonds for the

Figure 37-3 Assumption of Mortgage

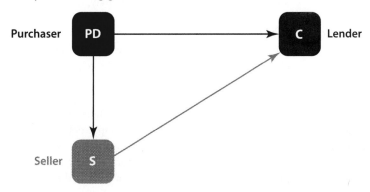

faithful performance of their duties. Such bonds obligate a surety for all losses an officer causes through negligence or through nonperformance of her duties. *Judicial bonds*, including attachment bonds, injunction bonds, and appeal bonds, represent a guaranty that the party required to furnish the bond will fulfill all of her obligations in connection with an aspect of the litigation process. In criminal proceedings, the purpose of a judicial bond, called a **bail bond**, is to ensure the appearance of the defendant in court.

Formation [37-7c]

Formation

the promise of the surety must satisfy all the elements of a contract and must also be in writing

The suretyship relationship is contractual and must satisfy all of the usual elements of a contract. No particular words are required to constitute a contract of suretyship or guaranty.

As discussed in Chapter 15, under the **statute of frauds**, the contractual promise of a surety to the creditor must be in writing to be enforceable. This requirement, which applies only to secondary or collateral promises, is subject to the exception known as the *main purpose doctrine*. Under this doctrine, if the leading object, or main purpose, of the promisor (surety) is to obtain an economic benefit that he did not previously enjoy, the promise is *not* within the statute of frauds.

The promise of a surety is *not* binding without consideration. Because the surety generally makes her promise to induce the creditor to confer a benefit on the principal debtor, the consideration that supports the principal debtor's promise usually supports the surety's promise as well. Thus, if Constance lends money to Philip on Sally's promise to act as a surety, Constance's extension of credit is the consideration to support not only Philip's promise to repay the loan but also Sally's suretyship undertaking. However, a surety's promise made *after* the principal debtor's receipt of the creditor's consideration must be supported by new consideration. Accordingly, if Constance has already sold goods on credit to Philip, a subsequent guaranty by Sally will not be binding unless new consideration is given.

Practical Advice

If you seek the additional security of a surety, obtain the surety's promise in writing. If you have already lent money to a debtor and then obtain a surety, new consideration must be given to the surety to make the promise binding.

DUTIES OF SURETY [37-8]

Duty of surety

upon default by the principal debtor, the creditor may proceed against the surety to enforce the surety's undertaking

Upon default by the principal debtor, the creditor may proceed against the surety to enforce the surety's undertaking or obligation. A surety or guarantor usually has *no* right to compel the creditor to collect from the principal debtor or to take action on collateral provided by the principal debtor. Nor is the creditor required to give the surety notice of the principal debtor's default unless the contract of suretyship provides otherwise. A guarantor of collection, on the other hand, has no liability until the creditor exhausts his legal remedies of collection against the principal debtor, including taking action on collateral provided by the principal debtor.

Up to the amount of each surety's undertaking, cosureties are *jointly and severally* liable for the principal debtor's default. The creditor may proceed against any or all of the **cosureties** and collect from any of them the amount that that surety has agreed to guarantee, up to and including the entire amount of the principal debtor's obligation.

Duty of cosurety

up to the amount of each surety's undertaking, cosureties are *jointly and severally* liable for the principal debtor's default

RIGHTS OF SURETY [37-9]

A surety whose principal debtor defaults has certain rights against the principal debtor, third parties, and cosureties. These rights include (1) exoneration, (2) reimbursement, (3) subrogation, and (4) contribution. These rights may, by agreement, be augmented, modified, or limited.

Exoneration [37-9a]

Exoneration

relief of surety's liability by requiring principal debtor to perform the underlying obligation

The ordinary expectation in a suretyship relation is that the principal debtor will perform the obligation and the surety will not be required to perform. Therefore, the surety has the right to require that her principal debtor perform the underlying obligation when that obligation is due. This right of the surety against the principal debtor, called the right of **exoneration**, is enforceable at equity. If the principal debtor fails to pay the creditor when the debt is due, the surety may obtain a decree ordering the principal debtor to pay the creditor. However, this remedy in no way affects the creditor's right to proceed against the surety. Unless otherwise agreed, collateral supplied by the principal debtor to secure the duty to reimburse the surety also secures the principal debtor's duty of exoneration owed to the surety.

A surety also has a right of exoneration against his cosureties. When the principal debtor's obligation becomes due, each surety owes every other cosurety the duty to pay her proportionate share of the principal debtor's obligation to the creditor. Accordingly, a surety may bring an action in equity to obtain an order requiring his cosureties to pay their share of the debt.

Reimbursement [37-9b]

Reimbursement
the right of a surety who has paid the creditor to be repaid by the principal debtor

When, on the default of the principal debtor, a surety pays the creditor, the surety has the right of **reimbursement** (repayment) against the principal debtor. This right arises, however, only when the surety actually has made payment and then applies only to the extent of the payment. Thus, a surety who advantageously negotiates a defaulted obligation and settles it at a compromise figure less than the original sum may recover from the principal debtor only the sum the surety actually paid, not the sum before negotiation. When collateral secures the obligations of the principal debtor to the surety, if the principal debtor fails to perform the duty of reimbursement, the surety can enforce her rights against the collateral.

Subrogation [37-9c]

Subrogation
surety's assumption of the creditor's rights

On payment of the principal debtor's *entire* obligation, the surety "steps into the shoes" of the creditor. Called **subrogation**, this confers on the surety all the rights the creditor has with respect to the underlying obligation. These include the creditor's rights

1. against the principal debtor, including the creditor's priorities with respect to those rights;
2. in collateral of the principal debtor, including the creditor's priorities with respect to that collateral;
3. against third parties, such as comakers, who also are obligated on the principal debtor's obligation; and
4. against cosureties.

Contribution [37-9d]

Contribution
payment from cosureties of their proportionate share

A surety who pays her principal debtor's obligation may require the cosureties to pay to her their proportionate shares of the obligation she paid. This right of **contribution** arises when a surety has paid more than her proportionate share of a debt, even though the cosureties originally were unaware of each other or were bound on separate instruments. They need be sureties only for the same principal debtor and the same obligation. The contractual agreement among the cosureties determines the right and extent of contribution for each. If no such agreement exists, sureties obligated for equal amounts share equally; when they are obligated for varying amounts, the proportion of the debt that each surety must contribute is determined by proration according to each surety's undertaking. For example, if X, Y, and Z are cosureties for PD to C in the amounts of $5,000, $10,000, and $15,000, respectively, which totals $30,000, then X's share of the total is one-sixth ($5,000/$30,000), Y's share is one-third ($10,000/$30,000), and Z's share is one-half ($15,000/$30,000).

DEFENSES OF SURETY AND PRINCIPAL DEBTOR [37-10]

The obligations the principal debtor and the surety owe to the creditor arise out of contracts. Accordingly, the usual contractual defenses apply, such as those that result from (1) the nonexistence of the principal debtor's obligation, (2) a discharge of the principal debtor's obligation, (3) a modification of the principal debtor's contract, or (4) a variation of the surety's risk. Some of these defenses are available only to the principal debtor, some only to the surety, and others to both parties (see Figure 37-4).

Personal Defenses of Principal Debtor [37-10a]

Personal defenses of principal debtor
defenses available only to the principal debtor: her incapacity, discharge in bankruptcy, and some setoffs

The defenses available *only* to a principal debtor are known as the **personal defenses of principal debtor**. For example, *incapacity* due to infancy or mental incompetency may serve as a defense for the principal debtor but *not* for the surety. If, however, the principal debtor disaffirms

Figure 37-4 Defenses of Surety and Principal Debtor

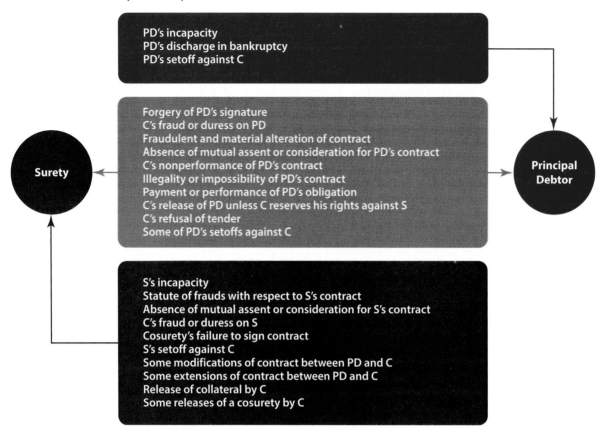

PD's incapacity
PD's discharge in bankruptcy
PD's setoff against C

Forgery of PD's signature
C's fraud or duress on PD
Fraudulent and material alteration of contract
Absence of mutual assent or consideration for PD's contract
C's nonperformance of PD's contract
Illegality or impossibility of PD's contract
Payment or performance of PD's obligation
C's release of PD unless C reserves his rights against S
C's refusal of tender
Some of PD's setoffs against C

Surety

Principal Debtor

S's incapacity
Statute of frauds with respect to S's contract
Absence of mutual assent or consideration for S's contract
C's fraud or duress on S
Cosurety's failure to sign contract
S's setoff against C
Some modifications of contract between PD and C
Some extensions of contract between PD and C
Release of collateral by C
Some releases of a cosurety by C

Note: C = Creditor; PD = Prinicipal Debtor; S = Surety.

the contract *and* returns the consideration he received from the creditor, the surety is discharged from his liability to the extent the value of the consideration equals the principal debtor's underlying obligation. A discharge of the principal debtor's obligation in bankruptcy does not discharge the surety's liability to the creditor on that obligation. The principal obligor may assert a claim against the creditor unrelated to the underlying obligation to the extent permitted under the law governing setoffs. Subject to several exceptions discussed later, the surety may *not* use as a setoff any unrelated claim that the principal debtor has against the creditor.

Personal Defenses of Surety [37-10b]

Personal defenses of surety

defenses available only to the surety, including her own incapacity, the statute of frauds, contract defenses to her suretyship undertaking, setoff, some modifications of the contract between the creditor and the principal debtor, and the creditor's release of collateral or a cosurety

Those defenses that only the surety may assert are called **personal defenses of surety**. They include defenses based on the surety's contract and those resulting from actions of the creditor after the formation of the surety's contract.

Surety's Contract The surety may use, as a defense, his own incapacity, noncompliance with the ***statute of frauds***, or the absence of mutual assent or consideration to support his obligation. ***Fraud*** (fraudulent or material misrepresentation) or ***duress*** practiced by the creditor on the surety is also a defense. Although, as a general rule, the creditor's nondisclosure of material facts to the surety is not fraud, there are two important exceptions. If a prospective surety requests information, the creditor must disclose it; the concealment of material facts will constitute fraud. Second, a creditor who (1) knows facts unknown to the surety that materially increase the surety's risk beyond that which the surety intends to assume and (2) has reason to believe the facts are unknown to the surety is under a duty to disclose this information; nondisclosure is considered fraud. Fraud on the part of the principal debtor may *not* be asserted against the creditor if the creditor is unaware of such fraud. Similarly, duress exerted by the principal debtor on the surety is not a defense against the creditor.

A surety is not liable if an intended cosurety, as named in the contract instrument, does not sign. A surety who has a claim against the creditor that is unrelated to the transaction giving rise to the surety's obligation may **set off** that claim against the surety's obligation.

American Manufacturing Mutual Insurance Company v. Tison Hog Market, Inc.
United States Court of Appeals, Eleventh Circuit, 1999
182 F.3d 1284, *cert. denied*, 531 U.S. 819, 121 S.Ct. 59, 148 L.Ed.2d 26 (2000)
http://scholar.google.com/scholar_case?case=13887389829730083003&q=182+F.3d+1284&hl=en&as_sdt=2,22

FACTS Every livestock dealer must execute and maintain a reasonable bond to secure the performance of its obligations. Thurston Paulk, doing business as Paulk Livestock Company (Paulk Livestock), and Coffee County Stockyard, Incorporated (Coffee County Livestock), both livestock dealers, applied to plaintiff American Manufacturing Mutual Insurance Company (American) to serve as a surety and issue bonds for them to meet their legal requirements. The applications for both bonds contained agreements to indemnify American for any losses that it might incur as a result of their issuance. The principal *debtor* on the first bond was Thurston Paulk, doing business as Paulk Livestock. The application was signed by Thurston Paulk in his role as the sole proprietor of Paulk Livestock. The indemnification agreement contained the purported signatures of Thurston Paulk and Betty Paulk. The principal *debtor* on the second bond was Coffee County Livestock. This application contained the signature of Thurston Paulk in his role as president of Coffee County Livestock and contained the purported signatures of Thurston Paulk, Betty Paulk, and Ashley Paulk.

After the bonds were issued, Paulk Livestock and Coffee County Livestock purchased numerous hogs from defendants Tison Hog Market, Inc.; Gainesville Livestock Market, Inc.; Townsend Livestock Market; South Carolina Farm Bureau Marketing Association; and Georgia Farm Bureau Marketing Association, Inc. When the defendant hog sellers did not receive payment for the hogs, they made claims against American on the surety bonds for the purchase money that they were owed. American conducted an investigation and learned that the bonds' indemnification agreements contained forged signatures of Ashley Paulk and Betty Paulk. American claimed that it would not have issued the bonds had it known that Betty and Ashley Paulk had not agreed to indemnify it, and it declared the bonds rescinded and returned all the premiums.

American then brought an action seeking a declaratory judgment relieving it from liability to the defendants on the ground that the bonds were void under Georgia insurance law due to the fraudulent and material misrepresentations of the bonds' principals. American argued that the principals had forged the signatures of Betty and Ashley Paulk on the indemnification agreements. The district court granted American's motion for summary judgment.

DECISION Summary judgment vacated and remanded for trial.

OPINION It is well established under the common law of suretyship that "fraud or misrepresentation practiced by the principal alone on the surety, without any knowledge or participation on the part of the creditor or obligee, in inducing the surety to enter into the suretyship contract will not affect the liability of the surety." From a practical standpoint, this common law treatment of a principal's fraud is the only one that makes sense. A creditor does business with a principal in reliance upon the existence of a bond. The bond provides security for the creditor because normally the creditor would have no way to know whether the principal is insolvent or otherwise an unreliable party with which to engage in business. If the creditor's ability to recover on a bond was dependent on the accuracy of the principal's representations to the surety, then the value of the bond to the creditor would be greatly lessened because the creditor would have no way to know what representations were made in the procurement of the bond. More important, this common law approach enables a livestock seller to deal freely with livestock dealers, knowing that the required bond will protect them in the event of a default even if the principal hid facts from the surety when obtaining the bond.

Georgia courts have applied the common law and held that a surety is still liable to a creditor even if the principal commits fraud so long as the creditor does not participate in the fraud. Applying the common law to the case at bar, there is no evidence that the defendants participated in any fraud. The fraud was committed solely by the principals. Under these circumstances, American is not relieved of liability on the bonds.

INTERPRETATION Fraud on the part of the principal debtor does not relieve the surety of its liability to the creditor on a surety bond if the creditor is unaware of such fraud.

ETHICAL QUESTION Is the court's decision fair to the surety? Explain.

CRITICAL THINKING QUESTION Should the fraud of the principal debtor relieve the surety of its obligation on the surety bond? Explain.

Variation of the Surety's Risk   If, after the surety enters into the secondary obligation, the creditor does an act that changes the risks that the surety assumed, there is the potential for a loss to the surety. In most cases, unless the surety agrees otherwise, the Restatement discharges the surety to the extent that such acts would cause the surety to suffer a loss; in some cases, the discharge is total.

If the principal debtor and the creditor agree to a *modification* (other than an extension of time or a release) of the underlying obligation, the surety is discharged *if* the modification creates a substituted contract or imposes risks on the surety fundamentally different from the surety's original undertaking. If the modification is not a substitute contract and does not fundamentally change the surety's risk, the surety is discharged to the extent that the modification would otherwise cause the surety a loss. The Restatement provides the following example of a fundamental change:

> P and O make a contract pursuant to which P promises to construct an office building on a designated site for $1,500,000. S issues payment and performance bonds with respect to the contract. Later, before the contract is performed, P and O agree to change the contract to provide that P will construct a factory on the site for $2,000,000. The change is so fundamental as to amount to a substituted contract. Therefore, S is discharged from its payment and performance bonds.

Unless the terms of the extension provide otherwise, if the creditor grants the principal debtor an *extension* of the time for performance of the underlying obligation (1) the extension also extends the time for performance of the principal debtor's duties of exoneration and reimbursement owed by the principal obligor to the secondary obligor, and (2) the surety is discharged to the extent that the extension would otherwise cause the surety a loss, and (3) the surety is entitled to have the extension apply to the time for performance of the surety's obligation.

On the other hand, if the terms of the extension expressly preserves the surety's recourse against the principal debtor as though no extension had been granted, the Restatement provides that the surety is *not* discharged unless the creditor's extension otherwise causes the surety to suffer a loss. If the creditor releases or impairs the value of collateral, the surety is discharged to the extent of the reduction in the value of the collateral. More generally, whenever the creditor brings about an impairment of the surety's recourse against the principal debtor, the surety is discharged from his duties to the creditor to the extent necessary to avoid this loss. An *impairment of recourse* includes an act by the creditor that increases the risk that the surety will be called upon to perform or that the surety will be unable to recover from the principal debtor. Similarly, if the creditor releases a cosurety, the other cosureties are discharged to the extent of the released surety's contributive share.

Defenses of Both Surety and Principal Debtor [37-10c]

Defenses of both surety and principal debtor include contract defenses to the contract between the creditor and the principal debtor except for the principal debtor's discharge in bankruptcy and incapacity

The surety may raise any defense of the principal obligor to the underlying obligation except the personal defenses of (1) the primary debtor's discharge of the underlying obligation in bankruptcy and (2) the unenforceability of the underlying obligation due to the principal debtor's lack of capacity. The surety may use as a setoff any unrelated claim that the principal debtor has against the creditor if (1) the creditor does not contest the principal debtor's claim asserted by the surety, (2) the principal debtor is made a party to the action, *or* (3) the principal debtor consents to the use of her claim by surety.

Examples of defenses available to both the surety and the principal debtor include the following. If the principal debtor's signature on an instrument is *forged* or if the creditor has exerted *fraud* or *duress* on the principal debtor, neither the principal debtor nor the surety is liable. Likewise, if the creditor has fraudulently and *materially altered* the contract instrument, both the principal debtor and the surety are discharged.

The absence of mutual assent or consideration to support the principal debtor's obligation is a defense for both the principal debtor and the surety. In addition, both may assert as defenses the *illegality* and the *impossibility* of performance of the principal debtor's contract.

Full *performance* of the underlying obligation by the principal debtor discharges both the principal debtor and the surety. If the principal debtor owes several debts to the creditor and makes a payment to the creditor without specifying the debt to which the payment should apply, the creditor is free to apply it to any one of them. For example, Pam owes Charles two debts, one for $5,000 and another for $10,000. Susan is a surety on the $10,000 debt. Pam sends Charles a payment in the amount of $3,500. If Pam directs Charles to apply the payment to the $10,000 debt, Charles must do so. Otherwise, Charles may, if he pleases, apply the payment to the $5,000 debt.

Unless the terms of the release provide otherwise, the creditor's *release* of the principal debtor from the underlying obligation affects all three relationships in a suretyship: (1) the principal debtor's duty to the creditor is discharged to the extent of the release, (2) the principal debtor's duties to the surety of exoneration and reimbursement are discharged, and (3) the surety is discharged. On the other hand, if the release expressly provides that the creditor retains the right to seek repayment of the remainder of the debt from the surety *and* that the surety retains her recourse against principal debtor, the Restatement provides that the surety is *not* discharged unless the creditor's release of the principal debtor otherwise causes the surety to suffer a loss. The reason for not discharging the surety is that the surety still has her rights against the principal debtor of exoneration, reimbursement, and subrogation.

The Restatement provides the following example:

> D borrows $1,000 from C. S guarantees D's obligation to C. As the due date of the debt approaches, it becomes obvious that D cannot repay the debt in full and may soon be facing bankruptcy. C, in order to collect as much as possible from D and lessen the need to collect from S, agrees to release D from the repayment obligation in exchange for $100 in cash. The agreement expressly provides that C retains the right to seek repayment of the remainder of the debt from S and that S retains its recourse against D. The agreement effects a preservation of S's recourse against D. As a result of the preservation of recourse, S suffers no loss flowing from unavailability of claims against D for performance, reimbursement, subrogation, or restitution because those claims continue as though the release had not been granted. Thus, unless C's release of D otherwise caused S to suffer a loss, S will not be discharged from its secondary obligation.

The creditor's refusal to accept the principal debtor's **tender** of *full* payment or performance of the underlying obligation completely discharges the surety. The creditor's refusal to accept the principal debtor's tender of *partial* payment or performance of the underlying obligation discharges the surety to the extent of the partial tender of performance. However, the creditor's refusal to accept a tender of payment by the principal debtor does not discharge the principal debtor. Rather, such refusal stops further accrual of interest on the debt and deprives the creditor of court costs on a subsequent suit by him to recover the amount due. If the creditor refuses the surety's tender of complete or partial performance of the surety's obligation, the surety's obligation is discharged to the extent that refusal of such tender causes the surety a loss.

ETHICAL DILEMMA

What Price Is "Reasonable" in Terms of Repossession?

Facts On credit, Jill Carr purchased a $1,000 television set at Ryko Appliance Store. The store's credit policy required Jill to give Ryko a security interest in the television set to secure her payment of the purchase price. Though she did not clearly comprehend the repossession procedures, Jill basically understood the terms; and she signed the credit slip and the security agreement on the reverse side.

Jill's payments to Ryko, $40.00 per month, were to extend for three years. Jill made the first six payments without a problem, but then, beset with large medical bills, she defaulted on the seventh payment. Her payments up to that point had reduced her principal balance by approximately $180. Ryko exercised its option to repossess the set.

Ryko's standard operating procedure was to offer repossessed sets at a special sale, to take the best price offered, and to make arrangements for the defaulting customer to pay any deficiency between the resale price and the balance due on the original selling price. But Marge Glass, the store manager, saw Jill's set and realized that it was just the type her husband wanted. She also knew that if she paid even a minimal price for the set, Ryko would eventually get the rest of the money from Jill. Thus, Marge paid Ryko $100 for the set and the store proceeded to make arrangements to collect the balance from Jill. Marge stated that $100 was the highest price anyone would have offered for the set and that her actions were, therefore, commercially reasonable.

Social, Policy, and Ethical Considerations

1. Is a store responsible for ensuring a customer's understanding of the nature and consequences of a sales transaction? Why? Why not?

2. Did Marge and Ryko act ethically or legally? Explain. In what ways would Jill's full understanding of the repossession process change your answer?

3. What ethical or social implications does Article 9 of the UCC have in this situation?

CHAPTER SUMMARY

Secured Transactions in Personal Property

Essentials of Secured Transactions

Definition of Secured Transaction an agreement by which one party obtains a security interest in the personal property of another to secure the payment of a debt

- *Debtor* person who has an interest in the collateral other than a security interest; typically the person obligated on the debt secured by the security interest
- *Secured Party* person in whose favor a security interest in the collateral is created or provided for under the security agreement
- *Collateral* property subject to a security interest
- *Security Agreement* agreement that creates or provides for a security interest
- *Security Interest* right in personal property that secures payment or performance of an obligation
- *Purchase Money Security Interest* security interest in goods purchased; interest is retained either by the seller of the goods or by a lender who advances the purchase price

Fundamental Rights of Debtor

- to redeem collateral by payment of the debt
- to possess general rights of ownership

Fundamental Rights of Secured Party

- to recover amount of debt
- to have collateral applied to payment of debt upon default

Classification of Collateral

Goods things that are movable when a security interest attaches

- *Consumer Goods* goods bought or used primarily for personal, family, or household purposes
- *Farm Products* goods that are part of a farming operation, including crops, livestock, or supplies used or produced in farming
- *Inventory* includes nonfarm product goods (1) held for sale, lease, or to be furnished under a service contract, or (2) that consist of raw materials, work in process, or materials used or consumed in a business
- *Equipment* goods not included in the definition of consumer goods, inventory, or farm products
- *Fixtures* goods that are so related to real property that they are considered part of the real estate
- *Accession* goods installed in or firmly affixed to personal property

Indispensable Paper

- *Chattel Paper* tangible or electronic record that evidences both a debt and a security interest in specific goods
- *Instruments* negotiable instruments or any other writing that evidences a right to payment of money that is transferable by delivery with any necessary indorsement
- *Documents* documents of title
- *Investment Property* investment security (stocks and bonds), security accounts, commodity contracts, and commodity accounts

Intangibles

- *Account* right to payment for (1) goods sold, leased, licensed, or otherwise disposed of; or (2) services rendered
- *General Intangibles* catchall category of collateral not otherwise covered; includes software, goodwill, literary rights, and interests in patents, trademarks, and copyrights

Other Kinds of Collateral

- *Proceeds* whatever is received upon sale, lease, license, exchange, or other disposition of collateral; the secured party, unless the security agreement states otherwise, has rights to the proceeds
- *Deposit Accounts* a demand, savings, time, or similar account maintained with a bank

Attachment	**Definition** security interest that is enforceable against the debtor
	Value consideration under contract law, a binding commitment to extend credit, or an antecedent debt
	Debtor's Rights in Collateral a debtor is deemed to have rights in personal property the debtor owns, possesses, is in the process of acquiring, or has the power to transfer rights to a secured party
	Security Agreement agreement between debtor and creditor creating a security interest: must be in a record authenticated by the debtor, unless, as in the case of most types of collateral, the secured party has possession of the collateral, and must contain a reasonable description of the collateral
	• *Authenticating Record*
	• *Consumer Goods* federal regulation prohibits a credit seller or lender from obtaining a consumer's grant of a nonpossessory security interest in household goods
	• *After-Acquired Property* a security agreement may cover property the debtor may acquire in the future
	• *Future Advances* a security agreement may include future advances
Perfection	**Definition** attachment plus any steps required for perfection
	Effect enforceable against most third parties
Methods of Perfecting	**Filing a Financing Statement** may be used for all collateral except deposit accounts, letter-of-credit rights, and money
	• *Financing Statement* document filed to provide notice of a security interest
	• *Duration of Filing* filing is effective for five years but may be continued by filing a continuation statement
	• *Place of Filing* statements, except for real-estate-related collateral, must be filed in a central location designated by the state.
	• *Subsequent Change of Debtor's Location*
	Possession by the secured party (a pledge); may be used for goods, instruments, money, negotiable documents, tangible chattel paper, or certificated securities
	Automatic Perfection perfection upon attachment; applies to a purchase money security interest in consumer goods and isolated assignments of accounts
	Temporary Perfection a security interest in certificated securities, instruments, and negotiable documents is automatically perfected for twenty days
	Control may be used to perfect a security interest in electronic chattel paper, investment property, non-consumer deposit accounts, and letter-of-credit rights
Priorities Among Competing Interests	*See Concept Review 37-3 for a summary of the priority rules.*
Default	**Repossession of Collateral** the secured party may take possession of the collateral on default without judicial process if it can be done without a breach of the peace
	Sale of Collateral the secured party may sell, lease, license, or otherwise dispose of any collateral
	Acceptance of Collateral the secured party, unless the debtor objects, may retain the collateral in full or partial satisfaction of the obligation (with the exception of the compulsory disposition of some consumer goods)

Suretyship

Nature and Formation	**Definition of Surety (Secondary Obligor)** a person who is obligated to perform an underlying obligation owed by the principal debtor to the creditor upon the principal debtor's failure to perform
	• *Principal Debtor* the party primarily liable on the obligation
	• *Guarantor* secondary obligor liable to a creditor immediately upon the default of a principal debtor
	• *Guarantor of Collection* secondary obligor liable to a creditor only after the creditor has exhausted the legal remedies against the principal debtor
	• *Surety* secondary obligor jointly and severally liable with the principal debtor to perform the underlying obligation
	• *Cosurety* each of two or more secondary obligors who are liable for the same debt of the principal debtor

Particular Kinds of Sureties

- *Party Assuming a Mortgage*
- *Fidelity Bonds*
- *Performance Bonds*
- *Official Bonds*
- *Judicial Bonds*

Formation the promise of the surety must satisfy all the elements of a contract and must also be in writing

Duties of Surety

Duty of Surety upon default by the principal debtor, the creditor may proceed against the surety to enforce the surety's undertaking

Duty of Cosurety up to the amount of each surety's undertaking, cosureties are *jointly and severally* liable for the principal debtor's default

Rights of Surety

Exoneration the right of a surety to be relieved of his obligation to the creditor by having the principal debtor perform the underlying obligation

Reimbursement the right of a surety who has paid the creditor to be repaid by the principal debtor

Subrogation the right of a surety who has paid the creditor to assume all the rights the creditor has with respect to the underlying obligation

Contribution the right to payment from each cosurety of her proportionate share of the amount paid to the creditor

Defenses of Surety and Principal Debtor

Personal Defenses of Principal Debtor defenses available only to the principal debtor, including her incapacity, discharge in bankruptcy, and some setoffs

Personal Defenses of Surety defenses available only to the surety, including her own incapacity, the statute of frauds, contract defenses to her suretyship undertaking, setoff, some modifications of the contract between the creditor and the principal debtor, and the creditor's release of collateral or a cosurety

Defenses of Both Surety and Principal Debtor include contract defenses to the contract between the creditor and the principal debtor except for the principal debtor's discharge in bankruptcy and incapacity

QUESTIONS

1. Victor sells to Bonnie a refrigerator for $600 payable in monthly installments of $30.00 for twenty months. Bonnie signs a security agreement granting Victor a security interest in the refrigerator. The refrigerator is installed in the kitchen of Bonnie's apartment. There is no filing of any financing statement. Assume that after Bonnie has made the first three monthly payments:
   a. Bonnie moves from her apartment and sells the refrigerator in place to the new occupant for $350 cash. What are the rights of Victor?
   b. Bonnie is adjudicated bankrupt, and her trustee in bankruptcy claims the refrigerator. What are the rights of the parties?

2. On January 2, Burt asked Logan to loan him money "against my diamond ring." Logan agreed to do so. To guard against intervening liens, Logan received permission to file a financing statement, and Burt and Logan signed a security agreement giving Logan an interest in the ring. Burt also signed a financing statement that Logan properly filed on January 3. On January 4, Burt borrowed money from Tillo, pledging his ring to secure the debt. Tillo took possession of the ring and paid Burt the money on the same day. The next day,

January 5, Logan loaned Burt the money under the assumption that Burt still had the ring. Who has priority, Logan or Tillo? Explain.

3. Joanna takes a security interest in the equipment in Jason Store and files a financing statement claiming "equipment and all after-acquired equipment." Berkeley later sells Jason Store a cash register, taking a security interest in the register and (a) files nine days after Jason receives the register, or (b) files twenty-five days after Jason receives the register. If Jason fails to pay both Joanna and Berkeley and they foreclose their security interests, who has priority on the cash register? Explain.

4. Finley Motor Company sells an automobile to Sara and retains a security interest in it. The automobile is insured, and Finley is named beneficiary. Three days after the automobile is totally destroyed in an accident, Sara files a petition in bankruptcy. As between Finley and Sara's trustee in bankruptcy, who is entitled to the insurance proceeds?

5. On September 5, Wanda, a widow who occasionally teaches piano and organ in her home, purchased an electric organ from Murphy's music store for $4,800, trading in her old

organ for $1,200 and promising in writing to pay the balance at $120 per month and granting to Murphy a security interest in the property in terms consistent with and incorporating provisions of the UCC. A financing statement covering the transaction was also properly filled out and signed, and Murphy properly filed it. After Wanda failed to make the December or January payments, Murphy went to her home to collect the payments or take the organ. Finding no one home and the door unlocked, he went in and took the organ. Two hours later, Tia, a third party and the present occupant of the house, who had purchased the organ for her own use, stormed into Murphy's store, demanding the return of the organ. She showed Murphy a bill of sale from Wanda to her, dated December 15, that listed the organ and other furnishings in the house.

   a. What are the rights of Murphy, Tia, and Wanda?

   b. Would your answer change if Murphy had not filed a financing statement? Why?

   c. Would your answer change if the organ had been principally used to give lessons?

6. On May 1, Lincoln lends Donaldson $200,000 and receives from Donaldson his agreement to pay this amount in two years and takes a security interest in the machinery and equipment in Donaldson's factory. A proper financing statement is filed with respect to the security agreement. On August 1, upon Lincoln's request, Donaldson executes an addendum to the security agreement covering after-acquired machinery and equipment in Donaldson's factory. A second financing statement covering the addendum is filed. In September, Donaldson acquires $50,000 worth of new equipment from Thompson, which Donaldson installs in his factory. In December, Carter, a judgment creditor of Donaldson, causes an attachment to issue against the new equipment. What are the rights of Lincoln, Donaldson, Carter, and Thompson? What can the parties do to best protect themselves?

7. Anita bought a television set from Bertrum for her personal use. Bertrum, who was out of security agreement forms, showed Anita a form he had executed with Nathan, another consumer. Anita and Bertrum orally agreed to the terms of the form. Anita subsequently defaulted on payment, and Bertrum sought to repossess the television.

   a. Explain who would prevail.

   b. Explain whether the result would differ if Bertrum had filed a financing statement.

   c. Explain whether the result would differ if Anita had subsequently sent Bertrum an e-mail that met all the requirements of an effective security agreement.

8. Aaron bought a television set for personal use from Penny. Aaron properly signed a security agreement and paid Penny $125 down, as their agreement required. Penny did not file, and subsequently Aaron sold the television for $800 to Clark, his neighbor, for use in Clark's hotel lobby.

   When Aaron fails to make the January and February payments, may Penny repossess the television from Clark?

   a. What if, instead of Aaron's selling the television set to Clark, a judgment creditor levied (sought possession) on the television? Who would prevail?

   b. What if Clark intended to use the television set in his home? Who would prevail?

9. Jones bought a used car from the A-Herts Car Rental System, which regularly sold its used equipment at the end of its fiscal year. First National Bank of Roxboro had previously obtained a perfected security interest in the car based upon its financing of A-Herts's automobiles. Upon A-Herts's failure to pay, First National is seeking to repossess the car from Jones. Does First National have an enforceable security interest in the car against Jones? Explain.

10. Allen, Barker, and Cooper are cosureties on a $750,000 loan by Durham National Bank to Kingston Manufacturing Co., Inc. The maximum liability of the sureties is as follows: Allen—$750,000, Barker—$300,000, and Cooper—$150,000. If Kingston defaults on the entire $750,000 loan, what are the liabilities of Allen, Barker, and Cooper?

11. Peter Diamond owed Carter $500,000 secured by a first mortgage on Diamond's plant and land. Stephens was a surety on this obligation in the amount of $250,000. After Diamond defaulted on the debt, Carter demanded and received payment of $250,000 from Stephens. Carter then foreclosed upon the mortgage and sold the property for $375,000. What rights, if any, does Stephens have in the proceeds from the sale of the property?

12. Paula Daniels purchased an automobile from Carey on credit. At the time of the sale, Scott agreed to be a surety for Paula, who is sixteen years old. The automobile's odometer stated fifty-two thousand miles, but Carey had turned it back from seventy-two thousand miles. Paula refuses to make any payments due on the car. Carey proceeds against Paula and Scott. What defenses, if any, are available to (a) Paula and (b) Scott?

13. Stafford Surety Co. agreed to act as the guarantor of collection on a debt owed by Preston Decker to Cole. Stafford was paid a premium by Preston to serve as surety. Preston defaults on the obligation. What are Cole's rights against Stafford Surety Co.?

14. Campbell loaned Perry Dixon $70,000, which was secured by a possessory security interest in stock owned by Perry. The stock had a market value of $40,000. In addition, Campbell insisted that Perry obtain a surety. For a premium, Sutton Surety Co. agreed to act as a surety for the full amount of the loan. Prior to the due date of the loan, Perry convinced Campbell to return the stock because its value had increased and he wished to sell it to realize the gain. Campbell released the stock and Perry subsequently defaulted. Is Sutton released from his liability?

15. Pamela Darden owed Clark $50,000 on an unsecured loan. On May 1, Pamela approached Clark for an additional loan of $30,000. Clark agreed to make the loan only if Pamela could obtain a surety. On May 5, Simpson agreed to be a surety on the $30,000 loan, which was granted that day. Both loans were due on October 1. On June 15, Pamela sent $10,000 to Clark but did not provide any instructions.

   a. What are Clark's rights?

   b. What are Simpson's rights?

16. Patrick Dillon applied for a $100,000 loan from Carlton Savings & Loan. Carlton required him to obtain a surety. Patrick approached Sinclair Surety Co., which insisted that Patrick provide it with a financial statement. Patrick did so, but the statement was materially false. In reliance upon the financial statement and in return for a premium, Sinclair agreed to act as surety. Upon Sinclair's commitment to act as surety, Carlton loaned Patrick the $100,000. After one payment of $4,000, Patrick defaulted. He then filed a voluntary petition in bankruptcy. Does Sinclair have any valid defense against Carlton?

17. On June 1, Smith contracted with Martin doing business as Martin Publishing Company to distribute Martin's newspapers and to account for the proceeds. As part of the contract, Smith agreed to furnish Martin a bond in the amount of $10,000 guaranteeing the payment of the proceeds. At the time the contract was executed and the credit extended, the bond was not furnished, and no mention was made as to the prospective sureties. On July 1, Smith signed the bond with Black and Blue signing as sureties. The bond recited the awarding of the contract for distribution of the newspapers as consideration for the bond.

On December 1, payment was due from Smith to Martin the sum of $3,600 under the distributor's contract. Demand for payment was made, but Smith failed to make payment. As a result, Martin brought an appropriate action against Black and Blue to recover the $3,600. What result?

18. Diggitt Construction Company was the low bidder on a well-digging job for the Village of Drytown. On April 15, Diggitt signed a contract with Drytown for the job at a price of $40,000. At the same time, pursuant to the notice of bidding, Diggitt prevailed upon Ace Surety Company to execute a performance bond indemnifying Drytown on the contract. On May 1, after Diggitt had put in three days on the job, the president of the company refigured his bid and realized that if his company were to complete the job it would lose $10,000. Accordingly, Diggitt notified Drytown that it was canceling the contract, effective immediately. What are the rights and duties of Ace Surety Company?

CASE PROBLEMS

19. Standridge purchased a Chevrolet automobile from Billy Deavers, an agent of Walker Motor Company. According to the sales contract, the balance due after the trade-in allowance was $2,282.50, to be paid in twelve weekly installments. Standridge claims that he was unable to make the second payment and that Billy Deavers orally agreed that he could make two payments the next week. The day after the double payment was due, Standridge still had not paid. That day Ronnie Deavers, Billy's brother, went to Standridge's place of employment to repossess the car, which the Walker Motor contract permitted. Rather than consenting to the repossession, Standridge drove the car to the Walker Motor Company's place of business and tendered the overdue payments. The Deavers refused to accept the late payment and instead demanded the entire unpaid balance. Standridge could not pay it. The Deavers then blocked Standridge's car with another car and told him he could just "walk his … home." Standridge brought suit, seeking damages for the Deavers's wrongful repossession of his car. The Deavers deny that they granted Standridge permission to make a double payment, that Standridge tendered the double payment, and that they rejected it. They claim that he made no payment and that, therefore, they were entitled to repossess the car. Discuss whether the car was properly repossessed.

20. National Acceptance Company loaned Ultra Precision Industries $692,000, and to secure repayment of the loan, Ultra executed a chattel mortgage security agreement on National's behalf on March 7, 2013. National perfected the security interest by timely filing a financing statement. Although the security interest covered specifically described equipment of Ultra, both the security agreement and the financing statement contained an after-acquired property clause that did not refer to any specific equipment.

Later in 2013 and in 2014, Ultra placed three separate orders for machines from Wolf Machinery Company. In each case it was agreed that after the machines had been shipped to Ultra and installed, Ultra would be given an opportunity to test them in operation for a reasonable period. If the machines passed inspection, Wolf would then provide financing that was satisfactory to Ultra and properly filed its financing statement. In all three cases, financing was arranged with Community Bank (Bank) and accepted, and a security interest was given in the machines. Furthermore, in each case a security agreement was entered into, and the secured parties then filed a financing statement within ten days. Ultra became bankrupt on October 7, 2015. National claimed that its security interest in the after-acquired machines should take priority over those of Wolf and Bank because their interests were not perfected by timely filed financing statements. Discuss who has priority in the disputed collateral.

21. Elizabeth Tilleraas received three student loans totaling $35,500 under the Federal Insured Student Loan Program (FISLP) of the Higher Education Act. These loans were secured by three promissory notes executed in favor of Dakota National Bank & Trust Co., Fargo, North Dakota. Under the terms of these student loans, periodic payments were required beginning twelve months after Tilleraas ceased to carry at least one-half of a full-time academic workload at an eligible institution. Her student status terminated on January 28, 2013, and the first installment payment thus became due January 28, 2014. She never made any payment on any of her loans. Under the provisions of the FISLP, the United States assured the lender bank repayment in event of any failure to pay by the borrower. The first payment due on the loans was in "default" on July 27, 2014, one hundred and eighty days after the failure to make the first installment payment. On December 17, 2014, Dakota National Bank & Trust sent notice of its election under the provisions of the loan to accelerate the maturity of the note. The bank demanded payment in full by December 27, 2015. It then filed FISLP insurance claims against the United States on May 6, 2016, and assigned the three Tilleraas notes to the United States on May 10, 2016. The government, in

turn, paid the bank's claim in full on July 5, 2016. The government subsequently filed suit against Tilleraas. Discuss whether the United States will prevail.

22. New West Fruit Corporation (New West) and Coastal Berry Corporation are both brokers of fresh strawberries. In the second half of 2008, New West's predecessor, Monc's Consolidated Produce, Inc., loaned money and strawberry plants to a group of strawberry growers known as Cooperativa La Paz (La Paz). In September 2013, Monc's and La Paz signed a "Sales and Marketing Agreement" to allow Monc's the exclusive right to market the strawberries grown by La Paz during the 2013–2014 season. The agreement did not mention the advances of money or plants, but did give Monc's a security interest in all crops and proceeds on specified property in the 2013–2014 season. The financing statement was properly signed and filed. Monc's closed down in January 2014, and its assets were assigned to New West. In April, New West learned that La Paz had agreed to market its 2014 crop through Coastal Berry. New West immediately arranged a meeting to advise the Coastal Berry officers of its contract with the growers. New West requested that Coastal Berry either pay New West the amounts owed by the growers or allow New West to market the berries to recover the money. Coastal Berry did not respond. After Coastal Berry began marketing the berries, New West sent letters demanding payment of the proceeds. In August 2014, New West filed suit against Coastal Berry, La Paz, the individual growers, and a berry-freezing company asserting that its security interest was valid and that it had duly notified Coastal Berry both through the financing statement on file and through the letters it had sent to Coastal Berry directly. Coastal Berry claimed that the security agreement was not effective because it did not specifically identify the debt (money and plants) being secured. Discuss.

TAKING SIDES

James Koontz agreed to purchase a Plymouth Sundance from Chrysler Credit Corporation (Chrysler) in exchange for sixty payments of $185.92. Koontz soon thereafter defaulted, and Chrysler notified Koontz that, unless he made the payments, it would repossess the vehicle. Koontz responded by notifying Chrysler that he would make every effort to make up missed payments, that he did not want the car repossessed, and that Chrysler was not to enter his private property to repossess the vehicle. A few weeks later, Chrysler sent the M & M Agency to repossess the vehicle.

When he heard the repossession in progress, Koontz, dressed only in his underwear, came outside and yelled, "Don't take it!" The repossessor ignored him and took the car anyway. Koontz did not physically challenge or threaten the repossessor.

a. Discuss the arguments that Chrysler legally repossessed the automobile.
b. Discuss arguments that Chrysler illegally repossessed the automobile.
c. Who should prevail?

Bankruptcy

CHAPTER 38

Always pay; for first or last you must pay your entire debt.

Ralph Waldo Emerson (1841)

CHAPTER OUTCOMES

After reading and studying this chapter, you should be able to:

1. Explain (a) the requirements for voluntary and involuntary bankruptcy cases, (b) the priorities of creditors' claims, (c) the debtor's exemptions, and (d) the debts that are not dischargeable in bankruptcy.

2. Explain the duties of a trustee and his rights (a) as a lien creditor, (b) to avoid preferential transfers, (c) to avoid fraudulent transfers, and (d) to avoid statutory liens.

3. Explain the procedure followed in distributing the debtor's estate under Chapter 7.

4. Compare the adjustment of debt proceedings under Chapters 11 and 13.

5. Identify and define the nonbankruptcy compromises between debtors and creditors.

A debt is an obligation to pay money owed by a debtor to a creditor. Debts are created daily by countless purchasers of goods at the consumer level; by retailers of goods in buying merchandise from a manufacturer, wholesaler, or distributor; by borrowers of funds from various lending institutions; and through the issuance and sale of debentures, corporate mortgage bonds, and other types of debt securities. Multitudes of business transactions are entered into daily on a credit basis. Commercial activity would be greatly restricted if credit were not readily obtainable or if needed funds were unavailable for lending.

Fortunately, most debts are paid when due, thus justifying the extension of credit and encouraging its continuation. Although defaults may create credit and collection problems, normally the total amount in default represents a very small percentage of the total amount of outstanding indebtedness. Nevertheless, both individuals and corporations encounter financial crises and business misfortune. An accumulation of debts that exceeds total assets may confront an individual as well as a business. Or these debtors might have assets in excess of total indebtedness but in such noncash form that they are unable to pay their debts as they mature. For both businesses and individuals, relief from pressing debt and from the threat of impending lawsuits by creditors is frequently necessary for economic survival.

The conflict between creditor rights and debtor relief has engendered various solutions, such as compromises requiring installment payments to creditors over a period of time during which they agree to withhold legal action. Other voluntary methods include compositions and assignments of assets by a debtor to a trustee or assignee for the benefit of creditors. In addition, creditors sometimes file equity receiverships or insolvency proceedings in a state court, according to statute. Nonetheless, the most adaptable and frequently used method of debtor relief—one that also affords protection to creditors—is a proceeding in a federal court under federal bankruptcy law.

FEDERAL BANKRUPTCY LAW

U.S. bankruptcy law serves a dual purpose: (1) to bring about a quick, *equitable distribution* of the debtor's property among her creditors and (2) to *discharge* the debtor from her debts, enabling the debtor to rehabilitate herself and to start afresh. Other purposes are to provide uniform treatment of similarly situated creditors, to preserve existing business relations, and to stabilize commercial usages.

The U.S. Bankruptcy Abuse Prevention and Consumer Protection Act of 2005 (2005 Act) contains the most extensive amendments to federal bankruptcy law since 1978. The U.S. Bankruptcy Code consists of nine chapters: eight odd-numbered chapters and one even-numbered chapter. Chapters 7, 9, 11, 12, and 13 provide five different types of proceedings; Chapters 1, 3, and 5 apply to those five proceedings unless otherwise specified. **Straight**, or ordinary, **bankruptcy** (Chapter 7) provides for the liquidation of the debtor's property, whereas the other proceedings provide for the **reorganization** and adjustment of the debtor's debts and, in the case of a business debtor, the continuance of the debtor's business. In reorganization cases, the creditors usually look to the debtor's future earnings, whereas in liquidation cases, the creditors look to the debtor's property at the commencement of the bankruptcy proceeding. Chapters 7, 11, 12, and 13 have provisions governing transfer of a case under that chapter to another chapter. The 2005 Act added Chapter 15 to the Bankruptcy Code for cross-border insolvency cases. Chapter 1 and certain sections of Chapters 3 and 5 apply to proceedings under Chapter 15.

1. Chapter 7 applies to all debtors, with the exception of railroads, insurance companies, banks, savings and loan associations, homestead associations, licensed small business investment companies, and credit unions. Moreover, Chapter 7 has special provisions for liquidating the estates of stockbrokers and commodity brokers. In the past several years, 70 to 75 percent of bankruptcies have been filed under Chapter 7.
2. Chapter 11 applies to railroads and any person who may be a debtor under Chapter 7 (except a stockbroker or a commodity broker). (Less than 1 percent of bankruptcies are filed under Chapter 11.)
3. Chapter 9 applies only to municipalities that are generally authorized to be debtors under that chapter, that are insolvent, and that desire to effect plans to adjust their debts.
4. Chapter 12 applies to individuals, or individuals and their spouses, engaged in farming if 50 percent of their gross income is from farming, their aggregate debts do not exceed $4,031,575, and at least 50 percent of their debts arise from farming operations. (Less than one-tenth of 1 percent of bankruptcies are filed under Chapter 12.) Corporations or partnerships may also qualify for Chapter 12. The 2005 Act made Chapter 12 permanent and extended its coverage to certain family fishermen if 50 percent of their gross income is from commercial fishing, their aggregate debts do not exceed $1,868,200, and at least 80 percent of their debts arise out of commercial fishing operations.
5. Chapter 13 applies to individuals with regular income who owe liquidated unsecured debts of less than $383,175 and secured debts of less than $1,149,525. In the past several years, 25 to 30 percent of bankruptcies have been filed under Chapter 13.
6. Chapter 15 covers cross-border (transnational) insolvencies and incorporates the Model Law on Cross-Border Insolvency, promulgated by the United Nations Commission on International Trade Law (UNCITRAL). These changes are intended to make cross-border filings easier to accomplish and to provide greater predictability. Chapter 15 encourages cooperation between the United States and foreign countries with respect to transnational insolvency cases.

This text will not further cover Chapters 9, 12, and 15.

The 1994 amendments to the Bankruptcy Act require that every three years, beginning in 1998, the U.S. Judicial Conference adjust for inflation the dollar amounts of certain provisions including eligibility for Chapters 12 and 13, requirements for filing involuntary cases, priorities, exemptions, and exceptions to discharge. The dollar amounts in this chapter reflect the adjustment that became effective on April 1, 2013.

GOING GLOBAL

What about transnational bankruptcies?

Enacted in 2005, Chapter 15 of the Bankruptcy Code covers cross-border (transnational) insolvencies and incorporates the Model Law on Cross-Border Insolvency, promulgated by the United Nations Commission on International Trade Law (UNCITRAL). The UNCITRAL Model Law has also been adopted in at least nineteen other countries including Canada, Mexico, Great Britain, Japan, and Australia.

The purpose of Chapter 15 is to provide effective mechanisms for dealing with cases of cross-border insolvency; that is, cases with debtors, assets, claimants, and other parties of interest involving more than one country. Chapter 15 specifies five objectives: (1) cooperation of the courts, trustees, and debtors in the United States with the courts and other competent authorities of foreign countries involved in cross-border insolvency cases; (2) greater legal certainty for trade and investment; (3) fair and efficient administration of cross-border insolvencies that protects the interests of all creditors and other interested entities, including the debtor; (4) protection and maximization of the value of the debtor's assets; and (5) facilitation of the rescue of financially troubled businesses, thereby protecting investment and preserving employment.

Chapter 15 allows proceedings for a foreign debtor or other related parties to access U.S. Bankruptcy Courts. Generally, a Chapter 15 case is ancillary (secondary) to a primary proceeding brought in another country, typically the debtor's home country. As an alternative, in some circumstances, the debtor or a creditor may commence a Chapter 7 or Chapter 11 case in the United States.

The Bankruptcy Code grants to U.S. District Courts original and exclusive jurisdiction over all bankruptcy cases and original, but not exclusive, jurisdiction over civil proceedings arising under bankruptcy cases. The district court must, however, abstain from related matters that, except for their relationship to bankruptcy, could not have been brought in a federal court. The district court in which a bankruptcy case is commenced has exclusive jurisdiction over all of the debtor's property. In addition, within each federal district court is established a bankruptcy court staffed by bankruptcy judges. Bankruptcy courts are authorized to hear certain matters specified by the Bankruptcy Code and to enter appropriate orders and judgments subject to review by the district court or, when established, by a panel of three bankruptcy judges. The federal circuit court of appeals has jurisdiction over appeals from the district court or panel. In all other matters, unless the parties agree otherwise, only the district court may issue a final order or judgment based upon proposed findings of fact and conclusions of law submitted to the court by the bankruptcy judge.

The U.S. trustees are government officials appointed by the U.S. Attorney General with administrative responsibilities in bankruptcy cases in almost all of the districts. For example, the U.S. trustee selects bankruptcy trustees and, in Chapter 11 proceedings, appoints the members of the unsecured creditors' committee. The 2005 Act gives the U.S. trustees added responsibilities in a number of areas.

CASE ADMINISTRATION—CHAPTER 3 [38-1]

Chapter 3 of the Bankruptcy Code contains provisions dealing with the commencement of a case in bankruptcy, the meetings of creditors, the officers who administer the case, and the officers' administrative powers.

Commencement of the Case [38-1a]

The filing of a voluntary or involuntary petition commences a bankruptcy case thereby beginning the jurisdiction of the bankruptcy court and the operation of the bankruptcy laws.

Voluntary Petitions

Commencement of the case
filing of a voluntary or involuntary petition begins jurisdiction of the bankruptcy court

Voluntary petition
available to any eligible debtor even if solvent

More than 99 percent of all bankruptcy petitions are filed voluntarily. Any person eligible to be a debtor under a given bankruptcy proceeding may file a **voluntary petition** under that chapter and need *not* be insolvent to do so. The commencement of a voluntary case constitutes an automatic ***order for relief***. The petition must include a list of all creditors (secured and unsecured), a list of all property the debtor owns, a list of property that the debtor claims is exempt, and a statement of the debtor's affairs.

The 2005 Act added a requirement that all individual debtors receive credit counseling from an approved nonprofit budget and credit counseling agency within the one-hundred-and-eighty-day period before filing the petition. This requirement does not apply to a debtor who (1) is exempted by the court or (2) resides in a district for which the U.S. trustee or the bankruptcy administrator determines that approved nonprofit budget and credit counseling agencies are not reasonably able to provide adequate services to the additional individuals who would seek required credit counseling. The role of the credit counseling agencies is to analyze the client's current financial condition, the factors that caused the financial distress, and how the client can develop a plan to respond to these problems.

Involuntary Petitions   An **involuntary petition** in bankruptcy may be filed only under Chapter 7 (liquidation) or Chapter 11 (reorganization). It may be filed (1) by three or more creditors who have undisputed unsecured claims that total $15,325 or more or (2) if the debtor has fewer than twelve creditors, by one or more creditors whose total undisputed unsecured claims equal $15,325 or more. An involuntary petition may not be filed against a farmer or against a banking, insurance, or nonprofit corporation.

> **Involuntary petition** may be filed only under Chapter 7 or 11 if the debtor is generally not paying his debts as they become due

Like a voluntary petition, the filing of an involuntary petition commences a case, but unlike a voluntary petition, it does not operate as an order for relief. The debtor has the right to answer. If the debtor does not timely contest the involuntary petition, the court will enter an order for relief against the debtor. However, if the debtor timely opposes the petition, the court may enter an order of relief only (1) if the debtor is generally not paying his debts as they become due or (2) if, within one hundred and twenty days before the filing of the petition, a custodian, assignee, or general receiver was appointed or took possession of substantially all of the debtor's property.

Dismissal [38-1b]

The court may dismiss a Chapter 7 case for cause after notice and a hearing. In a case filed by an individual debtor whose debts are primarily consumer debts, the court may dismiss the case or, with the debtor's consent, convert the case to one under Chapter 11 or 13, if the court finds that granting relief would be an abuse of the provisions of Chapter 7. A court can find abuse in one of two ways: (1) on general grounds based on whether the debtor filed the petition in bad faith or the totality of the circumstances of the debtor's financial situation demonstrates abuse or (2) an unrebutted presumption of abuse based on the means test established by the 2005 Act. The means test will be discussed later in this chapter.

> **Dismissal** the court may dismiss a case for cause after notice and a hearing; under Chapter 13, the debtor has an absolute right to have his case dismissed

Under Chapter 11, the court may dismiss a case for cause after notice and a hearing. Under Chapter 13, the debtor has an absolute right to have his case dismissed. Under Chapter 13, if a motion to dismiss is filed by an interested party other than the debtor, the court may dismiss the case only for cause after notice and a hearing.

Automatic Stays [38-1c]

The filing of a voluntary or involuntary petition operates as a stay against (i.e., it prevents) attempts by creditors to begin or continue to recover claims against the debtor, to enforce judgments against the debtor, or to create or enforce liens against property of the debtor. This stay applies to both secured and unsecured creditors, although a secured creditor may petition the court to terminate the stay as to her security on showing that she lacks adequate protection in the secured property. An automatic stay ends when the bankruptcy case is closed or dismissed or when the debtor receives a discharge.

> **Automatic stays** prevent attempts by creditors to recover claims against the debtor

> *Practical Advice*
>
> If you file a bankruptcy petition, you are protected from creditors' pursuing their claims against you except through the bankruptcy proceeding; this may be advantageous in that it requires all claims to be heard in one court at one time.

Trustees [38-1d]

A **trustee** is the representative of an estate and has the capacity to sue and be sued on behalf of the estate. In proceedings under Chapter 7, trustees are selected by a vote of the creditors. The 1994 amendments allow the creditors to elect a trustee in a Chapter 11 proceeding if the court orders the appointment of a trustee for cause. In Chapter 13 the trustee is appointed. Responsible, under Chapter 7, for collecting, liquidating, and distributing the debtor's estate, the trustee

> **Trustee** responsible for collecting, liquidating, and distributing the debtor's estate

has, among others, the following duties and powers: (1) collecting the property of the estate; (2) challenging certain transfers of property of the estate; (3) using, selling, or leasing property of the estate; (4) depositing or investing money of the estate; (5) employing attorneys, accountants, appraisers, or auctioneers; (6) assuming or rejecting any executory contract or unexpired lease of the debtor; (7) objecting to creditors' claims that are improper; and (8) opposing, if advisable, the debtor's discharge. Trustees under Chapters 11 and 13 perform some but not all of the duties of a Chapter 7 trustee.

Meetings of Creditors [38-1e]

Within a reasonable time after relief is ordered, a meeting of creditors must be held. Although the court may not attend this meeting, the debtor must appear and submit to an examination of his financial situation by the creditors and the trustee. In a proceeding under Chapter 7, qualified creditors at this meeting elect a permanent trustee.

CREDITORS, THE DEBTOR, AND THE ESTATE—CHAPTER 5 [38-2]

Creditors [38-2a]

The Bankruptcy Code defines a **creditor** as any entity having a claim against the debtor that arose at the time of or before the order for relief. A **claim** is a right to payment.

Proofs of Claim Creditors who wish to participate in the distribution of the debtor's estate may file a proof of claim. If a creditor does not do so in a timely manner, the debtor or trustee may file a proof of such claim. By doing this the debtor may prevent a claim from becoming nondischargeable. Filed claims are allowed unless a party who has an interest objects. If an objection is made, the court determines, after a hearing, the amount and validity of the claim. The court will not allow any claim that (1) is unenforceable against the debtor or her property, (2) is for unmatured interest, (3) may be offset against a debt owing the debtor, or (4) is for insider or attorney services in excess of the reasonable value of such services. An **insider** includes a relative or general partner of a debtor, as well as a partnership in which the debtor is a general partner or a corporation of which the debtor is a director, officer, or person in control.

Secured and Unsecured Claims A **lien** is a charge or interest in property to secure payment of an obligation and must be satisfied before the property is available to satisfy the claims of unsecured creditors. An allowed claim of a creditor who has a lien on property of the estate is a **secured claim** to the extent of the value of the creditor's interest in the property. The creditor's claim is an **unsecured claim** to the extent of the difference between the value of his secured interest and the allowed amount of his claim. Thus, if Alice has an allowed claim of $5,000 against the estate of debtor Bart and has a security interest in property of the estate that is valued at $3,000, Alice has a secured claim in the amount of $3,000 and an unsecured claim for $2,000.

A lien or secured claim can arise by agreement, judicial proceeding, common law, or statute. Consensual security interests in personal property are governed by Article 9 of the Uniform Commercial Code (UCC) and are discussed in Chapter 37. Consensual security interests in real property, called mortgages or deeds of trust, are covered in Chapter 49. A **judicial lien** is obtained by a judgment, a levy, or some other legal or equitable process. The common law grants to certain creditors, including innkeepers and common carriers, a possessory lien on property of their debtors that is in the creditor's possession or on the creditor's premises. Finally, a number of federal and state statutes grant liens to specified creditors.

Priority of Claims After secured claims have been satisfied, the remaining assets are distributed among creditors with unsecured claims. Certain classes of unsecured claims, however, have a *priority*, which means that they must be paid in full before any distribution is made to claims of lesser rank. Each claimant within a priority class shares *pro rata* if the assets are

---

Meeting of creditors
debtor must appear and submit to an examination of her financial situation

Creditor
any entity that has a claim against the debtor

Claim
a right to payment

Practical Advice

If you are a debtor in a bankruptcy proceeding, file a proof of claim for any creditor who does not file on her own. Such a filing may enable you to receive a discharge from that claim.

Insider
relative or general partner of debtor, partnership in which debtor is a partner, or corporation in which debtor is an officer, director, or controlling person

Lien
charge or interest in property to secure payment of a debt or performance of an obligation

Secured claim
claim with a lien on the property of the debtor

Unsecured claim
portion of a claim that exceeds the value of any property securing that claim

Judicial lien
property interest obtained by judgment, a levy, or some other legal or equitable process

Priority of claim
the right of certain claims to be paid before claims of lesser rank

CHAPTER 38 Bankruptcy **769**

insufficient to satisfy all claims in that class. The claims having a priority and the order of their priority are as follows:

1. *Domestic support obligations* (debts owed to a spouse, former spouse, or child of the debtor in the nature of alimony, maintenance, or support) subject to the expenses of a trustee in administering assets that otherwise can be used to pay support obligation;
2. *Expenses of administration* of the debtor's estate, including the filing fees paid by creditors in involuntary cases, the expenses of creditors in recovering concealed assets for the benefit of the bankrupt's estate, the trustee's necessary expenses, and reasonable compensation to receivers, trustees, and their attorneys, as allowed by the court;
3. Unsecured claims in an involuntary case arising in the ordinary course of the debtor's business after the commencement of the case but before the earlier of either the appointment of the trustee or the entering of the order for relief (such claimants are referred to as "*gap" creditors*);
4. Allowed, unsecured claims up to $12,475 for *wages, salaries, or commissions* earned within one hundred and eighty days before the filing of the petition or before the date on which the debtor's business ceases, whichever comes first;
5. Allowed, unsecured claims for contributions to *employee benefit plans* arising from services rendered within one hundred and eighty days before the filing of the petition or the cessation of the debtor's business, whichever occurs first, but limited to $12,475 multiplied by the number of employees covered by the plan, less the aggregate amount paid to such employees under number 3;
6. Allowed, unsecured claims up to $6,150 for *grain* or *fish producers* against a storage facility;
7. Allowed, unsecured claims up to $2,775 for *consumer deposits*; that is, moneys deposited in connection with the purchase, lease, or rental of property or the purchase of services for personal, family, or household use;
8. Specified income, property, employment, or excise *taxes owed to governmental units*; and
9. Allowed claims for death or personal injuries resulting from the debtor's operation of a motor vehicle or vessel while legally intoxicated from using alcohol, a drug, or other substance.

After creditors with secured claims and creditors with claims having a priority have been satisfied, creditors with allowed, unsecured claims share proportionately in any remaining assets.

Subordination of Claims A subordination agreement is enforceable under the Bankruptcy Code to the same extent that it is enforceable under nonbankruptcy law. In addition to statutory and contract priorities, the bankruptcy court itself can, at its discretion in proper cases, apply equitable priorities. The court accomplishes this through the doctrine of subordination of claims, whereby, assuming two claims of equal statutory priority, the court declares that one claim must be paid in full before the other claim can be paid anything. Bankruptcy courts apply subordination when allowing a claim in full, such as the inflated salary claims of officers in a closely held corporation, would be unfair and inequitable to other creditors. In such cases, the court does not disallow the claim but merely orders that it be paid after all other claims are paid in full. For example, the court may subordinate the claim of a parent corporation against its bankrupt subsidiary to the claims of the subsidiary's other creditors if the parent has so mismanaged the subsidiary to the detriment of its innocent creditors that this unconscionable conduct precludes the parent from seeking the court's aid.

Debtors [38-2b]

As indicated, the purpose of the Bankruptcy Code is to bring about an equitable distribution of the debtor's assets and to provide him a discharge. Accordingly, the Code explicitly subjects the debtor to specified duties, while exempting some of his property and discharging most of his debts.

Debtor's duties
the debtor must file specified information, cooperate with the trustee, and surrender all property of the estate

Debtor's Duties Under the Bankruptcy Code, the debtor must file a list of creditors, a schedule of assets and liabilities, a schedule of current income and expenditures, and a statement of her financial affairs. In any case in which a trustee is serving, the debtor must cooperate with the trustee and surrender to the trustee all property of the estate and all records relating to such property.

Debtor's exemptions

determined by state or
federal law, depending upon
the state

Debtor's Exemptions

The Bankruptcy Code exempts specified property of an individual debtor from bankruptcy proceedings, including the following: (1) up to $22,975 in equity in property used as a residence or burial plot; (2) up to $3,675 in equity in one motor vehicle; (3) up to $575 for any particular item of household furnishings, household goods, wearing apparel, appliances, books, animals, crops, or musical instruments that are primarily for personal, family, or household use with an aggregate limitation of $12,250; (4) up to $1,550 in jewelry; (5) any property up to $1,225 plus up to $11,500 of any unused amount of the first exemption; (6) up to $2,300 in implements, professional books, or tools of the debtor's trade; (7) unmatured life insurance contracts owned by the debtor, other than a credit life insurance contract; (8) professionally prescribed health aids; (9) social security, veteran's, and disability benefits; (10) unemployment compensation; (11) alimony and support payments, including child support; (12) payments from pension, profit-sharing, and annuity plans; (13) tax-exempt retirement funds; and (14) payments from an award under a crime victim's reparation law, a wrongful death award, and up to $22,975, not including compensation for pain and suffering or for actual pecuniary loss, from a personal injury award. In addition, the debtor may avoid judicial liens on any exempt property and nonpossessory, nonpurchase money security interests on certain household goods, tools of the trade, and professionally prescribed health aids.

The debtor has the option of using either the exemptions provided by the Bankruptcy Code or those available under state law. Nevertheless, a state may, by specific legislative action, limit its citizens to the exemptions provided by state law. More than three-quarters of the states have enacted such legislation. The 2005 Act specifies that a debtor's exemption is governed by the law of the state where the debtor was domiciled for seven hundred and thirty days immediately before filing. If the debtor did not maintain a domicile in a single state for the seven-hundred-and-thirty-day period, then the governing law is of the state where the debtor was domiciled for one hundred and eighty days immediately preceding the seven-hundred-and-thirty-day period (or for a longer portion of such one-hundred-and-eighty-day period than in any other state).

Whether or not federal or state exemptions apply, the 2005 Act provides that tax-exempt retirement accounts are exempt. Individual retirement accounts (IRAs) are subject to a $1,245,475 cap periodically adjusted for inflation. Nevertheless, the 2005 Act makes exempt property liable for nondischargeable domestic support obligations.

The 2005 Act also imposes limits on the use of state homestead exemptions. First, to the extent that the homestead was obtained through fraudulent conversion of nonexempt assets during the ten-year period before filing the petition, the exemption is reduced by that amount. Second, regardless of the level of the state exemption, a debtor may only exempt up to $155,675 of an interest in a homestead that was acquired during the 1,215-day period prior to the filing, but this limitation does not apply to any equity that has been transferred from the debtor's principal residence acquired more than 1,215 days before filing to the debtor's current principal residence if both residences are located in the same state. Third, a debtor may not exempt more than $155,675 if (1) the debtor has been convicted of a felony which under the circumstances demonstrates that the filing of the case was an abuse of the Bankruptcy Code or (2) the debtor owes a debt arising from (a) any violation of state or federal securities laws; (b) fraud, deceit, or manipulation in a fiduciary capacity or in connection with the purchase or sale of securities registered under the Securities Exchange Act of 1934; or (c) any criminal act, intentional tort, or willful or reckless misconduct that caused serious physical injury or death to another individual in the preceding five years. The $155,675 limitation is to be adjusted periodically for inflation.

Practical Advice

If you intend to enter bankruptcy, determine what property is exempt from the debtor's estate in your state and take appropriate action.

Discharge

relief from liability for all debts except those the Bankruptcy Code specifies as not dischargeable

Discharge

Discharge relieves the debtor from liability for all his dischargeable debts. A discharge of a debt voids any judgment obtained at any time concerning that debt and operates as an injunction against the commencement or continuation of any action to recover it.

No private employer may terminate the employment of, or discriminate with respect to employment against, an individual who is or has been a debtor under the Bankruptcy Code solely because such debtor (1) is or has been such a debtor, (2) has been insolvent before the commencement of a case or during the case, or (3) has not paid a debt that is dischargeable in a case under the Bankruptcy Code.

A reaffirmation agreement between a debtor and a creditor permitting the creditor to enforce a discharged debt is enforceable to the extent state law permits but only if (1) the agreement was made before the discharge has been granted; (2) the debtor received the required disclosures, which must be written, clear, and conspicuous, at or before the time at which the debtor signed the agreement; (3) the agreement has been filed with the court, accompanied, if applicable, by a declaration or an affidavit of the attorney who represented the debtor during the course of negotiating the agreement, which states that such agreement represents a fully informed and voluntary agreement by the debtor and imposes no undue hardship on her; (4) the debtor has not rescinded the agreement at any time prior to discharge or within sixty days after the agreement is filed with the court, whichever occurs later; (5) the court has informed a debtor who is an individual that he is not required to enter into such an agreement and has explained the legal effect of the agreement; and (6) in a case concerning an individual who was not represented by an attorney during the course of negotiating the agreement, the court has approved such agreement as imposing no undue hardship on the debtor and being in her best interests.

The Bankruptcy Code provides that certain debts of an individual are ***not dischargeable*** in bankruptcy. This provision applies to individuals receiving discharges under Chapters 7, 11, and, as discussed later in this chapter, the "hardship discharge" provision of Chapter 13. (The 2005 Act makes *most* of these apply to the standard discharge provision of Chapter 13.) The nondischargeable debts include the following:

1. Certain taxes and customs duties and debt incurred to pay such taxes or custom duties
2. Legal liabilities resulting from obtaining money, property, or services by false pretenses, false representations, or actual fraud
3. Legal liability for willful and malicious injuries to the person or property of another
4. Domestic support obligations and property settlements arising from divorce or separation proceedings
5. Debts not scheduled, unless the creditor knew of the bankruptcy
6. Debts the debtor created by fraud or embezzlement while acting in a fiduciary capacity
7. Student loans unless excluding the debt from discharge would impose undue hardship
8. Debts that were or could have been listed in a previous bankruptcy in which the debtor waived or was denied a discharge
9. Consumer debts for luxury goods or services in excess of $650 per creditor, if incurred by an individual debtor on or within ninety days before the order for relief, are presumed to be nondischargeable
10. Cash advances aggregating more than $925 obtained by an individual debtor under an open-ended credit plan within seventy days before the order for relief are presumed to be nondischargeable
11. Liability for death or personal injury based upon the debtor's operation of a motor vehicle, vessel, or aircraft while legally intoxicated
12. Fines, penalties, or forfeitures owed to a governmental entity
13. Certain debts incurred for violations of securities fraud law (This provision was added by the Sarbanes-Oxley Act.)

The following example illustrates the operation of discharge. Donaldson files a petition in bankruptcy. Donaldson owes Anders $1,500, Boynton $2,500, and Conroy $3,000. Assume that Anders's claim is not dischargeable in bankruptcy, while Boynton's and Conroy's are. Anders receives $180 from the liquidation of Donaldson's bankruptcy estate, Boynton receives $300, and Conroy receives $360. If Donaldson receives a bankruptcy discharge, Boynton and Conroy will be precluded from pursuing Donaldson for the remainder of their claims ($2,200 and $2,640, respectively). Anders, on the other hand, because his debt is not dischargeable, may pursue Donaldson for the remaining $1,320, subject to the applicable statute of limitations. If Donaldson does not receive a discharge, Anders, Boynton, and Conroy may all pursue Donaldson for the unpaid portions of their claims.

The Estate [38-2c]

Estate

all legal and equitable
interests of a debtor in
nonexempt property

The commencement of a bankruptcy case creates an **estate**, which is treated as a separate legal entity, distinct from the debtor. The estate consists of all legal and equitable interests of the debtor in nonexempt property at that time. The estate also includes property that the debtor acquires, within one hundred and eighty days after the filing of the petition, by inheritance, by a property settlement, by divorce decree, or as a beneficiary of a life insurance policy. In addition, the estate includes proceeds, rents, and profits from property of the estate and any interest in property that the estate acquires after the case commences. The 2005 Act *excludes* from the estate savings for postsecondary education through education IRAs and 529 plans if certain criteria are met. Finally, the estate includes property that the trustee recovers under her powers (1) as a lien creditor, (2) to avoid voidable preferences, (3) to avoid fraudulent transfers, and (4) to avoid statutory liens. Although in a Chapter 7 case the estate does not include earnings from services an individual debtor performs after the case commences, it does include, in a Chapter 11 or Chapter 13 case, wages an individual debtor earns and property she acquires after the case commences.

Trustee as lien creditor

trustee gains the rights and
powers of a creditor with
a judicial lien

Trustee as Lien Creditor When the case commences, the trustee gains the rights and powers of any creditor with a judicial lien against the debtor that is returned unsatisfied, whether such a creditor exists or not. The trustee is made an ideal creditor possessing every right and power conferred by the law of the state on its most favored creditor who has acquired a lien by legal or equitable proceedings. Because the trustee assumes the rights and powers of a purely hypothetical lien creditor, she need not locate an actual existing lien creditor.

Thus, under the UCC and the Bankruptcy Code, the trustee, as a hypothetical lien creditor, has priority over a creditor with a security interest that was not perfected when the bankruptcy petition was filed. A creditor with a purchase money security interest who files within the grace period allowed under state law, which in most states is twenty days after the debtor receives the collateral, however, will defeat the trustee, even if the petition is gap-filed before the creditor perfects and after the security interest is created. For example, Donald borrows $5,000 from Cathy on September 1 and gives her a security interest in the equipment he purchases with the borrowed funds. On October 3, before Cathy perfects her security interest, Donald files for bankruptcy. The trustee in bankruptcy can invalidate Cathy's security interest because it was unperfected when the bankruptcy petition was filed. Cathy would be able to assert a claim as an unsecured creditor. If, however, Donald had filed for bankruptcy on September 18 and Cathy had perfected the security interest on September 19, Cathy would prevail because she perfected her purchase money security interest within twenty days after Donald received the equipment.

Voidable preferences

Bankruptcy Code
invalidates certain
preferential transfers
made before the date of
bankruptcy from the debtor
to favored creditors

Voidable Preferences The Bankruptcy Code invalidates certain preferential transfers from the debtor to favored creditors before the date of bankruptcy. A creditor who has received a transfer invalidated as preferential may still make a claim for the unpaid debt, but the property he received under the preferential transfer becomes a part of the debtor's estate to be shared by all creditors. The trustee may recover any *transfer* of the debtor's property (1) to or for the benefit of a creditor; (2) for or on account of an antecedent debt the debtor owed before the transfer was made; (3) made while the debtor was insolvent; (4) made on or within ninety days before the date of the filing of the petition or, if the creditor was an "insider" (as defined earlier), within one year of the date of the filing of the petition; and (5) that enables such creditor to receive more than he would have received under Chapter 7.

A transfer is any means, direct or indirect, voluntary or involuntary, of disposing of property or an interest in property, including the retention of title as a security interest. The Bankruptcy Code presumes that the debtor has been insolvent on and during the ninety days immediately preceding the date of the filing of the petition. **Insolvency** is a financial condition such that the sum of one's debts exceeds the sum of all one's property at fair valuation.

Insolvency

financial condition in which
debts exceed fair value of
assets

For example, on March 3, David borrows $15,000 from Carla, promising to repay the loan on April 3. David repays Carla on April 3. Then, on June 1, David files a petition in bankruptcy. His assets are sufficient to pay general creditors only $0.40 on the dollar. David's repayment of the loan is a voidable preference, which the trustee may recover from Carla. The transfer (repayment) on April 3 (1) was to a creditor (Carla), (2) was on account of an antecedent debt (the $15,000 loan made on March 3), (3) was made while the debtor was insolvent (the debtor is presumed insolvent for the ninety days preceding the filing of the bankruptcy petition—June 1), (4) was made within ninety days of bankruptcy (April 3 is less than ninety days before June 1), and (5) enabled the creditor to receive more than she would have received under Chapter 7 (Carla received $15,000; she would have received 0.40 × $15,000 = $6,000 in bankruptcy). After returning the property to the trustee, Carla would have an unsecured claim of $15,000 against David's estate in bankruptcy, for which she would receive $6,000.

Consider another example. On April 16, Debra buys and receives merchandise from Stuart and gives him a security interest in the goods for the unpaid price of $20,000. On May 25, Stuart files a financing statement. On August 1, Debra files a petition for bankruptcy. The trustee in bankruptcy may avoid the perfected security interest as a preferential transfer. (1) The transfer of the perfected security interest on May 25 was to benefit a creditor (Stuart), (2) the transfer was on account of an antecedent debt (the $20,000 owed from the sale of the merchandise), (3) the debtor was insolvent at the time (the debtor's insolvency is presumed for the ninety days preceding the filing of the bankruptcy petition—August 1), (4) the transfer was made within ninety days of bankruptcy (May 25 is less than ninety days before August 1), and (5) the transfer enabled the creditor to receive more than he would have received in bankruptcy (on his secured claim, Stuart would recover more than he would on an unsecured claim).

Nevertheless, not all transfers made within ninety days of bankruptcy are voidable. The Bankruptcy Code makes exceptions for certain prebankruptcy transfers, including the following:

1. *Exchanges for new value.* If, for example, within ninety days before the petition is filed, the debtor purchases an automobile for $9,000, this transfer of property (i.e., the $9,000) is not voidable because it was not made for an antecedent debt but as a substantially contemporaneous exchange for new value.
2. *Enabling security interests.* If the creditor gives the debtor new value that the debtor uses to acquire property in which he grants the creditor a security interest, the security interest is not voidable if the creditor perfects it within thirty days after the debtor receives possession of the property. For example, if within ninety days of the filing of the petition, the debtor purchases a refrigerator on credit and grants the seller or lender a security interest in the refrigerator, the transfer of that interest is not voidable if the secured party perfects within thirty days after the debtor receives possession of the property.
3. *Payments in ordinary course.* The trustee may not avoid a transfer in payment of a debt incurred in the ordinary course of business or financial affairs of the debtor and the transferee and either (a) made in the ordinary course of business or financial affairs of the debtor and transferee or (b) made according to ordinary business terms.
4. *Consumer debts.* If the debtor is an individual whose debts are primarily consumer debts, the trustee may not avoid any transfer of property valued at less than $650.
5. *Nonconsumer debts.* In a case filed by a debtor whose debts are not primarily consumer debts, the trustee may not avoid any transfer of property valued at less than $6,225.
6. *Domestic support obligations.* The trustee may not avoid any transfer that is a bona fide payment of a debt for a domestic support obligation.

Fraudulent transfers

trustee may avoid fraudulent transfers made on or within two years before the date of bankruptcy

Fraudulent Transfers The trustee may avoid **fraudulent transfers** made on or within two years before the date of the filing of the petition. One type of fraudulent transfer consists of the debtor's transferring property with the actual intent to hinder, delay, or defraud any of her creditors. Another consists of the debtor's transferring property for less than a reasonably equivalent consideration when she is insolvent or when the transfer would make her so. For example, Carol, who is in debt, transfers title to her house to Wallace, her father, without any payment by Wallace to Carol and with the understanding that when the house is no longer in danger of seizure by creditors, Wallace will reconvey it to Carol. Carol's transfer of the house is a fraudulent transfer. The 2005 Act specifies that a fraudulent transfer includes a payment to an insider under an employment contract that is not in the ordinary course of business. A 1998 amendment to the Bankruptcy Code provides that a transfer of a charitable contribution to a qualified religious or charitable entity or organization will not be considered a fraudulent transfer if the amount of that contribution does not exceed 15 percent of the gross annual income of the debtor for the year in which the transfer is made. Transfers that exceed 15 percent are protected if they are "consistent with the practices of the debtor in making charitable contributions."

In addition, the trustee may avoid transfers of the debtor's property if the transfer is voidable under state law by a creditor with an allowable, unsecured claim. This section allows a trustee to avoid transfers that violate state fraudulent conveyance statutes, which make it illegal to transfer property to another party to defer, hinder, or defraud creditors. These statutes generally provide a three- to six-year limitations period, which the trustee can utilize. At least forty-three states have adopted the Uniform Fraudulent Transfer Act, which has a four-year statute of limitations.

Statutory liens
trustee may avoid statutory liens that first become effective on insolvency, are not perfected at commencement of the case, or are for rent

Statutory Liens A **statutory lien** arises solely by force of a statute and does not include a security interest or judicial lien. The trustee may avoid a statutory lien on property of the debtor if the lien (1) first becomes effective when the debtor becomes insolvent, (2) is not perfected or enforceable against a *bona fide* purchaser on the date the petition was filed, or (3) is for rent.

LIQUIDATION—CHAPTER 7 [38-3]

Purpose of Chapter 7
to distribute equitably the debtor's nonexempt assets and usually to discharge all dischargeable debts of the debtor

To accomplish its dual goals of distributing the debtor's property fairly and providing the debtor with a fresh start, the Bankruptcy Code has established two approaches: liquidation and adjustment of debts. Chapter 7 uses liquidation, whereas Chapters 11 and 13, discussed later, use the adjustment of debts. Liquidation involves terminating the business of the debtor, distributing his nonexempt assets, and, usually, discharging all his dischargeable debts.

Proceedings [38-3a]

Proceedings under Chapter 7 apply to all debtors except railroads, insurance companies, banks, savings and loan associations, homestead associations, and credit unions. A petition commencing a case under Chapter 7 may be either voluntary or involuntary. After the order for relief, an interim trustee is appointed, who serves until the creditors select a permanent trustee. If the creditors do not elect a trustee, the interim trustee becomes the permanent trustee. Under Chapter 7, the trustee collects and reduces to money the property of the estate; accounts for all property received; investigates the financial affairs of the debtor; examines and, if appropriate, challenges proofs of claims; opposes, if advisable, the discharge of the debtor; and makes a final report of the administration of the estate.

The creditors also may elect a committee of not fewer than three and not more than eleven unsecured creditors to consult with the trustee, to make recommendations to him, and to submit questions to the court.

Conversion [38-3b]

The debtor may convert a case under Chapter 7 to Chapter 11 or Chapter 13; moreover, any waiver of this right is unenforceable. Moreover, on request of a party in interest and after notice and a hearing, the court may convert a case under Chapter 7 to Chapter 11. The court also may convert a case under Chapter 7 to Chapter 13, but this can occur only upon the debtor's request. Any conversion to another chapter can only occur if the debtor may also be a debtor under that chapter.

Marrama v. Citizens Bank
Supreme Court of the United States, 2007
549 U.S. 365, 127 S.Ct. 1105, 166 L.Ed.2d 956
http://scholar.google.com/scholar_case?case=1525401286002576802&q=549+U.S.+365&hl=en&as_sdt=2,34

FACTS Robert Marrama filed a voluntary bankruptcy petition under Chapter 7. In the filing Marrama made a number of statements about his principal asset, a house in Maine, which were misleading or inaccurate. He reported that he was the sole beneficiary of the trust that owned the property and he listed its value as zero. He also denied that he had transferred any property other than in the ordinary course of business during the year preceding the filing of his petition. In fact, the Maine property had substantial value, and Marrama had transferred it into the newly created trust for no consideration seven months prior to filing his petition. Marrama later admitted that the purpose of the transfer was to protect the property from his creditors.

The trustee stated that he intended to recover the Maine property as an asset of the estate. Thereafter, Marrama sought to convert to Chapter 13, but both the trustee and Marrama's principal creditor objected, contending that the request to convert was made in bad faith and would constitute an abuse of the bankruptcy process.

The bankruptcy judge rejected the debtor's arguments, ruled that the facts established a "bad faith" case, and denied the request for conversion. Marrama's principal argument on appeal to the Bankruptcy Appellate Panel for the First Circuit was that he had an absolute right to convert his case from Chapter 7 to Chapter 13 under the language of Section 706(a) of the Code. The panel affirmed the decision of the bankruptcy court and the Court of Appeals for the First Circuit affirmed this ruling. The Supreme Court granted *certiorari*.

DECISION The judgment of the Court of Appeals is affirmed.

OPINION The principal purpose of the Bankruptcy Code is to grant a "fresh start" to the "honest but unfortunate debtor." Both Chapter 7 and Chapter 13 of the Code permit an insolvent individual to discharge certain unpaid debts toward that end. Chapter 7 authorizes a discharge of prepetition debts following the liquidation of the debtor's assets by a bankruptcy trustee, who then distributes the proceeds to creditors. Chapter 13 authorizes an individual with regular income to obtain a discharge after the successful completion of a payment plan approved by the bankruptcy

court. Under Chapter 7 the debtor's nonexempt assets are controlled by the bankruptcy trustee; under Chapter 13 the debtor retains possession of his property. A proceeding that is commenced under Chapter 7 may be converted to a Chapter 13 proceeding and vice versa.

The class of honest but unfortunate debtors who do possess an absolute right to convert their cases from Chapter 7 to Chapter 13 includes the vast majority of the hundreds of thousands of individuals who file Chapter 7 petitions each year. Congress sought to give these individuals the chance to repay their debts should they acquire the means to do so. Moreover, the unenforceability of a waiver of the right to convert functions as a consumer protection provision against contracts requiring a debtor to give up the right to convert to Chapter 13 as a nonnegotiable condition.

A statutory provision protecting a borrower from waiver, however, is not a shield against forfeiture. Nothing in the text of Section 706(a) of the Bankruptcy Code limits the authority of the court to take appropriate action in response to fraudulent conduct by the atypical litigant who has demonstrated that he is not entitled to the relief available to the typical debtor. On the contrary, the broad authority granted to bankruptcy judges to take any action that is necessary or appropriate "to prevent an abuse of process" is adequate to authorize an immediate denial of a motion to convert filed under Section 706(a) of the Bankruptcy Code in lieu of a conversion order that merely postpones the allowance of equivalent relief and may provide a debtor with an opportunity to take action prejudicial to creditors.

INTERPRETATION Prepetition bad-faith conduct may cause a forfeiture of the right to convert a Chapter 7 proceeding into a Chapter 13 case.

CRITICAL THINKING QUESTION Do you agree with the Court's reasoning and its policy arguments? Explain.

ETHICAL QUESTION Did the debtor act ethically? If he did not, should he be entitled to any relief under the Bankruptcy Code? Explain.

Dismissal [38-3c]

The court may dismiss a Chapter 7 case for cause after notice and a hearing. In a case filed by an individual debtor whose debts are primarily consumer debts the court may dismiss a case, or, with the debtor's consent, convert the case to one under Chapter 11 or 13, if the court finds that granting relief would be an abuse of the provisions of Chapter 7. A court can find abuse based on (1) general grounds based on whether the debtor filed the petition in bad faith or the totality of the circumstances of the debtor's financial situation demonstrates abuse *or* (2) an unrebutted presumption of abuse based on a new means test established by the 2005 Act.

Under the **means test** abuse is presumed (i.e., the debtor is not eligible for Chapter 7) for an individual debtor whose net current monthly income is greater than the state median income *and* if either (1) the debtor has available net income (income after deducting allowed expenses) for repayment to creditors over five years totaling at least $12,475, or (2) the available net income for repayment to creditors over five years is between $7,475 and $12,475 and such available net income is at least 25 percent of nonpriority unsecured claims. The means test can be explained by the following scenarios:

1. If the debtor's net current monthly income is less than or equal to the state median income, no presumption of abuse arises.
2. If the debtor's net current monthly income is greater than the state median income *and* the debtor's current monthly income less allowed expenses is less than $124.58 per month, no presumption of abuse arises.
3. If the debtor's net current monthly income is greater than the state median income *and* the debtor's current monthly income less allowed expenses is at least $124.58 per month, a presumption of abuse arises *if* the current monthly income less allowed expenses is sufficient to pay 25 percent of the debtor's nonpriority unsecured claims over sixty months.
4. If the debtor's net current monthly income is greater than the state median income *and* the debtor's current monthly income less allowed expenses is at least $207.92 per month, a presumption of abuse arises without regard to the amount of nonpriority unsecured claims.

For example, Debra's net current monthly income is greater than the state median income. After deducting allowed expenses her monthly income is $150, which places her in the third situation. If her nonpriority unsecured claims are $35,000, a presumption of abuse will arise because $150 multiplied by sixty equals $9,000, which is greater than 25 percent of $35,000, which equals $8,750. On the other hand, Debra would be eligible to file under Chapter 7 if her nonpriority unsecured claims are $36,100, because $150 multiplied by sixty equals $9,000, which is less than 25 percent of $36,100, which equals $9,025.

Distribution of the Estate [38-3d]

Distribution of the estate

in the following order: (1) secured creditors, (2) creditors entitled to a priority, (3) unsecured creditors, and (4) the debtor

After the trustee has collected all the assets of the debtor's estate, she distributes them to the creditors (and, if any assets remain, to the debtor) in the following order:

1. Secured creditors, on their security interests;
2. Creditors entitled to a priority, in the order provided;
3. Unsecured creditors who filed their claims on time (or tardily, if they did not have notice or actual knowledge of the bankruptcy);
4. Unsecured creditors who filed their claims late;
5. Claims for fines and multiple, exemplary, or punitive damages;
6. Interest at the legal rate from the date of the filing of the petition, to all of these claimants; and
7. Whatever property remains, to the debtor.

Claims of the same rank are paid proportionately. For example, Donley has filed a petition for a Chapter 7 proceeding. The total value of Donley's estate after paying the expenses of administration is $25,000. Evans, who is owed $15,000, has a security interest in property valued at $10,000. Fishel has an unsecured claim of $6,000, which is entitled to a priority of $2,000. The United States has a claim for income taxes of $4,000. Green has an unsecured claim of $9,000 that was filed on time. Hiller has an unsecured claim of $12,000 that was filed on time. Jerdee has a claim of $8,000 that was filed late. The distribution would be as follows: (1) Evans receives $11,500, (2) Fishel receives $3,200, (3) the United States receives $4,000, (4) Green receives $2,700, (5) Hiller receives $3,600, and (6) Jerdee receives $0.

Let us analyze this distribution: Evans receives $10,000 as a secured creditor and has an unsecured claim of $5,000. Fishel receives $2,000 on the portion of his claim entitled to a priority and has an unsecured claim of $4,000. The United States has a priority of $4,000. After paying $10,000 to Evans, $2,000 to Fishel, and $4,000 to the United States, there remains $9,000 ($25,000 − $10,000 − $2,000 − $4,000) to be distributed *pro rata* to unsecured creditors who filed on time. Their claims total $30,000 (Evans = $5,000, Fishel = $4,000, Green = $9,000, and Hiller = $12,000). Therefore,

APPLYING THE LAW

Bankruptcy

Facts Maria and Trent Jordan have accumulated $356,327 in unsecured debt on fifty-nine different credit cards, in several cases on six or seven different cards issued by the same financial institutions. Their large debt stems almost exclusively from remodeling their home. While most of the charges relate to purchases of materials, a substantial portion of the total credit card balance represents accrued interest and large cash advances they obtained from some of the cards to enable them to make minimum payments on other cards.

Maria is employed as a nurse, making $45,000 a year. Trent is a carpenter by trade. Though he is healthy and able, for the last three years he has not had outside employment, instead working exclusively on the remodeling project and managing the couple's finances. The median annual income for a two-person family in Florida, where they live, is approximately $47,000.

At this point, the annual interest accruing on the Jordans' credit card balances is about $36,000. They have never made a late payment on any of the credit cards, and they stopped using them six months ago. Their home is still only partially remodeled and is valued at about $115,000, with an outstanding mortgage of approximately $102,000. When the remodeling is complete, the home will be worth in excess of $350,000. However, given its partially completed state, the Jordans' current equity in the house is far less than Florida's homestead exemption. They own two modest automobiles that are subject to purchase money security interests, and they have no other assets of any value.

Earlier this year, the Jordans filed a petition for Chapter 7 bankruptcy relief. The U.S. trustee has now filed a motion to dismiss their case for abuse.

Issue Will the Jordans' petition in bankruptcy be dismissed?

Rule of Law If the court finds that granting relief to an individual debtor with primarily consumer debts would be an abuse of Chapter 7's provisions, the court may dismiss the debtor's bankruptcy case after notice and a hearing. Abuse may be established in one of three situations. First, the debtor may be unable to rebut a statutory presumption of abuse based on the means test established by the Bankruptcy Abuse Prevention and Consumer Protection Act of 2005 (2005 Act). The statutory presumption of abuse, however, does not arise in a case in which the debtor's income is less than the applicable state median income figure. Second, the court may dismiss the debtor's case for abuse if the filing was made in bad faith. Finally, the court might dismiss the bankruptcy case if the totality of the circumstances of the debtor's financial situation reflects abuse.

Application The Jordans are clearly unable to pay their debts, as the annual interest on their credit cards alone nearly engulfs their annual income. Nonetheless, their case may be subject to dismissal for abuse. The first possibility is the statutory presumption of abuse, but because their annual income of $45,000 is less than the state median income of $47,000, the statutory presumption under the 2005 Act does not arise. Next we assess the Jordans' good or bad faith in seeking bankruptcy relief. Their debt does appear to be voluntarily and deliberately incurred; it is not the result of a personal calamity like uninsured illness, involuntary loss of employment, or gambling compulsion. On the other hand, there is no evidence the Jordans made large "eve of bankruptcy" purchases or repeated bankruptcy filings, nor is there any indication they have misrepresented their income or expenses. Therefore, there does not seem to be any basis for a finding of bad faith.

The third potential basis for dismissal is the totality of the debtor's financial circumstances. The Jordans have clearly put themselves in an impossible financial situation. For at least three years before filing they systematically extended themselves far beyond their means. While it belies common sense that any credit card issuer would continue to extend credit to them under their financial circumstances, the fact remains that the Jordans took advantage of credit applications—solicited or unsolicited—to request and obtain fifty-nine different credit card accounts, carefully sustaining only the short-term obligations of each while somehow running up total unsecured debt of eight times their annual income. A court could certainly find that these debtors are using bankruptcy as part of a scheme to avoid obligations they never intended to satisfy. They appear to have made no significant attempt to address their enormous financial obligation. Indeed, it appears as though Mr. Jordan's management of the couple's finances may have become something of a complex game, using a combination of meager income and new cards with available cash advances to placate the demands of growing balances on older cards. Moreover, the couple has sought bankruptcy protection at a time when their remodeling project is still incomplete and their home's potential equity is still unavailable to satisfy the unsecured creditors. While Chapter 7 bankruptcy is a solution for the honest debtor who is hopelessly indebted, bankruptcy for the Jordans instead seems to be just the final step of a calculated process to avoid meaningful financial responsibility.

Conclusion A finding of substantial abuse due to the "totality of the debtor's financial circumstances" is within the discretion of the court. Here, it is likely that a court would dismiss the Jordans' bankruptcy case based on a finding that their intentional, irresponsible choices constitute abuse.

each will receive $9,000/$30,000, or $0.30 on the dollar. Accordingly, Evans receives an additional $1,500, Fishel receives an additional $1,200, Green receives $2,700, and Hiller receives $3,600. Because the assets were insufficient to pay all unsecured claimants who filed on time, Jerdee, who filed tardily, receives nothing. However, if Jerdee's claim were filed late because Donley had failed to

Figure 38-1 Collection and Distribution of the Debtor's Estate

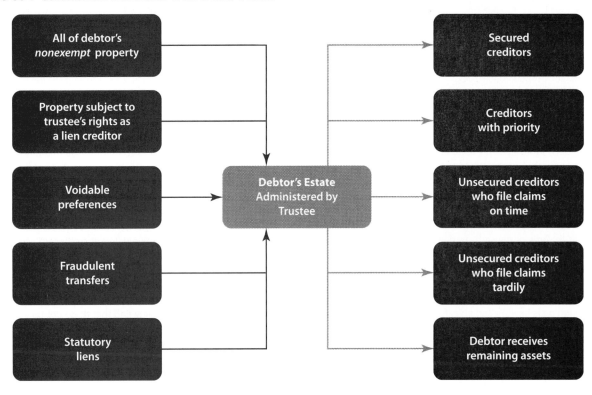

schedule the claim, Donley's debt to Jerdee would not be discharged unless Jerdee knew or had notice of the bankruptcy.

Figure 38-1 summarizes the collection and distribution of the debtor's estate.

Discharge [38-3e]

Discharge

granted by the court unless the debtor has committed an offense under the Bankruptcy Code or has received a discharge (1) within eight years under Chapter 7 or Chapter 11 or (2) subject to exceptions, within six years under Chapter 13

A **discharge** under Chapter 7 relieves the debtor of all debts that arose before the date of the order for relief, except for those debts that are not dischargeable. After distribution of the estate, the court will grant the debtor a discharge unless the debtor (1) is not an individual (partnerships and corporations may not receive a discharge under Chapter 7); (2) has destroyed, falsified, concealed, or failed to keep records and books of account; (3) has knowingly and fraudulently made a false oath or account, presented or used a false claim, or given or received bribes; (4) has transferred, removed, destroyed, or concealed any of his property with intent to hinder, delay, or defraud his creditors within twelve months before the filing of the bankruptcy petition; (5) has within eight years before the bankruptcy been granted a discharge under Chapter 7 or 11; (6) has refused to obey any lawful order of the court or to answer any question approved by the court; (7) has failed to explain satisfactorily any losses of assets or any deficiency of assets to meet his liabilities; or (8) has executed a written waiver of discharge approved by the court. A debtor also will be denied a discharge under Chapter 7 if she received a discharge under Chapter 13 within the past six years, unless payments under that chapter's plan totaled at least (1) 100 percent of the allowed unsecured claims or (2) 70 percent of such claims and the plan was the debtor's best effort.

The 2005 Act denies a discharge to an individual debtor who fails to complete a personal financial management course. This provision, however, does not apply if the debtor resides in a district for which the U.S. trustee or the bankruptcy administrator has determined that the approved instructional courses are not adequate to service the additional individuals who would be required to complete these instructional courses.

On request of the trustee or a creditor and after notice and a hearing, the court may revoke within one year a discharge the debtor obtained through fraud.

REORGANIZATION—CHAPTER 11 [38-4]

Reorganization is the process of correcting or eliminating the factors that caused the distress of a business enterprise to achieve the **purpose of reorganization**: to preserve both the distressed enterprise and its value as a going concern. Chapter 11 of the Bankruptcy Code governs reorganization of eligible debtors—including partnerships, corporations, and individuals—and permits the restructuring of their finances. A number of large corporations have made use of Chapter 11, including WorldCom, Enron, Kmart, Texaco, A. H. Robins, Johns Manville, Allied Stores, Global Crossing, Pacific Gas and Electric, CIT, Conseco, Lehman Brothers, Circuit City, Linens 'n Things, General Motors, and Chrysler. The main objective of a reorganization proceeding is to develop and carry out a fair, equitable, and feasible plan of reorganization.

Purpose of reorganization
to preserve a distressed enterprise and its value as a going concern

After a plan has been prepared and filed, a hearing held before the court determines whether or not it will be confirmed. Chapter 11 permits but does not require a sale of assets. Rather, it contemplates that the debtor will keep its assets and use them to generate earnings that will pay creditors under the terms of the plan confirmed by the court.

The 1994 and 2005 amendments provide for streamlined and more flexible procedures in a small business case, which is any case under Chapter 11 filed by a small business. The amendments define *small business* to include (1) persons engaged in commercial or business activities whose aggregate, noncontingent, liquidated debts do not exceed $2,490,925 (subject to periodic adjustments for inflation); and (2) cases in which the U.S. trustee has not appointed a committee of unsecured creditors or the court has determined that the committee of unsecured creditors is not sufficiently active and representative to provide effective oversight of the debtor. Under a small business case, the U.S. trustee has additional oversight duties, and the debtor has additional reporting requirements, although the plan process can be simpler and the time periods and deadlines are different.

Proceedings [38-4a]

Any person who may be a debtor under Chapter 7 (except a stockbroker or a commodity broker) and railroads may be debtors under Chapter 11. Petitions may be voluntary or involuntary.

As soon as possible after the order for relief, a committee of unsecured creditors (usually those who hold the seven largest unsecured claims against the debtor) is appointed. In addition, the court may order the appointment of additional committees of creditors or of equity security holders, if necessary, to ensure adequate representation. The committee may, with the court's approval, employ attorneys, accountants, and other agents to represent or perform services for the committee. The committee should consult with the debtor or trustee concerning the administration of the case and may investigate the debtor's affairs and participate in formulating a reorganization plan.

The debtor remains in possession and management of the property of the estate unless the court orders the appointment of a trustee, who may then operate the debtor's business. The court orders the appointment of a trustee only for cause (including fraud, dishonesty, incompetence, or gross mismanagement of the debtor's affairs) or if the appointment is in the interests of creditors or equity security holders. The 1994 amendments allow the creditors to elect the trustee.

The duties of a trustee in a case under Chapter 11 include the following: (1) to be accountable for all property received, (2) to examine proofs of claims, (3) to furnish information to all parties with an interest, (4) to provide the court and taxing authorities with financial reports of the debtor's business operations, (5) to make a final report and account of the administration of the estate, (6) to investigate the debtor's financial condition and to determine whether continuing the debtor's business is desirable, and (7) to file a plan or to file a report explaining why there will be no plan or to recommend either dismissal of the case or its conversion to Chapter 7.

At any time before confirming a plan, the court may terminate the trustee's appointment and restore the debtor to possession and management of the estate property and the operation of the debtor's business. When a trustee has not been appointed, which is usually the case, the debtor in possession performs many of the functions and duties of a trustee, with the principal exception of (self-)investigation.

The Bankruptcy Code provides that subsequent to filing and prior to seeking the rejection of union-drafted collective bargaining agreements, the trustee or debtor-in-possession must propose the necessary labor contract modifications that will enable the debtor to reorganize and that will also provide for the fair and equitable treatment of all parties concerned. The Code also requires that good faith meetings to reach a mutually satisfactory agreement be held between management and the union. It authorizes the court to approve rejection of the collective bargaining agreement only if the court finds that the proposal for rejection was made in accordance with these conditions, that the union refused the proposal without good cause, and that the balance of equities clearly favors rejection.

Plan of Reorganization [38-4b]

The debtor may file a plan at any time and has the exclusive right to file a plan during the one hundred and twenty days after the order for relief, unless a trustee has been appointed. Then other parties in interest, including the trustee, if one has been appointed, or a creditors' committee, may file a plan. On request of an interested party and after notice and a hearing, the court may for cause reduce or increase the one-hundred-and-twenty-day or one-hundred-and-eighty-day periods. The 2005 Act provides, however, that the one-hundred-and-twenty-day period may not be extended beyond eighteen months and the one-hundred-and-eighty-day period may not be extended beyond twenty months.

A plan of reorganization must divide creditors' claims and shareholders' interests into classes, specify how each class will be treated, deal with claims within each class equally, and provide adequate means for implementing the plan. After a plan has been filed, the plan and a written disclosure statement approved by the court as containing adequate information must be transmitted to each holder of a claim before seeking acceptance or rejection of the plan. Adequate information is that which would enable a hypothetical reasonable investor to make an informed judgment about the plan.

Acceptance of Plan [38-4c]

Acceptance of plan requires a specified proportion of creditors to approve the plan

Each class of claims and interests has the opportunity to accept or reject the proposed plan. To be accepted by a *class of claims*, a plan must be accepted by creditors that hold at least two-thirds in amount and more than one-half in number of the allowed claims of such class that actually voted on the plan. Acceptance of a plan by a *class of interests*, such as shareholders, requires acceptance by holders of at least two-thirds in amount of the allowed interests of such class that actually voted on the plan.

A class that is not impaired under a plan is deemed to have accepted the plan. Basically, a class is not impaired if the plan leaves unaltered the legal, equitable, and contractual rights to which the holder of such claim or interest is entitled. However, a class that will receive no distribution under a plan is automatically deemed not to have accepted the plan.

Confirmation of Plan [38-4d]

Confirmation of plan requires (1) good faith, (2) feasibility, (3) cash payments to certain priority creditors, and (4) usually acceptance by creditors

The court must confirm a plan before it is binding on any parties, and a court will confirm only a plan that meets all the requirements of the Bankruptcy Code. The following requirements are the most important:

1. The plan must have been proposed in good faith.
2. The court must find that confirmation of the plan is feasible and not likely to be followed by the debtor's liquidation or by its need for further financial reorganization.
3. Unless the claim holder agrees otherwise, certain priority creditors must have their allowed claims paid in full in cash immediately or, in some instances, on a deferred basis. These priority claims include domestic support obligations, the expenses of administration, gap creditors, claims for wages and salaries, employee benefits, and consumer deposits.
4. The plan must be accepted by at least one class of claims, and with respect to each class, each holder must either accept the plan or receive not less than the amount he would have received under Chapter 7. In addition, each class must accept the plan or be unimpaired by it. Nonetheless, under certain circumstances, the court may confirm a plan that is not accepted by all impaired classes by determining that the plan does not discriminate

unfairly and that it is fair and equitable. Under these circumstances, a class of claims or interests may, despite its objections, be subjected to the provisions of a plan. "Fair and equitable" with respect to secured creditors requires that they (1) retain their security interest and receive deferred cash payments, the present value of which is at least equal to their claims; (2) receive a lien on the proceeds of the sale of their collateral if the collateral is sold free and clear of their lien; or (3) realize the "indubitable equivalent" of their claims. Fair and equitable with respect to unsecured creditors means that such creditors are to receive property of value equivalent to the full amount of their claim or that no junior claim or interest is to receive anything. With respect to a class of interests, a plan is fair and equitable if the holders receive full value or if no junior interest receives anything at all.

In the case of a debtor who is an individual, the 2005 Act requires that the plan provide for payments to be made out of the debtor's future earnings from personal services or other future income. It also imposes an additional requirement for confirmation if an unsecured creditor objects to confirmation of the plan: the value of property distributed on account of that claim must not be less than (1) the amount of that claim or (2) the debtor's projected disposable income to be received during the longer of (a) the five-year period beginning on the first payment due date or (b) the plan's term.

RadLAX Gateway Hotel, LLC v. Amalgamated Bank
Supreme Court of the United States, 2012
566 U.S. ____, 132 S.Ct. 2065, 182 L.Ed.2d 967
http://scholar.google.com/scholar_case?q=132+S.CT.+2065+&hl=en&as_sdt=2,34&case=15917701183349776872&scilh=0

FACTS In 2007, RadLAX Gateway Hotel, LLC and RadLAX Gateway Deck, LLC (debtors) purchased the Radisson Hotel at Los Angeles International Airport, together with an adjacent lot on which the debtors planned to build a parking structure. To finance the purchase, the renovation of the hotel, and construction of the parking structure, the debtors obtained a $142 million loan from Longview Ultra Construction Loan Investment Fund, for which Amalgamated Bank (creditor or Bank) served as trustee. The lenders obtained a blanket lien on all of the debtors' assets to secure the loan.

Within two years the debtors had run out of funds and were forced to stop construction. By August 2009, they owed more than $120 million on the loan, with over $1 million in interest accruing every month and no prospect for obtaining additional funds to complete the project. Both debtors filed voluntary petitions under Chapter 11 of the Bankruptcy Code.

Pursuant to Section 1129(b)(2)(A) of the Bankruptcy Code, the debtors sought to confirm a "cramdown" bankruptcy plan over the Bank's objection. That plan proposed selling substantially all of the debtors' property at an auction and using the sale proceeds to repay the Bank. Under the debtors' proposed auction procedures, however, the Bank would not be permitted to bid for the property using the debt it was owed to offset the purchase price, a practice known as "credit-bidding." Instead, the Bank would be forced to bid cash. The Bankruptcy Court denied the debtors' request, concluding that the auction procedures did not comply with the Bankruptcy Code's requirements for cramdown plans. The Seventh Circuit affirmed, holding that Section 1129(b)(2)(A) does not permit debtors to sell an encumbered asset free and clear of a lien without permitting the lienholder to credit-bid.

DECISION Judgment of the Court of Appeals affirmed.

OPINION A Chapter 11 bankruptcy is implemented according to a "plan," typically proposed by the debtor, which divides claims against the debtor into separate "classes" and specifies the treatment each class will receive. Generally, a bankruptcy court may confirm a Chapter 11 plan only if each class of creditors affected by the plan consents. Section 1129(b) creates an exception to that general rule, permitting confirmation of nonconsensual plans—commonly known as "cramdown" plans—if "the plan does not discriminate unfairly, and is fair and equitable, with respect to each class of claims or interests that is impaired under, and has not accepted, the plan." Section 1129(b)(2)(A) establishes criteria for determining whether a cramdown plan is "fair and equitable" with respect to secured claims like the Bank's.

A Chapter 11 plan confirmed over the objection of a "class of secured claims" must meet one of three requirements in order to be deemed "fair and equitable" with respect to the nonconsenting creditor's claim. Section 1129(b)(2)(A) requires that the plan provide:

(i) (I) that the holders of such claims retain the liens securing such claims, whether the property subject to such liens is retained by the debtor or transferred to another entity, to the extent of the allowed amount of such claims; and (II) that each holder of a claim of such class receive on account of such claim deferred cash payments totaling at least the allowed amount of such claim, of a value, as of the effective date of the plan, of at least the value of such holder's interest in the estate's interest in such property;
(ii) for the sale, subject to section 363(k) of this title, of any property that is subject to the liens securing such claims, free and clear of such liens, with such liens to attach to the proceeds of such sale, and the treatment of such liens on proceeds under clause (i) or (iii) of this subparagraph; or
(iii) for the realization by such holders of the indubitable equivalent of such claims.

Under clause (i), the secured creditor retains its lien on the property and receives deferred cash payments. Under clause (ii), the property is sold free and clear of the lien, "subject to section 363(k)," and the creditor receives a lien on the proceeds of the sale. Section 363(k), in turn, provides that "unless the court for cause orders otherwise the holder of such claim may bid at such sale, and, if the holder of such claim purchases such property, such holder may offset such claim against the purchase price of such property"—*i.e.*, the creditor may credit-bid at the sale, up to the amount of its claim. Finally, under clause (iii), the plan provides the secured creditor with the "indubitable equivalent" of its claim.

The debtors in this case have proposed to sell their property free and clear of the Bank's liens, and to repay the Bank using the sale proceeds—precisely, it would seem, the disposition contemplated by clause (ii). Yet since the debtors' proposed auction procedures do not permit the Bank to credit-bid, the proposed sale cannot satisfy the requirements of clause (ii). Recognizing this problem, the debtors instead seek plan confirmation pursuant to clause (iii), which—unlike clause (ii)—does not expressly foreclose the possibility of a sale without credit-bidding. According to the debtors, their plan can satisfy clause (iii) by ultimately providing the Bank with the "indubitable equivalent" of its secured claim, in the form of cash generated by the auction.

The debtors' reading of §1129(b)(2)(A)—under which clause (iii) permits precisely what clause (ii) proscribes—is hyperliteral and contrary to common sense. Here, clause (ii) is a detailed provision that spells out the requirements for selling collateral free of liens, while clause (iii) is a broadly worded provision that says nothing about such a sale. The canon of statutory construction that the specific governs the general explains that the "general language" of clause (iii), "although broad enough to include it, will not be held to apply to a matter specifically dealt with" in clause (ii).

The structure here suggests that (i) is the rule for plans under which the creditor's lien remains on the property, (ii) is the rule for plans under which the property is sold free and clear of the creditor's lien, and (iii) is a residual provision covering dispositions under all other plans—for example, one under which the creditor receives the property itself, the "indubitable equivalent" of its secured claim. Thus, debtors may not sell their property free of liens under §1129(b)(2)(A) without allowing lienholders to credit-bid, as required by clause (ii).

INTERPRETATION A Chapter 11 bankruptcy plan may *not* be confirmed over the objection of a secured creditor if the plan provides for the sale of collateral free and clear of the creditor's lien but does not permit the creditor to "credit-bid" at the sale.

CRITICAL THINKING QUESTION How would the creditor be disadvantaged if it were required to accept the "indubitable equivalent" of its secured claim in the form of cash generated by the auction?

Effect of confirmation

binds the debtor and creditors and discharges the debtor

Effect of Confirmation [38-4e]

After its confirmation, the plan governs the debtor's performance obligations. The plan binds the debtor and any creditor, equity security holder, or general partner of the debtor. After the entry of a final decree closing the proceedings, a debtor that is *not* an individual is discharged from all of its debts and liabilities that arose before the date the plan was confirmed, except as otherwise provided in the plan, the order of confirmation, or the Bankruptcy Code. Unlike Chapter 7, partnerships and corporations may receive a discharge under Chapter 11 unless the plan calls for the liquidation of the business entity's property and termination of its business. The 2005 Act excepts from the discharge of any corporate debtor any debt (1) owed to the government as a result of fraud or (2) arising from a fraudulent tax return or willful evasion of taxes.

An *individual* debtor is not discharged until all plan payments have been made. However, if the debtor fails to make all payments, the court may, after a hearing, grant a "hardship discharge" if the value of property actually distributed is not less than what the creditors would have received under Chapter 7 and modification of the plan is not practicable. A discharge under Chapter 11 does not discharge an *individual* debtor from debts that are not dischargeable.

ADJUSTMENT OF DEBTS OF INDIVIDUALS—CHAPTER 13 [38-5]

Purpose of Chapter 13

to permit an individual debtor to file a repayment plan that will discharge her from most debts

The **purpose of Chapter 13** of the Bankruptcy Code is to permit an individual debtor to file a repayment plan that, if confirmed by the court, will discharge him from almost all of his debts upon completion of the payments under the plan. If, as occurs in many cases, the debtor does not make the required payments under the plan, the case will be converted to Chapter 7 or dismissed.

Proceedings [38-5a]

Chapter 13 provides a procedure for the adjustment of debts of an individual with regular income who owes liquidated, unsecured debts of less than $383,175 and secured debts of less than \$1,149,525. Sole proprietorships that meet these debt limitations are also eligible; partnerships and corporations are not. Only a voluntary petition may initiate a case under Chapter 13, and a trustee is appointed in every Chapter 13 case. Property of the estate in Chapter 13 includes wages the debtor earned and property she acquired after the Chapter 13 filing.

Conversion or Dismissal [38-5b]

The debtor may convert a case under Chapter 13 to Chapter 7. On request of the debtor, if the case has not been previously converted from Chapter 7 or Chapter 11, the court shall dismiss a case under Chapter 13. On request of a party in interest or the U.S. trustee, and after notice and a hearing, the court may convert a case under Chapter 13 to Chapter 7 *or* may dismiss a case under Chapter 13, whichever is in the best interests of creditors and the estate, for cause, including (1) unreasonable delay by the debtor, (2) failure of the debtor to file a plan timely, (3) denial of confirmation of a plan, or (4) material default by the debtor with respect to a term of a confirmed plan. Before the confirmation of a plan, on request of a party in interest or the U.S. trustee and after notice and a hearing, the court may convert a case under Chapter 13 to Chapter 11. Nonetheless, a case may *not* be converted to another chapter unless the debtor may be a debtor under that chapter.

The Plan [38-5c]

The debtor files the plan and may modify it at any time before confirmation. The plan must meet three requirements:

1. It must require the debtor to submit all or any portion of her future earnings or income, as is necessary for the execution of the plan, to the trustee's supervision and control.
2. It must provide for full payment on a deferred basis of all claims entitled to a priority unless a holder of a claim agrees to a different treatment of such claim.
3. If the plan classifies claims, it must provide the same treatment for each claim in the same class.

In addition, the plan may modify the rights of unsecured creditors and the rights of secured creditors, except those secured only by a security interest in the debtor's principal residence. If the debtor's net current monthly income is equal to or greater than the state median income, the plan may not provide for payments over a period longer than five years. If the debtor's net current monthly income is less than the state median income, the plan may not provide for payments over a period longer than three years, unless the court approves, for cause, a longer period not to exceed five years.

Confirmation of Plan [38-5d]

Confirmation of plan
requires that (1) it be made in good faith; (2) the present value of property distributed to unsecured creditors not be less than the amount that would be paid them under Chapter 7; (3) secured creditors accept the plan, keep their collateral, or retain their security interest and the present value of the property to be distributed to them is not less than the allowed amount of their claim; and (4) the debtor be able to make all payments and comply with the plan

To be confirmed by the court, the plan must meet certain requirements. First, the filing of the case must have been in good faith, and the plan must comply with applicable law and be proposed in good faith. Second, the present value of the property to be distributed to unsecured creditors must not be less than the amount they would receive under Chapter 7. Third, either the secured creditors must accept the plan, the plan must provide that the debtor will surrender the collateral to the secured creditors, or the plan must permit the secured creditors to retain their security interests and the present value of the property to be distributed to them is not less than the allowed amount of their claim. Fourth, the debtor must be able to make all payments and comply with the plan. Fifth, if the trustee or the holder of an unsecured claim objects to the plan's confirmation, then the plan must either provide for payments the present value of which is not less than the amount of that claim or provide that all of the debtor's disposable income for three years will be paid to unsecured creditors under the plan. If, however, the debtor's net current monthly income is equal to or greater than the state median income, the debtor's disposable income for not less than five years must be committed to pay unsecured creditors. For purposes of this provision, *disposable income* means current monthly income received by the debtor that is not reasonably necessary for the maintenance or support of the debtor or a dependent of the debtor, for domestic support obligations, and, if the debtor is engaged in business, for the payment of expenditures necessary for continuing, preserving, and operating the business. Sixth, if a debtor is required by judicial or administrative order or statute to pay a domestic support obligation, then the debtor must pay all such obligations that became payable after the filing.

Hamilton v. Lanning
Supreme Court of the United States, 2010
560 U.S. 505, 130 S.Ct. 2464, 177 L.Ed.2d 23
http://scholar.google.com/scholar_case?q=130+S.Ct.+2464&hl=en&as_sdt=2,34&case=7122148824674520754&scilh=0

FACTS The debtor (respondent) had $36,793.36 in unsecured debt when she filed for Chapter 13 bankruptcy protection in October 2006. In the six months before her filing, she had received a onetime buyout from her former employer, and this payment greatly inflated her gross income for April 2006 (to $11,990.03) and for May 2006 (to $15,356.42). As a result of these payments, respondent's current monthly income, as averaged from April through October 2006, was $5,343.70—a figure that exceeds the median income for a family of one in Kansas. The respondent's monthly expenses were $4,228.71. She reported a monthly "disposable income" of $1,114.98 on Form 22C.

On the form used for reporting monthly income (Schedule I), she reported income from her new job of $1,922 per month—which is below the state median. On the form used for reporting monthly expenses (Schedule J), she reported actual monthly expenses of $1,772.97. Subtracting the Schedule J figure from the Schedule I figure resulted in monthly disposable income of $149.03.

The respondent filed a plan that would have required her to pay $144 per month for 36 months. The petitioner, a private Chapter 13 trustee, objected to confirmation of the plan because the amount the respondent proposed to pay was less than the full amount of the claims against her, and because, in the petitioner's view, the respondent was not committing all of her "projected disposable income" to the repayment of creditors. The petitioner argues that the proper way to calculate projected disposable income was simply to multiply disposable income, as calculated on Form 22C, by the number of months in the commitment period. Employing this mechanical approach, the petitioner calculated that creditors would be paid in full if the respondent made monthly payments of $756 for a period of sixty months. Both parties agree that the respondent's actual income was insufficient to make payments in that amount.

The Bankruptcy Court endorsed the respondent's proposed monthly payment of $144 but required a sixty-month plan period. The court agreed that the word "projected" in Section 1325(b)(1)(B) of the Bankruptcy Code requires courts "to consider at confirmation the debtor's *actual* income as it was reported on Schedule I." The Bankruptcy Court reasoned that this conclusion was warranted by the text of Section 1325(b)(1) and was necessary to avoid the absurd result of denying bankruptcy protection to individuals with deteriorating finances in the six months before filing. The petitioner appealed to the Tenth Circuit Bankruptcy Appellate Panel, which affirmed. The Tenth Circuit also affirmed. The trustee appealed to the U.S. Supreme Court.

DECISION The decision of the Court of Appeals is affirmed.

OPINION Chapter 13 of the Bankruptcy Code provides bankruptcy protection to "individual[s] with regular income" whose debts fall within statutory limits. Unlike debtors who file under Chapter 7 and must liquidate their nonexempt assets to pay creditors, Chapter 13 debtors are permitted to keep their property, but they must agree to a court-approved plan under which they pay creditors out of their future income. A bankruptcy trustee oversees the filing and execution of a Chapter 13 debtor's plan.

Section 1325 of the Bankruptcy Code specifies circumstances under which a bankruptcy court "shall" and "may not" confirm a plan. If an unsecured creditor or the bankruptcy trustee objects to confirmation, Section 1325(b)(1) requires the debtor either to pay unsecured creditors in full or to pay all "projected disposable income" to be received by the debtor over the duration of the plan.

Before the enactment of the Bankruptcy Abuse Prevention and Consumer Protection Act of 2005 (BAPCPA), the Bankruptcy Code loosely defined "disposable income" as "income which is received by the debtor and which is not reasonably necessary to be expended" for the "maintenance or support of the debtor," for qualifying charitable contributions, or for business expenditures. The Code did not define the term "projected disposable income," and in most cases, bankruptcy courts used a mechanical approach in calculating projected disposable income. That is, they first multiplied monthly income by the number of months in the plan and then determined what portion of the result was "excess" or "disposable." In exceptional cases, however, bankruptcy courts took into account foreseeable changes in a debtor's income or expenses.

BAPCPA left the term "projected disposable income" undefined but specified in some detail how "disposable income" is to be calculated. "Disposable income" is now defined as "current monthly income received by the debtor" less "amounts reasonably necessary to be expended" for the debtor's maintenance and support, for qualifying charitable contributions, and for business expenditures. "Current monthly income," in turn, is calculated by averaging the debtor's monthly income during what the parties refer to as the six-month look-back period, which generally consists of the six full months preceding the filing of the bankruptcy petition. The phrase "amounts reasonably necessary to be expended" in Section 1325(b)(2) is also newly defined. For a debtor whose income is below the median for his or her state, the phrase includes the full amount needed for "maintenance or support," but for a debtor with income that exceeds the state median, only certain specified expenses are included.

Petitioner, advocating the mechanical approach, contends that "projected disposable income" means past average monthly disposable income multiplied by the number of months in a debtor's plan. Respondent, who favors the forward-looking approach, agrees that the method outlined by petitioner should be determinative in most cases, but she argues that in exceptional cases, where significant changes in a debtor's financial circumstances are known or virtually certain, a bankruptcy court has discretion to make an appropriate adjustment. Respondent has the stronger argument.

First, respondent's argument is supported by the ordinary meaning of the term "projected." "When terms used in a statute are undefined, [the courts] give them their ordinary meaning." Here, the term "projected" is not defined, and in ordinary usage future occurrences are not "projected" based on the assumption that the past will necessarily repeat itself. While a projection takes past events into account, adjustments are often made based on other factors that may affect the final outcome.

Second, the word "projected" appears in many federal statutes, yet Congress rarely has used it to mean simple multiplication. By contrast, as the Bankruptcy Code shows, Congress can make its mandate of simple multiplication, unambiguously—most commonly by using the term "multiplied."

Third, pre-BAPCPA case law points in favor of the "forward-looking" approach.

In cases in which a debtor's disposable income during the six-month look-back period is either substantially lower or higher than the debtor's disposable income during the plan period, the mechanical approach would produce senseless results that Congress did not intend. In cases in which the debtor's disposable income is higher during the plan period, the mechanical approach would deny creditors payments that the debtor could easily make. And where, as in the present case, the debtor's disposable income during the plan period is substantially lower, the mechanical approach would deny the protection of Chapter 13 to debtors who meet the chapter's main eligibility requirements.

INTERPRETATION When a bankruptcy court calculates a Chapter 13 debtor's projected disposable income, the court may account for changes in the debtor's income or expenses that are known or virtually certain at the time of confirmation.

CRITICAL THINKING QUESTION Does this ruling make it possible for debtors to time the filing of the Chapter 13 petition in order to lower the required payments under the Chapter 13 plan?

Effect of Confirmation [38-5e]

The provisions of a confirmed plan bind the debtor and all of her creditors. The confirmation of a plan vests in the debtor all property of the estate free and clear of any creditor's claim or interest for which the plan provides, except as otherwise provided in the plan or in the order confirming the plan. A plan may be modified after confirmation at the request of the debtor, the trustee, or a holder of an unsecured claim.

Discharge [38-5f]

Before the 2005 Act the discharge under Chapter 13 was considerably more extensive than that granted under Chapter 7. The 2005 Act, however, made the discharge of debts under Chapter 13 less extensive than previously. As a result Chapter 13 discharges only a few types of debts that are not also discharged under Chapter 7.

After a debtor completes all payments under the plan and of certain postpetition domestic support obligations, the court will grant him a discharge of all debts for which the plan provides, except the nondischargeable debts for (1) unfiled, late-filed, and fraudulent tax returns; (2) legal liabilities resulting from obtaining money, property, or services by false pretenses, false representations, or actual fraud; (3) legal liability for willful *or* malicious conduct that caused personal injury to an individual; (4) domestic support obligations; (5) debts not scheduled unless the creditor knew of the bankruptcy; (6) debts the debtor created by fraud or embezzlement while acting in a fiduciary capacity; (7) most student loans; (8) consumer debts for luxury goods or services in excess of $650 per creditor if incurred by an individual debtor on or within ninety days before the order for relief; (9) cash advances aggregating more than $925 obtained by an individual debtor under an open-ended credit plan within seventy days before the order for relief; (10) liability for death or personal injury based upon the debtor's operation of a motor vehicle, vessel, or aircraft while legally intoxicated; (11) restitution or criminal fine included in a sentence for a criminal conviction; and (12) certain long-term obligations on which payments extend beyond the term of the plan.

Even if the debtor fails to make all payments, the court may, after a hearing, grant a "hardship discharge" if the debtor's failure is due to circumstances for which the debtor is not justly accountable, the value of property actually distributed is not less than what the creditors would have received under Chapter 7, and modification of the plan is not practicable. This discharge is subject, however, to the same exceptions for nondischargeable debts as a discharge under Chapter 7.

The 2005 Act denies a discharge under Chapter 13 to a debtor who has received a discharge (1) in a prior Chapter 7 or Chapter 11 case filed during the four-year period preceding the filing of the Chapter 13 case or (2) in a prior Chapter 13 case filed during the two-year

CONCEPT REVIEW 38-1

Comparison of Bankruptcy Proceedings

	Chapter 7	Chapter 11	Chapter 12	Chapter 13
Objective	Liquidation	Reorganization	Adjustment	Adjustment
Eligible Debtors	Most debtors	Most debtors, including railroads	Family farmer who meets certain debt limitations	Individual with regular income who meets certain debt limitations
Type of Petition	Voluntary or involuntary	Voluntary or involuntary	Voluntary	Voluntary
Trustee	Usually selected by creditors; otherwise appointed	Only if court orders appointment for cause; creditors then may select trustee	Appointed	Appointed

period preceding the date of filing the subsequent Chapter 13 case. It also denies a discharge to a debtor who fails to complete a personal financial management course. This provision, however, does not apply if the debtor resides in a district for which the U.S. trustee or the bankruptcy administrator has determined that the approved instructional courses are not adequate to service the additional individuals who would be required to complete these required instructional courses.

CREDITORS' RIGHTS AND DEBTORS' RELIEF OUTSIDE OF BANKRUPTCY

The rights and remedies of debtors and creditors outside of bankruptcy are governed mainly by state law. Because of the expense and notoriety associated with bankruptcy, resolving claims outside of a bankruptcy proceeding is often in the best interests of both debtor and creditor. Accordingly, bankruptcy is usually considered a last resort.

Outside of bankruptcy, the rights and remedies of creditors are varied. In the first part of this section, we will examine the basic right of all creditors to pursue their overdue claims to judgment and to satisfy that judgment out of property belonging to the debtor. (Other rights and remedies are discussed elsewhere in this book.) The second part of this section will describe the various forms of nonbankruptcy compromises that provide relief to debtors who have become overextended and who are unable to pay all of their creditors.

CREDITORS' RIGHTS [38-6]

When a debtor fails to pay a debt, the creditor may file suit to collect it. The goal is to obtain a judgment against the debtor and to collect on that judgment.

Prejudgment Remedies [38-6a]

Attachment

seizure of property to bring it under the custody of the court

Because litigation takes time, a creditor attempting to collect on a claim through the judicial process almost always experiences delay in obtaining judgment. To prevent the debtor from meanwhile disposing of his assets, the creditor may use, when available, certain prejudgment remedies. The most important of these is **attachment**, the process of seizing property, through a judicial order, and bringing the property into the court's custody to secure satisfaction of the judgment ultimately to be entered in the action. Most states limit attachment to specified grounds and provide the debtor an opportunity for a hearing before a judge prior to the issuance of a writ of execution. In addition, the plaintiff generally must post a bond to compensate the defendant for loss should the plaintiff not prevail in the cause of action.

Garnishment

proceeding by a creditor against a third person who owes money to debtor

Similar in purpose is the remedy of prejudgment **garnishment**, which is a statutory proceeding directed at a third person who owes a debt to the debtor or who has property belonging to the debtor. Garnishment is most commonly used against the debtor's employer and the bank in which the debtor has a savings or checking account. Garnished property remains in the hands of the third party pending the outcome of the suit.

Postjudgment Remedies [38-6b]

If the debtor still has not paid the claim, the creditor may proceed to trial and try to obtain a court judgment against the debtor. Although necessary, obtaining a judgment is, nevertheless, only the first step. If the debtor does not voluntarily pay the judgment, the creditor will have to take additional steps to collect on it. These steps are called postjudgment remedies.

Writ of execution

order served by sheriff upon debtor demanding payment of a court judgment against debtor

First, the judgment creditor will have the court clerk issue a **writ of execution** demanding payment of the judgment, which is served by the sheriff upon the defendant debtor. Upon return of the writ "unsatisfied," the judgment creditor may post bond or other security and order a levy on and sale of specified nonexempt property belonging to the defendant debtor, which is then seized by the sheriff, advertised for sale, and sold at public sale under the writ of execution.

The writ of execution is limited to nonexempt property of the debtor. All states restrict creditors from recourse to certain property, the type and amount of which varies greatly from state to state.

If the proceeds of the sale do not produce funds sufficient to pay the judgment, the creditor may institute a *supplementary proceeding* in an attempt to locate money or other property belonging to the defendant. She may also proceed by *garnishment* against the debtor's employer or against a bank in which the debtor has an account. As discussed in Chapter 44, state and federal statutes contain exemption provisions that limit the amount of wages subject to garnishment.

Debtors' Relief [38-7]

The rights of creditors and the debtor's need for relief involve inherent conflicts arising from the following: (1) the right of diligent creditors to pursue their claims to judgment and to satisfy their judgments by sale of property of the debtor, (2) the right of unsecured creditors who have refrained from suing the debtor, and (3) the social policy of giving relief to a debtor who has contracted debts beyond his ability to pay and who therefore may carry a lifetime burden. Various forms of nonbankruptcy compromises have been developed to resolve these conflicts.

Compositions [38-7a]

Composition

agreement between debtor and two or more of her creditors that each will take a portion of his claim as full payment

A common law or nonstatutory **composition** (or "workout") is an ordinary contract or agreement between the debtor and two or more of her creditors under which the creditors receive a proportional part of their claims and the debtor is discharged from the balance of the claims. A composition is the state law analogue of Chapter 11 of the Bankruptcy Act. As a contract, it requires contractual formalities. For example, debtor D, owing debts of $5,000 to A, $2,000 to B, and $1,000 to C, offers to settle these claims by paying a total of $4,000 to A, B, and C. If A, B, and C accept the offer, a composition results, with A receiving $2,500, B $1,000, and C $500. The consideration for the promise of A to forgive the balance of his claim consists of the promises of B and C to forgive the balance of their claims. By avoiding a conflict among themselves to obtain the debtor's limited assets, all the creditors benefit.

We should note, however, that the debtor in a composition is discharged from liability only on the claims of those creditors who voluntarily consent to the composition. If, in this illustration, C had refused to accept the offer of composition and had refused to take the $500, he could attempt to collect his full $1,000 claim. Likewise, if D owed additional debts to X, Y, and Z, these creditors would not be bound by the agreement between D and A, B, and C. Another disadvantage of the composition is the fact that any creditor can attach the debtor's assets during the bargaining period that usually precedes the execution of the composition agreement. For instance, once D had advised A, B, and C that he was offering to compose the claims, any one of the creditors could seize D's property.

A variation of the composition is an extension agreement, developed by the debtor and two or more of her creditors, that provides an extended period of time for payment of her debts either in full or proportionately reduced.

Assignments for Benefit of Creditors [38-7b]

Assignment for benefit of creditors

voluntary transfer by the debtor of his property to a trustee, who applies the property to the payment of all the debtor's debts

A common law or nonstatutory **assignment for the benefit of creditors**, or a general assignment, as it is sometimes called, is a debtor's voluntary transfer of her property to a trustee, who applies the property to the payment of all the debtor's debts. For instance, debtor D transfers title to her property to trustee T, who converts the property into money and pays it to all of the creditors on a *pro rata* basis. An assignment for the benefit of creditors is a state law analogue of Chapter 7 of the Bankruptcy Act.

In most states, statutes now govern assignments for the benefit of creditors. These statutes typically require recording of the assignment, filing schedules of assets and liabilities, and providing notice to the creditors. Almost all of the statutes require that all creditors be treated equally, except those with liens or statutorily created priorities.

The advantage of an assignment over a composition is that it prevents the debtor's assets from being attached or executed and halts diligent creditors in their race to attach. An assignment does not require the creditors' consent, and the trustee's payment of part of the claims does not discharge the debtor from the balance of them. Thus, in the previous example, even after T pays A $2,500, B $1,000, and C $500 (and makes appropriate payments to all other creditors), A, B, and C and the other creditors may still attempt to collect the balance of their claims. Moreover, an assignment for the benefit of creditors is a ground for sustaining an involuntary petition for bankruptcy.

Because assignments benefit creditors by protecting the debtor's assets from attachment, some statutory enactments have endeavored to combine the idea of the assignment with a corresponding benefit that would discharge the debtor from the balance of his debts. However, because the U.S. Constitution prohibits a state from impairing a contractual obligation between private citizens, it is impossible for a state to force all creditors to discharge a debtor on a *pro rata* distribution of assets, although, as previously discussed, the federal government does have such power and exercises it in the Bankruptcy Code. Accordingly, the states generally have enacted assignment statutes permitting the debtor to obtain voluntary releases of the balance of claims from creditors who accept partial payments, thus combining the advantages of common law compositions and assignments.

Equity Receiverships [38-7c]

Equity receivership

receiver is a disinterested person appointed by the court to collect and preserve the debtor's assets and income and to dispose of them at the direction of the court

One of the oldest remedies in equity is the court's appointment of a receiver, a disinterested person who collects and preserves the debtor's assets and income and disposes of them at the court's direction. The court may instruct the receiver (1) to liquidate the assets by public or private sale, (2) to operate the business as a going concern temporarily, or (3) to conserve the assets until final disposition of the matter before the court.

A receiver will be appointed on the petition (1) of a secured creditor seeking foreclosure of his security, (2) of a judgment creditor who has exhausted legal remedies to satisfy the judgment, or (3) of a shareholder of a corporate debtor whose assets will likely be dissipated by fraud or mismanagement. The receiver is always appointed at the discretion of the court. Insolvency, in the equity sense of the debtor's inability to pay her debts as they mature, is one of the factors the court considers in appointing a receiver.

ETHICAL DILEMMA

For a Company Contemplating Bankruptcy, When Is Disclosure the Best Policy?

Facts Doris Williams is a senior executive for Foundation Insurance Corporation, a publicly held insurance company that issues a broad range of policies. Early in January, Williams was appointed to serve on a management team composed of herself and four other executive officers. The team reviews and finalizes recommendations for establishing loss reserves, recommendations regarding dividend payments to shareholders, and proposals for press releases.

For the past few years, Foundation has experienced increasingly alarming financial difficulties. Ten years ago, in order to compete with alternative investments, the company developed many innovative life insurance products to provide both traditional insurance and an attractive savings vehicle for the insured. However, to meet the high interest payments on these new insurance products, management invested in risky real estate ventures that promised—but often failed

to deliver—high returns. Foundation's property and casualty lines also experienced increased losses due to poor actuarial decisions and an unexpected rise in workers' compensation claims.

Toward the end of the first quarter, during the management team's review of dividend payments, Williams recommended slashing dividend payments, bolstering loss reserves, and publicly disclosing the company's growing financial problems. The four other committee members disagreed. They feared that the public would panic and that the effect on the market would be disastrous. They wanted more time to attempt to turn around the business. Williams went along with the committee for the first and second quarters. By the third quarter, however, the committee could no longer avoid recommending an unprecedented reduction in dividends and a dramatic increase in reserves. By the end of the year, the company, having

become insolvent, filed for bankruptcy protection. The current management team now wishes to reorganize the company.

Social, Political, and Ethical Considerations

1. Was it ethical for Williams to acquiesce with regard to the first and second quarters? Consider the interests of the consumer/policyholder, the company, the shareholders, and the members of the committee. Was there merit to the committee's request for more time to remedy the company's problems?

2. Should bankrupt insurers be treated differently from other bankrupt corporations? What role, if any, should government play in insuring insurance companies?

3. Should the old management team be allowed to retain control of Foundation? Why? Why not?

CHAPTER SUMMARY

Federal Bankruptcy Law

Case Administration— Chapter 3

Commencement of the Case the filing of a voluntary or involuntary petition begins jurisdiction of the bankruptcy court

- *Voluntary Petitions* available to any eligible debtor even if solvent
- *Involuntary Petitions* may be filed only under Chapter 7 or Chapter 11 if the debtor is generally not paying his debts as they become due

Dismissal the court may dismiss a case for cause after notice and a hearing; under Chapter 13, the debtor has an absolute right to have his case dismissed

Automatic Stay prevents attempts by creditors to recover claims against the debtor

Trustee responsible for collecting, liquidating, and distributing the debtor's estate

Meeting of Creditors debtor must appear and submit to an examination of her financial situation

Creditors, the Debtor, and the Estate— Chapter 5

Creditor any entity that has a claim against the debtor

- *Claim* a right to payment
- *Lien* charge or interest in property to secure payment of a debt or performance of an obligation
- *Secured Claim* claim with a lien on property of the debtor
- *Unsecured Claim* portion of a claim that exceeds the value of any property securing that claim
- *Priority of Claim* the right of certain claims to be paid before claims of lesser rank

Debtors

- *Debtor's Duties* the debtor must file specified information, cooperate with the trustee, and surrender all property of the estate
- *Debtor's Exemptions* determined by state or federal law, depending upon the state
- *Discharge* relief from liability for all debts except those the Bankruptcy Code specifies as not dischargeable

The Estate all legal and equitable interests of a debtor in nonexempt property

- *Trustee as Lien Creditor* trustee gains the rights and powers of a creditor with a judicial lien (an interest in property, obtained by court action, to secure payment of a debt)
- *Voidable Preferences* Bankruptcy Code invalidates certain preferential transfers made before the date of bankruptcy from the debtor to favored creditors
- *Fraudulent Transfers* trustee may avoid fraudulent transfers made on or within two years before the date of bankruptcy
- *Statutory Liens* trustee may avoid statutory liens that first become effective on insolvency, are not perfected at commencement of the case, or are for rent

Liquidation—Chapter 7

Purpose to distribute equitably the debtor's nonexempt assets and usually to discharge all dischargeable debts of the debtor

Proceedings apply to most debtors

Conversion a Chapter 7 case may be voluntarily converted to Chapter 11 or Chapter 13; a Chapter 7 case may be involuntarily converted by the court to Chapter 11

Dismissal the court may dismiss a case on general grounds *and* in a case filed by an individual debtor based on a means test

Distribution of the Estate in the following order: (1) secured creditors, (2) creditors entitled to a priority, (3) unsecured creditors, and (4) the debtor

Discharge granted by the court unless the debtor has committed an offense under the Bankruptcy Code or has received a discharge (1) within eight years under Chapter 7 or Chapter 11 or (2) subject to exceptions, within six years under Chapter 13

Reorganization—Chapter 11

Purpose to preserve a distressed enterprise and its value as a going concern

Proceedings debtor usually remains in possession of the property of the estate

Acceptance of Plan requires a specified proportion of creditors to approve the plan

Confirmation of Plan requires (1) good faith, (2) feasibility, (3) cash payments to certain priority creditors, and (4) usually acceptance by creditors

Effect of Confirmation binds the debtor and creditors and discharges the debtor

Adjustment of Debts of Individuals—Chapter 13

Purpose to permit an individual debtor to file a repayment plan that will discharge her from most debts

Conversion or Dismissal a Chapter 13 case may be voluntarily or involuntarily dismissed or converted to Chapter 7 or Chapter 11

Confirmation of Plan requires (1) that it be made in good faith; (2) that the present value of property distributed to unsecured creditors not be less than the amount that would be paid them under Chapter 7; (3) that secured creditors accept the plan, keep their collateral, or retain their security interest, and the present value of the property to be distributed to them is not less than the allowed amount of their claim; and (4) that the debtor be able to make all payments and comply with the plan

Discharge after a debtor completes all payments under the plan

Creditors' Rights and Debtors' Relief Outside Bankruptcy

Creditors' Rights

Prejudgment Remedies include attachment and garnishment

Postjudgment Remedies include writ of execution and garnishment

Debtors' Relief

Compositions agreement between debtor and two or more of her creditors that each will take a portion of his claim as full payment

Assignment for Benefit of Creditors voluntary transfer by the debtor of his property to a trustee, who applies the property to the payment of all the debtor's debts

Equity Receivership receiver is a disinterested person appointed by the court to collect and preserve the debtor's assets and income and to dispose of them at the direction of the court

QUESTIONS

1. **a.** Benson goes into bankruptcy. His estate is not sufficient to pay all taxes owed. Explain whether Benson's taxes are discharged by the proceedings.
   b. Benson obtained property from Anderson on credit by representing that he was solvent when in fact he knew he was insolvent. Explain whether Benson's debt to Anderson is discharged by Benson's discharge in bankruptcy.

2. Bradley goes into bankruptcy under Chapter 7 owing $25,000 as wages to his four employees. There is enough in his estate to pay all costs of administration and enough to pay his employees, but nothing will be left for general creditors. Do the employees take all the estate? If so, under what conditions? If the general creditors received nothing at all, would these debts be discharged?

3. Jessica sold goods to Stacy for $2,500 and retained a security interest in them. Two months later, Stacy filed a voluntary petition in bankruptcy under Chapter 7. At this time, Stacy still owed Jessica $2,000 for the purchase price of the goods, the value of which was $1,500.
   a. May the trustee invalidate Jessica's security interest? If so, under what provision?
   b. If the security interest is invalidated, what is Jessica's status in the bankruptcy proceeding?
   c. If the security interest is not invalidated, what is Jessica's status in the bankruptcy proceeding?

4. A debtor went through bankruptcy under Chapter 7 and received his discharge. Which of the following debts were completely discharged, and which remain as future debts against him?
   a. A claim of $9,000 for wages earned within five months immediately prior to bankruptcy.
   b. A judgment of $3,000 against the debtor for breach of contract.
   c. Sales taxes of $1,800.
   d. $1,000 for past domestic support obligations.
   e. A judgment of $4,000 for injuries received because of the debtor's negligent operation of an automobile.

5. Rosinoff and his wife, who were business partners, entered bankruptcy. A creditor, Baldwin, objected to their discharge in bankruptcy on the grounds that
   a. the partners had obtained credit from Baldwin on the basis of a false financial statement;
   b. the partners had failed to keep books of account and records from which their financial condition could be determined; and

   c. Rosinoff had falsely sworn that he had taken $70.00 from the partnership account when he had actually taken $700. Were the debtors entitled to a discharge?

6. X Corporation is a debtor in a reorganization proceeding under Chapter 11 of the Bankruptcy Code. By fair and proper valuation, its assets are worth $100,000. The indebtedness of the corporation is $105,000, and it has outstanding preferred stock of par value of $20,000 and common stock of par value of $75,000. The plan of reorganization submitted by the trustees would eliminate the common shareholders and would issue new bonds of the face amount of $5,000 to the creditors and new common stock in the ratio of 84 percent to the creditors and 16 percent to the preferred shareholders. Should this plan be confirmed?

7. Alex is a wage earner with a regular income. He has unsecured debts of $42,000 and secured debts owing to Betty, Connie, David, and Eunice totaling $120,000. Eunice's debt is secured only by a mortgage on Alex's house. Alex files a petition under Chapter 13 and a plan providing payment as follows: (a) 60 percent of all taxes owed; (b) 35 percent of all unsecured debts; and (c) $100,000 in total to Betty, Connie, David, and Eunice. Should the court confirm the plan? If not, how must the plan be modified or what other conditions must be satisfied?

8. John Bunker has assets of $130,000 and liabilities of $185,000 owed to nine creditors. Nonetheless, his cash flow is positive and he is making payment on all of his obligations as they become due. I. M. Flintheart, who is owed $22,000 by Bunker, files an involuntary petition in bankruptcy under Chapter 7 against Bunker. Bunker contests the petition. What will be the result? Explain.

9. Karen has filed a voluntary petition for a Chapter 7 proceeding. The total value of Karen's estate is $35,000. Ben, who is owed $18,000, has a security interest in property valued at $12,000. Lauren has an unsecured claim of $9,000, which is entitled to a priority of $2,000. The United States has a claim for income taxes of $7,000. Steve has an unsecured claim of $10,000 that was filed on time. Sarah has an unsecured claim of $17,000 that was filed on time. Wally has a claim of $14,000 that he filed late, even though Wally was aware of the bankruptcy proceedings. What should each of the creditors receive in a distribution under Chapter 7?

CASE PROBLEMS

10. Landmark at Plaza Park, Ltd., filed a plan of reorganization under Chapter 11 of the Bankruptcy Code. Landmark is a limited partnership whose only substantial asset is a two-hundred-unit garden apartment complex. City Federal holds the first mortgage on the property in the face amount of $2,250,000. The mortgage is due and payable six years from now.

Landmark has proposed a plan of reorganization under which the property now in possession of City Federal would be returned. Landmark will then deliver a nonrecourse note, payable in three years, in the face amount of $2,705,820.31 to City Federal in substitution of all of the partnership's existing liabilities. On the sixteenth month through the thirty-sixth month after the effective date of the plan, Landmark will make monthly interest payments computed on a property value of $2,260,000 at a rate of 3 percent above the original mortgage rate but 2.5 percent below the market rate for loans of similar risk. Finally, the note will be secured by the existing mortgage. Landmark's theory is that the note will be paid off at the end of thirty-six months by a combination of refinancing and accumulation of cash from the project. The key is Landmark's proposal to obtain a new first mortgage in three years in the face amount of $2,400,000.

City Federal is a first mortgagee without recourse that has been collecting rents pursuant to a rent assignment agreement since the default on the mortgage eleven months ago. City Federal is impaired by the plan and has rejected it. May it complete its foreclosure action? Explain.

11. Freelin Conn filed a voluntary petition under Chapter 7 of the Bankruptcy Code on September 30, 2015. Conn listed BancOhio National Bank as having a claim incurred in October of 2014 in the amount of $4,000 secured by an eight-year-old Oldsmobile. The car is listed as having a market value of $4,100. During the period from June 30, 2015, to September 30, 2015, Conn made three payments totaling $439.17 to BancOhio. May the trustee in bankruptcy set aside those three payments as voidable preferences? Explain.

12. David files a bankruptcy petition under Chapter 13. After the claims of secured and priority creditors have been satisfied, David's remaining bankruptcy estate has a value of $100,000. David's creditors with allowed unsecured claims are owed $250,000 in total. Chris, an unsecured creditor, is owed $13,500. David's Chapter 13 plan proposes to pay Chris $150 per month for three years. Should the bankruptcy court confirm David's plan? Explain.

13. Yolanda Christophe filed a bankruptcy petition under Chapter 13. Her scheduled debts consist of $11,100 of secured debt, $9,300 owed on an unsecured student loan, and $6,960 of other unsecured debt. Christophe asserts that the student loan is nondischargeable and that assertion has not been questioned. Christophe's proposed amended Chapter 13 plan calls for fifty-six monthly payments of $440 a month. The questioned provision in that plan is the division of the unsecured creditors into two classes. Under Christophe's proposed plan, the general unsecured creditors would receive 32 percent and the separately classified student loan creditor would receive 100 percent. Should this plan be confirmed?

14. On December 17 ZZZZ Best Co., Inc. (the debtor), borrowed $7 million from Union Bank (the bank). On July 8 of the following year the debtor filed a voluntary petition for bankruptcy under Chapter 7. During the preceding ninety days, the debtor had made interest payments of $100,000 to the bank on the loan. The trustee of the debtor's estate filed a complaint against the bank to recover those payments as a voidable preference. The bank asserts that the payments were not voidable because they came within the ordinary course of business exception. The trustee maintains that the exception applies only to short-term, not long-term, debt. Who is correct? Explain.

15. A landlord owned several residential properties, one of which was subject to a local rent control ordinance. The local rent control administrator determined that the landlord had been charging rents above the levels permitted by the ordinance and ordered him to refund the wrongfully collected rents to the affected tenants. The landlord did not comply with the order. The landlord subsequently filed for relief under Chapter 7 of the Bankruptcy Code, seeking to discharge his debts. The tenants filed an adversary proceeding against the landlord in the bankruptcy court, arguing that the debt owed to them arose from rent payments obtained by "actual fraud" and that the debt was therefore nondischargeable under the Bankruptcy Code. They also sought treble damages and attorneys' fees and costs pursuant to the state Consumer Fraud Act. The bankruptcy court ruled in favor of the tenants, finding that the landlord had committed "actual fraud" and that his conduct violated state law. The court therefore awarded the tenants treble damages totaling $94,147.50. Does the Bankruptcy Code bar the discharge of treble damages awarded on account of the debtor's fraud? Explain.

TAKING SIDES

Leonard and Arlene Warner sold the Warner Manufacturing Company to Elliott and Carol Archer for $610,000. A few months later the Archers sued the Warners in a state court for fraud connected with the sale. The parties settled the lawsuit for $300,000. The Warners paid the Archers $200,000 and executed a promissory note for the remaining $100,000. After the Warners failed to make the first payment on the $100,000 promissory note, the Archers sued for the payment in state court. The Warners then filed for bankruptcy under Chapter 7 of the Bankruptcy Code. The Archers claimed that the $100,000 debt was nondischarge-able because it was for "money obtained by fraud." Arlene Warner claimed that the $100,000 debt was dischargeable in bankruptcy because it was a new debt for money promised in a settlement contract and thus it was not a debt for money obtained by fraud.

a. What are the arguments that the debt is dischargeable in bankruptcy?

b. What are the arguments that the debt is *not* dischargeable in bankruptcy?

c. Explain whether the debt is dischargeable in bankruptcy.

Securities Regulation

The merchandise of securities is really traffic in the economic and social welfare of our people. Such traffic demands the utmost good and fair dealing on the part of those engaged in it. If the country is to flourish, capital must be invested in the enterprise.

Franklin D. Roosevelt

CHAPTER OUTCOMES

After reading and studying this chapter, you should be able to:

1. Explain the disclosure requirements of the 1933 Act, including which securities and transactions are exempt from these disclosure requirements.

2. Explain the potential civil liabilities under the 1933 Act.

3. List which provisions of the 1934 Act apply only to publicly held companies and which apply to all companies.

4. Explain the disclosure requirements of the 1934 Act.

5. Explain the potential civil liabilities under the 1934 Act.

The primary purpose of federal securities regulation is to prevent fraudulent practices in the sale of securities and thereby to foster public confidence in the securities market. Federal securities law consists principally of two statutes: the Securities Act of 1933, which focuses on the issuance of securities, and the Securities Exchange Act of 1934, which deals mainly with trading in issued securities. These "secondary" transactions greatly exceed in number and dollar value the original offerings by issuers.

The 1933 Act has two basic objectives: (1) to provide investors with material information concerning securities offered for sale to the public and (2) to prohibit misrepresentation, deceit, and other fraudulent acts and unfair practices in the sale of securities generally, whether or not they are required to be registered.

The 1934 Act extends protection to investors trading in securities that are already issued and outstanding. The 1934 Act also imposes disclosure requirements on publicly held corporations as well as regulating tender offers and proxy solicitations.

Both statutes are administered by the Securities and Exchange Commission (SEC), an independent, quasi-judicial agency consisting of five commissioners. The responsibilities of the SEC include interpreting federal securities laws; issuing new rules and amending existing rules; and coordinating U.S. securities regulation with federal, state, and foreign authorities. In 1996 Congress enacted legislation requiring the SEC, when making rules under either of the securities statutes, to consider, in addition to the protection of investors, whether its action will promote efficiency, competition, and capital formation.

In July 2010, President Obama signed into law the Dodd-Frank Wall Street Reform and Consumer Protection Act (Dodd-Frank Act), the most significant change to U.S. financial regulation since the New Deal in the 1930s. One of the many standalone statutes included in the Dodd-Frank Act is the Investor Protection and Securities Reform Act of 2010, which imposes new corporate governance and investor protection rules on publicly held companies. Corporate governance and investor protection provisions of the Dodd-Frank Act are discussed in this chapter as well as in Chapters 34, 35, 36, and 46.

The SEC has the power to seek civil injunctions and civil monetary penalties for violation of the statutes. (The maximum amount of civil monetary penalties must be adjusted for inflation at least once every four years.) The SEC also can recommend that the Justice Department bring criminal prosecutions. In addition, the SEC can issue orders censuring, suspending, or expelling broker-dealers, investment advisers, and investment companies. The Securities Enforcement Remedies and Penny Stock Reform Act of 1990 granted the SEC the power to issue cease-and-desist orders and, in any cease-and-desist proceeding, to impose civil monetary penalties up to the amount of $775,000, as adjusted for inflation in March 2013. Congress enacted the Private Securities Litigation Reform Act of 1995 (1995 Reform Act) to amend both the 1933 Act and the 1934 Act. One of its provisions grants authority to the SEC to bring civil actions for specified violations of the 1934 Act against aiders and abettors (those who knowingly provide substantial assistance to a person who violates the statute). The Dodd-Frank Act has extended this authority in two ways: (1) the Dodd-Frank Act empowers the SEC to bring enforcement actions under the 1933 Act against aiders and abettors and (2) the Dodd-Frank Act amends the 1933 and 1934 Acts to allow *recklessness* as well as knowledge to satisfy the mental state required for the SEC to bring aiding and abetting cases.

The 1995 Reform Act sought to prevent abuses in private securities fraud lawsuits. To prevent certain state private securities class action lawsuits alleging fraud from being used to frustrate the objectives of the 1995 Reform Act, Congress enacted the Securities Litigation Uniform Standards Act of 1998. The 1998 Act sets national standards for securities class action lawsuits involving nationally traded securities while it preserves the appropriate enforcement powers of state securities regulators but does not change the current treatment of individual lawsuits. The 1998 Act amends both the 1933 Act and the 1934 Act by prohibiting any private class action suit in state or federal court by any private party based upon state statutory or common law alleging (1) an untrue statement or omission in connection with the purchase or sale of a covered security or (2) that the defendant used any manipulative or deceptive device in connection with such a transaction.

In response to the business scandals involving companies such as Enron, WorldCom, Global Crossing, Adelphia, and Arthur Andersen in 2002, Congress passed the Sarbanes-Oxley Act, which amends the securities acts in a number of significant respects. The Act allows the SEC to add civil monetary penalties to a disgorgement fund for the benefit of victims of violations of the 1933 Act or the 1934 Act. Other provisions of the Act are discussed later in this chapter as well as in Chapters 6, 35, and 43. In addition, the Dodd-Frank Act requires the SEC to make an award to eligible whistleblowers who voluntarily provide original information that leads to a successful enforcement action in which the SEC imposes monetary sanctions in excess of $1 million. The amount of the award must be between 10 percent and 30 percent of funds collected as monetary sanctions, as determined by the SEC. The Dodd-Frank Act also prohibits retaliation by employers against individuals who provide the SEC with information about possible securities violations.

To increase U.S. job creation and economic growth by improving access to the public capital markets for emerging growth companies, Congress enacted the Jumpstart Our Business Startups Act of 2012 (JOBS Act). As discussed later in this chapter, the JOBS Act amends both the 1933 Act and the 1934 Act to provide reduced disclosure requirements for emerging growth companies (defined as companies with total annual gross revenues of less than $1 billion during their last completed fiscal year) and to expand the availability of exemptions from registering securities under the 1933 Act.

The SEC has recognized that the "use of electronic media also enhances the efficiency of the securities markets by allowing for the rapid dissemination of information to investors and financial markets in a more cost-efficient, widespread, and equitable manner than traditional paper-based methods." The SEC has provided interpretative guidance for the use of electronic media for the delivery of information required by the federal securities laws. The SEC defined *electronic media* to include audiotapes, videotapes, facsimiles, CD-ROM, electronic mail, bulletin boards, Internet websites, and computer networks. Basically, electronic delivery must provide notice, access, and evidence of delivery comparable to that provided by paper delivery.

The SEC has established the EDGAR (Electronic Data Gathering, Analysis, and Retrieval) computer system, which performs automated collection, validation, indexing, acceptance, and dissemination of reports required to be filed with the SEC. Its primary purpose is to increase the efficiency and fairness of the securities market for the benefit of investors, corporations, and the economy by speeding up the receipt, acceptance, dissemination, and analysis of corporate information filed with the SEC. The SEC requires all public domestic companies to make their filings on EDGAR, except filings exempted for hardship. EDGAR filings are posted at the SEC's website twenty-four hours after the date of filing.

In addition to the federal laws regulating the sale of securities, each state has its own laws regulating such sales within its borders. Commonly called Blue Sky Laws, these statutes all have provisions prohibiting fraud in the sale of securities. In addition, most states require the registration of securities and regulate brokers and dealers. The Uniform Securities Act of 1956 has been adopted at one time or another, in whole or in part, by 37 jurisdictions, whereas the Revised Uniform Securities Act of 1985 has been adopted in only a few states. Both Acts, however, have been preempted in part by the National Securities Markets Improvement Act of 1996 and the Securities Litigation Uniform Standards Act of 1998. In 2002 the Uniform Law Commission promulgated a new Uniform Securities Act, which has been adopted by at least seventeen states. The 2002 Uniform Securities Act seeks to give states regulatory and enforcement authority that minimizes duplication of regulatory resources and that blends with federal regulation and enforcement.

Any person who sells securities must comply with the federal securities laws as well as with the securities laws of each state in which he intends to offer his securities. However, in 1996 Congress enacted the National Securities Markets Improvements Act, which preempted state regulation of many offerings of securities. Because state securities laws vary greatly, we will discuss only the 1933 Act and the 1934 Act in this chapter.

THE SECURITIES ACT OF 1933

The 1933 Act, also called the "Truth in Securities Act," requires that a registration statement be filed with the SEC and that it become effective before any securities may be offered for sale to the public, unless either the transaction in which the securities are offered or the securities themselves are exempt from registration. The purpose of registration is to disclose financial and other information about the issuer and those who control it, so that potential investors may consider the merits of the securities. The 1933 Act also requires that potential investors be furnished with a *prospectus* (a document offering the securities for sale to interested buyers) containing the important data set forth in the registration statement. The 1933 Act prohibits fraud in *all* sales of securities involving interstate commerce or the mails, even if the securities are exempt from the 1933 Act's registration and disclosure requirements. Civil and criminal liability may be imposed for violations of the 1933 Act.

The National Securities Markets Improvements Act of 1996 broadly authorized the SEC to issue regulations or rules exempting any person, security, or transaction from any of the provisions of the 1933 Act or the SEC's rules promulgated under that Act. This authorization extends so far as such exemption is necessary or appropriate in the public interest and is consistent with the protection of investors.

DEFINITION OF A SECURITY [39-1]

Security
includes any note, stock, bond, preorganization subscription, and investment contract

The 1933 Act defines the term **security** to include any note; stock; bond; debenture; evidence of indebtedness; preorganization certificate or subscription; investment contract; voting-trust certificate; fractional undivided interest in oil, gas, or other mineral rights; or, in general, any interest or instrument commonly known as a security. This definition broadly includes the many types of instruments that fall within the ordinary concept of a security. Furthermore, the courts generally have interpreted the statutory definition to include nontraditional forms of investments. The Supreme Court, more specifically, employs a two-tier analysis to identify securities. Under this analysis, the Court will presumptively treat as a security a financial instrument designated as a note, stock, bond, or other instrument specifically named in the 1933 Act.

Investment contract

any investment of money or property made in expectation of receiving a financial return solely from the efforts of others

Practical Advice

Because securities are so broadly defined, if you plan to sell any type of financial investment, be sure to obtain legal counsel to assist you in complying with the requirements of the securities laws.

On the other hand, if a financial transaction lacks the traditional characteristics of an instrument specifically named in the 1933 Act, the Court has used a three-part test, derived from *Securities and Exchange Commission v. W. J. Howey Co.*, to determine whether that financial transaction constitutes an investment contract and thus a security. Under the *Howey* test, a financial instrument or transaction constitutes an **investment contract** if it involves (1) an investment in a common venture (2) premised on a reasonable expectation of profit (3) to be derived from the entrepreneurial or managerial efforts of others. Thus, limited partnership interests are usually considered securities because limited partners may not participate in management or control of the limited partnership. On the other hand, general partnership interests are usually held not to be securities because general partners have the right to participate in management of the general partnership. Thus, interests in limited liability companies (LLCs) are considered securities when the members do not take part in management (manager-managed LLCs) but are not deemed securities when the members exercise control of the company (member-managed LLCs). In certain circumstances, investments in citrus groves, whiskey warehouse receipts, real estate condominiums, cattle, franchises, and pyramid schemes have been held to be securities under the *Howey* test.

Securities and Exchange Commission v. Edwards
Supreme Court of the United States, 2004
540 U.S. 389, 124 S.Ct. 892, 157 L.Ed.2d 813
http://scholar.google.com/scholar_case?q=540+U.S.+389&hl=en&as_sdt=2,34&case=14322712118728699297&scilh=0

FACTS Charles Edwards was the chairman, CEO, and sole shareholder of ETS Payphones, Inc. (ETS), which sold payphones to the public via independent distributors. The payphones were offered with a site lease, a five-year leaseback and management agreement, and a buyback agreement. The purchase price for the payphone packages was approximately $7,000. Under the leaseback and management agreement, purchasers received $82 per month, a 14 percent annual return. Purchasers were not involved in the day-to-day operation of the payphones they owned as ETS selected the site for the phone, installed the equipment, arranged for connection and long-distance service, collected coin revenues, and maintained and repaired the phones. Under the buyback agreement, ETS promised to refund the full purchase price of the package at the end of the lease or within one hundred and eighty days of a purchaser's request.

In its marketing materials and on its website, ETS trumpeted the "incomparable pay phone" as "an exciting business opportunity," in which recent deregulation had "open[ed] the door for profits for individual pay phone owners and operators." According to ETS, very "few business opportunities can offer the potential for ongoing revenue generation that is available in today's pay telephone industry." Ten thousand people invested a total of $300 million in the payphone sale-and-leaseback arrangements.

The payphones did not generate enough revenue for ETS to make the payments required by the leaseback agreements, so the company depended on funds from new investors to meet its obligations. After ETS filed for bankruptcy protection, the Securities and Exchange Commission (SEC) brought this civil enforcement action. It alleged that Edwards and ETS had violated the registration requirements and antifraud provisions of the Securities Act of 1933, as well as Section 10(b) of the Securities Exchange Act of 1934 and Rule 10b-5 under that section.

The district court concluded that the payphone sale-and-leaseback arrangement was an investment contract and therefore was subject to the federal securities laws. The Court of Appeals reversed, holding that the respondent's scheme was not an investment contract.

DECISION The judgment of the U.S. Court of Appeals is reversed, and the case is remanded.

OPINION Congress's purpose in enacting the securities laws was to regulate *investments*, in whatever form they are made and by whatever name they are called. To that end, it enacted a broad definition of "security," sufficient to encompass virtually any instrument that might be sold as an investment. The 1993 Act and the 1934 Act define "security" to include any note, stock, treasury stock, security future, bond, debenture, investment contract, or any instrument commonly known as a security. "Investment contract" is not itself defined.

Under the Supreme Court decision in *SEC v. W. J. Howey Co.* the test for whether a particular scheme is an investment contract is "whether the scheme involves an investment of money in a common enterprise with profits to come solely from the efforts of others." This definition "embodies a flexible rather than a static principle, one that is capable of adaptation to meet the countless and variable schemes devised by those who seek the use of the money of others on the promise of profits." "Profits" was used in the sense of income or return, to include, for example, dividends, other periodic payments, or the increased value of the investment.

There is no reason to distinguish between promises of fixed returns and promises of variable returns for purposes of the test. In both cases, the investing public is attracted by representations of investment income, as purchasers were in this case by ETS's invitation to "watch the profits add up." Moreover, investments pitched as low risk (such as those offering a "guaranteed" fixed return) are particularly attractive to individuals more vulnerable to investment fraud, including older and less sophisticated investors. An investment scheme promising a fixed rate of return can be an "investment contract" and thus a "security" subject to the federal securities laws.

INTERPRETATION An investment scheme promising a fixed rate of return can be an "investment contract" and thus a "security" subject to the federal securities laws.

CRITICAL THINKING QUESTION How would you define a security? Explain.

Registration of securities

disclosure of accurate material information required in all public offerings of nonexempt securities unless offering is an exempt transaction

Practical Advice

When deciding whether to invest in a publicly offered security, keep in mind that the SEC does not pass on the merits of the securities nor does it guarantee the accuracy of the statements made in the registration statement or prospectus.

REGISTRATION OF SECURITIES [39-2]

The 1933 Act prohibits the offer or sale of any security through the use of the mails or any means of interstate commerce unless a registration statement for the securities being offered is in effect or the issuer secures an exemption from registration. The purpose of registration is to adequately and accurately disclose financial and other information on which investors may judge the merits of securities. However, registration does not insure investors against loss—the SEC does not judge the financial merits of any security. Moreover, the SEC does not guarantee the accuracy of the information presented in the registration statement.

Disclosure Requirements [39-2a]

In general, registration (Form S-1) calls for disclosure of information such as (1) a description of the registrant's properties, business, and competition; (2) a description of the significant provisions of the security to be offered for sale and its relationship to the registrant's other capital securities; (3) information about the management of the registrant; and (4) financial statements certified by independent public accountants. In 1992, the SEC imposed new disclosure requirements regarding compensation paid to senior executives and directors. In 2006 the SEC amended these rules to mandate clearer and more complete disclosure of compensation paid to directors, the CEO, the CFO, and the three other highest paid executive officers. The registration statement must be signed by the issuer, its CEO, its CFO, its chief accounting officer, and a majority of its board of directors.

A registration statement and the prospectus become public immediately on filing with the SEC, and investors can access them using EDGAR. The effective date of a registration statement is the twentieth day after filing, although the commission, at its discretion, may advance the effective date or require an amendment to the filing, which will begin a new twenty-day period. After the effective date, the issuer may make sales, provided the purchaser has received a final prospectus. The SEC has adopted rules to provide for an "access equals delivery" prospectus delivery model: the final prospectus delivery obligations are satisfied without printing and actually delivering final prospectuses if the issuer timely filed a final prospectus with the SEC.

In 1998 the SEC issued a rule requiring issuers to write and design the cover page, summary, and risk factors section of their prospectuses in plain English. In these sections, issuers must use short sentences; definite, concrete, everyday language; tabular presentation of complex information; no legal or business jargon; and no multiple negatives. Issuers also must design these sections to make them inviting to the reader and free from legalese and repetition that blur important information.

Integrated Disclosure [39-2b]

The disclosure system under the 1933 Act developed independently of that required by the 1934 Act, which will be discussed later in this chapter. As a result, issuers subject to both statutes were compelled to provide duplicative or overlapping disclosure. Then, in 1982, the SEC, in an effort to reduce or eliminate unnecessary duplication of corporate reporting, adopted an integrated system that provides for different levels of disclosure, depending on the issuer's reporting history and market following. All issuers may use the detailed form (Form S-1) described previously. The SEC has amended these rules to recognize four categories of issuers: nonreporting issuers, unseasoned issuers, seasoned issuers, and well-known seasoned issuers.

1. A nonreporting issuer is an issuer that is not required to file reports under the 1934 Act. Such an issuer must use Form S-1.
2. An unseasoned issuer is an issuer that has reported continuously under the 1934 Act for at least three years. Such an issuer must use Form S-1 but is permitted to disclose less detailed information and to incorporate some information by reference to reports filed under the 1934 Act.
3. A seasoned issuer is an issuer that has filed continuously under the 1934 Act for at least one year and has a minimum market value of publicly held voting and nonvoting stock of $75 million. Such an issuer is permitted to use Form S-3, thus disclosing even less detail in the 1933 Act registration and incorporating even more information by reference to 1934 Act reports. An issuer that does not meet the $75 million public float requirement can use Form S-3 if it (a) has a class of common equity securities listed and

registered on a national securities exchange, (b) has a class of securities registered under the 1934 Act, (c) has filed continuously under the 1934 Act for at least one year, and (d) does not sell more than the equivalent of one-third of its public float in primary offerings over any period of twelve calendar months. "Public float" means the value of a company's outstanding shares that is in the hands of public investors, as opposed to company officers, directors, or controlling-interest investors.

4. A well-known seasoned issuer is an issuer that has filed continuously under the 1934 Act for at least one year and has either (a) a minimum worldwide market value of its outstanding publicly held voting and nonvoting stock of $700 million or (b) $1 billion of nonconvertible debt or preferred stock that have been issued for cash in a registered offering within the preceding three years. A well-known seasoned issuer is also eligible to use Form S-3.

In 1992, the SEC established an integrated registration and reporting system for small business issuers. These rules are intended to facilitate access to the public financial markets for startup and developing companies and to reduce costs for small business issuers wishing to have their securities traded in public markets. As amended in 2008, the rules define a small business issuer as a noninvestment company with less than $75 million in public float. When a company is unable to calculate public float, however, the standard is less than $50 million in revenue in the last fiscal year.

Shelf Registrations [39-2c]

As amended in 2005, shelf registrations permit seasoned and well-known seasoned issuers to register unlimited amounts of securities that are to be offered and sold "off the shelf" on a delayed or continuous basis in the future. The information in the original registration must be kept accurate and current and the issuer must reasonably expect that the securities will be sold within three years of the effective date of the registration. Well-known seasoned issuers are eligible for a more streamlined shelf-registration process and automatic effectiveness of shelf registration statements upon filing. Shelf registrations allow issuers to respond more quickly to market conditions such as changes in stock prices and interest rates.

Communications [39-2d]

The SEC's 2005 revisions greatly liberalize the rules regarding written communications before and during registered securities offerings. These rules create a new type of written communication, called a "free-writing prospectus," which is any written offer, including electronic communications, other than a statutory prospectus. The flexibility provided under the new rules depends upon the characteristics of the issuer, including the type of issuer, the issuer's history of reporting, and the issuer's market capitalization.

1. Well-known seasoned issuers may engage at any time in oral and written communications, including a free-writing prospectus, subject to certain conditions.
2. All reporting issuers (unseasoned issuers, seasoned issuers, and well-known seasoned issuers) may at any time continue to publish regularly released factual business information and forward-looking information (predictions).
3. Nonreporting issuers may at any time continue to publish factual business information that is regularly released and intended for use by persons other than in their capacity as investors or potential investors.
4. Communications by issuers more than thirty days before filing a registration statement are permitted so long as they do not refer to a securities offering that is the subject of a registration statement.
5. All issuers may use a free-writing prospectus after the filing of the registration statement, subject to certain conditions.

Emerging Growth Companies (EGCs) [39-2e]

Emerging growth companies (EGCs) have reduced disclosure requirements and expanded permissible communications

The JOBS Act defines an emerging growth company (EGC) as a domestic or foreign issuer with total annual gross revenues of less than $1 billion (periodically adjusted for inflation) during its most recently completed fiscal year *if* that issuer did not first sell common equity securities in an initial public offering (IPO) on or before December 8, 2011. An issuer continues to be deemed to be an EGC until the earliest of the following: (1) it has annual gross revenues of $1 billion, as adjusted for inflation, or more; (2) five years after its IPO; (3) the date on which the issuer has, or had during the previous three-year period, issued more than $1 billion in nonconvertible debt; and (4) the date on which it is deemed to be a "large accelerated filer" pursuant to SEC rules.

The JOBS Act reduces the financial reporting requirements, and therefore the cost, in connection with an EGC's IPO. The JOBS Act also authorizes an EGC, before its IPO date, to submit to the SEC a draft registration statement for *confidential nonpublic review* by SEC staff before the public filing, provided that the initial confidential submission is publicly filed with the SEC no later than twenty-one days before the issuer conducts a "road show." (A "road show" is an offer that contains a presentation regarding an offering by one or more members of the issuer's management and includes discussion of the issuer, its management, and/or the securities being offered.) In addition, EGCs may engage in oral or written communications with potential investors that are qualified institutional buyers or *institutional* accredited investors prior to the filing of a registration statement to determine whether such investors might have an interest in a contemplated securities offering. The JOBS Act also liberalizes the use of research reports on EGCs.

EXEMPT SECURITIES [39-3]

Exempt securities
securities not subject to the registration requirements of the 1933 Act

The 1933 Act exempts a number of specific securities (called exempt securities) from its registration requirements. Because these exemptions apply to the securities themselves, they also may be resold without registration.

Short-Term Commercial Paper [39-3a]

The Act exempts any note, draft, or bankers' acceptance (a draft accepted by a bank), issued for working capital, that has a maturity of not more than nine months when issued. This exemption is not available, however, if the proceeds are to be used for permanent purposes, such as the acquisition of a plant, or if the paper is of a type not ordinarily purchased by the general public.

Other Exempt Securities [39-3b]

The 1933 Act also exempts the following kinds of securities from registration: (1) securities issued or guaranteed by domestic government organizations, such as municipal bonds; (2) securities of domestic banks and savings and loan associations; (3) securities of nonprofit charitable organizations; (4) certain securities issued by federally regulated common carriers; and (5) insurance policies and annuity contracts issued by state-regulated insurance companies.

EXEMPT TRANSACTIONS FOR ISSUERS [39-4]

Exempt transactions for issuers
issuance of securities not subject to the registration requirements of the 1933 Act

In addition to exempting specific types of securities, the 1933 Act also exempts *issuers* from the registration requirements for certain kinds of transactions. These **exempt transactions for issuers** include (1) private placements (Rule 506), (2) limited offers not exceeding $5 million (Rule 505), (3) limited offers not exceeding $1 million (Rule 504), and (4) limited offers solely to accredited investors. Except for some issuances under Rule 504, these registration exemptions apply only to the transaction in which the securities are issued; therefore, any resale must be made by registration, unless the resale qualifies as an exempt transaction. Moreover, these transactions are *not* exempt from the antifraud, civil liability, or other provisions of the federal securities laws.

The JOBS Act added a new crowdfunding exemption from registration that will allow eligible, domestic, nonpublic issuers to raise up to $1 million (periodically adjusted for inflation) annually.

In addition, the 1933 Act identifies a number of securities exemptions that are in effect transaction exemptions. These include intrastate issues, exchanges between an issuer and its security holders, and reorganization securities issued and exchanged with court or other government approval. Moreover, the Bankruptcy Act exempts securities issued by a debtor if they are offered under a reorganization plan in exchange for a claim or interest in the debtor. These exemptions apply only to the original issuance, and resales may be made only by registration, unless the resale qualifies as an exempt transaction.

Another transaction exemption is Regulation A, which permits an issuer to sell a limited amount of securities in an unregistered public offering, if certain conditions are met. Unlike

Practical Advice

If you plan to issue securities, carefully explore the possibility of using a transaction that is exempt from registration.

Figure 39-1 Registration and Exemptions Under the 1933 Act

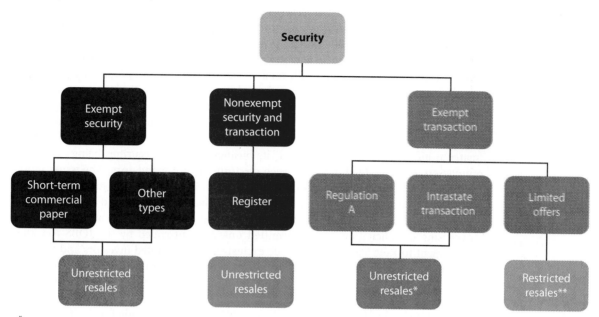

* Under intrastate exemption, resales to nonresidents may only be made nine months after the last sale in the initial issuance.
** Except some issuances under Rule 504.

other transaction exemptions, Regulation A places no restrictions upon the resale of securities issued pursuant to it.

Figure 39-1 illustrates registration and exemptions from registration under the 1933 Act.

Limited Offers [39-4a]

The 1933 Act exempts, or authorizes the SEC to exempt, transactions that do not require the protection of registration because they either involve a small amount of money or are made in a limited manner. Promulgated in 1982 to simplify and clarify these transaction exemptions, *Regulation D* contains three separate exemptions (Rules 504, 505, and 506), each involving limited offers. Limited offers made solely to accredited investors is a companion provision of the 1933 Act to the exemptions under Regulation D. Each of these four exemptions requires the issuer to file a Form D with the SEC online within fifteen days after the first sale of securities in the offering.

Securities sold pursuant to these exemptions (with the exception of some sold pursuant to Rule 504) are considered **restricted securities** and may be resold only by registration or in another transaction exempt from registration. An issuer who uses these exemptions must take reasonable care to prevent nonexempt, unregistered resales of restricted securities. Reasonable care includes, but is not limited to, the following: (1) making a reasonable inquiry to determine whether the purchaser is acquiring the securities for herself or for other persons; (2) providing written disclosure, prior to the sale to each purchaser, that the securities have not been registered and therefore cannot be resold unless they are registered or unless an exemption from registration is available; and (3) placing a legend on the securities certificate stating that the securities have not been registered and that they are restricted securities.

Restricted securities
securities issued under an
exempt transaction and
subject to resale
restrictions

Private Placements The most important transaction exemption for issuers is the so-called private placement provision of the 1933 Act, which exempts "transactions by an issuer not involving any public offering." SEC *Rule 506* establishes for all issuers a nonexclusive safe harbor for limited offers and sales without regard to the dollar amount of the offering. Satisfying the rule ensures the exemption, but there is no presumption that the exemption is unavailable for transactions that do not comply with the rule. Rule 506 is by far the most widely used Regulation D exemption, accounting for more than 90 percent of all Regulation D offerings and more than 99 percent of capital raised in Regulation D offerings.

Securities sold under this exemption are restricted securities and may be resold only by registration or in a transaction exempt from registration. The issue may be purchased by an unlimited number of "accredited investors" and by no more than thirty-five other purchasers. *Accredited investors* include banks, insurance companies, investment companies, executive officers or directors of the issuer, savings and loan associations, registered broker-dealers, certain employee benefit plans with total assets in excess of $5 million, any person whose net worth exceeds $1 million (excluding the value of the person's primary residence), and any person whose income exceeded $200,000 in each of the two preceding years and who reasonably expects an income in excess of $200,000 in the current year. If the sale involves any nonaccredited investors, the issuer must, before the sale, give such purchasers specified material information about the issuer, its business, and the securities being offered. If all the purchasers are accredited investors, such disclosure is not mandatory. The issuer must reasonably believe that each purchaser who is not an accredited investor has sufficient knowledge and experience in financial and business matters to evaluate the merits and risks of the investment or has the services of a representative who possesses such knowledge and experience. General advertising or solicitation is not permitted unless, as provided by the JOBS Act and a 2013 amendment to Rule 506, sales are made exclusively to accredited investors and the issuer takes reasonable steps to verify that such purchasers are accredited investors. The issuer must notify the SEC of sales made under the exemption and must take precautions against nonexempt, unregistered resales.

As required by the Dodd-Frank Act, in 2013 the SEC amended Rule 506 to impose "bad actor" disqualification requirements on offerings under Rule 506. "Bad actor" disqualification requirements disqualify securities offerings from reliance on exemptions if the issuer or other relevant persons have been convicted of, or are subject to court or administrative sanctions for, securities fraud or other violations of specified laws. Under the 2013 amendment to Rule 506, disqualifying conduct includes conviction of any felony or misdemeanor (1) in connection with the purchase or sale of any security or (2) involving the making of any false filing with the SEC.

Limited Offers Not Exceeding $5 Million

SEC *Rule 505* exempts from registration those offerings by noninvestment company issuers that do not exceed $5 million over twelve months. Rule 505 offerings are subject to bad actor disqualification provisions. Securities sold under this exemption are restricted securities and may be resold only by registration or in a transaction exempt from registration. General advertising or general solicitation is not permitted. The issue may be purchased by an unlimited number of accredited investors and by no more than thirty-five other purchasers. If the sale involves any nonaccredited investors, the issuer must, before the sale, give them specified material information about the issuer, its business, and the securities being offered; otherwise, such disclosure is not required. Unlike the issuer under Rule 506, however, the issuer under Rule 505 is *not* required to believe reasonably that each nonaccredited investor, either alone or with his representative, has sufficient knowledge and experience in financial matters to be capable of evaluating the investment's merits and risks. As under Rule 506, the issuer must take precautions against nonexempt, unregistered resales and must notify the SEC of sales made under the exemption.

Limited Offers Not Exceeding $1 Million

As amended in 1999, SEC *Rule 504* provides private, noninvestment company issuers with an exemption from registration for issues not exceeding $1 million within twelve months. (Issuers required to report under the 1934 Act and investment companies may not use Rule 504.) The issuer is to notify the SEC of sales under the rule, which permits sales to an unlimited number of investors and does not require the issuer to furnish any information to them.

If the issuance meets certain conditions, Rule 504 permits general solicitations, and acquired shares are freely transferable. The conditions are that the issuance is either (1) registered under state law requiring public filing and delivery of a disclosure document to investors before sale or (2) exempted under state law permitting general solicitation and advertising so long as sales are made only to accredited investors.

If the issuance does not meet these conditions, general solicitation and advertising are not permitted. Moreover, the securities issued are restricted, and the issuer must take precautions against nonexempt, unregistered resales.

Limited Offers Solely to Accredited Investors   In 1980, Congress added a section that exempts from registration offers and sales of securities solely to accredited investors if the total offering price is less than $5 million. General advertising or public solicitation is not permitted. As with Rules 505 and 506, an unlimited number of accredited investors may purchase the issue; however, this exemption allows no unaccredited investors to purchase. No information is required to be furnished to the purchasers. Securities sold under this exemption are restricted securities and may be resold only by registration or in a transaction exempt from registration. The issuer must notify the SEC of sales made under the exemption and must take precautions against nonexempt, unregistered resales.

Crowdfunding Exemption [39-4b]

Crowdfunding exemption

allows eligible, domestic, nonpublic issuers to raise up to $1 million annually by sales of limited amounts of stock to a large number of individuals, whether accredited or not, through brokers or funding portals

Crowdfunding is the use of the Internet to raise small amounts of money from a large number of contributors. The JOBS Act requires the SEC to adopt rules to implement a new **crowdfunding exemption** from registration that will allow eligible, domestic, nonpublic issuers to raise up to $1 million (periodically adjusted for inflation at least every five years) annually. This crowdfunding exemption permits the sale of limited amounts of stock to a large number of individuals, whether accredited or not, through brokers or a new category of intermediaries, funding portals. A funding portal is a crowdfunding intermediary registered with the SEC that displays securities on its Internet website. (Crowdfunding portals include Kickstarter, RocketHub, peerbackers, and Indeigogo.) The issuer must file with the SEC and disclose to investors certain basic information, including a description of the company's business, risk factors, the company's financial statements, the target offering amount, and the intended use of the funds raised through the offering. Investors' annual combined investments in securities sold under this exemption are limited based on an income and net worth test. The purchaser may not transfer securities issued pursuant to this exemption for one year after purchase except for transfers to the issuer, accredited investors, or as part of an offering registered with the SEC. The JOBS Act adds a new private right of action for a purchaser of a security in an exempted crowdfunding transaction for negligence-based liability for oral or written communications containing material misrepresentations or omissions made in the offering or sale of a security in that transaction. The suit may be brought against the "issuer," which is defined broadly to include any director, partner, principal executive, principal financial officer, and certain other officers, as well as any person who offers and sells securities on behalf of the issuer. On October 23, 2013, the SEC proposed a crowdfunding rule to implement the JOBS Act but the SEC had not issued a final rule by the time this book went to press.

Regulation A [39-4c]

Regulation A permits U.S. and Canadian issuers to offer up to $5 million of securities in any twelve-month period without registering them, provided that the issuer files an offering statement on paper with the SEC prior to the sale of the securities. An offering circular must also be provided to offerees and purchasers. The issuer may make offers upon filing the offering statement but may make sales only after the SEC has qualified it. (Issuers required to report under the 1934 Act and investment companies may not use Regulation A.) Regulation A filings are less detailed and time consuming than full registration statements, and the required financial statements are simpler and need not be audited unless the issuer has audited financial statements prepared for other purposes. Issuers now may use an optional, simplified question-and-answer disclosure document. Regulation A permits issuers to communicate with potential investors, or "test the waters" for potential interest in the offering, before filing the offering statement. Regulation A offerings are subject to bad actor disqualification provisions.

Regulation A sets no restrictions regarding the number or qualifications of investors who may purchase securities under its provisions. Regulation A offerings are public offerings, with no prohibition on general solicitation and general advertising. Securities sold under Regulation A are not restricted securities and, therefore, are not subject to the limitations on resale that apply to securities sold in private offerings. Because Regulation A offerings are exempt from the registration requirements of the 1933 Act, the liability provisions of Section 11 of the 1933 Act, discussed later, do not apply.

To expand the availability of Regulation A for issuers, the JOBS Act directs the SEC to amend Regulation A, or adopt a similar exemption, with the following terms:

1. The aggregate offering amount of all securities offered and sold within the prior twelve-month period in reliance on the exemption shall not exceed $50 million.
2. The securities may be offered and sold publicly.
3. The securities shall not be restricted securities.
4. The civil liability provision in section 12(a)(2), discussed later in this chapter, shall apply to any person offering or selling such securities.
5. The issuer must file audited financial statements with the SEC annually and such other periodic disclosures as the SEC may require.

On December 18, 2013, the SEC proposed to implement the JOBS Act mandate by expanding Regulation A into two tiers: Tier 1, for offerings of up to $5 million; and Tier 2, for offerings of up to $50 million. The proposals for offerings under Tier 1 and Tier 2 build on current Regulation A, and preserve, with some modifications, existing provisions regarding issuer eligibility, offering circular contents, testing the waters, and "bad actor" disqualification. The SEC had not issued a final rule by the time this book went to press.

Intrastate Issues [39-4d]

The 1933 Act also exempts from registration any security that is a part of an issue offered and sold only to persons who live in a single state where the issuer of such security is a resident and doing business. This exemption is intended to apply to local issues representing local financing carried out by local persons through local investments. The exemption does not apply if any offeree, who need not become a purchaser, is not a resident of the state in which the issuer is a resident.

The courts and the SEC have interpreted the exemption narrowly. *Rule 147*, promulgated by the SEC, provides a nonexclusive safe harbor for securing the intrastate exemption. Although satisfying the rule ensures the exemption, the exemption is not presumed to be unavailable for transactions that do not comply with the rule. Rule 147 requires that (1) the issuer be incorporated or organized in the state in which the issuance occurs; (2) the issuer be doing business principally in that state, meaning that the issuer must derive 80 percent of its gross revenues from that state, 80 percent of its assets must be located in that state, and 80 percent of the net proceeds from the issue must be used in that state; (3) all of the offerees and purchasers be residents of that state; (4) no resales to nonresidents be made during the period of sale and for nine months after the last sale; and (5) the issuer take precautions against interstate distributions. Such precautions include (1) placing on the security certificate a legend stating that the securities have not been registered and that resales can be made only to residents of the state and (2) obtaining a written statement of residence from each purchaser.

See Concept Review 39-1.

EXEMPT TRANSACTIONS FOR NONISSUERS [39-5]

Exempt transactions for nonissuers
resales by persons other than the issuer that are exempted from the registration requirements of the 1933 Act

The 1933 Act requires registration for any sale by *any* person (including nonissuers) of any nonexempt security, unless a statutory exemption can be found for the transaction. The Act, however, provides a transaction exemption for any person other than an issuer, underwriter, or dealer. In addition, the Act exempts most transactions by dealers and brokers. These three provisions exempt from the registration requirements of the 1933 Act most secondary transactions, that is, the numerous resales that occur on an exchange or in the over-the-counter market. Nevertheless, these exemptions do not extend to some situations involving resales by nonissuers, in particular to (1) resales of restricted securities acquired under Regulation D (Rules 506, 505, or 504) or limited offers solely to accredited investors and (2) sales of restricted or nonrestricted securities by affiliates. Such sales must be made pursuant to registration, Rule 144, or Regulation

---

CONCEPT REVIEW 39-1

Exempt Transactions for Issuers Under the 1933 Act

Exemption	Price Limitation	Information Required	Limitations on Purchasers	Resales
Regulation A	$5 million	Offering circular	None	Unrestricted
Expanded Regulation A	$50 million	Offering circular; Annual audited financial statements	None	Unrestricted
Intrastate Rule 147	None	None	Intrastate only	Only to residents before nine months
Rule 506	None	Material information to unaccredited purchasers	Unlimited accredited; thirty-five unaccredited	Restricted
Rule 505	$5 million	Material information to unaccredited purchasers	Unlimited accredited; thirty-five unaccredited	Restricted
Rule 504	$1 million	None	None	Restricted*
Limited Offers Solely to Accredited Investors	$5 million	None	Only accredited	Restricted
Crowdfunding	$1 million	Specified basic information	Unlimited in number; Amount purchased limited based on purchaser's net worth and income	Restricted

* Unrestricted if under state law the issuance is either (1) registered or (2) exempted with sales only to accredited investors.

Affiliate
one who controls, is controlled by, or is under common control with the issuer

Control
the direct or indirect possession of the power to direct the management and policies of a person through ownership of securities, by contract, or otherwise

---

Practical Advice

If you acquire restricted securities, do not resell them until you register them—which is rarely feasible—or you comply with an exemption for nonissuers.

A, subject to the limited exception provided to some issuances by Rule 504. An **affiliate** is a person who controls, is controlled by, or is under common control with the issuer. **Control** is the direct or indirect possession of the power to direct the management and policies of a person through ownership of securities, by contract, or otherwise.

Rule 144 [39-5a]

Rule 144 of the SEC sets forth conditions that, if met by an affiliate or by any person selling restricted securities, exempt her from registering such securities. As amended in 2008, the rule imposes less strict requirements on resales of securities of issuers that are subject to the reporting requirements of the 1934 Act than on resales of securities of nonreporting issuers.

Nonreporting Issuers   Amended Rule 144 requires for an affiliate selling *restricted* securities that there be adequate current public information about the issuer, that the affiliate selling under the rule have owned the restricted securities for at least one year, that she sell them only in limited amounts in unsolicited brokers' transactions, and that notice of the sale be provided to the SEC. An affiliate selling *nonrestricted* securities is subject to the same requirements except that the one-year holding period does not apply.

A person who is *not* an affiliate of the issuer when the *restricted* securities are sold and who has owned the restricted securities for at least one year, may sell them in unlimited amounts and is not subject to any of the other requirements of Rule 144.

Reporting Issuers   Amended Rule 144 requires for an affiliate selling *restricted* securities that there be adequate current public information about the issuer, that the affiliate selling under the rule have owned the restricted securities for at least six months, that he sell them only in limited amounts in unsolicited brokers' transactions, and that notice of the sale be provided to the

SEC. An affiliate selling *nonrestricted* securities is subject to the same requirements except there is no holding period.

If there is adequate current public information about the issuer, a person who is *not* an affiliate of the issuer when the *restricted* securities are sold and has owned the restricted securities for at least six months may sell them in unlimited amounts and is not subject to any of the other requirements of Rule 144. After one year, the nonaffiliate selling *restricted* securities need not comply with the current information requirement of Rule 144.

Regulation A [39-5b]

Regulation A also provides an exemption for nonissuers. The regulation places a $1.5 million limit on the total amount of securities sold by all nonissuers in any twelve-month period. Use of this exemption requires compliance with all of the conditions Regulation A imposes upon issuers, as discussed previously.

LIABILITY [39-6]

To implement its objectives of providing full disclosure and preventing fraud in the sale of securities, the 1933 Act imposes a number of sanctions for noncompliance with its requirements. These sanctions include administrative remedies by the SEC, civil liability to injured investors, and criminal penalties. In addition, the court may award attorneys' fees against any party who brings suit or asserts a defense without merit.

The 1995 Reform Act provides "forward-looking" statements (predictions) a "safe harbor" under the 1933 Act from civil liability that is based on an untrue statement of material fact or an omission of a material fact necessary to make the statement not misleading. The safe harbor applies only to issuers required to report under the 1934 Act. The safe harbor eliminates civil liability if a forward-looking statement is (1) immaterial, (2) made without actual knowledge that it was false or misleading, or (3) identified as a forward-looking statement and is accompanied by meaningful cautionary statements identifying important factors that could cause actual results to differ materially from those predicted. "Forward-looking" statements include projections of revenues, income, earnings per share, capital expenditures, dividends, or capital structure; management's plans and objectives for future operations; and statements of future economic performance. The safe harbor provision, however, does not cover statements made in connection with an IPO, a tender offer, a going private transaction, or offerings by a partnership or an LLC.

Unregistered Sales [39-6a]

Section 12(a)(1) of the Act imposes express civil liability for the sale of an unregistered security that is required to be registered, the sale of a registered security without delivery of a prospectus, the sale of a security by use of an outdated prospectus, or the offer of a sale before the filing of the registration statement. Liability is strict or absolute, because there are no defenses. The person who purchases a security sold in violation of this provision has the right to tender it back to the seller and recover the purchase price. If the purchaser no longer owns the security, he may recover monetary damages from the seller.

False Registration Statements [39-6b]

When securities have been sold subject to a registration statement, Section 11 of the 1933 Act imposes express liability on those who have included any untrue statement of a material fact in the registration statement or who have omitted any material fact from it. **Material** matters are those to which a reasonable investor would be substantially likely to attach importance in determining whether to purchase the security registered. Usually, proof of reliance upon the misstatement or omission is not required. The section imposes liability on (1) the issuer; (2) all persons who signed the registration statement, including the principal executive officer, principal financial officer, and principal accounting officer; (3) every person who was a director or partner; (4) every accountant, engineer, appraiser, or expert who prepared or certified any part of the registration statement; and (5) all underwriters. These persons generally are jointly and severally liable for the amount paid for the security, less either its value at the time of suit or the price for which

Unregistered sales
Section 12(a)(1) imposes absolute civil liability; there are no defenses

False registration statements
Section 11 imposes liability on the issuer, all persons who signed the statement, every director or partner, experts who prepared or certified any part of the statement, and all underwriters; defendants other than issuer may assert the defense of due diligence

Material
matters to which a reasonable investor would attach importance in deciding whether to purchase a security

it was sold, to any person who acquires the security without knowledge of the untruth or omission. A defendant is not liable for any or the entire amount otherwise recoverable under Section 11 that the defendant proves was caused by something other than the defective disclosure.

Due diligence defense

defense to liability for false registration statements available to defendants who had a reasonable (non-negligent) belief that there were no untrue statements and no material omissions

An expert is liable only for misstatements or omissions in the portion of the registration that she prepared or certified. Moreover, any defendant, other than the issuer (who has strict liability), may assert the defense of due diligence. The **due diligence defense** generally requires the defendant to show that he had reasonable grounds to believe and did believe that there were no untrue statements or material omissions. In some instances, due diligence requires a reasonable investigation to determine grounds for belief. The standard of reasonableness for such investigation and such grounds is that required of a prudent person in the management of his own property.

Escott v. BarChris Const. Corp.
U.S. District Court, Southern District of New York, 1968
283 F.Supp. 643
http://scholar.google.com/scholar_case?case=13642266152052517214&q=283+F.Supp.+643&hl=en&as_sdt=2,34

FACTS BarChris Construction Corporation sold shares of common stock to the public in December 1959. By early 1961, BarChris needed additional working capital and sold debentures to meet this need. A registration statement was filed with the Securities and Exchange Commission (SEC) in March 1961, with amendments filed in May. By the time BarChris received the net proceeds of this sale, it was experiencing financial difficulties. Eventually BarChris filed for bankruptcy. Escott, a purchaser of the debentures, brought suit under the Securities Act of 1933 against BarChris, the underwriters, the company's auditors (Peat, Marwick, Mitchell & Co.), and the persons who signed the registration, alleging that the registration statement contained materially false statements and material omissions. The defendants denied the falsity of the statements and their materiality. Furthermore, all of the defendants, except BarChris, claimed that they individually had exercised due diligence in connection with the statement so as to be free from liability under the statute.

DECISION Judgment for Escott granted.

OPINION The registration statement contained a number of false statements and omissions, many of which were material. Although the 1933 Act does provide a "due diligence" defense to all defendants other than the issuer, BarChris, none of them

sustained the burden of proving this defense. A nonexpert (the defendants other than the auditor) is not liable for material misstatements or omissions in a registration statement not based on an expert's authority if the nonexpert made a reasonable investigation from which he had reasonable grounds to believe the statements were true. A nonexpert is not liable for material misstatements or omissions made on the authority of an expert if the nonexpert had reasonable grounds to believe and did believe they were true. The due diligence defense for an expert, such as the auditors, requires reasonable grounds to believe that there were no material misstatements or omissions based upon a reasonable investigation. The standard of reasonableness is that of a prudent person in the management of his or her own property.

INTERPRETATION The 1933 Act imposes liability for material misstatements and omissions in a registration statement on the issuer, the directors, certain officers, experts, and the underwriters. These parties, except the issuer, may avoid liability by proving that they exercised due diligence in executing their duties with respect to the registration process.

CRITICAL THINKING QUESTION Do you agree with the court's decision? Explain.

Antifraud Provisions [39-6c]

Section 12(a)(2)

imposes liability upon the seller to the immediate purchaser, provided the purchaser did not know of the untruth or omission; but the seller is not liable if he did not know, and in the exercise of reasonable care could not have known, of the untrue statement or omission

The 1933 Act also contains two antifraud provisions: Section 12(a)(2) and Section 17(a). In addition, Rule 10b-5 of the 1934 Act applies to the issuance or sale of all securities, even those exempted by the 1933 Act. Rule 10b-5 is discussed later in this chapter.

Section 12(a)(2) imposes express liability on any person who offers or sells a security by means of a prospectus or oral communication that contains an untrue statement of material fact or omits a material fact. This liability extends only to the immediate purchaser, provided she did not know of the untruth or omission. The seller may avoid liability by proving that he did not know, and in the exercise of reasonable care could not have known, of the untrue statement or omission. The seller is liable to the purchaser for the amount paid on tender of the security. If the purchaser no longer owns the security, she may recover damages from the seller. A defendant is not liable for any portion of or the entire amount otherwise recoverable under Section 12(a)(2) that the defendant proves was caused by something other than the defective disclosure.

Section 17(a)

broadly prohibits fraud in the sale of securities

Section 17(a) makes it unlawful for any person in the offer or sale of any securities, whether registered or not, to do any of the following when using any means of transportation or communication in interstate commerce or the mails: (1) employ any device, scheme, or artifice to defraud; (2) obtain money or property by means of any untrue statement of a material fact or any statement that omits a material fact, without which the information is misleading; or (3) engage in any transaction, practice, or course of business that operates or would operate as a fraud or deceit upon the purchaser. There is considerable doubt whether the courts may imply a private right of action for persons injured by violations of this section. The Supreme Court has reserved this question, and most lower courts have denied the existence of a private remedy. The SEC, however, may bring enforcement actions under Section 17(a).

Criminal Sanctions [39-6d]

Criminal sanctions

willful violations are subject to a fine of not more than $10,000 and/or imprisonment of not more than five years

The 1933 Act imposes **criminal sanctions** on any person who willfully violates any of the provisions of the Act or the rules and regulations promulgated by the SEC pursuant to the Act. Conviction may carry a fine of not more than $10,000 or imprisonment of not more than five years, or both. Moreover, under the Federal Alternative Fines Act, if any person derives pecuniary gain from the offense, or if the offense results in pecuniary loss to a person other than the defendant, the defendant may be fined up to the greater of twice the gross gain or twice the gross loss.

The registration and liability provisions of the 1933 Act are summarized in Figure 39-2.

THE SECURITIES EXCHANGE ACT OF 1934

The Securities Exchange Act of 1934 deals mainly with the secondary distribution (resale) of securities. The 1934 Act's definition of a security is substantially the same as that of the 1933 Act. The 1934 Act seeks to ensure fair and orderly securities markets by establishing rules for market operations and by prohibiting fraudulent and manipulative practices. As amended

Figure 39-2 Registration and Liability Provisions of the 1933 Act

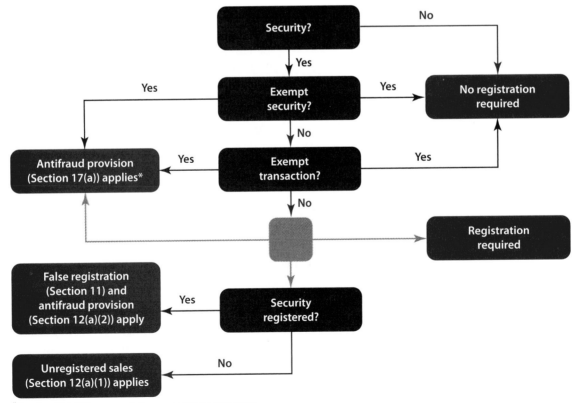

*Section 12 (a)(2) *may* apply to some of these issuances.

Figure 39-3 Applicability of the 1934 Act

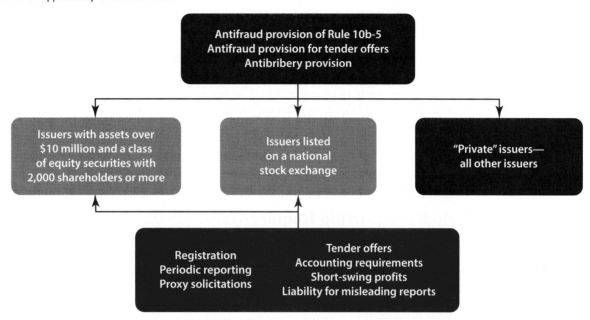

by the JOBS Act, the 1934 Act requires registration of all securities listed on national exchanges, as well as equity securities of companies (1) whose assets exceed $10 million and (2) whose equity securities include a class of equity securities held by either (a) two thousand or more persons or (b) five hundred or more persons who are not accredited investors. Issuers who must register such securities are also subject to the 1934 Act's periodic reporting requirements, short-swing profits provision, tender offer provisions, and proxy solicitation provisions, as well as the internal control and recordkeeping requirements of the Foreign Corrupt Practices Act. In addition, issuers of securities, whether registered under the 1934 Act or not, must comply with the antifraud and antibribery provisions of the Act. Figure 39-3 illustrates the applicability of the 1934 Act's provisions to different types of issuers.

The National Securities Markets Improvements Act of 1996 broadly authorized the SEC to issue regulations, rules, or orders exempting any person, security, or transaction from any of the provisions of the 1934 Act or the SEC's rules promulgated under that Act. This authorization extends so far as such exemption is necessary or appropriate in the public interest and is consistent with the protection of investors. This exemptive authority does not, however, extend to the regulation of government securities broker-dealers.

DISCLOSURE [39-7]

The 1934 Act imposes significant disclosure requirements upon reporting companies. These include the filing of securities registrations, periodic reports, disclosure statements for proxy solicitations, and disclosure statements for tender offers, as well as complying with the accounting requirements imposed by the Foreign Corrupt Practices Act. As part of its integrated registration and reporting system for small business issuers, in 1992 the SEC developed a new series of forms for qualifying issuers to use for registration and periodic reporting under the 1934 Act. Also in 1992, the SEC required disclosure of the compensation paid to senior executives and directors in registration statements, periodic reports, and proxy statements. As noted, in 2006 the SEC amended these rules to mandate clearer and more complete disclosure of compensation paid to directors, the CEO, the CFO, and the three other highest-paid executive officers. The issuer must disclose executive compensation over the last three years, including salary, bonus, a dollar value for stock and option awards, amount of compensation under nonequity incentive plans, annual change in present value of accumulated pension benefits and above-market earnings on nonqualified deferred compensation, and all other compensation including perquisites.

Similar disclosure is required for director compensation for the last fiscal year. Effective in 2000, a plain-English summary term sheet is required in all tender offers, mergers, and going private transactions.

Registration Requirements for Securities [39-7a]

The 1934 Act requires all regulated publicly held companies to register with the SEC. These one-time registrations apply to an entire class of securities. Thus, they differ from registrations under the Securities Act of 1933, which relate only to the securities involved in a specific offering. Registration requires disclosure of information such as the organization, financial structure, and nature of the business; the terms, positions, rights, and privileges of the different classes of outstanding securities; the names of the directors, officers, and underwriters and of each security holder owning more than 10 percent of any class of nonexempt equity security; bonus and profit-sharing arrangements; and balance sheets and profit-and-loss statements for the three preceding fiscal years.

Periodic Reporting Requirements [39-7b]

Following registration, an issuer must file specified annual and periodic reports to update the information contained in the original registration. The SEC has adopted rules under the Sarbanes-Oxley Act requiring an issuer's CEO and CFO to *certify* the financial and other information contained in the issuer's annual and quarterly reports. Moreover, the Act requires that each periodic report shall be *accompanied* by a written statement by the CEO and the CFO of the issuer certifying that the periodic report fully complies with the requirements of the 1934 Act and that information contained in the periodic report fairly presents, in all material respects, the financial condition and results of operations of the issuer. A CEO or CFO who certifies while *knowing* that the report does not comply with the Act is subject to a fine of not more than $1 million or imprisonment of not more than ten years, or both. A CEO or CFO who *willfully* certifies a statement knowing it does not comply with the Act shall be fined not more than $5 million or be imprisoned not more than twenty years, or both.

The Sarbanes-Oxley Act requires that issuers disclose in plain English to the public on a rapid and current basis such additional information concerning material changes in the financial condition or operations of the issuer as the SEC determines is necessary or useful for the protection of investors and in the public interest.

The 1934 Act, as amended by the Dodd-Frank Act, requires that each director, each officer, and any person who owns more than 10 percent of a registered equity security file reports with the SEC within ten days after he or she becomes such beneficial owner, director, or officer, or within such shorter time as the SEC may establish by rule. The 1934 Act also requires that each director, each officer, and any person who owns more than 10 percent of a registered equity security file reports with the SEC for any month in which changes in his ownership of such equity securities have occurred before the end of the second business day following the day on which the transaction was executed unless the SEC establishes a different deadline. The 1934 Act also requires that these filings reporting changes in ownership be made electronically on EDGAR, that the SEC make them publicly available on its Internet site, and that issuers make them available on their corporate websites if they maintain one.

Effective in 2010, the SEC adopted new requirements to improve the disclosure shareholders of public companies receive regarding compensation and corporate governance. These new rules require disclosure of (1) the qualifications of directors and nominees for director, and the reasons why that person should serve as a director of the issuer; (2) any directorships held by each director and nominee at any time during the past five years at any public company or registered investment company; (3) the consideration of diversity in the process by which candidates for director are considered for nomination by an issuer's nominating committee; (4) an issuer's board leadership structure and the board's role in the oversight of risk; (5) the aggregate grant date fair value of stock awards and option awards granted in the fiscal year computed in accordance with the Financial Accounting Standards Board; and (6) the issuer's compensation policies or practices as they relate to risk management and risk-taking incentives that can affect the issuer's risk and management of that risk, to the extent that risks arising from a issuer's compensation policies and practices for employees are reasonably likely to have a material adverse effect on the issuer.

Practical Advice

If you are a director, officer, or own more than 10 percent of a registered security, be sure to report to the SEC any sales or purchases you make of the company's equity securities.

Proxy Solicitations [39-7c]

Proxy

a signed writing by a
shareholder authorizing a
named person to vote her
stock at a specified meeting
of shareholders

A **proxy** is a writing signed by a shareholder authorizing a named person to vote his shares of stock at a specified shareholders' meeting. To ensure that shareholders have adequate information upon which to vote and an opportunity to participate effectively at shareholder meetings, the 1934 Act regulates the proxy solicitation process. The 1934 Act makes it unlawful for any person to solicit any proxy concerning any registered security "in contravention of such rules and regulations as the Commission may prescribe." *Solicitation* includes any request for a proxy, any request not to execute a proxy, or any request to revoke a proxy. The SEC has issued comprehensive and detailed rules prescribing the solicitation process and the disclosure of information about the issuer.

Proxy statements

proxy disclosure
statements are required
when proxies are solicited
or an issuer submits a
matter to a shareholder
vote

Proxy Statements   The 1934 Act prohibits solicitation of a proxy unless each person solicited has been furnished with a written **proxy statement** containing specified information. An issuer making solicitations must furnish security holders with a proxy statement describing all material facts concerning the matters being submitted to their vote, together with a proxy form on which the security holders can indicate their approval or disapproval of each proposal to be presented. Even a company that does not solicit proxies from its shareholders but submits a matter to their vote must provide them with information substantially equivalent to that which would appear in a proxy statement. With few exceptions, the issuer must file preliminary copies of a proxy statement and proxy form with the SEC at least ten days prior to the first date on which the forms are to be sent. In addition, in an election of directors, solicitations of proxies by a person other than the issuer are subject to similar disclosure requirements. The issuer in such an election also must include an annual report with the proxy statement. Effective in 2010, the SEC requires in proxy materials relating to the election of directors that the issuer disclose the qualifications of nominees for director and the reasons why that person should serve as a director of the issuer. The same information is required in the proxy materials prepared with respect to nominees for director nominated by others. Moreover, the Dodd-Frank Act authorizes the SEC to issue rules requiring that an issuer's proxy solicitation include nominations for the board of directors submitted by shareholders. Under the Dodd-Frank Act, the SEC must issue rules requiring issuers to disclose in annual proxy statements the reasons why the issuer has chosen to separate or combine the positions of chairman of the board of directors and CEO.

The Dodd-Frank Act contains several provisions regarding executive compensation. First, at least once every three years, issuers must include a provision in certain proxy statements for a nonbinding shareholder vote on the compensation of executives. In a separate resolution, shareholders determine whether this "say on pay" vote should be held every one, two, or three years. Second, the SEC must issue rules requiring issuers to describe clearly in annual proxy statements information that shows the relationship between executive compensation actually paid and the financial performance of the issuer, taking into account any change in the value of the shares of stock and dividends of the issuer and any distributions. Third, the SEC must issue rules requiring the disclosure of (1) the median of the annual total compensation of all issuer's employees except the CEO, (2) the annual total compensation of the CEO, and (3) the ratio of the amount described in (1) to the amount described in (2). Fourth, companies soliciting votes to approve merger or acquisition transactions must provide disclosure of certain "golden parachute" compensation arrangements (executive compensation that is based on or relates to the merger or acquisition transaction) and, in certain circumstances, to conduct a separate shareholder advisory vote to approve the golden parachute compensation arrangements. The JOBS Act exempts EGCs from the requirement for separate shareholder approval of executive compensation, including golden parachute compensation.

Effective March 30, 2007, the SEC amended its proxy rules to provide an alternative method for issuers and other persons to furnish proxy materials to shareholders: posting them on an Internet website and providing shareholders with notice of the availability of the proxy materials. Issuers must make paper or e-mail copies of the proxy materials available without charge to shareholders on request.

Shareholder Proposals   When management makes a solicitation, any security holder entitled to vote has the opportunity to communicate with other security holders. On written request, the corporation must mail the communication at the security holder's expense or, at its option, promptly furnish to that security holder a current list of security holders.

If an eligible security holder entitled to vote submits a timely and appropriate proposal for action at a forthcoming meeting, management must include the proposal in its proxy statement along with a brief statement explaining the shareholder's reasons for making the proposal. Management may omit a proposal if, among other things, (1) under state law it is not a proper subject for shareholder action, (2) it would require the company to violate any law, (3) it is beyond the issuer's power or authority to accomplish, (4) it relates to the conduct of the issuer's ordinary business operations, or (5) it relates to a nomination or an election for membership on the issuer's board of directors or to a procedure for such nomination or election. However, in 2010, the SEC amended the last exclusion by providing shareholders, under certain circumstances, the power to include in an issuer's proxy materials a shareholder proposal that seeks to establish in the issuer's governing documents a procedure for the inclusion in the proxy materials of director nominees selected by a shareholder or group of shareholders. In July 2011, the U.S. Court of Appeals for the District of Columbia invalidated this new proxy access provision based on the court's conclusion that the SEC had violated the Administrative Procedure Act by failing adequately to assess the economic effects of the new rule as required by the 1934 Act. The SEC decided not to seek a rehearing or review by the U.S. Supreme Court of this court decision. Unaffected by this court decision is a companion SEC rule adopted in 2010 permitting eligible shareholders to require companies to include shareholder proposals regarding proxy access procedures in company proxy materials. Under this new rule, companies will no longer be able to exclude a proposal seeking to establish a procedure in a company's governing documents for the inclusion of one or more shareholder nominees for director in the company's proxy materials.

Tender Offers [39-7d]

Tender offer
a general invitation to shareholders to purchase their shares at a specified price for a specified time

A **tender offer** is a general invitation to a company's shareholders to purchase their shares at a specified price for a specified time. In 1968, Congress enacted the Williams Act, which amended the 1934 Act to extend reporting and disclosure requirements to tender offers and other block acquisitions. The purpose of the Williams Act is to provide public shareholders with full disclosure by both the bidder and the target company so that the shareholders may make an informed decision.

Disclosure requirements
a statement disclosing specified information must be filed with the Securities and Exchange Commission and furnished to each offeree

Disclosure Requirements The 1934 Act imposes **disclosure requirements** in three situations: (1) when a person or group acquires more than 5 percent of a class of voting securities registered under the 1934 Act, (2) when a person makes a tender offer for more than 5 percent of a class of registered equity securities, or (3) when the issuer makes an offer to repurchase its own registered shares. Although different rules govern each situation, the disclosure required is substantially the same. The acquiring entity must file with the SEC a statement containing (1) the acquisitor's background; (2) the source of the funds it will use to acquire the securities; (3) the purpose of the acquisition, including any plans to liquidate the company or to make major changes in the corporate structure; (4) the number of shares the acquisitor owns; (5) the terms of the transaction; and (6) any relevant contracts, arrangements, or understandings. This disclosure is also required of anyone soliciting shareholders to accept or reject a tender offer. A copy of the statement must be furnished to each offeree and sent to the issuer.

The target company has ten days in which to respond to the bidder's tender offer by (1) recommending acceptance or rejection, (2) expressing no opinion and remaining neutral, or (3) stating that it is unable to take a position. The target company's response must include the reasons for the position it takes.

Required Practices A tender offer either by a third party or by the issuer is subject to the following rules: the initial tender offer must be kept open for at least twenty business days and for at least ten days after any change in terms. Shareholders who tender their shares may withdraw them at any time during the offering period. The tender offer must be open to all holders of the class of shares subject to the offer. All shares tendered must be purchased for the same price; thus, if an offering price is increased, both those who have tendered and those who have yet to tender will receive the benefit of the increase. A tender offeror who offers to purchase fewer than all of the outstanding securities of the target must accept, on a *pro rata* basis, securities tendered during the offer. During the tender offer, the bidder may buy shares of the target only through that tender offer. In a tender offer for all outstanding shares of a class, a tender offeror may provide a subsequent offering period of three to twenty days after completion of a tender offer, during which time security holders can tender shares without withdrawal rights.

Defensive Tactics   When confronted by an uninvited takeover bid—or by a potential uninvited bid—management of the target company may decide either to oppose the bid or to seek to prevent it. The defensive tactics management employs to prevent or defend against undesired tender offers have developed (and are still evolving) into a highly ingenious, and metaphorically named, set of maneuvers, some of which require considerable planning—and some of which are of questionable legality.

State Regulation   More than forty states have enacted statutes regulating tender offers. Although they vary greatly, most of these statutes tend to protect the target company from an unwanted tender offer. Some empower the state to review the merits of the offer or the adequacy of disclosure. Many impose waiting periods before the tender offer becomes effective. The state statutes generally require disclosures more detailed than those the Williams Act requires, and many of them exempt tender offers supported by the target company's management. A number of states have adopted fair price statutes, which require the acquisitor to pay to all shareholders the highest price paid to any shareholder. Some states have enacted business combination statutes prohibiting transactions with an acquisitor for a specified period after a change in control, unless disinterested shareholders approve.

See Concept Review 39-2.

CONCEPT REVIEW 39-2

Disclosure Under the 1934 Act

	Initial Registration	Periodic Reporting	Insider Reporting	Proxy Statement	Tender Offer
Registrant	Issuer if regulated, publicly held company	Issuer if regulated, publicly held company	Statutory insiders (directors, officers, and principal stockholders)	Issuer and other persons soliciting proxies	5 percent stockholder, tender offeror, or issuer
Information	Nature of business; Financial structure; Directors and executive officers; Financial statements	Annual, quarterly, or current report updating information in initial registration	Initial statement of beneficial ownership of equity securities; Changes in beneficial ownership	Details of solicitation; Legal terms of proxy; Annual report (if directors to be elected)	Identity and background; Terms of transaction; Source of funds; Intentions
Filing Date	Within 120 days after becoming a reporting company	Annual: within 90 days[1] after year's end; Quarterly: within 45 days[2] after quarter's end; Current: within 15 days after any material change	Within 10 days of becoming a statutory insider; Within 2 days after a change in ownership takes place	10 days before final proxy statement is distributed	5 percent stockholder: within 10 days after acquiring more than 5 percent of a class of registered securities; Tender offeror: before tender offer is made; Issuer: before offer to repurchase
Purpose of Disclosure	Adequate and accurate disclosure of material facts regarding securities listed on a national exchange or traded publicly over the counter	Update information contained in initial registration	Prevent unfair use of information that may have been obtained by a statutory insider	Full disclosure of material information; Facilitation of shareholder proposals	Adequate and accurate disclosure of material facts; Opportunity to reach uncoerced decision

[1] Certain issuers must file within sixty or seventy-five days.
[2] Certain issuers must file within forty days.

BUSINESS LAW **IN ACTION**

Since late 1995, U.S. corporations have been covered by the Private Securities Litigation Reform Act's "safe harbor," which enables publicly traded companies to publish their forward-looking statements without fear of liability for securities fraud in the event their well-grounded predictions do not materialize. Using the safe harbor, companies that report to the Securities and Exchange Commission (SEC) under the 1934 Act can now safely script their public statements—conference calls with securities analysts and shareholders, executives' interviews with financial news programs or magazines, annual reports to shareholders, and paper or Web-based press releases—to include forward-looking statements like earnings estimates and plans for new products or business combinations.

The safe harbor reflects two competing premises. On the one hand, predictions by management can be very valuable to the capital markets. On the other, this type of information also poses the risk that it will be misinterpreted as fact. Therefore, to pro-actively insulate qualifying forward-looking statements under the safe harbor, the company must identify its predictions and projections as forward-looking and must accompany them with meaningful cautionary language identifying important factors that could cause actual results to differ materially from those predicted.

Many companies therefore are now routinely including so-called safe harbor warnings in their public statements.

To satisfy the law, a company's public disclosure refers expressly to the statute and many then delineate the topics of the statement that might include forward-looking information. Some companies caution that the use of words similar to "should," "expect," and "see" indicates forward-looking information. To provide the necessary "meaningful cautionary language," the safe harbor warnings then articulate at great length those risk factors or uncertainties that could cause the company's actual performance or achievements to differ materially from those anticipated. For these risk factors effectively to protect the forward-looking statements, they must be carefully tailored to the specific disclosures being made.

Foreign Corrupt Practices Act

imposes internal control requirements on companies with securities registered under the 1934 Act

Foreign Corrupt Practices Act [39-7e]

In 1977, Congress enacted the Foreign Corrupt Practices Act (FCPA) as an amendment to the 1934 Act. Amended in 1988 and 1998, the FCPA (1) imposes internal control requirements on issuers with securities registered under the 1934 Act and (2) prohibits all U.S. persons, and certain foreign issuers of securities, from bribing foreign government or political officials (an activity that is discussed later in this chapter). The accounting requirements of the FCPA reflect the ideas that accurate recordkeeping is essential to managerial responsibility and that investors should be able to rely on the financial reports they receive. Accordingly, the accounting requirements were enacted (1) to ensure that an issuer's books accurately reflect financial transactions, (2) to protect the integrity of independent audits of financial statements, and (3) to promote the reliability of financial information required by the 1934 Act.

LIABILITY [39-8]

To implement its objectives, the 1934 Act imposes sanctions for noncompliance with its disclosure and antifraud requirements. These sanctions include civil monetary liability to injured investors and issuers, civil penalties, and criminal penalties.

The 1995 Reform Act contains several provisions that affect civil liability under the 1934 Act. First, the 1995 Reform Act imposes on a plaintiff in any private action under the 1934 Act the burden of proving that the defendant's alleged violation of the 1934 Act caused the loss for which the plaintiff seeks to recover damages. Second, the 1995 Reform Act imposes a limit on the amount of damages a plaintiff can recover in any private action under the 1934 Act based on a material misstatement or omission in which she seeks to establish damages by reference to the market price of a security. The plaintiff may not recover damage in excess of the difference between the purchase or sale price she paid or received for the security and the mean trading price of that security during the ninety-day period beginning on the date when the information correcting the misstatement or omission is disseminated to the market. Third, the 1995 Reform Act provides a "safe harbor" under the 1934 Act from civil liability based on an untrue statement of material fact or an omission of a material fact necessary to make the statement not misleading. The safe harbor applies to issuers required to report under the 1934

Act and who make "forward-looking" statements (predictions) if the statements meet specified requirements. The requirements of the safe harbor and the transactions to which it does not apply were discussed earlier in this chapter.

Misleading Statements in Reports [39-8a]

Misleading statements in reports
Section 18 imposes civil liability for any false or misleading statement made in a registration or report filed with the Securities and Exchange Commission

Section 18 imposes express civil liability upon any person who makes or causes to be made any false or misleading statement with respect to any material fact in any application, report, document, or registration filed with the SEC under the 1934 Act. Any person who purchased or sold a security in reliance upon such a false or misleading statement without knowing that it was false or misleading may recover under this section. A person is not liable, however, if she proves that she acted in good faith and had no knowledge that such statement was false or misleading. The court may award attorneys' fees against either the plaintiff or the defendant.

Short-Swing Profits [39-8b]

Short-swing profits
Section 16(b) imposes liability on certain insiders (directors, officers, and shareholders owning more than 10 percent of the stock of a corporation) for all profits made on sales and purchases within six months of each other, with any recovery going to the issuer

Section 16(b) of the 1934 Act imposes express liability upon insiders—directors, officers, and any person owning more than 10 percent of the stock of a corporation listed on a national stock exchange or registered with the SEC—for all profits resulting from their "short-swing" trading in such stock. If any insider sells such stock within six months from the date of its purchase or purchases such stock within six months from the date of a sale of the stock, the corporation is entitled to recover any and all profit the insider realizes from these transactions. The "profit" recoverable is calculated by matching the highest sale price against the lowest purchase price within the relevant six-month period. Losses cannot be offset against profits. Suit to recover such profit may be brought by the issuer or by the owner of any security of the issuer in the name and on behalf of the issuer if the issuer fails or refuses to bring such suit within sixty days of the owner's request.

Antifraud Provision [39-8c]

Antifraud provision
Rule 10b-5 makes it unlawful to (1) employ any device, scheme, or artifice to defraud; (2) make any untrue statement of a material fact; (3) omit to state a material fact; or (4) engage in any act that operates as a fraud

Section 10(b) of the 1934 Act and *SEC Rule 10b-5* make it unlawful for any person using the mails or facilities of interstate commerce in connection with the purchase or sale of any security (1) to employ any device, scheme, or artifice to defraud; (2) to make any untrue statement of a material fact; (3) to omit to state a material fact necessary to make the statements made not misleading; or (4) to engage in any act, practice, or course of business that operates or would operate as a fraud or deceit upon any person.

Rule 10b-5 applies to any purchase or sale of *any* security, whether it is registered under the 1934 Act or not, whether it is publicly traded or closely held, whether it is listed on an exchange or sold over the counter, or whether it is part of an initial issuance or a secondary distribution. There are *no* exemptions. The implied liability under Rule 10b-5 applies to purchaser as well as seller misconduct and allows both defrauded sellers and buyers to recover.

Requisites of Rule 10b-5
recovery requires (1) a misstatement or omission, (2) materiality, (3) *scienter* (intentional and knowing conduct), (4) reliance, (5) connection with the purchase or sale of a security, and (6) economic loss

Scienter
intentional and knowing conduct

Requisites of Rule 10b-5   Recovery of damages under Rule 10b-5 requires proof of (1) a misstatement or omission (2) that is material, (3) made with *scienter*, (4) relied upon (5) in connection with the purchase or sale of a security, and (6) that causes economic loss. This rule differs from common law fraud in that Rule 10b-5 imposes an affirmative duty of disclosure. A misstatement or omission is **material** if there is a substantial likelihood that a reasonable investor would consider it important in deciding whether to purchase or sell the security. Examples of material facts include substantial changes in dividends or earnings, significant misstatements of asset value, and the fact that the issuer is about to become a target of a tender offer. In an action for damages under Rule 10b-5, it must be shown that the violation was committed with **scienter**, or intentional misconduct. Negligence is not sufficient. Although the Supreme Court has not yet decided whether reckless conduct is sufficient to satisfy the requirement of *scienter*, the vast majority of circuit and district courts have held recklessness to be sufficient. Reliance upon the misstatement or omission is required, although in some circumstances it may be satisfied by the presumption of reliance upon the marketplace.

Direct reliance may be difficult to prove in an action brought under Rule 10b-5 because the buyer and seller usually do not negotiate their deal face to face. Recognizing the special nature of securities market transactions, the Supreme Court adopted the fraud-on-the-market theory, which establishes a rebuttable presumption of reliance based on the premise that the market price of a stock reflects any misstatement or omission and that the fraudulently affected market price has injured the plaintiff. Thus, a person who bought or sold a corporation's shares on a securities exchange after the issuance of a materially misleading statement by the corporation may invoke a rebuttable presumption that, in trading, he relied on the integrity of the price set by the market.

Remedies for Rule 10b-5 violations include rescission, damages, and injunctions. The courts, however, are divided over the measure of damages to impose.

Matrixx Initiatives, Inc. v. Siracusano
Supreme Court of the United States, 2011
563 U.S. 4, 131 S.Ct. 1309, 179 L.Ed.2d 398
http://scholar.google.com/scholar_case?q=131+S.+Ct.+1309&hl=en&as_sdt=2,34&case=15831619199744263593&scilh=0

FACTS Matrixx develops, manufactures, and markets over-the-counter pharmaceutical products. Zicam products are its main products. Zicam products are used to treat the common cold and associated symptoms. At the time of the events in question, one of Matrixx's products was Zicam Cold Remedy, which came in several forms including nasal spray and gel. The active ingredient in Zicam Cold Remedy was zinc gluconate. Plaintiffs allege that Zicam Cold Remedy accounted for approximately 70 percent of Matrixx's sales.

Plaintiffs initiated this securities fraud class action against Matrixx on behalf of individuals who purchased Matrixx securities between October 22, 2003, and February 6, 2004. The action principally arises out of statements that Matrixx made during that period relating to revenues and product safety. Plaintiffs claim that Matrixx's statements were misleading in light of reports that Matrixx had received, but did not disclose, about consumers who had lost their sense of smell (a condition called anosmia) after using Zicam Cold Remedy nasal spray or gel.

On January 30, 2004, Dow Jones Newswires reported that the Food and Drug Administration (FDA) was "looking into complaints that an over-the-counter common-cold medicine manufactured by a unit of Matrixx Initiatives, Inc. (MTXX) may be causing some users to lose their sense of smell" in light of at least three product liability lawsuits. Matrixx's stock fell from $13.55 to $11.97 per share after the report. In response, on February 2, Matrixx issued a press release:

All Zicam products are manufactured and marketed according to FDA guidelines for homeopathic medicine. Our primary concern is the health and safety of our customers and the distribution of factual information about our products. Matrixx believes statements alleging that intranasal Zicam products caused anosmia (loss of smell) are completely unfounded and misleading.

In no clinical trial of intranasal zinc gluconate gel products has there been a single report of lost or diminished olfactory function (sense of smell). Rather, the safety and efficacy of zinc gluconate for the treatment of symptoms related to the common cold have been well established in two double-blind, placebo-controlled, randomized clinical trials. In fact, in neither study were there any reports of anosmia related to the use of this compound. The overall incidence of adverse events associated with zinc gluconate was

extremely low, with no statistically significant difference between the adverse event rates for the treated and placebo subsets.

The day after Matrixx issued this press release, its stock price rebounded to $13.40 per share.

On February 19, 2004, Matrixx filed a Form 8-K with the SEC stating that it had "convened a two-day meeting of physicians and scientists to review current information on smell disorders" and that "[i]n the opinion of the panel, there is insufficient scientific evidence at this time to determine if zinc gluconate, when used as recommended, affects a person's ability to smell."

Plaintiffs claimed that Matrixx violated Section 10(b) of the Securities Exchange Act and SEC Rule 10b-5 by making untrue statements of fact and failing to disclose material facts necessary to make the statements not misleading in an effort to maintain artificially high prices for Matrixx securities. Matrixx moved to dismiss the complaint. The District Court granted the motion to dismiss, holding that the plaintiffs had not alleged a statistically significant correlation between the use of Zicam and anosmia so as to make failure to publicly disclose complaints and a medical study a material omission. The Court of Appeals for the Ninth Circuit reversed, holding that the District Court had erred in requiring an allegation of statistical significance to establish materiality. It concluded that the complaint adequately alleged "information regarding the possible link between Zicam and anosmia" that would have been significant to a reasonable investor.

DECISION The judgment of the Court of Appeals for the Ninth Circuit is affirmed.

OPINION Section 10(b) of the Securities Exchange Act makes it unlawful for any person to "use or employ, in connection with the purchase or sale of any security ... any manipulative or deceptive device or contrivance in contravention of such rules and regulations as the Commission may prescribe as necessary or appropriate in the public interest or for the protection of investors." SEC Rule 10b-5 implements this provision by making it unlawful to, among other things, "make any untrue statement of a material fact or to omit to state a material fact necessary in order to make the statements made, in the light of the circumstances under which they were made, not misleading." The U.S. Supreme Court has implied a private cause of action from the text and purpose of Section 10(b).

To prevail on their claim that Matrixx made material misrepresentations or omissions in violation of Section 10(b) and Rule 10b-5, the plaintiffs must prove "(1) a material misrepresentation or omission by the defendant; (2) scienter; (3) a connection between the misrepresentation or omission and the purchase or sale of a security; (4) reliance upon the misrepresentation or omission; (5) economic loss; and (6) loss causation."

To prevail on a Section 10(b) claim, a plaintiff must show that the defendant made a statement that was *misleading* as to a *material* fact, which requires a substantial likelihood that the disclosure of the omitted fact would have been viewed by the reasonable investor as having significantly altered the "total mix" of information made available.

Given that medical professionals and regulators act on the basis of evidence of causation that is not statistically significant, it stands to reason that in certain cases reasonable investors would as well. As a result, assessing the materiality of adverse event reports is a "fact-specific" inquiry that requires consideration of the source, content, and context of the reports. This is not to say that statistical significance (or the lack thereof) is irrelevant—only that it is not dispositive of every case.

Application of the "total mix" standard does not mean that pharmaceutical manufacturers must disclose all reports of adverse events. The fact that a user of a drug has suffered an adverse event, standing alone, does not mean that the drug caused that event. The question remains whether a *reasonable* investor would have viewed the nondisclosed information "'as having *significantly* altered the "total mix" of information made available.'" Applying the "total mix" standard in this case, the plaintiffs have adequately pleaded materiality. Viewing the allegations of the complaint as a whole, the complaint alleges facts suggesting a significant risk to the commercial viability of Matrixx's leading product. Assuming the facts to be true, these were material facts "necessary in order to make the statements made, in the light of the circumstances under which they were made, not misleading."

INTERPRETATION The materiality requirement for a Section 10(b) claim is satisfied when there is a substantial likelihood that the disclosure of the omitted fact would have been viewed by the reasonable investor as having significantly altered the "total mix" of information made available.

CRITICAL THINKING QUESTION Do you agree that the lack of statistical significance of adverse event reports should not necessarily preclude those reports from being material to reasonable investors? Explain.

Insider trading

"insiders" are liable under Rule 10b-5 for failing to disclose material, nonpublic information before trading on the information

Insiders

directors, officers, employees, and agents of the issuer, as well as those with whom the issuer has entrusted information solely for corporate purposes

---

Practical Advice

If you confidentially acquire any nonpublic information about a company, do not trade in that company's securities until that information has become public.

Insider Trading Rule 10b-5 applies to sales or purchases of securities made by an "insider" who possesses material information that is not available to the general public. An insider who fails to disclose such information before trading on it will be liable under Rule 10b-5 unless he waits for the information to become public. Under SEC Rule 10b5-1, a purchase or sale of an issuer's security is based on material nonpublic information about that security or issuer if the person making the purchase or sale was *aware* of the information when the person entered into the transaction. **Insiders**, for the purpose of Rule 10b-5, include directors, officers, employees, and agents of the security issuer, as well as those with whom the issuer has entrusted information solely for corporate purposes, such as underwriters, accountants, lawyers, and consultants. In some instances, the rule also precludes persons who receive material, nonpublic information from insiders—tippees—from trading on that information. A tippee is under a duty not to trade on inside information from an insider who has breached his fiduciary duty to the shareholders by disclosing the information to the tippee, who knows or should know that such a breach has occurred. (See Figure 39-4, which illustrates which parties are forbidden to trade on inside information.) In the case that follows, *United States v. O'Hagan*, the U.S. Supreme Court upholds the misappropriation theory as an additional and complementary basis for imposing liability for insider trading. Under this theory, a person who trades in securities for personal profit using confidential information misappropriated in breach of a fiduciary duty to the source of the information may be held liable for insider trading under Rule 10b-5. This liability applies even though the source of information is not the issuer of the securities that were traded. SEC Rule 10b5-2 adopts the misappropriation theory of liability: a violation of Section 10(b) includes the purchase or sale of a security of an issuer on the basis of material nonpublic information about that security or issuer in breach of trust or confidence that is owed to the issuer, the shareholders of that issuer, or *any other person who is the source of the material nonpublic information*. Under SEC Rule 10b5-2, a person has a duty of trust or confidence for purposes of the misappropriation theory of liability when (1) a person agrees to maintain information in confidence; (2) two people have a history, pattern, or practice of sharing confidences such that the recipient of the information knows or

Figure 39-4 Parties Forbidden to Trade on Inside Information

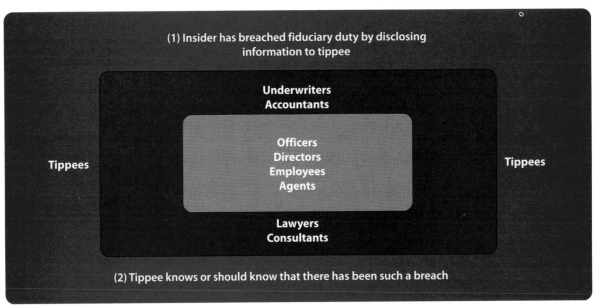

reasonably should know that the person communicating the material nonpublic information expects that the recipient will maintain its confidentiality; or (3) a person receives or obtains material nonpublic information from his or her spouse, parent, child, or sibling.

The Stop Trading on Congressional Knowledge Act of 2012 prohibits the purchase or sale of securities of any issuer by a person in possession of material nonpublic information regarding pending or prospective legislative action relating to the issuer of the securities if the information was obtained (1) by reason of being a member or employee of Congress or (2) knowingly from a member or employee of Congress. The Act also prohibits the purchase or sale of securities of any issuer by a person in possession of material nonpublic information derived from federal employment and relating to the issuer of the securities if the information was obtained (1) by reason of being a federal employee or (2) knowingly from a federal employee.

Under SEC Regulation FD (for "fair disclosure"), regulated issuers who disclose material nonpublic information to specified persons (primarily securities market professionals such as analysts and mutual fund managers) must make public disclosure of that information. If the selective disclosure was intentional or reckless, the issuer must make public disclosure simultaneously; for a nonintentional disclosure, the issuer must make public disclosure promptly, usually within twenty-four hours. In 2013, the SEC issued a report (1) confirming that Regulation FD applies to social media and other emerging means of communication used by public companies the same way it applies to company websites and (2) clarifying that issuers can use social media outlets like Facebook and Twitter to announce key information in compliance with Regulation FD so long as investors have been alerted about which social media will be used to disseminate such information. With a few exceptions, Regulation FD does not apply to disclosures made in connection with securities offerings registered under the 1933 Act. The SEC can enforce this rule by bringing an administrative action seeking a cease-and-desist order or a civil action seeking an injunction and/or civil monetary penalties.

Although both Section 16(b) and Rule 10b-5 address the problem of insider trading and both may apply to the same transaction, they differ in several respects. First, Section 16(b) applies only to transactions involving registered equity securities; Rule 10b-5 applies to all securities. Second, the definition of *insider* under Rule 10b-5 extends beyond directors, officers, and owners of more than 10 percent of a company's stock, whereas the definition under

Section 16(b) does not. Third, Section 16(b) does not require that the insider possess material, nonpublic information; liability is strict. Rule 10b-5 applies to insider trading only when such information is not disclosed. Fourth, Section 16(b) applies only to transactions occurring within six months of each other; Rule 10b-5 has no such limitation. Fifth, under Rule 10b-5, injured investors may recover damages on their own behalf; under Section 16(b), although shareholders may bring suit, any recovery is on behalf of the corporation.

United States v. O'Hagan
Supreme Court of the United States, 1997
521 U.S. 642, 117 S.Ct. 2199, 138 L.Ed.2d 724
http://scholar.google.com/scholar_case?q=117+S.CT.+2199&hl=en&as_sdt=2,34&case=287189961484150105&scilh=0

FACTS James Herman O'Hagan was a partner in the law firm of Dorsey & Whitney in Minneapolis, Minnesota. In July 1988, Grand Metropolitan PLC (Grand Met), a company based in London, England, retained Dorsey & Whitney as local counsel to represent Grand Met regarding a potential tender offer for the common stock of the Pillsbury Company, headquartered in Minneapolis. Both Grand Met and Dorsey & Whitney took precautions to protect the confidentiality of Grand Met's tender offer plans. O'Hagan did no work on the Grand Met representation. On August 18, 1988, O'Hagan began purchasing call options for Pillsbury stock. Each option gave him the right to purchase one hundred shares of Pillsbury stock by a specified date in September 1988. Later in August and in September, O'Hagan made additional purchases of Pillsbury call options. By the end of September, he owned two thousand five hundred unexpired Pillsbury options, apparently more than any other individual investor. O'Hagan also purchased, in September 1988, some five thousand shares of Pillsbury common stock, at a price just under $39 per share. When Grand Met announced its tender offer in October, the price of Pillsbury stock rose to nearly $60 per share. O'Hagan then sold his Pillsbury call options and common stock, making a profit of more than $4.3 million.

The Securities and Exchange Commission (SEC) initiated an investigation into O'Hagan's transactions, resulting in an indictment alleging that O'Hagan defrauded his law firm and its client, Grand Met, by using for his own trading purposes material, nonpublic information regarding Grand Met's planned tender offer in violation of Section 10(b) of the Securities Exchange Act of 1934 and SEC Rule 10b-5. A jury convicted O'Hagan and he was sentenced to a forty-one-month term of imprisonment. A divided panel of the Court of Appeals for the Eighth Circuit reversed O'Hagan's conviction, holding that liability under Section 10(b) and Rule 10b-5 may not be grounded on the "misappropriation theory" of securities fraud on which the prosecution relied.

DECISION Judgment of the Court of Appeals for the Eighth Circuit is reversed and remanded.

OPINION Under the "traditional" or "classical theory" of insider trading liability, Section 10(b) and Rule 10b-5 are violated when a corporate insider trades in the securities of his corporation on the basis of material, nonpublic information. Trading on such information qualifies as a "deceptive device" under Section 10(b) because "a relationship of trust and confidence [exists] between the shareholders of a corporation and those insiders who have obtained confidential information by reason of their position with that corporation." The classical theory applies not only to officers, directors, and other permanent insiders of a corporation but also to attorneys, accountants, consultants, and others who temporarily become fiduciaries of a corporation.

The "misappropriation theory" holds that a person commits fraud "in connection with" a securities transaction, and thereby violates Section 10(b) and Rule 10b-5, when he misappropriates confidential information for securities trading purposes, in breach of a duty owed to the source of the information. Under this theory, a fiduciary's undisclosed, self-serving use of a principal's information to purchase or sell securities, in breach of a duty of loyalty and confidentiality, defrauds the principal of the exclusive use of that information. In lieu of premising liability on a fiduciary relationship between a company insider and the purchaser or seller of the company's stock, the misappropriation theory premises liability on a fiduciary-turned-trader's deception of those who entrusted him with access to confidential information.

The two theories are complementary, each addressing efforts to capitalize on nonpublic information through the purchase or sale of securities.

In this case, the indictment alleged that O'Hagan, in breach of a duty of trust and confidence he owed to his law firm, Dorsey & Whitney, and to its client, Grand Met, traded on the basis of nonpublic information regarding Grand Met's planned tender offer for Pillsbury common stock. This conduct, the government charged, constituted a fraudulent device in connection with the purchase and sale of securities. The misappropriation at issue here was properly made the subject of a Section 10(b) charge because it meets the statutory requirement that there be "deceptive conduct" "in connection with" securities transactions.

INTERPRETATION A person who trades in securities for personal profit using confidential information misappropriated in breach of a fiduciary duty to the source of the information may be held liable for insider trading under Rule 10b-5.

ETHICAL QUESTION Did the defendant act unethically? Explain.

CRITICAL THINKING QUESTION What are the arguments for and against the misappropriation theory? With which position do you agree? Explain.

GOING GLOBAL

What about international securities regulation?

The securities markets have become increasingly internationalized, thereby raising questions regarding which country's law governs a particular transaction in securities. Foreign issuers who issue securities in the United States must register them under the 1933 Act unless an exemption is available. Foreign issuers whose securities are sold in the secondary market in the United States must register under the 1934 Act unless the issuer is exempt. Some nonexempt foreign issuers may avoid registration under the 1934 Act by providing the Securities and Exchange Commission (SEC) with copies of all information material to investors that they have made public in their home country. Regulation S provides a safe harbor from the 1933 Act registration requirements for offshore sales of equity securities of U.S. issuers.

The antifraud provisions of the U.S. securities laws apply to securities sold by the use of any means or instrumentality of interstate commerce. In determining the extraterritorial application of these provisions, the lower courts had generally found jurisdiction in cases in which there was either *conduct* or *effects* in the United States relating to a violation of the federal securities laws. In the 2010 case of *Morrison v. National Australia Bank Ltd.*, the U.S.

Supreme Court rejected these cases, holding that Section 10(b) and Rule 10b-5 of the Securities Exchange Act of 1934 do not apply extraterritorially but *only* reach the use of a manipulative or deceptive device or contrivance in connection with (1) the purchase or sale of a security listed on a U.S. stock exchange or (2) the purchase or sale of any other security in the United States. The Supreme Court held that Section 10(b) and Rule 10b-5 do not provide a cause of action to foreign plaintiffs suing foreign or U.S. defendants for misconduct in connection with securities traded on foreign exchanges.

The Dodd-Frank Act extends the reach of the antifraud provisions of the 1933 and 1934 Acts with respect to actions brought by the U.S. Justice Department and the SEC. In such actions, jurisdiction would include "(1) conduct within the United States that constitutes significant steps in furtherance of the violation, even if the violation is committed by a foreign adviser and involves only foreign investors; or (2) conduct occurring outside the United States that has a foreseeable substantial effect within the United States." The Dodd-Frank Act also requires the SEC to study the extent to which private rights of action under the antifraud provisions of the 1934 Act should be governed by these new

standards. On April 11, 2012, the SEC delivered to Congress its "Study on the Cross-Border Scope of the Private Right of Action Under Section 10(b) of the Securities Exchange Act of 1934," which provides several options but no specific recommendations. To date Congress has not taken any action. Thus the Dodd-Frank Act appears to restore to the SEC and the Department of Justice—but not private litigants—the right to bring proceedings to enforce the antifraud provisions of the U.S. securities laws in cases with an extraterritorial component.

The International Organization of Securities Commissions has a membership of more than two hundred national securities agencies and exchanges, which regulate more than 95 percent of the world's securities markets. The member agencies have agreed (1) to cooperate to promote high standards of regulation to maintain just, efficient, and sound markets; (2) to exchange information to promote the development of domestic markets; (3) to work together to establish standards and effective surveillance of international securities transactions; and (4) to provide support to promote the integrity of the markets by a rigorous application of the standards and by effective enforcement against offenses.

Express insider trading liability is imposed on any person who sells or buys a security while in possession of inside information

Express Insider Trading Liability [39-8d]

Section 20A imposes express civil liability upon any person who violates the Act by purchasing or selling a security while in possession of material, nonpublic information. Any person who contemporaneously sold or purchased securities of the same class as those improperly traded may bring a private action against the trader to recover damages for the violation. The total amount of damages may not exceed the profit gained or loss avoided by the violation, diminished by any amount the violator disgorges to the SEC pursuant to a court order. The action must be brought within five years after the date of the last transaction that is the subject of the violation. Tippers are jointly and severally liable with tippees who commit a violation by trading on the inside information.

Civil monetary penalties for insider trading may be imposed on inside traders in an amount up to three times the gains they made or losses they avoided

Civil Monetary Penalties for Insider Trading [39-8e]

In addition to the remedies discussed previously, the SEC is authorized to bring an action in a U.S. district court to have a civil monetary penalty imposed upon any person who purchases or sells a security while in possession of material, nonpublic information. Liability also extends to any person who by communicating material, nonpublic information aids and abets another person in such a violation. Liability also may be imposed on any person who directly or indirectly controlled a person who ultimately committed a violation if the controlling person knew or recklessly disregarded the likelihood that the controlled person would commit a violation and consequently failed to take appropriate steps to prevent the transgression. Under this provision, law firms, accounting firms, issuers, financial printers, news media, and others must implement policies to prevent insider trading. The violating transaction must be on or through the facilities of a national securities exchange or from or through a broker or dealer. Purchases that are part of a public offering by an issuer of securities are not subject to this provision.

The civil monetary penalty for a person who trades on inside information is determined by the court in light of the facts and circumstances but may not exceed three times the profit gained or loss avoided as a result of the unlawful purchase or sale. The maximum amount that may be imposed upon a controlling person is the greater of $1,525,000 (as adjusted for inflation in March 2013) or three times the profit gained or loss avoided as a result of the controlled person's violation. If that violation consists of tipping inside information, the court measures the controller's liability by the profit gained or loss avoided by the person to whom the controlled person directed the tip. For the purpose of this provision, "profit gained" or "loss avoided" is "the difference between the purchase or sale price of the security and the value of that security as measured by the trading price of the security a reasonable period after public dissemination of the nonpublic information."

Civil monetary penalties for insider trading are payable into the U.S. Treasury. An action to recover a penalty must be brought within five years after the date of the purchase or sale. The SEC is authorized to award bounties of up to 10 percent of a recovered penalty to informants who provide information leading to the imposition of the penalty. However, the Dodd-Frank Act has expanded whistleblower awards: the SEC now must award eligible whistleblowers who voluntarily provide original information that leads to *any* successful enforcement action in which the SEC imposes monetary sanctions in excess of $1 million. The amount of the award must be between 10 percent and 30 percent of funds collected as monetary sanctions, as determined by the SEC.

Misleading Proxy Statements [39-8f]

Misleading proxy statement

any person who distributes a false or misleading proxy statement is liable to injured investors

Any person who distributes a materially false or misleading proxy statement may be liable to a shareholder who relies upon the statement in purchasing or selling a security and consequently suffers a loss. In this context, a misstatement or omission is material if there is a substantial likelihood that a reasonable shareholder would consider it important in deciding how to vote. A number of courts have held that negligence is sufficient for an action under the proxy rule's antifraud provisions. In addition, when the proxy disclosure or filing requirement has been violated, a court may, if appropriate, enjoin a shareholder meeting or any action taken at that meeting. Other remedies are rescission, damages, and attorneys' fees. Since a proxy statement is filed with the SEC, a materially false or misleading proxy statement may also give rise to liability under Section 18, discussed earlier. In addition, Rule 10b-5 also applies to misstatements in proxy statements. Moreover, most proxy statements used with mergers and sales of assets are also considered 1933 Act registration statements subject to civil liability under Section 11 of the 1933 Act.

Fraudulent Tender Offers [39-8g]

Fraudulent tender offers

Section 14(e) imposes civil liability for false and material statements or omissions or fraudulent, deceptive, or manipulative practices in connection with any tender offer

Section 14(e) makes it unlawful for any person to make any untrue statement of material fact, to omit to state any material fact, or to engage in any fraudulent, deceptive, or manipulative practices in connection with any tender offer. This provision applies even if the target company is not subject to the 1934 Act's reporting requirements. Insider trading during a tender offer is prohibited by Rule 14e-3, which has been upheld by the U.S. Supreme Court in the case of *United States v. O'Hagan* presented previously.

Some courts have implied civil liability for violations of Section 14(e). Because of the small number of cases, however, the requirements for such an action are not entirely clear. A target company may seek an injunction, and a shareholder of the target may be able to recover damages or obtain rescission. The courts are likely to require *scienter*.

See Concept Review 39-3.

Schreiber v. Burlington Northern, Inc.
Supreme Court of the United States, 1985
472 U.S. 1, 105 S.Ct. 2458, 86 L.Ed.2d 1
http://scholar.google.com/scholar_case?q=105+S.Ct.+2458&hl=en&as_sdt=2,34&case=1407924312497176128&scilh=0

FACTS On December 21, 1982, Burlington Northern, Inc., made a hostile tender offer for El Paso Gas Co., proposing to purchase 25.1 million El Paso shares at $24 per share. The shareholders of El Paso fully subscribed the offer by the December 30, 1982, deadline. Burlington refused to accept those tendered shares and instead announced the terms of a new and friendly takeover agreement on January 10, 1983. Under this agreement, Burlington withdrew the December tender offer and substituted a new tender offer for 21 million shares at $24 per share. More than 40 million shares were tendered in response to this offer. Thus, the new offer disadvantaged those shareholders who had tendered during the first offer, for those who retendered were subject to substantial proration and hence received a diminished payment. Barbara Schreiber, one of the disadvantaged shareholders, brought an action against Burlington, El Paso, and members of El Paso's board, claiming that Burlington's rescission of the first tender offer and substitution of the new one was a "manipulative" distortion of the market for El Paso stock, which is prohibited by Section 14(e) of the Securities Exchange Act. The district court dismissed the suit for failure to state a claim, and the Court of Appeals affirmed.

DECISION Judgment of the Court of Appeals affirmed.

OPINION Section 14(e) of the Securities Exchange Act forbids "fraudulent, deceptive or manipulative acts or practices … in connection with any tender offer." Shreiber interprets the prohibition of "manipulative acts or practices" to include fully disclosed acts that nonetheless "artificially" affect the price of the takeover target's stock. This interpretation conflicts with the usual meaning of the term "manipulative." In a prior decision, the word "manipulative" was held to refer to "intentional or willful conduct designed to deceive or defraud investors by controlling or artificially affecting the price of securities." Thus, the term "manipulative" requires some sort of misrepresentation or nondisclosure. Moreover, Section 14(e) was added to the Securities Exchange Act simply to make sure that public shareholders have sufficient information with which to respond to a cash tender offer for their stock. The section does not attempt to address the substantive fairness of tender offers. It imposes upon a tender offeror only an obligation to disclose fully all material information, and Burlington complied with this requirement. Since Burlington's cancellation of the first tender offer was not accompanied by any misrepresentation, nondisclosure, or deception, no violation of Section 14(e) of the Securities Exchange Act occurred.

INTERPRETATION Shareholders have a right to full and accurate disclosure of information from those making tender offers to them.

ETHICAL QUESTION Did the defendants act unethically? Explain.

CRITICAL THINKING QUESTION Do you agree with the Court's interpretation of "manipulative"? Explain.

Antibribery provision of FCPA

prohibited bribery can result in civil monetary penalties, fines, and imprisonment

Antibribery Provision of FCPA [39-8h]

The FCPA generally prohibits a U.S. person, and certain foreign issuers of securities, from paying bribes to foreign officials to assist in obtaining or retaining business. Since 1998, the antibribery provisions also apply to foreign firms and persons who take any act in furtherance of such a corrupt payment while in the United States.

The FCPA makes it unlawful for any U.S. person, and certain foreign issuers of securities, or any of its officers, directors, employees, or agents to offer or give anything of value directly or indirectly to any foreign official, political party, or political official for the purpose of (1) influencing any act or decision of that person or party in his, or its, official capacity; (2) inducing an act or omission in violation of his, or its, lawful duty; or (3) inducing such person or party to use his, or its, influence to affect a decision of a foreign government to assist the person in obtaining or retaining business. An offer or promise to make a prohibited payment is a violation even if the offer is not accepted or the promise is not performed. The 1988 amendments to the Act explicitly excluded routine government action not involving the official's discretion, such as obtaining permits or processing applications. They also added an affirmative defense for payments that are lawful under the written laws or regulations of the foreign officials' country.

Violations can result in fines of up to $2 million for corporations and other business entities; individuals may be fined a maximum of $100,000 or be imprisoned for up to five years, or both. Moreover, under the Alternative Fines Act, the actual fine may be up to twice the benefit that the person sought to obtain by making the corrupt payment. Fines imposed upon individuals may not be paid directly or indirectly by the corporation or other business entity

CONCEPT REVIEW 39-3

Civil Liability Under the 1933 and 1934 Acts

Provision	Conduct	Plaintiffs	Defendants	Standard of Culpability	Reliance Required	Type of Liability	Remedies
Section 12(a)(1) 1933 Act	Unregistered sale or sale without prospectus	Purchasers from a violator	Sellers in violation	Strict liability	No	Express	Rescission Damages
Section 11 1933 Act	Registration statement containing material misstatement or omission	Purchasers of registered security	Issuer Directors Signers Underwriters Experts	Strict liability for issuer; Negligence for others	No	Express	Damages Attorneys' fees
Section 12(a)(2) 1933 Act	Material misstatement or omission	Purchasers from a violator	Sellers in violation	Negligence	No	Express	Rescission Damages
Section 18 1934 Act	False or misleading statements in a document filed with SEC	Purchasers or sellers	Persons making filing in violation	Knowledge or bad faith	Yes	Express	Damages Attorneys' fees
Section 16(b) 1934 Act	Short-swing profit by insider	Issuer; Shareholder of issuer	Directors; Officers; 10 percent shareholders	Strict liability	No	Express	Damages
Rule 10b-5 1934 Act	Deception or material misstatement or omission	Purchasers or sellers	Purchasers or sellers in violation	*Scienter*	Yes	Implied	Rescission Damages Injunction
Section 20A 1934 Act	Insider trading	Contemporaneous purchasers or sellers	Inside traders	*Scienter*	No	Express	Damages
Section 14(a) 1934 Act	Materially false or misleading proxy solicitation	Shareholders	Persons making proxy solicitation in violation	Negligence (probably)	Probably	Implied	Rescission Damages Injunction Attorneys' fees
Section 14(e) 1934 Act	Tender offer with deception or manipulation or material misstatement or omission	Target company; Shareholders of target	Persons making tender offer in violation	*Scienter* (probably)	Probably	Implied	Rescission Damages Injunction

on whose behalf the individuals acted. In addition, civil monetary penalties up to $16,000, as adjusted for inflation in March 2013, may be imposed.

In 1997 the United States signed the Organisation for Economic Co-operation and Development Convention on Combating Bribery of Foreign Public Officials in International Business Transactions (OECD Convention). The OECD Convention has been adopted by at least forty-one nations. In 1998 Congress enacted the International Anti-Bribery and Fair Competition Act of 1998 to conform the FCPA to the OECD Convention. The 1998 Act expands the FCPA to

ETHICAL DILEMMA

What Information May a Corporate Employee Disclose?

Facts Sam Thompson is the director of tax research in the tax department of Anna Louise, Inc., a publicly traded clothing manufacturer. Formed by James and Anna Louise around the turn of the century, the corporation has been managed ever since by family members, who still own a controlling interest.

While studying certain tax matters in connection with a highly sensitive marketing project, Sam learned that an international company had offered to purchase a controlling interest in Anna Louise. Later, while he was having lunch with Mike, his good friend and stockbroker, Mike began pressuring Sam

for information about the offer. Mike is ambitious and is attempting to build a solid client base. He is a diligent worker, performs extensive research to support recommendations to clients, and socializes a great deal with the business community. Mike told Sam that he could tell something special was going on at Sam's office. Sam had been working overtime and for the past two weeks had been unable to meet Mike as usual on Friday evening for drinks after work.

Social, Policy, and Ethical Considerations

1. What are Sam's ethical responsibilities to his employer with regard to

information he obtains at work? How should he respond to Mike's requests for information?
2. If Sam took Mike into his confidence, what ethical responsibilities would Mike have to Sam to keep the information to himself?
3. Does Mike have any duties of loyalty to Sam's employer?
4. As a practical matter, to what extent must one keep in confidence information obtained in one's employment? Is it "safe" for example, to discuss matters with one's closest friends or one's spouse?

include (1) payments made to "secure any improper advantage" from foreign officials, (2) all foreign persons who commit an act in furtherance of a foreign bribe while in the United States, and (3) officials of public international organizations within the definition of a "foreign official." A public international organization is defined as either an organization designated by executive order pursuant to the International Organizations Immunities Act, or any other international organization designated by executive order of the president.

Criminal Sanctions [39-8i]

Criminal sanctions
individuals who willfully violate the 1934 Act are subject to a fine of not more than $5 million and/or imprisonment of not more than twenty years

Section 32 of the 1934 Act imposes **criminal sanctions** on any person who willfully violates any provision of the Act (except the antibribery provision) or the rules and regulations promulgated by the SEC pursuant to the Act. As amended by the Sarbanes-Oxley Act, for individuals, conviction may carry a fine of not more than $5 million or imprisonment of not more than twenty years, or both, with one exception: a person who proves she had no knowledge of the rule or regulation is not subject to imprisonment. If the person, however, is not a natural person (e.g., a corporation), a fine not exceeding $25 million may be imposed. Moreover, under the federal Alternative Fines Act, if any person derives pecuniary gain from the offense, or if the offense results in pecuniary loss to a person other than the defendant, the defendant may be fined up to the greater of twice the gross gain or twice the gross loss.

CHAPTER SUMMARY

The Securities Act of 1933

Definition of a Security

Security includes any note, stock, bond, preorganization subscription, and investment contract

Investment Contract any investment of money or property made in expectation of receiving a financial return solely from the efforts of others

Registration of Securities

Disclosure Requirements disclosure of accurate material information required in all public offerings of nonexempt securities unless offering is an exempt transaction

Integrated Disclosure and Shelf Registrations permitted for certain qualified issuers

Emerging Growth Companies have reduced disclosure requirements and expanded permissible communications

Exempt Securities	**Definition** securities not subject to the registration requirements of the 1933 Act
	Types exempt securities include short-term commercial paper, municipal bonds, and certain insurance policies and annuity contracts
Exempt Transactions for Issuers	**Definition** issuance of securities not subject to the registration requirements of the 1933 Act
	Types exempt transactions for issuers include limited offers under Regulation D, limited offers solely to accredited investors, crowdfunding, Regulation A, and intrastate issues
Exempt Transactions for Nonissuers	**Definition** resales by persons other than the issuer that are exempted from the registration requirements of the 1933 Act
	Types exempt transactions for nonissuers include Rule 144 and Regulation A
Liability	**Unregistered Sales** Section 12(a)(1) imposes absolute civil liability; there are no defenses
	False Registration Statements Section 11 imposes liability on the issuer, all persons who signed the statement, every director or partner, experts who prepared or certified any part of the statement, and all underwriters; defendants other than the issuer may assert the defense of due diligence
	Antifraud Provisions Section 12(a)(2) imposes liability upon the seller to the immediate purchaser, provided the purchaser did not know of the untruth or omission; but the seller is not liable if he did not know, and in the exercise of reasonable care could not have known, of the untrue statement or omission. Section 17(a) broadly prohibits fraud in the sale of securities
	Criminal Sanctions willful violations are subject to a fine of not more than $10,000 and/or imprisonment of not more than five years

The Securities Exchange Act of 1934

Disclosure	**Registration and Periodic Reporting Requirements** apply to all regulated, publicly held companies and include one-time registration as well as annual, quarterly, and monthly reports
	Proxy Solicitations
	• *Definition of a Proxy* a signed writing by a shareholder authorizing a named person to vote her stock at a specified meeting of shareholders
	• *Proxy Statements* proxy disclosure statements are required when proxies are solicited or an issuer submits a matter to a shareholder vote
	Tender Offers
	• *Definition of a Tender Offer* a general invitation to shareholders to purchase their shares at a specified price for a specified time
	• *Disclosure Requirements* a statement disclosing specified information must be filed with the Securities and Exchange Commission and furnished to each offeree
	Foreign Corrupt Practices Act imposes internal control requirements on issuers with securities registered under the 1934 Act
Liability	**Misleading Statements in Reports** Section 18 imposes civil liability for any false or misleading statement made in a registration or report filed with the Securities and Exchange Commission
	Short-Swing Profits Section 16(b) imposes liability on certain insiders (directors, officers, and shareholders owning more than 10 percent of the stock of a corporation) for all profits made on sales and purchases within six months of each other, with any recovery going to the issuer
	Antifraud Provision Rule 10b-5 makes it unlawful to (1) employ any device, scheme, or artifice to defraud; (2) make any untrue statement of a material fact; (3) omit to state a material fact; or (4) engage in any act that operates as a fraud
	• *Requisites of Rule 10b-5* recovery requires (1) a misstatement or omission, (2) materiality, (3) *scienter* (intentional and knowing conduct), (4) reliance, (5) connection with the purchase or sale of a security, and (6) economic loss
	• *Insider Trading* "insiders" are liable under Rule 10b-5 for failing to disclose material, nonpublic information before trading on the information
	Express Insider Trading Liability is imposed on any person who sells or buys a security while in possession of inside information

Civil Monetary Penalties for Inside Trading may be imposed on inside traders in an amount up to three times the gains they made or losses they avoided

Misleading Proxy Statement any person who distributes a false or misleading proxy statement is liable to injured investors

Fraudulent Tender Offers Section 14(e) imposes civil liability for false and material statements or omissions or fraudulent, deceptive, or manipulative practices in connection with any tender offer

Antibribery Provision of FCPA prohibited bribery can result in civil monetary penalties, fines, and imprisonment

Criminal Sanctions individuals who willfully violate the 1934 Act are subject to a fine of not more than $5 million and/or imprisonment of not more than twenty years

QUESTIONS

1. Acme Realty, a real estate development company, is a limited partnership organized in Georgia. It is planning to develop a two-hundred-acre parcel of land for a regional shopping center and needs to raise $1.25 million. As part of its financing, Acme plans to offer $1.25 million worth of limited partnership interests to about one hundred prospective investors in the southeastern United States. It anticipates that about forty to fifty private investors will purchase the limited partnership interests.
   a. Must Acme register this offering? Why or why not?
   b. If Acme must register but fails to do so, what are the legal consequences?

2. Bigelow Corporation has total assets of $850,000, sales of $1,350,000, and one class of common stock with 375 shareholders and a class of preferred stock with 250 shareholders, both of which are traded over the counter. Which provisions of the Securities Exchange Act of 1934 apply to Bigelow Corporation?

3. Capricorn, Inc., is planning to "go public" by offering its common stock, which previously had been owned by only three shareholders. The company intends to limit the number of purchasers to twenty-five persons resident in the state of its incorporation. All of Capricorn's business and all of its assets are located in its state of incorporation. Based on these facts, what exemptions from registration, if any, are available to Capricorn, and what conditions would each of these available exemptions impose on the terms of the offer?

4. The boards of directors of DuMont Corp. and Epsot, Inc., agreed to enter into a friendly merger, with DuMont Corp. to be the surviving entity. The stock of both corporations was listed on a national stock exchange. In connection with the merger, both corporations distributed to their shareholders proxy statements seeking approval of the proposed merger. The shareholders of both corporations voted to approve the merger. About three weeks after the merger was consummated, the price of DuMont stock fell from $25.00 to $13.00 as a result of the discovery that Epsot had entered into several unprofitable long-term contracts two months before the merger had been proposed. The contracts will result in substantial losses from Epsot's operations for at least the next four years. The existence and effect of these contracts, although known to both corporations at the time of the proposed merger, were not disclosed in the proxy statements of either corporation. Can the shareholders of DuMont recover in a suit against DuMont under the 1934 Act? Explain.

5. Farthing is a director and vice president of Garp, Inc., whose common stock is listed on the New York Stock Exchange. Farthing engaged in the following transactions in the same calendar year: on January 2, Farthing sold five hundred shares at $30.00 per share; on January 15, she purchased three hundred shares at $30.00 per share; on February 1, she purchased two hundred shares at $45.00 per share; on March 1, she purchased three hundred shares at $60.00 per share; on March 15, she sold two hundred shares at $55.00 per share; and on April 1, she sold one hundred shares at $40.00 per share. Howell brings suit on behalf of Garp, alleging that Farthing has violated the Securities Act of 1934. Farthing defends on the ground that she lost money on the transactions in question. Is Farthing liable? If so, under which provisions and for what amount of money?

6. Intercontinental Widgets, Inc., had applied for a patent for a new state-of-the-art widget that, if patented, would significantly increase the value of Intercontinental's shares. On September 1, the Patent Office notified Jackson, the attorney for Intercontinental, that the patent application had been approved. After informing Kingsley, the company's president, of the good news, Jackson called his broker and purchased one thousand shares of Intercontinental at $18.00 per share. He also told his partner, Lucas, who immediately proceeded to purchase five hundred shares at $19.00 per share. Lucas then called his brother-in-law, Mammon, and told him the news. On September 3, Mammon bought four thousand shares at $21.00 per share. On September 4, Kingsley issued a press release that accurately reported that a patent had been granted to Intercontinental. On the next day, Intercontinental's stock soared to $38.00 per share. A class action suit is brought against Jackson, Lucas, Mammon, and Intercontinental for violations of Rule 10b-5. Who, if anyone, is liable?

7. Nova, Inc., sought to sell a new issue of common stock. It registered the issue with the Securities and Exchange Commission but included false information in both the registration statement and the prospectus. The issue was

underwritten by Omega & Sons and was sold in its entirety by Periwinkle, Rameses, and Sheffield, Inc., a securities broker-dealer. Telford, who was unaware of the falsity of this information, purchased five hundred shares at $6.00 per share. Three months later, the falsity of the information contained in the prospectus was made public, and the price of the shares fell to $1.00 per share. The following week, Telford brought suit against Nova, Inc.; Omega & Sons; and Periwinkle, Rameses, and Sheffield, Inc., under the Securities Act of 1933.

   a. Who, if anyone, is liable under the 1933 Act? If liable, under which provisions?

   b. What defenses, if any, are available to the various defendants?

8. Tanaka, a director and officer of Deep Hole Oil Company, telephoned Romani for the purpose of buying two hundred shares of Deep Hole Company stock owned by Romani. During the period of negotiations, Tanaka concealed his identity and did not disclose the fact that earlier in the day he had received a report of two rich oil strikes on the oil company's property. Romani sold his two hundred shares to Tanaka for $10.00 per share. Taking into consideration the new strikes, the fair value of the stock was approximately $20.00 per share. Romani sues Tanaka to recover damages. Is Tanaka liable? If so, under which provisions and for what amount of money?

9. Venable Corporation has seven hundred and fifty thousand shares of common stock outstanding, which are owned by 2,640 shareholders. The assets of Venable Corporation are valued at more than $10 million. In March, Underhill began purchasing shares of Venable's common stock in the open market. By April, he had acquired forty thousand shares at prices ranging from $12.00 to $14.00. Upon discovering Underhill's activities in late April, the directors of Venable had the corporation purchase the forty thousand shares from Underhill for $18.00 per share. Which provisions of the 1934 Act, if any, have been violated?

CASE PROBLEMS

10. Dirks was an officer of a New York broker-dealer firm who specialized in providing investment analysis of insurance company securities to institutional investors. On March 6, Dirks received information from Ronald Secrist, a former officer of Equity Funding of America. Secrist alleged that the assets of Equity Funding, a diversified corporation primarily engaged in selling life insurance and mutual funds, were vastly overstated as the result of fraudulent corporate practices. Dirks decided to investigate the allegations. He visited Equity Funding's headquarters in Los Angeles and interviewed several officers and employees of the corporation. The senior management denied any wrongdoing, but certain corporation employees corroborated the charges of fraud. Neither Dirks nor his firm owned or traded any Equity Funding stock, but throughout his investigation he openly discussed the information he had obtained with a number of clients and investors. Some of these persons sold their holdings of Equity Funding securities, including five investment advisers who liquidated holdings of more than $16 million.

While Dirks was in Los Angeles, he was in touch regularly with William Blundell, *The Wall Street Journal*'s Los Angeles bureau chief. Dirks urged Blundell to write a story on the fraud allegations. Blundell did not believe, however, that such a massive fraud could go undetected and declined to write the story. He feared that publishing such damaging hearsay might be libelous.

During the two-week period in which Dirks pursued his investigation and spread word of Secrist's charges, the price of Equity Funding stock fell from $26.00 per share to less than $15.00 per share. This led the New York Stock Exchange to halt trading on March 27. Shortly thereafter, California insurance authorities impounded Equity Funding's records and uncovered evidence of the fraud. Only then did the Securities and Exchange Commission (SEC) file a complaint against Equity Funding.

The SEC began an investigation into Dirks's role in the exposure of the fraud. After a hearing by an administrative law judge, the SEC found that Dirks had aided and abetted violations of Section 10(b) of the Securities Exchange Act of 1934 and SEC Rule 10b-5 by repeating the allegations of fraud to members of the investment community who later sold their Equity Funding stock. Has Dirks violated Section 10(b) and Rule 10b-5? Explain.

11. Texas Gulf Sulphur Company (TGS) was a corporation engaged in exploring for and mining certain minerals. A particular tract of Canadian land looked very promising as a source of desired minerals, and TGS drilled a test hole on November 8. Because the core sample of the hole contained minerals of amazing quality, TGS began to acquire surrounding tracts of land. Stevens, the president of TGS, instructed all on-site personnel to keep the find a secret. Because subsequent test drillings were performed, the amount of activity surrounding the drilling had resulted in rumors as to the size and quality of the find. To counteract these rumors, Stevens authorized a press release denying the validity of the rumors and describing them as excessively optimistic. The release was issued on April 12 of the following year, though drilling continued through April 15. In the meantime, several officers, directors, and employees had purchased or accepted options to purchase additional TGS stock on the basis of the information concerning the drilling. They also recommended similar purchases to outsiders without divulging the inside information to the public. At 10:00 A.M. on April 16, an accurate report on the find was finally released to the American financial press. The Securities and Exchange Commission brought an action against TGS and several of its officers, directors, and employees to enjoin conduct alleged to violate Section 10(b) of the Securities Act of 1934 and to compel rescission by the individual defendants of securities transactions assertedly conducted in violation of Rule 10b-5. Have any of the defendants violated Section 10(b)? Explain.

12. W. J. Howey Co. and Howey-in-the-Hills Service, Inc. were Florida corporations under direct common control and management. The Howey Company owned large tracts of citrus acreage in Florida. The service company cultivated, harvested, and marketed the crops. For several years, Howey Company offered one-half of its planted acreage to the public to help it "finance additional development." Each prospective customer was offered both a land sales contract and a service contract with Howey-in-the-Hills after being told that it was not feasible to invest in the grove without a service arrangement. Upon payment of the purchase price, the land was conveyed by warranty deed. The service company was given full discretion over cultivating and marketing the crop. The purchaser had no right of entry to market the crop. The service company also was accountable only for an allocation of the net profits after the companies pooled the produce. The purchasers were predominantly nonresident businesspersons attracted by the expectation of substantial profits. Contending that this arrangement was an investment contract within the coverage of the Securities Act of 1933, the Securities and Exchange Commission (SEC) brought an action against the two companies to restrain them from using the mails and instrumentalities of interstate commerce in the offer and sale of unregistered and nonexempt securities. Should the SEC succeed?

TAKING SIDES

Basic, Inc. was a publicly traded company. Combustion Engineering, Inc. and Basic began discussions concerning the possibility of a merger of the two companies. During the next two years, Basic made three public statements denying that it was engaged in merger negotiations. In December of the second year, Basic publicly announced its approval of Combustion's offer for all its outstanding shares. Former owners of Basic stock who sold their shares after Basic publicly denied that it was engaged in merger negotiations brought a class action suit against Basic and its directors for having released false or misleading information in violation of Section 10(b) of the 1934 Act and Rule 10b-5. The plaintiffs claimed that they were injured by selling their shares at prices that were artificially depressed as a consequence of Basic's misleading public statements. The defendants claimed that the plaintiffs had not proven that the plaintiffs had, in fact, relied upon the misleading statements in selling their stock.

a. What are the arguments that the plaintiffs have satisfied the reliance requirement of Section 10(b) of the 1934 Act and Rule 10b-5?

b. What are the arguments that the plaintiffs have *not* satisfied the reliance requirement of Section 10(b) of the 1934 Act and Rule 10b-5?

c. Which side should prevail?

Intellectual Property

CHAPTER 40

And he that invents a machine augments the power of a man and the well-being of mankind.

Henry Ward Beecher (1870)

CHAPTER OUTCOMES

After reading and studying this chapter, you should be able to:

1. Explain what trade secrets protect and how they may be infringed.

2. Distinguish among the various types of trade symbols.

3. Explain the extent to which trade names are protected.

4. Explain what copyrights protect and the remedies for infringement.

5. Explain what patents protect and the remedies for infringement.

Infringement

unauthorized use of intellectual property

Intellectual property (IP) is an economically significant type of intangible personal property that includes trade secrets, trade symbols, copyrights, and patents. These interests are protected from **infringement**, or unauthorized use, by others. Such protection is essential to the conduct of business. For example, a company would be far less willing to invest considerable resources in research and development if resulting discoveries, inventions, and processes were not protected by patents and by regulations safeguarding trade secrets. Similarly, a company would not be secure in devoting time and money to marketing its products and services without laws to defend its trade symbols and trade names. Moreover, without copyright protection, the publishing, entertainment, and computer software industries would be vulnerable to piracy, both by competitors and by the general public. In this chapter, we will discuss the law protecting (1) trade secrets; (2) trade symbols, including trademarks, service marks, certification marks, collective marks, and trade names; (3) copyrights; and (4) patents.

TRADE SECRETS [40-1]

Every business has secret information. Such information may include customer lists or contracts with suppliers and customers; it may also consist of secret formulas, processes, and production methods that are vital to the successful operation of the business. A business may disclose a trade secret in confidence to an employee with the understanding that the employee will not, in turn, reveal the information. To the extent the owner of the information obtains a patent on it, it is no longer a trade secret but is protected by patent law. Some businesses, however, choose not to obtain a patent because it provides protection for only a limited time, whereas state trade secret law protects a trade secret as long as it is kept secret. Moreover, if the courts invalidate a patent, the information will have been disclosed to competitors without the owner of the information obtaining any benefit. The Uniform Trade Secrets Act, promulgated in 1979 and amended in 1985, has been adopted by at least 47 states.

Definition [40-1a]

Trade secret
Commercially valuable,
secret information

Basically, a **trade secret** is commercially valuable information that is guarded from disclosure and is not general knowledge. The Uniform Trade Secrets Act defines a trade secret as

> information, including a formula, pattern, compilation, program, device, method, technique, or process that:
>
> (i) derives independent economic value, actual or potential, from not being generally known to, and not being readily ascertainable by proper means by, other persons who can obtain economic value from its disclosure or use, and
>
> (ii) is the subject of efforts that are reasonable under the circumstances to maintain its secrecy.

A famous example of a trade secret is the formula for Coca-Cola.

Misappropriation [40-1b]

Misappropriation
wrongful use

Misappropriation of a trade secret is the wrongful use of a trade secret. A person misappropriates a trade secret of another (1) by knowingly acquiring it through improper means or (2) by disclosing or using it without consent, if his knowledge of the trade secret came under circumstances giving rise to a duty to maintain secrecy or came from a person who used improper means or who owed the owner of the trade secret a duty to maintain secrecy. Trade secrets most frequently are misappropriated in two ways: (1) an employee wrongfully uses or discloses such secrets or (2) a competitor wrongfully obtains them.

An employee is under a duty of loyalty to his employer, which, among other things, charges the employee not to disclose trade secrets to competitors. It is wrongful, in turn, for a competitor to obtain vital secret trade information from an employee through bribery or other means. Besides breaching the duty of loyalty, the faithless employee who divulges secret trade information also commits a tort. In the absence of a contract restriction, an employee is under no duty upon termination of her employment to refrain from working for a competitor of, or competing with, a former employer; however, she may not use trade secrets or disclose them to third persons. The employee is entitled, nevertheless, to use the skill, knowledge, and general information she acquired during the previous employment relationship.

Practical Advice

Before disclosing a trade secret to another, require that person to sign a nondisclosure agreement.

Another improper method of acquiring trade secrets is industrial espionage conducted through methods such as electronic surveillance or spying. Improper means of acquiring another person's trade secrets also include theft, bribery, fraud, unauthorized interception of communications, and inducement or knowing participation in a breach of confidence. In the broadest sense, discovering another's trade secrets by any means other than independent research or personal inspection of the publicly available finished product is improper unless the other party voluntarily discloses the secret or fails to take reasonable precautions to protect its secrecy.

Remedies [40-1c]

Remedies
owner of a trade secret
may obtain damages or
injunctive relief when the
secret is misappropriated
by an employee or a
competitor

Remedies for misappropriation of trade secrets are damages and, when appropriate, injunctive relief. Damages are awarded in the amount of either the pecuniary loss to the plaintiff caused by the misappropriation or the pecuniary gain to the defendant, whichever is greater. A court will grant an injunction to prevent a continuing or threatened misappropriation of a trade secret for as long as is necessary to protect the plaintiff from any harm attributable to the misappropriation and to deprive the defendant of any economic advantage attributable to the misappropriation.

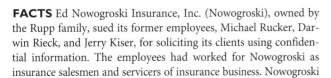

Ed Nowogroski Insurance, Inc. v. Rucker
Supreme Court of Washington, 1999
137 Wash.2d 427, 971 P.2d 936
http://scholar.google.com/scholar_case?q=971+P.2d+936+&hl=en&as_sdt=6,34&case=15515769364715143148&scilh=0

FACTS Ed Nowogroski Insurance, Inc. (Nowogroski), owned by the Rupp family, sued its former employees, Michael Rucker, Darwin Rieck, and Jerry Kiser, for soliciting its clients using confidential information. The employees had worked for Nowogroski as insurance salesmen and servicers of insurance business. Nowogroski also sued Potter, Leonard and Cahan, Inc., a rival insurance agency, for which employees Rucker, Rieck, and Kiser commenced work when they left their employment with Nowogroski. The trial court found that the employees had misappropriated Nowogroski's trade secrets by retaining and using confidential client lists and other information. However, the court did not award damages for one employee's solicitation of clients through the use of memorized client information. Nowogroski appealed. The Washington Court of Appeals held that there was no legal distinction between written and memorized information under the Washington Uniform Trade Secrets Act and remanded for a recalculation of damages. The Supreme Court of Washington granted this review.

DECISION Court of Appeals' decision is affirmed.

OPINION As a general rule, an employee who has not signed an agreement not to compete is free, upon leaving employment, to engage in competitive employment. In so doing, the former employee may freely use general knowledge, skills, and experience acquired under his or her former employer. However, the former employee, even in the absence of an enforceable covenant not to compete, remains under a duty not to use or disclose, to the detriment of the former employer, trade secrets acquired in the course of their employment. Where the former employee seeks to use the trade secrets of the former employer in order to obtain a competitive advantage, then competitive activity can be enjoined or result in an award of damages.

Briefly expressed, whether a customer list is protected as a trade secret depends on three factual inquiries: (1) whether the list is a compilation of information, (2) whether it is valuable because it is unknown to others, and (3) whether the owner has made reasonable attempts to keep the information secret. There is no dispute in this case that the customer names, expiration dates, coverage information, and related information is a compilation of information. The trial court found that the customer list and associated information

derived independent economic value from not being known, or readily ascertainable by proper means, by other persons who can obtain economic value from its disclosure or use and that Nowogroski undertook reasonable steps to protect its secrecy.

The question raised by this case is whether the fact that the customer information was in an employee's memory allows him to use with impunity the information that was otherwise a trade secret under the statute. The Uniform Trade Secrets Act does not distinguish between written and memorized information. The Act does not require a plaintiff to prove actual theft or conversion of physical documents embodying the trade secret information to prove misappropriation. As the Court of Appeals noted, two types of information mentioned in the Uniform Trade Secrets Act as examples of trade secrets include "method" and "technique;" these do not imply the requirement of written documents. While customer lists may or may not be trade secrets depending on the facts of the case, trade secret protection does not depend on whether the list is taken in written form or memorized.

INTERPRETATION Although a former employee may use general knowledge, skills, and experience acquired during the prior employment in competing with a former employer, the employee may not use or disclose trade secrets belonging to the former employer to actively solicit customers from a confidential customer list, whether written or memorized.

ETHICAL QUESTION Did any of the parties act unethically? Explain.

CRITICAL THINKING QUESTION What factors should be considered in determining whether a trade secret exists? Explain.

Criminal penalties

federal law imposes criminal penalties for the theft of trade secrets

Criminal Penalties [40-1d]

As amended in 2012, the Economic Espionage Act of 1996 prohibits the theft of trade secrets, as well as attempts and conspiracies to steal trade secrets, if the trade secret is related to a product or service used in or intended for use in interstate or foreign commerce. The Act imposes criminal penalties for violations but does not provide any civil remedies. The U.S. Attorney General, however, may bring a civil action to obtain appropriate injunctive relief against any violation of the Act. The statute defines trade secrets to mean

> [A]ll forms and types of financial, business, scientific, technical, economic, or engineering information, including patterns, plans, compilations, program devices, formulas, designs, prototypes, methods, techniques, processes, procedures, programs, or codes, whether tangible or intangible, and whether or how stored, compiled, or memorialized physically, electronically, graphically, photographically, or in writing if (a) the owner thereof has taken reasonable measures to keep such information secret; and (b) the information derives independent economic value, actual or potential, from not being generally known to, and not being readily ascertainable through proper means by the public.

The Act broadly defines theft to include all types of intentional conversion of trade secrets, including the following:

1. stealing, obtaining by fraud, or concealing such information;
2. without authorization copying, duplicating, sketching, drawing, photographing, downloading, uploading, photocopying, mailing, or conveying such information; and
3. purchasing or possessing a trade secret with knowledge that it has been stolen.

The Act punishes individuals who knowingly violate the Act with fines of up to $500,000, imprisonment for up to ten years, or both. Organizations that knowingly violate the Act are subject to fines of up to $5 million.

The Act imposes more severe penalties on persons who knowingly violate the Act intending or knowing that the offense will benefit any foreign government, foreign instrumentality, or foreign agent. Such individuals may be fined up to $5 million, imprisoned for up to fifteen years, or both; such organizations are subject to fines of not more than the greater of (1) $10 million or (2) three times the value of the stolen trade secret to the organization violating the Act.

TRADE SYMBOLS [40-2]

One of the earliest forms of unfair competition was the fraudulent marketing of one person's goods as those of another. Still common, this unlawful practice is sometimes referred to as "passing off" or "palming off." Basically, "cashing in" fraudulently on the goodwill, good name, and reputation of a competitor and his products deceives the public and deprives honest businesses of trade. Section 43(a) of the Federal Trademark Act (the Lanham Act) prohibits a person from using a false designation of origin in connection with any goods or services in interstate commerce. This section also prohibits a person from making a false or misleading description or representation of her own goods, services, or commercial activities. In 1988, Congress amended this section to prohibit the misrepresentation of *another* person's goods, services, or commercial activities. As a result Section 43(a) also forbids "reverse palming off," by which a producer misrepresents someone else's goods as his own. Accordingly, James would violate Section 43(a) by passing off his product as Sally's or by reverse passing off Sally's product as his. A violator of Section 43(a) is liable in a civil action to any person who is, or is likely to be, injured by the violation. The remedies are (1) injunctive relief, (2) an accounting for profits, (3) damages, (4) destruction of infringing articles, (5) costs, and (6) attorneys' fees in exceptional cases.

The Lanham Act also established federal registration of trade symbols and protection against misuse or infringement by injunctive relief and a right of action for damages against the infringer. An infringement involves passing off one's goods or services as those of the owner of the mark in a manner that deceives the public and constitutes unfair competition. Thus, trade symbol infringement law protects both consumers from being misled by the use of infringing trade symbols as well as producers from unfair practices by competitors.

Types of Trade Symbols [40-2a]

Trademark
Distinctive symbol, word, or design on a good that is used to identify the manufacturer

The Lanham Act recognizes four types of trade symbols or ***marks***. A **trademark** is a *distinctive* symbol, word, name, device, letter, number, design, picture, or combination in any arrangement that a person adopts or uses to identify the goods he manufactures or sells, as well as to distinguish them from those manufactured or sold by others. Examples of trademarks include Kodak, Xerox, and the rainbow apple logo on Apple computers. A trademark can also consist of goods' "trade dress," which is the appearance or image of goods as presented to prospective purchasers. Trade dress would include the distinctive but nonfunctional design of packaging labels, containers, and the product itself or its features. Examples include the Campbell Soup label and the shape of the Coca-Cola bottle. Internet domain names that are used to identify and distinguish the goods or services of one person from the goods or services of others and to indicate the source of the goods and services may be registered as a trademark. To qualify, an applicant must show that it offers services via the Internet and that it uses the Internet domain name as a source identifier.

Some trademarks are embodied in sounds, scents, and other formats that cannot be represented by a drawing. Examples of distinctive sound marks are MGM's lion's roar, NBC's chimes, the Harlem Globetrotters' theme song "Sweet Georgia Brown," Intel's chimes, and Lucasfilm's THX logo theme.

Service mark
distinctive symbol, word, or design that is used to identify a provider's services

Similar in function to the trademark, which identifies tangible goods and products, is a **service mark**, used to identify and distinguish the services of one person from those of others. For example, the titles, character names, and other distinctive elements of radio and television shows may be registered as service marks. Service marks may also consist of trade dress such as the decor or shape of buildings in which services are provided. Examples include McDonald's yellow arches and the shape of the old Coca-Cola bottle.

Certification mark
distinctive symbol, word, or design used with goods or services to certify specific characteristics

A **certification mark** is used on or in connection with goods or services to certify their regional or other origin, composition, mode of manufacture, quality, accuracy, or other characteristics, or that the work or labor in the goods or services was performed by members of a union or other organization. The marks "Good Housekeeping Seal of Approval" and "Underwriter's

Laboratory" are examples of certification marks. The owner of the certification mark does *not* produce or provide the goods or services with which the mark is used.

A **collective mark** is a distinctive mark or symbol used to indicate either that the producer or provider belongs to a trade union, trade association, fraternal society, or other organization, or that members of a collective group produce the goods or services. Like the owner of a certification mark, the owner of a collective mark is not the producer or provider but rather is the group of which the producer or provider is a member. An example of a collective mark is the union mark that indicates a product's manufacture by a unionized company.

Collective mark

distinctive symbol used to indicate membership in an organization

Registration [40-2b]

To be protected by the Lanham Act, a mark must be distinctive enough to identify clearly the origin of goods or services; it may not be immoral, deceptive, or scandalous. A trade symbol may satisfy the distinctiveness requirement in either of two ways. First, it may be *inherently distinctive* if prospective purchasers are likely to associate it with the product or service it designates because of the nature of the designation and the context in which it is used. Fanciful, arbitrary, or suggestive marks satisfy the distinctiveness requirement. In contrast, a descriptive or geographic designation is not inherently distinctive. Such a designation is one that is likely to be perceived by prospective purchasers as merely descriptive of the nature, qualities, or other characteristics of the goods or service with which it is used. Thus, the word Apple cannot be a trademark for apples, although it may be a trademark for computers.

Descriptive or geographic designations, however, may satisfy the distinctiveness requirement through the second method: acquiring distinctiveness through a "secondary meaning." A designation acquires a **secondary meaning** when a substantial number of prospective purchasers associate the designation with the product or service it identifies. The trademark office may accept proof of substantially exclusive and continuous use of a mark for five years as *prima facie* evidence of secondary meaning.

A **generic name** is one that is understood by prospective purchasers to denominate the general category, type, or class of goods or services with which it is used. A user cannot acquire rights in a generic name as a trade symbol. Moreover, a trade symbol will lose its eligibility for protection if prospective purchasers come to perceive a trade symbol primarily as a generic name for the category, type, or class of goods or services with which it is used. Under the Lanham Act, the test for when this has occurred is "the primary significance of the registered mark to the relevant public rather than purchaser motivation." Examples of marks that have lost protection because they became generic include "aspirin," "thermos," "escalator," and "cellophane."

Federal registration is denied to marks that are immoral, deceptive, or scandalous. Marks may not be registered if they disparage or falsely suggest a connection with persons, living or dead; institutions; beliefs; or national symbols. In addition, a trademark may not consist of the flag, coat of arms, or other insignia of the United States or of any state, municipality, or foreign nation. Moreover, a mark will not be registered if it so resembles a registered or previously used mark such that it would be likely to cause confusion, mistake, or deceit.

To obtain federal protection, which has a ten-year term with unlimited ten-year renewals, the mark must be registered with the U.S. Patent and Trademark Office. The registrant must either (1) have actually used the mark in commerce or (2) demonstrate a *bona fide* intent to use the mark in commerce and actually use it within six months, which period may be extended.

Federal registration is not required to establish rights in a mark, nor is it required to begin using a mark. Registration, however, provides numerous advantages. It gives nationwide constructive notice of the mark to all later users. It permits the registrant to use the federal courts to enforce the mark and constitutes *prima facie* evidence of the registrant's exclusive right to use the mark. This right becomes incontestable, subject to certain specified limitations, after five years. Finally, registration provides the registrant with Customs Bureau protection against imports that threaten to infringe upon the mark. A U.S. trade symbol registration provides protection only in the United States. However, in 2002 Congress enacted legislation implementing the Madrid Protocol, a procedural agreement allowing U.S. trademark owners to file for registration in at least 91 member countries by filing a single application.

Registration

to be registered and thus protected by the Lanham Act, a mark must be distinctive and not immoral, deceptive, or scandalous

Practical Advice

Guard against losing your trade symbol's distinctiveness by advertising the proper use of it, as the owners of Teflon, Kleenex, and Xerox have done.

Practical Advice

Give notice of your registered marks by displaying with the mark the words "Registered in U.S. Patent and Trademark Office" or the abbreviation "Reg. U.S. Pat. & Tm. Off." or the symbol ®.

To retain trademark protection, the owner of a mark must not abandon it by failing to make *bona fide* use of it in the ordinary course of trade. Abandonment occurs when an owner does not use a mark and no longer intends to use it. Three years of nonuse raises a presumption of abandonment, which the owner may rebut by proving her intent to resume use.

Anyone who claims rights in a mark may use the ^TM (trademark) or ^SM (service mark) designation, even if the mark is not registered. Only owners of registered marks may use the symbol ®.

Wal-Mart Stores, Inc. v. Samara Brothers, Inc.
Supreme Court of the United States, 2000
529 U.S. 205, 120 S.Ct. 1339, 146 L.Ed.2d 182
http://scholar.google.com/scholar_case?case=11551321958641509496&hl=en&as_sdt=2&as_vis=1&oi=scholarr

FACTS Samara Brothers, Inc. designs and manufactures children's clothing. Its primary product is a line of spring/summer one piece seersucker outfits decorated with appliques of hearts, flowers, fruits, and the like. A number of chain stores, including JCPenney, sell this line of clothing under contract with Samara. In 1995, Wal-Mart contracted with one of its suppliers, Judy-Philippine, Inc., to manufacture a line of children's outfits for sale in the 1996 spring/summer season. Wal-Mart sent Judy-Philippine photographs of a number of garments from Samara's line, on which Judy-Philippine's garments were to be based; Judy-Philippine duly copied, with only minor modifications, sixteen of Samara's garments, many of which contained copyrighted elements. In 1996, Wal-Mart briskly sold the so-called knockoffs, generating more than $1.15 million in gross profits. Samara officials launched an investigation, which disclosed that Wal-Mart and several other major retailers—Kmart, Caldor, Hills, and Goody's—were selling the knockoffs of Samara's outfits produced by Judy-Philippine.

Samara brought an action against Wal-Mart, Judy-Philippine, Kmart, Caldor, Hills, and Goody's for copyright infringement under federal law and infringement of unregistered trade dress under Section 43(a) of the Lanham Act. All of the defendants except Wal-Mart settled before trial. After a weeklong trial, the jury found in favor of Samara on all of its claims. The district court awarded Samara damages, interest, costs, and fees totaling almost $1.6 million, together with injunctive relief. The Second Circuit affirmed, and the U.S. Supreme Court granted *certiorari*.

DECISION Judgment of Court of Appeals reversed and case remanded.

OPINION The Lanham Act provides for the registration of trademarks, which include "any word, name, symbol, or device, or any combination thereof [used or intended to be used] to identify and distinguish [a producer's] goods ... from those manufactured or sold by others and to indicate the source of the goods." Registration of a mark under the Act enables the owner to sue an infringer. In addition to protecting registered marks, the Lanham Act, in Section 43(a), gives a producer a cause of action for the use by any person of "any word, term, name, symbol, or device, or any combination thereof ... which ... is likely to cause confusion ... as to the origin, sponsorship, or approval of his or her goods."

The breadth of the definition of marks registrable under the Act has been held to embrace not just word marks, such as "Nike," and symbol marks, such as Nike's "swoosh" symbol, but also "trade dress"—a category that originally included only the packaging, or

"dressing," of a product, but in recent years has been expanded by many courts of appeals to encompass the design of a product. The text of Section 43(a) provides little guidance as to the circumstances under which unregistered trade dress may be protected. It does require that a producer show that the allegedly infringing feature is not "functional" and is likely to cause confusion with the product for which protection is sought. Courts have universally required a producer to show that its trade dress is distinctive, since without distinctiveness the trade dress would not "cause confusion ... as to the origin, sponsorship, or approval of [the] goods."

The judicial differentiation between marks that are inherently distinctive and those that have developed secondary meaning has solid foundation in the statute itself. The Act requires that registration be granted to any trademark "by which the goods of the applicant may be distinguished from the goods of others"—subject to various limited exceptions. It also provides, again with limited exceptions, that "nothing in this chapter shall prevent the registration of a mark used by the applicant which has become distinctive of the applicant's goods in commerce"—that is, which is not inherently distinctive but has become so only through secondary meaning. Indeed, with respect to at least one category of mark—colors—we have held that no mark can ever be inherently distinctive. The Supreme Court has held that a color could be protected as a trademark, but only upon a showing of secondary meaning. Design, like color, is not inherently distinctive. In the case of product design, as in the case of color, consumer predisposition to equate the feature with the source does not exist.

To the extent there are close cases, courts should err on the side of caution and classify ambiguous trade dress as product design, thereby requiring secondary meaning. The very closeness will suggest the existence of relatively small utility in adopting an inherent-distinctiveness principle, and relatively great consumer benefit in requiring a demonstration of secondary meaning. In an action for infringement of unregistered trade dress under Section 43(a) of the Lanham Act, a product's design is distinctive, and therefore eligible for protection, only upon a showing of secondary meaning.

INTERPRETATION Unregistered trade dress is protected in a Section 43(a) action for infringement only upon a showing of secondary meaning for the product's design.

ETHICAL QUESTION Did any of the parties act unethically? Explain.

CRITICAL THINKING QUESTION Do you agree with the Court's decision? Explain.

Infringement [40-2c]

Infringement

occurs when a person
without authorization uses
a substantially
indistinguishable mark that
is likely to cause confusion,
mistake, or deception

Infringement of a mark occurs when a person without authorization uses an identical or substantially indistinguishable mark that is likely to cause confusion, to cause mistake, or to deceive. The intention to confuse is not required, nor is proof of actual confusion, although likelihood of confusion may be inferred from either. In a case involving consumer confusion, infringement occurs if an appreciable number of ordinarily prudent purchasers are *likely* to be misled or confused as to the source of the goods or services. In deciding whether infringement has occurred, the courts consider various factors, including the strength of the mark, the intent of the unauthorized user, the degree of similarity between the two marks, the relation between the two products or services the marks identify, and the marketing channels through which the goods or services are purchased.

The Federal Trademark Dilution Act of 1995 amended the Lanham Act to protect famous marks from dilution of their distinctive quality. The term **dilution** means the lessening of the capacity of a famous mark to identify and distinguish goods or services even if (1) there is no competition between the owner of the famous mark and the other party using the mark or (2) the other party's use of the mark does not result in the likelihood of confusion, mistake, or deception. Examples of dilution would include Microsoft shoes, Toyota aspirin, and Rolex cameras. In determining whether a mark is distinctive and famous, a court may consider factors such as (1) the degree of inherent or acquired distinctiveness of the mark; (2) the degree of recognition of the mark; (3) the duration and extent of the use, advertising, and publicity of the mark; (4) the geographical extent of the trading area in which the mark is used; and (5) the channels of trade for the goods or services with which the mark is used. The amendment exempts fair use of a famous mark in comparative commercial advertising, noncommercial use of a mark, and mention of a famous mark in news reporting.

The Trademark Cyberpiracy Prevention Act of 1999 amended the Lanham Act to protect the owner of a trademark or service mark from any person who, with a bad faith intent to profit from the mark, registers, traffics in, or uses a domain name which, at the time of its registration, is (1) identical or confusingly similar to a distinctive mark, (2) dilutive of a famous mark, or (3) is a protected trademark, word, or name. The Act specifies factors a court may consider in determining bad faith intent but prohibits such a determination if the defendant believed, with reasonable grounds, that the use of the domain name was fair or otherwise lawful. It further authorizes a court to order cancellation of the domain name or its transfer to the owner of the mark. In addition to injunctive relief, the Act makes available remedies that include recovery of the defendant's profits, actual damages, attorneys' fees, and court costs. It also provides for statutory damages in an amount of at least $1,000 and up to $100,000 per domain name. The Act shields a registrar, registry, or other registration authority from liability for damages for the registration or maintenance of a domain name for another, unless there is a showing of bad faith intent to profit from such registration or maintenance of the domain name registration.

Remedies [40-2d]

Remedies

the Lanham Act provides
the following remedies for
infringement: injunctive
relief, profits, damages,
destruction of infringing
articles, costs, and, in
exceptional cases,
attorneys' fees

The Lanham Act provides several **remedies** for infringement: (1) injunctive relief, (2) an accounting for profits, (3) damages, (4) destruction of infringing articles, (5) attorneys' fees in exceptional cases, and (6) costs. In assessing profits, the plaintiff has only to prove the gross sales made by the defendant; the defendant, in contrast, must prove any costs to be deducted in determining profits. If the court finds that the amount of recovery based on profits is either inadequate or excessive, the court may, in its discretion, award an amount it determines to be just. In assessing damages, the court *may* award up to three times the actual damages, according to the circumstances of the case. When an infringement is knowing and intentional, the court *shall* award attorneys' fees plus the greater of treble profits or treble damages, unless there are extenuating circumstances. In an action under the Federal Trademark Dilution Act of 1995, the owner of the famous mark can obtain only injunctive relief unless the person against whom the injunction is sought willfully intended to trade on the owner's reputation or to cause dilution of the famous mark. If willful intent is proven, the owner of the famous mark also may obtain the other remedies discussed.

When a person intentionally traffics in goods or services known to bear a counterfeit mark, both civil and criminal remedies are available. In addition, goods bearing the counterfeit mark may be seized and destroyed. A *counterfeit mark* means a spurious mark that is identical with, or substantially indistinguishable from, a registered mark and the use of which is likely to cause confusion, to cause mistake, or to deceive. In assessing damages for trademark counterfeiting the court shall, unless it finds extenuating circumstances, enter judgment for three times the defendant's profits or the plaintiff's damages, whichever is greater, plus reasonable attorneys' fees. Instead of actual damages and profits, the plaintiff may elect to receive an award of statutory damages, in an amount the court considers just, between $1,000 and $200,000 per counterfeit mark or, if the use of the counterfeit mark was willful, not more than $2 million per counterfeit mark. Criminal sanctions include a fine of up to $2 million or imprisonment of up to ten years, or both. For a repeat offense, the limits are $5 million and twenty years, respectively. For an offender who is not an individual (e.g., a corporation), the fine may be up to $5 million for a first offense and up to $15 million for a repeat offense.

TRADE NAMES [40-3]

Trade name
any name used to identify a business, vocation, or occupation

Remedies
damages and injunctions are available if infringement of a trade name occurs

A **trade name** is any name used to identify a business, vocation, or occupation. Descriptive and generic words, and personal and generic names, although not proper trademarks, may become protected as trade names upon acquiring a special significance in the trade. A name acquires such significance, frequently referred to as a "secondary meaning," through its continuing and extended use in connection with specific goods or services, whereby the name's acquired meaning eclipses its primary meaning in the minds of many purchasers or users. Although they may not be federally registered under the Lanham Act, trade names are protected, and a person who palms off her goods or services under the trade name of another is liable in damages and also may be enjoined from doing so.

COPYRIGHTS [40-4]

Copyright is a form of protection provided by the Federal Copyright Act to authors of original works, which include literary, musical, and dramatic works; pantomimes; choreographic works; pictorial, graphic, and sculptural works; motion picture and other audiovisual works; sound recordings; and architectural works. This listing is illustrative but not exhaustive; the Act extends copyright protection to "original works of authorship in any tangible medium of expression, now known or later developed." Moreover, in 1980, the Copyright Act was amended to extend copyright protection to computer programs. Furthermore, the Semiconductor Chip Protection Act of 1984 extended protection for ten years to safeguard mask works embodied in a semiconductor chip product.

On March 1, 1989, the United States joined the Berne Convention, an international treaty protecting copyrighted works. In 1998 Congress enacted the Digital Millennium Copyright Act (DMCA), which amended the Copyright Act to implement the World Intellectual Property Organization (WIPO) Copyright Treaty and the WIPO Performances and Phonograms Treaty of 1996 by extending U.S. copyright protection to works required to be protected under these two treaties. The WIPO treaty called for adequate legal protection and effective legal remedies against the circumvention of effective technological measures that are used by copyright owners to prevent unauthorized exercise of their copyrights. The DMCA contains three principal anticircumvention provisions.

The first provision of the DMCA prohibits circumventing a technological protection measure put in place by a copyright owner to control *access* to a copyrighted work. Under the DMCA, "to circumvent a technological measure" means "to descramble a scrambled work, to decrypt an encrypted work, or otherwise to avoid, bypass, remove, deactivate, or impair a technological measure, without the authority of the copyright owner." The second provision prohibits creating or making available technologies developed or advertised to defeat technological protections against unauthorized *access* to a copyrighted work. The third provision prohibits creating or making available technologies developed or advertised to defeat technological protections against unauthorized *copying* or other infringements of the exclusive rights of the copyright owner in a copyrighted work. Thus, the first two prohibitions deal with access controls while the third prohibition deals with copy controls. They make it illegal, for example, to create or distribute a computer program that can break the access or copy protection security code on an electronic book or a DVD movie. The Act provides civil remedies including injunctions, damages (actual and statutory), attorneys' fees, and destruction of the offending device. It also imposes criminal penalties of fines or imprisonment or both.

In no case does the copyright protection for an original work of authorship protect also any idea, procedure, process, system, method of operation, concept, principle, or discovery, regardless of the form in which it is described, explained, illustrated, or embodied in such work. Copyright protection extends only to an *original expression* of an idea. For example, the idea of interfamily feuding cannot be copyrighted, but a particular expression of that idea in the form of a novel, drama, movie, or opera may be thus protected.

Registration [40-4a]

Copyright applications are filed with the Register of Copyrights in Washington, D.C. Although registration of the copyright is not required, because copyright protection begins automatically as soon as the work is fixed in a tangible medium, registration is advisable, being a condition of the remedies of statutory damages and attorneys' fees for copyright infringement. When a work is published, it is advisable, though no longer required, to place a copyright notice on all publicly distributed copies, so as to notify users about the copyright claim. If proper notice appears on the published copies to which a defendant in a copyright infringement case had access, the defendant will be unable to mitigate actual or statutory damages by asserting a defense of innocent infringement. Innocent infringement occurs when the infringer did not realize that the work was protected.

Rights [40-4b]

As amended in 1998 by the Sonny Bono Copyright Extension Act, in most instances, copyright protection lasts the duration of the author's life plus an additional seventy years. The Copyright Act gives the **copyright** owner the exclusive right, and the right to authorize others, to reproduce the copyrighted work, prepare derivative works based upon the copyrighted work, distribute copies or recordings of the copyrighted work, perform the work publicly, and display the work publicly.

These broad rights are subject, however, to several limitations, the most important of which are "compulsory licenses," "fair use," and the "first sale doctrine." *Compulsory licenses* permit certain limited uses of copyrighted material upon the payment of specified royalties and compliance with statutory conditions. The Copyright Act provides that the *fair use* of a copyrighted work for purposes such as criticism, comment, news reporting, teaching (including multiple copies for classroom use), scholarship, or research is not an infringement of copyright. In determining whether the use made of a work in any particular case is fair, the courts consider the following factors: (1) the purpose and character of the use, including whether such use is of a commercial nature or is for nonprofit educational purposes; (2) the nature of the copyrighted work; (3) the amount and substantiality of the portion used in relation to the copyrighted work as a whole; and (4) the effect of the use upon the potential market for or value of the copyrighted work.

The *first sale doctrine* limits the copyright owner's exclusive right of distribution by allowing the owner of a particular lawfully made copy of a work to sell or otherwise dispose of possession of that copy without authority of the copyright owner. In 1990, amendments to this provision created an exception to the first sale doctrine by prohibiting the rental, lease, or commercial lending of sound recordings and computer programs for direct or indirect commercial advantage unless authorized by the copyright owner.

Registration
is not required but provides additional remedies for infringement

Practical Advice

You should register your copyrights and place a copyright notice on all publicly distributed copies. Notice consists of three elements: (1) the symbol © or the word Copyright or the abbreviation Copr.; (2) the year of first publication of the work; and (3) the name of the owner of the copyright in the work.

Copyright
exclusive right granted to original works of authorship, usually for the author's life plus seventy years, to (1) reproduce the copyrighted work, (2) prepare derivative works based on the work, (3) distribute copies of the work, and (4) perform or display the work publicly

Kirtsaeng v. John Wiley & Sons, Inc.
Supreme Court of the United States, 2013
568 U.S. ____, 133 S.Ct. 1351, 185 L.Ed.2d 392
http://scholar.google.com/scholar_case?case=17500823935382016021&q=Kirtsaeng+v.+John+
Wiley+%26+Sons,+Inc.&hl=en&as_sdt=4000006

FACTS John Wiley & Sons, Inc.'s business includes publishing academic textbooks. Wiley often assigns to its wholly owned foreign subsidiary, Wiley Asia, rights to publish, print, and sell a foreign edition of Wiley's English language textbooks abroad. Each copy of a Wiley Asia foreign edition likely contains language making it clear that the copy is to be sold only in a particular country or geographical region outside the United States. Thus there are two essentially equivalent versions of a Wiley textbook, each version manufactured and sold with Wiley's permission: (1) a U.S. version printed and sold in the United States, and (2) a foreign version manufactured and sold abroad. Wiley makes certain that copies of the foreign version state that they are not to be taken without permission into the United States.

Petitioner, Supap Kirtsaeng, a citizen of Thailand, moved to the United States in 1997 to study mathematics at Cornell University. He paid for his education with the help of a Thai Government scholarship, which required him to teach in Thailand for ten years on his return. Kirtsaeng successfully completed his undergraduate courses at Cornell, successfully completed a Ph.D. program in mathematics at the University of Southern California, and then, as promised, returned to Thailand to teach. While he was studying in the United States, Kirtsaeng asked his friends and family in Thailand to buy copies of foreign edition English language textbooks at Thai bookstores, where they sold at low prices, and mail them to him in the United States. Kirtsaeng would then sell them, reimburse his family and friends, and keep the profit.

In 2008, Wiley brought this federal lawsuit against Kirtsaeng for copyright infringement. Wiley claimed that Kirtsaeng's unauthorized importation of its English language books and his later resale of those books amounted to an infringement of Wiley's exclusive right to distribute under the Copyright Act as well as the Act's related import prohibition. Kirtsaeng replied that the books he had acquired were "lawfully made" and that he had acquired them legitimately. Thus, in his view, the Copyright Act's "first sale" doctrine permitted him to resell or otherwise dispose of the books without the copyright owner's permission.

The District Court held that Kirtsaeng could not assert the "first sale" defense because that doctrine does not apply to "foreign-manufactured goods." The jury then found that Kirtsaeng had willfully infringed Wiley's American copyrights by selling and importing without authorization copies of eight of Wiley's copyrighted titles and assessed statutory damages of $600,000 ($75,000 per work). On appeal, the Second Circuit Court of Appeals affirmed, concluding that the "first sale" doctrine does not apply to copies of American copyrighted works manufactured abroad.

DECISION The judgment of the Court of Appeals is reversed, and the case is remanded for further proceedings.

OPINION Section 106 of the Copyright Act grants "the owner of copyright under this title" certain "exclusive rights," including the right "to distribute copies … of the copyrighted work to the public by sale or other transfer of ownership." These rights are qualified, however, by the application of various limitations set forth in §§ 107 through 122. Those sections, typically entitled "Limitations on exclusive rights," include, for example, the principle of "fair use," permission for limited library archival reproduction, and the "first sale" doctrine.

Section 109(a) sets forth the "first sale" doctrine: Notwithstanding the provisions of § 106(3), which grants the copyright owner exclusive distribution rights, the owner of a particular copy or phonorecord "lawfully made under this title" is entitled, without the permission of the copyright owner, to sell or otherwise dispose of possession of that copy or phonorecord. Thus, even though § 106(3) forbids distribution of a copy of a copyrighted novel without the copyright owner's permission, § 109(a) adds that, once a copy of that novel has been lawfully sold or its ownership otherwise lawfully transferred, the buyer of *that copy* and subsequent owners are free to dispose of it as they wish. In copyright jargon, the "first sale" has "exhausted" the copyright owner's § 106(3) exclusive distribution right.

In addition, § 602(a)(1) provides that importing a copy without permission violates the copyright owner's exclusive distribution right. But § 602(a)(1) refers explicitly to the § 106(3) exclusive distribution right, and § 106, by its terms, is subject to the various doctrines and principles contained in §§ 107 through 122, including § 109(a)'s "first sale" limitation. Do those same modifications apply—in particular, does the "first sale" modification apply—when considering whether § 602(a)(1) prohibits importing a copy?

The Supreme Court held that the "first sale" doctrine applies to copies of a copyrighted work lawfully made abroad. The Court reasoned that § 109(a)'s language, its context, and the common-law history of the "first sale" doctrine, taken together, favor an interpretation that imposes no geographical restrictions. The language of § 109(a) read literally favors a nongeographical interpretation, namely, that "lawfully made under this title" means made "in accordance with" or "in compliance with" the Copyright Act. The language of § 109(a) says nothing about geography.

INTERPRETATION The first sale doctrine applies to copies of a copyrighted work lawfully made abroad.

CRITICAL THINKING QUESTION Explain what effect this decision will have on the importation and sale of copyrighted works that have been *unlawfully* made abroad.

Ownership

the author of the copyrighted work is usually the owner of the copyright, which may be transferred in whole or in part

Ownership [40-4c]

The author of a creative work owns the entire copyright. Although the actual creator of a work is usually the author, in two situations under the doctrine of **works for hire**, she is not considered the author. First, if an employee prepares a work within the scope of her employment, her employer is considered the author of the work. Second, if a work is specially ordered or commissioned for certain purposes specified in the copyright statute and the parties expressly agree in writing that the work shall be considered a work for hire, the person commissioning the work is deemed to be the author. The kinds of works subject to becoming works for hire by commission include contributions to collective works; parts of motion pictures or other audiovisual works; translations; supplementary works such as prefaces, illustrations, or afterwords; compilations; instructional texts; and tests. In a work made for hire, the copyright lasts for a term of ninety-five years from the year of its first publication, or a term of one hundred and twenty years from the year of its creation, whichever expires first.

The ownership of a copyright may be transferred in whole or in part by conveyance, will, or intestate succession. However, a transfer of copyright ownership, other than by operation of law, is not valid unless a note or memorandum chronicles the transfer in writing and is signed by the owner of the rights conveyed or by the owner's duly authorized agent. An author may terminate any transfer of copyright ownership, other than that of a work for hire, during the five-year period beginning thirty-five years after the transfer was granted.

Ownership of a copyright, or of any of the exclusive rights under a copyright, is distinct from the ownership of any material object that embodies the work. The transfer of ownership of any material object, including the copy or recording in which the work was first fixed, does not in itself convey any rights in the copyrighted work the object embodies; nor, in the absence of an agreement, does the transfer of copyright ownership or of any exclusive rights under a copyright convey property rights in any material object. Thus, the purchase of this textbook neither affects the publisher's copyright nor authorizes the purchaser to make and sell copies of the book. Under the first sale doctrine, however, the purchaser may rent, lend, or resell the book. Were this a recorded text, however, the purchaser's latter rights would be somewhat more limited: in 1990, amendments to the Copyright Act prohibited the rental, lease, or commercial lending of sound recordings and computer programs unless authorized by the copyright owner.

Infringement and Remedies [40-4d]

Infringement
occurs when someone exercises the copyright owner's rights without authorization

Infringement occurs whenever somebody exercises, without authorization, the rights exclusively reserved for the copyright owner. Infringement need not be intentional. To prove infringement, the plaintiff must simply establish that he owns the copyright and that the defendant violated one or more of the plaintiff's exclusive rights under the copyright. Proof of infringement usually consists of showing that the allegedly infringing work is substantially similar to the copyrighted work and that the alleged infringer had access to the copyrighted work. The DMCA amended the Copyright Act to create limitations on the liability of online providers for copyright infringement when engaging in certain activities.

Remedies
if infringement occurs after registration, the following remedies are available: (1) injunction, (2) impoundment and possible destruction of infringing articles, (3) actual damages plus profits or statutory damages, (4) costs, and (5) criminal penalties

For the owner to sue for infringement, the copyright must be registered with the Copyright Office, unless the work is a Berne Convention work whose country of origin is not the United States. For an infringement occurring after registration, the following **remedies** are available: (1) injunction; (2) impoundment and possible destruction of infringing articles; (3) actual damages plus profits made by the infringer that are additional to those damages, *or* statutory damages of at least $750 but no more than $30,000 (though the ceiling may reach $150,000 if the infringement is willful), according to what the court determines to be just; (4) in the court's discretion, costs including reasonable attorneys' fees to the prevailing party; or (5) criminal penalties of a fine and/or up to one year's imprisonment for willful infringement for purposes of commercial advantage or private financial gain.

In 1997, Congress enacted the No Electronic Theft Act (NET Act) to close a loophole in the Copyright Act, which permitted infringers to pirate copyrighted works willfully and knowingly, so long as they did not do so for profit. The NET Act amended federal copyright law to define "financial gain" to include the receipt of anything of value, including the receipt of other copyrighted works. The NET Act also clarified that when Internet users or any other individuals distribute copyrighted works broadly, even if they do not intend to profit personally, they have violated the Copyright Act. The Act accomplished this by imposing penalties for willfully infringing a copyright (1) for purposes of commercial advantage or private financial gain or (2) by reproducing or distributing, including by electronic means, during any 180-day period, one or more copies of one or more copyrighted works with a total retail value of more than $1,000. It also extended the statute of limitations for criminal copyright infringement from three to five years. Finally, it increased criminal penalties for certain copyright violations. Imprisonment for up to five years (ten years for subsequent offenses) may be imposed for willful infringement if at least ten copies with a total retail value of more than $2,500 in a 180-day period are reproduced or distributed.

The Family Entertainment and Copyright Act of 2005 established criminal penalties for willful copyright infringement by the distribution of a computer program, musical work, motion picture or other audiovisual work, or sound recording being prepared for commercial distribution by making it available on a computer network accessible to members of the public, if the person knew or should have known that the work was intended for commercial distribution. In essence, it prohibits (1) bootlegging of copyrighted audio and video material or (2) recording a cinema-released film on videotape from the audience (the primary way bootleggers make illegal copies of recently released movies). The bill does, however, allow for the sale and use of technology that can skip content of films in order to edit out language, violence, or sex. The criminal penalties are a fine and/or imprisonment for up to three years (six years for subsequent offenses), but if the infringement was for purposes of commercial advantage or private financial gain, then imprisonment may be imposed for up to five years (ten years for subsequent offenses).

The Anti-counterfeiting Amendments Act of 2004 prohibits knowingly trafficking in (1) a counterfeit or illicit label of a copy of a computer program, motion picture (or other audiovisual work), literary work, or pictorial, graphic, or sculptural work, a phonorecord, a work of visual art, or documentation or packaging; or (2) counterfeit documentation or packaging. Violators are subject to fines and/or imprisonment of up to five years. In addition, a copyright owner who is injured, or threatened with injury, may bring a civil action to obtain (1) an injunction; (2) impoundment and possible destruction of infringing articles; (3) reasonable attorneys' fees and costs; and (4) actual damages and any additional profits of the violator *or* statutory damages of at least $2,500 but no more than $25,000. Moreover, the court may increase an award of damages by three times the amount that would otherwise be awarded for a violation occurring within three years after a final judgment was entered for a previous violation.

PATENTS [40-5]

Patent

the exclusive right to an invention for twenty years from the date of application for utility and plant patents; fourteen years from grant for design patents

The U.S. Constitution grants Congress the power "to promote the Progress of Science and useful Arts, by securing for limited Times to … Inventors the exclusive Right to their … Discoveries." Through a **patent**, the federal government grants an inventor a monopolistic right to make, use, or sell an invention to the absolute exclusion of others for the period of the patent. The patent owner may also profit by selling the patent or by licensing others to use the patent on a royalty basis. However, the patent may not be renewed: upon expiration, the invention enters the "public domain," and anyone may then use it.

On September 16, 2011, President Obama signed into law the Leahy-Smith America Invents Act, which represents the most significant reform of the Patent Act since 1952. Most of its provisions apply to any patent issued on or after September 16, 2012. The legislation is intended to establish a more efficient patent system that will improve patent quality and limit unnecessary litigation costs. Subject to some exceptions, the America Invents Act provides that the United States will no longer award a patent to the first person to create an invention but instead will award the patent to the first inventor to file an application for the invention. Converting from a "first to invent" to a "first inventor to file" patent registration system is intended to simplify the application system and to harmonize the U.S. patent system with systems commonly used in other countries with which the United States conducts trade. The "first inventor to file" provision went into effect on March 16, 2013.

Patentability [40-5a]

Patentability

to be patentable as a utility patent, the invention must be (1) novel, (2) useful, and (3) not obvious

The Patent Act specifies those inventions that may be patented as **utility patents**: any new and useful process, machine, manufacture, or composition of matter or any new and useful improvement thereof. Thus, naturally occurring substances are not patentable, as the invention must be made or modified by humans. For example, the discovery of a bacterium with useful properties is not patentable, whereas the manufacture of a genetically engineered bacterium is. By the same

GOING GLOBAL

How is intellectual property protected internationally?

The U.S. laws protecting intellectual property do not apply to transactions in other countries. Generally, the owner of an intellectual property right must comply with each country's requirements to obtain from that country whatever protection is available. The requirements vary substantially from country to country, as does the degree of protection. The United States, however, belongs to multinational treaties that try to coordinate the application of member nations' intellectual property laws.

The Trade-Related Aspects of Intellectual Property Rights (TRIPS) portion of the World Trade Organization (WTO) Agreement states how the range of intellectual property should be protected when trade is involved. The World

Intellectual Property Organization (WIPO), one of the specialized agencies of the United Nations, attempts to promote—through cooperation among nations—the protection of intellectual property throughout the world. WIPO administers twenty-six international treaties dealing with intellectual property protection and includes more than 185 nations as member states.

- *Patents.* The principal treaties for patent protection are the Paris Convention for the Protection of Industrial Property (at least 175 nations), the Patent Cooperation Treaty (at least 148 nations), and the Patent Law Treaty (PLT) of 2000 (at least 36 nations).

- *Trademarks.* International treaties protecting trademarks are the Paris

Convention, the Trademark Law Treaty, the Arrangement of Nice Concerning the International Classification of Goods and Services (at least eighty-four nations), the Madrid Protocol of 1989 (at least ninety-one nations), the 1973 Vienna Trademark Agreement (at least thirty-two nations), and the Trademark Law Treaty of 1994 (at least fifty-three nations).

- *Copyrights.* The principal treaties covering copyrights are the 1952 Universal Copyright Convention, revised in 1971, the Berne Convention for the Protection of Literary and Artistic Works of 1886 (at least 167 nations), and the WIPO Copyright Treaty of 1996 (at least ninety-two nations).

token, laws of nature, principles, bookkeeping systems, fundamental truths, calculation methods, and ideas are not patentable. Accordingly, Einstein could not have patented his law that $E = mc^2$; nor could Newton have patented the law of gravity. Similarly, isolated computer programs are not patentable, although, as mentioned previously, they may be copyrighted.

To be patentable as a utility patent, the process, machine, manufacture, or composition of matter must meet three criteria: (1) novelty, (2) utility, and (3) nonobviousness.

In addition to utility patents, the Patent Act provides for plant patents and design patents. A ***plant patent*** protects the exclusive right to reproduce a new and distinctive variety of asexually producing plant. Asexually propagated plants are those that are reproduced by means other than from seeds, such as by the rooting of cuttings as well as by layering, budding, or grafting. Plant patents require (1) novelty, (2) distinctiveness, and (3) nonobviousness. A ***design patent*** protects a new, original, ornamental design for an article of manufacture. A design patent protects only the appearance of an article but not its structural or functional features. Design patents require (1) novelty, (2) ornamentality, and (3) nonobviousness.

Utility and plant patents have a term that begins on the date of the patent's grant and ends twenty years from the date of application, subject to extensions for statutorily specified delays. Design patents have a term of fourteen years from the date of grant.

Association for Molecular Pathology v. Myriad Genetics, Inc.
Supreme Court of the United States, 2013
569 U.S. ____, 133 S.Ct. 2107, 186 L.Ed.2d 124
http://scholar.google.com/scholar_case?q=133+S.Ct.+2107&hl=en&as_sdt=6,34&case=18430796342509149206&scilh=0

FACTS DNA's informational sequences and processes occur naturally within cells. Scientists can, however, extract DNA from cells using well-known laboratory methods. These methods allow scientists to isolate specific segments of DNA—for instance, a particular gene or part of a gene—which can then be studied, manipulated, or used. It is also possible to create DNA synthetically through processes similarly well-known in the field of genetics. This synthetic DNA created in the laboratory is known as complementary DNA (cDNA).

Myriad Genetics, Inc. discovered the precise location and sequence of what are now known as the BRCA1 and BRCA2 genes. Mutations in these genes can dramatically increase an individual's risk of developing breast and ovarian cancer. The average American woman has a 12 to 13 percent risk of developing breast cancer, but for women with certain genetic mutations, the risk can range between 50 and 80 percent for breast cancer and between 20 and 50 percent for ovarian cancer.

Knowledge of the location and sequence of the BRCA1 and BRCA2 genes enabled Myriad to develop medical tests that are useful for detecting mutations in a patient's BRCA1 and BRCA2 genes and thereby assessing whether the patient has an increased risk of cancer. Myriad then sought and obtained a number of patents, which would, if valid, give it the exclusive right to isolate an individual's BRCA1 and BRCA2 genes. The patents would also give Myriad the exclusive right to synthetically create BRCA cDNA. In Myriad's view, manipulating BRCA DNA in either of these fashions triggers its "right to exclude others from making" its patented composition of matter under the Patent Act.

The plaintiffs, including medical patients, advocacy groups, and doctors, filed this lawsuit in U.S. District Court seeking a declaration that Myriad's patents are invalid. The District Court granted summary judgment to the plaintiffs based on its conclusion that Myriad's claims, including claims related to cDNA, were invalid because they covered products of nature. The U.S. Court of Appeals for the Federal Circuit initially reversed, but on remand the Federal Circuit found both isolated DNA and cDNA eligible for a patent.

DECISION The judgment of the U.S. Court of Appeals for the Federal Circuit is affirmed in part and reversed in part.

OPINION The U.S. Supreme Court has long held that laws of nature, natural phenomena, and abstract ideas are not patentable. Rather, "they are the basic tools of scientific and technological work" that lie beyond the domain of patent protection. As the Supreme Court has explained, without this exception, there would be considerable danger that the grant of patents would "tie up" the use of such tools and thereby "inhibit future innovation premised upon them." This would be at odds with the very point of patents, which exist to promote creation.

The rule against patents on naturally occurring things is not without limits, however, for "all inventions at some level embody, use, reflect, rest upon, or apply laws of nature, natural phenomena, or abstract ideas," and "too broad an interpretation of this exclusionary principle could eviscerate patent law." Patent protection strikes a delicate balance between creating "incentives that lead to creation, invention, and discovery" and "imped[ing] the flow of information that might permit, indeed spur, invention." This well-established standard must be applied to determine whether Myriad's patents claim any "new and useful … composition of matter," § 101, or instead claim naturally occurring phenomena.

It is undisputed that Myriad did not create or alter any of the genetic information encoded in the BRCA1 and BRCA2 genes. The location and order of the nucleotides existed in nature before Myriad found them. Nor did Myriad create or alter the genetic structure of DNA. Instead, Myriad's principal contribution was uncovering the precise location and genetic sequence of the BRCA1 and BRCA2 genes. The question is whether this renders the genes patentable.

Myriad did not create anything. To be sure, it found an important and useful gene, but separating that gene from its surrounding genetic material is not an act of invention. Groundbreaking, innovative, or even brilliant discovery does not by itself satisfy the § 101 inquiry. Myriad found the location of the BRCA1 and BRCA2 genes, but that discovery, by itself, does not render the BRCA genes "new … composition[s] of matter," § 101, that are patent eligible. For these reasons, a naturally occurring DNA segment is a product of nature and not eligible for a patent merely because it has been isolated.

On the other hand, cDNA does not present the same obstacles to patentability as naturally occurring, isolated DNA segments. Creation of a cDNA sequence results in a molecule that is not naturally occurring in that "the non-coding regions have been removed." The lab technician unquestionably creates something new when cDNA is made. As a result, cDNA is not a "product of nature" and is eligible for a patent under § 101, except insofar as very short series of DNA may be indistinguishable from natural DNA.

INTERPRETATION Because laws of nature, natural phenomena, and abstract ideas are not patentable, a naturally occurring DNA segment is a product of nature and *not* eligible for a patent merely because it has been isolated whereas synthetically created cDNA is eligible for a patent because it is not naturally occurring.

CRITICAL THINKING QUESTION Do you agree with the U.S. Supreme Court's distinction between naturally occurring DNA and synthetically created DNA with respect to eligibility for a patent? Explain.

Issuance of patents

patents are issued upon application to and after examination by the U.S. Patent and Trademark Office

Issuance of Patents [40-5b]

The U.S. Patent and Trademark Office (USPTO) issues a patent upon the basis of a patent application containing a specification, which describes how the invention works, and claims, which describe the features that make the invention patentable. Prior to the 2011 America Invents Act, the applicant must have been the inventor. Under the America Invents Act, a person to whom the inventor has assigned, or is under an obligation to assign, the invention may file a patent application. Before granting a patent, the USPTO carefully and thoroughly examines the prior art and determines whether the submitted invention has novelty (does not conflict with a prior pending application or a previously issued patent) and utility, and is nonobvious. A patent application is confidential, and the USPTO will not divulge its contents. This confidentiality ends, however, upon the granting of the patent. Unlike rights under a copyright, no monopoly rights arise until the USPTO actually issues a patent. Therefore, anyone is free to make, use, and sell an invention for which a patent application is filed until the patent has been granted.

The rights granted by a U.S. patent extend only to the United States. A person desiring a patent in another country must apply for a patent in that country. The Patent Cooperation Treaty, adhered to by the United States and at least 147 other countries, facilitates the filing of applications for patents on the same invention in member countries by providing for centralized filing procedures and a standardized application format.

Congress previously amended the Patent Act to require the publication of certain utility and plant patent applications eighteen months after filing even if the patent has not yet been granted. This requirement applies only to those patent applications that are filed in other countries that require publication after eighteen months or under the Patent Cooperation Treaty. An applicant may obtain a reasonable royalty from a third party who between publication and issuance of the patent infringes it, provided the third party had actual notice of the published application.

An applicant whose application is rejected may apply for reexamination. If the application is again rejected, the applicant may appeal to the USPTO's Patent Trial and Appeal Board (previously called the Board of Patent Appeals and Interferences), and from there may appeal to the federal courts.

Infringement [40-5c]

Infringement

occurs when anyone without permission makes, uses, or sells a patented invention

Anyone who, without permission, makes, uses, or sells a patented invention is a *direct infringer*, whereas a person who actively encourages another to make, use, offer to sell, or sell a patented invention without permission is an *indirect infringer*. A *contributory infringer* is one who knowingly sells, or offers to sell, a part or component of a patented invention, unless the component is a staple or commodity or is suitable for a substantial noninfringing use. Though good faith and ignorance are defenses to contributory infringement, they are not defenses to direct infringement. To recover damages, a patent owner must (1) give actual notice to an infringer or (2) give constructive notice by marking a patented article with the word "Patent" and the number of the patent. The America Invents Act permits patent holders to "virtually mark" a product by providing the address of a publicly available website that associates the patented article with the number of the patent. This provision went into effect on September 16, 2011.

Practical Advice

Give notice of your patented articles by fixing on them the word patent or the abbreviation pat., together with (1) the number of the patent or (2) a reference to an Internet address.

Remedies [40-5d]

Remedies

for infringement of a patent are (1) injunctive relief; (2) damages; (3) treble damages, when appropriate; (4) attorneys' fees; and (5) costs

If a patent is infringed, the patent owner may sue for relief in federal court. The **remedies** for infringement under the Patent Act are (1) injunctive relief; (2) damages adequate to compensate the plaintiff but "in no event less than a reasonable royalty for the use made of the invention by the infringer"; (3) treble damages, when appropriate; (4) attorneys' fees in exceptional cases, such as those that involve knowing infringement; and (5) costs.

CONCEPT REVIEW 40-1

Intellectual Property

	Trade Secrets	Trade Symbols	Copyright	Patents
What Is Protected	Information	Mark	Work of authorship	Invention
Rights Protected	Use or sell	Use or sell	Reproduce, prepare derivative works, distribute, perform, or display	Make, use, or sell
Duration	Until disclosed	Until abandoned	Usually author's life plus seventy years	For utility and plant patents, twenty years from application; For design patents fourteen years from grant
Federally Protected	No	Yes	Yes	Yes
Requirements for Protection	Valuable secret	Distinctive	Original and fixed	Novel, useful, and nonobvious

ETHICAL DILEMMA

Who Holds the Copyright on Lecture Notes?

Facts Tom Rigsby considers himself a young, aspiring entrepreneur. At twenty-three, he has already established a highly successful small business, Take Note, which provides students at the University of the Midwest with detailed class notes for approximately seventy-five university courses, covering subjects that range from business law to modern literature. For each of his note sets, Rigsby charges $35.00.

He also offers, for $25.00, an exam package that includes summary notes as well as exam questions that professors have used in the past, which many fraternities on campus already keep on file exclusively for their members.

To make a profit, Rigsby has concentrated on the university's more popular courses, which often pack up to five hundred students into a single lecture hall. At present, he is grossing about $400,000 a year.

Most students who have used Rigsby's notes consider them to be of exceptionally high quality. Many believe that the notes have made the difference between an "A" and a "B" in their courses.

Rigsby received his degree from the University of the Midwest, where he graduated summa cum laude. Until recently, when he expanded his business, he based his Take Note packages either on notes he had taken while a regular student or on notes from classes he audited after he graduated. Now, he has hired two additional notetakers, both 4.0 students at the university. He pays them each a small salary plus royalties of 12 percent on every sale of their notes that he makes.

To the dismay of many professors at the university, though, Rigsby has never sought their permission to distribute notes of their classes. He does not see why he should. In fact, he believes that any question of copyright here should be answered in favor of the notetaker, not the professor. He acknowledges that in other states, businesses such as his pay royalties to professors, but he thinks such expenditures unnecessary.

Now, on behalf of the University of the Midwest and its professors, lawyers for the university have sued Rigsby for copyright infringement. He, in turn, has filed a countersuit, charging disparagement. Rigsby was planning to expand his business to three other Midwestern states, but now he says the university has disrupted his business with false accusations.

Social, Policy, and Ethical Considerations

1. Who does hold the copyright in this case? Did Rigsby act ethically in not seeking the professors' permission? Should he be required to share a part of his profits as royalties with the professors whose classes are covered by his Take Note packages?

2. Are the students acting ethically in buying Rigsby's Take Note packages? Does using one of Rigsby's exam packages constitute cheating? Does employing someone else's notes or old exam questions to study for an exam differ from using someone else's notes or outline to write a term paper?

3. Is the University of the Midwest acting responsibly in scheduling such large classes? What responsibility does it have to protect students from an impersonal or inadequate education? Is the university acting responsibly toward its professors? How should the university protect a professor's intellectual work?

CHAPTER SUMMARY

Trade Secrets

Definition of Trade Secret commercially valuable, secret information

Protection owner of a trade secret may obtain damages or injunctive relief when the secret is misappropriated (wrongfully used) by an employee or a competitor

Criminal Penalties federal law imposes penalties for the theft of trade secrets

Trade Symbols

Types of Trade Symbols

- *Trademark* distinctive symbol, word, or design on a good that is used to identify the manufacturer
- *Service Mark* distinctive symbol, word, or design that is used to identify a provider's services
- *Certification Mark* distinctive symbol, word, or design used with goods or services to certify specific characteristics
- *Collective Mark* distinctive symbol used to indicate membership in an organization

Registration to be registered and thus protected by the Lanham Act, a mark must be distinctive and not immoral, deceptive, or scandalous

Infringement occurs when a person without authorization uses a substantially indistinguishable mark that is likely to cause confusion, mistake, or deception

Remedies the Lanham Act provides the following remedies for infringement: injunctive relief, profits, damages, destruction of infringing articles, costs, and, in exceptional cases, attorneys' fees

Trade Names	**Definition of Trade Name** any name used to identify a business, vocation, or occupation
	Protection may not be registered under the Lanham Act, but infringement is prohibited
	Remedies damages and injunctions are available if infringement occurs
Copyrights	**Definition of Copyright** exclusive right, usually for the author's life plus seventy years, to original works of authorship
	Registration registration is not required but provides additional remedies for infringement
	Rights copyright protection provides the exclusive right to (1) reproduce the copyrighted work, (2) prepare derivative works based on the work, (3) distribute copies of the work, and (4) perform or display the work publicly
	Ownership the author of the copyrighted work is usually the owner of the copyright, which may be transferred in whole or in part
	Infringement occurs when someone exercises the copyright owner's rights without authorization
	Remedies if infringement occurs after registration, the following remedies are available: (1) injunction, (2) impoundment and possible destruction of infringing articles, (3) actual damages plus profits or statutory damages, (4) costs, and (5) criminal penalties
Patents	**Definition of Patent** the exclusive right to an invention for twenty years from the date of application for utility and plant patents; fourteen years from grant for design patents
	Patentability to be patentable, the invention must be (1) novel, (2) useful, and (3) not obvious
	Issuance of Patents patents are issued upon application to and after examination by the U.S. Patent and Trademark Office
	Infringement occurs when anyone without permission makes, uses, or sells a patented invention
	Remedies for infringement of a patent are (1) injunctive relief; (2) damages; (3) treble damages, when appropriate; (4) attorneys' fees; and (5) costs

QUESTIONS

1. Keller, a professor of legal studies at Rhodes University, is a diligent instructor. Late one night, while reading a newly published, copyrighted treatise of one thousand eight hundred pages written by Gilbert, he came across a three-page section discussing the subject matter he intended to cover in class the next day. Keller considered the treatment to be illuminating and therefore photocopied the three pages and distributed the copies to his class. One of Keller's students is a second cousin of Gilbert, the author of the treatise, and she showed Gilbert the copies. May Gilbert recover from Keller for copyright infringement? Explain.

2. Jennings conceived a secret process for the continuous freeze-drying of foodstuffs and related products and constructed a small pilot plant that practiced the process. However, Jennings lacked the financing necessary to develop the commercial potential of the process and, in hopes of obtaining a contract for its development and the payment of royalties, disclosed it in confidence to Merrick, a coffee manufacturer, who signed an agreement not to disclose it to anyone else. At the same time, Jennings signed an agreement not to disclose the process to any other person as long as Jennings and Merrick were considering a contract for its development. Upon Jennings's disclosure of the process, Merrick became extremely interested and offered to pay Jennings the sum of $1.75 million if, upon further development, the process proved to be commercially feasible. While negotiations between Jennings and Merrick were in progress, Nelson, a competitor of Merrick, learned of the process and requested a disclosure from Jennings, who informed Nelson that the process could not be disclosed to anyone unless negotiations with Merrick were broken off. Nelson offered to pay Jennings $2.5 million for the process, provided it met certain defined objective performance criteria. A contract was prepared and executed between Jennings and Nelson on this basis, without any prior disclosure of the process to Nelson. Upon the making of this contract, Jennings rejected Merrick's offer. The process was thereupon disclosed to Nelson, and demonstration runs of the pilot plant in the presence of Nelson's representatives were conducted under varying conditions. After three weeks of observing experimental demonstrations, compiling data, and analyzing results, Nelson informed Jennings that the process did not meet the performance criteria in the contract and that for this reason Nelson was rejecting the process. Two years later, Nelson placed on the market freeze-dried coffee that resembled in color, appearance, and texture the product of Jennings's pilot plant. What are the rights of the parties?

3. Stella, a chemist, was employed by Johnson, a manufacturer, to work on a secret process for Johnson's product under an exclusive three-year contract. Johnson employed Dabney, a sales person, on a week-to-week basis. Stella and Dabney resigned their employment with Johnson and accepted employment in their respective capacities with Washington, a rival manufacturer. Dabney began soliciting patronage from Johnson's former customers, whose names he had memorized. What are the rights of the parties in (a) a suit by Johnson to enjoin Stella from working

for Washington and (b) a suit by Johnson to enjoin Dabney from soliciting Johnson's customers?

4. Conrad and Darby were competitors in the business of dehairing raw cashmere, the fleece of certain Asiatic goats. Dehairing is the process of separating the commercially valuable soft down from the matted mass of raw fleece, which contains long coarse guard hairs and other impurities. Machinery for this process is not readily available on the open market. Each company in the business designed and built its own machinery and kept the nature of its process secret. Conrad contracted with Lawton, the owner of a small machine shop, to build and install new improved dehairing machinery of increased efficiency for which Conrad furnished designs, drawings, and instructions. Lawton, who knew that the machinery design was confidential, agreed that he would manufacture the machinery exclusively for Conrad and that he would not reproduce the machinery or any of its essential parts for anyone else. Darby purchased from Lawton a copy of the dehairing machinery that Conrad had specially designed. What are Conrad's rights, if any, against (a) Darby and (b) Lawton? Explain.

5. Sally, having filed locally an affidavit required under the assumed name statute, has been operating and advertising her exclusive toy store for twenty years in Centerville, Illinois. Her advertising has consisted of large signs on her premises reading "The Toy Mart." Bob, after operating a store in Chicago under the name of "The Chicago Toy Mart," relocated in Centerville, Illinois, and erected a large sign reading "TOY MART" with the word "Centerville" written underneath in substantially smaller letters. Thereafter, Sally's sales declined,

and many of Sally's customers patronized Bob's store, thinking it to be a branch of Sally's business. What are the rights of the parties?

6. Ryan Corporation manufactures and sells a variety of household cleaning products in interstate commerce. On national television, Ryan falsely advertises that its laundry liquid is biodegradable. Has Ryan violated the Lanham Act?

7. Gibbons, Inc., and Marvin Corporation are manufacturers who sell a variety of household cleaning products in interstate commerce. On national television Gibbons states that its laundry liquid is biodegradable and that Marvin's is not. In fact, both products are biodegradable. Has Gibbons violated the Lanham Act?

8. George McCoy of Florida has been manufacturing and distributing a cheesecake for more than five years, labeling his product with a picture of a cheesecake, which serves as a background for a Florida bathing beauty and under which is written the slogan "McCoy All Spice Florida Cheese Cake." George McCoy has not registered his trademark. Subsequently, Leo McCoy of California begins manufacturing a similar product on the West Coast using a label similar in appearance to that of George McCoy, containing a picture of a Hollywood star and the words "McCoy's All Spice Cheese Cake." Leo McCoy begins marketing his products in the eastern United States, using labels with the word "Florida" added, as in George McCoy's label. Leo McCoy has registered his product under the Federal Trademark Act. To what relief, if any, is George McCoy entitled?

CASE PROBLEMS

9. Sony Corporation manufactured and sold home video recorders, specifically Betamax videotape recorders (VTRs). Universal City Studios, Inc. (Universal) owned the copyrights on some programs aired on commercially sponsored television. Individual Betamax owners frequently used the device to record some of Universal's copyrighted television programs for their own noncommercial use. Universal brought suit, claiming that the sale of the Betamax VTRs to the general public violated its rights under the Copyright Act. It sought no relief against any Betamax consumer. Instead, Universal sued Sony for contributory infringement of its copyrights, seeking money damages, an equitable accounting of profits, and an injunction against the manufacture and sale of Betamax VTRs. Explain whether Universal will prevail in its action.

10. The Coca-Cola Company manufactures a carbonated beverage, Coke, made from coca leaves and cola nuts. The Koke Company of America introduced into the beverage market a similar product named Koke. The Coca-Cola Company brought a trademark infringement action against Koke. Coca-Cola claimed unfair competition within the beverage business due to Koke's imitation of the Coca-Cola product and Koke's attempt to reap the benefit of consumer identification with the Coke name. Should Coca-Cola succeed? Explain.

11. Vuitton, a French corporation, manufactures high-quality handbags, luggage, and accessories. Crown Handbags, a New York corporation, manufactures and distributes ladies' handbags. Vuitton handbags are sold exclusively in expensive department stores, and distribution is strictly controlled to maintain a certain retail selling price. The Vuitton bags bear a registered trademark and a distinctive design. Crown's handbags appear identical to the Vuitton bags but are of inferior quality. May Vuitton recover from Crown for manufacturing counterfeit handbags and selling them at a discount? Explain.

12. T.G.I. Friday's, a New York corporation and registered service mark, entered into an exclusive licensing agreement with Tiffany & Co. that allowed Tiffany to open a Friday's restaurant in Jackson, Mississippi. International Restaurant Group, operated by the owners of Tiffany, applied for a license to open a Friday's in Baton Rouge, Louisiana, but was refused. In Baton Rouge, International then opened a restaurant, called E.L. Saturday's, or Ever Lovin' Saturday's, which had the same type of menu and decor as Friday's. Friday's sues International for trademark infringement. Explain who will prevail.

13. As part of its business, Kinko's Graphics Corporation (Kinko's) copied excerpts from books, compiled them in "packets," and sold the packets to college students. Kinko's did this without permission from the owners of the copyrights to the books and

without paying copyright fees or royalties. Kinko's has more than two hundred stores nationwide and reported $15 million in assets and $3 million in profits for 1989. Basic Books, Harper & Row, John Wiley & Sons, and others (plaintiffs) sued Kinko's for violation of the Copyright Act. The plaintiffs owned copyrights to the works copied and sold by Kinko's and derived substantial income from royalties. They argued that Kinko's had infringed on their copyrights by copying excerpts from their books and selling the copies to college students for profit. Kinko's admitted that it had copied excerpts without permission and had sold them in packets to students, but it contended that its actions constituted a fair use of the works in question under the Copyright Act. What is the result? Explain.

14. In 1967, a Chicago brewer, Meister Brau, Inc., began making and selling a reduced-calorie, reduced-carbohydrate beer under the name "LITE." Late in 1968, that company filed applications to register "LITE" as a trademark in the U.S. Patent Office, which ultimately approved three registrations of labels containing the name "LITE" for "beer with no available carbohydrates." In 1972, Meister Brau sold its interest in the "LITE" trademarks and the accompanying goodwill to Miller Brewing Company. Miller decided to expand its marketing of beer under the brand "LITE." It developed a modified recipe, which resulted in a beer lower in calories than Miller's regular beer but not without available carbohydrates. The label was revised, and one of the registrations was amended to show "LITE" printed rather than in script. In addition, Miller undertook an extensive advertising campaign. From 1973 through 1976, Miller expanded its annual sales of "LITE" from fifty thousand barrels to 4 million barrels and increased its annual advertising expenditures from $500,000 to more than $12 million.

Beginning in early 1975, a number of other brewers, including G. Heileman Brewing Company, introduced reduced-calorie beers labeled or described as "light." In response, Miller began filing trademark infringement actions against competitors to enjoin the use of the word "light." Should Miller be granted the injunction? Explain.

15. B. C. Ziegler and Company (Ziegler) was a securities company located in West Bend. It had established an internal procedure by which its customer lists were treated confidentially. This procedure included burning or shredding any paper to be disposed of that contained a customer name or information. Nonetheless, Ziegler delivered a number of boxes of unshredded scrap paper to Lynn's Waste Paper Company for disposal. One of Lynn's employees, Ehren, who had been in the securities business and had worked for two of Ziegler's competitors, noticed the information contained in

the delivery from Ziegler and purchased six boxes of the Ziegler wastepaper for $16.75 from Lynn's. Shortly thereafter, Ehren and his daughter sorted through the information and ultimately obtained 11,600 envelopes of information on Ziegler's customers, including names, account summaries, and other information. Ehren sold this information to Thorson, a broker in competition with Ziegler. Thorson then sent a mailing to the Ziegler customers to solicit security sales for his firm and obtained an abnormally high response rate as a result. Ziegler, with the help of the West Bend Police Department, traced the dissemination of this information to Ehren and sought from the court a permanent injunction against Ehren using or disclosing the information regarding Ziegler's clients. What is the result?

16. Since the 1950s Qualitex Company has used a special shade of green-gold color on the pads that it makes and sells to dry cleaning firms for use on dry cleaning presses. In 1989 Jacobson Products (a Qualitex rival) began to sell its own press pads to dry cleaning firms, and it colored those pads a similar green-gold. In 1991 Qualitex registered the special green-gold color on press pads with the Patent and Trademark Office as a trademark. Qualitex sued Jacobson for trademark infringement. Jacobson argues that the Lanham Act does not permit registering "color alone" as a trademark. Explain whether a trademark violation has been committed.

17. Napster, Inc. (Napster) facilitates the transmission of MP3 files between and among its users. Through a process commonly called "peer-to-peer" file sharing, Napster allows its users to (a) make MP3 music files stored on individual computer hard drives available for copying by other Napster users; (b) search for MP3 music files stored on other users' computers; and (c) transfer exact copies of the contents of other users' MP3 files from one computer to another via the Internet. These functions are made possible by Napster's MusicShare software, available free of charge from Napster's Internet site, and Napster's network servers and server-side software. The plaintiffs include A&M Records, Geffen Records, Sony Music Entertainment, MCA Records, Atlantic Recording Corporation, Motown Record Company, and Capitol Records. The plaintiffs are engaged in the commercial recording, distribution, and sale of copyrighted musical compositions and sound recordings. The plaintiffs allege that Napster is a contributory and vicarious copyright infringer. Explain whether Napster should be enjoined "from engaging in, or facilitating others in copying, downloading, uploading, transmitting, or distributing plaintiffs' copyrighted musical compositions and sound recordings, protected by either federal or state law, without express permission of the rights owner."

TAKING SIDES

Southwire Company and Essex Group, Inc. are direct competitors in the cable and wire industry. Southwire's logistics system is a warehouse organizational system with components extending from architectural layout features to customized equipment and modified computer software. Southwire's logistics system was

primarily designed over a three-year period, with a development cost exceeding $2 million, by a project team headed by Richard McMichael. In addition to self-testing and a trial-and-error learning process, development of Southwire's logistics system also included modifications based on observation of logistics systems in other industries and the adaptation of commercially available components. The selection and arrangement of components and equipment in the new logistics system is unique to the Southwire logistics system. The new logistics system has resulted in substantial efficiencies to Southwire, with annual savings of $12 million. Because Southwire and its competitors produce basically identical goods for sale, the marketing advantage gained by the important efficiencies that have resulted from the new logistics system has proved especially valuable for Southwire. Essex hired McMichael, and Southwire brought suit against its former employee, McMichael, and his new employer, Essex, to enjoin McMichael from disclosing to Essex any Southwire trade secrets, particularly, trade secrets involving Southwire's logistics system.

a. What are the arguments in favor of the court *not* issuing the injunction?

b. What are the arguments in favor of the court issuing the injunction?

c. Explain whether the court should issue the injunction.

Employment Law

CHAPTER 41

I'm sticking to the union till the day I die.

Woody Guthrie
"Union Maid" (1946)

CHAPTER OUTCOMES

After reading and studying this chapter, you should be able to:

1. List and describe the major labor law statutes.

2. List and describe the major laws prohibiting employment discrimination.

3. Discuss the defenses available to employers under the various laws prohibiting discrimination in employment.

4. Explain the doctrine of employment at will and the laws protecting employee privacy.

5. Explain (a) the Occupational Safety and Health Administration (OSHA) and the Occupational Safety and Health Act, (b) workers' compensation, (c) unemployment compensation, (d) social security, (e) the Fair Labor Standards Act, (f) the Worker Adjustment and Retraining Notification Act, and (g) the Family and Medical Leave Act.

Though the common law originally governed the relationship between employer and employee in terms of tort and contract duties (rules that are a part of the law of agency, as discussed in Chapter 28, Relationship of Principal and Agent), this common law has been supplemented—and in some instances replaced—by statutory enactments, principally at the federal level. In fact, government regulation now affects the balance and working relationship between employers and employees in three principal areas. First, the general framework in which management and labor negotiate the terms of employment is regulated by federal statutes designed to promote both labor-management harmony and the welfare of society at large. Second, federal law has been enacted to prohibit employment discrimination based upon race, sex, religion, age, disability, or national origin. Finally, Congress, in response to the changing nature of American industry and the tremendous number of industrial accidents, has intervened by mandating that employers provide their employees with a safe and healthy work environment. Moreover, all of the states have adopted workers' compensation acts to provide compensation to employees injured during the course of employment.

In this chapter, we will focus on these three categories of government regulation of the employment relationship: (1) labor law, (2) employment discrimination law, and (3) employee protection.

LABOR LAW [41-1]

Labor law
provides the general framework in which management and labor negotiate terms of employment

Traditionally, **labor law** opposed concerted activities by workers (such as strikes, picketing, and refusals to deal) to obtain higher wages and better working conditions. At various times, such activities were found to constitute criminal conspiracy, tortious conduct, and violation of antitrust law. Eventually, public pressure in response to the adverse treatment accorded labor forced Congress to intervene.

Norris-La Guardia Act

established as U.S. policy the full freedom of labor to form labor unions without employer interference and withdrew from the federal courts the power to issue injunctions in nonviolent labor disputes

Labor dispute

any controversy concerning terms or conditions of employment or union representation

National Labor Relations Act (NLRA)

the Act (1) declares it a federally protected right of employees to unionize and to bargain collectively, (2) identifies five unfair labor practices by an employer, and (3) was created to administer these rights

Unfair labor practice

conduct in which an employer or union is prohibited from engaging

Unfair employer practice

conduct in which an employer is prohibited from engaging

Practical Advice

Treat all employees with appropriate respect and dignity.

Labor-Management Relations Act

the Act (1) prohibits unfair labor practices by a union, (2) prohibits closed shops, and (3) allows union shops

Unfair union practice

conduct in which a union is prohibited from engaging

Closed shop

employer can hire only union members

Norris-La Guardia Act [41-1a]

Congress enacted the **Norris-La Guardia Act** (also known as the Anti-Injunction Bill) in 1932 in response to growing criticism of the use of injunctions in peaceful labor disputes. The Act withdrew from the federal courts the power to issue injunctions in nonviolent **labor disputes**, broadly defined to include any controversy concerning terms or conditions of employment or union representation, regardless of whether the parties stood in an employer–employee relationship. More significantly, the Act declared it to be U.S. policy that labor was to have full freedom to form unions, without employer interference. Accordingly, the Act prohibited the so-called yellow dog contracts through which employers coerced their employees into promising that they would not join a union.

National Labor Relations Act [41-1b]

Enacted in 1935, the **National Labor Relations Act (NLRA)**, or the *Wagner Act*, marked the federal government's effort to support collective bargaining and unionization. The Act provides that "the right to self-organization, to form, join or assist labor organizations, to bargain collectively through representatives of their own choosing, and to engage in concerted activities for the purpose of collective bargaining or other mutual aid or protection" is, for workers, a federally protected right. Thus, the Act gave employees the right to union representation when negotiating employment terms with their employers.

Moreover, the Act sought to enforce the collective bargaining right by prohibiting certain employer and union activities deemed to be **unfair labor practices**. For example, the Act identifies the following activities as **unfair employer practices**: (1) to interfere with employees' rights to unionize and bargain collectively, (2) to dominate the union, (3) to discriminate against union members, (4) to discriminate against an employee who has filed charges or testified under the NLRA, and (5) to refuse to bargain in good faith with duly established employee representatives.

Labor-Management Relations Act [41-1c]

Following the passage of the NLRA, the country underwent a tremendous increase in union membership and labor unrest. In response to this trend, Congress passed the **Labor-Management Relations Act** (the LMRA, or Taft-Hartley Act) in 1947. The Act prohibits certain **unfair union practices** and separates the prosecutorial and adjudicative functions of the National Labor Relations Board (NLRB). More specifically, the Act amended the NLRA by declaring the following seven union activities of the NLRB to be ***unfair labor practices***: (1) coercing an employee to join a union, (2) causing an employer to discharge or discriminate against a nonunion employee, (3) refusing to bargain in good faith, (4) levying excessive or discriminatory dues or fees, (5) causing an employer to pay for work not performed ("featherbedding"), (6) picketing an employer to require it to recognize an uncertified union, and (7) engaging in secondary activities. A secondary activity is a boycott, strike, or picketing of an employer with whom a union has no labor dispute to persuade the employer to cease doing business with the company that is the target of the labor dispute. For example, assume that a union is engaged in a labor dispute with Anderson Company. To coerce Anderson into resolving the dispute in the union's favor, the union organizes a strike against Brooking Company, with which the union has no labor dispute. The union agrees to cease striking Brooking Company if Brooking agrees to cease doing business with Anderson. The strike against Brooking is a secondary activity prohibited as an unfair labor practice. See Concept Review 41-1 for a summary of union and employer unfair labor practices.

In addition to prohibiting unfair union practices, the Act also fosters employer free speech by declaring that unions or employees wishing to identify an employer's labor practice as unfair cannot use as proof any employer statement of opinion or argument that contains no threat of reprisal.

The LMRA also prohibits the closed shop but permits union shops, unless a state right-to-work law prohibits the latter. A **closed shop** contract requires the employer to hire only union

> ## CONCEPT REVIEW 41-1
>
> ### *Unfair Labor Practices*
>
> | Unfair Employer Practices | Unfair Union Practices |
> | --- | --- |
> | • Interfering with right to unionize
• Refusing to bargain in good faith
• Discriminating against union members
• Dominating the union
• Discriminating against an employee | • Coercing an employee to join the union
• Refusing to bargain in good faith
• Causing an employer to discriminate against a nonunion employee
• Featherbedding
• Picketing an employer to require recognition of an uncertified union
• Engaging in secondary activity
• Levying excessive or discriminatory dues |

Union shop

employer can hire nonunion members, but the employee must join the union

Right-to-work law

state statute that prohibits union shop contracts

members. A **union shop** contract permits the employer to hire nonunion members but requires the employee to become a union member within a specified time after gaining employment and to remain a member in good standing as a condition of employment. A **right-to-work law** is a state statute that prohibits union shop contracts. However, most states permit the existence of union shops.

Finally, the Act reinstates the availability of civil injunctions in labor disputes if requested of the NLRB to prevent an unfair labor practice. The Act also empowers the President of the United States to obtain an injunction for an eighty-day cooling-off period for a strike that is likely to endanger the national health or safety.

Labor-Management Reporting and Disclosure Act [41-1d]

Labor-Management Reporting and Disclosure Act

aimed at eliminating corruption in labor unions

The **Labor-Management Reporting and Disclosure Act**, also known as the *Landrum-Griffin Act*, is aimed at eliminating corruption in labor unions. The Act attempts to eradicate corruption through an elaborate reporting system and a union "bill of rights" designed to make unions more democratic. The latter provides union members with the right to nominate candidates for union offices, to vote in elections, to attend membership meetings, to participate in union business, to express themselves freely at union meetings and conventions, and to be accorded a full and fair hearing before the union takes any disciplinary action against them.

EMPLOYMENT DISCRIMINATION LAW [41-2]

Equal Employment Opportunity Commission (EEOC)

enforcement agency for federal laws that make it illegal to discriminate against a job applicant or an employee because of the person's race, color, religion, sex, national origin, age, disability, or genetic information

A number of federal statutes prohibit discrimination in employment on the basis of race, sex, religion, national origin, age, disability, and genetic information. The cornerstone of federal employment discrimination law is Title VII of the 1964 Civil Rights Act, but other statutes and regulations are significant as well, including the *Civil Rights Act of 1991* and the *Americans with Disabilities Act (ADA)*. In addition, most states have enacted similar laws prohibiting discrimination based on race, sex, religion, national origin, and disability. Title VII of the Civil Rights Act of 1964, the Americans with Disabilities Act, and the Age Discrimination in Employment Act apply to U.S. citizens working for U.S.-owned or U.S.-controlled companies in foreign countries. The **Equal Employment Opportunity Commission (EEOC)** is the enforcement agency for federal laws that make it illegal to discriminate against a job applicant or an employee because of the person's race, color, religion, sex, national origin, age, disability, or genetic information.

Equal Pay Act [41-2a]

Equal Pay Act

prohibits an employer from discriminating between employees on the basis of gender by paying unequal wages for the same work

The **Equal Pay Act** prohibits an employer from discriminating between employees on the basis of *gender* by paying unequal wages for the same work. The Act forbids an employer from paying wages at a rate less than the rate at which he pays wages to employees of the opposite sex for equal work at the same establishment. Most courts define *equal work* to mean "substantially equal" rather than identical. The burden of proof is on the claimant to make a *prima facie* showing that the employer pays unequal wages for work requiring equal skill, effort, and responsibility under similar working conditions. Once the employee has demonstrated that the employer pays unequal wages for *equal* work to members of the opposite sex, the burden shifts to the employer to prove that the pay differential is based on (1) a seniority system, (2) a merit system, (3) a system that measures earnings by quantity or quality of production, or (4) any factor except gender.

Remedies include awarding back pay, awarding liquidated damages (an additional amount equal to back pay), and enjoining the employer from further unlawful conduct. Though the Department of Labor was the federal agency originally designated by the statute to interpret and enforce the Act, these functions subsequently have been transferred to the EEOC.

Civil Rights Act of 1964 prohibits employment discrimination on the basis of race, color, gender, religion, or national origin

Employment discrimination hiring, firing, compensating, promoting, or training of employees based on race, color, gender, religion, or national origin

Civil Rights Act of 1964 [41-2b]

Title VII of the **Civil Rights Act of 1964** *prohibits* **employment discrimination** on the basis of race, color, gender, religion, or national origin in hiring, firing, compensating, promoting, training, and other employment-related processes. Harassment based on any of these characteristics is also prohibited. The definition of "religion" includes all aspects of religious observance and practice; the statute provides that an employer must make reasonable efforts to accommodate an employee's religious belief. The Act applies to employers engaged in an industry affecting commerce and having fifteen or more employees. The Act also covers federal, state, and local governments as well as labor organizations with fifteen or more members. The Act contains an antiretaliation provision that forbids an employer from discriminating against an employee who has brought a claim or proceeding under Title VII or who has testified, assisted, or participated in such an action.

Burlington Northern & Santa Fe Railway Company v. White
Supreme Court of the United States, 2006
548 U.S. 53, 126 S.Ct. 2405, 165 L.Ed.2d 345
http://scholar.google.com/scholar_case?case=11917239100694445813&q=548+U.S.+53&hl=en&as_sdt=2,34

FACTS Sheila White was hired by Burlington Northern & Santa Fe Railway Company (Burlington) in June 1997 as a "track laborer," a job that involves removing and replacing track components, transporting track material, cutting brush, and clearing litter and cargo spillage from the right-of-way. White's primary responsibility soon became operating a forklift; however, she also performed some of the track laborer tasks. White was the only woman working in the Maintenance of Way department. In September of 1997, White reported to Burlington officials that Bill Joiner (Joiner), her immediate supervisor, had repeatedly told her that women should not be working in the Maintenance of Way department and also had made insulting and inappropriate remarks to her in front of other colleagues. After Burlington conducted an internal investigation, Joiner was suspended for ten days and required to attend sexual-harassment training. Marvin Brown, a Burlington manager, then reassigned White to standard track laborer tasks and completely removed her from forklift duty. Brown explained that the reassignment reflected coworker's complaints that, in fairness, a "more senior man" should have the "less arduous and cleaner job" of forklift operator.

On October 10, White filed a complaint with the Equal Employment Opportunity Commission (EEOC). She claimed that the reassignment of her duties amounted to unlawful gender-based discrimination and retaliation for her having earlier complained about Joiner. In early December, White filed a second retaliation charge with the Commission, claiming that Brown had placed her under surveillance and was monitoring her daily activities. A few days later, White and her immediate supervisor, Percy Sharkey, had a disagreement. Sharkey told Brown that White had been insubordinate. Brown suspended White without

pay prompting White to initiate internal grievance procedures that eventually led Burlington to conclude White had not been insubordinate. White was reinstated, with thirty-seven days' back pay for the time she was suspended. Based on the suspension she then filed another EEOC charge for retaliation.

White filed a Title VII action against Burlington in federal court. A jury found in White's favor awarding her $43,500 in damages for her claims of unlawful retaliation. Burlington appealed arguing White did not suffer any harm from these acts of retaliation since she received back pay. The Sixth Circuit affirmed the district court's judgment for White. The U.S. Supreme Court granted *certiorari*.

DECISION Judgment of the Court of Appeals is affirmed.

OPINION Title VII's antidiscrimination provision seeks a workplace in which individuals are not discriminated against because of their racial, ethnic, religious, or gender-based status. The antiretaliation provision seeks to prevent an employer from interfering through retaliation with an employee's efforts to secure or advance enforcement of the Act's basic guarantees. The antiretaliation provision, unlike the antidiscrimination provision, is not limited to discriminatory actions that affect the terms and conditions of employment. Thus, the scope of the antiretaliation provision is broader than the antidiscrimination provision and extends beyond workplace-related or employment-related retaliatory acts and harm.

The antiretaliation provision protects an individual not from all retaliation, but rather from retaliation that produces an injury or harm. To prevail a plaintiff must show that a reasonable employee would have found the challenged action materially adverse, "which in this context means it well might have 'dissuaded a reasonable worker from making or supporting a charge of discrimination.'" The antiretaliation provision seeks to prevent employer interference with "unfettered access" to Title VII's remedial mechanisms. It does so by prohibiting employer actions that are likely "to deter victims of discrimination from complaining to the EEOC," the courts, and their employers. Normally petty slights, minor annoyances, and simple lack of good manners will not create such deterrence. A *reasonable* employee is the provision's standard for judging harm: an objective standard. Such a standard avoids the uncertainties and unfair discrepancies that can plague a judicial effort to determine a plaintiff's unusual subjective feelings. In this case, the jury found that two of Burlington's actions amounted to retaliation: the reassignment of White from forklift duty to standard track laborer tasks and the thirty-seven-day suspension without pay. Here, the jury had before it considerable evidence that the track labor duties were "by all accounts more arduous and dirtier"; that the "forklift operator position required more qualifications, which is an indication of prestige"; and that "the forklift operator position was objectively considered a better job and the male employees resented White for occupying it."

Based on this record, a jury could reasonably conclude that the reassignment of responsibilities would have been materially adverse to a reasonable employee.

White did receive back pay. But White and her family had to live for thirty-seven days without income. Many reasonable employees would find a month without a paycheck to be a serious hardship. And White described to the jury the physical and emotional hardship that thirty-seven days of having "no income, no money" in fact caused. Moreover, she obtained medical treatment for her emotional distress. A reasonable employee facing the choice between retaining her job (and paycheck) and filing a discrimination complaint might well choose the former.

INTERPRETATION Title VII's antiretaliation provision forbids employer actions against an employee that are materially adverse, and this prohibition extends beyond workplace-related or employment-related retaliatory acts and harm.

CRITICAL THINKING Do you agree with the rationale for the antiretaliation provision's extending beyond the antidiscrimination provision? Explain.

When Congress passed the ***Pregnancy Discrimination Act***, it extended the benefits of Title VII to pregnant women. Under the Act, an employer cannot refuse to hire a pregnant woman, fire her, or force her to take maternity leave unless the employer can establish a *bona fide* occupational qualification (BFOQ) defense (discussed later in this section). The Act, which protects the job reinstatement rights of women returning from maternity leave, requires employers to treat pregnancy as they would a temporary disability.

The enforcement agency for Title VII is the EEOC, which is empowered (1) to file legal actions in its own name or to intervene in actions filed by third parties, (2) to attempt to resolve alleged violations through informal means prior to bringing suit, (3) to investigate all charges of discrimination, and (4) to issue guidelines and regulations concerning enforcement policy.

Practical Advice

Issue a strong company policy against all types of prohibited discrimination and ensure that all business decisions comply with your policy.

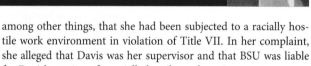

Vance v. Ball State University
Supreme Court of the United States, 2013
570 U.S. ____, 133 S.Ct. 2434, 186 L.Ed.2d 565
http://scholar.google.com/scholar_case?case=14881304984289805523&hl=en&as_sdt=6&as_vis=1&oi=scholarr

FACTS Maetta Vance, an African-American woman, began working for Ball State University (BSU) in 1989 as a substitute server in the University Banquet and Catering division of Dining Services. In 1991, BSU promoted Vance to a part-time catering assistant position, and in 2007 she applied and was selected for a position as a full-time catering assistant. Over the course of her employment with BSU, Vance lodged numerous complaints of racial discrimination and retaliation. In particular, Vance contended that Saundra Davis, a white woman who served as a catering specialist, had made Vance's life at work unpleasant through physical acts and racial harassment. Vance complained that Davis "gave her a hard time at work by glaring at her, slamming pots and pans around her, and intimidating her." She alleged that she was "left alone in the kitchen with Davis, who smiled at her"; that Davis "blocked" her on an elevator and "stood there with her cart smiling"; and that Davis often gave her "weird" looks. Vance's workplace issues persisted despite BSU's attempts to address the problem. As a result, Vance filed this lawsuit in 2006 in the U.S. District Court for the Southern District of Indiana, claiming,

among other things, that she had been subjected to a racially hostile work environment in violation of Title VII. In her complaint, she alleged that Davis was her supervisor and that BSU was liable for Davis' creation of a racially hostile work environment.

Both parties moved for summary judgment, and the District Court entered summary judgment in favor of BSU. The court explained that BSU could not be held vicariously liable for Davis' alleged racial harassment because Davis could not "hire, fire, demote, promote, transfer, or discipline" Vance and, as a result, was not Vance's The court further held that BSU could not be liable in negligence because it responded reasonably to the incidents of which it was aware. The Seventh Circuit affirmed and the Supreme Court granted *certiorari*.

DECISION Judgment affirmed.

OPINION Title VII of the Civil Rights Act of 1964 makes it "an unlawful employment practice for an employer … to discriminate against any individual with respect to his compensation, terms, conditions, or privileges of employment, because of such individual's race, color, religion, sex, or national origin." This provision obviously prohibits discrimination with respect to employment decisions that have direct economic consequences, such as termination, demotion, and pay cuts. But not long after Title VII was enacted, the lower courts held that Title VII also reaches the creation or perpetuation of a discriminatory work environment, and the U.S. Supreme Court agreed that Title VII prohibits the creation of a hostile work environment. In such cases, the Court has held, the plaintiff must show that the work environment was so pervaded by discrimination that the terms and conditions of employment were altered. Under Title VII, an employer's liability for such harassment may depend on the status of the harasser. If the harassing employee is the victim's co-worker, the employer is liable only if it was negligent in controlling working conditions. In cases in which the harasser is a "supervisor" and harassment culminates in a tangible employment action, the employer is strictly liable. But if no tangible employment action is taken, the employer escapes liability by establishing, as an affirmative defense, that (1) the employer exercised reasonable care to prevent and correct any harassing behavior and (2) that the plaintiff unreasonably failed to take advantage of the preventive or corrective opportunities that the employer provided. Thus it matters whether a harasser is a "supervisor" or simply a co-worker.

An employee is a "supervisor" for purposes of vicarious liability under Title VII if he or she is empowered by the employer to take tangible employment actions against the victim. Here the alleged harasser did not have the power or authority to take tangible employment actions with regard to the plaintiff. There is simply no evidence that Davis directed petitioner's day-to-day activities. The record indicates that Bill Kimes (the general manager of the Catering Division) and the chef assigned petitioner's daily tasks, which were given to her on "prep lists." The fact that Davis sometimes may have handed prep lists to petitioner is insufficient to confer supervisor status. Moreover, there is no evidence of negligence by BSU in monitoring Davis's behavior.

INTERPRETATION A person is a supervisor for purposes of vicarious liability under Title VII only if he is empowered by the employer to take tangible employment actions against the victim.

CRITICAL THINKING QUESTION Do you agree with the court's ruling? Explain.

Discrimination

prohibited by the Civil Rights Act; includes (1) using proscribed criteria to produce disparate treatment, (2) engaging in nondiscriminatory conduct that perpetuates past discrimination, and (3) adopting neutral rules that have a disparate impact

Proving Discrimination Each of the following constitutes discriminatory conduct prohibited by the Act:

1. **Disparate Treatment.** An individual shows that an employer used a prohibited criterion in making an employment decision by treating some people less favorably than others. Liability is based on proving that the employer's decision was motivated by the protected characteristic or trait. The Supreme Court has held that the plaintiff will have shown a *prima facie* case of discrimination if (a) she is within a protected class, (b) she had applied for an open position, (c) she was qualified for the position, (d) she was denied the job, and (e) the employer continued to try to fill the position from a pool of applicants with the complainant's qualifications. Once the plaintiff establishes a *prima facie* case, the burden shifts to the defendant to "articulate legitimate and nondiscriminatory reasons for the plaintiff's rejection." If the defendant so rebuts, the plaintiff then has the opportunity to demonstrate that the employer's stated reason was merely a pretext.

   If the employer's decision was based on a "mixed motive" (the employer used both lawful and unlawful reasons in making its decision), the courts employ a shifting burden of proof standard. First, the plaintiff must prove by a preponderance of the evidence that the employer used the protected characteristic as a motivating factor. The defendant, however, can limit the remedies available to the plaintiff by proving by a preponderance of the evidence that the defendant would have made the same decision even without the forbidden motivating factor. If the defendant sustains its burden of proof, under the Civil Rights Act of 1991 the remedies are limited to declaratory relief, certain types of injunctive relief, and attorneys' fees and costs.

2. **Present Effects of Past Discrimination.** Such effects result when an employer engages in conduct that on its face is "neutral"—that is, nondiscriminatory—but that actually perpetuates past discriminatory practices. For example, it has been held illegal for a union that previously had limited its membership to whites to adopt a requirement that new members be related to or recommended by existing members.

3. **Disparate Impact.** This occurs when an employer adopts "neutral" rules that adversely affect a protected class and that are not justified as being necessary to the business. Despite the employee's proof of disparate impact, the employer may prevail if it can demonstrate that the challenged practice is "job related for the position in question and

consistent with business necessity." Thus, all requirements that might have a disparate impact upon women, such as height and weight requirements, must be shown to be job related. Nevertheless, under the Civil Rights Act of 1991, even if the employer can demonstrate the business necessity of the questioned practice, the complainant will still prevail if she shows that a nondiscriminatory alternative practice exists.

Defenses   The Act provides several basic defenses: (1) a *bona fide* seniority or merit system, (2) a professionally developed ability test, (3) a compensation system based on performance results, and (4) a BFOQ. The BFOQ defense does not apply to discrimination based on race. A fifth defense, business necessity, is available in a disparate impact case. In addition, a defendant can reduce damages in a mixed-motive case by showing that it would have discharged the plaintiff for legal reasons.

Ricci v. Destefano
Supreme Court of the United States, 2009
557 U.S. 557, 129 S.Ct. 2658, 174 L.Ed.2d 490
http://scholar.google.com/scholar_case?case=8509283780298736470&q=557+U.S+.557&hl=en&as_sdt=40000006

FACTS In 2003, one hundred eighteen New Haven, Connecticut firefighters took examinations to qualify for promotion over the next two years to the rank of lieutenant or captain. Promotion examinations in New Haven were infrequent, so the stakes were high. Many firefighters studied for months, at considerable personal and financial cost. When the examination results showed that white candidates had outperformed minority candidates, the mayor and other local politicians opened a public debate that turned rancorous. Some firefighters argued the tests should be discarded because the results showed the tests to be discriminatory. Other firefighters said the exams were neutral and fair. The City took the side of those who protested the test results. It threw out the examinations.

Certain white and Hispanic firefighters who likely would have been promoted on the basis of their good test performance sued the City and some of its officials. The suit alleges that, by discarding the test results, the defendants discriminated against the plaintiffs based on their race, in violation of both Title VII of the Civil Rights Act of 1964 and the Equal Protection Clause of the Fourteenth Amendment. The City and the officials defended their actions, arguing that if they had certified the results, they could have faced liability under Title VII for adopting a practice that had a disparate impact on the minority firefighters. The District Court granted summary judgment for the defendants, and the Court of Appeals affirmed. The Supreme Court granted *certiorari*.

DECISION The judgment of the Court of Appeals is reversed, and the case is remanded for further proceedings.

OPINION Title VII of the Civil Rights Act of 1964 prohibits employment discrimination on the basis of race, color, religion, sex, or national origin. Title VII prohibits both intentional discrimination (disparate treatment) as well as practices that are not intended to discriminate but in fact have a disproportionately adverse effect on minorities (disparate impact). Disparate-treatment cases present "the most easily understood type of discrimination," and occur in cases in which an employer has "treated [a] particular person less favorably than others because of a protected trait."

The Civil Rights Act of 1964 did not include an express prohibition on policies or practices that produce a disparate impact. However, the Civil Rights Act of 1991 was enacted and included a provision codifying the prohibition on disparate-impact discrimination. Under the disparate-impact statute, a plaintiff establishes a *prima facie* violation by showing that an employer uses "a particular employment practice that causes a disparate impact on the basis of race, color, religion, sex, or national origin." An employer may defend against liability by demonstrating that the practice is "job related for the position in question and consistent with business necessity." Even if the employer meets that burden, however, a plaintiff may still succeed by showing that the employer refuses to adopt an available alternative employment practice that has less disparate impact and serves the employer's legitimate needs.

Previous Supreme Court decisions have held that certain government actions to remedy past racial discrimination—actions that are themselves based on race—are constitutional only in cases in which a "strong basis in evidence" indicates that the remedial actions were necessary. Applying this strong-basis-in-evidence standard to Title VII gives effect to both the disparate-treatment and disparate-impact provisions, allowing violations of one in the name of compliance with the other only in certain, narrow circumstances. Therefore, race-based action like the City's in this case is impermissible under Title VII unless the employer can demonstrate a strong basis in evidence that, had it not taken the action, it would have been liable under the disparate-impact statute.

Resolving the statutory conflict in this way allows the disparate-impact prohibition to work in a manner that is consistent with other provisions of Title VII, including the prohibition on adjusting employment-related test scores on the basis of race. Examinations like those administered by the City create legitimate expectations on the part of those who took the tests. As is the case with any promotion exam, some of the firefighters here invested substantial time, money, and personal commitment in preparing for the tests. Employment tests can be an important part of a neutral selection system that safeguards against the very racial animosities Title VII was intended to prevent. If an employer cannot rescore a test based on the candidates' race, then it follows *a fortiori* that it may not take the greater step of discarding the test altogether to achieve a more desirable racial distribution of promotion-eligible candidates—absent a strong basis in evidence that the test was deficient and that discarding the results is necessary to avoid violating the disparate impact provision. Thus, under Title VII, before an employer can engage in intentional discrimination for the asserted purpose of avoiding or remedying an unintentional disparate impact, the employer must have a strong basis in evidence to believe it will be subject to disparate-impact liability if it fails to take the race-conscious, discriminatory action.

On the basis of the degree of adverse impact reflected in the results, the City was compelled to take a hard look at the examinations to determine whether certifying the results would have had an impermissible disparate impact. The City could be liable for disparate-impact discrimination only (1) if the examinations were not job related and consistent with business necessity or (2) if there existed an equally valid, less-discriminatory alternative that served the City's needs but that the City refused to adopt. Here there is no strong basis in evidence to establish that the test was deficient in either of these respects.

INTERPRETATION Race-based disparate treatment is impermissible under Title VII unless the employer can demonstrate a strong basis in evidence that, had it not taken the action, it would have been liable under the disparate-impact statute.

ETHICAL QUESTION Did the City act unethically? Explain.

CRITICAL THINKING QUESTION Do you agree with the Supreme Court's decision? Explain.

Affirmative action

active recruitment of a designated group of applicants

Remedies Remedies for violation of the Act include enjoining the employer from engaging in the unlawful behavior, taking appropriate affirmative action, and reinstating employees to their rightful place (which may include promotion) and awarding them back pay from a date not more than two years prior to the filing of the charge with the EEOC. First promulgated by executive order, as discussed below, **affirmative action** generally means the active recruitment of minority applicants, although courts also have used the remedy to impose numerical hiring ratios (quotas) and hiring goals based on race and gender. The EEOC has defined affirmative action in employment as "actions appropriate to overcome the effects of past or present practices, policies, or other barriers to equal employment opportunity."

Prior to 1991, only victims of racial discrimination could recover compensatory and punitive damages from the courts. Today, however, under the Civil Rights Act of 1991, all victims of intentional discrimination based on race, gender, religion, national origin, or disability can recover compensatory and punitive damages, except in cases involving disparate impact. In cases not involving race, the Act limits the amount of recoverable damages according to the number of persons the defendant employs. Companies with 15 to 100 employees are required to pay no more than $50,000; companies with 101 to 200 employees, no more than $100,000; those with 201 to 500 employees, no more than $200,000; and those with 501 or more employees, no more than $300,000. Either party may demand a jury trial. Victims of racial discrimination are still entitled to recover unlimited compensatory and punitive damages.

Reverse discrimination

employment decisions taking into account race or gender to remedy past discrimination

Reverse Discrimination A major controversy has arisen over the use of **reverse discrimination** in achieving affirmative action. In this context, reverse discrimination refers to affirmative action that directs an employer to remedy the underrepresentation of a given race or gender in a traditionally segregated job by considering an individual's race or gender when hiring or promoting. An example would be an employer who discriminates against white males to increase the proportion of females or racial minority members in a company's workforce.

Due to the absence of state action, challenges to affirmative action plans adopted by private employers—those that are not government units at the local, state, or federal level—are tested under Title VII of the Civil Rights Act of 1964, not under the Equal Protection Clause of the U.S. Constitution. The U.S. Supreme Court has upheld an employer's right under Title VII to promote a female employee rather than a white male employee who had scored higher on a qualifying examination.

When a state or local government adopts an affirmative action plan that is challenged as constituting illegal reverse discrimination, the plan is subject to strict scrutiny under the *Equal Protection Clause* of the Fourteenth Amendment. Under the strict scrutiny test, the subject classification must (1) be justified by a compelling governmental interest and (2) be the least intrusive means available. (For a fuller discussion of the Equal Protection Clause and the standards of review, see Chapter 4.)

Practical Advice

In attempting to promote equal opportunity, respect the rights of nonminority applicants and employees.

With regard to racial discrimination, the U.S. Supreme Court has ruled that the federal government has "unique remedial powers" far exceeding those of state and local governments and that federal programs enacted to address such discrimination "are subject to a different [and less burdensome] standard than such classifications prescribed by state and local governments." However, the U.S. Supreme Court has placed significant constraints upon the federal government's ability to create programs favoring minority-owned businesses over white-owned businesses and appeared to apply the same strict standard to federal programs as to those required of state and local governments. Following this decision, the EEOC issued a statement which provided that "affirmative action is lawful only when it is designed to respond to a demonstrated and serious imbalance in the workforce, is flexible, time-limited, applies only to qualified workers, and respects the rights of non-minorities and men."

Sexual Harassment   The EEOC has defined **sexual harassment** as follows:

Sexual harassment

is an illegal form of sexual discrimination that includes unwelcome sexual advances, requests for sexual favors, and other verbal or physical conduct of a sexual nature

Unwelcome sexual advances, requests for sexual favors, and other verbal or physical conduct of a sexual nature constitute sexual harassment when

1. submission to such conduct is made either explicitly or implicitly a term or condition of an individual's employment,
2. submission to or rejection of such conduct by an individual is used as the basis for employment decisions affecting such individual, or
3. such conduct has the purpose or effect of reasonably interfering with an individual's work performance or creating an intimidating, hostile or offensive working environment.

Practical Advice

Issue a strong company policy against sexual harassment and thoroughly investigate any charge of a violation of such policy.

The courts, including the Supreme Court, have held that sexual harassment may constitute illegal sexual discrimination in violation of Title VII. Moreover, an employer will be held liable for sexual harassment committed by one of its employees if it does not take immediate action when it knows or should have known of the harassment. When the employee engaging in sexual harassment is an agent of the employer or holds a supervisory position over the victim, the employer may be liable without knowledge or reason to know.

The U.S. Supreme Court has also concluded that sex discrimination consisting of same-sex harassment is actionable under Title VII.

 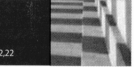

Faragher v. City of Boca Raton
Supreme Court of the United States, 1998
524 U.S. 775, 118 S.Ct. 2275, 141 L.Ed.2d 662
http://scholar.google.com/scholar_case?case=15103611360542350644&q=524+U.S.+775&hl=en&as_sdt=2,22

FACTS Between 1985 and 1990, while attending college, petitioner Beth Ann Faragher worked as an ocean lifeguard for the Marine Safety Section of the Parks and Recreation Department of the City of Boca Raton, Florida (City). During this period, Faragher's immediate supervisors were Bill Terry, David Silverman, and Robert Gordon. In June 1990, Faragher resigned.

In 1986, the City had adopted a sexual harassment policy. Although the City actually may have circulated the memo and statement to some employees, it failed to disseminate its policy among employees of the Marine Safety Section, with the result that Terry, Silverman, Gordon, and many lifeguards were unaware of it. From time to time over the course of Faragher's tenure at the Marine Safety Section, between four and six of the forty to fifty lifeguards were women. During that five-year period, Terry repeatedly touched the bodies of female employees without invitation and made crudely demeaning references to women and once commented disparagingly on Faragher's shape. During a job interview with a woman he hired as a lifeguard, Terry said that the female lifeguards had sex with their male counterparts and asked whether she would do the same.

Silverman behaved in similar ways. He once tackled Faragher and remarked that, but for a physical characteristic he found unattractive, he would readily have had sexual relations with her. Another time, he pantomimed an act of oral sex. Within earshot of the female lifeguards, Silverman made frequent, vulgar references to women and sexual matters, commented on the bodies of female lifeguards and beachgoers, and at least twice told female lifeguards that he would like to engage in sex with them.

Faragher did not complain to higher management about Terry or Silverman. Although she spoke of their behavior to Gordon, she did not regard these discussions as formal complaints to a supervisor but as conversations with a person she held in high esteem. Other female lifeguards had similarly informal talks with Gordon, but because Gordon did not feel that it was his place to do so, he did not report these complaints to Terry, his own supervisor, or to any other city official. In April 1990, however, two months before Faragher's resignation, Nancy Ewanchew, a former lifeguard, wrote to Richard Bender, the city's personnel director, complaining that Terry and Silverman had harassed her and other female lifeguards. The City found that Terry and Silverman had behaved improperly, reprimanded them, and required them to choose between a suspension without pay or the forfeiture of annual leave. On the basis of these findings, the district court concluded that the conduct of Terry and Silverman was discriminatory harassment sufficiently serious to alter the conditions of Faragher's employment and constitute an abusive working environment. The district court then ruled that there were three justifications for holding the City liable. First, the harassment was pervasive enough to support an inference that the City had "knowledge, or constructive knowledge" of it. Next, the City was liable under traditional agency principles because Terry and Silverman were acting as its agents. Finally, Gordon's knowledge of the harassment, combined with his inaction, "provides a further basis for imputing liability on the City." The Court of Appeals had "no trouble concluding that Terry's and Silverman's conduct ... was severe and pervasive enough to create an objectively abusive work environment," but it overturned the district court's conclusion that the City was liable.

DECISION The judgment of the Court of Appeals is reversed, and the case is remanded for reinstatement of the judgment of the district court.

OPINION Sexual harassment so "severe or pervasive" as to alter the conditions of the victim's employment and create an abusive working environment violates Title VII. To be actionable under the statute, a sexually objectionable environment must be both objectively and subjectively offensive, one that a reasonable person would find hostile or abusive, and one that the victim in fact did perceive to be so. To determine whether an environment is sufficiently hostile or abusive, a court must look at all the circumstances, including the "frequency of the discriminatory conduct; its severity; whether it is physically threatening or humiliating, or a mere offensive utterance; and whether it unreasonably interferes with an employee's work performance." Title VII does not prohibit "genuine but innocuous differences in the ways men and women routinely interact with members of the same sex and of the opposite sex"; simple teasing, offhand comments, and isolated

incidents (unless extremely serious) will not amount to discriminatory changes in the "terms and conditions of employment."

In implementing Title VII, it makes sense to hold an employer vicariously liable for some tortious conduct of a supervisor made possible by abuse of his supervisory authority. An employer is subject to vicarious liability to a victimized employee for an actionable hostile environment created by a supervisor with immediate (or successively higher) authority over the employee. When no tangible employment action is taken, a defending employer may raise an affirmative defense to liability or damages, subject to proof by a preponderance of the evidence. The defense includes two necessary elements: (1) that the employer exercised reasonable care to prevent and correct promptly any sexually harassing behavior and (2) that the plaintiff employee unreasonably failed to take advantage of any preventive or corrective opportunities provided by the employer or to avoid harm otherwise. No affirmative defense is available, however, when the supervisor's harassment culminates in a tangible employment action, such as discharge, demotion, or undesirable reassignment.

Applying these rules here, the judgment of the Court of Appeals must be reversed. The district court found that the degree of hostility in the work environment rose to the actionable level and was attributable to Silverman and Terry. It is undisputed that these supervisors "were granted virtually unchecked authority" over their subordinates, "directly controll[ing] and supervis[ing] all aspects of [Faragher's] day-to-day activities." It is also clear that Faragher and her colleagues were "completely isolated from the City's higher management."

INTERPRETATION Employers may become liable for the sexual harassment committed by their agents despite lack of knowledge.

ETHICAL QUESTION Should Faragher be allowed to prevail against the City when she had made no formal complaint? Explain.

CRITICAL THINKING QUESTION Do you agree with the court's decision? Explain.

Comparable Worth Industrial statistics on salaries indicate that women earn significantly less money than men do. Because the Equal Pay Act only requires equal pay for equal work, it does not apply to different jobs even if they are comparable. Thus, that statute provides no remedy for women who have been systematically undervalued and underpaid in "traditional" occupations, such as secretary, teacher, or nurse. As a result, women have sought redress under Title VII by arguing that the failure to pay comparable worth is discrimination on the basis of gender. The concept of **comparable worth** provides that employers should measure the relative values of different jobs through a job evaluation rating system that is free of any potential gender bias. Theoretically, the consistent application of objective criteria (including factors such as skill, effort, working conditions, responsibility, and mental demands) across job categories will ensure fair payment for all employees. For example, if evaluation under such a system found the jobs of truck driver and nurse to be at the same level, workers in both jobs would receive the same pay.

Comparable worth
equal pay for jobs of equal value to the employer

The Supreme Court has ruled that a claim of discriminatory undercompensation based on sex could be brought under Title VII, even when female plaintiffs were performing jobs different than those of their male counterparts. As the Court noted, however, the case involved a situation in which the defendant intentionally discriminated in wages; and the defendant, not the courts, had compared the jobs in terms of value. The Court also held that the four defenses available under the Equal Pay Act would apply to a Title VII claim. Since this decision, the concept of comparable worth has met with limited success in the courts. Nonetheless, more than a dozen states have adopted legislation requiring public and private employers to pay equally for comparable work.

Executive Order [41-2c]

Executive order

prohibits discrimination by federal contractors on the basis of race, color, gender, religion, or national origin on any work the contractors perform during the period of the federal contract

In 1965, President Johnson issued an **executive order** that prohibits discrimination by federal contractors on the basis of race, color, gender, religion, or national origin in employment on *any work* the contractor performs during the period of the federal contract. Federal contractors are also required to take affirmative action in recruiting. The secretary of labor, Office of Federal Contract Compliance Programs (OFCCP), administers enforcement of the program.

The program applies to all contractors and all of their subcontractors in excess of $10,000 who enter into a federal contract to be performed in the United States. Compliance with the affirmative action requirement differs for construction and nonconstruction contractors. All *nonconstruction* contractors with fifty or more employees or with contracts for more than $50,000 must have a written affirmative action plan to be in compliance. The plan must include a workforce analysis; planned corrective action, if necessary, with specific goals and timetables; and procedures for auditing and reporting. The director of the OFCCP periodically issues goals and timetables for each segment of the construction industry in each region of the country. As a condition precedent to bidding on a federal contract, a contractor must agree to make a good faith effort to achieve current published goals.

Age Discrimination in Employment Act [41-2d]

Age Discrimination in Employment Act (ADEA)

prohibits discrimination on the basis of age in hiring, firing, or compensating

The **Age Discrimination in Employment Act (ADEA)** prohibits discrimination on the basis of age in employment areas that include hiring, firing, and compensating. The Act applies to private employers having twenty or more employees and to all government units, regardless of size. The Act also prohibits mandatory retirement for most employees, no matter what their age, unless the retirement is justified by a suitable defense. In 2004 the U.S. Supreme Court held that the ADEA does not prevent an employer from favoring an older employee over a younger employee.

In 2009, the U.S. Supreme Court held that the ADEA's text does not authorize an alleged mixed-motives age discrimination claim that would result in a shifting burden-of-proof standard as previously discussed. Accordingly,

> a plaintiff bringing a disparate-treatment claim pursuant to the ADEA must prove, by a preponderance of the evidence, that age was the 'but-for' cause of the challenged adverse employment action. The burden of persuasion does not shift to the employer to show that it would have taken the action regardless of age, even when a plaintiff has produced some evidence that age was one motivating factor in that decision. *Gross v. FBL Financial Services, Inc.*, 557 U.S. 167, 129 S.Ct. 2343, 174 L.Ed.2d 119.

The major statutory defenses include (1) a BFOQ; (2) a *bona fide* seniority system; and (3) any other reasonable action, including the voluntary retirement of an individual. Remedies include back pay, injunctive relief, affirmative action, and liquidated damages equal to the amount of the award for "willful" violations. Furthermore, an ADEA claimant is entitled to a jury trial.

Disability Law [41-2e]

Disability law

several federal acts, including the Americans with Disabilities Act, provide assistance to the disabled in obtaining rehabilitation training, access to public facilities, and employment

The *Rehabilitation Act* attempts to assist the handicapped in obtaining rehabilitation training, access to public facilities, and employment. The Act requires federal contractors and federal agencies to take affirmative action to hire qualified handicapped persons. It also prohibits discrimination on the basis of handicap in federal programs and programs receiving federal financial assistance.

A *handicapped person* is defined as an individual who (1) has a physical or mental impairment that substantially affects one or more of her major life activities, (2) has a history of major life activity impairment, or (3) is regarded as having such an impairment. Major life activities include functions such as caring for oneself, seeing, speaking, or walking. Alcohol and drug abuses are not considered handicapping conditions for the purposes of this statute.

The *ADA* forbids an employer from discriminating against any person with a disability with regard to "hiring or discharge … employee compensation, advancement, job training and other terms, conditions and privileges of employment." In addition, businesses must make special accommodations, such as installing wheelchair-accessible bathrooms, for workers and customers with disabilities unless the cost is unduly burdensome. An employer may use qualification standards, tests, or selection criteria that screen out workers with disabilities if these measures are job related and consistent with business necessity and if no reasonable accommodation is possible. Remedies for violation of the ADA are those generally allowed under Title VII and include injunctive relief, reinstatement, back pay, and, for intentional discrimination, compensatory and punitive damages (capped according to company size by the Civil Rights Act of 1991).

On September 25, 2008, President George W. Bush signed into law the ADA Amendments Act of 2008 (ADAAA). This gave broader protections for disabled workers and "turn[ed] back the clock" on court rulings which Congress deemed too restrictive. The ADAAA includes a list of *major life activities*, including "caring for oneself, performing manual tasks, seeing, hearing, eating, sleeping, walking, standing, lifting, bending, speaking, breathing, learning, reading, concentrating, thinking, communicating, and working" as well as the operation of several specified "major bodily functions." The ADAAA overturned a 1999 U.S. Supreme Court case that held that an employee was not disabled if the impairment could be corrected by mitigating measures; the ADAAA specifically provides that such impairment must be determined without considering such ameliorative measures. Another judicially imposed restriction overturned by the ADAAA is the interpretation that an impairment that substantially limits one major life activity must also limit others to be considered a disability.

In addition, the ***Vietnam Veterans Readjustment Act*** requires firms having $10,000 or more in federal contracts to engage in affirmative action for disabled veterans and Vietnam-era veterans.

Practical Advice

Make reasonable accommodation for individuals with disabilities.

 Toyota Motor Manufacturing, Kentucky, Inc. v. Williams
Supreme Court of the United States, 2002
534 U.S. 184, 122 S.Ct. 681, 151 L.Ed.2d 615
http://scholar.google.com/scholar_case?case=3382304874478067867&q=122+S.Ct.+681&hl=en&as_sdt=40000006

FACTS Ella Williams began working at Toyota's automobile manufacturing plant in Georgetown, Kentucky, in August 1990. She was soon placed on an engine fabrication assembly line, where her duties included work with pneumatic tools. Use of these tools eventually caused pain in her hands, wrists, and arms. She sought treatment at Toyota's in-house medical service, where she was diagnosed with bilateral carpal tunnel syndrome and bilateral tendinitis. Williams consulted a personal physician who placed her on permanent work restrictions that precluded her from lifting more than twenty pounds or from "frequently lifting or carrying of objects weighing up to ten pounds," engaging in "constant repetitive … flexion or extension of [her] wrists or elbows," performing "overhead work," or using "vibratory or pneumatic tools."

In light of these restrictions, for the next two years Toyota assigned Williams to various modified duty jobs. Nonetheless,

Williams missed some work for medical leave, and eventually filed a claim under the Kentucky Workers' Compensation Act. The parties settled this claim, and Williams returned to work. She was unsatisfied by Toyota's efforts to accommodate her work restrictions, however, and responded by bringing an action in the U.S. District Court alleging that Toyota had violated the Americans with Disabilities Act (ADA) by refusing to accommodate her disability. That suit was also settled, and as part of the settlement, Williams returned to work in December 1993.

Upon her return, Toyota placed Williams on a team in Quality Control Inspection Operations (QCIO). In this position, she visually inspected painted cars moving slowly down a conveyor. When Williams began working in QCIO, inspection team members were required to open and shut the doors, trunk, and hood of each passing car. Sometime during Williams's tenure, however, the position was modified to include only visual inspection with few or no manual tasks. This position also required team members to use their hands to wipe each painted car with a glove as it moved along a conveyor. The parties agree that Williams was physically capable of performing both of these jobs and that her performance was satisfactory.

During the fall of 1996, Toyota announced that it wanted QCIO employees to be able to rotate through all four of the QCIO processes. (Williams had previously been on a team that did only two of the processes.) In part of the expanded job responsibilities, Williams was to apply a highlight oil to the hood, fender, doors, rear quarter panel, and trunk of passing cars at a rate of approximately one car per minute. Wiping the cars required Williams to hold her hands and arms up around shoulder height for several hours at a time.

A short while later, Williams began to experience pain in her neck and shoulders, and she again sought care at Toyota's in-house medical service, where she was diagnosed with an inflammation of the muscles and tendons around both of her shoulder blades and a condition that causes pain in the nerves that lead to the upper extremities. Williams requested that Toyota accommodate her medical conditions by allowing her to return to doing only her original two jobs in QCIO, which Williams claimed she could still perform without difficulty.

The parties disagree about what happened next. According to Williams, Toyota refused her request and forced her to continue working in the shell body audit job, which caused her even greater physical injury. According to Toyota, Williams simply began missing work on a regular basis. Regardless, it is clear that on December 6, 1996, the last day Williams worked at Toyota's plant, she was placed under a no-work-of-any-kind restriction by her treating physicians. On January 27, 1997, Williams received a letter from Toyota that terminated her employment, citing her poor attendance record.

Williams, claiming to be disabled because of her carpal tunnel syndrome and other related impairments, sued Toyota for failing to provide her with a reasonable accommodation as required by the ADA. The district court granted summary judgment to Toyota, finding that Williams's impairments did not substantially limit any of her major life activities. The Court of Appeals reversed.

DECISION The Court of Appeals' judgment granting partial summary judgment to Williams is reversed, and the case remanded for further proceedings.

OPINION Williams based her claim that she was "disabled" under the ADA on the ground that her physical impairments substantially limited her in (1) manual tasks; (2) housework; (3) gardening; (4) playing with her children; (5) lifting; and (6) working, all of which, she argued, constituted major life activities under the Act. Williams also argued, in the alternative, that she was disabled under the ADA because she had a record of a substantially limiting impairment and because she was regarded as having such an impairment.

Under the ADA, a physical impairment that "substantially limits one or more … major life activities" is a "disability." The question before this court is whether or not Williams's impairment substantially limits her major life activities and whether or not the Court of Appeals used the proper standard in making this determination.

"Substantially" in the phrase "substantially limits" suggests "considerable" or "to a large degree." The word "substantial" thus clearly precludes impairments that interfere in only a minor way with the performance of manual tasks from qualifying as disabilities.

"Major" in the phrase "major life activities" means important. "Major life activities" thus refers to those activities that are of central importance to daily life. For performing manual tasks to fit into this category—a category that includes such basic abilities as walking, seeing, and hearing—the manual tasks in question must be central to daily life.

The district court noted that at the time Williams sought an accommodation from Toyota, she admitted that she was able to do the manual tasks required by her original two jobs in QCIO. In addition, according to Williams's deposition testimony, even after her condition worsened, she could still brush her teeth, wash her face, bathe, tend her flower garden, fix breakfast, do laundry, and pick up around the house.

While the Court of Appeals in this case addressed the different major life activities of performing manual tasks, its analysis focused on Williams's inability to perform manual tasks associated only with her job. This was error. When addressing the major life activity of performing manual tasks, the central inquiry must be whether the claimant is unable to perform the variety of tasks central to most people's daily lives, not whether the claimant is unable to perform the tasks associated with her specific job. The Court held that to be substantially limited in performing manual tasks, an individual must have an impairment that prevents or severely restricts the individual from doing activities that are of central importance to most people's daily lives. The impairment's impact must also be permanent or long term.

The Supreme Court concluded that the Court of Appeals did not apply the proper standard in making its determination because it analyzed only a limited class of manual tasks and failed to ask whether Williams's impairments prevented or restricted her from performing tasks that are of central importance to most people's daily lives. The Court held that on this record, it was inappropriate for the Court of Appeals to grant partial summary judgment to Williams on the issue of whether she was substantially limited in performing manual tasks, and its decision to do so was reversed.

INTERPRETATION To be substantially limited in performing manual tasks, an individual must have an impairment that prevents or severely restricts the individual from doing activities that are of central importance to most people's daily lives. The impairment's impact must also be permanent or long term.

ETHICAL QUESTION Was the company ethical in its refusal to accommodate Williams? Explain.

CRITICAL THINKING QUESTION Should the specific tasks of the job be considered in determining disability?

BUSINESS LAW **IN ACTION**

Whitney & Whitney is a large American consulting service with both domestic and European clients. As such, the firm has offices in several U.S. cities and branches in both London and Prague. In the British and Czech Republic locations, Whitney & Whitney employs a number of U.S. citizens as well as foreign nationals. As a result, managers in the two European offices must comply with both local and U.S. employment discrimination laws. This is because Title VII of the Civil Rights Act, the Age Discrimination in Employment Act (ADEA), and the Americans with Disabilities Act (ADA) protect American citizens working for U.S.-controlled entities abroad, unless a foreign law mandates discriminatory conduct by the employer.

Only U.S. citizens working overseas are protected by U.S. discrimination laws. Foreign nationals working for Whitney & Whitney cannot take advantage of Title VII, the ADEA, or the ADA, but instead will have to look to British, Czech, or even European Union (EU) law if they have complaints about the firm's employment practices. Whitney & Whitney managers, thus, must comply with local antidiscrimination laws when dealing with their foreign employees or employment applicants and U.S. laws when dealing with U.S. employees or employment applicants.

Nonetheless, if a law of the United Kingdom or Czech Republic, or an EU directive requires Whitney & Whitney to treat all employees in a way that would violate Title VII, the ADEA, or the ADA, the firm will have to follow that foreign law. This is because U.S. law cannot be extended abroad in such a way that compels U.S.-controlled employers to comply with mutually inconsistent laws. So, for example, if a Czech labor regulation were to require exclusion of women from certain jobs posts, Whitney & Whitney would be required to follow this regulation in its Prague office, even though this same conduct would violate the rights of its female U.S. employees if they were working for the firm on American soil.

Genetic Information Discrimination [41-2f]

Genetic Information Nondiscrimination Act

forbids discrimination on the basis of genetic information with respect to any aspect of employment

The **Genetic Information Nondiscrimination Act** of 2008 (GINA) forbids discrimination on the basis of genetic information with respect to any aspect of employment, including hiring, firing, pay, job assignments, promotions, layoffs, training, fringe benefits, or any other term or condition of employment. The Act explicitly states that disparate impact on the basis of genetic information does not establish a cause of action. Under GINA, it is also illegal to (1) harass a person because of his or her genetic information and (2) retaliate against an applicant or employee because the person complained about discrimination, filed a charge of genetic discrimination, or participated in an employment discrimination investigation or lawsuit. Genetic information includes information about an individual's genetic tests and the genetic tests of an individual's family members, as well as information about any disease, disorder, or condition of an individual's family members (i.e., an individual's family medical history). Remedies for violation of GINA are those generally allowed under Title VII and include injunctive relief, reinstatement, back pay, and, for intentional discrimination, compensatory and punitive damages (capped according to company size by the Civil Rights Act of 1991). The EEOC enforces the GINA's provisions dealing with genetic discrimination in employment.

See Figure 41-1 for the number of charges filed with the EEOC in 2007–2013.

Figure 41-1 Charges Filed with the EEOC in 2007–2013

Category	Number of Charges						
	2007	2008	2009	2010	2011	2012	2013
Race	30,510	33,937	33,579	35,890	35,395	33,512	33,068
Sex	24,826	28,372	28,028	29,029	28,534	30,356	27,687
National Origin	9,396	10,601	11,134	11,304	11,833	10,883	10,642
Religion	2,880	3,273	3,386	3,790	4,151	3,811	3,721
Retaliation	26,663	32,960	33,613	36,258	37,334	31,208	31,478
Age	19,103	24,582	22,778	23,264	23,465	22,857	21,396
Disability	17,734	19,453	21,451	25,165	25,742	26,379	25,957
Equal Pay Act	818	954	942	1,044	919	1,082	1,019
Genetic Information				201	245	280	333

Source: EEOC, http://www.eeoc.gov/eeoc/statistics/enforcement/charges.cfm.

GOING GLOBAL

Do the antidiscrimination laws apply outside the United States?

Title VII of the Civil Rights Act of 1964, the Americans with Disabilities Act, and the Age Discrimination in Employment Act apply to U.S. citizens employed abroad by U.S. employers or by foreign companies controlled by U.S. employers. Employers, however, are not required to comply with these employment discrimination laws if compliance would violate the law of the foreign country in which the workplace is located.

CONCEPT REVIEW 41-2

Federal Employment Discrimination Laws

	Protected Characteristics	Prohibited Conduct	Defenses	Remedies
Equal Pay Act	Gender	Wages	Seniority Merit Quality or quantity measures Any factor other than sex	Back pay Injunction Liquidated damages Attorneys' fees
Title VII of Civil Rights Act	Race Color Gender Religion National origin	Terms, conditions, or privileges of employment	Seniority Ability test BFOQ (except for race) Business necessity (disparate impact only)	Back pay Injunction Reinstatement Compensatory and punitive damages for intentional discrimination • unlimited for race • limited for all others Attorney's fees
Age Discrimination in Employment Act	Age	Terms, conditions, or privileges of employment	Seniority BFOQ Any other reasonable Act	Back pay Injunction Reinstatement Liquidated damages for willful violation Attorneys' fees
Americans with Disabilities Act	Disability	Terms, conditions, or privileges of employment	Undue hardship Job-related criteria and business necessity Risk to public health and safety	Back pay Injunction Reinstatement Compensatory and punitive damages for intentional discrimination (limited) Attorneys' fees
Genetic Information Nondiscrimination Act	Genetic information	Terms, conditions, or privileges of employment	None	Back pay Injunction Reinstatement Compensatory and punitive damages for intentional discrimination (limited) Attorneys' fees

Note: BFOQ = *bona fide* occupational qualification.

EMPLOYEE PROTECTION [41-3]

Employees are accorded a number of job-related protections. These include a limited right not to be unfairly dismissed, a right to a safe and healthy workplace, compensation for injuries sustained in the workplace, and some financial security upon retirement or loss of employment. This section discusses (1) employee termination at will, (2) occupational safety and health, (3) employee privacy, (4) workers' compensation, (5) Social Security and unemployment insurance, (6) the Fair Labor Standards Act (FLSA), (7) employee notice of termination or layoff, and (8) family and health leave.

Employee Termination at Will [41-3a]

Employee termination at will
under the common law, a contract of employment for other than a definite term is terminable at will by either party

Under the common law, a contract of employment is terminable at will by either party unless the employment is for a definite term or the employee is represented by a labor union. Accordingly, under the common law, employers may "dismiss their employees at will for good cause, for no cause or even for cause morally wrong, without being thereby guilty of legal wrong." In recent years, however, a growing number of judicial exceptions to the rule, based on implied contract, tort, and public policy, have developed. A number of federal and state statutes enacted in the last sixty years also limit the rule, which may in addition be restricted by contractual agreement between employer and employee. In particular, most collective bargaining agreements negotiated through union representatives contain a provision prohibiting dismissal "without cause."

Statutory limitations
have been enacted by the federal government and some states

Statutory Limitations Federal legislation has been passed that limits the employer's right to discharge. These statutes fall into three categories: (1) those protecting certain employees from discriminatory discharge, (2) those protecting certain employees in their exercise of statutory rights, and (3) those protecting certain employees from discharge without cause.

At the state level, statutes protect workers from discriminatory discharge for filing workers' compensation claims. Also, many state statutes parallel federal legislation. Some states have adopted statutes similar to the NLRA, and many states prohibit discrimination in employment on the basis of factors such as race, creed, nationality, gender, or age. In addition, some states have statutes prohibiting discharge or other punitive actions taken for the purpose of influencing voting or, in some states, political activity.

Judicial limitations
based on contract law, tort law, or public policy

Judicial Limitations Judicial limitations on the employment-at-will doctrine have been based on contract law, tort law, and public policy. Cases founded in contract theory have relied on arguments maintaining, among other things, (1) that the dismissal was improper because the employee had detrimentally relied on the employer's promise of work for a reasonable time; (2) that the employment was not at will because of implied-in-fact promises of employment for a specific duration, which meant that the employer could not terminate the employee without just cause; (3) that the employment contract implied or expressly provided that the employee would not be dismissed so long as he satisfactorily performed his work; (4) that the employer had assured the employee that he would not be dismissed except for cause; or (5) that, upon entering into the employment contract, the employee gave consideration over and above the performance of services to support a promise of job security.

Courts have also created exceptions to the employment-at-will doctrine by imposing tort obligations on employers, most particularly with respect to the torts of intentional infliction of emotional distress and of interference with employment relations.

A majority of states now consider a discharge as wrongful if it violates a statutory or other established public policy. In general, this public-policy exception renders a discharge wrongful if it involves a dismissal for (1) refusing to violate a statute, (2) exercising a statutory right, (3) performing a statutory obligation, or (4) reporting an alleged violation of a statute that is of public interest ("whistle-blowing").

Jasper v. H. Nizam, Inc.
Supreme Court of Iowa, 2009
761 N.W.2d 751
http://scholar.google.com/scholar_case?case=2832611353601787809&hl=en&as_sdt=2&as_vis=1 &oi=scholarr

FACTS Kimberly Jasper was terminated from her employment at Kid University as the director of a child care facility in Johnston, Iowa. The center was owned by H. Nizam, Inc. Mohsin Hussain was the president of the corporation. Zakia Hussain, Mohsin's wife, was the vice president. Mohsin Hussain was a special education teacher for the Des Moines School District and was not involved in the day-to-day operation of the center. Jasper began her employment as director of the center in late August 2003. She was paid an hourly wage. There was no specific term of employment. A few weeks after Jasper started her employment, she and her husband agreed to rent a home owned by the Hussains. The house had four bedrooms and two bathrooms, but it had sustained substantial water damage and was in a general state of disrepair. The agreed monthly rent was $10.00, plus utilities, and the Jaspers were required to make all repairs to the house at their own expense.

Within a short time after Jasper started her employment, Hussain told her the center was not making enough money to justify the size of the staff. He also encouraged Jasper to attract more children to the center. Jasper responded by telling Hussain that any staff cuts would place the center in jeopardy of violating state regulations governing the minimum ratios between staff and children. Hussain was aware of the staffing requirements imposed by state regulations. The staff-to-child ratio became a frequent subject of conversation, and friction, between Hussain and Jasper. During one meeting with the Hussains and Jasper in early November, staff reductions were again discussed. Jasper claimed Zakia Hussain said, "What [the department of human services consultant] doesn't know won't hurt her." At a meeting between Hussain and Jasper later in November, Hussain proposed that Jasper and her assistant director begin to work as staff in the classrooms occupied by the children as a means to cut staff and reduce expenses. Jasper objected to the plan as unreasonable. She believed it would prevent her from performing her duties as director of the center and risk placing the center in violation of the ratio regulations. On December 1, 2003, Hussain terminated Jasper from her employment with Kid University. She was handed a written letter listing the reasons for the termination and was escorted outside the building. A confrontation followed after she was told she could not return to the building to remove her children from the day-care center, and police were called. Hussain also brought a forcible entry and detainer action against the Jaspers for failing to pay the December rent. Jasper and her family subsequently moved from the house, and she obtained new employment with another child care facility in April 2004.

Jasper brought a wrongful discharge action against the corporation and Hussain individually. She claimed Hussain terminated her employment because she refused to violate the staff-to-child ratios, in violation of public policy of Iowa. At trial, Jasper presented testimony that the center violated the staff-to-child ratios shortly after she was terminated. This violation occurred when one staff member was left in a classroom to supervise five or more children between the ages of one and two years old. The jury returned a verdict for Jasper, based on the tort of wrongful discharge in violation of public policy. The jury awarded Jasper lost wages of $26,915 and past pain and suffering of $100,000. It awarded her $39,507.25 for expenses relating to the house and additional services and expenses. The court of appeals affirmed the judgment but found the award of damages to be excessive.

DECISION Judgment affirmed in part and reversed in part.

OPINION Iowa follows the common-law employment-at-will doctrine but with the public-policy exception that there is a cause of action for wrongful discharge from employment when the reasons for the discharge contravene public policy. The elements of this action are (1) existence of a clearly defined public policy that protects employee activity; (2) the public policy would be jeopardized by the discharge from employment; (3) the employee engaged in the protected activity, and this conduct was the reason for the employee's discharge; and (4) there was no overriding business justification for the termination.

Wrongful discharge in violation of public policy can generally be aligned into four categories of statutorily protected activities: (1) exercising a statutory right or privilege, (2) refusing to commit an unlawful act, (3) performing a statutory obligation, and (4) reporting a statutory violation. The use of statutes as a source of public policy helps provide the essential notice to employers and employees of conduct that can lead to dismissal, as well as conduct that can lead to tort liability. The public-policy exception was adopted to place a limitation on an employer's discretion to discharge an employee when the public policy is so clear and well defined that it should be understood and accepted in our society as a benchmark.

Administrative regulations also may be used as a source of public policy to support the tort of wrongful discharge. In this case, the legislature clearly delegated authority to the department of human services to promulgate specific rules concerning the proper staff-to-child ratios as a means "to assure the health, safety, and welfare of children" in child care facilities. Without question, the protection of children is a matter of fundamental public interest. The particular administrative rule at issue in this case supports a clear and well-defined public policy that gives rise to the tort of wrongful discharge. The ratios were implemented at the specific direction of the legislature to protect the health, safety, and welfare of those children in Iowa who attend day care facilities. Additionally, the legislature intended for the ratios to be an important component of the larger public policy to protect children and, in turn, established a basic, important component of the operation of a day care center in Iowa. Staffing a child care facility below the minimum requirements established by an administrative rule is not a legitimate business concern.

INTERPRETATION Wrongful discharge exists when an employer's termination of an employee violates public policy as evidenced in the Constitution, in legislation, in an administrative regulation, or in a judicial decision.

CRITICAL THINKING QUESTION Do you agree with the principle of termination at will? Explain.

Occupational Safety and Health Act [41-3b]

Occupational Safety and Health Act

enacted to ensure workers a safe and healthful work environment

Congress enacted the **Occupational Safety and Health Act** to ensure, as far as possible, a safe and healthful working environment for every worker. The Act established the *Occupational Safety and Health Administration (OSHA)* to develop standards, conduct inspections, monitor compliance, and institute enforcement actions against those who are not in compliance.

Upon each employer who is engaged in a business affecting interstate commerce, the Act imposes a general duty to provide a work environment that is "free from recognized hazards that are causing or likely to cause death or serious physical harm to his employees." In addition to this general duty, the employer must comply with specific OSHA-promulgated safety rules. The Act also requires employees to comply with all OSHA rules and regulations. Finally, the Act prohibits any employer from discharging or discriminating against an employee who exercises her rights under the Act.

Enforcing the Act generally involves OSHA inspections and citations of employers, as appropriate, for (1) breach of the general duty obligation, (2) breach of specific safety and health standards, or (3) failure to keep records, make reports, or post notices required by the Act.

When a violation is discovered, the offending employer receives a written citation, a proposed penalty, and a date by which the employer must remedy the breach. Citations may be contested; in such cases, the Occupational Safety and Health Review Commission assigns administrative law judges to hold hearings. The commission, at its discretion, may grant review of an administrative law judge's decision; review is not a matter of right. If no such review occurs, the judge's decision becomes the commission's final order thirty days after receipt, and the aggrieved party may then appeal the order to the appropriate U.S. Circuit Court of Appeals.

Penalties for violations are both civil and criminal. In cases involving civil penalties, serious violations require that a penalty be proposed; in contrast, for nonserious violations, penalties are discretionary and rarely proposed. The Act further empowers the secretary of labor to obtain temporary restraining orders in situations in which regular OSHA procedures are insufficient to halt imminently hazardous or deadly business operations.

Practical Advice

Ensure your workers a safe and healthy work environment.

One stated purpose of the Act is to encourage state participation in regulating safety and health. The Act therefore permits a state to regulate the safety and health of the work environment within its borders, provided that OSHA approves the plan. The Act sets minimum acceptable standards for the states to impose but does not require that a state plan be identical to the OSHA guidelines. More than half of the states regulate health and safety in the workplace through state-promulgated plans.

Employee Privacy [41-3c]

Over the past two decades, employee privacy has become a major issue. The fundamental right to privacy is a product of common law protection, discussed in Chapter 7. Thus, the tort of invasion of privacy safeguards employees from unwanted searches, electronic monitoring and other forms of surveillance, and disclosure of confidential records. The tort actually consists of four different torts: (1) unreasonable intrusion into the seclusion of another, (2) unreasonable public disclosure of private facts, (3) unreasonable publicity that places another in a false light, and (4) appropriation of a person's name or likeness. In addition, the federal government and some states have legislatively supplemented the common law in certain areas.

Drug and alcohol tests

some states either prohibit such tests or prescribe certain scientific and procedural safeguards

Drug and Alcohol Testing
Although no federal legislation deals comprehensively with **drug and alcohol tests**, legislation in a number of states either prohibits such tests altogether or prescribes certain scientific and procedural standards for conducting them. In the absence of a state statute, *private* sector employees have little or no protection from such tests. The NLRB has held, however, that drug and alcohol testing in a union setting is a mandatory subject of collective bargaining.

The U.S. Supreme Court has ruled that the employer of a *public* sector employee whose position involved public health or safety or national security could subject the employee to a drug or alcohol test without either first obtaining a search warrant or having reasonable grounds to believe the individual had engaged in any wrongdoing. Based on Supreme Court and lower court decisions, it appears that a government employer may use (1) random or universal testing when the public health or safety or national security is involved and (2) selective drug testing when there is sufficient cause to believe an employee has a drug problem.

Lie Detector Tests The *Federal Employee Polygraph Protection Act* prohibits private employers from requiring employees or prospective employees to undergo a **lie detector test**, inquiring about the results of such a test, or using the results of such a test or the refusal to be tested as grounds for an adverse employment decision. The Act exempts government employers and, in certain situations, Energy Department contractors or persons providing consulting services for federal intelligence agencies. In addition, security firms and manufacturers of controlled substances may use a polygraph to test prospective employees. Moreover, an employer, as part of an ongoing investigation of economic loss or injury to its business, may use a polygraph test. Nevertheless, the use of the test must meet the following requirements: (1) it must be designed to investigate a specific incident or activity, not to document a chronic problem; (2) the employee to be tested must have had access to the property that is the subject of the investigation; and (3) the employer must have reason to suspect the particular employee.

Employees and prospective employees tested under any of these exemptions cannot be terminated, disciplined, or denied employment solely as a result of the test. The Act further provides that those subjected to a polygraph test (1) cannot be asked intrusive or degrading questions regarding topics such as their religious beliefs, opinions as to racial matters, political views, or sexual preferences or behaviors; (2) must be given the right to review all questions before the test and to terminate the test at any time; and (3) must receive a complete copy of the test results.

Workers' Compensation [41-3d]

To provide speedier and more certain relief to injured employees, all states have adopted statutes providing for **workers' compensation**. (Several states, however, exempt specified employers from workers' compensation statutes.) These statutes create commissions or boards that determine whether an injured employee is entitled to receive compensation and, if so, how much. The basis of recovery under workers' compensation is strict liability: the employee does not have to prove that the employer was negligent. The common law defenses of contributory negligence, voluntary assumption of risk, and the fellow servant rule (which covers injury caused by the negligence of a fellow employee) are *not* available to employers in workers' compensation proceedings. Such defenses are *abolished*. The *only* requirement is that the employee be injured and that the injury arises out of and in the course of his employment. The amounts recoverable are fixed by statute for each type of injury and are lower than the amounts a court or jury would probably award in an action at common law. The courts, therefore, do not have jurisdiction over such cases, except to review decisions of the board or commission; even then, the courts may determine only whether such decisions are in accordance with the statute. If a third party, however, causes the injury, the employee may bring a tort action against that third party.

Early workers' compensation laws did not provide coverage for occupational disease, and most courts held that occupational injury did not include disease. Today, virtually all states provide general compensation coverage for occupational diseases, although the coverage varies greatly from state to state.

Social Security and Unemployment Insurance [41-3e]

Social Security was enacted in 1935 in an attempt to provide limited retirement and death benefits to certain employees. Since then, the benefits have greatly increased, and the federal Social Security system, which has expanded to cover almost all employees, now contains four major benefit programs: (1) Old-Age and Survivors Insurance (OASI) (providing retirement and survivor benefits), (2) Disability Insurance (DI), (3) Hospitalization Insurance (Medicare), and (4) Supplemental Security Income (SSI).

The system is financed by contributions (taxes) paid by employers, employees, and self-employed individuals. Employees and employers pay matching contributions. It is the employer's responsibility to withhold the employee's contribution and to forward the full amount of the tax

---

Lie detector tests

federal statute prohibits private employers from requiring employees or prospective employees to take such tests

---

Practical Advice

Be careful to respect the privacy of employees.

Workers' compensation

compensation awarded to an injured employee whose injury arose out of and in the course of his employment

---

Social Security

measures by which the government provides economic assistance to disabled or retired employees and their dependents

to the Internal Revenue Service. Employee-made contributions are not tax deductible by the employee, whereas those made by the employer are. Self-employed persons are also required to report their taxable income and to pay the combined employer and employee amount of Social Security tax.

The federal *unemployment insurance* system was initially created by Title IX of the Social Security Act of 1935. Subsequently, Title IX was supplemented by the Federal Unemployment Tax Act and by numerous other federal statutes. This complex system depends upon the cooperation of state and federal programs. Federal law provides the general guidelines, standards, and requirements, while the states administer the program through their own employment laws. The system is funded by employer taxes: federal taxes generally pay the program's administrative costs, and state contributions pay for the actual benefits.

The purpose of the Federal Unemployment Tax Act is to provide **unemployment compensation** to workers who have lost their jobs, usually through no fault of their own, and who cannot find other employment. Payments, generally made weekly, are based on a particular state's formula.

Unemployment compensation
compensation awarded to workers who have lost their jobs and cannot find other employment

Fair Labor Standards Act [41-3f]

The FLSA regulates the employment of child labor outside of agriculture. The Act prohibits the employment of anyone under fourteen years of age in nonfarm work, except for newspaper deliverers and child actors. Fourteen- and fifteen-year-olds may work for a limited number of hours outside of school hours, under specific conditions, in certain *nonhazardous* occupations. Sixteen- and seventeen-year-olds may work in any *nonhazardous* job, while persons eighteen years old or older may work in *any* job, whether it is hazardous or not. The secretary of labor determines which occupations are considered hazardous.

In addition, the FLSA imposes wage and hour requirements upon covered employers. The Act provides for a minimum hourly wage and overtime pay of time-and-a-half for hours worked in excess of forty hours per week. However, the FLSA exempts certain workers from both its minimum wage and overtime provisions; those excluded include professionals, managers, and outside salespersons.

Fair Labor Standards Act
regulates the employment of child labor outside of agriculture

Worker Adjustment and Retraining Notification Act [41-3g]

The **Worker Adjustment and Retraining Notification Act (WARN)** requires an employer to provide sixty days' advance notice of a plant closing or mass layoff. A "plant closing" is defined as the permanent or temporary shutting down of a single site or units within a site if the shutdown results in fifty or more employees losing employment during any thirty-day period. A "mass layoff" is defined as a loss of employment during a thirty-day period either for five hundred employees or for at least one-third of the employees at a given site, if that one-third equals or exceeds fifty employees. WARN requires that notification be given to specified state and local officials as well as to the affected employees or their union representatives. The Act, which reduces the notification period with regard to failing companies and emergency situations, applies to employers with a total of one hundred or more employees who in the aggregate work at least two thousand hours per week, not including overtime.

Worker Adjustment and Retraining Notification Act (WARN)
federal statute that requires an employer to provide sixty days' advance notice of a plant closing or mass layoff

Family and Medical Leave Act [41-3h]

The **Family and Medical Leave Act** requires employers with fifty or more employees and governments at the federal, state, and local levels to grant eligible employees up to twelve weeks of leave during any twelve-month period for the birth of a child; adopting or gaining foster care of a child; or the care of a spouse, child, or parent who suffers from a serious health condition. The Act defines a "serious health condition" as an "illness, injury, impairment or physical or mental condition" that involves inpatient medical care at a hospital, hospice, or residential care facility or continuing medical treatment by a health-care provider. Employees are eligible for such leave if they have been employed by their present employer for at least twelve months and have worked at least 1,250 hours for their employer during the twelve months preceding the leave request. The requested leave may be paid, unpaid, or a combination of both.

Family and Medical Leave Act
requires some employers to grant employees leave for serious health conditions or certain other events

ETHICAL DILEMMA

What (Unwritten) Right to a Job Does an Employee Have?

Facts Gary Johnson was a six-year employee of Simon Corporation, a manufacturer of small appliances. Gary worked part of the time on the production line, where he manufactured fruit juicers, and the rest of the time as a quality control inspector.

Two years ago, the line foreman, James Sullivan, Gary's good and longstanding friend, observed that Gary was intoxicated on the job. James warned his friend privately against drinking on the job. Two months later, James again noticed that Gary was intoxicated; again he warned Gary that such conduct could not be tolerated. Because of the high unemployment in the area, James was worried about causing his friend to lose his job and therefore remained silent. Finally, after another month passed and James again noticed that Gary was intoxicated, he reported the problem to his supervisor.

The company's employee handbook explained that alcohol and drugs were prohibited on the job and that all employees identified as drug or alcohol dependent were to attend an alcohol and drug dependence program. After talking to James, the supervisor informed Gary that he must attend the company's program. Gary refused to cooperate and was fired.

Simon Corporation had regularly rehired employees who had been fired for intoxication but who had subsequently overcome their addiction. Although the rehiring practice was not spelled out in the handbook, the corporation had consistently followed the unwritten policy for ten years. Although Gary eventually overcame his addiction, the corporation refused to rehire him. Gary is now suing the company to rehire him, alleging that his original employment contract implied that he would be rehired if he demonstrated that he had overcome an addiction.

Social, Policy, and Ethical Considerations

1. Should James have waited so long before reporting the problem to his supervisor? Explain.
2. Does the nature of the product and the role of the employee affect the ethical considerations in such a decision? Assume, for example, that the juicer Gary produced would be potentially harmful if defective and consider, as well, his role in quality control.
3. How should a company handle alcohol and drug abuse among its employees?
4. Compare the goal of supporting recovering addicts with the need to ensure that the best employees are selected to perform a job.
5. How, if at all, should the state or federal government be involved in this type of situation?

CHAPTER SUMMARY

Labor Law

Purpose to provide the general framework in which management and labor negotiate terms of employment

Norris-La Guardia Act established as U.S. policy the full freedom of labor to form labor unions without employer interference and withdrew from the federal courts the power to issue injunctions in nonviolent labor disputes (any controversy concerning terms or conditions of employment or union representation)

National Labor Relations Act

- *Right to Unionize* declares it a federally protected right of employees to unionize and to bargain collectively
- *Prohibits Unfair Employer Practices* the Act identifies five unfair labor practices by an employer
- *National Labor Relations Board* created to administer these rights

Labor-Management Relations Act

- *Prohibits Unfair Union Practices* the Act identifies seven unfair labor practices by a union
- *Prohibits Closed Shops* agreements that mandate that an employer can hire only union members
- *Allows Union Shops* an employer can hire nonunion members, but the employee must join the union

Labor-Management Reporting and Disclosure Act aimed at eliminating corruption in labor unions

Employment Discrimination Law

Equal Employment Opportunity Commission enforcement agency for federal laws that make it illegal to discriminate against a job applicant or an employee because of the person's race, color, religion, sex, national origin, age, disability, or genetic information

Equal Pay Act prohibits an employer from discriminating between employees on the basis of gender by paying unequal wages for the same work

Civil Rights Act of 1964 prohibits employment discrimination on the basis of race, color, gender, religion, or national origin

- *Pregnancy Discrimination Act* extends the benefits of the Civil Rights Act to pregnant women
- *Affirmative Action* the active recruitment of a designated group of applicants
- *Discrimination* the Act provides four defenses (1) a *bona fide* seniority or merit system, (2) a professionally developed ability test, (3) a compensation system based on performance results, and (4) a *bona fide* occupational qualification
- *Reverse Discrimination* affirmative action that directs an employer to consider an individual's race or gender when hiring or promoting for the purpose of remedying underrepresentation of that race or gender in traditionally segregated jobs
- *Sexual Harassment* is an illegal form of sexual discrimination that includes unwelcome sexual advances, requests for sexual favors, and other verbal or physical conduct of a sexual nature
- *Comparable Worth* equal pay for jobs that are of equal value to the employer

Executive Order prohibits discrimination by federal contractors on the basis of race, color, gender, religion, or national origin on any work the contractors perform during the period of the federal contract

Age Discrimination in Employment Act prohibits discrimination on the basis of age in hiring, firing, or compensating

Disability Law several federal acts, including the Americans with Disabilities Act, provide assistance to people with disabilities in obtaining rehabilitation training, access to public facilities, and employment

Genetic Information Nondiscrimination Act forbids discrimination on the basis of genetic information with respect to any aspect of employment

Employee Protection

Employee Termination at Will under the common law, a contract of employment for other than a definite term is terminable at will by either party

- *Statutory Limitations* have been enacted by the federal government and some states
- *Judicial Limitations* based on contract law, tort law, or public policy
- *Limitations Imposed by Union Contract*

Occupational Safety and Health Act enacted to ensure workers a safe and healthful work environment

Employee Privacy

- *Drug and Alcohol Testing* some states either prohibit such tests or prescribe certain scientific and procedural safeguards
- *Lie Detector Tests* federal statute prohibits private employers from requiring employees or prospective employees to take such tests

Workers' Compensation compensation awarded to an employee who is injured in the course of his or her employment

Social Security measures by which the government provides economic assistance to disabled or retired employees and their dependents

Unemployment Compensation compensation awarded to workers who have lost their jobs and cannot find other employment

Fair Labor Standards Act regulates the employment of child labor outside of agriculture

Worker Adjustment and Retraining Notification Act federal statute that requires an employer to provide sixty days' advance notice of a plant closing or mass layoff

Family and Medical Leave Act requires some employers to grant employees leave for serious health conditions or certain other events

QUESTIONS

1. Gooddecade manufactures and sells automobile parts throughout the eastern part of the United States. Among its full-time employees are 220 fourteen- and fifteen-year-olds. These teenagers are employed throughout the company and are paid at an hourly wage rate of $3.00 per hour. Discuss the legality of this arrangement.

2. Janet, a twenty-year-old woman, applied for a position driving a truck for Federal Trucking, Inc. Janet, who is 5′4″ tall and weighs 135 pounds, was denied the job because the company requires that all employees be at least 5′6″ tall and weigh at least 150 pounds. Federal justifies this requirement on the basis that its drivers are frequently forced to move heavy

loads in making pickups and deliveries. Janet brings a cause of action. Has Federal Trucking violated the Civil Rights Act? Explain.

3. N. I. S. promoted John, a forty-two-year-old employee, to a supervisor's position while passing over James, a fifty-eight-year-old employee. N. I. S. told James he was too old for the job and that it preferred a younger man. Discuss whether James will succeed if he brings a cause of action.

4. Anthony was employed as a forklift operator for Blackburn Construction Company. While on the job, he operated the forklift in a manner that was careless and in direct violation of Blackburn's procedural manual and, as a result, caused himself severe injury. Blackburn denies liability based on Anthony's (a) gross negligence, (b) disobedience of the procedural manual, and (c) written waiver of liability. Can Anthony recover for his injury? Explain.

5. Hazelwood School District is located in Sleepy Hollow Township. It is being sued by several teachers who applied for teaching positions with the school but were rejected. The plaintiffs, who are all African Americans, produce the following evidence:
   a. 1.8 percent of the Hazelwood School District's certified teachers are African Americans, whereas 15.4 percent of the certified teachers in Sleepy Hollow Township are African Americans; and
   b. the hiring decisions by Hazelwood School District are based solely on subjective criteria. What decision should be made?

6. T. W. E., a large manufacturer, prohibited its employees from distributing union leaflets to other employees while on the company's property. Richard, an employee of T. W. E., disregarded the prohibition and passed out the leaflets before his work shift began. T. W. E. discharged Richard for his actions. Has T. W. E. committed an unfair labor practice?

7. Erwick was dismissed from her job at the C&T Steel Company because she was "an unsatisfactory employee." At the time, Erwick was active in an effort to organize a union at C&T. Is the dismissal valid?

8. Johnson, president of the First National Bank of A, believes that it is appropriate to employ only female tellers. Hence, First National refuses to employ Ken Baker as a teller but does offer him a maintenance position at the same salary. Baker brings a cause of action against First National Bank. Is First National illegally discriminating based on gender? Why?

9. Section 103 of the Federal Public Works Employment Act establishes the Minority Business Enterprise program and requires that, absent a waiver by the secretary of commerce, 10 percent of all federal grants given by the Economic Development Administration be used to purchase services or supplies from businesses owned and controlled by U.S. citizens belonging to one of six minority groups: African American, Spanish speaking, Asian, Native American, Eskimo, and Aleut. White owners of businesses contend the Act constitutes illegal reverse discrimination. Discuss.

CASE PROBLEMS

10. Worth H. Percivil, a mechanical engineer, was employed by General Motors (GM) for twenty-six years until he was discharged. At the time his employment was terminated, Percivil was head of GM's Mechanical Development Department. Percivil sued GM for wrongful discharge. He contends that he was discharged as a result of a conspiracy among his fellow executives to force him out of his employment because of his age, because he had legitimately complained about certain deceptive practices of GM, because he had refused to give the government false information although urged to do so by his superiors, and because he had, on the contrary, undertaken to correct certain alleged misrepresentations made to the government. GM claims that Percivil's employment was terminable at the will of GM for any reason and with or without cause, provided that the discharge was not prohibited by statute. Has Percivil been wrongly discharged? Why?

11. Samsoc brought an action against the Sailors' Union alleging that the Union induced and encouraged employees of Moore Dry Dock Company to engage in a strike or concerted refusal in the course of their employment to perform services for Moore in connection with the conversion into a bulk gypsum carrier of the *S. S. Phopho*, a vessel owned by Samsoc, the object being to force Moore to cease doing business with Samsoc and thus force Samsoc to resolve its dispute with the respondent. Has an unfair labor practice been committed? Explain.

12. The United Steelworkers of America and Kaiser Aluminum entered into a master collective bargaining agreement covering terms and conditions of employment at fifteen Kaiser plants. The agreement contained an affirmative action plan designed to eliminate conspicuous racial imbalances in Kaiser's then almost exclusively white craftwork forces. African-American craft-hiring goals were set for each Kaiser plant equal to the percentage of African Americans in the respective local labor forces. To meet these goals, on-the-job training programs were established to teach unskilled production workers—African Americans and whites—the skills necessary to become craftworkers. The plan reserved for African-American employees 50 percent of the openings in these newly created in-plant training programs.

   Pursuant to the national agreement, Kaiser altered its craft-hiring practice in its Gramercy, Louisiana, plant by establishing a program to train its production workers to fill craft openings. Selection of craft trainees was made on the basis of seniority. At least 50 percent of the new trainees were to be African American until the percentage of African-American skilled craftworkers in the Gramercy plant approximated the percentage of African Americans in the local labor force. During this affirmative action plan's first year of operation, thirteen craft trainees (seven African American, six white) were selected from Gramercy's production workforce. The most senior African American selected had less seniority than several white production workers who were denied admission to the program. Does the affirmative action plan wrongfully discriminate against white employees and therefore violate the Civil Rights Act of 1964? Justify your decision.

13. At Whirlpool's manufacturing plant in Ohio, overhead conveyors transported household appliance components throughout the plant. A wire mesh screen was positioned below the conveyors in order to catch falling components and debris. Maintenance employees frequently had to stand on the screens to clean them. Whirlpool began installing heavier wire because several employees had fallen partly through the old screens, and one had fallen completely through to the plant floor. At this time, the company warned workers to walk only on the frames beneath the wire but not on the wire itself. Before the heavier wire had been completely installed, a worker fell to his death through the old screen. A short time after this incident, Deemer and Cornwell, two plant employees, met with the plant safety director to discuss the mesh; to voice their concerns; and to obtain the name, address, and telephone number of the local Occupational Safety and Health Administration representative. The next day, the two employees refused to clean a portion of the old screen. They were then ordered to punch out for the remainder of the shift without pay and received written reprimands, which were placed in their employment files. Does Whirlpool's actions against Deemer and Cornwell constitute discrimination in violation of the Occupational Safety and Health Act? Explain.

14. The defendant, Berger Transfer and Storage, operated a national moving and transfer business employing approximately forty persons. In May and June, Local 705 of the International Brotherhood of Teamsters spoke with a number of Berger employees, obtaining twenty-eight cards signed in support of the union. The management of Berger, unwilling to work with the union, attempted to prevent it from representing Berger employees. The company first assigned all work to those with high seniority, in effect temporarily laying off low-seniority employees. The management then threatened to lay off permanently those with low seniority and threatened all employees with a total closedown of the plant. The management interrogated several employees about their union involvement and attempted to extract information about other employees' activities. When the union presented the company with the signed cards and recognition agreement, Berger refused to acknowledge the union's existence or its right to bargain on behalf of the employees. The union then called a strike, with employees picketing the Berger warehouse. During the picketing, the company threatened to terminate the picketers if they did not return to work. Later, one manager on two occasions recklessly drove a truck through the picket line, striking employees. Finally, the company contacted several of the employees and offered them the "grievance procedures and job security" the union would provide. The employees refused the offer. On June 15, the strike ended, with most of the picketers returning to work. Local 705 filed a complaint with the National Labor Relations Board, alleging that Berger had committed unfair labor practices in violation of the National Labor Relations Act. Will Local 705 succeed? Explain.

15. City of Richmond, Virginia (the City), adopted a Minority Business Utilization Plan requiring prime contractors awarded city construction contracts to subcontract at least 30 percent of the dollar amount of each contract to one or more Minority Business Enterprises (MBEs). The plan defined an MBE to include a business from anywhere in the United States that is at least 51 percent owned and controlled by African American, Spanish speaking, Asian, Native American, Eskimo, or Aleut citizens. Although the plan declared that it was "remedial" in nature, it was adopted after a public hearing at which no direct evidence was presented that the City had discriminated on the basis of race in letting contracts or that its prime contractors had discriminated against minority subcontractors. The evidence introduced in support of the plan included a statistical study indicating that, although the City's population was 50 percent African American, less than 1 percent of its prime construction contracts had been awarded to minority businesses in recent years. Additional evidence showed that a variety of local contractors' trade associations had virtually no MBE members. J. A. Croson Co., the sole bidder on a city contract, was denied a waiver and lost its contract because of the plan. Discuss the legality of the plan.

16. Burdine, a woman, was hired by the Texas Department of Community Affairs as a clerk in the Public Service Careers (PSC) Division. The PSC provides training and employment opportunities for unskilled workers. At the time she was hired, Burdine already had several years' experience in employment training. She was soon promoted, and later, when her supervisor resigned, she performed additional duties that usually had been assigned to the supervisor. Burdine applied for the position of supervisor, but the position remained unfilled for six months, until a male employee from another division was brought in to fill it. Burdine alleges discrimination violating Title VII of the 1964 Civil Rights Act. The defendant, Texas Department of Community Affairs, responds that nondiscriminatory evaluation criteria were used to choose the new supervisor. To comply with Title VII, must the Texas Department of Community Affairs hire Burdine as supervisor if she and the male candidate are equally qualified? Explain.

17. Wise was fired from her job at the Mead Corporation after she was involved in a fight with a coworker. On four other unrelated occasions, fights had occurred between male coworkers. Only one of the males was fired, but this was after his second fight, in which he seriously injured another employee. There is no dispute that Wise was qualified and performed her duties adequately. Wise successfully established a *prima facie* case of discrimination. However, the defendant, Mead Corporation, met its burden to "articulate legitimate and nondiscriminatory reasons" for firing Wise. Can she prevail? Explain.

18. John Novosel was employed by Nationwide Insurance Company for fifteen years. Novosel had been a model employee and, at the time of discharge, was a district claims manager and a candidate for the position of division claims manager. During Novosel's fifteenth year of employment, Nationwide circulated a memorandum requesting the participation of all employees in an effort to lobby the Pennsylvania state legislature for the passage of a certain bill before the body. Novosel,

who had privately indicated his disagreement with Nationwide's political views, refused to lend his support to the lobby, and his employment with Nationwide was terminated. Novosel brought two separate claims against Nationwide, arguing, first, that his discharge for refusing to lobby the state legislature on behalf of Nationwide constituted the tort of wrongful discharge in that it was arbitrary, malicious, and contrary to public policy. Novosel also contended that Nationwide breached an implied contract guaranteeing continued employment so long as his job performance was satisfactory. What decision as to each claim?

19. During the years prior to the passage of the Civil Rights Act of 1964, Duke Power openly discriminated against African Americans by allowing them to work only in the labor department of the plant's five departments. The highest paying job in the labor department paid less than the lowest paying jobs in the other four "operating" departments in which only whites were employed. In 1955, the company began requiring a high school education for initial assignment to any department except labor. However, when Duke Power stopped restricting African Americans to the labor department in 1965, it made completion of high school a prerequisite to transfer from labor to any other department. White employees hired before the high school education requirement was adopted continued to perform satisfactorily and to achieve promotions in the "operating" departments.

    In 1965, the company also began requiring new employees in the departments other than labor to register satisfactory scores on two professionally prepared aptitude tests, in addition to having a high school education. In September 1965, Duke Power began to permit employees to qualify for transfer to another department from labor by passing either of the two tests, neither of which was directed or intended to measure the ability to learn to perform a particular job or category of jobs. Griggs brought suit against Duke Power, claiming that the high school education and testing requirements were discriminatory and therefore prohibited by the Civil Rights Act of 1964. Is Griggs correct? Why?

20. Michelle Vinson was an employee of Meritor Savings Bank for approximately four years. Beginning as a teller-trainee, she ultimately advanced to the position of assistant branch manager. Her promotions were based solely upon merit. Sidney Taylor, a vice president of the bank and manager of the branch office in which Vinson worked, was Vinson's supervisor throughout her employment with the bank. After the bank fired Vinson for her abusive use of sick leave, she brought an action against Taylor and the bank, alleging that during her employment she had "constantly been subjected to sexual harassment" by Taylor in violation of Title VII of the Civil Rights Act of 1964. At trial, Vinson introduced evidence that Taylor repeatedly demanded sexual favors from her, fondled her in front of other employees, and forcibly raped her on a number of occasions. Taylor and the bank categorically denied Vinson's allegations. Does the conduct constitute sexual harassment? Explain.

21. Plaintiff, Beth Lyons, a staff attorney for the Legal Aid Society (Legal Aid) brought suit against her employer, alleging that Legal Aid violated the Americans with Disabilities Act (ADA) and the Rehabilitation Act by failing to provide her with a parking space near her office. Plaintiff worked for defendant in its lower Manhattan office.

    Lyon's disability was the result of being struck and nearly killed by an automobile. For six years from the date of the accident, Lyons was on disability leave from Legal Aid; she underwent multiple reconstructive surgeries and received "constant" physical therapy. Since the accident, Lyons has been able to walk only by using walking devices, including walkers, canes, and crutches. Since returning to work Lyons has performed her job duties successfully. Nevertheless, her condition severely limits her ability to walk long distances either at one time or during the course of a day.

    Before returning to work, Lyons asked Legal Aid to accommodate her disability by providing her a parking space near her office and the courts in which she would practice. She stated that this would be necessary because she is unable to take public transportation from her home in New Jersey to the Legal Aid office in Manhattan because such "commuting would require her to walk distances, climb stairs, and on occasion to remain standing for extended periods of time," thereby "overtax[ing] her limited physical capabilities." Lyons's physician advised Legal Aid by letter that such a parking space was "necessary to enable [Lyons] to return to work." Legal Aid informed Lyons that it would not pay for a parking space for her. Accordingly, Lyons has spent $300 to $520 a month, representing 15 percent to 26 percent of her monthly net salary, for a parking space adjacent to her office building. Are the accommodations requested by Lyons unreasonable? Why?

22. The Steamship Clerks Union has approximately 124 members, 80 of whom are classified as active. Members serve as steamship clerks who, during the loading and unloading of vessels in the port of Boston, check cargo against inventory lists provided by shippers and consignees. The work is not taxing; it requires little in the way of particular skills. On October 1, the Union formally adopted the membership sponsorship policy (the MSP), which provided that any applicant for membership in the Union (other than an injured longshoreman) had to be sponsored by an existing member for his application to be considered. The record reveals, without contradiction, that (1) the Union had no African American or Hispanic members when it adopted the MSP; (2) blacks and Hispanics constituted from 8 percent to 27 percent of the relevant labor pool in the Boston area; (3) the Union welcomed at least thirty new members over the next six years and then closed the membership rolls; (4) all "sponsored" applicants during this period and, hence, all the new members, were Caucasian; and (5) every recruit was related to (usually the son or brother of) a Union member.

    After conducting an investigation and instituting administrative proceedings, the Equal Employment Opportunity Commission (EEOC) brought suit, alleging that the Union had discriminated against African Americans and Hispanics by means of the MSP. Explain whether or not the EEOC will prevail.

23. Johnson Controls implemented a policy that women who are pregnant or who are capable of bearing children would not be placed into jobs involving lead exposure. Employees filed a class action lawsuit challenging Johnson Controls'

fetal-protection policy as sex discrimination that violated Title VII of the Civil Rights Act of 1964. Among the individual plaintiffs were Mary Craig, who had chosen to be sterilized to avoid losing her job; Elsie Nason, a fifty-year-old divorcee, who had suffered a loss in compensation when she was transferred out of a job that exposed her to lead; and Donald Penney, who had been denied a request for a leave of absence for the purpose of lowering his lead level because he intended to become a father. Discuss whether the plaintiffs have a valid cause of action.

TAKING SIDES

Mark Hunger was the safety director at Grand Central Sanitation. On September 7, Hunger "became aware" that hazardous materials consisting of blasting caps were being deposited into garbage containers at Shu-Deb, Inc. Grand Central collected garbage from these containers and dumped it at a dump site. Hunger knew that Grand Central was not licensed to dispose of hazardous materials and believed that it would violate state and/or federal law if the company transported or disposed of hazardous materials. Hunger also became concerned about the safety of company employees from the danger of transporting blasting caps. On September 9, Hunger informed Grand Central's owner and vice president, Gary Perin, of the information he received about the blasting caps. On September 12, Hunger, accompanied by Pennsylvania state police and agents of the Federal Bureau of Alcohol, Tobacco, and Firearms, went to search the contents of Shu-Deb's containers. However, the garbage had already been collected, so Hunger and the police located the garbage truck that had collected the garbage and searched it. No hazardous materials were found in the truck. On October 4, Hunger was terminated because of the incident. Hunger sued Grand Central for wrongful termination.

a. What are the arguments that Hunger was wrongfully terminated?

b. What are the arguments that Hunger was legally terminated?

c. Will Hunger prevail? Explain.

Antitrust

CHAPTER 42

Monopolies are odious, contrary to the spirit of free government and the principles of commerce, and ought not to be suffered.

Maryland Declaration of 1776

CHAPTER OUTCOMES

After reading and studying this chapter, you should be able to:

1. Describe and explain horizontal restraints of trade.

2. Describe and explain vertical restraints of trade.

3. Explain monopolization, attempts to monopolize, and conspiracies to monopolies and why they are illegal.

4. Explain the Clayton Act and its rules governing (a) tying contracts, (b) exclusive dealing, (c) horizontal mergers, (d) vertical mergers, and (e) conglomerate mergers.

5. Describe (a) the Robinson-Patman Act and the various defenses to it and (b) the Federal Trade Commission Act.

The economic community is best served in normal times by free competition in trade and industry. It is in the public interest that quality, price, and service in an open, competitive market for goods and services be determining factors in the business rivalry for the customer's dollar. Rather than compete, however, businesses would prefer to eliminate their competition and, consequently, to enjoy a position from which they could dictate both the price of their goods and the quantity they produce. Although eliminating competition by producing a better product is the proper goal of a business, some businesses effect this elimination through illegitimate means, such as fixing prices and allocating exclusive territories to certain competitors within an industry. The law of antitrust prohibits such activities and attempts to ensure free and fair competition in the marketplace.

The common law has traditionally favored competition and has held that agreements and contracts in restraint of trade are illegal and unenforceable. In addition, although several states enacted antitrust statutes during the 1800s, the latter half of the nineteenth century revealed concentrations of economic power in the form of "trusts" and "combinations" that were too powerful and widespread to be curbed effectively by state action. In 1890, this awesome and uncontrollable growth of power prompted Congress to enact the Sherman Antitrust Act, the first federal statute in this field. Since then, Congress has enacted other antitrust statutes, including the Clayton Act, the Robinson-Patman Act, and the Federal Trade Commission Act. These statutes prohibit anticompetitive practices and seek to prevent unreasonable concentrations of economic power that stifle or weaken competition.

SHERMAN ANTITRUST ACT [42-1]

Section 1 of the Sherman Act prohibits contracts, combinations, and conspiracies that restrain trade, while Section 2 outlaws both monopolies and attempts to monopolize.

Failure to comply with either section is a criminal violation and subjects the offender to fine or imprisonment or both. As amended by the Standards Development Organization Advancement Act of 2004, the Sherman Act subjects individual offenders to imprisonment of up to ten years and fines of up to $1 million, while corporate offenders are subject to fines of up to $100 million per violation. Moreover, under the federal Alternative Fines Act, the maximum fine may be increased to twice the amount the conspirators gained from the illegal acts or twice the money lost by the victims of the crime, if either of those amounts is over $100 million. In addition, the Sherman Act empowers the federal district courts to issue injunctions restraining violations, and anyone injured by a violation is entitled to recover in a civil action **treble damages** (i.e., three times the amount of the actual loss sustained). The U.S. Department of Justice and the Federal Trade Commission (FTC) have the duty to institute appropriate enforcement proceedings other than treble damages actions.

The Justice Department has expanded its enforcement policy regarding the Sherman Act to cover conduct by foreign companies that harms U.S. exports. Under this policy, the department examines conduct to determine whether it would violate the law if it occurred within borders of the United States. The department has indicated that it will focus primarily on boycotts and cartels that injure the export of U.S. products and services.

Restraint of Trade [42-1a]

Section 1 of the Sherman Act provides that "[e]very contract, combination in the form of trust or otherwise, or conspiracy, in restraint of trade or commerce among the several states, or with foreign nations is hereby declared to be illegal." Because the section's language is so broad, identifying the elements that constitute a violation has been largely a product of judicial interpretation.

Standards As noted, Section 1 prohibits every contract, combination, or conspiracy in restraint of trade. Taken literally, this prohibition would invalidate every unperformed contract. To avoid such an unrealistic application, the courts have interpreted this section to invalidate only *unreasonable* restraints of trade. This standard is known as the **rule of reason** test, a flexible standard under which the courts, in determining whether a challenged practice unreasonably restricts competition, consider a variety of factors, including the makeup of the relevant industry, the defendants' positions within that industry, the ability of the defendants' competitors to respond to the challenged practice, and the defendants' purpose in adopting the restraint. After reviewing the various factors, a court determines whether the challenged restraint unreasonably restricts competition.

By requiring the courts to balance the *anticompetitive* effects of every questioned restraint against its *procompetitive* effects, this standard placed a substantial burden upon the judicial system. The Supreme Court addressed this problem by declaring certain categories of restraints

---

Treble damages

three times actual loss

Practical Advice

Be advised that a violation of the Sherman Antitrust Act carries both criminal penalties and civil liability including treble damages.

Restraint of trade

Section 1 prohibits contracts, combinations, and conspiracies that restrain trade

---

Rule of reason

standard that balances the restraint's anticompetitive effects against its procompetitive effects

---

GOING GLOBAL

Do the antitrust laws apply outside the United States?

Section 1 of the Sherman Act provides that U.S. antitrust laws shall have a broad, extraterritorial reach. As discussed above, contracts, combinations, or conspiracies that restrain trade with foreign nations, as well as among the domestic states, are deemed illegal. Therefore, agreements among competitors to increase the cost of imports, as well as arrangements to exclude imports from U.S. domestic markets in exchange for agreements not to

compete in other countries, clearly violate U.S. antitrust laws. The antitrust provisions are also designed to protect U.S. exports from privately imposed restrictions seeking to exclude U.S. competitors from foreign markets. Amendments to the Sherman Act and the Federal Trade Commission Act limit their application to unfair methods of competition that have a direct, substantial, and reasonably foreseeable effect on U.S. domestic commerce, U.S. import

commerce, or U.S. export commerce. The U.S. Supreme Court has held that where price-fixing conduct significantly and adversely affects customers outside and inside the United States, but the foreign injury is separate from the domestic injury, the Sherman Act does not apply to a claim based solely on the foreign injury. *Hoffmann-La Roche Ltd v. Empagran S.A.,* 542 U.S. 155, 124 S.Ct. 2359, 159 L.Ed.2d 226 (2004).

Illegal *per se*

conclusively presumed
unreasonable and therefore
illegal

Practical Advice

Recognize that certain types
of conduct, due to their
pernicious effect on
competition and their lack
of any redeeming virtue, are
conclusively presumed to be
unreasonable and therefore
are illegal *per se*.

Horizontal restraints

agreements among
competitors

Vertical restraints

agreements among parties
at different levels in the
chain of distribution

Conscious parallelism

similar patterns of conduct
among competitors

to be unreasonable by their very nature, that is, **illegal *per se***. Characterizing a type of restraint as *per se* illegal significantly affects the prosecution of an antitrust suit. In such a case, the plaintiff need only show that the type of restraint occurred; she need not prove that the restraint limited competition. The defendants, in turn, may not defend on the basis that the restraint is reasonable. Furthermore, the court is not required to conduct extensive, and often difficult, economic analysis.

More recently, a third, intermediate test has been frequently used when the *per se* approach is not appropriate for the situation but the challenged conduct has obvious anticompetitive effects. Under this "quick look" rule of reason analysis, the courts will apply an abbreviated rule of reason standard rather than using the extensive analysis required by a full-blown rule of reason test. However, the extensiveness of the legal analysis required under the quick look test will vary based upon the circumstances, details, and logic of the restraint being reviewed. See *American Needle, Inc. v. National Football League*, later in this chapter.

Horizontal and Vertical Restraints
A trade restraint may be classified as either horizontal or vertical. A **horizontal restraint** involves collaboration among competitors at the same level in the chain of distribution. For example, an agreement among manufacturers, among wholesalers, or among retailers would be horizontal.

On the other hand, an agreement among parties who are not in direct competition at the same distribution level is a **vertical restraint**. Thus, an agreement between a manufacturer and a wholesaler is vertical. Although the distinction between horizontal and vertical restraints can become blurred, it often determines whether a restraint is illegal *per se* or should be judged by the rule of reason test. For instance, horizontal market allocations are illegal *per se*, whereas vertical market allocations are subject to the rule of reason test.

Concerted Action
Section 1 does not prohibit *unilateral* conduct; rather, it forbids *concerted* action. Thus, one person or business by itself cannot violate the section. As the U.S. Supreme Court held in *Monsanto Co. v. Spray-Rite Service Corporation* (1984), an organization has the "right to deal, or refuse to deal, with whomever it likes, as long as it does so independently." For example, if a manufacturer announces its resale prices in advance and refuses to deal with those who disagree with the pricing, there is no violation of Section 1 because the manufacturer has acted alone. On the other hand, if a manufacturer and its retailers together agree that the manufacturer will sell only to those retailers who agree to sell at a specified price, a violation of Section 1 may exist.

For purposes of the concerted action requirement, the courts view a firm and its employees as one entity. The same is also true for a corporation and its wholly owned subsidiaries; thus, the Sherman Act is not violated when a parent and its wholly owned subsidiary agree to a restraint in trade.

The concerted action requirement may be established by an express agreement. Not surprisingly, however, express agreements often are nonexistent, leaving the court to infer an interparty agreement from circumstantial evidence. Nonetheless, similar patterns of conduct among competitors, called **conscious parallelism**, are not sufficient in themselves to imply a conspiracy in violation of Section 1. Actual conspiracy requires an *additional* factor—such as complex actions that would benefit each competitor only if all of them acted—or indications of a traditional conspiracy—such as identical sealed bids from each competitor.

Joint ventures (discussed in Chapter 30) are a form of business association organized to carry out a particular business enterprise. Competitors frequently pool their resources to share costs and to eliminate wasteful redundancy. The validity under antitrust law of a joint venture generally depends on the competitors' primary purpose in forming it. A joint venture that was not formed to fix prices or divide markets will be judged under the rule of reason.

However, because uncertainty about the legality of joint ventures seemed to discourage their use for joint research and development, Congress passed the National Cooperative Research Act to facilitate such applications. The Act provides that the courts must judge joint ventures in the research and development of new technology under the rule of reason test and that treble damages do *not* apply to ventures formed in violation of Section 1 if those forming the venture have notified the Justice Department and the FTC of their intent to form the joint venture.

American Needle, Inc. v. National Football League
Supreme Court of the United States, 2010
560 U.S. 183, 130 S.Ct. 2201, 176 L.Ed.2d 947
http://scholar.google.com/scholar_case?case=7494086478657562944&q=130+S.Ct.+2201&hl=en&as_sdt=40000006

FACTS Originally organized in 1920, the National Football League (NFL) is an unincorporated association that encompasses 32 separately owned professional football teams. Each team has its own name, colors, and logo, and owns related intellectual property. Prior to 1963, the teams made their own arrangements for licensing their intellectual property and marketing trademarked items such as caps and jerseys. In 1963, the teams formed National Football League Properties (NFLP) to develop, license, and market their intellectual property. Most, but not all, of the substantial revenues generated by NFLP have either been given to charity or shared equally among the teams. However, the teams are able to and have at times sought to withdraw from this arrangement.

Between 1963 and 2000, NFLP granted nonexclusive licenses to a number of vendors, permitting them to manufacture and sell apparel bearing team insignias. American Needle, Inc., was one of those licensees. In December 2000, the teams voted to authorize NFLP to grant exclusive licenses, and NFLP granted Reebok International Ltd. an exclusive ten-year license to manufacture and sell trademarked headwear for all thirty-two teams. It thereafter declined to renew American Needle's nonexclusive license.

American Needle filed this action in the Northern District of Illinois, alleging that the agreements between the NFL, its teams, NFLP, and Reebok violated Sections 1 and 2 of the Sherman Act. In their answer to the complaint, the defendants asserted that the teams, NFL, and NFLP were incapable of conspiring within the meaning of Section 1 "because they are a single economic enterprise, at least with respect to the conduct challenged." The District Court granted summary judgment for the NFL. The Court of Appeals for the Seventh Circuit affirmed.

DECISION The judgment of the Court of Appeals is reversed, and the case is remanded for further proceedings.

OPINION This case involves only a narrow issue: whether the NFL and its individual teams are capable of engaging in a "contract, combination ..., or conspiracy" as defined by Section 1 of the Sherman Act, or whether the activity of the NFL "must be viewed as that of a single enterprise for purposes of §1." Section 1 applies only to concerted action that restrains trade.

It has long been held that concerted action under Section 1 does not turn simply on whether the parties involved are legally distinct entities. Instead, the courts have avoided such formalistic

distinctions in favor of a functional consideration of how the parties involved in the alleged anticompetitive conduct actually operate. The relevant question, is thus whether there is a "contract, combination ... or conspiracy" among "separate economic actors pursuing separate economic interests," such that the agreement "deprives the marketplace of independent centers of decisionmaking," and therefore of "diversity of entrepreneurial interests." The question is whether the agreement joins together "independent centers of decisionmaking."

Each NFL teams is a substantial, independently owned, and independently managed business. The teams compete with one another, not only on the playing field but also to attract fans, for gate receipts, and for contracts with managerial and playing personnel. Each team competes in the market for intellectual property. To a firm making hats, the Saints and the Colts are two potentially competing suppliers of valuable trademarks. When each NFL team licenses its intellectual property, it is not pursuing the "common interests of the whole" league but is instead pursuing interests of each corporation itself. Although NFL teams have common interests such as promoting the NFL brand, they are still separate, profit-maximizing entities, and their interests in licensing team trademarks are not necessarily aligned. The NFL is thirty-two potential competitors. Unlike typical decisions by corporate shareholders, NFLP licensing decisions effectively require the assent of more than a mere majority of shareholders. And each team's decision reflects not only an interest in NFLP's profits but also an interest in the team's individual profits. But the conduct at issue is still concerted activity under the Sherman Act that is subject to Section 1 analysis.

When "restraints on competition are essential if the product is to be available at all," *per se* rules of illegality are inapplicable, and instead the restraint must be judged according to the flexible Rule of Reason.

INTERPRETATION Section 1 of the Sherman Act applies only to *concerted* action that unreasonably restrains trade.

ETHICAL QUESTION Did any of the parties act unethically? Explain.

CRITICAL THINKING QUESTION Do you agree that the parties in this case engaged in concerted action? Explain.

Price fixing

an agreement with the purpose or effect of inhibiting price competition

Price Fixing
Price fixing is an agreement with the purpose or effect of inhibiting price competition; such agreements may, among other things, raise, depress, fix, peg, or stabilize prices. Price fixing is the primary and most serious example of a *per se* violation under the Sherman Act. All *horizontal* price-fixing agreements are illegal *per se*. This prohibition covers any agreement by which sellers establish *maximum* prices at which certain commodities or services are to be offered for sale, as well as those by which they set *minimum* prices. The law also prohibits sellers' agreements to change the prices of certain commodities or services simultaneously or to not advertise their prices.

The U.S. Supreme Court has condemned not only agreements among horizontal competitors that directly fix prices but also agreements that affect price indirectly. For example, in finding an agreement among beer wholesalers to eliminate interest-free short-term credit on sales to beer retailers to be illegal *per se*, the Court viewed the credit terms "as an inseparable part of price" and concluded that the agreement to eliminate interest-free short-term credit was equivalent to an agreement to eliminate discounts and, thus, was an agreement to fix prices.

In a 2007 case, *Leegin Creative Leather Products, Inc v. PSKS, Inc.*, 551 U.S 877, 127 S.Ct. 2705, 168 L.Ed.2d 623, the U.S. Supreme Court ruled that vertical price restraints (vertical minimum resale price maintenance agreements) are to be judged by the rule of reason. This decision overruled a 1911 U.S. Supreme Court decision that established the rule that it is *per se* illegal under Section 1 of the Sherman Act for a manufacturer to agree with its retailers to set the minimum price the retailer can charge for the manufacturer's goods. Although many states harmonize their antitrust laws with federal antitrust law, some states specifically prohibit vertical price fixing and at least one state's supreme court has held that minimum, vertical price fixing is illegal *per se* under that state's antitrust laws.

Leegin Creative Leather Products, Inc. v. PSKS, Inc.
Supreme Court of the United States, 2007
551 U.S. 877, 127 S.Ct. 2705, 168 L.Ed.2d 623
http://scholar.google.com/scholar_case?case=15925807009998997000&q=127+S.Ct.+2705&hl=en&as_sdt=40000006

FACTS Leegin Creative Leather Products, Inc. designs, manufactures, and distributes leather goods and accessories. In 1991, Leegin began to sell belts under the brand name "Brighton." The Brighton brand has now expanded into a variety of women's fashion accessories. It is sold across the United States in more than five thousand retail establishments, mostly independent, small boutiques and specialty stores. Leegin's business strategy is to use small retailers because they treat customers better, provide customers more services, and make their shopping experience more satisfactory than do larger, often impersonal retailers. PSKS, Inc. operates Kay's Kloset, a women's apparel store in Lewisville, Texas. Kay's Kloset buys from about seventy-five different manufacturers and at one time sold the Brighton brand. It first started purchasing Brighton goods from Leegin in 1995. Once it began selling the brand, the store promoted Brighton. Brighton was the store's most important brand and once accounted for 40 to 50 percent of its profits.

In 1997, Leegin instituted the "Brighton Retail Pricing and Promotion Policy." Following the policy, Leegin refused to sell to retailers that discounted Brighton goods below suggested prices. The policy contained an exception for products not selling well that the retailer did not plan on reordering. Leegin adopted the policy to give its retailers sufficient margins to provide customers the service central to its distribution strategy. It also expressed concern that discounting harmed Brighton's brand image and reputation. In December 2002, Leegin discovered Kay's Kloset had been marking down Brighton's entire line by 20 percent. Kay's Kloset contended it placed Brighton products on sale to compete with nearby retailers who also were undercutting Leegin's suggested prices. Leegin, nonetheless, requested that Kay's Kloset cease discounting. Its request refused, Leegin stopped selling to the store. The loss of the Brighton brand had a considerable negative impact on the store's revenue from sales.

PSKS sued Leegin claiming that Leegin had violated the antitrust laws. The jury agreed with PSKS and awarded it $1.2 million. The district court trebled the damages and reimbursed PSKS for its attorneys' fees and costs. It entered judgment against Leegin in the amount of $3,975,000.80. The Court of Appeals for the Fifth

Circuit affirmed. *Certiorari* was granted to determine whether vertical minimum resale price maintenance agreements should continue to be treated as *per se* unlawful.

DECISION The judgment of the Court of Appeals reversed.

OPINION The rule of reason is the accepted standard for testing whether a practice restrains trade in violation of Section 1 of the Sherman Act. Under this rule, the fact-finder weighs all of the circumstances of a case in deciding whether a restrictive practice should be prohibited as imposing an unreasonable restraint on competition. Appropriate factors to take into account include "specific information about the relevant business" and "the restraint's history, nature, and effect." Whether the businesses involved have market power is a further, significant consideration. In its design and function the rule distinguishes between restraints with anticompetitive effect that are harmful to the consumer and restraints stimulating competition that are in the consumer's best interest.

The rule of reason, however, does not govern all restraints. Some types "are deemed unlawful *per se*." The *per se* rule, treating categories of restraints as necessarily illegal, eliminates the need to study the reasonableness of an individual restraint in light of the real market forces at work and can give clear guidance for certain conduct. Restraints that are *per se* unlawful include horizontal agreements among competitors to fix prices or to divide markets. To justify a *per se* prohibition, a restraint must have "manifestly anticompetitive" effects and "lack any redeeming virtue,"

Minimum resale price maintenance can stimulate interbrand competition—the competition among manufacturers selling different brands of the same type of product—by reducing intrabrand competition—the competition among retailers selling the same brand. The promotion of interbrand competition is important because the primary purpose of the antitrust laws is to protect this type of competition. A single manufacturer's use of vertical price restraints tends to eliminate intrabrand price competition; this in turn encourages retailers to invest in tangible or intangible services or promotional efforts that aid the manufacturer's position against rival manufacturers. Resale price maintenance also has the potential to give consumers more options so that they can choose among low-price, low-service brands; high-price, high-service brands; and brands that fall in between.

While vertical agreements setting minimum resale prices can have procompetitive justifications, they may have anticompetitive effects in other cases; and unlawful price fixing, designed solely to obtain monopoly profits, is an ever-present temptation. Resale price maintenance may, for example, facilitate a manufacturer cartel. Vertical price restraints also "might be used to organize cartels at the retailer level." (A horizontal cartel among competing manufacturers or competing retailers that decreases output or reduces competition in order to increase price is *per se* unlawful.)

Thus, vertical agreements establishing minimum resale prices can have either procompetitive or anticompetitive effects, depending upon the circumstances in which they are formed. Therefore, they should be judged by the rule of reason standard, not a *per se* rule of unlawfulness.

INTERPRETATION Minimum vertical price fixing is judged by a rule of reason standard.

CRITICAL THINKING QUESTION Do you agree with the court's decision? Explain.

Market allocation

division of markets by customers, geographic location, or products

Market Allocations Direct price fixing is not the only way to control prices. Another method is through **market allocation**, whereby competitors agree not to compete with each other in specific markets, which may be defined by geographic area, customer type, or product class. All *horizontal* agreements to divide markets have been declared illegal *per se* because they grant to the firm remaining in the market a monopolistic control over price. Thus, if RAC and Sonny, both manufacturers of televisions, agree that RAC shall have the exclusive right to sell televisions in Illinois and Iowa and that Sonny shall have the exclusive right in Minnesota and Wisconsin, RAC and Sonny have committed a *per se* violation of Section 1 of the Sherman Act. Likewise, if RAC and Sonny agree that RAC shall have the exclusive right to sell televisions to Walmart and that Sonny shall sell exclusively to Target or that RAC shall have exclusive rights to manufacture twenty-seven-inch televisions and that Sonny shall manufacture thirty-inch sets, they are also in *per se* violation of Section 1 of the Sherman Antitrust Act.

No longer illegal *per se*, vertical territorial and customer restrictions are now judged by the rule of reason. This change in approach results from the Supreme Court's decision in *Continental T.V., Inc. v. GTE Sylvania, Inc.* (1977), which mandated the lower federal courts to balance the positive effect of vertical market restrictions on interbrand competition against the negative effects on intrabrand competition. Consequently, in some situations, vertical territorial restrictions will be found legitimate if, on balance, they do not inhibit competition in the relevant market.

The U.S. Department of Justice issued a "market structure screen," under which the department will challenge no restraints by a firm having a less than 10 percent share of the relevant market or a "Vertical Restraint Index" (a measure of relative market share), indicating that neither collusion nor exclusion is possible. The concept of relevant market will be discussed later in the section on monopolization.

Boycott

agreement among parties not to deal with a third party

Boycotts As noted earlier, Section 1 of the Sherman Act applies not to unilateral action but only to agreements or combinations. Accordingly, a seller's refusal to deal with any particular buyer does not violate the Act; and a manufacturer can thus refuse to sell to a retailer who persists in selling below the manufacturer's suggested retail price. On the other hand, when two or more firms agree not to deal with a third party, their agreement represents a *concerted refusal to deal*, or a group **boycott**, which may violate Section 1 of the Sherman Act. Such a boycott may be clearly anticompetitive, eliminating competition or reducing market entry.

Practical Advice

When attending trade association meetings or other conferences with competitors, be extremely careful not to discuss pricing, refusals to deal with certain customers, and territorial emphases.

Some group boycotts are illegal *per se* while others are subject to the rule of reason. Group boycotts designed to eliminate a competitor or to force that competitor to meet a group standard are illegal *per se* if the group has market power. On the other hand, cooperative arrangements "designed to increase economic efficiency and render markets more, rather than less, competitive" are subject to the rule of reason. Finally, most courts hold that the *per se* rule of illegality for concerted refusals to deal extends only to horizontal boycotts, not to vertical refusals to deal. Most courts have held that a rule of reason test should govern all nonprice vertical restraints, including concerted refusals to deal.

Tying arrangement

prohibited if it tends to create a monopoly or may substantially lessen competition

Tying Arrangements A **tying arrangement** occurs when the seller of a product, service, or intangible (the "tying" product) conditions its sale on the buyer's purchasing a second product, service, or intangible (the "tied" product) from the seller. For example, imagine that Xerox, a major manufacturer of photocopying equipment, required all purchasers of its photocopiers also to purchase from Xerox all of the paper they would use with the copiers. Xerox would thereby tie the sale of its photocopier—the *tying* product—to the sale of paper—the *tied* product.

Because tying arrangements limit buyers' freedom of choice and may exclude competitors, the law closely scrutinizes such agreements. A tying arrangement exists in situations in which a seller exploits its economic power in one market to expand its empire into another market. When the seller has considerable economic power in the tying product and more than an insubstantial amount of interstate commerce is affected in the tied product, the tying arrangement will be *per se* illegal. Economic power may be demonstrated by showing that (1) the seller occupied a dominant position in the tying market; (2) the seller's product enjoys an advantage not shared by its competitors in the tying market; or (3) a substantial number of customers have accepted the tying arrangement, and the only explanation for their willingness to comply is the seller's economic power in the tying market. If the seller lacks economic power, the tying arrangement is judged by the rule of reason test.

See the Ethical Dilemma at the end of this chapter.

Eastman Kodak Co. v. Image Technical Services, Inc.
Supreme Court of the United States, 1992
504 U.S. 451, 112 S.Ct. 2072, 119 L.Ed.2d 265
http://scholar.google.com/scholar_case?case=6652719385155799724&q=504+U.S.+451&hl=en&as_sdt=2,22

FACTS Eastman Kodak Co. manufactures and sells photocopiers and micrographic equipment. Kodak also services the equipment and sells replacement parts. Image Technical Services, Inc., is a group of independent service organizations (ISOs) that in the early 1980s began servicing Kodak equipment. Kodak subsequently established policies of selling parts only to buyers of the Kodak equipment who used Kodak service or who repaired their own machines. As part of the same policy, Kodak sought to limit ISO access to other sources of Kodak parts (such as those manufactured by original equipment manufacturers [OEMs]). Kodak made an agreement with the OEMs not to sell parts to ISOs and pressured individual equipment owners and independent parts distributors not to sell Kodak parts. Kodak succeeded in its intention to restrict ISOs from servicing Kodak machines. Some ISOs were forced out of business; others lost significant revenue. Customers were forced to switch to Kodak service, even if they preferred ISO service.

In 1987, the ISOs filed an action alleging that Kodak had unlawfully tied the sale of service to the sale of parts, in violation of Section 1 of the Sherman Act, and had unlawfully monopolized and attempted to monopolize the sale of service for Kodak machines, in violation of Section 2 of the Sherman Act. Kodak filed for summary judgment.

DECISION Summary judgment denied.

OPINION To defeat Kodak's motion for summary judgment, the ISOs must demonstrate, first, that service and parts are two distinct products and therefore able to be tied and, second, that Kodak had indeed tied the two products. Evidence presented showed that, historically, service and parts have been sold separately and, therefore, that they are separate products. The question remains whether Kodak possessed significant economic power in the tying market. The ISOs claim that because some parts are available only from Kodak, Kodak has excluded service competition, boosted service

prices, and forced unwilling consumption of Kodak service. This evidence alone is sufficient to entitle respondents to a trial on their market power claim. Kodak counters, however, that because it does not possess market power in the equipment market, it cannot possess market power in the parts sales and service market. Its logic is that if it were to boost prices in the parts sales and service markets, it would lose sales in the equipment market—its main sales area—because customers would buy equipment with more attractive service costs. This, however, must be determined by the economic realities of the marketplace, not by Kodak's theoretical disclaimers.

Regarding the second part of the allegations—that Kodak has monopolized or attempted to monopolize the service and parts market—it is clear that Kodak has succeeded in controlling almost 100 percent of the market of Kodak parts. The question remains as to whether controlling one brand of parts constitutes a market. Kodak claims that one brand cannot define a market, but the respondents claim that because the parts are not interchangeable with other brands, Kodak parts are, from the consumer's perspective, the entire relevant product market.

In the end, it may be decided that Kodak's parts, service, and equipment are one unified market or that the equipment market competition does discipline the aftermarkets of service and parts so that all three are competitively priced. Nonetheless, in this case, when we weigh the risk of deterring procompetitive behavior by proceeding to trial against the risk that illegal behavior will go unpunished, the balance tips against summary judgment.

INTERPRETATION One who possesses sufficient economic power in one market will not be permitted to gain unfair advantage in a different or tied market.

CRITICAL THINKING QUESTION Do you think tying arrangements are anticompetitive?

CONCEPT REVIEW 42-1

Restraints of Trade Under Sherman Act

Type of Restraint	Standard	
	Per Se Illegal	Rule of Reason
Price fixing	Horizontal	Vertical
Market allocations	Horizontal	Vertical
Group boycotts or refusals to deal	Horizontal Vertical (Minority)	Vertical (Majority)
Tying arrangements	If seller has economic power in tying product and affects a substantial amount of interstate commerce in the tied product	If seller lacks economic power in tying product

Monopolies [42-1b]

Economic analysis indicates that a monopolist will use its power to limit production and increase prices. Therefore, a monopolistic market will produce fewer goods than a competitive market would and will sell these goods at higher prices. Addressing the problem of monopolization, Section 2 of the Sherman Act prohibits **monopolies** and any attempts or conspiracies to monopolize. Thus, Section 2 prohibits both agreements among businesses and, unlike Section 1, unilateral conduct by one firm.

Monopolization   Although the language of Section 2 ostensibly prohibits *all* monopolies, the courts have required that a firm not only must possess market power but also must have attained the monopoly power unfairly or abused that power, once attained. By itself, the possession of monopoly power is not considered a violation of Section 2 because a firm may have obtained such power through its skills in developing, marketing, and selling products—that is, through the very competitive conduct that the antitrust laws are designed to promote.

Because it is extremely rare to find an unregulated industry with only one firm, determining the presence of monopoly power involves defining the degree of market dominance that constitutes such power. **Monopoly power** is the ability to control price or to exclude competitors from the marketplace. In grappling with this question of power, the courts have developed a number of criteria; but the most common test is market share. A market share greater than 75 percent generally indicates monopoly power, whereas a share less than 50 percent does not. A share between 50 and 75 percent is, in itself, inconclusive.

Market share is a firm's fractional share of the total relevant product and geographic markets, but defining these relevant markets is often a difficult and subjective project for the courts. The relevant *product market*, as demonstrated in the following case, includes products that are substitutable for the firm's product on the basis of price, quality, and adaptability for other purposes. For example, although brick and wood siding are both used on building exteriors, it is unlikely they would be considered part of the same product market. On the other hand, Coca-Cola and Seven-Up are both soft drinks and would be considered part of the same product market.

Monopolies

Section 2 prohibits monopolization, attempts to monopolize, and conspiracies to monopolize

Monopolization

requires market power (ability to control or exclude others from the marketplace) plus either the unfair attainment of the power or the abuse of such power

Monopoly power

ability to control price or exclude others from the marketplace

United States v. E. I. du Pont de Nemours & Co.
Supreme Court of the United States, 1956
351 U.S. 377, 76 S.Ct. 994, 100 L.Ed. 1264
http://scholar.google.com/scholar_case?q=76+S.Ct.+994&hl=en&as_sdt=6,34&case=11618050296866736407&scilh=0

FACTS In 1923, E. I. du Pont was granted the exclusive right to make and sell cellophane in North America. In 1927, the company introduced a moisture proof brand of cellophane that was ideal for various wrapping needs. Although more expensive than most competing wrapping, it offered a desired combination of transparency, strength, and cost. Except for its permeability to gases, however, cellophane had no qualities that a number of competing materials did not possess as well. Cellophane sales increased dramatically, and by 1950, du Pont produced almost 75 percent of the cellophane sold in the United States. Nevertheless, sales of the material constituted less than 20 percent of the sales of "flexible packaging materials."

The United States brought this action, contending that by so dominating cellophane production, du Pont had monopolized a part of trade or commerce in violation of the Sherman Act. Du Pont argued that it had not monopolized because it did not have the power to control the price of cellophane or to exclude competitors from the market for flexible wrapping materials. The government took a direct appeal from a ruling in favor of du Pont.

DECISION Judgment for du Pont affirmed.

OPINION The first step in determining whether du Pont has monopolized is to determine whether the company has monopoly power in the relevant market. Monopoly power is the power to control prices or to exclude competition in the relevant market.

The relevant market consists of commodities reasonably interchangeable by consumers for the same purposes. Control of the relevant market, in turn, depends on the availability and interchangeability of competing products. A measure of this interchangeability is the cross-elasticity of demand between cellophane and the other wrappings—that is, the responsiveness of the sales of cellophane to changes in the price of other wrapping materials. Here, the evidence shows that sales of the other materials were highly sensitive to changes in the price of cellophane, thus indicating that the products compete in the same market. In other words, the interchangeability of cellophane with other wrapping materials suffices to define the relevant market for purposes of determining whether du Pont has monopolized the market for all flexible wrapping materials. Although it accounted for more than 17 percent of the sales in that larger market, du Pont cannot be said, by that proportion of sales, to have the power to control prices or exclude competition.

INTERPRETATION The relevant product includes products that are substituted for the firm's product on the basis of price, quality, and adaptability.

ETHICAL QUESTION Did the Court fairly decide this case? Explain.

CRITICAL THINKING QUESTION What factors should be considered in deciding the interchangeability of products? Explain.

The relevant *geographic market* is the territory in which the firm sells its products or services. This may be at the local, regional, or national level. For instance, the relevant geographic market for the manufacture and sale of aluminum might be national, whereas that of a taxi company would be local. The scope of a geographic market depends on factors such as transportation costs, the type of product or service, and the location of competitors and customers.

If sufficient monopoly power has been proved, the law must then show that the firm has engaged in **unfair conduct**. However, the courts have yet to agree on what constitutes such conduct. One judicial approach is to place upon a firm possessing monopoly power the burden of proving that it acquired such power passively or that the power was "thrust" upon it. An alternative view is that monopoly power, combined with conduct designed to exclude competitors, violates Section 1. A third approach requires monopoly power plus some type of predatory practice, such as pricing below marginal costs. For example, one case that adopted the third approach held that a firm does not violate Section 2 of the Sherman Act if it attained its market share (1) through research, technical innovation, or a superior product or (2) through ordinary marketing methods available to all. In a decision that appears to combine these approaches, the Supreme Court has held that "[i]f a firm has been attempting to exclude rivals on some basis other than efficiency, it is fair to characterize its behavior as predatory."

To date, however, the U.S. Supreme Court has yet to identify the exact conduct, beyond the mere possession of monopoly power, that violates Section 2. To do so, the Court must resolve the complex and conflicting market and business policies that this most basic question of monopolies involves.

Attempts to monopolize specific intent to monopolize, plus a dangerous probability of success

Attempts to Monopolize

Section 2 also prohibits **attempts to monopolize**. As with monopolization, the courts have had difficulty developing a standard that distinguishes undesirable conduct likely to engender a monopoly from healthy, competitive conduct. The standard test applied by the courts requires proof of a specific intent to monopolize plus a dangerous probability of success; however, among other things, this test neither defines "intent" nor offers a standard of power by which to measure "success." Recent cases suggest that the greater the measure of market power a firm acquires, the less flagrant must its conduct be to constitute an attempt. These cases, however, do not specify any threshold level of market power.

Conspiracies to Monopolize Section 2 also condemns conspiracies to monopolize. Few cases involve this offense alone, as any conspiracy to monopolize would also constitute, in violation of Section 1, a combination in restraint of trade.

CLAYTON ACT [42-2]

In 1914, Congress strengthened the Sherman Act by adopting the Clayton Act, which was expressly designed "to supplement existing laws against unlawful restraints and monopolies." The Clayton Act provides only for civil actions, not for criminal penalties. Private parties may bring civil actions in federal court for treble damages and attorneys' fees. In addition, the Justice Department and the FTC are authorized to bring civil actions, including proceedings in equity, to prevent and restrict violations of the Act.

The major provisions of the Clayton Act deal with price discrimination, tying contracts, exclusive dealing, and mergers. Section 2, which deals with price discrimination, was amended and rewritten by the Robinson-Patman Act, which will be discussed later in this chapter. The Clayton Act exempts labor, agricultural, and horticultural organizations from all antitrust laws.

Tying Contracts and Exclusive Dealing [42-2a]

Tying arrangement
conditioning a sale of a desired product (tying product) on the buyer's purchasing a second product (tied product)

Section 3 of the Clayton Act prohibits **tying arrangements** and exclusive dealing, selling, or leasing arrangements that prevent purchasers from dealing with the seller's competitors when such arrangements *may* substantially lessen competition or *tend* to create a monopoly. This section is intended to stifle fledgling anticompetitive practices before they grow into violations of Section 1 or 2 of the Sherman Act. Unlike the Sherman Act, however, Section 3 applies only to practices involving commodities, not to those that involve services, intangibles, or land.

Tying arrangements, discussed earlier, have been labeled by the Supreme Court as serving "hardly any purpose beyond the suppression of competition." Although the Court at one time indicated that the standards applied under the Sherman Act differed from those applied under the Clayton Act, recent lower court cases suggest that the same rules now govern both types of actions.

Exclusive dealing arrangement
seller or lessor conditions agreement upon the buyer's or lessee's promise not to deal in competing goods

Exclusive dealing arrangements are agreements by which the seller or lessor of a product conditions the agreement upon the buyer's or lessee's promise not to deal in a competitor's goods. For example, a manufacturer of razors might require retailers wishing to sell its line of shaving equipment to agree not to carry competing merchandise. Such conduct, although treated more leniently than tying arrangements, violates Section 3 if it tends to create a monopoly or may substantially lessen competition. The courts treat exclusive dealing arrangements more leniently because such arrangements may bolster competition to the extent that they benefit buyers, and thus, indirectly, the ultimate consumers, by ensuring supplies, deterring price increases, and enabling long-term planning on the basis of known costs.

Merger
prohibited if it tends to create a monopoly or may substantially lessen competition

Horizontal merger
acquisition by one company of a competing company

Vertical merger
acquisition by one company of one of its suppliers or customers

Mergers [42-2b]

In the United States, corporate mergers have helped to reshape both corporate structure and our economic system. **Mergers** are horizontal, vertical, or conglomerate, depending on the relationship between the acquirer and the company acquired. A **horizontal merger** involves a company's acquisition of all or part of the stock or assets of a competing company. For example, if IBM were to acquire Apple, this would be a horizontal merger. A **vertical merger** is a company's acquisition of one of its customers or suppliers. A vertical merger is a *forward* merger if the acquiring company purchases a *customer*, such as the purchase of Revco Discount Drug Stores by Procter & Gamble Company. A vertical merger is a *backward* merger if the acquiring company

Conglomerate merger
an acquisition by one company of another that is not a competitor, customer, or supplier

purchases a supplier, for example, if Best Buy were to purchase Whirlpool Corporation. The third type of merger, the **conglomerate merger**, is a catchall category that covers all acquisitions not involving a competitor, customer, or supplier.

Section 7 of the Clayton Act prohibits a corporation from merging or acquiring another corporation's stock or assets when such an action would substantially lessen competition or would tend to create a monopoly. Currently, the law regarding horizontal, vertical, and conglomerate mergers is, particularly with respect to the last two, in a state of flux.

The principal objective of the antitrust law governing mergers is to maintain competition. Accordingly, the courts scrutinize the legality of horizontal mergers most carefully. Factors that affect this review include the market share of each of the merging firms, the degree of industry concentration, the number of firms in the industry, entry barriers, market trends, the vigor and strength of other competitors in the industry, the character and history of the merging firms, market demand, and the extent of industry price competition. The leading Supreme Court cases on horizontal mergers date from the 1960s and early 1970s. Since then, lower federal courts, the Department of Justice, and the FTC have emphasized antitrust law's goal of promoting economic efficiency. Accordingly, while the Supreme Court cases remain the law of the land, recent lower court decisions reflect a greater willingness to tolerate industry concentrations. Nevertheless, the government continues to prosecute, and the courts continue to condemn, horizontal mergers that are likely to harm consumers. Since 2009, there has been a significant increase in the merger oversight activities of the Department of Justice and the FTC.

Hospital Corp. of America v. FTC
United States Court of Appeals, Seventh Circuit, 1986
807 F.2d 1381
http://scholar.google.com/scholar_case?case=2172341578258873948&q=807+F.2d Þ 1381&hl=en&as_sdt=2,34

FACTS Hospital Corporation of America (HCA), the largest proprietary hospital chain in the United States, originally owned one hospital in the Chattanooga, Tennessee, area. Between 1981 and 1982, at a cost of $700 million, HCA acquired two hospital corporations, which also owned or managed hospitals in the Chattanooga area. After this acquisition, HCA owned or managed five of the eleven hospitals in the area. This acquisition also raised HCA's market share in the Chattanooga area from 14 percent to 26 percent. This made HCA the second-largest provider of hospital services in a highly concentrated market where the four largest firms now had a collective market share of 91 percent, compared with a preacquisition share of 79 percent. After investigation, the Federal Trade Commission (FTC) ruled that the acquisitions by HCA violated Section 7 of the Clayton Act. HCA appealed.

DECISION Judgment for the FTC affirmed.

OPINION Section 7 of the Clayton Act prohibits a merger or acquisition by a corporation that may lessen competition substantially or tend to create a monopoly. The application of Section 7 necessarily requires a prediction of the merger's impact, both present and future, on competition. The U.S. Supreme Court has repeatedly said that the economic concept of competition, rather than any desire to preserve rivals as such, is the lodestar that shall guide the application of the antitrust laws, including Section 7 of the Clayton Act. In applying Section 7, the FTC is required to judge whether the challenged acquisition is likely to hurt consumers by making it easier for the firms in the market to collude, expressly or tacitly, and thereby force prices above the competitive level. Section 7 does not require proof that a merger or other acquisition has created higher prices in the affected market. All that is necessary is that the merger create an appreciable danger of such consequences in the future. The challenged acquisition gave four firms control over an entire market, and as a result they would have little to fear if they raised prices above the competitive level.

INTERPRETATION A merger is illegal if it tends to create a monopoly or would substantially lessen competition.

ETHICAL QUESTION Did the court fairly decide this case? Explain.

CRITICAL THINKING QUESTION Do you agree that the government sufficiently proved its case? Explain.

Though far less likely to challenge vertical mergers, the Justice Department and the FTC will attack vertical mergers that are likely to raise entry barriers in the industry or to bar other firms in the acquiring firm's industry from competitively significant customers or suppliers. Although the Supreme Court has not decided a vertical merger case since 1972, recent decisions indicate that at least some lower courts have been willing to condemn only those vertical mergers that clearly show anticompetitive effects.

Finally, conglomerate mergers have been challenged only (1) when one of the merging firms would be highly likely to enter the other firm's market or (2) when the merged company would be disproportionately large, compared with the largest competitors in its industry.

The Justice Department and the FTC have both indicated that they will be primarily concerned with horizontal mergers in highly or moderately concentrated industries and that they question the benefits of challenging vertical and conglomerate mergers. Both the Justice Department and the FTC have justified this policy on the basis that the latter two types of mergers are necessary to transfer assets to their most productive use and that any challenge to such mergers would impose costs on consumers without corresponding benefits.

Antitrust law, as currently applied, focuses on the size of the merged firm in relation to the relevant market, not on the resulting entity's absolute size. In 1992 (subsequently revised in 1997 and 2010), the Justice Department and the FTC jointly issued new Horizontal Merger Guidelines to replace their separate guidelines originally issued in 1968. In doing so, the two agencies sought to prevent market power that results in "a transfer of wealth from buyers to sellers or a misallocation of resources." The guidelines are designed to provide an analytical framework to judge the impact of potential mergers.

The 2010 guidelines are intended to identify harmful mergers while avoiding unnecessary interference with those mergers that are economically beneficial or likely will have no competitive effect on the market: "These guidelines are intended to assist the business community ... by increasing the transparency of the analytical process." The 2010 guidelines clarify that "merger analysis does not use a single methodology but rather is a fact-specific process through which the agencies employ a variety of tools to analyze the evidence to determine whether a merger may substantially lessen competition." In addition, the 2010 rules explain (1) what sources of evidence and categories of evidence the agencies have found to be informative, (2) that market definition is not an end in itself or a necessary starting point of merger analysis, and (3) that market concentration is a useful tool to the extent it illuminates the merger's likely competitive effects. The 2010 guidelines add a new section dealing with mergers of powerful buyers and mergers between competing buyers.

The 1992, 1997, and 2010 guidelines, like their earlier counterparts, quantify market concentration through the Herfindahl-Hirschman Index (HHI) and measure a horizontal merger's impact on the index. This concentration index is calculated by summing the squares of the individual market shares of all firms in the market. An industry with only one firm would have an HHI of ten thousand (100^2). With two firms of equal size, the index would be five thousand ($50^2 + 50^2$); with five firms of equal size, the result would be two thousand ($20^2 + 20^2 + 20^2 + 20^2 + 20^2$). The increase a merger would cause in the index is calculated by doubling the product of the merging firms' market shares. For example, the merger of two firms with market shares of 5 percent and 10 percent respectively would increase the index by one hundred ($5 \times 10 \times 2 = 100$).

The 2010 guidelines classify an HHI of less than one thousand five hundred as an unconcentrated market, an HHI between one thousand five hundred and two thousand five hundred as a moderately concentrated market, and an HHI above two thousand five hundred as a highly concentrated market. The 2010 guidelines indicate that the FTC and Department of Justice employ the following general standards for the relevant markets they have defined:

Small Change in Concentration: Mergers involving an increase in the HHI of less than 100 points are unlikely to have adverse competitive effects and ordinarily require no further analysis.

Unconcentrated Markets: Mergers resulting in unconcentrated markets are unlikely to have adverse competitive effects and ordinarily require no further analysis.

Moderately Concentrated Markets: Mergers resulting in moderately concentrated markets that involve an increase in the HHI of more than 100 points potentially raise significant competitive concerns and often warrant scrutiny.

Highly Concentrated Markets: Mergers resulting in highly concentrated markets that involve an increase in the HHI of between 100 points and 200 points potentially raise significant competitive concerns and often warrant scrutiny. Mergers resulting in highly concentrated markets that involve an increase in the HHI of more than 200 points will be presumed to be likely to enhance market power. The presumption may be rebutted by persuasive evidence showing that the merger is unlikely to enhance market power.

Practical Advice

When considering potential merger targets, make sure to take into consideration the Herfindahl-Hirschman Index and the impact of the merger on the Index.

The 2010 guidelines explain that the purpose of these thresholds is to provide one way to identify some mergers unlikely to raise competitive concerns and some others for which it is particularly important to examine whether other competitive factors confirm, reinforce, or counteract the potentially harmful effects of increased concentration. The higher the postmerger HHI and the increase in the HHI, the greater are the Agencies' potential competitive concerns and the greater is the likelihood that the Agencies will request additional information to conduct their analysis.

The National Association of Attorneys General, composed of the attorneys general of the fifty states and five U.S. territories and protectorates, has also promulgated its own set of guidelines for horizontal mergers. Intended to apply to enforcement actions brought by the state attorneys general under federal and state antitrust statutes, the state guidelines place a greater emphasis on preventing transfers of wealth from consumers to producers than do the federal guidelines. Accordingly, the state attorneys general would be more likely to challenge certain mergers than would the federal government.

ROBINSON-PATMAN ACT [42-3]

Originally, Section 2 of the Clayton Act prohibited sellers only from differentially pricing their products in order to injure local or regional competitors. In 1936, in an attempt to limit the power of large purchasers, Congress amended Section 2 of the Clayton Act by adopting the Robinson-Patman Act, which further prohibits **price discrimination** in interstate commerce concerning commodities of like grade and quality. More specifically, the Act prohibits buyers from inducing and sellers from granting discrimination in prices. To constitute a violation, the price discrimination must substantially lessen competition or tend to create a monopoly.

Under this Act, a seller of goods may not grant discounts to buyers, including allowances for advertisements, counter displays, and samples, unless the seller offers the same discounts to all other purchasers on proportionately equal terms. The Act also prohibits other types of discounts, rebates, and allowances and makes it unlawful to sell goods at unreasonably low prices for the purpose of destroying competition or eliminating a competitor. The Act also makes it unlawful for a person knowingly to "induce or receive" an illegal discrimination in price, thus imposing liability on the buyer as well as the seller. Violation of the Robinson-Patman Act, with limited exceptions, is civil, not criminal, in nature. Price differentials may be justified by proof of either a cost savings to the seller or a good faith price reduction to meet a competitor's lawful price.

Primary-Line Injury [42-3a]

In enacting Section 2 of the Clayton Act in 1914, Congress was concerned with sellers who sought to harm or eliminate their competitors through price discrimination. Injuries accruing to a seller's competitors are called **primary-line injuries**. Because the Act forbids price discrimination only when such discrimination may substantially lessen competition or may tend to create a monopoly, the plaintiff in a Robinson-Patman primary-line injury case either must show that the defendant, with the intention of harming competition, has engaged in predatory pricing or must present a detailed market analysis that demonstrates how the defendant's price discrimination actually harmed competition. To prove predatory intent, a plaintiff may rely either on direct evidence of such intent or, more commonly, on inferences drawn from the defendant's conduct, such as below-cost or unprofitable pricing for a significant period of time. A predatory pricing scheme may also be challenged under the Sherman Act.

Secondary- and Tertiary-Line Injury [42-3b]

In amending Section 2 of the Clayton Act through the adoption of the Robinson-Patman Act, Congress was concerned primarily with small buyers, who were harmed by the discounts that sellers granted to large buyers. Injuries that accrue to some buyers because of the lower prices granted to others are called "secondary-line" injuries. To prove the required harm to competition, a plaintiff in a **secondary-line injury** case either must show substantial and sustained intramarket price differentials or must offer a detailed market analysis that demonstrates actual harm to competition. Because courts have been willing in secondary-line injury cases to infer harm to

Price discrimination
price differential

Primary-line injury
injury to a seller's competitors

Secondary-line injury
injury to competitors of the buyers

competition from a sustained and substantial price differential, proving a secondary-line injury is generally easier than proving a primary-line injury.

Tertiary-line injury occurs when the recipient of a favored price passes the benefits of the lower price on to the next level of distribution. Purchasers from other secondary-line sellers are injured in that they do not receive the benefits of the lower price; these purchasers may recover damages from the original discriminating seller.

Tertiary-line injury

injury to purchasers from
other secondary-line sellers

Cost Justification [42-3c]

If a seller can show that it costs less to sell a product to a particular buyer, the seller may lawfully pass along the cost savings. Section 2(a) provides that the Clayton Act does not "prevent differentials which make only due allowance for differences in the cost of manufacture, sale, or delivery resulting from the differing methods or quantities in which … commodities are … sold or delivered." For example, if Retailer A orders goods from Seller X by the carload, whereas Retailer B orders in small quantities, Seller X, who delivers F.O.B. (free on board) buyer's warehouse, may pass along the transportation savings to Retailer A. Nonetheless, although it is possible to pass along transportation savings, passing along alleged savings in manufacturing or distribution is extremely difficult because calculating and proving such savings is a complex task. Therefore, sellers rarely rely upon the defense of cost justification.

Meeting Competition [42-3d]

A seller may lower its price in a good faith attempt to meet competition. To illustrate:

1. Manufacturer X sells its motor oil to retail outlets for $0.65 per can. Manufacturer Y approaches A, one of Manufacturer X's customers, and offers to sell a comparable type of motor oil for $0.60 per can. Manufacturer X will be permitted to lower its price to A to $0.60 per can and need not lower its price to its other retail customers—B, C, and D. However, Manufacturer X may *not* lower its price to A to $0.55 unless it also offers this price to B, C, and D.
2. Manufacturer X will not be permitted to lower its price to A without also lowering its price to B, C, and D, in order to allow A to meet the lower price A's competitor, N, charges when selling Manufacturer Y's oil. The "meeting competition" defense is available only to meet the competition of the seller: the defense does not extend to a competitor's price to a specific, individual purchaser (see Figure 42-1).

A seller may beat its competitor's price, however, if it does not know the competitor's price, cannot reasonably determine the competitor's price, and acts reasonably in setting its own price.

FEDERAL TRADE COMMISSION ACT [42-4]

Federal Trade Commission Act

to prevent unfair methods of competition and unfair or deceptive practices, actions may be brought by the Federal Trade Commission, not by private individuals

In 1914, through the enactment of the **Federal Trade Commission Act**, Congress created the FTC, charged with preventing unfair methods of competition and unfair or deceptive acts or practices in commerce. To this end, the five-member commission is empowered to conduct appropriate investigations and hearings and to issue against violators cease-and-desist orders that are enforceable in the federal courts. The Supreme Court has commented on the breadth of the commission's power:

The "unfair methods of competition," which are condemned by … the Act, are not confined to those that were illegal at common law or that were condemned by the Sherman Act.… It is also clear that the Federal Trade Commission Act was designed to supplement and bolster the Sherman Act and the Clayton Act … to *stop in their incipiency acts and practices which, when full blown, would violate those Acts.* (Emphasis added.)

Complaints may be instituted by the FTC, which, after a hearing, "has wide latitude for judgment and the courts will not interfere except where the remedy selected has no reasonable relation to the unlawful practices found to exist." Although the FTC most frequently enters a cease-and-desist order having the effect of an injunction, it may order other relief, such as affirmative disclosure, corrective advertising, and the granting of patent licenses on a reasonable

Figure 42-1 Meeting Competition Defense

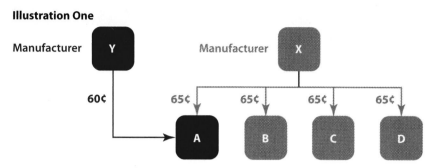

Illustration One

Result: Manufacturer **X** may lower its price to A to 60¢ without lowering its price to B, C, and D.

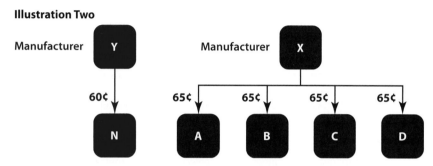

Illustration Two

Result: Manufacturer **X** may *not* lower its price to A to 60¢ without lowering its price to B, C, and D.

royalty basis. Appeals may be taken from orders of the FTC to the U.S. Courts of Appeals, which have exclusive jurisdiction to enforce, set aside, or modify FTC orders.

In performing its duties, the FTC investigates not only possible violations of the antitrust laws but also unfair methods of competition. For a more detailed discussion of the FTC and its powers, see Chapter 44.

ETHICAL DILEMMA

When Is an Agreement Anticompetitive?

Facts Robert Crane has been hired as a manager of Sandra Renee, Inc., a prosperous fashion design manufacturer. A maker of women's dresses, Sandra Renee specializes in formal gowns. An important and growing segment of its business consists of renting gowns to retail chains. Because high prices often deter consumers from purchasing formalwear, the design industry as a whole has been benefiting from formal gown rentals. Under its rental arrangement, Sandra Renee receives a percentage from each rental. The rental also provides increased exposure and advertising for Sandra Renee.

Robert was sent to a meeting of the Association of Fashion Design Manufacturers. At the meeting, representatives from

throughout the industry discussed the advantages of rentals; two members raised the question of what action should be taken if a retailer sold one of the gowns. After a brief debate, the members agreed that gowns should no longer be provided to such retailers. The representatives also discussed the different pricing mechanisms their respective firms used in dealing with renting retailers. They generally agreed that a flat dollar fee plus a significant percentage of the rental fee was the best pricing scheme.

Robert grew concerned that this discussion was inappropriate. But because he was new to the association, he was uncertain what to do. He considered voicing his objection, leaving the meeting, or staying but remaining silent.

Social, Policy, and Ethical Considerations

1. Was Robert's sense of discomfort with the discussion justified? Explain.

2. What action should Robert have taken?

3. Whose interests were at stake at this meeting? How might such a meeting affect the public, Sandra Renee, and the company's competitors?

4. To what extent should employees be informed about the ethical and legal obligations of trade associations before attending meetings such as this?

5. What actions are open to an employee who disagrees with a company position that violates the law?

CHAPTER SUMMARY

Sherman Antitrust Act

Restraint of Trade Section 1 prohibits contracts, combinations, and conspiracies that restrain trade

- *Rule of Reason* standard that balances the anticompetitive effects against the procompetitive effects of the restraint
- *Per Se Violations* conclusively presumed unreasonable and therefore illegal
- *Quick Look Standard* a modified or abbreviated rule of reason standard
- *Horizontal Restraints* agreements among competitors
- *Vertical Restraints* agreements among parties at different levels in the chain of distribution

Application of Section 1

- *Price Fixing* an agreement with the purpose or effect of inhibiting price competition; horizontal agreements are *per se* illegal, while vertical price fixing is judged by the rule of reason
- *Market Allocation* division of markets by customer type, geography, or products; horizontal agreements are *per se* illegal, while vertical agreements are judged by the rule of reason standard
- *Boycott* agreement among competitors not to deal with a supplier or customer; *per se* illegal
- *Tying Arrangement* conditioning a sale of a desired product (tying product) on the buyer's purchasing a second product (tied product); *per se* illegal if the seller has considerable power in the tying product or affects a more than insubstantial amount of interstate commerce in the tied product

Monopolies Section 2 prohibits monopolization, attempts to monopolize, and conspiracies to monopolize

- *Monopolization* requires market power (ability to control or exclude others from the marketplace) plus either the unfair attainment of the power or the abuse of such power
- *Attempt to Monopolize* specific intent to monopolize, plus a dangerous probability of success
- *Conspiracies to Monopolize*

Sanctions

- *Civil Liability* injured parties may recover treble damages (three times actual loss)
- *Criminal Penalties*

Clayton Act

Tying Arrangement prohibited if it tends to create a monopoly or may substantially lessen competition

Exclusive Dealing arrangement by which a party has sole right to a market; prohibited if it tends to create a monopoly or may substantially lessen competition

Merger prohibited if it tends to create a monopoly or may substantially lessen competition

- *Horizontal Merger* one company's acquisition of a competing company
- *Vertical Merger* a company's acquisition of one of its suppliers or customers
- *Conglomerate Merger* the acquisition of a company that is not a competitor, customer, or supplier

Sanctions civil actions may be brought for treble damages and injunctions

Robinson-Patman Act

Price Discrimination the Act prohibits buyers from inducing or sellers from giving different prices to buyers of commodities of similar grade and quality

Injury plaintiff may prove injury to competitors of the seller (primary-line injury), to competitors of other buyers (secondary-line injury), or to purchasers from other secondary-line sellers (tertiary-line injury)

Defenses (1) cost justification, (2) meeting competition, and (3) functional discounts

Sanctions civil liability (treble damages); criminal penalties in limited situations

Federal Trade Commission Act

Purpose to prevent unfair methods of competition and unfair or deceptive practices

Sanctions actions may be brought by the Federal Trade Commission, not by private individuals

QUESTIONS

1. Discuss the validity and effect of each of the following situations:
   a. A, B, and C, manufacturers of radios, orally agree that due to the disastrous, cutthroat competition in the market, they will establish a reasonable price to charge their purchasers.
   b. A, B, C, and D, newspaper publishers, agree not to charge their customers more than $0.30 per newspaper.
   c. A, a distiller of liquor, and B, A's retail distributor, agree that B should charge a price of $5.00 per bottle.

2. Discuss the validity of the following:
   a. A territorial allocation agreement between two manufacturers of the same type of products, whereby neither will sell its products in the area allocated to the other.
   b. An agreement between manufacturer and distributor not to sell a dealer a particular product or parts necessary for the product's repair.

3. Universal Video sells video recording equipment in the United States, and its sales constitute 40 percent of the total sales of such equipment in the United States. One-half of Universal's sales are to Giant Retailer, a company that possesses 50 percent of the retail market. Giant is presently seeking (1) to obtain an exclusive dealing arrangement with Universal or (2) to acquire Universal. Advise Giant as to the validity of its alternatives.

4. Z sells cameras to A, B, C, and D for $160 per camera. Y, one of Z's competitors, sells a comparable camera to A for $148.50. Z, in response to this competitive pressure from Y, lowers its price to A to $148.50. B, C, and D insist that Z lower its price to them to $148.50, but Z refuses. B, C, and D sue Z for unlawful price discrimination. Decision? Would your answer differ if Z reduced its price to A to $140?

5. Discount is a discount appliance chain store that continually sells goods at a price below manufacturers' suggested retail prices. A, B, and C, the three largest manufacturers of appliances, agree that unless Discount ceases its discount pricing, they will no longer sell to Discount. Discount refuses, and A, B, and C refuse to sell to Discount. Discount contends that A, B, and C are in violation of antitrust law. Explain whether Discount is correct.

6. Taylor Company produces 77 percent of the coal used in the United States. Coal provides 25 percent of the energy used in the United States. In a suit brought by the United States against Taylor for violation of the antitrust laws, what is the result?

7. Whirlpool Corporation manufactured vacuum cleaners under both its own name and under the Kenmore name. Oreck exclusively distributed the vacuum cleaners sold under the Whirlpool name. Sears, Roebuck & Co. exclusively distributed the Kenmore vacuum cleaners. Oreck alleged that its exclusive distributorship agreement with Whirlpool was not renewed because an unlawful conspiracy existed between Whirlpool and Sears. Oreck further contended that a *per se* rule was applicable because the agreement was (a) price fixing or (b) a group boycott, or (c) both. Who should prevail? Why?

8. Indian Coffee of Pittsburgh, Pennsylvania, marketed vacuum-packed coffee under the Breakfast Cheer brand name in the Pittsburgh and Cleveland, Ohio, areas. Folger Coffee, a leading coffee seller, began selling coffee in Pittsburgh. To make inroads into the new territory, Folger sold its coffee at greatly reduced prices. At first, Indian Coffee met Folger's prices but could not continue operating at such a reduced price and was forced out of the market. Indian Coffee brings an antitrust action. Explain whether Folger has violated the Sherman Act.

9. Justin Manufacturing Company sells high-fashion clothing under the prestigious "Justin" label. The company has a firm policy that it will not deal with any company that sells below its suggested retail price. Justin is informed by one of its customers, XYZ, that its competitor, Duplex, is selling the "Justin" line at a great discount. Justin now demands that Duplex comply with the agreement not to sell the "Justin" line below the suggested retail price. Discuss the implications of this situation.

10. Jay Corporation, the largest manufacturer of bicycles in the United States with 40 percent of the market, has recently entered into an agreement with Retail Bike, the largest retailer of bicycles in the United States with 37 percent of the market, under which Jay will furnish its bicycles only to Retail, and Retail will sell only Jay's bicycles. The government is now questioning this agreement. Discuss.

CASE PROBLEMS

11. Von's Grocery, a large retail grocery chain in Los Angeles, sought to acquire Shopping Bag Food Stores, a direct competitor. At the time of the proposed merger, Von's sales ranked third in the Los Angeles area and Shopping Bag's ranked sixth. Both chains were increasing their number of stores. The merger would have created the second-largest grocery chain in Los Angeles, with total sales in excess of $170 million. Prior to the proposed merger, the number of owners operating single stores declined from 5,365 to 3,590 over a thirteen-year period. During this same period, the number of chains with two or more stores rose from 96 to 150. The United States brought suit against Von's to prevent the merger, claiming that the proposed merger violated Section 7 of the Clayton Act in that it could result in the substantial lessening of competition or could tend to create a monopoly. What should be the result?

12. Boise Cascade Corporation is a wholesaler and retailer of office products. The Federal Trade Commission issued a complaint charging that Boise had violated the Robinson-Patman Act by receiving a wholesaler's discount from certain suppliers on products that Boise resold at retail, in competition with other

retailers that could not obtain wholesale discounts. Has the Robinson-Patman Act been violated? Explain.

13. Great Atlantic and Pacific Tea Company desired to achieve cost savings by switching to the sale of "private label" milk. A&P asked Borden Company, its longtime supplier of "brand label" milk, to submit a bid to supply certain A&P private label dairy products. A&P was not satisfied with Borden's bid, however, so it solicited other offers. Bowman Dairy, a competitor of Borden's, submitted a lower bid. At this point, A&P contacted Borden and asked it to rebid on the private label contract. A&P included a warning that Borden would have to lower its original bid substantially to undercut Bowman's bid. Borden offered a bid that doubled A&P's potential annual cost savings. A&P accepted Borden's bid. The Federal Trade Commission (FTC) then brought this action, charging that A&P had violated the Robinson-Patman Act by knowingly inducing or receiving illegal price discrimination from Borden. Discuss whether the FTC is correct in its allegations.

14. Clorox is the nation's leading manufacturer of household liquid bleach (accounting for 49 percent—$40 million—of sales annually) and is the only brand sold nationally. Clorox and its next largest competitor, Purex, hold 65 percent of national sales; and the top four bleach manufacturers control 80 percent of sales. Because all bleach is chemically identical, Clorox spends more than $5 million each year in advertising to attract and keep customers.

Procter & Gamble is the dominant national manufacturer of household cleaning products, with yearly sales of $1.1 billion. As with bleach, advertising is vital in the household cleaning products industry. Procter & Gamble annually spends more than $127 million in advertising and promotions. Procter & Gamble decided to diversify into the bleach business because its household cleaning products and bleach are both low-cost, high-turnover consumer goods, are dependent on mass advertising, and are sold to the same customers at the same stores by the same merchandising methods. Procter & Gamble decided to merge with Clorox, rather than start its own bleach division, in order to secure the dominant position in the bleach market immediately. Should the Federal Trade Commission take action against this merger, and, if so, what decision should it make?

15. The National Collegiate Athletic Association (NCAA) adopted a plan for televising college football games to reduce the adverse effect of television coverage on spectator attendance. The plan limited the total number of televised intercollegiate football games and the number of games any one school could televise. No member of the NCAA was permitted to sell any television rights except in accordance with the plan. As part of the plan, the NCAA had agreements with the American Broadcasting Company (ABC) and the Columbia Broadcasting System (CBS) to pay to each school at least a specified minimum price for televising football games. Several member universities now join to bring suit against the NCAA, claiming the new plan is a horizontal price-fixing agreement and an output limitation and as such is illegal *per se*. The NCAA counters that the existence of the product, college football, depends upon member compliance with restrictions and regulations. According to the NCAA, its restrictions, including the television plan, have a procompetitive effect. Is the television plan a reasonable restraint? Explain.

16. The National Society of Professional Engineers (Society) had an ethics rule that prohibited member engineers from disclosing or discussing price/fee information with customers until after the customer had hired a particular engineer. This rule against competitive bidding was designed to maintain high standards in the field of engineering. The Society felt that competitive pressure to offer engineering services at the lowest possible price would encourage engineers to design and specify inefficient, unsafe, and unnecessarily expensive structures and construction methods. According to the Society, awarding engineering contracts to the lowest bidder, regardless of quality, would be dangerous to the public health, safety, and welfare. The Society emphasizes that the rule is not an agreement to fix prices. Rather, it claims the rule was drafted by experienced, highly trained professional engineers to prevent public harm and is therefore reasonable. Does the rule unreasonably restrain trade and thus violate Section 1 of the Sherman Act? Why?

17. During a period of a few years, intense price competition characterized both the retail and the wholesale oil markets. At times, prices in the wholesale market fell below the manufacturer's cost. One cause of the volatile situation was the supply of "distress gasoline" placed on the market by seventeen independent refiners. These independent refiners had no retail sales outlets and little storage capacity, so they were forced to sell their product at "distress prices." In spite of their unprofitable operations, they could not afford to shut down, for, if they did so, they would be apt to lose both their oil connections in the field and their regular customers.

In an attempt to remedy this problem, the major oil companies entered into an informal agreement whereby each selected as its "dancing partner" one or more independent refiners having distress gasoline. The major oil company would then assume responsibility for purchasing the independent's distress supply at the "fair going market price." As a result, the market price of oil rose and the spot market became stable. Have the companies engaged in horizontal price fixing in violation of the Sherman Act? Why?

18. As part of a corporate plan to stimulate sagging television sales, GTE Sylvania began to phase out its wholesale distributors and began to sell its television sets directly to a smaller and more select group of franchised retailers. To this end, Sylvania limited the number of franchises granted for any given area and required each franchisee to sell Sylvania products only from the location or locations at which he was franchised. A franchise did not constitute an exclusive territory, and Sylvania retained sole discretion to increase the number of retailers in an area in light of the success or failure of existing retailers. The strategy apparently was successful, as Sylvania's national market share increased from less than 2 percent to 5 percent.

In the course of carrying out its plan, Sylvania franchised Young Brothers as a television retailer at a San Francisco location one mile from that of Continental T.V., Inc., one of Sylvania's most successful franchisees. A course of feuding began between Sylvania and Continental that reached a head when Continental requested permission to open a store in Sacramento, and Sylvania refused. Continental opened the Sacramento store anyway and began shipping merchandise there from its San Jose warehouse. Shortly thereafter, Sylvania terminated Continental's franchise. Is the franchise location restriction a *per se* violation of the Sherman Act? Explain.

TAKING SIDES

The California Dental Association (CDA) is a voluntary nonprofit association of local dental societies to which some nineteen thousand dentists belong, about three-quarters of those practicing in the state. The CDA lobbies on behalf of its members' interests and conducts marketing and public relations campaigns for their benefit. The dentists who belong to the CDA through these associations agree to abide by a Code of Ethics (Code), which includes a regulation limiting their right to advertise. Responsibility for enforcing the Code rests in the first instance with the local dental societies. Applicants who refuse to withdraw or revise objectionable advertisements may be denied membership, and members are subject to censure, suspension, or expulsion from the CDA.

The Federal Trade Commission (FTC) brought a complaint against the CDA, alleging that it applied its Code so as to restrict truthful, nondeceptive advertising and therefore violated Section 5 of the FTC Act. The FTC alleged that the CDA unreasonably restricted price advertising—particularly discounted fees—and advertising relating to the quality of dental services.

a. What are the arguments that the *per se* standard applies to this case?

b. What are the arguments that a rule of reason standard applies to this case?

c. Which standard should apply to this case? Explain.

Accountants' Legal Liability

CHAPTER 43

It is not uncommon these days to hear expressions of grave concern within our [the accounting] profession about excessive competition, unrestrained solicitation, concentration and a general decline in intra-professional courtesy. ... These concerns have led some to worry that our professionalism is either dead or teetering on the brink of extinction.

Wallace E. Olson
"Is Professionalism Dead?" *The Journal of Accountancy* (July 1978)

CHAPTER OUTCOMES

After reading and studying this chapter, you should be able to:

1. Describe the contract liability of an accountant to her client.

2. Describe for what and to whom an accountant has tort liability.

3. Describe who owns the working papers an accountant generates and whether client information is privileged.

4. Discuss the potential civil and criminal liability of an accountant under the 1933 Securities Act.

5. Discuss the potential civil and criminal liability of an accountant under the 1934 Securities Act.

A n accountant is subject to potential civil liability arising from the professional services he provides to his clients and third parties. This legal liability is imposed by both the common law at the state level and by federal securities laws. In addition, an accountant may violate federal and state criminal law through the performance of his professional activities. In this chapter, we will discuss accountants' legal liability under both state and federal law.

COMMON LAW [43-1]

An accountant's legal responsibility under state law may be based on (1) contract law, (2) tort law, or (3) criminal law. In addition, the common law gives accountants certain rights and privileges; in particular, the ownership of their working papers and, in some states, a limited accountant–client privilege.

Contract Liability [43-1a]

The employment contract between an accountant and client is subject to the general principles of contract law. All of the requirements of a common law contract must be present for the contract to be binding, including offer and acceptance, capacity, consideration, legality, and a writing if, as is often the case, the agreement falls within the one-year provision of the statute of frauds.

On entering into a binding contract (frequently referred to as an **engagement**), the accountant is bound to perform all **explicit duties** she agrees to provide under the contract. For example, if an accountant agrees to complete the audit of a client by October 15 so that the client may release its annual report on time, the accountant is under a contractual obligation to do so. Likewise, an accountant who contractually promises to conduct an audit to detect possible embezzlement is under a contractual obligation to provide for her client an expanded audit *beyond* generally accepted auditing standards (GAAS).

Contract liability
the employment contract between an accountant and her client is subject to the general principles of contract law

Engagement
binding contract for an accountant's services

Explicit duties
the accountant is bound to perform all the duties she expressly agrees to provide

Implicit duties

the accountant impliedly agrees to perform the contract in a competent and professional manner

Practical Advice

As an auditor, always exercise due diligence when auditing a client's financial statements. Moreover, be sure to issue the appropriate opinion.

Third-party beneficiary

noncontracting party whom the contracting parties intend to receive a primary benefit; contract liability extends to the client/ contracting party and to third-party beneficiaries

Breach of contract

general contract law principles apply

Practical Advice

In your engagement letter, clearly specify the terms of your contract and the parties for whom the financial statements are being prepared.

Tort

a private or civil wrong or injury other than a breach of contract

Negligence

an accountant is liable for failing to exercise the degree of care a reasonably competent accountant would exercise under the circumstances

Privity

contractual relationship

Foreseen users

those who the accountant knew would use the work or those who use the work for a purpose of which the accountant knew

By entering into a contract, an accountant also **implicitly** agrees to perform the contract in a competent and professional manner. By agreeing to render professional services, an accountant is held to those standards that are generally accepted by the accounting profession, such as GAAS and generally accepted accounting principles (GAAP). Although accountants need not ensure the absolute accuracy of their work, they must exercise the care of a reasonably skilled professional.

An accountant who breaches his contract will incur liability not only to the client but also to certain third-party beneficiaries. As discussed in Chapter 16, a **third-party beneficiary** is a noncontracting party whom the contracting parties intend to receive the primary benefit under the contract. For example, Otis Manufacturing Co. hires Adler, an accountant, to prepare a financial statement for Otis to use in obtaining a loan from Chemical Bank. Chemical Bank is a third-party beneficiary of the contract between Otis and Adler. Another example of a potential third party is an investor considering the purchase of part or all of a particular company. For a more detailed discussion of third-party beneficiaries, see Chapter 16.

Following general contract principles, an accountant who **materially breaches** his contract will be entitled to no compensation. Thus, if an accountant does not perform an audit on time when time is of the essence, or completes only 60 percent of the audit, she has committed a material breach. On the other hand, an accountant who *substantially performs* her contractual duties is generally entitled to be compensated for the contractually agreed-upon fee, less any damages or loss her nonmaterial breach has caused the client (see Chapter 18).

Tort Liability [43-1b]

In performing his professional services, an accountant may incur tort liability to his client or third parties for negligence or fraud. A **tort**, as discussed in Chapter 7, is a private or civil wrong or injury, other than a breach of contract, for which the courts will provide a remedy in the form of an action for damages.

Negligence An accountant is negligent if she does not exercise the degree of care a reasonably competent accountant would exercise under the circumstances. For example, Arthur, an accountant, is engaged to audit the books of Zebra Corporation. During the audit, Olivia, an officer of Zebra Corporation, notifies Arthur that she suspects that Terrance, the company's treasurer, is engaged in a scheme to embezzle from the corporation. Previously informed that Olivia and Terrance are on bad terms, Arthur does not pursue the matter. Terrance is, in fact, engaged in a commonly used embezzlement scheme. Arthur is negligent for failing to conduct a reasonable investigation of the alleged defalcation. Nonetheless, as mentioned earlier, an accountant is *not* liable for honest inaccuracies or errors of judgment, so long as she exercises reasonable care in performing her duties. Moreover, an accountant need *not guarantee* the accuracy of her reports, provided she acts in a reasonably competent and professional manner.

Most courts do not permit an accountant to raise the defense of the plaintiff's contributory (or comparative) negligence. Nevertheless, a few courts do permit such a defense despite the fact that they recognize "that professional malpractice actions pose peculiar problems and that the comparison of fault between a layperson and a professional should be approached with caution."

Historically, an accountant's liability for negligence extended only to the client and to third-party beneficiaries. Under this view, **privity** of contract was a requirement for a cause of action based on negligence. This approach was established by the landmark case of *Ultramares Corp. v. Touche.*

In recent years, a majority of the states have adopted a **foreseen users** or **foreseen class of users test**. This approach, which also has been adopted by the Second Restatement of Torts, expands the class of protected individuals to include those whom the accountant knew would use the work product *or* those who use the accountant's work for a purpose for which the accountant knew the work would be used. For instance, Denise, an accountant, knows that her client will use a work product to try to obtain a bank loan from Bank of America. Even if the client uses the audited financial statements to obtain a loan from a different bank, Denise would be liable to that second bank for any negligent misrepresentations in the financial statements. This class of protected individuals does not, however, include potential investors and the general public.

Figure 43-1 Accountants' Liability to Third Parties for Negligent Misrepresentation

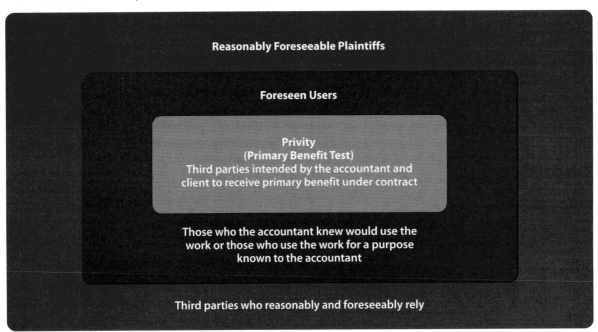

Reasonably Foreseeable Plaintiffs

Foreseen Users

Privity
(Primary Benefit Test)
Third parties intended by the accountant and
client to receive primary benefit under contract

Those who the accountant knew would use the
work or those who use the work for a purpose
known to the accountant

Third parties who reasonably and foreseeably rely

Fraud

an accountant who
commits a fraudulent act
is liable for both
compensatory and punitive
damages to any person
whom he should have
reasonably foreseen would
be injured; a fraudulent act
is a false representation of
fact that is material, is made
with knowledge of its falsity
and with the intention to
deceive, and is justifiably
relied on

Some courts have extended liability to benefit an even broader group: reasonably foreseeable plaintiffs, including those who are neither known to the accountant nor are members of a class of intended recipients. A few states have adopted this test, which requires only that the accountant reasonably foresee that such an individual might use the financial statements. The rationale behind the foreseeability standard of the law of negligence is that a tortfeasor should be fully liable for all the reasonably foreseeable consequences of her conduct. See Figure 43-1 for the various tests applied to accountants' liability to third parties for negligent misrepresentation.

Fraud An accountant who commits a fraudulent act is liable to any person the accountant *should have* reasonably foreseen would be injured through justifiable reliance on the misrepresentation. The required elements of **fraud**, which were more fully discussed in Chapter 11, are (1) a false representation (2) of fact (3) that is material and (4) made with knowledge of its falsity and with the intention to deceive, (5) is justifiably relied on, and (6) causes injury to the plaintiff. An accountant who commits fraud may be held liable for *both* compensatory and punitive damages.

Accountants also have been subject to a number of civil lawsuits based on the Racketeering Influenced and Corrupt Organizations Act (RICO). For a discussion of this act, see Chapter 6.

Murphy v. BDO Seidman, LLP
Court of Appeal, Second District, 2003
113 Cal.App.4th 687, 6 Cal.Rptr.3d 770
http://scholar.google.com/scholar_case?case=6493495192376414472&hl=en&as_sdt=2&as_vis=1

FACTS In November 1995, the defendant accounting firm Logan, Throop & Company (Logan) prepared a financial statement for World Interactive Networks, Inc. (WIN), a non-publicly-traded corporation, for the period ending in August 1995. The statement misrepresented the value of various WIN assets, claiming they were worth $145 million when in fact they amounted to only $30 million. Logan also claimed the financial statement complied with generally accepted accounting principles (GAAP) when it did not. In February 1996, Logan repeated essentially the same misrepresentations in its auditors' report of WIN's

1995 balance sheet. The same month that Logan released its auditors' report, the defendant accounting firm BDO Seidman, LLP (BDO) issued WIN's audited financial statement for 1995. In the statement, BDO misrepresented the value of WIN's assets, claiming they were worth slightly more than $121 million, when they were truly worth only $6.9 million. In addition, BDO misrepresented WIN's shareholder equity as $88 million, when the company was worthless. Several months later, BDO repeated essentially the same misrepresentations when it released its review of WIN's quarterly balance sheet for the period ending March 1996.

Struthers Industries, Inc. was a publicly traded corporation. In 1995, WIN and Struthers agreed to a reverse merger, subject to shareholder approval, in which WIN would sell its assets to Struthers in return for Struthers stock, following which Struthers would become WIN's subsidiary. While the proposed merger was pending, BDO prepared a *pro forma* financial statement of Struthers and WIN as a combined entity, which substantially repeated, from BDO's earlier audit of WIN, the same false asset values and misrepresentations about complying with GAAP. In January 1997, BDO sent the *pro forma* statement to the Securities and Exchange Commission (SEC). The SEC told Struthers the *pro forma* statement did not comply with GAAP because it did not properly account for the inherent uncertainty of the proposed merger. BDO did not tell plaintiffs, all of whom either owned or later bought WIN or Struthers stock, about the SEC's rejection of BDO's accounting for the proposed merger.

In March 1998, WIN and Struthers filed for bankruptcy, and the plaintiffs, who allege they relied on BDO's and Logan's financial statements to buy stock in the companies, lost their investments. Consequently, the plaintiffs sued both accounting firms, alleging causes of action for negligent and intentional misrepresentation. The defendants demurred to the complaint, which the court granted. This appeal followed.

DECISION The trial court's judgment is reversed in part and affirmed in part.

OPINION The defendants argue that their liability for any inaccuracies in the financial statements was only to their clients, WIN and Struthers, not to third parties.

In *Bily v. Arthur Young & Co.* the California Supreme Court formulated a hierarchy of duty for accountants who prepare inaccurate financial statements. Casting an ever-widening circle of obligation,

Bily established that the more egregious the misstatement, the broader the duty: (1) ordinary negligence—*no duty* to third parties; (2) negligent misrepresentation—duty to third parties who would be known with *substantial certainty* to rely on the misrepresentation; and (3) intentional misrepresentation—duty to third parties who could be *reasonably foreseen* to rely on the misrepresentation.

In their complaint regarding negligent misrepresentation, the plaintiffs allege that the defendants were aware that their report would be used by potential investors. This allegation is sufficient to satisfy the test for negligent misrepresentation. Second, the complaint also alleges that the defendants either intentionally or recklessly misstated the value of WIN's assets and shareholder equity and that the defendants should have foreseen that current and future investors in WIN and Struthers would rely on the misstated values in deciding whether to invest in those companies and to approve their merger. This allegation is sufficient for intentional misrepresentations. Accordingly, the plaintiffs made sufficient allegations regarding the defendant's duty to them as shareholders of Struthers, making the defendants liable for their misrepresentations.

INTERPRETATION Accountants owe a duty to anyone whom they (1) should have reasonably foreseen would rely on their intentional misrepresentations or (2) knew with substantial certainty would rely on their negligent misrepresentations.

ETHICAL QUESTION Did the court fairly decide this case? Explain.

CRITICAL THINKING QUESTION What is the appropriate test for determining an accountant's liability to third parties? Explain.

Criminal Liability [43-1c]

Criminal liability
state law imposes criminal liability on accountants for willfully certifying false documents, altering or tampering with accounting records, using false financial reports, giving false testimony, and committing forgery

An accountant's potential **criminal liability** in rendering professional services is based primarily on the federal law of securities regulation and taxation. Nonetheless, an accountant would violate state criminal law by knowingly and willfully certifying false documents, altering or tampering with accounting records, using false financial reports, giving false testimony under oath, or committing forgery. Criminal sanctions may be imposed under the Internal Revenue Code for knowingly preparing false or fraudulent tax returns or documents used in connection with a tax return. Such liability also extends to willfully assisting or advising a client or others to prepare a false return. Penalties for tax fraud may be a fine not to exceed $250,000 ($500,000 for a corporation) or three years' imprisonment, or both. Moreover, under the federal Alternative Fines Act, if any person derives pecuniary gain from the offense, or if the offense results in pecuniary loss to a person other than the defendant, the defendant may be fined up to the greater of twice the gross gain or twice the gross loss.

Client Information [43-1d]

In providing services for his client, an accountant necessarily obtains information concerning the client's business affairs. Two legal issues arise concerning this client information: (1) who owns the working papers the accountant generates and (2) whether the information is privileged.

Working papers
an accountant is considered the owner of his working papers but may not disclose their contents unless the client agrees or a court orders the disclosure

Working Papers
Audit **working papers** include an auditor's records of the procedures she followed, the tests she performed, the information she obtained, and the conclusions she reached in connection with an audit. All relevant information that pertains to the examination should be included in the working papers. Because an accountant is held to be the owner of his working papers, he need not surrender them to his client. Nevertheless, the accountant may not disclose the contents of these papers unless (1) the client consents or (2) a court orders the disclosure.

Accountant–Client Privilege

Accountant–Client Privilege   The issue of confidentiality as it concerns accountant–client communication is important, for if such information is considered to be privileged, it may not be admitted into evidence over the objection of the person possessing the privilege. The question of a possible **accountant–client privilege** frequently arises in tax disputes, criminal prosecution, and civil litigation.

Neither the common law nor federal law recognizes a general privilege. Nevertheless, some states have adopted statutes granting some form of accountant–client privilege. Most of these statutes grant the privilege to the client, although a few extend the prerogative to the accountant. In addition, the Internal Revenue Service (IRS) Restructuring and Reform Act grants accountants, who are authorized under federal law to practice before the IRS, the privilege of confidentiality for tax advice given to their client-taxpayers with respect to Internal Revenue Code matters. Regardless of whether or not the privilege exists, it is generally considered to be professionally unethical for an accountant to disclose confidential communications from a client unless the disclosure is in accordance with (1) American Institute of Certified Public Accountants (AICPA) or GAAS requirements, (2) a court order, or (3) the client's request.

FEDERAL SECURITIES LAW [43-2]

Accountants may be both civilly and criminally liable under provisions of the 1933 and 1934 Acts. (Chapter 39 contains a fuller discussion of the securities laws.) This liability is more extensive and has fewer limitations than liability under the common law. Securities and Exchange Commission (SEC) regulations require that auditors are qualified and independent of their audit clients both in fact and in appearance. Accordingly, Rule 2-01 of SEC Regulation S-X imposes restrictions on financial, employment, and business relationships between an accountant and an audit client and restrictions on an accountant providing certain nonaudit services to an audit client.

1933 Act [43-2a]

Accountants are subject to express **civil liability** under Section 11 of the 1933 Act if the financial statements they prepare or certify for inclusion in a registration statement contain any untrue statement or omit any material fact. This liability extends to anyone who acquires the security without knowledge of the untruth or omission. Not only does such liability require no proof of privity between the accountant and the purchasers, but proof of reliance on the financial statements also is not usually required under Section 11. An accountant will not be liable, however, if he can prove "due diligence." The defense of *due diligence* requires that the accountant had, after reasonable investigation, reasonable grounds to believe and did believe, at the *time* the registration statement became *effective*, that the financial statements were true, complete, and accurate. The standard of reasonableness is that required of a prudent person in the management of his or her own property. Thus, Section 11 imposes liability on accountants for *negligence* in the conduct of an audit or in the presentation of information in the financial statements. In addition, an accountant is not liable for any or the entire amount otherwise recoverable under Section 11 that the defendant proves was caused by something other than the defective disclosure.

Moreover, an accountant who willfully violates this section may be held **criminally liable** for a fine of not more than $10,000 or imprisonment of not more than five years, or both. Moreover, under the federal Alternative Fines Act, if any person derives pecuniary gain from the offense, or if the offense results in pecuniary loss to a person other than the defendant, the defendant may be fined up to the greater of twice the gross gain or twice the gross loss.

1934 Act [43-2b]

Civil Liability   **Section 18** of the 1934 Act imposes express *civil* liability on an accountant who makes or causes to be made any false or misleading statement about any material fact in any application, report, document, or registration filed with the SEC under the 1934 Act. Liability extends to any person who purchased or sold a security in reliance on that statement without knowing that it was false or misleading. An accountant is not liable, however, if she proves that she acted in good faith and had no knowledge that such statement was false or misleading. Thus, an accountant is not liable for false or misleading statements that result from good faith negligence.

Accountants may also be held civilly liable for violations of **Rule 10b-5**. Rule 10b-5, as discussed in Chapter 39, is extremely broad in that it applies to both oral and written

---

Accountant–client privilege

not recognized by the common law or federal law, although some states have adopted statutes granting some form of privilege

Civil liability

Section 11 imposes express civil liability on accountants if the financial statements they prepare or certify for a registration statement contain any untrue statement or omit any material fact, unless the accountant proves his due diligence defense

Criminal liability

a willful violator of Section 11 is subject to fines of not more than $10,000 and/or imprisonment of not more than five years

Section 18

imposes express civil liability on an accountant who knowingly makes any false or misleading statement about any material fact in any report, document, or registration filed with the Securities and Exchange Commission

Rule 10b-5

an accountant is civilly liable under this rule if he acts with *scienter* in making oral or written misstatements or omissions of material fact in connection with the purchase or sale of a security

APPLYING THE LAW

Accountants' Legal Liability

Facts For years, Eldon Jacobsen LLP prepared, certified, and audited the financial records of a large publicly traded telecom company called TeleNon. In 2014, TeleNon acquired a smaller telecom company known as TDT. When accounting for the TDT acquisition, TeleNon allocated a large portion of the purchase price to goodwill, which the company reported on its 2014 Form 10K would thereafter be amortized on a straight-line basis over forty years. Eldon Jacobsen certified that this treatment was in accordance with generally accepted accounting principles (GAAP) and generally accepted auditing standards (GAAS) and, accordingly, that the company's financial statements fairly represented TeleNon's financial position in all material respects. Eldon Jacobsen assigned the forty-year useful life to TDT's goodwill based on its detailed review of GAAP and GAAS, on the fact that most other telecom companies did so at the time, and also on the fact the Securities and Exchange Commission (SEC) did not object to a letter Eldon Jacobsen sent in early 2014 detailing the reasons behind its proposed choice of a forty-year depreciation period.

Subsequently, an internal audit of TeleNon's capital expenditure accounting revealed that a fifteen-year amortization period was more appropriate than forty. This and some other changes in accounting treatment led to a fairly massive restatement of TeleNon's 2014 financials. Unfortunately, TeleNon had issued some debt in 2014. The registration statement filed in connection with that bond offering included the financials certified by Eldon Jacobsen. A year after TeleNon's accounting restatement, purchasers of the bonds sued Eldon Jacobsen and others, alleging among other things that the registration statement misrepresented

TeleNon's true financial picture by understating its expenses.

Issue Has Eldon Jacobsen violated Section 11 of the 1933 Securities Act?

Rule of Law If the financial statements prepared or certified by an accounting firm for inclusion in a registration statement contain any untrue statement or omit any material fact, the accounting firm may be subject to civil liability under Section 11 of the 1933 Act. Anyone who purchases the security without knowledge of the falsehood can bring a civil suit for damages, whether or not the purchaser relied on the misstatement in the registration statement. The accounting firm, however, has a due diligence defense available to it. Proof of due diligence requires the accountants to have conducted a reasonable investigation and, therefore, to have had reasonable grounds to believe, and to have in fact believed at the time the registration became effective, that the financial statements they prepared or certified were true, accurate, and complete. In essence this amounts to a negligence standard, requiring the accountants to show they had an objectively reasonable basis for their accounting decisions.

Application An accounting firm has responsibility under Section 11 of the 1933 Act for the accuracy of the financial statements it certifies. If TeleNon's and Eldon Jacobsen's choice of a forty-year useful life for goodwill in the 2014 financials was not in conformity with GAAP and GAAS as understood at that time, the financial statements and Eldon Jacobsen's certification thereof were inaccurate. Therefore, unless Eldon Jacobsen can prove due diligence, it will be held liable to the bondholders. To do so, first the firm must be able to show that it conducted a

reasonable investigation before choosing the depreciation period. It appears here that, at a minimum, Eldon Jacobsen specifically researched GAAP and GAAS relative to the depreciation of goodwill, that it studied the convention then in use by "most other" telecom companies, and that it sought the SEC's input into its choice of this intangible asset's useful life. This seems to be an objectively reasonable approach, especially if there is expert testimony that this is the extent to which a reasonably skilled accountant would go in assessing the appropriate depreciation period under these circumstances.

Furthermore, the firm must be able to show that it had reasonable grounds to believe, and in fact did believe, that the financials were accurate, true, and correct as of the effective date of the registration statement. With no evidence of fraudulent intent present, it is reasonable to assume that the firm was convinced it was in compliance with GAAP and GAAS by virtue of its own research, the trend in the industry, and the Commission's failure to object to its letter setting forth the basis for choosing the forty-year depreciation period. Presumably, the Eldon Jacobsen accountants who were on the engagement will testify that they in fact believed their choice to be supported by and in conformity with GAAP and GAAS, as interpreted in 2014 when the registration statement became effective.

Conclusion Eldon Jacobsen can prove the due diligence defense in connection with its preparation of TeleNon's 2014 financial statements and their certification for inclusion in the registration statement attendant to the bond offering. Therefore, Eldon Jacobsen will not be held liable to the bondholders who are suing under Section 11 of the 33 Act.

Scienter
intentional or knowing conduct

misstatements or omissions of material fact and to *all* securities. An accountant may be liable for a violation of the rule to those who rely on the misstatement or omission of material fact when purchasing or selling a security. However, liability is imposed only if the accountant acted with **scienter**, or intentional or knowing conduct. Therefore, accountants are not liable under Rule 10b-5 for mere negligence, although most courts have held that reckless disregard of the truth is sufficient. See Concept Review 43-1 for a summary of accountants' civil liability under the federal securities laws.

Ernst & Ernst v. Hochfelder
Supreme Court of the United States, 1976
425 U.S. 185, 96 S.Ct. 1375, 47 L.Ed.2d 668
http://scholar.google.com/scholar_case?case=4219834259989886465&hl=en&as_sdt=2&as_vis=1&oi=scholarr

FACTS The defendant, Ernst & Ernst, was an accounting firm. From 1946 through 1967, it was retained by First Securities Company of Chicago, a small brokerage firm and member of the Midwest Stock Exchange and the National Association of Securities Dealers, to perform periodic audits of the firm's books and records. In connection with these audits, Ernst & Ernst prepared for filing with the Securities and Exchange Commission (SEC) the annual reports required of First Securities under the 1934 Act. It also prepared First Securities' responses to the financial questionnaires of the Midwest Stock Exchange.

Hochfelder and others (plaintiffs) were customers of First Securities who invested in a fraudulent securities scheme perpetrated by Leston B. Nay, president of the firm and owner of 92 percent of its stock. This fraud came to light in 1968 when Nay committed suicide, leaving a note that described First Securities as bankrupt and the escrow accounts as "spurious." Plaintiffs subsequently filed this action for damages against Ernst & Ernst under Section 10(b) of the 1934 Act. The complaint charged that Nay's escrow scheme violated Section 10(b) and Commission Rule 10b-5 and that Ernst & Ernst had "aided and abetted" Nay's violations by its "failure" to conduct proper audits of First Securities. The plaintiffs' cause of action rested on a theory of negligent nonfeasance—that, by failing to use "appropriate auditing procedures" in its audits of First Securities, Ernst & Ernst had thereby failed to discover internal practices of the firm said to prevent an effective audit. The district court dismissed the action, but the Court of Appeals reversed and remanded.

DECISION Judgment of the Court of Appeals reversed.

OPINION Section 10(b) of the 1934 Act and SEC Rule 10b-5 apply only to intentional conduct, not negligence. The legislative intent of the Act was to promote ethical standards of honesty and fair dealing by requiring regular accounting reports from corporations listed on national securities exchanges. In addition, Section 10 speaks specifically in terms of manipulation and deception and of implementing devices and contrivances. This is the commonly understood terminology of intentional wrongdoing. Based on this language and legislative history, the Supreme Court refused to expand the statute's scope to include negligent conduct. Because Ernst & Ernst's misconduct was merely negligent, not intentional, it is not liable to Hochfelder and the other shareholders.

INTERPRETATION Accountants are not liable under Rule 10b-5 for mere negligence.

CRITICAL THINKING QUESTION Do you agree with the court's decision in this case? Explain.

Criminal liability
a willful violator of either Section 18 or Rule 10b-5 is subject to fines of not more than $5 million and/or imprisonment of not more than twenty years

Criminal Liability Those who willfully violate Section 18 or Rule 10b-5 also may be held criminally liable. As amended by the Sarbanes-Oxley Act, for an accountant, conviction may carry a fine of not more than $5 million or imprisonment for not more than twenty years, or both, while an accounting firm may be fined up to $25 million. Moreover, under the federal Alternative Fines Act, if any person derives pecuniary gain from the offense, or if the offense results in pecuniary loss to a person other than the defendant, the defendant may be fined up to the greater of twice the gross gain or twice the gross loss.

CONCEPT REVIEW 43-1

Accountants' Liability Under Federal Securities Law

	Section 11 (1933 Act)	Section 18 (1934 Act)	Rule 10b-5 (1934 Act)
Conduct	Registration statement containing material misstatement or omission	False or misleading statements in a document filed with SEC	Deception or material misstatement or opinion
Fault	Negligence	Knowledge or bad faith	*Scienter*
Plaintiff's knowledge is a defense	Yes	Yes	Yes
Reliance required	No	Yes	Yes
Privity required	No	No	No

Note: SEC = Securities and Exchange Commission.

Sarbanes-Oxley Act [43-2c]

In response to the business scandals involving companies such as Enron, WorldCom, Global Crossing, and the accounting firm of Arthur Andersen, in 2002 Congress passed the **Sarbanes-Oxley Act**, which amends the securities acts in a number of significant respects to protect investors by improving the accuracy and reliability of corporate disclosures. The Act provides for the establishment of the five-member Public Company Accounting Oversight Board to oversee the audit of public companies to further the public interest in the preparation of informative, accurate, and independent audit reports for public companies. The SEC has oversight and enforcement authority over the Board. The Board enforces the Sarbanes-Oxley Act, the Federal securities laws, the SEC's rules, the Board's rules, and professional accounting standards. The duties of the Board include (1) registering public accounting firms that prepare audit reports for issuers; (2) overseeing the audit of public companies; (3) establishing audit report standards and rules; and (4) inspecting, investigating, and enforcing compliance on the part of registered public accounting firms and their associated persons. The Act directs the Board to establish or modify the auditing and related attestation standards, quality control standards, and ethics standards used by registered public accounting firms to prepare and issue audit reports. The willful violation of any Board rule is treated as a willful violation of the 1934 Act. Moreover, the Board can impose sanctions in its disciplinary proceedings, including the permanent revocation of an accounting firm's registration, a permanent ban on a person's associating with any registered firm, and civil monetary penalties of $15,825,000 for an accounting firm and $800,000 for a natural person, as adjusted for inflation in 2013.

To make auditors more independent from their clients, the Act prohibits accounting firms from performing eight specified nonaudit services for audit clients, including bookkeeping or other services related to the accounting records or financial statements; financial information systems design and implementation; appraisal or valuation services; fairness opinions; management functions or human resources; and actuarial services. Accounting firms may perform other nonaudit services not expressly forbidden by the Act if the company's audit committee grants prior approval and the approval by the audit committee is disclosed to investors in periodic reports. The lead audit partner having primary responsibility for the audit and the audit partner responsible for reviewing the audit must rotate at least every five years.

Auditors must report directly to the company's audit committee and make timely disclosure of accounting issues concerning (1) critical accounting policies and practices used in the audit; (2) alternative treatments and their ramifications within GAAP that have been discussed with management officials and the treatment preferred by the auditor; and (3) other material written communications between the auditor and management.

Audit Requirements

The Private Securities Litigation Reform Act of 1995 (Reform Act) imposed a significant set of obligations upon independent public accountants who audit financial statements required by the 1934 Act. The Reform Act authorizes the SEC to adopt rules that modify or supplement the practices or procedures followed by auditors in the conduct of an audit. Moreover, the Act requires auditors to establish procedures capable of detecting material illegal acts, identifying material related to party transactions, and evaluating whether there is a substantial doubt about the issuer's ability to continue as a going concern during the next fiscal year.

If the auditor becomes aware of information indicating an illegal act, it must determine whether an illegal act occurred and the illegal act's possible effect on the issuer's financial statements. Then the auditor must inform the issuer's management about any illegal activity and assure itself that the audit committee of the board of directors is adequately informed. If the auditor concludes that (1) the illegal act has a material effect on the issuer's financial statement, (2) neither senior management nor the board has taken timely and appropriate remedial action, *and* (3) the failure to take remedial action is reasonably expected to warrant departure from a standard auditor report or warrant resignation from the auditor's engagement, then the auditor promptly must report its conclusions to the issuer's board.

Within one day of receiving such report, the issuer must notify the SEC and furnish the auditor with a copy of that notice. If the auditor does not receive such notice, then the auditor must either resign or furnish the SEC with its report to the board. If the auditor resigns, it must furnish the SEC with a copy of its report.

Sarbanes-Oxley Act

establishes a new regulatory body to oversee public company auditors, makes auditors more independent from their clients, and places direct responsibility for the audit relationship on audit committees

---

Practical Advice

Recognize that civil liability for accountants under the federal securities laws extends to a greater range of misconduct and third parties than under common law.

Audit requirements

auditors must establish procedures capable of detecting material illegal acts, identifying material-related party transactions, and evaluating whether there is a substantial doubt about the issuer's ability to continue as a going concern during the next fiscal year

The Reform Act provides that an auditor shall not be held liable in a private action for any finding, conclusion, or statement expressed in the report the Act requires the auditor to make to the SEC. The SEC can impose civil penalties against an auditor who willfully violates the Reform Act by failing to resign or to furnish a report to the SEC.

CHAPTER SUMMARY

Common Law

Contract Liability the employment contract between an accountant and her client is subject to the general principles of contract law

- *Explicit Duties* the accountant is bound to perform all the duties she expressly agrees to provide
- *Implicit Duties* the accountant impliedly agrees to perform the contract in a competent and professional manner
- *Beneficiaries* contract liability extends to the client or contracting party and to third-party beneficiaries (noncontracting parties intended by the contracting parties to receive the primary benefit under the contract)
- *Breach of Contract* general contract law principles apply

Tort Liability a tort is a private or civil wrong or injury other than a breach of contract

- *Negligence* an accountant is liable for failing to exercise the degree of care a reasonably competent accountant would exercise under the circumstances; most courts have extended an accountant's liability for negligence beyond the client and third-party beneficiaries to foreseen third parties
- *Fraud* an accountant who commits a fraudulent act is liable for both compensatory and punitive damages to any person whom he should have reasonably foreseen would be injured; a fraudulent act is a false representation of fact that is material, is made with knowledge of its falsity and with the intention to deceive, and is justifiably relied on

Criminal Liability state law imposes criminal liability on accountants for willfully certifying false documents, altering or tampering with accounting records, using false financial reports, giving false testimony, and committing forgery

Client Information

- *Working Papers* an accountant is considered the owner of his working papers but may not disclose their contents unless the client agrees or a court orders the disclosure
- *Accountant–Client Privilege* not recognized generally by the common law or federal law, although some states have adopted statutes granting some form of privilege, and accountants authorized to practice before the Internal Revenue Service have privilege for tax advice given to their client-taxpayers with respect to Internal Revenue Code matters

Federal Securities Law

1933 Act

- *Civil Liability* Section 11 imposes express civil liability upon accountants if the financial statements they prepare or certify for a registration statement contain any untrue statement or omit any material fact, unless the accountant proves his due diligence defense, which requires that the accountant had, after reasonable investigation, reasonable grounds to believe and did believe that the financial statements were true, complete, and accurate
- *Criminal Liability* a willful violator of Section 11 is subject to fines of not more than $10,000 and/or imprisonment of not more than five years

1934 Act

- *Section 18* imposes express civil liability on an accountant who knowingly makes any false or misleading statement about any material fact in any report, document, or registration filed with the Securities and Exchange Commission
- *Rule 10b-5* an accountant is civilly liable under this rule if he acts with *scienter* in making oral or written misstatements or omissions of material fact in connection with the purchase or sale of a security
- *Criminal Liability* a willful violator of either Section 18 or Rule 10b-5 is subject to fines of not more than $5 million and/or imprisonment of not more than twenty years

Sarbanes-Oxley Act establishes a new regulatory body to oversee public company auditors, makes auditors more independent from their clients, and places direct responsibility for the audit relationship on audit committees

Audit Requirements auditors must establish procedures capable of detecting material illegal acts, identifying material related to party transactions, and evaluating whether there is a substantial doubt about the issuer's ability to continue as a going concern during the next fiscal year

QUESTIONS

1. Baldwin Corporation made a public offering of $250 million of convertible debentures and registered the offering with the Securities and Exchange Commission. The registration statement contained financial statements certified by Adams and Allen, Certified Public Accountants. The financial statements overstated Baldwin's net income and assets by 20 percent and understated the company's liability by 15 percent. Because Adams and Allen did not carefully follow generally accepted accounting standards, it failed to detect these inaccuracies, the discovery of which has caused the bond prices to drop from their original selling price of $1,000 per bond to $720. Can Conrad, who purchased $10,000 of the debentures, collect from Adams and Allen for his damages? Explain.

2. Ingram is a Certified Public Accountant (CPA) employed by Jordan, Keller, and Lane, CPAs, to audit Martin Enterprises, Inc., a fast-growing service firm that went public two years ago. The financial statements that Ingram audited were included in a proxy statement proposing a merger with several other firms. The proxy statement was filed with the Securities and Exchange Commission and included several inaccuracies. First, approximately $10 million, or more than 20 percent, of the previous year's "net sales originally reported" had proven nonexistent by the time the proxy statement was filed and had been written off on Martin's own books. This was not disclosed in the proxy statement, in violation of *Accounting Board Opinion Number 9*. Second, Martin's net sales for the current year were stated as $110,300,000, when in truth they were less than $100,500,000. Third, Martin's net profits for the current year were reported as $1,700,000, when in fact the firm had no earnings at all.
   a. What civil liability, if any, does Ingram have?
   b. What criminal liability, if any, does Ingram have?

3. Girard & Company, CPAs, audited the financial statements included in the annual report submitted by PMG Enterprises, Inc., to the Securities and Exchange Commission (SEC). The audit failed to detect numerous false and misleading statements contained in the financial statements.
   a. Investors who subsequently purchased PMG stock have brought suit against Girard under Section 18 of the 1934 Act. What defenses, if any, are available to Girard?
   b. The SEC has initiated criminal proceedings under the 1934 Act against Girard. What must be proven for Girard to be held criminally liable?

4. Dryden, a certified public accountant, audited the books of Elixir, Inc., and certified incorrect financial statements in a form that was filed with the Securities and Exchange Commission. Shortly thereafter, Elixir, Inc., went bankrupt. Investigation into the bankruptcy disclosed that through an intricate and clever embezzlement scheme, Kraft, the president of Elixir, had siphoned off substantial sums of money that now support Kraft in a luxurious lifestyle in South America. Investors who purchased shares of Elixir have brought suit against Dryden under Rule 10b-5. At trial, Dryden produces evidence that demonstrates that his failure to discover the embezzlement resulted merely from negligence on his part and that he had no knowledge of the fraudulent conduct. Is Dryden liable under the Securities Exchange Act of 1934? Why?

5. Johnson Enterprises, Inc., contracted with the accounting firm of P, A & E to perform an audit of Johnson. The accounting firm performed its duty in a nonnegligent, competent manner but failed to discover a novel embezzlement scheme perpetrated by Johnson's treasurer. Shortly thereafter, Johnson's treasurer disappeared with $175,000 of the company's money. Johnson now refuses to pay P, A & E its $50,000 audit fee and is seeking to recover $175,000 from P, A & E.
   a. What are the rights and liabilities of P, A & E and Johnson? Explain.
   b. Would your answer to (a) differ if the scheme was a common embezzlement scheme that generally accepted accounting standards should have disclosed? Explain.

6. The accounting firm of T, W & S was engaged to perform an audit of Progate Manufacturing Company. During the course of its investigation, T, W & S discovered that the company had overvalued its inventory by carrying the inventory on the books at the previous year's prices, which were significantly higher than current prices. When T, W & S approached Progate's president, Lehman, about the improper valuation of inventory, Lehman became enraged and told T, W & S that unless the firm accepted the valuation, Progate would sue T, W & S. Although T, W & S knew that Progate's suit was frivolous and unfounded, it wished to avoid the negative publicity that would arise from any suit brought against it. Therefore, on the assumption that the overvaluation would not harm anybody, T, W & S accepted Progate's inflated valuation of inventory. Progate subsequently went bankrupt, and T, W & S is now being sued by (1) First National Bank, a bank that relied upon T, W & S's statement to loan money to Progate; and (2) Thomas, an investor who purchased 20 percent of Progate's stock after receiving T, W & S's statement. What are the rights and liabilities of First National Bank, Thomas, and T, W & S?

7. J, B & J, CPAs, has audited the Highcredit Corporation for the past five years. Recently, the Securities and Exchange Commission (SEC) has commenced an investigation of

Highcredit for possible violations of federal securities law. The SEC has subpoenaed all of J, B & J's working papers pertinent to the audit of Highcredit. Highcredit insists that J, B & J not turn over the documents to the SEC. What action should J, B & J take? Why?

8. On February 1, the Gazette Corporation hired Susan Sharp to conduct an audit of its books and to prepare financial statements for the corporation's annual meeting on July 1. Sharp made every reasonable attempt to comply with the deadline but could not finish the report on time due to delays in receiving needed information from Gazette. Gazette now refuses to pay Sharp for her audit and is threatening to bring a cause of action against Sharp. What course of action should Sharp pursue? Why?

CASE PROBLEMS

9. John P. Butler Accountancy Corporation agreed to audit the financial statements of Westside Mortgage, Inc., a mortgage company that arranged financing for real property, for the year ending December 31, 2013. On March 22, 2014, after completing the audit, Butler issued unqualified audited financial statements listing Westside's corporate net worth as $175,036. The primary asset on the balance sheet was a $100,000 note receivable that had, in reality, been rendered worthless in August 2011 when the trust deed on real property securing the note was wiped out by a prior foreclosure of a superior deed of trust. The note constituted 57 percent of Westside's net worth and was thus material to an accurate representation of Westside's financial position. In October 2014, International Mortgage Company (IMC) approached Westside for the purpose of buying and selling loans on the secondary market. IMC signed an agreement with Westside in December after reviewing Westside's audited financial statements. In June 2015, Westside issued a $475,293 promissory note to IMC, on which it ultimately defaulted. IMC brought an action against Westside, its owners, principals, and Butler. IMC alleged negligence and negligent misrepresentation against Butler in auditing and issuing without qualification the defective financial statements on which IMC relied in deciding to do business with Westside. Butler moved for summary judgment, claiming that it owed no duty of care to IMC, a third party who was not specifically known to Butler as an intended recipient of the audited financial statements. The trial court granted Butler's motion, and IMC appealed. Decision?

10. Equisure, Inc., was required to file audited financial statements when it applied to have its stock listed on the American Stock Exchange (AmEx). It retained an accounting firm, defendant Stirtz Bernards Boyden Surdel & Larter, P.A. (Stirtz). Stirtz issued a favorable interim audit report that Equisure used to gain listing on the stock exchange. Subsequently, Equisure retained Stirtz to audit the financial statements required for Equisure's Form 10 filing with the U.S. Securities and Exchange Commission (SEC). Stirtz's auditor knew that the audit was for the SEC reports. Stirtz issued a "clean" audit opinion, which, with the audited financial statements, was included in Equisure's SEC filing and made available to the public. NorAm Investment Services, Inc., also known as Equity Securities Trading Company, Inc. (NorAm), a securities broker, began lending margin credit to purchasers of Equisure stock. These purchasers advanced only a portion of the purchase price; NorAm extended credit (a margin loan) for the balance and held the stock as collateral for the loan, charging interest on the balance. When NorAm had loaned approximately $900,000 in margin credit, its president, Nathan Newman, reviewed Stirtz's audit report and the audited financial statements. Based on his review, NorAm extended more than $1.6 million of additional margin credit for the purchase of Equisure shares. When AmEx stopped trading Equisure stock due to allegations of insider trading and possible stock manipulation, the stock became worthless. NorAm was left without collateral for more than $2.5 million in margin loans. Stirtz resigned as auditor of Equisure and warned that its audit report might be misleading and should no longer be relied upon. NorAm sued Stirtz for negligent misrepresentation and negligence. Explain whether or not NorAm will prevail.

TAKING SIDES

Arthur Young & Co., a firm of certified public accountants, was the independent auditor for Amerada Hess Corporation. During its review of Amerada's financial statements as required by federal securities laws, Young confirmed Amerada's statement of its contingent tax liabilities and prepared tax accrual work papers. These work papers, which pertained to Young's evaluation of Amerada's reserves for contingent tax liabilities, included discussions of questionable positions Amerada might have taken on its tax returns. The Internal Revenue Service (IRS) initiated a criminal investigation of Amerada's tax returns when, during a routine audit, it discovered questionable payments made by Amerada from a "special disbursement account." The IRS summoned Young to make available all its information relating to Amerada, including the tax accrual work papers. Amerada instructed Young not to obey the summons. The IRS then brought an action against Young to enforce the administrative summons.

a. What are the arguments that Young must turn over the work papers?

b. What are the arguments that the work papers are protected from government summons?

c. Who should prevail? Explain.

Consumer Protection

CHAPTER 44

Consumption is the sole end and purpose of production; and the interest of the producer ought to be attended to only so far as it may be necessary for promoting that of the consumer.

Adam Smith
Wealth of Nations (1776)

CHAPTER OUTCOMES

After reading and studying this chapter, you should be able to:

1. Describe the role of the Federal Trade Commission (FTC) and the major enforcement sanctions that it may use.

2. Describe the role and workings of (a) the Consumer Product Safety Commission (CPSC) and (b) the Consumer Financial Protection Bureau (CFPB).

3. Explain the principal provisions of the Magnuson-Moss Warranty Act and distinguish between a full and a limited warranty.

4. Describe what information a creditor must provide a consumer before the consumer incurs the obligation.

5. Outline the major remedies that are available to a creditor.

Consumer transactions have increased enormously since World War II. As of March 30, 2014, total consumer indebtedness was more than $11 trillion; nonmortgage consumer debt was over $3 trillion; and home mortgages (including home equity loans) exceeded $8 trillion. Although the definition varies, a consumer transaction generally involves goods, credit, services, or land acquired for personal, household, or family purposes. Historically, consumers were subject to the rule of *caveat emptor*—let the buyer beware. The law, however, has largely abandoned this principle and now offers greater protection to consumers. Most of this protection takes the form of statutory enactments at both the state and federal levels, and a number of government agencies are charged with enforcing these statutes. This enforcement varies enormously. In some cases, only government agencies may exercise enforcement rights, through the imposition of criminal penalties, civil penalties, injunctions, and cease-and-desist orders. In other cases, in addition to government's enforcement rights, consumers may privately seek the rescission of contracts and damages for harm resulting from violations of consumer protection laws. Finally, under certain consumer protection statutes such as state "lemon laws," consumers alone may exercise enforcement rights. In this chapter, we will examine state and federal consumer protection agencies and consumer protection statutes.

STATE AND FEDERAL CONSUMER PROTECTION AGENCIES [44-1]

Through the enactment of laws and regulations, legislatures and administrative bodies at the federal, state, and local levels all actively seek to shield consumers from an enormous range of harm. The most common abuses involving consumer transactions occur in the extension of credit, deceptive trade practices, unsafe products, and unfair pricing.

State and Local Consumer Protection Agencies [44-1a]

The many consumer protection agencies at the state and local levels typically deal with fraudulent and deceptive trade practices and fraudulent sales practices, such as false statements about a product's value or quality. In most jurisdictions, consumer protection agencies also help to resolve consumer complaints about defective goods or poor service.

Most state attorneys general facilitate consumer protection by enforcing laws against consumer fraud through judicially imposed injunctions and restitution. In recent years, as the federal government's role in consumer protection has diminished in response to the deregulatory movement, the states have correspondingly expanded their role. The National Association of Attorneys General (NAAG) has been active in coordinating lawsuits among the states. Under NAAG's guidance, several states will often simultaneously file lawsuits against a company that has been engaging in fraudulent acts involving more than one state.

In some instances, however, states have not coordinated their efforts and, instead, have acted inconsistently with respect to consumer protection, especially in health and safety matters. This lack of coordination can present serious problems to companies that sell large numbers of products in interstate commerce.

The Federal Trade Commission [44-1b]

Federal Trade Commission (FTC) prevents unfair methods of competition and unfair or deceptive acts or practices

At the federal level, the most significant consumer protection agency is the **Federal Trade Commission (FTC)**. Established in 1914, the FTC has two major functions: (1) under its mandate to prevent "unfair methods of competition in commerce," it and the Antitrust Division of the Department of Justice are responsible for antitrust enforcement at the federal level (the FTC's role in antitrust enforcement is discussed in Chapter 42); and (2) under its mandate to prevent "unfair and deceptive" trade practices, it is responsible for stopping fraudulent sales techniques.

In addressing unfair and deceptive trade practices, the five-member commission (no more than three of these members may be from the same political party) has the power to issue substantive industry-wide "trade regulation rules" and to conduct appropriate investigations and hearings. Among the rules it has issued so far are those regulating used car sales, franchising and business opportunity ventures, funeral home services, and the issuance of consumer credit, as well as those requiring a "cooling-off" period for door-to-door sales (discussed later in this chapter).

In many instances, the agency, in considering a deceptive trade practice, may seek a cease-and-desist order rather than issue a substantive industry-wide trade regulation rule. A **cease-and-desist order** directs a party to stop a certain practice or face punishment, such as a fine. In a typical situation, the FTC staff discovers a potentially deceptive practice, investigates the matter, and files (if appropriate) a complaint against the alleged offender (usually referred to as the respondent). After a hearing in front of an administrative law judge (ALJ) to determine whether a violation of the law has occurred, the FTC obtains a cease-and-desist order if the ALJ finds that one is necessary. The respondent may appeal to the FTC commissioners to reverse or modify the order. Appeals from orders issued by the commissioners go to the U.S. Courts of Appeals, which have exclusive jurisdiction to enforce, set aside, or modify orders of the commission.

Cease-and-desist order orders a party to stop a certain practice

Standards   Though the FTC Act does not define the words *unfair* or *deceptive*, the commission has issued three policy statements addressing the meaning of **unfairness** and has provided that an injury is unfair if it is substantial, not outweighed by any benefits to consumers or competition, and is one that consumers themselves could not reasonably have avoided. The standard, therefore, applies a cost-benefit analysis to the issue of unfairness.

The second policy statement deals with the meaning of **deception**—the basis of most FTC consumer protection actions—by providing that the commission will find deception in a misrepresentation, omission, or practice that is likely to mislead a consumer acting reasonably in the circumstances, to the consumer's detriment.

Deception may occur either through false representation or material omission. Examples of deceptive practices have included advertising that a certain product would save consumers 25 percent on their automotive motor oil, when the product simply replaced a quart of oil in the engine (which normally contains four quarts of oil) and was, in fact, more expensive than the oil it replaced; placing marbles in a bowl of vegetable soup to displace the vegetables from the

Unfairness requires injury to be (1) substantial, (2) not outweighed by any countervailing benefit, and (3) unavoidable by reasonable consumer action

Deception misrepresentation, omission, or practice that is likely to mislead the consumer acting reasonably in the circumstances

bottom of the bowl and therefore make the soup look thicker; and claiming that one drug provided greater pain relief than another named drug, when evidence actually was insufficient to prove the claim to the medical community.

To ensure that the FTC's guidance for online advertisers stays current with changes in digital media and Internet searches, in June 2013, the FTC sent letters to search engine companies to update guidance published in 2002 on distinguishing paid search results and other forms of advertising from natural search results. The letters note that in recent years paid search results have become less distinguishable as advertising, and the FTC is urging the search industry to make sure the distinction is clear. Failing clearly and prominently to distinguish advertising from natural search results could be a deceptive practice.

Deception can also occur through a failure to *disclose* important product information if such disclosure is necessary to correct a false and material expectation created in the consumer's mind by the product or by the circumstances of sale. For example, the FTC has insisted that the failure to disclose a product's country of origin constitutes a deceptive omission, based on the agency's view that consumers assume the United States to be the country of origin of a product that bears no other country's name.

Ad substantiation

requires advertisers to have a reasonable basis for their claims

The third policy statement issued by the commission involves **ad substantiation**. This policy requires that advertisers have a reasonable basis for their claims at the time they make such claims. Moreover, in determining the reasonableness of a claim, the commission places great weight on the cost and benefits of substantiation.

Federal Trade Commission v. Cyberspace.com LLC
United States Court of Appeals, Ninth Circuit, 2006
453 F.3d 1196
http://scholar.google.com/scholar_case?case=4160583678645707830&q=453+F.3d+1196&hl=en&as_sclt=2,22

FACTS In the late 1990s, Ian Eisenberg and Chris Hebard formed Electronic Publishing Ventures, LLC (EPV) and its four subsidiaries: Cyberspace.com, LLC, Essex Enterprises, LLC, Surfnet Services, LLC, and Splashnet.net, LLC. Two offshore entities, French Dreams Investments, N.V. (collectively *EFO* and owned by Eisenberg) and Coto Settlement (controlled by *Hebard*) owned EPV in equal parts. Between January 1999 and mid-2000, EPV's four subsidiaries mailed approximately 4.4 million solicitations offering Internet access to individuals and small businesses. The solicitations included a check, usually for $3.50, attached to a form resembling an invoice designed to be detached from the check by tearing at the perforated line. The check was addressed to the recipient and the recipient's phone number appeared on the "re" line. The back of the check and invoice contained small-print disclosures revealing that cashing or depositing the check would constitute agreement to pay a monthly fee for Internet access, but the front of the check and the invoice contained no such disclosures. The mailing explained in small print that a monthly fee would be billed to the customer's local phone bill after the check was cashed or deposited. At least 225,000 small businesses and individuals cashed or deposited the solicitation checks. The EPV subsidiaries used a billing aggregation service to place charges for $19.95 or $29.95 a month on the small businesses' and individuals' ordinary telephone bills. Internet usage records show, however, that less than 1 percent of the 225,000 individuals and businesses billed for Internet service actually logged on to the service.

Eisenberg and Hebard were aware that the solicitation had misled some consumers. The companies received complaints from recipients of the solicitations, which indicated that some customers had deposited the solicitation check without realizing that they had contracted

for Internet services. Materials that Eisenberg and Hebard prepared in an attempt to sell one of the subsidiaries in 1999 informed prospective buyers that "the Company believes that a number of customers sign up for the [sic] without realizing that when they deposit the check that they have ordered Internet service."

Based on its belief that the solicitations were deceptive in violation of Section 5 of the Federal Trade Commission Act (FTCA), the Federal Trade Commission (FTC) sought an injunction and consumer redress in the district court. The district court entered two stipulated permanent injunctions in which the defendants agreed to cease the practices at issue without admitting to a FTCA Section 5 violation. The parties then filed cross-motions for summary judgment on the issues of liability and consumer redress. After denying the defendants' motions for summary judgment, the district court granted the FTC's motion in part concluding that the proper amount of consumer redress was $17,676,897. EFO and Hebard appealed.

DECISION Judgment affirmed.

OPINION Section 5 of the FTCA prohibits "deceptive acts or practices in or affecting commerce." A practice falls within this prohibition (1) if it is likely to mislead consumers acting reasonably under the circumstances (2) in a way that is material. In this case, Hebard and EFO wrongfully contend that the fine print notices they placed on the reverse side of the check, invoice, and marketing insert preclude liability under FTCA Section 5. A solicitation may be likely to mislead by virtue of the net impression it creates even though the solicitation also contains truthful disclosures. Hebard and EFO's mailing created the deceptive impression that the $3.50 check was simply a refund or rebate rather than an offer for services. The front of the check and invoice lacked any indication that by cashing the check, the consumer was contracting to pay a monthly fee. This solicitation was likely to deceive consumers acting reasonably under the circumstances. This conclusion is bolstered by undisputed evidence indicating that Hebard and EFO's solicitation actually deceived nearly 225,000 individuals and small businesses. Hebard and EFO billed each of these consumers for a service that less than 1 percent of them ever attempted to use. It is reasonable to infer that most of the remaining 99 percent did not realize they had contracted for Internet service when they cashed or deposited the solicitation check. Clearly, the solicitation was likely to mislead

in a way that is material. A misleading impression created by a solicitation is material if it "involves information that is important to consumers and, hence, likely to affect their choice of, or conduct regarding, a product."

INTERPRETATION An act or practice is deceptive if (1) there is a representation, omission, or practice that, (2) is likely to mislead consumers acting reasonably under the circumstances, and (3) the representation, omission, or practice is material.

CRITICAL THINKING QUESTION Do you agree with the court's decision? Explain.

Remedies [44-1c]

In addition to the remedies discussed above, the FTC has employed three other remedies: (1) affirmative disclosure, (2) corrective advertising, and (3) multiple product orders. **Affirmative disclosure**, a remedy frequently employed by the FTC, requires an offender to include in its advertisements certain information that will prevent the ads from being considered deceptive.

Corrective advertising goes beyond affirmative disclosure by requiring an advertiser who has made a deceptive claim to disclose in future advertisements that such prior claims were in fact untrue. The theory behind this requirement is that a previous deception's effects will continue until expressly corrected.

Multiple product orders require a deceptive advertiser to cease and desist from any future deception not only in regard to the product in question but also in regard to all products sold by the company. This remedy is particularly useful in dealing with companies that have repeatedly violated the law.

In addition to these traditional remedies, the FTC also relies on direct court action in lieu of administrative proceedings. The FTC has the power to seek in a federal district court a preliminary injunction, pending completion of administrative proceedings, whenever the agency has reason to believe that a person has been violating FTC laws or rules. First used to stop mergers, this authority is now often invoked in consumer protection cases. The same provision also grants the agency authority to seek a permanent injunction "in proper cases" without a prior administrative finding that FTC law has been violated.

The Consumer Product Safety Commission [44-1d]

The **Consumer Product Safety Act (CPSA)** established an independent federal regulatory agency, the Consumer Product Safety Commission (CPSC). The purposes of the CPSA are (1) to protect the public against unreasonable risks of injury associated with consumer products, (2) to assist consumers in evaluating the comparative safety of consumer products, (3) to develop uniform safety standards for consumer products and to minimize conflicting state and local regulations, and (4) to promote research and investigation into the causes and prevention of product-related deaths, illnesses, and injuries. According to the CPSC, deaths, injuries, and property damage from consumer product incidents cost the United States more than $1 trillion annually.

Consisting of five commissioners, no more than three of whom can be from the same political party, the CPSC has authority to set safety standards for consumer products; to ban unsafe products; to issue administrative recall orders to compel repair, replacement, or refunds for products found to present substantial hazards; and to seek court orders requiring the recall of "imminently hazardous" products. In addition, Congress requires businesses under CPSC jurisdiction to notify the agency of any information indicating that their products contain defects that "could create" substantial product hazards. By triggering investigations that may lead to product recalls, these reports play a major role in the agency's regulatory activities. While the CPSC has jurisdiction over more than 15,000 kinds of consumer products, it does not have jurisdiction over some categories of products, including automobiles and other on-road vehicles, tires, boats, alcohol, tobacco, firearms, food, drugs, cosmetics, pesticides, and medical devices.

Affirmative disclosure
requirement that an advertiser include in its advertisements information that will render the ads nondeceptive

Corrective advertising
disclosure in an advertisement that previous ads were deceptive

Multiple product order
requires advertiser to cease and desist from deceptive statements on all products it sells

Consumer Product Safety Act (CPSA)
federal statute enacted to (1) protect public against unsafe products, (2) assist consumers in evaluating products, (3) develop uniform safety standards, and (4) promote safety research

The CPSC also enforces four statutes previously enforced by other agencies. These acts, commonly referred to as the "transferred acts," are the Federal Hazardous Substances Act, the Flammable Fabrics Act, the Poison Prevention Packaging Act, and the Refrigerator Safety Act. When the CPSC can regulate a product under one of these specific acts, rather than under the more general CPSA, the agency is directed to do so unless it specifically finds that regulation under the CPSA is in the public interest. Thus, a large number of CPSC regulations, such as those for toys, children's flammable sleepwear, and hazard warnings on household chemical products, arise under the transferred acts rather than under the CPSA.

When first established, the CPSC promulgated a number of *mandatory safety standards*; manufacturers either must follow these rules, which regulate product design, packaging, and warning labels, or face legal sanctions. To save time and money, the agency began to rely on the industry to establish *voluntary safety standards*—rules for which noncompliance does not violate the law—reserving mandatory standards for those instances in which voluntary standards proved inadequate. In 1981, Congress enacted legislation requiring the CPSC to rely on voluntary standards "whenever compliance with such voluntary standards would eliminate or adequately reduce the risk of injury addressed and there is substantial compliance with such voluntary standards." Although the 1981 amendments do not bar the CPSC from writing mandatory standards, the CPSC has promulgated few such standards since the law was amended.

In 2008, Congress enacted the Consumer Product Safety Improvement Act (CPSIA). To provide the public with immediate access to safety information about consumer products, one of the CPSIA's provisions requires the CPSC to create a searchable public database of reports of harm related to the use of products within the CPSC's jurisdiction. Members of the public can search the CPSC's Publicly Available Consumer Product Safety Information Database for safety information about products. Product manufacturers that are identified in a report may submit comments to be displayed in the database along with the report. Information about product recalls is also available in the database.

Consumer Financial Protection Bureau [44-1e]

In July 2010, President Obama signed into law the Dodd-Frank Wall Street Reform and Consumer Protection Act (Dodd-Frank Act), the most significant change to U.S. financial regulation since the New Deal. The Dodd-Frank Act establishes the Consumer Financial Protection Bureau (CFPB), an independent executive agency, which began operation on July 21, 2011, housed within the Federal Reserve, to regulate the offering and provision of consumer financial products or services under the existing federal consumer financial laws, most of which are discussed in this chapter. The primary goal of the CFPB is to ensure that all consumers have access to markets for consumer financial products and services and that markets for consumer financial services and products are fair, transparent, and competitive. The CFPB replaces the current federal consumer financial regulatory system, which had been split among seven different agencies: Office of the Comptroller of the Currency, Office of Thrift Supervision, Federal Deposit Insurance Corporation, Federal Reserve, National Credit Union Administration, Department of Housing and Urban Development (HUD), and the FTC.

The CFPB has broad rulemaking, supervisory, and enforcement authority over persons engaged in offering or providing a consumer financial product or service. A *consumer financial product or service* is a financial product or service that is "offered or provided for use primarily for personal, family, or household purposes." Financial products and services include the following: extending credit and servicing loans; engaging in deposit-taking activities; transmitting or exchanging funds; providing most real estate settlement services; providing stored value or payment instruments; providing check cashing, check collection, or check guaranty services; providing consumer credit reports; and collecting debt related to any consumer financial product or service. The Act excludes certain activities and parties from the CFPB's authority, including auto dealers, real estate brokerage activities, sellers of nonfinancial goods and services, legal practitioners, employee benefit plans, and persons regulated by the U.S. Securities and Exchange Commission, the U.S. Commodity Futures Trading Commission, or a State Securities Commission.

The CFPB may impose civil penalties for violations of a law, rule, or final order or condition. These penalties are imposed in writing by the CFPB in the following amounts: (1) up to $5,000 per day for any violation, (2) up to $25,000 per day for reckless violations, and (3) up $1 million per day for knowing violations. Civil penalties are paid into the CFPB Civil Penalty Fund established by the Dodd-Frank Act. In 2013, the CFPB issued a rule creating a process for allocating money from the Fund to compensate victims harmed by a person or company that was fined in an enforcement action brought by the CFPB.

Other Federal Consumer Protection Agencies [44-1f]

Among the many other federal agencies that play a major consumer protection role are the *National Highway Traffic Safety Administration (NHTSA)* and the *Food and Drug Administration (FDA)*.

Congress established the NHTSA to reduce the number of deaths and injuries resulting from highway crashes. Highway crashes in the United States kill approximately thirty-five thousand people each year and inflict injuries on more than 2 million others. Under authority similar to that of the CPSC, the NHTSA sets motor vehicle safety standards that promote crash prevention (e.g., rules for safer tires and brakes) and crashworthiness (e.g., interior padding, safety belts, and collapsible steering columns). As with the CPSC, manufacturers are required to report possible safety defects, and the agency may seek a recall if it determines that a particular automobile model presents a sufficiently great hazard. In addition, NHTSA is charged with establishing theft-resistance regulations and fuel-economy standards for motor vehicles. The NHTSA also is authorized to provide grants-in-aid for state highway safety programs and to conduct research on improving highway safety.

The FDA is the oldest federal consumer protection agency, dating back to 1906. The FDA enforces the Food, Drug and Cosmetic Act, enacted in 1938, which authorizes the agency to regulate "adulterated and misbranded" products. The FDA, an agency of the U.S Department of Health and Human Services, is responsible for protecting and promoting public health through the regulation and supervision of food safety, tobacco products, dietary supplements, prescription and over-the-counter pharmaceutical drugs, vaccines, biopharmaceuticals, blood transfusions, medical devices, electromagnetic radiation emitting devices, veterinary products, and cosmetics. The FDA uses two basic enforcement methods: it sets standards for products or requires their premarket approval. The products most often subject to premarket approval are drugs. Since 1976, the agency also has had the authority to subject medical devices such as pacemakers and intrauterine devices to premarket approval; it recently has been requiring a large and increasing number of such devices to undergo this approval process.

Although the FTC, CFPB, CPSC, NHTSA, and FDA are perhaps the best-known federal consumer protection agencies, numerous others play important roles. For example, the U.S. Postal Service brings many cases every year to close down mail fraud operations and the SEC, as discussed in Chapter 39, protects consumers against fraud in the sale of securities. In addition, many other agencies assist consumers with specific types of problems that fall within an agency's scope.

The Gramm-Leach-Bliley Financial Modernization Act (GLB Act) contains provisions to protect consumers' personal financial information held by financial institutions and originally gave authority to eight federal agencies and the states to administer and enforce its provisions. In 2011, the Dodd-Frank Act transferred GLBA privacy notice rulemaking authority from some of these agencies to the CFPB. The authority to promulgate GLBA privacy rules is vested for (1) depository institutions and many nondepository institutions in the CFPB; (2) securities and futures-related companies in the SEC and the Commodity Futures Trading Commission, respectively; and (3) certain motor vehicle dealers in the FTC.

The GLB Act requires financial institutions to give their customers privacy notices that explain the financial institution's information collection and sharing practices. Customers then have the right to limit sharing some of their personal financial information. Also, financial institutions and other companies that receive personal financial information from a financial institution may be limited in their ability to use that information.

CONSUMER PURCHASES [44-2]

When a consumer purchases a product or obtains a service, certain rights and obligations arise. (The extent to which these rights and obligations apply to all contracts was discussed more fully in Chapters 9 through 18; the extent to which they apply to a sale of goods under the Uniform Commercial Code [UCC] was discussed in Chapters 19 through 23.) Although a number of consumer protection laws have been enacted in recent years, they still leave much of a consumer's rights and duties to state contract law. In particular, Article 2 of the UCC provides the basic rules governing when a contract for the sale of goods is formed, what constitutes a breach of contract, and what rights an innocent party has against a party who commits a breach. Though many consumer protection laws add rights the UCC does not contain, they still use its tenets as building blocks. For example, many states have passed so-called lemon laws to provide additional contract cancellation rights to dissatisfied automobile purchasers. In 2012, the American Law Institute began a new project: the Restatement of the Law of Consumer Contracts. This new project will focus on the rules of contract law that treat consumer contracts differently from commercial contracts. It includes regulatory rules that are prominently applied in consumer protection law. The project will cover common law as well as statutory and regulatory law.

Federal Warranty Protection [44-2a]

A **warranty** creates a duty on the seller's part to assure that the goods or services she sells will conform to certain qualities, characteristics, or conditions. A seller is not required, however, to warrant what she sells; and in general she may, by appropriate words, disclaim (exclude) or modify a particular warranty or all warranties. Because a seller's power to disclaim or modify is so flexible, consumer protection laws have been enacted to ensure that consumers understand the warranty protection provided them.

To protect buyers and to prevent deception in selling, Congress enacted the **Magnuson-Moss Warranty Act**, which requires sellers of consumer products to provide adequate information about warranties. The FTC administers and enforces the Act, which provides for (1) disclosure in clear and understandable language of the warranty that is to be offered, (2) a description of the warranty as either "full" or "limited," (3) a prohibition against disclaiming implied warranties if a written warranty is given, and (4) an optional informal settlement mechanism.

The Act applies to consumer products with *written warranties*. A **consumer product** is any item of tangible personal property that is *normally* used for family, household, or personal use and that is distributed in commerce. The Act does *not* protect commercial purchasers, partly because they are considered sufficiently knowledgeable, in terms of contracting, to protect themselves. Also, they are able to employ their own attorneys to protect themselves and, in the marketplace, can spread the cost of their injuries.

Presale Disclosures   The Act contains **presale disclosure** provisions calculated to prevent confusion and deception and to enable purchasers to make educated product comparisons. A person making a warranty must, to the extent required by the rules of the FTC, fully and conspicuously disclose in simple and readily understood language the terms and conditions of such warranty. Separate rules apply to mail-order, catalog, and door-to-door sales.

Labeling Requirements   The Act further divides written warranties into two categories—limited and full—either of which, for any product costing more than $10, must be designated on the written warranty itself. The purpose of this provision is to enable the consumer to make an initial comparison of the legal rights under certain warranties. Under a **warranty** designated as **full**, the warrantor must agree to repair the product, without charge, to conform with the warranty; no limitation may be placed on the duration of any implied warranty; the consumer must be given the option of a refund or replacement if repair is unsuccessful; and consequential damages may be excluded only if the warranty conspicuously indicates their exclusion. A limited warranty is any warranty not designated as full.

Limitations on Disclaimers   Most significantly, the Act provides that a *written* warranty, whether full or limited, may ***not disclaim any implied warranty***. Specifically, a full warranty may not disclaim, modify, or limit any implied warranty. A limited warranty may not disclaim or modify any implied warranty but may limit its duration to that of the written warranty, provided that the limitation is reasonable, conscionable, and conspicuously displayed. Some states, however, do not allow limitations in the duration of implied warranties.

Federal warranty protection
applies to sellers of consumer goods who give written warranties

Warranty
creates a duty on the seller's part to assure certain features of goods or services

Consumer product
tangible personal property normally used for family, household, or personal purposes

Presale disclosure
requires terms of warranty to be simple and readily understood and to be made available before the sale

Labeling requirement
requires warrantor to inform consumers of their legal rights under a warranty (full or limited)

Full warranty
one under which warrantor will repair the product and, if unsuccessful, will replace or refund

Disclaimer limitation
prohibits a written warranty from disclaiming any implied warranty

Practical Advice

As a consumer, check to
see if the product you are
purchasing is covered by
a full or limited warranty.
If the warranty is limited,
ascertain the coverage and
terms of the warranty.

State "lemon laws"

state laws that attempt to
provide new car purchasers
with rights similar to full
warranties under the
Magnuson-Moss
Warranty Act

**Consumer right
of rescission**

in certain instances a
consumer is granted a brief
period of time during which
she may rescind (cancel) an
otherwise binding obligation

Rescission

right to cancel

Practical Advice

As a consumer, recognize
that in certain situations
you have a period of time in
which you may rescind your
contract.

For example, GE sells consumer goods to Barry for $150 and provides a written warranty regarding the quality of the goods. GE must designate the warranty as full or limited, depending on the warranty's characteristics, and may not disclaim or modify any implied warranty. On the other hand, had GE not provided Barry with a written warranty, the Magnuson-Moss Warranty Act would not apply; and GE could disclaim any and all implied warranties (see Figure 44-1).

State "Lemon Laws" [44-2b]

A number of state legislatures have enacted **lemon laws** that attempt to provide new car purchasers with rights that are similar to full warranties under the Magnuson-Moss Warranty Act. (Some states have broadened their laws to cover used cars; some also cover motorcycles.) There are many different lemon laws, but most define a *lemon* as a car that continues to have a defect that substantially impairs its use, value, or safety, even after the manufacturer has made reasonable attempts to correct the problem. If a consumer can prove that her car is a lemon, most lemon laws require the manufacturer either to replace the car or to refund its retail price, less an allowance for the consumer's use of the car. In addition, most lemon laws provide that the consumer may recover attorneys' fees and expenses if the case goes to litigation.

Consumer Right of Rescission [44-2c]

In most cases, a consumer is legally obligated once he has signed a contract. Many states, however, have statutes allowing a consumer a brief period—generally two or three days—during which he may rescind an otherwise binding credit obligation if the sale was solicited in his home. Moreover, the FTC has also set forth a trade regulation that applies to door-to-door sales, leases, or rentals of goods and services for $25.00 or more, whether the sale is for cash or on credit. The regulation permits a consumer to rescind a contract within *three days* of signing.

The right of **rescission** also exists under the *Federal Consumer Credit Protection Act* (discussed more fully in the next section), which allows a consumer three days during which he may withdraw from any credit obligation secured by a mortgage on his home, unless the extension of credit was made to acquire the dwelling. After the consumer rescinds, the creditor has twenty days to return any money or property he has received from the consumer.

The *Interstate Land Sales Full Disclosure Act* requires a developer of unimproved land to file a detailed statement of record containing specified information about specified subdivisions with the Department of Housing and Urban Development before offering the lots for sale or lease. The developer must provide a property report (a condensed version of the statement of record) to each prospective purchaser or lessee. The Act provides that a purchaser or lessee may revoke any contract or agreement for sale or lease at her option within seven days of signing the contract, and that the contract must clearly provide this right. A purchaser or lessee who does not receive a property report before signing a contract may revoke the contract within two years from the date of signing.

Figure 44-1 Magnuson-Moss Warranty Act

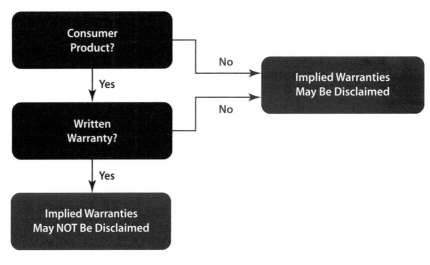

CONCEPT REVIEW 44-1

Consumer Rescission Rights

Law	Rescission Period	Door-to-Door Solicitation Required?	Credit or Cash
State "cooling-off" laws	Varies	Yes	Varies
Federal Trade Commission trade regulation	Within three days of signing the contract	Yes	Both
Consumer Credit Protection Act (CCPA)	Within three days of signing the contract	No	Credit only
Interstate Land Sales Full Disclosure Act	Within seven days of signing the contract	No	Both

CONSUMER CREDIT TRANSACTIONS [44-3]

Consumer credit transaction

any credit transaction involving goods, services, or land for personal, household, or family purposes

In the absence of special regulation, consumer credit transactions are governed by the laws that regulate commercial transactions generally. A **consumer credit transaction** is customarily defined as any credit transaction involving goods, services, or land acquired for personal, household, or family purposes. The following examples illustrate consumer credit transactions: Atkins borrows $600 from a bank to pay a dentist bill or to take a vacation; Bevins buys a refrigerator for her home from a department store and agrees to pay the purchase price in twelve equal monthly installments; Carpenter has an oil company credit card with which he purchases gasoline and tires for his family car.

Regulation of consumer credit has increased considerably because of the dramatic expansion of consumer credit and the numerous abuses in credit transactions, including misleading credit disclosures, unfair marketing practices, and oppressive collection methods. In response to concerns about consumer credit, Congress passed the *Federal Consumer Credit Protection Act (FCCPA)*, which requires creditors to disclose finance charges (including interest and other charges) and credit extension charges, and sets limits on garnishment proceedings. Since enacting the FCCPA, Congress has added titles to this law. In 1968 the National Conference of Commissioners on Uniform State Laws (now known as the Uniform Law Commission) promulgated the Uniform Consumer Credit Code (UCCC), which consolidated into one recommended law the regulation of all consumer credit transactions—loans and purchases on credit. Although only eleven states have adopted the UCCC, its impact on the development of consumer credit has extended well beyond their borders.

Access to the Market [44-3a]

Access to the market

discrimination in extending credit on the basis of gender, marital status, race, color, religion, national origin, or age is prohibited

The *Equal Credit Opportunity Act (ECOA)* prohibits all businesses that regularly extend credit from discriminating against any applicant for credit on the basis of race, color, sex, marital status, religion, national origin, age, or receipt of public assistance. When originally enacted, the ECOA gave the Federal Reserve Board (Fed) responsibility for prescribing the implementing regulation. The Fed issued *Regulation B* to implement the ECOA. The Dodd-Frank Act transferred *rulemaking* authority under the ECOA to the Consumer Financial Protection Bureau.

Under the ECOA, a creditor must notify an applicant, within thirty days of receiving an application, of the action the creditor has taken and must give specific reasons for denying credit. Although several federal agencies administer and enforce the ECOA, the FTC has overall *enforcement* authority. A credit applicant aggrieved by a violation of the ECOA may recover actual and punitive damages, plus attorneys' fees. Failure to comply with Regulation B can subject a financial institution to civil liability for actual and punitive damages in individual or class action suits. Liability for punitive damages can be (1) $10,000 in individual actions and (2) the lesser of $500,000 or 1 percent of the creditor's net worth in class action suits.

The *Home Mortgage Disclosure Act (HMDA)* was enacted by Congress along with the *Community Reinvestment Act (CRA)* to emphasize to financial institutions the importance of their reinvesting funds in the communities that they serve. Through the HMDA, Congress outlawed geographic discrimination, or *redlining*, the process by which financial institutions refuse to provide reasonable home financing terms to qualified applicants whose homes are located in geographic areas of declining value. In addition, the HMDA requires public disclosure of the financial institution's geographic pattern of mortgage lending. The CRA, by comparison, was intended to encourage financial institutions to meet the credit needs of their local communities.

Amendments to the HMDA and the CRA in 1989 expanded the disclosure and reporting requirements for all mortgage lenders and mandated that federal regulating agencies evaluate and rate CRA performance reports. In addition, in 2008 Congress enacted the **Troubled Asset Relief Program**, commonly referred to as **TARP**. TARP is a program of the U.S. government that purchases assets and equity from financial institutions to strengthen the U.S. financial sector. As of March 31, 2014, cumulative collections under TARP, together with the U.S. Treasury's additional proceeds from the sale of non-TARP shares of AIG, exceed total disbursements by more than $13 billion. The Dodd-Frank Act requires repaid TARP funds to be used for deficit reduction.

Disclosure Requirements [44-3b]

**Disclosure requirements
(Truth-in-Lending Act)**
requires creditor to
provide certain information
about contract terms to
the consumer before he
formally incurs the
obligation

Title One of the FCCPA, also known as the **Truth-in-Lending Act (TILA)**, as amended by the Dodd-Frank Act, has superseded state disclosure requirements relating to credit terms for both consumer loans and credit sales. Exempted from its provisions are loans greater than $53,000, as adjusted annually for inflation in January 2013. The Act does not cover credit transactions for business, commercial, or agricultural purposes. Creditors in every state not specifically exempted by the Fed must comply with federal disclosure standards. The Bankruptcy Abuse Prevention and Consumer Protection Act of 2005, discussed in Chapter 38, made a number of amendments to the TILA.

Before a consumer formally incurs a contractual obligation for credit, both state and federal statutes require the creditor to present to the consumer a written statement containing certain information about contract terms. Generally, the required disclosure concerns the cost of credit, that is, interest or sales finance charges. An important requirement in the TILA is that sales finance and interest rates must be quoted in terms of an **APR** (*annual percentage rate*) and must be calculated on a uniform basis. Congress required disclosure of this information to encourage consumers to compare credit terms, to increase competition among financial institutions, and to facilitate economic stability. Enforcement and interpretation of the TILA was assigned to the Fed, which issued **Regulation Z** to carry out this responsibility. However, as of July 21, 2011, these functions were transferred to the CFPB.

APR
annual percentage rate

Practical Advice

As a lender, make sure that
you disclose the annual
percentage rate (including
all appropriate costs) and all
other required information
prior to closing the loan.

The **Fair Credit and Charge Card Disclosure Act** adds to the TILA a new section requiring all credit and charge card applications and solicitations to include extensive disclosures whose requirements depend on the type of card involved and whether the application or solicitation is by mail, telephone, or other means.

Credit Accounts   Under the TILA a creditor must inform consumers who open revolving or open-ended credit accounts about how the finance charge is computed and when it is charged, what other charges may be imposed, and whether the creditor retains or acquires a security interest. Moreover, in 2000 the Fed published a rule requiring marketing material to display clearly a table that shows the APR and other important information such as the annual fee. The Bankruptcy Act of 2005 further requires a disclosure of any low or discounted introductory rates, how long these rates will apply, and the rates that will take effect upon the termination of the introductory rate. It further requires billing statements to disclose all late payment charges and the date that the payment is due. To be included in the billing statement is a warning that making only the minimum payment will increase the amount of interest that must be paid and the time it takes to repay the balance. In addition, the billing statement must include an example to show the consumer how long it will take to pay off a stated balance at a specified interest rate if she makes only the minimum payment required.

Open-ended credit
account permitting debtor
to enter into a series of
credit transactions

An **open-ended credit** account is one that permits the debtor to enter into a series of credit transactions that he may pay off either in installments or in a lump sum. Examples of this type of credit include most department store credit cards, most gasoline credit cards, VISA cards, and

Closed-ended credit

credit extended to debtor for a specified time

MasterCards. With this type of credit, the creditor is also required to provide a statement of account for each billing period. **Closed-ended credit**, in contrast, is credit extended for a specified time, during which the debtor generally makes periodic payments in an amount and at a time agreed upon in advance. Examples of this type of credit include most automobile financing agreements, most real estate mortgages, and numerous other major purchases. For nonrevolving or closed-ended credit accounts, the creditor must provide the consumer with information about the total amount financed; the cash price; the number, amount, and due date of installments; delinquency charges; and a description of the security, if any.

If solicitation for a credit card appears on the Internet or other interactive computer service, the provider must clearly and conspicuously disclose all information required by the TILA. These disclosures must be readily accessible to the consumer and be current.

Household Credit Services, Inc. v. Pfennig
Supreme Court of the United States, 2004
541 U.S. 232, 124 S.Ct. 1741, 158 L.Ed.2d 450
http://scholar.google.com/scholar_case?case=6616956060046722608&q=124+S.Ct.+1741&hl=en&as_sdt=40006

FACTS Sharon Pfennig holds a credit card initially issued by Household Credit Services, Inc. but in which MBNA America Bank, N.A., now holds an interest through the acquisition of Household's credit card operation. Although the terms of Pfennig's credit card agreement set her credit limit at $2,000, Pfennig was able to make charges exceeding that limit, subject to a $29 "over-limit fee" for each month in which her balance exceeded $2,000.

On August 24, 1999, Pfennig filed a complaint in the U.S. District Court for the Southern District of Ohio on behalf of a purported nationwide class of all consumers who were charged over-limit fees by Household or MBNA (defendants). Pfennig alleged that defendants allowed her and the other members of the class to exceed their credit limits, thereby subjecting them to over-limit fees. Pfennig claims the defendants violated the Truth-in-Lending Act (TILA) by failing to classify the over-limit fees as "finance charges" and thereby "misrepresented the true cost of credit." Defendants moved to dismiss the complaint on the ground that Regulation Z specifically excludes over-limit fees from the definition of "finance charge." The district court granted defendants' motion to dismiss. On appeal, Pfennig argued, and the Court of Appeals agreed, that Regulation Z's explicit exclusion of over-limit fees from the definition of "finance charge" conflicts with the TILA.

DECISION The judgment of the Court of Appeals for the Sixth Circuit is reversed.

OPINION The TILA regulates the substance and form of disclosures that creditors offering "open-ended consumer credit plans" (a term that includes credit card accounts) must make to consumers, and provides a civil remedy for consumers who suffer damages as a result of a creditor's failure to comply with TILA's provisions. When a creditor and a consumer enter into an open-ended consumer credit plan, the creditor is required to provide to the consumer a statement for each billing cycle for which there is an outstanding balance due. The statement must include the account's outstanding balance at the end of the billing period, and "the amount of any finance charge added to the account during the period, itemized to show the amounts, if any, due to the application of percentage rates and the amount, if any, imposed as a minimum or fixed charge." A "finance charge" is an amount "payable directly or indirectly by the person to whom the credit is extended, and imposed directly or indirectly by the creditor as an incident to the extension of credit." The Board has interpreted this definition to exclude "charges … for exceeding a credit limit" (Regulation Z). Thus, although respondent's billing statement disclosed the imposition of an over-limit fee when she exceeded her $2,000 credit limit, consistent with Regulation Z, the amount was not included as part of the "finance charge."

The Court of Appeals concluded that the over-limit fees in this case were imposed "incident to the extension of credit" and therefore fell squarely within the Act's definition of "finance charge." The Court of Appeals' characterization of the transaction in this case, however, is not supported by the facts. Pfennig alleged in her complaint that the over-limit fee is imposed for each month in which her balance exceeds the original credit limit. If this were true the over-limit fee would be imposed not as a direct result of an extension of credit for a purchase that caused respondent to exceed her $2,000 limit, but rather as a result of the fact that her charges exceeded her $2,000 limit at the time her monthly charges were calculated. Because over-limit fees, regardless of a creditor's particular billing practices, are imposed only when a consumer exceeds her credit limit, it is appropriate to characterize an over-limit fee not as a charge imposed for obtaining an extension of credit over a consumer's credit limit, but rather as a penalty for violating the credit agreement. Because over-limit fees, which are imposed only when a consumer breaches the terms of her credit agreement, can be characterized as a penalty for defaulting on the credit agreement, the decision to exclude them from the term "finance charge" is correct.

INTERPRETATION The TILA requires credit providers to disclose finance charges of loans but does not require all fees associated with loans to be classified as finance costs.

ETHICAL QUESTION Did any of the parties act unethically? Explain.

CRITICAL THINKING QUESTION Do you agree with the court's decision? Explain.

ARMs The Fed has amended Regulation Z to deal with variable or adjustable rate mortgages (ARMs). The *ARM disclosure rules* apply to any loan that is (1) a closed-ended consumer transaction, (2) secured by the consumer's principal residence, (3) longer than one year in duration, and (4) subject to interest rate variation. This coverage excludes open-ended lines of credit secured by the consumer's principal dwelling. The disclosures must be made when a creditor furnishes an application to a prospective borrower or before the creditor receives payment of a nonrefundable fee, whichever occurs first. The ARM disclosure rules require that the creditor provide the consumer with a consumer handbook on ARMs and a loan program disclosure statement covering the terms of each ARM that the creditor offers.

Home Equity Loans A home equity loan is a loan for a fixed amount of money that is secured by the consumer's home. A home equity line of credit is a revolving line of credit using the consumer's home as collateral for the loan. Under a line of credit, payments are owed only on the amount actually borrowed, not the full amount available. To regulate the disclosures and advertising of these loans, Congress enacted the ***Home Equity Loan Consumer Protection Act (HELCPA)***. HELCPA amends the TILA to require that lenders provide a disclosure statement and consumer pamphlet at (or, in some limited instances, within three days of) the time they provide an application to a prospective consumer borrower. HELCPA applies to all open-ended credit plans for consumer loans that are secured by the consumer's principal dwelling. Unlike other TILA statutes, HELCPA defines a principal dwelling to include second or vacation homes. The disclosure statement must include a statement that (1) a default on the loan may result in the consumer's loss of the dwelling; (2) some conditions must be met, such as a time by which the consumer must submit an application to obtain the specific terms; and (3) the creditor, under certain circumstances, may terminate the plan and accelerate the outstanding balance, prohibit further extension of credit, reduce the plan's credit limit, or impose fees upon the termination of the account. In addition, if the plan contains a fixed interest rate, the creditor must disclose each APR imposed. If the plan involves an ARM, it must include how the rate is computed, the manner in which rates will be changed, the initial rate and how it was determined, the maximum rate change that may occur in any one year, the maximum rate that can be charged under the plan, the earliest time at which the maximum interest can be reached, and an itemization of all fees the plan imposes. Regulation Z provides the consumer with the right to rescind such a plan until midnight of the third day following the opening of the plan, until delivery of a notice of the right to rescind, or until delivery of all material disclosures, whichever comes last. When the loan amount exceeds the fair market value of the house, the Bankruptcy Act of 2005 requires the lender to inform a consumer that the amount in excess of the fair market value is not tax deductible for federal income tax purposes.

Billing Errors The *Fair Credit Billing Act* attempts to relieve some of the problems and abuses associated with credit card billing errors. The Act establishes procedures for the consumer to follow in making complaints about specified billing errors and requires the creditor to explain or correct such errors. Until it responds to the complaint, the creditor may not take any action to collect the disputed amount, restrict the use of an open-ended credit account because the disputed amount is unpaid, or report the disputed amount as delinquent.

Settlement Charges Congress enacted the ***Real Estate Settlement Procedures Act (RESPA)*** to provide consumer home purchasers with greater and timelier information on the nature and costs of the settlement process and to protect them from unnecessarily high settlement charges. RESPA, which applies to all federally related mortgage loans, requires advance disclosure to home buyers and sellers of all settlement costs, including attorneys' fees, credit reports, title insurance, and, if relevant, an initial escrow account statement. Nearly all first mortgage loans fall within the scope of the Act. RESPA prohibits kickbacks and referral fees and limits the amount homebuyers must place in escrow accounts to ensure payment of real estate taxes and insurance. In 1990, the National Affordable Housing Act amended RESPA to require an annual analysis of escrow accounts. RESPA was administered and enforced by the secretary of housing and urban development until July 21, 2011, when these functions were transferred to the CFPB.

In 2013, the CFPB amended Regulation X (issued under the RESPA) and Regulation Z (issued under the TILA) to implement provisions of the Dodd-Frank Act regarding mortgage loan servicing. Effective on January 10, 2014, the new rules implement laws to protect consumers from detrimental actions by mortgage loan servicers and to provide consumers with better tools and information when dealing with mortgage loan servicers.

Mortgage Reform and Anti-Predatory Lending Act   One of the many standalone statutes included in the Dodd-Frank Act is the Mortgage Reform and Anti-Predatory Lending Act of 2010. It sets minimum underwriting standards for mortgages by requiring lenders to verify reasonably and in good faith that consumer-borrowers have a reasonable ability to repay the loan at the time the mortgage is granted. It also prohibits mandatory arbitration clauses and prepayment penalties for ARMs.

Contract Terms [44-3c]

Contract terms statutory and judicial limitations have been imposed on consumer obligations

Consumer credit is marketed on a mass basis. Frequently, contract documents are printed forms containing blank spaces to accommodate the contractual details the creditor will normally negotiate at the time she extends credit. Standardization and uniformity of contract terms facilitate the transfer of the creditor's rights (in most situations, those of a seller) to a third party, usually a bank or finance company.

Almost all states impose statutory ceilings on the amount that creditors may charge for the extension of consumer credit. Statutes regulating rates also specify what other charges may be made. Most statutes require a creditor to permit the debtor to pay her obligation in full at any time before the maturity date of the final installment. If the interest charge for the loan period was computed in advance and added to the principal of the loan, a debtor who prepays in full is entitled to a refund of the unearned interest already paid.

In the past, certain purchases involving consumer goods were financed in such a way that a consumer was legally obligated to make full payment of the price to a third party, even though the dealer from whom she bought the goods had committed fraud or the goods were defective. This occurred when the purchaser executed and delivered to the seller a negotiable instrument (a promissory note, draft, or check), and the seller negotiated it to a holder in due course, who purchased the note for value, in good faith, and without notice that it was overdue or that it had any defenses or claims attached to it. Though valid against the seller, the buyer's defenses—that the goods were defective or that the seller had committed fraud—were not valid against a holder in due course of the note. To preserve the claims and defenses of consumer buyers and borrowers and to make such claims and defenses available against holders in due course, the FTC adopted a rule that limits the rights of a holder in due course of an instrument evidencing a debt that arises out of a *consumer credit contract*. The rule, which was discussed in Chapter 25, applies to sellers and lessors of goods.

A similar rule applies to credit card issuers under the *Fair Credit Billing Act*. The Act preserves a consumer's defense against the issuer (provided the consumer has made a good faith attempt to resolve the dispute with the seller), but only if (1) the seller is controlled by the card issuer or is under common control with the issuer, (2) the issuer has included the seller's promotional literature in the monthly billing statements sent to the card holder, or (3) the sale involves more than $50 and the consumer's billing address is in the same state as, or within one hundred miles of, the seller's place of business.

Consumer Credit Card Fraud [44-3d]

Credit Card Fraud Act prohibits certain fraudulent practices and limits a card holder's liability for unauthorized use of a credit card to $50.00

Consumer credit card fraud, including stolen credit cards or card numbers, identity theft, skimming, and phishing, has become an increasingly serious problem and now totals billions of dollars each year. Congress enacted the **Credit Card Fraud Act**, which closed many loopholes in prior law. The Act prohibits the following practices: (1) possessing unauthorized cards, (2) counterfeiting or altering credit cards, (3) using account numbers alone, and (4) using cards obtained from a third party with his consent, even if the third party conspires to report the cards as stolen. It also imposes stiffer, criminal penalties for violation.

The FCCPA protects the *credit card holder* from loss by limiting to $50.00 the card holder's liability for another's unauthorized use of the holder's card. However, the card issuer may collect up to that amount for unauthorized use only if (1) the holder has accepted the card, (2) the issuer has furnished adequate notice of potential liability to the card holder, (3) the issuer has provided the card holder with a statement describing the means by which the holder may notify the card issuer of the loss or theft of the credit card, (4) the unauthorized use occurs before the card holder has notified the card issuer of the loss or theft, and (5) the card issuer has provided a method by which the person using the card can be identified as the person authorized to use the card.

Fair credit reporting consumer credit reports are prohibited from containing inaccurate or obsolete information

Fair Reportage [44-3e]

Because creditors usually grant consumers credit only after investigating their creditworthiness, it is essential that the information on which creditors base such decisions is accurate and current. To this end, Congress enacted the *Fair Credit Reporting Act (FRCA)*, which applies to consumer reports used to secure employment, insurance, and credit. The Act prohibits the inclusion of inaccurate or specified obsolete information in consumer reports and requires consumer reporting agencies to give consumers written advance notice before making an investigative report.

Practical Advice

The consumer may request information regarding the nature and substance of all information in the consumer reporting agency's files, the source of the information, and the names of all who received the consumer reports furnished for employment purposes within the preceding two years and for other purposes within the preceding six months.

If the consumer does not agree that the information in the file is accurate and complete, and so notifies the agency, the agency must then reinvestigate the matter within a reasonable time, unless the complaint is frivolous or irrelevant. If reinvestigation proves that the information is inaccurate, it must promptly be deleted. If the dispute remains unresolved after reinvestigation, the consumer may submit to the agency a brief statement setting forth the nature of the dispute, and this statement must be incorporated into the report.

Congress has amended the Act to restrict the use of credit reports by employers. An employer must now notify a job applicant or current employee that a report may be used and must obtain the applicant's consent prior to requesting an individual's credit report from a credit bureau. In addition, prior to taking an adverse action (refusal to hire, reassignment or termination, or denying a promotion) against the applicant or employee, the employer must provide the individual with a "pre-adverse action disclosure," which must contain the credit report and a copy of the CFPB's "A Summary of Your Rights Under the Fair Credit Reporting Act."

A recent amendment to the FCRA requires each of the nationwide consumer reporting companies to provide upon an individual's request a free copy of her credit report once every twelve months. Beginning January 1, 2013, the responsibility of interpreting and enforcing requirements under the FCRA shifted from the FTC to the CFPB.

Freeman v. Quicken Loans, Inc.
Supreme Court of the United States, 2012
___ U.S. ___, 132 S.Ct. 2034, 182 L.Ed.2d 398
http://scholar.google.com/scholar_case?case=7226073435610733022&hl=en&as_sdt=6&as_vis=1&oi=scholarr

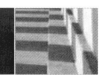

FACTS The Freemans, Bennetts, and Smiths (plaintiffs) are three married couples who obtained mortgage loans from defendant Quicken Loans, Inc. In 2008, they filed separate actions alleging that the defendant had violated a provision of the Real Estate Settlement Procedures Act (RESPA) by charging them fees for which no services were provided. In particular, the Freemans and Bennetts allege that they were charged loan discount fees of $980 and $1,100, respectively, but that the defendant did not give them lower interest rates in return. The Smiths' allegations focus on a $575 loan "processing fee" and a "loan origination" fee of more than $5,100. The U.S. District Court granted summary judgment in favor of the defendant because the plaintiffs did not allege any splitting of fees. The U.S. Court of Appeals for the Fifth Circuit affirmed. The U.S. Supreme Court granted *certiorari*.

DECISION Judgment of the U.S. Court of Appeals is affirmed.

OPINION Enacted in 1974, RESPA regulates the market for real estate "settlement services," a term defined by statute to include

"any service provided in connection with a real estate settlement," such as "title searches, … title insurance, services rendered by an attorney, the preparation of documents, property surveys, the rendering of credit reports or appraisals, … services rendered by a real estate agent or broker, the origination of a federally related mortgage loan …, and the handling of the processing, and closing or settlement." One of RESPA's consumer-protection provisions seeks to eliminate kickbacks or referral fees that tend to increase unnecessarily the costs of certain settlement services.

"No person shall give and no person shall accept any portion, split, or percentage of any charge made or received for the rendering of a real estate settlement service … other than for services actually performed." The dispute between the parties boils down to whether this provision prohibits the collection of an unearned charge by a single settlement-service provider—what might be called an undivided unearned fee—or whether it covers only transactions in which a provider shares a part of a settlement-service charge with one or more other persons who did nothing to earn that part.

By providing that no person "shall give" or "shall accept" a "portion, split, or percentage" of a "charge" that has been "made or received," "other than for services actually performed," RESPA clearly describes two distinct exchanges. First, a "charge" is "made" to or "received" from a consumer by a settlement-service provider. That provider then "give[s]," and another person "accept[s]," a "portion, split, or percentage" of the charge. Congress's use of different sets of verbs, with distinct tenses, to distinguish between the consumer-provider transaction (the "charge" that is "made or received") and the fee-sharing transaction (the "portion, split, or percentage" that is "give[n]" or "accept[ed]") would be pointless if, as the plaintiffs contend, the two transactions could be collapsed into one.

Plaintiffs try to merge the two stages by arguing that a settlement-service provider can "make" a charge (stage one) and then "accept" (stage two) the portion of the charge consisting of 100 percent. But then is not the provider also "receiv[ing]" the charge at the same time he is "accept[ing]" the portion of it? And who "give[s]" the portion of the charge consisting of 100 percent? The same provider who "accept[s]" it? This reading does not avoid collapsing the sequential relationship of the two stages, and it would simply destroy the tandem character of activities that the text envisions at stage two (*i.e.*, a giving and accepting).

In order to establish a violation, a plaintiff must demonstrate that a charge for settlement services was divided between two or more persons. Because plaintiffs do not contend that defendant split the challenged charges with anyone else, summary judgment was properly granted in favor of defendant.

INTERPRETATION RESPA does *not* prohibit the collection of an unearned charge by a single settlement-service provider but, instead, covers only a provider's splitting a fee with one or more other persons.

CRITICAL THINKING QUESTION Is the Supreme Court's decision fair and reasonable? Explain.

Credit Card Bill of Rights [44-3f]

On May 22, 2009, President Obama signed into law the *Credit Card Accountability, Responsibility, and Disclosure Act* (also known as the Credit Card Bill of Rights or CARD). The 2009 Act amends the TILA to establish fair and transparent practices relating to credit cards. The Act delegated regulation to the Fed (as of July 21, 2011, administration of CARD was transferred to the CFPB). The Fed issued regulations in three stages, the latest in June 2010. These regulations include the following:

1. Credit card issuers generally cannot raise interest rates, or any fees, during the first year an account is open, except when a variable rate changes, a promotional rate ends, or a required minimum payment is more than sixty days late.
2. After the first year, forty-five days' advance notice is required to (a) raise the interest rate on future purchases; (b) make certain changes in terms, such as increased annual fees, cash advance fees, and late fees; and (c) increase the minimum payment.
3. If a credit card issuer lawfully imposes a rate increase on a customer, the rate must be restored to the prior rate if the customer pays the minimum balance on time for the next six months.
4. Credit card issuers are prohibited from giving credit cards to a full-time college student under twenty-one years of age unless that student can prove that she has the means to pay or a parent or guardian cosigns for the card.
5. Credit card issuers may not raise the credit limit on accounts held by a college student under twenty-one and a cosigner without written permission from the cosigner.
6. Credit card agreements must be posted online and no fees can be charged to make a payment online, by phone, mail, or any other means.
7. Credit card issuers must mail account statements twenty-one days prior to the payment due date.
8. Credit card issuers must apply excess payments received to the balance with the highest interest rate first.
9. If the credit card issuer receives payment by 5:00 P.M. on the due date, the payment must be considered on time.
10. Credit card issuers must obtain the customer's permission before allowing the customer to spend more than the credit limit.
11. Card holders cannot be charged over-limit fees unless they give express permission ("opt in") to the card issuer to approve transactions that exceed their credit limits.
12. First-year fees required to open a credit card account cannot total more than 25 percent of the initial credit limit. This restriction applies to annual fees, application fees, and processing fees, but not to penalty fees, such as penalties for late payments.

BUSINESS LAW **IN ACTION**

Cash Store operates loan establishments that specialize in making short-term, high-interest "payday loans," typically two weeks in duration and carrying annual percentage rates greater than 500 percent. When a Cash Store customer is granted a loan, she writes out a check, postdated to the end of the loan period, for the full amount that she is obligated to pay. At the end of the two-week period, she has the option of paying the loan off or continuing for another two-week period by paying the interest. Cash Store customers sign a standard form called "Consumer Loan Agreement." Upon entering into or renewing each loan, Cash Store was in the practice of stapling to the top of the loan agreement a receipt that labeled the finance charge in red ink as either a "deferred deposit extension fee" or a "deferred deposit check fee," depending on whether the transaction was a renewal or an original loan.

To Cash Store's surprise, it was sued in a class action lawsuit alleging violations of the Truth-in-Lending Act (TILA) and Regulation Z. Specifically, plaintiffs claimed that the cash register receipt stapled to Cash Store's loan agreements physically covered up some of the required TILA disclosures. Plaintiffs further challenged the use of the term "deferred deposit fee" rather than "finance charge." The lawsuit maintained that these two practices rendered Cash Store's TILA disclosures neither clear nor conspicuous, as required by law.

Arguably, the practice of stapling a small receipt to TILA disclosures does not mislead borrowers as to the terms of a loan. But a federal appellate court refused to find this to be true as a matter of law and therefore sent the case to a jury to assess Cash Store's TILA disclosures from the perspective of the ordinary consumer. Regardless of the outcome of this jury trial, the lesson is clear: creditors should not affix anything to loan documents that even partially obscures TILA mandated disclosures. It is probably also advisable to refer to financing charges on loan documentation as just that, rather than devising another term that may not be deemed synonymous. Any possible efficiency or marketing advantage that may be achieved is not worth the cost of potential litigation.

13. If the account is closed or canceled by the consumer, the closed account will not be considered in default and the card issuer cannot require immediate repayment of the entire balance. Issuers also cannot charge monthly maintenance fees on closed accounts.

14. Penalty fees, such as late fees and over-limit fees must be "reasonable and proportional to the omission or violation" of the card agreement.

15. Gift cards or certificates may not expire sooner than five years after issuance.

16. Ads that make promotional offers for free credit reports must state that free credit reports are available under federal law at AnnualCreditReport.com. The disclosure must read: "You have the right to a free credit report from AnnualCreditReport.com or 877-322-8228, the ONLY authorized source under federal law."

CREDITORS' REMEDIES [44-4]

A primary concern of creditors involves their rights should a debtor default or become late in payment. When the credit charge is precomputed, the creditor may impose a delinquency charge for late payments, subject to statutory limits for such charges. If, instead of being delinquent, the consumer defaults, the creditor may declare the entire balance of the debt immediately due and payable and may sue on the debt. The other courses of action that are open to the creditor depend on his security. Security provisions in consumer credit contracts may require a cosigner, an assignment of wages, a security interest in the goods sold, a security interest in other real or personal property of the debtor, and a confession of judgment clause (i.e., a clause by the defendant giving the plaintiff power to enter judgment against the defendant).

Wage Assignments and Garnishment [44-4a]

Wage assignments and garnishment most states limit the amount that may be deducted from an individual's wages through either assignment or garnishment

Wage assignments are prohibited by some states. In most states and under the FCCPA, a limitation is imposed on the amount that may be deducted from an individual's wages during any pay period. In addition, the FCCPA prohibits an employer from discharging an employee solely because of a creditor's exercise of an assignment of wages in connection with any one debt.

Even in cases in which wage assignments are prohibited, the creditor may still reach a consumer's wages through garnishment. But garnishment is available only in a court proceeding to enforce the collection of a judgment. The FCCPA and state statutes contain exemption provisions that limit the amount of wages subject to garnishment.

Security Interest in Goods [44-4b]

Security interest in goods

seller may retain a security interest in goods sold or other collateral of the buyer, although some restrictions are imposed

In the case of credit sales, the seller may retain a security interest in the goods sold. Many states impose restrictions on other security the creditor may obtain. Where the debt is secured by property as collateral, the creditor, on default by the debtor, may take possession of the property and, subject to the provisions of the UCC, either retain it in full satisfaction of the debt or sell it and, if the proceeds are less than the outstanding debt, sue the debtor for the balance and obtain a deficiency judgment. The UCC provides that when a buyer of goods has paid 60 percent of the purchase price or 60 percent of a loan secured by consumer goods, the secured creditor may not retain the property in full satisfaction but must sell the goods and pay to the buyer that part of the sale proceeds in excess of the balance due. (Secured transactions are discussed in Chapter 37.) In addition, federal regulation prohibits a credit seller or lender from obtaining a consumer's grant of a nonpossessory security interest in household goods. Household goods include clothing, furniture, appliances, kitchenware, personal effects, one radio, and one television; such goods specifically exclude works of art, other electronic entertainment equipment, antiques, and jewelry. This rule, which does not apply to purchase money security interests or to pledges, prevents a lender or seller from obtaining a nonpurchase money security interest covering the consumer's household goods.

Debt Collection Practices [44-4c]

Debt collection practices

abusive, deceptive, and unfair practices by debt collectors in collecting consumer debts are prohibited by the Fair Debt Collection Practices Act

Abuses by some collection agencies led Congress to pass the *Fair Debt Collection Practices Act (FDCPA)*, which makes abusive, deceptive, and unfair practices by debt collectors in collecting consumer debts illegal. As of July 21, 2011, *administration* of the FDCPA was transferred from the FTC to the CFPB. Both the CFPB and the FTC have law *enforcement* powers under the FDCPA. The FDCPA does not apply to creditors themselves. Rather, the FDCPA provides that any debt collector who communicates with a person other than the consumer for the purpose of acquiring information about the consumer's location may not state that the consumer owes any debt. Moreover, the Dodd-Frank Act and Section 5 of the FTC Act prohibit creditors from engaging in unfair, deceptive, or abusive practices in their own collection activity.

The FDCPA prohibits a number of abusive collection practices, including (1) communication with the consumer at unusual or inconvenient hours; (2) communication with the consumer if she is represented by an attorney; (3) harassing, oppressive, or abusive conduct, such as obscene language or threats of violence; (4) false, deceptive, or misleading representations or means of collection; and (5) unfair or unconscionable means to collect any debt.

The FDCPA requires a debt collector, within five days of the initial communication with a consumer, to provide the consumer with a written notice that includes (1) the amount of the debt, (2) the name of the current creditor, and (3) a statement informing the consumer that she can request verification of the alleged debt. The consumer may recover damages from the collection agency for violations of the FDCPA.

Practical Advice

As a creditor carefully refrain from harassing or abusing a debtor and make sure that all contacts with the debtor strictly comply with all laws and regulations.

Jerman v. Carlisle, McNellie, Rini, Kramer & Ulrich LPA
United States Supreme Court, 2010
559 U.S. ___, 130 S.Ct. 1605, 176 L.Ed.2d 519
http://scholar.google.com/scholar_case?case=10408914555667566662&q=559+U.S.___,+130+S.Ct.+1605,+176+
L.Ed.2d+519&hl=en&as_sdt=4000006

FACTS Karen L. Jerman filed this suit against a law firm, Carlisle, McNellie, Rini, Kramer & Ulrich, L.P.A., and one of its attorneys, Adrienne S. Foster (collectively Carlisle). In April 2006, Carlisle filed a complaint in Ohio state court on behalf of a client, Countrywide Home Loans, Inc., seeking foreclosure of a mortgage held by Countrywide in real property owned by Jerman. The complaint included a "Notice," later served on Jerman, stating that the mortgage debt would be assumed to be valid unless Jerman disputed it in writing. Jerman's lawyer sent a letter disputing the debt, and Carlisle sought verification from Countrywide. When Countrywide acknowledged that Jerman had, in fact, already paid the debt in full, Carlisle withdrew the foreclosure lawsuit. Jerman then filed this lawsuit seeking class certification and damages under the Fair Debt Collection Practices Act (FDCPA), contending that Carlisle violated Section 1692g by stating that her debt would be assumed valid unless she disputed it in writing. The District Court held that Carlisle had violated Section 1692g by requiring Jerman to dispute the debt in writing. The court ultimately granted summary judgment to Carlisle, however, concluding that Section 1692k(c) shielded it from liability because the violation was not intentional, resulted from a *bona fide* error, and occurred despite the maintenance of procedures reasonably adapted to avoid any such error. The Court of Appeals for the Sixth Circuit affirmed.

DECISION The judgment of the U.S. Court of Appeals for the Sixth Circuit is reversed.

OPINION Congress enacted the FDCPA to eliminate abusive debt collection practices. The FDCPA regulates interactions between consumer debtors and debt collectors. Among other things, the FDCPA prohibits debt collectors from making false representations as to a debt's character, amount, or legal status; communicating with consumers at an "unusual time or place" likely to be inconvenient to the consumer; or using obscene or profane language or violence or the threat thereof. The FDCPA provides that a debt collector is not liable in an action brought under the FDCPA if she can show the violation was not intentional and resulted from a *bona fide* error. The FDCPA also states that none of its provisions imposing liability shall apply to any act done or omitted in good faith in conformity with any advisory opinion of the Federal Trade Commission. Jerman contends that when a debt collector intentionally commits the act giving rise to the violation (here, sending a notice that included the "in writing" language), a misunderstanding about what the FDCPA requires cannot render the violation "not intentional," given the general rule that mistake or ignorance of law is no defense. Carlisle, in contrast, argued that nothing in the statutory text excludes legal errors from the category of "*bona fide* error[s]" and noted that the FDCPA refers not to an unintentional "act" but rather an unintentional "violation."

The Supreme Court concluded that the *bona fide* error defense does not include mistaken interpretations of the FDCPA. The Court concluded that neither the text nor the legislative history of the FDCPA revealed an intent by Congress to provide a defense for mistakes of law.

The broad statutory requirement of procedures reasonably designed to avoid "any" *bona fide* error indicates that the relevant procedures are ones that help to avoid errors like clerical or factual mistakes. Such procedures are more likely to avoid error than those applicable to legal reasoning, particularly in the context of a comprehensive and complex federal statute such as the FDCPA.

INTERPRETATION The FDCPA was enacted to eliminate abusive debt collection practices and does not provide a defense for violations that result from mistakes of law.

ETHICAL QUESTION Did any of the parties act unethically? Explain.

CRITICAL THINKING QUESTION Do you agree with the Supreme Court's decision? Explain.

ETHICAL DILEMMA

Should Some Be Protected from High-Pressure Sales?

Facts Glen Thomas, a recent college graduate, was hired as a rental agent by New Vistas Condominiums, Inc., of Old Saybrook, Connecticut. Initially responsible for handling rentals on two apartment buildings, Glen was also assigned to an aggressive sales program for new time-share condominiums to be developed in Florida.

Under the new sales program, Glen was to be trained as a marketing specialist. His boss, Sabrina Cassey, explained that the marketing plan would target those between the ages of sixty and eighty. The condominiums would feature an attractive communal social program that would include swimming exercises, Friday night bingo games, and monthly movies. Also available, for additional fees, would be special services, such as food delivery, shopping, and domestic help.

In the following months, in marketing the new condominiums, New Vistas made particular efforts to interest those who had recently lost their spouses. The company

devised a system for following obituaries and purchased lists that directed its marketing personnel to recent widows and widowers at certain income levels.

For the new condominiums, Sabrina's marketing team has concocted a presentation she terms "lethal." The program begins with a direct mailing. Thereafter, individuals are invited to a party and are promised free prizes. A movie is shown that features elderly people socializing around a pool, playing cards, and having intimate candlelight dinners. Wine and dessert are served afterward. Then, once the terms of the condominium purchase have been explained, New Vistas salespeople distribute contracts and pressure the attendees to sign the contracts before the distribution of gifts. At the meetings, Sabrina's job is to explain the condominiums; Glen's role is to get the contracts signed.

On the first night of the sales promotion, Glen meets Irving Sherman, who happens to be the father of a girl Glen

dated in high school. Irving tells Glen that his wife has recently died, succumbing to a three-year battle with cancer. Glen knows that Irving has been through quite an ordeal; Irving himself had suffered from colon cancer several years earlier. When it comes time to press for signatures on the contracts, Glen becomes very uncomfortable and wants to leave.

Social, Policy, and Ethical Considerations

1. What should Glen do? Why? What alternative sales methods are available?

2. Is there anything ethically wrong with gearing sales to a special segment of the population? Should certain segments of the population be protected from high-powered sales programs?

3. Can the public ever be overprotected with regard to sales promotions? To what extent, if any, should individuals be limited in the nonfraudulent marketing of their products?

CHAPTER SUMMARY

Federal Trade Commission

Purpose to prevent unfair methods of competition and unfair or deceptive acts or practices

Standards
- *Unfairness* requires injury to be (1) substantial, (2) not outweighed by any countervailing benefit, and (3) unavoidable by reasonable consumer action
- *Deception* misrepresentation, omission, or practice that is likely to mislead the consumer acting reasonably in the circumstances
- *Ad Substantiation* requires advertisers to have a reasonable basis for their claims

Remedies
- *Cease-and-Desist Order* command to stop doing the act in question
- *Affirmative Disclosure* requires an advertiser to include certain information in its ad so that the ad is not deceptive
- *Corrective Advertising* requires an advertiser to disclose that previous ads were deceptive
- *Multiple Product Order* requires an advertiser to cease and desist from deceptive statements regarding all products it sells

Consumer Health, Safety, and Financial Protection

Consumer Product Safety Act federal statute enacted to
- *Protect Public Against Unsafe Products*
- *Assist Consumers in Evaluating Products*
- *Develop Uniform Safety Standards*
- *Promote Safety Research*

Consumer Financial Protection Bureau (CFPB) an independent executive agency housed within the Federal Reserve with broad rulemaking, supervisory, and enforcement authority over persons engaged in offering or providing a consumer financial product or service

Other Federal Consumer Protection Agencies

Consumer Purchases

Federal Warranty Protection applies to sellers of consumer goods who give written warranties
- *Presale Disclosure* requires terms of warranty to be simple and readily understood and to be made available before the sale
- *Labeling Requirement* requires warrantor to inform consumers of their legal rights under a warranty (full or limited)
- *Disclaimer Limitation* prohibits a written warranty from disclaiming any implied warranty

State "Lemon Laws" state laws that attempt to provide new car purchasers with rights similar to full warranties under the Magnuson-Moss Warranty Act

Consumer Right of Rescission in certain instances a consumer is granted a brief period of time during which she may rescind (cancel) an otherwise binding obligation

Consumer Credit Transactions

Definition any credit transaction involving goods, services, or land for personal, household, or family purposes

Access to the Market discrimination in extending credit on the basis of race, color, gender, marital status, race, color, religion, national origin, or age is prohibited

Disclosure Requirements (Truth-in-Lending Act) requires creditor to provide certain information about contract terms, including APR (annual percentage rate), to the consumer before he formally incurs the obligation

Contract Terms statutory, administrative, and judicial limitations have been imposed on consumer obligations

Credit Card Fraud Act prohibits certain fraudulent practices and limits a card holder's liability for unauthorized use of a credit card to $50.00

Fair Credit Reporting consumer credit reports are prohibited from containing inaccurate or obsolete information

Credit Card Bill of Rights (CARD) The 2009 Act amends the Truth-in-Lending Act to establish fair and transparent practices relating to credit cards

Creditors' Remedies **Wage Assignments and Garnishment** most states limit the amount that may be deducted from an individual's wages through either assignment or garnishment

Security Interest in Goods seller may retain a security interest in goods sold or other collateral of the buyer, although some restrictions are imposed

Debt Collection Practices abusive, deceptive, and unfair practices by debt collectors in collecting consumer debts are prohibited by the Fair Debt Collection Practices Act

QUESTIONS

1. The Federal Trade Commission (FTC) brings a deceptive trade practice action against Beneficial Finance Company based on Beneficial's use of its "instant tax refund" slogan. The FTC argues that Beneficial's advertising a tax refund loan or instant tax refund is deceptive in that the loan is not in any way connected with a tax refund but is merely Beneficial's everyday loan based on the applicant's credit worthiness. Is this an unfair or deceptive trade practice? Explain.

2. Brenda borrows $1,000 from Lincoln for one year, agreeing to pay Lincoln $200 in interest on the loan and to repay the loan in twelve monthly installments of $100. The contract that Lincoln provides and Brenda signs specifies that the annual percentage rate is 20 percent. Does this contract violate the Federal Consumer Credit Protection Act? Why?

3. A consumer entered into an agreement with Rent-It Corporation for the rental of a television set at a charge of $17.00 per week. The agreement also provides that if the renter chooses to rent the set for seventy-eight consecutive weeks, title will be transferred. The consumer now contends that the agreement is really a sales agreement, not a lease, and therefore is a credit sale subject to the Truth-in-Lending Act. Explain whether the consumer is correct.

4. Central Adjustment Bureau allegedly threatened Consumer with a lawsuit, service at his office, and attachment and sale of his property in order to collect a debt, although it did not intend to carry out the threat and did not have the authority to commence litigation. On some notices sent to Consumer, Central failed to disclose that it was attempting to collect a debt. In addition, Consumer contends that Central sent notices demanding payment that were purportedly from attorneys but were written, signed, and sent by Central. Has Central violated the Fair Debt Collection Act? Explain.

5. The Giant Development Company undertakes a massive real estate venture to sell 9,000 one-acre unimproved lots in Utah. The company advertises the project nationally. Arrington, a resident of New York, learns of the opportunity and requests information about the project. The company provides Arrington with a small advertising brochure that contains no information about the developer and the land. The brochure consists of vague descriptions of the joys of homeownership and nothing else. Arrington purchases a lot. Two weeks after entering into the agreement, Arrington wishes to rescind the contract. Will Arrington prevail?

6. Jane Jones, a married woman, applies for a credit card from Exxon but is refused credit. Jane is bewildered as to why she was turned down. What are her legal rights in this situation?

7. On a beautiful Saturday in October, Francie decides to take the twenty-mile ride from her home in New Jersey into New York City to do some shopping. Francie finds that Brown's Retail Sales, Inc., has a terrific sale on televisions and decides to surprise her husband with a new high-definition television. She purchases the set from Brown's on her VISA card for $1,450. When the set is delivered, Francie discovers that it does not work. Brown's refuses to repair or replace it or to credit Francie's account. Francie therefore refuses to pay VISA for the television. VISA brings a suit against Francie. Will VISA prevail? Why?

8. Frank finds Thomas's wallet, which contains many credit cards and Thomas's identification. By using Thomas's identification and VISA card, Frank goes on a shopping spree and runs up $5,000 in charges. Thomas does not discover that he has lost his wallet until the following day, when he promptly notifies his VISA bank. How much can VISA collect from Thomas?

9. Robert applies to Northern National Bank for a loan. Before granting the loan, Northern requests that Callis Credit Agency provide it with a credit report on Robert. Callis reports that three years earlier, Robert had embezzled money from his employer. Based on this report, Northern rejects Robert's loan application.
   a. Robert demands to know why the loan was rejected, but Northern refuses to divulge the information, arguing that it is privileged. Is Robert entitled to the information?
   b. Assume that Robert obtains the information and alleges that it is inaccurate. What recourse does Robert have?

CASE PROBLEMS

10. Colgate-Palmolive Co. produced a television advertisement that dramatically demonstrated the effectiveness of its Rapid Shave shaving cream. The ad purported to show the shaving cream being used to shave sandpaper. But because actual sandpaper appeared on television to be regular colored paper, Colgate substituted a sheet of Plexiglas with sand sprinkled on it. The Federal Trade Commission brought an action against Colgate, claiming that Colgate's ad was deceptive. Colgate defended on the ground that the consumer was merely being shown a representation of the actual test. Explain whether Colgate has engaged in an unfair or deceptive trade practice.

11. Several manufacturers introduced into the American market a product known as all-terrain vehicles (ATVs). ATVs are motorized bikes that sit on three or four low-pressure balloon tires and are meant to be driven off paved roads. Almost immediately, the Consumer Product Safety Commission (CPSC) began receiving reports of deaths and serious injuries. As the number of injuries and deaths increased, the CPSC began investigating ATV hazards. According to CPSC staff, children under the age of sixteen accounted for roughly half the deaths and injuries associated with this product. What type of rule, if any, may the CPSC issue for ATVs?

12. Sears formulated a plan to increase sales of its top-of-the-line Lady Kenmore brand dishwasher. Sears's plan sought to change the Lady Kenmore's image without reengineering or making any mechanical improvements in the dishwasher itself. To accomplish this, Sears undertook a four-year $8 million advertising campaign that claimed that the Lady Kenmore completely eliminated the need to prerinse and prescrape dishes. As a result of this campaign, sales rose by more than 300 percent. The "no scraping, no prerinsing" claim was not true, however; and Sears had no reasonable basis for asserting the claim. In addition, the owner's manual that customers received after they purchased the dishwasher contradicted the claim.

After a thorough investigation, the Federal Trade Commission (FTC) filed a complaint against Sears, alleging that the advertisements were false and misleading. The final FTC order required Sears to stop making the "no scraping, no prerinsing" claim. The order also prevented Sears from (1) making any "performance claims" for "major home appliances" without first possessing a reasonable basis consisting of substantiating tests or other evidence; (2) misrepresenting any test, survey, or demonstration regarding "major home appliances"; and (3) making any advertising statements not consistent with statements in postpurchase materials supplied to purchasers of "major home appliances." Sears contends the order is too broad, because it covers appliances other than dishwashers and includes "performance claims" as well. Explain whether Sears is correct.

13. Onondaga Bureau of Medical Economics (OBME), a collection agency for physicians, sent the plaintiff, Seabrook, a letter demanding payment for a $198 physician's bill. In addition to demanding payment, the letter stated that the bureau's client could commence against Seabrook a legal action that could result in a garnishment of his wages. Does OBME's letter violate the Fair Debt Collection Practices Act in that it (a) does not give Seabrook the required notice or (b) threatened legal action against him?

14. William Thompson was denied credit based on an inaccurate credit report compiled by the San Antonio Retail Merchant's Association. The Association confused Thompson's credit history with that of another William Thompson and failed to use Social Security numbers to distinguish the two men. The second Mr. Thompson had a poor credit history. Thompson made numerous attempts to have the Association correct its mistake, but the error was never corrected. Has the Association violated the Fair Credit Reporting Act? Explain.

15. Thompson Medical Company manufactures and sells Aspercreme, a topical analgesic. Aspercreme is a pain reliever that contains no aspirin. Thompson's advertisements strongly suggest that Aspercreme is related to aspirin, however, by claiming that it provides "the strong relief of aspirin right where you hurt." Is Thompson's advertisement for Aspercreme false and misleading? Explain.

16. Mary Smith bought a car from Doug Chapman under an installment sales contract. Smith carried the insurance on the car, as required by the contract. Shortly after Smith purchased the car, it was wrecked in an accident. Smith's insurance company paid Chapman the installments still owed on the car, as well as Smith's equity in the car. Smith requested a new car from Chapman under an installment plan that was the same as the one under which she had purchased the first car. Chapman refused, claiming that the contract for the first car allowed him to retain the equity amount as security interest and that Smith understood this as a term of the contract. The provision relating to the security interest appeared on the back of the contract, although the Truth-in-Lending Act required it to be on the front side. The front side had a notice referring to provisions on the back side. Explain whether Chapman's contract violates the Truth-in-Lending Act.

17. The Federal Trade Commission (FTC) ordered Warner-Lambert to cease and desist from advertising that its product, Listerine antiseptic mouthwash, prevents, cures, or alleviates the common cold and sore throats. The order further required Warner-Lambert to disclose in future advertisements that "[c]ontrary to prior advertising, Listerine will not help prevent colds or sore throats or lessen their severity." Warner-Lambert contended that even if its past advertising claims were false, the corrective advertising portion of the order exceeded the FTC's statutory power. The FTC claimed that corrective advertising was necessary in light of Warner-Lambert's one hundred years of false claims and the resulting persistence of erroneous consumer beliefs. Explain whether the FTC is correct.

18. Lenvil Miller owed $2,501.61 to the Star Bank of Cincinnati. Star Bank referred collection of Miller's account to Payco-General American Credits, Inc. (Payco), a debt collection agency. Payco sent Miller a collection form. Across the top of the form was the caption, "DEMAND FOR PAYMENT," in large, red, boldface type. The middle of the page stated "THIS IS A DEMAND FOR IMMEDIATE FULL PAYMENT OF YOUR DEBT," also in large, red, boldface type. That statement was followed in bold by "YOUR SERIOUSLY PAST DUE ACCOUNT HAS BEEN GIVEN TO US FOR IMMEDIATE ACTION. YOU HAVE HAD AMPLE TIME TO PAY YOUR DEBT, BUT YOU HAVE NOT. IF THERE IS A VALID REASON, PHONE US AT [***] TODAY. IF NOT, PAY US—NOW." The word "NOW" covered the bottom third of the form. At the very bottom in the smallest type to appear on the form was the statement, "NOTICE: SEE REVERSE SIDE FOR IMPORTANT INFORMATION." The notice was printed in white against a red background. On the reverse side were four paragraphs in gray ink. The last three paragraphs contained the validation notice required by the Fair Debt Collection Practices Act (FDCPA) to inform the consumer how to obtain verification of the debt.

    Miller sued Payco on the ground that the validation notice did not comply with the FDCPA. Miller argued that even though the validation notice contained all the necessary information, it violated the FDCPA because it contradicted other parts of the collection letter, was overshadowed by the demands for payment, and was not effectively conveyed to the consumer. Discuss whether Payco has violated the FDCPA.

19. Greg Henson sold his Chevrolet Camaro Z-28 to his brother, Jeff Henson. To purchase the car, Jeff secured a loan with Cosco Federal Credit Union (Cosco). Soon thereafter, the car was stolen and Jeff stopped making payments on his loan from Cosco. At the time, Cosco was unsure whether Greg retained an interest in the car so Cosco sued both Jeff and Greg for possession of the car. The trial court rendered a default judgment against Jeff and ruled that Greg had no longer any interest in the car. The court further entered a deficiency judgment against Jeff in the amount of $4,076. However, the clerk erroneously noted in the judgment docket that the money judgment had been rendered against Greg as well as against Jeff. However, the official record of judgments and orders correctly reflected that only Jeff was affected by the money judgment. Two credit agencies, CSC Credit Services (CSC) and Trans Union Corporation (Trans Union), relied on the state court judgment docket and indicated in Greg's credit report that he owed the money judgment. Greg and his wife, Mary Henson, allege that they then "contacted Trans [Union] twice, in writing, to correct this horrible injustice." When Trans Union did not respond, the Hensons brought an action alleging violations of the Federal Credit Reporting Act. Explain whether the Hensons should prevail.

20. Pantron I Corporation and Hal Z. Lederman market a product known as the Helsinki Formula. This product supposedly arrests hair loss and stimulates hair regrowth in baldness sufferers. The formula consists of a conditioner and a shampoo, and it sells at a list price of $49.95 for a three-month supply. The ingredients that allegedly cause the advertised effects are polysorbate 60 and polysorbate 80. Pantron offers a full money-back guarantee for those who are not satisfied with the product. The Federal Trade Commission (FTC) challenged both Pantron's claims that the formula arrested hair loss and promoted growth of new hair as unfair and deceptive trade practices. The FTC presented a variety of evidence that tended to show that the Helsinki Formula had no effectiveness other than its placebo effect (achieving results due solely to belief that the product will work). The FTC introduced expert testimony of a dermatologist and two other experts who denied there was any scientific evidence that the Helsinki Formula would be in any way useful in treating hair loss. Finally, the FTC introduced evidence of two studies that had determined that polysorbate-based products were ineffective in stopping hair loss and promoting regrowth. In response, Pantron introduced evidence that users of the Helsinki Formula were satisfied that it was effective. It offered testimony of eighteen users who had experienced hair regrowth or a reduction in hair loss after using the formula. It also introduced evidence of a "consumer satisfaction survey" it had conducted. Pantron also introduced evidence that more than half of its orders come from repeat purchasers, that it had received very few written complaints, and that very few of Pantron's customers (less than 3 percent) had redeemed the money-back guarantee. Pantron finally introduced several clinical studies of its own, none performed in the United States or under U.S. standards for scientific studies. The evidence from these studies did show effectiveness, but the studies were not random, blind-reviewed studies, and thus did not take into account the placebo effect. Discuss.

TAKING SIDES

Kevin Miller bought a house in Atlanta in 2007 and took out a mortgage. He lived in the house until 2010, when he accepted a job in Chicago; from then on, he rented the house. He received a letter demanding payment from a law firm on behalf of the mortgage company in 2012. By this time, Miller was renting the property to strangers and thus was making a business use of the property. Miller claimed that the law firm had violated the Fair Debt Collection Practices Act. The law firm replied that the letter is outside the scope of the Act because it was trying to collect a business debt rather than a consumer debt.

a. What are the arguments that the debt is a consumer debt?
b. What are the arguments that the debt is a business debt?
c. Which arguments would prevail? Explain.

Environmental Law

CHAPTER 45

Only within the moment of time represented by the present century has one species—man—acquired significant power to alter the nature of the world.

Rachel Carson
Silent Spring (1962)

CHAPTER OUTCOMES

After reading and studying this chapter, you should be able to:

1. Outline and explain the common law actions for environmental damage and the difficulties in prevailing in such actions.

2. Explain the major substantive provisions of the National Environmental Policy Act.

3. Explain the regulatory scheme of the Clean Air Act.

4. Explain the regulation of both point and nonpoint sources of pollution by the Clean Water Act.

5. Explain (a) the Federal Insecticide, Fungicide, and Rodenticide Act; (b) the Toxic Substances Control Act; (c) the Resource Conservation and Recovery Act; (d) the Superfund; (e) the Montreal Protocol; and (f) the Kyoto Protocol.

As technology has advanced and people have become more urbanized, their effect on the environment has increased. Our air has become dirtier; our waters have become more polluted. Although individuals and environmental groups have brought private actions against some polluters, the common law has proved unable to control environmental damage. Because of this inadequacy, the federal and state governments have enacted a variety of statutes designed to promote environmental concerns and prevent environmental harm. Although in recent years certain industrial countries, such as the United States, have made significant progress in controlling pollutants, such is not the case worldwide. Moreover, even as we have enjoyed some success in controlling some pollutants, a new generation of environmental problems has arisen. One of the more recent environmental issues is the regulation of high-volume horizontal hydraulic fracturing (fracking) for oil and gas. In this chapter, we will discuss both common law causes of action for environmental damage and federal regulation of the environment.

COMMON LAW ACTIONS FOR ENVIRONMENTAL DAMAGE

Private tort actions may be used to recover for harm to the environment. For example, if Alice's land is polluted by the mill next door, Alice may sue the mill in tort for the damage to her land. In suing to recover for environmental damage, plaintiffs generally have relied on the theories of nuisance, trespass, and strict liability.

NUISANCE [45-1]

The term *nuisance* encompasses two distinct types of wrong: private nuisance and public nuisance. A private nuisance involves an interference with a person's use and enjoyment of his or her land; a public nuisance is an act that interferes with a public right.

Private Nuisance [45-1a]

Private nuisance
interference with use and
enjoyment of a person's
land

To establish a **private nuisance**, plaintiff must show that the defendant has substantially and unreasonably interfered with the use and enjoyment of the plaintiff's land. In an action for damages, the plaintiff need not prove that the defendant's conduct was unreasonable, only that the interference was unreasonable. Thus, assuming all other requirements are met, the question in a private nuisance suit for damages is whether the defendant should pay for the harm it caused the plaintiff, even if the defendant's action was not unreasonable. For example, in one case, an electric utility using a coal-burning electric generator that employed the latest scientific methods for reducing emissions was held liable for the harm it caused its neighbor's alfalfa crops, even though the utility was performing the socially useful function of creating electric power.

Although a plaintiff need not prove the defendant's conduct is unreasonable to recover in a private nuisance action for damages, such reasonableness is an issue when the plaintiff sues for an injunction. In determining whether an injunction against a nuisance is appropriate, a court will "balance the equities" by considering a number of factors, including the gravity of the harm to the plaintiff, the social value of the defendant's activity that is causing the harm, the feasibility and costs of avoiding the harm, and the public interest, if any.

The need to balance the equities has meant that courts often deny injunctions when the defendant is engaged in a socially useful activity. Additionally, injunctions are frequently denied because the defendant successfully raises an equitable defense. Consequently, private nuisance actions have been of limited value in controlling environmental damage.

Public Nuisance [45-1b]

Public nuisance
interference with health,
safety, or comfort of the
public

To be treated as a **public nuisance**, an activity must somehow interfere with the health, safety, or comfort of the public. For example, the actions of an industrial plant in polluting a stream will be treated as a private nuisance if such actions inconvenience only the owners of land downstream but will be treated as a public nuisance if they kill the stream's marine life. Generally, only a public representative, such as the attorney general, may sue to stop a public nuisance. If, however, the nuisance inflicts upon an individual some unique harm that the general populace does not suffer, that individual may also sue to halt the nuisance. Out of concern about the economic impact of closing an industrial operation, public representatives frequently are unwilling to sue to abate a public nuisance. Consequently, because these representatives often will not, and private parties may not, sue, relatively few public nuisance actions have been brought against polluters.

Trespass to Land [45-2]

Trespass to land
interference with the right
of exclusive possession of
the property

To establish **trespass to land**, a plaintiff must show an invasion that interferes with the plaintiff's right of exclusive possession of the property and that is the direct result of an action by the defendant. For example, entering or throwing trash on someone else's land without permission constitutes a trespass. Trespass differs from private nuisance in that trespass requires an interference with the plaintiff's possession of the land. Thus, sending smoke or gas onto another's property may constitute a private nuisance but does not constitute a trespass.

Trespass often is difficult to establish in actions for environmental damage, either because the plaintiff is not in possession of the property or because the injury does not stem from an invasion of the property. Trespass actions have thus been of limited benefit in halting environmental damage. For a more complete discussion of trespass, see Chapter 8.

Strict Liability for Abnormally Dangerous Activities [45-3]

Strict liability
liability without fault for an
individual who engages in an
unduly dangerous activity in
an inappropriate location

Although they generally base tort liability on fault, the courts may hold **strictly liable**, that is, liable without fault, a person engaged in an abnormally dangerous activity. To establish such strict liability, a plaintiff must show that the defendant is carrying on an unduly dangerous activity in an inappropriate location and that the plaintiff has suffered damage because of this activity.

For example, a person who operates an oil refinery in a densely populated area may be held strictly liable for any damage the refinery causes. The requirement that the activity engaged in be (1) ultrahazardous and (2) inappropriate for its locale has limited the number of strict liability actions brought against polluters.

PROBLEMS COMMON TO PRIVATE CAUSES OF ACTION [45-4]

In addition to the shortcomings of each tort theory discussed previously, using a private cause of action to control environmental damage presents its own problems. The costs associated with private litigation (including the payment of one's own legal fees) are high, and although overall the environmental damage may be considerable, the extent of any particular injury may not warrant pursuing a private lawsuit. Furthermore, tort actions generally do not provide relief for aesthetic, as opposed to physical, injury. Additionally, in many tort actions, a significant issue of causation arises. For example, if a landowner lives near several plants, each of which emits pollution and none of which, by itself, would cause the amount of damage the landowner's property has suffered, the landowner may have difficulty recovering from any of the plant owners. Finally, even if a private plaintiff is successful, his recovery may be limited to monetary damages, leaving the defendant free to continue to pollute.

FEDERAL REGULATION OF THE ENVIRONMENT

Because private causes of action have proved inadequate to recompense and prevent environmental damage, the federal, state, and some local governments have enacted statutes designed to protect the environment. In this chapter, we will consider some of the more important federal environmental laws. In addition, the Environmental Protection Agency (EPA) has encouraged companies to conduct voluntary environmental audits. One of the key issues surrounding such self-audits is whether these audits are discoverable by state or federal prosecutors.

THE NATIONAL ENVIRONMENTAL POLICY ACT [45-5]

National Environmental Policy Act (NEPA) establishes environmental protection as a goal of federal policy

Congress enacted the **National Environmental Policy Act (NEPA)** to establish environmental protection as a goal of federal policy. The NEPA's declaration of national environmental policy states:

> The Congress, recognizing the profound impact of man's activity on the interrelations of all components of the natural environment, particularly the profound influences of population growth, high-density urbanization, industrial expansion, resource exploitation, and new and expanding technological advances, and recognizing further the critical importance of restoring and maintaining environmental quality to the overall welfare and development of man, declares that it is the continuing policy of the Federal Government, in cooperation with State and local governments … to use all practicable means and measures … in a manner calculated to foster and promote the general welfare, to create and maintain conditions under which man and nature can exist in productive harmony, and fulfill the social, economic and other requirements of present and future generations of Americans.

Thus, NEPA imposes the responsibility for maintaining the environment on all federal agencies. It is the responsibility of the federal government to consider the environmental consequences of all of its actions and to administer all of its programs in an environmentally sound manner.

Environmental impact statement (EIS) detailed statement concerning the environmental impact of a proposed federal action

The NEPA has two major substantive sections, one creating the Council on Environmental Quality and the other requiring that each federal agency, when recommending or reporting on proposals for legislation or other major federal action, prepare an **environmental impact statement (EIS)** if the legislation or federal action will have a significant environmental effect.

The Council on Environmental Quality [45-5a]

Council on Environmental Quality (CEQ)

three-member advisory group in the Executive Office of the President that makes recommendations to the President on environmental matters

The **Council on Environmental Quality (CEQ)**, a three-member advisory group, is not a separate administrative agency but rather is part of the Executive Office of the President; as such, it makes recommendations to the President on environmental matters and prepares annual reports on the condition of the environment. Although not expressly authorized to do so by statute, the CEQ, acting under a series of executive orders, has issued regulations regarding the content and preparation of environmental impact statements. The federal courts generally have deferred to these regulations.

Environmental Impact Statements [45-5b]

Unlike most federal environmental statutes, the NEPA does not focus on a particular type of environmental damage or harmful substance but instead expresses the federal government's continuing concern with protection of the environment. The NEPA's promotion of environmental considerations is effected through the EIS requirement. An EIS is required if the proposed action (1) is federal, (2) is considered "major," and (3) has a significant environmental impact.

Procedure for Preparing an EIS
When proposing legislation or considering a major federal action, the CEQ regulations require that a federal agency initially make an "environmental assessment," which is a short analysis of the need for an EIS. If the agency decides that no EIS is required, it must make this decision available to the public. If, on the other hand, the agency concludes that an EIS is required, the agency must engage in "scoping," which consists of consulting other relevant federal agencies and the public to determine the significant issues the EIS will address and the statement's appropriate scope. After scoping, the agency prepares a draft EIS, for which there is a comment period. After the comment period ends and revisions, if necessary, are made, a final EIS is published.

Scope of EIS Requirement
The EIS requirement of the NEPA applies to a broad range of projects:

Scope

The National Environmental Policy Act applies to a broad range of activities, including direct action by a federal agency as well as any action by a federal agency that permits action by other parties that will affect the quality of the environment

> [T]here is "Federal action" within the meaning of the statute not only when an agency proposes to build a facility itself, but also whenever an agency makes a decision which permits action by other parties which will affect the quality of the environment. NEPA's impact statement procedure has been held to apply where a federal agency approves a lease of land to private parties, grants licenses and permits to private parties, or approves and funds state highway projects. In each of these instances the federal agency took action affecting the environment in the sense that the agency made a decision which permitted some other party—private or governmental—to take action affecting the environment.

The NEPA's EIS requirement applies not only to a broad range of projects but also to a broad range of environmental effects. The NEPA has been held to apply not only to the natural environment but also to the urban environment, including impact on crime, esthetics, and socioeconomics.

The Act [NEPA] must be construed to include protection of the quality of life for city residents. Noise, traffic, overburdened mass transportation systems, crime, congestion and even availability of drugs all affect the urban "environment" and are surely results of the "profound influences of … high-density urbanization [and] industrial expansion." Although effects on health, including psychological health, are considered environmental effects under the NEPA, the Supreme Court has held that an effect is environmental only if it has a reasonably close causal relation to an impact on the physical environment.

Content of an EIS
The NEPA requires that an EIS describe in detail the environmental impact of a proposed action, any adverse environmental effects that could not be avoided if the proposal were implemented, alternatives to the proposed action, the relationship between local short-term uses of the environment and the maintenance and enhancement of long-term productivity, and any irreversible and irretrievable commitments of resources the proposed action would involve if it were implemented. Impact statements provide a basis for evaluating the benefits of a proposed project in light of its environmental risks and for comparing its environmental

Content

the environmental impact statement must contain, among other items, a detailed statement of the environmental impact of the proposed action, any adverse environmental effects that cannot be avoided, and alternative proposals

risks with those of alternatives. The Supreme Court has held that a federal agency is required to consider all *reasonable* alternatives in its EIS (a rule of reason standard). One reasonable alternative that always must be considered is doing nothing.

Nature of EIS Requirement   Whether the NEPA was solely procedural or whether it had a substantive component was initially unclear. The Supreme Court resolved the issue by holding that the NEPA's requirements are primarily procedural and that the NEPA does not require that the relevant federal agency attempt to mitigate the adverse effects of a proposed federal action. Rather, the NEPA attempts to prohibit uninformed decisions, not unwise agency actions.

THE CLEAN AIR ACT [45-6]

Clean Air Act
enacted to control and reduce air pollution

Initially, the federal government's role in controlling air pollution was quite limited. The states had primary responsibility for air pollution control, and the federal government merely supervised their efforts and offered technical and financial assistance. When state efforts proved inadequate to alleviate the problem, Congress enacted the **Clean Air Act** Amendments of 1970, greatly expanding the federal role in antipollution efforts. Major revisions to the Clean Air Act were enacted in 1977 and 1990. In March 2011, the EPA issued the Second Prospective Report that looked at the results of the Clean Air Act from 1990 to 2020. According to this study, the direct benefits from the 1990 Clean Air Act Amendments are estimated to reach almost $2 trillion for the year 2020 and to prevent 230,000 early deaths. Direct costs of implementation are estimated at $65 billion.

The Act establishes two regulatory schemes, one for existing sources and one for new stationary sources. The states retain primary responsibility for regulating existing stationary sources and motor vehicles then in use (i.e., in use when the Act, or its subsequently enacted amendments, took effect), whereas the federal government regulates new sources, new vehicles, and hazardous air pollutants. In June 2014, the EPA proposed a regulation that would require power plants by 2030 to cut U.S. carbon-dioxide emissions 30 percent below 2005 levels.

Under the Act, the EPA may impose civil penalties, as adjusted for inflation in December 2013, of up to $37,500 per day of violation. Criminal penalties, which depend on the type of violation, vary greatly, providing for a maximum fine of $1 million per violation and/or fifteen years' imprisonment for a knowing violation that endangers a person. For repeat convictions, the Act doubles the maximum punishments. Moreover, under the Federal Alternative Fines Act, if any person derives pecuniary gain from the offense, or if the offense results in pecuniary loss to a person other than the defendant, the defendant may be fined up to the greater of twice the gross gain or twice the gross loss.

Existing Stationary Sources and Motor Vehicles Then in Use [45-6a]

Because the states had not managed adequately to control air pollution, the 1970 amendments provided that, with respect to existing stationary sources and motor vehicles then in use, the federal government would set national air quality standards that the states would be primarily responsible for achieving.

 **Environmental Protection Agency v. EME Homer City Generation, L. P.**
Supreme Court of the United States, 2014
572 U.S. ___, 134 S.Ct. 1584
http://scholar.google.com/scholar_case?case=4963561081264543804&q=134+S.+Ct.+1584&hl=en&as_sdt=6,34

FACTS The Clean Air Act creates a federal-state partnership that aims to control air pollution in the United States. The Clean Air Act requires the Environmental Protection Agency (EPA) to establish air quality standards and gives the states significant freedom to implement their own plans (State Implementation Plan or SIP) in order to meet the standards. Among the problems the Act sought to prevent was the possible spread of air pollution from "upwind" states to "downwind" states. To address this problem, Congress included a Good Neighbor Provision in the Act, which instructs states to prohibit in-state sources "from emitting any air pollutant in amounts which will … contribute significantly" to downwind states' "nonattainment …, or interfere with maintenance," of any EPA-promulgated national air quality standard.

Interpreting the Good Neighbor Provision, in 2011, the EPA issued the Cross-State Air Pollution Rule (Transport Rule), which sets emission reduction standards for nitrogen oxide (NO_X) and sulfur dioxide (SO_2) emissions in 27 "upwind" states based on the air quality standards in "downwind" states. The rule calls for consideration of costs, among other factors, when determining the emission reductions an upwind state must make to improve air quality in polluted downwind areas. Various states, local governments, industry groups, and labor organizations brought suit in the U.S. Court of Appeals for the District of Columbia Circuit challenging the Transport Rule. The court vacated the rule in its entirety, holding the EPA's interpretation of the Good Neighbor Provision unreasonable and concluding that the EPA must disregard costs and consider exclusively each upwind state's physically proportionate responsibility for air quality problems downwind. The U.S. Supreme Court granted *certiorari*.

DECISION Judgment is reversed and case is remanded.

OPINION Air pollution is transient, heedless of state boundaries. As the pollution travels out of state, upwind states are relieved of the associated costs. Those costs are borne instead by the downwind states, whose ability to achieve and maintain satisfactory air quality is hampered by the steady stream of infiltrating pollution. For several reasons, curtailing interstate air pollution poses a complex challenge for environmental regulators. First, identifying the upwind origin of downwind air pollution is not easy. Further complicating the problem, pollutants do not emerge from the smokestacks of an upwind state and uniformly migrate downwind. Some pollutants stay within upwind states' borders, the wind carries others to downwind states, and some subset of that group drifts to states without air quality problems. In crafting a solution to the problem of interstate air pollution, regulators must account for the vagaries of the wind. Finally, upwind pollutants that find their way downwind are not left unaltered by the journey. Rather, as the gases emitted by upwind polluters are carried downwind, they are transformed, through various chemical processes, into altogether different pollutants.

Under the Transport Rule, EPA employed a "two-step approach" to determine when upwind states contributed significantly to nonattainment, and the amounts that had to be eliminated. At step one, called the "screening" analysis, the Agency excluded as *de minimis* any upwind state that contributed less than one percent of the three NAAQS to any downwind state.

The remaining states were subjected to a second inquiry, which the EPA called the "control" analysis. At this stage, the EPA sought to generate a cost-effective allocation of emission reductions among those upwind states "screened in" at step one. The EPA first calculated, for each upwind state, the quantity of emissions the state could eliminate at each of several cost thresholds. Cost for these purposes is measured as cost per ton of emissions prevented, for instance, by installing scrubbers on powerplant smokestacks. With this information, EPA conducted complex modeling to establish the combined effect the upwind reductions projected at each cost threshold would have on air quality in downwind states. Finally, EPA translated the cost thresholds it had selected into amounts of emissions upwind states would be required to eliminate. For each regulated upwind state, EPA created an annual emissions "budget." These budgets represented the quantity of pollution an upwind state would produce in a given year if its in-state sources implemented all pollution controls available at the chosen cost thresholds. If EPA's projected improvements to downwind air quality were to be realized, an upwind state's emissions could not exceed the level this budget allocated to it, subject to certain adjustments not relevant here.

Taken together, the screening and control inquiries defined the EPA's understanding of which upwind emissions were within the Good Neighbor Provision's ambit. In short, under the Transport Rule, an upwind state "contribute[d] significantly" to downwind nonattainment to the extent its exported pollution both (1) produced one percent or more of a NAAQS in at least one downwind state (step one) and (2) could be eliminated cost-effectively, as determined by EPA (step two).

The Act supports the EPA's position. Once the EPA has found a SIP inadequate, the EPA has a statutory duty to correct the deficiency. The Good Neighbor Provision delegates authority to the EPA to reduce upwind pollution, but only in "amounts" that push a downwind state's pollution concentrations above the relevant NAAQS. However, the nonattainment of downwind states results from the collective and interwoven contributions of multiple upwind states. Using costs in the Transport Rule calculus makes good sense. Eliminating those amounts that can cost-effectively be reduced is an efficient and equitable solution to the allocation problem the Good Neighbor Provision requires the EPA to address.

INTERPRETATION The Transport Rule is a permissible, workable, and equitable interpretation of the Good Neighbor Provision's requirement to balance the possibility of under- and over-control of emissions standards between states.

CRITICAL THINKING QUESTION Do you agree with the Court's decision? Explain.

National ambient air quality standards (NAAQS)
allowable limits for air pollutants that endanger the public health and welfare

National Ambient Air Quality Standards

Under the Act, the EPA administrator is required to establish **national ambient air quality standards (NAAQS)** for air pollutants that endanger the public health and welfare. The EPA administrator must establish "primary" standards to protect the public health, allowing for an adequate safety margin, and "secondary" standards to protect elements relating to the public welfare, such as animals, crops, and structures. The NAAQS for a particular pollutant specifies the concentration of that pollutant that will be allowed in the outside air over designated periods of time.

The EPA administrator established quality standards for seven major classes of pollutants—carbon monoxide, particulates, sulfur dioxide, nitrogen dioxide, hydrocarbons, ozone, and lead. The hydrocarbon NAAQS was subsequently withdrawn because it was no longer necessary.

The 1990 amendments to the Act sought to hasten attainment of the standards and provided that the EPA must establish new standards for major pollutants every five years. The amendments also imposed tighter standards with regard to ozone pollution.

State Implementation Plans

State implementation plan (SIP)

plan detailing how a state will implement and maintain an NAAQS within its borders

Once the EPA promulgates a new NAAQS, each state must submit to the agency a **state implementation plan (SIP)** detailing how the state will implement and maintain the NAAQS within the state. If the state adopted the SIP after public hearings and the SIP meets certain statutory conditions, the EPA is required to approve it. Foremost among the statutory conditions is the requirement that under the SIP the state will attain primary standards as soon as practicable but in any case within three years after the EPA approves the SIP. If the EPA determines that under a SIP a state will not attain an NAAQS within the designated time and the state fails to make the necessary amendments, the EPA is authorized to make amendments that will be binding on the state.

Under the 1990 amendments, the EPA also must decide whether an SIP is complete. If it is not, the EPA may treat the plan as a nullity in whole or in part. If it is complete, the EPA must approve or disapprove the plan within a year. Once the EPA approves an SIP, the plan is regarded as both state and federal law, enforceable by either its state of implementation or the federal government.

Prevention of Significant Deterioration Areas

Prevention of significant deterioration (PSD) areas

areas where air quality is higher than required

Soon after enactment of the Act, an issue arose as to whether air that was cleaner than required by an applicable NAAQS would be allowed to deteriorate to the NAAQS level. This issue was significant because much of the United States, particularly land in the southwest, had air whose quality was higher than that required by applicable standards. Responding to this issue, Congress, in the 1977 amendments, established a policy to prevent the quality of such air from deteriorating. To effectuate this policy, Congress established rules for areas whose air quality was higher than the applicable NAAQS required it to be or for which information was insufficient to determine the air quality (so-called **prevention of significant deterioration [PSD] areas**). Because the rules classified an area on a pollutant-by-pollutant basis, a particular area might be a PSD area with respect to one pollutant and an area that had not met the applicable NAAQS with respect to another pollutant.

In PSD areas, only limited increases in air pollution are allowed. Before a major stationary source in a PSD area may be constructed or modified, the owner or operator of the source must receive a permit from the applicable state regulator. To receive a permit, the owner or operator must demonstrate that the source will not increase pollution beyond permitted levels and must show that the source will use the best control technology available. These rules were modified in January 2011 to cover additional construction projects.

Nonattainment Areas

Nonattainment areas

areas that do not meet national ambient air quality standards

The 1977 and 1990 amendments also established special rules for areas that did not meet applicable NAAQS, so-called **nonattainment areas**. Before a major stationary source may be constructed or modified in a nonattainment area, the owner or operator of the source must receive a permit from the applicable state regulator. To receive a permit, the owner or operator must show that the source will comply with the lowest achievable emission rate, which is the more stringent of either the most stringent emission limitation contained in any SIP or the most stringent emission limitation actually achieved. Additionally, total emissions from existing stationary sources and the proposed new or modified source together must be less than the total emissions allowed from existing sources at the time the permit is sought. Thus, to obtain a permit in a nonattainment area, an owner or operator must in some way reduce total emissions from all sources (existing and new or modified). Under the 1990 amendments, the reduction required varies with the severity of the area's nonattainment problem. One way to reduce total emissions from all sources is to pay the owner or operator of another source to reduce its emissions by either installing more advanced emission control technology or closing its source. Alternatively, an owner or operator may reduce its own total emissions by altering the mix of emission controls at its plant. Under the EPA's "**bubble concept**," an entire plant is viewed as one source; consequently, the permit process applies only if total emissions from the plant increase. If, instead, the EPA treated each unit at a plant as a separate source, the

Practical Advice

When considering where to locate a facility that will emit pollution, carefully scrutinize pollution levels in those locations.

Bubble concept

views an entire plant as one source of pollution

owner/operator would be required to obtain a permit whenever it made a change to one unit. The bubble concept thus enables an owner or operator to bypass the permit process in some instances. Though environmental groups challenged the concept on this basis, the Supreme Court upheld the bubble concept, finding the regulation to be a reasonable exercise of the EPA's discretion.

New Source Standards [45-6b]

The scheme of the federal NAAQS and state SIPs applies to existing stationary sources and to motor vehicles then in use. In contrast, the Clean Air Act authorizes the federal government to establish national emission standards for new stationary sources, hazardous air pollutants, and new vehicles.

New stationary sources owner or operator must employ the best technological system of continuous emission reduction that has been adequately demonstrated

New Stationary Sources
The Act requires the EPA administrator to establish performance standards for stationary sources that are constructed or modified after the publication of applicable regulations. The standard of performance must "reflect the degree of emission limitation and percentage reduction achievable through application of the best technological system of continuous emission reduction which … has been adequately demonstrated." The standard governing new sources is more stringent than the standard governing existing sources; accordingly, from industry's perspective, it is better to be considered an existing source than a new or modified one.

New vehicles extensive emission standards are established

New Vehicles
The Clean Air Act requires the EPA administrator to establish emission standards for new motor vehicles and new motor vehicle engines. The Act also requires the use of reformulated automotive fuels to reduce ozone and carbon monoxide pollution. The reformulated gasoline must contain more oxygen and less volatile organic compounds.

Hazardous air pollutants to protect the public health, the EPA administrator must establish for hazardous air pollutants standards that provide ample safety margins

Hazardous Air Pollutants
The Act authorizes the EPA administrator to establish national emission standards for hazardous or toxic air pollutants, defined as "air pollutant[s] … caus[ing], or contribut[ing] to, air pollution which may reasonably be anticipated to result in an increase in mortality or an increase in serious irreversible, or incapacitating reversible, illness." The standard must be set at a level that "provides an ample margin of safety to protect the public health."

Acid rain standards are established to protect against acid rain (precipitation that contains high levels of sulfuric or nitric acid)

Acid Rain
The 1990 amendments attempt to halt environmental destruction caused by **acid rain**—precipitation that contains high levels of sulfuric or nitric acid. Because sulfur dioxide (which forms sulfuric acid in the atmosphere and comes back as acid rain) is primarily released into the atmosphere by electric utilities, the 1990 amendments regulate such utilities by allotting them emission allowances with regard to the amount of sulfur dioxide they may release into the atmosphere, based upon past emissions and fuel consumption. The amendments establish an allowance schedule that will significantly reduce emissions of sulfur dioxide and nitrous oxides. The amendments also permit each utility to bank or sell its emission allowances.

Greenhouse Gases
In 2007, as previously discussed, the U.S. Supreme Court held that the Clean Air Act's sweeping definition of "air pollutant" includes greenhouse gases and, therefore, the EPA has statutory authority to regulate such gases from new motor vehicles. *Massachusetts v. Environmental Protection Agency*, 549 U.S. 497, 127 S.Ct. 1438, 167 L.Ed.2d 248. Effective on January 2, 2011, the EPA promulgated greenhouse gas emission standards for new passenger cars, light-duty trucks, and medium-duty passenger vehicles. In addition, the EPA issued regulations subjecting stationary sources to PSD permitting based on their potential to emit greenhouse gases. This regulation was challenged, and the U.S. Supreme Court largely upheld the EPA's authority to regulate greenhouse gas emissions from stationary sources. The Court held that the EPA may continue to treat greenhouse gases as a pollutant subject to regulation for purposes of requiring permits for power plants and other large stationary pollution sources that would need permits based on their emission of conventional pollutants. *Utility Air Regulatory Group v. EPA*, 573 U.S. ____ (2014).

THE CLEAN WATER ACT [45-7]

Clean Water Act
enacted to protect against water pollution

As with air pollution control, the primary responsibility for controlling water pollution fell initially to the states. When their efforts proved inadequate, Congress fundamentally revised the nation's water pollution laws in its 1972 amendments to the Federal Water Pollution Control Act (subsequently renamed the **Clean Water Act**). Substantially amended again in 1977, 1981, and 1987, the Act attempts comprehensively to restore and maintain the chemical, physical, and biological integrity of the nation's waters.

The EPA may impose civil penalties, as adjusted for inflation in December 2013, of up to $37,500 per day for each violation. Criminal penalties for knowing violations are not less than $5,000 nor more than $50,000 per day of violation and/or three years' imprisonment. For repeat convictions, the maximum punishments are doubled. Moreover, under the Federal Alternative Fines Act, if any person derives pecuniary gain from the offense, or if the offense results in pecuniary loss to a person other than the defendant, the defendant may be fined up to the greater of twice the gross gain or twice the gross loss.

Point source
any discernible, confined, and discrete conveyance from which pollutants are or may be discharged

Nonpoint source
land use that causes pollution

Like the Clean Air Act, the Clean Water Act establishes different schemes for existing sources and new sources. Additionally, the Act provides different programs for point and nonpoint sources of pollution. A **point source** is "any discernible, confined and discrete conveyance ... from which pollutants are or may be discharged." A **nonpoint source**, in contrast, is a land use that causes pollution, such as a pesticide runoff from farming operations.

The scope of the Act is extremely broad, applying not only to all navigable waters in the United States but also to tributaries of navigable waters, interstate waters and their tributaries, the use of nonnavigable intrastate waters (if their misuse could affect interstate commerce), and freshwater wetlands. (See *Sackett v. Environmental Protection Agency* in Chapter 5.) The most recent and expensive case involving violations of the U.S. Clean Water Act was the Deepwater Horizon oil-drilling rig that burned and sunk in April 2010, spilling oil into the Gulf of Mexico. It was the largest U.S. offshore oil spill. BP chartered the rig from Transocean, its owner. Transocean pleaded guilty in federal district court to violating the U.S. Clean Water Act for its role and was sentenced to pay a $400 million criminal fine and $1 billion in civil penalties. In addition, BP settled a class-action suit brought by businesses and individuals damaged by the oil spill. In settling, BP agreed to create a $20 billion compensation fund, but the settlement does not have a cap. The federal trial of BP for liability under the Clean Water Act had not concluded at press time. However, in a criminal action for manslaughter charges stemming from the Deepwater Horizon explosion but not based on the Clean Water Act, BP pleaded guilty in federal court and agreed to pay $4.5 billion in criminal penalties. In March 2014, the EPA ended its ban on BP obtaining government contracts.

Point Sources [45-7a]

The Act mandates that the EPA administrator establish effluent limitations for categories of existing point sources. An **effluent limitation** is a technology-based standard that limits the amount of a pollutant that a point source may discharge into a body of water. The Act effectuates such limitations through the *National Pollutant Discharge Elimination System (NPDES)*, a permit system.

Effluent limitation
technology-based standard that limits the amount of pollutant that a point source may discharge

Effluent Limitations   Under the 1972 amendments, effluent limitations for existing point sources, other than publicly owned treatment works, required application of the best practicable control technology currently available (**BPT**) by 1977 and application of the best available technology economically achievable (**BAT**) by 1983. According to the EPA, BPT is "the average of the best existing performance by well-operated plants within each industrial category or sub-category," while BAT is "the very best control and treatment measures that have been or are capable of being achieved." Somewhat different standards apply to publicly owned treatment works.

BPT
best practicable control technology currently available

BAT
best available technology economically achievable

The National Pollutant Discharge Elimination System   The NPDES, the permit system through which effluent limitations are to be achieved, requires that any person responsible for the discharge from a point source of a pollutant into U.S. waters must obtain a

Practical Advice

If your plant will discharge effluents into a body of water, make sure that you obtain all necessary permits.

discharge permit from the EPA, the Army Corps of Engineers, or, in some circumstances, the relevant state. An NPDES permit incorporates the applicable effluent limitations and establishes a schedule for compliance. The holder of an NPDES permit is required to notify the appropriate authority if the holder will not meet its obligations under the permit. A discharge not in compliance with a permit is unlawful. With limited exceptions, new permits for existing facilities cannot be less stringent than current permits.

South Florida Water Management District v. Miccosukee Tribe of Indians
Supreme Court of the United States, 2004
541 U.S. 95, 124 S.Ct. 1537, 158 L.Ed.2
http://scholar.google.com/scholar_case?q=124+S.Ct.+1537&hl=en&as_sdt=2,34&case=2885126139617306748&scilh=0

FACTS South Florida Water Management District (District) operates a pumping facility that transfers water from a canal into a reservoir a short distance away. The Central and South Florida Flood Control Project (Project) consists of a vast array of levees, canals, pumps, and water impoundment areas in the land between south Florida's coastal hills and the Everglades. Historically, that land was itself part of the Everglades, and its water flowed in an unchanneled sheet. Starting in the early 1900s, however, the state began to build canals to drain the wetlands and make them suitable for cultivation. These canals proved to be a source of trouble: they lowered the water table, allowing salt water to intrude upon coastal wells, and they proved incapable of controlling flooding. Congress established the Project in 1948 to address these problems. It gave the U.S. Army Corps of Engineers the task of constructing a comprehensive network of levees, water storage areas, pumps, and canal improvements. These improvements fundamentally altered the hydrology (movement and quality of water) of the Everglades, changing the natural sheet flow of ground and surface water. The local sponsor and day-to-day operator of the Project is the District.

Five discrete elements of the Project are at issue: a canal called "C–11," which collects groundwater and rainwater from a 104-square-mile area that is home to 136,000 people; a large pump station known as "S–9," which pumps water out of the C–11 canal; (3) a large undeveloped wetland area called "WCA–3," the largest of several "water conservation areas"; and (4) and (5) two levees, L–33 and L–37. Using pump stations like S–9, the District maintains the water table in WCA–3 at a level significantly higher than that in the developed lands drained by the C–11 canal to the east. Absent human intervention, that water would simply flow back east, where it would rejoin the waters of the canal and flood the populated areas of the C–11 basin. That return flow is prevented or, more accurately, slowed by levees that hold back the surface waters of WCA–3. The combined effect of L–33 and L–37, C–11, and S–9 is artificially to separate the C–11 basin from WCA–3; left to nature, the two areas would be a single wetland covered in an undifferentiated body of surface and ground water flowing slowly southward.

The Project has wrought large-scale hydrologic and environmental change in South Florida, some deliberate and some accidental. Its most obvious environmental impact has been the conversion of what were once wetlands into areas suitable for human use. But the Project also has affected areas that remain wetlands.

Rain on the western side of the L–33 and L–37 levees falls into the wetland ecosystem of WCA–3. Rain on the eastern side of the levees, on the other hand, falls on agricultural, urban, and residential land. Before it enters the C–11 canal that rainwater absorbs contaminants produced by human activities. The water in C–11

therefore differs chemically from that in WCA–3. Of particular interest here, C–11 water contains elevated levels of phosphorus, which is found in fertilizers used by farmers in the C–11 basin. When water from C–11 is pumped across the levees, the phosphorus it contains alters the balance of WCA–3's ecosystem and stimulates the growth of algae and plants foreign to the Everglades ecosystem.

Plaintiffs Miccosukee Tribe of Indians and the Friends of the Everglades brought a citizen suit under the Clean Water Act contending that the pumping facility is required to obtain a discharge permit under the National Pollutant Discharge Elimination System (NPDES). The district court agreed and granted summary judgment to the plaintiffs. The U.S. Court of Appeals for the Eleventh Circuit affirmed. Both the district court and the Eleventh Circuit rested their holdings on the predicate determination that the canal and reservoir are two distinct water bodies.

DECISION The judgment of the U.S. Court of Appeals for the Eleventh Circuit is vacated, and the case is remanded for further development of the factual record.

OPINION Congress enacted the Clean Water Act (the Act) in 1972. Its stated objective was "to restore and maintain the chemical, physical, and biological integrity of the Nation's waters." To serve those ends, the Act prohibits "the discharge of any pollutant by any person" unless done in compliance with some provision of the Act. The relevant provision establishes the NPDES. Generally speaking, the NPDES requires dischargers to obtain permits that place limits on the type and quantity of pollutants that can be released into the nation's waters. The Act defines the phrase "discharge of a pollutant" to mean "any addition of any pollutant to navigable waters from any point source." A "point source," in turn, is defined as "any discernible, confined and discrete conveyance," such as a pipe, ditch, channel, or tunnel, "from which pollutants are or may be discharged."

According to the Tribe, the District cannot operate S–9 without an NPDES permit because the pump station moves phosphorus-laden water from C–11 into WCA–3. The District does not dispute that phosphorus is a pollutant, or that C–11 and WCA–3 are "navigable waters" within the meaning of the Act. The question, it contends, is whether the operation of the S–9 pump constitutes the "discharge of [a] pollutant" within the meaning of the Act.

The District and the federal government advance three separate arguments, any of which would, if accepted, lead to the conclusion that the S–9 pump station does not require a point source discharge permit under the NPDES program. Two of these arguments involve the application of disputed contentions of law to agreed-upon facts, while the third involves the application of agreed-upon law to disputed facts. The Supreme Court declined to resolve all of the parties' legal disagreements and instead remanded the case for further proceedings regarding their factual dispute.

For purposes of determining whether there has been "any addition of any pollutant to navigable waters from any point source," the government contends that all the water bodies that fall within the Act's definition of "navigable waters" (i.e., all "the waters of the United States, including the territorial seas") should be viewed unitarily for purposes of NPDES permitting requirements. Because the Act requires NPDES permits only when there is an addition of a pollutant "to navigable waters," the government's approach would lead to the conclusion that such permits are not required when water from one navigable water body is discharged, unaltered, into another navigable water body. That would be true even if one water body were polluted and the other pristine, and the two would not otherwise mix. Under this "unitary waters" approach, the S–9 pump station would not need an NPDES permit.

In this case, the District further contends that the C–11 canal and WCA–3 impoundment area are not distinct water bodies at all, but instead are two hydrologically indistinguishable parts of a single water body. The government agrees with the District on this point. The Tribe does not dispute that if C–11 and WCA–3 are simply two parts of the same water body, pumping water from one into the other cannot constitute an "addition" of pollutants.

The record leaves some factual issues unresolved. The district court was correct to characterize the flow through the S–9 pump station as a nonnatural one, propelled as it is by diesel-fired motors against the pull of gravity. And it also appears true that if S–9 were shut down, the water in the C–11 canal might for a brief time flow east, rather than west, as it now does. But the effects of shutting down the pump might extend beyond that. The limited record suggests that if S–9 were shut down, the area drained by C–11 would flood quite quickly. That flooding might mean that C–11 would no longer be a distinct body of navigable water, but part of a larger water body extending over WCA–3 and the C–11 basin. It also might call into question the Eleventh Circuit's conclusion that S–9 is the cause in fact of phosphorus addition to WCA–3. Nothing in the record suggests that the district court considered these issues when it granted summary judgment. Thus, the trial court must resolve the factual dispute over the validity of the distinction between C–11 and WCA–3.

INTERPRETATION NPDES requires dischargers to obtain permits that place limits on the type and quantity of pollutants that can be released into the nation's waters, but does not apply to a discharge of unaltered water from one navigable body of water to another navigable body of water.

ETHICAL QUESTION Did the court fairly decide this case? Explain.

CRITICAL THINKING QUESTION Should the NPDES be so strictly interpreted? Explain.

The 1977 Amendments Recognizing that the application deadlines it had set in the 1972 amendments would not be met, Congress extended and modified the deadlines in 1977. The 1977 amendments to the Clean Water Act divided pollutants into three categories—toxic, conventional, and nonconventional (any pollutants that are neither toxic nor conventional)—and established different deadlines and standards for each category. For conventional pollutants, a new standard, best conventional pollution control technology (**BCT**), was to be achieved.

BCT

best conventional pollution control technology

Nonpoint Source Pollution [45-7b]

Controlling nonpoint source pollution—such as agricultural and urban runoff—is inherently more difficult than controlling point source pollution. According to the EPA:

> There is no effective way as yet, other than land use control, by which you can intercept that runoff and control it in a way that you do a point source. We have not yet developed technology to deal with that kind of a problem. We need to find ways to deal with it, because a great quantity of pollutants [are] discharged by runoff, not only from agriculture but from construction sites, from streets, from parking lots, and so on, and we have to be concerned with developing controls for them.

Although Congress tried to address the problem of nonpoint source pollution in the 1972 amendments, little effective control of nonsource pollution occurred before 1987. The 1987 amendments require states to identify state waters that will not meet the Act's requirements without the management of nonpoint sources of pollution and to institute "best management practices" to control such sources. The EPA must approve each state's management plan.

New Source Performance Standards [45-7c]

The Act requires the EPA administrator to establish federal performance standards for new sources. A performance standard should "reflect the greatest degree of effluent reduction ... achievable through application of the best available demonstrated control technology." The preferred standard for new sources is one "permitting no discharge of pollutants." Violation of a standard by an owner or operator of a new source is unlawful.

HAZARDOUS SUBSTANCES [45-8]

Technological advances have enabled human beings to produce numerous artificial substances, some of which have proven extremely hazardous to health. As the potential and actual harm from these latter substances became clear, Congress responded by enacting various substances-related statutes. In this section, we will consider some of the most important federal statutes governing hazardous substances: the Federal Insecticide, Fungicide, and Rodenticide Act (FIFRA); the Toxic Substances Control Act (TSCA); the Resource Conservation and Recovery Act (RCRA); the Comprehensive Environmental Response, Compensation, and Liability Act (CER-CLA, or the Superfund); and the Superfund Amendments and Reauthorization Act (SARA).

The Federal Insecticide, Fungicide, and Rodenticide Act [45-8a]

FIFRA

the Federal Insecticide, Fungicide, and Rodenticide Act regulates the sale and distribution of pesticides

The federal government began regulating pesticides in 1910 and greatly expanded its control over such substances in 1947 with the passage of the **FIFRA**. Concern about pesticides increased dramatically after the publication in 1962 of *Silent Spring*, by Rachel Carson, and Congress has amended the FIFRA several times.

The FIFRA requires that a pesticide be registered with the EPA before any person in any state may distribute it. Such registration is legal only if the pesticide's composition warrants the claims its manufacturer proposes for it, the pesticide will perform its intended function without "unreasonable adverse effects on the environment," the pesticide generally will not cause unreasonably adverse environmental effects when used in accordance with widespread and commonly recognized practice, and the pesticide complies with FIFRA labeling requirements. The FIFRA defines "unreasonable adverse effects on the environment" as any unreasonable risk to humans or the environment, taking into account the economic, social, and environmental costs and benefits of the use of any pesticide. Thus, unlike many environmental statutes, the FIFRA expressly requires the EPA to consider the costs of the action it takes under the statute.

If a pesticide is registered and subsequent data reveal additional hazards, the EPA may cancel the registration after an administrative hearing. The 1988 amendments placed upon industry the cost of disposing of canceled pesticides. Cancellation proceedings typically take years, both because of the numerous stages of the administrative process and because of the required use of a scientific advisory committee. While the cancellation process is in progress, the pesticide may be manufactured and sold. If additional hazard is imminent, however, the product's registration may be suspended until the cancellation proceeding is completed. Once its registration has been suspended, the pesticide may not be manufactured or distributed.

Until recently, the FIFRA did not adequately address the problem of old pesticides that had been registered under earlier and less strict standards. Concerned that these pesticides did not meet current standards, Congress in 1988 amended the FIFRA to require the reregistration of pesticides registered before 1984. U.S. exports are not subject to most of the Act's requirements, though an exported pesticide not registered under the FIFRA must bear a label stating "Not Registered for Use in the United States of America."

To establish a more consistent, protective regulatory scheme, in 1996 Congress enacted the Food Quality Protection Act (FQPA), which amended FIFRA and the Federal Food, Drug, and Cosmetic Act. The FQPA imposed stricter safety standards, especially for infants and children, and a complete reassessment of all existing pesticide tolerances.

The EPA may impose civil penalties, as adjusted for inflation in December 2013, of up to $7,500 for each offense. Maximum criminal penalties for knowing violations are a $50,000 fine and/or one year's imprisonment. Moreover, under the Federal Alternative Fines Act, if any person derives pecuniary gain from the offense, or if the offense results in pecuniary loss to a person other than the defendant, the defendant may be fined up to the greater of twice the gross gain or twice the gross loss.

The Toxic Substances Control Act [45-8b]

TSCA

the Toxic Substances Control Act provides a comprehensive scheme for regulation of toxic substances

Congress passed the **TSCA** in an effort to provide a comprehensive scheme for regulating toxic substances. The TSCA contains provisions on the manufacture of new chemicals, the testing of suspect chemicals, the regulation of chemicals that present an unreasonable risk of injury to health and the environment, and the inventorying of all chemicals.

Under the Act, a manufacturer must notify the EPA before it manufactures a new chemical or makes a significant new use of an existing chemical. If the EPA administrator concludes that the information submitted is insufficient to permit a reasoned evaluation of the health and environmental effects of the chemical and the chemical may present an unreasonable risk of injury to health or the environment, the administrator may limit or prohibit the chemical's manufacture or distribution.

The Act authorizes the EPA to require the testing of any substance, whether existing or new, if (1) the manufacture or distribution of the substance may present an unreasonable risk of injury to health or the environment, (2) the data on the effects of the substance on health and the environment are insufficient, and (3) testing is necessary to develop such data.

Because of the many substances that might be subject to testing under the statutory standard, the TSCA mandates that the EPA establish a priority list for testing that contains no more than fifty substances at any time. This list is established by a committee whose members come from eight specified agencies.

Once the EPA determines, either through its testing program or through the premanufacturing notice process, that a substance "presents or will present an unreasonable risk of injury to health or the environment," the agency may restrict or prohibit use of the substance.

If the EPA administrator believes that a substance presents an imminent hazard, he is authorized to bring an action in federal district court for seizure of the substance or other appropriate relief. The statute defines an "imminently hazardous chemical substance or mixture" as one that presents an unreasonable risk of serious or widespread injury to health or the environment.

The TSCA requires the EPA to compile and keep current a list of each chemical substance manufactured or processed in the United States. The EPA's initial inventory of existing chemicals listed approximately fifty-five thousand substances. A chemical not listed on the inventory is subject to premanufacture review, even if it was in fact previously manufactured. Although not explicitly required to do so by the TSCA, the EPA reviews the substances on the inventory to determine their safety.

The EPA may impose civil penalties, as adjusted for inflation in December 2013, of up to $37,500 per day for a violation of the TSCA. Maximum criminal penalties for knowing violations are $25,000 fines for each day of violation and/or one year's imprisonment. Moreover, under the Federal Alternative Fines Act, if any person derives pecuniary gain from the offense, or if the offense results in pecuniary loss to a person other than the defendant, the defendant may be fined up to the greater of twice the gross gain or twice the gross loss.

The European Union enacted a new law effective on June 1, 2007—Registration, Evaluation and Authorization of Chemicals (REACH), which requires companies producing more than specified quantities of chemicals to investigate the potential hazards to human health and the environment. This differs from TSCA in that it applies to all chemicals commercially available in the European Union. REACH requires EU manufacturers and importers to gather information on the properties of their substances, which will help them manage them safely, and to register the information in a central database. The European Chemicals Agency will act as the central point in the REACH system: it will run the databases necessary to operate the system, coordinate the in-depth evaluation of suspicious chemicals, and run a public database in which consumers and professionals can find hazard information. REACH also calls for the progressive substitution of the most dangerous chemicals when suitable alternatives have been identified.

The Resource Conservation and Recovery Act [45-8c]

RCRA

the Resource Conservation and Recovery Act provides a comprehensive scheme for treatment of solid waste, particularly hazardous waste

Congress enacted the **RCRA** to provide a comprehensive scheme for the treatment of solid waste, particularly hazardous waste. The statute provides that the states are primarily responsible for nonhazardous waste, and the EPA regulates all phases of hazardous waste—generation, transportation, and disposal. Under the Act, the federal government must establish criteria for identifying hazardous waste, taking into account factors that include toxicity, persistence, degradability, flammability, and corrosiveness.

The Act prescribes for generators (entities that produce hazardous waste) standards concerning recordkeeping, labeling, the use of appropriate containers, and reporting. The statute requires the EPA to establish a **manifest system** to be used by generators. A *manifest* is a form on which the generator must specify the quantity, composition, origin, routing, and destination of hazardous waste. On the manifest the generator also must certify that the volume and toxicity of the waste have been reduced to the greatest degree economically practicable and that the method of treatment, storage, and disposal minimizes the threat to health and the environment.

Transporters must maintain records and properly label the waste they transport. Furthermore, they must comply with manifests and may transport hazardous waste only to facilities that have an RCRA hazardous waste facility permit.

Owners and operators of hazardous waste treatment, storage, and disposal sites must maintain records and comply with generator manifests. Facilities for hazardous waste treatment, storage, and disposal must obtain an RCRA hazardous waste facility permit. To obtain a permit, a facility must comply with relevant EPA standards. Failure to comply may subject the owner or operator to civil or criminal penalties.

The Act authorizes the EPA administrator to sue in federal court for an injunction if the administrator has evidence that "the past or present handling, storage, treatment, transportation or disposal of any solid waste or hazardous waste may present an imminent and substantial endangerment to health or the environment." Moreover, the EPA may impose civil penalties, as adjusted for inflation in December 2013, of up to $37,500 per day of violation. Maximum criminal penalties for knowing violations are $50,000 for each day of violation and/or five years' imprisonment. When a knowing violation endangers a person, the maximum criminal penalty is a $1 million fine and/or fifteen years' imprisonment. Moreover, under the Federal Alternative Fines Act, if any person derives pecuniary gain from the offense, or if the offense results in pecuniary loss to a person other than the defendant, the defendant may be fined up to the greater of twice the gross gain or twice the gross loss.

The Superfund [45-8d]

Although the RCRA regulates current and future generation, transportation, and disposal of hazardous waste, the Act provides only limited authority for the cleanup of abandoned or inactive hazardous waste sites. To fill this gap and to respond to the serious environmental and health risks posed by industrial pollution, Congress in 1980 enacted the Comprehensive Environmental Response, Compensation, and Liability Act (CERCLA, or the Superfund). CERCLA was also designed to have the polluter bear the expense of the cleanup. By 1986, the EPA, working under the Act, had spent $1.6 billion and had begun the cleanup of only eight sites. This record and other problems with the initial legislation prompted Congress to amend the CERCLA by enacting the Superfund Amendments and Reauthorization Act (SARA). The EPA has cleaned up more than a thousand National Priorities List sites, but funds in the Superfund are nearly exhausted.

Under CERCLA, when the EPA determines that an environmental cleanup is necessary at a contaminated site, the agency has four options: (1) enter into a settlement with potentially responsible parties (PRPs); (2) conduct the cleanup with Superfund money and then file suit to obtain reimbursement from the PRPs; (3) file an abatement action in a federal district court to compel the PRPs to conduct the cleanup; or (4) issue a unilateral administrative order instructing the PRPs to clean the site.

CERCLA requires the federal government to establish a National Contingency Plan (NCP) prescribing procedures and standards for responding to hazardous substance releases. The NCP specifies criteria for determining the priority of sites to be cleaned. The plan also identifies, on at least an annual basis, the sites that most require immediate cleanup. As adjusted for inflation in December 2013, the EPA may impose a civil penalty of up to $37,500 per day of violation; for repeat violations, the penalty may reach up to $117,500 per day of violation.

CERCLA establishes a trust fund to pay for hazardous waste removal and other remedial actions. The trust fund is financed in part by a surtax on businesses with annual incomes over $2 million, a tax on petroleum, and a tax on chemical feedstocks. An additional part of the trust fund comes from money recovered from persons responsible for the release of hazardous

---

Practical Advice

Make sure that you maintain proper records, apply proper labels, and obtain all necessary permits for the generation, transportation, and disposal of all hazardous waste material.

The Superfund

the Comprehensive Environmental Response, Compensation, and Liability Act (CERCLA) establishes (1) the National Contingency Plan for responding to releases of hazardous substances and (2) a trust fund to pay for removal and cleanup of hazardous waste substances. These parties include the owners and operators of a hazardous waste disposal facility from which there has been a release, as well as any generator of hazardous wastes that were disposed of at that facility.

Because CERCLA initially imposed liability on all owners of contaminated property, some parties were held liable even though they had acquired the land either involuntarily or without knowledge of the hazardous wastes stored there. For example, after foreclosing on a mortgage of $335,000 and taking title to a piece of property, a bank was held liable for Superfund costs of more than $555,000. Responding to the inequity of such situations, Congress in SARA established a new defense to CERCLA liability for "innocent landowners." To qualify as an innocent landowner, one "must have undertaken, at the time of acquisition, all appropriate inquiry into the previous ownership and uses of the property consistent with good commercial or customary practice in an effort to minimize liability." In addition, under the Superfund Recycling Act, recyclers are exempt from liability to third parties, although they remain liable in suits brought by the federal or state governments.

In 2002, President Bush signed into law the Small Business Liability Relief and Brownfields Revitalization Act. The purpose of the Act is to promote the purchase, development, and use of brownfields, which are industrially polluted properties that are not sufficiently contaminated to be classified as a priority by either the EPA or state environmental agencies. The Act attempts to accomplish this purpose by providing protection from liability under CERCLA to any purchaser of contaminated property, to owners and developers who clean up property under state voluntary cleanup programs, and to owners of property that has become contaminated by migrating pollutants.

United States v. Bestfoods
Supreme Court of the United States, 1998
524 U.S. 51, 118 S.Ct. 1876, 141 L.Ed.2d 43
http://scholar.google.com/scholar_case?case=10493022136789272816&q=524+U.S.+51&hl=en&as_sdt=40006

FACTS In 1957, Ott Chemical Co. (Ott I) began manufacturing chemicals at a plant near Muskegon, Michigan, and its intentional and unintentional dumping of hazardous substances significantly polluted the soil and ground water at the site. In 1965, CPC International Inc. (Bestfoods) incorporated a wholly owned subsidiary to buy Ott I's assets in exchange for CPC stock. The new company, Ott Chemical Co. (Ott II), continued chemical manufacturing at the site, and continued to pollute its surroundings. CPC kept the managers of Ott I, including its founder, president, and principal shareholder, Arnold Ott, on board as officers of Ott II. Arnold Ott and several other Ott II officers and directors were also given positions at CPC, and they performed duties for both corporations. In 1972, CPC sold Ott II to Story Chemical Company, which operated the Muskegon plant until its bankruptcy in 1977. Shortly thereafter, the Michigan Department of Natural Resources (MDNR) examined the site for environmental damage. It found the land littered with thousands of leaking and even exploding drums of waste, and the soil and water saturated with noxious chemicals. MDNR sought a buyer for the property who would be willing to contribute toward its cleanup, and after extensive negotiations, Aerojet-General Corp. arranged for transfer of the site from the Story bankruptcy trustee in 1977. Aerojet created a wholly owned California subsidiary, Cordova Chemical Company (Cordova/California), to purchase the property, and Cordova/California in turn created a wholly owned Michigan subsidiary, Cordova Chemical Company of Michigan (Cordova/Michigan), which manufactured chemicals at the site until 1986.

By 1981, the federal Environmental Protection Agency had undertaken to oversee the cleanup of the site, and its long-term remedial plan called for expenditures well into the tens of millions of dollars. To recover some of that money, the United States filed this action in 1989, naming five defendants as responsible parties: CPC, Aerojet, Cordova/California, Cordova/Michigan, and Arnold Ott. (By that time, Ott I and Ott II were defunct.) The district court held a fifteen-day bench trial on the issue of liability. The trial focused on the issues of whether CPC and Aerojet, as the parent corporations of Ott II and the Cordova companies, had "owned or operated" the facility within the meaning of statute, and the court held them both to be operators. Applying Michigan veil-piercing law, the Court of Appeals decided that neither CPC nor Aerojet was liable for controlling the actions of its subsidiaries, since the parent and subsidiary corporations maintained separate personalities and the parents did not utilize the subsidiary corporate form to perpetrate fraud or subvert justice.

DECISION The judgment of the Court of Appeals is vacated, and the case is remanded with instructions to return it to the district court for further proceedings consistent with this opinion.

OPINION The issue in this case, under the Comprehensive Environmental Response, Compensation, and Liability Act of 1980 (CERCLA), is whether a parent corporation may be held liable for pollution caused by its subsidiary. In most cases, the answer is "no," but there are some exceptions.

The first of these exceptions is when the corporate form is misused to accomplish certain wrongful purposes, most notably fraud, on the shareholder's behalf. In these cases, the corporate veil may be pierced and the shareholder (parent company) held liable for the corporation's (subsidiary's) conduct.

Additionally, a corporate parent that actively participated in, and exercised control over, the operations of the facility itself may be held directly liable in its own right as an operator of the facility. It is this direct liability that is the issue in this case.

Under the plain language of the statute, any person who operates a polluting facility is directly liable for the costs of cleaning up the pollution. This is so regardless of whether that person is the facility's owner, the owner's parent corporation or business partner, or even a saboteur who sneaks into the facility at night to discharge its poisons out of malice. If any such act of operating a corporate subsidiary's facility is done on behalf of a parent corporation, the parent company may be found liable.

Under CERCLA, an operator is simply someone who directs the workings of, manages, or conducts the affairs of a facility. To sharpen the definition for purposes of CERCLA's concern with environmental contamination, an operator must manage, direct, or conduct operations specifically related to pollution, that is, operations having to do with the leakage or disposal of hazardous waste, or decisions about compliance with environmental regulations. A parent can also be held directly liable when the parent operates the facility in the stead of its subsidiary or alongside the subsidiary in some sort of a joint venture.

The further difficulty with this case comes in the fact that some corporate officers served on both corporations' boards. In imposing direct liability, the district court failed to recognize that "it is entirely appropriate for directors of a parent corporation to serve as directors of its subsidiary, and that fact alone may not serve to expose the parent corporation to liability for its subsidiary's acts." It is a "well established principle [of corporate law] that directors and officers holding positions with a parent and its subsidiary can and do 'change hats' to represent the two corporations separately, despite their common ownership."

Thus, the Court of Appeals was correct in holding that a participation-and-control test looking to the parent's supervision over the subsidiary, especially one that assumes that dual officers always act on behalf of the parent, cannot be used to identify operation of a facility resulting in direct parental liability. Nonetheless, a return to the ordinary meaning of the word "operate" in the organizational sense will indicate why we think that the Sixth Circuit stopped short when it confined its examples of direct parental operation to exclusive or joint ventures, and declined to find at least the possibility of direct operation by CPC in this case.

There is, in fact, some evidence that CPC engaged in just this type and degree of activity at the Muskegon plant. The district court's opinion speaks of an agent of CPC alone who played a conspicuous part in dealing with the toxic risks emanating from the operation of the plant. G.R.D. Williams worked only for CPC; he was not an employee, officer, or director of Ott II, and thus, his actions were of necessity taken only on behalf of CPC. The district court found that "CPC became directly involved in environmental and regulatory matters through the work of … Williams, CPC's governmental and environmental affairs director. Williams … became heavily involved in environmental issues at Ott II." He "actively participated in and exerted control over a variety of Ott II environmental matters," and he "issued directives regarding Ott II's responses to regulatory inquiries."

These findings are enough to raise an issue of CPC's operation of the facility through Williams's actions, though no ultimate conclusion from these findings can be drawn at this point.

INTERPRETATION Direct parental liability under CERCLA's operator provision is not limited to a corporate parent's sole or joint venture operation with subsidiary.

CRITICAL THINKING QUESTION Who should be responsible for the clean up of these polluted sites? Explain.

INTERNATIONAL PROTECTION OF THE OZONE LAYER [45-9]

Montreal Protocol
treaty by which countries agreed to cut production of chlorofluorocarbons by 50 percent

In 1987, the United States and twenty-three other countries entered into the **Montreal Protocol** on Substances that Deplete the Ozone Layer, a treaty designed to prevent pollution that harms the ozone layer. At least 197 parties have ratified the treaty. The treaty requires all signatories to reduce their production and consumption of all chemicals, in particular chlorofluorocarbons (CFCs, more commonly called Freon), which deplete the ozone layer. Although having excessive ozone in the air we breathe can be hazardous, the ozone layer in the stratosphere helps to protect the earth from harmful ultraviolet radiation.

CFCs, halocarbons, carbon dioxide, methane, and nitrous oxide are extremely potent "greenhouse gases," which trap heat and thereby warm the earth. Human activities, however, have increased the release of greenhouse gases, resulting in the serious threat of global warming. If this occurs, the levels of the seas will rise and the climate will change over most of the earth, causing severe flooding and disruptions of agricultural production.

To combat this predicted climate change, 165 nations in 1992 negotiated an international treaty on global warming at the United Nations Framework Convention on Climate Change (UNFCCC) in Rio de Janeiro. The Convention sets an overall framework for intergovernmental efforts to address the challenge posed by climate change. The treaty's ultimate objective is to

CONCEPT REVIEW 45-1

Major Federal Environmental Statutes

Act	Major Purpose	Maximum Civil Penalty**	Maximum Criminal Penalty
National Environmental Policy Act (NEPA)	• Establish environmental protection as a major national goal • Mandate environmental impact statements be prepared prior to federal action having a significant environmental effect	None	None
Clean Air Act	• Control and reduce air pollution • Establish National Ambient Air Quality Standards	$37,500 per day of violation	$1 million fine per violation and/or fifteen years' imprisonment*
Clean Water Act	• Protect against water pollution • Establish effluent limitations	$37,500 per day of violation	$50,000 per day of violation and/or three years' imprisonment*
Federal Insecticide, Fungicide, and Rodenticide Act (FIFRA)	• Regulate the sale and distribution of pesticides • Prevent pesticides having an unreasonably adverse effect on the environment	$7,500 per offense of pesticides	$50,000 fine and/or one year of imprisonment
Toxic Substances Control Act (TSCA)	• Regulate toxic substances • Prevent unreasonable risk of injury to health and the environment from toxic substances	$37,500 per day of violation	$25,000 fine per day of violation and/or one year of imprisonment
Resource Conservation and Recovery Act (RCRA)	• Regulate the disposal of solid waste • Establish standards to protect human health and the environment from hazardous wastes	$37,500 per day of violation	$1 million fine and/or fifteen years' imprisonment
Comprehensive Environmental Response, Compensation, and Liability Act (CERCLA, or the Superfund) and Superfund Amendments and Reauthorization Act (SARA)	• Establish a national contingency plan for responding to releases of hazardous substances • Establish a trust fund to pay for removal of hazardous waste and other remedial actions	$37,500 per day of violation; $117,500 for repeat violations	None

*Doubled for repeat convictions.
**As adjusted for inflation in December 2013.

stabilize the "greenhouse gas concentration in the atmosphere at a level that would prevent dangerous anthropogenic [human-induced] interference with the climate system." At least 195 parties have ratified the treaty, which went into effect on March 21, 1994. The UNFCCC calls for all signatory countries to develop and update national inventories of all greenhouse gases not otherwise covered by the Montreal Protocol.

At a subsequent UNFCCC, held in Kyoto, Japan, in December 1997, the participating nations proposed the **Kyoto Protocol**, which is a set of binding greenhouse gas emission targets for industrial nations. The Kyoto Protocol is an amendment to the UNFCCC. The Protocol's first commitment period started in 2008 and ended in 2012. At the conference of the parties in Durban in 2011, governments of the parties to the Kyoto Protocol decided that a second commitment period, beginning in 2013, would seamlessly follow the end of the first commitment period. The length of the second commitment period is to be determined. At least 192 parties

Kyoto Protocol
resolution on greenhouse gases

have ratified the Kyoto Protocol. The United States is the only signatory to the Kyoto Protocol not to ratify the protocol. However, on July 27, 2005, the United States and five Asia-Pacific nations (Australia, China, India, Japan, and the Republic of Korea) announced a pact, the Asia-Pacific Partnership on Clean Development, which is designed to reduce global warming. This "Beyond Kyoto" pact promotes the development of nuclear and solar power to reduce greenhouse gases without harming economic development. The partnership brings together the world's two largest polluters—the United States and China.

ETHICAL DILEMMA

Distant Concerns

Facts In February 1990, an American chemical manufacturer gave the Environmental Protection Agency (EPA) test results suggesting that one of the company's chemicals causes tumors and reproductive problems in laboratory mice. The chemical, known as R-11 [scientific name-2,3,4,5-Bis (2 butylene) tetrahydro-2 furaldehyde], repelled biting flies and was sold by its manufacturer to other companies that made and marketed insecticides for human use. Such insecticides included familiar national brands sold in drugstores and other retail outlets to families, anglers, boaters, hikers, and campers.

The U.S. makers of name-brand insecticides immediately stopped adding R-11 to their products, and they notified retailers to take products containing it off their shelves. (The maker of R-11 had already stopped shipping it to the insecticide manufacturers.) In early April 1990, the Canadian government banned the use of R-11 in Canada. In late April, the EPA issued a public warning to U.S. consumers not to use products containing

the chemical. By the end of April, the EPA had not yet banned the chemical but was expected to do so any day. After the ban, retail stores would have just sixty days to get rid of any products containing R-11.

J. Randolph Ewing, a U.S. entrepreneur with trading partners in the Caribbean and South America, had contracted with a small manufacturer of insecticides for a shipment of mosquito and biting-fly repellent containing R-11. Ewing planned to sell the insecticide, through his trading partners, under a variety of his own labels. He took delivery in the United States April 1 and shipped about half of the insecticides out at once. He heard about the EPA warning in late April. Anticipating a ban, Ewing thought about what to do next. He had several thousand dollars invested in the insecticides. Should he ship the rest of the insecticides overseas immediately and not mention the EPA warning to his foreign trading partners? Should he tell his trading partners about the warning and offer to take the product back? Should he be concerned at all?

Social, Policy, and Ethical Considerations
1. What should Ewing do?
2. Would your advice to Ewing be any different if R-11 were already banned in the United States?
3. If a chemical is banned in the United States but not in certain foreign nations, should the U.S. government prohibit the manufacturer from making the chemical here and exporting it to countries where it's not banned? What about a U.S. company that manufactures a banned chemical offshore, for example, in joint venture with a foreign partner?
4. In answering Question 3, would you take a chemical-by-chemical approach? Or would you stand for or against an export ban based on the principle that what's not safe enough for Americans is not safe enough for others?
5. What, if any, would be the justifications for a double standard of safety for Americans and the rest of the world's citizens?

CHAPTER SUMMARY

Common Law Actions for Environmental Damage

Nuisance

Private Nuisance substantial and unreasonable interference with the use and enjoyment of a person's land

Public Nuisance interference with the health, safety, or comfort of the public

Other Common Law Actions

Trespass an invasion of land that interferes with the right of exclusive possession of the property

Strict Liability for Abnormally Dangerous Activities liability without fault for an individual who engages in an unduly dangerous activity in an inappropriate location

Federal Regulation of the Environment

National Environmental Policy Act (NEPA)	**Purpose** to establish environmental protection as a goal of federal policy

Council on Environmental Quality three-member advisory group in the Executive Office of the President that makes recommendations to the President on environmental matters

Environmental Impact Statement a detailed statement concerning the environmental impact of a proposed federal action

- *Scope* the National Environmental Policy Act applies to a broad range of activities, including direct action by a federal agency as well as any action by a federal agency that permits action by other parties that will affect the quality of the environment
- *Content* the environmental impact statement must contain, among other items, a detailed statement of the environmental impact of the proposed action, any adverse environmental effects that cannot be avoided, and alternative proposals

Clean Air Act

Purpose to control and reduce air pollution

Existing Sources

- *National Ambient Air Quality Standards (NAAQS)* the Environmental Protection Agency must establish NAAQS for air pollutants that endanger the public health and welfare
- *State Implementation Plan (SIP)* each state must submit a plan for each National Ambient Air Quality Standards detailing how the state will implement and maintain the standard

New Sources

- *New Stationary Sources* owner or operator must employ the best technological system of continuous emission reduction that has been adequately demonstrated
- *New Vehicles* extensive emission standards are established
- *Hazardous Air Pollutants* to protect the public health, the Environmental Protection Agency administrator must establish for hazardous air pollutants standards that provide ample safety margins
- *Acid Rain* standards are established to protect against acid rain (precipitation that contains high levels of sulfuric or nitric acid)
- *Greenhouse Gases* air pollutant includes greenhouse gases and, therefore, the EPA has statutory authority to regulate such gases

Clean Water Act

Purpose protect against water pollution

Point Sources Act establishes National Pollutant Discharge Elimination System (NPDES), a permit system, to control the amount of pollutants that may be discharged by a point source into U.S. waters

Nonpoint Sources Act requires the states to use the best management practices to control water runoff from agricultural and urban areas

Hazardous Substances

FIFRA the Federal Insecticide, Fungicide, and Rodenticide Act regulates the sale and distribution of pesticides

TSCA the Toxic Substances Control Act provides a comprehensive scheme for regulation of toxic substances

RCRA the Resource Conservation and Recovery Act provides a comprehensive scheme for treatment of solid waste, particularly hazardous waste

Superfund the Comprehensive Environmental Response, Compensation, and Liability Act (CERCLA) establishes (1) a National Contingency Plan for responding to releases of hazardous substances and (2) a trust fund to pay for removal and cleanup of hazardous waste

International Protection of the Ozone Layer

Montreal Protocol treaty by which countries agreed to cut production of chlorofluorocarbons (CFCs) by 50 percent

United Nations Framework Convention on Climate Change (UNFCCC) treaty sets an overall framework for intergovernmental efforts to address the challenge posed by climate change with the objective of preventing dangerous human interference of the climate system

Kyoto Protocol international agreement linked to UNFCCC establishing a set of binding greenhouse gas emission targets for developed nations

QUESTIONS

1. Atlantic Cement operated a large cement plant. Neighboring landowners sued for damages and an injunction, claiming that their properties were injured by the dirt, smoke, and vibrations coming from the plant. The lower court found that the plant constituted a nuisance and granted temporary damages but refused to grant an injunction because the benefits of operating the plant outweighed the harm to the plaintiffs' properties. The landowners appealed. Does the plant constitute a nuisance? Should it be shut down?

2. Seindenberg and Hutchinson (the site owners) leased a four-acre tract of land (the Bluff Road site) to a chemical manufacturing corporation (COCC). While the lease initially was for the sole purpose of allowing COCC to store raw materials and finished products in a warehouse on the land, COCC later expanded its business to include the brokering and recycling of chemical waste generated by third parties. COCC's owners subsequently formed a new corporation, South Carolina Recycling and Disposal, Inc. (SCRDI), for the purpose of taking over COCC's waste-handling business. The site owners accepted rent from SCRDI. The waste stored at Bluff Road contained many chemical substances that federal law defines as hazardous. Subsequently, the Environmental Protection Agency concluded that the site was a major fire hazard. The federal government contracted with a third party to perform a partial cleanup of the site. The state of South Carolina completed the cleanup. The federal government and the state sued SCRDI, COCC, the site owners, and three third-party generators as responsible parties under the Resource Conservation and Recovery Act and Comprehensive Environmental Response, Compensation, and Liability Act. Explain whether the federal government and the state of South Carolina will prevail.

3. The state of Y submits a plan under the Clean Air Act to attain national ambient air quality standards. Can the Environmental Protection Agency administrator deny approval of the state plan because it is (a) less stringent or (b) more stringent than the agency believes is feasible? Explain.

CASE PROBLEMS

4. Kennecott Copper Corp. brings this challenge to an Environmental Protection Agency (EPA) order that rejected a portion of the state of Nevada's implementation plan dealing with the control of stationary sources of sulfur dioxide (SO_2). All of the SO_2 emissions come from a single source—the Kennecott copper smelter at McGill. The EPA based its decision on the belief that the Clean Air Act national ambient air quality standards (NAAQS) must be met by continuous emission limitations to the maximum extent possible and that the Act permits the intermittent use of emission controls only when continuous controls are not economically feasible. Kennecott contends that the EPA must approve any state implementation plan that will attain and maintain an NAAQS within the statutory time period. Who will prevail? Why?

5. The Environmental Protection Agency (EPA) administrator issued an order suspending the registration of the pesticides heptachlor and chlordane under the Federal Insecticide, Fungicide, and Rodenticide Act (FIFRA). Velsicol Chemical Corp., located in Oklahoma, is the sole manufacturer of these pesticides and brings this action, contending that the evidence does not support the administrator's contention that the continued use of these chemicals poses an imminent hazard to human health. Velsicol and the U.S. Department of Agriculture (USDA) contend (a) that the EPA's laboratory tests on mice and rats do not "conclusively" show that either chemical is carcinogenic, (b) that mice are too prone to tumors to be reliable test subjects, and (c) that human exposure to these chemicals is insufficient to create a risk. Nonetheless, human epidemiology studies on both chemicals provide no basis for concluding that either pesticide is safe. The administrator based part of his claim on residues of these chemicals found in soil, air, and the aquatic ecosystem over long periods of time and on the presence of these chemicals in the human diet and human tissue. Does FIFRA apply in this situation? Explain.

6. The U.S. Department of the Interior filed an environmental impact statement (EIS) with regard to its proposal to lease approximately eighty tracts of submerged land, primarily located off the coast of Louisiana, for oil and gas exploration. Adjacent to the proposed area is the greatest estuarine coastal marsh in the United States. This marsh provides rich nutrients for the Gulf of Mexico, the most productive fishing region of the country. The EIS focused primarily on oil pollution and its negative environmental effect. Three conservation groups contend that the EIS is insufficient in that it does not properly discuss alternatives. The government contends that (a) it need only provide a detailed statement of the alternatives, not a discussion of their environmental impact, and (b) the only alternatives the National Environmental Policy Act requires it to discuss are those that can be adopted and implemented by the agency issuing the impact statement. Is the government correct in its contentions? Why?

7. Chemical Manufacturers Association (CMA) and four companies that manufacture chemicals challenged a test rule promulgated by the Environmental Protection Agency (EPA) under the Toxic Substances Control Act (TSCA). The plaintiffs asserted that the EPA must find that the existence of an unreasonable risk of injury to health is more probable than not before it may issue a test rule under the Act. In response, the EPA claimed that it may issue a test rule under the TSCA if the agency determines that there is a substantial probability of an unreasonable risk of injury to health. The test rule required toxicological testing to determine the health effects of the chemical, 2-ethylhexanoic acid, and imposed on exporters of this chemical a duty to file certain notices with the EPA. What standard should be applied? Why?

8. National-Southwire Aluminum Company (NSA) owns and operates a plant that emits fluoride. When its wet scrubbers were turned off as part of its regular maintenance program, NSA discovered no appreciable change in ambient fluoride levels. Because of the expense of operating the scrubbers and its belief that using the scrubbers did not significantly affect ambient fluoride levels, NSA desired to turn the scrubbers off permanently. Accordingly, NSA sought a determination from the Environmental Protection Agency (EPA) that turning off the scrubbers would not constitute a modification requiring the application of new source performance standards to the plant. Turning off the scrubbers would result in an increase of more than 1,100 tons per year of fluoride emissions with no decrease in the emission of any other pollutant. This increase was nearly four hundred times the level the EPA had established as inconsequential. The EPA determined that turning off the scrubbers would constitute a "new source" modification. Accordingly, NSA was required either to leave the scrubbers on or to install new pollutant control equipment. Is the EPA correct in its assertion? Explain.

9. The city of Fayetteville, Arkansas, received a National Pollutant Discharge Elimination System permit from the Environmental Protection Agency (EPA) for the discharge of sewage into a stream that ultimately reaches the Illinois River, twenty-two miles upstream from the Oklahoma border. The EPA permit limited the effluent discharge to comply with Oklahoma water quality standards, but the EPA stated that those standards would be violated only if the discharge would cause an actual, detectable violation of Oklahoma standards. Oklahoma appealed the permit, arguing that the permit violated Oklahoma water quality standards, which allow no degradation of water quality. Explain whether the permit should be granted.

10. A group of nineteen private organizations filed a rulemaking petition asking the Environmental Protection Agency (EPA) to regulate greenhouse gas emissions from new motor vehicles under the Clean Air Act. Fifteen months after the petition's submission, EPA requested public comment on all the issues raised in the petition, adding a "particular" request for comments on "any scientific, technical, legal, economic or other aspect of these issues that may be relevant to EPA's consideration of this petition." EPA received more than fifty thousand comments over the next five months. The EPA entered an order denying the rulemaking petition. The agency gave two reasons for its decision: (1) that contrary to the opinions of its former general counsels, the Clean Air Act does not authorize EPA to issue mandatory regulations to address global climate change; and (2) that even if the agency had the authority to set greenhouse gas emission standards, it would be unwise to do so at this time. In concluding that it lacked statutory authority over greenhouse gases, EPA observed that Congress "was well aware of the global climate change issue when it last comprehensively amended the [Clean Air Act] in 1990," yet it declined to adopt a proposed amendment establishing binding emissions limitations. Calling global warming "the most pressing environmental challenge of our time," twelve states, local governments, and private organizations, alleged that the EPA has abdicated its responsibility under the Clean Air Act to regulate the emissions of four greenhouse gases, including carbon dioxide, and brought this lawsuit. Who should prevail? Why?

TAKING SIDES

When considering an application for a special use permit to develop and operate a ski resort at Sandy Butte, a mountain in Washington that is part of a national forest, the Forest Service prepared an environmental impact statement (EIS). The EIS recommended the issuance of a special use permit for what was to be a sixteen-lift ski area, and the forest service issued the permit as recommended. Four organizations sued, claiming that the EIS was inadequate. The lower court held that the EIS was adequate, but the Court of Appeals reversed, concluding that the National Environmental Policy Act required that actions be taken to mitigate the adverse effects of a major federal action and that the EIS contain a detailed mitigation plan.

a. What are the arguments that the EIS should only take a hard look at the relevant environmental consequences?

b. What are the arguments that the EIS should propose actions that mitigate the relevant environmental consequences?

c. What should the EIS include in this situation?

International Business Law

CHAPTER 46

Peace, commerce, and honest friendship with all nations, entangling alliances with none.

Thomas Jefferson (1801)

CHAPTER OUTCOMES

After reading and studying this chapter, you should be able to:

1. Describe the purposes and major features of regional trade communities (especially the European Union and North American Free Trade Agreement [NAFTA]) and the World Trade Organization (General Agreement on Tariffs and Trade [GATT]).

2. Explain sovereign immunity, the act of state doctrine, expropriation, and confiscation.

3. Explain the legal controls imposed on the flow of trade, labor, and capital across national borders.

4. Explain the international dimensions of antitrust law, securities regulation, and the protection of intellectual property.

5. List and describe the forms in which a multinational enterprise may conduct its business in a foreign country.

I n the twenty-first century, every aspect of business, including business law, requires some understanding of international business practices. Since World War II, the global economy has become increasingly interconnected. Many U.S. corporations now have investments or manufacturing facilities in other countries; simultaneously, the number of foreign corporations with business operations in the United States has increased dramatically. Furthermore, whether a domestic corporation exports goods or not, it competes with imports from many other countries. For example, U.S. firms face competition from Japanese electronics and automobiles, Chinese electronics and textiles, Korean automobiles and electronics, French wines and fashions, German machinery, and Indian software programmers and call centers. To compete effectively, U.S. firms need to be aware of international business practices and developments.

Laws vary greatly from country to country: what one nation requires by law, another may forbid. To complicate matters, there is no single authority in international law that can compel countries to act. When the laws of two or more nations conflict, or when one party has violated an agreement and the other party wishes to enforce it or to recover damages, establishing who will adjudicate the matter, which laws will be applied, what remedies will be available, or where the matter should be decided often is very confusing. Nonetheless, given the growing impact of the global economy, a basic understanding of international business law is essential.

THE INTERNATIONAL ENVIRONMENT [46-1]

International law deals with the conduct and relations between nation-states and international organizations, as well as some of their relations with persons. Unlike domestic law, international law generally cannot be enforced. Consequently, international courts do not have compulsory jurisdiction, though they do have authority to

International law
includes law that deals with the conduct and relations of nation-states and international organizations as well as some of their relations with persons; such law is enforceable by the courts of a nation that has adopted the international law as domestic law

resolve an international dispute if the parties to the dispute accept the court's jurisdiction over the matter. Furthermore, a sovereign nation that has adopted an international law will enforce that law to the same extent as all of its domestic laws. In this section, we will examine some of the sources and institutions of international law.

International Court of Justice [46-1a]

International Court of Justice (ICJ)

judicial branch of the United Nations having voluntary jurisdiction over nations

The United Nations (U.N.), with at least 193 member states, has a judiciary branch called the **International Court of Justice (ICJ)**. The ICJ consists of fifteen judges, no two of whom may be from the same sovereign state, elected for nine-year terms by a majority of both the U.N. General Assembly and the U.N. Security Council. The usefulness of the ICJ is limited, however, because only nations (not private individuals or corporations) may be parties to an action before the court. Furthermore, the ICJ has contentious jurisdiction only over nation-parties who agree both to allow the ICJ to decide the case and to be bound by its decision. Moreover, because the ICJ cannot enforce its rulings, countries displeased with an ICJ decision may simply ignore it. Consequently, few nations submit their disputes to the ICJ.

The ICJ also has advisory jurisdiction if requested by a U.N. organ or specialized U.N. agency. Neither sovereign states nor individuals may request an advisory opinion. These opinions are nonbinding, and the U.N. agency requesting the opinion usually votes to decide whether to follow it.

Regional Trade Communities [46-1b]

Regional trade communities

international organizations, conferences, and treaties focusing on business and trade regulations; the EU (European Union) is the most prominent of these

Of much greater significance are international organizations, conferences, and treaties that focus on business and trade regulation. **Regional trade communities**, such as the European Union (EU), promote common trade policies among member nations. Other important regional trade communities include the Central American Common Market (CACM), the Caribbean Community Market (CARICOM), the Association of South East Asian Nations (ASEAN), the Andean Common Market (ANCOM), the Common Market for Eastern and Southern Africa (COMESA), the Asian Pacific Economic Cooperation (APEC), *Mercado Comun del Cono Sur* (Latin American Trading Group, MERCO-SUR), the Gulf Cooperation Council (GCC), *Alianza del Pacífico* (Pacific Alliance), and the Economic Community of West African States (ECOWAS).

European Union   The European Community (EC), the predecessor to the European Union, was formed in 1967 through a merger between the European Economic Community (better known as the Common Market), the European Coal and Steel Community, and the European Atomic Energy Community (Euratom). The EC worked to remove trade barriers among its member nations and to unify their economic policies. The EC had the power to make rules that bound member nations and that preempted its members' domestic laws.

In 1993, the Treaty on European Union (popularly called the Maastricht Treaty) took effect. It changed the name of the EC to the European Union (EU) and stated the EU's objectives to include (1) promoting economic and social progress by creating an area without internal borders and by establishing an economic and monetary union, (2) asserting its identity on the international scene by implementing a common foreign and security policy, (3) strengthening the protection of the rights and interests of citizens of its member states, and (4) developing close cooperation on justice and home affairs. The euro (€) is the single currency currently shared by eighteen of the EU's members, which together make up the euro area.

Until May 2004, the EU had fifteen members: Austria, Belgium, Denmark, Finland, France, Germany, Greece, Ireland, Italy, Luxembourg, the Netherlands, Portugal, Spain, Sweden, and the United Kingdom. In May 2004, the EU admitted ten eastern and southern European countries: Cyprus, the Czech Republic, Estonia, Hungary, Latvia, Lithuania, Malta, Poland, the Slovak Republic, and Slovenia. On January 1, 2007, Bulgaria and Romania became EU members, bringing the total number of members to twenty-seven. Croatia became the EU's twenty-eighth member on July 1, 2013. Five more countries have applied for EU membership: Iceland, Montenegro, Serbia, Turkey, and the Republic of Macedonia. The EU's total population is approximately 500 million (7 percent of the world's population) while its trade with the rest of the world accounts for approximately 20 percent of global exports and imports.

NAFTA The North American Free Trade Agreement (NAFTA), which took effect in 1994, established a free trade area among the United States, Canada, and Mexico. Its objectives are to (1) eliminate trade barriers to the movement of goods and services across the borders, (2) promote conditions of fair competition in the free trade area, (3) increase investment opportunities in the area, and (4) provide adequate and effective enforcement of intellectual property rights. In 2008 NAFTA's last transitional restrictions governing agricultural trade were removed.

International Treaties [46-1c]

International treaties
agreements between or
among independent nations,
such as the General
Agreement on Tariffs and
Trade (GATT), now called
the World Trade
Organization (WTO), and
the United Nations
Convention on the Law of
the Sea (UNCLOS)

A treaty is an agreement between or among independent nations. As discussed in Chapter 1, the U.S. Constitution authorizes the President to enter into treaties with the advice and consent of the Senate "providing two-thirds of the Senators present concur." The U.S. Constitution provides that all valid treaties are "the law of the land," having the legal force of a federal statute.

Nations have entered into bilateral and multilateral treaties to facilitate and regulate trade and to protect their national interests. In addition, treaties have been used to serve as constitutions of international organizations, to establish general international law, to transfer territory, to settle disputes, to secure human rights, and to protect investments. The Treaty Section of the Office of Legal Affairs within the United Nations Secretariat is responsible for registering and publishing treaties and agreements among member nations. Since its inception in 1946, the U.N. Secretariat has registered and published more than thirty thousand treaties that expressly or indirectly concern international business.

**World Trade
Organization (WTO)**
global international
organization dealing with
the rules of trade among
nations

World Trade Organization (WTO) The WTO is the only global international organization dealing with the rules of trade among nations. Probably the most important multilateral trade treaty is the General Agreement on Tariffs and Trade (GATT), which the WTO replaced as an international organization. The WTO officially commenced on January 1, 1995, and has at least 160 members accounting for more than 97 percent of world trade. (Approximately twenty-five countries are observers and are seeking membership.) Its basic purpose is to facilitate the flow of trade by establishing agreements on potential trade barriers such as import quotas, customs, export regulations, antidumping restrictions (the prohibition against selling goods for less than their fair market value), subsidies, and import fees. The WTO administers trade agreements, acts as a forum for trade negotiations, handles trade disputes, monitors national trade policies, and provides technical assistance and training for developing countries.

Under GATT's *most favored nation provision*, all signatories must treat each other as favorably as they treat any other country. Thus, any privilege, immunity, or favor given to one country must be given to all. Nevertheless, nations may give preferential treatment to developing nations and may enter into free trade areas with one or more other nations. A free trade area permits countries to discriminate in favor of their free trade partners, provided that the agreement covers substantially all trade among the partners. A second important principle adopted by GATT is that the protection offered domestic industries should take the form of customs tariffs, rather than other, more trade-inhibiting measures.

The most recent set of accords, adopted in 1994, included multilateral trade agreements on such matters as agricultural products, textiles and clothing, technical barriers to trade, trade-related investment measures, customs valuation, subsidies and countervailing measures, trade in services, antidumping measures, and protection of intellectual property rights. It also created the Dispute Settlement Body and increased the scope of GATT's dispute resolution process.

**United Nations
Convention on the Law
of the Sea (UNCLOS)**
establishes a comprehensive
set of rules governing all
uses of the oceans and their
resources

United Nations Convention on the Law of the Sea (UNCLOS) The United Nations Convention on the Law of the Sea (UNCLOS) establishes a comprehensive set of rules governing all uses of the oceans and their resources. UNCLOS also provides the framework for further development of specific areas of the law of the sea. UNCLOS entered into force in 1994 and has been ratified by at least 165 nations.

UNCLOS governs all aspects of the ocean, including economic and commercial activities, transfer of technology, environmental control, scientific research, and the settlement of disputes relating to ocean matters. A key feature of UNCLOS is that coastal nations have (1) sovereignty over their territorial sea up to a limit not to exceed twelve nautical miles, (2) sovereign rights in a 200-nautical mile exclusive economic zone (EEZ) with respect to natural resources and certain economic activities, and (3) sovereign rights to the continental shelf (the national area of the seabed) for exploring and exploiting it. The shelf can extend at least 200 nautical miles from the shore, and more under specified circumstances, but coastal nations share with the international community part of the revenue derived from exploiting resources from any part of their shelf beyond 200 miles.

Disputes can be submitted to the International Tribunal for the Law of the Sea established under UNCLOS, to the International Court of Justice, or to arbitration. The Tribunal has exclusive jurisdiction over deep seabed mining disputes.

JURISDICTION OVER ACTIONS OF FOREIGN GOVERNMENTS [46-2]

In this section, we will focus on a sovereign nation's power—and the factors limiting that nation's power—to exercise jurisdiction over a foreign nation or to take over property owned by foreign citizens. More specifically, we will examine state immunities (the principle of sovereign immunity and the act of state doctrine) and the power of a state to take foreign investment property.

Sovereign Immunity [46-2a]

Sovereign immunity
foreign country's freedom from a host country's laws

One of the oldest concepts in international law is that each nation has absolute and total authority over the events occurring within its territory. It has also been long recognized, however, that to maintain international relations and trade, a host country must refrain from imposing its laws on a foreign sovereign nation present within its borders. This absolute immunity from the courts of a host country is known as **sovereign immunity**. Originally, all acts of a foreign sovereign nation within a host country were considered immune from the host country's laws. In modern times, however, international law distinguishes between a foreign nation's public acts and its commercial ones. Only public acts, such as those concerning diplomatic activity, internal administration, or armed forces, will be granted sovereign immunity. By engaging in trade or commercial activities, a foreign nation subjects itself to the jurisdiction of its host country's courts with respect to any disputes that arise out of those commercial activities.

In 1976, Congress enacted the Foreign Sovereign Immunities Act to establish exactly the circumstances under which the United States would extend immunity to foreign nations. Under the Act, a "foreign state shall be immune from the jurisdiction of the courts of the United States and of the States" unless one of several statutorily defined exceptions applies. The most significant of the Act's exceptions is the "commercial" exception which applies if the suit is based upon (1) a commercial activity conducted in the United States by the foreign state, (2) an act that the foreign state performed in the United States in connection with a commercial activity it conducted elsewhere, or (3) a commercial activity performed outside the United States that nonetheless directly affects the United States. If an activity is one that a private party could normally carry on, it is commercial, and a foreign government engaging in that activity is not immune. On the other hand, if the activity is one that only governments can undertake, it is noncommercial under the Act. Examples of commercial activities include a contract by a foreign government to buy provisions or equipment for its armed forces; a foreign government's contract to construct or repair a government building; and a foreign government's sale of a service or a product or its leasing of property, borrowing of money, or investing in a security of a U.S. corporation. Examples of public (noncommercial) activities to which sovereign immunity would extend include nationalizing a corporation, determining limitations upon the use of the foreign state's natural resources, and the granting of licenses to export a natural resource.

Saudi Arabia v. Nelson
Supreme Court of the United States, 1993
507 U.S. 349, 113 S.Ct. 1471, 123 L.Ed.2d 47
http://scholar.google.com/scholar_case?q=113+S.Ct.+1471&hl=en&as_sdt=6,34&case=15997705832480823650&scilh=0

FACTS The Kingdom of Saudi Arabia owns and operates King Faisal Specialist Hospital in Riyadh (Hospital). The Hospital Corporation of America, Ltd. (HCA), an independent corporation existing under the laws of the Cayman Islands, recruits Americans for employment at the Hospital under an agreement signed with Saudi Arabia in 1973. HCA placed an advertisement in a periodical seeking applicants for a monitoring systems engineer position at the Hospital. Scott Nelson saw the ad in September 1983 while he was in the United States. After interviewing for the position in Saudi Arabia, Nelson returned to the United States, where he signed an employment contract with the Hospital, satisfied personnel processing requirements, and attended an orientation session that HCA conducted for Hospital employees. In December 1983, Nelson went to Saudi Arabia and began work at the Hospital. In March 1984, he discovered safety defects in the Hospital's oxygen and nitrous oxide lines that posed fire hazards. Nelson repeatedly advised Hospital officials of the safety defects and reported the defects to a Saudi government commission. On September 27, 1984 the Saudi government arrested him. Agents transported Nelson to a jail cell, where they shackled, tortured, and beat him and kept him for four days without food. Government agents forced him to sign a statement written in Arabic, which language Nelson did not know. Two days later, government agents transferred Nelson to the Al Sijan Prison to await trial. Nelson was confined in an overcrowded cell infested with rats, where he had to fight other prisoners for food and from which he was taken only once a week for fresh air and exercise. Only after the personal request of a U.S. senator did the Saudi government release Nelson, thirty-nine days after his arrest. Seven days later, the Saudi government allowed him to leave the country.

In 1988, Nelson filed suit against Saudi Arabia in the U.S. District Court for the Southern District of Florida, seeking damages for personal injury. The district court dismissed the case for lack of subject matter jurisdiction under the Foreign Sovereign Immunities Act of 1976. The Court of Appeals reversed, holding that under the Act, a foreign state is not immune from the jurisdiction of U.S. courts in any case involving an action based upon a commercial activity carried on in the United States by the foreign state. It concluded that Nelson's recruitment and hiring were commercial activities of Saudi Arabia and the Hospital carried on in the United States.

DECISION Decision of the Court of Appeals reversed.

OPINION The Foreign Sovereign Immunities Act provides the sole basis for obtaining jurisdiction over a foreign state in the courts of this country. Under the Act, a foreign state is presumptively immune from the jurisdiction of U.S. courts. The Act, however, provides an exception for commercial activities carried on by a foreign state and having substantial contact with the United States. The statute provides that such a commercial activity may be either a regular course of commercial conduct or a particular commercial transaction or act. The commercial character of the conduct or act is determined by reference to its "nature," rather than its "purpose." A state engages in commercial activity when it exercises only those powers that also can be exercised by private citizens. Thus, a foreign state engages in commercial activity only when it acts in the manner of a private player within the market. Whether a state acts in the manner of a private party is a question of behavior, not motivation. The question is not whether the foreign government is motivated by profit or by the desire to fulfill uniquely sovereign objectives. Rather, the issue is whether the particular actions that the foreign state performs are of the type by which a private party engages in trade or commerce.

In this case, Saudi Arabia recruited and signed an employment contract with Nelson in the United States. While these activities led to the conduct that eventually injured Nelson, they are not the basis for the suit. Nelson has not alleged breach of contract but personal injuries caused by Saudi Arabia's intentional wrongs. Nevertheless, such intentional conduct cannot qualify as commercial activity under the Act. The conduct boils down to the Saudi government's abuse of the power of its police, and however monstrous such abuse undoubtedly may be, a foreign state's exercise of the powers of its police and penal officers has long been understood to be sovereign in nature. The exercise of such powers is not the sort of action by which private parties can engage in commerce. Such acts as legislation, or the expulsion of an alien, or a denial of justice cannot be performed by an individual acting in his own name. They can be performed only by the state acting as such.

INTERPRETATION Only lawsuits based on the commercial activities of a foreign state are subject to the jurisdiction of the state or federal courts in the United States.

CRITICAL THINKING QUESTION What are the public policy arguments supporting and opposing the Court's approach in this case? Explain.

Act of State Doctrine [46-2b]

Act of state doctrine
rule that a court should not
question the validity of
actions taken by a foreign
government in its own
country

The **act of state doctrine** provides that a nation's judicial branch should not question the validity of the actions a foreign government takes within that foreign sovereign's own borders. In 1897, the U.S. Supreme Court described the act of state doctrine in terms that still remain valid: "Every sovereign State is bound to respect the independence of every other sovereign State, and the courts of one country will not sit in judgment on the acts of the government of another done within its own territory."

In the United States, there are several possible exceptions to the act of state doctrine. Some courts hold (1) that a sovereign may waive its right to raise the act of state defense and (2) that the doctrine may be inapplicable to commercial activities of a foreign sovereign. In addition, by federal statute, courts will not apply the act of state doctrine to a claim to specific property located in the United States when such a claim is based on the assertion that a foreign state confiscated the property in violation of international law, unless the President of the United States determines that the doctrine should be applied to that particular case.

Taking of Foreign Investment Property [46-2c]

Investing in foreign states involves the risk that the host nation's government may take the investment property. An **expropriation** or nationalization occurs when a government seizes foreign-owned property or assets for a public purpose and pays the owner just compensation for what is taken. In contrast, **confiscation** occurs when a government offers no payment (or a highly inadequate payment) in exchange for seized property, or seizes it for a nonpublic purpose. Confiscations violate generally observed principles of international law, whereas expropriations do not. In either case, few remedies are available to injured parties.

One precaution that U.S. firms can take is to obtain insurance from a private insurer or from the Overseas Private Investment Corporation (OPIC), an independent U.S. government agency. OPIC was established to facilitate the participation of U.S. private capital and skills in the economic and social development of developing countries and countries in transition from nonmarket to market economies. OPIC, which charges market-based fees for its products, accomplishes this by helping U.S. businesses to invest overseas by complementing the private sector in managing risks associated with foreign direct investment. Currently, OPIC services are available for new and expanding business enterprises in more than 150 countries worldwide. To date, OPIC has supported more than $200 billion of investment in more than 4,000 projects, generated an estimated $75 billion in U.S. exports, and supported more than 275,000 U.S. jobs.

The World Bank established the Multilateral Investment Guarantee Agency (MIGA) to encourage increased investment in developing nations. The MIGA has at least 180 member countries. MIGA's mission is to promote foreign direct investment into developing countries to help support economic growth, reduce poverty, and improve people's lives. It does this by providing political risk insurance (guarantees) to the private sector for such noncommercial risks as deprivation of ownership or control by government actions, breach of contract by a government when there is no judicial recourse, and loss from military action or civil disturbance.

TRANSACTING BUSINESS ABROAD [46-3]

Transacting business abroad may involve activities such as selling goods, information, or services; investing capital; or arranging for the movement of labor. Because these transactions may affect the national security, economy, foreign policy, and interests of both the exporting and importing countries, nations have imposed measures to restrict or encourage such transactions. In this section, we will examine the legal controls imposed upon the flow of trade, labor, and capital across national borders.

Flow of Trade [46-3a]

Advances in modern technology, communication, transportation, and production methods have swelled the flow of goods across national boundaries. The governments within each country thereby face a dilemma. On the one hand, they wish to protect and stimulate domestic industry. On the other hand, they want to provide their citizens with the best quality goods at the lowest possible prices and to encourage exports from their own countries.

Governments have used a variety of trade barriers to protect domestic businesses. A frequently applied device is the **tariff**, which is a duty or tax imposed on goods moving into or out of a country. Tariffs raise the price of imported goods, prompting some consumers to purchase less expensive, domestically produced items. Governments can also use **nontariff barriers** to give local industries a competitive advantage. Examples of nontariff barriers include unilateral or bilateral import quotas; import bans; overly restrictive safety, health, or manufacturing standards; environmental laws; complicated and time-consuming customs procedures; and subsidies to local industry.

Expropriation
governmental taking of foreign-owned property for a public purpose and with payment of just compensation

Confiscation
governmental taking of foreign-owned property without payment (or for a highly inadequate payment) or for a nonpublic purpose

Practical Advice

If you invest in foreign states, consider obtaining expropriation insurance from a private insurer or from the Overseas Private Investment Corporation (OPIC), an agency of the U.S. government.

Flow of trade
controlled by trade barriers on imports and exports

Tariff
duty or tax imposed on goods moving into or out of a country

Nontariff barriers
include quotas, bans, safety standards, and subsidies

Practical Advice

If you export goods, be sure to determine whether you must obtain an export license from the U.S. government and what import barriers, such as tariffs, you must satisfy in the countries to which you are sending the goods.

Dumping is the sale of exported goods from one country to another country at less than normal value. Under the WTO's Antidumping Code, "normal value" is the price that would be charged for the same or a similar product in the ordinary course of trade for domestic consumption in the exporting country. Dumping violates the GATT "if it causes or threatens material injury to an established industry in the territory of a contracting party or materially retards the establishment of a domestic industry."

Governments also control the flow of goods out of their countries by imposing quotas, tariffs, or total prohibitions. *Export controls* or restrictions usually result from important policy considerations, such as national defense, foreign policy, or the protection of scarce national resources. For example, the United States passed the Export Administration Act of 1979, which, as amended in 1985 and 1988, restricts the flow of technologically advanced goods and data from the United States to other countries. (The Act has been in lapse since August 21, 2001, but Presidents have extended control over exports by invoking their emergency powers under the International Emergency Economic Powers Act.) Nonetheless, to assist domestic businesses, countries generally encourage exports through the use of *export incentives* and *export subsidies*.

Flow of Labor [46-3b]

Flow of labor

controlled through passport, visa, and immigration regulations

The **flow of labor** across national borders generates policy questions concerning the employment needs of local workers. Each country has its own immigration policies and regulations. Almost all countries require that foreigners obtain valid passports before entering their borders; citizens, in turn, usually must have passports to leave or reenter the country. In addition, a country may issue foreign citizens visas that permit them to enter the country for identified purposes or for specific periods of time. For example, the U.S. Citizenship and Immigration Services (USCIS), a component of the Department of Homeland Security, oversees lawful immigration.

Flow of Capital [46-3c]

Flow of capital

the International Monetary Fund facilitates the expansion and balanced growth of international trade, assists in eliminating foreign exchange restrictions, and smooths the international balance of payments

Multinational businesses frequently need to transfer funds to, and receive money from, operations in other countries. Because there is no international currency, nations have sought to ease the **flow of capital** among themselves. In 1945, the International Monetary Fund (IMF) was established to promote international monetary cooperation, to facilitate the expansion and balanced growth of international trade, to assist in the elimination of foreign exchange restrictions that hamper such growth, and to shorten the duration and ease the disequilibrium in the international balance of payments among the members of the fund. Currently, at least 188 countries are members of the IMF.

Many nations have laws regulating foreign investment. Restrictions on the establishment of foreign investment tend to limit the amount of equity and the amount of control allowed to foreign investors. They may also restrict the way in which the investment is created, such as limiting or prohibiting investment by acquiring an existing locally owned business. At least 159 nations have signed the Convention on the Settlement of Investment Disputes Between States and Nationals of Other States. The Convention created the International Centre for the Settlement of Investment Disputes, which offers conciliation and arbitration for investment disputes between governments and foreign investors to promote increased flows of international investment.

Nations also have cooperated in forming international and regional banks to facilitate the flow of capital and trade. Such banks include the International Bank for Reconstruction and Development (part of the World Bank), the African Development Bank, the Asian Development Bank, the European Investment Bank, and the Inter-American Development Bank.

International Contracts [46-3d]

International contracts

involve additional issues beyond those in domestic contracts, such as differences in language, legal systems, and currency

The legal issues inherent in domestic commercial contracts also arise in **international contracts**. Moreover, additional issues, such as differences in language, customs, legal systems, and currency, are peculiar to international contracts. Such a contract should specify its official language and include definitions for all the significant legal terms used in it. In addition, it should specify the acceptable currency (or currencies) and payment method. The contract should include a choice of law clause designating which law will govern any breach or dispute regarding the contract, and a choice of forum clause designating whether the parties will resolve disputes through

Practical Advice

When you enter into international contracts, be sure that your contracts include provisions for payment, including acceptable currencies, choice of law, choice of forum, and *force majeure*.

CISG

United Nations Convention on Contracts for the International Sales of Goods governs all contracts for international sales of goods between parties located in different nations that have ratified the CISG

Letter of credit

bank's promise to pay the seller, provided certain conditions are met; used to manage the payment risks in international trade

one nation's court system or through third-party arbitration. (The United Nations Committee on International Trade Law and the International Chamber of Commerce have promulgated arbitration rules that have won broad international acceptance.) Finally, the contract should include a *force majeure* (unavoidable superior force) clause apportioning the parties' liabilities and responsibilities in the event of an unforeseeable occurrence, such as a typhoon, tornado, flood, earthquake, war, or nuclear disaster.

The United Nations Commission on International Trade Law (UNCITRAL) was established by the U.N. General Assembly to further the progressive harmonization and unification of the law of international trade. The Commission is composed of sixty member states elected by the General Assembly and is structured to be representative of the world's various geographic regions and its principal economic and legal systems. One of its primary functions is to develop conventions, model laws, and rules that are acceptable worldwide. One example is the United Nations Convention on Contracts for the International Sales of Goods (CISG) (discussed in the following section and in Chapters 19–23) and the arbitration rules mentioned earlier. Another is the UNCITRAL Model Law on Electronic Commerce, adopted in 1996, which is intended to facilitate the use of modern means of communications and storage of information. Legislation based on it has been adopted in more than sixty nations and, in the United States, it has influenced the Uniform Electronic Transactions Act, promulgated by the Uniform Law Commission (ULC) in 1999 and adopted by nearly all of the states. In 2001, the UNCITRAL Model Law on Electronic Signatures was adopted to bring additional legal certainty regarding the use of electronic signatures. Following a technology-neutral approach, the Act establishes a presumption that electronic signatures, which meet certain criteria of technical reliability, shall be treated as equivalent to handwritten signatures. Legislation based on it has been adopted in at least twenty-nine nations.

CISG The **CISG**, which has been ratified by the United States and at least seventy-nine other countries, governs all contracts for the international sales of goods between parties located in different nations that have ratified the CISG. Because treaties are federal law, the CISG supersedes the Uniform Commercial Code in any situation to which either could apply. The CISG includes provisions dealing with interpretation, trade usage, contract formation, obligations, and remedies of sellers and buyers, and risk of loss. Parties to an international sales contract may, however, expressly exclude CISG governance from their contract. The CISG specifically excludes sales of (1) goods bought for personal, family, or household use; (2) ships or aircraft; and (3) electricity. In addition, it does not apply to contracts in which the primary obligation of the party furnishing the goods consists of supplying labor or services. The CISG is discussed in Chapters 19 through 23.

Letters of Credit International trade involves a number of risks not usually encountered in domestic trade, most notably government controls over the export or import of goods and currency. The most effective means of managing these risks—as well as the ordinary trade risks of nonperformance by seller and buyer—is the irrevocable documentary letter of credit. Most international letters of credit are governed by the Uniform Customs and Practices for Documentary Credits, a document drafted by commercial law experts from many countries and adopted by the International Chamber of Commerce. A **letter of credit** is a promise by a buyer's bank to pay the seller, provided certain conditions are met. The letter of credit transaction involves three or four different parties and three underlying contracts. To illustrate: a U.S. business wishes to sell computers to a Belgian company. The U.S. and Belgian firms enter into a sales agreement that includes details such as the number of computers, the features they will have, and the date they will be shipped. The buyer then enters into a second contract with a local bank, called an *issuer*, committing the bank to pay the agreed price upon receiving specified documents. These documents normally include a bill of lading (proving that the seller has delivered the goods for shipment), a commercial invoice listing the purchase terms, proof of insurance, and a customs certificate indicating that customs officials have cleared the goods for export. The buyer's bank's commitment to pay is the irrevocable letter of credit. Typically, a *correspondent* or *paying bank* located in the seller's country makes payment to the seller. Here, the Belgian issuing bank arranges to pay the U.S. correspondent bank the agreed sum of money in exchange for the

BUSINESS LAW **IN ACTION**

Over the years Eastern Ship and Shore has sold marine products to a number of customers in South America. Now that it has a website featuring its wares, though, Eastern is beginning to receive more and more orders from overseas. So far, foreign customers have paid for smaller shipments in advance. However, Eastern needs a strategy for facilitating larger sales, particularly in those countries in which access to U.S. dollars is limited. A number of potential customers have requested credit terms, but Eastern is unprepared to take the risk associated with credit sales abroad. Likewise, Eastern has been hesitant to accept payment in foreign currencies. Consequently it

has had to forego some fairly profitable international transactions.

One solution might be the use of documentary letters of credit, also simply known as L/Cs or commercial credits. This financing device inserts a domestic and a foreign bank into the collection process. The exchange of money in the foreign country for a bill of lading and other documents evidencing the actual shipment of the contract goods is not a simultaneous exchange of money for merchandise. Nonetheless, it can give the foreign buyer paying a local bank for the goods in advance of their arrival some comfort that they are in the hands of a reputable transport company

and on their way. Similarly Eastern can be confident its invoice will be paid by a U.S. bank soon after shipment.

In addition to providing some assurance of the other party's contract performance, the letter of credit solves both of the problems that have foiled Eastern's unsuccessful foreign sales. The letter of credit permits a buyer to pay for the goods in local currency. Or if the buyer needs credit, it can borrow the funds to buy the goods from its local bank as part of the letter of credit transaction. In either instance the foreign bank will transfer funds to a U.S. bank, and Eastern will get paid in dollars shortly after shipment of the merchandise.

documents. The issuer then sends the U.S. computer firm the letter of credit. When the U.S. firm obtains all the necessary documents, it presents them to the U.S. correspondent bank, which verifies the documents, pays the computer company in U.S. dollars, and sends the documents to the Belgian issuing bank. Upon receiving the required documents, the issuing bank pays the correspondent bank and then presents the documents to the buyer. In our example, the Belgian buyer pays the issuing bank in Belgian francs for the letter of credit when the buyer receives the specified documents from the bank.

Antitrust Laws [46-3e]

Antitrust laws of the United States apply to unfair methods of competition that have a direct, substantial, and reasonably foreseeable effect on the domestic, import, or export commerce of the United States

Section 1 of the Sherman Act provides that U.S. **antitrust laws** shall have a broad, extraterritorial reach. As discussed in Chapter 42, contracts, combinations, or conspiracies that restrain trade with foreign nations, as well as among the domestic states, are deemed illegal. Therefore, agreements among competitors to increase the cost of imports, as well as arrangements to exclude imports from U.S. domestic markets in exchange for agreements not to compete in other countries, clearly violate U.S. antitrust laws. The antitrust provisions are also designed to protect U.S. exports when privately imposed restrictions seek to exclude U.S. competitors from foreign markets. Amendments to the Sherman Act and the Federal Trade Commission Act limit their application to unfair methods of competition that have a direct, substantial, and reasonably foreseeable effect on U.S. domestic commerce, U.S. import commerce, or U.S. export commerce. The U.S. Supreme Court has held that where price-fixing conduct significantly and adversely affects customers outside and inside the United States, but the foreign injury is separate from the domestic injury, the Sherman Act does not apply to a claim based solely on the foreign injury. *Hoffmann-La Roche Ltd v. Empagran S.A.*, 542 U.S. 155, 124 S.Ct. 2359, 159 L.Ed.2d 226 (2004).

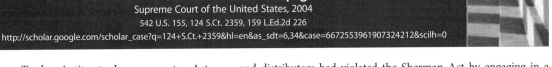

F. Hoffmann-La Roche Ltd v. Empagran S.A.
Supreme Court of the United States, 2004
542 U.S. 155, 124 S.Ct. 2359, 159 L.Ed.2d 226
http://scholar.google.com/scholar_case?q=124+S.Ct.+2359&hl=en&as_sdt=6,34&case=6672553961907324212&scilh=0

FACTS The Foreign Trade Antitrust Improvements Act (FTAIA) provides that the Sherman Act "shall not apply to conduct involving trade or commerce … with foreign nations," but creates exceptions for conduct that significantly harms imports, domestic commerce, or U.S. exporters. In this case, vitamin purchasers filed a class action alleging that vitamin manufacturers

and distributors had violated the Sherman Act by engaging in a price-fixing conspiracy thereby raising vitamin prices in the United States and foreign countries. The manufacturers and distributors moved to dismiss the suit as to some foreign-purchasers located in Ukraine, Australia, Ecuador, and Panama, each of which allegedly bought vitamins for delivery outside the United

States. The district court applied the FTAIA and dismissed the foreign purchasers' claims.

On appeal, the U.S. Court of Appeals for the District of Columbia Circuit reversed, holding that the FTAIA's general exclusionary rule applied to the case but the FTAIA's domestic-injury exception also applied. The U.S. Supreme court granted *certiorari*.

DECISION The judgment of the Court of Appeals is vacated, and the case is remanded.

OPINION The issue concerns (1) significant foreign anticompetitive conduct with (2) an adverse domestic effect and (3) an independent foreign effect giving rise to the claim. The FTAIA exception does not apply (and thus the Sherman Act does not apply) in this case for two reasons. First, the court ordinarily construes ambiguous statutes to avoid unreasonable interference with the sovereign authority of other nations. This rule of construction reflects principles of customary international law and cautions courts to assume that legislators take account of the legitimate sovereign interests of other nations when they write U.S. laws.

U.S. antitrust laws, when applied to foreign conduct, can interfere with a foreign nation's ability independently to regulate its own commercial affairs. However, our courts have long held that application of our antitrust laws to foreign anticompetitive conduct is nonetheless reasonable, and hence consistent with principles of prescriptive comity, insofar as they reflect a legislative effort to redress *domestic* antitrust injury that foreign anticompetitive conduct has caused.

On the other hand, it is not reasonable to apply those laws to foreign conduct insofar as that conduct causes independent foreign harm and that foreign harm alone gives rise to the plaintiff's claim. Principles of comity provide Congress greater leeway when it seeks to control through legislation the actions of *U.S.* companies, and some of the anticompetitive price-fixing conduct alleged here took place in *the United States*. But the higher foreign prices of which the foreign plaintiffs here complain are not the consequence of any domestic anticompetitive conduct that Congress sought to forbid. Rather Congress sought to *release* domestic (and foreign) anticompetitive conduct from Sherman Act constraints when that conduct causes foreign harm. Congress, of course, did make an exception in cases in which that conduct also causes domestic harm.

Second, the FTAIA's language and history suggest that Congress designed the FTAIA to clarify, perhaps to limit, but not *to expand* in any significant way, the Sherman Act's scope as applied to foreign commerce. There is no significant indication that at the time Congress wrote this statute courts would have thought the Sherman Act applicable in these circumstances.

INTERPRETATION Where price-fixing conduct significantly and adversely affects customers outside and inside the United States, but the foreign injury is separate from the domestic injury, the Sherman Act does not apply to a claim based solely on the foreign injury.

ETHICAL QUESTION Did the defendants act unethically? Explain.

CRITICAL THINKING QUESTION Do you agree with the Court's decision? Explain.

Securities regulation foreign issuers who issue securities in the United States, or whose securities are sold in the secondary market in the United States, must register them unless an exemption is available

Securities Regulation [46-3f]

The securities markets have become increasingly internationalized, thereby raising questions regarding which country's law governs a particular transaction in securities. (U.S. federal securities laws are discussed in Chapter 39.) Foreign issuers who issue securities in the United States must register them under the 1933 Act unless an exemption is available. Foreign issuers whose securities are sold in the secondary market in the United States must register under the 1934 Act unless the issuer is exempt. Some nonexempt foreign issuers may avoid registration under the 1934 Act by providing the Securities and Exchange Commission (SEC) with copies of all information material to investors that they have made public in their home country. Regulation S provides a safe harbor from the 1933 Act registration requirements for offshore sales of equity securities of U.S. issuers.

The antifraud provisions of the U.S. securities laws apply to securities sold by the use of any means or instrumentality of interstate commerce. In determining the extraterritorial application of these provisions, the lower courts had generally found jurisdiction in cases in which there was either *conduct* or *effects* in the United States relating to a violation of the federal securities laws. In the 2010 case of *Morrison v. National Australia Bank Ltd.* (see the following case), the U.S. Supreme Court rejected these cases, holding that Section 10(b) and Rule 10b-5 of the Securities Exchange Act of 1934 do not apply extraterritorially but *only* reach the use of a manipulative or deceptive device or contrivance in connection with (1) the purchase or sale of a security listed on a U.S. stock exchange or (2) the purchase or sale of any other security in the United States. The Supreme Court held that Section 10(b) and Rule 10b-5 do not provide a cause of action to foreign plaintiffs suing foreign or U.S. defendants for misconduct in connection with securities traded on foreign exchanges.

The Dodd-Frank Wall Street Reform and Consumer Protection Act of 2010 (Dodd-Frank Act), discussed in Chapter 39, extends the reach of the antifraud provisions of the 1933 and 1934 Acts with respect to actions brought by the U.S. Justice Department and the SEC. In such actions, jurisdiction would include "(1) conduct within the United States that constitutes significant steps in furtherance of the violation, even if the violation is committed by a foreign adviser and involves only foreign investors; or (2) conduct occurring outside the United States that has a foreseeable substantial effect within the United States." The Dodd-Frank Act also requires the SEC to study the extent to which private rights of action under the antifraud provisions of the 1934 Act should be governed by these new standards. On April 11, 2012, the SEC delivered to Congress its "Study on the Cross-Border Scope of the Private Right of Action Under Section 10(b) of the Securities Exchange Act of 1934," which provides several options but no specific recommendations. To date Congress has not taken any action. Thus the Dodd-Frank Act appears to restore to the SEC and the Department of Justice—but not private litigants—the right to bring proceedings to enforce the antifraud provisions of the U.S. securities laws in cases with an extraterritorial component.

The International Organization of Securities Commissions has a membership of more than two hundred national securities agencies and exchanges, which regulate more than 95 percent of the world's securities markets. The member agencies have agreed (1) to cooperate to promote high standards of regulation to maintain just, efficient, and sound markets; (2) to exchange information to promote the development of domestic markets; (3) to work together to establish standards and effective surveillance of international securities transactions; and (4) to provide support to promote the integrity of the markets by a rigorous application of the standards and by effective enforcement against offenses.

Morrison v. National Australia Bank Ltd.
Supreme Court of the United States, 2010
561 U.S. 247, 130 S.Ct. 2869, 177 L.Ed.2d 535
http://scholar.google.com/scholar_case?case=3519216444119666685&hl=en&as_sdt=2&as_vis=1&oi=scholarr

FACTS National Australia Bank Limited was the largest bank in Australia. Its ordinary shares (common stock) are not traded on any exchange in the United States. National's American Depositary Receipts (ADRs), which represent the right to receive a specified number of National's ordinary shares, however, are listed on the New York Stock Exchange. In February 1998, National bought HomeSide Lending, Inc., a mortgage servicing company headquartered in Florida. HomeSide's business was to receive fees for servicing mortgages. The rights to receive those fees, so-called mortgage-servicing rights, can provide a valuable income stream. How valuable each of the rights is depends, in part, on the likelihood that the mortgage to which it applies will be fully repaid before it is due, terminating the need for servicing. HomeSide calculated the present value of its mortgage-servicing rights by using valuation models designed to take this likelihood into account. It recorded the value of its assets, and the numbers appeared in National's financial statements. From 1998 until 2001, National's annual reports and other public documents touted the success of HomeSide's business, and senior executives of National and HomeSide did the same in public statements. But on July 5, 2001, National announced that it was writing down the value of Home-Side's assets by $450 million; and then again on September 3, by an additional $1.75 billion. The prices of both ordinary shares and ADRs declined.

Russell Leslie Owen and Brian and Geraldine Silverlock, all Australians, purchased National's ordinary shares in 2000 and 2001, before the write-downs. They sued National, HomeSide, National's CEO, and three HomeSide executives in the United States District Court for alleged violations of Sections 10(b) and 20(a) of the Securities and Exchange Act of 1934. According to the complaint, HomeSide and three of its executive officers had manipulated HomeSide's financial models to make the rates of early repayment unrealistically low in order to cause the mortgage-servicing rights to appear more valuable than they really were. The complaint also alleges that National and its CEO were aware of this deception by July 2000, but did nothing about it. Defendants moved to dismiss for lack of subject-matter jurisdiction and for failure to state a claim on which relief can be granted. The District Court granted the motion to dismiss for lack of subject matter jurisdiction. The Court of Appeals for the Second Circuit affirmed on similar grounds. The U.S. Supreme Court granted *certiorari*.

DECISION The Court of Appeal's dismissal of the complaint is affirmed on other grounds.

OPINION The Second Circuit erred in considering the extraterritorial reach of Section 10(b) to raise a question of subject-matter jurisdiction and affirming the District Court's dismissal. The District Court had subject-matter jurisdiction to adjudicate the question whether Section 10(b) applies to National's conduct. Since nothing in the lower courts' analysis turned on the mistake, the Supreme Court addressed whether the plaintiffs' allegations state a claim on which relief can be granted.

It is a "longstanding principle of American law 'that legislation of Congress, unless a contrary intent appears, is meant to apply only within the territorial jurisdiction of the United States.'" When a statute gives no clear indication of an extraterritorial application, it has none.

Because Rule 10b-5, the regulation under which petitioners have brought suit, was promulgated under Section 10(b), it does not extend beyond conduct encompassed by Section 10(b)'s prohibition. Therefore, if Section 10(b) is not extraterritorial, neither is Rule 10b-5. On its face, Section 10(b) contains nothing to suggest it applies abroad. Contrary to the argument of the plaintiffs, a general reference to foreign commerce in the definition of "interstate commerce" does not defeat the presumption against extraterritoriality. In short, there is no affirmative indication in the Exchange Act that Section 10(b) applies extraterritorially, and therefore it does not.

Plaintiffs contend that they seek no more than domestic application anyway, since Florida is where HomeSide and its senior executives engaged in the deceptive conduct of manipulating HomeSide's financial models and where the executives made misleading public statements there. The focus of the Exchange Act is not upon the place where the deception originated, but upon purchases and sales of securities in the United States. Section 10(b) does not punish deceptive conduct, but only deceptive conduct "in connection with the purchase or sale of any security registered on a national securities exchange or any security not so registered." And it is only transactions in securities listed on domestic exchanges, and domestic transactions in other securities, to which Section 10(b) applies. Thus Section 10(b) reaches the use of a manipulative or deceptive device or contrivance only in connec-

tion with the purchase or sale of a security listed on a U.S. stock exchange, and the purchase or sale of any other security in the United States. This case involves no securities listed on a domestic exchange, and all aspects of the purchases complained of by these petitioners occurred outside the United States.

INTERPRETATION Section 10(b) of the Securities Exchange Act of 1934 reaches the use of a manipulative or deceptive device or contrivance only in connection with the purchase or sale of a security listed on a U.S. stock exchange, and the purchase or sale of any other security in the United States; thus it does not provide a cause of action to foreign plaintiffs suing foreign and U.S. defendants for misconduct in connection with securities traded on foreign exchanges.

CRITICAL THINKING QUESTION What effect does the Supreme Court's decision have on the United States' interest in remedying frauds that are carried out in the United States?

Protection of intellectual property
the owner of an intellectual property right must comply with each country's requirements to obtain from that country whatever protection is available

Protection of Intellectual Property [46-3g]

The U.S. laws protecting intellectual property (discussed in Chapter 40) do not apply to transactions in other countries. Generally, the owner of an intellectual property right must comply with each country's requirements to obtain from that country whatever protection is available. The requirements vary substantially from country to country, as does the degree of protection. The United States belongs to multinational treaties that try to coordinate the application of member nations' intellectual property laws.

1. *Patents.* The principal treaties for patent protection are the Paris Convention for the Protection of Industrial Property (at least 175 nations), the Patent Cooperation Treaty (at least 148 nations), and the Patent Law Treaty (PLT) of 2000, which seeks to harmonize and streamline formal procedures in national and regional patent applications and patents. The PLT is in force in at least thirty-six nations.

2. *Trademarks.* International treaties protecting trademarks are the Paris Convention, the Trademark Law Treaty, the Arrangement of Nice Concerning the International Classification of Goods and Services (at least eighty-four nations), the Madrid Protocol of 1989 (at least ninety-one nations), and the 1973 Vienna Trademark Agreement (at least thirty-two nations). In 2002 Congress enacted legislation implementing the Madrid Protocol, a procedural agreement allowing U.S. trademark owners to file for registration in any number of more than ninety member countries by filing a single application in English and paying a single fee. The Trademark Law Treaty of 1994 seeks to streamline national and regional trademark registration procedures. It has been adopted by at least fifty-three nations.

3. *Copyrights.* The principal treaties covering copyrights are the 1952 Universal Copyright Convention, revised in 1971, and the Berne Convention for the Protection of Literary and Artistic Works of 1886 (at least 167 nations). The World Intellectual Property Organization (WIPO) Copyright Treaty of 1996 is a special agreement under the Berne Convention, signed by at least ninety-two nations, which extended copyright protection to computer programs and compilations of data and granted new rights corresponding to new forms for works in the digital environment.

The Trade-Related Aspects of Intellectual Property Rights (TRIPS) portion of the WTO Agreement states how the range of intellectual property should be protected when trade is involved. The WIPO, one of the specialized agencies of the United Nations, attempts to promote—through cooperation among nations—the protection of intellectual property throughout the world. WIPO administers twenty-six international treaties dealing with intellectual property protection and includes more than 185 nations as member states.

Foreign Corrupt Practices Act [46-3h]

Foreign Corrupt Practices Act (FCPA) prohibits all U.S. companies and certain foreign issuers of securities from bribing foreign government or political officials to assist in obtaining or retaining business

In 1977, Congress enacted the **Foreign Corrupt Practices Act (FCPA)** prohibiting any U.S. person, and certain foreign issuers of securities, from bribing foreign government or political officials to assist in obtaining or retaining business. Since 1998, the antibribery provisions also apply to foreign firms and persons who take any act in furtherance of such a corrupt payment while in the United States. The FCPA makes it unlawful for any U.S. person, and certain foreign issuers of securities, or any of its officers, directors, employees, or agents to offer or give anything of value directly or indirectly to any foreign official, political party, or political official for the purpose of (1) influencing any act or decision of that person or party in his or its official capacity, (2) inducing an act or omission in violation of his or its lawful duty, or (3) inducing such person or party to use his or its influence to affect a decision of a foreign government to assist the person in obtaining or retaining business. An offer or promise to make a prohibited payment is a violation even if the offer is not accepted or the promise is not performed. The 1988 amendments to the FCPA explicitly excluded routine government actions not involving the discretion of the official, such as obtaining permits or processing applications. This exclusion does *not* cover any decision by a foreign official whether, or on what terms, to award new business or to continue business with a particular party. The amendments also added an affirmative defense for payments that are lawful under the written laws or regulations of the foreign official's country.

Violations can result in fines of up to $2 million for corporations and other business entities; individuals may be fined a maximum of $100,000 or imprisoned up to five years, or both. Moreover, under the Alternative Fines Act, the actual fine may be up to twice the benefit that the person sought to obtain by making the corrupt payment. Fines imposed upon individuals may not be paid directly or indirectly by the corporation or other business entity on whose behalf the individuals acted. In addition, the courts may impose civil penalties of up to $16,000, as adjusted for inflation in March 2013.

Practical Advice

Take care to instruct your employees and agents not to bribe foreign officials, political parties, or political officials. Moreover, train them to distinguish between bribes, which are prohibited, and nondiscretionary facilitating payments, which are permitted.

In 1997 the United States signed the Organisation for Economic Co-operation and Development Convention on Combating Bribery of Foreign Public Officials in International Business Transactions (OECD Convention). The OECD Convention has been adopted by at least forty-one nations. In 1998 Congress enacted the International Anti-Bribery and Fair Competition Act of 1998 to conform the FCPA to the OECD Convention. The 1998 Act expands the FCPA to include (1) payments made to "secure any improper advantage" from foreign officials, (2) all foreign persons who commit an act in furtherance of a foreign bribe while in the United States, and (3) officials of public international organizations within the definition of a "foreign official." A public international organization is defined as either an organization designated by executive order pursuant to the International Organizations Immunities Act or any other international organization designated by executive order of the President.

Employment Discrimination [46-3i]

Title VII of the Civil Rights Act of 1964, the Americans with Disabilities Act, and the Age Discrimination in Employment Act, discussed in Chapter 41, apply to U.S. citizens employed abroad by U.S. employers or by foreign companies controlled by U.S. employers. Employers, however, are not required to comply with these employment discrimination laws if compliance would violate the law of the foreign country in which the workplace is located.

FORMS OF MULTINATIONAL ENTERPRISES [46-4]

Multinational enterprise (MNE) any business that engages in transactions involving the movement of goods, information, money, people, or services across national borders

The term **multinational enterprise (MNE)** refers to any business that engages in transactions involving the movement of goods, information, money, people, or services across national borders. Such an enterprise may conduct its business in any of several forms: through direct sales, foreign agents, distributorships, licensing, joint ventures, and wholly owned subsidiaries. A number of considerations determine which form of business organization would be best to use in conducting international transactions. These factors include financing, tax consequences, legal restrictions imposed by the host country, and the degree to which the MNE wishes to control the business.

Direct Export Sales [46-4a]

Under a **direct export sale**, the seller contracts directly with the buyer in the other country. This is the simplest and least involved MNE.

Direct export sales
seller contracts directly with the buyer in the other country

Foreign Agents [46-4b]

An agency relationship often is used by MNEs seeking limited involvement in an international market. The principal firm will appoint a local agent, who may be empowered to enter into contracts in the agent's country on the principal's behalf or who may be authorized only to solicit and take orders. The agent generally does not take title to the merchandise.

Foreign agents
a local agent in the host country is used to provide limited involvement for a multinational enterprise

Distributorships [46-4c]

A commonly used form of MNE is the **distributorship**, in which a producer of goods appoints a foreign distributor. Unlike an agent, a distributor takes title to the merchandise it receives; in other words, the distributor, not the producer, bears many of the risks connected with commercial sales. The distributorship format, however, is especially susceptible to antitrust violations. Therefore, both the producer and the distributor must take special care to ensure that the arrangement does not violate the antitrust laws of their respective governments.

Distributorship
multinational enterprise sells to a foreign distributor who takes title to the merchandise

Licensing [46-4d]

An MNE wishing to exploit an intellectual property right—such as a patent, trademark, trade secret, or an unpatented but innovative production technology—may choose to sell a foreign company the right to use such property, rather than enter the foreign market itself. The sale of such rights, called **licensing**, is one of the major means by which technology and information are transferred among nations. Normally, the foreign firm will pay royalties in exchange for the information, technology, or patent. Franchising is a form of licensing in which the owner of intellectual property grants permission to a foreign business under carefully specified conditions.

Licensing
multinational enterprise sells a foreign company the right to use technology or information

Joint Ventures [46-4e]

In a **joint venture**, two or more independent businesses from different countries agree to coordinate their efforts to achieve a common result. The sharing of profits and liabilities, as well as the delegation of responsibilities, is fixed by contract. One advantage of the joint venture is that each company can be responsible for that which it does best. To promote local ownership of investments, several developing nations and regional groups have enacted legislation that prohibits foreign businesses from owning more than 49 percent of any business enterprise in those countries. In addition, each country may require that its citizens comprise the majority of an enterprise's management.

Joint ventures
two independent businesses from different countries share profits, liabilities, and duties

Wholly Owned Subsidiaries [46-4f]

By far, **wholly owned subsidiaries** require the most active participation by a parent firm. Nevertheless, creating a foreign wholly owned subsidiary corporation can offer a firm numerous advantages, most significantly, the ability to retain authority and control over all phases of operation. This is especially attractive to businesses wishing to safeguard their technology.

Wholly owned subsidiary
enables a multinational enterprise to retain control and authority over all phases of operation

 Bulova Watch Company, Inc. v. K. Hattori & Co.
U.S. District Court, Eastern District of New York, 1981
508 F.Supp. 1322
http://scholar.google.com/scholar_case?case=3577482263610830702&q=508+F.Supp.+1322&hl=en&as_sdt=2,34

FACTS The plaintiff, Bulova Watch Company, was a New York corporation with its principal place of business in Flushing, New York. As both a manufacturer and seller of watches, Bulova claimed to have the largest direct sales marketing system in the watch business. The defendant, K. Hattori & Company (Hattori), incorporated under the laws of Japan with its principal office in

Tokyo, was the parent company of the wholly owned subsidiary Seiko Corporation of America (SCA), a New York corporation. SCA, in turn, owned all the stock of three "subsubsidiaries"—namely, Seiko Time Corp., Pulsar Time, and SPD Precision Inc.—all of which were incorporated under New York law. While the United States was Hattori's largest market, accounting for more than $500 million in sales, Hattori distributed its products in more than one hundred countries, using wholly owned subsidiaries in ten of those countries. For the remaining countries, Hattori employed independent distributors who conducted their own marketing and advertising activities and maintained their own repair centers. Desiring to expand the markets of its U.S.-based wholly owned subsidiaries, Hattori masterminded certain advertising campaigns and began recruiting and hiring several high-level direct sales marketing personnel from the Bulova company. Bulova filed this action against Hattori, alleging unfair competition, disparagement, and conspiracy to raid the plaintiff's marketing personnel. The defendant moved to dismiss the case for lack of jurisdiction, claiming that the Japanese parent company, Hattori, was an entity distinct and separate from its U.S. subsidiaries and therefore lacked sufficient control over the subsidiaries to satisfy jurisdictional requirements.

DECISION Motion to dismiss denied.

OPINION Recognizing that the means by which a multinational corporation exercises control over its widely dispersed components may vary, the court emphasized that the degree and nature of control may depend upon such factors as the nationality of the corporate parent, the type and range of products being sold, and the age and stage of corporate evolution attained by those connected to the parent corporation. The choice among the various modes of entering a market (such as licensing arrangement, joint venture, minority-, majority-, or wholly owned subsidiary) has significant implications for the control exercised by the parent. A wholly owned, marketing-based subsidiary is used where retaining unambiguous control of foreign operations is critical to the firm's strategy. Furthermore, enterprises with narrow product lines, such as Hattori with its exclusive manufacture of timepieces, tend to organize their operations on a highly integrated basis, linking production and marketing into tight strategic patterns. Again, the use of the wholly owned subsidiary form here reflects the desire for unambiguous control over sales and marketing to ensure uniform quality and promotion of the product sold. Finally, although Hattori's various subsidiaries may likely evolve into more autonomous units, characteristic of the later stages of multinational enterprise development, Hattori is currently a highly effective export manufacturer, more akin to the hub at the center of a wheel, with its various foreign subsidiaries and distributors as spokes. Accordingly, Hattori enjoys sufficient control over the activities of its wholly owned U.S. subsidiaries to support jurisdiction of U.S. courts in the action filed by the Bulova Watch Company.

INTERPRETATION Wholly owned subsidiaries are established by a parent company seeking to retain unambiguous control over the subsidiary's operation. Such control over a U.S. subsidiary may be sufficient to support jurisdiction by the U.S. courts over the parent.

ETHICAL QUESTION Was the court's decision fair to all of the parties? Explain.

CRITICAL THINKING QUESTION What factors should be relevant in deciding whether a company exercises sufficient control over a U.S. subsidiary to support U.S. jurisdiction over the parent? Explain.

ETHICAL DILEMMA

Who May Seek Economic Shelter Under U.S. Trade Law?

Facts Stanlon, Inc., a U.S. manufacturer of educational computer software for children, has grown into a major employer in New England. Over the past eight years, Stanlon has developed programs on reading readiness and basic phonics aimed at preschool children. This innovative software, which recognizes the cultural diversity in the United States, sells for an average price of $150. Stanlon sells its products primarily through several subsidiary companies that retail children's educational toys. The retailers accept cash, checks, and major credit cards. They have no arrangements for installment sales. Over the past eight years, Stanlon, Inc., has enjoyed an excellent sales record.

Two years ago, Soeki, Ltd., a Japanese corporation, entered the market. Soeki sells substantially similar products for $75.00 per software package. In addition, the retail stores through which Soeki sells offer liberal credit terms, including installment sales. Soeki's stores are located in neighborhoods of various social and economic classes, and several are located near stores operated by Stanlon, whose retailers are located primarily in affluent neighborhoods.

Since Soeki entered the market, Stanlon's sales have plummeted. Now, having begun to lay off substantial numbers of workers, Stanlon has instituted a lawsuit against Soeki, Ltd., alleging that Soeki is selling its software at unprofitable prices in order to drive Stanlon from the market.

Social, Policy, and Ethical Considerations

1. Should a foreign corporation be free to sell goods at the lowest price possible? What is the social policy behind laws that prohibit foreign companies from selling below cost? What cost should be considered fair?

2. Is it in U.S. consumers' interest to encourage all competition from foreign enterprises?

3. How would your answers change if a foreign drug company were selling a medically valuable drug at a price significantly below that charged by its U.S. competitors?

CHAPTER SUMMARY

The International Environment	**International Law** includes law that deals with the conduct and relations of nation-states and international organizations as well as some of their relations with persons; such law is enforceable by the courts of a nation that has adopted the international law as domestic law
	International Court of Justice judicial branch of the United Nations having voluntary jurisdiction over nations
	Regional Trade Communities international organizations, conferences, and treaties focusing on business and trade regulations; the European Union (EU) is the most prominent of these
	International Treaties agreements between or among independent nations, such as the General Agreement on Tariffs and Trade (GATT), now called the World Trade Organization (WTO), and the United Nations Convention on the Law of the Sea (UNCLOS)
	• *World Trade Organization (WTO)* global international organization dealing with the rules of trade among nations
	• *United Nations Convention on the Law of the Sea (UNCLOS)* establishes a comprehensive set of rules governing all uses of the oceans and their resources
Jurisdiction over Actions of Foreign Governments	**Sovereign Immunity** foreign country's freedom from a host country's laws
	Act of State Doctrine rule that a court should not question the validity of actions taken by a foreign government in its own country
	Taking of Foreign Investment Property
	• *Expropriation* governmental taking of foreign-owned property for a public purpose and with payment of just compensation
	• *Confiscation* governmental taking of foreign-owned property without payment (or for a highly inadequate payment) or for a nonpublic purpose
Transacting Business Abroad	**Flow of Trade** controlled by trade barriers on imports and exports
	• *Tariff* duty or tax imposed on goods moving into or out of a country
	• *Nontariff Barriers* include quotas, bans, safety standards, and subsidies
	Flow of Labor controlled through passport, visa, and immigration regulations
	Flow of Capital the International Monetary Fund facilitates the expansion and balanced growth of international trade, assists in eliminating foreign exchange restrictions, and smooths the international balance of payments
	International Contracts involve additional issues beyond those in domestic contracts, such as differences in language, legal systems, and currency
	• *CISG* United Nations Convention on Contracts for the International Sales of Goods governs all contracts for international sales of goods between parties located in different nations that have ratified the CISG
	• *Letter of Credit* bank's promise to pay the seller, provided certain conditions are met; used to manage the payment risks in international trade
	Antitrust Laws of the United States apply to unfair methods of competition that have a direct, substantial, and reasonably foreseeable effect on the domestic, import, or export commerce of the United States
	Securities Regulation foreign issuers who issue securities in the United States, or whose securities are sold in the secondary market in the United States, must register them unless an exemption is available
	Protection of Intellectual Property the owner of an intellectual property right must comply with each country's requirements to obtain from that country whatever protection is available
	Foreign Corrupt Practices Act prohibits all U.S. persons and certain foreign issuers of securities from bribing foreign government or political officials to assist in obtaining or retaining business
	Employment Discrimination Title VII of the Civil Rights Act of 1964, the Americans with Disabilities Act, and the Age Discrimination in Employment Act apply to U.S. citizens employed in foreign countries by U.S.-owned or U.S.-controlled companies

Forms of Multinational Enterprises

Definition of Multinational Enterprise (MNE) any business that engages in transactions involving the movement of goods, information, money, people, or services across national borders

Forms of MNE the choice of form depends on a number of factors, including financing considerations, tax consequences, and degree of control

- *Direct Export Sales* seller contracts directly with the buyer in the other country
- *Foreign Agents* a local agent in the host country is used to provide limited involvement for an MNE
- *Distributorship* MNE sells to a foreign distributor who takes title to the merchandise
- *Licensing* MNE sells a foreign company the right to use technology or information
- *Joint Ventures* two independent businesses from different countries share profits, liabilities, and duties
- *Wholly Owned Subsidiary* enables an MNE to retain control and authority over all phases of operation

QUESTIONS

1. Three banks that are wholly owned by the Republic of Costa Rica had issued promissory notes, payable in U.S. dollars in New York City. The notes are now in default due solely to actions of the Costa Rican government, which had suspended all payments of external debt because of escalating economic problems. Efforts by Costa Rica to curb foreign debt payment difficulties conflicted with U.S. policy for debt resolution procedures as conducted under the auspices of the International Monetary Fund. A syndicate of U.S. banks brought suit to recover on the promissory notes. The three Costa Rican banks assert the act of state doctrine as a defense. Should the doctrine apply? Explain.

2. Six U.S. manufacturers of broad-spectrum antibiotics derived a large percentage of their sales from overseas markets, including India, Iran, the Philippines, Spain, the Republic of Korea, Germany, Colombia, and Kuwait. The manufacturers agreed to a common plan of marketing, whereby territories were divided and prices for products were set. The plan members also agreed not to grant foreign producers licenses to the manufacturing technology of any of their "big money" drugs. May the above foreign countries recover treble damages for violation of the U.S. antitrust laws? Why?

3. After reading attractive brochures advertising a package tour of the Dominican Republic, a U.S. family decided to purchase tickets for the family vacation plan. The tour was a product of four different business entities, two domestic (U.S.) and two foreign. Sheraton Hotels & Inns, World Corporation, was to provide food and lodging; Dominicana Airlines, wholly owned by the government of the Dominican Republic, which routinely flew into Miami International Airport and sold tickets within the United States, was to provide roundtrip air transportation and "tourist cards" necessary for entry into the Dominican Republic; and two U.S. firms organized and sold the tour. Problems for the family began when their Dominicana flight landed in the Dominican Republic, and immigration officials denied them entry. Forced to leave, the family was shuttled first to Puerto Rico and then to Haiti, where they had to secure their own passage back to the United States at additional expense. The family brings suit for battery, false imprisonment, breach of warranty, and breach of contract against all four different business entities. The Dominicana Airlines asserts the act of state doctrine as a defense. Explain whether this defense applies in this situation.

4. A privately owned business in a developing country determines that current computer technology could solve many of the problems faced by its country's private and public sectors. This business, however, lacks the capital resources necessary for research and development to acquire such computer technology, even if trained personnel were available. Furthermore, despite a sense of patriotism, the business concludes that its national government could not efficiently or effectively handle such a development project. What business forms are available to this business for acquiring sophisticated computer technology? What are the advantages and problems inherent in the various options?

5. King Faisal II of Iraq was killed on July 14, 1958, in the midst of a revolution in that country that led to the establishment of a republic subsequently recognized by the U.S. government. On July 19, 1958, the new republic issued a decree that all property of the former ruling dynasty, regardless of location, should be confiscated. Subsequently, the Republic of Iraq brought suit in the United States to obtain possession of money and stocks deposited in the deceased king's U.S. bank account in New York City. Explain whether Iraq will be able to collect the funds.

6. A business entity incorporated under the laws of one of the European Union (EU) member nations contracts with the government of a developing nation to form a joint venture for the mining and refining of a scarce raw material used by several industrial nations in the manufacture of highly sensitive weapons systems. The contract calls for the EU-based corporation to invest money and technology that will be used to build permanent refinery plants that will eventually revert to the developing nation. The developing nation also reserves the right to set quotas on sales of this scarce resource and to choose the destination of exports. Due to political conflicts, the developing nation refuses to allow any exports of the scarce material to the United States. This causes a sharp price increase in exports to the United States by other suppliers. The United States asserts antitrust violations against the EU-based corporation for the effects produced within the United States. Should the United States succeed? Explain.

CASE PROBLEMS

7. A Panamanian corporation lends money to a Turkish enterprise, which issues a promissory note. The loan contract specifies that payment on the interest and principal shall be made to the Chemical Bank of New York City, where both parties maintain accounts. The loan contract contains no choice of law designation, but the Panamanian and Turkish companies have referred to the Chemical Bank in New York as their "legal address." As a result of a contractual performance dispute, the Turkish company suspends payments on the loan. The Panamanian corporation then brings suit in the United States to recover the balance of the payments due. What possible options for choice of law apply?

8. New England Petroleum Corporation (NEPCO), a New York corporation, was in the business of selling fuel oil in the United States. PETCO, a refinery incorporated in the Bahamas, was a wholly owned subsidiary of NEPCO. In 1968, PETCO entered into a long-term contract to purchase crude oil from Chevron Oil Trading (COT), which held 50 percent of an oil concession in Libya. In 1973, Libya nationalized COT and several other foreign-owned oil concessions, thereby forcing COT to terminate its contract with PETCO. To secure needed oil supplies, PETCO entered into a new contract with National Oil Corporation (NOC), which was wholly owned by the Libyan government. This contract was at a substantially higher price than the original contract with COT. The following month, Libya declared an oil embargo on exports to the United States, the Netherlands, and the Bahamas. Accordingly, NOC canceled its contracts with PETCO. After oil prices rose dramatically, NOC accepted bids for new contracts to replace the ones inactivated by the embargo. NEPCO brought suit in a U.S. district court against the Libyan government and NOC, alleging breach of contract. Does the district court have jurisdiction? Explain.

9. Nigeria, experiencing an economic boom due to exports of high-grade oil, embarked on an infrastructure development plan. Accordingly, Nigeria entered into at least 109 contracts with 68 suppliers for the purchase of cement at a price of almost $1 billion. Among the contracting suppliers were four U.S. corporations, including Texas Trading & Milling Corporation. Nigeria misjudged the cement market (having anticipated only a 20 percent fulfillment rate) and was forced to repudiate most of the contracts. Texas Trading & Milling Corporation and three other U.S. companies brought suit, alleging anticipatory breach of contract. Nigeria claimed immunity under the Foreign Sovereign Immunities Act. Is Nigeria's claim correct? Explain.

10. Prior to 1918, a Russian corporation had deposited sums of money with August Belmont, a private banker doing business in New York City. In 1918, the Soviet government nationalized the corporation and appropriated all of the corporation's property and assets, including the deposit account with Belmont. The deposit became the property of the Soviet government until 1933, when it was released and assigned to the U.S. government as part of an international compact between the United States and the former Soviet Union. The purpose of this arrangement was to bring about a final settlement of the claims and counterclaims between the two countries. The United States brought an action to recover the deposit from Belmont. Belmont resists, arguing that the act of nationalization by the Soviets was a confiscation prohibited by the Fifth Amendment to the U.S. Constitution and was also a violation of New York public policy. Explain who will prevail.

11. A federal grand jury handed down an indictment naming as a defendant Nippon Paper Industries Co., Ltd. (NPI), a Japanese manufacturer of facsimile paper. The indictment alleged that five years earlier NPI and certain unnamed coconspirators held a number of meetings in Japan, which culminated in an agreement to fix the price of thermal fax paper throughout North America. NPI and other manufacturers who were involved in the scheme purportedly accomplished their objective by selling the paper in Japan to unaffiliated trading houses on the condition that the latter charge specified (inflated) prices for the paper when they resold it in North America. The trading houses then shipped and sold the paper to their U.S. subsidiaries, which in turn sold it to U.S. consumers at inflated prices. The indictment further states that, to ensure the success of the venture, NPI monitored the paper trail and confirmed that the prices charged to end users were those that it had arranged. The indictment maintains that these activities had a substantial adverse effect on commerce in the United States and unreasonably restrained trade in violation of the Sherman Act. Does the Sherman Act apply to this conduct? Explain.

TAKING SIDES

The Commercial Office of Spain hired Enrique Segni to develop a market for Spanish wines in the U.S. Midwest. The Commercial Office is an arm of the Spanish government. Seven months later, Segni was fired, whereupon he filed a lawsuit in a U.S. district court charging that the Commercial Office had breached the contract and seeking payment for the remainder of the contract term as damages. The Commercial Office moved for dismissal, claiming immunity from suit under the terms of the Foreign Sovereign Immunities Act (FSIA).

a. What are the arguments that Spain is immune from suit under the FSIA?

b. What are the arguments that Spain is *not* immune from suit under the FSIA?

c. Explain which party should prevail.

Introduction to Property, Property Insurance, Bailments, and Documents of Title

CHAPTER 47

Property and law are born together, and die together. Before laws were made there was no property; take away laws, and property ceases.

Jeremy Bentham (English jurist and philosopher, 1748–1832)

CHAPTER OUTCOMES

After reading and studying this chapter, you should be able to:

1. Define (a) tangible and intangible property, (b) real and personal property, and (c) a fixture.

2. Explain (a) the ways to transfer title to personal property; (b) the three elements of a valid gift; and (c) the difference in the law's treatment of abandoned property, lost property, and mislaid property.

3. With respect to property insurance, explain (a) the different types of fires, (b) co-insurance clauses, (c) other insurance clauses, (d) insurable interest, (e) valued and open policies, and (f) the defenses of misrepresentation, breach of warranty, concealment, waiver, and estoppel.

4. Define the essential elements of a bailment and describe the rights and duties of the bailor and bailee.

5. (a) Explain what a document of title is and (b) identify and describe the various types of documents of title.

A lthough many U.S. rules of property stem directly from English law, in the United States, property occupies a unique status because of the protection expressly granted it by the U.S. Constitution and by most state constitutions as well. The Fifth Amendment to the federal Constitution provides that "No person shall be … deprived of life, liberty, or property, without due process of law; nor shall private property be taken for public use, without just compensation." The Fourteenth Amendment contains a similar requirement: "No State shall … deprive any person of life, liberty, or property, without due process of law." Under the police power, however, this protection afforded to property owners is subject to regulation for the public good.

The first part of this chapter provides a general introduction to the law governing real and personal property. The second part of this chapter deals specifically with personal property; the third part covers property insurance. The fourth part of the chapter covers bailments and the last part of the chapter discusses documents of title.

INTRODUCTION TO PROPERTY AND PERSONAL PROPERTY

Property

interest that is legally protected

Property is a legally protected interest or group of interests. It is valuable only because our law provides that certain consequences follow from the ownership of it. The right to use property, to sell it, and to control to whom it shall pass on the death of the owner are all included within the term *property*. Thus, a person who speaks of "owning property" may have one of two separate ideas in mind: (1) the *physical thing itself*, as when a homeowner says, "I just bought a piece of property in Oakland," meaning complete ownership of a physically identifiable parcel of land, or (2) a *right or interest* in a physical object (e.g., with respect to land, a tenant under a lease has a property interest in the leased land, although he does not own the land).

KINDS OF PROPERTY [47-1]

Property may be classified as (1) tangible or intangible and (2) real or personal, but these classifications are not mutually exclusive.

Tangible and Intangible [47-1a]

Tangible property is a legally protected interest in *physical* objects such as a farm, a chair, and a household pet. **Intangible property**, in contrast, is a legally protected interest in things that do not exist in a physical form. For example, the rights represented by a stock certificate, a promissory note, and a deed granting Jones a right-of-way over Smith's land are intangible property. Each represents certain rights that defy reduction to physical possession but have a legal reality in that the courts will protect them.

The same item may be the object of both tangible and intangible property rights. Suppose Ann purchases a book published by Brown & Sons. On the first page is the statement "Copyright 2015 by Brown & Sons." Ann owns the volume she has purchased. She has the right to exclusive physical possession and use of that particular copy. It is tangible property of which she is the owner. Brown & Sons, however, has the exclusive right to publish copies of the book, a right granted the publisher by the copyright laws. The courts will protect this intangible property of Brown & Sons, as well as Ann's tangible property right to her particular volume.

Real and Personal [47-1b]

The most significant practical distinction between types of property is the classification into real and personal property. To define this distinction simply, land and all interests in it are **real property** (also called *realty*), and every other thing or interest identified as property is **personal property** (also called *chattel*). This easy description encompasses most property, with the exception of certain physical objects that are personal property under most circumstances but that may, because of their attachment to land or their use in connection with land, become a form of real property called *fixtures*.

Fixtures [47-1c]

As noted, a **fixture** is an article or piece of property that was formerly treated as personal property but has been attached in such a manner to land or a building that it is now designated as real property even though it retains its original identity. The intent of the parties to convert the property to real property from personal property is usually shown by the permanent manner of affixation or the adaptation of the affixed object to the property. For example, building materials are clearly personal property; however, when worked into a building as its construction progresses, such materials become real property, as buildings are a part of the land they occupy. Thus, clay in its natural state is, of course, real property; when made into bricks, it becomes personal property; and if the bricks are then built into the wall of a house, the "clay" once again becomes real property.

Although doing so may be difficult, determining whether various items are personal property or real property may be the only way to settle certain conflicting ownership claims. Unless otherwise provided by agreement, personal property remains the property of the person who placed it on the real estate. On the other hand, property that has been affixed so as to become a fixture (an actual part of the real estate) becomes the property of the real estate owner.

In determining whether personal property has become a fixture, the intention of the parties, as expressed in their agreement, will control the settlement of conflicting claims. In the absence

Tangible property
legally protected interest in physical objects

Intangible property
legally protected interest in nonphysical things

Real property
land and interests in land

Personal property
all property that is not real property

Fixture
personal property so firmly attached to real property that an interest in it arises under real property law

Practical Advice

Specify in your contracts for the sale of real estate which fixtures stay with the property and which fixtures may be removed by the seller.

CONCEPT REVIEW 47-1

Kinds of Property

	Personal	Real
Tangible	Goods	Land Buildings Fixtures
Intangible	Negotiable instruments Stock certificates Contract rights Copyrights Patents	Leases Easements Mortgages

of an agreement, the following factors are relevant in determining whether any particular item is a fixture:

1. the physical relationship of the item to the land or building;
2. the intention of the person who attached the item to the land or building;
3. the purpose the item serves in relation to the land or building and in relation to the person who brought it there; and
4. the interest of that person in the land or building at the time of the item's attachment.

Although physical attachment is significant, a more important test is whether the item can be removed without causing material injury to the land or building on the land. If it *cannot* be so removed, the item is generally held to have become part of the realty.

By comparison, the test of purpose or use applies only if the item (1) is affixed to the realty in some way but (2) can be removed without material injury to the realty. In such a situation, if the use or purpose of the item is peculiar to a particular owner or occupant of the premises, the courts will tend to let him remove the item when he leaves. Accordingly, in the law of land-lord and tenant, the tenant may remove *trade fixtures* (i.e., items used in connection with a trade but not intended to become part of the realty), provided that she can accomplish this without material injury to the realty. On the other hand, doors may be removed without injury to the structure; yet, because they are necessary to the ordinary use of the building and are not peculiar to the use of the occupant, they are considered to be fixtures and thus part of the real property.

Practical Advice

When placing on real property a permanently affixed structure, such as a billboard, provide in your agreement with the owner of the land terms specifying who owns the structure and whether you have the right to remove it upon termination of the lease.

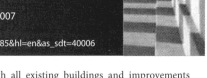

Freeman v. Barrs
Missouri Court of Appeals, Southern District, Division One, 2007
237 S.W.3d 285
http://scholar.google.com/scholar_case?case=15396954506601672605&q=237+S.W.3d+285&hl=en&as_sdt=40006

FACTS Plaintiff, Francis B. Freeman, Jr., brought this action to recover a cattle scale from defendant, Mary Ann Barrs. In 2005, Barrs purchased a tract of real estate consisting of approximately four thousand acres from plaintiff for $3.5 million. There were four residences on the property, two barns, and a covered pole barn with open sides. The pole barn housed the cattle scale that that plaintiff seeks to recover. The defendant claims that the cattle scale was a fixture that was part of the real estate and passed to the buyer in the sale.

Paragraph 2 of the form contract states—

INCLUSIONS, EXCLUSIONS AND EXCEPTIONS. The Property *includes* any and all rights, privileges and easements appurtenant

thereto, together with all existing buildings and improvements and all affixed equipment now located thereon, *if any*, including all mechanical, HVAC [heating, ventilation, and air condition-ing], electrical and plumbing systems, fixtures and equipment, fencing and other attached fixtures, trees, bushes, shrubs and plants, feed bunks in the fence, installed fences and gates, pro-pane tanks not under lease, water association rights and telephone rights where applicable, hog and cattle waterers in the fence or permanently installed, grain storage buildings and hog and cattle shades on permanent foundations, auger and conveyor systems. All grain, crops, livestock, hay, silage, and non-affixed personal property on the real estate are reserved by Seller or Seller's tenant.

The plaintiff purchased the cattle scale in June 2001 for $11,000. The scale was sold as a portable model. Plaintiff placed the scale in the pole-type barn on a concrete pad poured for the scale, then poured concrete ramps which would allow cattle to enter and exit the scale. Plaintiff further welded an iron fence into place to help funnel the cattle through the scale area. The scale was designed to be portable, and 70 percent of the scales sold were installed the same way as the plaintiff. The scale could be moved by cutting away a welded metal fence and lifting the scale with heavy machinery. The removal of the fence would take approximately one hour with use of a cutting torch, after which the scale could be moved within fifteen minutes. The trial court entered judgment in favor of the defendant.

DECISION Judgment of the trial court is affirmed.

OPINION Paragraph 2 of the real estate contract clearly provides that the sale included all affixed equipment located on the property. Thus, the question to be answered is whether the scale is a fixture. A fixture is an article of personal property that has been so annexed to the realty that it is regarded as part of the land and belongs to the person owning the land. The test for determining whether property has become a fixture is threefold, consisting of (1) the annexation to the realty, (2) the adaptation to the use to which the realty is devoted, and (3) the intent that the object become a permanent accession to the land. The latter two elements, adaptation and intent, are more important in determining whether a chattel became a fixture than the method by which the chattel is affixed to a freehold.

With respect to annexation, the scale weighs approximately six thousand five hundred pounds. A fence and gates within the structure had to be cut off in order to install the scale. A concrete slab was poured in the structure for placement of the scale. The size and shape of the slab were designed to accommodate the scale. Concrete ramps were installed on two sides of the scale and fencing was constructed to direct cattle onto the scale. The concrete construction (other than the slab) and the metal pipe fencing were completed after the scale was placed on the slab in the pole barn. The metal posts for the fence were set in the concrete. The scale has remained in place since its installation.

With respect to adaptation, Ray Stone had been ranch manager for plaintiff. He told the trial court that the scale was integral to a cattle-working facility. The scale was used to weigh cattle for sale and to determine required dosages of medicine administered to cattle.

With respect to intent, the scale was described as portable by its manufacturer. The manufacturer sold peripheral items that permitted the scale to be moved. This included a trailer and an inverter. Plaintiff did not buy that equipment. Ray Stone told the trial court that the scale was purchased "to be stationary whether it was portable or not."

A six-thousand-five-hundred-pound scale placed on a specially sized concrete pad and surrounded by metal pole fencing set in the concrete is annexed to the real estate on which the concrete pad is poured. The scale was put in place to facilitate the cattle operation on the premises. Its adaptation for that purpose enhanced the operation of the cattle ranch. The evidence demonstrates the plaintiff's intent for the scale to be a permanent installation. Therefore the scale is a fixture and, accordingly, the sale of the real estate on which the scale was situated included the sale of the scale.

INTERPRETATION A fixture is personal property so firmly attached to real property that an interest in it arises under real property.

ETHICAL QUESTION Did the court fairly decide this case? Explain.

CRITICAL THINKING QUESTION When should personal property become a fixture? What criteria should be used in the determination? Explain.

TRANSFER OF TITLE TO PERSONAL PROPERTY [47-2]

The transfer of title to real property typically is a formal affair. In contrast, title to personal property may be acquired and transferred with relative ease and little formality. Such facility with regard to the transfer of personal property is essential within a society whose trade and industry are based principally on transactions in personal property, which must be sold with minimal delay.

The law concerning personal property has been largely codified. The Uniform Commercial Code (UCC or the Code) includes the law of sales of goods (Article 2), as well as the law governing the transfer and negotiation of negotiable instruments (Article 3) and of investment securities (Article 8). Nonetheless, the Code does not cover a number of issues (addressed in the remainder of this chapter) involving the ownership and transfer of title to personal property. In addition, personal property may be, and often is, acquired by producing the item, rather than by selling or transferring it.

By Sale [47-2a]

Sale
transfer of property for consideration

By definition, a **sale** of *tangible* personal property (goods) is a transfer of title to specified existing goods for a consideration known as the price. Title passes when the parties intend it to pass, and transfer of possession is not required for a transfer of title. For a discussion of transfer of title, see Chapter 21.

Sales of *intangible* personal property also involve the transfer of title. Many of these sales also are governed by UCC provisions, while some, such as sales of copyrights and patents, are governed by specialized federal legislation.

By Gift [47-2b]

Gift
transfer of property
without consideration

Donor
maker of a gift

Donee
recipient of a gift

Delivery
includes both manual
transfer of the item and
constructive delivery

Constructive delivery
delivery of something that
symbolizes control over
the item

Practical Advice

As a donee of a gift,
attempt to receive actual or
constructive delivery of the
item as quickly as possible.

A **gift** is a transfer of title to property from one person to another without consideration. This lack of consideration is the basic distinction between a gift and a sale. Because a gift involves no consideration or compensation, it must be completed by delivery of the gift to be effective. A gratuitous promise to make a gift is not binding. In addition, there must be intent on the part of the maker (the **donor**) of the gift to make a present transfer, and there must be acceptance by the recipient (the **donee**) of the gift.

Delivery   Delivery is essential to a valid gift. The term **delivery** has a very special meaning that includes, but is not limited to, the manual transfer of the item to the donee. A donor may effect an irrevocable delivery by, for example, turning an item over to a third person with instructions to give it to the donee. Frequently, an item, because of its size, location, or intangibility, is incapable of immediate manual delivery. In such cases, an irrevocable gift may be effected through the delivery of something that symbolizes dominion over the item. This is referred to as **constructive delivery**. For example, if Joanne declares that she gives an antique desk and all its contents to Barry and hands Barry the key to the desk, in many states a valid gift has been made.

Intent   The law also provides clearly that the donor must intend to make a gift of the property. Thus, if Jack leaves a packet of stocks and bonds with Joan, her acquiring good title to them depends on whether Jack intended to make a gift of them or simply intended to place them in Joan's hands for safekeeping. A voluntary, uncompensated delivery made with the intent to give the recipient title constitutes a gift when the donee accepts the delivery. If these conditions are met, the donor has no further claim to the property.

Gifts, therefore, cannot be conditional. There is, however, one major exception to this rule: an engagement gift given in anticipation of marriage. If the marriage does not take place, the donor usually can recover the gift unless the donor broke the engagement without justification. But the courts will not apply the exception when a marriage is called off due to the death of one of the engaged parties.

Acceptance   The final requirement of a valid gift is acceptance by the donee. In most instances, of course, the donee will accept the gift gratefully. Accordingly, the law usually presumes that the donee has accepted. But certain circumstances may render acceptance objectionable, such as when a gift would impose a burden upon the donee. In such cases, the law will not require the recipient to accept an unwanted gift. For example, a donee may prudently reject a gift of an elephant or a wrecked car in need of extensive repairs.

Classification   Gifts may be either *inter vivos* or *causa mortis*. An *inter vivos* gift is a gift made by a donor during her lifetime. A gift *causa mortis* is a gift made by a donor in contemplation of her imminent death. A gift *causa mortis* is a conditional gift, contingent upon (1) the donor's death as she anticipated, (2) the donor's not revoking the gift prior to her death, and (3) the donee's surviving the donor.

 Mirvish v. Mott
Court of Appeals of New York, 2012
18 N.Y.3d 510, 965 N.E.2d 906
http://scholar.google.com/scholar_case?case=11454752601126833165&q=18+N.Y.3d+510+%282012%29&hl=en&as_sdt=4000006

FACTS Jacques Lipchitz, a Russian-born cubist sculptor, died in 1973 at the age of eighty-one. He was survived by his wife, Yulla H. Lipchitz, who inherited many valuable works of art from her highly successful husband, including "The Cry," a 1,100–pound bronze sculpture. After she was widowed, Yulla began a relationship with Biond Fury as early as 1980; the two of them lived together for seventeen years before her death on July 20, 2003, at the age of ninety-two.

From time to time, Yulla would make gifts to Fury, including art created by her late husband. She memorialized these gifts by giving Fury a picture of the artwork with a writing describing the piece and declaring that it was a gift. After Yulla's death, Fury produced a photograph of "The Cry" with the following notation on the back, in Yulla's handwriting: "I gave this sculpture 'The Cry' to my good friend Biond Fury in appreciation for all he did for me during my long illness. With love and my warm wishes for a Happy Future, Yulla Lipchitz October 2, 1997, New York." At the time, "The Cry" was in storage in New York in the custody of the Marlborough Gallery, Inc., a Manhattan art dealer.

About a year later, the French minister of culture and communication approached Pierre Levai, Marlborough's president, to ask about the possibility of placing "The Cry" on exhibit in Paris near the Louvre Museum for a period of five years, "with a view to its ultimately being purchased." On November 11, 1998, Levai wrote the minister that he had discussed the French government's request "with the Lipchitz family," who agreed to loan the sculpture for three years, unless Yulla died earlier. At the conclusion of the loan, Levai continued, the family was "prepared to negotiate a sale of the work," but if "[a]t the conclusion of the loan, … the sculpture [was] not purchased, it [was] to be returned to the Lipchitz family in New York at the borrower's cost."

Levai discussed the loan of "The Cry" to the French government only with Hanno Mott, Yulla's son, never with Yulla. Mott, who at the time did not know about the handwritten gift instrument conveying "The Cry" to Fury, is the executor and a residuary beneficiary of one third of his mother's estate. He is an attorney, and he handled Yulla's financial affairs and held power of attorney from her for many years prior to her death.

According to Mott, he talked to his mother about the loan and, on her behalf, "consented that ['The Cry'] should be put on display … in Paris and it was and it had [Yulla's] name on the loan." The French government at some point also inquired if, once the exhibition was over, Yulla was willing to make a gift of "The Cry." Mott testified that Yulla told him "No, of course not, but if they want to buy it, they can buy it"—i.e., that "we would [give] … a right of first refusal." "The Cry" was in Paris, subject to this agreement, when Yulla died. Her will did not mention "The Cry" or any other specific work of art. Fury claims not to have known that the sculpture was loaned to the French government in 1998.

On March 9, 2004, Fury's attorney sent a letter and a copy of the deed of gift to Mott's attorney, demanding immediate delivery of "The Cry" to Fury. Mott claims to have sold "The Cry" and three other sculptures in a package deal in July 2004 to Marlborough International Fine Art Establishment (Marlborough International) for $1 million. But in a letter to the French minister dated January 10, 2005, six months *after* the purported sale of "The Cry" to Marlborough International, Mott informed the minister that Yulla had passed away in 2003; noted that "the agreement for the loan also provided that at its conclusion the Lipchitz family would be prepared to negotiate a sale of the Sculpture"; and inquired "[o]n behalf of the family … whether the Ministry [had] any interest in acquiring the Sculpture at this time before arrangements are made for its return."

On September 15, 2005, Fury sold his interest in "The Cry" to David Mirvish, an art collector and gallery owner in Toronto, for

$220,000. On October 4, 2005, Mirvish's attorney notified Mott of the sale and demanded possession of the sculpture. In a letter dated October 14, 2005, the estate's attorney refused this demand, asserting "the Estate was the true owner of ['The Cry'], which was never subject of a valid *inter vivos* gift from [Yulla] to Biond Fury."

Both Mott, as executor of Yulla's estate, and Mirvish filed petitions with the Surrogate's Court seeking resolution of their conflicting claims of ownership of "The Cry." The Surrogate's Court ruled in favor of Mirvish, concluding that Yulla had made a valid *inter vivos* gift of "The Cry" to Fury because the wording of the deed of gift was "in the past tense, *i.e.,* 'I gave this sculpture "The Cry" to my good friend Biond Fury,'" which was not only "indicative of an antecedent transfer," but also "clearly identifie[d] the intended object and [was] consistent with [Yulla's] long pattern of making gifts of similar items to her companion." The Appellate Division reversed the Surrogate Court's decree.

DECISION The order of the Appellate Division is reversed, and the order of the Surrogate's Court is reinstated.

OPINION The principles of law that control the outcome of this appeal are

> First, to make a valid *inter vivos* gift there must exist the intent on the part of the donor to make a present transfer; delivery of the gift, either actual or constructive to the donee; and acceptance by the donee. Second, the proponent of a gift has the burden of proving each of these elements by clear and convincing evidence.

Relatedly, mere possession of a gift after the donor's death creates a presumption of delivery to the donee during the donor's lifetime.

Yulla's intent to make a present transfer of "The Cry" was clear on the face of the gift instrument, as the surrogate concluded. There is no suggestion Yulla was coerced; there is no question about her capacity. Nor is there any dispute that Fury accepted the gift. Mott has not raised a triable issue of fact overcoming the presumption of delivery. Thus, Mirvish has established by clear and convincing evidence each of the elements of a valid *inter vivos* gift—intent, delivery and acceptance.

INTERPRETATION The elements of a valid *inter vivos* gift are intent, delivery, and acceptance.

CRITICAL THINKING QUESTION When should the making of a gift be considered complete? Explain.

By Will or Descent [47-2c]

Title to personal property frequently is acquired by inheritance from a person who dies, either with or without a will. This method of acquiring title will be discussed in Chapter 50.

By Accession [47-2d]

Accession means the right of the owner of property to any increase in it, whether natural or human-made. For example, the owner of a cow acquires title by accession to any calves born to that cow.

By Confusion [47-2e]

Confusion arises when identical goods belonging to different people become so *commingled* (mixed) that the owners cannot identify their own property except as part of a mass of like goods. For example, Hereford cattle belonging to Benton become mixed with Hereford cattle belonging to Armstrong, and neither can specifically identify his herd as a result; or grain owned

Accession

right of the owner of property to any increase in it

Confusion

intermixing of goods belonging to two or more owners such that none of them can identify their property except as part of a mass of like goods

by Courts is combined inseparably with similar grain owned by Reichel. Confusion may result from accident, mistake, willful act, or agreement of the parties. If the goods can be apportioned, each owner who can prove his proportion of the whole is entitled to receive his share. If, however, the confusion results from the willful and wrongful act of one of the parties, he will lose his entire interest if unable to prove his share. Frequently, problems arise not because the owners cannot prove their original interests but because there is not enough left to distribute a full share to each. In such cases, if the confusion was due to mistake, accident, or agreement, each owner will bear the loss in proportion to his share. If the confusion resulted from an intentional and unauthorized act, the wrongdoer will first bear any loss.

By Possession [47-2f]

Possession
a person may acquire title by taking possession of property

Abandoned property
intentionally disposed of by the owner

Lost property
unintentionally left by the owner

Mislaid property
intentionally placed by the owner but unintentionally left

Treasure trove
coins or currency concealed by the owner for such a length of time that the owner is probably dead

Sometimes a person may acquire title to movable personal property by taking **possession** of it. If the property has been intentionally **abandoned** (intentionally disposed of), a finder is entitled to the property. Moreover, under the general rule, a *finder* is entitled to **lost** (unintentionally left) **property** against everyone except the true *owner*. Suppose Zenner, the owner of an apartment complex, leases a kitchenette apartment to Terrell. One night, Waters, Terrell's mother-in-law, is invited to sleep in the convertible bed in the living room. In the course of preparing the bed, Waters finds an emerald ring caught on the springs under the mattress. She turns the ring over to the police, but diligent inquiry fails to ascertain the true owner. As the finder, Waters will be entitled to the ring.

A different rule applies when the lost property is in the ground. Here, the owner of the land has a claim superior to that of the finder. For example, Josephs employs Kasarda to excavate a lateral sewer. Kasarda uncovers ancient Native American artifacts. Josephs, not Kasarda, has the superior claim.

A further exception to the rule gives the finder first claim against all but the true owner. If property is intentionally placed somewhere by the owner, who then unintentionally leaves it, it becomes **mislaid property**. Most courts hold that if property has been mislaid, not lost, then the owner of the premises, not the finder, has first claim if the true owner is not discovered. This doctrine is frequently invoked in cases involving items found in restaurants or on trains, buses, or airplanes.

Another category of property is the **treasure trove**, which consists of coins or currency concealed by the owner. To be classified as treasure trove, the property must have been hidden or concealed for such a length of time that the owner is probably dead or undiscoverable. Treasure trove belongs to the finder as against all but the true owner.

Many states now have statutes that provide a means of vesting title to lost property in the finder where a prescribed search for the owner proves fruitless.

PROPERTY INSURANCE

Insurance
contractual arrangement that distributes risk of loss among a large number of people (the insureds) through an insurance company (the insurer)

Insurance covers a vast range of contracts, each of which distributes risk among a large number of members (the insureds) through an insurance company (the insurer). Insurance is a contractual undertaking by the insurer to pay a sum of money or give something of value to the insured or a beneficiary upon the happening of a contingency or fortuitous event that is beyond the control of the contracting parties.

Insurance coverage of one form or another affects every commercial activity. Through insurance, a business can safeguard its tangible assets against almost any form of damage or destruction, whether resulting from natural causes or from the accidental or improper actions of people. Insurance may also protect a business from tort liability, including assertions involving strict liability, negligence, or the intentional acts of its representatives. A business may procure credit insurance to guard against losses from poor credit risks and fidelity bonds to secure it against losses incurred through employee defalcations. If a business hires a famous pianist, it may insure the latter's hands; if it decides to present an outdoor concert, it may insure against the possibility of rain. A business may purchase life insurance on its key executives to reimburse it for financial losses arising from their deaths, or it may purchase such life insurance payable to the families of executives as part of their compensation. An additional, increasingly important use of insurance is to carry out pension commitments arising from agreements with employees. Nonetheless, the remaining sections of this chapter will focus on the insurance of property.

The McCarran-Ferguson Act, enacted by Congress in 1945, left insurance regulation to the states. Statutes in each state regulate domestic insurance companies and establish standards for foreign (out-of-state) insurance companies wishing to do business within the state. Most state legislation relates to the incorporation, licensing, supervision, and liquidation of insurers and to the licensing and supervision of agents and brokers.

Because the insurance relationship arises from a contract of insurance between the insurer and the insured, the law of insurance is a branch of contract law. For this reason, the doctrines of offer and acceptance, consideration, and other rules applicable to contracts in general are equally applicable to insurance contracts. Beyond that, however, insurance law, like the law of sales, bailments, negotiable instruments, or other specialized types of contracts, contains numerous modifications of fundamental contract law, which are examined in the following sections.

FIRE AND PROPERTY INSURANCE [47-3]

Fire (property) insurance

provides protection against loss due to fire or other related perils

Fire and property insurance protects the owner (or another person with an insurable interest, such as a secured creditor or mortgagee) of real or personal property against loss resulting from damage to or destruction of the property by fire and certain related perils. Most fire insurance policies also cover damage caused by lightning, explosion, earthquake, water, wind, rain, collision, and riot.

Fire insurance policies are standardized in the United States, either by statute or by order of the state insurance departments, but their coverage is frequently enlarged through an "endorsement" or "rider" to include other perils or to benefit the insured in ways the provisions in the standard form do not. These policies normally are written for periods of one or three years.

Types of Fire Covered [47-3a]

Practical Advice

Maintain, off the premises, a detailed inventory of your insured property in case you must file a claim for loss.

Fire insurance policies usually are held to cover damage from "hostile" fires, but they do not cover losses caused by "friendly" fires. A **friendly fire** is one contained in its intended location (e.g., a fire in a fireplace, furnace, or stove). A **hostile fire** is any other fire—all fires outside their intended or usual locales. Thus, a friendly fire becomes hostile if it escapes from its usual confines.

Friendly fire

fire contained where it is intended to be

A standard insurance policy therefore will not cover heat or soot damage to a fireplace resulting from its continual use or damage done to personal property accidentally thrown into a stove. Damages caused by smoke, soot, water, and heat from a hostile fire are covered by the standard fire insurance policy, whereas such damages caused by a friendly fire generally are not. Moreover, most policies do not cover recovery for business interruption, unless they contain endorsements specifically covering such loss.

Hostile fire

any fire outside its intended or usual place

Co-insurance Clauses [47-3b]

Co-insurance

reduction in benefits for underinsuring the value of the property based on a percentage stated in the insurance policy and the amount underinsured

Co-insurance is an arrangement common in property insurance to share the risk between insurer and insured. **Co-insurance** is a reduction in benefits for underinsuring the value of the property based on a percentage stated in the insurance policy and the amount underinsured. For example, under the typical 80 percent co-insurance clause, the insured may recover the full amount of loss, not to exceed the face amount of the policy, provided the policy is for an amount not less than 80 percent of the property's insurable value. If the policy is for less than 80 percent, the insured recovers that proportion of the loss that the amount of the policy bears, up to 80 percent of the insurable value. The formula for recovery is as follows:

$$\text{Recovery} = \frac{\text{Face Value of Policy}}{\text{Fair Market Value of Property} \times \text{Co-insurance \%}} \times \text{Loss}$$

Practical Advice

When purchasing property insurance, determine whether there is a coinsurance clause and, if so, what the co-insurance percentage is.

Thus, if the co-insurance percentage is 80 percent, the value of the property is $100,000, and the policy is for $80,000 or more, the insured is fully protected against loss not to exceed the policy amount. If the policy amount is less than 80 percent of the property value, however, the insured receives only the proportion of the loss amount as determined in the previous formula. Thus, in the previous example, if the fire policy was for $60,000 and the property was 50 percent destroyed, the loss would be $50,000, of which the insurer would pay $37,500, which is $60,000/($100,000 \times 80\%)$ of $50,000. On a total loss, the recovery could not, of course, exceed the face amount of the policy.

Some states do not favor co-insurance clauses and strictly construe the applicable statute against their validity. In addition, property insurance is not held to be co-insurance unless the policy specifically so provides.

Multiple Insurers [47-3c]

Multiple insurers

if multiple insurers are involved, liability generally is distributed *pro rata*

Property insurance policies generally require that liability be distributed *pro rata* among **multiple insurers**. For example, Alexander insures his $120,000 building with Hamilton Insurance Co. for $60,000 and Jefferson Insurance Co. for $90,000. Alexander's building is partially destroyed by fire, causing Alexander $20,000 in damages. Alexander will collect two-fifths ($60,000/$150,000) of his damages from Hamilton ($8,000) and three-fifths ($90,000/$150,000) from Jefferson ($12,000).

BUSINESS LAW **IN ACTION**

Here's a little quiz. Which of the following do you think are examples of insurance fraud? Who, if anyone, should be punished?

A show horse, insured for several hundred thousand dollars, turns out to be a loser on the show-jumping circuit. The horse costs a lot to feed and train, and its selling price would be far less than the amount for which it's currently insured. The owner hires a hit man to electrocute the horse, a death that resembles death from colic. The owner collects the insurance and pays the hit man.

A bus rear-ends another vehicle in heavy city traffic. Several people standing on the sidewalk see the accident and jump onto the bus. They then claim to have been injured in the accident and get cooperative doctors to diagnose accident-related injuries.

Several apartment managers, having the power to pick contractors to repair fire- and accident-related damage to their buildings, charge their chosen contractors 10 percent kickbacks for being awarded repair jobs. The contractors, in turn, jack up their charges to cover the cost of the kickbacks.

An insurance company calculates the pay of an independent insurance adjuster as a percentage of each claim she evaluates. The adjuster persuades policyholders to inflate their claims so that she—and they—can collect more money. She also bribes employees of the insurance company to approve the claims.

Auto owners in states X and Y insure their cars in nearby state Z, which has lower auto insurance rates. The cars, of course, are kept at the owners' residences in states X and Y and are driven almost exclusively in those states.

A beachside restaurant goes up in flames one night at the end of summer. No

one can prove arson, but the owner has been floundering in cash flow problems.

Insurance fraud is a huge problem in the United States (and a growing problem in Europe). Part of the problem is that people use a double standard to judge insurance fraud. People think it's outrageous when a ring of crooks sets small fires in shops (after bribing the owners), makes inflated claims, bribes insurance brokers and adjusters as part of the scheme, and pockets millions. But, ironically, many can't see the harm in padding their own claims just a little when they lose property by theft or fire. After all, some faraway, faceless company is the one who pays.

Wrong. Everyone with insurance pays. Ten to fifteen cents of every dollar spent to purchase property and casualty insurance goes toward covering the cost of fraud. Insurers in the United States have stepped up their fight against claims made for staged accidents, padded body shop repair bills, faked bodily injury reports, falsely reported stolen cars, and actual auto theft. Insurers are pressing the battle on two fronts: public opinion and criminal investigation. Of the two, insurance companies believe that public opinion will make the bigger difference—*if* attitudes really can be changed.

Behavioral tip-offs—a person's eagerness for a quick settlement, use of a post office box or hotel as an address, or insistence on pursuing a claim in person rather than by mail or over the phone—lead insurers to investigate claims for fraud. They likewise become suspicious when a surprisingly large number of people submit medical bills from the same doctor or clinic.

However, insurance companies would very much like to win the hearts and

minds of the public in fighting insurance fraud—first, so that ordinary law-abiding citizens resist the temptation to cheat (it is generally accepted that more than 21 percent of claims submitted are padded) and, second, to encourage the honest majority to report those who do cheat. For example, one insurer advises its policyholders to do the following to fight fraud:

- If you're in an accident, report it to the police. If you witness an accident, report it. Your report can help to determine whether or not a claim is legitimate.

- When you've been in an accident, call your insurer immediately. Obtain a police report and get the other driver's name, address, and license number and his car's registration number. Write down what happened while your memory is fresh.

- Call the police and your insurance company if someone tells you about a doctor or lawyer who will help you to falsify or inflate a claim. Do the same if a body shop says it can inflate its estimate for you.

- Pay attention when you're car shopping: don't buy a car that you suspect may be stolen. You should look at the vehicle identification number to see whether it appears to have been changed. Other red flags: a new paint job, remade keys, and a lack of title or registration.

- Make yourself heard with your state legislators. Ask them to support antifraud legislation and regulations. If you suspect fraud, report it.

Types of Policies [47-3d]

Property insurance may be either a valued policy or an open policy. A **valued policy** is one providing for the full value of the property, upon which value the insured and the insurer specifically agree at the time the policy is issued. Should total loss occur, the insurer must pay this amount, not the actual or fair market value of the property. By comparison, no agreement in an **open policy** specifies the property's value; instead, the insurer pays the fair market value of the property calculated immediately prior to its loss. Thus, if Latrisha insures her building for $650,000 and at the time of its loss the property is valued at $600,000, under an open policy Latrisha would recover $600,000, while under a valued policy she would recover $650,000. If she insured the building for $700,000, and it was valued at that amount just prior to being blown apart by a tornado, under both types of policies Latrisha would recover $700,000. Insurance of property under a marine policy (insurance covering marine vessels and cargo) is generally considered to be valued, whereas nonmarine property insurance is presumed to be unvalued or open.

NATURE OF INSURANCE CONTRACTS [47-4]

The basic principles of *contract* law apply to insurance policies. Furthermore, because insurance companies engage in a large volume of business over wide areas, they tend to standardize their policies. In some states, standardization is required by statute. This usually means that the insured must accept a given policy or do without the desired insurance.

Offer and Acceptance [47-4a]

No matter how many stories tell of insurance agents aggressively soliciting would-be insureds to take out policies, the applicant usually makes the offer, and the contract is created when the insurance company accepts that offer. The company may condition its acceptance—upon payment of the premium, for instance. It also may write a policy that differs from the application, thereby making a counteroffer that the applicant may or may not choose to accept.

In fire and casualty insurance, agents often have authority to make the insurance effective immediately, when needed, by means of a **binder**, which is a temporary, preliminary insurance contact that is legally binding until the completion of the formal insurance contract. Should a loss occur before the company actually issues a policy, the binder will be effective on the same terms and conditions the policy would have had if it had been issued.

In general, insurance contracts have not been held to be subject to the statute of frauds; thus, courts have held oral contracts for insurance to be enforceable. As a practical matter, however, oral contracts for insurance are rare.

Insurable Interest [47-4b]

The concept of insurable interest has been developed over many years, primarily to eliminate gambling and to lessen the moral hazard. If a person could obtain an enforceable fire insurance policy on property that he did not own or in which he had no interest, he would be in a position to profit unfairly by the destruction of such property. An **insurable interest** is a relationship a person has with respect to certain property such that the happening of a possible, specific, damage-causing contingency would result in direct loss or injury to her. The purpose of insurance is protection against the risk of loss that would result from such a happening, not the realization of gain or profit.

Whether sole or concurrent, ownership obviously creates an insurable interest in property. Moreover, a right deriving from a contract concerning the property also gives rise to an insurable interest. For instance, shareholders in a closely held corporation have been held to have an insurable interest in the corporation's property to the extent of their interest. Likewise, lessees of property have insurable interests, as do holders of security interests, such as mortgagees or sellers with a purchase money security interest. Most courts have gone beyond the requirement of a legally recognized interest and apply a factual expectancy test. Under this test, the determinative question is whether the insured will obtain a benefit from the continued existence of the property or suffer a loss from its destruction. Thus, an individual who buys and insures a stolen automobile without knowledge that the automobile is stolen has an insurable interest in the automobile.

Practical Advice

When purchasing property insurance, make sure you have an insurable interest in the property and terminate the policy once you cease to have an insurable interest.

The insurable interest must exist at the time the property *loss* occurs, although some courts speak in terms of having the insurable interest at the time of insuring *and* at the time of loss. Property insurance policies are freely assignable after, but not before, a loss occurs.

Premiums [47-4c]

Premiums
amount to be paid for an insurance policy

Premiums are the consideration paid for an insurance policy. State law regulates the rates that may be charged for fire and various kinds of casualty insurance. The regulatory authorities are under a duty to require that the companies' rates be reasonable, not unfairly discriminatory, and neither excessively high nor inordinately low.

Defenses of the Insurer [47-4d]

An insurer may assert the ordinary defenses available to any contract. In addition, the terms of the insurance contract may provide specific defenses, such as the subject matter of the policy, types of perils covered, amount of coverage, and period of coverage. Moreover, the insurer may assert the closely related defenses of misrepresentation, breach of warranty, and concealment.

Misrepresentation
false representation of a material fact made by the insured that is justifiably relied upon by the insurer

Misrepresentation
A representation is a statement made by or on behalf of an applicant for insurance to induce an insurer to enter into a contract. The representation is not a part of the insurance contract, but if the application containing the representation is incorporated by reference into the contract, the representation becomes a warranty. For a **misrepresentation** to have legal consequences, it must be material, the insurer must have justifiably relied on it as an inducement to enter into the contract, and it must either have been substantially false when the insured made it or have become so, to the insured's knowledge, before the contract was created. The principal remedy of the insurer on discovery of the material misrepresentation is rescission of the contract. To rescind the contract, the insurer must tender to the insured all premiums that have been paid, unless the misrepresentation was fraudulent. To be effective, rescission must be made as soon as possible after discovery of the misrepresentation.

Breach of warranty
the failure of a required condition; generally an insurer may avoid liability for a breach of warranty only if the breach is material

Breach of Warranty
Warranties are of great importance in insurance contracts because they operate as conditions that must exist before the contract is effective or before the insurer's promise to pay is enforceable. If such is the case, the insurer does not merely have a defense against payment of the policy but can void the policy.

Failure of the condition to exist or to occur relieves the insurer from any obligation to perform its promise. Broadly speaking, a condition is simply an event whose happening or failure to happen either precedes the existence of a legal relationship or terminates one previously existing. Conditions are either precedent or subsequent. For example, payment of the premium is a condition precedent to the enforcement of the insurer's promise, as is the happening of the insured event. A condition subsequent is an operative event the happening of which terminates an existing, matured legal obligation. A provision in a policy to the effect that the insured shall not be liable unless suit is brought within twelve months from the date on which the loss occurs is an example of a condition subsequent.

To be a warranty, the provision must be expressly included in the insurance contract or clearly incorporated by reference. Usually, the policy statements that the insurer considers to be express warranties are characterized by words such as *warrant, on condition that, provided that,* or words of similar import. Other statements important to the risk assumed, such as the address of a building in a case in which personal property at a particular location is insured against fire, are sometimes held to be informal warranties.

Generally, it is becoming more difficult for an insurer to avoid liability on a policy when an insured breaches a warranty. For example, a number of states now require a breach to be material before the insurer may avoid liability.

Concealment
fraudulent failure to disclose a material fact

Concealment
Similar to material misrepresentation, **concealment** is the failure of an applicant for insurance to disclose material facts that the insurer does not know. The nondisclosure normally must be fraudulent as well as material to invalidate the policy; the applicant must have had reason to believe the fact was material; and its disclosure must have affected the

insurer's acceptance of the risk. The principal remedy of the insurer on discovery of concealment is rescission of the contract.

Waiver and Estoppel [47-4e]

In certain instances, an insurer who normally would be entitled to deny liability under a policy because of a misrepresentation, breach of condition, or concealment is "estopped" from taking advantage of the defense or else is said to have "waived" the right to rely on it because of other facts.

The terms *waiver* and *estoppel* are used interchangeably, although by definition they are not synonymous. As generally defined, **waiver** is the intentional relinquishment of a known right; and **estoppel** means that a person is prevented by his own conduct from asserting a position inconsistent with such conduct, on which another person has justifiably relied.

Because a corporation such as an insurance company can act only through agents, situations involving waiver invariably are based on an agent's conduct. The higher the agent's position in the company's organization, the more likely his conduct is to bind the company, as an agent acting within the scope of his authority binds his principal. Insureds have the right to rely on representations made by the insurer's employees, and when such representations reasonably induce or cause the insured to change her position or prevent her from causing a condition to occur, the insurer may not assert as a defense the condition's failure to occur, whether the term applied to her situation be waiver or estoppel. Companies have tried with little success to limit the authority of local selling agents to bind the company through waiver or estoppel.

Waiver
intentional relinquishment of a known right

Estoppel
person is prevented by his own conduct from asserting a position

Termination [47-4f]

Most insurance contracts are performed according to their terms, and due *performance* terminates the insurer's obligation. Normally, the insurer pays the principal sum due and the contract is thereby performed and discharged.

Cancellation by mutual consent is another way of terminating an insurance contract. Cancellation by the insurer alone means that the insurer remains liable, according to the terms of the policy, until such time as the cancellation is effective. To cancel a policy, the insurer must tender the unearned portion of the premium to the insured.

Termination
an insurance contract may be terminated by due performance or cancellation

BAILMENTS AND DOCUMENTS OF TITLE

BAILMENTS [47-5]

A **bailment** is the relationship created when one person (the **bailor**) transfers the possession of personal property by delivery, without transfer of title, to another (the **bailee**) for the accomplishment of a certain purpose, after which the bailee is to return the property to the bailor or dispose of it according to the bailor's directions. One of the most common occurrences in everyday life, bailments are of great commercial importance. Bailments include the transportation, storage, repair, and rental of goods, which together involve billions of dollars in transactions each year. The following are common examples of bailments: keeping a car in a public garage; leaving a car, a watch, or any other article to be repaired; renting a car or truck; checking a hat or coat at a theater or restaurant; leaving clothes to be laundered; delivering jewelry, stocks, bonds, or other valuables to secure the payment of a debt; storing goods in a warehouse; and shipping goods by public or private transportation.

The benefit of a bailment may, by its terms, accrue solely to the bailor, solely to the bailee, or to both parties. A bailment may be with or without compensation. On these bases, bailments are classified as follows:

Bailment
the temporary transfer of personal property by one party to another

Bailor
transferor of the bailed property

Bailee
recipient of the bailed property

1. *Bailments for the bailor's sole benefit* include the gratuitous custody of personal property and the gratuitous services that involve custody of personal property, such as repairs or transportation. For example, if Sherry stores, repairs, or transports Tim's goods without compensation, this is a bailment for the sole benefit of the bailor, Tim.
2. *Bailments for the bailee's sole benefit* are usually limited to the gratuitous loan of personal property for use by the bailee, as where Tim, without compensation, lends his car, lawn mower, or book to Sherry for her use.

3. *Bailments for the mutual benefit of both parties* include ordinary commercial bailments, such as the delivery of goods to a person for repair, jewels to a pawnbroker, or an automobile to a parking lot attendant.

Essential Elements of a Bailment [47-5a]

Essential elements of a bailment

(1) delivery of possession;
(2) personal property;
(3) possession, but not ownership, for a determinable time; and (4) restoration of possession to the bailor

The **essential elements of a bailment** are (1) the delivery of possession from a bailor to a bailee; (2) the delivery of personal property, not real property; (3) possession without ownership by the bailee for a determinable period; and (4) an absolute duty on the bailee to return the property to the bailor or to dispose of it according to the bailor's directions.

In most cases, two simple elements determine the existence of a bailment: (1) a separation of ownership and possession of the property (possession without ownership) and (2) a duty on the party in possession to redeliver the identical property to the owner or to dispose of it according to the owner's directions. Since a bailment need not be a contract, consideration is not required. A bailment may be created by operation of law from the facts of a particular situation; thus, a bailment may be *implied* or *constructive*.

Delivery of Possession
Possession by a bailee involves (1) the bailee's power to control the personal property and (2) either the bailee's intention to control the property or her awareness that the rightful possessor has given up physical control of it. Thus, for example, when a restaurant customer hangs his hat or coat on a hook furnished for that purpose, the hat or coat is within an area under the restaurant owner's physical control. But the restaurant owner is not a bailee of the hat or coat unless he clearly signifies an intention to exercise control over the hat or coat. On the other hand, when a clerk in a store helps a customer to remove his coat to try on a new one, the owner of the store usually is held to have become a bailee of the old coat through the clerk, her employee. Here, the clerk has signified an intention to control the coat by taking it from the customer, and a bailment results.

Personal Property
The bailment relationship can exist only with respect to personal property. The delivery of possession of real property by the owner to another is covered by real property law. Bailed property need not be tangible. Intangible property, such as the rights represented by promissory notes, corporate bonds, shares of stock, documents of title, and life insurance policies that are evidenced by written instruments and are thus capable of delivery, may be and frequently are the subject matter of bailments.

Possession for a Determinable Time
To establish a bailment relationship, the person receiving possession must be under a duty to return the personal property and must not obtain title to it. If the identical property transferred is to be returned, even in an altered form, the transaction is a bailment; however, if other property of equal value or the money value of the original property may be returned, a transfer of title has occurred, and the transaction is a sale.

Restoration of Possession to the Bailor
The bailee is legally obligated to restore the property to the bailor's possession when the bailment period ends. Normally, the bailee is required to return the identical goods bailed, although their condition may be changed because of the work that the bailee was required to perform on them. An exception to this rule concerns **fungible goods**, such as grain, which, for all practical purposes, consist of particles that are the equivalent of every other particle and are expected to be mingled with other like goods during a bailment. Given such goods, a bailee obviously cannot be required to return the identical goods bailed. His obligation is simply to return goods of the same quality and quantity.

Fungible goods

equivalent goods, each unit being the equivalent of every other unit

A bailee has a duty to return the property to the right person. Her mistake in delivering property to the wrong person does not excuse her, even when the bailor's negligence induces the mistake. A bailee who, through mistake or intention, misdelivers the property to a third person who has no right to its possession is guilty of conversion and is liable to the bailor.

Rights and Duties of Bailor and Bailee [47-5b]

The bailment relationship creates rights and duties on the part of the bailor and the bailee. The bailee is under a duty to exercise due care for the safety of the property and to return it to the right person; conversely, the bailee has the exclusive right to possess the property for the term of the bailment. In addition, depending on the nature of the transaction, a bailee may have the right to limit his liability, as well as to receive compensation and reimbursement of expenses. The bailor, in turn, has certain duties with respect to the condition of the bailed goods.

Bailee's duty to exercise due care

the bailee must exercise reasonable care to protect the safety of the property and to return it to the proper person

Commercial bailment

parties derive a mutual benefit

Bailee's Duty to Exercise Due Care   The bailee must exercise due care not to permit injury to or destruction of the property by the bailee or by third parties. The degree of care depends on the nature of the bailment relationship and the character of the property. In the context of a **commercial bailment**, from which the parties derive a mutual benefit, the law requires the bailee to exercise the care that a reasonably prudent person would exercise under the same circumstances. When the bailment benefits the bailee alone (Tim's borrowing Michael's truck without payment would be an example), the law requires more-than-reasonable care of the bailee. On the other hand, in cases in which the bailee accepts the property for the bailor's sole benefit, the law requires a lesser degree of care. Nevertheless, the amount of care required to satisfy any of the standards will vary with the character of the property.

When the property is lost, damaged, or destroyed while in the bailee's possession, it is often impossible for the bailor to obtain enough information to show that the loss or damage was due to the bailee's failure to exercise required care. The law aids the bailor in this respect by *presuming* that the bailee was at fault. The bailor is merely required to show that certain property was delivered by way of bailment and that the bailee either has failed to return it or has returned it in a damaged condition. The burden is then on the bailee to prove that he exercised the degree of care required.

Hadfield v. Gilchrist
Court of Appeals of South Carolina, 2000
343 S.C. 88, 538 S.E.2d 268
http://scholar.google.com/scholar_case?case=10116899322085945623&q=538+S.E.2d+268&hl=en&as_sclt=2,34

FACTS Sam Gilchrist owns a motor vehicle towing service and maintains a storage facility for the retention of the towed vehicles. Gilchrist operates under a license issued by the City of Charleston.

Mark Hadfield, a medical student at Medical University of South Carolina (MUSC), went to retrieve his 1988 Lincoln Continental from the parking spot where his wife parked the vehicle. The parking spot, located near MUSC, was on private property owned by Allen Saffer. Hadfield's wife parked the vehicle on Saffer's property without Saffer's permission. The vehicle was not in the parking spot when Hadfield arrived because Saffer had called Gilchrist to have the vehicle removed.

Gilchrist towed Hadfield's car to his storage facility. Gilchrist maintained a chain link fence around the storage area and had an employee on the lot around the clock. The employees' duties included periodically leaving the office to check on the storage area, which was some distance away from the office.

Hadfield called to retrieve his vehicle but was informed he would have to wait until the next morning and pay towing and storage fees. Upon Hadfield's arrival to pick up his car the following morning, he discovered the vehicle had been extensively vandalized. The vandals stole the radio/compact disc player, smashed windows, and pulled many electrical wires out of the dashboard. The vehicle depended heavily upon computers and never functioned properly after the incident. The vandals entered the storage area by cutting a hole in the fence. They vandalized between six and eight vehicles on the lot that night.

Hadfield's attempts to persuade Gilchrist to pay for the damages were futile. Hadfield secured estimates for the damage to the automobile at $4,021.43. After more than sixty days elapsed, Hadfield sold the vehicle for $1,000. The magistrate found Gilchrist liable for the damages as a bailee and entered judgment in favor of Hadfield for $4,035. Gilchrist appealed to the Circuit Court, which affirmed the decision of the magistrate.

DECISION The decision of the magistrate is affirmed.

OPINION The type of bailment created may determine the standard of care the bailee, Gilchrist, must meet. A bailment is created by the delivery of personal property by one person to another in trust, pursuant to an express or implied contract. Bailments are generally classified as being for (1) the sole benefit of the bailor, (2) the sole benefit of the bailee, or (3) the mutual benefit of both. Gratuitous bailments, those for the benefit of only one party, impose less liability on the bailee.

Although a bailment is ordinarily created by the agreement of the parties, a bailment may arise by operation of law when one person has lawfully acquired possession of another's personal property, other than by a contract, and holds it under such circumstances that the law imposes on the recipient of the property the obligation to keep it safely and redeliver it to the owner.

Gilchrist argues he towed the vehicle pursuant to the Charleston Municipal Ordinances and the ordinances are for the sole benefit of the vehicle owners. Accordingly, he contends, the relationship created is a gratuitous bailment. This is not correct. Clearly, Gilchrist benefited from the bailment in the form of towing and storage fees. Hadfield should have benefited in the form of safekeeping of his car. Thus a constructive bailment for the mutual benefit of Hadfield and Gilchrist was created.

The degree of care required of a bailee for mutual benefit is defined as ordinary care, or due care, or the degree of care that would be exercised by a person of ordinary care in the protection of his own property. In a bailment action alleging a breach of the duty of care, the bailor is entitled to be compensated for all losses that are the natural consequence and proximate result of the bailee's negligence.

The fact that Gilchrist's guard was in the office and not on duty at the impound lot, and considering the only other security for the vehicles was the chain link fence which was obviously easy

to cut through, the magistrate and Circuit Court judge rightly concluded Gilchrist failed to exercise ordinary care.

INTERPRETATION A bailment for mutual benefit confers a responsibility upon the bailee to exercise due care in protection of the property.

ETHICAL QUESTION Was Gilchrist negligent in his care of the automobiles on his lot?

CRITICAL THINKING QUESTION Would Hadfield have taken any better care of his car if it had been parked in his driveway at home? Why is Gilchrist held to a higher standard of care?

Bailee's absolute liability

occurs when (1) the parties so agree; (2) the custom of the industry requires the bailee to insure the property against the risk in question, but he fails to do so; or (3) the bailee uses the bailed property in an unauthorized manner

---

Practical Advice

As a bailee, exercise appropriate care to protect the safety of the property and to return it to its true owner.

Bailee's right to limit liability

certain bailees are not permitted to limit their liability for breach of their duties, except as provided by statute

---

Practical Advice

When dealing with bailees, be alert as to whether they are attempting to limit their liability, and if they are, carefully consider whether you are comfortable with the limitations.

Bailee's right to compensation

entitled to reasonable compensation for work or services performed on the bailed goods

Bailee's Absolute Liability to Return Property

As discussed, the bailee is free from liability if she exercised the degree of care required of her under the particular bailment while the property was within her control. This general rule has certain important exceptions that impose an absolute duty on the bailee to return the property undamaged to the proper person.

When the bailee has an obligation by express agreement with the bailor or by custom to insure the property against certain risks but fails to do so, and the property is destroyed or damaged through such risks, she is liable for the damage or nondelivery, even if she has exercised due care.

When the bailee uses the bailed property in a manner not authorized by the bailor or by the character of the bailment, and during the course of such use the property is damaged or destroyed, without fault on the bailee's part, the bailee is nonetheless absolutely (strictly) liable for the damage or destruction. The wrongful use by the bailee automatically terminates her lawful possession: she becomes a trespasser as to the property and, as such, is absolutely liable for whatever harm befalls it.

Bailee's Right to Limit Liability

Certain bailees—namely, common carriers, public warehousers, and innkeepers—may limit their liability for breach of their duties to the bailor only as provided by statute. Other bailees, however, may vary their duties and liabilities by contract with the bailor. When liability may be limited by contract, the law requires that any such limitation be properly brought to the bailor's attention before he bails the property. This is especially true in the case of "professional bailees," such as repair garages, who make it their business to act as bailees and who deal with the public on a uniform, rather than on an individual, basis. Thus, a variation or limitation in writing, contained, for example, in a claim check or stub given to the bailor or posted on the walls of the bailee's place of business, ordinarily will not bind the bailor unless (1) the bailee draws the bailor's attention to the writing, (2) the bailee informs the bailor that it contains a limitation or variation of liability, and (3) the limitation is not the result of unequal bargaining power. Some states do not permit professional bailees (who commonly include warehousers, garagers, and parking lot owners) to disclaim liability for their own negligence.

Bailee's Right to Compensation

A bailee who by express or implied agreement undertakes to perform work on or render services in connection with the bailed goods is entitled to reasonable compensation for those services or that work. In most cases, the agreement between bailor and bailee fixes the amount of compensation and provides how it shall be paid. In the absence of a contrary agreement, the compensation is payable when the bailee completes the work or performs the services. If, after such completion or performance but before the redelivery of the goods to the bailor, the goods are lost or damaged through no fault of the bailee, the bailee is still entitled to compensation for his work and services.

Most bailees who are entitled to compensation for work and services performed in connection with bailed goods acquire a possessory lien on the goods to secure the payment of such compensation. In most jurisdictions, the bailee has a statutory right to obtain a judicial foreclosure of his lien and a sale of the goods. Many statutes also provide that the bailee does not lose his lien

---

CONCEPT REVIEW 47-2

Duties in a Bailment

Bailor's Duty	Type of Bailment	Bailee's Duty of Care
For sole benefit of bailor	Slight care	To warn of defects of which she knew or should have known
For sole benefit of bailee	Utmost care	To warn of known defects
For mutual benefit	Ordinary care	To warn of defects of which she knew or should have known

---

Practical Advice

If you are a bailee, specify in your contract what your compensation will be.

Bailor's duties

in bailment for sole benefit of bailee, the bailor warrants that she is unaware of any defects; in all other bailments, the bailor has a duty to warn of all known defects and all defects she should discover upon a reasonable inspection

Ordinary bailee

one who must exercise due care

Extraordinary bailee

one who is absolutely liable for the safety of the bailed property without regard to the cause of any loss

Pledge

security interest by possession

Warehouser

storer of goods for compensation

on redelivery of the goods to the bailor, as was the case at common law. Instead, the lien will continue for a specified period after redelivery, if the bailee timely records with the proper authorities an instrument claiming such a lien.

Bailor's Duties   In a bailment for the sole benefit of the bailee, the bailor warrants that she is unaware of any defects in the bailed property. In all other instances, the bailor has a duty to warn the bailee of all defects she knows of or should have discovered upon a reasonable inspection of the bailed property. A number of courts have extended strict liability in tort and the implied warranties under Article 2 of the UCC to leases and bailments. Article 2A imposes implied warranties on the lease of goods.

Special Types of Bailments [47-5c]

Although the general principles that apply to all bailees govern pledgees, warehousers, and safe deposit companies, certain special features about the transactions in which they respectively engage subject them to extraordinary duties of care and liability. Innkeepers and common carriers also may be said to be *extraordinary* bailees, whereas all other bailees are *ordinary* bailees. This distinction is based on the character and extent of the liability of these two classes of bailees for the loss of or injury to bailed goods. As we have seen, an **ordinary bailee** is liable only for the loss or injury that results from his failure to exercise ordinary or reasonable care. The liability of the extraordinary bailee, on the other hand, is, in general, *absolute*. Just as an insurer, in general, becomes automatically liable to the insured on the happening of the hazard insured against, regardless of the cause, the **extraordinary bailee** becomes liable to the bailor for any loss or injury to the goods, regardless of the cause and without regard to the question of his care or negligence. Thus, he insures the safety of the goods.

Pledges   A **pledge** is a bailment for security in which the owner gives possession of her personal property to another (the secured party) to secure a debt or the performance of some obligation. The secured party does not have title to the property involved but merely a possessory security interest. Pledges of most types of personal property for security purposes are governed by Article 9 of the UCC, which was discussed in Chapter 37. In most respects, the secured party's duties and liabilities are the same as those of a bailee for compensation.

Warehousing   A **warehouser** is a bailee who, for compensation, receives goods to be stored in a warehouse. Under the common law, his duties and liabilities were identical to those of the ordinary bailee for compensation. Today, because a strong public interest affects their activities, warehousers are subject to extensive state and federal regulation. Warehousers also must be distinguished from ordinary bailees in that the receipts they issue for storage have acquired a special status in commerce. Regarded as documents of title, these receipts are governed by Article 7 of the UCC (documents of title will be discussed later in this chapter).

Safe Deposit Boxes   A majority of states hold that a person who rents a safe deposit box from a bank enters into a bailment relationship. As this constitutes a bailment for the parties' mutual benefit, the bailee bank owes the customer the duty to act with ordinary due care and is liable only if negligent.

Carriers of Goods   In the broadest sense, anyone who transports goods from one place to another, either gratuitously or for compensation, is a **carrier**. Carriers are classified primarily as common carriers and private carriers. A **common carrier** offers its services and facilities to the public on terms and under circumstances indicating that the offering is made to all persons. Stated somewhat differently, the criteria that define common carriers are as follows: (1) the carriage must be part of its business, (2) the carriage must be for remuneration, and (3) the carrier must represent to the general public that it is willing to serve the public in the transportation of property. Common carriers of goods include railroad, steamship, aircraft, public trucking, and pipeline companies. In contrast, a **private** or **contract carrier** is one who carries the goods of another on isolated occasions or who serves a limited number of customers under individual contracts without offering the same or similar contracts to the public at large.

The person who delivers goods to a carrier for shipment is known as the **consignor** or shipper. The person to whom the carrier is to deliver the goods is known as the **consignee**. The instrument containing the terms of the contract of transportation, which the carrier issues to the shipper, is called a *bill of lading* (discussed later in this chapter).

A common carrier is under a duty to serve the public to the limits of its capacity and, within those limits, to accept for carriage goods of the kind that it normally transports. A private carrier, by comparison, has no duty to accept goods for carriage, except where it agrees by contract to do so. Whether common or private, the carrier is under an absolute duty to deliver the goods to the person to whom the shipper has consigned them.

A private carrier, in the absence of special contract terms, is liable as a bailee for the goods it undertakes to carry. The liability of a common carrier, on the other hand, approaches that of an insurer of the safety of the goods, except when loss or damage is caused by an act of God, an act of a public enemy, the acts or fault of the shipper, the inherent nature of or a defect in the goods, or an act of public authority. The carrier, however, is permitted, through its contract with the shipper, to limit its liability, provided the carrier gives the shipper notice of this limitation and the opportunity to declare a higher value for the goods.

Innkeepers   At common law, **innkeepers** (better known as hotel and motel owners or operators) are held to the same *strict* or *absolute liability* for their guests' belongings as are common carriers for the goods they carry. This rule of strict liability applies only to those who furnish lodging to the public for compensation as a regular business and extends only to the belongings of lodgers who are guests. In almost all jurisdictions, case law and statute have substantially modified the innkeeper's strict liability under common law.

Documents of Title [47-6]

A **document of title**, which includes warehouse receipts and bills of lading, is a record evidencing a right to receive, control, hold, and dispose of the record *and* the goods it covers. Documents of title thus represent title to goods. To be a document of title, a document must be issued by or addressed to a bailee and must cover goods in the bailee's possession that are either identified or are fungible portions of an identified mass.

Briefly, a document of title symbolizes ownership of the goods it describes. Because of the document's legal characteristics, its ownership is equivalent to the ownership or control of the goods it represents, without the necessity of actual or physical possession of the goods. Likewise, it transfers the ownership or control of the goods without necessitating the physical transfer of the goods themselves. For these reasons, documents of title are a convenient means of handling the billions of dollars' worth of goods that are transported by carriers or are stored with warehousers. Documents of title also facilitate the transfer of title to goods and the creation of a security interest in goods. Article 7 of the UCC governs documents of title. In 2003 a revision of

---

Carrier
transporter of goods

Common carrier
carrier that offers its services to the general public

Private (or contract) carrier
carrier that limits its services and does not offer them to the general public

Consignor
shipper of goods

Consignee
person to whom the goods are to be shipped

Innkeeper
hotel or motel operator

Document of title
instrument evidencing ownership of the record and the goods it covers

UCC Article 7 was promulgated to update the original Article 7 and provide a framework for the further development of electronic documents of title. At least forty-five states have adopted Revised Article 7. This chapter covers Revised Article 7.

Types of Documents of Title [47-6a]

To facilitate electronic documents of title, several definitions in Article 1 have been revised including "bearer," "bill of lading," "delivery," "document of title," "holder," and "warehouse receipt." The term "electronic document of title" means "a document of title evidenced by a record consisting of information stored in an electronic medium." The term "tangible document of title" means "a document of title evidenced by a record consisting of information that is inscribed in a tangible medium." "Record" means "information that is inscribed on a tangible medium or that is stored in an electronic or other medium and is retrievable in perceivable form." The concept of an electronic document of title, according to Revised Article 7, allows for commercial practice to determine whether records issued by bailees are "in the regular course of business or financing" and are "treated as adequately evidencing that the person in possession or control of the record is entitled to receive, control, hold, and dispose of the record and the goods the record covers."

Warehouse Receipts   A **warehouse receipt** is a document of title issued by a person engaged in the business of storing goods for hire. A warehouser is liable for damages for loss or injury to the goods caused by his failure to exercise such care in regard to them as a reasonably careful person would exercise under the circumstances. The warehouser must deliver the goods to the person entitled to receive them under the terms of the warehouse receipt. Though a warehouser may limit his liability through a provision in the warehouse receipt fixing a specific maximum liability per article or item or unit of weight, this limitation does not apply when a warehouser converts goods to his own use.

To enforce the payment of her charges and necessary expenses in connection with keeping and handling the goods, a warehouser has a lien on the goods that enables her to sell them at public or private sale after notice and to apply the net proceeds of the sale to the amount of her charges. The Code, moreover, provides the warehouser a definite procedure for enforcing her lien against the goods stored and in her possession.

Bills of Lading   A **bill of lading** is a document of title evidencing the receipt of goods issued by a person engaged in the business of directly or indirectly transporting or forwarding goods. It serves a threefold function: (1) as a receipt for the goods, (2) as evidence of the contract of carriage, and (3) as a document of title. A bill of lading is negotiable if, by its terms, the goods are deliverable to bearer or to the order of a named person. Any other document is nonnegotiable.

Under the Code, bills of lading may be issued not only by common carriers but also by contract carriers, freight forwarders, or any person engaged in the business of transporting or forwarding goods.

The carrier must deliver the goods to the person entitled to receive them under the terms of the bill of lading. Common carriers are extraordinary bailees under the law and are subject to greater liability than are ordinary bailees, such as warehousers.

The Code allows a carrier to limit its liability by contract in all cases in which its rates depend on the value of the goods and the carrier allows the shipper an opportunity to declare a higher value. The limitation does not apply, however, when the carrier converts goods to its own use. Good faith under both Revised Article 1 and Revised Article 7 means "honesty in fact and the observance of reasonable commercial standards of fair dealing."

On goods in its possession that are covered by a bill of lading, the carrier has a lien for the charges and expenses necessary for its preservation of such goods. Against a purchaser for value of a negotiable bill of lading, this lien is limited to charges stated in the bill or in the applicable published tariff or, if no charges are so stated, to a reasonable charge.

The carrier may enforce its lien by public or private sale of the goods after notice to all persons known by the carrier to claim an interest in them. The sale must be on terms that are "commercially reasonable," and the carrier must conduct it in a "commercially reasonable manner."

Warehouse receipt

receipt issued by a person storing goods

Practical Advice

When dealing with warehousers, be alert as to whether they are attempting to limit their liability, and if they are, carefully consider whether you are comfortable with the limitations.

Bill of lading

document issued to the shipper by the carrier

Practical Advice

When dealing with common carriers, be alert as to whether they are attempting to limit their liability, and if they are, carefully consider whether you are comfortable with the limitations.

A purchaser in good faith of goods sold to enforce the lien takes those goods free of any rights of persons against whom the lien was valid, even if the enforcement of the lien does not comply with Code requirements. This rule applies both to carrier's and to warehouser's liens.

Negotiability of Documents of Title [47-6b]

Negotiability

a document of title is negotiable if, by its terms, the goods are to be delivered to bearer or to the order of a named person

The concept of **negotiability** has long been established in law. It is important not only in connection with documents of title but also in connection with commercial paper and investment securities, topics treated in other chapters of this book.

Revised Article 7 provides that a document of title is negotiable if by its terms the goods are to be delivered to bearer or to the order of a named person. Any other document is nonnegotiable. The negotiability of a document is determined at its time of issue. Revised Article 7 further provides for the integration of electronic documents of title and, to the extent possible, applies the same rules for electronic and tangible document of title.

A nonnegotiable document, such as a straight bill of lading or a warehouse receipt under which the goods are deliverable only to a person named in the bill, not to the order of any person or to bearer, may be transferred by assignment but may not be negotiated. Only a negotiable document or instrument may be negotiated.

An individual, under Revised Article 7, has "control" of an *electronic document of title* "if a system employed for evidencing the transfer of interests in the electronic document reliably establishes that person as the person to which the electronic document was issued or transferred." Control of an electronic document of title replaces the concept of possession and indorsement applicable to a tangible document of title. Thus, a person with a tangible document of title delivers the document by voluntarily transferring *possession*, while a person with an electronic document of title delivers the document by voluntarily transferring *control*. The key to having a system of control under Revised Article 7 is the ability to show at any point in time the one person entitled to the goods under the electronic document. Revised Article 7 leaves to the marketplace the creation of systems that meet this standard.

Due Negotiation [47-6c]

The Code sets forth the manner in which a negotiable document of title may be negotiated and the requirements of due negotiation. Under Revised Article 7, an order form negotiable *tangible* document of title running to the order of a named person is negotiated by her indorsement and delivery. Delivery of a tangible document of title means voluntary transfer of possession. After such indorsement in blank or to bearer, the document may be negotiated by delivery alone. A special indorsement, by which the document is indorsed over to a specified person, requires the indorsement of the special indorsee as well as delivery to accomplish a further negotiation.

Under Revised Article 7, a negotiable *electronic* document of title running to the order of a named person *or* to bearer is negotiated by delivery. Indorsement by the named person is not required to negotiate an electronic document of title. Delivery of an electronic document of title means voluntary transfer of control.

Due negotiation

delivery of a negotiable document in the regular course of business to a holder who takes it in good faith, without notice of any defense or claim, and for value

Due negotiation, a term peculiar to Article 7, requires not only that the purchaser of the negotiable document take it in good faith, without notice of any adverse claim or defense, and pay value, but also that she take it in the regular course of business or financing, not in settlement or payment of a money obligation (in essence, a holder by due negotiation). Thus, a transfer for value of a negotiable document of title to a nonbanker or to a person not in business, such as a college professor or student, would not be a due negotiation.

Due negotiation creates new rights in the holder of the document. The transferee does not stand in the shoes of his transferor; in other words, the defects and defenses available against the transferor are not available against the new holder. Newly created by the negotiation, his rights are free of such defects and defenses. This enables bankers and businesspersons to extend credit on documents of title without concern about possible adverse claims or the rights of third parties.

The rights of a holder of a negotiable document of title to whom it has been duly negotiated include (1) title to the document; (2) title to the goods; (3) all rights accruing under the law of agency or estoppel, including rights to goods delivered to the bailee after the document was issued; and (4) the issuer's direct obligation to hold or deliver the goods according to the document's terms.

Warranties

a person who negotiates or delivers a document of title for value, other than a collecting bank or other intermediary, incurs certain warranty obligations unless otherwise agreed

Warranties [47-6d]

A person, other than a collecting bank or other intermediary, who either negotiates or delivers a document of title for value incurs certain warranty obligations, unless otherwise agreed. Such transferor warrants to her immediate purchaser (1) that the document is genuine, (2) that she had no knowledge of any fact that would impair its validity or worth, and (3) that her negotiation or delivery is rightful and fully effective with respect to the title to the document and the goods it represents. Revised Article 7 makes it clear that these warranties only arise in the case of voluntary transfer of possession or control for value.

Ineffective documents

for a person to obtain title to goods by negotiation of a document, the goods must have been delivered to the issuer of the document by their owner or by one to whom the owner has entrusted actual or apparent authority

Ineffective Documents of Title [47-6e]

For a person to obtain title to goods through the negotiation of a document to him, the goods must have been delivered to the document's issuer by their owner or by either one to whom the owner has delivered the goods or one whom the owner has entrusted with actual or apparent authority to ship, store, or sell them. A warehouser or carrier, however, may deliver goods according to the terms of the document that it has issued or otherwise dispose of the goods as provided in the Code without incurring liability, even if the document did not represent title to the goods. The warehouser or carrier need only have acted in good faith and complied with reasonable commercial standards in both the receipt and delivery or other disposition of the goods. Such a bailee has no liability even though the person from whom the bailee received the goods had no authority to obtain the issuance of the document or to dispose of the goods, and the person to whom it delivered the goods had no authority to receive them.

Thus, a carrier or warehouser who receives goods from a thief or finder and later delivers them to a person to whom the thief or finder ordered them to be delivered is not liable to the true owner of the goods. Even a sale of the goods by the carrier or warehouser to enforce a lien for transportation or storage charges and expenses would not subject it to liability.

ETHICAL DILEMMA

Who Is Responsible for the Operation of Rental Property?

Facts Bobby Jones, a schoolteacher from a suburb of Atlanta, rents a fourteen-foot aluminum boat for the three-day Memorial Day weekend from Riverside Canoe and Boat Rentals on the Chattahoochee River. The manager of boat rentals gives Jones general instructions concerning the use of the craft and provides him with a booklet entitled "Boating Safety Rules." The manager also follows the routine procedure of examining the fuel line of the boat and starting the motor to ensure its serviceability.

On Memorial Day, while Jones is operating the boat on the Chattahoochee River, the motor stalls, forcing Jones to row the boat back to shore. Later that same day, Jones takes six minor children out in the boat to give them a ride on the river. Jones has been drinking beer nonstop since 8:00 A.M., and at the time of the afternoon boat ride his blood alcohol level is 0.22 percent. Jones recklessly moves into the swift current and heads toward a concrete dam and spillway. When he finally tries to reverse course, the motor stalls again, the boat is swept over the dam, and all of the children drown. Improbably, Jones lives.

Social, Policy, and Ethical Considerations

1. Could the boat rental company (and manager) have done more to prevent the accident that resulted in the children's deaths? Should the manager have done more?

2. Much rental property, including boats, cars, and power tools such as mowers and saws, is either potentially or inherently dangerous. What is the responsibility of the owner of such equipment to the renter of it? What, if anything, is the responsibility of the renter to the owner? Should the owner be held strictly liable for the renter's accidents with the property, regardless of fault? Why or why not? Who do you think was at fault in this accident?

3. Jones's neighbors, the Corcorans and Duvals, are the parents of four of the drowned children. Together, in their anger, they consult a lawyer to explore the idea of suing either Jones or Riverside Canoe and Boat Rentals, or both. What cause might their lawyer try to make against Jones? Against Riverside Canoe and Boat Rentals? Do you think they should sue? Why or why not?

4. Are some items of equipment so dangerous that state legislatures should pass laws forbidding their rental? If so, what items?

CHAPTER SUMMARY

Introduction to Property and Personal Property

Kinds of Property

Definition interest, or group of interests, that is legally protected

Tangible Property physical objects

Intangible Property property that does not exist in a physical form

Real Property land and interests in land

Personal Property all property that is not real property

Fixture personal property so firmly attached to real property that an interest in it arises under real property law

Transfer of Title to Personal Property

Sale transfer of property for consideration (price)

Gift transfer of property without consideration

- *Delivery* includes both manual transfer of the item and constructive delivery (delivery of something that symbolizes control over the item)
- *Intent*
- *Acceptance*
- *Classification*

Will right to property acquired upon death of the owner

Accession right of a property owner to any increase in such property

Confusion intermixing of goods belonging to two or more owners such that they can identify their individual property only as part of a mass of like goods

- If due to mistake, accident, or agreement, loss shared proportionately
- If caused by an intentional or unauthorized act, wrongdoer bears loss

Possession a person may acquire title by taking possession of property

- *Abandoned Property* intentionally disposed of by the owner; the finder is entitled to the property
- *Lost Property* unintentionally left by the owner; the finder is generally entitled to the property
- *Mislaid Property* intentionally placed by the owner but unintentionally left; the owner of the premises is generally entitled to the property
- *Treasure Trove* coins or currency concealed by the owner for such a length of time that the owner is probably dead or undiscoverable; the finder is entitled to the property

Property Insurance

Fire and Property Insurance

General Definition of Insurance contractual arrangement that distributes risk of loss among a large number of members (the insureds) through an insurance company (the insurer)

Coverage of fire and property insurance provides protection against loss due to fire or related perils

Types of Fire

- *Friendly Fire* fire contained in its intended location
- *Hostile Fire* any fire outside its intended or usual location

Co-insurance a reduction in benefits for underinsuring the value of the property based on a percentage stated in the insurance policy and the amount underinsured

Multiple Insurers if multiple insurers are involved, liability generally is distributed *pro rata*

Types of Policies

- *Valued Policy* covers full value of property as agreed upon by the parties at the time the policy is issued
- *Open Policy* covers fair market value of property as calculated immediately prior to the loss

Nature of Insurance Contracts

General Contract Law basic principles of contract law apply

Insurable Interest a financial interest or a factual expectancy in someone's property that justifies insuring the property; the interest must exist at the time the property loss occurs

Premiums amount to be paid for an insurance policy

Defenses of the Insurer

- *Misrepresentation* false representation of a material fact made by the insured that is justifiably relied upon by the insurer; enables the insurer to rescind the contract within a specified time
- *Breach of Warranty* the failure of a required condition; generally an insurer may avoid liability for a breach of warranty only if the breach is material
- *Concealment* fraudulent failure of an applicant for insurance to disclose material facts that the insurer does not know; allows the insurer to rescind the contract
- *Waiver* an insurer intentionally relinquishes the right to deny liability
- *Estoppel* an insurer is prevented by its own conduct from asserting a defense

Termination an insurance contract may be terminated by due performance or cancellation

---

Bailments and Documents of Title

Bailments

Definition the temporary transfer of personal property by one party (the bailor) to another (the bailee)

Classification of Bailments

- *For the Bailor's Sole Benefit*
- *For the Bailee's Sole Benefit*
- *For Mutual Benefit* includes ordinary commercial bailments

Essential Elements

- *Delivery of Possession*
- *Personal Property*
- *Possession, but Not Ownership, for a Determinable Time*
- *Restoration of Possession to the Bailor*

Rights and Duties

- *Bailee's Duty to Exercise Due Care* the bailee must exercise reasonable care to protect the safety of the property and to return it to the proper person
- *Bailee's Absolute Liability* occurs when (1) the parties so agree; (2) the custom of the industry requires the bailee to insure the property against the risk in question, but he fails to do so; or (3) the bailee uses the bailed property in an unauthorized manner
- *Bailee's Right to Limit Liability* certain bailees are not permitted to limit their liability for breach of their duties, except as provided by statute
- *Bailee's Right to Compensation* entitled to reasonable compensation for work or services performed on the bailed goods
- *Bailor's Duties* in bailment for sole benefit of bailee, the bailor warrants that she is unaware of any defects; in all other bailments, the bailor has a duty to warn of all known defects and all defects she should discover upon a reasonable inspection

Special Types

- *Pledge* security interest by possession
- *Warehouser* storer of goods for compensation; warehouser must exercise reasonable care to protect the safety of the stored goods and to deliver them to the proper person
- *Carrier of Goods* transporter of goods; a common carrier is an extraordinary bailee, and a private carrier is an ordinary bailee
- *Innkeeper* hotel or motel operator; is an extraordinary bailee except as limited by statute or case law

Documents of Title

Definition an instrument evidencing ownership of the record and the goods it covers

Types

- *Warehouse Receipt* receipt issued by person storing goods
- *Bill of Lading* document issued to the shipper by the carrier (1) as a receipt for the goods, (2) as evidence of their carriage contract, and (3) as a document of title

Negotiability a document of title is negotiable if, by its terms, the goods are to be delivered to bearer or to the order of a named person

Due Negotiation delivery of a negotiable document in the regular course of business to a holder, who takes in good faith, for value, and without notice of any defense or claim

Warranties a person who negotiates or delivers a document of title for value, other than a collecting bank or other intermediary, incurs certain warranty obligations unless otherwise agreed

Ineffective Documents for a person to obtain title to goods by negotiation of a document, the goods must have been delivered to the issuer of the document by their owner or by one to whom the owner has entrusted actual or apparent authority

QUESTIONS

1. In January, Roger Burke loaned his favorite nephew, Jimmy White, his valuable Picasso painting. Knowing that Jimmy would celebrate his twenty-first birthday on May 15, Burke sent a letter to Jimmy on April 14 stating:

   > Dear Jimmy,
   > Tomorrow I leave on my annual trip to Europe, and I want to make you a fitting birthday gift, which I do by sending you my enclosed promissory note. Also I want you to keep the Picasso that I loaned you last January, and you may now consider it yours. Happy birthday!
   > Affectionately,
   > Uncle Roger

   The negotiable promissory note for $5,000 sent with the letter was signed by Roger Burke, payable to Jimmy White or bearer, and dated May 15. On May 21, Burke was killed in an automobile accident while motoring in France.

   First Bank was appointed administrator of Burke's estate. Jimmy presented the note to the administrator and demanded payment, which was refused. Jimmy brought an action against First Bank as administrator, seeking recovery on the note. The administrator in turn brought an action against Jimmy, seeking the return of the Picasso.
   a. What decision in the action on the note?
   b. What decision in the action to recover the painting?

2. Several years ago, Pierce purchased a tract of land on which stood an old, vacant house. Recently, Pierce employed Fried, a carpenter, to repair and remodel the house. While Fried was tearing out a partition to enlarge one of the rooms, he found a metal box hidden in the wall. After breaking open the box and discovering that it contained $2,000 in gold and silver coins and old-style bills, Fried took the box and its contents to Pierce and told her where he had found it. When Fried handed the box and the money over to Pierce, he said, "If you do not find the owner, I claim the money." Pierce placed the money in an envelope and deposited it in her safe deposit box, where it presently remains. No one has ever claimed the money, but Pierce refuses to give it to Fried. Will Fried be able to recover the money from Pierce? Why?

3. Gable, the owner of a lumber company, was cutting trees over the boundary line between his property and property owned by Lane. Although he realized he had crossed onto Lane's property, Gable continued to cut trees of the same kind as those he had cut on his own land. While on Lane's property, he found a diamond ring on the ground, which he took home. All of the timber Gable cut that day was commingled. What are Lane's rights, if any (a) in the timber and (b) in the ring?

4. Decide each of the following problems.
   a. A chimney sweep found a jewel and took it to a goldsmith, whose apprentice removed the stone and refused to return it. The chimney sweep sues the goldsmith.
   b. One of several boys walking along a railroad track found an old stocking. All started playing with it until it burst in the hands of its discoverer, revealing several hundred dollars. The original discoverer claims all of the money; the other boys claim it should be divided equally.
   c. A traveling salesperson leaving a store notices a parcel of bank notes on the floor. He picks them up and gives them to the owner of the store to keep for the true owner. After three years, they have not been reclaimed, and the salesperson sues the storekeeper.
   d. Frank is hired to clean the swimming pool at the country club. He finds a diamond ring on the bottom of the pool. The true owner cannot be found. The country club sues Frank for possession of the ring.
   e. A customer found a pocketbook lying on a barber's table. He gave it to the barber to hold for the true owner, who failed to appear. The customer sues the barber.

5. Jones had fifty crates of oranges equally divided among grades A, B, and C, grade A being the highest quality and C being the lowest. Smith had one thousand crates of oranges,

about 90 percent of which were grade A, but some of which were grades B and C, the exact percentage of each being unknown. Smith willfully mixed Jones's crates with his own so that it was impossible to identify any particular crate. Jones seized the whole lot. Smith demanded nine hundred crates of grade A and fifty crates each of grades B and C. Jones refused to give them up unless Smith could identify particular crates. This Smith could not do. Smith brought an action against Jones to recover what he demanded or its value. Judgment for whom, and why?

6. Barnes, the owner and operator of Blackacre, decided to cease farming operations and liquidate his holdings. Barnes sold fifty head of yearling Merino sheep to Billing and then sold Blackacre to Clifton. He executed and delivered to Billing a bill of sale for the sheep and was paid for them. It was understood that Billing would send a truck for the sheep within a few days. At the same time, Barnes executed a warranty deed conveying Blackacre to Clifton. Clifton took possession of the farm and brought along one hundred head of his yearling Merino sheep and turned them into the pasture, not knowing the sheep Barnes sold Billing were still in the pasture. After the sheep were mixed, it was impossible to identify the fifty head belonging to Billing. Explain whether Billing will recover the fifty head of sheep from Clifton.

7. Susan permitted Kevin to take her very old grandfather clock on the basis of Kevin's representations that he was skilled at repairing such clocks and restoring them to their original condition and could do the job for $60.00. The clock had been badly damaged for years. Kevin immediately sold the clock to Fixit Shop for $30.00. Fixit Shop was in the business of repairing a large variety of items and also sold used articles. Three months later, Susan was in the Fixit Shop and clearly identified a grandfather clock Fixit Shop had for sale as the one she had given Kevin to repair. Fixit Shop had replaced more than half of the moving parts by having exact duplicates custom-made; the clock's exterior had been restored by a skilled cabinetmaker; and the clock's face had been replaced by a duplicate. All materials belonged to Fixit Shop, and its employees accomplished the work. Fixit Shop asserts it bought the clock in the normal course of business from Kevin, who represented that it belonged to him. The fair market value of the clock in its damaged condition was $30.00, and the value of repairs made is $220.

   Susan sued Fixit Shop for return of the clock. Fixit Shop defended that it then had title to the clock and, in the alternative, that Susan must pay the value of the repairs if she is entitled to regain possession. Who will prevail? Why?

8. Under an oral agreement, Hyer rented from Bateman a vacant lot for a filling station. Hyer placed on the lot a lightly constructed building bolted to a concrete slab and several storage tanks laid on the ground in a shallow excavation. Later, Hyer prepared a lease that contained a provision allowing him to remove the equipment at the termination of the lease. This lease was not executed, having been rejected by Bateman due to a renewal clause it contained. Several years later, another lease was prepared, which both Hyer and Bateman did sign. This lease did not mention removal of the equipment. At the termination of this lease, Hyer removed

the equipment, and Bateman brought an action to recover possession of the equipment. What judgment?

9. Elvers sold a parcel of real estate, describing it by its legal description and making no mention of any improvements or fixtures on it. The land had upon it a residence, a barn, a rail fence, a stack of hay, some growing corn, and a windmill. The residence had a mirror built into the west wall of the living room and a heating system consisting of a furnace, steam pipes, and coils. In the house were chairs, beds, tables, and other furniture. On the house was a lightning rod. In the basement were screens for the windows. Which of these things passed by the deed and which did not?

10. John Swan rented a safe deposit box at the Tenth Citizens Bank of Emanon, State of X. On December 17, 2014, Swan went to the bank with stock certificates to place in the safe deposit box. After he was admitted to the vault and had placed the stock certificates in the box, Swan found lying on a chair in the privacy booth of the vault a $5,000 negotiable bearer bond issued by the State of Wisconsin with coupons attached, due June 30, 2019. Swan picked up the bond and, observing that it did not carry the name of the owner, left the vault and went to the office of the president of the bank. He told the president what had occurred and delivered the bond to the president only after obtaining his promise that, should the owner not call for the bond or become known to the bank by June 30, 2015, the bank would redeliver the bond to Swan. On July 1, 2015, Swan learned that the owner of the bond had not called for it, nor was his identity known to the bank. Swan then asked that the bond be returned to him. The bank refused, stating that it would continue to hold the bond until the owner claimed it. Explain whether Swan will prevail in his action to recover possession of the bond.

11. Lile, an insurance broker who handled all insurance for Tempo Co., purchased a fire policy from Insurance Company insuring Tempo Co.'s factory against fire in the amount of $750,000. Before the policy was delivered to Tempo and while it was still in Lile's hands, Tempo advised Lile to cancel the policy. Prior to cancellation, however, Tempo suffered a loss. Tempo now makes a claim against Insurance Company on the policy. The premium had been billed to Lile but was unpaid at the time of loss. In an action by Tempo Co. against Insurance Company, what judgment?

12. On July 15, Adler purchased in Chicago a Buick sedan, intending to drive it that day to St. Louis, Missouri. He telephoned a friend, Maruchek, who was in the insurance business, and told him that he wanted liability insurance on the automobile, limited in amount to $50,000 for injuries to one person and to $100,000 for any one accident. Maruchek took the order and told Adler over the telephone that he was covered and that his policy would be written by the Young Insurance Company. Later that same day and before Maruchek had informed the Young Insurance Company of Adler's application, Adler negligently operated the automobile and seriously injured Brown, who brings suit against Adler. Is Adler covered by liability insurance?

13. Graham owns a building having a fair market value of $120,000. She takes out a fire insurance policy from the

Bentley Insurance Company for $72,000; the policy contains an 80 percent co-insurance clause. The building is damaged by fire to the extent of $48,000. How much insurance is Graham entitled to collect?

14. Phil was the owner of a herd of twenty highly bred dairy cows. He was a prosperous farmer, but his health was very poor. On the advice of his doctor, Phil decided to winter in Arizona. Before he left, he made an agreement with Freya under which Freya was to keep the cows on Freya's farm through the winter, be paid the sum of $800 by Phil, and return to Phil the twenty cows at the close of the winter. For reasons that Freya thought made good farming sense, Freya sold six of the cows and replaced them with six other cows. After winter was over, Phil returned from Arizona. Is Freya liable for conversion of the original six cows? Why?

15. Hines stored her furniture, including a grand piano, in Arnett's warehouse. Needing more space, Arnett stored Hines's piano in Butler's warehouse next door. As a result of a fire, which occurred without any fault of Arnett or Butler, both warehouses and their contents were destroyed. Is Arnett liable to Hines for the value of her piano and furniture? Explain.

16. Curtis rented a safe deposit box from Reliable Safe Deposit Company, in which he deposited valuable securities and $4,000 in cash. Later, after opening the box and discovering $1,000 missing, Curtis brought an action against Reliable. At the trial, the company showed that its customary procedure was as follows: that there were two keys for each box furnished to each renter; that if a key was lost, the lock was changed; that new keys were provided for each lock each time a box was rented; that there were two clerks in charge of the vault; and that one of the clerks was always present to open the box. Reliable Safe Deposit Company also proved that two keys were given to Curtis at the time he rented his box; that his box could not be opened without the use of one of the keys in his possession; and that the company had issued no other keys to Curtis's box. Explain whether Reliable is obligated to pay Curtis for the missing $1,000.

17. A, B, and C each stored five thousand bushels of yellow corn in the same bin in X's warehouse. X wrongfully sold ten thousand bushels of this corn to Y. A contends that inasmuch as his five thousand bushels of corn were placed in the bin first, the remaining five thousand bushels belong to him. What are the rights of the parties?

18. a. On April 1, Mary Rich, at the solicitation of Super Fur Company, delivered a $3,000 mink coat to the company at its place of business for storage in its vaults until November 1. On the same day, she paid the company its customary charge of $20 for such storage. After Mary left the store, the general manager of the company, on finding that its storage vaults were already filled to capacity, delivered Mary's coat to Swift Trucking Company for shipment to Fur Storage Company. En route, the truck in which Mary's coat was being transported was badly damaged by fire caused by the driver's negligence, and Mary's coat was totally destroyed. Is Super Fur Company liable to Mary for the value of her coat? Why?

b. Would your answer be the same if Mary's coat had been safely delivered to Fur Storage Company and had been stolen from the company's storage vaults without negligence on its part? Why?

19. Rich, a club member, left his golf clubs with Bogan, the pro at the Happy Hours Country Club, to be refinished at Bogan's pro shop. The refinisher employed by Bogan suddenly left town, taking Rich's clubs with him. The refinisher had previously been above suspicion, although Bogan had never checked on the man's character references. A valuable sand wedge that Bogan had borrowed from another member, Smith, for his own use in an important tournament was also stolen by the refinisher, as well as several pairs of golf shoes that Bogan had checked for members without charge as an accommodation. The club members concerned each made claims against Bogan for their losses. Can (a) Rich, (b) Smith, and (c) the other members compel Bogan to make good their respective losses?

20. Donna drove an automobile into Terry's garage and requested him to make repairs for which the charge would be $125. Donna, however, never returned to get the automobile. Two months later, Carla saw the automobile in Terry's garage and claimed it as her own, asserting that it had been stolen from her. Terry told Carla that she could have the automobile if she paid for the repairs and storage, which Carla did. One week later, Molly appeared and proved that the automobile was hers, that it had been stolen from her, and that neither Donna nor Carla had any rights in it. Discuss whether Terry is liable for conversion of the automobile.

21. On June 1, Cain delivered his 2010 automobile to Barr, the operator of a repair shop, for necessary repairs. Barr put the car in his lot on Main Street. The lot, which is fenced on all sides except along Main Street, holds one hundred cars and is unguarded at night, although the police make periodic checks. The lot is well lighted. The cars do not have the keys in them when left out overnight. At some time during the night of June 4, the hood, starter, alternator, and gearshift were stolen from Cain's car. The car remained on the lot, and during the evening of June 5, the transmission was stolen from the car. Did Barr exercise due care in taking care of the automobile?

22. Seton in Phoenix, according to a contract with Rider in New York, ships to Rider goods conforming to the contract and takes from the carrier the bill of lading for a shipper's order that Seton indorses in blank and forwards by mail to Clemson, his agent in New York, with instructions to deliver the bill of lading to Rider on receipt of payment of the price for the goods. Forest, a thief, steals the bill of lading from Clemson and transfers it for value to Pace, a *bona fide* purchaser. Before the goods arrive in New York, Rider is insolvent. What are the rights of the parties?

CASE PROBLEMS

23. Scarola purchased an automobile for value and without knowledge that it was stolen. After he insured the car with Insurance Company of North America (INA), the car was stolen once again. When INA refused to reimburse Scarola for the loss, contending that he did not have an insurable interest in the car, Scarola brought an action. Did Scarola have an insurable interest in the automobile? Why?

24. Sears had sold to and installed in the Seven Palms Motor Inn a number of furnishings, including drapes and bedspreads, in connection with the construction of a motel on land Seven Palms owned. Sears did not receive payment in full for the materials and labor and brought suit to recover $8,357.49, with interest, and to establish a mechanic's lien on the motel and land for the unpaid portion of the furnishings. Seven Palms asserted that neither the drapes nor bedspreads were fixtures and that, thus, Sears could not obtain a mechanic's lien on them. Explain whether the drapes and bedspreads are fixtures.

25. David E. Ross, his two brothers, and their families operated and owned the entire stock of five businesses. Ross had three children: Rod, David II, and Betsy. David II and Betsy were not involved in the operation of the companies, but Rod began working for one of the firms, Equitable Life and Casualty Insurance Company, in 2008. Between 2010 and 2014, the elder Ross informed a number of persons of his desire to reward Rod for his work with Equitable Life by giving him stock in addition to the stock he would inherit. He subsequently executed several stock transfers to Rod, representing shares in various family businesses, which were reflected by appropriate entries on the corporate books. Certificates were issued in Rod's name and placed in an envelope identified with the name Rod Ross, but they were kept with the other family stock certificates in an office safe to which Rod did not have access. In all, one-fourth of the stock holdings of David E. Ross were transferred to Rod in this manner. This fact is consistent with the elder Ross's expressed intention that Rod should ultimately receive a total of one-half of the stock upon his father's death. David E. died in April 2014. His will divided the estate equally among the three children and made no reference to prior gifts of stock to Rod. David II and Betsy brought an action contesting the validity of the stock transfers. Are the *inter vivos* gifts of the stock valid? Explain.

26. Mrs. Laval was a patient of Dr. Leopold, a practicing psychiatrist. Dr. Leopold shared an office with two associates practicing in the same field. No receptionist or other employee attended the office. Mrs. Laval placed her coat in the clothes closet that was placed in the reception area for the use of the patients. Later, when she returned to retrieve the coat to leave, she found it missing. Is Dr. Leopold liable to Mrs. Laval for the value of her coat? Explain.

27. Mr. Sewall left his car in a parking lot owned by Fitz-Inn Auto Parks, Inc. The lot was approximately one hundred by two hundred feet in size and had a chain link fence along the rear boundary to separate the lot from a facility of the Massachusetts Bay Transportation Authority. Although the normal entrance and exit were located at the front of the lot, it was also possible to leave by way of small side streets on either side of the lot. Upon entering the lot, the driver would pay the attendant on duty a fee of $5.00 to park. The attendant's duties were limited to collecting money from patrons and directing them to parking spaces. Ordinarily, the attendant remained on duty until 11:00 A.M., after which time the lot was left unattended. Furthermore, a patron could remove his car from the lot at any time without interference by any employee of the parking lot.

On the morning of April 15, Sewall entered the lot, paid the $5.00 fee, parked his car in a space designated by the attendant, locked it, and took the keys with him. This was a routine he had followed for several years. When he returned to the unattended lot that evening, however, he found that his car was gone, apparently having been stolen by an unidentified third person. Is Fitz-Inn, the owner of the lot, liable for the value of the car? Why?

28. Mrs. Mieske delivered thirty-two 50-foot reels of developed movie film to the Bartell Drug Company to be spliced together into four reels for viewing convenience. She placed the films, which contained irreplaceable pictures of her family's activities over a period of years, into the order in which they were to be spliced and then delivered them to the manager of Bartell. The manager placed a film processing packet on the bag of films and gave Mrs. Mieske a receipt that stated, "We assume no responsibility beyond retail cost of film unless otherwise agreed to in writing." Although the disclaimer was not discussed, Mrs. Mieske's parting words to the store manager were, "Don't lose these. They are my life."

Bartell sent the film to its processing agent, GAF Corporation, which intended to send them to another processing lab for splicing. While at the GAF laboratory, however, the film was accidentally placed in the garbage dumpster and was never recovered. Upon learning of the loss of their film, the Mieskes brought action to recover damages from Bartell and GAF. The defendants argued that their liability was limited to the cost of the unexposed film. Are GAF or Bartell liable to the Mieskes? If so, for how much?

29. Plaintiff, Heath Benjamin (Benjamin), found more than $18,000 in currency inside the wing of an airplane. At the time of this discovery, State Central Bank (State) owned the plane and it was being serviced by Lindner Aviation, Inc. (Lindner). Benjamin at the time was employed by Lindner and was conducting a routine annual inspection of the plane.

As part of the inspection, Benjamin removed panels from the underside of the wings. Although these panels were to be removed annually as part of the routine inspection, a couple of the screws holding the panel on the left wing were so rusty that Benjamin had to use a drill to remove them. Benjamin testified that the panel probably had not been removed for several years. Inside the left wing Benjamin discovered two packets approximately four inches high and wrapped in aluminum foil. He removed the packets from the wing and took off the foil wrapping. Inside the foil was approximately $18,000, tied in string and wrapped in handkerchiefs. The money was eventually turned over to the Keokuk police department. No one came forward within twelve months thereafter claiming to be the true owner of the money. Explain who is entitled to the currency.

30. Calvin Klein, Ltd., a New York clothing company, had used the services of Trylon Trucking Corporation for more than three years, involving hundreds of shipments. After completing each carriage, Trylon would forward to Calvin Klein an invoice that contained a limitation of liability provision. The provision stated,

> In consideration of the rate charged, the shipper agrees that the carrier shall not be liable for more than $50.00 on any shipment accepted for delivery to one consignee unless a greater value is declared, in writing, upon receipt at time of shipment and charge for such greater value paid, or agreed to be paid, by shipper.

On April 2, Trylon dispatched its driver Jamahl Jefferson to the J.F.K. International Airport to pick up 2,833 blouses sent from Hong Kong, China, to Calvin Klein. The driver disappeared, stealing both the truck and the blouses. Calvin Klein sued Trylon for the full value of the blouses. Does the limitation of liability provision extend to the shipment? Explain.

TAKING SIDES

The plaintiffs are public utilities providing telecommunications services in New Hampshire. The plaintiffs commenced separate actions for abatement of real estate taxes against sixteen municipalities. The plaintiffs disputed the defendants' treatment of its communications equipment as real estate, thereby challenging their authority to tax its equipment. The communications equipment at issue involves two basic categories: (1) distribution plant, which includes telephone poles, wires, and underground conduits; and (2) central office equipment, consisting of frames, switches, and other power equipment.

The plaintiffs submitted affidavits setting forth the following facts. All of the plaintiffs' poles, wires, and underground conduits located in the municipalities are placed either on public rights of way or on private property owned by third parties. Approximately 90 percent of the poles are located on public rights of way pursuant to licenses issued by the state or the municipalities. The remaining 10 percent of the poles are placed on private property either by consent of the property owner or pursuant to an easement. The poles, wires, and underground conduits are installed in a manner that permits and facilitates their removal and relocation. Consequently, removal of that equipment is neither complicated nor time consuming, and does not harm the underlying land or change its usefulness. The plaintiffs remove and relocate their poles, wires,

and underground conduits at the request of the state or the applicable private landowner or municipality. In obtaining the licenses, consents, or easements for their poles, wires, and underground conduits, the plaintiffs insist on maintaining ownership of that equipment and refuse any requests to make the equipment a permanent part of the realty. The plaintiffs' central office equipment, most of which is located in buildings owned by the plaintiffs, is both portable and designed to permit removal and relocation. The plaintiffs' practice and policy is to move pieces of central office equipment among buildings in response to changes in technology or system use. Although certain frames are bolted to the buildings, their removal is achieved without affecting the usefulness of the buildings or the frames themselves. When the plaintiffs ultimately vacate a building used as a central office, they remove all of their equipment and merely transfer the building "as a shell." The vacated building, though devoid of central office equipment, retains utility for other commercial or professional uses. The defendants did not dispute the specific facts set forth by the plaintiffs.

a. What are the arguments that the property is not real property and therefore not subject to taxation by the municipalities?

b. What are the arguments that the property is real property and can be taxed by the municipalities?

c. Who is correct? Explain.

Interests in Real Property

CHAPTER 48

Aedificare in tuo proprio solo non licet quod alteri noceat. To build upon your land what may injure another is not lawful.

Legal Maxim

CHAPTER OUTCOMES

After reading and studying this chapter, you should be able to:

1. Identify and explain the freehold interests: (a) fee simple estate, (b) qualified fee estate, (c) life estate, (d) remainder interest, and (e) reversionary interest.

2. Distinguish between a vested and contingent remainder.

3. Explain the primary rights and obligations of landlords and tenants.

4. Identify and explain the various forms of concurrent ownership of real property.

5. Identify and describe the various ways in which an easement may be created.

Interests in real property may be divided into possessory and nonpossessory interests. Possessory interests in real property, called estates, are classified, according to the quantity, nature, and extent of the rights they involve, into two major categories: freehold estates (those existing for an indefinite time or for the life of a person) and estates less than freehold (those that exist for a predetermined time), called leasehold estates. Both freehold estates and leasehold estates are regarded as possessory interests in property. In addition, there are several nonpossessory interests in property, including easements and *profits á prendre*. In addition, a person may have a privilege or license to go on property for a certain purpose. The ownership of interests in property may be held by one individual or concurrently by two or more persons, each of whom is entitled to an undivided interest in the entire property. We will consider all of these topics in this chapter.

FREEHOLD ESTATES [48-1]

Freehold estate

ownership of real property for an indefinite time or for the life of a person

As stated previously, a **freehold estate** is a right of ownership of real property for an indefinite time (fee estate) or for the life of a person (life estate). Of all the estates in real property, the most valuable are usually those present estates that combine the enjoyment of immediate possession with ownership at least for life. These estates are either some form of fee estates or estates for life. In addition, either type of estate may be created without immediate right to possession; such an estate is known as a future interest. Estates are classified according to their duration.

Fee Estates [48-1a]

Fee estate

right to immediate possession for an indefinite period of time

Fee estates include the right to immediate possession for an indefinite time and the right to transfer the interest by deed or will. Fee estates include both fee simple and qualified fee estates.

Fee Simple Estate

Fee simple estate

absolute ownership of property, which can be sold or passed on by will or inheritance

Fee Simple Estate   A **fee simple estate** means that the property is owned absolutely and can be sold or passed on by will or inheritance; this estate provides the greatest possible ownership interest. The absolute rights to transfer ownership and to transmit such ownership through inheritance are basic characteristics of a fee simple estate. Fee simple is the most extensive and comprehensive estate in land; all other estates are derived from it.

A fee simple is created by any words that indicate an intent to convey absolute ownership. "To B in fee simple" will accomplish the purpose, as will "to B forever." The general presumption is that a conveyance is intended to convey full and absolute title in the absence of a clear intent to the contrary. The grantor must possess, or have the right to transfer, a fee simple interest to transfer such an interest.

Qualified fee estate

Ownership subject to its being terminated upon the happening of a contingent event

Qualified or Base Fee Estate   A **qualified fee estate** is an estate in land that is less than a fee simple estate because it will terminate on the happening of a contingent event. A qualified fee estate is also known as a base fee, conditional fee, or fee simple defeasible. For example, Abe may provide in his will that his daughter is to have his house and lot in "fee simple forever so long as she does not use it to sell alcoholic beverages, in which case the house shall revert to Abe's estate." If his daughter dies without using the house to sell alcoholic beverages, the property is transferred to her heirs as if she had owned it absolutely. However, if she uses the house to sell alcoholic beverages, the daughter would lose her title to the land, and it would revert to Abe's heirs.

The holder of a qualified fee interest may transfer the property by deed or will, and the property will pass by intestate succession. All transferees, however, take the property subject to the initial condition imposed upon the interest.

Life Estates [48-1b]

Life estate

ownership right for the life of a designated person

Remainder

ownership estate that takes effect when the prior estate terminates

A **life estate** is an ownership right in property for the life of a designated individual; a **remainder** is the ownership estate that takes effect when the prior life estate terminates. For example, a grant or a devise (grant by will) "to Alex for life" creates in Alex an estate that terminates on his death. Such a provision may stand alone, in which case the property will revert to the grantor and his heirs; or, as is more likely, the provision will be followed by a subsequent grant to another party, such as "to Alex for life and then to Mario and his heirs." Alex is the *life tenant*, and Mario generally is described as the *remainderman*. Alex's life, however, need not be the measure of his life estate, as where an estate is granted "to Alex for the life of Bob." On Bob's death, Alex's interest terminates; if Alex dies before Bob, Alex's interest passes to his heirs or as he directs in his will for the remainder of Bob's life.

Practical Advice

The use of a life estate with a remainder is a useful way of providing income to one person with the ability to control the distribution of the corpus upon the termination of the life estate.

No particular words are necessary to create a life estate, as long as the words chosen clearly reflect the grantor's intent. Life estates arise most frequently in connection with the creation of trusts, which will be discussed in Chapter 50.

Generally, a life tenant may make reasonable use of the property as long as he does not commit "waste." Any act or omission that permanently injures the realty or unreasonably changes its characteristics or value constitutes **waste**. For example, the failure to repair a building, the unreasonable cutting of timber, or the neglect of an adequate conservation policy may subject the life tenant to an action by the remainderman to recover damages for waste.

Waste

any act or omission that permanently injures the realty or unreasonably changes its value

A conveyance by the life tenant passes only her interest. The life tenant and the remainderman may, however, join in a conveyance to pass the entire fee to the property, or the life tenant may terminate her interest by conveying it to the remainderman.

Future Interests [48-1c]

Not all interests in property carry the right to immediate possession, even though the right and title to the interest are absolute. Thus, where property is conveyed or devised by will "to A during his life and then to B and her heirs," B has a definite, existing *interest* in the property, but she is not entitled to immediate *possession*. This right and similar rights, generically referred to as future interests, are of two principal types: reversions and remainders.

Reversion

grantor's right to property upon termination of another estate

Reversions   If Anderson conveys property "to Benson for life" and makes no disposition of the remainder of the estate, Anderson holds the **reversion**—the grantor's right to the property on the death of the life tenant. Thus, Anderson would regain ownership to the property when

Benson dies. However, because Anderson has only to await the termination of his grantee's estate before he regains ownership, a reversion in Anderson is also created if he conveys property "to Caldwell for ten years." Reversions may be transferred by deed or will and pass by intestate succession.

Possibility of reverter
conditional reversionary
interest

A conditional reversionary interest, a **possibility of reverter** exists when property may return to the grantor or his successor in interest because an event on which a fee simple estate was to terminate has occurred. This potential reversion is present in the grant of a base or qualified fee, previously discussed in this chapter. Thus, Karlene has a possibility of reverter if she dedicates property to a public use "so long as it is used as a park" and indicates that if it is not so used, it will revert to her heirs. If, in one hundred years, the city ceases to use the property for a park, Karlene's heirs will be entitled to the property. A possibility of a reverter may pass by will or intestate succession. In some states, it may be transferred by deed.

Remainders A remainder, as discussed, is an estate in property that, like a reversion, will take effect in possession, if at all, on the termination of a prior estate created by the *same instrument*. Unlike a reversion, a remainder is held by a person other than the grantor or his successors. A grant from Gwen "to Lew for his life and then to Robert and his heirs" creates a remainder in Robert. On the termination of the life estate, Robert will be entitled to possession as remainderman, taking his title not from Lew but from the original grantor, Gwen.

Vested remainder
unconditional remainder
that is a fixed, present
interest to be enjoyed in
the future

A **vested remainder** is one in which the only contingency to possession by the remainderman is the termination of all preceding estates created by the transferor. When Richard has a remainder in fee, subject only to a life estate in Laura, the only obstacle to the right of immediate possession by Robert or his heirs is Laura's life. Laura's death is sufficient and necessary to place Robert in possession. The law considers this unconditional or vested remainder as a fixed, *present* interest to be enjoyed in the future.

Contingent remainder
remainder interest
conditional upon the
happening of an event in
addition to the termination
of the preceding estate

By comparison, a **contingent remainder** is one in which the right to possession is dependent or conditional on the happening of some event *in addition* to the termination of the preceding estates. The contingent remainder may be conditioned on the existence of someone yet to be born or on the happening of an event that may never occur. A provision in a will "to David for life and then to his children, but if he has no children then to Julie" creates contingent remainders both as to the children and as to Julie. Transferable by deed in most states, a contingent remainder is also inheritable, unless limited to termination prior to the death of the remainderman.

CONCEPT REVIEW 48-1

Freehold Estates

Interest	Complementary Estate	Duration	Transfer by Deed	Transfer by Will or Intestacy
Fee Simple	None	Perpetual	Yes	Yes
Qualified Fee	Possibility of reverter	Until contingency occurs	Yes	Yes
Life Estate	Reversion or remainder	Life of indicated person	Yes	No, unless measuring life is not life tenant's
Reversion	Life estate	Perpetual	Yes	Yes
Possibility of Reverter	Qualified fee	Perpetual if contingency occurs	In some states	Yes
Vested Remainder	Life estate	Perpetual	Yes	Yes
Contingent Remainder	Life estate	Perpetual if contingency occurs	In most states	Yes, unless it is limited such that it terminates before the death of the remainderman

Leasehold Estates [48-2]

A lease is both a contract and a grant of an estate in land. It is a contract, express or implied, by which the owner of the land, the **landlord** (lessor), grants to another, the **tenant** (lessee), an exclusive right to use and possess the land for a definite or ascertainable period or term. The possessory term thus granted is a nonfreehold estate in land called a **leasehold estate**. The landlord retains an interest, or a *reversion*, in the property. A leasehold estate has two principal characteristics: it continues for a definite or ascertainable term and carries with it the tenant's obligation to pay rent to the landlord. Thus, if Linda, the owner of a house and lot, rents both to Ted for a year, Linda, of course, still holds title to the property; but she has sold to Ted the right to occupy it. Ted's right to occupy the property is superior to that of Linda, and as long as Ted occupies the property according to the terms of the lease contract, he has, as a practical matter, exclusive possession against all the world as though he were the actual owner.

The law of leasehold estates has changed considerably over the past few decades. Traditionally, the common law viewed a leasehold estate less as a contract than as a conveyance of the use of land. In the twenty-first century, the landlord-tenant relationship is primarily viewed as a contract and therefore subject to the contract doctrines of unconscionability, implied warranties, and constructive conditions.

Moreover, numerous ordinances and statutes, such as the Uniform Residential Landlord and Tenant Act enacted by at least twenty-one states, now protect tenants' rights, thereby further modifying the landlord–tenant relationship. The Uniform Residential Landlord and Tenant Act, which was promulgated by the Uniform Law Commission, provides a comprehensive system for regulating the relationship between landlords and tenants and governs most persons who reside in rental housing. The Act does not apply to commercial or industrial properties, the occupancy of hotels or motels, mobile home park tenants, and recreational vehicle long-term tenants. The Act contains detailed requirements regarding the landlord's obligations (restrictions on security deposits and methods for providing notices to tenants and prohibitions on certain provisions in rental agreements), the landlord's rights (collection of rent, eviction, entering the premises, and termination of the lease), the tenant's obligations (payment of rent and compliance with rules), and the tenant's rights (possession, termination of the lease, receipt of essential services, and avoidance of unlawful eviction). Finally, the Act provides remedies for noncompliance by either the landlord or tenant.

Creation and Duration [48-2a]

Because leaseholds are created by contract, the usual requirements for contract formation therefore apply. In most jurisdictions, leases for a term longer than a statutorily specified period, generally fixed at either one or three years, must be in writing. A few states require that all leases be in writing. Leasehold interests have historically been divided into four categories: (1) definite term, (2) periodic tenancy, (3) tenancy at will, and (4) tenancy at sufferance. These tenancies most significantly vary in their duration and their manner of termination.

Definite Term　A lease for a **definite term** automatically expires at the end of the term. Such a lease is frequently termed a tenancy for years, even though its duration may be one year or less. It is created by express agreement, oral or written. No notice to terminate is required since the lease established its termination date.

Periodic Tenancy　A **periodic tenancy** is a lease of indefinite duration that continues for successive periods unless terminated by notice to the other party. For example, a lease "to Ted from month to month" or "from year to year" creates a periodic tenancy. Periodic tenancies are generally express, oral or written, but they also arise by implication. This creates a tenancy at will. If Ted pays rent to Laura at the beginning of each month (or some other regular time) and Laura accepts such payments, most courts would hold that the tenancy at will has been transformed into a tenancy from month to month.

Either party may terminate a periodic tenancy at the expiration of any one period, but only on adequate notice to the other party. If the lease contains no specific agreement, the common law requires six months' notice in tenancies from year to year. However, in most jurisdictions,

---

Landlord
owner of land who grants a leasehold interest to another

Tenant
possessor of the leasehold interest

Leasehold estate
right to possess real property for a period of time

Definite term
lease that automatically expires at the end of the term

Periodic tenancy
lease that continues for successive periods unless terminated by notice to the other party

this period has been shortened by statute to periods ranging between thirty and ninety days in duration. In periodic tenancies involving periods of less than one year, the notice required at common law is one full period in advance; but, again, this may be subject to statutory regulation.

Tenancy at will

lease that is terminable at any time

Tenancy at Will   A lease containing a provision that either party may terminate at any time creates a **tenancy at will**. A lease that does not specify a duration also creates a tenancy at will. At common law, such tenancies were terminable without any prior notice, but many jurisdictions now have statutes requiring a period of notice before termination, usually ten to ninety days.

Tenancy at sufferance

possession of real property without a valid lease

Tenancy at Sufferance   A **tenancy at sufferance** arises when a tenant fails to vacate the premises when the lease expires and thereby becomes a holdover tenant. Under the common law, the landlord may elect either to dispossess such tenant or to hold her for another term. Until the landlord makes this election, a tenancy at sufferance exists.

Transfer of Interests [48-2b]

Practical Advice

When entering into a lease, specify the duration of the lease and any optional periods of extension.

Both the tenant's possessory interest in the leasehold and the landlord's reversionary interest in the property may be freely transferred in the absence of contractual or statutory prohibition. This general rule is subject to one major exception: the tenancy at will. Any attempt by either party to transfer her interest is usually considered an expression of the intent (will) to terminate the tenancy.

Transfers by Landlord   After conveying the leasehold interest, a landlord is left with a reversionary interest in the property plus the right to rent and other benefits acquired under the lease. The landlord may transfer either or both of these interests. The party to whom the reversion is transferred takes the property subject to the tenant's leasehold interest, if the transferee has actual *or* constructive notice of the lease. For example, Linda leases Whiteacre to Tina for five years, and Tina records the lease with the register of deeds. Linda then sells Whiteacre to Arthur. Tina's lease is still valid and enforceable against Arthur, whose right to possession of Whiteacre begins only after the lease expires.

Transfers by Tenant   In the absence of a prohibitive lease or statutory provision, a tenant, except for a tenant at will, may dispose of his interest either by (1) assignment or (2) sublease, and in the absence of a lease provision to the contrary, the tenant may do both. As a result, most standard leases expressly require the landlord's consent to an assignment or subletting of the premises. However, under the majority view, a covenant against assignment of a lease does not prohibit the tenant from subleasing the premises; conversely, a prohibition against subleasing does not restrict the right to assign the lease.

Assignment

transfer of all of a tenant's interest in the leasehold

Covenants

express promises

Sublease

transfer of less than all of the tenant's interest in the leasehold

A tenant who transfers all interest in a leasehold (consequently forfeiting her reversionary rights) has made an **assignment**. The tenant's agreement to pay rent and certain other contractual **covenants** (express promises) pass to and obligate the assignee of the lease as long as the assignee remains in possession of the leasehold estate. Although the assignee is thus bound to pay rent, the original tenant is not relieved of her contractual obligation to do so. If the assignee fails to pay the stipulated rent, the original tenant will have to pay, though she will have a right to be reimbursed by the assignee. Thus, after an assignment of a tenant's interest, both the original tenant and the assignee are liable to the landlord for failure to pay rent.

A **sublease** differs from an assignment in that the tenant transfers less than all her rights in the lease and thereby retains a reversion in the leasehold (see Figure 48-1). For example, T is a tenant under a lease from L that is to terminate on December 31, 2015. If T leases the premises to SL for a shorter period than that covered by her own lease, say, until November 30, 2015, T, in transferring less than her whole interest in the lease, has subleased the premises.

Practical Advice

As the landlord, clearly specify in the lease whether it may be assigned or sublet and, if so, whether your written consent is required.

The legal effects of a sublease are entirely different from those of an assignment. In a sublease, the sublessee, SL in the previous example, has no obligation to T's landlord, L. SL's obligations run solely to T, the original tenant; and T is not relieved of any of her obligations under the lease. Thus, L has no right of action against T's sublessee, SL, under any covenants contained in the original lease between him and T, because that lease has not been assigned to SL. T, of course, remains liable to L for the rent and for all other covenants in the original lease.

Figure 48-1 Assignment Compared with Sublease

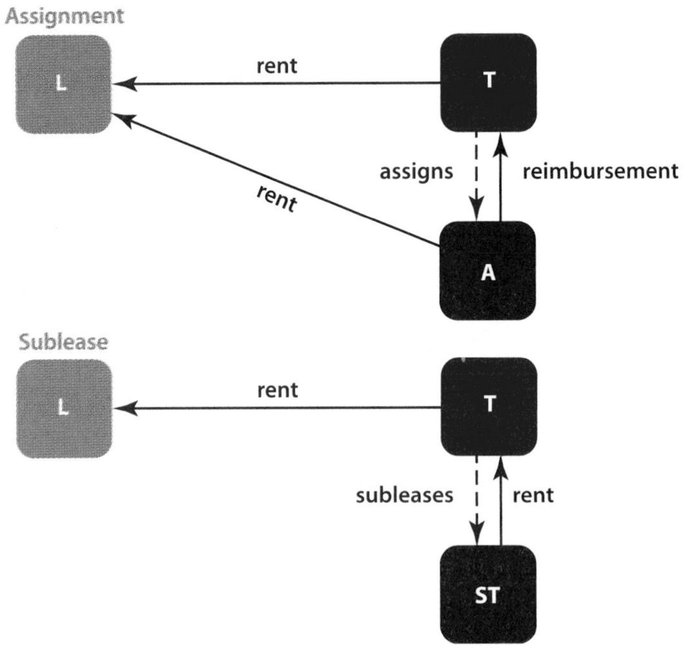

Tenant's Obligations [48-2c]

Tenant's obligations

the tenant has an obligation to pay a specified rent at specified times or, if none is specified, to pay a reasonable amount at the end of the term

Although the leasehold estate carries with it only an implied obligation on the part of the tenant to pay reasonable rent, the lease contract almost always contains an express promise or covenant by the tenant to pay rent in specified amounts at specified times. In the absence of a covenant specifying the rent amount and payment times, the rent will be a *reasonable* amount *payable only at the end of the term.*

Most leases provide that if the tenant breaches any of the covenants in the lease, the landlord may declare the lease at an end and regain possession of the premises. The tenant's express undertaking to pay rent thus becomes one of the covenants on which this provision can operate. If a lease contains no such provision, at common law, the tenant's failure to pay rent when due gives the landlord only the right to recover a judgment for the amount of such rent; it does not give him the right to oust the tenant from the premises. In most jurisdictions, however, statutory changes to the common law rule allow the landlord to dispossess the tenant for nonpayment of rent, even if the lease does not provide the landlord with such a right.

Unless the lease specifically provides otherwise, a tenant is under no duty to make any repairs to the leased premises. He is not obliged to repair or restore substantial or extraordinary damage occurring without his fault, nor to repair damage caused by ordinary wear and tear. However, the tenant is obliged to use the premises so that no substantial injury is caused them. The law imposes this duty; it need not be expressly stated in the lease. For example, a tenant who overloads an electrical connection and consequently shorts out a wiring system is liable to the landlord.

Destruction of the premises

under the common law, if the premises are destroyed, the tenant is not relieved of his obligation to pay rent and cannot terminate the lease

Destruction of the Premises   When the tenant leases land together with a building, and the building is destroyed by fire or some other chance event, the common law does not relieve him of his obligation to pay rent or permit him to terminate the lease. Most states, however, have statutorily modified the rule to exclude tenants who occupy only a portion of a building and who have no interest in the building as a whole, such as apartment tenants. Most leases contain clauses covering the accidental destruction of the premises.

Eviction

if the tenant breaches one of the covenants of her lease, the landlord may terminate the lease and evict (remove) her from the premises

Eviction   When the tenant breaches a covenant in her lease, such as the covenant to pay rent, and the landlord evicts or removes the tenant from the premises according to a specific lease provision or under a statute authorizing him to do so, the lease is terminated. Because breaching the covenant to pay rent does not injure the premises and because the landlord's action in evicting the tenant terminates the lease, the evicted tenant normally is not liable to the landlord for any future rent installments. Most long-term leases, however, contain a survival clause providing that the tenant's eviction for nonpayment of rent will not relieve her of liability for damages equal to the difference between the rent specified in the lease and the rent the landlord is able to obtain when reletting the premises. The landlord generally can terminate the tenancy if a tenant repeatedly disturbs other tenants and neighbors, such as by throwing loud parties or selling drugs, or otherwise violates the lease or the law. If the landlord wrongfully evicts the tenant, the tenant's obligations under the lease are terminated, and, as will be discussed, the landlord is liable for breach of the tenant's right of quiet enjoyment.

Unlike authorized eviction, the landlord's wrongful eviction of the tenant terminates the tenant's obligations under the lease. Moreover, as discussed later, the landlord is liable for breach of the tenant's right of quiet enjoyment.

Abandonment
if the tenant abandons the property and the landlord reenters or relets it, the tenant's obligation to pay rent terminates

Abandonment

Abandonment   If the tenant wrongfully abandons the premises before the lease term expires and the landlord reenters the premises or relets them to another, a majority of the courts hold that the tenant's obligation to pay rent terminates after such reentry. ("Reenter" in this case means to occupy the premises.) The landlord who desires to hold the tenant to his obligation to pay rent must either leave the premises vacant or have another "survival clause" in the lease that covers this situation.

Landlord's Obligations [48-2d]

Under the Federal Fair Housing Act, a landlord cannot discriminate against a tenant with regard to race, color, gender, religion, national origin, disability, or familial status (except under the housing for older persons exception). Nevertheless, unless the lease contains specific provisions, the landlord, under the common law, has few obligations to her tenant. Under the majority rule (the American rule), at the beginning of the lease, the landlord has only to give the tenant the right to possession. In a minority of states (the English rule), she has to give actual possession.

Quiet enjoyment
tenant's right to physical possession of the premises free of interference by the landlord

Constructive eviction
failure by the landlord in any obligation under the lease that causes a substantial and lasting injury to the tenant's enjoyment of the premises

Quiet Enjoyment

Quiet Enjoyment   The landlord may not interfere with the tenant's right to physical possession, use, and enjoyment of the premises. Rather, the landlord is bound to provide the tenant with quiet and peaceful enjoyment, a duty known as the landlord's covenant of **quiet enjoyment**. The landlord breaches this covenant, which arises by implication, whenever he wrongfully evicts the tenant. The law also regards the landlord as having breached this covenant if someone having better title to the property than the landlord evicts the tenant. The landlord is not responsible, however, for the wrongful acts of third parties unless they are done with his assent and under his direction.

Eviction need not be actual. Under the doctrine of **constructive eviction**, a failure by the landlord in any of her obligations under the lease that causes a substantial and lasting injury to the tenant's beneficial enjoyment of the premises is regarded as being, in effect, an eviction of the tenant. Under such circumstances, the courts permit the tenant to abandon the premises and terminate the lease. However, to claim that a constructive eviction occurred, the tenant must abandon possession within a reasonable time.

Home Rentals Corp. v. Curtis
Appellate Court of Illinois, Fifth District, 1992
236 Ill.App.3d 994, 602 N.E.2d 859, 176 Ill.Dec. 913
http://scholar.google.com/scholar_case?case=12032393052396288209&hl=en&as_sdt=2&as_vis=1&oi=scholarr

FACTS In February 1989, Home Rentals agreed to rent a single-family residence to Chris Curtis, Ed Domaracki, Mike Fraser, and Carson Flugstad (tenants), all of whom were students at Southern Illinois University. The terms of the written lease stated that the lease was to commence on August 17, 1989, and to expire on August 13, 1990. The tenants were to receive the premises in "good order and repair," rent was to be $740 per month, and a $500 deposit was required. The tenants initially paid $1,980 to cover the deposit and advance rent for the last two months of the lease. Although the house was fine when the tenants signed the lease in February, when they arrived on August 15, it was not. The electricity had not yet been turned on. Roaches had overrun the rooms, and the kitchen was so filthy and so infested by bugs that food could not be stored there. The carpet smelled, and one could see outside through holes in the wall. The bathrooms were unsanitary, no toilets worked, one of the bathtubs did not drain, and an open sewage drain emptied bathroom wastewater onto the basement floor. The tenants notified Home Rentals on the 16th that the place was uninhabitable because of the filth and roaches. Home Rentals responded that the tenants should just clean the place up and that it would reimburse them. Accordingly, the tenants attempted to clean the house, but the roach problem continued even after professional extermination, and Home Rentals did nothing about the plumbing. The tenants were never able to stay in the house. On August 21, the tenants finally sought housing elsewhere. They advised Home Rentals that they would not be living in the house, returned the keys, and reported the condition of the house to the city of Carbondale's Code Enforcement Division. The city notified Home Rentals on August 25, 1989, that it had found numerous city code violations and warned the corporation that the house would be posted "occupancy prohibited" unless all violations were corrected within 72 hours. By August 28, 1989, eleven days after the tenants' lease was to have commenced, Home Rentals had finally remedied all the violations. The city withdrew its threat, but Home Rentals did not rent the house to anyone else. Instead, it sued the tenants for breach of the lease and claimed $6,900 for all twelve months under the lease, less the deposit. The tenants denied the allegations and raised as affirmative defenses breach of the implied warranty of habitability and constructive eviction. Based on the latter theory, they asserted a counterclaim seeking the return of the $500 deposit and the $1,480 they had paid in advance rent. The trial court found for the tenants in the amount of $1,980, and Home Rentals appealed.

DECISION Judgment for the tenants affirmed.

OPINION A constructive eviction occurs when a landlord has done something grave and permanent with the intention of depriving the tenant of enjoyment of the premises. Constructive eviction does not require a finding that the landlord had the express intention to compel a tenant to leave the leased premises or to deprive him of their beneficial enjoyment. The landlord need only have committed acts or omissions that have rendered the leased premises useless to the tenant or that have deprived the tenant of the possession and enjoyment of the premises, in whole or part, making it necessary for the tenant to move.

The house did not meet the tenants' expectations: it did not have flushing toilets, its basement was full of sewage, and its kitchen was overrun by roaches. Basically, Home Rentals provided a house that was clearly unfit for people to occupy. It is true that a tenant may not abandon premises under the theory of constructive eviction without first affording the landlord a reasonable opportunity to correct the defects in the property. However, such an opportunity existed here. Considering the magnitude of the problem, four days was opportunity enough for Home Rentals to act.

INTERPRETATION If a landlord's failure to meet any of his obligations under a lease causes a substantial and lasting injury to the tenant's beneficial enjoyment of the premises, that failure, in effect, is a constructive and wrongful eviction of the tenant.

ETHICAL QUESTION Did Home Rentals act unethically? Explain.

CRITICAL THINKING QUESTION Did the court correctly decide this case? Explain.

Fitness for Use   Because the lease's primary value to the tenant is land, the landlord, under the common law, is under no obligation to provide or maintain the premises in a livable condition or to make them fit for any purpose, unless the lease specifically so provides. Most courts, however, have abandoned this rule in residential leases, instead imposing an **implied warranty of habitability** that requires leased premises to be habitable, that is, fit for ordinary residential purposes having adequate weatherproofing; heat, water, and electricity, *as well as* being clean, sanitary, and structurally safe. These courts also have held that the covenant to pay rent is conditioned on the landlord's performance of this warranty. Courts reaching these results have emphasized that the tenant's interest is in a place to live, not merely in land.

A number of states have statutes requiring landlords to keep residential premises fit for occupation. Zoning ordinances, health and safety regulations, and building and housing codes also may impose certain duties on the landlord.

Implied warranty of habitability
warranty that the leased premises are fit for ordinary residential purposes

Tucker v. Hayford
Court of Appeals of Washington, Division Three, 2003
118 Wash.App. 246, 75 P.3d 980
http://scholar.google.com/scholar_case?case=4713939053717898068&hl=en&as_sdt=2&as_vis=1&oi=scholarr

FACTS Robert Hayford bought a lot and mobile home in Kennewick, Washington, from Mike Kirby in 1994. The water to the home was supplied by a well, which was tested on December 8, 1993. On March 15, 1994, the Benton Franklin District Health Department wrote to Mr. Kirby that (1) the nitrate level of the well water was elevated; (2) the well was free of bacterial contamination; (3) the sanitary seal was improperly installed and maintained; and (4) chemicals were stored within one hundred feet of the well. To protect and improve the water system, the health department recommended that (1) the sanitary seal be properly installed, and (2) the chemicals be stored at least one hundred feet from the well. The health department also recommended that the well be tested yearly for bacteria.

Hayford leased the home to Don and Shalee Tucker in October of 1998. The Tuckers asked if the well water was drinkable. Hayford said it was as long as a water filter was used. He said that the nitrates were a bit high.

The Tuckers signed a written residential lease prepared by Hayford. They ultimately extended the tenancy through August 1, 2000. The Tucker family, including their four children, all became ill. The family's pediatric nurse practitioner suggested that they test their well water. The test, dated March 28, 2000, showed bacteria in the water. The Tuckers told Hayford of the problem, and Hayford had the well repaired. The Tuckers, nevertheless, moved out of the home on May 15, 2000. They sued Hayford for damages for personal injury arising from contaminated water. Hayford moved for summary judgment. The trial court granted the motion.

DECISION   The trial court's summary judgment order is reversed.

OPINION   The Tuckers sued for damages based on their contract (obligation to perform major maintenance and repair and covenant of quiet enjoyment), violation of the Landlord-Tenant Act, and negligent misrepresentation as to the water quality.

Obligations Imposed by the Contract   The tenant may recover for personal injuries caused by the landlord's breach of a repair covenant only if the unrepaired defect created an unreasonable risk of harm to the tenant. Here the lease includes (1) an express covenant of quiet enjoyment and (2) requires that the lessor maintain and repair the leased premises. Thus, the factual question is whether the condition of this well interfered with the tenant's quiet enjoyment of the home, *or* whether the well required "major maintenance" as spelled out in the lease agreement.

Quiet Enjoyment   No Washington case directly addresses the impact of drinking water on a tenant's quiet enjoyment of his home. Washington does, however, recognize that without water, a property is uninhabitable. The Tuckers have made out an actionable claim for breach of the covenant of quiet enjoyment.

Major Maintenance and Repair   A health inspector recommended that this well be tested at least annually for bacteria. The question then is whether a reasonable person knew or in the exercise of ordinary care should have known that this well should have been tested annually—as part of the major maintenance of this home.

Again, the evidence, viewed in a light most favorable to the Tuckers, includes high nitrate levels together with a recommendation for yearly bacteria testing. That is a sufficient showing to support a breach of the major maintenance and repair covenant of this lease.

Traditional Common Law Landlord Liability   Common law landlord liability requires proof of "(1) latent or hidden defects in the leasehold (2) that existed at the commencement of the leasehold (3) of which the landlord had actual knowledge (4) and of which the landlord failed to inform the tenant." The condition of the water was certainly hidden or latent as to the Tuckers. Furthermore, Hayford did not warn the Tuckers, and he was aware of the report that required the annual testing. The Tuckers have then raised an issue of fact—whether Hayford knew or should have known of this latent defect.

Implied Warranty of Habitability   A landlord is subject to liability for physical harm caused to the tenant and others upon the leased property with the consent of the tenant or his subtenant by a dangerous condition existing before or arising after the tenant has taken possession, if the landlord has failed to exercise reasonable care to repair the condition.

Washington's Landlord-Tenant Act   The Landlord-Tenant Act requires the landlord to "keep the premises fit for human habitation" and in particular to maintain the premises in substantial compliance with health or safety codes for the benefit of the tenant. It requires the landlord to make repairs, except in the case of normal wear and tear, "necessary to put and keep the premises in as good condition as it by law or rental agreement should have been, at the commencement of the tenancy."

INTERPRETATION   Most states require leased residential premises to be fit for ordinary residential purposes.

ETHICAL QUESTION   Did the court fairly decide this case? Explain.

CRITICAL THINKING QUESTION   When should the law require that premises be habitable? Explain.

Repair
unless there is a statute or specific provision in the lease, the landlord has no duty to repair or restore the premises

Repair   Under the common law, unless there is a specific provision in the lease or a statutory duty to do so, the landlord has no obligation to repair or restore the premises. The landlord does, however, have a duty to maintain, repair, and keep in safe condition those parts of the premises that remain under her control. For example, an apartment house owner who controls the building's stairways, elevators, lobbies, and other common areas is liable for keeping them maintained and repaired and is responsible for injuries that occur because of her failure to do so. With respect to apartment buildings, the courts presume that any portion of the premises that is not specifically leased to the tenants remains under the landlord's control. Thus, in such cases, the landlord is liable for making external repairs, including repairs to the roof. The courts have further expanded the "common areas" rule to individual rental unit equipment that is connected to a central system, such as central heating and air conditioning, hot water, and plumbing and electrical systems. For a discussion of a landlord's duties and tort liabilities to a tenant in common areas, see the section on duties of possessors in Chapter 8.

Although at common law the landlord is under no duty to repair, restore, or keep the premises in a livable condition, she may and often does assume those duties in the lease. However, her breach of such obligations under a lease does not entitle a tenant to abandon the premises and refuse to pay rent. Unless the lease specifically provides the tenant this right, the common law

Practical Advice

In your written lease, attempt to provide for the landlord's duty to repair, the landlord's liability to third parties, and the landlord's obligation to maintain the premises in habitable condition.

allows him only an action for damages. As mentioned, a number of states now have statutes that require the landlord to keep residential premises fit for occupancy and accordingly have imposed upon the landlord a duty to repair those items.

Landlord's Liability for Injury Caused by Third Parties   Some states hold landlords liable for injuries their tenants and others suffer as a result of the foreseeable criminal conduct of third parties. Although landlords cannot ensure their tenants' safety, courts have held landlords liable for failure "to take minimal precautions to protect members of the public from the reasonably foreseeable criminal acts of third persons."

Concurrent Ownership [48-3]

Both real and personal property may be owned by one individual or by two or more persons concurrently. Two or more persons who hold title concurrently generally are known as **co-tenants**. Each is entitled to an undivided interest in the entire property, and neither has a claim to any specific part of it. Each may have an equal undivided interest, or one may have a larger undivided share than the other.

The two major types of concurrent ownership are joint tenancy and tenancy in common. Both provide an undivided interest in the whole, the right of both tenants to possession, and the right of either to sell his interest during life and thus terminate the original relationship. Other forms of concurrent ownership of both real and personal property are tenancy by the entireties and community property. In addition, real property may be owned concurrently in the form of condominiums and cooperatives.

Co-tenants

persons who hold title concurrently

Tenancy in Common [48-3a]

Under a **tenancy in common**, the most frequently used form of concurrent ownership, each co-owner has both an undivided interest in the property with no right of survivorship and the right to possession, but none claims any specific portion of the property. Tenants in common need not have acquired their interests at the same time or by the same instrument, and their interests may differ as to duration and scope. Because there is no right of survivorship, the interests of tenants in common may be devised by will or pass by intestate succession. By statute in all states, a transfer of title to two or more persons is presumed to create a tenancy in common.

Partition is a physical division of the property that changes undivided interests into smaller, individually owned parcels. The size of the individual parcels is based upon the size of the owners' prior shares of the undivided interest. If physical division of the property (e.g., a house) is not practicable, the property will be sold and the proceeds will be divided.

Tenancy in common

co-ownership whereby each tenant holds an undivided interest with no right of survivorship

Partition

physical division of undivided property into smaller, individually owned parcels

Joint Tenancy [48-3b]

A **joint tenancy** is co-ownership whereby each tenant holds an undivided interest with a right of survivorship. The most significant feature of joint tenancy is the right of *survivorship*. On the death of a joint tenant, title to the entire property passes by operation of law to the survivor or survivors. Neither the heirs of the deceased joint tenant nor his general creditors have a claim to his interest after his death, and a joint tenant cannot transfer his interest by executing a will. Any joint tenant may sever the joint tenancy, however, by conveying or mortgaging his interest to a third party. Furthermore, the interest of either co-tenant is subject to levy and sale on execution. To *sever* a joint tenancy is to forfeit the right of survivorship: following severance, the tenancy becomes a tenancy in common among the remaining joint tenants and the transferee.

To sustain a joint tenancy, the common law requires the presence of what are known as the **four unities** of time, title, interest, and possession. The unity of time means that all the tenants' interests must take effect at the same time; the unity of title means that all the tenants must acquire title by the same instrument; the unity of interest means that the tenants' interests must be identical in duration and scope; and the unity of possession means that the tenants have identical rights of possession and enjoyment. The absence of any unity will prevent the creation of a joint tenancy. The presence of the fourth unity and any two of the others, however, will result in the creation of a tenancy in common, because the only unity required of a tenancy in common is the unity of possession.

Joint tenancy

co-ownership with the presence of the four unities and the right of survivorship

Four unities

time, title, interest, and possession

Practical Advice

If you jointly hold property with another, specify the type of joint ownership.

Kettler v. Security Nat. Bank of Sioux City
Court of Appeals of Iowa, 2011
805 N.W.2d 817
http://scholar.google.com/scholar_case?q=805+N.W.2D+817+&hl=en&as_sdt=6,34&case=4793469912787190935&scilh=0

FACTS Fay and Loretta O'Connell were married in 1940 and owned their residence along with several bank accounts as joint tenants with rights of survivorship. They had no children. Loretta had a sister, Mary Ann Raher, and two brothers, Milo Kettler and Robert Kettler. On November 21, 2005, the couple executed wills, both directing the residue of their estates pass to the survivor. On the second death, after certain specific bequests, the residual estate would pass to Milo and Robert. Loretta's sister was not included as a beneficiary in the residual estate of either Fay or Loretta, but was to receive $10,000 under Loretta's will. On that same date, Loretta signed a power of attorney form, appointing Fay as her attorney-in-fact, with Milo and Robert as successor attorneys-in-fact. In the summer of 2007, Loretta began suffering the debilitating effects of Alzheimer's disease, while Fay suffered from a terminal illness. Milo and Loretta's niece, Margaret Woolworth, filed an application alleging Fay was seriously mentally impaired. After an examination by a physician and a finding of no serious mental impairment, the application was dismissed. While Fay was involuntarily held for seventy-two hours, Milo and Margaret moved Loretta into a nursing home. It appears this motivated Fay to take action to change his will and take full control of the couple's assets.

Fay requested that Mary Ann come from her home in the state of Washington to Iowa and paid for her travel. While accompanied by Mary Ann, Fay went to the banks where he and Loretta had joint accounts and withdrew all the funds from those accounts. Fay deposited the funds into new accounts in his name alone and designated all but the money market account as payable-on-death to Mary Ann. Additionally, Fay executed a general power of attorney designating Mary Ann as Fay's attorney in fact. He also changed his will by setting up a trust for the care of Loretta, if she survived him. If Loretta did not survive him or upon Loretta's death, after certain bequests, the balance of the trust assets was left to Mary Ann. Milo and Robert were no longer beneficiaries under the new will, and Fay's attorney later testified that Fay "was very insistent he wanted nothing to go to them. And that was one of the reasons for the change in his will." The Security National Bank (SNB) was nominated as executor and trustee.

Fay died on August 9, 2007. In October 2007, Loretta, Milo, and Robert filed a petition naming the personal representative of Fay's estate, Security National Bank (SNB), and Mary Ann as defendants alleging conversion of Loretta's property by Fay and Mary Ann. In February 2009, the district court issued a summary judgment ruling. The district court found that because Fay did not intend to sever and could not destroy the joint tenancy, the assets remained held in joint tenancy with rights of survivorship in Loretta. The district court held that one co-tenant had no right to withdraw all or substantially all of the funds in an account, unless specifically authorized by the other joint tenants. An unauthorized, unilateral withdrawal of account funds is essentially a void action, and the parties' rights to the monies and the joint tenancy endure. The district court held that the transfers of ownership effectuated by Fay O'Connell prior to his death in regard to the bank accounts and certificates of deposit are void. Mary Ann and SNB appealed from this order.

DECISION The district court's ruling invalidating the withdrawals is reversed and remanded; Loretta's claim for conversion is upheld for her proportional interest (50 percent) of the withdrawn funds.

OPINION "Joint tenancy property is property held by two or more parties jointly, with equal rights to share in the enjoyment of the whole property during their lives, and a right of survivorship which allows the surviving party to enjoy the entire estate." A joint tenant's right to the joint tenancy property can be described as "an undivided interest in the entire estate to which is attached the right of survivorship." There are two separate features of joint tenancy: the "proportional interest" in the undivided interest in the property and the "accretive interest" in the right of survivorship.

A joint tenancy may be severed by the actions of one or both of the joint tenants. Any severance of joint tenancy creates a tenancy in common. Traditionally, Iowa followed the four unities of title test: to create a joint tenancy the four unities had to be present—interest, title, time, and possession. "To sever or terminate a joint tenancy, a joint tenant simply had to destroy one of the unities." That changed and Iowa adopted an "intent-based approach" in determining whether a joint tenancy had been created, severed, or terminated. Under the intent-based test, a court is not permitted "to determine the intent of a party under the facts and then fulfill it." "Instead, it seems fundamental that intent must be derived from an instrument effectuating the intent to sever the joint tenancy."

In the present case, the bank accounts were held in joint tenancy, with both Fay and Loretta having an undivided interest in the entire estate. Each joint tenant was permitted to make withdrawals from the account, as was specified in the account agreement. Ultimately, one joint tenant was permitted to deplete the account. Consequently, the withdrawals of funds was valid and could support the termination of the joint tenancy. Fay clearly demonstrated his intent that the funds no longer be held in the joint tenancies. First, he withdrew all of the funds. He then deposited both his and Loretta's proportional interests into accounts in his name only and payable-on-death to Mary Ann.

In a case where a joint tenant makes a valid withdrawal of more than his proportional share, the remedy is not to invalidate the entire transaction. Rather, the remedy is a suit between the joint tenants to recover the funds taken in excess of the withdrawing joint tenant's proportional share.

Even though the withdrawals from the joint tenancy accounts were valid transactions, this does not determine nor destroy the proportional interests as between Fay and Loretta. Fay had a right to withdraw all of the funds and even to take control of all of the funds. However, he did so at the risk of Loretta claiming her proportionate share. The presumption is that each party has an interest in one-half of the funds in a joint tenancy account.

INTERPRETATION In the case of a joint tenancy in personal property (which is severable), one of the joint tenants may sever the tenancy, putting an end to the incident of survivorship, by taking and using his share of the common property; if a joint tenant withdraws from the account in excess of his interest, he is liable to the other joint tenant for the excess amount withdrawn.

CRITICAL THINKING QUESTION Do you agree with court's decision in this case? Explain.

CONCEPT REVIEW 48-2

Rights of Concurrent Owners

	Undivided Interest	Right to Possession	Right to Sell	Right to Mortgage	Levy by Creditors	Right to Will	Right of Survivorship
Joint Tenancy	Yes	Yes	Yes	Yes	Yes	No	Yes
Tenancy in Common	Yes	Yes	Yes	Yes	Yes	Yes	No
Tenancy by Entireties	Yes	Yes	No	No	No	No	Yes

Tenancy by the Entireties [48-3c]

Tenancy by the entireties, recognized in some, but not all states, is created only by a conveyance to a husband and wife. It is distinguished from joint tenancy by the inability of either spouse to convey separately his or her interest during life and thus destroy the right of survivorship. Likewise, creditors cannot attach the interest of either spouse. By the nature of the tenancy, divorce would terminate the relationship, and partition would then be available as a method of creating separate interests in the property.

Community Property [48-3d]

In Arizona, California, Idaho, Louisiana, Nevada, New Mexico, Puerto Rico, Texas, Washington, and Wisconsin, under the **community property** system, one-half of any property acquired by either the husband or the wife belongs to each spouse. In most instances, the only property that belongs separately to either spouse is any property acquired before the marriage or acquired subsequent to it by gift or inheritance. On the death of either spouse, one-half of the community property belongs outright to the survivor, and the interest of the deceased spouse in the other half may go to the heirs of the decedent or as directed by will.

Condominiums [48-3e]

Condominiums embody a form of concurrent ownership now common in the United States. All states have enacted statutes authorizing this form of ownership. The purchaser of a **condominium** acquires separate ownership to the unit and becomes a tenant in common with respect to its common facilities, such as the land on which the project is built, recreational facilities, hallways, parking areas, and spaces between the units. A condominium association, funded by assessments levied on each unit, maintains the common elements. The transfer of a condominium conveys both the separate ownership of the unit and the share in the common elements.

Cooperatives [48-3f]

Cooperatives involve an indirect form of common ownership. A **cooperative**, usually a corporation, purchases or constructs dwelling units and then leases the units to its shareholders as tenants, who acquire the right to use and occupy their units.

NONPOSSESSORY INTERESTS [48-4]

Although a nonpossessory interest in land entitles the holder to use the land or to take something from it, the interest does not give him the right to possess the land. Nonpossessory interests include easements, *profits à prendre*, and licenses, all of which differ from a tenancy because the tenant has an exclusive *possessory* interest.

Definition of Easements [48-4a]

An **easement** is a *limited right* to use another's land in a specific manner that is created by the acts of the parties or by operation of law and that has all the attributes of an estate in the land itself. The easement can involve all or a specific portion of the property. For example, a typical easement exists when Liz sells part of her land to Bill and expressly provides in the same document or in a separate one that Bill, as the adjoining landowner, shall have a right-of-way over a

---

Tenancy by the entireties

co-ownership by spouses in which neither may convey his or her interest during life

Community property

rights of each spouse in property acquired by the other during marriage

Condominium

separate ownership of an individual unit with tenancy in common with respect to common areas

Cooperative

the corporate owner of the property leases units to its shareholders as tenants

Easement

right to use the land of another in a specific manner

Dominant parcel
land whose owner has rights in other land

Servient parcel
land subject to an easement

strip of Liz's remaining parcel of land. Bill's land is said to be the **dominant parcel** (land whose owner has rights in other land), and Liz's land, which is subject to the easement, is the **servient parcel**. Easements may, of course, exist for many different uses, as, for example, the right to run a ditch across another's land, to lay pipe under the surface, to erect power lines, or, in the case of adjacent buildings, to use a stairway or a common or "party" wall.

Types of Easements [48-4b]

Appurtenant easements
an easement interest that attaches to land and passes with it

Easements fall into two classes: easements appurtenant and easements in gross. **Appurtenant easements** are by far the more common, and, as the name indicates, the rights and duties they create pertain to the land itself, not to the individuals who have created such easements. Therefore, the easement usually stays with the land when it is sold. For example, continuing with the illustration of Liz and Bill, if Liz sells her servient parcel to Kyle, who has actual notice of the easement for the benefit of Bill's land or constructive notice through a local recording act, Kyle takes the parcel subject to the easement. Likewise, if Bill sells his dominant parcel to Daniel, the deed from Bill to Daniel does not need to refer specifically to the easement in order to give to Daniel, as the dominant parcel's new owner, the right to use the right-of-way over the servient parcel.

Easement in gross
personal right to use another's land

The second type of easement is an **easement in gross**, which is personal to the particular individual who receives the right. In effect, it amounts to little more than an irrevocable personal right to use another's land.

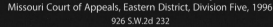

Borton v. Forest Hills Country Club
Missouri Court of Appeals, Eastern District, Division Five, 1996
926 S.W.2d 232
http://scholar.google.com/scholar_case?case=18361502037276936849&hl=en&as_sdt=2&as_vis=1&oi=scholarr

FACTS Plaintiffs, Gene and Deborah Borton, owners of a home which was adjacent to golf course, brought nuisance action against country club seeking injunctive relief and money damages based on golf balls which were hit onto their property. The defendant, Forest Hills Country Club, filed a counterclaim seeking declaration of easement allowing members to enter the plaintiff's property to retrieve errant golf balls.

The developer of defendant's golf course began to sell lots for residential use adjacent to the golf course in 1963. The developer filed and recorded a set of deed restrictions on all the residential lots adjacent to the golf course. Paragraph 11 of these deed restrictions recites:

> All owners and occupants of any lot in the Forest Hills Club Estates Subdivision shall extend to one person, in a group of members or guests playing a normal game of golf on the Forest Hills Golf and Country Club, or their caddy, the courtesy of allowing such person or caddy the privilege of retrieving any and all errant golf balls which may have landed or remained on any lot in the subdivision. However, care shall be exercised in the retrieving of such golf ball to prevent damage to any lawn, flowers, shrubbery, or other improvement on the lot.

Plaintiffs purchased a residence adjacent to the fairway on the eleventh hole on defendant's golf course in March 1994. The general warranty deed to plaintiffs provided that the property was subject to the set of deed restrictions and covenants. Because of the proximity of the tee boxes on the eleventh hole to plaintiffs' home, thousands of errant golf balls have been hit onto plaintiffs' property since they purchased their residence.

The trial court granted summary judgment in favor of defendant on plaintiff's claim and its counterclaim. Plaintiff appeals.

DECISION Affirmed in part and reversed and remanded in part.

OPINION Plaintiffs concede that paragraph 11 of the deed restriction gives defendant and its members some right with respect to

retrieving errant golf balls. Plaintiffs argue, however, that the right created in paragraph 11 is simply a license. Defendant contends it has an easement over the Bortons's property, either by express grant via paragraph 11 in the deed restriction or by prescription.

Both a license and easement give the grantee the right to go onto the grantor's property for a limited use. A license is a personal right and as such, may be revoked at the will of the licensor. An easement, by contrast, gives the grantee an interest in the property of the grantor and thus runs with the land and is binding upon successive landowners.

In this case, since the original developer of the property properly recorded and filed the deed restrictions, those restrictions created interests that run with the land and are binding on successive owners. Thus, plaintiffs do not have the power to revoke or modify the rights granted to defendant in paragraph 11 of the deed restrictions. Therefore, the deed restrictions in paragraph 11 are in the nature of an easement in favor of defendant and its members to retrieve errant golf balls hit onto plaintiffs' property during a normal game of golf.

Plaintiffs may recover if they can demonstrate that defendant's current use of the easement constitutes a greater burden to their land than what was contemplated or intended. The defendant did not address plaintiffs' claims in its cross motion for summary judgment and did not submit summary judgment facts to demonstrate that there is no material issue of fact in dispute as to this issue. Thus, the trial court's dismissal of plaintiffs' claim was premature.

INTERPRETATION Most easements give the grantee an interest in property of the grantor and run with the land and are binding upon successive landowners.

CRITICAL THINKING QUESTION Should the plaintiff be able to get out of the deed restriction? Explain.

APPLYING THE LAW

Interests in Real Property

Facts In 1992, the Padgetts bought a two-acre lot in the mountains from the Morgans. Almost immediately, the Padgetts built a weatherized cabin on the property, which they used every summer for a few months and every winter for a few weeks. They also built a small barn on the eastern edge of the property, behind their garage. After a couple years, the Padgetts improved their access to the barn by extending the gravel drive that started at the street to beyond the garage, along the property's eastern border, and into the barn.

About the time the Padgetts built the barn, the property owners to their east—the Martingales—built a summer home on their one-acre parcel, with a three-car garage in the far westernmost corner of their property. While the Martingales had originally envisioned accessing their garage by way of a spur off the concrete circular drive in front of the house, they did not immediately build the garage access driveway because two huge trees needed to be removed to do so. In the interim, easy access to the Martingale garage was available via the Padgetts' driveway, and the Padgetts did not seem to mind Mrs. Martingale driving the length of their gravel drive and then cutting back onto her own property behind the large trees.

The Martingales and Padgetts were quite friendly. More often than not, when Mrs. Martingale used the Padgetts' gravel drive to get to her garage, Mrs. Padgett would be out gardening. Mrs. Martingale would stop and talk to Mrs. Padgett for a few minutes and then continue driving back to the garage. The subject of Mrs. Martingale's use of the gravel drive never came up in conversation.

The Martingales never removed the big trees and never built any formal access to their garage. Then, in late 2014, the Padgetts converted their vacation home in the mountains to their primary residence. They demolished the barn and built a bigger one on the other side of their property. In the spring of 2015, Mrs. Padgett had the gravel leading to the spot where the barn had been removed, and she planted a vegetable garden in the area where the driveway had previously existed. When Mrs. Martingale arrived for her twenty-second consecutive summer in the mountains, she could no longer access her garage.

Issue Does Mrs. Martingale have an easement over the Padgetts' property?

Rule of Law Easements arise in several ways. First, and most commonly, easements are granted expressly by the landowner. Second, they can arise by implication if an owner of adjacent properties establishes a use that is apparent and permanent, and then conveys one of the properties without mention of the easement. Easements can also spring from necessity; conveyance of a portion of a parcel with no access to roads may require the seller also to convey an easement across his remaining land, to give the purchaser ingress and egress. Lastly, the law of most states contemplates easements by prescription. To establish a prescriptive easement, the one claiming it must prove that she has regularly used the other's land openly and adversely over a specific time period established by the relevant state's adverse possession laws.

Application The Padgetts did not expressly grant the Martingales an easement over their land. Moreover, no easement by implication can be established because the Padgetts did not buy their land from the Martingales, nor did the gravel driveway or the Martingale's garage exist until a few years after each couple had purchased their parcels. Furthermore, necessity cannot be shown since the Martingale property has street frontage, and all that would be required to give the Martingales easy vehicular access to their garage is removal of two trees on their own property.

The only possibility of establishing a permanent legal right of way across the Padgetts' land, perhaps suggested by the decades over which Mrs. Martingale used the gravel drive, is easement by prescription. The first requirement, open and generally known use, presents no hurdle here. Mrs. Padgett was quite aware of Mrs. Martingale's use of the gravel drive because the two women spoke briefly almost every time Mrs. Martingale drove down the Padgetts' gravel path to her own garage. Second, the use must have been adverse to that of the owner. Adverse use of an easement does not require exclusion of the owner. However, it does require that the use be hostile to the wishes of the rightful owner. Thus, if permission is given, the "adverse" element cannot be proven. Here, Mrs. Padgett apparently approved of Mrs. Martingale's use. Therefore, it cannot be said Mrs. Martingale's use was adverse. The third element of a prescriptive easement is use, consistent with the nature of the right of way, without interruption over the statutorily established prescription period. The prescriptive periods in most states are between five and twenty years. If Mrs. Martingale successfully used the Padgetts' gravel drive every time she drove into her garage over a twenty-one year interval, she has probably satisfied the time requirement in even the state with the longest prescriptive period.

Conclusion The Martingales' use of the Padgetts' gravel drive was not adverse. Therefore, the Martingales cannot establish an easement over the Padgetts' former gravel drive, despite Mrs. Martingale's openly using the right of way regularly for a period of twenty-one years.

Creation of Easements [48-4c]

The most common way to create an easement is by express grant or reservation. In an easement by ***express grant***, one party expressly transfers the easement to another party. For example, when Amy sells part of her land to Robert, she may, in the same deed, expressly grant him an easement over her remaining property. In an easement by ***reservation***, one party expressly reserves the right to retain an easement in property that is being transferred.

Easements by *implication* arise whenever an owner of adjacent properties establishes an *apparent* and *permanent* use in the nature of an easement and then conveys one of the properties without mention of any easement. An easement may also arise by *necessity*: if Andrew conveys part of his land to Sharon, and the part conveyed to Sharon is so situated that she would have no access to it except across Andrew's remaining land, the law implies a grant by Andrew to Sharon of an easement by necessity across his remaining land.

Finally, an easement may arise by *prescription* in most states if certain required conditions are met. To obtain an easement by prescription, a person must use a portion of land owned by another in a way (1) that is adverse to the rightful owner's use, (2) that is open and generally known, and (3) that continues, uninterrupted, for a specific period that varies from state to state. The claimant acquires no easement by prescription, however, if given the owner's permission to use the land.

Practical Advice

Be sure to have any easement you obtain put in writing and properly file it with the recorder of deeds.

Profits á Prendre [48-4d]

Profit á prendre

right to remove natural resources from another's land

Coming from the French, the phrase **profit á prendre** means the right to remove natural resources, such as petroleum, minerals, timber, and wild game, from another's land. An example would be the grant by B to A, an adjoining landowner, of the right to remove coal, fish, or timber from B's land or to graze his cattle on B's land. Like an easement, a *profit á prendre* may arise by prescription, but if it comes about through an act of the parties, it must be created with all the formalities accorded the grant of an estate in real property. Unless the right is clearly designated as exclusive, the owner of the land is entitled to exercise it as well. Unlike A in the previous example, even those who do not own adjacent land may hold the right to take profits. Thus, C may have a right to remove crushed gravel from B's acreage even though C lives in another part of the county.

Licenses [48-4e]

License

permission to use another's land

A **license**, which is created by a contract granting permission to use an owner's land, does not create an interest in the property. A license is usually exercised only at the will of the owner and subject to revocation by him at any time. For example, if Adams tells Ebone she may cut across Adams's land to pick hickory nuts, Ebone has nothing but a license subject to revocation at any time. Nonetheless, should Ebone, on the basis of that license, expend funds to exercise the right, the courts may prevent Adams from revoking the license simply because penalizing Ebone would be unfair, given the circumstances. In such a case, Ebone's interest would be, in practice, indistinguishable from an easement.

A common example of a license is a theater ticket or the use of a hotel room. No interest is acquired in the premises; there is simply a right of use for a given length of time, subject to good behavior. No formality is required to create a license; a shopkeeper licenses persons to enter his establishment merely by being open for business.

CHAPTER SUMMARY

Freehold Estates

Fee Estates right to immediate possession of real property for an indefinite time

- *Fee Simple Estate* absolute ownership of property, which can be sold or passed on by will or inheritance
- *Qualified Fee Estate* ownership of property subject to its termination upon the happening of a contingent event

Life Estates ownership right in property for the life of a designated person, while the remainder is the ownership estate that takes effect when the prior estate terminates

Future Interests

- *Reversion* grantor's right to property upon termination of another estate
- *Remainders* are of two kinds: (1) vested remainders (unconditional remainder that is a fixed, present interest to be enjoyed in the future) and (2) contingent remainders (remainder interest conditional upon the happening of an event in addition to the termination of the preceding estate)

Leasehold Estates

Lease both (1) a contract for use and possession of land and (2) a grant of an estate in land for a period of time

- **Landlord** owner of land who grants a leasehold interest to another while retaining a reversionary interest in the property
- **Tenant** possessor of the leasehold interest in the land

Duration of Leases

- **Definite Term** lease that automatically expires at the end of the term
- **Periodic Tenancy** lease that continues for successive periods unless terminated by notice to the other party
- **Tenancy at Will** lease that is terminable at any time
- **Tenancy at Sufferance** possession of real property without a lease

Transfer of Tenant's Interest

- **Assignment** transfer of all of the tenant's interest in the leasehold
- **Sublease** transfer of less than all of the tenant's interest in the leasehold

Tenant's Obligations the tenant has an obligation to pay a specified rent at specified times or, if none is specified, to pay a reasonable amount at the end of the term

- **Destruction of the Premises** under the common law, if the premises are destroyed, the tenant is not relieved of his obligation to pay rent and cannot terminate the lease
- **Eviction** if the tenant breaches one of the covenants of her lease, the landlord may terminate the lease and evict (remove) her from the premises
- **Abandonment** if tenant abandons property and the landlord reenters or relets it, tenant's obligation to pay rent terminates

Landlord's Obligations

- **Quiet Enjoyment** the right of the tenant to have physical possession of the premises free of landlord interference
- **Fitness for Use** most courts impose for residential leases an implied warranty of habitability that the leased premises are fit for ordinary residential purposes
- **Repair** unless there is a statute or a specific provision in the lease, the landlord has no duty to repair or restore the premises

Concurrent Ownership

Tenancy in Common co-ownership in which each tenant holds an undivided interest with no right of survivorship

Joint Tenancy co-ownership with the right of survivorship; requires the presence of the four unities (time, title, interest, and possession)

Tenancy by the Entireties co-ownership by spouses in which neither may convey his or her interest during life

Community Property spouses' rights in property acquired by the other during their marriage

Condominium separate ownership of an individual unit with tenancy in common with respect to common areas

Cooperative the corporate owner of the property leases units to its shareholders as tenants

Nonpossessory Interest

Easement limited right to use the land of another in a specified manner

- **Appurtenant** rights and duties created by the easement pertain to and run with the land of the owner of the easement (dominant parcel) and the land subject to the easement (servient parcel)
- **In Gross** rights and duties created by the easement are personal to the individual who received the right
- **Creation of Easements** easements may be created by (1) express grant or reservation, (2) implied grant or reservation, (3) necessity, and (4) prescription (adverse use)

Profit á Prendre right to remove natural resources from the land of another

Licenses permission to use the land of another

QUESTIONS

1. Kirkland conveyed a farm to Sandler to have and to hold for and during his life and on Sandler's death to Rubin. Some years thereafter, oil was discovered in the vicinity. Sandler thereupon made an oil and gas lease, and the oil company set up its machinery to begin drilling operations. Rubin then filed suit to enjoin the operations. Assuming an injunction to be the proper form of remedy, what decision?

2. Smith owned Blackacre in fee simple absolute. In section 3 of a properly executed will, Smith devised Blackacre as follows: "I devise my farm Blackacre to my son Darwin so long as it is used as a farm." Sections 5 and 6 of the will made gifts to persons other than Darwin. The last and residuary clause of Smith's will provided: "All the residue of my real and personal property not disposed of heretofore in this will, I devise and bequeath to Stanford University." What interests in Blackacre were created by Smith's will?

3. Panessi leased to Barnes, for a term of ten years beginning May 1, certain premises that were improved with a three-story building, the first floor being occupied by stores and the upper stories by apartments. On May 1 of the following year, Barnes leased one of the apartments to Clinton for one year. On July 5, a fire destroyed the second and third floors of the building. The first floor was not burned but was rendered unusable. Neither the lease from Panessi to Barnes nor the lease from Barnes to Clinton contained any provision regarding loss by fire. Discuss the liability of Barnes and Clinton to continue to pay rent.

4. Ames leased an apartment to Boor for $600 a month, payable the last day of each month. The term of the written lease was from January 1, 2014, through April 30, 2015. On March 15, 2014, Boor moved out, telling Ames that he disliked all the other tenants. Ames replied, "Well, you're no prize as a tenant; I can probably get more rent from someone more agreeable." Ames and Boor then had a minor physical altercation in which neither was injured. Boor sent the apartment keys to Ames by mail. Ames wrote Boor, "It will be my pleasure to hold you for every penny you owe me. I am renting the apartment on your behalf to Clay until April 30, 2015, at $425 a month." Boor had paid his rent through February 28, 2014. Clay entered the premises on April 1, 2014. How much rent, if any, may Ames recover from Boor?

5. Jay signed a two-year lease containing a clause that expressly prohibited subletting. After six months, Jay asked the landlord for permission to sublet the apartment for one year. The landlord refused. This angered Jay, and he immediately assigned his right under the lease to Kay. Kay was a distinguished gentleman, and Jay knew that everyone would consider him a desirable tenant. Is Jay's assignment of his lease to Kay valid?

6. In 2003, Roy Martin and his wife, Alice; their son, Hiram; and Hiram's wife, Myrna, acquired title to a 240-acre farm. The deed ran to Roy Martin and Alice Martin, the father and mother, as joint tenants with the right of survivorship, and to Hiram Martin and Myrna Martin, the son and his wife, as joint tenants with the right of survivorship. Alice Martin died in 2011, and in 2014, Roy Martin married Agnes Martin. By his will, Roy Martin bequeathed and devised his entire estate to Agnes Martin. When Roy Martin died in 2016, Hiram and Myrna Martin assumed complete control of the farm. State the interest in the farm, if any, of Agnes, Hiram, and Myrna Martin on the death of Roy Martin.

7. In her will, Teressa granted a life estate to Amos in certain real estate, with remainder to Brenda and Clive in joint tenancy. All the rest of Teressa's estate was left to Hillman College. While going to Teressa's funeral, the car in which Amos, Brenda, and Clive were riding was wrecked. Brenda was killed, Clive died a few minutes later, and Amos died on his way to the hospital. Who is entitled to the real estate in question?

8. Otis Olson, the owner of two adjoining city lots, A and B, built a house on each. He laid a drainpipe from lot B across lot A to the main sewer pipe under the alley beyond lot A. Olson then sold and conveyed lot A to Fred Ford. The deed, which made no mention of the drainpipe, was promptly recorded. Ford had no actual knowledge or notice of the drainpipe, although it would have been apparent to anyone inspecting the premises because it was only partially buried. Later, Olson sold and conveyed lot B to Luke Lane. This deed also made no reference to the drainpipe and was promptly recorded. A few weeks later, Ford discovered the drainpipe across lot A and removed it. Did he have the right to do so?

9. At the time of his marriage to Ann, Robert owned several parcels of real estate in joint tenancy with his brother, Sam. During his marriage, Robert purchased a house and put the title in his name and his wife's name as joint tenants, not as tenants in common. Robert died; within a month of his death, Smith obtained a judgment against Robert's estate. What are the relative rights of Sam, Smith, and Ann?

CASE PROBLEMS

10. In 1988, Ogle owned two adjoining lots numbered 6 and 7 fronting at the north on a city street. In that year, she laid out and built a concrete driveway along and two feet in front of what she erroneously believed to be the west boundary of lot 7. Ogle used the driveway for access to buildings situated at the southern end of both lots. Later in the same year, she conveyed lot 7 to Dale, and thereafter in the same year, she conveyed lot 6 to Pace. Neither deed made any reference to the driveway, and after the conveyance, Dale used it exclusively for access to lot 7. In 2015, a survey by Pace established that the driveway overlapped six inches on lot 6, and he brought an appropriate action to establish his lawful ownership

of the strip on which the driveway approaches, to enjoin its use by Dale, and to require Dale to remove the overlap. Will Pace prevail? Why?

11. Temco, Inc., conveyed to the Wynns certain property adjoining an apartment complex being developed by Sonnett Realty Company. Although nothing to this effect was contained in the deed, the sales contract gave the purchaser of the property use of the apartment's swimming pool. Temco's sales agent also emphasized that use of the pool would be a desirable feature in the event that the Wynns decided to sell the property.

Seven years later, the Bunns contracted to buy the property from the Wynns through the latter's agent, Sonnett Realty. Although both the Wynns and Sonnett Realty's agent told the Bunns that use of the apartment's pool went with the purchased property, neither the contract nor the deed subsequently conveyed to the Bunns so provided. When the Bunns requested pool passes from Temco and Offutt, the company that owned the apartments, their request was refused. Discuss whether the Bunns have a right to use the apartment's pool.

12. In 1972, a deed for land in Pitt County, North Carolina, was executed and delivered by Joel and Louisa Tyson unto M. H. Jackson and wife Maggie Jackson, for and during the term of their natural lives and after their death to the children of the said M. H. Jackson and Maggie Jackson that shall be born to their intermarriage as shall survive them to them and their heirs and assigns in fee simple forever.

Thelma Jackson Vester, a daughter of M. H. and Maggie Jackson, died in 2014, survived by three children. M. H. Jackson, who survived his wife, Maggie Jackson, died in 2015, survived by four sons. The children of Thelma Jackson Vester brought this action against M. P. Jackson, a son of and executor of the will of M. H. Jackson. The children of Vester contended that through their deceased mother they were entitled to a one-fifth interest in the land conveyed by the deed of 1972. The executor contended that the deed conveyed a contingent remainder and that only those children who survived the parents took an interest in the land. Discuss the contentions of both of the parties.

13. Robert and Marjorie Wake owned land that they used as both a cattle ranch and a farm. Each spring and autumn, the Wakes would drive their cattle from the ranch portion of the operation across an access road on the farmland to Butler Springs, which was also on the farmland.

In December 1992, the Wakes sold the farm to Jesse and Maud Hess but retained for themselves a right-of-way over the farm access road and the right to use Butler Springs for watering their livestock. In 1999, the Hesses sold the farm to the Johnsons, granting them uninterrupted possession of the property "excepting only that permissive use of the premises" owned by the Wakes.

The Wakes continued to use the access road and Butler Springs until 2000, when they sold their ranch and granted the new owners "their rights to the water of Butler Springs," but they said nothing about the access road. The ranch was subsequently sold several times, and all the owners used the access road and watering hole. In 2013, the Nelsons purchased the ranch. Shortly thereafter, the Johnsons notified the Nelsons that they had revoked the Nelsons' right to use the access road and Butler Springs. In 2015, the Johnsons closed the access road by locking the gates across the road. The Nelsons brought this action, claiming easements to both the access road and Butler Springs. The trial court ruled in favor of the Nelsons, and the Johnsons appealed. Does an easement in favor of the Nelsons exist? Why?

14. Clayton and Margie Gulledge owned a house at 532 Somerset Place, N.W. (the Somerset property) as tenants by the entirety. They had three children: Bernis Gulledge, Johnsie Walker, and Marion Watkins. When Margie Gulledge died in 1987, Clayton became the sole owner of the Somerset property. The following year, Clayton remarried, but the marriage was unsuccessful. To avoid a possible loss of the Somerset property, Bernis forwarded Clayton funds to satisfy the second wife's financial demands. In exchange, Clayton conveyed the property to Bernis and himself as joint tenants. In 2008, Clayton conveyed his interest in the Somerset property to his daughter, Marion Watkins. In 2008, Clayton died. Bernis died in 2014, and Johnsie Walker died in 2014. Marion Watkins claims to be a tenant in common with the estate of Bernis Gulledge. The estate claims that when Clayton died, Watkins' interest was extinguished, and Bernis became the sole owner of the Somerset property. Who is correct? Why?

15. By separate leases, Javins and a few others rented an apartment at the Clifton Terrace apartment complex. When they defaulted on their rent payments, the landlord, First National Realty, brought an action to evict them. The tenants admitted to the default but defended on the ground that the landlord had failed to maintain the premises in compliance with the Washington, D.C., Housing Code. They alleged that approximately one thousand five hundred violations of this code had arisen since the term of their lease began. Discuss the merits of this case.

16. On January 1, Mrs. Irene Kern leased an apartment from Colonial Court Apartments, Inc., for a one-year term. When the lease was entered into, Mrs. Kern asked for a quiet apartment, and Colonial assured her that the assigned apartment was in a quiet, well-insulated building. In fact, however, the apartment above Mrs. Kern's was occupied by a young couple, the Lindgrens. From the start of her occupancy, Mrs. Kern complained of their twice-weekly parties and other actions that so disturbed her sleep that she had to go elsewhere for rest. After Mrs. Kern had lodged several complaints, Colonial terminated the Lindgrens's lease effective February 28. The termination of the lease was prolonged, however, and Mrs. Kern vacated her apartment, claiming that she was no longer able to endure the continued disturbances. Colonial then brought this action to recover rent owed by Mrs. Kern. Will Colonial prevail? Has Mrs. Kern been constructively evicted? Explain.

17. On January 14, 2011, Eura Mae Redmon deeded land to her daughter, Melba Taylor, and two sons, W. C. Sewell and Billy Sewell, "jointly and severally, and unto their heirs, assigns and successors forever," with the grantor retaining a life estate. W. C. Sewell died on November 18, 2011, and Billy Sewell died on May 11, 2013. Mrs. Redmon died on February 17, 2015. Melba Taylor then sought a declaration that her mother had intended to convey the property to the grantees as joint tenants, thereby making her, by virtue of her brothers' deaths, sole owner of the property. Descendants of W. C. and Billy Sewell opposed the complaint on the ground that the deed created a tenancy in common among the grantees. Who is correct? Explain.

TAKING SIDES

On June 30, 2006, Martin Hendrickson and Solveig Hendrickson were married, and on January 3, 2007, a home previously owned by Martin was conveyed to them as joint tenants and not as tenants in common. Solveig Hendrickson paid no part of the consideration for the premises. On August 3, 2014, Martin Hendrickson duly executed a Declaration of Election to Sever Survivorship of Joint Tenancy by which he endeavored to preserve an interest in the premises for Ruth Halbert, his daughter by a previous marriage. On the same day, he executed his last will and testament, by the terms of which he directed that his wife, Solveig Hendrickson, receive the minimum amount to which she was entitled under the laws of the State of Minnesota. Martin Hendrickson died with a valid will on October 9, 2014.

a. What are the arguments that the joint ownership was severed by Martin Hendrickson's declaration thus creating a tenancy in common?

b. What are the arguments that the joint tenancy was not severed by Martin Hendrickson's declaration and thus the property passed to Solveig Hendrickson by survivorship upon Martin Hendrickson's death?

c. Which argument should prevail? Explain.

Transfer and Control of Real Property

CHAPTER 49

The right of property has not made poverty, but it has powerfully contributed to make wealth.

J. R. McCulloch
Principles of Political Economy

CHAPTER OUTCOMES

After reading and studying this chapter, you should be able to:

1. Explain (a) the essential elements of a contract of sale of an interest in real property, (b) the meaning and importance of marketable title, and (c) the concept of implied warranty of habitability.

2. Describe the fundamental requirements of a valid deed and distinguish among warranty, special warranty, and quitclaim deeds.

3. (a) Describe the elements of a secured transaction, (b) distinguish between a mortgage and a deed, and (c) distinguish between an assumption of a mortgage and buying subject to a mortgage.

4. Define and give examples of (a) adverse possession, (b) a variance, (c) a nonconforming use, and (d) eminent domain.

5. Describe the nature and types of restrictive covenants.

The law has always been extremely cautious about the transfer of title to real estate. Personal property may, for the most part, be passed easily and informally from owner to owner, but real property can be transferred only through compliance with a variety of formalities.

Title to land may be transferred in three principal ways: (1) by deed; (2) by will or by the law of descent on the death of the owner; and (3) by open, continuous, and adverse possession by a nonowner for a statutorily prescribed period of time. In this chapter, we will discuss the first and third methods of transfer; we will cover the second method in Chapter 50.

In addition to the legal restrictions placed on the transfer of real property, a number of other controls apply to the use of privately owned property. Government units impose some of these, including zoning and the taking of property by eminent domain. Private parties through restrictive covenants impose others. We will consider these three controls in the second part of this chapter.

TRANSFER OF REAL PROPERTY

The transfer of real property occurs most commonly by deed. Such transfers usually involve a contract for the sale of the land, the subsequent delivery of the deed, and the payment of the agreed-upon consideration. The transfer of real estate by deed, however, does not require consideration to be valid; it may be made as a gift. In most cases, the real estate purchaser must borrow part of the purchase price, using the real property as security. An unusual and far less common method of transferring title, adverse possession, requires no contract, deed, or other formality.

CONTRACT OF SALE [49-1]

As indicated in the chapters on general contracts, general contract law governs the sale of real property. In general, the seller agrees to convey the land and the buyer agrees to pay for it. In addition, the Federal Fair Housing Act (Title VIII of the Civil Rights Act, as amended) prohibits discrimination in the real estate market on the basis of race, color, religion, gender, national origin, disability, or familial status. The Act exempts the sale or rental of a single-family house owned by a private individual who owns fewer than four houses, provided that the owner does not use a broker or discriminatory advertising. Nevertheless, these exemptions do not apply to discrimination based on race or color; in the sale or rental of property, the Act prohibits all discrimination based on these factors.

Formation [49-1a]

Formation
a contract to transfer any interest in land must be in writing to be enforceable

Because an oral agreement for the sale of an interest in land is not enforceable under the statute of frauds, the buyer and seller not only must reduce the agreement to writing but also must have it signed by the other party in order to be able to enforce the agreement against that party. The simplest agreement should contain (1) the names and addresses of the parties, (2) a description of the property to be conveyed, (3) the time for the conveyance (called the *closing*), (4) the type of deed to be given, and (5) the price and manner of payment. To avoid dispute and to ensure adequately both parties' rights, a properly drawn contract for the sale of land will cover many other points as well.

Marketable Title [49-1b]

Marketable title
title free from any defects or encumbrances

Practical Advice

Before title to the property passes, the buyer should ensure that she is receiving good title by having the title searched.

Practical Advice

As a buyer, obtain title insurance on the property to be purchased to insure against loss from defective title.

The law of conveyancing firmly establishes that a contract for the sale of land carries with it an *implied* obligation on the part of the seller to transfer marketable title. **Marketable title** means that the title is free from (1) encumbrances (such as mortgages, easements, liens, leases, and restrictive covenants); (2) defects in the chain of title appearing in the land records (such as a prior recorded conveyance of the same property by the seller); and (3) events that deprive the seller of title, such as adverse possession or eminent domain. The obligation to convey marketable title is significant: if the title search reveals any defect not *specifically* excepted in the contract, the seller has materially breached the contract. The buyer's remedies for breach include specific performance with a price reduction, rescission and restitution, or damages for loss of bargain.

A title search involves examining prior transfers of and encumbrances to the property. Such an examination does not, however, guarantee rightful ownership; consequently, most buyers purchase title insurance as well. Issued in the amount of the purchase price of the property, **title insurance** indemnifies the owner against any loss due to defects in the title to the property or due to liens or encumbrances, except for those the policy identifies as existing when the policy was issued. Such policies also may be issued to protect the interests of mortgagees or tenants of property.

Implied Warranty of Habitability [49-1c]

Implied warranty of habitability
in a majority of states, the builder-seller of a dwelling impliedly warrants that a newly constructed house is free from latent defects

Practical Advice

As a buyer, carefully inspect any dwelling prior to purchasing it. Also seek to have the seller expressly warrant the dwelling's condition and habitability.

Because the obligation to transfer marketable title covers only the title to the property conveyed, such an obligation does not apply to the quality of any improvements to the land. The traditional common law rule is *caveat emptor*—let the buyer beware. Under this rigid maxim, the buyer must thoroughly inspect the property before the sale is completed, as any undiscovered defect would not be the seller's responsibility. The seller is liable only for any misrepresentations or express warranties he may have made about the property.

A majority of states have relaxed the harshness of the common law in sales made by one who builds and then sells residential dwellings. In such a sale, the builder-seller *impliedly* warrants a newly constructed house to be free of latent defects, that is, those defects not apparent upon a reasonable inspection of the house at the time of sale. In some states, this implied warranty of habitability benefits only the original purchaser; other states have extended it to subsequent purchasers for a reasonable period of time. In addition, many jurisdictions now require *all* sellers to disclose hidden defects that materially affect the property's value if reasonable examination would not reveal such defects. (See Chapter 11 for a discussion of misrepresentation.)

VonHoldt v. Barba & Barba Construction, Inc.
Supreme Court of Illinois, 1997
175 Ill.2d 426, 677 N.E.2d 836, 222 Ill.Dec. 302
http://scholar.google.com/scholar_case?case=17693796651563455274&q=677+N.E.2D+836&hl=en&as_sdt=2,34

FACTS In August 1982, defendant, Barba & Barba Construction, Inc., constructed a multilevel addition to a single-family house in Glenview, Illinois. Before the addition, the residence consisted of approximately two thousand three hundred square feet. After the addition, the house consisted of approximately three thousand two hundred square feet. More than eleven years later, on November 5, 1993, plaintiff, John W. VonHoldt, purchased the house.

Shortly after taking occupancy, plaintiff noticed a deflection of the wood flooring at the partition wall separating the master bedroom from an adjoining bathroom. This deflection created a depression in the floor plane. Plaintiff maintained that, due to the thickness of the carpet, the depression was nearly concealed. An investigation revealed that the addition had not been constructed in accordance with the architectural plans approved by the Village of Glenview or the Glenview Building Code. This variance resulted in excessive stress on the floor joists and inadequate support for a portion of the roof and ceiling causing a greater-than-expected floor deflection.

The plaintiff brought the present action against defendant alleging that defendant breached an implied warranty of habitability. The trial judge dismissed plaintiff's complaint for failure to state a cause of action. Plaintiff appealed and the appellate court affirmed.

DECISION Judgment affirmed due to the fact that plaintiff's action was barred by the ten-year statute of repose.

OPINION The implied warranty of habitability is a judicially created doctrine designed to avoid the unjust results of *caveat emptor* and the doctrine of merger. Initially, Illinois courts applied the doctrine to the sale of new homes to protect innocent purchasers who were not able to determine whether the house they purchased contained latent or hidden defects. The owner needs this protection because he is making a major investment, in many instances the largest single investment of his life. The owner usually relies on the integrity and skill of the builder, who is in the business of building houses, and has a right to expect to receive a house that is reasonably fit for use as a residence.

The implied warranty of habitability does include actions against a builder brought by a subsequent purchaser for latent defects in an addition to a home. When a builder makes a significant addition to a previously built home, an action for damages resulting from latent defects affecting habitability exists under the doctrine of implied warranty of habitability. An owner claiming that latent defects exist in a major addition to a structure should be provided the same protection for the addition as that given to the original owners. The purchaser of both a completed home and an addition places the same trust in the builder that the structure being erected is suitable for living. Furthermore, the ordinary buyer is not in a position to discover hidden defects in a structure even through the exercise of ordinary and reasonable care.

However, because here the action was time barred, plaintiff's complaint was properly dismissed.

INTERPRETATION The implied warranty of habitability applies to a subsequent purchase against a builder who makes a significant addition to a previously built home.

CRITICAL THINKING QUESTION Under what conditions should the implied warranty of habitability be applied? Explain.

DEEDS [49-2]

A **deed** is a formal document transferring any interest in land upon delivery and acceptance. The party who transfers property by a deed is called the **grantor**; the transferee of the property is the **grantee**.

Types of Deeds [49-2a]

The rights a deed conveys depend on the type of deed used. Deeds are of three basic types: warranty, special warranty, and quitclaim.

Warranty Deed

By a **warranty deed** (also called a general warranty deed), the grantor promises the grantee that the grantor has a valid title to the property. In addition, under a warranty deed, the grantor, either expressly or implicitly, obliges herself to make the grantee whole for any damage the grantee suffers should the grantor's title prove defective. A warranty deed includes certain promises or covenants, the most usual of which are *title, against encumbrances, quiet enjoyment*, and *warranty*. These various covenants constitute an assurance that the grantee will have undisturbed possession of the land and will, in turn, be able to transfer it without adverse claims of third parties. A phrase common in a warranty deed is "convey and warrant," although in a number of states the phrase "grant, bargain, and sell" is used, together with the seller's covenant (appearing later in the deed) that she will "warrant and defend the title."

Deed
a formal document transferring any type of interest in land

Grantor
party transferring property by a deed

Grantee
transferee of property transferred by deed

Warranty deed
grantor promises that she has valid title

Special Warranty Deed   Whereas a warranty deed contains a general warranty of title, a **special warranty deed** warrants only that the title has not been impaired, encumbered, or made defective because of any act or omission *of the grantor*. The grantor merely warrants the title so far as it concerns his acts or omissions. He does *not* warrant title as to the acts or omissions of others.

Quitclaim Deed   By a **quitclaim deed**, the grantor, in effect, says no more than "I make no promise as to what interest I do have in this land, but whatever it is, I convey it to you." A quitclaim deed usually provides that the grantor "conveys and quitclaims" or more simply "quitclaims all interest" in the property. Quitclaim deeds are used most frequently in transfers requiring persons who appear to have an interest in land to release their interest.

Formal Requirements [49-2b]

As noted, any transfer of an interest in land that is of more than a limited duration falls within the statute of frauds and must therefore be in writing. Almost every deed, whatever the type, contains substantially similar wording.

Often, the deed will first describe the land. The description must be sufficiently clear to permit identification of the property conveyed. After describing the property, the deed usually will proceed to describe the quantity of estate conveyed to the grantee. Deeds generally end with the grantor's signature, a seal, and an acknowledgment before a notary public or other official authorized to verify the authenticity of documents.

Delivery of Deeds [49-2c]

A deed does not transfer title to land until it is delivered. **Delivery**, or an *intent* that the deed is to take effect, is evidenced by the acts or statements of the grantor. Physical transfer of the deed is usually the best evidence of this intent, but it is not necessary. Frequently, in a transfer known as an **escrow**, a grantor will turn a deed over to a third party (the escrow agent) to hold until the grantee performs certain conditions. When the grantee so performs, the escrow agent must give her the deed.

Recordation [49-2d]

In almost all states, recording a deed is not necessary to pass title from grantor to grantee. Unless the grantee has the deed recorded, however, a subsequent good faith purchaser for value of the property will acquire title superior to that of the grantee. **Recordation** consists of delivering a duly executed and acknowledged deed to the recorder's office in the county where the property is located. There, a copy of the instrument is inserted in the current deed book and indexed.

In some states, called *notice* states, unrecorded instruments are invalid against any subsequent purchaser without notice. In *notice-race* states, an unrecorded deed is invalid against any subsequent purchaser without notice of who recorded first. Finally, in a few states, called *race* states, an unrecorded deed is invalid against any deed recorded before it.

At least twenty-eight states have adopted the Uniform Real Property Electronic Recording Act. This Act permits the electronic filing of real property instruments as well as systems for searching for and retrieving these land records.

SECURED TRANSACTIONS [49-3]

As discussed in Chapter 37, a **secured transaction** essentially involves two elements: (1) a debt or obligation to pay money and (2) the creditor's interest in specific property that secures performance of the obligation. A security interest in property cannot exist apart from the debt it secures: discharging the debt in any manner terminates the interest. Transactions involving the use of real estate as security for a debt are subject to real estate law, which consists of statutes and rules developed through common law interpretations of mortgages and trust deeds. In these cases, the real estate itself is used to secure the obligation, which is evidenced by a note and by either a mortgage or deed of trust. The debtor is referred to as the

---

Special warranty deed
grantor promises that he has not impaired title

Quitclaim deed
grantor transfers whatever interest she has in the property

Practical Advice

As a buyer, have the seller grant a general warranty deed that specifically provides for the seller's liability if the title is defective.

Delivery
intent that the deed take effect, as evidenced by acts or statements of the grantor

Escrow
holding by a third party of a document or funds

Recordation
required to protect the grantee's interest against third parties; consists of delivery of a duly executed and acknowledged deed to the appropriate recorder's office

Practical Advice

Promptly record your deed with the recorder of deeds; if possible, do this before or simultaneously with the seller's receipt of the purchase price.

Secured transaction
a secured transaction involves (1) a debt or obligation to pay money, (2) an interest of the creditor in specific property that secures performance, and (3) the debtor's right to redeem the property by paying the debt

Mortgagor

debtor who uses real estate to secure an obligation

Mortgagee

creditor of a secured transaction involving real estate

Mortgage

interest in land created by a written document that provides security for payment of a debt

Deed of trust

interest in real property which is conveyed to a third person as trustee for the creditor

mortgagor; the creditor is the **mortgagee**. The Uniform Commercial Code does *not* apply to real estate mortgages or deeds of trust.

Form of Mortgages [49-3a]

A **mortgage** is a security interest in land. The instrument that embodies a mortgage must meet all the requirements for such a document: it must be in writing, it must contain an adequate description of the property, and it must be executed and delivered. Nearly identical to a mortgage, a **deed of trust** contains one major difference: under a deed of trust, the property is conveyed not to the creditor as security but to a third person, who acts as trustee for the benefit of the creditor. The deed of trust creates rights almost the same as those created by a mortgage. In some states, it is customary to use a deed of trust in lieu of the ordinary form of mortgage.

As with all interests in realty, the mortgage or deed of trust should be promptly recorded to protect the mortgagee's rights against third persons who acquire an interest in the mortgaged property without knowledge of the mortgage.

Rights and Duties [49-3b]

The rights and duties of the parties to a mortgage may depend on whether it is considered to create a lien or to transfer legal title to the mortgagee. Most states have adopted the *lien* theory. The mortgagor retains title and, even in the absence of any stipulation in the mortgage, is entitled to possession of the premises to the exclusion of the mortgagee, even if the mortgagor defaults. Only through foreclosure (sale) or through the court appointment of a receiver can the right of possession be taken from the mortgagor. Other states have adopted the common law *title* theory, which gives the mortgagee the right of ownership and possession. In most cases, as a practical matter, the mortgagor retains possession simply because the mortgagee does not care about possession unless the mortgagor defaults.

Even though the mortgagor generally is entitled to possession and to many of the advantages of unrestricted ownership, he has a responsibility to deal with the property in a manner that will not impair the security. In most instances, *waste* (impairment of the security) results from the mortgagor's failure to prevent the actual or threatened actions of third parties against the land. For example, the debtor's failure to pay taxes or to discharge a prior lien may seriously impair the mortgagee's security. In such cases, the courts usually permit the mortgagee to pay the obligation and add it to his claim against the mortgagor.

The mortgagor may relieve his property from a mortgage lien by paying the debt that the mortgage secures. Characteristic of a mortgage, this right of **redemption** can be defeated only by operation of law. The right to redeem carries with it the obligation to pay the debt, and payment in full, with interest, is prerequisite to redemption. See Figure 49-1 for the fundamental rights of the mortgagor and mortgagee.

Redemption

debtor's right to remove the mortgage by paying the debt

Mortgage Regulation [49-3c]

In July 2010, President Obama signed into law the Dodd-Frank Wall Street Reform and Consumer Protection Act (Dodd-Frank), the most significant change to U.S. financial regulation since the New Deal during the 1930s. One of the many standalone statutes included in the Dodd-Frank is the Mortgage Reform and Anti-Predatory Lending Act of 2010, which modifies

Figure 49-1 Fundamental Rights of Mortgagor and Mortgagee

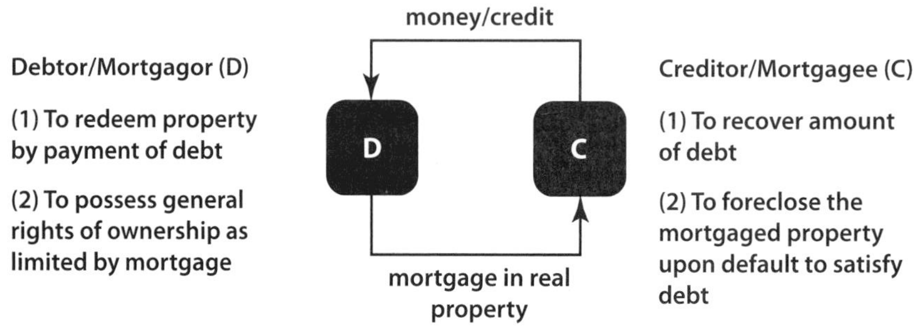

Practical Advice

An assignee of a mortgage is well advised to obtain the assignment in a writing duly executed by the mortgagee and to record it promptly with the proper public official. This will protect her rights against persons who subsequently acquire an interest in the mortgaged property without knowledge of the assignment.

Assumes the mortgage
purchaser of mortgaged property becomes personally liable to pay the debt

Subject to the mortgage
purchaser is not personally obligated to pay the debt, but the property remains subject to the mortgage

Foreclosure
sale of the mortgaged property upon default to satisfy the debt

Adverse possession
acquisition of title to land by open, continuous, and adverse occupancy for a statutorily prescribed period

Possession
must be actual and without intervening dominion by true owner

Practical Advice

If you own real property, inspect it on a regular basis and exercise control over it in order to prevent any person from obtaining adverse possession.

the Truth-in-Lending Act to make mortgage brokers and lenders more accountable for the loans that they make. The Dodd-Frank requires that lenders ensure a borrower's reasonable ability to repay the loan; prohibits unfair and deceptive lending practices (especially with respect to subprime mortgages); expands protection for borrowers of high-cost loans; and requires lenders to disclose the maximum amount a consumer could pay on a variable rate mortgage, with a warning that payments will vary based on interest rate changes.

Transfer of the Interests Under the Mortgage [49-3d]

The interests of the original mortgagor and mortgagee can be transferred, and the rights and obligations of their assignees will depend primarily on (1) the agreement of the parties to the assignment and (2) the legal rules protecting the interest of one who is party to the mortgage but not to the transfer.

If the *mortgagor* conveys the land, the purchaser is *not* personally liable for the mortgage debt unless she expressly **assumes the mortgage**. If she assumes the mortgage, she is personally obligated to pay the debt the mortgagor owes to the mortgagee. Furthermore, the mortgagee can also hold the mortgagor on his promise to pay. In contrast, a transfer of mortgaged property **"subject to" the mortgage** does *not* personally obligate the transferee to pay the mortgage debt. In such a case, the transferee's risk of loss is limited to the property.

A *mortgagee* has the right to assign the mortgage to another person without the mortgagor's consent.

Foreclosure [49-3e]

The right to foreclose usually arises upon default by the mortgagor. **Foreclosure** is an action through which the mortgage holder takes the property from the mortgagor, ends the mortgagor's rights in the property, and sells the property to pay the mortgage debt. If the proceeds are not sufficient to satisfy the debt in full, the debtor-mortgagor remains liable for paying the balance. Generally, the mortgagee will obtain a *deficiency judgment* for any unsatisfied balance of the debt and may proceed to enforce the payment of this amount out of the mortgagor's other assets. The mortgagor's default by nonperformance of other promises in the mortgage also may give the mortgagee the right to foreclose. For example, a mortgage may provide that the mortgagor's failure to pay taxes is a default that permits foreclosure. Mortgages also commonly provide that default in the payment of an installment makes the entire unpaid balance of the debt immediately due and payable, permitting foreclosure for the entire amount.

ADVERSE POSSESSION [49-4]

It is possible, although very rare, that title to land may be transferred involuntarily, without any deed or other formality, through adverse possession. In most states, a person who openly and continuously occupies the land of another for a statutorily prescribed period, typically twenty years, will gain title to the land by **adverse possession**. The **possession** must be actual. Courts have held that living on land, farming it, building on it, or maintaining structures on it is sufficient to constitute possession. However, the possession must be adverse. In other words, any act of dominion by the true owner, such as her entry on the land or assertion of ownership, will stop the period from running. Once broken, the statutory period would have to begin again, from the point at which the owner interrupted it. By statute, some jurisdictions have established shorter periods of adverse possession when possession exists in conjunction with some other claim, such as the payment of taxes for seven years and an apparent claim of title, even if it is not valid.

PUBLIC AND PRIVATE CONTROLS

In exercising its police power for the benefit of the community, the state can and does place controls on the use of privately owned land. Furthermore, the state does not compensate the owner for loss or damage he sustains because of such legitimate controls. The enforcement of zoning laws, which is a proper exercise of the police power, is not a taking of property but a regulation of its use. The taking of private property for a public use or purpose under the state's power of eminent domain is not, however, an exercise of police power, and the owners of the property so taken are entitled to be paid its fair and reasonable value. In addition, by means of restrictive covenants, which we will also consider in this section, the use of privately owned property may be privately controlled.

ZONING [49-5]

Zoning
public control over private land use

Zoning is the principal method of public control over land use. The validity of zoning is rooted in the police power of the state, the inherent power of government to provide for the public health, safety, morals, and welfare. Police power can be used only to regulate private property, never to "take" it. It is firmly established that regulation having no reasonable relation to public health, safety, morals, or welfare is unconstitutional as a denial of due process of law.

Enabling Acts and Zoning Ordinances [49-5a]

Enabling acts
the power to zone is generally delegated to local authorities by statutes known as enabling acts

The power to zone generally is delegated to local city and village authorities by statutes known as **enabling acts**. A typical enabling statute grants municipalities the following powers: (1) to regulate and limit the height and bulk of buildings to be erected; (2) to establish, regulate, and limit the building or setback lines on or along any street, trafficway, drive, or parkway; (3) to regulate and limit the intensity of the use of lot areas and to regulate and determine the area of open spaces within and around buildings; (4) to classify, regulate, and restrict the location of trades and industries and the location of buildings designated for specified industrial, business, residential, and other uses; (5) to divide the entire municipality into districts of such number, shape, area, and class (or classes) as may be deemed best suited to carry out the purposes of the statute; and (6) to set standards to which buildings or structures must conform.

Under these powers, the local authorities may enact zoning ordinances, consisting of a map and its accompanying descriptive text. The map divides the municipality into districts designated principally as industrial, commercial, or residential, with possible subclassifications. A well-drafted zoning ordinance will carefully define the uses permitted in each area. A special use (also called a conditional use or special exception) is a use authorized by the zoning ordinance but only upon specific approval by the zoning authorities on a case-by-case basis. Special uses include churches, schools, hospitals, homes for the disabled, and cemeteries.

Variance [49-5b]

Variance
a use differing from that provided in the zoning ordinance and granted in order to avoid undue hardship

Enabling statutes permit zoning authorities to grant variances when application of a zoning ordinance to specific property would cause its owner "particular hardship" unique or peculiar to the property. A **variance** permits a deviation from the zoning ordinance. Special circumstances applicable to particular property might include its unusual shape, topography, size, location, or surroundings. A variance is not available, however, if the hardship is caused by conditions general to the neighborhood or by the actions of the property owner. It must affirmatively appear that the property as presently zoned cannot yield a reasonable return on the owner's investment.

Practical Advice

Prior to buying or developing real property, make sure that your plans conform with all zoning ordinances and private restrictive covenants.

Nonconforming Uses [49-5c]

Nonconforming use
preexisting use not in accordance with the zoning ordinance

A zoning ordinance may not immediately terminate a lawful use that existed before the ordinance was enacted. Rather, this **nonconforming use** must be permitted to continue for at least a reasonable time. Most ordinances provide that a nonconforming use may be terminated (1) when the use is discontinued, (2) when a nonconforming structure is destroyed or substantially damaged, or (3) when a nonconforming structure has been permitted to exist for the period of its useful life, as fixed by municipal authorities.

Judicial Review of Zoning [49-5d]

Judicial review of zoning
zoning ordinances may be reviewed to determine if they are invalid or a confiscation of property

Although the zoning process traditionally is considered as legislative, it is subject to judicial review on several grounds, including the following: (1) that the resulting zoning ordinance is invalid; (2) that the ordinance has been applied unreasonably; and (3) that the ordinance amounts to a confiscation, or taking, of property. For example, a zoning ordinance may be invalid as a whole either because it bears no reasonable relation to public health, safety, morals, or welfare or because it involves the exercise of powers that the enabling act has not granted to the municipality.

Subdivision Master Plans [49-5e]

Most states have legislation enabling local authorities to require municipality approval of every land subdivision plat. These enabling statutes provide penalties for failure to secure such approval when required by local ordinance. Some statutes make it a criminal offense to sell lots by reference to unrecorded plats and provide that such plats may not be recorded unless approved by the local planning board. Other statutes provide that building permits will not be issued unless the plat is approved and recorded.

EMINENT DOMAIN [49-6]

Eminent domain
power to take (buy) private property for public use

The power to take private property for public use, known as the power of **eminent domain**, is recognized as one of the inherent powers of government both in the U.S. Constitution and in state constitutions. Nevertheless, this power is carefully circumscribed and controlled. The Fifth Amendment to the federal Constitution provides, "[N]or shall private property be taken for public use without just compensation," and the constitutions of the states contain similar or identical provisions. Consequently, constitutional provisions directly prohibit the taking of private property without just compensation and implicitly prohibit the taking of private property for other than public use. Moreover, both federal and state constitutions entitle to due process of law the individual from whom property is to be taken.

Public Use [49-6a]

Public use
public advantage

As noted, there is an implicit constitutional prohibition against taking private property for other than public use. Most states interpret **public use** to mean "public advantage." Thus, the power of eminent domain may be delegated to railroad and public utility companies. Because it enables such companies to offer continued and improved service to the public, the reasonable exercise of such power is upheld as a public advantage. As society grows more complex, other public purposes become legitimate grounds for exercising the power of eminent domain. One such use is in the area of urban renewal. Most states have legislation permitting the establishment of housing authorities with the power to condemn slum, blighted, and vacant areas and to finance, construct, and maintain housing projects. Some states have recently gone further by allowing private companies to exercise the power of eminent domain, provided the use is primarily for the public benefit, including the alleviation of unemployment or economic decay within the community.

Kelo v. City of New London
Supreme Court of the United States, 2005
545 U.S. 469, 125 S.Ct. 2655, 162 L.Ed.2d 439
http://scholar.google.com/scholar_case?case=1101424605047973909&q = 545+U.S. = 469&hl=en&as_sdt=2,10

FACTS In 2000, the city of New London approved a development plan that was "projected to create in excess of one thousand jobs, to increase tax and other revenues, and to revitalize an economically distressed city, including its downtown and waterfront areas." The plan proposed to replace a faded residential neighborhood—Fort Trumbull—with office space for research and development, a conference hotel, new residences, and a pedestrian "riverwalk" along the Thames River. The project, to be built by private developers, is intended to build upon a $350 million research center built nearby by the Pfizer pharmaceutical company.

In assembling the land needed for this project, the city's development agent has purchased property from willing sellers and proposes to use the power of eminent domain to acquire the remainder of the property from unwilling owners of fifteen properties in exchange for just compensation. The unwilling owners claimed that the taking of their properties would violate the "public use" restriction in the Fifth Amendment of the U.S. Constitution. The trial court granted a permanent restraining order prohibiting the taking of some of the properties located in parcel. The Supreme Court of Connecticut held that all of the city's proposed takings were valid. The U.S. Supreme Court granted *certiorari* to determine whether a city's decision to take property for the purpose of economic development satisfies the "public use" requirement of the Fifth Amendment.

DECISION Judgment of the Connecticut Supreme Court affirmed.

OPINION The disposition of this case turns on the question whether the city's development plan serves a "public purpose."

Without exception, U.S. Supreme Court cases have defined that concept broadly, reflecting a policy of deference to legislative judgments in this field.

Those who govern the city were not confronted with the need to remove blight in the contested area of Fort Trumbull, but their determination that the area was sufficiently distressed to justify a program of economic rejuvenation is entitled to deference. The city has carefully formulated an economic development plan that it believes will provide appreciable benefits to the community, including new jobs and increased tax revenue. As with other exercises in urban planning and development, the city is endeavoring to coordinate a variety of commercial, residential, and recreational uses of land, with the hope that they will form a whole greater than the sum of its parts. To effectuate this plan, the city has used the power of eminent domain to promote economic development. Given the comprehensive character of the plan and that the plan unquestionably serves a public purpose, the takings satisfy the public use requirement of the Fifth Amendment.

Promoting economic development is a traditional and long-accepted function of government. There is, moreover, no principled way of distinguishing economic development from the other public purposes that have been recognized. In prior cases, the Supreme Court has (1) upheld takings that facilitated agriculture and mining, (2) endorsed the purpose of transforming a blighted area into a "well-balanced" community through redevelopment, (3) upheld the interest in breaking up a land oligopoly that "created artificial deterrents to the normal functioning of the state's residential land market," and (4) accepted Congress's purpose of eliminating a significant barrier to entry in the particular market. It would be incorrect to rule that the city's interest in the economic benefits to be derived from the development of the Fort Trumbull area has less of a public character than those other interests. Clearly, there is no basis for exempting economic development from the traditionally broad understanding of public purpose.

The government's pursuit of a public purpose will often benefit individual private parties. Public ownership is not the sole method of promoting the public purposes of community redevelopment projects.

Alternatively, the owners maintain that for takings of this kind the law should require a "reasonable certainty" that the expected public benefits will actually accrue. Such a rule, however, would represent a great departure from the law. A constitutional rule that required postponement of the judicial approval of every condemnation until the likelihood of success of the plan had been ensured would unquestionably impose a significant impediment to the successful consummation of many such plans.

Just as the court should not second-guess the city's considered judgments about the efficacy of its development plan, the court should also not second-guess the city's determinations as to what lands it needs to acquire to effectuate the project. It is not for the courts to oversee the choice of the boundary line nor to sit in review on the size of a particular project area. Once the question of the public purpose has been decided, the amount and character of land to be taken for the project and the need for a particular tract to complete the integrated plan rests in the discretion of the legislative branch.

In affirming the city's authority to take petitioners' properties, the court does not minimize the hardship that condemnations may entail, notwithstanding the payment of just compensation. States are free to place further restrictions on its exercise of the takings power. Indeed, many states already impose "public use" requirements that are stricter than the federal baseline.

INTERPRETATION Governments have broad discretion in taking private property for a public purpose, which includes economic development.

CRITICAL THINKING QUESTION Do you agree with the court's decision? Explain.

Just Compensation [49-6b]

Just compensation
the owner of the property taken by eminent domain must be paid the fair market value of the property

When the power of eminent domain is exercised, the owners of the property taken must receive just compensation. The measure of **just compensation** is the fair market value of the property as of the time of taking. The compensation goes to holders of vested interests in the condemned property.

For an overview of eminent domain, see Figure 49-2.

PRIVATE RESTRICTIONS ON LAND USE [49-7]

Restrictive covenant
private restriction on property contained in a conveyance

Owners of real property may impose private restrictions, called **restrictive covenants** (or negative covenants), on the use of land. Historically, two types of private restrictions developed—real covenants and equitable servitudes. The two had different, although overlapping, requirements. Equitable servitudes now have nearly replaced real covenants. Accordingly, this section will cover only equitable servitudes, which we will identify by the more general term *restrictive covenant*.

Covenants Running with the Land [49-7a]

Covenants running with the land
covenants that bind not only the original parties but also subsequent owners of the property

If certain conditions are satisfied, a restrictive covenant will bind not only the original parties to it but also remote parties who subsequently acquire the property. A restrictive covenant that binds remote parties is said to "run with the land." To run with the land, the covenant must involve promises that are enforceable under the law of contracts. Accordingly, a majority of courts hold that restrictive covenants must be in writing. The parties who agree to the restrictive

Figure 49-2 Eminent Domain

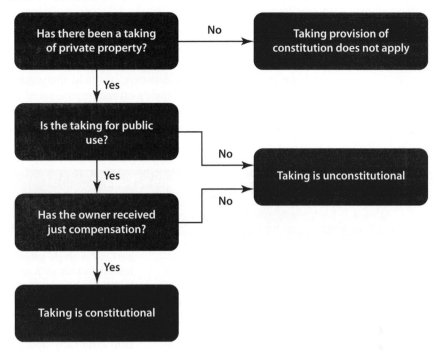

covenant must intend that the covenant will bind their successors. Moreover, the covenant must "touch and concern" the land, affecting its use, utility, or value. Finally, a restrictive covenant will bind only those successors who have had actual or constructive notice of the covenant.

Restrictive Covenants in Subdivisions [49-7b]

Covenants in subdivision
bind purchasers of lots in the subdivision as if the restrictions had been inserted in their own deeds

Restrictive covenants are widely used in subdivisions. The owners of lots are subject to restrictive covenants that, if actually brought to the attention of subsequent purchasers or recorded by original deed or by means of a recorded plat or separate agreement, bind purchasers of lots in the subdivision as though the restrictions had actually been inserted in their own deeds. If the entire subdivision has been subjected to a general building plan designed to benefit all of the lots, any lot owner in the subdivision has the right to enforce the restriction against a purchaser whose title descends from a common grantor. If a restriction is clearly intended to benefit an entire tract, the covenant will be enforced against a subsequent purchaser of one of the lots in the tract if (1) the restriction was apparently intended to benefit the purchaser of any lot in the tract and (2) the restriction appears somewhere in the chain of title to which the lot is subject.

Subdivisions may involve many types of restrictive covenants. The more common ones limit the use of property to residential purposes, restrict the area of the lot on which a structure can be built, or provide for a special type of architecture. Frequently, a subdivider will specify a minimum size for each house in an attempt to maintain structural unity in a neighborhood.

Restrictive covenants are construed strictly against the party asserting their applicability.

Termination of Restrictive Covenants [49-7c]

A restrictive covenant may end by the terms of the original agreement. For example, the developer of a subdivision may provide that the restrictive covenant will terminate after thirty-five years unless a specified majority of the property owners reaffirm the covenant. In addition, a court will not enforce a restrictive covenant if changed circumstances make enforcement inequitable and oppressive. Evidence of *changed conditions* may be found either within the tract covered by the original covenant or within the area adjacent to or surrounding the tract.

Validity of Restrictive Covenants [49-7d]

Although restrictions on land use have never been popular in the law, the courts will enforce a restriction that apparently will operate to the general benefit of the owners of all the land the restriction will affect. The usual method of enforcing such agreements is by injunction to restrain a violation.

The law for many years, however, has held that under the Fourteenth Amendment to the Constitution, a state or municipality cannot impose racial restrictions by statute or ordinance. In 1947 the Supreme Court extended this prohibition by holding that state courts, as an arm of state government, cannot enforce private racial restrictive covenants.

Cappo v. Suda
Appellate Court of Connecticut, 2011
126 Conn.App. 1, 10 A.3d 560
http://scholar.google.com/scholar_case?q=10+A.3D+560+&hl=en&as_sdt=6,34&case=871487323647805637&scilh=0

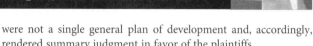

FACTS Plaintiffs, Thomas Cappo and certain other neighbors who reside on Ox Yoke Lane in Norwalk, Connecticut, seek to enforce a restrictive covenant against the defendants, Mark and Michelle Suda, from resubdividing the defendants' property and from constructing a second dwelling. The defendants admit that the properties belonging to the plaintiffs and the defendants are depicted on a "Map Showing Section Two of Cricklewood, Norwalk … as Map No. 3714" (Section Two) and admit that their deed contains a reference to restrictive covenants of the Norwalk land records. This restriction, as provided in their warranty deed, states, "Said tract is subject to the following restrictions: 1. No more than one dwelling together with an attached garage shall be constructed thereon." The trial court granted summary judgment in favor of the plaintiffs, and the defendants appealed.

DECISION The judgment is affirmed.

OPINION In general, restrictive covenants fall into three classes: (1) mutual covenants in deeds exchanged by adjoining landowners; (2) uniform covenants contained in deeds executed by the owner of property who is dividing his property into building lots under a general development scheme; and (3) covenants exacted by a grantor from his grantee presumptively or actually for the benefit and protection of his adjoining land which he retains. With respect to the second class of covenants, which is at issue in this case, any grantee under such a general or uniform development scheme may enforce the restrictions against any other grantee.

The defendants claim that, although a restrictive covenant that prohibits resubdivision for the purpose of building an additional dwelling was contained in their deed, that restriction has been abandoned because resubdivisions have occurred in surrounding properties, which the defendants contend are part of the same subdivision as their property. The parties reside in a subdivision referred to as Section Two. All thirteen of the lots in Section Two have been developed, and none of the lots contain more than one dwelling. Two other parcels originating from the same grantor and developed into abutting subdivisions exist, namely, "Cricklewood" and "Bow End Road." Resubdivisions have occurred in Cricklewood. The district court correctly held the three subdivisions, Section Two, Cricklewood and Bow End Road,

were not a single general plan of development and, accordingly, rendered summary judgment in favor of the plaintiffs.

When uniform covenants are contained in deeds executed by the owner of property who is dividing his property into building lots under a general development scheme, any grantee under such a general or uniform development scheme may enforce the restrictions against any other grantee.

Once a common scheme has been established, it is possible to find that the restrictive covenants are not enforceable because they have been abandoned.

"[W]hen presented with a violation of a restrictive covenant, the court is obligated to enforce the covenant unless the defendant can show that enforcement would be inequitable…. [A] [c]hange in circumstances … may justify the withholding of equitable relief to enforce a covenant…. Such a change in circumstances is decided on a case by case basis, and the test is whether the circumstances show an abandonment of the original restriction making enforcement inequitable because of the altered condition of the property involved."

The defendants admitted that the thirteen parcels in Section Two were developed under a common scheme using substantially uniform restrictions. Excepting the defendants' property, none of the owners of the parcels in Section Two have sought or received resubdivision approval, nor have repeated violations of the restrictions occurred in Section Two. Thus, the deed restrictions have not been abandoned.

The restrictions in the Section Two deeds have not been extinguished or abandoned as a result of resubdivisions that occurred in Cricklewood since the two subdivisions were not developed under a common scheme.

INTERPRETATION When uniform restrictive covenants are contained in deeds executed by the owner of property who is dividing his property into building lots under a general development scheme, any grantee under such a general or uniform development scheme may enforce the restrictions against any other grantee.

CRITICAL THINKING QUESTION What limits should the law place on the extent and duration of private restrictive covenants? Explain.

ETHICAL DILEMMA

Where Should Cities House the Disadvantaged?

Facts Susan Kate is a member of the city council in Wissahicken City. The Clinton Living Center, Inc., has just applied for a special use permit to allow the center to lease a building to use as a group home for the emotionally ill. The home will provide supervised group living quarters for individuals who have suffered from a wide range of emotional problems, including depression, anxiety, substance abuse, and sexual disorders. A small percentage of the proposed occupants will be criminal offenders embarking on the rehabilitative phase of their sentencing, with the ultimate goal of reentering the community. Many of the members will attend school and other job-training programs under supervision during the day.

The Wissahicken zoning ordinance requires that a special permit be obtained annually for hospitals for the insane, the mentally disabled, alcoholics, or drug addicts and for penal or correctional institutions. The building the center wishes to lease is in an R-3 zone that expressly permits apartment houses, multiple dwellings, hospitals, or nursing homes, but excludes penal institutions and homes for the insane, the mentally disabled, alcoholics, or drug addicts. In addition, the building is not far from an upper-middle-class neighborhood consisting of single-family homes. The home would be across the street from a middle school.

Public hearings have been held, and there is widespread community opposition to the proposed lease. Susan Kate, a new and politically ambitious member of the city council, must cast the deciding vote as to whether the special permit should be issued.

Social, Policy, and Ethical Considerations

1. What are the goals of zoning classifications?
2. Is there any justification for requiring a special permit under the circumstances? What are the community's concerns? Are these concerns justified?
3. What is the social policy behind placing rehabilitative group homes in the heart of a thriving community rather than in an isolated neighborhood?
4. Should a permit be refused for the purpose of preserving property values? Consider the concerns of a sixty-year-old couple who is close to retirement, has modest cash savings, and has always planned to sell their house in their mid-sixties and move to an apartment. Consider also the concerns of a young, newly married couple in search of affordable housing in a stable, established neighborhood.
5. Would your answers change if the special permit request were for a meeting home for homosexuals or for a group home for the profoundly retarded?

CHAPTER SUMMARY

Transfer of Real Property

Contract of Sale

Formation a contract to transfer any interest in land must be in writing to be enforceable

Marketable Title the seller must transfer marketable title, which is a title free from any defects or encumbrances

Quality of Improvements
- *Common Law Rule* under *caveat emptor* ("let the buyer beware"), the seller is not liable for any undiscovered defects
- *Implied Warranty of Habitability* in a majority of states, the builder-seller of a dwelling impliedly warrants that a newly constructed house is free from latent defects

Deeds

Definition a formal document transferring any type of interest in land

Types
- *Warranty Deed* the grantor (seller) promises the grantee (buyer) that she has valid title to the property without defect
- *Special Warranty Deed* the grantor promises that he has not impaired the title
- *Quitclaim Deed* the grantor transfers whatever interest she has in the property

Requirements the deed must (1) be written; (2) contain certain words of conveyance and a description of the property; (3) end with the signature of the grantor, a seal, and an acknowledgment before a notary public; and (4) be delivered

Delivery intent that the deed take effect, as evidenced by acts or statements of the grantor

Recordation required to protect the transferee's interest against third parties; consists of delivery of a duly executed and acknowledged deed to the appropriate recorder's office

Secured Transactions

Elements a secured transaction involves (1) a debt or obligation to pay money, (2) an interest of the creditor in specific property that secures performance, and (3) the debtor's right to redeem the property (remove the security interest) by paying the debt

Mortgage interest in land created by a written document that provides security to the mortgagee (secured party) for payment of the mortgagor's debt

Deed of Trust an interest in real property that is conveyed to a third person as trustee for the benefit of the creditor

Transfer of Interest

- *Assumes the Mortgage* the purchaser of mortgaged property becomes personally liable to pay the debt
- *Subject to the Mortgage* purchaser is not personally liable to pay the debt, but the property remains subject to the mortgage

Foreclosure upon default, sale of the mortgaged property to satisfy the debt

Adverse Possession

Definition acquisition of title to land by open, continuous, and adverse occupancy for a statutorily prescribed period

Possession must be actual and without intervening dominion by true owner

---

Public and Private Controls

Zoning

Definition principal method of public control over private land use, involves regulation of land but may not constitute a taking of the property

Authority the power to zone is generally delegated to local authorities by statutes known as enabling acts

Variance a use differing from that provided in the zoning ordinance and granted in order to avoid undue hardship

Nonconforming Use a use not in accordance with, but existing prior to, a zoning ordinance; permitted to continue for at least a reasonable time

Judicial Review zoning ordinances may be reviewed to determine whether they are invalid or a confiscation of property

Eminent Domain

Definition the power of a government to take (buy) private land for public use

Public Use public advantage

Just Compensation the owner of the property taken by eminent domain must be paid the fair market value of the property

Private Restrictions on Land Use

Definition private restrictions on property contained in a conveyance

Covenants Running with the Land covenants that bind not only the original parties but also subsequent owners of the property

Covenants in Subdivision bind purchasers of lots in the subdivision as if the restrictions had been inserted in their own deeds

---

QUESTIONS

1. Arthur was the father of Bridgette, Clay, and Dana and the owner of Redacre, Blackacre, and Greenacre.

Arthur made and executed a warranty deed conveying Redacre to Bridgette. The deed provided that "this deed shall become effective only on the death of the grantor." Arthur retained possession of the deed and died, leaving the deed in his safe deposit box.

Arthur made and executed a warranty deed conveying Blackacre to Clay. This deed also provided that "this deed shall become effective only on the death of the grantor."

Arthur delivered the deed to Clay. After Arthur died, Clay recorded the deed.

Arthur made and executed a warranty deed conveying Greenacre to Dana. Arthur delivered the deed to Lesley with specific instructions to deliver the deed to Dana on Arthur's death. Lesley duly delivered the deed to Dana when Arthur died.

a. What is the interest of Bridgette in Redacre, if any?

b. What is the interest of Clay in Blackacre, if any?

c. What is the interest of Dana in Greenacre, if any?

2. Arkin, the owner of Redacre, executed a real estate mortgage to the Shawnee Bank and Trust Company for $100,000. After the mortgage was executed and recorded, Arkin constructed a dwelling on the premises and planted a corn crop. After Arkin defaulted in the payment of the mortgage debt, the bank proceeded to foreclose the mortgage. At the time of the foreclosure sale, the corn crop was mature and unharvested. Arkin contends (a) that the value of the dwelling should be credited to him and (b) that he is entitled to the corn crop. Explain whether Arkin is correct.

3. Robert and Stanley held legal title of record to adjacent tracts of land, each consisting of a number of five acres. Stanley fenced his five acres in 1985, placing his east fence fifteen feet onto Robert's property. Thereafter, he was in possession of this fifteen-foot strip of land and kept it fenced and cultivated continuously until he sold his tract of land to Nathan on March 1, 1994. Nathan took possession under deed from Stanley, and continued possession and cultivation of the fifteen-foot strip that was on Robert's land until May 27, 2013, when Robert, having on several occasions strenuously objected to Nathan's possession, brought suit against Nathan for trespass. Explain whether Nathan has gained title by adverse possession.

4. Marcia executed a mortgage of Blackacre to secure her indebtedness to Ajax Savings and Loan Association in the amount of $125,000. Later, Marcia sold Blackacre to Morton. The deed contained the following provision: "This deed is subject to the mortgage executed by the Grantor herein to Ajax Savings and Loan Association."

   The sale price of Blackacre to Morton was $150,000. Morton paid $25,000 in cash, deducting the $125,000 mortgage debt from the purchase price. On default in the payment of the mortgage debt, Ajax brings an action against Marcia and Morton to recover a judgment for the amount of the mortgage debt and to foreclose the mortgage. Can Ajax recover from Marcia and Morton? Explain.

5. On January 1, 2014, Davis and Hershey owned Blackacre as tenants in common. On July 1, 2014, Davis made a written contract to sell Blackacre to Dibbert for $125,000. Pursuant to this contract, Dibbert paid Davis $125,000 on August 1, 2014, and Davis executed and delivered to Dibbert a warranty deed to Blackacre. On May 1, 2015, Hershey quitclaimed his interest in Blackacre to Davis. Dibbert brings an action against Davis for breach of warranty of title. What judgment?

6. In adjoining locations along one side of a single suburban village block, Barker operated a retail bakery; Davidson, a drug store; Farrell, a food store; Gibson, a gift shop; and Harper, a hardware store. As the population grew, the business section developed at the other end of the village, and the establishments of Barker, Davidson, Farrell, Gibson, and Harper were surrounded for at least a mile in each direction solely by residences. A zoning ordinance with the usual provisions was adopted by the village, and the area including the five stores was declared to be a "residential district for single-family dwellings." Thereafter, Barker tore down the frame building that housed the bakery and began to construct a modern brick bakery. Davidson found her business increasing to such an extent that she began to build an addition on the drugstore to extend it to the rear alley. Farrell's building was destroyed by fire, and he started to reconstruct it to restore it to its former condition. Gibson changed the gift shop into a sporting goods store and after six months of operation decided to go back into the gift shop business. Harper sold his hardware store to Hempstead. The village building commission brings an action under the zoning ordinance to enjoin the construction work of Barker, Davidson, and Farrell and to enjoin the carrying on of any business by Gibson and Hempstead. Assume the ordinance is valid. What result?

7. Alda and Mattingly are residents of Unit I of Chimney Hills Subdivision. The lots owned by Alda and Mattingly are subject to the following restrictive covenant: "Lots shall be for single-family residence purposes only." Alda intends to convert her carport into a beauty shop, and Mattingly brings suit against Alda to enjoin her from doing so. Alda argues that the covenant restricts only the type of building that can be constructed, not the incidental use to which residential structures are put. Will Alda be able to operate a beauty shop on the property? Why or why not?

CASE PROBLEMS

8. The City of Boston sought to condemn land in fee simple for use in constructing an entrance to an underground terminal for a subway. The owners of the land contend that no more than surface and subsurface easements are necessary for the terminal entrance and seek to retain air rights above thirty-six feet. The city argues that any building using this airspace would require structural supports that would interfere with the city's plan for the terminal. The city concedes that the properties around the condemned property could be assembled and structures could be designed to span over the condemned property, in which case the air rights would be quite valuable. Can the city condemn the property?

9. For seven years, Desford Potts had owned a six-acre tract of land within the corporate limits of the city of Franklin. The tract contained a livestock barn in which Potts stored lumber and other building materials. Bricks were also stored in stacks four or five feet high outside and behind the barn. Franklin passed a zoning ordinance by virtue of which Potts's lot was classified as residential property. Soon afterward, Potts moved some sawn logs onto his back lot, and the city complained that Potts's use of his property for storage of building materials was a "nonconforming use." Potts then brought an action to enjoin interference by the city of Franklin. Explain whether Potts will prevail.

10. In May 2005, Fred Parramore executed four deeds, each conveying a life estate in his land to him and his wife and a remainder interest in one-fourth of his land to each of his four children: Alney, Eudell, Bernice, and Iris. Although Fred executed and acknowledged the four deeds as part of his plan to distribute his estate at his death, he did not deliver them to his children at this time. Instead, he placed the deeds with his will in a safe deposit box and instructed the children to pick up their deeds at his death. Fred later conveyed Alney's deed to Alney, thereby vesting Alney's interest in that parcel, but Eudell, Bernice, and Iris's deeds were never handed over to them during Fred's lifetime. Fred, however, acted as if the land was beyond his control, and on one occasion told a prospective buyer that the land had already been deeded away. When Fred died in November 2015, Alney brought this action, claiming that the deeds to Eudell, Bernice, and Iris were ineffective because they had never been handed over during Fred's lifetime. Accordingly, Alney argued the remaining land should pass in equal shares to each of the four children under the residuary clause of Fred's will. Who will prevail? Why?

11. The Gerwitz family resides on a piece of land known as Lot 24 of the Belleville tract, which they acquired by deed in 1995. Shortly thereafter, the Gerwitzes began to use the adjacent vacant Lot 25. At various times they planted grass seed, flowers, and shrubs on the land and used it for picnics and cook-outs. In 2015, Gelsomin acquired Lot 25 and constructed a foundation on it so that he could place a house there. The Gerwitzes then brought this action to stop him, claiming title to Lot 25 by adverse possession. Discuss whether the Gerwitzes have obtained title by adverse possession.

12. Leo owned a one-story, one-family dwelling in a single-family residential zoning district in Detroit. He attempted to sell the house with its adjoining lot for $138,500. Houses in the neighborhood generally sold for $120,000 to $125,000. Immediately to the west of Leo's property was a gasoline service station. In addition, Leo's property was located on a corner frequented with heavy traffic. After he received no offers from residential use buyers during the period of more than a year that the property was listed and offered for sale, Leo applied to the board of zoning appeals for a variance to permit the use of the property as a dental and medical clinic and to use the side yard for off-street parking. The variance would be subject to certain conditions, including the preservation of the building's exterior as that of a one-family dwelling. Puritan-Greenfield Improvement Association, a nonprofit corporation, filed a complaint against Leo's variance request. Discuss whether the variance should be granted.

13. The Glendale Church purchased a twenty-one-acre parcel of land in a canyon along the banks of Mill Creek in Angeles National Forest. The church used the twelve flat acres next to the stream to operate a campground for disabled children. This area had a number of improved buildings located on it. In July, a forest fire destroyed all ground cover upstream from the church's campground, and a subsequent flood destroyed all the buildings. In response, the county of Los Angeles enacted an interim ordinance that temporarily prohibited the church from constructing new buildings. Is the church entitled to compensation for a temporary taking of its property? Why?

14. Robert V. Gross owned certain land on which he proposed to construct an eighty-three-unit apartment house. The land, however, was subject to a restriction imposed by a prior deed to a predecessor in title that provided that no part of the premises could be used for business purposes other than raising, growing, and selling live bait, fishing tackle, and sporting goods. Explain whether the restriction prohibits the construction and operation of an apartment house.

15. Sam and Eleanor Gaito purchased a home from Howard Frank Auman, Jr., in the spring of 2013. Auman had completed the construction of the house in November 2008. In the interim, three different parties had lived in the house for brief periods, but Auman had retained ownership. The last tenants, the Ashleys, experienced difficulties with the home's air-conditioning system. Repairs were attempted, but no effort was made to change the capacity of the air-conditioning unit.

When the Gaitos moved into the house in June 2013 they too had problems with the air-conditioning. The system created only a ten-degree difference between the outside and inside temperatures. The Gaitos complained to Auman on a number of occasions, but extensive repairs failed to correct the cooling problem. In May 2016, the Gaitos brought an action against Auman, alleging that the purchase price of the home included central air-conditioning and that Auman had breached the implied warranty of habitability. At trial, an expert in the field of heating and air-conditioning testified that a four-ton air-conditioning system, rather than the three-and-a-half-ton system originally installed, was appropriate for the Gaitos's house. The jury returned a verdict in favor of the Gaitos in the amount of $3,655. Explain whether this decision is correct.

16. In 1972, South Carolina enacted a Coastal Zone Management Act requiring any person using land in a "critical area" to obtain a permit for any uses other than those to which the critical area was devoted when the Act went into effect on September 28, 1977. In 1986, Lucas paid $975,000 for two residential lots on Isle of Palms in Charleston County, South Carolina, on which he intended to develop a residential subdivision known as "Beachwood East." Because no portion of those lots was included in a "critical area" at that time, Lucas was not required to obtain a permit. In 1988, however, South Carolina enacted the Beachfront Management Act, which established a "baseline" for the landward-most points of erosion and in effect barred the erection of any permanent habitable structures on his two parcels. Lucas filed suit in state court, claiming that the new statute violated his Fifth and Fourteenth Amendment rights by taking property without compensation. Is he entitled to just compensation for his property? Explain.

TAKING SIDES

Playtime Theaters and Sea-First Properties purchased two theaters in Renton, Washington, with the intention of exhibiting adult films. About the same time, they filed suit seeking injunctive relief and a declaratory judgment that the First and Fourteenth Amendments were violated by a city of Renton ordinance that prohibits adult motion picture theaters from locating within one thousand feet of any residential zone, single- or multiple-family dwelling, church, park, or school.

a. What are the arguments that the city has the right to enforce such an ordinance?

b. What are the arguments that the city does *not* have the right to enforce such an ordinance?

c. What result? Explain.

Trusts and Wills

CHAPTER 50

It was said ... many years ago that the parents of the trust were fraud and fear and that the court of conscience was its nurse.

George T. Bogert
Trusts, 6th ed. (1987)

CHAPTER OUTCOMES

After reading and studying this chapter, you should be able to:

1. Describe and explain the following types of trusts: (a) express, (b) testamentary, (c) *inter vivos*, (d) charitable, (e) spendthrift, (f) totten, (g) implied, (h) constructive, and (i) resulting.

2. Describe the powers and duties of a trustee.

3. Explain the formal requirements for making a valid will and the various ways in which a will may be revoked.

4. Define the following types of wills: (a) nuncupative, (b) holographic, and (c) soldiers' and sailors' wills.

5. Describe intestate succession and the administration of decedents' estates.

I n previous chapters, we have seen that real and personal property may be transferred in a number of ways, including by sale and by gift. Another important way in which a person may convey property or allow others to use or benefit from it is through trusts and wills. Trusts may take effect during the transferor's lifetime, or, when used in a will, they may become effective upon his death. Wills enable individuals to control the transfer of their property at their death. Upon a person's death, his or her property must pass to someone, and individuals are well advised to decide how their property should be distributed. Except for the statutory or common law rights of spouses, the law permits individuals to make such distributions by sale, gift, trust, and will. If, however, an individual dies without a will—that is, intestate—state law prescribes who shall be entitled to the property that the individual owned at death. In this chapter, we will examine trusts and wills, as well as the manner in which property descends when a person dies intestate.

TRUSTS

Trust
transfer of property to one party for the benefit of another

Settlor
creator of the trust

Trustee
holder of legal title to property for the benefit of another

Beneficiary
equitable owner of trust property

A **trust** is a *fiduciary relationship* in which one or more persons hold legal title to property while its use, enjoyment, and benefit (equitable title) belong to another. Allowed to serve any purpose that is not against the law or public policy, a trust may be created by agreement of the parties, by a grant in a will, or by a court decree. However fashioned, the relationship is known as a trust. The party creating the trust is the *creator* or **settlor**, the party holding the legal title to the property is the **trustee** of the trust, and the person who receives the benefit of the trust is the **beneficiary** (see Figure 50-1).

TYPES OF TRUSTS [50-1]

Although there are many varieties, all trusts fall into one of two major groups: express or implied. The implied trusts, which are imposed upon property by court order, are categorized as either "constructive" or "resulting" trusts.

Figure 50-1 Trusts

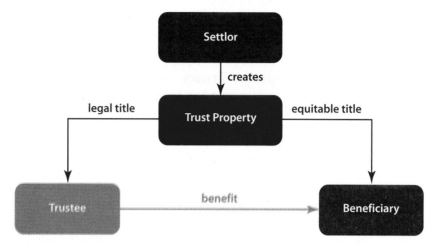

Express Trusts [50-1a]

Express trust

a trust established by voluntary action; usually in writing, although it may be oral

An **express trust** is, as the name indicates, a trust established by voluntary action and is represented either by a written document or, under some conditions, by an oral statement or conduct of the settlor. In a majority of jurisdictions, an express trust of real property must be in writing to meet the requirements of the statute of frauds.

No particular words are necessary to create a trust, provided that the settlor's intent to establish a trust is unmistakable. Determining whether a settlor really intended to create a trust is not always easy. Sometimes, in connection with a gift, a settlor will use words of request or recommendation that imply or express hope that the gift should or will be used for a particular purpose. Thus, instead of leaving properly "to X for the benefit and use of Y," a settlor may leave property to X "in full confidence and with hope that he will care for Y." Such a **precatory** (wishful) expression may be so definite as to impose a trust upon the property for Y's benefit. Whether the expression will create a trust or will constitutes nothing more than a gratuitous wish depends on whether the court believes from all the facts that the settlor genuinely intended a trust.

Precatory

expressing a wish

Testamentary trust

trust established by a will

Inter vivos **trust**

trust established during the settlor's lifetime

Testamentary Trust   Trusts employed in wills are known as **testamentary trusts** because they become effective after the settlor's death.

Inter Vivos **Trust**   A trust established during the settlor's lifetime is referred to as an *inter vivos* ("between-the-living") **trust**.

Practical Advice

As your estate grows, you should determine whether tax or other legal considerations make it beneficial to use a trust as a vehicle to distribute your assets.

Charitable Trusts   Almost any trust that has for its purpose the improvement of the whole or a class of humankind is a **charitable trust**, unless it is so vague that it cannot be enforced. Gifts for public museums, for park maintenance, and for the dissemination of a particular political doctrine or religious belief have been upheld as charitable.

Charitable trust

trust designed to benefit humankind

Spendthrift trust

trust designed to remove the trust estate from the beneficiary's control

Totten trust

a tentative trust consisting of a joint bank account opened by the settlor

Spendthrift Trusts   A settlor who believes that a beneficiary cannot be trusted to preserve even the limited rights granted her as beneficiary may provide in the trust instrument that the beneficiary cannot, by assignment or otherwise, impair her rights to receive principal or income and that creditors of the beneficiary cannot attach the fund or the income. Such a trust is called a **spendthrift trust**. Spendthrift provisions are valid in most states. However, once the beneficiary actually receives income from the trust, creditors may seize it or the beneficiary may use it as she pleases.

Totten Trusts   A **totten trust** or savings account trust involves a joint bank account opened by the trust settlor. For example, Sally deposits a sum of money into a savings account in the name of "Sally, in trust for Justin." Sally may make additional deposits into the account and may withdraw money from it whenever she pleases. Because the settlor may revoke a totten trust by withdrawing the funds or by changing the form of the account, such a trust is tentative. Usually the transfer of ownership becomes complete only on the depositor's death.

Implied Trusts [50-1b]

Implied trust
a trust created by operation of law

In some cases, the courts, in the absence of any expressed intent to create a trust, will impose a trust on property because the parties' acts appear to warrant such a construction. An **implied trust** owes its existence to the law.

Constructive trust
trust arising by operation of law to prevent unjust enrichment

Constructive Trusts

A **constructive trust** results when a court imposes a trust on property to rectify misconduct, to prevent unjust enrichment, or to undo a morally wrongful situation. The Restatement (Third) of Restitution and Unjust Enrichment provides that "[i]f a defendant is unjustly enriched by the acquisition of title to identifiable property at the expense of the claimant or in violation of the claimant's rights, the defendant may be declared a constructive trustee, for the benefit of the claimant, of the property in question and its traceable product."

A court will establish a constructive trust when a confidential relationship has been abused or where actual fraud or duress constitutes an equitable ground for creating the trust. The mere existence of a confidential relationship prohibits the trustee from seeking any personal benefit during the course of the relationship. For example, a director of a corporation who takes advantage of a "corporate opportunity" or who makes an undisclosed profit in a transaction with the corporation will be treated as a trustee for the corporation with respect to the property or profits he has acquired. Likewise, a trustee under an express trust who permits a lease held by the trust to expire and then acquires a new lease of the property in his individual capacity will be required to hold the new lease in a confidential trust for the beneficiary.

Keeney v. Keeney
Court of Appeals of Kentucky, 2007
223 S.W.3d 843
http://scholar.google.com/scholar_case?case=17154555324430393535&q=223+S.W.3d+843&hl=en&as_sdt=2,22

FACTS Barbara Keeney filed a petition for divorce against her husband, Milton Keeney, and joined her husband's parents as defendants, asserting that her husband had put real property in his parents' names to avoid payment on a prior unrelated judgment against her husband. Barbara asserts that the property was marital property and is seeking to establish her rights to the 6.6629 acres tract (Barlow Property), which is presently titled in the name of Milton's parents, Winfred and Ruth Kenney. Barbara claims that Milton, aided by Winfred and Ruth, intentionally avoided direct ownership of real and personal property in Milton's name in order to defraud a creditor with a prior judgment against Milton.

On June 22, 1982, Barbara and Milton were married. Before and during their marriage, Milton was self-employed in a business known as K-Bar Trailer Manufacturing Company, which built cattle, horse, and flat-bed trailers. Barbara worked with her husband on many of his K-Bar ventures. In February of 1983, and without Barbara's knowledge, Milton and his father purchased the Barlow property for $61,700. Although the purchase price was paid directly from the K-Bar checking account—the only checking account Barbara or Milton owned—the property was deeded to Winfred and Ruth.

Barbara and Milton separated in January 1995 and she filed for divorce on April 17, 1995. It was not until then that Milton informed Barbara that his parents actually owned the Barlow property. The trial court imposed a constructive trust, ordered that the real property be sold and the proceeds divided between the husband and wife, and awarded the wife half of the proceeds from the inventory sale.

DECISION Judgment affirmed.

OPINION A constructive trust is created by equity regardless of any actual or presumed intention of the parties to create a trust where the legal title to property is obtained through fraud, misrepresentation, concealment, undue influence, or through similar means or circumstances rendering it unconscionable for the holder of the legal title to retain the property. A constructive trust may also be imposed where title is taken under "circumstances of circumvention [or] imposition." When legal title to property has been acquired or held under such circumstances, the holder of that legal title may not in good conscience retain the beneficial interest and equity converts him into a trustee.

In this case there is no reason to believe that the trial court was clearly erroneous in any of its findings of fact. The collaboration of Milton and his parents to avoid a creditor's judgment unquestionably falls in that category of behavior described variously in our case law as "unconscientious," "unconscionable," and "violating equity in good conscience." These were certainly circumstances of circumvention. Winfred's and Ruth's efforts to hide Milton's beneficial ownership of property from a creditor had an obvious and even greater dispossessory effect on Barbara than it had on the creditor. Even if defrauding Barbara of her beneficial interest was not Winfred's and Ruth's original intention, it became so when she decided to divorce their son. Their retention of the property thus deprived Barbara of her beneficial ownership of the marital residence. Winfred and Ruth paid nothing for the property, and they would have been unjustly enriched if allowed to keep the property. Under such circumstances equity should impose a constructive trust in favor of the wronged party—Barbara.

INTERPRETATION Courts create constructive trusts in cases in which the legal title to property has been acquired by fraud, misrepresentation, concealment, or undue influence, or through similar means or circumstances rendering it unconscionable for the holder of the legal title to retain the property.

CRITICAL THINKING QUESTION When should a court impose a constructive trust? Explain.

Resulting trust

trust arising to fulfill the parties' presumed intent

Resulting Trusts   A **resulting trust** serves to effect the inferred or presumed *intent* of parties who have inadequately expressed their actual wishes. A resulting trust does not depend on contract or agreement but on presumed intent, as evidenced by the parties' acts. Because a resulting trust is created by implication and operation of law, it need not be evidenced in writing. The essence of a resulting trust is the presumption made by the law that the holder of legal title does not hold the property personally but as a trustee for another party. The most common example of a resulting trust is the case of Joel, who pays the purchase price for property and takes title in Ellen's name. Here, the courts presume that the parties intended Ellen to hold the property for Joel's benefit, and Ellen will be treated as a trustee. A second example of a resulting trust occurs when an express trust fails; then the trustee holds the property in trust for the settlor, to whom the property reverts.

CREATION OF TRUSTS [50-2]

Each trust has (1) a creator or settlor, (2) a "corpus" or trust property, (3) a trustee, and (4) a beneficiary. No particular words are necessary to create a trust, provided that the settlor's intent to establish a trust is unmistakable. Consideration is not essential to an enforceable trust.

Settlor [50-2a]

Any person legally capable of making a contract may create a trust. But if a settlor's conveyance would be voidable or void because of infancy, incompetency, or some other reason, the settlor's declaration of trust is also voidable or void.

Subject Matter [50-2b]

One major requirement of a trust is that the trust corpus or *res* must consist of property that is definite and specific. A trust cannot be effective immediately for property not yet in existence or yet to be acquired.

Trustee [50-2c]

Anyone legally capable of holding title to and dealing with property may be a trustee. The lack of a trustee, however, will not destroy a trust. The court will appoint an individual or institution to act as trustee if the settlor neglects to appoint one, if the named trustee does not qualify, or if the named trustee declines to serve.

Duties of trustee

the three primary duties of a trustee are to (1) carry out the purposes of the trust, (2) act prudently, and (3) act with utmost loyalty

Duties of the Trustee   A trustee has three primary duties: (1) to carry out the purposes of the trust, (2) to administer the trust prudently and carefully, and (3) to exercise a high degree of loyalty toward the beneficiary.

Ordinarily, no special skills are required of a trustee, who is required simply to act with the same degree of care that a **prudent person** would use to carry out his or her personal affairs. The trustee has a duty to make the trust property productive and thus to invest it in income-producing assets. Given the myriad circumstances of any particular case, what constitutes the care of a "prudent person" is, of course, not easy to generalize.

The duty of loyalty arises from the fiduciary character of the relationship between the trustee and the beneficiary. In all his dealings with the trust property, the beneficiary, and third parties, the trustee must act exclusively in the beneficiary's interest.

In the Matter of the Estate of Rowe
Supreme Court, Appellate Division, Third Department, New York, 2000
274 A.D.2d 87, 712 N.Y.S.2d 662; *appeal denied*, 96 N.Y.2d 707, 749 N.E.2d 206, 725 N.Y.S.2d 637 (2001)
http://scholar.google.com/scholar_case?case=7935201553540489298&q=712+N.YS.2d+662&hl=en&as_sdt=2,34

FACTS The petitioner, Wilber National Bank, was appointed trustee of a charitable trust created under the will of Frances E. Rowe (decedent). The trust was funded solely by thirty thousand shares of International Business Machines (IBM) common stock, which was trading for approximately $113 per share at the time of decedent's death in April 1989 and approximately $117 per share when the trust was funded in September 1989. Under the terms of the trust, the petitioner was required to make annual distributions to qualified charities of 8 percent of the estate trust assets, or $270,300; at the end of fifteen years, the balance remaining in the trust, if any, was payable to the respondents, who are the decedent's nieces, or their children.

In August 1994, the respondents made a demand that the petitioner file an intermediate accounting, claiming that the petitioner's failure to diversify the trust assets had resulted in a decline in yield and forced sales of trust principal, thereby threatening the assets of the trust. In December 1994, the Surrogate's Court required the petitioner to prepare an intermediate accounting. The petitioner filed its accounting and then commenced this proceeding for a judicial settlement. The respondents objected to the accounting upon the grounds that the petitioner's failure to diversify the trust was imprudent in that it violated the petitioner's own policy requiring diversification, the policy of the Comptroller of Currency, and regulations of the Federal Reserve Bank.

Because the value of the stock had dropped from the time the trust was funded, the Petitioner Trust Committee felt that it would be imprudent to diversify immediately, but gave its approval to a plan of diversifying at a later time when the stock had reached a higher price. In the meantime, the petitioner generated some income by selling various call options, and several small sales and in-kind distributions were made of IBM stock to fulfill the annual payout requirements. The first move toward diversification came in February 1991, when the petitioner sold 5,000 shares of IBM stock at $125 per share and an additional 2,959 shares at $136 per share. As of the close of the accounting period on December 31, 1994, the petitioner still held 19,398 shares of IBM stock valued at $74 per share. Over the course of the accounting period, the market value of the trust assets had dropped from $3,521,250 to $1,853,937.

In August 1997, the Surrogate's Court rendered its decision that, from the period September 8, 1989, to December 31, 1994, the petitioner had been negligent, that it had violated its own policy manual, and that it should have diversified most of the trust's holdings in IBM in January 1990. The Surrogate's Court ordered the petitioner to refund its commissions to the trust and directed that the petitioner pay damages of $496,259, together with $133,990 in interest, for a total of $630,249. The petitioner appealed.

DECISION Judgment affirmed.

OPINION The evidence showed that the petitioner's own written policy at the time of the original funding of the trust in 1989 required diversification of the trust assets. The policy became even more specific in 1994, requiring that "the Investment staff adhere to the principles of the 'Prudent Investor' rule by using modern portfolio theory and following a balanced and diversified approach in the management of those fund[s]." Furthermore, the 1994 policy advised that existing holdings exceeding 10 percent of a portfolio should be trimmed down over a period of time.

All of the facts and circumstances of the case must be examined to determine whether a concentration of a particular stock in an estate's portfolio violates the prudent person standard. Furthermore, each individual investment decision should be examined in relation to the entire portfolio as an entity, and a trustee can be found to have been imprudent for losses resulting from negligent inattentiveness, inaction, or indifference.

At trial, the respondent's expert expressed the strong opinion that the petitioner had acted imprudently in failing to diversify the trust's assets immediately upon receipt of the IBM stock, in furtherance of its initial goal of creating a diversified portfolio of fixed income-oriented assets and equity or growth assets. According to this expert, both the fifteen-year duration of the trust and the 8 percent annual payout requirement made the investment in IBM stock particularly inappropriate. First, IBM's dividends of less than $5 per share fell far short of satisfying the "extremely heavy burden" of having to pay out "an unvarying $270,300 a year" to charities, thereby requiring that capital be depleted to supplement the shortfall. Second, the extreme volatility and overall downward trend of IBM stock during this period and the fact that IBM itself was undergoing an "extremely stressful time" made it unsuitable for fulfilling the trust's investment goals. Moreover, the petitioner's tactic of waiting for the IBM stock to rise was based on "wishful hoping" and that any hesitancy on the part of petitioner to sell the IBM stock below acquisition costs was a "cosmetic kind of consideration."

In addition to the expert's testimony describing the petitioner's decision to delay diversification as unwise and unreasonably risky, the evidence reveals that the petitioner failed to follow its own internal protocol during the administration of the trust up to the time of the intermediate accounting, that the petitioner failed to conduct more than routine reviews of the IBM stock, and that the target prices set for the trust's IBM stock were department-wide positions affecting many accounts, giving no particular consideration to the unique needs of this particular trust.

INTERPRETATION A trustee is under a duty to manage trust assets with prudence and care and to act exclusively in the beneficiary's interest.

ETHICAL QUESTION Did the court fairly decide this case? Explain.

CRITICAL THINKING QUESTION What criteria should a court apply in scrutinizing the trustee's use, disposition, and distribution of the trust's assets? Explain.

Powers

generally established by the trust instrument and state law

Practical Advice

When creating a trust, carefully consider which powers you grant to your trustee in the trust instrument.

Powers of the Trustee

The **powers** of a trustee are determined by (1) the authority granted him by the settlor in the instrument creating the trust and (2) the rules of law in the jurisdiction in which the trust is established. State laws affecting the powers of trustees have their greatest impact on the investments a trustee may make with trust funds. Most states prescribe a prudent investor rule. Some, however, still follow the historical test, which prescribes a list of types of securities qualified for trust investment. In some jurisdictions, this list is permissive; in others, it is mandatory. If the list is permissive, the trustee may invest in securities of types not listed, though he carries the burden of showing that he made a prudent choice. The trust instrument itself may give the trustee wide discretion as to investments, in which case the trustee need not adhere to the list deemed advisable under the statute.

Allocation of Principal and Income Trusts often settle a life estate in the trust corpus on one beneficiary and a remainder interest on another beneficiary. For example, on his death, Bill leaves his property to a trustee who is instructed to pay the income from the property to Bill's widow during her life and to distribute the property to his children when she dies. In an instance such as this, the trustee must distribute the principal to one party (the remainderman) and the income to another (the life tenant or income beneficiary). The trustee must also allocate receipts and charge expenses between the income beneficiary and the remainderman. If the trust agreement does not specify how the funds should be allocated, the trustee is provided statutory guidance, derived in at least forty-six states from the *Revised Uniform Principal and Income Act*. This Act was amended and updated in 2008 to implement technical changes related to developments and interpretations relating to tax matters. At least thirty-five states have adopted the 2008 amendments. A trustee who fails to comply with the trust agreement or the statute is personally liable for any loss.

The general rule in allocating benefits and burdens between income beneficiaries and remaindermen is that ordinary or current receipts and expenses are chargeable to the income beneficiary, whereas extraordinary receipts and expenses are allocated to the remainderman. (Concept Review 50-1 illustrates these four types of allocations.) Ordinary income is money paid for the use of trust property and any gain or profit from such use, while either property received as a substitute for or a change in the form of the original trust property is trust principal.

Beneficiary [50-2d]

There are very few restrictions on who (or what) may be a beneficiary. Charitable uses are a common purpose of trusts, and if the settlor's object does not outrage public policy or morals, the courts will uphold almost any purpose that happens to strike a settlor's fancy.

A person named as a trust beneficiary may accept or reject the trust. In the absence of restrictive provisions in the trust instrument, such as a spendthrift clause, a beneficiary's interest may be reached by his creditors, or the beneficiary may sell or dispose of his interest. Upon death, if the beneficiary held more than a life estate in the trust, the beneficiary's interest, unless disposed of by his will, passes to his heirs or personal representatives.

Termination of a trust

the general rule is that the trust is irrevocable unless a power of revocation is reserved in the trust instrument

TERMINATION OF A TRUST [50-3]

Unless the settlor reserves a power of revocation, the general rule is that a trust, once validly created, is irrevocable. If so reserved, the trust may be terminated at the settlor's discretion.

Normally, the instrument creating a trust establishes the date on which the trust will terminate. The instrument may specify a period of years for which the trust is to last, or the settlor

---

CONCEPT REVIEW 50-1

Allocation of Principal and Income

	Expenses	Receipts
Ordinary—Income Beneficiary	Rents Royalties Cash dividends (regular and extraordinary) Interest	Interest payments Insurance Ordinary taxes Ordinary repairs Depreciation
Extraordinary—Remainderman	Stock dividends Stock splits Proceeds from sale or exchange of corpus Settlement of claims for injury to corpus	Extraordinary repairs Long-term improvements Principal amortization Costs incurred in the sale or purchase of corpus Business losses

may provide that the trust shall continue during the life of a named individual. The death of the trustee or beneficiary does not terminate the trust if neither of their lives is the measure of the trust's duration.

Though a court will usually decree a trust terminated if the beneficiary acquires legal title to the trust assets, courts will not order the termination of a trust simply because all of the beneficiaries petition the court to do so. The purposes the settlor set forth in the trust instrument, not the beneficiaries' wishes, will govern the court's actions.

If the same beneficiary holds both the equitable and legal title, the *merger doctrine* applies and the beneficiary holds the property outright. In order for a trust to exist, the trustee and beneficiary must be different persons.

DECEDENT'S ESTATES

Testament

will

Intestate

dying without a will

The assets (the estate) of a person who dies leaving a valid will are to be distributed according to the directions contained in the will. A will is also called a **testament**; the maker of a will is called a testator; and gifts made in a will are called devises or bequests. If a person dies without leaving a will, her property will pass to her heirs and next of kin in the proportions provided in the applicable state statute. This is known as **intestate** (dying-without-a-will) succession. If a person dies without a will and leaves no heirs or next of kin, her property *escheats* (reverts) to the state. Nonetheless, not all of the decedent's property will pass through the probate estate (the distribution of a decedent's estate to her successors). Certain property will pass through arrangements unaffected by distribution. For instance, the decedent's life insurance policy or pension plan will pass to the beneficiary of the policy or plan, property the decedent jointly owned with a right of survivorship will pass to the survivor, and property subject to a trust will be governed by the trust instrument.

WILLS [50-4]

Will

a properly executed written instrument whereby a person makes a disposition of his property to take effect after his death

---

Practical Advice

All adults should have a will that disposes of their assets in accordance with their wishes.

A **will** is a written instrument, executed according to statutorily dictated formalities, whereby a person makes a disposition of his property, which is to take effect after his death. One major characteristic of a will sets it apart from other transactions such as deeds and contracts: a will is revocable at any time during life. There is no such thing as an irrevocable will. A will takes effect only on the death of the testator.

In 1969, the Uniform Law Commission and the American Bar Association approved the Uniform Probate Code (UPC), an attempt to encourage throughout the United States the adoption of a uniform, flexible, speedy, and efficient system of settling a decedent's estate. At least seventeen states have adopted the UPC, which has been updated a number of times.

Mental Capacity [50-4a]

The law of wills is based upon implementing the testator's intent and therefore requires that the testator have the mental capacity to form such an intent. Thus, a minor does not have the legal capacity to make a will.

Testamentary capacity

for a will to be valid, the testator must be sufficiently competent to intend the document to be her will

Testamentary Capacity For a will to be valid the testator must be capable of (1) knowing and understanding in a general way (a) the nature and extent of his or her property, (b) the natural objects of his or her bounty, and (c) the disposition that he or she is making of that property; and (2) relating these elements to one another and forming an orderly desire regarding the disposition of the property. *Restatement (Third) of Property*: Wills and Other Donative Transfers.

Conduct invalidating a will

a will that is the product of duress, undue influence, or fraud is invalid and of no legal effect

Conduct Invalidating a Will Any document that appears to be a will but reflects an intent other than the testator's is not a valid will. This is the basis for the rule that a transfer of property by will is invalid to the extent the transfer was a result of duress, undue influence, or fraud. A party contesting a will on one of these grounds has the burden of establishing duress, undue influence, or fraud.

A transfer of property by will is invalidated by **duress** if a person threatened to perform or did perform a wrongful act that coerced the testator into making a transfer that the testator would not otherwise have made. *Restatement (Third) of Property*: Wills and Other Donative Transfers.

A transfer of property by will is invalidated by **undue influence** if a person exerted such influence over the testator that it overcame the testator's free will and caused the testator to make a transfer that the testator would not otherwise have made. "In the absence of direct evidence of undue influence, circumstantial evidence is sufficient to raise an inference of undue influence if the contestant proves that (1) the donor was susceptible to undue influence, (2) the alleged wrongdoer had an opportunity to exert undue influence, (3) the alleged wrongdoer had a disposition to exert undue influence, and (4) there was a result appearing to be the effect of the undue influence." *Restatement (Third) of Property*: Wills and Other Donative Transfers.

A transfer of property by will is invalidated by **fraud** if a person knowingly or recklessly made a false representation to the testator about a material fact that was intended to and did lead the testator to make a transfer that the testator would not otherwise have made. *Restatement (Third) of Property*: Wills and Other Donative Transfers. For example, Brian dies leaving all his property to Mark upon Mark's representation that he is Brian's long-lost son. Mark in fact is not Brian's son. In such a case, the will may be set aside because the misrepresentation was made with the intent to deceive, and Brian justifiably relied upon it. (See Chapter 11 for a more complete discussion of duress, undue influence, and fraud.)

Prine v. Blanton
Supreme Court of Georgia, 2012
290 Ga. 307, 720 S.E.2d 600
http://scholar.google.com/scholar_case?q=720+S.E.2D+600&hl=en&as_sdt=6,34&case=14249744099186000603&scilh=0

FACTS Testator Melvin H. Blanton's 1990 will and family trust divided the majority of his assets equally among his four surviving children and a granddaughter who was the child of his deceased daughter. In August 2008, Blanton met with his attorney and directed him to change his will and trust to exclude Debra Prine, his one surviving daughter. On September 17, 2008, while in the hospital, Blanton executed a new will and trust that left most of his property to his three sons through the Blanton Trust and excluded Debra Prine as a beneficiary. The following day, Blanton was placed in intensive care. He was discharged three weeks later to hospice care and died in February 2009. Blanton's sons and co-executors, Timmy M. Blanton and Greg Blanton, filed a petition to probate the will. Debra Prine challenged the validity of her father's will on the grounds that he lacked testamentary capacity and was operating under undue influence. Following a bench trial, the probate court found that Melvin Blanton was of sufficient sound and disposing mind and was not subjected to undue or illegal influence at the time he executed his will and trust amendment. Debra Prine appealed to the superior court, and the executors filed a motion for summary judgment, which the superior court granted.

DECISION Judgment of the superior court affirmed.

OPINION A testator possesses the mental capacity to make a will if he understands that he is executing a document that will dispose of his property after death, is capable of remembering the property that is subject to his disposition and the persons related to him by blood and affection, and "has sufficient intellect to enable him to have a decided and rational desire as to the disposition of his property." The controlling question is whether the testator had sufficient testamentary capacity at the time of executing the will.

The affidavit of the attorney who drafted and witnessed the will stated that Blanton was of a sufficient sound and disposing mind and memory at the time he instructed the attorney on how to prepare the will and at the time he executed it. The other subscribing witness and the notary public who executed the self-proving affidavit attached to the will also verified that Blanton knew he was signing his last will and testament and he appeared to be of sound and disposing mind and memory at the time.

His treating physician testified in a deposition that during office visits in 2008 Blanton was "sharp as a tack," showing no symptoms of mental instability, confusion, dementia, hallucinations, or declining mental condition. Blanton was admitted to the hospital on September 15, 2008, after he complained of abdominal pain and fever. Two days later he executed the new will and trust amendment. His physician testified that Blanton was his usual self on the morning the will was executed, his condition was improving, and his medications would not have affected his mental ability. During his rounds on the following morning, the physician found that Blanton had declined sharply and referred him to a specialist for a neurology consultation and admitted him into the hospital's intensive care unit.

In opposing the will Debra Pine relies on the affidavits of four lay witnesses. These witnesses either did not see Blanton until after he was admitted into intensive care or were vague about when they had seen him confused or hallucinating. Debra Prine testified that she did not see her father in the hospital until after work on the day he executed his will, he knew who she was at that time, and she had no knowledge of his mental condition earlier in the day. Evidence that the testator was aged, ill, and in pain when he executed his will or that his medical condition deteriorated while he was in the hospital does not show lack of testamentary capacity to make a will. Debra Prime has not presented a genuine issue of material fact that the testator lacked the requisite mental capacity when he signed his will.

To invalidate a will, undue influence must amount to deception or coercion that destroys the testator's free agency. The testator's choice of naming one relative instead of another as the favored beneficiary is an insufficient reason to deny probate of the will.

INTERPRETATION A testator possesses the mental capacity to make a will if he understands that he is executing a document that will dispose of his property after death, is capable of remembering the property that is subject to his disposition and the persons related to him by blood and affection, and has sufficient intellect to enable him to have a decided and rational desire as to the disposition of his property; to invalidate a will, undue influence must amount to deception or coercion that destroys the testator's free agency.

ETHICAL QUESTION Did the court fairly decide this case? Explain.

CRITICAL THINKING QUESTION Do you agree with the court's definition of mental capacity to make a will? Explain.

Formal requirements of a will

a will must be (1) in writing, (2) signed, and (3) attested to by witnesses

Formal Requirements of a Will [50-4b]

By statute in all jurisdictions, a will must comply with certain formalities to be valid. Such formalities are necessary not only to indicate that the testator understood what she was doing but also to help prevent fraud.

Writing A basic requirement for a valid will is that it be in writing. The writing may be informal, as long as it substantially meets the basic statutory formalities. Pencil, ink, and photocopy are equally valid media, and valid wills have been made on scratch paper and on an envelope.

It is also valid to incorporate into a will by reference another document that in itself is not a will because it was improperly executed. To incorporate a memorandum into a will by reference, the following four conditions must exist: (1) the memorandum must be in writing, (2) it must be in existence when the will is executed, (3) it must be adequately described in the will, and (4) it must be described in the will as being in existence.

Signature The testator (or someone else in the testator's name in the presence of the testator and at the direction of the testator) must sign her will; the signature verifies that the will has been executed. Most statutes require the signature to be at the end of the will. Even in jurisdictions that do not so specify, an ending signature will preclude the charge that the portions of the will that follow the signature were written after its execution and are therefore invalid.

Practical Advice

Store your will in a safe place and make sure that others know where it is kept. In addition, place an inventory of your assets where you store your will.

Attestation With the exception of a few isolated types of wills (noted later in this chapter) that are valid in a limited number of jurisdictions, a written will must be attested, or certified, by witnesses. The number and qualifications of witnesses and the manner of attestation generally are determined by statute. Usually, two or three witnesses are required.

Witnesses serve to acknowledge that the testator did execute the will and that she had the required intent and capacity. It is important that the testator sign first in the presence of all the witnesses; each witness should then sign in the testator's presence and in the presence of the other witnesses.

The most common restriction on a person's ability to act as a witness is that a witness must not have any interest under the will. At least two types of statute express this requirement. One type disqualifies a witness who is also a beneficiary under the will. The other voids the bequest or devise to the interested witness, thus making him a disinterested, and thereby qualified, witness.

Revocation

a will is revocable by the testator and under certain circumstances may be revoked by operation of law

Revocation of a Will [50-4c]

By definition, a will is revocable by the testator. Under certain circumstances, a will may be revoked by operation of law. Nevertheless, certain formalities are still necessary to effect a revocation. Most jurisdictions specify by statute the methods by which a will may be revoked. The five generally accepted methods for revoking a will are as follows.

Destruction or Alteration   Tearing, burning, or otherwise destroying a will is a strong sign that the testator intended to revoke it, and, unless such destruction is proven to be inadvertent, it is an effective way of revoking a will. In some states, partial revocation may be accomplished by erasing or obliterating part of the will. But substituted or additional bequests inserted between the written or printed lines of a will are not effective without reexecution and reattestation.

Golini v. Bolton
Court of Appeals of South Carolina, 1997
326 S.C. 333, 482 S.E.2d 784
http://scholar.google.com/scholar_case?case=1467799972510374304&q=482+S.E.2d+784&hl=en&as_sdt=2,34

FACTS   Willie Mae Arant executed her Last Will and Testament on August 5, 1992, in her home with two witnesses present. The original will could not be found after Arant's death, so a copy of the will was filed and admitted in Calhoun County Probate Court. The will left the bulk of the estate to Melvin Bolton, Arant's nephew, and Kent Sutcliffe, Arant's grandson. Mary Lou Golini, Arant's only surviving daughter, filed suit challenging the probate of the will on the ground that because the original will could not be found, it had been destroyed with the intent to revoke.

The probate court found Arant's will had not been revoked because it was returned to her attorney's office after it was executed and it was lost sometime after that. Furthermore, the probate court found that Arant thought she had the original in her possession but did not. The probate court found that Arant always indicated where her will was located and copies of her will were found in those locations after her death. Golini appealed to circuit court. The circuit court affirmed the probate court.

DECISION   Judgment affirmed.

OPINION   All parties agree that Arant properly executed her will. The dispute arises over what happened to the original will after its execution. Golini claims the evidence proves that Arant was the last person to have possession of her will because the will was executed in Arant's home and the witnesses to it testified they left the will with Arant after it was executed. Bolton claims, and the lower courts agreed, the evidence tended to show the last verifiable location of the will was in Arant's attorney's office, and therefore, the presumption of *animo revocandi* (intent to revoke) did not apply. "A will or any part thereof is revoked … by being burned, torn, canceled, obliterated, or destroyed, with the intent and for the purpose of revoking it by the testator or by another person in his presence and by his direction." Revocation by an act or by a subsequent instrument must be accompanied by an intention to revoke, and, without the intention, revocation does not take place.

Generally, those contesting a will have the burden of establishing revocation. However, when the testator takes possession of his will and it cannot be found at his death, the law presumes rebuttably that the testator destroyed the will with intent to revoke. The evidence to rebut the presumption must be clear and convincing.

The evidence reasonably supports the findings of the probate court that Arant was not in possession of her will. Both witnesses to the will's execution testified they were the only ones present when Arant signed her will and Arant had possession of the will when they left her home. Arant told the witnesses to the will she intended to have the will taken to her attorney's office.

Attorney Thomas Culclasure drafted two wills for Arant. He prepared the first will, which also excluded Golini, in 1988. He prepared the second will in 1992 after Arant's daughter, Sally, died. The second will Culclasure drafted was picked up from his office. After it was executed, Culclasure testified the will was returned to his office.

"Proof that a testator, whose will cannot be found after his death, entertained a kindly or loving feeling toward the beneficiaries under the will carries weight and tends toward the conclusion of nonrevocation of the will by the testator." Numerous witnesses testified as to the love and affection that existed between Arant and Bolton and Bolton's daily visits with Arant as well as his cooking her meals and running her errands. Even Golini testified Bolton was "like a son" to Arant. Before she died, Arant gave Bolton her power of attorney. Numerous witnesses also testified that Arant and Golini did not get along and that Arant stated on numerous occasions she intended to leave Golini out of her will.

INTERPRETATION   Revocation of a will must be accompanied by an intention to revoke it.

CRITICAL THINKING QUESTION   What criteria should be considered in determining whether a lost will was revoked? Explain.

Practical Advice

If you wish to revoke a previous will (1) make sure that your new will indicates that it revokes all prior wills, (2) destroy or cancel all prior wills, and (3) make sure that your witnesses and others know that you have intentionally revoked all prior wills.

Subsequent Will   The execution of a second will does not in itself constitute a revocation of an earlier will. The first will is revoked to the extent that the second will is inconsistent with the first. The most certain manner of revocation is through the execution of a later will containing a declaration that all former wills are revoked. In some, but not all, jurisdictions, a testator may revoke a will by a written declaration to this effect in a subsequent document, such as a letter, even if that document does not meet the formal requirements of a will.

Codicil

an addition to or revision of a will executed with all the formalities of a will

Practical Advice

If you wish to alter your will, you will need to either execute a codicil or a new will. In either case you need to comply with all the requirements of a new will.

Codicil

Codicil   A **codicil** is a written amendment or addition to an existing will executed with all the formal requirements of a will. The most frequent problem such an instrument raises involves the extent to which its terms, if not absolutely clear, revoke or alter provisions in the will. For the purpose of determining the testator's intent, the codicil and the will are regarded as a single instrument.

Operation of Law   A *marriage* generally revokes a will executed before the marriage. *Divorce*, on the other hand, generally does *not* revoke a provision in the will of one party for the benefit of the other.

The **birth** of a child after a will's execution may revoke the will, at least as far as that child is concerned, if the testator apparently has omitted a provision for the child. In some jurisdictions, the subsequent birth of a child will not revoke the will, if the child's omission from it is not apparently intentional; however, the share to which the child is entitled is equal to the share he would have received if the testator had died without a will.

Renunciation by the Surviving Spouse   Statutes generally provide a surviving spouse the right to renounce a will and describe the method by which the spouse may do so. Such statutory provisions enable the spouse to decide which method of taking—under the will or under intestate succession—would be most advantageous.

Special Types of Wills [50-4d]

There are many special types of wills, including nuncupative wills, holographic wills, soldiers' and sailors' wills, and living wills.

Nuncupative Wills   A nuncupative will is an unwritten oral declaration made before witnesses. In the few jurisdictions that authorize them, such declarations usually may be made only by a testator in his last illness. Under most statutes permitting nuncupative wills, only limited amounts of personal property may be passed by such wills.

Holographic Wills   In approximately one-half of the jurisdictions, a will entirely in the handwriting of the testator is a valid testamentary document even if the will is not witnessed. Such an instrument, referred to as a holographic will, must comply strictly with the statutory requirements for such wills.

BUSINESS LAW **IN ACTION**

Dr. Mason died, leaving behind a widow, two married sons, six grandchildren, and a thriving medical practice. At his death, Dr. Mason had considerable assets and a number of debts and other obligations. He had balances totaling about $5,000 on several credit cards, owed nearly $15,000 for minor renovations he had recently made to his home, and was under contract to sell a parcel of undeveloped real property he owned in another state to the adjacent landowner. One malpractice complaint was pending against Dr. Mason, brought by a former patient who alleged that he negligently sutured a laceration on her face, causing a large scar that had to be repaired by a plastic surgeon.

In his will, Dr. Mason made rather typical bequests, including certain specific items of personal property to his heirs and a large donation to the Humane Society. His will also named his sister, Frances, as the executrix of his estate.

Under the probate court's supervision, Frances must now carry out the duties of gathering Dr. Mason's assets, paying his debts, and generally winding up his affairs. First she will pay any costs associated with his final illness and burial and the expenses of administration of the estate, including a fee to which Frances is entitled for her services as personal representative. Creditors who have filed claims must then be satisfied, requiring Frances to pay Dr. Mason's credit card accounts, the outstanding home improvement invoices, and any state and federal tax liabilities. Finally, Frances must also complete the real estate sale and continue the defense of the malpractice claim to its conclusion. It is only then that Frances may distribute what remains of Dr. Mason's estate according to the wishes he expressed in his will.

Soldiers' and Sailors' Wills   For soldiers on active duty and sailors at sea, most statutes relax the formal requirements for a will and permit a testamentary disposition to be valid regardless of the informality of the document. In most jurisdictions, however, such a will cannot pass title to real estate.

Living Wills   Almost all states have adopted statutes that permit an individual to execute a living will. A living will is a form of advance health care directive by which individuals specify what actions should be taken for their health if they are no longer able to make decisions for themselves because of illness or incapacity. (A living will is not a *will* that acts as a disposition of property after death but rather a *directive* about medical care to be provided before death.) Through a living will and other forms of advance directives, which must comply with applicable statutory requirements, an individual may reject the use of life-prolonging procedures that artificially delay the dying process and ask to be allowed to die naturally should she contract an incurable illness or suffer an incurable injury. See the Ethical Dilemma at the end of this chapter.

Practical Advice

You should prepare a living will that specifically states your wishes concerning extraordinary medical treatment to preserve your life.

Intestate

person who dies without a valid will

Course of descent

each state prescribes rules for the passage of property not governed by a valid will; as a general rule the property passes in equal shares to each child after the widow's statutory rights have been settled

Per stirpes

a class or group of distributees takes the share to which their deceased ancestor would have been entitled, taking thus by its right of representing such ancestor and not as so many individuals

Per capita

an equal share is given to each of several persons, all of whom stand in equal degree to the decedent, without reference to the right of representation

INTESTATE SUCCESSION [50-5]

Property not effectively disposed of before death or by will passes in accordance with the law of intestate succession. (**Intestate** means dying without a valid will.) The rules set forth in statutes for determining, in cases involving intestacy, to whom the decedent's property shall be distributed not only ensure an orderly transfer of title to property but also purport to effect what probably would be the decedent's wishes. However, even if its requirements run contrary to the clear intention of the decedent, the intestacy statute will still govern the distribution.

The rules specifying the **course of descent** vary widely from state to state, but as a general rule and except for the specific statutory rights of the widow, the intestate property passes in equal shares to each child of the decedent living at the time of his death, with the share of any child who dies before the decedent to be divided equally among that child's children. For example, if A dies intestate, leaving a widow and children, his widow generally will receive one-third of his real estate and personal property, and the remainder will pass to his children in the manner stated above. If his wife does not survive A, his entire estate passes to their children. If A dies and leaves two surviving children, B and C, and two grandchildren, D1 and D2, the children of a predeceased child D, the estate will go one-third to B, one-third to C, and one-sixth each to D1 and D2, the grandchildren, who divide equally their parent's one-third share. This result is described legally by the statement that *lineal* descendants of predeceased children take property **per stirpes**, or by representation of their parent. If A had executed a will, he may have provided that all his lineal descendants, regardless of generation, would share equally. In that case, A's estate would be divided into four equal parts, and his descendants would be said to take the property **per capita** (see Figure 50-2).

If only the widow and relatives other than children survive the decedent, a larger share usually is allotted the widow. She may receive all the decedent's personal property and one-half his real estate or, in some states, his entire estate.

At common law, property could not lineally ascend; parents of an intestate decedent did not share in his estate. Today, in many states, if a decedent has no lineal descendants or a surviving spouse, the statute provides that parents are the next to share.

Most statutes make some provision for brothers and sisters in the event that no spouse, parents, or children survive the decedent. Brothers and sisters, together with nieces, nephews, aunts, and uncles, are termed *collateral* heirs. Beyond these limits, most statutes provide that, if there are no survivors in the named classes, the property shall be distributed equally among the next of kin in equal degree.

The common law did not consider a *stepchild* as an heir or next of kin, that is, as one to whom property would descend by operation of law; and this rule prevails today. Legally adopted children are, however, recognized as lawful heirs of their *adoptive* parents.

Figure 50-2 *Per Stirpes* and *Per Capita*

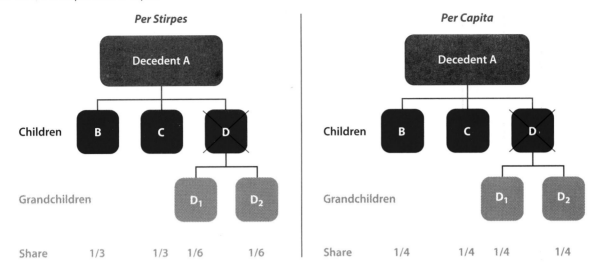

These generalities should be accepted as such; few fields of the law of property are so strictly a matter of statute, and the rights of heirs cannot reasonably be predicted without a knowledge of the exact terms of the applicable statute.

ADMINISTRATION OF ESTATES [50-6]

The rules and procedures controlling the management of a decedent's estate are statutory and therefore vary somewhat from state to state. In all jurisdictions, the estate is managed and finally disbursed under the supervision of a court. The procedure of managing the distribution of decedents' estates is referred to as **probate**, and the court that supervises the procedure is often designated the probate court.

The first legal step after death is usually to determine whether the deceased left a will. If a will exists, the testator has likely named her **executor** in it. If there is no will or if there is a will that fails to name an executor, the court will, on petition, appoint an **administrator**. The closest adult relative who is a resident of the state is entitled to this appointment.

Once approved or appointed by the court, the **role of the executor or administrator** is to collect the decedent's assets, pay the decedent's debts, and disburse the remainder of the decedent's estate according to the will or intestate statute.

If there is a will, the witnesses must prove it before the court by testifying to the signing of the will by all signatories and by confirming the mental condition of the testator at the time she executed the will. If the witnesses are dead, proof of their handwriting is necessary. If satisfied that the will is proved, the court will enter a formal decree admitting the will to probate.

Soon after the admission of the will to probate, the decedent's personal representative—the executor or administrator—must file an inventory of the estate. The personal representative will then begin his duties of collecting the assets, paying the debts, and disbursing the remainder. The executor or administrator occupies a fiduciary position not unlike that of a trustee, and his responsibility for investing proceeds and otherwise managing the estate is just as demanding.

The administration of every estate involves probate expenses, as well as fees to be paid to the executor or administrator and to the attorney who handles the estate. In addition, taxes are imposed at death by both the federal and state governments. The federal government imposes an *estate tax* on the transfer of property at death, whereas most state governments impose an *inheritance tax* on the privilege of an heir or beneficiary to receive the property. These taxes are separate from the basic income tax that the estate must pay on income received during estate administration.

Probate

the procedure for distributing a decedent's estate

Executor

the person named in the will and appointed by the court to administer the will

Administrator

a person appointed by the court to administer the estate when there is no will or when the person named in the will fails to qualify

Role of executor or administrator

responsible for collecting the decedent's assets, paying the decedent's debts, and disbursing the remainder of the decedent's estate according to the will or intestate statute

ETHICAL DILEMMA

When Should Life Support Cease?

Facts Marge Hilton, an inhalation therapist at Lankard Hospital, was recently assigned to a unit that has been treating Leslie Andrews. Andrews, a single, twenty-eight-year-old woman, was in a car accident two weeks ago and remains in a coma. All of her nutrition and hydration must be administered through a gastrostomy tube. Andrews, who was a dental assistant, has no known relatives, no medical insurance, and no significant assets.

Her medical condition offers no hope for recovery. Andrews does not have a living will, and the only evidence concerning whether she would wish to have life-sustaining efforts continued

is a casual statement, related to Lankard's administrator by two of her friends, that she "would not want to live like that." She had said this after the three attended a movie in which a young female character had been comatose for many years.

When Hilton was performing inhalation therapy for Andrews, she observed Andrews groan. She brought this to the attention of two physicians. The doctors explained that this did not indicate Andrews was showing signs of recovery or was regaining consciousness. The doctors did state that the patient may be experiencing discomfort, but

reassured Hilton that properly administered medication should take care of any pain.

Social, Policy, and Ethical Considerations
1. Under what circumstances should life-sustaining mechanisms be removed? Who should make the decision?
2. How would your answer change if Andrews were discovered to be six months pregnant?
3. If attending physicians must make the decision, should they be subject to civil or criminal liability arising out of their actions?

CHAPTER SUMMARY

Trusts

Types of Trusts

Definition of a Trust a fiduciary relationship in which legal title to property is held by one or more parties (the trustee) for the use, enjoyment, and benefit of another (the beneficiary)

Express Trust a trust established by voluntary action; usually in writing, although it may be oral
- *Testamentary Trust* a trust employed in a will; becomes effective after the creator's death
- *Inter Vivos Trust* a trust established during the settlor's lifetime
- *Charitable Trust* a trust that has as its purpose the benefit of humankind
- *Spendthrift Trust* a trust designed to remove the trust estate from the beneficiary's control and from liability for his individual debts
- *Totten Trust* a tentative trust consisting of a joint bank account opened by the settlor (creator of the trust)

Implied Trust a trust created by operation of law
- *Constructive Trust* an implied trust imposed to rectify fraud or to prevent unjust enrichment
- *Resulting Trust* an implied trust imposed to fulfill the presumed intent of the settlor

Creation and Termination of Trusts

Settlor creator of a trust; anyone legally capable of making a contract may be a settlor

Trustee anyone legally capable of holding title to and dealing with property may be a trustee
- *Duties* the three primary duties of a trustee are to (1) carry out the purposes of the trust, (2) act prudently, and (3) act with utmost loyalty
- *Powers* generally established by the trust instrument and state law
- *Allocation of Principal and Income* See Concept Review 50-1.

Beneficiary equitable owner of the trust property for whose use, enjoyment, and benefit the trust was created

Termination the general rule is that a trust is irrevocable unless a power of revocation is reserved in the trust instrument

Decedent's Estate

Wills

Definition a will (or testament) is a written instrument, executed with the formalities required by statute, whereby a person makes a disposition of his property to take effect after his death

Mental Capacity

- *Testamentary Capacity* for a will to be valid the testator must be sufficiently competent to intend the document to be her will

- *Conduct Invalidating a Will* a will that is the product of duress, undue influence, or fraud is invalid and of no effect

Formal Requirements a will must be (1) in writing, (2) signed, and (3) attested to by witnesses

Revocation a will is revocable by the testator and under certain circumstances may be revoked by operation of law

- *Destruction or Alteration* revokes a will

- *Subsequent Will* revokes prior wills to the extent they are inconsistent

- *Codicil* an addition to or revision of a will executed with all the formalities of a will

- *Marriage* generally revokes a will executed before the marriage

- *Birth of a Child* may revoke a will at least as far as that child is concerned

- *Renunciation by Surviving Spouse* surviving spouse may elect to take under laws of descent

Special Types of Wills generally binding only in specific situations and may have limitations upon their use

Intestate Succession

Intestate person who dies without a valid will

Course of Descent each state prescribes rules for the passage of property not governed by a valid will; as a general rule, the property passes in equal shares to each child after the widow's statutory rights have been settled

Administration of Estates

Probate the court's supervision of the management and distribution of the estate

Executor or Administrator a person who is responsible for collecting the decedent's assets, paying the decedent's debts, and disbursing the remainder of the decedent's estate according to the will or the intestate statute

- *Executor* the person named in the will and appointed by the court to administer the will

- *Administrator* a person appointed by the court to administer the estate when there is no will or when the person named in the will fails to qualify

QUESTIONS

1. State whether or not a trust is created in each of the following situations:
   a. A declares herself trustee of "the bulk of my securities" in trust for B.
   b. A, the owner of Blackacre, purports to convey to B in trust for C "a small part" of Blackacre.
   c. A deposits $100,000 in a savings bank. He declares himself trustee of the deposit in trust to pay B $50,000 out of the deposit, reserving the power to withdraw from the deposit any amounts not in excess of $50,000.

2. Testator gives property to Timothy in trust for Barney's benefit, providing that Barney cannot assign or pledge future trust income. Barney borrows money from Linda, assigning his future income under the trust for a stated period. Can Linda obtain any judicial relief to prevent Barney from collecting this income?

3. Collins was trustee for the beneficiary Indolent under the will of Indolent's father. Indolent, a middle-age doctor,

gave little concern to the management of the trust fund, contenting himself with receiving the income paid to him by the trustee. Among the assets of the trust were one hundred shares of ABC Corporation and one hundred shares of XYZ Corporation. About two years before the termination of the trust, Collins purchased the ABC stock from the trust at a fair price and after a full explanation to Indolent. At the same time, but without saying anything to Indolent, he purchased the XYZ stock at a price higher than its current market value. At the termination of the trust, both stocks had advanced in market value well beyond the prices paid by Collins, and Indolent demanded that Collins either account for this advance in the value of both stocks or replace the stocks. What are Indolent's rights?

4. Joe Brown gave $350,000 to his wife, Mary, with which to buy real property. They orally agreed that title to the real property should be taken in the name of Mary Brown but that she should hold the property in trust for Joe Brown. There were two witnesses to the oral agreement, both of

whom are still living. Mary purchased the property on September 2, and a deed to it with Mary Brown as the grantee was delivered.

Mary died ten years later, without a will. The real property is now worth $1 million. Joe Brown is claiming the property as the beneficiary of a trust. Mary's children are claiming that the property belongs to Mary's estate and have pleaded the statute of limitations and the statute of frauds as defenses to Joe's claim. There is no evidence to prove whether Mary would or would not have conveyed the property to Joe during her lifetime if she had been requested to do so. What are Joe's ownership rights to this particular real property?

5. On March 10, John Carver executed his will, which was witnessed by William Hobson and Sam Witt. By his will, Carver devised his farm, Stonecrest, to his nephew, Roy White. The residue of his estate was given to his sister, Florence Carver.

A codicil to his will executed on April 15 of that year, provided that $50,000 be given to Carver's niece, Mary Jordan, and $50,000 to Wanda White, Roy White's wife. The codicil was witnessed by Roy White and Harold Brown. John Carver died on September 1, of that year, and the will and codicil were admitted to probate. How should Carver's estate be distributed?

6. Edwin Fuller, a bachelor, prepared his will in his office. The will, which contained no residuary clause, provided that one-third of his estate would go to his nephew, Tom Fuller, one-third to the city of Emanon to be used for park improvements, and one-third to his brother, Kurt.

He signed the will in his office and then went to the office of his nephew, Tom Fuller, who signed the will as a witness at Edwin's request. No other persons were available in Tom's office, so Edwin then went to the bank, where Frank Cash, the cashier, also signed as a witness at Edwin's request. In each instance, Edwin stated that he had signed the document but did not state that it was his will.

Edwin returned to his office and placed the will in his safe. Subsequently, Edwin died, survived by Kurt, his only heir-at-law. How should the estate be distributed?

7. Arnold executed a one-page will in which he devised his farm to Burton. Later, after a quarrel with Burton, Arnold wrote the words "I hereby cancel and revoke this will /s/ Arnold" in the margin of the will but did not destroy the will. Arnold then executed a deed to the farm, naming Connie as grantee, and placed the deed and will in his safe. Shortly afterward, Arnold married Donna, with whom he had one child, Ernest. Arnold died some time later, and the deed and will were found in his safe. Burton, Connie, and Ernest claim the farm, and Donna claims dower. Discuss the validity of each claim.

8. The validly executed will of John Dane contained the following provision: "I give and devise to my daughter, Mary, Redacre for and during her natural life and, at her death, the remainder to go to Wilmore College." The will also provided that the residue of his estate should go to Wilmore College. Thereafter, Dane sold Redacre and then added a validly executed codicil to his will, "Due to the fact that I have sold Redacre, which I previously gave to my daughter, Mary, I now give and devise Blackacre to Mary in place and instead of Redacre."

Another clause of the codicil provided: "I give my one-half interest in the oil business that I own in common with William Steele to my son, Henry." Subsequently, Dane acquired all of the interest in the oil business from his partner, Steele, and, at the time of his death, Dane owned the entire oil business. The will and codicil have been admitted to probate.

a. What interest, if any, does Mary acquire in Blackacre?

b. What interest, if any, does Henry acquire in the oil business?

9. Leonard Wolfe was killed in an automobile accident while driving his Toyota Camry. The car was rendered a total loss, and Wolfe's insurance carrier paid his estate $17,550 for damage to the vehicle. Under the terms of Wolfe's will, any car owned at his death was to be given to his brother, David. Wolfe's daughter, Carol, however, brought an action, claiming that the gift of the car to David was adeemed by its total destruction and that she, as the residuary legatee under the will, was entitled to the insurance proceeds. Who is entitled to the insurance proceeds?

10. Grace Peterson, a spinster then aged seventy-four, asked Chester Gustafson, a Minneapolis attorney, to draw a will for her. Gustafson, who had also probated Peterson's sister's estate, drew this first will and six subsequent wills and codicils free of charge because he claimed that she had no money to pay for his services. Over the five-year period during which Gustafson redrew Peterson's will, an increasing amount of property was devised to Gustafson's children, until, finally, the seventh will so devised Peterson's entire estate. Peterson, however, hardly knew the children except from several chance encounters ten years before. She died five years later, without ever having changed the seventh will, and Gustafson, who was named as executor, now seeks to have the will admitted to probate. Discuss whether the seventh will should be probated.

CASE PROBLEMS

11. By his last will and testament, Henry Nussbaum made a residual bequest and devise of his estate to his niece, Jane Blair, as trustee, in trust for the education of his grandchildren. If the trust could not be fulfilled, the residue was to revert to the plaintiff, Dorothy Witmer. After Nussbaum died in 2003, the plaintiff contended that the trustee had breached her fiduciary duty by failing to invest the trust corpus. A considerable portion of the trust funds were held in a checking account from 2006 to 2015. The trustee claimed that the will failed to specify when and what investments were to be made and, hence, such matters were left to her good-faith discretion. She also explained the large checking account balances by the fact that she thought she would need access to the funds to pay for college in the near future. Decision?

12. Rodney Sharp was a fifty-six-year-old dairy farmer whose education did not go beyond the eighth grade. Upon the death of his wife of thirty-two years, Sharp developed a very close relationship with Jean Kosmalski, a schoolteacher sixteen years his junior. Sharp eventually proposed to Kosmalski, but when she refused, he continued to make gifts to her in hope of changing her mind. He also gave her access to his bank account, from which she withdrew substantial amounts of money; made a will naming her as sole beneficiary; and executed a deed naming her as a joint owner of his farm. Then, in September 2013, Sharp transferred his remaining joint interest in the farm to Kosmalski. In February 2015, Kosmalski ordered Sharp to move out of his home and to vacate the farm. She then took possession of both, leaving Sharp with assets of $3,000. Discuss whether a constructive trust should be imposed on the property transferred to Kosmalski.

13. John Hobelsberger lived alone on his farm near Kranzburg, South Dakota. A grandniece, Phyllis Raml, and her husband, Ralph, lived on and operated a farm about two miles away. Hobelsberger and the Ramls had a friendly and cordial relationship. The Ramls visited him rather frequently and largely cared for him during his later years. Hobelsberger was hospitalized on October 23 and his condition was diagnosed as intermittent cerebral insufficiency. During his hospitalization, he requested that the Ramls send an attorney to see him about the preparation of a will. Thomas Green, an attorney, interviewed the testator on or about November 10 and prepared a will in compliance with his instructions.

   Hobelsberger was transferred to a nursing home on November 19. On November 22, Green and a secretary went to the nursing home and witnessed his signing of the will. Hobelsberger was then eighty years old. He subscribed the will with a mark because he was having trouble with his hands. Hobelsberger died on July 19 of the following year, survived by twenty-seven nieces and nephews and seven grandnieces and grandnephews. The will, after providing for the payment of debts and funeral expenses, left Hobelsberger's entire estate to Phyllis Raml. Nine of the nieces and nephews contested the will, claiming lack of testamentary capacity, undue influence by the Ramls, and improper execution. The county court admitted the will to probate, the circuit court affirmed, and the contestants appealed. Decision?

14. Mamie Henry, a widow, died leaving no children but she was survived by several nieces and nephews. At first no will was found, and Joe Barksdale, a nephew, was appointed administrator of Mrs. Henry's estate. Later, Rita Pendergrass produced a copy of a will allegedly made by Mrs. Henry. The will left all of Mrs. Henry's property to Mrs. Pendergrass and appointed her as executrix. When Mrs. Pendergrass sought to have the will admitted to probate, Joe Barksdale and Olen Barksdale filed a contest on the grounds that the purported will was never duly executed, or, if executed, was destroyed by Mrs. Henry prior to her death. Should the will be probated? Explain.

15. George Washington Croom died testate. In his will Croom left various bequests of real and personal property to his children and a grandchild. In Item Eight of his will Croom stated, "I leave nothing whatsoever to my daughter Kathryn Elizabeth Turner, and my son Ernest Edward Croom." At his death, Croom also left three optional share certificates in Carolina Savings and Loan Association issued to George W. Croom or Kimberly Joyce Croom, the deceased's minor daughter. Each of these certificates had attached to it an "Agreement Concerning Stock in Carolina Savings and Loan Association," which purported to create a joint account with a right of survivorship. Two of these agreements were signed by George Croom only and the third agreement was not signed at all. None of these certificates were specifically devised by Croom's will and the will contained no residuary clause. Who is entitled to share in these assets?

TAKING SIDES

Upon George Welch's death, he was survived by his third wife, Dorothy Welch, and his daughter by his first marriage, Patricia Fisher. At the time George and Dorothy were married, George was in very poor health and he relied on Dorothy to care for him. George was suicidal and an alcoholic and suffered from severe depression. During the eight months George and Dorothy were married, George became isolated from his family and his health deteriorated. Prior to his death, George transferred the bulk of his assets to Dorothy. Dorothy assisted in the transfer of George's assets and often completed checks and other papers for George's signature. Although George and Dorothy had executed a prenuptial agreement, during the month preceding his death George made a new will that named Dorothy as his sole beneficiary. Patricia had been the sole beneficiary of his prior will. Through the transfers of assets and the new will, Dorothy received $570,000.

a. What are the arguments that Patricia is entitled to the $570,000?

b. What are the arguments that Dorothy is entitled to the $570,000?

c. Who should prevail? Why?

Appendices

Appendix A
The Constitution of the United States of America

We the People of the United States, in Order to form a more perfect Union, establish Justice, insure domestic Tranquility, provide for the common defense, promote the general Welfare, and secure the Blessings of Liberty to ourselves and our Posterity, do ordain and establish this Constitution for the United States of America.

ARTICLE I
Section 1
All legislative Powers herein granted shall be vested in a Congress of the United States, which shall consist of a Senate and House of Representatives.

Section 2
The House of Representatives shall be composed of Members chosen every second Year by the People of the several States, and the Electors in each State shall have the Qualifications requisite for Electors of the most numerous Branch of the State Legislature.

No Person shall be a Representative who shall not have attained to the Age of twenty five Years, and been seven Years a Citizen of the United States, and who shall not, when elected, be an Inhabitant of that State in which he shall be chosen.

Representatives and direct Taxes shall be apportioned among the several States which may be included within this Union, according to their respective Numbers, which shall be determined by adding to the whole Number of free Persons, including those bound to Service for a Term of Years, and excluding Indians not taxed, three fifths of all other Persons. The actual Enumeration shall be made within three Years after the first Meeting of the Congress of the United States, and within every subsequent Term of ten Years, in such Manner as they shall by Law direct. The number of Representatives shall not exceed one for every thirty Thousand, but each State shall have at Least one Representative; and until such enumeration shall be made, the State of New Hampshire shall be entitled to chuse three, Massachusetts eight, Rhode Island and Providence Plantations one, Connecticut five, New-York six, New Jersey four, Pennsylvania eight, Delaware one, Maryland six, Virginia ten, North Carolina five, South Carolina five, and Georgia three. When vacancies happen in the Representation from any State, the Executive Authority thereof shall issue Writs of Election to fill such vacancies.

The House of Representatives shall chuse their Speaker and other Officers; and shall have the sole Power of Impeachment.

Section 3
The Senate of the United States shall be composed of two Senators from each State, chosen by the Legislature thereof, for six Years; and each Senator shall have one Vote.

Immediately after they shall be assembled in Consequence of the first Election, they shall be divided as equally as may be into three Classes. The Seats of the Senators of the first Class shall be vacated at the Expiration of the second Year, of the second Class at the Expiration of the fourth Year, and of the third Class at the Expiration of the sixth Year, so that one third may be chosen every second Year; and if Vacancies happen by Resignation or otherwise, during the Recess of the Legislature of any State, the Executive thereof may make temporary Appointments until the next Meeting of the Legislature, which shall then fill such Vacancies.

No Person shall be a Senator who shall not have attained to the Age of thirty Years, and been nine Years a Citizen of the United States, and who shall not, when elected, be an Inhabitant of that State for which he shall be chosen.

The Vice President of the United States shall be President of the Senate, but shall have no Vote, unless they be equally divided.

The Senate shall chuse their other Officers, and also a President pro tempore, in the Absence of the Vice President, or when he shall exercise the Office of President of the United States.

The Senate shall have the sole power to try all Impeachments. When sitting for that Purpose, they shall be an Oath or Affirmation. When the President of the United States is tried, the Chief Justice shall preside: And no Person shall be convicted without the Concurrence of two thirds of the Members present.

Judgment in Cases of Impeachment shall not extend further than to removal from Office, and disqualification to hold and enjoy any Office of honor, Trust or Profit under the United States: but the Party convicted shall nevertheless be liable and subject to Indictment, Trial, Judgment and Punishment, according to Law.

Section 4
The Times, Places and Manner of holding Elections for Senators and Representatives, shall be prescribed in each State by the Legislature thereof: but the Congress may at any time by Law make or alter such Regulations, except as to the Places of chusing Senators.

The Congress shall assemble at least once in every Year, and such Meeting shall be on the first Monday in December, unless they shall by Law appoint a different Day.

Section 5
Each House shall be the Judge of the Elections, Returns and Qualifications of its own Members, and a Majority of each shall constitute a Quorum to do Business; but a smaller Number may adjourn from day to day, and may be authorized to compel the Attendance of absent Members, in such Manner, and under such Penalties as each House may provide.

Each House may determine the Rules of its Proceedings, punish its Members for disorderly Behaviour, and, with the Concurrence of two thirds, expel a Member.

Each House shall keep a Journal of its Proceedings, and from time to time publish the same, excepting such Parts as may in their Judgment require Secrecy; and the Yeas and Nays of the Members of either House on any question shall, at the Desire of one fifth of those Present, be entered on the Journal.

Neither House, during the Session of Congress, shall, without the Consent of the other, adjourn for more than three days, nor to any other Place than that in which the two Houses shall be sitting.

Section 6
The Senators and Representatives shall receive a Compensation for their Services, to be ascertained by Law, and paid out of the Treasury of the United States. They shall in all Cases, except Treason, Felony and Breach of the Peace, be privileged from Arrest and Breach of the Peace, be privileged from Arrest during their Attendance at the Session of their respective Houses, and

in going to and returning from the same; and for any Speech or Debate in either House, they shall not be questioned in any other Place.

No Senator or Representative shall, during the Time for which he was elected, be appointed to any civil Office under the Authority of the United States, which shall have been created, or the Emoluments whereof shall have been encreased during such time; and no Person holding any Office under the United States, shall be a Member of either House during his Continuance in Office.

Section 7

All Bills for raising Revenue shall originate in the House of Representatives; but the Senate may propose or concur with Amendments as on other Bills.

Every Bill which shall have passed the House of Representatives and the Senate, shall, before it become a Law, be presented to the President of the United States; If he approve he shall sign it, but if not he shall return it, with his Objections to that House in which it shall have originated, who shall enter the Objections at large on their Journal, and proceed to reconsider it. If after such Reconsideration two thirds of that House shall agree to pass the Bill, it shall be sent, together with the Objections, to the other House, by which it shall likewise be reconsidered, and if approved by two thirds of that House, it shall become a Law. But in all such Cases the Votes of both Houses shall be determined by Yeas and Nays, and the Names of the Persons voting for and against the Bill shall be entered on the Journal of each House respectively. If any Bill shall not be returned by the President within ten Days (Sundays excepted) after it shall have been presented to him, the Same shall be a Law, in like Manner as if he had signed it, unless the Congress by their Adjournment prevent its Return, in which Case it shall not be a Law.

Every Order, Resolution, or Vote to which the Concurrence of the Senate and House of Representatives may be necessary (except on a question of Adjournment) shall be presented to the President of the United States; and before the Same shall take Effect, shall be approved by him, or being disapproved by him, shall be repassed by two thirds of the Senate and House of Representatives, according to the Rules and Limitations prescribed in the Case of a Bill.

Section 8

The Congress shall have Power to lay and collect Taxes, Duties, Imposts and Excises, to pay the Debts and provide for the common Defense and general Welfare of the United States; but all Duties, Imposts and Excises shall be uniform throughout the United States;

To borrow Money on the credit of the United States;

To regulate Commerce with foreign Nations, and among the several States, and with the Indian Tribes;

To establish an uniform Rule of Naturalization, and uniform Laws on the subject of Bankruptcies throughout the United States;

To coin Money, regulate the Value thereof, and of foreign Coin, and fix the Standard of Weights and Measures;

To provide for the Punishment of counterfeiting the Securities and current Coin of the United States;

To establish Post Offices and post Roads;

To promote the Progress of Science and useful Arts, by securing for limited Times to Authors and Inventors the exclusive Right to their respective Writings and Discoveries;

To constitute Tribunals inferior to the supreme Court;

To define and punish Piracies and Felonies committed on the high Seas, and Offenses against the Law of Nations;

To declare War, grant Letters of Marque and Reprisal, and make Rules concerning Captures on Land and Water;

To raise and support Armies, but no Appropriation of Money to that Use shall be for a longer Term than two Years;

To provide and maintain a Navy;

To make Rules for the Government and Regulation of the land and naval Forces;

To provide for calling forth the Militia to execute the Laws of the Union, suppress Insurrections and repel Invasions;

To provide for organizing, arming, and disciplining, the Militia, and for governing such Part of them as may be employed in the Service of the United States, reserving to the States respectively, the Appointment of the Officers, and the Authority of training the Militia according to the discipline described by Congress;

To exercise exclusive Legislation in all Cases whatsoever, over such District (not exceeding ten Miles square) as may, by Cession of particular States, and the Acceptance of Congress, become the Seat of the Government of the United States, and to exercise like Authority over all Places purchased by the Consent of the Legislature of the State in which the Same shall be, for the Erection of Forts, Magazines, Arsenals, dock-Yards, and other needful Buildings;—And

To make all Laws which shall be necessary and proper for carrying into Execution the foregoing Powers, and all other Powers vested by this Constitution in the Government of the United States, or in any Department or Officer thereof.

Section 9

The Migration or Importation of such Persons as any of the States now existing shall think proper to admit, shall not be prohibited by the Congress prior to the Year one thousand eight hundred and eight, but a Tax of Duty may be imposed on such Importation, not exceeding ten dollars for each Person.

The Privilege of the Writ of Habeas Corpus shall not be suspended, unless when in Cases of Rebellion or Invasion the public Safety may require it.

No Bill of Attainder or ex post facto Law shall be passed.

No Capitation, or other direct, Tax shall be laid, unless in Proportion to the Census or Enumeration herein before directed to be taken.

No Tax or Duty shall be laid on Articles exported from any State.

No Preference shall be given by any Regulation of Commerce or Revenue to the Ports of one State over those of another; nor shall Vessels bound to, or from, one State, be obliged to enter, clear, or pay Duties in another.

No Money shall be drawn from the Treasury, but in Consequence of Appropriations made by Laws; and a regular Statement and Account of the Receipts and Expenditures of all public Money shall be published from time to time.

No Title of Nobility shall be granted by the United States: And no Person holding any Office of Profit or Trust under them, shall, without the Consent of the Congress, accept of any present, Emolument, Office, or Title, of any kind whatever, from any King, Prince, or foreign State.

Section 10

No State shall enter into any Treaty, Alliance, or Confederation; grant Letters of Marque and Reprisal; coin Money; emit Bills of Credit; make any Thing but gold and silver Coin a Tender in Payment of Debts; pass any Bill of Attainder, ex post facto Law, or Law impairing the Obligation of Contracts, or grant any Title of Nobility.

No State shall, without the Consent of the Congress, lay any Imposts or Duties on Imports or Exports, except what may be absolutely necessary for executing its inspection Laws: and the net Produce of all Duties and Imposts, laid by any State on Imports or Exports, shall be for the Use of the Treasury of the United States; and all such Laws shall be subject to the Revision and Controul of the Congress.

No State shall, without the Consent of Congress, lay any Duty of Tonnage, keep Troops, or Ships of War in time of Peace, enter into any Agreement or Compact with another State, or with a foreign Power, or engage in War, unless actually invaded, or in such imminent Danger as will not admit of delay.

ARTICLE II
Section 1

The executive Power shall be vested in a President of the United States of America. He shall hold his Office during the Term of four Years, and, together with the Vice President, chosen for the same Term, be elected, as follows:

Each State shall appoint, in such Manner as the Legislature thereof may direct, a Number of Electors, equal to the whole Number of Senators and Representatives to which the State may be entitled in the Congress: but no Senator or Representative, or Person holding an Office of Trust or Profit under the United States, shall be appointed an Elector.

The Electors shall meet in their respective States, and vote by Ballot for two Persons, of whom one at least shall not be an Inhabitant of the same State with themselves. And they shall make a list of all the Persons voted for, and of the Number of Votes for each; which List they shall sign and certify, and transmit sealed to the Seat of the Government of the United States, directed to the President of the Senate. The President of the Senate shall, in the presence of the Senate and House of Representatives, open all the Certificates, and the Votes shall be counted. The Person having the greatest Number of Votes shall be the President, if such Number be a Majority of the whole Number of Electors appointed; and if there be more than one who have such Majority, and have an equal Number of Votes, then the House of Representatives shall immediately chuse by Ballot one of them for President; and if no Person have a Majority, then from the five highest on the List the said House shall in like Manner chuse the President. But in chusing the President, the Votes shall be taken by States, the Representation from each State having one Vote; A quorum for this Purpose shall consist of a Member or Members from two thirds of the States, and a Majority of all the States shall be necessary to a Choice. In every Case, after the Choice of the President, the Person having the Greatest Number of Votes of the Electors shall be the Vice President. But if there should remain two or more who have equal Votes, the Senate shall chuse from them by Ballot the Vice President.

The Congress may determine the Time of Chusing the Electors, and the Day on which they shall give their Votes; which Day shall be the same throughout the United States.

No Person except a natural born Citizen, or a Citizen of the United States, at the time of the Adoption of this Constitution, shall be eligible to the Office of President; neither shall any Person be eligible to that Office who shall not have attained to the Age of thirty five Years, and been fourteen Years a Resident within the United States.

In Case of the Removal of the President from Office, or of his Death, Resignation, or Inability to discharge the Powers and Duties of the said Office, the Same shall devolve on the Vice President, and the Congress may by Law provide for the Case of Removal, Death, Resignation or Inability, both of the President and Vice President, declaring what Officer shall then act as President, and such Officer shall act accordingly, until the Disability be removed, or a President shall be elected.

The President shall, at stated Times, receive for his Services, a Compensation, which shall neither be encreased nor diminished during the Period for which he shall have been elected, and he shall not receive within that Period any other Emolument from the United States, or any of them.

Before he enter on the Execution of his Office, he shall take the following Oath or Affirmation:—"I do solemnly swear (or affirm) that I will faithfully execute the Office of President of the United States, and will to the best of my Ability, preserve, protect and defend the Constitution of the United States."

Section 2

The President shall be Commander in Chief of the Army and Navy of the United States, and of the Militia of the several States, when called into the actual Service of the United States; he may require the Opinion, in writing, of the principal Officer in each of the executive Departments, upon any Subject relating to the Duties of their respective Offices, and he shall have Power to grant Reprieves and Pardons for Offences against the United States, except in Cases of Impeachment.

He shall have Power, by and with the Advice and Consent of the Senate, to make Treaties, providing two thirds of the Senators present concur; and he shall nominate, and by and with the Advice and Consent of the Senate, shall appoint Ambassadors, other public Ministers and Consuls, Judges of the supreme Court, and all other Officers of the United States, whose Appointments are not herein otherwise provided for, and which shall be established by Law: but the Congress may by Law vest the Appointment of such inferior Officers, as they think proper, in the President alone, in the Courts of Law, or in the Heads of Departments.

The President shall have Power to fill up all Vacancies that may happen during the Recess of the Senate, by granting Commissions which shall expire at the End of their next Session.

Section 3

He shall from time to time give to the Congress Information of the State of the Union, and recommend to their Consideration such Measures as he shall judge necessary and expedient; he may, on extraordinary Occasions, convene both Houses, or either of them, and in Case of Disagreement between them, with Respect to the Time of Adjournment, he may adjourn them to such Time as he shall think proper, he shall receive Ambassadors and other public Ministers; he shall take Care that the Laws be faithfully executed, and shall Commission all the Offices of the United States.

Section 4

The President, Vice President and all civil Officers of the United States, shall be removed from Office on Impeachment for, and Conviction of, Treason, Bribery, or other high Crimes and Misdemeanors.

ARTICLE III
Section 1

The judicial Power of the United States, shall be vested in one supreme Court, and in such inferior Courts as the Congress may from time to time ordain and establish. The Judges, both of the supreme and inferior Courts, shall hold their Offices during good Behaviour, and shall, at Times, receive for their Services, a Compensation, which shall not be diminished during their Continuance in Office.

Section 2

The judicial Power shall extend to all Cases, in Law and Equity, arising under this Constitution, the Laws of the United States, and Treaties made, or which shall be made, under their Authority;—to all Cases affecting Ambassadors, other public Ministers and Consuls;—to all Cases of admiralty and maritime Jurisdiction;—to Controversies to which the United States shall be a Party;—to controversies between two or more States;—between a State and Citizens of another State;— between Citizens of different States;—between Citizens of the same State claiming Lands under Grants of different States; and between a State, or the Citizens thereof, and foreign States, Citizens or Subjects.

In all Cases affecting Ambassadors, other public Ministers and Consuls, and those in which a State shall be Party, the supreme Court shall have original Jurisdiction. In all the other Cases before mentioned, the supreme Court shall have appellate Jurisdiction, both as to Law and Fact, with such Exceptions, and under such Regulations as the Congress shall make.

The Trial of all Crimes, except in Cases of Impeachment, shall be by Jury; and such Trial shall be held in the State where the said Crimes shall have been committed; but when not committed within any State, the Trial shall be at such Place or Places as the Congress may by Law have directed.

Section 3

Treason against the United States, shall consist only in levying War against them, or in adhering to their Enemies, giving them Aid and Comfort. No Person shall be convicted of Treason unless on the Testimony of two Witnesses to the same overt Act, or on Confession in open Court.

The Congress shall have Power to declare the Punishment of Treason, but no Attainder of Treason shall work Corruption of Blood, or Forfeiture except during the Life of the Person attainted.

ARTICLE IV
Section 1

Full Faith and Credit shall be given in each State to the public Acts, Records, and judicial Proceedings of every other State. And the Congress may by general Laws prescribe the Manner in which such Arts, Records and Proceedings shall be proved, and the Effect thereof.

Section 2

The Citizens of each State shall be entitled to all Privileges and Immunities of Citizens in the several States.

A Person charged in any State with Treason, Felony, or other Crime, who shall flee from Justice, and be found in another State, shall on Demand of the executive Authority of the State from which he fled, be delivered up, to be removed to the State having Jurisdiction of the Crime.

No Person held to Service or Labour in one State, under the Laws thereof, escaping into another, shall, in Consequence of any Law or Regulation therein, be discharged from such Service or Labour, but shall be delivered up on Claim of the Party to whom such Service or Labour may be due.

Section 3

New States may be admitted by the Congress into this Union; but no new State shall be formed or erected within the Jurisdiction of any other State; nor any State be formed by the Junction of two or more States, or Parts of States, without the Consent of the Legislatures of the States concerned as well as the Congress.

The Congress shall have Power to dispose of and make all needful Rules and Regulations respecting the Territory or other Property belonging to the United States; and nothing in this Constitution shall be so construed as to Prejudice any Claims of the United States, or of any particular State.

Section 4

The United States shall guarantee to every State in this Union a Republican Form of Government, and shall protect each of them against Invasion; and on Application of the Legislature, or of the Executive (when the Legislature cannot be convened) against domestic Violence.

ARTICLE V

The Congress, whenever two thirds of both Houses shall deem it necessary, shall propose Amendments to this Constitution, or, on the Application of the Legislatures of two thirds of the several States, shall call a Convention for proposing Amendments, which, in either Case, shall be valid to all Intents and Purposes, as Part of this Constitution, when ratified by the Legislatures of three fourths of the several States, or by Conventions in three fourths thereof, as the one or the other Mode of Ratification may be proposed by the Congress; Provided that no Amendment which may be made prior to the Year One thousand eight hundred and eight shall in any Manner affect the first and fourth Clauses in the Ninth Section of the first Article; and that no State, without its Consent, shall be deprived of its equal Suffrage in the Senate.

ARTICLE VI

All Debts contracted and Engagements entered into, before the Adoption of this Constitution, shall be as valid against the United States under this Constitution, as under the Confederation.

This Constitution, and the Laws of the United States which shall be made in Pursuance thereof; and all Treaties made, or which shall be made, under the Authority of the United States, shall be the supreme Law of the Land; and the Judges in every State shall be bound thereby, any Thing in the Constitution or Laws of any State to the Contrary notwithstanding.

The Senators and Representatives before mentioned, and the Members of the several State Legislatures, and all executive and judicial Officers, both of the United States and of the Several States, shall be bound by Oath or Affirmation, to support this Constitution; but no religious Test shall ever be required as a Qualification to any Office or public Trust under the United States.

ARTICLE VII

The Ratification of the Conventions of nine States, shall be sufficient for the Establishment of this Constitution between the States so ratifying the Same.

Amendment I [1791]

Congress shall make no law respecting an establishment of religion, or prohibiting the free exercise thereof; or abridging the freedom of speech, or the press; or the right of the people peaceably to assemble, and to petition the Government for a redress of grievances.

Amendment II [1791]

A well regulated Militia, being necessary to the security for a free State, the right of the people to keep and bear Arms, shall not be infringed.

Amendment III [1791]

No Soldier shall, in time of peace be quartered in any house, without the consent of the Owner, nor in time of war, but in a manner to be prescribed by law.

Amendment IV [1791]

The right of the people to be secure in their persons, houses, papers, and effects, against unreasonable searches and seizures, shall not be violated, and no Warrants shall issue, but upon probable cause, supported by Oath or Affirmation, and particularly describing the place to be searched, and the persons or things to be seized.

Amendment V [1791]

No person shall be held to answer for a capital, or otherwise infamous crime, unless on a presentment or indictment of a Grand Jury, except in cases arising in the land or naval forces, or in the Militia, when in actual service in time of War or public danger; nor shall any person be subject for the same offense to be twice put in jeopardy of life or limb; nor shall be compelled in any criminal case to be a witness against himself, nor be deprived of life, liberty, or property, without due process of law; nor shall private property be taken for public use, without just compensation.

Amendment VI [1791]

In all criminal prosecutions, the accused shall enjoy the right to a speedy and public trial, by an impartial jury of the State and district wherein the crime shall have been committed, which district shall have been previously ascertained by law, and to be informed of the nature and cause of the accusation; to be confronted with the Witnesses against him; to have compulsory process for obtaining witnesses in his favor, and to have the Assistance of counsel for his defense.

Amendment VII [1791]

In suits at common law, where the value in controversy shall exceed twenty dollars, the right of trial by jury shall be preserved, and no fact tried by a jury, shall be otherwise re-examined in any Court of the United States, than according to the rules of the common law.

Amendment VIII [1791]

Excessive bail shall not be required, no excessive fines imposed, nor cruel and unusual punishments inflicted.

Amendment IX [1791]

The enumeration in the Constitution, of certain rights, shall not be construed to deny or disparage others retained by the people.

Amendment X [1791]

The powers not delegated to the United States by the Constitution, nor prohibited by it to the States, are reserved to the States respectively, or to the people.

Amendment XI [1798]

The judicial power of the United States shall not be construed to extend to any suit in law or equity, commenced or prosecuted against one of the United States by Citizens of another State, or by Citizens or Subjects of any Foreign State.

Amendment XII [1804]

The Electors shall meet in their respective states and vote by ballot for President and Vice-President, one of whom, at least, shall not be an inhabitant of the same state with themselves; they shall name in their ballots the person voted for as President, and in distinct ballots the person voted for as Vice-President, and they shall make distinct lists of all persons voted for as President, and of all persons voted for as Vice-President, and of the number of votes for each, which lists they shall sign and certify, and transmit sealed to the seat of the government of the United States, directed to the President of the Senate;—The President of the Senate shall, in the presence of the Senate and House of Representatives, open all the certificates and the votes shall then be counted;—The person having the greatest number of votes for President, shall be the President, if such a number be a majority of the whole number of Electors appointed; and if no person have such majority, then from the persons having the highest numbers not exceeding three on the list of those voted for as President, the House of Representatives shall choose immediately, by ballot, the President. But in choosing the President, the votes shall be taken by states, the representation from each state having one vote; a quorum for this purpose shall consist of a member or members from two-thirds of the states, and a majority of all the states shall be necessary to a choice. And if the House of Representatives shall not choose a President whenever the right of choice shall devolve upon them, before the fourth day of March next following, then the Vice-President shall act as President, as in the case of the death or other constitutional disability of the President. The person having the greatest number of votes as Vice-President, shall be the Vice-President, if such number be a majority of the whole number of Electors appointed, and if no person have a majority, then from the two highest numbers on the list, the Senate shall choose the Vice-President; a quorum for the purpose shall consist of two-thirds of the whole number of Senators, and a majority of the whole number shall be necessary to a choice. But no person constitutionally ineligible to the office of President shall be eligible to that of the Vice-President of the United States.

Amendment XIII [1865]
Section 1

Neither slavery nor involuntary servitude, except as a punishment for crime whereof the party shall have been duly convicted, shall exist within the United States, or any place subject to their jurisdiction.

Section 2

Congress shall have power to enforce this article by appropriate legislation.

Amendment XIV [1868]
Section 1

All persons born or naturalized in the United States, and subject to the jurisdiction thereof, are citizens of the United States and of the State wherein they reside. No State shall make or enforce any law which shall abridge the privileges or immunities of citizens of the United States; nor shall any State deprive any person of life, liberty, or property, without due process of law; nor deny to any person within its jurisdiction the equal protection of the laws.

Section 2

Representatives shall be appointed among the several States according to their respective numbers, counting the whole number of persons in each State, excluding Indians not taxed. But when the right to vote at any election for the choice of electors for President and Vice President of the United States, Representatives in Congress, the Executive and Judicial officers of a State, or the members of the Legislature thereof, is denied to any of the male inhabitants of such State, being twenty-one years of age, and citizens of the United States, or in any way abridged, except for participation in rebellion, or other crime, the basis of representation therein shall be reduced in the proportion which the number of such male citizens shall bear the whole number of male citizens twenty-one years of age in such State.

Section 3

No person shall be a Senator or Representative in Congress, or elector of President and Vice President, or hold any office, civil or military, under the United States, or under any State, who, having previously taken an oath, as a member of Congress, or as an officer of the United States, or as a member of any State legislature, or as an executive or judicial officer of any State, to support the Constitution of the United States, shall have engaged in insurrection or rebellion against the same, or given aid or comfort to the enemies thereof. But Congress may by a vote of two-thirds of each House, remove such disability.

Section 4

The validity of the public debt of the United States, authorized by law, including debts incurred for payment of pensions and bounties for services in suppressing insurrection or rebellion, shall not be questioned. But neither the United States nor any State shall assume or pay any debt or obligation incurred in aid of insurrection of rebellion against the United States, or any claim for the loss or emancipation of any slave; but all such debts, obligations and claims shall be held illegal and void.

Section 5

The Congress shall have power to enforce, by appropriate legislation, the provisions of this article.

Amendment XV [1870]
Section 1

The right of citizens of the United States to vote shall not be denied or abridged by the United States or by any State on account of race, color, or previous condition of servitude.

Section 2

The Congress shall have power to enforce this article by appropriate legislation.

Amendment XVI [1913]

The Congress shall have power to lay and collect taxes on incomes, from whatever source derived, without apportionment among the several States, and without regard to any census or enumeration.

Amendment XVII [1913]

The Senate of the United States shall be composed of two Senators from each State, elected by the people thereof, for six years; and each Senator shall have one vote. The electors in each State shall have the qualifications requisite for electors of the most numerous branch of the State legislatures.

When vacancies happen in the representation of any State in the Senate, the executive authority of each State shall issue writs of election to fill such vacancies; Provided, That the legislature of any State may empower the executive thereof to make temporary appointments until the people fill the vacancies by election as the legislature may direct.

This amendment shall not be construed as to affect the election or term of any Senator chosen before it becomes valid as part of the Constitution.

Amendment XVIII [1919]
Section 1

After one year from the ratification of this article the manufacture, sale, or transportation of intoxicating liquors within, the importation thereof into, or the exportation thereof from the United States and all territory subject to the jurisdiction thereof for beverage purposes is hereby prohibited.

Section 2

The Congress and the several States shall have concurrent power to enforce this article by appropriate legislation.

Section 3

This article shall be inoperative unless it shall have been ratified as an amendment to the Constitution by the legislatures of the several States, as provided in the Constitution, within seven years from the date of the submission hereof to the States by the Congress.

Amendment XIX [1920]

The right of citizens of the United States to vote shall not be denied or abridged by the United States or by any State on account of sex.

Congress shall have power to enforce this article by appropriate legislation.

Amendment XX [1933]
Section 1

The terms of the President and Vice President shall end at noon on the 20th day of January, and the terms of Senators and Representatives at noon on the 3d day of January, of the years in which such terms would have ended if this article had not been ratified; and the terms of their successors shall then begin.

Section 2

The Congress shall assemble at least once in every year, and such meeting shall begin at noon on the 3d day of January, unless they shall by law appoint a different day.

Section 3

If, at the time fixed for the beginning of the term of the President, the President elect shall have died, the Vice President elect shall become President. If a President shall not have been chosen before the time fixed for the beginning of his term, or if the President elect shall have failed to qualify, then the Vice President elect shall act as President until a President shall have qualified; and the Congress may by law provide for the case wherein neither a President elect nor a Vice President elect shall have qualified, declaring who shall then act as President, or the manner in which one who is to act shall be selected, and such person shall act accordingly until a President or Vice President shall have qualified.

Section 4

The Congress may by law provide for the case of the death of any of the persons from whom the House of Representatives may choose a President whenever the right of choice shall have devolved upon them, and for the case of the death of any of the persons from whom the Senate may choose a Vice President whenever the right of choice shall have devolved upon them.

Section 5

Sections 1 and 2 shall take effect on the 15th day of October following the ratification of this article.

Section 6

This article shall be inoperative unless it shall have been ratified as an amendment to the Constitution by the legislatures of three-fourths of the several States within seven years from the date of its submission.

Amendment XXI [1933]
Section 1

The eighteenth article of amendment to the Constitution of the United States is hereby repealed.

Section 2

The transportation or importation into any State, Territory, or possession of the United States for delivery or use therein of intoxicating liquors, in violation of the laws thereof, is hereby prohibited.

Section 3

This article shall be inoperative unless it shall have been ratified as an amendment to the Constitution by conventions in the several States, as provided in the Constitution, within seven years from the date of the submission hereof to the States by the Congress.

Amendment XXII [1951]
Section 1

No person shall be elected to the office of the President more than twice, and no person who has held the office of President, or acted as President, for more than two years of a term to which some other person was elected President shall be elected to the office of the President more than once. But this Article shall not apply to any person holding the office of President when this Article was proposed by the Congress, and shall not prevent any person who may be holding the office of President, or acting as President, during the term within which this Article becomes operative from holding the office of President, or acting as President during the remainder of such term.

Section 2

This article shall be inoperative unless it shall have been ratified as an amendment to the Constitution by the legislatures of three-fourths of the several States within seven years from the date of its submission to the States by the Congress.

Amendment XXIII [1961]
Section 1

The District constituting the seat of Government of the United States shall appoint in such manner as the Congress may direct:

A number of electors of President and Vice President equal to the whole number of Senators and Representatives in Congress to which the District would be entitled if it were a State, but in no event more than the least populous State; they shall be in addition to those appointed by the States, but they shall be considered, for the purposes of the election of President and Vice President, to be electors appointed by a State; and they shall meet in the District and perform such duties as provided by the twelfth article of amendment.

Section 2

The Congress shall have power to enforce this article by appropriate legislation.

Amendment XXIV [1964]
Section 1

The right of citizens of the United States to vote in any primary or other election for President or Vice President, for electors for President or Vice President or for Senator or Representative in Congress, shall not be denied or abridged by the United States or any State by reason of failure to pay any poll tax or other tax.

Section 2

The Congress shall have power to enforce this article by appropriate legislation.

Amendment XXV [1967]
Section 1

In case of the removal of the President from office or of his death or resignation, the Vice President shall become President.

Section 2

Whenever there is a vacancy in the office of the Vice President, the President shall nominate a Vice President who shall take office upon confirmation by a majority vote of both Houses of Congress.

Section 3

Whenever the President transmits to the President pro tempore of the Senate and the Speaker of the House of Representatives his written declaration that he is unable to discharge the powers and duties of his office, and until he transmits to them a written declaration to the contrary, such powers and duties shall be discharged by the Vice President as Acting President.

Section 4

Whenever the Vice President and a majority of either the principal officers of the executive departments or of such other body as Congress may by law provide, transmit to the President pro tempore of the Senate and the Speaker of the House of Representatives their written declaration that the President is unable to discharge the powers and duties of his office, the Vice President shall immediately assume the powers and duties of the office as Acting President.

Thereafter, when the President transmits to the President pro tempore of the Senate and the Speaker of the House of Representatives his written declaration that no inability exists, he shall resume the powers and duties of his office unless the Vice President and a majority of either the principal officers of the executive department or of such other body as Congress may by law provide, transmit within four days to the President pro tempore of the Senate and the Speaker of the House of Representatives their written declaration that the President is unable to discharge the powers and duties of his office. Thereupon Congress shall decide the issue, assembling within forty-eight hours for that purpose if not in session. If the Congress, within twenty-one days after receipt of the latter written declaration, or, if Congress is not in session, within twenty-one days after Congress is required to assemble, determines by two-thirds vote of both Houses that the President is unable to discharge the powers and duties of his office, the Vice President shall continue to discharge the same as Acting President; otherwise, the President shall resume the powers and duties of his office.

Amendment XXVI [1971]

Section 1

The right of citizens of the United States, who are eighteen years of age or older, to vote shall not be denied or abridged by the United States or by any State on account of age.

Section 2

The Congress shall have power to enforce this article by appropriate legislation.

Amendment XXVII [1992]

No law, varying the compensation for the services of the Senators and Representatives, shall take effect, until an election of Representatives shall have intervened.

The Code consists of the following Articles:
1. General Provisions
2. Sales
2A. Leases
3. Commercial Paper
4. Bank Deposits and Collections
4A. Funds Transfers
5. Letters of Credit
6. Bulk Transfers
7. Warehouse Receipts, Bills of Lading and Other Documents of Title
8. Investment Securities
9. Secured Transactions: Sales of Accounts, Contract Rights and Chattel Paper
10. Effective Date and Repealer
11. Effective Date and Transition Provisions

REVISED ARTICLE 1: GENERAL PROVISIONS
Part 1—General Provisions
§ 1–101. Short Titles.
(a) This [Act] may be cited as the Uniform Commercial Code.
(b) This article may be cited as Uniform Commercial Code—General Provisions.

§ 1–102. Scope of Article.
This article applies to a transaction to the extent that it is governed by another article of [the Uniform Commercial Code].

§ 1–103. Construction of [Uniform Commercial Code] to Promote Its Purposes and Policies; Applicability of Supplemental Principles of Law.
(a) [The Uniform Commercial Code] must be liberally construed and applied to promote its underlying purposes and policies, which are:
　(1) to simplify, clarify, and modernize the law governing commercial transactions;
　(2) to permit the continued expansion of commercial practices through custom, usage, and agreement of the parties; and
　(3) to make uniform the law among the various jurisdictions.
(b) Unless displaced by the particular provisions of [the Uniform Commercial Code], the principles of law and equity, including the law merchant and the law relative to capacity to contract, principal and agent, estoppel, fraud, misrepresentation, duress, coercion, mistake, bankruptcy, and other validating or invalidating cause supplement its provisions.

§ 1–104. Construction Against Implied Repeal.
[The Uniform Commercial Code] being a general act intended as a unified coverage of its subject matter, no part of it shall be deemed to be impliedly repealed by subsequent legislation if such construction can reasonably be avoided.

§ 1–105. Severability.
If any provision or clause of [the Uniform Commercial Code] or its application to any person or circumstance is held invalid, the invalidity does not affect other provisions or applications of [the Uniform Commercial Code] which can be given effect without the invalid provision or application, and to this end the provisions of [the Uniform Commercial Code] are severable.

§ 1–106. Use of Singular and Plural; Gender.
In [the Uniform Commercial Code], unless the statutory context otherwise requires:
(1) words in the singular number include the plural, and those in the plural include the singular; and
(2) words of any gender also refer to any other gender.

§ 1–107. Section Captions.
Section captions are part of [the Uniform Commercial Code].

§ 1–108. Relation to Electronic Signatures in Global and National Commerce Act.
This article modifies, limits, and supersedes the federal Electronic Signatures in Global and National Commerce Act, 15 U.S.C. Section 7001 et seq., except that nothing in this article modifies, limits, or supersedes Section 7001(c) of that Act or authorizes electronic delivery of any of the notices described in Section 7003(b) of that Act.

Part 2—General Definitions and Principles of Interpretation
§ 1–201. General Definitions.
(a) Unless the context otherwise requires, words or phrases defined in this section, or in the additional definitions contained in other articles of [the Uniform Commercial Code] that apply to particular articles or parts thereof, have the meanings stated.
(b) Subject to definitions contained in other articles of [the Uniform Commercial Code] that apply to particular articles or parts thereof:
　(1) "Action", in the sense of a judicial proceeding, includes recoupment, counterclaim, set-off, suit in equity, and any other proceeding in which rights are determined.
　(2) "Aggrieved party" means a party entitled to pursue a remedy.
　(3) "Agreement", as distinguished from "contract", means the bargain of the parties in fact, as found in their language or inferred from other circumstances, including course of performance, course of dealing, or usage of trade as provided in Section 1-303.
　(4) "Bank" means a person engaged in the business of banking and includes a savings bank, savings and loan association, credit union, and trust company.
　(5) "Bearer" means a person in possession of a negotiable instrument, document of title, or certificated security that is payable to bearer or indorsed in blank.

*Copyright © 2007 by The American Law Institutue and the National Conference of Commissioners on Uniform State Laws. Reproduced with the permission of the Permanent Editorial Board for the Uniform Commercial Code. All rights reserved.

(6) "Bill of lading" means a document evidencing the receipt of goods for shipment issued by a person engaged in the business of transporting or forwarding goods.

(7) "Branch" includes a separately incorporated foreign branch of a bank.

(8) "Burden of establishing" a fact means the burden of persuading the trier of fact that the existence of the fact is more probable than its nonexistence.

(9) "Buyer in ordinary course of business" means a person that buys goods in good faith, without knowledge that the sale violates the rights of another person in the goods, and in the ordinary course from a person, other than a pawnbroker, in the business of selling goods of that kind. A person buys goods in the ordinary course if the sale to the person comports with the usual or customary practices in the kind of business in which the seller is engaged or with the seller's own usual or customary practices. A person that sells oil, gas, or other minerals at the wellhead or minehead is a person in the business of selling goods of that kind. A buyer in ordinary course of business may buy for cash, by exchange of other property, or on secured or unsecured credit, and may acquire goods or documents of title under a preexisting contract for sale. Only a buyer that takes possession of the goods or has a right to recover the goods from the seller under Article 2 may be a buyer in ordinary course of business. "Buyer in ordinary course of business" does not include a person that acquires goods in a transfer in bulk or as security for or in total or partial satisfaction of a money debt.

(10) "Conspicuous", with reference to a term, means so written, displayed, or presented that a reasonable person against which it is to operate ought to have noticed it. Whether a term is "conspicuous" or not is a decision for the court. Conspicuous terms include the following:

(A) a heading in capitals equal to or greater in size than the surrounding text, or in contrasting type, font, or color to the surrounding text of the same or lesser size; and

(B) language in the body of a record or display in larger type than the surrounding text, or in contrasting type, font, or color to the surrounding text of the same size, or set off from surrounding text of the same size by symbols or other marks that call attention to the language.

(11) "Consumer" means an individual who enters into a transaction primarily for personal, family, or household purposes.

(12) "Contract", as distinguished from "agreement", means the total legal obligation that results from the parties' agreement as determined by [the Uniform Commercial Code] as supplemented by any other applicable laws.

(13) "Creditor" includes a general creditor, a secured creditor, a lien creditor, and any representative of creditors, including an assignee for the benefit of creditors, a trustee in bankruptcy, a receiver in equity, and an executor or administrator of an insolvent debtor's or assignor's estate.

(14) "Defendant" includes a person in the position of defendant in a counterclaim, cross-claim, or third-party claim.

(15) "Delivery", with respect to an instrument, document of title, or chattel paper, means voluntary transfer of possession.

(16) "Document of title" includes bill of lading, dock warrant, dock receipt, warehouse receipt or order for the delivery of goods, and also any other document which in the regular course of business or financing is treated as adequately evidencing that the person in possession of it is entitled to receive, hold, and dispose of the document and the goods it covers. To be a document of title, a document must purport to be issued by or addressed to a bailee and purport to cover goods in the bailee's possession which are either identified or are fungible portions of an identified mass.

(17) "Fault" means a default, breach, or wrongful act or omission.

(18) "Fungible goods" means:

(A) goods of which any unit, by nature or usage of trade, is the equivalent of any other like unit; or

(B) goods that by agreement are treated as equivalent.

(19) "Genuine" means free of forgery or counterfeiting.

(20) "Good faith," except as otherwise provided in Article 5, means honesty in fact and the observance of reasonable commercial standards of fair dealing.

(21) "Holder" means:

(A) the person in possession of a negotiable instrument that is payable either to bearer or to an identified person that is the person in possession; or

(B) the person in possession of a document of title if the goods are deliverable either to bearer or to the order of the person in possession.

(22) "Insolvency proceeding" includes an assignment for the benefit of creditors or other proceeding intended to liquidate or rehabilitate the estate of the person involved.

(23) "Insolvent" means:

(A) having generally ceased to pay debts in the ordinary course of business other than as a result of bona fide dispute;

(B) being unable to pay debts as they become due; or

(C) being insolvent within the meaning of federal bankruptcy law.

(24) "Money" means a medium of exchange currently authorized or adopted by a domestic or foreign government. The term includes a monetary unit of account established by an intergovernmental organization or by agreement between two or more countries.

(25) "Organization" means a person other than an individual.

(26) "Party", as distinguished from "third party", means a person that has engaged in a transaction or made an agreement subject to [the Uniform Commercial Code].

(27) "Person" means an individual, corporation, business trust, estate, trust, partnership, limited liability company, association, joint venture, government, governmental subdivision, agency, or instrumentality, public corporation, or any other legal or commercial entity.

(28) "Present value" means the amount as of a date certain of one or more sums payable in the future, discounted to the date certain by use of either an interest rate specified by the parties if that rate is not manifestly unreasonable at the time the transaction is entered into or, if an interest rate is not so specified, a commercially reasonable rate that takes into account the facts and circumstances at the time the transaction is entered into.

(29) "Purchase" means taking by sale, lease, discount, negotiation, mortgage, pledge, lien, security interest, issue or reissue, gift, or any other voluntary transaction creating an interest in property.

(30) "Purchaser" means a person that takes by purchase.

(31) "Record" means information that is inscribed on a tangible medium or that is stored in an electronic or other medium and is retrievable in perceivable form.

(32) "Remedy" means any remedial right to which an aggrieved party is entitled with or without resort to a tribunal.

(33) "Representative" means a person empowered to act for another, including an agent, an officer of a corporation or association, and a trustee, executor, or administrator of an estate.

(34) "Right" includes remedy.

(35) "Security interest" means an interest in personal property or fixtures which secures payment or performance of an obligation. "Security interest" includes any interest of a consignor and a buyer of accounts, chattel paper, a payment intangible, or a promissory note in a transaction that is subject to Article 9. "Security interest" does not include the special property interest of a buyer of goods on identification of those goods to a contract for sale under Section 2-401, but a buyer may also acquire a "security interest" by complying with Article 9. Except as otherwise provided in Section 2-505, the right of a seller or lessor of goods under Article 2 or 2A to retain or acquire possession of the goods is not a "security interest", but a seller or lessor may also acquire a "security interest" by complying with Article 9. The retention or reservation of title by a seller of goods notwithstanding shipment or delivery to the buyer under Section 2-401 is limited in effect to a reservation of a "security interest." Whether a transaction in the form of a lease creates a "security interest" is determined pursuant to Section 1-203.

(36) "Send" in connection with a writing, record, or notice means:

(A) to deposit in the mail or deliver for transmission by any other usual means of communication with postage or cost of transmission provided for and properly addressed and, in the case of an instrument, to an address specified thereon or otherwise agreed, or if there be none to any address reasonable under the circumstances; or

(B)   in any other way to cause to be received any record or notice within the time it would have arrived if properly sent.

(37) "Signed" includes using any symbol executed or adopted with present intention to adopt or accept a writing.

(38) "State" means a State of the United States, the District of Columbia, Puerto Rico, the United States Virgin Islands, or any territory or insular possession subject to the jurisdiction of the United States.

(39) "Surety" includes a guarantor or other secondary obligor.

(40) "Term" means a portion of an agreement that relates to a particular matter.

(41) "Unauthorized signature" means a signature made without actual, implied, or apparent authority. The term includes a forgery.

(42) "Warehouse receipt" means a receipt issued by a person engaged in the business of storing goods for hire.

(43) "Writing" includes printing, typewriting, or any other intentional reduction to tangible form. "Written" has a corresponding meaning.

§ 1–202. Notice; Knowledge.

(a)   Subject to subsection (f), a person has "notice" of a fact if the person:

(1)   has actual knowledge of it;

(2)   has received a notice or notification of it; or

(3)   from all the facts and circumstances known to the person at the time in question, has reason to know that it exists.

(b)   "Knowledge" means actual knowledge. "Knows" has a corresponding meaning.

(c)   "Discover", "learn", or words of similar import refer to knowledge rather than to reason to know.

(d)   A person "notifies" or "gives" a notice or notification to another person by taking such steps as may be reasonably required to inform the other person in ordinary course, whether or not the other person actually comes to know of it.

(e)   Subject to subsection (f), a person "receives" a notice or notification when:

(1)   it comes to that person's attention; or

(2)   it is duly delivered in a form reasonable under the circumstances at the place of business through which the contract was made or at another location held out by that person as the place for receipt of such communications.

(f)   Notice, knowledge, or a notice or notification received by an organization is effective for a particular transaction from the time it is brought to the attention of the individual conducting that transaction and, in any event, from the time it would have been brought to the individual's attention if the organization had exercised due diligence. An organization exercises due diligence if it maintains reasonable routines for communicating significant information to the person conducting the transaction and there is reasonable compliance with the routines. Due diligence does not require an individual acting for the organization to communicate information unless the communication is part of the individual's regular duties or the individual has reason to know of the transaction and that the transaction would be materially affected by the information.

§ 1–203. Lease Distinguished from Security Interest.

(a)   Whether a transaction in the form of a lease creates a lease or security interest is determined by the facts of each case.

(b)   A transaction in the form of a lease creates a security interest if the consideration that the lessee is to pay the lessor for the right to possession and use of the goods is an obligation for the term of the lease and is not subject to termination by the lessee, and:

(1)   the original term of the lease is equal to or greater than the remaining economic life of the goods;

(2)   the lessee is bound to renew the lease for the remaining economic life of the goods or is bound to become the owner of the goods;

(3)   the lessee has an option to renew the lease for the remaining economic life of the goods for no additional consideration or for nominal additional consideration upon compliance with the lease agreement; or

(4)   the lessee has an option to become the owner of the goods for no additional consideration or for nominal additional consideration upon compliance with the lease agreement.

(c)   A transaction in the form of a lease does not create a security interest merely because:

(1)   the present value of the consideration the lessee is obligated to pay the lessor for the right to possession and use of the goods is substantially equal to or is greater than the fair market value of the goods at the time the lease is entered into;

(2)   the lessee assumes risk of loss of the goods;

(3)   the lessee agrees to pay, with respect to the goods, taxes, insurance, filing, recording, or registration fees, or service or maintenance costs;

(4)   the lessee has an option to renew the lease or to become the owner of the goods;

(5)   the lessee has an option to renew the lease for a fixed rent that is equal to or greater than the reasonably predictable fair market rent for the use of the goods for the term of the renewal at the time the option is to be performed; or

(6)   the lessee has an option to become the owner of the goods for a fixed price that is equal to or greater than the reasonably predictable fair market value of the goods at the time the option is to be performed.

(d)   Additional consideration is nominal if it is less than the lessee's reasonably predictable cost of performing under the lease agreement if the option is not exercised. Additional consideration is not nominal if:

(1)   when the option to renew the lease is granted to the lessee, the rent is stated to be the fair market rent for the use of the goods for the term of the renewal determined at the time the option is to be performed; or

(2)   when the option to become the owner of the goods is granted to the lessee, the price is stated to be the fair market value of the goods determined at the time the option is to be performed.

(e)   The "remaining economic life of the goods" and "reasonably predictable" fair market rent, fair market value, or cost of performing under the lease agreement must be determined with reference to the facts and circumstances at the time the transaction is entered into.

§ 1–204. Value.

Except as otherwise provided in Articles 3, 4, [and] 5, [and 6], a person gives value for rights if the person acquires them:

(1)   in return for a binding commitment to extend credit or for the extension of immediately available credit, whether or not drawn upon and whether or not a charge-back is provided for in the event of difficulties in collection;

(2)   as security for, or in total or partial satisfaction of, a preexisting claim;

(3)   by accepting delivery under a preexisting contract for purchase; or

(4)   in return for any consideration sufficient to support a simple contract.

§ 1–205. Reasonable Time; Seasonableness.

(a)   Whether a time for taking an action required by [the Uniform Commercial Code] is reasonable depends on the nature, purpose, and circumstances of the action.

(b)   An action is taken seasonably if it is taken at or within the time agreed or, if no time is agreed, at or within a reasonable time.

§ 1–206. Presumptions.

Whenever [the Uniform Commercial Code] creates a "presumption" with respect to a fact, or provides that a fact is "presumed," the trier of fact must find the existence of the fact unless and until evidence is introduced that supports a finding of its nonexistence.

Part 3—Territorial Applicability and General Rules
§ 1–301. Territorial Applicability; Parties' Power to Choose Applicable Law.

(a)   In this section:

(1)   "Domestic transaction" means a transaction other than an international transaction.

(2)   "International transaction" means a transaction that bears a reasonable relation to a country other than the United States.

(b) This section applies to a transaction to the extent that it is governed by another article of the [Uniform Commercial Code].

(c) Except as otherwise provided in this section:

(1) an agreement by parties to a domestic transaction that any or all of their rights and obligations are to be determined by the law of this State or of another State is effective, whether or not the transaction bears a relation to the State designated; and

(2) an agreement by parties to an international transaction that any or all of their rights and obligations are to be determined by the law of this State or of another State or country is effective, whether or not the transaction bears a relation to the State or country designated.

(d) In the absence of an agreement effective under subsection (c), and except as provided in subsections (e) and (g), the rights and obligations of the parties are determined by the law that would be selected by application of this State's conflict of laws principles.

(e) If one of the parties to a transaction is a consumer, the following rules apply:

(1) An agreement referred to in subsection (c) is not effective unless the transaction bears a reasonable relation to the State or country designated.

(2) Application of the law of the State or country determined pursuant to subsection (c) or (d) may not deprive the consumer of the protection of any rule of law governing a matter within the scope of this section, which both is protective of consumers and may not be varied by agreement:

(A) of the State or country in which the consumer principally resides, unless subparagraph (B) applies; or

(B) if the transaction is a sale of goods, of the State or country in which the consumer both makes the contract and takes delivery of those goods, if such State or country is not the State or country in which the consumer principally resides.

(f) An agreement otherwise effective under subsection (c) is not effective to the extent that application of the law of the State or country designated would be contrary to a fundamental policy of the State or country whose law would govern in the absence of agreement under subsection (d).

(g) To the extent that [the Uniform Commercial Code] governs a transaction, if one of the following provisions of [the Uniform Commercial Code] specifies the applicable law, that provision governs and a contrary agreement is effective only to the extent permitted by the law so specified:

(1) Section 2-402;

(2) Sections 2A-105 and 2A-106;

(3) Section 4-102;

(4) Section 4A-507;

(5) Section 5-116;

(6) Section 6-103;

(7) Section 8-110;

(8) Sections 9-301 through 9-307.

§ 1–302. Variation by Agreement.

(a) Except as otherwise provided in subsection (b) or elsewhere in [the Uniform Commercial Code], the effect of provisions of [the Uniform Commercial Code] may be varied by agreement.

(b) The obligations of good faith, diligence, reasonableness, and care prescribed by [the Uniform Commercial Code] may not be disclaimed by agreement. The parties, by agreement, may determine the standards by which the performance of those obligations is to be measured if those standards are not manifestly unreasonable. Whenever [the Uniform Commercial Code] requires an action to be taken within a reasonable time, a time that is not manifestly unreasonable may be fixed by agreement.

(c) The presence in certain provisions of [the Uniform Commercial Code] of the phrase "unless otherwise agreed", or words of similar import, does not imply that the effect of other provisions may not be varied by agreement under this section.

§ 1–303. Course of Performance, Course of Dealing, and Usage of Trade.

(a) A "course of performance" is a sequence of conduct between the parties to a particular transaction that exists if:

(1) the agreement of the parties with respect to the transaction involves repeated occasions for performance by a party; and

(2) the other party, with knowledge of the nature of the performance and opportunity for objection to it, accepts the performance or acquiesces in it without objection.

(b) A "course of dealing" is a sequence of conduct concerning previous transactions between the parties to a particular transaction that is fairly to be regarded as establishing a common basis of understanding for interpreting their expressions and other conduct.

(c) A "usage of trade" is any practice or method of dealing having such regularity of observance in a place, vocation, or trade as to justify an expectation that it will be observed with respect to the transaction in question. The existence and scope of such a usage must be proved as facts. If it is established that such a usage is embodied in a trade code or similar record, the interpretation of the record is a question of law.

(d) A course of performance or course of dealing between the parties or usage of trade in the vocation or trade in which they are engaged or of which they are or should be aware is relevant in ascertaining the meaning of the parties' agreement, may give particular meaning to specific terms of the agreement, and may supplement or qualify the terms of the agreement. A usage of trade applicable in the place in which part of the performance under the agreement is to occur may be so utilized as to that part of the performance.

(e) Except as otherwise provided in subsection (f), the express terms of an agreement and any applicable course of performance, course of dealing, or usage of trade must be construed whenever reasonable as consistent with each other. If such a construction is unreasonable:

(1) express terms prevail over course of performance, course of dealing, and usage of trade;

(2) course of performance prevails over course of dealing and usage of trade; and

(3) course of dealing prevails over usage of trade.

(f) Subject to Section 2-209, a course of performance is relevant to show a waiver or modification of any term inconsistent with the course of performance.

(g) Evidence of a relevant usage of trade offered by one party is not admissible unless that party has given the other party notice that the court finds sufficient to prevent unfair surprise to the other party.

§ 1–304. Obligation of Good Faith.

Every contract or duty within [the Uniform Commercial Code] imposes an obligation of good faith in its performance and enforcement.

§ 1–305. Remedies to Be Liberally Administered.

(a) The remedies provided by [the Uniform Commercial Code] must be liberally administered to the end that the aggrieved party may be put in as good a position as if the other party had fully performed but neither consequential or special damages nor penal damages may be had except as specifically provided in [the Uniform Commercial Code] or by other rule of law.

(b) Any right or obligation declared by [the Uniform Commercial Code] is enforceable by action unless the provision declaring it specifies a different and limited effect.

§ 1–306. Waiver or Renunciation of Claim or Right After Breach.

A claim or right arising out of an alleged breach may be discharged in whole or in part without consideration by agreement of the aggrieved party in an authenticated record.

§ 1–307. Prima Facie Evidence by Third-party Documents.

A document in due form purporting to be a bill of lading, policy or certificate of insurance, official weigher's or inspector's certificate, consular invoice, or any other document authorized or required by the contract to be issued by a third party is prima facie evidence of its own authenticity and genuineness and of the facts stated in the document by the third party.

§ 1–308. Performance or Acceptance Under Reservation of Rights.

(a) A party that with explicit reservation of rights performs or promises performance or assents to performance in a manner demanded or offered by the other party does not thereby prejudice the rights reserved. Such words as "without prejudice," "under protest," or the like are sufficient.

(b) Subsection (a) does not apply to an accord and satisfaction.

§ 1–309. Option to Accelerate at Will.

A term providing that one party or that party's successor in interest may accelerate payment or performance or require collateral or additional collateral "at will" or when the party "deems itself insecure," or words of similar import, means that the party has power to do so only if that party in good faith believes that the prospect of payment or performance is impaired. The burden of establishing lack of good faith is on the party against which the power has been exercised.

§ 1–310. Subordinated Obligations.

An obligation may be issued as subordinated to performance of another obligation of the person obligated, or a creditor may subordinate its right to performance of an obligation by agreement with either the person obligated or another creditor of the person obligated. Subordination does not create a security interest as against either the common debtor or a subordinated creditor.

ARTICLE 2: SALES
Part 1—Short Title, Construction and Subject Matter
§ 2–101. Short Title.

This Article shall be known and may be cited as Uniform Commercial Code—Sales.

§ 2–102. Scope; Certain Security and Other Transactions Excluded From This Article.

Unless the context otherwise requires, this Article applies to transactions in goods; it does not apply to any transaction which although in the form of an unconditional contract to sell or present sale is intended to operate only as a security transaction nor does this Article impair or repeal any statute regulating sales to consumers, farmers or other specified classes of buyers.

§ 2–103. Definitions and Index of Definitions.

(1) In this Article unless the context otherwise requires
    (a) "Buyer" means a person who buys or contracts to buy goods.
    (b) "Good faith" in the case of a merchant means honesty in fact and the observance of reasonable commercial standards of fair dealing in the trade.
    (c) "Receipt" of goods means taking physical possession of them.
    (d) "Seller" means a person who sells or contracts to sell goods.

(2) Other definitions applying to this Article or to specified Parts thereof, and the sections in which they appear are:
"Acceptance". Section 2–606.
"Banker's credit". Section 2–325.
"Between merchants". Section 2–104.
"Cancellation". Section 2–106(4).
"Commercial unit". Section 2–105.
"Confirmed credit". Section 2–325.
"Conforming to contract". Section 2–106.
"Contract for sale". Section 2–106.
"Cover". Section 2–712.
"Entrusting". Section 2–403.
"Financing agency". Section 2–104.
"Future goods". Section 2–105.
"Goods". Section 2–105.
"Identification". Section 2–501.
"Installment contract". Section 2–612.
"Letter of Credit". Section 2–325.
"Lot". Section 2–105.
"Merchant". Section 2–104.
"Overseas". Section 2–323.
"Person in position of seller". Section 2–707.
"Present sale". Section 2–106.
"Sale". Section 2–106.

"Sale on approval". Section 2–326.
"Sale or return". Section 2–326.
"Termination". Section 2–106.

(3) The following definitions in other Articles apply to this Article:
"Check". Section 3–104.
"Consignee". Section 7–102.
"Consignor". Section 7–102.
"Consumer goods". Section 9–109.
"Dishonor". Section 3–507.
"Draft". Section 3–104.

(4) In addition Article 1 contains general definitions and principles of construction and interpretation applicable throughout this Article.

§ 2–104. Definitions: "Merchant"; "Between Merchants"; "Financing Agency".

(1) "Merchant" means a person who deals in goods of the kind or otherwise by his occupation holds himself out as having knowledge or skill peculiar to the practices or goods involved in the transaction or to whom such knowledge or skill may be attributed by his employment of an agent or broker or other intermediary who by his occupation holds himself out as having such knowledge or skill.

(2) "Financing agency" means a bank, finance company or other person who in the ordinary course of business makes advances against goods or documents of title or who by arrangement with either the seller or the buyer intervenes in ordinary course to make or collect payment due or claimed under the contract for sale, as by purchasing or paying the seller's draft or making advances against it or by merely taking it for collection whether or not documents of title accompany the draft. "Financing agency" includes also a bank or other person who similarly intervenes between persons who are in the position of seller and buyer in respect to the goods (Section 2–707).

(3) "Between merchants" means in any transaction with respect to which both parties are chargeable with the knowledge or skill of merchants.

§ 2–105. Definitions: Transferability; "Goods"; "Future" Goods; "Lot"; "Commercial Unit".

(1) "Goods" means all things (including specially manufactured goods) which are movable at the time of identification to the contract for sale other than the money in which the price is to be paid, investment securities (Article 8) and things in action. "Goods" also includes the unborn young of animals and growing crops and other identified things attached to realty as described in the section on goods to be severed from realty (Section 2–107).

(2) Goods must be both existing and identified before any interest in them can pass. Goods which are not both existing and identified are "future" goods. A purported present sale of future goods or of any interest therein operates as a contract to sell.

(3) There may be a sale of a part interest in existing identified goods.

(4) An undivided share in an identified bulk of fungible goods is sufficiently identified to be sold although the quantity of the bulk is not determined. Any agreed proportion of such a bulk or any quantity thereof agreed upon by number, weight or other measure may to the extent of the seller's interest in the bulk be sold to the buyer who then becomes an owner in common.

(5) "Lot" means a parcel or a single article which is the subject matter of a separate sale or delivery, whether or not it is sufficient to perform the contract.

(6) "Commercial unit" means such a unit of goods as by commercial usage is a single whole for purposes of sale and division of which materially impairs its character or value on the market or in use. A commercial unit may be a single article (as a machine) or a set of articles (as a suite of furniture or an assortment of sizes) or a quantity (as a bale, gross, or carload) or any other unit treated in use or in the relevant market as a single whole.

§ 2–106. Definitions: "Contract"; "Agreement"; "Contract for Sale"; "Sale"; "Present Sale"; "Conforming" to Contract; "Termination"; "Cancellation".

(1) In this Article unless the context otherwise requires "contract" and "agreement" are limited to those relating to the present or future sale of goods. "Contract for sale" includes both a present sale of goods and a contract to sell goods at a future time. A "sale" consists in the passing of title from the seller to the buyer for a price (Section 2–401). A "present sale" means a sale which is accomplished by the making of the contract.

(2) Goods or conduct including any part of a performance are "conforming" or conform to the contract when they are in accordance with the obligations under the contract.

(3) "Termination" occurs when either party pursuant to a power created by agreement or law puts an end to the contract otherwise than for its breach. On "termination" all obligations which are still executory on both sides are discharged but any right based on prior breach or performance survives.

(4) "Cancellation" occurs when either party puts an end to the contract for breach by the other and its effect is the same as that of "termination" except that the cancelling party also retains any remedy for breach of the whole contract or any unperformed balance.

§ 2–107. Goods to Be Severed From Realty: Recording.

(1) A contract for the sale of minerals or the like (including oil and gas) or a structure or its materials to be removed from realty is a contract for the sale of goods within this Article if they are to be severed by the seller but until severance a purported present sale thereof which is not effective as a transfer of an interest in land is effective only as a contract to sell.

(2) A contract for the sale apart from the land of growing crops or other things attached to realty and capable of severance without material harm thereto but not described in subsection (1) or of timber to be cut is a contract for the sale of goods within this Article whether the subject matter is to be severed by the buyer or by the seller even though it forms part of the realty at the time of contracting, and the parties can by identification effect a present sale before severance.

(3) The provisions of this section are subject to any third party rights provided by the law relating to realty records, and the contract for sale may be executed and recorded as a document transferring an interest in land and shall then constitute notice to third parties of the buyer's rights under the contract for sale.

Part 2—Form, Formation and Readjustment of Contract
§ 2–201. Formal Requirements; Statute of Frauds.

(1) Except as otherwise provided in this section a contract for the sale of goods for the price of $500 or more is not enforceable by way of action or defense unless there is some writing sufficient to indicate that a contract for sale has been made between the parties and signed by the party against whom enforcement is sought or by his authorized agent or broker. A writing is not insufficient because it omits or incorrectly states a term agreed upon but the contract is not enforceable under this paragraph beyond the quantity of goods shown in such writing.

(2) Between merchants if within a reasonable time a writing in confirmation of the contract and sufficient against the sender is received and the party receiving it has reason to know its contents, it satisfies the requirements of subsection (1) against such party unless written notice of objection to its contents is given within ten days after it is received.

(3) A contract which does not satisfy the requirements of subsection (1) but which is valid in other respects is enforceable

    (a) if the goods are to be specially manufactured for the buyer and are not suitable for sale to others in the ordinary course of the seller's business and the seller, before notice of repudiation is received and under circumstances which reasonably indicate that the goods are for the buyer, has made either a substantial beginning of their manufacture or commitments for their procurement; or

    (b) if the party against whom enforcement is sought admits in his pleading, testimony or otherwise in court that a contract for sale was made, but the contract is not enforceable under this provision beyond the quantity of goods admitted; or

    (c) with respect to goods for which payment has been made and accepted or which have been received and accepted (Sec. 2–606).

§ 2–202. Final Written Expression: Parol or Extrinsic Evidence.

Terms with respect to which the confirmatory memoranda of the parties agree or which are otherwise set forth in a writing intended by the parties as a final expression of their agreement with respect to such terms as are included therein may not be contradicted by evidence of any prior agreement or of a contemporaneous oral agreement but may be explained or supplemented

    (a) by course of dealing or usage of trade (Section 1–205) or by course of performance (Section 2–208); and

    (b) by evidence of consistent additional terms unless the court finds the writing to have been intended also as a complete and exclusive statement of the terms of the agreement.

§ 2–203. Seals Inoperative.

The affixing of a seal to a writing evidencing a contract for sale or an offer to buy or sell goods does not constitute the writing a sealed instrument and the law with respect to sealed instruments does not apply to such a contract or offer.

§ 2–204. Formation in General.

(1) A contract for sale of goods may be made in any manner sufficient to show agreement, including conduct by both parties which recognizes the existence of such a contract.

(2) An agreement sufficient to constitute a contract for sale may be found even though the moment of its making is undetermined.

(3) Even though one or more terms are left open a contract for sale does not fail for indefiniteness if the parties have intended to make a contract and there is a reasonably certain basis for giving an appropriate remedy.

§ 2–205. Firm Offers.

An offer by a merchant to buy or sell goods in a signed writing which by its terms gives assurance that it will be held open is not revocable, for lack of consideration, during the time stated or if no time is stated for reasonable time, but in no event may such period of irrevocability exceed three months; but any such term of assurance on a form supplied by the offeree must be separately signed by the offeror.

§ 2–206. Offer and Acceptance in Formation of Contract.

(1) Unless other unambiguously indicated by the language or circumstances

    (a) an offer to make a contract shall be construed as inviting acceptance in any manner and by any medium reasonable in the circumstances;

    (b) an order or other offer to buy goods for prompt or current shipment shall be construed as inviting acceptance either by a prompt promise to ship or by the prompt or current shipment of conforming or non-conforming goods, but such a shipment of non-conforming goods does not constitute an acceptance if the seller seasonably notifies the buyer that the shipment is offered only as an accommodation to the buyer.

(2) Where the beginning of a requested performance is a reasonable mode of acceptance an offeror who is not notified of acceptance within a reasonable time may treat the offer as having lapsed before acceptance.

§ 2–207. Additional Terms in Acceptance or Confirmation.

(1) A definite and seasonable expression of acceptance or a written confirmation which is sent within a reasonable time operates as an acceptance even though it states terms additional to or different from those offered or agreed upon, unless acceptance is expressly made conditional on assent to the additional or different terms.

(2) The additional terms are to be construed as proposals for addition to the contract. Between merchants such terms become part of the contract unless:

    (a) the offer expressly limits acceptance to the terms of the offer;

    (b) they materially alter it; or

    (c) notification of objection to them has already been given or is given within a reasonable time after notice of them is received.

(3) Conduct by both parties which recognizes the existence of a contract is sufficient to establish a contract for sale although the writings of the parties do not otherwise establish a contract. In such case the terms of the particular contract consist of those terms on which the writings of the parties agree, together with any supplementary terms incorporated under any other provisions of this Act.

§ 2–208. Course of Performance or Practical Construction.

(1) Where the contract for sale involves repeated occasions for performance by either party with knowledge of the nature of the performance and opportunity for objection to it by the other, any course of performance accepted or acquiesced in without objection shall be relevant to determine the meaning of the agreement.

(2) The express terms of the agreement and any such course of performance, as well as any course of dealing and usage of trade, shall be construed whenever reasonable as consistent with each other; but when such construction is unreasonable, express terms shall control course of performance and course of performance shall control both course of dealing and usage of trade (Section 1–205).

(3) Subject to the provisions of the next section on modification and waiver, such course of performance shall be relevant to show a waiver or modification of any term inconsistent with such course of performance.

§ 2–209. Modification, Rescission and Waiver.

(1) An agreement modifying a contract within this Article needs no consideration to be binding.

(2) A signed agreement which excludes modification or rescission except by a signed writing cannot be otherwise modified or rescinded, but except as between merchants such a requirement on a form supplied by the merchant must be separately signed by the other party.

(3) The requirements of the statute of frauds section of this Article (Section 2–201) must be satisfied if the contract as modified is within its provisions.

(4) Although an attempt at modification or rescission does not satisfy the requirements of subsection (2) or (3) it can operate as a waiver.

(5) A party who has made a waiver affecting an executory portion of the contract may retract the waiver by reasonable notification received by the other party that strict performance will be required of any term waived, unless the retraction would be unjust in view of a material change of position in reliance on the waiver.

§ 2–210. Delegation of Performance; Assignment of Rights.

(1) A party may perform his duty through a delegate unless otherwise agreed or unless the other party has a substantial interest in having his original promisor perform or control the acts required by the contract. No delegation of performance relieves the party delegating of any duty to perform or any liability for breach.

(2) Unless otherwise agreed all rights of either seller or buyer can be assigned except where the assignment would materially change the duty of the other party, or increase materially the burden or risk imposed on him by his contract, or impair materially his chance of obtaining return performance. A right to damages for breach of the whole contract or a right arising out of the assignor's due performance of his entire obligation can be assigned despite agreement otherwise.

(3) Unless the circumstances indicate the contrary a prohibition of assignment of "the contract" is to be construed as barring only the delegation to the assignee of the assignor's performance.

(4) An assignment of "the contract" or of "all my rights under the contract" or an assignment in similar general terms is an assignment of rights and unless the language or the circumstances (as in an assignment for security) indicate the contrary, it is a delegation of performance of the duties of the assignor and its acceptance by the assignee constitutes a promise by him to perform those duties. This promise is enforceable by either the assignor or the other party to the original contract.

(5) The other party may treat any assignment which delegates performance as creating reasonable grounds for insecurity and may without prejudice to his rights against the assignor demand assurances from the assignee (Section 2–609).

Part 3—General Obligation and Construction of Contract
§ 2–301. General Obligations of Parties.

The obligation of the seller is to transfer and deliver and that of the buyer is to accept and pay in accordance with the contract.

§ 2–302. Unconscionable Contract or Clause.

(1) If the court as a matter of law finds the contract or any clause of the contract to have been unconscionable at the time it was made the court may refuse to enforce the contract, or it may enforce the remainder of the contract without the unconscionable clause, or it may so limit the application of any unconscionable clause as to avoid any unconscionable result.

(2) When it is claimed or appears to the court that the contract or any clause thereof may be unconscionable the parties shall be afforded a reasonable opportunity to present evidence as to its commercial setting, purpose and effect to aid the court in making the determination.

§ 2–303. Allocation or Division of Risks.

Where this Article allocates a risk or a burden as between the parties "unless otherwise agreed", the agreement may not only shift the allocation, but may also divide the risk or burden.

§ 2–304. Price Payable in Money, Goods, Realty, or Otherwise.

(1) The price can be made payable in money or otherwise. If it is payable in whole or in part in goods each party is a seller of the goods which he is to transfer.

(2) Even though all or part of the price is payable in an interest in realty the transfer of the goods and the seller's obligations with reference to them are subject to this Article, but not the transfer of the interest in realty or the transferor's obligations in connection therewith.

§ 2–305. Open Price Term.

(1) The parties if they so intend can conclude a contract for sale even though the price is not settled. In such a case the price is a reasonable price at the time for delivery if

  (a) nothing is said as to price; or

  (b) the price is left to be agreed by the parties and they fail to agree; or

  (c) the price is to be fixed in terms of some agreed market or other standard as set or recorded by a third person or agency and it is not so set or recorded.

(2) A price to be fixed by the seller or by the buyer means a price for him to fix in good faith.

(3) When a price left to be fixed otherwise than by agreement of the parties fails to be fixed through fault of one party the other may at his option treat the contract as cancelled or himself fix a reasonable price.

(4) Where, however, the parties intend not to be bound unless the price be fixed or agreed and it is not fixed or agreed there is no contract. In such a case the buyer must return any goods already received or if unable so to do must pay their reasonable value at the time of delivery and the seller must return any portion of the price paid on account.

§ 2–306. Output, Requirements and Exclusive Dealings.

(1) A term which measures the quantity by the output of the seller or the requirements of the buyer means such actual output or requirements as may occur in good faith, except that no quantity unreasonably disproportionate to any stated estimate or in the absence of a stated estimate to any normal or otherwise comparable prior output or requirements may be tendered or demanded.

(2) A lawful agreement by either the seller or the buyer for exclusive dealing in the kind of goods concerned imposes unless otherwise agreed an obligation by the seller to use best efforts to supply the goods and by the buyer to use best efforts to promote their sale.

§ 2–307. Delivery in Single Lot or Several Lots.

Unless otherwise agreed all goods called for by a contract for sale must be tendered in a single delivery and payment is due only on such tender but where the circumstances give either party the right to make or demand delivery in lots the price if it can be apportioned may be demanded for each lot.

§ 2–308. Absence of Specified Place for Delivery.

Unless otherwise agreed

  (a) the place for delivery of goods is the seller's place of business or if he has none his residence; but

  (b) in a contract for sale of identified goods which to the knowledge of the parties at the time of contracting are in some other place, that place is the place for their delivery; and

  (c) documents of title may be delivered through customary banking channels.

§ 2–309. Absence of Specific Time Provisions; Notice of Termination.

(1) The time for shipment or delivery or any other action under a contract if not provided in this Article or agreed upon shall be a reasonable time.

(2) Where the contract provides for successive performances but is indefinite in duration it is valid for a reasonable time but unless otherwise agreed may be terminated at any time by either party.

(3) Termination of a contract by one party except on the happening of an agreed event requires that reasonable notification be received by the other party and an agreement dispensing with notification is invalid if its operation would be unconscionable.

§ 2–310. Open Time for Payment or Running of Credit; Authority to Ship Under Reservation.

Unless otherwise agreed

(a) payment is due at the time and place at which the buyer is to receive the goods even though the place of shipment is the place of delivery; and

(b) if the seller is authorized to send the goods he may ship them under reservation, and may tender the documents of title, but the buyer may inspect the goods after their arrival before payment is due unless such inspection is inconsistent with the terms of the contract (Section 2–513); and

(c) if delivery is authorized and made by way of documents of title otherwise than by subsection (b) then payment is due at the time and place at which the buyer is to receive the documents regardless of where the goods are to be received; and

(d) where the seller is required or authorized to ship the goods on credit the credit period runs from the time of shipment but post-dating the invoice or delaying its dispatch will correspondingly delay the starting of the credit period.

§ 2–311. Options and Cooperation Respecting Performance.

(1) An agreement for sale which is otherwise sufficiently definite (subsection (3) of Section 2–204) to be a contract is not made invalid by the fact that it leaves particulars of performance to be specified by one of the parties. Any such specification must be made in good faith and within limits set by commercial reasonableness.

(2) Unless otherwise agreed specifications relating to assortment of the goods are at the buyer's option and except as otherwise provided in subsections (1)(c) and (3) of Section 2–319 specifications or arrangements relating to shipment are at the seller's option.

(3) Where such specification would materially affect the other party's performance but is not seasonably made or where one party's cooperation is necessary to the agreed performance of the other but is not seasonably forthcoming, the other party in addition to all other remedies

    (a) is excused for any resulting delay in his own performance; and

    (b) may also either proceed to perform in any reasonable manner or after the time for a material part of his own performance treat the failure to specify or to cooperate as a breach by failure to deliver or accept the goods.

§ 2–312. Warranty of Title and Against Infringement; Buyer's Obligation Against Infringement.

(1) Subject to subsection (2) there is in a contract for sale a warranty by the seller that

    (a) the title conveyed shall be good, and its transfer rightful; and

    (b) the goods shall be delivered free from any security interest or other lien or encumbrance of which the buyer at the time of contracting has no knowledge.

(2) A warranty under subsection (1) will be excluded or modified only by specific language or by circumstances which give the buyer reason to know that the person selling does not claim title in himself or that he is purporting to sell only such right or title as he or a third person may have.

(3) Unless otherwise agreed a seller who is a merchant regularly dealing in goods of the kind warrants that the goods shall be delivered free of the rightful claim of any third person by way of infringement or the like but a buyer who furnishes specifications to the seller must hold the seller harmless against any such claim which arises out of compliance with the specifications.

§ 2–313. Express Warranties by Affirmation, Promise, Description, Sample.

(1) Express warranties by the seller are created as follows:

    (a) Any affirmation of fact or promise made by the seller to the buyer which relates to the goods and becomes part of the basis of the bargain creates an express warranty that the goods shall conform to the affirmation or promise.

    (b) Any description of the goods which is made part of the basis of the bargain creates an express warranty that the goods shall conform to the description.

    (c) Any sample or model which is made part of the basis of the bargain creates an express warranty that the whole of the goods shall conform to the sample or model.

(2) It is not necessary to the creation of an express warranty that the seller use formal words such as "warrant" or "guarantee" or that he have a specific intention to make a warranty, but an affirmation merely of the value of the goods or a statement purporting to be merely the seller's opinion or commendation of the goods does not create a warranty.

§ 2–314. Implied Warranty: Merchantability; Usage of Trade.

(1) Unless excluded or modified (Section 2–316), a warranty that the goods shall be merchantable is implied in a contract for their sale if the seller is a merchant with respect to goods of that kind. Under this section the serving for value of food or drink to be consumed either on the premises or elsewhere is a sale.

(2) Goods to be merchantable must be at least such as

    (a) pass without objection in the trade under the contract description; and

    (b) in the case of fungible goods, are of fair average quality within the description; and

    (c) are fit for the ordinary purpose for which such goods are used; and

    (d) run, within the variations permitted by the agreement, of even kind, quality and quantity within each unit and among all units involved; and

    (e) are adequately contained, packaged, and labeled as the agreement may require; and

    (f) conform to the promises or affirmations of fact made on the container or label if any.

(3) Unless excluded or modified (Section 2–316) other implied warranties may arise from course of dealing or usage of trade.

§ 2–315. Implied Warranty: Fitness for Particular Purpose.

Where the seller at the time of contracting has reason to know any particular purpose for which the goods are required and that the buyer is relying on the seller's skill or judgment to select or furnish suitable goods, there is unless excluded or modified under the next section an implied warranty that the goods shall be fit for such purpose.

§ 2–316. Exclusion or Modification of Warranties.

(1) Words or conduct relevant to the creation of an express warranty and words or conduct tending to negate or limit warranty shall be construed wherever reasonable as consistent with each other, but subject to the provisions of this Article on parol or extrinsic evidence (Section 2–202) negation or limitation is inoperative to the extent that such construction is unreasonable.

(2) Subject to subsection (3), to exclude or modify the implied warranty of merchantability or any part of it the language must mention merchantability and in case of a writing must be conspicuous, and to exclude or modify any implied warranty of fitness the exclusion must be by a writing and conspicuous. Language to exclude all implied warranties of fitness is sufficient if it states, for example, that "There are no warranties which extend beyond the description on the face hereof."

(3) Notwithstanding subsection (2)

    (a) unless the circumstances indicate otherwise, all implied warranties are excluded by expressions like "as is", "with all faults" or other language which in common understanding calls the buyer's attention to the exclusion of warranties and makes plain that there is no implied warranty; and

(b) when the buyer before entering into the contract has examined the goods or the sample or model as fully as he desired or has refused to examine the goods there is no implied warranty with regard to defects which an examination ought in the circumstances to have revealed to him; and

(c) an implied warranty can also be excluded or modified by course of dealing or course of performance or usage of trade.

(4) Remedies for breach of warranty can be limited in accordance with the provisions of this Article on liquidation or limitation of damages and on contractual modification of remedy (Sections 2–718 and 2–719).

§ 2–317. Cumulation and Conflict of Warranties Express or Implied.

Warranties whether express or implied shall be construed as consistent with each other and as cumulative, but if such construction is unreasonable the intention of the parties shall determine which warranty is dominant. In ascertaining that intention the following rules apply:

(a) Exact or technical specifications displace an inconsistent sample or model or general language of description.

(b) A sample from an existing bulk displaces inconsistent general language of description.

(c) Express warranties displace inconsistent implied warranties other than an implied warranty of fitness for a particular purpose.

§ 2–318. Third Party Beneficiaries of Warranties Express or Implied.

Note: *If this Act is introduced in the Congress of the United States this section should be omitted. (States to select one alternative.)*

Alternative A A seller's warranty whether express or implied extends to any natural person who is in the family or household of his buyer or who is a guest in his home if it is reasonable to expect that such person may use, consume or be affected by the goods and who is injured in person by breach of the warranty. A seller may not exclude or limit the operation of this section.

Alternative B A seller's warranty whether express or implied extends to any natural person who may reasonably be expected to use, consume or be affected by the goods and who is injured in person by breach of the warranty. A seller may not exclude or limit the operation of this section.

Alternative C A seller's warranty whether express or implied extends to any person who may reasonably be expected to use, consume or be affected by the goods and who is injured by breach of the warranty. A seller may not exclude or limit the operation of this section with respect to injury to the person of an individual to whom the warranty extends.

§ 2–319. F.O.B. and F.A.S. Terms.

(1) Unless otherwise agreed the term F.O.B. (which means "free on board") at a named place, even though used only in connection with the stated price, is a delivery term under which

(a) when the term is F.O.B. the place of shipment, the seller must at that place ship the goods in the manner provided in this Article (Section 2–504) and bear the expense and risk of putting them into the possession of the carrier; or

(b) when the term is F.O.B. the place of destination, the seller must at his own expense and risk transport the goods to that place and there tender delivery of them in the manner provided in this Article (Section 2–503);

(c) when under either (a) or (b) the term is also F.O.B. vessel, car or other vehicle, the seller must in addition at his own expense and risk load the goods on board. If the term is F.O.B. vessel the buyer must name the vessel and in an appropriate case the seller must comply with the provisions of this Article on the form of bill of lading (Section 2–323).

(2) Unless otherwise agreed the term F.A.S. vessel (which means "free alongside") at a named port, even though used only in connection with the stated price, is a delivery term under which the seller must

(a) at his own expense and risk deliver the goods alongside the vessel in the manner usual in that port or on a dock designated and provided by the buyer; and

(b) obtain and tender a receipt for the goods in exchange for which the carrier is under a duty to issue a bill of lading.

(3) Unless otherwise agreed in any case falling within subsection (1) (a) or (c) or subsection (2) the buyer must seasonably give any needed instructions for making delivery, including when the term is F.A.S. or F.O.B. the loading berth of the vessel and in an appropriate case its name and sailing date. The seller may treat the failure of needed instructions as a failure of cooperation under this Article (Section 2–311). He may also at his option move the goods in any reasonable manner preparatory to delivery or shipment.

(4) Under the term F.O.B. vessel or F.A.S. unless otherwise agreed the buyer must make payment against tender of the required documents and the seller may not tender nor the buyer demand delivery of the goods in substitution for the documents.

§ 2–320. C.I.F. and C. & F. Terms.

(1) The term C.I.F. means that the price includes in a lump sum the cost of the goods and the insurance and freight to the named destination. The term C. & F. or C.F. means that the price so includes cost and freight to the named destination.

(2) Unless otherwise agreed and even though used only in connection with the stated price and destination, the term C.I.F. destination or its equivalent requires the seller at his own expense and risk to

(a) put the goods into the possession of a carrier at the port for shipment and obtain a negotiable bill or bills of lading covering the entire transportation to the named destination; and

(b) load the goods and obtain a receipt from the carrier (which may be contained in the bill of lading) showing that the freight has been paid or provided for; and

(c) obtain a policy or certificate of insurance, including any war risk insurance, of a kind and on terms then current at the port of shipment in the usual amount, in the currency of the contract, shown to cover the same goods covered by the bill of lading and providing for payment of loss to the order of the buyer or for the account of whom it may concern; but the seller may add to the price the amount of premium for any such war risk insurance; and

(d) prepare an invoice of the goods and procure any other documents required to effect shipment or to comply with the contract; and

(e) forward and tender with commercial promptness all the documents in due form and with any indorsement necessary to perfect the buyer's rights.

(3) Unless otherwise agreed the term C. & F. or its equivalent has the same effect and imposes upon the seller the same obligations and risks as a C.I.F. term except the obligation as to insurance.

(4) Under the term C.I.F. or C. & F. unless otherwise agreed the buyer must make payment against tender of the required documents and the seller may not tender nor the buyer demand delivery of the goods in substitution for the documents.

§ 2–321. C.I.F. or C. & F.: "Net Landed Weights"; "Payment on Arrival"; Warranty of Condition on Arrival.

Under a contract containing a term C.I.F. or C. & F.

(1) Where the price is based on or is to be adjusted according to "net landed weights", "delivered weights", "out turn" quantity or quality or the like, unless otherwise agreed the seller must reasonably estimate the price. The payment due on tender of the documents called for by the contract is the amount so estimated, but after final adjustment of the price a settlement must be made with commercial promptness.

(2) An agreement described in subsection (1) or any warranty of quality or condition of the goods on arrival places upon the seller the risk of ordinary deterioration, shrinkage and the like in transportation but has no effect on the place or time of identification to the contract for sale or delivery or on the passing of the risk of loss.

(3) Unless otherwise agreed where the contract provides for payment on or after arrival of the goods the seller must before payment allow such preliminary inspection as is feasible; but if the goods are lost delivery of the documents and payment are due when the goods should have arrived.

§ 2–322. Delivery "Ex-Ship".

(1) Unless otherwise agreed a term for delivery of goods "ex-ship" (which means from the carrying vessel) or in equivalent language is not restricted to a particular ship and requires delivery from a ship which has reached a place at the named port of destination where goods of the kind are usually discharged.

(2) Under such a term unless otherwise agreed

(a) the seller must discharge all liens arising out of the carriage and furnish the buyer with a direction which puts the carrier under a duty to deliver the goods; and

(b) the risk of loss does not pass to the buyer until the goods leave the ship's tackle or are otherwise properly unloaded.

§ 2–323. Form of Bill of Lading Required in Overseas Shipment; "Overseas".

(1) Where the contract contemplates overseas shipment and contains a term C.I.F. or C. & F. or F.O.B. vessel, the seller unless otherwise agreed must obtain a negotiable bill of lading stating that the goods have been loaded on board or, in the case of a term C.I.F. or C. & F., received for shipment.

(2) Where in a case within subsection (1) a bill of lading has been issued in a set of parts, unless otherwise agreed if the documents are not to be sent from abroad the buyer may demand tender of the full set; otherwise only one part of the bill of lading need be tendered. Even if the agreement expressly requires a full set

(a) due tender of a single part is acceptable within the provisions of this Article on cure of improper delivery (subsection (1) of Section 2–508); and

(b) even though the full set is demanded, if the documents are sent from abroad the person tendering an incomplete set may nevertheless require payment upon furnishing an indemnity which the buyer in good faith deems adequate.

(3) A shipment by water or by air or a contract contemplating such shipment is "overseas" insofar as by usage of trade or agreement it is subject to the commercial, financing or shipping practices characteristic of international deep water commerce.

§ 2–324. "No Arrival, No Sale" Term.

Under a term "no arrival, no sale" or terms of like meaning, unless otherwise agreed,

(a) the seller must properly ship conforming goods and if they arrive by any means he must tender them on arrival but he assumes no obligation that the goods will arrive unless he has caused the non-arrival; and

(b) where without fault of the seller the goods are in part lost or have so deteriorated as no longer to conform to the contract or arrive after the contract time, the buyer may proceed as if there had been casualty to identified goods (Section 2–613).

§ 2–325. "Letter of Credit" Term; "Confirmed Credit".

(1) Failure of the buyer seasonably to furnish an agreed letter of credit is a breach of the contract for sale.

(2) The delivery to seller of a proper letter of credit suspends the buyer's obligation to pay. If the letter of credit is dishonored, the seller may on seasonable notification to the buyer require payment directly from him.

(3) Unless otherwise agreed the term "letter of credit" or "banker's credit" in a contract for sale means an irrevocable credit issued by a financing agency of good repute and, where the shipment is overseas, of good international repute. The term "confirmed credit" means that the credit must also carry the direct obligation of such an agency which does business in the seller's financial market.

§ 2–326. Sale on Approval and Sale or Return; Consignment Sales and Rights of Creditors.

(1) Unless otherwise agreed, if delivered goods may be returned by the buyer even though they conform to the contract, the transaction is

(a) a "sale on approval" if the goods are delivered primarily for use, and

(b) a "sale or return" if the goods are delivered primarily for resale.

(2) Except as provided in subsection (3), goods held on approval are not subject to the claims of the buyer's creditors until acceptance; goods held on sale or return are subject to such claims while in the buyer's possession.

(3) Where goods are delivered to a person for sale and such person maintains a place of business at which he deals in goods of the kind involved, under a name other than the name of the person making delivery, then with respect to claims of creditors of the person conducting the business the goods are deemed to be on sale or return. The provisions of this subsection are applicable even though an agreement purports to reserve title to the person making delivery until payment or resale or uses such words as "on consignment" or "on memorandum". However, this subsection is not applicable if the person making delivery

(a) complies with an applicable law providing for a consignor's interest or the like to be evidenced by a sign, or

(b) establishes that the person conducting the business is generally known by his creditors to be substantially engaged in selling the goods of others, or

(c) complies with the filing provisions of the Article on Secured Transactions (Article 9).

(4) Any "or return" term of a contract for sale is to be treated as a separate contract for sale within the statute of frauds section of this Article (Section 2–201) and as contradicting the sale aspect of the contract within the provisions of this Article on parol or extrinsic evidence (Section 2–202).

§ 2–327. Special Incidents of Sale on Approval and Sale or Return.

(1) Under a sale on approval unless otherwise agreed

(a) although the goods are identified to the contract the risk of loss and the title do not pass to the buyer until acceptance; and

(b) use of the goods consistent with the purpose of trial is not acceptance but failure seasonably to notify the seller of election to return the goods is acceptance, and if the goods conform to the contract acceptance of any part is acceptance of the whole; and

(c) after due notification of election to return, the return is at the seller's risk and expense but a merchant buyer must follow any reasonable instructions.

(2) Under a sale or return unless otherwise agreed

(a) the option to return extends to the whole or any commercial unit of the goods while in substantially their original condition, but must be exercised seasonably; and

(b) the return is at the buyer's risk and expense.

§ 2–328. Sale by Auction.

(1) In a sale by auction if goods are put up in lots each lot is the subject of a separate sale.

(2) A sale by auction is complete when the auctioneer so announces by the fall of the hammer or in other customary manner. Where a bid is made while the hammer is falling in acceptance of a prior bid the auctioneer may in his discretion reopen the bidding or declare the goods sold under the bid on which the hammer was falling.

(3) Such a sale is with reserve unless the goods are in explicit terms put up without reserve. In an auction with reserve the auctioneer may withdraw the goods at any time until he announces completion of the sale. In an auction without reserve, after the auctioneer calls for bids on an article or lot, that article or lot cannot be withdrawn unless no bid is made within a reasonable time. In either case a bidder may retract his bid until the auctioneer's announcement of completion of the sale, but a bidder's retraction does not revive any previous bid.

(4) If the auctioneer knowingly receives a bid on the seller's behalf or the seller makes or procures such a bid, and notice has not been given that liberty for such bidding is reserved, the buyer may at his option avoid the sale or take the goods at the price of the last good faith bid prior to the completion of the sale. This subsection shall not apply to any bid at a forced sale.

Part 4—Title, Creditors and Good Faith Purchasers
§ 2–401. Passing of Title; Reservation for Security; Limited Application of This Section.

Each provision of this Article with regard to the rights, obligations and remedies of the seller, the buyer, purchasers or other third parties applies irrespective of title to the goods except where the provision refers to such title. Insofar as situations are not covered by the other provisions of this Article and matters concerning title became material the following rules apply:

(1) Title to goods cannot pass under a contract for sale prior to their identification to the contract (Section 2–501), and unless otherwise explicitly agreed the buyer acquires by their identification a special property as limited by this Act. Any retention or reservation by the seller of the title (property) in goods shipped or delivered to the buyer is limited in effect to a reservation of a security interest. Subject to these provisions and to the provisions of the Article on Secured Transactions (Article 9), title to goods passes from the seller to the buyer in any manner and on any conditions explicitly agreed on by the parties.

(2) Unless otherwise explicitly agreed title passes to the buyer at the time and place at which the seller completes his performance with reference to the physical delivery of the goods, despite any reservation of a security interest and even though a document of title is to be delivered at a different time or place; and in particular and despite any reservation of a security interest by the bill of lading

   (a) if the contract requires or authorizes the seller to send the goods to the buyer but does not require him to deliver them at destination, title passes to the buyer at the time and place of shipment; but

   (b) if the contract requires delivery at destination, title passes on tender there.

(3) Unless otherwise explicitly agreed where delivery is to be made without moving the goods,

   (a) if the seller is to deliver a document of title, title passes at the time when and the place where he delivers such documents; or

   (b) if the goods are at the time of contracting already identified and no documents are to be delivered, title passes at the time and place of contracting.

(4) A rejection or other refusal by the buyer to receive or retain the goods, whether or not justified, or a justified revocation of acceptance revests title to the goods in the seller. Such revesting occurs by operation of law and is not a "sale".

§ 2–402. Rights of Seller's Creditors Against Sold Goods.

(1) Except as provided in subsections (2) and (3), rights of unsecured creditors of the seller with respect to goods which have been identified to a contract for sale are subject to the buyer's rights to recover the goods under this Article (Sections 2–502 and 2–716).

(2) A creditor of the seller may treat a sale or an identification of goods to a contract for sale as void if as against him a retention of possession by the seller is fraudulent under any rule of law of the state where the goods are situated, except that retention of possession in good faith and current course of trade by a merchant-seller for a commercially reasonable time after a sale or identification is not fraudulent.

(3) Nothing in this Article shall be deemed to impair the rights of creditors of the seller

   (a) under the provisions of the Article on Secured Transactions (Article 9); or

   (b) where identification to the contract or delivery is made not in current course of trade but in satisfaction of or as security for a pre-existing claim for money, security or the like and is made under circumstances which under any rule of law of the state where the goods are situated would apart from this Article constitute the transaction a fraudulent transfer or voidable preference.

§ 2–403. Power to Transfer; Good Faith Purchase of Goods; "Entrusting".

(1) A purchaser of goods acquires all title which his transferor had or had power to transfer except that a purchaser of a limited interest acquires rights only to the extent of the interest purchased. A person with voidable title has power to transfer a good title to a good faith purchaser for value. When goods have been delivered under a transaction of purchase the purchaser has such power even though

   (a) the transferor was deceived as to the identity of the purchaser, or

   (b) the delivery was in exchange for a check which is later dishonored, or

   (c) it was agreed that the transaction was to be a "cash sale", or

   (d) the delivery was procured through fraud punishable as larcenous under the criminal law.

(2) Any entrusting of possession of goods to a merchant who deals in goods of that kind gives him power to transfer all rights of the entruster to a buyer in ordinary course of business.

(3) "Entrusting" includes any delivery and any acquiescence in retention of possession regardless of any condition expressed between the parties to the delivery or acquiescence and regardless of whether the procurement of the entrusting or the possessor's disposition of the goods have been such as to be larcenous under the criminal law.

(4) The rights of other purchasers of goods and of lien creditors are governed by the Articles on Secured Transactions (Article 9), Bulk Transfers (Article 6) and Documents of Title (Article 7).

Part 5—Performance

§ 2–501. Insurable Interest in Goods; Manner of Identification of Goods.

(1) The buyer obtains a special property and an insurable interest in goods by identification of existing goods as goods to which the contract refers even though the goods so identified are nonconforming and he has an option to return or reject them. Such identification can be made at any time and in any manner explicitly agreed to by the parties. In the absence of explicit agreement identification occurs

   (a) when the contract is made if it is for the sale of goods already existing and identified;

   (b) if the contract is for the sale of future goods other than those described in paragraph (c), when goods are shipped, marked or otherwise designated by the seller as goods to which the contract refers;

   (c) when the crops are planted or otherwise become growing crops or the young are conceived if the contract is for the sale of unborn young to be born within twelve months after contracting or for the sale of crops to be harvested within twelve months or the next normal harvest season after contracting whichever is longer.

(2) The seller retains an insurable interest in goods so long as title to or any security interest in the goods remains in him and where the identification is by the seller alone he may until default or insolvency or notification to the buyer that the identification is final substitute other goods for those identified.

(3) Nothing in this section impairs any insurable interest recognized under any other statute or rule of law.

§ 2–502. Buyer's Right to Goods on Seller's Insolvency.

(1) Subject to subsection (2) and even though the goods have not been shipped a buyer who has paid a part or all of the price of goods in which he has a special property under the provisions of the immediately preceding section may on making and keeping good a tender of any unpaid portion of their price recover them from the seller if the seller becomes insolvent within ten days after receipt of the first installment on their price.

(2) If the identification creating his special property has been made by the buyer he acquires the right to recover the goods only if they conform to the contract for sale.

§ 2–503. Manner of Seller's Tender of Delivery.

(1) Tender of delivery requires that the seller put and hold conforming goods at the buyer's disposition and give the buyer any notification reasonably necessary to enable him to take delivery. The manner, time and place for tender are determined by the agreement and this Article, and in particular

   (a) tender must be at a reasonable hour, and if it is of goods they must be kept available for the period reasonably necessary to enable the buyer to take possession; but

   (b) unless otherwise agreed the buyer must furnish facilities reasonably suited to the receipt of the goods.

(2) Where the case is within the next section respecting shipment tender requires that the seller comply with its provisions.

(3) Where the seller is required to deliver at a particular destination tender requires that he comply with subsection (1) and also in any appropriate case tender documents as described in subsections (4) and (5) of this section.

(4) Where goods are in the possession of a bailee and are to be delivered without being moved

    (a) tender requires that the seller either tender a negotiable document of title covering such goods or procure acknowledgment by the bailee of the buyer's right to possession of the goods; but

    (b) tender to the buyer of a non-negotiable document of title or of a written direction to the bailee to deliver is sufficient tender unless the buyer seasonably objects, and receipt by the bailee of notification of the buyer's rights fixes those rights as against the bailee and all third persons; but risk of loss of the goods and of any failure by the bailee to honor the non-negotiable document of title or to obey the direction remains on the seller until the buyer has had a reasonable time to present the document or direction, and a refusal by the bailee to honor the document or to obey the direction defeats the tender.

(5) Where the contract requires the seller to deliver documents

    (a) he must tender all such documents in correct form, except as provided in this Article with respect to bills of lading in a set (subsection (2) of Section 2–323); and

    (b) tender through customary banking channels is sufficient and dishonor of a draft accompanying the documents constitutes non-acceptance or rejection.

§ 2–504. Shipment by Seller.

Where the seller is required or authorized to send the goods to the buyer and the contract does not require him to deliver them at a particular destination, then unless otherwise agreed he must

(a) put the goods in the possession of such a carrier and make such a contract for their transportation as may be reasonable having regard to the nature of the goods and other circumstances of the case; and

(b) obtain and promptly deliver or tender in due form any document necessary to enable the buyer to obtain possession of the goods or otherwise required by the agreement or by usage of trade; and

(c) promptly notify the buyer of the shipment.

Failure to notify the buyer under paragraph (c) or to make a proper contract under paragraph (a) is a ground for rejection only if material delay or loss ensues.

§ 2–505. Seller's Shipment Under Reservation.

(1) Where the seller has identified goods to the contract by or before shipment:

    (a) his procurement of a negotiable bill of lading to his own order or otherwise reserves in him a security interest in the goods. His procurement of the bill to the order of a financing agency or of the buyer indicates in addition only the seller's expectation of transferring that interest to the person named.

    (b) a non-negotiable bill of lading to himself or his nominee reserves possession of the goods as security but except in a case of conditional delivery (subsection (2) of Section 2–507) a non-negotiable bill of lading naming the buyer as consignee reserves no security interest even though the seller retains possession of the bill of lading.

(2) When shipment by the seller with reservation of a security interest is in violation of the contract for sale it constitutes an improper contract for transportation within the preceding section but impairs neither the rights given to the buyer by shipment and identification of the goods to the contract nor the seller's powers as a holder of a negotiable document.

§ 2–506. Rights of Financing Agency.

(1) A financing agency by paying or purchasing for value a draft which relates to a shipment of goods acquires to the extent of the payment or purchase and in addition to its own rights under the draft and any document of title securing it any rights of the shipper in the goods including the right to stop delivery and the shipper's right to have the draft honored by the buyer.

(2) The right to reimbursement of a financing agency which has in good faith honored or purchased the draft under commitment to or authority from the buyer is not impaired by subsequent discovery of defects with reference to any relevant document which was apparently regular on its face.

§ 2–507. Effect of Seller's Tender; Delivery on Condition.

(1) Tender of delivery is a condition to the buyer's duty to accept the goods and, unless otherwise agreed, to his duty to pay for them. Tender entitles the seller to acceptance of the goods and to payment according to the contract.

(2) Where payment is due and demanded on the delivery to the buyer of goods or documents of title, his right as against the seller to retain or dispose of them is conditional upon his making the payment due.

§ 2–508. Cure by Seller of Improper Tender or Delivery; Replacement.

(1) Where any tender or delivery by the seller is rejected because non-conforming and the time for performance has not yet expired, the seller may seasonably notify the buyer of his intention to cure and may then within the contract time make a conforming delivery.

(2) Where the buyer rejects a non-conforming tender which the seller had reasonable grounds to believe would be acceptable with or without money allowance the seller may if he seasonably notifies the buyer have a further reasonable time to substitute a conforming tender.

§ 2–509. Risk of Loss in the Absence of Breach.

(1) Where the contract requires or authorizes the seller to ship the goods by carrier

    (a) if it does not require him to deliver them at a particular destination, the risk of loss passes to the buyer when the goods are duly delivered to the carrier even though the shipment is under reservation (Section 2–505); but

    (b) if it does require him to deliver them at a particular destination and the goods are there duly tendered while in the possession of the carrier, the risk of loss passes to the buyer when the goods are there duly so tendered as to enable the buyer to take delivery.

(2) Where the goods are held by a bailee to be delivered without being moved, the risk of loss passes to the buyer

    (a) on his receipt of a negotiable document of title covering the goods; or

    (b) on acknowledgment by the bailee of the buyer's right to possession of the goods; or

    (c) after his receipt of a non-negotiable document of title or other written direction to deliver, as provided in subsection (4)(b) of Section 2–503.

(3) In any case not within subsection (1) or (2), the risk of loss passes to the buyer on his receipt of the goods if the seller is a merchant; otherwise, the risk passes to the buyer on tender of delivery.

(4) The provisions of this section are subject to contrary agreement of the parties and to the provisions of this Article on sale on approval (Section 2–327) and on effect of breach on risk of loss (Section 2–510).

§ 2–510. Effect of Breach on Risk of Loss.

(1) Where a tender or delivery of goods so fails to conform to the contract as to give a right of rejection the risk of their loss remains on the seller until cure or acceptance.

(2) Where the buyer rightfully revokes acceptance he may to the extent of any deficiency in his effective insurance coverage treat the risk of loss as having rested on the seller from the beginning.

(3) Where the buyer as to conforming goods already identified to the contract for sale repudiates or is otherwise in breach before risk of their loss has passed to him, the seller may to the extent of any deficiency in his effective insurance coverage treat the risk of loss as resting on the buyer for a commercially reasonable time.

§ 2–511. Tender of Payment by Buyer; Payment by Check.

(1) Unless otherwise agreed tender of payment is a condition to the seller's duty to tender and complete any delivery.

(2) Tender of payment is sufficient when made by any means or in any manner current in the ordinary course of business unless the seller demands payment in legal tender and gives any extension of time reasonably necessary to procure it.

(3) Subject to the provisions of this Act on the effect of an instrument on an obligation (Section 3–802), payment by check is conditional and is defeated as between the parties by dishonor of the check on due presentment.

§ 2–512. Payment by Buyer Before Inspection.

(1) Where the contract requires payment before inspection non-conformity of the goods does not excuse the buyer from so making payment unless

(a) the non-conformity appears without inspection; or

(b) despite tender of the required documents the circumstances would justify injunction against honor under the provisions of this Act (Section 5–114).

(2) Payment pursuant to subsection (1) does not constitute an acceptance of goods or impair the buyer's right to inspect or any of his remedies.

§ 2–513. Buyer's Right to Inspection of Goods.

(1) Unless otherwise agreed and subject to subsection (3), where goods are tendered or delivered or identified to the contract for sale, the buyer has a right before payment or acceptance to inspect them at any reasonable place and time and in any reasonable manner. When the seller is required or authorized to send the goods to the buyer, the inspection may be after their arrival.

(2) Expenses of inspection must be borne by the buyer but may be recovered from the seller if the goods do not conform and are rejected.

(3) Unless otherwise agreed and subject to the provisions of this Article on C.I.F. contracts (subsection (3) of Section 2–321), the buyer is not entitled to inspect the goods before payment of the price when the contract provides

(a) for delivery "C.O.D." or on other like terms; or

(b) for payment against documents of title, except where such payment is due only after the goods are to become available for inspection.

(4) A place or method of inspection fixed by the parties is presumed to be exclusive but unless otherwise expressly agreed it does not postpone identification or shift the place for delivery or for passing the risk of loss. If compliance becomes impossible, inspection shall be as provided in this section unless the place or method fixed was clearly intended as an indispensable condition failure of which avoids the contract.

§ 2–514. When Documents Deliverable on Acceptance; When on Payment.

Unless otherwise agreed documents against which a draft is drawn are to be delivered to the drawee on acceptance of the draft if it is payable more than three days after presentment; otherwise, only on payment.

§ 2–515. Preserving Evidence of Goods in Dispute.

In furtherance of the adjustment of any claim or dispute

(a) either party on reasonable notification to the other and for the purpose of ascertaining the facts and preserving evidence has the right to inspect, test and sample the goods including such of them as may be in the possession or control of the other; and

(b) the parties may agree to a third party inspection or survey to determine the conformity or condition of the goods and may agree that the findings shall be binding upon them in any subsequent litigation or adjustment.

Part 6—Breach, Repudiation and Excuse
§ 2–601. Buyer's Rights on Improper Delivery.

Subject to the provisions of this Article on breach in installment contracts (Section 2–612) and unless otherwise agreed under the sections on contractual limitations of remedy (Sections 2–718 and 2–719), if the goods or the tender of delivery fail in any respect to conform to the contract, the buyer may

(a) reject the whole; or

(b) accept the whole; or

(c) accept any commercial unit or units and reject the rest.

§ 2–602. Manner and Effect of Rightful Rejection.

(1) Rejection of goods must be within a reasonable time after their delivery or tender. It is ineffective unless the buyer seasonably notifies the seller.

(2) Subject to the provisions of the two following sections on rejected goods (Sections 2–603 and 2–604),

(a) after rejection any exercise of ownership by the buyer with respect to any commercial unit is wrongful as against the seller; and

(b) if the buyer has before rejection taken physical possession of goods in which he does not have a security interest under the provisions of this Article (subsection (3) of Section 2–711), he is under a duty after rejection to hold them with reasonable care at the seller's disposition for a time sufficient to permit the seller to remove them; but

(c) the buyer has no further obligations with regard to goods rightfully rejected.

(3) The seller's rights with respect to goods wrongfully rejected are governed by the provisions of this Article on seller's remedies in general (Section 2–703).

§ 2–603. Merchant Buyer's Duties as to Rightfully Rejected Goods.

(1) Subject to any security interest in the buyer (subsection (3) of Section 2–711), when the seller has no agent or place of business at the market of rejection a merchant buyer is under a duty after rejection of goods in his possession or control to follow any reasonable instructions received from the seller with respect to the goods and in the absence of such instructions to make reasonable efforts to sell them for the seller's account if they are perishable or threaten to decline in value speedily. Instructions are not reasonable if on demand indemnity for expenses is not forthcoming.

(2) When the buyer sells goods under subsection (1), he is entitled to reimbursement from the seller or out of the proceeds for reasonable expenses of caring for and selling them, and if the expenses include no selling commission then to such commission as is usual in the trade or if there is none to a reasonable sum not exceeding ten per cent on the gross proceeds.

(3) In complying with this section the buyer is held only to good faith and good faith conduct hereunder is neither acceptance nor conversion nor the basis of an action for damages.

§ 2–604. Buyer's Options as to Salvage of Rightfully Rejected Goods.

Subject to the provisions of the immediately preceding section on perishables if the seller gives no instructions within a reasonable time after notification of rejection the buyer may store the rejected goods for the seller's account or reship them to him or resell them for the seller's account with reimbursement as provided in the preceding section. Such action is not acceptance or conversion.

§ 2–605. Waiver of Buyer's Objections by Failure to Particularize.

(1) The buyer's failure to state in connection with rejection a particular defect which is ascertainable by reasonable inspection precludes him from relying on the unstated defect to justify rejection or to establish breach

(a) where the seller could have cured it if stated seasonably; or

(b) between merchants when the seller has after rejection made a request in writing for a full and final written statement of all defects on which the buyer proposes to rely.

(2) Payment against documents made without reservation of rights precludes recovery of the payment for defects apparent on the face of the documents.

§ 2–606. What Constitutes Acceptance of Goods.

(1) Acceptance of goods occurs when the buyer

(a) after a reasonable opportunity to inspect the goods signifies to the seller that the goods are conforming or that he will take or retain them in spite of their nonconformity; or

(b) fails to make an effective rejection (subsection (1) of Section 2–602), but such acceptance does not occur until the buyer has had a reasonable opportunity to inspect them; or

(c) does any act inconsistent with the seller's ownership; but if such act is wrongful as against the seller it is an acceptance only if ratified by him.

(2) Acceptance of a part of any commercial unit is acceptance of that entire unit.

§ 2–607. Effect of Acceptance; Notice of Breach; Burden of Establishing Breach After Acceptance; Notice of Claim or Litigation to Person Answerable Over.

(1) The buyer must pay at the contract rate for any goods accepted.

(2) Acceptance of goods by the buyer precludes rejection of the goods accepted and if made with knowledge of a non-conformity cannot be revoked because of it unless the acceptance was on the reasonable assumption that the non-conformity would be seasonably cured but acceptance does not of itself impair any other remedy provided by this Article for non-conformity.

(3) Where a tender has been accepted

    (a) the buyer must within a reasonable time after he discovers or should have discovered any breach notify the seller of breach or be barred from any remedy; and

    (b) if the claim is one for infringement or the like (subsection (3) of Section 2–312) and the buyer is sued as a result of such a breach he must so notify the seller within a reasonable time after he receives notice of the litigation or be barred from any remedy over for liability established by the litigation.

(4) The burden is on the buyer to establish any breach with respect to the goods accepted.

(5) Where the buyer is sued for breach of a warranty or other obligation for which his seller is answerable over

    (a) he may give his seller written notice of the litigation. If the notice states that the seller may come in and defend and that if the seller does not do so he will be bound in any action against him by his buyer by any determination of fact common to the two litigations, then unless the seller after seasonable receipt of the notice does come in and defend he is so bound.

    (b) if the claim is one for infringement or the like (subsection (3) of Section 2–312) the original seller may demand in writing that his buyer turn over to him control of the litigation including settlement or else be barred from any remedy over and if he also agrees to bear all expense and to satisfy any adverse judgment, then unless the buyer after seasonable receipt of the demand does turn over control the buyer is so barred.

(6) The provisions of subsections (3), (4) and (5) apply to any obligation of a buyer to hold the seller harmless against infringement or the like (subsection (3) of Section 2–312).

§ 2–608. Revocation of Acceptance in Whole or in Part.

(1) The buyer may revoke his acceptance of a lot or commercial unit whose non-conformity substantially impairs its value to him if he has accepted it

    (a) on the reasonable assumption that its non-conformity would be cured and it has not been seasonably cured; or

    (b) without discovery of such non-conformity if his acceptance was reasonably induced either by the difficulty of discovery before acceptance or by the seller's assurances.

(2) Revocation of acceptance must occur within a reasonable time after the buyer discovers or should have discovered the ground for it and before any substantial change in condition of the goods which is not caused by their own defects. It is not effective until the buyer notifies the seller of it.

(3) A buyer who so revokes has the same rights and duties with regard to the goods involved as if he had rejected them.

§ 2–609. Right to Adequate Assurance of Performance.

(1) A contract for sale imposes an obligation on each party that the other's expectation of receiving due performance will not be impaired. When reasonable grounds for insecurity arise with respect to the performance of either party the other may in writing demand adequate assurance of due performance and until he receives such assurance may if commercially reasonable suspend any performance for which he has not already received the agreed return.

(2) Between merchants the reasonableness of grounds for insecurity and the adequacy of any assurance offered shall be determined according to commercial standards.

(3) Acceptance of any improper delivery or payment does not prejudice the aggrieved party's right to demand adequate assurance of future performance.

(4) After receipt of a justified demand failure to provide within a reasonable time not exceeding thirty days such assurance of due performance as is adequate under the circumstances of the particular case is a repudiation of the contract.

§ 2–610. Anticipatory Repudiation.

When either party repudiates the contract with respect to a performance not yet due the loss of which will substantially impair the value of the contract to the other, the aggrieved party may

(a) for a commercially reasonable time await performance by the repudiating party; or

(b) resort to any remedy for breach (Section 2–703 or Section 2–711), even though he has notified the repudiating party that he would await the latter's performance and has urged retraction; and

(c) in either case suspend his own performance or proceed in accordance with the provisions of this Article on the seller's right to identify goods to the contract notwithstanding breach or to salvage unfinished goods (Section 2–704).

§ 2–611. Retraction of Anticipatory Repudiation.

(1) Until the repudiating party's next performance is due he can retract his repudiation unless the aggrieved party has since the repudiation cancelled or materially changed his position or otherwise indicated that he considers the repudiation final.

(2) Retraction may be by any method which clearly indicates to the aggrieved party that the repudiating party intends to perform, but must include any assurance justifiably demanded under the provisions of this Article (Section 2–609).

(3) Retraction reinstates the repudiating party's rights under the contract with due excuse and allowance to the aggrieved party for any delay occasioned by the repudiation.

§ 2–612. "Installment Contract"; Breach.

(1) An "installment contract" is one which requires or authorizes the delivery of goods in separate lots to be separately accepted, even though the contract contains a clause "each delivery is a separate contract" or its equivalent.

(2) The buyer may reject any installment which is non-conforming if the non-conformity substantially impairs the value of that installment and cannot be cured or if the non-conformity is a defect in the required documents; but if the non-conformity does not fall within subsection (3) and the seller gives adequate assurance of its cure the buyer must accept that installment.

(3) Whenever non-conformity or default with respect to one or more installments substantially impairs the value of the whole contract there is a breach of the whole. But the aggrieved party reinstates the contract if he accepts a non-conforming installment without seasonably notifying of cancellation or if he brings an action with respect only to past installments or demands performance as to future installments.

§ 2–613. Casualty to Identified Goods.

Where the contract requires for its performance goods identified when the contract is made, and the goods suffer casualty without fault of either party before the risk of loss passes to the buyer, or in a proper case under a "no arrival, no sale" term (Section 2–324) then

(a) if the loss is total the contract is avoided; and

(b) if the loss is partial or the goods have so deteriorated as no longer to conform to the contract the buyer may nevertheless demand inspection and at his option either treat the contract as avoided or accept the goods with due allowance from the contract price for the deterioration or the deficiency in quantity but without further right against the seller.

§ 2–614. Substituted Performance.

(1) Where without fault of either party the agreed berthing, loading, or unloading facilities fail or an agreed type of carrier becomes unavailable or the agreed manner of delivery otherwise becomes commercially impracticable but a commercially reasonable substitute is available, such substitute performance must be tendered and accepted.

(2) If the agreed means or manner of payment fails because of domestic or foreign governmental regulation, the seller may withhold or stop delivery unless the buyer provides a means or manner of payment which is commercially a substantial equivalent. If delivery has already been taken, payment by the means or in the manner provided by the regulation discharges the buyer's obligation unless the regulation is discriminatory, oppressive or predatory.

§ 2–615. Excuse by Failure of Presupposed Conditions.

Except so far as a seller may have assumed a greater obligation and subject to the preceding section on substituted performance:

(a) Delay in delivery or non-delivery in whole or in part by a seller who complies with paragraphs (b) and (c) is not a breach of his duty under a contract for sale if performance as agreed has been made impracticable by the occurrence of a contingency the non-occurrence of which was a basic assumption on which the contract was made or by compliance in good faith with any applicable foreign or domestic governmental regulation or order whether or not it later proves to be invalid.

(b) Where the causes mentioned in paragraph (a) affect only a part of the seller's capacity to perform, he must allocate production and deliveries among his customers but may at his option include regular customers not then under contract as well as his own requirements for further manufacture. He may so allocate in any manner which is fair and reasonable.

(c) The seller must notify the buyer seasonably that there will be delay or non-delivery and, when allocation is required under paragraph (b), of the estimated quota thus made available for the buyer.

§ 2–616. Procedure on Notice Claiming Excuse.

(1) Where the buyer receives notification of a material or indefinite delay or an allocation justified under the preceding section he may by written notification to the seller as to any delivery concerned, and where the prospective deficiency substantially impairs the value of the whole contract under the provisions of this Article relating to breach of installment contracts (Section 2–612), then also as to the whole,

    (a) terminate and thereby discharge any unexecuted portion of the contract; or

    (b) modify the contract by agreeing to take his available quota in substitution.

(2) If after receipt of such notification from the seller the buyer fails so to modify the contract within a reasonable time not exceeding thirty days the contract lapses with respect to any deliveries affected.

(3) The provisions of this section may not be negated by agreement except in so far as the seller has assumed a greater obligation under the preceding section.

Part 7—Remedies

§ 2–701. Remedies for Breach of Collateral Contracts Not Impaired.

Remedies for breach of any obligation or promise collateral or ancillary to a contract for sale are not impaired by the provisions of this Article.

§ 2–702. Seller's Remedies on Discovery of Buyer's Insolvency.

(1) Where the seller discovers the buyer to be insolvent he may refuse delivery except for cash including payment for all goods theretofore delivered under the contract, and stop delivery under this Article (Section 2–705).

(2) Where the seller discovers that the buyer has received goods on credit while insolvent he may reclaim the goods upon demand made within ten days after the receipt, but if misrepresentation of solvency has been made to the particular seller in writing within three months before delivery the ten day limitation does not apply. Except as provided in this subsection the seller may not base a right to reclaim goods on the buyer's fraudulent or innocent misrepresentation of solvency or of intent to pay.

(3) The seller's right to reclaim under subsection (2) is subject to the rights of a buyer in ordinary course or other good faith purchaser under this Article (Section 2–403). Successful reclamation of goods excludes all other remedies with respect to them.

§ 2–703. Seller's Remedies in General.

Where the buyer wrongfully rejects or revokes acceptance of goods or fails to make a payment due on or before delivery or repudiates with respect to a part or the whole, then with respect to any goods directly affected and, if the breach is of the whole contract (Section 2–612), then also with respect to the whole undelivered balance, the aggrieved seller may

    (a) withhold delivery of such goods;

    (b) stop delivery by any bailee as hereafter provided (Section 2–705);

    (c) proceed under the next section respecting goods still unidentified to the contract;

    (d) resell and recover damages as hereafter provided (Section 2–706);

    (e) recover damages for non-acceptance (Section 2–708) or in a proper case the price (Section 2–709);

    (f) cancel.

§ 2–704. Seller's Right to Identify Goods to the Contract Notwithstanding Breach or to Salvage Unfinished Goods.

(1) An aggrieved seller under the preceding section may

    (a) identify to the contract conforming goods not already identified if at the time he learned of the breach they are in his possession or control;

    (b) treat as the subject of resale goods which have demonstrably been intended for the particular contract even though those goods are unfinished.

(2) Where the goods are unfinished an aggrieved seller may in the exercise of reasonable commercial judgment for the purposes of avoiding loss and of effective realization either complete the manufacture and wholly identify the goods to the contract or cease manufacture and resell for scrap or salvage value or proceed in any other reasonable manner.

§ 2–705. Seller's Stoppage of Delivery in Transit or Otherwise.

(1) The seller may stop delivery of goods in the possession of a carrier or other bailee when he discovers the buyer to be insolvent (Section 2–702) and may stop delivery of carload, truckload, planeload or larger shipments of express or freight when the buyer repudiates or fails to make a payment due before delivery or if for any other reason the seller has a right to withhold or reclaim the goods.

(2) As against such buyer the seller may stop delivery until

    (a) receipt of the goods by the buyer; or

    (b) acknowledgment to the buyer by any bailee of the goods except a carrier that the bailee holds the goods for the buyer; or

    (c) such acknowledgment to the buyer by a carrier by reshipment or as warehouseman; or

    (d) negotiation to the buyer of any negotiable document of title covering the goods.

(3) (a) To stop delivery the seller must so notify as to enable the bailee by reasonable diligence to prevent delivery of the goods.

    (b) After such notification the bailee must hold and deliver the goods according to the directions of the seller but the seller is liable to the bailee for any ensuing charges or damages.

    (c) If a negotiable document of title has been issued for goods the bailee is not obliged to obey a notification to stop until surrender of the document.

    (d) A carrier who has issued a non-negotiable bill of lading is not obliged to obey a notification to stop received from a person other than the consignor.

§ 2–706. Seller's Resale Including Contract for Resale.

(1) Under the conditions stated in Section 2–703 on seller's remedies, the seller may resell the goods concerned or the undelivered balance thereof. Where the resale is made in good faith and in a commercially reasonable manner the seller may recover the difference between the resale price and the contract price together with any incidental damages allowed under the provisions of this Article (Section 2–710), but less expenses saved in consequence of the buyer's breach.

(2) Except as otherwise provided in subsection (3) or unless otherwise agreed resale may be at public or private sale including sale by way of one or more contracts to sell or of identification to an existing contract of the seller. Sale may be as a unit or in parcels and at any time and place and on any terms but every aspect of the sale including the method, manner, time, place and terms must be commercially reasonable. The resale must be reasonably identified as referring to the broken contract, but it is not necessary that the goods be in existence or that any or all of them have been identified to the contract before the breach.

(3) Where the resale is at private sale the seller must give the buyer reasonable notification of his intention to resell.

(4) Where the resale is at public sale

   (a) only identified goods can be sold except where there is a recognized market for a public sale of futures in goods of the kind; and

   (b) it must be made at a usual place or market for public sale if one is reasonably available and except in the case of goods which are perishable or threaten to decline in value speedily the seller must give the buyer reasonable notice of the time and place of the resale; and

   (c) if the goods are not to be within the view of those attending the sale the notification of sale must state the place where the goods are located and provide for their reasonable inspection by prospective bidders; and

   (d) the seller may buy.

(5) A purchaser who buys in good faith at a resale takes the goods free of any rights of the original buyer even though the seller fails to comply with one or more of the requirements of this section.

(6) The seller is not accountable to the buyer for any profit made on any resale. A person in the position of a seller (Section 2–707) or a buyer who has rightfully rejected or justifiably revoked acceptance must account for any excess over the amount of his security interest, as hereinafter defined (subsection (3) of Section 2–711).

§ 2–707. "Person in the Position of a Seller".

(1) A "person in the position of a seller" includes as against a principal an agent who has paid or become responsible for the price of goods on behalf of his principal or anyone who otherwise holds a security interest or other right in goods similar to that of a seller.

(2) A person in the position of a seller may as provided in this Article withhold or stop delivery (Section 2–705) and resell (Section 2–706) and recover incidental damages (Section 2–710).

§ 2–708. Seller's Damages for Non-Acceptance or Repudiation.

(1) Subject to subsection (2) and to the provisions of this Article with respect to proof of market price (Section 2–723), the measure of damages for non-acceptance or repudiation by the buyer is the difference between the market price at the time and place for tender and the unpaid contract price together with any incidental damages provided in this Article (Section 2–710), but less expenses saved in consequence of the buyer's breach.

(2) If the measure of damages provided in subsection (1) is inadequate to put the seller in as good a position as performance would have done then the measure of damages is the profit (including reasonable overhead) which the seller would have made from full performance by the buyer, together with any incidental damages provided in this Article (Section 2–710), due allowance for costs reasonably incurred and due credit for payments or proceeds of resale.

§ 2–709. Action for the Price.

(1) When the buyer fails to pay the price as it becomes due the seller may recover, together with any incidental damages under the next section, the price

   (a) of goods accepted or of conforming goods lost or damaged within a commercially reasonable time after risk of their loss has passed to the buyer; and

   (b) of goods identified to the contract if the seller is unable after reasonable effort to resell them at a reasonable price or the circumstances reasonably indicate that such effort will be unavailing.

(2) Where the seller sues for the price he must hold for the buyer any goods which have been identified to the contract and are still in his control except that if resale becomes possible he may resell them at any time prior to the collection of the judgment. The net proceeds of any such resale must be credited to the buyer and payment of the judgment entitles him to any goods not resold.

(3) After the buyer has wrongfully rejected or revoked acceptance of the goods or has failed to make a payment due or has repudiated (Section 2–610), a seller who is held not entitled to the price under this section shall nevertheless be awarded damages for non-acceptance under the preceding section.

§ 2–710. Seller's Incidental Damages.

Incidental damages to an aggrieved seller include any commercially reasonable charges, expenses or commissions incurred in stopping delivery, in the transportation, care and custody of goods after the buyer's breach, in connection with return or resale of the goods or otherwise resulting from the breach.

§ 2–711. Buyer's Remedies in General; Buyer's Security Interest in Rejected Goods.

(1) Where the seller fails to make delivery or repudiates or the buyer rightfully rejects or justifiably revokes acceptance then with respect to any goods involved, and with respect to the whole if the breach goes to the whole contract (Section 2–612), the buyer may cancel and whether or not he has done so may in addition to recovering so much of the price as has been paid

   (a) "cover" and have damages under the next section as to all the goods affected whether or not they have been identified to the contract; or

   (b) recover damages for non-delivery as provided in this Article (Section 2–713).

(2) Where the seller fails to deliver or repudiates the buyer may also

   (a) if the goods have been identified recover them as provided in this Article (Section 2–502); or

   (b) in a proper case obtain specific performance or replevy the goods as provided in this Article (Section 2–716).

(3) On rightful rejection or justifiable revocation of acceptance a buyer has a security interest in goods in his possession or control for any payments made on their price and any expenses reasonably incurred in their inspection, receipt, transportation, care and custody and may hold such goods and resell them in like manner as an aggrieved seller (Section 2–706).

§ 2–712. "Cover"; Buyer's Procurement of Substitute Goods.

(1) After a breach within the preceding section the buyer may "cover" by making in good faith and without unreasonable delay any reasonable purchase of or contract to purchase goods in substitution for those due from the seller.

(2) The buyer may recover from the seller as damages the difference between the cost of cover and the contract price together with any incidental or consequential damages as hereinafter defined (Section 2–715), but less expenses saved in consequence of the seller's breach.

(3) Failure of the buyer to effect cover within this section does not bar him from any other remedy.

§ 2–713. Buyer's Damages for Non-Delivery or Repudiation.

(1) Subject to provisions of this Article with respect to the proof of market price (Section 2–723), the measure of damages for non-delivery or repudiation by the seller is the difference between the market price at the time when the buyer learned of the breach and the contract price together with any incidental and consequential damages provided in this Article (Section 2–715), but less expenses saved in consequence of the seller's breach.

(2) Market price is to be determined as of the place for tender or, in cases of rejection after arrival or revocation of acceptance, as of the place of arrival.

§ 2–714. Buyer's Damages for Breach in Regard to Accepted Goods.

(1) Where the buyer has accepted goods and given notification (subsection (3) of Section 2–607) he may recover as damages for any non-conformity of tender the loss resulting in the ordinary course of events from the seller's breach as determined in any manner which is reasonable.

(2) The measure of damages for breach of warranty is the difference at the time and place of acceptance between the value of the goods accepted and the value they would have had if they had been as warranted, unless special circumstances show proximate damages of a different amount.

(3) In a proper case any incidental and consequential damages under the next section may be recovered.

§ 2–715. Buyer's Incidental and Consequential Damages.

(1) Incidental damages resulting from the seller's breach include expenses reasonably incurred in inspection, receipt, transportation and care and custody of goods rightfully rejected, any commercially reasonable charges, expenses or commissions in connection with effecting cover and any other reasonable expense incident to the delay or other breach.

(2) Consequential damages resulting from the seller's breach include

(a) any loss resulting from general or particular requirements and needs of which the seller at the time of contracting had reason to know and which could not reasonably be prevented by cover or otherwise; and

(b) injury to person or property proximately resulting from any breach of warranty.

§ 2–716. Buyer's Right to Specific Performance or Replevin.

(1) Specific performance may be decreed where the goods are unique or in other proper circumstances.

(2) The decree for specific performance may include such terms and conditions as to payment of the price, damages, or other relief as the court may deem just.

(3) The buyer has a right of replevin for goods identified to the contract if after reasonable effort he is unable to effect cover for such goods or the circumstances reasonably indicate that such effort will be unavailing or if the goods have been shipped under reservation and satisfaction of the security interest in them has been made or tendered.

§ 2–717. Deduction of Damages From the Price.

The buyer on notifying the seller of his intention to do so may deduct all or any part of the damages resulting from any breach of the contract from any part of the price still due under the same contract.

§ 2–718. Liquidation or Limitation of Damages; Deposits.

(1) Damages for breach by either party may be liquidated in the agreement but only at an amount which is reasonable in the light of the anticipated or actual harm caused by the breach, the difficulties of proof of loss, and the inconvenience or nonfeasibility of otherwise obtaining an adequate remedy. A term fixing unreasonably large liquidated damages is void as a penalty.

(2) Where the seller justifiably withholds delivery of goods because of the buyer's breach, the buyer is entitled to restitution of any amount by which the sum of his payments exceeds

(a) the amount to which the seller is entitled by virtue of terms liquidating the seller's damages in accordance with subsection (1), or

(b) in the absence of such terms, twenty per cent of the value of the total performance for which the buyer is obligated under the contract or $500, whichever is smaller.

(3) The buyer's right to restitution under subsection (2) is subject to offset to the extent that the seller establishes

(a) a right to recover damages under the provisions of this Article other than subsection (1), and

(b) the amount or value of any benefits received by the buyer directly or indirectly by reason of the contract.

(4) Where a seller has received payment in goods their reasonable value or the proceeds of their resale shall be treated as payments for the purposes of subsection (2); but if the seller has notice of the buyer's breach before reselling goods received in part performance, his resale is subject to the conditions laid down in this Article on resale by an aggrieved seller (Section 2–706).

§ 2–719. Contractual Modification or Limitation of Remedy.

(1) Subject to the provisions of subsection (2) and (3) of this section and of the preceding section on liquidation and limitation of damages,

(a) the agreement may provide for remedies in addition to or in substitution for those provided in this Article and may limit or alter the measure of damages recoverable under this Article, as by limiting the buyer's remedies to return of the goods and repayment of the price or to repair and replacement of non-conforming goods or parts; and

(b) resort to a remedy as provided is optional unless the remedy is expressly agreed to be exclusive, in which case it is the sole remedy.

(2) Where circumstances cause an exclusive or limited remedy to fail of its essential purpose, remedy may be had as provided in this Act.

(3) Consequential damages may be limited or excluded unless the limitation or exclusion is unconscionable. Limitation of consequential damages for injury to the person in the case of consumer goods is prima facie unconscionable but limitation of damages where the loss is commercial is not.

§ 2–720. Effect of "Cancellation" or "Rescission" on Claims for Antecedent Breach.

Unless the contrary intention clearly appears, expressions of "cancellation" or "rescission" of the contract or the like shall not be construed as a renunciation or discharge of any claim in damages for an antecedent breach.

§ 2–721. Remedies for Fraud.

Remedies for material misrepresentation or fraud include all remedies available under this Article for non-fraudulent breach. Neither rescission or a claim for rescission of the contract for sale nor rejection or return of the goods shall bar or be deemed inconsistent with a claim for damages or other remedy.

§ 2–722. Who Can Sue Third Parties for Injury to Goods.

Where a third party so deals with goods which have been identified to a contract for sale as to cause actionable injury to a party to that contract

(a) a right of action against the third party is in either party to the contract for sale who has title to or a security interest or a special property or an insurable interest in the goods; and if the goods have been destroyed or converted a right of action is also in the party who either bore the risk of loss under the contract for sale or has since the injury assumed that risk as against the other;

(b) if at the time of the injury the party plaintiff did not bear the risk of loss as against the other party to the contract for sale and there is no arrangement between them for disposition of the recovery, his suit or settlement is subject to his own interest, as a fiduciary for the other party to the contract;

(c) either party may with the consent of the other sue for the benefit of whom it may concern.

§ 2–723. Proof of Market Price: Time and Place.

(1) If an action based on anticipatory repudiation comes to trial before the time for performance with respect to some or all of the goods, any damages based on market price (Section 2–708 or Section 2–713) shall be determined according to the price of such goods prevailing at the time when the aggrieved party learned of the repudiation.

(2) If evidence of a price prevailing at the times or places described in this Article is not readily available the price prevailing within any reasonable time before or after the time described or at any other place which in commercial judgment or under usage of trade would serve as a reasonable substitute for the one described may be used, making any proper allowance for the cost of transporting the goods to or from such other place.

(3) Evidence of a relevant price prevailing at a time or place other than the one described in this Article offered by one party is not admissible unless and until he has given the other party such notice as the court finds sufficient to prevent unfair surprise.

§ 2–724. Admissibility of Market Quotations.

Whenever the prevailing price or value of any goods regularly bought and sold in any established commodity market is in issue, reports in official publications or trade journals or in newspapers or periodicals of general circulation published as the reports of such market shall be admissible in evidence. The circumstances of the preparation of such a report may be shown to affect its weight but not its admissibility.

§ 2–725. Statute of Limitations in Contracts for Sale.

(1) An action for breach of any contract for sale must be commenced within four years after the cause of action has accrued. By the original agreement the parties may reduce the period of limitation to not less than one year but may not extend it.

(2) A cause of action occurs when the breach occurs, regardless of the aggrieved party's lack of knowledge of the breach. A breach of warranty occurs when tender of delivery is made, except that where a warranty explicitly extends to future performance of the goods and discovery of the breach must await the time of such performance the cause of action accrues when the breach is or should have been discovered.

(3) Where an action commenced within the time limited by subsection (1) is so terminated as to leave available a remedy by another action for the same breach such other action may be commenced after the expiration of the time limited and within six months after the termination of the first action unless the termination resulted from voluntary discontinuance or from dismissal for failure or neglect to prosecute.

(4) This section does not alter the law on tolling of the statute of limitations nor does it apply to causes of action which have accrued before this Act becomes effective.

ARTICLE 2A: LEASES
Part 1—General Provisions
§ 2A–101. Short Title.

This Article shall be known and may be cited as the Uniform Commercial Code—Leases.

§ 2A–102. Scope.

This Article applies to any transaction, regardless of form, that creates a lease.

§ 2A–103. Definitions and Index of Definitions.

(1) In this Article unless the context otherwise requires:

(a) "Buyer in ordinary course of business" means a person who in good faith and without knowledge that the sale to him [or her] is in violation of the ownership rights or security interest or leasehold interest of a third party in the goods buys in ordinary course from a person in the business of selling goods of that kind but does not include a pawnbroker. "Buying" may be for cash or by exchange of other property or on secured or unsecured credit and includes receiving goods or documents of title under a pre-existing contract for sale but does not include a transfer in bulk or as security for or in total or partial satisfaction of a money debt.

(b) "Cancellation" occurs when either party puts an end to the lease contract for default by the other party.

(c) "Commercial unit" means such a unit of goods as by commercial usage is a single whole for purposes of lease and division of which materially impairs its character or value on the market or in use. A commercial unit may be a single article, as a machine, or a set of articles, as a suite of furniture or a line of machinery, or a quantity, as a gross or carload, or any other unit treated in use or in the relevant market as a single whole.

(d) "Conforming" goods or performance under a lease contract means goods or performance that are in accordance with the obligations under the lease contract.

(e) "Consumer lease" means a lease that a lessor regularly engaged in the business of leasing or selling makes to a lessee who is an individual and who takes under the lease primarily for a personal, family, or household purpose [, if the total payments to be made under the lease contract, excluding payments for options to renew or buy, do not exceed $_____].

(f) "Fault" means wrongful act, omission, breach, or default.

(g) "Finance lease" means a lease with respect to which:

(i) the lessor does not select, manufacture, or supply the goods;

(ii) the lessor acquires the goods or the right to possession and use of the goods in connection with the lease; and

(iii) one of the following occurs:

(A) the lessee receives a copy of the contract by which the lessor acquired the goods or the right to possession and use of the goods before signing the lease contract;

(B) the lessee's approval of the contract by which the lessor acquired the goods or the right to possession and use of the goods is a condition to effectiveness of the lease contract;

(C) the lessee, before signing the lease contract, receives an accurate and complete statement designating the promises and warranties, and any disclaimers of warranties, limitations or modifications of remedies, or liquidated damages, including those of a third party, such as the manufacturer of the goods, provided to the lessor by the person supplying the goods in connection with or as part of the contract by which the lessor acquired the goods or the right to possession and use of the goods; or

(D) if the lease is not a consumer lease, the lessor, before the lessee signs the lease contract, informs the lessee in writing (a) of the identity of the person supplying the goods to the lessor, unless the lessee has selected that person and directed the lessor to acquire the goods or the right to possession and use of the goods from that person, (b) that the lessee is entitled under this Article to the promises and warranties, including those of any third party, provided to the lessor by the person supplying the goods in connection with or as part of the contract by which the lessor acquired the goods or the right to possession and use of the goods, and (c) that the lessee may communicate with the person supplying the goods to the lessor and receive an accurate and complete statement of those promises and warranties, including any disclaimers and limitations of them or of remedies.

(h) "Goods" means all things that are movable at the time of identification to the lease contract, or are fixtures (Section 2A–309), but the term does not include money, documents, instruments, accounts, chattel paper, general intangibles, or minerals or the like, including oil and gas, before extraction. The term also includes the unborn young of animals.

(i) "Installment lease contract" means a lease contract that authorizes or requires the delivery of goods in separate lots to be separately accepted, even though the lease contract contains a clause "each delivery is a separate lease" or its equivalent.

(j) "Lease" means a transfer of the right to possession and use of goods for a term in return for consideration, but a sale, including a sale on approval or a sale or return, or retention or creation of a security interest is not a lease. Unless the context clearly indicates otherwise, the term includes a sublease.

(k) "Lease agreement" means the bargain, with respect to the lease, of the lessor and the lessee in fact as found in their language or by implication from other circumstances including course of dealing or usage of trade or course of performance as provided in this Article. Unless the context clearly indicates otherwise, the term includes a sublease agreement.

(l) "Lease contract" means the total legal obligation that results from the lease agreement as affected by this Article and any other applicable rules of law. Unless the context clearly indicates otherwise, the term includes a sublease contract.

(m) "Leasehold interest" means the interest of the lessor or the lessee under a lease contract.

(n) "Lessee" means a person who acquires the right to possession and use of goods under a lease. Unless the context clearly indicates otherwise, the term includes a sublessee.

(o) "Lessee in ordinary course of business" means a person who in good faith and without knowledge that the lease to him [or her] is in violation of the ownership rights or security interest or leasehold interest of a third party in the goods, leases in ordinary course from a person in the business of selling or leasing goods of that kind but does not include a pawnbroker. "Leasing" may be for cash or by exchange of other property or on secured or unsecured credit and includes receiving goods or documents of title under a pre-existing lease contract but does not include a transfer in bulk or as security for or in total or partial satisfaction of a money debt.

(p) "Lessor" means a person who transfers the right to possession and use of goods under a lease. Unless the context clearly indicates otherwise, the term includes a sublessor.

(q) "Lessor's residual interest" means the lessor's interest in the goods after expiration, termination, or cancellation of the lease contract.

(r) "Lien" means a charge against or interest in goods to secure payment of a debt or performance of an obligation, but the term does not include a security interest.

(s) "Lot" means a parcel or a single article that is the subject matter of a separate lease or delivery, whether or not it is sufficient to perform the lease contract.

(t) "Merchant lessee" means a lessee that is a merchant with respect to goods of the kind subject to the lease.

(u) "Present value" means the amount as of a date certain of one or more sums payable in the future, discounted to the date certain. The discount is determined by the interest rate specified by the parties if the rate was not manifestly unreasonable at the time the transaction was entered into; otherwise, the discount is determined by a commercially reasonable rate that takes into account the facts and circumstances of each case at the time the transaction was entered into.

(v) "Purchase" includes taking by sale, lease, mortgage, security interest, pledge, gift, or any other voluntary transaction creating an interest in goods.

(w) "Sublease" means a lease of goods the right to possession and use of which was acquired by the lessor as a lessee under an existing lease.

(x) "Supplier" means a person from whom a lessor buys or leases goods to be leased under a finance lease.

(y) "Supply contract" means a contract under which a lessor buys or leases goods to be leased.

(z) "Termination" occurs when either party pursuant to a power created by agreement or law puts an end to the lease contract otherwise than for default.

(2) Other definitions applying to this Article and the sections in which they appear are:

"Accessions". Section 2A–310(1).
"Construction mortgage". Section 2A–309(1)(d).
"Encumbrance". Section 2A–309(1)(e).
"Fixtures". Section 2A–309(1)(a).
"Fixture filing". Section 2A–309(1)(b).
"Purchase money lease". Section 2A–309(1)(c).

(3) The following definitions in other Articles apply to this Article:

"Account". Section 9–106.
"Between merchants". Section 2–104(3).
"Buyer". Section 2–103(1)(a).
"Chattel paper". Section 9–105(1)(b).
"Consumer goods". Section 9–109(1).
"Document". Section 9–105(1)(f).
"Entrusting". Section 2–403(3).
"General intangibles". Section 9–106.
"Good faith". Section 2–103(1)(b).
"Instrument". Section 9–105(1)(i).
"Merchant". Section 2–104(1).
"Mortgage". Sect 9–105(1)(j).
"Pursuant to commitment". Section 9–105(1)(k).
"Receipt". Section 2–103(1)(c).
"Sale". Section 2–106(1).
"Sale on approval". Section 2–326.
"Sale or return". Section 2–326.
"Seller". Section 2–103(1)(d).

(4) In addition Article 1 contains general definitions and principles of construction and interpretation applicable throughout this Article.

As amended in 1990.

§ 2A–104. Leases Subject to Other Law.

(1) A lease, although subject to this Article, is also subject to any applicable:

(a) certificate of title statute of this State: (list any certificate of title statutes covering automobiles, trailers, mobile homes, boats, farm tractors, and the like);

(b) certificate of title statute of another jurisdiction (Section 2A–105); or

(c) consumer protection statute of this State, or final consumer protection decision of a court of this State existing on the effective date of this Article.

(2) In case of conflict between this Article, other than Sections 2A–105, 2A–304(3), and 2A–305(3), and a statute or decision referred to in subsection (1), the statute or decision controls.

(3) Failure to comply with an applicable law has only the effect specified therein.

As amended in 1990.

§ 2A–108. Unconscionability.

(1) If the court as a matter of law finds a lease contract or any clause of a lease contract to have been unconscionable at the time it was made the court may refuse to enforce the lease contract, or it may enforce the remainder of the lease contract without the unconscionable clause, or it may so limit the application of any unconscionable clause as to avoid any unconscionable result.

(2) With respect to a consumer lease, if the court as a matter of law finds that a lease contract or any clause of a lease contract has been induced by unconscionable conduct or that unconscionable conduct has occurred in the collection of a claim arising from a lease contract, the court may grant appropriate relief.

(3) Before making a finding of unconscionability under subsection (1) or (2), the court, on its own motion or that of a party, shall afford the parties a reasonable opportunity to present evidence as to the setting, purpose, and effect of the lease contract or clause thereof, or of the conduct.

(4) In an action in which the lessee claims unconscionability with respect to a consumer lease:

(a) If the court finds unconscionability under subsection (1) or (2), the court shall award reasonable attorney's fees to the lessee.

(b) If the court does not find unconscionability and the lessee claiming unconscionability has brought or maintained an action he [or she] knew to be groundless, the court shall award reasonable attorney's fees to the party against whom the claim is made.

(c) In determining attorney's fees, the amount of the recovery on behalf of the claimant under subsections (1) and (2) is not controlling.

Part 2—Formation and Construction of Lease Contract
§ 2A–201. Statute of Frauds.

(1) A lease contract is not enforceable by way of action or defense unless:

(a) the total payments to be made under the lease contract, excluding payments for options to renew or buy, are less than $1,000; or

(b) there is a writing, signed by the party against whom enforcement is sought or by that party's authorized agent, sufficient to indicate that a lease contract has been made between the parties and to describe the goods leased and the lease term.

(2) Any description of leased goods or of the lease term is sufficient and satisfies subsection (1)(b), whether or not it is specific, if it reasonably identifies what is described.

(3) A writing is not insufficient because it omits or incorrectly states a term agreed upon, but the lease contract is not enforceable under subsection (1)(b) beyond the lease term and the quantity of goods shown in the writing.

(4) A lease contract that does not satisfy the requirements of subsection (1), but which is valid in other respects, is enforceable:

(a) if the goods are to be specially manufactured or obtained for the lessee and are not suitable for lease or sale to others in the ordinary course of the lessor's business, and the lessor, before notice of repudiation is received and under circumstances that reasonably indicate that the goods are for the lessee, has made either a substantial beginning of their manufacture or commitments for their procurement;

(b) if the party against whom enforcement is sought admits in that party's pleading, testimony or otherwise in court that a lease contract was made, but the lease contract is not enforceable under this provision beyond the quantity of goods admitted; or

(c) with respect to goods that have been received and accepted by the lessee.

(5) The lease term under a lease contract referred to in subsection (4) is:

(a) if there is a writing signed by the party against whom enforcement is sought or by that party's authorized agent specifying the lease term, the term so specified;

(b) if the party against whom enforcement is sought admits in that party's pleading, testimony, or otherwise in court a lease term, the term so admitted; or

(c) a reasonable lease term.

§ 2A–202. Final Written Expression: Parol or Extrinsic Evidence.

Terms with respect to which the confirmatory memoranda of the parties agree or which are otherwise set forth in a writing intended by the parties as a final expression of their agreement with respect to such terms as are included therein may not be contradicted by evidence of any prior agreement or of a contemporaneous oral agreement but may be explained or supplemented:

(a) by course of dealing or usage of trade or by course of performance; and

(b) by evidence of consistent additional terms unless the court finds the writing to have been intended also as a complete and exclusive statement of the terms of the agreement.

§ 2A–204. Formation in General.

(1) A lease contract may be made in any manner sufficient to show agreement, including conduct by both parties which recognizes the existence of a lease contract.

(2) An agreement sufficient to constitute a lease contract may be found although the moment of its making is undetermined.

(3) Although one or more terms are left open, a lease contract does not fail for indefiniteness if the parties have intended to make a lease contract and there is a reasonably certain basis for giving an appropriate remedy.

§ 2A–205. Firm Offers.

An offer by a merchant to lease goods to or from another person in a signed writing that by its terms gives assurance it will be held open is not revocable, for lack of consideration, during the time stated or, if no time is stated, for a reasonable time, but in no event may the period of irrevocability exceed 3 months. Any such term of assurance on a form supplied by the offeree must be separately signed by the offeror.

§ 2A–206. Offer and Acceptance in Formation of Lease Contract.

(1) Unless otherwise unambiguously indicated by the language or circumstances, an offer to make a lease contract must be construed as inviting acceptance in any manner and by any medium reasonable in the circumstances.

(2) If the beginning of a requested performance is a reasonable mode of acceptance, an offeror who is not notified of acceptance within a reasonable time may treat the offer as having lapsed before acceptance.

§ 2A–207. Course of Performance or Practical Construction.

(1) If a lease contract involves repeated occasions for performance by either party with knowledge of the nature of the performance and opportunity for objection to it by the other, any course of performance accepted or acquiesced in without objection is relevant to determine the meaning of the lease agreement.

(2) The express terms of a lease agreement and any course of performance, as well as any course of dealing and usage of trade, must be construed whenever reasonable as consistent with each other; but if that construction is unreasonable, express terms control course of performance, course of performance controls both course of dealing and usage of trade, and course of dealing controls usage of trade.

(3) Subject to the provisions of Section 2A–208 on modification and waiver, course of performance is relevant to show a waiver or modification of any term inconsistent with the course of performance.

§ 2A–208. Modification, Rescission and Waiver.

(1) An agreement modifying a lease contract needs no consideration to be binding.

(2) A signed lease agreement that excludes modification or rescission except by a signed writing may not be otherwise modified or rescinded, but, except as between merchants, such a requirement on a form supplied by a merchant must be separately signed by the other party.

(3) Although an attempt at modification or rescission does not satisfy the requirements of subsection (2), it may operate as a waiver.

(4) A party who has made a waiver affecting an executory portion of a lease contract may retract the waiver by reasonable notification received by the other party that strict performance will be required of any term waived, unless the retraction would be unjust in view of a material change of position in reliance on the waiver.

§ 2A–209. Lessee Under Finance Lease as Beneficiary of Supply Contract.

(1) The benefit of a supplier's promises to the lessor under the supply contract and of all warranties, whether express or implied, including those of any third party provided in connection with or as part of the supply contract, extends to the lessee to the extent of the lessee's leasehold interest under a finance lease related to the supply contract, but is subject to the terms of the warranty and of the supply contract and all defenses or claims arising therefrom.

(2) The extension of the benefit of a supplier's promises and of warranties to the lessee (Section 2A–209(1)) does not: (i) modify the rights and obligations of the parties to the supply contract, whether arising therefrom or otherwise, or (ii) impose any duty or liability under the supply contract on the lessee.

(3) Any modification or rescission of the supply contract by the supplier and the lessor is effective between the supplier and the lessee unless, before the modification or rescission, the supplier has received notice that the lessee has entered into a finance lease related to the supply contract. If the modification or rescission is effective between the supplier and the lessee, the lessor is deemed to have assumed, in addition to the obligations of the lessor to the lessee under the lease contract, promises of the supplier to the lessor and warranties that were so modified or rescinded as they existed and were available to the lessee before modification or rescission.

(4) In addition to the extension of the benefit of the supplier's promises and of warranties to the lessee under subsection (1), the lessee retains all rights that the lessee may have against the supplier which arise from an agreement between the lessee and the supplier or under other law.

As amended in 1990.

§ 2A–210. Express Warranties.

(1) Express warranties by the lessor are created as follows:

(a) Any affirmation of fact or promise made by the lessor to the lessee which relates to the goods and becomes part of the basis of the bargain creates an express warranty that the goods will conform to the affirmation or promise.

(b) Any description of the goods which is made part of the basis of the bargain creates an express warranty that the goods will conform to the description.

(c) Any sample or model that is made part of the basis of the bargain creates an express warranty that the whole of the goods will conform to the sample or model.

(2) It is not necessary to the creation of an express warranty that the lessor use formal words, such as "warrant" or "guarantee," or that the lessor have a specific intention to make a warranty, but an affirmation merely of the value of the goods or a statement purporting to be merely the lessor's opinion or commendation of the goods does not create a warranty.

§ 2A–211. Warranties Against Interference and Against Infringement; Lessee's Obligation Against Infringement.

(1) There is in a lease contract a warranty that for the lease term no person holds a claim to or interest in the goods that arose from an act or omission of the lessor, other than a claim by way of infringement or the like, which will interfere with the lessee's enjoyment of its leasehold interest.

(2) Except in a finance lease there is in a lease contract by a lessor who is a merchant regularly dealing in goods of the kind a warranty that the goods are delivered free of the rightful claim of any person by way of infringement or the like.

(3) A lessee who furnishes specifications to a lessor or a supplier shall hold the lessor and the supplier harmless against any claim by way of infringement or the like that arises out of compliance with the specifications.

§ 2A–212. Implied Warranty of Merchantability.

(1) Except in a finance lease, a warranty that the goods will be merchantable is implied in a lease contract if the lessor is a merchant with respect to goods of that kind.

(2) Goods to be merchantable must be at least such as

(a) pass without objection in the trade under the description in the lease agreement;

(b) in the case of fungible goods, are of fair average quality within the description;

(c) are fit for the ordinary purposes for which goods of that type are used;

(d) run, within the variation permitted by the lease agreement, of even kind, quality, and quantity within each unit and among all units involved;

(e) are adequately contained, packaged, and labeled as the lease agreement may require; and

(f) conform to any promises or affirmations of fact made on the container or label.

(3) Other implied warranties may arise from course of dealing or usage of trade.

§ 2A–213. Implied Warranty of Fitness for Particular Purpose.

Except in a finance lease, if the lessor at the time the lease contract is made has reason to know of any particular purpose for which the goods are required and that the lessee is relying on the lessor's skill or judgment to select or furnish suitable goods, there is in the lease contract an implied warranty that the goods will be fit for that purpose.

§ 2A–214. Exclusion or Modification of Warranties.

(1) Words or conduct relevant to the creation of an express warranty and words or conduct tending to negate or limit a warranty must be construed wherever reasonable as consistent with each other; but, subject to the provisions of Section 2A–202 on parol or extrinsic evidence, negation or limitation is inoperative to the extent that the construction is unreasonable.

(2) Subject to subsection (3), to exclude or modify the implied warranty of merchantability or any part of it the language must mention "merchantability", be by a writing, and be conspicuous. Subject to subsection (3), to exclude or modify any implied warranty of fitness the exclusion must be by a writing and be conspicuous. Language to exclude all implied warranties of fitness is sufficient if it is in writing, is conspicuous and states, for example, "There is no warranty that the goods will be fit for a particular purpose".

(3) Notwithstanding subsection (2), but subject to subsection (4),

(a) unless the circumstances indicate otherwise, all implied warranties are excluded by expressions like "as is," or "with all faults," or by other language that in common understanding calls the lessee's attention to the exclusion of warranties and makes plain that there is no implied warranty, if in writing and conspicuous;

(b) if the lessee before entering into the lease contract has examined the goods or the sample or model as fully as desired or has refused to examine the goods, there is no implied warranty with regard to defects that an examination ought in the circumstances to have revealed; and

(c) an implied warranty may also be excluded or modified by course of dealing, course of performance, or usage of trade.

(4) To exclude or modify a warranty against interference or against infringement (Section 2A–211) or any part of it, the language must be specific, be by a writing, and be conspicuous, unless the circumstances, including course of performance, course of dealing, or usage of trade, give the lessee reason to know that the goods are being leased subject to a claim or interest of any person.

§ 2A–215. Cumulation and Conflict of Warranties Express or Implied.

Warranties, whether express or implied, must be construed as consistent with each other and as cumulative, but if that construction is unreasonable, the intention of the parties determines which warranty is dominant. In ascertaining that intention the following rules apply:

(a) Exact or technical specifications displace an inconsistent sample or model or general language of description.

(b) A sample from an existing bulk displaces inconsistent general language of description.

(c) Express warranties displace inconsistent implied warranties other than an implied warranty of fitness for a particular purpose.

§ 2A–216. Third-Party Beneficiaries of Express and Implied Warranties.

Alternative A A warranty to or for the benefit of a lessee under this Article, whether express or implied, extends to any natural person who is in the family or household of the lessee or who is a guest in the lessee's home if it is reasonable to expect that such person may use, consume, or be affected by the goods and who is injured in person by breach of the warranty. This section does not displace principles of law and equity that extend a warranty to or for the benefit of a lessee to other persons. The operation of this section may not be excluded, modified, or limited, but an exclusion, modification, or limitation of the warranty, including any with respect to rights and remedies, effective against the lessee is also effective against any beneficiary designated under this section.

Alternative B A warranty to or for the benefit of a lessee under this Article, whether express or implied, extends to any natural person who may reasonably be expected to use, consume, or be affected by the goods and who is injured in person by breach of the warranty. This section does not displace principles of law and equity that extend a warranty to or for the benefit of a lessee to other persons. The operation of this section may not be excluded, modified, or limited, but an exclusion, modification, or limitation of the warranty, including any with respect to rights and remedies, effective against the lessee is also effective against the beneficiary designated under this section.

Alternative C A warranty to or for the benefit of a lessee under this Article, whether express or implied, extends to any person who may reasonably be expected to use, consume, or be affected by the goods and who is injured by breach of the warranty. The operation of this section may not be excluded, modified, or limited with respect to injury to the person of an individual to whom the warranty extends, but an exclusion, modification, or limitation of the warranty, including any with respect to rights and remedies, effective against the lessee is also effective against the beneficiary designated under this section.

§ 2A–219. Risk of Loss.

(1) Except in the case of a finance lease, risk of loss is retained by the lessor and does not pass to the lessee. In the case of a finance lease, risk of loss passes to the lessee.

(2) Subject to the provisions of this Article on the effect of default on risk of loss (Section 2A–220), if risk of loss is to pass to the lessee and the time of passage is not stated, the following rules apply:

(a) If the lease contract requires or authorizes the goods to be shipped by carrier

(i) and it does not require delivery at a particular destination, the risk of loss passes to the lessee when the goods are duly delivered to the carrier; but

(ii) if it does require delivery at a particular destination and the goods are there duly tendered while in the possession of the carrier, the risk of loss passes to the lessee when the goods are there duly so tendered as to enable the lessee to take delivery.

(b) If the goods are held by a bailee to be delivered without being moved, the risk of loss passes to the lessee on acknowledgment by the bailee of the lessee's right to possession of the goods.

(c) In any case not within subsection (a) or (b), the risk of loss passes to the lessee on the lessee's receipt of the goods if the lessor, or, in the case of a finance lease, the supplier, is a merchant; otherwise the risk passes to the lessee on tender of delivery.

Part 3—Effect of Lease Contract
§ 2A–302. Title to and Possession of Goods.
Except as otherwise provided in this Article, each provision of this Article applies whether the lessor or a third party has title to the goods, and whether the lessor, the lessee, or a third party has possession of the goods, notwithstanding any statute or rule of law that possession or the absence of possession is fraudulent.

§ 2A–303. Alienability of Party's Interest Under Lease Contract or of Lessor's Residual Interest in Goods; Delegation of Performance; Transfer of Rights.
(1) As used in this section, "creation of a security interest" includes the sale of a lease contract that is subject to Article 9, Secured Transactions, by reason of Section 9–102(1)(b).

(2) Except as provided in subsections (3) and (4), a provision in a lease agreement which (i) prohibits the voluntary or involuntary transfer, including a transfer by sale, sublease, creation or enforcement of a security interest, or attachment, levy, or other judicial process, of an interest of a party under the lease contract or of the lessor's residual interest in the goods, or (ii) makes such a transfer an event of default, gives rise to the rights and remedies provided in subsection (5), but a transfer that is prohibited or is an event of default under the lease agreement is otherwise effective.

(3) A provision in a lease agreement which (i) prohibits the creation or enforcement of a security interest in an interest of a party under the lease contract or in the lessor's residual interest in the goods, or (ii) makes such a transfer an event of default, is not enforceable unless, and then only to the extent that, there is an actual transfer by the lessee of the lessee's right of possession or use of the goods in violation of the provision or an actual delegation of a material performance of either party to the lease contract in violation of the provision. Neither the granting nor the enforcement of a security interest in (i) the lessor's interest under the lease contract or (ii) the lessor's residual interest in the goods is a transfer that materially impairs the prospect of obtaining return performance by, materially changes the duty of, or materially increases the burden or risk imposed on, the lessee within the purview of subsection (5) unless, and then only to the extent that, there is an actual delegation of a material performance of the lessor.

(4) A provision in a lease agreement which (i) prohibits a transfer of a right to damages for default with respect to the whole lease contract or of a right to payment arising out of the transferor's due performance of the transferor's entire obligation, or (ii) makes such a transfer an event of default, is not enforceable, and such a transfer is not a transfer that materially impairs the prospect of obtaining return performance by, materially changes the duty of, or materially increases the burden or risk imposed on, the other party to the lease contract within the purview of subsection

(5) Subject to subsections (3) and (4):

(a) if a transfer is made which is made an event of default under a lease agreement, the party to the lease contract not making the transfer, unless that party waives the default or otherwise agrees, has the rights and remedies described in Section 2A–501(2);

(b) if paragraph (a) is not applicable and if a transfer is made that (i) is prohibited under a lease agreement or (ii) materially impairs the prospect of obtaining return performance by, materially changes the duty of, or materially increases the burden or risk imposed on, the other party to the lease contract, unless the party not making the transfer agrees at any time to the transfer in the lease contract or otherwise, then, except as limited by contract, (i) the transferor is liable to the party not making the transfer for damages caused by the transfer to the extent that the damages could not reasonably be prevented by the party not making the transfer and (ii) a court having jurisdiction may grant other appropriate relief, including cancellation of the lease contract or an injunction against the transfer.

(6) A transfer of "the lease" or of "all my rights under the lease", or a transfer in similar general terms, is a transfer of rights and, unless the language or the circumstances, as in a transfer for security, indicate the contrary, the transfer is a delegation of duties by the transferor to the transferee. Acceptance by the transferee constitutes a promise by the transferee to perform those duties. The promise is enforceable by either the transferor or the other party to the lease contract.

(7) Unless otherwise agreed by the lessor and the lessee, a delegation of performance does not relieve the transferor as against the other party of any duty to perform or of any liability for default.

(8) In a consumer lease, to prohibit the transfer of an interest of a party under the lease contract or to make a transfer an event of default, the language must be specific, by a writing, and conspicuous.

As amended in 1990.

§ 2A–304. Subsequent Lease of Goods by Lessor.
(1) Subject to Section 2A–303, a subsequent lessee from a lessor of goods under an existing lease contract obtains, to the extent of the leasehold interest transferred, the leasehold interest in the goods that the lessor had or had power to transfer, and except as provided in subsection (2) and Section 2A–527(4), takes subject to the existing lease contract. A lessor with voidable title has power to transfer a good leasehold interest to a good faith subsequent lessee for value, but only to the extent set forth in the preceding sentence. If goods have been delivered under a transaction of purchase, the lessor has that power even though:

(a) the lessor's transferor was deceived as to the identity of the lessor;

(b) the delivery was in exchange for a check which is later dishonored;

(c) it was agreed that the transaction was to be a "cash sale"; or

(d) the delivery was procured through fraud punishable as larcenous under the criminal law.

(2) A subsequent lessee in the ordinary course of business from a lessor who is a merchant dealing in goods of that kind to whom the goods were entrusted by the existing lessee of that lessor before the interest of the subsequent lessee became enforceable against that lessor obtains, to the extent of the leasehold interest transferred, all of that lessor's and the existing lessee's rights to the goods, and takes free of the existing lease contract.

(3) A subsequent lessee from the lessor of goods that are subject to an existing lease contract and are covered by a certificate of title issued under a statute of this State or of another jurisdiction takes no greater rights than those provided both by this section and by the certificate of title statute.

As amended in 1990.

§ 2A–307. Priority of Liens Arising by Attachment or Levy on, Security Interests in, and Other Claims to Goods.
(1) Except as otherwise provided in Section 2A–306, a creditor of a lessee takes subject to the lease contract.

(2) Except as otherwise provided in subsections (3) and (4) and in Sections 2A–306 and 2A–308, a creditor of a lessor takes subject to the lease contract unless:

(a) the creditor holds a lien that attached to the goods before the lease contract became enforceable;

(b) the creditor holds a security interest in the goods and the lessee did not give value and receive delivery of the goods without knowledge of the security interest; or

(c) the creditor holds a security interest in the goods which was perfected (Section 9–303) before the lease contract became enforceable.

(3) A lessee in the ordinary course of business takes the leasehold interest free of a security interest in the goods created by the lessor even though the security interest is perfected (Section 9–303) and the lessee knows of its existence.

(4) A lessee other than a lessee in the ordinary course of business takes the leasehold interest free of a security interest to the extent that it secures future advances made after the secured party acquires knowledge of the lease or more than 45 days after the lease contract becomes enforceable, whichever first occurs, unless the future advances are made pursuant to a commitment entered into without knowledge of the lease and before the expiration of the 45-day period.

As amended in 1990.

§ 2A–308. Special Rights of Creditors.
(1) A creditor of a lessor in possession of goods subject to a lease contract may treat the lease contract as void if as against the creditor retention of

possession by the lessor is fraudulent under any statute or rule of law, but retention of possession in good faith and current course of trade by the lessor for a commercially reasonable time after the lease contract becomes enforceable is not fraudulent.

(2) Nothing in this Article impairs the rights of creditors of a lessor if the lease contract (a) becomes enforceable, not in current course of trade but in satisfaction of or as security for a pre-existing claim for money, security, or the like, and (b) is made under circumstances which under any statute or rule of law apart from this Article would constitute the transaction a fraudulent transfer or voidable preference.

(3) A creditor of a seller may treat a sale or an identification of goods to a contract for sale as void if as against the creditor retention of possession by the seller is fraudulent under any statute or rule of law, but retention of possession of the goods pursuant to a lease contract entered into by the seller as lessee and the buyer as lessor in connection with the sale or identification of the goods is not fraudulent if the buyer bought for value and in good faith.

Part 4—Performance of Lease Contract: Repudiated, Substituted and Excused

§ 2A–407. Irrevocable Promises: Finance Leases.

(1) In the case of a finance lease that is not a consumer lease the lessee's promises under the lease contract become irrevocable and independent upon the lessee's acceptance of the goods.

(2) A promise that has become irrevocable and independent under subsection (1):

(a) is effective and enforceable between the parties, and by or against third parties including assignees of the parties; and

(b) is not subject to cancellation, termination, modification, repudiation, excuse, or substitution without the consent of the party to whom the promise runs.

(3) This section does not affect the validity under any other law of a covenant in any lease contract making the lessee's promises irrevocable and independent upon the lessee's acceptance of the goods.

As amended in 1990.

Part 5—Default

A. In General

§ 2A–503. Modification or Impairment of Rights and Remedies.

(1) Except as otherwise provided in this Article, the lease agreement may include rights and remedies for default in addition to or in substitution for those provided in this Article and may limit or alter the measure of damages recoverable under this Article.

(2) Resort to a remedy provided under this Article or in the lease agreement is optional unless the remedy is expressly agreed to be exclusive. If circumstances cause an exclusive or limited remedy to fail of its essential purpose, or provision for an exclusive remedy is unconscionable, remedy may be had as provided in this Article.

(3) Consequential damages may be liquidated under Section 2A–504, or may otherwise be limited, altered, or excluded unless the limitation, alteration, or exclusion is unconscionable. Limitation, alteration, or exclusion of consequential damages for injury to the person in the case of consumer goods is prima facie unconscionable but limitation, alteration, or exclusion of damages where the loss is commercial is not prima facie unconscionable.

(4) Rights and remedies on default by the lessor or the lessee with respect to any obligation or promise collateral or ancillary to the lease contract are not impaired by this Article.

As amended in 1990.

§ 2A–504. Liquidation of Damages.

(1) Damages payable by either party for default, or any other act or omission, including indemnity for loss or diminution of anticipated tax benefits or loss or damage to lessor's residual interest, may be liquidated in the lease agreement but only at an amount or by a formula that is reasonable in light of the then anticipated harm caused by the default or other act or omission.

(2) If the lease agreement provides for liquidation of damages, and such provision does not comply with subsection (1), or such provision is an exclusive or limited remedy that circumstances cause to fail of its essential purpose, remedy may be had as provided in this Article.

(3) If the lessor justifiably withholds or stops delivery of goods because of the lessee's default or insolvency (Section 2A–525 or 2A–526), the lessee is entitled to restitution of any amount by which the sum of his [or her] payments exceeds:

(a) the amount to which the lessor is entitled by virtue of terms liquidating the lessor's damages in accordance with subsection (1); or

(b) in the absence of those terms, 20 percent of the then present value of the total rent the lessee was obligated to pay for the balance of the lease term, or, in the case of a consumer lease, the lesser of such amount or $500.

(4) A lessee's right to restitution under subsection (3) is subject to offset to the extent the lessor establishes:

(a) a right to recover damages under the provisions of this Article other than subsection (1); and

(b) the amount or value of any benefits received by the lessee directly or indirectly by reason of the lease contract.

§ 2A–507. Proof of Market Rent: Time and Place.

(1) Damages based on market rent (Section 2A–519 or 2A–528) are determined according to the rent for the use of the goods concerned for a lease term identical to the remaining lease term of the original lease agreement and prevailing at the times specified in Sections 2A–519 and 2A–528.

(2) If evidence of rent for the use of the goods concerned for a lease term identical to the remaining lease term of the original lease agreement and prevailing at the times or places described in this Article is not readily available, the rent prevailing within any reasonable time before or after the time described or at any other place or for a different lease term which in commercial judgment or under usage of trade would serve as a reasonable substitute for the one described may be used, making any proper allowance for the difference, including the cost of transporting the goods to or from the other place.

(3) Evidence of a relevant rent prevailing at a time or place or for a lease term other than the one described in this Article offered by one party is not admissible unless and until he [or she] has given the other party notice the court finds sufficient to prevent unfair surprise.

(4) If the prevailing rent or value of any goods regularly leased in any established market is in issue, reports in official publications or trade journals or in newspapers or periodicals of general circulation published as the reports of that market are admissible in evidence. The circumstances of the preparation of the report may be shown to affect its weight but not its admissibility.

As amended in 1990.

B. Default by Lessor

§ 2A–508. Lessee's Remedies.

(1) If a lessor fails to deliver the goods in conformity to the lease contract (Section 2A–509) or repudiates the lease contract (Section 2A–402), or a lessee rightfully rejects the goods (Section 2A–509) or justifiably revokes acceptance of the goods (Section 2A–517), then with respect to any goods involved, and with respect to all of the goods if under an installment lease contract the value of the whole lease contract is substantially impaired (Section 2A–510), the lessor is in default under the lease contract and the lessee may:

(a) cancel the lease contract (Section 2A–505(1));

(b) recover so much of the rent and security as has been paid and is just under the circumstances;

(c) cover and recover damages as to all goods affected whether or not they have been identified to the lease contract (Sections 2A–518 and 2A–520), or recover damages for nondelivery (Sections 2A–519 and 2A–520);

(d) exercise any other rights or pursue any other remedies provided in the lease contract.

(2) If a lessor fails to deliver the goods in conformity to the lease contract or repudiates the lease contract, the lessee may also:

(a) if the goods have been identified, recover them (Section 2A–522); or

(b) in a proper case, obtain specific performance or replevy the goods (Section 2A–521).

(3) If a lessor is otherwise in default under a lease contract, the lessee may exercise the rights and pursue the remedies provided in the lease contract, which may include a right to cancel the lease, and in Section 2A–519(3).

(4) If a lessor has breached a warranty, whether express or implied, the lessee may recover damages (Section 2A–519(4)).

(5) On rightful rejection or justifiable revocation of acceptance, a lessee has a security interest in goods in the lessee's possession or control for any rent and security that has been paid and any expenses reasonably incurred in their inspection, receipt, transportation, and care and custody and may hold those goods and dispose of them in good faith and in a commercially reasonable manner, subject to Section 2A–527(5).

(6) Subject to the provisions of Section 2A–407, a lessee, on notifying the lessor of the lessee's intention to do so, may deduct all or any part of the damages resulting from any default under the lease contract from any part of the rent still due under the same lease contract.

As amended in 1990.

§ 2A–509. Lessee's Rights on Improper Delivery; Rightful Rejection.

(1) Subject to the provisions of Section 2A–510 on default in installment lease contracts, if the goods or the tender or delivery fail in any respect to conform to the lease contract, the lessee may reject or accept the goods or accept any commercial unit or units and reject the rest of the goods.

(2) Rejection of goods is ineffective unless it is within a reasonable time after tender or delivery of the goods and the lessee seasonably notifies the lessor.

§ 2A–510. Installment Lease Contracts: Rejection and Default.

(1) Under an installment lease contract a lessee may reject any delivery that is nonconforming if the nonconformity substantially impairs the value of that delivery and cannot be cured or the nonconformity is a defect in the required documents; but if the nonconformity does not fall within subsection (2) and the lessor or the supplier gives adequate assurance of its cure, the lessee must accept that delivery.

(2) Whenever nonconformity or default with respect to one or more deliveries substantially impairs the value of the installment lease contract as a whole there is a default with respect to the whole. But, the aggrieved party reinstates the installment lease contract as a whole if the aggrieved party accepts a nonconforming delivery without seasonably notifying of cancellation or brings an action with respect only to past deliveries or demands performance as to future deliveries.

§ 2A–511. Merchant Lessee's Duties as to Rightfully Rejected Goods.

(1) Subject to any security interest of a lessee (Section 2A–508(5)), if a lessor or a supplier has no agent or place of business at the market of rejection, a merchant lessee, after rejection of goods in his [or her] possession or control, shall follow any reasonable instructions received from the lessor or the supplier with respect to the goods. In the absence of those instructions, a merchant lessee shall make reasonable efforts to sell, lease, or otherwise dispose of the goods for the lessor's account if they threaten to decline in value speedily. Instructions are not reasonable if on demand indemnity for expenses is not forthcoming.

(2) If a merchant lessee (subsection (1)) or any other lessee (Section 2A–512) disposes of goods, he [or she] is entitled to reimbursement either from the lessor or the supplier or out of the proceeds for reasonable expenses of caring for and disposing of the goods and, if the expenses include no disposition commission, to such commission as is usual in the trade, or if there is none, to a reasonable sum not exceeding 10 percent of the gross proceeds.

(3) In complying with this section or Section 2A–512, the lessee is held only to good faith. Good faith conduct hereunder is neither acceptance or conversion nor the basis of an action for damages.

(4) A purchaser who purchases in good faith from a lessee pursuant to this section or Section 2A–512 takes the goods free of any rights of the lessor and the supplier even though the lessee fails to comply with one or more of the requirements of this Article.

§ 2A–512. Lessee's Duties as to Rightfully Rejected Goods.

(1) Except as otherwise provided with respect to goods that threaten to decline in value speedily (Section 2A–511) and subject to any security interest of a lessee (Section 2A–508(5)):

    (a) the lessee, after rejection of goods in the lessee's possession, shall hold them with reasonable care at the lessor's or the supplier's disposition for a reasonable time after the lessee's seasonable notification of rejection;

    (b) if the lessor or the supplier gives no instructions within a reasonable time after notification of rejection, the lessee may store the rejected goods for the lessor's or the supplier's account or ship them to the lessor or the supplier or dispose of them for the lessor's or the supplier's account with reimbursement in the manner provided in Section 2A–511; but

    (c) the lessee has no further obligations with regard to goods rightfully rejected.

(2) Action by the lessee pursuant to subsection (1) is not acceptance or conversion.

§ 2A–513. Cure by Lessor of Improper Tender or Delivery; Replacement.

(1) If any tender or delivery by the lessor or the supplier is rejected because nonconforming and the time for performance has not yet expired, the lessor or the supplier may seasonably notify the lessee of the lessor's or the supplier's intention to cure and may then make a conforming delivery within the time provided in the lease contract.

(2) If the lessee rejects a nonconforming tender that the lessor or the supplier had reasonable grounds to believe would be acceptable with or without money allowance, the lessor or the supplier may have a further reasonable time to substitute a conforming tender if he [or she] seasonably notifies the lessee.

§ 2A–515. Acceptance of Goods.

(1) Acceptance of goods occurs after the lessee has had a reasonable opportunity to inspect the goods and

    (a) the lessee signifies or acts with respect to the goods in a manner that signifies to the lessor or the supplier that the goods are conforming or that the lessee will take or retain them in spite of their nonconformity; or

    (b) the lessee fails to make an effective rejection of the goods (Section 2A–509(2)).

(2) Acceptance of a part of any commercial unit is acceptance of that entire unit.

§ 2A–517. Revocation of Acceptance of Goods.

(1) A lessee may revoke acceptance of a lot or commercial unit whose nonconformity substantially impairs its value to the lessee if the lessee has accepted it:

    (a) except in the case of a finance lease, on the reasonable assumption that its nonconformity would be cured and it has not been seasonably cured; or

    (b) without discovery of the nonconformity if the lessee's acceptance was reasonably induced either by the lessor's assurances or, except in the case of a finance lease, by the difficulty of discovery before acceptance.

(2) Except in the case of a finance lease that is not a consumer lease, a lessee may revoke acceptance of a lot or commercial unit if the lessor defaults under the lease contract and the default substantially impairs the value of that lot or commercial unit to the lessee.

(3) If the lease agreement so provides, the lessee may revoke acceptance of a lot or commercial unit because of other defaults by the lessor.

(4) Revocation of acceptance must occur within a reasonable time after the lessee discovers or should have discovered the ground for it and before any substantial change in condition of the goods which is not caused by the nonconformity. Revocation is not effective until the lessee notifies the lessor.

(5) A lessee who so revokes has the same rights and duties with regard to the goods involved as if the lessee had rejected them.

As amended in 1990.

§ 2A–518. Cover; Substitute Goods.

(1) After a default by a lessor under the lease contract of the type described in Section 2A–508(1), or, if agreed, after other default by the lessor, the lessee may cover by making any purchase or lease of or contract to purchase or lease goods in substitution for those due from the lessor.

(2) Except as otherwise provided with respect to damages liquidated in the lease agreement (Section 2A–504) or otherwise determined pursuant to agreement of the parties (Sections 1–102(3) and 2A–503), if a lessee's cover is by a lease agreement substantially similar to the original lease agreement and the new lease agreement is made in good faith and in a commercially reasonable manner, the lessee may recover from the lessor as damages (i) the present value, as of the date of the commencement of the term of the new lease agreement, of the rent under the new lease agreement applicable to that period of the new lease term which is comparable to the then remaining term of the original lease agreement minus the present value as of the same date of the total rent for the then remaining lease term of the original lease agreement, and (ii) any incidental or consequential damages, less expenses saved in consequence of the lessor's default.

(3) If a lessee's cover is by lease agreement that for any reason does not qualify for treatment under subsection (2), or is by purchase or otherwise, the lessee may recover from the lessor as if the lessee had elected not to cover and Section 2A–519 governs.

As amended in 1990.

§ 2A–519. Lessee's Damages for Non-delivery, Repudiation, Default, and Breach of Warranty in Regard to Accepted Goods.

(1) Except as otherwise provided with respect to damages liquidated in the lease agreement (Section 2A–504) or otherwise determined pursuant to agreement of the parties (Sections 1–102(3) and 2A–503), if a lessee elects not to cover or a lessee elects to cover and the cover is by lease agreement that for any reason does not qualify for treatment under Section 2A–518(2), or is by purchase or otherwise, the measure of damages for non-delivery or repudiation by the lessor or for rejection or revocation of acceptance by the lessee is the present value, as of the date of the default, of the then market rent minus the present value as of the same date of the original rent, computed for the remaining lease term of the original lease agreement, together with incidental and consequential damages, less expenses saved in consequence of the lessor's default.

(2) Market rent is to be determined as of the place for tender or, in cases of rejection after arrival or revocation of acceptance, as of the place of arrival.

(3) Except as otherwise agreed, if the lessee has accepted goods and given notification (Section 2A–516(3)), the measure of damages for non-conforming tender or delivery or other default by a lessor is the loss resulting in the ordinary course of events from the lessor's default as determined in any manner that is reasonable together with incidental and consequential damages, less expenses saved in consequence of the lessor's default.

(4) Except as otherwise agreed, the measure of damages for breach of warranty is the present value at the time and place of acceptance of the difference between the value of the use of the goods accepted and the value if they had been as warranted for the lease term, unless special circumstances show proximate damages of a different amount, together with incidental and consequential damages, less expenses saved in consequence of the lessor's default or breach of warranty.

As amended in 1990.

§ 2A–520. Lessee's Incidental and Consequential Damages.

(1) Incidental damages resulting from a lessor's default include expenses reasonably incurred in inspection, receipt, transportation, and care and custody of goods rightfully rejected or goods the acceptance of which is justifiably revoked, any commercially reasonable charges, expenses or commissions in connection with effecting cover, and any other reasonable expense incident to the default.

(2) Consequential damages resulting from a lessor's default include:

    (a) any loss resulting from general or particular requirements and needs of which the lessor at the time of contracting had reason to know and which could not reasonably be prevented by cover or otherwise; and

    (b) injury to person or property proximately resulting from any breach of warranty.

§ 2A–521. Lessee's Right to Specific Performance or Replevin.

(1) Specific performance may be decreed if the goods are unique or in other proper circumstances.

(2) A decree for specific performance may include any terms and conditions as to payment of the rent, damages, or other relief that the court deems just.

(3) A lessee has a right of replevin, detinue, sequestration, claim and delivery, or the like for goods identified to the lease contract if after reasonable effort the lessee is unable to effect cover for those goods or the circumstances reasonably indicate that the effort will be unavailing.

§ 2A–522. Lessee's Right to Goods on Lessor's Insolvency.

(1) Subject to subsection (2) and even though the goods have not been shipped, a lessee who has paid a part or all of the rent and security for goods identified to a lease contract (Section 2A–217) on making and keeping good a tender of any unpaid portion of the rent and security due under the lease contract may recover the goods identified from the lessor if the lessor becomes insolvent within 10 days after receipt of the first installment of rent and security.

(2) A lessee acquires the right to recover goods identified to a lease contract only if they conform to the lease contract.

C. Default by Lessee
§ 2A–523. Lessor's Remedies.

(1) If a lessee wrongfully rejects or revokes acceptance of goods or fails to make a payment when due or repudiates with respect to a part or the whole, then, with respect to any goods involved, and with respect to all of the goods if under an installment lease contract the value of the whole lease contract is substantially impaired (Section 2A–510), the lessee is in default under the lease contract and the lessor may:

    (a) cancel the lease contract (Section 2A–505(1));

    (b) proceed respecting goods not identified to the lease contract (Section 2A–524);

    (c) withhold delivery of the goods and take possession of goods previously delivered (Section 2A–525);

    (d) stop delivery of the goods by any bailee (Section 2A–526);

    (e) dispose of the goods and recover damages (Section 2A–527), or retain the goods and recover damages (Section 2A–528), or in a proper case recover rent (Section 2A–529);

    (f) exercise any other rights or pursue any other remedies provided in the lease contract.

(2) If a lessor does not fully exercise a right or obtain a remedy to which the lessor is entitled under subsection (1), the lessor may recover the loss resulting in the ordinary course of events from the lessee's default as determined in any reasonable manner, together with incidental damages, less expenses saved in consequence of the lessee's default.

(3) If a lessee is otherwise in default under a lease contract, the lessor may exercise the rights and pursue the remedies provided in the lease contract, which may include a right to cancel the lease. In addition, unless otherwise provided in the lease contract:

    (a) if the default substantially impairs the value of the lease contract to the lessor, the lessor may exercise the rights and pursue the remedies provided in subsections (1) or (2); or

    (b) if the default does not substantially impair the value of the lease contract to the lessor, the lessor may recover as provided in subsection (2).

As amended in 1990.

§ 2A–524. Lessor's Right to Identify Goods to Lease Contract.

(1) After default by the lessee under the lease contract of the type described in Section 2A–523(1) or 2A–523(3)(a) or, if agreed, after other default by the lessee, the lessor may:

    (a) identify to the lease contract conforming goods not already identified if at the time the lessor learned of the default they were in the lessor's or the supplier's possession or control; and

(b) dispose of goods (Section 2A–527(1)) that demonstrably have been intended for the particular lease contract even though those goods are unfinished.

(2) If the goods are unfinished, in the exercise of reasonable commercial judgment for the purposes of avoiding loss and of effective realization, an aggrieved lessor or the supplier may either complete manufacture and wholly identify the goods to the lease contract or cease manufacture and lease, sell, or otherwise dispose of the goods for scrap or salvage value or proceed in any other reasonable manner.

As amended in 1990.

§ 2A–525. Lessor's Right to Possession of Goods.

(1) If a lessor discovers the lessee to be insolvent, the lessor may refuse to deliver the goods.

(2) After a default by the lessee under the lease contract of the type described in Section 2A–523(1) or 2A–523(3)(a) or, if agreed, after other default by the lessee, the lessor has the right to take possession of the goods. If the lease contract so provides, the lessor may require the lessee to assemble the goods and make them available to the lessor at a place to be designated by the lessor which is reasonably convenient to both parties. Without removal, the lessor may render unusable any goods employed in trade or business, and may dispose of goods on the lessee's premises (Section 2A–527).

(3) The lessor may proceed under subsection (2) without judicial process if it can be done without breach of the peace or the lessor may proceed by action.

As amended in 1990.

§ 2A–526. Lessor's Stoppage of Delivery in Transit or Otherwise.

(1) A lessor may stop delivery of goods in the possession of a carrier or other bailee if the lessor discovers the lessee to be insolvent and may stop delivery of carload, truckload, planeload, or larger shipments of express or freight if the lessee repudiates or fails to make a payment due before delivery, whether for rent, security or otherwise under the lease contract, or for any other reason the lessor has a right to withhold or take possession of the goods.

(2) In pursuing its remedies under subsection (1), the lessor may stop delivery until

    (a) receipt of the goods by the lessee;

    (b) acknowledgment to the lessee by any bailee of the goods, except a carrier, that the bailee holds the goods for the lessee; or

    (c) such an acknowledgment to the lessee by a carrier via reshipment or as warehouseman.

(3) (a) To stop delivery, a lessor shall so notify as to enable the bailee by reasonable diligence to prevent delivery of the goods.

    (b) After notification, the bailee shall hold and deliver the goods according to the directions of the lessor, but the lessor is liable to the bailee for any ensuing charges or damages.

    (c) A carrier who has issued a nonnegotiable bill of lading is not obliged to obey a notification to stop received from a person other than the consignor.

§ 2A–527. Lessor's Rights to Dispose of Goods.

(1) After a default by a lessee under the lease contract of the type described in Section 2A–523(1) or 2A–523(3)(a) or after the lessor refuses to deliver or takes possession of goods (Section 2A–525 or 2A–526), or, if agreed, after other default by a lessee, the lessor may dispose of the goods concerned or the undelivered balance thereof by lease, sale, or otherwise.

(2) Except as otherwise provided with respect to damages liquidated in the lease agreement (Section 2A–504) or otherwise determined pursuant to agreement of the parties (Sections 1–102(3) and 2A–503), if the disposition is by lease agreement substantially similar to the original lease agreement and the new lease agreement is made in good faith and in a commercially reasonable manner, the lessor may recover from the lessee as damages (i) accrued and unpaid rent as of the date of the commencement of the term of the new lease agreement, (ii) the present value, as of the same date, of the total rent for the then remaining lease term of the original lease agreement minus the present value, as of the same date, of the rent under the new lease agreement applicable to that period of the

new lease term which is comparable to the then remaining term of the original lease agreement, and (iii) any incidental damages allowed under Section 2A–530, less expenses saved in consequence of the lessee's default.

(3) If the lessor's disposition is by lease agreement that for any reason does not qualify for treatment under subsection (2), or is by sale or otherwise, the lessor may recover from the lessee as if the lessor had elected not to dispose of the goods and Section 2A–528 governs.

(4) A subsequent buyer or lessee who buys or leases from the lessor in good faith for value as a result of a disposition under this section takes the goods free of the original lease contract and any rights of the original lessee even though the lessor fails to comply with one or more of the requirements of this Article.

(5) The lessor is not accountable to the lessee for any profit made on any disposition. A lessee who has rightfully rejected or justifiably revoked acceptance shall account to the lessor for any excess over the amount of the lessee's security interest (Section 2A–508(5)).

As amended in 1990.

§ 2A–528. Lessor's Damages for Non-acceptance, Failure to Pay, Repudiation, or Other Default.

(1) Except as otherwise provided with respect to damages liquidated in the lease agreement (Section 2A–504) or otherwise determined pursuant to agreement of the parties (Sections 1–102(3) and 2A–503), if a lessor elects to retain the goods or a lessor elects to dispose of the goods and the disposition is by lease agreement that for any reason does not qualify for treatment under Section 2A–527(2), or is by sale or otherwise, the lessor may recover from the lessee as damages for a default of the type described in Section 2A–523(1) or 2A–523(3)(a), or, if agreed, for other default of the lessee, (i) accrued and unpaid rent as of the date of default if the lessee has never taken possession of the goods, or, if the lessee has taken possession of the goods, as of the date the lessor repossesses the goods or an earlier date on which the lessee makes a tender of the goods to the lessor, (ii) the present value as of the date determined under clause (i) of the total rent for the then remaining lease term of the original lease agreement minus the present value as of the same date of the market rent at the place where the goods are located computed for the same lease term, and (iii) any incidental damages allowed under Section 2A–530, less expenses saved in consequence of the lessee's default.

(2) If the measure of damages provided in subsection (1) is inadequate to put a lessor in as good a position as performance would have, the measure of damages is the present value of the profit, including reasonable overhead, the lessor would have made from full performance by the lessee, together with any incidental damages allowed under Section 2A–530, due allowance for costs reasonably incurred and due credit for payments or proceeds of disposition.

As amended in 1990.

§ 2A–529. Lessor's Action for the Rent.

(1) After default by the lessee under the lease contract of the type described in Section 2A–523(1) or 2A–523(3)(a) or, if agreed, after other default by the lessee, if the lessor complies with subsection (2), the lessor may recover from the lessee as damages:

    (a) for goods accepted by the lessee and not repossessed by or tendered to the lessor, and for conforming goods lost or damaged within a commercially reasonable time after risk of loss passes to the lessee (Section 2A–219), (i) accrued and unpaid rent as of the date of entry of judgment in favor of the lessor, (ii) the present value as of the same date of the rent for the then remaining lease term of the lease agreement, and (iii) any incidental damages allowed under Section 2A–530, less expenses saved in consequence of the lessee's default; and

    (b) for goods identified to the lease contract if the lessor is unable after reasonable effort to dispose of them at a reasonable price or the circumstances reasonably indicate that effort will be unavailing, (i) accrued and unpaid rent as of the date of entry of judgment in favor of the lessor, (ii) the present value as of the same date of the rent for the then remaining lease term of the lease agreement, and (iii) any incidental damages allowed under Section 2A–530, less expenses saved in consequence of the lessee's default.

(2) Except as provided in subsection (3), the lessor shall hold for the lessee for the remaining lease term of the lease agreement any goods that have been identified to the lease contract and are in the lessor's control.

(3) The lessor may dispose of the goods at any time before collection of the judgment for damages obtained pursuant to subsection (1). If the disposition is before the end of the remaining lease term of the lease agreement, the lessor's recovery against the lessee for damages is governed by Section 2A–527 or Section 2A–528, and the lessor will cause an appropriate credit to be provided against a judgment for damages to the extent that the amount of the judgment exceeds the recovery available pursuant to Section 2A–527 or 2A–528.

(4) Payment of the judgment for damages obtained pursuant to subsection (1) entitles the lessee to the use and possession of the goods not then disposed of for the remaining lease term of and in accordance with the lease agreement.

(5) After default by the lessee under the lease contract of the type described in Section 2A–523(1) or Section 2A–523(3)(a) or, if agreed, after other default by the lessee, a lessor who is held not entitled to rent under this section must nevertheless be awarded damages for non-acceptance under Section 2A–527 or Section 2A–528.

As amended in 1990.

§ 2A–530. Lessor's Incidental Damages.
Incidental damages to an aggrieved lessor include any commercially reasonable charges, expenses, or commissions incurred in stopping delivery, in the transportation, care and custody of goods after the lessee's default, in connection with return or disposition of the goods, or otherwise resulting from the default.

ARTICLE 3: NEGOTIABLE INSTRUMENTS
Part 1—General Provisions and Definitions
§ 3–101. Short Title.
This Article may be cited as Uniform Commercial Code—Negotiable Instruments.

§ 3–102. Subject Matter.
(a) This Article applies to negotiable instruments. It does not apply to money or to payment orders governed by Article 4A. A negotiable instrument that is also a certificated security under Section 8–102(1)(a) is subject to Article 8 and to this Article.

(b) In the event of conflict between the provisions of this Article and those of Article 4, Article 8, or Article 9, the provisions of Article 4, Article 8 and Article 9 prevail over those of this Article.

(c) Regulations of the Board of Governors of the Federal Reserve System and operating circulars of the Federal Reserve Banks supersede any inconsistent provision of this Article to the extent of the inconsistency.

§ 3–103. Definitions.
(a) In this Article:

(1) "Acceptor" means a drawee that has accepted a draft.

(2) "Drawee" means a person ordered in a draft to make payment.

(3) "Drawer" means a person that signs a draft as a person ordering payment.

(4) "Good faith" means honesty in fact and the observance of reasonable commercial standards of fair dealing.

(5) "Maker" means a person that signs a note as promisor of payment.

(6) "Order" means a written instruction to pay money signed by the person giving the instruction. The instruction may be addressed to any person, including the person giving the instruction, or to one or more persons jointly or in the alternative but not in succession. An authorization to pay is not an order unless the person authorized to pay is also instructed to pay.

(7) "Ordinary care" in the case of a person engaged in business means observance of reasonable commercial standards, prevailing in the area in which that person is located, with respect to the business in which that person is engaged. In the case of a bank that takes an instrument for processing for collection or payment by automated

means, reasonable commercial standards do not require the bank to examine the instrument if the failure to examine does not violate the bank's prescribed procedures and the bank's procedures do not vary unreasonably from general banking usage not disapproved by this Article or Article 4.

(8) "Party" means party to an instrument.

(9) "Promise" means a written undertaking to pay money signed by the person undertaking to pay. An acknowledgment of an obligation by the obligor is not a promise unless the obligor also undertakes to pay the obligation.

(10) "Prove" with respect to a fact means to meet the burden of establishing the fact (Section 1–201(8)).

(11) "Remitter" means a person that purchases an instrument from its issuer if the instrument is payable to an identified person other than the purchaser.

(b) Other definitions applying to this Article and the sections in which they appear are:

"Acceptance" Section 3–409.
"Accommodated party" Section 3–419.
"Accommodation indorsement" Section 3–205.
"Accommodation party" Section 3–419.
"Alteration" Section 3–407.
"Blank indorsement" Section 3–205.
"Cashier's check" Section 3–104.
"Certificate of deposit" Section 3–104.
"Certified check" Section 3–409.
"Check" Section 3–104.
"Consideration" Section 3–303.
"Draft" Section 3–104.
"Fiduciary" Section 3–307.
"Guarantor" Section 3–417.
"Holder in due course" Section 3–302.
"Incomplete instrument" Section 3–115.
"Indorsement" Section 3–204.
"Indorser" Section 3–204.
"Instrument" Section 3–104.
"Issue" Section 3–105.
"Issuer" Section 3–105.
"Negotiable instrument" Section 3–104.
"Negotiation" Section 3–201.
"Note" Section 3–104.
"Payable at a definite time" Section 3–108.
"Payable on demand" Section 3–108.
"Payable to bearer" Section 3–109.
"Payable to order" Section 3–110.
"Payment" Section 3–603.
"Person entitled to enforce" Section 3–301.
"Presentment" Section 3–501.
"Reacquisition" Section 3–207.
"Represented person" Section 3–307.
"Special indorsement" Section 3–205.
"Teller's check" Section 3–104.
"Traveler's check" Section 3–104.
"Value" Section 3–303.

(c) The following definitions in other Articles apply to this Article:
"Bank" Section 4–105.
"Banking day" Section 4–104.
"Clearing house" Section 4–104.
"Collecting bank" Section 4–105.
"Customer" Section 4–104.
"Depositary bank" Section 4–105.
"Documentary draft" Section 4–104.
"Intermediary bank" Section 4–105.
"Item" Section 4–104.
"Midnight deadline" Section 4–104.
"Payor bank" Section 4–105.
"Suspends payments" Section 4–104.

(d) In addition, Article 1 contains general definitions and principles of construction and interpretation applicable throughout this Article.

§ 3–104. Negotiable Instrument.

(a) "Negotiable instrument" means an unconditional promise or order to pay a fixed amount of money, with or without interest or other charges described in the promise or order, if it:

(1) is payable to bearer or to order at the time it is issued or first comes into possession of a holder;

(2) is payable on demand or at a definite time; and

(3) does not state any other undertaking or instruction by the person promising or ordering payment to do any act in addition to the payment of money except that the promise or order may contain (i) an undertaking or power to give, maintain, or protect collateral to secure payment, (ii) an authorization or power to the holder to confess judgment or realize on or dispose of collateral, or (iii) a waiver of the benefit of any law intended for the advantage or protection of any obligor.

(b) "Instrument" means negotiable instrument.

(c) An order that meets all of the requirements of subsection (a) except subparagraph (1) and otherwise falls within the definition of "check" in subsection (f) is a negotiable instrument and a check.

(d) Notwithstanding subsection (a), a promise or order other than a check is not an instrument if, at the time it is issued or first comes into possession of a holder, it contains a conspicuous statement, however expressed, indicating that the writing is not an instrument governed by this Article.

(e) An instrument is a "note" if it is a promise, and is a "draft" if it is an order. If an instrument falls within the definition of both "note" and "draft," the person entitled to enforce the instrument may treat it as either.

(f) "Check" means (i) a draft, other than a documentary draft, payable on demand and drawn on a bank or (ii) a cashier's check or teller's check. An instrument may be a check even though it is described on its face by another term such as "money order."

(g) "Cashier's check" means a draft with respect to which the drawer and drawee are the same bank or branches of the same bank.

(h) "Teller's check" means a draft drawn by a bank (i) on another bank, or (ii) payable at or through a bank.

(i) "Traveler's check" means an instrument that (i) is payable on demand, (ii) is drawn on or payable at or through a bank, (iii) is designated by the term "traveler's check" or by a substantially similar term, and (iv) requires, as a condition to payment, a countersignature by a person whose specimen signature appears on the instrument.

(j) "Certificate of deposit" means an instrument containing an acknowledgment by a bank that a sum of money has been received by the bank, and a promise by the bank to repay the sum of money. A certificate of deposit is a note of the bank.

§ 3–105. Issue of Instrument.

(a) "Issue" means the first delivery of an instrument by the maker or drawer, whether to a holder or nonholder, for the purpose of giving rights on the instrument to any person.

(b) An unissued instrument, or an unissued incomplete instrument (Section 3–115) that is completed, is binding on the maker or drawer, but nonissuance is a defense. An instrument that is conditionally issued or is issued for a special purpose is binding on the maker or drawer, but failure of the condition or special purpose to be fulfilled is a defense.

(c) "Issuer" applies to issued and unissued instruments and means any person that signs an instrument as maker or drawer.

§ 3–106. Unconditional Promise or Order.

(a) Except as provided in subsections (b) and (c), for the purposes of Section 3–104(a), a promise or order is unconditional unless it states (i) an express condition to payment or (ii) that the promise or order is subject to or governed by another writing, or that rights or obligations with respect to the promise or order are stated in another writing; however, a mere reference to another writing does not make the promise or order conditional.

(b) A promise or order is not made conditional (i) by a reference to another writing for a statement of rights with respect to collateral, prepayment, or acceleration, or (ii) because payment is limited to resort to a particular fund or source.

(c) If a promise or order requires, as a condition to payment, a countersignature by a person whose specimen signature appears on the promise or order, the condition does not make the promise or order conditional for the purposes of Section 3–104(a). If the person whose specimen signature appears on an instrument fails to countersign the instrument, the failure to countersign is a defense to the obligation of the issuer, but the failure does not prevent a transferee of the instrument from becoming a holder of the instrument.

(d) If a promise or order at the time it is issued or first comes into possession of a holder contains a statement, required by applicable statutory or administrative law, to the effect that the rights of a holder or transferee are subject to claims or defenses that the issuer could assert against the original payee, the promise or order is not thereby made conditional for the purposes of Section 3–104(a), but there cannot be a holder in due course of the promise or order.

§ 3–107. Instrument Payable in Foreign Money.

Unless the instrument otherwise provides, an instrument that states the amount payable in foreign money may be paid in the foreign money or in an equivalent amount in dollars calculated by using the current bank-offered spot rate at the place of payment for the purchase of dollars on the day on which the instrument is paid.

§ 3–108. Payable on Demand or at a Definite Time.

(a) A promise or order is "payable on demand" if (i) it states that it is payable on demand or at sight, or otherwise indicates that it is payable at the will of the holder, or (ii) it does not state any time of payment.

(b) A promise or order is "payable at a definite time" if it is payable on elapse of a definite period of time after sight or acceptance or at a fixed date or dates or at a time or times readily ascertainable at the time the promise or order is issued, subject to rights of (i) prepayment, (ii) acceleration, or (iii) extension at the option of the holder or (iv) extension to a further definite time at the option of the maker or acceptor or automatically upon or after a specified act or event.

(c) If an instrument, payable at a fixed date, is also payable upon demand made before the fixed date, the instrument is payable on demand until the fixed date and, if demand for payment is not made before that date, becomes payable at a definite time on the fixed date.

§ 3–109. Payable to Bearer or to Order.

(a) A promise or order is payable to bearer if it:

(1) states that it is payable to bearer or to the order of bearer or otherwise indicates that the person in possession of the promise or order is entitled to payment,

(2) does not state a payee, or

(3) states that it is payable to or to the order of cash or otherwise indicates that it is not payable to an identified person.

(b) A promise or order that is not payable to bearer is payable to order if it is payable (i) to the order of an identified person or (ii) to an identified person or order. A promise or order that is payable to order is payable to the identified person.

(c) An instrument payable to bearer may become payable to an identified person if it is specially indorsed as stated in Section 3–205(a). An instrument payable to an identified person may become payable to bearer if it is indorsed in blank as stated in Section 3–205(b).

§ 3–110. Identification of Person to Whom Instrument Is Payable.

(a) A person to whom an instrument is payable is determined by the intent of the person, whether or not authorized, signing as, or in the name or behalf of, the maker or drawer. The instrument is payable to the person intended by the signer even if that person is identified in the instrument by a name or other identification that is not that of the intended person. If more than one person signs in the name or behalf of the maker or drawer and all the signers do not intend the same person as payee, the instrument is payable to any person intended by one or more of the signers.

(b) If the signature of the maker or drawer of an instrument is made by automated means such as a check-writing machine, the payee of the instrument is determined by the intent of the person who supplied the name or identification of the payee, whether or not authorized to do so.

(c) A person to whom an instrument is payable may be identified in any way including by name, identifying number, office, or account number. For the purpose of determining the holder of an instrument, the following rules apply:

    (1) If an instrument is payable to an account and the account is identified only by number, the instrument is payable to the person to whom the account is payable. If an instrument is payable to an account identified by number and by the name of a person, the instrument is payable to the named person, whether or not that person is the owner of the account identified by number.

    (2) If an instrument is payable to:

        (i) a trust, estate, or a person described as trustee or representative of a trust or estate, the instrument is payable to the trustee, the representative, or a successor of either, whether or not the beneficiary or estate is also named;

        (ii) a person described as agent or similar representative of a named or identified person, the instrument is payable either to the represented person, the representative, or a successor of the representative;

        (iii) a fund or organization that is not a legal entity, the instrument is payable to a representative of the members of the fund or organization; or

        (iv) an office or to a person described as holding an office, the instrument is payable to the named person, the incumbent of the office, or a successor to the incumbent.

(d) If an instrument is payable to two or more persons alternatively, it is payable to any of them and may be negotiated, discharged, or enforced by any of them in possession of the instrument. If an instrument is payable to two or more persons not alternatively, it is payable to all of them and may be negotiated, discharged, or enforced only by all of them. If an instrument payable to two or more persons is ambiguous as to whether it is payable to the persons alternatively, the instrument is payable to the persons alternatively.

§ 3–111. Place of Payment.

Except as otherwise provided for items in Article 4, an instrument is payable at the place of payment stated in the instrument. If no place of payment is stated, an instrument is payable at the address of the drawee or maker stated in the instrument. If no address is stated, the place of payment is the place of business of the drawee or maker. If a drawee or maker has more than one place of business, the place of payment is any place of business of the drawee or maker chosen by the person entitled to enforce the instrument. If the drawee or maker has no place of business, the place of payment is the residence of the drawee or maker.

§ 3–112. Interest.

(a) Unless otherwise provided in the instrument, (i) an instrument is not payable with interest, and (ii) interest on an interest-bearing instrument is payable from the date of the instrument.

(b) Interest may be stated in an instrument as a fixed or variable amount of money or it may be expressed as a fixed or variable rate or rates. The amount or rate of interest may be stated or described in the instrument in any manner and may require reference to information not contained in the instrument. If an instrument provides for interest but the amount of interest payable cannot be ascertained from the description, interest is payable at the judgment rate in effect at the place of payment of the instrument and at the time interest first accrues.

§ 3–113. Date of Instrument.

(a) An instrument may be antedated or postdated. The date stated determines the time of payment if the instrument is payable at a fixed period after date. Except as provided in Section 4–401(3), an instrument payable on demand is not payable before the date of the instrument.

(b) If an instrument is undated, its date is the date of its issue or, in the case of an unissued instrument, the date it first comes into possession of a holder.

§ 3–114. Contradictory Terms of Instrument.

If an instrument contains contradictory terms, typewritten terms prevail over printed terms, handwritten terms prevail over both, and words prevail over numbers.

§ 3–115. Incomplete Instrument.

(a) "Incomplete instrument" means a signed writing, whether or not issued by the signer, the contents of which show at the time of signing that it is incomplete but that the signer intended it to be completed by the addition of words or numbers.

(b) Subject to subsection (c), if an incomplete instrument is an instrument under Section 3–104, it may be enforced (i) according to its terms if it is not completed, or (ii) according to its terms as augmented by completion. If an incomplete instrument is not an instrument under Section 3–104 but, after completion, the requirements of Section 3–104 are met, the instrument may be enforced according to its terms as augmented by completion.

(c) If words or numbers are added to an incomplete instrument without authority of the signer, there is an alteration of the incomplete instrument governed by Section 3–407.

(d) The burden of establishing that words or numbers were added to an incomplete instrument without authority of the signer is on the person asserting the lack of authority.

§ 3–116. Joint and Several Liability; Contribution.

(a) Except as otherwise provided in the instrument, two or more persons who have the same liability on an instrument as makers, drawers, acceptors, indorsers who are indorsing joint payees, or anomalous indorsers, are jointly and severally liable in the capacity in which they sign.

(b) Except as provided in Section 3–417(e) or by agreement of the affected parties, a party with joint and several liability that pays the instrument is entitled to receive from any party with the same joint and several liability contribution in accordance with applicable law.

(c) Discharge of one party with joint and several liability by a person entitled to enforce the instrument does not affect the right under subsection (b) of a party with the same joint and several liability to receive contribution from the party discharged.

§ 3–117. Other Agreements Affecting an Instrument.

Subject to applicable law regarding exclusion of proof of contemporaneous or prior agreements, the obligation of a party to an instrument to pay the instrument may be modified, supplemented, or nullified by a separate agreement of the obligor and a person entitled to enforce the instrument if the instrument is issued or the obligation is incurred in reliance on the agreement or as part of the same transaction giving rise to the agreement. To the extent an obligation is modified, supplemented, or nullified by an agreement under this section, the agreement is a defense to the obligation.

§ 3–118. Statute of Limitations.

(a) Except as provided in subsection (e), an action to enforce the obligation of a party to pay a note payable at a definite time must be commenced within six years after the payment date or dates stated in the note or, if a payment date is accelerated, within six years after the accelerated payment date.

(b) Except as provided in subsection (d) or (e), if demand for payment is made to the maker of a note payable on demand, an action to enforce the obligation of a party to pay the note must be commenced within six years after the demand. If no demand for payment is made to the maker, an action to enforce the note is barred if neither principal nor interest on the note has been paid for a continuous period of 10 years.

(c) Except as provided in subsection (d), an action to enforce the obligation of a party to an unaccepted draft to pay the draft must be commenced within six years after dishonor of the draft or 10 years after the date of the draft, whichever period expires first.

(d) An action to enforce the obligation of the acceptor of a certified check or the issuer of a teller's check, cashier's check, or traveler's check must be commenced within six years after demand for payment is made to the acceptor or issuer, as the case may be.

(e) An action to enforce the obligation of a party to a certificate of deposit to pay the instrument must be commenced within six years after demand for payment is made to the maker, but if the instrument states a maturity date and the maker is not required to pay before that date, the six-year period begins when a demand for payment is in effect and the maturity date has passed.

(f) This subsection applies to an action to enforce the obligation of a party to pay an accepted draft, other than a certified check. If the obligation of the acceptor is payable at a definite time, the action must be commenced within six years after the payment date or dates stated in the draft or acceptance. If the obligation of the acceptor is payable on demand, the action must be commenced within six years after the date of the acceptance.

(g) Unless governed by other law regarding claims for indemnity or contribution, an action (i) for conversion of an instrument, for money had and received, or like action based on conversion, (ii) for breach of warranty, or (iii) to enforce an obligation, duty, or right arising under this Article and not governed by this section must be commenced within three years after the cause of action accrues.

§ 3–119. Notice of Right to Defend Action.

In an action for breach of an obligation for which a third person is answerable over pursuant to this Article or Article 4, the defendant may give the third person written notice of the litigation, and the person notified may then give similar notice to any other person who is answerable over. If the notice states (i) that the person notified may come in and defend and (ii) that failure to do so will bind the person notified in an action later brought by the person giving the notice as to any determination of fact common to the two litigations, the person notified is so bound unless after seasonable receipt of the notice the person notified does come in and defend.

Part 2—Negotiation, Transfer and Indorsement

§ 3–201. Negotiation.

(a) "Negotiation" means a transfer of possession, whether voluntary or involuntary, of an instrument to a person who thereby becomes its holder if possession is obtained from a person other than the issuer of the instrument.

(b) Except for a negotiation by a remitter, if an instrument is payable to an identified person, negotiation requires transfer of possession of the instrument and its indorsement by the holder. If an instrument is payable to bearer, it may be negotiated by transfer of possession alone.

§ 3–202. Negotiation Subject to Rescission.

(a) Negotiation is effective even if obtained (i) from an infant, a corporation exceeding its powers, or a person without capacity, or (ii) by fraud, duress, or mistake, or in breach of duty or as part of an illegal transaction.

(b) To the extent permitted by law, negotiation may be rescinded or may be subject to other remedies, but those remedies may not be asserted against a subsequent holder in due course or a person paying the instrument in good faith and without knowledge of facts that are a basis for rescission or other remedy.

§ 3–203. Rights Acquired by Transfer.

(a) An instrument is transferred when it is delivered by a person other than its issuer for the purpose of giving to the person receiving delivery the right to enforce the instrument.

(b) Transfer of an instrument, regardless of whether the transfer is a negotiation, vests in the transferee any right of the transferor to enforce the instrument, including any right as a holder in due course, but the transferee cannot acquire rights of a holder in due course by a transfer, directly or indirectly, from a holder in due course if the purchaser engaged in fraud or illegality affecting the instrument.

(c) Unless otherwise agreed, if an instrument is transferred for value and the transferee does not become a holder because of lack of indorsement by the transferor, the transferee has a specifically enforceable right to the unqualified indorsement of the transferor, but negotiation of the instrument does not occur until the indorsement is made.

(d) If a transferor purports to transfer less than the entire instrument, negotiation of the instrument does not occur. The transferee obtains no rights under this Article and has only the rights of a partial assignee.

§ 3–204. Indorsement.

(a) "Indorsement" means a signature, other than that of a maker, drawer, or acceptor, that alone or accompanied by other words, is made on an instrument for the purpose of (i) negotiating the instrument, (ii) restricting payment of the instrument, or (iii) incurring indorser's liability on the instrument, but regardless of the intent of the signer, a signature and its accompanying words is an indorsement unless the accompanying words, the terms of the instrument, the place of the signature, or other circumstances unambiguously indicate that the signature was made for a purpose other than indorsement. For the purpose of determining whether a signature is made on an instrument, a paper affixed to the instrument is a part of the instrument.

(b) "Indorser" means a person who makes an indorsement.

(c) For the purpose of determining whether the transferee of an instrument is a holder, an indorsement that transfers a security interest in the instrument is effective as an unqualified indorsement of the instrument.

(d) If an instrument is payable to a holder under a name that is not the name of the holder, indorsement may be made by the holder in the name stated in the instrument or in the holder's name or both, but signature in both names may be required by a person paying or taking the instrument for value or collection.

§ 3–205. Special Indorsement; Blank Indorsement; Anomalous Indorsement.

(a) If an indorsement is made by the holder of an instrument, whether payable to an identified person or payable to bearer, and the indorsement identifies a person to whom it makes the instrument payable, it is a "special indorsement." When specially indorsed, an instrument becomes payable to the identified person and may be negotiated only by the indorsement of that person. The principles stated in Section 3–110 apply to special indorsements.

(b) If an indorsement is made by the holder of an instrument and it is not a special indorsement, it is a "blank indorsement." When indorsed in blank, an instrument becomes payable to bearer and may be negotiated by transfer of possession alone until specially indorsed.

(c) The holder may convert a blank indorsement that consists only of a signature into a special indorsement by writing, above the signature of the indorser, words identifying the person to whom the instrument is made payable.

(d) "Anomalous indorsement" means an indorsement made by a person that is not the holder of the instrument. An anomalous indorsement does not affect the manner in which the instrument may be negotiated.

§ 3–206. Restrictive Indorsement.

(a) An indorsement limiting payment to a particular person or otherwise prohibiting further transfer or negotiation of the instrument is not effective to prevent further transfer or negotiation of the instrument.

(b) An indorsement stating a condition to the right of the indorsee to receive payment does not affect the right of the indorsee to enforce the instrument. A person paying the instrument or taking it for value or collection may disregard the condition, and the rights and liabilities of that person are not affected by whether the condition has been fulfilled.

(c) The following rules apply to an instrument bearing an indorsement (i) described in Section 4–201(2), or (ii) in blank or to a particular bank using the words "for deposit," "for collection," or other words indicating a purpose of having the instrument collected for the indorser or for a particular account:

  (1) A person, other than a bank, that purchases the instrument when so indorsed converts the instrument unless the proceeds of the instrument are received by the indorser or are applied consistently with the indorsement.

  (2) A depositary bank that purchases the instrument or takes it for collection when so indorsed converts the instrument unless the proceeds of the instrument are received by the indorser or applied consistently with the indorsement.

  (3) A payor bank that is also the depositary bank or that takes the instrument for immediate payment over the counter from a person other than a collecting bank converts the instrument unless the proceeds of the instrument are received by the indorser or applied consistently with the indorsement.

  (4) Except as otherwise provided in paragraph (3), a payor bank or intermediary bank may disregard the indorsement and is not liable if the proceeds of the instrument are not received by the indorser or applied consistently with the indorsement.

(d)   Except for an indorsement covered by subsection (c), the following rules apply to an instrument bearing an indorsement using words to the effect that payment is to be made to the indorsee as agent, trustee, or other fiduciary for the benefit of the indorser or another person.

> **(1)**   Unless there is notice of breach of fiduciary duty as provided in Section 3–307, a person that purchases the instrument from the indorsee or takes the instrument from the indorsee for collection or payment may pay the proceeds of payment or the value given for the instrument to the indorsee without regard to whether the indorsee violates a fiduciary duty to the indorser.
>
> **(2)**   A later transferee of the instrument or person that pays the instrument is neither given notice nor otherwise affected by the restriction in the indorsement unless the transferee or payor knows that the fiduciary dealt with the instrument or its proceeds in breach of fiduciary duty.

(e)   Purchase of an instrument bearing an indorsement to which this section applies does not prevent the purchaser from becoming a holder in due course of the instrument unless the purchaser is a converter under subsection (c).

(f)   In an action to enforce the obligation of a party to pay the instrument, the obligor has a defense if payment would violate an indorsement to which this section applies and the payment is not permitted by this section.

§ 3–207. Reacquisition.

Reacquisition of an instrument occurs if it is transferred, by negotiation or otherwise, to a former holder. A former holder that reacquires the instrument may cancel indorsements made after the reacquirer first became a holder of the instrument. If the cancellation causes the instrument to be payable to the reacquirer or to bearer, the reacquirer may negotiate the instrument. An indorser whose indorsement is canceled is discharged, and the discharge is effective against any later holder.

Part 3—Enforcement of Instruments
§ 3–301. Person Entitled to Enforce Instrument.

"Person entitled to enforce" an instrument means (i) the holder of the instrument, (ii) a nonholder in possession of the instrument who has the rights of a holder, or (iii) a person not in possession of the instrument who is entitled to enforce the instrument pursuant to Section 3–309. A person may be a person entitled to enforce the instrument even though the person is not the owner of the instrument or is in wrongful possession of the instrument.

§ 3–302. Holder in Due Course.

(a)   Subject to subsection (c) and Section 3–106(d), "holder in due course" means the holder of an instrument if:

> **(1)**   the instrument when issued or negotiated to the holder does not bear such apparent evidence of forgery or alteration or is not otherwise so irregular or incomplete as to call into question its authenticity, and
>
> **(2)**   the holder took the instrument (i) for value, (ii) in good faith, (iii) without notice that the instrument is overdue or has been dishonored or that there is an uncured default with respect to payment of another instrument issued as part of the same series, (iv) without notice that the instrument contains an unauthorized signature or has been altered, (v) without notice of any claim to the instrument stated in Section 3–306, and (vi) without notice that any party to the instrument has any defense or claim in recoupment stated in Section 3–305(a).

(b)   Notice of discharge of a party to the instrument, other than discharge in an insolvency proceeding, is not notice of a defense under subsection (a), but discharge is effective against a person who became a holder in due course with notice of the discharge. Public filing or recording of a document does not of itself constitute notice of a defense, claim in recoupment, or claim to the instrument.

(c)   Except to the extent a transferor or predecessor in interest has rights as a holder in due course, a person does not acquire rights of a holder in due course of an instrument taken (i) by legal process or by purchase at an execution, bankruptcy, or creditor's sale or similar proceeding, (ii) by purchase as part of a bulk transaction not in ordinary course of business of the transferor, or (iii) as the successor in interest to an estate or other organization.

(d)   If, under Section 3–303(a)(1), the promise of performance that is the consideration for an instrument has been partially performed, the holder may assert rights as a holder in due course of the instrument only to the fraction of the amount payable under the instrument equal to the value of the partial performance divided by the value of the promised performance.

(e)   If (i) the person entitled to enforce an instrument has only a security interest in the instrument and (ii) the person obliged to pay the instrument has a defense, claim in recoupment or claim to the instrument that may be asserted against the person who granted the security interest, the person entitled to enforce the instrument may assert rights as a holder in due course only to an amount payable under the instrument which, at the time of enforcement of the instrument, does not exceed the amount of the unpaid obligation secured.

(f)   To be effective, notice must be received at such time and in such manner as to give a reasonable opportunity to act on it.

(g)   This section is subject to any law limiting status as a holder in due course in particular classes of transactions.

§ 3–303. Value and Consideration.

(a)   An instrument is issued or transferred for value if:

> **(1)**   the instrument is issued or transferred for a promise of performance, to the extent the promise has been performed;
>
> **(2)**   the transferee acquires a security interest or other lien in the instrument other than a lien obtained by judicial proceedings;
>
> **(3)**   the instrument is issued or transferred as payment of, or as security for, an existing obligation of any person, whether or not the obligation is due;
>
> **(4)**   the instrument is issued or transferred in exchange for a negotiable instrument; or
>
> **(5)**   the instrument is issued or transferred in exchange for the incurring of an irrevocable obligation to a third party by the person taking the instrument.

(b)   "Consideration" means any consideration sufficient to support a simple contract. The drawer or maker of an instrument has a defense if the instrument is issued without consideration. If an instrument is issued for a promise of performance, the drawer or maker has a defense to the extent performance of the promise is due and the promise has not been performed. If an instrument is issued for value as stated in subsection (a), the instrument is also issued for consideration.

§ 3–304. Overdue Instrument.

(a)   An instrument payable on demand becomes overdue at the earliest of the following times:

> **(1)**   on the day after the day demand for payment is duly made;
>
> **(2)**   if the instrument is a check, 90 days after its date; or
>
> **(3)**   if the instrument is not a check, when the instrument has been outstanding for a period of time after its date which is unreasonably long under the circumstances of the particular case in light of the nature of the instrument and trade usage.

(b)   With respect to an instrument payable at a definite time the following rules apply: (1) If the principal is payable in installments and a due date has not been accelerated, the instrument becomes overdue upon default under the instrument for nonpayment of an installment, and the instrument remains overdue until the default is cured. (2) If the principal is not payable in installments and the due date has not been accelerated, the instrument becomes overdue on the day after the due date. (3) If a due date with respect to principal has been accelerated, the instrument becomes overdue on the day after the accelerated due date.

(c)   Unless the due date of principal has been accelerated, an instrument does not become overdue if there is default in payment of interest but no default in payment of principal.

§ 3–305. Defenses and Claims in Recoupment.

(a)   Except as stated in subsection (b), the right to enforce the obligation of a party to pay the instrument is subject to the following:

> **(1)**   A defense of the obligor based on (i) infancy of the obligor to the extent it is a defense to a simple contract, (ii) duress, lack of legal capacity, or illegality of the transaction that nullifies the obligation of the obligor, (iii) fraud that induced the obligor to sign the instrument with neither knowledge nor reasonable opportunity to learn of its character

or its essential terms, or (iv) discharge of the obligor in insolvency proceedings.

(2) A defense of the obligor stated in another section of this Article or a defense of the obligor that would be available if the person entitled to enforce the instrument were enforcing a right to payment under a simple contract.

(3) A claim in recoupment of the obligor against the original payee of the instrument if the claim arose from the transaction that gave rise to the instrument. The claim of the obligor may be asserted against a transferee of the instrument only to reduce the amount owing on the instrument at the time the action is brought.

(b) The right of a holder in due course to enforce the obligation of a party to pay the instrument is subject to defenses of the obligor stated in subsection (a)(1), but is not subject to defenses of the obligor stated in subsection (a)(2) or claims in recoupment stated in subsection (a)(3) against a person other than the holder.

(c) Except as stated in subsection (d), in an action to enforce the obligation of a party to pay the instrument, the obligor may not assert against the person entitled to enforce the instrument a defense, claim in recoupment, or claim to the instrument (Section 3–306) of another person, but the other person's claim to the instrument may be asserted by the obligor if the other person is joined in the action and personally asserts the claim against the person entitled to enforce the instrument. An obligor is not obliged to pay the instrument if the person seeking enforcement of the instrument does not have rights of a holder in due course and the obligor proves that the instrument is a lost or stolen instrument.

(d) In an action to enforce the obligation of an accommodation party to pay an instrument, the accommodation party may assert against the person entitled to enforce the instrument any defense or claim in recoupment under subsection (a) that the accommodated party could assert against the person entitled to enforce the instrument, except the defenses of discharge in insolvency proceedings, infancy, or lack of legal capacity.

§ 3–306. Claims to an Instrument.

A person taking an instrument, other than a person having rights of a holder in due course, is subject to a claim of a property or possessory right in the instrument or its proceeds, including a claim to rescind a negotiation and to recover the instrument or its proceeds. A person having rights of a holder in due course takes free of the claim to the instrument.

§ 3–307. Notice of Breach of Fiduciary Duty.

(a) This section applies if (i) an instrument is taken from a fiduciary for payment or collection or for value, (ii) the taker has knowledge of the fiduciary status of the fiduciary, and (iii) the represented person makes a claim to the instrument or its proceeds on the basis that the transaction of the fiduciary is a breach of fiduciary duty. Notice of breach of fiduciary duty by the fiduciary is notice of the claim of the represented person. "Fiduciary" means an agent, trustee, partner, corporation officer or director, or other representative owing a fiduciary duty with respect to the instrument. "Represented person" means the principal, beneficiary, partnership, corporation, or other person to whom the duty is owed.

(b) If the instrument is payable to the fiduciary, as such, or to the represented person, the taker has notice of the breach of fiduciary duty if the instrument is (i) taken in payment of or as security for a debt known by the taker to be the personal debt of the fiduciary, (ii) taken in a transaction known by the taker to be for the personal benefit of the fiduciary, or (iii) deposited to an account other than an account of the fiduciary, as such, or an account of the represented person.

(c) If the instrument is made or drawn by the fiduciary, as such, payable to the fiduciary personally, the taker does not have notice of the breach of fiduciary duty unless the taker knows of the breach of fiduciary duty.

(d) If the instrument is made or drawn by or on behalf of the represented person to the taker as payee, the taker has notice of the breach of fiduciary duty if the instrument is (i) taken in payment of or as security for a debt known by the taker to be the personal debt of the fiduciary, (ii) taken in a transaction known by the taker to be for the personal benefit of the fiduciary, or (iii) deposited to an account other than an account of the fiduciary, as such, or an account of the represented person.

§ 3–308. Proof of Signatures and Status as Holder in Due Course.

(a) In an action with respect to an instrument, the authenticity of, and authority to make, each signature on the instrument is admitted unless specifically denied in the pleadings. If the validity of a signature is denied in the pleadings, the burden of establishing validity is on the person claiming validity, but the signature is presumed to be authentic and authorized unless the action is to enforce the liability of the purported signer and the signer is dead or incompetent at the time of trial of the issue of validity of the signature. If an action to enforce the instrument is brought against a person as the undisclosed principal of a person who signed the instrument as a party to the instrument, the plaintiff has the burden of establishing that the defendant is liable on the instrument as a represented person pursuant to Section 3–402(a).

(b) If the validity of signatures is admitted or proved and there is compliance with subsection (a), a plaintiff producing the instrument is entitled to payment if the plaintiff proves entitlement to enforce the instrument under Section 3–301, unless the defendant proves a defense or claim in recoupment. If a defense or claim in recoupment is proved, the right to payment of the plaintiff is subject to the defense or claim except to the extent the plaintiff proves that the plaintiff has rights of a holder in due course which are not subject to the defense or claim.

§ 3–309. Enforcement of Lost, Destroyed, or Stolen Instrument.

(a) A person not in possession of an instrument is entitled to enforce the instrument if (i) that person was in rightful possession of the instrument and entitled to enforce it when loss of possession occurred, (ii) the loss of possession was not the result of a voluntary transfer by that person or a lawful seizure, and (iii) that person cannot reasonably obtain possession of the instrument because the instrument was destroyed, its whereabouts cannot be determined, or it is in the wrongful possession of an unknown person or a person that cannot be found or is not amenable to service of process.

(b) A person seeking enforcement of an instrument pursuant to subsection (a) must prove the terms of the instrument and the person's right to enforce the instrument. If that proof is made, Section 3–308 applies to the case as though the person seeking enforcement had produced the instrument. The court may not enter judgment in favor of the person seeking enforcement unless it finds that the person required to pay the instrument is adequately protected against loss that might occur by reason of a claim by another person to enforce the instrument. Adequate protection may be provided by any reasonable means.

§ 3–310. Effect of Instrument on Obligation for Which Taken.

(a) Unless otherwise agreed, if a certified check, cashier's check, or teller's check is taken for an obligation, the obligation is discharged to the same extent discharge would result if an amount of money equal to the amount of the instrument were taken in payment of the obligation. Discharge of the obligation does not affect any liability that the obligor may have as an indorser of the instrument.

(b) Unless otherwise agreed and except as provided in subsection (a), if a note or an uncertified check is taken for an obligation, the obligation is suspended to the same extent the obligation would be discharged if an amount of money equal to the amount of the instrument were taken.

(1) In the case of an uncertified check, suspension of the obligation continues until dishonor of the check or until it is paid or certified. Payment or certification of the check results in discharge of the obligation to the extent of the amount of the check.

(2) In the case of a note, suspension of the obligation continues until dishonor of the note or until it is paid. Payment of the note results in discharge of the obligation to the extent of the payment.

(3) If the check or note is dishonored and the obligee of the obligation for which the instrument was taken has possession of the instrument, the obligee may enforce either the instrument or the obligation. In the case of an instrument of a third person which is negotiated to the obligee by the obligor, discharge of the obligor on the instrument also discharges the obligation.

(4) If the person entitled to enforce the instrument taken for an obligation is a person other than the obligee, the obligee may not enforce the obligation to the extent the obligation is suspended. If the obligee is the person entitled to enforce the instrument but no longer has possession of it because it was lost, stolen, or destroyed, the obligation may not be enforced to the extent of the amount payable on the instrument, and to that extent the obligee's rights against the obligor are limited to enforcement of the instrument.

(c) If an instrument other than one described in subsection (a) or (b) is taken for an obligation, the effect is (i) that stated in subsection (a) if the instrument is one on which a bank is liable as maker or acceptor, or (ii) that stated in subsection (b) in any other case.

§ 3–311. Accord and Satisfaction by Use of Instrument.

(a) This section applies if a person against whom a claim is asserted proves that (i) that person in good faith tendered an instrument to the claimant as full satisfaction of the claim, (ii) the amount of the claim was unliquidated or subject to a bona fide dispute, and (iii) the claimant obtained payment of the instrument.

(b) Unless subsection (c) applies, the claim is discharged if the person against whom the claim is asserted proves that the instrument or an accompanying written communication contained a conspicuous statement to the effect that the instrument was tendered as full satisfaction of the claim.

(c) Subject to subsection (d), a claim is not discharged under subsection (b) if the claimant is an organization and proves that within a reasonable time before the tender, the claimant sent a conspicuous statement to the person against whom the claim is asserted that communications concerning disputed debts, including an instrument tendered as full satisfaction of a debt, are to be sent to a designated person, office or place, and the instrument or accompanying communication was not received by that designated person, office, or place.

(d) Notwithstanding subsection (c), a claim is discharged under subsection (b) if the person against whom the claim is asserted proves that within a reasonable time before collection of the instrument was initiated, an agent of the claimant having direct responsibility with respect to the disputed obligation knew that the instrument was tendered in full satisfaction of the claim, or received the instrument and any accompanying written communication.

Part 4—Liability of Parties
§ 3–401. Signature.

(a) A person is not liable on an instrument unless (i) the person signed the instrument, or (ii) the person is represented by an agent or representative who signed the instrument and the signature is binding on the represented person under Section 3–402.

(b) A signature may be made (i) manually or by means of a device or machine, and (ii) by the use of any name, including any trade or assumed name, or by any word, mark, or symbol executed or adopted by a person with present intention to authenticate a writing.

§ 3–402. Signature by Representative.

(a) If a person acting, or purporting to act, as a representative signs an instrument by signing either the name of the represented person or the name of the signer, the represented person is bound by the signature to the same extent the represented person would be bound if the signature were on a simple contract. If the represented person is bound, the signature of the representative is the "authorized signature of the represented person" and the represented person is liable on the instrument, whether or not identified in the instrument.

(b) If a representative signs the name of the representative to an instrument and that signature is an authorized signature of the represented person, the following rules apply:

(1) If the form of the signature shows unambiguously that the signature is made on behalf of the represented person who is identified in the instrument, the representative is not liable on the instrument.

(2) Subject to subsection (c), if (i) the form of the signature does not show unambiguously that the signature is made in a representative capacity or (ii) the represented person is not identified in the instrument, the representative is liable on the instrument to a holder in due course that took the instrument without notice that the representative was not intended to be liable on the instrument. With respect to any other person, the representative is liable on the instrument unless the

representative proves that the original parties to the instrument did not intend the representative to be liable on the instrument.

(c) If a representative signs the name of the representative as drawer of a check without indication of the representative status and the check is payable from an account of the represented person who is identified on the check, the signer is not liable on the check if the signature is an authorized signature of the represented person.

§ 3–403. Unauthorized Signature.

(a) Except as otherwise provided in this Article, an unauthorized signature is ineffective except as the signature of the unauthorized signer in favor of a person who in good faith pays the instrument or takes it for value. An unauthorized signature may be ratified for all purposes of this Article.

(b) If the signature of more than one person is required to constitute the authorized signature of an organization, the signature of the organization is unauthorized if one of the required signatures is missing.

(c) The civil or criminal liability of a person who makes an unauthorized signature is not affected by any provision of this Article that makes the unauthorized signature effective for the purposes of this Article.

§ 3–404. Impostors; Fictitious Payees.

(a) If an impostor by use of the mails or otherwise induces the maker or drawer of an instrument to issue the instrument to the impostor, or to a person acting in concert with the impostor, by impersonating the payee of the instrument or a person authorized to act for the payee, an indorsement of the instrument by any person in the name of the payee is effective as the indorsement of the payee in favor of any person that in good faith pays the instrument or takes it for value or for collection.

(b) If (i) a person whose intent determines to whom an instrument is payable (Section 3–110(a) or (b)) does not intend the person identified as payee to have any interest in the instrument, or (ii) the person identified as payee of the instrument is a fictitious person, the following rules apply until the instrument is negotiated by special indorsement:

(1) Any person in possession of the instrument is its holder.

(2) An indorsement by any person in the name of the payee stated in the instrument is effective as the indorsement of the payee in favor of any person that in good faith pays the instrument or takes it for value or for collection.

(c) Under subsection (a) or (b) an indorsement is made in the name of a payee if (i) it is made in a name substantially similar to that of the payee or (ii) the instrument, whether or not indorsed, is deposited in a depositary bank to an account in a name substantially similar to that of the payee.

(d) With respect to an instrument to which subsection (a) or (b) applies, if a person paying the instrument or taking it for value or for collection fails to exercise ordinary care in paying or taking the instrument and that failure substantially contributes to loss resulting from payment of the instrument, the person bearing the loss may recover from the person failing to exercise ordinary care to the extent the failure to exercise ordinary care contributed to the loss.

§ 3–405. Employer Responsibility for Fraudulent Indorsement by Employee.

(a) This section applies to fraudulent indorsements of instruments with respect to which an employer has entrusted an employee with responsibility as part of the employee's duties. The following definitions apply to this section:

(1) "Employee" includes, in addition to an employee of an employer, an independent contractor and employee of an independent contractor retained by the employer.

(2) "Fraudulent indorsement" means (i) in the case of an instrument payable to the employer, a forged indorsement purporting to be that of the employer, or (ii) in the case of an instrument with respect to which the employer is drawer or maker, a forged indorsement purporting to be that of the person identified as payee.

(3) "Responsibility" with respect to instruments means authority (i) to sign or indorse instruments on behalf of the employer, (ii) to process instruments received by the employer for bookkeeping purposes, for deposit to an account, or for other disposition, (iii) to prepare or process instruments for issue in the name of the employer, (iv) to supply information determining the names or addresses of payees of instruments to be issued in the name of the employer, (v) to control the disposition of instruments to be issued in the name of the employer, or (vi) to otherwise act with respect to instruments in a responsible capacity. "Responsibility" does not include the assignment of duties that merely allow an employee to have access to instruments or blank or incomplete instrument forms that are being stored or transported or are part of incoming or outgoing mail, or similar access.

(b) For the purpose of determining the rights and liabilities of a person who, in good faith, pays an instrument or takes it for value or for collection, if an employee entrusted with responsibility with respect to the instrument or a person acting in concert with the employee makes a fraudulent indorsement to the instrument, the indorsement is effective as the indorsement of the person to whom the instrument is payable if it is made in the name of that person. If the person paying the instrument or taking it for value or for collection fails to exercise ordinary care in paying or taking the instrument and that failure substantially contributes to loss resulting from the fraud, the person bearing the loss may recover from the person failing to exercise ordinary care to the extent the failure to exercise ordinary care contributed to the loss.

(c) Under subsection (b) an indorsement is made in the name of the person to whom an instrument is payable if (i) it is made in a name substantially similar to the name of that person or (ii) the instrument, whether or not indorsed, is deposited in a depositary bank to an account in a name substantially similar to the name of that person.

§ 3–406. Negligence Contributing to Forged Signature or Alteration of Instrument.

(a) A person whose failure to exercise ordinary care substantially contributes to an alteration of an instrument or to the making of a forged signature on an instrument is precluded from asserting the alteration or the forgery against a person that, in good faith, pays the instrument or takes it for value.

(b) If the person asserting the preclusion fails to exercise ordinary care in paying or taking the instrument and that failure substantially contributes to loss, the loss is allocated between the person precluded and the person asserting the preclusion according to the extent to which the failure of each to exercise ordinary care contributed to the loss.

(c) Under subsection (a) the burden of proving failure to exercise ordinary care is on the person asserting the preclusion. Under subsection (d) the burden of proving failure to exercise ordinary care is on the person precluded.

§ 3–407. Alteration.

(a) "Alteration" means (i) an unauthorized change in an instrument that purports to modify in any respect the obligation of a party to the instrument, or (ii) an unauthorized addition of words or numbers or other change to an incomplete instrument relating to the obligation of any party to the instrument.

(b) Except as provided in subsection (c), an alteration fraudulently made by the holder discharges any party to whose obligation the alteration applies unless that party assents or is precluded from asserting the alteration. No other alteration discharges any party, and the instrument may be enforced according to its original terms.

(c) If an instrument that has been fraudulently altered is acquired by a person having rights of a holder in due course, it may be enforced by that person according to its original terms. If an incomplete instrument is completed and is then acquired by a person having rights of a holder in due course, it may be enforced by that person as completed, whether or not the completion is a fraudulent alteration.

§ 3–408. Drawee Not Liable on Unaccepted Draft.

A check or other draft does not of itself operate as an assignment of funds in the hands of the drawee available for its payment, and the drawee is not liable on the instrument until the drawee accepts it.

§ 3–409. Acceptance of Draft; Certified Check.

(a) "Acceptance" means the drawee's signed agreement to pay a draft as presented. It must be written on the draft and may consist of the drawee's signature alone. Acceptance may be made at any time and becomes effective when notification pursuant to instructions is given or the accepted draft is delivered for the purpose of giving rights on the acceptance to any person.

(b) A draft may be accepted although it has not been signed by the drawer, is otherwise incomplete, is overdue, or has been dishonored.

(c) If a draft is payable at a fixed period after sight and the acceptor fails to date the acceptance, the holder may complete the acceptance by supplying a date in good faith.

(d) "Certified check" means a check accepted by the bank on which it is drawn. Acceptance may be made as stated in subsection (a) or by a writing on the check which indicates that the check is certified. The drawee of a check has no obligation to certify the check, and refusal to certify is not dishonor of the check.

§ 3–410. Acceptance Varying Draft.

(a) If the terms of a drawee's acceptance vary from the terms of the draft as presented, the holder may refuse the acceptance and treat the draft as dishonored. In that case, the drawee may cancel the acceptance.

(b) The terms of a draft are not varied by an acceptance to pay at a particular bank or place in the United States, unless the acceptance states that the draft is to be paid only at that bank or place.

(c) If the holder assents to an acceptance varying the terms of a draft, the obligation of each drawer and indorser that does not expressly assent to the acceptance is discharged.

§ 3–411. Refusal to Pay Cashier's Checks, Teller's Checks, and Certified Checks.

(a) In this section, "obligated bank" means the acceptor of a certified check or the issuer of a cashier's check or teller's check bought from the issuer.

(b) If the obligated bank wrongfully (i) refuses to pay a cashier's check or certified check, (ii) stops payment of a teller's check, or (iii) refuses to pay a dishonored teller's check, the person asserting the right to enforce the check is entitled to compensation for expenses and loss of interest resulting from the nonpayment and may recover consequential damages if the obligated bank refused to pay after receiving notice of particular circumstances giving rise to the damages.

(c) Expenses or consequential damages under subsection (b) are not recoverable if the refusal of the obligated bank to pay occurs because (i) the bank suspends payments, (ii) the obligated bank is asserting a claim or defense of the bank that it has reasonable grounds to believe is available against the person entitled to enforce the instrument, (iii) the obligated bank has a reasonable doubt whether the person demanding payment is the person entitled to enforce the instrument, or (iv) payment is prohibited by law.

§ 3–412. Obligation of Maker.

A maker of a note is obliged to pay the note (i) according to its terms at the time it was issued or, if not issued, at the time it first came into possession of a holder, or (ii) if the maker signed an incomplete instrument, according to its terms when completed as stated in Sections 3–115 and 3–407. The obligation is owed to a person entitled to enforce the note or to an indorser that paid the note pursuant to Section 3–415.

§ 3–413. Obligation of Acceptor.

(a) An acceptor of a draft is obliged to pay the draft (i) according to its terms at the time it was accepted, even though the acceptance states that the draft is payable "as originally drawn" or equivalent terms, (ii) if the acceptance varies the terms of the draft, according to the terms of the draft as varied, or (iii) if the acceptance is of a draft that is an incomplete instrument, according to its terms when completed as stated in Sections 3–115 and 3–407. The obligation is owed to a person entitled to enforce the draft or to the drawer or an indorser that paid the draft pursuant to Section 3–414 or 3–415.

(b) If the certification of a check or other acceptance of a draft states the amount certified or accepted, the obligation of the acceptor is that amount. If (i) the certification or acceptance does not state an amount, (ii) the instrument is subsequently altered by raising its amount, and (iii) the instrument is then negotiated to a holder in due course, the obligation of the acceptor is the amount of the instrument at the time it was negotiated to the holder in due course.

§ 3–414. Obligation of Drawer.

(a) If an unaccepted draft is dishonored, the drawer is obliged to pay the draft (i) according to its terms at the time it was issued or, if not issued, at the time it first came into possession of a holder, or (ii) if the drawer signed an incomplete instrument, according to its terms when completed as stated in Sections 3–115 and 3–407. The obligation is owed to a person entitled to enforce the draft or to an indorser that paid the draft pursuant to Section 3–415.

(b) If a draft is accepted by a bank and the acceptor dishonors the draft, the drawer has no obligation to pay the draft because of the dishonor, regardless of when or by whom acceptance was obtained.

(c) If a draft is accepted and the acceptor is not a bank, the obligation of the drawer to pay the draft if the draft is dishonored by the acceptor is the same as the obligation of an indorser stated in Section 3–415(a) and (c).

(d) Words in a draft indicating that the draft is drawn without recourse are effective to disclaim all liability of the drawer to pay the draft if the draft is not a check or a teller's check, but they are not effective to disclaim the obligation stated in subsection (a) if the draft is a check or a teller's check.

(e) If (i) a check is not presented for payment or given to a depositary bank for collection within 30 days after its date, (ii) the drawee suspends payments after expiration of the 30-day period without paying the check, and (iii) because of the suspension of payments the drawer is deprived of funds maintained with the drawee to cover payment of the check, the drawer to the extent deprived of funds may discharge its obligation to pay the check by assigning to the person entitled to enforce the check the rights of the drawer against the drawee with respect to the funds.

§ 3–415. Obligation of Indorser.

(a) Subject to subsections (b), (c) and (d) and to Section 3–419(d), if an instrument is dishonored, an indorser is obliged to pay the amount due on the instrument (i) according to the terms of the instrument at the time it was indorsed, or (ii) if the indorser indorsed an incomplete instrument, according to its terms when completed as stated in Sections 3–115 and 3–407. The obligation of the indorser is owed to a person entitled to enforce the instrument or to a subsequent indorser that paid the instrument pursuant to this section.

(b) If an indorsement states that it is made "without recourse" or otherwise disclaims liability of the indorser, the indorser is not liable under subsection (a) to pay the instrument.

(c) If notice of dishonor of an instrument is required by Section 3–503 and notice of dishonor complying with that section is not given to an indorser, the liability of the indorser under subsection (a) is discharged.

(d) If a draft is accepted by a bank after an indorsement was made and the acceptor dishonors the draft, the indorser is not liable under subsection (a) to pay the instrument.

(e) If an indorser of a check is liable under subsection (a) and the check is not presented for payment, or given to a depositary bank for collection, within 30 days after the day the indorsement was made, the liability of the indorser under subsection (a) is discharged.

§ 3–416. Transfer Warranties.

(a) A person that transfers an instrument for consideration warrants to the transferee and, if the transfer is by indorsement, to any subsequent transferee that:

> **(1)** the warrantor is a person entitled to enforce the instrument,
>
> **(2)** all signatures on the instrument are authentic and authorized,
>
> **(3)** the instrument has not been altered,
>
> **(4)** the instrument is not subject to a defense or claim in recoupment stated in Section 3–305(a) of any party that can be asserted against the warrantor, and
>
> **(5)** the warrantor has no knowledge of any insolvency proceeding commenced with respect to the maker or acceptor or, in the case of an unaccepted draft, the drawer.

(b) A person to whom the warranties under subsection (a) are made and who took the instrument in good faith may recover from the warrantor as damages for breach of warranty an amount equal to the loss suffered as a result of the breach, but not more than the amount of the instrument plus expenses and loss of interest incurred as a result of the breach.

(c) The warranties stated in subsection (a) cannot be disclaimed with respect to checks. Unless notice of a claim for breach of warranty is given to the warrantor within 30 days after the claimant has reason to know of the breach and the identity of the warrantor, the warrantor is discharged to the extent of any loss caused by the delay in giving notice of the claim.

(d) A cause of action for breach of warranty under this section accrues when the claimant has reason to know of the breach.

§ 3–417. Presentment Warranties.

(a) If an unaccepted draft is presented to the drawee for payment or acceptance and the drawee pays or accepts the draft, (i) the person obtaining payment or acceptance, at the time of presentment, and (ii) a previous transferor of the draft, at the time of transfer, warrant to the drawee making payment or accepting the draft in good faith that:

> **(1)** the warrantor is or was, at the time the warrantor transferred the draft, a person entitled to enforce the draft or authorized to obtain payment or acceptance of the draft on behalf of a person entitled to enforce the draft;
>
> **(2)** the draft has not been altered; and
>
> **(3)** the warrantor has no knowledge that the signature of the purported drawer of the draft is unauthorized.

(b) A drawee making payment may recover from any warrantor damages for breach of warranty equal to the amount paid by the drawee less the amount the drawee received or is entitled to receive from the drawer because of payment of the draft. In addition the drawee is entitled to compensation for expenses and loss of interest resulting from the breach. The right of the drawee to recover damages under this subsection is not affected by any failure of the drawee to exercise ordinary care in making payment. If the drawee accepts the draft (i) breach of warranty is a defense to the obligation of the acceptor, and (ii) if the acceptor makes payment with respect to the draft, the acceptor is entitled to recover from any warrantor for breach of warranty the amounts stated in the first two sentences of this subsection.

(c) If a drawee asserts a claim for breach of warranty under subsection (a) based on an unauthorized indorsement of the draft or an alteration of the draft, the warrantor may defend by proving that the indorsement is effective under Section 3–404 or 3–405 or the drawer is precluded under Section 3–406 or 4–406 from asserting against the drawee the unauthorized indorsement or alteration.

(d) This subsection applies if (i) a dishonored draft is presented for payment to the drawer or an indorser or (ii) any other instrument is presented for payment to a party obliged to pay the instrument, and payment is received. The person obtaining payment and a prior transferor of the instrument warrant to the person making payment in good faith that the warrantor is or was, at the time the warrantor transferred the instrument, a person entitled to enforce the instrument or authorized to obtain payment on behalf of a person entitled to enforce the instrument. The person making payment may recover from any warrantor for breach of warranty an amount equal to the amount paid plus expenses and loss of interest resulting from the breach.

(e) The warranties stated in subsections (a) and (d) cannot be disclaimed with respect to checks. Unless notice of a claim for breach of warranty is given to the warrantor within 30 days after the claimant has reason to know of the breach and the identity of the warrantor, the warrantor is discharged to the extent of any loss caused by the delay in giving notice of the claim.

(f) A cause of action for breach of warranty under this section accrues when the claimant has reason to know of the breach.

§ 3–418. Payment or Acceptance by Mistake.

(a) Except as provided in subsection (c), if the drawee of a draft pays or accepts the draft and the drawee acted on the mistaken belief that (i) payment of the draft had not been stopped under Section 4–403, (ii) the signature of the purported drawer of the draft was authorized, or (iii) the balance in the drawer's account with the drawee represented available funds, the drawee may recover the amount paid from the person to whom or for whose benefit payment was made or, in the case of acceptance, may revoke the acceptance. Rights of the drawee under this subsection are not affected by failure of the drawee to exercise ordinary care in paying or accepting the draft.

(b) Except as provided in subsection (c), if an instrument has been paid or accepted by mistake and the case is not covered by subsection (a), the person paying or accepting may recover the amount paid or revoke acceptance to the extent allowed by the law governing mistake and restitution.

(c) The remedies provided by subsection (a) or (b) may not be asserted against a person who took the instrument in good faith and for value. This subsection does not limit remedies provided by Section 3–417 for breach of warranty.

§ 3–419. Instruments Signed for Accommodation.

(a) If an instrument is issued for value given for the benefit of a party to the instrument ("accommodated party") and another party to the instrument ("accommodation party") signs the instrument for the purpose of incurring liability on the instrument without being a direct beneficiary of the value given for the instrument, the instrument is signed by the accommodation party "for accommodation."

(b) An accommodation party may sign the instrument as maker, drawer, acceptor, or indorser and, subject to subsection (d), is obliged to pay the instrument in the capacity in which the accommodation party signs. The obligation of an accommodation party may be enforced notwithstanding any statute of frauds and regardless of whether the accommodation party receives consideration for the accommodation.

(c) A person signing an instrument is presumed to be an accommodation party and there is notice that the instrument is signed for accommodation if the signature is an anomalous indorsement or is accompanied by words indicating that the signer is acting as surety or guarantor with respect to the obligation of another party to the instrument. Except as provided in Section 3-606, the obligation of an accommodation party to pay the instrument is not affected by the fact that the person enforcing the obligation had notice when the instrument was taken by that person that the accommodation party signed the instrument for accommodation.

(d) If the signature of a party to an instrument is accompanied by words indicating unambiguously that the party is guaranteeing collection rather than payment of the obligation of another party to the instrument, the signer is obliged to pay the amount due on the instrument to a person entitled to enforce the instrument only if (i) execution of judgment against the other party has been returned unsatisfied, (ii) the other party is insolvent or in an insolvency proceeding, (iii) the other party cannot be served with process, or (iv) it is otherwise apparent that payment cannot be obtained from the party whose obligation is guaranteed.

(e) An accommodation party that pays the instrument is entitled to reimbursement from the accommodated party and is entitled to enforce the instrument against the accommodated party. An accommodated party that pays the instrument has no right of recourse against, and is not entitled to contribution from, an accommodation party.

§ 3–420. Conversion of Instrument.

(a) The law applicable to conversion of personal property applies to instruments. An instrument is also converted if the instrument lacks an indorsement necessary for negotiation and it is purchased or taken for collection or the drawee takes the instrument and makes payment to a person not entitled to receive payment. An action for conversion of an instrument may not be brought by (i) the maker, drawer, or acceptor of the instrument or (ii) a payee or indorsee who did not receive delivery of the instrument either directly or through delivery to an agent or a co-payee.

(b) In an action under subsection (a), the measure of liability is presumed to be the amount payable on the instrument, but recovery may not exceed the amount of the plaintiff's interest in the instrument.

(c) A representative, other than a depositary bank, that has in good faith dealt with an instrument or its proceeds on behalf of one who was not the person entitled to enforce the instrument is not liable in conversion to that person beyond the amount of any proceeds that it has not paid out.

Part 5—Dishonor

§ 3–501. Presentment.

(a) "Presentment" means a demand (i) to pay an instrument made to the maker, drawee, or acceptor or, in the case of a note or accepted draft payable at a bank, to the bank, or (ii) to accept a draft made to the drawee, by a person entitled to enforce the instrument.

(b) Subject to Article 4, agreement of the parties, clearing house rules and the like,

(1) presentment may be made at the place of payment of the instrument and must be made at the place of payment if the instrument is payable at a bank in the United States; may be made by any commercially reasonable means, including an oral, written, or electronic communication; is effective when the demand for payment or acceptance is received by the person to whom presentment is made; is effective if made to any one of two or more makers, acceptors, drawees or other payors; and

(2) without dishonoring the instrument, the party to whom presentment is made may (i) treat presentment as occurring on the next business day after the day of presentment if the party to whom presentment is made has established a cut-off hour not earlier than 2 p.m. for the receipt and processing of instruments presented for payment or acceptance and presentment is made after the cut-off hour, (ii) require exhibition of the instrument, (iii) require reasonable identification of the person making presentment and evidence of authority to make it if made on behalf of another person, (iv) require a signed receipt on the instrument for any payment made or surrender of the instrument if full payment is made, (v) return the instrument for lack of a necessary indorsement, or (vi) refuse payment or acceptance for failure of the presentment to comply with the terms of the instrument, an agreement of the parties, or other law or applicable rule.

§ 3–502. Dishonor.

(a) Dishonor of a note is governed by the following rules:

(1) If the note is payable on demand, the note is dishonored if presentment is duly made and the note is not paid on the day of presentment.

(2) If the note is not payable on demand and is payable at or through a bank or the terms of the note require presentment, the note is dishonored if presentment is duly made and the note is not paid on the day it becomes payable or the day of presentment, whichever is later.

(3) If the note is not payable on demand and subparagraph (2) does not apply, the note is dishonored if it is not paid on the day it becomes payable.

(b) Dishonor of an unaccepted draft other than a documentary draft is governed by the following rules:

(1) If a check is presented for payment otherwise than for immediate payment over the counter, the check is dishonored if the payor bank makes timely return of the check or sends timely notice of dishonor or nonpayment under Section 4–301 or 4–302, or becomes accountable for the amount of the check under Section 4–302.

(2) If the draft is payable on demand and subparagraph (1) does not apply, the draft is dishonored if presentment for payment is duly made and the draft is not paid on the day of presentment.

(3) If the draft is payable on a date stated in the draft, the draft is dishonored if (i) presentment for payment is duly made and payment is not made on the day the draft becomes payable or the day of presentment, whichever is later, or (ii) presentment for acceptance is duly made before the day the draft becomes payable and the draft is not accepted on the day of presentment.

(4) If the draft is payable on elapse of a period of time after sight or acceptance, the draft is dishonored if presentment for acceptance is duly made and the draft is not accepted on the day of presentment.

(c) Dishonor of an unaccepted documentary draft occurs according to the rules stated in subparagraphs (2), (3), and (4) of subsection (b) except that payment or acceptance may be delayed without dishonor until no later than the close of the third business day of the drawee following the day on which payment or acceptance is required by those subparagraphs.

(d) Dishonor of an accepted draft is governed by the following rules:

(1) If the draft is payable on demand, the draft is dishonored if presentment for payment is duly made and the draft is not paid on the day of presentment.

(2) If the draft is not payable on demand, the draft is dishonored if presentment for payment is duly made and payment is not made on the day it becomes payable or the day of presentment, whichever is later.

(e) In any case in which presentment is otherwise required for dishonor under this section and presentment is excused under Section 3–504, dishonor occurs without presentment if the instrument is not duly accepted or paid.

(f)   If a draft is dishonored because timely acceptance of the draft was not made and the person entitled to demand acceptance consents to a late acceptance, from the time of acceptance the draft is treated as never having been dishonored.

§ 3–503. Notice of Dishonor.

(a)   The obligation of an indorser stated in Section 3–415(a) and the obligation of a drawer stated in Section 3–414(c) may not be enforced unless (i) the indorser or drawer is given notice of dishonor of the instrument complying with this section or (ii) notice of dishonor is excused under Section 3–504(c).

(b)   Notice of dishonor may be given by any person; may be given by any commercially reasonable means including an oral, written, or electronic communication; is sufficient if it reasonably identifies the instrument and indicates that the instrument has been dishonored or has not been paid or accepted. Return of an instrument given to a bank for collection is a sufficient notice of dishonor.

(c)   Subject to Section 3–504(d), with respect to an instrument taken for collection by a collecting bank, notice of dishonor must be given (i) by the bank before midnight of the next banking day following the banking day on which the bank receives notice of dishonor of the instrument, and (ii) by any other person within 30 days following the day on which the person receives notice of dishonor. With respect to any other instrument, notice of dishonor must be given within 30 days following the day on which dishonor occurs.

§ 3–504. Excused Presentment and Notice of Dishonor.

(a)   Presentment for payment or acceptance of an instrument is excused if (i) the person entitled to present the instrument cannot with reasonable diligence make presentment, (ii) the maker or acceptor has repudiated an obligation to pay the instrument or is dead or in insolvency proceedings, (iii) by the terms of the instrument presentment is not necessary to enforce the obligation of indorsers or the drawer, or (iv) the drawer or indorser whose obligation is being enforced waived presentment or otherwise had no reason to expect or right to require that the instrument be paid or accepted.

(b)   Presentment for payment or acceptance of a draft is also excused if the drawer instructed the drawee not to pay or accept the draft or the drawee was not obligated to the drawer to pay the draft.

(c)   Notice of dishonor is excused if (i) by the terms of the instrument notice of dishonor is not necessary to enforce the obligation of a party to pay the instrument, or (ii) the party whose obligation is being enforced waived notice of dishonor. A waiver of presentment is also a waiver of notice of dishonor.

(d)   Delay in giving notice of dishonor is excused if the delay was caused by circumstances beyond the control of the person giving the notice and the person giving the notice exercised reasonable diligence after the cause of the delay ceased to operate.

§ 3–505. Evidence of Dishonor.

(a)   The following are admissible as evidence and create a presumption of dishonor and of any notice of dishonor stated:

(1)   a document regular in form as provided in subsection (b) which purports to be a protest;

(2)   a purported stamp or writing of the drawee, payor bank, or presenting bank on or accompanying the instrument stating that acceptance or payment has been refused unless reasons for the refusal are stated and the reasons are not consistent with dishonor;

(3)   a book or record of the drawee, payor bank, or collecting bank, kept in the usual course of business which shows dishonor, even if there is no evidence of who made the entry.

(b)   A protest is a certificate of dishonor made by a United States consul or vice consul, or a notary public or other person authorized to administer oaths by the law of the place where dishonor occurs. It may be made upon information satisfactory to that person. The protest must identify the instrument and certify either that presentment has been made or, if not made, the reason why it was not made, and that the instrument has been dishonored by nonacceptance or nonpayment. The protest may also certify that notice of dishonor has been given to some or all parties.

Part 6—Discharge and Payment

§ 3–601. Discharge and Effect of Discharge.

(a)   The obligation of a party to pay the instrument is discharged as stated in this Article or by an act or agreement with the party which would discharge an obligation to pay money under a simple contract.

(b)   Discharge of the obligation of a party is not effective against a person acquiring rights of a holder in due course of the instrument without notice of the discharge.

§ 3–602. Payment.

(a)   Subject to subsection (b), an instrument is paid to the extent payment is made (i) by or on behalf of a party obliged to pay the instrument, and (ii) to a person entitled to enforce the instrument. To the extent of the payment, the obligation of the party obliged to pay the instrument is discharged even though payment is made with knowledge of a claim to the instrument under Section 3–306 by another person.

(b)   The obligation of a party to pay the instrument is not discharged under subsection (a) if:

(1)   a claim to the instrument under Section 3–306 is enforceable against the party receiving payment and (i) payment is made with knowledge by the payor that payment is prohibited by injunction or similar process of a court of competent jurisdiction, or (ii) in the case of an instrument other than a cashier's check, teller's check, or certified check, the party making payment accepted, from the person having a claim to the instrument, indemnity against loss resulting from refusal to pay the person entitled to enforce the instrument, or

(2)   the person making payment knows that the instrument is a stolen instrument and pays a person that it knows is in wrongful possession of the instrument.

§ 3–603. Tender of Payment.

(a)   If tender of payment of an obligation of a party to an instrument is made to a person entitled to enforce the obligation, the effect of tender is governed by principles of law applicable to tender of payment of an obligation under a simple contract.

(b)   If tender of payment of an obligation to pay the instrument is made to a person entitled to enforce the instrument and the tender is refused, there is discharge, to the extent of the amount of the tender, of the obligation of an indorser or accommodation party having a right of recourse against the obligor making the tender.

(c)   If tender of payment of an amount due on an instrument is made by or on behalf of the obligor to the person entitled to enforce the instrument, the obligation of the obligor to pay interest after the due date on the amount tendered is discharged. If presentment is required with respect to an instrument and the obligor is able and ready to pay on the due date at every place of payment stated in the instrument, the obligor is deemed to have made tender of payment on the due date to the person entitled to enforce the instrument.

§ 3–604. Discharge by Cancellation or Renunciation.

(a)   A person entitled to enforce an instrument may, with or without consideration, discharge the obligation of a party to pay the instrument (i) by an intentional voluntary act such as surrender of the instrument to the party, destruction, mutilation, or cancellation of the instrument, cancellation or striking out of the party's signature, or the addition of words to the instrument indicating discharge, or (ii) by agreeing not to sue or otherwise renouncing rights against the party by a signed writing.

(b)   Cancellation or striking out of an indorsement pursuant to subsection (a) does not affect the status and rights of a party derived from the indorsement.

§ 3–605. Discharge of Indorsers and Accommodation Parties.

(a)   For the purposes of this section, the term "indorser" includes a drawer having the obligation stated in Section 3–414(c).

(b)   Discharge of the obligation of a party to the instrument under Section 3–605 does not discharge the obligation of an indorser or accommodation party having a right of recourse against the discharged party.

(c)   If a person entitled to enforce an instrument agrees, with or without consideration, to a material modification of the obligation of a party to the instrument, including an extension of the due date, there is discharge of the obligation of an indorser or accommodation party having a right of recourse against the person whose obligation is modified to the extent the modification causes loss to the indorser or accommodation party with respect to the right of recourse. The indorser or accommodation party is deemed to have suffered loss as a result of the modification equal to the amount of the right of recourse unless the person enforcing the instrument proves that no loss was caused by the modification or that the loss caused by the modification was less than the amount of the right of recourse.

(d) If the obligation of a party to an instrument is secured by an interest in collateral and impairment of the value of the interest is caused by a person entitled to enforce the instrument, there is discharge of the obligation of an indorser or accommodation party having a right of recourse against the obligor to the extent of the impairment. The value of an interest in collateral is impaired to the extent (i) the value of the interest is reduced to an amount less than the amount of the right of recourse of the party asserting discharge, or (ii) the reduction in value of the interest causes an increase in the amount by which the amount of the right of recourse exceeds the value of the interest. The burden of proving impairment is on the party asserting discharge.

(e) If the obligation of a party to an instrument is secured by an interest in collateral not provided by an accommodation party and the value of the interest is impaired by a person entitled to enforce the instrument, the obligation of any party who is jointly and severally liable with respect to the secured obligation is discharged to the extent the impairment causes the party asserting discharge to pay more than that party would have been obliged to pay, taking into account rights of contribution, if impairment had not occurred. If the party asserting discharge is an accommodation party not entitled to discharge under subsection (d), the party is deemed to have a right to contribution based on joint and several liability rather than a right to reimbursement. The burden of proving impairment is on the party asserting discharge.

(f) Under subsection (d) or (e) causation of impairment includes (i) failure to obtain or maintain perfection or recordation of the interest in collateral, (ii) release of collateral without substitution of collateral of equal value, (iii) failure to perform a duty to preserve the value of collateral owed, under Article 9 or other law, to a debtor or surety or other person secondarily liable, or (iv) failure to comply with applicable law in disposing of collateral.

(g) An accommodation party is not discharged under subsection (c) or (d) unless the person agreeing to the modification or causing the impairment knows of the accommodation or has notice under Section 3–419(c) that the instrument was signed for accommodation. There is no discharge of any party under subsection (c), (d), or (e) if (i) the party asserting discharge consents to the event or conduct that is the basis of the discharge, or (ii) the instrument or a separate agreement of the party provides for waiver of discharge under this section either specifically or by general language indicating that parties to the instrument waive defenses based on suretyship or impairment of collateral.

ARTICLE 4: BANK DEPOSITS AND COLLECTIONS
Part 1—General Provisions and Definitions
§ 4–101. Short Title.
This Article shall be known and may be cited as Uniform Commercial Code—Bank Deposits and Collections.

§ 4–102. Applicability.
(1) To the extent that items within this Article are also within the scope of Articles 3 and 8, they are subject to the provisions of those Articles. In the event of conflict the provisions of this Article govern those of Article 3 but the provisions of Article 8 govern those of this Article.

(2) The liability of a bank for action or non-action with respect to any item handled by it for purposes of presentment, payment or collection is governed by the law of the place where the bank is located. In the case of action or non-action by or at a branch or separate office of a bank, its liability is governed by the law of the place where the branch or separate office is located.

§ 4–103. Variation by Agreement; Measure of Damages; Certain Action Constituting Ordinary Care.
(1) The effect of the provisions of this Article may be varied by agreement except that no agreement can disclaim a bank's responsibility for its own lack of good faith or failure to exercise ordinary care or can limit the measure of damages for such lack or failure; but the parties may by agreement determine the standards by which such responsibility is to be measured if such standards are not manifestly unreasonable.

(2) Federal Reserve regulations and operating letters, clearing house rules, and the like, have the effect of agreements under subsection (1), whether or not specifically assented to by all parties interested in items handled.

(3) Action or non-action approved by this Article or pursuant to Federal Reserve regulations or operating letters constitutes the exercise of ordinary care and, in the absence of special instructions, action or non-action consistent with clearing house rules and the like or with a general banking usage not disapproved by this Article, prima facie constitutes the exercise of ordinary care.

(4) The specification or approval of certain procedures by this Article does not constitute disapproval of other procedures which may be reasonable under the circumstances.

(5) The measure of damages for failure to exercise ordinary care in handling an item is the amount of the item reduced by an amount which could not have been realized by the use of ordinary care, and where there is bad faith it includes other damages, if any, suffered by the party as a proximate consequence.

§ 4–104. Definitions and Index of Definitions.
(1) In this Article unless the context otherwise requires
    (a) "Account" means any account with a bank and includes a checking, time, interest or savings account;
    (b) "Afternoon" means the period of a day between noon and midnight;
    (c) "Banking day" means that part of any day on which a bank is open to the public for carrying on substantially all of its banking functions;
    (d) "Clearing house" means any association of banks or other payors regularly clearing items;
    (e) "Customer" means any person having an account with a bank or for whom a bank has agreed to collect items and includes a bank carrying an account with another bank;
    (f) "Documentary draft" means any negotiable or non-negotiable draft with accompanying documents, securities or other papers to be delivered against honor of the draft;
    (g) "Item" means any instrument for the payment of money even though it is not negotiable but does not include money;
    (h) "Midnight deadline" with respect to a bank is midnight on its next banking day following the banking day on which it receives the relevant item or notice or from which the time for taking action commences to run, whichever is later;
    (i) "Properly payable" includes the availability of funds for payment at the time of decision to pay or dishonor;
    (j) "Settle" means to pay in cash, by clearing house settlement, in a charge or credit or by remittance, or otherwise as instructed. A settlement may be either provisional or final;
    (k) "Suspends payments" with respect to a bank means that it has been closed by order of the supervisory authorities, that a public officer has been appointed to take it over or that it ceases or refuses to make payments in the ordinary course of business.

(2) Other definitions applying to this Article and the sections in which they appear are:
    "Collecting bank" Section 4–105.
    "Depositary bank" Section 4–105.
    "Intermediary bank" Section 4–105.
    "Payor bank" Section 4–105.
    "Presenting bank" Section 4–105.
    "Remitting bank" Section 4–105.

(3) The following definitions in other Articles apply to this Article:
    "Acceptance" Section 3–410.
    "Certificate of deposit" Section 3–104.
    "Certification" Section 3–411.
    "Check" Section 3–104.
    "Draft" Section 3–104.
    "Holder in due course" Section 3–302.
    "Notice of dishonor" Section 3–508.
    "Presentment" Section 3–504.
    "Protest" Section 3–509.
    "Secondary party" Section 3–102.

(4) In addition Article 1 contains general definitions and principles of construction and interpretation applicable throughout this Article.

§ 4–105. "Depositary Bank"; "Intermediary Bank"; "Collecting Bank"; "Payor Bank"; "Presenting Bank"; "Remitting Bank".

In this Article unless the context otherwise requires:

(a) "Depositary bank" means the first bank to which an item is transferred for collection even though it is also the payor bank;

(b) "Payor bank" means a bank by which an item is payable as drawn or accepted;

(c) "Intermediary bank" means any bank to which an item is transferred in course of collection except the depositary or payor bank;

(d) "Collecting bank" means any bank handling the item for collection except the payor bank;

(e) "Presenting bank" means any bank presenting an item except a payor bank;

(f) "Remitting bank" means any payor or intermediary bank remitting for an item.

§ 4–106. Separate Office of a Bank.

A branch or separate office of a bank [maintaining its own deposit ledgers] is a separate bank for the purpose of computing the time within which and determining the place at or to which action may be taken or notices or orders shall be given under this Article and under Article 3.

Note: *The brackets are to make it optional with the several states whether to require a branch to maintain its own deposit ledgers in order to be considered to be a separate bank for certain purposes under Article 4. In some states "maintaining its own deposit ledgers" is a satisfactory test. In others branch banking practices are such that this test would not be suitable.*

§ 4–107. Time of Receipt of Items.

(1) For the purpose of allowing time to process items, prove balances and make the necessary entries on its books to determine its position for the day, a bank may fix an afternoon hour of two p.m. or later as a cut-off hour for the handling of money and items and the making of entries on its books.

(2) Any item or deposit of money received on any day after a cut-off hour so fixed or after the close of the banking day may be treated as being received at the opening of the next banking day.

§ 4–108. Delays.

(1) Unless otherwise instructed, a collecting bank in a good faith effort to secure payment may, in the case of specific items and with or without the approval of any person involved, waive, modify or extend time limits imposed or permitted by this Act for a period not in excess of an additional banking day without discharge of secondary parties and without liability to its transferor or any prior party.

(2) Delay by a collecting bank or payor bank beyond time limits prescribed or permitted by this Act or by instructions is excused if caused by interruption of communication facilities, suspension of payments by another bank, war, emergency conditions or other circumstances beyond the control of the bank provided it exercises such diligence as the circumstances require.

§ 4–109. Process of Posting.

The "process of posting" means the usual procedure followed by a payor bank in determining to pay an item and in recording the payment including one or more of the following or other steps as determined by the bank:

(a) verification of any signature;

(b) ascertaining that sufficient funds are available;

(c) affixing a "paid" or other stamp;

(d) entering a charge or entry to a customer's account;

(e) correcting or reversing an entry or erroneous action with respect to the item.

Part 2—Collection of Items: Depositary and Collecting Banks

§ 4–201. Presumption and Duration of Agency Status of Collecting Banks and Provisional Status of Credits; Applicability of Article; Item Indorsed "Pay Any Bank".

(1) Unless a contrary intent clearly appears and prior to the time that a settlement given by a collecting bank for an item is or becomes final (subsection (3) of Section 4–211 and Sections 4–212 and 4–213) the bank is an agent or sub-agent of the owner of the item and any settlement given for the item is provisional. This provision applies regardless of the form of indorsement or lack of indorsement and even though credit given for the item is subject to immediate withdrawal as of right or is in fact withdrawn; but the continuance of ownership of an item by its owner and any rights of the owner to proceeds of the item are subject to rights of a collecting bank such as those resulting from outstanding advances on the item and valid rights of setoff. When an item is handled by banks for purposes of presentment, payment and collection, the relevant provisions of this Article apply even though action of parties clearly establishes that a particular bank has purchased the item and is the owner of it.

(2) After an item has been indorsed with the words "pay any bank" or the like, only a bank may acquire the rights of a holder

(a) until the item has been returned to the customer initiating collection; or

(b) until the item has been specially indorsed by a bank to a person who is not a bank.

§ 4–202. Responsibility for Collection; When Action Seasonable.

(1) A collecting bank must use ordinary care in

(a) presenting an item or sending it for presentment; and

(b) sending notice of dishonor or non-payment or returning an item other than a documentary draft to the bank's transferor [or directly to the depositary bank under subsection (2) of Section 4–212] (*see note to Section 4–212*) after learning that the item has not been paid or accepted as the case may be; and

(c) settling for an item when the bank receives final settlement; and

(d) making or providing for any necessary protest; and

(e) notifying its transferor of any loss or delay in transit within a reasonable time after discovery thereof.

(2) A collecting bank taking proper action before its midnight deadline following receipt of an item, notice or payment acts seasonably; taking proper action within a reasonably longer time may be seasonable but the bank has the burden of so establishing.

(3) Subject to subsection (1)(a), a bank is not liable for the insolvency, neglect, misconduct, mistake or default of another bank or person or for loss or destruction of an item in transit or in the possession of others.

§ 4–203. Effect of Instructions.

Subject to the provisions of Article 3 concerning conversion of instruments (Section 3–419) and the provisions of both Article 3 and this Article concerning restrictive indorsements only a collecting bank's transferor can give instructions which affect the bank or constitute notice to it and a collecting bank is not liable to prior parties for any action taken pursuant to such instructions or in accordance with any agreement with its transferor.

§ 4–204. Methods of Sending and Presenting; Sending Direct to Payor Bank.

(1) A collecting bank must send items by reasonably prompt method taking into consideration any relevant instructions, the nature of the item, the number of such items on hand, and the cost of collection involved and the method generally used by it or others to present such items.

(2) A collecting bank may send

(a) any item direct to the payor bank;

(b) any item to any non-bank payor if authorized by its transferor; and

(c) any item other than documentary drafts to any non-bank payor, if authorized by Federal Reserve regulation or operating letter, clearing house rule or the like.

(3) Presentment may be made by a presenting bank at a place where the payor bank has requested that presentment be made.

§ 4–205. Supplying Missing Indorsement; No Notice from Prior Indorsement.

(1) A depositary bank which has taken an item for collection may supply any indorsement of the customer which is necessary to title unless the item contains the words "payee's indorsement required" or the like. In the absence of such a requirement a statement placed on the item by the depositary bank to the effect that the item was deposited by a customer or credited to his account is effective as the customer's indorsement.

(2) An intermediary bank, or payor bank which is not a depositary bank, is neither given notice nor otherwise affected by a restrictive indorsement of any person except the bank's immediate transferor.

§ 4–206. Transfer Between Banks.

Any agreed method which identifies the transferor bank is sufficient for the item's further transfer to another bank.

§ 4–207. Warranties of Customer and Collecting Bank on Transfer or Presentment of Items; Time for Claims.

(1) Each customer or collecting bank who obtains payment or acceptance of an item and each prior customer and collecting bank warrants to the payor bank or other payor who in good faith pays or accepts the item that

    (a) he has a good title to the item or is authorized to obtain payment or acceptance on behalf of one who has a good title; and

    (b) he has no knowledge that the signature of the maker or drawer is unauthorized, except that this warranty is not given by any customer or collecting bank that is a holder in due course and acts in good faith

        (i) to a maker with respect to the maker's own signature; or

        (ii) to a drawer with respect to the drawer's own signature, whether or not the drawer is also the drawee; or

        (iii) to an acceptor of an item if the holder in due course took the item after the acceptance or obtained the acceptance without knowledge that the drawer's signature was unauthorized; and

    (c) the item has not been materially altered, except that this warranty is not given by any customer or collecting bank that is a holder in due course and acts in good faith

        (i) to the maker of a note; or

        (ii) to the drawer of a draft whether or not the drawer is also the drawee; or

        (iii) to the acceptor of an item with respect to an alteration made prior to the acceptance if the holder in due course took the item after the acceptance, even though the acceptance provided "payable as originally drawn" or equivalent terms; or

        (iv) to the acceptor of an item with respect to an alteration made after the acceptance.

(2) Each customer and collecting bank who transfers an item and receives a settlement or other consideration for it warrants to his transferee and to any subsequent collecting bank who takes the item in good faith that

    (a) he has a good title to the item or is authorized to obtain payment or acceptance on behalf of one who has a good title and the transfer is otherwise rightful; and

    (b) all signatures are genuine or authorized; and

    (c) the item has not been materially altered; and

    (d) no defense of any party is good against him; and

    (e) he has no knowledge of any insolvency proceeding instituted with respect to the maker or acceptor or the drawer of an unaccepted item.

In addition each customer and collecting bank so transferring an item and receiving a settlement or other consideration engages that upon dishonor and any necessary notice of dishonor and protest he will take up the item.

(3) The warranties and the engagement to honor set forth in the two preceding subsections arise notwithstanding the absence of indorsement or words of guaranty or warranty in the transfer or presentment and a collecting bank remains liable for their breach despite remittance to its transferor. Damages for breach of such warranties or engagement to honor shall not exceed the consideration received by the customer or collecting bank responsible plus finance charges and expenses related to the item, if any.

(4) Unless a claim for breach of warranty under this section is made within a reasonable time after the person claiming learns of the breach, the person liable is discharged to the extent of any loss caused by the delay in making claim.

§ 4–208. Security Interest of Collecting Bank in Items, Accompanying Documents and Proceeds.

(1) A bank has a security interest in an item and any accompanying documents or the proceeds of either

    (a) in case of an item deposited in an account to the extent to which credit given for the item has been withdrawn or applied;

    (b) in case of an item for which it has given credit available for withdrawal as of right, to the extent of the credit given whether or not the credit is drawn upon and whether or not there is a right of charge-back; or

    (c) if it makes an advance on or against the item.

(2) When credit which has been given for several items received at one time or pursuant to a single agreement is withdrawn or applied in part the security interest remains upon all the items, any accompanying documents or the proceeds of either. For the purpose of this section, credits first given are first withdrawn.

(3) Receipt by a collecting bank of a final settlement for an item is a realization on its security interest in the item, accompanying documents and proceeds. To the extent and so long as the bank does not receive final settlement for the item or give up possession of the item or accompanying documents for purposes other than collection, the security interest continues and is subject to the provisions of Article 9 except that

    (a) no security agreement is necessary to make the security interest enforceable (subsection (1)(b) of Section 9–203); and

    (b) no filing is required to perfect the security interest; and

    (c) the security interest has priority over conflicting perfected security interests in the item, accompanying documents or proceeds.

§ 4–209. When Bank Gives Value for Purposes of Holder in Due Course.

For purposes of determining its status as a holder in due course, the bank has given value to the extent that it has a security interest in an item provided that the bank otherwise complies with the requirements of Section 3–302 on what constitutes a holder in due course.

§ 4–210. Presentment by Notice of Item Not Payable by, Through or at a Bank; Liability of Secondary Parties.

(1) Unless otherwise instructed, a collecting bank may present an item not payable by, through or at a bank by sending to the party to accept or pay a written notice that the bank holds the item for acceptance or payment. The notice must be sent in time to be received on or before the day when presentment is due and the bank must meet any requirement of the party to accept or pay under Section 3–505 by the close of the bank's next banking day after it knows of the requirement.

(2) Where presentment is made by notice and neither honor nor request for compliance with a requirement under Section 3–505 is received by the close of business on the day after maturity or in the case of demand items by the close of business on the third banking day after notice was sent, the presenting bank may treat the item as dishonored and charge any secondary party by sending him notice of the facts.

§ 4–211. Media of Remittance; Provisional and Final Settlement in Remittance Cases.

(1) A collecting bank may take in settlement of an item

    (a) a check of the remitting bank or of another bank on any bank except the remitting bank; or

    (b) a cashier's check or similar primary obligation of a remitting bank which is a member of or clears through a member of the same clearing house or group as the collecting bank; or

    (c) appropriate authority to charge an account of the remitting bank or of another bank with the collecting bank; or

    (d) if the item is drawn upon or payable by a person other than a bank, a cashier's check, certified check or other bank check or obligation.

(2) If before its midnight deadline the collecting bank properly dishonors a remittance check or authorization to charge on itself or presents or forwards for collection a remittance instrument of or on another bank which is of a kind approved by subsection (1) or has not been authorized by it, the collecting bank is not liable to prior parties in the event of the dishonor of such check, instrument or authorization.

(3) A settlement for an item by means of a remittance instrument or authorization to charge is or becomes a final settlement as to both the person making and the person receiving the settlement

    (a) if the remittance instrument or authorization to charge is of a kind approved by subsection (1) or has not been authorized by the person receiving the settlement and in either case the person receiving the settlement acts seasonably before its midnight deadline in presenting, forwarding for collection or paying the instrument or authorization,—at the time the remittance instrument or authorization is finally paid by the payor by which it is payable;

(b) if the person receiving the settlement has authorized remittance by a non-bank check or obligation or by a cashier's check or similar primary obligation of or a check upon the payor or other remitting bank which is not of a kind approved by subsection (1)(b),—at the time of the receipt of such remittance check or obligation; or

(c) if in a case not covered by sub-paragraphs (a) or (b) the person receiving the settlement fails to seasonably present, forward for collection, pay or return a remittance instrument or authorization to it to charge before its midnight deadline,—at such midnight deadline.

§ 4–212. Right of Charge-Back or Refund.

(1) If a collecting bank has made provisional settlement with its customer for an item and itself fails by reason of dishonor, suspension of payments by a bank or otherwise to receive a settlement for the item which is or becomes final, the bank may revoke the settlement given by it, charge-back the amount of any credit given for the item to its customer's account or obtain refund from its customer whether or not it is able to return the items if by its midnight deadline or within a longer reasonable time after it learns the facts it returns the item or sends notification of the facts. These rights to revoke, charge-back and obtain refund terminate if and when a settlement for the item received by the bank is or becomes final (subsection (3) of Section 4–211 and subsections (2) and (3) of Section 4–213).

(2) [Within the time and manner prescribed by this section and Section 4–301, an intermediary or payor bank, as the case may be, may return an unpaid item directly to the depositary bank and may send for collection a draft on the depositary bank and obtain reimbursement. In such case, if the depositary bank has received provisional settlement for the item, it must reimburse the bank drawing the draft and any provisional credits for the item between banks shall become and remain final.]

Note: *Direct returns is recognized as an innovation that is not yet established bank practice, and therefore, Paragraph 2 has been bracketed. Some lawyers have doubts whether it should be included in legislation or left to development by agreement.*

(3) A depositary bank which is also the payor may charge-back the amount of an item to its customer's account or obtain refund in accordance with the section governing return of an item received by a payor bank for credit on its books (Section 4–301).

(4) The right to charge-back is not affected by

(a) prior use of the credit given for the item; or

(b) failure by any bank to exercise ordinary care with respect to the item but any bank so failing remains liable.

(5) A failure to charge-back or claim refund does not affect other rights of the bank against the customer or any other party.

(6) If credit is given in dollars as the equivalent of the value of an item payable in a foreign currency the dollar amount of any charge-back or refund shall be calculated on the basis of the buying sight rate for the foreign currency prevailing on the day when the person entitled to the charge-back or refund learns that it will not receive payment in ordinary course.

§ 4–213. Final Payment of Item by Payor Bank; When Provisional Debits and Credits Become Final; When Certain Credits Become Available for Withdrawal.

(1) An item is finally paid by a payor bank when the bank has done any of the following, whichever happens first:

(a) paid the item in cash; or

(b) settled for the item without reserving a right to revoke the settlement and without having such right under statute, clearing house rule or agreement; or

(c) completed the process of posting the item to the indicated account of the drawer, maker or other person to be charged therewith; or

(d) made a provisional settlement for the item and failed to revoke the settlement in the time and manner permitted by statute, clearing house rule or agreement.

Upon a final payment under subparagraphs (b), (c), or (d) the payor bank shall be accountable for the amount of the item.

(2) If provisional settlement for an item between the presenting and payor banks is made through a clearing house or by debits or credits in an account between them, then to the extent that provisional debits or credits for the item are entered in accounts between the presenting and payor banks or between the presenting and successive prior collecting banks seriatim, they become final upon final payment of the item by the payor bank.

(3) If a collecting bank receives a settlement for an item which is or becomes final (subsection (3) of Section 4–211, subsection (2) of Section 4–213) the bank is accountable to its customer for the amount of the item and any provisional credit given for the item in an account with its customer becomes final.

(4) Subject to any right of the bank to apply the credit to an obligation of the customer, credit given by a bank for an item in an account with its customer becomes available for withdrawal as of right

(a) in any case where the bank has received a provisional settlement for the item,—when such settlement becomes final and the bank has had a reasonable time to learn that the settlement is final;

(b) in any case where the bank is both a depositary bank and a payor bank and the item is finally paid,—at the opening of the bank's second banking day following receipt of the item.

(5) A deposit of money in a bank is final when made but, subject to any right of the bank to apply the deposit to an obligation of the customer, the deposit becomes available for withdrawal as of right at the opening of the bank's next banking day following receipt of the deposit.

§ 4–214. Insolvency and Preference.

(1) Any item in or coming into the possession of a payor or collecting bank which suspends payment and which item is not finally paid shall be returned by the receiver, trustee or agent in charge of the closed bank to the presenting bank or the closed bank's customer.

(2) If a payor bank finally pays an item and suspends payments without making a settlement for the item with its customer or the presenting bank which settlement is or becomes final, the owner of the item has a preferred claim against the payor bank.

(3) If a payor bank gives or a collecting bank gives or receives a provisional settlement for an item and thereafter suspends payments, the suspension does not prevent or interfere with the settlement becoming final if such finality occurs automatically upon the lapse of certain time or the happening of certain events (subsection (3) of Section 4–211, subsections (1)(d), (2) and (3) of Section 4–213).

(4) If a collecting bank receives from subsequent parties settlement for an item which settlement is or becomes final and suspends payments without making a settlement for the item with its customer which is or becomes final, the owner of the item has a preferred claim against such collecting bank.

Part 3—Collection of Items: Payor Banks
§ 4–301. Deferred Posting; Recovery of Payment by Return of Items; Time of Dishonor.

(1) Where an authorized settlement for a demand item (other than a documentary draft) received by a payor bank otherwise than for immediate payment over the counter has been made before midnight of the banking day of receipt the payor bank may revoke the settlement and recover any payment if before it has made final payment (subsection (1) of Section 4–213) and before its midnight deadline it

(a) returns the item; or

(b) sends written notice of dishonor or nonpayment if the item is held for protest or is otherwise unavailable for return.

(2) If a demand item is received by a payor bank for credit on its books it may return such item or send notice of dishonor and may revoke any credit given or recover the amount thereof withdrawn by its customer, if it acts within the time limit and in the manner specified in the preceding subsection.

(3) Unless previous notice of dishonor has been sent an item is dishonored at the time when for purposes of dishonor it is returned or notice sent in accordance with this section.

(4) An item is returned:

(a) as to an item received through a clearing house when it is delivered to the presenting or last collecting bank or to the clearing house or is sent or delivered in accordance with its rules; or

(b) in all other cases, when it is sent or delivered to the bank's customer or transferor or pursuant to his instructions.

§ 4–302. Payor Bank's Responsibility for Late Return of Item.
In the absence of a valid defense such as breach of a presentment warranty (subsection (1) of Section 4–207), settlement effected or the like, if an item is presented on and received by a payor bank the bank is accountable for the amount of

(a) a demand item other than a documentary draft whether properly payable or not if the bank, in any case where it is not also the depositary bank, retains the item beyond midnight of the banking day of receipt without settling for it or, regardless of whether it is also the depositary bank, does not pay or return the item or send notice of dishonor until after its midnight deadline; or

(b) any other properly payable item unless within the time allowed for acceptance or payment of that item the bank either accepts or pays the item or returns it and accompanying documents.

§ 4–303. When Items Subject to Notice, Stop-Order, Legal Process or Setoff; Order in Which Items May Be Charged or Certified.
(1) Any knowledge, notice or stop-order received by, legal process served upon or setoff exercised by a payor bank, whether or not effective under other rules of law to terminate, suspend or modify the bank's right or duty to pay an item or to charge its customer's account for the item, comes too late to so terminate, suspend or modify such right or duty if the knowledge, notice, stop-order or legal process is received or served and a reasonable time for the bank to act thereon expires or the setoff is exercised after the bank has done any of the following:

(a) accepted or certified the item;

(b) paid the item in cash;

(c) settled for the item without reserving a right to revoke the settlement and without having such right under statute, clearing house rule or agreement;

(d) completed the process of posting the item to the indicated account of the drawer, maker, or other person to be charged therewith or otherwise has evidenced by examination of such indicated account and by action its decision to pay the item; or

(e) become accountable for the amount of the item under subsection (1)(d) of Section 4–213 and Section 4–302 dealing with the payor bank's responsibility for late return of items.

(2) Subject to the provisions of subsection (1) items may be accepted, paid, certified or charged to the indicated account of its customer in any order convenient to the bank.

Part 4—Relationship Between Payor Bank and Its Customer
§ 4–401. When Bank May Charge Customer's Account.
(1) As against its customer, a bank may charge against his account any item which is otherwise properly payable from that account even though the charge creates an overdraft.

(2) A bank which in good faith makes payment to a holder may charge the indicated account of its customer according to

(a) the original tenor of his altered item; or

(b) the tenor of his completed item, even though the bank knows the item has been completed unless the bank has notice that the completion was improper.

§ 4–402. Bank's Liability to Customer for Wrongful Dishonor.
A payor bank is liable to its customer for damages proximately caused by the wrongful dishonor of an item. When the dishonor occurs through mistake liability is limited to actual damages proved. If so proximately caused and proved damages may include damages for an arrest or prosecution of the customer or other consequential damages. Whether any consequential damages are proximately caused by the wrongful dishonor is a question of fact to be determined in each case.

§ 4–403. Customer's Right to Stop Payment; Burden of Proof of Loss.
(1) A customer may by order to his bank stop payment of any item payable for his account but the order must be received at such time and in such manner as to afford the bank a reasonable opportunity to act on it prior to any action by the bank with respect to the item described in Section 4–303.

(2) An oral order is binding upon the bank only for fourteen calendar days unless confirmed in writing within that period. A written order is effective for only six months unless renewed in writing.

(3) The burden of establishing the fact and amount of loss resulting from the payment of an item contrary to a binding stop payment order is on the customer.

§ 4–404. Bank Not Obligated to Pay Check More Than Six Months Old.
A bank is under no obligation to a customer having a checking account to pay a check, other than a certified check, which is presented more than six months after its date, but it may charge its customer's account for a payment made thereafter in good faith.

§ 4–405. Death or Incompetence of Customer.
(1) A payor or collecting bank's authority to accept, pay or collect an item or to account for proceeds of its collection if otherwise effective is not rendered ineffective by incompetence of a customer of either bank existing at the time the item is issued or its collection is undertaken if the bank does not know of an adjudication of incompetence. Neither death nor incompetence of a customer revokes such authority to accept, pay, collect or account until the bank knows of the fact of death or of an adjudication of incompetence and has reasonable opportunity to act on it.

(2) Even with knowledge a bank may for ten days after the date of death pay or certify checks drawn on or prior to that date unless ordered to stop payment by a person claiming an interest in the account.

§ 4–406. Customer's Duty to Discover and Report Unauthorized Signature or Alteration.
(1) When a bank sends to its customer a statement of account accompanied by items paid in good faith in support of the debit entries or holds the statement and items pursuant to a request or instructions of its customer or otherwise in a reasonable manner makes the statement and items available to the customer, the customer must exercise reasonable care and promptness to examine the statement and items to discover his unauthorized signature or any alteration on an item and must notify the bank promptly after discovery thereof.

(2) If the bank establishes that the customer failed with respect to an item to comply with the duties imposed on the customer by subsection (1) the customer is precluded from asserting against the bank

(a) his unauthorized signature or any alteration on the item if the bank also establishes that it suffered a loss by reason of such failure; and

(b) an unauthorized signature or alteration by the same wrongdoer on any other item paid in good faith by the bank after the first item and statement was available to the customer for a reasonable period not exceeding fourteen calendar days and before the bank receives notification from the customer of any such unauthorized signature or alteration.

(3) The preclusion under subsection (2) does not apply if the customer establishes lack of ordinary care on the part of the bank in paying the item(s).

(4) Without regard to care or lack of care of either the customer or the bank a customer who does not within one year from the time the statement and items are made available to the customer (subsection (1)) discover and report his unauthorized signature or any alteration on the face or back of the item or does not within three years from that time discover and report any unauthorized indorsement is precluded from asserting against the bank such unauthorized signature or indorsement or such alteration.

(5) If under this section a payor bank has a valid defense against a claim of a customer upon or resulting from payment of an item and waives or fails upon request to assert the defense the bank may not assert against any collecting bank or other prior party presenting or transferring the item a claim based upon the unauthorized signature or alteration giving rise to the customer's claim.

§ 4–407. Payor Bank's Right to Subrogation on Improper Payment.

If a payor bank has paid an item over the stop payment order of the drawer or maker or otherwise under circumstances giving a basis for objection by the drawer or maker, to prevent unjust enrichment and only to the extent necessary to prevent loss to the bank by reason of its payment of the item, the payor bank shall be subrogated to the rights.

> **(a)** of any holder in due course on the item against the drawer or maker; and
>
> **(b)** of the payee or any other holder of the item against the drawer or maker either on the item or under the transaction out of which the item arose; and
>
> **(c)** of the drawer or maker against the payee or any other holder of the item with respect to the transaction out of which the item arose.

Part 5—Collection of Documentary Drafts

§ 4–501. Handling of Documentary Drafts; Duty to Send for Presentment and to Notify Customer of Dishonor.

A bank which takes a documentary draft for collection must present or send the draft and accompanying documents for presentment and upon learning that the draft has not been paid or accepted in due course must seasonably notify its customer of such fact even though it may have discounted or bought the draft or extended credit available for withdrawal as of right.

§ 4–502. Presentment of "On Arrival" Drafts.

When a draft or the relevant instructions require presentment "on arrival", "when goods arrive" or the like, the collecting bank need not present until in its judgment a reasonable time for arrival of the goods has expired. Refusal to pay or accept because the goods have not arrived is not dishonor; the bank must notify its transferor of such refusal but need not present the draft again until it is instructed to do so or learns of the arrival of the goods.

§ 4–503. Responsibility of Presenting Bank for Documents and Goods; Report of Reasons for Dishonor; Referee in Case of Need.

Unless otherwise instructed and except as provided in Article 5 a bank presenting a documentary draft

> **(a)** must deliver the documents to the drawee on acceptance of the draft if it is payable more than three days after presentment; otherwise, only on payment; and
>
> **(b)** upon dishonor, either in the case of presentment for acceptance or presentment for payment, may seek and follow instructions from any referee in case of need designated in the draft or if the presenting bank does not choose to utilize his services it must use diligence and good faith to ascertain the reason for dishonor, must notify its transferor of the dishonor and of the results of its effort to ascertain the reasons therefor and must request instructions.

But the presenting bank is under no obligation with respect to goods represented by the documents except to follow any reasonable instructions seasonably received; it has a right to reimbursement for any expense incurred in following instructions and to prepayment of or indemnity for such expenses.

§ 4–504. Privilege of Presenting Bank to Deal With Goods; Security Interest for Expenses.

(1) A presenting bank which, following the dishonor of a documentary draft, has seasonably requested instructions but does not receive them within a reasonable time may store, sell, or otherwise deal with the goods in any reasonable manner.

(2) For its reasonable expenses incurred by action under subsection (1) the presenting bank has a lien upon the goods or their proceeds, which may be foreclosed in the same manner as an unpaid seller's lien.

REVISED ARTICLE 9: SECURED TRANSACTIONS
Part 1—General Provisions
§ 9–101. Short Title.

This article may be cited as Uniform Commercial Code—Secured Transactions.

§ 9–102. Definitions and Index of Definitions.

(a) [Article 9 definitions.] In this article:

(1) "Accession" means goods that are physically united with other goods in such a manner that the identity of the original goods is not lost.

(2) "Account", except as used in "account for", means a right to payment of a monetary obligation, whether or not earned by performance, (i) for property that has been or is to be sold, leased, licensed, assigned, or otherwise disposed of, (ii) for services rendered or to be rendered, (iii) for a policy of insurance issued or to be issued, (iv) for a secondary obligation incurred or to be incurred, (v) for energy provided or to be provided, (vi) for the use or hire of a vessel under a charter or other contract, (vii) arising out of the use of a credit or charge card or information contained on or for use with the card, or (viii) as winnings in a lottery or other game of chance operated or sponsored by a State, governmental unit of a State, or person licensed or authorized to operate the game by a State or governmental unit of a State. The term includes health-care-insurance receivables. The term does not include (i) rights to payment evidenced by chattel paper or an instrument, (ii) commercial tort claims, (iii) deposit accounts, (iv) investment property, (v) letter-of-credit rights or letters of credit, or (vi) rights to payment for money or funds advanced or sold, other than rights arising out of the use of a credit or charge card or information contained on or for use with the card.

(3) "Account debtor" means a person obligated on an account, chattel paper, or general intangible. The term does not include persons obligated to pay a negotiable instrument, even if the instrument constitutes part of chattel paper.

(4) "Accounting", except as used in "accounting for", means a record:

> **(A)** authenticated by a secured party;
>
> **(B)** indicating the aggregate unpaid secured obligations as of a date not more than 35 days earlier or 35 days later than the date of the record; and
>
> **(C)** identifying the components of the obligations in reasonable detail.

(5) "Agricultural lien" means an interest, other than a security interest, in farm products:

> **(A)** which secures payment or performance of an obligation for:
>> **(i)** goods or services furnished in connection with a debtor's farming operation; or
>>
>> **(ii)** rent on real property leased by a debtor in connection with its farming operation;
>
> **(B)** which is created by statute in favor of a person that:
>> **(i)** in the ordinary course of its business furnished goods or services to a debtor in connection with a debtor's farming operation; or
>>
>> **(ii)** leased real property to a debtor in connection with the debtor's farming operation; and
>
> **(C)** whose effectiveness does not depend on the person's possession of the personal property.

(6) "As-extracted collateral" means:

> **(A)** oil, gas, or other minerals that are subject to a security interest that:
>> **(i)** is created by a debtor having an interest in the minerals before extraction; and
>>
>> **(ii)** attaches to the minerals as extracted; or
>
> **(B)** accounts arising out of the sale at the wellhead or minehead of oil, gas, or other minerals in which the debtor had an interest before extraction.

(7) "Authenticate" means:

> **(A)** to sign; or
>
> **(B)** to execute or otherwise adopt a symbol, or encrypt or similarly process a record in whole or in part, with the present intent of the authenticating person to identify the person and adopt or accept a record.

(8) "Bank" means an organization that is engaged in the business of banking. The term includes savings banks, savings and loan associations, credit unions, and trust companies.

(9) "Cash proceeds" means proceeds that are money, checks, deposit accounts, or the like.

(10) "Certificate of title" means a certificate of title with respect to which a statute provides for the security interest in question to be indicated on the certificate as a condition or result of the security interest's obtaining priority over the rights of a lien creditor with respect to the collateral.

(11) "Chattel paper" means a record or records that evidence both a monetary obligation and a security interest in specific goods, a security interest in specific goods and software used in the goods, a security interest in specific goods and license of software used in the goods, a lease of specific goods, or a lease of specific goods and license of software used in the goods. In this paragraph, "monetary obligation" means a monetary obligation secured by the goods or owed under a lease of the goods and includes a monetary obligation with respect to software used in the goods. The term does not include (i) charters or other contracts involving the use or hire of a vessel or (ii) records that evidence a right to payment arising out of the use of a credit or charge card or information contained on or for use with the card. If a transaction is evidenced by records that include an instrument or series of instruments, the group of records taken together constitutes chattel paper.

(12) "Collateral" means the property subject to a security interest or agricultural lien. The term includes:

(A) proceeds to which a security interest attaches;

(B) accounts, chattel paper, payment intangibles, and promissory notes that have been sold; and

(C) goods that are the subject of a consignment.

(13) "Commercial tort claim" means a claim arising in tort with respect to which:

(A) the claimant is an organization; or

(B) the claimant is an individual and the claim:

(i) arose in the course of the claimant's business or profession; and

(ii) does not include damages arising out of personal injury to or the death of an individual.

(14) "Commodity account" means an account maintained by a commodity intermediary in which a commodity contract is carried for a commodity customer.

(15) "Commodity contract" means a commodity futures contract, an option on a commodity futures contract, a commodity option, or another contract if the contract or option is:

(A) traded on or subject to the rules of a board of trade that has been designated as a contract market for such a contract pursuant to federal commodities laws; or

(B) traded on a foreign commodity board of trade, exchange, or market, and is carried on the books of a commodity intermediary for a commodity customer.

(16) "Commodity customer" means a person for which a commodity intermediary carries a commodity contract on its books.

(17) "Commodity intermediary" means a person that:

(A) is registered as a futures commission merchant under federal commodities law; or

(B) in the ordinary course of its business provides clearance or settlement services for a board of trade that has been designated as a contract market pursuant to federal commodities law.

(18) "Communicate" means:

(A) to send a written or other tangible record;

(B) to transmit a record by any means agreed upon by the persons sending and receiving the record; or

(C) in the case of transmission of a record to or by a filing office, to transmit a record by any means prescribed by filing-office rule.

(19) "Consignee" means a merchant to which goods are delivered in a consignment.

(20) "Consignment" means a transaction, regardless of its form, in which a person delivers goods to a merchant for the purpose of sale and:

(A) the merchant:

(i) deals in goods of that kind under a name other than the name of the person making delivery;

(ii) is not an auctioneer; and

(iii) is not generally known by its creditors to be substantially engaged in selling the goods of others;

(B) with respect to each delivery, the aggregate value of the goods is $1,000 or more at the time of delivery;

(C) the goods are not consumer goods immediately before delivery; and

(D) the transaction does not create a security interest that secures an obligation.

(21) "Consignor" means a person that delivers goods to a consignee in a consignment.

(22) "Consumer debtor" means a debtor in a consumer transaction.

(23) "Consumer goods" means goods that are used or bought for use primarily for personal, family, or household purposes.

(24) "Consumer-goods transaction" means a consumer transaction in which:

(A) an individual incurs an obligation primarily for personal, family, or household purposes; and

(B) a security interest in consumer goods secures the obligation.

(25) "Consumer obligor" means an obligor who is an individual and who incurred the obligation as part of a transaction entered into primarily for personal, family, or household purposes.

(26) "Consumer transaction" means a transaction in which (i) an individual incurs an obligation primarily for personal, family, or household purposes, (ii) a security interest secures the obligation, and (iii) the collateral is held or acquired primarily for personal, family, or household purposes. The term includes consumer-goods transactions.

(27) "Continuation statement" means an amendment of a financing statement which:

(A) identifies, by its file number, the initial financing statement to which it relates; and

(B) indicates that it is a continuation statement for, or that it is filed to continue the effectiveness of, the identified financing statement.

(28) "Debtor" means:

(A) a person having an interest, other than a security interest or other lien, in the collateral, whether or not the person is an obligor;

(B) a seller of accounts, chattel paper, payment intangibles, or promissory notes; or

(C) a consignee.

(29) "Deposit account" means a demand, time, savings, passbook, or similar account maintained with a bank. The term does not include investment property or accounts evidenced by an instrument.

(30) "Document" means a document of title or a receipt of the type described in Section 7–201(2).

(31) "Electronic chattel paper" means chattel paper evidenced by a record or records consisting of information stored in an electronic medium.

(32) "Encumbrance" means a right, other than an ownership interest, in real property. The term includes mortgages and other liens on real property.

(33) "Equipment" means goods other than inventory, farm products, or consumer goods.

(34) "Farm products" means goods, other than standing timber, with respect to which the debtor is engaged in a farming operation and which are:

(A) crops grown, growing, or to be grown, including:

(i) crops produced on trees, vines, and bushes; and

(ii) aquatic goods produced in aquacultural operations;

(B) livestock, born or unborn, including aquatic goods produced in aquacultural operations;

(C) supplies used or produced in a farming operation; or

(D) products of crops or livestock in their unmanufactured states.

(35) "Farming operation" means raising, cultivating, propagating, fattening, grazing, or any other farming, livestock, or aquacultural operation.

(36) "File number" means the number assigned to an initial financing statement pursuant to Section 9–519(a).

(37) "Filing office" means an office designated in Section 9–501 as the place to file a financing statement.

(38) "Filing–office rule" means a rule adopted pursuant to Section 9–526.

(39) "Financing statement" means a record or records composed of an initial financing statement and any filed record relating to the initial financing statement.

(40) "Fixture filing" means the filing of a financing statement covering goods that are or are to become fixtures and satisfying Section 9–502(a) and (b). The term includes the filing of a financing statement covering goods of a transmitting utility which are or are to become fixtures.

(41) "Fixtures" means goods that have become so related to particular real property that an interest in them arises under real property law.

(42) "General intangible" means any personal property, including things in action, other than accounts, chattel paper, commercial tort claims, deposit accounts, documents, goods, instruments, investment property, letter-of-credit rights, letters of credit, money, and oil, gas, or other minerals before extraction. The term includes payment intangibles and software.

(43) "Good faith" means honesty in fact and the observance of reasonable commercial standards of fair dealing.

(44) "Goods" means all things that are movable when a security interest attaches. The term includes (i) fixtures, (ii) standing timber that is to be cut and removed under a conveyance or contract for sale, (iii) the unborn young of animals, (iv) crops grown, growing, or to be grown, even if the crops are produced on trees, vines, or bushes, and (v) manufactured homes. The term also includes a computer program embedded in goods and any supporting information provided in connection with a transaction relating to the program if (i) the program is associated with the goods in such a manner that it customarily is considered part of the goods, or (ii) by becoming the owner of the goods, a person acquires a right to use the program in connection with the goods. The term does not include a computer program embedded in goods that consist solely of the medium in which the program is embedded. The term also does not include accounts, chattel paper, commercial tort claims, deposit accounts, documents, general intangibles, instruments, investment property, letter-of-credit rights, letters of credit, money, or oil, gas, or other minerals before extraction.

(45) "Governmental unit" means a subdivision, agency, department, county, parish, municipality, or other unit of the government of the United States, a State, or a foreign country. The term includes an organization having a separate corporate existence if the organization is eligible to issue debt on which interest is exempt from income taxation under the laws of the United States.

(46) "Health-care-insurance receivable" means an interest in or claim under a policy of insurance which is a right to payment of a monetary obligation for health-care goods or services provided.

(47) "Instrument" means a negotiable instrument or any other writing that evidences a right to the payment of a monetary obligation, is not itself a security agreement or lease, and is of a type that in ordinary course of business is transferred by delivery with any necessary indorsement or assignment. The term does not include (i) investment property, (ii) letters of credit, or (iii) writings that evidence a right to payment arising out of the use of a credit or charge card or information contained on or for use with the card.

(48) "Inventory" means goods, other than farm products, which:

   (A) are leased by a person as lessor;

   (B) are held by a person for sale or lease or to be furnished under a contract of service;

   (C) are furnished by a person under a contract of service; or

   (D) consist of raw materials, work in process, or materials used or consumed in a business.

(49) "Investment property" means a security, whether certificated or uncertificated, security entitlement, securities account, commodity contract, or commodity account.

(50) "Jurisdiction of organization", with respect to a registered organization, means the jurisdiction under whose law the organization is organized.

(51) "Letter-of-credit right" means a right to payment or performance under a letter of credit, whether or not the beneficiary has demanded or is at the time entitled to demand payment or performance. The term does not include the right of a beneficiary to demand payment or performance under a letter of credit.

(52) "Lien creditor" means:

   (A) a creditor that has acquired a lien on the property involved by attachment, levy, or the like;

   (B) an assignee for benefit of creditors from the time of assignment;

   (C) a trustee in bankruptcy from the date of the filing of the petition; or

   (D) a receiver in equity from the time of appointment.

(53) "Manufactured home" means a structure, transportable in one or more sections, which, in the traveling mode, is eight body feet or more in width or 40 body feet or more in length, or, when erected on site, is 320 or more square feet, and which is built on a permanent chassis and designed to be used as a dwelling with or without a permanent foundation when connected to the required utilities, and includes the plumbing, heating, air-conditioning, and electrical systems contained therein. The term includes any structure that meets all of the requirements of this paragraph except the size requirements and with respect to which the manufacturer voluntarily files a certification required by the United States Secretary of Housing and Urban Development and complies with the standards established under Title 42 of the United States Code.

(54) "Manufactured-home transaction" means a secured transaction:

   (A) that creates a purchase-money security interest in a manufactured home, other than a manufactured home held as inventory; or

   (B) in which a manufactured home, other than a manufactured home held as inventory, is the primary collateral.

(55) "Mortgage" means a consensual interest in real property, including fixtures, which secures payment or performance of an obligation.

(56) "New debtor" means a person that becomes bound as debtor under Section 9–203(d) by a security agreement previously entered into by another person.

(57) "New value" means (i) money, (ii) money's worth in property, services, or new credit, or (iii) release by a transferee of an interest in property previously transferred to the transferee. The term does not include an obligation substituted for another obligation.

(58) "Noncash proceeds" means proceeds other than cash proceeds.

(59) "Obligor" means a person that, with respect to an obligation secured by a security interest in or an agricultural lien on the collateral, (i) owes payment or other performance of the obligation, (ii) has provided property other than the collateral to secure payment or other performance of the obligation, or (iii) is otherwise accountable in whole or in part for payment or other performance of the obligation. The term does not include issuers or nominated persons under a letter of credit.

(60) "Original debtor", except as used in Section 9–310(c), means a person that, as debtor, entered into a security agreement to which a new debtor has become bound under Section 9–203(d).

(61) "Payment intangible" means a general intangible under which the account debtor's principal obligation is a monetary obligation.

(62) "Person related to", with respect to an individual, means:

   (A) the spouse of the individual;

   (B) a brother, brother-in-law, sister, or sister-in-law of the individual;

   (C) an ancestor or lineal descendant of the individual or the individual's spouse; or

   (D) any other relative, by blood or marriage, of the individual or the individual's spouse who shares the same home with the individual.

(63) "Person related to", with respect to an organization, means:

   (A) a person directly or indirectly controlling, controlled by, or under common control with the organization;

   (B) an officer or director of, or a person performing similar functions with respect to, the organization;

   (C) an officer or director of, or a person performing similar functions with respect to, a person described in subparagraph (A);

   (D) the spouse of an individual described in subparagraph (A), (B), or (C); or

(E) an individual who is related by blood or marriage to an individual described in subparagraph (A), (B), (C), or (D) and shares the same home with the individual.

(64) "Proceeds", except as used in Section 9–609(b), means the following property:

(A) whatever is acquired upon the sale, lease, license, exchange, or other disposition of collateral;

(B) whatever is collected on, or distributed on account of, collateral;

(C) rights arising out of collateral;

(D) to the extent of the value of collateral, claims arising out of the loss, nonconformity, or interference with the use of, defects or infringement of rights in, or damage to, the collateral; or

(E) to the extent of the value of collateral and to the extent payable to the debtor or the secured party, insurance payable by reason of the loss or nonconformity of, defects or infringement of rights in, or damage to, the collateral.

(65) "Promissory note" means an instrument that evidences a promise to pay a monetary obligation, does not evidence an order to pay, and does not contain an acknowledgment by a bank that the bank has received for deposit a sum of money or funds.

(66) "Proposal" means a record authenticated by a secured party which includes the terms on which the secured party is willing to accept collateral in full or partial satisfaction of the obligation it secures pursuant to Sections 9–620, 9–621, and 9–622.

(67) "Public-finance transaction" means a secured transaction in connection with which:

(A) debt securities are issued;

(B) all or a portion of the securities issued have an initial stated maturity of at least 20 years; and

(C) the debtor, obligor, secured party, account debtor or other person obligated on collateral, assignor or assignee of a secured obligation, or assignor or assignee of a security interest is a State or a governmental unit of a State.

(68) "Pursuant to commitment", with respect to an advance made or other value given by a secured party, means pursuant to the secured party's obligation, whether or not a subsequent event of default or other event not within the secured party's control has relieved or may relieve the secured party from its obligation.

(69) "Record", except as used in "for record", "of record", "record or legal title", and "record owner", means information that is inscribed on a tangible medium or which is stored in an electronic or other medium and is retrievable in perceivable form.

(70) "Registered organization" means an organization organized solely under the law of a single State or the United States and as to which the State or the United States must maintain a public record showing the organization to have been organized.

(71) "Secondary obligor" means an obligor to the extent that:

(A) the obligor's obligation is secondary; or

(B) the obligor has a right of recourse with respect to an obligation secured by collateral against the debtor, another obligor, or property of either.

(72) "Secured party" means:

(A) a person in whose favor a security interest is created or provided for under a security agreement, whether or not any obligation to be secured is outstanding;

(B) a person that holds an agricultural lien;

(C) a consignor;

(D) a person to which accounts, chattel paper, payment intangibles, or promissory notes have been sold;

(E) a trustee, indenture trustee, agent, collateral agent, or other representative in whose favor a security interest or agricultural lien is created or provided for; or

(F) a person that holds a security interest arising under Section 2–401, 2–505, 2–711(3), 2A–508(5), 4–210, or 5–118.

(73) "Security agreement" means an agreement that creates or provides for a security interest.

(74) "Send", in connection with a record or notification, means:

(A) to deposit in the mail, deliver for transmission, or transmit by any other usual means of communication, with postage or cost of transmission provided for, addressed to any address reasonable under the circumstances; or

(B) to cause the record or notification to be received within the time that it would have been received if properly sent under subparagraph (A).

(75) "Software" means a computer program and any supporting information provided in connection with a transaction relating to the program. The term does not include a computer program that is included in the definition of goods.

(76) "State" means a State of the United States, the District of Columbia, Puerto Rico, the United States Virgin Islands, or any territory or insular possession subject to the jurisdiction of the United States.

(77) "Supporting obligation" means a letter-of-credit right or secondary obligation that supports the payment or performance of an account, chattel paper, a document, a general intangible, an instrument, or investment property.

(78) "Tangible chattel paper" means chattel paper evidenced by a record or records consisting of information that is inscribed on a tangible medium.

(79) "Termination statement" means an amendment of a financing statement which:

(A) identifies, by its file number, the initial financing statement to which it relates; and

(B) indicates either that it is a termination statement or that the identified financing statement is no longer effective.

(80) "Transmitting utility" means a person primarily engaged in the business of:

(A) operating a railroad, subway, street railway, or trolley bus;

(B) transmitting communications electrically, electromagnetically, or by light;

(C) transmitting goods by pipeline or sewer; or

(D) transmitting or producing and transmitting electricity, steam, gas, or water.

(b) [**Definitions in other articles.**] The following definitions in other articles apply to this article:

"Applicant" Section 5–102.

"Beneficiary" Section 5–102.

"Broker" Section 8–102.

"Certificated security" Section 8–102.

"Check" Section 3–104.

"Clearing corporation" Section 8–102.

"Contract for sale" Section 2–106.

"Customer" Section 4–104.

"Entitlement holder" Section 8–102.

"Financial asset" Section 8–102.

"Holder in due course" Section 3–302.

"Issuer" (with respect to a letter of credit or letter-of-credit right) Section 5–102.

"Issuer" (with respect to a security) Section 8–201.

"Lease" Section 2A–103.

"Lease agreement" Section 2A–103.

"Lease contract" Section 2A–103.

"Leasehold interest" Section 2A–103.

"Lessee" Section 2A–103.

"Lessee in ordinary course of business" Section 2A–103.

"Lessor" Section 2A–103.

"Lessor's residual interest" Section 2A–103.

"Letter of credit" Section 5–102.

"Merchant" Section 2–104.

"Negotiable instrument" Section 3–104.

"Nominated person" Section 5–102.

"Note" Section 3–104.

"Proceeds of a letter of credit" Section 5–114.

"Prove" Section 3–103.

"Sale" Section 2–106.

"Securities account" Section 8–501.

"Securities intermediary" Section 8–102.
"Security" Section 8–102.
"Security certificate" Section 8–102.
"Security entitlement" Section 8–102.
"Uncertificated security" Section 8–102.

(c) [**Article 1 definitions and principles.**] Article 1 contains general definitions and principles of construction and interpretation applicable throughout this article.

§ 9–103. Purchase-Money Security Interest; Application of Payments; Burden of Establishing.

(a) [**Definitions.**] In this section:

  (1) "purchase-money collateral" means goods or software that secures a purchase-money obligation incurred with respect to that collateral; and

  (2) "purchase-money obligation" means an obligation of an obligor incurred as all or part of the price of the collateral or for value given to enable the debtor to acquire rights in or the use of the collateral if the value is in fact so used.

(b) [**Purchase-money security interest in goods.**] A security interest in goods is a purchase-money security interest:

  (1) to the extent that the goods are purchase-money collateral with respect to that security interest;

  (2) if the security interest is in inventory that is or was purchase-money collateral, also to the extent that the security interest secures a purchase-money obligation incurred with respect to other inventory in which the secured party holds or held a purchase-money security interest; and

  (3) also to the extent that the security interest secures a purchase-money obligation incurred with respect to software in which the secured party holds or held a purchase-money security interest.

(c) [**Purchase-money security interest in software.**] A security interest in software is a purchase-money security interest to the extent that the security interest also secures a purchase-money obligation incurred with respect to goods in which the secured party holds or held a purchase-money security interest if:

  (1) the debtor acquired its interest in the software in an integrated transaction in which it acquired an interest in the goods; and

  (2) the debtor acquired its interest in the software for the principal purpose of using the software in the goods.

(d) [**Consignor's inventory purchase-money security interest.**] The security interest of a consignor in goods that are the subject of a consignment is a purchase-money security interest in inventory.

(e) [**Application of payment in non-consumer-goods transaction.**] In a transaction other than a consumer-goods transaction, if the extent to which a security interest is a purchase-money security interest depends on the application of a payment to a particular obligation, the payment must be applied:

  (1) in accordance with any reasonable method of application to which the parties agree;

  (2) in the absence of the parties' agreement to a reasonable method, in accordance with any intention of the obligor manifested at or before the time of payment; or

  (3) in the absence of an agreement to a reasonable method and a timely manifestation of the obligor's intention, in the following order:

    (A) to obligations that are not secured; and

    (B) if more than one obligation is secured, to obligations secured by purchase-money security interests in the order in which those obligations were incurred.

(f) [**No loss of status of purchase-money security interest in non-consumer-goods transaction.**] In a transaction other than a consumer-goods transaction, a purchase-money security interest does not lose its status as such, even if:

  (1) the purchase-money collateral also secures an obligation that is not a purchase-money obligation;

  (2) collateral that is not purchase-money collateral also secures the purchase-money obligation; or

  (3) the purchase-money obligation has been renewed, refinanced, consolidated, or restructured.

(g) [**Burden of proof in non-consumer-goods transaction.**] In a transaction other than a consumer-goods transaction, a secured party claiming a purchase-money security interest has the burden of establishing the extent to which the security interest is a purchase-money security interest.

(h) [**Non-consumer-goods transactions; no inference.**] The limitation of the rules in subsections (e), (f), and (g) to transactions other than consumer-goods transactions is intended to leave to the court the determination of the proper rules in consumer-goods transactions. The court may not infer from that limitation the nature of the proper rule in consumer-goods transactions and may continue to apply established approaches.

§ 9–104. Control of Deposit Account.

(a) [**Requirements for control.**] A secured party has control of a deposit account if:

  (1) the secured party is the bank with which the deposit account is maintained;

  (2) the debtor, secured party, and bank have agreed in an authenticated record that the bank will comply with instructions originated by the secured party directing disposition of the funds in the deposit account without further consent by the debtor; or

  (3) the secured party becomes the bank's customer with respect to the deposit account.

(b) [**Debtor's right to direct disposition.**] A secured party that has satisfied subsection (a) has control, even if the debtor retains the right to direct the disposition of funds from the deposit account.

§ 9–105. Control of Electronic Chattel Paper.

A secured party has control of electronic chattel paper if the record or records comprising the chattel paper are created, stored, and assigned in such a manner that:

(1) a single authoritative copy of the record or records exists which is unique, identifiable and, except as otherwise provided in paragraphs (4), (5), and (6), unalterable;

(2) the authoritative copy identifies the secured party as the assignee of the record or records;

(3) the authoritative copy is communicated to and maintained by the secured party or its designated custodian;

(4) copies or revisions that add or change an identified assignee of the authoritative copy can be made only with the participation of the secured party;

(5) each copy of the authoritative copy and any copy of a copy is readily identifiable as a copy that is not the authoritative copy; and

(6) any revision of the authoritative copy is readily identifiable as an authorized or unauthorized revision.

§ 9–106. Control of Investment Property.

(a) [**Control under Section 8–106.**] A person has control of a certificated security, uncertificated security, or security entitlement as provided in Section 8–106.

(b) [**Control of commodity contract.**] A secured party has control of a commodity contract if:

  (1) the secured party is the commodity intermediary with which the commodity contract is carried; or

  (2) the commodity customer, secured party, and commodity intermediary have agreed that the commodity intermediary will apply any value distributed on account of the commodity contract as directed by the secured party without further consent by the commodity customer.

(c) [**Effect of control of securities account or commodity account.**] A secured party having control of all security entitlements or commodity contracts carried in a securities account or commodity account has control over the securities account or commodity account.

§ 9–107. Control of Letter-of-Credit Right.

A secured party has control of a letter-of-credit right to the extent of any right to payment or performance by the issuer or any nominated person if the issuer or nominated person has consented to an assignment of proceeds of the letter of credit under Section 5–114(c) or otherwise applicable law or practice.

§ 9–108. Sufficiency of Description.

(a) [**Sufficiency of description.**] Except as otherwise provided in subsections (c), (d), and (e), a description of personal or real property is sufficient, whether or not it is specific, if it reasonably identifies what is described.

(b) [**Examples of reasonable identification.**] Except as otherwise provided in subsection (d), a description of collateral reasonably identifies the collateral if it identifies the collateral by:

(1) specific listing;

(2) category;

(3) except as otherwise provided in subsection (e), a type of collateral defined in [the Uniform Commercial Code];

(4) quantity;

(5) computational or allocational formula or procedure; or

(6) except as otherwise provided in subsection (c), any other method, if the identity of the collateral is objectively determinable.

(c) [**Supergeneric description not sufficient.**] A description of collateral as "all the debtor's assets" or "all the debtor's personal property" or using words of similar import does not reasonably identify the collateral.

(d) [**Investment property.**] Except as otherwise provided in subsection (e), a description of a security entitlement, securities account, or commodity account is sufficient if it describes:

(1) the collateral by those terms or as investment property; or

(2) the underlying financial asset or commodity contract.

(e) [**When description by type insufficient.**] A description only by type of collateral defined in [the Uniform Commercial Code] is an insufficient description of:

(1) a commercial tort claim; or

(2) in a consumer transaction, consumer goods, a security entitlement, a securities account, or a commodity account.

§ 9–109. Scope.

(a) [**General scope of article.**] Except as otherwise provided in subsections (c) and (d), this article applies to:

(1) a transaction, regardless of its form, that creates a security interest in personal property or fixtures by contract;

(2) an agricultural lien;

(3) a sale of accounts, chattel paper, payment intangibles, or promissory notes;

(4) a consignment;

(5) a security interest arising under Section 2–401, 2–505, 2–711(3), or 2A–508(5), as provided in Section 9–110; and

(6) a security interest arising under Section 4–210 or 5–118.

(b) [**Security interest in secured obligation.**] The application of this article to a security interest in a secured obligation is not affected by the fact that the obligation is itself secured by a transaction or interest to which this article does not apply.

(c) [**Extent to which article does not apply.**] This article does not apply to the extent that:

(1) a statute, regulation, or treaty of the United States preempts this article;

(2) another statute of this State expressly governs the creation, perfection, priority, or enforcement of a security interest created by this State or a governmental unit of this State;

(3) a statute of another State, a foreign country, or a governmental unit of another State or a foreign country, other than a statute generally applicable to security interests, expressly governs creation, perfection, priority, or enforcement of a security interest created by the State, country, or governmental unit; or

(4) the rights of a transferee beneficiary or nominated person under a letter of credit are independent and superior under Section 5–114.

(d) [**Inapplicability of article.**] This article does not apply to:

(1) a landlord's lien, other than an agricultural lien;

(2) a lien, other than an agricultural lien, given by statute or other rule of law for services or materials, but Section 9–333 applies with respect to priority of the lien;

(3) an assignment of a claim for wages, salary, or other compensation of an employee;

(4) a sale of accounts, chattel paper, payment intangibles, or promissory notes as part of a sale of the business out of which they arose;

(5) an assignment of accounts, chattel paper, payment intangibles, or promissory notes which is for the purpose of collection only;

(6) an assignment of a right to payment under a contract to an assignee that is also obligated to perform under the contract;

(7) an assignment of a single account, payment intangible, or promissory note to an assignee in full or partial satisfaction of a preexisting indebtedness;

(8) a transfer of an interest in or an assignment of a claim under a policy of insurance, other than an assignment by or to a health-care provider of a health-care-insurance receivable and any subsequent assignment of the right to payment, but Sections 9–315 and 9–322 apply with respect to proceeds and priorities in proceeds;

(9) an assignment of a right represented by a judgment, other than a judgment taken on a right to payment that was collateral;

(10) a right of recoupment or set-off, but:

(A) Section 9–340 applies with respect to the effectiveness of rights of recoupment or set-off against deposit accounts; and

(B) Section 9–404 applies with respect to defenses or claims of an account debtor;

(11) the creation or transfer of an interest in or lien on real property, including a lease or rents thereunder, except to the extent that provision is made for:

(A) liens on real property in Sections 9–203 and 9–308;

(B) fixtures in Section 9–334;

(C) fixture filings in Sections 9–501, 9–502, 9–512, 9–516, and 9–519; and

(D) security agreements covering personal and real property in Section 9–604;

(12) an assignment of a claim arising in tort, other than a commercial tort claim, but Sections 9–315 and 9–322 apply with respect to proceeds and priorities in proceeds; or

(13) an assignment of a deposit account in a consumer transaction, but Sections 9–315 and 9–322 apply with respect to proceeds and priorities in proceeds.

§ 9–110. Security Interests Arising under Article 2 or 2A.

A security interest arising under Section 2–401, 2–505, 2–711(3), or 2A–508(5) is subject to this article. However, until the debtor obtains possession of the goods:

(1) the security interest is enforceable, even if Section 9–203(b)(3) has not been satisfied;

(2) filing is not required to perfect the security interest;

(3) the rights of the secured party after default by the debtor are governed by Article 2 or 2A; and

(4) the security interest has priority over a conflicting security interest created by the debtor.

Part 2—Effectiveness of Security Agreement; Attachment of Security Interest; Rights of Parties to Security Agreement
§ 9–201. General Effectiveness of Security Agreement.

(a) [**General effectiveness.**] Except as otherwise provided in [the Uniform Commercial Code], a security agreement is effective according to its terms between the parties, against purchasers of the collateral, and against creditors.

(b) [**Applicable consumer laws and other law.**] A transaction subject to this article is subject to any applicable rule of law which establishes a different rule for consumers and [insert reference to (i) any other statute or regulation that regulates the rates, charges, agreements, and practices for loans, credit sales, or other extensions of credit and (ii) any consumer-protection statute or regulation].

(c) [**Other applicable law controls.**] In case of conflict between this article and a rule of law, statute, or regulation described in subsection (b), the rule of law, statute, or regulation controls. Failure to comply with a statute or regulation described in subsection (b) has only the effect the statute or regulation specifies.

(d) [**Further deference to other applicable law.**] This article does not:

(1) validate any rate, charge, agreement, or practice that violates a rule of law, statute, or regulation described in subsection (b); or

(2) extend the application of the rule of law, statute, or regulation to a transaction not otherwise subject to it.

§ 9–203. Attachment and Enforceability of Security Interest; Proceeds; Supporting Obligations; Formal Requisites.

(a) [**Attachment.**] A security interest attaches to collateral when it becomes enforceable against the debtor with respect to the collateral, unless an agreement expressly postpones the time of attachment.

(b) [**Enforceability.**] Except as otherwise provided in subsections (c) through (i), a security interest is enforceable against the debtor and third parties with respect to the collateral only if:

(1) value has been given;

(2) the debtor has rights in the collateral or the power to transfer rights in the collateral to a secured party; and

(3) one of the following conditions is met:

(A) the debtor has authenticated a security agreement that provides a description of the collateral and, if the security interest covers timber to be cut, a description of the land concerned;

(B) the collateral is not a certificated security and is in the possession of the secured party under Section 9–313 pursuant to the debtor's security agreement;

(C) the collateral is a certificated security in registered form and the security certificate has been delivered to the secured party under Section 8–301 pursuant to the debtor's security agreement; or

(D) the collateral is deposit accounts, electronic chattel paper, investment property, or letter-of-credit rights, and the secured party has control under Section 9–104, 9–105, 9–106, or 9–107 pursuant to the debtor's security agreement.

(c) [**Other UCC provisions.**] Subsection (b) is subject to Section 4–210 on the security interest of a collecting bank, Section 5–118 on the security interest of a letter-of-credit issuer or nominated person, Section 9–110 on a security interest arising under Article 2 or 2A, and Section 9–206 on security interests in investment property.

(d) [**When person becomes bound by another person's security agreement.**] A person becomes bound as debtor by a security agreement entered into by another person if, by operation of law other than this article or by contract:

(1) the security agreement becomes effective to create a security interest in the person's property; or

(2) the person becomes generally obligated for the obligations of the other person, including the obligation secured under the security agreement, and acquires or succeeds to all or substantially all of the assets of the other person.

(e) [**Effect of new debtor becoming bound.**] If a new debtor becomes bound as debtor by a security agreement entered into by another person:

(1) the agreement satisfies subsection (b)(3) with respect to existing or after-acquired property of the new debtor to the extent the property is described in the agreement; and

(2) another agreement is not necessary to make a security interest in the property enforceable.

(f) [**Proceeds and supporting obligations.**] The attachment of a security interest in collateral gives the secured party the rights to proceeds provided by Section 9–315 and is also attachment of a security interest in a supporting obligation for the collateral.

(g) [**Lien securing right to payment.**] The attachment of a security interest in a right to payment or performance secured by a security interest or other lien on personal or real property is also attachment of a security interest in the security interest, mortgage, or other lien.

(h) [**Security entitlement carried in securities account.**] The attachment of a security interest in a securities account is also attachment of a security interest in the security entitlements carried in the securities account.

(i) [**Commodity contracts carried in commodity account.**] The attachment of a security interest in a commodity account is also attachment of a security interest in the commodity contracts carried in the commodity account.

§ 9–204. After-Acquired Property; Future Advances.

(a) [**After-acquired collateral.**] Except as otherwise provided in subsection (b), a security agreement may create or provide for a security interest in after-acquired collateral.

(b) [**When after-acquired property clause not effective.**] A security interest does not attach under a term constituting an after-acquired property clause to:

(1) consumer goods, other than an accession when given as additional security, unless the debtor acquires rights in them within 10 days after the secured party gives value; or

(2) a commercial tort claim.

(c) [**Future advances and other value.**] A security agreement may provide that collateral secures, or that accounts, chattel paper, payment intangibles, or promissory notes are sold in connection with, future advances or other value, whether or not the advances or value are given pursuant to commitment.

§ 9–205. Use or Disposition of Collateral Permissible.

(a) [**When security interest not invalid or fraudulent.**] A security interest is not invalid or fraudulent against creditors solely because:

(1) the debtor has the right or ability to:

(A) use, commingle, or dispose of all or part of the collateral, including returned or repossessed goods;

(B) collect, compromise, enforce, or otherwise deal with collateral;

(C) accept the return of collateral or make repossessions; or

(D) use, commingle, or dispose of proceeds; or

(2) the secured party fails to require the debtor to account for proceeds or replace collateral.

(b) [**Requirements of possession not relaxed.**] This section does not relax the requirements of possession if attachment, perfection, or enforcement of a security interest depends upon possession of the collateral by the secured party.

Part 3—Perfection and Priority
§ 9–301. Law Governing Perfection and Priority of Security Interests.

Except as otherwise provided in Sections 9–303 through 9–306, the following rules determine the law governing perfection, the effect of perfection or nonperfection, and the priority of a security interest in collateral:

(1) Except as otherwise provided in this section, while a debtor is located in a jurisdiction, the local law of that jurisdiction governs perfection, the effect of perfection or nonperfection, and the priority of a security interest in collateral.

(2) While collateral is located in a jurisdiction, the local law of that jurisdiction governs perfection, the effect of perfection or nonperfection, and the priority of a possessory security interest in that collateral.

(3) Except as otherwise provided in paragraph (4), while negotiable documents, goods, instruments, money, or tangible chattel paper is located in a jurisdiction, the local law of that jurisdiction governs:

(A) perfection of a security interest in the goods by filing a fixture filing;

(B) perfection of a security interest in timber to be cut; and

(C) the effect of perfection or nonperfection and the priority of a nonpossessory security interest in the collateral.

(4) The local law of the jurisdiction in which the wellhead or minehead is located governs perfection, the effect of perfection or nonperfection, and the priority of a security interest in as-extracted collateral.

§ 9–302. Law Governing Perfection and Priority of Agricultural Liens.

While farm products are located in a jurisdiction, the local law of that jurisdiction governs perfection, the effect of perfection or nonperfection, and the priority of an agricultural lien on the farm products.

§ 9–303. Law Governing Perfection and Priority of Security Interests in Goods Covered by a Certificate of Title.

(a) [**Applicability of section.**] This section applies to goods covered by a certificate of title, even if there is no other relationship between the jurisdiction under whose certificate of title the goods are covered and the goods or the debtor.

(b) [**When goods covered by certificate of title.**] Goods become covered by a certificate of title when a valid application for the certificate of title and the applicable fee are delivered to the appropriate authority. Goods cease to be covered by a certificate of title at the earlier of the time the certificate of title ceases to be effective under the law of the issuing jurisdiction or the time the goods become covered subsequently by a certificate of title issued by another jurisdiction.

(c) [**Applicable law.**] The local law of the jurisdiction under whose certificate of title the goods are covered governs perfection, the effect of perfection or nonperfection, and the priority of a security interest in goods covered by a certificate of title from the time the goods become covered by the certificate of title until the goods cease to be covered by the certificate of title.

§ 9–307. Location of Debtor.

(a) [**"Place of business."**] In this section, "place of business" means a place where a debtor conducts its affairs.

(b) [**Debtor's location: general rules.**] Except as otherwise provided in this section, the following rules determine a debtor's location:

    (1) A debtor who is an individual is located at the individual's principal residence.

    (2) A debtor that is an organization and has only one place of business is located at its place of business.

    (3) A debtor that is an organization and has more than one place of business is located at its chief executive office.

(c) [**Limitation of applicability of subsection (b).**] Subsection (b) applies only if a debtor's residence, place of business, or chief executive office, as applicable, is located in a jurisdiction whose law generally requires information concerning the existence of a nonpossessory security interest to be made generally available in a filing, recording, or registration system as a condition or result of the security interest's obtaining priority over the rights of a lien creditor with respect to the collateral. If subsection (b) does not apply, the debtor is located in the District of Columbia.

(d) [**Continuation of location: cessation of existence, etc.**] A person that ceases to exist, have a residence, or have a place of business continues to be located in the jurisdiction specified by subsections (b) and (c).

(e) [**Location of registered organization organized under State law.**] A registered organization that is organized under the law of a State is located in that State.

(f) [**Location of registered organization organized under federal law; bank branches and agencies.**] Except as otherwise provided in subsection (i), a registered organization that is organized under the law of the United States and a branch or agency of a bank that is not organized under the law of the United States or a State are located:

    (1) in the State that the law of the United States designates, if the law designates a State of location;

    (2) in the State that the registered organization, branch, or agency designates, if the law of the United States authorizes the registered organization, branch, or agency to designate its State of location; or

    (3) in the District of Columbia, if neither paragraph (1) nor paragraph (2) applies.

(g) [**Continuation of location: change in status of registered organization.**] A registered organization continues to be located in the jurisdiction specified by subsection (e) or (f) notwithstanding:

    (1) the suspension, revocation, forfeiture, or lapse of the registered organization's status as such in its jurisdiction of organization; or

    (2) the dissolution, winding up, or cancellation of the existence of the registered organization.

(h) [**Location of United States.**] The United States is located in the District of Columbia.

(i) [**Location of foreign bank branch or agency if licensed in only one state.**] A branch or agency of a bank that is not organized under the law of the United States or a State is located in the State in which the branch or agency is licensed, if all branches and agencies of the bank are licensed in only one State.

(j) [**Location of foreign air carrier.**] A foreign air carrier under the Federal Aviation Act of 1958, as amended, is located at the designated office of the agent upon which service of process may be made on behalf of the carrier.

(k) [**Section applies only to this part.**] This section applies only for purposes of this part.

§ 9–308. When Security Interest or Agricultural Lien Is Perfected; Continuity of Perfection.

(a) [**Perfection of security interest.**] Except as otherwise provided in this section and Section 9–309, a security interest is perfected if it has attached and all of the applicable requirements for perfection in Sections 9–310 through 9–316 have been satisfied. A security interest is perfected when it attaches if the applicable requirements are satisfied before the security interest attaches.

(b) [**Perfection of agricultural lien.**] An agricultural lien is perfected if it has become effective and all of the applicable requirements for perfection in Section 9–310 have been satisfied. An agricultural lien is perfected when it becomes effective if the applicable requirements are satisfied before the agricultural lien becomes effective.

(c) [**Continuous perfection; perfection by different methods.**] A security interest or agricultural lien is perfected continuously if it is originally perfected by one method under this article and is later perfected by another method under this article, without an intermediate period when it was unperfected.

(d) [**Supporting obligation.**] Perfection of a security interest in collateral also perfects a security interest in a supporting obligation for the collateral.

(e) [**Lien securing right to payment.**] Perfection of a security interest in a right to payment or performance also perfects a security interest in a security interest, mortgage, or other lien on personal or real property securing the right.

(f) [**Security entitlement carried in securities account.**] Perfection of a security interest in a securities account also perfects a security interest in the security entitlements carried in the securities account.

(g) [**Commodity contract carried in commodity account.**] Perfection of a security interest in a commodity account also perfects a security interest in the commodity contracts carried in the commodity account.

§ 9–309. Security Interest Perfected Upon Attachment.

The following security interests are perfected when they attach:

(1) a purchase-money security interest in consumer goods, except as otherwise provided in Section 9–311(b) with respect to consumer goods that are subject to a statute or treaty described in Section 9–311(a);

(2) an assignment of accounts or payment intangibles which does not by itself or in conjunction with other assignments to the same assignee transfer a significant part of the assignor's outstanding accounts or payment intangibles;

(3) a sale of a payment intangible;

(4) a sale of a promissory note;

(5) a security interest created by the assignment of a health-care-insurance receivable to the provider of the health-care goods or services;

(6) a security interest arising under Section 2–401, 2–505, 2–711(3), or 2A–508(5), until the debtor obtains possession of the collateral;

(7) a security interest of a collecting bank arising under Section 4–210;

(8) a security interest of an issuer or nominated person arising under Section 5–118;

(9) a security interest arising in the delivery of a financial asset under Section 9–206(c);

(10) a security interest in investment property created by a broker or securities intermediary;

(11) a security interest in a commodity contract or a commodity account created by a commodity intermediary;

(12) an assignment for the benefit of all creditors of the transferor and subsequent transfers by the assignee thereunder; and

(13) a security interest created by an assignment of a beneficial interest in a decedent's estate.

§ 9–310. When Filing Required to Perfect Security Interest or Agricultural Lien; Security Interests and Agricultural Liens to Which Filing Provisions Do Not Apply.

(a) [**General rule: perfection by filing.**] Except as otherwise provided in subsection (b) and Section 9–312(b), a financing statement must be filed to perfect all security interests and agricultural liens.

(b) [**Exceptions: filing not necessary.**] The filing of a financing statement is not necessary to perfect a security interest:

   (1) that is perfected under Section 9–308(d), (e), (f), or (g);

   (2) that is perfected under Section 9–309 when it attaches;

   (3) in property subject to a statute, regulation, or treaty described in Section 9–311(a);

   (4) in goods in possession of a bailee which is perfected under Section 9–312(d)(1) or (2);

   (5) in certificated securities, documents, goods, or instruments which is perfected without filing or possession under Section 9–312(e), (f), or (g);

   (6) in collateral in the secured party's possession under Section 9–313;

   (7) in a certificated security which is perfected by delivery of the security certificate to the secured party under Section 9–313;

   (8) in deposit accounts, electronic chattel paper, investment property, or letter-of-credit rights which is perfected by control under Section 9–314;

   (9) in proceeds which is perfected under Section 9–315; or

   (10) that is perfected under Section 9–316.

(c) [**Assignment of perfected security interest.**] If a secured party assigns a perfected security interest or agricultural lien, a filing under this article is not required to continue the perfected status of the security interest against creditors of and transferees from the original debtor.

§ 9–311. Perfection of Security Interests in Property Subject to Certain Statutes, Regulations, and Treaties.

(a) [**Security interest subject to other law.**] Except as otherwise provided in subsection (d), the filing of a financing statement is not necessary or effective to perfect a security interest in property subject to:

   (1) a statute, regulation, or treaty of the United States whose requirements for a security interest's obtaining priority over the rights of a lien creditor with respect to the property preempt Section 9–310(a);

   (2) [list any certificate-of-title statute covering automobiles, trailers, mobile homes, boats, farm tractors, or the like, which provides for a security interest to be indicated on the certificate as a condition or result of perfection, and any non-Uniform Commercial Code central filing statute]; or

   (3) a certificate-of-title statute of another jurisdiction which provides for a security interest to be indicated on the certificate as a condition or result of the security interest's obtaining priority over the rights of a lien creditor with respect to the property.

(b) [**Compliance with other law.**] Compliance with the requirements of a statute, regulation, or treaty described in subsection (a) for obtaining priority over the rights of a lien creditor is equivalent to the filing of a financing statement under this article. Except as otherwise provided in subsection (d) and Sections 9–313 and 9–316(d) and (e) for goods covered by a certificate of title, a security interest in property subject to a statute, regulation, or treaty described in subsection (a) may be perfected only by compliance with those requirements, and a security interest so perfected remains perfected notwithstanding a change in the use or transfer of possession of the collateral.

(c) [**Duration and renewal of perfection.**] Except as otherwise provided in subsection (d) and Section 9–316(d) and (e), duration and renewal of perfection of a security interest perfected by compliance with the requirements prescribed by a statute, regulation, or treaty described in subsection (a) are governed by the statute, regulation, or treaty. In other respects, the security interest is subject to this article.

(d) [**Inapplicability to certain inventory.**] During any period in which collateral subject to a statute specified in subsection (a)(2) is inventory held for sale or lease by a person or leased by that person as lessor and that person is in the business of selling goods of that kind, this section does not apply to a security interest in that collateral created by that person.

§ 9–312. Perfection of Security Interests in Chattel Paper, Deposit Accounts, Documents, Goods Covered by Documents, Instruments, Investment Property, Letter-of-Credit Rights, and Money; Perfection by Permissive Filing; Temporary Perfection Without Filing or Transfer of Possession.

(a) [**Perfection by filing permitted.**] A security interest in chattel paper, negotiable documents, instruments, or investment property may be perfected by filing.

(b) [**Control or possession of certain collateral.**] Except as otherwise provided in Section 9–315(c) and (d) for proceeds:

   (1) a security interest in a deposit account may be perfected only by control under Section 9–314;

   (2) and except as otherwise provided in Section 9–308(d), a security interest in a letter–of-credit right may be perfected only by control under Section 9–314; and

   (3) a security interest in money may be perfected only by the secured party's taking possession under Section 9–313.

(c) [**Goods covered by negotiable document.**] While goods are in the possession of a bailee that has issued a negotiable document covering the goods:

   (1) a security interest in the goods may be perfected by perfecting a security interest in the document; and

   (2) a security interest perfected in the document has priority over any security interest that becomes perfected in the goods by another method during that time.

(d) [**Goods covered by nonnegotiable document.**] While goods are in the possession of a bailee that has issued a nonnegotiable document covering the goods, a security interest in the goods may be perfected by:

   (1) issuance of a document in the name of the secured party;

   (2) the bailee's receipt of notification of the secured party's interest; or

   (3) filing as to the goods.

(e) [**Temporary perfection: new value.**] A security interest in certificated securities, negotiable documents, or instruments is perfected without filing or the taking of possession for a period of 20 days from the time it attaches to the extent that it arises for new value given under an authenticated security agreement.

(f) [**Temporary perfection: goods or documents made available to debtor.**] A perfected security interest in a negotiable document or goods in possession of a bailee, other than one that has issued a negotiable document for the goods, remains perfected for 20 days without filing if the secured party makes available to the debtor the goods or documents representing the goods for the purpose of:

   (1) ultimate sale or exchange; or

   (2) loading, unloading, storing, shipping, transshipping, manufacturing, processing, or otherwise dealing with them in a manner preliminary to their sale or exchange.

(g) [**Temporary perfection: delivery of security certificate or instrument to debtor.**] A perfected security interest in a certificated security or instrument remains perfected for 20 days without filing if the secured party delivers the security certificate or instrument to the debtor for the purpose of:

   (1) ultimate sale or exchange; or

   (2) presentation, collection, enforcement, renewal, or registration of transfer.

(h) [**Expiration of temporary perfection.**] After the 20–day period specified in subsection (e), (f), or (g) expires, perfection depends upon compliance with this article.

§ 9–313. When Possession by or Delivery to Secured Party Perfects Security Interest Without Filing.

(a) [**Perfection by possession or delivery.**] Except as otherwise provided in subsection (b), a secured party may perfect a security interest in negotiable documents, goods, instruments, money, or tangible chattel paper by taking possession of the collateral. A secured party may perfect a security interest in certificated securities by taking delivery of the certificated securities under Section 8–301.

(b) [**Goods covered by certificate of title.**] With respect to goods covered by a certificate of title issued by this State, a secured party may perfect a security interest in the goods by taking possession of the goods only in the circumstances described in Section 9–316(d).

(c) [**Collateral in possession of person other than debtor.**] With respect to collateral other than certificated securities and goods covered by a document, a secured party takes possession of collateral in the possession of a person other than the debtor, the secured party, or a lessee of the collateral from the debtor in the ordinary course of the debtor's business, when:

    (1) the person in possession authenticates a record acknowledging that it holds possession of the collateral for the secured party's benefit; or

    (2) the person takes possession of the collateral after having authenticated a record acknowledging that it will hold possession of collateral for the secured party's benefit.

(d) [**Time of perfection by possession; continuation of perfection.**] If perfection of a security interest depends upon possession of the collateral by a secured party, perfection occurs no earlier than the time the secured party takes possession and continues only while the secured party retains possession.

(e) [**Time of perfection by delivery; continuation of perfection.**] A security interest in a certificated security in registered form is perfected by delivery when delivery of the certificated security occurs under Section 8–301 and remains perfected by delivery until the debtor obtains possession of the security certificate.

(f) [**Acknowledgment not required.**] A person in possession of collateral is not required to acknowledge that it holds possession for a secured party's benefit.

(g) [**Effectiveness of acknowledgment; no duties or confirmation.**] If a person acknowledges that it holds possession for the secured party's benefit:

    (1) the acknowledgment is effective under subsection (c) or Section 8–301(a), even if the acknowledgment violates the rights of a debtor; and

    (2) unless the person otherwise agrees or law other than this article otherwise provides, the person does not owe any duty to the secured party and is not required to confirm the acknowledgment to another person.

(h) [**Secured party's delivery to person other than debtor.**] A secured party having possession of collateral does not relinquish possession by delivering the collateral to a person other than the debtor or a lessee of the collateral from the debtor in the ordinary course of the debtor's business if the person was instructed before the delivery or is instructed contemporaneously with the delivery:

    (1) to hold possession of the collateral for the secured party's benefit; or

    (2) to redeliver the collateral to the secured party.

(i) [**Effect of delivery under subsection (h); no duties or confirmation.**] A secured party does not relinquish possession, even if a delivery under subsection (h) violates the rights of a debtor. A person to which collateral is delivered under subsection (h) does not owe any duty to the secured party and is not required to confirm the delivery to another person unless the person otherwise agrees or law other than this article otherwise provides.

§ 9–314. Perfection by Control.

(a) [**Perfection by control.**] A security interest in investment property, deposit accounts, letter-of-credit rights, or electronic chattel paper may be perfected by control of the collateral under Section 9–104, 9–105, 9–106, or 9–107.

(b) [**Specified collateral: time of perfection by control; continuation of perfection.**] A security interest in deposit accounts, electronic chattel paper, or letter-of-credit rights is perfected by control under Section 9–104, 9–105, or 9–107 when the secured party obtains control and remains perfected by control only while the secured party retains control.

(c) [**Investment property: time of perfection by control; continuation of perfection.**] A security interest in investment property is perfected by control under Section 9–106 from the time the secured party obtains control and remains perfected by control until:

    (1) the secured party does not have control; and

    (2) one of the following occurs:

        (A) if the collateral is a certificated security, the debtor has or acquires possession of the security certificate;

        (B) if the collateral is an uncertificated security, the issuer has registered or registers the debtor as the registered owner; or

        (C) if the collateral is a security entitlement, the debtor is or becomes the entitlement holder.

§ 9–315. Secured Party's Rights on Disposition of Collateral and in Proceeds.

(a) [**Disposition of collateral: continuation of security interest or agricultural lien; proceeds.**] Except as otherwise provided in this article and in Section 2–403(2):

    (1) a security interest or agricultural lien continues in collateral notwithstanding sale, lease, license, exchange, or other disposition thereof unless the secured party authorized the disposition free of the security interest or agricultural lien; and

    (2) a security interest attaches to any identifiable proceeds of collateral.

(b) [**When commingled proceeds identifiable.**] Proceeds that are commingled with other property are identifiable proceeds:

    (1) if the proceeds are goods, to the extent provided by Section 9–336; and

    (2) if the proceeds are not goods, to the extent that the secured party identifies the proceeds by a method of tracing, including application of equitable principles, that is permitted under law other than this article with respect to commingled property of the type involved.

(c) [**Perfection of security interest in proceeds.**] A security interest in proceeds is a perfected security interest if the security interest in the original collateral was perfected.

(d) [**Continuation of perfection.**] A perfected security interest in proceeds becomes unperfected on the 21st day after the security interest attaches to the proceeds unless:

    (1) the following conditions are satisfied:

        (A) a filed financing statement covers the original collateral;

        (B) the proceeds are collateral in which a security interest may be perfected by filing in the office in which the financing statement has been filed; and

        (C) the proceeds are not acquired with cash proceeds;

    (2) the proceeds are identifiable cash proceeds; or

    (3) the security interest in the proceeds is perfected other than under subsection (c) when the security interest attaches to the proceeds or within 20 days thereafter.

(e) [**When perfected security interest in proceeds becomes unperfected.**] If a filed financing statement covers the original collateral, a security interest in proceeds which remains perfected under subsection (d)(1) becomes unperfected at the later of:

    (1) when the effectiveness of the filed financing statement lapses under Section 9–515 or is terminated under Section 9–513; or

    (2) the 21st day after the security interest attaches to the proceeds.

§ 9–316. Continued Perfection of Security Interest Following Change in Governing Law.

(a) [**General rule: effect on perfection of change in governing law.**] A security interest perfected pursuant to the law of the jurisdiction designated in Section 9–301(1) or 9–305(c) remains perfected until the earliest of:

    (1) the time perfection would have ceased under the law of that jurisdiction;

    (2) the expiration of four months after a change of the debtor's location to another jurisdiction; or

    (3) the expiration of one year after a transfer of collateral to a person that thereby becomes a debtor and is located in another jurisdiction.

(b) [**Security interest perfected or unperfected under law of new jurisdiction.**] If a security interest described in subsection (a) becomes perfected under the law of the other jurisdiction before the earliest time or event described in that subsection, it remains perfected thereafter. If the security interest does not become perfected under the law of the other jurisdiction before the earliest time or event, it becomes unperfected and is deemed never to have been perfected as against a purchaser of the collateral for value.

(c) [**Possessory security interest in collateral moved to new jurisdiction.**] A possessory security interest in collateral, other than goods covered by a certificate of title and as-extracted collateral consisting of goods, remains continuously perfected if:

(1) the collateral is located in one jurisdiction and subject to a security interest perfected under the law of that jurisdiction;

(2) thereafter the collateral is brought into another jurisdiction; and

(3) upon entry into the other jurisdiction, the security interest is perfected under the law of the other jurisdiction.

(d) [**Goods covered by certificate of title from this state.**] Except as otherwise provided in subsection (e), a security interest in goods covered by a certificate of title which is perfected by any method under the law of another jurisdiction when the goods become covered by a certificate of title from this State remains perfected until the security interest would have become unperfected under the law of the other jurisdiction had the goods not become so covered.

(e) [**When subsection (d) security interest becomes unperfected against purchasers.**] A security interest described in subsection (d) becomes unperfected as against a purchaser of the goods for value and is deemed never to have been perfected as against a purchaser of the goods for value if the applicable requirements for perfection under Section 9–311(b) or 9–313 are not satisfied before the earlier of:

(1) the time the security interest would have become unperfected under the law of the other jurisdiction had the goods not become covered by a certificate of title from this State; or

(2) the expiration of four months after the goods had become so covered.

(f) [**Change in jurisdiction of bank, issuer, nominated person, securities intermediary, or commodity intermediary.**] A security interest in deposit accounts, letter-of-credit rights, or investment property which is perfected under the law of the bank's jurisdiction, the issuer's jurisdiction, a nominated person's jurisdiction, the securities intermediary's jurisdiction, or the commodity intermediary's jurisdiction, as applicable, remains perfected until the earlier of:

(1) the time the security interest would have become unperfected under the law of that jurisdiction; or

(2) the expiration of four months after a change of the applicable jurisdiction to another jurisdiction.

(g) [**Subsection (f) security interest perfected or unperfected under law of new jurisdiction.**] If a security interest described in subsection (f) becomes perfected under the law of the other jurisdiction before the earlier of the time or the end of the period described in that subsection, it remains perfected thereafter. If the security interest does not become perfected under the law of the other jurisdiction before the earlier of that time or the end of that period, it becomes unperfected and is deemed never to have been perfected as against a purchaser of the collateral for value.

§ 9–317. Interests That Take Priority over or Take Free of Security Interest or Agricultural Lien.

(a) [**Conflicting security interests and rights of lien creditors.**] A security interest or agricultural lien is subordinate to the rights of:

(1) a person entitled to priority under Section 9–322; and

(2) except as otherwise provided in subsection (e), a person that becomes a lien creditor before the earlier of the time:

(A) the security interest or agricultural lien is perfected; or

(B) one of the conditions specified in Section 9–203(b)(3) is met and a financing statement covering the collateral is filed.

(b) [**Buyers that receive delivery.**] Except as otherwise provided in subsection (e), a buyer, other than a secured party, of tangible chattel paper, documents, goods, instruments, or a security certificate takes free of a security interest or agricultural lien if the buyer gives value and receives delivery of the collateral without knowledge of the security interest or agricultural lien and before it is perfected.

(c) [**Lessees that receive delivery.**] Except as otherwise provided in subsection (e), a lessee of goods takes free of a security interest or agricultural lien if the lessee gives value and receives delivery of the collateral without knowledge of the security interest or agricultural lien and before it is perfected.

(d) [**Licensees and buyers of certain collateral.**] A licensee of a general intangible or a buyer, other than a secured party, of accounts, electronic chattel paper, general intangibles, or investment property other than a certificated security takes free of a security interest if the licensee or buyer gives value without knowledge of the security interest and before it is perfected.

(e) [**Purchase-money security interest.**] Except as otherwise provided in Sections 9–320 and 9–321, if a person files a financing statement with respect to a purchase-money security interest before or within 20 days after the debtor receives delivery of the collateral, the security interest takes priority over the rights of a buyer, lessee, or lien creditor which arise between the time the security interest attaches and the time of filing.

§ 9–320. Buyer of Goods.

(a) [**Buyer in ordinary course of business.**] Except as otherwise provided in subsection (e), a buyer in ordinary course of business, other than a person buying farm products from a person engaged in farming operations, takes free of a security interest created by the buyer's seller, even if the security interest is perfected and the buyer knows of its existence.

(b) [**Buyer of consumer goods.**] Except as otherwise provided in subsection (e), a buyer of goods from a person who used or bought the goods for use primarily for personal, family, or household purposes takes free of a security interest, even if perfected, if the buyer buys:

(1) without knowledge of the security interest;

(2) for value;

(3) primarily for the buyer's personal, family, or household purposes; and

(4) before the filing of a financing statement covering the goods.

(c) [**Effectiveness of filing for subsection (b).**] To the extent that it affects the priority of a security interest over a buyer of goods under subsection (b), the period of effectiveness of a filing made in the jurisdiction in which the seller is located is governed by Section 9–316(a) and (b).

(d) [**Buyer in ordinary course of business at wellhead or minehead.**] A buyer in ordinary course of business buying oil, gas, or other minerals at the wellhead or minehead or after extraction takes free of an interest arising out of an encumbrance.

(e) [**Possessory security interest not affected.**] Subsections (a) and (b) do not affect a security interest in goods in the possession of the secured party under Section 9–313.

§ 9–322. Priorities among Conflicting Security Interests in and Agricultural Liens on Same Collateral.

(a) [**General priority rules.**] Except as otherwise provided in this section, priority among conflicting security interests and agricultural liens in the same collateral is determined according to the following rules:

(1) Conflicting perfected security interests and agricultural liens rank according to priority in time of filing or perfection. Priority dates from the earlier of the time a filing covering the collateral is first made or the security interest or agricultural lien is first perfected, if there is no period thereafter when there is neither filing nor perfection.

(2) A perfected security interest or agricultural lien has priority over a conflicting unperfected security interest or agricultural lien.

(3) The first security interest or agricultural lien to attach or become effective has priority if conflicting security interests and agricultural liens are unperfected.

(b) [**Time of perfection: proceeds and supporting obligations.**] For the purposes of subsection (a)(1):

(1) the time of filing or perfection as to a security interest in collateral is also the time of filing or perfection as to a security interest in proceeds; and

(2) the time of filing or perfection as to a security interest in collateral supported by a supporting obligation is also the time of filing or perfection as to a security interest in the supporting obligation.

(c) [**Special priority rules: proceeds and supporting obligations.**] Except as otherwise provided in subsection (f), a security interest in collateral which qualifies for priority over a conflicting security interest under Section 9–327, 9–328, 9–329, 9–330, or 9–331 also has priority over a conflicting security interest in:

(1) any supporting obligation for the collateral; and

(2) proceeds of the collateral if:

(A) the security interest in proceeds is perfected;

(B) the proceeds are cash proceeds or of the same type as the collateral; and

(C) in the case of proceeds that are proceeds of proceeds, all intervening proceeds are cash proceeds, proceeds of the same type as the collateral, or an account relating to the collateral.

(d) [**First-to-file priority rule for certain collateral.**] Subject to subsection (e) and except as otherwise provided in subsection (f), if a security interest in chattel paper, deposit accounts, negotiable documents, instruments, investment property, or letter-of-credit rights is perfected by a method other than filing, conflicting perfected security interests in proceeds of the collateral rank according to priority in time of filing.

(e) [**Applicability of subsection (d).**] Subsection (d) applies only if the proceeds of the collateral are not cash proceeds, chattel paper, negotiable documents, instruments, investment property, or letter-of-credit rights.

(f) [**Limitations on subsections (a) through (e).**] Subsections (a) through (e) are subject to:

(1) subsection (g) and the other provisions of this part;

(2) Section 4–210 with respect to a security interest of a collecting bank;

(3) Section 5–118 with respect to a security interest of an issuer or nominated person; and

(4) Section 9–110 with respect to a security interest arising under Article 2 or 2A.

(g) [**Priority under agricultural lien statute.**] A perfected agricultural lien on collateral has priority over a conflicting security interest in or agricultural lien on the same collateral if the statute creating the agricultural lien so provides.

§ 9–323. Future Advances.

(a) [**When priority based on time of advance.**] Except as otherwise provided in subsection (c), for purposes of determining the priority of a perfected security interest under Section 9–322(a)(1), perfection of the security interest dates from the time an advance is made to the extent that the security interest secures an advance that:

(1) is made while the security interest is perfected only:

(A) under Section 9–309 when it attaches; or

(B) temporarily under Section 9–312(e), (f), or (g); and

(2) is not made pursuant to a commitment entered into before or while the security interest is perfected by a method other than under Section 9–309 or 9–312(e), (f), or (g).

(b) [**Lien creditor.**] Except as otherwise provided in subsection (c), a security interest is subordinate to the rights of a person that becomes a lien creditor to the extent that the security interest secures an advance made more than 45 days after the person becomes a lien creditor unless the advance is made:

(1) without knowledge of the lien; or

(2) pursuant to a commitment entered into without knowledge of the lien.

(c) [**Buyer of receivables.**] Subsections (a) and (b) do not apply to a security interest held by a secured party that is a buyer of accounts, chattel paper, payment intangibles, or promissory notes or a consignor.

(d) [**Buyer of goods.**] Except as otherwise provided in subsection (e), a buyer of goods other than a buyer in ordinary course of business takes free of a security interest to the extent that it secures advances made after the earlier of:

(1) the time the secured party acquires knowledge of the buyer's purchase; or

(2) 45 days after the purchase.

(e) [**Advances made pursuant to commitment: priority of buyer of goods.**] Subsection (d) does not apply if the advance is made pursuant to a commitment entered into without knowledge of the buyer's purchase and before the expiration of the 45-day period.

(f) [**Lessee of goods.**] Except as otherwise provided in subsection (g), a lessee of goods, other than a lessee in ordinary course of business, takes the leasehold interest free of a security interest to the extent that it secures advances made after the earlier of:

(1) the time the secured party acquires knowledge of the lease; or

(2) 45 days after the lease contract becomes enforceable.

(g) [**Advances made pursuant to commitment: priority of lessee of goods.**] Subsection (f) does not apply if the advance is made pursuant to a commitment entered into without knowledge of the lease and before the expiration of the 45-day period.

§ 9–324. Priority of Purchase-Money Security Interests.

(a) [**General rule: purchase-money priority.**] Except as otherwise provided in subsection (g), a perfected purchase-money security interest in goods other than inventory or livestock has priority over a conflicting security interest in the same goods, and, except as otherwise provided in Section 9–327, a perfected security interest in its identifiable proceeds also has priority, if the purchase-money security interest is perfected when the debtor receives possession of the collateral or within 20 days thereafter.

(b) [**Inventory purchase-money priority.**] Subject to subsection (c) and except as otherwise provided in subsection (g), a perfected purchase-money security interest in inventory has priority over a conflicting security interest in the same inventory, has priority over a conflicting security interest in chattel paper or an instrument constituting proceeds of the inventory and in proceeds of the chattel paper, if so provided in Section 9–330, and, except as otherwise provided in Section 9–327, also has priority in identifiable cash proceeds of the inventory to the extent the identifiable cash proceeds are received on or before the delivery of the inventory to a buyer, if:

(1) the purchase-money security interest is perfected when the debtor receives possession of the inventory;

(2) the purchase-money secured party sends an authenticated notification to the holder of the conflicting security interest;

(3) the holder of the conflicting security interest receives the notification within five years before the debtor receives possession of the inventory; and

(4) the notification states that the person sending the notification has or expects to acquire a purchase-money security interest in inventory of the debtor and describes the inventory.

(c) [**Holders of conflicting inventory security interests to be notified.**] Subsections (b)(2) through (4) apply only if the holder of the conflicting security interest had filed a financing statement covering the same types of inventory:

(1) if the purchase-money security interest is perfected by filing, before the date of the filing; or

(2) if the purchase-money security interest is temporarily perfected without filing or possession under Section 9–312(f), before the beginning of the 20–day period thereunder.

(d) [**Livestock purchase-money priority.**] Subject to subsection (e) and except as otherwise provided in subsection (g), a perfected purchase-money security interest in livestock that are farm products has priority over a conflicting security interest in the same livestock, and, except as otherwise provided in Section 9–327, a perfected security interest in their identifiable proceeds and identifiable products in their unmanufactured states also has priority, if:

(1) the purchase-money security interest is perfected when the debtor receives possession of the livestock;

(2) the purchase-money secured party sends an authenticated notification to the holder of the conflicting security interest;

(3) the holder of the conflicting security interest receives the notification within six months before the debtor receives possession of the livestock; and

(4) the notification states that the person sending the notification has or expects to acquire a purchase-money security interest in livestock of the debtor and describes the livestock.

(e) [**Holders of conflicting livestock security interests to be notified.**] Subsections (d)(2) through (4) apply only if the holder of the conflicting security interest had filed a financing statement covering the same types of livestock:

(1) if the purchase-money security interest is perfected by filing, before the date of the filing; or

(2) if the purchase-money security interest is temporarily perfected without filing or possession under Section 9–312(f), before the beginning of the 20–day period thereunder.

(f) [**Software purchase-money priority.**] Except as otherwise provided in subsection (g), a perfected purchase-money security interest in software has priority over a conflicting security interest in the same collateral, and, except as otherwise provided in Section 9–327, a perfected security interest in its identifiable proceeds also has priority, to the extent that the purchase-money security interest in the goods in which the software was acquired for use has priority in the goods and proceeds of the goods under this section.

(g) [**Conflicting purchase-money security interests.**] If more than one security interest qualifies for priority in the same collateral under subsection (a), (b), (d), or (f):

(1) a security interest securing an obligation incurred as all or part of the price of the collateral has priority over a security interest securing an obligation incurred for value given to enable the debtor to acquire rights in or the use of collateral; and

(2) in all other cases, Section 9–322(a) applies to the qualifying security interests.

§ 9–325. Priority of Security Interests in Transferred Collateral.

(a) [**Subordination of security interest in transferred collateral.**] Except as otherwise provided in subsection (b), a security interest created by a debtor is subordinate to a security interest in the same collateral created by another person if:

(1) the debtor acquired the collateral subject to the security interest created by the other person;

(2) the security interest created by the other person was perfected when the debtor acquired the collateral; and

(3) there is no period thereafter when the security interest is unperfected.

(b) [**Limitation of subsection (a) subordination.**] Subsection (a) subordinates a security interest only if the security interest:

(1) otherwise would have priority solely under Section 9–322(a) or 9–324; or

(2) arose solely under Section 2–711(3) or 2A–508(5).

§ 9–327. Priority of Security Interests in Deposit Account.

The following rules govern priority among conflicting security interests in the same deposit account:

(1) A security interest held by a secured party having control of the deposit account under Section 9–104 has priority over a conflicting security interest held by a secured party that does not have control.

(2) Except as otherwise provided in paragraphs (3) and (4), security interests perfected by control under Section 9–314 rank according to priority in time of obtaining control.

(3) Except as otherwise provided in paragraph (4), a security interest held by the bank with which the deposit account is maintained has priority over a conflicting security interest held by another secured party.

(4) A security interest perfected by control under Section 9–104(a)(3) has priority over a security interest held by the bank with which the deposit account is maintained.

§ 9–328. Priority of Security Interests in Investment Property.

The following rules govern priority among conflicting security interests in the same investment property:

(1) A security interest held by a secured party having control of investment property under Section 9–106 has priority over a security interest held by a secured party that does not have control of the investment property.

(2) Except as otherwise provided in paragraphs (3) and (4), conflicting security interests held by secured parties each of which has control under Section 9–106 rank according to priority in time of:

(A) if the collateral is a security, obtaining control;

(B) if the collateral is a security entitlement carried in a securities account and:

(i) if the secured party obtained control under Section 8–106(d)(1), the secured party's becoming the person for which the securities account is maintained;

(ii) if the secured party obtained control under Section 8–106(d)(2), the securities intermediary's agreement to comply

with the secured party's entitlement orders with respect to security entitlements carried or to be carried in the securities account; or

(iii) if the secured party obtained control through another person under Section 8–106(d)(3), the time on which priority would be based under this paragraph if the other person were the secured party; or

(C) if the collateral is a commodity contract carried with a commodity intermediary, the satisfaction of the requirement for control specified in Section 9–106(b)(2) with respect to commodity contracts carried or to be carried with the commodity intermediary.

(3) A security interest held by a securities intermediary in a security entitlement or a securities account maintained with the securities intermediary has priority over a conflicting security interest held by another secured party.

(4) A security interest held by a commodity intermediary in a commodity contract or a commodity account maintained with the commodity intermediary has priority over a conflicting security interest held by another secured party.

(5) A security interest in a certificated security in registered form which is perfected by taking delivery under Section 9–313(a) and not by control under Section 9–314 has priority over a conflicting security interest perfected by a method other than control.

(6) Conflicting security interests created by a broker, securities intermediary, or commodity intermediary which are perfected without control under Section 9–106 rank equally.

(7) In all other cases, priority among conflicting security interests in investment property is governed by Sections 9–322 and 9–323.

§ 9–329. Priority of Security Interests in Letter-of-Credit Right.

The following rules govern priority among conflicting security interests in the same letter-of-credit right:

(1) A security interest held by a secured party having control of the letter-of-credit right under Section 9–107 has priority to the extent of its control over a conflicting security interest held by a secured party that does not have control.

(2) Security interests perfected by control under Section 9–314 rank according to priority in time of obtaining control.

§ 9–330. Priority of Purchaser of Chattel Paper or Instrument.

(a) [**Purchaser's priority: security interest claimed merely as proceeds.**] A purchaser of chattel paper has priority over a security interest in the chattel paper which is claimed merely as proceeds of inventory subject to a security interest if:

(1) in good faith and in the ordinary course of the purchaser's business, the purchaser gives new value and takes possession of the chattel paper or obtains control of the chattel paper under Section 9–105; and

(2) the chattel paper does not indicate that it has been assigned to an identified assignee other than the purchaser.

(b) [**Purchaser's priority: other security interests.**] A purchaser of chattel paper has priority over a security interest in the chattel paper which is claimed other than merely as proceeds of inventory subject to a security interest if the purchaser gives new value and takes possession of the chattel paper or obtains control of the chattel paper under Section 9–105 in good faith, in the ordinary course of the purchaser's business, and without knowledge that the purchase violates the rights of the secured party.

(c) [**Chattel paper purchaser's priority in proceeds.**] Except as otherwise provided in Section 9–327, a purchaser having priority in chattel paper under subsection (a) or (b) also has priority in proceeds of the chattel paper to the extent that:

(1) Section 9–322 provides for priority in the proceeds; or

(2) the proceeds consist of the specific goods covered by the chattel paper or cash proceeds of the specific goods, even if the purchaser's security interest in the proceeds is unperfected.

(d) [**Instrument purchaser's priority.**] Except as otherwise provided in Section 9–331(a), a purchaser of an instrument has priority over a security interest in the instrument perfected by a method other than possession if the purchaser gives value and takes possession of the instrument in good faith and without knowledge that the purchase violates the rights of the secured party.

(e) [**Holder of purchase-money security interest gives new value.**] For purposes of subsections (a) and (b), the holder of a purchase-money security interest in inventory gives new value for chattel paper constituting proceeds of the inventory.

(f) [**Indication of assignment gives knowledge.**] For purposes of subsections (b) and (d), if chattel paper or an instrument indicates that it has been assigned to an identified secured party other than the purchaser, a purchaser of the chattel paper or instrument has knowledge that the purchase violates the rights of the secured party.

§ 9–331. Priority of Rights of Purchasers of Instruments, Documents, and Securities under Other Articles; Priority of Interests in Financial Assets and Security Entitlements under Article 8.

(a) [**Rights under Articles 3, 7, and 8 not limited.**] This article does not limit the rights of a holder in due course of a negotiable instrument, a holder to which a negotiable document of title has been duly negotiated, or a protected purchaser of a security. These holders or purchasers take priority over an earlier security interest, even if perfected, to the extent provided in Articles 3, 7, and 8.

(b) [**Protection under Article 8.**] This article does not limit the rights of or impose liability on a person to the extent that the person is protected against the assertion of a claim under Article 8.

(c) [**Filing not notice.**] Filing under this article does not constitute notice of a claim or defense to the holders, or purchasers, or persons described in subsections (a) and (b).

§ 9–332. Transfer of Money; Transfer of Funds from Deposit Account.

(a) [**Transferee of money.**] A transferee of money takes the money free of a security interest unless the transferee acts in collusion with the debtor in violating the rights of the secured party.

(b) [**Transferee of funds from deposit account.**] A transferee of funds from a deposit account takes the funds free of a security interest in the deposit account unless the transferee acts in collusion with the debtor in violating the rights of the secured party.

§ 9–333. Priority of Certain Liens Arising by Operation of Law.

(a) [**"Possessory lien."**] In this section, "possessory lien" means an interest, other than a security interest or an agricultural lien:

(1) which secures payment or performance of an obligation for services or materials furnished with respect to goods by a person in the ordinary course of the person's business;

(2) which is created by statute or rule of law in favor of the person; and

(3) whose effectiveness depends on the person's possession of the goods.

(b) [**Priority of possessory lien.**] A possessory lien on goods has priority over a security interest in the goods unless the lien is created by a statute that expressly provides otherwise.

§ 9–334. Priority of Security Interests in Fixtures and Crops.

(a) [**Security interest in fixtures under this article.**] A security interest under this article may be created in goods that are fixtures or may continue in goods that become fixtures. A security interest does not exist under this article in ordinary building materials incorporated into an improvement on land.

(b) [**Security interest in fixtures under real-property law.**] This article does not prevent creation of an encumbrance upon fixtures under real property law.

(c) [**General rule: subordination of security interest in fixtures.**] In cases not governed by subsections (d) through (h), a security interest in fixtures is subordinate to a conflicting interest of an encumbrancer or owner of the related real property other than the debtor.

(d) [**Fixtures purchase-money priority.**] Except as otherwise provided in subsection (h), a perfected security interest in fixtures has priority over a conflicting interest of an encumbrancer or owner of the real property if the debtor has an interest of record in or is in possession of the real property and:

(1) the security interest is a purchase-money security interest;

(2) the interest of the encumbrancer or owner arises before the goods become fixtures; and

(3) the security interest is perfected by a fixture filing before the goods become fixtures or within 20 days thereafter.

(e) [**Priority of security interest in fixtures over interests in real property.**] A perfected security interest in fixtures has priority over a conflicting interest of an encumbrancer or owner of the real property if:

(1) the debtor has an interest of record in the real property or is in possession of the real property and the security interest:

(A) is perfected by a fixture filing before the interest of the encumbrancer or owner is of record; and

(B) has priority over any conflicting interest of a predecessor in title of the encumbrancer or owner;

(2) before the goods become fixtures, the security interest is perfected by any method permitted by this article and the fixtures are readily removable:

(A) factory or office machines;

(B) equipment that is not primarily used or leased for use in the operation of the real property; or

(C) replacements of domestic appliances that are consumer goods;

(3) the conflicting interest is a lien on the real property obtained by legal or equitable proceedings after the security interest was perfected by any method permitted by this article; or

(4) the security interest is:

(A) created in a manufactured home in a manufactured-home transaction; and

(B) perfected pursuant to a statute described in Section 9–311(a)(2).

(f) [**Priority based on consent, disclaimer, or right to remove.**] A security interest in fixtures, whether or not perfected, has priority over a conflicting interest of an encumbrancer or owner of the real property if:

(1) the encumbrancer or owner has, in an authenticated record, consented to the security interest or disclaimed an interest in the goods as fixtures; or

(2) the debtor has a right to remove the goods as against the encumbrancer or owner.

(g) [**Continuation of paragraph (f)(2) priority.**] The priority of the security interest under paragraph (f)(2) continues for a reasonable time if the debtor's right to remove the goods as against the encumbrancer or owner terminates.

(h) [**Priority of construction mortgage.**] A mortgage is a construction mortgage to the extent that it secures an obligation incurred for the construction of an improvement on land, including the acquisition cost of the land, if a recorded record of the mortgage so indicates. Except as otherwise provided in subsections (e) and (f), a security interest in fixtures is subordinate to a construction mortgage if a record of the mortgage is recorded before the goods become fixtures and the goods become fixtures before the completion of the construction. A mortgage has this priority to the same extent as a construction mortgage to the extent that it is given to refinance a construction mortgage.

(i) [**Priority of security interest in crops.**] A perfected security interest in crops growing on real property has priority over a conflicting interest of an encumbrancer or owner of the real property if the debtor has an interest of record in or is in possession of the real property.

(j) [**Subsection (i) prevails.**] Subsection (i) prevails over any inconsistent provisions of the following statutes:

§ 9-335. Accessions.

(a) [**Creation of security interest in accession.**] A security interest may be created in an accession and continues in collateral that becomes an accession.

(b) [**Perfection of security interest.**] If a security interest is perfected when the collateral becomes an accession, the security interest remains perfected in the collateral.

(c) [**Priority of security interest.**] Except as otherwise provided in subsection (d), the other provisions of this part determine the priority of a security interest in an accession.

(d) [**Compliance with certificate-of-title statute.**] A security interest in an accession is subordinate to a security interest in the whole which is perfected by compliance with the requirements of a certificate-of-title statute under Section 9–311(b).

(e) [**Removal of accession after default.**] After default, subject to Part 6, a secured party may remove an accession from other goods if the security interest in the accession has priority over the claims of every person having an interest in the whole.

(f) [**Reimbursement following removal.**] A secured party that removes an accession from other goods under subsection (e) shall promptly reimburse any holder of a security interest or other lien on, or owner of, the whole or of the other goods, other than the debtor, for the cost of repair of any physical injury to the whole or the other goods. The secured party need not reimburse the holder or owner for any diminution in value of the whole or the other goods caused by the absence of the accession removed or by any necessity for replacing it. A person entitled to reimbursement may refuse permission to remove until the secured party gives adequate assurance for the performance of the obligation to reimburse.

§ 9–336. Commingled Goods.

(a) [**"Commingled goods."**] In this section, "commingled goods" means goods that are physically united with other goods in such a manner that their identity is lost in a product or mass.

(b) [**No security interest in commingled goods as such.**] A security interest does not exist in commingled goods as such. However, a security interest may attach to a product or mass that results when goods become commingled goods.

(c) [**Attachment of security interest to product or mass.**] If collateral becomes commingled goods, a security interest attaches to the product or mass.

(d) [**Perfection of security interest.**] If a security interest in collateral is perfected before the collateral becomes commingled goods, the security interest that attaches to the product or mass under subsection (c) is perfected.

(e) [**Priority of security interest.**] Except as otherwise provided in subsection (f), the other provisions of this part determine the priority of a security interest that attaches to the product or mass under subsection (c).

(f) [**Conflicting security interests in product or mass**] If more than one security interest attaches to the product or mass under subsection (c), the following rules determine priority:

   (1) A security interest that is perfected under subsection (d) has priority over a security interest that is unperfected at the time the collateral becomes commingled goods.

   (2) If more than one security interest is perfected under subsection (d), the security interests rank equally in proportion to the value of the collateral at the time it became commingled goods.

§ 9–337. Priority of Security Interests in Goods Covered by Certificate of Title.

If, while a security interest in goods is perfected by any method under the law of another jurisdiction, this State issues a certificate of title that does not show that the goods are subject to the security interest or contain a statement that they may be subject to security interests not shown on the certificate:

   (1) a buyer of the goods, other than a person in the business of selling goods of that kind, takes free of the security interest if the buyer gives value and receives delivery of the goods after issuance of the certificate and without knowledge of the security interest; and

   (2) the security interest is subordinate to a conflicting security interest in the goods that attaches, and is perfected under Section 9–311(b), after issuance of the certificate and without the conflicting secured party's knowledge of the security interest.

Part 5—Filing
§ 9–501. Filing Office.

(a) [**Filing offices.**] Except as otherwise provided in subsection (b), if the local law of this State governs perfection of a security interest or agricultural lien, the office in which to file a financing statement to perfect the security interest or agricultural lien is:

   (1) the office designated for the filing or recording of a record of a mortgage on the related real property, if:

      (A) the collateral is as-extracted collateral or timber to be cut; or

      (B) the financing statement is filed as a fixture filing and the collateral is goods that are or are to become fixtures; or

   (2) the office of [ ] [or any office duly authorized by [ ]], in all other cases, including a case in which the collateral is goods that are or are to become fixtures and the financing statement is not filed as a fixture filing.

(b) [**Filing office for transmitting utilities.**] The office in which to file a financing statement to perfect a security interest in collateral, including fixtures, of a transmitting utility is the office of [ ]. The financing statement also constitutes a fixture filing as to the collateral indicated in the financing statement which is or is to become fixtures.

§ 9–502. Contents of Financing Statement; Record of Mortgage as Financing Statement; Time of Filing Financing Statement.

(a) [**Sufficiency of financing statement.**] Subject to subsection (b), a financing statement is sufficient only if it:

   (1) provides the name of the debtor;

   (2) provides the name of the secured party or a representative of the secured party; and

   (3) indicates the collateral covered by the financing statement.

(b) [**Real-property-related financing statements.**] Except as otherwise provided in Section 9–501(b), to be sufficient, a financing statement that covers as-extracted collateral or timber to be cut, or which is filed as a fixture filing and covers goods that are or are to become fixtures, must satisfy subsection (a) and also:

   (1) indicate that it covers this type of collateral;

   (2) indicate that it is to be filed [for record] in the real property records;

   (3) provide a description of the real property to which the collateral is related [sufficient to give constructive notice of a mortgage under the law of this State if the description were contained in a record of the mortgage of the real property]; and

   (4) if the debtor does not have an interest of record in the real property, provide the name of a record owner.

(c) [**Record of mortgage as financing statement.**] A record of a mortgage is effective, from the date of recording, as a financing statement filed as a fixture filing or as a financing statement covering as-extracted collateral or timber to be cut only if:

   (1) the record indicates the goods or accounts that it covers;

   (2) the goods are or are to become fixtures related to the real property described in the record or the collateral is related to the real property described in the record and is as-extracted collateral or timber to be cut;

   (3) the record satisfies the requirements for a financing statement in this section other than an indication that it is to be filed in the real property records; and

   (4) the record is [duly] recorded.

(d) [**Filing before security agreement or attachment.**] A financing statement may be filed before a security agreement is made or a security interest otherwise attaches.

§ 9–503. Name of Debtor and Secured Party.

(a) [**Sufficiency of debtor's name.**] A financing statement sufficiently provides the name of the debtor:

   (1) if the debtor is a registered organization, only if the financing statement provides the name of the debtor indicated on the public record of the debtor's jurisdiction of organization which shows the debtor to have been organized;

   (2) if the debtor is a decedent's estate, only if the financing statement provides the name of the decedent and indicates that the debtor is an estate;

   (3) if the debtor is a trust or a trustee acting with respect to property held in trust, only if the financing statement:

(A) provides the name specified for the trust in its organic documents or, if no name is specified, provides the name of the settlor and additional information sufficient to distinguish the debtor from other trusts having one or more of the same settlors; and

(B) indicates, in the debtor's name or otherwise, that the debtor is a trust or is a trustee acting with respect to property held in trust; and

(4) in other cases:

(A) if the debtor has a name, only if it provides the individual or organizational name of the debtor; and

(B) if the debtor does not have a name, only if it provides the names of the partners, members, associates, or other persons comprising the debtor.

(b) [**Additional debtor-related information.**] A financing statement that provides the name of the debtor in accordance with subsection (a) is not rendered ineffective by the absence of:

(1) a trade name or other name of the debtor; or

(2) unless required under subsection (a)(4)(B), names of partners, members, associates, or other persons comprising the debtor.

(c) [**Debtor's trade name insufficient.**] A financing statement that provides only the debtor's trade name does not sufficiently provide the name of the debtor.

(d) [**Representative capacity.**] Failure to indicate the representative capacity of a secured party or representative of a secured party does not affect the sufficiency of a financing statement.

(e) [**Multiple debtors and secured parties.**] A financing statement may provide the name of more than one debtor and the name of more than one secured party.

§ 9–504. Indication of Collateral.

A financing statement sufficiently indicates the collateral that it covers if the financing statement provides:

(1) a description of the collateral pursuant to Section 9–108; or

(2) an indication that the financing statement covers all assets or all personal property.

§ 9–506. Effect of Errors or Omissions.

(a) [**Minor errors and omissions.**] A financing statement substantially satisfying the requirements of this part is effective, even if it has minor errors or omissions, unless the errors or omissions make the financing statement seriously misleading.

(b) [**Financing statement seriously misleading.**] Except as otherwise provided in subsection (c), a financing statement that fails sufficiently to provide the name of the debtor in accordance with Section 9–503(a) is seriously misleading.

(c) [**Financing statement not seriously misleading.**] If a search of the records of the filing office under the debtor's correct name, using the filing office's standard search logic, if any, would disclose a financing statement that fails sufficiently to provide the name of the debtor in accordance with Section 9–503(a), the name provided does not make the financing statement seriously misleading.

(d) [**"Debtor's correct name."**] For purposes of Section 9–508(b), the "debtor's correct name" in subsection (c) means the correct name of the new debtor.

§ 9–512. Amendment of Financing Statement.
[Alternative A]

(a) [**Amendment of information in financing statement.**] Subject to Section 9–509, a person may add or delete collateral covered by, continue or terminate the effectiveness of, or, subject to subsection (e), otherwise amend the information provided in, a financing statement by filing an amendment that:

(1) identifies, by its file number, the initial financing statement to which the amendment relates; and

(2) if the amendment relates to an initial financing statement filed [or recorded] in a filing office described in Section 9–501(a)(1), provides the information specified in Section 9–502(b).

[Alternative B]

(a) [**Amendment of information in financing statement.**] Subject to Section 9–509, a person may add or delete collateral covered by, continue or terminate the effectiveness of, or, subject to subsection (e), otherwise amend the information provided in, a financing statement by filing an amendment that:

(1) identifies, by its file number, the initial financing statement to which the amendment relates; and

(2) if the amendment relates to an initial financing statement filed [or recorded] in a filing office described in Section 9–501(a)(1), provides the date [and time] that the initial financing statement was filed [or recorded] and the information specified in Section 9–502(b).

[End of Alternatives]

(b) [**Period of effectiveness not affected.**] Except as otherwise provided in Section 9–515, the filing of an amendment does not extend the period of effectiveness of the financing statement.

(c) [**Effectiveness of amendment adding collateral.**] A financing statement that is amended by an amendment that adds collateral is effective as to the added collateral only from the date of the filing of the amendment.

(d) [**Effectiveness of amendment adding debtor.**] A financing statement that is amended by an amendment that adds a debtor is effective as to the added debtor only from the date of the filing of the amendment.

(e) [**Certain amendments ineffective.**] An amendment is ineffective to the extent it:

(1) purports to delete all debtors and fails to provide the name of a debtor to be covered by the financing statement; or

(2) purports to delete all secured parties of record and fails to provide the name of a new secured party of record.

§ 9–515. Duration and Effectiveness of Financing Statement; Effect of Lapsed Financing Statement.

(a) [**Five-year effectiveness.**] Except as otherwise provided in subsections (b), (e), (f), and (g), a filed financing statement is effective for a period of five years after the date of filing.

(b) [**Public-finance or manufactured-home transaction.**] Except as otherwise provided in subsections (e), (f), and (g), an initial financing statement filed in connection with a public-finance transaction or manufactured-home transaction is effective for a period of 30 years after the date of filing if it indicates that it is filed in connection with a public-finance transaction or manufactured-home transaction.

(c) [**Lapse and continuation of financing statement.**] The effectiveness of a filed financing statement lapses on the expiration of the period of its effectiveness unless before the lapse a continuation statement is filed pursuant to subsection (d). Upon lapse, a financing statement ceases to be effective and any security interest or agricultural lien that was perfected by the financing statement becomes unperfected, unless the security interest is perfected otherwise. If the security interest or agricultural lien becomes unperfected upon lapse, it is deemed never to have been perfected as against a purchaser of the collateral for value.

(d) [**When continuation statement may be filed.**] A continuation statement may be filed only within six months before the expiration of the five-year period specified in subsection (a) or the 30-year period specified in subsection (b), whichever is applicable.

(e) [**Effect of filing continuation statement.**] Except as otherwise provided in Section 9–510, upon timely filing of a continuation statement, the effectiveness of the initial financing statement continues for a period of five years commencing on the day on which the financing statement would have become ineffective in the absence of the filing. Upon the expiration of the five-year period, the financing statement lapses in the same manner as provided in subsection (c), unless, before the lapse, another continuation statement is filed pursuant to subsection (d). Succeeding continuation statements may be filed in the same manner to continue the effectiveness of the initial financing statement.

(f) [**Transmitting utility financing statement.**] If a debtor is a transmitting utility and a filed financing statement so indicates, the financing statement is effective until a termination statement is filed.

(g) [**Record of mortgage as financing statement.**] A record of a mortgage that is effective as a financing statement filed as a fixture filing under Section 9–502(c) remains effective as a financing statement filed as a fixture filing until the mortgage is released or satisfied of record or its effectiveness otherwise terminates as to the real property.

§ 9–516. What Constitutes Filing; Effectiveness of Filing.

(a) [**What constitutes filing.**] Except as otherwise provided in subsection (b), communication of a record to a filing office and tender of the filing fee or acceptance of the record by the filing office constitutes filing.

(b) [**Refusal to accept record; filing does not occur.**] Filing does not occur with respect to a record that a filing office refuses to accept because:

   (1) the record is not communicated by a method or medium of communication authorized by the filing office;

   (2) an amount equal to or greater than the applicable filing fee is not tendered;

   (3) the filing office is unable to index the record because:

      (A) in the case of an initial financing statement, the record does not provide a name for the debtor;

      (B) in the case of an amendment or correction statement, the record:

         (i) does not identify the initial financing statement as required by Section 9–512 or 9–518, as applicable; or

         (ii) identifies an initial financing statement whose effectiveness has lapsed under Section 9–515;

      (C) in the case of an initial financing statement that provides the name of a debtor identified as an individual or an amendment that provides a name of a debtor identified as an individual which was not previously provided in the financing statement to which the record relates, the record does not identify the debtor's last name; or

      (D) in the case of a record filed [or recorded] in the filing office described in Section 9–501(a)(1), the record does not provide a sufficient description of the real property to which it relates;

   (4) in the case of an initial financing statement or an amendment that adds a secured party of record, the record does not provide a name and mailing address for the secured party of record;

   (5) in the case of an initial financing statement or an amendment that provides a name of a debtor which was not previously provided in the financing statement to which the amendment relates, the record does not:

      (A) provide a mailing address for the debtor;

      (B) indicate whether the debtor is an individual or an organization; or

      (C) if the financing statement indicates that the debtor is an organization, provide:

         (i) a type of organization for the debtor;

         (ii) a jurisdiction of organization for the debtor; or

         (iii) an organizational identification number for the debtor or indicate that the debtor has none;

   (6) in the case of an assignment reflected in an initial financing statement under Section 9–514(a) or an amendment filed under Section 9–514(b), the record does not provide a name and mailing address for the assignee; or

   (7) in the case of a continuation statement, the record is not filed within the six-month period prescribed by Section 9–515(d).

(c) [**Rules applicable to subsection (b).**] For purposes of subsection (b):

   (1) a record does not provide information if the filing office is unable to read or decipher the information; and

   (2) a record that does not indicate that it is an amendment or identify an initial financing statement to which it relates, as required by Section 9–512, 9–514, or 9–518, is an initial financing statement.

(d) [**Refusal to accept record; record effective as filed record.**] A record that is communicated to the filing office with tender of the filing fee, but which the filing office refuses to accept for a reason other than one set forth in subsection (b), is effective as a filed record except as against a purchaser of the collateral which gives value in reasonable reliance upon the absence of the record from the files.

§ 9–520. Acceptance and Refusal to Accept Record.

(a) [**Mandatory refusal to accept record.**] A filing office shall refuse to accept a record for filing for a reason set forth in Section 9–516(b) and may refuse to accept a record for filing only for a reason set forth in Section 9–516(b).

(b) [**Communication concerning refusal.**] If a filing office refuses to accept a record for filing, it shall communicate to the person that presented the record the fact of and reason for the refusal and the date and time the record would have been filed had the filing office accepted it. The communication must be made at the time and in the manner prescribed by filing-office rule but [, in the case of a filing office described in Section 9–501(a)(2),] in no event more than two business days after the filing office receives the record.

(c) [**When filed financing statement effective.**] A filed financing statement satisfying Section 9–502(a) and (b) is effective, even if the filing office is required to refuse to accept it for filing under subsection (a). However, Section 9–338 applies to a filed financing statement providing information described in Section 9–516(b)(5) which is incorrect at the time the financing statement is filed.

(d) [**Separate application to multiple debtors.**] If a record communicated to a filing office provides information that relates to more than one debtor, this part applies as to each debtor separately.

Part 6—Default
§ 9–601. Rights after Default; Judicial Enforcement; Consignor or Buyer of Accounts, Chattel Paper, Payment Intangibles, or Promissory Notes.

(a) [**Rights of secured party after default.**] After default, a secured party has the rights provided in this part and, except as otherwise provided in Section 9–602, those provided by agreement of the parties. A secured party:

   (1) may reduce a claim to judgment, foreclose, or otherwise enforce the claim, security interest, or agricultural lien by any available judicial procedure; and

   (2) if the collateral is documents, may proceed either as to the documents or as to the goods they cover.

(b) [**Rights and duties of secured party in possession or control.**] A secured party in possession of collateral or control of collateral under Section 9–104, 9–105, 9–106, or 9–107 has the rights and duties provided in Section 9–207.

(c) [**Rights cumulative; simultaneous exercise.**] The rights under subsections (a) and (b) are cumulative and may be exercised simultaneously.

(d) [**Rights of debtor and obligor.**] Except as otherwise provided in subsection (g) and Section 9–605, after default, a debtor and an obligor have the rights provided in this part and by agreement of the parties.

(e) [**Lien of levy after judgment.**] If a secured party has reduced its claim to judgment, the lien of any levy that may be made upon the collateral by virtue of an execution based upon the judgment relates back to the earliest of:

   (1) the date of perfection of the security interest or agricultural lien in the collateral;

   (2) the date of filing a financing statement covering the collateral; or

   (3) any date specified in a statute under which the agricultural lien was created.

(f) [**Execution sale.**] A sale pursuant to an execution is a foreclosure of the security interest or agricultural lien by judicial procedure within the meaning of this section. A secured party may purchase at the sale and thereafter hold the collateral free of any other requirements of this article.

(g) [**Consignor or buyer of certain rights to payment.**] Except as otherwise provided in Section 9–607(c), this part imposes no duties upon a secured party that is a consignor or is a buyer of accounts, chattel paper, payment intangibles, or promissory notes.

§ 9–607. Collection and Enforcement by Secured Party.

(a) [**Collection and enforcement generally.**] If so agreed, and in any event after default, a secured party:

   (1) may notify an account debtor or other person obligated on collateral to make payment or otherwise render performance to or for the benefit of the secured party;

(2) may take any proceeds to which the secured party is entitled under Section 9–315;

(3) may enforce the obligations of an account debtor or other person obligated on collateral and exercise the rights of the debtor with respect to the obligation of the account debtor or other person obligated on collateral to make payment or otherwise render performance to the debtor, and with respect to any property that secures the obligations of the account debtor or other person obligated on the collateral;

(4) if it holds a security interest in a deposit account perfected by control under Section 9–104(a)(1), may apply the balance of the deposit account to the obligation secured by the deposit account; and

(5) if it holds a security interest in a deposit account perfected by control under Section 9–104(a)(2) or (3), may instruct the bank to pay the balance of the deposit account to or for the benefit of the secured party.

(b) [**Nonjudicial enforcement of mortgage.**] If necessary to enable a secured party to exercise under subsection (a)(3) the right of a debtor to enforce a mortgage nonjudicially, the secured party may record in the office in which a record of the mortgage is recorded:

(1) a copy of the security agreement that creates or provides for a security interest in the obligation secured by the mortgage; and

(2) the secured party's sworn affidavit in recordable form stating that:

(A) a default has occurred; and

(B) the secured party is entitled to enforce the mortgage nonjudicially.

(c) [**Commercially reasonable collection and enforcement.**] A secured party shall proceed in a commercially reasonable manner if the secured party:

(1) undertakes to collect from or enforce an obligation of an account debtor or other person obligated on collateral; and

(2) is entitled to charge back uncollected collateral or otherwise to full or limited recourse against the debtor or a secondary obligor.

(d) [**Expenses of collection and enforcement.**] A secured party may deduct from the collections made pursuant to subsection (c) reasonable expenses of collection and enforcement, including reasonable attorney's fees and legal expenses incurred by the secured party.

(e) [**Duties to secured party not affected.**] This section does not determine whether an account debtor, bank, or other person obligated on collateral owes a duty to a secured party.

§ 9–608. Application of Proceeds of Collection or Enforcement; Liability for Deficiency and Right to Surplus.

(a) [**Application of proceeds, surplus, and deficiency if obligation secured.**] If a security interest or agricultural lien secures payment or performance of an obligation, the following rules apply:

(1) A secured party shall apply or pay over for application the cash proceeds of collection or enforcement under Section 9–607 in the following order to:

(A) the reasonable expenses of collection and enforcement and, to the extent provided for by agreement and not prohibited by law, reasonable attorney's fees and legal expenses incurred by the secured party;

(B) the satisfaction of obligations secured by the security interest or agricultural lien under which the collection or enforcement is made; and

(C) the satisfaction of obligations secured by any subordinate security interest in or other lien on the collateral subject to the security interest or agricultural lien under which the collection or enforcement is made if the secured party receives an authenticated demand for proceeds before distribution of the proceeds is completed.

(2) If requested by a secured party, a holder of a subordinate security interest or other lien shall furnish reasonable proof of the interest or lien within a reasonable time. Unless the holder complies, the secured party need not comply with the holder's demand under paragraph (1)(C).

(3) A secured party need not apply or pay over for application noncash proceeds of collection and enforcement under Section 9–607 unless the failure to do so would be commercially unreasonable. A secured party that applies or pays over for application noncash proceeds shall do so in a commercially reasonable manner.

(4) A secured party shall account to and pay a debtor for any surplus, and the obligor is liable for any deficiency.

(b) [**No surplus or deficiency in sales of certain rights to payment.**] If the underlying transaction is a sale of accounts, chattel paper, payment intangibles, or promissory notes, the debtor is not entitled to any surplus, and the obligor is not liable for any deficiency.

§ 9–609. Secured Party's Right to Take Possession after Default.

(a) [**Possession; rendering equipment unusable; disposition on debtor's premises.**] After default, a secured party:

(1) may take possession of the collateral; and

(2) without removal, may render equipment unusable and dispose of collateral on a debtor's premises under Section 9–610.

(b) [**Judicial and nonjudicial process.**] A secured party may proceed under subsection (a):

(1) pursuant to judicial process; or

(2) without judicial process, if it proceeds without breach of the peace.

(c) [**Assembly of collateral.**] If so agreed, and in any event after default, a secured party may require the debtor to assemble the collateral and make it available to the secured party at a place to be designated by the secured party which is reasonably convenient to both parties.

§ 9–610. Disposition of Collateral after Default.

(a) [**Disposition after default.**] After default, a secured party may sell, lease, license, or otherwise dispose of any or all of the collateral in its present condition or following any commercially reasonable preparation or processing.

(b) [**Commercially reasonable disposition.**] Every aspect of a disposition of collateral, including the method, manner, time, place, and other terms, must be commercially reasonable. If commercially reasonable, a secured party may dispose of collateral by public or private proceedings, by one or more contracts, as a unit or in parcels, and at any time and place and on any terms.

(c) [**Purchase by secured party.**] A secured party may purchase collateral:

(1) at a public disposition; or

(2) at a private disposition only if the collateral is of a kind that is customarily sold on a recognized market or the subject of widely distributed standard price quotations.

(d) [**Warranties on disposition.**] A contract for sale, lease, license, or other disposition includes the warranties relating to title, possession, quiet enjoyment, and the like which by operation of law accompany a voluntary disposition of property of the kind subject to the contract.

(e) [**Disclaimer of warranties.**] A secured party may disclaim or modify warranties under subsection (d):

(1) in a manner that would be effective to disclaim or modify the warranties in a voluntary disposition of property of the kind subject to the contract of disposition; or

(2) by communicating to the purchaser a record evidencing the contract for disposition and including an express disclaimer or modification of the warranties.

(f) [**Record sufficient to disclaim warranties.**] A record is sufficient to disclaim warranties under subsection (e) if it indicates "There is no warranty relating to title, possession, quiet enjoyment, or the like in this disposition" or uses words of similar import.

§ 9–611. Notification Before Disposition of Collateral.

(a) [**"Notification date."**] In this section, "notification date" means the earlier of the date on which:

(1) a secured party sends to the debtor and any secondary obligor an authenticated notification of disposition; or

(2) the debtor and any secondary obligor waive the right to notification.

(b) [**Notification of disposition required.**] Except as otherwise provided in subsection (d), a secured party that disposes of collateral under Section 9–610 shall send to the persons specified in subsection (c) a reasonable authenticated notification of disposition.

(c) [**Persons to be notified.**] To comply with subsection (b), the secured party shall send an authenticated notification of disposition to:

(1) the debtor;

(2) any secondary obligor; and

(3) if the collateral is other than consumer goods:

    (A) any other person from which the secured party has received, before the notification date, an authenticated notification of a claim of an interest in the collateral;

    (B) any other secured party or lienholder that, 10 days before the notification date, held a security interest in or other lien on the collateral perfected by the filing of a financing statement that:

        (i) identified the collateral;

        (ii) was indexed under the debtor's name as of that date; and

        (iii) was filed in the office in which to file a financing statement against the debtor covering the collateral as of that date; and

    (C) any other secured party that, 10 days before the notification date, held a security interest in the collateral perfected by compliance with a statute, regulation, or treaty described in Section 9–311(a).

(d) [**Subsection (b) inapplicable: perishable collateral; recognized market.**] Subsection (b) does not apply if the collateral is perishable or threatens to decline speedily in value or is of a type customarily sold on a recognized market.

(e) [**Compliance with subsection (c)(3)(b).**] A secured party complies with the requirement for notification prescribed by subsection (c)(3)(B) if:

(1) not later than 20 days or earlier than 30 days before the notification date, the secured party requests, in a commercially reasonable manner, information concerning financing statements indexed under the debtor's name in the office indicated in subsection (c)(3)(B); and

(2) before the notification date, the secured party:

    (A) did not receive a response to the request for information; or

    (B) received a response to the request for information and sent an authenticated notification of disposition to each secured party or other lienholder named in that response whose financing statement covered the collateral.

§ 9–615. Application of Proceeds of Disposition; Liability for Deficiency and Right to Surplus.

(a) [**Application of proceeds.**] A secured party shall apply or pay over for application the cash proceeds of disposition under Section 9–610 in the following order to:

(1) the reasonable expenses of retaking, holding, preparing for disposition, processing, and disposing, and, to the extent provided for by agreement and not prohibited by law, reasonable attorney's fees and legal expenses incurred by the secured party;

(2) the satisfaction of obligations secured by the security interest or agricultural lien under which the disposition is made;

(3) the satisfaction of obligations secured by any subordinate security interest in or other subordinate lien on the collateral if:

    (A) the secured party receives from the holder of the subordinate security interest or other lien an authenticated demand for proceeds before distribution of the proceeds is completed; and

    (B) in a case in which a consignor has an interest in the collateral, the subordinate security interest or other lien is senior to the interest of the consignor; and

(4) a secured party that is a consignor of the collateral if the secured party receives from the consignor an authenticated demand for proceeds before distribution of the proceeds is completed.

(b) [**Proof of subordinate interest.**] If requested by a secured party, a holder of a subordinate security interest or other lien shall furnish reasonable proof of the interest or lien within a reasonable time. Unless the holder does so, the secured party need not comply with the holder's demand under subsection (a)(3).

(c) [**Application of noncash proceeds.**] A secured party need not apply or pay over for application noncash proceeds of disposition under Section 9–610 unless the failure to do so would be commercially unreasonable. A secured party that applies or pays over for application noncash proceeds shall do so in a commercially reasonable manner.

(d) [**Surplus or deficiency if obligation secured.**] If the security interest under which a disposition is made secures payment or performance of an obligation, after making the payments and applications required by subsection (a) and permitted by subsection (c):

(1) unless subsection (a)(4) requires the secured party to apply or pay over cash proceeds to a consignor, the secured party shall account to and pay a debtor for any surplus; and

(2) the obligor is liable for any deficiency.

(e) [**No surplus or deficiency in sales of certain rights to payment.**] If the underlying transaction is a sale of accounts, chattel paper, payment intangibles, or promissory notes:

(1) the debtor is not entitled to any surplus; and

(2) the obligor is not liable for any deficiency.

(f) [**Calculation of surplus or deficiency in disposition to person related to secured party.**] The surplus or deficiency following a disposition is calculated based on the amount of proceeds that would have been realized in a disposition complying with this part to a transferee other than the secured party, a person related to the secured party, or a secondary obligor if:

(1) the transferee in the disposition is the secured party, a person related to the secured party, or a secondary obligor; and

(2) the amount of proceeds of the disposition is significantly below the range of proceeds that a complying disposition to a person other than the secured party, a person related to the secured party, or a secondary obligor would have brought.

(g) [**Cash proceeds received by junior secured party.**] A secured party that receives cash proceeds of a disposition in good faith and without knowledge that the receipt violates the rights of the holder of a security interest or other lien that is not subordinate to the security interest or agricultural lien under which the disposition is made:

(1) takes the cash proceeds free of the security interest or other lien;

(2) is not obligated to apply the proceeds of the disposition to the satisfaction of obligations secured by the security interest or other lien; and

(3) is not obligated to account to or pay the holder of the security interest or other lien for any surplus.

§ 9–616. Explanation of Calculation of Surplus or Deficiency.

(a) [**Definitions.**] In this section:

(1) "Explanation" means a writing that:

    (A) states the amount of the surplus or deficiency;

    (B) provides an explanation in accordance with subsection (c) of how the secured party calculated the surplus or deficiency;

    (C) states, if applicable, that future debits, credits, charges, including additional credit service charges or interest, rebates, and expenses may affect the amount of the surplus or deficiency; and

    (D) provides a telephone number or mailing address from which additional information concerning the transaction is available.

(2) "Request" means a record:

    (A) authenticated by a debtor or consumer obligor;

    (B) requesting that the recipient provide an explanation; and

    (C) sent after disposition of the collateral under Section 9–610.

(b) [**Explanation of calculation.**] In a consumer-goods transaction in which the debtor is entitled to a surplus or a consumer obligor is liable for a deficiency under Section 9–615, the secured party shall:

(1) send an explanation to the debtor or consumer obligor, as applicable, after the disposition and:

    (A) before or when the secured party accounts to the debtor and pays any surplus or first makes written demand on the consumer obligor after the disposition for payment of the deficiency; and

    (B) within 14 days after receipt of a request; or

(2) in the case of a consumer obligor who is liable for a deficiency, within 14 days after receipt of a request, send to the consumer obligor a record waiving the secured party's right to a deficiency.

(c) [**Required information.**] To comply with subsection (a)(1)(B), a writing must provide the following information in the following order:

(1) the aggregate amount of obligations secured by the security interest under which the disposition was made, and, if the amount reflects a rebate of unearned interest or credit service charge, an indication of that fact, calculated as of a specified date:

(A) if the secured party takes or receives possession of the collateral after default, not more than 35 days before the secured party takes or receives possession; or

(B) if the secured party takes or receives possession of the collateral before default or does not take possession of the collateral, not more than 35 days before the disposition;

(2) the amount of proceeds of the disposition;

(3) the aggregate amount of the obligations after deducting the amount of proceeds;

(4) the amount, in the aggregate or by type, and types of expenses, including expenses of retaking, holding, preparing for disposition, processing, and disposing of the collateral, and attorney's fees secured by the collateral which are known to the secured party and relate to the current disposition;

(5) the amount, in the aggregate or by type, and types of credits, including rebates of interest or credit service charges, to which the obligor is known to be entitled and which are not reflected in the amount in paragraph (1); and

(6) the amount of the surplus or deficiency.

(d) [**Substantial compliance.**] A particular phrasing of the explanation is not required. An explanation complying substantially with the requirements of subsection (a) is sufficient, even if it includes minor errors that are not seriously misleading.

(e) [**Charges for responses.**] A debtor or consumer obligor is entitled without charge to one response to a request under this section during any six-month period in which the secured party did not send to the debtor or consumer obligor an explanation pursuant to subsection (b)(1). The secured party may require payment of a charge not exceeding $25 for each additional response.

§ 9–617. Rights of Transferee of Collateral.

(a) [**Effects of disposition.**] A secured party's disposition of collateral after default:

(1) transfers to a transferee for value all of the debtor's rights in the collateral;

(2) discharges the security interest under which the disposition is made; and

(3) discharges any subordinate security interest or other subordinate lien [other than liens created under [cite acts or statutes providing for liens, if any, that are not to be discharged]].

(b) [**Rights of good-faith transferee.**] A transferee that acts in good faith takes free of the rights and interests described in subsection (a), even if the secured party fails to comply with this article or the requirements of any judicial proceeding.

(c) [**Rights of other transferee.**] If a transferee does not take free of the rights and interests described in subsection (a), the transferee takes the collateral subject to:

(1) the debtor's rights in the collateral;

(2) the security interest or agricultural lien under which the disposition is made; and

(3) any other security interest or other lien.

§ 9–620. Acceptance of Collateral in Full or Partial Satisfaction of Obligation; Compulsory Disposition of Collateral.

(a) [**Conditions to acceptance in satisfaction.**] Except as otherwise provided in subsection (g), a secured party may accept collateral in full or partial satisfaction of the obligation it secures only if:

(1) the debtor consents to the acceptance under subsection (c);

(2) the secured party does not receive, within the time set forth in subsection (d), a notification of objection to the proposal authenticated by:

(A) a person to which the secured party was required to send a proposal under Section 9–621; or

(B) any other person, other than the debtor, holding an interest in the collateral subordinate to the security interest that is the subject of the proposal;

(3) if the collateral is consumer goods, the collateral is not in the possession of the debtor when the debtor consents to the acceptance; and

(4) subsection (e) does not require the secured party to dispose of the collateral or the debtor waives the requirement pursuant to Section 9–624.

(b) [**Purported acceptance ineffective.**] A purported or apparent acceptance of collateral under this section is ineffective unless:

(1) the secured party consents to the acceptance in an authenticated record or sends a proposal to the debtor; and

(2) the conditions of subsection (a) are met.

(c) [**Debtor's consent.**] For purposes of this section:

(1) a debtor consents to an acceptance of collateral in partial satisfaction of the obligation it secures only if the debtor agrees to the terms of the acceptance in a record authenticated after default; and

(2) a debtor consents to an acceptance of collateral in full satisfaction of the obligation it secures only if the debtor agrees to the terms of the acceptance in a record authenticated after default or the secured party:

(A) sends to the debtor after default a proposal that is unconditional or subject only to a condition that collateral not in the possession of the secured party be preserved or maintained;

(B) in the proposal, proposes to accept collateral in full satisfaction of the obligation it secures; and

(C) does not receive a notification of objection authenticated by the debtor within 20 days after the proposal is sent.

(d) [**Effectiveness of notification.**] To be effective under subsection (a)(2), a notification of objection must be received by the secured party:

(1) in the case of a person to which the proposal was sent pursuant to Section 9–621, within 20 days after notification was sent to that person; and

(2) in other cases:

(A) within 20 days after the last notification was sent pursuant to Section 9–621; or

(B) if a notification was not sent, before the debtor consents to the acceptance under subsection (c).

(e) [**Mandatory disposition of consumer goods.**] A secured party that has taken possession of collateral shall dispose of the collateral pursuant to Section 9–610 within the time specified in subsection (f) if:

(1) 60 percent of the cash price has been paid in the case of a purchase-money security interest in consumer goods; or

(2) 60 percent of the principal amount of the obligation secured has been paid in the case of a non-purchase-money security interest in consumer goods.

(f) [**Compliance with mandatory disposition requirement.**] To comply with subsection (e), the secured party shall dispose of the collateral:

(1) within 90 days after taking possession; or

(2) within any longer period to which the debtor and all secondary obligors have agreed in an agreement to that effect entered into and authenticated after default.

(g) [**No partial satisfaction in consumer transaction.**] In a consumer transaction, a secured party may not accept collateral in partial satisfaction of the obligation it secures.

§ 9–621. Notification of Proposal to Accept Collateral.

(a) [**Persons to which proposal to be sent.**] A secured party that desires to accept collateral in full or partial satisfaction of the obligation it secures shall send its proposal to:

(1) any person from which the secured party has received, before the debtor consented to the acceptance, an authenticated notification of a claim of an interest in the collateral;

(2) any other secured party or lienholder that, 10 days before the debtor consented to the acceptance, held a security interest in or other lien on the collateral perfected by the filing of a financing statement that:

(A) identified the collateral;

(B) was indexed under the debtor's name as of that date; and

(C) was filed in the office or offices in which to file a financing statement against the debtor covering the collateral as of that date; and

(3) any other secured party that, 10 days before the debtor consented to the acceptance, held a security interest in the collateral perfected by compliance with a statute, regulation, or treaty described in Section 9–311(a).

(b) [**Proposal to be sent to secondary obligor in partial satisfaction.**] A secured party that desires to accept collateral in partial satisfaction of the obligation it secures shall send its proposal to any secondary obligor in addition to the persons described in subsection (a).

§ 9–622. Effect of Acceptance of Collateral.

(a) [**Effect of acceptance.**] A secured party's acceptance of collateral in full or partial satisfaction of the obligation it secures:

(1) discharges the obligation to the extent consented to by the debtor;

(2) transfers to the secured party all of a debtor's rights in the collateral;

(3) discharges the security interest or agricultural lien that is the subject of the debtor's consent and any subordinate security interest or other subordinate lien; and

(4) terminates any other subordinate interest.

(b) [**Discharge of subordinate interest notwithstanding noncompliance.**] A subordinate interest is discharged or terminated under subsection (a), even if the secured party fails to comply with this article.

§ 9–623. Right to Redeem Collateral.

(a) [**Persons that may redeem.**] A debtor, any secondary obligor, or any other secured party or lienholder may redeem collateral.

(b) [**Requirements for redemption.**] To redeem collateral, a person shall tender:

(1) fulfillment of all obligations secured by the collateral; and

(2) the reasonable expenses and attorney's fees described in Section 9–615(a)(1).

(c) [**When redemption may occur.**] A redemption may occur at any time before a secured party:

(1) has collected collateral under Section 9–607;

(2) has disposed of collateral or entered into a contract for its disposition under Section 9–610; or

(3) has accepted collateral in full or partial satisfaction of the obligation it secures under Section 9–622.

§ 9–624. Waiver.

(a) [**Waiver of disposition notification.**] A debtor or secondary obligor may waive the right to notification of disposition of collateral under Section 9–611 only by an agreement to that effect entered into and authenticated after default.

(b) [**Waiver of mandatory disposition.**] A debtor may waive the right to require disposition of collateral under Section 9–620(e) only by an agreement to that effect entered into and authenticated after default.

(c) [**Waiver of redemption right.**] Except in a consumer-goods transaction, a debtor or secondary obligor may waive the right to redeem collateral under Section 9–623 only by an agreement to that effect entered into and authenticated after default.

§ 9–625. Remedies for Secured Party's Failure to Comply with Article.

(a) [**Judicial orders concerning noncompliance.**] If it is established that a secured party is not proceeding in accordance with this article, a court may order or restrain collection, enforcement, or disposition of collateral on appropriate terms and conditions.

(b) [**Damages for noncompliance.**] Subject to subsections (c), (d), and (f), a person is liable for damages in the amount of any loss caused by a failure to comply with this article. Loss caused by a failure to comply may include loss resulting from the debtor's inability to obtain, or increased costs of, alternative financing.

(c) [**Persons entitled to recover damages; statutory damages in consumer-goods transaction.**] Except as otherwise provided in Section 9–628:

(1) a person that, at the time of the failure, was a debtor, was an obligor, or held a security interest in or other lien on the collateral may recover damages under subsection (b) for its loss; and

(2) if the collateral is consumer goods, a person that was a debtor or a secondary obligor at the time a secured party failed to comply with this part may recover for that failure in any event an amount not less than the credit service charge plus 10 percent of the principal amount of the obligation or the time-price differential plus 10 percent of the cash price.

(d) [**Recovery when deficiency eliminated or reduced.**] A debtor whose deficiency is eliminated under Section 9–626 may recover damages for the loss of any surplus. However, a debtor or secondary obligor whose deficiency is eliminated or reduced under Section 9–626 may not otherwise recover under subsection (b) for noncompliance with the provisions of this part relating to collection, enforcement, disposition, or acceptance.

(e) [**Statutory damages: noncompliance with specified provisions.**] In addition to any damages recoverable under subsection (b), the debtor, consumer obligor, or person named as a debtor in a filed record, as applicable, may recover $500 in each case from a person that:

(1) fails to comply with Section 9–208;

(2) fails to comply with Section 9–209;

(3) files a record that the person is not entitled to file under Section 9–509(a);

(4) fails to cause the secured party of record to file or send a termination statement as required by Section 9–513(a) or (c);

(5) fails to comply with Section 9–616(b)(1) and whose failure is part of a pattern, or consistent with a practice, of noncompliance; or

(6) fails to comply with Section 9–616(b)(2).

(f) [**Statutory damages: noncompliance with Section 9–210.**] A debtor or consumer obligor may recover damages under subsection (b) and, in addition, $500 in each case from a person that, without reasonable cause, fails to comply with a request under Section 9–210. A recipient of a request under Section 9–210 which never claimed an interest in the collateral or obligations that are the subject of a request under that section has a reasonable excuse for failure to comply with the request within the meaning of this subsection.

(g) [**Limitation of security interest: noncompliance with Section 9–210.**] If a secured party fails to comply with a request regarding a list of collateral or a statement of account under Section 9–210, the secured party may claim a security interest only as shown in the list or statement included in the request as against a person that is reasonably misled by the failure.

§ 9–626. Action in Which Deficiency or Surplus Is in Issue.

(a) [**Applicable rules if amount of deficiency or surplus in issue.**] In an action arising from a transaction, other than a consumer transaction, in which the amount of a deficiency or surplus is in issue, the following rules apply:

(1) A secured party need not prove compliance with the provisions of this part relating to collection, enforcement, disposition, or acceptance unless the debtor or a secondary obligor places the secured party's compliance in issue.

(2) If the secured party's compliance is placed in issue, the secured party has the burden of establishing that the collection, enforcement, disposition, or acceptance was conducted in accordance with this part.

(3) Except as otherwise provided in Section 9–628, if a secured party fails to prove that the collection, enforcement, disposition, or acceptance was conducted in accordance with the provisions of this part relating to collection, enforcement, disposition, or acceptance, the liability of a debtor or a secondary obligor for a deficiency is limited to an amount by which the sum of the secured obligation, expenses, and attorney's fees exceeds the greater of:

(A) the proceeds of the collection, enforcement, disposition, or acceptance; or

(B) the amount of proceeds that would have been realized had the noncomplying secured party proceeded in accordance with the provisions of this part relating to collection, enforcement, disposition, or acceptance.

(4) For purposes of paragraph (3)(B), the amount of proceeds that would have been realized is equal to the sum of the secured obligation, expenses, and attorney's fees unless the secured party proves that the amount is less than that sum.

(5) If a deficiency or surplus is calculated under Section 9–615(f), the debtor or obligor has the burden of establishing that the amount of proceeds of the disposition is significantly below the range of prices that a complying disposition to a person other than the secured party, a person related to the secured party, or a secondary obligor would have brought.

(b) [**Non-consumer transactions; no inference.**] The limitation of the rules in subsection (a) to transactions other than consumer transactions is intended to leave to the court the determination of the proper rules in consumer transactions. The court may not infer from that limitation the nature of the proper rule in consumer transactions and may continue to apply established approaches.

§ 9–627. Determination of Whether Conduct Was Commercially Reasonable.

(a) [**Greater amount obtainable under other circumstances; no preclusion of commercial reasonableness.**] The fact that a greater amount could have been obtained by a collection, enforcement, disposition, or acceptance at a different time or in a different method from that selected by the secured party is not of itself sufficient to preclude the secured party from establishing that the collection, enforcement, disposition, or acceptance was made in a commercially reasonable manner.

(b) [**Dispositions that are commercially reasonable.**] A disposition of collateral is made in a commercially reasonable manner if the disposition is made:

    (1) in the usual manner on any recognized market;

    (2) at the price current in any recognized market at the time of the disposition; or

    (3) otherwise in conformity with reasonable commercial practices among dealers in the type of property that was the subject of the disposition.

(c) [**Approval by court or on behalf of creditors.**] A collection, enforcement, disposition, or acceptance is commercially reasonable if it has been approved:

    (1) in a judicial proceeding;

    (2) by a bona fide creditors' committee;

    (3) by a representative of creditors; or

    (4) by an assignee for the benefit of creditors.

(d) [**Approval under subsection (c) not necessary; absence of approval has no effect.**] Approval under subsection (c) need not be obtained, and lack of approval does not mean that the collection, enforcement, disposition, or acceptance is not commercially reasonable.

A

abatement Reduction or elimination of gifts by category upon the reduction in value of the estate.

absolute surety Surety liable to a creditor immediately upon the default of the principal debtor.

acceptance *Commercial paper* Acceptance is the drawee's signed engagement to honor the draft as presented. It becomes operative when completed by delivery or notification.
Contracts Compliance by offeree with terms and conditions of offer.
Sale of goods The UCC provides three ways a buyer can accept goods: (1) by signifying to the seller that the goods are conforming or that he will accept them in spite of their nonconformity, (2) by failing to make an effective rejection, and (3) by doing an act inconsistent with the seller's ownership.

acceptor Drawee who has accepted an instrument.

accession An addition to one's property by increase of the original property or by production from such property; *e.g.,* A innocently converts the wheat of B into bread. The UCC changes the common law where a perfected security interest is involved.

accident and health insurance Provides protection from losses due to accident or sickness.

accommodation An arrangement made as a favor to another, usually involving a loan of money or commercial paper. While a party's intent may be to aid a maker of a note by lending his credit, if he seeks to accomplish thereby legitimate objects of his own and not simply to aid the maker, the act is not for accommodation.

accommodation indorser Signer not in the chain of title.

accommodation party A person who signs commercial paper in any capacity for the purpose of lending his name to another party to an instrument.

accord and satisfaction A method of discharging a claim whereby the parties agree to accept something in settlement, the "accord" being the agreement and the "satisfaction" its execution or performance. It is a new contract that is substituted for an old contract, which is thereby discharged, or for an obligation or cause of action and that must have all of the elements of a valid contract.

account Any account with a bank, including a checking, time, interest or savings account. Also, any right to payment, for goods or services, that is not evidenced by an instrument or chattel paper; *e.g.,* account receivable.

accounting Equitable proceeding for a complete settlement of all partnership affairs.

act of state doctrine Rule that a court should not question the validity of actions taken by a foreign government in its own country.

actual authority Power conferred upon agent by actual consent given by principal.

actual express authority Actual authority derived from written or spoken words of principal.

actual implied authority Actual authority inferred from words or conduct manifested to agent by principal.

actual notice Knowledge actually and expressly communicated.

actus reas Wrongful or overt act.

ademption The removal or extinction of a devise by act of the testator.

adequacy of consideration Not required where parties have freely agreed to the exchange.

adhesion contract Standard "form" contract, usually between a large retailer and a consumer, in which the weaker party has no realistic choice or opportunity to bargain.

adjudication The giving or pronouncing of a judgment in a case; also, the judgment given.

administrative agency Governmental entity (other than courts and legislatures) having authority to affect the rights of private parties.

administrative law Law dealing with the establishment, duties, and powers of agencies in the executive branch of government.

administrative process Entire set of activities engaged in by administrative agencies while carrying out their rulemaking, enforcement, and adjudicative functions.

administrator A person appointed by the court to manage the assets and liabilities of an intestate (a person dying without a will). A person named in the will of a testator (a person dying with a will) is called the executor. Female designations are administratrix and executrix.

adversary system System in which opposing parties initiate and present their cases.

adverse possession A method of acquiring title to real property by possession for a statutory period under certain conditions. The periods of time may differ, depending on whether the adverse possessor has color of title.

affidavit A written statement of facts, made voluntarily, confirmed by oath or affirmation of the party making it, and taken before an authorized officer.

affiliate Person who controls, is controlled by, or is under common control with the issuer.

affirm Uphold the lower court's judgment.

affirmative action Active recruitment of minority applicants.

affirmative defense A response that attacks the plaintiff's legal right to bring an action as opposed to attacking the truth of the claim; *e.g.,* accord and satisfaction; assumption of risk; contributory negligence; duress; estoppel.

affirmative disclosure Requirement that an advertiser include certain information in its advertisement so that the ad is not deceptive.

after-acquired property Property the debtor may acquire at some time after the security interest attaches.

agency Relation in which one person acts for or represents another by the latter's authority.
Actual agency Exists where the agent is really employed by the principal.
Agency by estoppel One created by operation of law and established by proof of such acts of the principal as reasonably lead to the conclusion of its existence.
Implied agency One created by acts of the parties and deduced from proof of other facts.

agent Person authorized to act on another's behalf.

allegation A statement of a party setting out what he expects to prove.

allonge Piece of paper firmly affixed to the instrument.

annuity contract Agreement to pay periodic sums to insured upon reaching a designated age.

annul To annul a judgment or judicial proceeding is to deprive it of all force and operation.

answer The answer is the formal written statement made by a defendant setting forth the ground of his defense.

antecedent debt Preexisting obligation.

anticipatory breach of contract (or **anticipatory repudiation**) The unjustified assertion by a party that he will not perform an obligation that he is contractually obligated to perform at a future time.

apparent authority Such principal power that a reasonable person would assume an agent has in light of the principal's conduct.

appeal Resort to a superior (appellate) court to review the decision of an inferior (trial) court or administrative agency.

appeal by right Mandatory review by a higher court.

appellant A party who takes an appeal from one court to another. He may be either the plaintiff or defendant in the original court proceeding.

appellee The party in a cause against whom an appeal is taken; that is, the party who has an interest adverse to setting aside or reversing the judgment. Sometimes also called the "respondent."

appropriation Unauthorized use of another person's name or likeness for one's own benefit.

appurtenances Things appurtenant pass as incident to the principal thing. Sometimes an easement consisting of a right of way over one piece of land will pass with another piece of land as being appurtenant to it.

APR Annual percentage rate.

arbitration The reference of a dispute to an impartial (third) person chosen by the parties, who agree in advance to abide by the arbitrator's award issued after a hearing at which both parties have an opportunity to be heard.

arraignment Accused is informed of the crime against him and enters a plea.

articles of incorporation (or **certificate of incorporation**) The instrument under which a corporation is formed. The contents are prescribed in the particular state's general incorporation statute.

articles of partnership A written agreement by which parties enter into a partnership, to be governed by the terms set forth therein.

as is Disclaimer of implied warranties.

assault Unlawful attempted battery; intentional infliction of apprehension of immediate bodily harm or offensive contact.

assignee Party to whom contract rights are assigned.

assignment A transfer of the rights to real or personal property, usually intangible property such as rights in a lease, mortgage, sale agreement, or partnership.

assignment of rights Voluntary transfer to a third party of the rights arising from a contract.

assignor Party making an assignment.

assumes Delegatee agrees to perform the contractual obligation of the delegator.

assumes the mortgage Purchaser of mortgaged property becomes personally liable to pay the debt.

assumption of risk Plaintiff's express or implied consent to encounter a known danger.

attachment The process of seizing property, by virtue of a writ, summons, or other judicial order, and bringing the same into the custody of the court for the purpose of securing satisfaction of the judgment ultimately to be entered in the action. While formerly the main objective was to coerce the defendant debtor to appear in court, today the writ of attachment is used primarily to seize the debtor's property in the event a judgment is rendered.

   Distinguished from execution See **execution**.

     Also, the process by which a security interest becomes enforceable. Attachment may occur upon the taking of possession or upon the signing of a security agreement by the person who is pledging the property as collateral.

authority Power of an agent to change the legal status of his principal.

authorized means Any reasonable means of communication.

automatic perfection Perfection upon attachment.

award The decision of an arbitrator.

B

bad checks Issuing a check with funds insufficient to cover it.

bailee The party to whom personal property is delivered under a contract of bailment.

   Extraordinary bailee Absolutely liable for the safety of the bailed property without regard to the cause of loss.

   Ordinary bailee Must exercise due care.

bailment A delivery of personal property in trust for the execution of a special object in relation to such goods, beneficial either to the bailor or bailee or both, and upon a contract to either redeliver the goods to the bailor or otherwise dispose of the same in conformity with the purpose of the trust.

bailor The party who delivers goods to another in the contract of bailment.

bankrupt The state or condition of one who is unable to pay his debts as they are, or become, due.

Bankruptcy Code The Act was substantially revised in 1978 and again in 2005. Straight bankruptcy is in the nature of a liquidation proceeding and involves the collection and distribution to creditors of all the bankrupt's nonexempt property by the trustee in the manner provided by the Act. The debtor rehabilitation provisions of the Act (Chapters 11 and 13) differ from straight bankruptcy in that the debtor looks to rehabilitation and reorganization, rather than liquidation, and the creditors look to future earnings of the bankrupt, rather than to property held by the bankrupt, to satisfy their claims.

bargain Negotiated exchange.

bargained exchange Mutually agreed-upon exchange.

basis of the bargain Part of the buyer's assumption underlying the sale.

battery Unlawful touching of another; intentional infliction of harmful or offensive bodily contact.

bearer Person in possession of an instrument.

bearer paper Payable to holder of the instrument.

beneficiary One who benefits from act of another. See also **third-party beneficiary**.

   Incidental A person who may derive benefit from performance on contract, though he is neither the promisee nor the one to whom performance is to be rendered. Since the incidental beneficiary is not a donee or creditor beneficiary (see **third-party beneficiary**), he has no right to enforce the contract.

   Intended beneficiary Third party intended by the two contracted parties to receive a benefit from their contract.

   Trust As it relates to trust beneficiaries, includes a person who has any present or future interest, vested or contingent, and also includes the owner of an interest by assignment or other transfer and, as it relates to a charitable trust, includes any person entitled to enforce the trust.

beyond a reasonable doubt Proof that is entirely convincing and satisfying to a moral certainty; criminal law standard.

bilateral contract Contract in which both parties exchange promises.

bill of lading Document evidencing receipt of goods for shipment issued by person engaged in business of transporting or forwarding goods; includes airbill.

   Through bill of lading A bill of lading which specifies at least one connecting carrier.

bill of sale A written agreement, formerly limited to one under seal, by which one person assigns or transfers his right to or interest in goods and personal chattels to another.

binder A written memorandum of the important terms of a contract of insurance which gives temporary protection to an insured pending investigation of risk by the insurance company or until a formal policy is issued.

blue law Prohibition of certain types of commercial activity on Sunday.

blue sky laws A popular name for state statutes providing for the regulation and supervision of securities offerings and sales, to protect citizen-investors from investing in fraudulent companies.

bona fide Latin. In good faith.

bond A certificate or evidence of a debt on which the issuing company or governmental body promises to pay the bondholders a specified amount of interest for a specified length of time and to repay the loan on the expiration date. In every case, a bond represents debt—its holder is a creditor of the corporation, not a part owner, as the shareholder is.

boycott Agreement among parties not to deal with a third party.

breach Wrongful failure to perform the terms of a contract.

Material breach Nonperformance which significantly impairs the aggrieved party's rights under the contract.

bribery Offering property to a public official to influence the official's decision.

bulk transfer Transfer not in the ordinary course of the transferor's business of a major part of his inventory.

burglary Breaking and entering the home of another at night with intent to commit a felony.

business judgment rule Protects directors from liability for honest mistakes of judgment.

business trust A trust (managed by a trustee for the benefit of a beneficiary) established to conduct a business for a profit.

but for rule Person's negligent conduct is a cause of an event if the event would not have occurred in the absence of that conduct.

buyer in ordinary course of business Person who buys in ordinary course, in good faith, and without knowledge that the sale to him is in violation of anyone's ownership rights or of a security interest.

by-laws Regulations, ordinances, rules, or laws adopted by an association or corporation for its government.

C

callable bond Bond that is subject to redemption (reacquisition) by the corporation.

cancellation One party's putting an end to a contract because of a breach by other party.

capital Accumulated goods, possessions, and assets, used for the production of profits and wealth. Owners' equity in a business. Also used to refer to the total assets of a business or to capital assets.

capital surplus Surplus other than earned surplus.

carrier Transporter of goods.

casualty insurance Covers property loss due to causes other than fire or the elements.

cause of action The ground on which an action may be sustained.

caveat emptor Latin. Let the buyer beware. This maxim is more applicable to judicial sales, auctions, and the like than to sales of consumer goods, where strict liability, warranty, and other laws protect.

certificate of deposit A written acknowledgment by a bank or banker of a deposit with promise to pay to depositor, to his order, or to some other person or to his order.

certificate of title Official representation of ownership.

certification Acceptance of a check by a drawee bank.

certification of incorporation See **articles of incorporation**.

certification mark Distinctive symbol, word, or design used with goods or services to certify specific characteristics.

certiorari Latin. To be informed of. A writ of common law origin issued by a superior to an inferior court requiring the latter to produce a certified record of a particular case tried therein. It is most commonly used to refer to the Supreme Court of the United States, which uses the writ of certiorari as a discretionary device to choose the cases it wishes to hear.

chancery Equity; equitable jurisdiction; a court of equity; the system of jurisprudence administered in courts of equity.

charging order Judicial lien against a partner's interest in the partnership.

charter An instrument emanating from the sovereign power, in the nature of a grant. A charter differs from a constitution in that the former is granted by the sovereign, while the latter is established by the people themselves.

Corporate law An act of a legislature creating a corporation or creating and defining the franchise of a corporation. Also a corporation's constitution or organic law; that is to say, the articles of incorporation taken in connection with the law under which the corporation was organized.

chattel mortgage A pre-Uniform Commercial Code security device whereby the mortgagee took a security interest in personal property of the mortgagor. Such security device has generally been superseded by other types of security agreements under UCC Article 9 (Secured Transactions).

chattel paper Writings that evidence both a debt and a security interest.

check A draft drawn upon a bank and payable on demand, signed by the maker or drawer, containing an unconditional promise to pay a sum certain in money to the order of the payee.

Cashier's check A bank's own check drawn on itself and signed by the cashier or other authorized official. It is a direct obligation of the bank.

C. & F. Cost and freight; a shipping contract.

C.I.F. Cost, insurance, and freight; a shipping contract.

civil law Laws concerned with civil or private rights and remedies, as contrasted with criminal laws.

The system of jurisprudence administered in the Roman empire, particularly as set forth in the compilation of Justinian and his successors, as distinguished from the common law of England and the canon law. The civil law (Civil Code) is followed by Louisiana.

claim A right to payment.

clearinghouse An association of banks for the purpose of settling accounts on a daily basis.

close corporation See **corporation**.

closed-ended credit Credit extended to debtor for a specific period of time.

closed shop An employer who can only hire union members.

C.O.D. Collect on delivery; generally a shipping contract.

code A compilation of all permanent laws in force consolidated and classified according to subject matter. Many states have published official codes of all laws in force, including the common law and statutes as judicially interpreted, which have been compiled by code commissions and enacted by the legislatures.

codicil A supplement or an addition to a will; it may explain, modify, add to, subtract from, qualify, alter, restrain, or revoke provisions in an existing will. It must be executed with the same formalities as a will.

cognovit judgment Written authority by debtor for entry of judgment against him in the event he defaults in payment. Such provision in a debt instrument on default confers judgment against the debtor.

collateral Secondarily liable; liable only if the party with primary liability does not perform.

collateral (security) Personal property subject to security interest.

Banking Some form of security in addition to the personal obligation of the borrower.

collateral promise Undertaking to be secondarily liable, that is, liable if the principal debtor does not perform.

collecting bank Any bank, except the payor bank, handling the item for collection.

collective mark Distinctive symbol used to indicate membership in an organization.

collision insurance Protects the owner of an automobile against damage due to contact with other vehicles or objects.

commerce power Exclusive power granted by the U.S. Constitution to the federal government to regulate commerce with foreign countries and among the states.

commercial bailment Bailment in which parties derive a mutual benefit.

commercial impracticability Performance can only be accomplished with unforeseen and unjust hardship.

commercial law A phrase used to designate the whole body of substantive jurisprudence (*e.g.*, Uniform Commercial Code; Truth in Lending Act) applicable to the rights, intercourse, and relations of persons engaged in commerce, trade, or mercantile pursuits. See **Uniform Commercial Code**.

commercial paper   Bills of exchange (*i.e.*, drafts), promissory notes, bank checks, and other negotiable instruments for the payment of money, which, by their form and on their face, purport to be such instruments. UCC Article 3 is the general law governing commercial paper.

commercial reasonableness   Judgment of reasonable persons familiar with the business transaction.

commercial speech   Expression related to the economic interests of the speaker and its audience.

common carrier   Carrier open to the general public.

common law   Body of law originating in England and derived from judicial decisions. As distinguished from statutory law created by the enactment of legislatures, the common law comprises the judgments and decrees of the courts recognizing, affirming, and enforcing usages and customs of immemorial antiquity.

community property   Rights of a spouse in property acquired by the other during marriage.

comparable worth   Equal pay for jobs of equal value to the employer.

comparative negligence   Under comparative negligence statutes or doctrines, negligence is measured in terms of percentage, and any damages allowed shall be diminished in proportion to amount of negligence attributable to the person for whose injury, damage, or death recovery is sought.

complainant   One who applies to the courts for legal redress by filing a complaint (*i.e.*, plaintiff).

complaint   The pleading which sets forth a claim for relief. Such complaint (whether it be the original claim, counterclaim, cross-claim, or third-party claim) shall contain (1) a short, plain statement of the grounds upon which the court's jurisdiction depends, unless the court already has jurisdiction and the claim needs no new grounds of jurisdiction to support it, (2) a short, plain statement of the claim showing that the pleader is entitled to relief, and (3) a demand for judgment for the relief to which he deems himself entitled. Fed.R. Civil P. 8(a). The complaint, together with the summons, is required to be served on the defendant. Rule 4.

composition   Agreement between debtor and two or more of her creditors that each will take a portion of his claim as full payment.

compulsory arbitration   Arbitration required by statute for specific types of disputes.

computer crime   Crime committed against or through the use of a computer or computer/services.

concealment   Fraudulent failure to disclose a material fact.

conciliation   Nonbinding process in which a third party acts as an intermediary between disputing parties.

concurrent jurisdiction   Authority of more than one court to hear the same case.

condition   An uncertain event which affects the duty of performance.
   Concurrent conditions   The parties are to perform simultaneously.
   Express condition   Performance is contingent on the happening or nonhappening of a stated event.

condition precedent   An event which must occur or not occur before performance is due; event or events (presentment, dishonor, notice of dishonor) which must occur to hold a secondary party liable to commercial paper.

condition subsequent   An event which terminates a duty of performance.

conditional acceptance   An acceptance of an offer contingent upon the acceptance of an additional or different term.

conditional contract   Obligations are contingent upon a stated event.

conditional guarantor of collection   Surety liable to creditor only after creditor exhausts his legal remedies against the principal debtor.

confession of judgment   Written agreement by debtor authorizing creditor to obtain a court judgment in the event debtor defaults. See also **cognovit judgment**.

confiscation   Governmental taking of foreign-owned property without payment.

conflict of laws   That branch of jurisprudence, arising from the diversity of the laws of different nations, states, or jurisdictions, that reconciles the inconsistencies, or decides which law is to govern in a particular case.

confusion   Results when goods belonging to two or more owners become so intermixed that the property of any of them no longer can be identified except as part of a mass of like goods.

consanguinity   Kinship; blood relationship; the connection or relation of persons descended from the same stock or common ancestor.

consensual arbitration   Arbitration voluntarily entered into by the parties.

consent   Voluntary and knowing willingness that an act should be done.

conservator   Appointed by court to manage affairs of incompetent or to liquidate business.

consideration   The cause, motive, price, or impelling influence which induces a contracting party to enter into a contract. Some right, interest, profit, or benefit accruing to one party or some forbearance, detriment, loss, or responsibility given, suffered, or undertaken by the other.

consignee   One to whom a consignment is made. Person named in bill of lading to whom or to whose order the bill promises delivery.

consignment   Ordinarily implies an agency; denotes that property is committed to the consignee for care or sale.

consignor   One who sends or makes a consignment; a shipper of goods. The person named in a bill of lading as the person from whom the goods have been received for shipment.

consolidation   In *corporate law*, the combination of two or more corporations into a newly created corporation. Thus, A Corporation and B Corporation consolidate to form C Corporation.

constitution   Fundamental law of a government establishing its powers and limitations.

constructive   That which is established by the mind of the law in its act of *construing* facts, conduct, circumstances, or instruments. That which has not in its essential nature the character assigned to it, but acquires such character in consequence of the way in which it is regarded by a rule or policy of law; hence, inferred, implied, or made out by legal interpretation; the word "legal" being sometimes used here in lieu of "constructive."

constructive assent   An assent or consent imputed to a party from a construction or interpretation of his conduct; as distinguished from one which he actually expresses.

constructive conditions   Conditions in contracts which are neither expressed nor implied but rather are imposed by law to meet the ends of justice.

constructive delivery   Term comprehending all those acts which, although not truly conferring a real possession of the vendee, have been held by construction of law to be equivalent to acts of real delivery.

constructive eviction   Failure by the landlord in any obligation under the lease that causes a substantial and lasting injury to the tenant's enjoyment of the premises.

constructive notice   Knowledge imputed by law.

constructive trust   Arising by operation of law to prevent unjust enrichment. See also **trustee**.

consumer goods   Goods bought or used for personal, family, or household purposes.

consumer product   Tangible personal property normally used for family, household, or personal purposes.

contingent remainder   Remainder interest, conditional upon the happening of an event in addition to the termination of the preceding estate.

contract   An agreement between two or more persons which creates an obligation to do or not to do a particular thing. Its essentials are competent parties, subject matter, a legal consideration, mutuality of agreement, and mutuality of obligation.

Destination contract Seller is required to tender delivery of the goods at a particular destination; seller bears the expense and risk of loss.

Executed contract Fully performed by all of the parties.

Executory contract Contract partially or entirely unperformed by one or more of the parties.

Express contract Agreement of parties that is expressed in words either in writing or orally.

Formal contract Agreement which is legally binding because of its particular form or mode or expression.

Implied-in-fact contract Contract where agreement of the parties is inferred from their conduct.

Informal contract All oral or written contracts other than formal contracts.

Installment contract Goods are delivered in separate lots.

Integrated contract Complete and total agreement.

Output contract A contract in which one party agrees to sell his entire output and the other agrees to buy it; it is not illusory, though it may be indefinite.

Quasi contract Obligation not based upon contract that is imposed to avoid injustice.

Requirements contract A contract in which one party agrees to purchase his total requirements from the other party; hence, such a contract is binding, not illusory.

Substituted contract An agreement between the parties to rescind their old contract and replace it with a new contract.

Unconscionable contract One which no sensible person not under delusion, duress, or in distress would make, and such as no honest and fair person would accept. A contract the terms of which are excessively unreasonable, overreaching, and one-sided.

Unenforceable contract Contract for the breach of which the law does not provide a remedy.

Unilateral and bilateral A unilateral contract is one in which one party makes an express engagement or undertakes a performance, without receiving in return any express engagement or promise of performance from the other. Bilateral (or reciprocal) contracts are those by which the parties expressly enter into mutual engagements.

contract clause Prohibition against the states' retroactively modifying public and private contracts.

contractual liability Obligation on a negotiable instrument, based upon signing the instrument.

contribution Payment from cosureties of their proportionate share.

contributory negligence An act or omission amounting to a want of ordinary care on the part of the complaining party, which, concurring with defendant's negligence, is proximate cause of injury.

The defense of contributory negligence is an absolute bar to any recovery in some states; because of this, it has been replaced by the doctrine of comparative negligence in many other states.

conversion Unauthorized and wrongful exercise of dominion and control over another's personal property, to exclusion of or inconsistent with rights of the owner.

convertible bond Bond that may be exchanged for other securities of the corporation.

copyright Exclusive right granted by federal government to authors of original works including literary, musical, dramatic, pictorial, graphic, sculptural, and film works.

corporation A legal entity ordinarily consisting of an association of numerous individuals. Such entity is regarded as having a personality and existence distinct from that of its several members and is vested with the capacity of continuous succession, irrespective of changes in its membership, either in perpetuity or for a limited term of years.

Closely held or close corporation Corporation that is owned by few shareholders and whose shares are not actively traded.

Corporation de facto One existing under color of law and in pursuance of an effort made in good faith to organize a corporation under the statute. Such a corporation is not subject to collateral attack.

Corporation de jure That which exists by reason of full compliance with requirements of an existing law permitting organization of such corporation.

Domestic corporation Corporation created under the laws of a given state.

Foreign corporation Corporation created under the laws of any other state, government, or country.

Publicly held corporation Corporation whose shares are owned by a large number of people and are widely traded.

Subchapter S corporation A small business corporation which, under certain conditions, may elect to have its undistributed taxable income taxed to its shareholders. Of major significance is the fact that Subchapter S status usually avoids the corporate income tax, and corporate losses can be claimed by the shareholders.

Subsidiary and parent Subsidiary corporation is one in which another corporation (called parent corporation) owns at least a majority of the shares and over which it thus has control.

corrective advertising Disclosure in an advertisement that previous ads were deceptive.

costs A pecuniary allowance, made to the successful party (and recoverable from the losing party), for his expenses in prosecuting or defending an action or a distinct proceeding within an action. Generally, "costs" do not include attorneys' fees unless such fees are by a statute denominated costs or are by statute allowed to be recovered as costs in the case.

cosureties Two or more sureties bound for the same debt of a principal debtor.

co-tenants Persons who hold title concurrently.

counterclaim A claim presented by a defendant in opposition to or deduction from the claim of the plaintiff.

counteroffer A statement by the offeree which has the legal effect of rejecting the offer and of proposing a new offer to the offeror. However, the provisions of the UCC modify this principle by providing that the "additional terms are to be construed as proposals for addition to the contract."

course of dealing A sequence of previous acts and conduct between the parties to a particular transaction which is fairly to be regarded as establishing a common basis of understanding for interpreting their expressions and other conduct.

course of performance Conduct between the parties concerning performance of the particular contract.

court above—court below In appellate practice, the "court above" is the one to which a cause is removed for review, whether by appeal, writ of error, or certiorari, while the "court below" is the one from which the case is being removed.

covenant Used primarily with respect to promises in conveyances or other instruments dealing with real estate.

Covenants against encumbrances A stipulation against all rights to or interests in the land which may subsist in third persons to the diminution of the value of the estate granted.

Covenant appurtenant A covenant which is connected with land of the grantor, not in gross. A covenant running with the land and binding heirs, executors, and assigns of the immediate parties.

Covenant for further assurance An undertaking, in the form of a covenant, on the part of the vendor of real estate to do such further acts for the purpose of perfecting the purchaser's title as the latter may reasonably require.

Covenant for possession A covenant by which the grantee or lessee is granted possession.

Covenant for quiet enjoyment An assurance against the consequences of a defective title, and against any disturbances thereupon.

Covenants for title Covenants usually inserted in a conveyance of land, on the part of the grantor, and binding him for the completeness, security, and continuance of the title transferred to the grantee. They comprise covenants for seisin, for right to convey, against encumbrances, or quiet enjoyment, sometimes for further assurance, and almost always of warranty.

Covenant in gross   Such as do not run with the land.

Covenant of right to convey   An assurance by the covenantor that the grantor has sufficient capacity and title to convey the estate which he by his deed undertakes to convey.

Covenant of seisin   An assurance to the purchaser that the grantor has the very estate in quantity and quality which he purports to convey.

Covenant of warranty   An assurance by the grantor of an estate that the grantee shall enjoy the same without interruption by virtue of paramount title.

Covenant running with land   A covenant which goes with the land, as being annexed to the estate, and which cannot be separated from the land or transferred without it. A covenant is said to run with the land when not only the original parties or their representatives, but each successive owner of the land, will be entitled to its benefit, or be liable (as the case may be) to its obligation. Such a covenant is said to be one which "touches and concerns" the land itself, so that its benefit or obligation passes with the ownership. Essentials are that the grantor and grantee must have intended that the covenant run with the land, the covenant must affect or concern the land with which it runs, and there must be privity of estate between the party claiming the benefit and the party who rests under the burden.

covenant not to compete   Agreement to refrain from entering into a competing trade, profession, or business.

cover   Buyer's purchase of goods in substitution for those not delivered by breaching seller.

credit beneficiary   See **third-party beneficiary**.

creditor   Any entity having a claim against the debtor.

crime   An act or omission in violation of a public law and punishable by the government.

criminal duress   Coercion by threat of serious bodily injury.

criminal intent   Desired or virtually certain consequences of one's conduct.

criminal law   The law that involves offenses against the entire community.

cure   The right of a seller under the UCC to correct a nonconforming delivery of goods to buyer within the contract period.

curtesy   Husband's estate in the real property of his wife.

cy-pres   As near (as possible). Rule for the construction of instruments in equity, by which the intention of the party is carried out *as near as may be*, when it would be impossible or illegal to give it literal effect.

D

damage   Loss, injury, or deterioration caused by the negligence, design, or accident of one person, with respect to another's person or property. The word is to be distinguished from its plural, "damages," which means a compensation in money for a loss or damage.

damages   Money sought as a remedy for breach of contract or for tortious acts.

Actual damages   Real, substantial, and just damages, or the amount awarded to a complainant in compensation for his actual and real loss or injury, as opposed, on the one hand, to "nominal" damages and, on the other, to "exemplary" or "punitive" damages. Synonymous with "compensatory damages" and "general damages."

Benefit-of-the-bargain damages   Difference between the value received and the value of the fraudulent party's performance as represented.

Compensatory damages   Compensatory damages are such as will compensate the injured party for the injury sustained, and nothing more; such as will simply make good or replace the loss caused by the wrong or injury.

Consequential damages   Such damage, loss, or injury as does not flow directly and immediately from the act of the party, but only from some of the consequences or results of such act. Consequential damages resulting from a seller's breach of contract include any loss resulting from general or particular requirements and needs of which the seller at the time of contracting had reason to know and which could not reasonably be prevented by cover or otherwise, and injury to person or property proximately resulting from any breach of warranty.

Exemplary or punitive damages   Damages other than compensatory damages which may be awarded against a person to punish him for outrageous conduct.

Expectancy damages   Calculable by subtracting the injured party's actual dollar position as a result of the breach from that party's projected dollar position had performance occurred.

Foreseeable damages   Loss of which the party in breach had reason to know when the contract was made.

Incidental damages   Under the UCC, such damages include any commercially reasonable charges, expenses, or commissions incurred in stopping delivery, in the transportation, care, and custody of goods after the buyer's breach, in connection with the return or resale of the goods, or otherwise resulting from the breach. Also, such damages, resulting from a seller's breach of contract, include expenses reasonably incurred in inspection, receipt, transportation, and care and custody of goods rightfully rejected, any commercially reasonable charges, expenses, or commissions in connection with effecting cover, and any other reasonable expense incident to the delay or other breach.

Irreparable damages   In the law pertaining to injunctions, damages for which no certain pecuniary standard exists for measurement.

Liquidated damages and penalties   Damages for breach by either party may be liquidated in the agreement but only at an amount which is reasonable in the light of the anticipated or actual harm caused by the breach, the difficulties of proof of loss, and the inconvenience or nonfeasibility of otherwise obtaining an adequate remedy. A term fixing unreasonably large liquidated damages is void as a penalty.

Mitigation of damages   A plaintiff may not recover damages for the effects of an injury which she reasonably could have avoided or substantially ameliorated. This limitation on recovery is generally denominated as "mitigation of damages" or "avoidance of consequences."

Nominal damages   A small sum awarded where a contract has been breached but the loss is negligible or unproven.

Out-of-pocket damages   Difference between the value received and the value given.

Reliance damages   Contract damages placing the injured party in as good a position as he would have been in had the contract not been made.

Treble damages   Three times actual loss.

de facto   In fact, in deed, actually. This phrase is used to characterize an officer, a government, a past action, or a state of affairs which must be accepted for all practical purposes but which is illegal or illegitimate. See also **corporation**, *corporation de facto*.

de jure   Descriptive of a condition in which there has been total compliance with all requirements of law. In this sense it is the contrary of *de facto*. See also **corporation**, *corporation de jure*.

de novo   Anew; afresh; a second time.

debenture   Unsecured bond.

debt security   Any form of corporate security reflected as debt on the books of the corporation in contrast to equity securities such as stock; *e.g.,* bonds, notes, and debentures are debt securities.

debtor   Person who owes payment or performance of an obligation.

deceit   A fraudulent and cheating misrepresentation, artifice, or device used to deceive and trick one who is ignorant of the true facts, to the prejudice and damage of the party imposed upon. See also **fraud**; **misrepresentation**.

decree   Decision of a court of equity.

deed   A conveyance of realty; a writing, signed by a grantor, whereby title to realty is transferred from one party to another.

deed of trust   Interest in real property which is conveyed to a third person as trustee for the creditor.

defamation Injury of a person's reputation by publication of false statements.

default judgment Judgment against a defendant who fails to respond to a complaint.

defendant The party against whom legal action is sought.

definite term Lease that automatically expires at end of the term.

delectus personae Partner's right to choose who may become a member of the partnership.

delegatee Third party to whom the delegator's duty is delegated.

delegation of duties Transferring to another all or part of one's duties arising under a contract.

delegator Party delegating his duty to a third party.

delivery The physical or constructive transfer of an instrument or of goods from one person to another. See also **constructive delivery**.

demand Request for payment made by the holder of the instrument.

demand paper Payable on request.

demurrer An allegation of a defendant that even if the facts as stated in the pleading to which objection is taken be true, their legal consequences are not such as to require the demurring party to answer them or to proceed further with the cause.

    The Federal Rules of Civil Procedure do not provide for the use of a demurrer, but provide an equivalent to a general demurrer in the motion to dismiss for failure to state a claim on which relief may be granted. Fed.R. Civil P. 12(b).

depositary bank The first bank to which an item is transferred for collection even though it may also be the payor bank.

deposition The testimony of a witness taken upon interrogatories, not in court, but intended to be used in court. See also **discovery**.

descent Succession to the ownership of an estate by inheritance or by any act of law, as distinguished from "purchase."

    Descents are of two sorts, lineal and collateral. Lineal descent is descent in a direct or right line, as from father or grandfather to son or grandson. Collateral descent is descent in a collateral or oblique line, that is, up to the common ancestor and then down from him, as from brother to brother, or between cousins.

design defect Plans or specifications inadequate to ensure the product's safety.

devise A testamentary disposition of land or realty; a gift of real property by the last will and testament of the donor. When used as a noun, means a testamentary disposition of real or personal property; when used as a verb, means to dispose of real or personal property by will.

dictum Generally used as an abbreviated form of *obiter dictum*, "a remark by the way"; that is, an observation or remark made by a judge which does not embody the resolution or determination of the court and which is made without argument or full consideration of the point.

directed verdict In a case in which the party with the burden of proof has failed to present a prima facie case for jury consideration, the trial judge may order the entry of a verdict without allowing the jury to consider it because, as a matter of law, there can be only one such verdict.

disaffirmance Avoidance of a contract.

discharge Termination of certain allowed claims against a debtor.

disclaimer Negation of warranty.

discount A discount by a bank means a drawback or deduction made upon its advances or loans of money, upon negotiable paper or other evidences of debt payable at a future day, which are transferred to the bank.

discovery The pretrial devices that can be used by one party to obtain facts and information about the case from the other party in order to assist the party's preparation for trial. Under the Federal Rules of Civil Procedure, tools of discovery include depositions upon oral and written questions, written interrogatories, production of documents or things, permission to enter upon land or other property, physical and mental examinations, and requests for admission.

dishonor To refuse to accept or pay a draft or to pay a promissory note when duly presented. See also **protest**.

disparagement Publication of false statements resulting in harm to another's monetary interests.

disputed debt Obligation whose existence or amount is contested.

dissenting shareholder One who opposes a fundamental change and has the right to receive the fair value of her shares.

dissolution The dissolution of a partnership is the change in the relation of the partners caused by any partner's ceasing to be associated with the carrying on, as distinguished from the winding up, of the business. See also **winding up**.

distribution Transfer of partnership property from the partnership to a partner; transfer of property from a corporation to any of its shareholders.

dividend The payment designated by the board of directors of a corporation to be distributed pro rata among a class or classes of the shares outstanding.

document Document of title.

document of title Instrument evidencing ownership of the document and the goods it covers.

domicile That place where a person has his true, fixed, and permanent home and principal establishment, and to which whenever he is absent he has the intention of returning.

dominant Land whose owner has rights in other land.

donee Recipient of a gift.

donee beneficiary See **third-party beneficiary**.

donor Maker of a gift.

dormant partner One who is both a silent and a secret partner.

dower A species of life-estate which a woman is, by law, entitled to claim on the death of her husband, in the lands and tenements of which he was seised in fee during the marriage, and which her issue, if any, might by possibility have inherited.

    Dower has been abolished in the majority of the states and materially altered in most of the others.

draft A written order by the first party, called the drawer, instructing a second party, called the drawee (such as a bank), to pay a third party, called the payee. An order to pay a sum certain in money, signed by a drawer, payable on demand or at a definite time, and to order or bearer.

drawee A person to whom a bill of exchange or draft is directed, and who is requested to pay the amount of money therein mentioned. The drawee of a check is the bank on which it is drawn.

    When a drawee accepts, he engages that he will pay the instrument according to its tenor at the time of his engagement or as completed.

drawer The person who draws a bill or draft. The drawer of a check is the person who signs it.

    The drawer engages that upon dishonor of the draft and any necessary notice of dishonor or protest, he will pay the amount of the draft to the holder or to any indorser who takes it up. The drawer may disclaim this liability by drawing without recourse.

due negotiation Transfer of a negotiable document in the regular course of business to a holder, who takes in good faith, without notice of any defense or claim, and for value.

duress Unlawful constraint exercised upon a person, whereby he is forced to do some act against his will.
Physical duress Coercion involving physical force or the threat of physical force.

duty Legal obligation requiring a person to perform or refrain from performing an act.

E

earned surplus Undistributed net profits, income, gains, and losses.

earnest The payment of a part of the price of goods sold, or the delivery of part of such goods, for the purpose of binding the contract.

easement A right in the owner of one parcel of land, by reason of such ownership, to use the land of another for a special purpose not inconsistent with a general property right in the owner. This right is distinguishable from a "license," which merely confers a personal privilege to do some act on the land.

Affirmative easement One where the servient estate must permit something to be done thereon, as to pass over it, or to discharge water on it.

Appurtenant easement An incorporeal right which is attached to a superior right and inheres in land to which it is attached and is in the nature of a covenant running with the land.

Easement by necessity Such arises by operation of law when land conveyed is completely shut off from access to any road by land retained by the grantor or by land of the grantor and that of a stranger.

Easement by prescription A mode of acquiring title to property by immemorial or long-continued enjoyment; refers to personal usage restricted to claimant and his ancestors or grantors.

Easement in gross An easement in gross is not appurtenant to any estate in land or does not belong to any person by virtue of ownership of an estate in other land but is a mere personal interest in or a right to use the land of another; it is purely personal and usually ends with death of grantee.

Easement of access Right of ingress and egress to and from the premises of a lot owner to a street appurtenant to the land of the lot owner.

ejectment An action to determine whether the title to certain land is in the plaintiff or is in the defendant.

electronic funds transfer A transaction with a financial institution by means of computer, telephone, or other electronic instrument.

emancipation The act by which an infant is liberated from the control of a parent or guardian and made his own master.

embezzlement The taking, in violation of a trust, of the property of one's employer.

emergency Sudden, unexpected event calling for immediate action.

eminent domain Right of the people or government to take private property for public use upon giving fair consideration.

employment discrimination Hiring, firing, compensating, promoting, or training of employees based on race, color, sex, religion, or national origin.

employment relationship One in which employer has right to control the physical conduct of employee.

endowment contract Agreement to pay insured a lump sum upon reaching a specified age or in event of death.

entirety Used to designate that which the law considers as a single whole incapable of being divided into parts.

entrapment Induced by a government official into committing a crime.

entrusting Transfer of possession of goods to a merchant who deals in goods of that kind and who may in turn transfer valid title to a buyer in the ordinary course of business.

equal pay Equivalent pay for the same work.

equal protection Requirement that similarly situated persons be treated similarly by government action.

equipment Goods used primarily in business.

equitable Just, fair, and right. Existing in equity; available or sustainable only in equity, or only upon the rules and principles of equity.

equity Justice administered according to fairness, as contrasted with the strictly formulated rules of common law. It is based on a system of rules and principles which originated in England as an alternative to the harsh rules of common law and which were based on what was fair in a particular situation.

equity of redemption The right of the mortgagor of an estate to redeem the same after it has been forfeited, at law, by a breach of the condition of the mortgage, upon paying the amount of debt, interest, and costs.

equity securities Stock or similar security, in contrast to debt securities such as bonds, notes, and debentures.

error A mistake of law, or a false or irregular application of it, such as vitiates legal proceedings and warrants reversal of the judgment.

Harmless error In appellate practice, an error committed in the progress of the trial below which was not prejudicial to the rights of the party assigning it and for which, therefore, the appellate court will not reverse the judgment.

Reversible error In appellate practice, such an error as warrants the appellate court's reversal of the judgment before it.

escrow A system of document transfer in which a deed, bond, or funds is or are delivered to a third person to hold until all conditions in a contract are fulfilled; *e.g.*, delivery of deed to escrow agent under installment land sale contract until full payment for land is made.

estate The degree, quantity, nature, and extent of interest which a person has in real and personal property. An estate in lands, tenements, and hereditaments signifies such interest as the tenant has therein.

Also, the total property of whatever kind that is owned by a decedent prior to the distribution of that property in accordance with the terms of a will or, when there is no will, by the laws of inheritance in the state of domicile of the decedent.

Future estate An estate limited to commence in possession at a future day, either without the intervention of a precedent estate or on the determination by lapse of time, or otherwise, of a precedent estate created at the same time. Examples include reversions and remainders.

estoppel A bar or impediment raised by the law which precludes a person from alleging or from denying a certain fact or state of facts, in consequence of his or her previous allegation, denial, conduct, or admission, or in consequence of a final adjudication of the matter in a court of law. See also **waiver**.

eviction Dispossession by process of law; the act of depriving a person of the possession of lands which he has held, pursuant to the judgment of a court.

evidence Any species of proof or probative matter legally presented at the trial of an issue by the act of the parties and through the medium of witnesses, records, documents, concrete objects, etc., for the purpose of inducing belief in the minds of the court or jury as to the parties' contention.

exception A formal objection to the action of the court, during the trial of a cause, in refusing a request or overruling an objection; implying that the party excepting does not acquiesce in the decision of the court but will seek to procure its reversal, and that he means to save the benefit of his request or objection in some future proceeding.

exclusionary rule Prohibition of illegally obtained evidence.

exclusive dealing Sole right to sell goods in a defined market.

exclusive jurisdiction Such jurisdiction that permits only one court (state or federal) to hear a case.

exculpatory clause Excusing oneself from fault or liability.

execution *Execution of contract* includes performance of all acts necessary to render it complete as an instrument; implies that nothing more need be done to make the contract complete and effective.

Execution upon a money judgment is the legal process of enforcing the judgment, usually by seizing and selling property of the debtor.

executive order Legislation issued by the president or a governor.

executor A person appointed by a testator to carry out the directions and requests in his will and to dispose of the property according to his testamentary provisions after his decease. The female designation is executrix. A person appointed by the court in an intestacy situation is called the administrator(rix).

executory That which is yet to be executed or performed; that which remains to be carried into operation or effect; incomplete; depending upon a future performance or event. The opposite of executed.

executory contract See **contracts**.

executory promise Unperformed obligation.

exemplary damages See **damages**.

exoneration Relieved of liability.

express Manifested by direct and appropriate language, as distinguished from that which is inferred from conduct. The word is usually contrasted with "implied."

express warranty Explicitly made contractual promise regarding property or contract rights transferred; in a sale of goods, an affirmation of fact or a promise about the goods or a description, including a sample, of goods which becomes part of the basis of the bargain.

expropriation Governmental taking of foreign-owned property for a public purpose and with payment.

ex-ship Risk of loss passes to buyer when the goods leave the ship. See also **F.A.S.**

extortion Making threats to obtain property.

F

fact An event that took place or a thing that exists.

false imprisonment Intentional interference with a person's freedom of movement by unlawful confinement.

false light Offensive publicity placing another in a false light.

false pretenses Intentional misrepresentation of fact in order to cheat another.

farm products Crops, livestock, or stock used or produced in farming.

F.A.S. Free alongside. Term used in sales price quotations indicating that the price includes all costs of transportation and delivery of the goods alongside the ship.

federal preemption First right of the federal government to regulate matters within its powers to the possible exclusion of state regulation.

federal question Any case arising under the Constitution, statutes, or treaties of the United States.

fee simple

   Absolute A fee simple absolute is an estate that is unlimited as to duration, disposition, and descendibility. It is the largest estate and most extensive interest that can be enjoyed in land.

   Conditional Type of transfer in which grantor conveys fee simple on condition that something be done or not done.

   Defeasible Type of fee grant which may be defeated on the happening of an event. An estate which may last forever, but which may end upon the happening of a specified event, is a "fee simple defeasible."

   Determinable Created by conveyance which contains words effective to create a fee simple and, in addition, a provision for automatic expiration of the estate on occurrence of stated event.

fee tail An estate of inheritance, descending only to a certain class or classes of heirs; *e.g.*, an estate is conveyed or devised "to A. and the heirs of his body," or "to A. and the heirs male of his body," or "to A. and the heirs female of his body."

fellow servant rule Common law defense relieving employer from liability to an employee for injuries caused by negligence of fellow employee.

felony Serious crime.

fiduciary A person or institution who manages money or property for another and who must exercise in such management activity a standard of care imposed by law or contract; *e.g.*, executor of estate; receiver in bankruptcy; trustee.

fiduciary duty Duty of utmost loyalty and good faith, such as that owed by a fiduciary such as an agent to her principal.

field warehouse Secured party takes possession of the goods but the debtor has access to the goods.

final credit Payment of the instrument by the payor bank.

financing statement Under the Uniform Commercial Code, a financing statement is used under Article 9 to reflect a public record that there is a security interest or claim to the goods in question to secure a debt. The financing statement is filed by the security holder with the secretary of state or with a similar public body; thus filed, it becomes public record. See also **secured transaction**.

fire (property) insurance Provides protection against loss due to fire or other related perils.

firm offer Irrevocable offer to sell or buy goods by a merchant in a signed writing which gives assurance that it will not be rescinded for up to three months.

fitness for a particular purpose Goods are fit for a stated purpose, provided that the seller selects the product knowing the buyer's intended use and that the buyer is relying on the seller's judgment.

fixture An article in the nature of personal property which has been so annexed to realty that it is regarded as a part of the land. Examples include a furnace affixed to a house or other building, counters permanently affixed to the floor of a store, and a sprinkler system installed in a building.

   Trade fixtures Such chattels as merchants usually possess and annex to the premises occupied by them to enable them to store, handle, and display their goods, which generally are removable without material injury to the premises.

F.O.B. Free on board at some location (for example, F.O.B. shipping point; F.O.B. destination); the invoice price includes delivery at seller's expense to that location. Title to goods usually passes from seller to buyer at the F.O.B. location.

foreclosure Procedure by which mortgaged property is sold on default of mortgagor in satisfaction of mortgage debt.

forgery Intentional falsification of a document with intent to defraud.

four unities Time, title, interest, and possession.

franchise A privilege granted or sold, such as to use a name or to sell products or services. The right given by a manufacturer or supplier to a retailer to use his products and name on terms and conditions mutually agreed upon.

fraud Elements include false representation; of a present or past fact; made by defendant; action in reliance thereon by plaintiff; and damage resulting to plaintiff from such misrepresentation.

fraud in the execution Misrepresentation that deceives the other party as to the nature of a document evidencing the contract.

fraud in the inducement Misrepresentation regarding the subject matter of a contract that induces the other party to enter into the contract.

fraudulent misrepresentation False statement made with knowledge of its falsity and intent to mislead.

freehold An estate for life or in fee. It must possess two qualities: (1) immobility, that is, the property must be either land or some interest issuing out of or annexed to land; and (2) indeterminate duration.

friendly fire Fire contained where it is intended to be.

frustration of purpose doctrine Excuses a promisor in certain situations when the objectives of contract have been utterly defeated by circumstances arising after formation of the agreement, and performance is excused under this rule even though there is no impediment to actual performance.

full warranty One under which warrantor will repair the product and, if unsuccessful, will replace it or refund its cost.

fungibles With respect to goods or securities, those of which any unit is, by nature or usage of trade, the equivalent of any other like unit; *e.g.,* a bushel of wheat or other grain.

future estate See **estate**.

G

garnishment A statutory proceeding whereby a person's property, money, or credits in the possession or control of another are applied to payment of the former's debt to a third person.

general intangible Catchall category for collateral not otherwise covered.

general partner Member of either a general or limited partnership with unlimited liability for its debts, full management powers, and a right to share in the profits.

gift A voluntary transfer of property to another made gratuitously and without consideration. Essential requisites of "gift" are capacity of donor, intention of donor to make gift, completed delivery to or for donee, and acceptance of gift by donee.

gift causa mortis A gift in view of death is one which is made in contemplation, fear, or peril of death and with the intent that it shall take effect only in case of the death of the giver.

good faith Honesty in fact and the observance of reasonable commercial standards of fair dealing.

good faith purchaser Buyer who acts honestly, gives value, and takes the goods without notice or knowledge of any defect in the title of his transferor.

goods A term of variable content and meaning. It may include every species of personal property, or it may be given a very restricted meaning. Sometimes the meaning of "goods" is extended to include all tangible items, as in the phrase "goods and services."

All things (including specially manufactured goods) which are movable at the time of identification to a contract for sale other than the money in which the price is to be paid, investment securities, and things in action.

grantee Transferee of property.

grantor A transferor of property. The creator of a trust is usually designated as the grantor of the trust.

gratuitous promise Promise made without consideration.

group insurance Covers a number of individuals.

guaranty A promise to answer for the payment of some debt, or the performance of some duty, in case of the failure of another person who, in the first instance, is liable for such payment or performance.

The terms *guaranty* and *suretyship* are sometimes used interchangeably; but they should not be confounded. The distinction between contract of suretyship and contract of guaranty is whether or not the undertaking is a joint undertaking with the principal or a separate and distinct contract; if it is the former, it is one of "suretyship," and if the latter, it is one of "guaranty." See also **surety**.

guardianship The relationship under which a person (the guardian) is appointed by a court to preserve and control the property of another (the ward).

H

heir A person who succeeds, by the rules of law, to an estate in lands, tenements, or hereditaments, upon the death of his ancestor, by descent and right of relationship.

holder Person who is in possession of a document of title or an instrument or an investment security drawn, issued, or indorsed to him or to his order, or to bearer, or in blank.

holder in due course A holder who takes an instrument for value, in good faith, and without notice that it is overdue or has been dishonored or of any defense against or claim to it on the part of any person.

holograph A will or deed written entirely by the testator or grantor with his own hand and not witnessed (attested). State laws vary with respect to the validity of the holographic will.

homicide Unlawful taking of another's life.

horizontal privity Who may bring a cause of action.

horizontal restraints Agreements among competitors.

hostile fire Any fire outside its intended or usual place.

I

identified goods Designated goods as a part of a particular contract.

illegal per se Conclusively presumed unreasonable and therefore illegal.

illusory promise Promise imposing no obligation on the promisor.

implied-in-fact condition Contingencies understood but not expressed by the parties.

implied-in-law condition Contingency that arises from operation of law.

implied warranty Obligation imposed by law upon the transferor of property or contract rights; implicit in the sale arising out of certain circumstances.

implied warranty of habitability Leased premises are fit for ordinary residential purposes.

impossibility Performance that cannot be done.

in personam Against the person. Action seeking judgment against a person involving his personal rights and based on jurisdiction of his person, as distinguished from a judgment against property (*i.e.*, in rem).

in personam jurisdiction Jurisdiction based on claims against a person, in contrast to jurisdiction over his property.

in re In the affair; in the matter of; concerning; regarding. This is the usual method of entitling a judicial proceeding in which there are no adversary parties, but merely some res concerning which judicial action is to be taken, such as a bankrupt's estate, an estate in the probate court, a proposed public highway, etc.

in rem A technical term used to designate proceedings or actions instituted *against the thing*, in contradistinction to personal actions, which are said to be *in personam*.

Quasi in rem A term applied to proceedings which are not strictly and purely *in rem*, but are brought against the defendant personally, though the real object is to deal with particular property or subject property to the discharge of claims asserted; for example, foreign attachment, or proceedings to foreclose a mortgage, remove a cloud from title, or effect a partition.

in rem jurisdiction Jurisdiction based on claims against property.

incidental beneficiary Third party whom the two parties to a contract have no intention of benefiting by their contract.

income bond Bond that conditions payment of interest on corporate earnings.

incontestability clause The prohibition of an insurer to avoid an insurance policy after a specified period of time.

indemnification Duty owed by principal to agent to pay agent for losses incurred while acting as directed by principal.

indemnify To reimburse one for a loss already incurred.

indenture A written agreement under which bonds and debentures are issued, setting forth maturity date, interest rate, and other terms.

independent contractor Person who contracts with another to do a particular job and who is not subject to the control of the other.

indicia Signs; indications. Circumstances which point to the existence of a given fact as probable, but not certain.

indictment Grand jury charge that the defendant should stand trial.

indispensable paper Chattel paper, instruments, and documents.

indorsee The person to whom a negotiable instrument, promissory note, bill of lading, etc., is assigned by indorsement.

indorsement The act of a payee, drawee, accommodation indorser, or holder of a bill, note, check, or other negotiable instrument, in writing his name upon the back of the same, with or without further or qualifying words, whereby the property in the same is assigned and transferred to another.

Blank indorsement No indorsee is specified.

Qualified indorsement Without recourse, limiting one's liability on the instrument.

Restrictive indorsement Limits the rights of the indorser in some manner.

Special indorsement Designates an indorsee to be paid.

infliction of emotional distress Extreme and outrageous conduct intentionally or recklessly causing severe emotional distress.

information Formal accusation of a crime brought by a prosecutor.

infringement Unauthorized use.

injunction An equitable remedy forbidding the party defendant from doing some act which he is threatening or attempting to commit, or restraining him in the continuance thereof, such act being unjust and inequitable, injurious to the plaintiff, and not such as can be adequately redressed by an action at law.

innkeeper Hotel or motel operator.

inquisitorial system System in which the judiciary initiates, conducts, and decides cases.

insider Relative or general partner of debtor, partnership in which debtor is a partner, or corporation in which debtor is an officer, director, or controlling person.

insiders Directors, officers, employees, and agents of the issuer as well as those the issuer has entrusted with information solely for corporate purposes.

insolvency Under the UCC, a person is insolvent who either has ceased to pay his debts in the ordinary course of business or cannot pay his debts as they fall due or is insolvent within the meaning of the Federal Bankruptcy Law.

Insolvency (bankruptcy) Total liabilities exceed total value of assets.

Insolvency (equity) Inability to pay debts in ordinary course of business or as they become due.

inspection Examination of goods to determine whether they conform to a contract.

instrument Negotiable instruments, stocks, bonds, and other investment securities.

insurable interest Exists where insured derives pecuniary benefit or advantage by preservation and continued existence of property or would sustain pecuniary loss from its destruction.

insurance A contract whereby, for a stipulated consideration, one party undertakes to compensate the other for loss on a specified subject by specified perils. The party agreeing to make the compensation is usually called the "insurer" or "underwriter"; the other, the "insured" or "assured"; the written contract, a "policy"; the events insured against, "risks" or "perils"; and the subject, right, or interest to be protected, the "insurable interest." Insurance is a contract whereby one undertakes to indemnify another against loss, damage, or liability arising from an unknown or contingent event.

Co-insurance A form of insurance in which a person insures property for less than its full or stated value and agrees to share the risk of loss.

Life insurance Payment of a specific sum of money to a designated beneficiary upon the death of the insured.

Ordinary life Life insurance with a savings component that runs for the life of the insured.

Term life Life insurance issued for a limited number of years that does not have a savings component.

intangible property Protected interests that are not physical.

intangibles Accounts and general intangibles.

intent Desire to cause the consequences of an act or knowledge that the consequences are substantially certain to result from the act.

inter alia Among other things.

inter se or **inter sese** Latin. Among or between themselves; used to distinguish rights or duties between two or more parties from their rights or duties to others.

interest in land Any right, privilege, power, or immunity in real property.

interest in partnership Partner's share in the partnership's profits and surplus.

interference with contractual relations Intentionally causing one of the parties to a contract not to perform the contract.

intermediary bank Any bank, except the depositary or payor bank, to which an item is transferred in the course of collection.

intermediate test Requirement that legislation have a substantial relationship to an important governmental objective.

international law Deals with the conduct and relations of nation-states and international organizations.

interpretation Construction or meaning of a contract.

interpretative rules Statements issued by an administrative agency indicating its construction of its governing statute.

intestate A person is said to die intestate when he dies without making a will. The word is also often used to signify the person himself. *Compare* **testator.**

intrusion Unreasonable and highly offensive interference with the seclusion of another.

inventory Goods held for sale or lease or consumed in a business.

invitee A person is an "invitee" on land of another if (1) he enters by invitation, express or implied, (2) his entry is connected with the owner's business or with an activity the owner conducts or permits to be conducted on his land, and (3) there is mutual benefit or a benefit to the owner.

J

joint liability Liability where creditor must sue all of the partners as a group.

joint and several liability Liability where creditor may sue partners jointly as a group or separately as individuals.

joint stock company A general partnership with some corporate attributes.

joint tenancy See **tenancy.**

joint venture An association of two or more persons to carry on a single business transaction for profit.

judgment The official and authentic decision of a court of justice upon the respective rights and claims of the parties to an action or suit therein litigated and submitted to its determination.

judgment in personam A judgment against a particular person, as distinguished from a judgment against a thing or a right or *status.*

judgment in rem An adjudication pronounced upon the status of some particular thing or subject matter, by a tribunal having competent authority.

judgment n.o.v. Judgment non obstante veredicto in its broadest sense is a judgment rendered in favor of one party notwithstanding the finding of a verdict in favor of the other party.

judgment notwithstanding the verdict A final binding determination on the merits made by the judge after and contrary to the jury's verdict.

judgment on the pleadings Final binding determination on the merits made by the judge after the pleadings.

judicial lien Interest in property that is obtained by court action to secure payment of a debt.

judicial review Power of the courts to determine the constitutionality of legislative and executive acts.

jurisdiction The right and power of a court to adjudicate concerning the subject matter in a given case.

jurisdiction over the parties Power of a court to bind the parties to a suit.

jury A body of persons selected and summoned by law and sworn to try the facts of a case and to find according to the law and the evidence. In general, the province of the jury is to find the facts in a case, while the judge passes upon pure questions of law. As a matter of fact, however, the jury must often pass upon mixed questions of law and fact in determining the case, and in all such cases the instructions of the judge as to the law become very important.

justifiable reliance Reasonably influenced by a misrepresentation.

L

labor dispute Any controversy concerning terms or conditions of employment or union representation.

laches Based upon the maxim that equity aids the vigilant and not those who slumber on their rights. It is defined as neglect to assert a right or claim which, taken together with a lapse of time and other circumstances causing prejudice to the adverse party, operates as a bar in a court of equity.

landlord The owner of an estate in land, or a rental property, who has leased it to another person, called the "tenant." Also called "lessor."

larceny Trespassory taking and carrying away of the goods of another with the intent to permanently deprive.

last clear chance Final opportunity to avoid an injury.

lease Any agreement which gives rise to relationship of landlord and tenant (real property) or lessor and lessee (real or personal property).
The person who conveys is termed the "lessor," and the person to whom conveyed, the "lessee"; and when the lessor conveys land or tenements to a lessee, he is said to lease, demise, or let them.

Sublease, or *underlease* One executed by the lessee of an estate to a third person, conveying the same estate for a shorter term than that for which the lessee holds it.

leasehold An estate in realty held under a lease. The four principal types of leasehold estates are the estate for years, periodic tenancy, tenancy at will, and tenancy at sufferance.

leasehold estate Right to possess real property.

legacy "Legacy" is a gift or bequest by will of personal property, whereas a "devise" is a testamentary disposition of real estate.

Demonstrative legacy A bequest of a certain sum of money, with a direction that it shall be paid out of a particular fund. It differs from a specific legacy in this respect: that, if the fund out of which it is payable fails for any cause, it is nevertheless entitled to come on the estate as a general legacy. And it differs from a general legacy in this: that it does not abate in that class, but in the class of specific legacies.

General legacy A pecuniary legacy, payable out of the general assets of a testator.

Residuary legacy A bequest of all the testator's personal estate not otherwise effectually disposed of by his will.

Specific legacy One which operates on property particularly designated. A legacy or gift by will of a particular specified thing, as of a horse, a piece of furniture, a term of years, and the like.

legal aggregate A group of individuals not having a legal existence separate from its members.

legal benefit Obtaining something to which one had no legal right.

legal detriment Doing an act one is not legally obligated to do or not doing an act one has a legal right to do.

legal entity An organization having a legal existence separate from that of its members.

legal sufficiency Benefit to promisor or detriment to promisee.

legislative rules Substantive rules issued by an administrative agency under the authority delegated to it by the legislature.

letter of credit An engagement by a bank or other person made at the request of a customer that the issuer will honor drafts or other demands for payment upon compliance with the conditions specified in the credit.

letters of administration Formal documents issued by probate court appointing one an administrator of an estate.

letters testamentary The formal instrument of authority and appointment given to an executor by the proper court, empowering him to enter upon the discharge of his office as executor. It corresponds to letters of administration granted to an administrator.

levy To assess; raise; execute; exact; tax; collect; gather; take up; seize. Thus, to levy (assess, exact, raise, or collect) a tax; to levy an execution, *i.e.*, to levy or collect a sum of money on an execution.

liability insurance Covers liability to others by reason of damage resulting from injuries to another's person or property.

liability without fault Crime to do a specific act or cause a certain result without regard to the care exercised.

libel Defamation communicated by writing, television, radio, or the like.

liberty Ability of individuals to engage in freedom of action and choice regarding their personal lives.

license License with respect to real property is a privilege to go on premises for a certain purpose, but does not operate to confer on or vest in the licensee any title, interest, or estate in such property.

licensee Person privileged to enter or remain on land by virtue of the consent of the lawful possessor.

lien A qualified right of property which a creditor has in or over specific property of his debtor, as security for the debt or charge or for performance of some act.

lien creditor A creditor who has acquired a lien on the property by attachment.

life estate An estate whose duration is limited to the life of the party holding it or of some other person. Upon the death of the life tenant, the property will go to the holder of the remainder interest or to the grantor by reversion.

limited liability Liability limited to amount invested in a business enterprise.

limited partner Member of a limited partnership with liability for its debts only to the extent of her capital contribution.

limited partnership See **partnership**.

limited partnership association A partnership which closely resembles a corporation.

liquidated Ascertained; determined; fixed; settled; made clear or manifest. Cleared away; paid; discharged.

liquidated damages See **damages**.

liquidated debt Obligation that is certain in amount.

liquidation The settling of financial affairs of a business or individual, usually by liquidating (turning to cash) all assets for distribution to creditors, heirs, etc. To be distinguished from dissolution.

loss of value Value of promised performance minus value of actual performance.

lost property Property with which the owner has involuntarily parted and which she does not know where to find or recover, not including property which she has intentionally concealed or deposited in a secret place for safekeeping. Distinguishable from mislaid property, which has been deliberately placed somewhere and forgotten.

M

main purpose rule Where object of promisor/surety is to provide an economic benefit for herself, the promise is considered outside of the statute of frauds.

maker One who makes or executes; as the maker of a promissory note. One who signs a check; in this context, synonymous with drawer. See **draft**.

mala in se Morally wrong.

mala prohibita Wrong by law.

mandamus Latin, we command. A legal writ compelling the defendant to do an official duty.

manslaughter Unlawful taking of another's life without malice.

Involuntary manslaughter Taking the life of another by criminal negligence or during the course of a misdemeanor.

Voluntary manslaughter Intentional killing of another under extenuating circumstances.

manufacturing defect Not produced according to specifications.

mark Trade symbol.

market allocations Division of market by customers, geographic location, or products.

marketable title Free from any defects, encumbrances, or reasonable objections to one's ownership.

marshaling of assets Segregating the assets and liabilities of a partnership from the assets and liabilities of the individual partners.

master See **principal**.

material Matters to which a reasonable investor would attach importance in deciding whether to purchase a security.

material alteration Any change that changes the contract of any party to an instrument.

maturity The date at which an obligation, such as the principal of a bond or a note, becomes due.

maxim A general legal principle.

mechanic's lien A claim created by state statutes for the purpose of securing priority of payment of the price or value of work performed and materials furnished in erecting or repairing a building or other structure; as such, attaches to the land as well as buildings and improvements erected thereon.

mediation Nonbinding process in which a third party acts as an intermediary between the disputing parties and proposes solutions for them to consider.

mens rea Criminal intent.

mentally incompetent Unable to understand the nature and effect of one's acts.

mercantile law An expression substantially equivalent to commercial law. It designates the system of rules, customs, and usages generally recognized and adopted by merchants and traders that, either in its simplicity or as modified by common law or statutes, constitutes the law for the regulation of their transactions and the solution of their controversies. The Uniform Commercial Code is the general body of law governing commercial or mercantile transactions.

merchant A person who deals in goods of the kind involved in a transaction or who otherwise by his occupation holds himself out as having knowledge or skill peculiar to the practices or goods involved in the transaction or to whom such knowledge or skill may be attributed by his employment of an agent or broker or other intermediary who by his occupation holds himself out as having such knowledge or skill.

merchantability Merchant seller guarantees that the goods are fit for their ordinary purpose.

merger The fusion or absorption of one thing or right into another. In corporate law, the absorption of one company by another, the latter retaining its own name and identity and acquiring the assets, liabilities, franchises, and powers of the former, which ceases to exist as separate business entity. It differs from a consolidation, wherein all the corporations terminate their separate existences and become parties to a new one.

Conglomerate merger An acquisition, which is not horizontal or vertical, by one company of another.

Horizontal merger Merger between business competitors, such as manufacturers of the same type of products or distributors selling competing products in the same market area.

Short-form merger Merger of a 90 percent subsidiary into its parent.

Vertical merger Union with corporate customer or supplier.

midnight deadline Midnight of the next banking day after receiving an item.

mining partnership A specific type of partnership for the purpose of extracting raw minerals.

minor Under the age of legal majority (usually eighteen).

mirror image rule An acceptance cannot deviate from the terms of the offer.

misdemeanor Less serious crime.

mislaid property Property which an owner has put deliberately in a certain place that she is unable to remember, as distinguished from lost property, which the owner has left unwittingly in a location she has forgotten. See also **lost property**.

misrepresentation Any manifestation by words or other conduct by one person to another that, under the circumstances, amounts to an assertion not in accordance with the facts. A "misrepresentation" that justifies the rescission of a contract is a false statement of a substantive fact, or any conduct which leads to a belief of a substantive fact material to proper understanding of the matter in hand. See also **deceit**; **fraud**.
  Fraudulent misrepresentation False statement made with knowledge of its falsity and intent to mislead.
  Innocent misrepresentation Misrepresentation made without knowledge of its falsity but with due care.
  Negligent misrepresentation Misrepresentation made without due care in ascertaining its falsity.

M'Naghten Rule Right/wrong test for criminal insanity.

modify Change the lower court's judgment.

money Medium of exchange issued by a government body.

monopoly Ability to control price or exclude others from the marketplace.

mortgage A mortgage is an interest in land created by a written instrument providing security for the performance of a duty or the payment of a debt.

mortgagor Debtor who uses real estate to secure an obligation.

multinational enterprise Business that engages in transactions involving the movement of goods, information, money, people, or services across national borders.

multiple product order Order requiring an advertiser to cease and desist from deceptive statements on all products it sells.

murder Unlawful and premeditated taking of another's life.

mutual mistake Where the common but erroneous belief of both parties forms the basis of a contract.

N

necessaries Items needed to maintain a person's station in life.

negligence The omission to do something which a reasonable person, guided by those ordinary considerations which ordinarily regulate human affairs, would do, or the doing of something which a reasonable and prudent person would not do.
  Culpable negligence Greater than ordinary negligence but less than gross negligence.

negligence per se Conclusive on the issue of negligence (duty of care and breach).

negotiable Legally capable of being transferred by indorsement or delivery. Usually said of checks and notes and sometimes of stocks and bearer bonds.

negotiable instrument Signed document (such as a check or promissory note) containing an unconditional promise to pay a "sum certain" of money at a definite time to order or bearer.

negotiation Transferee becomes a holder.

net assets Total assets minus total debts.

no arrival, no sale A destination contract, but if goods do not arrive, seller is excused from liability unless such is due to the seller's fault.

no-fault insurance Compensates victims of automobile accidents regardless of fault.

nonconforming use Preexisting use not in accordance with a zoning ordinance.

nonprofit corporation One whose profits must be used exclusively for the charitable, educational, or scientific purpose for which it was formed.

nonsuit Action in form of a judgment taken against a plaintiff who has failed to appear to prosecute his action or failed to prove his case.

note See **promissory note**.

novation A novation substitutes a new party and discharges one of the original parties to a contract by agreement of all three parties. A new contract is created with the same terms as the original one; only the parties have changed.

nuisance Nuisance is that activity which arises from the unreasonable, unwarranted, or unlawful use by a person of his own property, working obstruction or injury to the right of another or to the public, and producing such material annoyance, inconvenience, and discomfort that law will presume resulting damage.

O

obiter dictum See **dictum**.

objective fault Gross deviation from reasonable conduct.

objective manifestation What a reasonable person under the circumstances would believe.

objective satisfaction Approval based upon whether a reasonable person would be satisfied.

objective standard What a reasonable person under the circumstances would reasonably believe or do.

obligee Party to whom a duty of performance is owed (by delegator and delegatee).

obligor Party owing a duty (to the assignor).

offer A manifestation of willingness to enter into a bargain, so made as to justify another person in understanding that his assent to that bargain is invited and will conclude it. Restatement, Second, Contracts, § 24.

offeree Recipient of the offer.

offeror Person making the offer.

open-ended credit Credit arrangement under which debtor has rights to enter into a series of credit transactions.

opinion Belief in the existence of a fact or a judgment as to value.

option Contract providing that an offer will stay open for a specified period of time.

order A final disposition made by an agency.

order paper Payable to a named person or to anyone designated by that person.

order to pay Direction or command to pay.

original promise Promise to become primarily liable.

output contract See **contracts**.

P

palpable unilateral mistake Erroneous belief by one party that is recognized by the other.

parent corporation Corporation which controls another corporation.

parol evidence Literally oral evidence, but now includes prior to and contemporaneous, oral, and written evidence.

parol evidence rule Under this rule, when parties put their agreement in writing, all previous oral agreements merge in the writing and the contract as written cannot be modified or changed by parol evidence, in the absence of a plea of mistake or fraud in the preparation of the writing. But the rule does not forbid a resort to parol evidence not inconsistent with the matters stated in the writing. Also, as regards sales of goods, such written agreement may be explained or supplemented by course of dealing, usage of trade, or course of conduct, and by evidence of consistent additional terms, unless the court finds the writing to have been intended also as a complete and exclusive statement of the terms of the agreement.

part performance In order to establish part performance taking an oral contract for the sale of realty out of the statute of frauds, the acts relied upon as part performance must be of such a character that they reasonably can be naturally accounted for in no other way than that they were performed in pursuance of the contract, and they must be in conformity with its provisions.

partial assignment Transfer of a portion of contractual rights to one or more assignees.

partition The dividing of lands held by joint tenants, copartners, or tenants in common into distinct portions, so that the parties may hold those lands in severalty.

partnership An association of two or more persons to carry on, as co-owners, a business for profit.

Partnerships are treated as a conduit and are, therefore, not subject to taxation. The various items of partnership income (gains and losses, etc.) flow through to the individual partners and are reported on their personal income tax returns.

Limited partnership Type of partnership comprised of one or more general partners who manage business and who are personally liable for partnership debts, and one or more limited partners who contribute capital and share in profits but who take no part in running business and incur no liability with respect to partnership obligations beyond contribution.

Partnership at will One with no definite term or specific undertaking.

partnership capital Total money and property contributed by partners for permanent use by the partnership.

partnership property Sum of all of the partnership's assets.

past consideration An act done before the contract is made.

patent Exclusive right to an invention.

payee The person in whose favor a bill of exchange, promissory note, or check is made or drawn.

payer or payor One who pays or who is to make a payment, particularly the person who is to make payment of a check, bill, or note. Correlative to "payee."

payor bank A bank by which an item is payable as drawn or accepted. Correlative to "Drawee bank."

per capita This term, derived from the civil law and much used in the law of descent and distribution, denotes that method of dividing an intestate estate by which an equal share is given to each of a number of persons, all of whom stand in equal degree to the decedent, without reference to their stocks or the right of representation. The opposite of *per stirpes.*

per stirpes This term, derived from the civil law and much used in the law of descent and distribution, denotes that method of dividing an intestate estate where a class or group of distributees takes the share to which its deceased would have been entitled, taking thus by its right of representing such ancestor and not as so many individuals. The opposite of *per capita.*

perfect tender rule Seller's tender of delivery must conform exactly to the contract.

perfection of security interest Acts required of a secured party in the way of giving at least constructive notice so as to make his security interest effective at least against lien creditors of the debtor. In most cases, the secured party may obtain perfection either by filing with the secretary of state or by taking possession of the collateral.

performance Fulfillment of one's contractual obligations. See also **part performance; specific performance.**

periodic tenancy Lease with a definite term that is to be continued.

personal defenses Contractual defenses which are good against holders but not holders in due course.

personal property Any property other than an interest in land.

petty crime Misdemeanor punishable by imprisonment of six months or less.

plaintiff The party who initiates a civil suit.

pleadings The formal allegations by the parties of their respective claims and defenses.

Rules or codes of civil procedure Unlike the rigid technical system of common law pleading, pleadings under federal and state rules or codes of civil procedure have a far more limited function, with determination and narrowing of facts and issues being left to discovery devices and pretrial conferences. In addition, the rules and codes permit liberal amendment and supplementation of pleadings.

Under rules of civil procedure, the pleadings consist of a complaint, an answer, a reply to a counterclaim, an answer to a cross-claim, a third-party complaint, and a third-party answer.

pledge A bailment of goods to a creditor as security for some debt or engagement.

Much of the law of pledges has been replaced by the provisions for secured transactions in Article 9 of the UCC.

possibility of reverter The interest which remains in a grantor or testator after the conveyance or devise of a fee simple determinable and which permits the grantor to be revested automatically of his estate on breach of the condition.

possibility test Under the statute of frauds, asks whether performance could possibly be completed within one year.

power of appointment A power of authority conferred by one person by deed or will upon another (called the "donee") to appoint, that is, to select and nominate, the person or persons who is or are to receive and enjoy an estate or an income therefrom or from a fund, after the testator's death, or the donee's death, or after the termination of an existing right or interest.

power of attorney An instrument authorizing a person to act as the agent or attorney of the person granting it.

power of termination The interest left in the grantor or testator after the conveyance or devise of a fee simple on condition subsequent or conditional fee.

precatory Expressing a wish.

precedent An adjudged case or decision of a court, considered as furnishing an example or authority for an identical or similar case afterwards arising or a similar question of law. See also **stare decisis**.

preemptive right The privilege of a stockholder to maintain a proportionate share of ownership by purchasing a proportionate share of any new stock issues.

preference The act of an insolvent debtor who, in distributing his property or in assigning it for the benefit of his creditors, pays or secures to one or more creditors the full amount of their claims or a larger amount than they would be entitled to receive on a *pro rata* distribution. The treatment of such preferential payments in bankruptcy is governed by the Bankruptcy Act.

preliminary hearing Determines whether there is probable cause.

premium The price for insurance protection for a specified period of exposure.

preponderance of the evidence Greater weight of the evidence; standard used in civil cases.

prescription Acquisition of a personal right to use a way, water, light, and air by reason of continuous usage. See also **easement**.

presenter's warranty Warranty given to any payor or acceptor of an instrument.

presentment The production of a negotiable instrument to the drawee for his acceptance, or to the drawer or acceptor for payment; or of a promissory note to the party liable, for payment of the same.

presumption A presumption is a rule of law, statutory or judicial, by which a finding of a basic fact gives rise to the existence of presumed fact, until presumption is rebutted. A presumption imposes on the party against whom it is directed the burden of going forward with evidence to rebut or meet the presumption, but does not shift to such party the burden of proof in the sense of the risk of nonpersuasion, which remains throughout the trial upon the party on whom it was originally cast.

price discrimination Price differential.

price fixing Any agreement for the purpose and effect of raising, depressing, fixing, pegging, or stabilizing prices.

prima facie Latin. At first sight; on the first appearance; on the face of it; so far as can be judged from the first disclosure; presumably; a fact presumed to be true unless disproved by some evidence to the contrary.

primary liability Absolute obligation to pay a negotiable instrument.

principal *Law of agency* The term "principal" describes one who has permitted or directed another (*i.e.*, an agent or a servant) to act for his benefit and subject to his direction and control. Principal includes in its meaning the term "master" or employer, a species of principal who, in addition to other control, has a right to control the physical conduct of the species of agents known as servants or employees, as to whom special rules are applicable with reference to harm caused by their physical acts.

Disclosed principal One whose existence and identity are known.

Partially disclosed principal One whose existence is known but whose identity is not known.

Undisclosed principal One whose existence and identity are not known.

principal debtor Person whose debt is being supported by a surety.

priority Precedence in order of right.

private carrier Carrier which limits its service and is not open to the general public.

private corporation One organized to conduct either a privately owned business enterprise for profit or a nonprofit corporation.

private law The law involving relationships among individuals and legal entities.

privilege Immunity from tort liability.

privity Contractual relationship.

privity of contract That connection or relationship which exists between two or more contracting parties. The absence of privity as a defense in actions for damages in contract and tort actions is generally no longer viable with the enactment of warranty statutes, acceptance by states of the doctrine of strict liability, and court decisions which have extended the right to sue to third-party beneficiaries and even innocent bystanders.

probable cause Reasonable belief of the offense charged.

probate Court procedure by which a will is proved to be valid or invalid, though in current usage this term has been expanded to include generally all matters and proceedings pertaining to administration of estates, guardianships, etc.

procedural due process Requirement that governmental action depriving a person of life, liberty, or property be done through a fair procedure.

procedural law Rules for enforcing substantive law.

procedural rules Rules issued by an administrative agency establishing its organization, method of operation, and rules of conduct for practice before it.

procedural unconscionability Unfair or irregular bargaining.

proceeds Consideration for the sale, exchange, or other disposition of collateral.

process *Judicial process* In a wide sense, this term may include all the acts of a court from the beginning to the end of its proceedings in a given cause; more specifically, it means the writ, summons, mandate, or other process which is used to inform the defendant of the institution of proceedings against him and to compel his appearance, in either civil or criminal cases.

Legal process This term is sometimes used as equivalent to "lawful process." Thus, it is said that legal process means process not merely fair on its face but valid in fact. But properly it means a summons, writ, warrant, mandate, or other process issuing from a court.

profit corporation One founded for the purpose of operating a business for profit.

profit à prendre Right to make some use of the soil of another, such as a right to mine metals; carries with it the right of entry and the right to remove.

promise to pay Undertaking to pay an existing obligation.

promisee Person to whom a promise is made.

promisor Person making a promise.

promissory estoppel Arises where there is a promise which promisor should reasonably expect to induce action or forbearance on part of promisee and which does induce such action or forbearance, and where injustice can be avoided only by enforcement of the promise.

promissory note An unconditional written promise to pay a specified sum of money on demand or at a specified date. Such a note is negotiable if signed by the maker and containing an unconditional promise to pay a sum certain in money either on demand or at a definite time and payable to order or bearer.

promoters In the law relating to corporations, those persons who first associate themselves for the purpose of organizing a company, issuing its prospectus, procuring subscriptions to the stock, securing a charter, etc.

property Interest that is legally protected.

Abandoned property Intentionally disposed of by the owner.

Lost property Unintentionally left by the owner.

Mislaid property Intentionally placed by the owner but unintentionally left.

prosecute To bring a criminal proceeding.

protest A formal declaration made by a person interested or concerned in some act about to be done, or already performed, whereby he expresses his dissent or disapproval or affirms the act against his will. The object of such a declaration usually is to preserve some right which would be lost to the protester if his assent could be implied, or to exonerate him from some responsibility which would attach to him unless he expressly negatived his assent.

Notice of protest A notice given by the holder of a bill or note to the drawer or indorser that the bill has been protested for refusal of payment or acceptance.

provisional credit Tentative credit for the deposit of an instrument until final credit is given.

proximate cause Where the act or omission played a substantial part in bringing about or actually causing the injury or damage and where the injury or damage was either a direct result or a reasonably probable consequence of the act or omission.

proxy (Contracted from "procuracy.") Written authorization given by one person to another so that the second person can act for the first, such as that given by a shareholder to someone else to represent him and vote his shares at a shareholders' meeting.

public corporation One created to administer a unit of local civil government or one created by the United States to conduct public business.

public disclosure of private facts Offensive publicity given to private information about another person.

public law The law dealing with the relationship between government and individuals.

puffery Sales talk that is considered general bragging or overstatement.

punitive damages Damages awarded in excess of normal compensation to punish a defendant for a serious civil wrong.

purchase money security interest Security interest retained by a seller of goods in goods purchased with the loaned money.

Q

qualified fee Ownership subject to its being taken away upon the happening of an event.

quantum meruit Expression "quantum meruit" means "as much as he deserves"; describes the extent of liability on a contract implied by law. Elements essential to recovery under quantum meruit are (1) valuable services rendered or materials furnished (2) for the person sought to be charged, (3) which services and materials such person accepted, used, and enjoyed, (4) under such circumstances as reasonably notified her that plaintiff, in performing such services, was expected to be paid by the person sought to be charged.

quasi Latin. As if; almost as it were; analogous to. Negatives the idea of identity but points out that the conceptions are sufficiently similar to be classed as equals of one another.

quasi contract Legal fiction invented by common law courts to permit recovery by contractual remedy in cases where, in fact, there is no contract, but where circumstances are such that justice warrants a recovery as though a promise had been made.

quasi in rem See **in rem**.

quasi in rem jurisdiction Jurisdiction over property not based on claims against it.

quiet enjoyment Right of a tenant not to have his physical possession of premises interfered with by the landlord.

quitclaim deed A deed of conveyance operating by way of release; that is, intended to pass any title, interest, or claim which the grantor may have in the premises but neither professing that such title is valid nor containing any warranty or covenants for title.

quorum When a committee, board of directors, meeting of shareholders, legislature, or other body of persons cannot act unless at least a certain number of them are present.

R

rape Unlawful, nonconsensual sexual intercourse.

ratification In a broad sense, the confirmation of a previous act done either by the party himself or by another; as, for example, confirmation of a voidable act.

In the law of principal and agent, the adoption and confirmation by one person, with knowledge of all material facts, of an act or contract performed or entered into in his behalf by another who at the time assumed without authority to act as his agent.

rational relationship test Requirement that legislation bear a rational relationship to a legitimate governmental interest.

real defenses Defenses that are valid against all holders, including holders in due course.

real property Land, and generally whatever is erected or growing upon or affixed to land. Also, rights issuing out of, annexed to, and exercisable within or about land. See also **fixture**.

reasonable man standard Duty of care required to avoid being negligent; one who is careful, diligent, and prudent.

receiver A fiduciary of the court, whose appointment is incident to other proceedings wherein certain ultimate relief is prayed. He is a trustee or ministerial officer representing the court, all parties in interest in the litigation, and the property or funds entrusted to him.

recognizance Formal acknowledgment of indebtedness made in court.

redemption (a) The realization of a right to have the title of property restored free and clear of a mortgage, performance of the mortgage obligation being essential for such purpose. (b) Repurchase by corporation of its own shares.

reformation Equitable remedy used to reframe written contracts to reflect accurately real agreement between contracting parties when, either through mutual mistake or unilateral mistake coupled with actual or equitable fraud by the other party, the writing does not embody the contract as actually made.

regulatory license Requirement to protect the public interest.

reimbursement Duty owed by principal to pay back authorized payments agent has made on principal's behalf. Duty owed by a principal debtor to repay surety who pays principal debtor's obligation.

rejection The refusal to accept an offer; manifestation of an unwillingness to accept the goods (sales).

release The relinquishment, concession, or giving up of a right, claim, or privilege, by the person in whom it exists or to whom it accrues, to the person against whom it might have been demanded or enforced.

remainder An estate limited to take effect and be enjoyed after another estate is determined.

remand To send back. The sending by the appellate court of a cause back to the same court out of which it came, for the purpose of having some further action taken on it there.

remedy The means by which the violation of a right is prevented, redressed, or compensated. Though a remedy may be by the act of the party injured, by operation of law, or by agreement between the injurer and the injured, we are chiefly concerned with one kind of remedy, the judicial remedy, which is by action or suit.

rent Consideration paid for use or occupation of property. In a broader sense, it is the compensation or fee paid, usually periodically, for the use of any property, land, buildings, equipment, etc.

replevin An action whereby the owner or person entitled to repossession of goods or chattels may recover those goods or chattels from one who has wrongfully distrained or taken such goods or chattels or who wrongfully detains them.

reply Plaintiff's pleading in response to the defendant's answer.

repudiation Repudiation of a contract means refusal to perform duty or obligation owed to other party.

requirements contract See **contracts**.

res ipsa loquitur "The thing speaks for itself"; permits the jury to infer both negligent conduct and causation.

rescission An equitable action in which a party seeks to be relieved of his obligations under a contract on the grounds of mutual mistake, fraud, impossibility, etc.

residuary Pertaining to the residue; constituting the residue; giving or bequeathing the residue; receiving or entitled to the residue. See also **legacy**, **residuary legacy**.

respondeat superior Latin. Let the master answer. This maxim means that a master or employer is liable in certain cases for the wrongful acts of his servant or employee, and a principal for those of his agent.

respondent In equity practice, the party who makes an answer to a bill or other proceeding. In appellate practice, the party who contends against an appeal (*i.e.*, the appellee). The party who appeals is called the "appellant."

restitution An equitable remedy under which a person who has rendered services to another seeks to be reimbursed for the costs of his acts (but not his profits) even though there was never a contract between the parties.

restraint on alienation A provision in an instrument of conveyance which prohibits the grantee from selling or transferring the property which is the subject of the conveyance. Many such restraints are unenforceable as against public policy and the law's policy of free alienability of land.

restraint of trade Agreement that eliminates or tends to eliminate competition.

restrictive covenant Private restriction on property contained in a conveyance.

revenue license Measure to raise money.

reverse An appellate court uses the term "reversed" to indicate that it annuls or avoids the judgment, or vacates the decree, of the trial court.

reverse discrimination Employment decisions taking into account race or gender in order to remedy past discrimination.

reversion The term reversion has two meanings. First, it designates the estate left in the grantor during the continuance of a particular estate; second, it denotes the residue left in grantor or his heirs after termination of a particular estate. It differs from a remainder in that it arises by an act of law, whereas a remainder arises by an act of the parties. A reversion, moreover, is the remnant left in the grantor, while a remainder is the remnant of the whole estate disposed of after a preceding part of the same has been given away.

revocation The recall of some power, authority, or thing granted, or a destroying or making void of some deed that had existence until the act of revocation made it void.

revocation of acceptance Rescission of one's acceptance of goods based upon a nonconformity of the goods which substantially impairs their value.

right Legal capacity to require another person to perform or refrain from performing an act.

right of entry The right to take or resume possession of land by entering on it in a peaceable manner.

right of redemption The right (granted by statute only) to free property from the encumbrance of a foreclosure or other judicial sale, or to recover the title passing thereby, by paying what is due, with interest, costs, etc. Not to be confounded with the "equity of redemption," which exists independently of statute but must be exercised before sale. See also **equity of redemption**.

right to work law State statute that prohibits union shop contracts.

rights in collateral Personal property the debtor owns, possesses, or is in the process of acquiring.

risk of loss Allocation of loss between seller and buyer where the goods have been damaged, destroyed, or lost.

robbery Larceny from a person by force or threat of force.

rule Agency statement of general or particular applicability designed to implement, interpret, or process law or policy.

rule against perpetuities Principle that no interest in property is good unless it must vest, if at all, not later than twenty-one years, plus period of gestation, after some life or lives in being at time of creation of interest.

rule of reason Balancing the anticompetitive effects of a restraint against its procompetitive effects.

S

sale Transfer of title to goods from seller to buyer for a price.

sale on approval Transfer of possession without title to buyer for trial period.

sale or return Sale where buyer has option to return goods to seller.

sanction Means of enforcing legal judgments.

satisfaction The discharge of an obligation by paying a party what is due to him (as on a mortgage, lien, or contract) or what has been awarded to him by the judgment of a court or otherwise. Thus, a judgment is satisfied by the payment of the amount due to the party who has recovered such judgment, or by his levying the amount. See also **accord and satisfaction**.

scienter Latin. Knowingly.

seal Symbol that authenticates a document.

secondary liability Obligation to pay is subject to the conditions of presentment, dishonor, notice of dishonor, and sometimes protest.

secret partner Partner whose membership in the partnership is not disclosed.

Section 402A Strict liability in tort.

secured bond A bond having a lien on specific property.

secured claim Claim with a lien on property of the debtor.

secured party Creditor who possesses a security interest in collateral.

secured transaction A transaction founded on a security agreement. Such agreement creates or provides for a security interest.

securities Stocks, bonds, notes, convertible debentures, warrants, or other documents that represent a share in a company or a debt owed by a company.

Certificated security Security represented by a certificate.

Exempt security Security not subject to registration requirements of 1933 Act.

Exempt transaction Issuance of securities not subject to the registration requirements of 1933 Act.

Restricted securities Securities issued under an exempt transaction.

Uncertificated security Security not represented by a certificate.

security agreement Agreement that grants a security interest.

security interest Right in personal property securing payment or performance of an obligation.

seisin Possession with an intent on the part of him who holds it to claim a freehold interest.

self-defense Force to protect oneself against attack.

separation of powers Allocation of powers among the legislative, executive, and judicial branches of government.

service mark Distinctive symbol, word, or design that is used to identify the services of a provider.

servient Land subject to an easement.

setoff A counterclaim demand which defendant holds against plaintiff, arising out of a transaction extrinsic to plaintiff's cause of action.

settlor Creator of a trust.

severance The destruction of any one of the unities of a joint tenancy. It is so called because the estate is no longer a joint tenancy, but is severed.

Term may also refer to the cutting of crops, such as corn, wheat, etc., or to the separation of anything from realty.

share A proportionate ownership interest in a corporation.

Shelley's case, rule in Where a person takes an estate of freehold, legally or equitably, under a deed, will, or other writing, and in the same instrument there is a limitation by way of remainder of any interest of the same legal or equitable quality to his heirs, or heirs of his body, as a class of persons to take in succession from generation to generation, the limitation to the heirs entitles the ancestor to the whole estate.

The rule was adopted as a part of the common law of this country, though it has long since been abolished by most states.

shelter rule Transferee gets rights of transferor.

shipment contract Seller is authorized or required only to bear the expense of placing goods with the common carrier and bears the risk of loss only up to such point.

short-swing profits Profits made by insider through sale or other disposition of corporate stock within six months after purchase.

sight draft An instrument payable on presentment.

signature Any symbol executed with intent to validate a writing.

silent partner Partner who takes no part in the partnership business.

slander Oral defamation.

small claims courts Inferior civil courts with jurisdiction limited by dollar amount.

social security Measures by which the government provides economic assistance to disabled or retired employees and their dependents.

sole proprietorship A form of business in which one person owns all the assets of the business, in contrast to a partnership or a corporation.

sovereign immunity Foreign country's freedom from a host country's laws.

special warranty deed Seller promises that he has not impaired title.

specific performance The doctrine of specific performance is that where damages would compensate inadequately for the breach of an agreement, the contractor or vendor will be compelled to perform specifically what he has agreed to do; *e.g.*, ordered to execute a specific conveyance of land.

With respect to the sale of goods, specific performance may be decreed where the goods are unique or in other proper circumstances. The decree for specific performance may include such terms and conditions as to payment of the price, damages, or other relief as the court may deem just.

standardized business form A preprinted contract.

stare decisis Doctrine that once a court has laid down a principle of law as applicable to a certain state of facts, it will adhere to that principle and apply it to all future cases having substantially the same facts, regardless of whether the parties and property are the same or not.

state action Actions by governments, as opposed to actions taken by private individuals.

state-of-the-art Made in accordance with the level of technology at the time the product is made.

stated capital Consideration, other than that allocated to capital surplus, received for issued stock.

statute of frauds A celebrated English statute, passed in 1677, which has been adopted, in a more or less modified form, in nearly all of the United States. Its chief characteristic is the provision that no action shall be brought on certain contracts unless there be a note or memorandum thereof in writing, signed by the party to be charged or by his authorized agent.

statute of limitation A statute prescribing limitations to the right of action on certain described causes of action; that is, declaring that no suit shall be maintained on such causes of action unless brought within a specified period after the right accrued.

statutory lien Interest in property, arising solely by statute, to secure payment of a debt.

stock "Stock" is distinguished from "bonds" and, ordinarily, from "debentures" in that it gives a right of ownership in part of the assets of a corporation and a right to interest in any surplus after the payment of debt. "Stock" in a corporation is an equity, representing an ownership interest. It is to be distinguished from obligations such as notes or bonds, which are not equities and represent no ownership interest.

Capital stock See **capital**.

Common stock Securities which represent an ownership interest in a corporation. If the company has also issued preferred stock, both common and preferred have ownership rights. Claims of both common and preferred stockholders are junior to claims of bondholders or other creditors of the company. Common stockholders assume the greater risk, but generally exercise the greater control and may gain the greater reward in the form of dividends and capital appreciation.

Convertible stock Stock which may be changed or converted into common stock.

Cumulative preferred Stock having a provision that if one or more dividends are omitted, the omitted dividends must be paid before dividends may be paid on the company's common stock.

Preferred stock is a separate portion or class of the stock of a corporation that is accorded, by the charter or by-laws, a preference or priority in respect to dividends, over the remainder of the stock of the corporation, which in that case is called *common stock*.

Stock warrant A certificate entitling the owner to buy a specified amount of stock at a specified time(s) for a specified price. Differs from a stock option only in that options are granted to employees and warrants are sold to the public.

Treasury stock Shares reacquired by a corporation.

stock option Contractual right to purchase stock from a corporation.

stop payment Order for a drawee not to pay an instrument.

strict liability A concept applied by the courts in product liability cases in which a seller is liable for any and all defective or hazardous products which unduly threaten a consumer's personal safety. This concept applies to all members involved in the manufacture and sale of any facet of the product.

strict scrutiny test Requirement that legislation be necessary to promote a compelling governmental interest.

subagent Person appointed by agent to perform agent's duties.

subject matter jurisdiction Authority of a court to decide a particular kind of case.

subject to the mortgage Purchaser is not personally obligated to pay the debt, but the property remains subject to the mortgage.

subjective fault Desired or virtually certain consequences of one's conduct.

subjective satisfaction Approval based upon a party's honestly held opinion.

sublease Transfer of less than all of a tenant's interest in a leasehold.

subpoena A subpoena is a command to appear at a certain time and place to give testimony upon a certain matter. A subpoena duces tecum requires production of books, papers, and other things.

subrogation The substitution of one thing for another, or of one person into the place of another with respect to rights, claims, or securities.

Subrogation denotes the putting of a third person who has paid a debt in the place of the creditor to whom he has paid it, so that he may exercise against the debtor all the rights which the creditor, if unpaid, might have exercised.

subscribe Literally, to write underneath, as one's name. To sign at the end of a document. Also, to agree in writing to furnish money or its equivalent, or to agree to purchase some initial stock in a corporation.

subscriber Person who agrees to purchase initial stock in a corporation.

subsidiary corporation Corporation controlled by another corporation.

substantial performance Equitable doctrine protects against forfeiture for technical inadvertence, trivial variations, or omissions in performance.

substantive due process Requirement that governmental action be compatible with individual liberties.

substantive law The basic law of rights and duties (contract law, criminal law, tort law, law of wills, etc.), as opposed to procedural law (law of pleading, law of evidence, law of jurisdiction, etc.).

substantive unconscionability Oppressive or grossly unfair contractual terms.

sue To begin a lawsuit in a court.

suit "Suit" is a generic term of comprehensive signification that applies to any proceeding in a court of justice in which the plaintiff pursues, in such court, the remedy which the law affords him for the redress of an injury or the recovery of a right.

Derivative suit Suit brought by a shareholder on behalf of a corporation to enforce a right belonging to the corporation.

Direct suit Suit brought by a shareholder against a corporation based upon his ownership of shares.

summary judgment Rule of Civil Procedure 56 permits any party to a civil action to move for a summary judgment on a claim, counterclaim, or cross-claim when he believes that there is no genuine issue of material fact and that he is entitled to prevail as a matter of law.

summons Writ or process directed to the sheriff or other proper officer, requiring him to notify the person named that an action has been commenced against him in the court from which the process has

issued and that he is required to appear, on a day named, and answer the complaint in such action.

superseding cause Intervening event that occurs after the defendant's negligent conduct and relieves him of liability.

supreme law Law that takes precedence over all conflicting laws.

surety One who undertakes to pay money or to do any other act in event that his principal debtor fails therein.

suretyship A guarantee of debts of another.

surplus Excess of net assets over stated capital.

T

tangible property Physical objects.

tariff Duty or tax imposed on goods moving into or out of a country.

tenancy Possession or occupancy of land or premises under lease.

Joint tenancy Joint tenants have one and the same interest, accruing by one and the same conveyance, commencing at one and the same time, and held by one and the same undivided possession. The primary incident of joint tenancy is survivorship, by which the entire tenancy on the decease of any joint tenant remains to the survivors, and at length to the last survivor.

Tenancy at sufferance Only naked possession which continues after tenant's right of possession has terminated.

Tenancy at will Possession of premises by permission of owner or landlord, but without a fixed term.

Tenancy by the entirety A tenancy which is created between a husband and wife and by which together they hold title to the whole with right of survivorship so that, upon death of either, the other takes the whole to the exclusion of the deceased's heirs. It is essentially a "joint tenancy," modified by the common law theory that husband and wife are one person.

Tenancy for a period A tenancy for years or for some fixed period.

Tenancy in common A form of ownership whereby each tenant (*i.e.,* owner) holds an undivided interest in property. Unlike the interest of a joint tenant or a tenant by the entirety, the interest of a tenant in common does not terminate upon his or her prior death (*i.e.,* there is no right of survivorship).

tenancy in partnership Type of joint ownership that determines partners' rights in specific partnership property.

tenant Possessor of a leasehold interest.

tender An offer of money; the act by which one produces and offers to a person holding a claim or demand against him the amount of money which he considers and admits to be due, in satisfaction of such claim or demand, without any stipulation or condition.

Also, there may be a tender of performance of a duty other than the payment of money.

tender of delivery Seller makes available to buyer goods conforming to the contract and so notifies the buyer.

tender offer General invitation to all shareholders to purchase their shares at a specified price.

testament Will.

testator One who makes or has made a testament or will; one who dies leaving a will.

third-party beneficiary One for whose benefit a promise is made in a contract but who is not a party to the contract.

Creditor beneficiary Where performance of a promise in a contract will benefit a person other than the promisee, that person is a creditor beneficiary if no purpose to make a gift appears from the terms of the promise, in view of the accompanying circumstances, and performance of the promise will satisfy an actual, supposed, or asserted duty of the promisee to the beneficiary.

Donee beneficiary The person who takes the benefit of the contract even though there is no privity between him and the contracting parties. A third-party beneficiary who is not a creditor beneficiary. See also **beneficiary**.

time paper Payable at definite time.

time-price doctrine Permits sellers to have different prices for cash sales and credit sales.

title The means whereby the owner of lands or of personalty has the just possession of his property.

title insurance Provides protection against defect in title to real property.

tort A private or civil wrong or injury, other than breach of contract, for which a court will provide a remedy in the form of an action for damages.

Three elements of every tort action are the existence of a legal duty from defendant to plaintiff, breach of that duty, and damage as proximate result.

tortfeasor One who commits a tort.

trade acceptance A draft drawn by a seller which is presented for signature (acceptance) to the buyer at the time goods are purchased and which then becomes the equivalent of a note receivable of the seller and the note payable of the buyer.

trade name Name used in trade or business to identify a particular business or manufacturer.

trade secrets Private business information.

trademark Distinctive insignia, word, or design of a good that is used to identify the manufacturer.

transferor's warranty Warranty given by any person who transfers an instrument and receives consideration.

treaty An agreement between or among independent nations.

treble damages Three times actual loss.

trespass At common law, trespass was a form of action brought to recover damages for any injury to one's person or property or relationship with another.

Trespass to chattels or personal property An unlawful and serious interference with the possessory rights of another to personal property.

Trespass to land At common law, every unauthorized and direct breach of the boundaries of another's land was an actionable trespass. The present prevailing position of the courts finds liability for trespass only in the case of intentional intrusion, or negligence, or some "abnormally dangerous activity" on the part of the defendant. *Compare* **nuisance**.

trespasser Person who enters or remains on the land of another without permission or privilege to do so.

trust Any arrangement whereby property is transferred with the intention that it be administered by a trustee for another's benefit.

A trust, as the term is used in the Restatement, when not qualified by the word "charitable," "resulting," or "constructive," is a fiduciary relationship with respect to property, subjecting the person by whom the title to the property is held to equitable duties to deal with the property for the benefit of another person, which arises through a manifestation of an intention to create such benefit.

Charitable trust To benefit humankind.

Constructive trust Wherever the circumstances of a transaction are such that the person who takes the legal estate in property cannot also enjoy the beneficial interest without necessarily violating some established principle of equity, the court will immediately raise a *constructive trust* and fasten it upon the conscience of the legal owner, so as to convert him into a trustee for the parties who in equity are entitled to the beneficial enjoyment.

Inter vivos trust Established during the settlor's lifetime.

Resulting trust One that arises by implication of law, where the legal estate in property is disposed of, conveyed, or transferred, but the intent appears or is inferred from the terms of the disposition, or from the accompanying facts and circumstances, that the beneficial interest is not to go or be enjoyed with the legal title.

Spendthrift trust Removal of the trust estate from the beneficiary's control.

Testamentary trust Established by a will.

Totten trust A tentative trust which is a joint bank account opened by the settlor.

Voting trust A trust which holds the voting rights to stock in a corporation. It is a useful device when a majority of the shareholders in a corporation cannot agree on corporate policy.

trustee In a strict sense, a "trustee" is one who holds the legal title to property for the benefit of another, while, in a broad sense, the term is sometimes applied to anyone standing in a fiduciary or confidential relation to another, such as agent, attorney, bailee, etc.

trustee in bankruptcy Representative of the estate in bankruptcy who is responsible for collecting, liquidating, and distributing the debtor's assets.

tying arrangement Conditioning a sale of a desired product (tying product) on the buyer's purchasing a second product (tied product).

U

ultra vires Acts beyond the scope of the powers of a corporation, as defined by its charter or by the laws of its state of incorporation. By the doctrine of ultra vires, a contract made by a corporation beyond the scope of its corporate powers is unlawful.

unconscionable Unfair or unduly harsh.

unconscionable contract See **contracts**.

underwriter Any person, banker, or syndicate that guarantees to furnish a definite sum of money by a definite date to a business or government in return for an issue of bonds or stock. In insurance, the one assuming a risk in return for the payment of a premium.

undisputed debt Obligation whose existence and amount are not contested.

undue influence Term refers to conduct by which a person, through his power over the mind of a testator, makes the latter's desires conform to his own, thereby overmastering the volition of the testator.

unemployment compensation Compensation awarded to workers who have lost their jobs and cannot find other employment.

unenforceable Contract under which neither party can recover.

unfair employer practice Conduct in which an employer is prohibited from engaging.

unfair labor practice Conduct in which an employer or union is prohibited from engaging.

unfair union practice Conduct in which a union is prohibited from engaging.

Uniform Commercial Code One of the Uniform Laws, drafted by the National Conference of Commissioners on Uniform State Laws, governing commercial transactions (sales of goods, commercial paper, bank deposits and collections, letters of credit, bulk transfers, warehouse receipts, bills of lading, investment securities, and secured transactions).

unilateral mistake Erroneous belief on the part of only one of the parties to a contract.

union shop Employer can hire nonunion members, but such employees must then join the union.

universal life Ordinary life divided into two components, a renewable term insurance policy and an investment portfolio.

unliquidated debt Obligation that is uncertain or contested in amount.

unqualified indorsement One that imposes liability upon the indorser.

unreasonably dangerous Danger beyond that which the ordinary consumer contemplates.

unrestrictive indorsement One that does not attempt to restrict the rights of the indorsee.

usage of trade Any practice or method of dealing having such regularity of observance in a place, vocation, or trade as to justify an expectation that it will be observed with respect to the transaction in question.

usury Collectively, the laws of a jurisdiction regulating the charging of interest rates. A usurious loan is one whose interest rates are determined to be in excess of those permitted by the usury laws.

V

value The performance of legal consideration, the forgiveness of an antecedent debt, the giving of a negotiable instrument, or the giving of an irrevocable commitment to a third party.

variance A use differing from that provided in a zoning ordinance in order to avoid undue hardship.

vendee A purchaser or buyer; one to whom anything is sold. See also **vendor**.

vendor The person who transfers property by sale, particularly real estate; "seller" being more commonly used for one who sells personalty. See also **vendee**.

venue "Jurisdiction" of the court means the inherent power to decide a case, whereas "venue" designates the particular county or city in which a court with jurisdiction may hear and determine the case.

verdict The formal and unanimous decision or finding of a jury, impaneled and sworn for the trial of a cause, upon the matters or questions duly submitted to it upon the trial.

vertical privity Who is liable to the plaintiff.

vertical restraints Agreements among parties at different levels of the distribution chain.

vested Fixed; accrued; settled; absolute. To be "vested," a right must be more than a mere expectation based on an anticipation of the continuance of an existing law; it must have become a title, legal or equitable, to the present or future enforcement of a demand, or a legal exemption from the demand of another.

vested remainder Unconditional remainder that is a fixed present interest to be enjoyed in the future.

vicarious liability Indirect legal responsibility; for example, the liability of an employer for the acts of an employee or that of a principal for the torts and contracts of an agent.

void Null; ineffectual; nugatory; having no legal force or binding effect; unable, in law, to support the purpose for which it was intended.

This difference separates the words "void" and "voidable": *void* in the strict sense means that an instrument or transaction is nugatory and ineffectual, so that nothing can cure it; *voidable* exists when an imperfection or defect can be cured by the act or confirmation of the person who could take advantage of it.

Frequently, the word "void" is used and construed as having the more liberal meaning of "voidable."

voidable Capable of being made void. See also **void**.

voir dire Preliminary examination of potential jurors.

voluntary Resulting from free choice. The word, especially in statutes, often implies knowledge of essential facts.

voting trust Transfer of corporate shares' voting rights to a trustee.

W

wager (gambling) Agreement that one party will win or lose depending upon the outcome of an event in which the only interest is the gain or loss.

waiver Terms "estoppel" and "waiver" are not synonymous; "waiver" means the voluntary, intentional relinquishment of a known right, and "estoppel" rests upon principle that, where anyone has done an act or made a statement that would be a fraud on his part to controvert or impair, because the other party has acted upon it in belief that what was done or said was true, conscience and honest dealing require that he not be permitted to repudiate his act or gainsay his statement. See also **estoppel**.

ward An infant or insane person placed by authority of law under the care of a guardian.

warehouse receipt Receipt issued by a person storing goods.

warehouser Storer of goods for compensation.

warrant In contracts, to engage or promise that a certain fact or state of facts, in relation to the subject matter, is, or shall be, as it is represented to be.

In conveyancing, to assure the title to property sold, by an express covenant to that effect in the deed of conveyance.

warranty A warranty is a statement or representation made by a seller of goods, contemporaneously with and as a part of a contract of sale, though collateral to express the object of the sale, having reference to the character, quality, or title of goods, and by which the seller promises or undertakes to ensure that certain facts are or shall be as he then represents them.

The general statutory law governing warranties on sales of goods is provided in the UCC. The three main types of warranties are (1) express warranty; (2) implied warranty of fitness; (3) implied warranty of merchantability.

warranty deed Deed in which grantor warrants good clear title. The usual covenants of title are warranties of seisin, quiet enjoyment, right to convey, freedom from encumbrances, and defense of title as to all claims.

Special warranty deed Seller warrants that he has not impaired title.

warranty liability Applies to persons who transfer an instrument or receive payment or acceptance.

warranty of title Obligation to convey the right to ownership without any lien.

waste Any act or omission that does permanent injury to the realty or unreasonably changes its value.

white-collar crime Corporate crime.

will A written instrument executed with the formalities required by statutes, whereby a person makes a disposition of his property to take effect after his death.

winding up To settle the accounts and liquidate the assets of a partnership or corporation, for the purpose of making distribution and terminating the concern.

without reserve Auctioneer may not withdraw the goods from the auction.

workers' compensation Compensation awarded to an employee who is injured, when the injury arose out of and in the course of his employment.

writ of certiorari Discretionary review by a higher court. See also **certiorari**.

writ of execution Order served by sheriff upon debtor demanding payment of a court judgment against debtor.

Z

zoning Public control over land use.

Many of the definitions are abridged and adapted from *Black's Law Dictionary*, 5th edition, West Publishing Company, 1979.

Index